STALIN

Stalin:
Paradoxes of Power, 1878–1928

Armageddon Averted:
The Soviet Collapse, 1970–2000

Magnetic Mountain:
Stalinism as a Civilization

Steeltown, USSR:
Soviet Society in the Gorbachev Era

Uncivil Society:
*1989 and the Implosion of the Communist
Establishment*

STALIN

WAITING FOR HITLER

1929–1941

STEPHEN KOTKIN

PENGUIN PRESS

NEW YORK | 2017

PENGUIN PRESS
An imprint of Penguin Random House LLC
375 Hudson Street
New York, New York 10014
penguin.com

Photograph credits appear on pages 1119–1120.

Kotkin, Stephen.
Stalin / Stephen Kotkin. volumes cm
Includes bibliographical references and index. Contents: Volume I.
Paradoxes of power, 1878–1928.
ISBN 9781594203794 (hardcover)
ISBN 9780143127864 (paperback)
Volume II. Waiting for Hitler, 1929–1941.
ISBN 9781594203800 (hardcover) / ISBN 9780735224483 (e-book)
1. Stalin, Joseph, 1879–1953.   2. Stalin, Joseph, 1879–1953—Psychology.
3. Heads of state—Soviet Union—Biography.   4. Dictators—Soviet
Union—Biography.   5. Soviet Union—Politics and
government—1917–1936.   6. Soviet Union—Politics and
government—1936–1953.   7. Political culture—Soviet Union—History.
8. Soviet Union—History—1925–1953. I. Title.
DK268.S8K65 2014
947.084"2092—dc23 [B]
2014032906

Printed in the United States of America
1   3   5   7   9   10   8   6   4   2

Book design by Marysarah Quinn
Maps by Jeffrey L. Ward

for Alex Levine and Joyce Howe
   who, beginning with the rough patches in graduate school, held me together

Midway on life's journey
I found myself in a dark wood,
for the straight path was lost.

DANTE ALIGHIERI,
The Divine Comedy, 1308–1321

It cannot be called virtue to kill one's
fellow citizens, betray one's friends,
be without faith, without pity, without
religion; by these methods one may
indeed gain power, but not glory.

NICCOLÒ MACHIAVELLI,
The Prince, 1513

CONTENTS

PREFACE

But if there isn't a tsar, who's going to rule Russia?

ALEXEI, 1917, *when his father, Nicholas II,*
abdicated for both of them

THROUGH THE FIRST THIRTY-NINE YEARS OF HIS LIFE, the achievements of Iosif Stalin (b. 1878) were meager. As a teenager, he had abandoned a successful trajectory, with high marks in school, to fight tsarist oppression, and published first-rate poems in a Georgian newspaper, which he recited in front of others. ("To this day his beautiful, sonorous lyrics echo in my ears," one person would recall.) But his profession—revolutionary—made for a "career" of hiding, prison, exile, escape, recapture, penury. It had gotten to the point, in far northern Siberia, that even escape had become impossible. He persevered, known only to the tsarist police and some of his fellow revolutionaries, who were dispersed in remote internal exile, like him, or in Europe. Only the world-shattering Great War, the shocking abdication of the tsar and tsarevich in February 1917, the return of Vladimir Lenin to Russia that April thanks to imperial German cynicism, the suicidal Russia-initiated military offensive in June, and a fatal pas de deux between Prime Minister Alexander Kerensky and Supreme Commander Lavr Kornilov in August had altered Stalin's life prospects. All of a sudden, he had become one of the four leading figures in an improbable Bolshevik regime. He played an outsized role in the 1918–21 civil war and territorial reconquest, and a foremost role in the invention of the Union of Soviet Socialist Republics. In 1922, five years removed from desolate isolation near the Arctic Circle, he found himself in the uncanny position of being able to build a personal dictatorship within the Bolshevik dictatorship, thanks to Lenin's appointing him Communist party general secretary (April), followed by Lenin's incapacitating stroke (May). Stalin seized that opportunity passionately and ruthlessly. By 1928, he had decided that 120 million peasants in Soviet Eurasia had to be forcibly collectivized. The years 1917–28 proved to be astonishingly eventful. But the years from 1929 through 1941—the period covered in this volume—would prove still more so.

This volume, too, examines Stalin's power in Russia, recast as the Soviet Union, and the Soviet Union's power in the world. But whereas in the preceding volume he was offstage for long stretches as global developments unfolded around him, now the opposite and, in fact, more difficult challenge of narration awaits: Stalin is present on nearly every page. He is now deep into the violent re-shaping of all Eurasia that he announced at the end of volume I, continuing to micromanage the ever-expanding party-state machinery, delving into the gran-ular details of armaments production and grain collections, while also conduct-ing a comprehensive foreign policy touching all corners of the planet and, for the first time, overseeing cultural affairs. But volume II takes place largely in his of-fice, and, indeed, in his mind. Whereas right through 1927, he had not appeared to be a sociopath in the eyes of those who worked most closely with him, by 1929–30 he was exhibiting an intense dark side. As the decade progresses, he will go from learning to be a dictator to becoming impatient with dictatorship and forging a despotism in mass bloodshed. Volume I's analytical burden of explain-ing where such power comes from remains, but volume II raises questions of why he arrested and murdered immense numbers of loyal people in his own commis-sariats, officer corps, secret police, embassies, spy networks, scientific and artis-tic circles, and party organizations. What could he have been thinking? How was this even possible?

Stalin's mass terror of 1936–38 was a central episode, but not *the* central epi-sode, of his regime in the period covered by this volume. That designation belongs, first, to the 1929–33 collectivization of agriculture, then to the 1939 Pact with Nazi Germany and its aftershocks. If Stalin's foil in volume I was Trotsky (who, though politically vanquished, will haunt him more than ever), now a second materializes, and not a foreign exile wielding little more than a pen, but another dictator pre-siding over the rearmament of the greatest power on the continent.

Adolf Hitler was eleven years Stalin's junior, born in 1889 in a frontier region of Austria-Hungary. He lost his father at age fifteen and his mother at eighteen. (The Jewish physician who tended to his mother would recall that in forty years he had never seen anyone as broken with grief over a mother's death as her son.) At age twenty, Hitler found himself on a breadline in Vienna, his inheritance and savings nearly spent. He had twice been rejected from Vienna's Academy of Fine Arts ("sample drawing unsatisfactory") and was staying in a homeless shelter behind a railway station. A vagrant on the next bed recalled that Hitler's "clothes were being cleaned of lice, since for days he had been wandering about without a roof and in a terribly neglected condition." The vagrant added that Hitler lived on various shelters' bread and soup and "discussed politics." With a small loan from an aunt, he got himself into better quarters, a men's home, and managed to find odd jobs, such as painting picture postcards and drafting advertisements. He also frequented the city's public libraries, where he read political tracts, newspapers, the philosopher Schopenhauer, and the fiction of Karl May set in the cowboys-and-Indians days of the American West or the exotic Near East. Hitler dodged the Austrian draft and the police. When they finally caught up with him, they judged the undernourished and gloomy youth to be unfit for service. He fled across the border to Munich, and in August 1914 he joined the German army as a private. He ended the Great War still a private, but its aftermath transformed his life prospects. He would be among the many who migrated from left to right in the chaotic wake of imperial Germany's defeat.

During the November 1918 leftist revolution in Munich, Hitler was in a hospital in Pomerania, but he was released and marched in the funeral cortège of provincial Bavaria's murdered leader, a Jewish Social Democrat; film footage captured Hitler wearing two armbands, one black (for mourning) and the other red. After Social Democrats and anarchists, in April 1919, formed a Bavarian Soviet Republic, the Communists quickly seized power; Hitler, who contemplated joining the Social Democrats, served as a delegate from his battalion's soviet (council). He had no profession to speak of, but appears to have taken part in leftist indoctrination of the troops. Ten days before Hitler's thirtieth birthday, the Bavarian Soviet was quickly crushed by the so-called Freikorps of war veterans. He remained in the military because a superior, the chief of the German army's "information" department, had the idea of sending him to an antileftist instructional course, then using him to infiltrate leftist groups. The officer recalled that Hitler "was like a tired stray dog looking for a master," and "ready to throw in his lot with anyone who would show him kindness." Be that as it may, the assignment as informant led to Hitler's involvement in a minuscule right-wing group, the German Workers' Party, which had been established to draw workers away from Communism and which Hitler, with the assistance of rabidly anti-Semitic émigrés from the former imperial Russia, would remake into the National Socialist German Workers' Party, or Nazis.

Now a transfixing far-right agitator, Hitler remained a marginal figure. When Stalin was the new general secretary of the Communist party of the largest state in the world, Hitler was in prison for a failed attempt, in 1923 in Munich, his adopted hometown, to seize power locally, which would be derided as the Beer Hall Putsch. To be sure, he had managed to turn his trial into a triumph. (One of the judges remarked, "What a tremendous chap, this Hitler!") Indeed, even though Hitler was an Austrian citizen and convicted, the presiding judge had refrained from having him deported, reasoning that the law "cannot apply to a man who thinks and feels as German as Hitler, who voluntarily served for four and a half years in the German army at war, who attained high military honors through outstanding bravery in the face of the enemy, was wounded." During his first two weeks in prison, Hitler refused to eat, believing he deserved to die, but letters arrived congratulating him as a national hero. Richard Wagner's daughter-in-law Winifred sent paper and pencil, encouraging him to write a book. Hitler had an attendant in confinement, Rudolf Hess, who typed his dictation, creating an autobiography dedicated to the sixteen Nazis killed in the failed putsch. In *Mein Kampf*, Hitler portrayed himself as a man of destiny and pledged to revive Germany as a great power and rid it of Jews, anointing himself "the destroyer of Marxism." In December 1924, after serving thirteen months of a five-year sentence, he was released, but his book sales disappointed, a second book failed to find a publisher, and his Nazi party proved ineffectual at the ballot box. Lord d'Abernon, the British ambassador to Berlin at the time, summarized Hitler's political life after his early release from prison as "thereafter fading into oblivion."

History is full of surprises. That this Austrian in a fringe political movement would become the dictator of Germany, and Stalin's principal nemesis, was scarcely imaginable. But Field Marshal Count Helmuth von Moltke the Elder (1800–91), chief of the Prussian and then German general staff for thirty-one years, had conceived of strategy as improvisation, a "system of expedients," an ability to turn unexpected developments created by others or by happenstance to one's advantage, and Hitler turned out to be just such a master improviser: often uncertain, a perpetrator of mistakes and a beneficiary of luck, but a man possessed of radical ideas who sensed where he was ultimately going and grasped opportunities that came his way. Stalin, too, was a strategist in von Moltke's sense, a man of radical ideas able to perceive and seize opportunities that he did not always create but turned to his advantage. The richest opportunities perceived by Stalin and Hitler were often supposedly urgent "threats" they inflated or invented. If history is driven by geopolitics, institutions, and ideas, especially that triad's interaction, it takes historical agents to set it all in motion.

No country had seemed capable of surpassing Great Britain, whose overseas empire would soon encompass a quarter of the globe, and whose power obsessed both Stalin and Hitler as the prime mover of the entire world. But Stalin had also grown up in an epoch when Germany had begun to stand out for having the best manufacturing processes and engineering schools. His direct experience of Germany consisted of just a few months in 1907 in Berlin, where he stopped on the way back to Russia from a Bolshevik meeting in London. He studied but never mastered the German language. But like several tsarist predecessors, especially Sergei Witte, Stalin was a Germanophile, admiring that country's industry and science—in a word, its modernity. For the longest time, though, Stalin had no idea of Hitler's existence.

Tsarist Russia had aimed in the Great War to destroy forever the threat of German power by breaking up the Hohenzollern and Habsburg realms and establishing a belt of Slavic states that would presumably be friendly to Russia. German and Austrian war aims, conversely, had sought to diminish a perceived Russian menace by stripping it of its western borderlands. If Russia had won the war, it would likely have enacted something like the German-imposed Brest-Litovsk Treaty in reverse. But Russia lost (on the eastern front), just as Germany and Austria-Hungary lost (on the western front), leading to the Versailles Peace. Contrary to received wisdom, Europe's postwar security system did not disintegrate because of spinelessness or blundering. Only the dual collapse of Russian and German power had made possible Versailles, which could have succeeded only if German and Russian power never rose again. (Britain effectively recognized the instability of Versailles, for, having failed to reach a modus vivendi with German power before the Great War clash, would spend the entire postwar period pursuing an accommodation.) The two Versailles pariahs, Germany and the Soviet Union, entered into clandestine military cooperation. Then, in 1933, as we shall see, Hitler was handed the wheel of the great state Stalin admired. The lives of the two dictators, as the biographer Alan Bullock wrote, had run in parallel. But it was the intersection that would matter: two very different men from the peripheries of Russian power and of German power, respectively, who were bloodily reviving and remaking their countries, while unknowingly and then knowingly drawing ever closer. It was not only the German people who turned out to be waiting for Hitler.

A BRIEF NOTE ON SOURCES

This is a book about authoritarian rule, coercion, manipulation of social divisions and invention of enemies, institutionalized prevarication, but it is based on research into facts. Stalin left an immense historical record. His surviving personal archive ("fond" or collection 558) exists in two parts, now brought together. The first ten sections (identified in Russian by "opis" or finding aid) consist of materials systematized from his own and other archives in connection with a biography planned for his sixtieth birthday in 1939 by the Marx-Engels-Lenin Institute (now called RGASPI). These include his personal photo albums, correspondence, and reminiscences about him. Books from his personal library (opis 4) would be added after his death. The more valuable second part consists of one vast section (opis 11), which was his working personal archive, located in the "special sector" of the apparatus, later called the Politburo (now the Presidential) Archive, but transferred to RGASPI in 1998–99. Stalin decided what would go into this working archive, but these materials do not always show him in the best light; on the contrary, many documents he kept demonstrate his policy mistakes and his gratuitous cruelty to his opponents and loyalists (who, despite their own crimes, sometimes emerge worthy of sympathy). Some of Stalin's personal archive—how much remains impossible to say—was destroyed by him and others. For example, he was known to make notes in two sets of notebooks, one black (for technology) and one red (for personnel), but none of these have turned up, save for a few pages. Files of compromising materials on the members of his inner circle, believed to have been in his Kremlin office safe or a cupboard at his Near Dacha, have not turned up. The invaluable logbooks for visitors to his two offices (Old Square and the Kremlin) have been published, but the ones for his Moscow dacha have not and are feared to have been lost or pulped. His enormous record collection vanished, and the bulk of his library was dispersed. Nonetheless, the amount of materials that has survived and become accessible is staggering.

Not only do we have Stalin's personal archive, but also colossal party and state archives, in the capital and in regions, while for foreign affairs there are the archives of other governments, too. Even though in Stalin's case we lack a *Mein Kampf,* recorded "table talks," or bona fide accounts by mistresses, we do have his voluminous correspondence while on holiday in Sochi or Gagra, when he issued detailed instructions to those running affairs on his behalf back in the capital. In addition, many other minions recorded his instructions—the boss of the film industry, the head of the Comintern, the notetaker for the government—in real time. Subsequent memoirs, some of which are revealing, enhance and sometimes unlock the archival materials. Regime transcripts for instructional dissemination were made of all party congresses, most of Stalin's extended remarks at Kremlin receptions, and a handful of key politburo and Central Committee meetings. The central press, which he tightly controlled, also affords excellent material on his thinking. Archives of the secret police, counterintelligence, and bodyguard directorate remain almost entirely closed, and those for the military and foreign policy arm can be very difficult to access, but these institutions have published enormous quantities of document collections, and those scholars who have enjoyed unusually good access, including to the secret police materials, have published monographs with extensive quotations. There is also the phenomenon of scanning, which permits the quiet sharing of documents. So the evidentiary record, while not complete, is astonishingly rich.

Many scholars have been working on these materials, and this volume is indebted to the excellent research produced by R. W. Davies on the economy, Oleg Khlevniuk on the party-state machinery, Vladimir Khaustov on the secret police, Matthew Lenoe on events surrounding Sergei Kirov, Vladimir Nevezhin on the conception of the Soviet state as a great power, Adam Tooze on Nazi Germany's grand strategy, Gabriel Gorodetsky on the British establishment and on Stalin's foreign policy, and countless others, acknowledged in the endnotes.

Words cannot express how much better this book became thanks to my U.S.-based editor, Scott Moyers, and the rest of the team at Penguin. It exists at all thanks to him and my agent, Andrew Wylie. Many others—alas, far too numerous to list—deserve to be singled out for their kindness and perspicacity. Let me here express my gratitude to all, particularly archivists, librarians, and fellow scholars in Russia. Oleg Budnitskii took me on as an associate senior researcher at his International Center for the History and Sociology of World War II and Its Consequences at the National Research University Higher School of Economics, in Moscow. I have also benefited tremendously from being a fellow at the Hoover Institution at Stanford University, whose Library and Archives are a treasure beyond belief, and I am deeply grateful to the L&A director, Eric Wakin. Above all, Princeton University has provided me a dream scholarly home and spectacular students for the better part of three decades.

STALIN

THE IMPERIAL SENATE (MOSCOW KREMLIN)

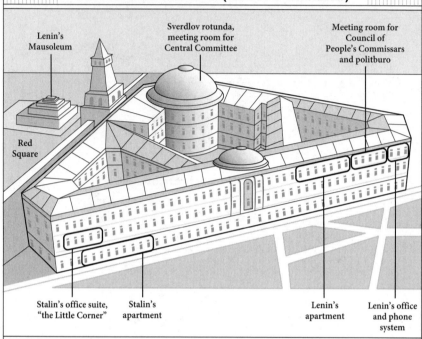

Lenin's Mausoleum

Sverdlov rotunda, meeting room for Central Committee

Meeting room for Council of People's Commissars and politburo

Red Square

Stalin's office suite, "the Little Corner"

Stalin's apartment

Lenin's apartment

Lenin's office and phone system

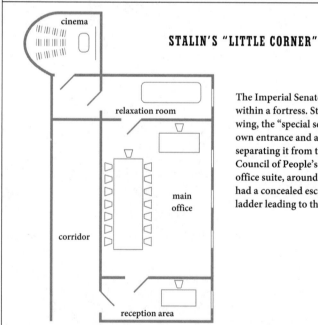

cinema

STALIN'S "LITTLE CORNER"

relaxation room

main office

corridor

reception area

The Imperial Senate was a fortress within a fortress. Stalin's expansive wing, the "special sector," had its own entrance and a special door separating it from the offices of the Council of People's Commissars. His office suite, around 1600 square feet, had a concealed escape shaft with a ladder leading to the basement.

© 2017 Jeffrey L. Ward

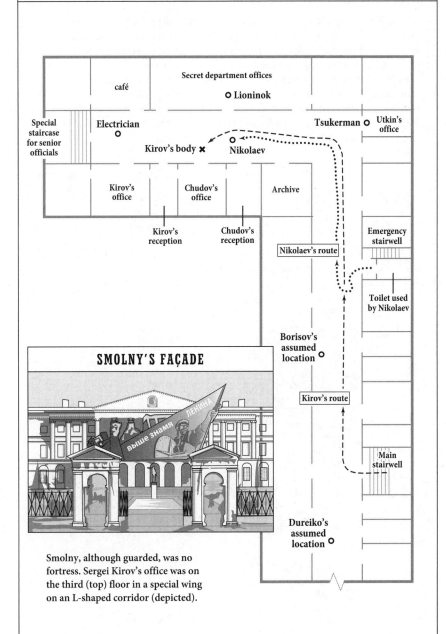

SMOLNY (LENINGRAD)

café

Secret department offices

O Lioninok

Special staircase for senior officials

Electrician O

Tsukerman O

Utkin's office

Kirov's body ✖ Nikolaev O

Kirov's office

Chudov's office

Archive

Kirov's reception

Chudov's reception

Nikolaev's route

Emergency stairwell

Toilet used by Nikolaev

Borisov's assumed location O

Kirov's route

SMOLNY'S FAÇADE

Main stairwell

Dureiko's assumed location O

Smolny, although guarded, was no fortress. Sergei Kirov's office was on the third (top) floor in a special wing on an L-shaped corridor (depicted).

Adapted from Alla Kirilina and Matthew Lenoe

This map offers a preliminary overview of the extent and severity of the famine. Soviet census and mortality/morbidity data can be uncertain because millions were on the move during this period. (The largest decline in population between the 1926 and 1937 censuses occurred in Saratov province, but this was not the place where the famine proved most severe.) Little information is available for some regions (Chuvash autonomous province, Northern province, Eastern Siberia). The famine did not begin and end at the same time in all places. The map offers estimated degrees of certainty based on what has been substantiated to date. *(Courtesy of Mark Tauger)*

Baltic Sea

SOVIET UKRAINE

ARKHANGELSK PROVINCE

CENTRAL BLACK EARTH

URALS

TATAR AUTONOMOUS REPUBLIC

Black Sea

RUSSIAN REPUBLIC

LOWER VOLGA MID-VOLGA

NORTH CAUCASUS

SOVIET GEORGIA

Caspian Sea

KAZAKH AUTONOMOUS REPUBLIC

0 Miles 1000
0 Kilometers 1000

CHINA

© 2017 Jeffrey L. Ward

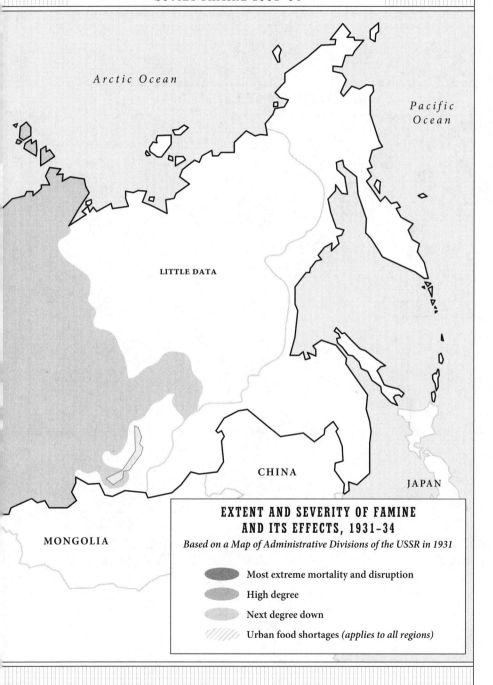

SOVIET FAMINE 1931–34

Arctic Ocean

Pacific Ocean

LITTLE DATA

CHINA

JAPAN

MONGOLIA

EXTENT AND SEVERITY OF FAMINE AND ITS EFFECTS, 1931–34

Based on a Map of Administrative Divisions of the USSR in 1931

Most extreme mortality and disruption

High degree

Next degree down

Urban food shortages *(applies to all regions)*

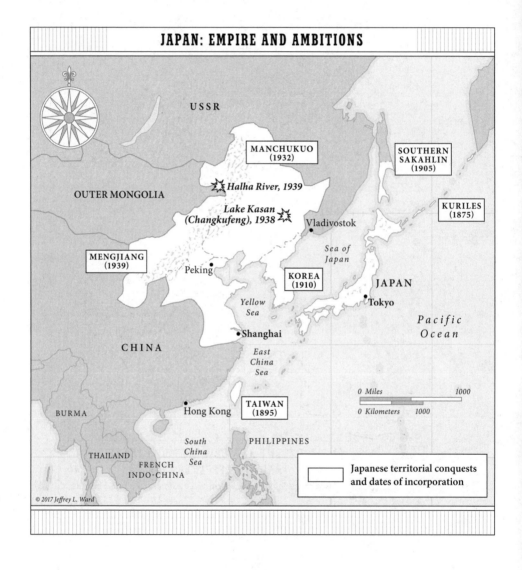

JAPAN: EMPIRE AND AMBITIONS

USSR

MANCHUKUO
(1932)

SOUTHERN
SAKAHLIN
(1905)

Halha River, 1939

OUTER MONGOLIA

Lake Kasan
(Changkufeng), 1938

KURILES
(1875)

Vladivostok

Sea of
Japan

MENGJIANG
(1939)

Peking

KOREA
(1910)

JAPAN

Tokyo

Yellow
Sea

Pacific
Ocean

Shanghai

CHINA

East
China
Sea

0 Miles   1000

0 Kilometers   1000

BURMA

Hong Kong

TAIWAN
(1895)

THAILAND

FRENCH
INDO-CHINA

South
China
Sea

PHILIPPINES

Japanese territorial conquests
and dates of incorporation

© 2017 Jeffrey L. Ward

CHINA: FOREIGN OCCUPATION AND CIVIL WAR

USSR

OUTER MONGOLIA
(Soviet puppet state)

MANCHURIA/
Manchukuo

CHINESE EASTERN
RAILROAD

Harbin

SOUTH MANCHURIAN
RAILROAD

Vladivostok

Mukden

Kuriles

XINJIANG
(de facto Soviet
protectorate)

*Marco Polo
Bridge (1937)*

Sea of
Japan

Yan'an (Shaanxi province)

JAPAN

Tokyo

*Route of
the Long March
(1934–35)*

Xi'an

Yellow
Sea

Nanking

Pacific
Ocean

CHINA

Wuhan

Shanghai

Chongqing

East
China
Sea

BURMA

Taiwan

Hong Kong

0 Miles   1000

0 Kilometers   1000

THAILAND

FRENCH
INDO-CHINA

South
China
Sea

PHILIPPINES

Areas occupied by the Japanese

© 2017 Jeffrey L. Ward

SPAIN: PUTSCH AND CIVIL WAR 1936–39

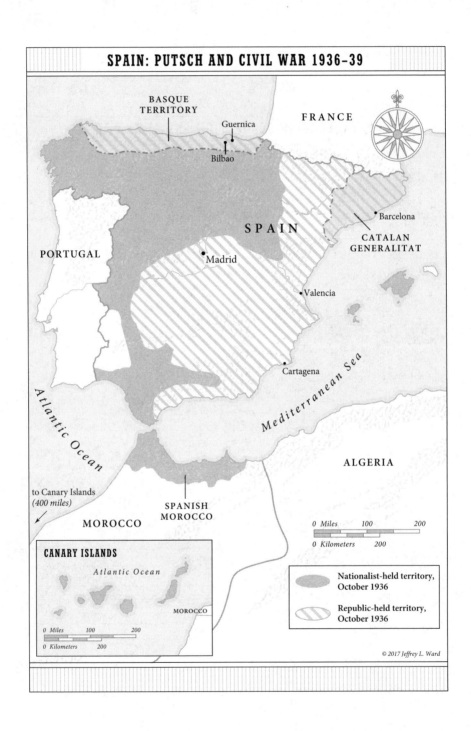

BASQUE
TERRITORY

Guernica

FRANCE

Bilbao

SPAIN

Barcelona

CATALAN
GENERALITAT

PORTUGAL

Madrid

Valencia

Cartagena

Mediterranean Sea

Atlantic Ocean

ALGERIA

to Canary Islands
(400 miles)

SPANISH
MOROCCO

MOROCCO

0 Miles   100   200

0 Kilometers   200

CANARY ISLANDS

Atlantic Ocean

MOROCCO

0 Miles   100   200

0 Kilometers   200

Nationalist-held territory,
October 1936

Republic-held territory,
October 1936

© 2017 Jeffrey L. Ward

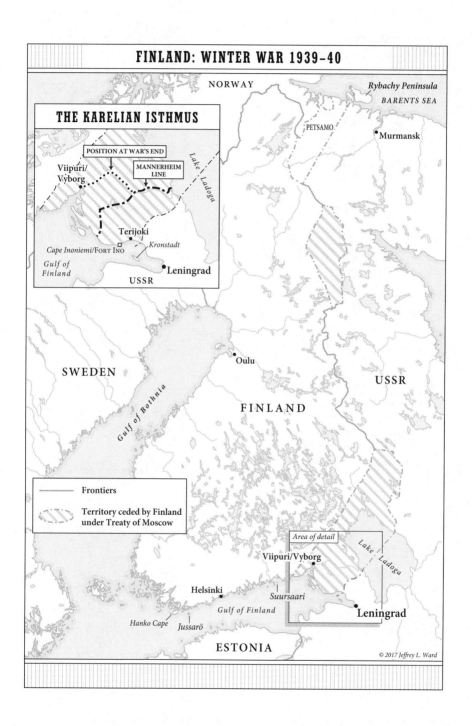

FINLAND: WINTER WAR 1939-40

NORWAY

Rybachy Peninsula

BARENTS SEA

PETSAMO

•Murmansk

THE KARELIAN ISTHMUS

POSITION AT WAR'S END

MANNERHEIM LINE

Viipuri/ Vyborg

Lake Ladoga

Terijoki

Kronstadt

Cape Inoniemi/FORT INO

Gulf of Finland

•Leningrad

USSR

•Oulu

SWEDEN

Gulf of Bothnia

FINLAND

USSR

Frontiers

Territory ceded by Finland under Treaty of Moscow

Area of detail

Lake Ladoga

Viipuri/Vyborg

Helsinki

Suursaari

Leningrad

Hanko Cape *Jussarö*

Gulf of Finland

ESTONIA

© 2017 Jeffrey L. Ward

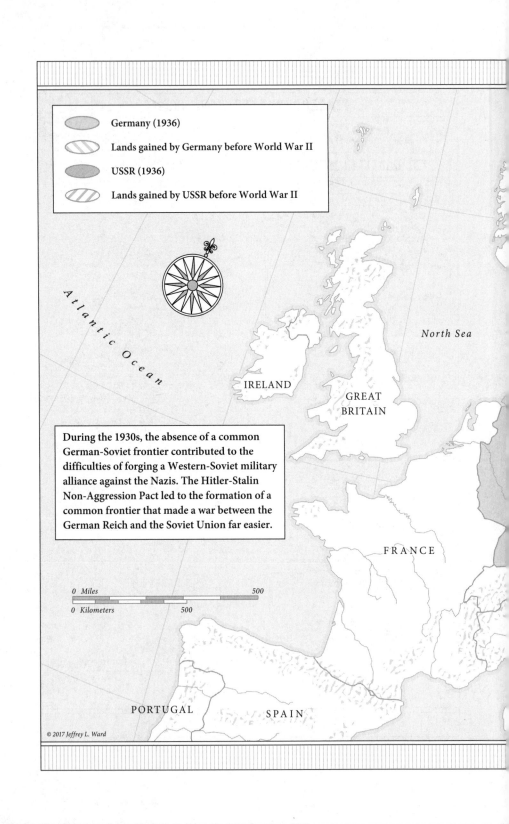

Germany (1936)

Lands gained by Germany before World War II

USSR (1936)

Lands gained by USSR before World War II

Atlantic Ocean

North Sea

IRELAND

GREAT
BRITAIN

During the 1930s, the absence of a common
German-Soviet frontier contributed to the
difficulties of forging a Western-Soviet military
alliance against the Nazis. The Hitler-Stalin
Non-Aggression Pact led to the formation of a
common frontier that made a war between the
German Reich and the Soviet Union far easier.

FRANCE

0 Miles   500

0 Kilometers   500

PORTUGAL   SPAIN

GREATER GERMAN REICH, EXPANDED SOVIET UNION

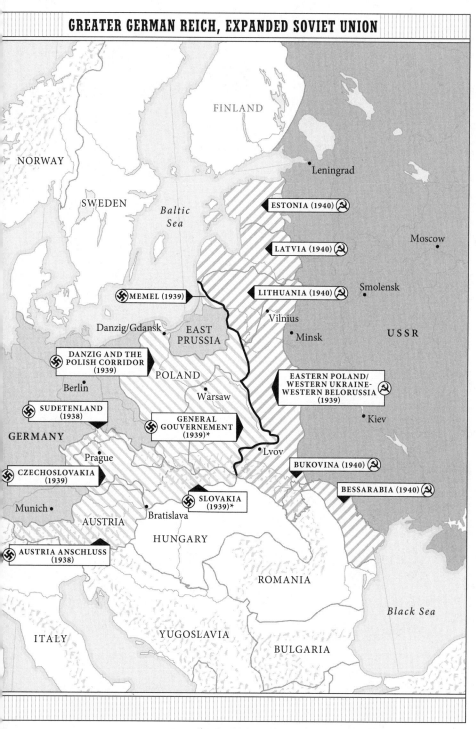

*Neither Slovakia nor the General Gouvernement was incorporated into the Reich.

EQUAL TO THE MYTH

Here he is, the greatest and most important of our contemporaries. . . . In his full size he towers over Europe and Asia, over the past and the present. He is the most famous and yet almost the least known man in the world.

HENRI BARBUSSE, Stalin, *1935*[1]

IOSIF STALIN WAS A HUMAN BEING. He collected watches.[2] He played skittles and billiards. He loved gardening and Russian steam baths.[3] He owned suits and ties but never wore them, unlike Lenin, and, unlike Bukharin, he did not fancy traditional peasant blouses or black leather jackets. He wore a semi-military tunic of either gray or khaki color, buttoned at the top, along with baggy khaki trousers that he tucked into his tall leather boots. He did not use a briefcase, but he sometimes carried documents inside folders or wrapped in newspapers.[4] He liked colored pencils—blue, red, green—manufactured by Moscow's Sacco and Vanzetti factory (originally built by the American Armand Hammer). He drank Borjomi mineral water and red Khvanchkara and white Tsinandali wines from his native Georgia. He smoked a pipe, using the tobacco from Herzegovina Flor brand cigarettes, which he would unroll and slide in, usually two cigarettes' worth. He kept his desk in order. His dachas had runners atop the carpets, and he strove to keep to the narrow coverings. "I remember, once he spilled a few ashes from his pipe on the carpet," recalled Artyom Sergeyev, who for a time lived in the Stalin household after his own father's death, "and he himself, with a brush and knife, gathered them up."[5]

Stalin had a passion for books, which he marked up and filled with placeholders to find passages. (His personal library would ultimately grow to more than

20,000 volumes.) He annotated works by Marx and Lenin, but also Plato and the German strategist Clausewitz in translation, as well as Alexander Svechin, a former tsarist officer whom Stalin never trusted but who demonstrated that the only constant in war was an absence of constants.[6] "Stalin read a great deal," noted Artyom. "And always, when we saw him, he would ask what I was reading and what I thought about it. At the entrance to his study, I recall, there was a mountain of books on the floor." Stalin recommended the classics—Gogol, Tolstoy—telling Artyom and Vasily that "during wartime there would be a lot of situations you had never encountered before in life. You will need to make decisions. But if you read a lot, then in your memory you will already have the answers how to conduct yourself and what to do. Literature will tell you."[7] Among Russian authors, Stalin's favorite was probably Chekhov, who, he felt, portrayed villains, not just heroes, in the round. Still, judging by the references scattered among his writings and speeches, he spent more time reading Soviet-era belles lettres.[8] His jottings in whatever he read were often irreverent: "Rubbish," "Fool," "Scumbag," "Piss off," "Ha-ha!"

His manners were coarse. When, on April 5, 1930, a top official in the economy drew a black-ink caricature of finance commissar Nikolai Bryukhanov hanging by his scrotum, Stalin wrote on it, "To members of the politburo: For all his current and future sins Bryukhanov is to be hung by the balls; if his balls hold, he is to be considered acquitted by the court; if his balls do not hold, he is to be drowned in the river."[9] But Stalin cultivated a statesmanlike appearance, editing out his jokes and foul language even from the transcripts of official gatherings that were meant to be circulated only internally.[10] He occasionally jabbed the air with his index finger for emphasis during speeches, but he usually avoided histrionics. "All Stalin's gestures were measured," Artyom recalled. "He never gesticulated severely." Artyom also found his adoptive father reserved in his compliments. "Stalin never used expressions of the highest degree: marvelous [*chudesno*], elegant [*shikarno*]. He said 'fine' [*khorosho*]. He never went higher than 'fine.' He could also say 'suitable' [*goditsia*]. 'Fine' was the highest compliment from his mouth."[11]

Stalin invoked God casually ("God forbid," "Lord forgive us") and referred to the Pharisees and other biblical subjects.[12] In his hometown of Gori, he had lived across from the cathedral, attended the parish school, sung beatifically in the choir, and set his sights on becoming a priest or a monk, earning entrance to the Tiflis seminary, where he prayed nine to ten times per day and completed the full course of study except for sitting his last year's final exams. By then he had become immersed in banned literature, beginning with Victor Hugo, evolving toward

Karl Marx, and had come to detest organized religion and abandoned his piety.[13] Rumors that Stalin attended church services in the 1930s have never been substantiated.[14] In Stalin's marginalia in works by Dostoevsky and Anatole France, he continued to be drawn to issues of God, the church, religion, and immortality, but the depth and nature of that interest remain difficult to fathom.[15] Be that as it may, he had long ago ceased to adhere to Christian notions of good and evil.[16] His moral universe was that of Marxism-Leninism.

He appears to have had few mistresses, and definitely no harem. His family life was neither particularly happy nor unhappy. His father, Beso, had died relatively young, not uncommon in the early twentieth century; his mother, Keke, lived alone in Tiflis. His first wife, Ketevan "Kato" Svanidze, a Georgian to whom he was married in 1906, had died in agony the next year of a common disease in Baku. He married again, to Nadezhda Alliluyeva, a Russian better known as Nadya, who had been born in Tiflis in 1901 and lived in Baku, too. Stalin had known her since she was a toddler. They had married in 1918, when he was officially thirty-nine (actually forty). She worked as his secretary, then as one of Lenin's secretaries, but she had higher ambitions. The couple had two healthy children, Vasily (b. 1921) and Svetlana (b. 1926). He also had a son from his first marriage, Yakov (b. 1907), whom he had abandoned to relatives in Georgia for the first fourteen years of the boy's life. Stalin avoided contact with his many blood relatives from his father's and mother's families. He did live among in-laws—Kato's and Nadya's many brothers and sisters and their spouses—but his interest in them would wane. Personal life was subsumed in politics.

STALIN WAS A COMMUNIST and a revolutionary. He was no Danton, the French firebrand who could mount a rostrum and ignite a crowd (until he was guillotined in 1794). Stalin spoke softly, sometimes inaudibly, because of a defect in his vocal cords. Nor was he the dashing type, like his contemporary the Italian aviator Italo Balbo (b. 1896), a Blackshirt *squadrista* who, a jaunty cigarette dangling from his lips, lived the fascist ideal of the "new man," leading armadas of planes in formation across the Mediterranean and then the Atlantic, attaining international renown (until he died in a crash caused by his own country's antiaircraft guns).[17] Stalin turned white during air travel and avoided it. He relished being called Koba, after the Georgian folk-hero avenger and the real-life benefactor who underwrote his education, but one childhood chum had called him Geza, a Gori-dialect term for the awkward gait Stalin had developed after an accident.

He had to swing his hip all the way around to walk.[18] This and other physical defects apparently weighed on him. Once, near his beloved medicinal baths at Matsesta, in the Caucasus, according to a bodyguard, Stalin encountered a boy of about six, "reached out his hand and asked, 'What's your name?' 'Valka,' the boy answered firmly. 'Well, my name is Smallpox-Pockmarks,' Stalin said to him. 'Now we are introduced.'"[19]

Like the twisted spine of Shakespeare's Richard III, it is tempting to find in such deformities the wellsprings of bloody tyranny: torment, self-loathing, inner rage, bluster, a mania for adulation. The boy at Matsesta was around the age Stalin had been when he had contracted the disease whose lifelong scars he bore on his nose, lower lip, chin, and cheeks. His pockmarks were airbrushed from public photographs, and his awkward stride kept from public view. (Film of him walking was prohibited.) People who met him saw the facial disfigurement and odd movement, as well as signs that he might be insecure. He loved jokes and caricatures, but never about himself. (Of course, the supposedly ultraconfident Lenin had refused to allow even friendly caricatures of himself to be printed.)[20] Stalin's sense of humor was perverse. Those who encountered him further discovered that he had a limp handshake and was not as tall as he appeared in photographs. (He stood five feet seven inches, or about 1.7 meters, roughly the same as Napoleon and one inch shorter than Hitler, who was 1.73 meters.)[21] And yet, despite their initial shock—could *this* be Stalin?—most first-time onlookers usually found that they could not take their gaze off him, especially his expressive eyes.[22] More than that, they witnessed him shouldering an immense load, under colossal pressure. Stalin possessed the skills and steeliness to rule a great country, unlike Shakespeare's Richard III. He radiated charisma, the charisma of dictatorial power.

Dictatorship, in the wake of the Great War, was widely understood to offer a transcendence of the mundane, a "state of exception," in the words of the future Nazi theorist Carl Schmitt.[23] For Soviet theorists, too, dictatorship promised political dynamism and the redemption of humanity. In April 1929, Vladimir Maksimovsky (b. 1887), who had known and once opposed Lenin (over the Treaty of Brest-Litovsk with imperial Germany) and had supported Trotsky's right to be heard, delivered a lecture on Niccolò Machiavelli that he published the same year in the USSR's main Marxist history journal. Maksimovsky turned the Renaissance Florentine into a theorist of "revolutionary bourgeois dictatorship," which the author deemed progressive in its day, in contrast to the reactionary dictatorship of Mussolini. The assessment rested on the class base. Thus, the working-class Soviet dictatorship was progressive, too. Maksimovsky, following Machiavelli, conceded that dictatorship could descend into tyranny, with a ruler pursuing purely personal interests.[24] But Maksimovsky did not explicitly address the question of a given dictator's personality, or how the process of exercising unlimited power affects a ruler's character. Subsequent scholars have rightly noted that only a near-permanent state of emergency—made possible by Communist ideology and practice—allowed Stalin to give free rein to his savagery. But what has been missed is that Stalin's sociopathology was to a degree an outgrowth of the experience of dictatorial rule.

Stalin's childhood, diseases and all, had been more or less normal; his years as general secretary were anything but.[25] He emerged from the 1920s a ruler of seemingly irreconcilable contradictions. He could flash burning anger, visible in yellowish eyes; he could glow with a soft, capacious smile. He could be utterly solicitous and charming; he could be unable to forget a perceived slight and compulsively contrive opportunities for revenge. He was single-minded and brooding, soft-spoken and foul-mouthed. He prided himself on his voracious reading and his ability to quote the wisdom of Marx or Lenin; he resented fancy-pants intellectuals who he thought put on airs. He possessed a phenomenal memory and a mind of scope; his intellectual horizons were severely circumscribed by primitive theories of class struggle and imperialism. He developed a feel for the aspirations of the masses and incipient elites; he almost never visited factories or farms, or even state agencies, reading about the country he ruled in secret reports and newspapers. He was a cynic about everyone's supposed base motives; he lived and breathed ideals. Above all, his core identity was as heir and leading pupil of Lenin, but Lenin's purported Testament had called for his removal, and from the time it first appeared, in the spring and summer of 1923, the document haunted him, provoking at least six resignations, all of which had been rejected but left him embattled, resentful, vengeful.

Stalin's painstaking creation of a personal dictatorship within the Leninist dictatorship had combined chance (the unexpected early death of Lenin) and aptitude: he had been the fifth secretary of the party, after Yakov Sverdlov (who also died prematurely), Yelena Stasova, Nikolai Krestinsky, and Vyacheslav Molotov. His self-fashioning as savior of cause and country who was menaced from every direction dovetailed with fears for the socialist revolution and Russia's revival as a great power menaced from every direction. Lenin's party, with its seizure of power in the former Russian empire, had enacted upon itself a condition of "capitalist encirclement," a structural paranoia that fed, and was fed by, Stalin's personal paranoia. But those feelings on his part, whatever their now untraceable origins, had ballooned in his accumulation and enactment of the power of life and death over hundreds of millions. Such were the paradoxes of power: the closer the country got to achieving socialism, the sharper the class struggle became; the more power Stalin personally wielded, the more he still needed. Triumph shadowed by treachery became the dynamic of both the revolution and Stalin's life. Beginning in 1929, as the might of the Soviet state and Stalin's personal dictatorship grew and grew, so, too, did the stakes. His drive to build socialism would prove both successful and shattering, and deeply reinforcing of his hypersuspicious, vindictive disposition.[26] "Power tends to corrupt, and absolute power corrupts absolutely," an English Catholic historian wrote in a private letter in reference to the Inquisition and the papacy.[27] Absolute power also shapes absolutely.

Communism was an idea, a dream palace whose attraction derived from its seeming fusion of science and utopia. In the Marxist conception, capitalism had created great wealth by replacing feudalism, but then it became a "fetter" that promoted only the interests of the exploiter class, at the expense of the rest of humanity. But once capitalism was overcome, the "forces of production" would be unleashed as never before. What is more, exploitation, colonies, and imperialist war would give way to solidarity, emancipation, and peace, as well as abundance. Concretely, socialism had been difficult to imagine.[28] But whatever it was, it could not be capitalism. Logically, socialism would be built by eradicating private property, the market, and "bourgeois" parliaments and putting in their place collective property, socialist planning, and people's power (or soviets). Of course, the capitalists would never allow themselves to be buried. They would fight to the death against socialism, using every means—wrecking, espionage, lies—because this was a war in which only one class could emerge victorious. The most terrible crimes became morally imperative acts in the name of creating paradise on earth.[29]

MASS VIOLENCE RECRUITED legions ready to battle implacable enemies who stood on the wrong side of history.[30] The purported science of Marxism-Leninism and the real-world construction of socialism, on the way toward Communism, offered ostensible answers to the biggest questions: why the world had so many problems (class) and how it could be made better (class warfare), with a role for all. People's otherwise insignificant lives became linked to building an entirely new world.[31] To collect grain forcibly or operate a lathe was to strike a hammer blow at world imperialism. It did not hurt that those who took part stood to gain personally: idealism and opportunism are always reinforcing.[32] Accumulated resentments, too, fueled the aspiration to become significant. People under the age of twenty-nine made up nearly half of the Soviet population, giving the country one of the younger demographic profiles in the world, and youth proved especially attracted to a vision that put them at the center of a struggle to build tomorrow today, to serve a higher truth.[33] The use of capitalism as antiworld also helps explain why, despite the improvisation, the socialism that would be built under Stalin coalesced into a "system" that could be readily explained within the framework of the October Revolution.

Stalin personified Communism's lofty vision. A cult would be built around him, singling him out as "*vozhd,*" an ancient word that denoted someone who had earned the leadership of a group of men through a demonstrated ability to acquire and dispense rewards, but had become tantamount to "supreme leader," the Russian equivalent of *duce* or *Führer.*[34] By acclaiming Stalin, people could acclaim the cause and themselves as devotees. He resisted the cult.[35] Stalin would call himself shit compared with Lenin.[36] In draft reportage for *Pravda* of his meeting with a collective farm delegation from Odessa province in November 1933, he inserted the names Mikhail Kalinin, Molotov, Lazar Kaganovich, simulating collective leadership.[37] Similarly, according to Anastas Mikoyan, Stalin rebuked Kaganovich, saying, "What is this? Why do you praise me alone, as if one man decides everything?"[38] Whether Stalin's objections reflected false modesty, genuine embarrassment, or just his inscrutable self remains hard to say, but he indulged the prolonged ovations.[39] Molotov would recall that "at first he resisted the cult of personality, but then he came to like it a bit."[40]

STALIN ALSO PERSONIFIED the multinational Union. The USSR, like imperial Russia, was a uniquely Eurasian sprawl across two continents, at home in neither. Stalin was skeptical that nationality would eventually wither, unlike many leftists who worshipped class.[41] Nation, for him, was both stubborn fact and opportunity, a device for overcoming perceived backwardness.[42] Implanting loyal party rule in, say, Ukraine or his native Georgia would preoccupy him, but not nearly as much as the history and geopolitics of Russia.[43] Russia had come to see itself as a providential power ordained by God, with a special mission in the world. Its court splendor surpassed any other monarchy, but for all its industrialization it had remained an agrarian empire resting on the backs of peasants. Resources never stretched as far as ambitions, a discrepancy compounded by the circumstance that Russia lacked natural boundaries. This had spurred conquest of neighboring lands, before they could be used as presumed springboards of invasion, thereby creating a dynamic of "defensive" expansionism. Such was the Russia that the Georgian inherited and wholly devoted himself to as the socialist motherland.

A human being, a Communist and revolutionary, a dictator encircled by enemies in a dictatorship encircled by enemies, a fearsome contriver of class warfare, an embodiment of the global Communist cause and the Eurasian multinational state, a ferocious champion of Russia's revival, Stalin did what acclaimed leaders do: he articulated and drove toward a consistent goal, in his case a powerful state backed by a unified society that eradicated capitalism and built industrial socialism.[44] "Murderous" and "mendacious" do not begin to describe the person readers will encounter in this volume. At the same time, Stalin galvanized millions. His colossal authority was rooted in a dedicated faction, which he forged, a formidable apparatus, which he built, and Marxist-Leninist ideology, which he helped synthesize. But his power was magnified many times over by ordinary people, who projected onto him their soaring ambitions for justice, peace, and abundance, as well as national greatness. Dictators who amass great power often retreat into pet pursuits, expounding interminably about their obsessions, paralyzing the state. But Stalin's fixation was a socialist great power. In the years 1929–36, covered in part III, he would build that socialist great power with a first-class military. Stalin was a myth, but he proved equal to the myth.

CHAPTER 1

TRIUMPH OF THE WILL

> We reject the concept of rule-of-law state. If a person
> seeking to claim the title of Marxist speaks seriously about
> a rule-of-law state and moreover uses the term
> "rule-of-law state" in connection with the *Soviet* state, this
> means he is led by bourgeois jurists. This means he
> departs from Marxist-Leninist teaching on the state.
>
> LAZAR KAGANOVICH, *Institute of Soviet
> Construction, November 4, 1929*[1]

> There, in Europe, let them meow, in full voice . . . about the
> USSR's "collapse." They will not alter one iota either our
> plans or our cause. The USSR will be a first-class country
> with the largest, technologically best-equipped industrial
> and agricultural production. Socialism is invincible. No
> longer will we have "*miserable*" Russia. An end to that!
> We'll have a powerful and prosperous *modern* Russia.
>
> *Stalin to Maxim Gorky, in Sorrento, December 1930*[2]

MAURICE HINDUS, an émigré who returned to his native village in southern
Ukraine to bear witness, grasped that Stalin's forced wholesale collectivization
and breakneck industrialization were "a stupendous gamble."[3] Twelve years earlier, a separate peasant revolution, parallel to the urban Bolshevik one, had expropriated most of Russia's gentry, as well as many peasant landholders, and
resulted in the creation of a smallholding population of 25 million peasant
households. Undoing this new socioeconomic landscape of de facto land ownership seemed a nearly unimaginable proposition. Lenin's quasimarket New Economic Policy had been a grudging concession to this peasant revolution, and
although the mass of Communists had little love for farmers, as the NEP's benefits were available to be appropriated, many Communists in the countryside had
come to accept peacefully growing into socialism. Ironically, this vision was
never stronger than at the height of central party actions—price regulation,

creeping statization, industrialization ambitions—that fatally undermined NEP's already faltering viability. Stalin repudiated pro-NEP Communists in the same way he lacerated European Social Democrats and their so-called parliamentary road to socialism. "Can we imagine that?" he wrote in the margins of an essay by Engels, republished in 1930, on the peaceful attainment of socialism in France and the United States. "No, that is incorrect!"[4]

Stalin insisted that small farms had to be consolidated to enable the mechanization and application of agronomy needed to achieve higher levels of output. All that was possible without collectivization, of course—it had happened in the United States, as Stalin himself pointed out, but there it had entailed large-scale, mechanized *private* farms, and for Marxist-Leninists, class and property relations ultimately determined political systems. Some politburo members did think or hope they could collectivize agriculture voluntarily, but as of 1928, voluntary collectivization had occurred on just 1 percent of the country's arable land. Coercion was the only way to attain wholesale collectivization. The extreme violence and dislocation would appall many Communists. But Stalin and his loyalists replied that critics wanted to make an omelet without breaking eggs. The only real alternative to forced collectivization was Communist acceptance of capitalist social relations and the long-term political consequences that entailed. Either the peasant revolution would be overcome or the regime would be under permanent threat. To these weighty considerations was added a do-or-die imperative to industrialize, which had to be financed somehow. Getting more grain, including for export, by squeezing the peasants seemed to be the answer and was dubbed primitive socialist accumulation. Russia had experienced centuries of cruelty toward peasants, but the inhumanity was now given supposed scientific and moral authority.[5]

Stalin was not head of the government (the Council of People's Commissars). He was general secretary of the Communist party, which controlled all regime communications, personnel appointments, the secret police, and the army, and supervised the government. (For elucidation of the workings of the Soviet party-state system, see the explanatory note on page 907.) From his office (Room 521) at party headquarters on Moscow's Old Square, he propelled the building of socialism in a furious storm of mass mobilization.[6] His actions in 1929–30 were improvised, but they sprang from deep Marxist premises.[7] Stalin, like Lenin, accepted the historical obsolescence of the "petit bourgeois" peasantry, the irredeemability of capitalism, the vileness of class enemies, the inevitability of violence in revolution, and the value of tactical flexibility amid firmness of will. He was Leninist to the core.[8] Stalin sharpened the sense of urgency to force-build socialism by banging on about the dangers of "capitalist encirclement." Millions of urbanites and some of the rural populace became entranced by the combination of real class warfare and modern machines. The mass appeal of taking part in the creation of a new and better world recruited a new generation of party activists, and captured imaginations worldwide.

The savage upheaval of building socialism would also further reveal, and further shape, the darkness within Stalin's mind. "Right deviationists," "social fascists," "liquidation of the kulaks," "wreckers," "right-left bloc," "terrorist acts," "military coup plots," "Trotskyites"—all these tropes, rooted in the Bolshevik repertoire, now took on an even more sinister edge. Stalin emerges in the documents as self-assured yet on a knife's edge, a supreme bully with a keen eye for others' weak spots yet roiling with resentment. Even his moments of satisfaction come across as laced with venom. No matter how much he crushed rivals, *he* was under siege. No matter how many enemies were deported, imprisoned, or executed, new ones emerged—and they were coming after *him*. No matter how much power he accumulated, *he* needed more. All the while, regime violence seemed to beget the very foes within and threat of war from without that secret police reports incessantly warned about. Stalin's chip-on-the-shoulder, suspect-the-worst persona fed into, and was fed by, the drive to build socialism in the overheated atmosphere he fostered. The revolution's destiny and Stalin's personality became increasingly difficult to distinguish.

THE VICTIM

For a man possessed by raison d'état, Stalin's actions were often highly personal. Nikolai Bukharin, unlike Trotsky, was close to the Soviet dictator. The two had met in Vienna in 1913, and from the mid-1920s Stalin had shown genuine affection for him. Alexei Balashov, who as a young man worked loyally in Stalin's inner secretariat, would recall, late in life, that "when they brought him the forms with the results of politburo member voting by telephone poll, frequently, without looking up from the document, Stalin would ask, 'How did Bukharin vote?— *For?*' Stalin, for a time, held Bukharin's views in high regard, and they informed the positions he himself would take."[9] Also unlike Trotsky, Bukharin had been careful not to come out in open opposition to Stalin. But in 1929, while forcing through his radical shift to coercive wholesale collectivization, Stalin charged

Bukharin and his allies with "deviation" from the party line. Thus did the dictator fashion for himself and the regime a new high-profile internal foe.[10]

Bukharin, who had been instrumental in enabling Stalin to smash Trotsky, inadvertently facilitated his own demonization by Stalin. The stepped-up attacks were set in motion by the sudden appearance of a pamphlet published by a shadowy Trotskyite underground on January 23, 1929, which carried Lev Kamenev's "notes," nominally for Zinoviev, of a clandestine meeting Bukharin had initiated with Kamenev back on July 11, 1928.[11] Bukharin was caught out: he had met on the sly with a former oppositionist and divulged to him internal party matters while privately voicing the opposite position to the July 1928 plenum resolutions that he himself had drafted. The incident went to the party's Central Control Commission, chaired by the Stalin loyalist Sergo Orjonikidze, who generally disliked Stalin's political vendettas and, till now, had tried to reconcile Bukharin and his patron. But Kamenev's "notes" had Bukharin asserting that Orjonikidze had bad-mouthed Stalin behind his back. Kamenev, for his part, submitted written testimony, which, like the "notes" themselves, proved damning of Bukharin, a further act of ingratiation with Stalin. Bukharin belatedly surmised that he had fallen into a trap, while Stalin gave the appearance of being pained to have to take action. ("Sad as it is, I must report the fact of . . .") At the first of two joint sessions of the politburo with the presidium of the Central Control Commission, on January 30, 1929, Stalin condemned Bukharin, as well as his associates Mikhail Tomsky and Alexei Rykov, as "a right deviationist, capitulationist group advocating not for the liquidation of capitalist elements of the city and countryside, but for their free development."[12]

Thus did opposition to *forced* collectivization and *coercive* grain collection become advocacy for capitalism. Bukharin, Rykov, and Tomsky wrote an appeal invoking Lenin's Testament—"since these words were written, this 'unbounded power' has become even more 'unbounded'"—but on February 9, 1929, with Orjonikidze in charge, the party censured Bukharin, for having met Kamenev, and Rykov and Tomsky, for having failed to report it.[13]

Stalin, in parallel, had been reading summaries by the secret police (OGPU) of the intercepted correspondence between Trotsky and his adherents exiled at the far ends of the USSR who were gloating that Stalin's radical turn had vindicated their long-standing leftist advocacy for class war against kulaks and NEPmen. Stalin read out excerpts at the politburo, which acceded to his pique and voted to deport Trotsky.[14] Turkey granted a visa, and on January 20, the OGPU appeared in Alma-Ata and loaded up the Trotsky family and their belongings.

On February 10 in Odessa, an OGPU convoy smuggled him, his wife, Natalya Sedova, and their elder son, Lev Sedov, aboard the steamship *Ilich.* Troops lined the harbor. There were no other passengers. The order for deportation was silent about Trotsky's personal archives—and if not expressly told to confiscate, the secret police did not confiscate. Trotsky managed to carry out crates of documents and books.[15] It took fewer than two weeks for two of his essays to appear in the "bourgeois" press. In "How Could This Happen?" Trotsky explained his defeat by allowing that Stalin was "gifted in a practical sense, endurance, and perseverance in the pursuit of outlined goals," but added that "his political horizon is inordinately narrow. His theoretical level is just as primitive. His pastiche booklet *Foundations of Leninism,* in which he tries to pay tribute to the party's theoretical traditions, teems with schoolboy errors. . . . What is Stalin?" Trotsky concluded. "The outstanding mediocrity in our party."[16]

Trotsky was evicted from his temporary residence at the Soviet consulate in Istanbul, and for safety he relocated to Prinkipo (Prince's Isle), twelve miles away, or an hour and a half by boat, in the Sea of Marmara. It had been used to exile rivals to the Byzantine emperors and now was mostly deserted except for summer holidaymakers.[17] He arrived at the "red-cliffed island set in deep blue" (in the words of Max Eastman) on March 8, 1929, and took up residence at a spacious, run-down villa in the outskirts of the main village. Turkish policemen stood guard outside the gates to the rented quarters, where there was little in the way of furniture. But, as in Soviet Sukhum, where Trotsky used to convalesce, a veranda faced the sea. Lev Sedov set up shop on the ground floor to keep track of the voluminous correspondence, and Trotsky began outfitting an office on the second floor. He tried to move on to Europe, but governments refused him a visa, beginning with Germany's Social Democrats, whom Trotsky had incessantly ridiculed.[18] From remote Prinkipo, his exposure of the Soviet regime's lies reverberated around the world—and inside Stalin's office.[19]

While still in the Soviet Union, Trotsky had lost any public voice, but abroad he not only wrote for periodicals in several European languages but also established a Russian-language *Bulletin of the Opposition (Leninist-Bolsheviks).* His inaugural publisher's note set out the party opposition's right to exist and promised facts and documents; in that vein, he wrote an open letter to the workers of the USSR denying that he had left the Soviet Union voluntarily.[20] The OGPU spread a rumor that Trotsky had been deported to enliven the revolutionary movement in the West, an invitation for émigré White Guards to assassinate him.[21] The *Bulletin,* printed in Paris in small print runs, was not legally available inside the USSR, though for a time some Soviet officials who traveled abroad would smuggle the exotic broadsheets home and pass them around.²² It carried an astonishingly well-informed account of the party sessions behind closed doors in Moscow involving Bukharin, who complained that "in the twelfth year of the revolution [there is] not a single elected provincial party chief; the party does not participate in decision making. Everything is done from above." Bukharin was shouted down: "Where did you pick that up—from whom? From Trotsky!"²³

Trotsky, in fact, refused common cause with Bukharin and those he deemed expressions of petit bourgeois class interests. "The rightists think that if one affords greater space to individual peasant economy, then the current difficulties can be overcome," he wrote in a March 1929 essay, also in the *Bulletin*'s inaugural issue. "A wager on the capitalist farmer (the European or Americanized kulak) would doubtless yield fruits, but they would be capitalist fruits that at some near-term stage would lead to the political downfall of Soviet power. . . . The course toward the capitalist farmer is absolutely incompatible with the dictatorship of the proletariat."²⁴ For Stalin, however, the "right deviation," which wanted to continue the existing party policy of the NEP, was in cahoots with the smashed left opposition, which had wanted to overturn the NEP. Both, in criticizing the party line, exposed disunity and therefore weakness, an invitation for the capitalist powers to intervene and overthrow socialism. And because Stalin incarnated party unity and the resolve to build socialism, he was, logically, their prime target of assassination. Thus did opposition to Stalin's policies become equated with terrorism, thanks also to a big hand from Wiaczesław Mężyński, chairman of the OGPU.²⁵

All the while, Stalin's inner circle craved his favor. On March 10, 1929, *Pravda* had published a report by Klim Voroshilov to a Leningrad provincial party conference analyzing the international situation, socialist construction, and the party opposition to collectivization, and four days later Voroshilov wrote to the dictator asking whether he had "screwed up 100 percent or just 75 percent." Stalin responded by praising his account as "a good, principled report," and, in reference to the U.S. president and the British foreign secretary, added, "All the Hoovers and Chamberlains and Bukharins got it in the ass."²⁶

Bukharin had grimly foreseen that Stalin would twist his words and label him a schismatic to extract political advantage, but Stalin's cruelty was something his friend would puzzle over for a long time. And no matter how underhandedly the dictator undercut Bukharin, Stalin was the victim. "Don't try to compel me to be quiet, or hide my opinion by your shouts that I 'want to teach everyone,'" Stalin wrote to Bukharin on April 16, 1929, the day of a politburo confrontation. "Will you at some point desist from the attacks against me?"[27]

NO PITY

Following the politburo session, on that same day, Stalin convened a punitive joint Central Committee–Central Control Commission plenum, lasting a week, at which his loyalists spewed venom at Bukharin.[28] On April 18, amid intense heckling, Bukharin launched a counterattack against Stalin's peasant policy for coercing poor and middle peasants, too, insisting that "the number of kulak households is few," and that "we can allow individual farming to develop without fear of rich peasants." Stalin did not formally respond until the evening session on April 22. "Friendship is friendship, but state service is service," he noted. "We all serve the interests of the working class, and if the interests of the working class diverge from the interests of personal friendship, then down with personal friendship."[29]

Stalin wielded a compelling strategic vision—accelerated, noncapitalist modernity—but he was at pains to deny that he was abrogating Lenin's NEP. (Otherwise, *he* would be the deviationist.) The NEP, he explained, had always had two sides—a retreat, to be followed by a renewed offensive—and "Bukharin's mistake is that he does not see the two-sided nature of NEP; he sees only the first side."[30] Stalin cited Lenin to the Manichaean effect that everything came down to "'who defeats whom,' us or the capitalists. . . . Every advance of capitalist elements is a loss for us," and that the peasantry was "the last capitalist class." He reminded attendees that Rykov and Bukharin had been the first to repudiate his offer to resign (back in December 1927), and he threw Lenin's Testament back in Bukharin's face, reading aloud the parts about Bukharin and commenting, "A theoretician without dialectics. A theoretician of our party about whom it can scarcely be said—with great doubts can it be said—that his outlook is fully Marxist." After all that, Stalin posed as conciliator, coming out "against the expulsion of Bukharin and Tomsky from the politburo."[31]

Stalin might not have had the votes for expulsion. All the same, Bukharin was sacked as editor of *Pravda,* and Tomsky quit as head of trade unions. Rykov remained head of the government, which coordinated the economy.[32] Stalin managed to have the plenum repudiate Rykov and Bukharin's policy alternatives, such as importing grain ("It is better to squeeze the kulak and extract from him surplus grain, which he has in no small quantity"), but plenum resolutions summarizing the right's position (even in condemnation) were not published.[33]

Developments in the countryside supported Stalin's critics. The 1928–29 harvest had come in at only 62–63 million tons (well below the official figure of 70–71 million), and total state grain collections amounted to only around 8 million tons—2 million less than the previous year.[34] Leningrad had already introduced food rationing in November 1928. Moscow soon followed, as did other industrial cities, going beyond bread to sugar and tea, then meat, dairy, and potatoes. But Stalin argued that the problems caused by his antimarket coercion required more coercion. In spring 1929, he dispatched Kaganovich as a plenipotentiary to the Urals and Western Siberia, some of the same districts the dictator himself had visited the year before. By summer 1929, however, food shortages loomed. The regime would need to spend scarce hard currency (the equivalent of 30 million convertible or gold rubles, or almost $15 million) to import a quarter million tons of grain.[35] Those were just facts. Stalin anticipated that the ramped-up coercion would serve as a device of political recruitment, cleaving off the poor and middle peasant from the kulak. This was a complement to his invention of a schismatic "right deviation," which forced his faction to redeclare its loyalty and held the party mass in check.[36]

Stalin's political opportunism was at the service of implanting socialism (noncapitalism) in the countryside and collecting grain to feed and finance noncapitalist industrialization in the cities. He had seized the gift of Bukharin's political amateurism, but in a larger way he had created his own moment, taking advantage of a crisis that his emergency measures had helped create to force through permanent emergency-ism. Mikoyan would admit, in June 1929, that "had it not been for the grain difficulties, the question of strong collective farms and of machine-tractor stations would not have been posed *precisely at this moment* with such vigor, scope, and breadth."[37] He had been appointed by Stalin a candidate member of the politburo already in 1926, at age thirty, as well as head of trade, making him the youngest people's commissar. In that capacity he worked directly under Rykov and, for a time, was close to Bukharin (like Stalin), but now Mikoyan emerged as one of Stalin's key minions who enacted the new hard line. And yet, Mikoyan remained the recipient of Stalin's relentless pressure. "No concessions in grain procurements," Stalin would soon write to him. "Hold the line and be maximally unyielding! If you now pity them and vacillate even one iota from our plan, . . . no one will pity either the Central Committee or the trade commissariat."[38]

GEOPOLITICAL DILEMMA

Upon the close of the plenum, the regime convened the 16th party conference (April 23–29, 1929), which once more ratified the "optimal" (maximalist) variant of the Five-Year Plan.[39] This wild-eyed scheme, which had officially commenced in October 1928, reversed the NEP-era loss of revolutionary élan and envisioned a nearly fourfold increase in investment in the state sector of the economy, to achieve a GDP leap of around 20 percent per annum.[40] The phantasmagorical document also foresaw an absolute increase in household consumption. Still, the emphasis fell upon machine building, or, in Marxist terms, expansion of the means of production, in order to emancipate the USSR from dependence on foreign capitalists.[41] That age-old dream, which predated the Bolshevik regime, always went unrealized, because the West possessed critical advanced technology that Russia needed in order to compete against the West. Stalin's gamble on collectivization and socialist industrialization to emancipate Russia depended on eliciting foreign capitalist cooperation as well.[42] But the Soviets broadcast an intention to overthrow capitalism globally.[43]

The young Soviet state had been unable to reclaim tsarist Poland, Finland, Estonia, Latvia, or Lithuania, which had become independent states; Bessarabia, which had been seized by Romania; or Kars and Ardahan, which were claimed by Turkey. Communist revolutions in Hungary and parts of Iran had been overturned or aborted; Communist coups had failed abjectly in Germany, Bulgaria, and Estonia. Attempts to forge a loyal ally out of Nationalist-governed China had blown up in Stalin's face. Traditional Russian influence had emerged enhanced in Mongolia, a Soviet satellite, but diminished in Korea and Manchuria (Japan had annexed the first and coveted the second). And so, even as the Soviets laid claim to being the antidote to the existing world order of imperialism, they found themselves pursuing a policy of coexistence, meaning trying to win recognition and trade from the capitalists.[44] Lenin had once boasted that the capitalists would sell the rope that the Communists would use to hang them, but because of his repudiation of tsarist and Provisional Government debts, the Soviets had not been able to secure long-term credits for foreign purchases.[45] Stalin's extreme violence and accompanying desecration of churches added to the reputational costs for capitalists if they sold to the Communists. It remained a mystery how Stalin was going to obtain blueprints, machines, and know-how from the advanced capitalist countries.

POPULISM

Soviet industry, construction, and transport employed, at most, 6 million workers in 1929—of whom 4.5 million performed manual labor—out of a working population of well more than 60 million.[46] Alongside familiar output norms, piece rates, and labor discipline, Soviet factories were supposed to be crucibles for new forms of socialist labor. "Shock work," connoting overfulfillment of work norms via all-out exertion and rationalization, spread during the Five-Year Plan in conjunction with so-called socialist competitions among brigades for honors and better rations.[47] In early 1929, *Pravda* had published "How to Organize Competition?" This previously unpublished article by Lenin, about unleashing workers' creative energies, was part of a campaign in which workers took vows, often in writing, not to slack off or show up drunk or go AWOL, and to fulfill the plan. Some work collectives were afforded Union-wide publicity.[48] Stalin had never really been a worker himself, had clashed bitterly with the one genuine worker in the politburo (Tomsky), and rarely visited factories. But he nurtured a deep populist streak.

A journalist for the newspaper *Female Peasant*, Yelena Mikulina (b. 1906), was having difficulty publishing her pamphlet, "Socialist Competition of the Masses," on textile workers in Ivanovo-Voznesensk. In early May 1929, she boldly dropped the manuscript off for Stalin at the party secretariat, imploring his aides for an audience. Stalin, surprising his functionaries, had his top aide, Ivan Tovstukha, summon her to Old Square on May 10. "You wanted to tell me something?" he was said to have asked Mikulina, who recalled answering, "'I have nothing to say, because I am frightfully afraid, and completely stunned.' . . . 'Ha, ha ha,' Stalin laughed. And in his laugh he showed his teeth. And his entire face, sown with large pockmarks, also laughed." They talked about where else Mikulina might venture to write firsthand about socialist construction—perhaps Kazakhstan, where the Turkestan–Siberian Railway was being built.[49] She asked Stalin to write a preface to her essays, which he did the next day, sending it by courier to her dormitory. The preface, which touted how "the powerful production rise of the toiling masses has begun," was published in *Pravda* (May 22, 1929). The state publishing house immediately issued Mikulina's pamphlet in a print run of 100,000. She sent Stalin an autographed copy, with the dedication "I cannot tell you how powerfully I love you."[50]

Stalin, in his preface, warned anyone who dared to impede "the creative initiative of the masses."[51] Then the reviews arrived. One, from a newspaper editor in Yaroslavl, told Stalin that "workers greet the pamphlet with mocking laughter," but nonetheless inquired whether his own censorious draft review (which he enclosed) merited publication.[52] Another, forwarded to Stalin by the party boss of Ivanovo-Voznesensk, provoked a response. "It is not so easy to take in comrade Stalin," the dictator wrote. "I am decisively against writing prefaces only for pamphlets and books of literary 'big-shots,' literary 'names.' . . . We have hundreds and thousands of young capable people, who are striving with all their might to rise up from below."[53]

"SOCIAL FASCISTS"

Bolshevism, like Italian fascism, was an insurrection against both a liberal constitutional order and European Social Democracy. In Stalin's formulation, codified at the Sixth Comintern Congress (1928), a bourgeoisie desperate to retain its hold on power sought to establish extreme fascist regimes by co-opting Social Democrats. Therefore, Social Democracy—which reconciled workers to capitalism, and thus lured them away from their supposed true home in the Communist party—constituted a handmaiden of fascism ("social fascism").[54] Social Democrats returned and often instigated the enmity, expelling Communists from trade unions and agitating against the Soviet regime. During clashes on May Day 1929, the German Social Democrat Party supported the police against banned worker street rallies encouraged by German Communists; 30 people were killed, nearly 200 injured, and more than 1,000 arrested.[55] The Comintern condemned the Berlin events as Social Democratic "terror." A German Communist party congress the next month resolved that "Social Democracy is preparing . . . the establishment of the fascist dictatorship."[56]

In Moscow, the Comintern opened its tenth expanded plenum on July 3, 1929, with seventy-two delegates, half of whom had voting rights. Otto Kuusinen, the Finnish-born Comintern secretary general, noted that "factories would determine the outcome of the next war and the next civil war," a summons to close ranks behind Soviet industrialization.[57] Stalin had inserted the following into the theses: "The Comintern executive committee plenum suggests paying special attention to strengthening the fight against the 'left' wing of Social Democracy, which is retarding the disintegration of Social Democracy by sowing illusions about this wing's opposition to the policies of Social Democracy's leadership, but in fact strongly supports social fascism."[58] Bukharin, formally chairman of the Comintern executive committee, had not even been showing up at headquarters, and on the plenum's final day (July 19) he was replaced by Molotov.[59] Privately, Clara Zetkin, the high-profile German Communist, had confided to a Swiss comrade that "the Comintern has turned from a living political body into a dead mechanism, which, on the one hand, is capable only of swallowing orders in Russian and, on the other, of regurgitating them in different languages." Publicly, she continued to lend her prestige to the cause by keeping her mouth shut.[60]

Other foreign Communists exulted in the Soviet party's militant turn under Stalin. Klement Gottwald, responding to allegations that the Czechoslovak Communist party was under Moscow's thumb, boasted to his country's National Assembly, "We go to Moscow to learn from the Russian Bolsheviks how to wring your necks. (Outcry). And you know the Russian Bolsheviks are masters at it! (Uproar)."[61]

ADVANCED TECHNOLOGY, ARRESTS

Voroshilov, as he wrote privately (June 8, 1929) to Orjonikidze, who was away convalescing, had gotten into a row with Bukharin at a politburo session. "I lost my self-control and blurted out in Little Nikolai's face, 'You liar, bastard, I'll punch you in the face,' and other such nonsense and all in front of a large number of people," he lamented. "Bukharin is trash and is capable of telling the vilest fabrications straight to your face. . . . Still, I did not behave properly. . . . After this scene Bukharin left the politburo meeting and did not return." Voroshilov had just voted to accommodate Bukharin's wishes in the matter of his next appointment, forming part of a rare politburo majority in that vote against Stalin.[62] Soon thereafter, Stalin had the politburo revisit the military aspect of industrialization, just months after formal approval of the maximalist variant of the Five-Year Plan. On July 15, two secret decrees were issued that, to a considerable degree, belatedly sided with Voroshilov and the Red Army against Rykov's fiscal prudence.[63]

The first decree underscored the long-standing view that all the states neighboring the USSR to the west needed to be viewed as a "likely enemy," which required attaining military parity with them. It also called for acceleration of the components of the Five-Year Plan that served defense (nonferrous metals, chemicals, machine building) by means of "foreign technical assistance and aid, and acquisition of the most vital prototype models."[64] Red Army growth was set to reach 643,700 active troops by the end of the Five-Year Plan. Improvements were mandated in soldiers' housing and vigilance against "kulak moods, anti-Semitism, [and] distorted disciplinary practices" (hazing). The second decree, on military factories proper, complained that they were overseen by "the caste of old tsarist-era specialists," many of whom stood accused of "wrecking." Voroshilov tasked the army staff—headed by Boris M. Shaposhnikov, a tsarist-era officer descended from Orenburg Cossacks—with redoing its economic plans and administration to facilitate mass production of advanced aircraft, artillery, and tanks.[65] "Everyone has a magnificent impression," the commissariat's business manager wrote to Voroshilov of the secret decrees. "Boris Mikhailovich even declared that he got more effect from this document than from his medical treatment in Germany."[66]

Secret military cooperation with Germany, in violation of the Versailles Treaty, had been under way for years. More than 100 Soviet officers had attended German general staff academy courses on state-of-the-art military science. (Some German officers, such as Friedrich von Paulus, presented guest lectures in Moscow.)[67] Most of the Soviet brass, including Mikhail Tukhachevsky, made brief trips to Germany, but a few, such as Jeronimas Uborevičius, known as Uborevich, studied there for long stretches (in his case, from late 1927 through early 1929).[68] A peasant from Lithuania (a land of free peasants) who had graduated from imperial Russia's artillery school, then joined the Bolsheviks in 1917, Uborevičius spoke fluent German, resembled a German general staff type—precise, punctual, professional—and admired that country's technology and organization. He became a favorite of the Reichswehr while enjoying Stalin's favor, who assigned him to the new armaments directorate.[69] The entire Red Army tank park numbered perhaps ninety units, mostly of Great War vintage, such as French-made tanks captured from the Whites. Artillery had been an area of rapid technological change since the Great War, but in August 1929 Stalin received yet another damning report deeming Red Army artillery "on the same technical level as in 1917, if not 1914," despite considerable expenditure.[70] In late summer and fall 1929, almost the entire artillery directorate and inspectorate were arrested for wrecking. Ten people were executed; others "testified" against tsarist-era military specialists beyond those in artillery, foreshadowing more arrests to come.[71]

TIGHT LEASH

All dictators risk overthrow when, for their own power, they empower a secret police. Kamenev's "notes" of his conversation with Bukharin included the latter's assertions about the OGPU's supposed sympathies ("Yagoda and Trilisser are with us"). Genrikh Yagoda and Meyer Trilisser, aka Mikhail Moskvin, the longtime head of OGPU foreign intelligence and, like Yagoda, an OGPU deputy chairman, had been compelled to submit explanations to Stalin, with a copy to Orjonikidze at the party Control Commission.[72] Yagoda had to admit that he met regularly with Rykov, who, after all, was the head of the government, including in Rykov's private apartment (in the same building as Stalin's). Yagoda and Rykov both hailed from the Volga region.[73]

Complicating the situation, the OGPU chairman, Mężyński, suffered numerous ailments, from severe asthma to a spinal injury as a result of a car accident in Paris. (He often received subordinates while half lying on a couch.) People whispered that he had never fully recovered his spirits after his young wife had died during surgery.[74] Stalin ignored his requests to resign. On April 21, 1929—precisely the moment of Stalin's machinations against the right deviation—Mężyński had a massive heart attack. He was ordered to curtail his smoking and sugar intake and to rest. After several months, on August 1, the doctors allowed him to return to work, but only if he went to the office every other day and for no more than five hours each time; Mężyński rejected these conditions and returned to Lubyanka anyway.[75] But his absences and continued illness heightened the already sharp jockeying in the secret police. With Yagoda down south on holiday, Trilisser, at a meeting of the Sokolniki ward of the Moscow party organization where OGPU officials were registered, demanded self-criticism to rid the secret police of unworthy people, and accused Yagoda of "retreating from the general line of the party with the right deviation."[76]

Police operatives had recently been instructed to omit the name and location of their branch even when signing their secret internal correspondence, so as to reduce any outsider's ability to decipher the organization's structure in case of a leak.[77] Now, Stalin wrote to Mężyński (September 16, 1929), "it turns out you (the Chekists) have taken a course toward full-bore self-criticism inside the GPU. In other words, the Chekists are committing the same mistakes that were committed not long ago in the military body. . . . Do not forget that the GPU is no less a militarized agency than the military body. . . . Would it be impossible to undertake decisive measures against this evil?"[78] Trilisser lost out, replaced by Stanisław Messing, who was close to his fellow Pole Mężyński. At the same time, the Stalin favorite, Yefim Yevdokimov, was brought from the North Caucasus to run the central OGPU secret-political directorate, which oversaw the secret, counterintelligence, special (army), informational (intelligence analysis), Eastern, and operative departments—a counterweight to Yagoda.[79]

Among the 2,000-odd operatives in the central OGPU at this time, Yevdokimov stood out. His North Caucasus bailiwick had become the most medal-bedecked in the Union, thanks to the protracted counterinsurgency against a well-armed populace ("bandit formations"), a civil war after the civil war.[80] What is more, the place where Stalin took his holidays fell within his jurisdiction. In conspiring with the dictator to manufacture the 1928 Shakhty trial, Yevdokimov had become an all-Union star (and in 1930 would receive his fourth Order of the Red Banner).[81] He looked after his subordinates' families and gathered them at his house for banquets and singing—Ukrainian choral songs, Cossack songs, Russian folk ditties—with one Chekist playing the piano and another the accordion. "Yevdokimov had formed a powerful group that would implement his any command," recalled one member. "By giving out awards, taking care of their daily life concerns, and corrupting their behavior, Yevdokimov had succeeded in forging a strong nucleus of Chekists loyal to him to the end. In turn, these people forged groups of operatives loyal to one another and, by extension, to Yevdokimov."[82]

There was no assignment from which Yevdokimov would shrink on behalf of *his* patron. Innocently, Stalin, in the letter to Mężyński on September 16, 1929, had written: "I got wind that Yevdokimov is being transferred to Moscow to secret-operative work (it seems in place of Deribas). Would it not follow to simultaneously make him a member of the OGPU collegium? It seems to me it would follow." Yevdokimov was named to the collegium even before his relocation to Moscow took effect.[83]

Stalin did not instigate this anti-Yagoda revolt. But he had again extracted advantage from others' actions. Yagoda was promoted to first deputy chairman of the OGPU, from merely "deputy," while Messing became a new second deputy chairman. But Stalin allowed Yevdokimov to implant his North Caucasus minions into the many departments in the capital that he now oversaw.[84] Yevdokimov's top deputy was now Jan Kulikowski, known as Olsky (b. 1898), another Pole of noble descent, who remained the head of the powerful counterintelligence department while becoming concurrently head of the special department for the army. Artur Artuzov, deputy chief of foreign intelligence and a long-standing Yagoda nemesis, became Yevdokimov's other top deputy.[85] Yagoda would have to overexert himself to demonstrate separation from the "right deviation" and loyalty to Stalin.

THE GENERAL SECRETARY'S WIFE—A RIGHTIST

All during the OGPU machinations, Stalin was on holiday down south, from the third week of July 1929, staying mostly at the Puzanovka dacha in Sochi. He had caught severe flu. He promoted "Bolshevik self-criticism" when it suited him, but in a letter of July 29 to Molotov, whom he had left in charge, he denounced some articles he had seen in *Communist Youth League Pravda* and the journal *Young Guard* as tantamount to "a call for a review of the general line of the party, for the undermining of the iron discipline of the party, for the turning of the party into a discussion club."[86] Stalin drafted politburo resolutions and instructions on foreign affairs, ordered that close attention be paid to the new iron- and steelworks under construction, and directed that the internal exile Cristian Rakovski, whose damning essay Stalin had read in the first issue of Trotsky's *Bulletin of the Opposition* (July 1929), be deported to an even more remote locale (which turned out to be Barnaul, Siberia). Stalin complained about low grain procurements and demanded surveillance over collective farm directors and arrests of urban "speculators." He congratulated Molotov (August 29) for savage attacks against Bukharin in *Pravda,* and reported, "I'm beginning to recuperate in Sochi."[87]

Stalin directed talks to restore diplomatic relations with Britain (severed in mid-1927). The negotiations, supported by British industrialists, were launched after the Labour party won elections and the Labourite Ramsay MacDonald was returned as prime minister (in June 1929). "No haste should be displayed on the British question," he instructed Molotov, denigrating deputy foreign affairs commissar Maxim Litvinov. "Remember we are waging a struggle (negotiations with enemies is struggle) not with England alone, but with the whole capitalist world, for the MacDonald government is the vanguard of the capitalist governments in the work of 'humiliating' and 'bridling' the Soviet government with 'new,' more 'diplomatic,' more 'masked,' in a word, more 'valid' methods. The MacDonald government wants to show the whole capitalist world that it can take more from us (with the help of 'soft' methods) than Mussolini, Poincaré, and Baldwin, that it can be a greater Shylock than the capitalist Shylock himself. And it wants this because only in this way can it win over the trust of its own bourgeoisie (and not only its bourgeoisie). We would be the bottom of the barrel if we could not manage to reply to these arrogant bastards briefly and to the point: '*You won't get a friggin' thing from us.*'"[88]

Stalin was assiduously courting Maxim Gorky, the Russian writer, to return permanently from Italy, and in 1929, for the second year in a row, he visited the USSR. "I heard Gorky evidently went to Sochi,"—Stalin's wife, Nadya, wrote to him on August 28.[89] "He will probably visit you, a pity, without me." After traveling down the Volga, Gorky made it to Tiflis and, apparently, Sochi, but soon began spitting blood and cut his trip short.[90] Nadya was in Moscow to sit entrance exams for the Industrial Academy. "I send you a big kiss, like the kiss you gave me when we parted," she wrote to her husband in the August 28 letter, delivered by airplane. He wrote the next day about how "I have already managed to take two medicinal baths. I think I'll take ten." On September 1, he wrote that he had evidently "been close to pneumonia," and still suffered from a persistent cough. "As soon as you get 6–7 free days, get down here to Sochi. How are things with the exam? I kiss you, my Tatka."[91]

Nadya wrote the next day of daily life in the capital, "I must say that the mood about food supplies, among students and teachers, is only so-so; everyone is worn out by the queues." She added knowingly, "Do not be angry at such details."[92] She had the further audacity to intervene on behalf of a member of *Pravda*'s editorial collegium, the secretary of its party cell, Kovalev, who had fallen afoul for publishing a critical article about the need for criticism, without seeking prior authorization from the Central Committee. But Kovalev had received authorization from higher-ups at *Pravda*. "I cannot be indifferent about the fate of such a good worker and comrade of mine," Nadya wrote to Stalin, revealing that she knew a politburo meeting had been scheduled to adjudicate the matter. (Nadya also wrote, "And, if you can, send 50 rubles, I do not have a kopeck left." Stalin sent her 120 rubles.) He accepted her account of Kovalev's scapegoating ("I think you are right") and sent a telegram to Molotov that same evening asking to delay any decision. The next day, Stalin instructed Orjonikidze and Molotov to establish firmer control over *Pravda*. Orjonikidze wrote to Stalin that "Kovalev has so far not been touched even though he committed a mass of idiocies. I agree with you that the leaders of *Pravda* are more at fault." (Kovalev would be fired from *Pravda* all the same.) Orjonikidze pointedly added, "I must say, the sooner you return, the better."[93]

Molotov and Orjonikidze had just written a joint letter to Stalin (September 13, 1929), pleading for newspaper criticism of leading officials to be reined in, but that same day, Stalin wrote back, "I consider your proposal risky in that it could objectively lead to curbing of self-criticism, which is unacceptable." The next day, he added that "full-on self-criticism activates the mass and creates a state of siege for all and all kinds of bureaucrats. This is a great achievement."[94]

Stalin read newspapers assiduously on holiday. After finding an account in *Pravda* of a mid-September Rykov speech, he erupted in a telegram he sent to Molotov, Voroshilov, and Orjonikidze, making known that at a minimum, he wanted Rykov removed from chairing politburo sessions. ("Can you not put an end to this comedy?")[95] Meanwhile, Nadya wrote to him from Moscow (September 27) that "without you it is very, very boring," and pleaded, "In a word, come back. It will be nice together. . . . I kiss you firmly, firmly." She detailed the infighting at the Industrial Academy, where she was studying chemical dyes and synthetic fibers for clothing applications. "Students here are graded as follows: kulak, middle peasant, poor peasant. There is such enormous laughter and argument every day. In a word, they have already put me down as a rightist."[96]

Stalin did not react to her naïve "joke" on the touchiest (for him) of subjects in his next letter (September 30), noting only that he would be back in Moscow in a week. On October 3, Britain and the USSR signed a one-page protocol restoring relations, without settling their outstanding disputes, just as Stalin had insisted.[97] With his return imminent, he wrote to Molotov (October 6), "It is necessary to think Bukharin will be kicked out of the politburo."[98] Stalin also revealed his prickliness yet again. "For some reason, recently, you have started praising me," he wrote to Nadya (October 8). "What does this mean? Good, or bad?"[99]

TREMORS

Stalin had not been abroad since 1913. "How good would it be if you, comrade Stalin, changing appearance, traveled for a certain time abroad with a genuine translator, not a tendentious one," foreign affairs commissar Georgy Chicherin had recently written. "You would see reality."[100] (Stalin would not set foot outside the USSR until 1943.) The dictator continued to direct intelligence officials to focus on threats posed by Britain, France, Germany, and Japan, as well as the "limitrophes," the immediate borderland states (Poland, Finland, Latvia, Lithuania, Estonia, Romania). They were reporting what he solicited.[101] "The Turkish general staff has received testimony from Germany, Poland, and England that war between the USSR and Poland will happen in early 1930," one report stated (October 11, 1929), in passages Stalin underlined. "Poland is seriously preparing for war. . . . Rumors are circulating as well among the [military] attachés in Moscow about a war coming soon."[102]

Gorky had returned to Sorrento already, and Stalin, back in Moscow, resumed his side of their correspondence via diplomatic pouch. "Things are not going badly here," he noted (October 24). "We're moving the cart along; of course, with creaking, but we're moving forward. . . . They say that you are writing a play about wrecking and that you would not be against receiving related materials. I gathered materials on wrecking and I'll send them to you presently. . . . How's your health?"[103] Other pressing business included dispatching central functionaries to oversee grain collections in the North Caucasus, Bashkiria, the Central and Lower Volga, and Ukraine.[104] Stalin was using the heavy-handed procurements to force peasants into collective farms. He and other regime officials either ignored the disposition of animals altogether or publicly insisted on immediate full socialization. Rather than hand their animals over to the collectives, peasants had been trying to sell them since summer, but markets were flooded and prices had cratered, so the peasants had begun slaughtering animals en masse in protest. The livestock that had been socialized were often up to their knees in dung, and dying.[105] A catastrophe was unfolding.

Also on October 24, the United States stock market lost 11 percent of its value at the opening bell. Trading on that "Black Thursday" was heavy, and the ticker tape could not keep up—people had no idea what stocks were worth. Bankers tried to arrest the slide with bulk purchases of blue chips above trading prices. But when the market opened on Monday, it fell 13 percent. "Black Tuesday" (October 29) saw a 12 percent drop amid record trading (a record not broken for four decades), which brought the Dow Jones to 40 percent below the peak it had reached in September. The Wall Street crash came after a speculative boom in which stocks were being purchased at an average price-to-earnings ratio of 32, far above historic levels, thanks partly to the invention of margin buying. When prices dropped, investors could not pay back the loans they had assumed to purchase the stocks. Just one in six U.S. households owned stocks, but the shock provoked business bankruptcies, credit contraction, worker layoffs, and psychological uncertainty. Most remarkable, the weeklong drop in share prices occurred almost instantaneously on all financial markets in the world except Japan—and the Soviet Union, which, of course, did not have a stock market.[106]

On November 5, 1929, following protracted negotiations between Britain and the Soviet Union, the House of Commons ratified restoration of diplomatic relations by a wide margin (324 to 199).[107] Each government continued to accuse the other of treachery, but for Stalin, diplomatic recognition by the world's "leading imperialist power" denoted acknowledgment of the Five-Year Plan for rapid industrialization.[108] That same day, a politburo decree ordered the execution of the OGPU espionage operative Yakov Blyumkin. His fatal act had been to meet on Prinkipo with Trotsky, his former patron, who revealed that he had managed to carry out secret documents, which he intended to publish to expose Stalin, and predicted the regime's downfall, averring that the underground "Bolshevik-Leninists" needed to strengthen their opposition. Blyumkin evidently sensed that Trotsky was fantasizing, yet he had agreed to carry messages to Moscow from Trotsky, written inside books in invisible ink.[109] He became one of the first Communist party members executed by the Soviet regime for a political crime.

A GREAT BREAK

The permanency, or not, of ad hoc regime violence in the countryside was set to be clarified at the year's second Central Committee plenum, scheduled to open November 10, 1929, and Stalin went on the offensive, with a newspaper article, "The Year of the Great Break," in *Pravda* on the revolution's anniversary (November 7). "We are going full speed ahead by means of industrialization to socialism, leaving behind our traditional 'Russian' backwardness," he declared. "We are becoming a country of metal, a country of the automobile, a country of the tractor." In the run-up to the plenum, regime officials had begun to boast of fulfilling the Five-Year Plan in just four years, and, at the plenum itself, this would become a "vow" attributed to "the proletariat" and, soon, a ubiquitous slogan—"5 in 4."[110] His article predicted giant new farms of 125,000 to 250,000 acres, larger than even the biggest U.S. farms of the time, and insisted that "the peasants are joining collective farms . . . as whole villages, whole counties, whole districts, even sub-provinces"—a supposed movement from below, refuting the rightists. He further boasted that "the country in something like three years will become one of the most grain-rich, if not *the* most grain-rich, in the world."[111] That would allow for vast grain exports, to pay for imported machinery.[112]

Local party committees, under intense central pressure, claimed to have doubled the number of collectivized households since June 1929—the basis of Stalin's plenum's assertions—but even so collectivization still amounted to only 7.6 percent of households.[113] And it was eyewash anyway. "We had wholesale collectivization on the territory of dozens of villages," the Ukraine party boss Stanisław Kosior admitted to the plenum, "and then it turned out that all of it was inflated, artificially created, and that the population did not take part and knew nothing." Critical comments were also uttered by Sergei Syrtsov, who had hosted Stalin in Siberia the year before and been brought back to Moscow by him in 1929, becoming a candidate member of the politburo and head of the Russian republic's Council of People's Commissars (Rykov's lesser position, taken away from him).[114] When Syrtsov bemoaned the lack of thought given to policy implementation, Stalin interrupted, "You think everything can be 'prepared beforehand'?"[115]

Stalin had the plenum compel a new capitulation from the rightists, which *Pravda* would publish ("We consider it our duty to declare that . . . the party and its Central Committee have proved right"), and on the final day (November 17) he prompted them to expel Bukharin from the politburo.[116] But the dictator, passing a handwritten note to Orjonikidze acknowledging the hall's sentiment, proved unable to finish off Rykov.[117] Still, plenum resolutions warned of "the sharpening of the class struggle and the stubborn resistance by capitalist elements to socialism on the offensive."[118] In fact, before the year was out, the secret police would record at least 1,300 spontaneous, uncoordinated peasant protests against party policy.[119] But Stalin forced through a decree that transformed his theretofore ad hoc pronouncements into an official mandate for wholesale Union-wide collectivization.[120]

SHOW OF FORCE

Also on November 17, 1929, the Soviet Union launched the second part of a major military operation in Manchuria. Stalin's China policy, a "united front" that forced the Chinese Communists into a junior partnership with the Soviet-supported "bourgeois" Nationalists (or Guomindang) to prioritize resistance to imperialism, had been in disarray. The Nationalist leader Chiang Kai-shek had massacred Chinese Communists, and had gone on to unify much of north and south China. The main exception was Manchuria, ruled by a warlord based in Mukden, Zhang Xueliang, known as the Young Marshal, who had taken over for his Japanese-assassinated father. In a conspiracy coordinated with Chiang, Zhang raided the Soviet consulate in Harbin, produced documents of Soviet subversion, and occupied the jointly managed Chinese Eastern Railway, a tsarist-built shortcut for the Trans-Siberian that afforded a sphere of influence.[121] Aiming to evict the Soviets, Zhang's troops violated the extraterritoriality granted by treaty and detained Soviet rail officials, charging them with spreading Communist propaganda and instigating rebellion. The USSR arrested Chinese merchants on Soviet soil and, in August 1929, broke off diplomatic relations.[122]

Stalin suspected that the Mukden warlord, no less than the Nationalist government in Nanking, was in the pay of the British, the Japanese, or the Americans (or all three), so that the railroad seizure might be a diversionary action. He authorized formation of a Special Far Eastern Army consisting of local conscripts (as well as some ethnic Germans from the Volga region, a separate ethnic Buryat cavalry division, and one battalion of Soviet Koreans). They were commanded by Vasily Blyukher, the former top military adviser to Chiang.[123]

Zhang's Mukden regulars and irregulars numbered up to a quarter million, aided by thousands of former émigré White Guards. Japanese troops were stationed just 125 miles south of Harbin, guarding a rail spur, the South Manchurian Railway, from Harbin down to Port Arthur, which tsarist Russia had also built, but ceded the lease to Japan as war spoils in 1905. (This area was known in its Chinese characters as Guāndōng or Kwantung, meaning "east of the mountain pass," beyond which lay Manchuria.)[124] Given these realities, Stalin had hesitated to punish the Chinese by force, despite Voroshilov's urgings, but after the Soviet consul general in Tokyo obtained assurances from a well-connected Japanese industrialist that Japan would not interfere in a Soviet showdown with China as long as Red Army forces did not move too deep into Manchuria, Stalin agreed to the strike.[125] More than 300,000 soldiers, sailors, and aviators were mobilized on the two sides, including Soviet reserves and border guards— approximately 20 percent of the entire Red Army ended up being sent to or near the front. Blyukher drew up the war plan (availing himself of pre-1917 archives); Voroshilov took up field headquarters in Chita, Siberia. Both Chiang and the Young Marshal had underestimated Soviet resolve and capabilities, such as their superior air power and battlefield command.

Blyukher's offensive was cleverly designed to annihilate the enemy before its full force could be mustered. Employing fast maneuvering in a combined sea-air-land operation, he encircled Chinese troops in just forty-eight hours, despite Soviet shortages of artillery. The Far Eastern Army had managed to operate on two salients separated by 600 miles and to synchronize three major operations: naval and amphibious assaults down the Sungari River (October 1929), a western thrust from Manzhouli, and an eastern one from Suifenhe (both in November 1929). The Soviets claimed to have had just 812 killed in action (though the toll was likely higher).[126] The Far Eastern Army was awarded the Order of the Red Banner.[127] Some foreign newspapers in the Far East lauded Blyukher as a "Red Napoleon."[128] China's government sued for peace, agreeing to restore Soviet co-control over the railroad and "disarm the White Guard detachments and expel their organizers and instigators from [China's] Three Eastern Provinces."[129] The Soviet military action beyond its borders reinforced deep anxieties among Polish and French diplomats. Japan's Kwantung Army command, for its part, was in no mind to accept Soviet successes in Manchuria. High officials in Tokyo—who had allowed the Soviets to weaken Chinese forces—now concluded that Chinese troops could be easily vanquished, an inference that, if acted upon, could bring Japan and the USSR into collision.[130]

Stalin was ecstatic. "Obviously our fellows from the Far East Army gave [the Chinese] a good scare," he crowed on December 5, 1929, to Molotov (now the one on holiday). "We rebuffed America and England and France rather rudely for their attempt to intervene. We could not have done otherwise. Let them know what Bolsheviks are like! I think the Chinese landowners will not forget the object lessons taught them by the Far East Army." Stalin added: "Grain procurements are progressing. We are raising the supply allocations for industrial cities like Ivanovo-Voznesensk, Kharkov, and so on. The collective farm movement is growing by leaps and bounds. Of course, there are not enough machines and tractors—how could it be otherwise?—but simply pooling peasant tools results in a colossal increase in sown acreage."[131]

EVERYWHERE, VICTORY

From December 5 through 10, 1929, the regime staged the First All-Union Congress of Shock Brigades. "Workers took to the podium and spoke not only about their factory, their plant—they spoke about planning in general, about standardization, about control figures, and so on," Valerian Kuibyshev, the head of the Supreme Council of the Economy, boasted from the dais. "That is how people can speak who feel themselves the masters of their country."[132]

On December 15, seven weeks after Black Tuesday on the New York Stock Exchange, a *Pravda* editorial declared that a general economic crisis had engulfed the United States. As other customers for large capital orders became scarcer, Stalin shopped the great capitalist department store. Starting with the American companies Freyn Engineering and Arthur McKee, Moscow signed "technical assistance" contracts to import the new American wide-strip steel mills and heavy blooming mills with which to build brand-new integrated steel plants at Magnitogorsk (Urals), equivalent in size to the flagship U.S. Steel plant in Gary, Indiana, as well as others in Kuznetsk (Siberia) and Zaporozhe (Ukraine). Additionally, the Soviets contracted with the Ford Motor Company to build an integrated mass-production facility in Nizhny Novgorod for cars and trucks, on the basis of recent Ford patents and its famed River Rouge plant. Caterpillar was engaged to re-equip factories in Kharkov and Leningrad to mass-produce tractors and harvesters, while giant tractor plants were contracted for Stalingrad and, very soon, Chelyabinsk, intended to be the largest in the world. Contracts would be signed with DuPont and Nitrogen Engineering to manufacture ammonia, nitric acid, and synthetic nitrogen, and Westvaco for chlorine. There would be ball-bearings technology from Sweden and Italy, advanced plastics and aircraft from France, turbines and electrical technology from Britain.[133] Virtually every contract would contain at least one turnkey installation—an entire plant from scratch to operation.[134] The Soviets had to pay with foreign-currency-earning exports (grain, timber, oil) or gold reserves.[135] But now Stalin's regime even managed to obtain foreign credits, which, although short term, were frequently on favorable terms with foreign government guarantees and did not even necessitate that they redeem the pre-Communist state debts.[136]

On December 21, 1929, Stalin officially turned fifty. *Pravda* had begun printing congratulations three days earlier, and on the actual day, the paeans occupied six and a half of the issue's eight pages, with some of the approximately 1,000 congratulatory telegrams coming from factories and organizations, but not from collective farmers.[137] Molotov sent a private note. "I know that you are diabolically busy," he wrote. "But I shake your fifty-year-old hand."[138] The state publishing house issued a collection of the tributes in an edition of 300,000 copies. "Wherever Stalin is," it stated, "there is success, victory."[139] The *Pravda* birthday issue carried the iconic photograph of Stalin with Lenin at the latter's dacha and hailed the dictator as "the best pupil, heir, and successor of Lenin." But that made him a target: "Stalin stands at the head of the Leninist Central Committee. Therefore he is invariably the object of savage abuse on the part of the world bourgeoisie and the Social Democrats."[140]

Stalin struck a modest pose in a published response (December 22), crediting the Leninist party and the working class, "which bore me and reared me in its own image and likeness," and making a solemn vow: "You need have no doubt, comrades, I am prepared to devote to the cause of the working class, the cause of the proletarian revolution and world Communism, all my strength, all my ability, and, if need be, all my blood, drop by drop."[141]

The newsreel agency produced a six-part silent amalgamation of Stalin moments caught on film: smiling, waving, graciously accepting accolades, wise, benevolent.[142] It conveyed his revolutionary bona fides with tsarist-police photographs and fingerprints and images of the shacks he inhabited during exile in Solvychegodsk and Kureika. Viewers also saw his birth hovel and hometown of Gori, with its medieval-fortress ruins on the hill, a pantheon of childhood photos, and a long interlude at the current Tiflis home of his bespectacled mother, Keke Geladze, as she assembled a care package with his beloved homemade walnut jam. Now Stalin also became the organizer of the Red Army, an innovation canonized in Voroshilov's birthday pamphlet, "Stalin and the Red Army." Trotsky was provoked to consider writing a history of the Red Army and the civil war in rebuttal, but that would not get done: a suspicious fire at his residence destroyed many of his papers and books on the subject.[143] Voroshilov's draft, meanwhile, had been sent to Stalin for prior approval. The defense commissar had written that Stalin made fewer mistakes than the others. Stalin wrote back, "Klim! There were no mistakes—cut that paragraph."[144]

CLOSE TO THE MASSES (METAPHYSICALLY)

Those who wanted to be part of the world-historical building of socialism would have to fall in line. "It is now completely clear that one cannot be for the party and *against* the present leadership," the Trotsky apostate and state bank head Georgy "Yuri" Pyatakov wrote in *Pravda* (December 23, 1929). "One cannot be for the Central Committee *and* against Stalin."[145] Unlike Italian fascism, however, Marxism had trouble *admitting* a cult of the leader. This delicate question was directly addressed—for perhaps the last time under Stalin—in the lead article of the journal *Party Construction,* published in connection with Stalin's jubilee. The author, K. Popov, characterized leadership as necessary and Stalin's as "armed with Marxist-Leninist revolutionary theory, forged by multiyear experience of the struggle for Leninism, hand in hand with Lenin." Popov referred to a "leading group" within the party and to Stalin as "the genuine 'first among equals,'" because, in his struggle for Leninism, he "invariably expresses the will of hundreds of thousands and millions." Stalin's illiberal regime, in other words, was democratic. Popov quoted Lenin to the effect that "one person can represent the will of hundreds and tens of thousands of people," and underscored the "democracy" of party congresses, whereby "the will of the collective party leadership and the will of the leaders merge with the will of the masses."[146]

Soviet newspapers had taken to berating actual Soviet workers as shirkers, absentees, and drunks, ruining the regime's industrial plan with indiscipline. The Menshevik émigré press speculated that "capitalist" types had regained control of the factories. Gorky, also abroad, was taken aback. "Negative reports must be balanced by positive reporting," he urged in a letter to Stalin in late 1929. "Progress in carrying out the Five-Year Plan must be reported on a week-to-week and month-to-month basis . . . : the construction of housing, factories, plants, bakeries, community centers, canteens, and schools. . . . The press should keep reminding itself and its readers . . . that socialism is being built in the USSR not by sloppy individuals, hooligans, and raving morons, but by a genuinely new and mighty force—the working class." Soon enough, updates on "socialist construction" and worker heroes—alongside the encomiums to Stalin and lurid tales of sabotage—would saturate the public sphere.[147]

LIQUIDATION OF THE KULAKS AS A CLASS

Already by early December 1929, the Soviet state had procured 13.5 million tons of grain—more than twice as much as in any preceding year of the regime.[148] But the state had to feed many more rural folk (who had previously purchased or traded for food on the market), set aside grain for ambitious surges in export, and meet the rationing norms for the industrial cities and construction sites, as well as the Red Army.[149] In that connection, the November 1929 plenum had created a new USSR land commissariat. Stalin appointed Yakov Epstein, known as Yakovlev, the editor of *Peasant Newspaper* and a member of the disciplinary Central Control Commission, as commissar.[150] He presided over a commission on the tempos of collectivization and forms of collectives, which decided not on the *kommuna*—full socialization of everything—but on an intermediate form, the *artel,* with socialization of land, labor, draft animals, and fundamental implements, but private ownership of cows, other livestock, and some everyday tools. Collectivized peasants were also to be allowed to retain household plots. The commission's thorniest question was whether the "class enemy" kulak would be permitted to join the new socialist agriculture. Disposition of kulaks had largely been left to locals, and many collective farms were admitting them. The Yakovlev commission warned against any blanket approach.[151]

Suddenly, however, in a speech on the last day (December 27, 1929) of a week-long Congress of Agrarians-Marxists, Stalin preempted the commission, thundering in words *Pravda* carried two days later that "we have gone over from a policy of *limiting* the exploiting tendencies of the kulak to a policy of *eliminating* the kulaks as a class." Liquidating an entire class? "Is it possible to accelerate tempos of our socialized industry more while having such an agricultural base as small peasant farms, incapable of expanding production and yet predominating in our economy?" he asked rhetorically. "No, not possible. Is it possible to continue for a more or less long period to base Soviet power and socialist construction on two different foundations—on the foundation of the largest and most consolidated socialist industry and on the foundation of the most subdivided and backward small-scale peasant economy? No, not possible." He continued: "What's the solution? The solution is to make agriculture large-scale, make it capable of accumulation, of expanding production, and in this way transform the agricultural base of our economy."[152] Stalin had a famously soft voice, but one audience member called his ultra-class-war speech "electrifying."[153]

Once again, the dictator had enacted a conspiracy within the regime: at Old Square, more than a month before, he had received the OGPU hierarchs—Yagoda, Messing, Yevdokimov, and others—as well as Georgy Blagonravov, the former head of the secret police transport department and now first deputy commissar of railroads.[154] This would be the kulak liquidation team.

Stalin also used his pencil to hand victory to the more rabid members of the Yakovlev commission: the partially socialized *artels* were no longer to be allowed as the main form of collectives indefinitely, but would be superseded by a leap to the "higher-form" *kommunas*. Stalin also crossed out mention of farmers retaining minor implements, chickens, or a milk cow and wrote in that collectivization was to be completed in just one to two years (depending on region), using dekulakization. All this became a politburo resolution approved on January 5, 1930.[155] Six days later, Yagoda asked his top subordinates how many people could be interned in existing labor camps and where new camps might be quickly established, encouraging them to "think creatively."[156] The upshot was that each territory would have a deportation quota.[157] "Not everyone has the nerves, strength, character, and understanding to appreciate the scenario of a tremendous breakup of the old and a feverish construction of the new," Stalin exulted in a letter to Gorky in Sorrento (January 17). "Naturally, with such a 'baffling turmoil,' we are bound to have those who are exhausted, distraught, worn out, despondent, and lagging—and those who go over to the enemy camp. These are the inevitable 'costs' of revolution."[158]

Stalin issued secret circulars to local party machines on the dekulakization of more than 2 million peasants, using every available instrument: the procuracy, courts, regular police (militia), secret police, party activists, urban workers, and, if necessary, soldiers.[159] Orjonikidze let slip the recklessness at the Central Control Commission on January 18: "Do not forget that in our conditions, what yesterday was considered correct today might already be incorrect."[160]

BUILDERS OF THE NEW WORLD

There were more than 500,000 settlements in just the European part of the Soviet Union. Newspaper articles and decrees made their way to the county level and even below, but the party-state lacked rural cadres that could see through consistent implementation.[161] Stalin, however, had an ace in his deck: a decision to recruit urban workers to build socialism in the countryside had been announced at the November 1929 plenum. Trade unions ("Time does not wait!") were recruiting "politically literate" workers who were to inject their superior "consciousness" into the vast "spontaneity" of the petit bourgeois countryside.[162] Worker volunteers were backed by considerable force. Red Army men would be used sparingly—the OGPU was warning of "kulak" moods even among poor peasant soldiers—but thousands of OGPU internal troops were deployed.[163] "Those who are joining the collective farm, sign up with me," one activist announced. "Those who do not want to join, sign up with the police chief."[164]

Of Stalin's many instruments, however, none was greater than the enchanted vision of building a new world. The regime had planned to mobilize up to 25,000 urban workers; more than 70,000 were said to have volunteered, and around 27,000 were accepted. More than two thirds were party members, and more than four fifths were from industrial regions. The vast majority had between five and twelve years' factory experience, but nearly half belonged to the 23–29 age cohort.[165] Only one in fourteen were female. "Your role is the role of the proletarian leader," Kaganovich told a group of Moscow and Leningrad "25,000ers" about to depart for villages. "There will be difficulties, there will be kulak resistance and sometimes even collective farmer resistance, but history is moving in our favor. . . . Either we destroy the kulaks as a class, or the kulaks will grow as a class of capitalists and liquidate the dictatorship of the proletariat."[166] Semyon Budyonny, the civil war cavalry hero, and Voroshilov had appeared at Moscow train stations to conduct send-offs to "the grain front."[167] One worker recruit was quoted as saying, "It has been necessary for a long time to carry out such a firm policy, the sooner to catch up to capitalist countries."[168]

The 25,000ers descended on the countryside in late January/early February 1930, in advance of the spring sowing drive.* They discovered that the regime-instigated class war was eliciting both social solidarity—poor peasants hiding or aiding kulaks—and peasant eagerness to benefit from expropriating those better off.[169] Peasant property, seized in the name of the state without compensation, was supposed to be turned over to the new collectives after settlement of outstanding debts of the household in question, and its value counted toward the joining fees for poor peasant members.[170] But activists (or onlookers) who evicted "kulaks" could take their possessions. One OGPU report stated that members "of lower echelons of the party-soviet apparatus deprived members of kulak and middle peasant households of their clothing and warm underwear (directly from their body), 'confiscated' headwear from children's heads, and removed shoes from people's feet."[171] A favored trick was the "auction": one new village party secretary managed to obtain a four-room house, valued at 700 rubles, for 25.[172]

The OGPU secretly reported that some of the volunteers tried to rape village women and lusted for power. ("If I command it, you must do it, whether to jump into water or fire, otherwise it's a bullet to the forehead.")[173] Administrative chaos ensued in many places. Even conscientious 25,000ers were not well versed in

---

* Like tsarist Russia, the Soviet Union had two sowing seasons: one in the spring, harvested in late summer/fall, accounting for about 60 percent of the year's crop (mostly wheat and barley); another in the fall, harvested in the spring, accounting for 40 percent (almost all the rye, some barley, and some wheat).

management or agronomy, and most faced material hardships on-site, as well as armed resistance. "Remember, you sons of bitches, we'll get even with you," read notes delivered to 25,000ers in their names.[174] Ambushes by peasants with axes and sawed-off shotguns spread fear, concretizing the Manichaean propaganda.[175] But the orgy of confiscation occurred alongside rampant idealism.[176] Some 25,000ers reported indignantly that *kommuna*—not *artel*—collective farms had been imposed; others wrote earnest letters about "violations of socialist legality" (to the very authorities who committed them), risking charges of playing into the "kulak's hands." Many of the 25,000ers had escaped villages not long before and imagined that they were helping to overcome darkness and bring modern life to the countryside.

WRATHFUL SPRING

Early OGPU reports had been channeling Stalin's delusion that "middle" and "poor" peasants were "turning toward the collective farm," but soon enough the secret police reported mass resistance. ("Down with collectivization!" "No one is taking an ounce of grain from here!") In March 1930 alone, the OGPU would register more than 6,500 spontaneous "anti-Soviet group protests."[177] Peasants could not coordinate their opposition across regions, had no transregional leaders or access to the press, and were armed, if at all, only with hunting rifles. This was by no means a "civil war." Of the 2.5 million peasants who joined protests, according to the secret police count for the year, most did so nonviolently, refusing to join the collectives. Still, peasants would assassinate more than 1,100 rural officials and activists in 1930. Another weapon was arson, "the Red Rooster," set loose on administrative buildings.[178] Most frequently, protesters destroyed their own livestock: already one quarter of the country's farm animals had been lost, a higher proportion than during the cataclysmic civil war. Almost half the mass peasant actions in 1930 would occur in Ukraine, where, in strategic regions bordering Poland, revolt overtook every inhabited settlement. Many villages elected their own leaders, ringing church bells to signal mobilization. Hundreds of leaflets were printed, in thousands of copies: "Down with Soviet power!" "Long live a free Ukraine!"[179]

Stalin had been warning of how "liquidation of the kulaks" and the "sharpening of the class struggle" would encourage "imperialist intervention" in the USSR.[180] Had the "imperialists" been anywhere near as aggressive as he and

Soviet propaganda painted them, they would have taken full advantage of his reckless destabilization.

Almost no one had foreseen Stalin's stunning turn to complete liquidation of the kulaks, but now came another bolt from the blue: on March 2, 1930, *Pravda* published his article "Dizzy with Success," castigating local functionaries as "blockheads" caught up in "communist vainglory" who "feared acknowledging their errors." Stalin took no responsibility himself for the dislocation. "The collective farm must not be imposed by force," he admonished. "That would be stupid and reactionary."[181]

Despite his apparent retreat, intended to ease the pressure, the OGPU reports on domestic rebellion kept coming: uprisings in Georgia, Armenia, Azerbaijan, the Central Black Earth region, Siberia's Barabinsk steppe.[182] Enraged especially about the overthrow of Soviet governing bodies along the frontier with Poland, Stalin privately ripped into the OGPU "to stop making speeches and act more decisively" (March 19, 1930). An offended Vsevolod Balytsky, Ukraine OGPU chief, claimed to the republic party boss, Kosior, that he was already doing just that, from a command post in the field. Orjonikidze, dispatched to the scene, wrote that peasant rebellions in border regions were being smashed "using machine guns and, in some places, cannons."[183]

Trotsky, of all people, published an open letter to the Communist party (dated March 23) condemning the "adventurism" of violent collectivization and breakneck industrialization. Very few Soviet Communists could read the exile's text, but they did not have to.[184] The *Pravda* issue with Stalin's article was reselling for 3, 4, or 5 rubles in the countryside, and peasants were gathering to listen to it being read.[185] One peasant in the Lower Volga observed, "We have two governments—one in the center that writes to take back everything and the other local one that does not want this."[186] In fact, some local officials did reject Stalin's retreat. "If they saw someone with a newspaper, they beat them harder and condemned: 'So, you're reading comrade Stalin's article,'" M. Kvasov wrote, in a letter published in *Peasant Newspaper*, apropos of a village assembly on March 27. "When the peasants showed the party cell secretary, Petrov, Stalin's article, they declared, 'You are concealing the party line.' But Petrov answered coldly: 'You, comrades, are non-party, and this does not concern you. Don't believe everything in the newspapers.'[187] Local officials began to accuse Stalin of "right deviationism."[188]

In the regime's urban strongholds, money was giving way to barter amid galloping inflation, coins (which contained silver) were being hoarded, and even

cigarettes could not be had. "At Moscow Tricotage no. 3," a trade union functionary wrote in his diary (March 14), "one worker gave a speech stating, 'Stalin wrote
a correct article, only late. Bukharin wrote about this half a year ago and now it
is being done Bukharin's way. Ilich was right, saying, "Don't trust Stalin, he will
ruin you."'"[189] Moscow provincial party boss Kārlis Baumanis—who had been
ahead of Stalin in publicly promoting wholesale collectivization—was now made
a sacrificial lamb, accused of extreme leftism. Kaganovich replaced him as party
boss for Moscow in April 1930, while remaining a Central Committee secretary.
Dispatched to Western Siberia that month (Roberts Eihe, the party boss there,
was said to have appendicitis), Kaganovich got an earful, but he forced the local
party bureau to adopt a secret resolution condemning as "leftist" their complaints against Stalin's scapegoating of them.[190]

Nikolai Kin, a worker in the southern Ukraine city of Kherson, sent Stalin a
blistering rebuttal to "Dizzy with Success," detailing how the Central Committee
was at fault, the party's authority was damaged, and regime policies were self-
defeating: "We are liquidating the kulak, and developing orphans and the indi-
gent, throwing the children of kulaks, who are guilty of nothing, on the street."
Stalin responded privately. "Time will pass, the fury will subside, and you will
understand that you are incorrect from beginning to end," he wrote (April 22),
admonishing Kin not to take pride in being a worker. "Among workers all kinds
of people are found, good ones, bad ones. I know old workers with long experience in production who are still following the Mensheviks and even now cannot
emancipate themselves from nostalgia for the old capitalist masters. Yes, comrade Kin, all kinds of workers are found on the earth."[191]

PROPAGANDA AND HUNGER

To immense fanfare, on April 25, 1930, the separate constructions of the northern and southern sections of the Turkestan–Siberian Railway, known as Turksib,
were joined at Aina-Bulak, some eight months ahead of schedule, using excavators
purchased abroad and gargantuan amounts of manual labor, amid climate ex-
tremes and self-generated chaos. The Soviets engaged and persecuted "bourgeois"
specialists and Kazakh *jataki* (horsemen without herds); unemployed Slavic workers had flocked in for the ration cards. The upshot would be Siberian grain imported to Central Asia to allow further expansion of cotton crops, and, in the short
term, a propaganda coup.[192] To the ceremony/banquet for thousands in the steppes

("Long Live Turksib! Long Live Stalin!"), a special train from Moscow carried officials and foreign guests, "a microcosm of the Soviet world . . . and its capitalist encirclement," quipped an American journalist.[193] A single Turksib could occlude many fiascoes, especially for people who wanted to believe. Not every person would be ideologized to the same depth, but life outside Communism was becoming unthinkable.[194]

The Rostov Agricultural Engineering Works followed, the largest of its kind in Europe, pronounced complete on June 1, 1930, after three years of construction.[195] An iconic power station, Dneprostroi, at the cataracts of the Dnieper in Soviet Ukraine, was under fevered construction. Never mind that, for a time, half the derricks were occupied picking up the other half: the symbolism of harnessing nature in order to power a new industrial complex of projected aluminum plants and an integrated steel plant at Zaporozhe was linked in saturation coverage to individual transformation. "We build the dam, and the dam builds us" became the oft-repeated slogan.[196] Epic constructions of the state-of-the-art steel blast furnaces—and of new people—at far-off Magnitogorsk and Kuznetsk were bathed in bright spotlights, too, attracting hordes of foreign correspondents, many of whom were moved to renounce their skepticism.

The sites also drew peasant laborers seeking to transform themselves, escape from dekulakization, or find food. Reports of spot food shortages and starvation-induced disease were most extensive already in summer 1930 and emerged from the Central Black Earth region, the North Caucasus, Ukraine, the Soviet Far East, and Western Siberia.[197] The authorities in Kiev implored Mikoyan to send emergency supplies ("All local resources have been used"). The OGPU noted that collective farmers in Ukraine were refusing to work because they were not being fed, threatening a vicious food-shortage circle.[198] But it was in the Kazakh autonomous republic that hunger and mass flight were most extensive in the summer of 1930. More than 150,000 Kazakhs, and their nearly 1 million head of livestock, were said to be heading for Siberia, Uzbekistan, Iran, Afghanistan, and China.[199] Propaganda notwithstanding, the collectivization that was supposed to finance industrialization was instead threatening to starve it.[200]

LUCK BEYOND BELIEF

Stalin kept up the pressure to suppress resistance; the OGPU had made 140,724 arrests between January 1 and April 15, 1930, and from the latter date through

September 30 it would make another 142,993. But he was powerless to reverse an anticollectivization wave unintentionally incited by his "Dizzy with Success" article.[201] The proportion of collectivized households, on paper, would collapse, from 56 percent as of March 1, 1930, to 24 percent by the summer.[202] In the Tatar autonomous republic, collectivized households fell from 83 to 13 percent. Altogether, perhaps 8 million households quit, taking 7 million draft animals. At the same time, at least 5 million households remained in collectives, and more than 4 million of them had joined only recently, meaning that this was their first agricultural season in the new way.[203] The regime's violence and the peasants' resistance had put the spring sowing and thus the fall harvest under threat, with consequences for industrialization. Stalin—and the country—needed a miracle.

Getting collective farms up and running was not for the squeamish. A few 25,000ers were able to pry loose scarce tools, scrap metal, construction materials for barns and silos, spare parts for machines, generators, books, tobacco, and workers from their home factories for their collective farms, and many put their skills to use as mechanics to repair inventory. Peasants went from threatening 25,000ers to protesting their transfers.[204] Tellingly, the vast majority of the volunteers would end up staying in the countryside as new rural officials. (On average, a 25,000er ended up in one of every three collective farms in the principal grain-growing regions, and in one of every five collective farms overall.) By and large, despite minimal regime support and their own ignorance, it seems they helped salvage the spring 1930 sowing season. One key contribution was their introduction of the brigade system into the fields.[205]

Regime concessions were even more consequential for the spring sowing. Peasants who quit collective farms were given back their seed grain if they promised to sow crops. Belatedly, the regime made clear that although the main fields, draft horses, and plows would be collectivized, some livestock could remain in households' possession. For those who stayed in the collectives, gigantomania, whereby entire counties were combined into a single collective farm, was abandoned.[206] Those who remained were also permitted to cultivate their own household plots of fruit and vegetables. Perhaps 33 percent of what these farmers grew in 1930 would come from these plots. The regime was keen to demonstrate the collectives' superiority to individual household farming and allowed the collective farms to retain a sizable 3.5 tons of grain per household. Stalin would never again countenance such a generous retention. What the farmers did not consume, they could sell. Stalin assumed that the collectively worked fields would soon render small household plots and the maintenance of animals uneconomical, but for now his regime sent out a decree to "forbid the closing of markets, reopen bazaars, and not hinder the sale of their products on the market by peasants, including collective farmers."[207]

Beyond 25,000er mobilization and grudging regime flexibility, local solutions to the chaos emerged. The central authorities had proved unable to settle on how collective farmers would be compensated, but the farmers sowed crops anyway as locales came up with their own compensation formulas.[208] Sheer luck made an incalculable contribution in the form of spectacularly favorable weather. "Nature gave us an extra month of spring," one official rejoiced, and, given how late the sowing campaign had begun, that month was crucial for the harvest.[209] With harvest projections suddenly going from doubtful to promising, grain exports to earn hard currency for machinery imports would be increased far beyond what the Five-Year Plan had anticipated for 1930, to more than 5 million tons. Mikoyan crowed at a Moscow regional party conference in early June that "one more year, and we shall not only secure ourselves enough grain, but become one of the largest grain producers in the whole world."[210]

LAUGHTER, APPLAUSE

In the early summer of 1930, Stalin had sent Nadya to German doctors in Karlsbad for a stomach ailment. "Tatka! . . . What was the journey like, what did you see, have you been to the doctors, what do they say about your health, write to me," he wrote on June 21. "We open the [party] congress on the 26th. Things are not too bad. I miss you very much. Tatochka, I am at home alone, like an owl. . . . Come home soon. I kiss you."[211] The 16th Party Congress opened as scheduled, the first since December 1927 and a massive affair, attended by 2,159 delegates, 1,268 of them with voting rights. Yet another purge had expelled more than 170,000 party members, especially in the countryside, for "passivity," drunkenness, "defects in personal life," "alien" social origins, or being "concealed" Trotskyites, and intimidated those who sympathized with the rightists.[212] But because of new recruitment of worker members, sometimes of entire factory shops, membership in 1930 would rise by more than 500,000, to 2.2 million. Still, that was 1.4 percent of a total population of perhaps 160 million. Only one quarter of state functionaries belonged to the party, and in industrial management it was significantly less.[213]

Stalin's lengthy political report, over both the morning and the afternoon

of June 27, proceeded in his now familiar catechism fashion of rhetorical questions, enumerated points, and key-phrase repetition, in a self-congratulatory
tone. "Today there is an economic crisis in nearly all the industrial countries of
capitalism," he gloated. "The illusions about the omnipotence of capitalism in
general, and about the omnipotence of North American capitalism in particular,
are collapsing." He deemed the crisis one of overproduction, and asserted that
capitalism's contradictions were sharpening, which goaded the bourgeoisie to
foreign adventurism. "Capitalist encirclement is not simply a geographical conception," he warned. "It means that around the USSR there are hostile class
forces, ready to support our class enemies within the USSR morally, materially,
by means of financial blockade, and, when the opportunity arises, by means of
military intervention." Stalin bragged, however, that the party's industrialization tempos were making the Trotskyite super-industrialists of the 1920s seem
"the most extreme minimalists and the most wretched capitulators. (Laughter.
Applause.)"[214]

Stalin remonstrated that "people who chatter about the necessity of reducing
the rate of development of industry are enemies of socialism, agents of our class
enemies (applause)." "Dizzy with Success" rural caution was abandoned: "Either
we vanquish and crush them, the exploiters, or they will vanquish and crush the
workers and peasants of the USSR."[215] Because the "socialist sector" had come to
dominate the economy, he declared, the USSR had entered "the period of socialism." Congress delegates enjoyed the right to purchase scarce goods at the restricted OGPU store, including fabric for a suit (3 meters for just 54 rubles), a
coat, a shirt, a pair of shoes, two pairs of underwear, two knitting needles, two
chunks of regular soap, and one of bath soap. They also received, gratis, 800
grams of meat, 800 grams of cheese, 1 kilo of smoked sausage, 80 grams of sugar,
100 grams of tea, and 125 cigarettes. "This is, of course, a blatant buy-off," observed Ivan Shitts, a Russified Baltic German (Shutz) and an editor at the *Great
Soviet Encyclopedia*, in his diary, noting that despite propaganda trumpeting the
"heady growth of production," the opportunity to buy mundane goods was
treated as a perquisite.[216]

Budyonny, the country's most famous horseman, joked at the congress that
"we will destroy the horse as a class." He had in mind not the peasants' destruction of livestock, which the regime had provoked, but the introduction of tractors. Just in time for the congress, the Stalingrad Tractor Factory, whose
construction had been rushed through the brutal winter, produced its first

tractor. Stalin had sent a congratulatory telegram, printed in *Pravda* on June 18, thanking "our teachers in technology, the American specialists and technicians," and lauding the plant's prospective annual tractor output as "50,000 missiles exploding the old bourgeois world, and laying the road to a new socialist order in the countryside."[217] This was the USSR's first conveyor belt plant, but only 60 percent of the machine tools had been installed. Instead of a planned 2,000 tractors in the July–September 1930 quarter, the factory would produce 43, and an American engineer on-site noted that "after 70 hours of work they begin to go to pieces." Soviet steel was awful, copper ribbon for radiators arrived scratched beyond use, thousands of the assembly-line workers were touching nuts and bolts for the first time. Two of the high-priced American engineers died from typhoid; others begged to go home.[218] Mastering Fordist assembly lines would take time. But a twenty-five-year-old *Pravda* correspondent, before he died of tuberculosis, gushed about the "uninterrupted flow of life, if you wish, the conveyor belt of History, the laws of its development in socialist conditions with all its breakdowns, terrible disruptions, savagery, filth, outrages."[219]

At pre-congress meetings in educational academies, factories, and major party organizations, sharp attacks had been leveled at party policy.[220] But rather than attempt to lead this widespread sentiment—that is, behave like an opposition—Rykov and Tomsky had traveled to party gatherings and warned of attempts by "petit bourgeois elements" in the village and the "bourgeoisie" abroad to take advantage of divisions inside the party. Their reward was to be rebuked at the congress for insufficient zeal in repudiating their potential followers.[221]

Bukharin, ill with pneumonia—what Trotsky contracted while under political assault—had gone to Crimea, where he hooked up with Anna Larina; she was sixteen, he was forty-one.[222] Rykov was left to shoulder the burden and, through vicious heckling, once again admitted his errors ("of tremendous political significance") but denied that he was part of any opposition.[223] During the proceedings, Stalin wrote to Nadya (July 2) in Germany, "Tatka! I got all three letters. I could not reply immediately, as I was very busy. Now at last I am free. The congress will end the 10–12th. I shall be expecting you, do not be too long coming home. But stay longer, if your health makes it necessary. . . . I kiss you."[224] The congress dragged on to the 13th. Tomsky, Bukharin, and Rykov were reelected to the Central Committee, which returned Rykov to the politburo. But Tomsky was left out of the politburo, and his people were systematically purged from trade union positions. "It could be said that this is a violation of proletarian democracy," Kaganovich told the congress delegates, apropos of the firings, "but comrades, it has long been known that for us Bolsheviks democracy is no fetish."[225]

Kaganovich was "elected" to full membership in the politburo. Voroshilov and Orjonikidze departed the capital immediately for holidays of around two months. On July 17, the Stalin loyalist Sergei Kirov reported on the party congress to the Leningrad party organization he oversaw. "In a word, do not be in a hurry," he said, mocking the rightists. "If the question arises that it is necessary to press the kulak, why do it? We are building socialism anyway, and sooner or later the kulak himself will disappear. . . . If we need to conduct grain collections, if the kulak must hand over his surplus, why squeeze him when the price paid could be raised and he will then give it over himself. . . . In a word, the rightists are for socialism, but without particular fuss, without struggle, without difficulties."[226]

Two days later, state bank chairman Pyatakov, the recanted Trotskyite, who had been talking heart to heart to Orjonikidze, wrote to Stalin detailing a fiscal crisis and runaway inflation from lack of attention to costs and promiscuous printing of money. He proposed radically streamlining imports, curbing exports of animal products, raising prices on many goods, and tightening expenditures at the wasteful iconic construction projects.[227] It was, effectively, a belated post-congress brief for a course correction. Stalin did not immediately respond.

AN ANTICAPITALIST SYSTEM
IN EMBRYO

Stalin's personal dictatorship—known as the party's "secret department"—got a new director on July 22, 1930: Alexander Poskryobyshev (b. 1891), whose father, like Stalin's, had been a cobbler and who had trained as a nurse before the revolution. "One day," the shaven-headed Poskryobyshev would recall, "Stalin summoned me and said, 'Poskryobyshev, you have a frightful look about you. You'll terrify people.' And he engaged me."[228] On July 23, Stalin departed for his annual southern holiday, taking Poskryobyshev with him. Molotov was left to mind the store in Moscow. Nadya, after visiting her brother Pavel Alliluyev, the Soviet trade representative in Berlin, had returned from Germany and joined her husband. On July 26, Stalin's Rolls-Royce, exiting the territory of the Puzanovka dacha, crashed into a car from the nearby resort Red Storm. Nadya, Budyonny, and Stalin's main bodyguard, Ivan Jūsis, were also in the vehicle. A piece of flying glass cut Stalin's left eyebrow.[229]

Stalin had been suffering occasional dizziness and a flaring of nerves, and doctors confirmed a diagnosis of neurasthenia.[230, 231] His medical record for 1930, signed by Usher Leib "Lev" Levin, a top Kremlin physician who had taken care of Lenin, characterized the ruler's living conditions ("good"), diet ("good"), work conditions ("intellectual, significant, interesting, indeterminate number of hours in the day"), drinking ("rare"), and smoking ("a lot"). It listed his appendectomy, which had left a scar, and illnesses over the years (chest pains, flu, polyarthritis, chronic tonsillitis, coughing). Stalin's outward appearance was noted as "fatigued"; his liver and spleen as not enlarged. He was said to have frequent pain in his left shoulder muscles, which were atrophying, a result of a childhood contusion. Down south, he had his usual joint and muscle aches and undertook sulfur baths at Matsesta, near Sochi, which worked wonders. "After the course of baths, K. E. Voroshilov came over for a walk, and they drank cold, naturally carbonated water," Stalin's physician, Ivan Valedinsky, recalled. "After the walk Stalin's throat hurt, [and he developed] so-called follicular sore throat with attacks and flaring." Stalin's temperature reached 102. It took four days to drop. After that, he complained of pains in his left leg. Valedinsky saw his patient every day for three weeks, and the dictator appreciated his company, speaking to him on a wide variety of topics: labor discipline, collective farms, the intelligentsia. When it was time for Valedinsky to depart, Stalin inquired how he could recompense him. "I asked for help in changing my apartment, which was a former merchant's horse stable," the doctor recalled. "Stalin smiled after this conversation. When I returned to Moscow, I was called by the Central Committee and told they would show me an 'object,' which turned out to be a five-room apartment."[232]

Stalin cherished his recuperative time on the Black Sea. On August 13, 1930, he notified Molotov, back in Moscow, "P.S. Bit by bit I'm getting better." Exactly one month later, he would write, "I'm now *completely* recovered."[233] But, as always, this was a working holiday, and he received ciphered telegrams every day, and fat packets of longer documents eight to twelve times a month. Many of the far-reaching changes to the country and the regime he set in motion the previous winter and spring were now consolidated.[234] The secret police enjoyed a further ballooning in personnel.[235] Strangely, there had been a reversal of fortunes between agriculture and industry. Meat and dairy production had fallen off a cliff, but the grain harvest—ultimately fixed at 77.2 million tons—turned out to be the best in Soviet history to date.[236] With the agricultural cooperatives that had been marketing peasant products transformed into collectors of grain, and machine tractor stations also facilitating collections, the regime would procure a whopping 22 million tons at state-set prices. (The peasants ate or sold the rest on the market.)[237] All the while, however, from July through September 1930, critical metal-producing and fuel industries declined, undermining industry as a whole. Labor supply became tight, railways devolved into bottlenecks, and inflation proceeded unabated. Glaring underproduction of tractors compared with plan targets and mass loss of livestock cast doubt on agriculture's future, too.

Already in the summer and fall of 1930, while luminaries such as H. G. Wells, the British science fiction writer, were lauding the Five-Year Plan as "the most important thing in the world today," the "planlessness" of Soviet planning was exposed in an incisive analysis by the Menshevik émigré newspaper *Socialist Herald,* which pointed out that setting maximal quantitative targets and goading each factory to meet them, where some would succeed and others not, and where even successes would be at varied levels, rendered coherence impossible. Overfulfilling the output target of nuts only led to waste if they exceeded the production of bolts; an increased supply of bricks provided no extra utility with insufficient mortar.[238] Hoarding and wheeling and dealing via illegal markets—a shadow economy—became indispensable to the working of the "planned" economy but rendered shortages and corruption endemic. "We buy up materials we do not need," noted the head of supply at Moscow's electrical engineering plant, "so that we can barter them for what we do need."[239] With no legal market mechanisms to control quality, defective goods proliferated. Even priority industrial customers suffered anywhere from 8 to 80 percent defective inputs, with no alternative suppliers, and one factory's poor inputs became another factory's low-quality output.[240]

Stalin was well informed about the problems.[241] But he understood next to nothing of the structural pathologies he had embedded by eliminating private property and legal market mechanisms. Unaccountable regional party machines, meanwhile, were consumed by skirmishing. After a collective denunciation had arrived from Western Siberia against Roberts Eihe, Stalin wrote to Molotov (August 13, 1930) that Siberia had just been divided into two regions, west and east, and that no one had complained about Eihe when he had run all of Siberia. "Suddenly Eihe turns out to be 'unable to cope' with his assignments? I have no doubt this is a crudely masked attempt to deceive the Central Committee and create 'their own' *artel*-like regional committee based on mutual protection. I advise you to kick out all the intriguers and . . . put full trust in Eihe."[242] Convoluted infighting near his holiday dacha, in the South Caucasus federation, involving Georgia, Armenia, and Azerbaijan party bosses, was giving Stalin fits.[243]

The dictator also kept a close eye on Mikhail Kalinin, who enjoyed a high profile because of his peasant origins and his role as ceremonial head of state (chairman of the Soviet central executive committee).[244] At the politburo, Kalinin occasionally allowed himself to vote against Stalin (as in the case of closing the cafeteria for the Society of Old Political Prisoners). Orjonikidze, at the party Control Commission, had received materials from the tsarist police archives to the effect that Kalinin, as well as Jānis Rudzutaks, had squealed while under arrest, leading to incarceration of other comrades in the underground.[245] Then, individuals accused of belonging to a fabricated "Laboring Peasant Party" testified in prison about their plans to include Kalinin in a replacement government. Molotov hesitated to circulate the extracted testimony. "That Kalinin has sinned cannot be doubted," Stalin insisted (August 23), intent on narrowing Kalinin's scope to act independently. "The Central Committee must definitely be informed about this in order to teach Kalinin never to get mixed up with such rascals again."[246]

Even as he attended to his personal power, Stalin drove the financing of industrialization. "We have one and a half months left to export grain: starting in late October (perhaps even earlier), American grain will come onto the market in massive quantities, and we will not be able to withstand that," he warned Molotov (August 23). "Once again: *we must force through grain exports with all our might*."[247] Stalin insisted on sales even though world grain prices had fallen 6 percent in 1929 and would fall another 49 percent in 1930. (The equivalent of a year's grain exports were being stockpiled across countries.) Prices for industrial machinery remained more or less stable, meaning that in 1930, twice as much Soviet grain had to be exported per unit of machinery imported than had been the case in 1928.[248] "Some clever people will come along and propose holding off on the shipments until the price of grain on the world markets rises 'to its ceiling,'" he cautioned Molotov in the August 23 letter. "There are quite a few of these clever people in trade. They ought to be horsewhipped, because they are dragging us into a trap. In order to hold out, we must have hard currency reserves. But we don't have them. . . . In short, we must push grain exports furiously."[249]

The Soviets would export just over 5 million tons of grain at an average price of only 30 rubles per ton (half that of 1926); they would earn 157.8 million foreign-currency rubles, equivalent to a bit more than $80 million.[250] But whereas Soviet cereals had effectively accounted for zero percent of world market share in 1928, before 1930 was over the USSR would capture fully 15 percent.[251]

Stalin continued to insist that the economic troubles in the capitalist world had only reinforced the dependence of Poland, Finland, and the Baltic states on the imperialist powers, which eyed these states as platforms for attacking the Soviet Union. In fact, the Polish government had secretly rebuffed the urgent entreaties of the Ukrainian national movement in Poland to invade the Soviet Union, evidently deterred by Soviet military measures on the frontier.[252] Still, Stalin warned Molotov about likely provocations by Poland or Romania and about Polish diplomacy. "The Poles are certain to be putting together (if they have not already done so) a bloc of Baltic states (Estonia, Latvia, Finland) in anticipation of a war against the USSR," he wrote (September 1, 1930). "To repulse both the Polish-Romanians and the Balts we should prepare to deploy (in the event of war) no fewer than 150 to 160 infantry divisions, that is, (at least) 40 to 50 divisions more than are provided for under our current guidelines. This means that we will have to bring our current army reserves up from 640,000 to 700,000 men." Otherwise, Stalin asserted, "we are not going to be able to defend Leningrad and the right bank of Ukraine."[253]

CONSPIRACY OF LOGIC

The bulkiest papers in Stalin's holiday mailbag had become OGPU reports of plots and accompanying protocols of interrogation. Thousands of specialists had been sentenced.[254] From Sochi, Stalin had instructed Molotov to circulate to Central Committee members new "testimony" extracted from specialists in two agencies (food supply and the statistical administration). That same day, in a belated and indirect response to Pyatakov's devastating memo on state finances, Stalin wrote to Mężyński demanding a report on "the struggle" against speculators.[255] He had also written to Molotov "that two or three dozen wreckers from the [finance commissariat] must be executed." He wanted them linked to the rightists, adding that "a whole group of wreckers in the meat industry must definitely be shot and their names published in the press."[256] *Pravda* (September 3) duly publicized arrests of prominent specialists. Executions would follow.

Privately, Stalin acknowledged his didactic purposes. "By the way," he wrote to Molotov, apropos of a "Menshevik Party" trial, "how about Misters Defendants admitting their *mistakes* and disgracing themselves politically, while simultaneously acknowledging the strength of the Soviet government and the correctness of the method of collectivization? It would not be a bad thing if they did."[257] A scapegoat dimension was also manifest: on September 13, he wrote that supply commissariat "wreckers" had plotted to "cause hunger in the country and provoke unrest among the broad masses and thus facilitate the overthrow of the dictatorship of the proletariat."[258] *Pravda* announced the executions of forty-eight "food wreckers," and the OGPU reported worker approval and intelligentsia disapproval of the sentences. ("In tsarist times there were also executions, but they were rare; now they look at people as if they are dogs.")[259] Stalin issued instructions for a trial of a "Union for the Liberation of the Ukraine," which was staged in Kharkov's Opera House with forty-five defendants: writers, theologians, philologists, schoolteachers, a librarian, medical personnel. "We ought not to hide the sins of our enemies from the workers," he wrote to the bosses of Soviet Ukraine. "In addition, let so-called 'Europe' know that the repressions against the counterrevolutionary part of the specialists who try to poison and infect Communists-patients are completely justified."[260]

The entire country, it seemed, was honeycombed with wreckers—including in the Red Army command: on September 10, 1930, Mężyński sent Stalin interrogation protocols incriminating Tukhachevsky and other high-placed military men in a conspiracy against the regime.[261]

Tukhachevsky had been demoted from chief of staff to commander of the Leningrad military district. He remained a polarizing figure, a former nobleman who mixed prominently with tsarist general staff types, even though he had never gone to the general staff academy. Many people deemed him, as one put it, "smart, energetic, firm, but vile to the last degree, nothing sacred besides his own direct advantage."[262] At a public book discussion, he had been the target of resentful shouts in the hall ("You should be hung for 1920," a reference to the Polish-Soviet War debacle).[263] Recently, he had submitted a fourteen-page memorandum to Voroshilov calling for massive increases in military industry. Tukhachevsky argued that no modern army could prevail without tanks, aircraft, chemical weapons, and parachute infantry for greater mobility. He called for annual production of no less than 50,000 tanks and 40,000 airplanes (which would rise in the future to 197,000 tanks and 122,500 aircraft). This unsolicited program had put Voroshilov—already anxious about Stalin's fondness for Uborevičius, another modernizer—on the spot.

Voroshilov had had the memo vivisected by the new chief of staff,

Shaposhnikov. Although Tukhachevsky had not specified the size of his proposed standing army, Shaposhnikov reckoned it at a preposterous 11 million, fully 7.5 percent of the Soviet population.[264] Then the defense commissar had sat on these materials for weeks.[265] Immediately after "Dizzy with Success" was published castigating excesses, Voroshilov had sent the original and Shaposhnikov's damning assessment to Stalin, noting that "Tukhachevsky wants to be original and . . . 'radical.'"[266] Stalin had answered, "You know that I greatly respect comrade Tukhachevsky as an especially capable comrade," a remarkable admission. But Stalin, too, dismissed Tukhachevsky's "'fantastic' plan" as out of touch with "the *real* possibilities of the economic, financial, and cultural order," and concluded that "to implement such a 'plan' would entail ruining both the country's economy and the army. It would be worse than any counterrevolution."[267]

Stalin's letter had deemed Tukhachevsky a victim of "faddish 'leftism,'" but in Mężyński's September 10, 1930, letter, he was accused of harboring "rightist" sentiments as the head of a military plot. Collectivization had provoked hints of wavering in the Red Army (something Voroshilov denied), and Stalin was preternaturally given to seeing an ideological affinity between the party right deviation and the tsarist-era officers. Police informants who suffused the military milieu reported gossip, on the basis of which the OGPU had arrested two military academy teachers close to Tukhachevsky.[268] At first their "testimony" was vague, involving his Gypsy lover (who might be working for foreign intelligence), but under police direction they began to "recollect" Tukhachevsky's possible links to "right deviationists," until soon enough they spoke of a monarchist-military plot to seize power.[269] "I reported this case to comrade Molotov and asked for authorization, while awaiting your directives," Mężyński wrote in his letter to Stalin, asking whether he should immediately arrest all the top military men named or await Stalin's return, which, given the alleged existence of a coup plot, could be risky. Stalin instructed Mężyński to "limit yourself to maximally careful surveillance."[270]

Had Stalin believed in the existence of a genuine military plot, could he have suggested waiting to arrest the plotters and remained on holiday, far from the capital, for another month? It is impossible to establish his thinking definitively. Still, it appears that for him the "coup plot" derived not from facts per se, but from Marxist-Leninist logic: criticism of collectivization ipso facto meant support for capitalism; support for capitalism meant colluding with the imperialists; furthering the cause of imperialism meant effectively plotting to overthrow the Soviet regime; plotting an overthrow perforce entailed assassinating Stalin, since he embodied the building of socialism.

Elections in Germany on September 14, 1930, meanwhile, delivered a sensation: the National Socialists received 6.37 million votes, 18.25 percent of the total, and increased their parliamentary deputies from 12 to 107, becoming the second-largest party in the Reichstag, after the Social Democrats, at 143. Communist deputies increased from 54 to 77. *Pravda* (September 16) deemed the vote a "temporary success of the bourgeoisie," even while noting that millions of those who had voted for the Nazis had rejected the existing order.

Stalin at this time seems to have been more fixated on his nemesis Rykov, complaining to Molotov (September 13) that "the Council of People's Commissars is paralyzed by Rykov's insipid and essentially anti-party speeches. . . . Clearly, this cannot continue. Radical measures are needed. As to what kind, I shall tell you when I get to Moscow." But Stalin could not wait, writing again from Sochi, "Rykov and his lot must go as well. This is now inevitable. . . . *But for the time being, this is just between you and me.*" By September 22, Stalin was urging Molotov to take Rykov's place as head of government. "With the arrangement I am proposing to you," Stalin noted, "we will finally have a perfect union between the top levels of the state and the party, and this will reinforce our power." Stalin instructed Molotov to discuss the idea "in a tight circle with close friends" and report any objections. He appears to have written the same to Kaganovich.[271] Stalin also showed deep frustration over circumvention of central directives, despite newspaper exposés. In the same letter, he proposed "a standing commission established for the sole purpose of systematically *checking up on implementation* of the center's decisions."[272]

From reports of eavesdropped conversations, Stalin could read that the populace was unhappy with the consequences of wholesale collectivization, dekulakization, and accelerated industrialization—which was why Rykov was especially dangerous: he was a leader who could rally the disaffected and the opportunistic. It was not Rykov alone, moreover: at a politburo meeting on September 16, 1930, the Stalin protégé Syrtsov, head of the Russian republic's Council of People's Commissars, had agreed with Rykov, head of the USSR Council of People's Commissars, regarding an accumulation of problems not being addressed, and supported Rykov's proposals to sell scarce goods, such as sugar, at market prices to stabilize state finances.[273] Molotov told the dictator that at the politburo meeting, Syrtsov had spoken "with frantic right-wing opportunist claims that it is not possible to solve acute economic problems with repressive 'OGPU' methods."[274] Despite Stalin's impatience, the removal of Rykov—an ethnic Russian with a peasant background, who had worked with Lenin, occupied

Lenin's former position, and refused to embrace the role of opposition—would be no simple matter.[275]

Stalin forwarded the OGPU interrogation protocols incriminating Tukhachevsky to Orjonikidze on September 24. "Read without delay the testimony," he suggested. "The material, as you see, is utterly secret, and Molotov, myself, and now you are the only ones to know about it. I do not know if Klim knows. It turned out that Tukhachevsky is a captive of anti-Soviet elements and was thoroughly worked over by anti-Soviet elements from the ranks of the rightists. . . . Is it possible? Of course, it is possible, since it is not excluded. . . . It seems the rightists are prepared to embark on the path of military dictatorship if only to escape from the Central Committee, collective and state farms, Bolshevik tempos of industrialization." Here, again, was that objective "logic" of conspiracy. And yet, Stalin concluded the letter ambiguously: "We cannot end this affair in the usual way (immediate arrest and so on). We need to think this through."[276]

On October 2, 1930, Mężyński sent Stalin interrogation materials relating to a clandestine Industrial Party. "To the OGPU, comrade Mężyński. In person only. From Stalin," the dictator wrote back, specifying the exact content of the conspiracies and demanding corroborating testimony, which, if extracted, "will be a serious victory for the OGPU." Stalin either believed or made it appear that he believed in the fabrications, instructing Mężyński's interrogators to ascertain: "1) Why was the [foreign military] intervention in 1930 put off? 2) Is it because Poland was not ready? 3) Perhaps because Romania was not ready? 4) Perhaps because the Baltic states and Romania have not yet come to terms with Poland? 5) Why have they put off the attack to 1931? 6) Might they put it off to 1932?" Stalin added that the confessions would be made available to "the workers of the world. We shall launch as broad a campaign as possible against interventionists and thwart them in their attempts for the next one or two years, which is of great significance to us. Everything understood?"[277]

RUN THE GOVERNMENT?

Nadya had already returned to Moscow in August. "How was your travel?" Stalin had written with tenderness (September 2, 1930). "Write about everything, my Tatochka. I'm getting a little better. Your Iosif." Writing again, he asked her to send his textbook for English.[278] On September 8, he had written her about his difficult dental work. He sent peaches and lemons from his Sochi orchard. But something was amiss. "The Molotovs scolded me for leaving you alone," she answered him (September 19). "I explained my departure by reference to my studies, but that of course was not the real reason. This summer I did not feel that you would like me if I prolonged my stay; quite the contrary. Last summer I felt very much that you would, but this time I did not. Of course, there was no point in staying in such a mood. Write, if my letter does not make you cross, but as you like. All the best. A Kiss. Nadya." Stalin (September 24) denied that her presence had been undesirable ("Tell the Molotovs from me that they are wrong") and assured her that, despite having had eight teeth filed down in a single day, "I am healthy and feel better than ever." On September 30, she wrote that she had required an operation on her throat and had been bedridden for days. On October 6, she complained that "for some reason I am not hearing anything from you. . . . Probably you are distracted by your quail-hunting trips. . . . I heard from a young, interesting lady that you are looking fantastic—she saw you at lunch at Kalinin's. She said that you were exceptionally jolly and gave no rest to everyone taken aback by your personage. I am glad to hear it."[279]

On October 7, Molotov, Voroshilov, Orjonikidze, Kuibyshev, Mikoyan, and Kaganovich—but not Kirov (in Leningrad), Kosior (in Ukraine), Rudzutaks, or Kalinin (both away on holiday and outside the innermost circle)—met without Stalin to discuss his proposal that Molotov replace Rykov.[280] The next day, Voroshilov wrote to Sochi that "Mikoyan, Molotov, Kaganovich, in part Kuibyshev, and I think that the best resolution would be unification of the leadership." He left out Orjonikidze. Voroshilov added that "as never before, the Council of People's Commissars needs someone with the strategist's gift." Stalin's episodic interventions in day-to-day government operations had a disruptive quality, and regularizing them could be beneficial.[281] It is also possible that they reasoned that having Stalin shoulder responsibility for the details of government could diminish his dictatorial behavior, for someone else would have to run the controlling party apparatus. Voroshilov admitted in his letter that "the most important, the most, from my point of view, acute question in the combination under discussion would be the party leadership."[282]

Mikoyan, in a separate letter, affirmed his support for "a consolidated leadership," "like what we had when Ilich was alive." Kaganovich wrote to Stalin (October 9) leaving it to him to decide, noting that "the most important strategic maneuvers in the economy and politics were determined, and would be determined, by you, wherever you might be. But will things get better if there is a change? I doubt it." He concluded that this argued for Molotov's appointment.

Molotov wrote that same day, listing the reasons he was unsuitable and encouraging Stalin to take the post, but acknowledging that party work and the Comintern would suffer. Unsurprisingly, Stalin decided to hold on to the party apparatus, which afforded him the final word on policy and personnel without the day-to-day burdens of the government. Orjonikidze had ascertained from private conversations that Stalin felt it was "inexpedient at the current time to have a complete (including externally, in front of the whole world) merger . . . of the party and Soviet leadership." Orjonikidze, perhaps the other obvious choice to replace Rykov, agreed with Stalin that Molotov should be the one. "He [Molotov] expressed doubts about how much authority he would hold for the likes of us," Orjonikidze wrote to Stalin, "but of course all that is nonsense."[283]

FICTION

Stalin returned to Moscow and, on October 14, 1930, received the OGPU hierarchs Mężyński and Olsky (the newly named head of the special department for the army).[284] That same day, Bukharin phoned him on Old Square, requesting a face-to-face meeting. Stalin had forwarded to Bukharin some Industrial Party interrogations that mentioned a terrorist plot against the dictator, with connections to the right deviation. On the phone, Stalin accused Bukharin of fostering an atmosphere for terrorist acts by criticizing the party line. Bukharin exploded that day in a private letter: "I consider your accusations monstrous, demented slander, wild and, in the last analysis, unintelligent." Stalin circulated the missive to the other politburo members.[285] On October 15, the politburo removed Pyatakov from the state bank but postponed a decision on Bukharin until he could appear in person.[286]

Formal politburo sessions continued to take place, as in the time of Lenin, in the rectangular meeting room on the third floor of the Kremlin's Imperial Senate, in front of Lenin's preserved corner office. But officials were bypassing formal structures to obtain Stalin's approval. Back from holiday, in his Old Square office, he received economics officials, the head of the railroads, a professor who had founded the Soviet biochemical industry, and the new head of foreign trade, Arkady Rosenholz (known as Rozengolts), in tandem with the foreign affairs commissar.[287] On October 17 and again on the eighteenth, Stalin received Vissarion "Beso" Lominadze, recently appointed South Caucasus party boss, whom he did not trust, and

Ruven "Vladimir" Polonsky, newly appointed Azerbaijan party boss. The second day's tête-à-tête to sort out the Caucasus infighting lasted three and a half hours.[288]

The politburo assembled again (October 20) and, with Syrtsov reporting, ordered the designation of several priority regions—Moscow, Leningrad, the Donbass, Baku—with higher norms of supply for workers.[289] The body also directed the OGPU to continue investigations of wrecking by alleged underground parties; decided to move the secret department of the central party apparatus from Old Square to the Imperial Senate, instructing Voroshilov to clean out undesirables still living in the Kremlin; and obliged Stalin to cease walking on foot in Moscow.[290] Bukharin seems to have asked what more was demanded of him, accused Stalin of violating their truce, and stormed out of the session. The politburo ruled that Stalin had been correct in refusing the one-on-one meeting. The dictator supposedly said, "I wanted to curse him out, but since he has left, there's nothing to say."[291]

Stalin was not the only one engaged in provocations. On October 21, Boris Reznikov, a student and party organizer at the Institute of Red Professors, who had worked under Syrtsov in Siberia as a deputy newspaper editor and had joined Syrtsov's group of intimates in Moscow, sat in the office of Lev Mekhlis, a Stalin aide and editor at *Pravda,* and wrote a denunciation of "factional activities" by Syrtsov as well as Lominadze. According to Reznikov, Syrtsov's "group" foresaw a collapse of Stalin's regime as a result of economic catastrophe. Mekhlis forwarded Reznikov's denunciation to Stalin that evening.[292] Reznikov, who nursed his own grievances against the dictator, played the role of agent provocateur, initiating a second informal meeting on October 22, in a private apartment, where he and Syrtsov again made critical remarks about the Stalin regime. Reznikov had aggressively solicited secret information from Syrtsov about the recent politburo meeting, and proposed that they link up with the right deviation, which profoundly worsened Syrtsov's indiscretions.[293] That same day, Stalin summoned Syrtsov to Central Committee HQ, on Old Square.[294] Those present when Syrtsov had spoken, summoned to a confrontation with Reznikov, repudiated his accusations, but all the same, they were expelled from the party and arrested, and they confessed. As Orjonikidze would put it, "They did not want to speak the truth to the Central Control Commission, but when they were imprisoned in the OGPU they bared their souls in front of comrade Mężyński (laughter)."[295]

Reznikov further claimed that Syrtsov had said that if push came to shove, a number of party secretaries, including Andrei Andreyev (North Caucasus),

Nikolai Kolotilov (Ivanovo-Voznesensk), and Roberts Eihe (Western Siberia), "might turn on Stalin." Syrtsov had also stated, according to Reznikov, that "a large share of party activists, deeply dissatisfied with the current policy and political regime, still believe a tradition of collective leadership exists in the politburo. . . . We need to dispel these illusions. The 'politburo' is a fiction. In reality, all decisions are made behind the backs of politburo members, by a small clique of party insiders, who meet in the Kremlin or in the former apartment of Clara Zetkin."[296]

The next day, Stalin forwarded the written denunciations by Reznikov against Syrtsov and Lominadze's factional group ("essentially right-deviationist") to Molotov—now the one away on holiday—commenting, "It is unimaginable vileness. Everything goes to show that Reznikov's reports correspond with reality. They played at staging a coup; they played at being the politburo."[297]

Meanwhile, Tukhachevsky, in the presence of Stalin, Voroshilov, Orjonikidze, and other politburo members, had been made to confront his two accusers from the military academy, and he, in turn, accused them of lying. It seems that Jan Gamarnik (head of the army political department), Iona Yakir (commander of the Ukrainian military district), and the latter's deputy, Ivan Dubovoi, were also present and vouched for Tukhachevsky.[298] Whether Stalin intended merely to intimidate the military men or had really wanted to incarcerate them remains unclear. In the October 23, 1930, letter to Molotov, he wrote, "As for the Tukhachevsky affair, he turns out to be 100 percent clean. This is very good."[299]

Syrtsov and Lominadze would not get off as easily. "I considered and consider Stalin's unwavering firmness in the struggle against Trotskyites and the right opposition an enormous historical service," Lominadze wrote in his defense (November 3, 1930). "But at the same time I thought that Stalin has a certain empiricism, a certain lack of ability to foresee. . . . Further, I did not like and do not like that sometimes (especially during the days of his 50th jubilee), in certain speeches in the press, Stalin was placed on the same plane as Lenin. If memory serves, I said this to comrade Orjonikidze and pointed to the corresponding places in the press." Lominadze's admission put Orjonikidze in a bind.[300]

Their cases were adjudicated at a joint session of the Central Committee and the Central Control Commission presidium (November 4), where Lominadze and Syrtsov both confessed to *engaging in political discussions with the other.* Syrtsov did not back down from claims that politburo decisions were predecided.[301] "I did not doubt for one minute the need for the liquidation of the kulaks as a class," he stated. "But I believe that, in addition to slogans, it is necessary and correct to have a detailed discussion of the implementation of these measures in a Central Committee plenum or a detailed meeting of the politburo. It seems to me we could have avoided many of the costs by doing so." For stating the achievements of regime policy but also the problems—the precipitous drop in workers' real wages, the shortages of goods ("an enormous counterrevolutionary danger emanates from queues"), the mass loss of livestock, inflation, budget shortfalls—and for suggesting the reintroduction of market mechanisms such as free trade, Syrtsov was accused of being a right opportunist and pro-capitalist, like Rykov.[302]

Stalin in his remarks denied using Clara Zetkin's unused Kremlin apartment in the Grand Kremlin Palace—except maybe a little, to avoid distracting phone calls as he composed his report to the party congress. "While I was working in this apartment at different times, Molotov, Kalinin, Sergo, Rudzutaks, and Mikoyan each came to see me once," he further divulged. "Did we, certain politburo members, occasionally meet? Yes, we did, mostly in the Central Committee building [on Old Square]. What is bad about that?" In a passage Stalin would edit out of the transcript, he inadvertently confirmed Syrtsov's charge, elaborating how the regime actually worked: "Sometimes a question arises, you phone Voroshilov: Are you home? Home. Come over, let's talk."[303]

So Syrtsov was right: the "politburo" had become a kind of fiction.

Stalin played the victim ("Let them abuse me. I'm used to that") and sought to accentuate the seriousness of the affair.[304] "School pupils gathered, fancied themselves big politicians, and decided to playact as the politburo—is it worth it for us to waste time on these pupils?" he asked. "In another time and under different circumstances, one could agree with that assessment. But in the current conditions, when the class struggle has sharpened to the ultimate degree, when every factional sally against the party leadership strengthens the front of our class enemies, and double-dealing of unprincipled people is transformed into the most dangerous evil of interparty life—in such conditions, such an assessment of the 'left'-right bloc would, at the least, be careless." He characterized talk that blamed him as an invitation to "a host of terrorists." Before closing, he turned his fangs on Rykov: "Your post does not exist for ceremonial purposes, but for implementing party orders on a daily basis. Is this the case now? Unfortunately not. . . . Such a state of affairs cannot last long."[305] When it came to the decision on Syrtsov and Lominadze, Stalin sought to appear the moderate, as usual, proposing only their demotion from full to candidate status. But a vote for expulsion from the Central Committee had already passed.[306]

SELLING OUT TO THE CAPITALISTS

Soviet newspapers (November 11, 1930) published lengthy indictments of prominent scientists and engineers accused of establishing a clandestine Industrial
Party. It was said to contain more than 2,000 members who had worked undetected for years to wreck Soviet industry and transport and, ultimately, overthrow
the regime with the assistance of foreign military intervention (by half a dozen
countries), thereby delivering Ukraine's wealth to Poland and France, and Caspian oil to Britain. "If the enemy does not surrender," Gorky, from Italy, obligingly
wrote in *Pravda* (November 15), "they will be annihilated."[307] Under klieg lights in
the chandeliered House of Trade Unions (the former nobility club) on November
25, in front of scores of Soviet and foreign correspondents, eight engineers stood
in the dock. Meetings at Soviet factories and the Academy of Sciences approved
resolutions demanding the death penalty. Columns of workers were marched
through snow in Moscow and other cities carrying banners: NO MERCY FOR THE
CLASS ENEMIES.[308] Thirteen days of delirium and treason tales ensued, with blanket coverage. The politburo decree specified the headlines, including "Our answer
to the class enemy—millions of workers in the ranks of shock workers."[309]

The problems faced by Soviet workers were all too real. An internal report
(November 10) from a secret OGPU survey of cafeterias noted that half were being patronized far beyond capacity, and that "in all cafeterias (even in restricted
ones) there are long queues, which causes worker dissatisfaction and negatively
affects labor discipline." The OGPU found rats (dead and alive), cockroaches,
and flies (including in the soup), a lack of spoons, forks, and knives (forcing long
waits for their reuse), lunches far below daily caloric norms, theft by employees,
and filth beyond description.[310]

Just as in the Shakhty trial two years earlier, the only "evidence" in the Industrial Party trial consisted of confessions recorded in secret police custody, which
were repeated at the proceedings. (The published indictments had noted that one
arrested engineer had "died under questioning.") No witnesses were called. All
eight defendants pleaded guilty. Leonid Ramzin, director of the All-Russian
Thermal Engineering Institute, confessed to leading the underground "party,"
and spoke of foreign panic at Soviet successes and of a pending invasion by Romania, to be joined by Poland, then France, and supported by the British Royal
Navy, with émigré collusion.[311] Two of the émigrés named had died before the
supposed meetings took place. Also, Ramzin named as the prospective head of a

replacement "bourgeois" republic a Russian engineer who admired Herbert Hoover (as an engineer) but who had already been executed, without a public trial, in a previous case.[312] Never mind: Nikolai Krylenko, the prosecutor, hinted at veiled links between the "bourgeois specialists" and rightists in the party. All in all, the published trial transcript might be the best extended record to date of the workings of Stalin's mind: the possible and the actual were fused into a narrative that could be—must be—true.[313]

Stalin's truculence, too, was evident. If in the Shakhty case he had willfully put several German citizens in the dock during negotiations for a Soviet-German trade agreement, now he targeted France, which he had recently called "the most aggressive and militarist country of all aggressive and militarist countries of the world."[314] France had imposed restrictions on Soviet imports; the Soviets had countered with reductions in imports from France.[315] Krylenko elicited laughter by reading out French news accounts of Russian émigrés in Paris gathering in protest of the proceedings: grand dukes, clergy, merchants—that is, "former people." But Ramzin testified at trial that he and other plotters had cooperated directly with none other than the former French president and prime minister Raymond Poincaré. The latter's office issued a denial, which was adduced at trial as "proof" of the plot.[316] A foreign affairs commissariat official tried to render the charges credible, giving a briefing for foreign representatives that waved off necessarily simplistic propaganda of an imminent military intervention but insisted that influential anti-Soviet circles in capitalist countries were inciting war through provocations such as assassinations of Soviet foreign envoys, seizure and publication of secret Soviet documents, and press campaigns about Soviet kidnappings abroad.[317]

Stalin needed no further evidence of such Western plots, but he had received a copy of a transcript of a recent confidential conversation between Winston Churchill, the former chancellor of the exchequer (out of office following the Labour party victory), and Prince Otto von Bismarck, a grandson of the famous chancellor. Churchill was recorded as telling the prince, who served in the German embassy in London, that "the growing industrialization of the Russian state presents all Europe with an extremely great danger, against which we can manage . . . only by creating a bloc of all the rest of Europe and America against Russia."[318] Behind the scenes, Czechoslovakia's foreign minister, Edvard Beneš, had sought to ingratiate himself with Moscow by telling the Soviet envoy in Prague (September 1930), "Confidentially, not long ago in Geneva, the French strongly insisted on action by Poland against the USSR with the active support of all members of the Little Entente" (an alliance of Czechoslovakia, Romania, and Yugoslavia, which the French hoped to direct against Germany and the members saw as directed against Hungary). Beneš shocked the Soviet foreign affairs commissariat by adding that if a military intervention against the USSR by France, Britain, and Italy took place, Czechoslovakia was "a member of the European states and will do the same that they do."[319]

Presiding judge Andrei Vyshinsky, as per instructions, read out guilty verdicts, sentencing three to prison terms and five, Ramzin included, to death. This came without right of appeal. The hall erupted in an ovation. Two days later, the regime announced that Soviet power was strong and had no need for revenge: the executions had been "commuted" to eight- or ten-year terms.[320] The morning after sentencing, Ramzin was spotted at his institute office cleaning out his desk, without apparent guard.[321] He was permitted to continue scientific work while serving his prison term.[322] Some Soviet workers saw through the "wrecking" burlesque.[323] But the leniency might have provoked the greater fury.[324] Even émigré enemies of the USSR acknowledged that a majority of workers accepted the guilt of the "bourgeois" specialists. "They got 3,000 [rubles per month] and traveled in cars, while we live on bread and potatoes," the well-informed Menshevik *Socialist Herald* quoted Soviet workers as saying. "They sold themselves to the capitalists."[325]

Lurking in the background was Stalin's long-standing personal nemesis, whose pen was once again prolifically engaged.[326] Now forty-eight years old, Trotsky in 1930 published *My Life: An Attempt at an Autobiography*, in Russian, German, English, and French, aiming to document how *he* was the true Leninist. He also wrote a stirring three-volume *History of the Russian Revolution*, in which his own and Lenin's roles were uppermost and Stalin's nonexistent; the book's preface was completed on Prinkipo on November 14, 1930. As it happened, that same day, Stalin returned a devoted young apparatchik of uncommon diligence to the central party apparatus as department head for economic personnel. His name was Nikolai Yezhov (b. 1895). Stalin received him on November 21, the first of what would be hundreds of private audiences connected to rooting out sabotage and treason.[327]

MYSTERY MAN

Rumors that Stalin had been killed were being spread out of independent Latvia, where many governments ran their intelligence operations against the Soviet

Union, and on November 22 Eugene Lyons, a Belorussia-born, New York–raised UPI correspondent in Moscow and a Soviet sympathizer, suddenly got summoned to Old Square for a seventy-minute audience. Stalin had last granted an interview four years earlier, to the American Jerome Davis, and was still pursuing the same aim of normalizing relations with the United States, which had become the USSR's third-largest trading partner, after Germany and Britain, but remained the only great power that withheld diplomatic recognition. In Stalin's office, Lyons noted portraits of Marx, Engels, and Lenin on the wall. "My pulse, I am sure, was high," he would recall. "No sooner, however, had I stepped across the threshold than diffidence and nervousness fell away. Stalin met me at the door and shook hands, smiling. . . . He was remarkably unlike the scowling, self-important dictator of popular imagination. . . . 'Comrade Stalin,' I began the interview, 'may I quote you to the effect that you have not been assassinated?' He laughed."

Lyons established for a foreign audience that Stalin had a wife and three children (the Soviet populace did not know), and that he could be charming. "Commenting on the fact that he is called Russia's Dictator," Lyons wrote, "Comrade Stalin exclaimed with another hearty laugh: 'It is just very funny!'"[328] Lyons was treated to tea and sandwiches in an adjacent room while typing his dispatch. Russia's dictator approved the typescript ("in general, more or less correct"), allowing it to be transmitted to New York, where the scoop created a sensation. Lyons returned to the United States for a twenty-city lecture tour. "One cannot live in the shadow of Stalin's legend," he observed, "without coming under its spell."[329]

The Soviet-friendly *New York Times* correspondent Walter Duranty erupted at his handlers over Lyons's scoop. Belatedly, Duranty, too, was granted an interview, also of seventy minutes, on November 27. He wrote that Stalin believed that the current global crisis in capitalism would deepen but not mark its demise, and yet the result would be a war over markets in the future, and the downfall of the the Versailles settlement.[330] "Stalin is the most interesting personality in the world," Duranty enthused in his telegram to the United States, which passed Soviet censors. "But of all national leaders he is the least known, he remains removed from everyone, mysterious, like a Tibetan Dalai Lama."[331]

A friend of Duranty's, H. R. Knickerbocker, got his own scoop: an interview with Stalin's mother, Keke Geladze, in Tiflis, for the *New York Evening Post* (December 1, 1930). "Revolutionary posters and the eternal appeal for harder work on the Five-Year Plan reminded one that all the way from Siberia to the edge of Persia the Soviet Union is dominated today by a single purpose, and a single will,"

Knickerbocker wrote. Keke, speaking through an interpreter of Georgian, took responsibility for Stalin's failure to finish the seminary: "He was not expelled. I took him out on account of his health. He did not want to go. I took him out. He was my only [surviving] son." She pointed at a pile of periodicals, all mentioning Stalin. "See how he works," she said. "All this he has done. He works too hard." The article was titled "Stalin Mystery Man Even to His Mother."[332]

STOUT INNER CIRCLE

All authoritarian regimes require a sense of being under siege by sinister "enemies." The inhabitants of the USSR found themselves exhorted to relentless vigilance against class enemies, supposedly longing for foreign military intervention to overturn the Soviet regime, restore capitalism, and exact revenge. Under such a vision, even diehard socialists could be denounced as "White Guards"—as Lenin and Trotsky had denounced the Kronstadt sailors in 1921—if they opposed the Soviet regime. Pervasive domestic difficulties rendered the treason tales plausible, press reports gave them life, and Stalin afforded them great intensity.[333] During the proceedings against Syrtsov and Lominadze, he had interrupted Mikoyan to say of his Communist party critics, "Now they are all White Guards."[334] Working intimately with the obliging Mężyński, he had elaborated a comprehensive scenario: a right deviation, a right-left bloc, "bourgeois specialist" wreckers, and a military conspiracy with right-deviation links, all of them with foreign ties, aiming to bring on war, reverse collectivization, sabotage industrialization, and remove him.[335] He was the fulcrum.

On December 1, 1930, Syrtsov became the first politburo official expelled by the method of merely polling Central Committee members over the phone, without a plenum.[336] During the whole year, not a single multiday Central Committee plenum had taken place. One had been postponed, perhaps because Stalin had to cajole members into accepting the sacking of Rykov.[337] Now Stalin wrote to Gorky in Sorrento, divulging Rykov's imminent replacement by Molotov, calling it "unpleasant business" while championing Molotov as "a bold, smart, utterly modern leader."[338] As for Bukharin, Stalin wrote to him on December 13, in his now customarily put-upon fashion, that "I have never refused a conversation with you. No matter how much you cursed me, I have never forgotten that friendship that we had. I am leaving aside the fact that the interests of the cause require each of us unconditional forgetting of any 'personal' insults. We can always talk, if you want."[339]

Finally, on December 17, 1930, the delayed plenum opened, and at the last minute it became a joint session of the Central Committee and the punitive Central Control Commission.[340] On the third day, after Rykov's report had been lacerated by all and sundry, Kosior suddenly proposed relieving Rykov of his post and nominated Molotov to head the government. No one could doubt who stood behind the move. The vote was unanimous.[341] "Until now I have had to work mostly as a party functionary," Molotov told the joint plenum. "I declare to you, comrades, that I go to the work in the Council of People's Commissars as a party functionary, as a conductor of the will of the party and its Central Committee."[342] Bukharin, in a speech also delivered on December 19, mocked himself and his allies and joked about executions of rich peasants and the shooting of party oppositionists, eliciting laughter, while still managing to score points about Stalin's wild-eyed industrialization and collectivization—a bravura performance. ("This is turning into an incoherent discussion. I am deeply sorry for this fact, but it is not my fault.")[343] Over repeated interruptions, Bukharin had finally just told Molotov that they would do whatever they wanted, since "all power and authority are in your hands."

Molotov had no prior experience in government, but he would prove himself up to the task. Born the ninth of ten children, in 1890, to a shop clerk in central Russia, under the name Skryabin (he was a nephew of the composer and pianist Alexander Skryabin), he had joined the Bolshevik faction in 1908 while a teenager, and in 1912 took the name Molotov ("Hammer"). Bukharin, speaking to Kamenev, had fumed about "that blockhead Molotov, who tries to teach me Marxism," but Molotov had attended the St. Petersburg Polytechnic and edited *Pravda* before Bukharin did. Molotov's underground hardening and diligence had attracted him to Lenin, who called him Comrade Filing Cabinet. An underling recalled that "everything he was given to do was done faultlessly, in time, and at any price."[344] Another observer, who described Molotov as "fully conscious of his importance and power," noted that he could sit for long hours of hard work and was informally called Stone Ass.[345]

On the final day (December 21), Rykov was expelled from the politburo; Orjonikidze assumed his spot on that supreme body.[346] Kaganovich assumed Molotov's place as Stalin's top deputy in the party. Whereas Molotov had been methodical and wooden, Kaganovich was dynamic and showy. The Menshevik *Socialist Herald* rightly judged the latter to be "of quite exceptional abilities," with an excellent memory for names and faces, "a quite exceptional ability to deal with people," an immense capacity for work, and willpower.[347] Kaganovich ran the orgburo, which oversaw personnel and ideology, but Molotov, as head of government, would now chair politburo meetings, by tradition going back to Lenin. Molotov had known Stalin since 1912, and Kaganovich had known Stalin since 1919.[348] "He was generally personally always against me," Molotov recalled of Kaganovich later in life. "Everybody knew this. He would say, 'You are soft, you are an *intelligent,* and I am from the workers.'" Molotov added, "Kaganovich, he is an administrator, but crude; therefore, not all can stand him. He not only pressurizes, but is somewhat personally self-regarding. He is strong and direct—a strong organizer and quite a good orator."[349]

Voroshilov and Orjonikidze were closer to Stalin personally (the former had known him since 1906, the latter since 1907), and while Voroshilov continued to oversee the military, Stalin appointed Orjonikidze head of the Supreme Council of the Economy, in place of the faltering loyal dog Kuibyshev, who was transferred to the state planning commission.[350] Kuibyshev had gone from voicing skepticism about lunatic plan targets to promoting them zealously; now Orjonikidze went from sharply criticizing industrial cadres to being their protector, and gathered around him capable "bourgeois" experts, even if they had been imprisoned for a time.[351] Sounding a bit like the sacked state bank chairman and former Trotsky supporter Pyatakov, whom Orjonikidze would make his deputy, he pointed out, in a long memorandum on industry in December 1930, that "money is being spent without any budget. . . . Accounting is exceptionally weak and muddled." Stalin made only superficial notes on the memo; these were Orjonikidze's worries now.[352]

None of the men in Stalin's faction had the revolutionary profiles of Zinoviev or Kamenev, let alone Trotsky, but the Stalinists were hardened Bolsheviks and, under the pressure of events, strove to enforce his line and resolve problems, sometimes presenting him with solutions.[353] He confided in them, writing scathingly about everyone else in the regime, and to an extent he allowed them room to work, reserving the right to reverse any of their decisions; they acknowledged his power to do so, knowing the burdens he shouldered. The heart of the regime remained awkwardly divided between party headquarters on Old Square, where Stalin had his principal office, and the Imperial Senate in the Kremlin, where the government had its offices but where the secret department of Stalin's apparatus had moved, the politburo met, and Central Committee plenums were held. Voroshilov, in his letter concerning Rykov's replacement, had noted that "having the headquarters and main command point" on Old Square was "cumbersome, inflexible, and . . . organizationally problematic," adding that "Lenin in the current situation would be sitting in the Council of People's Commissars" in the Kremlin.[354] Clara Zetkin's empty apartment in the Kremlin had served as a kind of transition to a permanent move to the Kremlin by Stalin, but this transition would be gradual; he continued to use his top-floor Old Square suite.[355] In any case, as Kaganovich had mentioned, the regime was now wherever Stalin's person happened to be.

INTO 1929, his seventh year as general secretary, Stalin had continued to enlarge his personal dictatorship within the Bolshevik dictatorship, and by the end of 1930 he had amassed still vaster power. This process of acquiring and exercising supreme power in the shadow of Lenin's supposed Testament calling for his removal and the criticisms in the party made Stalin who he was.

Around the time of the December 1930 plenum, Iona and Alexander Pereprygin, two of the six siblings of Lydiya Pereprygina—the orphaned, scandalously young teenager with whom Stalin had had a long cohabitation during his last Siberian exile—were arrested for long-ago White Army service. They wrote an appeal to Stalin, reminding him of the "former friendship you nourished with us."[356] The brothers did not mention the son (Alexander) whom Stalin had allegedly fathered with Pereprygina and abandoned, but it is possible that one of Pereprygina's sons was Stalin's. ("Ësif was a jolly fellow, singing and dancing well," Anfisa Taraseyeva, of Kureika village, would recall. "He desired girls and had a son here, with one of my relatives.")[357] Pereprygina, who had married a local fisherman, was now a widow with numerous children; Stalin never assisted her. What action, if any, he took in response to her brothers' letter remains unknown.[358] When doodling, Stalin would sometimes draw wolves, but his days in a remote eight-log-cabin settlement among the indigenous Evenki on the Arctic Circle—where he almost died in sudden blizzards while hunting or fishing through holes cut in the ice—were a world away.

What Stalin forced through all across Eurasia was flabbergasting, using newspaper articles, secret circulars, plenipotentiaries, party discipline, a few plenums, a party congress, the secret police and internal troops, major foreign technology companies and foreign customers for Soviet primary goods, tens of thousands of urban worker volunteers and a tiny handful of top politburo officials, and the dream of a new world. Trotsky perceived him as an opportunist and cynic, a representative of the class interests of the bureaucracy, a person bereft of convictions. With Rykov's expulsion from the politburo, Trotsky even predicted, in his *Bulletin of the Opposition,* that "just as the rout of the left opposition at the 15th Party Congress [in 1927] . . . preceded the turn to the left . . . the rout of the right opposition presages an inevitable turn to the right."[359] Others in the emigration knew better. "Stalin is acting logically in the new peasant policy," Boris Bakhmeteff, the former Provisional Government ambassador to Washington and a civil engineering professor at Columbia University, had observed of collectivization to a fellow émigré as early as February 12, 1929. "If I were a consistent Communist, I would be doing the same." No less shrewdly, he added, "Stalin is capable of adapting, and, in contrast to other Bolshevik politicians, possesses tactical gifts. But it seems to me wrong to think that he is an opportunist and that for him Communism is a mere name."[360]

The Soviet state, no less than its tsarist predecessor, sought control over grain supplies to finance imports of machinery to survive in the international system, but Stalin ideologically excluded the "capitalist path." His vision was one of anticapitalist modernity. The perpetual emergency rule required to build socialism afforded free rein to his inner demons as well. Stalin's persecution of his friend Bukharin in 1929–30 revealed new depths of malice, as well as self-pity.[361] At the same time, his deft political neutering of Bukharin, Tomsky, and Rykov had demanded considerable exertion.[362] The rightists possessed an alternative program that—whether or not it could possibly work to achieve socialism—commanded support. Indeed, it is striking how much potential power the right wing of the party had possessed *within the politburo,* and how Stalin crushed them anyway.[363] They were hard pressed to match his cunning, and immobilized by their own aversion to schism: amid the mass peasant revolts that Rykov himself had predicted, the rightists shrank from too public a challenge to the party line.[364] Tactics aside, the rightists were handcuffed by party structures and practices: they had no way to capitalize on the deep disillusionment in the army and the secret police, except via a conspiracy, even when they were still members of the politburo. Rykov was respected but had made no friends throttling army budgets, and, unlike Stalin, had not earned plaudits at the front in the civil war.[365]

Stalin had adroitly positioned himself as the incarnation of the popular will and historical necessity, but his resounding political triumph of 1929–30 had demonstrated a certain dependency, beyond even the luck of the harvest. His power rested on Mężyński and Yagoda, who were in operational command of the secret police and not personally close to him, though keen to demonstrate their loyalty—but could Stalin be sure? Not for nothing had he promoted Yevdokimov. More fundamentally, Stalin's power rested upon just four fellow politburo members: Molotov, Kaganovich, Orjonikidze, and Voroshilov. The first two seemed unlikely ever to waver. But Orjonikidze and Voroshilov? Had they acted on their knowledge of the dangerous muddle Stalin had created with his "Great Break" and embraced the well-founded critiques put forward by the Stalin protégé Syrtsov and the Orjonikidze protégé Lominadze, the two authoritative figures in the politburo could have taken Stalin down. Of course, the question would have been, Who could replace him? No one in Stalin's faction appeared to consider himself the dictator's equal. Still, what if, going forward, they changed their minds? What if further difficulties arose, and this time foreign capitalists selling their state-of-the-art technology, and the peasants and the weather delivering a bounteous harvest, did not come to Stalin's rescue?

CHAPTER 2

APOCALYPSE

> Using deception, slander, and cunning against party
> members, with the aid of unbelievable acts of violence and
> terror, under the guise of a struggle to uphold the purity
> of Bolshevik principles and party unity, and using a
> powerful centralized party apparatus as his base, Stalin
> has over the past five years cut off and eliminated from
> positions of leadership all the best, genuinely Bolshevik
> cadres in the party and has established his personal
> dictatorship within the party and throughout the country
> as a whole, breaking with Leninism and taking a path of
> the most unbridled adventurism and uncontrolled
> personal tyranny, bringing the Soviet Union to the brink
> of the abyss.
>
> MARTEMYAN RYUTIN, *Communist party*
> *official, August–September 1932*[1]

IN THE FALL OF 1930, Japan celebrated the twenty-fifth anniversary of its victory in the Russo-Japanese War with fanfare, paying tribute to Admiral Tōgō (who was still active) and other "war gods" and reenacting Port Arthur's capture at the Kabuki Theater. "As a father," a general declares in the play, spurring wild applause, "I am pleased with the death of my two sons for the emperor."[2] That same fall, as soon as the surprise harvest bounty had been gathered, Stalin renewed his all-out forced collectivization and kulak deportations.[3] The December 1930 Central Committee plenum rubber-stamped his extremism, demanding 80 percent collectivization over the course of the next year in top grain-growing areas (Ukraine, North Caucasus, Lower Volga, Central Volga), and 50 percent in the next group (Central Black Earth, Siberia, Urals, steppes of Ukraine, Kazakhstan).[4] When the Eastern Siberians balked, Stalin replied that 50 percent was "a minimum target."[5] The plenum had also formally approved fulfillment of the Five-Year Plan within four years (by the end of 1932), while stipulating that 1931 would see the most ambitious industrial leap yet: a 35 percent rise in GDP, and a 45 percent jump in industry.[6] Stalin was spearheading a depiction of industrialization as class war, a revolutionary upsurge against a stepped-up offensive by alien elements, which struck a deep chord.[7] Some contemporaries did note the obvious falseness of the regime's ubiquitous slogans, but other observers, such as the American journalist Eugene Lyons, would remark that "these boys are geniuses for advertising."[8]

Mikhail Koltsov, the journalist-propagandist, boasted in *Pravda* (January 1, 1931) that "we are welcoming this new year happily and joyfully, without vacillations and doubts."[9] To enforce that steadfastness amid his distrust, Stalin used the police and party discipline.[10] He also turned to the bully pulpit, decrying the inept factory boss, the consummate red-tapist, the windbag, all of whom were successes at profusions of loyalty but failures at delivering the goods. More ominously, he would warn of deliberate deception, collusion, double-dealing, and sabotage. But the dictator himself would turn out to be the grand saboteur, leading the country and his own regime into catastrophe in 1931–33, despite the intense zeal for building a new world.[11] Peasants would speak of the biblical Apocalypse, some saying that the Virgin Mary had sent a letter in golden script warning that bands of horsemen would descend and destroy the collective farms.[12] Instead, the Four Horsemen arrived in the form of the enforcement of the collectives and mass starvation. Rumblings within the party would surface, demanding Stalin's removal.

BULLY'S MIND-SET

Henry Ford popularized the fact that manufacturing could be revolutionized by large capital investments and superior organization, throwing up a direct challenge for industry throughout the world economy. Mass manufacturing required costly, risky, up-front investments and a large market, but the Soviet statized economy removed competition (internal and foreign) and manipulated domestic demand, enabling industry to take advantage of assembly lines.[13] During the Five-Year Plan, the USSR would erect from scratch or wholly rebuild more than 1,000 factories, many in Fordist fashion.[14] All the advanced technology, with the exception of synthetic rubber, would be imported from leading foreign companies, and had to be paid for in hard currency.[15] The imports were assimilated with difficulty, and limited to priority sectors, such as steelmaking, chemicals, and machine building. The construction industry continued to use brick and timber rather than concrete; steam, not electricity, continued to power railways.[16] And even where blast furnaces or turbines were installed, auxiliary work was often still performed by hand or with primitive tools. Still, industry expanded significantly, and simultaneously with a plunge in production all across the capitalist world. Tsarist Russia had produced almost no machine tools in 1914; the Soviet Union, in 1932, produced 20,000.[17]

Under the slogan "Catch and Overtake" (the capitalists), the regime was on its way to acquiring not just a new industrial base but, finally, a substantial working class.[18] Already in 1930, employed labor nearly reached the plan target for 1932–33. Full employment, a magical idea, resonated globally. By the end of 1930, unemployment had reached 2.5 million in Great Britain, more than 3 million in Germany (it soon doubled from that), and more than 4 million in the United States (it soon tripled). But the disappearance of the unemployed in the USSR gave rise to unprecedented labor turnover—workers had options—which in turn provoked draconian laws such as prison sentences for violations of labor discipline or perceived negligence, and mandatory labor books to track workers.[19] Many workers and some managers fell into the inconsistently applied dragnet, but the excess of demand over worker supply subverted regime efforts to "plan" labor allocation. The flux was staggering: as many as 12 million rural folk permanently resettled in cities or at construction sites that became cities during the plan. (Moscow, which received migrants from other cities, too, swelled from 2 million to 3.7 million.)[20] Many tramped from place to place.[21]

No central decree explicitly outlawed private trade, but Stalin incited attacks against NEPmen (traders).[22] The number of shops and kiosks shrank from more than 600,000 in 1928 to 140,000. Party-state pressure also squeezed out individual artisans. (Molotov then decried the severe scarcity of wooden spoons at factory canteens and the sheer impossibility of having clothes or shoes mended.)[23] Many NEPmen disappeared back to villages, but a large number found employment in supply departments, enjoying privileged positions in the new socialist order.[24] Meanwhile, with rationing for bread and other staples already introduced in major cities, Stalin had placed the Achilles' heel of worker provisioning on the December 1930 plenum's agenda. The gathering endorsed a practice, initiated at some factories, to form "closed" cooperatives inside the gates to distribute groceries and clothes. The larger factories would soon establish their own farms, granaries, and goods warehouses, an unplanned yet foreseeable result of the suppression of legal private trade and private enterprise.[25]

Simply by virtue of its monopoly over politics and the public sphere and its dynamic mass organizations, the Soviet party-state stood out from other contemporary authoritarian regimes, but piecemeal introduction of a socioeconomic monopoly, too, added another major dimension to fulfilling the aspirations of totalitarian control. Centralized procurement and distribution imposed a nearly impossible administrative burden, and vast corruption and everyday ingenuity afforded people space to maneuver. Still, the Soviet state now asserted sway over not just people's political activities and thoughts but also their employment, housing, children's schooling, even their caloric intake—effectively, their families' life chances.[26]

The state itself was in upheaval, undergoing headlong expansion, thanks to elimination of private property, and political purging.[27] Skilled workers were promoted to fill many of the vacancies created by expansion and arrests.[28] This altered the demographics of the apparatus (but not its behavior) and of the working class, pushing the ratio of workers in large-scale industry aged twenty-two and under up to one third; the percentage of female workers rose as well.[29] New managers and engineers would have far more hands-on experience than tsarist-era ones, but for now, competence was in short supply and, combined with the frenzied pace, caused an epidemic of accidents and waste.[30] Some high-profile projects had to be shelved. Orjonikidze opened an All-Union Conference of Leading Personnel of Socialist Industry (January 30–February 4, 1931) with a speech that defended quantitative output targets but called for controlling costs, supplementing centralized allocation with direct factory-to-factory contract relations for additional supplies, and holding managers accountable for financial results and output quality. Further, he defended the "bourgeois" specialists, who for eighteen months had been subjected to withering public denunciations and trials for wrecking.[31]

But on the final day, Stalin arrived in the hall. "It is sometimes asked whether the pace can be reduced a bit, and the speed of development restrained," he stated. "No, this is impossible!" His reasoning was revealing: "To slacken the tempo would mean falling behind. And those who fall behind get beat up. But we do not want to get beat up! One feature of the history of old Russia was the continual beatings she suffered because of her backwardness. She was beaten up by the Mongol khans. She was beaten up by the Turkish beys. She was beaten up by the Swedish barons. She was beaten up by the Polish-Lithuanian pans. She was beaten up by the Anglo-French capitalists. She was beaten up by the Japanese lords. All beat her—because of her backwardness, her military backwardness, cultural backwardness, political backwardness, industrial backwardness, agricultural backwardness. Such is the law of the exploiters: beat up and rob the backward and the weak, capitalism's law of the jungle. You are backward, you are weak—and therefore you are wrong; therefore you can be beaten up and enslaved. You are mighty, therefore you are right, therefore we must handle you carefully." He concluded: "We are a hundred years behind the advanced countries. . . . We must make good this gap in ten years. Either we do it, or they will crush us."[32]

The dictator tapped into Russia's perennial torment over relative weakness vis-à-vis the West, and more recent fears of foreign forces ganging up on the socialist motherland. One participant would recall that Stalin "literally opened a valve through which the steam could be released."[33] But he challenged bosses to get out of their offices. "There are many people among us who think that management is synonymous with signing papers," he said. "This is sad, but true. . . . How is it that we Bolsheviks, . . . who emerged victorious from the bitter civil war, who have solved the tremendous task of building a modern industry, who have swung the peasantry on to the path of socialism—how is it that in the matter of the management of production, we bow to a slip of paper? The reason is that it is easier to sign papers than to manage production." He enjoined them to "look into everything, let nothing escape you, learn and learn again. . . . Master technology. It is time Bolsheviks themselves became experts. . . . Technology decides everything. And an economic manager who does not want to study technology, who does not want to master technology, is a joke and not a manager."[34]

DROUGHT AND REGIME SABOTAGE

Who, precisely, was a kulak—an owner of three cows? Four cows? Criteria could be murky. But centrally imposed quotas forced answers.[35] Naming "kulaks" often involved preemptively denouncing others to save oneself or settling old scores. "Socialism was a religion of hatred, envy, enmity between people," a group from Kalinin province (formerly Tver) wrote to *Socialist Husbandry* (March–April 1931).[36] Some peasants were motivated by class-war sentiments, but the quotas could be met only if many middle and poor peasants suddenly got classified as "kulaks." Those who refused to join the collectives became "kulaks," no matter how poor. The designation "kulak henchman" made anyone fair game, and ambitious secret police officials exceeded their quotas.[37] According to the OGPU's own classifications, many of those swept up in antikulak operations were petty traders, "former people," priests, or random "anti-Soviet elements."[38] The haste, arbitrariness, and wanton violence facilitated the operation by inciting chaos and fears of things slipping out of control, spurring further harsh measures.[39] Stalin ordered a second wave of internal deportations beginning in late May (through early fall 1931), which proved nearly twice as large as the previous year's.[40] He relied on local party bosses but especially the OGPU, and on the barbed rivalry between Yagoda and Yevdokimov for his favor.[41]

All told, around 5 million people were "dekulakized"—by the police, by their fellow peasants, or by choosing to flee, with an untold number perishing during deportation or not long after. Up to 30,000 heads of households were summarily executed. OGPU operatives improvised colonization villages, soon rechristened "special settlements," which were intended to be self-sufficient, but despite a torrent of decrees, actual settlements with housing would be formed only belatedly.[42] The dispossessed who survived the journeys in cold, dark cattle cars to the taiga had to make it through the first winter in tents or under the open sky.[43] They helped build the Magnitogorsk Metallurgical Combine, the Chelyabinsk Tractor Plant, and other Five-Year Plan showcases. The self-dekulakized and peasants who were dispossessed but not internally deported sought livelihoods at the same construction sites, provoking accusations of "infiltration."[44] The deputy OGPU plenipotentiary to Eastern Siberia reported mass flight from the special settlements, too, because of "severe living conditions and the food situation," as well as "epidemic diseases and high mortality among children." People, he wrote, "were completely covered in filth."[45]

All the while, the regime was supposed to be facilitating the planting for the next harvest, the first in which the collective and state farms would predominate.[46] The Five-Year Plan had originally envisioned a 1931 harvest of 96 million tons, and as late as the end of 1930 the harvest was estimated at 98.6 million, far larger than the best prerevolutionary harvests.[47] But in 1931, a cold spring followed by a summer drought—a fatal combination—struck the Kazakh steppes, Siberia, the Urals, the Volga, and Ukraine.[48]

Stalin got warnings of lagging harvest preparation as well as locust infestation and ordered some actions, but the regime seems not to have perceived the danger.[49] Kalinin wrote to the holidaying Avel Yenukidze (May 27, 1931), the secretary of the central executive committee of the Soviet, about the "unprecedented weather" in Moscow ("It's just like the hot south; rain is rare and brief") yet still asserted that "by all data the harvest should be good."[50] He made no mention of the devastating loss of draft animals (slaughtered animals do not consume grain, but they do not pull plows, either).[51] Matters were most dire in Russia's Kazakh autonomous republic, where the regime had decided that, in order to overcome "backwardness," it would force-settle nomads.[52] This region was the country's main meat supplier, but it was made a destination for several hundred thousand deported kulaks, further diminishing land for herds and increasing claimants on local food. State procurements took such a large proportion of the grain grown here that herders and their animals were effectively left to starve.[53] Reports reached Moscow of significant deaths among Kazakhs from famine and of mass flight to Uzbekistan, Siberia, Turkmenistan, Iran, and China in search of food.[54] Only the mountain territories of Dagestan matched the depth of starvation and epidemics seen again in 1931 in the Kazakh autonomous republic, a territory larger than Western Europe.[55]

Urban rationing, meanwhile, was mired in bureaucracy, while investment in housing, health care, and education took a backseat. Stalin attended both days of a conference of industrial managers (June 22–23, 1931).[56] In a rousing closing speech, he stressed no-excuses fulfillment of plan targets, while enumerating six conditions for industrial development, such as promoting higher-education graduates and factory workers into administration, and observed that "no ruling class has managed without its own intelligentsia," a euphemism for the emerging Soviet elite. His other conditions included expanding trade and differentiating workers' wages to stimulate productivity. "Socialism," Stalin concluded, "is the systematic improvement of the position of the working class," without which the worker "will spit on your socialism."[57]

"SPRINGTIME"

Control over the military is always an issue in a dictatorship. OGPU special departments continued to maintain watch lists for officers with tsarist pasts. Anti-Soviet émigré organizations, in parallel, strained to perceive tensions within the Red Army and infused their correspondence with fantasies about an officers' anti-Communist putsch. But the OGPU had infiltrated émigré groups and created front organizations to intercept their correspondence, track agents infiltrating from abroad, and entrap disaffected military men at home.[58] Many former tsarist General Staff Academy graduates would have been glad to see the Communist regime evolve into something else, but, having been relegated to administrative or teaching posts, they were in no position to work for an overthrow.[59] The smarter ones feared a foreign military intervention, precisely because the regime would round them up as presumed traitors (or, conversely, the occupiers would not forgive them for serving the Reds).[60] Voroshilov, the only quasimilitary figure in Stalin's politburo, beat back the OGPU provocations to dredge up "enemies," including against his own aide-de-camp.[61] Still, dossiers accumulated.[62] The central special department, in a kind of military equivalent to the Industrial Party trial, brought together initially disparate arrests, alleging a plot for a putsch in coordination with a military attack by the old Entente powers in spring 1931. Hence, the counterintelligence operation was code-named Springtime.

Mężyński certainly knew how to please Stalin, but he might have received direct instructions.[63] Stalin suspected Red Army commanders, few of whom were proletarians, to be "rightist" sympathizers secretly opposed to collectivization who would prove "opportunistic" in the event of an aggression from without. The roots of the "plot" were placed in Ukraine, even though the head of the Ukraine OGPU, Balytsky, had initially not taken to the task—until Mężyński reminded him that Ukraine's Chekists had missed the Shakhty Affair (a "discovery" of the North Caucasus OGPU).[64] Balytsky telegrammed Moscow (February 15, 1931) about a "counterrevolutionary military organization" in Kharkov. "Ivanovsky talked about the existence of a general operational plan for an uprising in Ukraine," he wrote of extracted testimony. "The plan was sketched on a map, which Ivanovsky destroyed during the Industrial Party Trial." Ivanovsky was also said to have corresponded with a parallel Moscow organization; that correspondence, too, had been burned.[65]

More than 3,000 former tsarist officers in Kharkov, Kiev, Moscow, and Leningrad were charged with conspiracy and espionage.[66] Shaposhnikov, the chief of staff of the army, whom Stalin had recently allowed to enter the party without the mandatory period of candidate status, was made to confront an arrested staff officer who accused him of belonging to the clandestine "organization." Shaposhnikov exposed his accuser as a slanderer, avoiding arrest but suffering demotion, in April 1931, to commander of the Volga military district.[67] Several score officers were not merely intimidated but executed. The sixty-six-year-old tsarist major general Andrei Snesarev—who, despite having joined the Reds, was Stalin's old nemesis during the Tsaritsyn days of 1918—was already in a labor camp on a death sentence commuted to ten years. Now he became one of the alleged plot's "leaders" and was resentenced to death in summer 1931, although, once again, the dictator commuted his sentence ("Klim! I think, for Snesarev, we could substitute ten years instead of the highest measure").[68]

Tukhachevsky's name, yet again, had surfaced in the "testimony" of those arrested. But Soviet intelligence had intercepted and decoded a telegram sent March 4, 1931, by the Japanese military attaché in Moscow, Lieutenant Colonel Yukio Kasahara, to the general staff in Tokyo, belittling the Red Army's capabilities, and urging "a speedy war" before the propitious moment passed.[69] After four discussions of Japan at the politburo, on June 10, in a surprise for the brass, Stalin returned Tukhachevsky from the Leningrad military district and promoted him to replace the head of armaments, Uborevičius (who went to the Belorussian military district).[70] As a deputy defense commissar to Voroshilov once more, Tukhachevsky made a summer inspection tour of strategic regions. Thus was the sweeping Springtime operation wound down, for now; the collection of compromising materials on Tukhachevsky and others did not cease.[71]

Stalin, in parallel, kept a watch on military technology. In mid-June 1931, with Voroshilov in tow, he visited the central aerodrome, in Moscow, to inspect Soviet aircraft, climbing into the cabin of the new Polikarpov I-5 fighter, under the direction of Alexander Turzhansky (b. 1898), of the Air Force Research Institute. "Listening to my explanations, Stalin suddenly asked, 'Where's the radio?'" Turzhansky recalled. "'On fighters there is no radio yet.' 'And how do you fight an air battle?' 'By maneuvering the aircraft.' 'That is unacceptable!'" A radio engineer hastened to the rescue, reporting that there was a prototype plane with a radio, but it awaited testing. Next up for inspection was a French Potez aircraft. Stalin asked, "'And the French plane has a radio?'" Turzhansky answered in the negative. "'Aha!' said a surprised Stalin. 'All the same, we need a radio on our fighters. And before them.'"[72]

UPHEAVAL

Some OGPU operatives looked askance at the primitive fabrications against what were unthreatening military administrators and teachers already on a short leash. Additionally, although Yagoda liked to advertise his office on the third floor of Lubyanka, 2, as open, many operatives despised him. Messing, the second deputy chief and head of foreign espionage, teamed up with Olsky, Yevdokimov, and Abram Levin (who oversaw the regular police and was known as Lev Belsky), to accuse Yagoda and Balytsky of artificially "inflating" cases.[73] The rebels were hardly strangers to fabrication (Yevdokimov and Olsky had recently framed a group of microbiologists).[74] But they saw Yagoda as walking on eggshells over alleged ties to the right deviation. Mężyński's continuing ill health helped spur the intrigue as well. His weight had ballooned to more than 250 pounds, exacerbating his heart condition, bronchial asthma, and endocrinal deficiency, and he had been reporting to work at Lubyanka perhaps twice a week for a few hours, before finally being sent to Crimea.[75] (He evidently spent time studying Persian, dreaming of reading the verses of the medieval polymath Omar Khayyám in the original.)[76] Mężyński returned to work only on June 8, 1931, and not at full strength.[77]

Stalin could have seized on the intrigues to promote a favorite, such as Yevdokimov. The latter knew Stalin had no fondness for Yagoda, but he had miscalculated the dictator's appetite for disorder in the organs, and for having Chekists force personnel decisions on him. On July 15, 1931, Stalin had Yevdokimov sent on holiday to the spa town of Kislovodsk and, ten days later, installed Ivan Akulov (a deputy head of the workers' and peasants' inspectorate) as first deputy chief of the OGPU. Yagoda nominally fell to second deputy. Stalin also advanced Balytsky to third deputy, a new post.[78] Akulov's appointment from outside was Stalin's response to the criticisms of OGPU illegalities.[79] Balytsky's spot in Ukraine was given to Stanisław Redens, Stalin's brother-in-law (through his first wife). Yevdokimov was assigned to run the OGPU in Leningrad in place of Filipp Medved (who was reassigned to Belorussia), but then the politburo reversed itself.[80] Medved stayed; Yevdokimov ended up in Central Asia.[81] The regime warned those transferred not "to bring along any functionary at all close to him from the regions they were leaving when transferring from one place to another," an entrenched practice of cliques that no decree could halt.[82] A clique was how Stalin had achieved and exercised power.

Global financial shocks were spiraling, but how much Stalin understood or paid attention remains uncertain. France and the United States together held two thirds of the world's gold, but their monetary authorities intervened to hold down the money supply, thereby failing to check the inflows of gold and causing global deflation. On July 6, 1931, France reluctantly accepted Herbert Hoover's proposal for a one-year moratorium on intergovernmental payments, including Germany's reparations. Hoover was concerned that Germany would default after the failure, in spring 1931, of Creditanstalt, Austria's largest bank, founded by the Rothschilds and considered impregnable (but lacking liquidity because of efforts to sustain the country's old industrial structure). That, in turn, had provoked bank runs in Hungary and Germany, too, and attacks on sterling. On July 8, strict controls were imposed on all German foreign exchange transactions, but five days later, one German bank collapsed. British officials fumed over France's perceived intransigence vis-à-vis Germany's hardship. "Again and again be it said," British prime minister Ramsay MacDonald confided to his diary (July 22), "France is the enemy."[83] British recognition of the need to "fix" the Versailles Treaty had only become more acute.

Despite the intense pressure on him, Stalin's flashes of anger were rarely seen, although at the politburo on August 5, 1931, he exploded in full view at a fellow Caucasus comrade for not removing a skullcap.[84] The next day, evidently his last in Moscow, he convoked an ad hoc politburo "commission" to draft a party circular on the OGPU events. It explained that the dismissed operatives had "conducted a completely intolerable group struggle against the leadership of the OGPU" by spreading rumors that "the wrecking case in the military was artificially 'inflated.'"[85] New rumors spread about what had really transpired.[86] Yagoda dispatched his own secret circular, approved by Stalin, admitting that "some individual operatives" had "forced the accused to give untrue testimony," but Yagoda denounced accusations of systematic falsification as slander by "our class and political enemies."[87]

HOLIDAY MAILBAG

Voroshilov traveled for more than two months in the summer of 1931, stopping in Khabarovsk, Vladivostok, Blagoveshchensk, Ulan Ude, Chita, Irkutsk, Novosibirsk, Chelyabinsk, and Magnitogorsk, and writing to Stalin about the benefits. "You are right: we do not always take into account the colossal significance of personal travel and firsthand familiarization with people, with business," Stalin answered. "We would gain a lot (and the cause would especially gain a lot) if we traveled more frequently to locales and got acquainted with people at work." But the dictator did not follow his own advice, leaving Moscow only for Sochi: "I did not want to leave on holiday, but then I surrendered (I got tired)."[88]

Stalin took full advantage of his southern holiday, writing to Yenukidze about having spent ten days in Tsqaltubo, in central-western Georgia, twelve miles from Kutaisi, where he had once sat in a tsarist prison. Its radon-carbonate springs boasted a natural temperature of 91 to 95 degrees Fahrenheit. "I took twenty baths," he observed. "The water was marvelous."[89] But field couriers delivered regime business in staggering volume: OGPU reports about Japan's aggressive behavior, fuel problems, foreign currency expenditures, forestry, nonferrous metals, politburo minutes.[90] Functionaries often sat paralyzed until he responded. His mailbag was the nexus of what normally would be called the policy-making process. He chose what to read (or not), and his preferences and habits profoundly shaped state behavior. He tended to go on holiday during harvest season and inquired often about grain procurements while paying little attention to the cultivation of crops or animal husbandry.[91] Stalin's non-holiday mail was also voluminous. In the six months leading up to August 1931, the apparatus processed 13,000 private letters in his name—enumerating each writer's identity, social origins, and employment and appending summaries of every letter, transferring most to the archives, sending some to government agencies for response, and forwarding 314 of them to Stalin.[92] His aides tended to pass him letters purporting to be from former acquaintances (requesting material aid or seeking the status of association with him); any that took up Marxist-Leninist theory; and those proposing scientific inventions (one letter from Egypt was forwarded with the annotation "not particularly trustworthy proposal for invention of 'death rays'").[93] Another type concerned allegations of abuse by officials. Stalin usually forwarded this filtered correspondence to responsible functionaries, expecting an answer. (In May 1931, a member of the Young Pioneers scouts group had written back to report that local officials had finally come through with a pair of boots, making school attendance possible, thanks to Stalin's intervention.)[94] "You are now all-powerful," wrote one correspondent. "Your word determines not only the life but even the freedom of a person."[95]

The holiday correspondence revealed that Stalin knew of the terrible food situation. "Now it is clear to me that Kartvelishvili and the Georgian Central Committee secretariat, with their reckless 'policy of harvest gathering,' have brought a number of regions in western Georgia *to famine*," he wrote to Kaganovich (August 17, 1931), using a word the regime would not publicly allow. "They do not understand that the Ukraine methods of harvest gathering, necessary and expedient in *grain-growing regions*, are not expedient and harmful in *non-grain-growing regions* that in addition lack *any* industrial proletariat. They're arresting people by the hundreds, including party members openly sympathizing with those dissatisfied and not sympathizing with the 'policy' of the Georgian Central Committee."[96] Stalin directed Mikoyan to send emergency grain to western Georgia.[97] One could never know which denunciation might catch Stalin's eye.[98] He could even rise to officials' defense when he perceived them to be victims of a vendetta.[99] Word reached him that one of his old Tiflis Theological Seminary teachers, seventy-three-year-old Nikolai Makhatadze, was imprisoned. "I know him from the seminary and I think he cannot present a danger for Soviet power," Stalin wrote to Kartvelishvili in Tiflis. "I request that the old man be released and that I be informed of the result."[100]

Kaganovich was now Stalin's top deputy in the party, and for the first time, the thirty-eight-year-old was managing affairs in the dictator's absence. Stalin took pride in what he called, to Kaganovich, "our leading group, which was formed historically in the struggle with all forms of opportunism," and reacted angrily to quarrels among them.[101] "I don't agree with you about Molotov," he wrote to Orjonikidze (September 11, 1931). "If he's giving you or the Supreme Economic Council a hard time, raise the matter in the politburo. You know perfectly well the politburo won't let Molotov or anyone else persecute you or the Supreme Council of the Economy. In any event, you're as much to blame as Molotov is. You called him a 'scoundrel.' That can't be allowed in a comradely environment. You ignore him, the Council of People's Commissars . . . Do you really think Molotov should be excluded from this ruling circle that has taken shape in the struggle against the Trotsky-Zinoviev and Bukharin-Rykov deviations? . . . Of course Molotov has his faults. But who doesn't have faults? We're all rich in faults. We have to work and struggle together—there's plenty of work to go around. We have to respect one another and deal with one another." Soon, an exasperated Stalin would reprimand Orjonikidze yet again: "We work together, come what may! The preservation of the unity and indivisibility of our ruling circle! Understood?"[102]

In Sochi, Stalin was staying up high at the Zenzinovka dacha and measuring temperature differences with the lower Puzanovka dacha, in a reprise of his youthful days as a weatherman at the Tiflis observatory. Nadya had again departed early; her fall classes were resuming. "Everything is according to the usual: a game of *gorodki*, a game of lawn bowling, another game of *gorodki*, and so on," he wrote, addressing her affectionately as "Tatka!" (September 9, 1931). Nadya replied that she had gotten safely back to a dreary capital. On the 14th, he wrote again: "I'm glad you've learned how to write substantive letters. There's nothing new in Sochi. The Molotovs have left. They say Kalinin is coming. . . . It's lonely. How are you doing? Have Satanka [Svetlana] write something to me. And Vaska, too. Continue to keep me 'informed.' I kiss you." Nine-year-old Vaska (Vasily) wrote to his father (September 21) about how he was riding his bike, raising guppies, and taking photos with a new camera. Stalin wrote to Nadya about a visit from Kirov. "I went one time (just once!) to the seaside. I went bathing. It was very good! I think I'll go again." Nadya wrote back, "I'm sending the book by Dmitrievsky (that defector) *On Stalin and Lenin*. . . . I read about it in the White press, where they say that it has the most interesting material about you. Curious?"[103]

MANCHURIAN SURPRISE

Instigator of mayhem at home, Stalin received a jolt from abroad. On the morning of September 18, 1931, an "explosion" just outside Mukden, on the South Manchurian Railway, disrupted a few yards of track; it did not even prevent the arrival of the latest train.[104] But within an hour, Japan's Kwantung Army had begun massacring Chinese garrison soldiers sleeping in their barracks in northern Mukden, and by September 19 the Japanese flag already flew over the Chinese city. Japan's military quickly seized other Chinese cities, revealing a premeditated plan.[105] Manchuria had long been a kind of Balkans of the east, a battleground in successive clashes dating back to the Sino-Japanese War (1894–95). Now, Japan claimed to be restoring stability following the supposed vacuum opened up by the Red Army withdrawal after its 1929 military confrontation with China over the Chinese Eastern Railway.[106] Half the world's soybeans were grown in Manchuria, which found a hungry market in Japan, while exports of Manchuria's iron ore enabled Japan to become the top steel producer in East Asia. Chiang Kai-shek's Nationalist government in Nanking, which faced opposition from Chinese Communists and a breakaway Nationalist faction in Canton, ordered no retaliation by the Manchurian warlord Zhang Xueliang, and sought recourse in the League of Nations.[107]

Soviet-Japanese relations had been tense, but Soviet exports to Japan had doubled between 1925 and 1931, while Japanese exports to the USSR, from a very low base, had increased tenfold. Still, Japan's actions in Manchuria violated the 1905 Treaty of Portsmouth, which recognized a Russian sphere of influence around the Chinese Eastern Railway. Tokyo pressured Moscow to allow it to use that rail line to move its troops against Chinese forces and, when Moscow refused, arrested some of the Soviet employees; one died in custody (from typhus, Japan claimed), another from supposed suicide. Belatedly, the Soviets acquiesced in Japan's use of the railroad to chase down Chinese resistance—right to the borders of the Soviet satellite Mongolia and the Soviet Union itself.[108] And so, after all the propaganda about looming "imperialist intervention" and the fabricated crimes of Red Army officers supposedly lying in wait to commit treason in the event of an external attack, an "imperialist" power had acted.

Stalin was preoccupied with the limitrophes, the former tsarist lands on the western frontier.[109] Soviet war plans took as their point of departure an enemy coalition of neighboring states, above all Poland (P) and Romania (R), which would be incited and supported by the Western imperialist powers. This "PR series" of contingency plans, drawn up in 1931–32, envisioned advancing in the Baltic region to protect Leningrad and the right flank, but mostly defending the presumed main axes, the center and the south, even retreating as far as the Dnieper River until full Soviet mobilization enabled a counteroffensive.[110] But Stalin was well aware of Soviet vulnerabilities in the Far Eastern theater, too. By 1931, Japan's Kwantung Army numbered 130,000, with another 127,000 Manchurian soldiers, out of a total Manchurian population of 30 million, versus fewer than 100,000 troops in the Soviet Far Eastern Army and a total Soviet Far East population of just 800,000, of whom one quarter were ethnic Koreans and Chinese.[111] Soviet rail capacity there was perhaps no more than four or five trains per day, too slight for mass reinforcements.[112] The Soviet Far Eastern Army had yet to acquire a fleet, air force, or storehouses in case the Trans-Siberian artery was cut off by enemy air strikes. Japan's military did not need to read the secret OGPU reports to know that collectivization and dekulakization had undermined Red Army morale. The Kwantung leadership judged the USSR incapable of real war, so that if the Red Army did engage, the Japanese would pounce—and if the civilian government in Tokyo opposed a full-scale clash, then let it fall.[113]

Stalin chose not to hurry back to Moscow. At the politburo, some officials demanded resolute action to uphold Soviet administration of the Chinese Eastern Railway, just as in 1929, but Stalin suspected other countries would take advantage of a Soviet-Japanese clash, especially after Kaganovich and Molotov informed him of the lack of reaction by the British and the French. "Most probably, Japan's intervention is being conducted by agreement with all or some of the great powers on the basis of the expansion and strengthening of spheres of influence in China," he speculated to his minions (September 23, 1931). "Our military intervention is, of course, excluded; even diplomatic involvement is now not expedient, since it would only unite the imperialists, when it is advantageous to us for them to quarrel."[114]

On October 1, 1931, the Council of People's Commissars quietly raised the investment plan for armaments. Production had barely increased in the first nine months of the year.[115] Stalin finally left Sochi for Moscow on October 7. Ten days later, the regime created a "committee of reserves" charged with stockpiling grain in anticipation of war. The ambitious export plans to pay for imported industrial machinery remained in place.[116] But heavy rains were hitting drought-stricken areas, ruining part of the harvested grain that had been stacked. Across the Union, the larger-than-expected bulge in the urban labor force had pushed the number of people on rations to 46 million by fall 1931, from 26 million at the start of 1930.[117] The army and the growing prison population, not to mention the bureaucratic hydra responsible for distribution of grain, had to be fed, too.[118] Grain stocks in the entire Soviet Far East amounted to a mere 190,000 tons.

GLOBAL EARTHQUAKE

On Monday morning, September 21, 1931—nearly simultaneously with the Japanese aggression in Manchuria—Great Britain stunned the world, abandoning the gold standard, even though it had not run out of reserves.[119] Within four weeks, eighteen countries followed the UK off gold. Stocks on the New York exchange lost half their value, the second crash in eighteen months. The pound's resulting devaluation had global consequences, because Britain, along with the United States, served as the world's principal short-term lender.[120] Soon London would embrace "imperial free trade," meaning free only for British dominions, alongside protectionist tariffs for other countries, and would improvise a sterling bloc. This effectively ended a long epoch of Britain upholding an open global economic order.[121]

Pravda (September 22, 1931) triumphantly deemed the gold-standard démarche "not only a weakening of Britain, but a weakening of international imperialism as a whole." Marxists like Stalin assumed the crisis inhered in the functioning of capitalism. In fact, human decisions transformed structural problems into what came to be known as the Great Depression. Central bankers and their acolytes had long believed in the necessity of convertibility between currencies and gold, but a fixed-exchange-rate system works only if there is convergence in the macroeconomic performance of the participants (similar levels of wage and price inflation, public and private deficits, competitiveness) and an absence of shocks. Now, confronted with a shock, monetary authorities chose to raise interest rates, exacerbating the problems. And finances became unglued anyway. By year's end, nearly 3,000 banks in the United States, the citadel of world finance, would fail or be taken over as confidence and GDP cratered, accompanied by deflation in asset and commodity prices, disruption of trade, and mass unemployment.[122]

The Depression's impact proved worse in Eastern Europe than in Western, because largely peasant countries were whiplashed by the commodity price crash while their governments (Czechoslovakia excepted) depended on foreign financing, which dried up. Most Eastern European countries hesitated to depreciate their currencies, for fear of a repeat of hyperinflation, but they closed banks, imposed foreign-exchange and trade controls, raised tariffs, and postponed or suspended foreign debt payments—moves toward autarchy that magnified arbitrary bureaucratic power at the expense of markets and imparted further impetus to authoritarianism, right-wing populism, and xenophobia.[123] The USSR was also a predominantly peasant country, and although capitalist economic troubles initially had allowed Stalin to enjoy nearly unfettered Western technology transfer, now he was caught out, dependent on commodity prices and foreign financing for those industrial purchases.[124]

Stalin had been preoccupied with a possible French-led collective boycott that could cut the Soviets off from all advanced technology, and Orjonikidze had bent over backward to a delegation of German industrial luminaries, while Stalin restrained the insurrectionist impulses of the German Communists.[125] Berlin, for its part, faced shrinking foreign markets and rising unemployment—and was coming around to the idea that Stalin's crazy building of socialism might work. A bilateral trade agreement had been signed that extended German government-guaranteed credits to the USSR for a period of twenty-eight months, longer than the usual. The Soviets were to use the funds to purchase an additional 300 million marks' worth of German industrial goods, at favorable prices.[126] The deal was supposed to underwrite the wild industrial leap of 1931 and put to rest, for now, the feared anti-Soviet boycott. German exports to the USSR would jump to double the level of 1929. But the agreement had not resolved the severe Soviet balance-of-payment problems.[127] The Soviets even failed to reap the benefits of the pound's devaluation because of their renewed economic reliance on Germany.[128]

Soviet reliance on expensive short-term credits—the only kind predominantly available to the Communist regime—imposed relentless pressure to retire maturing debt and obtain new loans. With Soviet foreign debt more than doubling in the period 1929–31 (it would increase 50 percent in 1931 alone), rumors of a pending default spread in the Western press. (Turkey and much of Latin America defaulted at this time.)[129] On October 6, 1931, the British chargé d'affaires in Moscow wrote to London that the severe Soviet balance-of-payments crisis, on top of the failures to meet 1931 output targets, would even compel Moscow to break off rapid industrialization and collectivization.[130] Wishful thinking aside, the worsening terms of trade and tariffs did force the Soviets to curtail imports of consumer and even capital goods.[131] But the Soviets meticulously paid their debts. The pressure to do so partly explains the regime's continued export of grain despite fears for the harvest and low global prices.[132] Only state-imposed deprivation allowed the USSR to avoid external default.

THE STRUGGLE AGAINST KULAK SABOTAGE

Compared with the robust 1930 harvest—officially estimated at 83.5 million tons, but closer to 73–77 million—the 1931 harvest would come in somewhere between 57 million and 65 million tons. A cutback in grain exports loomed, but Stalin stalled the reckoning, continuing to lash out at the "liberalism" of rural officialdom for failing to extirpate "the kulak."[133] He also countenanced intensified religious persecution and ruination of churches.[134] Still, he had grudgingly allowed a slight reduction in procurement targets for the Volga, the Urals, Siberia, and Kazakhstan, the most drought-stricken regions, while holding the line on Ukraine's targets and raising the quotas for the North Caucasus (which had largely escaped the drought).[135] Mikoyan, on October 31, 1931, told a Central Committee plenum that on the eve of the harvest, "we had awaited the season of the grain collections with rainbow perspectives."[136] Regional party bosses, given the floor, uttered the truth: drought and a poor harvest had rendered even the reduced quotas impossible. Stalin—who got his back up when officials cited natural causes as excuses—exploded, sarcastically mocking one speaker's "exactitude" in adducing data on lower crop yields.[137] And yet, the dictator agreed to gather separately with plenum delegates from the grain-growing regions, which resulted in additional procurement reductions.[138]

Growers were reluctant to sell even what they had at the regime's punishingly low prices: in 1931, the market price per tsentner of rye was 61.53 rubles, versus the state price of 5.50; for wheat, the disparity was greater still.[139] But now, procurement agents grabbed even the food for minimal consumption. State collections in fall 1931 (and into early 1932) would leave farmers with less grain, meat, and dairy than in any year since the mid-1920s. "Comrade Stalin, I ask you to look into how collective farmers live on the collective farms," urged one of the countless letters pouring in about the starvation. "At the meetings it is impossible to speak up; if you do speak up, then they say you are an opportunist."[140]

Stalin was the sole bulwark against retreat from building socialism. On November 16, 1931, as he was walking the short distance between party headquarters on Old Square and the Kremlin, down Ilinka Street, a former White officer and presumed British agent, whom the OGPU had under surveillance, chanced upon him.[141] The man, who used the alias Yakov Ogarev, was said to have been so startled that he failed to pull his revolver from under his heavy overcoat. In another telling, the OGPU operative shadowing him had grabbed the enemy's hand. Either way, Ogarev was arrested. "I recognized [Stalin] immediately from the likeness to his portraits I had seen," he would testify. "He appeared shorter than I expected. He was moving slowly and looked at me intently. I also did not take my eyes off him." There was no trial, no mention in the press.[142] The politburo issued another secret resolution forbidding Stalin from walking Moscow on foot. The chance encounter somewhat recalled that of Gavrilo Princip and Franz Ferdinand on a Sarajevo street outside Moritz Schiller's Delicatessen in 1914. But the armed Ogarev was no Princip.

QUEST FOR NONAGGRESSION

Japan, with its invasion of Manchuria, had seized an industrial territory larger than Germany, France, and Austria combined, while losing just 3,000 killed, 5,000 wounded, and 2,500 frostbitten.[143] "Japan plans to seize not only Manchuria but also Peking," Stalin wrote presciently to Voroshilov (November 27, 1931), adding, "It is not impossible and even likely that they will seize the Soviet Far East and Mongolia to soothe the feelings of the Chinese clients with territory captured at our expense." He further surmised that the Japanese would claim to be safeguarding the region from "Bolshevik infection" while creating their own economic base on the mainland, without which Japan would be boxed in by "militarizing America, revolutionizing China, and the fast-developing USSR."[144] Stalin supported "serious preventive measures of a military and nonmilitary character," including additional units for the Soviet Far East, walking a fine line between showing weakness, which might invite attack, and overly strong measures, which might offer a casus belli.[145] He also reinforced Soviet efforts to conclude nonaggression pacts with countries on the western frontier. Such a pact had been signed with

Lithuania (1926), but he sought them with Latvia, Estonia, Finland, Romania, and, above all, Poland.[146]

Amid reports that the French government was encouraging Japan to launch a war against the USSR and trying to insert a clause into its draft bilateral pact with Moscow that would be invalidated by just such a third-party attack—all of which fit Stalin's cynical view of the imperialist powers—he suffered an unpleasant surprise: fierce resistance to a nonaggression pact with Poland from inside the foreign affairs commissariat.[147]

Stalin, finally, had replaced foreign affairs commissar Chicherin—a hypochondriac frequently absent abroad for treatment—with his deputy, Maxim Litvinov.[148] (In a bitter parting memorandum, Chicherin fulminated against Litvinov, the Comintern, and "the GPU, [which] deals with the foreign affairs commissariat as with a class enemy.")[149] Litvinov, never a close associate of Stalin's, became the face of the USSR abroad.[150] Whereas Chicherin was aristocratic and urbane, Litvinov was rough hewn. He was also Jewish. He had lived in exile in the UK from 1907 through early 1918 and afterward as a midlevel embassy counselor, spoke fluent accented English, and had married an English writer, Ivy Low, the daughter of a prominent Jewish family, whom he called his *bourgeoise*. He continued Chicherin's orientation on Germany while seeking to make all of Europe his bailiwick, but Stalin subdivided the department and inserted rivals.[151] Still, issues of Stalin's control remained (foreign affairs personnel, about one third of whom were Jews, were better educated than functionaries of any other government body).[152] A Polish offer to Litvinov to resume talks for a nonaggression pact had been rebuffed—and Stalin had been informed only ex post facto.[153]

The dictator was convinced that Poland's ruler, Józef Piłsudski, was secretly working to undermine Ukraine, but also that, without Poland, a major imperialist attack on the Soviet Union would be far less feasible.[154] A Polonophobe himself, he nonetheless warned Kaganovich not to be taken in by the foreign affairs commissariat's "anti-Polonism."[155] Stalin discovered, however, that any decrease in tensions with Poland threatened bilateral relations with Germany: the Reichswehr chief of staff, on a visit to Moscow, expressed fears that a Soviet-Polish nonaggression pact would guarantee Poland's existing borders.[156]

Litvinov was also working assiduously, alongside his deputy Lev Karakhan, for a nonaggression pact with Japan, hewing to Stalin's line to stress Soviet noninterference and to make concessions.[157] On December 13, 1931, the OGPU decoded and forwarded to Stalin an intercepted transcript of a conversation between the Japanese military attaché in Moscow, Kasahara, and his superior (visiting from

Tokyo), advocating for war before the USSR became too strong and underscoring that "the countries on the Soviet western border (i.e., at a minimum Poland and Romania) are in a position to act with us."[158] The attaché added that the Japanese ambassador to Moscow, Kōki Hirota, thought "the cardinal objective of this war must lay not so much in protecting Japan from Communism as in seizing the Soviet Far East and Eastern Siberia." Stalin circled these territories and circulated the intercept to the politburo and the military command, advising that the Soviet Union risked becoming, like China, a rag doll of the imperialists.[159]

Also on December 13, Stalin sat for a two-hour interview with the German psychoanalytical writer Emil Ludwig. When Ludwig noted "a bowing before all things American" in the USSR, Stalin accused him of exaggerating. "We do respect American business-like manner in everything—in industry, in technology, in literature, in life," the dictator allowed, adding: "The mores there in industry, the habits in production, contain something democratic, which you cannot say of the old European capitalist countries, where, still today, feudal aristocrat haughtiness lives." Still, in terms of "our sympathies for any one nation, . . . I'd have to say it would be the Germans." Stalin had been exiled in Siberia, and Ludwig delicately suggested a contrast with Lenin's European emigration. "I know many comrades who were abroad for twenty years," Stalin answered, "lived somewhere in Charlottenburg [Berlin] or the Latin Quarter [Paris], sat for years in cafés and drank beer, and yet did not manage to acquire a knowledge of Europe and failed to understand it."[160] Ludwig inquired whether Stalin believed in fate. "Bolsheviks, Marxists, do not believe in fate," he answered. "The very notion of fate, of *Schicksal*, is a prejudice, nonsense, a survival of mythology, the mythology of the ancient Greeks." Ludwig pressed: "So the fact that you did not die is an accident?" Stalin: "There are internal and external factors whose totality led to the circumstance that I did not die. But utterly independent of that, another could have been in my place, because someone had to sit right here."[161]

CONCEALED MILITARIZATION

Despite Soviet groveling, the Japanese government did not bother to reply through diplomatic channels to renewed offers of a nonaggression pact.[162] Voroshilov, in a note to his deputy Gamarnik (January 13, 1932), parroted Stalin's line of a likely Japanese invasion, yet added skepticism. "The creation of a Far Eastern Russian government is being projected and other claptrap," he noted. "All of this is rumor, very symptomatic."[163] On January 29, Artuzov forwarded to Stalin a secret report (obtained via a mole) by French military intelligence, which envisioned four scenarios for the outbreak of a war: German occupation of the Rhineland, following a possible Nazi revolution; an Italian strike against Yugoslavia, drawing in France; a grudge match between Poland and Germany; and "a conflict with the USSR agreed by many countries."[164] The fourth scenario—Stalin's fixation—was supported by other reports of France supplying Japan and Franco-German rapprochement.[165] Anti-Soviet circles in Paris were fantasizing that Japan would make available liberated Soviet territory for the émigrés' triumphal return.[166] Molotov, at the 17th party conference (January 30–February 4, 1932)—lower in stature than a congress—warned that "the danger of imperialist attack has considerably increased."[167]

A pseudonymous "letter from Moscow" published in Trotsky's *Bulletin* abroad reported that at the party conference, Stalin had been largely silent. "After every sitting, delegates and visitors were asked, 'What did Stalin say?'" the report claimed. "'Nothing.'"[168] True enough. Secretly, however, Stalin had embarked on energetic steps. Japan had changed his mind.

Whereas Tukhachevsky and the brass had long wanted to prioritize military production, Stalin prioritized heavy industry in general—the base of a modern economy, in his view—but now, just six months after having rejected Tukhachevsky's wild spending requests, Stalin was himself demanding forced creation of 40 to 50 new divisions.[169] Following the replacement (January 5) of the Supreme Council of the Economy by three commissariats—heavy industry, light industry, and forestry—the regime created a unified main mobilization directorate in heavy industry for the defense factories.[170] On January 19, Stalin agreed to a commission on "tankification" of the Red Army, on which he placed Tukhachevsky, and rammed through a plan for 10,000 tanks in 1932. Fewer than 2,000 had been manufactured in 1931, but Stalin wielded the preposterous new target to force expansion of assembly lines and creation of systematic tank-building capability at tractor and automobile factories, too.[171]

Stalin needed advanced tank designs—and, amazingly, he got them. The Soviet trade mission in Britain had secured permission to purchase 15 Vickers-Armstrong medium (six-ton) tanks, 26 Carden Loyd light armored machine-gun carriers, and 8 Carden Loyd amphibious tanks, as well as a license for production and blueprints.[172] In parallel, working undercover at the Soviet trade organization in New York, the OGPU had overcome the lack of diplomatic relations and a legal injunction to procure specifications for the Christie M1931 tank. (J. Walter

Christie was an engineer, who sometimes tested his designs with race car driving, and his dual-drive tank designs were notable for their innovative suspension and speed; he had offered to sell the technology to the U.S. military, but it had declined.) Two "tractors" shipped out of New York were in reality Christie tanks without the turrets, which became the basis for production of the Soviet track-wheeled "BT" at the Kharkov Locomotive Plant.[173] The imported designs demanded more sophisticated motors, gearboxes, chassis, caterpillar tracks, optics, traversing mechanisms, and armor plating than Soviet industry had been producing.[174] Still, by the end of 1932, the Soviets, who had been incapable of producing a single decent tank, would manufacture 2,600.[175] Soviet military spending would skyrocket in 1932 to 2.2 billion rubles, from 845 million—all of which Stalin kept concealed.[176]

OMINOUS SIGNS

Japanese troops entered Harbin, the main Soviet railway junction in China, on February 5, 1932, to the euphoria of anti-Soviet émigrés.[177] In late February, Soviet intelligence delivered another intercepted Kasahara letter to Tokyo promising that "if we were to attack the USSR, Poland, Romania, and the Baltic states would join (but not immediately), supported actively by the French and the not inconsiderable force of White Russians along the border."[178] Japanese military aircraft were violating Soviet airspace; Stalin ordered Soviet forces not to yield to the provocations of warmongers.[179] Still, the regime established the Far Eastern Fleet as a separate command and ordered up additional submarines.[180] On March 4, 1932, *Izvestiya* published excerpts from the decrypted secret Japanese telegrams calling for seizure of Siberia and the Soviet Far East. (Evidently, the Japanese had discovered that the Soviets had broken their codes.) *Izvestiya* underscored that, while Moscow maintained neutrality in the Sino-Japanese conflict, "the Soviet Union will not permit anyone to violate Soviet borders, advance into its territory, and capture even a tiny parcel of Soviet soil."[181] Tukhachevsky revisited the "PR" war plan, with preemptive destruction of Poland by "heavy bomber strikes in the Warsaw region" and tank armies on the ground.[182]

Japan did not annex Manchuria, as it had the far smaller Taiwan and Korean Peninsula, but it orchestrated the proclamation of a puppet state of Manchukuo (Manchu Land) and, on March 9, installed Henry Pu-Yi, the deposed last Qing emperor (whom the Japanese had recently kidnapped), as head of state in what was the Qing ancestral homeland.[183] Ten days later, Karakhan offered assurances of Soviet restraint to Japan's ambassador Hirota, who secretly advised Tokyo that it could do as it pleased in Manchuria.[184] Quietly, the Soviets were offering to recognize Manchukuo, sell Japan the Chinese Eastern Railway, and negotiate fishing rights, oil leases, and trade, in exchange for a Japanese halt to sponsorship of anti-Soviet émigré groups, but Tokyo displayed indifference. The Soviet envoy in Tokyo was instructed to convey that Moscow would not be intimidated.[185] Stalin's options were narrow, however. Negotiations for nonaggression pacts had been concluded with Finland (January 21, 1932) and Latvia (February 5), and one would be signed with Estonia (May 4), but talks with Romania deadlocked over its disputed annexation of Bessarabia.[186] Negotiations with France were torturous and would not succeed until late fall.[187]

Stalin received fresh reports that Warsaw had not desisted from attempts to destabilize Ukraine or cooperate with Japan in a possible military strike against the USSR.[188] Even so, negotiations with Poland would bear fruit in late summer, albeit in a pact valid for just three years. German fears were borne out: Stalin would bow to Poland's insistence to insert a clause about the inviolability of the latter's frontiers.[189] But Voroshilov had complained bitterly in a letter (March 12, 1932) to the Soviet envoy in Berlin that only because of necessity were the Reichswehr high commanders "'friendly' with us (hating us in their hearts)."[190] The pacts with Poland and France would effectively mark a break in the Soviet pursuit of the elusive special relationship with Germany predicated on Versailles pariah status. This posture had always been aimed at preemption of an anti-Soviet bloc, which the 1931 trade agreement with Berlin and the 1932 nonaggression pacts with Warsaw and Paris would manage to accomplish, for now.[191] Still, Soviet intelligence, obsessed with the emigration, had difficulty discerning the motives of foreign governments.[192] And the USSR had no alliances. Nonaggression pacts were signed between enemies.[193]

PRESSURE FOR RETREAT

A land commissariat internal report in early 1932 noted that peasants were quitting the collectives by the hundreds of thousands to roam industrial sites in search of food.[194] The politburo shrank the bread allocation in cities for people on the lower-priority ration lists (numbers 2 and 3), affecting 20 million souls. There was little to ration.[195] Stalin knew. But every time he conceded grain procurement reductions, every time he allowed strategic reserves to go unfilled, the already low rations for workers had to be lowered and grain was not exported, putting the military-industrial buildup at risk. The much delayed first blast furnace at the Magnitogorsk Metallurgical Combine had been started up early 1932, in a furious rush in horrendous frosts, to coincide with the 17th party conference. Two giant chemical factories, the first aluminum factory, and a ball-bearing plant were started up, and the first four trucks rolled off the line at the Nizhny Novgorod auto factory. But these were political startups. At Magnitogorsk, the new blast furnace's cone caved in; it had to be completely rebuilt. Industrial output began to stagnate or even decline in spring 1932.[196]

Voices were being raised. "Although you, comrade Stalin, are a pupil of Lenin, your behavior is not Leninist," the delegate Fedorintseva of the rural soviet "Soldier," in the Black Earth region, wrote to *Izvestiya* in spring 1932. "Lenin taught: factories to the workers, land to the peasants, and what do you do? You confiscate not only land but livestock, huts, and possessions from the middle and poor peasants. You threw out Trotsky and call him a counterrevolutionary, but you, comrade Stalin, are the real and first Trotskyite, and a pupil not of Lenin but of Trotsky. Why? They taught us in political circle that Trotsky proposed to build socialism with force at the expense of the muzhik."[197] Trotsky added his own voice. "Separated from the apparatus, Stalin is . . . a nullity, an empty void," he wrote in a new "open letter" to the party, in his *Bulletin of the Opposition* (March 1, 1932), predicting that "the man who yesterday was the symbol of the might of the apparatus tomorrow might become in everyone's eyes the symbol of its bankruptcy."[198]

Suddenly, the regime backed down from socialization of all livestock, with a decree (March 26, 1932) initiated by land commissar Yakovlev and accepted by Stalin. Functionaries in the commissariat interpreted it as a retreat from collectivization—some asked whether it contained a typo—but the aim was tactical: to end flight from the collectives. Local officials did not hurry to return collectivized animals.[199]

Not coincidentally, speculation about the dictator's health, typical in any dictatorship, intensified. "This is not the first time that false rumors that I am ill have circulated in the bourgeois press," Stalin wrote in a letter published in *Pravda* (April 3). "Sad though it may be, the fact is that I am in perfect health."[200]

Ukraine party boss Kosior reported to Stalin that one quarter of the republic's horses had died, and that the surviving ones were "skin and bones."[201] The OGPU reported that in Borisov, in the Belorussian republic, a crowd had seized grain warehouses, and several hundred women and children had marched on the local

Red Army barracks ("signs of commiseration could be seen among the soldiers and officers").[202] In the textile mills of the Ivanovo region, ration cuts of up to one half, on top of labor intensification measures, provoked strikes and spontaneous assemblies.[203] A sign placed in a shopwindow read "Even as the starving workers of Vichuga and Teikovo were being fired upon because they agitated for bread, here, behind the store's drawn curtains, Communist functionaries and Red police of the GPU were fattening themselves up."[204] Ten thousand demonstrators ransacked the party and police buildings ("Toss the Communists . . . out the window"). Stalin dispatched Kaganovich, who mobilized local party agitators to speak with workers and himself heard out their grievances.[205]

Ivanovo's striking workers did not reject socialism, only its building at their expense, and mostly blamed local officials for their plight.[206] They shared a resolute anticapitalism with the Soviet regime, but that anticapitalism afforded the regime bureaucratic control over workers' employment, housing, and food. The strikers were further stymied by the state monopoly over newspapers, radio, and the public sphere. More profoundly still, the strikers were trapped in the socialist vocabulary of class war.[207] Kaganovich's report for Stalin unfurled clichés, but, unlike the workers, the regime drew power from Bolshevik language: in conditions of "capitalist encirclement," Kaganovich could equate worker criticism with playing into the imperialists' hands. He managed to browbeat most strikers back to the shop floor, after which the OGPU arrested worker organizers and officials accused of worker sympathies.[208]

GRUDGING CONCESSIONS, PRIVATE APOLOGY

In parades on the May Day holiday in 1932, the Soviets offered the first public demonstrations of the Red Army's mechanization—not only in Moscow, but in Leningrad, Kharkov, Kiev, Tiflis, and Khabarovsk.[209] That same day, the first stage of the Dneprostroi hydroelectric dam supplied power, and this launch would prove durable. ("We are talking to you from the roof of an immense Bolshevik triumph!" gushed Soviet radio.)[210] Still, workers could not eat or clothe themselves with tanks and electricity.[211] On May 4, Stalin led a politburo discussion that culminated in reduced procurement targets and acceptance of a commission's recommendation to purchase hundreds of thousands of livestock from Mongolia, western China, Iran, and Turkey.[212] On May 6 and 10, the regime issued decrees announcing the grain procurement reductions for collective farmers and the remaining individual household farmers, from 22.4 million to 18.1 million tons. The targets for state farms were raised, from 1.7 to 2.5 million, for a new overall target of 20.6 million. This was just 81 percent of actual 1931 procurements. The decrees even forbade further liquidation of individual household farms, ordered the return of confiscated livestock and an end to lawlessness, and stipulated that, after peasants had met procurement quotas for the harvest (deadline: January 15, 1933), they could freely trade in any surplus directly with consumers at "collective farm markets."[213]

Could it be? As recently as the October 1931 party plenum, Mikoyan, speaking for Stalin, had flatly rejected suggestions to permit rural trade at market prices after fulfillment of state obligations.[214] But now peasants were permitted to maintain their own cows (though not horses), cultivate household plots, and sell a significant portion of the fruits of their labor at market prices.[215] To be sure, private property in the means of production remained outlawed (household plots could not be sold or inherited). Still, it turned out that peasants had to be incentivized with private livestock holdings and market sales of even some of their collective farm output. Workers, too, had to be provided incentives through wage differentiation.[216] State-owned and state-managed factories were not permitted to engage in direct marketlike relations with one another, but they did so illegally. "The necessity of avoiding a break in production," one official at Magnitogorsk explained, "will compel the receiving factory to seek the necessary materials from other sources by every possible means."[217]

The surprises kept coming. Stalin returned Shaposhnikov to a high-profile post in the capital, as director of the Frunze Military Academy, and on May 7, 1932, he even sent a *written* apology to Tukhachevsky for having denounced his January 1930 super-rearmament memorandum as Red militarism. "Two years later," Stalin wrote, with a copy to Voroshilov, "when some unclear matters have become clearer for me, I must confess that my judgment was too severe, and that the conclusions of my letter were not correct in all respects." Stalin noted that Tukhachevsky had been suggesting a peacetime army not of 11 million (per Shaposhnikov's accusations) but of "8 million souls" and suggested that 6 million well-supplied, well-organized troops were "more or less within our capabilities." (Soviet forces still numbered fewer than 1 million.) Stalin added: "Do not curse me for the fact that I corrected these shortcomings outlined in my [1930] letter with a certain tardiness."[218]

What was next? Stalin had long forbidden directing more consumer goods to villages to incentivize the flow of grain, but now he acquiesced in this, too.[219] He even agreed to importing grain ("54,000 tons of grain have already been purchased in Canada," he telegrammed the party boss of Eastern Siberia on May 8. "You will get your share").[220] Tellingly, however, Stalin does not appear to have initiated a single one of these concessions, and invariably he issued barbed reminders of the need for unconditional fulfillment of centrally assigned procurement targets and the perfidy of capitalism.[221] Unlike Lenin in 1921, Stalin was not willing to admit a "retreat" or neo-NEP.[222] This reflected his touchiness about admitting *any* mistakes, desire to maintain his authority at the system's apex, and nonnegotiable ideological commitment.[223]

Mongolia, the Soviet satellite, provides a stark contrast. Zealots of the Mongolian People's Party, egged on by Comintern advisers, had launched a "class war" against "feudalism," confiscating estates, ransacking Buddhist lamaseries, killing nobles and lamas, and collectivizing herders.[224] At least one third of the livestock—the country's main wealth—was lost. Inflation soared, shortages proliferated. In spring 1932, revolts led by lamas overtook four provinces in the northwest, amid rumors that either the elderly Panchen Lama (from Tibetan exile) or the Japanese would arrive with troops to liberate Mongolia from Communist occupation.[225] The uprisings took Stalin by surprise ("The latest telegrams reported successes; therefore, such an unexpected and sharp deterioration is incomprehensible"). The Soviets dispatched consumer goods and ten fighter planes, which strafed the rebels; about 1,500 would be killed. Facing annihilation, rebels engaged in murder and cannibalism.[226] On May 16, the politburo condemned the Mongolian party for "blindly copying the policy of Soviet power in the USSR." Mongolian ruling officials were ordered to abandon collectivization of nomads, proclaim an "all-people's government," and publicly repudiate the noncapitalist path in Mongolia's current conditions. The shift would be confirmed at a Mongolian People's Party plenum and be dubbed the New Course.[227] It was the full reversal Stalin would not countenance at home.

PANIC AROUND HIM

Whether the grudging concessions could save the situation was uncertain. "Stalin figured out trade with collective farms late," the OGPU reported of one worker's reaction in Minsk. "If he had thought about this in 1929–30, it would have been better, but now nothing will come of it, because the peasants have nothing;

everything was destroyed."[228] Union-wide stocks of food and fodder amounted to perhaps a month's supply, with less than that in Ukraine, the North Caucasus, and the Lower Volga. A rattled Kuibyshev handwrote a supersecret memo in blue pencil on May 23, 1932, proposing to slice rations even for those with absolute highest priority ("special list" and "list 1"). The politburo rejected this, but it reduced allocations to the Red Army by 16 percent and resolved to accelerate grain imports from Persia.[229] Molotov led a commission to Ukraine that reported (May 26) that "the situation is worse than we supposed," and suggested granting still more "loans" of seed, fodder, and food. Stalin conceded release of another 41,000 tons of seeds from the strategic reserves in Ukraine and Belorussia.[230] These loans—which would reach 1.267 million tons Union-wide for the year, three times the amount provided in spring 1931—were supposed to be returned from the pending 1932 harvest, seed for seed.[231]

In late May, Stalin departed for his annual southern holiday, which would be especially prolonged (through late August). "The number of politburo inquiries has no effect on my health," he wrote from Sochi. "You can send as many inquiries as you like—I'll happily answer them with pleasure."[232] He rebuffed requests to send Red Army troops to Mongolia. "We cannot conflate Mongolia with Kazakhstan or Buryatia," he instructed Kaganovich (June 4), adding that Mongolian officials "should announce that the leaders of the rebellion are agents of the Chinese and especially the Japanese imperialists, who are seeking to strip Mongolia of its freedom and independence."[233] He also ordered documents concerning Soviet-Mongolian relations evacuated from Ulan Bator.[234] "The Japanese, of course (of course!), are preparing for war against the USSR," he wrote to Orjonikidze in June 1932, "and we need to be ready (for sure!) for everything."[235] Stalin kept up the pressure. "Will our industrialists produce the planned number of tanks, airplanes, antitank weapons?" he wrote to Voroshilov (June 9). "Have the bombers been sent to the East? Where, exactly, and how many? The trip on the Volga was interesting—I'll say more: magnificent. A great river, the Volga. Damn."[236]

Stalin's mood oscillated. "It seems I shall not be getting better anytime soon," he complained to Kaganovich in mid-June. "A general weakness and real sense of fatigue are only now becoming evident. Just when I think I am beginning to get better, it turns out that I have a long way to go. I am not having rheumatic symptoms (they disappeared somewhere), but the overall weakness is not going away."[237] He was chauffeured to his usual polyarthritis salt baths at nearby Matsesta. While on the terrace or out fishing, he would tell tales of the revolutionary underground and prison. He tended to his mandarins, berries, and grapes and played badminton or skittles with a cook against a bodyguard. Evenings, he competed in billiards, and the losers, which included himself, crawled under the table to absorb the winners' banging from above. Gypsy dances and other performances accompanied the late-evening meals and drinking. The lights usually went out in his quarters at 2:00 or 3:00 a.m.

Stalin's holiday mailbag delivered increasingly dire news. "Because of the general famine, as you know, villagers have started flocking" to train stations, the Stalin loyalist Hryhory Petrovsky, in Ukraine, wrote on June 10, 1932. "In some cases, two thirds of the men had left their villages in search of bread."[238] (Yagoda reported on construction of a dacha settlement in the environs of Moscow using state funds for the grain collection commissariat.)[239] Stalin held firm, proposing (June 18) the convocation of party secretaries from the main grain-growing provinces and republics to ensure "unconditional fulfillment of the plan."[240] He ordered up an editorial in *Pravda* demonstrating "with documentation the complete victory of the collective and state farms in agriculture, since the weight of the individual farming sector this year does not even reach 20 percent" (a reference to sown acreage). He added, "It is necessary to curse rudely and sharply all the lackeys of capitalism—Mensheviks, SRs [Socialist Revolutionaries], Trotskyites, and right deviationists—stating that the attempts of the enemies of the toilers to return the USSR to the capitalist path have been decisively defeated and turned into ashes, that the USSR has irreversibly adopted the new socialist path, that the decisive victory of socialism in the USSR can be considered already finalized."[241] The editorial duly appeared (June 26, 1932). That same day, Stalin conceded a significant reduction in grain exports for the third quarter.[242]

The first mass-produced Soviet heavy bomber, the four-engine TB-3, had been tested in the air, but Voroshilov reported ("Dear Koba") that just four had been manufactured, and that even these had malfunctioning radiators.[243] He also had to inform Stalin about a shocking number of crashes in training: eleven aircraft downed just between June 5 and 20, killing thirty crew members. Voroshilov asked permission to join Stalin for a few days down south ("I have not been sleeping normally for a long time"). Stalin wrote back on June 24: "The most worrisome are the crashes and the deaths of our aviators. The loss of airplanes is not as scary (the hell with them) as the loss of living people, aviators. Live human beings are the most valuable and most important thing in our entire cause, especially in aviation."[244, 245]

Regional party bosses gathered in Moscow on June 28, 1932, and Molotov read out Stalin's stern letter (sent ten days earlier): "In Ukraine, despite a harvest that was not bad, a number of districts with good harvests turned out to be in a state of ruin and famine."[246] This was the second known documented instance when Stalin used the word "famine" (*golod*).[247] Molotov and Kaganovich approved only a slight reduction in procurements.[248] Stalin, in two telegrams (July 1 and 2, 1932), spewed venom on Ukraine's leadership ("demobilizers") and ordered both of his top minions to attend Ukraine's upcoming party conference.[249] At that gathering (July 6–9), Kosior (a USSR politburo member) pointed out that some regions were already starving, while Ukraine government head Vlas Chubar (a candidate USSR politburo member) challenged Molotov and Kaganovich to go out and see for themselves.[250] Afterward, Kaganovich wrote to Stalin that "all members of the [Ukraine] politburo . . . spoke in favor of lowering the plan" for deliveries, but "we categorically turned aside a revision."[251]

Then, on July 24, Stalin undermined their hard work. "Our governing directive that the grain collection plan for the USSR be fulfilled unconditionally is correct," he wrote to Kaganovich and Molotov. "But bear in mind that an exception must be made for the districts in Ukraine that have suffered especially. This is necessary not solely from the point of view of justness, but also in view of the special condition of Ukraine and its common frontier with Poland."[252] The next day, he again tried to explain his turnabout, suggesting that at the time of the Ukraine party conference he had not wanted "to derail the grain procurements." What Kaganovich and Molotov made of Stalin's zigzagging remains unknown. Stalin was banking on the harvest, whose "prospects," he wrote, "will become clear (they have already become clear!): they are doubtless good for the USSR as a whole." But the harvest was being overreported, and Stalin latched on to what he wanted to hear.[253]

Sown acreage had shrunk noticeably. Tractive power, seed grain, and fodder were scarce. The spring sowing season had proved short, and wheat sown beginning in late May always produced lower yields and was more susceptible to August rains, which would descend torrentially as early as the beginning of the month. Rust epiphytotics damaged a significant part of the wheat harvest, to the surprise of officials who had failed to identify it.[254] Demoralized farmers forced into collectives were threshing and using manure sloppily and showing disregard for collectivized animals.[255] Voroshilov had been granted his holiday, and on July 26 he wrote to Stalin about what he saw traveling south: "a scandalous infestation of the grain with weeds" in the North Caucasus.

The defense commissar appeared to be buckling under the pressure, complaining that "when one sees our military cadres, it is enough to make one a misanthrope," and adding: "I cannot even say that these people do not work; on the contrary, they work until they are exhausted, but with no results."[256] Stalin kept up the pressure. "Six bombers for the Far East is nothing," he responded (July 30). "We need to send no fewer than 50 to 60 TB-3s. And this needs to be done as soon as possible. Without this, the defense of the Far East is only an empty phrase."[257]

An OGPU report to the "Central Committee" (August 1, 1932) estimated rifles at just 85 percent of needs, stationary machine guns at 68 percent, hand grenades at 55, revolvers at 36, modernized howitzers at 26 percent, 107-millimeter shells at 16 percent, and 76-millimeter shells at 7. Only a third of the projected 150 divisions could be fully outfitted.[258] Nonetheless, that same day, the politburo confirmed Kuibyshev's recommendation to reduce capital investments by a whopping 10 percent—more than that in heavy industry. Orjonikidze exploded. Kaganovich sought to conciliate him ("My friend, the financial situation required it") while making clear that Stalin had signed on ("We wrote to our chief friend, and he thought it absolutely correct and timely to make cuts").[259] In mid-August, yet another Chinese commander resisting the Japanese managed to flee to Soviet territory, but the Japanese army pursued him. The war minister in Tokyo was said to have been barely restrained from launching an attack on the USSR.[260]

SUMMER DOOM

Telegrams, letters, and reports swamped Sochi with news of mass death of horses, mass failure to sow crops, mass starvation, mass flight from collective farms, and a bewildering lack of government response.[261] Andrew Cairns, a Scottish Canadian agricultural expert sent by the Empire Marketing Board, in London, to determine if Western farmers might learn something from Soviet collectivization, managed to travel around Ukraine, Crimea, the North Caucasus lowlands, and the Volga valley from May through August 1932, and he observed women pulling up grass to make soup. Of urban canteens he noted, "As each worker finished his meal there was a scramble of children and one or two women and men for their soup plates to lick, and their fish bones to eat."[262] Throughout August 1932, unsigned editorials in *Pravda* lashed out at kulak "machinations" and grain "speculators."

Stalin also received reports that "spoilage" was exaggerated and that grain was being stolen from slow-moving freight trains or slipped into ample pockets during mowing, stacking, or threshing, or just not being gathered (remaining in the fields to be eaten). He insisted to Kaganovich that just as private property under capitalism was sacred, so state property under socialism had to be recognized as "sacred and inviolable."[263] The dictator drafted a law, issued on August 7, 1932, that imposed the death penalty for the minutest theft of collective farm grain.[264] He congratulated himself ("It is good") and ordered a follow-up secret directive on the law sent to party organizations.[265] *Pravda* (August 8) placed the pitiless law on an inside page; Kaganovich corrected this the next day with a front-page editorial.[266] Other articles called for firing squads no matter the size of the theft. (One could view the compulsory state grain procurements—paying a mere 4.5 to 6.1 rubles per 100 kilos of rye, and 7.1 to 8.4 rubles for wheat, below production costs—as a form of grand theft, even as this enabled black bread to be sold in cities for just 8 to 12 kopecks a kilo.)[267] Some politburo members had objected to the law in draft, but in reporting the objections to Sochi, Kaganovich had omitted names.[268]

Stalin exploded at Kaganovich (August 11) over fresh requests from Ukraine to lower procurement targets yet again. "Things in Ukraine have hit rock bottom . . . about fifty county party committees having spoken out against the grain procurement plan, deeming it unrealistic. . . . This is not a party but a parliament, a caricature of a parliament." He demanded removal of Kosior and Chubar, and the demotion of Ukraine OGPU chief Redens. "Bear in mind that Piłsudski is not daydreaming, and his agent network in Ukraine is much stronger than Redens or Kosior think," Stalin noted. "Also keep in mind that the Ukrainian Communist party (500,000 members, ha-ha) contains quite a few (yes, many!) rotten elements, conscious and unconscious Petliurites [a reference to the civil war Ukrainian nationalist], even direct agents of Piłsudski. If things get worse, these elements will not hesitate to open a front inside (and outside) the party, against the party." Stalin warned direly: "Without these and similar measures (economic and political strengthening of Ukraine, in the first place in its *border districts* and so on), I repeat, we may lose Ukraine."[269]

Polish spies were infiltrating the USSR, and being caught.[270] At the same time, the Polish government had just signed the three-year bilateral nonaggression pact with Stalin, easing the pressure.[271] Perhaps he was using the threat to sustain Kaganovich's severity or just could not let go of his fixation on an imperialist intervention provoked by internal difficulties. In the same note, Stalin informed

Kaganovich that he had decided to appoint Balytsky as OGPU plenipotentiary in Ukraine and had already spoken with Mężyński. On the sacking of Kosior and Chubar, however, the crafty Kaganovich pushed back, ever so gently—"It is harder for me to judge than you"—and Stalin relented.[272] Belatedly, the dictator also accepted land commissar Yakovlev's critique of excessive expansion of sown area, which disrupted crop rotation, and he reluctantly allowed a slowing to enable crop rotation to be reintroduced.[273] But when, on August 20, 1932, Boris Sheboldayev, party boss in the North Caucasus, telegrammed to report that the harvest had turned out even lower, and farmers were in revolt, Stalin answered, with a copy to Kaganovich: "Either the local party committee is being diplomatic toward the population or it is leading the Central Committee by the nose."[274]

Nadya had again accompanied him to Sochi, with the children, Vasily (then ten) and Svetlana (five), but she again returned to Moscow before he did. "We have built a marvelous little house," Stalin wrote of a new Sochi dacha, to the man in Moscow responsible for such properties down south, Yenukidze, just as his holiday was coming to a close.[275]

"GRAVEDIGGER OF THE REVOLUTION AND OF RUSSIA"

Stalin had made the USSR more vulnerable to its enemies, especially Japan. Collectivization-dekulakization was his policy, which all party officials knew, having been bombarded by extremist directives in his name. They also knew that the right deviation had predicted calamity. Individual efforts to get Stalin to ease up provoked his rage. Officials' ability to act collectively was limited to Central Committee plenums, but those took place under the watchful eye of his hard-line loyalists, the secret police, and the stool pigeons who chauffeured vehicles and staffed hotels. Conspiratorially, late one night in August 1932, a few veterans of the revolution and the civil war gathered in a private apartment near Moscow's Belorussia train station that belonged to Martemyan Ryutin (b. 1890), an editor at *Red Star*, the army newspaper, to discuss the crisis.[276] Stalin had promoted the peasant-born Siberian to candidate membership in the Central Committee—the top elite (then 121 people)—but then in 1928 had sacked him for a "conciliatory attitude toward the right opposition." Not long thereafter, he had Ryutin expelled from the party.[277] Now, Ryutin and the party members Vasily Kayurov, a department chief in the state archives, Mikhail Ivanov, an employee of the Russian Soviet Federated Socialist Republic (RSFSR) workers' and peasants' inspectorate, and Kayurov's son Alexander, a senior inspector in the USSR supply commissariat, had channeled their worries into a seven-page "Appeal to All Members of the All-Union Communist Party (Bolsheviks)," which labeled Stalin an "unprincipled intriguer," "a sophist, a political trickster, and actor," "theoretically worthless," "a dictator" like "Mussolini, Napoleon, Piłsudski, Horthy, Primo de Rivera, Chiang Kai-shek," and "the gravedigger of the revolution in Russia."[278]

"Gravedigger" was the epithet that Trotsky had once hurled at Stalin. Ryutin, infamously, had been a Trotsky scourge.[279]

Secretly, at a hut in a village about forty miles outside Moscow, on August 21, 1932, Ryutin presented the "Appeal to All Members" as well as a much longer document, "Stalin and the Crisis of the Proletarian Dictatorship," to perhaps fifteen middling officials in various bureaucratic entities.[280] They constituted themselves as the Union of Marxist-Leninists and held elections to leadership posts. One of them hosted a follow-up meeting in his apartment, where it was decided that the documents should be circulated hand to hand. Jānis Stens, an ethnic Latvian professor at the Institute of Red Professors, passed copies to Kamenev and Zinoviev at the dacha they shared outside Moscow. Another conspirator passed copies to Trotskyites in Kharkov. A copy got to the disgraced former Moscow party boss Nikolai Uglanov (Ryutin's former patron), who was close to Bukharin. (Bukharin would later deny that he had received a copy or knew of the Ryutin group.)

Ryutin's nearly 200-page "Stalin and the Crisis of the Proletarian Dictatorship" was a marvel. It condemned the "adventuristic rate of industrialization" and "adventuristic collectivization with the aid of unbelievable acts of violence and terror," defended Trotsky as a genuine revolutionary despite his shortcomings, and excoriated the rightists for capitulation, yet underscored how "the right wing has proved correct in the economic field." Ryutin brimmed with rage at Stalin's muzzling of party members, and with idealism about Marx and Lenin. ("To place the name of Lenin alongside the name of Stalin is like placing Mount Elbrus alongside a heap of dung.")[281] He proposed twenty-five concrete measures, from new elections to party organs on the basis of intraparty democracy to a mass purge of the OGPU, from dispersal of coercively formed collective farms and loss-making state farms to ending dekulakization, state procurements of grain and livestock, and agricultural exports.[282] Ryutin's prerequisite for these proposals was fulfilling Lenin's Testament. He concluded that "putting an end to Stalin the dictator and his clique" was "the primary duty of every honest Bolshevik."[283]

There it was *again*. Remove Stalin. Lenin's Testament. The subject of endless party discussions that had prompted Stalin to offer to resign at least six times between 1923 and December 1927.

Ryutin acknowledged that "the removal of Stalin and his clique via the normal democratic means guaranteed by the rules of the party and the Soviet Constitution is completely impossible" and explained that "the party has two choices: to continue meekly to endure the mockery of Leninism and the terror, and wait calmly for the final collapse of the proletarian dictatorship; or to remove this clique by force and save the cause of Communism."[284] But his text, even in the version of the document typed up by the OGPU, made no direct call for assassination. And he undertook no such preparations.[285] Instead, having diagnosed the party as the instrument of oppression, he imagined it as the instrument of liberation.[286] Two party members with knowledge of Ryutin's texts sent a written denunciation to the apparatus on September 14, 1932.[287] Stalin was informed the next day. Arrests followed. Ryutin was hauled in on September 22. That same day, Kamenev and Zinoviev were summoned to explain why, having read the Ryutin documents, they had failed to report them, a party crime.[288]

Ryutin was not alone. In its September 1932 issue, Trotsky's *Bulletin* published a "draft platform" (missing the first page) attributed to unnamed members of a "left opposition" underground in the USSR. It declared a "crisis of the Soviet economy" and called for fixing (in Marxist terms) the imbalance between industry and agriculture by reducing expenditures on industry to ease inflation, dispersing nonviable collective farms, ceasing the coerced liquidation of kulaks, and attracting foreign capital through the old practice of leases (or foreign concessions). Quixotically, the authors even offered to cooperate with "the faction that is ruling at present," as part of a shift from "the current obviously unhealthy and obviously nonviable regime to a regime of party democracy."[289] That same month, a traveling Soviet official passed a second text, by Ivan Smirnov, a onetime Trotsky supporter who worked as deputy head for transport equipment in the state planning commission, to Trotsky's son Lev Sedov, in Berlin, who amplified it and published it in the *Bulletin*. It consisted of selected material from an internal state planning commission report on the first six months of 1932. "In view of the inability of the present leadership to extricate itself from the economic and political blind alley," the published article concluded, "the conviction is growing in the party that it is necessary to replace the leadership."[290]

Sedov wrote to his father—in invisible ink—that a "bloc" had formed inside the USSR of "Zinovievites, the Sten-Lominadze group, and Trotskyites," an apparent reference to the small Ryutin conspiracy. But Trotsky fretted that the "left" was incorrectly throwing its lot in with the "rightists" and instructed Lev that, with the émigré Constitutional Democrat "Milyukov, the Mensheviks and Thermidorians of all sorts" demanding Stalin's removal, "we may temporarily have to support him. . . . The slogan 'Down with Stalin' is ambiguous and should not be raised as a war cry at this moment."[291]

THE FOUR HORSEMEN

In September 1932, back from his three-month holiday, Stalin quietly softened his August 7 law: no death penalty for theft of tiny amounts of grain, just sentences of ten years.[292] The 1932 harvest was coming in at fewer than 60 million tons, and possibly as low as 50 million, which was close to the horrific result in the famine year of 1921.[293] Reports to Stalin would peg the harvest as bad but much higher than reality, up to 69 million tons, a discrepancy he never came to appreciate.[294]

Half of all Kazakhs—as many as 2 million—had picked up their tents and remaining herds and fled the collectives. Half of the party functionaries in that republic were said to have deserted their posts.[295] One official report to Stalin in August had noted that the Kazakh autonomous republic now counted 6 million head of livestock, down from 40 million in 1929.[296] Finally, on September 17, he presented a decree for a politburo voice vote that loosened the form of collective farms in Kazakh territories, allowing each household to own eight to ten cattle, up to 100 sheep and goats, and three to five camels, but still insisted that forced settlement would continue "to eradicate economic and cultural anachronisms."[297] He also authorized reductions in grain collections for the Kazakh regions (47,000 tons), along with food assistance (33,000) and postponement of repayment of seed and food advances (98,000)—which together totaled more than one quarter of their original procurement plan.[298] Quotas had already been reduced for Ukraine, but "it is completely incontrovertible that Ukraine will not deliver this amount of grain," the Ukraine official Mendel Khatayevich had courageously written to

Stalin, who underlined this passage in red pencil.[299] At the end of September, the North Caucasus received a massive 660,000-ton grain procurement reduction, albeit to a level still unattainable.[300]

Exports cratered. In 1932, the regime would export just 1.73 million tons of grain, down from 5.06 million in 1931 and 4.76 in 1930. Tsarist Russia in 1913 had exported more than 9 million tons of grain.[301]

With the country in famine's death grip, Stalin convened a joint Central Committee–Central Control Commission plenum (September 28–October 2, 1932) devoted to trade, consumer goods, and ferrous metallurgy. With the harvest over, he aimed to reduce the spring concessions to household plots and private markets. The plenum also condemned the Ryutin group "as traitors to the party and to the working class who, under the flag of a spurious 'Marxism-Leninism,' have attempted to create a bourgeois-kulak organization for the restoration of capitalism and particularly kulakdom in the USSR." Ryutin, under OGPU interrogation, had claimed sole authorship, to shield his comrades. The plenum adopted Stalin's resolution calling for immediate expulsion of all who knew about but did not report the group.[302] Zinoviev, Kamenev, and Uglanov, who visibly wept, repented yet again, but they were nevertheless kicked out of the party yet again and sentenced to internal exile for three years (Zinoviev to Kustanai, Kazakhstan; Kamenev to Minusinsk, Eastern Siberia).[303]

Several tons of meat, sausage, chicken, and fish, 300 kilos of caviar, 600 kilos of cheeses, and large amounts of fruit, vegetables, and mushrooms had been ordered up for the plenum, some of which the attendees were allowed to haul home.

Gossip in Moscow had Stalin tendering his resignation, only to have it rejected.[304] In fact, the inner circle closed ranks behind him. "Now," Kirov stated in a report (October 8, 1932) on the plenum to the Leningrad party, published in *Pravda,* "everyone can see that we were utterly correct, that the further we proceed on the path of constructing socialism, the more manifest is the counterrevolutionary character of every oppositionist tendency." Ryutin got ten years. He was remanded to the prison near the large Urals village of Verkhne-Uralsk, joining Trotskyites he had once condemned.[305] On November 7, 1932, the revolution's fifteenth anniversary, in the first of Ryutin's many letters from prison to his wife, Yevdokiya—aware that any correspondence was read by the authorities—he wrote, "I live now only in the hope that the party and the Central Committee will in the end forgive their prodigal son." He added, "You will not be touched. I have signed everything."[306]

A PERSONAL BLOW

For someone building a new world, Stalin's home life was unremarkable. As only insiders knew, he lived in an apartment on the second floor of the three-story Amusement Palace, the Kremlin's only surviving seventeenth-century boyar residence, with vaulted ceilings and wood-burning stoves. He slept on a divan in an undersized bedroom. Nadya had her own, more ample room, with an oriental carpet of distinct color, a Georgian *takhta* (divan) on which she placed embroidered pillows, as well as a bed, desk, and drawing table. Her window opened onto the Kremlin's Alexander Garden and scenic Kutafya Tower. Between the couple's bedrooms was the dining room, "large enough to have a grand piano in it," their daughter, Svetlana, would recall. Down a hall were bedrooms for Svetlana and Vasily; Svetlana shared hers with a nanny, Alexandra Bychkova. ("If it hadn't been for the even, steady warmth given off by this large and kindly person," Svetlana would later write, "I might long ago have gone out of my mind.")[307] Vasily bunked with Artyom, known as Tom (also the nickname for the boy's deceased father). Stalin's grown son from his first marriage, Yakov, no longer lived with them. Farther down the same hall, the governesses had a room, as did Karolina Til, an ethnic German from Latvia who oversaw the household. The children could see their father everywhere—on posters and newspaper front pages—but not so much at home.

Most visitors to the Kremlin apartment were regime officials. Stalin had no surviving siblings, and his father was deceased. Keke, his mother, lived alone in Tiflis; Nadya, in letters, expressed regret that Keke could not come to Moscow because of the severe climate. The one surviving letter from Keke to her son, from the 1920s, has her wishing him complete annihilation of his enemies.[308] Eighteen of Stalin's letters to her (in Georgian) have survived, containing a word about his health and the children and wishes for her health and long life, all brief and signed "Your Soso."[309] They invariably included an apology for their rarity ("I, of course, am guilty").[310] Stalin had nothing to do with his mother's or father's relations. Relatives from both of Stalin's marriages would stop by the Kremlin apartment: Alexander Svanidze (the brother of Stalin's deceased first wife, Kato) and his wife, Maria, a former opera singer from a well-off Jewish family; Kato's sisters, Mariko and Sashiko; Nadya's father, Sergei Alliluyev, and mother, Olga; Nadya's brothers, Fyodor and Pavel, and the latter's fetching wife, Yevgeniya (Zhenya); and Nadya's sister Anna, who had married Redens (they lived in Kharkov).[311] Several of them lived at the Zubalovo dacha complex, where the Stalins had a dacha that they had remodeled, adding a balcony to the second floor and an outdoor bathhouse. He planted an orchard, and raised pheasants, guinea fowl, and ducks, and liked to lie down on the warm tiled stove in the kitchen to alleviate the pain in his joints.[312] He also liked to wind up the player piano or gramophone and sing. While Kirov, Voroshilov, and even Molotov danced, he watched.[313]

Nadya made occasional use of her husband's position, but she refused to play the smiling wife of the leader, an opportunity other Kremlin wives would have killed for.[314] "We spoke among ourselves, and many times to Nadya, that she was not a match for him," recalled Galina Serebryakova, the spouse of a regime official. "He needed a different wife!"[315] She attended the Industrial Academy under her maiden name, Alliluyeva, and it remains unclear whether her fellow students knew she was Stalin's wife.[316] (Nadya belonged to the party, and Nikita Khrushchev, the academy's party secretary, learned her husband's identity.) The effects of her exposure to the student milieu—young women in the city selling themselves to make ends meet; students with ties to the famine-stricken countryside—remain difficult to gauge. She kept an emotional distance.[317] She dressed simply: a white blouse, navy blue skirt below the knee, low-heeled shoes, little jewelry, no perfume. "There was nothing striking about her," recalled Irina Gogua, who worked in the Kremlin. "In Iosif's presence she seemed plain; it was obvious that she was tense."[318] Svetlana would later try to recollect moments of tenderness, or even attention, from her mother but could not.[319] "A woman of very strong character," Karl Pauker, the head of regime bodyguards, was said to have told a Kremlin doctor. "She is like a flint. The Master is very rough with her, but even he is afraid of her sometimes. Especially when the smile disappears from her face."[320]

Nadya was diagnosed with a defective heart valve, angina, and general exhaustion and suffered from migraines, evidently from a cranial impairment that the best doctors could not alleviate. (Some observers thought she had clinical depression or schizophrenia.)[321] Regime intimates witnessed shouting matches between her and Stalin, laced with his obscenities. But there were episodes of affection, too. "Once, after a party at the Industrial Academy, where Nadezhda was studying, she returned home severely ill from having drunk some wine, and she felt badly," Vladimir Alliluyev, the son of Anna and Stanisław Redens, recalled. "Stalin laid her down, comforted her, and Nadezhda said, 'Anyway, you love me a little bit.'"[322]

Nadya rarely revealed the stress of their almost parallel lives. "Altogether, we have terribly little free time, both Iosif and I," she had written to Keke. "You have probably heard that I have gone back to school (in my old age). I do not find studying in itself difficult. But it is pretty difficult trying to fit it in with duties at home. . . . Still, I am not complaining, and so far I am coping with it all quite successfully. Iosif has promised to write to you himself. As far as his health is concerned, I can say that I marvel at his strength and his energy. Only a really healthy man could stand the amount of work he gets through."[323]

In November 1932, Nadya was weeks from graduation and facing exams.[324] On November 7, Svetlana, Vasily, and Artyom watched the Revolution Day parade on Red Square. Nadya marched with the Industrial Academy delegates. "It was cold, and Stalin was on the Mausoleum, as always, in an overcoat," recalled Khrushchev, who marched with her. When the wind gusted, she said to him, "Look at mine: he did not bring his scarf, he'll catch a cold and again be sick."[325] After joining her children, according to Artyom, Nadya complained of a headache and went home early. The children were taken to the Sokolovka dacha, another state facility used by the family, where they could ski. On November 8, Stalin was in his office between 2:30 and 8:05 p.m., which resulted in a menacing circular to Ukrainian officials that cut off all consumer goods until grain flowed again, and a telegram to the Kazakh leadership accusing it of providing low harvest numbers aimed at "deceiving the state."[326]

Nadya was in the apartment, preparing for the customary holiday banquet that evening in the Voroshilov residence in the Grand Kremlin Palace.[327] She put on an unusually stylish (for her) black dress of fabric imported from Berlin, with embroidered red roses, and placed a red tea rose in her dark hair. She was thirty-one years old; her husband was turning fifty-four.[328] Stalin, it seems, sat across from her and drank more than usual. Some witnesses say he flirted with Galina Yegorova, the thirty-four-year-old actress wife of his military crony Alexander Yegorov. There had been much talk of dalliances (a hairdresser; a pretty woman who worked in protocol).[329] Voroshilov tried to ease the tension, but an eruption occurred. Stalin threw something at Nadya (a bread crust, an orange peel, a cigarette butt).[330] She stormed out. Molotov's wife, Pearl Karpovskaya, known as Polina Zhemchuzhina, followed her. Witnesses mostly cite Stalin's rudeness; Molotov faulted Nadya. "Alliluyeva was already something of a psychopath at that time," he would recall. "She left the gathering with my wife. They took a walk on the Kremlin grounds. It was late at night, and she complained to my wife: 'I do not like this, I do not like that. . . .' She spoke about the young female barber Stalin saw. It was all simple: Stalin had drunk a little too much, he made some jokes. Nothing special, but it had an effect on her."[331]

On the morning of November 9, Karolina Til found Nadya in a pool of blood in her room, near a small toy-sized pistol. (It fit into a lady's handbag; her brother Pavel had brought it from Germany as a gift.) When Stalin emerged from his room into the dining room, Til evidently told him, "Nadya is no longer with us."[332]

Nadya had shot herself in the heart.[333] A call came in to the Sokolovka dacha to prepare the children for return to Moscow; apparently, Voroshilov went to pick up Vasily and Artyom and tried to talk to Svetlana, who was six and a half, but he kept breaking down in tears. Svetlana appears to have remained behind with her nanny.[334] Nadya's open casket was placed upstairs in a nonpublic section of the State Department Store (GUM), across from the Kremlin on Red Square, where the central executive committee presidium, run by Yenukidze, had offices. "Early morning for the ceremony of bidding farewell, we climbed the second floor of GUM," Artyom recalled. "Vasily and I climbed the stairs ahead of Stalin. He moved in silence. He was glum. I remember: as soon as Iosif Vissarionovich approached the casket, he began simply to cry, he broke down in tears. . . . Vasily literally hung on to him and said, 'Papa, don't cry, Papa, don't.'"[335] Molotov recalled, "I had never seen Stalin weeping before, but as he stood there by the coffin, tears ran down his cheeks. She loved Stalin very much—that is a fact. . . . He went up to [the coffin] and said, 'I did not take enough care of you.'"[336]

Pravda (November 10, 1932) announced the death of Nadezhda Sergeyevna Alliluyeva in what was the first mention in the Soviet press of Stalin's marriage.[337] No cause was given.[338] She had been diagnosed with acute appendicitis but had put off the operation until after her exams, and this became the unofficial cause of death, spread by the secret police.[339] Rumors that Stalin shot her over political disagreements were instantaneous. Some people claimed they heard from a Kremlin doctor or a servant that Nadya's screams for him to stop had been heard by neighbors (through impossibly thick walls).[340] Others whispered that he had driven her to suicide.[341] Still other rumors had Stalin marrying Kaganovich's sister Rosa (no such person existed).[342] Kirov and Orjonikidze, Stalin's two closest comrades, were said to have stayed in the Kremlin apartment with him the night of her death. Bukharin, who used to visit Nadya in the apartment, would offer to exchange Kremlin apartments with Stalin. Stalin accepted. Soon, however, he and the children instead moved into the Imperial Senate, to an apartment one floor below his Kremlin office. It comprised seven rooms on a long corridor, with rooms for servants and bodyguards at each end and windows looking out onto the Arsenal.[343]

The casket was placed on a white catafalque for an unhurried procession to the Novodevichy Cemetery on November 12. The newspaper had announced the schedule, and Moscow's streets were lined with people (many of them plainclothes police). Stalin exited the Kremlin on foot, behind the horse-drawn hearse. Whether he marched the full four miles, through many narrow and winding streets, is uncertain.[344] TASS announced that grave-site eulogies were delivered by Bukharin (for the Krasnaya Presnya ward party committee, Nadya's primary party organization) and Kaganovich (Moscow party boss). "We are burying one of the best, most loyal members of our party," Kaganovich stated. "Raised in the family of an old Bolshevik proletarian, going forward after the revolution for many years in a state of the greatest loyalty to the cause of the working class, Nadezhda Sergeyevna was organically linked with the worker movement, with our party. . . . We, close friends and comrades, understand the severity of the loss of comrade Stalin, and we know what duties this imposes on us with respect to comrade Stalin."[345]

After Nadya was lowered into the grave, "Stalin threw a handful of dirt on it," Artyom recalled. "He told Vasily and me to do likewise. Returning home, we had lunch. Stalin sat silently, contemplatively. Soon he left for a meeting of the government."[346] *Pravda* published a grace note from the dictator (November 18) offering "heartfelt gratitude to all organizations, comrades, and individuals who had expressed their condolences on the occasion of the death of my close friend and comrade Nadezhda Sergeyevna Alliluyeva-Stalina." He exhibited remorse and self-pity, fury and his sense of victimhood.[347] Svetlana's subsequent account, unreliable in most respects, rightly surmised that her father "was too intelligent not to know that people always commit suicide to punish someone."[348]

ENEMY WITH A PARTY CARD

Secret reports were now mentioning a threat of starvation even for Moscow and Leningrad.[349] Military intelligence estimated that Japan had a standing army of 1,880,000, Poland 1,772,000, Romania 1,180,000, Finland 163,000, Estonia 75,000, and Latvia 114,000.[350] Absorbing his personal loss, his subjects starving, his eastern and western borders facing formidable enemies, Stalin could have been moved to carve out a breathing space. But the spring 1932 concessions had failed to produce a harvest miracle, and now he ratcheted up the repression again to squeeze blood from a stone.[351] He had formed a commission to purge the party in the North Caucasus, sending Kaganovich there to bang heads, and returned Yevdokimov to its capital, Rostov, ordering that villages that failed to fulfill grain quotas be deported in their entirety. (Their houses and fields were to be taken by "conscientious Red Army collective farmers who have too little land or bad land in other regions.")[352] Molotov was dispatched to Ukraine, whence he complained to Stalin (November 21) that in the "opportunist, bourgeois, kulak situation," local functionaries were urging that farmers' consumption needs be met before more grain went to the state.[353] That same day, Stalin accused the party boss in the Kazakh republic, Filipp Goloshchokin, of having surrendered despite "a maximal reduction" in procurement quotas, and ordered him to "strike those Communists in counties and below who are in the hands of petit bourgeois anarchy and have slid onto the rails of kulak sabotage."[354]

The Soviet agricultural press in November 1932 carried headlines of peasants dying from starvation in Poland ("It is not a crisis; it is a catastrophe"), Czechoslovakia ("dying villages"), China ("hunger despite a good harvest"), and the United States ("poverty and ruin").[355] Not a word about the famine in the Soviet Union.

Once again, the party "opposition" played into Stalin's hands: he received a denunciation (on or before November 19) against two officials, Nikolai Eismont, commissar of food for the RSFSR, and Vladimir Tolmachev, head of road transport for the RSFSR, who, in connection with the Revolution Day holiday, had been drinking in Eismont's apartment. They gathered again the next day with Alexander Smirnov, a former agriculture commissar who had been demoted to a position in forestry, and criticized anew Stalin's destructive policies. Smirnov had become a Central Committee member back in 1912, the same year as Stalin. Eismont had been on the recent commission to the North Caucasus led by Kaganovich and had seen the swarms of starving refugees at railroad stations. Under the influence, the trio had discussed possible replacements for the general secretary: Voroshilov, Kalinin, even Smirnov.

There it was, *yet again*. Remove Stalin.

The Central Control Commission, now overseen by the Stalin minion Jānis Rudzutaks, deemed the lubricated conversations a "counterrevolutionary grouping."[356] Stalin added the disgraced rightist Mikhail Tomsky (head of the state publishing house) to the "conspiracy," and summoned a joint session of the politburo and the Control Commission presidium on November 27. "These people," the attack dog Yemelyan Yaroslavsky fulminated, "are like the Ryutin group, only in a different form." By now, though, the crisis under Stalin's rule was pervasive and even some arch-loyalists shrank from full-throated condemnation of their loose-tongued comrades. Kuibyshev referred to Smirnov by his nickname ("Foma") and recalled their long association, dating back to Narym exile. (Stalin had been there, too, and Smirnov had fed him.) Mikoyan, who used to be Eismont's boss, awkwardly said almost nothing (until the very end).[357]

Rumors again circulated that Stalin had verbally offered to resign, and that after an awkward silence Molotov had spoken up to reassure him he had the party's confidence.[358] Be that as it may, Stalin found himself defending his policies.[359] He grumbled that the conspirators "represent matters as if Stalin were guilty of everything" and warned that the choice was between becoming a victim of the imperialists—the fate of China—or a socialist industrial power that could defend itself. "What matters is not Stalin, but the party," he concluded. "You can remove Stalin, but things will continue just as they are."[360]

Eismont and Tolmachev were the ones expelled from the party, and Smirnov from the Central Committee, although they were not arrested.[361] Stalin had a transcript of the proceedings made for circulation to party organizations. He sent another vituperative telegram (also signed by Molotov), this one to officials in the Urals (December 7, 1932), condemning as "unpersuasive" their explanations for local state farms' failures to fulfill procurement quotas. "The provincial leadership cannot escape its responsibility," it said, asking for names of the state farm directors. "Announce to the directors that a party card will not save them from arrest, that an enemy with a party card warrants greater attention than an enemy without a party card."[362]

SHARPENING THE CLASS STRUGGLE

On December 12, 1932, the Soviet Union restored diplomatic relations with Chiang Kai-shek's government in Nanking. The next day, Japan belatedly replied to the Soviet offer of a nonaggression pact in a note to Soviet envoy Alexander Troyanovsky with a rejection.[363] The Japanese leaked distorted versions of the exchange; the Soviet press published the originals, aiming to demonstrate Japan's belligerence.[364] Stalin, meanwhile, decided to widen the party purge he had imposed on the North Caucasus: on December 11, *Pravda* had carried a resolution in the name of the Central Committee announcing a multiregion party cleansing for 1933.[365] His mood was captured in his greeting to the secret police on the fifteenth anniversary of their founding, December 20, which *Pravda* printed that day—"I wish you success in your difficult task of extirpating the enemies of the dictatorship of the proletariat!"[366]

Stalin also took the time to repudiate Thomas Campbell, an agricultural expert from Montana who several years earlier had been afforded an audience, and had now published a book about his experiences and meeting with Stalin ("piercing black eyes which concentrate on you even while talking through an interpreter"). It was mostly sympathetic, but on the touchy subject of Comintern subversion, he wrote that Stalin had "unhesitatingly admitted, with disarming frankness, that under Trotsky there had been an attempt to spread Communism throughout the world. He said this was the primary cause of his break with Trotsky. . . . He explained that they had neither the time nor the money to try to communize the whole world, even should they wish to do so." In his published repudiation (December 23, 1932), Stalin denied that Trotsky's name had come up, and noted that Campbell's book mentioned a transcript of their conversation but shrank from including it. Stalin's rebuttal contained a purported transcript, which had him stressing the need for diplomatic recognition to normalize trade relations and had Campbell mentioning meeting with then President-elect Herbert Hoover prior to setting out for the Soviet Union and promising to convey the Stalin conversation back to Hoover.[367]

Before the year was out, Stalin pushed through a decree on an internal passport system to purge urban areas of "alien" and "non-laboring elements."[368] Recipients were to include permanent residents aged sixteen or older in cities and towns, and at construction sites, as well as transport workers and state-farm laborers, but not collective farmers. He aimed to diminish the pressure on the urban food supply and force peasants back into the collectives.[369] On December 29, 1932, a furious directive in the name of the politburo threatened collective farms that failed to meet procurement quotas with a compulsory early repayment of credits, a cutoff from machine-tractor-station equipment, and confiscation of "all the grain they had, including the so-called seed funds"—the basis for the spring sowing campaign.[370]

Despite the greater repression, procurements as of January 1, 1933, had reached only 17.4 million tons, 3.7 million fewer than collected by the same time the previous year (and 3 million below the plan).[371] On January 7, Stalin opened another joint plenum of the Central Committee and the Central Control Commission, boasting that "we had no iron and steel industry. . . . We now have one. We had no tractor industry. We now have one. We had no automobile industry"—and so on, through aircraft and more. He admitted that the first Five-Year Plan prioritized heavy industry but baldly asserted that living standards had improved. He had reduced industrial growth targets for the second Five-Year Plan to a more realistic 13–14 percent per annum.[372]

Stalin's most important declaration concerned a sharpening of the class struggle as the country got closer to socialism, a cudgel he had used against Bukharin in 1928 (and a concept Trotsky had articulated a decade earlier). "We need to keep in mind that the increase in the power of the Soviet state will strengthen the resistance of the last holdovers of dying classes," Stalin asserted. "Precisely because they are dying out and in their last days, they will switch from some forms of striking to other, sharper forms, appealing to the backward strata of the population. . . . On this soil, smashed groups of old counterrevolutionary parties of SRs and Mensheviks, bourgeois nationalists of the center and periphery, may stir and come to life, shards of counterrevolutionary elements of Trotskyites and right deviationists may stir and come to life." He added: "This, of course, is not scary. But all this needs to be kept in mind if we want to do away with these elements quickly and without especially large numbers of victims."[373]

Opposition, according to Stalin, now worked "on the sly," masked behind simulated loyalty. In a second set of remarks to the plenum (January 11), he asserted—in line with the reports he received—that "our harvest was not worse, but better than in the previous year." He blamed any problems on "anti-Soviet elements" and concealed "nests of counterrevolution." "They sit right in the collective farm, holding positions as storemen, business managers, bookkeepers, secretaries, and so on," he averred. "They will never say 'Down with the collective farm.' They are 'for' the collective farm."[374]

Trotsky was ever present—his writings had been demanding that 1933 be the year of the major overhaul, an otherwise obscure proposal condemned at the plenum as "slander."[375]

The politburo closed ranks around the dictator, and the others fell in line. "We, as members of the Central Committee, vote for Stalin because he is ours. (Applause.)," declared Rudzutaks. "You won't find a single instance when Comrade Stalin hesitated or retreated. That is why we are with him. Yes, he vigorously chops off what is rotten, he chops off what is slated for destruction. If he didn't do this, he would not be a Leninist." Similarly, the disgraced Bukharin stated, "We have won dazzling victories in the building up of the Five-Year Plan. We are currently at war and must exercise the strictest discipline. . . . That is why such groupings must be hacked off without the slightest mercy, without being in the slightest troubled by any sentimental considerations concerning the past, concerning personal friendships." Smirnov, in futile self-defense, denied that he or any other party member could have uttered the words about the need to "remove comrade

Stalin": "I think that only someone drunk out of his mind or insane could ever say such a thing."[376]

At the plenum's close (January 12), the regime announced suspension of recruitment into the party and the pending purge. That same day, Stalin permitted the politburo to approve, in a poll vote, another reduction in the yearly grain procurement for Ukraine, of 457,000 tons; other regions got smaller reductions. Twelve days later, the dictator sacked the party bosses in Ukraine's Dnepropetrovsk, Odessa, and Kharkov provinces.[377] He did the same to the party boss of the Kazakh republic.[378] Yagoda reported that eighty-seven "Trotskyites" had been rounded up or soon would be.[379] Regime decision making was becoming more and more informal, with most key matters adjudicated in Stalin's office.[380] Secret police reports were claiming an ever greater share of his paperwork.[381] He floated the notion with the OGPU of deporting another 3 million peasants, a target soon sliced to 2 million, then 500,000, and finally only half of that.[382]

The OGPU, in any case, was consumed with forming local detachments to enforce a draconian decree, on January 22, 1933, ordering interdiction of peasant flight from grain-growing regions and blaming local authorities for allowing an exodus, which had helped spread epidemics and become a weapon for discrediting regime policies.[383] Railway ticket sales were suspended and dragnets set up from the Caucasus to the Urals on one side and along the western borderlands on the other.[384] Perhaps Stalin feared an unraveling of the collective farm order. In any case, the decree showed that he was very anxious to prevent the spread of further discontent to the urban socialist core. He also had to feed the cities, which could become death traps. Overall, the number of fleeing peasants captured and sent back would be relatively small (low hundreds of thousands, when there were 17 million peasants in collective farms in Ukraine alone). Many farmers were already trapped in regions without adequate food.[385]

Molotov, meanwhile, gloated to the central executive committee of the Soviet on January 23, 1933, that more and more capitalist states were recognizing the Soviet Union. "Some clever ones still consider further 'study' of the USSR necessary (i.e., to delay recognition)," he stated. "It should not be difficult to guess how Soviet might has increased, how our economy is expanding, how much the international weight of the USSR has grown. Those who are full of useless and empty phrases about further study of the USSR are the ones who have the most to lose from the absence of diplomatic ties."[386] Stalin sent a congratulatory note: "The confident-contemptuous tone with respect to the 'Great Powers,' the belief in our own strength, the simple spitting in the pot of the swaggering 'Great Powers'—very good. Let them 'eat it.'"[387]

GEOPOLITICAL CATASTROPHE

The Nazis had lost thirty-four seats in Germany's November 1932 parliamentary elections, seeing their vote drop by 2 million—to 33.1 percent, from 37.4 percent in July 1932.[388] The party, an amalgam of territorial organizations and divergent interests, was wracked by dissension and defections, partly triggered by Adolf Hitler's refusal, even after the electoral reversal, of any post short of chancellor.[389] A key driver of Nazi support, the Depression, had bottomed out, and a slow recovery was under way. And yet, traditional conservatives desperate for stability and order proved unable to fashion a parliamentary majority that achieved their goal of excluding the Social Democrats and defanging the trade union movement and the Communists.[390] The maladroit octogenarian president, former field marshal Paul von Hindenburg, had appointed defense minister Kurt von Schleicher, another soldier turned politician, as chancellor in early December 1932, elbowing aside the ambitious archconservative Franz von Papen. But when Hindenburg refused to declare a state of emergency and allow Schleicher to dissolve the Reichstag to avoid a no-confidence vote, the chancellor resigned. Schleicher colluded with Hitler to try to stop the return of his nemesis von Papen, while the latter persuaded Hindenburg to appoint Hitler, even though the field marshal had trounced the Nazi in elections to the presidency and mocked him as a mere corporal.[391] Traditional conservatives imagined that they could "tame" Hitler and the radical right while achieving a broadened anti-left coalition. On January 30, 1933, von Papen—having secured the vice chancellorship for himself—escorted the Nazi ruffian into the Chancellery, for the oath of office, through a rear door.[392]

"A stubby little Austrian with a flabby handshake, shifty brown eyes, and a Charlie Chaplin mustache," wrote the world's best-selling daily newspaper, the London *Daily Herald*. "What sort of man is this to lead a great nation?"[393]

Nazi ranks were electrified. "Hitler is Reich Chancellor," marveled Joseph Goebbels. "Just like a fairy-tale."[394] Goebbels improvised a torchlight parade through Berlin, playacting a seizure of power, even though Hitler had come to power legally (just like Italy's Mussolini).[395] Success had not come out of nowhere, however. By 1929, the Nazis had 3,400 party branches around the country and were mounting countless public rallies, sponsoring concerts, putting up Christmas trees and maypoles, spotlighting local heroes. They spoke to German people's fears and prejudices, but also to their aspirations and interests, promising a reckoning with the disgraceful recent past and a future of national unity and rebirth.[396] Paramilitary Nazi Brownshirts, known as the SA, engaged in street brawling with the Social Democrats and the Communists (who fought each other as well). The Nazi leadership encouraged violence and lawlessness, just as the Bolsheviks had on their path to power, but the Nazis accused the Communists of fomenting the chaos and called for order.[397] Organized opposition to the Nazis was either irresolute or at loggerheads.[398] The Reichswehr was focused on rearmament.[399]

There was one political force that could compete with Nazi storm troopers in the streets—the Communists—but they proactively subverted Weimar democracy, even knowing that this facilitated Nazi aims. Through the Comintern, Stalin was enforcing a struggle to the death—with Social Democracy. "The Nazi tree should not hide the Social Democrat forest," the German Communist leader Ernst Thälmann had warned.[400] The catastrophe of the Comintern policy of "social fascism" was vividly brought home in the November 1932 elections, when German Communists had garnered nearly 6 million votes, and the Social Democrats more than 7 million, as compared with the Nazis' 11.7 million. In no free and fair election did the Nazis ever win more votes than the Communists and Social Democrats combined.[401]

Many Communists imagined Nazism, which they labeled "fascism," to be the terminal stage of the crisis of "monopoly capitalism," so that the turmoil in Germany would eventually redound to them, which meant they needed to make themselves ready by outbattling their rivals on the left.[402] Some Communists even welcomed the Nazi accession to power. Stalin did not.[403] Still, he appears to have underestimated Hitler, as many—but not all—contemporaries did. He interpreted Hitler and Nazism as creatures of finance capital, a class-based analysis, and assumed that German militarists would continue to shape state policy. Secret German-Soviet military cooperation had been failing.[404] But Stalin hoped it would be renewed.[405] Werner von Blomberg, who had played a hand in Hindenburg's appointment of Hitler and stayed on as war minister, would pass on to the Soviet embassy that "a change in Soviet-German relations is out of the question under any circumstances."[406] But Nazism's appeal to German workers was manifest, and its intense ideological radicalism was directed at the Soviet Union.[407]

RADICAL REALIGNMENTS

As the Nazis reveled in Hitler's chancellorship, Stalin's regime staged the First all-Union Congress of Collective Farm Shock Workers (February 15–19, 1933), attended by more than 1,500 delegates, nearly 900 of whom held no bureaucratic office and half of whom were not party or Communist Youth League members. They were recognized for labor performance.[408] Kaganovich addressed them in a folksy manner, reciting peasant proverbs, while praising the vicious injunction against theft of socialist property as a *"great law."* He boasted of the creation of 200,000 collective farms and 5,000 state farms, asserting that only collectiviza-tion had made possible industrialization and the preemption of foreign military intervention.[409] One collective farm brigadier, who had been asked by Kaganovich whether the collectivized system was better, answered, "Things are, of course, bet-ter now. Still, before I was master of my fate, and now I am not the master."[410]

On the final day, Stalin, putting on a folksy air, too, warned biblically that he who did not work would not eat, but promised that each collective farmer would have a cow ("prolonged applause").[411] He scolded those who underestimated women ("Women on the collective farms are a great force"). He acknowledged that "quite a number of people, including collective farmers," had been skeptical of party policy, but dismissed the idea of a third way, individual farming without capitalists and landowners, because it would inevitably give rise to a "kulak-capitalist regime." Silent on the famine, he asserted that "the multi-million-mass poor peasants, previously living half starving, have now become middle peasants in the collective farms, they have become well-off. This is an achievement that the world has not seen before."[412]

On February 27, a fire consumed the German Reichstag, and a young, unem-ployed bricklayer, recently arrived from the Netherlands, was found inside and arrested. He was a member of the Dutch Communist party. The Nazi party was still a minority in the parliament, but now Hitler persuaded President Hinden-burg to sign an emergency decree suspending the governments of Germany's fed-eral states and most civil liberties "as a defensive measure against the Communists."[413] Dissolution of parliament and snap elections, which were scheduled for March 5, afforded Hitler a campaign of intense hysteria about Communist subversion. The Nazis still won only 43.9 percent (288 of 647 seats), but with their partners, the German National People's Party, who won 8 percent, they had a governing majority.[414] Hitler had been handed power, but now he seized it, proposing an Enabling Act to promulgate laws on his authority as chancellor without the Reichstag for a period of four years. It required a two-thirds vote. Only the Social Democrats, twelve of whose deputies had been imprisoned, voted against the measure, which passed 441 to 94.[415] Soon the Nazis were the sole legal party in Germany.

Hitler—who had become a German citizen only in 1932—was dictator of the country, upending the traditional conservatives.[416] "With few exceptions, the men who are running this government are of a mentality that you and I cannot understand," the American consul general wrote in a message to the state department. "Some of them are psychopathic cases and would ordinarily be receiving treatment somewhere."[417]

Elements in the Nazi movement—assisted by colluding police—exuded fanatical delight in physically annihilating leftist property, institutions, and people. Hitler fulminated against "Judeo-Bolshevism" as a worldwide conspiracy.[418] At the same time, he received the Soviet envoy, Lev Khinchuk, on April 28, 1933, and shortly thereafter allowed Germany to ratify the long-delayed extension of the 1926 Berlin treaty, ostensibly reaffirming good bilateral relations.[419] "The cornerstone of Soviet foreign policy is the maintenance of peace," *Izvestiya* editorialized (May 6). "In this spirit, the Soviet Union does not wish to alter anything in its attitude to Germany." But Radek penned an essay in *Pravda* (May 10) noting that the fascist regimes led the way in "revision of the robber baron peace of Versailles," and warning that this would entail "the creation of a worse Brest-Litovsk peace." He hinted at a Soviet effort to cozy up to Poland.[420]

Communist parties outside the USSR numbered 910,000 members, and the German party had accounted for 330,000 of them, the second largest after China (350,000).[421] But Hitler crushed them. This left the French and Czechoslovak parties, with just 34,000 and 60,000 members, respectively, as the next largest. Communists in France and Czechoslovakia pressured Moscow to abandon the "social fascism" policy. But in spring 1933, when seven Social Democratic parties issued a joint public appeal for a nonaggression pact with Communists, Stalin approved instructions "to step up the campaign against the Second International," arguing that "it is necessary to emphasize the flight of Social Democracy to the fascist camp." This stance was shared by many of the foreign Communists he had gathered at Comintern HQ.[422] The long-standing civil war on the left persisted.[423]

EDUCATION OF A TRUE BELIEVER

Upward of 50 million Soviet inhabitants, perhaps as many as 70 million, were caught in regions with little or no food.[424] More than a million cases of typhus would be registered in 1932–33, and half a million of typhoid fever.[425] The OGPU claimed in a report to Stalin (March 1933) that it had interdicted 219,460 runaways in search of food, sending 186,588 back to their points of origin and arresting the others.[426] Human and animal corpses littered county roads, railroad tracks, the open steppe, the frontiers. Peasants ate dogs and cats, exhumed horse carcasses, boiled gophers. The Dnepropetrovsk OGPU reported to Kharkov (March 5, 1933) "on the rising cases of tumefaction and death on the basis of famine, verified and confirmed in documents by physician observation." The regional OGPU boss sent tables with the numbers of starving families by county, and named conscientious laborers who were starving, adding that a traveling commission had delivered grain from the reserves to the suffering areas.[427] It was, of course, too little too late.

Death and disease wracked the entire Soviet wheat belt—Ukraine (including the Moldavian autonomous republic), the North Caucasus (including the Kuban, Stavropol, and Don provinces), the Middle and Lower Volga valley (from Nizhny Novgorod to Astrakhan, including the Volga German autonomous republic), and the Central Black Earth region—but also Vologda and Arkhangelsk in the north, the Urals, and the Kazakh autonomous republic.[428] Party officials begged for emergency aid to "save the lives of many people from starvation death," as the ethnic Kazakh official Turar Ryskulov wrote to Stalin (March 9, 1933).[429] An OGPU operative assembled a summary of starvation *in the cities* in the Urals, Volga valley, and North Caucasus, underscoring the negative effects on workers' political mood.[430] Reports of cannibalism in Ukraine were averaging ten per day. Parents were killing one child and feeding it to the others; some prepared soup stock and salted the remaining flesh in barrels to preserve it.[431] The secret police reported on cannibal bands that targeted orphans: "This group cut up and consumed as food three children, including an eleven-year-old son and an orphan whose parents perished from starvation."[432]

Reports and letters to Stalin's office were graphic.[433] The documents show that he became livid not when he learned that people were driven to eating human flesh but when he learned that an American correspondent was given permission to travel to famine-stricken regions ("We already have enough spies in the USSR").[434]

When even the unsqueamish Kaganovich confirmed the catastrophe, it evidently got through to the dictator.[435] On March 20, 1933, the politburo, with Stalin signing the protocol, resolved to supply more tractors (though fewer than requested), send more food aid to Ukraine, allow free trade in foodstuffs in Kharkov and Kiev, and mobilize all internal resources for the sowing campaign.[436] (That same day, the politburo directed the OGPU to remove guns from the population.)[437]

Voroshilov, on holiday again, had written to Stalin complaining of insomnia and stomach problems. Stalin answered, "I still feel poorly, sleep little, and am not getting better, but this is not manifested in work." Orjonikidze wrote to Voroshilov (April 9) that he was sick and exhausted and complained about how his first deputy, Pyatakov, worked hard but did not believe in the party's strategy, and how Orjonikidze needed a trusted deputy who could relieve him as commissar, because "I am rather ill and cannot make it much longer."[438]

How did the regime not come apart altogether? How did higher-ups writing and receiving the reports not concede that the situation called for repudiation of regime policies? How did local officials persist in implementing orders?

Lev Kopelev (b. 1912) was a Communist Youth League militant, the editor in chief of an agitation paper, and a 25,000er requisitioning grain in his native Ukraine from late 1932 into spring 1933. He had been arrested, for ten days in 1929, for putting out leaflets defending the "Bolshevik-Leninists" (as Trotskyites called themselves).[439] Young and naïve, he had admitted his error. His life rippled with meaning. "The grain front!" he recalled of the procurement campaigns. "Stalin said the struggle for grain was the struggle for socialism. I was convinced we were warriors on an invisible front, fighting kulak sabotage for the grain which was needed by the country, by the Five-Year Plan." Kopelev noted how a local OGPU operative was the son of a miner and had worked in a mine himself ("We believed him without reservation"), while meetings with villagers took place under religious icons. "Every time I began to speak, I wanted to prove to these people that they were making a serious mistake by hiding the grain"—after all, workers in the cities were putting in two and three shifts yet did not have enough food; Japanese militarists and now German fascists surrounded the country. Villagers were eating grass and gnawing on twigs, denying that they had grain to give, before being hauled off—"and I persuaded myself, explained to myself: I mustn't give in to debilitating pity," Kopelev said. He convinced himself that "the famine was caused by the opposition of suicidally unconscientious peasants, enemy intriguers, and the inexperience and weakness of the lower ranks of [party and soviet] workers."[440]

Kopelev was "speaking Bolshevik," or making the revolution personal, internalizing its inescapable vocabulary, worldview, and presentations of self. The regime compelled people to write and recite autobiographies using prescribed categories and ways of thinking. Kopelev was a true believer, but it was not necessary to believe. It was, however, necessary to appear to believe and even the reluctant came to employ the language and thought processes of the regime to view the world through party directives and official reportage—class and enemies, factory output, and imperialist threats, false versus genuine consciousness. This is what gave Stalin's regime its extraordinary power.[441]

Even in the hospital with diarrhea, Kopelev devoured the reportage of Five-Year Plan triumphs and Stalin's catechismal speeches. If doubts crept in, he took inspiration from role models—like the orphaned son of a hired farm laborer who had worked for "kulaks" but become chairman of a village soviet. Stalin purged the Ukrainian party apparatus and replaced the Kharkov party boss with Pavel Postyshev, a Bolshevik originally from industrial Ivanovo-Voznesensk, who now became the number two in Ukraine. Postyshev, Kopelev wrote, "stood in line at grocery stores, cafeterias, bathhouses, and he sat with petitioners in the waiting rooms of various government establishments." Postyshev opened cafés in factory shops, had flowers planted, and viciously condemned Ukrainian intellectuals as bourgeois nationalists and agents of fascism. "For me, Postyshev became a hero, a leader, a paragon of the true Bolshevik—and not for me alone."[442] In newspaper photographs of turbines and tractors, in live glimpses of freight cars loaded with steel, Kopelev saw the new world coming into being. When a peasant tried to burn down a collectivized barn, Kopelev was confirmed in his conviction that sabotage existed. Capitalist encirclement was a fact. In 1933, he was awarded a coveted place at Kharkov University.[443] "I believed," Kopelev wrote, "because I wanted to believe."[444]

CONSEQUENCES

Hay carts were going round to gather the corpses, as during the medieval plagues.[445] "I saw things that are impossible to forget until one's death," the Cossack novelist Mikhail Sholokhov wrote to Stalin (April 4, 1933) of his native Don River valley. Stalin responded (May 6) that he had directed that the area be provided food aid and that the information in Sholokhov's letter should be investigated, but he stood his ground. "Your letters create a somewhat one-sided impression," Stalin wrote. "The esteemed grain growers of your region (and not only your region) carried out a 'sit-down strike' (sabotage!) and would not have minded leaving the workers and the Red Army without grain." He deemed their actions "a 'quiet' war with Soviet power. A war of attrition, dear comrade Sholokhov."[446]

Stalin was indeed at war—with the peasantry, and with his own Communist party for supposedly going soft at this perilous hour. On May 4, he had received a report from Yagoda on how newly arrived emaciated conscripts were eager for the promised bread toasts and a lump of sugar, while relatives trailed them, looking for handouts. One was overheard to say, "When there were no collective farms, peasants lived a lot better. Now, with collective farms, everyone is starving. If war breaks out, no one will defend Soviet power; everyone will go against it."[447]

Japan's Kwantung Army attempted to seize Jehol, in Inner Mongolia, a springboard for attacking both Peking (Beijing) and Outer Mongolia, the Soviet satellite.[448] Chiang Kai-shek's earlier appeal to the League of Nations had merely resulted in Japan quitting that body, which Tokyo had come to see as a racist Anglo-American conspiracy to emasculate it.[449] On the last day of May 1933, Kwantung generals signed a truce with "local" officials in the port of Tientsin (Tianjin), in northern China, that extended Manchukuo's borders to the Great Wall, gave Japan control of the strategic mountain pass, and created a demilitarized zone extending sixty miles south of the wall and just north of the Peking-Tientsin district.[450] Stalin suspected that Chiang, whose signature was not on the truce, was secretly negotiating an end to the war, which would free up Japan to attack him. Presumed Japanese saboteurs were crossing into Soviet territory.[451] The dictator received intercepted communications between the British ambassador in Tokyo and the foreign office in London, asserting that Japan's military buildup went beyond its aims in China and that Japanese army observers viewed war with the Soviet Union as inevitable.[452] Stalin had Soviet newspapers publish intelligence excerpts, in disguised form, to expose Tokyo's aggressive desires.[453]

The party journal *Bolshevik* tried to rebut a sense of "the capitulation of the Soviet Union in the face of world imperialism in general and Japanese imperialism in particular."[454] But whether the USSR could even fight a war had become doubtful. On May 7, 1933, the politburo had prohibited the OGPU from imposing the death penalty—the Soviet Far East was granted an exception—and the next day Stalin and Molotov had issued a secret directive to party organizations and OGPU branches suspending mass peasant deportations and ordering release of Gulag inmates guilty of lesser infractions, in light of "the three-year struggle that has destroyed our class enemies in the village."[455] "The moment has arrived when we no longer need mass repressions," the decree explained, conceding that further "severe forms of repression" could "bring the influence of our party in the village to zero."[456] But then, when Kosior and others in Ukraine had reported on severe repression being undertaken against peasants there, Stalin responded (May 31), "Finally you are beginning to apply yourself in Bolshevik fashion."[457]

Early June brought a small measure of relief: berries, green onions, young potatoes, carrots, and beets became ready for consumption, for those who maintained household gardens (and guarded them round the clock).[458] Hungry children who were discovered rooting around in the plots were sometimes killed, then and there, by farmers protecting their families' food.[459] The regime was purchasing livestock from western China and again reducing grain exports. For 1933, it would end up at 1.68 million tons, when the original plan had been for 6.2 million. Exports in 1933 would bring in a mere 31.2 million gold rubles, a fivefold revenue plunge since 1930.[460] The general crisis forced a halt to the generous increases in military expenditures, which would decrease in 1933 to 2 billion rubles (from 2.2 billion).[461]

On June 1, 1933, the announced party purge commenced. The procedures specified ferreting out self-seekers, the politically passive, and the morally depraved, but also—in a conspicuous indication of Stalin's hand—"open and hidden violators of party discipline, who do not fulfill party and state decisions, subjecting to doubt and discrediting the plans by the party with nonsense about their 'unreality' and 'unattainability.'" The party journal explained that the enemy, unable to proceed openly and frontally (like the class-alien targets of the previous general purges), deceitfully penetrated the party and hid behind a party card to sabotage socialism from within ("double-dealers").[462]

During the Five-Year Plan, membership had ballooned by more than 2 million, to 3.55 million (2.2 million full members, 1.35 million candidates). Each party organization established its own purge commission, and every Communist—this now included Central Committee members—had to place their party cards on the table, recite their autobiographies, and submit to interrogation. The commissions usually had records of previous autobiographies and any denunciations; the proceedings were open to non-party workmates to chime in. The previous purge, in 1929–30, had expelled around one in ten. Now, nearly one in five would be expelled, and nearly as many would quit rather than submit to the procedure, bringing the total number who did not keep party cards to more than 800,000.[463]

Expulsion was not cause for arrest, which required accusations of a crime, but Stalin's commentary implied guilt until proven innocent.[464]

STALIN'S FAMINE

Before 1917, to import machinery, Russia had been exporting more than would have seemed permissible, given domestic consumption needs. ("We will not eat our fill, but we will export," Alexander III's finance minister had remarked.)[465] A famine had broken out in 1891–92. In the four years prior, Russia had exported about 10 million tons of grain, but then a dry autumn, which delayed fall planting, severely cold winter temperatures without the usual snowfalls, a windy spring that blew away topsoil, and a long and dry summer damaged the harvest. The tsarist state had contributed to the vulnerability by reducing the rural workforce (conscripting young males), enforcing peasant redemption payments for former gentry land in connection with the serf emancipation, and having tax collectors seize vital livestock if payments fell short. Even after crop failure and hunger were evident, grain exports continued for a time. And the finance minister had opposed even this belated stoppage. The tsarist government refused to use the word "famine" (*golod*), admitting to only a "failed harvest" (*neurozhai*); censors prevented newspapers from reporting about it. Around 500,000 people died, primarily from cholera epidemics triggered by starvation.[466]

Stalin's famine, involving extirpation of capitalism and denomadization, was incomparably worse. In 1931–33, famine and related epidemics probably killed between 5 and 7 million people. Perhaps 10 million more starved nearly to death.[467] "I don't know how they stood it!" Molotov would say later in his long life. In the Kazakh autonomous republic, starvation and disease probably claimed between 1.2 and 1.4 million people, the vast majority of them ethnic Kazakhs, from a population of roughly 6.5 million (of whom perhaps 4.12 million were ethnic Kazakhs). This was the highest death ratio in the Soviet Union.[468] In Ukraine, the death toll was around 3.5 million, out of a population of 33 million. Statistics on livestock were not published in the Soviet press in 1932 or 1933, but the country likely lost half of its cattle and pigs and two thirds of its sheep. The horse population declined from 32.6 million to around 16 million; by 1933, tractors supplied only 3.6 million to 5.4 million horsepower equivalents. Kazakh livestock losses were beyond staggering: camels from 1.06 million to 73,000, sheep from 21.9 million to 1.7 million, cattle herds from 7.5 million to 1.6 million.[469] By 1933, a Kazakh family owned, on average, just 3.7 cattle, compared with 22.6 in 1929. And Kazakhs ended up only nominally collectivized: the regime reinstituted private control of animals, and the majority of Kazakhs worked household plots and failed to work the requisite number of days for the collectives. But the damage to the USSR's meat supply was done, and enduring.[470]

Many contemporaries, such as the Italian ambassador, who traveled through Ukraine in summer 1933, deemed the famine deliberate.[471] Monstrously, Stalin himself made the same accusation—accusing peasants of not wanting to work.[472] Regime propaganda castigated the starving refugees besieging towns for "passing themselves off as ruined collective farmers."[473] Nonetheless, the famine was not intentional.[474] It resulted from Stalin's policies of forced collectivization-dekulakization, as well as the pitiless and incompetent management of the sowing and procurement campaigns, all of which put the country on a knife-edge, highly susceptible to drought and sudden torrential rains.[475] Stalin appears to have genuinely imagined that increasing the scale of farms, mechanization, and collective efficiency would boost agricultural output. He dismissed the loss of better-off peasants from villages, only belatedly recognized the crucial role of incentives, and wildly overestimated the influx of machines. He twice deluded himself—partly from false reporting by frightened statisticians, partly from his own magical thinking—that the country was on the verge of a recovery harvest.

Always grudgingly, Stalin approved, and in some cases initiated, reductions in grain exports, beginning already in September 1931; in 1932 and 1933 he signed reduced grain collection quotas for Ukraine, the North Caucasus, the Volga valley, Crimea, the Urals, the Central Black Earth region, the Kazakh autonomous republic, and Eastern Siberia on nine occasions.[476] The 1933 grain procurement target fell from 24.3 to 19.6 million tons; the actual amount collected would be around 18.5 million tons.[477, 478] Altogether, the regime returned about 5.7 million tons of grain back to agriculture, including 2 million tons from reserves and 3.5 million from procurements. Stalin also approved clandestine purchase of grain and livestock abroad using scarce hard currency.[479] Just between February and July 1933, he signed or countenanced nearly three dozen small allocations of food aid to the countryside, primarily to the North Caucasus and Ukraine, as well as the Kazakh lands (which necessitated sharp reductions in the bread rations for city dwellers, many of whom were put on the brink of starvation). All of these actions were woefully insufficient for avoiding the mass starvation in the countryside caused by his policies, in the face of challenging natural conditions. Still, these actions do not indicate that he was trying to exterminate peasants or ethnic Ukrainians.[480] In the Kazakh autonomous republic, probably between 35 and 40 percent of the titular nation—as compared with 8 to 9 percent of Slavs there—perished from starvation or disease, not because the regime targeted Kazakhs by ethnicity, but because regime policy there consisted of forced denomadization. Similarly, there was no "Ukrainian" famine; the famine was Soviet.[481]

In the spring of 1933, officials gave the famine a self-justifying pedagogical gloss. Ukrainian party leader Kosior wrote that "the unsatisfactory preparation for sowing in the worst affected regions shows that the hunger has not yet taught many collective farmers good sense."[482] In the same vein, an official report to Stalin and Molotov from Dnepropetrovsk claimed that collective farmer attitudes had improved as a result of "the understanding that . . . bad work in the collective farm leads to hunger."[483] Such reports followed Stalin's lead. He admitted privately to Colonel Raymond Robins of the American Red Cross (May 13, 1933)—who had met with Lenin during the acknowledged Soviet famine of 1921–23—that "a certain part of the peasantry is starving now." Stalin claimed that hardworking peasants were incensed at the indolent ones who caused the famine. "The collective farmers roundly curse us. It is not right to help the lazy—let them perish. Such are the morals." It was ventriloquism.[484]

Once Stalin had caused the horror, even complete termination of exports would not have been enough to prevent famine. The regime had no strategic grain reserves left, having released them.[485] Only more aggressive purchases of food abroad and open appeals for international assistance could have averted many (and perhaps most) of the deaths. The world had plenty of food in 1933—indeed, the glut was depressing global prices for grain—but Stalin refused to reveal vulnerability, which, in his mind, would incite enemies. Admission also would have been a global propaganda debacle, undermining the boasts about the Five-Year Plan and the collective farms.

STALIN HAD CAUSED A DOMESTIC CALAMITY and rendered the Soviet Union vulnerable in the face of Japan's expansionism, while contributing significantly to the ascent in Germany of Hitler, who threatened expansionism, and provoking blistering internal critiques.[486] But his faction felt compelled to rally around him. "Loyalty to Stalin," wrote a military official who later defected, "was based principally on the conviction that there was no one to take his place, that any change in the leadership would be extremely dangerous, and that the country must continue in its present course, since to stop now or attempt a retreat would mean the loss of everything."[487] A correspondent wrote to Trotsky on Prinkipo, in early spring 1933, that "they all speak about Stalin's isolation and the general hatred of him, but they often add: 'If it were not for that (we omit the strong epithet), everything would have fallen to pieces by now. It is he who keeps everything together.'"[488]

Resolute in extremis, Stalin ordered the forced return of peasant escapees, the blacklisting of entire counties (they would suffer the highest mortality), and the banning of fishing in state waters or even private charity—anything that would have made it possible to avoid the collectives.[489] The OGPU arrested 505,000 people in 1933, as compared with 410,000 the year before.[490] Some farmers were still refusing to sow crops, since the regime would only take the harvested grain away.[491] But most weeded the fields, sowed, and brought in the harvest. "All the collective farm workers now say: 'We understand our mistakes and we are ready to work,'" one local report noted. "'We will do everything expected of us.'"[492] Officials concluded that they had broken the peasants' will, indirectly suggesting the regime had partnered with famine to achieve subjugation.[493] Indeed, it was the famished peasants who would lift the regime and the country out of starvation, producing between 70 and 77 million tons of grain in 1933, a bumper crop comparable to the miracle of 1930.[494] The peasants, in their land hunger and separate revolution, had made possible the advent of a Bolshevik regime in 1917–18; now enslaved, the peasants saved Stalin's rule.[495]

Through it all, he had revealed escalating rage and pathological suspicion, to the point that not only bourgeois specialists or former tsarist officers were considered as enemies, but many workers and party loyalists. At once self-righteous and self-pitying, the aggressor who somehow was always the victim, full of rage, Stalin could display affection as well. He wrote (June 25, 1933) to Avel Yenukidze, the overseer of Kremlin affairs, who had gone to Germany for treatment of a heart condition, recommending he avoid fats. "Try to observe a diet, move about more, and get fully healthy," Stalin wrote. "We extended the length of your holiday by a month, and now it's up to you." The dictator exhibited his own good spirits. "We have ramped up agriculture and coal," he added. "Now we're going to ramp up rail transport. Harvest gathering in the south has already begun. In Ukraine and the North Caucasus, the harvest is taken care of. This is the main thing. In other regions, the outlook so far is good. I'm healthy. Greetings! Your Stalin."[496]

CHAPTER 3

VICTORY

Imagine that a house is being built, and when it is finished
it will be a magnificent palace. But it is still not finished,
and you draw it in this condition and say, "There's your
socialism"—and there's no roof. You will be a realist, of
course—you will be telling the truth. But it is immediately
apparent that this truth is in actual fact an untruth. Only
the person who understands what kind of house is being
built, how it is being built, and who understands that it
will have a roof can utter socialist truth.

ANATOLY LUNACHARSKY, *former
commissar of enlightenment, 1933*[1]

MARXIST IMPERATIVES OF transcending capitalism—combined with inordinate willpower—brought apocalypse. During the first Five-Year Plan, the volume
of investment quadrupled, to 44 percent of GDP by 1932 (measured in 1928
prices), but none of the massive net increase in investment came from higher
agricultural surpluses.[2] Grain exports did not end up paying for imports of machinery.[3] Soviet agriculture made no net contribution to industrialization; on the
contrary, it was a net recipient of resources during the plan. True, a key driver of
the industrial spurt was new labor power from villages, but the statist system
used those workers grossly inefficiently. Another key driver of the spurt was brutally suppressed consumption (reinforced by that thief called inflation).[4] Should
we view peasant starvation as a source of "investment"? Even if we did, collectivization and dekulakization lowered agricultural output dramatically.[5] Stalin's
policies did expand state procurement of grain, potatoes, and vegetables, but at
breathtaking economic, to say nothing of human, cost. Collectivization involved
the arrest, execution, internal deportation, or incarceration of 4 to 5 million
peasants; the effective enslavement of another 100 million; and the loss of tens of
millions of head of livestock. The industrialization and accompanying militarization began to revive the Soviet Union as a great power, a necessity for

survival in the international system, but collectivization was not "necessary" to "modernize" a peasant economy or industrialize.[6]

Collectivization *was* necessary from the point of view of Marxism-Leninism, which asserted that only a noncapitalist "mode of production" could undergird a Communist regime.[7] Once the fall 1933 harvest proved to be good, and the unbalanced investments of the first Five-Year Plan finally produced results in the second plan, even skeptics gave Stalin his due: his lunatic gamble had panned out. Socialism (anticapitalism) was victorious in the countryside as well as the city. But culture, too, for Marxists, was an integral aspect of any system of class relations, and in culture Stalin was still groping his way. Letters from cultural figures got to his desk quickly—his aides understood his interest—and, as in foreign policy, he made just about every significant decision (unlike in the economy, for want of time or interest).[8] But the challenges proved different, not amenable to blunt class warfare. Culture did not offer the equivalent of capitalist private property or "bourgeois" parliaments to eradicate as the path to socialism. Certainly for Stalin, the party had the right to determine the disposition of all writers and artists, but not in a clumsy way.

This chapter examines the period from summer 1933 to early fall 1934, although at times it will track back in time to illuminate the trajectory of Stalin's engagement with the artistic intelligentsia, while weaving in the workings of the Union and continuing developments in foreign affairs. Trotsky, early on, had argued that the literary sphere had its own relatively autonomous dynamic and therefore should not be administered the same way as the economy or politics ("Art must make its own way and by its own means").[9] He had objected to a drive for an exclusively "proletarian" culture, championed the works of "fellow travelers," a term he coined for those who did not join the party but sympathized with the cause, and defined the party's task in culture as ensuring that influential fellow travelers did not go over to the side of "the bourgeoisie."[10] Stalin had taken exactly the same position. A politburo decree had denied a monopoly to the early movement for proletarian culture, and supported a "society for the development of Russian culture," to be headed by a non-party "Soviet-minded" writer of stature.[11] Stalin approved a proposal for a non-party writers' periodical, *Literary Newspaper*.[12] The militant culture movement endured under the name Russian Association of Proletarian Writers.[13] Factions for and against an exclusively proletarian culture, with the former tending to be Russocentric and the latter tending to see themselves as internationalist, dragged Stalin into their political-aesthetic and personal vendettas.[14] But in culture, he blocked in-transigent enforcement of Communist ideology, groping his way to a socialist aesthetic.

PHARAOH

Solovki, the regime's original prison labor camp, which provided timber and fish, got displaced in the early 1930s by giant new forced labor complexes, such as one in northern Kazakhstan for ore mining and metals.[15] Most ambitiously, in the harsh Chukotka territory, the Far Northern Construction Trust, or Dalstroi, was formed to extract gold.[16] Prisoners traveled in cattle cars across the length of the USSR, then, from the railway terminus at Vladivostok, by ship more than 1,700 miles across the Sea of Okhotsk to Nagayevo Bay and the settlement of Magadan. The first slave labor ships had arrived there in June 1932, mostly with thieves, bandits, and murderers, almost half of whom failed to survive the journey.[17] To reach the gold-digging areas, Dalstroi used tank crews to clear a path northward up the Okhotsk coast and in along the Kolyma River, then had prisoners lay road-beds of logs over frozen earth, shortening what had been multiweek trips by rein-deer. Thanks partly to a relatively rational treatment of slave laborers, more than 100 million rubles' worth of gold would be mined each year.[18] Beyond Dalstroi, though, the expected savings on cheap prison labor were often undone by low productivity and high administrative costs.[19] Still, the Gulag was crucial for de-veloping remote areas. The Union was not only an ethnoterritorial but also an economic structure.

Stalin did not visit the slave labor complexes, with one notable exception: the White Sea–Baltic Canal. Declared finished on June 20, 1933, after just twenty-one months, it extended for 155 miles, longer than the Panama and Suez canals, through difficult terrain.[20] Under Yagoda's chaperoning, from July 18 to 25, Sta-lin, Voroshilov, Kirov, and Yenukidze sailed the entire canal, also touring the Kola Peninsula, the Northern Fleet, and the polar port of Murmansk. Kirov had driven to Moscow and chauffeured his guests to Leningrad.[21] Stalin's fellow Georgian Orjonikidze was the dictator's oldest close friend in the regime, but Kirov—a Russian who had spent the underground years in the Caucasus—had become even closer.[22] Stalin called him Mironych, an affectionate diminutive of his patronymic, and sometimes Kirych.[23] As a new general secretary, Stalin had given him a copy of his *On Lenin and Leninism,* inscribed TO MY FRIEND AND MY BELOVED BROTHER.[24] Stalin had transferred Kirov from Baku to replace Zinoviev as head of the Leningrad party organization, the most important after Moscow, a posting Kirov had resisted, yielding only after Stalin agreed it would be temporary (allowing him to return to the Caucasus). Kirov stayed on to rout the entrenched Zinoviev machine.[25] It was partly the chance to spend time with Kirov that drew Stalin to visit the canal.

Kirov's personal qualities—straightforward, amiable—endeared him to more conniving Bolsheviks. "Stalin loved and respected Kirov above all others," a longtime bodyguard would recall. "He loved him with a kind of touching, tender love. Kirov's trips to Moscow and the south were for Stalin a genuine holiday. Sergei Mironovich would come for a week, two. In Moscow he would stay at Stalin's apartment, and Stalin would literally not separate from him."[26] "Stalin loved him," Molotov recalled. "He was Stalin's favorite."[27] Kirov stood a mere five feet five inches (1.64 meters), shorter than the dictator.[28] He sent game he hunted to Stalin and, following Nadya's death, stayed with him when in the capital (Kirov had earlier bunked with Orjonikidze). "Kirov had the ability to dissipate misunderstandings, to convert them into jokes, to break the ice," recalled Artyom (whose deceased father had also been friendly with Kirov). "He was astonishingly bright-natured, a person like a beam of light, and at home they loved him very much, the members of [Stalin's] family and the service personnel. They always waited upon his appearances . . . and called him Uncle Kirov." Kirov jestingly called Stalin "the Great Leader of All Peoples of All Times," according to Artyom, and Stalin "would retort that Kirov was the 'Most Loved Leader of the Leningrad Proletariat.'"[29]

The canal held strategic promise for developing mineral-rich Soviet Karelia and opening a reliable pathway from Leningrad to the north, but it ran a mere sixty feet deep and eighty feet wide, limiting its use. Stalin was said to have been disappointed, finding it "shallow and narrow."[30] Nonetheless, the pharaonic visit was recorded on Soviet newsreels. Kremlinologists noted Yagoda's prominence in the footage, even though Mężyński remained OGPU chairman. Overseeing such construction was Yagoda's forte, and he would receive the Order of Lenin for the canal. More than 126,000 forced laborers did the work, almost entirely without machines, and probably at least 12,000 died doing so, while orchestras played in the background. Some of the surviving builders were "amnestied" with fanfare; others were transferred to construction of a Moscow–Volga Canal.[31]

GOLDEN FLEECE

Nine-year-old Svetlana had gone ahead to Sochi with her nanny. "Hello, my Dear Daddy," she wrote on August 5, 1933. "I received your letter and I am happy that you allowed me to stay here and wait for you. . . . When you come, you will not recognize me. I got really tanned. Every night I hear the howling of the coyotes. I wait for you in Sochi. I kiss you. Your Setanka."[32] On August 18, the dictator boarded a train with his son Vasily, Artyom, and Voroshilov for Nizhny Novgorod, whence they embarked with local party boss Andrei Zhdanov on the steamship *Clara Zetkin* down the Volga for four days. From Stalingrad, the group traversed the steppes by automobile to Sochi, reaching the resort on August 25, after a 2,000-mile journey. "Yet again," Voroshilov wrote to Yenukidze, "I sensed the whole limitlessness of our expanses, the whole greatness of the proletariat's conquests."[33, 34] No more than an hour after having arrived in Sochi, Stalin set out in his car with Voroshilov on a drive to Green Grove, near Matsesta. At the Riviera Bridge, in Sochi's center, they collided with a truck. It was dark, and the road unlit. Stalin's guard detail, in the trailing car, immediately opened fire. The truck driver, who appears to have been drunk, fled in the darkness. It is unclear how severe the collision was, but Stalin was unharmed.

Stalin was remarkably hardy, all things considered. (A medical report covering family history listed incidences of "tuberculosis, syphilis, alcoholism, drug abuse, epilepsy, mental difficulties, suicide, metabolic disorders, malignant tumors, diseases of the endocrine glands.") This was his first southern sojourn following Nadya's death, but third consecutive one during the famine. He and his entourage had passed through settlements emptied by an absence of food and an abundance of typhus, but whether they took note remains uncertain. "Koba and I visited one (of the ten) of our horse state farms near the cities of Salsk and Proletarskaya," Voroshilov continued in the letter to Yenukidze about Rostov province. "There we saw the most splendid horses—mothers and foals, foals and working horses. We saw magnificent merino sheep, livestock of good Kalmyk (red) lineage, geese, chickens, pigs. All this is well cared for, and the steppes are fully assimilated." Voroshilov took up residence at Sochi's second-best dacha, Blinovka (where his wife awaited him), but complained of dubious types being accommodated at neighboring facilities, as well as bacteria in the water, and the medical staff, especially Degtyarev ("He's a doctor in the way that you and I are astronomers!"). Yenukidze answered (August 30, 1933) that officials all went south at the same time and things got overrun. "Koba has been feeling wonderfully the whole time, but the fourth day now he's complaining of his teeth," Voroshilov wrote back (September 7).[35] A dentist (Shapiro) had arrived to attend to Stalin's mouth.[36]

Stalin finally had secure high-frequency phone lines in Sochi, though he still used telegrams and field couriers, too.[37] In Moscow, officials were convening in his Old Square office, usually with Kaganovich presiding.[38] Of the 1,038 politburo decisions taken that summer, Stalin would intervene in 119, the vast majority at prompts from Kaganovich, whose correspondence was filled with plaintive requests for more guidance. "I cannot and should not have to decide any and all questions that concern the politburo," Stalin replied (September 5, 1933). "You yourselves can consider matters and work them out."[39] This instruction came immediately upon the heels of a scolding. Orjonikidze, along with land commissar Yakovlev, had objected to criminal prosecutions for managers who had shipped agricultural combines without the full complement of parts. They had the politburo formally rebuke the USSR deputy procurator general, Vyshinsky. Stalin exploded. "Sergo's behavior can only be characterized as antiparty," he wrote, "because its goal is to protect reactionary elements of the party against the Central Committee." They reversed their decision.[40]

On September 22, Stalin left the Puzanovka dacha to inspect a new one being built for him near Gagra, a small resort on Abkhazia's northern Black Sea coast.[41] He fell in love with this land, close by the site, according to ancient Greek legend, of the ram with a golden fleece, a symbol of authority and kingship.[42] Entirely mountainous, with passes up to 10,000 feet above sea level and deep valleys cut by crystal-clear rivers, this seaside haven enjoyed ample moisture, and, because the mountains came almost up to the coast, Sukhum, its gracious capital, was shielded from cold northern air masses. Abkhazia had the warmest winters in the USSR. Its mountains teemed with wild boars for hunting, and its rivers and plentiful lakes with fish. Its naturally carbonated sulfur springs added to its allure. Local Bolsheviks had nationalized the neglected, malaria-infested prerevolutionary resorts, but officials in Moscow sought to claim them as well. The revived spas, as well as the citrus groves, grapevines, and tobacco fields, would forge a link to the far-off Eurasian capital. The man who would build that link was a native son, Nestor Lakoba.[43]

"I AM KOBA, YOU ARE LAKOBA"

Short and deaf, with refined features and a cropped mustache, Lakoba carried himself with elegance. He did not pound a fist on the table or shout profanities, like his hotheaded friend Orjonikidze. Whereas Bolshevik rule in ethnic Georgian regions had, for a time, been dicey—a mass uprising had broken out in the 1920s—in Abkhazia it looked firm. Lakoba won wide popularity through the customary patronage (apartments, dachas, scarce goods), but also by attentiveness to ordinary people. He cultivated social harmony, downplaying the peasantry's supposed social stratification, and managed to delay collectivization of the citrus groves and tobacco fields and even avoid dekulakization, otherwise unheard of. Almost uniquely among local bosses, his power base was not in the party. The Abkhaz Communist party was merely a provincial organization of the Georgian party, but the Soviet state was federal, and Lakoba served as chairman of the Abkhaz government (Council of People's Commissars) in the 1920s, and after 1930 as chairman of the Abkhaz soviet's central executive committee.[44] Often, he skipped meetings of the party organization.[45]

Wits dubbed Abkhazia "Lakobistan." A traveling commission had complained that such "a personalized regime is always a bad thing, always kills social life and weakens organizations, demoralizes cadres and encourages a slavish passivity among them."[46] But Orjonikidze sent Lakoba regular telegrams about taking care of high-level Moscow visitors at the spas.[47] Trotsky (who had recuperated often in Sukhum) admired Lakoba, though he noted that, "despite the special sound amplifier he carried in his pocket, conversing with him was not easy."[48] (The regime soon acquired a new, bulky Phonophor hearing device for him from Siemens.) Stalin called him the Deaf One, and loved that Lakoba could whip top Soviet military men at billiards and shoot like a sniper. "When Lakoba came to Moscow, you would always see him at Stalin's place, either at the apartment or at the dacha," Khrushchev would recall, adding, "Stalin trusted him completely."[49] Artyom recalled that visits by Lakoba brightened up the house, noting: Stalin "loved Lakoba very much."[50] The dictator was said to joke, "I am Koba, and you are Lakoba."

The two men shared a great deal. Lakoba (b. 1893) did not remember his father, who had died of a bullet wound. Two stepfathers had died as well. His mother, after many tries, got him into a religious school and then the Tiflis seminary— where Stalin had studied more than a decade earlier—and whence Lakoba, too, was expelled. Lakoba had helped lead the Red Army's civil war reconquest and Bolshevization of Abkhazia, while Stalin had egged on Orjonikidze to do the same in Georgia.[51] The Abkhaz had become a minority in Georgia-controlled Abkhazia, but Lakoba and other Abkhaz Bolsheviks were determined to redress this by remaining independent.[52] Stalin had ended up caught between the Abkhaz, who proclaimed their own republic, and the Georgians, who tried to force the territory back into Georgia.[53] He had approved a fudge recognizing Abkhazia as a "treaty republic." Such decisions among competing claims had to be made across the Union, given the more than one hundred languages and the threescore recognized "nations."[54]

The USSR consisted of three levels: (1) Union republics, initially reserved for Russia, Ukraine, Belorussia, and the South Caucasus Federation (Georgia, Armenia, Azerbaijan), then Uzbekistan and Turkmenistan; (2) autonomous republics inside Union republics for concentrated populations such as the Tatars, Bashkirs, and Yakuts in the RSFSR; the Moldavians in Ukraine; and (3) autonomous provinces, many of them in the RSFSR and the South Caucasus Federation.[55] In former tsarist Turkestan, the inhabitants, who were often multilingual, had been compelled to choose one national identity, then fought over territory. The prize cities of Bukhara and Samarkand, despite populations categorized as predominantly Tajik (Persian), had gone to Uzbekistan (Turkic), thanks to Uzbek leaders' dynamism and Tajik leaders' fumbling.[56] But then Stalin had acceded to Tajik demands for equal status, upgrading their autonomous republic in Uzbekistan to a self-standing Union republic.[57] Uzbeks seized the opportunity to become a national elite and aligned their future with the central regime, coercing their cereal-growing republic toward intensive cotton production. Mosques were forcibly shuttered.[58] Power was centralized in Moscow, but there were internal ethnoterritorial borders, local state institutions, vernacular official languages, and growing ranks of indigenous Communists.[59] The regime fostered not nationalism per se but Soviet nations, with Communist institutions and ways of thinking.

With the "treaty republic" status, Stalin had allowed the Abkhaz to perceive themselves as akin to a Union republic but not join the USSR as a fourth constituent of the South Caucasus Federation. His dispensation stemmed from his wariness of Georgian nationalism, his admiration for Lakoba, and Abkhazia's uniqueness as the Soviet Union's only subtropical region. But belated collectivization in the region's Gudauta district had provoked a mass peasant uprising.[60] Lakoba negotiated a settlement without bloodshed, but Stalin terminated the "treaty republic" designation, specifying it as an "autonomous republic" in

Georgia.[61] This spurred further protests, including in Lakoba's home village of Lykhny; the local party boss blamed Lakoba's indulgence of "kulaks."[62] Lakoba managed to disperse the crowds peacefully again, promising to travel to Moscow on their behalf.[63] The OGPU arrested putative ringleaders, but Lakoba did manage to see Stalin and extract an accommodation: collectivization would resume, yet exclude horses.[64] Still, Stalin's upheaval affected governing structures, too, and empowered a man who emerged as Lakoba's cunning rival: Lavrenti Beria.[65]

"A GOOD ORGANIZER"

Beria's Mingrelian family was descended from a feudal prince, but he was born, in 1899, to modest circumstances in a hillside village in Abkhazia. He attended Sukhum's city school, whose subjects included Russian, Orthodox theology, arithmetic, and science. His mother, Marta, like Keke Geladze, worked as a seamstress to pay for school; Beria, also like Stalin, might have been helped by a rich patron (a textile merchant who employed Marta as a domestic). Beria joined the party after the tsar's abdication, served in the army, and graduated from high school with honors.[66] He missed the revolution, and spent part of the civil war on the wrong side: the Musavat ("Equality") party of Azerbaijani nationalists had established an independent republic through the meddling of Ottoman and then British occupation forces, and after the British left, Beria joined Musavat counterintelligence.[67] Following the Bolshevik reconquest, he was arrested. A meeting was called and Orjonikidze and others ruled that the party had likely assigned Beria to infiltrate the "bourgeois nationalists."[68] Beria enrolled at the newly established Polytechnic University, on the premises of his old high school, with a state stipend, to fulfill his dream of becoming an engineer, but Mircafar Bagirov (b. 1896), the twenty-four-year-old head of the Azerbaijan Cheka, recruited Beria and, after a few weeks, named him deputy secret police chief, at age twenty-one.[69]

Beria's Soviet secret police dirty work provoked numerous investigations for abuses.[70] "I feel that everyone dislikes me," he wrote to Orjonikidze (May 1930). "In the minds of many comrades, I am the prime cause of all the unpleasantries that befell comrades over the recent period, and I figure almost like a stool pigeon."[71] Underhandedly, Beria attacked everyone else, but *he* felt perpetually put upon—just like Stalin.

In fact, Beria had become a legend. His early top boss, Solomon Mogilevsky, chairman of the South Caucasus OGPU, had died in a mysterious plane crash whose cause could not be established by three separate commissions of inquiry.[72] His next boss, Ivan Pavlunovsky, pleaded at staff meetings for his deputy Beria to cease the intrigues against him.[73] Stalin replaced Pavlunovsky with Redens, an ethnic Pole, who knew none of the Caucasus languages or personnel. In the wee hours on March 29, 1931, after a sloshy birthday gathering for Beria at a private apartment, a drunk Redens departed—with no bodyguard detail. He made his way to the building of a young female OGPU operative who had previously rebuffed his advances; Redens tried to break down her door, and neighbors called the regular police, who arrested the disorderly drunk. His identity was established only at the station house. Word of the humiliation spread inordinately quickly. Beria immediately phoned Stalin, who transferred Redens to Belorussia (and shortly thereafter to Ukraine). Stalin was said to have delighted in Beria's artfulness at compromising the dictator's hapless brother-in-law.[74] Beria was promoted to chief of the South Caucasus OGPU, overseeing Azerbaijan, Armenia, and Georgia, including Abkhazia.[75] Mężyński noted, on the tenth anniversary of the Georgian branch of the OGPU, that "comrade Beria always finds his bearings precisely, even in the most complex circumstances."[76]

Lakoba, six years Beria's senior, had everything the young secret police operative did not: heroic prerevolutionary and civil war exploits, colossal popularity among the masses, and intimate ties to Stalin.[77] But Stalin's southern holidays were beset by epic local infighting: Georgians against Armenians, Georgians against Georgians. Stalin blamed locals' ability to appeal to Orjonikidze, and wrote to Kaganovich that "if we don't intervene, these people by their stupidity may ruin things."[78] Orjonikidze was pushing for the restoration as party boss of Mamiya Orakhelashvili, a protégé (who had the university diploma Beria coveted), while Lakoba pushed for Beria (and sent him a transcript of a three-way conversation he'd had with Stalin and Orjonikidze).[79] Lakoba midwifed a three-day Beria visit to Abkhazia to see Stalin.[80] Beria soon got appointed first secretary of Georgia and concurrently second secretary of the South Caucasus Federation (under Orakhelashvili).[81] He could now see Stalin during the dictator's holidays without special intercession.[82] In summer 1932, Beria poured poison in the dictator's ear about Orakhelashvili.[83] The latter begged Stalin, and especially Orjonikidze, to be relieved of his post as Beria's nominal superior.[84]

Nothing rankled Stalin more than the suspicion that provincial officials sabotaged central directives, but in his homeland he had found someone who fulfilled orders to the letter. "Beria makes a good impression," Stalin wrote to Kaganovich

(August 12, 1932). "He's a good organizer, a businesslike, capable functionary." Stalin also prized Beria's antagonism to Orjonikidze and the Georgian old guard. "In looking over South Caucasus affairs, I have become all the more convinced that in personnel selection, Sergo is an irredeemable bungler," Stalin's note concluded. Kaganovich wrote back (August 16): "Beria came to see me. He does indeed make a good impression as a top-level functionary."[85] On October 9, Orakhelashvili was relieved of his post, and Beria promoted to first secretary of the South Caucasus Federation, while remaining party boss of Georgia.[86] Beria was recorded as being in Stalin's office for the first time on November 9, just after the holiday celebrations.[87] On December 21, Beria had the Georgian party issue a formal reprimand to Lakoba.[88]

NEAR-FATAL LAUNCH

The three-story dacha under construction in Gagra that Stalin visited with Lakoba on September 23, 1933, stood only twenty-five miles from Sochi. It had been carved right into the steep cliff, 700 feet above sea level, and was well concealed by tree cover, blending in with its green paint.[89] The rooms had parquet flooring, wooden ceilings in patterns, wooden furniture, and a wood-paneled cinema. Handwoven Caucasus rugs graced the floors, and nets wrapped the chandeliers to protect from possible falling glass. Each room had an emergency button. The smallish bedrooms had mattresses filled with seaweed and medicinal herbs. Salt water was piped into the bath. An auxiliary structure housed a billiard room, kitchen, and pantry. The menu consisted largely of freshly slaughtered animals, especially lambs, held live on the grounds. Lemon trees, guard booths, and a rocky hillside of fragrant eucalyptus, cypress, and cherry trees surrounded the villa; tobacco was planted as well. Guards also circled the property with truncheons, on the lookout for snakes. During the day, donkeys could be seen, and at night, jackals. Down below lay a stone beach. A small, rapid stream at the dacha gave it its name: Cold Spring. Here, Lakoba would organize a hunting party. First, however, on the day of his arrival, Stalin and entourage went for a boat ride on the Black Sea.

Yagoda had had a launch sent in, the *Red Star,* used on the Neva River in Leningrad. Small and unseaworthy, it had only some glass over the cabin, through which everyone was visible. At around 1:30 p.m., the group pushed off southward—Stalin, Voroshilov, and Beria, along with Vlasik and L. T. Bogdanov (bodyguards) and S. F. Chechulin (cipher specialist). "We headed for the Pitsunda Cape," Vlasik would recall. "Entering the pier, we disembarked on the shore, relaxed, drank and snacked, walked about, spending a few hours on the shore." Their picnic, beginning around 4:00 p.m., included Abkhaz wine. "Then we embarked again and headed back," Vlasik continued. "At the Pitsunda Cape, there is a lighthouse and, nearby on the shore, a border post. When we exited the pier and turned in the direction of Gagra, there were rifle shots from the shore." The boat was some 600 to 700 yards out. Vlasik claimed that he and Bogdanov covered Stalin and returned fire; Beria would claim that he covered Stalin's body with his own. The bullets from the shore (three in total) landed in the water. The boat pulled farther from the coast. High waves rose up—a storm was in the offing—and it took the launch three harrowing hours to make it back to the Old Gagra pier.[90]

Stalin, according to Chechulin, had initially joked that the Abkhaz were accustomed to greeting guests with gunshots, but after returning to Cold Spring, he sent Bogdanov back to Pitsunda to investigate. A few days later, Chechulin handed Stalin a letter from a local border guard who asked to be forgiven for shooting at the unregistered launch, which he had taken to be a foreign vessel. Sergeant N. I. Lavrov, commander of the border post, further explained that the boat had entered the restricted zone, so, as per regulations, they signaled it to stop, and when it kept going they fired warning shots in the air. Stalin did not label the incident an attempted assassination.[91] Beria had Sergo Goglidze, the head of border guards for the South Caucasus, "investigate," and he brought forward "witnesses" who testified that the shots were fired at the launch itself, blame for which, in Abkhazia, could be laid on Lakoba.[92] But Yagoda evidently instructed Beria to portray it as a misunderstanding (in line with Stalin's preference). The Georgian secret police sacked the Abkhaz OGPU chief and punished six Abkhaz border guards with two to three years in the Gulag; Lavrov got five.[93] Goglidze was soon named OGPU chief for Georgia. Legends circulated that Beria had organized hoodlums to stage the incident to discredit Lakoba, after which Beria's henchmen had executed the perpetrators.[94, 95]

GERMAN GAMBIT

While Stalin was in remote Gagra, a trial for the Reichstag fire was taking place in Leipzig. It had opened on September 21, 1933, and among the accused were the German Communist party leader Ernst Thälmann and Georgi Dimitrov, a Bulgarian and undercover head of the Comintern's Western European Bureau in Berlin. One of eight children from a workers' family, Dimitrov had been sentenced to death for his political activities in his native country after he escaped to Yugoslavia. In Germany he operated in obscurity, but in the Leipzig courtroom he outdueled the state witnesses, Goebbels and Hermann Göring, and made the three-month trial an international antifascist sensation. (The Nazis did not have prearranged scripts for defendants who were broken to confess publicly.) "I am defending myself, an accused Communist," Dimitrov said from the dock. "I am defending my political honor, my honor as a revolutionary. I am defending my Communist ideology, my ideals." Germany's high court would convict only the Dutch Communist apprehended at the scene, who would be guillotined just shy of his twenty-fifth birthday. Dimitrov would be acquitted for lack of evidence. Journalists from the world over were admitted to the proceedings, but two Soviet reporters seeking access were arrested, leading to a diplomatic row. Mikhail Koltsov, however, reported out of Paris for *Pravda* (September, 25, 26, 28, 29, 30), transforming Dimitrov into a household name in the USSR and fostering the legend of Communists as courageous opponents rather than facilitators of the rise of Nazism.[96]

At the Reich Chancellery on September 26, at a meeting of department heads, the state secretary (the number two) at the foreign ministry insisted that Germany had little to gain from a breach with the USSR, given the countries' economic compatibility. Hitler concurred on avoiding handing Moscow a pretext to sever relations, but he warned officials not to indulge in delusions ("The Russians were always lying") and predicted that the Soviet government would never forgive the smashing of German Communism and that the new order in Germany had crushed every hope of world revolution.[97] Hitler was furtively accelerating a military buildup set in motion by his predecessors, in violation of Versailles restrictions, and told every Briton he could reach that German expansionism would be at Soviet expense and that Germany's purely continental interests did not conflict with Britain's global empire. He disavowed wanting to annex Austria (a wish that pre-1933 German governments had not disguised).[98] He would also insist to an interviewer for *Le Matin* that he wanted to live in peace with France.[99] Stalin followed the least hints of Franco-German as well as Anglo-German rapprochement, and of supposed British instigation of Poland and Japan and Polish-Japanese collusion.[100] He saw danger not in "superstructure" ideologies in any single capitalist country, such as Nazi Germany, but in the underlying "class interests" of all capitalist powers, led by Britain and France, which, axiomatically, strove to catalyze an anti-Soviet bloc.

On September 28, amid Soviet negotiations to sell the Chinese Eastern Railway to Manchukuo, the Japanese had Manchukuo authorities arrest six Soviet employees. The Japanese were evidently trying to force a sale at a rock-bottom price. The Soviets had requested 250 million rubles; the Japanese offered the equivalent of one tenth that sum: 50 million paper yen.[110] Stalin terminated the negotiations. He also ordered up a propaganda offensive against Japanese "militarism"—not something he did vis-à-vis Nazi Germany.[101]

Yenukidze, a Germanophile and Stalin confidant, concocted a scheme with German ambassador Herbert von Dirksen to find a modus vivendi by sending someone with stature to Hitler, even without formal invitation. They decided that the Jewish Nikolai Krestinsky, a former Soviet ambassador to Germany who was fluent in the language and was taking a rest cure at Kissingen, was to stop over in Berlin on the way home. Litvinov advised against such a move, but Molotov and Kaganovich favored it. Stalin agreed. Hitler reluctantly acceded to his foreign ministry's urgings to receive the "Judeo-Bolshevik" envoy.[102] Right then (October 14, 1933), however, the Führer declared on the radio that Germany would pull out of the League of Nations.[103] France erupted with loose talk of launching a preventive war.[104] Molotov and Kaganovich wrote to Stalin (October 16), reversing their support for Krestinsky's Berlin stopover. "It is incomprehensible why Krestinsky's trip should be called off," the dictator fired back that same day. "What do we care about the League, and why should we conduct a demonstration in honor of an insult to the League and against its insult of Germany?"[105] But the foreign affairs commissariat had already backed out of the gambit.[106]

AMERICAN GAMBIT

Stalin had traveled again, a few miles south of the Pitsunda Cape, arriving on October 9, 1933, at Mysra (Myussera in Russian), site of a secluded seaside Romano-Greek estate recently owned by an Armenian oil magnate.[107] Nearby, Lakoba had instigated construction of yet another luxury dacha for Stalin. (Only the urinals were of domestic make.)[108] The next day, in New York, Henry Morgenthau Jr., acting treasury secretary, had brought a Philadelphia millionaire and Franklin Roosevelt confidant, William Bullitt, to a meeting with an unofficial Soviet representative. Roosevelt was eager to find common cause in containing

Japanese expansionism, concerned about Hitler, and being lobbied by U.S. business for continued access to the Soviet market, after orders from that country had shrunk. Bullitt delivered a draft letter from the president, addressed to Kalinin (formal head of state), containing an invitation to Washington for a chosen representative. Stalin, who had hurried back to Gagra, instructed Molotov to accept and recommended sending Litvinov. The latter begged off in a cipher, but Stalin and Kalinin wrote to Molotov and Kaganovich (October 17) insisting on Litvinov and urging them to "act more boldly and without delay, since now the situation is favorable."[109]

On November 2, 1933, Stalin finally left Sochi for Moscow.[110] Yagoda soon reported to Voroshilov that, in connection with a "counterrevolutionary terrorist monarchist plot" to assassinate Stalin, twenty-six arrests had been made, almost all former gentry and a lot of them women. One was said to have "connections" through children to people living in the Kremlin.[111] (During 1933, there would be at least ten serious attempts on Hitler's life.)[112]

In mid-November Litvinov managed what he himself had doubted: U.S. recognition, after sixteen years of no relations. He had conceded nothing on repudiated tsarist and Provisional Government debts, other than a willingness to discuss them, and made an empty pledge that the Soviets would not interfere in U.S. domestic affairs by supporting American Communists.[113] Molotov took to publicly praising Litvinov.[114] Stalin awarded him a state dacha and a bodyguard detail, a mark of Litvinov's rising value—and the need to keep him under 24/7 surveillance. Anxieties in Tokyo about U.S.-Soviet collusion in the Far East intensified.[115] Japan, without allies and in violation of international covenants, pursued hegemony in its region, which entailed formidable simultaneous military burdens: defeat of the Red Army in a possible war; subjugation of mainland China; and attainment of home-island security against the U.S. Navy.[116] But for now, the depth of any U.S.-Soviet cooperation remained uncertain.[117]

The Americans promptly dispatched their own Marx to the USSR, Harpo, on a pantomime goodwill tour. His act brought the house down. (After he convinced a Soviet family that he had not pilfered their silver, they shook hands, and 300 table knives cascaded to the floor from his sleeves.)[118] Bullitt had arrived as ambassador on December 11, 1933, and Litvinov immediately dropped the bombshell that the USSR, in anticipation of war with Japan, wished to join the League of Nations.[119] On December 20, at a banquet in Bullitt's honor at Voroshilov's apartment, Bullitt was taken by the charm of the "cherub" host; the pair danced a medley of Caucasus moves and American foxtrot.[120] Stalin attended and asked

Bullitt for 250,000 tons of steel rails to complete strategic double-tracking of the Trans-Siberian. "If you want to see me at any time, day or night, you have only to let me know and I will see you at once," the dictator volunteered. "President Roosevelt is today, in spite of being a leader of a capitalist country, one of the most popular men in the Soviet Union." Then Stalin planted a wet kiss on Bullitt's cheek.[121]

At this very moment, the Comintern executive committee approved theses for the American Communist party's upcoming convention in Cleveland (to be held in the spring). "The 'New Deal' of Roosevelt is the aggressive effort of the bankers and trusts to find a way out of the crisis at the expense of the millions of toilers," the theses stated. "Under cover of the most shameless demagogy, Roosevelt and the capitalists carry through drastic attacks upon the living standards of the masses, increased terrorism against the Negro masses. . . . The 'New Deal' is a program of fascistization and the most intense preparations for imperialist war."[122]

Granting an interview to the reliably pro-Soviet Walter Duranty (December 25, 1933), Stalin spoke publicly about his diplomatic coup with the United States. Sitting between portraits of Marx and Lenin, with a drawing of a projected 1,312-foot Palace of the Soviets that was supposed to eclipse the Empire State Building, the dictator lauded Roosevelt as "by all appearances . . . a courageous statesman." He assured American business that the Soviets paid their debts ("Confidence, as everyone knows, is the basis of credit"). He put Japan on notice as well. Then, when Duranty, on cue, inquired of the Soviet stance vis-à-vis the League of Nations, Stalin responded, "We do not always and in all conditions take a negative attitude toward the League," adding that "the League may well become a break upon or an obstacle to war."[123]

The United States was not a member of the League. Any Soviet bid would have to be shepherded by France, and three days later the Soviet envoy in Paris communicated Moscow's terms for joining the League as well as a regional alliance.[124] Franco-Soviet talks would proceed glacially. Distrust ran deep.[125] Édouard Herriot, who had signed the Franco-Soviet nonaggression pact and now wanted to counter Hitler, had demonstrated the price of rapprochement when, in summer-fall 1933, he had visited the USSR during the famine, disembarking at Odessa. Just before he reached Kiev, streets were washed, corpses removed, shops with windows stocked with goods (the populace was not allowed in), and a "festive crowd" assembled from OGPU and Communist Youth League personnel. In Kharkov, he was shown a "model" children's facility, the tractor factory, and a museum devoted to the Ukrainian writer Taras Shevchenko. He asked to see the countryside and was taken to a collective farm where he again encountered activists and operatives, this time disguised as farmers. Everywhere, he ate his fill. Soviet Ukraine was "like a garden in full bloom," Herriot observed in *Pravda*. "When one believes that the Ukraine is devastated by famine, allow me to shrug my shoulders."[126]

LAMAS AND WOLVES

Duranty had been followed into Stalin's office by the co-chairs of the politburo's Mongolia commission, Voroshilov and Sokolnikov, and two Mongolian officials, a deputy prime minister for finance and a leftist party scourge of the lamas. Mongolia served as a Soviet showcase and experimental laboratory for the colonial world and, even more important, a territory that supplied defense in depth for the southern Siberian border, meat and raw materials for the Soviet economy (paralleling Kazakhstan), and a link with China, should war with Japan break out.[127] Since imposing the "New Course" retreat stabilization, Stalin had worried that Mongolia's NEP equivalent had allowed a revival of traders (NEPmen) and better-off nomads (kulaks), and persistent sway of the lama "class." Voroshilov told the Mongols that, against a population of just 700,000, there were still 120,000 lamas with undue influence ("Beyond that, the lamas engage in homosexuality, corrupting the youth who return to them"). Stalin asked how the lamas supported themselves. The Mongols answered that lamas drew substantial income from the lamaseries and served as spiritual leaders, physicians, traders, and advisers to the *arats* (common people). "It's a state within a state," Stalin interjected. "Chinggis Khan would not have permitted that. He would have cut them all down."

Soviet proconsuls were instigating a terror against fabricated Japanese spies, which destroyed the head of the Mongolian People's Party and brought perhaps 2,000 arrests.[128] Stalin asked about the budget, and the Mongols replied that their GDP totaled just 82 million tugriks, while the state budget was 33 million; the Soviets extended a loan of 10 million, but the army alone cost 13 million. "A large part of your budget is being swallowed up by white-collar employees," Stalin admonished. "Can it be impossible to get away with fewer?"[129]

Sometime either before or after Stalin received these two Mongols, he met with Mongolian prime minister Peljidiin Genden, but in Molotov's office. The dictator would write Genden in a courtesy follow-up note, "I am very glad that your Republic has, finally, taken the correct path, that your internal affairs are succeeding, that you are strengthening your international might and strengthening your independence." He advised that Mongolia needed "full unity" in the leadership, full support of the *arats,* and an army on the highest level, and promised continued fraternal assistance. "In that, you should have no doubts," he concluded. "Voroshilov, Molotov, and I together thank you for the gifts you sent." The Soviet Union was reciprocating with new automatic rifles. "They will come in handy in a battle against wolves of all types, two-legged and four-legged."[130]

WHITES AND REDS

In the field of culture—unlike foreign affairs and nationalities—Stalin had long hesitated to make his instructions public. "What kind of a critic am I, the devil take me!" he had written in response to Gorky's urgings in 1930.[131] When Konstantin Stanislavsky sought approval for staging *The Suicide,* by Nikolai Erdman (b. 1900), Stalin had replied, "I am a dilettante in these matters."[132] The dictator began to work out how he would manage the artistic intelligentsia with the Kiev-born writer Mikhail Bulgakov (b. 1891), who in the 1920s serialized a novel depicting a family of Kiev White Guardists, the Turbins, during the civil war, which muddied the red-white, good-evil picture.[133] Only two thirds of the work appeared before it helped prompt the journal's closing, but it proved a sensation.[134] Bulgakov turned it into a play titled *The Days of the Turbins.* Directed by Stanislavsky and Vladimir Nemirovich-Danchenko, it revived the fortunes of the Moscow Art Theater, which the pair had founded in 1898, premiering Chekhov's *The Seagull.* Muscovites queued day and night for Bulgakov's portrayal of the tragedy that befell those who had joined the counterrevolution in Ukraine.[135]

Bulgakov's daring work had no Reds at all, and his portrayal of the Whites as human beings provoked slander that he was a White Guardist enabling "former people" who had lost loved ones and possessions to mourn. Party militants likened him to the "rightists."[136] Stalin acquiesced to the outcries to ban Bulgakov's play *Flight,* another civil war story, about a family that opted to emigrate rather than live under Bolshevism.[137] But the dictator went to see *Turbins,* privately approved it, and publicly defended it.[138] At a meeting with irate pro-regime Ukrainian writers, Stalin pointed out that "it won't do to write only about Communism. We have a population of 140 million, and there are only one and a half million Communists." Bulgakov, Stalin allowed, was "alien," "not ours," for failing to depict exploitation properly, but he insisted that *The Days of the Turbins* remained "useful" to the cause, whatever the author's intent.[139] The furious polemics would not cease, however, and Stalin finally let the play be shuttered. Censors now prohibited even publication of Bulgakov's works, and he wrote the first of several despairing letters to the authorities asking to be deported abroad with his wife, to no avail.[140]

Bulgakov wrote again "to the government" on March 28, 1930, pointing out that he had unearthed 301 reviews of his work over a decade, three of which had been positive, and pleading again to be allowed to emigrate with his wife or, failing that, to be appointed as an assistant director at the Moscow Art Theater; failing that, as a supernumerary there or, failing that, as a stagehand.[141] On April 18, one of Stalin's top aides phoned the poet at his Moscow apartment, asking his wife, who answered, to summon him. Bulgakov thought the call a prank. (This happened to be Good Friday, a significant day for Bulgakov, son of a theologian.) Stalin came on the line. "We received your letter," he stated. "And read it with the comrades. You will get a favorable answer to it. . . . Perhaps we really should permit you to travel abroad? What, have we irritated you so much?" Bulgakov: "I have thought a great deal recently about whether a Russian writer can live outside his homeland, and it seems to me he cannot." Stalin: "You are correct."[142] What motivated Stalin to make his first phone call to a major non-party writer remains uncertain. But four days earlier, the greatest poet in the revolution, Vladimir Mayakovsky, who was mercilessly heckled at his public recitations, fatally shot himself in the heart. ("Seriously, there is nothing to be done," he wrote in a suicide note, as if echoing Chernyshevsky. "Goodbye.")[143]

Bulgakov got appointed as a stage director's assistant. One writer sent him a fake summons to the Central Committee, a poor joke about his desperate petitioning. Bulgakov developed neurasthenia.[144] Bereft of a public, he was said to be narrating stories at his apartment over tea. One such story, according to a fellow writer, involved Bulgakov sending long letters nearly every day to Stalin, signed "Tarzan" to disguise himself. Stalin, frightened, ordered that the letter writer be identified. Bulgakov was found out, brought to the Kremlin, and confessed. Stalin noticed his shabby trousers and shoes and summoned the commissar of supply. "Your people can steal, all right," Stalin yelled at the minion, "but when it comes to clothing a writer, they're not up to it!" Bulgakov, in the story, took to visiting Stalin in the Kremlin regularly and noticed he was depressed. "You see, they all keep screaming: Genius, genius! And yet there's no one I could have a glass of brandy with, even!" When Stalin phoned the Moscow Art Theater on Bulgakov's behalf, he was told the theater director had died—that very minute. "People are so nervous these days!" Stalin was depicted as saying. "No sense of humor."[145]

Like Bulgakov, Yefim Pridvorov (b. 1883), known as Demyan Bedny (*bedny* meaning "the poor one," though many called him Bedny [Poor] Demyan), had been born in Ukraine and made his mark in Moscow, but while Bulgakov sought no more than a modus vivendi, Bedny tirelessly served the regime. He traveled the sites of the Five-Year Plan, declaiming verse to workers, and acquired a personal Ford and a sumptuous apartment in the Grand Kremlin Palace (his wife, children, mother-in-law, and nanny lived with him).[146] Bedny knew Stalin before the revolution and, like him, had published his first verse as a teenager (and was dogged by rumors of uncertain parentage). He flaunted his access to the dictator.[147] But two of Bedny's poem-feuilletons irked the dictator deeply, one for mocking Russian national traditions (peasants sleeping on their warm stoves, which Stalin also did), and the dictator promulgated a resolution criticizing him. Bedny wrote to him melodramatically ("The hour of my catastrophe has come").[148] Stalin exploded. "Dozens of poets and writers have been rebuked by the Central Committee when they made mistakes," he answered. "All this you considered normal and understandable. But when the Central Committee found itself compelled to criticize your mistakes, you suddenly started to fume and shout about a 'noose.' . . . Is your poetry perhaps above criticism?"[149]

Voroshilov protected his Grand Kremlin Palace neighbor Bedny, whose sloshy charm and erudition played well with the defense commissar.[150] But on September 1, 1932, the politburo heard a report on the poet's debauched life, and Stalin had him evicted from the Kremlin. Bedny apologized to the dictator for his "life befouled with egotistic, greedy, evil, false, cunning, vengeful philistinism," but begged for an equivalent-sized apartment for his private library, the largest in the regime, perhaps 30,000 volumes; Stalin promised space for it. (Yenukidze allocated Bedny an apartment in a small building at Rozhdestvensky Boulevard, 15, which the poet, in a sarcastic note to him, called "a rat's barn.")[151] Bedny had worsened his predicament by indiscretion: one regular at his Kremlin apartment had recorded (and distorted) the often inebriated poet's table talks, including a complaint that when he loaned books to Stalin, they came back stained with greasy finger marks.[152] Stalin allowed Bedny to receive the Order of Lenin in connection with the poet's fiftieth birthday, accompanied by a citation recognizing him as an "outstanding proletarian poet."[153] Bedny had just written to Stalin, "I am afraid of nothing more than my letters. Especially my letters to you."[154]

HUMAN SOULS

As Bedny sank, Gorky rose. ("Previously," the gifted children's writer Nikolai Korneychukov, known as Korney Chukovsky, punned slyly in his diary, "literature was impoverished [*o-bed-nena*]; now it is embittered [*o-gor-chena*].")[155] Stalin, with OGPU assistance, had finally coaxed Gorky, already a literary giant before the revolution, permanently back from fascist Italy. Preparing the ground, on April 23, 1932, the dictator, without warning, had disbanded the Russian Association of Proletarian Writers.[156] The zeal of the self-styled proletarians—such as Bedny—with each striving to expose the tiniest ideological deviation in rivals, was outweighed by their lack of creative achievement. At the same time, the deep political suspicion about the non-party writers—such as Bulgakov—was balanced by their usually superior abilities. The abolition decree also established a committee to organize a founding congress for a new Union of Soviet Writers, open to non-party members. (Other arts were supposed to be organized in similar fashion.) Stalin wanted Gorky, whom the Association of Proletarian Writers had denounced as "a man without class consciousness," to be its head.

Alexander Fadeyev, one of the chairmen of the dissolved Association of Proletarian Writers, wrote in indignation to Kaganovich (May 10).[157] The next day, Stalin sat in his office with Fadeyev, two other leaders of the proletarian writers' association, two culture apparatchiks, and Kaganovich, for more than five hours. On May 29, the dictator met with some of them again for thirty minutes, just before departing for his long summer holiday.[158] Ivan Gronsky, one of the attendees, would later explain that Stalin had no intention of revisiting the dissolution of the proletarians, but had asked what creative method to propose. Gronsky claimed he had answered that prerevolutionary realism had been "progressive" in its "bourgeois-democratic" day, producing many great works, but now they required a literature to advance the "proletarian socialist" stage, and he suggested "proletarian socialist realism" or "Communist realism." Stalin countered that they needed an artistic method to unite all cultural figures, and supposedly suggested "socialist realism" for its brevity, intelligibility, and inclusiveness. Whether or not it was actually the dictator who came up with this formulation, he made the decision to adopt it.[159]

Stalin named Gorky honorary chairman of the organizing committee for the proposed new writers' union.[160] On September 17, 1932, the regime awarded Gorky the Order of Lenin, renamed Moscow's central Tverskaya Street, the Volga city of Nizhny Novgorod (Gorky's birthplace), and the Moscow Art Theater for him. It also launched a weeklong celebration of forty years of his artistic production, culminating on September 25 in the Bolshoi. Gronsky would later claim he had objected to such excessive adulation, to which Stalin supposedly replied, "He is an ambitious man. It is necessary to bind him to the party."[161]

Not long thereafter, Stalin attended two meetings with writers—not at Central Committee headquarters on Old Square, but at the luxurious mansion granted to Gorky in central Moscow (Malaya Nikitskaya, 6), an art moderne masterpiece expropriated from the prerevolutionary industrialist and art patron Stepan Ryabushinsky. At the first session (October 20, 1932), Stalin and entourage met with writers who belonged to the party, and he explained the party decision to disband the Association of Proletarian Writers. He praised the superior power of live theater, citing Alexander Afinogenov's *Fear*, which was seen by millions and dramatizes waverers among intellectuals, but has a party organizer saying, "We are fearless in the class struggle—and merciless with the class enemy," while an angel child asks, "Papa, which is the greater menace—a left deviation or a right deviation? I think the greatest menace is double-dealers."[162] But Stalin was trying to urge the gathered party loyalists toward tutelage. "The sea of non-party writers is multiplying, but no one leads them, no one helps them; they are orphans," he stated. "At one time, I was also non-party and did not understand many things. But senior comrades did not push me away; they taught me how to master the dialectic."[163]

Six days later, non-party writers were included in a second gathering with the dictator and his entourage. Invitations had gone out only over the phone, with the proviso not to divulge the information, perhaps in order to enhance the sense of being chosen. (Neither Bedny nor Bulgakov was invited.) Few of the fifty assembled literary figures had ever met Stalin, let alone spent an intimate evening with him. Emotions ran high. At the first break, they surrounded Stalin, and one asked about state dachas. "From under his bushy eyebrows, his eyes quickly and carefully survey the rows of those present," the literary critic Koreli Zelinsky wrote in a private account the next day. "When Stalin laughs—and he does so often and quickly—he squints and bends over the table, his eyebrows and mustache run apart, and his visage becomes sly. . . . What the portraits do not at all convey is that Stalin is very mobile. . . . He is very sensitive to the objections and in general strangely attentive to everything said around him. It seems he does not listen or forget. But, no, it turns out he caught everything at all wavelengths in the radio station of his mind. The answer is ready at once, in the forehead, straightforward, yes or no. Then you understand that he is always ready for combat. And, at the same time, watch out if he wants to please. There is a vast gamut of hypnotic tools at his disposal."[164]

Stalin wanted to conjure into being a coterie of writers of stature whose utterances would carry weight and yet who could be more or less controlled. "I forgot to talk about what you are 'producing,'" he remarked, after allowing many writers to speak. "There are various forms of production: artillery, locomotives, automobiles, trucks. You also produce 'commodities,' 'works,' 'products.' . . . You are engineers of human souls. . . . As some here rightly said, the writer cannot sit still; he must get to know the life of the country. Rightly said. People are transforming life. That is why I propose a toast: 'To Engineers of Human Souls.'"[165] Voroshilov interjected, "Not really." Everyone applauded. Stalin turned his whole body to the defense commissar: "Your tanks would be worth little if the souls inside them were rotten. No, the production of souls is more important than the production of tanks."

During a second break, the tables were laid with food and drink (this was still during the famine time), and Fadeyev importuned Stalin to repeat what he had told the Communist writers at the earlier gathering: intimate details of Lenin's last days. Stalin stood, raised his glass, and said, "To a great man, to a great man," then repeated it again, as if a little drunk. "Lenin knew he was dying," Stalin said, and "asked me once when we were alone together to bring him a cyanide capsule. 'You are the most severe person in the party,' Lenin said. 'You are able to do it.' At first I promised him, but then I could not do it. How could I give Ilich poison? I felt bad. And then, you never know how the illness will progress. So I didn't give it to him." There were further toasts, and the atmosphere became ever more visionary (an entire writers' city; no more paper shortages). "I still remember how Gorky bid farewell to Stalin, kissing like a man on the mustaches," Zelinsky wrote. "Gorky, tall, stooped to Stalin, who stood straight like a soldier. Gorky's eyes shone and, ashamedly, unnoticeably, he wiped away a small tear."[166]

Fadeyev followed the meeting with a diatribe in *Literary Newspaper* against his former comrades in the Association of Proletarian Writers and preserved his position of influence with the regime. Gorky faced opportunities and dilemmas he had not encountered back in Sorrento.[167] One of the first major services he performed, on August 17, 1933, was to lead a "brigade" of 120 writers who followed Stalin's tour to the White Sea–Baltic Canal with their own OGPU-supervised visit and glorified slave labor, in the name of a supposedly higher humanism. "I saw grandiose structures—dams, sluices, and a new waterway," the satirist Mikhail Zoshchenko wrote in one of the many thank-you notes to Yagoda (August 22). "But I was taken more by the people, who worked there and who organized the work. I saw thieves and bandits (now shock workers), who gave speeches in a human tongue, summoning their comrades at work to follow their example. Previously I had not seen the OGPU in the role of educator, and what I saw was for me extraordinarily joyful."[168]

WHO WOULD WRITE THE BIOGRAPHY?

Distribution of Stalin's writings inside the USSR reached an estimated 16.5 million copies as of early 1934.[169] His *Questions of Leninism* alone had been issued, in 17 languages, in more than 8 million copies by then. But the problem of Stalin's biography remained acute: the only Russian-language text, written by his aide Tovstukha, dated back to the 1920s and was the length of a newspaper essay.[170] Although Mikhail Koltsov had written a lively *Life of Stalin* for serialization in the *Village Newspaper*, it remained unpublished, evidently because Stalin had rejected it.[171]

Foreign publications, meanwhile, were making the leader of the world proletariat into a bandit/bank robber, and recounting his alleged betrayals of comrades as an undercover agent for the tsarist secret police.[172] A psychoanalytic memoir by a Gori and Tiflis classmate (who had emigrated) alleged that Stalin's father, Beso, had beaten him, so that, "from childhood on, the realization of his thoughts of revenge became the aim to which everything was subordinated."[173] A Comintern official in Germany wrote alarmingly to Moscow about the sullying of Stalin's image by enemies, singling out in particular Essad Bey.[174] A Baku-born Jew (1905) whose birth name was Lev Nussimbaum, Bey had gone to a Russian gymnasium in Berlin, taken classes in Turkish and Arabic at Friedrich Wilhelm University, begun wearing a turban, reinvented himself as a Muslim prince, and become a bestselling author who frequented the Café Megalomania. His colorful *Stalin*, published in Berlin in 1931, portrayed an outlaw in vivid orientalist strokes and embellished or invented evidence so that the dubious became possible, the possible probable, and the probable certain. "The difference between poetry and truth," he wrote, "is not yet recognized in the mountains."[175]

Bey's competition proved to be another orientalist-fabulist: Beria. No sooner had the regional party organization fallen under his control than it established a Stalin Institute to collect materials pertinent to "Stalin's biography and his role as theoretician and organizer" of the party in the South Caucasus.[176] But Stalin's aide Tovstukha, deputy director of the Marx-Engels-Lenin Institute in Moscow, started trying to transfer all original Stalin-related materials from Georgia.[177] Regime officials, meanwhile, had sounded out Gorky to write the biography, but he demurred.[178] Instead, the apparatus accepted a proposal by the French writer Henri Barbusse to write a book about Stalin, with oversight by Tovstukha (to ensure the desired depiction of the struggle against Trotsky).[179] Anyone taking on Stalin's life had to confront his constant discouragement. When the latest *History of the All-Union Communist Party (Bolsheviks)* referred to him in standard parlance as "the wise leader of all the toilers," Stalin wrote, "An apotheosis of individuals? What happened to Marxism?"[180] He rejected the Society of Old Bolsheviks' plan to mount an exhibit about his life as "strengthening a 'cult of the personality,' which is harmful and incompatible with the spirit of our party."[181]

"CONGRESS OF VICTORS"

The year 1934 dawned. Soviet industry was booming. The capitalist world remained mired in the Great Depression. The United States had recognized the Soviet Union. The famine was mostly over. It was time to gloat. In "The Architect of Socialist Society" (*Pravda,* January 1, 1934), sycophant supreme Karl Radek depicted a future historian giving lectures in the revolution's fiftieth year at the School of Interplanetary Communications. The lecturer, looking back from 1967, would emphasize the surprise among the world bourgeoisie that a new leader had succeeded Lenin and built socialism, at a necessarily furious pace, against the fierce resistance of capitalist elements and their facilitators. Stalin was called "the great pupil of great teachers who himself had now become the teacher, . . . the exemplar of the Leninist Party, bone of its bone, blood of its blood." His success was attributed to his "creative Marxism," his proximity to cadres, his resolve, and his fealty to Lenin. "He knew that he had fulfilled the oath taken ten years earlier over Lenin's casket," the essay observed. "And all the working people of the world and the world revolutionary proletariat knew it, too."[182]

Ten years to the day after Stalin had been sworn that oath, January 26, the 17th Party Congress opened in the Grand Kremlin Palace, bringing together 1,225 voting and 739 nonvoting delegates, representing 2.8 million members and candidates. Party statutes had specified an annual congress, but three and a half years had elapsed, the longest interval yet.[183] *Pravda* headlined it as the "Congress of Victors." Magnanimously, the dictator had allowed high-profile opposition figures back into the party after they had again publicly admitted their errors.

From the rostrum they issued self-flagellating calls for "unity," with Kamenev defending Stalin's personal dictatorship (in contrast to his bold denunciation of it back at the 14th Party Congress).[184] Bukharin, whom Stalin would appoint editor of *Izvestiya*, told the congress regarding the right deviation: "Our grouping was unavoidably becoming the focus for all the forces fighting against the socialist offensive, and primarily for the strata most threatened by the socialist offensive—the kulaks and their urban intellectual ideologists," which had heightened the danger of "an untimely foreign intervention." He praised the plan and quipped, "Hitler wants to drive us into Siberia, and the Japanese imperialists want to drive us from Siberia, so the entire 160 million population of our country would have to be located on one of the blast furnaces of Magnitogorsk."[185]

Stalin delivered a five-hour keynote on opening night. "He spoke unhurriedly, as if conversing," one witness wrote in his diary. "He was witty. The more he spoke, the closer he became to the audience. Ovations. Explosions of laughter. Full-blooded. But a practical, working speech."[186] The dictator issued a call to accountability, speaking of "difficulties of our organizational work, difficulties of our organizational leadership. They are concentrated in us ourselves, in our leading functionaries, in our organizations. . . . The responsibility for our failures and shortcomings rests, in nine out of ten cases, not on 'objective conditions' but on ourselves and only on ourselves." He denounced chancellery methods of management ("resolutions and decrees") and called for criticism from below, worker competitions, getting bosses into the factories and farms, getting skilled workers out of offices and into production, and refusing to tolerate people who failed to implement directives. "We must not hesitate to remove them from their leading posts, regardless of their services in the past."[187]

After the applause died down, Stalin offered an example of empty-words leadership:

STALIN: How goes the sowing?

FUNCTIONARY: The sowing, comrade Stalin? We have mobilized.

   (Laughter.)

STALIN: And?

FUNCTIONARY: We posed the question squarely. (Laughter.)

STALIN: And then?

FUNCTIONARY: We have a breakthrough, comrade Stalin, soon there'll be
   a breakthrough.

   (Laughter.)

STALIN: And in fact?

FUNCTIONARY: There is movement. (Laughter.)

STALIN: But in fact, how goes the sowing?

FUNCTIONARY: So far, the sowing is not happening, comrade Stalin.
(General guffaws.)[188]

Stalin pointedly added that provincial officials, "like feudal princes, think the laws were written not for them but for fools."

Against capitalism's "raging waves of economic shocks and military-political catastrophes," Stalin contrasted how "the USSR stands apart, like an anchor, continuing its socialist construction and struggle for keeping the peace." He accused the capitalists, without irony, of "deepening their exploitation via strengthening the intensity of their labor, and at the expense of farmers, by further reduction in the prices of products of their labor." Fascism, and especially National Socialism, he averred, "contained not an atom of socialism," and "should be seen as a sign of the bourgeoisie's weakness, of its lack of power to rule by the old parliamentary methods, forcing it to turn internally to terrorist methods of rule" and externally to a "policy of war." Without naming the likely aggressor, he foresaw a "new imperialist war" that "will certainly unleash revolution and place the very existence of capitalism in question in a number of countries, as happened during the first imperialist war."[189]

Stalin observed that fascism in Italy had not prohibited good bilateral relations with the USSR, and dismissed as "imaginary" German complaints that the Soviet Union's many nonaggression pacts signified a "reorientation" toward Western Europe. "We never had any orientation toward Germany, nor have we [now] any orientation toward Poland and France," he insisted. "We were oriented in the past and are oriented in the present only on the USSR. (Stormy applause.)" He also warned Japan: "Those who desire good peace and relations would always meet a positive response, but those who try to attack our country will receive a crushing rebuff to teach them in future not to poke their pig snouts into our Soviet garden. (Thunderous applause.)"[190]

RUDELY INTERRUPTED

As Stalin basked in the Grand Kremlin Palace spectacle, Hitler intruded, announcing a ten-year nonaggression "declaration" with Poland. The text contained no recognition of existing borders, but, sensationally, each side vowed not to "resort to force in the settlement of such disputes" as might arise between them.[191] Hitler's foreign policy adviser, Alfred Rosenberg, had vowed to annihilate Poland. Poland's participation was no less head spinning: it had a military alliance with France as well as a defensive alliance with Romania (both dating to 1921). But Poland had only a poorly equipped army to defend long borders facing two dynamic dictatorships, both of whose predecessors had made the country disappear from the map. Adding to that sense of vulnerability, the Versailles Treaty had made the predominantly ethnic German city of Danzig an autonomous "free city" under the League of Nations, leaving Poland without a Baltic port, and placed a so-called Corridor of Polish territory between German East Prussia and the rest of Germany, a recipe for instability.[192]

Even though the declaration did not legally invalidate the Franco-Polish alliance, Hitler had effectively broken the encirclement ring. Poland's political class, meanwhile, dreamed of playing an independent role in European affairs. "It was," one interwar observer noted, "a tragedy for Poland to have been reborn too weak to be a power, and strong enough to aspire to more than the status of a small state."[193] French officials privately called Poland a bigamist.[194] But of course, Paris was in talks with Berlin as well. Piłsudski received the French ambassador after the signing (January 29, 1934), explaining that "he had hesitated, had dragged things on, but the Franco-German negotiations had made him decide to expedite them, because if the [French] proposals were accepted by Germany, France would openly abandon the [Versailles] peace treaty."[195] The nonaggression declaration with Germany promised Poland reduced economic tensions as well (an end to trade and tariff wars). Moreover, even though France based its security on relations with Britain, not its eastern alliances, French foreign ministers now finally began to visit Warsaw.[196]

Stalin was caught out worse than the French. Seeking to keep Poland out of any anti-Soviet alliance, he had allowed the Galicia-born Radek to meet secretly with Polish officials. Radek insisted that Poland's private gestures toward Moscow constituted "an about-face and not a maneuver."[197] Artur Artuzov, the intelligence official, tried to puncture this wishful thinking, arguing that the Poles were flirting with the USSR solely to raise Germany's interest in a bilateral deal, but Stalin accused Artuzov of "misinforming the politburo."[198] Voroshilov, too, had gotten into the act, requesting a meeting with the sympathetic German ambassador, Rudolf Nadolny, and dwelling "a particularly long time on Hitler's *Mein Kampf,* in which connection he finally said that two words of the chancellor's in public would be enough [to dispel] the impression that the anti-Soviet tendency of the book still had validity today."[199]

Hitler's intelligence reports had warned of a pending Polish-Soviet alliance—Radek's back-channel flattery and calculated leaks had done the work for Piłsudski.[200] Stalin, ready to betray Germany to Poland and Poland to Germany, had been one-upped by both.[201]

Piłsudski had made plain to a German interlocutor that "Poland would never under any circumstances respond to any German attempts to turn Polish efforts toward Russian Ukraine."[202] But in Moscow, suspicions were rife that the anodyne German-Polish declaration contained secret military and territorial clauses.[203] Colonel Józef Beck—who had helped Piłsudski carry out his 1926 military coup—made the first visit to the Soviet Union by a Polish foreign minister since their state's reestablishment. He had little love for Poland's ally France (having once been ejected from that country as persona non grata) and prided himself on being able to handle Germany, but he wanted to avoid appearing to tilt between Poland's two big neighbors. He was hosted at a luncheon by Voroshilov, and engaged thrice by Litvinov (February 13, 14, and 15, 1934), who noted that his Polish counterpart "does not see danger on the part of Germany or general danger of war in Europe at this time." The Polish-born Litvinov gloated that when he reminded Beck that Poland had signed nonaggression pacts with the USSR for three years, and with Germany for ten, "Beck became manifestly embarrassed (the one time during our entire conversation)." But the minister vowed this could be fixed, and indeed their bilateral pact would soon be extended to ten years (and their legations upgraded to embassies). Beck returned from Moscow with pleurisy.[204]

KIROV AND OTHERS ACCLAIM THE LEADER

The party congress had continued through February 10. Stalin belatedly acknowledged the livestock losses (his report carried a table), which he attributed to kulak sabotage, yet he urged that "1934 must and can be a breakthrough year to growth of the whole livestock economy." The dearth of meat was widely felt.[205] Orjonikidze proposed that industrial production plans be cut, rather than increased, and the congress approved a resolution for the rest of the second plan, stipulating 18.5 percent growth in consumer goods, versus 14.5 for producer goods. Many speakers underscored the imperative to ramp up retail trade and living standards.[206] But Kaganovich affirmed that Stalin's "revolution from above was the greatest revolution human history has known, a revolution that smashed the old economic structure and created a new collective farm system."[207] Even Yevgeny Preobrazhensky, the erstwhile ardent Trotsky supporter, marveled from the rostrum, "Collectivization—that is the heart of the matter! Did I predict collectivization? I did not."[208]

Kirov, afforded the honor of closing out discussion of Stalin's report, celebrated all that had been achieved, assuring delegates that "the chief difficulties are behind us," while reminding them to keep shoulders to the wheel. His oratory elicited repeated clapping, especially when he proposed that every word of Stalin's political report be approved as marching orders. "Comrades, ten years ago, we buried the man who founded our party, who founded our proletarian state," Kirov concluded. "We, comrades, can say with pride before Lenin's memory: we fulfilled that vow; we in future, too, shall fulfill that vow, because that vow was made by the grand strategist of the liberation of the toilers of our country and the whole world, comrade Stalin. (Stormy, prolonged applause, a warm ovation by the entire hall, all stand.)"[209]

Stalin declined to give the heretofore customary reply to the discussion, citing "no disagreements at all."[210] He dictated the composition of the new Central Committee: seventy-one members and sixty-eight candidates. The number of candidates he permitted to stand equaled the number of slots, although, by party tradition, delegates could cross out anyone they opposed. In the voting on February 9, 1934, only 1,059 of 1,225 ballots ended up in the record. (At the previous congress, 134 voting delegates had not returned ballots.)[211] Only Kalinin and Ivan Kodatsky (Leningrad province soviet chairman) were elected unanimously in the official accounting. Three votes went against Stalin, though apparatchiks might have tossed out a few negatives. Kirov received four against. (Back at the 16th Congress, Stalin, like Kirov, had officially received nine votes against.)[212]

Rumors circulated in Moscow and then abroad about some provincial party bosses having sought to have the aw-shucks Kirov replace Stalin.[213] Lev Shaumyan (b. 1904), a newspaper editor (and the unofficially adopted son of Mikoyan), would later assert that "the thought ripened in the minds of certain congress delegates, primarily those who remembered Lenin's Testament well, that it was time to transfer Stalin from the post of general secretary to other work."[214] But the idea that Kirov was widely viewed as worthy of replacing Stalin, or that he led a "moderate faction" opposed to Stalin, is contradicted by the evidence.[215] Kirov seemed a provincial by comparison with his predecessor in the second capital, Zinoviev, who had worked closely with Lenin and headed the Comintern. At the same time, Kirov had turned out a lot like Zinoviev: a talker, a bon vivant. Still, there was a difference. "At meetings, he never once said anything about any question," Mikoyan told Khrushchev of Kirov. "He sat silent, and that was it."[216] Selecting the general secretary, moreover, fell not to the congress but to the one-day plenum of the newly elected Central Committee afterward. Another gloss on the whispering was provided by the Leningrad delegate Mikhail Rosliakov. "Generally," he would recall, "the talk was that the party had matured, grown stronger, that there were even people capable of replacing Stalin if the necessity arose."[217]

A congress report by the apparatchik Yezhov revealed that 10 percent of the party membership had joined during the civil war or before 1917, but that this profile applied to 80 percent of the congress delegates. In other words, 1,646 of the 1,966 delegates had become Communists when Lenin was the leader.[218] But Lenin-era Communists showed loyalty to Stalin. One was Veniamin Furer (b. 1904), a talented organizer in a mining town of Ukraine who had been given the floor at the congress during the February 7 session. "At the 16th Party Congress, comrade Stalin spoke of those reserves that lurk in the depths of our Soviet system," Furer said in his remarks at the 17th. "If one breaks the bureaucratic knot, if one advances organizational work, these reserves would surface. . . . These reserves are the creative energy, the creative initiative of the mass." He hit all the Stalin notes: "Thousands of new people have grown in the Donbass and constitute the proletarians of the Stalinist epoch. . . . They present to us, to our organizational work, to our leadership, more demands, demands that are more complex. . . . Our new worker judges us, in localities, on concrete questions: apartment repair, club organization, development of shops and canteens. . . . This party congress, opening a new plane of battle for socialism, should task the entire party and each Communist with the fighting task of studying and fully mastering the Stalinist style of work. (Applause.)"[219]

MERE SECRETARY

A military-industrial parade on Red Square punctuated the victors' congress. On February 10, 1934, Stalin and his inner circle met, apparently before the Central Committee plenum that evening, and he proposed that Kirov relocate to Moscow as a Central Committee secretary. "What are you talking about?!" Molotov later recalled of Kirov's response. "I'll be no good here. In Leningrad I can do as well as you, but what can I do here?" Some evidence suggests that Orjonikidze supported Kirov's refusal, Stalin stalked out, and Kirov went to mollify him.[220] A compromise ensued: Kirov would become a Central Committee secretary but remain party boss in Leningrad.[221]

This provoked the hasty transfer of Andrei Zhdanov from Gorky (Nizhny Novgorod) to Moscow as Central Committee secretary.[222] Born in Mariupol (1896), Zhdanov was the grandson of a priest and the son of a school inspector (who had died when the boy was just three) and a classical pianist (who had health issues after giving birth to him).[223] He affected the trappings of an intellectual, had an easy demeanor in Stalin's presence, and was a Russian nationalist. Khrushchev recalled him as a charming fellow who would carry out any assignment.[224] Zhdanov was not even a politburo candidate member, but, in the absence of the dictator or Kaganovich, he would sign politburo meeting protocols.[225]

Working sessions of the politburo were giving way to "commissions" (an invention of Kaganovich), while the use of telephone polls for approving politburo decisions had grown to between 1,000 and 3,000 times a year. Even so, Stalin was often just dictating "politburo" decrees to Poskryobyshev or his other top aide Boris Dvinsky. (Ever the functionaries, they would note, "No telephone polling of politburo members taken.")[226]

Further reflecting the changes wrought by collectivization-dekulakization, Stalin elevated several secret police officials to full membership in the Central Committee without prior candidate status: Yagoda (43 years old), Yevdokimov (43), Balytsky (42), and Beria (35). Yezhov (39) and Khrushchev (39) also became full members without having been candidates. Zhdanov (38) was promoted from candidate to full member; Poskryobyshev and Mekhlis became candidate members, even though they had not even been congress delegates.[227] The post-congress Central Committee returned all members of the politburo from the previous congress, in 1930, except for Rykov.[228] Stalin's name came first on the list of members of the politburo, the orgburo, and the secretariat (after the 16th Congress, his name had appeared alphabetically). His portrait in the gallery of politburo members was rendered far larger, and his khakis lightened to make him stand out. Tellingly, however, Stalin decided that he should be formally listed as merely a "secretary," in what looks like yet another indication of the long shadow of Lenin's Testament about removing him as "general secretary."[229]

PRIVATE LIFE

Inside the triangular Kremlin, the Imperial Senate formed its own triangular fortress, and Stalin's wing was a fortress within the fortress. Even the regime personnel given regular Kremlin passes for state business needed a special pass for
Stalin's wing. Located one floor below where Lenin's had been and on the building's opposite side, it came to be known to regime insiders as "the Little Corner."[230] Stalin had marked his permanent shift to the Kremlin by having the
interiors redone. The walls in the offices were lined with shoulder-height wood
paneling, under the theory that wood vapors enhanced air quality, and the elevators were paneled with mahogany. The tiled stove in Stalin's office yielded to
central heating. Behind his working desk hung a portrait of Lenin. In a corner, on
a small table, stood a display case with Lenin's death mask. Another small table
held several telephones ("Stalin," he would answer). Next to the desk was a stand
with a vase holding fresh fruit. In the rear was a door that led to a room for relaxation, rarely used, with oversized hanging maps and a giant globe. In the main
office, between two of the three large windows that let in afternoon sun, sat a
black leather couch where, in his better moods, Stalin and guests sipped tea with
lemon. In the country's darkest moments he could exude optimism, but when, to
others, matters seemed brightest, he could become gloomy, withdrawn.

Ten miles away, in Volynskoe village, near the town of Kuntsevo on the right
bank of the Moscow River, the OGPU completed construction on a new dacha for
him in 1934—within just a year, using fiberboard panels (not long-lasting, but
easy to put up).[231] In contrast to the neo-Gothic style of Zubalovo, Meran Merzh-
anyants, known as Miron Merzhanov, an ethnic Armenian and the head architect for the central executive committee, adopted a simpler neoclassicism for the
one-story, seven-room villa with sundeck and veranda.[232] The Near Dacha, as it
became known, sat on thirty acres in a deep wood and was encircled by a solid
wall made of plywood, four to five meters high, which was painted green, like the
residence, to blend in. The site proved easy to secure but at first noisy (to one side
lay the village of Davydkovo, which filled with drunken men at night, and to
another, the Kiev Station freight depot).[233] For a time, Stalin continued to sleep at
his new Kremlin apartment and use the Zubalovo dacha, but Nadya's absence
weighed on him at places they had shared. Soon he decided on the Near Dacha as
his permanent residence.[234]

Hitler lived at the eighteenth-century Palais Schulenburg, at 77 Wilhelm-strasse, the chancellor's residence since 1871, which during the Weimar Republic had acquired a modernist addition, where Hitler had his formal office. The Führer had the palace part remodeled, recovering the original grandeur but with an elegant simplicity. He would also have his Munich apartment (16 Prinz-regentenplatz) refurbished in rectilinear forms, opening up larger light-filled, strikingly modern and spare spaces. These interiors were photographed for the German public. Additionally, Hitler vastly expanded the chalet-style farmhouse in the alpine border town of Berchtesgaden, in the Obersalzberg, where he had stayed on holiday. It had been rechristened the Berghof ("mountain farm") and now had more than thirty rooms.[235] An ample dining room, study, and great hall were built with Swiss stone and pinewood paneling, and the Teutonic furniture, too, was deliberately oversized. Picture windows and an open-air terrace afforded panoramic views of the snowcapped Bavarian Alps and Austria in the distance. Over time, the entire mountain area would be closed in a wide security perimeter with a high fence, but the loss of physical accessibility was compensated for by images of Hitler's domestic life published in periodicals. Commercially available photo albums also depicted him hiking in the pure mountain air with his dog or entertaining blond children at his mountain retreat. Postcards for sale showed him feeding deer on the terrace—a private, softer Führer.[236]

No public mention was made of the existence, let alone location, of Stalin's private Moscow residence, even as the entire regime became organized around it. A team of chauffeurs remained on twenty-four-hour call at the special Kremlin garage, which was jammed with foreign makes. Stalin had acquired a 1929 Rolls-Royce but was usually driven in a Packard, a premier luxury brand he had come to love since the Tsaritsyn days (when he rode in a Packard Twin Six "touring car").[237] In 1933, the regime had purchased the new Packard Twelve in the United States (Stalin would travel with the top down, from Sochi to Abkhazia and back, just for the ride). He preferred the jump seat, facing forward, which he pulled down himself. One guard sat on the backseat, and another next to the driver. Stalin's Packard drove right up to his entrance of the Imperial Senate; exiting the Kremlin, at the Borovitskaya Gates, he traveled west along Znamenka, then the Arbat, Smolensk Square, Borodino Bridge, Great Dorogomilov Street, and onto the old Mozhaisk Highway to a hidden sharp left turnoff at Volynskoe. Service personnel nicknamed the route "the Georgian Military Highway," in reference to the actual road in the Caucasus.

Inside the dacha, Stalin and his guests, by custom, wore slippers (he tucked his trousers into his socks). An intercom connected all the rooms. The hot water heater was imported. A separate building, some 200 yards from the principal residence, housed a kitchen, which had a traditional Russian-style stove, which beckoned when his rheumatism acted up. The auxiliary structure contained a Russian-style bathhouse and billiard room, too. Master artisans from around the country fabricated much of the furniture, doors, and wall paneling at Moscow's Lux Factory. A wooden bed that workmen had used became Stalin's. Contrary to legend, he slept in the bedroom (some 200 square feet). The floors were also made of wood. The dining room, off to the right of the entrance, had a long table, an upright piano, and a gramophone. Stalin collected records, favoring the danceable light romances of Pyotr Leshchenko and especially the émigré Alexander Vertinsky.[238] During and after meals, he convened regime meetings. According to Mikoyan, the dictator ate slowly but had a healthy appetite. "Stalin loved a variety of fish dishes," he wrote. "Danube herring he loved very much. . . . He loved poultry: guinea fowl, duck, flattened young chicken. He loved thin rack of lamb cooked on a spit. . . . Thin bones, a little meat, dry-broiled."[239] Lakoba would bring racks of lamb from Abkhazia.

The Near Dacha was built with children's bedrooms, but Vasily (age thirteen) and Svetlana (eight) continued to live in the Kremlin apartment below their father's office and to spend weekends and summers at Zubalovo.[240] (Yakov Jughashvili, age twenty-six, lived at Granovsky, 3.) Full-time care of the children fell to Til as well as Pauker, who had been born in Habsburg Lemberg (Lwów, Lviv, Lvov), of Jewish extraction, the son of a barber, from whom he had learned the trade.[241] Vasily, red haired like his mother, with a pimply face, initially was sent to School No. 20; Svetlana began at No. 25, a model school known for "very tough, strict discipline," as Pauker reported to Stalin. (Vasily was transferred there.)[242] Their father's portrait hung in the school, which offered radio and electrotechnology, airplane and automobile modeling, ballroom dancing, theater, a rifle team, parachute jumping, volleyball, hockey, excursions to the State Tretyakov Gallery, summer camps in Crimea. Perhaps 85 percent of the teaching staff did not belong to the party. Vasily's closest friend was nicknamed "Collective Farm Boy" (his mother, from a village, scrubbed the school's floors). But his friends could not visit him at home. Stalin would sometimes read aloud to Vasily and Artyom. "Once he almost laughed to the point of tears," Artyom recalled of a reading of the satirist Mikhail Zoshchenko, "and then he said, 'And here comrade Zoshchenko remembered about the GPU and changed the ending!'"[243]

Stalin's own son was a rambunctious type, signing his letters "Red Vaska." Perhaps he misbehaved, at least in part, to get his father's attention. "With a reluctant heart," the bodyguard Vlasik would recall, "we had to report his behavior to his father, ruining his mood."[244] Vasily observed how his father doted on his younger sister, with constant reminders that Svetlana was a good example.[245] Svetlana studied hard under the guidance of her nanny, Bychkova.[246] "Stalin, someone who absolutely lacked sentimentalism, expressed such untypical gentleness toward his daughter," recalled Candide Charkviani, a Georgian official. "'My Little Hostess,' Stalin would say, and seat Svetlana on his lap and give her kisses. 'Since she lost her mother, I have kept telling her that she is the mistress of the house,' Stalin told us."[247] Stalin instructed her to issue orders, and she would address written commands to "Secretary No. 1," and he would answer, "I submit." She also recalled, however, that he was absent. "Once in a while," she wrote, "he enjoyed the sounds of children playing." Stalin would overnight at the Near Dacha. "Sometimes before he left, he'd come to my room in his overcoat to kiss me good night as I lay sleeping," Svetlana added. "He liked kissing me while I was little, and I'll never forget how tender he was to me."[248] She was heard to utter, "Let the whole world hate me, as long as Papa loves me. If Papa tells me to go to the moon, I'll go."[249, 250]

Into the public vacuum about Stalin's personal life stepped Kyrill Kakabadze, a Soviet trade representative in Berlin for Georgia's manganese mines, who had defected and published a defamatory essay in the British *Sunday Express* (April 8, 1934) that purported to describe Stalin's "orgies" at a "personal estate" in Zubalovo of 300,000 acres. "Stalin lives like a tsar," he wrote, supposedly costing the state £300,000 a year and 1,000 lives a day. "Stalin took for himself huge apartments that had once been inhabited by Ivan the Terrible." Soviet representatives in London begged for compromising material on Kakabadze for release to the British press (the OGPU went to work, discovering that he was from a merchant family), then the German press republished the Kakabadze articles.[251] Stalin took it out on Beria, his minion for all things Georgian, writing (April 14) that, "besides the Georgian carousers and scamps arrested in Moscow hotels, there is another large group in Leningrad. The dissoluteness of so-called representatives of Georgian economic organizations has placed shame on the South Caucasus organizations. We oblige you to take immediate measures to liquidate the unseemliness, if you do not want the South Caucasus to end up in the court of the Central Committee."[252]

COMMON ENEMIES

Stalin had fixed a covetous eye on Chinese Turkestan, or Xinjiang ("New Territory"). From January through April 1934, he fought a small war there. Renewal of a mass Muslim rebellion had spurred Comintern operatives to contemplate pushing for a socialist revolution, but Soviet military intelligence had pointed out that, even though the rebels commanded the loyalty of almost the entire Muslim population (90 percent), a successful Muslim independence struggle in Chinese Turkestan could inspire the Kazakhs and Kyrgyz in Soviet Turkestan or even the Mongols. Stalin had decided to send about 7,000 OGPU and Red Army soldiers, as well as airplanes, artillery, mustard gas, and Soviet Uzbek Communists, to defend the Chinese warlord. Remarkably, he allowed Soviet forces to combine with former White Army soldiers abroad, who were promised amnesty and Soviet citizenship. A possible Muslim rebel victory turned into a defeat. Unlike the Japanese in Manchuria, Stalin did not set up an independent state, but he solidified his informal hold on Xinjiang, setting up military bases, sending advisers, and gaining coal, oil, tungsten, and tin concessions. Some 85 percent of Xinjiang's trade was with the USSR.[253] British and Japanese observers and Chinese newspapers railed against Soviet "imperialism."[254] Chiang Kai-shek became dependent on Soviet goodwill to communicate with Xinjiang's capital, Ürümqi.[255]

Ambassador Bullitt, who had returned to the United States after his brief December whirlwind in Moscow, came back. "The honeymoon atmosphere had evaporated completely before I arrived," he wrote to Roosevelt (April 13, 1934).[256] That very day, the U.S. Congress passed the Johnson Act, which prohibited foreign nations in default from marketing bonds in the United States, effectively preempting Roosevelt's government from underwriting loans to the Soviet Union as negotiations proceeded for belated repayment of tsarist and Provisional Government debt.[257]

For Stalin, in any case, the threat of an immediate Japanese attack had receded.[258] Hitler's Germany was the greater puzzle.[259] On April 19, Stalin's spies delivered a copy of a secret document sent by the British ambassador in Berlin, Eric Phipps, to London, quoting Hitler to the effect that "it's better to be respected and unloved than weak and loved." Phipps asserted that "in relation to Russia, however, Hitler is ready to leave personal feelings aside and conduct a policy of realism."[260] A follow-up intercepted assessment from Phipps stated, in Russian translation, "The [Nazi] regime is solid, and the storm troopers are so disciplined that [Hitler] can be endangered only as a result of a serious uprising or a slow process of internal decay." Stalin underlined this passage.[261] Balytsky, OGPU chief in Soviet Ukraine, sent Stalin a report on the German consulates in Kharkov, Kiev, and Odessa, which were now run by Nazi party members who were said to be recruiting Nazi youth and storm troopers on Soviet territory among the half million ethnic Germans in Soviet Ukraine. Balytsky initiated arrests of Soviet "fascists."[262]

On May 5, 1934, Polish foreign minister Beck, as promised, signed an early renewal of the nonaggression pact with the Soviet Union.[263] But Stalin took talk of Poland trying to maintain neutrality vis-à-vis both its giant neighbors as disinformation, and behind Poland—indeed, behind every Soviet foe—he saw Britain. Stalin could not or would not grasp that "imperialist" Britain had the same enemies as the USSR: Nazi Germany in Europe and militaristic Japan in Asia.[264] British-Soviet relations were poor.[265] The British embassy official Sir William Strang had reported from Moscow that *Pravda* was calling the Nazi ideologue Rosenberg "a lackey of British imperialism."[266] Officials in London were also incredulous at Soviet assertions that the British were "the real force behind German and Japanese fascism," as the Comintern's Dmytro Manuilsky had put it at the 17th Party Congress. The son of an Orthodox priest from Ukraine, he had charged, in typical contradictions-of-capitalism fashion, that Britain was instigating these two powers against the Soviet Union to avoid a new intra-imperialist war over colonies.[267] Even the tsarist-era military men Alexander Svechin and Boris Shaposhnikov wrote that Poland, Romania, and other limitrophe states were ultimately subordinated to the will of London and Paris.[268]

Internally, Tukhachevsky urged that, since Poland or Romania was sure to attack at some point, the Red Army ought to take advantage of the poor state of these implacable enemies' railways to deliver a knockout blow before they could fully mobilize. The appeal of such preemptive war had been enhanced by a perceived shift toward military attacks without formal war declarations.[269] But for all the talk about the inevitability of war, Stalin was not looking to fight one.[270]

Neither was Britain. Although Japan eyed British-controlled parts of Southeast and South Asia, it was preoccupied with China, but Germany under Hitler looked less contained—and British credibility was on the line.[271] British society, however, was overwhelmingly desirous of avoiding another catastrophic war and mostly sympathetic to Germany's grievances against the Versailles Treaty. Added to this was the political-ideological challenge of the Comintern and, behind it, the Soviet Union, whose industrialization—contrary to British expectations—had seemed to succeed. For London, no less than for Stalin, some sort of accommodation with Nazi Germany seemed the path to security.

POET TO POET

The poet Osip Mandelstam, outraged over the famine, had composed sixteen lines that blamed Stalin. The verses, which he read to a handful of intimates, did not mention the dictator by name, but mocked a "Kremlin highlander" with oily fingers, a criminal underworld past, and part Ossetian descent. In April 1934, Mandelstam saw fellow poet Boris Pasternak on the street—the two had known each other since 1922—and he recited the rhymed invective to him. Hearsay has Pasternak deeming the lines an act of suicide, responding, "I didn't hear this; you didn't recite it to me."[272] On the night of May 16–17, Mandelstam was arrested at his apartment, where the police confiscated manuscripts, letters, and his address book. The poet was allowed to take a few personal items and books. He was said to have selected Dante's *Inferno*.[273]

The admission process to the new union of writers had commenced, and on May 15, Fadeyev, Bedny, Pasternak, and others were inducted.[274] A devastated Pasternak now learned of Mandelstam's arrest from Anna Gorenko (b. 1889), known as Akhmatova, who had arrived from Leningrad that evening. He went to see Mandelstam's wife, Nadezhda, and they evidently tried to call Bedny, who had once promised to defend Mandelstam if necessary, but had ceased to have contact with Stalin and deemed intervention useless.[275] Nadezhda managed to get into the Kremlin to see Yenukidze, but also with no results. It seems Pasternak went to *Izvestiya* and implored Bukharin to intercede. (Pasternak was doing literary translations for the newspaper as a source of income.)[276] According to the woman who later would become Pasternak's lover, he "raced frantically all over town, telling everybody that he was not to blame and denying responsibility for Mandelstam's disappearance." In fact, Pasternak did not know but Mandelstam, under interrogation, had not named all the people to whom he had recited the poem—only those already known to the interrogator—and omitted Pasternak.[277] At the other extreme, the short-story writer Pyotr Pavlenko boasted to acquaintances that he'd been allowed to listen secretly to Mandelstam's interrogation at Lubyanka, evidently from behind a door in an adjacent room.[278]

In a surprise, Mandelstam was sentenced not to death or even a Gulag camp, but exile in Cherdyn (northern Urals), and allowed to take his wife. In early June 1934, he attempted suicide, jumping out a window. Bukharin wrote to Stalin about the poet's frail psychology, noting that "Boris Pasternak is utterly at a loss over Mandelstam's arrest and no one knows anything."[279] Then, on June 13, Pasternak was summoned to the phone at his communal apartment on Volkhonka Street. The caller said Stalin would be getting on the line, but Pasternak, like Bulgakov some years earlier, thought it a prank and hung up. The phone rang again, the same voice stating the call was from Stalin's office and, to eliminate disbelief, dictated a special number to call. Pasternak dialed it and soon heard, "Stalin speaking."

Stalin told Pasternak that Mandelstam's case had been reexamined and the result would be favorable. (The sentence was commuted to mere banishment from the largest cities; he and his wife moved to Voronezh.) Stalin asked if Mandelstam was Pasternak's friend—a tricky question. If Pasternak said yes, he could be implicated; if he said no, he was betraying Mandelstam. "Poets rarely make friends," he answered. "They envy each other." Stalin told him that if something terrible had befallen one of his friends, he would go to the wall to aid him. Then Stalin asked if Mandelstam was genuinely a "master." Again, tricky: this could have referred to the verses about the "Kremlin highlander." What Pasternak answered remains a matter of dispute. He seems to have suggested that they meet face-to-face. Stalin hung up. Pasternak dialed the number again, asking Poskryobyshev to reconnect him, but Stalin's aide said the dictator was busy. Pasternak asked whether he could tell others of the call; Poskryobyshev said he would leave it to him.[280] That very day, Pasternak told Ilya Ehrenburg (who was living in Paris with a Soviet passport but had just arrived in Moscow with André Malraux). Ehrenburg spread the sensational news to select other writers.[281] For Pasternak, the call had happened extremely quickly, but it would reverberate in his head for a lifetime.

A NEW AUTHORITY

Georgi Dimitrov, the acquitted but still imprisoned Bulgarian Comintern operative, had finally been deported from Germany. He arrived in Moscow by plane (February 27, 1934), and Stalin afforded him a hero's welcome and Soviet citizenship.[282] "It is difficult to imagine," Dimitrov recorded in his diary, "a more grandiose reception or more sympathy and love."[283] He had become the best-known

Communist internationally after Stalin.[284] Dimitrov was given an apartment at the Comintern's Hotel Lux, which also housed a young Yugoslav named Josip Broz Tito and a Vietnamese named Nguyen Ai Cuoc, later known as Ho Chi Minh.[285] (Dimitrov would soon obtain one of the 550 grand apartments in the new Government House, an elite complex colloquially known as the House on the Embankment, designed by Boris Yofan and built by Yagoda, on the site of wine warehouses along the Moscow River, a stone's throw from the Kremlin walls.)[286] Stalin took to phoning him. Convalescing outside Moscow at a dacha in Arkhangelskoe, on the former estates of Princes Golitsyn and Yusupov, Dimitrov requested an audience. On April 6, Stalin had him named to the Comintern executive committee, and the next day he received him in the Little Corner, one on one.[287]

Some Communists, including Germans who had managed to escape into exile from Nazi terror, were lobbying for a shift toward cooperation with other parties on the left.[288] But Stalin stressed the need to win over European workers from parliamentarism, whose absence had allowed Russian workers to be revolutionary in 1917. "In all countries, the bourgeoisie will proceed to fascism," he told Dimitrov, which he presented as an opportunity for Communists to win workers' allegiance, provided the latter were made to understand that the era of parliamentarism was ending, meaning Social Democrats could be outmaneuvered. Still, he concluded that "we cannot immediately and easily win millions of workers in Europe." In the meantime, he encouraged Dimitrov to seize leadership inside the Comintern: "Kuusinen is good, but an academic; Manuilsky—agitator; [Wilhelm] Knorin—propagandist! [Osip] Pyatnitsky—narrow . . . Who says that this 'foursome' must remain [in charge]?" Molotov chimed in: "You have looked the enemy in the face. And after prison, you now take the work into your hands."[289]

At the 1934 May Day parade, Stalin motioned Dimitrov to come up to the dictator's side on the Mausoleum, a Kremlinological sign for all. Dimitrov seized the moment, asking to be received again privately when convenient; Stalin agreed to an audience the next day. "Select *yourself* where and *how* to appear and what to write," he instructed him in the Little Corner. "Don't let yourself be talked into anything."[290] Dimitrov drew inspiration from recent events in France, where workers, in response to antiparliamentary riots by far right, monarchist, and fascist leagues, had ignored party divisions on the left and united in a general strike to prevent France from following Germany's path.[291] "The wall between Communist workers and Social Democrats should be demolished," Dimitrov told the visiting Maurice Thorez, the French Communist party leader, on May 11. But this was a call not to cooperate with Social Democrat party leaders but to redouble efforts to reclaim their rank and file.[292] Additional urgency arrived on May 19, when a fascist-inflected coup succeeded in Dimitrov's native Bulgaria. And yet, not only Stalin but also Pyatnitsky (real surname Tarshis), Béla Kun, Wilhelm Knorin, Solomon Lozovsky (Dridzo), and Jenő Varga detested Social Democrats and opposed a broad leftist front to combat fascism.

BUNGLING

Stalin summoned Artuzov, who had predicted Poland's behavior, to a series of discussions in the Little Corner. (Litvinov exited when the intelligence officials entered.)[293] Soviet military intelligence in Europe had suffered a string of catastrophic exposures several years running, as a result of violating elementary tradecraft: recruiting agents among local Communist party members (who were under police surveillance).[294] A list compiled by Yagoda for Stalin and Voroshilov of every agent exposure with names, dates, and causes, covered ten pages and highlighted "infestation by traitors," "recruitment of foreign cadres among dubious elements," and "non-observance of the rules of conspiracy," all of which had resulted in the USSR being fed "a mass of disinformation."[295] On May 26, 1934, Stalin appointed Artuzov deputy chief of military intelligence, concurrent with his post as head of OGPU foreign intelligence, an unprecedented combination.[296]

Within a month, Artuzov had written a detailed analysis—one copy to Stalin, one to Voroshilov, and none to Jan Berzin, the nominal military intelligence chief—detailing that the Soviets now had essentially no military intelligence operations in Romania, Latvia, Estonia, Finland, France, or Italy. His solution was to prohibit, once again, recruitment of foreign Communists as spies and to improve the pay and housing of operatives abroad. Fatefully, Stalin also accepted Artuzov's recommendation to liquidate military intelligence's department for analysis, the one central clearinghouse for assessing the mass of all incoming information. Artuzov pointed out that there was no such all-knowing and therefore risky department of analysis in the OGPU foreign directorate (which was one of its weaknesses).[297] Military intelligence was subordinated directly to the defense commissar, who emerged with enhanced powers.[298]

In terms of counterintelligence, the secret police claimed that a Soviet spy in Chinese Harbin was a double agent who had helped Japan roll up part of the Soviet espionage network in the Far East.[299] Stalin demanded to know from Yagoda which Soviet operative had recruited the spy.[300] A far more important case remains confounding. The OGPU had put the head of Red Army external relations, Colonel Vasily Smagin, under observation on the basis of intercepted deciphered telegrams from the Japanese military attaché Torashirō Kawabe. "We have precisely established that Smagin in January 1934, using the possibilities in his position, took from a rank-and-file operative in the Fourth Department [military intelligence] fifty-seven file cards of secret agent material about Japan and twenty-nine about China to his home for three days," Yagoda wrote. "This had nothing in common with his official duties." Stalin underlined this passage, and another about Smagin's closeness to Kawabe. Smagin, however, was only sacked and left unemployed—and eventually given a teaching position.[301]

LONG KNIVES

Hitler's renunciation of the League of Nations had begun to lift the postwar taboo in France on the idea of any "alliance."[302] Since Hitler's takeover, Litvinov had been urging a regional pact against him, borrowing the phrase "collective security" from the League and arguing that "peace is indivisible" (i.e., either every country had peace or none had it). Lenin had sized up Litvinov as "the most crocodile-like of our diplomats," who tore into and held on to people.[303] Stalin, however, was not keen on a regional pact that, without Germany, would come across as anti-German while not even guaranteeing Soviet border security on the Baltic Sea. He also wanted to avoid giving a pretext for a Polish-German bloc on his immediate border.[304] Still, he viewed talks with Paris as a useful instrument for his talks with Berlin, exactly as the French did.[305]

The USSR won diplomatic recognition on June 9, 1934, from Czechoslovakia and Romania, members of the Little Entente, and by the 27th draft of a comprehensive Eastern Pact—France, the Soviet Union, the Little Entente, the Baltic states, Germany, Poland, Finland—was being circulated alongside a separate Franco-Soviet agreement.[306] On June 29, Stalin received an OGPU intelligence report ("from a serious Polish source") asserting that, by having invited Goebbels to Warsaw, Piłsudski was showing Paris he had options to discourage the latter's bruited alliance with Moscow.[307]

The counterpart to a Soviet security deal centered on France was a Comintern shift toward a united front with Social Democrats against fascism. Dimitrov wrote cryptically in his diary (June 29), "Stalin: I never answered you. I had no time. On this question, there is still nothing in my head. Something must be prepared!" (Dimitrov also wrote to himself, "So lonely and personally unhappy! It's almost more difficult for me now than last year in prison." But then Dimitrov, despite being married to the cause, addressed his personal loneliness, resuming correspondence with Rosa Fleischmann, a Jewish Communist from Czechoslovakia's Sudetenland whom he had met in Vienna years earlier, and who would soon become his second wife and companion, something Stalin did not have.)[308]

The Central Committee was holding a plenum, the first such full meeting since the party congress, devoted to meat supply and livestock.[309] Early on the morning of June 30, 1934, Hitler arrested Captain Ernst Röhm, chief of staff of the street-fighting SA (Sturmabteilung), in a Bavarian resort town; as many as 2,000 more arrests ensued. Surly and overweight, with a prominent scar on his left cheek, and openly homosexual, Röhm was one of the few who used the familiar *du* ("thou") with Hitler. He led some 3 million SA members, poorly armed and disorganized, but more than were in the Nazi party, and nearly thirty times the size of the Reichswehr (limited by the Versailles Treaty).[310] His Brownshirt militia sought a permanent place in the Nazi order as a reward for helping bring Hitler to power and targeting Nazi enemies (leftists, Jews), but he had toned down his rhetoric of a continuing revolution and accepted Hitler's request to go on medical leave and send the Brownshirts on leave as well (most were due to return in August). But Reichswehr generals—who reported to Hindenburg, not the chancellor Hitler—were adamant that the paramilitary SA be neutered. The Nazi Schutzstaffel, or SS (Heinrich Himmler), Sicherheitsdienst, or SD (Reinhard Heydrich), and Gestapo (also Heydrich) had no love for their SA rivals, either. Rumors of a pending crackdown against the SA had spurred the latter to yet another drunken rampage in Munich on the evening of June 29.[311] At the same time, Hitler had been told that President Hindenburg was ready to declare martial law and receive the former conservative prime minister Franz von Papen on June 30. In the end, after much stalling, the Führer felt compelled to move against both the SA and the traditional conservatives.

The army brass put its resources in SS hands, and left the latter to fabricate the damning evidence of a supposed SA "putsch" with the aid of an unnamed foreign country.[312] Still, it was awkward: the SA had been just as crucial (and just as dispensable) to the Nazi revolution as the Kronstadt sailors had been to the Bolshevik revolution in Russia. In a two-hour, radio-broadcast speech to the Reichstag (twelve of whose members would be among those to be executed), Hitler highlighted storm trooper moral laxity and Röhm's homosexuality and declared that he had acted patriotically to preempt a planned SA "Night of the Long Knives."[313]

Stalin was said to have badgered his newly arrived envoy in Berlin for details of the "bloodbath."[314] *Izvestiya* dedicated four columns on its front page to Hitler's Reichstag speech about the Night of the Long Knives.[315] "What a guy [*molodets*]," Stalin exclaimed to his inner circle, according to Mikoyan's later recollections. "Well done. Knows how to act!"[316] A Comintern instant analysis, clueless about the dynamics of the Nazi regime, wrote that the "monopolist big bourgeoisie" had crushed the "petit-bourgeois strata."[317] *Pravda* (July 2, 1934) editorialized that "German fascism once again revealed itself as the agent of finance capital." British intelligence did little better, misperceiving a triumph of the Reichswehr over the party and a "return of the Rapallo line" of closeness to the Soviet Union.[318] In fact, the episode solidified a Nazi accord with the army and large-scale industry on Hitler's terms, while clearing the way for him to merge the chancellorship with the presidency upon Hindenburg's passing. The SS would be even more radical, ideologically, than the SA.

If the hearsay about Stalin's enthusiastic reaction is correct, he was also wrong. This was the first (and would be the sole) violent regime purge of Hitler's rule. The Führer had agreed to dispatch Röhm only under pressure from Göring, Himmler, and Heydrich, yet he still hoped Röhm could be persuaded to do the deed himself. (The Brownshirt fighter did not touch the pistol left for him in his prison cell and had to be executed.)[319] For all the sensation, a mere eighty-five known people were summarily executed without legal proceedings, and just fifty of them even belonged to the SA. Some individual scores were settled.[320] What Stalin and British intelligence most failed to grasp was the consolidation of the Nazi regime's anti-Bolshevism.[321]

Stalin, however, was not ready to surrender on winning over Nazi Germany. On July 1, 1934, following the conclusion of the Central Committee plenum, Dimitrov sent him a draft of his political report for a proposed 7th Comintern Congress (scheduled for the fall). Dimitrov could defy Hitler, Göring, and Goebbels, but he remained inordinately deferential toward the Soviet dictator. Stalin, in turn, asked that Dimitrov "consider" his suggestions, and his marginal comments indicate that he was far from letting go of his thesis on Social Democracy as the left wing of fascism. Dimitrov's text asked "whether it is correct to refer to Social Democracy *indiscriminately* as social fascism," and "Are Social Democrats always and everywhere the main social bulwark of the bourgeoisie?" Stalin wrote in the margins, "As to the leadership—yes, but not 'indiscriminate.'" Beyond this tiny concession, where Dimitrov gently tried to rehabilitate some Social Democrats as a basis for cooperation in the struggle against fascism, Stalin pointedly inserted,

"Against whom is this thesis?"[322] On July 5, the politburo was informed that Germany, still suffering the effects of the Depression, had raised the prospect of a 200-million-mark credit for the purchase of German machinery.[323] Dimitrov, suffering from latent malaria, chronic gastritis, and other illnesses, departed for two months to Georgia on medical leave.

STRENGTHENING SOCIALIST LEGALITY

On July 10, 1934, after six months of internal back-and-forth, the regime announced the replacement of the OGPU by the NKVD (the people's commissariat of internal affairs).[324] Mężyński had appealed to Stalin yet again in early 1934 to be allowed to resign. ("No activities. Only lying down 24 hours a day," he had written in his notebook in Kislovodsk. "This is death. You lie all day in the hammock, and death sits across from you.")[325] Stalin proposed that Kaganovich confer with him and possibly accept his request. Then, on May 10, Mężyński's heart had stopped. Four days later, his ashes were interred in the Kremlin Wall, with an artillery salute.[326] Rumors had Stalin set to appoint Mikoyan, which frightened Yagoda's gang and brightened other Chekists who appreciated Mikoyan's sly humor and lectures at their club.[327] But Stalin named Yagoda commissar and Yankel Sorenson, known as Yakov Agranov, his first deputy.[328] The regime had just expanded Article 58 of the RSFSR criminal code (regarding counterrevolutionary activities) with new subarticles (2–13) to cover attempts to seize power, espionage, anti-Soviet propaganda and agitation, and Trotskyism.[329] As Stalin had proposed, military desertion was now punished as treason, with sentences of execution or, in extenuating circumstances, ten years in confinement.[330] Nonetheless, the formation of the NKVD was conceived as a genuine legal reform.[331] The politburo would soon decree a parallel expansion in the number of judges and procuracy personnel, with pay raises.[332] Kaganovich explained that "the reorganization of the OGPU means that, as we are in more normal times, we can punish through the court and not resort to extrajudicial repression, as we have until now."[333]

This new mandate had to be explained to police operatives.[334] "In capitalist countries, instead of the 'celebrated' bourgeois order, there is chaos, a sea of blood, extrajudicial executions, gas, machine guns and armored cars on the streets," Yagoda told them in a speech at the NKVD's founding. "If now, in the village, we do not have expansive kulak formations that we had previously, if in the city the counterrevolution does not have the character it had before, the question arises: What guises, what forms are possible for the activities of coun-terrevolutionary agents?" He answered that former parties (SRs, Mensheviks, bourgeois nationalists) could reanimate and link up with Communist opposition-ist elements (Trotskyites, rightists) for espionage and sabotage, requiring the NKVD to abjure mass arrests in favor of "subtle, painstaking, and probing inves-tigations."[335] Investigations had to be conducted with greater observance of proce-dural rules.[336] Ultimately, the reform was aimed at better coherence of the state, under the slogan "strengthening revolutionary legality."[337] But none of this meant imposing limits on Stalin's power, whose extralegal operation caused many of the very problems of arbitrariness about which he complained.[338]

ARTISTS AND THE STATE

Technically, the Union of Soviet Writers was a civic organization, but it was bla-tantly an arm of the state.[339] It was spending almost no time on aesthetics.[340] Its main activity, in the run-up to the anticipated founding congress, consisted of endless meetings of its governing board and manifold committees, and enter-tainment. The union's headquarters occupied a nineteenth-century mansion on Vorovsky (formerly Cooks') Street, in what had been Moscow's most aristocratic neighborhood, part of the ancient Dolgorukov estate. (This figured in Tolstoy's *War and Peace* as the Rostov estate.) Known as the "Central House of the Writ-ers," the HQ had a library with newspapers and journals, a restaurant, a compet-itive billiards team, sport groups for tennis, chess, and horseback riding, and study sections for thematic subjects and foreign languages. It also took over a fledgling dacha colony, at Peredelkino, which, like the Moscow HQ, would afford a certain degree of self-organized intellectual life (circles, house visits), although this was shadowed by willing and blackmailed informants.[341]

Two years after the politburo decree announcing it, the writers' union's found-ing congress had still not met, having been postponed several times. Gorky had been set to deliver the keynote, but on May 11, 1934, his son Maxim Peshkov passed away, at age thirty-eight. He had taken part in a drinking binge with some secret police operatives at a May Day picnic, been left to sleep it off outside on a bench, and been diagnosed with influenza. He was buried at Novodevichy Ceme-tery on May 12 (the day before Mężyński's body was placed on view at the House of Trade Unions). Gorky was shattered. "He no longer belonged to himself, and seemed that he was not a person but an institution," obliged to carry on, noted one close friend.[342] Gossips speculated that the regime had killed Gorky's son to intimidate him.[343] But as the congress's new opening date approached, Gorky would write a forceful letter to Stalin, asking to be relieved of his role as chairman, and would submit a heated article for *Pravda* lashing out at party hacks trying to control literature (which Kaganovich authorized Mekhlis to hold back). "Literary affairs are sharpening," Kaganovich would write to Stalin, who, preoccupied with other matters on which Kaganovich sought guidance (Japan, grain procurements), would answer, three days later, "It must be explained to all Communist writers that the Master in literature, as in all other areas, is only the Central Committee, and that they are obliged to subordinate themselves unconditionally to the latter."[344]

A Literary Fund was established on July 28, 1934, with the aim of subsidizing cultural figures in need, including up-and-coming writers, formalizing an ad hoc practice whereby they were granted shoes or winter coats. The money came from 10 percent deductions in the honoraria paid by publishing houses, as well as 0.5 to 2 percent of the fees for live performances. Additionally, the state budget contributed 25 percent of the Literary Fund's resources. Soon, about 100,000 requests for aid accumulated (many writers submitted multiple petitions).[345] Behind closed doors, writers disagreed vehemently on whether such subsidies enhanced productivity or blocked it by removing hunger.[346] The Literary Fund obtained permission to build more dachas at Peredelkino as well. Of the three dozen writers' families initially granted residency, few were Communist party members. Most writers failed to pay the nominal rent.[347]

WRITING HISTORY

On July 23, 1934, Stalin received the British writer H. G. Wells—who had interviewed Lenin—and they argued the world.[348] (Radek would send Stalin a translation of passages about the dictator in Wells's autobiography, published the same year, noting, "We didn't manage to seduce the girl.")[349] Stalin's last meeting in Moscow was July 29. Vlasik arranged for their special train to stop at Sochi's remote freight yard for security reasons, but Stalin—for all his security anxieties—detested having to hide and insisted on detraining at the regular passenger station. His black Rolls-Royce awaited him, but he enjoyed walking a bit on foot, startling onlookers.[350] That summer, he planned to work on a new history textbook. A few years back, in a letter to the journal *Proletarian Revolution*, he had exploded in fury at one historian's criticisms of Lenin for supposedly having insufficiently criticized the danger of centrism in German Social Democracy before the Great War. Stalin, right on the facts, had tendentiously exaggerated the author's argument, and called the article "anti-party and semi-Trotskyite." Stalin also rejected the author's claim that more documents remained to be uncovered. "Who besides hopeless bureaucrats would rely only on paper documents?" he wrote. "Who besides archival rats do not understand that the party and its leaders need to be assessed above all by their actions, and not only by their declarations?"[351]

Not long thereafter, the politburo had formed a commission to write a new history of the party. But even the textbook drafted by the lapdog Yaroslavsky had been rejected, for lacking vivid individual heroes.[352] Stalin had his minions force the issue.[353] Functionaries assembled a large group of historians. "We went into the hall like geese," Sergei Piontkovsky recorded in his diary. "In all, there were about 100 people in the room. . . . Stalin stood up frequently, puffed on his pipe, and wandered between the tables." He interrupted the main speaker and finally just took the floor. "Stalin spoke very quietly. He held the secondary school textbooks in his hand and spoke with a slight accent, striking the textbooks with his hand, proclaiming, 'These textbooks are good for nothing. What the heck is the "feudal epoch," "the epoch of industrial capitalism," "the epoch of formations"— it's all epochs and no facts, no events, no people, no concrete information, no names, no titles, no content.'" Piontkovsky's diary continued: "Stalin said what we need are textbooks with facts, events, names. History should be history."[354]

Of course, behind closed doors, Stalin was using just such a schematic vocabulary: *feudal epoch, capitalist mode of production, bourgeois democracy.*[355]

In Sochi, the dictator summoned Kirov, who arrived in early August and stayed at the Zenzinovka dacha (where Rykov used to stay). Writing history was not exactly Kirov's forte. But Stalin also summoned Zhdanov, the dictator's youngest favorite. Speaking to Alexandra Kollontai, Soviet envoy to Sweden, before departing Moscow, Stalin had playfully posed as a "right deviationist," contrasting himself with Zhdanov, a "left deviationist," a statement less about Stalin's politics than Zhdanov's extremism.[356] Vasily and Artyom were also in Sochi all July and August, and Stalin gave them the draft history to test it. Zhdanov's fifteen-year-old son, Yuri, invited to join the group for lunch, recalls that Stalin, to general laughter, observed that historians divided history into three successive schemata: matriarchate, patriarchate, and secretariat.[357]

After work, Stalin and Kirov grilled kebabs, sang old songs ("There's a Cliff on the Volga"), and worked the garden with shovels, while Kirov chased the ducks and guinea fowl. Stalin did not like to swim (he was from the mountains), but Kirov did, and Stalin would wait for him at the shore. Stalin even permitted Kirov to go with him to the Russian steam bath, where they pounded each other with birch leaves.[358] The dictator permitted no mistresses or prostitutes. Kirov got bored. "I am devilishly sick of this place," he wrote to his wife back in Leningrad, complaining that they could not even play skittles. "We had intense heat, then six days and nights of intense rain. . . . Now, again, tedious heat has struck."[359] Stalin could not be torn from his beloved Sochi, but Kirov was back in Leningrad already by August 30, 1934, having departed in a train with Andrei Andreyev's family. "He had a strong suntan," recalled Natalya Andreyeva, the functionary's daughter. "His teeth were white; he smiled often."[360]

Grain procurements were severely lagging, despite the comparatively good harvest, and Kaganovich and Molotov wrote to Stalin about easing the burden on transport by purchasing 100,000 tons of Argentine and Australian wheat for the Soviet Far East. "Wheat imports now, when abroad they are shouting about the lack of wheat in the USSR, can only be a political minus," he objected.[361] Instead he proposed they apply "maximum pressure." Molotov was deployed to Siberia, Kaganovich to Ukraine, Mikoyan to Kursk and Voronezh, Chubar to the Middle Volga, and Zhdanov to Stalingrad province. Voroshilov, on fall maneuvers, was instructed to look into harvest gathering in Belorussia and the western province.[362] Kirov was sent to Kazakhstan to ensure harvest collection under his former protégé, local party boss Levon Mirzoyan. Stalin was now taking a restrained approach to the Kazakhs. Kirov got the head procurator for East Kazakhstan fired for abuses and asked Yagoda to remove police operatives for mistreating collective farmers.[363] But when Kaganovich wrote to Stalin requesting a reduced procurement quota for Ukraine, Stalin warned him and the inner circle of a slippery slope.[364]

EXTRAVAGANZA

Finally, the founding congress of the Union of Soviet Writers had opened on August 17, 1934, with 597 delegates (377 with voting rights) and 40 foreign guests.[365] The union had admitted around 1,500 members and 1,000 candidate members, of whom 1,535 lived in the Russian republic, including slightly more than 500 in Moscow, 206 in Ukraine, around 100 in Belorussia, 90 in Armenia, 79 in

Azerbaijan, and 26 in Turkmenistan. About one third of the total membership and one half of the congress attendees belonged to the party.[366] "Literally all writers submitted applications to join the writers' union," the newly appointed deputy head of the Central Committee culture department stated at a pre-congress gathering of the union's party members. "Not a single writer did not submit an application, except Anna Akhmatova."[367] An exaggeration, but not by much. "On the threshold of its opening, the question unexpectedly arose of how to decorate the Columned Hall of the House of Trade Unions," recalled one playwright of the venue. "Several of the projects were completely fantastic and unacceptable. At the last meeting, which took place in [culture and propaganda chief Alexei] Stetsky's office, . . . I suggested we hang portraits of the classic writers. Stetsky stood, shook my hand, and said the question was decided."[368]

A grandiose affair, broadcast over the radio and shown on newsreels, the congress lasted sixteen days. Crowds massed outside the hall to catch glimpses of the famous writers. Inside, an ovation greeted Gorky's appearance to launch the proceedings. His report, "On Soviet Literature," offered a potted history of literature from the dawn of writing that did not take up a single Soviet writer and, vaguely, called for a "folklore of the toiling people."[369] Samuil Marshak gave a report on children's literature (August 19), Radek on the literature of dying capitalism (August 24), Aleksei Tolstoy on dramaturgy (August 27).[370] "Everyone is consumed by the congress; the West through government glasses," the literary critic Mikhail Kuzmin laconically wrote of the long speeches.[371] Zhdanov informed Sochi (August 28) that "everyone praises the congress right up to the incorrigible skeptics and ironists, who are not few in the writers' milieu."[372] By contrast, Chekists reported from informants that Mikhail Prishvin and Pantaleymon Romanov had ridiculed the "outstanding boredom and bureaucratism," while the romanticist P. Rozhkov called the congress "a sleepy kingdom." Isaac Babel labeled it "a literary wake."[373]

One revelation emerged from the report (August 20) on literature in the Georgian republic, delivered by the university rector Malakia Toroshelidze, who at Stalin's insistence began with the Middle Ages. It attracted the most attention of all the reports on national literatures in the USSR, and sparked discussion about ignored achievements, given the obsession with Europe.[374] The Frenchman Malraux, the most prestigious foreigner in attendance, in prepared remarks read by an interpreter, noted that "if writers are really engineers of human souls, do not forget that an engineer's highest calling is to invent. Art is not submission; art is conquest. (Applause.)" He added, "You should know that only really new works can sustain the cultural prestige of the Soviet Union abroad, the way Mayakovsky sustained it, the way Pasternak does. (Applause.)"[375] This was the nub of the dilemma Stalin faced.

When novelist Fyodor Gladkov invited Ivan Kirilenko (b. 1902), an infamous hard-liner, and other Ukrainian writers to "tea," they declined, fearing it would be seen as "a grouping."[376] An NKVD analysis of the delegates turned up several former SRs, anarchists, nationalists, and members of anti-Soviet "organizations." Someone distributed an unauthorized leaflet to the foreign delegates; nine copies were found, written in pencil, and the NKVD tried handwriting analysis to identify the anonymous author. "You organize various committees to aid the victims of fascism, you gather the antiwar congresses, you establish libraries of books burned by Hitler, all that is wonderful," the leaflet stated. "But why do we not see your activity in connection with aiding the victims of our Soviet fascism, carried out by Stalin. . . . Why do you not establish libraries to rescue Russian literature. . . . Personally we worry that in a year or two Iosif Jughashvili (Stalin), who did not finish seminary, will not be satisfied with the title of world philosopher and demand, on the example of Nebuchadnezzar, that he be considered, at least, a 'sacred cow.'"

Stalin, from Sochi, intervened with his whip hand so that the politburo decreed coverage by more than just *Evening Moscow* and *Literary Newspaper*.[377] "It is necessary for *Pravda* or *Izvestiya* to print the speeches of the representatives of Ukraine, Belorussia, the Tatar autonomous republic, Georgia, and other republics," he had written to Kaganovich and Zhdanov (August 21, 1934). "They need to be printed fully or at a minimum two thirds of each speech. The speeches of the nationals are no less important than others. Without their publication, the congress of writers would be colorless and uninteresting. If this requires that we supplement the number of newspaper pages, then it should be done, without regard for paper."[378] The dictator also expressed outrage at the party organizations of Buryat-Mongolia, Yakutia, the Volga Germans, and Bashkiria for not taking the gathering seriously. "The writers' congress is a very important matter, for it unites and strengthens the intelligentsia of the peoples of the USSR under the flag of the Soviets, under the flag of socialism. This is very important for us, very important for socialism. The above-named republics turned out to be in the tail of events, they turned out cut off from the living cause and disgraced themselves. We cannot overlook such a failure."[379]

The congress would cost 1.2 million rubles, significantly over budget, with breakfasts, lunches, and dinners amounting to about 40 rubles per day per attendee. The average cost of a canteen lunch for a worker was 84 kopecks, for a white-collar employee 1.75 rubles; lunch in a commercial restaurant cost 5.84 rubles.[380] (In 1934, worker salaries averaged 125 rubles per month, schoolteacher salaries around 100.)

Delegates could avail themselves of a tour of Moscow's Museum of Western Painting, an excursion to the planetarium, a trip to the cinema for *The Way of the Enthusiasts* or Dziga Vertov's *Three Songs About Lenin*. A Moscow theater was staging *The Miraculous Alloy,* Vladimir Kirshon's comedy of optimistic youth. Pasternak and his company tried Moscow's recently opened Georgian restaurant, Aragvi, where a meal cost a small fortune. The vast majority of delegates took part in Aviation Day festivies (August 18). Gorky hosted soirées at his dacha for foreign guests and intimates.[381] Delegates were also afforded a special showing of the documentary *Chelyuskin,* about 104 people on an Arctic research mission whose icebreaker of that name had sunk, stranding them on an ice floe for months, until their rescue (on the twenty-eighth landing) by daring Soviet aviators, who were then given a ticker tape parade in Moscow.[382] Stalin had gone to greet the returning *Chelyuskin* expedition scientists and sailors at Moscow's Belorussia train station. Soviet radio had focused world attention on the expedition's plight, but the dictator evidently had declined an American offer of assistance.[383]

FAIRY TALE

Zhdanov, in his speech at the congress, had called for literary depictions of "reality in its revolutionary development," geared toward "the ideological remolding and education of the toilers in the spirit of socialism." He demanded "a combination of the most austere, sober, practical work, with supreme heroism and the most grandiose prospects."[384] Some speakers urged multiple ways to achieve this. "We should tell our artists, 'Everything is permitted,'" urged the thirty-four-year-old screenwriter Natan Zarkhi. "Everything that serves the defense of the motherland, its strengthening, the victory of Communism, Bolshevik ideas, everything that leads to the development of Soviet culture and the flourishing of the creative individuality of the people, growing not in spite of the collective but because of it."[385]

Socialist realism's precise forms, in other words, remained to be adjudicated even just in literature.[386] Any definition for music was deferred without end. Musicians effectively lost the ability to experiment at the composition level but could pursue refinement of instrumental and vocal techniques. Many "class enemies" (sons of former tsarist generals, nephews of tsarist interior ministers, daughters of former nobles, former ladies-in-waiting) were allowed to remain at positions in music and conduct training, a tolerance perhaps reflecting Stalin's intense interest in quality traditional music.[387] Painting had its own specificities. Standard realism had already triumphed by the 1920s, but many painters had little experience in narrative forms and had trouble finding a place in the new order.[388] Stalin, who in the underground days had collected postcards of famous paintings, in power chose not to live surrounded by oil paintings on the walls. (On the contrary, he had allowed the sale abroad of "bourgeois" artworks accumulated in tsarist Russia, altogether some four thousand paintings, including forty-four of the highest order—Rembrandt, Rubens, Raphael, Titian, van Eyck—until meager receipts and international scandal prompted an end to the fire sales.)[389, 390]

Pasternak had harbored illusions about the likely philosophical level of the congress. "I am murderously downtrodden," he was said to have repeated in intimate company. "You understand: murderously."[391] Many writers who disagreed vehemently about aesthetics agreed on the need for top-down imposition of a single approach for everyone. They were also zealous about getting state recognition, as opposed to public favor, and not a few lobbied for or welcomed repressive measures against rivals. Socialist realism served as an administration system as much as an aesthetic: party directives, censorship, prizes, apartments, dachas, travel—or their denial—as well as myriad personnel employed as cultural apparatchiks, editors, and censors, what Bulgakov called "people with ideological eyes."[392]

On August 29, 1934, with the congress set to draw to a close in three days and "elections" imminent for the position of writers' union secretary (or party controller), Zhdanov and Kaganovich wrote to Sochi proposing candidates.[393] Stalin narrowed their list to two, and they selected the bespectacled Alexander Shcherbakov (b. 1901), whose education at the Communist Academy and the Institute of Red Professors had been interrupted (on official documents he wrote: "according to my education, a teacher of the history of the party").[394] Summoned out of the blue by Kaganovich, Shcherbakov arrived to find Zhdanov with him. "Here's the thing," they told him. "We want to assign you work that is extremely important and difficult; you probably will be stunned when I tell you what kind of work it is." He was contemplating northeastern Kazakhstan. "I was genuinely stunned," Shcherbakov recorded in his diary. They dispatched him directly from Old Square to the writers' milieu. "I spent a half hour at the congress. I left. Nauseating."[395]

Aleksei Tolstoy, author of science fiction, historical novels, and children's books, would call Shcherbakov "a rabbit who swallowed a boa constrictor."[396] Tolstoy (b. 1883), a distant relative of Leo Tolstoy and Ivan Turgenev, embodied many of the paradoxes Stalin faced with writers. He had emigrated to Paris with the Whites but returned in 1923 to a hero's welcome, supporting the revolution. He took up residence in a villa with servants in Tsarskoye Selo, where Nicholas and Alexandra had lived, earning the nickname "the workers-and-peasants' count." (Stalin first met him in 1932 at Gorky's.) After the success of the first two installments of Tolstoy's novel *Peter the First* (1934), which celebrated the founding of the Russian empire and compared Peter to Stalin, he was told to relocate to Moscow, where he got a state apartment and a dacha in elite Barvikha. ("He collected mahogany and birch pieces made during Paul I's reign" to furnish his residences, one Soviet musician wrote.)[397] The count wore a fur-lined coat with beaver collar, caroused in Moscow's restaurants with a rat pack, married his young secretary (his fourth wife), and enjoyed permission to travel to Europe at state expense. "The great trait of the personality of Aleksei Tolstoy," the contemporary literary historian Dmitry Svyatopolk-Mirsky observed, "was the astonishing combination of enormous natural gifts with a complete lack of brains."[398] But he toed the line.

Writing to Zhdanov from Sochi, Stalin, based on newspaper accounts, deemed Gorky's congress speech "a bit pale from the point of view of *Soviet* literature," and complained that Bukharin's speech had introduced "an element of hysteria," but concluded that "in general the congress went well."[399] The congress concluded on September 1, 1934, by "electing" thirty-seven preapproved members of the union's governing body chaired by Gorky, which that same day "elected" Shcherbakov as head of its secretariat.[400] The NKVD secretly reported that the writers were busying themselves with personal matters: purchase of cars, construction of dachas, departures on writing trips or holidays, some doing so even before the final day of the congress. "What is striking, above all," the operative noted, "is that after the congress the writers talk very little about it. It is as if everyone conspired to keep silent."[401] In fact, the writers expended considerable energy parsing the power of this or that person on the governing board, who was up, who down, what it would mean for their careers and the course of literature. Many viewed Gorky as a guarantee of literary values, and a balance of power among egos and tendencies.

. . .

TSARIST CENSORS HAD SUPPRESSED parts of the work of the bravura satirist Mikhail Saltykov-Shchedrin, and in the early 1930s, Leningrad writers had issued *Unpublished Shchedrin,* a compilation Stalin acquired and assiduously marked up in red and blue pencil, indicating multiple readings of its vivid passages about bureaucrats, scoundrels, debauches. "Write your denunciations, wretches," Stalin underlined. "Grief goes to that city whose boss showers it with decrees without thinking, but still greater grief occurs when the boss is unable to apply any decrees at all."[402] In a gesture calculated to win intelligentsia favor, he allocated state funds to the son of Saltykov-Shchedrin, and the OGPU compiled a report on conversations among Leningrad writers about it. The critic V. Medvedev was quoted to the effect that Stalin was "a most decisive and severe politician," but also "a great liberal and patron in the best sense of that word. Every day we hear about a conversation between Stalin and some writers, or about some assistance rendered at his initiative to one of the mass of writers. In Stalin, literature and writers have a great friend."[403] That was precisely how the dictator wanted to be seen.

Stalin's success in getting the creative intelligentsia in line had been uncanny. Every major cultural figure in the USSR in the 1930s had his or her own love affair with him. They exaggerated their own significance, and the attention he paid to them. The best ones, however, were correct: he did oversee them personally. Stalin tended not to imprison or execute those he considered the highest talents (Bulgakov, Akhmatova, Pasternak, even Andrei Platonov), and would accept a lightening of the sentences of those on whom punishment seemed unavoidable, such as with Mandelstam's exile. Many cultural figures were lied to and coerced to conjure up a socialist paradise of joy and plenty.[404] But blandishments and the prospect of a mass audience proved effective in recruitment as well. The prestigious names, like Tolstoy, who were neither Communist nor anti-Communist but cynics, were precisely whom Stalin had in mind when he insisted that art could best be categorized as loyal (or disloyal), that is, as Soviet (or anti-Soviet). The problem, however, was artistic quality. Blast furnaces and even collective farms turned out to be a lot easier than novels, poems, or plays, let alone symphonies or canvases.[405] That said, much of the mass Soviet public—who wanted to believe in a brighter future—embraced socialist realism.[406] As the opening line had it in a hit song, "Everything Higher: Aviation March," by Pavel German and Ilya "Yuli" Khait, which would prove popular only in the 1930s: "We were born to turn fairy tale into reality."

Yenukidze sent Stalin a long, upbeat account of Moscow affairs (September 5, 1934), beginning with the writers' congress, which he predicted would have "gigantic consequences for the writers of all our republics and not less for the foreign proletarian and in general advanced writers." He congratulated Stalin on his wisdom for having the speeches published and his advice to Toroshelidze concerning the report on Georgian literature, which Yenukidze, a fellow Georgian writing to Stalin in Russian, singled out for special praise. He touched on the removal of the ancient Kitaigorod walls in front of Old Square, where Stalin had kept his party office, and on reconstruction work inside the Kremlin, where Stalin had his now predominant office. Yenukidze was having the Kremlin walls repainted, the roofs fixed, and interior lawns replaced. He lauded construction of the metro, the liveliness of Moscow streets, the opening of the theater season, and the good weather, lamenting only the pending departure of his close friend Voroshilov for a holiday in Sochi. "The children arrived fine," Yenukidze concluded in reference to Vasily and Svetlana. "I saw them three times. They are going to school. I'm ending, otherwise you will curse me for these prolix trivialities. Be healthy."[407]

CHAPTER 4

TERRORISM

Yesterday I was at the NKVD. . . . I understood that, in
order to demonstrate my loyalty, I need to work harder for
the NKVD. He said that if I work well, everything will
remain a secret, but otherwise I could be deported from
Moscow. I was given three main tasks in my work . . . the
October Revolution celebrations and conversations. Is an
assassination attempt against Stalin not being
prepared . . . By the way, in front of him lay a file two
fingers high all about me.

Informant's notes, November 1934[1]

STALIN'S UNDERSTANDING OF WORLD markets remained amateurish, but he
had a keen appreciation for technology. As of 1934, the Soviets possessed 3,500
tanks (T-26s, BTs, T-28s), as well as another 4,000 armored vehicles (T-27s). Fighter
planes of Soviet make and mobile artillery were also coming off assembly lines in
numbers. Even radios were beginning to spread widely in the armed forces (in
1930, there had been zero among the field units). Overall troop strength had
grown from 586,000 in 1927 to nearly a million. The command staff was more
educated, having completed courses at the many military academies.[2] From August 30 to September 4, 1934, the Red Army conducted its annual fall maneuvers
in Ukraine, which the Polish consul in Kiev interpreted as "a demonstration
against foreign countries, particularly Japan." The exercises went badly, though.
Mechanization presented underappreciated organizational and logistical challenges, raising the stakes for Soviet diplomacy.[3]

Much of Stalin's holiday back-and-forth with Moscow, from Gagra and Sochi,
in September 1934 concerned his customary pressure on the harvest collection
but also foreign affairs.[4] Over the summer, Czechoslovakia, Latvia, Estonia, and
Lithuania had conveyed their readiness to sign on to the Franco-Soviet proposal
for a broad Eastern Pact, but Estonia and Latvia made their membership conditional on Germany's and Poland's. So did Britain, which also made its support for

a parallel Franco-Soviet alliance conditional on Germany's inclusion in that.[5] On September 11, 1934, Hitler definitively rejected any Eastern Pact. Poland's rejection would soon follow. Stalin was urged to grasp the French option without Germany, embracing an antifascist coalition.[6] Negotiations for the large state credit from the German government, initiated at Berlin's request, had bogged down. But Stalin reassured Kuibyshev (September 14), in a telegram, which, as usual, became a politburo decree, that "the Germans will not walk away from us, because they need a [trade] agreement with us more than we need one from them."[7] Nonetheless, on September 18, the Soviet Union formally joined the League of Nations, after intensive diplomacy to line up other countries' votes.[8] Many Communist party and Youth League members cringed at joining the Versailles imperialist order.[9] Stalin himself had once denounced the League as "an anti-working-class comedy."[10]

Soviet newspapers explained that some imperialist powers, although ill-disposed toward socialism, did not want to see an anti-Soviet military intervention, for fear it would spark a world war directed at themselves.[11] Joining the League was also a prerequisite to alliance with France or a broader regional security structure. Nonetheless, at Stalin's urging, the politburo resolved (September 23), "Do not hurry with the initiative of an [Eastern] Pact without Germany and Poland." France slowed for its own reasons.[12] It was courting Mussolini in a common front to guarantee Austria's sovereignty against Nazi pressure, part of which involved France's help in normalizing Italo-Yugoslav relations. On October 9, Yugoslavia's King Alexander I landed on a state visit at the Marseilles harbor, where he was promptly assassinated. French foreign minister Louis Barthou was killed in the police cross fire. The assassin, beaten to death on the spot, was Macedonian and a member of the Croatian terrorist ring, the Ustaše, led by Ante Pavelić and protected by Mussolini.[13] Soviet intelligence suspected the Nazi secret police of aiming to destabilize Yugoslavia and to liquidate a bulwark of friendly Franco-Soviet relations. Stalin wrote to Kaganovich and Molotov, "In my opinion, the murder of Barthou and Alexander is the work of the hand of German-Polish intelligence."[14]

Inside the Comintern, Dimitrov, supported by Manuilsky, Kuusinen, Thorez, and Wilhelm Pieck, continued pushing for a shift to a popular front, while Pyatnitsky, Knorin, Kun, and others held to the anti–Social Democrat line. Dimitrov implored Stalin for assistance in changing the structure and personnel of the Comintern's "leading organs." Eventually Stalin got around to sending a handwritten note. "As you can see, I am late in replying, and I apologize for that," he wrote. "Here on holiday, I do not sit in one place, but move from one location to another. . . . I entirely agree with you regarding the review of the methods of work of the Comintern organs, their reorganization and the changes in their composition. I have already mentioned this to you during our meeting at the Central Committee. . . . I hope to see you soon and to discuss all in detail. I have no doubt that the politburo will support you. Greetings!"[15] The planned 7th Comintern Congress was postponed yet again.[16]

The zigs and zags were seen domestically, too. A group at the Stalin metallurgical factory in Novokuznetsk, Siberia, had been arrested, and Stalin instructed Kaganovich that "all those drawn into spying on behalf of Japan be shot." Local party head Eihe was empowered to approve executions on his own from September through November.[17] The same power was soon granted to party bosses in Chelyabinsk and in Central Asia, in connection with alleged sabotage of the cotton campaign.[18] At the same time, petitions reached Stalin from people in the Gulag convicted in fabricated cases of wrecking and espionage on behalf of Japan, and the dictator (September 11, 1934) redirected the claims of confessions extracted under torture to Kuibyshev and Zhdanov, noting that "it is possible the content of both documents corresponds to reality," and called for a commission to "cleanse the ranks of the secret police of bearers of certain 'interrogation devices' and punish the latter regardless of who it might be." The commission upheld the two petitions and brought additional cases, detailing, in an October 1934 report, how NKVD operatives were detaining those accused in freezing cells for days on end, holding them in suffocating positions, and threatening to shoot them until they "confessed." Stalin approved a suggestion to send plenipotentiaries to Azerbaijan for a "thorough investigation" of efforts to advance careers through sheer quantity of confessions extracted.[19]

A need for recovery and reconciliation following the famine had been evident, and in that regard the conciliatory "Congress of Victors" had been a success. But now a vague sense of a bigger shift—League of Nations membership, a less hectic second Five-Year Plan, a stress on legality—gained momentum. To be sure, reconciliation hardly suited Stalin's character or his theory of rule: the sharpening of the class struggle as socialism became successful; the special danger of enemies with party cards.[20] Nonetheless, secret police arrests started declining precipitously.[21] A relative relaxation was visible in culture as well, even beyond Stalin's indulgence of non-party writers. "Not long ago a music critic, seeing in his dream a saxophone or [Leonid] Utyosov, would have awoken in a cold sweat and run to *Soviet Art* to confess his errors," wrote the militant *Komsomol Pravda* (October 27,

1934) about the Soviet Union's newly famous jazz band. "Now? Now there is no refuge from 'My Masha.' Wherever you go, she sits 'At the Samovar.'"[22]

Stalin finally returned to Moscow on October 29, 1934.[23] While he was away, 1,038 of that year's 3,945 politburo agenda items had been decided, most with his approval; sixteen of the year's forty-six politburo meetings had taken place in his absence.[24] Litvinov again wrote to Stalin and Molotov (November 1) insisting that Germany's rebuilt military power would assuredly be used against the USSR, with the support of Poland, Finland, and Japan. The next day, Stalin relented: the politburo authorized negotiations for an Eastern Pact with just France and Czechoslovakia, or even France alone, an apparent concession to "collective security."[25] Stalin remained attentive to his own security as well. Inside his suite at Old Square, in his wing in the Kremlin's Imperial Senate, and at his Moscow and southern dachas, only NKVD personnel were permitted to carry weapons. Those whom Stalin received were supposed to check any weapons they had upon entering the premises. (Some were searched.)[26] Propaganda notwithstanding, the prospect of an assassination—akin to what had happened to the Yugoslav king in Marseilles—seemed utterly remote.

KIROV AND *CHAPAYEV*

Stalin's return from southern holidays was still being marked by informal gatherings initiated by members of his extended family, who showed up at his apartment in the Imperial Senate at suppertime and played with the children, waiting, hoping to catch him. "Yesterday, after a three-month interval, I saw Iosif," Maria Svanidze, his first wife's sister-in-law, wrote in her diary (November 4, 1934). "He looked well, tanned, but he had lost weight. He suffered from flu there. . . . I[osif] joked with Zhenya, that she had again filled out, and he was very tender with her," Svanidze added. "Now, when I know everything, I observed them." Yevgeniya "Zhenya" Alliluyeva, an actress, was married to Pavel Alliluyev (the brother of Stalin's second wife, Nadya), and a jealous Svanidze suspected an affair. Stalin had deeper interests. "After the meal Iosif was in a very good-natured mood," she continued. "He took the Intercity *vertushka* and called Kirov, joking with him about the end of rationing and the price rise for bread. He advised Kirov to come to Moscow immediately, in order to defend the interests of Leningrad province against an even higher price rise than in other provinces. Evidently Kirov demurred, and Iosif gave the phone to Kaganovich, who urged Kirov to come for a day. Iosif loves Kirov and after returning from Sochi really wanted to see him, steam in a Russian bath together."[27]

The revolution's seventeenth anniversary approached. At the Bolshoi on the evening before the November 7 parade, the ballerina Marina Semyonova (b. 1908) performed a Caucasus dance. "She danced in a light gray Circassian vest and light gray Astrakhan 'Kubanka,' and when, with the last gesture, she held back her Kubanka on her head, her blond hair sprayed down her shoulders," Artyom recalled. "This made a colossal impression on the audience; everyone shouted 'Bravo, encore.'" Semyonova went to curtsy at the left loge, where Stalin sat, over the orchestra, practically on the stage. He bent down to the ballerina and said something. "She nodded, gave the orchestra a signal, and repeated the dance." After the concert, Stalin said to his entourage, "Semyonova is the best of all."[28] She was the common-law wife of Karakhan, the former first deputy foreign affairs commissar, demoted by Stalin to ambassador to Turkey; rumors spread of her affair with Stalin.[29]

Stalin's bachelor life was not all rumors. Kirov did come, after the November holiday. In the evenings, now that Nadya was gone, Stalin had taken to watching films with his entourage.[30] On November 10 (and into the morning of the 11th), Boris Shumyatsky, head of the motion picture industry, screened the new film *Chapayev* for the dictator, Kirov, and Molotov.[31] Shumyatsky had been born in Ulan Ude (1886) near Lake Baikal, was a former Soviet envoy to Iran and former rector of the Communist University of the Toilers of the East, and had replaced Martemyan Ryutin as head of the film industry back when it was considered a backwater, but had built it up. At the Kremlin cinema soft chairs with ample armrests and high backs, concealing who was in them, were placed three across, in several rows. The floor was covered in a drab gray cloth, over which was placed a runner, muffling noise from movement. Stalin issued comments during the screenings, in the dark, and afterward when the lights were back on. Tables for Georgian mineral water and wines sat alongside each chair.[32] "We used to go after dinner, about nine in the evening," Svetlana recalled. "It was late for me, of course, but I begged so hard that my father couldn't refuse. He'd push me to the front with a laugh: 'You show us how to get there, House Mistress. Without you to guide us, we'd never find it!'" Stalin often watched more than one film, and Svetlana would go to bed sometimes after midnight, even on school nights. "I'd get out of the movie late and go racing home through the empty, quiet Kremlin. The next day at school, I could think of nothing but the heroes I'd seen on film the night before."[33]

Chapayev portrayed the civil war hero of that name as a real human being, warts and all, and the Whites as worthy foes. Stalin had already seen it twice and fallen in love with its down-home details. "You should be congratulated," he had said to the always anxious Shumyatsky. "It's done very well, cleverly and tactfully. Chapayev, Furmanov, and Petka are good. The film will have great educational significance. It's a nice gift for the holiday." *Chapayev* induced Stalin to push for construction of sound cinemas all across the Union (there were just 400 to 500 of them, out of some 30,000 film-showing installations).[34] "I will be taking a greater interest in this than previously," he had told Shumyatsky on November 9–10.[35] At the November 10–11 screening, Stalin turned to Kirov and accused him of never visiting the film studio in Leningrad (*Chapayev* was their production). "You know, here people are speaking about your Leningrad films, and you don't even know them. You don't know the riches lurking there, probably you never even watch films." Kirov, Stalin joked, had "bureaucratized."[36]

Stalin invited Shumyatsky to stay for supper. The film boss seized the moment to point out that the state planning commission was being tight with funding, allocating 50 million rubles for the next year instead of the "minimal" 92 million requested. "You hear that, Molotov? That's not the way," Stalin said. "Look into it." Shumyatsky also mentioned that initial reviews of *Chapayev* were favorable but had stressed the wrong themes.[37] "Akh, those critics," Stalin responded. "They disorient people." The dictator phoned Mekhlis and ordered something more glowing, which *Pravda* published the next day (November 12). Stalin—now also joined by Kalinin and Molotov's wife, Zhemchuzhina—decided to view *Chapayev* for a second time that night. "The more you watch it," he said, "the better it seems, the more you find new aspects in it." The evening lasted until 2:00 a.m.[38] On November 13, after work, Kirov accompanied Stalin to the Zubalovo dacha, where they played billiards and watched a puppet show put on by Svetlana and other children, before repairing to Stalin's new Near Dacha for supper. At Zubalovo, the Stalin family dined on the smelt and whitefish Kirov had brought. "With Kirov," Svanidze noted, Svetlana "has a great friendship, because I[osif] is especially close and good with him."[39]

UNDER THE GUN

Filipp Medved's nerves were on edge. An ethnic Belorussian (b. 1889), he had joined the party in 1907 (one of his recommenders was Felix Dzierżyński) and had recently helped organize the White Sea–Baltic Canal construction. Now he headed the secret police in Leningrad, an international port and frontier city swimming with foreign consulates and military factories. Known to relish banquets, Medved had put on weight and taken to drink (Armenian brandy), while his wife, Raisa Kopylovskaya, came on to other men in public. (Rumors had Medved imprisoning the Leningrad *torgsin* shop manager after Raisa flirted with him; she might have been involved in self-enrichment schemes, too.) Whisperings about Medved's supposed homosexuality (he had kissed the openly gay jazzman Utyosov on the mouth in public) further undermined his authority.[40] His first deputy, Ivan Zaporozhets, was widely seen as Yagoda's "spy."[41] And those were the least of Medved's worries.

Stalin had no confidence in him. The dictator continued to be frustrated over a perceived NKVD mishmash of promiscuous arrests and indolence against enemies.[42] Yagoda ("in accordance with your instructions") had sent a team of operatives to investigate the Leningrad and Siberian NKVD branches. "The facts that were uncovered," he had reported to Stalin (September 1934), "convinced me that [Nikolai] Alekseyev (Western Siberian NKVD) and Medved are absolutely incapable of leading our work in the new conditions and providing that sharp turnabout in state security management methods now necessary." Yagoda proposed sacking the two branch chiefs, to set examples, and recommended a chessboard of transfers, which would bring Henriks Štubis (b. 1894), an ethnic Latvian known as Leonid Zakovsky ("unquestionably a strong and capable operative"), from Belorussia to Leningrad, with Medved recalled to Moscow to determine "if he is still fit for work in the NKVD or utterly burned out."[43]

This was the second time Medved's transfer had been bruited; the first, in 1931, Kirov had blocked. The Leningrad party boss socialized with him (the childless Kirov was especially fond of Medved's boy Misha).[44] Kirov was also an infamous womanizer, whose carousing was a matter of citywide gossip. Kirov's wife, Maria Markus (b. early 1880s), was Jewish (like the wives of Molotov, Voroshilov, Andreyev, Kuibyshev, and Poskryobyshev). They had met in Vladikavkaz in 1909, at the offices of the newspaper *Terek*, where she worked as a bookkeeper. She suffered from headaches, insomnia, and a hormonal disorder, frequently screamed, and threatened to kill herself; her windows had been barred. She'd had a few small strokes and was effectively confined to a state rest home in suburban Tolmachevo.[45] To what extent she knew of her husband's extramarital affairs— ballerinas, young women in the apparatus—remains unclear, but they were certainly Medved's worry: he had to help conceal them, even as he was under severe pressure from Pauker in Moscow to strengthen Kirov's protection.[46] Kirov's personal guard had ballooned from three to as many as fifteen men after Stalin's visit to Leningrad in summer 1933, and Kirov's office had been relocated to a less accessible location.[47]

MONGOLS AND KIROV

On November 15, 1934, Stalin received a delegation led by Mongolian prime minister Genden, the latter's third annual audience with Stalin, an unusual number for any foreign leader, but impoverished, landlocked Mongolia was the Soviet Union's sole "ally." As a result of purges and mass quitting, the Mongolian People's Party, already severely outnumbered by lamas, had dropped to half its peak strength of 40,000.[48] Stalin, over the course of three hours, pressed Genden on the lamas: How numerous and powerful were the monks? Did the people follow them or the Communists? How did the monks finance their activities? These issues, Genden tried to answer, were "complex," "subtle." "In a war in which you cannot defeat the enemy by a frontal assault, you should use roundabout maneuvering," Stalin advised. "Your first action should be to put your own teachers in the schools to battle the monks for influence among the youth. Teachers and activists must be the direct conduits of your policy. . . . The government must build more water wells to show the people that they, not the monks, are more concerned about their economic needs." He also advised producing films and promoting theater in the Mongolian language and building a strong army of functionally and politically literate conscripts.

Stalin divulged his theory of rule. "In connection with the big lamas who commit this or that political crime, you need to punish them, bringing them to court for treason against the motherland, and not for general indictment of counterrevolutionary work," he explained. "In such cases, you need open trials so that the commoners, the *arats,* understand that the lamas are linked to foreign enemies; they betrayed the motherland. But you can do this only from time to time at this point." He added: "Foreign powers will not recognize you as long as it is unclear who is stronger, you or the monks. After you strengthen your government and army and raise the economic and cultural level of your people, the imperialist powers will acknowledge you. If they do not, now being strong, you can spit in their faces."[49]

This was how Stalin was ruling the Soviet Union.

Genden, the offspring of a poor nomad family who had learned to read and write, was a gifted politician with a feel for the masses, and full of guile. Trying to ingratiate himself, he announced that the illiterate Choibalsan (b. 1895), minister of livestock and agriculture, who had spent considerable time in Moscow being groomed by Voroshilov, would become first deputy prime minister. Choibalsan was already serving as a Soviet agent in the Mongolian leadership.[50]

Agranov forwarded to Stalin a decrypted intercept of a telegram (November 17, 1934) from ambassador Joseph Grew, in Tokyo, to the U.S. State Department, concerning a conversation with Japanese foreign minister Kōki Hirota, who had stated that, given the various agreements among European powers, Japan could not remain isolated and would have to follow suit. "A decision was taken such that the foreign ministry would search for an ally," Hirota was quoted as saying of the cabinet. "The chosen country should above all have no specific interests in Asia. In this category could be included Russia or England." Stalin underlined that passage. "But the USSR is completely excluded as a potential ally because of its aggressive position toward Japan and its interests." By contrast, Hirota thought a deal could be reached with Britain over weapons sales and trade, provided Japanese interests were recognized in China. The United States was also on Hirota's potential ally list, and he concluded what Grew deemed an "unusual conversation" with a desire for friendly relations. Stalin wrote on the document, "And so it happens, it's become tough for Hirota. Interesting."[51]

On November 27, Stalin received the Mongols again, this time with Kirov in tow, even though he was not a member of the politburo's Mongolia commission. Stalin began by noting that he was forgiving all of Mongolia's debt as of January 1, 1934—30 million tugriks, the equivalent of almost 10 million gold rubles (at the official exchange rate)—and half the debt accumulated in the coming year: another 33 million tugriks, with the other half to be paid starting in 1941. "If you do not have a good army, the imperialists, Japan, will swallow you," he said, pointing out that the Mongolian army numbered only 10,000. He said their army budget was 14 million tugriks but offered to pay 6 million a year for five years for expansion, and advised the Mongols to pay their portion with state monopolies on tobacco, salt, and matches, alongside alcohol. He also informed them that they needed to sign bilateral pacts of nonaggression and of mutual assistance, but that the second, for now, would not be published, a message for Japan, but not an overly provocative one.[52] The nonpublic pact would allow the Red Army to defend the USSR by reassuming advance positions on Mongolian territory. "There should be a difference between Soviet assistance in wartime and in peacetime,"

Demid, a graduate of the prestigious Officers' Cavalry School in Tver, urged.[53] Resistance proved futile, however.[54] Soon, some 2,000 Red Army troops would reenter Mongolia.

Kirov had returned to Moscow because of a Central Committee plenum, the third and final of the year, from November 25 to 28, 1934. It dealt with the end of bread rationing, which involved some 50 million people, a costly subsidy and administrative expense amid financial challenges. Rye bread, which cost 50 kopecks per kilo in a state store with a ration coupon (and 1 ruble 50 kopecks at commercial shops), would now cost 1 ruble, a significant increase for workers.[55] "What is the idea of the policy of abolition of the rationing system?" Stalin remarked at the plenum. "The cash economy is one of the few bourgeois economic mechanisms that we socialists must make full use of. . . . It is very flexible, and we need it."[56] Kirov said little, as usual. Afterward, Stalin took a small group, including Kirov, to the Kremlin cinema, where Shumyatsky showed *Chapayev,* which Stalin said he was seeing for the eleventh time. Orjonikidze, meanwhile, was suffering from heart palpitations and stomach pains. He had been the only member of the inner circle left out of that fall's harvest mobilization, and had had his holiday extended. Stalin had compelled him to stay away from the capital until November 29. By the time Orjonikidze returned to Moscow, his friend Kirov had left.[57] Stalin saw Kirov off at the station.[58]

A TERRORIST

Leonid Nikolayev (b. 1904) was a misfit. He had been born in Leningrad, the son of an alcoholic (who died when the boy was three or four), suffered from rickets as a toddler, and developed bowed legs. He left school around age twelve, when his mother, a night cleaning woman at a tram depot, apprenticed him to a watch repairman. But 1917 had revolutionized Nikolayev's fortunes: he served as a village soviet chairman in 1919–20, while barely a teenager; became a candidate and, within a month, a full member of the party in 1924 (during the "levy" following Lenin's death); and got appointed as a Communist Youth League functionary in Zinoviev's Leningrad machine.[59] Nikolayev was sent to the nearby town of Luga, where he met and, in 1925, married Milda Draule (b. 1901), an ethnic Latvian and gymnasium graduate, petite, round-faced, with brown hair, who worked as a bookkeeper in the county party apparatus and was a zealot, too. She and Leonid moved in with his mother, grandmother, unmarried sister, married sister, and brother-in-law in Leningrad, and in 1927 the couple had their first child, whom they named Karl Marx ("Marx" for short). Milda quit working for a time. The Five-Year Plan had opened further horizons for working-class offspring such as Nikolayev, but matters went sour. He had a quarrelsome nature. In 1929, he was fired from his latest job (as a clerk at the Red Arsenal Factory), and then from another factory, and in spring 1930 he was mobilized by the party to Eastern Siberia for the sowing and harvest campaigns.

Milda got hired as a bookkeeper in the Leningrad provincial party apparatus, now under Kirov, and was soon promoted to the department for light industry personnel. Nikolayev returned from Siberia in 1931, and in April he got a position as an assessor in the provincial party apparatus. In November 1931, the couple had a second child, Leonid. They were able to obtain a three-room apartment in a fee-based cooperative. Her elderly, infirm parents lived with them.[60] But in the meantime he had been shifted to the Youth League's Down with Illiteracy Society, his thirteenth place of work (as recorded in his official labor book).[61] Acquaintances got him a post in the workers' and peasants' inspectorate, but he was fired in October 1932. Draule had lost her provincial party sinecure, being transferred in August 1933 to the provincial heavy-industry bookkeeping squad, at first as a temporary worker, though she obtained regular status in January 1934 and was awarded prizes. Nikolayev signed on as an itinerant lecturer for the Institute of Party History, in the provincial party organization, but on March 31, 1934, he was summoned before a party commission for refusing "mobilization" to transport (to give lectures to railroad workers). A party meeting deemed him "rude, extremely unrestrained, hysterical." After he spoke, one of the members asked, "Is Nikolayev's psychological condition normal?"[62]

Nikolayev was expelled from the party and fired, losing his ration coupons. On appeal, his expulsion was reversed in May 1934, and replaced by a severe reprimand—still a black mark in his file. Out of work, angry at perceived party slights, and reduced to living off his wife's earnings, he petitioned like a demon to overturn his reprimand and secure what he regarded as suitable employment for a working-class Communist—as an apparatchik. In July 1934, he wrote to Kirov, and on August 25 to Stalin, only to have his letters rerouted to the perceived source of his troubles: the Leningrad party machine.[63] On October 9, with his family facing eviction from their cooperative apartment, a despairing Nikolayev wrote to the politburo, "I request that I be given in the first instance, in the shortest possible time, treatment at a sanatorium-resort, but if such a possibility does not exist, then I must give up belief and hope in a rescue." This letter, too, was rerouted to the Leningrad party.[64] Nikolayev began stalking Kirov. On October 15, he trailed him on the long walk from the Uritsky (Tauride) Palace to the Trinity Bridge and on toward his residence, in the elite building at Red Dawn Street, 26–28. (Chekhov had lived there before the revolution.) The guard detained Nikolayev and took him to NKVD headquarters ("the House of Tears," as he called it).

Nikolayev's torn attaché case was found to contain newspapers and books. He had a party card and his old pass from when he had worked at party HQ. "He was a member of the party, had earlier worked in Smolny, and (only) tried to approach Kirov with a request for help in getting a job," surmised the responsible operative Alexander Gubin, who, after a subordinate's oral report, ordered Nikolayev's release.[65] Like many civil war veterans, Nikolayev owned a Nagant revolver—1895 model, 1912 issue—which he had obtained in 1918 and reregistered in 1924 and 1930 (both times allowing the registration to lapse). But whether he was carrying the gun that day remains uncertain.[66] On October 19, 1934, Nikolayev was in Smolny but failed once more to obtain an audience with Kirov. He was increasingly incensed at the discrepancy between the workers' state and the state of workers, as reflected in his own life.

Nikolayev had been keeping a notebook/diary about himself and Milda, devout Communists living through world-historical times, which originally was intended for their children's edification but now became a place to ponder his options. His text contained grammatical errors, but Nikolayev read Aleksei Tolstoy and Gorky, imagining he could impart a literary quality to his writings.[67] He wrote of Milda as "my only true companion" but began to reproach her, too, recording, on October 26, "M., you could have prevented much, but you did not wish to," evidently disappointed she had not used her connections to land him a position. "Wrote to everyone, no one left, wrote to Kirov, Stalin, politburo, party Control Commission, but no one pays attention," he recorded, portraying himself as one of the few brave people ready to sacrifice himself "for the sake of (all of) humanity."[68]

Three days later, an entry averred that "the time for action has arrived" and evoked the organizer of Alexander II's assassination, Andrei Zhelyabov of the People's Will, who had been executed (Lenin had compared him to Robespierre). "As a soldier of the revolution, no death frightens me. I am ready for anything now, and no one has the power to preempt that." Nikolayev appeared to be using his diary writing to steel his resolve, and contemplated going over the heads of the party bureaucracy to the working masses, to teach the party a lesson.[69]

Nikolayev diagrammed Kirov's routes, some possible shot angles and methods of assassination: "After first shot, run to his car: a) smash window and fire; b) open door." He also continued to write plaintive letters seeking recourse, while underscoring the plight of workers stuck in queues versus the good life of speculators. On November 5, 1934, he glimpsed Kirov's passing car but did not shoot through the glass.[70] On November 14, Nikolayev went to Leningrad's Moscow Station yet again, looking for Kirov to arrive on the overnight train; this time Kirov did disembark, but Nikolayev could not get close. On November 21 he wrote another farewell to Milda ("My days are numbered, no one is coming to our aid. . . . Forgive me for everything").[71] After Kirov departed for the plenum in Moscow, Nikolayev stalked the station once more, but on November 29, when Kirov returned, he again could not get close. As it happened, however, Nikolayev read in that day's *Leningrad Pravda* that at 6:00 p.m. on December 1, in the old Tauride Palace, Kirov would be reporting on the recent plenum in Moscow to the Leningrad "party active."

HISTORIC OPPORTUNITY

On the morning of Kirov's speech, Nikolayev called Milda at work, twice, for assistance in getting a ticket. By 1:00 p.m. he had learned that she could not or would not deliver. He went to the ward party committee around 1:30 p.m. One official suggested he could get him a ticket by the end of the day. For insurance, Nikolayev went to Smolny to try his luck with former co-workers. Smolny was an entire complex of buildings where 1,829 people worked and thousands more came and went. Besides the province and city party machines, more than fifteen organizations had offices there, including a department for the disfranchised and the workers' and peasants' inspectorate (on the second floor), where Nikolayev had worked. The inner courtyard connected to a residential building that housed 160 families, and there was a pigsty for supplying the cafeteria. The door to the building's north wing, where top officials had offices on the third floor, required a special key, but it was given out freely: there was a hairdresser on the first floor, through the same entryway.[72] Access to the third floor was governed by mere possession of a party card (for non-party members, a special pass). Nikolayev showed his party card and for an hour traipsed from office to office. His acquaintances rebuffed his pleadings for a ticket, but one promised to come through at the end of the day. Nikolayev exited and walked around. Close to

4:30 p.m., he returned and climbed to the third floor. He stopped off at the toilet, to relieve himself or hide (or both). He claimed that when he came out, he unexpectedly saw Kirov in the long corridor, coming toward him, fifteen to twenty paces away, unaccompanied.[73]

Whether Kirov was expected at Smolny that day—a Saturday—before his speech remains uncertain. His purpose in stopping by also remains unclear. One story has it that he wanted to inquire about the preparations for the end of rationing, which was generating social anxiety. Mikhail Chudov, the second secretary, was chairing a meeting of some twenty apparatchiks at 3:00 p.m. to draft resolutions for a Leningrad party plenum on rationing that was scheduled for the day after Kirov's ticketed speech. Or maybe Kirov wanted to touch up his speech one last time with his deputy.[74] Be that as it may, at 4:00 p.m. Kirov had exited his apartment building, walked toward the Trinity Bridge, and gotten into his chauffeured car. He was trailed by the usual escort car with two guards, but at what distance remains unclear: Kirov would hound Medved after he had spotted a trailing vehicle. The traveling guard was supposed to deliver Kirov to other members of the detail once at Smolny. Inside, Kirov's head bodyguard, Mikhail Borisov—who had started in Kirov's detail in the 1920s—was to accompany him everywhere and, when Kirov entered his office, to remain in the reception room with Kirov's top aide, Nikolai Sveshnikov. But the guard detail had been complaining to superiors that Kirov interfered with their duties (their latest complaint had been on November 16, 1934, to Pauker).

Kirov—a politburo member—insisted that the guards stay back and not cross his vision.[75] On December 1, the fifty-three-year-old Borisov, who was not in good physical form, was maintaining a fair distance, as many as thirty paces. The corridor was L-shaped, and, after Kirov turned left onto the shorter part, where his office had been relocated for safety, Borisov could not see him.[76]

Kirov's two-room suite at the far end of the short corridor was near a special stairwell and elevator protected by a lockable glass door (many people had keys), but he refused to use this special side entrance established for him. His back room, accessible only from his front one, was used not just by him but also as a private lunch space by leaders of the provincial and city party committees and provincial and city soviets. Directly across the hall was a canteen that attracted traffic, too. Workmen were coming and going on the third floor that day. As Kirov approached Nikolayev in the long part of the L-corridor, Nikolayev turned his back. Kirov passed. The corridor was dim. (Kirov was farsighted yet refused to wear glasses in public, wary of resembling a member of the intelligentsia.)[77]

Nikolayev looked around and, he claimed, saw no one else. "When he turned left toward his office, whose disposition I knew well, the entire half of the [short] corridor was empty—I rushed forward five steps, pulled the Nagant revolver out of my pocket on the run, brought the muzzle to Kirov's head, and fired one shot into his forehead," Nikolayev would testify. "Kirov immediately fell face first." Nikolayev then tried to shoot himself but either was foiled by an electrician who had heard the first gunshot or lost consciousness and slid down the wall next to Kirov's body, now in a pool of blood.[78]

Medved was two miles from Smolny, at NKVD headquarters (Volodarsky, formerly Liteiny, Boulevard, no. 4), when the call came in. He threw down the receiver and exclaimed, "Kirov's been shot."[79] First deputy Zaporozhets was away (he had broken his leg by falling from a horse during an equestrian competition and, after his cast was removed, had been given a holiday on November 13 at an NKVD resort in Sochi).[80] Medved and second deputy Fyodor Fomin (an old Yevdokimov protégé) dashed over to Smolny. Kirov had been shot between 4:30 and 4:37 and found to have no pulse seconds later. Testimony suggests that he was carried into his office around seven or eight minutes later and laid on the conference table, where doctors vainly attempted to resuscitate him.[81] Local security personnel, having heard the shot, claimed that they had secured Smolny's third floor and that very soon the general alarm had been activated, a signal to seal the entire building. About twenty minutes after Medved had hastened out of the NKVD building, he ordered a contingent of thirty NKVD operatives dispatched to Smolny to detain and question everyone inside. But already, in Chudov's office, adjacent to Kirov's, the first interrogation was recorded as having commenced at 4:45, just minutes after the shooting—it was the questioning of Milda Draule. If this was accurate, she had to have been on-site when the shooting occurred.[82]

Ten or so witnesses on the third floor that day—bodyguards, an electrician attending to circuit breakers after some lights went out, a stockman, the director of the circus awaiting a meeting, various functionaries, Nikolayev himself—all placed the shooting in the corridor outside Chudov's office. Kirov was said to have been found on the floor facedown, head toward the back stairwell, Nikolayev on the floor faceup, head the other way.[83] But a special forensic analysis performed by a Russian defense ministry team in 2004 on the bullet hole in the rear of Kirov's cap concluded, from the angle of entry, that either Nikolayev was lying on the floor when he fired the gun or Kirov was lying down. The forensic analysis also turned up large stains from dried semen on the underpants that Kirov had been wearing (on the front top, inside). In theory, NKVD interrogators could have arranged the testimony of even multiple witnesses to disguise the morally damaging circumstance that an esteemed leader had not been carried to the conference table in his office but was already on it, in flagrante delicto.[84, 85] Crucially, however, there was no way to prove the exact position of the cap while it was on Kirov's head.

Two shots had been fired. (All seven bullets in the gun were accounted for: five were still inside the revolver.) Kirov was hit by only one bullet (later extracted from his head), which was confirmed to have been fired from the Nagant registered to Nikolayev.[86] The second bullet was recovered from the floor (a ricochet mark was found on a cornice where wall and ceiling met). The upward angle of the bullet entry, fired from behind at close range, can likely be explained by the fact that although Kirov was short, Nikolayev was even shorter.[87]

As for the semen, already on the night of December 1 rumors were circulating—tracked by the NKVD—of a liaison with Draule having caused Kirov's demise. Despite arrests, this gossip persisted. At one enterprise, the non-party Khasanov was overheard to say, "Nikolayev killed comrade Kirov because he lived with his wife." A candidate member of the party, Gubler, when asked why Nikolayev had killed Kirov, responded, "Because of tarts." At the Leningrad timber company: "Rumors are circulating that Kirov was killed because of personal score-settling, since he lived with Nikolayev's wife." An employee of the Southern Water Station: "I know why they killed Kirov—I spoke with Kirov's cook and she told me that it was because of a woman, because of jealousy."[88] The pants semen does seem to indicate some sort of tryst the day of the assassination, but that would have been far easier to arrange and hide at Kirov's residence, where he spent most of the day, with his wife away at Tolmachevo. (Kirov answered the door when a courier delivered documents.)[89] As we saw, Draule was in Smolny. The rumors seem to reflect a timeworn trope of the jealous husband and Kirov's general reputation rather than specifics.[90] Of course, even if nothing happened that afternoon between Kirov and Draule, the pair could have been lovers. Draule, under interrogation, denied an affair with Kirov.[91] But if she was lying, it is still striking that neither Nikolayev's handwritten notebook/diary nor his testimony alluded to being cuckolded by Kirov.[92]

Nikolayev had been bundled into a side office on the third floor, whence he was whisked to NKVD headquarters, where he alternated between wailing uncontrollably and falling silent while staring at a single point. He was carried on a stretcher to the NKVD's internal clinic for examination at around 6:40 p.m.[93]

Only around 10:00 or 11:00 p.m. could the NKVD interrogate him. Besides the gun, Nikolayev had been carrying his attaché case and was found to be in possession of a party card, a pass to the Smolny cafeteria (from his workers' and peasants' inspectorate days), which was how his identity was quickly established, and an address book, which is how his relatives were quickly found. At searches of his and his mother's apartments, operatives found copies of his various letters to the authorities, the numerous notebooks comprising a diary, the sketch of Kirov's routes, a fragmentary plan of assassination, secret letters to his wife about his plotting and willingness to die, and instructions on where to find these letters— the kind of treasure trove of documentary evidence never adduced at any of the countless fabricated trials.

"I prepared the whole thing myself," Nikolayev was recorded as having told Medved, Fomin, and other Leningrad operatives the night of the assassination, "and I never let anyone know of my intentions." He added: "There was a single reason—estrangement from the party, from which the events in the Leningrad Institute of Party History pushed me away, my unemployment, and the lack of material and, above all, moral assistance from the party organizations. My whole situation reverberated from the moment I was expelled from the party (eight months ago), which discredited me in the eyes of party organizations." Nikolayev enumerated all his fruitless letters for redress, adding, "There was a single aim of the assassination: for it to become a political signal to the party that over the past eight to ten years on my path of life and work, there has accumulated the baggage of unjust treatment of a living person on the part of certain state persons. . . . This historic mission has been accomplished by me. I had to show the whole party where they had brought Nikolayev."[94]

CAVALCADE

Medved had the unenviable task of informing Yagoda, his superior. In the office of the second secretary of the Leningrad city party committee, he composed a telegram: "On December 1, 16:30 in Smolny, third floor, twenty paces from comrade Kirov's office, Kirov was shot in the head by an unknown assailant who approached him and who, according to party documents, is Leonid Nikolayev, b. 1904, party member since 1924. Kirov is in his office. With him are professors of surgery . . . and other doctors." The message mentioned that "several functionaries at Smolny recognized Nikolayev . . . as someone who had earlier worked" there, and that an arrest warrant had been issued for his wife, misnamed as Graule. Medved lied that Borisov "had accompanied Kirov to the point of the incident," concealing NKVD negligence. Inexplicably, the message was stamped as sent at 6:20 p.m. and received and decoded in Moscow by 7:15 p.m.[95] Already just after 5:00 p.m., Chudov had called Stalin's office number; Poskryobyshev picked up.[96]

As Kirov lay dead, shot by an assassin at party headquarters in Leningrad, Stalin was in his office at party headquarters in Moscow. Members of the inner circle—Molotov, Voroshilov, Kaganovich, Zhdanov—had entered the dictator's suite on Old Square at 3:05 p.m. When the news from Leningrad arrived, according to Kaganovich, Stalin "was shocked at first."[97] Yagoda appeared at 5:50 p.m. and called the Leningrad NKVD twice, likely from Stalin's office, to inquire whether Nikolayev was wearing foreign clothing (he was not).[98] Molotov, later in life, recalled that Stalin had rebuked Medved over the phone ("Incompetents!").[99] At 6:15, Pauker arrived with his deputy and the Kremlin commandant Rudolf Peterson; ten minutes later, they were dismissed to prepare a special train for that evening. Others began arriving: Kalinin, Mikoyan, and Orjonikidze at 6:20, Andreyev at 6:25, Chubar at 6:30, Yenukidze at 6:45. They all cleared out except for Yagoda, who stayed until 8:10, when Mekhlis (editor of *Pravda*), Bukharin (*Izvestiya*), Stetsky (culture and propaganda department), and Mikhail Suslov (a Control Commission functionary) entered, staying ten minutes. Stalin edited the text of a bulletin that would run in central newspapers under the names of all politburo members. "You were dear to us all, comrade Kirov, as a true friend, a true comrade, a dependable comrade-in-arms," it stated, using the familiar *ty* ("thou") inserted by Stalin. "You were always with us in the years of our hard struggles for the triumph of socialism in our country, you were always with us in the years of wavering and trouble inside our party, you lived through all the difficulties of the last years with us. . . . Farewell, our dear friend and comrade, Sergei!"[100]

Stalin then held back Yagoda, alone, for twenty minutes, until 8:30 p.m.[101] At some point the dictator had drafted a short, vaguely worded law stipulating expedited handling of terrorist cases, with immediate implementation of the death penalty and no right of appeal, which Yenukidze signed as secretary of the Soviet's central executive committee (and which, subsequently, Kalinin signed as chairman of that body).[102] Leningrad party officials, convening their own meeting in Smolny at 6:00 p.m., drafted their own announcement, formed their own

funeral commission, and instructed lower-level party committees to call meetings at factories that very night.[103]

Soviet radio announced Kirov's murder at 11:30 p.m.; workers heard over factory loudspeakers. Newspaper editors around the country were called. Meanwhile, another coded telegram had arrived from Medved at 10:30 p.m., with a
short record of Draule's interrogation, which had only basic information about
her, as if just her role as Nikolayev's wife was of interest. She was quoted as stressing his sense of grievance. ("From the moment of his party expulsion, he descended into a down mood, waiting the whole time for rectification of his status
and reprimand and not wanting to work anywhere.") A third Medved telegram,
forty minutes after midnight, indicating that the NKVD had started analysis of
the materials seized in searches, quoted Nikolayev's "political testament" (letter
to the politburo) about his efforts to assassinate Kirov, and reported that his address book contained entries for the German consulate (Herzen Street, 43; telephone, 1-69-82) and the Latvian consulate (telephone, 5-50-63).[104] Yagoda was
already on the train with Stalin.

Kaganovich had summoned Khrushchev to lead a Moscow delegation of some
sixty party officials and workers. The grandson of a serf and the son of a coal
miner, Khrushchev (b. 1894) had attended a village school for four years and become a skilled metalworker in the Donbass town of Yuzovka (the name was
changed in 1924 to Stalino), where he had hankered after further study while rising in the apparatus, catching the eye of Kaganovich (then Ukraine party boss),
who promoted him to the Ukrainian capital. At the 14th Party Congress, in Moscow in 1925, Khrushchev would later recall, he had encountered Stalin for the first
time and was surprised to meet a general secretary with a modest demeanor, proletarian plainness, even abrasiveness—a stirring role model for working-class
Communists such as the ambitious Khrushchev. "He dreamed of being a factory
director," one contemporary recalled of Khrushchev. "I'll go to Moscow, I'll try to
get in the Industrial Academy, and if I do I'll make a good factory manager."
Thanks to Kaganovich, he had been able to enroll, despite meager academic qual-
ifications. In a mere year and a half, Khrushchev had leapt from the Donbass coal
region to Kharkov to Kiev to Moscow. Now he was leading a train, in parallel to
Stalin's train, to Leningrad. Stalin made Kaganovich stay behind in Moscow.
Khrushchev recalled tears in Kaganovich's eyes.[105] Stalin also refused to allow Orjonikidze to go on the train (ostensibly over worries for his weak heart).

Around 10:00 or so that morning of December 2, Stalin and entourage—
Molotov, Voroshilov, Zhdanov, Yezhov, Alexander Kosaryov, a large contingent of

NKVD operatives, and at least 200 armed men (the Dzierżyński regiment)—alighted at Leningrad's Moscow Station. Enveloped by the massive security force, the group proceeded to the Sverdlov Hospital morgue, then to Smolny, where they took over Kirov's office. "I saw a group approaching," one Communist Youth League functionary recalled. "I saw Stalin in the middle; in front of him was Genrikh Yagoda with a revolver in his raised hand. The latter gave an order: 'Everyone, faces to the wall! Hands on your trouser seams!'"[106]

Agranov ordered Fomin to accompany him to Leningrad NKVD HQ, where he commandeered Medved's office and all the case materials.[107] A shattered Borisov, the bodyguard—who had been interrogated the previous night but proved nearly unable to speak (his service revolver had been discovered still unloaded in its holster)—was summoned in the opposite direction, to Smolny.[108] As he was being driven, his head smashed into the wall of a building at around 10:50 a.m. and he died almost instantly. Neither the driver nor the three NKVD operatives accompanying him were hurt. The NKVD had used a one-and-a-half-ton Ford truck to transport Borisov, who was placed in the truck bed. Apparently, no other vehicles were available at the garage because of the cavalcade that had descended from Moscow. A spring on the truck's front suspension was known to be defective and jerry-rigged, although deemed safe to drive at slow speeds. The driver might have been speeding—the summons was urgent—when he crossed tram tracks in the road. The truck swerved rightward violently. The driver tried to compensate by steering left. A tire blew. The truck ran a sidewalk and struck a building on the side where Borisov happened to be. A piece of his overcoat was caught by a metal clamp holding a drainpipe.[109] It is conceivable that he smashed his own head against the wall once the vehicle swung. It is also possible, though even less likely, that the Leningrad NKVD killed Borisov to hide evidence of incompetence—which was what Stalin suspected.[110]

Nikolayev was brought before Stalin.[111] The dictator had a hard time accepting that anyone ever acted alone.[112] But it was especially difficult to believe the pathetic Nikolayev could have carried out such a momentous assassination by himself. He stood a hair over five feet (1.53 meters), with "simian arms" down to his knees and very short legs, and, though he was only thirty years old, was a physical and emotional wreck. By then he was also severely sleep deprived. "An unprepossessing appearance. A clerk. Not tall. Scraggly," recalled Molotov. "I think he was, it seems, angry with something, expelled from the party, aggrieved."[113] What Stalin managed to extract from the petulant, megalomanical, delirious Nikolayev remains unclear. (A rumor in Smolny suggested that Nikolayev had failed to recognize Stalin until he was shown an official portrait alongside the person before him.) Taken to a waiting vehicle on the street, where people were going about their business, Nikolayev was said to have shouted, "Remember me—I am the assassin. Let the people know who killed Kirov!"[114]

FAREWELL

Kirov's open casket was placed for public viewing in the vestibule of the former Tauride Palace on December 2 for two days. His widow, Leningrad and Moscow officials, and delegations of workers from the two capitals paid their respects, many through tears. Initially, *Pravda* (December 2) accused "enemies of the working class and Soviet power, White Guards." The next day, the newspaper identified the assassin as Nikolayev, labeling him a former employee of the workers' and peasants' inspectorate, omitting his employment in the party committee and his party membership.[115] The NKVD was investigating foreign involvement: Nikolayev had visited the German consulate a few times and the Latvian once. He testified that he had found their numbers in the phone book and hoped to be introduced to foreign journalists, but had been brushed off by the German consul while trying to sell anti-Soviet documents (his writings) for money.[116] Nikolayev might have sought a visa to Latvia for escape. Also on December 3, at a detached house in Leningrad's Stone Island neighborhood that Stalin and his entourage were using, the dictator dressed down Medved and Fomin. (Yagoda that day issued an indictment of them and six other Leningrad NKVD operatives.) "The murder of Kirov is the hand of an organization," Stalin told Medved and Fomin, "but which organization is difficult to say right now."[117]

Around 10:00 p.m. on December 3, Stalin claimed Kirov's casket and led a processional to the station, where his special train departed after midnight. It was met in Moscow by an air force squadron overhead. On December 4 and 5, Kirov's casket was placed for viewing in Moscow's Columned Hall of the House of Trade Unions. That afternoon and evening, Stalin received a large number of officials in his office and, among other business, appointed a new trade representative to Hitler's Berlin, David Kandelaki. Normally, Soviet trade representatives never met with Stalin, but Kandelaki, who was Georgia born and Germany educated, would be received an inordinate number of times in the Little Corner starting in late 1934.[118] "Kandelaki," noted the Soviet press officer at the Berlin embassy, "clearly gave us the impression that he had confidential instructions from Stalin personally, and the power to go beyond economic subjects in talks with the Germans."[119]

Departing his office that night of December 5 at 10:00, Stalin arrived at the House of Trade Unions for a final farewell as the Bolshoi Orchestra played Chopin's funeral march. He evidently kissed the dead Kirov on the lips and stated, "Farewell, dear friend."[120] The body was taken to be cremated. Back at the Kremlin, Shumyatsky showed Stalin, Voroshilov, Molotov, Orjonikidze, Mikoyan, Kaganovich, and Zhdanov clips from a documentary by Yakov Bliokh of Kirov's life and death. "Koba especially tensely watched those parts depicting the deceased Kirov in motion," Shumyatsky noted, using Stalin's nickname. "When they showed the episodes of the population reading the sad news, everyone noted that the reaction to the event was depicted powerfully and clearly. . . . Koba and the others watched especially tensely the parts in Leningrad—in the Tauride Palace, at the casket, and the accompanying of the casket with the body to the train station." It was silent footage, but Shumyatsky had also brought film of two of Kirov's speeches. Stalin liked Kirov's speech at the last Leningrad provincial party conference, where he had spoken about Marxist-Leninist education.[121]

On Red Square the next day, a full military funeral took place. A devastated Orjonikidze was afforded the honor of interring the urn in the Kremlin Wall. Stalin also allowed Orjonikidze's signature to be placed second under Kirov's obituary in *Pravda*, after the dictator's, out of the usual hierarchy.[122] Molotov delivered a eulogy (Stalin complimented him on it). Stalin had the orchestra play a Kirov favorite, Shatrov's "On the Hills of Manchuria," which dated to the Russo-Japanese War of 1904–5: "The crosses for magnificent bygone heroes show their whiteness, and the shades of the past circle about, hardening us about those who fell in vain. . . . But believe me, we will avenge you and celebrate a bloody funeral feast."[123] *Pravda* that morning (December 6) had already announced that seventy persons were being tried in other cases on charges of "preparing terrorist actions against Soviet authorities." The inner circle repaired to Stalin's apartment in the Imperial Senate for a luncheon. The dictator, full of grief, according to Artyom, said Kirov had been an optimist, a lover of life, so if anyone was to cry, to "let out snot," they would be dishonoring his memory. He played songs on the gramophone Kirov loved. "Everyone there was in a crushed mood." Stalin requested that they watch the Kirov documentary footage again and invited Vasily and Svetlana, calling her the Mistress of the House and asking her to direct the viewing. Stalin again reminded Shumyatsky to insert footage of the liveliness of the streets and squares as Kirov's casket was brought to the capital. Postyshev said Shumyatsky needed to include a speech by Stalin, whose voice had not yet appeared in sound footage. "Film is a powerful instrument for propaganda and agitation," Stalin intoned. Then they watched *Chapayev* until 1:00 a.m.[124]

Unlike the pioneer Mussolini, the Soviet dictator chose not to speak directly on radio.[134] The twenty-year-old Yuri Levitan had become Stalin's voice from around the time of the 17th Party Congress, when he had read the five-hour congress speech over the radio. On December 6, 1934, Levitan was on the air when Kirov's ashes were interred in the Kremlin Wall: "Farewell, pupil of Lenin and friend of Stalin, leader of the Leningrad proletariat, farewell!"[125] That night, after the film screening, Pavel Alliluyev stayed at the Near Dacha to keep an eye on his brother-in-law. "I'm an utter orphan," the dictator supposedly told him, putting his head in his hands. Stalin also said Kirov had looked after him as one does for a child.[126]

THE INVESTIGATION

At Stalin's suggestion, to get Nikolayev to admit complicity in a "group," he was plied with food, cigarettes, and the usual promises to spare his own and his family members' lives. Interrogators lied that Milda had not (yet) been arrested. Agranov and his team were making suggestions to him about "ties," and Nikolayev began to go along, admitting that he did belong to a "group." He also tried to jump out the window. The interrogators were now interested in his acquaintances Ivan Kotolynov and Nikolai Shatsky, both at one time expelled from the party and figures in Nikolayev's notebook/diary. Kotolynov was being called a Trotskyite, but, as it happened, he and others had been Communist Youth League functionaries when Zinoviev was party boss.[127] Voilà. The names of Zinoviev as well as Kamenev started to crop up in the interrogation protocols, which Agranov was forwarding to Stalin.[128] (In the Kirov case, the dictator would receive at least 260 interrogation protocols, a new genre of belles lettres.)[129]

The NKVD drafted a scenario, which Stalin edited, of parallel terrorist organizations, a "Leningrad Center" and a "Moscow Center." None of this had been part of the interrogations before December 4, 1934, when Stalin had summoned a large group to his office, including prosecutors, court officials, secret police operatives, and Agranov, who came from Leningrad.[130] During discussions over the next several days, Stalin shifted Zinoviev and Kamenev from the Leningrad to the guiding Moscow Center. The Leningrad Center was now said to be led by Nikolayev, Kotolynov, and their associates.[131]

Amid a mood for bloodthirsty revenge, the ethnic Pole party boss of Ukraine, Kosior, wanted to respond to the assassination with directives for mass relocations of Soviet ethnic Poles from the frontier. But a calculating Stalin softened a secret circular sent by party channels (December 7, 1934) to both Ukraine and Belorussia regarding their ethnic Polish border populations, evidently to avoid complications in Soviet-Polish and Soviet-German relations. By contrast, in response to a plan to deport 5,000 "socially alien" families from the Karelian autonomous republic and Leningrad province—both near the Finnish border, where geopolitical complications were largely absent—Stalin wrote, "Why not more?"[132]

On December 9, after meetings in his office with the prosecutors, judges, and NKVD officials, among many others, until 7:30 p.m., Stalin suppered one floor below at his Kremlin apartment with Kaganovich, Zhdanov, Orjonikidze, and Molotov, a practice that was becoming increasingly routine. The relatives had come over on the pretext of giving Svetlana, said to be distraught over Kirov's death, some gifts to cheer her up. "It broke my heart to look at him," Maria Svanidze wrote in her diary of Stalin at the table. "He is suffering greatly."[133]

In Leningrad, fourteen people—all save Shatsky—testified that they had participated in an underground Zinovievite "group," but all denied complicity in the assassination except Nikolayev. Interrogators had tried to get him to admit that his working-class father had hired laborers, making him the offspring of a class alien, but he refused. Nonetheless, Nikolayev, a working-class Communist of conviction—precisely why he had killed Kirov—somehow had to be turned into a "class enemy." Over time, the wily Agranov seems to have persuaded him that he could realize one more great deed: the destruction of the Zinovievites. Nikolayev apparently would not fully realize until later that this task on behalf of the cause required retrospectively making *him* a member of the 1920s Zinoviev opposition.

Accused Zinovievites were arrested in waves, and one turned out to be hiding the archives of the Zinoviev opposition. (All told, 843 "former Zinovievites" would be arrested by the NKVD in the ten weeks after the murder; thousands would be exiled administratively.) The few core genuine supporters of Zinoviev did not hide their critical feelings toward Stalin and his policies: they believed, for example, that Hitler's rise in Germany had resulted from Comintern passivity.[134] They also freely admitted that they occasionally met and discussed these views. And so it was "an organization" and "anti-party." They were also found to have copies of Lenin's Testament and the Ryutin appeal calling for Stalin's removal, and almost every one of them turned out to have a gun at home, sometimes more than one, usually acquired and held legally since civil war days. And so it was "terrorism," too.

Was it not plausible that these former party oppositionists—armed and, by their own admission, meeting to criticize Stalin—would in shadowy ways have taken part in the killing of Kirov, who, after all, had displaced their patron Zinoviev?[135] Kotolynov, according to one interrogation protocol (December 12), would admit only that "our organization bears the *political and moral responsibility* for the murder of Kirov by Nikolayev, having reared Nikolayev in *an atmosphere of embittered relations* to the leaders of the Soviet Communist Party." Here was one formula.[136] On December 16, Zinoviev and Kamenev were arrested.[137] Zinoviev confessed to a host of fictitious crimes, and agreed to name "all those I can and will remember as former participants in the anti-party struggle."[138] *Pravda* and *Leningrad Pravda* (December 17) ran the same front-page editorial asserting that Nikolayev had been *directed* by the former Leningrad opposition "Zinovievites" to kill Kirov. Here was a different formula.

FIRST TRIAL

Stalin sent Zhdanov to replace Kirov as first secretary. With the regime and much of the country in mourning, the dictator ordered that his official birthday, on December 21, 1934—his fifty-fifth—not be celebrated publicly. Nonetheless, the apparatchiks gathered the obligatory well-wishes.[139] On the day itself, Agranov, Vyshinsky, and Akulov arrived from Leningrad and, along with Yagoda and Ulrich, were in Stalin's office for an hour, until 8:30 p.m., evidently to go over the pending trial.[140] Then a private celebration took place at the Near Dacha, in the company of the in-laws from both deceased wives and the inner circle. They had to add a second table. Stalin, Artyom would recall, "read the birthday congratulations in the newspapers, and commented on them humorously."[141]

Orjonikidze pronounced a toast for Kirov, which, according to Maria Svanidze's diary, elicited tears and a moment of silence. Someone mentioned that Dora Khazan-Andreyeva had attended the Industrial Academy with Nadya. Stalin stood. "Since the Academy was mentioned," he said, "permit me to drink to Nadya." "All stood and silently approached Iosif to clink their glasses," Svanidze wrote. Around 1:00 a.m., they got up from the table and Stalin put on the gramophone and people danced—the Caucasus lezginka or Cossack hopak—though there was not much room. Budyonny played the accordion, Zhdanov the piano. "The Caucasus people," Svanidze recorded, "sang sad songs, polyphonic—the Master sang in a high tenor."[142]

Newspapers announced the next morning that the NKVD had turned over the investigatory results for trial. But on December 23, *Pravda*, shockingly, announced that "the NKVD has established a lack of sufficient evidence to turn Zinoviev and Kamenev over to the courts." Stalin also decided against a public trial of the remaining "Zinovievites," perhaps because the extracted confessions were of anti-Stalin conversations, not plotting terrorism. The indictments published in *Pravda* and *Leningrad Pravda* of fourteen people headed by Nikolayev mentioned a connection to a foreign consulate but stopped short of naming it, as if afraid to have to prove it, or wary of involving Nazi Germany in discussions of Kirov's murder.[143]

In Leningrad, Ulrich opened the closed trial on December 28 at 2:20 p.m., and read the guilty verdicts before dawn the next morning: death penalty. Not a single Smolny witness had been summoned to the trial. (Nearly fourscore of them— every witness to the events that day and many others—would soon be transferred to other work, expelled from the party, or exiled.) "Nikolayev shouted, 'Severe,'" according to one of Agranov's soft-pedaling telegrams to Stalin, which failed to report that Nikolayev and others recanted their testimony.[144] The executions were carried out within an hour; the head executioner was said to have broken down in tears at memories of the fallen Kirov.[145] Kotolynov was shot last. "This whole trial is rubbish," he had told Agranov and Vyshinsky. "People have been executed. Now I'll be executed, too. But all of us, with the exception of Nikolayev, are not guilty of anything."[146]

Hundreds more would be shot, none of whom had any link to the murder. (Union-wide, as many as 6,500 people might have been arrested and charged under the December 1 antiterror law in the first month alone.)[147] "It's hard to believe that in the twentieth century there is a corner of Europe where medieval barbarians have taken up residence, where savage concepts are accompanied so strangely by science, art, and culture," Nina Lugovskaya, an atypical fifteen-year-old student in Moscow, the daughter of a persecuted "bourgeois" economist, recorded in her diary (December 30). "To call Nikolayev a coward! He went willingly to his death for what he believed in, he was better than all those so-called leaders of the working class put together!"[148]

REWRITING THE CAUCASUS

Beria had been pressing his minions in Tiflis to produce a Stalin hagiography. He had ordered systematic gathering of "recollections" of Stalin in the underground years and appointed Toroshelidze, chairman of the Writers' Union of Georgia, Tiflis University rector, and director of the Stalin Institute, to galvanize the work. The "reminiscences" were assembled, but the "scholarly" biography did not materialize.[149] Lakoba, meanwhile, had been active, too. Hashim Smyrba, an old brigand, had once hidden Stalin in his hut a few miles outside Batum, in the Muslim region of Ajaristan, in 1901–2, when Stalin and his accomplices, disguised with veils to look like Muslim women, transported illegal leaflets to Batum in fruit baskets. Hashim had died in 1922, at age eighty-one. Lakoba had an ethnographer collect material and forwarded to Stalin a pamphlet, *Stalin and Hashim, the Years 1901–1902: Episodes from the Batum Underground.* "Comrade Lakoba!" he wrote back. "Your Caucasus essay makes a good impression. And Hashim, as in life, is simple, naïve, but honest and devoted. Such helpmates were not few in the revolution; with their hearts they felt the truth."[150] Lakoba published the pamphlet in Abkhazia, in a print run of 20,000. (Kaganovich sent the paper.) It called Stalin "a person such as history gives to humanity just once in a hundred or two hundred years."

Playfully, the pamphlet noted that Hashim and other villagers had surmised that "Soso" was counterfeiting money and asked for some, but the business turned out to be revolutionary leaflets. Hashim: "You're a good man, Soso. Only it's a pity that you are not a Muslim." Stalin: "And what would happen if I were a Muslim?" Hashim: "If you converted to Islam, I would give you in marriage seven beauties the likes of which you probably never, ever saw. Do you want to be a Muslim?" "Comrade Stalin answered with a smile, 'OK!' and shook Hashim's hand." (Stalin ended up being imprisoned.)[151]

Lakoba wrote the preface to the Hashim pamphlet, emphasizing that Stalin, too, was simple, close to the masses—a winning formula.[152] By contrast, Beria had a far more ambitious and difficult aim—not two years in Batum, but the entire Caucasus before 1917, and falsification of a past that many people knew firsthand.[153] One of those people was Yenukidze, who was the godfather of the deceased Nadya by virtue of his acquaintance with her father, the worker-revolutionary Sergei Alliluyev. Yenukidze was also a founding member of the Baku group of the party (spring 1901) and had established the illegal printing press in the Caucasus—

code-named "Nino" (Nina in Russian), with his cousin Trifon—that had re-printed the exiled Lenin's illegal *Iskra* newspaper. Known in the underground as the Little Golden Fish, Yenukidze had serialized his autobiographical *Our Underground Printing Presses in the Caucasus* in a journal in 1923 and had not artificially magnified Stalin's role.[154] As business manager of regime affairs from early on, he had served Stalin faithfully.[155] But Mekhlis, writing to Stalin (January 4, 1935), listed a number of "mistakes" in a Yenukidze *Pravda* article (December 29, 1934) on the thirtieth anniversary of the 1904 Baku strike, and criticized his book on the illegal printing press, whose third edition had just been published. Stalin had Mekhlis's denunciation of Yenukidze circulated to the politburo, and marked up the text himself: When was the Baku party committee established? Who created the printing press? Yenukidze seemed to be placing himself above the martyr Lado Ketskhoveli, the youth who had introduced Stalin to Marxism.[156]

LAUGHTER

Long focused on the impact of live theater, Stalin had not grasped the full power of film immediately.[157] But Shumyatsky had persisted, and goaded the party to issue a directive to film all major events in the USSR, design handheld cameras to be put into wide production, and have regional officials treat newsreels the way they treated the press. Stalin began to review the newsreels at the Kremlin cinema sessions.[158] But it had really been *Chapayev* that transformed him—a person accustomed to working with written texts—from someone who occasionally viewed films for diversion to their executive producer, from the backgrounds of scenes to the dialogue and score. The dictator played a decisive role in supporting not just subjects of political import but also farce. In that regard, an enormous breakthrough was wrought by a young assistant to the virtuoso Sergei Eisenstein, after the latter's scandalous failure to finish a film in Mexico.[159] Shumyatsky had suggested that Eisenstein next make a Soviet comedy, but the director showed little interest. But his assistant, Grigory Alexandrov, using every Hollywood trick he had learned in their travels, cowrote and directed *Jolly Fellows,* which became a smash hit.[160]

Stalin's inner circle had divided over the appropriateness of comedy. When Shumyatsky was set to premiere *Jolly Fellows* in the Kremlin, Voroshilov, who had seen it, stated, "It's an interesting, jolly, thoroughly musical film featuring Utyosov and his jazz." Kaganovich objected that Utyosov had no voice; Zhdanov complained that Utyosov was a master only of criminal underworld songs. "You'll see," Voroshilov countered, "he's a very gifted actor, an extraordinary humorist, and sings delightfully in the film." He was right. "Brilliantly conceived," Stalin said to Voroshilov after viewing one scene with a jazz orchestra rehearsal that devolves into a hilarious fight, and another with collective farm livestock run amok. "The film allows you to relax in an interesting, entertaining fashion. We experienced the exact feeling one has after a day off. It's the first time I have experienced such a feeling from viewing our films, among which have been very good ones." After watching another film, Stalin returned to discussion of *Jolly Fellows,* lauding the bold acting of the female lead, Lyubov Orlova, and male lead, Utyosov, as well as the excellent jazz. "He talked about the songs," Shumyatsky wrote. "Turning to comrade Voroshilov, he pointed out that the march would go to the masses, and began to recall the melody and ask about the words."[161]

A new genre, the Soviet musical comedy, was born.[162] Shumyatsky's determination had paid off.[163] He had witnessed a live performance of Utyosov's band—whose musicians sang, danced, and acted—and had suggested they team up with the director Alexandrov. Utyosov, for his part, had insisted on music by Isaac Dunayevsky (b. 1900), a graduate of the Kharkov Conservatory who had made a name for himself at the Moscow Satire Theater and more recently the Leningrad Music Hall. Vasily Lebedev-Kumach (b. 1898), the son of a Moscow cobbler and himself a writer at the satirical periodical *Crocodile,* composed the lyrics. When ideologues attacked the resulting work, Shumyatsky galvanized Stalin's support.[164] *Jolly Fellows* had gone into final editing, following the dictator's suggestions, but its public opening was delayed by Kirov's assassination. It premiered publicly on December 25, at Moscow's Shock Worker cinema, where Orlova, Utyosov, and Alexandrov were in the audience. A banquet followed at the Metropole. General release took place in January 1935, and soon an astonishing 6,000 copies of the film were in circulation Union-wide. The publicity campaign, unprecedented for the Soviet Union, borrowed American techniques, with postcards of scenes from the film and phonographic records of the songs. Shumyatsky even had sheet music of the score published with an attractive cover, and there were tie-in cookies from the baking trust and cigarettes from the tobacco trust. The film's stars featured in radio appearances.

Many cultural figures collaborated with the Soviet party-state precisely for its wherewithal to deliver mass audiences.[165] To be sure, whereas listeners in Britain or Germany could tune in to several stations, including some that originated from abroad, the Soviets invested in cable (wire) radio, which was inexpensive and durable, enabling mass production, and imposed far stricter state control over content, since the wires delivered just the two official stations.[166] Only the privileged had hard-to-procure wireless receivers with tuners. Wire radios were installed in outdoor public spaces, factories, meeting halls, clubs, and dormitories. The Soviet Union had 2.5 million radio reception points already by 1934.[167] Radio Moscow and Radio Comintern were broadcasting approximately eighteen hours per day, creating an ambient Sovietness.[168]

"Boring agitation is counter-agitation," one Soviet film critic argued.[169] Surveys of radio listeners' letters showed that they wanted fewer symphonies and more humor, information about the outside world, advice on childrearing, medical issues, and other daily life concerns, and entertainment, such as folk music, Gypsy romances, jazz, operettas (not operas), and songs from the latest films.[170] While Germany had Marlene Dietrich, and America Greta Garbo, the Soviets had Orlova, promoted in the press, books, and fan postcards.[171] (She and Alexandrov would begin a love affair and later marry.) The songs proved to be easily and widely memorized. From streets to shop, almost the entire USSR was singing "Such a Lot of Nice Girls" (or the tango version, "Heart," released by Pyotr Leshchenko) and the march ("A happy song lightens your heart"). Even in profoundly anti-Soviet Poland *Jolly Fellows* would find popularity. The comic master Chaplin would praise the film as better propaganda for the Soviet cause than executions.[172]

Stalin authorized an all-Union Creative Conference of Workers in Soviet Cinema (January 8–13, 1935), albeit without formation of a formal union such as the writers had. Eisenstein was awarded the task of delivering the keynote. "When I heard Eisenstein's report, I was afraid that he knows so much, and his head is so clear that, it is obvious, he'll never make another film," director Oleksandr Dovzhenko said in his follow-up speech. "If I knew as much as he does, I would literally die. (Laughter, applause.)"[173] *Pravda* (January 11) published a congratulatory note from Stalin to Shumyatsky. "Greetings and best wishes to the workers of Soviet cinema on the day of its glorious fifteenth anniversary," the note stated. "Soviet power expects from you new successes—new films that, like *Chapayev,* proclaim the greatness of the historic cause of the struggle for power of the workers and peasants of the Soviet Union, mobilize for the attainment of new tasks, and remind us of both the achievements and difficulties of socialist construction."[174]

That same day, Stalin attended the ceremony at the Bolshoi where, for the first time, state awards were handed out to film workers. He had edited the proposed awards list: Orders of Lenin were given to the Leningrad Film Studio, Shumyatsky, Pavel Tager (who had helped introduce sound to Soviet films), and numerous directors. Eisenstein had been proposed for the lesser Order of the Red Banner, which Stalin crossed out, substituting something lesser still: "honored artist."[175] After this humiliation, Eisenstein had to offer the closing remarks. "No one here has had to listen to so many compliments about highbrow wisdom as I," he stated. "The crux—and this you know—is that I have not been engaged in film production for several years, and I consider the [awards] decision a signal from the party and government that I must enter production."[176] The gathering concluded with a performance of the third act of *Swan Lake*.[177]

Shumyatsky did not speak at the ceremony or at the conference, but *Pravda* (January 11) published an excerpt from his forthcoming book, *Cinema for the Millions*. "The victorious class wants to laugh with joy," he wrote. "That is its right, and Soviet cinema must provide its audiences with this joyful Soviet laughter." He admitted, however, that "we have no common view on such fundamental and decisive problems of our art as the interrelationship between form and content, as plot, as the pace and rhythm of a film, the role of the script, the techniques of cinema."[178] In fact, all he and other film people had to go on was Stalin's utterances or their own intuition about what might please him.

THE SECOND TRIAL

On January 13, 1935, a plebiscite took place in a small region on the western side of the Rhine known as the Saar, which the Versailles Treaty had taken from Germany and put under the League of Nations, stipulating such a vote after fifteen years. Some 445,000 Saarlanders, 90.35 percent, freely voted to join Germany under Nazi dictatorship rather than France or remain under the League. The French and British expected this removal of a German grievance to be followed by German compliance. Hitler perceived only a removal of restraint, and would exult that "blood is stronger than any document or mere paper. What ink has written will one day be blotted out in blood." Large ethnic German populations resided in Czechoslovakia, Poland, Hungary, Romania, and even the Soviet Union.[179]

The Kirov documentary opened publicly on January 14.[180] The NKVD had been planning a second public trial of eight "Zinovievites" willing to incriminate themselves, with Draule testifying about their links to Nikolayev. In the event, she would be tried in camera, while several high-profile Zinovievites were added to the eight unknowns for a public trial, which took place January 15–16. The nineteen defendants, now headlined by Zinoviev himself, Kamenev, and Grigory Yevdokimov, were charged with fostering a "moral atmosphere" conducive to the terrorism that had resulted in Kirov's death. They had been promised their lives if they fulfilled their party duty and publicly confessed. Zinoviev admitted that he'd had conversations with people whom the NKVD called the Leningrad Center, for example with Vladimir Levin back in 1932, during his work in livestock requisitions. Kamenev at first refused to go along with the canard that his private conversations signified participation in a so-called Moscow Center or had somehow inspired acts of terrorism.[181] Yevdokimov confessed to having suggested that collectivization was a mad adventure, that the tempos of industrialization would turn the working class against the party, and that there was no party anymore, since Stalin had usurped its role.[182] Zinoviev was sentenced to ten years, Yevdokimov to eight, Kamenev to five.[183]

Pravda's trial report (January 18, 1935) acknowledged that incitement of the Kirov murder by the Moscow Center had not been proven, but insisted that the Moscow Center had known about the "terrorist sentiments" of Nikolayev and his Leningrad Center. That same day, Stalin sent an explanatory letter to all party organizations, which accused the former Zinoviev opposition of "two-facedness," equated them with "White Guard wreckers, spies, and provocateurs," and deemed expulsion from the party insufficient: they needed to be imprisoned so they could no longer pursue sabotage. The circular excoriated the Zinoviev opposition's concealment of its views in professions of loyalty, and blamed the NKVD for complacency. ("Is it that difficult for a Chekist to understand that a party card can be forged or stolen from its owner?") The circular called for better teaching of party history, especially the foul deeds of the various oppositions, and instructed local party organizations to seek enemies among any party members who had ever expressed criticism of Stalin and his ruling group.[184] The NKVD distributed its own secret circular to branches explaining that Nikolayev's long-existing "center" for terrorism had eluded the Leningrad NKVD because of the latter's failure to heed Yagoda's instructions to strengthen Kirov's guard.[185]

Three days later, regime favorites assembled for the anniversary of Lenin's death.[186] Shumyatsky showed a new documentary about Lenin, to which was added the speaking footage from the Kirov documentary—the first time a recorded speech had been heard at the Bolshoi. "The whole hall at first went silent," the cinema boss wrote, "then people could not contain themselves, and stormy applause, from the heart, eclipsed the inspiring speech of Mironych about the significance of Marxist-Leninist rearing." When the sound parts ended and the silent parts resumed, the orchestra started playing but could not be heard. "The end of the film, with the appearance of I. V. Stalin, was drowned out in a stormy ovation." Stalin had Shumyatsky summoned to the imperial box and "again reiterated the exceptional power of film."[187]

The regime held a closed trial of the Leningrad NKVD on January 23, 1935. Borisov's death was ruled an accident, and four operatives were released. Twelve others were convicted, including Medved and Zaporozhets (three years each), as well as Gubin and Fomin (two years). Almost all ended up serving their time as commandants at the Dalstroi gold camps in the far northeast.[188] Three days later, 663 former Zinovievites in Leningrad were exiled to Siberia, and 325 others transferred to jobs in other regions. In the meantime, on January 25, Valerian Kuibyshev died of heart failure, at age forty-six. The autopsy would find arteriosclerosis and blood clots. His heavy drinking had resulted in unpredictable work absences, a constant refrain in Stalin's correspondence.[189] He was cremated, and the urn with his ashes interred in the Kremlin Wall, adjacent to Kirov's.[190]

NAZISM'S WINDFALL

Soviet military intelligence, for all its blowups and failures, amassed a breathtaking network in Warsaw—thanks to Hitler. Rudolf Herrnstadt, born in the Silesian town of Gleiwitz (1903), a correspondent for the left-wing *Berliner Tageblatt* and a Jew, had joined the German Communist party as Rudolf Arbin, began working for Soviet intelligence around 1931, and fled the Nazis to Warsaw in 1933 with his lover, also a Soviet agent. He maintained journalist cover and recruited Gerhard Kegel ("X"), a junior banker and journalist (b. 1907) also from Upper Silesia, who had joined the German Socialist Party and then the Communists and now worked in the trade department of Germany's embassy in Warsaw. Herrnstadt's lover, the angular-faced Ilse Stöbe (b. 1911), code-named "Alta," the daughter of working-class parents in Berlin, had worked for the same newspaper as Herrnstadt. She had been directed to join the Nazi party and, in mid-1934, was named a cultural attaché of the Nazi party's foreign office in Poland. Stöbe would recruit the Silesia-born (1897) Rudolf von Scheliha ("Aryan"), the son of a Prussian squire, who joined the Nazi party at the suggestion of Soviet intelligence and in late 1934 had gotten himself named as the top aide in Warsaw to German ambassador Hans-Adolf von Moltke. Other recruits included the radioman Kurt Schulze ("Berg," b. 1894), Kurt Welkisch ("ABC," b. 1910), a German journalist and diplomat, and his wife, Margarita Welkisch ("LCL," b. 1913).[191] They were linked in their anti-Nazism.

Inside Nazi Germany, Wilhelm "Willy" Lehmann (b. 1884), code-named "Breitenbach," a long-serving Berlin policeman, had been secretly recruited even before the Nazis came to power, then moved into the Gestapo, where he was assigned to nothing less than counterintelligence against the Soviet Union. (He had been tasked with summary executions during the Night of the Long Knives, which helped solidify his bona fides.) Lehmann passed to Moscow details of German intelligence's organizational structure and forthcoming operations and, in 1935, of early German rocket tests. That same year, Harro Schulze-Boysen (b. 1909), a Prussian aristocrat officer at Göring's Luftwaffe, contacted the Soviet embassy offering his services; he was given the code name "Elder." Not long thereafter, Arvid Harnack (b. 1901), a senior official in the Nazi economics ministry and onetime leftist youth organizer, also made contact with the Soviet embassy; he was advised to join the Nazi party and given the code name "Corsican." No other country would field such an undercover network in the halls of the Third Reich.

Another remarkable anti-Nazi Soviet spy was in Tokyo, Richard Sorge, the offspring of a Russian mother and a German father, who, in preparation for assignment to Japan, had traveled to Germany and happened to meet the publisher of the *Journal of Geopolitics,* a zealous Nazi who gave him a contract as a stringer and a letter of introduction to the German embassy in Tokyo. Sorge, code-named "Ramsay," joined the Nazi party, took with him a radio operator, and charmed the ambassador in Japan, Herbert von Dirksen. Other contacts gave Sorge entrée to Colonel Eugen Ott, who became the German military attaché (and would one day replace Dirksen). Sorge also had spectacular success penetrating Japanese officialdom, partly thanks to the esteem in which the Germans held him. German diplomats discovered that the journalist stringer Sorge had better information about Japan than they did, and they let him help compile embassy reports to Berlin, copies of which surreptitiously went to Moscow.[192]

Soviet intelligence enjoyed gobsmacking success in the UK, too. Harold Philby, nicknamed "Kim" after the Rudyard Kipling character, had been born in British India (1912); his father was an adviser to the Saudi king, and the son aimed to join the foreign office. As a student at Cambridge University, Philby had been helped by Maurice Dobb, an economics lecturer and an early British Communist party member, to go abroad and work for the World Committee for the Relief of the Victims of German Fascism. Aiding refugees from Nazism in Austria, Philby married a Hungarian-Jewish divorcée who belonged to the Austrian Communist party and came to the attention of Tivadar (Theodore) Maly, a Hungary-born Soviet intelligence operative who secretly recommended him for recruitment. Back in London, a friend of Philby's wife set up a meeting in Regent's Park with the Artuzov protégé Arnold Deutsch, a chemical engineer born in Habsburg Slovakia, of Jewish extraction, who had joined the Austrian Communist party and relocated to the Soviet Union, before being posted as station chief to the UK.[193] Deutsch transformed Philby, a budding journalist, into a play-acting right-winger and reliable courier with a valuable British passport. Through Philby, Soviet intelligence recruited Guy Burgess (b. 1911), another Cambridge University student; Anthony Blunt, a Cambridge student and then tutor in art history; and the invaluable Donald Maclean, a fourth Cambridge University graduate who entered the British foreign office in 1935. Artuzov's team would even penetrate MI6.[194]

All the while, Soviet counterintelligence was spending as much or more time on its own diplomats and military officers as on foreign governments. NKVD special department operatives for watching the Red Army had ballooned to an all-time record of 3,769 by January 1935.[195] Mark Stokland, known as Gai, the head of the special department, received yet another phantasmagorical secret "report" from the informant Tatyana Zaionchkovskaya, who socialized with Tukhachevsky, among others, and asserted that the "counterrevolution" inside the USSR was counting on former officers to shoot Stalin. "This is complete rubbish of a stupid old woman who has lost her mind," Gai wrote. But such "reports" kept coming.[196]

What use Stalin and the Soviet regime would make of the intelligence windfall inadvertently delivered by Hitler and Nazism, meanwhile, remained to be seen. Hermann Göring, under the pretext of a hunting trip, was invited to undertake a diplomatic trip to Poland from January 26 to 31, 1935. He had just spent several days with Hitler in the Obersalzberg, and now, on the anniversary of the nonaggression declaration with Poland, he told Beck that Germany would not sign a broad Eastern Pact or any treaty with the Soviet Union, and that "the chancellor has decided to continue the policy of developing good neighborly relations with Poland." Göring told Józef Lipski, the Polish envoy to Berlin, who was back in Warsaw for the occasion, that Germany would have to expand, but not at Polish expense, and that Poland might acquire more Lithuanian territory in any deal over the Polish Corridor. At a reception in his honor, Göring tried to prove a lack of aggression toward Poland by pointing out that, for Germany, creating a common border with the USSR would be "highly dangerous." At the former tsarist family hunting grounds in the Białowieza (Belovezh) Forest, in the presence of two Polish generals, Göring "almost proposed an anti-Soviet alliance, and a joint march on Moscow," according to the Polish record. "Ukraine would be a Polish sphere of influence, while northwestern Russia would go to Germany." Göring conveyed something similar in his audience with President Piłsudski, even offering that the marshal could command a joint Polish-German attack on the USSR. The elderly president answered that Poland, having a 600-mile border with the Soviet Union, needed peace.[197]

Public knowledge of Göring's visit, combined with the secretiveness of its substance, sparked all manner of speculation.[198] On January 30, Stalin had Tukhachevsky—who had a sky-high profile abroad—deliver a policy speech to the 2,000 delegates of the 7th USSR Congress of Soviets. He declared that the Red Army was concentrating soldiers in the Far East and, in general, was a force not to be underestimated, revealing for the first time that the military budget had risen to more than 5 billion rubles—10 percent of total expenditures—and was projected to reach 6.5 billion in 1935. In fact, 1934 outlays had amounted to a gargantuan 5.8 billion (as compared with 417 million a decade before), and internal projections for 1935 were 7.5 billion.[199] But even the deliberately lowball figures were impressive. Tukhachevsky added, accurately, that troop strength had increased to 940,000. "We are working for the development of mobility and daring, for the development of initiative, independence, persistence—to put it crudely, 'nerve,'" he explained of the new military doctrine, adding that commanders accustomed since the civil war to cavalry had had to "adjust to a new level, to be able to utilize the mobility of aviation and our mechanized troops and tanks. [It] is not so simple." Both when he had first appeared on the dais and after he finished, the entire hall stood in applause for a good long time. "The ovation was marked out from others by its force and sincerity," one attendee recalled. "Tukhachevsky was a good orator, and his speech stirred the audience to its depths."[200] The rousing account of Red Army might was published in *Pravda* (January 31) along with a photograph of Stalin, Voroshilov, and other politburo members listening to Tukhachevsky.[201]

LITTLE BLACKBERRY

Nikolai Yezhov, along with Agranov, was the point man on the Kirov assassination fallout. Stalin convened a one-day Central Committee plenum on February 1, 1935, to formalize Yezhov's appointment as a Central Committee secretary. Officially, he had been born (1895) to a working-class family in industrial St. Petersburg, but he hailed from Mariampol, in tsarist Lithuania, and his father was a musician, then a forest warden, brothel ("tearoom") owner, and housepainter. His mother was the maid of the musical ensemble's conductor and either an ethnic Lithuanian or a Russian who grew up in Lithuania. (Yezhov spoke Lithuanian and Polish, which he hid.) Having completed only first grade, he went to the imperial Russian capital at age eleven to apprentice to a tailor, before signing on to the Putilov Works and then being conscripted. He joined the Bolshevik party in 1917 (before October) and served as a military commissar during the civil war, after which his star rose as a regional party functionary in Tatarstan, then in Mari-El (east-central Russia), where he provoked anger for running roughshod over the local ethnics, and then in the Kazakh steppe (Semipalatinsk).[202] Yezhov enjoyed playing guitar, composing verse, reading—he had been dubbed Kolya the Book Lover—and building model ships.[203] He was nervous and shy, and developed a reputation as mild-mannered, but he stood out for his uncommon energy.[204] In 1927, Ivan Moskvin, the head of the Central Committee's assignments and records department, had brought Yezhov into the central apparatus (they had met in the hotel at the 14th Party Congress). "I don't know a more ideal worker, or rather executive," Moskvin wrote to his son-in-law. "If you entrust him with anything, you need not check up: you can be sure, he will do it. Yezhov has only one fault, admittedly a fundamental one: he doesn't know where to stop. . . . And sometimes one has to keep an eye on him in order to stop him in time."[205]

Yezhov displaced his mentor Moskvin as head of assignments and records. The dictator had taken a shine to him, nicknaming him the Little Blackberry (Yezhevichka), and allowed him to attend politburo sessions, oversee personnel in the economy, and help run the orgburo.[206] In late 1933, the émigré *Socialist Herald* had published a revealing essay on "the dictator's inner circle" that ridiculed Yezhov. "Short in stature, nearly a dwarf, with thin curved legs, an asymmetric face, bearing the marks of his birth (his father was a hereditary alcoholic), with evil eyes, a thin squeaky voice, and a severely sarcastic tongue," read the profile, calling him "a typical representative of the Petersburg lower-foreman type, whose determining character trait was rage against those born in better circumstances . . . enormous rage against the intelligentsia, including the party intelligentsia."[207] The ridicule confirmed Yezhov's meteoric rise. Now a Central Committee secretary, he enjoyed a grand office on Old Square, on the top floor near the dictator's, and use of a three-story villa with a private cinema, tennis court, nanny, and staff, in Meshcherino, the prerevolutionary artists' and writers' colony on the Pra River just outside Moscow. (Yezhov had divorced his first wife and married Yevgeniya Feigenberg Khayutina Gladun, a social climber whom he met at a government resort in Sochi—it was her third marriage—and she began to convene literary salons.)[208]

Stalin also promoted Chubar and Mikoyan, longtime candidate members of the politburo, to full membership, giving them the voting slots of Kirov and Kuibyshev. Zhdanov and Eihe became candidate politburo members.[209] On February 27, 1935, Kaganovich replaced Andreyev as transport commissar, who became a Central Committee secretary. The railways had long been a bottleneck, and others posted there had not fared well (including Andreyev). On February 28, Stalin convened another one-day Central Committee plenum to formalize Andreyev's promotion. Khrushchev got Kaganovich's post as head of the Moscow party. Yezhov was put in charge of party personnel and local party organizations and freed from overseeing industry and managing the orgburo (responsibilities transferred to Andreyev). Yezhov also took over chairmanship of the party Control Commission from his mentor Kaganovich.[210] In a word, Kaganovich's protégés in the apparatus became Stalin's, and instead of the powerful post of de facto second secretary, held first by Molotov and then Kaganovich, Stalin now had a troika of three younger apparatchik deputies: Yezhov, Zhdanov, and Andreyev, of whom only Andreyev had met him before 1917.[211] The most frequent visitors to Stalin's Kremlin apartment for meals were now Molotov, Voroshilov, Kaganovich, Mikoyan, and Andreyev.[212] But the Little Blackberry spent more and more time in Stalin's office.

SOMETHING TO TALK ABOUT

Henri Barbusse's *Stalin: A New World Seen Through One Man* came out in French in February 1935. The Frenchman was the sole foreign intellectual who had met Stalin both recently and in the past (1927, 1932, 1933, 1934), and at both his office and his apartment.[213] His draft manuscript had been submitted for review to the Soviet functionary Stetsky, who faced a dilemma: the book not only mentioned

Trotsky, but also portrayed him as a thinker, while not portraying Stalin as such.[214] In a delicate dance to avoid alienating Barbusse, Stetsky managed to obtain changes. "Stalin is the Lenin of our day," the final text felicitously stated. "Stalin is a person with a scholar's mind, a worker's figure, and a simple soldier's dress." Barbusse portrayed the cult, much maligned in Western Europe, as a natural phenomenon arising from the depths ("If Stalin believes in the masses, the masses believe in him"), and humanized the dictator. "It is not so much that his expression is a little wild as that there seems to be a perpetual twinkle in his eye," Barbusse wrote. "He laughs like a child," and "people who laugh like children love children."[215]

Barbusse made his motivations plain, writing that "every state except one is moving through fascism towards ruin." But his knowledge of Soviet realities was dim.

Collective farms had stabilized, and the size of the harvests improved, in part from belated mechanization, in part from fortunate weather, but also from regime concessions to the farmers, who had been allowed to maintain "household plots" and personal cows, pigs, sheep, and chickens (though not horses, a sore point). In the Grand Kremlin Palace from February 11 to 17, 1935, the regime convened a Second all-Union Congress of Collective Farm Shock Workers, attended by 1,433 delegates, the majority of whom were not party members. Crop growers, herders, and tractor drivers were given the floor.[216] Maria Demchenko, of the Comintern Collective Farm in Kiev province, pledged to harvest 500 centners of sugar beets per hectare ("We must bombard the country with sugar"), which the regime made into a "movement" of 500ers (the average at her farm was 245). Stalin did not deliver a formal speech, but came and went all seven days. "Iosif Vissarionovich," Demchenko told the delegates, "laughs with us, converses with us, shares his thoughts with us on how to work on the collective farm and how we can live better."[217] One Kazakh tractor driver, Beken Tankin, a former nomad whose Russian was shaky, had been put in the position of chairing one of the nine sessions and became bewildered when delegates started shouting "Hurrah!" The ovation persisted. Finally, someone came up from behind and turned Tankin around: Stalin had reentered the congress presidium. Smiling, the dictator pointed to a button on the table for Tankin to press for quiet. "I'll go home to my collective farm," he said to himself, "with something to talk about."[218]

Delegates "elected" a commission of 170 members to consider a new charter for collective farms drafted by the Central Committee agriculture department.[219] At the commission, on February 16, Stalin went through the text point by point, grandly asserting that members were not taking into account the interests of collective farmers. Instead of the 0.10–0.12 hectare for household plots some people were recommending, he proposed 0.25 to 0.5, and even up to 1 hectare in some regions, depending on conditions, as well as up to one cow and two calves, one sow and its progeny, up to ten sheep and goats, unlimited poultry, and twenty beehives. "Comrade Stalin," Kalinin objected, "we do not have enough land." Voroshilov interjected that those getting 0.5 hectare would in any case be "a minority." Stalin disagreed: "Our country is big, the conditions are very various."[220] He also recommended maternity leave of two months (at half average pay), a nod to the outsized role that ambitious women such as Demchenko played.[221] The final charter, approved on February 17, granted the leave, personal livestock, and household plots of the size Stalin suggested, and the press let the rural laborers know who was responsible for the ostensible largesse.[222] In fact, Stalin despised the household plots, and his regime strove to contain them.[223]

One contemporary émigré analyst deemed the 1935 household-plot-size concessions a "collective farm NEP," but still likened the collective farms to the Gulag system, only larger.[224] The state dominated the grain trade, imposing very heavy quotas and very low state prices, paying collective farmers subsistence wages, predominantly in kind, and forcing them to work in brigades—a demotion from peasant to laborer, which encouraged dependency and sloth.[225] The regime also imposed unpaid obligations for roadwork, timber felling, and hauling, and required rural laborers (unlike urban workers) to deliver quotas of meat, milk, and eggs from their household plots, even if they did not own a cow or livestock. But after all the blood and tears of dekulakization, the new charter belatedly conceded legal entry into collective farms to former kulaks, albeit supposedly only "after a strict check to ensure that wolves in sheep's clothing were not getting in on the pretext of being reformed characters."[226] The Soviet village ended up stratified, with rich and poor, based on bureaucratic position.[227]

"FORMERS"

Three women in their early twenties who worked as cleaning personnel in the Kremlin had sat down to "tea" and gossiped. One supposedly said, "Stalin has people do the work for him—that's why he's so fat. He has servants and luxuries." The second: "Stalin killed his wife. He's not Russian but Armenian, very evil, and never looks at anyone with a nice glance." The third: "Comrade Stalin gets a lot of money and he misleads us, saying that he only makes 200 rubles [per month]." Rudolf Peterson, the Kremlin commandant—who had been one of the first to see Nadya's body after she shot herself and was said to have given her vanished suicide note to Stalin—passed a report of these conversations to Yenukidze, who did nothing.[228] But another denunciation came forward, and on January 20, 1935, the NKVD's Pauker, Georgy Molchanov, and Genrikh Lyushkov, all of whom were involved in the investigation of Kirov's murder on the NKVD's watch, conducted interrogations. Yagoda sent Stalin a report that day about cleaning personnel who were said to belong to "a counterrevolutionary group" in the Kremlin.[229]

Yezhov, meanwhile, had invited the dictator to join him at a closed-door operational gathering of all NKVD central and provincial bosses on February 3; Stalin accepted, and delivered a speech on vigilance.[230] At the gathering, Agranov contradicted the official line on the Kirov murder, stating, accurately, that "Nikolayev was gripped by ecstasy over fulfilling an historical mission, comparing himself to Zhelyabov and [Alexander] Radishchev." Agranov went on to issue a mea culpa: "We did not succeed in proving that the 'Moscow Center' knew and prepared a terrorist act against comrade Kirov."[231]

In the testimony of Kremlin employees, each person mentioned other names, leading to new arrests, and on February 5, Yagoda sent Stalin a report with interrogation protocols containing confessions of private complaints about daily life and a lack of democracy, as well as "Trotskyite interpretations of Lenin's so-called Testament" and speculation about how Stalin's wife had really died.[232] While interrogating Kremlin janitors, the NKVD heard about some daughters of former nobles who worked as librarians in the Kremlin, transporting books back and forth from the private residences. Yagoda's power ended at the Kremlin walls—inside, Yenukidze's central executive committee apparatus and Voroshilov's defense commissariat ruled—and the NKVD chief evidently made professions that he could not be responsible for the safety of the leadership with such women going about using special passes. Testimony was spun into the existence of an "aristocratic nest" around Nina Rozenfeld, an ethnic Armenian, educated at gymnasium, who was said to have boasted of her descent from an ancient Muscovy clan. (One arrested colleague defended her as "a Soviet-inclined person.")[233] Stalin read, numbered, and marked up the voluminous interrogation protocols with queries or comments. On one, where it was noted that the accused had initially been a cleaning lady before becoming a Kremlin librarian, he underlined the sentence and wrote, "Ha-ha, cleaner-librarian?"[234]

These were indeed small fry.[235] Nonetheless, on February 14, the politburo substituted the NKVD for the central executive committee as the defense commissariat's partner for oversight of the Kremlin.[236] The NKVD took over the reconstruction of the Grand Kremlin Palace's Andreyev and Alexandrov halls and of the Sverdlov Hall in the Imperial Senate. This looked like a triumph for Yagoda, but on February 22, the politburo directed Yezhov, not Yagoda, to conduct a verification of the central executive committee apparatus. NKVD interrogation protocols in the "Kremlin Affair" had to be sent to him.[237] Zinoviev, meanwhile, had been hauled out of prison and re-interrogated in Moscow on February 19 in connection with the Kirov murder. "To Kamenev belongs the winged formulation on how 'Marxism is now whatever is convenient for Stalin,'" he testified. "Kamenev and I did discuss Stalin's removal, but we thought only in terms of his being replaced in the post of general secretary. . . . I did not hear declarations by Kamenev about a terrorist act in the struggle with the party leadership."[238] Yezhov had work to do. Soon the politburo would formally task him with reviewing the statutes governing the NKVD: further pressure on Yagoda.[239]

Yezhov praised Zakovsky, whose Leningrad Chekists were poring over pre-revolutionary archives, address lists, and phone books, stringing together people like beads to form counterrevolutionary "organizations" of former nobles, merchants, factory owners, rentiers, old regime functionaries, priests, and family members.[240] Zakovsky had been a Red Guard protecting Smolny during the October Revolution, and his Cheka service dated from its founding, in December 1917 (he was said to have been invited to join by Dzierżyński). He had completed just two years of schooling, yet he was credited with compiling the internal NKVD training textbook. He had reported to Yagoda on the more than 11,000 "former people" employed in the city's party and government institutions.[241] Yagoda, in a note to Stalin (February 26), objected to indiscriminate roundups of "formers," unless they were proven counterrevolutionaries, because of the potential for a negative press campaign abroad, but Stalin brushed the memo aside ("to the archive").[242] Beginning on February 28, Zakovsky and his minions began "cleansing" the former people, the universities, and the border zones, requesting authorization for ever more arrests in "unmasked" conspiracies and boasting of preventing terrorist acts against the new Leningrad party boss, Zhdanov.[243]

FOREIGN MODELS

Bulgakov's *The Days of the Turbins* had been returned to theaters, partly as a result of Gorky's determination and political weight.[244] By some accounts, Stalin saw it fifteen times.[245] In 1935, he sent the fourteen-year-olds Vasily and Artyom to see it. Artyom recalled not comprehending the play, because it showed no Reds, only Whites, and the latter fought among themselves. Stalin explained that "between the Reds and the Whites there was a spectrum from almost Red to almost White, so that the people who fight in the play, some are very White, others a bit pink, but not Red. They could not get along, so they fought. Never think that you can divide people between purely Red and purely White. That is only leaders, the more literate, conscious people. The masses follow these or those, frequently confusing them, and do not go where they are supposed to go."[246]

Stalin approved an International Film Festival in Moscow (February 21–March 2, 1935) and allowed the world-renowned Eisenstein to chair the jury. Captions under photographs of the Soviet participants read "director," while Eisenstein's read "Extraordinary World-Class Director," but speakers pointedly asked why he had not made a film in six years, accusing him of silence about Soviet achievements.[247] Walt Disney animations—*Three Little Pigs, Peculiar Penguins*—were featured (and, before the year was out, shown to the Soviet public).[248] An American film about Mexico called *Viva, Villa!* was also screened, prompting the poet Alexander Bezymensky to accuse *Jolly Fellows* of having plagiarized its music from this film. This spurred renewed ideological attacks against mere laughter. "*Jolly Fellows* creates the impression that some bourgeois directors sneaked into the studios at night and secretly shot the film using a Soviet stage set," a French critic remarked, as quoted in the Soviet press.[249] Stalin ordered Mekhlis at *Pravda* to defend Shumyatsky, and the attack dog editorialized, without irony, that "both editors [of *Izvestiya* and *Literary Newspaper*] have apparently forgotten the elementary rules of decency essential to Soviet newspapers."[250]

At the concluding ceremony in the Columned Hall of the House of Trade Unions, Leningrad Film took first prize, primarily for *Chapayev; The Last Billionaire* by the French-born René-Lucien Chomette, known as René Clair, took second; and Disney third.[251] Clair's film, a commercial flop in France, portrays a nearly bankrupt fictional European kingdom ("Casinaria") that begs for help from the earth's richest man ("Monsieur Banco"), who, upon arrival, is accidentally hit in the head and awakens a babbling imbecile. Casinaria soon becomes a dictatorship.[252]

Certain types of foreign literature were being translated, and, once in Russian (or another Soviet language), they could be incorporated, alongside Lev Tolstoy, into the Soviet canon as "classics of world literature." This included Cervantes, Molière, Balzac, Goethe, and especially Shakespeare, all of whom were often translated freely, rather than literally.[253] "Shakespearize More!" (an exhortation credited to Marx) had been revived, with propagandists characterizing him as a "people's bard."[254] For a March 1935 international theater festival in Moscow— Bertolt Brecht, Kurt Eisler, and Edward Gordon Craig participated—the featured Soviet entrant was Shakespeare's *King Lear,* which had premiered at the Moscow State Jewish Theater in Yiddish, with Solomon Mikhoels playing Lear.[255] Of course, Lear had lost all his territory and descended into insanity.[256]

TAKE CARE

Local officials all around the Union were reporting to Stalin on steel, chemicals, military hardware. Beria was reporting on Baku oil and Georgian rare metals, the boost in manganese output at Chiatura, the performance of the Tiflis railway shops now named for Stalin, and the output of new plants: the Tiflis machine-tool factory, now named for Kirov; Zestafoni Ferroalloy Plant; Inguri Pulp and Paper.[257] Lakoba's reports concerned tea, citrus, tobacco, and geraniums. He sent crates of tangerines and lemons to Stalin and Orjonikidze in Moscow. But Abkhazia's resorts left a lot to be desired. "Authority, comrades, does not arise by itself; it needs to be won. It arises where living people get things done, not from books, not from formulas," he had told the 7th Congress of Soviets of the Abkhaz autonomous republic in March 1935. "You know, comrades, in resort construction we still look very weak.. . . . We have not managed to reestablish our old resorts fully."[258] Nonetheless, the Abkhaz autonomous republic was awarded the Order of Lenin, partly for tobacco production (which was largely the work of family farms, not collectives).[259]

As the NKVD interrogated ever more Kremlin personnel, Yenukidze's name inevitably came up.[260] Well liked, he ran a regime of favors, doling out unique state resources and using his status as Stalin's intimate to take care of old friends and solve sticky matters involving elite households.[261] The fifty-eight-year-old had never married and had not himself moved into the Kremlin, continuing to live in the Metropole, where the central executive committee had had its original offices, but if he was trying to keep his bedding of underage females out of sight, he failed.

During testimony, some arrested Kremlin employees mentioned Yenukidze's "girls." Irina Gogua, another Kremlin employee who fell into the NKVD's net, was the daughter of an old Menshevik who had gone to school with Yenukidze in Tiflis. "He was a fantastic guy, very charming, a flaming redhead who, thanks to graying, had become such a soft blond," she would recall of Yenukidze. "True, his face was pockmarked, even more so than Iosif Vissarionovich's. . . . You see, it was a paradox. He was accused of debauchery, devil knows what. But he was a very warm person. He had one quality: he hated to say no, he helped people, independent of who they were. He had one weakness: girls who married his closest friends with whom he would fall in love."[262]

What really got Yenukidze into trouble was his quiet disbursal of state funds to help the often destitute families of non-Bolshevik revolutionaries from the underground years, former Communist party oppositionists (Kamenev's relatives), even former nobles (like himself) for whom he found jobs in the sprawling central executive committee. Kirov's assassination had made such actions especially sinister but, protected by Voroshilov, Yenukidze was merely demoted on March 3, 1935, to a position in the central executive committee of the South Caucasus.[263] Ivan Akulov, USSR procurator general, became secretary of the central executive committee; Andrei Vyshinsky took over as USSR procurator general.

The Kirov and Kremlin Affair investigations were now running in parallel. In Leningrad on March 10, Draule was tried and executed, along with her sister and brother-in-law; there was no public announcement.[264] The next day, a secret NKVD circular observed that enemies had been smashed mercilessly but as a result had "gone deep underground," so operatives had to dig deeper to find them.[265] In Moscow, in further testimony (March 11), Nina Rozenfeld was said to have attributed Nadya Alliluyeva's death to differences over party policy, while complaining about the removal of Zinoviev and Kamenev and a lack of democracy. Rozenfeld happened to be the former wife of Lev Kamenev's brother Nikolai, and their son, Boris N. Rozenfeld, was labeled a Trotskyite.[266] Nikolai Kamenev had been arrested, and found to have painted watercolors of Stalin. Finally, Lev Kamenev was interrogated (March 21) and asked about his brother, who Lev was told had confessed to planning to kill Stalin. Lev Kamenev said that after the arrests of the Zinoviev followers Ivan Bakayev and Grigory Yevdokimov in the wake of the Kirov murder, an agitated Zinoviev had come to him expressing fears of an action like Germany's Night of the Long Knives against him and others. Stalin circulated the document to Molotov, Kaganovich, Voroshilov, and Yezhov, writing, "Idiotic interrogation of Kamenev."[267]

Stalin had the politburo approve by telephone poll a secret party circular absolving Yenukidze of knowing of plans to assassinate the dictator, but deeming him to have been used by the class enemy. His demotion to the South Caucasus was judged too light a punishment.[268] Gorky was following press accounts of the Kremlin Affair. "What is striking is not so much the behavior of Yenukidze, but the shameful indifference to this behavior of the party-ites," he wrote ingratiatingly to Stalin (March 23, 1935). "Even the non-party people long ago knew and spoke about how the old man was surrounded by nobles, Mensheviks, and, in general, shitty flies." Gorky asserted that the strangely well-informed émigré *Socialist Herald* got its inside information from Yenukidze's staff. "The closer we get to war, the stronger will be the efforts of these jokers of all suits to try to assassinate you, in order to decapitate the Union," Gorky stated in his letter, which Stalin circulated to the politburo. "This is natural, for the enemies see well: there is no one who could take your place. With your colossal and wise work, you have inculcated in millions of people trust and love to you—that's a fact. . . . Take care of yourself."[269]

Also on March 23, after protracted negotiations, the Soviets sold the Chinese Eastern Railway to Manchukuo for the convertible currency equivalent of 140 million yen, a fraction of its market (let alone strategic) value.[270] (Stalin's regime left behind a network of undercover agents.) On the same day, the politburo decreed that the payment would be used for more equipment purchases in the United States, Britain, and Germany for Moscow's ZIS Factory, which manufactured heavy trucks and, soon, luxury sedans.[271] Chinese patriots said the railroad was not the Soviets' to sell, and the Nationalist government in Nanking lodged an official protest. Chiang Kai-shek had opened semiofficial negotiations for a friendship treaty with Japan's representative, who proposed a Sino-Japanese alliance. As a dedicated anti-Communist, Chiang would have been a natural ally of Japan (as well as Germany) against the Soviet Union.[272] But "Chiang Kai-shek did not go for this," the Soviet chargé d'affaires in China had reported of the alliance proposal. Chiang did raise the Japanese legation to the status of an embassy, and the two countries announced an exchange of ambassadors. This provoked anti-Japanese protests in Tientsin and Peking. Japan, leaping on the "insult" of the protests, had its garrison in Tientsin expel the Chinese Nationalist authorities and soldiers from Hebei province, and then from the Chahar province of Inner

Mongolia, as it spread its control over northern China. Japan would also ramp up pressure on the Soviet satellite Outer Mongolia.[273] The Soviet chargé d'affaires, in the same report about Chiang, warned that another faction in the Nanking government "favors an alliance" with Japan.[274]

JOYRIDE

On April 22, 1935, after concluding meetings in the Little Corner at 7:00 p.m., Stalin went downstairs to his apartment for supper. It was the birthday of Svetlana's governess, and the relatives had come by. Stalin was said to be in a good mood. During the toasts, Svetlana said she wanted to ride on the new Moscow metro. Her governess, Maria Svanidze, and others were to accompany her and Vasily; Kaganovich sent the party with his deputy. Suddenly Stalin said he wanted to go, too. Molotov was phoned to join. "Everybody was terribly concerned," Svanidze wrote in her diary. "There was a lot of whispering about the danger of such an outing without proper preparation."

A now pale Kaganovich suggested that they wait until midnight, when the metro shut down. Stalin insisted they go immediately. They drove in three cars to Moscow's Crimea Square and descended into the station, waiting for what turned out to be twenty minutes; a train arrived already packed. Workers decoupled the car with the motor and Stalin's group was off, to Hunters' Row, the station closest to the Kremlin, where he inspected the station and the escalator; onlookers erupted. Stalin ended up surrounded by well-wishers. Bodyguards and police had arrived and tried to bring order. The crowd smashed an enormous metal lamp. Svanidze was nearly smothered against a column. Vasily was scared for his life. Svetlana was so frightened, she stayed in the train car. We "were intimidated by the uninhibited ecstasy of the crowd," Svanidze wrote. "Iosif was merry."

This was an unstaged moment catalyzed by his daughter. Stalin reboarded, traveling to the end of the line, Sokolniki, where he was supposed to get into a waiting automobile, but he decided to stay on board and return to Smolensk Square, where no vehicles were waiting (the train beat them). He and his entourage went on foot toward the Arbat as rain descended and puddles formed. A car finally arrived. Svetlana and Vasily were taken to the Kremlin apartment, where Vasily "threw himself on the bed and cried hysterically." Stalin headed to the Near Dacha. Evidently, his obsession with possible assassination was in abeyance that evening: regular passengers had been allowed to ride in the train carriage with him from Hunters' Row.[275] "Iosif smiled affectionately the whole time," Svanidze wrote in her diary. "I think that, despite all his sobriety, he was touched by the people's love and attention to their Supreme Leader. . . . He once said about the ovations offered to him that people need a tsar, that is, someone to revere and in whose name to live and labor."[276]

COULD STALIN HAVE MURDERED HIS CLOSEST FRIEND? He was capable of anything.[277] But who, precisely, would have carried out that mission for him? Medved, who was incompetent, and would himself go to his grave suspecting that Yagoda had organized the murder on Stalin's behalf?[278] Zaporozhets, who broke his leg, took no part in any operational matters after September 1934, and had left town on an extended holiday in the weeks leading up to the critical deed? Borisov, a near invalid who had gotten his bodyguard job only because he was of working-class origin and, for a time, had been a night watchman and was a faithful dog to Kirov? A mystery second gunman in the corridor, who eluded every single witness, as well as the lockdown imposed after the shots were heard? There is no evidence whatsoever that Stalin killed Kirov (despite the work of several commissions under Khrushchev aimed at discrediting the dictator). And there is copious evidence, recorded right before and after the assassination, that Nikolayev did it, and managed to pull it off because of his determination and shoddy NKVD security practices that were, ultimately, traceable to Kirov himself.[279] Nikolayev had motive, and opportunity.[280] He roiled with grievance and summoned resolve from revolutionary terrorist history and Soviet ideals of a workers' state and social justice. He plotted out numerous attempts, all of which failed, until finally a combination of planning and luck gave him the chance to fulfill a wish to exact revenge and make history.

While Nikolayev reclaimed a sense of higher purpose from his despair, Stalin's regime made the Kirov assassination into an epoch-defining event. Most people in Leningrad and elsewhere, living in communal apartments, barracks, and mud huts, were preoccupied with material hardship. Apparatchiks complained that the discussions they were ordered to oversee of Kirov's murder were overtaken by the pending end of bread rationing and threatened price increases.[281] The end of rationing had generated significant anxiety and resentment.[282] All the while, conspiracy theories flourished: Medved had slipped Nikolayev a pass to Smolny; Chudov had ordered a hit to take Kirov's place; foreign agents had penetrated the building; it was Stalin's doing (a rumor that grew over time). Police informants hastened to capture or invent such gossip. In Leningrad: "I like brave men like Ni-kolayev who must have gone to a certain death." "It's clear not all the Zhelyabovs have disappeared in Rus; the struggle for freedom goes on." "The murderer wanted good for the people, that's why he killed Kirov." In the miners' region of Donetsk: "Kirov was killed; it's not enough; Stalin should have also been killed."[283]

Speculation that the affable provincial party leader constituted a threatening political rival to Stalin is without foundation.[284] Similarly, the regime folklore that Yagoda's NKVD had "resisted" the direction of the investigation was largely invented. Yagoda had no issues with framing Zinoviev and "Zinovievites," a scenario that Stalin, in any case, did not come to immediately. The dictator drove an overkill response to the murder, relying not just on the hyper-ingratiating Yezhov, Agranov, and Zakovsky, but also on Yagoda. Yagoda had suggested the foreign angle—textbook Stalinist practice—calling from Stalin's office the first night.[285] It was Stalin who had chosen not to investigate Nikolayev's visits and telephone calls to the German and Latvian consulates. The fabrications, moreover, exacerbated the professional degradation of the secret police, which enraged Stalin, and for which he had recently abolished the OGPU in favor of the NKVD. The fabrications also hurt the USSR's reputation internationally, to which Stalin had become more sensitive. At the same time, it is wrong to assert that Stalin "took advantage" of the Kirov assassination. He needed no such pretext to act as he chose. He pushed for fierce revenge against "enemies" and prevention of recurrences out of anger, and loss.

One of Stalin's prime fixations was confirmed: the NKVD was asleep on the job. In a city teeming with foreigners and presumed foreign agents, with innumerable "former people" and other presumed class enemies, with even much of the lower orders disaffected by the sacrifices of building socialism, Leningrad's secret-operative department had only a short, pathetic list of potential terrorists—and did not even share that list with the bodyguard department.[286] A parallel obsession of Stalin's was also confirmed: an enemy terrorist in possession of a party card, taking advantage of ties to party members, had penetrated security with ease and assassinated a top leader.[287] In fact, Nikolayev had been purged, for a time, but the episode had only rendered him more dangerous, just as Stalin was warning (the "class struggle" sharpened). But Stalin chose not to make this the object of the investigation and trials. Nikolayev's individual terrorism—which had grown from his violated sense of worker empowerment and Communist justice—was altered, at Stalin's behest, into the mythology that Zinoviev and Kamenev, both powerless, were somehow behind the assassination. Then Stalin remained bothered by their sentencing for creating a "moral atmosphere" conducive to terrorism, because it had fallen short of convictions for direct preparation in terrorist acts by his old critics or direct links to his arch-nemesis Trotsky, who remained out of reach in foreign exile.[288]

Stalin increasingly was alone. Not only had both of his wives died, but now his closest friend was gone. Henceforth he went to the steam bath alone. Relations with Orjonikidze had become strained, and Stalin's ardor for Lakoba was cooling, partly as a result of Beria's intrigues. Stalin's newer associates, Andreyev, Yezhov, and Zhdanov, were minions, not social peers, and he was not socially close to the unlettered Kaganovich or the stiff Molotov. But Stalin had the Soviet state, which he had helped build into a major military power.[289] Still, despite joining the League of Nations, the Soviet state was also to a considerable extent alone. And, more and more, the militarized state and its ruler were being stalked from afar by a nemesis the likes of which, inside the party, Stalin had never faced: Adolf Hitler.

CHAPTER 5

A GREAT POWER

They talk about it in Soviet institutions, factory smoking
rooms, student dormitories, and commuter trains. The
most widespread sentiment is the feeling of national pride.
Russia has again become a Great Power whose friendship
even such powerful states as France desire. . . . In Soviet
institutions the philistine functionaries, silent for years,
now speak confidently about national patriotism, about
the historical mission of Russia, about the revival of the
Franco-Russian alliance.

Émigré Socialist Herald, *May 1935*[1]

FRANCE AND BRITAIN, to the west, and the Soviet Union, to the east, had a
Hitler problem. All the powers were slowly coming to grips with the Nazi leader,
whose turgid masterpiece, *Mein Kampf* (a crisp title suggested by his publisher),
had been reissued after he became chancellor.[2] The prison-dictated autobiography, first published in 1925–26, had been issued in English translation only in
1933, and in abridged form, cleansed of "offensive" paragraphs; Britain's foreign
office possessed a single copy of an unexpurgated edition (which it misplaced for
a time). A French translation had finally appeared only in 1934 (few French politicians read German).[3] A Russian translation would be published only in 1935,
and only in the Shanghai emigration.[4] Soviet foreign affairs commissariat personnel, many of whom were Jewish, could read the original German with all the
"Drang nach Osten" and "Judeo-Bolshevism" riffs.[5] Still, people were unsure what
to make of the book's ravings in policy terms. Hitler's calls for rearmament could
be misread as standard German nationalism. His radical anti-Semitism could be
misconstrued as in line with remarks by Kaiser Wilhelm II, who had blamed the
Jews for the Great War.[6] Even the Führer's expansionist *Lebensraum* could be
stretched to resemble a defensible, if emotional, reaction to the circumstance that
so many German speakers had been left out of Bismarck's "unified" Germany.

While Hitler exploited a national politics of salvation and an international politics of national self-determination, Stalin was conjuring up a domestic politics of siege and anticapitalist mobilization and an international politics of anti-imperialism. But he did no better than his British and French counterparts in taking the measure of the Nazi regime. Between January and March 1935, the newspaper *Red Star* published a series of articles about supposed tensions between Hitler and his Nazi entourage, on one side, and the German military on the other. The German army supposedly "sought to reestablish the old relations with Russia," and German generals "foresee a military clash with France in the first instance."[7] Alongside this provocation—or was it a fantasy?—the Soviet war plan for the western theater still identified Poland as the main enemy, anticipating that Romania would join Poland's side, but assuming that Germany, because it coveted Polish territory, would at least indirectly support Soviet defense by threatening Poland's rear. Soviet intelligence, however, forwarded a report of intensified rumors of a Franco-German rapprochement, possibly leading to a larger bloc with Poland—supposedly Piłsudski's dream—and maybe drawing in Finland, Hungary, Romania, even Italy.[8] In fact, Poland had no intention of sacrificing its precious independence to the victor of a German-Soviet clash, continuing its neutrality toward both of its giant neighbors, along with separate alliances with France and Romania—in short, bilateralism, not multilateralism.[9] This was a truth the British understood, the French regretted, Hitler relished, and Stalin never accepted.

Finally, during two unusually long sessions with the military men in the Little Corner (February 28, March 8), Stalin acknowledged reality.[10] The regime resolved to be more forceful in standing up to Japan, and admitted that Germany might start a war against the Soviet Union not opportunistically, waiting for Japan to act, but on its own initiative.[11] Above all, the PR (Poland-Romania) war plan was displaced by a new GP (Germany-Poland) plan, in which Poland as well as Romania remained enemies, but only as auxiliaries: Nazi Germany eclipsed them.[12] Soviet diplomacy, predicated upon disruption of European solidarity and avoidance of commitments, was even slower to turn. Membership in the League of Nations had brought little, and negotiations for the regional security system known as the Eastern Pact were effectively dead, but time and again the politburo instructed the Soviet envoy Vladimir Potyomkin in Paris, "Do not rush ahead and thereby foster the misconception that we need the [Franco-Soviet bilateral alliance] more than the French. We are not as weak as some suggest."[13] By spring 1935, however, Soviet foreign policy more seriously contemplated securing the country against Nazi Germany.[14] Stalin both countenanced and exerted a break on that shift, refusing to abandon pursuit of closer economic, and ultimately political, ties with Berlin. At the same time, he wanted the world to recognize that the country he led was a revived great power.

THE HITLER PROBLEM

British officials feared that an arms race would derail its fragile economic recovery, and that another war would no better solve the German problem than had the Great War. Hitler had invited foreign secretary Sir John Simon as well as Lord Privy Seal Anthony Eden to Berlin. On March 7, 1935, three days before the scheduled visit, London published a policy paper urging a sheepishly modest £11 million increase in military spending, citing German rearmament and bellicosity. Hitler developed a "cold," and the visit was put off ("Those ruling England *must* get used to dealing with us on an equal footing").[15] On March 9, Göring assembled foreign military attachés to announce the existence of a German air force, which was prohibited by Versailles. On March 15, the French National Assembly debated a doubling of army service, from one to two years. Using this as a pretext, the next day, in a further flouting of Versailles, Hitler declared reintroduction of conscription for the Reichswehr—renamed the Wehrmacht—tripling its size to 300,000, which was to rise at some unspecified date to 550,000 (pundits predicted 3 million). *Pravda* prominently reported Nazi Germany's actions.[16] On March 17, representatives of France, Britain, Italy, and the Soviet Union discussed "protesting" Hitler's actions at the League, but Britain and France demurred.[17] That same day, Heroes' Memorial Day in Germany, Hitler celebrated the rebirth of the German army in the State Opera House, and afterward staged a review of the Wehrmacht, effectively a military parade, to jubilant crowds.[18] Belatedly, the Führer now deigned to receive Simon and Eden after all. The pair, rather than cancel in protest, paid the first visit by British high officials to Hitler as chancellor.

Hitler met them in the morning and the afternoon on both March 25 and 26, wearing a brown tunic with a red swastika armband, and launched with a monologue on the menace of Bolshevism and Soviet expansionism, insisting that he merely wanted to improve the welfare of the German people, who had been through a bitter fifteen years. He further declaimed that Germany's exit from the League of Nations had been approved by 94 percent of the people, and that no one in Germany imagined annexing Austria, given the principles of state sovereignty and noninterference. He raised hopes for a bilateral naval pact by accepting that his fleet be limited to no more than 35 percent the size of Britain's—three times the size of the Versailles restrictions—provided the Soviet Union did not expand its own military even more than it had. He also boasted that he had already achieved air parity with Britain, a falsehood that, when leaked, would set off a storm in London. "He emphasized his words with jerky, energetic gestures of the right hand, sometimes clenching his fist," Hitler's interpreter wrote. "He impressed me as a man who advanced his arguments intelligently and skillfully."[19]

Hitler parried the Britons' efforts to draw Germany into any multilateral agreement, such as a pact covering Austria or German readmission to the League of Nations. He noted that he "could give the British ministers the assurance that Germany would never declare war on Russia," but added that Bolshevik doctrine, political aims, and military capabilities meant that "from Russia there was greater probability of war than from other countries. Moreover, the risks for Russia in a possible war were smaller than those for other powers. Russia could with impunity allow the occupation of great tracts of her territory as large as Germany; she could permit bombardment of great regions; she could therefore wage war without risking destruction." It was a shrewd lament, and revealed Hitler's deepest preoccupations.

A skeptical Eden voiced doubts that the Soviet Union would initiate a war. Hitler pronounced himself "firmly convinced that one day cooperation and solidarity would be urgently necessary to defend Europe against the Asiatic and Bolshevik menace." The Führer thanked his guests and voiced hope that they had understood his efforts to raise his country to equal status with other nations. "The British ministers," according to their record, avowed that they "would take away very pleasant memories of the kindness and hospitality shown them."[20] In the evening, Hitler, in tails, hosted a banquet and concert at the Chancellery. Press accounts made it hard to discern what, if anything, had transpired. But the mere fact of the visit conveyed British readiness to renegotiate already imposed treaty obligations.

Stalin's spies in London (the Irish John King, a cipher clerk at the foreign office, recruited in mid-February 1935) and in Rome (Francesco Constantini, an Italian employee at the British embassy) each delivered copies of the British foreign office record of the conversation, which ran to 23,000 words. But NKVD intelligence forwarded a severely condensed Russian translation of just 4,000 words, selecting only certain statements, which they removed from context, to form a new single stream. Their editing made it seem that the British had given

Hitler carte blanche to annex Austria and schemed to instigate a Nazi-Soviet clash.[21] "Mister Hitler," the NKVD version of the British record had the Nazi stating, "would not sign an agreement he could not accept, but if he did take on obligations, he would never violate them."[22]

Being fed what he craved, Stalin's suspicions were further incited by the fact that Eden, on the way to Berlin, had stopped over in Paris to sound out the French about readmitting Germany into the League and a possible arms limitation agreement. French foreign minister Pierre Laval, Stalin knew, had been noncommittal. "Laval told Eden France could renounce aid from the Little Entente and the USSR only if England signed a military alliance, a Franco-English military alliance," according to an intelligence report about the conversation from a Soviet agent in the French foreign ministry, on which Stalin wrote, "Important. (Truthful.) My archive."[23]

Laval waved the Soviet card to break through British hesitation, but the British establishment was cool even to the "entente" it had signed with France in 1932, let alone to a real bilateral alliance.[24] British secret services, starved of resources, a bit old-fashioned, and uncoordinated, contributed to government ignorance, sometimes willful, of the capabilities, let alone the intentions, of Hitler's regime.[25] Never mind that Hitler's boasting that Germany would be a "world power" or nothing uncannily echoed British declarations about their own empire: many British officials believed or wanted to believe that German rearmament was, or would be, limited, gradual.[26] The fright over Hitler's assertion of air parity did consolidate moves to some British rearmament.[27] But even those Brits who took a dark view of Nazi Germany remained eager to nip the developing arms race in the bud with some sort of accommodation.

STRANGE PEOPLE

Simon did not bother to travel to Moscow, instead returning home to report on Hitler to the cabinet; Eden was transported from the German border in a Soviet-supplied luxury rail coach equipped with a phonograph that played English jazz. From his car window he found Moscow drab, the people poorly dressed. On the day of his arrival, March 28, Litvinov and Soviet envoy to Britain Ivan Maisky received him, along with British ambassador Lord Chilston and Strang of the foreign office, who had been with Eden in Berlin. Eden conveyed that Hitler had harped on the Soviet threat and how Germany was the bulwark of "European civilization" and needed to be permitted to rearm. "We do not have the slightest doubt about German aggression," Litvinov answered, according to the Soviet notetaker. "German foreign policy is inspired by two main ideas—*revanche* and domination in Europe." Litvinov elucidated that the Soviets wanted "mutual assistance" against Germany and possibly Poland, according to the British notetaker. When the British offered congratulations on the Soviet sale of the Chinese Eastern Railway, Litvinov remarked, "In Japan, even in military circles, a tendency to maintain peaceful relations with the USSR is growing rapidly."[28]

That evening, Litvinov hosted a banquet in Eden's honor at the Neo-Gothic Spiridonovka, an expropriated merchant's mansion, and made a speech in English about the ominous state of the world.[29] The next day, the group returned to the German theme, with Eden again stressing that people in Britain were less convinced than those in the USSR of Nazism's aggressiveness. Litvinov answered: "The original German plan had been to attack France and then to attack in the East. . . . The plan now apparently is to leave France alone, but to attack in the East only."[30] Eden raised the perennial complaint about Comintern propaganda abroad. Litvinov, in the Soviet account, responded, "What in reality is 'propaganda'? Is what the British press publishes about the USSR propaganda?"[31] Eden and entourage were taken to view the collections of priceless jewels, silver sent from Queen Elizabeth to Ivan the Terrible, and the wedding dress of Catherine the Great in the Kremlin, which Eden called "Aladdin's cave glittering with history." They walked over to Catherine's former Imperial Senate, where, in Molotov's office, Eden became the first high Western official to be received by Stalin.

Eden opened with a statement about the integrity of Soviet state borders and said that the same should apply to the British empire, then asked for Stalin's views on the current situation; Stalin replied by asking for Eden's. He volunteered that matters were "anxious but not alarming," and commended the League of Nations, which the world had lacked before the Great War. "I think the situation now is worse than in 1913," Stalin answered, "because in 1913 there was only one center of military danger—Germany—and now there are two: Germany and Japan." Contradicting the previous day's remarks by Litvinov (present now), Stalin stated that "the situation in the Far East is extremely alarming," and any recent "improvement temporary."

The main topic was the Hitler problem. "We are not trying to isolate Germany," Stalin explained. "On the contrary, we want to live with Germany in friendly relations. The Germans are a great and valiant people. We will never forget that. It was impossible to hold that people down for long in the chains of the Versailles Treaty. Sooner or later the German people had to liberate themselves from the Versailles chains." He added that the Soviet Union would not defend Versailles but stressed that the way Germany overcame its pariah status mattered. He inquired of Eden's impressions from his Berlin visit and, after a short, evasive answer, stated, "Strange people sit there in Berlin. For example, about a year ago the German government proposed a 200-million mark loan to us. We agreed and began negotiations, and after that the German government suddenly started spreading rumors that Tukhachevsky and Göring were secretly meeting to work out a joint plan to attack France. Is that really a state policy? That is trivial policy."[32] When Stalin asked whether, as Litvinov reported of his own conversations with Eden, Hitler had raved about a Soviet threat, Eden answered affirmatively. Stalin: "Well, you know, at the same time the German government has agreed, in connection with the loan, to sell us products about which it is awkward to talk openly—arms, chemicals, and so on." Eden claimed to be incredulous. "Completely true," Stalin replied. "Really, is this a state policy? Is this serious policy? No; trifling, clumsy people sit there in Berlin."[33]

Molotov invited everyone to the long table for tea. Eden, taking in the USSR map on the wall, remarked (according to the Soviet notetaker), "What a wonderful map and such a huge country." Then Eden "looked at the place on the map occupied by Great Britain and added, 'England is such a small island.' Comrade Stalin looked at Great Britain and said, 'Yes, a small island, but a lot depends on it. If this small island tells Germany, "We will not give you money, raw materials, metal," peace in Europe would be guaranteed.' Eden did not reply to this."[34]

LEVERAGE

The Red Army's new GP war plan entailed significant advances, based on covert mobilization, surprise, and preemption. Rigorous internal debate had reaffirmed the value of the offensive and what were known as deep operations—that is, efforts that combined armor, motorized infantry, and close air support to smash through fixed enemy defenses, exploiting gaps to strike deep in the enemy's rear and cause disarray, so as to preempt regrouping and counterattacking and to radically shorten the length of engagement.[35] Covert troop buildups for quick strikes and penetration, to disrupt enemy mobilization, made irrelevant traditional mobilization or declarations of war: attacking armies that had achieved tactical surprise could complete deployments of mobilized reserves on enemy territory. Preemptive seizure of Poland, to deny its use to Germany, now loomed large in the Soviet ability to disrupt the latter's mobilization and counterattacking strength.[36]

A shift to recognition of Germany as the enemy surfaced publicly on March 31, 1935, when *Pravda* published a sensational essay under Tukhachevsky's by-line: "The Military Plans of Today's Germany." Stalin had softened the title from the even more provocative "The Military Plans of Hitler." Still, the article, quoting extensively from *Mein Kampf*, presenting figures on German rearmament, and spelling out new German war doctrines, exploded like a bomb.[37]

Tukhachevsky believed mid-1930s Europe to be in a state similar to that on the eve of the Great War, with Poland playing the role of Austria-Hungary, but whereas Germany in that war had made the mistake of attacking France before Russia, this time around it would strike the USSR first, believing it needed to go after the stronger force, then take on a weak France. Stalin twisted this around: Germany's first strike would be against France and Czechoslovakia, and only after an *Anschluss* with ethnic German regions would Hitler attack the USSR. Thus, Tukhachevsky's article, in a new ending the dictator had inserted, stated that behind the "convenient screen" of anti-Soviet fulminations, Germany was really plotting to attack in the west (France and Belgium, for ore and ports) and in the center (the Polish Corridor, Czechoslovakia, Austria). Stalin further inserted that "in order to realize its plans of *revanche* and conquest, Germany by this summer will have an army of 849,000, that is, 40 percent larger than that of France, and almost as large as that of the USSR. (The USSR has 940,000, considering all types of forces.) And that will be despite the fact that the USSR has 2.5 times the population and ten times the territory."[38] German diplomats indignantly protested to Moscow.[39]

Eden's Moscow visit came to a close. *Pravda* (April 1, 1935) and *The Times* of London (April 1) published a joint communiqué: "Mr. Eden and MM. Stalin, Molotov, and Litvinov were of the opinion that in the present international situation it was more than ever necessary to pursue the endeavor to promote the building up of a system of collective security in Europe . . . in conformity with the principle of the League of Nations." Eden's telegrams to London reported that Stalin showed "a remarkable knowledge and understanding of international affairs," that Stalin's "sympathies seemed broader than those of M. Litvinov," and that "he displayed no emotion whatever except for an occasional chuckle or flash of wit." The dictator had struck Eden as "a man of strong oriental traits of character with unshakeable assurance and control whose courtesy in no way hid from us an implacable ruthlessness."[40] Later, in his memoirs, Eden amplified these impressions: "Stalin's personality made itself felt without effort or exaggeration. He had natural good manners, perhaps a Georgian inheritance. Though I knew him to be a man without mercy, I respected the quality of his mind and even felt a sympathy which I have never been able entirely to analyze." Eden concluded, "I have never known a man handle himself better in conference. Seldom raising his voice, a good listener, prone to doodling."[41]

In Berlin on April 9, the Soviet trade representative, Kandelaki, and the Reichsbank president, Hjalmar Schacht, finally concluded the proposed loan agreement, which extended a 200-million-mark credit for five years, at 2 percent interest. Stalin had been right: the Germans, needing to supply the rearming Wehrmacht, had made the concessions. The USSR pledged to place new orders with German industrial firms, as well as to complete within eighteen months current orders for German industrial goods and contracts for German shipping. Soviet payments would take the form of 100 million marks in gold and foreign currency and 100 million marks' worth of raw materials: naphtha, timber, furs, manganese ores.[42] So much for Stalin's warning to Eden not to supply Hitler. Sergei Bessonov, a counselor with a trade profile at the USSR's Berlin embassy, who wore a Hitler mustache, reported to Moscow that "Schacht reiterated to both me and comrade Kandelaki that his course of rapprochement with the USSR was being carried out with the consent and approval of Hitler."[43] Only now did the French cabinet approve going forward with a treaty with the Soviets; Laval informed Potyomkin and issued a public statement.[44]

STAGING GROUNDS

On Red Square on May 1, 1935, upward of 30,000 tank drivers, artillerymen, cavalry, and infantry marched past the Mausoleum as 800 warplanes flew in a choreographed formation.[45] The next day, Voroshilov presided over the annual banquet for select participants in the Grand Kremlin Palace.[46] The palace had been built under Nicholas I and dedicated in 1849 as the residence of the tsars when they visited the old capital. Its construction had folded in parts of nine churches, including Moscow's oldest extant structure, the Church of the Resurrection of Lazarus (1393), and the Palace of Facets (1491), which had been used by Ivan the Terrible. The 150-foot-high building had two stories, despite appearing to have a third (the upper floor contained two sets of windows). Its main entranceway opened to a stunning sixty-six-step staircase and a gigantic mural by

Ilya Repin, "Alexander III Receiving Rural District Elders in the Courtyard of Petrovsky Palace" (1886), which depicted the strapping sovereign in full-dress uniform. The ground floor, facing the front façade, was taken up by the royal apartments (where Voroshilov lived). One floor up were five dazzling halls named for the High Orders of the empire: the St. George, the Vladimir, the Alexander, the Andreyev, and the Catherine. The Soviets had combined the St. Andrew and St. Alexander, creating a larger, plainer space for party congresses. A raised stage was added to the St. George's Hall, the main venue for banquets, which boasted dazzling white marble, fifty-foot ceilings, eighteen columns bearing allegories of imperial Russian military victories, and hundreds of marble plaques with the names of military heroes.[47]

Inside, no more than one in fifteen parade participants could be accommodated for an experience that would reverberate over a lifetime. Around 800 places could be set at tables in the St. George's Hall, with spillover accommodated in the adjacent Facets (which could hold around 400) and the rose-marbled St. Vladimir Octagon, linking the two. Seats were preassigned, the most prestigious being those closest to Stalin's table, known as the Presidium, where Molotov occupied seat number 2 and Voroshilov 3. Each table, holding twenty to thirty people, was piled with caviar, fish, game, fresh vegetables, and fruit, although the food could seem incidental to the finest-flavored vodkas, brandies, wines, and Crimean champagne. One or two NKVD officers in civilian dress sat at each table (identifiable by the glaring circumstance that they did not drink) and listened attentively to the conversations, but enough actresses and other eye candy were distributed about to counteract some of the intimidation. The well-lubricated affairs had been publicly, albeit laconically, reported in *Pravda*.[48] The imperial splendor—giant fireplaces and mirrors, chandeliers, antique furniture, parquet floors polished to a brilliant shine—stirred embarrassment in the worker and peasant state.[49] Stalin exhibited no such qualms.

N.B. (a thinly disguised Nikolai Bukharin) reported in *Izvestiya* that upon Stalin's entrance "suddenly the applause, which grew like a snowstorm, covered everything, and became a blizzard, thunder, blustery spontaneous joy and ecstasy." During the endless toasts, Stalin sipped red wine, a glass of mineral water nearby.[50] (Voroshilov preferred vodka; after each shot he would cut off a slice of butter from a mound and swallow it.)[51] The dictator customarily delivered a speech in the form of his own toast, and now proposed that glasses be raised to the health of the Red Army rank and file ("Bolsheviks in the party and nonparty"). Then, trailed by his entourage, he made the rounds, personally greeting attendees. Suddenly, a few exuberant types lifted him up and carried him about the hall, putting him down at each table for a toast. Ubiquitous NKVD guards in full-dress uniform had proved powerless in the face of the hall's fervor and Stalin's desire to soak it up.[52]

At events like these, after the dictator and his retinue departed, the tables would be removed and functionaries and military officers in uniform approached the actresses and ballerinas to ask them for a dance.[53] Before exiting, Stalin might duck into the kitchen to congratulate the chefs, after which they—like his bodyguards, drivers, or film projectionists—would walk through fire for him.[54] But it was the artists at these events, often non-party members, whom he worked most to bend to his will. Stalin addressed them with the formal *vy* ("you"), paid attention to their performances amid the din, and invited some to drink at his table, inquiring whether they might have requests of him for themselves or their organizations. Relaxed, convivial, he engaged in freewheeling conversation.[55]

Earlier that same day of May 2, the Soviet envoy to Paris had signed a mutual assistance pact with France—the Soviet Union's first formal alliance. *Pravda* hailed it as a triumph.[56] It had taken nearly eight months of negotiations since the Soviet Union had been voted into the League of Nations. Article 2 stipulated "immediate aid and assistance" if either country became the victim of unprovoked attack and the Council of the League of Nations failed to reach a unanimous decision, but the "immediate" was diluted in an accompanying protocol that, at French insistence, left out any time limit to act while the council deliberated.[57] The treaty dumbfounded many Soviet Communist party members.[58] The Soviet press reported that Stalin approved of French imperialism's military buildup "at the level consonant with its security."[59] French domestic audiences were better prepared, thanks to a drawn-out public discussion. France's ally Poland was angry, even though it shared responsibility for catalyzing the treaty.[60] In Hitler's Chancellery, the reaction was incandescent rage. The Führer now obsessed over the "Bolshevization of France" and "Judeo-Bolshevik encirclement" of Germany the way Stalin obsessed over an "anti-Soviet imperialist bloc" and "capitalist encirclement."

"CADRES DECIDE EVERYTHING"

On May 4, 1935, Voroshilov, with Stalin in attendance, was back presiding in the Grand Kremlin Palace amid a sea of dress uniforms, this time over the annual graduation of military academies. The defense commissar issued "an order" for everyone to fill their glasses, then toasted Stalin at length, stirring the standing hall to frenzy. The orchestra played a flourish. Molotov was next. "You already know, comrades, about our new success in the struggle for peace," he said. "You already know from newspapers about the agreement on mutual assistance, which the Soviet Union has signed with one of the most visible powers of Europe—France. . . . The signing of the Soviet-French Agreement became possible because of the growth and strengthening of the power of our country and the force of our Red Army under the genius leadership of our party, comrade Stalin. Our enormous growth has become plain to our friends and to those whom it is impossible to call friends." Molotov, along with Stalin, went up to Voroshilov and exchanged kisses.[61] Stalin sounded his now habitual populism.

"Comrades, now, when our achievements are great in all branches of industry and governance—now it has become typical to speak a lot about leaders, bosses of the upper echelon, to credit the successes to them," he stated. "This is incorrect." The Soviet people had triumphed over backwardness, he continued, which had required "great sacrifices, great efforts, . . . and patience, patience." Some had lacked stamina. "There is a saying, 'Let bygones be bygones,' but all the same, a person's memory retains things." Stalin rebuked those who, he remembered, had wanted to expend scarce resources on consumer goods and "all kinds of trifles," instead of "tractors, automobiles, airplanes, tanks. . . . You will recall the declarations, from leaders of the Central Committee, that 'you are embarking on adventurism'; you heard such speeches, indeed it was not only speeches. . . . Others threatened to kill some of us, they wanted to break apart the leadership. It's plain as day we are people forged in fire, unbreakable, and did not retreat. (Stormy applause.)"

Stalin opened himself up: "It's plain as day that, back then, we did not retreat; we are Bolsheviks, people, so to speak, of a special cut. Lenin forged us, and Lenin was a man who did not know and did not acknowledge fear; this man was our teacher, our educator, our father—this was a person who, the more enemies raged and the more opponents inside the party fell into hysterics, the more he gathered force and the more resolutely he went forward. We learned a bit from him, this person. . . . We did not retreat; we went forward to attack and smashed some people. I must admit, I also had a hand in that."[62]

He could not let the thought go: the fork in the road, supposedly either a more comfortable life, with small-scale, backward agriculture and no security, or large-scale mechanized farms and a socialist great power. "There were victims—it is true—some of us fell by the wayside, others from a bullet." The country overcame its "famine of technology," he said, using a resonant word. "But now we have a new famine: a famine of people. . . . If, earlier, technology decided everything, now people decide everything, because now we have the technology. . . . Cadres are the most valuable capital. Not everyone in our country understands this, unfortunately." He told a story about his exile days in Turukhansk, how at the time of the spring flood, when a group went out to pilfer some of the giant pine logs being floated down the Yenisei, one man went missing, but no one bothered to look for him. "If a cow had disappeared, they would have gone searching, but a person perished, a trifle. . . . We do not value people. People can always be produced, but a mare, go try. (Stormy applause.)"[63]

Stalin, an avid gardener, had already been instructing officials to "cultivate people with care and attention, the way a gardener cultivates a beloved fruit tree," a skill he had shown since his youth.[64] As the hall quieted again, he continued: "I drink to you, to the higher cadres of our Red Army, and wish you every success in the organization of the defense of our country, in the practical leadership of this defense, because you will lead it. We, here, will lead the speechifying, but you will lead the practical work. (Stormy applause.)" His toast concluded: "Only those good cadres who are not afraid and do not hide from difficulties, but overcome them. Only in the struggle with difficulties can one grow genuine cadres who are not afraid of difficulties. Then our army will be invincible. (Stormy applause of the entire hall. Everyone stands and addresses comrade Stalin with loud shouts of Hurrah and applause.)"[65]

Stalin edited the above raw transcript with his stenographer on May 5, producing the version published in *Pravda* the next day, sharpening the key point, a shift in slogans from "Technology decides everything" to "Cadres decide everything."[66] The newspaper version enjoined officials to "show the greatest concern for our functionaries, 'great' and 'small,' . . . help them when they need support, encourage them when they show their first success, move them forward," and warned, "We have a whole series of instances of soulless, bureaucratic and outright scandalous attitudes toward workers."[67] On May 9, Stalin's in-laws received permission to pay him a late-night visit at the Near Dacha. The dictator recalled his elder son Yakov's attempted suicide and groused, "How could Nadya, condemning Yakov's act, shoot herself. She did a very bad thing, she maimed me for life. Let's drink to Nadya!" Those gathered got to reminiscing about the recent spontaneous metro ride, "the ecstasy of the crowd, the enthusiasm. Iosif again expressed his thought on the fetishism of the people's psyche, on the striving to have a tsar," Maria Svanidze noted. "Iosif was in a down mood; more accurately, he was preoccupied, something was occupying him to the depths, for which he had not yet found the answer."[68]

REVEALED PREFERENCES

Stalin's tête-à-tête with Eden had yielded nothing. French foreign minister Laval, who, in signing the nominal alliance with Moscow, still hoped to goad London into a real one, belatedly traveled to Moscow, but conspicuously stopped in Warsaw, where he informed Beck that France's new alliance was neither anti-German nor even pro-Soviet. In the Soviet capital for three days, beginning May 13, 1935, Laval met with Litvinov, Molotov, and Stalin.[69] The politburo had just decreed a Red Army expansion to 1.094 million troops by the end of 1936, and before the summer was out, Stalin would accept Voroshilov's proposal to lower the conscription age by six months each year (dropping it from twenty-one to nineteen by 1939).[70] Laval was brought to a military airfield for a demonstration. When he appeared at the Bolshoi on May 15, he drew an ovation.[71] But barely a week after the treaty with France had been signed, Litvinov informed the new German ambassador, Werner von der Schulenburg, that a bilateral nonaggression pact was urgently needed and would "lessen the significance of the Franco-Soviet alliance."[72]

Maisky, in London, was brought into the loop, and he recorded in his diary that Stalin had asked Laval about his recent trip to Poland and, when Laval proceeded to predict a shift in Warsaw away from pro-German attitudes, had cut him off: "You are friends of the Poles, so try to persuade them that they are playing a dangerous game that will bring disaster on themselves. The Germans will trick them and sell them short. They will involve Poland in some adventure, and when she weakens, they will either seize her or share her with another power."[73]

Stalin had something the tsar never had—control over a political party in France's parliament—and he acceded to Laval's request to stop the French Communists from opposing France's military budget and its new two-year service law. French Communists turned on a dime.[74] Stalin, in return, told Laval that he thought it prudent to prepare for the worst and wanted to add concrete military obligations to their treaty. Reluctantly, Laval agreed to open talks after the Soviets reached an accord with France's ally Czechoslovakia.[75] That very day in

Prague, May 16, foreign minister Beneš and Soviet envoy Sergei Alexandrovsky signed a mutual assistance pact. Beneš had drafted the text. He, understandably, did not want to dilute France's obligations and was anxious not to allow the Soviets to invoke the pact on their own and possibly draw Czechoslovakia into a Soviet-Polish conflict. The Soviets, predictably, were keen to have France retain the main burden and themselves avoid being drawn into a possible German-Czechoslovak conflict over Austria. And so, even though the Czechoslovak-Soviet treaty carried the same obligation of mutual assistance in the event of a third-party attack as did the Franco-Soviet pact, a special clause stated that the Soviets were obliged to act only if the French fulfilled their obligations first.[76]

Laval, again, stopped in Poland, where Piłsudski had died of liver cancer on May 12, 1935. "Stalin," Laval told one Polish confidant, "is wise, cold, detached, and ruthless." To another he said, "Oh, oh! Very strong. He is a grand figure, but an Asiatic conqueror type, a species of Tamerlane."[77] At Piłsudski's funeral, in Kraków (May 18), Laval assured Göring, who was representing Hitler, of France's good intentions. Göring, for his part, renewed his wooing of the Poles with tall tales of Soviet air bases about to appear in Czechoslovakia.[78] In Berlin, at St. Hedwig's Cathedral, in a sensational gesture, Hitler attended a holy mass, with a symbolic coffin draped in a Polish flag in honor of the deceased Polish president. On May 21, in another long speech to the Reichstag, the Führer held out the prospect of nonaggression pacts with all of Germany's neighbors except Lithuania ("What else could I wish for other than calm and peace?"). He criticized the Franco-Soviet treaty, while stating in a moderate tone that, in the matter of rearmament, Germany expected to be treated equally by Britain.[79]

Soviet military intelligence, meanwhile, had suffered another self-inflicted disaster by violating tradecraft yet again, recruiting agents among Communists under police surveillance—this time in Denmark, which ran the Soviet agents in Nazi Germany. Danish police had gone looking for a suspected spy on charges of raping a chambermaid (possibly an invented pretext) and netted the current and former station chiefs for Germany, as well as cash, fake passports, and codes. In early May, over several sessions in the Little Corner with Voroshilov, among others, Stalin promoted Semyon Uritsky from deputy head of the tank armor directorate to chief of military intelligence, retaining Artuzov as deputy head. (Artuzov would be replaced on May 21 as concurrent head of NKVD espionage by his deputy, Abram Slutsky.) Stalin told the Jewish Uritsky to recruit operatives and agents among ethnic Russians, Ukrainians, Belorussians, Latvians, and Jews, but to avoid Poles, Finns, Estonians, Hungarians, and Austrians. As spies in the field risked their lives to combat fascism, Uritsky went to war to force out Artuzov, seething that he "would be the idiot with the genius deputy."[80]

CONNECTING THE DOTS

All this while, Stalin was reading interrogation protocols about elaborate terrorist "centers" of cleaning ladies and librarians plotting his assassination. By now, only nine persons hired by Yenukidze remained on the Kremlin staff.[81] On May 12, 1935, Yagoda had sent Stalin proposals for punishment of the 112 people who had been arrested in the Kremlin Affair. Yagoda left blank Lev Kamenev's sentence; Stalin wrote in ten years for him, and execution instead of ten years for Nina Rozenfeld.[82] The next day, Yenukidze was named central executive committee plenipotentiary for the resorts group in the North Caucasus, which included elite Kislovodsk, second after Sochi.[83] Stalin also dispatched a secret circular to all party organizations announcing a party card verification campaign to "introduce Bolshevik order in our house."[84] Over the years, 200,000 duplicate cards had been issued for those reported lost or stolen. Nearly 15,000 party cards in the Donbass and 13,000 in Central Asia were still unaccounted for. (Several months later, the verification campaign would miss its completion deadline, inciting Stalin to irate charges of "family-ness," or self-protection, by colluding local elites.)[85]

Yezhov had drafted the circular and was overseeing the verification. In parallel, he was demanding stronger oversight of foreigners in the USSR, calling them spies.[86] He also asked Stalin to read his ambitious theoretical manuscript, "From Factional Activity to Open Counterrevolution (On the Zinovievite Counterrevolutionary Organization)." It set out how the Zinovievites, right deviationists, and Trotskyites were working together for a coup.[87] Stalin received the draft on May 17 and underlined various passages ("The Zinovievite counterrevolutionary band definitively chooses terror as its weapon in this battle against the party and working class"). Whether he had instigated the work remains unknown; Yezhov had pretensions and had absorbed Stalin's worldview. "There is no doubt that the Trotskyites were also informed about the terrorist side of the activity conducted by the Zinoviev organization," Yezhov's text asserted, concluding that "from testimony . . . we have established that [the Trotskyites] had also embarked on the path of terrorist groups."[88]

Trotsky had predicted, almost immediately after his expulsion from the territory of the Soviet Union, that "there remains only one thing for Stalin: to try to draw a line of blood between the official party and the opposition. He absolutely must connect the opposition with assassination attempts, and preparations for armed insurrections."[89]

Stalin had decided to devote a Central Committee plenum (June 5 and 7, 1935)—one of only two during the year that lasted more than a day—to the Kremlin Affair. He assigned the main report not to Yagoda but to Yezhov, who began not with Yenukidze but with Kirov, explaining that the "embittered" Zinovievite-Kamenevite-Trotskyite "group" had been driven "to the most extreme forms of struggle—namely, terror," and charged the rightists with complicity, citing attempts to link up with the Zinovievites in 1932. Yezhov deemed Yenukidze "a corrupt and self-complacent Communist" who had unwittingly allowed White Guards to infiltrate the citadel of power. Yenukidze, given the floor on the second day, averred that all hiring in the Kremlin "was carried out with the participation of the NKVD," prompting Yagoda to interject from the floor, "That's not true." Yenukidze insisted on the point, denied cohabiting with the arrested women, and seemed incredulous that helping former Menshevik families could be treason. Yagoda charged him with creating "his own parallel 'GPU'" in the Kremlin and called for his expulsion from the party, going beyond Yezhov's call for expulsion from the Central Committee.[90]

Stalin had kept strangely silent, but he finally professed himself unable to abandon a good friend with whom he had spent many a holiday, so he suggested that Yenukidze be expelled from the Central Committee and the party but not handed over to the NKVD.[91] Attendees voted unanimously for expulsion from the Central Committee and voted—with some hands raised in objection—for expulsion from the party for "political and personal dissoluteness." The minutes for internal circulation and *Pravda*'s public report were falsified to conceal the objections.[92] Yenukidze became the first Bolshevik who had joined the party before the revolution and who had never joined an opposition afterward to be expelled.[93]

WISHFUL THINKING

Hitler was zealously driving a revision of the Versailles order; Stalin did not oppose revision, provided it did not come at Soviet expense. As the sequential visits in spring 1935 of Eden and Simon to Berlin and Eden to Moscow had shown, each dictator was central to the other's grand strategy, but in differing ways. For Hitler, the Soviet Union was the principal evil, and Britain his principal wedge. For Stalin, Britain was the principal evil, and Germany his principal wedge. For France, the courting of the Soviet Union, a step that Britain disliked, was a way to woo a hard-to-get Britain. For Britain, the Soviet Union and Nazi Germany were both evil, but avoiding the costs of direct confrontation with Germany was paramount. Britain signed the proposed naval pact with Germany on June 18, 1935, which happened to be the anniversary of Waterloo.

Britain possessed the largest maritime force in world history, but it faced shipyard capacity limits and treasury austerity. The pact formally limited Germany's fleet to 35 percent of Britain's, while ostensibly locking Germany into a quality standstill. (Eden in Moscow had assured Stalin that Germany's 35 percent demand was out of the question.) But Hitler's special envoy, Joachim von Ribbentrop, had negotiated for Germany to have 45 percent as many submarines as the British did at that time, and to eventually reach parity, a giveaway of true intentions.[94] Hitler gave the go-ahead for two already planned super-battleships, the *Bismarck* and the *Tirpitz,* both exceeding the treaty's quality limits.[95] Ribbentrop had been invited to lunch the day before the signing by an influential journalist at *The Times* and told him he was keen for prime minister Stanley Baldwin (who had just assumed that office for the third time) to meet the Führer, because he wanted "Baldwin to hear Hitler's ideas about Western solidarity against Bolshevism."[96]

FRENCH CONNECTIONS

In reply to Nazism, a group of French intellectuals who had attended the Soviet writers' congress—André Malraux, André Gide, Louis Aragon—decided to mount an International Congress of Writers for the Defense of Culture, which was scheduled to open at the 3,000-seat Maison de Mutualité, in the Latin Quarter, on June 21, 1935, and run for five days. Around 250 invitations went out to writers in thirty-eight countries, including many political émigrés.[97] Koltsov arrived early to assist in the organizing and deliver the secret financing (20,000 gold rubles). Thanks to Ehrenburg, Gide, and Malraux, Isaac Babel (who had once lived in Paris) and Boris Pasternak (whose poems were untranslated, but whose name was well known) got added as late as June 19. (They arrived late, in new suits specially sewn for them.) Gorky declined Stalin's urgings to attend, citing poor health.[98] About a week before the opening, outside a Paris café, André Breton encountered Ehrenburg—who was infamous for having denounced surrealism as "onanism, pederasty, exhibitionism, and even bestiality"—and smashed him in the face. Ehrenburg cut Breton from the speaker list.[99]

From the podium, Malraux declared that "the humanism we want to create . . . finds its expression in the line of thought running from Voltaire to Marx," while Gide averred that "one can be profoundly internationalist while remaining profoundly French." Aldous Huxley deplored the "endless Communist demagogy," while E. M. Forster would write that he'd had "to hear the name of Karl Marx detonate again and again like a well-placed charge, and draw after it the falling masonry of applause."[100]

During the congress, the leftist French writer, dramatist, and musicologist Romain Rolland traveled the other way—to the USSR, at Gorky's invitation. After rounds of theater, cinema, and banquets, on June 28, he enjoyed a long audience in the Little Corner.[101] Wispy, compulsive, puritanical, Rolland (b. 1866) had won the Nobel Prize in Literature "as a tribute to the lofty idealism of his literary production and to the sympathy and love of truth with which he has described different types of human beings." His masterwork, a ten-volume novel cycle, *Jean-Christophe*, depicts a German-French friendship. He also harbored a long-standing fascination with the Russian Revolution and once observed that "this order is all bloody and soiled like a human baby just wrested from his mother's womb," but, "in spite of disgust, in spite of the horror of ferocious crimes, I go up to the child, I embrace the newly-born: he is hope, the miserable hope of the human future. He is yours in spite of you!"[102]

Rolland told Stalin that he saw him as the embodiment of the "new humanism."[103] He observed that Westerners shared the idealism inside the USSR but had trouble comprehending, for example, the news in the Soviet press that, as of April 7, 1935, criminal law was being applied to children twelve and up, and that minors could be executed. After letting Rolland speak for twenty minutes, Stalin requested permission to respond. "We had to pass this repressive law threatening the death penalty for child criminals, especially their instigators," he answered. "In fact, we will not enforce this law. I hope that it will not be enforced. Naturally, publicly, we cannot admit this; the desired effect would be lost, the effect of intimidation."[104] The dictator deployed his customary flattery ("I am happy to chat with the greatest writer in the world"), but came across as genuinely enamored of the *grand écrivain* even while throwing dust in Rolland's eyes.[105] Stalin called in the "Kremlin photographer" to record the event for propaganda purposes. But he would refuse all of Rolland's entreaties to publish the transcript.[106]

On June 30, Rolland, a guest on the Mausoleum at a physical culture parade involving 127,000 participants, was taken aback by the idolatry of the "emperor"—including the airplanes writing Stalin's name in the sky—but also by the dynamism of the young people of the revolutionary epoch. His surprise reflected reading about Soviet failures before his arrival. "The economic situation, it seems, is good," he wrote in a letter from Moscow to a literary critic friend in France. "During the last year, the conditions of life have improved significantly. This gargantuan city, which now numbers four million inhabitants, is a waterfall of life, healthy, warm, well-ordered. Among this crowd of strong, mobile, well-nourished people, you and I would look like strangers from a famine land."[107]

At a soirée at Gorky's mansion, Rolland supped with the inner circle. Here, Stalin came across as "a jester, a bit rude and peasant in his jokes, relentlessly showering this or that person with pleasantries, laughing heartily." This was a coarser side to the decorous dictator encountered in the Little Corner, yet still self-disciplined. "Stalin eats and drinks thoroughly, but he knows well when to stop," Rolland added. "After a reasonable number of full glasses"—toasts to all and sundry—"Stalin unexpectedly stops, refusing refills and further helpings. . . . He sucks his small wooden pipe with pleasure."[108]

PROFLIGACY

Poland's foreign minister Beck paid a visit to Berlin (July 3–4, 1935), where he was received one-on-one by Hitler, who complimented the genius of Piłsudski, averred that Poland should never be pushed from the Baltic, and enlarged upon the Soviet menace.[109] On July 5, Stalin received Kandelaki, back from Berlin, where Schacht had proposed a whopping new ten-year, 1-billion-mark loan, reasoning that Soviet counter-deliveries of raw materials could solve Germany's shortages without overly taxing precious hard currency reserves.[110] Internal jostling had begun among the Soviets over their own economic plan for the next year, and the total amount of investment was the key state decision.[111] For three years running, capital investment had been allowed only modest increases, and when the commissariats fought back, the hard-nosed Molotov—backed by the finance commissariat, the state bank, and Stalin—had held the line, warning against higher inflation and imbalances. On July 19, the chairman of the state planning commission, Valērijs Mežlauks, the son of a Latvian nobleman and a German mother, proposed that 1936 capital investment be slashed by 25 percent, to 17.7 billion rubles.[112] He explained that the reduction would facilitate a budget surplus and the goals of "increasing real wages and gradually reducing [retail] prices."

Stalin's involvement in the nitty-gritty of economic policy had tapered as he allowed Molotov and others to carry the burden. Molotov happened to be on holiday, and two days after Mežlauks's opening gambit, Stalin convened a meeting in his Old Square office. By now, Mežlauks's investment plan had already been forced up to 19 billion. He was present for just an hour and twenty minutes, and fifty minutes of that overlapped with the military men (Voroshilov, Yegorov, Tukhachevsky).[113] That evening, Stalin reported to Molotov that he had decided on 22 billion. "We shall see," Stalin observed. "There are some things which we must not cut: the defense commissariat; repair of rail track and rolling stock, plus the payment for new wagons and locomotives (railroad commissariat); the building of schools (enlightenment commissariat); re-equipment (light industry); paper and cellulose factories (timber); and certain very necessary enterprises: coal, oil, open-hearth furnaces, rolling mills, viscose factories, power stations, chemistry (heavy industry commissariat). This makes it more difficult."[114]

Molotov replied (July 25) by trying to hold the line at 22 billion rubles ("It's possible and necessary"). Mežlauks wrote to Stalin and Chubar (Molotov's deputy), acknowledging the difficulties that 22 billion would present for the industrial commissariats but insisting that this had to be the ceiling "for financial reasons." On July 28, Stalin convened a politburo meeting, summoning some seventy-five people.[115] The group voted a 1936 investment plan of 27.3 billion, while stipulating that the commissariats reduce their construction costs (somehow) so that the actual number would turn out to be 25.1 billion. Stalin wrote to Molotov that "22 billion was not enough and, as can be seen, could not be enough." None of the economic officials had resisted Stalin, and Molotov, too, bit the bullet ("I would have preferred a smaller amount of capital construction").[116] The decree was published and, as usual, the tenacious lobbying persisted. Stalin continued to indulge it. The final 1936 investment plan would be 32.635 billion, not a 25 percent decrease from 1935 but a nearly 40 percent increase.[117] It appears that Stalin had gained confidence in the economic system, which was having its second-straight good year, and, despite the risks of inflation, yearned to have more of both guns and butter.[118]

ANTIFASCIST FRONT

Stalin, sensing his leverage, had sent Kandelaki back to Berlin, and on July 15, 1935, according to Schacht, Kandelaki told him he had just spoken with Stalin, Molotov, and foreign trade commissar Rosenholz, and that German obstruction and price gouging had prevented the USSR from fully utilizing the existing 200-million-mark credit, but Kandelaki "expressed the hope that it might also be possible to improve German-Russian political relations. I replied that we had indeed already previously agreed that a brisk exchange of goods would be a good starting point for the improvement of general relations, but that I was not able to enter into political negotiation."[119]

The much-delayed 7th Comintern Congress, the first in seven years, opened on July 25 in the House of Trade Unions with 513 delegates (371 with the right to vote), representing sixty-five Communist parties. The last party member at liberty in Japan had just been arrested. German Communists had dwindled to a tiny group.[120] Wilhelm Pieck, a German in Soviet exile, delivered the opening report, but Dimitrov made the key speech, formally announcing a policy shift to "a broad people's antifascist front." Dimitrov explained that an alliance with non-Communist leftists was a temporary expedient in response to a special threat. "Fascism in power, comrades, . . . is the openly terrorist dictatorship of the more reactionary, more chauvinist, more imperialist elements of finance capital," he observed. "The most reactionary variant of fascism is fascism of the German type." He called Nazism impudent for claiming to be socialist when "it has nothing in common with socialism. . . . It is a government system of political banditry, a system of provocations and torture of the working class and the revolutionary elements of the peasantry, petit bourgeoisie, and intelligentsia. It is medieval barbarism and atrocity. It is unbridled aggression against other nations and countries."

Dimitrov cautioned that "Soviet power and only Soviet power can bring salvation!" but exhorted the delegates to learn "the parliamentary game."[121] A photograph of Stalin with the Comintern delegates was published in *Pravda,* but he did not deign to deliver a speech.[122] Yezhov was soliciting reports on hidden spies among resident foreign Communists and other political émigrés. (There were 4,600 Germanophone expatriates alone, thanks to Nazism.)[123] While the congress continued, on July 27, the USSR military collegium passed sentences in the Kremlin Affair on thirty people: two got the death penalty, and the rest between two and eight years in camps. The NKVD special board had sentenced eighty others in the case. Lev Kamenev, already serving a five-year term for the Kirov case, got another ten.[124]

Beria delivered a sensation. He had sacked Toroshelidze as head of his Stalin project, in favor of Yermolai "Erik" Bedia, Georgia's enlightenment commissar, who set to work on "The Rise and Development of Bolshevik Organizations in the South Caucasus." Documents of the conspiratorial underground years were few, so people were invited to reminisce, sometimes writing their own texts, often allowing Beria's apparatchiks to write or type them up. Those who participated were usually given envelopes of cash ("Comrade Stalin remembers you and asked me to convey this"). Vsevolod Merkulov, Beria's top aide, shaped the final text, and on July 21–22, 1935, in a special meeting of the South Caucasus party active, with some 2,000 attendees, Beria read it aloud. The audience spent much of the five hours standing and applauding each mention of "the Great Stalin." *Dawn of the East* published the full text, under Beria's byline, in two issues (July 24–25).[125] *Pravda* reprinted it over the course of eight days, making Beria famous in the party *outside* the Caucasus.[126] The text was also issued as a stand-alone pamphlet in a print run that would reach 35 million.[127] The central apparatus instructed all party organizations to organize study groups on Beria's report, which "offered the richest material on the role of Stalin as a Supreme Leader and theorist of our party."[128]

Also during the Comintern Congress, on July 30, following a five-day conference of 400 railroad industry personnel, Stalin hosted a banquet in the St. George's Hall. He rose to speak "under the thunder of applause, and an ovation that long did not let up," according to the account he edited for *Pravda*. "He said that the existence and development of our state, which exceeds in its size any other state in the world, including England and its colonies (excluding its dominions), is unthinkable without well-laid-down rail transport connecting the gigantic provinces of our country into a single state whole. . . . England, as a state, would be unthinkable without its first-class sea transport, which connects its myriad territories into a single whole. Exactly the same way the USSR, as a state, would be unthinkable without first-class rail transport, connecting its myriad provinces and territories into a single whole."[129] Left unsaid was that precisely the underdeveloped rail network posed the gravest impediment to Soviet war planning. In the western theater, the most glaring rail vulnerability lay at one of the most strategic points, south of the Pripet Marshes, along the Kiev military district frontier, while in the Far Eastern theater, throughput deficiency was still worse: a mere twelve pairs of trains per day, a level not much improved since the Russo-Japanese War defeat in 1904–5.[130]

Stalin inserted a remarkable political paragraph when editing the transcript. "In capitalist countries there are several parties—for example, England: Liberals, Conservatives, Labourites," he wrote. "There's not much difference between them—all of them stand for the continuation of exploitation—but one party criticizes the other. When the party in power missteps and the masses begin to get disaffected, that party is replaced by another. . . . We do not need such a lightning rod. We have a one-party system, but this system has its darker side—there's no one to criticize us, even gently—so we have to criticize ourselves, check, not be afraid of our shortcomings, difficulties, confront them. We all should teach the masses, but also learn from the 'little people,' listen to them. . . . Self-criticism, that's the key to our successes. The bourgeoisie put forward their smartest and most skillful people to govern the state: Roosevelt, Baldwin, Hitler—he's a talented person—Mussolini, Laval, but nothing comes of it. We have victories, and these victories come not from the genius of someone; that's stupidity. We do not have geniuses. We had one genius: Lenin. We are all people of middling capabilities, but we Bolsheviks take correct stances and implement them—that's why we gain victories."[131]

The Comintern Congress rolled on, celebrating the fortieth anniversary of Engels's death at the session on August 5.[132] Four days later, Ivan Tovstukha, deputy director of the Marx-Engels-Lenin Institute, died from tuberculosis, at age forty-six. His obituary provided what might have been the first public information on Stalin's group of top aides who actually ran the country.[133] Internally, Tovstukha had sabotaged the efforts of Yaroslavsky to write a comprehensive Stalin biography. Now Yaroslavsky appealed directly to the dictator, but Stalin wrote across his letter: "I am against the idea of a biography about me. Maxim Gorky had a plan like yours, and he asked me, too, but I have backed away from this matter. I don't think the time has come for a Stalin biography."[134]

That very summer, a foreign author struck again: Boris Lifshitz, who had been born in Kiev (1895), moved with his family to Paris at age two, helped found the French Communist party, went by the name Souvarine, and had been expelled from the Comintern for voicing his and his comrades' anger at the persecution of Trotsky (with whom Souvarine eventually fell out). Souvarine exacted revenge by publishing *Stalin: A Critical Study of Bolshevism* in French, which portrayed Stalin as both devoted to the cause and painstaking in intrigue, a doer rather than a thinker like Lenin or Trotsky, a man who struggled long and hard for recognition amid supposed insignificance in the revolutionary movement and overcame seemingly insuperable obstacles, such as Lenin's Testament calling for his removal. Souvarine demonstrated the moral bankruptcy of Stalin's successful political ruthlessness.[135]

The Comintern Congress ratified the new line of Communist–Social Democrat cooperation in Europe. In Asia, Stalin had long been forcing Communist-"bourgeois" cooperation against Japanese imperialists in a "united front." But Chiang Kai-shek had launched the fifth in a series of encirclement campaigns against the Chinese Communists, most of whom had found refuge at a mountain redoubt far southwest of Shanghai, adapting the precepts of Sun Tzu's *The Art of War* ("The enemy attacks, we retreat; the enemy halts, we harass; the enemy retreats, we pursue"). With Nationalist troops pressing the final annihilation, about 130,000 rank-and-file Communist troops and civilians had managed to break out, fleeing on a horrendous "Long March" into the deep interior. (Survivors of the rout-retreats would straggle first into Sichuan province, then Yan'an, in Shaanxi province, covering 3,700 miles over 370 days.) With the Long March still under way, a Chinese Communist delegation had set out for the Comintern Congress, but would arrive only after it had concluded. Meanwhile, the congress ordered the Chinese Communists to link up with "cooperative" Nationalists, whom they were to somehow cleave off from Chiang.[136]

Stalin was satisfied. "The Comintern Congress turned out not so bad," he had written to the holidaying Molotov. "The delegates made a good impression. The resolutions came out not bad." Stalin also divulged ("I think it's time") that he was going to hand the organization over to Dimitrov. "I really am a bit tired. I've had to spend time with the Comintern-ites, the investment plan for '36, all sorts of issues—you get tired, willy-nilly. No big deal. Fatigue passes quickly, if you relax for a day or even a few hours."[137] On August 10, the politburo approved creation of a Comintern secretariat, with Dimitrov as general secretary.[138] That same day, Stalin departed for his southern holiday. Although he had eliminated the de facto second secretary post in favor of multiple deputies, he left Kaganovich in charge again. The inner circle had solidified over several years: Molotov at the government, Kaganovich at the party, Voroshilov at the military, Orjonikidze at heavy industry, Mikoyan at trade. Kaganovich and Molotov had inevitably become rivals for his favor, and officials below them divided between the "Lazariches" (sons of Lazar) and the "Vyacheslaviches" (sons of Vyacheslav). Both men were indispensable—Molotov as the principal confidant, Kaganovich as the ultimate troubleshooter—and both shouldered immense burdens, following the example Stalin set.[139]

Before the congress adjourned (on August 21, 1935), it formally "elected" Dimitrov to the new Comintern executive committee, which in turn "elected" him as Comintern general secretary.[140] An American delegation led by Earl Browder had attended, even though the U.S. secretary of state had warned the Soviet ambassador that any American participation would be taken as yet another violation of their diplomatic recognition agreement.[141] After Browder boasted at the congress of the revolutionary movement's progress in the United States under his guidance, Bullitt recommended closing Soviet consulates in San Francisco, curtailing visas, and having President Roosevelt lay the case of Soviet violations before the American people.[142] The president opted to protest in writing, and on August 25 Bullitt handed a strongly worded note to Krestinsky, who rejected it out of hand but informed Stalin, Molotov, Voroshilov, and Kaganovich that the note threatened a break in relations.[143]

Soviet officials blamed domestic American politics; one surmised that Bullitt had been trying to make his career on improved relations but, failing that, had turned to anti-Soviet careerism.[144] Stalin did not overreact.[145] He had already given up on any kind of pact with the United States against Japan. Negotiations over repayment of tsarist and Provisional Government debts had failed, with no long-term credits extended to Moscow to purchase American goods.[146] Predictably, the Soviets denied any control over Comintern affairs (even though the congress met in Moscow in a government facility, and its official bulletins were issued by TASS). An irate Bullitt soon left for a holiday back home.[147]

HOLIDAY COMMANDS

The dictator would be away from Moscow for nearly three months.[148] From Sochi, he telegrammed Kaganovich that "Svetlana, Mistress of the House, will be in Moscow August 27. She demands permission to leave for Moscow soon, in order to supervise her secretaries."[149] About Vasily he said nothing. In Moscow on August 30, Henri Barbusse, who had contracted pneumonia, passed away.[150] Soviet officials had waffled on whether to publish a Russian translation of his *Stalin,* but finally would do so posthumously, in a print run of 100,000.[151] Both the spring sowing and the fall gathering had been organized in a timelier, more efficient manner than in years past, and the 1935 harvest would be good: 79 million tons. The state would procure 23.9 million tons, up from 19.7 million the previous year.[152] Stalin finally would be able to build a substantial strategic grain reserve

(9.4 million tons). "What is happening with grain procurements this year is our completely unprecedented stunning victory," Kaganovich exulted to the holiday-ing Orjonikidze (September 4), "a victory of Stalinism." Of Stalin he wrote, "He's holidaying now, it seems, none too badly. Klim [Voroshilov] is with him now. He went to settle some military matters."[153]

On September 5, 1935, Kaganovich reported to Sochi that Kandelaki had re-turned to Moscow and conveyed that only 25 million of the 200-million-mark credit had been spent, because of the complexity of Soviet orders. "It seems af-fairs in Germany are not going very badly," Stalin wrote back. "Give Comrade Kandelaki my regards and tell him to insist on getting from the Germans *every-thing* we need with regard to the military and dyes."[154]

Stalin sent a ciphered telegram (September 7) directing that Yenukidze be posted elsewhere ("to Kharkov, Rostov, Novosibirsk or another place, but not Moscow or Leningrad"), after learning that he had been visiting with Orjoni-kidze and Orakhelashvili when they were on holiday and "talked politics with them day and night."[155] The next day Stalin wrote again, to Kaganovich, that Agranov had sent him a note about "a Yenukidze group of 'old Bolsheviks' ('old farts' in Lenin's expression). Yenukidze is a person alien to us. It is strange that Sergo and Orakhelashvili continue to be friends with him." A politburo decree ordered Yenukidze immediately transferred to Kharkov road transportation.[156] Yezhov, meanwhile, wrote to boast to the dictator, regarding his investigation of terrorism plots against the leadership, that "only in the past months have I suc-ceeded in dragging the NKVD into this work, and it is beginning to yield re-sults."[157] But Yezhov's conspiracy to uncover conspiracies would have to wait: he was ill. "You should leave on holiday as soon as possible—for a resort in the USSR or abroad, whichever you prefer, or whatever the doctors say," Stalin ordered (September 10). "Go on holiday as soon as possible, unless you want me to raise a big ruckus."[158, 159]

A medical report (September 1935) by the Kremlin's Dr. Levin noted Stalin's completion of a course of medicinal baths at Matsesta, and his being advised to curtail his smoking. Stalin seems to have felt vulnerable during his own medical exams. He asked one of the physicians who attended him, Miron Shneiderovich, if he read newspapers, to which the doctor replied that he read *Pravda* and *Izvest-iya*. Stalin supposedly told him, "Doctor, you're a smart man, and you should understand, there's not a word of truth in them." Typical Stalin mischief: the dictator laughed, but then asked, "Doctor, tell me, but the truth, do you sometimes have the desire to poison me?" Shneiderovich went silent. Stalin: "I know, doctor, that you are a timid person, weak, that you would never do that, but I have enemies who are capable of doing it."[160]

The same ostensible paranoiac took a drive and then a stroll in Sochi. "Why are you leaving, comrades?" he said to a group of Soviet holidaymakers shocked to encounter him, according to one's recollections. "Why are you so proud that you shun our company? Come here. Where are you from?" They approached. "Well, let's get acquainted," Stalin said. "This is comrade Kalinin, this is the wife of comrade Molotov . . . and this is I, Stalin." He shook hands. Stalin called over his bodyguard-photographers, mocking them as "mortal enemies," and instructed them to photograph not just himself but "all the people." He invited over a woman at a kiosk selling apples and a salesclerk from a food stand. The latter hesitated to leave her post, but finally did so. When an empty public bus happened to pull up, Stalin invited the driver and the ticket taker to have their photos taken, too.[161]

FALL MANEUVERS

Red Army maneuvers were held (September 12–15, 1935) in the Kiev military district, commanded by Iona Yakir.[162] The exercises entailed a lightning counteroffensive supported by tanks, fighter aircraft, and artillery, directed both frontally and at the enemy's rear, in a variant on "deep operations," to employ speed and mobility to punch through enemy lines. The scale and armor were staggering: 65,000 troops, 10,000 tanks, 600 aircraft, and 300 artillery pieces, covering an area of nearly 150 by 120 miles on the western border.[163] Tanks were organized in mechanized corps for slashing attacks, while for the first time 1,188 parachutists were dropped from TB-3 bombers. Just 10 of the 4,000-plus motorized machines that saw action suffered any kind of breakage. "The French, Czechs, and Italians who attended the maneuvers felt our power, definitely, to the fullest," Voroshilov boasted to Sochi (September 16). "Our commanders who have returned from French, Czech, and Italian maneuvers report that the difference in our favor is definitely very substantial."[164]

General Lucien Loizeau, deputy chief of the French general staff and head of their delegation, was quoted in *Red Star* (September 18) offering high praise. "I saw a mighty, serious army, of very high quality in terms of both technology and morale," he stated. "I think it would be right to consider the Red Army first in the world in terms of tanks. The paratrooper drops of large units that I observed in Kiev I consider a fact that has no precedent in the world."[165] In his secret summary for the French staff, Loizeau concluded, "This army appeared to me therefore capable of a great initial effort, which would permit it to retain on the eastern front important countervailing forces during the period so critical as the beginning of a conflict."[166]

Loizeau's eyewitness assessment would be rejected at French staff headquarters by skeptics opposed to a binding military convention in the Franco-Soviet alliance. The proud Soviets would send films of the maneuvers to their embassies to be shown to foreign governments. The immediate official internal report praised the mechanized corps and three tank battalions, which had averaged a speed of 15 miles an hour and in some cases covered 400 miles. But later, in his final summary, Voroshilov would criticize the separate armored forces and praise the role of the unmotorized infantry.[167] This quiet reversal reflected the defense commissar's threat perception—from his forward-looking subordinates, Uborevičius and Tukhachevsky, whose stature was rising even higher.

Nazi Germany was not invited to send a delegation to the Soviet maneuvers, but the consulate in Kiev sent Berlin a report, evidently based on informants, which highlighted the Red Army's maneuverability.[168] Almost simultaneously, from September 10 through 16, 1935, the Nazis staged a party congress at Nuremberg. Hundreds of thousands celebrated the reintroduction of compulsory military service and emancipation from Versailles diktat. Leni Riefenstahl delivered her third annual documentary, *Day of Freedom: Our Wehrmacht,* which culminated in a montage of Nazi flags and German fighter planes flying in a swastika formation to the national anthem, with its refrain "Deutschland, Deutschland über alles." Hitler delivered seventeen separate speeches.[169] On September 15, the Reichstag unanimously passed hastily composed laws forbidding marriages and extramarital intercourse between Jews and Germans, and establishing that only those of German or related blood could be citizens.[170] Hitler gave his first remarks expressly on the "Jewish Question" since becoming chancellor and called what became known as the Nuremberg laws defensive, congratulated himself for using legal means, and warned that if "Jewish elements" persisted in their agitation and provocations, the issue would have "to be transferred to the final solution of the National Socialist party."[171] Goebbels cited Bolshevism as motive and justification.[172]

Also on September 15, Kaganovich and Molotov wrote to Stalin of rumors among Berlin journalists that Germany would sever diplomatic relations. "Do not allow hysterical noise in our press, and do not succumb to the hysteria of our journalists," Stalin advised. "Nuremberg is the answer to our Comintern congress. The Hitlerites could not *not* curse us if one takes into account that the Comintern congress poured latrine filth over them. Let *Pravda* criticize them on principle and politically, without street vulgarity. *Pravda* could say that Nuremberg confirms the Comintern assessment of National Socialism as the most primitive form of chauvinism, that anti-Semitism is the animal form of chauvinism and hatred of humans, that anti-Semitism from the point of view of the history of culture is a return to cannibalism, that National Socialism in that light is not even original, for it slavishly repeats the Russian pogromists of the tsarist period of Tsar Nicholas II and Rasputin."[173]

STRATIFICATION

Fourteen-year-old Vasily Stalin was having a crisis. He had taken to smoking. Although he had enough wits not to touch his father's cigarette box, his primitive efforts to hide the odor on his breath by sucking candy failed. His grades had sunk even lower. One day at school, several boys teamed up to thrash him. Stalin called the teacher and asked if Vasily had provoked his assailants; she reported that he had made them angry. "So be it," he said. "I won't bother you any longer."[174] Vasily played soccer after school, which became an excuse for him to skip homework (too tired), according to a note from the Zubalovo dacha commandant to Vlasik (September 22, 1935). "Vasily thinks he is an adult," the commandant wrote, "and insistently demands we fulfill his wishes, which are often stupid."[175] Stalin gave his son two months to get his act together, threatening to replace him at home with other boys of exemplary behavior.[176]

A letter from seventy-year-old Fekla Korshunova, who lived on her husband's pension from the "Leader of the Proletariat" peat plant, was forwarded to Stalin in Sochi. She wanted to give him one of her cows as a gift but was unsure that it was a good idea ("That will be clearer to you"). She signed off by noting that she used to receive 15 rubles 64 kopecks per month in pension, but now got 24 rubles. Stalin wrote back (September 30), "Thank you, mama, for your kind letter. I do not need a cow, because I do not have any farmland—I'm just a white-collar employee, I serve the people the best that I can, and white-collar types rarely do their own farming. I advise you, mama, to keep the cow yourself and maintain it in my memory. Respecting You, I. Stalin."[177]

More than 10 million women were employed outside the home—in retail, local soviets, schools, traditional textiles—but they had also barged into industrial employment, a consequence, one trade union official said, of "massive desire."[178] On October 1, the regime abolished rationing for meat, fish, sugar, fats, and potatoes, portending price rises, but lowered the retail price of bread. The party mobilized agitators at workplaces to impart the "correct" understanding.[179] One typical couple in Leningrad, he a hauler and she a teacher, lived in a room of 150 square feet, the husband and wife sleeping on the bed, the elder son on a cot, two younger daughters sharing another cot (foot to head), and the youngest girl on an ottoman. "That's how we lived for ten years," the son, who did homework in the magnificent prerevolutionary Saltykov-Shchedrin Library until midnight, would recall. "And we were happy in our way. The main thing: everyone was studying— even Mama at forty-five years old finished the pedagogical night school."[180]

Amid the endemic shortages, the regime manipulated consumer goods as reward or punishment.[181] Elites enjoyed privileged access to staples and luxuries such as restaurant meals or fashionable winter coats.[182] Purchase of desirable goods usually required a special coupon as well as money, and a leather jacket bought for 300 rubles in a subsidized state store by those awarded coupons could be resold at the market for three times that or more—which technically was a crime, but also a way of life. Midlevel NKVD operatives were paid just 150–350 rubles per month (an overcoat cost 700 rubles in 1935), and they, too, had to buy "voluntary" government bonds, usually at a cost of a month's salary. True, operatives received subsidized meals at work, but higher-ups made at least five times as much in salary and received nearly a thousand rubles extra per month in cash "bonuses." Bosses' high living was a constant refrain in secret reports. "That's enough laughing at the workers, enough starving, enough teasing them like dogs" read an anonymous letter to Zhdanov in 1935. "Our enemies are our aristocrats who harm the working people."

FOREIGN POLICY REVEALED

Stalin exposed his grasp of world affairs to Kaganovich and Molotov in connection with a crisis developing over East Africa, where, on October 3, 1935, after prolonged tensions and border clashes, a large Italian army stationed in Eritrea invaded Abyssinia (Ethiopia) without a declaration of war. This was the Second Italo-Abyssinian War: Italy had lost the African territory in 1896 in a humiliating military defeat at Adwa. Italian forces, meeting fierce resistance, used aerial bombardment of villages and mustard gas against tribesmen.[183] On October 7, the League of Nations pronounced Italy the aggressor and began the process of imposing sanctions, but the League's failure to punish Italy would soon be manifest. During the League debate, a Czechoslovak spectator shot himself.

Stalin was taking it in stride. "Kalinin reports that the foreign affairs commissariat doubts the possibility of grain exports and other products from the USSR to Italy in view of the dispute in Abyssinia," he wrote from Sochi during the buildup to the invasion. "I think that these doubts of the foreign affairs commissariat derive from their non-understanding of the international situation. The conflict is not so much between Italy and Abyssinia as between Italy and France, on one side, and England on the other. The old Entente is no more. In its place, two ententes are forming: the entente of Italy and France on one side and the entente between England and Germany on the other. The worse the brawl between them, the better for the USSR. We can sell grain to one and the other, so they can fight. It is not at all advantageous for us now if one side smashes the other. For us it is advantageous for their brawl to be as long as possible, without a quick victory by one over the other."[184]

In reality, Britain and France were on one side, and, increasingly, Italy and Germany on the other.

When Litvinov had requested permission to walk demonstratively out of the Assembly of the League of Nations to protest its failure to elect the USSR representative (himself) as one of the six vice presidents, Stalin had agreed ("Let the Assembly eat the Abyssinian kasha"). But when Litvinov's walkout induced the British and French to scramble to include him in the League's presidium, Stalin erupted to Kaganovich and Molotov over the easy acceptance of the face-saving gesture. "Litvinov was frightened by his own proposal and hurried to extinguish the incident," he fumed. "Litvinov wants to follow the British line, but we have our own line." Stalin called the League's leadership "thieves" who "did not treat the USSR with the proper respect," and charged Litvinov with being guided "not so much by the interests of the USSR as by his own overwhelming pride."[185]

On October 26, Tukhachevsky—not seen at the German embassy since Hitler's ascent—appeared at the farewell reception for departing counselor Fritz von Twardowski. "Tukhachevsky was unusually frank and cordial," Twardowski reported. "His remarks were full of the greatest respect for the German army, its officer corps, and its organizational capacity, which led him to express the view that the new German Reich army would be fully prepared for war already this year, or at latest next year." Twardowski pushed back against such an idea, but the deputy defense commissar persisted: "If it should come to war between Germany and the Soviet Union, which would be an appalling misfortune for both nations, Germany would no longer be confronted with the old Russia; the Red Army had learned a great deal and done a great deal of work." Twardowski noted that Tukhachevsky had volunteered that "if Germany and the Soviet Union still had the same friendly political relations they used to have, they would be in a position to dictate peace to the world."[186]

KEKE

On holiday, Stalin again suffered from stomach pains and caught influenza.[187] Very unusually, he stopped in to see his septuagenarian mother.[188] Since he had become a widower for the second time, his letters to Keke had changed. "Greetings, Mother Dear, I got the jam, the ginger, and the churchkhela [Georgian candle-shaped candy]," he had written in 1934. "The children are very pleased and send you their thanks. I am well, so don't worry about me. I can bear my burden. I do not know whether or not you need money. I am sending you 500 rubles just in case. . . . Keep well, dear mother, and keep your spirits up. A kiss. Your son, Soso. P.S. The children genuflect to you. After Nadya's death, my private life has been very hard, but a strong man must always be manly."[189]

Stalin was in the company of Beria, who had erected a grandiose marble pavilion over the dictator's wooden birth hovel in Gori and opened it to the public.[190] Beria also instigated approval for construction of a Stalin museum in Gori, next to which were supposed to be a cinema, drama theater, library, hotel, and House of the Collective Farmer. The low estimate for the total cost nearly equaled Gori's annual budget (900,000 rubles).[191] Keke was still living under Beria's care, in the single room on the ground floor of the former tsarist viceroy's palace, where Georgia's Council of People's Commissars had its offices. She ventured to the market dressed in black, a widow for more than a quarter century now, and shadowed by secret police. Beria's wife, Nino, visited her regularly. In June 1935, Svetlana and Vasily had paid a visit. The children were staying with "Uncle Lavrenti" for a week and, according to Svetlana, saw their grandma for half an hour. Neither Svetlana nor Vasily understood Georgian; they communicated through their half brother, Yakov. Svetlana would recall being shocked at the sight of Keke's spartan metal bed. Keke was ill (she received them while in bed, as demonstrated by photographs, which Stalin permitted to be published).[192] Stalin's own visit—a further indication that she was ill—took place on October 17. There is plausible hearsay from her attending physician that Stalin asked, "Mother, why did you beat me so hard?" and that she responded, "That's why you turned out so well."[193]

Stalin's Georgian origins had been muted over time, with his features softened in photographs (his long pointed nose was reduced, his arched left eyebrow lowered, his chin moved forward, his face made oval).[194] Three days after the visit, *Pravda*'s correspondent interviewed Keke, and on October 21 Poskryobyshev passed a draft of his article to the dictator with a request to publish it. "I won't undertake to approve or reject," Stalin answered. "It's not my business."[195] The article appeared in *Pravda* (October 23). "The 75-year-old Keke is affable, cheerful. . . . 'He came unexpectedly, without warning. The door opens and he walks in. He kissed me a long time, and I reciprocated. How do you like our Tiflis? I asked him.'" The newspaper further quoted her as saying, "'I worked each day and raised a son. It was hard. . . . We ate poorly. . . . An exemplary son! . . . I wish everyone such a son!'"[196]

Pravda followed up (October 27) with additional details from Keke: "'Our Lavrenti came and announced that Soso had arrived and that he was already here and coming in. . . . The door opened, and there he stood on the threshold: it's him, my own. . . . I look and I can't believe my eyes.'" She notices that he has gray hair. "'What's that, son, have you gone gray?'" Stalin answers: "'It's nothing, Mother, a little gray. It's not important. I feel terrific, and you should not doubt it.'"[197] (The account omitted the part where she said, "What a shame that you didn't become a priest," which Stalin, according to Svetlana, liked to repeat.) Keke was quoted as revealing that Stalin's father had removed him from school to apprentice him to a shoemaker, against her strenuous objections. On October 29, Stalin exploded. "I ask that you prohibit the vulgar rubbish that infiltrated our central and local press, publishing an 'interview' with my mother and sundry other promotional nonsense right up to portraits," he wrote from Sochi to Molotov, Kaganovich, Andreyev, Zhdanov, and Boris Tal (head of publishing in the apparatus). "I ask that you spare me from the promotional hoopla of these scum."[198]

LIFE BECOMES MORE JOYOUS

Stalin's first order of business back in Moscow, on November 2, 1935, was to receive Kandelaki, just returned from a meeting in Berlin with Schacht, who had revisited the proposal for a large new credit, now half a billion marks, while Kandelaki had again raised the need for political rapprochement and reemphasized Soviet interest in state-of-the-art military technology (automatic piloting of aircraft, remote control of vessels). France's Laval, who had concurrently become prime minister, was also working all channels to secure rapprochement with Germany while delaying formal ratification of the Soviet alliance. Hitler perceived weakness.[199] Schulenburg, Germany's ambassador, reported that at the dinner for the diplomatic corps on Revolution Day, Litvinov had raised his glass and loudly proclaimed, "I drink to the rebirth of our friendship!" Schulenburg added, "The British ambassador, who was sitting opposite, said: 'Well, that's a fine toast.'"[200]

The capital was having its usual chilly, white winter, but at the November 7, 1935, parade, for the first time, Voroshilov, Tukhachevsky, and others appeared with gold shoulder boards. Not long thereafter, Stalin allowed the reintroduction of the snapped-hand salute and formal ranks.[201] The dictator named five "marshals": Voroshilov, Yegorov, Tukhachevsky, Blyukher, and Budyonny.[202] In the process of awarding ranks for thousands of others, some officers were effectively demoted because it was remembered that they happened to be the sons of priests or gentry or had once run afoul of a bigwig.[203] The NKVD also got ranks. Zakovsky, conductor of the post-Kirov meat grinder in Leningrad, became commissar of state security first rank, equivalent to general in the army; Stalin had raised this from the proposal in the draft. Yagoda became general commissar of state security, the sole person in that rank.[204] Grasping for rank, uniforms, and medals, as well as grand apartments, dachas, and cash bonuses, the new elite was becoming ever more conspicuous.[205]

On November 8, the extended family of the Alliluyevs and Svanidzes gathered for the third consecutive year in memory of Nadya. The night before Stalin had spent with the cronies until 3:00 a.m. Now, concerned about the dictator's mood on the occasion, Molotov called to suggest watching a film together, but Stalin begged off.[206] His elder son, Yakov, had found a new woman, Judith Meltzer (b. 1911), a ballerina from Odessa who went by Yulia. Yakov had been cohabiting with and gotten engaged to Olga Golysheva (b. 1909), a fellow student at the Moscow Aviation School from Stalingrad province, but they broke up and she went home.[207] Meltzer had evidently come to Yakov's attention at a Moscow restaurant, where he had an altercation with her second husband, Nikolai Bessarab, an NKVD officer who served as an aide to Redens, Stalin's brother-in-law and now head of the Moscow province NKVD. "She is a fine woman,

30–32 years old, coquettish, speaks stupidities with aplomb, reads novels, gave herself the goal of leaving her husband and making a 'career,' and succeeded," Maria Svanidze acidly wrote of Meltzer at the holiday dinner. "She already lives with Yasha, but her belongings are with her husband."[208]

Between November 14 and 17, 1935, the regime held the First All-Union Conference of Stakhanovites in the Grand Kremlin Palace. Pressure for labor intensification had been high even before Stalin's approval of capital investment increases—but an apparent solution fell into the regime's lap. At the Central-Irmino mine in Kadievka (Donbass), Alexei Stakhanov (b. 1906), a jackhammer operator, hewed 102 tons of coal in a single overnight shift, more than fourteen times his quota of seven. At 6:00 a.m., the mine's party cell voted to award Stakhanov bonus pay of 220 rubles (a month's salary) and give him permanent passes to the workers' club. *Pravda* carried a report of Stakhanov's feat (September 2); the next day he had a new apartment. Stakhanov's innovation was to ask that hewers like himself be freed from periodically setting down their jackhammers in order to prop the coal face. Additionally, a local party organizer had hauled in extra equipment and workers, whose names went unmentioned in the shower of publicity he arranged. Orjonikidze, in Kislovodsk, read the *Pravda* account and telephoned aides in Moscow and the coal trust in Kadievka. *Pravda* (September 11) launched a "movement" across industrial sectors and into the Gulag.[209]

Record chasing often left follow-on shifts bereft of supplies and labor to meet, let alone exceed, norms, provoked breakdowns and injuries, and exacerbated tensions among workers. But managers who tried to contain Stakhanovism's deleterious consequences risked accusations of sabotaging worker initiative.[210] (The mine director at Central-Irmino would be arrested for "wrecking"; his place would be taken by the party organizer.)[211] Stakhanovism became a truncheon against both managers and workers, forcing norms upward. At the Stakhanovite conference, Orjonikidze, as always, stressed the need to raise quality, not just quantity.[212] On the closing day, as Voroshilov regaled the Stakhanovites with the paratrooper exploits at the recent army maneuvers, Stalin walked in, inciting delirium.

The dictator soon took the podium, attributing the "profoundly revolutionary" movement to initiative from below, in the country's new conditions. "Life has become better, comrades," he observed. "Life has become more joyous. And whenever life is joyful, work goes better." (Earlier in the proceedings, the 3,000 attendees had spontaneously broken out into the catchy march from *Jolly Fellows*.) "If there had been a crisis in our country, if there had been unemployment—that scourge of the working class—if people in our country lived badly, drably, joylessly, there would have been nothing like the Stakhanovite movement. (Applause.) . . . If there is a shortage of bread, a shortage of butter and fats, a shortage of textiles, and if housing conditions are bad, freedom will not carry you very far. It is very difficult, comrades, to live on freedom alone. (Shouts of approval. Applause.)"[213]

Stalin closed by asking for approval to reward the country's best workers with the highest state honor, again inciting delirium. Stakhanov would be awarded the Order of Lenin, admitted to the party, promoted into mine management, and made the author of texts extolling Stalin for originating his movement.[214] He would take to drinking, lose his Order of Lenin and party card in a drunken brawl, smash the mirrored walls at the Metropole Hotel restaurant, and wed a fourteen-year-old. Stalin would lose interest in Stakhanovism, but he now paid still more attention to the cultivation of public heroes.

DIPLOMATIC DELUSIONS

The Soviet envoy to Bulgaria, Fyodor Ilin, the son of a priest and himself a storied Bolshevik, who adopted the surname Raskolnikov (from Dostoevsky's character), was in Moscow in late November 1935. He and his wife decided to see Oleksandr Korniychuk's play *Platon Krechet*, about the new Soviet intelligentsia's quest for genuine humanism and social justice, at the affiliate of the Moscow Art Theater on Theological Lane. Unexpectedly, Raskolnikov encountered Stalin and Molotov. (The pair had first gone to the Moscow Art Theater, but the show they went to see had been switched out.) During intermission, Stalin engaged Raskolnikov in a discussion of Soviet policy in Bulgaria. Molotov took note of Stalin's respect for Raskolnikov, and the next morning Zhemchuzhina, Molotov's wife, phoned to invite Raskolnikov and his wife to their dacha. During billiards, drinking, and dancing, the men discussed the threat of fascism, and Molotov exclaimed, "Our main enemy is England!"[215]

At the theater, Stalin had asked Raskolnikov to visit him in his office, but when the envoy phoned from the foreign affairs commissariat, a disbelieving Poskryobyshev gave him the runaround. Once, when Raskolnikov dialed Stalin's number, the dictator himself picked up—and invited him over right then. It was December 9, 1935. Raskolnikov got twenty minutes one-on-one, his first (and sole) visit to the Little Corner. "Stalin's working office in the recently refurbished

Kremlin building was furnished, point for point, the same way as his office on the top floor of the immense building of the Central Committee on Old Square," Raskolnikov noted. The dictator came out from behind the desk, placed Raskolnikov at the large felt table, took a seat, and, after pinching some tobacco, lit his pipe. Raskolnikov relayed that his superiors had declined Sofia's request to buy Soviet weapons. "A mistake!" Stalin interjected, adding that the Bulgarians would just buy them from the Germans. Raskolnikov received authorization to report Stalin's view at the commissariat. The conversation widened. "'England now stands for peace!' Stalin stated ironically, opening his palms wide, animatedly approaching me," Raskolnikov recalled. "'England now will be plucked. Its colonies are spread around the whole world. Defending them is unthinkable: they would need 100 navies to do that. It's not like us, where everything is gathered in a single space. Therefore, England, of course, stands for peace.'"[216]

Behind the scenes, Litvinov persisted in his anti-Nazism, writing to Stalin to confirm a TASS report that Schacht had confided to a French banker that Germany intended to partition Soviet Ukraine with Poland. Litvinov urged that the dictator issue "a directive about opening a systematic counter-campaign against German fascism and fascists," whose attacks on Bolshevism had reached "Homeric proportions." But other foreign affairs personnel pushed in Stalin's preferred direction. Twardowski, back in the German foreign ministry, phoned Yakov Surits, the Soviet envoy to Berlin, to arrange a courtesy appointment—and suddenly Sergei Bessonov, the embassy counselor for trade, called asking to be received before Surits. Twardowski arranged to see them separately on December 10. Bessonov, given the first meeting, bluntly opened: "How could German-Soviet relations be improved?" Surits posed the same question in the guise of seeking advice. Bessonov wrote to the foreign affairs commissariat that his conversations confirmed "the existence of strata and groups in Germany interested, for various reasons, in normalizing relations," singling out big business and the old-line military, and said they were looking for concrete steps from the USSR to help them in domestic policy battles.[217]

Hitler had his own idées fixes. On December 13, he received UK ambassador Sir Eric Phipps at the latter's request to discuss stalled air force limitations talks. Germany's decision to build a fleet and the ensuing naval arms race had helped precipitate the Great War, but British officialdom feared an air arms race even more.[218] Phipps had been telling himself that the feral Führer was more reasonable than the lunatic entourage surrounding him. But Hitler launched a tirade, condemning the Franco-Soviet pact as a "military alliance unmistakably directed against Germany" (according to the German notetaker) and observing (according to the British notetaker) "that Berlin might easily in a few hours be reduced to [a] heap of ashes by a Russian air attack." He lashed out at British diplomatic engagement with Moscow, asserting that Whitehall was cozying up to the Soviet Union only because it wanted a counterweight to Japan. Phipps denied this, and insisted that "we are living in the same house" with the Soviet Union and could not ignore it. Hitler countered that the Soviets were "a foul and unclean inhabitant of the house with whom the other dwellers should have no political truck whatsoever."

Hitler, ever more darkly and loudly, raged on that Communist pledges in bilateral pacts not to interfere in the affairs of other countries were belied by Moscow's "most aggressive and insolent underground interference in the affairs of all civilized states, not excluding the British empire." He shouted that he had resisted internal demands to request a fleet half the size of the British navy, taking only one third, yet Britain still tolerated the French alliance with Bolshevism and was contemplating one of its own. "At one moment Herr Hitler referred savagely to Lithuania, declaring that neither that country nor the Baltic states in general would present any obstacle to a Russian attack on Germany," Phipps noted in his summary, adding that "even when pretending to fear a Russian attack, he spoke of Russia with supreme contempt, and declared his conviction that Germany was vastly superior to her both militarily and technically. At times he ground the floor with his heel."[219]

SMASHED PIPE

Moscow's Triumphal Square was renamed for Mayakovsky.[220] Lily Brik, who lived in Leningrad caring for Mayakovsky's archive, had written to Stalin in despair that the dead poet's books were nearly impossible to obtain, a special room at the Communist Academy promised for his literary heritage had never been provided, and a request to turn his last residence in a small wooden house into a library had never been supported. "I alone cannot overcome this bureaucratic indifference and resistance—and after six years of work I am turning to you, since I see no other means to realize the enormous revolutionary bequest of Mayakovsky," she wrote. Stalin instructed Yezhov that "Mayakovsky was and remains the best, most talented poet of our Soviet epoch. The indifference to his memory or his works is a crime. Brik's complaints are correct."[221] Suddenly,

Pravda (December 5, 1935) published a laudatory essay on the poet, citing Stalin calling him "talented" (an intentional toning down, which would be corrected).[222] Pasternak wrote privately to the dictator expressing gratitude for the recognition of his fellow poet ("warmly loving you and loyal to you").[223]

Japan was busy confirming Stalin's prescience about its vaulting ambitions.[224] In Manchukuo, it had gone on to create a vast autonomous province for ethnic Mongols and fostered preservation of traditional lifestyles, the opposite of Soviet social engineering in its Mongolian satellite.[225] Chiang Kai-shek had conceded territory to the Japanese occupiers, planning to take them on decisively after he had annihilated the Communists, but the Communist escape to the interior had put off that reckoning. Surviving Communists had united in a new sanctuary in impoverished Shaanxi province, where Mao, carried on a palanquin during the Long March, emerged as the paramount leader.[226] Chiang approached the Soviet envoy Dimitri Bogomolov asking for weapons, as if the Nationalists were finally going to launch a war to evict the Japanese. "From all my conversations, I am left with the impression that they would like to precipitate a possible conflict between ourselves and Japan," Bogomolov informed Moscow (December 9, 1935). Stalin agreed to ship the arms (via Xinjiang), worried that Chiang might otherwise cut a side deal with Japan. On December 9, the Comintern's "united front" policy was stretched to include cooperation with Chiang—unbeknownst to Mao in the remote interior, who would erupt when apprised.[227]

A Soviet official "close to the Kremlin" told U.S. embassy personnel that any moves by Japan against Mongolia would be regarded as a threat to Soviet territorial integrity, but a week later Japanese-Manchukuo forces burned down a Mongolian frontier post, killing or kidnapping several Mongolian border guards, and this drew only a protest.[228] In the meantime, on December 12, a Mongolian delegation arrived in Moscow, again led by Prime Minister Genden, who was dragging his feet over Stalin's orders to extirpate lama influence and enlarge the penurious country's military budget.[229] Genden was quick-tempered, and known to indulge in wine, women, and indiscreet song. Before his departure from Ulan Bator, he had supposedly boasted, "I'll deal with that Georgian with the knife-tipped nose. . . . I'll enjoy a quarrel with him."[230]

The Mongols in Moscow had to cool their heels. On Stalin's official fifty-sixth birthday (December 21, 1935) at the Near Dacha, the Alliluyevs and Svanidzes discovered that they were now outnumbered by politburo officials. "Zhdanov played the accordion beautifully, but it broke down on him a few times," Maria Svanidze recorded in her diary. "They sang graceful Abkhaz and Ukrainian songs, old student songs, and some plain silly ones. Postyshev was in high spirits. He was jokingly dancing the Russian national dance with Molotov, spoke to him in Kazakh, and this pair entertained I[osif] and all the guests. After supper, everyone went through to the study (the large room). I[osif] wound up the gramophone and people danced the Russian dance, Anastas Ivanovich [Mikoyan] danced the lezginka, wildly, and sometimes lost the rhythm. As usual, we danced the foxtrot. . . . We asked I[osif] to join in, but he said that since the death of Nadya he no longer danced."[231]

The regime held a Central Committee plenum from December 21 to 25, and on the final day Yezhov reported on the ongoing party card verification campaign: of the 2.34 million members and candidate members, 1.915 million had gone through the process, and of those, 175,166 had been expelled. Two thirds of the expulsions were for "passivity," that is, failing to attend meetings, pay dues, or study. Some 20 percent were dropped as White Guards or kulaks, 8.5 percent as swindlers and scoundrels, and some 1 percent as foreign spies. Around 3 percent, 5,500 party members, were expelled as "Trotskyites and Zinovievites."[232] About 15,000 of those expelled would also be arrested. The process, still not complete, was now to be followed by a physical exchange of party cards, old for new. Yezhov congratulated himself.[233] On the plenum's eve, resistance to Stakhanovism had been designated as terrorism.[234] At a heavy industry conference the day after the plenum, Orjonikidze conspicuously mentioned nothing of sabotage.[235]

Stalin had decided to allow, for the first time, the genuine number for projected Soviet military spending for the coming year to be released—a staggering, meant-to-impress 14.8 billion rubles, 16 percent of the state budget.[236]

Late on December 30, he and his inner circle received the delegation from Mongolia in Molotov's office, and took an aggressive posture. Molotov: "You, Genden, when drunk, all the time speak anti-Soviet provocations. We know that before your departure to come here, you said that we would recommend a long stay in the Kremlin hospital or holiday in Crimea, 'in connection with your health.'" Stalin reprimanded Genden for spending only 25 percent of the state budget on the military, asserting that the USSR would spend 70–80 percent when necessary, and demanding that Mongolia spend 50–60 percent. "If you, Genden, are not concerned with the defense of your country, and you think that Mongolia suffers from its ties to the USSR, which you think cheats and takes advantage of Mongolia, and you want to get friendly with Japan, then go ahead!" Stalin declared disingenuously. "We do not compel you to have relations with us if you do not want to." He added: "You do nothing about the lamas. . . . They can undermine a good army and the rear."[237]

Molotov declared a break and invited them to "tea" (often code for spirits). Demid, the defense minister, understood that his country could not manage against possible Japanese aggression without Soviet assistance, while Genden preferred to rely on the country's own army, with more Soviet weapons, even as he feared excessive debt to, and therefore dependence on, Moscow.[238] Whether at this Kremlin session or a New Year's reception at the Mongolian embassy, Genden, in a drunken state, did something no one else ever had or would—he snatched Stalin's pipe and smashed it.[239]

"INTERESTING"

Stalin welcomed the year 1936 with a larger crowd than usual at the Near Dacha: the inner circle and nearly all the people's commissars as well as his relatives.[240] "The country has never lived so full-blooded a life as at present," *Pravda* announced in an editorial (January 1, 1936). "Vivacity, confidence, and optimism are universally dominant. The people are, as it were, taking to wing. The country is in the process of becoming not only the richest but also the most cultured in the entire world. The advance of the working class to the level of professional engineers and technicians is on the agenda." The editorial, "The Stakhanovite Year," was accompanied by an oversized portrait of Stalin smiling and smoking a pipe.

Molotov boasted to the central executive committee, as reported by the Soviet press, that "representatives of the German government had raised the question of a new and larger credit facility covering a ten-year period."[241] In Berlin, Kandelaki presented a list of desiderata that included submarines, IG Farben chemical patents, and Zeiss optical technology.[242] The British embassy in Berlin warned the foreign office about a grand deal in the offing.[243] Schacht, who had originally deflected Kandelaki's attempts to shift their conversations to political matters, now remarked to him, "If a meeting between Stalin and Hitler could take place, it would change many things." Stalin wrote on his copy of the secret report: "Interesting."[244]

"Trotskyites" had also seized attention. Valentin Olberg, a provincial teacher who happened to have just returned from Germany, was arrested by the NKVD (January 5, 1936), which extracted "testimony" from him that he had come back with a special task assigned to him by none other than Trotsky: a "terrorist act" against Stalin. Olberg named other "terrorists" he had "recruited"; arrests followed.[245] By spring the NKVD would arrest 508 "Trotskyites," one of whom was found in possession of Trotsky's personal archive for 1927. Stalin ordered the NKVD to furnish Yezhov with copies of all documents pertaining to Trotskyites and freed him from overseeing party organs, a task passed to Yezhov's deputy, Georgy Malenkov (b. 1902). Yezhov now oversaw the NKVD full time.[246]

In Ulan Bator on January 20, Choibalsan, minister of livestock and agriculture, made an impassioned speech in favor of accepting Soviet "proposals." Many of the top Mongolian party officials present were reluctant to submit to Stalin's diktat; some perhaps even favored negotiations with Japan, but they knew someone would immediately inform Moscow. They approved a formal invitation to the USSR for two army brigades, and resolved to increase their own army to 17,000 and their national guard to 2,500.[247]

Also on January 20, King George V died near midnight, at age eighty-three, after being administered a lethal dose of morphine and cocaine to put him out of his suffering and, according to his physician, to allow his death to feature in the morning rather than the afternoon papers.[248] Stalin named Tukhachevsky, alongside Litvinov, to the Soviet delegation for the funeral, in Windsor Castle on January 28. Tukhachevsky traveled by train via Berlin, where he stopped off for a few hours, setting off a speculative frenzy about meetings with the German general staff. The Soviet press was silent about the stopover; Germany denied the rumors.[249] Stalin does seem to have tried to contrive a meeting.[250]

Tukhachevsky had visited Germany nine times, but despite his respect for German military achievements, he distrusted that country.[251] In Britain, where he spent not hours but thirteen days, he met French general Maurice Gamelin, also in London for the funeral, who hosted him at an embassy reception, where the Soviet commander met officers who had been interned with him in the German POW camp. Gamelin invited him to stop in Paris, where Tukhachevsky was afforded a lavish program of meetings and military inspections. In long hours with Gamelin, Tukhachevsky made plain his concern over the threat of German aggression.[252] Maisky and Litvinov were urging Eden, newly named foreign secretary, to use the League of Nations and other instruments to halt the German danger before it came to war. Eden wrote in an internal memo that he told them he was "unable to imagine what else could be done," and to Litvinov's suggestion for a Soviet-British-French bloc against Germany, he responded, "I cannot imagine how that could be done."[253]

"FRIENDSHIP OF PEOPLES"

On January 27, 1936, Stalin and his entourage received a sixty-seven-person del-egation of milkmaids, artists, and functionaries from Buryat-Mongolia in the Russian republic. A report sent by the region's leaders in advance noted that the autonomous republic had 82 percent collectivization and stood first in the Union among national republics in livestock per capita, with 3.36 cows, 3.91 sheep, 0.9 goat, and 0.23 pig held collectively per household. (The numbers for Kazakhstan were 0.84, 1.47, 6.9, and 0.09.)[254] *Pravda*'s coverage of the Kremlin reception in-cluded a photograph of Stalin in Buryat robes, with a dagger in his sash. These receptions for national groups in traditional dress constituted a recent inven-tion.[255] *Pravda* had hit upon the slogan, enunciated at one such reception, of the "Friendship of Peoples."[256]

In the Buryat-Mongolia coverage, there was also a photo of Stalin with Engel-sina "Gelya" Markizova, a seven-year-old Buryat girl wearing a brand-new sail-or's outfit and beaming in his arms.[257] Named for Engels (her brother was named Vladlen, after Vladimir Lenin), she was the daughter of a Buryat-Mongolia offi-cial and lived on Stalin Street in Ulan Ude. She had presented him with two bouquets that her mother, a student at the Moscow Institute of Medicine, had thought to purchase (one was supposed to be for Voroshilov). Stalin had picked her up, and she had wrapped her arms around his shoulders, creating an indelible image.[258] Stalin's daughter, Svetlana, had recently appeared with him in a photo-graph in *Pravda* (he was shown looking down, cupping her head with his good arm, her bright face smiling).[259] Stalin also permitted a photograph of Vasily and Svetlana together in *Pioneer Pravda* (which he instructed Svetlana to "trea-sure").[260] Thereafter, his two younger children faded from public view. But the images with children persisted, creating a sense of a paternal leader. The depic-tions of traditional dances and rural females—which had once conveyed the backwardness to be overcome—now signified supposed harmony in diversity, embodied by a happy father figure.[261]

Russians, too, constituted a nation, but their folklore was presented as imperial culture.[262] Even as workers remained the vanguard class, Russians became the vanguard nation.[263] "All the peoples, participants in the great socialist construc-tion, can take pride in the results of their work," *Pravda* editorialized (February 1, 1936). "But first among equals are the Russian people, the Russian workers, the Russian toilers, whose role throughout the whole Great Proletarian Socialist

Revolution has been exceptionally large, from the first victories to the present day's brilliant period of development." Celebration of the expansion of the state from Muscovy allowed restoration of even Ivan the Terrible to a pedestal. Stalin's leftist critics decried what they perceived as his abandonment of pure Marxism, a perception of retreat that Stalin's rightist critics shared but welcomed.[264] In fact, Stalin's embrace of the imperial Russian inheritance was selective, showing little concern for churches, large numbers of which had been destroyed. (Kaganovich had dynamited Moscow's Cathedral of Christ the Savior, the world's largest Orthodox church, built in the nineteenth century to commemorate the victory over Napoleon.)[265] The absence of private property, the leading role of the party, and the red flag with hammer and sickle amply reinforced the fact that this was a Communist regime. But Stalin's willingness—and ability—to blend imperial Russian *étatisme* with Marxist-Leninist class approaches strengthened the socialist state.[266]

MUDDLE

Stalin revealed his theory of cultural oversight in a letter to Shcherbakov's deputy, Vladimir Kirpichnikov, known as Stavsky. "Take a look at comrade Sobolev," the dictator instructed. "He is, unquestionably, a major talent (judging by his book *Capital Repairs*). He is, as you see from his letter, capricious and uneven. . . . But these traits, in my view, could be found in any giant literary talent (perhaps with a few exceptions). It is not necessary to oblige him to write a second *Capital Repairs*. Such an obligation would lead to nothing. It is not necessary to oblige him to write about collective farms or Magnitostroi. It is impossible to write about such matters under obligation. Let him write what and when he wants. In a word, let him. And take care of him."[267] But apparatchiks capable of nurturing talent as well as loyalty were rare. Stories of poorly educated censors forbidding the music of someone named Schubert over the radio because he might be a "Trotskyite" were the least of it.[268] The censor (*glavlit*) had obtained power over plays, films, ballets, broadcasts, and even circus acts, as well as literature, but it was often overwhelmed and had the NKVD and party commissions looking over its shoulder. Taking chances (saying yes) carried no upside; prohibition was the safest recourse, leading to round after round of supplication, paperwork, and foot dragging, unless someone with sufficient authority and confidence put an end to the runaround and said yes.[269]

Shcherbakov admitted to Stalin that, after fifteen months as secretary of the writers' union, he was being criticized for not being sufficiently on top of things.[270] But Stalin was besieged, and trying to preserve himself to oversee only the most outstanding cultural figures. Finally, on his initiative, the politburo approved the creation of an all-Union Committee for Artistic Affairs, placed not in the party apparatus but in the Council of People's Commissars, with Platon Lebedev, known as Kerzhentsev (b. 1881), as chairman. The son of a physician–cum–tsarist Duma deputy, he had been educated at gymnasium and then Moscow University, was a prolific writer on topics ranging from the new science of time management to the Paris Commune, and an experienced functionary, whose most recent appointment had been as head of Soviet radio.[271]

Kerzhentsev arrived just when a storm broke in music. During the entire previous year, only three long-playing records with Soviet music had been issued, and only one was symphonic: the score of Dmitry Shostakovich (b. 1906) for *Hamlet*. As for opera, Shcherbakov had written to Stalin, Andreyev, and Zhdanov (January 11, 1936) that Leningrad's Maly Opera Theater was, "in essence, the sole theater that vigorously and systematically is working out the extremely important problem of the Soviet theater—namely, the creation of a contemporary musical spectacle." He cited *Lady Macbeth of Mtsensk*, by Shostakovich; *Quiet Flows the Don*, by Ivan Dzerzhinsky (b. 1909); and two works by Valery Zhelobinsky (b. 1913). Shcherbakov proposed that the Leningrad theater be renamed the State New Academy Opera Theater, and that its personnel receive state awards and pay raises to the level of the Kirov Ballet. Stalin redirected Shcherbakov's letter to Kerzhentsev.[272] The Leningrad theater was not renamed, but its ambitious conductor, Samuil Samosud, was anointed a "people's artist" of the RSFSR and got approval to showcase his theater at a festival in Moscow. On opening night, much of Moscow's creative intelligentsia showed for *Quiet Flows the Don*, based on the novel by Sholokhov. The opera—a patriotic glorification of the Don Cossacks' immutable spirit and readiness to defend the motherland—proved a crowd-pleaser, with its lyrical and accessible music. After the final act, Stalin edged forward in the imperial box, making himself visible, and applauded demonstratively.

Stalin summoned Samosud to his box, and the discussion ended up lasting two hours; TASS distributed an account, heralding the advent of a Soviet opera repertoire. On January 17, 1936, Stalin ordered the director of the Bolshoi to stage its own production of *Quiet Flows the Don*, and the director decided to stage all the Samosud works, engaging Fyodor Lopukhov as principal dancer (he had danced the operas in Leningrad). The Bolshoi opened with *Lady Macbeth*, which was easier to mount than the other two. On January 26, Stalin and entourage attended. Unlike *Quiet Flows the Don,* Shostakovich's music was subversive of operatic convention, with discord and hyper-naturalistic portrayals of rape and murder. Stalin exited before the final curtain. This afforded Kerzhentsev a chance to establish his authority as the head of the new committee, at the expense of the existing culture power brokers, above all Shcherbakov. An unsigned denunciation, "A Muddle Instead of Music," appeared in *Pravda* (January 28). (Kerzhentsev was the likely author, not Stalin, as rumored.)[273] Only a short while before, *Pravda* had been over the top in praising the same opera. Even though Samosud had originated the production of the Shostakovich opera, the dictator had seen the Bolshoi version. He named him artistic director of the Bolshoi effective immediately.[274]

Shumyatsky, who remained head of Soviet cinema (and became Kerzhentsev's second deputy), learned that Stalin viewed the *Pravda* article as "programmatic," a demand "not for rebuses and riddles," but music accessible to the masses, citing the "realistic music" of great Soviet films, especially *Jolly Fellows,* in which "all the songs are good, simple, melodic."[275] The "signal" got across. ("Don't you read the papers?" a voice from the audience shouted at a speaker during a meeting of the Moscow Artists' Union, referring to the denunciation of Shostakovich.)[276] Shostakovich inveigled an audience with Kerzhentsev (February 7), and accepted "the majority" of the criticisms. Kerzhentsev advised the composer to travel around villages and acquaint himself with the folk music of Russia, Ukraine, Belorussia, and Georgia, as Rimsky-Korsakov had once done. Shostakovich promised to do so, while noting that composers would appreciate a meeting with Stalin.[277] The press launched a vicious campaign against "formalists," which targeted not only Shostakovich but also Eisenstein and theater director Vsevolod Meyerhold, leaders of the 1920s avant-garde. Kerzhentsev soon took the initiative to purge avant-garde works in museums.[278]

Bulgakov had two plays about to run: *Molière* (originally titled *The Cabal of Hypocrites*), at the Moscow Art Theater, which was to premiere on February 15, 1936, and *Ivan Vasilevich,* which was in final revisions for the Theater of Satire. *Molière* opened to a packed hall and wild applause.[279] Behind the scenes, Kerzhentsev pointed out to Stalin and Molotov that Bulgakov had written *Molière* back when most of his works were banned and that, in the travails of a writer under the Sun King (Louis XIV), he intended to evoke what it was like when a playwright's ideas "went against the political system and plays were prohibited." He conceded the brilliance of the play, which "skillfully, in the lush netherbloom, carries poisonous drops," and recommended killing it with damning reviews.[280]

Pravda ran just such a damning article ("external brilliance and false content").[281] *Molière* closed after seven successful performances. *Ivan Vasilevich*—a comedy mocking Ivan the Terrible—never opened, a blow to the writer but also, given Stalin's views, a blessing.[282] On February 19, after a month in his new post, Kerzhentsev wrote to Stalin and Molotov proposing a competition for a play and screenplay on 1917, promising to "show the role of Lenin and Stalin in the preparation and implementation of the October Revolution." Stalin took a pencil and crossed out his own name.[283]

AMERICAN MIRROR

Being a great power meant looking into the American mirror. Shumyatsky had launched the idea of a Soviet Hollywood. A severe lack of factory capacity meant that Soviet film prints were in short supply—usually fewer than forty copies per film for the entire country—and he wanted a film industry capable of producing its own quality film stock, cameras, projectors, sound-recording machines, and lighting, all of which were expensive to import.[284] He had headed an eight-person commission to Paris, London, Rochester (Eastman Kodak), and Los Angeles, whence he published stories about his film viewings and meetings, returning determined to found a Soviet Cinema City in the mild, sunlit climate on the Black Sea, permitting year-round work.[285] At a Kremlin screening, he had gotten Stalin to approve the Hollywood idea. "Opponents cannot see farther than their own noses," the dictator had intoned. "We need not only good pictures but also more of them, in quantity and in distribution. It becomes obnoxious when the same films remain in all the theaters for months on end."[286] At a follow-up screening, when Stalin saw *Chapayev* for the thirty-eighth time, the dictator said he had heard that Mussolini would build his Cinecittà outside Rome in just two years. But despite Stalin's verbal support, the expensive Hollywood on the Black Sea never materialized.[287]

Opposition came not just from industrial and budget officials. Yechi'el-Leyb Faynzilberg, known as Ilya Ilf, and Yevgeny Katayev, known as Petrov, wrote a letter to Stalin opposing the Soviet Hollywood idea (February 26, 1936).[288] Already household names for their satirical novels *The Twelve Chairs* and *The Little Golden Calf,* featuring the con man Ostap Bender, Ilf and Petrov had just returned from several months in the United States and would write *One-Story America,* which was about not only the "girls who are half naked, three-quarters naked, and nine-tenths naked [who] dance, or act," but the real America—that of working people, a country of democracy if not of socialism. Their book related details of traveling in a Ford through twenty-five states with set pieces about skyscrapers, well-paved roads, vending machines, Mark Twain's hometown, hunters, cowboys, boxers, farmers, Negroes, Indians—an unimaginable world for a Soviet audience.[289]

America surfaced in Yagoda's reports, too. Gulag camps and colonies together held around 1.2 million forced laborers, while exiled "kulaks" in "special settlements" numbered around 900,000.[290] Camps were releasing invalids, which burnished mortality statistics, and Yagoda pressed for financial accountability and better sanitation.[291] Gold output in the Kolyma camps would jump to 36.77 tons in 1936 (from 15.94 the year before), which, an internal report stressed, beat California.[292] Mass arrests by the NKVD in 1936 would decline to 131,168, as compared with 505,256 in 1933 (and with 205,173 in 1934 and 193,093 in 1935). In March 1936 Yagoda bragged at the Council of People's Commissars that, because of increased professionalism, reorganization, and new methods, criminality had been sharply reduced, and the problem of mass social unrest (such as during collectivization) resolved. He conceded that organized hooliganism, robbery, and theft of socialist property persisted, and that ordinary police did not feel safe patrolling working-class districts in mushrooming industrial cities. He also admitted that crime rates were not diminishing as noticeably in rural settlements, where police were almost absent. Still, in the previous year, he gloated, there had been fewer reported murders across the Soviet Union than in the city of Chicago.[293]

HITLER, AGAIN

Hitler continued his manipulative mastery. On February 21, 1936, he granted an interview to Bertrand de Jouvenel for *Paris-Midi,* stressing his policy of peace, the unifying threat of Bolshevism, and the folly of Franco-German enmity. "Let us be friends," the Führer pleaded, calling his *Mein Kampf* outdated and promising "correction of certain pages."[294] (Unlike Stalin, with his useful idiots, Hitler did not get to edit the transcripts.) A few days later, the Führer sought out Arnold Toynbee, a philosopher of history who was in Berlin to address the Nazi Law Society. "I want England's friendship, and if you English will make friends with us, you may name your conditions—including, if you like, conditions about Eastern Europe," he told the professor, who predicted to the foreign office that "any response from the British side . . . would produce an enormous counter-response from Hitler."[295] Göring, hunting in Poland again (February 19–24), proclaimed at a luncheon hosted by Beck, "in the name of the Führer and chancellor, that any rumors that Germany intended to enter into closer relations with the Soviet Union were unfounded."[296]

In Mongolia on February 26, Choibalsan was named head of a new interior ministry (the NKVD equivalent) and, along with Demid, promoted to marshal. (Soviet personnel accounted for one quarter of Mongolian interior ministry personnel.) That same day, in Tokyo, young officers of the Imperial Japanese Army staged a putsch, intending to submit demands to the emperor for the dismissal of their rivals and the appointment of a new prime minister and military-dominated cabinet. They occupied central Tokyo and assassinated two former prime ministers and other high officials, but failed to capture the sitting prime minister or the Imperial Palace. The emperor opposed the action; on February 29 the rebels surrendered.[297]

On March 1, 1936, Stalin granted an interview to Roy Howard, president of Scripps-Howard News, which, unlike his earlier exchanges with foreigners, he allowed to be published in mass-circulation newspapers. Stalin observed that the situation in Japan after the recent putsch remained unclear, but that "for the time being, the Far Eastern hotbed of danger shows the greatest activity," and issued an unequivocal public warning: "If Japan should venture to attack the Mongolian People's Republic and encroach upon its independence, we will have to help." Howard suggested that the Italian fascists and the German Nazis characterized their systems as state-centric, and the Soviets had built "state socialism." Stalin rejected the term ("inexact") and any comparison: "Primarily, this is because the private ownership of the factories and works—of the land, the banks, transport, and so on—has remained intact, and therefore capitalism remains in full force in Germany and in Italy." Howard pressed Stalin about world revolution. Stalin: "We never had such plans and intentions." Howard countered with examples. Stalin: "This is all the result of a misunderstanding." Howard: "A tragic misunderstanding?" Stalin: "No, a comic, or, perhaps, a *tragicomic* one."[298]

Stalin gestured toward Rome, telling Howard that fascist Italy's much-condemned invasion of Abyssinia was a mere "episode," but he noted that, even as Hitler spoke about peace, the Führer could not "avoid issuing threats"—Stalin's first unequivocal public rebuke of Nazism. He added that Germany might join with Poland or the Baltic states against the USSR, just as it had in the Great War against Russia.[299]

Hitler excelled at the bold gesture. On March 7, 1936, which happened to be two days after *Pravda* and *Izvestiya* published Stalin's interview, the Führer sent troops into a zone on the left bank of the Rhine River that bordered France and had been demilitarized for an indefinite period by the Versailles Treaty. His wooing of Britain had partially succeeded, getting him the Anglo-German naval pact, which fell short of the total acquiescence he sought but put some distance between Britain and France. His scheming to drive a wedge between Italy and France had failed—until Mussolini moved to realize long-standing designs by invading Abyssinia, opening a rift between Rome and the Western powers. True, Hitler's maneuvering with Poland had helped provoke the Franco-Soviet pact, but that agreement seemed only to have spurred more Soviet approaches to him. In the Rhineland occupation, Hitler had overcome his foreign ministry's opposition and his own usual last-minute attack of nerves.[300] "Fortune favors the brave!" Goebbels had written in his diary the day Hitler informed him of the decision for the Rhineland action. "He who dares nothing wins nothing."[301]

British officials were exasperated: they had been about to *offer* Germany remilitarization, but, as Eden told the cabinet (March 9), "Hitler has deprived us of the possibility of making to him a concession which might otherwise have been a useful bargaining counter in our hands in the general negotiations with Germany which we had it in contemplation to initiate."[302] London appealed pro forma to the League of Nations (March 12) and strenuously worked to restrain any French response.[303] French ruling circles lacked the confidence to stand up to Germany alone.[304] Only a small contingent of the fledgling Wehrmacht had entered the demilitarized zone, ostensibly so as not to give the impression of a Western invasion. One or two French divisions would have sufficed to drive them out.[305] Instead, German industry could now be organized for war without concern for the security of the Rhine and the Ruhr. France was humiliated. "In these three years," Hitler exulted at a hastily summoned session of the neutered Reichstag in the Kroll Opera House, "Germany has regained its honor, found belief again, overcome its greatest economic distress, and finally ushered in a new cultural ascent." He cited the recently ratified Franco-Soviet alliance as justification for his remilitarization. "The revolution may take place in France tomorrow," he added. "In that case, Paris would be nothing more than a branch office of the Communist International."[306]

France managed to get Britain to sign a diplomatic note specifying that in the event of a German attack on France, the two Western powers would enter into general staff talks, which fell short of automatic military assistance but was a step.[307] Stalin locked down his Mongolian vassals in a Treaty of Friendship and Cooperation, signed in Ulan Bator (March 12), which formalized the already imposed military alliance for a ten-year period.[308] Some observers also expected Hitler's action to deepen Franco-Soviet ties, but French officials complained that Stalin was more interested in provoking war between France and Germany than in cooperating with France to fight.[309]

Stalin just did not view the French as offering anything remotely comparable to Germany economically. (Thanks to a well-placed spy, Karl Behrens, the Soviets were receiving technical blueprints from AEG, Germany's preeminent heavy electrical engineering firm.) Also, the Rhineland's remilitarization indicated that the USSR might not be the principal target of German aggrandizement.[310, 311] Molotov gave an extended interview in Moscow to the editor of the influential French newspaper *Le Temps* (March 19, 1936) stating that Germany might start a war—in the west. He did reaffirm the Franco-Soviet pact and admit that "a certain part of the Soviet people" felt implacable hostility toward Germany's current rulers, but he volunteered, unartfully, that the "chief tendency, determining the policy of Soviet power, thinks an improvement in Soviet-German relations possible . . . yes, even Hitler's Germany."[312]

CHARISMATIC POWER

A Georgian delegation was received in the Kremlin, also on March 19, and Molotov greeted them in Georgian: "*Amkhanagebo!* (Stormy applause, turning into an ovation.)" When he noted that they had given the country Stalin, there was "an eruption of applause" that would not cease.[313] In the Grand Kremlin Palace between April 11 and 21, the Communist Youth League 10th Congress took place. "Stalin had yet to make an appearance," the writer Konstantin Paustovsky wrote of the final day. "We want comrade Stalin, Stalin, Stalin," the delegates shouted, stamping their feet. "And then it happened! Stalin emerged suddenly and silently out of the wall behind the Presidium table. . . . Everyone jumped. There was frenzied applause. . . . Unhurriedly, Stalin came up to the table, stopped, and, with hands linked on his stomach, gazed at the hall. . . . The first thing that struck me was that he did not resemble the thousands of portraits and official photographs, which set out to flatter him. The man who stood before me was stumpy and stocky, with a heavy face, reddish hair, low forehead, and a thick mustache. . . . The hall rocked with all the shouting. People applauded, holding their hands high over their heads. At any moment, one felt, the ceiling would come crashing down. Stalin raised a hand. Immediately there was a deathly hush. In that hush, Stalin shouted abruptly and in a rather hoarse voice, with a strong Georgian accent, 'Long Live Soviet youth!'"[314]

The children's writer Chukovsky was close to the front (sixth or seventh row). "What took place in the hall! HE stood, a bit fatigued, engrossed in thought, titanic," Chukovsky noted in his diary. "One sensed the immense habituation to power, the force, and at the same time something female, soft. I looked around: everyone had loving faces, kind, inspirational, and smiling faces. Just to see— simply see—was happiness for us all." Chukovsky, too, had sensed the power. "Never," he concluded, "did I think I was capable of such feelings."[315]

On May 1, 1936, the regime staged the massive military display on Red Square, and the next day the emotive Voroshilov once again served as a deft master of ceremonies. "Comrades, by the ancient Soviet custom, it is proposed that we fill our glasses," he told a boisterous hall in the Grand Kremlin Palace, proceeding with toast after toast (for Stalin, Molotov, Kalinin, Orjonikidze, Kaganovich). Before each pronouncement, Voroshilov employed Soviet jargon, tongue in cheek: "Comrades, I do not doubt your vigilance in general, but in this case a check is needed. How's the situation with glasses?" (Refills, quickly.) And on it went, until Stalin rose to toast Voroshilov, and Molotov rose to toast "the Great Stalin," whereupon the entire room of cadets and officers stood as one.[316]

The Red Army, across 1935 and 1936, acquired a staggering 7,800 tanks, 4,200 airplanes, 9,600 artillery systems, and 6.7 million rounds of ammunition, and soon reached 1.423 million men, on a par with the tsarist army in peacetime. The USSR's spring 1936 war games again had Nazi Germany as the main enemy, but the exercises revealed that pre-positioning of massive forces on the frontier would not be enough: without a prior Soviet occupation of the independent Baltic states to seize the strategic initiative from Germany, victory could be elusive.[317] But Stalin would not countenance such aggressive preemptive moves. It was, in any case, doubtful whether the Red Army could even launch a preemptive war, even as its massive size and disposition made it seem poised to do so.[318] Such combat would have put to a severe test the Soviet rail network, known both at home and abroad to be a weak point.[319] Also, the military expansion, overly rapid and incoherent, had led to a critical dearth of well-trained junior officers.[320] Stalin, who received Tukhachevsky nine times in the Little Corner in 1936, including on April 3 and May 28, with a slew of military brass and intelligence officials, had moved him from running armaments to a reorganized directorate for military training.[321]

BLINDERS

In Berlin on May 4, the Soviet embassy hosted a banquet to celebrate a recently signed modest new bilateral trade protocol, without new credits—the existing 200-million-mark loan remained to be drawn down—but with procedures to fix short-term clearing of accounts (inhibited by currency regulations).[322] Bessonov told a German foreign ministry official of Soviet readiness to do what was necessary to create the "preconditions of (Soviet-German) détente."[323] Hitler had appointed Herbert Göring head of a new office for raw material and foreign exchange, crucial for the rearmament economy.[324] The indefatigable Kandelaki managed to obtain an audience with him (May 13) through a cousin of the Luftwaffe head, during which an amiable Göring promised to make inquiries about Kandelaki's request for assistance in obtaining the military technology he sought, and professed delight at the recent trade protocol. Göring also pledged that "all his efforts were directed toward making closer contacts with Russia again, politically, too, and he thought the best way would be through intensifying and expanding mutual trade relations." He added, "If the Russian gentlemen encountered difficulties in Germany or were faced with questions with which they were making no headway, he most cordially invited them to turn to him at any time. He was always ready to receive them and assist them by word and deed."[325] Schacht, the next day, tried to downplay Göring's remarks, but Kandelaki departed immediately to report in Moscow.[326] A few days later, Göring would agree with a group of German industrialists that business with the Soviet Union was important and promised at some point to bring the issue up with Hitler, "whose attitude to it, admittedly, was not very sympathetic."[327]

Göring wanted no more from the Soviets than raw materials in a strictly nonpolitical trade relationship, and he played a complex game. The day after meeting Kandelaki, he received Polish foreign minister Beck and informed him that the Soviet representative had been insisting on a meeting and, finally, had been granted one, during which Kandelaki had made "a concrete proposal for the purchase of several warships and armaments in Germany. The Soviet delegation gave us to understand that Stalin, in contrast to Litvinov, is positively inclined to

Germany." Göring claimed he had presented the Soviet enticements to "the chancellor," who "energetically spoke against such suggestions." That was what the Poles wanted to hear. Still, Beck had to understand that Soviet-German rapprochement was at least under discussion. Thus did Göring put pressure on Warsaw to improve Polish-German relations—on Berlin's terms—while continuing to sabotage any possible Polish-Soviet rapprochement by dangling the possibility of German-Polish joint military action, should the Red Army attack.[328]

Inside the Soviet regime, the British remained the fixation. "Fascism's strength is not in Berlin, fascism's strength is not in Rome," Kalinin, head of the Soviet state, said in May 1936, echoing comments by Molotov. "Fascism's strength is in London, and not even in London per se but in five London banks."[329] Mussolini—infuriated by League of Nations sanctions over his Abyssinian invasion—had threatened to quit that body, but it hardly mattered. He publicly drew closer to Nazi Germany.[330] On the battlefield, Italy had snatched victory from what briefly looked like possible defeat, and in early May 1936, Emperor Haile Selassie, although refusing to vacate the throne, fled into exile. Italy would merge Abyssinia with Eritrea and Somaliland, forming Italian East Africa; King Victor Emmanuel III would be proclaimed emperor. Mussolini was denounced as the worst of the dictators, a "mad dog act," or, in the words of Britain's Anthony Eden, a "gangster"—language that was not heard publicly from Whitehall about Hitler.[331] A smiling Hitler told British ambassador Phipps, in regard to Mussolini's aggression in Abyssinia (May 14), "With dictators, nothing succeeds like success."[332] Four days later, Germany's foreign minister, Konstantin von Neurath, confidently told William Bullitt, now the U.S. ambassador in Berlin, that Germany would annex Austria at some point, and no one would stop it.[333]

CULTURAL TRIUMPHS, TROTSKYITES

Sergei Prokofyev's *Little Peter and the Wolf*, commissioned by the Central Children's Theater run by Natalya Sats, had premiered at the Moscow Philharmonic on May 2, 1936, before moving to the children's venue.[334] Although Soviet functionaries had failed to cajole the self-exiles Igor Stravinsky and Sergei Rachmaninov to return, they had succeeded in retrieving Prokofyev, who lived among the constellation of émigré luminaries in Paris with his Spanish wife, Lina Codina, and their Paris-born children. He would receive a four-room apartment in an elite neo-constructivist building (Zemlyanoy Val, 14) and immediately set to work on a plethora of commissions. He had never gravitated to vaudeville or the Hollywood musical, and he took Shostakovich's public humiliation as promising that there would be ample space for his own diatonic melodies, determined, as he was, to become a central player in what was a serious musical culture. Prokofyev underestimated the bureaucratic deadweight (approval committees made up of third- and fourth-rate musical talent would rewrite his works), but in the meantime the orchestral storytelling of his *Little Peter and the Wolf* enchanted young audiences.[335]

Alexandrov, Eisenstein's former assistant, had done it again: his film *Circus* premiered on May 23, 1936. Alexandrov, who had once been a circus performer himself, based the film on the Ilf and Petrov play *Under the Big Top*, from the Moscow Music Hall. *Circus* lacked the disorganized zaniness of *Jolly Fellows*: the cameraman had been to Hollywood with Shumyatsky and introduced American storyboarding and Disney's matching of sound and image. *Circus* followed the winning Hollywood formula of the transformation of a spunky underdog into a smash success. The female lead, Marion Dixon (played by Lyubov Orlova), a name evocative of Marlene Dietrich, is a performer in an American circus that comes to the USSR on tour. She had given birth to a son with a black lover and suffered racism in the United States; in the USSR, she falls for a Russian performer named Ivan and defects, which spurs the circus director to threaten to expose her illegitimate black child, but the Moscow audience embraces him, and Marion remains in Moscow with her Ivan. The film climaxes with a lullaby sung, in turn, by representatives of the various Soviet nationalities. (The final kiss cliché, characteristic of American comedies, between the little black boy, Jimmy, and a little white girl was cut.) Dunayevsky supplied six catchy songs, performed by Yakov Skomorovsky's jazz band, including the colossally popular, easily memorized "Song of the Motherland," with lyrics by Lebedev-Kumach ("I know of no other country where a person breathes this freely!"). The film's final production number has Orlova dancing at the pinnacle of a multilayered cake structure. One million people saw *Circus* during just its first two weeks in Moscow. Orlova crisscrossed the country. In Chelyabinsk, she was awarded a piston ring from the factory foundry engraved with lyrics from the *Jolly Fellows* march: "Song helps us build and live."[336]

Party Card, directed by Ivan Pyryev, had premiered in Moscow on April 7, 1936. In the film, the year is 1932 and Pavel Kurganov, from Siberia, the son of a kulak, signs on at a Moscow factory. Becoming a shock worker there, he seduces and marries a young woman, Anna Kulikova, an outstanding assembly-line worker and loyal party member. Unbeknownst to Anna (played brilliantly by Ada Voitsik), Pavel (Andrei Abrikosov) has murdered a Communist Youth League activist, to take over his identity, while secretly working for foreign intelligence, which assigned him the task of obtaining a party member's card to commit sabotage. Despite her initial lack of vigilance, which Anna's party colleagues at work denounce, she teams up with her former sweetheart to expose her husband as an embittered kulak enemy. The lesson: Pavel, a peasant lad, had looked trustworthy, but no one can be trusted. The most dangerous enemy is the one with a party card.[337] In the initial draft of the screenplay (by Yekaterina Vinogradskaya), titled *Little Anna,* Pavel had not been a spy. Stalin helped recast it.[338] Party cards, long a sign of status in the Soviet Union, allowing holders to attend secret meetings, receive secret information, and shoulder extra responsibilities, now endangered those who held them.

Yagoda had written to Stalin recommending that the multitude of "Trotskyites" in custody be executed, in accordance with the Kirov assassination antiterror law.[339] Some were said to have "ties" to the Gestapo. He reported that two arrested Trotskyites had been found to have thirteen issues of the *Bulletin of the Opposition* in a suitcase hidden in the wall—Stalin kept his in a cupboard—as well as a copy of the defector Grigory Besedovsky's book *On the Road to Thermidor.* The NKVD had also found an address book—more "Trotskyites" to arrest.[340] On May 20, 1936, pointing to "the unceasing counterrevolutionary activity of Trotskyites in internal exile, and of those expelled from the party," the politburo stipulated that more than 600 "Trotskyites" should be sent to remote concentration camps, while those found to have engaged in terrorism were to be executed.[341] Yagoda furnished Stalin with additional testimony about "Trotskyite-Zinovievite organizations" on June 1.[342]

From June 1 to 4, 1936, the Central Committee held its first plenum of the year. It was devoted to agriculture, the pending adoption of a new constitution, and the appeals/reinstatement process for party members expelled during the recent verification campaign (more than 200,000 total). With the regime under severe financial pressure, Stalin had reduced the interest paid on government bonds subscribed to by ordinary people from 8–10 percent to 4 percent, with maturity extended from 10 to 20 years, which he now felt compelled to mention. Some 50 million Soviet inhabitants were affected, most of whom had "subscribed" only under severe pressure from trade unions and party organizers. "As you are well aware, we spend an alarming amount of money on things that cannot be postponed," he told the plenum attendees (June 3), who would have to face the people's resentment back in their locales. "Much money has been spent, and is being spent, on such matters as building schools, teachers' pay, urban improvement, irrigation, afforestation of a number of parts of the country, . . . and constructing canals. Money is being spent on defense and even more will be spent in the future. . . . We do not yet have a navy, and a new one must be established. . . . This is the situation, comrades."[343]

These remarks were not reported in the press. *Pravda*, however, did castigate provincial-level party bosses for "mistakes" made in party expulsions.[344] Yezhov in his report had admitted that far from everyone expelled was an enemy, but he ominously stated that "we ought not to think that the enemy, who yesterday was still in the party, will rest content with being expelled from the party and quietly wait for 'better times.'" Stalin made some rambling interjections about clearer procedures for appeals, and allowed Yenukidze to be reinstated in the party. Several matters were not recorded even in the rough draft materials of the plenum, including an exchange between Yagoda and Stalin on the "Trotskyite-Zinovievite bloc."[345]

Gorky had taken gravely ill during the plenum, four days after visiting his son Maxim's grave in Novodevichy Cemetery. "We came to see you at 2:00 a.m.," Stalin, Molotov, and Voroshilov wrote in a short note (June 10). "They said your pulse was excellent (82, more or less). The doctors forbade us from seeing you. We had to comply. Greetings from all of us, a big greeting."[346] On the morning of June 18, he died at his dacha. Levitan, on Soviet radio, called him "a great Russian writer, brilliant artist of the word, friend of workers, and fighter for the victory of Communism." Gorky's brain was removed and taken in a bucket, by his secretary, to Moscow's Brain Research Institute, which housed the brains of Lenin and Mayakovsky. That day and the next, the brainless body lay in state as half a million people paid their respects. (When Stalin entered for the solemn farewell, applause broke out, which was shown on newsreels.)[347] On June 20, at the state funeral, Gide, on the Mausoleum, delivered one of the eulogies, along with Aleksei Tolstoy and Molotov. Rolland sent a letter from Switzerland, published in *Pravda* (June 20): "I recall his youthful ardor, his sparkling enthusiasm when he spoke of the new world in whose building he took part. I recall his goodness and the sorrow hidden in its depth."

Gorky's ashes were interred in the Kremlin Wall. Stalin afforded Andreyev, his apparatchik for culture, the honor of placing the urn. The regime seized the writer's archive (Yagoda especially was in for infuriating surprises).[348] Rumors circulated of poisoning. One of those accused was Gorky's former mistress Baroness Moura Budberg, who got her surname through marriage to an Estonian aristocrat, started an affair with H. G. Wells, and was thought to be a double British and Soviet agent. But the main suspect in the whisperings was Stalin.[349] In fact, Gorky, who was sixty-eight, had been extremely sick, and was properly diagnosed and treated by a battery of top physicians.[350] His autopsy revealed bronchitis, tuberculosis, and a damaged left lung. The writer had smoked nearly three packs of cigarettes a day, and needed an oxygen tank. *Pravda* gave the cause of death as "a cardiac arrest and paralysis of the lungs." Gorky had never spiritually recovered from his son Maxim's untimely death.[351] "What has brought you to the Bolsheviks?" Yekaterina Kuskova, Gorky's lifelong friend, recalled asking him once, in an obituary published in the emigration (June 26). "Do you remember how I began to read Marx with you in Nizhny Novgorod, and you proposed to throw the 'German philistine' into the fire?"[352]

THE MARXIST-LENINIST REGIME that emerged in the blood and fever dreams of the years 1929–36 was buffeted by global structural forces, from fluctuations in commodity prices to innovations in tank designs, and by the deepening of a new historical conjuncture, the mass age. The most powerful countries achieved and maintained their great-power status by mastery of a set of modern attributes: mass production, mass consumption, mass culture, mass politics. Great Britain had not only powerful ships and airplanes, engineers and trained military officers, but also a broad-based political system, an integrated national culture, and a deep degree of societal cohesion. Every other aspiring great power had to achieve its own mass-based version of modernity, which imparted new impetus and form to their geopolitical rivalries. That competition took place not just across the liberal-illiberal divide but among the democratizing parliamentary countries Britain, France, and the United States, and among avowedly authoritarian regimes: fascist Italy, Nazi Germany, Imperial Japan, and the Soviet Union. All of them either had to match the others in some way or risk becoming, like the rest of the world, colonies. Modernity was not a sociological but a geopolitical process.[353]

Stalin forced into being a *socialist* modernity, presiding over the creation of a mass-production economy, a Soviet mass culture, an integrated society, and a mass politics without private property.[354, 355]

This upheaval, in addition to geopolitics and ideology, reflected Russia's long-standing sense of world-historical destiny combined with profound insecurity and relative weakness vis-à-vis the European powers. This gap had long goaded Russia into catch-up acquisition of Western technology to protect the country's non-Western identity, borrowing not ideas and institutions of liberty but technology for industry and techniques for administration of resources and population—the social-engineering part of the Enlightenment. But even as Russia advanced, the West did not stand still and remained richer, more advanced, more powerful. Still, under Stalin the Soviets had imported and copied Western technology and skills, enforced deprivation on the populace, and created a massive land army and air force that would be the envy of other powers—just as imperial Russia had done.[356] Stalin's use of the state to force-modernize the country was far more radical and violent than that of his tsarist predecessors because of the Great War conjuncture, which accelerated the use of violence for political ends, and the anticapitalism, which coercion alone could achieve. Thanks to the Great Depression, Stalin was also able to secure technology transfer with greater independence from foreign desiderata.[357]

In imperial Russia, only a strong personality—a Sergei Witte, a Pyotr Stolypin—had been able to impose something of a unified will on the ministries, while toiling to implant loyalists across the entire bureaucracy, but the tsar and his agents deliberately undermined strong central government, because that threatened the prerogatives of the autocrat. Stolypin, arguably Russia's greatest statesman, had occupied the position of prime minister, but Stalin occupied the position of supreme ruler, like the tsar, and he favored unified government.[358] Through Molotov and others, he achieved coordination, and over a much larger apparatus. And while Stolypin had had to contend with a quasiparliament to legalize his policies, the Congress of Soviets possessed none of the powers even of the tsarist Duma. To be sure, Stalin had to obtain politburo approval. But he either manipulated the members or just acted unilaterally. He possessed instruments Stolypin could not have dreamed of: a single-party machine that enveloped the whole country, a Soviet secret police that vastly exceeded the tsarist *okhranka* in personnel and acceptable practice, a galvanizing ideology that morally justified any and all means, and housebroken nationalisms as well as a supranational Soviet identity that bound the peoples of the former Russian empire to the regime.[359]

Perhaps the biggest difference was that the Soviet regime mobilized the masses on its behalf. Machiavelli had suggested that princes aim to restrict or eliminate access to public spaces—amphitheaters and squares, town halls and auditoriums, streets and even parks—but Stalin flooded them. His state's power was magnified by a host of mass organizations: the party and Youth League, the army and civil defense associations, trade unions that dispensed social welfare, a kind of mass conscription society.[360] The dictator coerced and cajoled the artistic intelligentsia into state service as well. His regime actively engaged the new Soviet society at every level, in identities and practices of everyday life, through which people became part of the system.[361] The populace absorbed the regime's language, ways of thinking, and modes of behavior. Aspirations, in turn, emerged from the new Soviet society, and Stalin became attentive to quality of life, consumer goods, entertainment, and pride. By the mid-1930s the revolution and Stalin's leadership were seen as having enabled a great country to take its rightful place among the powers, with a supposedly morally and economically superior system.[362] "In Germany bayonets do not terrorize a people," Hitler had boasted in spring 1936. "Here a government is supported by the confidence of the entire people. . . . I have not been imposed by anyone upon this people. From the people I have grown up, in the people I have remained, to the people I return. My pride is that I know no statesman in the world who with greater right than I can say that he is representative of his people."[363] Similarly, Stalin had boasted to Roy Howard that same spring of 1936 that the USSR was "a truly popular system, which grew up from within the people."[364]

Stalin had improvised his way toward attainment of the modern authoritarian dream: incorporating the masses without empowering them. Europe's democratic great powers were put on the defensive by the dynamic mass politics and stated aspirations of the authoritarian regimes. France's dilemma was particularly stark. Fearful of revived German power, it had turned to a pact with the Communist USSR, but its willingness to do so was based precisely upon the pact's absence of a military convention, alongside a desperately desired deepening of cooperation with Britain, as well as mollification of Italy and the marginalization of the French Communists.[365] In the event, Britain had shown itself ready to surrender the continental guarantees that France viewed as bedrock, France's precarious placation of a prickly Mussolini was failing, and France's Communist party was growing significantly in strength, winning more than 15 percent of the vote and seventy-two seats in spring 1936 (versus 8 percent and ten seats four years earlier). All of this damaged Paris's already weak commitment to alliance with Moscow.

Stalin's dilemma was no less stark. Suspicious that the imperialists Britain and France would galvanize an anti-Soviet front and goad countries on his border into attacking, he had worked to neutralize Poland and recruit Germany, keeping them out of the feared anti-Soviet coalition. On his eastern flank, Japan had seized the Soviet sphere of influence in Manchuria and taken other parts of northern China, directly threatening Soviet territory. All of this had spurred his turn toward outright militarization, membership in the League of Nations, an antifascist front in the Comintern, and mutual assistance pacts with France and its ally Czechoslovakia. But Stalin, like the tsarist conservative and Germanophile Pyotr Durnovó, questioned the wisdom of such an orientation. He held to his quest for rapprochement with Nazi Germany, to acquire advanced technology while preventing a broad anti-Soviet coalition. Hitler, however, increasingly named the Soviet Union as his principal target. Stalin's options were to deter or deflect the penetration in his direction of Germany and Japan, via an alliance with binding military obligations; secure some form of accommodation (nonaggression pacts); or fight Germany and Japan on his own, perhaps simultaneously, a two-front nightmare the tsars had not faced.[366]

Russia's perennial quest to build a strong state, to match an ever-superior West, had culminated, yet again, in personal rule. That person was extraordinary, a man of deep Marxist-Leninist convictions and iron will, but dogged by Lenin's purported Testament calling for his removal and internal opposition over the searing episode of forced collectivization-dekulakization. At least 5,000 "Trotskyites" and "Zinovievites" were arrested in the first half of 1936 (as compared with 631 in all of 1934). Before the year was out, the total would reach 23,279.[367] And that would be the beginning. A fixation on former oppositionists, above all Trotsky, would begin to consume the country. None of that was caused by the foreign policy dilemmas, but it would exacerbate them. Could Bolshevism's avatar Stalin solve the deep challenges of Russian history that, along with anticapitalism and the mass age, had produced him and his epigones?

PART II

TERROR AS STATECRAFT

Will future generations understand it all? Will they understand what is happening? It is terrifying living through it.

ALEXANDRA KOLLONTAI,
Soviet envoy to Sweden, notes written at a European
spa on hotel stationery, March 25, 1938[1]

IN HIS *HERO WITH A THOUSAND FACES,* Joseph Campbell would indirectly explain the archetype in world mythologies that Soviet regime propagandists much earlier had applied to Stalin: humble origins (a man of the people), a call to greatness on the people's behalf, a demonstration of separation (slaying of dragons, i.e., of the party opposition), a crushing setback and near defeat (peasant and party resistance to collectivization), a mythic rebound of resilience and fortitude, culminating in triumph (Congress of Victors; a socialist great power).[2] With Soviet hagiographers competing to portray Stalin as just such a humble man of the people and their instrument of destiny, Beria, in particular, intuited the dividends from depicting him as the Lenin of the Caucasus. This portrait, for all its blatant falsehoods, captured Stalin's obsession with menace, something Campbell's archetype could not do, but also Stalin's archetypal commitment to a transcendent mission for the supposed greater good. Realizing the dream of socialism had seemed improbable for decades. But after the abdication of the tsar, in 1917, the decision by Russia's Provisional Government to continue the war—like imperial Germany's decision to launch the U-boat campaign that provoked U.S. entry and tipped the war's balance—had changed the course of humanity. Socialism was no longer just libraries full of pamphlets, songs, marches, meetings, and schisms, but a country.

In power, socialism swelled the state and destroyed not just the "bourgeoisie" but the small-business owner, the family farmer, the artisan.[3] All of this shocked non-Leninist socialists who hoped to end exploitation and alienation and break through to social democracy while still insisting on their class approach. These Marxists repudiated the Soviet Union as not socialism but a deformation, because of Russia, or Lenin, or Stalin. After all, Marx had never advocated mass murder, but freedom. Nowhere did he say there should be collective farms formed by secret police coercion, mass deportations to frozen wastes, terrible famine.[4] Of course, Marx had insisted that wage labor was "wage slavery," private capital "exploitation" and "alienation," the market "chaos," and therefore that, to achieve lasting abundance and freedom, capitalism had to be "transcended." The tragedy began unfolding with the very invention of "capitalism."[5] Once markets and private property were named and blamed as the source of evil, statization would be the consequence. A few socialists began, painfully, to recognize that there could be no freedom without markets and private property, but they were denounced as apostates. Compounding the tragedy of the left, traditional conservatives committed the gross error of inviting the fascists and Nazis to power in no small part because of the leftist threat and the hard-nosed view that differences between anticapitalist democratic socialists and Leninists were delusion. To top it all off, Social Democrats and Communists fought a bitter civil war over workers' allegiance.

When Hegel famously referred to history as a "slaughter bench," he had no idea what he was talking about, and yet he was right. Partly that was because of the influence of Hegel's hazardous ideas on the Marxists: the sophistry known as the dialectic, the idolatry of the state, the supposed historical "progress" through the "necessary" actions of great men.[6]

It was no accident, as Hegelian-inspired Marxists might say (and as Trotsky had predicted already in 1904), that a single leader had emerged atop a single-party system that, on the basis of class analysis, denied legitimacy to political opposition.[7] It was also no accident that this single leader was Stalin, at once a militant Communist and an unprincipled intriguer, an ideologue and an opportunist—the Leninist fusion—who, like his mentor, possessed extreme willpower, which was the prerequisite for attaining what only unspeakable bloodshed could: the elimination of capitalism.[8] Stalin could not boast the effortless success of those to the manor born. He had to be, and was, a relentless striver. He also happened to carry a gargantuan chip on his shoulder, for although he had benefited immeasurably from Lenin's patronage, he then suffered the unending humiliation of Lenin's supposed call for his removal, which was thrown at him by his rivals and whispered across the entire party. Stalin emerged as a leader of acute political intelligence and bottomless personal resentment. The collectivization that he forced through to the end, famine notwithstanding, provoked criticism in the party—Syrtsov on the fiction of the politburo; Ryutin on his amoral dictatorship—magnifying Stalin's righteousness and resentment. To an extent, power reveals who a person is. But the *effects* on Stalin of accruing and exercising power unconstrained by law or constitutional limits—the power of life and death over hundreds of millions—were immense. Alongside the nature of Bolshevism, the setting of his regime—Russia, with its fraught history and geopolitics, its sense of historic mission and grievance, which were given new impetus and form by socialism's fixation on capitalist encirclement—also indelibly shaped who he became.

Without Stalin there would have been no socialism, and without socialism, no Stalin.[9] That said, his demonic disposition, which the experience of *this* kind of rule in *this* place heightened, never overwhelmed his ability to function at the highest level. Physically, he continued to suffer from frequent bouts of flu and fever, stomach ailments, dental problems, and severe pain in his joints, but he proved hearty enough to be a hands-on ruler of one sixth of the earth's surface. His capacity for work was prodigious, his zeal for detail unquenchable.[10] He received 100 or even 200 documents a day, some of substantial length, and he read many of them, often to the end, scribbling comments or instructions on them.[11] He initiated or approved untold personnel appointments, goaded minions in relentless campaigns, attended myriad congresses and ceremonies bearing the burden of instruction, assiduously followed the public and private statements of cultural figures, edited novels and plays, and prescreened films. He pored over a voluminous flow of intelligence reports and lengthy interrogation protocols of accused spies, wreckers, counterrevolutionaries, traitors. He wrote and rewrote the texts of decrees, newspaper editorials, and his own speeches, confident in his abilities. Very occasionally he made grammatical mistakes in Russian, his second language, but he wrote accessibly, using rhetorical questions, catchphrases, enumeration.[12] The fools were the ones who took him for a fool.

Pravda taught Soviet inhabitants indebtedness to the state and to Stalin personally, depicting everything they had—food, clothing, education, joy—as gifts ("Thank you, comrade Stalin!").[13] In newsreels he came across as the epitome of wise leadership, photogenic in his signature tunic. "In his speeches Stalin was categorical, but simple," recalled the loyalist writer Konstantin Simonov (b. 1915).

"With people—this we sometimes saw in the newsreels—he conducted himself simply. He dressed simply, identically. There was nothing showy about him, no external pretensions to greatness or a sense of being chosen. This corresponded to our impressions of how a person standing at the head of the party should be. Altogether this was Stalin: all these feelings, all these positive traits, real and drawn by us, of the leader of the party and state."[14] Stalin's leader cult was manufactured—acquiring the character of an arms race, as proponents strove to outdo one another—but not artificial.[15] If Hitler, despite the forelock that fell into his face, the near ridiculous mustache, and the constant chewing of his finger-nails, could hold his country in thrall, the reason lay at least as much in the German people as in the Führer's gifts. Stalin, too, possessed a weird magnetism, derived from his ability to personify socialist modernity and Soviet might, to inspire and validate people's aspirations. The cult's power was that it was not just about Stalin; it was about *them*.[16]

LOOKED AT SOBERLY, Stalin's anticapitalist experiment resembled a vast camp of deliberately deprived workers, indentured farmers, and slave laborers toiling for the benefit of an unacknowledged elite.[17] But the Soviet Union was a fairy tale. Unrelenting optimism spread alongside famine, arrests, deportations, executions, camps, censorship, sealed borders.[18] Newsreels that showed Stalin also featured belching smokestacks—Soviet inhabitants came to know factories by name and sight—tanks and bombers, giant icebreakers, fecund farms, the friendship of peoples, and vigorous, marching, smiling masses, a tableau of modernity, progress, socialism. Many Soviet inhabitants—especially, but not only, the young—craved a transcendent purpose, and in the swirl of ambition, fanaticism, and opportunism they willingly endured hardships, finding personal fulfillment, even liberation, in *submission* to the state-led struggle in the name of social justice, abundance, and peace. The relentless demands for public professions of loyalty risked eliciting playacting and sullen obedience. But the cause offered the possibility of belonging. Many embraced violence and cruelty as unavoidable in bringing about a new world, and they keenly soaked up the propaganda. To manage contradictions and conscience, they had the transcendent truth of Marxism-Leninism, and the personal example of "comrade Stalin." People of this era who were looking for a brighter future, a chance to be part of something larger than themselves, found it.[19] "The tiniest little fish," one woman would enthuse in her diary, "can stir the depths of the ocean."[20]

In the USSR, an entire generation was coming of age in what seemed like the most heroic epoch in history, acquiring skills, education, apartments—building and living socialism. New or wholly reconstructed factories abounded, their production celebrated daily. The famine had been left behind, and rationing was abolished. In the economy, the years 1934–36 turned out to be relatively good, as the country consolidated its investments.[21] Waste was colossal, of course, but most of the rest of the world was still mired in the effects of the Great Depression. The regime had also eased up on the state of emergency, the extrajudicial and judicial executions. And yet, the land of Soviets remained deeply insecure. When the Russian scientist Ivan Pavlov fed a dog, it salivated, and the scientist rang a bell. After many repetitions, Pavlov stopped the feeding but continued the ringing—and the animal salivated anyway. Pavlov had conditioned the dog to respond to the bell as if the sound were the smell and taste of food. The Soviet populace, too, had been conditioned: the "bell" sounded by the regime was "capitalist encirclement," and the people's reflexive response was fear of foreign invasion and war.[22]

Nonetheless, the Soviet population was unprepared for what struck the country during its hour of triumph beginning in 1936. Even by Stalinist standards, the carnage would be breathtaking.[23] The peak year for Soviet executions—20,201 of them—had been 1930, during dekulakization. In the three years from 1934 to 1936, a time that included mass reprisals for the Kirov murder, the NKVD reported arresting 529,434 people, including 290,479 for counterrevolutionary crimes, and executing 4,402 of them. But for the two years 1937 and 1938, the NKVD would report 1,575,259 arrests, 87 percent of them for political offenses, and 681,692 executions. (The country's working-age population was around 100 million.) Because an untold number of people sentenced to incarceration were actually executed, and many others died during interrogation or transit and fell outside of execution tabulations, the total who perished directly at the hands of the Soviet secret police in 1937–38 was likely closer to 830,000.[24]

No such numbers were publicly divulged, and as a result almost no one could fathom the full scale of what was transpiring. Nor could people comprehend the reasons. In many industrial sectors, output plans were not being met, and queues for bread would appear as a result of a poor harvest in 1936, but a sense of the world-beating success of industrialization and stabilization of the collective farm system remained pervasive. (Even privately, the regime evinced no special anxiety about the economic situation.)[25] Substantial popular discontent persisted, as under all authoritarian regimes, but it was not *increasing,* and it certainly did not threaten the regime.[26] Soviet society had astonishingly little overt political opposition of any kind. No possibility existed of establishing any genuine *organization* independent of the regime, let alone of overthrowing it—that would be possible only via military defeat and occupation. The threat of such a war, and on two fronts—west (Germany) and east (Japan)—did continue to loom large in 1937–38, but it already had for several years without provoking any remotely comparable domestic bloodshed. Indeed, the years 1937 and 1938 would bring the long-feared bloodbath—but it did not come on account of war. No foreign power attacked.[27] There was no immediate threat—social, economic, political—to the country or to the regime's legitimacy or stability, no crisis. But then, suddenly, there was total crisis.

SCHOLARS HAVE APPROACHED the enigma of the Great Terror in a variety of ways. Robert Conquest, who gave the episode its proper name (1968, 1990), remains the point of departure, having definitively shown Stalin's central role decades before archives were declassified. Conquest, though, did not really attempt an explanation (he wrote more or less under the assumption that a Communist regime, and Stalin personally, would inevitably get around to inflicting mass terror in pursuit of ever-greater power).[28] Alexander Gerschenkron, in a review of Conquest's *The Great Terror,* quoted his argument that "the nature of the whole purge depends in the last analysis on the personal and political drives of Stalin," then observed that all dictators exhibit a drive to increase their power, and that any modern dictatorship "which is supported neither by an ancient tradition (or close alliance with an ancient power, such as the Church) nor by the active consent of the governed must at all times justify its continuation in power." Stalin's dictatorship, too, would be expected to foster "a permanent condition of stress by creating enemies at home and abroad and/or by imposing upon the population gigantic tasks that would be unlikely to be carried out in the absence of the dictatorship," as well as "a charismatic image of the dictator," "a utopian goal, carefully kept in a remote future," and "proscription of any deviating values, supported by threats and acts of repression."[29]

Stalin instigated an epic version of the time-honored authoritarian device of trumped-up conspiracies linking internal with external "enemies," but the Soviet case differed in more than just scale.[30] Roy Medvedev, author of the other monumental work on the terror (1971, 1989), endeavored to separate Stalin from the sacred Lenin and depicted him as a traditional tyrant, but he similarly asserted that Stalin was motivated by "lust for power, boundless ambition," as if all tyrants murdered their own elites not just on such a scale but also with forced confessions to fantastical crimes they had not committed.[31] Trotsky imagined Stalin's motivations as jealousy and pettiness, while the biographer Robert C. Tucker saw a pursuit of fame and glory. Moshe Lewin surmised that a paranoid "Stalin actually *became the system* and his personality acquired therefore a 'systemic' dimension," an apt description, though not an analysis.[32] Hiroaki Kuromiya incisively dissected Stalin's cold-blooded logic regarding opponents and enemies, while Erik van Ree revealed Stalin as a Marxist-Leninist true believer, and Arfon Rees showed him to be a combination revolutionary and Machiavellian.[33] These insights were not offered as explanations for the murderous episode of 1937–38. "There is in Stalin's Terror an element of sheer preposterousness which defies explanation," Adam Ulam conceded, after trying.[34]

A few analysts have stressed not intentions but the chronic dysfunctionality of the political system, as if all authoritarian regimes—which are all dysfunctional to a great degree—do what Stalin's did.[35] In Nazi Germany, Hitler went after the Jews (less than 1 percent of the population), Communists, and Social Democrats, but in the USSR Stalin savaged his own loyal elites across the board. To be sure, the greater number of victims were ordinary Soviet people, but what regime liquidates colossal numbers of *loyal* officials? Could Hitler—had he been so inclined—have compelled the imprisonment or execution of huge swaths of Nazi factory and farm bosses, as well as almost all Nazi provincial Gauleiters and their staffs, several times over? Could he have executed the personnel of Nazi central ministries, thousands of his Wehrmacht officers—including almost his entire high command—as well as the Reich's diplomatic corps and its espionage agents, its celebrated cultural figures, and the leadership of Nazi parties throughout the world (had such parties existed)? Could Hitler also have decimated the Gestapo even *while* it was carrying out a mass bloodletting? And could the German people have been told, and would the German people have found plausible, that almost everyone who had come to power with the Nazi revolution turned out to be a foreign agent and saboteur?[36] Even among ideological dictatorships, Communism stands out.

Special features inherent in the Soviet system made a mass and participatory terror between 1936 and 1938 possible. The existence of an extensive police apparatus equipped to arrest and sentence in assembly-line fashion was necessary but not sufficient. Still more important was the existence of the shadowy Communist party, which had cells in all of the country's institutions, making heresy hunting possible, and an ideology, a class-war practice, and a conspiratorial modus operandi that proved readily conducive to mass murder in the name of reasserting the party's special mission and purity. All of this was buttressed by the adversarial nature of Soviet noncapitalist industrialization and collectivization, which was linked to an increase in the ranks of enemies; the regime's censorship (strict control over information and assiduous promotion of certain ways of thinking); widespread resentment of the new elite, which under socialism was not supposed to exist; and widespread belief in a grand crusade, building socialism, in whose name the terror was conducted.[37] The masses became complicit as a result of party cell, factory, and farm meetings, and especially their written denunciations, informing, and extracted confessions. That said, the slaughter was neither self-generating nor self-sustaining. Soviet state power was enacted by millions of people—not just those within the formal administrative machinery—but guided by a single individual.

Did Stalin have reason to fear for his power? He had built socialism, a feat even his loyalists had thought unlikely. His personal authority was so secure that, as we shall see, in August 1936 he could once again abandon the capital for more than two months, going on holiday to Sochi. There was no repetition of the blistering Ryutin condemnation in a text circulated hand to hand. No one in his inner circle pretended to be on the same level. Nonetheless, it was clear to him that his "unbounded power" remained oddly contingent. He was the supreme leader by virtue of his position as head of the party, reinforced by his acclamation as the "Lenin of our day."[38] But voting politburo members held the right to nominate someone else as the top secretary of the party, a recommendation that would be forwarded for formal ratification to the first plenum of the Central Committee newly chosen by a party congress. Stalin was thus a dictator on conditional contract. His faction had stood by him through thick and thin. But would the voting nine—Molotov, Kaganovich, Voroshilov, Orjonikidze, Kalinin, Andreyev, Kosior, Mikoyan, and Chubar—continue to do so? Even if Stalin remained certain of their obeisance, he was eager, like all dictators, to convert his dictatorship into despotism.[39] For the men in his own loyal faction, in which Stalin had long taken evident pride, this meant breaking their will. Herein lay a key motivation for the fantastic terror of 1936–38.

And yet, considerations of personal power alone do not explain Stalin or the terror. Certainly he pursued power with a vengeance—on behalf of the cause, which in his mind was the same thing as his personal rule—but he had taken gambles with his power, also on behalf of the cause, and was sometimes defiant when it would have been more power enhancing to be prudent. At times he could not be sure what would enhance his power. For him, the terror constituted a form of rule, a matter of statecraft.

Stalin was a liar, a chameleon, who talked out of both sides of his mouth and often said what interlocutors wanted to hear. But more than any other secretive dictator, except perhaps Hitler, he repeatedly explained himself. Everything Stalin did during the years 1936–38 he had been talking about for years. Some things he said only privately, such as his instructions to a Mongolia delegation to stage trials of lamas not merely as counterrevolutionaries but as spies for Mongolia's foreign enemy Japan, because the lamas could become traitors in the rear in the event of war. Publicly, however, Stalin had stated that he was building socialism against all manner of implacable class enemies; that the class struggle sharpened as the country got closer to the full victory of socialism; that enemies with party cards were the most dangerous because they could secretly burrow into the heart of the system; that those who opposed collectivization wanted to restore capitalism; that all foreigners were spies; that the Zinovievites, Trotskyites, and the right deviation were interlinked and tied to the military; that the rightists wanted to remove him in a putsch, establish a puppet government, hand over Soviet territories, and make a rump USSR into a colony of Germany or Japan (or was it Poland or Romania?); that enemies had become desperate and resorted to all-out terror; that the big bosses were not as valuable as the lower levels; that legions of new people (a "Soviet intelligentsia") needed to be promoted and nurtured in Marxism-Leninism; that a new imperialist war was inevitable; that the Soviet Union had to avoid becoming the target of an anti-Soviet bloc; that the country needed to become a great power with a military to match the imperialists; that a new imperialist war could enable socialism to expand the same way the previous imperialist war had enabled the Russian Revolution; that the British stood behind the entire imperialist order; that Hitler was an intelligent leader; and that Trotsky and his supposed followers were the most diabolical threat to socialism and the Soviet state.[40] These various enunciations fit into a grisly logical whole, and Stalin had the untrammeled power to act on them.

CHAPTER 6

ON A BLUFF

The cause of Spain is not solely the cause of the Spaniards, but the cause of all progressive and advanced humanity.

STALIN, *open telegram to José Díaz,*
published in Pravda, *October 16, 1936,*
republished in Mundo Obrero, *October 17*

Stalin conducts a struggle on a totally different plane. He seeks to strike not at the ideas of an opponent, but at his skull.

TROTSKY, *journal entry en route to Mexico on*
a Norwegian oil tanker, December 30, 1936[1]

STALIN DEPARTED FOR SOCHI ON AUGUST 14, 1936, and would remain down south through October 25. His absences from Moscow since 1930 (this holiday included) averaged seventy-eight days per annum. His Sochi dacha was not in the town proper, but on a zigzagging road about a mile up and in from the Black Sea. North led to Sochi, south to the sulfur baths of Matsesta (farther on were Gagra and Sukhum, in Abkhazia). The pristine setting offered the smell of pine trees and salty air, while the compound contained guest villas, tennis courts (where Nadya used to play), and a detached billiards hall, all surrounded by NKVD troops. The main dacha was an unpretentious wooden structure with an open-air veranda that Stalin prized. Matsesta's curative sulfur waters were now being pumped in, obviating the trip. The staff and guards equipped the residence with the usual pianolas and phonographs, but holidays were not downtime. While away from the capital in 1930, Stalin had remade the Soviet government structure, and the next year he reorganized management of foreign affairs. The 1936 southern holiday would prove to be his most momentous yet as he further radicalized his pursuit of Trotskyites with his most frenzied public trial to date and upended international politics with a military intervention on the Iberian Peninsula.

Spain had been Europe's only major country to avoid the Great War, and the

Second Spanish Republic, born in April 1931, bucked the authoritarian trend engulfing the continent. That year, amid a resounding Radical Republican Party victory in municipal elections, King Alfonso XIII, who had reigned since his birth, in 1886, fled abroad (without formal abdication), inspiring hopes among the country's peasants and workers and fears among the propertied and the Church establishment. But the Republic had managed only timid land reform, while Spain's few pockets of industry remained gripped by the Depression. A third of the population could neither read nor write, and more than half of its children had no access to education. The Cortes, Spain's parliament, was roiled by raw, irreconcilable emotions—for and against the Church and the army, for and against socialism. A military coup in August 1932 had been foiled by a general strike, but it confirmed the army's lack of loyalty to the Republic. Spain experienced wild electoral swings from left (1931) to right (1933) and back on February 18, 1936, when a leftist coalition known as the Popular Front defeated the ruling coalition of rightist parties (the National Front). A quirk in the election law magnified the Popular Front's narrow victory and gave them a solid majority of 264 representatives—162 Left Republicans and independents, 88 Socialists, 14 Communists—versus 156 for the right and 54 for the center (including many Catalans and the Basques).[2] The Popular Front's majority, moreover, stemmed from working-class parties, but the Socialists, Communists, and anarchists did not take government portfolios. At the same time, the Basques in the north and the Catalans in the northeast strove for autonomy, while the central government possessed no reliable provincial officialdom and was hard pressed to live up to soaring expectations for social reform. Some electoral fraud on behalf of the Popular Front also contributed to the instability. More vivid were sensational fables of "Red massacres" of clergy and landowners, mob actions, and rural unrest. The upshot was a cauldron of antigovernment conspiracies.[3]

Spain would be torn apart by a civil war during which the country of 25 million people would see 1.7 million fighters conscripted by the Republic and 1.2 million by the Nationalists, and up to 200,000 battlefield deaths, over the course of nearly three years of combat over class, religion, region, and governance. Perhaps as many as 49,000 civilians would perish in the Republic's zone, where the leftists would perpetrate or indulge mob killings of "reactionaries" and "fascists." How many civilians died in the Nationalists' bombing of Republic-controlled cities remains unknown (perhaps 10,000), but the Nationalists would end up summarily executing some 130,000 people in a deliberate strategy of anticivilian terror.[4] During the same period, Stalin would execute or cause the death of up to 1 million people, from a total population of close to 170 million. But the conspiracies in the Soviet Union were invented.

Some scholars have argued that events in Spain helped precipitate or at least radicalize Stalin's domestic terror of 1936–38, which they portray as a sincere, if wildly excessive, attempt to eradicate suspected real and potential saboteurs lying in wait to assist externally launched aggression.[5] But Stalin had decided in 1935 to reopen the Kirov murder case and instigate a new wave of arrests of "Trotskyites" around the country. On June 29, 1936—before any hint of Spain—Yagoda had reported to Stalin, Molotov, and Yezhov on "very important" interrogation testimony obtained from arrested "Trotskyites": Yefim Dreitser, Trotsky's former bodyguard; Richard Pikel, former head of Zinoviev's secretariat; and Isaac Esterman. Stalin circulated the report to the politburo.[6] Furious preparations were under way for a showcase trial (pokazatelnyi protess) involving these and other "Trotskyites" in Moscow. Spain would turn out to be important for Stalin's mass bloodletting less as cause than as added rationalization.[7]

In the summer and early fall of 1936, the Soviet leader made no speeches; indeed, he did not even appear in public. He sat on his Sochi veranda, reading stacks of well-ordered secret documents, then dictated some telegrams to aides with him on the Black Sea coast, which technicians coded and relayed to Kaganovich in Moscow. Kaganovich, who had never finished elementary school and could not write grammatical Russian, in turn formulated Stalin's instructions as politburo decrees, which he had coded and dispatched to the tens of thousands of party committees that existed in every single Soviet locality and factory, and a majority of collective and state farms. Comintern secretary general Dimitrov did the same for every Communist party in the world. This produced orchestrated mass meetings all across Eurasia and beyond, at which preselected speakers issued demands for execution, even before convictions had been pronounced, while others in attendance raised their hands in agreement. The Soviet press, in ideological lockstep, delivered saturation coverage to thousands of towns and tens of thousands of villages, whipping up intense hysteria. The power of Stalin's regime—resting upon the telegraph, a tiny handful of aides, the Communist party machine, the secret police, the military, and the dream of a better world—was breathtaking.

While atop his bluff overlooking the Black Sea, 850 miles from Moscow, Stalin would also decide after much hesitation to intervene in the Spanish civil war.[8]

He ordered no strategic analyses of the pros and cons or formal policy-making discussions.[9] He seems to have consulted next to no one. Molotov, head of the government, was himself on holiday (July 27–September 1, 1936). Mikoyan was in the United States (August–September) to study the food industry, with more than $600,000 in hard currency to acquire model machinery.[10] When the intervention details were finalized, Orjonikidze, head of heavy industry, was on holiday (September 5–November 5).[11] To be sure, Kaganovich was in Moscow, and in frequent contact with Sochi (referring to Stalin as "our parent"). Voroshilov was also in the capital and communicated with Stalin on the high-frequency phone and by ciphered telegram. But the decision to take action in Spain, like the earlier reopening of the Kirov case and preparations for a grand trial of Trotskyites, was Stalin's alone. We shall puzzle it out, including limits he imposed.[12] Soviet military hardware sent to Spain would be voluminous and state of the art, but Soviet personnel would never exceed 700 or so at any time, two thirds of them in lower-level positions: pilots, tank drivers, technicians. It was not Spain but Trotsky that riveted Stalin's attention, including much of the attention he paid to Spain.

Never an optimist about revolution abroad, Stalin had nonetheless said that the critical ingredient was war, which Spain would have, making it a test of his own theory of geopolitics. The question of revolution in Spain also intensified his rivalry with his long-standing nemesis. Not long after King Alfonso's flight, Trotsky had written an unsolicited letter (April 27, 1931) to the Soviet politburo advising that the fate of "the revolution" in Spain depended on whether a combat-capable and authoritative Communist party was formed there. He had also warned that worker-peasant defeat "would lead almost automatically to the establishment in Spain of a genuine fascism in the style of Mussolini." Stalin had distributed the letter to the inner circle, writing on it, "I think this impudent and Menshevik charlatan citizen Trotsky should get a blow to the head from the Comintern executive committee. Let him know his place."[13]

COLONIAL EXPERIENCE

Britain had acceded to French ambitions in Morocco in 1904, provided that weaker Spain retained control over the Moroccan territory directly opposite British-controlled Gibraltar, which was crucial to Britain's dominant position in the Mediterranean. Francisco Franco y Bahamonde had arrived in Spanish

Morocco in 1912 and cofounded a Spanish Legion there. (His counterpart, the French commander in North Africa, was Philippe Pétain.) A provincial like Stalin and Hitler, Franco had grown up in Spanish Galicia, where he was marinated in peasant pragmatism and bullied by his father. He was short in stature at five feet five inches (1.64 meters)—two inches shorter than Stalin and three than Hitler—and very slight, earning the nickname Cerillito ("Little Matchstick"). At age fourteen, unable to enroll at the Naval Academy, Franco had entered an infantry academy, where, in 1910, he graduated 251st in a class of 312. In quick succession, however, he would become Spain's youngest captain, major, colonel, and general (the first in his graduating class), thanks to his exploits in colonial Morocco. In 1916, Franco took a bullet to the lower abdomen—a fraction of an inch in any direction and, like most soldiers with stomach wounds in Africa, he would have died. But after ten years of ruthless counterinsurgency, he secured the Moroccan ruler's surrender, the deed that earned him a general's rank at thirty-three, which made him the youngest general ever in the Spanish army and at the time the youngest in Europe. "My years in Africa live within me with indescribable force," he would later tell a newspaper editor. "There was born the possibility of rescuing a Great Spain."[14]

The man who would make Spain great again was a poor public speaker, with a high-pitched voice. In Morocco, he had come to detest the leftists back in Spain who, in his mind, failed to appreciate the grand colonial enterprise.[15] In 1935, Franco was promoted to chief of staff in Madrid, and in February 1936, when elections brought to power the Popular Front, the general told a confidant it was a Trojan horse to smuggle Communism into Spain and offered his assistance to the defeated rightist prime minister, should the latter want to annul the vote.[16] The Republic's civilian president smelled a rat and reassigned Franco to the Canary Islands, off the Atlantic coast. In fact, Spain's military *was* engaged in a plot. But Franco's participation was not confirmed until the very eve of their putsch, and even then he voiced uncertainty. The prime mover in the coup was the Cuban-born general Emilio Mola. (Cuba had been a province of Spain.) The forty-eight-year-old Mola had recently been reassigned to a backwater with a small garrison to counteract his suspected plotting. His main accomplice was the sixty-four-year-old general José Sanjurjo, who, along with some 15,000 Spaniards (mostly monarchists and conservatives), was living under asylum in Portugal, courtesy of António de Oliveira Salazar's dictatorship. Salazar ignored the Spanish Republic's pleas to prevent Sanjurjo's return, but on July 20, the latter's small plane crashed en route: it seems the general's clothes trunk was too heavy.[17] Sanjurjo's unexpected death elevated the forty-three-year-old Franco as Mola's main partner and rival. "Franco," Sanjurjo had warned, still bitter that during his 1932 coup the younger man had stood on the sidelines, "will do nothing to commit himself; he will always be in the shadows, because he is crafty [*cuco*]."[18]

Franco had flown from the Grand Canary—on a chartered British plane—to Morocco, where he rallied Spain's best fighting force, the ruthless Army of Africa (5,000 men of the Spanish Foreign Legion, 17,000 Moorish troops, and 17,000 Spanish conscripts).[19] On July 17, they rose up in the coordinated coup. But on the mainland, the Nationalists gained the support of only about half of the Territorial Army, some 60,000 soldiers. Garrisons in key industrial cities—Madrid, Barcelona, Valencia, Bilbao—refused to join the rebellion. But the military plotters would not accept defeat. Mola became the rebel Nationalist commander in the north, Franco in the south. Colonial experience could cut in very different ways: Gandhi had gone to South Africa and returned to British India with the idea of a Congress Party and peaceful protest; Franco, from Spanish Morocco, brought back brutal counterinsurgency. He and Mola enacted the savage political cleansing (*limpieza*) of Franco's Moroccan colonial war—only this time against fellow Spaniards.[20] To induce Republic-held territory to surrender, Nationalist troops engaged in gang rapes of women, marching with panties flying from their bayonets. Women in the tens of thousands had their hair shaved off and their mouths force-fed castor oil, a laxative, so that, when paraded through the streets, they would soil themselves. Men were just shot, especially if found in possession of a trade union card. All the while, Franco obsessed over supposed international conspiracies of Freemasons, Jews, Communists.

Spain had last experienced major armed conflict when resisting Napoleon Bonaparte. Now, Catalonia used the military's putsch to carry out its own regional coup d'état against rule by Madrid, splitting the resistance. In Barcelona, in what was christened the Catalan Generalitat, a newly formed Unified Socialist Party of Catalonia competed with anarchists to arm workers in resistance, while the Republic government in Madrid reluctantly armed workers. These new militias radicalized domestic politics—the very outcome that the military putsch was supposed to forestall. Worker syndicates seized factories, and farmers formed collectives or redistributed land to individuals.[21] In the greatest twist, despite the weakness of Spain's right-wing party, inspired by fascism, the Falange (Phalanx), and its Communist party—each possessed fewer than 30,000 members in July

1936—Spain became a battleground in the international struggle between fascism and Communism.[22]

GREAT POWER MACHINATIONS

Spain and the Soviet Union were remote from each other (the USSR accounted for 0.9 percent of Spain's trade in the first half of 1936).[23] The Spanish Republic maintained normal diplomatic relations with just about every country in the world except the Soviet Union, and the putsch had looked unlikely to alter any of that.[24] France ought to have been Spain's natural partner, especially after the June 1936 formation of a Popular Front government in Paris, which included Communists as well as Socialists under Prime Minister Léon Blum. Spain's Popular Front government had already appealed to France's Popular Front for military aid by July 18, and got a positive initial response from Blum, but pro-Franco personnel in Spain's embassy in Paris leaked the request to France's right-wing press, which launched a vicious campaign against Blum (a Jew as well as a Socialist). On a visit to London, moreover, Blum discovered that Britain opposed helping Spain's elected government.[25] Britain had a great deal at stake: it accounted for 40 percent of total foreign investment in Spain, including the Rio Tinto mining conglomerate. But Prime Minister Stanley Baldwin sought to avoid new government commitments, given the costs of maintaining the empire, or unwittingly facilitating a Communist takeover in Spain.[26] His stance was shared by even most of the Labour party and the trade union bosses.[27] Many British Catholics, meanwhile, admired General Franco's stated program; much of British business sided with him as well. And so, on July 25, Blum reversed himself and agreed to join Britain's policy of "non-intervention." The hope was that the gambit would also take in Germany and Italy.[28]

The Spanish putschists, however, themselves had appealed to Hitler and Mussolini. Franco, bereft of an air force, was cut off from the mainland, but his appeal to the German government failed. He had recourse to a second channel: German expatriates in Spanish Morocco. A nondescript German sales director at a trading firm (kitchen equipment) who was a member of the Nazi Party Abroad wanted to demonstrate his own importance and that of the fledgling organization, and he flew Franco's emissaries to Berlin, using Nazi party channels to reach Deputy Führer Rudolf Hess on holiday at his country estate. On July 25,

Hess, one of the few people to address Hitler with the familiar *du*, received the emissaries and phoned Hitler, who was at the summer Wagner Festival. Hess dispatched the Spaniards and Morocco-based Nazis by car to Bayreuth, and, following the conclusion of *Siegfried*, the group hand-delivered Franco's request for military aid at the Wagner family residence. Hitler had shown no interest in supporting the coup before the generals had acted, and now seemed unsure—his own rearmament had a ways to go—but he launched a monologue and worked himself into a lather. ("If Spain really goes Communist, France in her present situation will also be Bolshevized in due course, and then Germany is finished.") That very day, support for Franco against the "international Jewish revolutionary headquarters in Moscow" was assured.[29] Hitler consulted only the minions in his company and made the decision against their objections.[30] "We're taking part a bit in Spain," Goebbels noted in his diary. "Not clear. Who knows what it's good for."[31]

Hitler appears to have been in a fine mood that evening: the aid to Spain would be dubbed Operation Magic Fire. ("Magic fire" music accompanies Siegfried's passage through the flames to liberate Brünnhilde.) The Führer even sent twice as many Junkers Ju 52 transport planes as Franco requested. Franco would have eventually gotten his troops over the Spanish Republic's naval blockade to the mainland, but Nazi assistance accelerated that movement, struck at the Republic's morale, and buttressed Franco's standing vis-à-vis Mola. Franco had also approached Italy for support, on July 22, 1936, and the new Italian foreign minister, Count Galeazzo Ciano (Mussolini's son-in-law), was gung-ho. The duce had mocked the Spanish Republic as "not a revolution but a plagiarism," and had been paying a small retainer to a leader of Spain's fascist equivalents while vaguely promising support to any would-be putschists.[32] Now, emboldened by reports of British acquiescence and French paralysis, he decided to provide substantial military assistance, without consulting his own military men. In parallel to his expansionism in Abyssinia, the duce dreamed of a still larger Italian Mediterranean empire at French expense, via a friendly government in Spain. He also derided Léon Blum as "one Jew who did not enjoy the gift of prophecy."[33] Spain would push Italy still closer to Germany.

Spain would also push France and the Soviet Union further apart. The French brass feared that any military support for the Spanish Popular Front could ignite a pan-European war, which, overestimating the German military, they felt France was in no position to fight successfully.[34] More broadly, French ruling circles viewed reliance on the Soviets to stand up to Nazi Germany as a provocation toward Berlin and an invitation to ideological contagion. "If defeated," the French foreign minister would note privately, France "would be Nazified. If victorious, it must, owing to the destruction of German power, submit, with the rest of Europe, to the overwhelming weight of the Slavic world, armed with the Communist flamethrower."[35]

FABRICATING A "UNITED" CENTER

Yagoda's NKVD was rounding up "Trotskyites," including in faraway Gulag camps. On June 19, 1936—again, well before the putsch in Spain—he and Vyshinsky had sent Stalin a list of eighty-two people accused of terrorism "links," recommending that they be tried by the military collegium and executed. Zinoviev and Kamenev were included. Stalin instructed Yezhov to have the NKVD prepare a trial against a *united* Trotskyite-Zinovievite "center."[36] On July 15, Yagoda sent a secret NKVD circular to every operative, severely criticizing the NKVD bosses in certain regions for "opportunistic kindheartedness, self-assurance, forgetfulness of old Chekist traditions, and inactivity" (i.e., failure to expose "Trotskyites").[37] Stalin was insisting on a high-profile public trial, broadcast live, and Yezhov applied pressure so that people under arrest began to be re-interrogated to build a story line of a "united center." Zinoviev, naïvely, had been writing groveling prison letters to Stalin asking for forgiveness; Kamenev had been trying to dissociate himself from Zinoviev.[38] In mid-July, the two were brought from prisons in the Urals to Moscow. Yezhov took part in their interrogations and appealed to their revolutionary patriotism, arguing that an international Trotskyite conspiracy in cahoots with Germany and Japan threatened the Soviet Union, and thus their confessions were necessary for the cause.

Zinoviev offered to comply if Stalin personally promised to spare him. Kamenev resisted ("You are observing Thermidor in pure form," he said during interrogation). The two were taken to see "the politburo," which turned out to be a meeting with Stalin and Voroshilov.[39] Stalin evidently flattered them, calling them comrades, followers of Lenin, whose cooperation was necessary to combat Trotsky.[40] No less germane was the fact that Kamenev had been informed that his son was under investigation. Kamenev and Zinoviev did begin to testify about their improbable plotting with Trotsky.[41] On July 23, 1936, Yakov Agranov, who, together with Yezhov, had handled the original Kirov investigation case against the "Zinovievites," personally re-interrogated the already imprisoned Dreitser (said to be the "head" of an underground "Trotskyite" organization) and Pikel, extracting the necessary "testimony" concerning a "united center."[42] On July 26, Stalin had the NKVD haul in Sokolnikov, who had once joined Zinoviev and Kamenev in questioning Stalin's absolute power in the role of general secretary. On the night of July 27–28, the NKVD arrested the ex-wife of Yuri Pyatakov, Orjonikidze's first deputy at heavy industry. Stalin's anti-Trotsky drive had its own dynamic prior to events in Spain.

TRYING TO STEM REVOLUTION

Bereft of an ambassador in Madrid, Stalin had next to no information about what was going on, beyond reports via Comintern channels.[43] On July 23, 1936, at a Comintern executive committee meeting, Dimitrov emphasized the value of the Spanish conflict for rallying international forces to a global popular front, and begged Stalin for comments on draft theses.[44] Stalin wrote "correct" on Dimitrov's instructions to the Spanish Communist party for restraint; on July 24, the secret orders went to Madrid for Spanish Communists "not to run ahead," that is, to contain their struggle to supporting the "bourgeois democratic republic" rather than pushing for a dictatorship of the proletariat. Dimitrov did allow that "when our positions have strengthened, we can go further."[45] By July 25 the Nazis and Italian fascists were already wielding the bogeyman of "Bolshevism" in Spain to justify supporting the putschists. That day, with Blum backing off his pledge to support Spain's Republic, the Spanish prime minister, in a letter to the Soviet envoy in Paris, conveyed his government's desire to purchase Soviet arms in quantity.[46] The Soviets did not reply. An Italian assessment out of Moscow on July 27 noted Soviet "embarrassment" over Spain and a likely pursuit of "prudent neutrality."[47]

Dimitrov was not received by Stalin during these days. Litvinov, who had recently celebrated his sixtieth birthday and received the Order of Lenin, was urging Stalin to maintain Soviet-French-Anglo "solidarity" by avoiding military aid to Spain's besieged Republic. The foreign affairs commissar finally got in to see the dictator on July 28 (Molotov and Voroshilov were absent). (Not until August 7 would Stalin again summon anyone to the Kremlin office.)[48] The antifascist popular front strategy (Dimitrov) and "collective security" (Litvinov), once seen as in sync, were deeply at odds, given France's position.

The Comintern executive committee was also discussing China—it aimed to rein in the Chinese Communists, who were not following the Comintern policy of cooperation with Chiang against the Japanese.[49] At the end of the Long March, Mao had arrived in Yan'an, in China's northwest, where the Communists set up a ministate. Chiang Kai-shek's Nationalist (Guomindang) government, based in Nanking, wanted to isolate the Reds, a task he assigned to Zhang Xueliang, whom the Japanese had chased from Manchuria. Zhang had his headquarters in Xi'an, 200 miles north of Mao, and commanded a sprawling force of perhaps 300,000. Only in late June or early July 1936, after an almost two-year hiatus, was a radio link reestablished between Moscow and the Chinese Communists in the remote interior, and the Chinese comrades asked the Comintern to provide $3 million monthly to cover military expenses, help organize contributions from the Chinese diaspora, and send Soviet aircraft, artillery, antiaircraft artillery, infantry rifles, machine guns, and pontoons, through either Xinjiang or Mongolia.[50] But at the July 23 Comintern meeting, Dimitrov insisted that "the task in China right now consists not in expanding the regions under soviets and the Chinese Red Army, but . . . unification of the vast majority of the Chinese people against the Japanese invaders." The goal was to "complete the bourgeois-democratic revolution," although eventually, "in the process of this struggle, the moment will come for the mass organization of the struggle for Soviet power."[51]

Four days later, Dimitrov submitted draft directives for the Chinese Communists to Stalin, who would take some time to return them. In the meantime, the Comintern directives to Spain's Communists to avoid revolution arrived just as the Spanish Republic state began to melt away. Jails were being cracked open, court records ransacked, village rents pronounced null and void, and businesses collectivized. Spain's moderate Socialists, together with Spain's Communists, could not contain the workers, peasants, and anarchists in the Republic's zone, especially in Catalonia, where 70 percent of industry would be collectivized in three heady months. "The first impression: armed workers, rifles on their shoulders, but wearing their civilian clothes," Franz Borkenau, an Austrian writer who had quit the German Communist party in protest over Stalin's rule and traveled to Spain, would observe. "And no 'bourgeoisie' whatever!"[52]

To stand by while the leftist Popular Front and popular revolution in Spain went down to "fascist" armed aggression would threaten Moscow's prestige. Sometime between July 27 and 29, 1936, the head of the Spanish Communist party sent a cipher responding in detail to Comintern questions about "the correlation of forces," which Dimitrov forwarded immediately to Stalin. "The adversary has the advantage that he has many spies in the government camp," the Spanish report concluded. "Despite that, if France will deliver the requested aid in the form of airplanes and ammunition, the adversary will be destroyed."[53] Would Stalin step into the breach? A genuine leftist revolution was unfolding in Spain against his instructions, and the Chinese Communists were pressing revolution against orders as well. Rendering this situation still more maddening was the circumstance that he was being *visibly* outflanked on the left by Trotsky.

THE TROTSKY CHALLENGE

Stalin hated Trotsky with a deep, emotional, blind, wild hate; he also feared him, in a way he feared no one else. Trotsky had long been under nearly total NKVD surveillance, first on an island in Turkey and then in France. The NKVD knew of or had inspired a plan by the anti-Soviet émigré Russian All-Military Union to assassinate him in 1934, but operational amateurism produced nothing beyond recriminations.[54] In 1935, Trotsky had accepted an offer of asylum from the new Norwegian Labor Party government, taking up residence with his wife as guests of the journalist, painter, and parliamentarian Konrad Knudsen in Oslo, where the NKVD had few resources.[55] But Trotsky's elder son, Lev Sedov, the nerve center of international Trotskyism (such as it was), had remained in Paris, where the Soviet secret police enjoyed a robust presence. Boris Atanasov, known as Afanasyev (b. 1902), an ethnic Bulgarian assassin and kidnapper who oversaw infiltration of émigré circles in Paris, had been tasked with penetration of Trotsky's Paris operation.

Afanasyev stumbled upon an unbelievably valuable agent: Mordka "Mark" Zborowski (b. 1908), who had been born in a Jewish family in imperial Russia and, after the revolution, resettled in Poland, where he eventually joined the Polish Communists. After an arrest and short prison sentence, Zborowski fled to Berlin, then to Grenoble, where he attended university, and was recruited into the NKVD in Paris around 1933.[56] Zborowski befriended Sedov's wife, who recommended him for the position of her husband's secretary. "At present the source meets with the son nearly every day," Zborowski's secret police handler reported to Moscow, which responded that "we caution that you do not go too far and thereby destroy all our plans in this machination."[57] The NKVD was able to install listening devices on the telephones in the apartments of Sedov and his collaborators. Zborowski also gained access to secret lists of, and correspondence with, trusted Trotsky loyalists worldwide, on the basis of which the NKVD compiled a card catalog. Zborowski, known to Sedov as Étienne, a fluent Russian speaker in an otherwise French-only milieu, took charge of Sedov's correspondence and helped edit Trotsky's Russian-language *Bulletin of the Opposition*. Stalin, therefore, could read not only Trotsky's mail but also drafts of his essays, sometimes before they were published.[58]

Knowing what Trotsky would publish did not help counter it, however. Events in Spain afforded him a grand new platform from which to bash Stalin still more—as a counterrevolutionary who failed to support not a theoretical but an actual revolution under direct attack by "fascism." On July 30, Trotsky, in high dudgeon, wrote that in "curbing the social revolution," Spain's Popular Front leaders "compel the workers and peasants to spill ten times as much of their own blood in a civil war. And to crown everything, these gentlemen expect to disarm the workers again after the victory and to force them to respect the sacred laws of private property."[59] By that date, Nazi German planes had not only airlifted Franco's *africanistas* to the Spanish mainland, but also begun strafing Madrid. Also on July 30, two of the initial Italian squadron of twelve Savoia-Marchetti medium bombers sent from Sardinia to Morocco to assist the Spanish insurgency had crash-landed in French Algeria, revealing Italian involvement.[60] The "fascists" had stolen the initiative. More than that even, with the Spanish Republic state dissolving, someone else could fill the vacuum. Stalin seemed to be facing a possibly victorious Trotskyism in Spain, where Trotsky was popular. The specter of Trotskyites capturing a physical redoubt in a real country would seize Stalin like the proverbial red cape in front of a bull.[61]

DICTATOR'S DILEMMA

Members of Stalin's inner circle strove to circumscribe the expanding effects of his reopening of the Kirov murder case. *Pravda*, back on June 2, 1936, had published a speech by Pavel Postyshev, a candidate member of the politburo and party boss of Kiev province, upbraiding Ukrainian officials for unwarranted repressions; five days later, the newspaper editorialized ("Lessons of the Donbass") that the coal plan fulfillment failures in Ukraine had resulted not from wrecking but from showy record-breaking labor stunts as well as the wrongful persecution of engineers.[62] This was a prominent theme of Orjonikidze's as well. "What kind ⌐⸍

saboteurs?" he defiantly exclaimed at a multiday meeting of the guiding council of the heavy industry commissariat on June 25. "During the 19-year existence of Soviet power, we . . . have graduated more than 100,000 engineers and a similar number of technicians. If all of them, and the old-regime engineers as well, whom we have reeducated, turned out to be saboteurs in 1936, then congratulate yourself with such success. What kind of saboteurs! They are not saboteurs, but good people, our sons, our brothers, our comrades. . . . They will die on the front of Soviet power, if this is required. . . . It is not sabotage—this is nonsense—but incompetence." Orjonikidze's spirited defense elicited "rousing and prolonged applause."[63]

Orjonikidze worked long hours under phenomenal strain, which strained his weak heart. (One time when he suffered from heart palpitations he lost consciousness in his office, inducing his assistants to summon a doctor from the Kremlin hospital.) He also had just one kidney. Gossips said his wife, Zinaida, had a difficult personality, compounding his problems.[64] On June 29, the culmination of the heavy industry gathering, the commissar's poor health had become visible for all to see. A foreign doctor was brought in to examine him.[65] Be that as it may, the key factor in exacerbating his health was his old friend and fellow Georgian, who was mercilessly, relentlessly driving the "saboteur" line. Kaganovich also did not see why manifestly loyal people needed to be arrested and executed. He had been defending top Ukrainian officials from Stalin's wrath since famine days. But he knew Stalin all too well. In early July 1936, the dictator had sent Kaganovich—then vacationing in Kislovodsk—protocols of the Dreitser and Pikel "interrogations"; he took the unsubtle hint. "Although this was clear even earlier, they have now revealed the true bandit face of those murderers and provocateurs Trotsky, Zinoviev, Kamenev," he had responded to Stalin on July 6. "The main instigator of this gang is that venal scum Trotsky. It is time to declare him an outlaw and to execute the rest of the lowlifes we have in jail. Regards as ever, Yours, L. Kaganovich."[66]

Stalin pressed for wider arrests, using the unique instruments only he commanded: he dispatched a secret circular (July 29, 1936)—drafted by Yezhov and edited by the dictator—to party organizations, which was to be read aloud to all party members and which quoted the "testimony" of the various accused "Trotskyites." "Confronted with the completely irrefutable successes of socialist construction, they initially hoped our party could not cope with the difficulties," the circular stated. "But seeing that the party was successfully overcoming difficulties, they wagered on the defeat of Soviet power in a forthcoming war, as a result of which they dreamed of seizing power." Then, "not seeing any prospects, in despair, they resorted to the last means of struggle—terror." The circular explained that the "Trotskyites" had colluded in terror with Zinoviev and Kamenev and that, after the imprisonment of the latter, "Trotsky had taken upon himself all direction of terrorist activity in the USSR." The document exhorted that "the essential mark of every Bolshevik in the current situation should be the ability to recognize and identify enemies of the party no matter how well they are able to disguise themselves." But who were these *hidden* enemies?[67] How did the circular jibe with other signals conveyed by Postyshev and Orjonikidze in the authoritative *Pravda*?

NKVD operatives would "unmask" enemies to win raises, medals, and promotions; informants, queried about a "Trotskyite" underground, would become eager to please. Regional party officials, in order to protect themselves and their closest people, targeted as "Trotskyites" lower-level types as well as economic managers—precisely the people Orjonikidze sought to protect.[68] But Kaganovich, responsible for rail transport—which had been suffering an inordinate number of accidents, driven by underinvestment and overexploitation—expressly rejected assertions of Trotskyites in his bailiwick. On July 30, 1936, the day after the secret party circular on hidden enemies, he presided over the country's inaugural all-Union Day of Transport, where, before 25,000 railway employees assembled at the outdoor Green Theater, in Gorky Park, as well as a Union-wide audience listening on radio, he delivered a two-hour oration on the daily loading of 81,214 freight cars, exceeding Stalin's directive to reach 80,000. "Here the way is not purging and repression," Kaganovich stated, noting the multitudes of railway workers who had received state awards. "No, for 99 percent of railway employees are honest people, who are committed to their work, who love their motherland."[69] Soviet newspapers prominently published photographs of Kaganovich and Orjonikidze together that summer of 1936.[70]

Multiple incentives impel dictators to try to convert their rule into despotism. Some lack the necessary means or personal traits to crush close allies. Stalin, of course, possessed both the wherewithal and the personality. But would he break Orjonikidze, Kaganovich, and other members of his innermost circle? Kaganovich was indispensable, still running the linchpin party apparatus in his absence, while Orjonikidze, no less vital, ran the critical heavy industry portfolio. Both of them removed a great burden from the far too burdened Stalin. At the same time, Orjonikidze's Union-wide fiefdom afforded him a political base second only to the dictator's. *Izvestiya* (still edited by Bukharin) did not shy from calling Orjonikidze "the people's favorite," the expression in Lenin's purported

Testament for Bukharin.[71] In fact, Orjonikidze *was* more accessible, and in many quarters more genuinely popular, than Stalin. And he enjoyed extremely warm relations with other core members of the ruling group, including defense commissar Voroshilov, as well as Kaganovich.

IMPROVISING A COURSE

Stalin maintained his nonresponse to Madrid's request for arms, but in the meantime the pressure to do *something* did not abate. On August 1, 1936—the opening day of the Summer Olympics in Nazi Berlin, not to mention the anniversary of the outbreak of the Great War—*Izvestiya* published an essay by Radek, which Stalin had approved, characterizing the civil war in Spain as part of a "meticulously" planned global aggression by "European fascists."[72] That same day, *Pravda* published Spanish reportage under the headline "Fascism Means War; Socialism Means Peace." August 2 in Moscow brought a temperature of 99 degrees Fahrenheit (37.2 Celsius), the highest in fifty-seven years.[73] That day, Boris Pasternak met André Gide at his dacha in the writers' colony of Peredelkino (where he had just moved in) and helped open the Frenchman's eyes to Soviet realities; Pasternak also warned his NKVD minder that Gide was preparing a critical work on the USSR.[74] The next day, which was not a Soviet holiday, a reported throng of more than 100,000 demonstrators assembled on Red Square. Adorned in summer whites in the suffocating heat, the dense crowd listened to songs and speeches calling for defense of the Spanish Republic. Six tanned sportswomen, holding hands, led chants of "Down with Franco! Down with Franco!" "Our hearts are with those who at this moment are giving up their lives in the mountains and streets of Spain, defending the liberty of their people," a female worker from the Red Dawn factory declared from the dais. "We say, 'Remember, you are not alone. We are with you.'"[75]

Soviet newspapers and radio placed Spain center stage, depicting Republic heroism against fascist aggression, and tying the Soviet Union to this cause.[76] *Pravda*—"Hands off the Spanish people!" . . . "Down with the fascist rebels and their German and Italian inspirers!"—reported that workers had been massed in front of the Winter Palace in Leningrad (100,000) and in Tashkent (100,000), Gorky (60,000), Rostov-on-Don (35,000), Minsk (30,000), Sverdlovsk (20,000), and Tiflis (10,000).[77] The Comintern resolved to "immediately undertake a wide campaign of solidarity for the fighters defending the Republic in Spain," including "collections of medicines, foodstuffs, gold," and enlistment of medical volunteers and purchases of ambulances.[78] The regime also announced "voluntary" deductions from workers' paychecks for humanitarian assistance to Spain.[79] "We see how quickly fascists from different states will unite when the task is the asphyxiation of the working class," one Soviet autoworker was quoted as stating in *Pravda*. "Through our relief aid . . . we will show the fascists that no country will be cut off from the workers of the rest of the world. The cause of Spain is our own cause."[80]

Would Stalin risk getting embroiled in foreign war? "A number of Soviet officials charged with the conduct of Soviet foreign relations were opposed to sending funds to Spain, since they felt that such action would be used by Italy and Germany to justify the aid given by themselves," one Soviet official told the U.S. chargé d'affaires in Moscow on August 3, 1936. "These objections were overruled, however, by the Soviet leaders who take the view that if the Soviet Union is to continue to maintain hegemony over the international revolutionary movement, it must not hesitate in periods of crisis to assume the leadership of that movement."[81] Tellingly, however, neither Stalin nor any of the members of the Soviet leadership attended the August 3 Moscow demonstration. Not even Comintern leaders were allowed to appear. The main speech was delivered by the head of the trade unions (Nikolai Shvernik), as if the process of gathering humanitarian aid were a spontaneous expression of worker solidarity.[82]

All the while, the geopolitical maneuvering was fast and furious. In early August, France approached Germany, Italy, the Soviet Union, and other countries about a formal collective "Non-Intervention Agreement" for Spain.[83] Britain had treated a *formal* agreement guardedly, but now it decided it could drive a wedge between France and Spain. On August 3, the Italian government promised to study the matter. On August 5, the French chargé d'affaires in Moscow approached the foreign affairs commissariat, reporting that Britain had signed on and that Germany had agreed to do so if the Soviets would. Litvinov was on holiday, and one of his deputies, Krestinsky, advised Stalin, "We cannot either not give an affirmative response or give an evasive response, because then this will be used by the Germans and Italians, who will justify their further support for the insurgents by our refusal." That evening, Krestinsky was able to reply that the USSR, too, would sign on, provided that not only Italy and Germany but Portugal's dictatorship did so as well.[84] The next day, Italy confirmed its support in principle.

Also on August 5, Trotsky, from Norway, sent his French and American publishers a manuscript that he had completed with only a little more than half a year's work: *The Revolution Betrayed: What Is the Soviet Union and Where Is It Going?* He sent a copy to his son Sedov in Paris for excerpting in the *Bulletin*. Thus did Soviet intelligence obtain a copy, while reporting that the text was to be translated into multiple foreign languages, which meant worldwide impact.[85] When Stalin saw the text remains uncertain, but it was likely not long after it had come into NKVD hands.[86] There is no known record of his reaction. Still, Trotsky's spirited wielding of Marxist analysis against the purported leader of world Marxists struck at the foundations of Stalin's legitimacy and self-identity. He portrayed Stalin's rule as a full-blown counterrevolution, or Thermidor, a consequence of an evil social compact between the new bureaucratic elite and the old bourgeoisie, a deformation of Leninism pejoratively labeled "Stalinism." Notwithstanding the building of socialism, therefore, the revolution had been betrayed.[87] Trotsky's analysis appeared with impeccable timing: Spain could be taken as proof of Stalin's betrayal of the entire world revolution. The book reinforced the convergence of the Trotsky problem and the Spanish problem.

FARCE

Preparations proceeded for a public trial in Moscow of "Trotskyites." On August 7, 1936, USSR procurator general Vyshinsky sent Stalin a draft indictment charging twelve people with establishing a terror organization aiming to assassinate the dictator and other members of the leadership. Stalin raised the number of defendants to sixteen, five of whom were Germans—members of the German Communist party who had fled to the USSR—thereby reinforcing his beloved foreign espionage story line. He also sharpened the "testimony" he received of the fabricated plot. "It is not enough to cut down the oak," he inserted in the testimony of one alleged would-be assassin. "You must cut down all the young that grow around the oak."[88]

The French Communist party had sent a reconnaissance delegation to Spain and, also on August 7, reported that "the situation is very critical because of non-availability of armaments," a conclusion confirmed by Soviet military intelligence. Comintern HQ in Moscow telegrammed Maurice Thorez, head of the French Communists, to pressure the French government to rescue the Spanish Republic and thereby the French Popular Front (and, perhaps, the USSR from having to intervene in Spain).[89] That same day, Krestinsky explained in a telegram to the Soviet envoy in Rome that "we understood Italy and Germany would continue arming the putschists" in Spain, but the USSR had to remove any justification for them to do so.[90] On August 10, the expression "malevolent neutrality," coined by Labour peer Lord Strabolgi in reference to British policy on Spain, appeared in the *Daily Herald*, the world's bestselling newspaper.

Stalin had little desire to follow in Britain's ignominious wake while being shown up by Mussolini and Hitler, cold-shouldered by the French Socialist Léon Blum, and squeezed between a whining Litvinov and a lacerating Trotsky. But if he rejected the Non-Intervention Agreement, Britain and France might unite with fascist Italy and Nazi Germany against the USSR in a four-power deal over Spain, and perhaps more broadly. (The British cabinet secretary had privately stated on July 20, 1936, "In the present state of Europe, with France and Spain menaced by Bolshevism, it is not inconceivable that before long it might pay us to throw in our lot with Germany and Italy.")[91] There was also, as ever, the commercial aspect. On August 19, Litvinov would write to the Soviet envoy Surits that Kandelaki, the Soviet trade representative in Berlin, would "inform the Germans about our demurral on the [credit] agreement so far. At the same time, he was authorized to ask if the Germans were agreed to selling us certain items that specially interest us and, if so, raise the question of a credit agreement anew."[92]

Nazi Germany, as Berlin's authoritative Institute for Business Cycle Research had recently noted in a report, faced depleted stocks of raw materials, which would seem to have argued for rapprochement with both the USSR and the Western powers.[93] But the Führer had other ideas, finalizing a Four-Year Plan in August 1936—one of the very few documents in Hitler's own hand—which began with a statement about history being a struggle among nations for existence. It insisted that Germany had to be ready for war within four years; otherwise, "those strata of mankind which have hitherto provided the leadership" would suffer "replacement by worldwide Jewry." Hitler added that "a victory of Bolshevism over Germany would lead . . . to the final destruction, indeed to the annihilation of the German people. . . . In the face of the necessity of defense against this danger, all other considerations must recede into the background as being completely irrelevant."[94] Soviet intelligence had obtained information that Germany would not be ready to launch a massive-scale war before 1939.[95] Still, as Hitler revealed in his Four-Year Plan, Germany's destiny would be realized through conquest, not trade.[96]

Soaring revolutionary sentiments, full of bluster but also raw emotion, were erupting in the press of the high-profile French Communist party and the reports out of Spain by Communists and pro-Comintern leftists. China was radicalizing as well. On August 13, Stalin finally returned Dimitrov's request for approval of the draft instructions for the Chinese Communists (he merely wrote "in favor"). Two days later, the instructions were radioed to Yan'an, concretizing the actions required under the united front policy, and warning, "It is incorrect to place Chiang Kai-shek on the same plane as the Japanese invaders."[97] Mao formally complied, writing to the Nationalists to request an end to their civil war and negotiations.[98] But Dimitrov would have his hands full trying to enforce Mao's compliance.

In Spain, the Soviet regime kept to the impression of providing only human-itarian aid voluntarily contributed by workers through trade unions (some 264 million rubles would be collected overall).[99] But on August 21, 1936, the thirty-year-old Soviet filmmaker Roman Karmen and his cinematographer Boris Makaseyev, who had been hastily dispatched to Spain by the politburo, managed to film a Canadian hunter (who had volunteered to fight for the Republic) shoot-ing down an Italian bomber that had been raining destruction on the Republic's side. A few days later, the world saw Karmen's documentary footage, which conclusively proved "fascist" support for the Spanish putschists working to over-throw the elected Republic.[100] On August 23, Italy cynically signed the Non-Intervention Agreement. The Soviets did so the same day. Germany would formally sign the next day. From this point, any violation of nonintervention by Moscow could serve as a pretext justifying Italian and German supply of arms to the insurgents.[101]

SHOWCASE TRIAL

Yezhov was furiously driving extraction of "testimony" for the trial of a "Trotskyite-Zinovievite Terrorist Center" in Moscow. On August 10, he con-fronted Pyatakov with documents from his opposition days that had been seized at the apartment of his arrested ex-wife. Pyatakov demanded a chance to prove his loyalty, requesting, as Yezhov wrote to Stalin, that "they allow him personally to shoot all those sentenced to be shot at the upcoming trial, including his former wife," an assignment Pyatakov wanted broadcast. Stalin was only interested that Pyatakov smear himself and others.[102] It was a few days later, late on the night of August 13, that the dictator, after holding a Kremlin banquet for Soviet aviators who had completed the first nonstop flight from Moscow to the Soviet Far East, departed for his annual southern holiday. That day, TASS issued a venomous press release about a trial for treason to commence in a few days with sixteen defendants, including Zinoviev and Kamenev and, in absentia, Trotsky (then fishing in a small Norwegian village). Stalin tasked Kaganovich with implementing the trial's final push. Before the trial, Vasily Ulrich, chairman of the military collegium of the USSR Supreme Court, presented drafts of the sentences, which Stalin approved, and the Soviet press demanded "no leniency for enemies of the people who have tried to deprive the people of their leaders."[103]

Also on August 14, the NKVD arrested Vitali Primakov, commander of the Leningrad military district and a hero of the civil war. Six days later, the same fate befell Vitovt Putna, Soviet military attaché to Great Britain (and before that to Japan, Germany, and Finland). Primakov and Putna were charged with "Trotskyism" and participation in a military "plot." Many Red Army officers had had interactions with them.

The five-day trial of the Trotskyite-Zinovievite center commenced on August 19, in the October Hall of white Corinthian columns in the House of Trade Unions.[104] The spectacle followed an extended period of behind-the-scenes torture, scripting, and rehearsing, and this time it would result not in mere exile or imprisonment. The defendants, besides the five German Communists who "confessed" to Gestapo ties, were eleven prominent Bolsheviks of the 1926–27 opposition.[105] Ten of the sixteen happened to be Jewish (this received no special attention). Invited audience members numbered some 150 people, including 30 handpicked foreign journalists and diplomats, as well as many plainclothes NKVD operatives, but not the relatives of the accused. Despite slipups that betrayed the fabrication, the defendants, all Communists, publicly confessed to being wreckers, spies, terrorists.[106] (Kaganovich made sure to add himself and Orjonikidze to the list of targets.)[107] "I, Kamenev, together with Zinoviev and Trotsky, organized and guided this conspiracy," Stalin's former close associate stated. "I had become convinced that the party's—Stalin's—policy was successful and victorious. We, the opposition, had banked on a split in the party, but this hope proved groundless. We could no longer count on any serious domestic difficulties to allow us to overthrow Stalin's leadership."

Some of the "testimony" had implicated rightists (Rykov, Bukharin, Tomsky), and Kaganovich and Yezhov (August 20) had jointly telegrammed Stalin in Sochi asking for instructions on that score. The next day, the dictator permitted mention at the trial of the rightists, as well as a yet-to-be-unveiled "parallel center" (Pyatakov, Sokolnikov, Radek). On that day, *Izvestiya* published an essay by Radek, who, as a former Trotsky supporter, lent his credibility to the wild charges against Trotsky, Kamenev, and Zinoviev, calling the attempts to assassinate the Soviet leader and the links to the Gestapo "a plot to restore capitalism in the USSR."[108] Stalin had also been prompted to remember the out-of-favor poet Demyan Bedny, who published "No Mercy!" in *Pravda* (August 21): "Here are the ones who murdered Kirov! . . . They were going for Stalin!"[109]

Testifying to these fixations, Stalin's holiday correspondence changed. It remained laconic and often ill-humored, sometimes downright scolding, with almost no personal information—just directives and responses to initiatives by Kaganovich (or Molotov). But content-wise, of the more than 140 letters and ciphered telegrams he exchanged during this holiday, a mere half dozen concerned the industrial economy, and most of those involved the dictator approving others' proposals, without comment.[110] Now the mailbag also included the transcript of a Tomsky speech, interrogation "protocols" of Kamenev, draft protocols of Sokolnikov's interrogation. (Stalin: "Did he not inform [the British journalist] of the plans for the assassination of Soviet leaders? Of course he did.") Such documents were pointing to a vast, phantasmagoric conspiracy, from party officials to military men. Bukharin, hiking the Pamirs in Central Asia, had hurried back to Moscow to find Stalin away on holiday, and would write the dictator a letter, which also found its way into the holiday mailbag, rabidly endorsing all the fabricated charges of the trial, except those about himself ("I embrace you, for I'm clean").[111] Trotsky, who hurriedly returned to Oslo from his fishing holiday, told the *New York Times* that the trial was fraudulent and "puts the Dreyfus scandal and the Reichstag fire trial in the shadow."[112]

As for Tomsky, when his driver arrived at his dacha outside Moscow to pick him up for his job as head of the state publishing house—bearing a copy of that morning's *Pravda* (August 22), which reported an investigation into Tomsky for counterrevolution—he shot himself. Tomsky prepared a suicide note ("Dear Comrade Stalin"), expressing his despair while protesting his innocence, and beseeching the dictator, whom he called his "old fighting comrade," not to believe Zinoviev's slander against him. Tomsky apologized, yet again, for his comment one evening in 1928 that someone would shoot Stalin. "Do not take seriously what I blurted out then—I have deeply regretted this always."[113] *Pravda* reported the suicide the next day as an admission of guilt.[114] In an act of attempted posthumous revenge that played on Stalin's conspiratorial bent, Tomsky cleverly implicated NKVD chief Yagoda as a rightist coconspirator, having his wife convey orally the "secret" that Yagoda was the person who had "recruited" Tomsky.[115]

Kamenev and Stalin had known each other for more than three decades. "Greetings, friend! I kiss you on the nose, Eskimo-style," Stalin had written to him in December 1912, evoking their Siberian exile. "For hell's sake! I miss you devilishly. I miss you—I swear by my dog. I have no one, no one to chat with, heart to heart, may the devil run you over."[116] On the eve of Kamenev's execution, Stalin wrote to Kaganovich that Kamenev, through his wife, had sounded out the French ambassador about supporting a possible Trotskyite-Zinovievite government. "I believe Kamenev also sounded out the English, German, and American ambassadors," Stalin added. "This means Kamenev was supposed to reveal to these foreigners the plans for the conspiracy and the murder of the leaders of the party. This also means Kamenev had already revealed the plans to them, for otherwise the foreigners would not have begun talking about the future Trotskyite-Zinovievite 'government' with him."[117] Did Stalin believe this? Was he straining to justify his political murders to Kaganovich? These questions remain unanswerable.

Stalin supervised the trial from afar, sternly instructing Kaganovich that the sentences had to mention Trotsky and Sedov. ("This carries enormous significance for Europe, both for the bourgeoisie and for the workers.")[118] A few hours after the court had adjourned on August 24, Ulrich, at 2:30 a.m., pronounced the defendants guilty and condemned all but one to death. Later that day, the regime staged a grand aviation display at Moscow's Tushinsky Aerodrome ("Glory to Stalinist aviation and the Stalinist falcons"). Planes flew difficult maneuvers. Parachutists dropped from the sky. "The enemies' schemes," a teacher in the Institute of World Economy and International Relations recorded in his diary, "cannot stop our enormous successes."[119] Kamenev and the others wrote appeals for mercy in the predawn hours. (Only one defendant expressly refused to do so.) Perhaps, as would be rumored, Stalin had promised them their lives in exchange for public "confessions" to crimes they had not committed.[120] But well before the end of the seventy-two-hour period for appeals specified in Soviet law, Kamenev, Zinoviev, and the rest were executed in the cellars.[121] Yezhov retrieved the bullet casings as souvenirs.

FORCING MASS HYSTERIA

The day after the August 13, 1936, discussion of Spain in the Little Corner, Stalin received a résumé of Soviet-Spanish diplomatic relations from Krestinsky, which accelerated a belated exchange of ambassadors. The choice fell to a twenty-year veteran of the Soviet diplomatic corps, Marcel Rosenberg, who was summoned from Karlsbad.[122] Litvinov had written to Kaganovich urging that people appointed as ambassadors in major countries should know the local language, while lamenting that the foreign affairs commissariat had only a single fluent Spanish speaker: Leonid Gaikis, a Lithuanian who had grown up in Argentina and was serving as consul general in Istanbul. Litvinov felt constrained to inform Kaganovich, with a copy to Stalin, that in 1923 Gaikis had voted for the Trotskyite platform. Stalin did not prevent Gaikis's appointment as an "adviser" in the embassy in Madrid, effectively Rosenberg's deputy.[123] A bit later, Stalin would consent to the establishment of a consulate in Catalonia and the appointment there of Vladimir Antonov-Ovseyenko, the hero of the 1917 storming of the Winter Palace—also a repentant former Trotsky sympathizer. The consul would tell Ilya Ehrenburg, who would go to Spain as an *Izvestiya* correspondent, that his key task would consist of making the Spanish anarchists "see reason."[124]

Before Stalin had gone on holiday, the politburo had first approved a *Pravda* request to send a special correspondent to Spain, Mikhail Koltsov, the Soviet Union's best-known journalist-propagandist.[125] During the 1920s and '30s, he had published more than a thousand stylistically free-flowing essays, including on collectivization ("Fortress in the Steppe"), driving a taxi in Moscow, and flying in the first Soviet-made airplane. Koltsov could do what almost no one else could: toe the Stalinist line while delivering enduring portraits of Soviet life. He had a sense of humor, too, founding *Crocodile,* the Soviet humor magazine, and had even been to Spain, following the fall of its monarchy, and published *Spanish Spring* (1933).[126] By August 8, 1936, he'd arrived in Madrid, and over the next several weeks he managed to compose twenty reports for *Pravda,* relayed by telephone to Moscow. "A stocky little Jew with a huge head and one of the most expressive faces of any man I ever met," Claud Cockburn, a British journalist who encountered Koltsov in Spain, would recall. "He unquestionably and positively enjoyed the sense of danger and sometimes—by his political indiscretions, for instance, or still more wildly indiscreet love affairs—deliberately created dangers which need not have existed."[127] Koltsov's engaging reportage for Soviet readers would render Spain's civil war immediate and in Stalin's preferred light: as a struggle not just against fascism per se but against Trotskyism—indeed, against a supposed linkup between Trotskyism and fascism.[128]

Was there Trotskyism in Spain? Spain's Popular Front government consisted of representatives of its Republican parties, which received support from the Spanish Socialist Workers' Party, the Unified Socialist Party of Catalonia (only nominally united), the Syndicalist Party and various anarchist formations (at least initially), Basque separatists, the Spanish Communist party, and the Workers Party of Marxist Unification (POUM). The latter, formed in 1935, consisted of breakaway left Communists and dissident Marxist-Leninists who demanded an immediate transition to a dictatorship of the proletariat in Spain, precisely Trotsky's position. The leading theorist of the POUM, Andreu Nin, had spent nine years in Moscow as secretary general of the Red International of Labor Unions (Profintern) and had sided with Trotsky's left opposition. Nin broke with Moscow and had a falling-out with the exiled Trotsky as well. In spring 1936, Trotsky had set his followers the task of exposing "the full wretchedness of the leadership of the 'Workers Party of Marxist Unification' and especially of the former 'Left Communists' . . . before the eyes of all the advanced workers."[129] On August 10, 1936, Victor Serge—an intellectual Stalin had released into foreign exile, who was now busy translating Trotsky's *The Revolution Betrayed* into French— begged Trotsky to take back his harsh words about the POUM, "to deny the bureaucracy any possibility whatsoever of turning the revolution into a prison for workers in the Stalinist manner." But Trotsky continued to lacerate the POUM for supposedly vacillating between support of the "bourgeois" democratic phase of Spain's revolution and of Trotsky's Fourth International (full-bore anticapitalist revolution).[130]

Koltsov's crafty reportage conveying a Trotsky-centric interpretation of events in Spain perfectly complemented the saturation coverage and orchestrated meetings all across the USSR over the Trotskyite showcase trial, together whipping up anti-Trotsky hysteria. In Stalin's worldview, Nin's hoary link to Trotsky alone rendered the POUM "Trotskyite." There was also the POUM's independence, criticizing the Stalinist line while claiming the mantle of Marxism. Some members of the POUM, moreover, openly admired Trotsky, and some of its officials discussed inviting him to take up residence in Barcelona. Sometimes fabricated nightmares have a way of coming true. The Trotsky bogey had long been one of Stalin's prime instruments for enforcing dictatorial rule; now, all of a sudden, he had to worry about a victory of the anti-Stalinist left— Trotskyism to him—in a real country. "Trotsky, and all that Trotsky represented, was Stalin's real fear," American diplomat George Kennan would surmise.[131] Kennan was speaking broadly, not in connection with Spain per se, but Spain had become *the* place.

"GREETINGS"

Public confessions by Lenin's former comrades to monstrous state crimes and the rabid saturation propaganda about hidden enemies had revolutionized the political atmosphere. The White émigré press rejoiced at the executions: "Sixteen is not enough! Give us forty more, give us hundreds, give us thousands." Alexander Kerensky, in exile in the United States, saw nothing surprising in accusations that Trotsky had collaborated with the Gestapo: after all, had not Lenin and Trotsky been German agents in 1917?[132] Lev Sedov, in a detailed exposé of the trial, called Lenin the "first terrorist": after all, his Testament had instructed, "Remove Stalin." Stalin, for his part, fumed at Kaganovich and Molotov (September 6) that *Pravda*'s trial coverage had "failed to produce a single article that provided a Marxist explanation," because "the newspaper wrapped everything in personal terms, that there are evil people who want to seize power and good people who are in power.... The articles should say that the struggle against Stalin, Voroshilov, Molotov, . . . and others is a struggle against the Soviets, against collectivization, against industrialization, a struggle, consequently, for the restoration of capitalism. . . . They should have said, finally, that the degradation of these scum to the level of White Guards and fascists is a logical outgrowth of their moral decline as [Communist] opposition leaders in the past."[133]

Pravda (September 4, 1936) had crowed that the number of "Trotskyites" was "microscopic," and that the "opposition" had been dealt a crushing blow. But Yezhov, in a letter (September 9) to Sochi with details of Tomsky's suicide, wrote that "without doubt the Trotskyites in the army have some unmasked cadres," adding that Trotskyite "ties" inside the secret police had yet to be investigated properly.[134]

Bukharin had written to Voroshilov, "I'm terribly glad the dogs were shot."[135] On September 10, 1936, *Pravda* suddenly announced that the procuracy had cleared Bukharin, as well as Rykov, of connections to terrorism.[136] But four days later, Kaganovich reported to Sochi the results of the "interrogations" of Bukharin, Rykov, and Sokolnikov, commenting that the latter—Kaganovich's once-close comrade back in Nizhny Novgorod and Turkestan—had been "in contact" with the "Trotskyite-Zinovievite Terrorist Center" and adding that it was good the USSR was exterminating "all these rats."[137] Bukharin wrote to Stalin again, claiming to be "mentally ill," under too much strain to "go on living," because his life had "become meaningless. . . . This is surely a paradox: the more I devote myself to serving the party with all my heart, the worse my unfortunate predicament becomes, and now I no longer have the strength to fight against the attacks anymore. . . . I urgently beg of you to allow me to come and see you. . . . Only you can cure me. If my fate is of any concern to you . . . then meet with me."[138] Stalin ignored this plea.

Orjonikidze, in early September 1936, had gone on his annual holiday to Kislovodsk. He wrote to Stalin (September 7) that he had listened to parts of the trial on the radio in Kaganovich's office. "Shooting them was not enough," he noted. "If it had been possible, they should have been shot at least ten times. . . . They caused tremendous harm to the party. Now, knowing what they're made of, you don't know who's telling the truth and who's lying, who's a friend and who's a double-dealer. This is the poison they injected into the party. . . . People don't know whether they can trust this or that former Trotskyite or Zinovievite." After condemning people who were already dead, he added pointedly: "I am very worried about the army. . . . A skillful enemy could deal us an irreparable blow here: they will start to spread rumors about people and instill distrust in the army. Here we need to be very careful." Orjonikidze also tried to shield his deputy Pyatakov: "If we do not arrest him, let us send him somewhere, or leave him in the Urals, as at present."[139] Stalin had Pyatakov expelled from the Central Committee and the party (September 9) without a meeting. In the NKVD inventory of his confiscated property were his Order of Lenin and his party card, no. 0000059—a low number, indicating very long membership (Pyatakov was one of only six figures mentioned in Lenin's Testament).[140] On September 11, Stalin answered Orjonikidze from Sochi: "1) Pyatakov is already under arrest. 2) It's possible Radek will be arrested. Toroshelidze and Budu [Mdivani] are thoroughly stained. They too could be arrested. . . . Greetings to Zina. I. Stalin."[141]

SUDDEN DECISION

Policy on Spain took a sudden turn. On August 29, 1936, the politburo had prohibited sending arms, ammunition, or planes to Spain, in accord with the Non-Intervention Agreement, a prohibition *Pravda* had announced (August 30). On September 2, in a telegram to the Soviet embassy in London, Litvinov had written that "guiding our relationship to the Spanish events is a striving in every possible way to impede the delivery of weapons to the Spanish insurgents and the necessity of strictly curtailing the activities of countries such as Germany, Italy, and Portugal."[142] But Spanish events were moving rapidly. On September 4, the first Soviet-produced newsreels from Spain were shown in Moscow, and soon they were distributed to other large cities.[143] That same day, Francisco Largo Caballero, a trade unionist, head of the Socialist Workers' Party, and Spain's most prominent civilian politician, became prime minister. The Spanish Communist party accepted an invitation to join the new cabinet in the Popular Front coalition (the anarchists declined).[144] For Moscow, the stakes had been raised. Already, prior to this in early September, the politburo had begun approving, by voice vote, plans for shipments of Soviet industrial goods to Spain. But now Stalin sent a telegram to Kaganovich (September 6, 1936) about how "it would be good" to sell Mexico fifty Soviet bombers, and possibly 20,000 rifles and 20 million cartridges, which could then get to Spain.[145] This short cipher—sent the same day Stalin dressed down the Soviet press summaries of the recent Moscow trial of Trotskyites—effectively set in motion a Soviet military intervention.

Stalin, with Voroshilov (communicating by high-frequency phone), had decided against committing regular Soviet troops.[146] But the politburo had already resolved to form volunteer "international brigades," to be organized in Paris under the leadership of André Marty, assisted by the Italian Communist party in exile, and funded by Moscow. Many of the volunteers—from the United States, the British Isles, Latin America, and the whole of the European continent, including Nazi Germany and fascist Italy—were not Communists but idealists or adventurers.[147] (The volunteers' passports would be taken for "safekeeping," a windfall for the NKVD.)[148] These Comintern brigades remained within the letter of the Non-Intervention Agreement. No Soviet nationals were allowed to join, although many volunteered to.

Now Stalin also approved the dispatch not just of propagandists and diplomats but military advisers.[149] The commander of a Soviet naval cruiser, Nikolai Kuznetsov, who was at sea, received a telegram summons to Moscow and, at the defense commissariat, discovered that he was being posted to Spain as naval attaché. ("What do you know about Spain?" he was asked.)[150] The top military adviser appointed to Spain was the Latvian Berzin, who had headed Soviet military intelligence until 1935. The Soviet military attaché to the Madrid front was Vladimir Gorev (b. 1900), a blond Belorussian peasant who had become a veteran undercover military intelligence operative with experience in China and the United States, spoke excellent English, and had exemplary manners.[151] The position of commercial attaché was soon filled by Artur Stashevsky [Hirschfeld], a Jew born in tsarist Latvia, who had been a driving force in the accumulation of Soviet gold reserves and who, in Spain, would serve as the top Soviet political operative.[152]

Already by early fall, there would be more than 550 Soviet personnel in-country, the highest ranking of whom took up residence in Madrid's Palace Hotel.[153]

Additionally, the NKVD sent Leiba Feldbein, who used the name Alexander Orlov, to gather intelligence and organize guerrilla warfare in Spain.[154] Orlov had been born (1895) in Belorussia and raised in an Orthodox Jewish family, joining Trotsky's group of leftist internationalists in 1917, fighting for the Reds in the Russian civil war, and in 1920, at age twenty-five, joining the party and the Cheka in Arkhangelsk, going on to work in the economic and transport sections of the secret police and undercover in Paris, Berlin, Vienna, Geneva, Copenhagen, and London. "He spoke English well, dressed dapperly, was good-looking and very intelligent," Louis Fischer would write.[155] Abram Slutsky, head of NKVD foreign intelligence, had evidently alighted upon his friend Orlov for posting to Spain partly to protect him: a young assistant in the NKVD with whom Orlov had been having an affair shot herself in front of Lubyanka HQ after he refused to leave his wife.[156] Orlov, his wife, and their daughter would cross the Soviet-Polish border en route to Spain on September 10, 1936.[157]

Ilya Ehrenburg, the *Izvestiya* correspondent, who arrived in Spain a few weeks after his rival *Pravda* correspondent Koltsov, wrote in a letter to Stalin (also on September 10), after having traveled more than 1,500 miles of Spanish territory, that "POUM (the Trotskyites) in Catalonia are weak. At the front, their column of 3,500 men is the most undisciplined. They have tense relations with the Unified Socialist Party of Catalonia (our party) and with the anarchists."[158] Stalin held the opposite view on the POUM's threat.

DIFFERENT SHOWS

In London on September 9, 1936, the Non-Intervention Committee held its first meeting, with twenty-seven European states represented. The session devolved into insults. Especially acrimonious exchanges took place between the Soviet ambassador (Ivan Maisky) and the German embassy counselor (Prince Otto von Bismarck, grandson of the chancellor).[159] But the deeper problem was the conveners' cynicism. "A piece of humbug," one senior British foreign office official observed of the committee. "Where humbug is the alternative to war, it is impossible to place too high a value upon it."[160] But given that the public heard every day about how Italy and Germany *were* intervening forcefully, British credibility suffered a blow.

Contemporaneously with the sorry spectacle in London, military attachés and specialists from France and Czechoslovakia, as well as Britain, had been invited to Red Army maneuvers (September 7–10)—a show to impress. This was the first time a British delegation had been invited. Held in the Belorussian military district, commanded by the capable Iona Yakir, the Bessarabian-born (1896) son of a Jewish pharmacist, the exercises assumed a German-Polish aggression against the Soviet Union.[161] All told, an astonishing 85,000 troops and auxiliaries and 1,136 tanks and armored vehicles took part. The "enemy" (blues) attacked with almost 37,000 men, 211 airplanes, and 453 combined-arms tanks, mostly T-28s but also T-27s (the Soviet variant of the Carden Loyd tankette), while the "friendly" forces (reds) possessed more than 42,000 men and 240 airplanes, as well as three mechanized brigades and several rifle and cavalry-tank units. The terrain was circumscribed in relation to the size of forces engaged and, without rivers or marshes, artificially ideal for tank warfare. After aviation created a smoke fog, the large mechanized units forged the Berezina River. One mechanized tank brigade completed a 125-mile march. The culmination entailed a parachute drop and reassembly, in battle formation, of some 1,800 men armed with machine guns and light artillery.[162] The scale, complexity, and coordination of the exercises, according to *Pravda* (September 10), duly impressed the onlookers. In fact, Britain's Lieutenant Colonel Giffard Martel, a well-known tank theorist at the war office, was put in mind of the tsarist army: great physical brutality with manifest "tactical clumsiness." Privately dismissing the exercise as "more like a tattoo than maneuvers," he deemed the training of junior officers weak, found radio communication not widely used, and saw little skill in the use of mechanized formations. Martel surmised that a well-equipped and well-commanded enemy could dodge the blow and inflict tremendous counterdamage.[163]

General Victor-Henri Schweisguth, who led the French delegation, told Voroshilov that Hitler saw the Soviet Union as the source of evil and was menacingly accusing Czechoslovakia of complicity in that evil. Voroshilov retorted that Hitler's anti-Soviet ravings masked his real intention of attacking France, and once again urged bilateral staff talks.[164] Schweisguth made a mental note that his Soviet counterparts claimed to want closer military cooperation with France yet seemed eager for Hitler to attack France first. In his confidential report upon return to Paris, he deemed the Red Army "insufficiently prepared for a war against a Great European Power," adding: "The circumstances of its employment against Germany remain very problematical." He warned that the Soviets hoped that "the storm burst first upon France," and that, because of the absence of a common frontier with Germany, the Soviet Union could stand aside, like the United States in 1918, "to arbitrate the situation in the face of a Europe exhausted by battle."[165] Schweisguth saw value in talks with the Soviets only as prevention against a Soviet-German military alliance.[166] The feelings were mutual: Yakir, who had just traveled to France, came back with a low regard for French military doctrine, technical level, operational-strategic thinking, and its army as a whole.[167]

Captain František Moravec, of Czechoslovak military intelligence, had arrived in Moscow before the maneuvers to cooperate with his Soviet counterparts in connection with their alliance treaty. Quartered at the Metropole and enveloped by Soviet counterintelligence, his six-man Czechoslovak team was received by Uritsky, head of military intelligence, becoming the first group of foreigners admitted to the "Chocolate House," the three-story mansion that served as HQ, and then by Tukhachevsky, chief of the general staff. There were banquets at Spiridonovka on gold plates with the tsar's monogram, stay-overs at the former Yusupov Palace in Arkhangelskoe, and a visit to the Moscow–Volga Canal Gulag site. He perceived his Soviet partners as ignorant of the Wehrmacht, noting that Soviet military intelligence "had not even organized proper supporting activities, such as the study of the German news media." Whether Moravec, who spoke Russian, was shown the breadth of Soviet capabilities remains uncertain (the Czechoslovaks were technically "White Guards"). Still, he was correct about the dearth of foreign-language expertise in a system that valued proletarian origins and sycophancy over expertise. "The unexpected inefficiency in the military intelligence service of a regime which had been nourished on clandestine undertakings," he concluded, "was surprising."[168] The men from Prague felt an urgency vis-à-vis their neighbor Nazi Germany that was not felt in Moscow.[169]

Most damaging of all the private reports on the maneuvers was Voroshilov's. At the banquet, in front of foreigners, he lauded the exercises. But while Tukhachevsky, acknowledging the shortcomings of tank performance in the rifle divisions, whose commanders still did not know how to use them to the fullest, deemed their efforts superior to what the Red Army had previously managed, Voroshilov internally denounced the tank formations and urged a doubling down on infantry.[170] Part of his motivation appears to have been long-standing envy at the superior abilities and reputations of Tukhachevsky, Yakir, and Uborevičius (commander of the Ukrainian military district), all modernizers, and more knowledgeable about Germany.[171]

OPERATION X

On September 13, 1936, the city of San Sebastián fell to Spain's putschists. The next day, Molotov, having just returned from holiday, followed up on Stalin's telegram to Kaganovich the week before and chaired a meeting devoted to, among other matters, Spain. Attendees included Yagoda, Slutsky (NKVD foreign intelligence), Uritsky (military intelligence), Meyer Trilisser (Comintern intelligence), and Dimitrov, who recorded an agenda item as "organization of aid to the Spanish (via a smuggling scheme)."[172] Later that day at Lubyanka, Yagoda presided over a meeting with Slutsky, Uritsky, Mikhail Frinovsky (head of NKVD border guards), and others to plan foreign military deliveries, including purchases abroad, for Spain. Before September 14 was out, Slutsky and Uritsky had presented Kaganovich with corrections to an operational plan, code-named Operation X.[173]

Also on September 14, the annual Nazi Nuremberg party rally concluded as Hitler announced further rearmament steps and unleashed his most rabid denunciation yet of the international Jewish conspiracy and the "infernal plague" of Bolshevism, which was "letting loose these wild beasts on the terrified and helpless world." He mentioned German designs on Ukraine. In response to this drumbeat, the Soviet state publishing house issued a collection of translated original German documents from the period of the Great War, *The Crash of the German Occupation in Ukraine,* underscoring the high costs then of Germany's attempted colonial enslavement of Ukraine and warning, "Let German fascists now try to poke their snouts onto Soviet land!"[174] The Führer still hoped to catalyze a broad anti-Bolshevik coalition, which would support, or at least not block, German expansionism eastward and continental domination. He portrayed the Soviet Union as intent on imminent attack, but his ravings made it seem as if Germany would march then and there.[175] The U.S. ambassador in Berlin thought the rally speeches might "make it difficult for the Soviet embassy to remain in Berlin."[176] Hitler mused that Stalin would be moved to break off diplomatic relations.[177] Litvinov urged a Soviet diplomatic protest to deter further invective.[178] Stalin, on the contrary, was soon renewing feelers to the Nazi regime.

Voroshilov sent detailed lists of all materials to be supplied in the Spanish operation to Stalin for approval.[179] Because of the Non-Intervention Agreement, the Soviets had initially aimed to provide only third-party and "surplus" weapons, but, given the urgency, Operation X specified also providing Soviet weapons—just as the Spanish government had been requesting. Soviet intelligence was estimating that the Republic possessed one rifle for every three soldiers.[180] On September 18, the first small-arms shipment, labeled CANNED MEAT, left a Soviet port. So did humanitarian cargo (flour, sugar, butter, canned goods, clothing, medicine).[181] Secret Soviet documents stipulated that for the weapons "the customer should pay their full price." Back on September 13, the Spanish Republic had secretly decided to evacuate the better part of the country's gold reserves from Madrid by train. Spain had the world's fourth-largest reserves, amounting to more than 2.3 trillion pesetas, or $783 million at prevailing exchange rates, a cache amassed by the crown over centuries: bullion bars, gold louis d'or, British sovereigns, rare Portuguese coins, Inca and Aztec treasure from the conquistador period. The crates began arriving at the port of Cartagena in the early hours of September 17, and for the next five and a half weeks remained in a hillside cave above the harbor. Prime Minister Largo Caballero had shipped the gold to the port at which Spain had agreed to receive Soviet cargo.

NKVD COUP

In Moscow, comic relief arrived on September 19, 1936, when regional party boss Kuzma Ryndin, after whom twenty collective farms and mines had been named, petitioned the dictator to rename Chelyabinsk—which roughly connoted "a pit"—into "Kaganovichgrad." Stalin wrote on the request: "Against."[182] The next day, the politburo formally rejected a proposal from Litvinov for an expanded *Soviet-led* bloc against Nazi Germany, but it reaffirmed the pursuit of "collective security."[183] Franco was busy establishing a regime. On the battlefield he took his time, transferring operations from urgent military objectives to political ones, perplexing the other generals. On September 21, in a hut on an airfield in Salamanca, citing the need for unified command in the war effort, Franco managed to get himself elevated to generalissimo of insurgent armies, even though he was junior to Mola. A week later, Franco manipulated matters further to get himself named chief of state with "absolute powers." Several of the colluding commanders envisioned his elevation as temporary, anticipating a return of the monarchy, but Franco remarked of the moment, "You have placed Spain in my hands." He did not even control Madrid.

Throughout Europe, significant doubts reverberated among leftist intellectuals about the alleged treason of the executed Bolshevik revolutionaries, but in Republic Spain, the POUM's *La Batalla* was almost the only newspaper to detail, let alone condemn, the Moscow showcase trial, labeling the Soviet Union a "bureaucratic regime of poisonous dictatorship." Tit for tat, the lead editorial in the September 1936 issue of *The Communist International,* issued in multiple European languages, condemned the POUM as fascist agents masquerading as leftists, with ties to Trotsky, Kamenev, Zinoviev, Franco, Mussolini, Hitler.[184]

Yezhov was bombarding Stalin with reports of secret police deficiencies and forwarded a denunciation of Yagoda by a provincial NKVD chief.[185] Stalin summoned Yezhov to the Black Sea.[186] Yagoda evidently knew, eavesdropping on Stalin's calls to Yezhov in Moscow.[187] Yefim Yevdokimov, whose bailiwick included Sochi, was also likely pouring poison into Stalin's ear about the detested Yagoda.[188] Suddenly, on the evening of September 25, 1936, Stalin sent a bombshell phonegram from Sochi to Kaganovich and Molotov, in Moscow, urging Yagoda's removal. The message was cosigned by Andrei Zhdanov, the dictator's new favorite, ten years younger than Kirov (and eighteen younger than Stalin), who was with him at the dacha. "Yagoda clearly turned out to be not up to the task of unmasking the Trotskyite-Zinovievite bloc," the secret message read. "The OGPU was four years late in this process."[189] "Four years" harked back to the meetings among a few party opposition members damning Stalin's rule, as a result of the catastrophe of collectivization and famine. Among the potential candidates to head the NKVD were the experienced Chekists Yevdokimov and Balytsky, who at one time had risen to number three in the secret police, before Yagoda squeezed him out of Moscow and sent him back to Ukraine. Yet another option was Lavrenti Beria, the (nominally) former Chekist running the South Caucasus party machine.[190] But Stalin picked his party-apparatus protégé Yezhov.

On the afternoon of September 26, Stalin and Voroshilov spoke on the phone to discuss military shipments to Spain; they noted that no Soviet trademarks should be discernible on the tanks.[191] Stalin also directed Voroshilov to read out the Sochi phonegram about Yagoda's dismissal to Yagoda at a Council of People's Commissars meeting. The commander of the Moscow military district and other officers accompanied Yagoda to Lubyanka to turn over his portfolio.[192] That day, Stalin dictated a second note for Yagoda, which the bodyguard Vlasik read to him over the phone, informing him of his transfer to the commissariat of communications: "It is a defense-oriented commissariat. I have no doubt you will be able to put this commissariat back on its feet. I urge you to agree"—as if Yagoda could decline.[193] The symbolism was ominous: Yagoda would be replacing Rykov, the disgraced rightist with whom his own name had been linked. Yagoda evidently hurtled to Sochi, where Pauker, the NKVD bodyguard directorate head, blocked his suddenly former boss from Stalin's compound.[194] Meanwhile, on September 27, Yagoda's photograph as the new people's commissar for communications appeared alongside Yezhov's in all the newspapers.

Yagoda would spend the next two months on sick leave; he did not make a run for it or try to organize an "accident" to eliminate Yezhov (let alone Stalin).

This was the first removal of an NKVD chief (Dzierżyński and Mężyński had died in office). "This wonderful, wise decision of our parent was ripe," Kaganovich wrote to Orjonikidze of the appointment of his former party underling. "Things will likely go well with Yezhov at the helm."[195] The middle and lower NKVD ranks also saluted the changeover, and not only from a careerist perspective: many perceived that Yezhov would restore Chekist professionalism (which speaks to their illusions). "The majority of old Chekists were convinced that with the coming to the NKVD of Yezhov we would at last return to the traditions of Dzierżyński, overcome the unhealthy atmosphere and the careerist, degenerating, and fabricating tendencies introduced in the organs during the last years of Yagoda," one operative recalled. "We thought that now the firm and reliable hand of the Central Committee would rein in the organs."[196] Yezhov moved into his new office at Lubyanka, 2, on September 29, 1936, and that very day Stalin approved a politburo resolution, drafted by his new NKVD chief, "On the Attitude Toward Counter-Revolutionary Trotskyite-Zinovievite Elements," which designated the latter as "foreign agents, spies, subversives, and wreckers on behalf of the foreign bourgeoisie in Europe."[197]

ARMING SPAIN, EYEING NAZI GERMANY

Soviet cargo traveled to Spain via the Black Sea, Bosporus, and Mediterranean, or, in a few instances, the Baltic and North seas, in disguised ships, with sailors wearing the tropical clothing of South Asia or the leisure wear of British cruise lines.[198] Spanish ports were blockaded, and ships were being attacked by the Nationalists; the undersized Soviet navy would be challenged.[199] Still, not a single ship with Soviet arms for Spain would be lost. On October 4, 1936, the first Soviet-supplied but not Soviet-manufactured war matériel secretly arrived at Cartagena: 150 light machine guns, 240 grenade throwers, 100,000 grenades, 20,000 rifles, 16.5 million bullets. Some of these arms turned out to be Great War relics. The rifles were from at least eight different countries of origin (Canada to Japan), of ten different types with six different calibers, making maintenance with spare parts difficult. Some of the best weaponry arrived in insufficient quantities (a mere six excellent Vickers light howitzers, with 6,000 shells). Still, overall the value for the weapons-starved Republic was substantial.[200] Three days later, the Soviet Union formally demanded an end to German, Italian, and Portuguese violations of the Non-Intervention Agreement or else the USSR would consider itself not bound by it.[201]

On October 11, Kaganovich sent Stalin a phonegram reminding him that "we have not communicated anything to Largo Caballero about our [weapons] shipments. We think we should have Gorev inform Largo Caballero officially, but conspiratorially, about the aid . . . that has already arrived, in detail, and when ships arrive in future." Stalin agreed.[202]

The next day, 50 Soviet-made light tanks and 51 "volunteer" tank specialists arrived at Cartagena—and the Spaniards raised their fists and shouted hurrah.[203] "It erupted to the point of mass hysteria from joy," wrote Gorev, the Soviet military attaché, in a report that reached Stalin via Voroshilov. "You needed to see it to feel it. Despite the fact that we were ready and are generally calm people, this affected even my subordinates. The euphoria was just exceptional."[204] The T-26B1 tanks, a heavier copy of the British Vickers six-ton model, updated with a Soviet turret and 45-millimeter dual-purpose gun, as well as the Polikarpov I-15 and I-16 aircraft, were of the highest international standards.[205] Three days later, fast Soviet Tupolev SB-2 bombers, which had only just gone into full production in early 1936 and were among the most powerful in their class in the world, arrived.[206] In the face of such hardware, it was easy to forget that the Soviet Union was in many ways still a poor country: as of October 1936, more than 33,000 young commanders beyond their tours of duty lacked apartments.[207]

The Soviets were keen to observe German and Italian weaponry in action, and to test their own in battle conditions. Nonetheless, Voroshilov would write privately to Stalin about the "pain" of parting with up-to-date Soviet aircraft, even at world market prices.[208]

The Spanish Republic had essentially no armaments industry, and even with Soviet production assistance it would need quite some time to produce its own tanks, armored vehicles, or planes.[209] Soviet advisers were especially aghast that anarchist-controlled factories produced not the most necessary military items but the most profitable.[210] A lack of Spanish government unity frustrated Soviets in-country. "There is no unified security service, since the [Republic] government does not consider this to be very moral," the NKVD liaison bureau in Spain reported (October 15, 1936). "Each [political] party has therefore created its own security apparatus. In the present government, there are many former policemen with pro-fascist sentiments. Our help is accepted politely, but the vital work that is necessary for the country's security is sabotaged."[211] Dimitrov and the Italian Communist Palmiro Togliatti were pushing for "an antifascist state" and a "new kind of democracy," which implied a pathway for transition to socialism in the Soviet sense.[212] But Stalin opposed even backdoor Sovietization.

In an open letter to Largo Caballero (also October 15) published in Soviet and Spanish newspapers, Stalin boasted of Soviet aid that "the workers of the USSR are doing no more than their duty in giving the help they are able to give to the Spanish revolutionary masses."[213] But he paid close attention to the economic costs. The Soviets had recently been informed about the Spanish gold. The Republic's finance minister, Juan Negrín, negotiated with Ambassador Rosenberg to hand off a large part of the gold reserves stashed in Cartagena for current and future payments. Rosenberg reported (October 15) that the matter had been agreed upon in principle.[214] In strictest secrecy, with Negrín on-site, the NKVD's English-speaking Orlov, posing as a representative of the U.S. Federal Reserve, oversaw the transfer from the caves, evidently enlisting the Soviet tankists who had arrived a few days earlier. On October 25, the same day Stalin was back in Moscow, they loaded 510 metric tons—around 7,800 crates, each weighing 145 pounds—collectively valued at $518 million, onto four ships bound for Odessa.[215]

Litvinov, for his part, lamented to Rosenberg that "the Spanish question has ruined our relations with England and France and sowed doubts in Bucharest and even Prague."[216] But Stalin would not be cowed: on October 23, the Soviet Union—without relinquishing membership in the Non-Intervention Committee—announced that because of others' violations, it was not bound by the Non-Intervention Agreement.[217] The French were incredulous. "Stalin has no ideals," complained the secretary general of the French foreign ministry to the British.[218] For Stalin, of course, everything was the other way around: the inactions of France and Britain, in the face of blatant Italian fascist and Nazi German violations, had soured *him* on the Western powers.[219]

That October of 1936, the German ambassador, Schulenburg, returned from summer leave—and encountered extraordinary warmth, from the Soviet border to the capital, "as if nothing whatsoever had happened." He informed Berlin that Krestinsky was "extremely friendly and did not refer to events at Nuremberg at all."[220] Stalin's shopping list for Germany included armored plating, aircraft catapults, underwater listening devices, and warships (costing 200 million reichsmarks), for which the Soviets were offering to pay largely in manganese and chromium ores on the basis of world prices, according to a German memo

(October 19).[221] On October 20, Hitler bestowed plenipotentiary powers on Hermann Göring to implement the Four-Year Plan by prioritizing weapons production, tightening state controls on exports, and achieving self-sufficiency in essential raw materials, all to reduce imports (costing scarce hard currency) and the impact of a possible blockade. Soviet trade officials were hopeful, as Göring appeared poised to assume a direct role in bilateral trade.[222]

HAPPY BIRTHDAY, SERGO

Orjonikidze's poor health was deteriorating further, and his autumn rest away from Moscow was proving relentlessly stressful, thanks to Stalin. Whereas a mere 11 of the 823 highest officials of the heavy industry commissariat who belonged to the *nomenklatura* (those officials who could not be removed without Central Committtee approval) had been fired during the party card verification campaign of spring–summer 1936—with just 9 of them suffering arrest—during the last four months of 1936, 44 senior officials would be fired, 37 of whom would lose their party cards and, with three exceptions, be arrested.[223] In October 1936, Stalin had Orjonikidze's elder brother Papuliya arrested, a first for a relative of a sitting politburo member. Orjonikidze demanded to see his brother, but Lavrenti Beria, the policeman turned party boss in Georgia, where Papuliya worked, said he could allow that only after concluding the investigation.[224] Orjonikidze understood that it was not Beria but Stalin who was behind the incarceration.[225] On October 8, Stalin had Kaganovich's deputy Yakov Livshits removed as deputy commissar of railways and, six days later, arrested.[226]

On October 24, the country effusively celebrated "Comrade Sergo's" fiftieth birthday in a Union-wide extravaganza. But the industry commissar did not attend the gala, staged near his holiday dacha in Kislovodsk. (His wife went on his behalf.)[227] Stalin ordered the arrests of Orjonikidze's former Caucasus associates Stepan Vardanyan, now party boss in Taganrog and the former leader of reconquered Bolshevik Georgia, and Levan Gogoberidze, party secretary at a factory in the Azov–Black Sea territory and a former party boss of Georgia.[228] Happy birthday, Sergo.

How far Stalin would go remained to be seen. On October 25—after two and a half months away—he returned to Moscow to discover an inquiry from the Associated Press in Moscow about rumors that he was ill or perhaps dead. Normally very touchy about discussions of his health, that very day he responded playfully.

"As far as I know from the foreign press, I long ago left this sinful world and moved on to the next," Stalin wrote to the correspondent. "As it is impossible not to trust the foreign press, if one does not want to be crossed out of the list of civilized people, I ask you to believe this report and not to disturb my peace in the silence of that other world." The delighted AP man dispatched a telegram to the United States on October 26, to the effect that "Stalin refused to deny the rumors of his death."[229]

The bulk of Spain's gold, reaching Odessa by November 2, went by train to Moscow, accompanied by Orlov's cousin, Ukraine NKVD operative Zinovy Katznelson. Another $155 million (some 2,000 crates) was shipped to Marseilles, as an advance for weapons the Spaniards hoped to purchase from France. A small remainder was taken to a cave in southern Spain. Some of the lot that arrived in the USSR was evidently deposited in the finance commissariat's precious metal vaults on Nastasinsky Lane on November 6, 1936, in time for Revolution Day.[230] Orlov, having accompanied the shipment to Soviet shores, was back in Spain already and, on November 7, celebrated the Bolshevik anniversary in the company of, among others, Koltsov and Gorev, in the latter's suite at Madrid's Palace Hotel.[231] In parallel, Trotsky had ordered his son in Paris to transfer his archives to the International Institute of Social History, on Rue Michelet in Amsterdam, headed by the Menshevik émigré Boris Nicolaevsky, but Zborowski tipped off the Soviets, and a few days later, on the night of November 6–7, the papers were stolen (cash was left untouched)—another Revolution Day gift for Stalin.

On November 6, Stalin took in the customary Revolution Day performance at the Bolshoi in the imperial box, and the next day he presided over the parade atop the Mausoleum. Bukharin, with his lover, the twenty-three-year-old Anna Larina, was living in Stalin's old Kremlin apartment, where Nadya had killed herself. He possessed a gun—given to him by Voroshilov, with the ironic inscription TO THE LEADER OF THE GREAT PROLETARIAN REVOLUTION—but did not attempt suicide. He was still listed on the masthead of *Izvestiya* as editor, so he received a pass to the Revolution Day celebration, in his case for the lowest level of the reviewing stand. Stalin caught sight of him and sent a guard to invite him and Larina up to the Mausoleum, a gesture for all to see—and misread as reconciliation. Not long thereafter, another story has it, Bukharin was being served with an eviction notice for the Kremlin apartment when, suddenly, the apartment's special Kremlin line rang: it was Stalin, just inquiring how things were going. Bukharin informed him of the eviction, and Stalin appeared to react angrily; the eviction was halted. Stalin was torturing him psychologically.[232]

Orjonikidze had returned to Moscow for Revolution Day, but on November 9 he would suffer a heart attack and lose consciousness for a time. Stalin responded by intensifying the pressure, driving a public trial of "Trotskyite" saboteurs for a mine explosion in Siberia, which would be afforded expansive press coverage and directly contravene Orjonikidze's stance on the causes behind industrial mishaps. Treason was made to appear ubiquitous. On November 5, Malenkov had reported to Stalin that 62 former "Trotskyites" had been found to be working in the central army apparatus and military academies. Ten days later, Gamarnik, head of the army's political administration, and deputy defense commissar, received a list of 92 "Trotskyites" in the Red Army. Altogether, 212 "Trotskyites" were arrested in the military between August and December 1936, but that included just 32 officers, very few of whom were ranked as a major or higher. Despite party pressure and the flow of denunciations, the command staff, concerned with destabilization, exhibited caution.[233]

NO PASARÁN!

Molotov and other speakers on Revolution Day had blustered about standing up to bullies and how, when confronted, the fascists would desist from further expansionism. But Hitler, after having decided, on emotional grounds, to assist Franco, had quickly imposed limits on his own. He had supplied some 100 planes (fighters, bombers) and nearly 6,500 well-equipped military personnel, the so-called Condor Legion, but he refused the massive troop commitments that Mussolini had made, instead allowing the Nazi intervention to become utterly subordinated to the German war economy. Germany found a place to sell its products and, thanks to monopoly positions with the putschists, obtained desperately needed raw materials and goods (iron ore, pyrites, copper, wolfram, foodstuffs) without having to sacrifice dwindling foreign exchange.[234]

On November 8, 1936, Franco's troops began their assault on Madrid from the south. He had put off the offensive, while working to make himself *caudillo,* a kind of Spanish equivalent of Führer or duce. The delay had allowed the Soviet military adviser Gorev to organize defenses. That day, the first troops of the International Brigades arrived in Madrid. But German and Italian planes had been bombing Spain for a hundred days and, with the Madrid front close to breaking, the Republic government had hastily fled for safety to Valencia. The capital, however, was to be defended. Banners were hung: NO PASARÁN ("They shall not pass"), a

Spanish translation of the French slogan of Pétain at Verdun in 1916. Mola's army, meanwhile, had begun to converge on Madrid from the northwest. Back in October 1936, when asked on the radio which of his four columns would take the capital, he had replied, "The fifth column." Mola meant that sympathizers to the Nationalists would subvert the Republic from within.[235]

Fear of such subversion had occurred naturally to Soviet personnel.[236] Koltsov had recorded in his diary (November 4–6, 1936) worries about "8,000 fascists who are locked up in several prisons around Madrid," although the Spanish Republic's interior minister seemed unconcerned and evacuated himself.[237] The logistics of evacuating several thousand prisoners were daunting. Inmates were tied together without their possessions and loaded onto transport—but then, down the road, forced off the buses, verbally abused, and executed by squads of Communists, anarchists, and regular-army men; villagers were press-ganged to dig mass-grave ditches. The executions, in fits and starts over several weeks, killed more than 2,000 prisoners from Madrid jails, without trial, in the worst of the many massacres in the Republic's zone perpetrated by leading Spanish Communists and their Soviet advisers, Gorev, Orlov, and Koltsov.[238] How many of these prisoners were Nationalist sympathizers prepared to take up arms if somehow given them will never be known. In the event, no fifth column materialized, but Mola's attempted witticism became immortal.[239]

Madrid came under withering assault for ten days as shrapnel and incendiary shells exploded in its plazas. But Soviet planes had broken the Nationalists' monopoly of the skies: there was no more bombing of Madrid from low altitude with impunity.[240] The Italian Fiat CR-32 and the German Heinkel He-51 proved no match for the more maneuverable I-15 and I-16, while the Soviet SB bomber outperformed the famed Junkers Ju 52. Soviet pilots demonstrated stamina and courage (while gaining invaluable experience: they had had little flight time in training back home). No less crucially, Soviet-led mechanized units, using the T-26, rendered any attempted advance by the Nationalists costly. Soviet tank men would suffer high casualties in Spain: thirty-four killed and nineteen missing in action, casualties of one in seven.[241] On November 18, Germany and Italy formally recognized Franco's Nationalist government, but five days later Franco called off his direct assault on Madrid.[242] Morale shifted. "We are finished," a Nationalist officer told a German military observer. "We cannot stand at any point if the Reds are capable of undertaking counterattacks."[243] In fact, the Republic's side was too depleted to mount what might have been the decisive counteroffensive.

However much he was motivated by his Trotsky fixation, the high-quality Soviet hardware Stalin sold to Spain showed a desire to strut his stuff.[244] In preventing Franco's seizure of Madrid, the Red Army had indeed demonstrated its mettle for all the world's skeptics. The French took notice of Soviet aircraft performance in Madrid's defense; the British, of the overall Soviet effort. "The Soviet government has saved the government in Madrid which everyone expected to collapse," concluded the undersecretary of state at the foreign office. "The Soviet intervention has indeed completely changed the situation."[245] The Soviet mood was ebullient. "And today," crowed Koltsov on November 25, 1936, "Franco did not enter the capital."

SOCIALIST "DEMOCRACY"

That same day, an Eighth Extraordinary Congress of Soviets, attended by 2,016 voting delegates (409 female), opened in the Grand Kremlin Palace in Moscow. Stalin's lengthy oration—broadcast live on Soviet radio for the first time, revealing his soft Georgian accent to millions—concerned a draft text of a new constitution, motivated, he argued, by changes in social structure.[246] He had started thinking about a new constitution no later than summer 1934. (On holiday then, he had requested a copy of the current 1924 constitution.)[247] He had had a commission approved, which he chaired and which studied foreign constitutions.[248] "Behind the Kremlin walls, work is going on to replace the Soviet constitution with a new one, which, according to the declarations of Stalin, Molotov, and others, will be the 'most democratic in the world,'" Trotsky had written in May 1936, adding that "no one is acquainted with the draft of the constitution as yet."[249] But in June 1936, Stalin had had the draft published for months of public commentary. Soviet propaganda delivered saturation coverage, and claimed that by fall 1936 half a million meetings had been held, encompassing 51 million people.

The new constitution ended legal discrimination against "former people" (kulaks, priests), to considerable complaint from the party rank and file.[250] It altered the electoral system for soviets from indirect to direct, from restricted to universal suffrage (returning the vote to former kulaks), and from open to secret balloting.[251] Most remarkable, it enumerated a plethora of individual and social rights (pensions, free medical care, education).[252] The Menshevik émigré press acknowledged that the terroristic Communist dictatorship was not going to self-liquidate, but nonetheless speculated that the constitution might unleash new political forces.[253]

Soviet officials worked to orchestrate the public discussions, but some people seized the moment. Collective farmers expressed hatred of the in-kind system of remuneration according to days worked and demanded to be paid in cash, like urban workers. One proposed that instead of the slogan "He who does not work does not eat," they substitute "He who works should eat."[254] A student at a medical school in Zaporozhie (Ukraine) was reported to have said, "In the USSR we have no democracy and will not have it; everything is done and will be done as Stalin dictates. We will be given neither freedom of the press nor freedom of speech." After his arrest, some fellow students tried to pass a letter to him in prison praising his courage.[255] The constitution's article on freedom of religion sparked petitions from Orthodox believers to reopen churches. Wishful misunderstandings abounded: that the constitution was reintroducing private property, that kulaks would be allowed to return to their villages, that farmers would "live as before," that Stalin might abolish the party, because he could not trust it, and institute presidential rule, which would provoke even more political terror (along the lines of Kirov's murder).[256]

The draft text omitted the category "the proletariat" in favor of "the people," which Trotsky disparaged as additional evidence of a retreat from socialism and consolidation of a new ruling class of functionaries (concealed in the term "intelligentsia").[257] "In a private conversation Stalin admitted that we did not have a dictatorship of the proletariat," Molotov would later recall. "He told me that personally, but not firmly."[258] Stalin's Eighth Congress speech was categorical, however. "In 1917, the peoples of the USSR overthrew the bourgeoisie and established a dictatorship of the proletariat, established Soviet power," he explained. "That is a fact, not a promise. Then the Soviet government eliminated the landlord class and transferred more than 150 million hectares of former landlord, state, and monastery lands to the peasants, and that was in addition to those lands already in peasant hands. That is a fact, not a promise. Then the Soviet government expropriated the capitalist class, took away their banks, factories, railroads, and other means of production, declared them socialist property, and put at the head of these enterprises the best members of the working class. That is a fact, not a promise." He added that industrialization and collectivization further transformed the social structure, giving the USSR two nonantagonistic classes (workers and peasants) and one stratum (the intelligentsia). This was the first fully authoritative analysis of Soviet society in class terms.

The constitution aspired to reinforce socialist legality—rule by law—a triumph for USSR procurator general Vyshinsky. It also further centralized the state machinery (this was largely omitted in public discussions). Successive drafts had stipulated that the USSR government would exercise jurisdiction over land, water, and natural resources, while decisions of the USSR Council of People's Commissars would be binding on the republics. The constitution replaced the periodic Congress of Soviets with a permanent USSR Supreme Soviet, to which all republic laws were to be subordinated. (Criminal codes remained the prerogative of republics.) Physically, the Russian Soviet Federated Socialist Republic was significantly shrunk as two of its autonomous ethnic republics became full-fledged Union republics—Kazakhstan and Kyrgyzstan—while a third (Karakalpak) was transferred to the Uzbek republic. This brought the number of Central Asian Union republics to five. Also, the South Caucasus Federation was dissolved in favor of the self-standing republics of Georgia, Armenia, and Azerbaijan, bringing the total number of Union republics to eleven. For the first time, a Soviet constitution also enshrined the Communist party as "the vanguard of the working people in their struggle to strengthen and develop the socialist system," and as "the leading core of all organizations of the working people, both public and state." This appeared not in the section on the state but the one on "public organizations."

In his speech, Stalin aimed to rebut criticisms in the "bourgeois" press, broadcasting damning views otherwise unavailable to the Soviet populace. Fascist critics, he revealed, dismissed the Soviet constitution as "an empty promise, calculated to pull off a well-known maneuver and deceive people." Stalin further revealed that "bourgeois" critics on the left were asserting a Soviet shift to the right, away from a dictatorship of the proletariat and toward the same camp as bourgeois countries. He countered that there had been not a shift but a "transformation . . . into a more flexible, . . . more powerful system of leadership of the state by society." Above all, Stalin said, "bourgeois" critics "talk about democracy. But what is democracy? Democracy in capitalist countries, where there are antagonistic classes, is, in the final analysis, democracy for the strong, democracy for the propertied minority. Democracy in the USSR, by contrast, is democracy for the toilers, that is, democracy for all." Thus, he concluded, "the USSR constitution is the only thoroughly democratic constitution in the world."[259]

Stalin's entrance to Catherine the Great's triangular Imperial Senate.

Inner sanctum:
Stalin's Kremlin office
(the "Little Corner"),
a photo taken by James
Abbé, April 13, 1932,
to counteract rumors
of the dictator's ill
health spread by foreign
intelligence services.

Happy times (left to right): Kirov, Kaganovich, Orjonikidze, Stalin, and Mikoyan on the Kremlin grounds in 1932 at the height of the Soviet famine.

In search of food: starvation in the Kazakh autonomous republic (Pavlodar province).

Н. С. Аллилуева-Сталина в гробу.

Nadya Alliluyeva, Stalin's second wife, November 1932. From the photo album of her father, Sergei (which would be confiscated after his arrest and placed in Stalin's archive).

Stalin and Co.: Lavrenti Beria holds Svetlana; Nestor Lakoba wears a bulky hearing aid. This is the first southern holiday without Nadya. Sochi, 1933.

Vasily and his widowed father with Nikolai Vlasik, bodyguard and photographer. Evidently Svetlana took this photo. Sochi, summer 1933.

Svetlana, Sergei Kirov, and Stalin. Sochi, summer 1934.

The 17th Party Congress—"Congress of Victors"—in the newly combined
Andreyev-Alexandrov hall. Grand Kremlin Palace, January–February 1934.

Boris Pasternak
(left) and the painter
Pavel Malkov,
First Congress
of the Union of
Soviet Writers,
August 29, 1934.

The Writers' Congress keynote speech was given by Maxim Gorky, whom Stalin had coaxed back from exile and pampered. Gorky helped the dictator conscript the artistic intelligentsia into state service.

Seducing the European cultural set: Nobel Laureate Romain Rolland (to Stalin's right) and Maria Kudryashova, Rolland's wife-translator; Stalin; and Soviet cultural minder Alexander Arosyev. Little Corner, June 28, 1935.

Stalin's cultural dilemmas: Demyan Bedny, a celebrated but mediocre proletarian poet loyal to the cause.

Mikhail Bulgakov, a suspected White Guardist, but supremely talented.

Mass entertainment: Grigory Alexandrov (center), acclaimed director of the hit musicals *Jolly Fellows* (1934), *Circus* (1936), and *Volga-Volga* (1938). Stalin supported musicals against ideological attack.

Leonid Utyosov (left) and his phenomenally popular jazz band.

Dmitri Shostakovich, composer.
Stalin's tastes in classical music ran
to the traditional, which caught out
Shostakovich, but more so-called former
people (of the old regime) survived in
music than in any other artistic pursuit,
partly because of Stalin's indulgence.

Ivan Kozlovsky, lyric tenor,
one of Stalin's favorites, 1933.

Fallen friend: Kirov's bier, flanked by Stalin and Kaganovich. Moscow, December 4, 1934.

Above: Leonid Nikolayev, terrorist.

Right: Filipp Medved, helping
to supervise construction of the
White Sea–Baltic canal, a Gulag
project, after which he was posted
to the Leningrad NKVD, making
him responsible for Kirov's security.

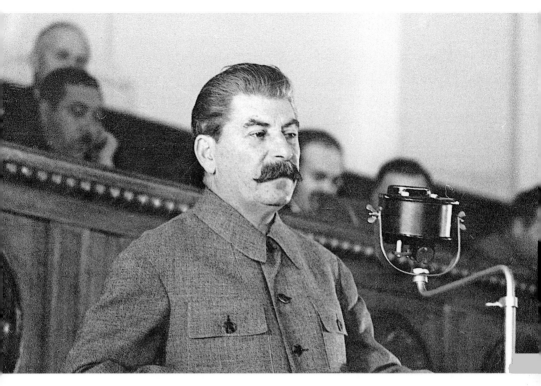

Candid images were not permitted for public reproduction: including Stalin in profile, his Georgian features manifest, Second all-Union Congress of Collective Farm Shock Workers, February, 1935.

Three marshals (left to right): Yegorov, Voroshilov, and Tukhachevsky,
with Stalin and Lakoba (far right) on holiday. Abkhazia, mid-1930s.

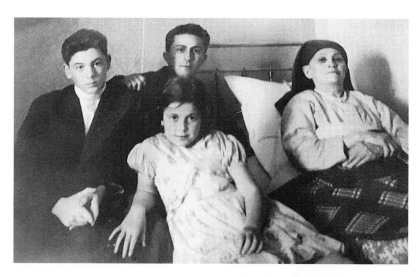

Vasily, Yakov, and Svetlana, with Stalin's mother,
an ill Keke Geladze, on her metal bed. Tiflis, June 1935.

The first meeting with a high Western official: Anthony Eden (left foreground), accompanied by British ambassador Viscount Chilston (right), all looking toward the British photographer. (Background) Ivan Maisky, Soviet ambassador to the Court of St. James's, is to the left of Molotov. Molotov's office, March 29, 1935.

A new Stalin favorite: Moscow party boss Nikita Khrushchev (in front of Stalin and in summer whites with a white worker's cap), flanked by Yagoda (left) and Andrei Andreyev (center, with black cap), on the Lenin Mausoleum, July 10, 1935.

Stalin and his indispensable servitors: Molotov and Alexander
Poskryobyshev (center), head of the secret department, January 1936.

Molotov presiding over the Council of People's Commissars, the cabinet-style government,
on the third floor of the Imperial Senate, in front of the door to the deceased Lenin's preserved office.

Man of the imperial borderlands, with Lazar Kaganovich (tucking his ear). Stalin celebrated the Russian nation's civilizing mission, ending Lenin's warnings about great Russian chauvinism. Kremlin reception for collective farmers from Tajikistan and Turkmenistan. Imperial Senate, December 4, 1935.

Matinee idol: Stalin at a gathering of wives of officials.
Grand Kremlin Palace, May 1936. Stalin kept few mistresses.

Long March: Chinese Communists find refuge from Chiang Kai-shek's encirclement campaigns in remote Shaanxi province, 1935. Right to left: Mao Zedong, Zhu De, Zhou Enlai, and Qin Bangxian (known as Bo Gu).

Putsch in Spain: General Francisco Franco trailed by General Emilio Mola (in glasses), August 19, 1936. Neither in China nor in Spain would Stalin instigate or countenance a Communist takeover.

EVERYTHING UNRAVELS

On the morning of the Congress's launch, *Pravda* had proclaimed Stalin the "genius of the new world, the wisest man of the epoch, the great leader of Communism," and then deemed his constitution speech a breakthrough for all humanity. While Stalin's report to the 16th Party Congress (1930) had been published in 11 million copies (twenty-four languages) and the one to the 17th Congress (1934) in 14 million copies (fifty languages), his Congress of Soviets speech was printed in 20 million copies. "No book in the world," *Pravda* added, "has ever been published in that kind of print run."[260]

In Berlin, on the very same day Stalin delivered his spirited constitution speech, Joachim von Ribbentrop, German ambassador to the UK but also minister plenipotentiary, formally signed an Anti-Comintern Pact with Japanese ambassador Kintomo Mushanokōji. The signing took place not in the foreign ministry but in the Büro Ribbentrop, to stress the pact's ideological salience.[261] Ribbentrop read a statement to the press (the eyewitness William Shirer called it a "harangue") declaring Germany and Japan "unwilling to tolerate any longer the machinations of the Communist agitators," and their pact "a turning point in the struggle of all law-abiding and civilized nations against the forces of disintegration."[262]

For Japan, keen to contain the Soviet Union while obtaining a free hand in China, this was its first major accord with a European power since abrogation of the Anglo-Japanese alliance, in 1920. Indeed, given the infighting, poor communications, deception, and jurisdictional ambiguity inside the Japanese government, the agreement constituted a mini miracle. Japanese newspapers conveyed a lack of enthusiasism ("making lukewarm friends at the expense of red-hot enemies," wrote *Nichi Nichi*).[263] Above all, Japan's army had zealously sought firm military commitments against the USSR, but had gotten only "consultations." Still, it did forge an intelligence liaison with the German staff, focused on the Red Army.[264]

Hitler relished the propaganda breakthrough, and hoped it would bring along Britain. According to Count Ciano, who had gone on his first official visit to Germany in October 1936, Hitler told him, "If England sees the gradual formation of a group of Powers which are willing to make common front with Germany and Italy under the banner of anti-Bolshevism, if England has the feeling that we have a common organized force in the Far East . . . , not only will she refrain from fighting against us, but she will seek means of agreement and common ground with this new political system."[265] For Stalin, the irony of such a pact was extreme, given how he had bridled the Comintern in both Spain and China.[266]

Stalin knew beforehand. Colonel Eugen Ott, the German military attaché in Tokyo, had learned in spring 1936, from his Japanese army contacts, of the secret negotiations under way in Berlin. Ott confided in Richard Sorge, the Soviet military intelligence spy in the German embassy in Tokyo, who had informed Moscow. The published text consisted of two short articles.[267] But Sorge had been reporting that it contained a secret article. Wrongly, he initially thought this pertained to a military alliance. But he would manage to photograph the full text and get it to Shanghai, whence it was picked up by a Soviet courier.[268] The secret section specified that, should either Germany or Japan "become the object of an unprovoked attack by the USSR," each "obliges itself to take no measures that would tend to ease the situation in the USSR." Most significantly, the secret clause also enjoined the two powers "to conclude no political treaties with the USSR contrary to the spirit of this agreement without mutual consent."[269]

Soviet-German relations sank to a nadir. Stalin had ordered arrest sweeps of German nationals in the USSR in November and seems to have contemplated a separate Moscow trial of some of them. Molotov, on November 29, told the delegates to the Congress of Soviets, "We have no feelings for the great German people other than friendship and genuine respect, but the gentlemen fascists would best be included in that nation, or 'nation,' or 'higher order,' which is called the 'nation' of modern cannibals."[270]

Goebbels, the day before Molotov's address, had crowed to a secret gathering of the Nazi press that Nazism and Bolshevism could never coexist: one must perish.[271] "There is no going back," he confided in his diary (December 1), apropos of Hitler's thinking. "He outlines the tactics of the Reds. Spain is elevated to a global question. France the next victim. Blum a convinced agent of the Soviets. Zionist and world destroyer. Whoever is victorious in Spain secures the prestige for himself. . . . The authoritarian states (Poland, Austria, Yugoslavia, Hungary) are not secure. The only committed anti-Bolshevik states are Germany, Italy, Japan. Therefore, agreements with them. England will come over when the crisis breaks out in France. Not a love match with Poland but a reasonable relationship."[272]

The British foreign office produced an internal memorandum in late November on the expropriation and collectivization of British firms in the Spanish Republic, concluding that it "shows quite clearly that the alternative to Franco is Communism tempered by anarchy; and . . . [it is] further believed that if this last regime is triumphant in Spain it will spread to other countries, notably France."[273]

Blum's Popular Front government, for its part, was engaged in heated internal debate about the future of the Franco-Soviet alliance, and Potyomkin, the Soviet envoy, cautioned patience to the foreign affairs commissariat. But Stalin's spies had supplied him with General Schweisguth's memorandum denigrating the Red Army. "On the basis of very reliable information in our possession, I have to inform you for your guidance that the French military authorities are vehemently opposed to a Franco-Soviet [military] pact and speak openly about it," Litvinov had written to Potyomkin. "We in no way want to speed up negotiations, nor do we wish them to suspect that we are backing away."[274] An unsigned editorial—written by Molotov—in *Izvestiya* condemned the Anti-Comintern Pact and defiantly noted, "We must believe exclusively in our own strength."[275]

ENIGMATIC PLENUM

In the face of the German-Japanese Anti-Comintern Pact, as well as the British and French efforts at accommodating Hitler, Mussolini, and now possibly Franco, on December 4, Stalin convoked a Central Committee plenum. It was, however, devoted not to the deepening challenges of foreign policy—something he almost never allowed to be discussed by the country's nominal policy-making body—but to virulent charges of treason. The day before, Yezhov had delivered a lengthy address to a conference of NKVD operatives in the capital, itself a telling assembly, and noted ominously, "I think we have not investigated the military Trotskyite line to the fullest. . . . You well know the efforts of imperialist intelligence HQ to create agent networks in our army. . . . We are uncovering diversionary-wrecking organizations in industry. What grounds are there to believe that it is impossible to carry out diversionary acts in the army? There are more opportunities, not fewer, here than in industry."[276]

Stalin assigned the main plenum report ("On Trotskyite and Rightist Anti-Soviet Organizations") to Yezhov, and during his excoriation of the Zinovievites and Trotskyites, someone interjected, "What about Bukharin?" Yezhov took up the prompt, which in turn almost immediately provoked Stalin to interrupt, "We need to talk about them [the rightists]." Beria interjected, "There's a scoundrel for you!" Stalin, in the July 29, 1936, secret circular, had denied any positive political program to the Trotskyites, but now he asserted that the leftist Trotskyites shared the rightists' "program" of capitalist restoration.[277] Bukharin plaintively asked how he could defend himself against such slanderers. "Do you really believe I could have anything in common with these subversives, with these saboteurs, with these scum, after thirty years in the party?" he exclaimed at Stalin. "This is nothing but madness." When Bukharin pointed out that he physically could not have been at the alleged meetings with the Zinovievites and Trotskyites, Molotov countered, "You are acting like a lawyer."[278]

When Yezhov referred to a transport official as "an enemy," Stalin interrupted to specify that the accused was "a German spy—he in fact got money for information from German intelligence—he was a spy." Addressing Bukharin, Stalin ridiculed suicide as opposition blackmail. "Here is one of the easiest means by which, right before death, leaving this world, one can spit in the face of the party, deceive the people, one last time," Stalin stated, mentioning Tomsky.[279] Another was the thirty-two-year-old apparatchik Veniamin Furer, who had committed suicide at a dacha in Osinki, outside Moscow, in fall 1936 after his friend Yakov Livshits—Kaganovich's top deputy at the railroad commissariat—had been arrested as a "Trotskyite." Furer, the rising star who had delivered a stirring ode to the Stalinist leadership style at the 17th Party Congress, left behind a long letter praising the Soviet leader while defending Livshits, who, like Furer, had briefly sided with Trotsky in 1923. Because Stalin was on holiday in Sochi, the letter had been brought to Kaganovich. "He walked up and down and then began to sob" out loud, Nikita Khrushchev, another Kaganovich protégé, would recall. "He was unable to collect himself for a long time after he read it." Kaganovich ordered the letter circulated to all politburo members. Now, at the plenum, Stalin cruelly mocked Kaganovich. "What a letter he left behind," he noted of Furer. "You read it and tears well up in your eyes."[280]

Also on December 4, 1936, in a memo circulated to all politburo members, Stalin dressed down Orjonikidze for having hidden long-ago correspondence with Beso Lominadze, who had been pronounced a posthumous enemy after committing suicide, while party boss, in Magnitogorsk the year before. The accusation of having concealed information from "the Central Committee" was one of Stalin's most threatening. What also rankled was that Lominadze's suicide note had been read over the telephone to Orjonikidze by Lominadze's deputy in Magnitogorsk, and that Orjonikidze was providing a pension to Lominadze's widow and money to their son (named Sergo, in Orjonikidze's honor). Stalin had reports that Orjonikidze was bad-mouthing him behind his back to his cronies Mamiya Orakhelashvili and Shalva Eliava.[281] At the plenum, Orjonikidze joined in the vicious attacks against Bukharin.

On the evening of December 5, the Congress of Soviets concluded by adopting the new constitution unanimously. The next day was devoted to a mass celebration of the adoption on Red Square. On December 7, the plenum resumed. Despite the venom, it ended without expulsions, let alone arrests. Stalin proposed "considering the matter of Bukharin and Rykov unfinished" and postponing a decision until the next plenum.[282] Adding to the mystery, this plenum, uniquely for the 1930s, went unmentioned in the press. That same press took to slandering Bukharin and Rykov still more ferociously. Especially noteworthy was that much of the bile flowed in *Izvestiya,* where Bukharin remained listed as editor. "My morale," Bukharin wrote in a letter (December 15), "is in such a state that I am half-alive."[283]

KIDNAP

Stalin judged that a Communist takeover in China would never produce a regime strong enough to hold off the Japanese military. After the Chinese comrades formed revolutionary soviets, against Moscow's advice, he had Dimitrov insist on "soviets—only in the cities, but not as organs of power, rather of organization of the masses. Without confiscations."[284] But the "united front" resembled a sandcastle on the beach. The Nationalists were not interested, either.[285] A Japanese envoy arrived on a warship at Nanking, the Nationalist capital, and demanded that China grant Japan the right to place troops anywhere in China to fight Communists. Chiang Kai-shek refused to conduct negotiations himself over the request, and the envoy's talks with Chiang's foreign minister went nowhere. (Chiang insisted that Japan respect China's administrative integrity in northern China, which Japan continued to violate.) But rumors of a possible Chinese entry into the Anti-Comintern Pact had alarmed Stalin. Chiang was also pressing his campaign to eradicate the Chinese Communist base in Shaanxi, while demanding, in negotiations with them in Shanghai, that they bring their Red Army strictly under his Nanking government.[286]

Events on the ground, however, had their own dynamic—and their import potentially exceeded that of Spain, for Stalin and for the world.

The warlord Zhang Xueliang, known as the Young Marshal, had traveled to Italy, then Germany, courting Mussolini, then Hitler and Göring, for help against Japan. In France he had met Litvinov, asking to be received by Stalin in Moscow;

Stalin declined, concerned about not complicating his relations with Japan.[287] Zhang had returned to China and eventually entered into negotiations with the Chinese Communists; one of his interlocutors was Zhou Enlai, who got the Young Marshal not only to cease operations against the Chinese Communists but to supply them with weapons. The Communists contemplated trying to secretly admit Zhang to the party.[288] In November 1936, Zhang wrote to Chiang Kai-shek, imploring him to pursue a united front with the Communists against Japan in earnest. In December, Zhang traveled to Nanking in person to report about the mutinous moods of his troops in Shaanxi, who were supposed to pursue the Communists, and renewed his pleading. Chiang told him, according to Zhang, that if the government pulled back from fighting the Chinese Communists to take on Japan, the Communists would eventually win hold of the nation.[289]

Chiang ordered Zhang to intensify the "bandit suppression" campaign to finish off the Communists.[290] But Zhang urged Chiang to go to Xi'an and talk to the Shaanxi and Manchurian soldiers. Chiang's entourage warned against such a trip, but exposure to danger had typically enhanced Chiang's stature, and he agreed to go. Back in Xi'an, Zhang reported on the conversation, in general terms, by radiogram to Mao, whose "party center" was holed up in dank caves (one bodyguard was stung by a scorpion).[291] Chiang flew off to Xi'an with an extra guard detail and contingent of officers, moving into a hot-springs resort, a small walled enclave ten miles outside the district town of Lintong. In an ancient one-story pavilion once used by the Tang emperor Xuanzong, Chiang received delegations of the Shaanxi and Northeast (Manchurian) armies.[292] At dawn on December 12, his scheduled day of departure, a 200-man contingent of Zhang's personal guard stormed the walled compound. A gun battle killed many of Chiang's bodyguards. He heard the shots, was told the attackers wore fur caps (the headgear of the Manchurian troops), crawled out a window, scaled the compound's high wall, and ran along a dry moat up a barren hill, accompanied by one bodyguard and one aide. He slipped and fell, losing his false teeth and injuring his back, and sought refuge in a cave on the snow-covered mountain. The next morning, the leader of China—shivering, toothless, barefoot, a robe over his nightshirt—was captured.

Whether Zhang acted on his own or in a conspiracy with the Communists remains uncertain. He was an opium-addled playboy—one mistress was Mussolini's daughter—but also an anti-Japanese patriot. Perhaps in his earnestness for a united front he had gotten caught up in the intrigues of Zhou and Mao. The wily Chiang, for his part, had been negotiating in bad faith with Zhou Enlai (Chiang's former political commissar at the Soviet-financed 1920s Whampoa Military Academy).[293] News of Chiang's pending arrest—or admonishment—in Xi'an had reached Mao's makeshift headquarters via the dilapidated village of Bao'an in the early-morning hours of December 12. His secretary passed him the radiogram. "After reading it, [he] joyfully exclaimed, 'How about that! Time for bed. Tomorrow there will be good news!'"[294]

Chiang, upon being taken into custody, was speechless. (He has himself telling his captors, "I am the Generalissimo. Kill me, but do not subject me to indignities.")[295] Zhang's head bodyguard carried Chiang to a car and set off for a government office in Xi'an. Zhang, standing at attention, addressed him as commander in chief. "I wish to lay my views before your excellency, the generalissimo," Zhang said to his captive, pleading with him to work with the Communists in a patriotic coalition. Zhang had aides draft formal proposals for a united "National Salvation" government, an immediate end to the civil war, and a release and pardon of all political prisoners. He also requested that the Chinese Communists receive an invitation to send a delegation to Xi'an.[296] Chiang repeatedly denounced him as a rebel. "Your bad temper," Zhang replied, "is always the cause of trouble."[297]

Chiang's surprise capture would seem to have offered Moscow a chance to discredit him as incompetent in the anti-Japanese crusade and to exact revenge. After all, this was the same Chiang who had humiliated Stalin with a massacre of Chinese Communists in 1927 and, subsequently, had nearly destroyed the Chinese Red Army in a series of ruthless encirclement campaigns. Word reached Moscow that same day of December 13. "Optimistic, favorable assessment regarding Zhang Xueliang," crowed the normally restrained Dimitrov, in his diary.[298] Dimitrov's Chinese assistant in the Comintern recalled that "you could not find anyone" who did not feel "Chiang must be finished off." Manuilsky, he added, "rubbed his hands, embraced me, and exclaimed, 'Our dear friend has been caught, aha!'"[299] That same day, Mao was even more gleeful. "Chiang has owed us a blood debt as high as a mountain," he was quoted as exclaiming at a meeting in his cave. "Now it is time to liquidate the blood debt. Chiang must be brought to Bao'an for a public trial."[300] Mao sent congratulations to Zhang, whom he called China's "national leader in resisting Japan."[301]

Stalin, to a considerable extent, held the fate of China and, indeed, Asia in his hands.

CHINA IN THE BALANCE

Dimitrov, on December 14, 1936, held a meeting of Comintern hierarchs, after which he wrote to Stalin that the Chinese Communists had become close to Zhang, despite Comintern warnings about his unreliability, and that "it was hard to imagine Zhang Xueliang would have undertaken his adventurist action without coordination with them."[302] Around midnight, Stalin phoned him: "Are these events in China occurring with your authorization? This is the greatest service to Japan anyone could possibly render. Who is this Wang Ming of yours? A provocateur? He wanted to file a telegram to have Chiang Kai-shek killed." (Wang Ming, born Chen Shaoyu in 1904, headed the Chinese Comintern delegation in Moscow.) When Dimitrov claimed innocence, Stalin stated, "I'll find you that telegram."[303] (There was likely no such telegram: Stalin was misinformed or trying to scare Dimitrov into pulling back.) Later still, Molotov phoned the Comintern head: "Come to Comrade Stalin's office tomorrow at 3:30; we'll discuss Ch[inese] affairs. Only you and Man[uilsky], nobody else!"[304] *Pravda* (December 14) and *Izvestiya* (December 15) condemned Chiang's kidnapping as playing into Japanese hands.

The Comintern officials were received on December 16, at 7:20 p.m., for fifty minutes.[305] Dimitrov and Manuilsky, along with Molotov, Kaganovich, Voroshilov, Orjonikidze, and Stalin, hammered out a telegram for the Chinese Communists that condemned Zhang's move, "whatever his intentions," as inciting Japanese aggression and a united imperialist bloc against China, and ordered the Chinese Communists to stand "decisively for a peaceful resolution of the conflict," while enjoining the Nationalists to cease their attempted destruction of the Chinese Red Army and to unite for the struggle against Japanese imperialism. This was precisely Zhang's position (which went unmentioned).[306] In Xi'an on December 16, Zhang addressed the public in the central square, explaining that he had served, and would continue to serve, under Chiang, but that the generalissimo must engage the struggle against the Japanese. "Chiang thinks that he is the government," Zhang stated. "Since he refuses to turn the guns against the enemy, and turns them against us, I had no alternative but to . . . arrest him."[307] The Nationalist executive committee and political council in Nanking, meanwhile, directed its Central Army toward Xi'an.[308]

Had Stalin been driven predominantly by vengeance, he would have ordered Chiang killed (or just let it happen). But Stalin acted from his sense of strategy. The same applied to his domestic terror.

Before being dismissed from Stalin's office, Dimitrov was privy to a denunciation of Blum ("a charlatan. He's no Largo Caballero") and a discussion of the NKVD's interrogation of Sokolnikov: "The investigation concludes that Trotsky abroad and the center of the bloc within the USSR entered into negotiations with the Hitlerite and Japanese governments . . . first, to provoke a war by Germany and Japan against the USSR; second, to promote the defeat of the USSR in that war and to take advantage of that defeat to achieve the transfer of power in the USSR to their government bloc; third, on behalf of the future bloc government, to guarantee territorial and economic concessions to the Hitlerite and Japanese governments." Sokolnikov had joined the party in 1905, at age seventeen, been with Lenin on the sealed train in April 1917, signed the Brest-Litovsk Treaty, which had ended up saving the fledgling regime in 1918, led the civil war reconquest of Turkestan in 1920, masterminded the NEP stabilization as finance commissar, and served as an effective ambassador to Britain. But it turned out he had *all along* been working to overthrow Soviet power. Sokolnikov was said to have confessed.[309]

Two days later, Dimitrov received the prominent German Jewish antifascist novelist Jacob Arje (b. 1884), known as Lion Feuchtwanger, and his common-law wife, Maria Osten (Gresshöner). "It is incomprehensible why the accused are admitting everything, knowing it will cost them their lives," Feuchtwanger pointed out, regarding the trial of Zinoviev, Kamenev, and others. "It is incomprehensible why, apart from the confessions of the accused, no sort of evidence has been produced." Feuchtwanger, a Soviet sympathizer, added that "the records of the trial" were "full of contradictions, unconvincing. The trial is conducted monstrously."[310]

Dimitrov's radiogram for the Chinese comrades arrived in Bao'an village on December 17 or 18. (Part of it had failed to transmit; Mao would read the full text only on December 20.) "Mao Zedong flew into a rage when the order came from Moscow to release Chiang" rather than to stage a trial and execution, wrote the youthful Communist sympathizer Edgar Snow, claiming to have heard from an eyewitness (the widow of Sun Yat-sen). "Mao swore and stamped his feet."[311] Mao, on December 19, said to an assembly of the Chinese politburo, "The Japanese say that the arrest [of Chiang] was arranged by the Soviet Union, while the Soviet Union says that it was contrived by the Japanese."[312] That day, the Chinese Communists issued a statement that Zhang and his men "had acted on the basis of patriotic motives, honestly and with sincere zealotry for the fate of the nation."[313] Mao detested Chiang and any appearance of buckling under to Moscow, but

Zhou, after trekking by donkey to see Mao, flew to Xi'an on a Zhang-supplied plane and ordered him not to harm Chiang, citing Stalin's direct orders. Zhang was to release him after somehow extracting a promise of a renewed united front.[314] Of course, this had been Zhang's plan all along.

"KAUTSKY"

Stalin and Britain effectively shared the same goal in the Far East—prevention of a Japanese conquest of China—but British-Soviet negotiations between May and December 1936, on London's initiative, for a bilateral pact on naval limitations failed. Britain continued to want to get other runners in the naval arms race to run more slowly, for a time, so that it could cross the finish line first. But the Soviets, like Nazi Germany, did not really want limitations. Even more, Moscow sought the most advanced British naval technology and technical assistance as part of its program to build an oceangoing fleet.[315] Cooperation, not just on the sea, proved elusive, even though Stalin, the world leader of Communism, paradoxically was serving as Britain's main bulwark against the spread of Communism: he was trying to force the Chinese Communists to help free Chiang and resume the coalition with the Nationalists against Japan, and having the Comintern direct the Spanish Communists to remain under the wing of the Popular Front government against Franco.

At the same time, Stalin ordered the Comintern to have the Spanish Communists intensify the "complete and final annihilation" of the Spanish "Trotskyites" as "agents of fascism."[316] Spain's Communists, with the collusion of the anarchists, forced the POUM leader, Andreu Nin, out of the Catalan regional government.[317] (The next month, Spain's Communists would set upon the anarchists, too, arresting or assassinating their leaders.) Koltsov's reportage in *Pravda* continued to fixate not on Franco but on the POUM, noting (December 17, 1936) that "the purge of the Trotskyite and anarcho-syndicalist elements" in Spain "will be carried out with the same energy as in the USSR."[318] Koltsov soon infiltrated the POUM to write a hatchet piece; in an especially piquant passage, he would assert that the POUM newspaper (*La Batalla*) had "found its sole object of hatred and daily attack . . . not General Franco, not General Mola, not Italian and German fascism, but the Soviet Union." Koltsov also wrote how Trotsky was supposedly giving directives to the POUM and how the POUM "had restructured in the usual

Trotskyite fashion" in order to engage in "terrorism" ("provocations, raids, and murders"). He accused the POUM "Trotskyites" of attracting only riffraff and scum.[319]

Tens of thousands of workers and people's militias who were sacrificing their lives to save the Republic were cowards and fascist hirelings.

That December of 1936, Stalin again suffered from a high temperature, as well as tonsillitis. It had been a while since he had countenanced medical observation. His staff summoned Dr. Ivan Valedinsky to the Near Dacha. Valedinsky, who had not seen Stalin since 1931, brought a heart specialist, Vladimir Vinogradov, and a throat infection specialist, Boris Preobrazhensky. They diagnosed a re-emergence of follicular angina from arteriosclerosis. The elevated temperature lasted five days.[320] But Stalin hosted a Kremlin reception for top NKVD opera-tives on December 20, 1936, the nineteenth anniversary of the founding of the Cheka, and that same day attended a congress of wives of Red Army command-ers in the Grand Kremlin Palace. On December 21, he celebrated his official fifty-seventh birthday with his inner circle, the military brass, and relatives, but without his children. "A mass of guests," Maria Svanidze wrote in her diary, "all dressed up, noisy, lively, dancing to the radio, went home toward 7:00 a.m."[321]

The dictator had managed some official business that day. In a letter to Prime Minister Largo Caballero, dated December 21, Stalin, Molotov, and Voroshilov reiterated that they wanted to "prevent the enemies of Spain from regarding it as a Communist Republic" and offered political advice, as if to a pupil ("Pay atten-tion to the peasants" and "Draw the petite and middle urban bourgeoisie onto the side of the government"). "It is quite possible," the message noted, "that in Spain, the parliamentary road will prove more appropriate toward revolutionary devel-opment than was the case in Russia."[322] The message dripped with Marxist revi-sionism. Consider that an evolutionary path somehow bringing about socialism was precisely what the Italian Comintern official Palmiro Togliatti believed in— and he was referred to in Soviet ciphered telegrams as "Kautsky," the German Social Democrat whom Lenin had denounced.[323]

WHAT MIGHT HAVE BEEN

Hermann Göring had invited Surits to his home on Leipziger Platz, according to the Soviet envoy, and on December 14, 1936, he delivered a monologue about

Germany's Four-Year Plan and how bilateral economic relations "should be built without regard to the state of our political relations," that is, "apoliticized." Göring allowed that some items on the list submitted by Kandelaki could be purchased, but most could have been expected only to elicit a negative response: no state could sell such top-secret objects to another. Surits protested. Göring mollified him, citing Bismarck regarding the need for strong ties between Germany and Russia.[324] Ten days later, Kandelaki and a colleague met fruitlessly with Schacht (whose star had waned with Göring's rise over the economy). To the now perpetual Soviet inquiries about a political rapprochement, Schacht retorted that it would be possible if the Soviets ended their "encirclement" of Germany by quitting Spain, France (in the guise of the Popular Front), and Czechoslovakia (the mutual assistance pact). Kandelaki returned to Moscow for consultations. The Soviet hopes incited by Göring's elevation to plenipotentiary looked illusory.

Mongolia served as Stalin's other linchpin in Soviet eastern defense, alongside China, and on December 23, 1936, he received yet another delegation from the livestock-herding nation, led by the new prime minister, Anandyn Amar, in Molotov's office. "In olden times the Mongols beat the Chinese," Stalin said. "Defending themselves against you, they built the Great Chinese Wall." Amar: "All the territory up to the Great Chinese Wall belonged to us, Mongols." Voroshilov (smiling): "You have imperialist aims."[325] The Soviets would have to spend still more money to shore up its feeble satellite.

In China, Zhou Enlai, aware of the Communists' utter dependence on the Soviet Union for weapons and supplies, was shrewd enough to follow Stalin's orders, not Mao's. Zhou also enjoyed unusual sway with Zhang, who listened to few others. Chiang, however, refused to negotiate his release by agreeing to a renewed united front. British and U.S. military attachés who went to Xi'an encouraged Chiang to draw out the standoff, and he gave hints that he might order resumption of his encirclement campaign. But the generalissimo finally relented. One source of pressure was his wayward son, Chiang Ching-kuo, who had denounced his father as an enemy and, with his Russian wife, was studying in the Soviet Union—that is, he was in Stalin's hands. A telegram was sent to the Chinese Communists stressing that in talks with Chiang the possible return of his son should be mentioned. On December 25 morning, Chiang belatedly received Zhou, who saluted his former commander, a sign of Communist obedience, and, on verbal promises of a renewed united front, agreed to his release.[326] As Chiang prepared to depart

Xi'an, at 2:00 p.m. on December 26, a coolie appeared, carrying a suitcase, followed by a guilt-ridden Zhang, who announced that he was surrendering and wanted to accompany Chiang and his entourage back to Nanking. Chiang appears to have pardoned him.[327] They took off in Zhang's Boeing, Chiang sitting in the copilot's seat.

Chiang had been right about the upside of his risky visit to Xi'an: throngs cheered his return to the Nanking capital that December 26. (Two months later, Chiang would compare his ordeal at Xi'an with the crucifixion of Jesus Christ.)[328] His inner circle now urged him to go on the offensive and wipe out the Communists once and for all.[329] The three Communist armies in the northern Shaanxi region totaled perhaps 50,000 troops, of whom fewer than 30,000 possessed weapons, and they had no air force. Chiang's armies numbered more than 2 million, of whom 300,000 had been trained by the Germans (many carried German-made weapons), with 314 fighter planes and 600 pilots. His political authority was also colossal. But the generalissimo's proven ability for treachery yielded before his recognition of China's need for foreign assistance, and he honored the promise he made to Zhou and Zhang to carry out Stalin's united front policy. Chiang assigned specific territory to the Communists and funded their separate administration and army, controlled by Mao. Stalin held Chiang's son to ensure the promises were kept.[330]

Had Chiang been killed, Chinese accommodation with Japan, at Soviet expense, was a likely outcome. With Chiang's death, the top Nationalist officials Wang Jingwei, who strenuously opposed cooperation with the USSR, and He Yingqin, China's war minister, a graduate of the Japanese Military Academy and one of the key architects of the civil war against the Communists, could have established a new government to cooperate with Japan. (Zhang Qun, the foreign minister in Chiang's government, had also been educated in Japan.) This could have resulted in a Japanese thrust northward, into Soviet territory, instead of southward in Asia—and therefore no Pearl Harbor or war with the United States.[331]

Conversely, had Chiang not gone to Xi'an and been kidnapped and ultimately released, he would likely have crushed the Chinese Communists and killed or chased Mao out to Mongolia or Siberia, without forfeiting Stalin's military aid. In the event, not only Chiang but also the Chinese Communists survived, even thrived, becoming more associated publicly with the national anti-Japanese struggle. These would prove to be momentous developments.

"POPPYCOCK"

On December 30, 1936, Stalin sent Bukharin a New Year's "gift": a packet of others' "testimony" incriminating him in foul deeds.[332] Stalin also held a banquet for his physicians and, amid toasts to Soviet medicine, suddenly announced that there were enemies among the doctors. Molotov stood and thanked the physician-professors for helping to make Stalin better while attributing his recovery to the dictator's robust constitution. After dinner, Stalin brought in a Radiola for dancing.[333] Meanwhile, the January 1937 editorial of *The Communist International,* written in Stalin's signature style of questions and answers, pointedly noted that "the Spanish Trotskyites conduct themselves like the advanced guard of the notorious 'fifth column' of Franco insurgents. Is it possible to support the heroic struggle of the Spanish popular masses without fighting against the traitorous Trotskyite band? No, it is impossible."[334] *La Batalla,* the POUM's organ, responded that "Stalin is destroying, without looking back, everything that opposes him. . . . Stalin maintains his incontestable power with terror."[335]

Stalin also managed to flush Trotsky out of Norway. As a condition of his asylum, Trotsky was under a gag order. But while he had been away from Oslo for that fishing holiday, the house where he lived had been set upon by fascist thugs led by Major Vidkun Quisling, and in Moscow Trotsky was being convicted in absentia of political terror. He now acceded to the insistent requests for interviews. "Trotsky declares that the Moscow charges are invented and fabricated," the headlines screamed in the Norwegian press. Litvinov demanded that Norway rescind Trotsky's asylum; the Soviets hinted that they would cease importing Norwegian herring. The Norwegian Labor government caved, placing Trotsky under house arrest. The government in Mexico offered him asylum, and he arrived there by ship on January 9, 1937. Trotsky was given use of a villa known as the Blue House, designed by the painter Diego Rivera as an inspirational refuge amid wildflowers and squawking parrots.[336] The quasimodernist, quasirustic compound, tended by servants, was located on Avenida Londres in the Mexico City suburb of Coyoacán.[337] Here, the NKVD's efforts to assassinate Trotsky resumed.

On January 8, Stalin had received Lion Feuchtwanger in the Little Corner. The dictator used these conversations with foreign sympathizers as mental calisthenics.[338] The German writer opened with a question about the glaring absence of criticism of the regime by Soviet intellectuals. Stalin did not deny it. "Up to 1933, few writers believed the peasant question could be solved on the basis of collective farms," he said. "There is no more of that criticism. Facts persuade. The wager of Soviet power on collectivization was won. . . . The problem of the mutual relations between the working class and the peasantry was the most important and has furnished the most worries to revolutionaries in all countries. The problem looked insoluble: the peasantry, reactionary, linked with private property, dragged backwards; the working class went forward. This contradiction undermined revolutions more than once. That's how the revolution in France [Paris Commune] perished in 1871."[339]

Feuchtwanger, telling Stalin he came across as modest, inquired of the adulation, "Is this not an extra burden on you?" Stalin: "I am in complete agreement with you. It's unpleasant when they exaggerate to hyperbolic scale." Attributing great strides to one individual, he explained, "is, of course, wrong—what can one person do?—[but] they see in me a unifying concept, and create foolish raptures around me." Beyond the masses, Stalin explained in this unscripted moment that Soviet functionaries "are afraid if they do not have a bust of Stalin, then either the newspaper or their superior will curse them, or a visitor will take notice. This is careerism, a form of bureaucrat 'self-defense': in order not to be touched, they must install a bust of Stalin. Every party that is victorious attracts alien elements, careerists. They try to defend themselves by mimicry: they install busts, they write slogans in which they do not believe."[340]

The conversation turned to the public trial of "Trotskyites," and Stalin tried to convey that domestic oppositionists and foreign imperialist powers had to be working together: after all, they wanted the same outcome. "They are for the USSR's defeat in war against Hitler and the Japanese," he said, promising that a pending new trial would reveal how oppositionists were connected to the Gestapo and negotiating with Hess, the deputy Führer. "For the power they would obtain in the downfall of the USSR in a war," he averred, the opposition had planned to "make concessions to capitalism: concede territory to Germany (Ukraine or a part thereof), to Japan (the Soviet Far East or a part thereof); open a wide path for German capital in the European part of the USSR, for Japanese capital in the Asian part . . . disband the greater part of the collective farms and allow 'private initiative,' as they express it, [and] reduce the state control over industry."

Feuchtwanger inquired whether the Soviet Union would publish the additional trial materials besides the confessions. Stalin: "What materials?" Feuchtwanger: "The results of the preliminary investigation. Everything that proves their guilt aside from confessions." Stalin: "Kirov was killed; this is a fact. Zinoviev, Kamenev, Trotsky were not there. But people implicated them for the crime, as inspirers of it. All of them are experienced conspirators—Trotsky, Zinoviev, Kamenev, and others. They do not leave behind such documents. When people caught them out in the confrontations [with witnesses], they had to admit their guilt." Stalin continued: "They say that people testify because they are promised their freedom. This is nonsense. These are all experienced people; they fully understand what it means to testify against oneself." At the same time, Stalin circumscribed the danger, noting that of the approximately 17,000 party members who had voted for the opposition platform in 1927, "there were 8,000 to 10,000 of them left."[341]

Stalin, under questioning, justified the new constitution's emphasis on democracy. "We do not just have democracy carried over from bourgeois countries," he told Feuchtwanger. "We have an unusual democracy, we have an addition: the word 'socialist' democracy." Stalin allowed that capitalism's lesser form of democracy was more progressive than fascism, and that the global popular front against fascism "is a struggle for democracy."[342] Still, he went on to note that in October 1917, many people in Russia had been afraid of the pending seizure of power, in 1918 of the Brest-Litovsk peace, in 1928–32 of collectivization, and now they were scared of fascism. "Fascism," Stalin stated, "is poppycock. It is a temporary phenomenon."[343]

NOISY NEW TRIAL

Determinations of who was an "enemy" were being made locally. Officials strained to protect their own people, while still demonstrating zeal. But Stalin began to go after provincial party bosses who had never been in any opposition. On January 2, 1937, Sheboldayev, party boss of the Azov–Black Sea region, was dismissed amid accusations of "Trotskyite wreckers in the party organization." On January 13, the Kiev provincial party committee was deemed "littered with an exceedingly great number of Trotskyites," and three days later Postyshev was replaced as Kiev province secretary by Sergei Kudryavtsev, while the Kharkov provincial party boss was replaced by Nikolai Gikalo. Both would press the destruction of sitting party officials.[344] Meanwhile, Stalin had Bukharin summoned to a confrontation with Radek and Pyatakov, who were delivered from prison. Bukharin told his wife that Radek had denounced him as a spy and terrorist with whom he had plotted Stalin's murder, and that Pyatakov resembled a "skeleton with its teeth knocked out."[345]

Also on January 13, Mao moved from his hideout in the caves near Bao'an back to the town of Yan'an (pop. 3,000), the now legally acknowledged Red capital, where, in a mountain valley surrounded by fortress walls and towers, the Communists occupied the former residences of landowners and merchants. In the Little Corner on January 19, two directives were finalized. One criticized the Chinese Communists for working to split the Nationalists. The second ordered them to reorganize governance in the areas under their control from "soviets" to a "national revolutionary" front of all "democratic" forces, renounce land confiscations, and "direct serious attention to the machinations of Trotskyite elements, who in Xi'an, as in all of China, try to undermine the cause of the united anti-Japanese front with their provocational activities and are servants of the Japanese aggressors."[346] Mao would slow-walk any second united front. The Comintern gave the Chinese Communists more than $800,000 and promised a similar sum to come.[347]

On January 23, 1937, a second trial in Moscow of a parallel "Anti-Soviet Trotskyite Center" opened, like the first, in the October Hall, after Stalin had hand-edited the charges.[348] Ten of the seventeen defendants worked in Orjoni-kidze's heavy industry commissariat.[349] "And here I stand before you in filth, crushed by my own crimes," Pyatakov publicly confessed, "bereft of everything through my own fault, a man who has lost his party, who has no friends, who has lost his family, who has lost his very self." Yezhov had personally forced his erstwhile drinking buddy, in thirty-three days of torture, to capitulate to accusations of Trotskyism and plotting with Germany.[350] (Yezhov was finally named to the highest rank, "general commissar of state security.")[351] Radek, in court, delivered a tour de force fabricated history of Trotskyism. His "features," an American correspondent observed, "seemed curiously out of focus, his teeth charred and uneven, his eyes very much alive behind thick glasses."[352] Soviet newspapers and radio afforded wire-to-wire coverage, accompanied by orchestrated meetings at factories and farms. "Why such a great fuss over the trial?" Feuchtwanger would ask Dimitrov. "Incomprehensible. An atmosphere has been created of extreme unrest among the population, mutual suspicion, denunciations, and so forth. Trotskyism has been killed—why such a campaign?"[353]

Feuchtwanger found the allegations preposterous. And yet the oppositionists *had* organized a conspiratorial meeting, in summer 1932, at Zinoviev's dacha, where expelled party members of the Leningrad opposition had discussed reviving their old links to Trotsky. A message from Trotsky to join forces *had* been carried into the Soviet Union. Stalin was also correct that the NKVD (then the

OGPU) had missed these contacts, which was evidently part of the basis for his statement, in the September 1936 dismissal of Yagoda, that the NKVD was four years behind.[354] Of course, this was a pathetic "bloc" incapable of consequential action (Smirnov, a supposed organizer of the conspiracy to murder Kirov in 1934, had been in prison since 1933).[355] But the meeting was not an invention. The "terror" charges, too, contained the minutest kernel of truth. After a decree had rescinded Trotsky's Soviet citizenship, he had written a spirited open letter to the central executive committee of the Soviet (which had nominal jurisdiction over citizenship) asserting that "Stalin has led us to a cul-de-sac. . . . It is necessary, at last, to carry out Lenin's last insistent advice: *remove Stalin.*"[356] Trotsky had not written "remove by assassination," but how else could it be done?[357]

In the middle of the trial, on January 26, Shumyatsky showed Stalin and the inner circle a special newsreel of the dictator's speech on the new constitution at the recent Eighth all-Union Extraordinary Congress of Soviets. The film depicted the Spassky Tower with its clock, the Grand Kremlin Palace interior, the congress delegates, Stalin's appearance and the resulting ovation with shouts of hurrah, and then his entire speech, accompanied by documentary footage of Soviet achievements—factories, collective farms, the military, culture. This was the first time Stalin had been filmed in sound. "After it ended they applauded for a long time," Shumyatsky noted. "I[osif] V[issarionovich] said: 'It turned out to be good stuff, and you know, I had wanted to burn the negative when you previewed the fragments.'"[358]

Stalin was also reading the screenplay for *A Great Citizen,* by Friedrich Ermler (in collaboration with Manuel Bolshintsov and Mikhail Bleiman), based on the life and assassination of Kirov, who in the film was known as Pyotr Shakhov, the party secretary of an unspecified region. Stalin (January 27, 1937) praised the screenplay to Shumyatsky—"it is politically literate, no question. The literary achievements are also indisputable"—but wanted changes, complaining that the party opposition seemed to have a longer party membership than the members of the Central Committee ("reality gives the opposite picture"). Stalin also wrote that "references to Stalin must be eliminated" in favor of "the Central Committee." The film's assassin (Bryantsev) was depicted as a former Trotskyite who, after the defeat of the opposition, wormed his way into the position of director of the Museum of the Revolution. Stalin proposed that the suspense be shifted from Shakhov's assassination to the larger forces behind it, instructing that "the struggle between the Trotskyites and the Soviet government should not resemble a struggle between two coteries for power, one of which 'got lucky' in the fight, the other 'did not,'" but a struggle between two programs: the socialist program, supported by the people, versus a Trotskyite program "for the restoration of capitalism in the USSR," at the behest of fascism that was "repudiated by the people."[359] He further demanded that the murder scene itself be excised (Ermler would instead shoot a dark corridor, with the sound of the gun going off).[360]

On January 28, 1937, Dimitrov had sent yet another telegram to Mao, reporting on the new trial in Moscow and concluding, "We await information on your concrete measures in the struggle against Trotskyites."[361] On the evening of the 29th, Orjonikidze visited his former first deputy Pyatakov in prison for the last time and observed his utterly smashed face. Several hours later, at 3:00 a.m. on the 30th, Vasily Ulrich read out the prearranged verdict at the trial: thirteen death sentences, including Pyatakov; four others convicted but not to be executed, including Radek (ten years of penal labor).[362] The party machine turned out a crowd on Red Square, reported at 200,000, in temperatures of 16 degrees below zero (27 below Celsius), for speeches by Khrushchev and Shvernik. The masses carried banners demanding immediate executions, which had already been implemented.[363]

In Berlin on the 29th, Kandelaki had passed to Schacht a proposal in Litvinov's name for political negotiations between diplomatic representatives, agreeing to treat them "as confidential and not to divulge anything, . . . if this is what the German government demands."[364] But Hitler's speeches more and more resembled declarations of war. "Any further treaty connections with the present Bolshevist Russia would be completely worthless for us," he told the Reichstag on the fourth anniversary of his chancellorship, on January 30. "It is out of the question that National Socialist Germany could ever be bound to protect Bolshevism or that we, on our side, could ever agree to accept the assistance of a Bolshevist state. For I fear that the moment any nation agreed to accept such assistance, it would thereby seal its own doom."

SOME ANALYSTS HAVE SPECULATED that Stalin used Spain in a war of wills with Hitler and Mussolini, a dramatic idea not supported by any evidence.[365] Others have asserted that, despite the long distance and difficult logistics, Stalin aimed to create a Communist regime on the Iberian Peninsula, precisely the opposite of what abundant evidence proves.[366] Still others have concluded that he pursued a Republic victory—which, for a time, he did.[367] His predicament was bizarre. *He* was the one who had saved the "bourgeois" democrat Chiang Kai-shek from execution by Chinese Communists and was defending "bourgeois" democracy in Spain against fascist aggression *and* Communist subversion. Working to prevent a Franco triumph put Stalin at loggerheads not only with Nazi Germany and fascist Italy, but also France and Britain. The Soviet dictator appears not to have been the least anxious about keeping in good standing with the latter, to maintain the declared policy of "collective security." But there are indications he suspected that the momentum of aggressive right-wing regimes in Europe would tempt Britain and France, under the influence of their own right-wing circles, into a self-protective international coalition with "fascism," at Soviet expense.[368]

The British had signed a declaration with Italy pledging to "respect the status quo on the Mediterranean" (which further complicated already difficult Soviet shipments to Republic Spain).[369] "He who sups with the devil," *Izvestiya* had huffed at Britain's accommodation of the Italian fascists, "should have a long spoon" (January 5, 1937).[370] What is more, Stalin learned—from intercepted and decoded U.S. State Department communications—that Britain was preparing to demand from the Soviet Union the creation of a classical liberal-conservative, rather than Republican-socialist, government in Spain, and, "if Moscow refuses, then cut a deal with Germany and Italy." That ultimatum never came, but Britain was seeking accommodation with Germany over Spain.[371] France also stepped up its efforts to overcome mutual hostility with Germany. The fear that the bourgeois-democratic capitalists (Britain, France) were keen to align with the fascist-capitalists (Germany, Italy, and a Francoist Spain) haunted Stalin.

His determination to counter the perceived danger of a Trotskyite beachhead on Spanish Republic territory, as well as Trotsky's relentless barrage of writings about the betrayal of the revolution, cannot be separated from these geopolitical concerns. Indeed, Trotskyism for Stalin *was* a geopolitical concern.[372] Trotskyites in Spain were few, insignificant, and under venomous attack even from Trotsky. But Stalin had a darkly expansive view of threats.[373] Moreover, Trotsky, though a single person, reached a worldwide audience. At the same time, Stalin would not have been Stalin had he not also perceived a threat as a grand opportunity. He had no more instigated the kidnapping of Chiang in China than he had the putsch by Sanjurjo, Mola, and Franco in Spain, but he had turned both actions to his advantage. The apparent necessity of preventing Trotskyism in Spain would conveniently provide Stalin with vivid justification for his annihilation of "enemies" at home as well. He transformed his Spanish challenge into a domestic cudgel. The place of Trotsky inside Stalin's head was immense, and Trotsky was occupying a similar enormity in the consciousness of the entire country and, to some extent, Spain—both nemesis and ever-handy instrument. But it also began with Stalin's determination to smash his inner circle, his instinct to bully and humiliate turning ever more vicious.

CHAPTER 7

ENEMIES HUNTING ENEMIES

"I think, I think, and I can't understand anything. What is
happening?" Koltsov used to repeat, walking up and down
in his office. . . . "These are people we have known for
years, with whom we lived next door! . . . I feel I'm going
crazy. I'm a member of the editorial board of *Pravda,* a
well-known journalist . . . it would seem I should be able
to explain to others the sense of what is happening, the
reasons for so many unmaskings and arrests. But in fact,
I, like the last terrified philistine, know nothing,
understand nothing, I'm bewildered, wander in the dark."

BORIS YEFIMOV, *Soviet caricaturist, talking about his
brother Mikhail Koltsov*[1]

INTO 1937, the Soviet colossus would seem to have been at the height of its
power, helping to stave off Franco's seizure of Madrid with its military hardware
and know-how, but the USSR itself had fallen under grim siege. The NKVD was
suffering a massacre—and not *after* it had arrested at least 1.6 million people but
all the while it was doing so. Between late 1936 and late 1938, arrests of NKVD
personnel exceeded 20,000. The NKVD's Main Directorate of State Security
(GUGB), which directly perpetrated the wholesale bloodletting, was decimated:
around 2,300 of the 22,000 state security operatives were arrested—269 in the
center and 2,064 in locales—of whom the great bulk (1,862) were charged with
"counterrevolution."[2] All eighteen "commissars of state security" (the top ranks)
who served under Yagoda would be shot, with a single exception (who would be
poisoned). Stalin also decimated his top military commanders, while constantly
reminding the public that an attack on the Soviet Union was imminent, indeed
that a new imperialist war had already started over Spain.

Even following the executions of Kamenev, Zinoviev, Pyatakov, and others in
the two public trials of August 1936 and late January 1937, massacres of NKVD
state security and Red Army officers would come as a shock. One high official,

though, did sense what was about to unfold. On January 11, Artur Artuzov, a onetime Stalin favorite, was sacked as deputy head of military intelligence, having been the target of relentless intrigue by military men as a person from the civilian side. Artuzov was transferred back to the NKVD, to a low-level position in the archives department, where he did all he could to return himself to favor, writing an overview of Soviet counterintelligence, which he had founded, and begging for an audience with Yezhov. Failing that, he wrote to Yezhov on January 25 that NKVD foreign intelligence possessed information from foreign sources, dating back many years but never forwarded to higher-ups, revealing a "Trotskyite organization" in the Red Army. Sensationally, the documents linked Marshal Tukhachevsky to foreign powers.[3] Artuzov knew full well how such compromising materials had been planted in Europe in order to make their way back to Moscow: in the 1920s he had helped lead just such an operation ("The Trust").[4] Now, to these fabricated documents he appended a list of thirty-four "Trotskyites" in military intelligence. His cynical efforts at ingratiation and revenge would not save his own life, but Artuzov had guessed right about Stalin's intentions.[5]

Explanations for Stalin's rampage through his own officer corps have ranged from his unquenchable thirst for power to the existence of an actual conspiracy.[6] Nearly every dictator lusts for power, and in this case there was no military conspiracy. Nor were the massacres a response to a pressing new international crisis in 1937–38. Even the potential fall of the Republic forces in Spain posed no direct threat to the Soviet Union or Stalin's regime. Another interpretation asserts that he "misperceived" a threat of foreign infiltration into the Soviet officer corps, owing to the barrage of intelligence reports he received, and decided to root out what he wrongly concluded were foreign agents throughout the officer corps, and then, as denunciations arrived in a flood, the process "escaped" his control. But Stalin demanded those very intelligence reports that allegedly led to his "misperceptions," issuing specific instructions and questions to intelligence officials, who came to understand what he wanted.[7] A spiral of denunciations certainly took place; this again was something Stalin could have tamped down, but instead fomented at every turn.

A few scholars have argued that Stalin was "tricked" into executing his military men.[8] Reinhard Heydrich, of the Nazi Sicherheitsdienst (SD), would later boast of his clever work to decapitate the Red Army by manufacturing compromising materials, but such machinations, if they took place, were of no consequence.[9] Soviet secret agents were tasked with spreading rumors in Europe of a pending military coup in Moscow, which other Soviet representatives abroad picked up and reported back to Moscow.[10] Uritsky, chief of military intelligence (who had squeezed out Artuzov), informed Stalin and Voroshilov about chatter in German military circles in Berlin concerning political opposition among Red Army generals (which Uritsky discounted).[11] Paris may have been the liveliest echo chamber: Beria (for whom the city was a long-standing field of operations) sent a relative of his wife there to spread rumors among Georgian Menshevik émigré circles of a pending military coup in Moscow. This, or another channel, prompted French minister of war Édouard Daladier to convey official word to the Soviet ambassador, who in turn sent a coded telegram to Moscow about a plot "by German circles to promote a coup d'état in the Soviet Union with the assistance of persons from the command staff of the Red Army."[12] Stalin—as the wily but doomed Artuzov surmised—was engaged in the very activity of which he accused the top army commanders: collaborating with foreign enemies.[13] A "Tukhachevsky plot" did exist: Stalin's, to smear and execute him.

Top military officers of any regime, in a war, could fall into enemy captivity or even choose to collaborate with foreign occupiers, and while it seems doubtful that Tukhachevsky or Iona Yakir or Jeronimas Uborevičius, the three most authoritative commanders in the Red Army, would have agreed to serve as puppets installed by foreign powers to control conquered Soviet territory, *in theory* they were among the very few who could have. Preemption of a replacement government could have been part of Stalin's motivation in liquidating these men, but he went far, far beyond that aim: out of approximately 144,000 officers, some 33,000 were removed in 1937–38, and Stalin ordered or incited the irreversible arrest of around 9,500 and the execution of perhaps 7,000 of them.[14] Of the 767 most high-ranking commanders, at least 503—and by some accounts more than 600—were executed or imprisoned. And among the highest rungs of 186 commanders of divisions, the carnage took 154, as well as 8 of the 9 admirals, 13 of the army's 15 full generals, and 3 of its 5 marshals. What great power has ever executed 90 percent of its top military officers? What regime, in doing so, could expect to survive? An assault on such scale, and without regime collapse, could only happen within the structures of a one-party Leninist regime and, ultimately, the conspiratorial worldview and logic of Communism, a Manichean universe of two camps and pervasive enemies. The combination of Communist ways of thinking and political practice with Stalin's demonic mind and political skill allowed for astonishing bloodletting.

BEDFELLOWS AND STRANGERS

Stalin's attack on military and NKVD bigwigs consumed enormous time and energy but otherwise presented few difficulties for him. He could even make light of it all, as if peacocking his power, repeating such stories as the one about the professor who embarrassed an ignoramus Chekist for not knowing the author of *Yevgeny Onegin* (Alexander Pushkin, Russia's national poet). The Chekist arrested the professor, then bragged, "I got the professor to confess! He wrote it!"[15] During the week of February 10, 1937, the entire country commemorated the hundredth anniversary of the *death* of Pushkin. The poet underwent a metamorphosis from aristocratic serf owner who fathered a child by one serf and sold others to the army to a radical-democrat bard of the people. *Pravda* (February 10) declared that Pushkin was "entirely ours, entirely Soviet, insofar as it is Soviet power that has inherited all the best in our people." Altogether, 13.4 million copies of Pushkin's works were published in some form—said to be one of every five books in Soviet libraries.[16] Before the year was out, the bitter joke would make the rounds that if Pushkin had been born in the twentieth century rather than the nineteenth, he still would have died in the year '37.

That same month of February 1937, China's Nationalist ruling group balked at approving the united front to which Chiang had agreed, proposing accommodation with the Japanese and suppression of the Communists, but Chiang overrode them, reconfirming the significance of Stalin's refusal to allow him to be executed after he had been taken hostage. Chinese Communists, flush with foreign currency from both Nanking and Moscow, had purchased a fleet of American-made trucks, making them much more mobile, and did not take well to a renewed alliance with the generalissimo.[17] The party leadership tried to quell the sentiment with a confidential communiqué to the ranks promising that the united front against the Japanese would allow the Communists to expand their influence a thousand times. Chiang was shown a copy.[18] Here was an act of treason not invented by the NKVD.

China had been afforded none of the centrality in the Soviet public sphere that Spain had. Stalin's bold projection of Soviet military power onto the Iberian Peninsula, in the name of international worker solidarity, had struck a chord. "The only thing that existed for us that year was Spain, the fight with the fascists," Alexei Adzhubei, a schoolboy in 1937 (and the future son-in-law of Khrushchev), would recall. "Spanish caps—blue with red edging on the visor—then came into fashion, and also big berets, which we tilted at a rakish angle."[19] NKVD informants reported some bitter remarks ("One's children don't see chocolate and butter, and we are sending them to Spanish workers") but found real solidarity.[20] Inside Spain, however, Soviet advisers appear not to have understood, or to have been willing to admit, that the Francoists had support among broad swaths of the Spanish population who were Catholic and conservative. Instead, the deputy chief of Soviet military intelligence in Spain contrasted the "overwhelming majority of the Spanish people" ("the working masses") with the "German and Italian interventionists and the military-fascist clique of Franco."

Soviet class suspicions extended to Spanish military men fighting for the Republic. The same intelligence summary noted that, "up to now, officers and generals who are politically unreliable have had great influence in the bureaucracy of the war ministry and on the general staff and the staffs of the fronts. They are hindering and sabotaging measures for the organization and a more rational use of the Republic's armed forces."[21] Complementing these class-politics suspicions was the Soviets' low opinion of the Spaniards' know-how.[22] "In the Spanish army, the situation was so bad that our advisers were required to perform both organizational and operational combat tasks," recalled Kirill Meretskov, a top Soviet military official in-country.[23] Of course, Soviet advisers knew little of Spanish history, mentalities, or language. Nikolai Kuznetsov, the chief naval adviser, had spent his first week wandering Madrid on his own, attempting to pick up a few words of the language, while evaluating the Republic's military situation. Often, no interpreter was available, or only a terrible one. Officials in Moscow initially refused to accept "White Guard" émigré Russians who volunteered for the Republic. Even after Moscow relented, no more than one interpreter per ten Soviets was ever found.[24]

Ignorance was only part of the challenge. Antonov-Ovseyenko nearly provoked the resignation of the Spanish finance minister, Negrín, who accused the Soviet representative in Barcelona of being "more Catalan than the Catalans."[25] Many Soviet advisers were said to emulate feudal lords, keeping villas, Spanish wine caches, and concubines.[26] Ambassador Rosenberg projected imperiousness, being escorted everywhere by half a dozen bodyguards. "If he stepped into a *pissoir* on the Cuatro Caminos," observed Louis Fischer, the fellow-traveling American journalist, "they surrounded its tin walls and waited."[27] Rosenberg would visit Largo Caballero, with his sprawling entourage, and, like a proconsul, issue explicit instructions ("It would be expedient to dismiss X").[28] The politburo, by telephone poll, had approved a directive that Rosenberg not force this or that decision on the Spanish government ("An ambassador is not a commissar, but at most an adviser"), but it was too late.[29] "Out you go! Go out!" Largo Caballero finally had shouted at Rosenberg, during a meeting in January 1937, loud enough for all those outside to hear. "You must learn, Señor Ambassador, that the Spaniards may be poor and need aid from abroad, but we are sufficiently proud not to accept that a foreign ambassador should try and impose his will on the head of the Spanish government."[30]

While Soviet condescension collided with local pride in Spain, in Moscow the Spanish Republic failed to finance its embassy during its first year or to keep its representative informed, even though Stalin afforded the ambassador, Dr. Marcelino Pascua—a medical statistician who spoke Russian—unusual access (as well as a two-story mansion, featuring eight bedrooms, four baths, two kitchens, and two salons). By protocol, Stalin did not receive foreign envoys, but in the Little Corner on February 3, 1937, he, along with Molotov and Voroshilov, received Pascua, who was carrying a personal letter from Largo Caballero (dated January 12).[31] The Soviet trio warned the envoy that Spanish Republic codes were easy to break and urged him to use couriers instead of telegrams. (Eight months later, Voroshilov was still issuing the warning.) Pascua, for his part, indicated that Spain would like to sign a treaty of friendship. Stalin rebuffed him, disingenuously stating that "if Spain distanced itself somewhat from the USSR," the Republic could "obtain aid from Britain."[32] The conversation lasted nearly five hours. Stalin asked Pascua to convey to the Spanish people his wishes "for a complete victory over the internal and external enemies of the Spanish Republic."[33]

The next day, Stalin convened an expansive internal gathering on the course of the war in Spain, summoning tankists, aviators, engineers, and others who had firsthand combat experience there. The conclusions reached remain unknown.[34] But later in the month of February, he had the politburo approve additional large sales of weapons to Spain, based upon lists submitted by Voroshilov and Uritsky. Stalin, at his tête-à-tête with Pascua, had spoken ill of his own diplomatic representatives in Spain. On February 9, the politburo voted by telephone poll to replace Rosenberg with his deputy Gaikis, who had been recalled for consultations and was on his way to Moscow; Gaikis, too, would vanish.[35] Just nine months after the appearance of a Soviet ambassador in Spain, Moscow would again be left without one. Spain, for its part, would withdraw and not replace its ambassador (the next year), leaving its Moscow embassy with more canines than Spanish nationals.[36] Republic Spain's old-line Socialists deeply distrusted Communists and looked on the Soviet Union as never more than a means to an end.

Soviet advisers themselves were often at daggers drawn. Koltsov freelanced as an adviser and Soviet agent with the Soviet military's connivance, thereby angering Comintern officials who denounced him to Moscow. Berzin complained to Voroshilov and Yezhov of the Spanish government's dissatisfaction with the decorated NKVD operative Alexander Orlov and recommended his recall. Orlov, who had been promoted to NKVD station chief in Spain, wrote to Moscow, in late February 1937, that Soviet military attaché "Gorev has no military experience. In war affairs he is a child. [Berzin] is a good party member, but he is not an expert—and this is the pinnacle of our command."[37] Gorev complained that "they all blame each other for thousands of mortal sins, gather facts, even the smallest ones, about each other, and accuse one another of interference." Here was the pot calling the kettle black, for Gorev had written to Voroshilov complaining of the chief Soviet tank commander, General Semyon Krivoshein, that he "has still not learned what can be discussed over the telephone and what is not permitted."[38] Soviet advisers, though, were often caught between a rock and a hard place. "Before my departure, comrade Voroshilov gave me a short directive on the work of our people," Grigory Stern, promoted to the senior Soviet military official in-country, would report. "Do not in any circumstance issue an order, but . . . do everything necessary for victory."[39]

Predictably, Voroshilov violated his own strictures, issuing specific orders, down to the movement of tanks, as he tried to direct entire military operations from Moscow.[40]

Whether because they came to understand what Stalin wanted to hear or themselves shared the conspiratorial worldview, Soviet military advisers increasingly wrote of treachery. "The fascist intervention in Spain and the Trotskyite-Bukharinite bands arming in our country are the link in a single chain," one adviser reported to Moscow. Similarly, Stashevsky, the top Soviet political operative in Spain, wrote to Moscow, "I am sure there are provocations everywhere, and it is not excluded that a fascist organization exists among the [Republic's] higher officers." Some actual or would-be agents of Italian intelligence and the Gestapo were being uncovered and arrested behind Republic lines, but it was hard to know if this was what Stashevsky meant.[41] Stalin demanded investigations, but he meant of treacherous *Soviet* advisers: "Check every cipher clerk, radio operator, and generally every employee in communications, and fill the headquarters with new people, loyal and fight-capable. . . . Without this radical measure the Republicans will certainly lose the war. This is our firm conviction."[42]

WAR OF ATTRITION

Stalin had scheduled the next Central Committee plenum for February 20. The agenda approved by the politburo on February 5 included a report on the Bukharin-Rykov case (Yezhov); three reports on wrecking and espionage in industry (Orjonikidze, Kaganovich, Yezhov); and a report on "the political education of party cadres and measures of the struggle against Trotskyism and other double-dealers in party organizations" (Stalin).[43] There would also be a report on elections to party organizations and to the new Supreme Soviet (Zhdanov), in line with the new constitution. Unbeknownst to the Central Committee members, in preparation for the gathering, Georgy Malenkov, a thirty-five-year-old apparatchik overseeing personnel, had secretly compiled inventories of "anti-Soviet elements." These consisted of all "formers": tsarist officials, military officers, police, merchants, and nobles; White officers and officials; SRs, Mensheviks, and kulaks—eighteen categories of people, all told, who were viewed as targets for recruitment by foreign adversaries. "It should be noted in particular," Malenkov underscored in a cover note to Stalin (February 15), "that there are currently more than 1.5 million former members and candidates of the party who have been expelled or lost their membership card over the course of events at various times dating to 1922." He designated more than 100,000 as "alien" or "socially harmful." Stalin underlined Malenkov's figures.[44]

Suddenly the number of putative enemies was colossal, and they were everywhere. At the Moscow Ball-Bearing Factory, for example, there were 1,084 expellees and only 452 current party members, an alarming picture that could be found at strategic enterprises all across the Union.[45] And it was in the big factories that the party was strongest. Of course, these were people who had been expelled by Stalin's purges and party card exchanges, so if any had become disloyal, the dictator had a big hand in making them so. As per usual practice, Central Committee members received a package of preparatory documents, and in them Stalin included "testimonies" being extracted in Lubyanka cellars implicating sitting Central Committee members. But Malenkov's inventories remained secret as the NKVD field couriers delivered the plenum packages to the Central Committee, the party Control Commission, and around fifty invited guests, including, unusually, some twenty operatives from the NKVD.[46]

Stalin edited Orjonikidze's draft report for the plenum, advising, "State with facts which branches are affected by sabotage and exactly how they are affected."[47] That same evening, arriving considerably late, Orjonikidze addressed the central directorate of his heavy industry commissariat. He admonished officials that worker deaths on the job used to elicit reactions even under the "Black Hundred" Duma of tsarist days, while in the USSR, twenty workers could be killed and buried and officials would report the working class in good spirits. He lashed out at them for failing to see wrecking ("Do you tell me how you'll end the wrecking and which measures you'll adopt?") while also employing Stalin's language to condemn his recently executed deputy Pyatakov. Orjonikidze was as familiar as anyone with Stalin's emotional bullying. During the first forty-seven days of 1937, he met Stalin in the Little Corner twenty-two times, for a total of almost seventy-two hours.[48] There were also phone calls, meals together, walks on the Kremlin grounds. The heavy industry commissar, careful to demonstrate his loyalty, was trying to soften the dictator's rule. Orjonikidze indicated to his staff that alleged incidents of sabotage should be investigated objectively, and decided to send his own commissions to look into the NKVD's three most sensational "wrecking cases," evidently hoping to present fresh reports to the Central Committee plenum and disprove the blanket allegations.[49]

On February 17, 1937, Orjonikidze arrived at his commissariat, across the way from Old Square, at 12:10 p.m., two hours later than usual; he seems to have gone over to talk to Stalin, being one of the few people who could enter the dictator's Kremlin apartment.[50] Upon returning to his own Kremlin apartment, in the same Amusement Palace, Orjonikidze evidently had a shouting match over the telephone with Stalin, with profanities in Russian and Georgian.[51] The NKVD had been searching Orjonikidze's apartment, an obvious provocation.[52] The remainder of Orjonikidze's day was occupied with meetings, including a politburo meeting at 3:00 p.m. to go over the plenum reports. Stalin hand-corrected Orjonikidze's draft resolution on sabotage, inserting passages about "Trotskyite wreckers." In the early evening, Orjonikidze made his way back to the commissariat for more meetings, leaving for home at 12:20 a.m. (February 18). Later that morning, he did not emerge from his bedroom to take breakfast. When one of his subordinates came by in the afternoon, he refused to receive him. At around dusk, his wife, Zinaida, heard a gunshot in the bedroom. Orjonikidze was dead.[53]

Informed on the apartment's Kremlin line by Zinaida, Stalin summoned the cronies to the Little Corner, whence they walked to Orjonikidze's apartment.

Then, at 8:55 p.m., Stalin, Molotov, Voroshilov, Kaganovich, Zhdanov, Mikoyan, Postyshev (recently sacked as Kiev party boss), and Yezhov—in essence, the inner regime at this point—assembled again in the Little Corner. Doctor Levin was summoned at 9:40, for five minutes. The group remained until 12:25 a.m. (February 19).[54] Stalin chose not to use the death to further his allegations of ubiquitous enemy agents. Instead, public accounts gave the cause as "heart failure," said to have occurred at 5:30 p.m. on February 18, during Orjonikidze's daily nap.

The opening of the plenum was delayed for three days. Out-of-town members had begun to arrive at the Metropole, Moskva, and National hotels only to discover Orjonikidze's untimely death, reported in Soviet newspapers (February 19). The country went into grief-stricken shock. Orjonikidze had been a mere fifty years old. "The Hall of Columns [in the House of Trade Unions], wreaths, music, the scent of flowers, tears, honor guards, thousands and thousands of people passing by the open casket," recalled one eyewitness.[55] Stalin stood in the honor guard. On February 21, following an extravagant state funeral, the urn with Orjonikidze's ashes was interred in the Kremlin Wall (adjacent to his friend Kirov). "Comrades, we have lost one of the best leaders of the Bolshevik party and the Soviet state," Molotov stated in the main eulogy, blaming "the Trotskyite degenerates," the "Pyatakovs," for hastening Orjonikidze's death.[56] But rumors spread in Moscow, picked up by the Menshevik *Socialist Herald* in Paris, that Stalin had either killed him or driven him to suicide.[57]

Probably the best chance to stop Stalin was gone. Orjonikidze had been beholden to the principle of party unity, and he had no independent access to the press or radio, and no levers over the NKVD or the army.[58] Still, he possessed colossal authority, having worked closely with Lenin, beginning before the revolution, with service as a courier between the European emigration and Russia, and for years supervising heavy industry, the regime's crowning achievement.[59] He could have tried to use this standing to force a showdown at the plenum over fabricated wrecking charges.[60] But even had he done so, only collective action could have succeeded, requiring Orjonikidze to possess resolve and cunning to organize all or most of the other top Stalinists—not only Voroshilov, Kaganovich, and Mikoyan, who had been close to Orjonikidze, but also Molotov, who was not—in unified action against Stalin. For any of them individually, broaching the subject of moving against Stalin would have been tantamount to political, and perhaps physical, death. Moreover, even if troubled by Stalin's gathering homicidal behavior, they all, including Orjonikidze, still recognized him as the leader.

It was Stalin who shouldered such complex matters as Spain, China, Nazi Germany, Britain and France, the party machine, ideology.

Orjonikidze had confided thoughts of suicide to Kaganovich and Mikoyan.[61] In published photographs taken near the body, Kaganovich was seen expressing visibly strong emotions: grief, anger. He had lost his soul mate, and he knew Stalin had been sadistically pressuring the infirm Orjonikidze. Kaganovich—tough as nails, explosive—was spiritually broken. Stalin went on to break Mikoyan, summoning him in 1937 to discuss the arrest of his subordinate in the food industry commissariat, Mark Belenky, then, after Mikoyan supposedly protested and Stalin called him blind in matters of personnel, summoning him again to show him protocols of Belenky's "confession." "Have a look: he confessed to wrecking," Stalin said. "You vouched for him. Go and read it!" Mikoyan called it "a blow against me."[62] Members of the inner circle were no longer comrades of the ruler. Stalin was no longer first among peers, but a despot.[63]

EXTIRPATION

Molotov opened the delayed Central Committee plenum on February 23 in the Sverdlov rotunda of Catherine the Great's Imperial Senate, and in the shadow of Orjonikidze's death. The sessions would last an unusual eleven days, longer than any other plenum.[64] NKVD officials from all around the country, most of them not members of the Central Committee, were conspicuous. Stalin set a tone of menace in his opening remarks, calling top officials who had been arrested "empty chatterboxes, lacking technical training," whose only claim to fame was "possession of a party card." He added that "current wreckers have no technical advantages over our people. On the contrary, in technical terms our people are better prepared." Sounding a cherished theme, he boasted that "we have tens of thousands of capable people, talented people. We need only to know them and promote them, so that they do not get stuck in the old place and begin to rot."[65]

The first order of business at the choreographed gathering, though, was Bukharin and Rykov. On the opening evening, Yezhov reported on the accusations of treason. Mikoyan reliably reinforced his points. Bukharin had written a long rebuttal of the press slander against him to the politburo and announced a hunger strike. Now, in a debilitated state, unshaven, wearing a rumpled suit, he was given the floor. He denied the charges but was mercilessly heckled. "Trotsky and his disciples Zinoviev and Kamenev once worked with Lenin, and now these people have reached an agreement with Hitler," Stalin interrupted. "After all that has happened with these men, these former comrades who have reached an agreement with Hitler in order to sell out the USSR, there are no more surprises in human life. You must prove everything. . . ."[66] Three days before the plenum, Bukharin had again abased himself in a letter to Stalin. "I really love you now dearly and with belated love," he wrote, praising Stalin's mistrust as a sign of "wisdom." Bukharin predicted that a still greater age would dawn, with Stalin as the very "world spirit" Hegel had imagined.[67]

Turar Ryskulov, an ethnic Kazakh candidate member of the Central Committee and the long-standing deputy chairman of the Council of People's Commissars for the Russian republic, quietly tried to persuade some plenum attendees to come to the defense of Rykov and Bukharin, but he could not manage to do so.[68]

At the plenum (February 24), Rykov denied the scurrilous accusations and called the mockery of him "a savage thing," given that he was already effectively condemned to death (he pointed out that others had confessed and been shot anyway). During Rykov's and Bukharin's speeches, nearly 1,000 interruptions were recorded. Not one was supportive. Stalin made the greatest number (100), followed by Molotov (82) and Postyshev (88).[69] More than half of those present never interjected, but for two more days (February 25–26), speakers took the dais to rip into the rightists. "Bukharin writes in his statement to the Central Committee that Ilich [Lenin] died in his arms," Yezhov shouted. "Rubbish! You're lying! Utterly false!" Bukharin responded that "those present when Ilich died were Maria Ilinichna [Ulyanova], Nadezhda Konstantinovna [Krupskaya], and myself"—and turned toward them for confirmation. Neither Lenin's wife nor his sister said anything. Bukharin continued: "Did I take Ilich's dead body in my arms, and kiss his feet?" Both women stayed silent.

Stalin intervened at the plenum (February 27) to recommend a seeming middle ground whereby Bukharin and Rykov would not be immediately put on trial, but turned over to the NKVD for further "investigation." Secret police operatives took Bukharin and Rykov away, the first time anyone had been arrested at a party plenum.[70] The pair spent the remainder of the proceedings at the Lubyanka inner prison while Stalin formed a special commission of the plenum to adjudicate their fate.[71] Bukharin's expulsion from the Central Committee and his disposition to the NKVD were duly upheld by the commission, whose members included Mikoyan (chairman), Maria Ulyanova, and Krupskaya.[72]

Perhaps Stalin might now be satiated? "It must be hoped," the Stalinist propagandist Yaroslavsky told the plenum, "that we are discussing in the Central Committee of our party the question of betrayal by members and candidate members of the Central Committee for the last time."[73] Such was the naïveté.

With Stalin's primary aim accomplished, the plenum switched gears. Zhdanov had reported (February 26) on the upcoming elections by secret ballot to party posts (for May), a way to mobilize pressure from below against sitting officials, as well as elections to soviets. "We lack the habits of direct elections and secret ballots," he admitted. One plenum attendee, trying to convey the immensity of the organizational undertaking, reminded the plenum of the 1917 vote for the Constituent Assembly. Stalin pointed out that the class enemy could be elected, especially given that some collective farms had no Communist party members. "Keep in mind that our country has two million Communists and a 'bit more' non-party people," Zhdanov noted of the scores of millions of non-party adults.[74] He even alluded to the days when Bolshevism had had to survive in the underground.[75] It was a surreal discussion: no one was forcing the monopoly regime to stage competitive elections by secret ballot.

On the morning of February 28, Molotov, in place of Orjonikidze, delivered the report on sabotage in industry, and ridiculed Orjonikidze's counterinvestigations that minimized wrecking. Kaganovich, falling in line, presented similar tales of sabotage, though he continued to try to push back ever so gently. "As you can see," he summarized, "we have had a rather serious cleansing of the ranks of politically dangerous people."[76]

February 28 also happened to be Svetlana Stalin's eleventh birthday. The relatives gathered in the Kremlin apartment without the despot. In her diary, Maria Svanidze, the sister-in-law of Stalin's first wife, Kato, bad-mouthed the "half-wit" and "idiot" relatives of Stalin's second wife, Nadya, and the couple's "lazy" son Vasily, concluding that "the only normal people present" were her, her husband (Alyosha Svanidze), Nadya's sister-in-law Zhenya, and "Little Svetlana, who makes up for all the rest." Maria also recorded that Stalin's elder son, Yakov, from his marriage to Kato, had arrived with his new wife, Judith "Yulia" Meltzer (b. 1911). "She is pretty, older than Yasha—he's her fifth husband, not counting other relationships—none too bright, little cultured. She trapped him, of course. . . . Too bad for I[osif]."[77] (In fact, Stalin's elder son was her third husband.[78]) Yakov was now studying at Moscow's Artillery Academy, but he could never manage to please his father. Be that as it may, two sons whom Stalin deemed disappointing and two dead wives were not the main factors keeping him away from the family scene, despite his fondness for Svetlana. His dislike for busybodies like Svanidze had grown. In any case, he was busy, forcing extirpation of "enemies and spies who had a party card in their pocket."[79]

"TRULY A HISTORIC PLENUM!"

Back at the interminable plenum, after a further flogging of industrial wrecking, Yezhov was at the dais again (March 2). He would speak a total of five times. (Molotov spoke thrice.) Now, Yezhov suddenly laced into Yagoda for sheltering spies and traitors at the NKVD, prompting Yagoda to shout denials ("Not true!"). But in the discussion that day and the next, numerous NKVD officials rose to condemn Yagoda, including his old nemesis Yevdokimov. The latter had three turns at the rostrum, and helpfully linked Yagoda to the rightists Bukharin and Rykov. That was precisely the testimony being beaten out of Georgy Molchanov, who until recently had headed the NKVD's secret-political department and who had been arrested in Minsk (following a demotion to the Belorussian NKVD). "I think," Yevdokimov thundered, "that matters are not limited to Molchanov alone." Yagoda: "What, have you gone out of your mind?" Yevdokimov: "We must put Yagoda on trial."[80] One participant asked why Yagoda had not already been arrested. "(Noise in the hall.)"[81] This is what a slaughterhouse would sound like if the pigs, cows, and sheep could talk.

Stalin, after innumerable interjections, finally delivered his own full address on March 3. "The more we advance, the more successes we have, the more embittered the remnants of the defeated and exploiting classes will become, the more rapidly they will go over to sharper forms of struggle, the more they will inflict damage on the Soviet state, the more they will seize on the most desperate means of struggle as the last resort of the doomed," he asserted, repeating his long-standing theory.[82] He chastised party and state officials—like the ones sitting there in the Sverdlov Hall—for "political blindness" on this score. "Some of our leading cadres, both in the center and locally, not only failed to discern the real countenance of these wreckers, diversionists, spies, and murderers," he stated, "but proved so unconcerned, complacent, and naïve that at times they themselves assisted in promoting the agents of foreign states to one or another responsible post." To anyone who might object, Stalin mockingly added, "Capitalist encirclement? Rubbish! What significance can some kind of capitalist encirclement have if we fulfill and surpass our economic plans? New forms of wrecking, the struggle with Trotskyism? Trifle! What significance can these trifles have if we fulfill and overfulfill our plan? . . . Our party's not shabby, the party's Central Committee is also not bad—what the hell more do we need? Strange people sit there in Moscow, in the Central Committee of the party: they think up all sorts of questions, instigate about some kind of wrecking. They themselves don't sleep and don't allow others to."[83]

Inside the sarcasm, Stalin had blurted out confirmation of the real driver behind the mass arrests and executions: *it was him.*

Mekhlis, in *Pravda* the next day, obediently ripped into the heretofore de rigueur toadying, ridiculing the rituals as "boot-licking therapy" and condemning the "supreme leaderism" of specific local party bosses.[84] The far-flung operations of Stalin's regime were riddled with cross-purposes, self-dealing, underfulfillment of economic targets, poor record keeping, reports of faked successes, pervasive misappropriation of state funds, and victimization of the weakest officials as scapegoats. The "system" was an unwieldy amalgam of competing clans and impossible rules, vast webs of relationships and red-tape procedures overlaid with a tableau of powerful myths (including the myth of the system itself). Stalin returned to the dais for a menacing summation (March 5). "People are sometimes selected based not on a political or business principle but on personal acquaintance, personal allegiance, friendships," he warned, citing the example of Levon Mirzoyan, who was said to have brought thirty people to Kazakhstan from postings in Azerbaijan and the Urals. "What does it mean to drag a whole group of cronies with you? . . . It means you have acquired a certain independence from local organizations and, if you will, a certain independence from the Central Committee."

Stalin would know: forming a political clan was precisely how he had built his personal dictatorship inside the Bolshevik dictatorship, and gained his own independence. Never mind. "Some comrades among us think that if they are a people's commissar, then they know everything," he added. "They believe that rank, in and of itself, affords very great, almost inexhaustible knowledge. Or they think: If I am a Central Committee member, then I am not one by accident, then I must know everything. This is not the case." He maligned even Orjonikidze, praising the fallen industry commissar as "one of the first and best politburo members among us," but accusing him of "wasting time and effort" defending enemies.[85] "Truly a historic plenum!" the Comintern's Dimitrov noted in his diary.[86]

SELF-SLAUGHTERHOUSE

The decisive question—what, precisely, would be the scope of the high-level arrests—remained unclear. Stalin, in his plenum summation, estimated the number of Trotskyites and Zinovievites, as well as rightists, at 30,000, of whom he said 12,000 had already been arrested. But of course, some officials were being arrested not for an opposition past but for insufficient vigilance against the opposition. And "testimony" never failed to produce more names. Already, large numbers of "rightists" were being subjected to torture at Lubyanka's internal prison (many declared hunger strikes, and not a few attempted suicide).[87] Most ominously, Stalin had alluded at the plenum to the inventories compiled by Malenkov: the 1.5 million former party members, expellees whom Stalin now called "grist for the mill of our enemies."[88]

Those who had sat in the Sverdlov Hall through the jaw-dropping plenum did not yet know, but "testimony" being compiled in NKVD cellars painted a scenario of a Red Army/NKVD plot to seize power in the Soviet Union, Franco style.[89] The NKVD, in a March 1937 draft document in connection with the plenum, asserted that foreign intelligence services had established a gigantic number of spy centers in the USSR, while conceding, "We do not know where they are or who belongs to the counterrevolutionary organizations created by foreign intelligence agencies, and as a result we cannot liquidate them at the necessary moment."[90] They could have been inside the NKVD itself.

Stalin's weapon against his own NKVD leadership was, as in all other institutions, the party. Following the despot's call to ramp up enemy hunting at the plenum, Yezhov, as per usual practice, convened a meeting of the NKVD "party active" at Lubyanka (March 19–21) to discuss the lessons. All top NKVD operatives were party members. Yezhov set the tone by lacerating Yagoda, then invited those present to speak up, a devastatingly simple way to elicit denunciations.[91] Gleeful revenge against Yagoda and others poured forth, but it was mixed with terrified self-preservation: how could the operatives denounce Yagoda, under whom they had all worked, without somehow implicating themselves? On March 29, Mikhail Frinovsky—who had a lot to prove, having been a top operative under Yagoda—led a team that arrested his former boss, and beat Yagoda demonstratively in the process.[92]

Yagoda's arrest was stunning.[93, 94] He knew that "Stalin treated [him] coolly and met with him just for official business" (as one of Stalin's top bodyguards would later put it).[95, 96] Still, Yagoda could be forgiven if he imagined himself to be indispensable, given his services to Stalin: millions of kulaks deported, countless priority construction objects completed, comprehensive surveillance imposed on the army, the party-state, cultural elites. Yagoda held the rank of "general commissar of state security" (equivalent to marshal), which he had retained even after being shunted over to the communications commissariat. Some NKVD operatives had taken to referring to the party apparatchik as Yezhov's "temporary posting" to the NKVD, as Kaganovich had informed Stalin.[97] But Yezhov finally had been named to that rank, which Yagoda lost. After seventeen years at the very top of the secret police, he was reduced to waiting for the despot to return him to favor.

Yagoda's passivity was not a given. He had controlled assassination squads, a poison laboratory, a plethora of safe houses (at home and abroad), even an ability to eavesdrop on Stalin. Because of the length of his service in the organs (from 1919), he had a network whose mutual loyalties predated Stalin's full power.[98] But Yagoda turned out to be a mere minion, while Stalin studied, fostered, and used the NKVD's natural rivalries and animosities to control him even before appointing Yezhov to supervise NKVD business on behalf of the unchallengeable party. Now Stalin used these internal antagonisms, as well as Yezhov, to annihilate Yagoda. Once the invitation came down from on high, score settling proved irresistible and self-preservation instincts kicked in.[99] In denunciations, Yagoda's subordinates revealed that they viewed him not as a Dzierżyński-like sword and shield of the revolution but as unprincipled, a cruel boss, a shady wheeler and dealer (commerçant).[100]

When Frinovsky's squad raked over Yagoda's Kremlin apartment (Miliutinsky Lane, 9) and his sumptuous dacha (Ozerki), they found 1,229 bottles of wine (the majority of foreign origin and dating to as early as 1897), 11,075 cigarettes of foreign make (Turkish and Egyptian), along with 8 boxes of foreign tobacco, 3,904 pornographic photos and 11 pornographic films, 21 men's overcoats, mostly foreign made, plus 4 fur coats and 4 leather overcoats, 11 foreign-made leather jackets, 22 men's suits, 31 pairs of imported women's shoes, and 22,997 rubles. The list went on (and on): 399 foreign music records, 101 imported children's games, 37 pairs of imported gloves, 17 large carpets, 7 medium-size carpets, 5 animal skin carpets (bear, leopard, wolf), a collection of 165 pipes (including some made of elephant tusks), 95 bottles of imported perfume, 542 examples of Trotskyite and fascist literature.[101] Only the infamous foreign jewelry Yagoda and his minion Alexander Lurye used to entrap foreigners and enrich themselves had failed to turn up. Word of the eye-popping inventory advanced through the rumor mill, further discrediting Yagoda and his closest associates.[102]

Yagoda was charged with embezzlement and leading a conspiracy on behalf of Nazi Germany to assassinate Stalin. Had Yagoda been a long-standing foreign agent, he let pass countless opportunities to have Stalin and entourage killed (such as the night of the Kirov assassination, when, as Yagoda knew, Stalin and his clique were all together on a train to Leningrad).

No one in Stalin's inner circle would defend Yagoda, who had relentlessly intruded into their commissariats and persecuted their personnel. "I repeat: I knew Voroshilov hated me," Yagoda would soon be quoted as testifying, when asked why he supposedly felt compelled to eavesdrop on Stalin's telephone conversations. "Molotov and Kaganovich held me in the same hostile regard."[103] The cronies were not so naïve as to imagine Yagoda had launched these proctology exams on their institutions of his own accord, but they could imagine that he had lobbied Stalin for his own initiatives to make their lives miserable. Kaganovich compared Yagoda with Joseph Fouché, the French Revolution's unscrupulous secret policeman who managed to survive four regimes (Jacobins, Directory, Napoleon, the Restoration) and became associated with counterrevolution.[104] Yagoda lacked a prerevolutionary Bolshevik underground past. "My whole life I went about with a mask," Yagoda was recorded as confessing, in interrogation protocols, "making myself out to be a staunch Bolshevik. In fact, in its real understanding, I was never a Bolshevik." Stalin underlined this passage, among others.[105] (An interrogation transcript of Avel Yenukidze arrived the same day as Yagoda's.) It is almost as if the endless hours of interrogations, and the lengthy written and signed protocols, were for *him*.

Other stunning arrests followed: the head of the NKVD special department for security in the military, Mark Gai, and the head of Stalin's bodyguards, Pauker.[106] They and many more were "unmasked" as fascist spies plotting to assassinate the leadership. Pauker could have withdrawn the Kremlin guard, leaving Stalin exposed. But he did not have to go to that trouble: Pauker shaved Stalin and could have slit his throat. Back when Yagoda had been sacked from the NKVD, Pauker had been the one to block his access to Stalin's dacha in Sochi, and now, just a few months later, he was supposed to have been been in a conspiracy with Yagoda against Stalin *all along*? Yezhov went further still, asserting to the NKVD bosses that "[Zakhar] Volovich, Pauker's deputy, specially planted an engineer, a German spy, as the head of the secret government telephone station. In such a way did the enemy learn of the telephone conversations between Stalin and Molotov."[107]

The fabrications and the beating of people to unconsciousness to extract pre-scripted testimony of assassination "plots" did, for some Chekists, violate professional pride. But the problem for them was not that, or not that alone; rather, they had all worked with Yagoda. Why had they not spoken earlier? Were they secretly in league with him? Operatives who initially survived Yagoda's sacking now became still more "vigilant": that is, they attempted to ward off their own arrests, magnifying the slaughterhouse. Back in February 1937, Yakov Agranov—the first deputy NKVD chief, who had taken over state security (GB) from the arrested Molchanov—had asked regional NKVD branches for lists of operatives and other staff who had been Trotskyites, Zinovievites, and rightists.[108] But in spring 1937, Agranov would be demoted to Saratov province. There, he proceeded to extract "confessions" left and right, including from his immediate local predecessor, Roman Pilar von Pilhau, who confessed to trying to organize Yezhov's assassination, the ultimate extracted accusation for someone like Agranov, seeking to ingratiate himself with the new boss. But with so many "Yagodaites" giving "testimony" under torture, denunciations against Agranov flowed like lava, and soon he, too, would be arrested.[109]

Through it all, the NKVD never broke down, let alone rebelled. The ease with which Yagoda was destroyed proved that there was no threat whatsoever to Stalin's rule. The secret police, even under assault, remained an utterly reliable instrument of his will, a testament to both the limits of the feared yet despised Yagoda's authority and the strength of Stalin's as supreme leader.

DEFT MANEUVERS

During the plenum of February 23–March 5, 1937, Voroshilov was given the floor at the March 2 morning session. Yezhov and Molotov had already delivered their reports on ubiquitous enemies. Stalin had considered assigning a separate report on the army but demurred. ("We had in mind the importance of the matter," according to Molotov, meaning the possible consequences.) Instead, Voroshilov spoke during discussion of Kaganovich's report, which covered sabotage on the railroads.[110] The defense commissar was one of Stalin's two most important minions.[111] He stood far closer to Stalin than any other military man or security official, having first met him in 1906 and having fought together with him during the civil war. But his position atop the massive Soviet military had hardly been foreordained. Back in November 1921, following bitter internal battles during the civil war over the shape of the military, he had begged Stalin to be released. "In Moscow I already told you of my intention to alter my field of play, and now I have firmly decided: I have grown tired of work in the military institution, and the center of gravity is not there now either," a then thirty-year-old Voroshilov had written. "I submit that I would be more useful in the civilian sphere. I await approval and friendly support from you at the Central Committee for my transfer. I'd like to work in the Donbass, where I ask the Central Committee to send me. I'll take any kind of work and I hope to buck up again, otherwise I'll start to decay (spiritually) here. You should pity me. A strong embrace, your Voroshilov."[112] Instead, within four years Stalin had named Voroshilov defense commissar.

As of June 21, 1935, the arrest of any officer from platoon level up required the approval of the defense commissar, which put Voroshilov front and center in Stalin's terror.

Stalin prized Voroshilov's canine fealty and avuncular sociability. A connoisseur of the opera, Voroshilov discovered a fondness for posing for oil portraits, too, sitting for long periods in the studio of Alexander Gerasimov. Gossip made the rounds that Voroshilov had acquired yet another villa (his third), at state expense, expressly for a ballerina, even as he reprimanded those below for doing the same.[113] The erstwhile metalworker and his wife, Golda Gorbman, a convert from Judaism who went by the name Yekaterina Voroshilova, had turned their apartment in the Grand Kremlin Palace into the regime's social epicenter.[114] Voroshilov was stormy and sentimental, given to tears even more readily than Franco, but, like the Spanish general, he had never acquired genuine military training. He had not served in the tsarist army, despite being the right age. Unlike the standouts Tukhachevsky, Yakir, and Uborevičius, Voroshilov had not been sent to study in Germany (although he had visited and met with top German officers). He usually chastised commanders as if their mistakes surprised him, and doled out praise, while marking milestones and awards with personal letters. Still, Voroshilov could not stanch the chitchat about his military incompetence.

Ivan Kutyakov, a party member since 1917 and the person who had taken command of the famous Chapayev's unit when the latter fell in 1919, recorded in his diary in 1937 that, "as long as 'the iron one' is in charge, we will have misconception, bootlicking, and everything stupid will be valued, everything smart will be devalued."[115] Kutyakov was too far from the center of power to understand that Voroshilov was a shrewd political operator who had developed a certain bureaucratic-procedural mastery, with which he had often kept the wolves of the NKVD's special department at bay, dismissing requests for arrest authorization with phrases like "It's not obligatory to arrest every fool; one can simply toss them from the Red Army."[116] But Kutyakov did understand that the fate not just of the top officers who looked down on Voroshilov but of the entire Red Army lay in the commissar's hands.

At the plenum, Voroshilov once more demonstrated his skillfulness as a crowd-pleasing orator. "Lazar Moiseyevich [Kaganovich], before I took the podium, said, 'Let's see how you will criticize yourself—that'll be interesting.' (General laughter.)," Voroshilov noted, before proceeding to sharply distinguish his area of responsibility from transport. "In the Worker-Peasant Red Army at the current moment, fortunately or unfortunately, and, I think, to grand fortune, we have not so far uncovered especially many enemies of the people," he asserted. He did not deny their presence but spent a great deal of time on the past, especially how Trotsky in the early 1920s had supposedly tried but failed to rally the army against the party and how, "without noise, and that was not necessary, we threw out a large number of unfit elements, including the Trotskyite-Zinovievite tail, including all manner of dubious riffraff." Specifically, he noted, "we cleaned out some 47,000 over the course of 12 to 13 years," almost half of them (22,000) just in the years 1934–36, including 5,000 "oppositionists." Around 10,000 of the discharges had been arrested, but few had been higher-ups. And tens of thousands of new officers, graduates of twelve military academies, as well as engineers, doctors, and political workers, were newly promoted. "The country gives it its best sons," Voroshilov concluded, and it "constitutes an armed force ready to fight and loyal to the party and state." He also reminded everyone of the army's singular importance ("the whole world is against us").[117]

Voroshilov's was a command performance. His assertion that there were few foreign agents or saboteurs in his bailiwick was precisely what his close friend Orjonikidze had been saying about heavy industry before his suicide. Like Orjonikidze (and others), Voroshilov fully shared Stalin's worldview but lacked the paranoiac bent or iron willingness to murder loyalists for some purported larger political end. And, despite Orjonikidze's manifest failure to protect industry, Voroshilov had not relinquished his delusion that he might deflect the guillotine from the Red Army. But he was subjected to intense pressure. Molotov had interjected, "If you think that situation in your area is fine and dandy, you're profoundly misguided."[118] Also, a contingent of military men was in attendance (Tukhachevsky, oddly, was absent, rumored to be on holiday in Sochi), and several railed against enemies, looking to save their own skins.[119] Nor could Voroshilov avoid having to convoke a follow-up meeting of the commanders to discuss the "lessons" of the plenum. He dared to tell them that "our main enemy is there, in the West, . . . the capitalists, the imperialists"—not in the hall where he was speaking. But as Voroshilov hesitated to denounce his own officer corps, others rushed in.[120]

Grigory Kulik, a peasant-born cavalry officer resentful of the noble-born Tukhachevsky and his ilk, had just returned from Spain and wrote to Voroshilov (April 29, 1937) demanding that enemies in the military be rooted out because "as a Bolshevik I do not wish that the precious blood of our people is spilled in a future war in excess because of careerists, hidden traitors, and talentless commanders." This was a self-characterization, albeit unintentionally so. But Kulik's vicious ambition ratcheted up the pressure on Voroshilov. (Kulik very soon attained his first audience in the Little Corner; Stalin promoted him to chief of artillery administration.)[121] Another immense point of pressure was that the Red Army personnel department required autobiographies, on which had been introduced a new question (in 1936): "With whom have you worked?" Trotsky had headed the army until January 1925—and who had not "worked" with him? Almost none of these men had been personally close to him, but they had the fatal association. Even those lucky enough to have joined after Trotsky's dismissal could still be brought low by the required autobiography in their own hand: all of a sudden, some person they knew would be arrested, and they would be liable for their association with an "enemy" and for having failed to report such an enemy, which was a capital crime.[122]

Above all, Voroshilov had no control over Yezhov, who hungered for Stalin's approval. In the Little Corner, the despot tutored Yezhov on portraying a conspiracy with a shadow government, ready to take over: Yagoda as head of the Council of People's Commissars, Tukhachevsky as defense commissar, Bukharin as general secretary of the party. (One wonders what went through the minds of those present at official discussions of such a prospect.) Their palace coup, on behalf of foreign powers, was said to involve Pauker, assisted by former Kremlin commandant Rudolf Peterson (sacked back in the Yenukidze affair), who were collectively going to help cut the Kremlin lights and toss grenades into the special cinema during a politburo viewing. (Another variant had them smushing poison onto Kremlin telephone receivers.)[123] Voroshilov was not going to defend the manifestly more talented Tukhachevsky, whom he despised, against Stalin's machinations, but what the defense commissar might not have fully understood was how indulging Tukhachevsky's annihilation could break open the bloodgates on the beloved army he was trying to protect.[124]

POPULAR FRONT ON THE RIGHT, CIVIL WAR ON THE LEFT

No general war had broken out over Spain because none of the major powers wanted one. Spain might have been the world's great cause, on one side or the other, but it was no outside country's principal concern. The global morality play, in fact, was deceiving. "I know that there are some people who believe that as the outcome of this civil war Spain inevitably must have a government either fascist or Communist," Anthony Eden, then Britain's foreign secretary, had told a Foreign Press Association dinner in early 1937. "That is not our belief. On the contrary, we believe that neither of these forms of government being indigenous to Spain, neither is likely to endure. Spain will in time evolve her own Spanish form of government." These self-serving remarks had a certain prescience.[125]

Nor were the often lurid rumors accurate. Nationalist agents had learned and leaked word of the Spanish Republic gold transfer to the "Reds" in Moscow, provoking an international scandal, as well as a steep drop in the peseta's value, which raised the costs of imports, but the holdings in Moscow were being used to pay down the Republic's imports of expensive weaponry.[126] Moscow gouged the Spaniards on the prices charged for some weapons (and charged for shipment). Even as the ruble held steady against the dollar, at 5.3 to $1, in transactions with Spain the Soviets converted the ruble at anywhere from 2.0 to 3.95 to $1, after which they then made the conversion of the ruble prices into pesetas; the Spaniards never saw the original ruble conversion rate. This chicanery probably added at least 25 percent to the prices Spain paid for Soviet weaponry. Still, the value of the Soviet weapons delivered did reach a substantial approximation of the value of gold the Soviets took in.[127]

Hitler, following Franco's failure to capture Madrid, had decided neither to increase nor to decrease his circumscribed commitment, but Mussolini had expanded the already expansive Italian contribution, thereby perhaps helping to prevent a Nationalist collapse. In February 1937, when Italy had nearly 50,000 troops on the ground in Spain, Mussolini had also dispatched Roberto Farinacci as a personal envoy. Farinacci tried to talk Franco into creating a fascist-style monopoly party and perhaps name a House of Savoy prince as king of Spain. But the more Farinacci saw, the more he was put off by the infighting and corruption. He judged Franco to be "timid," and characterized his massacres of political prisoners as "politically senseless." The Nationalists' secret police overheard Farinacci concluding that Mussolini would have to take over Spain and appoint him as proconsul.[128] Franco did adopt the slogan "Una Patria, Un Estado, Un Caudillo" (evoking "Ein Volk, Ein Reich, Ein Führer"), but there would be no Spanish fascist regime. When King Vittorio Emanuele had made Mussolini prime minister, back in 1922, the Italian fascist party counted 320,000 members, ten times the number of Spanish Falangists in 1936. Spain's homegrown fascists would lose 60 percent of this not very robust membership in civil war combat.[129]

Farinacci complained further to Rome that Franco "has no idea of what the Spain of tomorrow should be like," an utterly mistaken assessment. Farinacci also wrote that Franco "is only interested in winning the war, and then for a long period after, in how to impose an authoritarian, or, better, dictatorial government to purge the nation of all those who have had any contact, direct or indirect, with the Reds," an observation that was spot-on. Franco understood the civil war not solely as a military endeavor but as a political project. During his counterinsurgency in Morocco, he had learned how to massacre a populace into submission *and* how to manipulate tribal leaders, pitting them against one another or finding their price, making them dependent on him. Now, in a similar battlefield gradualism in the homeland—refusing all entreaties for a mediated peace, killing or chasing out implacable elements in the Spanish population en masse, training a keen eye on rival rebel officers—the caudillo baffled and infuriated his foreign fascist supporters. Yet the *cuco* Franco had a ready answer. "I will occupy Spain town by town, village by village, railway by railway," he snapped at an impatient Italian ambassador. "Nothing will make me abandon this gradual program. It will bring me less glory but internal peace. . . . I can assure you that I am not interested in territory but in inhabitants. . . . I must have the certainty of being able to found a regime."[130]

Such a statement could be taken as excuse making for Franco's mediocrity in the new conditions of modern combat, which required combined use of air, armor, and infantry (in German-style warfare, which Soviet advisers also knew). But a quick military conquest of Spain would not have been easy.[131] Among the Soviet-sponsored International Brigades, casualty rates would be high, up to 75 percent in some units, while home leave was denied and desertion would become prevalent. But Spain's regular Republic's People's Army had become formidable, the majority of its field commands held by regular officers, many of them accomplished. Franco, however, would win the grinding civil war not only because he attained a unified military command. On the political battlefield, as it were, he forged a loose but effective coalition, an integrative strategy of no enemies to the right, co-opting Spanish fascists, who were more housebroken than their Italian counterparts.[132] Thus, whereas in Italy and then Germany the traditional right, fearing the left, had invited the radical right to power, in Spain Franco built a successful popular front—on the right.

Franco re-created the ancien régime court, with processions to church under a canopy surrounded by bishops.[133] Beneath this powerful symbolism, he also forced into being a single legal political organization, relying on his young brother-in-law, Ramón Serrano Súñer, who had escaped from a Republic prison, to oversee the political amalgam.[134] This was no simple feat: the monarchists alone were split, with more than one presumptive heir waiting in the wings.[135] But the Francoist political party managed to bring into coalition seemingly incompatible groupings of Alfonso monarchists and the Carlist monarchists, along with Catholics, upper officer corps, and the Falange Blueshirts. Fissures remained, but they were not enough to split the coalition, while being just enough to facilitate Franco's staying power.

This contrasted starkly with the Republic. Many Spaniards suspected both indigenous Communists and Moscow of the worst, but with Communists working against broad nationalization of private industry, many of Spain's shopkeepers, farmers, and lesser civil servants cooperated with them in defense of the Republic. Yet the Republic could not take full advantage. It lacked not only a vigorous parliamentary life during the civil war but unified leadership, comprising as it did three governments in three capitals: Valencia (after evacuation from Madrid), Bilbao (Basques), and Barcelona (the Catalan Generalitat). Anarchists, who were concentrated in Barcelona, pursued a strategy of winning the war via grassroots revolution, but in areas where revolution had been effected, the Nationalist rebel forces sliced through the lines with ease.[136] Even if the Nationalists had disintegrated, it is hard to see how the leftist victors could have avoided a civil war, which simmered and occasionally boiled on the left nearly the entire time they were battling Franco.[137]

The Spanish left was irreparably divided against itself. Beyond the usual tableau of anarchist leaders and many anarchist rank and file splintering over issues, or the factions within the Communist movement treating one another as enemies, the Communists and the POUM wanted to eliminate each other, as did the

Communists and the anarchists. No less an unbridgeable gulf existed between the Communists and the Socialists, who stood ready to kill each other (and not just in Spain). That and the other divisions help explain why Spain's Republic would not win, despite holding the strategic interior, coasts, and many ports. Stalin did not initiate these profound mutual enmities. He contributed to them, but he also struggled to overcome them, refusing to indulge the calls for a Communist coup and insisting on upholding the Popular Front under the Socialist party prime minister.[138] But Communism was ultimately an either-or proposition. Put another way, Socialists could give up anticapitalism and become "meliorists" (or redistributionists) within a parliamentary market system; Communists could never do so and remain Communists. Thus, despite the soaring passion of the antifascist crusade, the leftist Popular Front was doomed.

As for Franco's techniques of war (insurgency-cum-counterinsurgency) and his vicious yet relatively adroit authoritarian rule, Stalin paid no special mind. The despot understood himself not as just another caudillo, but as an ideas-based leader. In practical terms, Spain's strong interest groups, and the need for Franco to not just manipulate but accommodate them, provided a stark contrast with the political terrain under the Soviet despot, who had crushed even the quasi-independence of his inner circle.[139] Franco, therefore, had nothing to teach him, except that a military-led putsch, assisted externally by fascists, could try to seize a whole country, a scenario that Stalin was manipulating to justify his own savage domestic counterinsurgency against an imaginary insurgency.

ELUSIVE GERMANY

In Moscow, the German Communist Wilhelm Pieck, at a meeting of the German commission of the Comintern secretariat on February 11, 1937, had contradicted Stalin's adviser Jenő Varga, a Hungarian Communist. Pieck argued that "the German bourgeoisie will not decide to go to war, and has grave doubts about Hitler's provocations, which he needs to raise his prestige." Varga interjected: "You think the German bourgeoisie does not want war?" Pieck: "No, not now. . . . We have information that the German army generals are against the provocational policy conducted by Hitler." Varga: "That means that the current fascist regime in Germany is not a regime of the haute bourgeoisie, the finance oligarchy, but Hitler's regime?" Pieck answered that "finance capital had understood that it could not dominate the masses with the help of Weimar democracy, but that did not mean fascism was merely an instrument. It is a force unto itself; we need to evaluate it as an independent force." Pieck claimed that he was not denying "finance capital's" power, but arguing that it had everything to lose from war, and thus that the Hitler regime was not reducible to finance capital. Varga was incredulous.[140]

In Berlin, Kandelaki's efforts to jump-start talks for bilateral political rapprochement had gone nowhere, and Stalin, through Litvinov, had tried to shift channels to the German foreign ministry. The Germans had raised questions about the Soviet request for absolute confidentiality; Litvinov, who loathed the idea of talks with Nazi Germany, smelled a rat, suspecting that, because of its economic straits, Germany was trying to simulate talks with Moscow to interest London and Paris in economic negotiations. But German foreign minister Neurath informed Schacht of similar suspicions: "Yesterday, during a personal report to the Führer, I spoke to him about your discussions with Mr. Kandelaki and especially about the declaration he made to you in the name of Stalin and Molotov. . . . I am in agreement with the Führer that at present these [talks] could lead to no result at all, and rather would be used by them to reach their desired goal of a military alliance with France and, if possible, a further rapprochement with England." He added that any Soviet declaration about reining in Comintern propaganda would be worth nothing, as had been shown by earlier Soviet promises to Britain. The only thing that would move the Führer would be a regime change away from Bolshevism toward military dictatorship in Moscow. "Heil Hitler! Your Neurath."[141]

Kandelaki, on his own initiative, approached Herbert Göring, an industrial adviser, SS officer, and cousin of the famous Luftwaffe head, and Herbert expressed delight at Moscow's willingness to enter direct talks and promised to inform his cousin, as if the same information conveyed by official channels weeks earlier would not have reached Hermann Göring. These talks also went nowhere. "Schacht managed only to whisper to me (literally whisper) that he does not see any possibility right now for altering our relations," Surits wrote Litvinov. "The young Göring also hinted not a word about our matters."[142] Stalin sent a ciphered telegram to Berlin (March 19, 1937) asking Kandelaki if he would agree to take over as ambassador to Germany in place of Surits—deemed by the American ambassador to Berlin "the brightest head among the diplomats here"—who was being transferred to Paris.[143] But on April 2, the Soviets announced that Kandelaki was being recalled from Berlin and promoted to deputy trade commissar.[144]

On April 1, 1937, the second Five-Year Plan had been pronounced complete—in just four years and three months, just like the first. (Ten days later, the third

Five-Year Plan would be officially approved.) On April 5, Surits left Berlin for consultations in Moscow; on April 7, he was officially transferred to Paris, but he returned to Germany to await his successor. On April 16, he wrote to Litvinov from Berlin: "Without exception, all the members of the diplomatic corps are fixed on the question of possible changes in Soviet-German relations. The rumors about the possibility of a rapprochement between Germany and the USSR have become widespread in Berlin's diplomatic circles, despite being refuted. Some even suggested that the relevant negotiations have already begun, which the Soviet side is keeping in strict confidence."[145] Litvinov's suspicions had been correct. Germany leaked the "negotiations," trying to drive a wedge between the USSR and France. On April 17, Litvinov telegrammed the Soviet chargé in Paris (Yevgeny Hirschfeld) and the envoy in Czechoslovakia (Alexandrovsky): "Inform the foreign ministry that the rumors circulating abroad about our rapprochement with Germany are without foundation. We did not conduct and are not conducting negotiations with the Germans, which should be clear if only from the simultaneous recall of our ambassador and trade representative."[146]

Hitler had unilaterally terminated the back-channel contacts with Soviet personnel. Stalin had the German nationals in the Soviet Union who had been arrested deported.[147] Also in April, on his initiative, the politburo formed two parallel quintets, which were dubbed permanent commissions: one for foreign policy and other top-secret matters (Stalin, Molotov, Voroshilov, Kaganovich, Yezhov) and one for urgent economic affairs (Molotov, Stalin, Chubar, Mikoyan, Kaganovich).[148] This institutionalized the narrower decision making in the name of the politburo that was already prevalent.

A DESPOT'S REALM

Terror had seized the privileged precincts of society—the postmidnight knock, the search and confiscations in the presence of summoned neighbors ("witnesses" were required by law), the wailing of spouses and children, the disappearances without trace, the fruitless pleading for information at NKVD reception windows, the desperate queues outside transit prisons and unheard screams inside, the bribes to guards for scraps of information on whereabouts.[149] But ordinary Soviet inhabitants mostly did not feel an immediate threat of arrest.[150] As the morbid joke had it, when uniformed men arrived and said "NKVD," people answered, "You've got the wrong apartment—the Communists live upstairs."[151]

Newspaper editorials complained that collective farmers were illegally enlarging household plots, reducing compulsory deliveries, and avoiding tax payments after the arrests of all their supervisors.[152] *Pravda* criticized workers, too, for supposedly taking advantage of the destruction of enemies by failing to show up on the job.[153] One provincial factory worker, the landlord to the exiled poet Osip Mandelstam and his wife, told the poet that the trials were an elite affair, "a fight for power among themselves."[154]

Soviet life proceeded on its course. Ilya Ilf and Evgeny Petrov published their entertaining *One-Story America,* about their travels to that far-off land, and the Bolshoi premiered Mikhail Glinka's *Ruslan and Lyudmila* (April 14, 1937). A week later the Moscow Art Theater premiered Tolstoy's *Anna Karenina,* in a staging by Nemirovich-Danchenko. Stalin attended, along with Molotov, Voroshilov, and Zhdanov. It depicted how the passionate love of Anna (played by Alla Tarasova) for Vronsky led to her suicide. The show concluded with a life-size train bearing down on the audience as Anna lay on the tracks.[155] Earlier that same day, Stalin had Yezhov invent the "discovery," via intelligence sources, of a foreign plot against Tukhachevsky's life, which prevented the marshal from accepting an invitation to the upcoming coronation in London of George VI. The Soviets announced that Tukhachevsky had a cold.[156]

On April 22, Stalin paid his third visit to a part of the eighty-mile canal linking the Moscow and Volga rivers; newsreels and newspapers showered the visit with publicity (several of the people captured on film would soon be arrested and erased).[157] For the canal's official opening, in summer, a flotilla of forty-four ships would deliver the supposed builder-Stakhanovites to the embankment at Moscow's Gorky Park, where a celebration took place.[158] The canal was built by Gulag laborers, more than 20,000 of whom likely perished. Agitators celebrated the achievement that Moscow was now linked to five seas: White, Black, Baltic, Caspian, and Azov.

Food hardships returned. Around 100 million rural folk, 97 percent of all rural households, were confined to 237,000 collective farms and compelled to supply the fruits of their labor—grain, meat, milk, eggs—to the state at prices that were more than ten times below those at "peasant" markets. At the same time, more than 38 percent of the country's vegetables and potatoes and 68 percent of its meat and dairy products in 1937 were produced on their small household plots for sale at those markets.[159] The state store network had grown considerably, but it still had fewer outlets and was more poorly managed than NEP-era retail.[160] Urban per capita consumption in 1937 was higher than it had been in 1928.[161] But the priority on heavy industry and the military depressed living standards.[162] Decent housing was especially scarce.[163] The effects of the poor 1936 harvest were being felt. Local newspapers referred to the queues for bread, indirectly acknowledging the shortages. Secret NKVD reports in 1937 noted "food difficulties"—collective farmers fleeing the most affected areas for the cities to try to get the food they had grown that had been confiscated from them, and spreading typhus.[164] Vyshinsky, the USSR procurator general, reported to Stalin in spring 1937 about peasants stealing the corpses of collapsed livestock, eating offal, potato roots, and fellow humans.[165]

The first Soviet rockets using liquid fuel were launched, traveling eight miles.[166] At the same time, in heavy industry and the defense industry, 585 people had been arrested. There were also arrests in the enlightenment commissariat (288), light industry (141), transport (137), agricultural commissariat (102), food commissariat (100), and the Academy of Sciences (77).[167] The forestry commissariat had, instead of the budgeted 2,480 personnel, just 1,024.[168] Meanwhile, provincial and republic NKVD "party actives" were being forced to follow the suicidal ritual of mutual denunciation. Stalin read an anonymous letter sent to him that claimed that many operatives in the NKVD feared arrest and could not comprehend how the entire NKVD leadership had consisted of thieves and traitors, imploring Stalin to check into the situation and stop the extermination of people.[169]

HINTS

Semyon Krivoshein, the tank commander in Spain, had written to Voroshilov urging that the Spanish Communists be allowed to seize power, in order to prosecute the war effectively. "Revolutionary Spain needs a strong government that is able to organize and guarantee the victory of the revolution," he stressed. "The Communist party ought to come to power even by force, if necessary." Voroshilov had passed Krivoshein's report to Stalin on March 10, 1937.[170] But on March 14, in the Little Corner, Stalin met with Molotov, Voroshilov, Kaganovich, Dimitrov, André Marty, and Togliatti and again expressed support for the Socialist trade unionist Largo Caballero as prime minister. The despot did agree it was best to have Largo Caballero relinquish the war minister portfolio.[171] Voroshilov wrote to Berzin and Gaikis on March 15, that, to overcome the tensions between the Spanish Socialists and Communists, Moscow would not object to a merger of the two in a united Socialist Workers' Party. The next day, Voroshilov instructed Berzin and Stern that the *Pravda* journalist Koltsov was to refrain from mocking Mussolini, so as not to provoke expanded Italian involvement in the war.[172] Dimitrov, for his part, had been imploring Stalin for another meeting before Marty left Moscow for Spain on March 16, and, that day, the Comintern chief, Togliatti, and Marty were received, along with the cronies, at the Near Dacha, "until 2:30 in the morning." Stalin cracked wise at Dimitrov's expense, unnerving him. The despot would not budge on the matter of Communist revolution in Spain.[173]

A Communist takeover had become entirely realistic. By spring 1937, Spain's Communist party—long one of Europe's smallest—reached 250,000 members, on its way to perhaps 400,000.[174] (French Communist party membership peaked at 330,000 in 1937; the British Communist party numbered fewer than 20,000.) Spain's Communists, moreover, were a fighting force: perhaps 130,000 of the 360,000 troops in the Republic's People's Army were Communists.[175] The entire POUM may have been 60,000 members, the anarchist groups 100,000, and the Socialist party 160,000. Civil war had made the Communists Republic Spain's dominant force. Indeed, Largo Caballero, a courageous if vain man, regretted this ever-growing influence of the Spanish Communists and of Moscow, and during the early-winter months of 1937 and into the spring, he floated versions of a war settlement through the Spanish ambassador in Paris. France would obtain the part of Morocco it did not control, Germany would be offered mines and other economic concessions, and Italy a naval base on Menorca, while the Soviets would be forced out.[176] Stalin would likely have known of such a proposal. He told Dimitrov that "if there is a decision for foreign forces to leave Spain, the International Brigades are to be disbanded."[177]

Stalin was reading his briefs closely, writing to Voroshilov (April 13, 1937) that Berzin, in Spain, "is mistaken in his assessment of the failed offensive of the blues [Republic forces] in the area of Casa de Campo [west of Madrid]. The cause of the failure above all consists in the circumstance that when the blues attacked Casa de Campo, the blue troops at Jarama [east of Madrid] remained silent, not even undertaking demonstration acts and giving the whites [Nationalists] the opportunity to throw in their reserves from Jarama against the blues in Casa de Campo. The blue troops are making analogous tactical mistakes constantly."[178] Right or wrong, it was a battlefield analysis not reliant on invocations of treason and conspiracy.

Franco had felt constrained to abandon, for now, the attempt to capture

Madrid, but forces under Mola were being massed to conquer Spain's Basque country. On April 26, 1937, the German Condor Legion, assisted by Italian aircraft, attacked Guernica, the ancient capital of the Basques, at the behest of the Nationalists, aiming to sow terror in the Republic's rear. The attack came on a Monday, market day. Not only was the civilian population of some 5,000 to 7,000 (including refugees) carpet-bombed, but as they tried to escape, they were strafed with machine guns mounted on Heinkel He-51s. Hundreds were killed. George Steer, a British journalist in the vicinity, stirred worldwide anger over the atrocities and German culpability with firsthand reportage (*Times,* April 28, 1937), which was reprinted in France. Nationalists muddied the waters, introducing the lie, propagated by British friends of Franco, that the Basques had blown up their own symbolic capital to discredit Nationalist forces.[179]

Also in April 1937, the NKVD intercepted and photographed a communication from the Japanese military attaché in Warsaw to the general staff in Tokyo. NKVD foreign intelligence could not read the Japanese and had to go to Lefortovo prison for assistance from R. N. Kim, a Soviet counterintelligence agent on Japan who had been arrested as a foreign spy. The document was composed in the hand of the Japanese attaché's aide—handwriting well known to Kim—and conveyed that "contact had been established with an emissary of Marshal Tukhachevsky." This secret message for Tokyo had been sent not by ciphered telegram but by diplomatic pouch, which traveled from Poland to Japan through the Soviet Union. Japanese intelligence appears to have intended the "secret" document to be "intercepted."[180]

MAY DAYS

A convoluted action also took place on May Day 1937, a holiday marked by a military parade through the seat of power. "Infantry, cavalry, tanks would sweep past while fighters and bombers roared overhead," one foreign observer noted. "Every now and then he [Stalin] would raise his hand, palm outstretched, with a little gesture that was at once a friendly wave, a benediction, and a salute."[181] Still, the regime undertook unprecedented precautions, even by Stalinist standards, enveloping Red Square in NKVD troops and plainclothes officers—as if a putsch were imminent. It was: Stalin's putsch. Right after the parade, in the normally convivial setting of the Voroshilovs' apartment, the despot warned the many military men present that unexposed enemies were in their midst.[182]

In Catalonia by this time, tensions were boiling over, because food prices had nearly doubled since the onset of civil war, many factories were operating far below capacity, and tit-for-tat political murders were taking place. The governing Socialists, not to mention the Communists, had long been eager to crush the anarchists, as well as the POUM and, along with them, Catalan regional autonomy. On May 2, when the civilian president of the Republic's government called the civilian president of the Catalan Generalitat, an operator at the anarchist-controlled main telephone station said the line needed to be kept open for more important business. The next day, government police seized the station. Workers in Barcelona laid down their tools, barricades went up, and, within hours, all political forces had mustered their militias. Later, Franco would boast that his agents had provoked the Barcelona anarchist uprising so as to disorganize the Republic's rear. No doubt his agents did try. The NKVD, too, had infiltrated the POUM to instigate an attempted "seizure of power"—as a pretext to crush it.[183] In fact, no one needed to instigate the events. The crackdown was brutal. On May 7, a special assault guard arrived from Valencia, some 6,000 men. The street combat left around 500 dead and 1,000 wounded.[184] On May 15, amid calls for harsh reprisals against "anarchist" violence, Largo Caballero resigned as prime minister.

During Barcelona's violent May Days, Koltsov was on a six-week trip back home. He had dug in with soldiers in trenches, witnessing the heroism and death of a real war. "There was something new in him, he became older, more severe, appeared pensive," one acquaintance recalled. "He had gotten thinner, his skin was tanned, the flame of war had literally burned him, charred him."[185] Koltsov's longtime coworkers at *Pravda* were being accused of monstrous crimes and being arrested. Around his luxury apartment at Government House (the House on the Embankment), the doors to his neighbors' apartments were sealed with wax, indicating that the residents had been hauled off by the NKVD.[186]

Stalin, joined by Molotov, Voroshilov, Kaganovich, and Yezhov, had granted Koltsov an audience in the Little Corner, his second. "He sincerely, profoundly, . . . fanatically believed in the wisdom of Stalin," Koltsov's brother Boris Yefimov would recall. "How many times, after meeting the Master, my brother would regale me in minute detail about his way of conversing, about his specific observations, phrases, jokes. He liked everything about Stalin."[187] Now the despot mocked Koltsov. "Stalin stood near me, put his hand on his heart, and bowed: 'What should one call you in Spanish, Mig-u-el?'" Koltsov told his brother after the audience. "Mig-el, Comrade Stalin." Stalin: "Right, then, Don Mig-el. We, noble Spaniards, heartily thank you for your interesting report. Goodbye for now, Don Mig-el." As Koltsov reached the door, Stalin called after him: "Have you a revolver, Comrade Koltsov?" "Yes, Comrade Stalin." "But you aren't planning to shoot yourself with it?" "Of course not." "Well, excellent! Excellent! Thank you again, Comrade Koltsov, goodbye, Don Mig-el."[188]

After Moscow's May Day, the *Pravda* correspondent made his way back to Spain. A new NKVD courier for the diplomatic pouch arrived from Moscow and casually told fellow operatives in Spain that Koltsov "had sold himself to the English."[189]

ASSASSINATIONS

Voroshilov approved a long list of medals for service in Spain, but the grind there was taking its toll on Soviet personnel.[190] Meanwhile, attempts to use death squads to assassinate Franco came to naught.[191] Still, Soviet intelligence officials in Moscow did not relinquish the fantasy. Theodore Maly, the Soviet spy chief in London, operating without diplomatic cover, had been instructed to send Kim Philby, the British-born Soviet agent, as a freelance war correspondent to Spain to infiltrate Franco's entourage so as to assassinate him. Philby (code-named "Söhnchen," "Little Sonny" in German) was to observe all details of Franco's bodyguard retinue. He expressed enthusiasm, but after some three months in Spain he was recalled to London. "The fact is that Little Sonny has come back in low spirits," Maly, who had doubted Moscow's scheme from the start, reported on May 24, 1937. "He has not even managed to get near to the 'interesting' objective." Maly added that even if Philby had somehow gotten near Franco, "he would not have been able to do what was required of him. Though devoted and ready to sacrifice himself, he does not possess the physical courage and other qualities necessary for this attempt."[192]

In the Barcelona cauldron, the assignments were more serious. The NKVD assassin Josifas "Juzik" Grigulevičius, known as Grigulevich, born in Wilno (Vilnius) in 1913 to a Russian mother and a Lithuanian-Jewish father and raised a Karaite, had assassinated police informers in his youth, been imprisoned in Poland in 1932–33 for Communist subversion, and then joined his émigré father in Argentina and picked up Spanish, to go with his native Polish, Lithuanian, and Russian, as well as French. "Max," as he would be known in Spain, had flown into Barcelona from Toulouse back in the fall, then made his way to Madrid, where he trained saboteurs and arsonists for work behind Franco's lines. He also liquidated

"Trotskyites."[193] Grigulevich had arrived in Barcelona with his death squad on May 3, 1937.[194] His primary target was Andreu Nin. The Soviet NKVD station chief Orlov forged a letter from a Nazi agent to Franco detailing Nin's supposed "infiltration" of the POUM for the Nationalists. An agent for the Soviets persuaded a bookshop known to support the POUM to take custody of a suitcase for a few days; government police promptly arrived and found the suitcase, which contained the supposed secret documents—the Orlov forgery of a POUM conspiracy with the "fascists." On May 23, Orlov pressed the case against the POUM, adducing the captured "document" he had fabricated, which was written in invisible ink and in code but was said to have been "deciphered" thanks to the capture of some of Franco's codebooks. Koltsov played up the "evidence" of the POUM treachery in *Pravda*.[195] The POUM was soon outlawed, its headquarters at Barcelona's Hotel Falcon converted into a house of detention.

After Nin was arrested, Orlov's thugs kidnapped him from Spanish prison and took him to a secret place of confinement maintained by the NKVD at Alcalá de Henares, the birthplace of Cervantes. There, they tortured him to get him to confess he was a "fascist agent." With much of the POUM leadership awaiting trial, such testimony was thought necessary to persuade the public to support death sentences. Nin refused to confess to treason, Trotskyism, or other crimes. He was executed in secret by Grigulevich's death squad on the Alcalá de Henares highway and buried there.[196] When people continued to inquire about his whereabouts, the Soviets replied that he must have gone off with his fascist hirelings. Orlov wrote a pamphlet, attributed to Nin, denouncing Trotskyism.[197] The NKVD operative had worked extra hard to prove his bona fides to Stalin. In carrying out Stalin's no-holds campaign against "Trotskyites" and "enemies" in Spain, the NKVD contingent there—which numbered no more than forty, and sometimes half that—gave the impression, wrongly, of attempted Sovietization.[198]

Soviet annihilation of the POUM also sowed deep disillusionment among those who identified with the antifascist cause of Spain's Republic. Eric Blair, better known as George Orwell, who, before discovering the Lancashire miners in 1936, had been only intermittently interested in politics, had gone to Spain in early 1937 and joined a militia associated with the POUM. "It was the first time that I had ever been in a town where the working class was in the saddle," he would write in *Homage to Catalonia*. "Practically every building of any size had been seized by the workers and was draped with red flags or with the red and black flag of the Anarchists; every wall was scrawled with the hammer and sickle and with the initials of the revolutionary parties; almost every church had been gutted and its images burnt. . . . Every shop and cafe had an inscription saying that it had been collectivised; even the bootblacks had been collectivised and their boxes painted red and black. Waiters and shop-walkers looked you in the face and treated you as an equal. . . . In outward appearance it was a town in which the wealthy classes had practically ceased to exist." But Orwell was shocked to discover that the Communists were fighting tooth and nail against this grassroots revolution. On May 20, 1937, he was shot in the throat by a sniper. With the banning of the POUM, he would flee across the border to France.[199]

In Paris, an International Exhibition opened on May 25 that would run for six months. In front of the Eiffel Tower, a neoclassical columned Nazi pavilion designed by Albert Speer and topped by an eagle faced a Soviet pavilion designed by Boris Yofan and topped by a statue designed by Vera Mukhina, of a male worker and a female peasant together thrusting a hammer and sickle. Nearby stood the Spanish pavilion, which, from summer 1937, would showcase Pablo Picasso's *Guernica*.[200] The besieged Basque country had surrendered.

STALIN'S TUKHACHEVSKY PLOT

Thanks to the endless purges and verifications, the Soviet armed forces counted just 150,000 party members among its 1.4 million men—half the number it had four years earlier. This spurred a move, in May 1937, to reintroduce political commissars and create three-person military soviets in units, to which local nonmilitary party secretaries were added.[201] But if Stalin was worried about a decline of party influence in the army, he himself was the cause.

Corps commander Primakov, nine months in Lefortovo, had refused to admit his "guilt," but finally on May 8, 1937, he "confessed" and implicated others.[202] On May 10, a politburo decree demoted Tukhachevsky from first deputy defense commissar to commander of the Volga military district. It also named Marshal Alexander Yegorov—Stalin's crony from the civil war—as the new first deputy commissar, returned Shaposhnikov as chief of the general staff, and shifted Yakir from Kiev to the Leningrad military district.[203] Stalin received Tukhachevsky in the Little Corner on May 13, in the presence of Voroshilov, Molotov, Yezhov, and Kaganovich, and reassured the marshal that everything would be sorted out, mentioning a problem with Tukhachevsky's lover, Yulia Kuzmina, who supposedly was a foreign agent.[204] Around this time, August Kork, head of the Frunze

Military Academy, was arrested and beaten into testifying. On May 15, Boris Feldman, head of the Red Army cadres department, was arrested, and, under severe torture, he incriminated Tukhachevsky (who the next day departed for his new posting in the rear, the city of Kuibyshev).[205] Yezhov was putting together the pieces in Stalin's scenario.

Tukhachevsky did himself few favors, stirring resentment (like Yagoda in the NKVD).[206] The marshal was the army's most brilliant military mind, and the first to let you know. Already in 1920, he had provoked the interest of the political police for willfulness as well as abuse of subordinates and funds.[207] In his grand apartment in Moscow's House on the Embankment, he hosted musicial evenings with the likes of Shostakovich and had the state military orchestra perform private parties at his state dacha, immodesties heightened by his aristocrat pedigree.[208] A serial womanizer, he lived with Kuzmina without having divorced his third wife, while also carrying on an affair with Natalya Sats, director of the Central Children's Theater. (He preferred intellectual beauties, not the youngish, buxom peasant girls who had once caught Stalin's eye.) Stalin exploited these appetites: Tukhachevsky shared at least two lovers with Yagoda, who helped keep tabs on the marshal—Shura Skoblina, the niece of the émigré White Guard general, and Nadezhda "Timosha" Peshkova, the widow of Gorky's son.[209] Most Soviet officials were afraid of even limited intercourse with foreigners, but Tukhachevsky enjoyed high-level contact with the German and French militaries (he spoke both languages), which of course had been authorized but nonetheless endangered him.[210] Yezhov would relate a tale of how, during a visit to France, Tukhachevsky had supposedly cut off a piece of fabric at Napoleon's grave and made himself an amulet. To all of this was added Voroshilov's long-standing ill will.[211]

Stalin was also fixated on the authority of the commanders of the country's two most strategic military districts on the western border: Yakir, who had headed the Kiev (Ukrainian) military district since 1926, and Uborevičius (b. 1896), the son of a Lithuanian peasant, who had commanded the western (Belorussian) since 1931 and had an extraordinary following among the officer corps.[212] Together, these two commands accounted for 25 of the Soviet Union's 90 infantry divisions and 12 of its 26 cavalry divisions. Only Blyukher, atop the Soviet Far Eastern Army, commanded comparable forces. Stalin had promoted the proletarian Blyukher to marshal while overlooking Yakir and Uborevičius, who were whispered to be jealous. Voroshilov, for his part, disliked Blyukher, perceiving a dangerous rival. (Amid rumors of Blyukher's pending promotion to deputy defense commissar, Voroshilov preemptively promoted a Blyukher deputy to the post.)[213] Such jockeying by outsize egos could be found in any large institution, but in Stalin's hands everyday tensions or indiscretions could become lethal. Through chauffeurs, bodyguards, cooks, maids, adjutants, secretarial staff, mistresses, and the NKVD special departments, the top military men were under a level of surveillance exceeding even that conducted on the foreign military attachés of Britain, Germany, Poland, Romania, or Japan.[214]

Also in Stalin's sights was Soviet military intelligence. Uritsky was out of his depth and bereft of talented people—such as Artuzov and Otto Steinbrück—whom he had forced out.[215] On May 20, Artuzov was arrested in his office (no. 201) on the second floor of Lubyanka and accused of being a rightist alongside Yagoda, as well as concealing material implicating Tukhachevsky (the very material he had *forwarded* to Yezhov). His interrogation protocols, which he signed with his own blood, would also assert that Yagoda had told him of widespread NKVD dissatisfaction with the Soviet leadership, "whose despotism stands in crying contradiction to declarations of Soviet democracy."[216] On May 21, Stalin received the interrogation protocols of Semyon Firin-Pupko, a longtime military intelligence operative with experience in Poland, France, and Germany and, most recently, a deputy chief of the Gulag, responsible for forced labor construction sites. Accused of being a *German* spy, Firin painted in his "testimony" an incredible portrait of the complete capture of Soviet military attachés abroad by *Polish* intelligence, which he said was also directing Soviet counterintelligence in Moscow.[217]

That same day, Stalin summoned Molotov, Voroshilov, Kaganovich, Yezhov, Frinovsky, Slutsky (head of NKVD foreign intelligence), Yakov Serebryansky (head of NKVD agents abroad without diplomatic cover), Uritsky, Mikhail Alexandrovsky (deputy chief of military intelligence, who had replaced Artuzov), and Alexander Nikonov (another Uritsky deputy) to the Little Corner for a two-and-a-half-hour session.[218] In an internal memorandum that day, addressed to Yezhov and Voroshilov, the despot ordered that all Soviet agents abroad and their handlers be rechecked, because "military intelligence and its apparatus have fallen into German hands." Stalin's memo noted that "from the point of view of intelligence, we cannot have friends; there are immediate enemies and potential enemies," and deemed the Czechoslovaks—with whom the Soviet Union had a mutual assistance pact—"the enemies of our enemies, nothing more." He ordered Soviet personnel not to share intelligence secrets with Czechoslovakia or any other country, and "to fully assimilate the lesson of the cooperation with the Germans," whereby "Rapallo, close ties, created the illusion of friendship. The Germans have remained our enemies, and they penetrated us and implanted their network." He added, "We have had enormous victories, we are stronger than all politically, we are stronger economically, but in intelligence we have been smashed. Understand, they smashed us in intelligence."[219]

Civil defense followed. Its head, the ethnic Latvian Roberts Eidemanis (shortened to Eideman), was arrested on May 22 and, under torture, "incriminated" twenty others. Yezhov had the interrogation protocols on Stalin's desk quickly. The despot wrote on them, "All those people named by Eideman in civil defense (center and periphery) immediately arrest"[220]—no verification of their specific spying activities and any damage caused.

Also on May 22, as if a putsch were imminent, troops of the Dzierżyński Regiment, guardians of the Kremlin, were brought to full alert and all Kremlin passes were invalidated. Out in Kuibyshev, Tukhachevsky was arrested and forced to remove his marshal's uniform.[221] Stalin, as promised, had him returned to Moscow, but by convoy guard. On the post-facto Central Committee resolution proposing Tukhachevsky's arrest, Marshal Budyonny wrote, "Unequivocally in favor. The scum should be executed."[222] In the cellars on May 26, a mere four days after his arrest, Tukhachevsky began to sign whatever interrogators put in front of him. Zinovy Ushakov, who prided himself on obtaining confessions no other investigator could extract, mercilessly beat Tukhachevsky, whose blood dripped onto the pages of a confession to crimes he did not commit. By some accounts, Tukhachevsky's teenage daughter, Svetlana, was brought to the prison, where the interrogators told him they would rape her.[223]

Even as he had the Soviet military brass tortured for being agents of fascism, on May 27, 1937, in the Little Corner, Stalin received Kandelaki, his erstwhile Berlin trade representative, who was trying to cut a deal with the German fascists.[224] Germany's military attaché in Moscow, General Ernst Köstring, was sending constant updates to Berlin, as Stalin knew. In Berlin's diplomatic circles, German officials "confidentially" whispered how not all of their spies in the Soviet armed forces had yet been caught, egging Stalin on.[225] He needed no such inducement, of course. On May 28–29, Yakir and Uborevičius were arrested. On May 30, eight days after Gamarnik had inscribed "in favor" on the post-facto arrest order for Tukhachevsky, he himself was dismissed. The next day he killed himself in his apartment on Bolshoi Rzhevsky Street.[226] (Kulik, who lived in the same building, would soon join a second apartment to his own: eight rooms for a three-person family. Shaposhnikov would get Gamarnik's dacha in Zubalovo.) Real and imagined associates, acquaintances, and relatives of the arrested men fell into the NKVD cellars. Stalin dictated, edited, and pored over the interrogation protocols, then circulated and referred to them as if they were factual.[227]

TERRORIZING THE NKVD

Plenty of NKVD personnel came forward to enact the carnage on coworkers. A key cooperative group centered on Yevdokimov, party boss of the North Caucasus territory. He had first met Yezhov at the Communist Academy in the 1920s. Stalin, around the time he issued the Sochi telegram replacing Yagoda with Yezhov, had consulted with Yevdokimov.[228] Yevdokimov had been among those who ripped into Yagoda at the February–March 1937 plenum.[229] He aspired to be Yezhov's new first deputy at the NKVD and head of the state security department (GB). Instead, Mikhail Frinovsky, whom Yezhov was consulting regularly over wet lunches, got the position.[230] Frinovsky had worked under Yevdokimov in his early career in Ukraine and the North Caucasus, but was his own man. He became one of the few Chekists closely tied to Yagoda (as chief of the USSR border guards) who would flourish under Yezhov. Yezhov did promote a slew of Yevdokimov people in the NKVD, including Israel Dagin, Yakov Deich, Sergei Mironov, Nikolai Nikolayev-Zhurid, and Vladimir Kursky, who replaced Pauker as head of bodyguards. (Kursky would shoot himself six days after receiving the Order of Lenin; Dagin would replace him.) All in all, fourteen of the sixty-odd regional NKVD bosses in 1937 were linked by service in the North Caucasus under Yevdokimov.[231] Thus did the enemies of Yezhov's enemy (Yagoda) become Yezhov's new friends—and the zealous implementers of the slaughter in the NKVD itself.

Despite the upheaval, Yezhov's NKVD, like Yagoda's, was made up of people of roughly the same generation, with Cheka service dating to Dzierżyński, overwhelmingly white-collar rather than working-class or peasant backgrounds, and heavily Jewish or non-Russian.[232] Yezhov's NKVD, similarly, was riven with distrust. When informing Frinovsky that he wanted to appoint him first deputy commissar, Yezhov asked him to recite his accumulated sins. "You have so many sins, you ought to be arrested right now," Yezhov told him, adding, "Well, so what, you'll work, and you'll be my person 100 percent."[233] Frinovsky further testified that "Yezhov demanded that I find investigators who were utterly dependent on us or had sins on their records, and they knew they had sins, which could be held over them."[234]

Stalin had more faith in his young protégé than he'd had in Yagoda, but Yezhov still had to clear NKVD personnel appointments with the despot. Yezhov wielded nearly unimaginable power and terrified a vast country, but he never felt at ease. "Coming to the NKVD organs, at first I found myself alone," he would later explain. "I did not even have an aide." This was a lie: Yezhov had imported loyalists from the party apparatus, including Mikhail Litvin, who got the critical post of head of NKVD personnel, and Isaak Shapiro, who became head of the NKVD secretariat. Still, Stalin would often compel him to destroy his own associates. And the chain-reaction arrests, including of many people Yezhov had newly promoted, did foster paranoia. "I tasked this or that NKVD department head with interrogating someone who had been arrested," Yezhov noted, "while thinking to myself: 'Today you interrogate him, tomorrow I'll arrest you.' All around were enemies of the people, my enemies."[235]

WEST ON THE WANE

Stalin had invested considerable time wooing Western intellectual sympathizers. But just as Pasternak had told the secret police, André Gide, in his *Return from the U.S.S.R.* (December 1936), published something critical, which noted, among other things, that "one fully literate worker asked if we also had schools in France."[236] Gide had also written a private "Report for My Friends on My Trip to the USSR," and, on a mimeographed copy of a Russian translation Zhdanov had written for Stalin, "Defender of homosexuals!"[237] The politburo wanted Koltsov to publish a rebuttal of Gide's book, but he was occupied in Spain, so the apparatchiks engaged Feuchtwanger, who answered with *Moscow, 1937.*[238] It was rushed into print in Russian in a print run of 200,000, and contained excerpts of Feuchtwanger's early 1937 conversation with Stalin. "In official portraits Stalin gives the impression of being a tall, wide-shouldered, imposing person," Feuchtwanger wrote. "In real life he is not very tall, thinnish, and, in the expanse of his Kremlin room where I met him, he was not very noticeable." He added: "Stalin speaks slowly, softly, in a bit of voiceless voice. During a conversation he paces back and forth in the room, then he suddenly comes upon his interlocutor and, directing the index finger of his handsome hand toward him, he clarifies, or expounds, while formulating thought-out phrases, draws patterns on a sheet of paper with a colored pencil."[239]

Simplicity—Stalin's beloved self-characterization—was the leitmotif. "Stalin speaks unpretentiously and is able to express complicated thoughts simply," Feuchtwanger continued. "Sometimes he speaks too simply, like a person who is used to formulating his thoughts so that they are understood from Moscow to Vladivostok. . . . He feels himself quite free in many areas [of knowledge] and cites by memory without preparation names, dates, facts always exactly." Feuchtwanger wrote that "of all the men I know who have power, Stalin is the most unpretentious." This was the cue to discuss the cult: "I spoke frankly to him about the vulgar and excessive cult made of him, and he replied with equal candor. . . . He thinks it is possible even that 'wreckers' may be behind it in an attempt to discredit him." The German sympathizer was bothered by the showcase trials and put into print the heresy that "it seemed the bullets which tore into Zinoviev and Kamenev killed not only them, but the new world." And yet, in the end, he ended up justifying the trials he knew to be falsified, on the basis of cultural snobbery (Russia was backward) and the political imperative to close ranks against fascism.[240]

Vsevolod Vishnevsky, the Soviet writer, found "a lot of European arrogance" in Feuchtwanger's text. "Neither Malraux nor all these Western 'public figures' are of any use to us," Vishnevsky wrote to Sergei Eisenstein (May 24, 1937). "Their historical value is much smaller than ours. . . . Let everything be ours. Let the law begin with us."[241]

STALIN'S ATTEMPT AT EXPLANATION

Stalin directed Voroshilov to summon an extraordinary session of the USSR's Main Military Council, which customarily met once annually, in November or December, but now convened June 1 to 4, 1937. Its 85 members were top army and fleet commanders and heads of military academies, many of whom had been arrested or discharged, leaving 53 to attend, but 116 nonmembers were invited, along with Yezhov, Frinovsky, and others of the NKVD.[242] Some invitees arrived from as far away as Vladivostok (a week's journey by train), while Kirill Meretskov had only just returned from Spain and, a naïf, expected to be asked to report on its key military lessons.[243] Instead, attendees were compelled to spend the first day reading interrogation protocols about a fantastic homegrown fascist military plot. "The testimonies were typed carbon copies on normal paper, some contained numeration, some not," one participant recalled. "The print on them was not always sharp, and reading them was difficult." Readings were hurried, and new pages kept coming, with insufficient copies to go around, forcing people to wait as sections were freed up (and to read them out of order). Some of the protocols implicated attendees in the hall. Finally, the formal session opened, not in the House of the Red Army, as previously stipulated, but in the Sverdlov Hall of the Kremlin's Imperial Senate building.[244] The mood was cemeterylike.

Stalin attended all four days. (He would not become a member of the Military Council until the next year, so the sessions were officially designated a joint meeting of the council and "the politburo.") Voroshilov had to deliver a report in the same room used for the February–March 1937 Central Committee plenum, but since then his deputy defense commissars (Tukhachevsky, Gamarnik) had turned out to be foreign agents: where had he been looking? In the presidium, Stalin "looked over the hall with interest, seeking familiar faces, and fixing his gaze on some," while Voroshilov "seemed to have shrunk in height," the participant recalled. "His hair had turned even grayer, wrinkles had appeared, and his voice, normally muffled, became completely hoarse."[245] Voroshilov complained that, back during the 1936 May Day celebrations, in a discussion in his apartment that devolved into recriminations over the 1920 Soviet-Polish War debacle, "Tukhachevsky said in the presence of comrades Stalin, Molotov, and many others that I and Budyonny had supposedly created a small clique of people around myself that controls policy. Two days later, Tukhachevsky took his words back." Voroshilov then tried to downplay his grudge-drenched remarks as merely "the usual squabbles," and to put distance between himself and the accused: "I, as you know, did not especially like, did not love Tukhachevsky. I had strained relations with him."[246]

Voroshilov's comments were almost beside the point. Stalin, on the second day (June 2), to a prolonged standing ovation, would deliver his most revealing remarks during his terror.

"Comrades, I hope no one doubts now that a military-political plot against Soviet power existed," he began. "Such an abundance of testimony by the criminals themselves and observations by comrades who work there, such a mass of them, that, indubitably, here we have a military-political plot against Soviet power, stimulated and financed by German fascists." The mere fact that he had to address possible doubts spoke volumes. Moreover, the usually systematic Stalin meandered, losing his train of thought. He denied that Tukhachevsky had been arrested because of noble lineage, reminding the audience that Engels was the son of a factory owner and asking if they knew that Lenin was from the nobility. Also disingenuously, Stalin asserted that no one was being arrested for having long ago voted with Trotsky. But then the despot contradicted himself. "Dzierżyński voted for Trotsky, and not only voted, but openly supported Trotsky, during Lenin's time, against Lenin," he told the military men. "This was a very active Trotskyite, and he wanted to bring the whole GPU to the defense of Trotsky. In this he did not succeed."[247] *Dzierżyński* a Trotskyite? Well, in fall 1925, Dzierżyński had very briefly flirted with joining Kamenev in opposition, before quickly repudiating Kamenev's initiative to recruit him. Almost no one knew besides Stalin.

With this outburst, Stalin was trying to underscore not social origins (Dzierżyński, too, had been gentry), but deeds. "Did you read his testimony?" he asked of Tukhachevsky. "He passed on our operational plans—our operational plans, the holy of holies—to the German army. He had dealings with representatives of the German Reichswehr. A spy? A spy." Stalin put out the idea that Tukhachevsky, as well as Yakir and others, had been entrapped by a seductress and blackmailed with threats of exposure. "There is an experienced agent in Germany, in Berlin . . . Josephine Heinze; maybe one of you knows her," Stalin said threateningly. "She is a beautiful woman. An old agent. She recruited Karakhan. She recruited him with the ways of a woman. She recruited Yenukidze. She helped recruit Tukhachevsky. She also had Rudzutaks in her hands. This Josephine Heinze is a very experienced agent. She is probably Danish and works for the German Reichswehr. A beautiful woman, who likes to cater to all men's desires."

A lot of work for one chanteuse. Stalin further explained to the closed-door gathering that foreign powers sought to conquer the Soviet Union because its successes had increased its value, while those same successes had induced Soviet officials to let down their guard.[248] As a result, he said, the top ranks of Soviet military intelligence actually worked for German, Japanese, and Polish intelligence.

"Collective farms," Stalin suddenly exclaimed. "What in the world do they [the arrested military brass] have to do with collective farms?" Indeed. In his rambling answer, he again contradicted himself. He told a story of aristocratic types (Yenukidze, Tukhachevsky) who supposedly preferred a gentry economy and opposed socialism in the village.[249] Here he revealed the centrality in his terror scenario of the right deviation, which in some ways was more important even than perfidious Trotskyism, because the right signified the possible *class* degeneration of the revolution: the political attitudes of the former tsarist officers, bourgeois specialists in industry, and the peasant mass—real social groups, for whom capitalism was not anathema but preferred. The right, therefore, was a *structural* threat, a false (or petit bourgeois) class consciousness.

Straining to persuade the attendees of the improbable charges, Stalin also appealed to current events, asserting that the Wehrmacht "wanted to make the USSR into a second Spain." This supposedly explained the vast scale of the Kremlin's response. All the same, the scale of arrests was unnerving. "People are saying that a mass of the military command structure is being taken out of commission," Stalin admitted. "I see some are perplexed about how we will replace them. . . . Our army has a wealth of talent. In our country, in our party, in our army there is a wealth of talent." After these assurances, he enjoined them to have the courage to promote these young people "more boldly; don't be afraid. (Prolonged applause.)"[250]

DIGESTING THE UNDIGESTIBLE

Stalin had displayed less than a full command of key military terms and issues, and he misstated people's names.[251] What the attendees, their lives on the line, made of his rambling remains unclear. Following a break, discussion ensued. Marshal Blyukher stated that in the units, "they are not speaking the way they should be. In a word, we'll have to explain to the troops what this is about." Stalin jumped on him: "You mean reconsider who has been arrested?" Blyukher tried to recover: "Not exactly that." Some back-and-forth ensued over a list that had been compiled, of 150 people to be promoted, and Voroshilov stated, "The list is somewhere." (The Red Army personnel chief who had compiled the list had been arrested.) Stalin interjected: "There's no need to look at the list, since half of those on it had been arrested."[252]

Throughout the four days of the Main Military Council gathering in the Kremlin, forty-two military men would take the floor; thirty-four of them would be arrested. All told, just ten of the eighty-five members as of 1937 would survive, the rest falling to "friendly fire."[253] (Sergei Kamenev, the civil-war-era commander in chief, had managed to cheat Stalin, dying of natural causes at age fifty-five, but he would be made a foreign agent posthumously.) Not a single speaker defended his arrested colleagues. On the contrary, they called them fascists and scum. Budyonny interrupted often, brutishly remarking that the civil war heroes Yakir and Uborevičius had been cowards back then. Shaposhnikov—wearing old-fashioned spectacles, his hair parted down the middle, unfailingly correct in manner—spoke only of his own shortcomings, an elegant stance, which did not spread and did nothing to halt the pandemonium.[254] None of the military officers, most of whom had battlefield experience, would try to stop Stalin's insanity. They were locked in Bolshevik ways of looking at the world, their own fear, and the grip of his person.

The day after Stalin's speech and the initial discussion, on June 3, 1937, General Emilio Mola—of "fifth column" fame—died when his plane hit a hillside in fog. Mola's crash (three months after Sanjurjo's) induced Franco to stop traveling by air. (He would tour the front by car.)[255] Franco attended Mola's funeral, where, in front of onlookers, the caudillo's uniform split at the armpit, a sign of his weight gain. But Franco, whose ambitions and pitilessness were evident, had not even murdered Mola, a genuine rival, let alone the bulk of Spain's upper officer corps.

On June 4, the final day, a diminished Voroshilov offered concluding remarks. Stalin interrupted, demanding to know why the Communist party members he had personally sent to the Red Army were not leading tank units. "They cannot be commanders right away," Voroshilov responded defensively. "We need to teach them." Stalin: "What, are you not teaching them?" Voroshilov: "We're teaching them, but in order to grow into a brigade commander, you must put in a rather significant amount of time."[256]

Late on the concluding evening, a telegram arrived reporting that Keke Geladze, Stalin's mother, had died in the Georgian capital. The cause was heart failure, according to the medical report; she was probably in her seventy-seventh year. (The morbid joke, whispered in Tiflis, that the guard outside her apartment was there to ensure she did not give birth to another Stalin, lost its topicality.)[257] Stalin did not interrupt his terror against his own army to attend the funeral, a terrible breach of custom for a Georgian; Beria represented him at the ceremony. *Pravda* reported that a wreath had been sent with the inscription, in Russian and Georgian, TO A DEAR AND BELOVED MOTHER, FROM YOUR SON IOSIF JUGHASHVILI (STALIN).[258] Keke's few personal effects went to one of her two female peasant companions who had known her in Gori; a tag on her iron bed bore the notation PROPERTY OF THE NKVD.[259] The funeral procession gave off the sound of stomping jackboots as nearly the entire Georgian secret police marched with her coffin.[260] A washerwoman and seamstress, she would be buried in Georgia's Mtatsminda (Holy Mountain) Pantheon of Writers and Public Figures.

IN CAMERA

Soviet borders were effectively closed (visas were required to exit). A privileged few were afforded occasional access to foreign newsreels. Juri Jelagin, a musician, recalled how members of his elite Vakhtangov Theater troupe were whisked to Mosfilm. "We watched American and German chronicles," he wrote. "We saw horse jumping in Paris, President Roosevelt's press conferences, Hitler's nighttime torchlight processions, Davis Cup tennis matches, Mussolini speaking from the balcony of the palace in Rome, and sittings of the English Parliament."[261] A few organizations had authorized access to foreign publications. Some Soviet inhabitants had relatives abroad, and though their correspondence passed through censorship, the latter struggled to keep up.[262] Information from foreign radio broadcasts such as the BBC was accessible, but only to the minority with dial radios in certain regions (even listening to foreign musical programs could get one denounced). The overwhelming majority of USSR inhabitants were cut off from the outside world, except for what the regime decided could be shown or heard.[263] Even in the foreign affairs commissariat, department heads for various regions of the world were frequently in the dark about specific world events.[264]

On top of the enforced isolation, a swirl of dark forces and shadowy machinations suffused the mentality of the time. The opaque regime had originated as a conspiracy and had never ceased being one, while fighting against what one scholar has aptly called the "omnipresent conspiracy."[265] The plots could be so convoluted that many of those involved did not even know about them. (As Macduff says in Shakespeare's *Macbeth*, "Cruel are the times when we are traitors / And do not know ourselves.") Some Soviet inhabitants saw through the smoke and mirrors. "Even the simplest fool knew that all those thousands were not 'traitors,' 'enemies of the people,' or 'spies,'" insisted Ismail Akhmedov, then a junior military intelligence officer (who would later defect).[266] But, in fact, the vast majority did not know.

On June 11, 1937, Soviet newspapers and radio stunned the country, announcing a trial, later that day, for Marshal Tukhachevsky and seven other high-ranking Red Army officers, for complicity in a "Trotskyite Anti-Soviet Military Organization" on behalf of foreign powers: Yakir, Uborevičius, Eideman, Kork,

Putna, Feldman, and Primakov. A ninth, the suicide Gamarnik, was posthumously named a Nazi spy and Gestapo agent as well. (Three of the nine "Gestapo agents" were Jews.)[267] Right before and after announcement of the "trial," *Pravda* serialized a Russian translation of Charles Russell's short *Espionage and Counter-Espionage, M.I-4* (1926), for study by party cadres.[268] Still, the Soviet populace had not been prepared by way of a long campaign culminating in a public trial.

Everything had taken place behind the scenes. On June 8, prison wardens had presented the eight defendants with their formal indictments, and the next day Yakir had addressed a petition for mercy to "Our Own Close Comrade Stalin," who wrote on it, "He is a scoundrel and a whore." Other politburo members had to read it as well. ("A perfectly precise definition. K. Voroshilov." "A scumbag and a whore, deserves only one kind of punishment, death. L. Kaganovich." Molotov affixed his name without elaborating.) After collecting the signatures, Stalin wrote on the document, "My archive."[269] Also on June 8, 1937, he sacked Uritsky as military intelligence chief after the latter wrote confessing that he had visited Yakir, Uborevičius, and other arrested enemies in their homes but desperately insisting, "I was not friends with them."[270] He was replaced by his predecessor, the disgraced Berzin, who had returned from Spain and, after Stalin had sung his praises, been decorated with the Order of Lenin. The forty-seven-year-old triumphantly returned to his old office in the Chocolate House, following a tryst the same morning with his Spanish mistress, Aurora Sánchez, who would very soon celebrate her twentieth birthday.[271]

Among the charges leveled against Tukhachevsky were that he desired to force into being more tank and mechanized divisions at the expense of cavalry (which was true) and that he and others *wished* to replace Voroshilov as defense commissar with a professional military man, a point the men did not deny.[272] NKVD interrogator-torturers had compelled Tukhachevsky to compose a post-facto war "plan of defeat," which amounted to a version of the sophisticated doctrines he had been advancing for years and the Soviets had been successfully practicing at maneuvers.[273] Not that anyone noticed, but the "Trotskyite" charge brimmed with irony: Tukhachevsky had repeatedly contradicted Trotsky, arguing that revolution had changed war fundamentally.[274]

The single-day trial of the military men took place in camera, near the Kremlin, on the second floor of the three-story military collegium building (October 25 Street).[275] In the chamber, collegium members could avail themselves of sausages, black caviar, pastries, chocolates, fruit. Chief military judge Vasily Ulrich was known to enjoy a brandy.[276] Seven high-ranking officers, including Marshals Blyukher and Budyonny (newly named commander of the Moscow military district), Pavel Dybenko (newly named commander of the Leningrad military district), Shaposhnikov, and others were added to the collegium for the trial.[277] Except for Voroshilov, the entire top brass, some fifty people in all, was either in the dock or on the court.[278] As specified under the December 1, 1934, anti-terrorist law, there were no witnesses and no defense counsel, and no right of appeal. At the "trial," Yakir acknowledged the existence of the "center" but shifted blame onto Tukhachevsky. Feldman did the same. When Kork tried to absolve himself and attack the others, they incriminated him, calling him a liar and provocateur. Primakov had volunteered an additional handwritten denunciation of commanders not yet arrested. Dybenko pressed Tukhachevsky for details about his planned palace coup, and Blyukher pressed Yakir to elaborate on Gamarnik's counterrevolutionary Trotskyite plotting.[279]

Budyonny reported that day to Voroshilov ("only personally"), in a nineteen-page memorandum, that "from the testimony of Tukhachevsky, Kork, Yakir, and Uborevičius it is evident that they decided to work out first on their own initiative the plan for the defeat of the Red Army during the war and only after that to clear it with the German general staff . . . [but] because of their arrest they did not finish." Still, Budyonny concluded, "I consider that nonetheless they passed it on to German intelligence" (parroting Stalin's closed-door speech of June 2).[280]

Ulrich, in the middle of the proceedings, pronounced a recess and rushed to the Little Corner, appearing at 4:00 p.m. and staying twenty minutes. At 4:50 p.m., Stalin sent a ciphered telegram to every Soviet locality to organize mass meetings of workers and peasants and Red Army garrisons to affirm the necessity of executions, informing them that the sentences would be published the next day.[281] Just before midnight, Ulrich sentenced all eight to death; the men were led down to the cellar, where the NKVD's head executioner, Vasily Blokhin, used German Walther pistols to execute the fascist hirelings.[282] Yuri Levitan, now twenty-three and a familiar voice, read the *Pravda* trial report over Soviet radio. Vehement approvals of the death sentences appeared under the names of famous Soviet scientists, such as the world-renowned plant specialist Nikolai Vavilov, and cultural figures, such as actress Alla Tarasova, a USSR People's Artist. *Izvestiya* on June 12 printed a collective letter from Soviet writers, led by Alexander Fadeyev, naming the eight Soviet commanders as fascist agents who "wore a mask for years" and decrying how "fascists destroy culture, they bring degeneration to humanity, rude, idiotic militarization. The fascists kill the world's best people."[283]

That same day, Maria Ulyanova, Lenin's sister, died of a cerebral hemorrhage at age fifty-nine. Stalin had her ashes interred in the Kremlin Wall, adjacent to Gorky's. This left Krupskaya, aged sixty-eight, alone in the Kremlin apartment they had shared with Lenin.[284] Alexander G. Solovyov, by now head of educational institutions in the commissariat of military industry, found Krupskaya sitting by Ulyanova's casket in the Council of People's Commissars club. "I asked what lay behind such an early death," Solovyov noted in his diary. "Krupskaya breathed heavily and said [Maria] could not survive the difficult conditions created around us. Look around more closely, she said: it is possible you do not notice our utterly abnormal situation, the poisoned life."[285]

It was on June 15, 1937, that Republic Spain's new prime minister had ordered the mass arrests of the POUM leadership in Barcelona. The final destruction of the Spanish "Trotskyites," including the NKVD's secret assassination of Andreu Nin, had become small potatoes, however satisfying to Stalin.

Pravda reported on a spectacular sixty-three-hour flight (June 18–20, 1937) by Valery Chkalov, copilot Georgy Baidukov, and navigator Alexander Belyakov, from Moscow to the Pacific coast of the United States. The trio landed in Vancouver, Washington, after a daring nonstop flight that covered a distance of more than 5,500 miles and pioneered the polar air route.[286] "He is our father," Chkalov said of Stalin after landing. "The aviators of the Soviet Union call Soviet aviation Stalinist aviation. He teaches us, nurtures us, warns us about risks like children who are close to his heart; he sets us on the right path, takes joy in our success."[287] The exploit showcased the airmen and the airplane: the wide wingspan on the Soviet-designed ANT-25, the work of A. N. Tupolev, had enabled great range and fuel efficiency. The risk of failure had been immense, but so was the reward: domestic and international acclaim. Tupolev was soon imprisoned on trumped-up charges.[288]

BREAKING KLIM

Pravda, unrelenting, urged ever more naming of names; Stalin was forwarding to the newspaper selections from the investigatory materials Yezhov was providing. The editor, forty-eight-year-old Lev Mekhlis, a former Menshevik, high strung, with a yellowish face, never took his cigarette from his mouth and was known behind his back as the Gloomy Demon.[289] "I never met someone with a more complex and contradictory character," one Soviet official wrote. "I also never heard any kind words about him or praise for his work"—except from the despot: "In Stalin's eyes Mekhlis was daring, insistent, diligent, and true."[290] Stalin soon named him head of the Red Army's political administration, which carried promotion to deputy defense commissar. Mekhlis would travel the many military districts, demanding arrests and executions. "The defense commissariat became like a kennel of mad dogs," Khrushchev would recall. "Mekhlis was one of the worst."[291]

To try to halt the savagery and save themselves, the top brass would have needed to be in a real conspiracy, but to them the idea of a military coup, such as in Spain, was anathema: they were Communists, and conscious of party discipline. Anyway, organizing a coup was an utterly remote proposition in the webs of surveillance and mutual denunciation.[292] Stalin wielded monopoly control over communications, the party cells and political administration in army units, the NKVD special departments for the army, and the public story in all newspapers and on the radio, which received ostensible confirmation of his narrative in real-life events in Spain. He also had a plethora of "vigilant" types in pursuit of reward or survival: the Kuliks and Budyonnys, the Little Blackberry Yezhov, the Gloomy Demon Mekhlis, and, in the end, Voroshilov, too.

On June 14, 1937, Voroshilov had sent a telegram to Novosibirsk reminding the locals that "only I personally sanction arrests of Trotskyites, double-dealers, and such."[293] He did not accede in every instance, especially when he was bucking Yezhov or Mekhlis rather than Stalin. Twice Yezhov sought Voroshilov's permission to arrest one of the latter's deputies, Andrei Khrulyov, head of military construction, but Voroshilov refused; the third time, Yezhov asked Stalin, who also refused.[294] But Soviet military archives contain nearly thirty volumes of lists with the names of military men charged with crimes that the special department sent to the defense commissar for approval. Voroshilov affixed his signature to each name or to the whole list: "I do not object" . . . "I agree" . . . "Arrest him." Sometimes he added vicious remarks: "Take all the scoundrels out" . . . "Round up the vermin."[295] Military officials dutifully conveyed to him the indignation that was supposedly emanating from the ranks over the revelations of treason ("These bastards should be chopped up alive, like pigs"). But their reports noted that "a few individuals have expressed panicked views that the fascist band that gave away many secrets to the Germans struck a blow against the fortress of the Red Army which will lead to defeat."[296] In fact, confusion broke out. One air brigade deputy commander destroyed all the portraits of top marshals and generals, and wanted to do the same for the portraits of the country's political leaders, because *no one* could now be trusted.[297]

Incarcerated Red Army men inundated the defense commissar with desperate letters about their torture, begging—*begging*—for his help. "Kliment Yefremovich! You must check how the cases against the commanders of the Red Army are being handled," a group of civil war comrades wrote to him. "You will find that materials are extracted from the arrested by means of force, threats, and turning men into limp rags."[298] Whether Voroshilov read these painful letters, which came in the many thousands, is unknown.[299] In a pathetic note to himself, he wrote, "It is possible to fall into an unpleasant situation: you defend someone and he turns out to be a true enemy, a fascist."[300] But Voroshilov told Kuznetsov, the naval commander, that he did not believe in the guilt of the commander of the Black Sea Fleet, who had been arrested. Kuznetsov wondered, "How is it possible to sleep, when hundreds and thousands of your subordinates are arrested, and you know this is wrong?" He added, "The longer things went on, the more he [Voroshilov] lost face."[301] In fact, evidence indicates that Voroshilov knew full well the charges were a lie.[302] He also comprehended the incalculable damage and dishonor wrought upon so many dedicated, patriotic military men as uniforms, chevrons, and medals were torn off and bullets fired into the backs of necks. "The authority of the army in the country is shaken," Voroshilov wrote, again in notes to himself. "The authority of the commanding group has been shaken. . . . This means that the methods of our work, the whole system of governing the army, my work as commissar, has suffered a shattering crash."[303]

Sixteen years after Voroshilov had implored Stalin, in vain, to move him to a civilian post, the former metalworker had come to cherish the Red Army, but his forced complicity in the massacre of loyal officers on the basis of fabricated charges and torture-extracted testimony psychologically pulverized him.[304] When Alexandra Kollontai returned from her ambassadorial post to Moscow in 1937, accompanying the Swedish foreign minister, she found the normally buoyant Voroshilov "sweating from suffering; he was unaccustomedly hunched over." She commiserated, telling him of the "terrible sorrow" that resulted from "losing faith" in the moral fiber of close friends. "You understand this?" he responded. "Terrible grief, yes, yes."[305]

People were at a loss. "Could Voroshilov really have been indifferent to the fate of these cadres, colleagues from the civil war?" wondered Colonel Ilya Dubinsky, a Soviet tank commander demoted to deputy head of a school in Kazan. "With whom did he intend to smash the arrogant Hitler?"[306] Trotsky, from afar, called Voroshilov "hopelessly compromised among all the thoughtful elements of the army."[307] Voroshilov carried a pistol and was an expert marksman. He lacked Orjonikidze's courage, however—if suicide can be called courage. Whether the defense commissar contemplated shooting Stalin, we shall never know. Voroshilov had to know he was no substitute leader.

FIFTH COLUMN STORY LINE

Stalin had one of the most exhilarating periods in his life in May–June 1937. He had plotted and carried out a conspiracy to invent a conspiracy, ridding himself of the few plausible alternate leaders, compelled the rest of the upper officer corps to take part, and broken Voroshilov like a dog, while having his handiwork relentlessly acclaimed in newspapers and on radio. But did Stalin understand the price? Unlike Voroshilov, he appreciated Tukhachevsky's exceptional talent. Stalin did not need Machiavelli to understand that a celebrated military man posed the gravest threat to a prince. (The Florentine had advised that such a commander should either be killed or discredited in the eyes of the army and the people.)[308] Molotov said late in life, apropos of Tukhachevsky, "We were not sure whether he would stay firmly on our side at a difficult moment, because he was a rightist" and, unlike Trotskyites, rightists concealed their views. Molotov added, "Had he [Tukhachevsky] not been caught, he would have been very dangerous. He was the most authoritative."[309] True enough, but Stalin could have just had the commander quietly exiled or shot. But the despot had deliberately cut a very wide swath. And he had insisted that the men's bodies be lacerated until they confessed to being foreign agents.

Mola's "fifth column" bon mot emerged as the main public justification for the terror offered by representatives of the Soviet regime: a prophylactic action, with inevitable excesses, against *potential* enemies lying in wait for a foreign aggression. "Is it not clear that as long as capitalist encirclement exists, there will continue to exist among us wreckers, spies, saboteurs, and murderers, sent into our hinterland by the agents of foreign states?" Stalin had asked rhetorically at the February–March 1937 plenum.[310] He had underlined a similar passage in the draft notes of Molotov's speech for the plenum, and interrupted Yezhov's speech with the instruction, about one accused enemy, "And he will save up his strength until the moment of war, when he will really do us a lot of harm."[311] Mikoyan, a quick learner, mentioned a "fifth column" explicitly in his second speech at the same plenum. Molotov, fifty years later, would explain that Stalin "took no chances. He pitied no one. . . . It was hard to determine the limit where to stop."[312]

This way of thinking went beyond Stalin and his henchmen. "I am happy that all this has been uncovered and that our agencies are in a position to expose so much rottenness before the outbreak of war so that we can emerge victorious," Bukharin, under vicious attack, had stated back at the December 1936 Central Committee plenum, in relation to terror against others, "because had we missed it at the outset and caught it only in the midst of war, that could have led to an extraordinary and terrible defeat for the entire socialist cause."[313] Foreign observers of the Soviet terror also picked up the fifth column rationale.[314] Many victims, too, linked their annihilation to a pending war (as well as to the "democratic" elections announced with the new constitution).[315] But Stalin's butchery was not triggered by the July 1936 military coup and the ensuing civil war in Spain.[316] Stalin himself almost never used Mola's piquant "fifth column" phrase. (Bukharin in December 1936 had not actually used the term, either.)

Insiders' treachery and the "foreign hand" had been core parts of Stalin's worldview and governing style since his warlord days in Tsaritsyn, his first real exercise of state power, when, in August 1918, he had twenty-one "class enemies" executed for allegedly plotting to assist, from within, the Whites' capture of the city from without, a bald attempt to galvanize the workers to fight to defend the city. He had explained this technique to the delegation from Mongolia in 1934 and again in 1935. Events in Spain in 1936 provided a dramatic story line, manipulated by him, for the ever greater scale of a domestic offensive against Zinovievites, Trotskyites, and rightists that predated Spain. Stalin acquired an additional way to justify arresting any official in heavy industry and completely unhinging weapons production: actually, he was improving Soviet security, because they wanted to turn the Soviet Union into a second Spain. He could eviscerate Soviet intelligence and diplomacy, but he was making the country more secure. Soviet borders were being penetrated, so he could shoot the border guards to make the country safer.[317] Stalin could murder anyone on the flimsiest of pretexts, or even without a pretext, and in doing so he could assert that he was fighting tooth and nail to defend socialism and the Soviet state against the kind of rightist military putsch he had been warning about for years, and that Spain concretized.

Spain was convenient but unnecessary for Stalin's terror. The ideas of capitalist encirclement and the enemy within had been born with the Bolshevik coup itself and become the basis of all Bolshevik propaganda in the 1920s. Stalin had been contemplating the destruction of Bukharin and Tukhachevsky in the precise scenario deployed in 1937 for years. "Is it possible?" he had written to Orjonikidze about interrogation protocols implicating Tukhachevsky in a coup plot with Bukharin, Rykov, and Tomsky. "Of course it is possible." Stalin had answered his own question: "It seems the rightists are prepared to take the path of military dictatorship if only to escape from the Central Committee, collective and state farms, Bolshevik tempos of industrialization." Here was the nub of 1937—but the letter had been sent September 24, 1930.[318]

PERCEIVED SECURITY IMPERATIVES and a need for absolute unity once again turned the quest in Russia to build a strong state into personal rule. The Soviet regime presented multiple paradoxes: gigantic administrative structures and their frequent abolition, re-creation, and reorganization; ponderous proceduralism and pervasive violation of those procedures. Some of this was by design: overlapping jurisdictions was one way Stalin tried to keep minions in check and himself abreast of information. But much of it was unintentional—dictatorship hamstringing itself. Bureaucracies came alive, or failed to do so, on the basis of their boss's personal dynamism and ability to build and galvanize a personal following. This was true at every level, and especially at the pinnacle.

Tyranny has a circular logic: once a dictator has achieved supreme power, he becomes keener still to hold it, driving him to weed his own ranks of even potential challengers. At the same time, plots linking domestic and foreign foes—who are supposedly caught in the nick of time—constitute one of the oldest devices in the authoritarian handbook. The content of the trumped-up plots is always specific to the culture in question, but the result is always some form of emergency rule, whereby political rivals and opponents are summarily eliminated. Under the interwar Romanian dictatorship, it was the ethnic Hungarian minority and their purported paymasters in Budapest, as well as the Gypsies; in the interwar Polish dictatorsip, it was the Ukrainians and their paymasters in Moscow and Kiev; and everywhere it was the Jews, the ultimate international conspiracy, especially for Hitler, who saw them as ready to engage in internal subversion, in league with Germany's foreign enemies. The ratcheting up of tensions to fever pitch over subversion scenarios helps galvanize and recruit supporters, burnish regime legitimacy, and tighten central control. Scapegoats promote solidarity. A sacrificial lamb can be a kind of gift from a ruler to followers. But the breathtaking scope, as well as the participation of the targeted, set Stalin's actions apart.

The Red Army was immense, and the self-inflicted losses—90 percent of the top ranks—represented just 0.5 percent of the whole. But a dearth of good officers to discipline, train, and lead conscripts was precisely its chief vulnerability.

Conscripts, for their part, could not be sure who among their commanders would soon be unmasked as a foreign agent. Moreover, all of the Soviet Union's foreign enemies were watching. On June 24, 1937, the organ of the Wehrmacht (*Deutsche Wehr*) wrote that in "shooting these well-known military brass of the Soviet Union, they self-consciously sacrificed fighting ability and leadership of the Red Army to politics. Tukhachevsky, unquestionably, was the most outstanding of all Red commanders and cannot be replaced. . . . Supposed espionage, of course, is just made up. If the Bolsheviks maintain that the 'accused' have confessed, that is, of course, a lie." The Nazi party organ, *Völkischer Beobachter,* wrote of the USSR that "a country with such a system of murder is still included in the group of 'civilized states.'" The Polish press gleefully pointed out that in light of the espionage charges in Moscow, the French general staff could expect that any secret military plans it might develop with the Soviets would be passed to the Germans.[319]

The Soviet general staff documented the foreign reactions. The damage was severe, but Stalin, far from being deterred, was just beginning.[320] By contrast, his involvement in Spain had effectively peaked as of May–June 1937. Despite the accusatory exaggerations against both the Soviet Union and Nazi Germany, Stalin, even more than Hitler, had deliberately kept his intervention on the Iberian Peninsula within limits. Altogether, between 1,150 and 1,500 Soviet combat personnel would see duty, including 772 pilots and 351 tank operators, a paltry number compared with the 19,000 Germans, let alone the 80,000 Italians who would fight.[321] Another 500 or so Soviet military advisers would also serve, but only 9 Soviet political workers were sent to Spain during the entire war.[322] Soviet deaths would be recorded at 125, plus another 43 missing in action.[323] German dead would be estimated at 300. Italy would suffer 16,650 dead, wounded, and missing in action and would expend at least 6.1 billion lira supporting Franco.[324] (The economic advantages anticipated for Italian support fell largely to Germany.)[325] Stalin's expenses would be significant (in the form of loans that would not be repaid) but contained.[326] Especially with the "Trotskyite" POUM crushed by spring–summer 1937, Stalin appears to have lost much of his interest.[327] After summer 1937, little new Soviet equipment would be sent or upgrades made, while Soviet pilots and tank crews would be withdrawn, diplomatic ties downgraded, and the heady cultural exchanges terminated.[328]

Propaganda on Spain did not disappear, but in Soviet newsreels, China gained ascendancy.[329] On this front as well, Stalin was annihilating his officers. NKVD bigwig Vsevolod Balytsky had been transferred from Ukraine to fabricate a

Trotskyite-fascist conspiracy in the Soviet Far Eastern Army, the country's critical line of defense against Japan; within a few weeks, on July 7, 1937, Balytsky himself was arrested as a Polish agent. He had been in Stalin's Little Corner more than twenty times in the 1930s. En route eastward, at a Siberian train station, he had unburdened himself of complaints about the terror to a fellow Chekist, who promptly denounced him to Yezhov. The assignment of eviscerating the Soviet Far Eastern Army fell to another butcher.[330] On the country's southern border, Georgia's Beria reported to Stalin (July 9) that he had uncovered his own "military conspiracy" in the South Caucasus military district. The next day, Joseph Goebbels recorded in his diary that Hitler judged Stalin "likely diseased in the brain. Otherwise one cannot explain his bloody rule."[331]

CHAPTER 8

"WHAT WENT ON IN NO. 1'S BRAIN?"

We cannot say that these were the deeds of a giddy despot.
He considered that this should be done in the interest of
the party, of the working masses, in the name of the
defense of the revolution's gains. In this lies the whole
tragedy!

Nikita Khrushchev[1]

Stalin thought very highly of Bukharin. Yes, he did.
Bukharin was very educated and cultivated. But what
should one do?

Vyacheslav Molotov[2]

Had Stalin aimed only to break his inner circle, utterly cow the
wider elite, and make himself a despot, he might have ended the terror with the
in-camera trial and executions of the military men and the arrests of Yagoda,
Pauker, and other NKVD higher-ups. Mission accomplished. But he had much
larger aims, with plans for more high-profile trials. In summer 1937, he vastly expanded the arrests and executions to nonelites. There was no "dynamic" forcing
him to do so, no "factional" fighting, no heightened threat abroad. The terror was
not spiraling out of his control. He just decided, himself, to approve quota-driven
eradication of entire categories of people in a *planned* indiscriminate terror known
as mass operations.[3] This momentous decision was complemented by a widening
of the annihilation of sitting elites, which was unveiled at yet another manic Central Committee plenum, this one from June 23 to 29, 1937. On the opening day,
Yezhov (according to his notes) enlarged on what he had said at the inconclusive
plenum of December 1936 and written up at length in his unpublished magnum
opus, "From Factionalism to Open Counterrevolution," submitted to his teacher
Stalin in May 1935: namely, that the USSR was mortally threatened by an immense
überconspiracy made up of innumerable intertwined conspiracies.

Yezhov, at the plenum, spelled out a military-fascist conspiracy, a rightist-fascist
plot in the NKVD, a Kremlin rightist-fascist group of plotters, an espionage

organization of the Polish military, Polish National Democrats in Belorussia, an anti-Soviet rightist-Trotskyite group in the Azov–Black Sea territory and another in Eastern Siberia, a rightist anti-Soviet group in the Urals, an anti-Soviet rightist-fascist group in Western Siberia, a rightist-Trotskyite espionage group in the Soviet Far East, an organization of rightists in Western Siberia united in a partisan-guerrilla uprising, an anti-Soviet Cossack organization in Orenburg, and a wrecking rightist-Trotskyite anti-Soviet group in the agriculture commissariat. "I enumerated only the most important," he allowed, adding that each was "linked in the closest possible way" and together constituted a "Center of Centers," which was colluding with "fascist government circles in Germany, Japan, and Poland, on the one hand, and, on the other, with representatives abroad of anti-Soviet parties of Trotskyites, Mensheviks, and SRs." The shared aim of all these leftist revolutionaries was said to be restoring capitalism in the USSR by way of "a palace coup, an armed uprising supported by foreign interventionists, the preparation of a Soviet defeat in the event of a war with fascist countries, and the coming to power of themselves as a result of political and territorial concessions to the fascists." Yezhov warned that the scale of the conspiracy emanating from "testimony" indicated that the USSR stood on the verge of civil war.[4]

What attendees said in response remains unknown—Yezhov's report and the follow-up discussion were not transcribed—but we do know that Trotsky interceded from afar. He sent a telegram from Mexico to the central executive committee of the Soviet, formally the highest organ of the state, declaring that "Stalin's policies are leading to a crushing defeat, both internally and externally. The only salvation is a turn in the direction of Soviet democracy, beginning with a public review of the last trials. I offer my full support in this endeavor." This document went to the NKVD, which forwarded it to Stalin. "Mug of a spy!" he wrote on Trotsky's text. "Brazen spy for Hitler!"[5]

Stalin's expansion of long-standing party purge practices required a surprisingly small degree of manipulation, and yet his terror was a spectacular feat in its own way. He would manage to annihilate not only nearly the entire upper ranks of the Soviet military and the secret police—in a police-military dictatorship—but much of the industrial managerial class, the regional party machines, and the cultural beau monde.[6] He also visited ruin upon Soviet military and civilian intelligence, military attachés and diplomats abroad, and foreign Communist parties, prime instruments that any dictatorship would cherish. What was he doing?

The only way into Stalin's serpentine mind—or, as Arthur Koestler put it in *Darkness at Noon,* "what went on in No. 1's brain?"—begins with public and private comments made by him and those he instructed.[7] Hitler turned out to be a brilliant actor, and the same has been said of Stalin, who dissembled shamelessly and playacted skillfully. But also like Hitler, who incessantly talked of his intentions (most people just did not believe him), Stalin proved extraordinarily voluble as well.[8] We can never know in the end what Stalin believed. We can, however, come to understand how his mind worked.

Sometimes his terror ruminations were extensive, such as at the June 2, 1937, closed session of the Main Military Council; other times they were brief. They emerged from his long-standing self-conception that those who opposed *him* were broadcasting disunity and weakness, thereby inviting foreign powers to attack—in other words, objectively supporting the USSR's enemies—while he, a selfless servant of the cause, under siege from uncomprehending critics, had been placed on this earth to defend the socialist revolution and the Soviet state. Therefore, he was not merely justified, but dutybound, to eradicate oppositionists and anyone taken in by them. The incarceration or physical liquidation of more than a million and a half human beings apparently posed no moral dilemmas for him. On the contrary, to pity class enemies would be to indulge sentiment over the laws of objective historical development. Ignorance of history could be fatal, Stalin argued, and he spent a great deal of time during the terror midwifing an accessible history of the Russian state, from its origins to the present, as a tool of mass civic training.[9] Stalin was a massacring pedagogue.

A TEACHER AND A PUPIL

In Boris Yefimov's celebrated cartoons, Yezhov was depicted with an oversized gloved fist crushing shrunken enemies. In person, he stood a mere five feet tall (1.51 meters), had a prominent scar on his right cheek (a civil war injury) and yellowish teeth (something he shared with Stalin), and walked with a pronounced limp, a gait even worse than the despot's. He was beset by a hacking cough from tuberculosis, myasthenia and neurasthenia, anemia, angina, sciatica, psoriasis, and even malnutrition, ailments of long standing. One old revolutionary said Yezhov reminded him of slum children whose favorite occupation was to tie paraffin-soaked paper to a cat's tail and set fire to it.[10] Around 1930, Yezhov had begun to indulge in drinking benders, to the point of losing consciousness. One of his drinking companions had been Fyodor Konar (Polashchuk), who used to bring along prostitutes. (Konar had been arrested in January 1933 as a Polish spy and executed two months later for "sabotage in agriculture.") Another drinking buddy, Lev Maryasin, a former coworker in the personnel department of the central apparatus who had become head of the state bank and deputy finance commissar, used to compete with Yezhov in farting competitions. (Maryasin, too, was arrested, by Yezhov's NKVD.)[11] Stalin allowed Yezhov various leaves, spending hard currency on treatments abroad, but the illnesses, along with Yezhov's propensity for daytime drinking, took a toll. "Yezhov not only drank," recalled Zinaida Glikina, a friend of Yezhov's wife, Yevgeniya. "In addition, he deteriorated and lost the visage not only of a Communist but of a human being."

As Yezhov fanatically prosecuted the terror, in early 1937 his teeth began to fall out. He suffered from appetite loss, dizziness, and insomnia. Doctors diagnosed overwork and ordered a long holiday, which Yezhov deemed out of the question.[12] In April 1937, one of his subordinates had suggested the cause might be meals at the NKVD canteen, where undiscovered enemies could be lurking. The Red Army's chemical warfare academy was called in and "found" trace elements of mercury in Yezhov's office. An NKVD employee was tortured and confessed, implicating Yagoda in an assassination attempt. Traces of mercury were suddenly found in Yezhov's former apartment (on Bolshoi Kiselny), in his new one (in the Kremlin), and at his dacha (in Meshcherino); all were ventilated, and the mercury vanished. No one explained how the inaccessible residences had become contaminated. But Yezhov now had his urine checked regularly, and switched offices inside NKVD headquarters.[13] He was reported to have created a circuitous, one-way route to his Lubyanka suite—up to the fifth floor, down to the first, then up to the third, as if he were under threat from the agency he commanded.[14]

Could this alcoholic, increasingly infirm, frightened Lilliputian creature have been responsible for Soviet state security? Yezhov, of course, was an instrument. It was not he—and not a rebellious military command, as in Spain—who originated the mass violence in the USSR.[15] But Stalin goaded him relentlessly: "Comrade Yezhov. Very important. It is necessary to go through the Udmurt, Mari-El, Chuvash, and Mordovian republics, to go through with a whip."[16]

Back in tsarist Russia, General Alexander Gerasimov, the head of the *okhranka* in St. Petersburg, met with Nicholas II just once during his entire career; political policing was viewed as necessary, but not necessarily honorable, work. That had changed: in 1935 and 1936, Yagoda had been in Stalin's office every month, sometimes more than once. From January 1937 through August 1938, an interval during which Stalin received visitors on 333 days, Yezhov would make 288 appearances, second only to Molotov. How often they additionally met at the Near

Dacha or spoke on the telephone remains unknown. Stalin sometimes played chess with him.[17] The Bloody Dwarf, as Yezhov was known in whispers, cleansed enemies out of conviction, but also to please his master, just as Yezhov's subordinates showed fanaticism in terror to please him. His three concurrent positions—NKVD chief, Central Committee secretary, chairman of the party Control Commission—rendered him as knowledgeable about Stalin's thinking as anyone.[18] "A teacher with a pupil, an eagle with an eaglet," the Stalinist writer-enforcer Alexander Fadeyev wrote of the despot and his protégé. "Stalin tends to him lovingly, like a gardener tends to a beloved tree."[19] Yezhov returned Stalin's favor with nonpareil zeal and brutality.[20]

As the ringleaders of the phantasmagorical "Center of Centers," Yezhov named Bukharin (who was writing desperate, groveling letters to Stalin), Rykov (who had failed to act decisively when he had his chance back in 1928–29), Tomsky (who shot himself rather than his tormentors), Zinoviev (who had been writing his own groveling letters to Stalin), Kamenev (who could have smothered the Bolshevik monopoly in its cradle in 1917 but shrank from doing so), émigré SR, Menshevik, and White Guard organizations (which were infiltrated and in some cases established by the NKVD), and Pyatakov (who begged to be the executioner of all the others, an offer Stalin declined, reasoning out loud at the Central Committee that "no one would believe that you voluntarily decided to do this, without being coerced, and besides, we have never announced the names of the people who carry out sentences").[21] This was a pathetic register of coup leaders. As for the supposedly threatening anti-Soviet émigré organizations, Yezhov's NKVD had thoroughly penetrated them. Some, such as the Helsinki branch of the Organization of Ukrainian Nationalists (OUN), were actually led by Soviet agents, while the leaders of others, such as General Evgeny Miller of the Russian All-Military Union, had been kidnapped.[22] "They present no value whatsoever," Sergey Spigelglas, deputy director of NKVD foreign espionage, reported, "since they have neither money, nor international connections, nor organization, nor people."[23]

Ultimately, however, Yezhov was right in one crucial way: a conspiratorial "Center of Centers" threatening the Soviet Union *did* exist: the Little Corner itself.

COMMUNISM'S EASE OF MASS MURDER

Throughout 1937 and 1938, there were on average nearly 2,200 arrests and more than 1,000 executions per day.[24] The NKVD extracted testimony under torture even from people who would not be tried publicly, because that was one way they met quotas—gathering ever more names of accomplices—but also, more fundamentally, because Stalin craved this. Even when "confessions" had been edited by him, he treated them as if they were real, underlining passages, circulating them to the politburo, and referring to "testimony." During the two frenzied, gruesome years of 1937 and 1938, Yezhov forwarded to him more than 15,000 written "special communications," an average of 20 per day, many of which Stalin marked up and returned with further instructions.[25]

The terror's scale would become crushing. More than 1 million prisoners were convoyed by overloaded rail transport in 1938 alone.[26] The Lubyanka's feared inner prison contained a mere 110 cells. (The building had been a hotel for visiting insurance executives and retained its parquet in the corridors. Most of the floors were aboveground, but the windows were bricked up; the cellars were reserved for priority prisoners and executions.)[27] But Butyrka, tsarist Russia's former central transit prison—whence the Cheka founder Felix Dzierżyński had once escaped—filled with 20,000 inmates, six times capacity. And Butyrka was considered a resort compared with Lefortovo, while the most feared of all, Sukhanovka, located at a former monastery just outside Moscow and known as the dacha, was still more jammed.[28] Some arrest sweeps had to be delayed or put off because of overcrowding.[29] Urgent requests to Moscow for instructions began to sit without response (by summer 1938, more than 100,000 unattended cases would languish).[30] Stalin, for two years running, felt constrained to skip his much-beloved annual southern holiday—even he struggled to keep the pace, despite his inhuman capacity for work.

Given the numbers involved, the state's violence against its own population inevitably was chaotic.[31] Stalin lost track of people, writing next to names in interrogation protocols, "Arrest," when they were already in custody, a point he came to recognize. ("Comrade Yezhov: The names identified by me in the text with the letters 'ar' are to be arrested, if they have not yet been arrested.")[32] Stalin would suddenly remember someone and inquire about his fate (some were dead, some not). People whose names sounded similar to someone else's would suffer misdirected arrests. Not everyone on the hundreds of lengthy execution lists was shot.[33] But for all this messiness, the process was systematic, driven by continuous orders and codified in updated antiterrorist laws and procedures. Mass murder does not somehow "break out," but must be set in motion, and then driven onward, as Stalin did, and be sustained by powerful drivers.

A number of factors made such a terror possible. The Communist party underwent periodic "purges" to root out those deemed unworthy—because of background, beliefs, or inability to carry out responsibilities—and these long-standing practices that normally led to expulsion and possible arrest were ramped up to certain arrest and likely execution. Moreover, the very fact of the long history of party expulsions, even without arrest, had created a multitude of individuals who could be seen as potentially dangerous. The terror was also propelled by the bureaucratic imperatives and careerism of a formidable repressive apparatus that had been built up over many years, especially as a result of collectivization-dekulakization, as well as a pervasive fear in the ranks of the NKVD for their own lives. Additionally, the highly organized monopoly public sphere could be—and now was—ordered to disseminate charges of mass sabotage and spying. Even in the largest cities, tiny numbers of correspondents and editors—local Mekhlis equivalents—could fan mass hysteria. Public receptiveness to the charges, in turn, was facilitated by the widely shared tenet that building socialism constituted an adversarial crusade against myriad "enemies" at home and abroad, and by the circumstance that the system was not supposed to have a new elite, but did. The new elite's apartments, cars, servants, concubines, and imported luxuries were often visible, while workers and farmers lived in hovels and went hungry. This did not mean that every ordinary Soviet inhabitant was eager for the blood of bigwigs, but few tears were shed.

The terror, like every aspect of Soviet reality, also depended upon isolation. Foreigners were kept from Soviet inhabitants, and the number permitted to go abroad, even on official business, shrank to the point that Stalin could examine delegation lists for approval (or not).[34] But the key to it all lay in the nature of Communism as a conspiracy to seize and hold power. Everywhere the mechanism for the terror was the same: a secret party circular from Stalin ordering a still more vigilant hunt for "enemies," a local party meeting, a summons to Bolshevik "criticism," further denunciations, pandemonium. Just a handful of "activists," who understood the vocabulary of invective or insinuation to tear down rivals and protect themselves, could precipitate chain reactions of annihilation in which millions became complicit in additional meetings in factories, farms, schools. This was intentional, to achieve scale. The frenzy never escaped Stalin's ability to shape and ultimately stop it. Still, often the denouncers were denounced right back by those they had aimed at, in a circular firing squad. And if a person *defended* someone accused of being an enemy of the people, well, then, that was proof that he or she, too, was an enemy.[35] Even if one merely inquired about a coworker who had suddenly stopped showing up, one could be accused of harboring "ties" or "sympathies."[36] Party and state officials, in other words, became trapped in the twisted logic of the system they had helped create. They accepted that foreign capitalist powers would never accept the success of the Soviet Union, that "dying classes" could not be expected to go quietly, that socialism had myriad enemies, but now these loyal Soviet officials were themselves the enemy.

STALIN AND THE STATE

The party's monopoly went hand in hand with administrative dysfunction. This was a state with awesome power, one that had the capacity to build competitive tanks and artillery in big batches, confiscate much of a harvest, deliver a coordinated propaganda message at every factory and farm, and internally deport whole nations but was largely unable to execute subtle tasks (except when functionaries knowingly behaved illegally).[37] The Soviet party-state was clumsy and pervasive, at its strongest in mobilization, suppression, and surveillance. The system gathered incredible quantities of information yet was often poorly informed.[38] Stalin expressed frustration at local officials' supposed narrow horizons and imagined that he alone upheld the interests of the revolution and state *tout court,* as against specific institutional or sectoral interests. He was cognizant of some limits on his freedom of action—great distances, primitive communication, low levels of education, the bureaucratism and self-dealing—but he nonetheless tried to force his way past them and often did so. He presumed the efficacy of administration and administrative methods and spent considerable time and energy in reorganizations of agencies and work flow.[39] But he frequently obviated those same agencies by calling in a plenipotentiary, delivering a pep talk, and having that person go out and bang heads to get things done, then report solely to him. He had come to understand that the ever-growing system of monitoring decision making was achieving less and less.[40] Still, he did not understand that organizations, particularly overly large ones, develop an often perverse dynamic beyond functionaries' self-interest.

Far from everything began with Stalin. The politburo adjudicated some 3,000 items per year in the 1930s.[41] Stalin did not really delegate, but the work flow exceeded his capacity to oversee every issue.[42] Some decisions under his signature (affixed by his staff) he never read. Molotov recalled that Stalin would approach the pile and ask which were the important ones.[43] Stalin could ask for guidance: "What to do?" he would sometimes write on documents. (Who knew if it was genuine or a test?) Others in the leadership and throughout the labyrinthine apparatus had no choice but to try to address issues that confronted them day in and day out. But he concentrated information and decision making at the top, which overwhelmed him and his top aides, drowned the central agencies in paperwork, and created massive logjams. The system was in constant pressure against itself—in information gathering and reporting, in coordination or refusal thereof, in pushing responsibility off and back on.[44] Stalin's interventions were perforce episodic, sometimes preceded by careful study, sometimes not. He unwittingly created bottlenecks, and narrowed the exchange of information even at the top of the regime. Coordination did take place across agencies in the Little Corner. But when he assigned spheres to individual plenipotentiaries, he sometimes did not inform them of one another's work. Everything rested upon the people Stalin chose to summon, or not, the reports he solicited and decided to read, or not, the decisions he rendered and how he did or even did not communicate them, and, ultimately, his ability to understand the country and the world.

Very early on in his rule, proper leadership had emerged as one of Stalin's most recurrent themes. For him it meant not declarations of decrees, but their implementation.[45] Stalin derived his sense of the country and the world predominantly from documents, as well as intuition.[46] But without irony he castigated "paper leadership" and "office leadership," functionaries who sat in their big suites and issued orders without familiarizing themselves with the situation in the factory shops or fields, who failed to inquire about people's experiences and difficulties in order to lend practical help in the tasks at hand. He had complained early and often of needing to "break through the wall of bureaucratism and improve the slipshod performance of our bureaucracies."[47] He had stressed the work of "checking up by punching people in the face" (September 2, 1930).[48] His view of power was deceptively simple: indicate the correct line, assign individuals to implement it, and goad and watch them. Less than 100 percent fulfillment meant rotten liberals showing leniency, playing into the hands of enemies, becoming enemies themselves. But even as his regime demanded unwavering implementation of central directives, it often provided little guidance in the rationales for policies as recorded in the minimalist politburo minutes that were circulated. This left officials poring over *Pravda*, especially the speeches of Stalin. He appears to have assumed that he was being crystal clear, leaving no room for ambiguity, so that misinterpretations had to be deliberate. He also does not appear to have appreciated the negative consequences of coercion.

Policy to Stalin was reduced to an exercise in obedience and resolve. But by constantly pushing to tighten the system and render it more hierarchical, Stalin had empowered the gatekeeping officials not only in his secretariat but also in the regions, whom he instinctively did not trust. Even allowing for secret police exaggeration, the provincial *nomenklatura* certainly dragged their feet over directives, failed to cope with the (impossible) demands placed upon them (as would their successors), covered their failures with deception, and brazenly feathered their own nests. Stalin closely followed the reports of self-dealing and local collusion ("family-ness"), flouting of central directives, scapegoating of rivals or underlings who had dared to heed the exhortations in the party press to criticize bosses.[49] He detested officials making excuses or covering up their failures and pretending they were succeeding, behavior he denounced as double-dealing. Stalin likely understood but would not admit that his own relentless pressure and exorbitant demands made the evasions and coping mechanisms pervasive. He wanted officials to perform well but to be constantly looking over their shoulders. He worked to identify or assign agents inside locales and institutions to report directly to him, bypassing administrative hierarchies, and empowered the secret police to stand above other institutions, yet he feared that the police might conspire against him, so he worked to trip them up, too.

Evasive, self-serving behavior by officialdom is endemic to every authoritarian state.[50] What was atypical—to put it mildly—was their mass extermination by their own regime. Stalin faced no imperative to murder them. He could sack or transfer any local satrap at will.[51] Instead, he not only put Soviet officials to death or had them deported to slave labor camps en masse, but, in a huge expenditure of state resources, had them tortured to confess and, incredibly, had these Communists confess not to being corrupt or incompetent, but to plotting to assassinate him and restore capitalism on behalf of foreign powers. And that was not all. In the Marxist worldview, entire classes—feudal lords, the bourgeoisie—had outlived their usefulness and become "fetters" on humanity's further development. ("Everyone is against us who has outlived the epoch allotted to him by history," Maxim Gorky had written in *Pravda* in November 1930.)[52] But Stalin took to applying notions of epochal obsolescence, not just presumptive disloyalty, to the body of experienced Soviet functionaries, as if they, too, were people of a bygone epoch and needed to make way. He would promote the young, to fix the pathologies of the state.

WE ARE THE ENEMY

As each phase of the seemingly endless party cleanings had unfolded, the focus of attack had moved ever closer to the centers of power. Whereas the 1933–34 party purge (expulsions largely without arrest) had targeted the rank and file, and the 1935 verification and exchange of party cards had affected to a great degree lower-level apparatchiks sacrificed by their superiors, the 1936–38 terror, which involved arrest as well as expulsion, consumed the big fish, those who had earlier implemented the expulsions of others, and decimated the *Stalinist* Central Committee.[53] Central Committee membership had always been a mark of the highest prestige and privilege. True, its members had long ago ceased to demonstrate any capacity for, let alone inclination toward, collective action.[54] They met only when summoned, and even then were ultracareful to avoid the appearance of gathering in subgroups. After they received the June 1937 plenum materials in advance (as per normal procedure), which included interrogation protocols of already arrested high officials, Central Committee members wrote to Stalin swearing their fealty, even if their own names were not (yet) mentioned in "testimonies." None wrote or spoke up to question the frame-ups.[55]

Upon the opening of the June plenum, of the seventy-one members and sixty-eight candidates for membership formally elected to the Central Committee at the previous party congress (1934), thirteen had been arrested (including Pyatakov, Bukharin, and Rykov), three had committed suicide (Tomsky, Orjonikidze, and Gamarnik), four had died of natural causes (Mężyński, Kuibyshev, Tovstukha, and Alexander Steinhart), and one had been assassinated (Kirov). During the plenum, Stalin sanctioned the destruction of at least another thirty-one, so that more than fifty of the 139 did not take part in or finish the sessions; several more would be arrested right after.[56] Altogether, around 100 of the 139 Central Committee members would not survive to the next party congress. The vast majority of them had not been Stalin's opponents in the oppositions of the 1920s. Nor had they run afoul of him subsequently. To be sure, a few, such as Sergei Syrtsov, party boss of Siberia during Stalin's 1928 visit, had been expelled from the Central Committee in 1930 for private criticism of him.[57] But most of those arrested now were stalwarts who had been loyal right through the fire of dekulakization-collectivization and beyond.[58] Their subordinates and associates were also destroyed—followed, in many cases, by their replacements.

Most astonishingly, sitting provincial party bosses were forced to organize their own annihilation by summoning party meetings and encouraging denunciations.[59] When, predictably, they tried to protect themselves and their associates by sacrificing other, often rival, officials, Stalin accused them of suppressing criticism. He had sent a ciphered telegram around the Union expressly warning that "some party secretaries of provinces, apparently wishing to escape blame, very eagerly give authorization to the NKVD organs to arrest certain leaders, directors, technical directors, engineers and technicians, mid-managers of factories and transport, and other sectors. The Central Committee reminds you that neither secretaries of a province or territory, nor secretaries of national parties, nor party-soviet leaders in locales have the right to authorize such arrests."[60] Such decisions were Stalin's alone and, to ensure compliance, he dispatched "Central Committee" plenipotentiaries: Kaganovich to Chelyabinsk, Yaroslavl, Ivanovo, and Ukraine; Zhdanov to Bashkiria, Tataria, and Orenburg; Malenkov to Belorussia, Armenia, Kazan, Tula, Omsk, and Tambov; Andreyev to Uzbekistan, Tajikistan, Saratov, and the North Caucasus; Shkiryatov to the Soviet Far East. In Kiev, chairing an assembly of the "party active," Kaganovich began, "Well, come on up and report whatever anyone knows about enemies of the people."[61]

There was no way to ensure one's survival, but people felt they could not just sit there and wait for the others to denounce them. Chain reactions spread—once triggered via these party meetings, rabid newspaper articles that vilified people by name, and Stalin's plenipotentiaries (who had to please him). Kaganovich had arrived in Ivanovo like the head of a foreign occupation, with a bodyguard detail of thirty, and been greeted by local NKVD bosses; the party machine had not even been apprised in advance. He phoned Stalin repeatedly to detail his impressive results: the arrest of nearly every leader in the local party (he had brought an entire replacement leadership with him). But Stalin demanded still more pressure "to stop liberalizing."[62] (At the train station, as Kaganovich was seen off, he made a point to thank all service personnel and handed out tips of 50 to 100 rubles each, identifying with the proletarians.)[63] In Kazakhstan, the entire party bureau—the republic equivalent of the politburo—was arrested. In Turkmenistan, no bureau existed for months.[64] Many party machines would be wiped out two and even three times. This could hardly render the provincial apparatus more responsive.[65] Rather than make examples of some disobedient regional functionaries in order to frighten the rest, the terror effectively paralyzed the entire, sprawling regional apparatus. "During the purges hundreds of thousands of bureaucrats shook in their boots," wrote the American eyewitness John Scott, who worked in provincial

Magnitogorsk. "Many people reacted by shunning responsibility. . . . Still other people became exasperated and bitter."[66]

A good number of upper-level functionaries had been working sixteen- to eighteen-hour shifts, often through the night, under tremendous strain. The commissar for domestic trade, Israel Veitser, was suffering from impaired health, according to the Kremlin medical team, partly because he usually arrived at the office around noon and departed between 3:00 and 5:00 a.m., taking papers home with him. (The Council of People's Commissars decreed that he should finish work by midnight.)[67] Veitser's deputies, advisers, and secretaries all worked similar hours. Veitser, who happened to be married to the theater director Natalya Sats (the onetime mistress of Tukhachevsky), was sacked and arrested. Twenty of twenty-eight members of the Council of People's Commissars would be arrested.[68] Soviet industrial production, the supposed lifeblood of the regime, took a hit. In the strategic coal industry, output in 1936 had stagnated; in the first quarter of 1937, the plan went unfulfilled. Almost the entire provincial Donbass party that was appointed in May 1937, seventy-six people, would be slaughtered.[69]

Sarkis Sarkisov (Danielyan), an ethnic Armenian who served as party boss in the Donetsk coal basin, had worked in Leningrad under Zinoviev. When attacked by the NKVD, he went on the offensive, becoming complicit in the sweeping arrests of his colleagues in the provincial machine, until he, too, was arrested and executed.[70] Eduards Prāmnieks, an ethnic Latvian stonemason who had succeeded Zhdanov as party boss in Nizhny Novgorod/Gorky, succeeded Sarkisov. "Many people cannot understand why the Donbass, which was always a fortress of Bolshevism, has become infiltrated by enemies and scum," Prāmnieks pontificated. "One must remember that, as an extremely important center, the Donbass will always be a target for enemies and spies."[71] His work was paralyzed. "With whom to work?" he confided to the writer Avdeyenko. "All the first and second secretaries of the city have turned out to be enemies of the people. . . . The directors of factories have turned out to be wreckers or spies. The chief engineers, chief technicians, even the chief doctors of some hospitals, are also from the ranks of scum."[72] Then, another wholesale liquidation struck the Donbass—at least 140 factory and mine directors, chief engineers, and party officials—and Prāmnieks, too, turned out to be "scum."[73] Kaganovich, at a Kremlin reception for the coal and metallurgy sectors, would state that as a result of the "wrecking by Trotskyite-Bukharinite hirelings," the coal industry had fallen into difficult straits. Stalin softened this dire verdict in the coal industry report that was published.[74] Still, he evidently deemed the production losses a price worth paying.

NESTS OF SPIES

There were some 10,000 foreign Communists in residence in the Soviet Union.[75] They and their counterparts abroad were feared the world over as subversives of bourgeois order, but in Stalin's mind they were a mortal danger to the Soviet Union. Back during the centennial celebration of Pushkin's death at the Bolshoi, he had blurted out to Dimitrov, "All of you there in the Comintern are playing into the enemy's hands." He called the Comintern a "nest of spies."[76] Foreign Communists talked. They could not fail to observe the abject subordination of all Communist parties to Moscow, the embourgeoisement of Soviet upper echelons, the opacity of decision making, the lack of commitment to world revolution (as opposed to Soviet state interests). But the overwhelming majority of foreign Communists had little to nothing of value to divulge to foreign governments. Formal structure in the Comintern had been abandoned: it was just the Little Corner, and just when Stalin got around to summoning or corresponding with Dimitrov. Dimitrov, who had stood up to Göring and Goebbels in a Leipzig courtroom, received foreign Communists' interrogation protocols containing ever new names and had to issue telegrams summoning some of these people from abroad to Moscow, where, he knew, they would be executed.[77]

The 400 rooms of the isolating Comintern residence, the perversely named Hotel Lux, were cleared out multiple times during the terror. None of it appears to have been policy driven. Pyatnitsky, Lozovsky, Knorin, and Kun had all supported the "social fascism" thesis close to Stalin's heart and they all perished; Dimitrov, Manuilsky, and Kuusinen had supported the broad leftist front, and they survived.

British, American, French, and Czechoslovak Communists largely escaped death or the Gulag; they belonged to legal parties and did not require refuge in the Soviet Union. Chinese Communists, in the deep interior of their country, also mostly escaped Stalin's cellars. But of the sixty-eight German Communists who managed to obtain refuge in the USSR after Hitler had come to power, Stalin had forty-one put to death. More members of the pre-1933 German Communist politburo were killed in the Stalinist terror (seven) than under Hitler (five).[78] Polish Communists in Soviet exile suffered the worst: an estimated 5,000 arrests just in spring–summer 1937. Stalin had the Polish Communist party formally dissolved, "owing to its saturation with spies and provocateurs." He wrote across Dimitrov's draft resolution, "The dissolution is about two years late."[79] (Many Polish

Communists would hear of the dissolution of their party by Moscow while wallowing in prisons in Poland.)[80] To be sure, Stalin was hardly alone in his suspicion of political émigrés: verification campaigns directed at foreigners living in the Soviet Union were long-standing and accepted as necessary, given the tense international situation and the shadowy nature of politics under Communism.[81] But the verifications did not establish facts. They began with presumed guilt and snowballed via all manner of slander and innuendo.

Planning went forward for a public trial of "Trotskyite-fascists" in the Comintern, and the tentative list of "Trotskyites" seems to have included Mao.[82] The trial never materialized. It was supposed to center on Pyatnitsky, an original member of the Russian Social Democratic Workers' Party (1898) who had never joined any opposition but was expelled from the Central Committee and placed "under investigation" during the June 1937 plenum. Despite being beaten to a pulp over the course of a full year, Pyatnitsky refused to slander himself.[83]

Stalin had Soviet diplomacy put up against the wall, too. On July 1, 1937, Vasily Korzhenko, deputy chief of the Stalingrad NKVD, was named business manager of the foreign affairs commissariat, which ushered him into a world of secret privilege. The commissariat building at Blacksmith Bridge comprised two wings. One was for amenities, such as a nursery for diplomats' children, a clinic for staff and foreign embassy officials, a library, hairdressing salon, tailor's shop, gastronome, and recreational facility. The other wing contained the office suites and private apartments of the higher officials. Korzhenko's office had four comfortable chairs, a divan, a Persian rug, and an ample mahogany working desk. Five telephones sat atop the desk, once a sign of status but now points of life-and-death pressure. The one with a red button was a direct line to Stalin's office. Pushing that with the receiver lifted elicited an immediate response from the Little Corner—and vice versa. Another, with a white button, was connected to the NKVD. Korzhenko, as he spoke, could see the secret police building across the way at Lubyanka Square through his office's three expansive French windows. Goaded by Yezhov and Frinovsky, Korzhenko acted much like a Gestapo officer who had been infiltrated into the Soviet foreign affairs commissariat. His daughter explained that her father "was not concerned with diplomacy but had absolute power over foreign [commissariat] employees from cipher clerks to ambassadors . . . not only in Moscow but throughout the world."[84]

Among the first to have been targeted were Nikolai Krestinsky and Lev Karakhan.[85] Because nearly everyone in foreign affairs had worked with these "enemies of the people," no one was safe from guilt by association. Vulnerability to arrest depended less on what people had done than on the sometimes random flow of denunciations, the caprice of Korzhenko and NKVD officials, and, ultimately, the authorization (or not) of Stalin. Personnel files with mandatory autobiographies were fatal: if you wrote out all of your associations, you were a goner; if you concealed even a single piece of information, you were a goner. When the NKVD station chief in Lithuania complained to Yezhov about the ambassador, Yezhov forwarded to Stalin material on the expenses of the embassy, two thirds of which went to refurbishing the ambassador's office. Yezhov further noted that the ambassador had left abruptly for a three-month "holiday," attempting to escape the arrest wave.[86] Litvinov at times tried to blunt the murderous rampage, but he, too, feared for his life.[87] Soviet embassies were emptied of personnel, and to the extent that dispatches were still being sent to Moscow, the paperwork often went unanswered from lack of personnel. Surviving officials, meanwhile, were "so patently in abject terror, that one must pity them," one American diplomat wrote to Washington. "They fear to talk on any subject and apparently dread meeting foreign visitors."[88]

"ANTI-SOVIET ELEMENTS"

Violence against the population was a hallmark of the Soviet state nearly from its inception, of course, and had reached its apogee in the collectivization-dekulakization. In that sense, the 1937–38 campaign against "anti-Soviet elements" afforded grisly continuity. But these new "mass operations" entailed not just large-scale deportations with some executions, but a preponderance of extrajudicial killing. They would account for 1.1 million of the 1.58 million arrests in 1937–38, and 634,000 of the 682,000 executions.[89] Unlike the state murders in the military, secret police, state agencies, and party, these sweeps captured almost none of Stalin's attention. Still, he relentlessly drove the astronomical numbers with memoranda, telephone directives, and quotas.[90] Local NKVD bosses, predictably, would petition to have their quotas raised, which the "Central Committee" invariably granted. Yezhov was now constantly in the Little Corner, sometimes remaining even after Molotov had departed, and often with his first deputy, Frinovsky. The quota method afforded wide scope to the pair as well as to local NKVD bosses in determining life or death.[91]

Miron Korol, who went by the name Sergei Mironov, had been born in Kiev (1894) to Jewish parents (his grandmother had owned a dairy shop on fashionable

Khreshchatyk Street). The young man graduated from a high school for commerce, fought in the tsarist army in the Great War, and, in the civil war, headed a unit of Budyonny's famous 1st Calvary Army before joining the Cheka (age twenty-seven) and, four years later, the party. Mironov cut his teeth in the North Caucasus, yet another Yevdokimovite, especially in Chechnya, where "banditism" was no mere slogan of abuse, and counterinsurgency was for real. By 1930, Mironov had climbed to deputy secret police head in Kazakhstan, where he managed influxes of "special resettlers" (deported "kulaks") and denomadization, which resulted in mass death and starvation. From September 1933 through 1936, he headed the OGPU-NKVD in industrial Dnepropetrovsk, living in a villa with a billiards room, cinema, and modernized bathhouse, emulating his superior, Ukraine NKVD chief Balytsky, who had an even more impressive villa on the Dnieper River, where in 1936 Mironov and his second wife, Agnessa, had their wedding, at state expense.[92] Vodka, champagne, and nighttime card playing for large sums mixed with surveillance over the party elite, under the guise of providing security. Yezhov, spurred by Frinovsky, promoted Mironov to NKVD chief of Western Siberia, where he took over the villa of the former tsarist governor general and continued the grand style of sumptuous banquets and a household of servants.

Mironov lived in the Chekist world. Once upon a time, that had meant defending Soviet power against armed enemies; now it entailed a deceitful game of unmasking "Trotskyites" and "spies" on railroads and at factories. In private conversations with Agnessa, Mironov called the high-profile November 1936 Kemerovo wrecking case (which predated his arrival) "fabrication" (*lipa*). Torture was known as physical methods or sanctions, with a "scribe" writing up interrogation protocols, often in the absence of the person interrogated and with cynical instructions. ("In this interrogation protocol, it'd be good to add a few little bombs, a touch of terrorism, a rebellion, throw in some diversionary action, then it would be full fledged.") A mass execution was known as a wedding. Chekists would joke that one of them had shot the wrong people but promised to "correct the mistake."[93] A profound brittleness underlay the dark humor: Mironov could not shake the thought that he, too, would end up in Novosibirsk's "bird house" (prison). In March 1937, he was promoted to commissar of state security (third rank), putting him in the elite of the elite. Once, playing billiards, he could see uniformed men approaching outside—and turned white. They proved to be just a rotation of the exterior guard. Mironov had served under the "enemy" Yagoda, and Mironov's deputy, Alexander Uspensky, was closer to Yezhov and could earn a promotion by taking down his new boss. According to Agnessa, "Seryozha said that he [Uspensky] was not a person but mucus."[94]

Such animal fear prompted varied reactions. Some NKVD personnel became inert, some threw themselves out the window, some strove to reconfirm their worth with rabid arrests. Mironov felt impelled to do the latter. He was the one who had telegrammed Yezhov with a denunciation of Balytsky while the latter had been traveling toward his new assignment in the Soviet Far East. Back on June 17, 1937, on the eve of the Central Committee plenum at which Yezhov would unveil the "Center of Centers," Mironov had "requested permission" to form a Western Siberian "troika," comprising the regional NKVD chief, the procurator, and the party boss, to expedite death sentences. He wrote that thousands of exiles were lying in wait to form a counterrevolutionary army. Troikas had been widely used for dekulakization and, before that, in the 1920s antibanditry operations of the North Caucasus, so they were familiar to Mironov. Deich (of the NKVD secretariat) or Frinovsky, knowing how much Stalin prized requests "from below," likely had suggested a troika revival to Mironov. Be that as it may, on June 22, Yezhov forwarded Mironov's "request" to Stalin.

As a respite from the Central Committee plenum, on June 25, 1937, Stalin, with the retinue in tow, went to the Moscow aerodrome to greet the returning crew of the first-ever airborne polar expedition to set up a scientific station on drift ice. In the summer heat, an improvised banquet took place in the Kremlin. "The tables were set in a way I had never before seen, since I had never been in a restaurant," observed a then twenty-five-year-old Sigurd Shmidt, whose father, Otto, was the head of the Arctic Institute.[95] Sergei Obraztsov, the Moscow Art Theater actor and puppeteer, debuted inventive verse about the explorers, which pleased Stalin no end. He invited Obraztsov to share some wine.[96]

Mironov, during the June 1937 "Center of Centers" plenum, privately complained to Frinovsky that all the fabrication was making it impossible to pursue real cases. "What are you doing philosophizing?" Frinovsky snapped. "Now the tempo is such that you need to show results not within months or years, but in days."[97] On June 28, even before the plenum had concluded, a sentencing troika was approved for Western Siberia. On July 2, Stalin authorized a resolution, "On Anti-Soviet Elements," directing all regions to reintroduce troikas to pass sentences without courts.[98] (The resolution was issued in the politburo's name, but formal meetings had ceased.)[99] It would become the most murderous single document of his regime. On July 3, a coded telegram in Yezhov's name went to all sixty-five NKVD republic and regional offices, demanding a fast inventory of previously deported kulaks, ordinary criminals, and former convicts.[100] As the calculations were being tabulated, on July 5, a decree was issued to incarcerate wives of enemies in camps for five to eight years—for being their wives.[101] The Uzbekistan leadership asked to be able to include "nationalist terrorists" (i.e., non-Uzbeks, especially Tajiks); Mironov's Western Siberia asked to include former SRs, former Mensheviks, former Whites, former priests—indeed, all "formers."[102] Permission was granted.[103] For those who required extra motivation, the NKVD bosses in Chelyabinsk and Tataria were arrested, which would prompt a sleepless night for Mironov; he had once worked under the Tatar head.[104]

There were carrots for the NKVD, too: in a single month, 179 operatives received state awards, including no fewer than forty-six Orders of Lenin (Mironov got one). On July 17, 1937, Yezhov was awarded the Order of Lenin, "for outstanding successes in leading the organs of the NKVD in the fulfillment of government tasks." That same day, the politburo formally approved substantial NKVD pay increases for state security personnel (GB) in Moscow, Leningrad, and Ukraine.[105] Rank-and-file operatives now got paid 500 to 800 rubles per month, while republic NKVD heads got 3,500 rubles per month, a jump of 300 percent. (By comparison, a provincial party boss got a salary of 2,000 rubles per month, not including the extra cash envelopes, and the head of the USSR Supreme Court got 1,200 rubles.) Additionally, while NKVD bosses had long enjoyed the use of villas with servants, like gentry, while their subordinates often lived in communal housing or dormitory beds, during the terror, many rank-and-file operatives acquired coveted apartments, as well as state dachas from arrested "enemies."[106] Possessions confiscated from enemies of the people, including cash, were considered fair game (some Chekists were known to complain when arrestees turned out to be "poor peasants"). Some of the loot would be legally resold through what were called special trading centers, which had been set up to bring in revenue from confiscations, but much was pocketed. Bosses not on the scene expected a cut.[107]

Once home from the Moscow gathering, Mironov instructed his subordinates (July 25) that the requirement of procuracy authorization for an arrest (Article 127 of the 1936 Constitution) had been "suspended," and that they should go out and secretly "find a place where the sentences can be carried out and the bodies buried."[108]

On July 26, 1937, Stalin hosted a Kremlin reception for the aviators Chkalov, Baidukov, and Belyakov, who had returned from North America and a White House reception. They had ridden to the Kremlin in open-top cars garlanded with flowers. Stalin embraced and kissed them. The heroes requested that the evening's concert program include jazz by Leonid Utyosov, whose band approached the stage singing "Heart," from the smash film *Jolly Fellows*. Despite the absence of microphones, the acoustics proved splendid in the intimate Palace of Facets. The jazzmen also played the American melody "Reflection in Water," with the verses in Russian, about a woman waiting for the return of her lover, which is said to have brought tears to Stalin's eyes. The despot rose to applaud, leading a long ovation. Utyosov played the number again, and once again visible tears ran down Stalin's cheeks; then a third encore. The supreme leader was moved to issue his own request, a manifesto of the criminal world called "From the Odessa Jail," replete with argot that had been officially banned.[109]

Frinovsky handled the dirty work, writing up NKVD Operational Order No. 00447 (dated July 31), which Stalin approved. (The 00 indicated supersecrecy.) "The organs of state security are faced with the task of mercilessly crushing this entire gang of anti-Soviet elements," the order noted, demanding "an end once and for all to the foul subversion of the Soviet state's foundations."[110] Every *potential* enemy—as determined by administrative fiat—was to be either executed (category 1) or sent to distant points of the Gulag (category 2). Regional and republic NKVD archivists updated their card catalogs of "anti-Soviet elements," former "kulaks," and "recidivist" criminals. Yezhov and Frinovsky used the submitted numbers to assign local arrest quotas totaling, Union-wide, 269,000 (76,000 to be shot, 193,000 to get eight to ten years in the Gulag).[111] Predictably, regional NKVD officials requested still higher quotas. Western Siberia had it easy, with among the densest concentration of exiled kulaks (more than 200,000), labor camps teeming with ordinary criminals, and large contingents of released inmates.[112] In Turkmenistan, the NKVD sent paddy wagons out to the bazaar to haul in people; in Sverdlovsk, in the office of an official arrested as a "counterrevolutionary," the NKVD found a list of Stakhanovites, a handy group to help meet the quota.[113] During just the first two weeks of August 1937, 100,000 people were arrested, far more than the number in the entire year since the Moscow public trial of August 1936.[114]

The NKVD sliced through the populace like a reaper through the wheat fields. Nothing fundamental had changed in "kulak sabotage," crime rates, or Gulag labor needs. Locally, the kulak operation sometimes had little to do with former kulaks. In the Perm region of the Urals province (where former KGB archives have been accessible), the majority of the targets were workers and white-collar functionaries. Here, supersecret order 00447 extended carte blanche to local operatives for eradicating "conspiracies" they were already "unmasking," as reflected in their mounting NKVD reports dating to fall 1936 and especially spring 1937 (following central plenums and directives). The local pattern resembled the spread of a virus—after one person got arrested, his or her associates got infected with their "guilt," a reaction that was then repeated, in an ever-widening way.[115]

At the same time regional secret police officials could no more start mass murdering the populace without central directives than they could continue to do so after central directives instructed them to halt.[116] What happened was that Stalin decided on mass murder, and he could count on Frinovsky at the center and the Mironovs in the locales to implement it.[117]

Parallel "national" operations did not use quotas, but a nationality itself was a kind of quota.[118] Every person among Soviet nationalities with a corresponding nation-state outside the USSR became a potential NKVD target. To be sure, sweeping ethnic deportations had begun earlier.[119] But such actions expanded exponentially: the entire population of ethnic Koreans in the Soviet Far East were deported to Kazakhstan and Uzbekistan, where they would dig holes for "housing." The sheer scale of the action against Soviet Koreans—135,000 deported by late October 1937 and as many as 185,000 eventually—gave rise to complications, which provoked Stalin's ire. "People who sabotage the action, no matter who they might be, arrest forthwith and punish," he wrote to the top officials in the Soviet Far East.[120] Regional NKVD offices also now put together "albums" of foreigners and ethnics in their localities, rating the personages by degree of suspicion. Soviet ethnic Poles were the main targets: 144,000 were arrested and 111,000 executed, nearly half of all the non-Russian nationals killed.[121, 122] (There were around 636,000 ethnic Poles in the Soviet Union.) "Very good!" the ethnic Georgian Stalin wrote on a report by Yezhov, a closet part ethnic Lithuanian. "Dig down and cleanse this Polish-espionage filth. Destroy it in the interests of the USSR!"[123]

Next were Soviet ethnic Germans: 55,000 arrested and nearly 42,000 executed.[124] Citizens of Germany were rounded up, too.[125] Frinovsky, on July 20, forwarded to Stalin a report from NKVD counterintelligence: "A crow was killed near Lake Ladoga. It had a ring with the number D-72291 and an inscription, 'Germany.' Simultaneously, a kite [a bird of prey] killed a crow near the village of Rusynya in the Batetsky area of the Leningrad region. This crow also had a ring with the number D-70398 with the same inscription, 'Germany.' Evidently, the Germans are studying wind directions by using crows, with the aim of using the winds for diversionary activity and bacteriological purposes (torching settlements, haystacks, and so on)."[126] What the NKVD had discovered was a research project of German ornithologists to study crow migration.

After Yezhov had posted Alexei Nasedkin to Smolensk as NKVD chief and advised him to "make arrests more boldly" of Soviet ethnic Poles and Germans, Nasedkin discovered, on-site, accumulated "testimony" on a "counterrevolutionary" Latvian cultural society. He rushed back to Moscow. "Yezhov livened up," Nasedkin recalled, and he asked, "Are there a lot of Latvians in Smolensk?" Nasedkin answered: 5,000, of whom he estimated 450 to 500 could be arrested. "Drivel," Yezhov said. "I'll discuss it with the Central Committee and we'll have to spill the blood of Latvians—arrest not fewer than 1,500–2,000. They are all nationalists." Nasedkin himself was received in the Little Corner to report on the "Latvian conspiracy." His "vigilance" helped spark the arrest of nearly every prominent Soviet Latvian: the talented head of the Red Air Force, Yakov Alksnis (Jēkabs Alksnis); the vexed chief of military intelligence, Jan Berzin (Pēteris Ķuzis); the celebrated Chekists Yakov Peters (Jēkabs Peterss) and Martin Latsis (Jānis Sudrabs); the first-ever Red Army supreme commander, Ioakim Vatsetis (Jukums Vācietis), who had saved the Bolshevik regime from the left SRs in 1918; Western Siberian party boss Roberts Eihe; politburo candidate member Jānis Rudzutaks.[127] All across the USSR, countless people suddenly became "Latvian," in the interests of meeting quotas. Nasedkin, back in Smolensk, inquired whether he could arrest Latvians in the absence of compromising material on them. "Material," answered Yezhov, "will arise in the course of interrogation."[128]

Yezhov would effectively take Rudzutaks's slot on the politburo; Zhdanov would get Rudzutaks's dacha.[129] "He did not admit anything!" Molotov recalled of his long-serving, loyal deputy Rudzutaks. "I think that he was not a conscious participant, but he liberalized with this fraternity, and believed that all this was nonsense, trifles. And that could not be forgiven. He did not understand the dangers. . . . A rather intelligent man, no question. He had a kind of non-Latvian flexibility. Latvians were not so much slow thinkers, but they simplified a bit. First-class thinkers in our party were not found among Latvians."[130]

ANNIHILATING MILITARY INTELLIGENCE

Yezhov received a translation of an intercepted report from a Western European military attaché in Moscow, stating that nearly all foreign representatives in Moscow viewed the charges against Tukhachevsky and other military men as preposterous, an artifact of Stalin's hypersuspiciousness, and concluded that the executions had damaged Soviet military might. Whether Yezhov had the courage to forward the document to Stalin remains unclear.[131] But another case demonstrates Stalin's disregard of consequences. In early 1937, Yezhov had sent him a detailed sketch of the German army's troop positioning for 1935–36, reporting that the valuable material had been photographed from the safe of the German military attaché, Ernst Köstring, without the latter's knowledge. Yezhov attributed the feat to the Soviet intelligence officer and ethnic Hungarian lieutenant Béla Bíró (b. 1891), whom he praised for "showing initiative, boldness, agility, and sangfroid." Stalin had approved Yezhov's recommendation that Bíró be awarded the Order of the Red Star "for special services." But then, on July 2, 1937, Yezhov's NKVD, with Stalin's approval, arrested Bíró, and on September 2 it would have him executed at its state farm killing field, "Kommunarka," for espionage.[132] Bíró's loss was repeated many times.[133, 134]

Mikhail Alexandrovsky, the just-named deputy of military intelligence, was arrested in July 1937. On August 1, Berzin—less than two months after Stalin had returned him as military intelligence chief—was replaced by his other deputy, Alexander Nikonov. Nikonov lasted a few days before his arrest. Under torture, each confessed and named more names. Stalin could have had their interrogations conducted to find out who (if anyone) had actually recruited them, what damage (if any) they had inflicted. Alternately, he could have kept them in place and had them shadowed to see what (if any) foreign contacts they had. None of that was done.[135] Military intelligence was handed to an NKVD counterintelligence operative beholden to Yezhov, as if the main task at hand were a police operation against the country's own intelligence.[136] Altogether, at least 300 military intelligence officers would be arrested in Moscow alone.[137] The head of personnel in military intelligence reported that half the allotted positions had become vacant. Maria Polyakova, an undercover operative in Switzerland who returned to Moscow in fall 1937, found no one to report to. "I could not understand what was going on, and I did not know whom to ask about it," she recalled. "I met the department staff, who were primarily [recent] graduates of the military academy and did not know languages or the work of our agency."[138]

Stalin explicitly rejected the notion that the arrests were cynical. In August 1937, at a gathering he attended of political functionaries in the military, the head of the Far Eastern Army's political department complained. "We cannot tell the party mass, the commanding staff, or the Red Army men what [specific] wrecking activities these wreckers committed," the man stated. "And by the way, the interest in this matter is enormous," having been incited by the NKVD's reading of excerpts of the interrogation protocols at Red Army party meetings. One official at the meeting interjected: "Would it not be sufficient just to say that they worked to restore capitalism?" Stalin: "All the same, the testimonies have significance."[139]

FAR EASTERN "IMPERIALIST WAR"

Japanese ground and air forces in the Manchukuo puppet state had violated the Soviet border more than 150 times in 1935 and again in 1936.[140] In 1937, a major incident took place over strategic islets in the Amur River.[141] Islands along a river boundary were normally adjudicated by their positioning relative to the channel of the main current. But since the Russo-Chinese border treaties of 1858 and 1860, storms and other natural causes had caused a shift in the Amur's main channel, so that a pair of small islets some sixty and fifty miles downstream from Blagoveshchensk, respectively, had moved to the Manchukuo side of the Amur's main current. The Soviets argued that the border marker should now be the river's deepest channel, which would put the islets back in Soviet territory. On June 19, 1937, the Japanese had reported that some twenty Soviet soldiers had landed at one of the two islets—known as Kanchazu in Manchu—on motorboats, removed buoys, and evicted Manchukuo gold panners, actions repeated at other Amur islets. Manchukuo government protests brought no resolution. The Japanese Kwantung Army was inclined to clear the Soviet troops by force, but Tokyo military brass decided, on June 28, 1937, that "the problem of these islands located so remotely did not warrant risking a major commitment of the national strength." That very day, however, a high Japanese military intelligence officer recently returned from Moscow published a report in an Osaka newspaper suggesting that the Soviet Union's executions of its own top military commanders threatened the Red Army with disintegration, meaning Japan had nothing to fear.[142]

Stalin's terror—proclaimed as vital in the face of a coming "inevitable war"— was potentially inviting that very war. With Tukhachevsky and the others dead a mere few weeks and the Red Army in turmoil, on June 29, Soviet diplomats informed the Japanese that Moscow would remove the troops from the Amur islets.

By now, though, three small Soviet gunboats had arrived on the scene, and on June 30 Japanese Kwantung Army forces opened fire, sinking one boat and damaging another; thirty-seven Soviet sailors died. Disgust at Tokyo's "timidity" and an urge to respond to the Soviet "buildup" were strong. Stalin had a diplomatic protest lodged, but he refrained from military retaliation. Japanese intelligence intercepted Blyukher's order from Khabarovsk to the Amur flotilla commander to withdraw. On July 3—the same day Yezhov's NKVD order went out to branches to prepare for "mass operations" against the USSR's own population—Soviet troops began to evacuate the islets. Manchukuo filled the vacuum on July 6, occupying the now evacuated (and until recently unoccupied) islets and converting Kanchazu into de facto Manchukuo territory, which still drew no Soviet response. Japanese intelligence could scarcely believe the near hysteria in intercepted Soviet military communications: a few artillery rounds seemed to have frightened the Red Army away, despite its three-to-one troop advantage in theater. "I think it was a really good 'reconnaissance' in force," a Japanese intelligence officer concluded of the unplanned skirmish. Thus, while the Amur incident had persuaded much of the Kwantung Army of Tokyo's timidity, the general staff in Tokyo had begun to discuss the hollowness of the Red Army.[143]

Japanese troops (numbering between 5,000 and 7,000) also controlled all the areas of China immediately north, east, and west of Peking—areas that faced the USSR and the Soviet satellite of Mongolia. On July 7, 1937, about 135 of those troops were engaged in night maneuvers ten miles west of Peking at the Marco Polo Bridge, an 800-year-old ancient granite structure once restored by the great Qing emperor Kangxi. The bridge, near a railway choke point, had long been coveted by Japan, because it served as the sole link between Peking and the rest of Nationalist-controlled China. Unusually, these Japanese night maneuvers took place without prior courtesy notice, and around 10:30 p.m., Chinese troops, perhaps fearing that an actual attack had commenced, fired some rifle shots. The Japanese returned fire. After mutual apologies for the minor firefight by the two sides' liaison officers on duty, as well as some bellicose statements, the Japanese brigade commander refused to back down and ordered an artillery barrage. The Chinese shelled the Japanese in return. Then, on July 9, the Japanese and Chinese commanders in the Marco Polo Bridge area agreed to a cease-fire and mutual pullback.

Chiang Kai-shek was at Lushan for a military conference and, on the basis of radio reports, could not judge whether the gunfire and shelling had been unplanned or constituted a Japanese provocation, on the order of the Mukden incident that had preceded the seizure of Manchuria. He felt constrained to deploy some of his best divisions, institute martial law, and order a general mobilization. Japan's government, now headed by prime minister Prince Fumimaro Konoe, deemed the incident a Chinese "provocation" and dispatched three divisions. When the Japanese troops arrived at Tientsin, on July 12, Chiang telegrammed his military in the field: "I am now determined to declare war on Japan."[144] On July 22, the Japanese commander at the Marco Polo Bridge announced a deadline for Chinese troop withdrawal; Chiang ordered his men to attack. Few in the Konoe cabinet were for all-out war, but few were against it. Tokyo announced, to popular acclamation, that it had been "forced to resort to resolute action."[145] With Emperor Hirohito's approval, the Japanese bombarded and seized Peking (July 28) and nearby Tientsin (July 30).[146]

Stalin was saved. His insistence on a "united front," instead of an attempted Communist takeover, now looked prescient, but he had to weigh continuing support for the anti-Japanese resistance in China against possibly provoking Japan into war against the Soviet Union. The Soviet department in Japanese military intelligence had correctly surmised that Moscow would not intervene in the event of a Japanese expedition to Peking.[147]

Japan's occupation of northern China was swift. Whether the war would spread beyond northern China remained uncertain. But Zhang Zhizhong, commander of the Shanghai-Nanking garrison and a former teacher at the Soviet-funded Whampoa Military Academy, who had been urging Chiang Kai-shek to attack vulnerable Japanese positions in Shanghai, staged his own incident: on August 9, 1937, a Chinese army unit shot and killed a Japanese lieutenant and private just outside the Shanghai airport. To make it seem as if the Japanese had fired first, a Chinese prisoner on death row was dressed in military uniform and executed at the airport gate. Zhang renewed his pressure on Chiang to engage in an all-out war with Japan, not just protect the north; Chiang demurred. Zhang staged bombing runs on Japanese ships, grounding aircraft and troops. Japanese reinforcements began to make their way to Shanghai. Chiang approached Moscow for a mutual assistance treaty. Stalin, wanting to prevent a Japanese conquest of China but not to entangle the Soviets in a direct war with Japan, agreed only to a nonaggression pact, which was signed in Nanking on August 21.[148] (This was the same day a joint decree of the Council of People's Commissars and the politburo ordered the deportation of all ethnic Koreans from the Soviet Far East.)[149] On August 22, Japanese forces arrived in Shanghai.

America's ambassador in Moscow reported to Washington that Litvinov had told Léon Blum that "he and the Soviet Union were perfectly delighted that Japan had attacked China," and that "the Soviet Union hoped that war between China and Japan would continue just as long as possible."[150] Some suggested that Zhang Zhizhong was a Soviet agent who had provoked war on Moscow's orders.[151] (Chiang would force Zhang to resign in September 1937, but would not accuse him of being a foreign agent.) On September 14, the Soviets and Chiang signed an additional accord for the supply of Soviet weapons on $50 million in credits, with the proviso that one quarter to one fifth would go to the Chinese Red Army.[152]

After his release from the hostage-taking incident, Chiang had conceded the legality of the Chinese Communist forces, but now they would not be subordinated to his orders. The Communist army in the north, centered on Yan'an and numbering 46,000, was renamed the Eighth Route Army. On September 23, Chiang acknowledged a public declaration of the Chinese Communists, published in the Nationalist press the day before—a form of legalization. Mao, while paying lip service to the united front, planned a guerrilla war in the north independently of the Nationalists, effectively keeping his army out of the main brunt of the fighting.

Stalin, too, took advantage. He had already sent 5,000 Soviet troops, dressed in Chinese uniforms, to Xinjiang, provoking a rebellion against the pro-Soviet local puppet but also increasing the Soviet foothold.[153] Chiang feared a Soviet pact with Japan to divide China—after all, the Soviets had already broken off Outer Mongolia from China—but he was more obliged than ever to tolerate Soviet encroachment.[154] That's because Stalin now agreed to sell desperately needed combat aircraft and to help with training, as in Spain, although in China's case he did so on credit (altogether extending three separate loans to the Chinese government, totaling $250 million, to cover the costs).[155] In the wake of Stalin's military pullback from the ongoing civil war in Spain (Operation X), at least 450 Soviet pilots would be in China before the year was out (Operation Z).[156] During the last few months of 1937, the USSR flew 297 fighter planes and bombers into Chinese airfields, while trucks and ships (via Canton) delivered nearly 300 cannons, 82 tanks, 400 vehicles, and a mass supply of arms and ammunition. Stalin also lent support to Chinese partisan units, to further tie down the Japanese, and ordered Comintern head Dimitrov, again, to rein in the revolutionary impulses of the Chinese Communist party.

Some 400 Uighur students, future Soviet agents for Chinese Xinjiang, were being schooled in Tashkent, but then the Uighurs were all executed in a single night. After murdering his own Xinjiang fifth column, Stalin blinded himself, recalling and executing his diplomats from half a dozen consulates across China's western interior, including Ürümqi and Kashgar. Still, his position in Xinjiang strengthened as the Soviets oversaw construction of a nearly 2,000-mile road, completed in just months with Chinese coolie labor, from Sary-Ozek, Kazakhstan, through Ürümqi to Lanzhou, to transport war supplies to China's anti-Japanese resistance.[157]

THE OTHER FRONT

Spain was still on fire. "The front stretches very far," *Pravda*'s Koltsov had lyricized in his Spanish diary (July 7, 1937). "It goes from Madrid's trenches, across Europe, across the entire world. It crosses countries, villages, cities, it crosses boisterous meeting halls, it courses quietly through the shelves of bookstores."[158] And apartments: Malenkov informed Stalin (August 16) of a denunciation from a Soviet official in Spain, who had written, "I do not know if it is known in Moscow that in Madrid Koltsov lives with his two wives with completely equal status (at least by outward appearance). There are very many conversations and troubling questions about this, including in Madrid. The matter does not just concern giving an answer to our Spanish friends whether polygamy is legal for Soviet writers, but also, for example, the apartment of Koltsov's [common-law] wife, Maria Osten, has been turned into a salon where high-profile comrades of various nationalities gather and where they discuss delicate questions in the presence of not fully verified comrades."[159]

Soviet advisers were trying to stave off defeat, reorganizing the International Brigades. In September 1937, Victorio Codovilla (b. 1894), an Italian-Argentine Comintern representative in Spain, was recalled to Moscow. Dimitrov forwarded to Stalin (September 8) a letter from Codovilla asking "what tactics should we advise the Comintern" for victory in Spain. Stalin wrote in the margin: "Together with the Socialists, without looking away from them, expose and smash the enemies of the united front." Where Codovilla noted that the parliament was not meeting, Stalin wrote, "Restore the parliament, the municipal governments." Where Codovilla re-proposed a merger of the Spanish Socialist and Communist parties, suggesting both names be used, Stalin wrote in the margin, "United Worker Party."[160]

FRONTLINE DEFENSE

Chiang Kai-shek did not capitulate to Japan. Still, Stalin might have been chastened at the prospect that China would fall, which would allow Japan to pivot toward the Soviet Union. A Japanese advance beyond Peking toward Kalgan in August 1937, on the old caravan route to Mongolia, threatened the Soviet satellite, a potential springboard for invading Eastern Siberia and cutting off the Soviet Far East. But Stalin pressed ahead with his destabilizing decapitation of the Red Army on trumped-up charges, including in the Soviet Far East. He also allowed his murderous "mass operations" to continue, which consumed vast industrial and transport resources. Most strikingly, he unleashed a rampage in Mongolia.[161]

On August 13, Stalin met in the Little Corner for four hours with Molotov, Voroshilov, Yezhov, Frinovsky, and Pyotr Smirnov, a newly minted deputy defense commissar; chief of staff Shaposhnikov joined the meeting late.[162] Yezhov reported on a pending "Japanese-sponsored" coup d'état in the Mongolian capital. (Genden, Mongolia's prime minister, who was suspected of being pro-Japanese, had already been arrested in Sochi.) Stalin decided to send a clandestine delegation headed by Frinovsky. He also named Mironov, the Western Siberian NKVD boss, plenipotentiary for Mongolia, in place of the Soviet ambassador (who was a Soviet intelligence operative but was arrested by the NKVD for being a Japanese spy). "As soon as his promotion occurred," Mironov's wife, Agnessa, noted, "Mirosha became manifestly cheerful, and his former self-confidence returned immediately." And yet, as Frinovsky and his armed gang traveled by train to pick him up on the way at Novosibirsk, Mironov started to fear that his promotion might be a ruse to effect his arrest.[163] Not this time. In Irkutsk, Eastern Siberia, Frinovsky beat a local official in the greeting party to a pulp in front of the rest of the local leadership, demonstrating how "enemies" were dealt with.[164] He and Mironov disembarked in Ulan Ude (Soviet Buryatia) and went the final 350 miles by car to Ulan Bator, which they reached on August 24, unannounced. It was not the Japanese but the Soviets who launched a coup d'état.

Marshal Demid, Mongolia's popular defense minister, untouchable inside his country, had been summoned for talks in Moscow and, en route, had stopped briefly in Irkutsk on August 20, around the same time that Frinovsky had arrived in the city. On August 22, near Taiga Station (close to Novosibirsk), Demid died of "food poisoning" from Soviet-supplied canned goods. His corpse continued all the way to Moscow, where it was met at Kazan Station by an honor guard, then dispatched to a crematorium.[165] Demid had played a key role in Genden's removal, at Moscow's bidding.[166] Stalin evidently did not expect Demid to acquiesce in the wholesale slaughter of the Mongolian officer corps he had appointed for being "Japanese agents." Demid's rival, the other Mongolian marshal, Interior Minister Khorloogiin Choibalsan, had staged five public trials between April 1936 and May 1937, of lamas as "Japanese and Chinese spies." "We fulfilled the advice of comrade Stalin," he had reported to Yezhov. But now, Frinovsky told Choibalsan of more spies and plots, and insisted that he invite in more Soviet troops. A formal invitation was issued on August 25; two days later, Molotov and Voroshilov telegrammed an affirmative response.[167] A Soviet army commanded by Ivan Konev, from the Transbaikal military district, had already crossed the frontier—nearly 30,000 well-equipped troops. Their mission was to deter Japan and prepare Mongolia as a supply hub for the Nationalists in China. (The Gobi Desert dunes, belatedly studied, would be revealed to be untraversable.)

Following Demid's funeral, Choibalsan became defense minister and supreme commander (September 2, 1937). With him, Frinovsky compiled a list of 115 "spies," reporting every detail to Yezhov. Demid, who held a Soviet Order of the Red Banner and numerous Mongolian military medals, became a Japanese spy posthumously. On September 10, sixty-five people on the list were rounded up. The next day, Mongolia's top brass were summoned to appear at Choibalsan's office in full regalia and, one by one, were arrested, transported to prison, and tortured to confess.[168] Frinovsky set up an "extraordinary commission," like a troika, to expedite sentencing-shootings, then departed for home.[169] The "diplomat" Mironov remained.

A public trial (October 4–7, 1937) of "reactionary lamas" charged with spying for Japan was staged in Ulan Bator's State Central Theater (which also functioned as the national parliament's building).[170] The theater overflowed with 1,323 people (against a capacity of 1,200), while public loudspeakers broadcast the proceedings and expansive coverage was given in the party newspaper *Ünen* (*Truth*). All twenty-three defendants, who had been burned with hot iron rods and promised their lives if they confessed, did so; four were sentenced to the Gulag, nineteen to death. They were shot in front of the theater. On October 18, in the same venue, a second public trial was staged, of fourteen high officials said to belong to a Genden-Demid "organization." Two days later, all fourteen were pronounced guilty; one was sent to a camp, and thirteen were taken to a valley outside the capital, where, with truck and car headlights illuminating the darkness, they were executed. Those Mongolian leaders who were not executed were forced to observe. Choibalsan, drunk, waved his pistol and shouted revolutionary slogans.[171]

LEADERS COME AND GO

Reveries of finding vast numbers of capable "new people" had periodically gripped Stalin, and now many young people, capable or otherwise, were vaulted into high places. Of the 12,500 graduates of higher-education institutions in the fourth quarter of 1937, 2,127 went directly to senior positions, including 278 promoted to directors or deputy directors of factories; another 22 became directors, deputy directors, heads, or deputy heads of departments in trusts; 294 became heads or deputy heads of departments or sectors in the Council of People's Commissars. Many were promoted again, quickly. In September 1937, M. S. Lazarev went from chief of a shop at the Gorky Automobile Plant to director of the Yaroslavl Electric Machine-Building Factory. "I literally had to go onto the site unprepared, because the management had been arrested and the apparatus was completely new," he would tell a Central Committee conference for the recently promoted. But then, on October 1, he was promoted again, becoming head of the tractor and motor industry in the machine building commissariat.[172] Not all of these newly promoted people could cope. "I want to say, honestly, that, despite nine months of work, I have failed to get into the rhythm of things and to develop appropriate economic skills," admitted S. M. Dobrokhotov, the deputy head and chief engineer of the strategic rubber industry, also in the machine building commissariat.

Even with such promotions, the Soviet system was not producing nearly enough young people to fill all the vacated positions, in the center or the locales, because right through the terror and beyond, the apparatus was ballooning.[173] In fall 1937, a floodlike 130,000 students were admitted to higher-education institutions.[174] On October 23, 1937, the politburo established a commission for assigning graduates of higher education directly via the Central Committee.[175]

On the evening of October 29, Stalin hosted a reception in the Kremlin's Palace of Facets, culminating a four-day conference of some 400 representatives of the metals-and-coal industry. He had already explicitly identified his rule with the expansive ranks of middling "cadres" in his resounding slogan "Cadres decide everything" (1935), but by 1937 he was singling out the up-and-coming generation more and more, receiving them in the magical inner sanctum, the Little Corner, or, as now, in the lustrous reception halls of the Kremlin.[176] "Leaders come and go, but the people remain," he told the coal-and-metals gathering. "Only the people are immortal. All the rest is transient. Therefore, it is necessary to be able to value the confidence of the people." He could not help divulging, "I am not sure, I apologize again, that there are not people among you who, although they work for the Soviet government, are not also taking care of themselves in the West by also working for some foreign intelligence services: Japanese, German, or Polish." (These lines were edited out of his remarks published in *Pravda*.) But he went on to accentuate the positive. "Comrades! My toast will be original and unusual," he continued. "We are accustomed to pronounce toasts for the health of leaders, bosses, *vozhdi*, people's commissars. This, of course, is not bad. But besides the big leaders, there are middling and lesser leaders. We have tens of thousands of these leaders, the middling and lesser ones. They are modest people, they do not push themselves out front, they are almost unnoticeable. But one would be blind not to notice them. Because the fate of production in our entire economy depends on them. . . . To the health of our middle and smaller economic leaders! (Ovation, shouts of Hurrah.)"[177]

Stalin's populism was addressed not to the workers but to the middle and lower-level functionaries, people he christened the "Soviet intelligentsia." He showed an uncanny knack for winning over people who, like himself, had risen from humble backgrounds, thanks to education. He identified with these up-and-comers, claiming them as his own, sentiments they keenly reciprocated. To be sure, Stalin bullied and dominated others, demanded unquestioning obedience, whose manifestation (or not) he alone judged. And yet, cruel and capricious though he was, Stalin could also be highly personable. "All his life he was very good at finding people and promoting them," recalled Svetlana, "and that is why so many remained devoted to him, often young people whom he would pull out and promote over the heads of the old guard. That was quite a part of him: his sociability and being with people."[178]

Galvanizing and molding young strivers fit Stalin's personality as much as pathological suspicion and wholesale murder. Ryutin, in his 1932 "Stalin and the Crisis of the Proletarian Dictatorship," had called for "new forces" from within the party and the working class to "destroy Stalin's dictatorship," but Stalin himself was conjuring these new forces to replace destroyed functionaries of his dictatorship.[179] Of course, if he felt he needed to clear space to promote a hard-charging younger generation, he could have forced sitting functionaries into retirement.[180] By having the new people take the place of the wantonly tortured and executed, he compromised them all.

PETER AND SOVIET PATRIOTISM

Not a single member of Stalin's politburo, going back to 1930, had completed university, the despot included, but he adhered ferociously to the transformative power of education, and for him Russian history was among the greatest pedagogical instruments. But his commission to produce a new history textbook for elementary schools had yielded only vague instructions, finalized and signed by him, Zhdanov, and Kirov at his Sochi dacha back in summer 1934; they were published only after significant delay in *Pravda* (January 27, 1936), which was followed by an open competition. On August 22, 1937, a second-place winner was announced (there was no first-place winner). It was a humble collective at the Moscow State Pedagogical Institute, led by Andrei Shestakov.[181] Shestakov (b. 1877) had grown up one of nine children, the son of a peasant and a fisherman on the White Sea littoral, and finished only the local five-year school before being hired on at the woodcutting factory, but he studied at night.[182] He had relocated to Moscow in 1921, by then a skilled mechanic, and took up the study of agrarian history, at age forty-four, at the Institute of Red Professors. By the 1930s, he had become deputy director and then director of the Museum of the Revolution.[183] His team worked on their manuscript, *A Short Course on the History of the USSR: A Textbook for the Third and Fourth Grades*, from March 1936 through July 1937, and, after political vetting, had it published in September 1937 for the start of the new school year and the run-up to the twentieth anniversary of the revolution.

While maintaining the Marxist core of class struggle, the book offered a nationalist narrative of Russia's "gathering of the lands"—from Kievan Rus, in the tenth century, through the Stalin Constitution of 1936—in the spirit of nineteenth-century historiography. "We love our country and we must know its wonderful history," the book noted. "Those who know history understand present-day life better, are better able to fight the enemies of our country, and make Socialism stronger."[184] In the last quarter of 1937, 6.5 million Russian-language copies were printed; it was simultaneously translated into the languages of the Soviet peoples.[185] Still, parents struggled to obtain copies.[186] The USSR counted some 30 million schoolchildren, and the Shestakov text was recommended beyond schools.[187] "Not only millions of children and young people will learn according to it," enthused the party journal *Bolshevik*, "but so will millions of workers and peasants and hundreds of thousands of party activists, propagandists, and agitators."[188] There were critics. "It has not turned out to be a history of the USSR at all," Volodymyr Zatonsky, Ukraine's commissar of enlightenment, wrote of the draft manuscript. "Basically, it is a history of the Russian state."[189] In celebrating a great power, not its nationalities, the text gave a prominent place to personalities, a rebuke to abstract schema such as "feudal epoch."[190] Shestakov portrayed Peter the Great not as an oppressor who built a baroque capital on the bones of the lower orders, but as a dynamic leader who had transformed Russia almost single-handedly by advancing technical training and military skills.[191]

Stalin had edited Shestakov's text closely, inserting in the section on ancient Rus that "Christianity in its time was a step forward in the development of Russia in comparison to paganism." Leafing through the page proofs of the manuscript, Stalin had struck out a reproduction of Ilya Repin's painting *Ivan the Terrible Killing His Son* and inserted a laudatory passage on the dreaded *oprichnina* for strengthening "the autocratic power in the Russian state by destroying the privileges of the boyars." This marked the Soviet despot's rethinking of how to fit Ivan, too, into the grand statist narrative.[192] Stalin deemed the centralizing Russian state as having been progressive in its time, allowing the Russian people to push forward on the road of capitalist development, while introducing enlightenment to backward regions, but the Soviets had rightly altered the state's class basis, enabling Soviet propaganda to glorify both the imperial Russian state and the revolutionary movement against it.

In parallel, Vladimir Petrov's film *Peter the First,* adapted from the popular novel by Aleksei Tolstoy, had premiered on September 1, 1937, the opening day of school.[193] It showed the tsar forging his new capital and cadres ruthlessly, decisively. "The epoch of Peter I was one of the greatest pages in the history of the Russian people," Tolstoy told workers at the Skorokhod factory (September 11). "The boyars' dark, uncultured Rus, with their backward technology and patriarchal beards, would have fallen to foreign invaders in no time. A revolution was necessary within the very life of the country, in order to lift Russia up to the level of the cultured European countries. Peter was able to accomplish this, and the Russian people were able to defend their independence."[194] One Soviet inhabitant proudly recorded in her diary, "The content and superb execution of our films arouse admiration even abroad. If you take such films as *Chapayev* [and] *Peter the First* . . . you simply forget that you're sitting in a movie theater, and not actually participating in what you are seeing."[195]

Stalin, like Peter (albeit without the extensive travels), had come to understand Europe as both a treasure trove of know-how and technology to be copied and a political and geopolitical threat to be kept at bay to protect Russia's non-Western identity and nondemocratic system. His recorded comments on Peter had been intermittent (1926, 1928, 1931), but all had emphasized the class nature of the tsar's rule. Now, too, incorporation of Peter in the Soviet pantheon did not vitiate the Marxist stance or class critique.[196] More broadly, Stalin did not reintroduce ritualized processionals accompanied by clergy. Instead of landed gentry and bureaucrats, the USSR had only functionaries; instead of peasant households and self-organized communes, it had statist collectives; instead of the Orthodox Church, Marxism-Leninism. Stalin did not elevate his children to be tsareviches. When he caught his son Vasily attempting to trade on his lineage, he exploded, "You're not Stalin and I'm not Stalin. Stalin is Soviet power. Stalin is what he is in the newspapers and the portraits, not you, no, not even me!"[197] In sum, notwithstanding superficial resemblances—a one-man autocracy, an overweening state, a functionary ethos, an obsession with security, a forced modernization drive—anyone who had lived under both systems, not only peasants and the pious, knew the differences.[198]

The Soviet Union even lacked a requirement to study Russian, and most non-Russian schoolchildren were illiterate in the language. When the enlightenment commissar of the Russian republic suggested a far-reaching Russification of schooling, Stalin objected, insisting that Russian become only a subject, not the medium of all instruction, to the detriment of vernacular languages.[199] Still, a state imperative was felt. "There is one language in which all citizens of the USSR can more or less express themselves—that is Russian," Stalin remarked at a Central Committee plenum (October 12, 1937). "So we concluded that it should be obligatory. It would be good if all citizens drafted into the army could express themselves in Russian just a little, so that if some division or other was transferred, say an Uzbek one to Samara, it could converse with the populace."[200]

LOOSE-TONGUED SELF-PORTRAIT

On November 6, 1937, the eve of the revolution's twentieth anniversary, at the Bolshoi, which was resplendent in red velvet and gold trim and sported an expensive new curtain, Mikhail Romm's *Lenin in October* premiered. This was the first feature film with Stalin as a lead character, played by Semyon Goldstab, a Jewish actor from Ukraine. The film depicted a likable, grandfatherly Lenin (played by Boris Shchukin) who relied on Stalin, while Kamenev and Zinoviev, Trotsky, the Mensheviks, and SRs were shown to be objects of Lenin's hatred and treasonous opponents of the seizure of power. After the showing, Stalin would have Romm reshoot the scenes involving the storming of the Winter Palace and the arrest of the Provisional Government by Antonov-Ovseyenko (who had recently returned from Spain and himself been arrested).[201] The film's message, like the press accounts of the anniversary, was that Stalin was Lenin's equal.

On November 7, as elite units of the Red Army massed near Red Square, dignitaries assembled on the reviewing stand. To the right of the Mausoleum stood the foreign diplomatic corps, in fur hats and fur-lined coats; to the left, Soviet high officialdom; on the Mausoleum itself, at the last minute, Stalin emerged, accompanied by the retinue. When the Savior's Tower chimes struck 10:00 a.m., Voroshilov, on a white horse, rode to the assembled troops and administered the oath of allegiance to each unit in turn. The formations, as they passed, turned sharply rightward toward the Mausoleum in unison. "It was extremely moving, regardless of where one stood politically," remarked an American observer. "I had heard the most cynical diplomats admit that this was 'stark drama.'"[202]

That night, in the privacy of Voroshilov's Kremlin apartment, two dozen or so regime intimates gathered, as per custom. Some thirty-odd toasts had already been pronounced by the time Stalin rose, and he rambled at length. "The Russian tsars did a great deal that was bad," he began his toast. "They robbed and enslaved the people. They waged wars and seized territories in the interests of landowners. But they did one thing that was good: they amassed an enormous state, all the way to Kamchatka. We have inherited that state." Here was an awesome responsibility—and an evidently inebriated Stalin added a warning. "Whoever attempts to destroy that unity of the socialist state, whoever seeks the separation of any of its parts or nationalities—that man is an enemy. . . . And we will destroy each and every such enemy; even if he was an old Bolshevik, we shall destroy all his kin, his family."[203]

Interrupted by shouts "To the great Stalin," he continued impatiently ("I have not finished my toast") and turned once more to the decisiveness of the middle cadres, over the objections of those present—*try to stay silent*—that his leadership was decisive: "A great deal is said about great leaders. But a cause is never won unless the right conditions exist. And the main thing here is the middle cadres—party, economic, military. They're the ones who choose the leader, explain our positions to the masses, and ensure the success of our cause. They don't try to climb above their station; you don't even notice them." Dimitrov again tried to object that Stalin was nonetheless more important, prompting him to insist yet again, "The fundamental thing is the middle cadres. That must be noted, and it must never be forgotten that, other conditions being equal, the middle cadres decide the outcome of our cause."[204]

Stalin then broached the most taboo of subjects. "Why did we prevail over Trotsky and the rest?" he asked. "Trotsky, as we know, was the most popular man in our country after Lenin." Trotsky—the number two! "Bukharin, Zinoviev, Rykov, Tomsky were all popular. We were little known—yours truly, Molotov, Voroshilov, and Kalinin—then."[205] Stalin went on to explain, however, that Trotsky had committed the fatal mistake of ignoring the middle cadres. "The party itself had wanted" the triumph of the lesser-knowns.

In yet another revealing gesture that tipsy night, Stalin indulged his man-of-the-borderlands persona, stating, "Comrade Dimitrov, I apologize for interrupting you; I am not a European, but a Russified Georgian-Asiatic."[206] We can only guess how émigré press portrayals of him rankled: a *kinto* (Georgian thug), a snitch for the tsarist *okhranka*, a nonentity, a usurper, an Asiatic.

Stalin in his toast referred to himself as just a "practical type" (*praktik*), unlike those famous personages. "Whom did we have?" he asked, answering, "Well, I led the organizational work in the Central Committee," as if it were the most humdrum, shoulder-to-the-wheel post. "But what was I in comparison with Ilich [Lenin]? A feeble specimen." He named his faction: "There were Molotov, Kalinin, Kaganovich, Voroshilov—all of whom were unknown. . . ." But, Stalin continued, "the people advance those who lead them to victory, personalities in history come and go, but the people remain, and the people do not make mistakes." The unerring folk: that was how the hardworking faction of "feeble specimens" had triumphed over the famous personages like Trotsky. "I remind you of the following," Stalin added, with evident pride. "In 1927, 700,000 party members voted for the Central Committee's line; such was the core who voted for us feeble specimens. Some 4,000 to 6,000 voted for Trotsky, and 20,000 abstained."[207] In closing, he recalled Kirov's death, a wake-up call: "Kirov, with his blood, opened the eyes of us idiots (excuse the blunt expression)."[208] After the toasts ran their course, they repaired to the Kremlin cinema for another viewing of Romm's *Lenin in October*.

POSTSCRIPT

On November 11, 1937, Stalin received Dimitrov and Wang Ming, a young rival to Mao, and told them, "Trotskyites [in China] must be hunted down, shot, destroyed. They are international provocateurs, fascism's most vicious agents!" Stalin also instructed them that "the main thing now is the war, not an agrarian revolution, not confiscation of land," and concluded, "neither England nor America wants China to win. They fear a Chinese victory because of their own imperialist ambitions." (Wang would immediately leave Moscow, where he had lived for six years, and, in China, insist on mounting a party congress, where he would deliver the political report.)[209] With the Comintern types, Stalin underscored how waverers in the party had faltered at every difficult moment: in 1905, in October 1917, Brest-Litovsk in 1918, the civil war, "and especially collectivization, a completely novel, historically unprecedented event. Various weak elements fell away from the party . . . they went underground. Powerless themselves, they linked up with external enemies, promised Ukraine to the Germans, Belorussia to the Poles, the Far East to the Japanese. They hoped for war and were especially insistent that the German fascists launch a war against the USSR as soon as possible." He continued: "They were planning an action for the beginning of this year. They lost their nerve. They were preparing in July [1937] to attack the politburo at the Kremlin. But they lost their nerve."[210]

Preposterous: longtime Communists had no such opportunity to "link up" with foreign enemies or attempt a coup. And yet, time and again, when volunteering thoughts on the mass arrests and executions, Stalin returned to the party opposition to collectivization in 1932, and the plots against him. *Time* magazine (November 15, 1937), of all places, mentioned alleged assassinaton attempts. "Our Sun!" the magazine wrote semifacetiously of the celebrations of Stalin not only in Moscow but also in Madrid and, in a lesser way, at Carnegie Hall in New York, in connection with the twentieth anniversary of the Russian Revolution, comparing Stalin to Louis XIV. *Time* highlighted Romm's new film, in which "it is not Lenin and Trotsky who make the revolution of 1917 but Lenin and Stalin," adding, "With Sun Stalin eclipsing Trotsky in Spain as well as in Russia, the Dictator felt strong enough to permit the bringing to light in court last week of two attempts to assassinate him years ago." This was a reference to two incidents, in 1933 and 1935, both in the Caucasus, neither (as we have seen) an attempt on Stalin's life, but both recently detailed as such in *Dawn of the East,* the Georgian party newspaper under Beria's control.[211]

STICKING WITH CHIANG

Stalin and his intermediaries continued to rebuff China's entreaties for the Soviets to declare war on Japan, but Moscow was shipping arms a great distance and at great difficulty, mostly through Xinjiang, to keep the fighting going.[212] Japan had forced Chiang into all-out war, which won him strong domestic support, perhaps the most for a Chinese ruler since the mid–Qing dynasty, but Chiang took considerable time to find a workable strategy of resistance. His frontal military battles led to catastrophe. In November 1937, the Japanese captured Shanghai, followed, on December 13, by Nanking, the Chinese Nationalist capital, where the Imperial troops proceeded to massacre up to 300,000 civilians. The Nationalist government fled to Wuhan, in the interior. Only now, after the devastation of even his crack troops, did Chiang turn from frontal engagements to a long war of attrition.[213]

Stalin stuck to his strategy of a Nationalist-led united front against Japan, reasoning that Japan could fight either China or the Soviet Union but not both, and using Dimitrov and Wang Ming to tamp down the Communists to the extent possible. Wang Ming went to Wuhan as the Chinese Communist liaison to the Nationalists; Mao stayed at Yan'an, where the Communist base would expand significantly, from perhaps 40,000 members in 1937 to 200,000 by the next year.[214] The desperate Long March to desolate Yan'an to escape Nationalist encirclement was proving to be a boon for survivors, now buffering the Communists from the brunt of the Imperial Japanese Army. Japan's war in China was unintentionally reordering the balance of power between Chiang's Nationalists and Mao's Communists to the latter's favor. In December 1937, Chiang—in yet another attempt to drag the Soviets directly into the war—publicly revealed that China was getting substantial Soviet military aid. "Chiang Kai-shek behaved not fully cautiously," Stalin wrote to Molotov and Voroshilov. "Well, the devil take him."[215] But Stalin held to him.

CELEBRATION AMID DEATH

In December 1937, the USSR held elections for the new bicameral Supreme Soviet, a permanent body to replace the Congress of Soviets. There were 569 seats in the soviet of the Union and 574 in the soviet of nationalities, both elected on the basis of universal suffrage.[216] The provision for multiple candidates had been unceremoniously dropped.[217] Stalin, too, ran for election, choosing to represent Moscow city's "Stalin ward," and delivered candidate remarks from the imperial box at the Bolshoi on December 11, 1937. ("Comrades, to tell you the truth, I had no intention of making a speech. But our respected Nikita Sergeyevich [Khrushchev] dragged me, so to speak, to this meeting. 'Make a good speech,' he said.") The next day, the uncontested balloting took place as the regime laid on food, drink, music, and dancing.[218] The process reached into every village, and no-show voters were monitored. The press reported that more than 91 million votes were cast—96.8 percent of those eligible—and that every candidate running was duly "elected."[219]

On December 20, the NKVD celebrated its twentieth anniversary. Sergei Mironov traveled from blood-soaked Mongolia, finding portraits of Dzierżyński and Yezhov adorning all Soviet newspapers and Young Pioneers competing for the honor of having their scout groups bear these names.[220] At the Bolshoi, Voroshilov, Zhdanov, Dimitrov, and others sat in the presidium. Kaganovich arrived late and was greeted by an ovation. So did Molotov (for him the hall stood while applauding). Mikoyan chaired the festivities and praised NKVD head Yezhov as "a talented and faithful pupil of Stalin . . . beloved by the Soviet people."[221] In *Pravda* that morning, Frinovsky had denounced the swine and fascist bandits inside the NKVD who had been arrested; Mikoyan's speech closed with praise for their replacements. "The NKVD has worked gloriously during this time," he noted. "Let us wish that the workers of the NKVD in future will work as gloriously as they have this year."[222] Another ten Orders of Lenin were awarded to NKVD operatives, to go with the forty-six from the summer.[223] Stalin joined for the post-speech concert.[224]

The next night, Shostakovich's Fifth Symphony premiered in Leningrad, in the white auditorium of the former Chamber Music Association. "Writers, poets, musicians, scientists, and army officers filled every seat," Jelagin recalled. "The younger people stood in the aisles along the walls. . . . The audience refused to leave, and the applause continued unabated. Shostakovich came out and took dozens of bows." He was no longer the "formalist."[225] This was also Stalin's official fifty-ninth birthday. He received Molotov, Yezhov, Voroshilov, Kaganovich, and Mikoyan for three hours, until 1:00 a.m. In media res, he summoned Pyotr Pumpur, head of aviation training in the Red Air Force, and Yakov Smushkevich, a thirty-five-year-old fighter pilot, both of them decorated Spanish civil war veterans who now oversaw the dispatch of Soviet pilots to China.[226] The NKVD was reporting devastating shortcomings in the air forces of the Red Army: not just egregious rations, loss of valuable equipment, alcoholism, and hazing, but a colossal number of aviation crashes. Stalin received interrogation protocols indicating that in the Soviet Far East, new aerodromes, poorly built, flooded in the rain and became unusable, forcing planes to be kept under an open sky. "Very important," Stalin wrote back to Yezhov.[227] The response, for now, would be more arrests, more executions.[228, 229, 230]

Stalin's last office visitors on the evening of December 23, members of the inner circle, departed at 10:05 p.m. Whether they accompanied him for supper at the Near Dacha remains unknown. At 5:00 a.m., he awoke with a temperature of 102 degrees Fahrenheit (38.9 Celsius), which had not fallen as of 12:20 p.m., ten minutes before he received Yezhov. An entry made that day in his medical record by Professor Valedinsky and Kremlin hospital chief Pyotr Mandryka noted "general weakness, slightly hyperemic nostrils, and conjunctiva. Not severe exterior pallor, some puffiness of the face. A heavy head. . . . A slight pain on the right when swallowing, serious congestion in the back on the right. Posterior wall of the pharynx is covered with mucus, slightly hyperemic." Their diagnosis was "follicular angina" (inflammation of the lymphoid ring in the throat) and "myasthenia" (chronic autoimmune neuromuscular disease). The illness proved to be prolonged. Stalin slept poorly. On December 30, for example, he awoke at 12:40 a.m., after four hours' rest. A urine sample was taken at 1:45 a.m. (these were frequent). He requested warm milk at 2:25 a.m. At 3:45 a.m. he requested a glass of hot water to shave. He brushed his teeth, went to the toilet. At 5:40 a.m. he fell back asleep, rising three hours later and asking for tea and breakfast. At 4:00 p.m. he fell back asleep until 8:20 p.m., drank some tea, and fell back asleep at 11:15 p.m. for twenty-five minutes, then had supper. He was further diagnosed with streptococcus. No visits were recorded in his office logbook from December 24 through January 6.

RED ARMY VERSUS WEHRMACHT

At the annual year-end gathering of the Main Military Council—which happened before Stalin took ill, but which he did not attend—the recently named commander of the South Caucasus military district (a strategic border area), Nikolai Kuibyshev, had pointed out that new commanders of divisions had never before led even a battalion. Voroshilov, who had to formally approve such appointments, feigned shock. "I assure you, Comrade People's Commissar, that we could not find anyone better," Kuibyshev stated, adding that everyone else was in the hands of the NKVD. It was a searing moment of truth. But it passed. Voroshilov, in his closing speech, noted that "the gangrene" had not been fully cut out. Kuibyshev soon fell among the victims.[231] To be sure, some Soviet military officers who were framed and shot had been more skilled at embezzling state funds than at commanding troops.[232] Still, their replacements—to the extent that vacant officer positions could even be filled—were not always more honest or competent.[233] The Red Army had problems before the terror; the massacres created more.

Hitler presented a stark contrast. German army officers swore their service oath to him personally, an innovation instituted by the war minister, Field Marshal Werner von Blomberg, but even so, Hitler, unlike Stalin, experienced significant loyalty issues with the brass. Behind the Führer's back, Wehrmacht officers did not shrink from discussing how his approach to matters of war was irresponsible and dilettantist. On November 5, 1937, Hitler convened a meeting in the Chancellery to discuss the jockeying over steel supplies between the Luftwaffe (Göring) and the navy (Erich Raeder); army chief Colonel General Werner von Fritsch and Foreign Minister Neurath were also invited. Instead of adjudicating the dispute, Hitler used the occasion to hold forth on Germany's position in the world, its need for raw materials, and *Lebensraum*. "The aim of German policy was to make secure and to preserve the racial community and to enlarge it," he said. "It was therefore a question of space." But this need for more space ran up against "two hate-inspired antagonists, Britain and France, to whom a German colossus in the center of Europe was a thorn in the flesh." The Führer outlined scenarios of when—not if—Germany would have to fight a general European war: not later than 1943–45, and possibly before. In the meantime, Hitler said he had "to settle the Czech and Austrian questions" through small wars of plunder, which, he predicted, Britain and France would not oppose militarily.

Two exceedingly noteworthy things happened during the four-hour harangue. First, Hitler mentioned the Soviet Union merely in passing, and he made no reference to "Judeo-Bolshevism." Second, Blomberg and Fritsch had the temerity to object to the Führer. They "repeatedly emphasized the necessity that Britain and France must not appear in the role of our enemies" (as Blomberg's adjutant recorded in his notes).[234] Within three months, both Blomberg and Fritsch would be removed, and the army, navy, and air force chiefs would be reporting directly to Hitler.[235] This turnabout was long in coming, but oddly triggered.

The sixty-year-old Blomberg, a widower with five children, got remarried on January 12, 1938; Göring served as best man and Hitler as witness. Shortly thereafter, the police revealed that the twenty-five-year-old bride had been under longtime "morals" surveillance, posed for pornographic photographs, and had a criminal record for prostitution; she was out on parole. Blomberg was afforded a chance to save his situation by annulling the marriage, but he refused, and on January 27 he was relieved of his post. "Worst crisis for the regime since the Röhm Affair," Goebbels recorded in his diary. "The Führer looks like a corpse."[236] Fritsch appeared to be next in line to succeed Blomberg, but Hitler became concerned about further scandal: there was a file from summer 1936, collected by SD chief Heydrich, on the bachelor Fritsch's alleged homosexuality. Hitler's military adjutant, who smelled a rat, disobeyed the Führer and showed the file to Fritsch. Hitler took his adjutant's disobedience in stride and summoned Fritsch's dubious accuser from an internment camp to the Chancellery's private library, where Fritsch (in cilivian clothes) confronted him. The Gestapo judged the accusations inconsistent. Still, Fritsch was forced to resign on February 3. (At trial, he would be exonerated on the basis of mistaken identity: Frisch instead of Fritsch.) Some figured that Heydrich had set Fritsch up, but if so, the SD had gained nothing; others surmised that Göring had been intriguing to subordinate the army to himself, but again, if that were true, he failed.

On February 4, 1938, a moody Hitler, heeding the advice of Goebbels, abolished the German war ministry and made himself de facto war minister, while appointing the "true as a dog" Wilhelm Keitel as chief of staff. Twelve German generals were removed, but, far from having them arrested and forced under torture to confess to treason on behalf of foreign enemies, Hitler gave them pensions. He sent Blomberg into exile for a year in Italy, with a golden handshake of 50,000 reichsmarks. The Führer was supreme in the military sphere, and the SS was now allowed to create its own armed force of up to 600,000 men—but without mass hysteria, let alone mass murder. Hitler had been concerned throughout about not just commander loyalties but also public perceptions and the standing of the German armed forces.[237]

INDISTINGUISHABLE ENEMIES

Stalin was being inundated by petitions about the NKVD's "illegal" arrests of party members. On January 7, 1938, he announced a Central Committee plenum, to begin four days hence, which would piggyback on the previously scheduled first-ever session of the USSR Supreme Soviet. (All Central Committee members had been "elected" to the pseudo-parliament.) The agenda for the plenum, which met January 11, 14, 18, and 20, was "mistakes committed by party organizations during the expulsion of Communists."[238] Party officials, given the chance, proved eager to claw back against the NKVD, a matter of (their) life and death. Malenkov divulged that 65,000 of the 100,000 members expelled in the last six months of 1937 had appealed.[239] Stalin allowed the wildness to be reined in: during the first six months of 1938, there would be "only" 37,000 expulsions of party members. In addition, in 1938, 77,000 Communists would be reinstated and 148,000 new members allowed to join (as compared with 32,000 the year before).[240] That said, there was no real reprieve. "The SR line (both left and right) has not been fully uncovered," Stalin wrote to Yezhov (January 17). "Can the NKVD account for the SRs ('formers') in the army? I would like to see a report promptly. Can the NKVD account for the 'former' SRs outside the army (in civil institutions)? I would also like a report in two-three weeks. . . . What has been done to expose and arrest all Iranians in Baku and Azerbaijan? . . . We must act more swiftly and intelligently."[241]

The new Supreme Soviet had opened to incredible fanfare on January 12, and three days later it announced an enlarged naval program and a measure authorizing its presidium, formally chaired by Kalinin, to declare a state of war (martial law) if necessary. Yezhov related a "request by the toilers" that Moscow be renamed Stalinodar; Stalin rejected it.[242] On January 17, Zhdanov gave a speech condemning spying by foreign consulates in Leningrad, approving the arrests of ethnic groups with compatriots abroad (Poles, Finns, Estonians, Latvians, Germans), hammering at the water transport commissariat under Rykov, and going after Kerzhentsev, head of the committee on artistic affairs, for permitting "alien" culture (such as Meyerhold's theater).[243] On January 20, at the Kremlin wrap-up reception for delegates, Stalin, during the course of five toasts, called Bukharin and Rykov "foreign agents" and members of a "rightist-Trotskyite anti-Soviet bloc."[244] The next night at the Bolshoi, on the fourteenth anniversary of Lenin's death, Moscow's Vakhtangov Theater performed the last act of *The Man with a Gun,* a play by Nikolai Pogodin about the October Revolution. The accomplished actor Ruben Simonov, an ethnic Armenian, played Stalin in his youthful days. Conscious of the occasion and audience, he had not been able to eat for days and lost control of his nerves. Nonetheless, Jelagin, playing in the orchestra pit, observed Stalin in the imperial box enthusiastically applauding Simonov as himself.[245]

A Great Citizen, based on the assassination of Kirov, premiered on February 13, 1938, after Stalin's edits. The Communist character (Katz) was given the last word at the hero's grave: "The party of Bolsheviks is building a new life, realizing the centuries' dream of humanity! And those who stand in the way, who try to prohibit this work, the people will destroy!" *Pravda*'s critic enthused that "*A Great Citizen* teaches vigilance and the ability to differentiate enemy from friend and friend from enemy." Besides Katz, nearly every party member who appeared in the film came across as a likely foreign agent.[246]

Also in mid-February, Trotsky's son Lev Sedov suffered an acute appendicitis attack and died after treatment in a private Paris clinic run by White Russian émigrés who had NKVD connections. Whether Sedov (b. 1906) could have died of natural causes remains unclear. Trotsky lost his most important follower and the main coordinator of his work, and the NKVD lost its nearly effortless total surveillance over Trotsky's operations.[247]

In late February 1938, after all the Spanish gold removed to the Soviet Union had been spent ($550 million) on weapons, an emissary from the Republic arrived to plead for Soviet credits to buy more. Stalin had already withdrawn his military advisers and tankists. Dimitrov, with Stalin's authorization, had had Spanish

Communists nondemonstratively quit the Popular Front government, partly to blunt Franco's propaganda line.[248] But Stalin extended the credits (which would never be repaid) to continue forestalling a Franco victory, even as he showed impatience. "You neither take seriously nor have a deep interest in your own production," he admonished the Spanish envoy, underscoring the economic benefits of military industry. "You could be doing much more. We'll give you the motorized equipment, since that is the most difficult. But you must develop your military industry."[249] Soviet military industry, despite investment 2.8 times as high as in 1933, was in disarray from Stalin's annihilations.

THIRD (AND FINAL) PUBLIC TRIAL

Stalin constantly urged more public trials. Dozens had been staged in fall 1937 throughout the provinces, following an express order by the despot, who complained that "liquidation of wreckers is being undertaken in secret by the NKVD, and collective farmers are not being mobilized in the struggle." He had dictated sentences by telegram ("shoot"), though a few local judges refused to impose the death penalty on their former party colleagues; prosecutors appealed the judges' displays of mercy (i.e., ten-year Gulag sentences).[250] Some Communists, despite brutalization in the NKVD cellars and threats to family members, refused to incriminate themselves. That included Martemyan Ryutin, author of the devastating internal condemnation of forced collectivization and Stalin's dictatorship. Back in October 1936, while serving a ten-year sentence, he had been rearrested in solitary confinement and transferred to Lubyanka to furnish "testimony" for a planned trial of right deviationists. (His condemnation of collectivization made him a "rightist" in Stalin's mind.) But Ryutin steadfastly denied the new charges of "terrorism," and his "retrial" had taken place in camera in the military collegium (January 10, 1937). It had lasted forty minutes, after which he was executed in the basement.[251] Ryutin had written to the central executive committee of the Soviet—not to the degenerated party—that "I do not intend to and will not confess things about myself that are untrue, whatever it will cost me."[252]

The Ryutin Platform had come up at the second Moscow trial in late January 1937, but it had not been a central aspect.[253] Bukharin, who was being blackmailed with threats against his wife and daughter, cooperated and was afforded the highest possible profile in Stalin's terror scenario. He had been in prison for almost a year, and at the prime of life (fifty years of age). During that period

(February 1937–March 1938), he wrote an autobiographical novel (*How It All Began*), a philosophical treatise, a collection of poems, and several rambling "Dear Koba" letters pleading for his life and asking why Stalin needed him to die. It was an excellent question, but one with a ready answer. Whereas Ryutin had been the actual implacable opponent and Bukharin had never joined a party opposition, Bukharin was the preeminent symbol.[254] Stalin's invention of the "right deviation"—a tacit admission that it was not an opponent per se—and his attacks that twisted their policy positions involved a *structural* threat, a false or petit bourgeois class consciousness. Ultimately, this made Bukharin and the rightists central to Stalin's terror scenario.

On March 2, 1938, the third Moscow trial finally commenced, like the first two, in the October Hall of the House of Trade Unions, in front of nearly 200 spectators, including the usual handpicked foreign journalists and diplomats. It lasted eighteen sittings. A total of twenty-one defendants, nine of whom had sat in the Central Committee, were in the dock. Three were doctors of the Kremlin medical staff. Stalin had edited chief procurator Vyshinsky's script. (Vyshinsky would also edit the transcript, removing remarks exculpating the accused and discussions of the law by the defense lawyers.) The accused had spent long hours memorizing their testimony. Bukharin, Krestinsky, Rykov, Cristian Rakovski—staunch Bolsheviks—confessed that they had plotted to assassinate Lenin and Stalin *since 1918;* had murdered Kirov, Mężyński, Kuibyshev, Gorky, Gorky's son Maxim; had conspired with Nazi Germany, Japan, and Great Britain to partition the Soviet Union, hand over territory (Ukraine, Belorussia), and abolish collective farms.[255] Yezhov had falsely promised at least some defendants their lives in exchange for self-incrimination.[256] NKVD interrogators sat in the first row, a reminder that "re-interrogation" could take place between sessions.[257] Krestinsky had been "beaten horribly," according to the head of the Lefortovo prison's hygiene department. "His entire back was a wound."[258] Still, on the first day, Krestinsky repudiated his confession and pleaded not guilty, causing a sensation. That night he was re-interrogated—he had a wife and children—and on the second day he nodded his assent when asked if he was guilty.[259] "It is now clear why there are interruptions of supplies here and there, why, with our riches and abundance of products, there is a shortage first of one thing, then of another," Vyshinsky thundered. "It is these traitors who are responsible for it."[260]

Stalin received from Yezhov daily summaries of reactions to the trial, assembled from NKVD branches around the Union, and some local secret police officials dared to convey comments about how unpersuasive the proceedings were.[261] In *Pravda,* and in equally vicious commentary on Soviet radio, Mikhail Koltsov, who had been recalled from Spain, fluently conveyed the party line on the trial, cursing the treasonous snakes, praising Yezhov to the skies. Privately, though, Koltsov was said to have told a fellow writer who had wanted to witness the spectacle live, "Don't go! . . . What is being done there the mind cannot conceive. . . . Very strange trial. Very strange."[262] The *New York Times* captured some of the insanity. "It is as if twenty years after Yorktown somebody in power at Washington found it necessary for the safety of the State to send to the scaffold Thomas Jefferson, Madison, John Adams, Hamilton, Jay and most of their associates," the paper wrote. "The charge against them would be that they conspired to hand over the United States to George III."[263]

Under the klieg lights in the wee hours on March 13, Vasily Ulrich read out the sentences individually. Three were for long Gulag terms. The other sentences—"to be shot"—echoed in the hall eighteen times. "I experienced profound shame, especially here in court, when I learned and understood the full counterrevolutionary infamy of the crimes of the Right-Trotskyite Bloc, in which I served as an assassin," Pyotr Kryuchkov, Gorky's former secretary (assigned to him by Yagoda), stated in his last word. He added, "I ask you, citizen judges, for a reduced sentence." On March 15, the condemned were executed one by one, with Yagoda and Bukharin rumored to have been last so as to have to witness the others' deaths.[264]

Yagoda had never risen higher than nonvoting candidate member of the Central Committee, and had never been much of a public face for the regime, absent from prominent public photographs (an exception was the White Sea–Baltic Canal book, which, however, was withdrawn). But his corpse was said to have been displayed on the grounds of his legendary dacha, located outside Moscow on the Kaluga highway, the site of a prerevolutionary estate that he had occupied in 1927. The complex had become part of the Kommunarka state farm and had served as a well-stocked country club for Yagoda's use, but then it became a killing field. Kommunarka shared that function with nearby Butovo, also just outside Moscow, a former stud farm that the NKVD had seized from its owner. Mass burials of ashes also took place at the former Donskoi Monastery (1591), whose crematorium (completed in October 1927) was the first in Russia or the Soviet Union. Tukhachevsky's ashes had been dumped here in a mass grave. Initially, victims' ashes were buried in the common graves using a shovel, but soon the

NKVD brought in an excavator and a bulldozer. At Kommunarka, up to 14,000 executions would take place, primarily of political, military, scientific, and cultural figures, whose bones were sometimes seen in the jaws of prowling dogs.[265]

FAILURES OF CONTEMPORARY KREMLINOLOGY

Contemporaries could not fathom what was going on. "Something incomprehensible is happening," the secretary of the party organization in the Novosibirsk NKVD, Sergei Plestsov, told an NKVD department chief in Ukraine who had returned briefly to Novosibirsk, his former place of employment, in fall 1937.[266] Orlov, NKVD station chief in Spain, also deemed the mass arrests unfathamoble.[267] "What for?" the deputy railways commissar, Livshits, had exclaimed when taken away, according to rumors in upper party circles.[268] This unanswered question was etched all across the Soviet space, into the walls of teeming prisons and labor camps, stamped on the souls of the children carted off to orphanages, heard echoing through the execution cellars, and repeated throughout society as people wondered if they would be next.[269] Victims who had had frequent contact with Stalin did no better. Stalin had included Rosenholz, the long-serving commissar of foreign trade (1930–37), in the March 1938 trial of the Trotskyite-rightist bloc. Rosenholz had told his interrogator-torturer that years earlier, when he had brought Stalin documents, the latter had asked just two or three questions before affixing his signature, trusting Rosenholz, but more recently Stalin's "suspiciousness had reached lunacy." He could only surmise that Stalin "was in a fit, a crazy fit of rage against treason, against baseness."[270] "Explaining the present regime in terms of Stalin's personal lust for power is too superficial," Trotsky wrote in May 1938. True enough, but he could not explain why such a terror annihilated the very apparatus in whose "class interest" it had supposedly been launched.[271]

Kremlinologists of all stripes absorbed every rumor and strained every nerve to decipher the puzzle. "Every bit of testimony at the [March 1938] Bukharin-Rykov trial was the subject of endless discussion in the Embassy," recalled Charles Bohlen, who attended as an interpreter for the new American ambassador, Joseph Davies. "There was speculation over the reason the purges were started, what they were trying to accomplish, whether Stalin was mad, whether he had some other sinister plan, how much truth there was in the accusations."[272] Few were as naïve as Davies, who accepted the trials at face value (and believed that the Soviet

Union was wending its way in the right direction and eager for cooperation with the capitalists). Bohlen, along with George Kennan, thought Marxism-Leninism had exacerbated whatever obscure power politics lay behind the trials. Most other foreign ambassadors—Werner von der Schulenburg (Germany), Robert Coulondre (France), and Viscount Chilston (Britain)—attributed the bizarre episode to power politics alone.[273] Davies's approach—to accept the accusations and confessions—was found in Soviet society. "Who would have benefited from sentencing and executing such people . . . if they were not guilty?" recalled the Soviet writer Konstantin Simonov of Tukhachevsky and other top officers. "Either they were guilty or what was happening was incomprehensible."[274]

Lifelong revolutionaries, who had been beaten by tsarist police for working on behalf of the revolution, were now being beaten with whips, blackjacks, and poles to confess to lifelong conspiracies *against* the revolution. Inside the party and among party widows, hearsay circulated about Stalin's special thirst for revenge and his vendetta against the "old Bolsheviks" (those who had joined the party before 1917), because they knew the real story of his past and Lenin's call for his removal.[275] Old Bolsheviks numbered 182,000 in 1934 and would number 125,000 in 1939, a decline of one third, which was roughly the annihilation ratio for all officials.[276] Another conjecture involved apparatchik fears of a supposed "transition to democracy," since the draft constitution had restored the right to vote to former kulaks and called for multicandidate elections.[277] Stalin had contemptuously dismissed any concerns, then threw out the multicandidate idea anyway. Probably the most widespread contemporary supposition about the terror involved a belief—or a desire to believe—that Stalin remained unaware. "We thought that Stalin did not know about the insane retribution against Communists, and the Soviet intelligentsia," the writer Ehrenburg recalled. Meyerhold said, "They hide it from Stalin." Pasternak said, "If only someone told all this to Stalin!"[278]

Functionaries inside the police harbored similar delusions. Israel Shreider, who went by Mikhail, a top official in the militia (the regular police), which was subordinated to the NKVD, observed that "at that time, I saw Stalin as a god and blindly believed that he did not know what was going on in the organs of the NKVD." Arrested himself, he was taken to Moscow's Butyrka prison, whose cells were crammed with big shots. They were beaten senseless during "interrogations." None wanted to speak to the others, suspecting that their cell mates were stool pigeons, and each demanded paper so they could write petitions to Stalin to profess their innocence. "Everyone wrote to Stalin," Shreider explained. "Naturally, in perpetually thinking of Stalin, we frequently saw him in our dreams, spoke with him, proved to him our innocence, complained about the torturer-interrogators." The next day, Shreider added, they noticed that those who had dreamed of Stalin were summoned to "interrogation" and beaten. "When someone began to report that he had seen Stalin in his dream," he noted, "the whole cell expressed sympathy." They noticed that their interrogators would place their petitions to Stalin on the desk during interrogations. "Does Stalin know?" they asked themselves again. "The petitions and complaints are not reaching him!"[279]

A corollary to the Stalin-did-not-know delusion was the legend of infiltration of the NKVD by enemies aiming to destroy good people. "Everyone more and more talks about the sickness or wrecking by the NKVD leaders," professor Vladimir Vernadsky (b. 1863), a renowned geochemist and member of the Soviet Academy of Sciences, wrote in his diary (January 25, 1938). "More and more heard about Yezhov's wrecking. Again unnecessary, infuriating severity all around. Again discussion of deliberate wrecking" (February 20).[280] A political commissar in the army in Vyazma, near Smolensk, told a military associate, "It looks like party cadres are being destroyed deliberately."[281]

These and other conjectures—which would echo in the subsequent scholarly literature—offer insight into Soviet mentalities of the time, but no explanation for the terror.[282] In Mongolia, there was no old Bolshevism or faux transition to democracy. Mironov had gone back to Ulan Bator, where he would personally help force the arrest of at least 10,000 Mongols in the sparsely populated country, including 300 ministerial officials and 180 military leaders, by the time he returned to Moscow for good in April 1938.[283] A onetime lowly ensign of the tsarist army and then a Soviet border guard, Mironov was promoted to deputy foreign affairs commissar responsible for the strategic Far East, moved into the House on the Embankment, obtaining a high-floor six-room apartment with a view to the Kremlin's onion domes, and fantasized about becoming foreign affairs commissar. His days were numbered.[284]

Altogether, at least 20,000 Mongols would be executed over the course of 1937–38. Much of its officialdom—Choibalsan excepted—was obliterated.[285] (In Spain, the Soviet terror was infinitesimal in comparison.) More than half of Mongolia's state budget was now being spent on the military, but the Soviets were forcing annihilation of the small number of Mongolian officers. And even after the massive destruction and replacement, Soviet personnel did not trust the Mongolian army—then again, the executions and lies aroused strong anti-Russian feelings.[286] The rampage seemed utterly senseless, insanity.

THE LOGIC OF A WARPED MIND

Back at the February–March 1937 plenum, Stalin had referred to "about 12,000 party members who sympathized with Trotsky to some extent or other [in 1927]. Here you see the total forces of the Trotskyite gentlemen."[287] Accurate or not, he presented this number in a way that was dismissive, not alarmist. Similarly, in his November 1936 opening of the 8th Congress of Soviets, apropos of allowing former kulaks to vote in the elections to the new Supreme Soviet, he had said, "Some say this is dangerous, because elements hostile to Soviet power could sneak into the highest offices, some of the former White Guardists, kulaks, priests, and so on. But really, what is there to fear? . . . For one thing, not all former kulaks, White Guardists, and priests are hostile to Soviet power."[288] Half a year later, he approved orders for mass executions of former kulaks because of the mortal danger they posed. "We have become convinced," Malenkov had revealingly explained on a trip to annihilate the leadership of the autonomous republic of Tatarstan, inside the Russian republic, "that where the tasks of the party and government are not being fulfilled, we must seek enemies."[289]

It sounded like complete cynicism: "seek" (or fabricate) enemies. But in Stalin's world, which his minions came to share, every allegation derived from a kernel of truth, no matter how minuscule. Tukhachevsky *did* have meetings with the German military brass (which were fully authorized). Republic and provincial party bosses *did* fail to implement central directives (which bordered on the impossible). Poland, Germany, and Japan *did* try to recruit spies on Soviet territory among non-Russian nationalities (standard international practice). Dekulakized peasants *did* have grievances against Soviet power (they had been dispossessed and deported to frozen wastes). Hostile powers *did* funnel disinformation into Soviet military intelligence (Stalin was proactively doing the same). Pro-Japanese sentiment *did* emerge in Mongolia (thanks to inhuman Soviet overlordship). "Bukharin met with Kamenev, they talked, they discussed the policies of the Central Committee and other things," Kaganovich, late in life, parroting Stalin, reasoned of their ill-advised July 1928 meeting. "Trotsky, who was a good organizer, could have headed a rebellion. . . . Who after all could believe that old, experienced conspirators, using all the experience of Bolshevik conspiratorial methods and Bolshevik organization, that these people would not establish ties among themselves and would not create an organization?"[290]

Above all, opposition to collectivization *had* taken place. Stalin seems to have been haunted not by the millions of peasants and nomads who had starved but by the Communist officials who had dared to criticize his rule because of it.[291] He repeatedly voiced his venom against them, charging that they had lacked the stomach to see through what was necessary. Opposition to collectivization became the leitmotif of the interrogation protocols he demanded and underlined, and of his private and public utterances. Stalin, interrupting Yezhov, had blurted out at the December 1936 plenum about the rightists, "They denied that they had any platform. They had a platform. What did it call for? For the restoration of private enterprise in industry, for the opening of our gates to foreign capital, especially to English capital. . . . For the restoration of private enterprise in agriculture, for the curtailment of the collective farms, for the restoration of the kulaks, for moving the Comintern out of the USSR."[292] It remained only to add a sense of the means for an internal putsch—the Red Army command (around Tukhachevsky), the NKVD leadership (around Yagoda), the Kremlin commandant and bodyguard directorate—to complete the narrative arc from criticism of collectivization to espionage, sabotage, coup.

Stalin presumed that the socialist system's survival depended on him and that his former comrades desperately wanted to get rid of him. If, additionally, one assumed—as he did—that a foreign military attack was inevitable, and that in the event of war his former comrades could become eager collaborators with the fascists and other foreign enemies—not just out of spite, revenge, or ambition but because only his removal could undo collectivization—then all these people, and anyone who sympathized with or thought like them, had to be eliminated before war broke out. Did critics not understand that all opposition was objectively serving foreign enemies? Who could deny that the Soviet Union faced enemies? Who could deny that the capitalists had intervened against the USSR in the civil war and would do so again? Who could deny that imperialism was aggressive and would stop at nothing? In Spain, "fascists" had risen up in a putsch, and they were being assisted by the foreign fascist powers, and not opposed by the "democratic" ones. What more did anyone need to know? If counterrevolution supported by aggressive foreign intervention could take place in Spain, was it not still more likely to be attempted against the Soviet Union, a strategic country with a fully socialist system? His critics either failed elementary logic or had "lost their minds."[293]

"SPIES"

Pravda had underscored, accurately, that both Japan and Germany were "anti-status-quo powers" and could attain their aims solely through a new world war, a flanking threat Stalin did not invent.[294] Soviet intelligence reported that Japan and Germany shared intelligence information about Soviet military capabilities with each other as well as with Poland, which was true. Finland was sharing intelligence with the Japanese about Soviet military capabilities, too. Japan had sent military observer missions to countries encircling the USSR—Romania, Latvia, Estonia, Finland, Poland, Latvia—and Stalin regularly received reports, culled from decoded Japanese military attaché communications, of a possible Japanese attack on the USSR. Admiral Wilhelm Canaris, of the Abwehr (German military intelligence), had met the Japanese military attaché to Berlin (Hiroshi Ōshima) in 1936, and the next year he met an intelligence official of the Finnish general staff (Antero Svensson). The Abwehr also extended financial assistance to Estonian intelligence.[295] Of course, all the powers in the interwar period were targeted by foreign espionage. The international situation in the 1930s posed a threat to every great power, but only one embarked on a wholesale domestic slaughter. Nazi Germany was crawling with spies, especially spies working on behalf of the Soviet Union, but again, Hitler did not put to death his own officials and intelligence officers.[296] Stalin had even his policy critics charged as "spies."

Stalin did not invent the hoary trope of the "foreign hand" (externally assisted conspiracy to undermine the state). Allegations of a foreign hand at court had contributed mightily to the erosion of Nicholas II's legitimacy during the Great War; Kerensky, nearly successfully, had leveled the foreign hand charge against Lenin and the Bolsheviks. It was a device straight out of the authoritarian handbook, playing to patriotic stirrings and insecurities—in Russia's case, of a complex geography—and it was powerfully reinforced by the Bolshevik division of the world into two hostile camps, socialism and capitalism. For years, Stalin had been driving Soviet propagandists and the NKVD to find the foreign hand behind everything: in the 1928 Shakhty trial (French and German agents), in Ukrainian resistance to collectivization (Polish agents, relying on the British and the French), in the 1932 rebellion in the satellite Mongolia (Japanese agents), in the Kirov murder (German agents, even as he had discouraged investigation of the actual leads to the Latvian and German consulates). But 1937–38 was different.

Nothing had prepared the Soviet populace for the explosion of spy mania that now engulfed the country.[297] Although Stalin's November 1934 instructions to the Mongols had stated that critics needed to be charged as spies, and his politburo resolution of September 29, 1936, had insisted that the Zinoviev-Trotskyite conspirators be seen as "intelligence agents, spies, subversives, and wreckers of the fascist bourgeoisie," in the second half of 1936—during the outbreak of the Spanish civil war and Stalin's decision to intervene there militarily—there had been no full-throated public campaign of *mass* charges of spying. Then, under Stalin's tutelage, *Pravda* carried a sensational article (May 4, 1937) across three pages, "On Certain Cunning Techniques of Recruitment by Foreign Intelligence," which Stalin had edited and which was widely reprinted and assigned for discussion at meetings throughout the country. It asserted that inside the USSR, Nazi Germany possessed "a reserve that could be called upon for espionage work."[298] Stalin had inserted a page of material into the draft about an alleged incident concerning a Soviet employee in Japan who had met a female "aristocrat" in a restaurant. Once, during their rendezvous, a Japanese in military uniform arrived to announce he was the woman's husband. Another Japanese man appeared and proposed that he could quiet the scandal by having the Soviet man sign a document promising to inform the Japanese about internal Soviet affairs. The truce maker, Stalin explained, was a Japanese intelligence operative. The Soviet man had unwittingly been recruited to spy for Japan. It could happen.[299]

But the number of accused spies was just too large for such a person-by-person recruitment. In 1935–36, the NKVD had arrested 9,965 foreign "spies." (By comparison, in France, 300 foreign passport holders and 48 French nationals were noted as *suspected* enemy agents in 1936.) Then, in 1937–38, the NKVD arrested 265,039 spies.[300] This included nearly 19,000 just for Latvia and 7,800 just for Romania. Who exactly could be running more than a quarter million spies among the Soviet populace? Who gave them their directives? To whom did they report? Stalin did not publicly address this issue of spy handlers, and it is easy to see why.

The small number of ordinary citizen foreign passport holders who remained resident in the USSR were registered and monitored.[301] As for accredited representatives of foreign governments, they numbered 1,129 at embassies in Moscow and some 400 at twenty-four consulates.[302] This foreign diplomatic community—as Stalin knew better than anyone—was under the most intense surveillance. The sixty-two employees of the German embassy in Moscow (as of 1938) were kept under unrelenting watch and nearly total isolation from the Soviet public.[303] Even leaving aside the fact that every Soviet inhabitant knew the inevitable consequences of any contact with foreigners, let alone with foreign diplomatic personnel, the idea that these few German employees could have recruited and handled 39,000 accused German spies among the Soviet populace in 1937–38 beggars belief. True, Germany also had a few foreign consulates, but Stalin, in a tit for tat, had forced one German mission after another to close: Leningrad, Kiev, Kharkov, Odessa, Novosibirsk.[304] By spring 1938, not just Germany, but Finland, Estonia, Latvia, Sweden, Norway, Denmark, Italy, Britain, and Afghanistan had all lost their consulates in the Soviet Union.

Not surprisingly, internal German foreign ministry records indicate that of the approximately 1,100 German nationals who would be arrested for intelligence operations in the USSR from 1936 to 1941, just two had any such involvement, and one vanished without trace.[305] The head of the security agency for the Wehrmacht admitted internally in 1938 that he lacked a firm idea of how Soviet military intelligence worked.[306]

The number of accused Polish spies was even greater than the number of German ones. In fact, Polish sabotage activities on Soviet territory had not suddenly increased; they had been going on, closely watched and interdicted, for a long time. Until 1937, Poland maintained consulates in Moscow, Leningrad, Kharkov, Kiev, Minsk, and Tiflis, but Poland managed to hold on to just two (Kiev, Minsk), in exchange for which the Soviet Union kept one in Poland (Lwów) and one in the Free City of Danzig (Gdańsk).[307] Stalin's counterintelligence measures apparently induced the Polish embassy and consulates on Soviet territory to desist from recruiting agents among Soviet ethnic Poles (who mostly did not live in Moscow, Kiev, or Minsk in any case).[308] But the arrest of Polish "spies" among Soviet inhabitants continued, exceeding 101,000 by the end of 1938, a spectacularly improbable workload for one embassy and two consulates.

Despite the mass arrests, Stalin had no idea whether he was catching any real foreign spies or, if he was, what harm they might have caused—and what is more, he made virtually no effort to find out. Japanese army intelligence did send small numbers of White Russian émigrés and Koreans across the barely marked frontiers to recruit or bribe the disaffected among the Soviet population.[309] But the NKVD arrested nearly 53,000 Soviet inhabitants as agents of Japan in 1937–38. All "testimony" about their espionage and sabotage was either suggested or outright written by their interrogators, in the pursuit of arrest quotas. "Spies" and "terrorists" captured at or near border crossings were lumped together with contrabandists (ordinary people engaged in petty trade).[310] Dubiously, the country for which an arrested Soviet inhabitant was allegedly engaged in acts of espionage and sabotage was often altered at the very last minute. If a person had an ethnic Polish wife or relative, he or she would usually be charged as a Polish spy, unless all of a sudden the accused was needed for a "case" involving German spies (or Japanese, or Romanian, and so on).[311] To be sure, an excuse for such sloppiness was at the ready: better to chop off some innocent heads than to let even one spy go free. War was coming. But then, as we shall see, in 1939 and 1940—after a new world war had commenced—the NKVD would arrest a measly 7,620 spies, a quarter million fewer than in 1937–38.[312]

The NKVD's egregious violation of elementary rules of counterintelligence craft in the treatment of alleged spies in 1937–38 mattered only if Stalin was primarily pursuing foreign agents in the conventional sense, meaning people who committed specific acts. But he had called every foreigner in the Soviet Union ipso facto a spy, beginning with humanitarian relief workers during the first Soviet famine of 1921–23.[313] For him, "spying" seems to have encompassed an extraordinarily wide variety of activities, including clipping newspapers.[314] At closed party meetings and sessions in the Little Corner, he mostly insisted that those arrested were actual spies engaged in specific acts.[315] He would tell minions that penetration by foreign spies was increasing, such information would then duly appear in intelligence reports sent to him, and he would cite the reports. At meetings, he scribbled notes about saboteurs, spies, and the like.[316] Did Stalin, at some level, convince himself that the USSR was crawling with spies and would-be spies ready to act when the opportunity presented itself? Perhaps he did, but his charges of espionage were based not on facts but on a political equation. Kaganovich absorbed Stalin's way of thinking, remarking at the February–March 1937 plenum that "if they stand for defeat [of the Soviet Union], it's clear they are spies."[317]

SYNOPSIS

World history had never before seen such carnage by a regime against itself, as well as its own people—not in the French Revolution, not under Italian fascism or Nazism. Although it was clear to no one at the time, the future bloodbath was latent in Stalin's policy battles with what he called the right deviation in 1928 and especially 1929, when he took evident pleasure in humiliating Bukharin. It was also manifest in Stalin's toying with the arrest of Tukhachevsky in 1930, and propelled by the opposition in the party during collectivization and the famine

in 1932. It was facilitated by Stalin's promotion of Yezhov inside the party apparatus, to oversee the NKVD and the reopening of the Kirov assassination case in
1935, followed by arrest waves of Trotskyites in late 1935 and early 1936.[318] Unsatisfied with the convictions of Zinoviev and Kamenev for creating a "moral atmosphere" conducive to Kirov's murder, Stalin had insisted that they be directly
implicated in the actual deed, and that Trotsky, in foreign exile, be directly implicated, too. From here it was a short step to the incited public hysteria of the first
Moscow showcase trial, staged in August 1936, of Zinovievites and Trotskyites,
which fixated on a meeting in 1932 when the two tiny, pathetic groupings had
attempted to coordinate, and resulted in the executions of Zinoviev and
Kamenev.

Stalin drove the process with his desire to break psychologically the loyalists in
his inner circle, above all Orjonikidze but also Kaganovich and Voroshilov, and he
further intensified it with his desire to counter Trotsky's condemnatory writings
about his betrayal of the revolution and interdict the possibility of a Trotskyite
beachhead in Spain under a dissident (non-Stalinist) Marxist party, the POUM,
some of whose members had once been associated with Trotsky or continued to
admire him. A second trial of "Trotskyites," in January 1937, was followed by Orjonikidze's suicide and an unprecedented eleven-day February–March 1937 Central Committee plenum, which included fatal smearing of Bukharin and Yagoda
and Stalin's threat to replace sitting elites wholesale; an early June 1937 special
session of the Main Military Council and a mid-June in-camera trial resulting in
executions of Tukhachevsky and the military brass; a late June 1937 party plenum
outlining a phantasmagorical "Center of Centers"; the launching, in July–August
1937, of "mass operations" with ever-expanding quotas; the annihilation of republic and provincial party machines, of the Comintern, foreign affairs commissariat, foreign intelligence, and military intelligence; the disruption of the industrial
economy, including military industry; the August 1937 coup-rampage in Mongolia; some forty provincial showcase trials, mostly in fall 1937, ordered up by central
directive; a January 1938 plenum's concessions to party wailings about NKVD
savagery, accompanied by extensions of the mass operations. The third Moscow
trial, in March 1938, seemed to mark a public culmination of sorts, but the carnage was far from over.

Mass terror by the regime against its own elites and masses, like collectivization, was both an inherent possibility within the Bolshevik revolutionary project
and a choice Stalin alone made—and saw through. Collectivization (a violent conscription of the peasantry to serve the state) and its attendant horrors were

necessary to consolidate the Bolshevik project of a political monopoly hell-bent on a noncapitalist modernity (collectivization would not be repudiated after Stalin's death). The mass terror constituted a gratuitous infliction of phenomenal violence, although for Stalin, in many ways, the party's recoil at the costs of collectivization precipitated his terror. The best indication that the terror inhered in Bolshevism was the relative ease with which Stalin could foist the bloodbath upon the political police, army, party-state, cultural elites, and indeed the entire country. The best indication of his singular role in doing so was the fact that it blindsided even his intimates. Molotov, no softie, did not see the *mass* arrests and executions coming (he was still vouching for some former repentant Trotskyites in fall 1936).[319] "Gradually," Molotov would explain later in life, "things came to light in a sharp struggle in various areas."[320] Stalin would have Molotov's top aides arrested in 1937–38. Orjonikidze, Kaganovich, and Voroshilov—Stalinists all—not only failed to foresee but resisted the wholesale expansion into their spheres of the wrecking-espionage mania, publicly stating that wreckers and spies were few.

There *could* have been no such terror without the Communist party and its ideology, but there *would* have been no such terror without Stalin, and his profoundly dark personality, immense strength of will, and political skill.[321] At least 383 execution lists signed by him have survived, containing the names of more than 43,000 "enemies of the people," mostly the highest-level officials and officers. The terror was centrally implemented by Nikolai Yezhov and Mikhail Frinovsky of the NKVD.[322] Molotov, Voroshilov, Kaganovich, Mikoyan, Zhdanov, Andreyev, and Malenkov cosigned the mass sentencing lists prepared for the "politburo," and traveled as emissaries to multiple locales to pour oil on the flames. *Pravda*, under the frenzied editorship of Lev Mekhlis—whose deeply tortured soul even Stalin remarked upon—served as an indispensable fulcrum of public direction of the terror. Of those who implemented the terror regionally, among the most rabid proved to be such NKVD operatives as Sergei Mironov (Western Siberia and Mongolia) and Leonid Zakovsky (Leningrad and Moscow). But Stalin relentlessly drove them.[323] Had he wanted only to break the will of his own inner circle, he could have accomplished that without mass graves. Had he, despite his dictatorial grip, felt a need to subjugate even more the secret police and the military brass, he could have done that with a surgical strike. Had he wanted to force supposedly noncompliant elites to become more obedient, he did not need to have so many sitting officials killed—and then, often, their replacements as well.

Stalin showed no sign that he was in the least tormented by the slaughter—he received an outpouring of furious or grief-stricken letters from wives, mothers, daughters, sons, brothers of the arrested, begging for his intercession to stop the madness, and he ignored them—but he did show awareness of the security conse- quences of what he was doing.[324] In August 1937, at a large gathering of political workers in the Red Army, he had asked the rapporteur "how Red Army soldiers were reacting to the fact that there were commanders who were trusted, and sud- denly criticized, and arrested?" The rapporteur was put on the spot—was the question a provocation? In response, he gently admitted the obvious: doubts were being expressed about the guilt of accused Red Army commanders. Stalin shot back: "Are there facts here of a loss of authority of the party, the authority of the military leadership?" Was it a rhetorical question, even a kind of confession? The despot continued: "Like this: One tries to parse this out, today one turns in so and so, and then they arrest him. God parse it out, whom to believe?" The rapporteur responded: "Comrade Stalin here put the question about whether the authority of the party, the authority of the army, has been undermined. I must say, no." Stalin interjected: "A little undermined."[325] He knew.

NONCAUSES

Very few people had come to know Stalin well, and those who did, he confounded. "Speaking about myself, I can say that I knew two Stalins," Mikoyan would write. "The first, whom I valued a great deal and respected as an old comrade, for the first ten years, and then a completely different person in the later period. . . . I was able to grasp the full measure of Stalin's dictatorial tendencies and actions only when it was already too late to struggle against him. Orjonikidze and Kirov, with whom I was very close and whose attitudes I understood, ended up in the same position of being deceived by the 'first' guise of Stalin." However self-exculpatory, Mikoyan's assessment rings true. Kaganovich, late in life, said much the same. "The postwar was a different Stalin," he remarked. "The prewar, different. Be- tween '32 and the '40s, different. Until '32, completely different. He changed. I saw no fewer than five-six different Stalins." Khrushchev, too, differentiated an earlier from a later ruler. "In the early 1930s, Stalin was very simple and accessi- ble," he recalled, but then Stalin changed, for reasons that Khrushchev, who con- tinued to worship him, never figured out.[326]

Stalin's darkening mental disposition has often been attributed to the 1932 protest-suicide of his second wife, Nadya. Some have also pointed to the Decem- ber 1934 assassination and loss of his rare close friend Sergei Kirov in Leningrad (for which Stalin was blamed). That these events had an outsized emotional impact on him is plausible. One of his bodyguards recalled late in life that Stalin would sit for long periods at Nadya's grave, in Moscow's Novodevichy Cemetery. Svetlana, who was six at the time of her mother's death and kept away from the funeral, asserted that her father never visited the grave, but she, too, insisted that her father never got over Nadya's death.[327] That said, *direct* evidence regarding the evolution of Stalin's psychology remains extremely thin. Moreover, much of the core terror scenario in Stalin's mind predated 1932, while the mass murders did not follow closely after the 1932 or 1934 events. So, although the assertion that he snapped in 1932 (or 1934) might well be true, it does not solve the riddle of why he launched and saw through such a mass killing several years later.

By far the simplest of all explanations would be to attribute the terror to paranoia, a kind of hallucinatory aria.[328] Stalin suspected the worst of people, and he received an endless stream of reports confirming his suspicions.[329] Never mind that he was the arch-plotter: *They* were out to get *him*. Never mind that he was an inveterate liar: *They* were lying to *him,* sabotaging his directives, covering up their mistakes. He suspected that the effusive affirmations of his leadership were two-faced, and that officials were privately thinking critical thoughts. Yezhov, like Yagoda before him, dutifully assembled overheard remarks (real or invented), and the despot read them.[330] The prisons, too, were eavesdropped on, and the transcripts delivered to Stalin.[331] Stalin was compulsively eager for denunciations (and therefore susceptible to people's efforts to annihilate rivals), and once he had read a denunciation about someone, he found it difficult to put it out of mind: *suspicions* had been raised. When informed that someone had bad-mouthed him behind his back, Stalin would undergo a "psychological metamorphosis," according to Svetlana. "At this point—and this was where his cruel, implacable nature showed itself—the past ceased to exist for him. Years of friendship and fighting side by side in a common cause might as well never have been. . . . 'So you've betrayed me,' some inner demon would whisper. 'I don't even know you anymore.'"[332]

Distrust is the disease of the tyrant. Stalin's "maniacal suspiciousness" was extreme even by those standards, something he himself would occasionally acknowledge.[333] And yet, even beyond the fact that none of the psychological diagnoses of him have been based upon direct medical evidence, the emphasis on his paranoia can be overdone. He showed tremendous self-control, rarely raised his voice, rarely displayed anger (and if so, usually with his eyes).[334] At the parades on Red Square, he did not wear a bulletproof vest under his overcoat.[335] He did not employ a double. His chief bodyguard would recall not only that "Stalin did not like it when he was accompanied by security," but that he would walk the streets of Sochi and greet the crowds, shaking hands. (We have already noted similar behavior in his one joyride on the metro.) Stalin's obsession over poison and assassination ran deep. But if he was paranoiac, he was also lucidly strategic. The evidence for an extremely high degree of calculation behind the terror is overwhelming.[336]

A THEORY AND PRACTICE OF RULE

The terror was not about some imagined Georgian national proclivity to violence, Stalin's supposed criminal energy, an outgrowth of beatings by his father, a result of the authoritarian snitch culture of the Tiflis seminary, feelings of inadequacy and shame before genuine Bolsheviks, the suicide of his wife, the death of Kirov, or Stalin's paranoiac streak. It was an outgrowth of his rule.

Stalin's great conundrum was the state. He studied the art of rule via books rather than contemporary examples, and was conversant with German philosophy (Fichte, Hegel), Russia's revolutionary tradition (nihilism, the People's Will, Plekhanov), and the French Revolution (Jacobinism, Robespierre, Thermidor).[337] Machiavelli was known to him via the socialist revolutionary tradition in a way that the Florentine was not for the Nazis. Stalin underlined a variety of passages in his 1869 Russian translation of *The Prince* ("It is unnatural that the armed should submit to the unarmed"; "Princes may, without dread, be severe in wartime").[338] He also underlined a passage noting that "Chinggis Khan killed many people, saying, 'The deaths of the vanquished are necessary for the conquerors' peace of mind.'"[339] But Stalin never extolled the Mongolian khan, except privately to Mongols, and he had discovered his saying in Vasily Klyuchevsky's *Course of Russian History* (1916). Stalin systematically studied works on autocratic rule, such as Vatslav Vorovsky's *On the Nature of Absolutism,* in volume 1 of his *Works* (1933) and Mikhail Olminsky's *The State, Bureaucracy, and Absolutism in the History of Russia,* third edition (1925).[340] He had become passionately devoted to the study of ancient Egypt, Persia, Greece, and Rome, marking up Robert Vipper's *Essays on the History of the Roman Empire* (originally Berlin, 1923), especially passages on Augustus.[341] Stalin had taken to studying up on how to be a despot.

Even as his reading had widened, it remained anchored in Marx and Lenin.[342] But of the many gaping holes in Marx's oeuvre, by far the greatest was the relative inattention to the state, and not just in the transition period from capitalism to socialism (and on to communism), but in general—a gap Lenin did not fill.[343] To the extent that Stalin allowed himself rare criticisms of Lenin, it was on the question of the state.[344] In his copy of a 1935 reissue of Lenin's *State and Revolution,* for example, Stalin had marked the passage about the survival (rather than withering) of the state in the initial stage of a classless society—so on that, Lenin was correct—but when Lenin quoted Engels about the class-oppressive nature of all states, including socialist ones, Stalin wrote in the margin, "No!"[345] In his copy of a 1937 reissue of Marx's *The Civil War in France,* next to the passage about how all states had a "class character," Stalin would write, "Not only."[346] But what else, exactly? And what to say about the issue of his personal dictatorship, which was not anticipated in Marxist theory, to put it mildly? In the ideologized Communist context, these questions demanded an answer. Marxism-Leninism did not explain the operation of "bureaucracy," except as an inherent degeneration that should not have existed in the first place.

Not coincidentally, the Soviet state and its functionaries happened to be the grand theme of Trotsky's anti-Stalin Marxist writings. Stalin was made to wonder: should he proactively prevent the consolidation of a bureaucratic "class" by deliberately upending it? If so, how would that help the Soviet state manage the economy or the country's defense? Should he ensure that the revolutionary regime not "degenerate," as revolutionaries turned into bureaucrats, and instead remove them so that new, younger leaders could come to the fore to regenerate the revolution?[347] In the event, Stalin decided to force a radical reinvention of the Soviet elite, in the mold of the young striver he had once been, executing or incarcerating those he deemed to be of a bygone epoch while promoting and nurturing hundreds of thousands of new people.[348]

Stalin's carnage made him more preoccupied than ever with identifying and promoting people, to fill the vacant positions in the mammoth and still growing apparatus.[349] He blended incited pandemonium and mass murder with an ambitious, people-centric exercise in statecraft. Statecraft may seem a bizarrely incongruous framework for understanding the mass murder of one's own people. To be clear, the challenges of running and conceptualizing the state under socialism did not cause the terror. His obsessions with criticism of collectivization, Trotsky, and the independence of his own inner circle were the key drivers. Still, the challenges of the state's operation and personnel were the context in which Stalin acted. He apparently hoped that younger, more energetic, and—ultimately—better-educated functionaries would better spur economic development, because of dynamism and superior political consciousness. Those who had been through the trials of revolution, collectivization, and industrialization were exhausted, morally and politically, susceptible to temptation, whether through blandishments proffered by foreign agents or the indulgence of the high life. Their replacements, no less significantly, would all be beholden to Stalin utterly.[350]

This went far beyond patronage. Instinctively didactic, Stalin was at heart a pedagogue. A critical core of his inner being consisted of an ethos and practice of self-improvement, a result of his initial leap at the Gori school, studies at the seminary, discovery of Marxism, path into punditry, and triumph over the intellectuals and pseudo-intellectuals atop the party. Stalin "worked very hard to improve himself," Molotov, the longest close observer, would later recall.[351] In turn, the advancement of new people to high positions, and their personal growth while in those positions, became defining elements in his self-conception as the leader who opened opportunity to them. Young cadres, he argued, could lead by mastering Marxist-Leninist orthodoxy and the ins and outs of technology. He latched on to younger people, those who represented the future, products of the soil and the shop floor, as well as of the evening technical and party courses, bootstrapping just as he had and in need of mentoring. The terror enabled him to play the role of teacher to a populous new generation of functionaries, a fundamental trait of his persona and of his conception of rule. He directed showcase trials, the content of confessions extracted even in the absence of trials, and newspaper reportage to tell stories and teach lessons.

All the while, Stalin purposefully ratcheted up fear to strengthen political control and mobilize the entire country to a state of high tension, a technique of rule undergirded by his connect-the-dots theory of party opposition to forced collectivization leading inexorably to a putsch on behalf of foreign powers—it was at once ludicrous and logical, and he repeated it over and over again, in public and in private. "In the face of the danger of military attack," he was quoted as saying in a 1938 book on "defense dramaturgy," by the theater critic Zinaida Chalaya, "our entire people must be kept in the condition of mobilization readiness, so that no 'accident' or tricks by our external enemies could catch us off guard."[352] Stalin worked tirelessly to put the country in the grip of fear, supposedly for its own benefit.

NO ONE HAD TALKED more about the coming war than Stalin, as he drove the country's military buildup, but then he attacked all the institutions critical for a war effort, and not just the armed forces. In the foreign affairs commissariat, at least one third of all staff would be either executed or imprisoned, including nearly two thirds of the upper echelons.[353] Soviet trade representatives abroad were also destroyed en masse, absurdly accused of embezzling and funneling hundreds of thousands of rubles to Trotsky and Sedov, even as NKVD foreign intelligence's agent in Paris lent Trotsky's son in Paris sums of 10 to 15 francs that he had trouble paying back.[354] In NKVD foreign intelligence, there would be nearly 100 arrests in 1937–38, including at least a dozen station chiefs abroad; in Berlin, Stalin cleaned house, arresting nearly every NKVD operative there. Military intelligence fared still worse, losing 182 operational staff to arrests in 1937–38. "You are aware that, in essence, there is no intelligence gathering," the head of the political administration in Soviet military intelligence reported to Mekhlis in 1938. "We have no military attaché in America, Japan, England, France, Italy, Czechoslovakia, Germany, Finland, Iran, Turkey, that is, in almost every major country."[355, 356] For 127 consecutive days in 1938, Stalin did not receive any information whatsoever from NKVD foreign intelligence.

Stalin's terror, not born of any fundamental crisis, caused multiple crises. Many officials who remained at large yearned for an end to the mass arrests, because they feared not just for themselves but for the country.[357] People at home and abroad who had not questioned Stalin's rule before now did so.[358] Would he come to see the scope of his damage? Would the "Center of Centers" operating out of the Little Corner just keep framing and murdering people indefinitely?

CHAPTER 9

MISSING PIECE

Beria sat in the presidium. Some of the speakers praised him highly, and then everyone stood up and clapped. Beria clapped, too. . . . I was prepared for the applause at every mention of Stalin's name and knew that if it came at the end of a speech, everyone rose to their feet. But now I was taken by surprise—who was this Beria?

> ILYA EHRENBURG, *Tbilisi, December 1937, 750th anniversary of Shota Rustaveli's Georgian epic poem,* The Knight in the Panther's Skin[1]

I exalted him for being unafraid to purge the party and thereby to unify it.

> NIKITA KHRUSHCHEV *on Stalin*[2]

DICTATORIAL POWER IS NEVER EFFICIENT, all-knowing, and all-controlling; it shows its strength by violently suppressing any hint of alternatives but is otherwise brutally inefficient. Stalin's conveyor-belt arrests and executions targeting enemies, however, generated not discipline and security, but disorder and insecurity. In the Kolyma gold-mining camps, productivity per prisoner, near the best in the Gulag, was dropping precipitously. Escapees from the bulging Karaganda camp complex were taking up residence in Alma-Ata, the Kazakhstan capital. Right in central Moscow, in April 1938, a mass protest broke out at the overflowing Taganka prison when thousands of inmates repudiated their torture-extracted testimony en masse; Yezhov and Frinovsky hurtled over to Moscow province NKVD offices to demand resolute countermeasures, deathly afraid that any bit of negative information might reach the Little Corner. (Rumors of the prison unrest were already sweeping Moscow.)[3] Then there was the matter of the NKVD's sheer sprawl. By spring 1938, despite mass arrests of police personnel, the ranks had swelled to a gargantuan 1 million. This included 54,000 in state security (GUGB) proper, both central and regional, which was more than double the number before the terror had started; 259,000 border guards and internal troops; 195,000 militia or ordinary police; 125,000 railroad and road police; and 132,000 who manned the far-flung points of the Gulag archipelago, with its 2 million inmates (even after all the executions).[4] Simply directing this huge state within the state was an urgent imperative. An overwhelmed Yezhov, getting drunk in the daytime with top staffers in his Lubyanka office, would drive out to Lefortovo to beat up prisoners during "interrogations," as Stalin knew.[5] Everyone who came into contact with the secret police chief could see his physical deterioration. Yezhov's sickly pallor, publicly attributed to an attempted poisoning, had been divulged at the March 1938 Bukharin-Rykov-Yagoda trial, which prompted naïve or careerist rank-and-file party loyalists to write to him "to take care."

A flow of petitions warned Stalin that the NKVD was engaged in a vast liquidation of loyal Soviet people. His initial response to the NKVD's faltering operations and legitimacy was to concurrently appoint Yezhov commissar of water transport, on April 8, 1938. The appointment made a certain sense, in that water transport, which stood second after railways in carrying freight, supplied a large number of the NKVD's Gulag camps and was poorly performing and needed help.[6] But Yezhov had never worked in water transport, and he was still supposed to be shouldering the responsibilities of a Central Committee secretary, on top of the NKVD. Stalin's pressure on him to maintain the domestic terror at fever pitch did not abate.[7] Such a workload would have crushed any official, let alone a neurasthenic and alcoholic. Stalin, therefore, could scarcely have expected Yezhov to set an additional commissariat right. Rather, the water appointment appears to have constituted a typically twisted maneuver in the despot's final destruction of Yezhov, just as Yagoda's final destruction had been preceded by his transfer to another commissariat—communications—where Yagoda had served another half a year before his arrest. The menacing moves against Yezhov were similarly ponderous, indirect.

On April 30, 1938, a top Yezhov deputy at the NKVD, Zakovsky, was arrested. He had been a Stalin favorite, the operative who had helped oversee Stalin's rare trip to the interior of the country (Siberia, in 1928), and had been appointed to exact retribution in Leningrad in the aftermath of Kirov's assassination. At the January 24, 1938, Moscow meeting of all top NKVD officials, Zakovsky's maniacal work had been praised to the skies, especially his high percentage of extracted confessions, which had brought a promotion to the central NKVD in Moscow.[8] (Zakovsky was said to have boasted that he could make Karl Marx confess to being Bismarck's agent.)[9] Yezhov, forced to explain Zakovsky's arrest to other NKVD operatives, averred that his award-winning underling had manufactured "pumped-up cases" and set outrageously high arrest quotas in Leningrad. Of course, these were the very reasons Zakovsky had been named a deputy chief of the USSR NKVD. Yezhov, moreover, told the assembled operatives that the rabid arrests would continue, further reinforcing the impression that Zakovsky had been destroyed against Yezhov's wishes.[10] A sense of doom began to close in on the secret police. On the eve of Zakovsky's removal, at Frinovsky's dacha, Vasily Karutsky, an operative recently promoted to the central NKVD, had "called Zakovsky a traitor and spy and said that he would soon be arrested" to Zakovsky's face, according to an eyewitness, who added that "Zakovsky, for his part, had called Karutsky a traitor and said that if he himself were arrested, it would only be after Karutsky."[11] Karutsky proved correct: he succeeded Zakovsky at the Moscow NKVD. On the second day on the job, he shot himself.[12]

Clouds darkened over the core Yezhovite group in the NKVD, the "clan" of Yevdokimov, whose collective promotions had facilitated the annihilation of the Yagodaites. Already, back on October 19, 1937, the Yevdokimov loyalist Alexander Kaul had been arrested in the North Caucasus, and although Frinovsky managed to get him transferred to Moscow and placed in the internal prison (to sit quietly without being interrogated), in fall 1937, *Pravda* reported on the connections of Yevdokimov, then head of the Rostov provincial party machine, to "enemies of the people." In November 1937, Stalin sent a valued top aide in his personal secretariat, Boris Dvinsky, to Rostov to serve as second secretary. Yezhov and Frinovsky had managed to get their person, Yakov Deich, appointed as NKVD chief in Rostov, but Deich shocked them, forwarding materials on Yevdokimov to Moscow. "Yezhov and Frinovsky . . . were so infuriated at Deich," Alexander Uspensky, another close Yezhov associate, would testify, that "Frinovsky told me personally he would shoot Deich."[13] Yezhov ordered Deich recalled, but the latter's replacement in the Rostov NKVD also chose to follow Dvinsky's instructions, not Yezhov's, and began to arrest more of Yevdokimov's associates. (Deich was arrested March 29, 1938.) On May 3, Stalin had Yevdokimov transferred to Moscow as the new first deputy at water transport, belatedly fulfilling Yevdokimov's dream of becoming Yezhov's deputy, only not at the NKVD. Yevdokimov exhorted Yezhov to rehabilitate him in Stalin's eyes, and Yezhov sent a "commission" to Rostov (headed by the trusted Litvin) that got the many Yevdokimov associates in prison to repudiate their fabricated testimony against their patron, for what that was worth.[14]

Yevdokimov's removal to Moscow and the accompanying onslaught against his cadres back in Rostov—which betrayed Stalin's hand—manifestly threatened Yezhov. Reasoning that even higher numbers of "enemies" could win back Stalin's favor, Yezhov urged Frinovsky to notch up the terror, but even Frinovsky began to drag his feet in implementing Yezhov's orders.[15] From March through May 1938, Kaganovich, who had previously felt compelled to collude in the execution of most of his own subordinates, now did not even respond to NKVD materials sent to him about the need for further arrests in rail transport; when those arrests were force ordered, Kaganovich sabotaged the NKVD's dirty work.[16] Yezhov threatened Molotov with arrest, telling him, "In your shoes, Vyacheslav Ivanovich, I would not be posing such questions to the competent organs. Do not forget that a chairman of the Council of People's Commissars, A. I. Rykov, was already in my institution." But Molotov went to Stalin, who advised him to demand an apology from Yezhov, which Molotov obtained.[17] Yezhov appeared to be a wounded animal, and the other animals were acting accordingly. But a secret police boss without fangs is destabilizing for a regime.

Even a despot has to have someone at the end of the phone or telegraph line to implement directives. Stalin's glaring need for elementary administrative capacity went well beyond the post of NKVD chief. At the top of the state's now nineteen commissariats, alongside Molotov (the chairman), only five others had survived: Voroshilov (defense), Kaganovich (rail transport plus heavy industry), Mikoyan (trade), Yezhov (NKVD plus water transport), and Litvinov (foreign affairs). Among the five secretaries of the Central Committee—who were supposed to oversee the vast state—two (Kaganovich and Yezhov) concurrently held two government portfolios each, which left, besides Stalin, just Andrei Zhdanov and Andrei Andreyev to oversee the day-to-day work of personnel and propaganda. And Zhdanov ran the huge Leningrad party organization. A glaring indication of the need for capacity at the top was provided by the fact that at the January 1938 Central Committee plenum, Malenkov had been tasked with the main report, and he was not even a member of the Central Committee. As head of the party department overseeing republic and provincial party machines, he was besieged with requests for cadres to fill the gaping vacancies produced by the arrests. And yet, he himself had to be concerned for his life—after all, Malenkov was Yezhov's former deputy in that same party department.

Given that Yezhov's days appeared numbered, that Kaganovich was overcommitted and slightly out of favor (owing partly to his closeness to Orjonikidze), and that Voroshilov was both out of his depth and spiritually smashed, Stalin was in urgent need of another top lieutenant alongside the redoubtable Molotov. The choice would fall upon the despot's Caucasus compatriot.

Lavrenti Beria had never served in Moscow. Still, he had a supreme achievement in the eyes of Stalin: Beria had crushed not just the Georgian Mensheviks but also the Georgian Bolsheviks. Moreover, he possessed none of the Union-wide standing of that other high-placed Georgian whom he displaced, Orjonikidze. Beria was quick to take offense and blame others, obsessive about perceived slights, and a keeper and settler of scores—just like Stalin. That similarity (or emulation) did not stem primarily from shared cultural proclivities, for although Stalin and Beria were both Georgians (in Beria's case, a Mingrelian assimilated to Georgia), and both were Russified, countless other Russified Georgians, even among the Bolsheviks, behaved nothing like these two. Rather, both men were products and consummate practitioners of a particular dictatorial system. Each had cultivated patrons in the highest places—Lenin for Stalin; Stalin for Beria—and each had shown an audacity against rivals, evidence of a thirst for power and a profound sense of their own destiny. Beria, unlike almost every other provincial party boss, not only survived the terror in his domain, but ran the terror locally, dictating lines of interrogation, summoning NKVD bosses to *party* headquarters. No other Soviet region was so dominated by a single figure. "Beria was the absolute-power master of Georgia, and all organizations and agencies, including the NKVD, implemented his demands unquestioningly," his closest minion, Bogdan "Bakhcho" Kobulov, would testify.[18] Beria ran the Caucasus the way Stalin ran the entire Soviet Union.

Beria would turn out to be the missing piece. The now thirty-nine-year-old was not the only discovery who would fill a void in Stalin's entourage and the inner regime; there was also a forty-four-year-old up-and-comer named Nikita Khrushchev, who became a core member of the inner circle and, as it turned out, best buddies with Beria. Still, no one encapsulated the evolution of Stalin's order better than the man he would transfer from Georgia to the Soviet capital in August 1938. And the move would come not a moment too soon. Just before Beria's transfer, on top of everything else, Stalin would experience his worst crisis since 1932: a very high-level defection from the Soviet Far East to Japan, which was armed to the teeth. In going back to trace Beria's path upward from Georgia to Moscow during the terror, it will be necessary to visit Ukraine and the Soviet Far East, too. Beria's move to the capital would reflect the profound changes to Stalin's regime, and bring its own.

"TURN THE ENEMIES OF
SOCIALISM TO ASHES!"

Beria ruled the three-republic South Caucasus Federation—Stalin's homeland—like a Persian shah.[19] At his well-appointed and beautifully maintained two-story villa in Krtsanisi, on a hilltop outside the Georgian capital, he served grand Sunday luncheons, in large company, of spicy Mingrelian and Georgian specialties for his favored police and party functionaries and their families, whom he invited over from their more modest cottages in the same dacha settlement. Another showcase for Beria's gifts as host and patron, and a jumping-off point for his ingratiating visits to the southern villas of the shah of shahs (Stalin), was the dacha Beria had built for himself on a raised point above the Black Sea at Gagra. There, Beria was observed to practice photography, excel at volleyball, swim the farthest, and behave especially affably toward children. "Beria attracted everyone back then by his inner power, his ineffable magnetism, the charisma of his personality," recalled a future daughter-in-law of Anastas Mikoyan, then a little girl, who observed a relaxed Beria at his dachas and his city apartment in 1935–36. "He was not handsome; he wore a pince-nez, which then was a rarity. His look was piercing, hawkish. His leadership, boldness, self-confidence, and pronounced Mingrelian accent stood out."[20]

Beria's takeover of the Caucasus would have been impossible without Stalin's patronage, but he was no mere satrap. He responded especially energetically to the summons to root out "Trotskyism." In Georgia, 30 percent of arrested Communists during the 1935–36 party verifications and card exchanges were designated as Trotskyites; by contrast, in Tatarstan, it was 7 percent.[21] He would make sure to satisfy Stalin, while clearing his own path.

Beria had removed Armenak Abulyan as Armenia's NKVD chief by promoting him to second deputy commissar of the South Caucasus secret police; Abulyan was then said to have died in a car accident (early 1935).[22] Mircafar Bagirov, party boss of Azerbaijan (since December 1933), was Beria's man, but Aghasi Khanjyan, party boss in Armenia (since 1930), was not. Beria appointed Georgi Tsaturov deputy NKVD chief in Armenia and, at supper in his apartment, tasked him with gathering compromising materials. "It is necessary to remove Khanjyan, but whoever I've sent has failed; it's necessary to do this skillfully," Beria instructed. As Tsaturov and those he recruited in Yerevan collected and manufactured the slander, Beria duplicitously distanced himself from the efforts: once, when Khanjyan was in Beria's office and Tsaturov came by, Beria made a show of cursing his minion for giving Khanjyan trouble. "He's a big-time figure and he must be safeguarded," Beria said, as if Tsaturov were a rogue.[23] At South Caucasus party meetings, too, Beria simulated magnanimity, pointing out that he preferred that Khanjyan correct his own mistakes (thereby reminding everyone that there were mistakes). These were ruses well known from Stalin's repertoire, and indeed the repertoire of any practicing authoritarian, though Beria excelled at them.

Nerses (Nersik) Stepanyan (b. 1898), the director of Armenia's Institute of Marxism-Leninism, and therefore Khanjyan's subordinate, secretly wrote a memoir aimed at correcting the falsehoods of Beria's claim to fame (his *On the History of the Bolshevik Organization in the South Caucasus*).[24] The NKVD arrested Stepanyan (May 21, 1936) as a "counterrevolutionary nationalist-Trotskyite," and Beria summoned a meeting of the South Caucasus party bureau on July 9 in Tiflis, now officially called by its Georgian name, Tbilisi. Goglidze, followed by Bagirov and Beria, assailed the "Armenian Central Committee" (meaning Khanjyan) for shielding the enemy Stepanyan and his "group."[25] When the session concluded, around 5:30 p.m., Khanjyan went to the offices maintained by the Armenian republic in Tbilisi. His two bodyguards testified that they found him in his room between 7:00 and 8:00 p.m. with a bullet wound to the head. The Tbilisi ambulance service registered a call at 9:25 p.m. Khanjyan was delivered to the emergency room at 10:25. He underwent "an operation" around 1:30 a.m. (July 10) but was pronounced dead, with a death date of July 9.[26]

Yet another official inconvenient to Beria was dead. Some Caucasus officials, as well as Armenian émigrés, many of whom viewed Khanjyan as a patriot, suspected that Beria, in his own office, had shot him in cold blood. But a visiting Moscow party Control Commission sat in the very next room and would have been able to hear and then observe such an incident. In fact, Khanjyan left suicide notes, at least one of which his wife accepted as her husband's handwriting. Beria was unscrupulous, but more calculating than impulsive. Khanjyan's removal as party boss of Armenia, in any case, was imminent. The relentless hounding and arrest preparations by Beria's henchmen were enough to drive someone to shoot himself.[27]

Beria informed Stalin on the high-frequency phone. The South Caucasus party bureau reassembled on July 10, for six hours, and resolved to telegram Stalin requesting a plenipotentiary to investigate. "The Central Committee," Stalin replied, "considers it unnecessary to send its own representative to ascertain the circumstances of Khanjyan's suicide, since in this matter everything is clear and no investigation is required."[28] Beria went on the offensive. On July 11, 1936, *Dawn of the East* announced that Khanjyan had taken his own life and labeled the act "a manifestation of cowardice especially unworthy of a leader of a party organization," while further noting that Khanjyan had "committed errors, demonstrating insufficient vigilance in the case of the discovery of nationalist, counterrevolutionary, and Trotskyite groups," and suffered from "a severe form of tuberculosis."[29] Khanjyan was buried without public ceremony under a cement grave in Yerevan; Armenian officials were swept up in arrests, some while allegedly trying to escape into Iran.[30] On July 20, *Dawn of the East,* under Beria's byline, carried a vicious attack on Stepanyan that announced the unmasking of "Trotskyite-Zinovievite terrorist groups" in Tbilisi, Baku, and Yerevan. "A Communist who shows conciliation and rotten liberalism in the face of double-dealing," Beria wrote, "commits the greatest crime before the party, Soviet power, and our motherland."[31]

On August 19, 1936, the opening day of the first public trial in Moscow of Trotskyites, *Pravda* reprinted Beria's article—"Turn the Enemies of Socialism to Ashes!" This was a lightning-bolt Kremlinological signal of his standing. Between 1935 and 1938, Beria would have eight articles printed in *Pravda,* unheard of for a provincial party secretary.[32]

Stalin's anti-Trotskyite campaign arrived like a gift for Beria. In Armenia in September 1936, a Beria tool (Amatouni Amatouni) was duly advanced from second secretary to party boss. It was the next month that Beria, on Stalin's orders, arrested Orjonikidze's brother Papuliya in Tbilisi—sweet revenge: no more "Dear Sergo" groveling.[33] The Mingrelian could further consolidate his grip over the Caucasus. Of course, just about every local party boss interpreted the eruption of the enemy campaign self-servingly: scores to be settled, kudos to be won, apartments and dachas to be freed up and doled out as patronage. But across the Union, of the sixty-five top bosses, few would survive: Zhdanov (Leningrad), Khrushchev (Moscow, Ukraine), Beria (Georgia), and his patron turned client, Bagirov (Azerbaijan). Both of the latter were career secret police officials running party machines.

A NIGHT AT THE OPERA

Stalin liked to needle Beria—who prided himself on being a sportsman—about how the diminutive "Deaf One," Nestor Lakoba, was a superior rifle shot and billiards player. Stalin would take Lakoba in his car, for all to see, and make Beria ride separately. At a speech in 1936 in Sukhum, Lakoba could say, rightfully, "The Supreme Leader of our party, the Supreme Leader of the working masses of the whole world, this supreme person, this extraordinary comrade, the friend of all toilers, Comrade Stalin, visits us almost every year."[34] Beria constantly connived to trip Lakoba up.[35] On a Sunday afternoon in spring 1936, Beria showed up unannounced at the Lakoba compound in Sukhum, 180 miles from Tbilisi, with his wife, Nino, as if it were a social visit, and started asking questions based on a denunciation from the father of a woman (Adile) who said she had been kidnapped, mountain style, as a teenage bride (she married one of the five brothers of Lakoba's wife, Sarie).[36] Another time, when Stalin and Beria were guests in Lakoba's native village and Sarie prepared the food, Beria switched his plate with Stalin's at the last minute, as if she might try to poison the leader.[37]

Lakoba had chased Alexei Agrba, secret police plenipotentiary, from Abkhazia, but Beria, using his power as head of the South Caucasus party committee, appointed Agrba first secretary of the Abkhazia provincial party committee, which gave Lakoba endless grief. During the summer of the anti-Trotskyite campaign and Spanish intervention in 1936, Stalin, on holiday in Sochi, visited his new dacha at Myussera, in Abkhazia, specially built by Lakoba, but the latter was nowhere to be seen. Stalin had his staff inquire, and Lakoba answered that Agrba had not granted him permission to exit the Abkhaz capital and that Stalin had instructed him (Lakoba) to submit to party discipline. Stalin granted permission, and directed Beria to recall Agrba to Tbilisi.[38] But on August 17, 1936, Beria managed to get Stalin to have the USSR central executive committee "Georgify" toponyms in Abkhazia: Sukhum officially became Sukhumi, a blow for Lakoba, who had refused even to distribute vehicle license plates in Abkhazia because they said "Georgia."

Lakoba and Sarie attended the 8th Congress of Soviets in Moscow (November 25–December 5, 1936). Hearsay indicates that Stalin, as per usual, sent a car to the Metropole Hotel to fetch them for dinner and that, in connection with the new Soviet constitution, Lakoba lobbied Stalin to transfer Abkhazia to the Krasnodar region of the RSFSR, out of Georgia, while bitterly complaining, as ever, about Beria.[39] Be that as it may, Beria summoned Lakoba to stand before the Georgian "party active," scheduled for December 28, 1936, and Lakoba set out from Sukhumi on December 26 and checked into Tbilisi's Hotel Orient, on Rustaveli Prospect.[40] The next day, he shared a meal (either lunch or supper; the sources conflict) with Beria and Nino at Beria's home or, according to Lakoba's driver and bodyguard Davlet Kandalia, at the home of the founder of a Georgian dance ensemble (Sukhishvili). After the meal, Lakoba attended a December 27 performance of the first Georgian ballet, *Mzechabuki* ("Sun-Like Youth"), composed by Andria Balanchivadze (brother of George Balanchine), at the Tbilisi's National Opera and Ballet Theater. Lakoba suddenly fell ill and, after the first act, returned just down the street to the Orient. There he died, at 4:20 a.m. (December 28).[41]

After Beria and his goons arrived on the scene, a doctor diagnosed a heart attack.[42] Lakoba had blood problems and was thought to be taking anticoagulants. A year-old confidential medical report from the Kremlin hospital, in Moscow (Vozdvizhenka, 6), had diagnosed him with flu and inflamed erysipelas in the area of the left auricle, which had spread to the nearby parts of the ear and the upper part of the neck, with chronic festering leading to his severe hearing reduction. It also found arteriosclerosis and cardiosclerosis (induration of the heart).[43] Still, whispers about a poisoning emerged immediately. Lakoba was forty-three years old.

Beria buried Lakoba with full honors, doubtless after consultation with the Little Corner. The body was brought to Abkhazia on December 29, 1936, and lay in state in Sukhumi's State Drama Theater. The Abkhaz provincial party committee bureau resolved to name the Sukhumi hydroelectric station, then under construction, after him and to establish ten student stipends in his name at the Sukhumi Pedagogical Institute, publishing word in the press, and to give his Lincoln automobile and a dacha under construction to his family.[44] Two days later, 13,000 people attended a state funeral; Beria served as a pallbearer. Lakoba was placed in a special crypt in the city's botanical garden.[45] Stalin did not send condolences. An NKVD squad from Tbilisi was rifling the Abkhaz archives. Already in January 1937, Lakoba's portraits began to be removed. His grave was moved outside the city proper, to the Mikhailov Cemetery; the prominent crypt was destroyed. Some whispered that Lakoba's entire innards—stomach, kidneys, brains, and even larynx—had been removed, and his body burned.[46] Lakoba's widow went to Moscow (staying with another recent widow, Zinaida Orjonikidze), but failed to gain an audience with Stalin.

Lakoba's suspicious death, after Khanjyan's suicide, enhanced Beria's mystique and power. Lakoba had been Stalin's close friend (and midwifed Beria's introduction to him), but Stalin appears not to have investigated Beria's plausible role in Lakoba's death, instead colluding in Beria's conversion of the genuinely popular Lakoba into a posthumous enemy of the people. He was accused of national deviation, having allowed Trotsky "to escape" into exile in Turkey in 1929, and of having plotted to kill Stalin and Beria. (A man who showed off his marks-manship in Stalin's presence during target practice with his Brauning scarcely needed to "plot" an assassination.) Beria would now systematically annihilate Lakoba's kin and associates.[47] Agrba, the Beria creature, was reinstalled as Ab-khazia's party boss.[48]

POWERS OF EXTRADITION

Beria had to request Central Committee authorization not just for appointments of province, county, and city party officials, but also factory directors and candi-dates for local soviet elections.[49] Orgburo directives (of October 15 and Decem-ber 26, 1936) now required regional party machines to submit six reports a year on their activities, an effort to enforce compliance with central directives, a Sta-lin obsession. Beria made sure that the Georgian party complied, submitting its full summary report for 1936 after making lower-level organizations do the same, but he used the occasion to point out to Stalin (February 17, 1937) that the new paper mandates had not released locals from submitting other required de-tailed reports or statistical summaries to the orgburo and various Central Com-mittee departments. "The Central Committee of the Communist party of Georgia is not certain that such reporting requirements could bring any kind of benefit," Beria wrote. "Instead of the utterly necessary permanent living link be-tween lower and upper party organizations, a written paper link is established, which takes up a lot of party organizations' time." The businesslike critique and accompanying illustrations were spot-on, yet astonishing. Stalin chose not to dis-cipline the impudence.[50]

Beria incarnated the terror-facilitated ascendancy of the NKVD vis-à-vis the party, but he had achieved that status years before. During stays in Moscow, he had gotten his own apartment in the NKVD residences on Troitsk Alley (near Samotyochnaya Square), where raucous drinking, singing, dancing, and women were observed in abundance, and which he retained after switching to the party apparatus.[51] Yagoda had continued to send a car from the central NKVD garage to pick up the Caucasus party boss. When Yagoda was arrested, Beria easily maneu-vered the changeover to Yezhov.[52] He had not worked for Yagoda over the course of many years, and when Yezhov had taken a holiday at Georgia's Abastumani sanatorium, Beria had played the consummate host; Yezhov reciprocated on Be-ria's visits to Moscow.[53] Yezhov knew that Beria received invitations to the Near

Dacha. At the February–March 1937 plenum in Moscow, Beria had to wait until one of the last speaking slots (morning session on March 4). He followed his winning approach of stating, multiple times, how comrade Stalin was correct.[54]

After the plenum, on March 20, Mekhlis, at *Pravda*, nipped at Beria's heels with a front-page article, "A Serious Warning to the Southern Regions," which mentioned Beria, among others, by name. In April 1937, the South Caucasus party committee was disbanded, which nominally sliced Beria's bailiwick down to just Georgia. In fact, he would extend his reach even beyond the Caucasus.

Beria had long detested how old Caucasus party comrades who despised him would gather at Orjonikidze's Kremlin apartment or dacha near Moscow (first in Volynskoe, then at Sosnovka) to badmouth him—another circumstance Beria shared with Stalin. But seizing the opportunity afforded by the terror, Beria had his Caucasus operative Vsevolod Merkulov go after the former Caucasus higher-ups now outside the region.[55] Levan Gogoberidze was arrested in the Azov region and extradited to Beria's custody. Bogdan Kobulov, the Beria protégé who headed the Georgian NKVD, reported in November 1936 that Gogoberidze had confessed to disseminating "counterrevolutionary and slanderous fabrications about the past of Comrade Beria . . . on the basis of what he had heard from Comrade Orjonikidze."[56] Mamiya Orakhelashvili, whom Beria had replaced as South Caucasus party boss and who had received sanctuary in Moscow as deputy director of the Marx-Engels-Lenin Institute, thanks to Orjonikidze, was exiled to Astrakhan in April 1937, several weeks after Orjonikidze's suicide; then he was arrested (June 26, 1937) and extradited to Beria. "I learned," Orakhelashvili was said to have testified, "that Sergo Orjonikidze had been joined by Levan Gogoberidze, Pyotr Anishvili, and Nestor Lakoba in waging the most active struggle against the secretary of the Communist party of Georgia, Lavrenti Beria, deliberately spreading slanderous and disturbing fabrications about him."[57]

Everywhere else, associates who had scattered to other provinces were rounded up and tortured to incriminate *sitting* provincial party bosses. Beria alone enjoyed powers of extradition, partly because of his own audacity, partly owing to the circumstance that his enemies were also Stalin's enemies. Orjonikidze stood at the center of the Stalin-Beria bond. Orakhelashvili further testified that "I made slanderous remarks about Stalin as the party's dictator and I considered his politics to be excessively harsh. In this regard, Sergo Orjonikidze exerted great influence on me; in 1936, when he was talking with me about Stalin's attitude toward the leaders of the Leningrad opposition at that time (Zinoviev, Kamenev, . . .), he said that, with his extreme cruelty, Stalin was leading the party to a split and in the end would drive the country into a blind alley."[58]

Beria had even been able to win a tug-of-war with Yezhov. Beria had arrested Polikarp "Budu" Mdivani, an old Stalin nemesis, but "testimony" in Moscow had implicated Mdivani, so Yezhov had forced his extradition to the capital, where he was reinterrogated at Lubyanka and "confessed."[59] But Beria evidently lobbied Stalin, for Mdivani was returned to Georgia. On April 12, 1937, Beria sent Stalin protocols of thirteen different interrogation sessions with Mdivani, extracted in Tbilisi's Metekhi fortress prison (where Stalin had done time under the tsarist regime). The dossier totaled more than 200 pages, and Stalin underlined several passages, then sent copies to Molotov, Kaganovich, and Voroshilov.[60] At Georgia's 10th Party Congress (May 15–21, 1937), Beria, under a portrait of himself, accused Mdivani and associates of having "chattered about a supposedly 'unbearable regime,' . . . about the use of some kind of 'Chekist' methods, about how the condition of the toilers in Georgia is worsening."[61]

Beria attempted to draw boundaries around some of his people. "We should fight all forms of counterrevolution; we must at the same time act wisely, in order to avoid falling from one extreme into another," he told Georgia's 10th Congress. "A blanket approach to all former nationalists and Trotskyists, some of whom happened by chance to be in their ranks but abandoned Trotskyism a long time ago, can only damage the cause of fighting with real Trotskyites, wreckers and spies." But pressure came from the redoubtable Mekhlis in the form of an article by *Pravda*'s Tbilisi correspondent following the last day of the Georgian congress (May 22, 1937), which reported "insufficient criticism and self-criticism" and "not a few Hallelujah speeches." Again, Beria differentiated himself: on May 27, he telegrammed Stalin about the "incorrect and tendentious" article, insisting that self-criticism had been extensive not only at the Georgian congress but at the lead-up district and city party conferences, whose intent, he wrote, had been "to profoundly and correctly explain to the party masses the decisions of the March [1937] plenum of the Central Committee and the speech of comrade Stalin."[62]

Beria even informed Stalin how he had eavesdropped on the communication with editors in Moscow of the said *Pravda* correspondent, Mikhail Mezenin, as if he were a foreign agent on Georgian soil.[63] Branding *Pravda*'s reportage a concerted effort to "discredit the work of the congress of the Communist party (Bolsheviks) of Georgia," Beria requested that the Central Committee direct the newspaper to familiarize itself with the materials of the Georgian congress and publish a correct report, enclosing transcripts for Stalin. It is hard to imagine another regional party boss engaging in, let alone getting away with, such push-back. Beria was permitted to publish his own article in *Pravda* (June 5, 1937) lauding the Georgian congress for its strict adherence to the party line against Trotskyists and other enemies. In the meantime, on May 31, the first of many enemy lists signed by Stalin and Molotov had arrived in Tbilisi, with 139 names under "first category" (execution) and 39 under "second category" (ten years).[64] This direct order Beria could not resist.

A DESPOT'S PREFERENCES

Beria's checkered civil-war-era biography continued to incite whispers. Grigory Gofman (known as Kaminsky), the USSR commissar for health, who, in that capacity, had signed the false heart-attack death certificate for Orjonikidze, blurted out at the June 1937 Central Committee plenum, in Moscow, that Beria had served in the bourgeois nationalist Musavat counterintelligence during the occupation of Baku by the British, making Beria an English spy.[65] Kaminsky, alone among the attendees, had actually been at the Baku party meeting in 1920 at which Beria's Musavat involvement had been formally discussed—Kaminsky was then the party secretary of Azerbaijan—so he also knew Beria had been exonerated. Some Central Committee members had not even known of the original accusations. The Sverdlov Hall was thunderstruck. "No one spoke up in refutation," recalled Khrushchev, an eyewitness. "Even Beria did not speak to offer some kind of clarification. Silence."[66] Stalin declared a break.

Kaminsky cut an extraordinary figure. Back in Tula, the original center of ancient Russia's armaments industry, Kaminsky (b. 1895), then a young, gifted Jewish firebrand, had edited the Bolshevik newspaper *Kommunar* between 1918 and 1920—roughly the same period when Beria served in Musavat bourgeois counterintelligence. The Tula newspaper had begun life with a print run of 300, but Kaminsky raised it above 10,000 by addressing himself to workers and peasants.[67] "*Kommunar* with one hand will help toilers organize life, fix the economy, summon to discipline, labor, and public order," he wrote in the very first issue (July 4, 1918), "and with the other hand it will mercilessly strangle the head of counterrevolution." Nineteen years later at the plenum, he became the "counter-revolution." Instead of allowing discussion of Beria's past, Stalin had Kaminsky arrested and expelled that very day.[68] The NKVD ransacked his apartment in the grand House on the Embankment and his state dacha in elite Barvikha, carting away the gypsum busts of him made by the renowned sculptor Vera Mukhina, as well as every photograph and piece of paper, including his eleven-year-old daughter's drawing of their dacha garden.[69] His two brothers were also arrested. His mother took to standing in the Alexander Garden, outside the Kremlin walls near closed-off Red Square, anticipating that "any minute Iosif Vissarionovich would come out and then she'd tell him her three sons had been arrested and he would take pity on her and release them."[70] Kaminsky got "ten years without the right of correspondence," which meant he was executed.[71]

Stalin was accepting "testimony" of fabricated events as real, but he chose to overlook actual deeds in Beria's life that, in the case of others, were made retroactively fatal. Kaminsky's outburst at the plenum appears to have precipitated a letter that same day (June 25) to Stalin from the former South Caucasus secret police chief, Ivan Pavlunovsky, whom Beria had pushed aside way back when. A candidate member of the Central Committee, Pavlunovsky (b. 1888) had served in the vital war mobilization department of the heavy industry commissariat (under Orjonikidze). His private letter to Stalin stated that when he had been named head of the South Caucasus GPU, back in 1926, Dzierżyński had called him in and told him that one of his new subordinates, Beria, had worked in Musavat counterintelligence, but that this should not be held against him, because he had done so on a party assignment. Pavlunovsky added that Orjonikidze had told him, "Comrade Stalin is aware of" Beria's past and that "he [Orjonikidze] had discussed it with Comrade Stalin."[72] Pavlunovsky's private defense of a Stalin favorite was an effort to save his own skin. It failed. He was arrested on June 28, part of Orjonikidze's "clan" that Stalin was extirpating.[73]

A MINI SUPREME LEADER

Yet another way Beria imitated Stalin was by setting himself up as sole "patron" of the arts in his domain. He was known to strut into rehearsals and summon actors and actresses for private audiences, and he made the intelligentsia understand that they existed for service to the state and panegyrics to the leadership.[74] This went fist in glove with a certain artistic preference. Whereas many Georgian Bolsheviks had argued that Shota Rustaveli was a "feudal," and Ilya Chavchavadze a "bourgeois idealist," Beria deemed them great national artists and had them published in new editions in huge print runs. He also made sure to assert his control over the

Rustaveli Theater, his Bolshoi equivalent. (The Rustaveli's rococo facility in the city's heart had been completed in 1901, with money from the Armenian oil magnate Aleksandr Mantashov, at whose concern a young Jughashvili had stirred political trouble.) First, Beria chased the Meyerhold of Georgia, the Rustaveli's high-handed, turbulent Sandro Akhmeteli (Akhmetelashvili), to Moscow (November 1935); then, when the anti-Trotskyite campaign afforded the opportunity, Beria had Akhmeteli arrested and extradited back to Georgia, charged with creating a terrorist organization in the Rustaveli. When Georgian culture took the spotlight for a ten-day festival, staged in both Leningrad and Moscow (January 4–13, 1937), Beria led the delegation and, at the Kremlin banquet (January 14), sat at the presidium table with Stalin.[75] Akhmeteli was tortured until paralyzed, and soon executed.[76]

Intimidated intellectuals can be still further cowed. In Beria's report to Georgia's 10th Party Congress in May 1937, he had called the arrested Akhmeteli "a fascist wrecker" and warned others still at liberty. "It would not be superfluous for [Paolo] Yashvili, [Konstantin] Gamsakhurdia, [Mikheil] Javakhishvili, and [Nikolo] Mitsishvili and several others to think seriously about their activity," Beria stated, adding that "Paolo is not being noble. . . . He is over forty now and it is time he came to his senses."[77] (The journal *Literary Georgia* printed the text of Beria's speech as if it were literature.) Beginning in late May, the Writers' Union of Georgia held a series of presidium meetings to enforce Beria's strictures upon itself. Long-standing animosities, jealousies, and infighting born of the intimacy of elite life in the shared courtyards off Tbilisi's Lermontov and Griboyedov streets, and of fear, fed a mutual denunciation frenzy.[78] Davit Demetradze, a mediocre critic, excoriated the time before Beria's reign when the Georgian classic authors Rustaveli and Chavchavadze had been banned, condemning the "leftist" extremism of the Russian and Georgian associations of proletarian writers, but also the European "bourgeois" decadence and carousing of the rightist Blue Horn symbolist poets (Yashvili and Titsian Tabidze) and the Academic Group of the novelist Gamsakhurdia. The latter, in response, noted, "I've committed every sin under the sun, but never with hooligans, thieves, and enemies of the people," which induced laughter.

Stalin had sent Alexander Fadeyev, the writer-functionary, to bring back a personal report from Georgia's 10th Party Congress. "We wrote what bothered us," recalled Fadeyev (who had taken along an assistant). "What bothered us was that a bust of Beria already stood on the square, and the Congress members stood every time Lavrenti Pavlovich walked in." Later, over supper at the Near Dacha,

Stalin would broach with Beria the matter of the latter's cult in Georgia. "Who's raising the steam in my bath?" the experienced Beria was said to have asked. Stalin evidently hinted that he had gotten his information from writers. By Fadeyev's account, Stalin let Beria read his personal letter.[79] If true, that action helped reinforce a permanent enmity between Beria and the head of the Union of Soviet Writers.

In Tbilisi on July 22, 1937, during yet another round called to deliberate Paolo Yashvili's expulsion, Yashvili smuggled a hunting gun into the building, climbed to the top floor, and shot himself dead, emptying both barrels. Outside, it was raining, and the poet Javakhishvili, in deep shock, was said to have paced the foyer muttering about needing a car to take him home so that his white suit would not be ruined.[80] Javakhishvili perished, too, as did Tabidze, the translator of Pasternak into Georgian (whom the Russian writer deemed "brilliant, polished, cultured, an amusing talker, European, and good-looking").[81] The faithful hatchet man Demetradze went down, too, but Gamsakhurdia, the intellectual with perhaps the longest list of transgressions, would survive. University educated in St. Petersburg and Berlin, where he had obtained a doctorate—a distinction Beria craved—Gamsakhurdia was a fellow Mingrelian and shared Beria's loathing of Orjonikidze and the cultural philistine Pilipe Makharadze. But Gamsakhurdia had been among those deported to Solovki in connection with the 1924 uprising, and after his release and return, Beria had had him rearrested for an affair with a young publishing executive arrested for Trotskyism. But then Beria pardoned him, observing that sexual intercourse with enemies of the people was permitted.[82]

SUPPLICANT

Beria's letters to Stalin in 1937 were often preoccupied with economic troubles, thus putting him in the position of supplicant. He was working with Mikoyan to reorganize light industry locally to increase consumer goods, but this required bending the USSR finance commissariat and the state planning commission, as well as the formidable Molotov.[83] Beria had written to Stalin and Molotov complaining that only 22,346 of 61,705 allocated automotive tires had been supplied to Georgia, and more than a tenth of what arrived was either unusable or inappropriate for Georgian conditions. That same month, he requested flour and grain beyond his central allocation quotas, citing a failed corn harvest he attributed to unfavorable weather in western Georgia, Abkhazia, and Ajaria, which caused prices to jump. (Beria informed Stalin he had already appealed to Molotov.) Beria wrote to Stalin and Molotov anticipating failures to meet milk supply quotas (revealing that most households in western Georgia had a single cow) and asked that Abkhazia, Ajaria, and western Georgia be exempted from milk supply quotas in 1937–38. He repeated his request for food aid and soon reported long queues for bread in Kutaisi, Sukhumi, Batum, Samtredia, Zestafoni, Chiatura, and Poti.[84]

Beria wrote to Stalin and Molotov about the Tkvib coal mines, which supplied industrial enterprises all across the South Caucasus and were supposed to produce 350,000 tons in 1937, but industrial growth was expected to raise local demand, while problems with the two main seams foreshadowed a decline in 1938 (and an end to all coal extraction by 1942). Back in 1935, the heavy industry commissariat had drawn up plans for exploiting new seams, which by 1939 were supposed to yield 800,000 tons, but neither blueprints nor financing existed even now. Beria asked for a commission to be sent immediately.[85] Similarly, the USSR Council of People's Commissars had approved construction of a 12,000-kilowatt hydroelectric station in Tbilisi in 1936, to be up and running before the end of that year, but turbines and boilers had not been delivered. Planned capacity was reduced to 8,000 kilowatts. Leningrad's Nevsky Factory was to deliver two turbines, but not until December 1937 and March 1938; boilers and other equipment had not been delivered, Beria reported, naming the negligent factory suppliers and predicting that if this continued, electricity shortages in 1937, as in 1936, would require occasional shutdowns of local factories. The completion of several new factories in 1937, moreover, would only exacerbate the energy problems.[86]

Beria lobbied tirelessly over supply challenges. "The Georgian SSR and in particular Tbilisi city are experiencing a severe shortage of industrial goods in the planned assortment, especially cotton and wool fabrics and leather shoes," he wrote to Stalin and Molotov on July 2, 1937, requesting that Tbilisi be raised to the supply category of Moscow, Leningrad, Kiev, and Minsk and that the USSR light industry commissariat open specialized fabric and leather shops in his republic. On August 15, 1937, he requested extra seed stocks, reporting to Stalin and Molotov that, because of hail covering more than 10,000 hectares, the harvest had failed in west-central Georgia and that collective farmers lacked seeds for the next planting. In late August, floods devastated parts of Georgia, especially South Ossetia, damaging bridges and roads, including the Georgian Military Highway, inducing Beria to request extra emergency funding.[87]

CARNAGE AND TRIUMPH

At some point during that summer of 1937, Beria traveled by car to Sukhumi, accompanied by his driver, a party functionary, and his bodyguard Boris Sokolov, as he did often, but this time they were accosted by three bandits with pistols. Sokolov was said to have covered Beria; the driver and functionary got out of the car. The bandits fled. Sokolov was taken to the hospital with bullet wounds in his hand. Beria's star rose higher still.[88]

Beria's winning ways entailed indefatigably seeking, implementing, and reporting on Stalin's directives (written, oral, or intuited). On July 20, 1937, he wrote to Stalin ("Dear Koba"), enumerating a long list of names of arrested officials, detailing supposed spying and wrecking and when they had established "ties" to the rightists Rykov and Bukharin. The litany encompassed just about every major figure since the mid-1920s in Georgia, Armenia, and Azerbaijan—except Beria. He quoted the victims testifying against each other: "G. Mgaloblishvili and Sh. Eliava gave expansive testimony about the espionage work of David Kandelaki." Stalin underlined that and other passages ("The scum and traitor Mamiya Orakhelashvili so far keeps silent. We are afraid to take him firmly in hand, since at every interrogation he faints"). Beria conveyed that 200 people had already been shot and that requests were pending with Yezhov to authorize 250 more arrests. "I think it will be necessary to execute not fewer than 1,000 people, including counterrevolutionary rightists, Trotskyites, spies, diversionaries, wreckers, and so on," Beria added (Stalin underlined this, too). Nor did Beria forget about the need to arrest Lakoba's wife and mother ("I ask for your directives").[89]

Mdivani had refused to incriminate himself publicly and had to be convicted and executed at a one-day "trial" in camera (July 9, 1937).[90] But Beria vigorously fulfilled Stalin's Union-wide instructions in summer–fall 1937 to stage public trials and engage "the toilers" with broadcasts on radio and agitators facilitating collective listening. One trial centered on Zekeri Lordkipanidze, an official in Georgia's Ajarian autonomous republic, who was said to be "linked" to émigré mullahs and the Turkish consulate in Batum and plotting to break off Muslim Ajarisa on Turkey's behalf.[91] Another trial in Abkhazia's State Drama Theater, which Beria himself attended, centered on relatives and associates of the deceased Lakoba, a "Trotskyite pygmy."[92] The prearranged death sentences were affirmed at collective farm assemblies, precisely in accordance with Stalin's circular. Concerning another public trial of "rightists" accused of attempting to restore capitalism in eastern

Georgia, Beria boasted to Stalin (August 29, 1937) that "the trial played an exceptionally important role in raising the awareness of the broad masses of workers about counterrevolution, sabotage, and subversion by enemies of the people."[93]

Stalin nonetheless saw fit to impart a lesson to Beria. On September 8, 1937, the despot sent a cipher to Armenia asserting that affairs were in an egregious state and Trotskyites were finding protection. Armenian party boss Amatouni Amatouni, the Beria creature, and Stepan Akopov, head of the Yerevan city party, had recently been reconfirmed in their posts, but there had been accusations against them of leniency toward enemies, which also raised questions about Armenia's NKVD chief, Khachik Moughdousi (Astvatsaturov), another Beria creature.[94] On September 15, Mikoyan and Malenkov arrived in Yerevan with a brigade of Chekists who arrested and tortured Moughdousi and his deputies. That day, at a plenum of the Armenian Central Committee, Malenkov read out Stalin's recent cipher to Armenia, spurring three days of circular-firing-squad "discussion." On September 18, seven of the nine members of the Armenian politburo were removed. That same day, Beria issued an order for the arrest of his protégé in Abkhazia, Alexei Agrba, now made into a counterrevolutionary bourgeois nationalist, and arrived in Yerevan.[95] "To my complete surprise, Beria suddenly appeared," Mikoyan recalled. "He entered the room as I was speaking at the podium. . . . I assumed Stalin had ordered him to come and arrest me there at the plenum. But I hope I was able to conceal my anxiety and he [Beria] did not notice."[96]

None of the sweeping expulsions at the Armenian party plenum, which continued to September 23, had been cleared with Beria. With the dissolution of the South Caucasus Federation, Armenia no longer fell under his jurisdiction. Still, he showed up to ensure that another protégé, the former head of the Tbilisi city party organization, Grigory Arutyunov, got named as the new party boss of Armenia. (He de-Russified his name back to Harutyunyan.)[97] In Sukhumi, too, where he sacrificed his Abkhaz plant, Agrba, Beria installed new clients.[98]

On December 10, 1937, in the Georgian National Theater of Opera and Ballet, Beria delivered a Yezhov "Center of Centers" speech, detailing a vast plot in the Caucasus, linking poets, theater directors, engineers, and functionaries who aimed to spread typhoid in Kakhetia (eastern Georgia), sell off Ajarisa to Turkey, and assassinate him. Georgia's intelligentsia responded with "prolonged applause."[99] Ten days later, Beria celebrated the twentieth anniversary of the founding of the Soviet Cheka, also in the Rustaveli, with his devoted gang (Merkulov, Goglidze, Kobulov, Vladimir Dekanozov, Solomon Milstein). The year culminated in celebrations of what Beria designated, with Stalin's approval, the 750th anniversary of Shota Rustaveli and his twelfth-century Georgian epic *The Knight in the Panther's Skin,* which brought a host of Moscow literati to Tbilisi, including Ilya Ehrenburg, who observed the Stalin-like ovations that Beria received.[100]

THE RECKONING

Georgia's population in 1937 was about 3.4 million, or 2 percent of the Soviet total, but of the approximately 40,000 names on the extant execution lists submitted by Yezhov and signed by Stalin, 3,485 names (9 percent) were from Georgia.[101] But the extent to which those names reflected Beria's input, versus Yezhov's or Stalin's, remains unclear. About 21,000 were sentenced by troika in the "mass operations" (three quarters were illiterate or barely literate), while another 3,165 were sentenced by the military collegium, numbers in line with the pattern of Soviet quotas.[102] But Ukraine, with nine times the population of Georgia, had almost forty-five times more people arrested than Georgia did in the national operations (89,700 to 2,100).[103] Of the 644 Communist party delegates to Georgia's 10th Party Congress, 425 would be arrested and sentenced either to death or the Gulag—66 percent, a figure in line with the destruction of the delegates to the USSR 17th Party Congress.[104] Scholars assert that one quarter of the Writers' Union of Georgia was exterminated, a very rough estimate.[105] In a report (October 28, 1937) about the unmasking of a counterrevolutionary espionage group of writers centered around Javakhishvili, Beria noted that sixty-one local NKVD operatives had been arrested.[106] And there was still a year of the bloodbath to go.[107]

This horrific picture was less sanguinary than in Armenia, which had one third the population of Georgia but suffered 4,530 executions in 1937–38, out of 8,837 arrests for counterrevolution. (Just one person had been executed in Soviet Armenia in 1936.)[108] Matters were bloodier still in Western Siberia, where at least 300,000 people were executed in 1937–38, about 4 percent of the adult male population there.[109] Proportionally, the slaughterhouse in the Soviet Far East was perhaps greater still.[110] Overall, Georgia had neither the softest nor the hardest terror.[111]

Abkhazia, the autonomous republic in Georgia where the ethnic Mingrelian Beria had been born, continued to be his special target.[112] Under him, the share of ethnic Abkhaz in the party declined from more than 21 percent to 15 percent. Ethnic Russians declined as well, from 29 to 16 percent, while ethnic Georgians in the Abkhaz party rose from 26 to 48 percent.[113] In the autonomous republic's overall population, ethnic Abkhaz would shrink from around 28 percent (in 1926) to 18 percent (by 1939), thanks to a state-sponsored mass influx of Georgians, especially Mingrelian settlers. In 1938, when the rest of the USSR's minority nations were switching from Latin letters to Cyrillic, Beria forced the Abkhaz to switch to the Georgian alphabet.[114] Beria had also written to Stalin complaining that the Muslim Ajarians had been designated a separate nation for the 1937 census, arguing that they "shared the same language, territory, economic life, and culture with Georgians" (omitting their Muslim religion) and requested a correcting directive.[115] Such nationalization efforts by party bosses in other national republics could have provoked punishment for "national deviation."

Besides Beria, one of the very few other regional party satraps to survive was his former patron, now protégé, in Azerbaijan, Bagirov, who also wrote to Stalin boasting of his arrests: Trotskyites and ethnic Iranians living in the frontier zones, not to mention anyone who had personally crossed him. More than 10,000 officials would be removed in Azerbaijan in 1937–38.[116] Stalin evinced special interest in the arrests in Nakhichevan, an autonomous republic inside Azerbaijan, bordering both Iran and Turkey, calling it "the most dangerous point in the whole South Caucasus." Bagirov obligingly bloodied it.[117] Of course, alongside the party boss, the head of the NKVD in Azerbaijan, Yuvelyan Sumbatov-Topuridze, also a Beria protégé (and a Georgian), ordered his subordinates to overfulfill arrest quotas. At the same time, Bagirov himself looked to be in danger, as Azerbaijan figured in Malenkov's report to the January 1938 party plenum on mistakes in the expulsions and arrests of Communists. An NKVD commission from Moscow, chaired by a high figure (Mikhail Litvin), came to Baku. But somehow, Bagirov managed to pin the blame on the local NKVD; Sumbatov-Topuridze was the one removed, on January 10, though not arrested (Beria managed to transfer him to the NKVD's economic administration in Moscow).[118] Bagirov, too, survived, likely thanks to Beria.

A FAVORITE FOR UKRAINE

Beria was not the only phenomenon to emerge. Just before Stalin switched Beria to the party from the secret police, Nikita Khrushchev in January 1932 became Kaganovich's deputy, number two in the huge Moscow party organization, with Kaganovich's guiding example of a superhuman work ethic to emulate. Khrushchev developed a reputation for bootlicking.[119] In January 1934, he became Moscow city party boss, and, in early 1935, concurrently, Moscow provincial party boss, a region equivalent in physical size to England and Wales. One official who knew him explained that, like Kaganovich, Khrushchev "compensated (not always successfully) for gaps in education and cultural development with intuition, improvisation, boldness, and great natural gifts."[120]

During the terror, in fall 1937, the Moscow party active assembled in the city's conservatory for a meeting presided over by Kaganovich (by then both heavy industry commissar and railroad commissar) and Khrushchev. Khrushchev spoke passionately, lost his place, mispronounced words, and made people laugh, epitomizing the lower-middle strata who had risen with the revolution and Stalin's rule. "A large head, a high forehead, light-colored hair, a wide-open smile—all this conveyed the impression of simplicity and goodwill," recalled one observer, seeing the golden boy for the first time. "And I, and my neighbors, glancing at Khrushchev, experienced not only satisfaction, but a kind of tender emotion: what a fellow, a regular miner, and he had become secretary of the Moscow party committee."[121]

But Iona Yakir, the arrested military officer, had visited Khrushchev at his Moscow dacha, part of the manor house on the estate of the former Moscow governor general, in Novo-Ogaryovo; Yakir had been there on the very eve of his arrest. Yakir's sister was married to Semyon Korytny, a close Khrushchev colleague in Moscow, who was also arrested in the hospital—the day after Khrushchev had visited him there. "I worried," Khrushchev recalled. "First, I pitied him. Second, they could come after me, too." Stalin ordered or allowed Yezhov to arrest two of Khrushchev's top aides in Moscow, both of whom Khrushchev viewed as exceptionally trustworthy. Stalin divulged to Khrushchev that each had testified against him, claiming that "Khrushchev" was not his real name but a mask, and hinted that such arrests might be the work of enemies who had infiltrated the NKVD, hardly comforting for Khrushchev's prospects.[122]

And then there was the biggest black spot: Khrushchev divulged to Kaganovich that, during his student days back in 1923, he had sympathized with Trotsky, information likely to come forward in an anonymous denunciation. Kaganovich "blanched." "Trotskyism" by his protégé threatened him, too, especially because Kaganovich himself had hints of Trotsky association: he had served in the civil war on the eastern front, among Trotsky supporters, not on the southern front, among Stalin supporters. He advised Khrushchev to inform Stalin immediately. Stalin, in response, told Khrushchev not to worry. The despot's absolution, Khrushchev would recall, "further strengthened my confidence in Stalin, and gave rise to a feeling of certainty that those who were being arrested really were enemies of the people."[123]

Khrushchev was more of a "Trotskyite" than myriad officials who were destroyed for it. If Stalin had suddenly changed his mind, nothing Khrushchev did, or did not do, could have saved his life. Of the thirty-eight highest officials in the Moscow provincial party organization, three survived, two of whom were Kaganovich and Khrushchev. As party boss of Moscow, Khrushchev had to "authorize" arrests, and, in connection with the onset of "mass operations," he'd had to submit a list of "criminal and kulak elements," which in his case carried an expansive 41,305 names; he marked 8,500 of them "first category" (execution).[124]

Stalin entrusted his star pupil with a big new assignment. In late January 1938, the Ukraine-born ethnic Russian Khrushchev replaced the ethnic Pole Stanisław Kosior as party boss of Ukraine.[125] He arrived in Kiev atop a mountain of corpses and took part in new arrest waves. By this time, the Communist party in Ukraine had been reduced by half, to 284,152 members (just 1 percent of the population), and the Ukrainian politburo and Central Committee had essentially ceased to function. Many provinces in Ukraine had no first or second secretaries, and none had a third secretary (with a single exception). Newspapers lacked editors. All eleven Ukrainian politburo members would perish without a trace. No one from the Ukrainian orgburo or the Ukrainian party Control Commission would survive, either. Just two of the sixty-two members and forty candidate members of the Ukrainian Central Committee would manage to escape execution or incarceration.[126] This state of affairs was not unique to Ukraine, but this was a strategic and industrial region roughly equal in size to France.

At least 160,000 victims, in Moscow and Ukraine, would be arrested under Khrushchev during the terror. Such rough figures should put to rest the notion that Beria was a singular monster, instead of an exceedingly ambitious figure, like Khrushchev, who developed ways to thrive in a monstrous system. It bears further remarking that Khrushchev, while working in Moscow, got along well with the party boss of the Caucasus. "I met Beria, it seems, in 1932," Khrushchev would recall. "We met to discuss personnel issues. . . . He came with Bagirov" (whom Khrushchev already knew). They talked about an Armenian (Ruben Mkrtichyan, known as Rubenov) who was party boss of a Moscow ward but being recommended for a higher position. "After the first encounter with Beria, I got closer to him," Khrushchev continued. "I liked Beria—a simple and sharp-witted person. Therefore, at Central Committee plenums, we often sat next to each other, exchanging opinions, scoffing at the orators. I liked Beria so much that in 1934, when I was on holiday in Sochi for the first time, I went to see him in Tiflis."[127]

Khrushchev, no less than Beria, albeit with a sunnier and more idealistic disposition, earnestly took to the role of pupil under the great teacher. Another Khrushchev subordinate, P. V. Lukashov, was arrested in Ukraine only a few weeks after Khrushchev had received Stalin's approval to promote him. "For me it was a moral blow," he recalled. "How could this be? I had seen this man, trusted him, respected him. But what could I do?" Lukashov, miraculously, was released, after which he described for Khrushchev the ways he had been tortured—to testify against Khrushchev. When Khrushchev mentioned Lukashov's arrest to Stalin, the latter said, "Yes, there are perversions. On me, as well, they're collecting material."[128]

During the terror of 1937–38, Khrushchev would turn out to be one of only two people promoted to candidate membership in the politburo, the other being Yezhov. And Khrushchev became the first person elevated to the politburo without prerevolutionary membership in the party.[129]

NKVD DEGRADATION

Ukraine also got a new NKVD boss, Alexander Uspensky, whose overkill in Orenburg province had recommended him.[130] "In January 1938, I went to a session of the USSR Supreme Soviet in Moscow," Uspensky testified. "Yezhov unexpectedly summoned me. . . . Yezhov was completely drunk. On the table next to him was a bottle of brandy. Yezhov said to me: Well, are you going to Ukraine?" The appointment took effect on January 25.[131] Uspensky replaced Israel Leplyovsky, who had run the NKVD special department and been the main organizer of the case materials in the annihilation of Tukhachevsky and the Red Army high command, then was demoted to Kiev, where he had exceeded the already sky-high arrest quotas for the republic, but Yezhov complained anyway.[132] Uspensky, for his part, also had a great deal to make up for: he had been deputy Kremlin commandant under Yagoda, back in fall 1937, when Stalin summoned him to the Little Corner, along with Yezhov, Molotov, and Zhdanov, for thirty minutes and asked point-blank, "Was he honest and not recruited by Yagoda?" Yezhov intervened and said that Uspensky had regularly reported to him at the party apparatus on irregularities in Kremlin security.[133] All the same, Yezhov, unsure how that visit to the Little Corner would turn, had instructed his secretariat to prepare a warrant for Uspensky's arrest. After Stalin relented, Yezhov used Uspensky's anxious ferocity in Orenburg to try to buttress his own standing.

In the first half of 1938, the NKVD "mass operations" were specially prolonged for the USSR's two most strategic territories. The Soviet Far East, facing Japan, received the highest new quota; Ukraine, facing Nazi Germany, the second highest.[134] Uspensky would send Moscow reams of reports about unmasked "plots," besting the totals of all other regional NKVD chieftains.[135] First, though, Yezhov went in person to Khrushchev's and Uspensky's new bailiwick to ratchet up the carnage. Just before departing for Kiev, on February 12, 1938, he had summoned several operatives. "Yezhov asked us, 'Who here speaks Ukrainian?'" one participant, Grigory Kobyzev, testified. "It turned out that those present knew almost no Ukrainian. Yezhov asked, 'How are we going to converse there in Ukraine?' Frinovsky laughed and loudly said, 'Over there, there is not a single Ukrainian, just Jew after Jew.'" Yezhov laughed as well. Kobyzev was named head of NKVD personnel in Ukraine and tasked with purging it of Jews. The spectacular ascent, as a result of the Bolshevik revolution, of people from the former Pale of Settlement was entering eclipse. "Oh, cadres, cadres, this is not Ukraine but a whole Birobijan," Yezhov further remarked, once he and Kobyzev were on-site, alluding to the special Soviet Jewish enclave in the Far East.

Yezhov went down the list of all Ukraine NKVD personnel, marking those for arrest or demotion (to tasks such as Gulag duty).[136] He also gave a speech lacerating the assembled NKVD men in Ukraine for allegedly having left large numbers of anti-Soviet elements at large. A cigarette dangled from his mouth the entire time he lectured; the scar on his face was starkly visible. "It was my first time at such a high-level gathering, and naturally I marveled at everything," testified Mikhail Zhabokritsky, the Jewish NKVD chief of the Moldavian autonomous republic, in Ukraine, who would be arrested a few days later. "But what astonished me the most was Yezhov himself—not tall, even dwarfish, thin, frail. When he sat in the chair, from the table one could only see his head." Although Yezhov was a general commissar of state security, equivalent to the rank of marshal, he dressed indifferently. "His self-confident pose, the independent tone of his speech, did not harmonize with his exterior and came across as ridiculous," observed Zhabokritsky. At the farewell banquet in Kiev, Yezhov got so drunk that his bodyguards had to carry him out in front of everyone.[137] "This year was a special one for the Soviet country," Khrushchev would summarize to the Ukrainian Communists at their next party congress, praising the mass arrests while adding that "after the trip to Ukraine by Nikolai Ivanovich Yezhov, and the arrival of comrade Uspensky in the Ukrainian SSR NKVD, a real rout of enemy nests began."[138]

While the wretched USSR NKVD chief was laying waste to Ukraine, morale, and his own reputation, on February 17, 1938, Frinovsky, in Moscow, summoned Abram Slutsky, head of NKVD foreign intelligence. The son of a Jewish railway worker from a Ukrainian village, Slutsky was the sole remaining central NKVD department head from Yagoda's time. He'd had an illustrious career in industrial espionage, pilfering the designs for ball bearings from Sweden in the late 1920s, then spent the 1930s purloining Trotsky's archives in Paris, infiltrating émigré groups, and overseeing assassinations on foreign soil.[139] But a torrent of denunciations had ramped up the pressure to take down the last Yagodaite. Yezhov and Frinovsky evidently worried that an arrest would induce NKVD operatives abroad to defect—before they could be recalled and executed—and so they had concocted an act worthy of a spy novel. As Slutsky and Frinovsky were talking in the latter's office, another operative entered and, pretending to be awaiting his turn to report, snuck up from behind and put a chloroform mask over Slutsky's face. Once he fell unconscious, a third operative emerged and injected Slutsky's right arm with poison. *Pravda,* giving the cause of death as a heart attack, published a laudatory obituary on February 18: "Farewell, trusted friend and comrade!" That night, the intelligence chief's body lay in state with an honor guard in the central NKVD club at Bolshaya Lubyanka, 14, the two-story eighteenth-century baroque palace that had been described in Tolstoy's *War and Peace.*

A MAN ALONE

On February 19, a grandchild was born to Stalin: Galina, the daughter of Yakov Jughashvili and his wife, Yulia Meltzer. A previous granddaughter, Yelena, the offspring of Yakov's first wife, had died not long after birth in 1929. A grandson, Yevgeny, had been born on January 10, 1936, in Uryupinsk, Stalingrad province, to Olga Golysheva, his former fiancée, and Yakov had not appeared for Yevgeny's birth; the mother had given the boy her own surname. When Yakov found out, evidently in 1938, he had interceded with the authorities to get the boy officially registered as Jughashvili. Stalin never recognized Yevgeny as his grandson.[140] Slutsky, meanwhile, was cremated and interred at the prestigious Novodevichy

Cemetery. Gossip reached Orlov, the NKVD station chief in Spain, to the effect that during the lying in state, colleagues noticed stains on Slutsky's face from hydrocyanic acid.[141] Whether this was true or not, they all understood that he had been killed. In any case, in April 1938, after the elaborate ruse concerning Slutsky's death to avoid provoking defections abroad, Stalin threw caution to the wind and allowed Slutsky to be declared "an enemy of the people" anyway.[142] He was playing with fire.

Stalin held no government position, did not attend diplomatic functions, and rarely met with foreigners.[143] He was largely inaccessible to most Soviet elites as well. He continued to reside at the Near Dacha, where he had helped plant an orchard of apple, cherry, linden, birch, pine, and maple trees, as well as grapevines, jasmine, viburnum, rose hips, petunias, lilies of the valley, lilacs, wallflowers, violets. But the hastily built structure, in its prefabricated original form, had not lasted even four years. It was replaced in spring 1938 by a building of bricks, which were stuccoed and painted the same dark green, evidently Stalin's preferred color, although this could have been for camouflage purposes, to blend into the forest. (Many dachas in Moscow's outskirts and down south were now painted green.) The rebuilt main building followed the same design: a single story with seven rooms and a solarium on the roof. A new, large auxiliary building, where the kitchen and staff operated, was connected to the main dacha by a long corridor. The grounds got a new canteen for the guards and staff, an office for the head bodyguard, rooms for medical personnel, and a cinema. The familiar small, cozy dining room—some 800 square feet, amply lit with tall windows, a fireplace in the corner, and seating for eight to ten—was where Stalin worked and took meals when alone or in small groups.

At his preferred seat, on the far left side of the table, there would be a generous collection of colored pencils and notebooks and a special deep ashtray of marble, where he could stand up his pipe. Stalin had an electric teapot that he operated himself. A round table, located between two of the four windows, held his multiple black telephones (made by Siemens) and a button to summon the staff. A high-frequency phone, the color of elephant tusk, allowed secure long-distance calls, especially for military and police purposes. Calls into the dacha were answered by a duty officer, who used an internal line to inform Stalin of the incoming call. The despot, if he so desired, would pick up, press the lever, and answer, "Stalin." One of the phones was an ordinary city line, which Stalin might have installed so callers could bypass the staff to reach him (people from telephone booths sometimes got the dacha accidentally, and eventually the city line would be removed).[144] The small dining room, like all the others, had a couch, where he did his reading, as well as a small writing desk. A door led from this room to the glass-enclosed northern veranda, which also had a work/dining table. It was neither luxurious nor ostentatious.

Benito Mussolini, on a typical day in 1938, spent an hour or two every afternoon in the downstairs private apartment in the Palazzo Venezia of Claretta Petacci, whom he called little Walewska, after Napoleon's mistress. The duce would have sex, nap, listen to music on the radio, eat some fruit, reminisce about his wild youth, complain about all the women vying for his attention (including his wife), and have Walewska dress him. Before and after the daily trysts—Mussolini had recently told his son-in-law that "genius lies in the genitals"—the duce would call Claretta a dozen times, to report on his travails and his ulcer. Claretta recorded his "thoughts" in her diary: Jews were "pigs . . . a people destined to be completely slaughtered"; the English were "a disgusting people . . . they think only with their asses"; the Spanish were "lazy, lethargic . . . eight centuries of Muslim domination, that's why." She also recorded their lovemaking and his reveries about her "delicious little body." Mussolini was not just head of state but head of five different ministries, yet Italy had only very small tanks, a navy whose ships could not leave port for want of air cover, and just ten total army divisions. In August 1938, he was shocked to learn that the finance minister knew of major shortages of artillery while he, the war minister, did not. At such moments, when Mussolini's inattention, inaccessibility, and incompetence were exposed, it was never his fault. Anyway, what was mere technology compared with spirit, character, will?[145]

Stalin's world was nothing like the virile Italian's. Women in his life remained very few. (There were almost none in positions of power, either.) He still did not keep a harem, despite ample opportunities.[146] Inevitably, rumors circulated of affairs: the wife of a deceased politburo member, code-named "Z" (i.e., Zinaida Orjonikidze); the sister of Kaganovich, Roza, who did not exist; a Bolshoi ballerina or singer.[147] If Stalin had a mistress, she may have been a Georgian aviator, Rusudan Pachkoriya, a beauty some twenty years his junior, whom he observed at an exhibition at Tushino airfield. She lived in Tbilisi and, while in Moscow, stayed at a sports dormitory (later, she obtained a prominent Gorky Street apartment). Stalin might have met her occasionally in private quarters, under the pretext of conducting aviation "consultations," according to one of his surviving bodyguards (the sole source on the matter).[148] But whatever pleasures Stalin occasionally took, he was married to Soviet state power. A widower twice over, he spent his time seeking succor not in the female body but in military technology and in cadres.

Karolina Til, the longtime Stalin family housekeeper, an ethnic German from Riga who had been the one to find Nadya's dead body, went on pension in 1938. In the fall, Vasily (age seventeen) would leave home to attend the Kachinsk Higher Military Aviation School, in Kucha, Crimea, near Sevastopol. Artyom, Stalin's informally adopted son, was in artillery school; Yakov Jughashvili was enrolled in the advanced Artillery Academy. Svetlana (age twelve) was still attending Moscow's Lepeshinsky Experimental School-Commune, on Ostozhenka; she lived in the Kremlin apartment. Stalin adored but rarely saw his lonely daughter. Following the arrests of the heads of the bodyguard directorates—Pauker and then Kursky and Dagin—in quick succession, a new person would enter the Stalin household: Nikolai Vlasik (b. 1896), the son of Belorussian peasants who himself had completed just a few years of school before becoming an unskilled laborer.[149] His modest education, short stature, and doglike loyalty seem to have made him unthreatening to Stalin. Vlasik's purview, like Pauker's, included Stalin's security, food, personal life, and children. Poskryobyshev continued to handle all regime matters and, inevitably, became close with Vlasik (who stood guard in the outer reception office). The promotion also put Vlasik in charge of the Bolshoi, as well as other top Moscow theaters (the Maly, the Arts, Vakhtangov), and he came to know many of the artists personally, especially the females.[150] Stalin saw more of Poskryobyshev and Vlasik than anyone else. Vlasik became Beria's venomous rival.

Stalin was profoundly alone in the sulfuric aquifers of his being. But he hated to be alone. His awkward character exacerbated the isolation that inevitably befalls a tyrant upon whom everyone's life depends. Not only had he driven his second wife to suicide, but most of his closest friends were gone: Kirov, Lakoba, Orjonikidze. Stalin was complicit in the death of the third, and perhaps of the second, while being blamed, in whispers, for the first. He had deliberately murdered almost all his comrades in arms, including those he had been genuinely fond of, such as Bukharin. The few who survived—Molotov, Voroshilov, Kaganovich, Mikoyan—had largely been reduced to minions. Beria would come into this group as a minion, too, but he would be more enterprising.

STALIN MANUFACTURES A TOP FOREIGN AGENT

Japan's ambassador to Moscow complained to Tokyo that Soviet counterintelligence officials "steal suitcases from military attachés."[151] But Japanese reconnaissance aircraft were flying over Vladivostok, Khabarovsk, and Komsomolsk on cloudy days, then shutting down their engines and gliding noiselessly, photographing Soviet military installations with their Fairchild cameras. With the assistance of Finnish cryptographers, the Japanese had broken the codes used in the Soviet Far East. They also had dug underground cables into Soviet territory from Manchukuo to eavesdrop on Soviet telephone conversations. Japanese intelligence rightly regarded Polish intelligence as the world's top anti-Soviet service and held joint military intelligence conferences with the Poles, in Harbin and Warsaw.[152] Stalin had the Japanese consulates in Odessa, Novosibirsk, Khabarovsk, and Blagoveshchensk shuttered.[153] But four Japanese consulates remained in the Soviet Far East (Vladivostok, Petropavlovsk, Okha, and Aleksandrovsk), while Manchukuo, Japan's puppet state, maintained consulates in Chita and Blagoveshchensk. Nonetheless, when *Pravda* characterized the Soviet Far East as riddled with spies (April 23 and 28, 1937), it meant Soviet military commanders.

Gamarnik, who had committed suicide just prior to his likely inclusion in the Tukhachevsky "trial," had been a commander in the Soviet Far East, and his former subordinates were being arrested. Insinuations of spying on behalf of the Japanese also implicated the current commander of the Soviet Far Eastern Army, Blyukher, whose subordinates were being arrested.[154] But it was not Gamarnik, Blyukher, other Soviet officials, or former kulaks who served the Japanese cause, but Stalin himself. His orders for sweeping arrests of Japanese "spies" ended up delivering windfall details of Soviet military capabilities, dislocation, and war plans to Tokyo.

Genrikh Lyushkov—described as "stout, black-haired, black-eyed, with a Charlie Chaplin mustache and a strongly Jewish cast of countenance"—was among the small number of NKVD bigwigs to enjoy an audience in the Little Corner during the terror.[155] Born in Odessa in 1900, the son of a Jewish tailor, he had joined the Cheka in 1920, learned good German, and conducted industrial espionage in Germany. He was also one of the few top Chekists with a higher degree in jurisprudence. He was, however, not a star (one colleague in Moscow recalled "a modest person and decent functionary") and had no major awards.[156] But in December 1934, in the wake of the Kirov assassination, Lyushkov, as deputy chief of the NKVD's secret-political department in Moscow, had arrived with Stalin's entourage in Leningrad and participated in the "interrogations," catching the eye of Yezhov (then still in the party apparatus). In August 1936, Yagoda had appointed Lyushkov NKVD boss of the Azov–Black Sea territory to produce compromising material on the party boss (and Yagoda nemesis) there, Yevdokimov. In

September, Yagoda was cashiered. All the same, Lyushkov went on a murderous rampage of trumped-up charges against the Yevdokimov clan, gaining a reputation with underlings as an arrogant bully. Frinovsky and Yezhov tried to rein him in, but Lyushkov had instructions directly from Stalin.[157]

During the flurry of prizes for those prosecuting the terror, on July 3, 1937, Lyushkov received the Order of Lenin.[158] He was transferred out of Rostov to take up the big terror assignment in the Soviet Far East that had been given (a few weeks earlier) to Balytsky.[159] On July 28, Lyushkov had a fifteen-minute audience in the Little Corner, and three days later he set out by train for Khabarovsk with a heavy entourage, arriving August 9.[160] He boasted in telegrams to Moscow about one unmasked "plot" after another; Stalin devoured the interrogation protocols, especially after Terenty Deribas (Balytsky's long-serving predecessor) was denounced for embezzling gold in a machination during which an NKVD officer fell under a train. (Stalin: "To Yezhov. Important. It's possible that Deribas, beyond everything already, was a serious ordinary criminal. This must be investigated.")[161] It was Lyushkov, in late summer–fall 1937, who conducted the deportation of some 170,000 Soviet Koreans; *Pravda* announced his award for implementing an important assignment "in the field of transport."[162] In December 1937, Stalin let him become one of the "elected" to the new USSR Supreme Soviet. "I'm fortunate," Lyushkov told the toilers who formally nominated him, "that I belong to the caste of functionaries of the punitive organs."[163]

Lyushkov was just beginning. Between December 1937 and May 1938, he imprisoned or deported 19,000 of the 25,000 ethnic Chinese in the Soviet Far East, including every last one in Vladivostok.[164] As a result of his "vigilance," he had to beg for translators in Asian languages, requesting the transfer to the NKVD of eight students by name from Far Eastern University.[165] He also begged Moscow for new operatives: thirty-seven NKVD officers were locked up in the local prison as foreign "spies." But Lyushkov had problems far bigger than lack of personnel: he had served in the organs under Yagoda. Of the forty-one NKVD officers under Yagoda who had held the title of commissar of state security (first, second, or third rank)—equivalent to general—only ten, including Lyushkov, remained alive and at liberty. One (Slutsky) had been poisoned, three had committed suicide, and the rest had been arrested and for the most part executed.[166] Lyushkov, in the capital for the January 1938 Supreme Soviet convocation, complained to Frinovsky that he was being tailed upon exiting his Moscow hotel. Frinovsky replied that Yezhov was just trying to safeguard him, which was true. The arrested Georgian Lordkipanidze had incriminated Lyushkov.

Instead of passing the Lordkipanidze interrogation protocols to Stalin, Yezhov had had Frinovsky reinterrogate Yagoda. The latter complied: Lyushkov had not been part of the "plot." Testimony against Lyushkov kept coming, however, and Frinovsky pressured Yezhov, asking why they were protecting this "Yagodaite," especially since, on the inside, people already knew of the "testimony" accumulated against him. Yezhov was in a bind. If Lyushkov were belatedly arrested, Yezhov would have to explain to Stalin why he had failed to forward the interrogation protocols earlier. Nonetheless, the pressure against Lyushkov built, and on April 16, 1938, Frinovsky ordered Lyushkov to send his deputy, Moisei Kagan, to Moscow, ostensibly to be assigned to another post. Lyushkov had secretly agreed with Kagan that the latter, upon arrival, would let him know everything was okay. Lyushkov heard nothing. (Kagan was arrested.)[167]

Another of Lyushkov's outsized problems was a man against whom he was supposed to be gathering compromising materials: Marshal Blyukher. Despite the German-sounding name (Blücher), evidently a nickname for his grandfather, Blyukher was an ethnic Russian, born to a peasant family, who had commanded the Soviet Far Eastern Army since its inception (1930), held the rank of marshal since its introduction (1935), and earned no fewer than five Orders of the Red Banner and two Orders of Lenin.[168] Following his complicity on the panel of judges in the 1937 in-camera trial and execution of Tukhachevsky and the other commanders, Blyukher had taken to drink, starting that very night in his room at the Hotel Moskva. Back in the Soviet Far East, his own top people were being arrested.[169] "Vasily Konstantinovich became more and more closed," Blyukher's young second wife, Glafira, would recall, "but he still believed Stalin would defend him, although, thinking out loud at home, he not infrequently said that the Master was too severe, idiosyncratic, at times wacky, and yet he believed in his party conscience."[170] In January 1938, Blyukher had led the Far Eastern delegation to the USSR Supreme Soviet in Moscow and, furthermore, was among the select few elected to the body's presidium. Lyushkov, for his part, knew that Stalin had lost confidence in Blyukher. "Blyukher is very ambitious for power," Lyushkov would later observe. "His role in the Far East does not satisfy him; he wants more. He considers himself above Voroshilov. Politically, it is doubtful whether he is satisfied with the general situation, although he is very careful. In the army he is more popular than Voroshilov."[171]

Blyukher, of course, knew that Lyushkov was gunning for him, and he went on the offensive, spreading rumors that Moscow had lost "political confidence" in Lyushkov.[172] Thus did each man's vulnerability contribute to the other's.

Stalin had gotten lucky in the Far East: Japan had become bogged down. "The situation in China splendid," Soviet deputy foreign affairs commissar Potyomkin remarked, as the French ambassador to Moscow Coulondre reported to Paris. Potyomkin "is counting on the resistance by this country for several years, after which Japan will be too enfeebled to be capable of attacking the USSR. This opinion appears to be shared by the Soviet leadership."[173] Stalin himself told a Chinese special envoy (the son of Sun Yat-sen) that "China was fighting Russia's battle as well as her own" and "that China would continue to receive all possible help from Russia in the form of munitions, airplanes, and other supplies."[174] But he avoided direct confrontation with Japan, sternly warning (April 7, 1938) the party boss in Soviet Northern Sakhalin to quit harassing Japanese economic operations there, since any trouble over the foreign concessions could serve as a casus belli. Similarly, in connection with the Japanese ambassador in London, Stalin instructed his envoy Maisky "not to avoid a meeting with [Shigeru] Yoshida, and if you get such a meeting listen to him attentively. Ask him to outline concrete measures for improving relations between Japan and the Soviet Union. State that the USSR strives for improved relations. On these points, report to me."[175]

Predictably, though, Stalin was pursuing his own intrigues. On April 12, 1938, Moscow notified Blyukher of an imminent Japanese attack against Soviet positions, based on information from Chiang Kai-shek.[176] Stalin could not help but understand that such "intelligence" reflected Chiang's indefatigable efforts to precipitate direct Soviet involvement in the war, but the despot could not resist using this Chinese provocation. Even as the Soviet Far Eastern Army was adding more than 100,000 troops from the Volga and Siberian military districts in 1938, as well as large numbers of planes and tanks, Stalin dispatched newly named deputy defense commissar Lev Mekhlis to Khabarovsk, with armed escorts and replacement military officers—referred to locally as the "Black Hundred" (like the vigilantes under tsarism).[177] It was the end of the line for the thirty-eight-year Soviet Far East NKVD boss, Lyushkov.

Lyushkov, however, failed to show up to greet Mekhlis. Yezhov had already formally relieved the loyal Lyushkov of his post (May 26, 1938), under the pretext of a future unspecified assignment in the central NKVD, but Lyushkov knew this constituted a death warrant and, taking advantage of his close relationship with Yezhov, managed to stall his return to Moscow. (Yezhov apparently sent an emissary to arrest him out in the Far East.) On June 9, Lyushkov told his deputy he had to travel to the frontier zone for a meeting with a very important agent. He went by train from Khabarovsk to Vladivostok, then by car to Posyet, inspected the local border guard detachments, and on June 12 went out to the purported agent-rendezvous spot. Leaving his one companion at a distance, and wearing "a disguise"—mufti and hunting cap, under which he wore his full dress NKVD uniform—Lyushkov got lost in the rain and darkness. Near the Hunchun River, however, he found two Manchukuo border guards and willingly gave himself up, revealing his officer's garments underneath. Imagine the lowly guards' frame of mind: in the middle of nowhere, out of the predawn morning mists, appeared not some wayward small-fry contraband trader, but a man wearing an NKVD uniform and carrying a party card, Supreme Soviet elected representative ID, and papers signed by Yezhov identifying him as commissar of state security, third rank, equivalent to a major general in the Imperial Japanese Army.

Moscow officialdom was shaken. Was there an explanatory note? Did the Japanese kidnap Lyushkov? Yezhov cried and cried, blurting out, "Now I'm lost."[178] He informed Stalin, but omitted mention of the interrogation "testimonies" against Lyushkov and of how he had long shielded him from arrest.[179] On June 15, 1938, Lyushkov's wife, Nina, was arrested in their Moscow apartment, and accused of having known about but failed to report her husband's planned defection.[180] That evening, Blyukher showed up in Yezhov's office to inquire about the Lyushkov situation and, no doubt, his own standing. Right at that moment, Yezhov was summoned to the Little Corner. Stalin decided to send the Lyushkov nemesis Frinovsky to Khabarovsk, more than 5,000 miles by train, to ascertain what had happened; he departed on June 17. Mekhlis, meanwhile, flew back from the Soviet Far East and, on June 20, gave a report in the Little Corner, after which Stalin immediately sent him eastward again, to further annihilate the cadres in the Siberian and Transbaikal military districts, on the way to renewed massacres of the Soviet Far Eastern Army.[181]

Whether by happenstance or calculation, the border point with Manchukuo that Lyushkov had crossed, some eighty miles southwest of Vladivostok, fell under the jurisdiction of the Japanese Korean Army, rather than the more rabid Kwantung Army, which might have refused to yield such a prize catch once they had determined his bona fides. The Korean Army's Russian-language linguist on-site concluded that Lyushkov constituted "the escape of the century" and radioed headquarters in Seoul; despite suspicions that he was a plant, Lyushkov was whisked to Tokyo. A Japanese Kwantung Army intelligence officer, chafing at his lack of opportunity to interrogate Lyushkov, leaked word of the defection to the Chinese-language press in Manchukuo on June 24; Polish military intelligence picked up the obscure newspaper sensation immediately, even before Frinovsky had a chance to clarify in person what had happened. Nazi newspapers reported the defection on July 1, thereby alerting Japanese diplomats in Moscow.

Japanese military intelligence released a statement by Lyushkov, which the *Yomiuri Shimbun* published on July 3, 1938. "Until recently, I committed great crimes against the people as I actively collaborated with Stalin in the conduct of his policy of deception and terror," the statement read. "I am genuinely a traitor. But I am a traitor only to Stalin." Lyushkov, from direct experience, called the Kirov murder investigation "fatal for the country, just as for the party," and divulged that the interrogation protocols for Kamenev and Zinoviev were lies. (Lyushkov would tell his Japanese interrogators that the fabrications in connection with the Kirov murder had launched his doubts about the Soviet system.) "Nikolayev did not belong to Zinoviev's group," Lyushkov's published statement read. "He was an abnormal person who suffered from megalomania. He decided to perish in order to become an historical hero. This is evident from his diary." Lyushkov labeled all the trials of 1936 through 1938 "utterly fabricated," a result of Stalin's "hypersuspiciousness" and "his firm determination to rid himself of all Trotskyites and rightists who . . . could present political danger in the future." And, Lyushkov added, hundreds of thousands of innocent people were being arrested. He further noted that Stalin had sought to provoke the war between China and Japan in order that each would weaken the other, with the ultimate aim of Bolshevizing China.[182] Lyushkov asserted that the arrests of so many alleged saboteurs had provoked actual, if silent, sabotage: people were working indifferently or giving in to carelessness on the railways and in factories because of anger at the arrest of innocents.[183]

WINDFALL FOR JAPANESE INTELLIGENCE

Stalin's terror, allegedly aimed at eliminating foreign agents inside the USSR, had manufactured one in Genrikh Lyushkov, now an invaluable spy/informant for the Japanese. Nothing had ever happened before to Stalin that reached this level—not the case of his former aide Boris Bazhanov, who had escaped abroad in 1928, not even Trotsky's foreign deportation in 1929. Lyushkov had carried with him a dramatic, damning letter addressed to the Central Committee from General Albert Lapin, a Far Eastern Air Force commander, who had committed suicide on September 21, 1937, in his cell at Khabarovsk prison. "I served the Soviet

Government faithfully for 17 years," Lapin wrote. "Do I deserve to be treated like this? I don't have the strength to endure anymore." Lapin's note was written in blood.[184]

Out of the public eye, Lyushkov gave the Japanese a detailed overview of the Soviet Far East, from the number of trucks and how many were out of commission to the condition of all railroads and airports, the training and use of Chinese and Korean agents, Soviet signals intelligence, and the exact numbers and locations of Red Army and NKVD troops east of Lake Baikal (400,000), along with the airplanes (nearly 2,000) and submarines (90). Lyushkov assessed the Soviet Far Eastern Army negatively, pointing to a lack of reserves and infrastructure, out-of-commission artillery and aviation, insufficient training, and dismal organization. He especially singled out an absence of senior command personnel, thanks to the rampages of Mekhlis. Lyushkov conceded that Blyukher believed these shortcomings could be remedied, but he attributed that to Blyukher's fears of allowing Moscow to learn the real situation. In any case, Lyushkov told the Japanese that Stalin had already lost confidence in Blyukher. Provocatively, he also told his Japanese handlers that Blyukher and even Voroshilov had concluded that the Soviets should launch a preemptive strike, because war with Japan was inevitable and Japan was vulnerable, owing to its invasion of China. Hence, the Soviet buildup was far from defensive. Lyushkov even outlined what he said were contingency plans for a Soviet attack. He evidently aimed to precipitate a Japanese-Soviet war to dislodge the murderous despot.

Lyushkov had rare firsthand information about the man in the Kremlin and his "abnormal suspicion," an assessment he said was widely shared among those who interacted with Stalin.[185] "In Stalin's [mind], there was fear of the lack of preparedness for war and chiefly an acute fear of plotters, especially in the army," Lyushkov surmised, adding that the despot feared that "a war might be utilized for revolution" *against* him. He stated that Stalin harbored little confidence in the stability of Chiang Kai-shek, and was worried about a possible attack in the west by Germany. Finally, Lyushkov said the Soviet leader suspected Japan was using second- and third-line divisions in China, saving its best for a fight against the USSR.[186]

Richard Sorge, the Soviet military intelligence asset in Nazi Germany's Tokyo embassy, confirmed the damage from the defection. Berlin had sent an intelligence officer to Tokyo to take part in debriefing Lyushkov, and Sorge obtained the German embassy's copy of the classified report, which showed that Lyushkov had told the Japanese of deep internal dissatisfaction with Stalin, and asserted that the Red Army "might collapse in a day" if Japan attacked.[187] Sorge reported that Lyushkov was laying bare for the USSR's mortal enemy how the Soviet system actually functioned, as well as what Soviet officials and ordinary folk actually thought—even what Stalin thought. Sorge concluded that "Lyushkov was an inexhaustible treasure trove of information about the Red Army, the NKVD, the party, and the dynamics of the Soviet people at large."[188]

And then it happened again: on July 9, 1938, the NKVD's Orlov, in Catalonia, received a coded telegram from Yezhov ordering him to a Soviet ship docked at Antwerp for a rendezvous with an unnamed person who would be known to him. Orlov removed $60,000 from the safe, a colossal sum in those days, and fled. According to one NKVD insider, Orlov had guessed wrong: he was being recalled not to be executed but to be named the latest head of NKVD foreign intelligence. Be that as it may, he stole away, with wife and daughter, to Canada and then the United States. Yezhov hesitated to inform Stalin of this second major terror-induced defection. Orlov knew a great deal, from the details of Soviet involvement in Spain, such as the murder of POUM leader Andreu Nin, to the identities of Soviet undercover agents in Europe.[189] But apparently he sent a personal letter to Yezhov about his desire merely to escape execution by his own side.[190] Orlov, a Jew and a dedicated leftist, defected not to Nazi Germany but to oblivion.[191] This was a stroke of luck Stalin did not deserve.

Even the most damaging defection Stalin had ever suffered, an act caused by his terror, did not induce him to relent. On the contrary, back in the Soviet Far East, Frinovsky and Mekhlis went on a post-Lyushkov rampage. If in 1937, 2,969 military officers in the Soviet Far East had been dismissed, of whom 383 had been arrested, in 1938 another 2,272 would be dismissed, of whom 865 would be arrested.[192] Frinovsky now also had the task of "reinforcing" Soviet borders in the east. The NKVD began evacuating every single inhabitant within two miles of the border and established a shoot-on-sight zone, rendering infiltration of would-be Japanese agents suicidal, which became equally true of further attempts at defection from the Soviet side.[193] But the Japanese already had the crown jewels. Sorge, in his reports with photographed documents to Moscow, underscored that, like German defectors from Nazism, Lyushkov exaggerated the extent to which the regime he deserted was ready to fall, but Sorge speculated that Japan and Germany, seizing upon the weaknesses that Lyushkov was spelling out, might take combined military action against the USSR.[194] That, of course, constituted the single most frightening scenario for Stalin, a possible outcome of his own wanton terror.

"THE INEVITABLE WAR" (NEARLY)

On July 6, 1938, Japanese Kwantung Army signal operators intercepted and were able to decode a message to Soviet Far Eastern Army headquarters in Khabarovsk from a frontier commander who recommended that Soviet border troops secure unoccupied high ground on the western edge of Lake Khasan. The Japanese government, already incensed at Soviet military aid to China, had its eye on the strategic heights.[195] The spot—near the confluence of the Soviet Union, Korea (a Japanese colony), and Manchukuo (a Japanese puppet state)—was known in Russian as Zaozernaya, meaning "Beyond the Lake" (in Chinese it was called Changkufeng, or "Tight Drum Peaks," and in Japanese, Chōkohō). This ill-defined waste, ten miles inland from the Sea of Japan and perilously close to Vladivostok, comprised marsh and sandy hills and suffered daytime temperatures up to 120 degrees Fahrenheit, with chilly nights. It was effectively uninhabited, but it overlooked the Korean port city of Rajin-Sonbong, as well as the strategic railways across northern Korea and into Manchukuo.[196] On July 9, in the name of "preventing the Japanese from taking the hilltop, given its advantageousness for surveillance over our territory," about thirty NKVD border troops seized Beyond the Lake, dug trenches, and strung barbed wire.[197]

Four days after the Soviet border action, Lyushkov gave an international press conference at the Sanno Hotel, in Tokyo, to refute the doubters of his bona fides, and further hammered at Stalin's prestige. "What caused you to betray your country?" an English correspondent asked. Lyushkov replied, "We need to kill Stalin."[198]

On July 15, Japan's military attaché and chargé d'affaires in Moscow demanded the removal of the new pillboxes on Beyond the Lake, claiming that they stood on Manchukuo territory (based on the Japanese interpretation of the 1860 Convention of Peking, between imperial Russia and the Qing empire). Blyukher sent his own army commission to the heights and, based on its findings, accused the NKVD's Frinovsky of having violated the Manchukuo frontier, dissension that the Japanese picked up.[199] Blyukher suspected a provocation by Frinovsky and Mekhlis to trap and bring him down by precipitating a war. His suspicions were far from crazy. The Soviet Far Eastern Army had not been involved in the action: Frinovsky had avoided coordinating anything with a soon-to-be enemy of the people. Blyukher angrily telegraphed Frinovsky, with a copy to Yezhov, warning that "some bastard might create a military conflict" and demanding that "all suspicious people who might intentionally aggravate the situation" be removed. Frinovsky, in turn, sent damning reports on Blyukher to Moscow.[200] On July 27, unbeknownst to Frinovsky or Mekhlis, Blyukher secretly telegrammed Voroshilov that the border violators were the NKVD, not the Japanese. But on July 28, Voroshilov strongly rebuffed Blyukher, insisting that the Japanese were the culprits, while pointedly addressing himself also to Frinovsky and Mekhlis, thereby revealing Blyukher's private communication. Voroshilov, behind both Frinovsky's and Blyukher's backs, directed Mekhlis to "investigate this case" and report on Blyukher.[201] This was how a great power conducted itself in the face of a potent military foe.[202]

By spring 1938, Japanese forces in Manchukuo numbered 300,000, which meant that, with a mobilization of reservists, the Japanese could now match the Soviet Far Eastern Army in numbers, if not in tanks and aircraft.[203] Moreover, Stalin knew that Japanese troops were massing near Lake Khasan. How they would respond to the Soviet border "strengthening" remained unclear.[204] Many officials in Tokyo viewed as inadvisable the launching of a second-front war against the Soviet Union before completing China's conquest. But because Stalin had backed down over the Amur River border incident in June 1937 and had murdered so many Red Army officers as "foreign agents," and because Lyushkov had just defected with a bonanza of information, others in Tokyo contemplated the benefits of testing Soviet resolve and reflexes.[205] Lake Khasan fell within the jurisdiction of the Japanese Korean Army, but hawks in the Japanese Kwantung Army indicated that they would step in should their counterparts shrink from taking action. "We still were not particularly enthusiastic," one Korean Army officer recalled, "but now the Kwantung Army came along and booted us in the ass." This could have been it: the war Stalin feared, precipitated by minions following his orders to arrest and murder his own loyal military men.

Emperor Hirohito appeared to come to Stalin's rescue: after a series of audiences in Tokyo on July 20, the emperor, finding himself unimpressed with the contradictory reports and wary of his military's adventurism, withheld authorization for a full-scale war.[206] Japanese soldiers were ordered to withdraw. Nonetheless, events spiraled: Soviet border guards occupied a second high point, referred to as "Nameless," and on July 29 a local Japanese border unit commander—without formal approval from Japanese Korean Army headquarters (in Seoul) or supreme headquarters (in Tokyo), but with the connivance of his local division commander—used the pretext of these additional Soviet patrols to cross the Tumen River with three battalions. In a firefight, the Japanese units were repulsed.[207] But citing this Soviet "provocation" and "buildup," the local Japanese garrison launched a second frontal assault, called by them a "counterattack," on the night of July 30–31, and this time they succeeded in driving off the NKVD border troops and capturing both Beyond the Lake and Nameless, with heavy losses on each side. Japanese headquarters accepted the fait accompli. Stalin perceived that To-kyo was deliberately testing his resolve and had Voroshilov issue an order, on July 31, to annihilate the enemy.[208]

Sorge apologized for having failed to forewarn Moscow that a Japanese action on the frontier was imminent (in fact, it had been an unforeseeable local initia-tive). In the same coded radio communication, on August 1, 1938, he conveyed that the German ambassador and military attaché had learned that the Japanese wanted to settle the dispute by diplomatic means, but only after seizing the heights.[209] When Sorge's communication reached Stalin, if at all, and what heed the despot might have paid to it remain unclear.[210] Stalin's hypersuspiciousness and categorical judgments were a long-standing problem for Soviet intelligence. He had previously dismissed vouchsafed information supplied by Sorge as "dis-orientation emanating from German circles."[211] In any case, Stalin was deter-mined to make up for his climbdown in summer 1937—when he had just launched the murders of Red Army commanders—and to erase doubts about the "purged" Red Army.

To unleash a concentrated assault, Blyukher had to import more troops to the remote frontier zone, which took time. He also had to contend with potentially deadly intrigues from the unprincipled Mekhlis, as well as Frinovsky, who exer-cised command over the NKVD border guard troops yet adamantly refused to coordinate; both were denouncing Blyukher behind his back to Stalin. On Au-gust 1, 1938, an accusatory Stalin called Blyukher on the high-frequency phone:

STALIN: Tell me, Blyukher, why is the order of the defense commissar for aerial bombardment of all our territory occupied by the Japanese including the Zaozernaya Heights not being implemented?

BLYUKHER: Reporting. The air force is ready to take off. The takeoff was delayed by adverse meteorological circumstances. This very minute [air force commander Pavel] Rychagov has ordered planes into the air to attack, not taking weather into account. . . . The aviation is taking off right now, but I fear that we will hit our own units and Korean settlements with this bombing.

STALIN: Tell me honestly, comrade Blyukher, do you wish to fight with the Japanese for real? If you do not have such a wish, tell me directly, as becomes a Communist; if you have such a desire, I would think you ought to go out to the site straightaway. I do not understand your fear that the bombing will hit the Korean population, and your fear that the air force cannot carry out its mission because of fog. . . . What do the Koreans matter to you, if the Japanese are hitting batches of our people? What does a little cloudiness mean for Bolshevik aviation if it is really going to defend the honor of its Motherland? I await an answer.

BLYUKHER: The air force has been ordered into the air. . . . Your directives are being implemented and will be implemented with Bolshevik precision.[212]

Not a hint of humanity: pitiless raison d'état.

Blyukher, without waiting for the full contingent of reinforcements, responded to Stalin's prompt: he assigned Grigory Stern, his new chief of staff and a veteran of the Spanish civil war whom Stalin esteemed, to evict the Japanese. But on August 2–3, 1938, the Japanese troops, holding the heights, forced the Soviets to advance through heavily exposed corridors, which, in addition, were inhospitable to tanks, and repelled Stern's assault. Stalin's insistence on immediate engagement had produced a Soviet bloodbath.

The Soviets rebuffed a Japanese proffer on August 4 of a cease-fire.[213] On August 7, Blyukher was ordered out of the combat zone. That same day and the next, Stern led a renewed air and land assault, this time massive. A total of more than 30,000 troops were deployed, counting both sides. But because of the Japanese emperor's refusal to countenance a possible wider war, even as the Soviet air force conducted large-scale bombing of Japanese rear positions in Korea, the Japanese did not employ air power or artillery even on the front lines. Still, on August 8, Sorge radioed from his sources out of Tokyo that "advocates of strong military action against the USSR are increasing."[214] The emperor was coming around to urgent pleas to allow stronger engagement, if only in self-defense. After the Japanese advanced more Kwantung Army units to the frontier—forces that could attack from the rear and trap Soviet forces on the heights "like a rat in a sack"—Stalin finally agreed to a cease-fire on August 11. Litvinov boasted to Soviet representatives abroad that "Japan has received a lesson, assured of our firmness and will to resist, and of the illusory nature of aid from Germany."[215] In fact, matters had gotten very close to full escalation. And what Nazi Germany might have done in those circumstances remains an open question.[216]

Be that as it may, Stalin and the Red Army were ultimately spared not by Soviet resolve or Japanese circumspection but by China. Soviet-Japanese hostilities took place concurrently with the titanic Battle of Wuhan (June–October 1938), where the Chinese government had shifted its military industries and where more than 1 million Chinese troops, commanded by Chiang himself, massed against Japanese forces who aimed for a decisive showdown. In the event, the Imperial Japanese Army would manage to seize Wuhan, China's second-largest city, but at a staggering cost of 100,000 Japanese casualties.[217] Tokyo, which militarily was now both mired in China and engaged with the Soviet Union, continued to beseech Berlin for conversion of the Anti-Comintern Pact into a formal military alliance directed against Moscow. Hitler was interested insofar as such an alliance would apply to Britain and France as well, thereby bringing them to heel in Europe by threatening their colonial empires in Asia. Stalin was privy to these talks from Sorge, in detail, including the many sticking points.[218]

Stalin's wager on Chiang had returned dividends. The Chinese leader had managed to stalemate Japan's land army. Chiang had also firmly rebuffed the Chinese Communists' demands to arm the workers for "revolutionary war" against the Japanese.[219] It is easy to see why. "The seizure of power by armed force, the settlement of the issue of war, is the central task and the highest form of revolution," Mao averred to a China Communist party plenum in the second half of 1938, adding that Chiang, whom the Communist leader deemed a counterrevolutionary, "has held firmly to the vital point that whoever has an army has power, that war decides everything. In this respect we ought to learn from him."[220] Stalin had no desire to see Chiang's Nationalists fall to the Japanese because of Chinese Communist treason behind the lines. Nor did he want to provoke Tokyo and Berlin into overcoming their differences. Still, he proved unyielding with Japan over the disputed border at Lake Khasan, insisting on the status quo antebellum, and, for now, got his way. The Japanese political leadership took a step back. At the same time, Japanese military hawks of a self-fashioned "north strike" school became more emboldened in their zeal to test the Red Army.[221] They would be back.

As Stalin well knew, it had taken the Red Army nearly ten days of ferocious combat to dislodge a limited number of Japanese troops, who, additionally, were fighting with their hands partly tied by their emperor. The Soviets lost 792 killed, 3,279 wounded; Japanese casualties amounted to 526 killed and 913 wounded—2,600 fewer.[222] "We were not sufficiently quick in our tactics, and particularly in combined operations, in dealing the enemy a concentrated blow," Voroshilov would observe, taking no responsibility himself. He added, again with no personal liability, "It was discovered that the Far Eastern theater was poorly prepared for war (roads, bridges, communications)."[223] Voroshilov could have noted further that the Soviet officer corps, including almost every one of Blyukher's deputies and aides, had been massacred and terrorized, and that Blyukher himself had been sandbagged and sidelined by his own side. Still, whether Blyukher, any more than those sitting in judgment of him, really was up to the challenges of modern warfare remained unclear.[224] On August 16, 1938, Voroshilov summoned the marshal to Moscow for an accounting. Six days later, Lavrenti Beria was named to a new post in the capital. Beria's and Blyukher's paths would soon cross.

FIRST DEPUTY NKVD USSR

Why Stalin let Yezhov remain at the helm for so long remains mysterious. By summer 1938, the insanity in the NKVD had gotten to the point that at least one newly appointed provincial NKVD chief released large numbers of prisoners and wrote to Lubyanka about the outrageous falsifications.[225] Vlas Chubar, the government deputy head, in a memo to Stalin, Molotov, and Voroshilov dated June 16, 1938, pointed out the glaring discrepancies between Soviet mobilization plans for war and the resources at hand.[226] That same day, Chubar was expelled from the politburo (the resolution cited "testimony" of arrested politburo candidate members).[227] The next day, he was demoted to the directorship of a pulp-and-paper factory construction site in Solikamsk, a Gulag camp. On June 25, Malenkov informed Stalin that Chubar, through the Central Committee book-ordering service, had requested copies of Trotsky's *Permanent Revolution,* as well as his *Stalin School of Falsification* and *My Life,* and several issues of the Menshevik émigré *Socialist Herald.*[228]

Yezhov had retreated to his dacha in Meshcherino and fallen into a near-perpetual bender. "I literally went out of my mind," he would write of Lyushkov's defection in a letter to Stalin. "I summoned Frinovsky and proposed that we together report to you. Alone I could not do it. At that time Frinovsky said, 'Now they will punish us big-time.'"[229] Frinovsky had been sent away from Moscow, leaving the NKVD without either a functioning commissar or a resident first deputy. Yezhov—resentful, even irate, at Stalin—schemed to name his own new first deputy, settling on Litvin, who by summer 1938 was running the Leningrad NKVD. Litvin had even come to Moscow a few times, expecting Yezhov to have the appointment finalized, but it never happened. Instead, Stalin had Malenkov, in the party apparatus's personnel department, compile a list of candidates.

Malenkov and his aides came up with Fyodor Kuznetsov (b. 1904), deputy head for political propaganda in the Red Army; Nikolai Gusarov (b. 1905), party secretary of Sverdlovsk city, in the Urals; Nikolai Pegov (b. 1905), a green apparatchik in Malenkov's department; and Sergei Kruglov (b. 1907), an even greener functionary in Malenkov's department.[230] These names, many of whom were creatures of Malenkov, constituted a ridiculous attempt to assert control over the NKVD. But Malenkov's otherwise self-serving list did include the one actual candidate.

Beria by now had seventeen years' experience in the highest executive ranks of the secret police and the party, in a major region. Frinovsky had served as secret police head in Azerbaijan in the early 1930s, so he knew Beria's abilities and character, and Frinovsky, with Yezhov, in their pathetic way, had been trying to assemble compromising materials on him, including a report (dated March 26, 1938) on abuses by Beria and his henchman Dekanozov in the Georgian party organization.[231] In May 1938, Yezhov and Frinovsky had sought to use former Azerbaijan NKVD chief Sumbatov-Topuridze to prepare a case against Beria. On July 1, one of Yezhov's department heads requested the files on the Menshevik government in Georgia, hoping to find evidence of Beria's activities for the wrong side. Frinovsky urged Yezhov to pass these materials to Stalin; Yezhov evidently did so.[232] Stalin could only have been grateful for additional compromising materials to hold over Beria's head.

Matters came to a head in connection with another USSR Supreme Soviet session, which was to open on August 10. Yezhov learned from Israel Dagin, chief of bodyguards, that Beria, who was in town for the Supreme Soviet, had been summoned to the Near Dacha. "That very day," Dagin would testify, "Yezhov phoned me incessantly and one time he started to ask, 'Do you know what they're talking about?' I answered: 'Nikolai Ivanovich, please!' Yezhov stopped speaking on that issue."[233] Eavesdropping on Stalin was a suicidal temptation, but Yezhov was close to that point. The Yezhov favorite Uspensky, NKVD boss of Ukraine, who was also in Moscow for the Supreme Soviet, said he had heard from Isaak Shapiro that "Yezhov has big troubles, since the Central Committee does not trust him. Then Shapiro told me that there are rumors Yezhov was about to get a deputy (he did not name him) whom he needed to beware of."[234]

On a recent occasion at the Near Dacha, according to Khrushchev, Stalin had already told those gathered, "It's necessary to strengthen the NKVD, assist comrade Yezhov, select a deputy for him," and he asked Yezhov for his preference. Yezhov requested Malenkov. "Stalin had the ability to pause in a conversation as if he were thinking over the answer, although he had long ago thought through each question," Khrushchev would observe. "Sure," Stalin finally replied, "Of course, Malenkov would be good, but we cannot give you Malenkov. Malenkov is at the Central Committee in charge of cadres, and then a new question would arise: who would we appoint there?" When Stalin asked for another recommendation, Yezhov said nothing. "So Stalin said, 'What would you think if we gave you Beria for a deputy?' Yezhov was severely startled, but he caught himself and said, 'That's a good candidate. Of course, comrade Beria can do the job, and not only as a deputy. He could be the commissar.'"[235]

On August 21, 1938, the "politburo" officially appointed Beria as first deputy chief of the NKVD under Yezhov. Malenkov, for his part, had a lot to fear, having once been Yezhov's deputy in the party apparatus and been close to him, visiting him at his apartment and dacha, and now Malenkov delivered a long, detailed denunciation of Yezhov to Poskryobyshev, marked FOR STALIN, PERSONALLY.[236] Molotov, meanwhile, had been after Khrushchev to return from Ukraine, where he had just been posted, to serve as Molotov's deputy chairman at the Council of People's Commissars; Stalin had agreed, but Khrushchev had pleaded to remain in Ukraine, and Stalin had yielded to him. At the Near Dacha, Beria had brushed off Khrushchev: "What are you congratulating me for? You yourself did not want to be Molotov's deputy. . . . I also did not want to transfer to Moscow. I'd be better off in Georgia."[237] One of Beria's closest minions, Merkulov, would also testify (in a letter to Khrushchev) that Beria was distraught at being named Yezhov's deputy.[238]

Neither *Pravda* nor *Izvestiya* reported the appointment. That same day, Stalin and Molotov signed the latest execution list (3,176 names). Yezhov received his new "deputy" in his Lubyanka office on the evening of August 22.[239] It must have been stupendously awkward. Yezhov would write to Stalin that "Beria has a power-mongering character. He does not abide subordination. He will never forgive that Budu Mdivani was 'broken' in Moscow and not in Tbilisi. He will never forgive the destruction in Armenia [in September 1937], because it was not his initiative." Yezhov also expressed regret for having allowed "many liberties for Georgia. It was suspicious that Beria wants to eliminate every Chekist who ever worked in Georgia."

Beria immediately departed Moscow for Tbilisi to wind up affairs, while Yezhov again vanished to his dacha in Meshcherino, complaining of headaches and insomnia, heart pain, and lack of appetite and summoning a doctor, who wrote out a prescription for rest. When the prescribed rest elapsed, Yezhov repeated the summons for a doctor and remained at the dacha, not reporting to work, through the end of August. On August 25, 1938, the Supreme Soviet presidium met to discuss a proposal to continue allowing early release from the Gulag for exemplary labor performance, but Stalin asked them to consider using awards instead. "Would it not be possible to keep people in a camp?" he objected. "If we free them, they will return to their old ways. In the camp the atmosphere is different; there it is hard to be spoiled." In time a decree would follow: "Convicts in USSR NKVD camps should serve their sentences in their entirety."[240]

Also on August 25, Frinovsky returned from the Far East to Moscow. At a train station outside the capital, the head of NKVD transport, Boris Berman, entered Frinovsky's carriage and told him he had been appointed naval commissar. Frinovsky responded that he already knew and that he would turn over the NKVD first deputy portfolio to Litvin. "I answered not to Litvin, but to Beria," Berman recalled telling him. "Beria, what?" Frinovsky responded. Right from the Moscow train terminal, he made for Yezhov's dacha. Yezhov greeted him with kisses on the cheek, something that had not happened before. "I had never seen Yezhov in such a depressed state," Frinovsky would testify.[241] Yezhov fantasized about "reorganizing" the NKVD, so as to reduce the power of a first deputy. More prosaically, Yevdokimov, seeking to rehabilitate himself by working like a demon as Yezhov's deputy at the water transport commissariat, warned Frinovsky that the NKVD operatives in prison who had not yet been shot could be reinterrogated, and their cases turned against the Yezhovites. A slew of hurried executions took place before Beria got back to Moscow.[242]

DILEMMAS

Peasants had rebelled en masse against the violence of forced collectivization and dekulakization, and even some party officials had protested. But the terror? A group of Kremlin bodyguards had been carrying loaded pistols on Red Square during the 1937 May Day festivities, within shooting distance of Stalin and the entire leadership; within a few months, they went meekly to their deaths, liquidated as an alleged "assassin corps" working for foreign agents.[243] This seeming passivity confounds to this day.[244] "Isn't it time we started thinking about what is happening in our country?" Pyotr Smorodin, the second secretary of the Leningrad provincial party committee, stated in company during a group lunch at a day resort for party activists. "We have to act before they take us all one at a time, like chickens from their roost!" Everyone present was stupefied. They began to get up and leave, except for a single old friend and the latter's stepdaughter.[245] Many tried to keep a low profile, hoping it would pass. "We all took the easy way out," Nadezhda Mandelstam, wife of the poet and a Gulag survivor, would observe, "by keeping silent in the hope that not we but our neighbors would be killed."[246]

In fact, many people took an active part, cynically or earnestly.[247] A Soviet worker needed to labor for sixty-two hours to purchase a loaf of bread, versus about seventeen minutes for an American—data that Soviet workers did not have, of course, but they all knew their bosses helped themselves to the best supplies and apartments and escaped prosecution for embezzlement or tyrannical comportment. Until now. "You're a wrecker yourself," workers jeered at higher-ups during the terror. "Tomorrow they'll come and arrest you. All you engineers and technicians are wreckers."[248] To be sure, many ordinary people were disgusted by the arrests and executions, and some felt the victims were targeted precisely because they wanted to help workers and peasants. But not a few reasoned that officials, whether or not they were foreign agents, deserved their comeuppance.[249] In 1938, the regime decreed a limit on the size of dacha that an official could have, "in light of the fact that . . . a number of arrested conspirators (Rudzutaks, Rosenholz, Antipov, Mezhlauk, Karakhan, Yagoda, and others) built themselves grandiose dacha-palaces with fifteen–twenty rooms or more, where they lived in luxury and spent the people's money."[250] Fatalism, too, abounded. Iosif Ostrovsky, who, as head of the NKVD administration-organization directorate, supervised construction (hospitals, the Hotel Moskva, the Council of People's Commissars building), was arrested. "You know I never would have thought that I would be incarcerated in the prison whose construction I directed," Ostrovsky was said to have mused in Lefortovo (originally erected in 1881 but expanded). "But the prison is very well constructed; you can't complain."[251] He was shot.

Part of what looks like passivity was ideological. The writer Alexander Afinogenov, expelled from the party and awaiting arrest at his dacha in the privileged Peredelkino writers' colony in Moscow's outskirts, his plays now banned, had recorded in his diary (December 25, 1937) that he "turned to the radio, for the latest news, and a strange thing happened: ordinary news about life in our country, our people, their words and aspirations, lifted me up immediately; it was as if I had washed in cold water after a day of exhausting reflections." He claimed that his sense of profound isolation was broken when he "engaged with the life of the whole country, again felt the grandeur of this life and understood the insignificance of my own minor difficulties."[252] As of 1938, the USSR had 1,838 sanatoriums, 1,270 recreational facilities, and 12,000 pioneer camps for children, and they were all in heavy usage. That year, Afinogenov was reinstated in the party.

People's fates were often random, and not because Stalin intentionally sought to sow still greater dread by arbitrariness, but with little apparent rhyme or reason.[253] Jenő Varga courageously wrote to the despot (March 28, 1938), with copies to Dimitrov and Yezhov, about the "dangerous atmosphere of panic" among foreigners whose children were cursed at school as fascists. "This demoralization is enveloping the majority of Comintern workers and is spreading even to individual members of the Executive Committee Secretariat," Varga wrote of the Hotel Lux. "Many foreigners gather up their belongings every evening in expectation of arrest. Many are half mad and incapable of working because of constant fear." Varga had served under Béla Kun in the Hungarian Soviet Republic. Kun was arrested and executed (August 29, 1938); Varga survived.[254] Similarly, while one Red Army commander extremely close to Stalin, the civil war crony Marshal Yegorov, was executed, another, Marshal Budyonny, was spared, even though both had been subjects of a torrent of denunciations (the Red Army men *not* shot had essentially identical files to those who were shot, often from the same "testimony").[255] Among regime literati, Mikhail Koltsov was arrested and executed ("Remember," he had instructed Louis Aragon, the leftist French writer, in Paris, "Stalin is always right").[256] But Ilya Ehrenburg, who, like Koltsov, had been in Spain and was secretly denounced by all and sundry, survived. "May I ask you something?" a young writer (who had been five years old in 1938) would later inquire of Ehrenburg. "How was it that you survived?" Ehrenburg answered, "I shall never know."[257]

Yet another person inexplicably not arrested was Demyan Bedny. The NKVD had produced a devastating overview of his "anti-Sovietism" on September 9, 1938, a few months after the poet was expelled from the party and the Union of Soviet Writers. "D. Bedny systematically expressed his resentment against comrades Stalin, Molotov, and other leaders. . . . 'I adhered to the party, 99.9 percent of which comprised spies and provocateurs. Stalin is a horrible person and often guided by personal accounts. All great leaders have always surrounded themselves with a galaxy of brilliant companions; who has Stalin created? He has annihilated everyone, there is no one, all destroyed. Such a situation occurred only under Ivan the Terrible.'" Bedny was said to have called the mass accusations baseless. "The army has been utterly destroyed; trust and command have been undermined; it is impossible to fight with such an army. Myself, under these conditions, I would concede half of Ukraine just to keep from being attacked.

Such a talented strategist as Tukhachevsky has been destroyed." Bedny called the new constitution a "fiction," and the elections to the Supreme Soviet a sham. He even criticized Stalin's holy of holies, the collective farms, for their absence of incentives. The NKVD concluded that "several times he expressed his intention to commit suicide." That Bedny said all these things was plausible, although the NKVD material did not need to be actually true in order for Stalin to act on it. For whatever reason, he refrained from ordering or authorizing an arrest.[258]

Of course, some people survived for abundantly clear reasons: Stalin deliberately spared the tarnished Khrushchev and Beria, among others, because he liked them. Stalin had allowed the writer Aleksei Tolstoy to be elected as a Supreme Soviet delegate from Leningrad.[259] Hundreds of Soviet inhabitants poured their hearts out to Tolstoy in his capacity as a deputy, and, for whatever reason, he held on to their acts of bravery. "Can it really be that there is no defense from careerists, toadies, and cowards who earn their bread on each slogan, yesterday for collectivization, today for vigilance?" wrote an architect whose brother had been arrested. "Can it really be that you, deputies, are created only in order to shout hurrah for Stalin and to applaud Yezhov?" The letter writer asked Tolstoy to pass his signed letter to Stalin. "I am not mad," he added. "I have a family, a son, work that I love. . . . But right now the feeling of truth is stronger than the fear of ten years in the camps." A woman wrote to pillory Tolstoy's story "Grain" for its mendacities and glorification of Stalin. "The best people, who are devoted to Lenin's ideas, honest and unbought, are sitting behind bars, arrested by the thousands, being executed," she told him, withholding her name. "They cannot bear the grandiose Baseness triumphing throughout the land. . . . And you, an engineer of the human soul, are cowardly turned inside out, and we saw the unseemly inside of a purchasable hack. . . . Fear: that's the dominant feeling that has seized citizens of the USSR. And you do not see that? . . . Where is the majestic pathos that in October [1917] moved millions to fight to the death? Overcome by the fetid breath of Stalin and of yes-men like you."[260]

Some targets of the terror had come to understand how the epoch stamped them. Theodore Maly, the Soviet spy, had been born in Temesvár (Timișoara), in the Austro-Hungarian empire, in 1894, studied to become a Catholic priest, got conscripted during the Great War, was imprisoned in a series of tsarist POW camps, and ended up in Siberia, where he joined the Cheka. The tall, urbane ethnic Hungarian was able to pose as an Austrian, German, Swiss, or Brit. In July 1937, when he received a summons to return to Moscow, he knew its import— execution—but he went back. Before doing so, he attempted to explain this decision to Elisabeth Poretsky, whose husband, Ignace Reiss (Ignace Poretsky), also worked in Soviet intelligence and would defect. "I saw all the horrors, young men with frozen limbs dying in the trenches" during the Great War, Maly told her. "We were all covered with vermin and many were dying of typhus. I lost my faith in God and when the revolution broke out I joined the Bolsheviks." During the civil war, Maly continued, "we would pass burning villages which had changed hands several times in a day. . . . Our Red detachments would 'clean up' villages exactly the way the Whites did. What was left of the inhabitants, old men, women, children, were machine-gunned for having given assistance to the enemy. I could not stand the wailing of women. I simply could not." Then came collectivization: "I knew what we were doing to the peasants, how many were deported, how many were shot."[261] Maly also had to know that the NKVD could easily kill him abroad (as would happen to Reiss, in Lausanne, Switzerland). After Maly returned to Moscow, he was duly arrested, "convicted" of spying for Germany, and executed (September 20, 1938).[262] Maly was among legions of functionaries who carried baggage.[263]

BERIA MEETS BLYUKHER

In Georgia, Beria tried to implant his protégé Valerian Bakradze as his successor, but Stalin blocked him. Instead, on August 31, 1938, he was replaced by Candide Charkviani, the third secretary, who was thirty-one years old and would try to erect his own local machine.[264] On August 31 in Moscow, Blyukher appeared before the Main Military Council, chaired by Voroshilov, with Budyonny, Kulik, and two other high military officers, as well as Molotov and Stalin. Frinovsky attended, too. The group roundly castigated the marshal for Lake Khasan's high casualties and disorganization, and for false reporting. Voroshilov and Frinovsky accused him of gross incompetence "bordering on conscious defeatism." Stalin removed Blyukher from the Far Eastern command.[265] Voroshilov recommended Blyukher take a holiday and await his next assignment and gave him his own dacha at Bocharov Ruchei, near Lake Ritsa.[266] On September 4, 1938, the semi-autonomous Far Eastern Army was divided into three separate armies, each subordinated directly to Voroshilov.[267] On September 8, Stalin officially named Frinovsky naval commissar. On September 13, Beria spent nearly two hours in the Little Corner with Molotov, Zhdanov, and Yezhov, beginning past midnight.[268] He got an office in Lubyanka on the third floor, next to Yezhov's. On

September 29, Beria would officially be named head of the NKVD Main Directorate of State Security (GUGB), the secret police within the secret police.

Pravda (October 3, 1938) published a photo of Mikheil Gelovani playing Stalin in *The Man with the Gun,* a film adaptation of the play about soldiers in the October Revolution. (Maxim Strauch played Lenin.) Gelovani (b. 1893), who worked at the Rustaveli, in Tbilisi, was descended from an ancient Georgian princely house. He had first played Stalin in *They Wanted Peace,* which also premiered in 1938 and was set in 1917, and displaced Semyon Goldstab, whom Stalin had not especially liked.[269] With makeup and fake mustache, Gelovani resembled Stalin closely, except for his height and his thin neck (which had to be hidden), and managed to mimic Stalin's Georgian accent to perfection. He brought the despot to life. Mikheil Chiaureli, the Georgian director and screenwriter, who had cast Gelovani, kept him from Stalin, trying to monopolize his own access. Chiaureli recalled the film's screening in the Kremlin cinema. Stalin sat in the front row; behind him were Molotov and Voroshilov, film boss Semyon Dukelsky, and the director. After the lights came on, a long, awkward silence ensued. Stalin, silently, got up to exit. At the door, he suddenly turned and said, "I didn't know—it turns out that I'm so charming. Well done!"[270]

Beria's appointment to Moscow invited conversations about Stalin's own Georgian origins. Whispers had long ago spread of a "Caucasus group" atop the regime: Stalin, Orjonikidze, Yenukidze, Mikoyan. In effect, Beria was taking Orjonikidze's place in the inner circle. "At that time I thought that Stalin wanted a Georgian in the NKVD," Khrushchev would recall. "We thought at the time that the whole matter was that he was from the Caucasus, a Georgian, closer to Stalin not only as a party member but as a person of the same ethnicity."[271] In fact, Stalin detested reminders of his Georgianness, and yet he was willing to incur this risk, demonstrating just how much he prized Gelovani—and valued and needed Beria.

Inside the Soviet police, first-class sadists were fewer than one might think. Boris Rodos, in that context, stood out, a "chopper" (*kolun*) who could reliably smash those under "interrogation" to *near* death. He would snap a whip across a prisoner's legs, continuing after he collapsed to the floor, pour freezing water over him, then force him to scoop his diarrhea with his tin cup and swallow, then shout, "Sign! Sign!"[272] ("An insignificant man with the mental horizon of a chicken," Khrushchev would later say.) Rodos's children, who knew nothing of their father's work, observed phone calls at all hours, prompting him to awake, shave, put on his uniform, and go downstairs for a waiting car; when he got home, sometimes only after several days, he would wash and wash his hands and arms up to his elbows, like a surgeon.[273] Rodos was assigned to people like the arch-Stalinist Roberts Eihe, an early winner of the Order of Lenin (1935) and a polit-buro candidate member who, in Western Siberia, had signed execution lists with tens of thousands of names, before his own turn came. From prison Eihe wrote to Stalin how, "throughout the entire time of my work in Siberia, I decisively and mercilessly implemented the party line"—a statement of pristine truth.[274] At the Sukhanovka prison, where Beria kept an office, Rodos beat Eihe senseless, not desisting even after Eihe crumbled into an unconscious heap. When Eihe was raised and again refused to admit to Beria, standing nearby, that he was a spy for Latvia, Rodos went after him again. One of Eihe's eyes popped out.[275]

Many targets like Eihe were beaten not only in Beria's presence but by Beria himself, something Stalin never did. "An intriguer, a careerist, a bloodthirsty, amoral debauchee," observed one high-level NKVD operative in Georgia who was arrested and sent to the Gulag. "If he [Beria] had to eliminate someone from his path, he removed him. If he had to occupy someone's place, he intrigued and compromised that person, achieving his removal."[276] Of course, such an unsa-vory reputation was a source of power: Who wanted to be on the wrong side of Beria? Minions gravitated toward a winner. They found Beria a severe, demand-ing boss, assigning tough tasks on strict deadlines and brooking no excuses. But for those who met the challenges, Beria afforded strong support and even some freedom of action, eliciting fierce loyalty. They feared but also admired him as a professional in police work and a patron. Beria got them apartments, the best provisions, and higher salaries and cash bonuses. He had no qualms about acting like a cold-blooded murderer, but, equally Stalin-like, he took care of his peo-ple.[277] He was a hangman, but far more. "Beria was an industrious person, not a loafer [*shaliai-valiai*]; he was a big-time functionary," recalled a member of the Egnatashvili clan—the clan of Stalin's surrogate father—who hated and feared Beria. "It's necessary to look truth in the eye: he was really capable of getting things done. It was another question at what price? But whatever was delegated to him, he carried it out."[278]

On October 22, 1938, NKVD operatives appeared at Voroshilov's dacha, where the thirty-nine-year-old Blyukher and his twenty-three-year-old wife were stay-ing. They arrested the couple and took them to Moscow.[279] Yezhov had signed the order, but Beria oversaw the interrogation in Lefortovo. Back in summer 1937, Stalin had said that Tukhachevsky and Gamarnik, on orders from the Japanese, had tried to remove Blyukher from command of the Soviet Far Eastern Army;

now, in fall 1938, Stalin had Blyukher accused of being a spy for the Japanese since 1922. Under "interrogation," Beria's men reduced Blyukher's face to a bloody pulp—he lost an eye—yet the marshal refused to confess. Blyukher would die under torture. Beria telephoned Stalin with the news, after which the marshal was cremated.[280] His death was never announced.[281]

Beria's value, as well as Khrushchev's, got magnified many times over by Stalin's hectic quest for leading personnel caused by his annihilations. Stalin had assigned Alexander Shcherbakov, Zhdanov's deputy in Leningrad, as party boss in Irkutsk, but in spring 1938 he received him again and appointed him party boss to the Donbass.[282] In fall 1938, Stalin would hand him the Moscow party organization, summoning Khrushchev from Ukraine to preside over the meeting to denounce the sitting Moscow party head as an enemy of the people and support Shcherbakov (who had once worked under Khrushchev in Ukraine). "There is also testimony against him," Khrushchev recalled telling Stalin of Shcherbakov, whom he deemed "poisonous, snakelike." Stalin resolved the matter by appointing a second secretary from Malenkov's circle to watch over Shcherbakov.[283]

Stalin's most important minion, Molotov, showed little ambition to cultivate his own power base.[284] Orjonikidze, by contrast, had built an immense semi-autonomous fiefdom in heavy industry, which Stalin had broken up into numerous economic commissariats. But now Stalin found himself constrained to facilitate the establishment of another fiefdom: Beria at the NKVD. A rivalry between Molotov and Beria for Stalin's favor assisted the despot in keeping an eye on both.[285] Still, Beria challenged him to stay on his toes, and Stalin would strive to institute all manner of checks on Beria, a process that had begun before his transfer to Moscow.[286] Unlike in the case of Voroshilov at the Red Army, Stalin had appointed not merely a loyalist, but a man exceptionally suited for his post. Beria would come to exercise immense power by dint of the organization he now headed de facto and his undeniable operational skill.

"TYRANTS DESTROYED," a short story published in Russian in 1936 by the émigré Vladimir Nabokov (the son of a Provisional Government scribe), imagined an egomaniac with the power to drive his subjects mad, in a kind of infectious psychosis.[287] Stalin knew the state of the country and the consequences of his actions. Compared with anyone else inside the USSR, he was exceptionally well informed, served by an information-gathering system that stretched across the vast country and, to an extent, the entire globe.[288] Still, it took intense effort on his part to ferret out information that officials did not want him to know. He sought accurate information, but for him that meant Marxist-Leninist ways of thinking refracted through a jaundiced view of people. Stalin exhibited a proclivity to depict the world as he wanted to see it, indeed, as he could and did shape it. He elicited intelligence about enemies, treason, vulnerabilities. It would be going too far to call him, or the Soviet system, a victim of its own trap.[289] An echo chamber effect shapes surveillance and reporting mechanisms in any authoritarian regime. Still, in the Soviet case the revolution was encircled, and Stalin's worldview reinforced that structural paranoia.

The USSR faced genuine foreign threats, and the terror was conducted in the name of state security, but mass arrests in the Red Army further emboldened foreign enemies, including Hitler and proponents of war in the Nazi regime, while rendering the USSR's already wary potential allies more wary. The vastly expanded hunt to root out enemies in 1936–38 helped unify the country around threats but spread deep fear and made many otherwise loyal Soviet people anti-Soviet. The mass annihilation of party and state functionaries, and the heightened dread among survivors, did nothing to alter the political system's inbuilt malperformance. Stalin smashed nearly every provincial party machine in 1937–38, but they would reappear.[290] He killed off heads of state bodies, too, and the state fiefdoms reappeared. Industry had been suffering genuine problems, but the mass arrests that were attributed to wrecking only lowered output further. Complicity in the mass murder of Red Army officers and loyal officials compromised all those who took part or benefited, including large numbers of new young people.

During the enemy mania of 1937 and 1938, no military graduation banquets took place (eleven of the fourteen military academy directors suffered arrest).[291] Still, the graduations themselves did take place. So did at least fifteen Kremlin banquets for other occasions, which eclipsed party gatherings in ceremony and—alongside the parades on Red Square for May Day, Revolution Day, and Physical Culture Day—became the principal staging ground of Stalin's rule.[292] He held banquets (large and small) for managers, engineers, and high-profile workers in various industrial branches; women; athletes; aviators; representatives of the Union republics. Marina Raskova, the aviator, was bundled along with the rest of the *Motherland* airplane crew to the Kremlin's Palace of Facets immediately upon their return to Moscow (October 27, 1938). When she encountered Stalin, she erupted in tears, unable to control herself; he comforted her, taking her by the shoulders, patting her head, seating her next to him. When Stalin rose to speak, the hall hushed, straining to hear his soft voice. He talked about the need to take special care of aviators, and about matriarchy back in the mists of time.[293] That same evening, he managed an appearance at the fortieth anniversary of the Moscow Art Theater, arriving with nearly his entire suite: Molotov, Voroshilov, Kaganovich, Andreyev, Mikoyan, Zhdanov, Yezhov, and Khrushchev, all of whom were photographed in the company of the leading actresses and actors. Medals were handed out liberally.[294] The ineffaceable evil was mixed with a grandeur that was celebrated with pride in the Grand Kremlin Palace and in localities alike.

Genius and madness may be two sides of the same coin (as Aristotle wrote), but Stalin was neither. He showed himself capable of immense foresight but also blindness. He was astonishingly hardworking yet often self-defeating, uncannily shrewd yet often narrow-minded and mulish. He possessed an inordinately strong will that brooked little or no challenge to his views.[295] This ferocious willpower emanated from a transcendent sense of personal destiny and of historical necessity. Stalin, too, intrigued ceaselessly, but he was utterly absorbed in the matter of Soviet statehood and statecraft. Moreover, he had authority, not just power. He *inhabited* the Kremlin—he filled the offices and the parade halls built by Catherine the Great and Alexander I. Combining the majesty of imperial Russian power with the seeming sureties of Marxism-Leninism, a great state with socialism, proved to be his masterwork.[296] Its expression was the new people, his people, not those of a bygone epoch destined to be crushed like whole classes under the wheels of history. It was a vision in which terror could make sense. And yet, what transpired in 1936–38 cannot be made wholly rational any more than absolute evil can.[297]

Stalin murdered from the Little Corner. He was a distant murderer. He took no part in the bloody rituals. He was not an assassin, nor a witness to assassinations, although he did sometimes witness the results of torture when the accused were brought before him and others of the politburo in so-called confrontations with their accusers. He wrote the execution directives and signed the lists of names. He did not allow the public to know of his signatures but made sure his inner circle, too, were implicated. He spoke to them all the time about the accusations in the same way as the propaganda related them in public—in terms of legions of hidden spies everywhere, traitors, and confessions to these crimes that he referred to literally—and instructed his police minions to employ torture, frequently using euphemisms, though sometimes being explicit ("Beat Ryabinin all over for not implicating Vareikis").[298]

Letters detailing torture, abuses, and injustices continued to reach Stalin.[299] Few grasped the depth of his malice.[300] Molotov came to see it and, further, to understand that it was not solely personal but rooted in a sense of raison d'état and core political convictions. Was showing pity to enemies and double-dealers

Marxist? Did alleged Marxists not understand capitalist encirclement? Did they not understand class struggle? Who would be responsible if pity were shown and Soviet power were defeated in war and overthrown? Stalin would be responsible. A light tenor, he continued to sing romantic songs such as the Georgian "Suliko" ("I sought my sweetheart's grave, but could not find it"), but running the Soviet state did not afford him much scope for sentimentality. His ruthlessness was dictated, in his own mind, by the laws of history and social development. Nonetheless, Stalin's terror went beyond reckless. And soon, he himself would indirectly recognize as much.

THREE-CARD MONTE

How horrible, fantastic, incredible it is, that we should be digging trenches and trying on gas masks here because of a quarrel in a faraway country between people of whom we know nothing.

> Prime Minister Neville Chamberlain,
> *radio broadcast, September 27, 1938, speaking of the*
> *Sudetenland in Czechoslovakia*[1]

Colonel Jean Delmas, French military attaché in Romania: "Do you not think it is time and possible to arrest Germany's expansion?"

Lieutenant General Gheorghe Ştefan Ionescu, Romanian chief of staff: "In my view, it is the last opportunity. If we let it pass, we can no longer contain Germany and, in that case, enormous sacrifices would be required, while today the victory appears certain." (September 28, 1938)[2]

Hitler was a force of nature because potential counterforces allowed him to be. For years he had been seeking an audience with one of his idols, Benito Mussolini, who had been handed power after a colossal bluff, the March on Rome, in 1922. Finally, in 1934, after the Führer, too, had been handed power—also by traditional conservatives wary of leftist revolution and desperate for an authoritarian mass base—the duce condescended to a meeting. Afterward, Mussolini reassured an Italian Jewish leader, "I know Mr. Hitler. He is an imbecile and a scoundrel; an endless talker." The duce added, "In the future there will be no remaining trace of Hitler while the Jews will still be a great people. . . . Mr. Hitler is a joke that will last only a few years."[3] On July 25, 1934, advantageously misconstruing a question that had been posed by Mussolini (who had conducted the conversation in his atrocious German), Hitler and his overzealous minions had colluded with Austrian Nazis in a putsch against Mussolini's friend the Austrian authoritarian leader Engelbert Dollfuss.[4] Even as his wife and family were guests of Mussolini's at his seaside villa in Riccione, Italy, the Austrian chancellor—known as the Jockey for his five-foot-two height—was slowly, agonizingly bleeding to death on his office couch in Vienna. An enraged duce mobilized 100,000 troops on the Brenner Pass to support the Austrian armed forces—and Hitler backed down. "If this group of criminals and pederasts should take over Europe," the duce fumed, "it would mean the end of our civilization."[5]

Mussolini had demonstrated that Hitler could be deterred. In the meantime, the Italian fascist had switched sides, because of his expansionism in Africa in 1935 and the next year's outbreak of the Spanish civil war, when the duce and the Führer found common cause supporting Franco.[6] On November 1, 1936, during a bombastic outburst in Milan, Mussolini had mused that a Rome-Berlin "Axis" had formed, around which all of Europe would be "reorganized." The British cartoonist David Low called Mussolini "the man who took the lid off."[7] Hitler and Mussolini became a corrosive duo, but hardly genuinely committed allies. Following a duce state visit to Berlin in September 1937, according to Albert Speer, Hitler pantomimed him. "His chin thrust forward, his legs spread, and his right hand jammed on his hip, Hitler, who spoke no foreign languages, bellowed Italian or Italian-sounding words like *giovinezza, patria, victoria, macaroni, belleza, bel canto,* and *basta.* Everyone around him made sure to laugh, and it was indeed very funny."[8] The histrionic duce would be derided as a cardboard Caesar presiding over a regime of gestures, from the Roman salute that replaced the handshake to the leader cult.[9] But his playacting about an Axis with Germany put a heavier onus on France and Britain. Even in the face of Hitler's illegal rearmament and public statements about expansionism, however, the Western powers strove to avoid a repeat of the horrors of the Great War.[10]

Most contemporary statesmen assumed that great powers acted out of self-interest, that international discord was the norm, that peace was provided for by balance of power, and that the overturning of the balance (or equilibrium) would bring consequences that even anti-status-quo (or revisionist) powers failed to foresee.[11] Here was the rub, however: the Versailles order had not been a genuine equilibrium. The treaty had been possible solely because of an anomaly in 1919: the simultaneous collapse of both German and Russian power. One or the other of these big countries was certain to come back strongly. In the event, both rose to be major military powers, and within a single generation. As if that were not enough, the old Habsburg buffer was gone. The revived Polish state and expanded Greater Romania exacerbated the instability with their barbed rivalries with, respectively, Czechoslovakia and Hungary. Lack of resolve on the part of the Western powers was in many ways a symptom, not a cause, of the death rattle of Versailles. Stalin, for his part, hardly objected to Versailles revisionism—the Bolsheviks had not even been invited to the peace conference—provided, of course, that any "new order" did not come at Soviet expense.[12] Versailles's obsolescence offered extraordinarily fertile ground for Hitler's appetites and, in his wake, for Stalin's opportunism.

The Führer could mesmerize people. Winston Churchill, the Tory politician, had written in September 1937 that "one may dislike Hitler's system and yet admire his patriotic achievement. If our country were defeated I hope we should find a champion as indomitable to restore our courage and lead us back to our place among nations."[13] Churchill would soon experience a drastic change of heart, coming around to the view that Hitler was serious about his martial and racialist aspirations.[14] But many observers, perhaps most, would continue to assume that, like all politicians, the Nazi, too, would eventually "come to see reason."

Hitler posed a profound danger to Stalin's personal dictatorship as the Führer not only rearmed his country but raged ever more rabidly against "Judeo-Bolshevism," transforming Germany from partner of convenience with the USSR during the Weimar years to menace. Stalin was bafflingly slow to come to grips with the centrality of ideology in the Nazi program. On the Soviet despot's Asian flank, meanwhile, the long-standing threat of an expansionist Japan had only strengthened. The symbolic November 1936 Anti-Comintern Pact between Germany and Japan, which Italy joined the next year, and the relentless Soviet border clashes with Japan, including the summer 1938 limited war at Lake Khasan, meant that the Soviet Union faced the prospect of a two-front war—and without allies.[15] Mongolia, the world's only other socialist state, had a total population far smaller than the Red Army. Stalin had signed a nonaggression pact with Chiang Kaishek's China, but a decade of bitterness and distrust was not easily overcome, and China's ability to continue holding off a Japanese military onslaught, while battling internal Communist subversion, remained uncertain. Could Stalin somehow achieve a military alliance with the Western capitalist democracies, even as he was conducting grisly mass executions at home and engaged in forms of Communist subversion of his potential partners abroad? Czechoslovakia provided the key test.

CZECHOSLOVAKIA CALLED TO MIND the old Habsburg empire in miniature—Mussolini dubbed it Czecho-Germano-Polono-Magyaro-Rutheno-Romano-Slovakia. Of the new country's approximately 15 million people, Czechs formed a bare majority, and the main minorities—3.25 million Germans, 3 million Slovaks, 750,000 Hungarians, 100,000 Ruthenians [Ukrainians], 100,000 Poles—chafed at real and perceived discrimination. Politically, the country remained a parliamentary democracy, but in some ways it was too divided, too nationalist, and even too small to sustain the limited stability that old Austria-Hungary had fitfully managed.[16] Hitler preyed upon these vulnerabilities, taking advantage of Czechoslovakia's democracy to subvert it: spreading lies to discredit its democratic institutions while claiming the protections of laws to defend freedom of expression; covertly funding pro-Nazi political groups while irately denouncing the evidence of its complicity fake, even inciting armed revolt by Czechoslovakia's German speakers, who were concentrated mostly in the horseshoe-shaped Sudetenland, contiguous with Germany. With regional tensions high, on February 24, 1938, the twentieth anniversary of the founding of the Red Army, the Soviet embassy in Prague threw a glittering reception for 350 guests. (The German, Italian, and Polish ambassadors stayed away.) General Ludvík Krejčí, chief of the Czechoslovak general staff, stated in the presence of journalists that if Germany were to attack, "We will fight and we will never fall to our knees." He added that the Czechoslovak general staff wanted relations with the Soviet general staff to be on a par with those it had with the French. Still, doubts existed in Prague about whether the USSR was really prepared to defend Czechoslovakia.[17]

Events moved very rapidly. On March 12, a different Habsburg successor state vanished when the Wehrmacht, unopposed, seized Austria, a country of 7 million predominantly German speakers. It was the first time since the Great War that a German army had crossed a state frontier for purposes of conquest, and, in and of itself, it constituted an event of perhaps greater import than the assassination of Archduke Franz Ferdinand, which had helped spark the Great War mobilizations in 1914.[18] The Versailles and Saint-Germain treaties of 1919 expressly forbade a forcible annexation of Austria by Germany, but Berlin deemed what it called *Anschluss* a "reunification" with the German speakers whom Bismarck had left out of his unified Germany. Even Germans not enamored of National Socialism rejoiced. Hitler overcame the stain of his failed 1934 putsch, and this time Mussolini, estranged from Britain and France and judging a deal with Hitler more prudent than paying the cost of opposing him, allied Italy to Germany's expansionism even as the latter threatened Italy's own territorial interests.

France, for its part, lacked a government on the day Hitler invaded Austria; the coalition cabinet had just resigned—again. (France would have sixteen governments over the eight years beginning in 1932.) British prime minister Neville Chamberlain's special envoy to Hitler, Edward Wood, First Earl of Halifax, leader of the House of Lords, had conveyed (back on November 19, 1937) that London would not stand in his way over Austria—or the ethnic-German-majority provinces of Czechoslovakia and Danzig—provided such revisions to the Versailles Treaty came through "peaceful evolution." In the conversation it had been Halifax, not Hitler, who first mentioned these other territories coveted by Nazi Germany.[19] Chamberlain (b. 1869) did publicly warn Germany not to attack Czechoslovakia, but he privately informed Paris that London would not join a military counteraction should Hitler repeat his aggression.[20] France wanted it both ways as well: it publicly affirmed its resolve to defend Czechoslovakia while privately wanting British pusillanimity as an excuse not to have to live up to its own treaty obligations.[21]

Rationalizations were to hand. The Versailles peace had been pummeled by pundits as unjust and self-defeating, while state borders in Eastern Europe were widely viewed as arbitrary, including by the East Europeans themselves. What would the powers be shedding blood to defend? All true, but Austria's disappearance should have and could have been stopped. Germany's mobilization was so sudden, ordered by the Führer at 7:00 p.m. on March 10, 1938, that it nearly collapsed. "Nothing had been done, nothing at all," chief of staff General Ludwig Beck fumed of the planning.[22] Only the long lists of Austrian Jews had been meticulously prepared. Once across the frontier, the German army had to purchase gasoline at private Austrian petrol stations; lucky for them, it was for sale. The Austrian leader, Kurt von Schuschnigg, had decided not to resist militarily, and yet, even without resistance, and in perfect weather, nearly one in six German tanks broke down before reaching Vienna. Many of the Wehrmacht's horses, meanwhile, lacked shoes: German farmers, forced to remit horses by quota, had turned over their most decrepit.[23] Fatefully, however, the improvised chaos of the German invasion was not immediately recognized as such. The French did not even have a military attaché on the ground to observe the near disaster.[24]

What outsiders did see was that much of the Austrian population greeted Hitler's show of force with euphoria: Nazi banners, Hitler salutes, flowers. By March 13, Austria was already officially a province of Germany, and the Austrian army had sworn an oath to Hitler personally. The Führer issued a decree banning all parties save the National Socialists on what had been Austrian territory. Many Jews were rounded up in Vienna, whose 176,000 citizens of that extraction (10 percent of the urban population) made it the largest Jewish city in the German-speaking world. The Gestapo arrived at Berggasse 19, the offices of Sigmund Freud, who possessed the wherewithal to get himself and some of his possessions out, to London, but others were not so lucky (his four sisters would all be murdered farther east). Much of the Austrian political class was deported to Dachau or an Austrian camp soon opened at the quarries in Mauthausen. Austrian gold and foreign currency reserves, including private holdings, were looted—780 million reichsmarks' worth, more than Germany's own.[25] On March 14, Hitler entered Vienna as conqueror, staying at the Imperial Hotel, near whose entrance he had shoveled snow many years earlier to earn a few Habsburg crowns.

For two days, Soviet newspapers did not even comment on the Nazi seizure of Austria: *Pravda* and *Izvestiya* were consumed with blaring the death sentences for Bukharin and other accused "war provocateurs."[26] When Hitler delivered a rousing speech before a quarter million people on Vienna's Heroes' Square on March 15, 1938, in Moscow Bukharin was made to watch as the other defendants from his "trial" were shot, and then he, too, was executed. Stalin took his colored pencils to the transcript of Bukharin's last statement in court, before it was published in the Soviet press, and crossed out several passages, including: "I accept responsibility even for those crimes about which I did not know or about which I did not have the slightest idea"; "I deny most of all the prosecutor's charge that I belonged to the group sitting on the court bench with me, because such a group never existed!"[27]

Czechoslovakia was now surrounded on three sides by German troops, and its western border defenses were gone. Back when Stalin had agreed to mutual assistance pacts with France and Czechoslovakia, he had pledged to come to the latter's aid *if France did so first*.[28] On the same day Hitler spoke in Vienna and Bukharin was executed, deputy foreign affairs commissar Potyomkin, who had taken over for the arrested Krestinsky, told the Czechoslovak ambassador that requests for reassurance should be addressed to Paris.[29] On March 21, 1938, Sergei Alexandrovsky, the Soviet envoy in Prague, warned his interlocutors that the defense of Czechoslovakia was not in the first instance the Red Army's responsibility.[30] On

March 26, Litvinov wrote to Alexandrovsky that "the Hitlerization of Austria has predetermined the fate of Czechoslovakia." That day he had been in Stalin's Little Corner, along with Molotov, Voroshilov, and others, for two hours.[31] By March 27, the despot was compelled to close the Soviet embassy in Vienna "in connection with the elimination of the Austrian state." Austria's legation in Moscow was signed over to Hitler. On March 28, Stalin sent Marshal Kulik to Prague. Krejčí was again ingratiating, joining denunciations of Trotsky and asking Kulik point-blank, "Will you help us if the Germans attack?" According to the Soviet note-taker, "Comrade Kulik answered 'that help will be forthcoming.'"[32] But on March 29, *Pravda* warned that "German aggression against Czechoslovakia will occur only if Germany is sure that the other powers will not intervene on the Czech side. Thus, everything depends on the attitude adopted by France and Britain."[33]

Over in Spain, Franco's forces reached the Mediterranean, slicing the Republic's zone in two. At the same time, French intelligence, citing a "top-secret and completely reliable" source, reported on Germany's war plans against Czechoslovakia.[34] On April 21, Stalin met in the Little Corner with Molotov, other minions, Litvinov, and Alexandrovsky, who was instructed to reaffirm that the Soviet Union stood with France and Czechoslovakia—a reminder of France's obligations.[35] Hitler traveled to Italy, his second visit since becoming chancellor, seeking Mussolini's assent to a Nazi plan to "take out" Czechoslovakia. Despite seven days of pomp, sightseeing, and spectacle recalling the visit of Holy Roman emperor Charles V in 1536, the Führer came away without a binding military pact.[36]

Czechoslovak president Edvard Beneš, who had studied for a law degree in France and had represented the new Czechoslovakia at Versailles, showed resolve, telling the Soviet envoy (May 18, 1938) that he would defend his state's frontiers and sovereignty "with all the means at his disposal" and urging that this message be conveyed personally to Stalin.[37] Between May 19 and 22, under the impression that a German strike was imminent, in a repeat of the Austrian scenario, Beneš called up reservists, 199,000 men, which doubled the force structure, and he repositioned troops to the front lines in the Sudetenland. The British issued a formal protest of Hitler's presumed war plans and evacuated nonessential staff from their Berlin embassy.[38] Whether a German offensive had been imminent remains uncertain; it appears that the Czechoslovaks had been fed disinformation.[39] The emergency Czechoslovak mobilization, in eliciting the warning from Britain to Germany, had made it seem as if Hitler had had to abandon his putsch at the last minute under pressure, which provoked his fury. In fact, Hitler had already decided on an attack, and the planning was well under way for a short war against

Czechoslovakia, but now those secret plans were given stronger impetus and refined (with a target completion date of October 1).[40] Even more consequentially, hyper-war-averse Britain had accidentally emerged as the ostensible roadblock to Hitler's continental *Lebensraum* and racial aspirations. French hostility—which Hitler took for granted—would be far more threatening if Britain stood shoulder to shoulder with France. The Führer began to contemplate the necessity of a war in the west as prelude to his eventual expansionism in the east.[41]

Germany's heightened spring–summer preparations against Czechoslovakia became known to Stalin, who ordered the Kiev and Belorussian military districts reorganized into a special military command (with a completion deadline of September 1), but to unspecified purpose. The Soviet high command internally noted that the Czechoslovak army and populace were in a fighting mood, and that President Beneš, who had been born to a peasant family, seemed inclined to stand up for his country.[42] But in Prague, the severe doubts about Moscow, which General Krejčí had expressed back in March, persisted. Would Stalin help defend them?

ALTHOUGH STALIN HAD SUCCESSFULLY stood up to the Japanese at Lake Khasan in summer 1938, that border war had exposed Soviet military weaknesses, which were aired at a meeting of the Main Military Council on August 31. Stalin had reduced Soviet involvement in the Spanish civil war, but he had ramped up military involvement on behalf of China and remained deeply preoccupied with shoring up defenses in the Soviet Far East while, paradoxically, continuing to massacre his own military personnel there.[43] He was also preoccupied with Polish-German collusion. Poland's leadership had been among the first to recognize the March 1938 German takeover of Austria. A few days after that, Poland itself took advantage, compelling independent Lithuania, in an ultimatum, to recognize Poland's annexation of Wilno (which the Poles had occupied militarily back in 1920–22). Lithuania had no defenders, west or east, but whereas Poland's power play did not turn Western opinion definitively against Warsaw, it reconfirmed Stalin's ingrained suspicions of likely German-Polish revisionist collaboration.[44] Potyomkin, under a pseudonym, had publicly mocked Polish fantasies of annexing all of Lithuania and predicted a coming German-inspired Polish invasion of the USSR. "Hitler wants to let Poland loose against the Soviet Union," he wrote, adding that the Führer "only wants [the Poles] to clear the road for Germany. . . . He is preparing Poland's fourth partition."[45]

Moscow's assistance to Prague faced formidable logistical challenges: Soviet territory was not contiguous with Czechoslovakia. Four of the five partially mobilized Soviet army groups were on the border with Poland, the best transit route, but Poland adamantly refused to permit a military crossing. Some contemporaries speculated that the Soviets could still have gone through Poland on a contrived League of Nations authorization.[46] Romania, also a Soviet enemy, provided a less advantageous but still valuable land route, along with overflight options, but discussions with Bucharest were inconclusive, partly because of Soviet claims to Romania-controlled Bessarabia and partly because of King Carol II's objections.[47] Even though Romania did not shut the door entirely to passage, the rail gauge differed, so the Red Army would have needed to change the undermount wheels at the border or obtain substantial European rolling stock from someone.[48]

London, Paris, and Berlin all judged the Red Army incapable of decisive intervention abroad—after all, Stalin had decapitated his own officer corps.[49] A Soviet spy secretly transmitted to Stalin the brutal internal intelligence assessment of his French ally to the effect that Soviet armed forces "were not capable of conducting an offensive war" and that the USSR had been "weakened by an internal crisis."[50] Officials in France and Britain began spreading self-exculpatory rumors that the Soviets would do nothing in defense of Czechoslovakia.[51] Stalin again had Kalinin publicly reaffirm that Moscow would honor its treaty obligations "to the last letter"—that is, take action provided France did so, a position that was announced on public radio loudspeakers throughout the Soviet Union. France had secretly warned the Czechoslovak government in July 1938 that it would not take up arms over the Sudeten issue under any circumstances.[52] In trying to back off their treaty obligations, the French grasped a convenient pretext: they knew that Germany had broken some British codes and that, therefore, thanks to telegrams out of Prague by the British special envoy Viscount Walter Runciman, Hitler could see how far—very far, indeed—the British would go to avert war.[53]

The Führer, ratcheting up the pressure, had ordered that the harvest be gathered as quickly as possible (to free up horses for the Wehrmacht), private trucks be requisitioned, border defenses with France be fully manned, and reserves be called up for fall "maneuvers" in East Prussia. But no peacetime market economy had ever managed Germany's level of military expenditures, and Germany was already the highest-taxed major economy, and approaching insolvency. The German stock market had dropped 13 percent between April and August 1938.[54] German military circles had begun plotting to remove the reckless Führer in a palace coup before he could embroil Germany in a new world war for which the country and the army were not ready.[55] Troops of the elite 23rd Infantry Division, stationed in Potsdam, were to occupy Berlin's ministries, its radio station, and the facilities of the regular police, the Gestapo, and the SS. Hitler's bodyguard division, the SS-Leibstandarte, who were stationed in Saxony near the border with Czechoslovakia, would be blocked on-site. A final action involved seizure of the Chancellery and of Hitler himself. The plotters were not fully coordinated, but some sort of putsch seemed to be coming to a head right after Hitler's Nuremberg rally closing speech on September 12, when many expected him to declare war on Czechoslovakia. He did not. Still, one conspirator told his brother on September 14 that "Hitler will be arrested tomorrow."[56]

Then the news broke: on September 15, Neville Chamberlain boarded an airplane for the second time in his sixty-nine years and, for the first time, would meet with Hitler. The British PM touched down only one day after the Nazi party had concluded its annual weeklong rally in Nuremberg, a ferocious, torchlit spectacle whose images were seen worldwide.

A MAJORITY OF THE BRITISH establishment believed, or wanted to believe, that an agreement with Germany over Czechoslovakia was possible.[57] But what kind? The PM proposed awarding Germany the Czechoslovak border territories with majority ethnic German populations in exchange for Hitler's not resorting to force and a great-power "guarantee" of rump Czechoslovakia's territorial integrity.[58] A diplomatic deal, even such a stunningly advantageous gift, was precisely what the war-thirsty Hitler feared. He had been startled by Chamberlain's offer to come to Berlin.[59] During a fortnight, as the Führer got ever more expansive in his demands, the elderly, unwell Chamberlain would fly to him three times. ("If at first you can't concede," went a nasty ditty that made the rounds, "fly, fly again.")[60] On the eve of the first encounter, Chamberlain had written to his sister Ida, "Is it not positively horrible to think that the fate of hundreds of millions depends on one man and he is half mad?"[61] Eight days later (September 19), he wrote to her again: "Here was a man who could be relied upon when he had given his word."[62]

Of course, Stalin had been straining to elicit his own deal with Hitler, who would have none of it. Sorge, the agent of Soviet military intelligence at the German embassy in Japan, was reporting on secret German-Japanese negotiations for a binding military alliance.[63] In Moscow, three meetings of the Main Military Council took place on September 19, with Stalin in attendance, and much of the discussion was taken up with shortcomings and planned construction in Soviet Far Eastern military districts.[64] That same day, Beneš, in receipt of Anglo-French proposals that day for territorial concessions to Germany—which he was inclined to reject—asked Alexandrovsky specifically if the Soviets would support Czechoslovakia should Germany attack *and* France fulfill its treaty obligations. Potyomkin telegrammed Alexandrovsky that the answer was yes, and that Moscow was transmitting the same answer immediately to Paris, all of which was conveyed to Beneš by telephone on September 20 while he was meeting with the Czechoslovak government.[65] Beneš, the next day, was aggressively pressured by Britain and France into accepting the "deal." From September 21 to 23, Stalin undertook a redeployment and partial mobilization in his western borderlands—which held 76 divisions—and had the Red Army troops informed that they would be defending Czechoslovakia.[66] On September 23, the Führer flat out rejected the British-French "compromise"—the prize of the Sudetenland without having to fight for it. France and Czechoslovakia partially mobilized.[67] The Soviet envoy in Paris briefed the French on intensified Soviet troop movements.[68]

Chamberlain again took the lead to defuse the bellicosity. "However much we may sympathize with a small nation confronted by a big and powerful neighbor, we cannot in all circumstances undertake to involve the whole British Empire in war simply on her account," the PM stated on the radio on September 27. "If we have to fight, it must be on larger issues than that."[69] That same day, the German general staff moved its troops to forward positions on the frontier with Czechoslovakia. The French and British governments reluctantly felt that they would be compelled to fight if the Wehrmacht forcibly seized Czechoslovakia. The Royal Navy was on full alert. Britain's populace was digging trenches and air-raid shelters and filling sandbags; the authorities were distributing gas masks. The mood was grim.[70] Hitler, in fact, was hours from ordering an invasion. But on September 28, Mussolini accepted a British entreaty to coordinate a disorganized four-power summit with Chamberlain (Britain), Édouard Daladier (France), and Hitler (Germany), with the duce (Italy) acting as dishonest broker.[71]

Hitler chose the site of the Führer Building in the Nazi movement's capital, Munich. The British and French governments consented to consigning the Czechoslovaks to an adjacent room, apart from the negotiations. The Soviet Union, despite its treaties with France and Czechoslovakia, was not even invited. Chamberlain, along with Daladier, agreed not only that Czechoslovakia would cede the Sudetenland but also that all fortifications and weapons there would be left intact. Hitler acceded to this granting of his original demands rather than unleash the war he had been promising, and the infamous Munich Pact was signed in the small hours on September 30 (it was dated the day before).[72] Wehrmacht troops marched into western Czechoslovakia with international authorization. Nazi Germany absorbed, gratis, industrial plants, coal and other natural resources, and 11,000 square miles of territory, on which lived 3 million Sudeten Germans and 800,000 Czechs. Non-German Sudeten inhabitants were given fewer than ten days to evacuate, and forced to relinquish everything—homes, household possessions, livestock. The German government was absolved from paying compensation.

Chamberlain allowed himself to imagine that he was "fixing" the Versailles Treaty by removing the supposed cause of German aggression: too many ethnic Germans living outside German borders. Hitler, recounting what he had told Chamberlain, had remarked in a public speech on September 26, 1938, at the Sports Palace in Berlin, that the Sudetenland was "the last territorial claim which I have to make in Europe, but it is a claim from which I will not swerve, and which I will satisfy, God willing. . . . And this I guarantee. We don't want any Czechs at all." That had been the straw that Chamberlain grasped. To win over Britain's head of state, George VI, to the deal with the distasteful Hitler, the PM had played up "the prospect of Germany and England as the two pillars of European peace and buttresses against Communism."[73] In fact, Chamberlain prioritized the higher purpose of preserving the British empire. (The self-governing dominions would, in any case, not join a war over Czechoslovakia.)[74] What Chamberlain and his ilk missed was that Germany was not militarily strong, but, if unopposed now, it would never be so weak again.

Daladier had heard from an adamant French general staff, which wanted more time to build up the military, that the Luftwaffe was too strong for France.[75] But if he understood how the French brass tended to exaggerate German capabilities, Daladier, a veteran of the Great War, also recognized the antiwar sentiment in French society, which, along with Germany, had borne the heaviest devastation in that conflict. Still, the former history teacher from Provence also understood that France had failed to honor its commitments. "No, I am not proud," Daladier told colleagues concerning Munich. "I do not know what you think, you others, but I, I will say it again, I am not proud."[76]

Whatever the worries in Paris and London over their own military unpreparedness, in fall 1938 the Wehrmacht was woefully unready for a major military clash against the combined forces of Czechoslovakia (36 already mobilized divisions), France, and possibly the Soviet Union. True, in Czechoslovakia, half the Sudeten German conscripts had deserted to Germany, and many ethnic Poles had failed to report to the colors, but more than 1 million troops, including reservists, were called to the colors.[77] Nazi Germany possessed around 70 divisions, but that included a great many rated second class, while some would have to remain home to protect Germany against an attack from the west. If Germany were forced to employ nearly the full weight of its army (and air force) in a war in Czechoslovakia, France might be left with as much as a seven-to-one advantage in Germany's west, at a time when Germany's Siegfried Line (or Westwall) was perhaps 5 percent complete (recently poured concrete had not yet set).[78] Chief of staff Ludwig Beck had been trying to rally the military brass to oppose Hitler's plans, curb the SS, and "reestablish orderly conditions in the Reich," because he feared that the French general could take advantage of adventurism in Czechoslovakia and strike a decisive blow from the other side.[79] To be sure, by August 1938, Beck had resigned, but his replacement, Lieutenant General Franz Halder, was perhaps even more anxious over the Wehrmacht's inadequacies and the German public's antiwar mood, and on September 28 he pleaded with military commander in chief General Walther von Brauchitsch to restart the coup against Hitler, to prevent war.[80] Brauchitsch, however, worried that such an act would divide the army, and in any case he and others were undercut by the announcement of the diplomatic gathering in Munich.

Stalin had a copy of the French intelligence assessment, via a Soviet spy, which indicated both German weaknesses and lack of French resolve stemming from worries about its own weakness.[81] The despot seemed off the hook. Nonetheless, he had had the Red Army augment its military preparedness: on September 28, Voroshilov reported that 246 high-speed bombers and 302 fighter planes were ready to take off within two days; some 330,000 Soviet reservists in the interior were called up. On September 29, chief of staff Shaposhnikov issued an order not to discharge Red Army soldiers and commanders who had completed service.[82] In the event, none of the mobilized troops or planes would see action. The cynical Germans had long anticipated that the absence of a common frontier with Czechoslovakia would serve as a convenient pretext for Stalin to demur on living up to his commitments and coming to Prague's rescue.[83] Beneš had had his own doubts on that score.[84] Still, we shall never know whether Stalin would have fulfilled his obligations, because France failed to fulfill its own treaty obligations, the precondition for Soviet action.

.   .   .

NOTHING IN THE TREATIES of mutual assistance with France and Czechoslovakia *precluded* unilateral Soviet action. We have no reliable record of Stalin's deliberations, if any occurred, over this question.[85] But indirect evidence is available. Back on September 19, 1938, after the French and British indicated that they would not go to war to defend Czechoslovakia, Beneš hoped to reverse Western policy by obtaining a unilateral Soviet commitment: he received the Soviet envoy Alexandrovsky, who encouraged the Czechoslovaks to fight the Germans come what may; in response, Beneš privately said to his secretary, "They naturally play their own game. We cannot trust them completely either. If they get us into it, they will leave us twisting in the air."[86] On September 25, Beneš had grilled the Soviet envoy point-blank about the specifics of possible Soviet military action under any circumstances—and Alexandrovsky had sat in stone silence. They met again the next day and the day after, and the Soviet envoy again offered nothing; on the contrary, he reported to Moscow that Beneš appeared to be trying to drag the Soviet Union into a war.[87] On September 28, the Czechoslovak legation in Moscow inquired directly; Beneš received no commitments. No Soviet official ever initiated or responded to Czechoslovak requests for elementary military coordination.

Stalin made no moves whatsoever toward unilateral military action to defend Czechoslovakia.[88] He never even issued an explicit warning to Germany. That did not mean, however, that Soviet troop movements constituted a ruse. They were directed, along with multiple diplomatic and public warnings, at Poland. Back on September 23, Potyomkin had roused the Polish chargé d'affaires at the undiplomatic hour of 4:00 a.m. to warn him that the Soviet Union would renounce their bilateral nonaggression pact if Poland attacked Czechoslovakia; that evening, the Polish diplomat responded in the name of his government that the Soviets ought not to get involved in matters that did not concern them.[89] *Izvestiya* (September 26) published the Soviet note to Poland, and the next day Polish diplomats stationed in Minsk reported to Warsaw on Soviet military preparations. Poland officially protested Soviet overflights of their common frontier.[90] The Soviets also asked the French for their views on a Soviet military response to a Polish armed attack on Czechoslovakia.[91]

Polish foreign minister Józef Beck wrote to the Polish ambassador in Berlin (September 28), about the Soviet military actions, that "the character of these demonstrations was distinctly political, and the forms at times outright comical. From the military point of view, this so far has no great significance."[92] When the

Polish ambassador inquired of Nazi foreign minister Ribbentrop how Germany would view a Polish military action against Czechoslovakia, Ribbentrop, according to the German account, responded supportively but also noted that "if the Soviet Union undertakes an offensive against Poland, which I, however, consider excluded, then a completely new situation in the Czechoslovak question would arise for Germany."[93]

Did Stalin fantasize about delivering a blow to Poland, in revenge for 1920, and achieving a new partition of that country—seizing Galicia, with its large Ukrainian and Belorussian populations—if the Czechoslovaks decided to fight alone and became embroiled in war against Germany?[94] The despot certainly inclined toward opportunism, and he had kept his options open. Conversely, he might have just wanted to deter any Polish or combined Polish-German military action against Ukraine. Or perhaps in mobilizing he was angling to ensure that France, not the Soviet Union, would be blamed for any debacle with Czechoslovakia. What we know for certain is that during the biggest foreign policy moment of his regime to date, Stalin went more than 100 hours—from very early on September 28 through late on October 2—without receiving visitors in the Little Corner.[95] "Have you received any advice, instructions, or comments on the part of comrade Stalin or the comrades in the politburo regarding our work in the current situation?" Dimitrov wrote, in a plaintive request to his Comintern deputies on September 29.[96] Where was Stalin? He was spending every day at a five-day gathering (September 27–October 1) of propagandists from Leningrad and Moscow to discuss a book, *The History of the all-Union Communist Party (Bolsheviks): Short Course.*[97]

NONE OF THE PRIOR EFFORTS to publish a new textbook for Marxist-Leninist ideological training had met Stalin's expectations. A revised draft of the *Short Course* party history (not to be confused with the *Short Course* USSR history) had been presented to him around the time of the Bukharin trial, and he had spent much of summer 1938 in Moscow rewriting it, forgoing his beloved annual Caucasus holiday.[98] Some pages he rewrote several times. Numerous passages betrayed his preoccupations. A reference to the Greek hero Antaeus, the half giant who had been invincible in battle until he lost physical contact with the earth, indicated his reading of ancient Greek history. (Stalin did not mention that Antaeus had been killing his enemies so as to amass their skulls for a temple dedicated to his father, Poseidon.)[99] Collectivization received a central place. "The originality of this revolution," the *Short Course* stated, "consisted in the circumstance that it was brought about from above, at the initiative of state power, with the direct support from below by the mass of millions of peasants."[100] Stalin cut much of the material about himself, but he left in Lenin's return from exile and April 1917 theses as "decisive moments in the history of the party."[101] Yaroslavsky, an author of the draft, lauded Stalin's deletions as demonstrating the "exceptionally great modesty that adorns a Bolshevik."[102] Stalin also cut details of the opposition's deeds—wrecking in industry, treachery in Spain—but highlighted how class enemies with a party card were the most dangerous of all and how "double-dealers" constituted "an unprincipled gang of political careerists who, having long ago lost the confidence of the people, strive to insinuate themselves once more into the people's confidence by deception, by chameleon-like changes of color, by fraud, by any means, only that they retain the title of political figures."[103] He inserted dense philosophical passages about dialectical materialism ("The essence is not in individuals but in ideas, in the theoretical tendency").[104]

Stalin circulated the revised text to his inner circle (only some dared make written suggestions) and then convoked a kind of book club in the Little Corner between September 8 and 18, 1938, to finalize the text, one chapter per day.[105] "I am interested now in the new intelligentsia from the workers, from the peasants," Stalin said, according to notes Zhdanov took. "Without our own intelligentsia we shall perish. We have to run the country. . . . The state has to be managed through white collar employees."[106] *Pravda* began serialization, using centerfolds, publishing the first chapter on September 9, 1938, and another chapter each day thereafter. The stand-alone book then went to press in a first print run of 6 million.[107]

At the opening of the propagandists' gathering, on September 27, Zhdanov delivered the greeting, but Stalin could not refrain from intervening at length already that first day. "If we speak about wrecking, about Trotskyites, then you should know that not all these wrecker Trotskyite-Bukharinites were spies," Stalin told the agitators, seeming to reverse everything he had previously said. "I would not say that they were spies; they were our people, but then they went astray. Why? They turned out not to be genuine Marxists; they were weak theoretically." Never mind that the NKVD had fabricated their crimes, tortured them to confess, and executed them whether they confessed or not: if only these middle and lower functionaries had been able to study the *Short Course,* they would still be alive.[108]

Stalin showed impatience, explaining that "religion had a positive significance during the time of Saint Vladimir; there was paganism then, and Christianity was a step forward. Now our geniuses speaking from the vantage point of the twentieth century claim that Vladimir was a scoundrel and the pagans were scoundrels, that religion is vile; that is, they do not want to evaluate events dialectically, such that everything in its time had its place."[109] He also denounced anti-intellectualism: "What is this savageness? This is not Marxism, not Leninism. This is old-bourgeoisism." During twenty years, "with God's help and with your help, we have created our intelligentsia," but, he complained, "there are people who, if someone left the ranks of the workers and no longer works at the factory, or left the ranks of the peasantry and no longer works in the fields, would consider him an alien. I repeat, this is savagery, this is dangerous savagery. . . . Not a single state without white collar [functionaries], a commanding corps in the economy, in politics, in culture; not a single state could govern the country that way. . . . Our state took over all of industry—almost all—our state took over the significant channels of agriculture. . . . How could we manage without an intelligentsia?"[110]

He evinced no fondness for workers—unless they had been promoted to white-collar functionaries.[111] "We have about 8 million officials," he continued. "Just imagine this. This is the apparatus, with whose assistance the workers govern the country. . . . How could we not cultivate this apparatus in the spirit of Marxism?" He insisted that theory was their weak point. "What is theory?" he asked, in his cathechismic style. "It is knowledge of the laws of society, knowledge that enables one to get oriented in a situation, but in this orientation process they turned out to be bad Marxists, bad because we raised them badly." The consequences, he re-peated, were dire: "If a fascist should show up, our cadres need to know how to struggle against him, and not be scared of him, and not to withdraw from and not to kowtow to him, as happened with a significant part of the Trotskyites and Bukharinites, formerly our people, who then went over to the other side." Stalin had been compelled again and again to battle against deviations: Communists kept losing their way. These were not petty squabbles among personalities, but battles over correct theory. People who misunderstood theory made mistakes, such as opposing collectivization. He told the propagandists not to fear if some comrades did not enter the kingdom of socialism.

"And so, to whom is this book addressed?" Stalin summarized. "To cadres, and to rank-and-file workers at factories—not to rank-and-file white-collar em-ployees in agencies, but to those cadres about whom Lenin said they are profes-sional revolutionaries. The book is addressed to leading cadres."[112] But in the discussion of Stalin's remarks, some attendees dared to note the difficulties of assimilating the text. A. B. Shlyonsky, for example, called the *Short Course* "an encyclopedia of everything known about matters of Marxism-Leninism," but he wondered where the heroes were. He suggested a need for materials to supplement the text with stories of individuals.[113] Stalin, mentioning Shlyonsky by name, retorted that "we were presented with this sort of draft text [with heroes] and we revised it fundamentally. The draft text was based for the most part on exemplary individuals—those who were the most heroic, those who escaped from exile and how many times they escaped, those who suffered in the name of the cause." But, Stalin continued, "can we really use such a thing to train and educate our cadres? We ought to base our cadres' training on ideas, on theory . . . knowledge of the laws of historical development. If we possess such knowledge, then we'll have real cadres, but if people do not possess this knowledge, they will not be cadres—they will be just empty spaces. . . . It is ideas that really matter, not individuals—ideas, in a theoretical context."[114]

ON SEPTEMBER 30, 1938, around 9:30 a.m. local time (11:30 a.m. in Moscow), eight hours after the signing of the Munich Pact but well before German troops had entered Czechoslovakia, Beneš phoned the Soviet ambassador and inquired whether the Czechoslovaks should take arms and, by implication, whether the USSR would back them in a war even without the French. He asked for an answer between 6:00 and 7:00 p.m. local time. Given the repeated negative signals over the previous two weeks, this action is not easy to comprehend. The Soviet ambassador drove to Prague Castle to seek further information, but Beneš was meeting with the cabinet and leaders of political parties. Around 11:45 a.m. local time, the Soviet legation cabled the Czechoslovak president's query to Moscow.[115] Before Moscow replied, Alexandrovsky cabled the foreign affairs commissariat again, at 1:40 p.m. Prague time, to report that Beneš had already accepted the Munich diktat (he had done so at 12:30 p.m. local time).[116] The foreign affairs commissariat suspected that Beneš had wanted to claim that his hand had been forced because of the absence of a Soviet reply.[117] He in fact made no such claim, though he had to have been tempted. More likely, Beneš did not want to give up. The Czechoslovak high command had told him that the army stood ready to fight, with or without allies. Had Beneš ordered the formidable Czechoslovak divisions into action against Germany, he might have forced Stalin's hand, and that of the French government, too. The Czechoslovak president chose not to take the gamble.[118]

Stalin remained at the gathering of propagandists, where his frustrations had been building daily, and on October 1, the concluding day, he vented in a lengthy soliloquy. "Comrades, I thought that the assembled comrades would help the

Central Committee and furnish some serious criticism," he remarked. "Unfortunately, I must say that the criticism turned out to be not serious, not deep, and straight-out unsatisfactory in places." He condemned the complaints that this or that fact was missing from the text, when the point was to capture the *general tendency*. "He who would study Leninism and Lenin should study Marx and Engels," he reiterated. "Lenin arrived at new thoughts because he stood on the shoulders of Marx and Engels." Stalin narrated the entire history of the party, in detail, from origins, like an agitator of the first rank. He could also turn playful. "It's often asked: What's the deal? Marx and Engels said that as soon as proletarian power is established and nationalizes the means of production, the state should wither. What the hell? It does not wither? Its death is overdue. We've lived twenty years, the means of production have been nationalized, and you don't want to wither. (Laughter.)" In fact, he explained, no one had foreseen that the revolution would give birth to a new form of power. "Of course, the Petersburg proletariat, when they created soviets [of people's deputies], did not think that they were conducting a turnabout in Marxist theory about the specific forms of the dictatorship of the proletariat. They just wanted to defend themselves against tsarism." In *The Communist Manifesto,* which Stalin deemed "one of the best if not the best writing of Marx and Engels," the founders had based their view of the state on the two months of the Paris Commune. "An experience of two months!" What would they have said, he asked, if they could study the twenty years of Soviet power?

Stalin had been wrestling with the problem of the state under socialism throughout the terror. Now he enumerated the state's functions: maximizing production and military defense by mobilizing the country's resources. Only a professional army, he pointed out, could stand up to the armies of the capitalists.[119] He made clear that success could not be guaranteed by his leadership alone, or by the 3,000 or so officials who composed what he called the "general staff" of the party-state. "Do not think that governing a country means just writing directives," he reiterated. "Bollocks. To govern means to do things for real, to be able to carry out the resolutions in practice, and even sometimes to improve the resolutions if they are bad." In other words, reading the *Short Course* was going to facilitate handling the confounding challenges of planning and running an entire industrial economy, the complicated operations and logistics of preparing a gigantic army for battle, ensuring that every school building and schoolchild was ready for the school year or graduation. "We need to direct this book to that intelligentsia, in order to give party members and non-party members, who are not worse than party members, the opportunity to acquire knowledge and raise their horizon, their political level. . . . That's everything. (Rousing applause. Shouts: Hurrah to the Wise Stalin.)"[120]

Pravda (October 1, 1938) had directed its wrath over Czechoslovakia at Poland, predicting a new Polish partition (it was "well known that the German fascists have long been keen on some parts of Poland"). In fact, that very day, the government in Warsaw delivered an ultimatum, with a twenty-four-hour deadline, to Czechoslovakia to hand over two thirds of that country's partially ethnic Polish territory in coal-rich Silesia known as Těšín (Cieszyn) and Fryštát (Freistadt); Prague capitulated, rendering a Polish attack unnecessary.[121] "An exceptionally bold action carried out in brilliant fashion," Göring enthused to the Polish ambassador. The Polish envoy in Germany imagined "that our step was deemed here such an expression of great strength and independent action that it is a true guarantee of our good relations with the government of the Reich."[122] Stalin knew that Poland's 1938 war games had been defensive in character, but the collusion in Czechoslovakia's dismemberment, in his thinking, put Poland on a plane with Nazi Germany.[123] Poland had ignored Soviet warnings, although the Polish ambassador to Moscow reassured the Soviets that "the guiding line of Polish foreign policy is the status quo: nothing with Germany against the USSR and nothing with the USSR against Germany."[124] Still, the Soviets let it be known that the Poles were engaged in a dangerous game: there were more than 6 million Ukrainians and 2 million Belorussians in Poland.

CZECHOSLOVAKIA, AFTER AUSTRIA, became the second great collective missed opportunity of 1938. Very late on the night of October 2, 1938, after Germany and now Poland had carved up Czechoslovakia, the Soviet Union—diplomatically silent for more than thirty-six hours—delivered an affirmative response to the Czechoslovak president's request for unilateral Soviet military support. Moscow's absurdly tardy response, the pinnacle of cynicism, even rebuked Beneš for having failed to fight Germany.[125] Japan's military brass were crestfallen that Munich had defused a European war, which they had hoped would diminish European backing for Chiang Kai-shek and compel his capitulation.[126] As for Hitler, despite the windfall of territory, population, and industry, he had been denied a battlefield triumph, settling for his ostensible aim (the Sudetenland), as opposed to his real one (all of Czechoslovakia).[127] France's perceptive military attaché in Berlin rightly reported to Paris that the Führer viewed Munich as a defeat, and that the Nazis wanted to ramp up propaganda to combat "the profound lassitude which the German people demonstrated when faced with the prospect of another war."[128]

Back in London, Chamberlain, appearing in front of exuberant crowds on the balcony of Buckingham Palace with the king and queen, and again outside his official residence at 10 Downing Street, hailed the Munich Pact as "peace for our time."[129] *Izvestiya* (October 4, 1938) acidly wrote, "It is the first time we know of that the seizure of someone else's territory, the shift of borders guaranteed by international treaties to foreign armies, is nothing less than a 'triumph' or 'victory' for peace." How often did the Soviet press carry the truth? But for Stalin, too, Munich was a defeat. The German ambassador to the Soviet Union had correctly reported to Berlin the sour mood in Moscow.[130] Soviet inaction—however the Kremlin justified it—damaged the country's international standing. Munich also starkly demonstrated Soviet international friendlessness while militarily opening a clear path eastward for Hitler. "History tells us," Stalin himself had observed in an interview with Roy Howard back in 1936, "that when a state wishes to attack a state with which it does not share a border, it begins to create new borders until it neighbors the state it wishes to attack."[131]

Hitler had aggressively shifted his borders farther eastward, in Stalin's direction, and the Western powers had acquiesced. "The second imperialist war has already started," reemphasized the twelfth and final chapter of the *Short Course*. "The characteristic aspect of the second imperialist war is that it is carried on and widened by the aggressive powers, while the other powers, the 'democratic' ones, against whom the war is being waged, pretend that the war does not concern them."[132] Shrewdly, the Polish ambassador to London, Count Edward Raczyński, likened the 1938 Munich Pact to a football match wherein Chamberlain had defended the British goal and shifted "play" to Stalin's side of the pitch. Litvinov was said to have exclaimed, according to the NKVD, that the deal handing Czechoslovakia's Sudetenland to the Nazis portended "an attack on us. . . . War is coming. The one small hope is that Germany somehow rethinks. Perhaps someone will persuade Hitler."[133]

Stalin's murderous rampage, however, had put out of action his nonpareil spy network in Germany. Zelman Passov (b. 1905), the recently appointed head of the NKVD intelligence, who had completed three grades of primary schooling, wrote that "during such sharpening of the international situation, such as the [German] preparations for the seizure of Austria [and] Czechoslovakia, the foreign department [espionage] did not have one agent communication, not a single piece of information, out of Germany."[134]

STALIN WAS NOT FINISHED with the *Short Course*. On October 11–12, 1938, he convened a two-day expanded session of the politburo (an ersatz Central Committee plenum), tasking Zhdanov with delivering the main report. For the first time since 1935, a stenographic record was kept of a politburo session, indicating an intention to circulate the discussion to party members not present. In attendance was the new crop of regional bosses, most of whose predecessors had been put to death. "Did everyone read it, we need to ask, and what are the remarks?" Stalin inquired of the textbook. Molotov chimed in: "Are there comrades who did not read the draft?" Voices: "No, everyone read it." Troshin, from the Gorky (Nizhny Novgorod) province party committee, spoke up: "Many propagandists and district secretaries at the courses say that they understand chapter 4 ["dialectical materialism"] . . . only with the greatest difficulty." Stalin angrily interjected: "That means they have read nothing—not Marx, not Engels." Molotov chided the Gorky comrades for not being able to find a few agitators capable of delivering explanatory lectures. But Oleksandr Khomenko, the head of the propaganda department in the Kiev province party, also said the text was not easy, citing a colleague. Molotov: "If the comrade had earlier read and really knew the history of the party, why are insurmountable difficulties arising for him now?" Khomenko: "He knew the history of the party, comrade Molotov, in terms of those textbooks which we had, and those textbooks were manifestly unsatisfactory." Stalin erupted again: "So it happens like this: some study the history of the party but do not consider themselves obliged to study Marx; others study dialectical materialism and do not consider themselves obliged to study the history of the party."

The party officials whom Stalin had promoted to replace those he had murdered were telling him the truth: they could not manage the *Short Course* intended especially for them.

Stalin asked for the floor. He stressed how, back before 1929, small individual household farms had become predominant, how the establishment of large-scale collectivized farms had been a matter of national survival, and how only Marxism-Leninism allowed one to understand all this. "If cadres determine everything, and that means cadres who work with their intellect, cadres who administer the country, and if these cadres turn out to be politically weakly grounded, that means the state is threatened with danger," he warned, giving as an example the Bukharin-ites, calling "their top layer" irredeemable foreign agents. "But besides the heads, Bukharin and others, there were masses of them, and not all of them were spies and foreign intelligence operatives." Stalin continued: "One may assume that 10,000, 15,000, 20,000, and more were people of Bukharin. One may assume that just as many, and maybe more, were people of Trotskyism. What do you think, were all of them spies? Of course not."

Here was a startling admission two years into a mass terror that had seen some 1.6 million arrests. "What had happened to them?" Stalin continued. "These were cadres who could not swallow the big changeover to the collective farm system, could not comprehend this big changeover, because they were not politically well grounded; they did not know the laws of development of society, the laws of economic development, the laws of political development." He allowed that "we lost many, but we acquired new cadres who won over the people to collectivization and won over the peasant. Only this explains why we were able so easily to replace yesterday's party elite."[135]

He returned, in conclusion, to collectivization: "The key is the chapter about why we went for collective farms. What was this? Was it the caprice of the leaders, the [ideological] itch of the leaders, who (so we are told) read through Marx, drew conclusions, and then, if you please, restructured the whole country according to those conclusions? Was collectivization just something invented—or was it necessity? Those who didn't understand a damn thing about economics—all those rightists, who didn't have the slightest understanding of our society either theoretically or economically, nor the slightest understanding of the laws of historical development, nor the essence of Marxism—they could say such things as suggesting that we turn away from the collective farms and take the capitalist path of development in agriculture."[136] The *Short Course* reconfirmed that the terror emanated from Stalin's mind, not as a response to crisis but as a theory of Soviet history and his rule: party opposition to collectivization, a new generation of functionaries, pedagogy.

THE SOVIET POLITICAL landscape resembled a huge forest full of charred stumps as a wildfire raged on ahead, but Stalin, who had set that fire, was still heaping oil on it long after its catastrophic consequences had become manifest. Finally, however, with the September–October 1938 rollout of the *Short Course*, the training manual for those who had been chosen to go forward (or just got lucky), the mass terror was, in an important sense, complete—and not a moment too soon. Stalin had been barefacedly manipulating the threat of war and foreign intervention to impose and justify this terror, but his murders had shaken the Red Army to its core.[137] And now Munich: not the threat of some abstract war at some point, but right here, right now.[138] The danger to the USSR evidently was grave enough that on October 8, 1938, not long after having demonstrably mobilized the Red Army for possible use against Poland, Stalin had Potyomkin tell the ambassador from Poland—which had just seized a piece of Czechoslovakia in the teeth of Moscow's warnings not to do so—that "no hand extended to the Soviets would be left hanging in the air."[139] So much for Stalin's threat to invalidate the Soviet-Polish nonaggression pact.[140] Poland, too, had been excluded from the deliberations at Munich, but Berlin and Warsaw were in talks.

Supplication of Poland was not Stalin's only conspicuous immediate post-Munich action: a mere eight days after the pact had slapped him across the face, he had also quietly formed a "commission" to investigate arrests by the NKVD. It was made up of the party functionaries Andreyev and Malenkov, as well as Beria and Vyshinsky, and nominally chaired by Yezhov.[141] This heralded the beginning of the end of the mass terror.

Yezhov's men understood that Stalin was moving to bring the Yezhov era at the NKVD to a close. On November 12, 1938, the same week as Marshal Blyukher's death at Beria's hands in Lefortovo prison, Mikhail Litvin, Yezhov's right hand, shot himself. Two days later, the Ukraine NKVD chief, Uspensky—who was also close to Yezhov—composed a suicide note, had his wife purchase him a train ticket eastward to Voronezh, deposited some clothes on the banks of the Dnieper, and fled to Moscow, bringing wads of rubles, to hide at his mistress's apartment. When the money ran out, she kicked him out, and Uspensky headed north to Arkhangelsk, hoping to sign up for logging work, anonymously. Stalin told Khrushchev in Kiev, over the phone, that Yezhov, taking advantage of the NKVD's responsibility for the security of the government communication system, must have listened in on the despot's previous call to Khrushchev about arresting Uspensky and then tipped him off.[142] The day after Uspensky's flight, Stalin, receiving his minions in the Little Corner, had a decree approved disbanding the assembly-line death sentence troikas.[143] On November 17, he summoned Vyshinsky for a "report," after which the despot issued another decree in the politburo's name, justifying the terror but blaming the NKVD for "a host of major deficiencies and distortions."[144]

Just like that, without public acknowledgment, with a few pieces of paper in the Little Corner, the mass terror was halted. Coincidence? The terror supposedly was aimed at rooting out enemies lying in wait for a war, but then, at what would appear to be maximum international war danger for the USSR, Stalin suddenly moved to end the mass arrests. Had he become less paranoid? Was it just that he had been waiting for completion of a *Short Course*? Or was he jolted by events portending actual danger?[145] We cannot definitively establish his motivations. But in the wake of Munich, the despot, in his sixty-first year, had reached a crossroads.

HENRY KISSINGER, IN his magisterial *Diplomacy* (1988), deemed Stalin "the supreme realist—patient, shrewd, and implacable."[146] That is not the Stalin readers have encountered in this book. He often showed himself to be a shrewd operator forced to make difficult choices to defend the interests of his country, but he was never that alone. Just as often, the hard choices that confronted him had been created by his own blunders and gratuitous mayhem. Stalin cannot plausibly be portrayed as a clear-eyed realpolitiker abroad and unhinged mass murderer at home; he was the same calculating, distrustful mind in both cases. Throughout the massacres, he remained thoroughly, passionately engaged in foreign policy, devoted in his way to the cause of the Soviet state and the cause of socialism. He was an ideologue and would-be statesman who forced socialism into being through massive violence—the only way complete anticapitalism could have been achieved—and this building of socialism, in turn, made him the full sociopath he became. Now collectivization was behind him, and the mass terror against his own elites and others mostly behind him, but Hitler was in front of him. Stalin was defiant toward the Western powers and solicitous toward Germany, but fearful of an all-imperialist anti-Soviet coalition incorporating Nazi Germany, too. The resulting pas de trois—Chamberlain, Hitler, Stalin—became, in effect, a Chamberlain-versus-Stalin contest to win over Hitler. Stalin would be put to the supreme test. The stakes were the survival not just of his regime but of the country.

HAMMER

They arrested my first secretary, then they arrested the
second. . . . They arrested my first aide. A Ukrainian, also
from the workers. He was not especially literate, but I
could rely on him as an honest person. They arrested him,
it seems they put a lot of pressure on him, but he did not
want to say a thing and threw himself down the elevator
shaft at the NKVD. That's the way it was with all my staff.

VYACHESLAV MOLOTOV ("Hammer")[1]

THE FORMER AVIATOR NIKOLAI SHPANOV, in his novella *The First Blow: A
Story About the Future War,* published in early 1939 in the thick journal *Banner,*
then as a book in the Library of a Commander series, named Nazi Germany as
the country's principal foe.[2] The action revolved around Soviet Air Force Day
(August 18) in an unspecified future year. People are observing a Soviet pilot's
exploits at an air show when suddenly, over loudspeakers, at precisely 5:00 p.m.,
they hear that Luftwaffe warplanes have violated the Soviet frontier. Within one
minute, Soviet fighters are challenging the Germans in the skies. Only twenty-
nine minutes later, the last surviving German plane has fled Soviet airspace. The
Red Air Force then mounts a lightning counterattack with 700 state-of-the-art
planes into Germany's industrial rear. As bombers reach an aircraft factory at
Nuremberg, German workers break out into "L'Internationale" in solidarity. Already the next morning, Soviet ground troops have smashed across the frontier.
Quick victory comes with little loss of Soviet life. Vsevolod Vishnevsky, in a review, deemed the book "valuable, interesting, profoundly germane," and explained
that "it entertainingly speaks about how the Soviet people will fight a just war
against aggressors, a war that will be fatal for the enemies of socialism."[3]

Outside this dream palace, Stalin faced a harsher, ideology-inflected version of
the security dilemma that had bedeviled his tsarist predecessors: a now even more
aggressive German power on the European continent and a now even more aggressive, militarist Japan moving onto the Asian mainland—two flanking powers

that were now formally allied. In Europe, he could keep trying to secure a deal with anti-Communist France and Britain, in order to try to deter Germany, or keep pursuing a deal somehow with Nazi Germany to try to redirect German ambitions westward. In the Far East, no such deal with the United States or Britain seemed even theoretically possible. Stalin had kept Litvinov in place, despite Yezhov's predations against the foreign affairs commissariat (which Beria would continue).[4] "We sometimes prefer to be isolated rather than to go along with the bad actions of others," Litvinov had written to Maisky in London, "and that is why isolation does not frighten us."[5] But such a retreat into "fortress Russia"—a temptation also indulged by the party's chief ideologue, Zhdanov—afforded Stalin little comfort: the British and the Nazis could join in a deal against the Soviet Union, turning Soviet "isolation" deadly. Had that not been the significance of Munich?[6]

German and Italian planes, following General Franco's directives, had sunk 10 British-registered merchant ships and seriously damaged 37 more that were en route to Spanish Republic ports, but even after outrage had erupted in the House of Commons, Neville Chamberlain had merely told his Tory cabinet that if Franco "must bomb the Spanish [Republic] government ports he must use discretion and that otherwise he might arouse a feeling in this country which would force the government to take action."[7] Franco had sent a letter to Chamberlain thanking him for his "friendship" and underscoring how both leaders stood for "world peace." In Stalin's mind, Spain had starkly illuminated not only the limits of Soviet relations with the West, but also the expansiveness of British-French accommodation with "fascism" (Germany, Italy, and a Francoist Spain). Conversely, the limited but bloody purges inside the Spanish Republic further reinforced doubts among the Western powers about security cooperation with Stalin.

Unlike Litvinov—no less a dyed-in-the-wool Marxist—Stalin refused to distinguish between the imperialists, as either "pacific" (democratic) or "aggressor" (fascist). He divided the world into just two camps, and for him, as for Lenin, all diplomacy amounted to two-faced intercourse with enemies.[8] This stance facilitated a flexible readiness to contemplate either of two diametric opposites: the expedient of "collective security" with the "democratic" capitalists, in Litvinov's parlance, or détente with the "fascists." Post-Munich, Stalin would renew the Soviet efforts at negotiations with Britain and France against Germany. Simultaneously, he would ramp up his so far failed stratagems to reach rapprochement with Hitler's Germany, despite the venom about "Judeo-Bolshevism" out of Berlin.[9] But the image of a wily Stalin brilliantly keeping his options open, to extract maximum advantage, is belied by the fact that neither Hitler nor Chamberlain proved at all forthcoming. Europe's collective security dilemma, drawing in Japan, had deep structural foundations.

PERSONALITIES, REGIMES

In London, far too many British officials labored under the delusion that "moderates," such as Göring, existed in the Nazi hierarchy and could act as restraining influences on Hitler.[10] Some British officials held the view, largely originating with Nevile Henderson, the ambassador to Berlin, that Hitler was like Jekyll and Hyde: normally cautious and reasonable, but given to flying off the handle if provoked or humiliated. Others speculated that, like all dictators, he engaged in "foreign adventurism" to quiet domestic dissatisfaction.[11] Still others subscribed to the view that his seemingly impetuous actions were driven by economic crisis, a view picked up from disaffected Germans.[12] In Moscow, too, next to nothing of Hitler's personality or the operation of his regime was well understood, beyond his uncanny success and Western indulgence of it.[13] Walter Krivitsky, a Soviet intelligence officer (born Samuel "Shmelka" Ginsberg in Austro-Hungarian Galicia), had defected to the West and, in 1938, in the most authoritative Russian émigré newspaper and then in *The Saturday Evening Post,* predicted an imminent deal between Stalin and Hitler. Krivitsky had divulged secret Soviet flirtations, aiming "to convince German leaders of the genuineness of Stalin's own intentions, of his readiness to commit himself quite far in bringing about a rapprochement."[14] But Krivitsky failed to acknowledge how all of Stalin's backdoor and front-door intermediaries with Nazi Germany had made no headway.

Hitler's early circumstances had been nowhere near as humble as Stalin's. (Hitler's father, a senior customs official in the Habsburg empire, earned roughly the same salary as a school principal, and then enjoyed a handsome pension.)[15] But Hitler, too, had not completed his basic education, let alone attended university. No less a striver than Stalin, he had assembled an extensive private library, but he delighted in melodramas, the occult, German translations of Shakespeare, Carlyle's biography of Frederick the Great, Henry Ford's four-volume *The International Jew: The World's Foremost Problem.*[16] (Albert Speer would dub Hitler a "genius of dilettantism.") The Führer showed little interest in foreign languages or travel beyond Germany. His passions were architecture, painting, cinema, classical music, boxing, roadside picnics, and high-speed motoring in his Mercedes-Benz, sitting up front next to his chauffeur. (Hitler could not drive.) He railed against those who put on what he perceived as intellectual airs, feared committing a faux pas among more refined people, basked in the least signs of others' approval, and did not hide his megalomania. "I believe," he had written, echoing Napoleon, "my life is the greatest novel in world history."

Some contemporaries attributed Hitler's interminably long monologues, with quivering lips, to an effort to conceal his inadequacies, rather than a proclivity to get carried away, for he could also restrain himself and come across as an amiable conversationalist. He felt most at ease at reunions of the Munich "street brawlers" from the years of Nazism's rise, but he saw them only once a year. He confided fully in no one. ("Just as I never got close to him, I never observed anyone else doing so, either," Joachim von Ribbentrop would recall.) Hitler enjoyed unguarded relations only with the Wagner clan in Bayreuth and the family of his photographer, Heinrich Hoffmann, through whom Hitler had met Eva Braun (when she was then seventeen, he forty). She eventually became his de facto wife and, although blond and blue-eyed, was secretly checked for Jewish ancestry on Hitler's orders. (She proved to be "Aryan.")[17] Hitler ate no meat, smoked no cigarettes, and rarely consumed alcohol, but he enjoyed cakes and lumping sugar into his tea (he suffered from dental problems). He exercised in order to hold his right arm upward for long stretches and, despising perspiration, took multiple baths each day. He had insomnia, eczema on his legs and feet (making it uncomfortable to wear boots), and gastric pains. A bout of stomach cramps would set him ranting about death from cancer. His mother had died at age forty-seven, and he told confidants he was fated to die young as well. (In May 1938, following the *Anschluss,* he dictated a private will.)[18] He ingested pills, prescribed by his quack doctor, but suspected that kitchen staff aimed to assassinate him (the pots were guarded). He carried a pistol, even as he was surrounded by commandos. He was given to uncontrolled farting.

Hitler can look like a crude and banal figure who inexplicably took over a highly industrialized, culturally advanced, politically sophisticated country, but he had proved to be an astute student of German mass sentiment. He attracted followers partly with his consummate acting skills. He cultivated an image of simplicity and humility, did not carry a wallet, and favored military uniforms, while forgoing any medals other than his Iron Cross First Class and Golden Party Emblem. He possessed a phenomenal memory. He also evinced a talent for mimicking people and situations. "In order to depict the barrage of the first day at the Battle of the Somme more vividly," Ernst "Putzi" Hanfstaengl would recall, "he used a large repertoire of the firing, descent, and impact noises made by French, English, and German howitzers and mortars, the general impression of which he would vividly augment by imitating the hammering tack-tack of the machine guns."[19]

The Führer had commissioned an imposing new chancellor's complex in Berlin, dismissing the existing one as "fit for a soap company." The monumental edifice, with 400 rooms, readied in less than a year, was fronted by square columns and seventeen-foot-high double doors, which were flanked by gilded bronze and stone eagles clutching swastikas in their talons. The building's 480-foot-long upper-floor Marble Gallery, which led to a grand hall for receptions, was twice the length of the Versailles Hall of Mirrors. "On the long walk from the entrance to the reception hall," Hitler boasted to his architect, Albert Speer, "they'll get a taste of the power and grandeur of the German Reich!" Hitler, meanwhile, lived in the old "soap" building, using its modest study as his main working office. But off the new Chancellery's Marble Gallery stood the Führer's vast "study," for the audiences he granted, with portraits of Prudence, Fortitude, Justice, and Wisdom above the four doors. Hitler's lengthy afternoon meals at the Chancellery (beginning at 2:00 or 3:00) involved up to fifty people; they merely had to telephone the adjutant to say they'd be coming—without being summoned. These were not Germany's military brass or industrialists, but the inner court of Reichsleiters and Gauleiters and old party comrades, often from Munich. Evening suppers were more intimate still, comprising six to eight persons—Hitler's doctor, photographer, pilot, radioman, private secretary (Martin Bormann)—where, according to Speer, "usually Hitler would tell stories about his life."[20]

Frequently, though, Hitler was absent from Berlin, seeking refuge at his Bavarian alpine retreat, the Berghof, where he relished holding forth on race and global conquest in table talks. Like Stalin, Hitler fretted about being alone. ("Hitler needs to have people around him," Goebbels had observed early on. "Otherwise he broods too much.")[21] But unlike Stalin, the Führer was unwilling or incapable of submitting to routine. Nazi Germany was a scrum of divergent interests—party, army, bureaucratic fiefdoms, private industry—with a proliferation of ad hoc agencies and plenipotentiaries.[22] Hitler refused to chair committees or agencies, and often went lengthy periods without summoning officials.[23] After February 5, 1938, the infrequent cabinet meetings had ceased altogether. Hitler's diligence went into preparing the texts for his speeches, which he rewrote with fountain pen after dictating a first draft, and into military affairs. But he awoke late and appeared at work well after noon, glancing through clippings assembled by the Reich press chief, then repairing to "breakfast" and avoiding his own officials. ("I asked myself often: when did he really work?" recalled Speer.)[24] His desk was empty, and he almost never worked at it. ("For him, desks were mere pieces of decoration," the head of the Hitler Youth recalled.) Reports went unread. "He disliked reading files," recalled Fritz Wiedemann, who in the 1930s served as Hitler's adjutant. "I got decisions out of him, even on very important matters, without his ever asking me for the relevant papers. He took the view that many things sorted themselves out if they were left alone."[25]

Stalin's regime, too, was beset by improvisation, but the despot devoured documents and, even when away from Moscow down south, used the telephone, telegraph, and field couriers assiduously.[26] One comes away flabbergasted not by learning what went on without Stalin's involvement, but by the quantity of information he managed to command and the number of spheres in which he intervened. He had terminated the increasingly infrequent formal meetings of the politburo, but he was as obsessively hands-on as Hitler was sometimes disengaged. Stalin read and affixed written directives; Hitler conducted state affairs mostly by talking, and his interlocutors—sometimes an oddly assembled bunch—would piece together decisions from the ramblings or try to get him to confirm them later. For all that, no small degree of coordination took place through the Chancellery and the Führer conferences. He hesitated to intervene in bureaucratic struggles to avoid being caught up in unpopular decisions and festering resentments.[27] On the issues of greatest importance to Hitler, from foreign affairs to the Jewish question, he encouraged the involvement of multiple agencies. He would sometimes set the players against one another, in "a carefully balanced system of mutual enmity," as Speer would note. Oscillating between freneticism and lethargy, Hitler tended to postpone the most difficult decisions, biting his fingernails while others waited and waited. "Sometimes," one secretary recalled, "he would stop and stare silently at Lenbach's portrait of Bismarck, lost in thought and collecting himself before he started to wander around again."[28]

Stalin sometimes took the wives of his top officials hostage and arrested and executed their aides; Hitler allowed pre-1933 comrades—Göring, Goebbels, Himmler, a few others—to build power centers within the state.[29] Hitler showed awareness of the need to indulge the preferences of elites and powerful bodies. Supposedly, his style of rule incited minions to forge ahead with initiatives in the hope of anticipating his wishes and earning favor, in what has been called "working toward the Führer," but that was possible only in certain spheres, and when Hitler became cognizant of underlings' efforts to take such initiatives, he often intervened to stop them.[30] Stalin's micromanagement and flashes of anger largely precluded proactive risk taking in the first place. Local officials almost always awaited explicit instructions, which, however, often turned out to be impossible to fulfill, so they began a process not of "working toward the *vozhd*," but cat and mouse (circumventions, prevarications, concealment), which drove Stalin's desire to clamp down further. The Soviet political machine often suffered paralysis not from Hitler-style ostensible aloofness but from extreme centralization and dependency on a single person who just could not do everything. In the end, whether at the Little Corner or the Near or Sochi dacha, the Chancellery or the Berghof mountain hideaway, everything revolved around the Person. Every functionary's dream was to serve as Hitler's or Stalin's personal representative—*the* authority for a designated sphere of activity.

BERIA'S TAKEOVER

Yezhov could have schemed to flee abroad, dealing a blow to the Soviet state and paying Stalin back for mistreatment, but instead he retreated to his dacha. On November 19, 1938, the "politburo" summoned the NKVD commissar to the Little Corner, where, from 11:10 p.m. until 4:20 a.m., they discussed a denunciation of him that Beria had orchestrated from a provincial NKVD boss (Viktor Zhuravlyov).[31] Yezhov wrote a letter to Stalin, which he likely ended up not sending, saying that "the past two years of tense, highly strung work have acutely strained my whole nervous system."[32] He was accused of having permitted foreign spies to capture Soviet espionage. On November 23, Yezhov was again in Stalin's office, where he had logged nearly 900 hours over the previous two years, but these three and a half would be his last: Stalin edited Yezhov's resignation.[33] On November 25, the despot sent a telegram to all regional party secretaries referring to Zhuravlyov's denunciation of NKVD errors and noting that "the Central Committee had granted Yezhov's request to resign."[34] *Pravda* printed a delayed announcement, on its back page (December 8). Executing the NKVD chief could throw into doubt the mass arrests and executions. For now, Stalin retained Yezhov as a Central Committee secretary, chairman of the party Control Commission, and water transport commissar.

Beria, even as deputy NKVD chief, had arrested 332 NKVD leadership personnel between September and December 1938, including 140 in the central apparatus and 18 of the NKVD commissars in Union and autonomous republics. NKVD operatives still on the job became disoriented.[35] So did military men. "Now, if you notice or unmask an enemy, there's no one to inform about it, because the higher the boss, the more likely he's an enemy of the people," one Red Army political worker complained. "You have to ask: Who can you believe, and to whom do you report?" Another asked who the enemy was: the person who got arrested or the person who did the arresting?[36] At the same time, hopeful letters poured in as people logically assumed that their cases—which had been falsified—would be overturned. At the defense commissariat alone, nearly 2,000 such letters were being received *every day*.

As NKVD chief, Beria insinuated himself deeply into the regime. Initially, he had brought just a handful of his gang to Moscow, including Vsevolod Merkulov, a graduate of St. Petersburg University and the son of an aristocrat tsarist officer, and son-in-law of a tsarist general (who had served as war minister in the Provisional Government). Merkulov was the only ethnic Russian among Beria's Caucasus subordinates, and Beria named him first deputy in Moscow. Another was Bogdan Kobulov (b. 1904), a Tbilisi Armenian who had been expelled from the Communist Youth League and arrested for rape in 1921, but became an informant for, and then an operative in, the secret police; Kobulov became deputy chief of the investigation department. But when annihilation of Yezhovites opened up expansive vistas for Beria's people, he summoned many others from the Caucasus: Lavrenti Janjava, known as Tsanava (b. 1900), who had been expelled from the party in 1922 for abducting a bride (he was reinstated the next year) and became NKVD chief in Belorussia; Goglidze (b. 1901), who would be given the Leningrad NKVD; Solomon Milstein (b. 1898), descended from a wealthy trading family of Vilnius Jews (most of whom had fled abroad after the revolution), who began as deputy head of investigation but would get the new NKVD rail transport department; and Vladimir Dekanozov (b. 1898), who would get a series of high posts.[37]

Georgians in the NKVD in Moscow would jump from 3.13 percent (January 1938)—already nearly double their weight in the overall population—to 7.84 percent (July 1939).[38] Georgians aside, Beria's NKVD saw a dramatic reduction in minorities, especially Jews, and promotion of ethnic Russians.[39] Regime officials who had once looked to Yezhov as someone who would clean up the antiparty actions and mistakes of his predecessor viewed Beria as someone who would do the same. Releases of some people arrested under Yezhov reinforced such illusions. Stalin got credit for correcting his mistaken trust in Yezhov, and for a new, vigorous, loyal top official.[40] Beria's power came to exist on a completely different plane from Yezhov's or Yagoda's. Stalin, however, made sure to have non-Beriaites inserted into key positions (Sergei Kruglov, who had been on Malenkov's list of possible NKVD first deputy chiefs, got the critical post of head of NKVD personnel).[41] Stalin also directed Beria to turn in the documents regarding his role in the Musavat; Beria had Merkulov collect and deliver them.[42]

BUCK-PASSING

Stalin had shattered his own remarkable spy network: of the 450 secret police officials stationed abroad, at least 275 had been arrested by his regime.[43] In January 1939, the despot was informed that "the USSR NKVD does not have a single spy coordinator [*rezident*] abroad and not one proven agent. The work of the NKVD foreign department practically is destroyed and in essence needs to be organized from scratch."[44] Similarly, the acting chief of the key western department of the separate agency for military intelligence reported that "the Red Army is essentially without an intelligence arm. The agent networks, which are the basis of intelligence, have almost all been liquidated."[45] In truth, recruited foreign agents and underground informants were still out there, but, with a few key exceptions, such as the German embassies in Warsaw and Tokyo, they lacked handlers to receive information. Beria would work to reconstitute espionage.

Even with good espionage, Hitler remained difficult to gauge: how far would he *actually* go? How far *could* he really go? He had started from tremendous relative weakness. Germany had lost a war, it lacked an army, navy, air force, or financial prowess, and Hitler's actions were necessarily full of zigs and zags, opportunistic, hard to read. He decried unfair treatment of his country, made "concessions," talked ceaselessly of nonaggression pacts and peace. His vision was vague enough to allow people to see it as just an overheated version of long-standing German nationalism.[46] Indeed, the Nazis' ultimate goals—eradicating a supposed global Jewish conspiracy; complete German racial dominance of Europe—seemed so improbable that even some minions in the know could scarcely believe Hitler actually meant them in full.[47] The Munich-born Konrad Heiden had published, in exile, the first serous biography of Hitler, in two volumes in 1936–37, arguing that Germany's raw materials and food base would be insufficient for taking on the European continent, especially because any new conflict, like the previous one, would be long. Heiden also predicted that Hitler's rearmament would provoke counter-rearmament and alliances against Germany.[48] But by early 1939, no such blocking coalition had formed.

For Stalin, rapprochement with the Western imperialists had always been a dangerous game full of illusions: the capitalists could never be trusted because they could never permanently accept the existence of Soviet power. Like Lenin, he held in contempt any promises the imperialists might make. Just as Poland's Pił-sudski had once used the Soviet Union's courtship to obtain a nonaggression declaration with the supposedly anti-Polish Nazi regime, the British would play the same game, using negotiations with Stalin to obtain a deal with Hitler. If Britain and Germany had joined forces before 1914, they could have destroyed Russia as a world power.[49] Preventing just such a mésalliance between London and Berlin had become Stalin's fixation. He had received a continuous flow of intelligence about the relentless British efforts to cozy up to Germany and divert it in the direction of the USSR almost from the moment of Hitler's accession to power.[50] British officials harbored the exact suspicion in reverse, perceiving Stalin's interest in negotiations with them as a ploy to win his own deal with Hitler while "stealthily and cunningly pulling all the strings behind the scenes to get us involved in war with Germany," as Chamberlain had privately remarked to one of his sisters), when the real quarrel, to British thinking, was between Nazism and Communism.[51]

Many members of the British establishment detested the Bolsheviks as incubators of colonial revolutionaries who threatened the British empire, and they viewed Russia as semibarbarous, run by people of the wrong sort. In the early 1930s, Reader Bullard, British consul general in the Soviet Union, described Litvinov—who had been born Meir Henoch Mojszewicz Wallach-Finkelstein, in 1876, to a well-off banking family in Białystok—as a "Warsaw Jew" and "shameless liar."[52] Beyond well-grounded suspicions of Russia and ingrained anti-Communism flavored by anti-Semitism, an alliance with the Soviet Union effectively constituted an admission that war could not be avoided.[53] Most ordinary Brits, in what was a democracy, were of a mind that the Great War slaughterhouse had claimed nearly 1 million subjects for naught. The war had increased the national debt tenfold in four years.[54] Most British conservatives—not just those in the Tory government—to a degree shared Chamberlain's preferred policy of negotiation with Hitler as a way of exerting influence over him.[55] A majority of the opposition Labour party remained pacifist throughout Nazi aggrandizement, opposing rearmament.[56] "Lose or win," one influential British journalist had observed, catching the general view, "a world war would be for England the end of everything."[57]

Britain felt overextended already, defending a global empire. The Scramble for Africa had never fully subsided, while in India, Palestine, Northern Ireland, and elsewhere, insurgencies drained resources and men. The Depression and misguided fiscal and monetary tightening had undercut confidence as well: real output in 1938 was no better than it had been in 1918 (annual GDP growth averaged 0.5 percent). Various worst-case scenarios in British intelligence reports—which for a long time had been underplaying Nazi Germany's capabilities but now grossly overestimated them—enhanced the appeal of negotiation. So did underestimation of the Red Army. On top of everything, Eastern Europe and even the continent as a whole were just not a British priority, notwithstanding the Versailles Treaty.[58] Chamberlain was, by conviction, fiscally conservative. He abjured investing in a continental expeditionary force, which to his mind would only embolden France to take risks against Germany and bankrupt the British treasury.[59] Still, he was investing in the Royal Air Force and the Royal Navy. If all else failed and Hitler tried to overrun Western Europe—which seemed unlikely, given the existence of the French land army—the British home isles, Chamberlain reasoned, could be defended.[60]

Chamberlain not only convinced himself that he could accede to grievances of Nazi Germany without infringing core British interests, but also the grievances of fascist Italy and Imperial Japan, and, via bilateral agreements, diminish these powers' incentives for trilateral cooperation as well.[61] His combination of diplomacy (engagement, conciliation) and a measure of deterrence (the threat of a massive bombing campaign)—what was known as appeasement (essentially to make peace)—occupied a venerable place in British policy, dating back to the nineteenth century. It offered a way of settling international quarrels by appealing to the other side's reasonableness and forging compromises, rather than opting for costly war.[62] Why stumble down the path of turning the latest equivalent of a Balkan squabble into a world war? A repeat threatened equally bloody futility, at a minimum, and potentially far worse: Communist subversion of the continent in the ruins.[63]

Germany's other great-power antagonist, France, was also the only other large democracy left in Europe. Its geopolitical position was unenviable. France had triumphed in the Great War, but the conflict had been fought to immense devastation on its soil, and, in the aftermath, it lacked the wherewithal to hold down a rising Germany. The United States had tipped the balance in the war and could have provided the security guarantees that would have allowed France, in the 1920s, to make the kinds of concessions to Germany that Britain advocated and stability required, but the Americans had had no desire to do so.[64] Instead, French postwar security had come to rest on three shakier pillars: a military occupation of Germany's Rhineland, military superiority over a disarmed Germany, and alliances with the newly independent small states on the eastern side of Germany. The first two had vanished. As for the third, Eastern Europe roiled with homegrown animosities and irredentism that undermined reliable security partnerships. France's alliance system with Poland and Czechoslovakia had hollowed out even before Hitler had put it to the test.[65] And so, behind the defenses of the Maginot Line (named for a defense minister who had launched its construction), France was thrown back onto its familiar options: alliance with the British or alliance with the Russians. Before the Munich Pact, the Tory government had exhibited ruthless caution toward entanglement with France, and after Munich it took only baby steps, initiating staff talks with France.[66]

Munich had almost pushed Stalin in the opposite direction: he contemplated denouncing the Franco-Soviet pact before reaffirming it.[67] But Stalin's on-and-off efforts to convert the 1935 Franco-Soviet mutual assistance treaty into a real military alliance against German power—following in the footsteps of Nicholas II—had produced only desultory military talks.[68] Britain staunchly opposed a Franco-Soviet military convention, and Paris would not break from London, even after the Munich debacle, and even after the French ambassador's warnings out of Moscow that the Soviet Union was not a colossus with feet of clay and could cozy up to Berlin.[69] The French general staff continued to dismiss the Red Army's value in a European war and to underscore the USSR's lack of common borders with Germany and the fact that Poland and Romania remained disinclined to grant transit routes.[70] Stalin's executions of three of his five marshals amid public accusations that they and others had given away battle plans and other secrets to the Nazis cast new doubt on the Red Army as a possible partner.[71] But even before the full denouement of the grisly executions, the French had backed away from the military talks.[72] For Prime Minister Daladier—the man who had granted Trotsky asylum in France back in 1933—another pan-European war would mean the "utter destruction of European civilization," opening a vacuum for "Cossack and Mongol hordes."[73]

So that was it: Germany foaming at the mouth with anti-Communism and anti-Slav racism, and now armed to the teeth; Britain cautious and aloof in the face of another continental war; and France even more exposed than Britain, yet deferring to London, and wary of its nominal ally, the USSR. Stalin was devastating his own country with mass murders and bald-faced mendacities, but the despot faced a genuine security impasse: German aggression and buck-passing by great powers—himself included.

MUSIC AND TORTURE

Secret police, in their smartest dress uniforms, lined the walls of the cavernous main hall and all the entrances of the Grand Kremlin Palace for the 1939 New Year's banquet. Soviet officials did not bring their wives unless the latter, too, held official positions, such as Molotov's Zhemchuzhina (fishing industry commissar). But much of the beau monde was intermarried: the actor Ivan Moskvin attended with his wife, Alla Tarasova, a star of the same theater; the filmmaker Alexandrov with his wife, the singer-starlet Lyubov Orlova; the dancer Igor Moiseyev with his common-law wife, the Bolshoi prima ballerina Nina Podgoretskaya. But Stalin himself could come off as the movie star: the mischievous grin, the lifted head, the pauses, nods, glances. During the toasts, when he called out Soviet triumphs and heroes, people clinked glasses, tapped knives and forks, and shouted his name. By the time the USSR State Jazz Band entered the anteroom of the Andreyev Hall, it was after 2:00 a.m. A Chekist, as the police liked to be called, summoned them to the stage following the Alexandrov Red Army Ensemble—240 singers and dancers—and Moiseyev's State Folk Dance Ensemble.

"We walked into the dimly lit, deserted Andreyev Hall, which is used by the Supreme Soviet for its meetings," recalled Juri Jelagin. "The hall was lined with rows of armchairs like a theater auditorium, or perhaps more like a university auditorium, because each chair was equipped with a small writing desk and a radio headset." They reached a door, behind which was a stage. "The bright lights blinded us. We were in the ornate, white [St. George's] Hall of the Kremlin. . . . The large tables were crowded with people, and a regular feast was in progress." In front of the stage, at a distance from the other tables, was the Presidium table, the seats facing the hall, backs to the performers. When the jazz musicians appeared on the stage, Stalin and his entourage turned and applauded. "Stalin was wearing a khaki tunic without any ribbons or decorations. He smiled at us and nodded encouragement. In front of him stood a half-empty glass of brandy." The jazzmen, with their female vocalist, Nina Donskaya, performed "Jewish Rhapsody," by Svyatoslav Knushevitsky, perhaps Moscow's top cellist. (He was married to Natalya Spiller, the Bolshoi soprano much admired by Stalin.) For whatever reason, according to Jelagin, Stalin paid no attention to Donskaya. "He turned away and began to eat."

The mass murderer was able to differentiate, within his conventional tastes, a sublime performance from a merely good one. He loved opera, and selections were invariably included from the prerevolutionary repertoire (Rimsky-Korsakov, Glinka, Mussorgsky, Borodin, Tchaikovsky) and the better-known Western classics (*Carmen, Faust,* and *Aida*). But his greatest passion was for Russian, Ukrainian, and Georgian folk songs.[74] After the jazz band had concluded its six approved numbers—among them Tchaikovsky's "Sentimental Waltz" and Stalin's sentimental favorite, "Suliko"—the Presidium table, according to Jelagin, "applauded long and vigorously." Only now, after exiting and storing their instruments, were the musicians invited to dine—in a separate hall for performers, one floor below, loaded with "caviar, hams, salads, fish, fresh vegetables [in winter], decanters of vodka, red and white wine, and fine Armenian brandy. There were about four hundred of us, but the tables could seat at least a thousand." Here, the Chekist servers wore their police uniforms. The musicians were addressed by the latest chairman of the committee on artistic affairs, Alexei Nazarov (b. 1905), who toasted Stalin as well as some of the most famous performers, such as the singer Ivan Kozlovsky.[75]

Kozlovsky (b. 1900), the virtuoso soloist at the Bolshoi (since 1926), would receive the Order of Lenin in 1939. (The next year, Stalin would make him a USSR People's Artist.) He possessed a transparent, even voice, with a beautiful and gentle timbre in the upper register, which was not particularly powerful yet filled the largest spaces. He hailed from a Ukrainian village and had a brother who had emigrated at the end of the civil war and ended up in the United States, which alone would have been enough to doom the tenor. Zealous Chekists went to Kozlovsky's native village to dig up dirt, but when Poskryobyshev handed Stalin thick files of compromising material, the despot was said to have observed, "Fine, we'll imprison comrade Kozlovsky—and who'll sing, you?"[76] Apocryphal or not, the despot was known to keep track of the schedule for the Bolshoi and to terminate meetings in the Little Corner to catch an aria sung by Kozlovsky, Maxim

Mikhailov (a bass), or Mark Reizen (also a bass), the lyrical tenor Sergei Lemeshev, the lyrical sopranos Spiller and Yelena Kruglikova, or the mezzo-soprano Vera Davydova.[77] At the New Year's gala, Kozlovsky, who acquired the reputation of being an unbearable person, sang "La Donna è Mobile," from *Rigoletto*, at Stalin's request.[78]

Two days later, Stalin informed USSR procurator general Vyshinsky that he wanted a public trial of those arrested in the NKVD.[79] "The enemies of the people who penetrated the organs of the NKVD," the commission on the secret police internally reported to Stalin—as if the secret police rampage had somehow occurred without his directives—"consciously distorted the punitive policy of Soviet power, conducting a mass of baseless arrests of people guilty of nothing, and at the same time protecting the activities of enemies of the people. . . . They urged that prisoners offer testimony about their supposed espionage activity for foreign intelligence, explaining that such invented testimony was necessary for the party and the government in order to discredit foreign states." The despot circulated the report to the inner circle: they needed to know how to interpret the terror, as the result of the infiltration of "spies in literally every [NKVD] department."[80] But for whatever reason, a public trial of the NKVD never took place. "I am very busy with work," Stalin wrote (January 6, 1939) to Afinogenov, the reprieved writer, who had sent a copy of his latest play to read. "I beg forgiveness."[81]

Beria issued a secret directive calling for NKVD branches to cease recruiting informants for surveillance of party and factory bosses, and to destroy, in their presence, the files compiled against them.[82] Provincial party bosses were even invited to scrutinize the dossiers of all NKVD personnel in their domains.[83] But Stalin had some second thoughts. "The Central Committee has learned," he wrote in a telegram to all locales (January 10, 1939), "that the secretaries of provinces and territories, checking on the work of the local NKVD, have charged them with using physical means of interrogation against those arrested as if it were a crime." He informed them that the "physical methods" had been approved by "the Central Committee" and agreed to by "the Communist parties of all the republics" (whose leaders had almost all been shot as foreign agents and wreckers). "It is known that all bourgeois intelligence services apply physical coercion with regard to representatives of the socialist proletariat, and in the ugliest forms," he stressed. "One might ask why the socialist intelligence service must be more humane with regard to inveterate agents of the bourgeoisie."[84]

COMPLICATING FACTORS

Stalin exacerbated but did not invent the hostility of his Eastern European neighbors. Lithuania, Latvia, Estonia, and Finland preferred neutrality but, if forced to choose, would opt for Berlin over Moscow.[85] Romania was openly pro-German. Poland, a nasty regime sandwiched directly between two nastier ones, sought a middle way. Some members of Polish ruling circles latched on to the idea of throwing in their lot with Hitler to deflect him farther eastward, even at the high cost of territorial concessions, and a few high-placed Poles fantasized about a joint Polish-Nazi attack on the USSR, an aggression in which they imagined Poland could wrest Ukraine from the Soviets, a delusion that Nazi officials cynically encouraged.[86] But Polish foreign minister Beck, who spoke good German, had met several times with Hitler, trying to reach an accommodation without sacrificing Poland's independence. In early 1939, Hitler summoned him to Berlin for one last effort to bully Poland into joining the Anti-Comintern Pact, which would have required that Poland allow the Wehrmacht to march across its territory and "return" to Germany the Free City of Danzig and the surrounding Polish Corridor (a chunk of territory that had belonged to Frederick the Great's East Prussia but, thanks to the Versailles Treaty, now belonged to Poland and lay between German East Prussia and the rest of Germany). Poland would have become economically dependent on (nonexistent) Nazi goodwill.[87]

Soviet intelligence, thanks to its penetration of the German embassy in Poland, reported (February 10, 1939) that Hitler had allegedly told Beck there was no need to seize Ukraine, for "the Soviet Union in two to three years would perish of its own internal contradictions and clear the path for Germany and Poland to reach a friendly resolution of the Ukrainian question." The Soviet report further observed that Hitler had bent over backward to ingratiate himself, which German diplomatic personnel in Poland interpreted as merely tactical, and that "Beck, it seems, had been left unsatisfied by the conversation and as before thinks the fundamental aim of German expansion remains the East, and in this connection Hitler does not plan on making any concessions to Poland."[88]

Nonetheless, Soviet military intelligence reported to Moscow that the German ambassador in Warsaw, Hans-Adolf von Moltke, had boasted to a German journalist on February 13 that "the situation is utterly clear. We know that in the event of a German-Soviet conflict, Poland would take our side."[89] The Western powers, too, suspected illiberal Poland of being pro-German and territorially revisionist.

But Beck had refused to make any firm commitments regarding Hitler's entreaties. He knew Western support for Poland was fragile—as did everyone, after Munich—and he feared a *Western* diktat over Danzig and the Corridor. But he nonetheless pinned Poland's security hopes on Britain and France. The alternative, a security alliance with the Soviet Union, was anathema. The Soviets returned the enmity, and had lacked even an ambassador in Warsaw since November 1937 (through June 1939).

Poland's best security guarantee was probably a full-scale war by Japan against the Soviet Union, and Polish military intelligence worked extremely closely with its Japanese counterpart, essentially conducting an extended tutorial on their common adversary. Japanese Manchukuo forces continued to engage Soviet and Mongolian troops in border clashes. The Soviet spy Sorge (codenamed "Ramsay") relayed to Moscow (January 23, 1939) an analysis of infighting among three factions in Japan. One demanded a ramping up of the all-out war with China; a second, the Kwantung Army, demanded a peace settlement with China to shift to all-out war with the Soviet Union; a third, in a variant on the second, urged winding down operations in central and south China and holding on to only northern China and Manchuria, to use as a base of operations for attacking the USSR. Sorge included the prime and war ministers in the third group and added that the only way for Japan to corral domestic radicalism was to turn the radicals' attention toward the USSR.[90]

Adding to the pressure on Moscow, anti-Soviet émigrés in Harbin, China, were using radio to debunk Soviet propaganda in broadcasts into eastern Soviet territories. Radio stations from German territory were also transmitting in Russian to the westernmost parts of the Soviet Union, whose equipment was not powerful enough to jam these foreign signals.[91]

Through it all, Hitler remained Stalin's most complicating factor. "One thing I should like to say on this day which may be memorable for others as well as for us Germans: In the course of my life I have very often been a prophet, and have usually been ridiculed for it," Hitler raved, deep into a speech on January 30, 1939, the sixth anniversary of his becoming chancellor. "Above all the Jewish people only laughed at my prophecies. I believe that such gales of laughter now stick in the throats of Jewry in Germany." He continued: "Today I will once more be a prophet: if the international finance Jewry inside and outside Europe should succeed in plunging the nations once more into a world war, then the result will not be the Bolshevization of the earth, and thus the victory of Jewry, but the annihilation of the Jewish race in Europe."[92] This revealing resentment-cum-threat was partly a belated response to Roosevelt and U.S. criticisms of the anti-Jewish pogrom Kristallnacht, as well as to bogged-down negotiations over restrictions for Jewish immigrants from Germany and Austria, and an equation of the United States with "the headquarters of world Jewry."[93] The Reichstag erupted in acclamation.

Hitler had achieved more than anyone—perhaps even he himself—had imagined, and he wielded his increasing power and confidence to raise the stakes. On February 13, 1939, he placed a laurel on the grave of Otto von Bismarck, and the next day he presided over the launching of the *Bismarck,* Germany's grandest new battleship. "As Führer of the German people and Chancellor of the Reich," he told the assembled crowd, "I can give this ship no finer name."[94] Of course, Bismarck, unifier of Germany, had proceeded from a sense of limits and a need for balance, not unlimited expansion, and had refrained from swallowing the Habsburg empire, while Hitler had already annexed Austria and Czechoslovakia's Sudetenland. At the same time, the prohibitive costs of Hitler's ongoing rearmament and military actions, as well as anxiety over raw material supply, were mounting. The national debt had tripled since his takeover.[95] Hitler ordered a reduction in the Wehrmacht budget for the first quarter of 1939. But the army, knowing the Führer, ignored the limit. Hitler did not make strategic decisions on the basis of economic considerations.[96] Still, more affordable supplies of raw materials for the war machine had to be found.[97] Germany had submitted to Moscow a request for formal trade talks, and Mikoyan handed the German ambassador two new shopping lists for industrial goods in February 1939.[98] *The USSR and the Capitalist Encirclement,* a book published that same month, asserted that the "ruling class" in Britain and France desired not an alliance with the USSR against "fascism," but a war between the Soviet Union and Germany.[99]

PURSUING REWARDS

Soviet prisons now held an estimated 350,000 inmates, while Gulag labor camps and colonies held 1.665 million. But the recorded proportion of prisoners who did not work in the period 1937–39 ranged from 16.6 percent to 27.1 percent. The camp complexes had accumulated ill, invalid, and idle "laborers."[100] The slave labor productivity exception had always been the gold-mining trust in the Kolyma River region of the far northeast. Stalin sent a telegram (January 24, 1939) praising Karp Pavlov, Dalstroi's head: "Let us reward all, starting with Pavlov, without embarrassment or false modesty." A two-decade veteran of the secret police, with service from Crimea to Krasnoyarsk, Pavlov had arrived two years before to replace the long-serving head of Dalstroi, who was executed as the head of a counterrevolutionary spy-diversionist Trotskyist organization.[101] On February 2, 1939, Pavlov received the Order of Lenin. That winter, thousands of gold diggers would again perish.

New influxes would double the Dalstroi population to 160,000 by the end of the year. (Soon Pavlov would be promoted to chief of mining and metallurgy for the entire Gulag.)[102] Dalstroi had acquired enough performers to form a local symphony and a musical comedy troupe, both of which entertained the bosses in the local "capital" of Magadan, a jumble of log cabins and transit prisons known as the Athens of Okhotsk.[103] Magadan could claim a higher concentration not just of musicians and actors, but of doctors, scholars, poets, novelists, photographers, and painters, than any urban center east of the Urals, and many to the west, but the terror had killed off the trust's technical specialists and lowered productivity.[104] Magadan officials begged to see Union-wide arrest lists so they could scour them for geologists, hydrologists, and other desperately needed "wreckers" and "Trotskyites."

Beria's NKVD discovered a self-styled "fascist organization" in Moscow, whose handful of members had evidently fashioned a flag, put up seventy posters on the eve of Red Army Day (February 23), drew some graffiti, and wrote poems. They seem to have discussed Nazism, anti-Semitism, and Russian nationalism. At least one turned informant, leading to four arrests. Three of the members turned out to have been nineteen when they joined the group; the organizer was seventeen. The NKVD produced five volumes on the case.[105]

ABSENT FATHER

Stalin received a troubling report in February 1939 from his son Vasily's military aviation school. Now almost eighteen, he had become a candidate member of the party, but not long before, Stalin had written to one of Vasily's teachers at his previous school that he was "a spoiled youth of middling capabilities, a wild beast (like the Scythians), not always truthful, loves to blackmail weak 'bosses,' not infrequently impudent, with a weak—more accurately—unorganized will. . . . He was spoiled by sundry 'godfathers' and 'godmothers,' who reinforced the circumstance that he is 'Stalin's son.'"[106] With Vasily's transfer to the military school in Crimea, Beria had reported to Stalin that the school's bosses had met him with pomp at the train station. Stalin had ordered that Vasily be moved to a regular barracks.[107] The latest report, cleverly worded, was framed in praise: "Politically literate. Dedicated to the cause of the party of Lenin-Stalin and our motherland. Actively interested and well versed in questions of the international and domestic situation." But it also noted that Vasily was given to cramming, occasionally reported unshaven for duty, and "reacts badly to snafus in flight."[108] His friends found him generous—and a target. "Despite a nondescript appearance (small stature, scrawny, redheaded, chalky)," one acquaintance recalled of him that "all kinds of sycophants and especially girls clung to him like flies to honey."[109]

Stalin continued to shower tenderness on his daughter, Svetlana—when he saw her. Now thirteen and without her brother or longtime housekeeper, Karolina Til, she continued to live in the Kremlin apartment, where her father appeared only for late-evening "lunches." The dining room "had a large, carved sideboard with my mother's cups on it and a table with the latest newspapers and magazines," she recalled. "Above it was a large portrait of my mother, a blown-up print of one of the photographs taken at our house." After the meal, Stalin would go back upstairs to the office or head out to the Near Dacha for the night. Svetlana spent summers partly at the old Zubalovo dacha, partly either in Sochi or Mukhalatka, Crimea. "Sometimes after school was out in the summer, he'd take me to Kuntsevo for three days or so," she would recall of the Near Dacha. "He enjoyed having me around. But it didn't work out, because it was impossible for anybody to fit in with his way of life. He'd have his first meal at two or three in the afternoon and lunch at eight in the evening. Then he'd sit up late at the table. . . . It was too much for me." They did go for walks in the Kuntsevo woods, and, thanks to her nurse's lessons, Svetlana would ace her father's oral quizzes on the names of flowers, grasses, and singing birds. But soon he would have to return to his paperwork. "At that point he didn't need me anymore," Svetlana continued. "I'd get restless and bored and long to leave as quickly as possible for Zubalovo, where I could take one of my friends with me and there were so many things I enjoyed. Meantime, my father thought it was being with him that bored me, and that hurt his feelings." Svetlana's nanny would advise her to ask forgiveness, and he would talk to her again. "I heard him mutter angrily, 'She went away! Imagine leaving her old father like that! Says she's bored!' But he was kissing me and had already forgiven me, for without me he had been lonelier than ever."[110]

18TH PARTY CONGRESS

Great powers, when menaced by a rising or aggressive power, usually build up their militaries and seek strategic alliances, but *leadership* in the international arena has always been costly, and each power had drawn the lesson from the Great War experience that defense trumped offense, such that any new war could not be won easily. The benefits of getting someone else to do the fighting appeared to be very high, while the risks of that other side succumbing quickly appeared to be low.[111] And so, Britain, France, and the Soviet Union were each keen to afford the others the "honor" of standing up to Germany. Stalin worried about a linkup of the others behind his back ("a united imperialist front against the USSR"). His energetic feelers for political rapprochement with Germany and, less energetically, for a binding military dimension to his mutual assistance pact with France had failed to make headway. Facing two blind alleys—Paris/London and Berlin—he opened the 18th Party Congress on March 10, in the combined Andreyev-Alexander hall of the Grand Kremlin Palace.

Stalin had not been compelled to convoke a congress. This was the first since the January 1934 "Congress of Victors," and thus the first to take place in the wake of his terror (a "congress of survivors," as it were). Back when admission to the party had been closed, in January 1933, membership had stood at 2.2 million, and although it had been reopened in November 1936, the ranks were still thinner by 700,000.[112] The congress was attended by 1,569 delegates with voting rights and another 466 without, who had been "elected" (without alternatives) in primary party organizations. Once in Moscow, as per custom, they sat with their province or republic delegations for formal photographs with Stalin and others in his inner circle. Their local newspapers, in turn, featured their presence at the congress. Factories and collective farms had sent greetings to Stalin and affirmations of the congress agenda. All this was captured in newsreels.[113] Identification of congress delegates by social origin (worker, peasant, white collar) ceased—the class question having supposedly been resolved—but markers for occupation, age, and education remained. Only 63 voting delegates worked in agriculture, 230 in industry, and 110 in transport. Military and NKVD made up the second-largest group, at 283 (18 percent), while the largest comprised apparatchiks—those for whom their sole occupation was party work—with 659 voting delegates (42 percent). Another 162 (10 percent) served as functionaries in trade unions and soviets. Nearly half the delegates were thirty-five years of age or under; four fifths were no older than forty. Just under half (46 percent) had not graduated from high school.[114]

Krupskaya missed the congress, having died in agony on February 27, 1939, one day after her seventieth birthday. She had been suffering from acute appendicitis, peritonitis, thrombosis, and arteriosclerosis and appears to have had an abdominal embolism, though the precise cause of death remains uncertain.[115] She was the only former avowed member of an opposition group in the party (in her case, from fall 1925 to fall 1926) to die naturally.[116] Olga Ulyanova (b. 1922), the daughter of Lenin's brother Dmitry, who lived in the Kremlin Cavalry Building, recalled that upon coming home from school, she would look up across the way to the apartment of her aunts, Krupskaya and Ulyanova, in the nearby Imperial Senate. If a light was on in the second window, it meant Krupskaya was in; if in the fifth, then Maria; if in the fourth, they were in the dining room. "I came home in the evening and looked at the window of their apartment," Olga recalled of late February 1939. "The windows were dark. They had no light, and no longer ever would."[117]

Krupskaya's hand in helping create a Lenin Testament had failed to slow Stalin's succession. He was among those who carried the urn of her ashes for burial in the Kremlin Wall on March 1. He allowed the newspapers to be filled with eulogies for a few days, but the highest-level official called upon to publish an obituary was the chairman of the RSFSR Supreme Soviet.[118] Trotsky, in exile, rendered his own. "In addition to being Lenin's wife—which, by the way, was not accidental—Krupskaya was an outstanding personality in her devotion to the cause, her energy and her purity of character," he wrote (March 4). "Lenin's illness and death—and this again was not accidental—coincided with the breaking point of the revolution and the beginning of Thermidor. Krupskaya became confused. . . . She made an attempt to oppose the Stalinist clique, and in 1926 she found herself for a brief interval in the ranks of the opposition. Frightened by the prospect of split, she broke away." As a member of the Central Committee, Krupskaya had approved the expulsions and death sentences of Trotsky, Zinoviev, Kamenev, and Bukharin.[119] With her death, Stalin had a chocolate factory named after her. Orders went out to the Soviet press: "Do not print another word about Krupskaya."[120] For the proposed ribbon on the official wreath, Stalin altered the text (with his red pencil) from "closest friend of Lenin" to "closest helpmate of Lenin."[121] Stalin was Lenin's "closest friend."

THE TERROR'S PROMOTIONS

At the party congress, Stalin received public credit for the mass arrests. "Comrade Stalin has directed the work of purging enemies who have wormed their way into the party," Matvei Shkiryatov, deputy head of the party Control Commission, noted in an understatement. "Comrade Stalin taught us how to fight wreckers in a new way; he taught us how to get rid of these hostile elements quickly and decisively." One female party member told a story of how she had mailed to Stalin a denunciation of "the gang" in the Communist Youth League leadership and how he moved to eradicate them, "although he was very busy."[122]

The full scope of the bloodletting was not revealed, but it was secretly recorded: 15,485 of the 32,899 positions in 1939 on the Central Committee *nomenklatura*—the highest officials—had been appointed in the years 1937–38, a turnover of nearly half.[123] Of the 10,902 party secretaries of counties, cities, and districts, 6,909 had been appointed in 1937–38. Of the 333 regional party bosses, 293 had assumed their posts since the 17th Congress, most since 1937–38; only six heads of regional machines were older than forty-six; 91 percent were between twenty-six and forty years of age. Forty-four of the 71 Central Committee members were new (by contrast, at the 17th Congress in 1934, 10 of the 71 had been new). The same picture obtained throughout industry: on the railways, 2,245 of 2,968 senior posts as of November 1938 had been at their positions just one year. In the NKVD, the average age of the upper ranks fell between 1937 and 1939, from around forty-three to thirty-five. Fully 85 percent of Red Army officers were under thirty-five years of age.[124] These people, inexperienced and young, were by and large graduates of technical education.[125] A mass of graduates (even greater numbers would now follow) helped make possible extermination of their predecessors.

Pravda deemed these new cadres "healthy young representatives of a healthy young people," one of Stalin's core tenets. They were manifestly one of his reasons for summoning the congress: to demonstrate that the purged party was alive and well. Alexei Kosygin (b. 1904), who had graduated from the Leningrad Textile Institute just four years earlier, would become commissar of textile production. Vyacheslav Malyshev (b. 1902), who had finished technical school in 1937, would become commissar of heavy machine building. The dashing Leonid Brezhnev (b. 1906), who had graduated from a metallurgical technicum in 1935, was promoted to party boss of his home region, Dnepropetrovsk (Ukraine). The village-born

Mikhail Suslov (b. 1902), who had joined the party in 1921 and taken a few training courses, had been sent in 1936 to Rostov province, where, in October 1937, after the arrest of the entire provincial leadership, he was named third and then second secretary. In February 1939, after the arrest of everyone in neighboring Orjonikidze (Stavropol) province, Suslov had been named first secretary there. "Understand it is only thanks to Stalin that we have all risen so high," he would later explain. "Everything we have is thanks to Stalin."[126]

No less striking was the expansionism. The number of officially designated "leading personnel" hit 1.6 million in 1939, a leap from 600,000 in 1928. Overall, there were now 7.5 million administrative personnel, as compared with 1.45 million in 1928.[127] These white-collar employees and their offspring had come to dominate the spaces in higher education.[128] They were also well fed: between 1937 and 1939, when overall employment rose 10 percent, the Soviet salary fund jumped 41 percent, largely because the salary fund for administrative positions rose 66.5 percent. Especially pronounced increases were observed in supply, procurement, and, inevitably, departments introduced to control costs.[129] Despotism, too, cannot function without functionaries.[130] The terror that murdered officials en masse accentuated the ascendancy of the functionary class.

When Stalin made his way to the rostrum to deliver the main political report, the 2,000-odd attendees stood in an ovation. Making eye contact with the many delegations, the despot motioned for silence, but the applause only intensified. People desisted only when he rang the cowbell. Under a spotlight, Stalin received a new model rifle, a gift from the "proletarians of Tula" (Russia's ancient armaments center), and he aimed it at the hall. Speaking softly, slowly, as usual, he conceded that there had been "more mistakes than might have been expected" in the cleansing of the ranks. But he pronounced the terror "unavoidable" and "beneficial." "Our party is now smaller in membership, but, on the other side, its quality is better," he told the beneficiaries.[131]

Stalin praised his creation. "As a result of the colossal cultural work conducted by the party and the Government, a burgeoning new Soviet intelligentsia was born and took shape, an intelligentsia that emerged from the ranks of the working class, peasantry, Soviet white-collar, the sweat and blood of our people, an intelligentsia that does not know the yoke of exploitation and despises exploiters and stands ready to serve the peoples of the USSR with belief and truth," he rhapsodized, underscoring that these "young healthy people" would be genuinely Marxist cadres. "There is scarcely any necessity to dwell on the serious importance of party propaganda, of the Marxist-Leninist rearing of our laboring employees," he told the delegates, adding, in the wake of the *Short Course,* that without a developed Marxist-Leninist consciousness, functionaries "will degenerate into pragmatist-pedants."[132]

NEW INNER CIRCLE

Stalin removed Petrovsky from candidate member of the politburo, but, uniquely, did not have him arrested.[133] He promoted Zhdanov and Khrushchev to full (voting) membership of the politburo, where they joined Molotov, Voroshilov, Kaganovich, Mikoyan, Andreyev, Kalinin, and the despot. Malenkov, in charge of personnel for years, finally became a member of the Central Committee, but, among party apparatchiks, Zhdanov alone enjoyed inner-circle status. In his speech to the congress on party affairs, he noted that masked enemies had infiltrated the ranks, slandered, and expelled honest Communists en masse, and singled out the new "Soviet" intelligentsia as the regime's political base.[134] Zhdanov traveled often from Leningrad to take part in the ad hoc sessions in the Little Corner. He had become a personal favorite of the despot, as much as if not more than "Mykita" (the Ukrainianized version of Khrushchev's name that Stalin used for his Ukraine party boss). "Only Zhdanov received from Stalin the same kind of treatment that Kirov enjoyed," Molotov would recall. "After Kirov, Stalin liked Zhdanov best."[135]

The party would continue to serve as the regime's indispensable ideological, personnel, and disciplinary instrument and charismatic symbol, but the state (government, military, secret police) gained more and more operational power, thanks to Molotov (government), the consigliere and longest-serving full politburo member after Stalin, Voroshilov (military), and Beria (secret police), nemesis of both Voroshilov and Molotov. Beria was elevated to one of two candidate member positions in the politburo, along with Shvernik, head of the trade unions (since 1930).[136] Stalin was uncommonly solicitous toward Beria, ordering, for example, that his household be given better accommodations after inspecting their first Moscow flat, with its shared kitchen. Beria ended up not at the Kremlin but in a two-story detached mansion, the former residence of General Alexei Kuropatkin, war minister during the Russo-Japanese War fiasco, at Little Nikitskaya Street, 28.[137] The Beria household also obtained use of a wooden dacha in the pine forest near Arkhangelskoe, but, the story goes, Stalin saw it, judged it a hovel, and moved them into the arrested Postyshev's newer, palatial country estate.[138] "Beria's dacha was sumptuous, immense," recalled Svetlana, who played there with Sergo Beria (fifteen months her senior). Beria's deputy Merkulov would later testify that "in Moscow, practically every evening, comrade Stalin summoned Beria" to the Near Dacha.[139]

SOCIALIST REALISM

Nearly 19 million peasant households belonged to collective farms. Investment in mechanization and infrastructure had increased from 1.5 billion rubles in the first Five-Year Plan to 6.3 billion in the second (the third, which had commenced in 1938, would see another 5 billion). But output of tractors and combines, after having risen exponentially, was declining as the number of tanks, made at the same factories, soared.[140] Official harvest figures for 1937 (120.2 million tons), 1938 (94.9 million), and 1939 (105.4 million) were exaggerated. Even these numbers signified output per head below the 1913 level.[141] Still, the state procured 36 million tons of the 1939 harvest (as compared with 10.8 million in 1928). The regime had reacted with assistance, rather than secret police barricades, to the regions that had suffered a major drought in 1936 and a lesser one in 1938, avoiding even a partial repeat of the famine of 1931–33.[142] The continued underperformance of the livestock and dairy sectors, still not recovered from dekulakization-denomadization, was publicly acknowledged.

In his congress report, Andreyev, now the Central Committee secretary responsible for agriculture, called for a reduction in the size of the farmers' household plots, which he claimed had been allowed to become their main occupation. To an extent, he was correct, although, according to official statistics, 77 percent of household plots conformed to size limits imposed by the February 1935 statute, 12 percent were below, and only 10 percent above.[143]

Molotov gave the congress report on industry and the third Five-Year Plan. The heavy industry commissariat had been further divided in early 1939 into many smaller ones, reducing the power of their commissars.[144] Industry remained a wreck as a result of Stalin's massacres. "If last year and today the majority of industries has not fulfilled their plan, the cause of this is our weak cadres, who were promoted to leading work during the past year," one brave official wrote to the despot in March 1939, adding that "the atmosphere of lack of confidence and oversuspiciousness . . . blunts the initiative and energy of the personnel, and has an extremely harmful effect on all the work."[145] Molotov, however, regaled the delegates with fantastic projections of annual growth in the third Five-Year Plan, of between 13.5 and 15.2 percent. Production of locomotives was supposed to reach 225 percent of the 1937 figure, coal 206 percent, electric power 200 percent. Nearly simultaneous with Molotov's congress speech, *Krokodil*—the Soviet satirical journal, printed a caricature of the Third Reich. "What are you doing to propagandize the Four-Year Plan?" Göring asks Goebbels. Answer: "Prohibit the population from laughing."[146]

During the Soviet party congress, *Industry of Socialism,* a monumental art exhibition, was mounted near the Park of Culture metro station. Artists working in photography, industrial design, and even graphic and poster art had been excluded in favor of oil painters. Originally slated to open on the revolution's twentieth anniversary, it had been mounted in an earlier form by November 1937 in a hard-to-reach hall on the Frunze Embankment, but it had not been open to the public—many of the figures depicted in the paintings had been (or were soon to be) arrested. Artists, too, were arrested, and even some of those not arrested had failed to produce their contracted works. (Soviet paints were known to be of miserable quality, and funds for purchasing foreign paints and canvases were unavailable, a fact that the artists wrote denunciations about.) Most of the works on exhibit in 1939 depicted railroads, canals, coal pits, and gold mines, as well as a Tajik weather station, Arctic exploration, and the good life of workers who enjoyed rewards like motorcycles for their labor exploits. Visitors encountered a gigantic mosaic of precious stones and metals that traced the infrastructure and natural resources of the USSR, Stalin's epic canvas. Newsreels gave a narrated tour of the works.[147] First prize went to Boris Yoganson's disconsolate *In an Old Urals Factory* (1937), which showed a muscular worker staring down the fat-cat owner. More innovative was Yuri Pimenov's *New Moscow* (1937), which depicted a new boulevard and a prosperous Soviet way of life, symbolized by automobiles and stylish attire, in a decidedly modern look reminiscent of a Cézanne. The painting's central figure was a woman in an open-top car—and in the driver's seat.[148]

HITLER INTRUDES

Stalin, in his congress report, had boasted that "it is necessary to recognize that the most important achievement in the sphere of public-political life during the reporting period . . . is the complete democratization of the country's public life."[149]

He mispronounced the name of the commissariat of agriculture—calling it the Narkomzyom, accenting the last syllable, instead of Narkomzyem—and every speaker who followed copied his mistake.[150] Occasionally raising his right index finger for emphasis, he pointed out that the country had to have "at its disposal a well-trained army, well-organized penal organs, and a strong intelligence service." He also underscored the system's political fastness. "In the event of a war, the rear and the front, in view of their homogeneity and internal unity, will be stronger than in any other country, which foreign lovers of military confrontation would do well to keep in mind," he observed, lauding himself for collectivization. "Some people in the Western press are claiming that the purge of spies, murderers, and wreckers from Soviet institutions—the likes of Trotsky, Zinoviev, Kamenev, Yakir, Tukhachevsky, Rosenholz, Bukharin, and other scum—has 'shaken' the Soviet system and brought disintegration," the despot added. "Such cheap gossip merits only our contempt."[151]

Foreign affairs took up about one quarter of Stalin's speech, and on this score he had thoroughly reworked the text from the draft supplied by aides. He noted that the League of Nations had proved useless but argued that, given the dangerous times, it "should not be ignored." He stressed the fact of a "new imperialist war," now in its second year, and named Germany, Italy, and Japan as aggressors, but warned that efforts at collective security were "in disarray" because "the "non-aggressor states," Britain and France, were playing a dangerous game. They were stronger than the fascist powers but shrank from meeting the threat, refusing to intervene in Spain, China, or Czechoslovakia "to save their own skins." Remarking on the hysteria in the Western press over supposed German designs on Soviet Ukraine, Stalin warned countries "accustomed to having others pull chestnuts out of the fire for them"—a reference to Britain and France—that they would not succeed in pushing the Soviet Union into war. "We stand for peace and strengthening of businesslike ties with all countries," he noted, but only "as long as these countries maintain similar relations with the Soviet Union and do not try to damage our country's interests."[152]

When Stalin finished—congratulating the victorious working class, the victorious collective farm peasantry, the Soviet intelligentsia—the entire Andreyev-Alexandrov hall stood in thunderous applause. Editorials in *Izvestiya*, the government newspaper, did not elaborate Stalin's statement that "collective security" was effectively dead or his hints that Moscow might even turn to Nazi Germany, as if that were an option.[153] Goebbels's propaganda ministry had instructed the German press (March 13, 1939) that "you can comment on the congress of

Communists in Moscow as a still greater strengthening of the Stalin-Kaganovich clique." (Kaganovich was Jewish.)[154]

The German ambassador, Schulenburg, was the son of a Prussian officer, tall, elegant, pious, an aristocrat of long pedigree, with a balding pate, white mustache, and impeccable manners. The childless, genial count had developed exceptionally good relations with the Soviets, as with his own staff.[155] He had also developed a rivalry with his predecessor in Moscow, Dirksen, now in London. They engaged in a parallel competition to normalize Soviet-German and Anglo-German relations, respectively.[156] Still, Schulenburg doubted that Stalin's speech signaled a policy shift, although he did note the absence of the customary denunciations of the fascist states.[157] Hitler's foreign minister showed the Führer a German translation of Stalin's speech, but the Nazi leader remained skeptical, and, in any case, he was preoccupied: right in the middle of Stalin's party congress, on March 15, 1939, the Wehrmacht seized the rest of truncated Czechoslovakia, making a mockery of the Munich Pact and Hitler's pretense of merely wanting to incorporate ethnic Germans. Among the prizes were the Czechoslovak army's advanced mechanized divisions and the famous Škoda Works, in the city of Plzeň (Pilsen), one of Europe's premier military factories. "Give me a kiss, girls!" Hitler told his secretaries. "This is the greatest day of my life. I shall enter history as the greatest German of them all."[158] The Führer annexed the Czech lands (Bohemia and Moravia) as a Third Reich "protectorate"; Slovakia became nominally independent, under a Nazi puppet. Czechoslovakia's eastern Subcarpathian Rusyn (Ruthene) province became an independent state—for thirty hours, until March 16, when Hungarian troops invaded and annexed the southern part; Polish troops seized the northern part and established a common border with Hungary.[159]

Hitler had intruded on Stalin's affirmation of Soviet unity and might. The despot had Litvinov convey to Schulenburg that "the Soviet government cannot recognize the inclusion of the Czech lands in the German empire, or that of Slovakia in any form."[160] An aide to the Soviet military attaché in Berlin reported, rightly, that Hitler had already achieved a windfall: advanced Czech weapons plants, advanced Czech mechanized divisions, storehouses of grain. Less positively for Germany, the attaché noted that the Nazis had absorbed a large non-German population that could create risks in Germany's rear if the Führer pushed still farther out. On that latter score, the Soviet military aide was unequivocal: Germany was gearing up for further expansion. The question was: in which direction, "east or west?"[161]

FIXATION

Trotsky had been writing about the creation of a Fourth International since at least 1933, but the founding congress had only taken place on September 3, 1938, and was attended by fewer than two dozen delegates, at a private home outside Paris. In October 1938, he had fantasized, in a speech in Mexico he recorded on a gramophone, that "in the course of the next ten years, the program of the Fourth International will become the program of millions, and these revolutionary millions will be able to take heaven and earth by storm."[162] However absurd his "movement," Trotsky's pen was another matter. Commenting the day after Stalin's political report to the 18th Party Congress, Trotsky scandalously surmised, like Krivitsky before him, that "Stalin is preparing to play with Hitler."[163] Around the time of the party congress, Stalin ordered renewed efforts to assassinate Trotsky.[164]

That Trotsky was still alive was almost inexplicable. He had been sentenced to execution in absentia at the first Moscow public trial (August 1936), but the attempts to have him killed probably dated to 1929 in Turkey. He had been hunted all the while he had been in Paris (1933–35) and after his relocation to Norway. The most recent effort, in 1938, led by veterans of the Spanish civil war dispatched to the United States and then Mexico, had petered out after their NKVD espionage overseers in Moscow (Sergei Spigelglas) and New York (Pyotr Guttsait) were arrested as supposed foreign spies.[165] A new plan would expressly forbid everyone previously involved in such efforts to take part, and would be put together by Pavel Sudoplatov (b. 1907) and Naum "Leonid" Eitingon (b. 1899), until recently the NKVD station chief in Republic Spain.[166]

Sudoplatov was a celebrated assassin, having liquidated Yevhen Konovalets, the leader of the fascistic émigré Organization of Ukrainian Nationalists (OUN). Sudoplatov hailed from Ukraine and spoke the language. The NKVD had penetrated the OUN and even ran its branches, but Konovalets, who had been born in Habsburg Galicia and studied in Lemberg (now Lwów), was viewed as a possible figurehead who could be used by foreign powers and had working ties to intelligence officers from Nazi Germany, as well as fascist Italy, Lithuania, and Poland.[167] On May 23, 1938, Sudoplatov had managed to blow Konovalets up in a Rotterdam restaurant with a box of chocolates that concealed a time bomb, escaping undetected. It was bravura wet work. In November 1938, after yet another NKVD foreign intelligence chief was arrested, the thirty-one-year-old Sudoplatov had briefly shot up to acting chief. But when Beria took over the NKVD, he installed as foreign intelligence chief his Caucasus crony Vladimir Dekanozov, whose principal experience was in food processing and supply, including self-supply.

Sudoplatov was moved back down to section director. Someone in Beria's entourage, perhaps Dekanozov, placed Sudoplatov under investigation for ties to "enemies" (i.e., the now-arrested NKVD bosses under whom Sudoplatov had worked). The assassin spent months fearing he was about to be liquidated. Damaging rumors were being spread about him, and he was not being shown documents or allowed to carry out assignments, even those Beria had expressly directed he be given. It appears that Beria contrived to firm up Sudoplatov's position using Kremlinology: he invited him to a soccer match between Spartacus (the trade union team) and Dynamo (the NKVD team) and had him sit in the government loge; Malenkov was there, along with the full canopy of Beria cronies. "I didn't utter a word," Sudoplatov explained, "but my mere presence in that elevated place signaled Kruglov, Serov, Tsanava, and others to stop spreading rumors about evidence against me in the archives."[168]

In March 1939, as Sudoplatov tells the story, Beria took him to the Little Corner to see Stalin and proposed that Sudoplatov be named deputy chief of NKVD foreign intelligence, in order to oversee global anti-Trotskyite operations. In this telling, as Stalin lit his pipe with a match and got up and paced, the assassin took note of "the simplicity of Stalin's reactions. It was hard to imagine that such a man could deceive you, his reactions were so natural, without the slightest sense of him posing." Stalin was indeed an actor, especially in the Little Corner. "There are no important political figures in the Trotskyite movement except Trotsky himself," he was said to have advised. "If Trotsky is finished, the threat will be eliminated." Obviously, the Nazis would never resort to using a Jew even as a figurehead. Nonetheless, Stalin supposedly added, "Without the elimination of Trotsky, as the Spanish experience shows, when the imperialists attack the Soviet Union, we cannot rely on our allies in the international Communist movement."[169]

According to Sudoplatov, he and Beria debated innumerable scenarios for what Stalin had called the "action." The chosen plan derived from events in civil war Spain, where, after murdering Konovalets, Sudoplatov had taken refuge and met up with Eitingon (the two knew each other from five years earlier, when they were "illegals," operating without diplomatic cover, in Soviet foreign intelligence). The Spanish- and English-speaking Eitingon had in his circle the twenty-year-old Ramón Mercader, a Spanish-born revolutionary who carried out sabotage missions behind Franco's lines. Back in Moscow, Eitingon did not know that he had been denounced as a British spy by arrested officials, but, thanks to his acquaintance with Sudoplatov, he was chosen to lead the latest field unit, with Mercader as its centerpiece, to penetrate the Blue House, in Coyoacán, Mexico, where Trotsky lived.[170]

A "GUARANTEE" FOR POLAND

Alliances are often about imposing brakes, not empowerment. The Anglo-French "entente" was unwritten, which caused tremendous anxiety in France, but this was essentially a way for Britain to restrain its partner without committing itself formally to continental war. French alliances with Poland and Czechoslovakia had been meant the same way (a means to limit the smaller countries' behavior while not fully committing France), but that arrangement had suited neither Poland nor Czechoslovakia. The Franco-Soviet-Czechoslovak alliance had afforded no such intra-alliance control and fooled no one, paving the way for the collective failure to prevent Germany's forbidden annexation of Austria and the dismemberment of the third partner, Czechoslovakia.[171] Germany's military had consumed 17 percent of national production in 1938, about the same as in the USSR but double the level in Britain or France; in 1939, the German percentage would rise to 20 percent. Militarily, Britain and France were still holding to a mostly defensive posture, leaving all the initiative in the hands of the aggressor.[172]

Even into 1939, Hitler's references to the injustices of Versailles and to his desire merely to "unite" all ethnic Germans had still been eliciting sympathy in Britain.[173] But his seizure of all the Czech lands, on March 15, 1939, and recognition of an independent Slovakia blew up British domestic politics. Rumors flew that Germany was preparing similar conquests of Romania, Hungary, and Ukraine.[174] A Soviet military intelligence assessment (March 17) concluded that "the seizure of Czechoslovakia is the first act, the threshold to further, larger happenings," and that even if, as some experts claimed, Germany's next moves would be westward, it would still need raw materials for its military from the east.[175] That same day, British ambassador Sir William Seeds asked Litvinov what the Soviet position would be in the event of a Nazi invasion of Romania. That same evening, after consulting Stalin, the foreign affairs commissar proposed a multipower diplomatic conference involving Britain, the USSR, Romania, Poland, and others. On March 18, a Saturday, the British cabinet met. "The Prime Minister said that until a week ago we had proceeded on the assumption that we should be able to continue with our policy of getting onto better terms with the Dictator Powers, and that although those powers had aims, those aims were limited," the minutes recorded, indicating a possible policy shift. But Chamberlain, who celebrated his seventieth birthday that day, insisted that they continue seeking to negotiate, although he did become far more willing to warn Hitler against future aggression.[176]

German war preparations became blatant. On March 20, Ribbentrop issued an ultimatum to Lithuania to transfer the Baltic Sea deepwater port of Memel (Klaipeda), which had been awarded to independent Lithuania at Versailles, or risk military occupation. Lithuania capitulated, and the leaders of the 40,000 ethnic Germans in that country stepped up their agitation for subordination of Lithuanian foreign policy to Germany. This magnified the Kremlin's high anxiety that the Baltic states would become staging grounds for an attack on the Soviet Union.[177] On March 21, Ribbentrop informed the Polish ambassador, Jan Lipski, that Poland's territorial desires vis-à-vis now nominally independent Slovakia might be satisfied if Poland handed Germany Danzig and allowed a German-controlled special transit route through Poland to and from East Prussia. Lipski was noncommittal. So as not to drive Poland into Britain's arms, Hitler informed his brass that no seizure of Danzig would be carried out and ordered Nazi ruffians in Danzig to desist from provocations for now. Germany would instead wear Poland down. On March 23, King Carol II, from whom no territory was sought, agreed to closely align Romania's economy with Germany's, creating joint-stock companies for Romanian oil, manganese, copper, and bauxite, as well as grain, corn, fodder, and pigs, to be exchanged for German armaments, machines, and investments in Romanian transport and communications. A secret protocol obliged Bucharest to expand oil production.[178]

An alarmed Moscow sought details. Soviet tensions with Romania had only intensified, but in 1939 the NKVD would arrest a mere fifty-nine Romanian "spies," as compared with 7,810 in 1937–38.[179] (Total NKVD arrests in 1939 would amount to 63,889, not only the fewest in the decade but a mere half of the next lowest year.) These statistics—compiled by the Soviet regime—give the lie to avowals that the terror constituted a campaign to root out a potential fifth column. More broadly, as Stalin also knew, the vast majority of former kulaks, national minorities, and recidivist criminals remained at large, meaning that the supposed potential fifth column of the wronged and resentful was still there, when the prospect of war surpassed that of the previous two years.

Back and forth the diplomatic volleys went. On March 25, 1939, the Polish government formally rejected Germany's demands. Hitler secretly began to contemplate attacking Poland, to reestablish the pre-1914 frontiers in East Prussia and evict the ethnic Polish population.[180] On March 28, Litvinov delivered official notes to Estonia and Latvia, warning that the Soviet Union would view any state agreement—made voluntarily or under duress—that diminished the Baltic states' independence or led to the political and economic hegemony of a third state over their territory and infrastructure as unacceptable, "with all the ensuing consequences."[181]

Then came the sensation: on March 31, Chamberlain, who had not stood up for democratic Czechoslovakia, announced a unilateral "guarantee" of Poland's independence in the House of Commons. His act was hardly sentimental: Poland was a dictatorship, albeit one without a dictator (since Piłsudski's death, in 1935). But British intelligence warned Chamberlain—wrongly, as it turned out—of an imminent coup in Danzig to turn the city over to Hitler. (Vernon Kell, head of MI5, also passed on a report that Hitler had mocked the Tory PM as an "asshole.")[182] Chamberlain had noted that the French government knew of the guarantee in advance and supported it, but the way he had made it public—in response to a parliamentary question about what the government would do in the event of a German attack on Poland—gave it the appearance of an improvisation.[183] Maisky reported to Moscow that David Lloyd George, the former PM, had been told by Chamberlain on March 31, when asked why he had given a guarantee to Poland, that, "according to the information at his disposal, neither the German general staff nor Hitler would ever risk war if they knew that they would have to fight simultaneously on two fronts—the West and the East."[184] That said, the British offered no specific military commitments to Poland (or, over time, to any country in Eastern Europe).[185]

Trotsky, who had been allowed to visit London in March 1939, bitingly observed that "Chamberlain would give away all the democracies of the world (there are not many left) for one tenth of India." Beyond personal foibles, Trotsky noted that "the fear of Great Britain and France before Hitler and Mussolini explains itself by the fact that the world position of these two colony-holding countries . . . no longer corresponds with their specific economic weight. The war can bring nothing to them, but can take a great deal from them."[186]

Even the appeasement-inclined governments in the British empire's dominions denounced Hitler's action. Britain's lively press had a field day with Chamberlain—the beak nose, the shiny top hat, the impeccably tailored overcoat, the umbrella. The prime minister had made a career in municipal politics in his native Birmingham, following an up-and-down business career, and had only become a member of Parliament at age forty-nine, rising to minister of health (twice) and chancellor of the exchequer (twice). He had become PM, in late May 1937, only when Baldwin had decided to resign (the Tories still commanded a majority in the House of Commons). Then sixty-eight, Chamberlain was the second-oldest person to become PM, and he was widely perceived as a caretaker until the next election. He saw himself as a reformer of domestic affairs, but he got entangled in trying to resolve international issues in order to pursue his domestic goals.[187]

Chamberlain's guarantee of Poland's independence, not its borders, presupposed further territorial revision, provided this was not achieved by force. The PM appears to have imagined that the British guarantee would strengthen Poland's hand in "negotiations" with Nazi Germany over Danzig and the Corridor. Chamberlain's idea was that London would be able to exert control in any possible Anglo-Polish alliance.[188] He warned Warsaw not to do anything rash to precipitate German military action—which, however, showed that, despite his assurances to the contrary at a cabinet meeting, the guarantee had, to an extent, placed the question of war or peace with Germany in the hands of a third country.[189] The dominant player in Poland's ruling triumvirate, Foreign Minister Beck, was not fully trusted in London (or in Paris), and his idea of what was "reasonable" in negotiations with Germany differed from Chamberlain's.

Chamberlain's announcement of a British guarantee for Poland, which was soon publicly joined by France, happened to occur the same day (April 1, 1939) that Madrid, the last Republic holdout in Spain, fell to Franco's forces.[190] Britain and France had already recognized his regime on February 27. On March 26, the caudillo had declared Spain's adherence to the Anti-Comintern Pact. Although he had forged a politically and militarily unified Nationalist cause, a successful Popular Front on the right, he had still required thirty-two months, some 100,000 combined Italian and German troops, immense quantities of foreign weaponry, disorganization and mini civil war in the Republic camp, the timidity of France, and the active collusion of Britain to triumph. Altogether, probably half a million perished on both sides combined, including civilians, but after his victory, Franco would put to death more people than had all the kings of Spain combined; he offered no amnesty, instead forcing still more Spaniards into labor battalions or exile (Stalin refused to take them in). The victorious Nationalists in the locales, too, exacted vengeance, mostly on the Republic's former rank-and-file officialdom (top leaders escaped).[191] Franco was a criminal. The putsch he helped launch and the methods he used to prosecute the ensuing civil war constituted massive crimes against humanity. But his illegal action had galvanized the very leftist threat he had wanted to preempt. Stalin had chosen to hold back the Spanish Communist party, for the time being, but because of the inexorable ascendancy of the Communists in just about any extreme situation in which they are present in force, a Franco victory had become the lesser evil (as the fullness of Spain's history would demonstrate). History rarely delivers moral clarities.

The British government and establishment were more or less pleased. But Britain's reputation had suffered, France had been weakened, and Italy had become alienated from France and Britain, which had opened the path to Germany's *Anschluss* with Austria. While the Spanish experience had further encouraged Chamberlain in his hopes that Britain could avoid war regardless of what happened on the continent, it had further convinced Hitler that Britain and France were afraid. Stalin had drawn the same conclusion.

Two weeks after Chamberlain's gesture toward Poland, he issued, under French pressure, a similar guarantee for Romania, also a dictatorship. But the PM resisted calls in Britain for a "grand alliance" against Hitler, meaning one that involved the Soviet Union. He argued that such a bloc too closely resembled the old alliances that catastrophically had spawned the Great War.[192] His domestic critics, numerous and vociferous, were neither consistent nor unified—not even just the conservatives—over a viable alternative policy.[193] In May 1939, the Bank of England would transfer to Nazi Germany gold valued at £6 million, held in London accounts by the erstwhile Czechoslovak National Bank.[194] Inside Whitehall, appeasement was far from dead, even after the debacle of Czechoslovakia: when the British cabinet discussed the guarantee for Poland, its members agreed that it would be operative only if the Poles did not demonstrate "provocative or stupid obstinacy" regarding Danzig and the Corridor.[195] The guarantee further required that the Poles themselves mobilize to fight the Germans, an action that London kept warning the Poles not to take. For all that, however, the guarantee had been publicly proclaimed. The nightmare Chamberlain had strenuously tried to avoid was now upon him: a possible second Europe-wide war.

Stalin was well informed about the brouhaha that had erupted in Britain over Hitler's seizure of all of Czechoslovakia. The despot also likely knew that the British cabinet had discussed the possibility of asking the Soviet Union to join a coalition against Hitler but that the Poles were refusing to countenance such a move. With the guarantee, Chamberlain had effectively chosen Poland over the Soviet Union.[196] But to make his guarantee credible, he needed a military commitment to the defense of Poland from the Soviet Union.[197] Suddenly, unintentionally, Chamberlain, who left day-to-day management of Soviet affairs largely to his foreign secretaries, had placed Stalin and the USSR at the center of European power politics.[198] Some British foreign policy officials ignorantly predicted that Stalin would now "stand aloof," failing to grasp the despot's fear of a Western-German alliance behind his back.[199] At the same time, Chamberlain's guarantee to Poland had given Hitler a powerful incentive to seek some sort of deal with the USSR, to secure his rear. London's turn to Poland, in other words, unintentionally heightened the British need to talk to Stalin—lest Hitler do so.[200]

A BELATED DEMISE

Beria's extreme urgency notwithstanding, the operation to murder Trotsky took time, and success was hardly assured. In the meantime, the NKVD commissar had ways of ingratiating himself: in the wee hours of April 6, 1939, Mikhail Frinovsky, Yezhov's former first deputy of the NKVD, was arrested, just after he had requested to be relieved as naval commissar, "in view of my ignorance of sea matters."[201] The regime sailed on. *Friendship of Peoples,* the first issue of an annual almanac, was issued in a print run of 10,000, for translations of the belles lettres of the Union republics into Russian. "The Soviet people sing," the editor's note observed. "Their songs speak of the joy of labor and victories, the successes of socialist construction. They do not know borders and are heard round the world. They talk of the miraculous flowering of the great constellation of eleven Union republics, each of which has become a bright, shining pearl. . . . The Soviet people have something to sing."[202]

Stalin's reading now extended to biographies of Ivan the Terrible and foreign affairs, including Yevgeny Tarle's *Talleyrand* (1939), published in the series *Lives of Remarkable People.*[203] In April 1939, not long after the Nazi occupation of rump Czechoslovakia, Stalin read an intercepted ciphered communication from the Japanese representative in Buenos Aires to Tokyo: "Taking into account that in a European war some 75 submarines of Germany would temporarily seek to paralyze England, what would happen if such powers as Japan, Germany, Italy, and Spain united?" Stalin underlined every word in this fantasy and wrote on it a quick count of the combined divisions (250) such an alliance would yield.[204]

On April 7, *Lenin in 1918,* Mikhail Romm's sequel to his *Lenin in October* (1937), premiered to acclaim in Moscow.[205] The film would be shown at Cannes and nominated for the Palme d'Or. The celebrated Shchukin again played Lenin, with what was regarded as even greater fidelity to his life.[206] Gelovani again successfully played Stalin, who despite the title was the central man of action, sent in 1918 to obtain grain in Tsaritsyn, where he shows himself to be a great military commander who feeds the two capitals in the north and saves the Soviet republic. Stalin had dictated changes to the original cut. Originally entitled *Assassination,* for the near-fatal attempt on Lenin's life that year, the film opens with Lenin asking Gorky, "What should we do with our enemies?" Gorky worries about "excessive severity," but Lenin retorts, "Severity nowadays is an essential condition of battle. Such severity will be understood."[207]

Many people who had been arrested under Yezhov were being released as victims of "enemies" who had infiltrated the NKVD. Also on April 7, the geochemist Vladimir Vernadsky noted in his diary that "Yezhov's portrait in the Lomonosov Institute was taken down." He added: "They say [it has happened] everywhere. This is a person who destroyed thousands, if not tens of thousands, of innocents."[208] The interrogator-torturers, who before had followed orders from Frinovsky, had set to beating out of him testimony against Yezhov, including how the latter had ordered that suspects be beaten to provide false testimony. Within a week Beria would send Stalin a forty-three-page confession written by Frinovsky; Stalin made notes on it.[209] On April 10, Yezhov himself finally was arrested, evidently in Malenkov's office on Old Square, where Yezhov had been summoned as a precaution, perhaps so that he would not commit suicide. Stalin was eating supper in his Kremlin apartment, below the Little Corner, with Khrushchev, among others, when Beria's call about the apprehension came through. Yezhov's arrest went unmentioned in the Soviet press.[210] "Despite all the major shortcomings and failures in my work," Yezhov would boast, in a letter to Stalin, "I must say that, with the daily guidance of the Central Committee, the NKVD really trounced the enemy."[211] Beria wanted Yezhov to confess to failing to cleanse the bodyguards of the enemy Karl Pauker's people, thereby putting Stalin at risk, a convenient pretext for Beria to try to stuff the Kremlin guards, now led by Vlasik, with his own people, but Stalin mostly thwarted this power grab.[212]

Beria personally oversaw Yezhov's interrogation at night at Sukhanovka, the most feared prison in the system, where Beria kept an office.[213] Almost no light ever penetrated the darkness of the five-by-seven-foot cells, some of which were located far underground. Prisoners were often not permitted to sleep or sit, but instead forced to stand all night. In the worst and tiniest cells, it was, in any case, impossible to stand, and freezing water was run through constantly. Executions took place in the site's former cathedral, where a crematorium had been set up. The Yagodaites and many thousands of others had been buried at Yagoda's former dacha complex, near the Kommunarka state farm, but the Yezhovites would meet their deaths at Sukhanovka cathedral, as well as at the nearby Butovo killing field. Altogether, more than 100 of the highest-ranking Yezhovites were massacred—all of his deputies, almost all department heads in the center, almost all NKVD heads in Union republics and provinces.[214]

Sukhanovka lay not far from Yezhov's luxurious dacha at Meshcherino (which now went to the Comintern chief Dimitrov). A search of the dacha, Yezhov's Lubyanka office, and his Kremlin apartment turned up juicy finds: an arsenal of guns, 115 books written by counterrevolutionaries and anti-Soviet émigrés—the kind of literature Stalin collected in abundance. "Behind the books in various places," the investigator noted, "were discovered three half-bottles (full) of wheat vodka, one half-bottle of vodka, half emptied, and two empty half-bottles of vodka." In the desk the NKVD investigator found four bullet casings, marked ZINOVIEV, KAMENEV, and SMIRNOV (two). Perhaps the greatest discovery was that in Yezhov's apartment—and not in his Lubyanka safe—he had kept a cache of documents from the tsarist-era Tiflis gendarmerie on "Koba." Whispers of a "file on Stalin" circulated throughout the upper ranks of the regime.[215] The nature of this file in Yezhov's possession remains unknown. For Beria, it was unclear which was more dangerous: to turn the material over to Stalin, and thus indicate that he had seen it, or to not turn it over.[216] Stalin supposedly flashed the material Yezhov had gathered on him at a politburo meeting, as if Yezhov had been acting on his own in the terror's excesses.[217]

Beria also obtained twenty pages of testimony from Yezhov that compromised his former party deputy Malenkov, which Beria evidently passed on to Stalin, but the despot chose not to allow Malenkov's destruction.[218] Still, Beria delivered still more pleasing news: on April 13, 1939, Merkulov, his first deputy, finally managed to produce testimony with the signature of the stout Yefim Yevdokimov. Beria had personally gone to arrest him at his apartment on Grand Kisel Lane, 5, off Great Lubyanka, but Yevdokimov had held out for seven months, through broken legs and unceasing torture, which had continued in the prison hospital.[219] When confronted by former colleagues, he shouted them down for confessing to fabricated crimes; investigators were compelled to cease such confrontations, for Yevdokimov sometimes convinced others to retract their statements. When the NKVD put one former colleague in his cell to cajole him into confessing, Yevdokimov cursed him as a lowlife and the supposed plot inside the NKVD as "fabrication." Another coaxer-informant reported that "during my stay together with Yevdokimov . . . he said that all he wanted was a bomb to blow up the investigative unit of the NKVD and fly with it up in the air, and that an apparatus that so cripples and destroys innocent people can only be called fascist."[220]

But after the arrests of Frinovsky and Yezhov, Yevdokimov evidently agreed to incriminate himself, along with them. Beria was on a roll: on April 16, his minions managed to track down former Ukrainian NKVD chief Alexander Uspensky, who, after having staged his own suicide, had evaded an all-Union manhunt for five months (in Arkhangelsk, Moscow, Kaluga, Kazan, Sverdlovsk). He was apprehended outside the luggage area of the train station at Miass, in the Urals.[221] The interrogation of Yezhov, meanwhile, would result in twenty fat volumes. He was charged with heading a "counterrevolutionary organization"—while heading the NKVD.

Stalin's former NKVD chief confessed to working for a veritable world gazetteer of enemy intelligence services: Germany, Britain, France, Japan, Poland. (Yezhov had in fact liquidated the Polish Communist party, on Stalin's orders.) On April 24, 1939, Yezhov "testified" about his "pederasty," meaning homosexual relations. As recorded in the protocols, he recounted that his first such experience dated to age fifteen or sixteen, when, along with other male youths, he was a tailor's apprentice. Yezhov named various Soviet officials, from the army and elsewhere, with whom he claimed to have cohabitated for months; many of his male partners were married but, conveniently, for service reasons, happened to be without their wives. Among the latter category, Yezhov named Filipp Goloshchokin, at the time party secretary in Kazakhstan. More recently, Yezhov had been on a long, alcohol-soaked debauch with Vladimir Konstantinov, one of his longtime lovers (along with Ivan Dementyev). Yezhov characterized his homosexual liaisons as "mutually active."[222] How much of this Beria embellished cannot be known. History does not record the prudish Stalin's reaction.

TRIPLE ALLIANCE PROPOSAL

Back on April 3, 1939, Poland's Beck had arrived in London, seeking recourse. That same day, Hitler ordered plans developed for a military attack on Poland that could begin no later than the early fall. On April 11, the Wehrmacht issued clarifying instructions that a war against Poland was to be avoided, if possible, but preparations would go forward.[223] On April 14, the British and French governments—separately—approached the Soviets. Foreign secretary Halifax asked Maisky whether the Soviet Union would make a public declaration to the effect that it would support countries that were "victims of aggression" if they resisted such an act, by providing aid "if desired . . . and in such a manner as would be found most convenient."[224] It was a small move in the direction of the Soviets by the British government.

Also on April 14, 1939, TASS sent a secret internal report, which reached Stalin, containing a Russian translation of an article in the *New York World-Telegram* by its editor, Roy Howard, who had achieved renown by attaining the interview with Stalin some years back. Howard's latest article, dispatched from Paris—beyond Soviet censors—called the Soviet Union a false "shop-window country" with ubiquitous surveillance, propaganda that covered over everything with lies, thousands of internally deported or executed political prisoners, and, as a result, a military and industry in disarray. Howard wrote that Communism had failed to find an alternative to capitalism's stimulation, and that the standard of living remained below that of Italy. He called the Soviet system—in passages underlined by Stalin—"oriental military despotism, the iron hand, and mercilessness" and concluded, in a paragraph crossed out by Stalin, that "at the present time, despite the gigantic army and air force, in the opinion of foreign military observers, including French and British officials, the USSR has lost hope as a factor in the pending combination of forces against fascism."[225]

The Soviets, in this context, upped the British ante; Litvinov (April 15) sent Stalin and Molotov a draft proposal for a formal alliance with Britain and France. Stalin edited the text, transforming it into a specific eight-point plan for an unequivocal anti-Nazi Triple Alliance.[226] Litvinov was received in the Little Corner on April 16, and the next day he conveyed the final text to the British, summoning Seeds from the theater in the middle of a play; the day after that, Litvinov passed it to the French. Scholars who continue to deny that Stalin ever wanted a military alliance with the West have to explain why he offered one, in written form. British officials, internally, judged the Soviet proposal "extremely inconvenient" and hurriedly worked to douse French interest in it; the French contemplated an independent policy vis-à-vis Moscow, but only briefly.[227]

Also on April 17, the newly appointed Soviet ambassador in Berlin, Aleksei Merekalov, called on Ernst von Weizsäcker, state secretary at the German foreign ministry, to complain about violations of Soviet trade contracts with the Škoda

Works since the Germans had taken it over. Merekalov, a former deputy commissar for trade (who spoke no German), observed that fulfillment of the contracts would indicate whether the German government was willing to "cultivate and expand economic relations with Russia." Weizsäcker shot back that, given reports of a possible British-French-Soviet military alliance, the atmosphere for delivering war matériel to Russia was not favorable. This prompted Merekalov to inquire about current events in Europe and Soviet-German relations. Weizsäcker, sticking to his brief, stated that Germany desired "mutually satisfactory commercial relations with Russia," to which Merekalov replied, "Russian policy has always moved in a straight line." The envoy further pointed out that ideological differences had scarcely affected Soviet-Italian relations and did not have to "prove a stumbling block" with Berlin, especially since the USSR had refrained from exploiting the tensions between Germany and the West. Merekalov concluded that normalizing bilateral relations was possible, the refrain of Soviet trade and diplomatic officials going on six years.[228]

Škoda was selling the Soviets antiaircraft guns, howitzers, and naval weapons, in exchange for iron and manganese ores, nickel, tungsten, copper, tin, and foodstuffs. Stalin viewed fulfillment of the orders as important in themselves, and as a revealing test of German intentions, which remained unclear. Hitler, during a long, rambling audience granted to Grigore Gafencu, the Romanian foreign minister, in the Chancellery (April 19, 1939), raved about the British, Danzig, and being forced into war. "In the end, victor or vanquished, we shall all be buried in the same ruins," he was said to have told Gafencu. "And the only one who will profit is that man in Moscow."[229]

Romania, like Poland, expressed concerns to London that any formal security treaty involving the USSR would provoke Hitler's wrath against them. Viscount Halifax, according to the well-informed Maisky, told Polish ambassador Raczyński that "the Soviet proposal, though serious, went further than the British government was prepared to go." Indeed, already on April 19, according to notes of a meeting of the British government's foreign policy committee taken by Sir Alexander Cadogan (who had replaced Robert Vansittart as the top foreign office bureaucrat), London had decided to reject the Soviet proposal without directly conveying as much. British officials reasoned that the Soviet military was in no position to extend support beyond its borders, and that friends of Britain would erupt in fury at an alliance with the bloody Communist menace. Cadogan, however, did note the risk, albeit "remote," that an outright British rejection of the Soviet proposal might provoke a Soviet-German agreement. He also deemed the Soviet proposal politically awkward. "We have taken the attitude that the Soviets preach us sermons on 'collective security' but make no practical proposals," Cadogan observed. "They have now made such, and they will rail at us for turning them down. And the Left in this country may be counted on to make the most of this."[230]

The British stalled any formal response, cloaking rejection in the form of "comments" (as a German official in London noted).[231] Litvinov had written to Merekalov in early April 1939, regarding Britain and France, that "later, our help will be sought, which will cost them more dearly, and they will have to recompense us."[232] But on April 19 and 21, Stalin convoked angry meetings in the Little Corner, having had the envoys to Britain (Maisky), Germany (Merekalov), and France (Surits) recalled. (Potyomkin, evidently protecting Surits, had him send a subordinate.)[233] Especially at the second session, on April 21, "collective security" was eviscerated.[234] "The atmosphere was strained to an extreme," recalled Maisky. "Although outwardly Stalin appeared calm, puffing on his pipe, it was evident he was extremely ill-disposed toward Litvinov." After almost six years, "collective security" had gotten nowhere. Litvinov evidently had written a resignation letter, though he did not submit it. "Molotov became vicious," Maisky added, "attacking Litvinov unremittingly, accusing him of every mortal sin."[235] Merekalov had been summoned to the April 21 meeting only for the last of the four hours. Fresh from meeting in Berlin with Weizsäcker, he insisted that Soviet-German rapprochement was possible; after all, Hitler needed Soviet neutrality. The British had still not replied to the Soviet offer of a Triple Alliance, but on April 26 they informed *Berlin* that they would not accept Moscow's proposal.[236] Stalin decided to bring in the Hammer.

SEIZING FOREIGN AFFAIRS

Ten years younger than the despot, Molotov was the second-most-senior member of the inner circle. He could play violin and took tango lessons (with Voroshilov), though he stammered and was infamous for being mulish. But he had never belonged to a party opposition or the Mensheviks, let alone fought for the Whites or worked in bourgeois counterintelligence (like Beria) and, almost uniquely, was completely untainted. There had been, essentially, just that March 1936 botched

Le Temps interview, after which Molotov's name disappeared from the targets of "enemy" assassination attempts for a time.[237] (Trotsky closely followed the absence, then reappearance, of Molotov's name, speculating on its significance; Molotov followed Trotsky's Kremlinological writings.)[238] All during the terror, when Stalin had sent Molotov "materials" on someone and asked what should be done, he had invariably leapt at the cue: "Arrest." Molotov sometimes crossed out "exile" and wrote "shoot." When Stalin murdered Molotov's aides, he acquiesced, and was not known to have tried to protect anyone except his wife.[239] One subordinate recalled that "Molotov was often agitated, and lost his temper over nothing."[240] That was especially the case after Stalin had read *him* the riot act. At the 18th Party Congress, Stalin had publicly humiliated his number two, approving the draft of Molotov's report beforehand but then, after he had delivered it, convening the politburo to criticize it, which Molotov then had to acknowledge to the ongoing congress.[241] Still, the indispensable Molotov proved unfailingly reliable, and possessed phenomenal grit.

Molotov had been present every single time Litvinov was summoned to the Little Corner between 1935 and 1939, with a mere two exceptions.[242] The chairman of the Council of People's Commissars did not hide his antipathy for the foreign affairs commissar. Zhdanov, whom Stalin had made head of the Supreme Soviet commission for foreign affairs, a platform for spewing additional venom about dens of foreign spies, was perhaps even more rabid in his dislike. A Russian nationalist whose virulently anticapitalist, anti-imperialist speeches appeared frequently in the press, Zhdanov came to be seen as the public antipode to the cosmopolitan, multilingual Litvinov. He publicly condemned the mutual assistance pact with France—the linchpin of Litvinov's foreign policy.[243] Still, Zhdanov worked in Leningrad, and Molotov was by far the most frequent presence in Stalin's Little Corner—logging three times the total hours of the next closest visitors (Voroshilov, Malenkov, Kaganovich, Beria, Mikoyan). In fact, Molotov not only met Stalin alone often but was present at three quarters of all recorded gatherings in the Little Corner. Few others in that regime, if any, could have borne the weight of such proximity to Stalin.

Stalin had long been directing foreign policy himself from his Little Corner, relying upon the NKVD, military intelligence, the Comintern, special envoys, and Molotov as head of government and member of the politburo commission on foreign policy.[244] The despot summoned foreign affairs commissariat staff and ambassadors from abroad without Litvinov being present, and he had ignored

Litvinov's warnings about intervening in Spain and much else. Litvinov must have feared for his own life.[245] Two terror waves had pulverized his commissariat, the first in spring 1937, the second in spring 1938 (which targeted those who had worked with him yet remained at large).[246] Foreigners looked to Litvinov's fortunes as a key to unlocking the enigma of Soviet foreign policy.[247] During the 1939 May Day parade, Stalin allowed him to appear atop the Lenin Mausoleum for all to see.[248] The next day, Maisky, in London, ruminating on the Soviet proposal for a grand alliance with Britain and France, concluded that "acceptance by the British Government can scarcely be doubted."[249] But that very night, Beria and Dekanozov, along with Molotov and Malenkov, arrived at the foreign affairs commissariat, in the form of a "Central committee commission," to interrogate the staff. Litvinov was forced to observe the humiliation.[250] On May 3, Litvinov received the British ambassador calmly, and Seeds, belatedly, answered the Soviet alliance proposal by reporting that Whitehall had still not come to a decision—after a fortnight.[251] That same evening, in Stalin's Little Corner, yet another flaying of collective security took place. As Litvinov sat there impassively, Molotov lost his composure, shouting as Litvinov departed, "You think we are all fools."[252]

During the Little Corner gathering, Beria had slipped out at 5:05 p.m., ten minutes before Litvinov was admitted. NKVD troops proceeded to surround the foreign affairs commissariat building on Blacksmith Bridge, diagonally across from the back side of Lubyanka. At 11:00 that night, Kremlin staff dispatched a coded message to Soviet ambassadors—which, unusually, was signed by Stalin himself—noting Litvinov's "disloyal attitude to the Council of People's Commissars" and the acceptance of his "request" to be relieved of his duties.[253] On the morning of May 4, at the foreign affairs commissariat, Molotov announced that he was taking over. In Litvinov's old office, he had to sort through his state papers, which lay in a disorganized pile, many unread, some smeared in butter from sandwiches—the kind of disarray the fastidious Molotov found especially distasteful.

Litvinov's 1939 dismissal marked Stalin's full emancipation from the foreign policy "specialists."[254] Unlike many Bolsheviks of his vintage, such as Litvinov, Molotov had never been part of the foreign emigration in Europe.[255] Also unlike Litvinov, Molotov enjoyed direct access to Soviet intelligence agencies, which he would employ alongside regular channels of diplomacy.[256] Among the cast of top minions, Molotov, further, was uniquely self-assured. "I would say," Khrushchev later recalled, "that he was the only person in the politburo who opposed Stalin on this or that question for the second time."[257] Georgy Zhukov, the military commander, later recalled that "at times it reached the point where Stalin raised his voice and even lost all self-control, and Molotov, smiling, rose from behind the table and held firm to his point of view." Zhukov added that Molotov "exerted a serious influence on Stalin, especially in foreign policy questions, in which Stalin at that time, before the war, considered him [Molotov] as competent."[258]

A ROUTED, TRANSFORMED COMMISSARIAT

Litvinov was put under investigation for high treason, partly based upon "testimony" from Yezhov, delivered to Stalin on April 27, to the effect that, while on holiday at Merano, Italy, Litvinov, while dancing a foxtrot, had told Yezhov that "our statesmen have absolutely no culture at all." Litvinov lost his Moscow apartment but kept his state dacha outside the city, which Beria had surrounded with NKVD troops. The story goes that Litvinov, finding his government phone disconnected, used a city line to call Beria, who "joked" that the goons were stationed there for his "protection."[259] Litvinov's house arrest reverberated throughout the foreign affairs commissariat as his closest associates still at large were arrested and tortured to build a "case" against their boss. "Beria and Kobulov put me on a chair and sat on either side and punched me in the head, playing 'swings,'" recalled Yevgeny Gnedin, the press officer of the foreign affairs commissariat. "They beat me horribly, with the full force of their arms, demanding I give testimony against Litvinov."[260] One foreign affairs commissariat insider who might not have been displeased at Litvinov's removal was Vasily Korzhenko. When he heard of Molotov's appointment as commissar, he anticipated a promotion; after all, Korzhenko had been helping direct carnage from the inside. But the Korzhenko family driver had been arrested as a Polish spy; his replacement, too, was arrested as a trumped-up spy.[261] The loyal hatchet man himself, rather than being given the expected promotion, was asked for his keys, and, back out in the corridor, NKVD operatives arrested him. He disappeared, now a victim as well as perpetrator.

Soviet diplomacy's image abroad was being devastated by the widely discussed disappearances. As in the case of the NKVD, however, a planned separate trial of foreign commissariat personnel would never take place.[262] The wet work of mopping up the remaining Litvinovites fell to the Beriaite Dekanozov, who had only recently been named head of NKVD foreign espionage but now became first deputy commissar of foreign affairs. Dekanozov's place was taken by Pavel Fitin (b. 1907), the son of Russian peasants in Siberia, who had attended a village middle school, then graduated as an agricultural engineer from the Tirmiryazev Academy, in Moscow, and became an editor at the state agricultural publisher. In March 1938, the party had him mobilized to the NKVD Central School, in Moscow, but not the newly opened NKVD School of Special Designation for training spies, outside the capital in the woods (he lacked knowledge of a foreign language). Nonetheless, by August 1938 he was an intern in the NKVD's espionage directorate, in the department for Trotskyites and rightists abroad. In January 1939, Fitin was named deputy head of Soviet civilian espionage, and on May 13, 1939, he would be promoted to the top position (while holding the rank of major).[263] Sudoplatov would be advanced to deputy chief under Fitin and given a grand office at Lubyanka HQ, on the seventh floor—the old office of Abram Slutsky, the former NKVD foreign intelligence chief who had been killed with poison by his own agency.[264]

Not everyone in foreign affairs was arrested. Alexandra Kollontai, a former member of the old Workers' Opposition and one of the world's first female ambassadors, survived. Why remains mysterious, though she did constantly seek out Stalin's guidance, allowing him to explain geopolitics to her, flattering his self-conception as the Lenin of our day, while also sucking up to Voroshilov, playing on his infamous sentimentality.[265] Equally remarkable, the Litvinovite Maisky, a former Menshevik who during the civil war had been a member of the anti-Bolshevik government in Samara, was not recalled. A few diplomatic personnel, when summoned home, escaped. Raskolnikov, Soviet envoy to Bulgaria, had received a telegram from Litvinov ordering him to Moscow in connection with an unspecified new appointment, but he dragged out his departure from Sofia and, en route to the Soviet Union, managed to switch trains and abscond to Paris. (In summer 1939, Raskolnikov would be convicted in absentia.) How often Litvinov had tried to protect people, versus how often he became complicit in their destruction, remains unclear.[266] He had written to Stalin that he was worried about nine ambassadorial vacancies (including Warsaw, Bucharest, Tokyo, and Washington), with more vacancies looming, and he underscored that "in some of these capitals there has not been an ambassador for a year."[267] NKVD station chiefs had been assigned to the ambassadorial positions in China and Mongolia—and they asked

Lubyanka headquarters if they could inform the foreign affairs commissariat of their diplomatic activities.

A number of those now arrested in foreign affairs were Jewish. Their deliberate removal in 1937–39 did not signify a *special* anti-Semitism, any more than their original mass promotion into the foreign affairs commissariat, or into the Cheka, had signaled a special Judeophilia.[268] The removal of Jews was aimed at altering the image of the regime and making way for promotion of the young, the humble, and the Slavic, as in the NKVD. Typical of the new men was twenty-four-year-old Vladimir Pavlov, an ethnic Russian who had graduated in spring 1939 from the Moscow Energy Institute and, already a candidate member of the party, found himself a top aide to Molotov. Pavlov soon became one of Stalin's interpreters.[269] Another example was Andrei Gromyko (b. 1909), a working-class militant from Belarus who had been trained as a Marxist economist and suddenly entered diplomatic service in spring 1939 as the new head of the foreign affairs commissariat's American department. (He had "virtually no knowledge of foreign affairs," American diplomats in Moscow surmised after a luncheon.)[270] Molotov would recall that Litvinov "was an intelligent man, an outstanding personality, but one did not trust him." By contrast, Molotov viewed Gromyko as "still young and inexperienced, but loyal."[271]

When Hitler had asserted control over his foreign ministry, which he had called an "intellectual garbage dump," by appointing the Nazi parvenu Ribbentrop to replace the old-line aristocrat Baron Konstantin von Neurath, the takeover was said to resemble a fight of the jackboots against the striped trousers.[272] The Soviet foreign affairs commissariat was rocked not just by the brawling over political orientation—Britain/France versus Germany—but by class and cultural antagonisms. Litvinov had once been a young firebrand, the man Lenin had called upon to fence the money that Kamo and Stalin had heisted from the mail coach on Yerevan Square in 1907. But Victor Serge, in France, characterized the dismissed sixty-three-year-old Litvinov as "a large diplomat with a lined face resembling a very wealthy diamond merchant from Antwerp or a City banker related to the Rothschilds."[273] No love was lost between the Litvinov caste of "bourgeois" Soviet diplomats of Western three-piece suits and clubby gestures— the very features that made him acceptable in the Western world—and the latest young appointees, who often came from the workbench or the plow, such as Pavlov and Gromyko. But Pavlov aside, the newly promoted were often monolingual (as Litvinov had complained to Stalin) and out of their depth.[274] A former textile plant manager would soon be appointed Soviet envoy to Berlin.

A POLISH HINGE?

On April 20, 1939, when Hitler celebrated his fiftieth birthday, he playfully wrote to Ribbentrop, "Please invite a series of foreign guests, among them as many cowardly civilians and democrats as possible," adding that he wanted these foreigners to see "a parade of the most modern of armies."[275] Some 20,000 guests were accommodated in the grandstand alone. Celebrations were also held in other German cities, and the Free City of Danzig. The birthday festivities had actually begun the day before, when Hitler rode at the head of a fifty-white-limousine cavalcade along Speer's newly constructed East-West Axis, the central boulevard of what was to be the transformed capital, decorated with Nazi banners and lit by torches. For the military parade, the Führer stood on the reviewing stand, flanked by generals, admirals, field marshals, and bodyguards. Arm extended in Nazi salute, he took in the largest display in Nazi Germany to date of goose-stepping columns—nearly 50,000 uniformed troops—along with tanks, artillery, antiaircraft guns, and Messerschmitt fighters and Heinkel bombers roaring overhead. According to one foreign eyewitness, Hitler "never took his eyes from the immense army on the march."[276]

All surrounding streets and other approaches had been sealed, of course, but the British military attaché in Berlin, Colonel Noel Mason-MacFarlane, had an apartment overlooking the reviewing stand. "Easy rifle shot," he had said to a colleague in the run-up to the Munich Pact. "I could pick the bastard off from here as easy as winking, and what's more I'm thinking of doing it. . . . There'd be all hell to pay, of course, and I'd be finished in every sense of the word. Still . . . with that lunatic out of the way . . ."[277] His superiors at the war office would have none of it. Again in March 1939, at the time of the invasion of rump Czechoslovakia, Mason-MacFarlane had urged headquarters in London to take energetic action, warning of catastrophe if Hitler was not "unexpectedly wafted to Valhalla." Now, during preparations for Hitler's birthday, he had been able to observe the swastika banners and other decorations going up. Assassination by a high-velocity rifle from his apartment remained feasible: his drawing-room window was no more than 100 yards from the reviewing stand. The noise of the crowds, not to mention the blare of the military band, could drown out any shots and allow an assassin a decent chance to escape. Again, however, the war office demurred.[278]

Following the parade, safely inside the Chancellery hall where Bismarck had presided over the Congress of Berlin in 1878, Hitler's inner circle presented him with bronze casts, Meissen porcelains, oil paintings (including a Titian), tapestries, antique weapons, rare coins, and kitschy Nazi memorabilia.[279] "The Führer is fêted as no other mortal has ever been," gushed Goebbels, the instigator of the grandiosity. A collector's luxury anniversary edition of *Mein Kampf* was published in both dark blue and red cases with stamped gold sword. Hitler, as state propaganda noted, had arisen from the lower ranks, and for his birthday, low-income Germans received 15 reichsmarks, plus 5 more for each dependent, as a onetime gift. Whatever the daily life hardships, Germans could be proud again. "A great man," one seventeen-year-old girl observed, speaking for millions, "a genius, a person sent to us from heaven."[280]

On April 28, 1939—two days after the British government had informed Berlin that it would not accept Soviet proposals for an alliance—the Führer denounced his nonaggression declaration with Poland as well as the Anglo-German naval accord, blaming the two countries, in a blistering two-hour speech at one of the fewer than a dozen Reichstag sessions since he had claimed power.

Hitler was furious over another letter from U.S. president Franklin Roosevelt pleading for assurances from the Nazi leader that he would not commit aggression against a long list of specified countries, promising him access to raw materials in return. The message had been disclosed to the *New York Times* before reaching Hitler, and he had summoned the 855 Reichstag deputies to the Kroll Opera House. "For the past six and a half years, I have lived day and night for the single task of awakening the powers of my people in the face of our desertion by the rest of the world," he gloated, in front of an immense Nazi eagle. "I have conquered chaos in Germany, reestablished order, immensely increased production in all branches of our national economy, produced, by strenuous efforts, substitutes for numerous materials which we lack, prepared the way for new inventions, . . . caused magnificent roads to be built and canals to be dug, created gigantic new factories." He congratulated himself for overcoming Versailles and reunifying Germany as well: "I have likewise endeavored to rid them of that treaty, page by page, which in its 448 articles contains the vilest oppression which has ever been inflicted on men and nations. I have brought back to the Reich the provinces stolen from us in 1919. . . . I have reunited the territories that have been German throughout a thousand years of history—and, Mr. Roosevelt, I have endeavored to attain all this without bloodshed and without bringing to my people, and so to others, the misery of war."[281]

Hitler's speech drew hearty applause and laughs, including when he implied that he would refrain from attacking the many countries that remained under the

British colonial yoke or had already been invaded by the United States over the course of its existence. His twisted thinking—calling dictatorship "order" and the Weimar Constitution "chaos"—did not vitiate the fact that Germany's vast pool of 6 million unemployed had been returned to the dignity of work, with an economic boom absent inflation (or strikes, which were outlawed), and that Germany had incorporated Austria, the Sudetenland, the Saarland, and Memel. A once great but prostrate country had in Nazi fashion become great again, in a single generation; a lifelong nonentity had become the world's central figure.[282]

Denunciation of the nonaggression declaration seemed to indicate a likely intention to attack Poland, for which Hitler might want to secure Soviet neutrality. His speech had conspicuously omitted the usual denunciations of "Judeo-Bolshevism," which Western observers duly noted. German press attacks against the USSR ceased, as the Soviets duly noted.[283] On May 3, 1939, General Karl Bodenschatz, Göring's adjutant, warned the French military attaché in Berlin that "something is up in the East." He repeated his warning to the Polish military attaché. (The next day was Litvinov's dismissal.) Four days later, Bodenschatz informed the French ambassador in Berlin, Robert Coulondre, that Hitler wanted an agreement with the Soviet Union.[284]

VISIONS OF A DEAL

On the evening of May 5, the delayed Kremlin banquet for May Day parade participants took place in the St. George's Hall, and among the artists summoned for the first time was Igor Ilinsky, the stage and film actor (of *Volga-Volga* fame), who read from Chekhov's comic writing. "Everyone ate, drank, conversed," Ilinsky complained, "and, it seemed, no one was listening to me."[285] Earlier that day, Merekalov had been recalled from Berlin, which left the embassy to Georgy Astakhov, the chargé d'affaires (rumored to be an NKVD intelligence operative). That same day, Karl Schnurre, head of the East European and Baltic section of the commercial policy department in the German foreign ministry, informed Astakhov, in a response to Merekalov's inquiry regarding the Škoda Works, that its new German director would fulfill Soviet orders.[286] Astakhov, according to the German notetaker, "was visibly gratified at the declaration and stressed the fact that for the Soviet Government the material side of the question was not of as great importance as the question of principle." Astakhov then asked whether negotiations might be resumed. When Schnurre was noncommittal, Astakhov stressed the significance of Molotov's replacement of Litvinov.[287] Astakhov reported to Moscow in detail on the reaction in Germany to Litvinov's dismissal, but he did not have access to Hitler.[288]

While Stalin's embassy in Berlin also sought to drive home the significance of the personnel change, Germany's embassy in Moscow buzzed with the implications of the dismissal of Litvinov (known on Nazi radio as "Litvinov-Finkelstein"). Each side's functionaries reported that the other side looked eager for rapprochement.[289] The timing was propitious: German economic planners were warning that Germany's war machine might fall critically short of oil, rubber, and manganese, all of which Stalin could supply.[290] But was *Hitler* interested? Internally, Göring had broached the idea of approaching Moscow, if only to frighten Warsaw into concessions.[291] Stalin had long suspected that Hitler might be simulating talks with Moscow in order to frighten London into cutting a deal with Berlin.

Britain's stance vis-à-vis the Soviet Union offered no greater clarity, given the nonanswer to Moscow's alliance proposal that Seeds had delivered to Litvinov (the day before the latter's ouster was announced in the press). Litvinov vanished from public view. He was said to be playing bridge, reading poetry, taking walks at his state dacha, and learning to type. But Stalin did not authorize an arrest.[292] No sentimentality was involved. Litvinov's destruction would have delivered an unequivocal signal abroad. Had the despot wanted to consign Britain and France to hell for good—and he did seem to want just that—he would be doing so with no security alternative at hand.[293] Most worrisome, if he abandoned Britain and France definitively, they might cut a nightmare deal with Hitler behind his back.

A German-Japanese anti-Soviet coalition remained a possibility as well. Japan posed a significant threat to the Western powers' colonies, and Germany sought to convert the Anti-Comintern Pact into a real military alliance with Japan in order to raise the cost of any British and French declaration of war against Germany on behalf of Poland. Sorge reported from Tokyo (May 5, 1939) that the Japanese side was divided: its navy sought to include as mutual enemies the United States and Britain, not just the Soviet Union, while Japan's army dreamed about a joint war with Nazi Germany against the USSR.[294] Germany was also hoping to sign binding military obligations with its Italian partner in the Axis. In Milan on May 6–7, Ribbentrop met Galeazzo Ciano, Mussolini's son-in-law and the foreign minister, to iron out final details for a bilateral "Pact of Steel" (Mussolini had wanted to call it the Pact of Blood). Japan had been given no advance notice, but Ribbentrop informed a skeptical Ciano that Germany wanted to include Japan.[295] For Stalin, getting some sort of deal with Hitler also promised to drive a crucial wedge between Tokyo and Berlin, and possibly with Italy, too.

NEGOTIATIONS, OF A SORT

On May 8, Molotov received British ambassador Seeds, a lifelong Russophile, as well as French ambassador Paul-Émile Naggiar, in his Kremlin office and assured them that the Soviet offer of an alliance conveyed by Litvinov still stood and that "collective security" negotiations would continue. The government chairman/foreign affairs commissar also bluntly accused the Western governments of wanting to talk "ad infinitum" and insisted that any political agreement had to be coupled with a formal military alliance. Seeds requested a public declaration of support for Britain and France in their guarantees to Poland and Romania, in a form agreeable to them, but said nothing of British and French military aid if the Soviet Union were attacked. "As you see," Molotov wrote in a telegram to Surits (Paris) and Maisky (London), "the English and French are demanding of us unilateral and gratuitous assistance with no intention of rendering us equivalent assistance." Maisky responded that a "relapse to the Munich policy" of capitulation to Hitler was evident in London. On May 11, as Molotov again received Seeds and Naggiar, Halifax told the Soviet ambassador in London that no three-way "guarantees" could be offered to the three Baltic states against an aggression, a central Soviet demand to remove these potential attack platforms.[296]

On May 10 at the Berghof, Hitler, with Ribbentrop in tow, received Gustav Hilger, from the Moscow embassy staff (resident in Moscow since June 1920), and Schnurre, the Soviet trade expert in the German foreign ministry, posing many questions and *listening*. "Will Stalin be prepared under well-known circumstances to come to an agreement with Germany?" Hitler asked, according to Schnurre.[297] Within a week, on the initiative of General Keitel, Hitler would also meet with his German military attaché to Moscow, General Ernst Köstring, who, like Hilger, had been born in Russia (1876) and knew the language, and who, no softy on Bolshevism, confirmed the positive interpretations of German-Soviet relations that Hilger and German ambassador Schulenburg had presented.[298] Perhaps Hitler relished an approach to Moscow as a way to upset and apply pressure against Poland and Britain, but he loathed the idea of sacrificing any war production to Stalin, which was what a deal with Moscow would have to entail. Ribbentrop was assiduously seeking Japan's signature to the military Pact of Steel, offering to allow the

Japanese to publicly portray the expansive agreement as if it were directed only at the USSR.[299]

Poland's tensions with Germany had even pushed the Warsaw leadership into wary discussions with the USSR. Also on May 10, deputy foreign affairs commissar Potyomkin met in Warsaw with Beck, at the latter's request. Haughty and deceitful as he might be, Beck had turned out not to be the Nazi stooge that Soviet stooges had portrayed him to be. "Peace is a thing precious and desirable," he had declared in a speech in the Polish parliament on May 5, carried live on radio, explaining his rejection of Hitler's demands. "Our generation, bloodied in wars, certainly deserves peace. But peace, like almost all things of this world, has its price, a high but a measurable one. We in Poland do not know the concept of peace at any price. There is only one thing in the lives of men, nations, and states that is without price—honor." An eyewitness recalled, in relation to the otherwise deeply unpopular foreign minister, "I saw women throwing flowers into Beck's car as he was returning from parliament"—testimony, perhaps, to the limits of Poland's room to have cut a deal.[300] Now, five days later, when Potyomkin hinted that Moscow would support Poland against Germany if the Poles so desired, Beck, in a rambling discourse on the "correlation of forces" in Europe and the lack of Anglo-French resolve, was said to have conceded that "Poland could not stand up to Germany without Soviet support."[301]

But the Poles backtracked immediately. On May 11, Molotov received the Polish ambassador, Wacław Grzybowski, who "clarified" his government's official response: Poland could not accept even a guarantee of its borders by Moscow, let alone a possible alliance treaty.[302] The next day, Poland signed a mutual assistance pact with France that, within a mere week, would produce written pledges of mutual military aid in the event of war.

Molotov demanded nothing less from Britain and France. On May 14, he responded to the British by reiterating the Soviet insistence on reciprocal security obligations, and on including trilateral guarantees for the territorial integrity of the Baltic states, too. But Latvia, Lithuania, and Estonia did not seek "guarantees" of their sovereignty, least of all from the Soviet Union, which they feared as much as or more than Nazi Germany, and Britain did not want to force them. At the same time, it remained highly uncertain whether Britain or France could persuade Poland and Romania to add the USSR to the British and French guarantees of their sovereignty or even grant unequivocal transit rights to the Red Army.[303] In this context, a secret Soviet memorandum of May 15, "English Diplomacy's Dark Maneuver in August 1914," recounted how London had promised

Berlin it would stand aside, and even secure France's neutrality, if Germany attacked Russia but not France. Molotov underlined several passages, as if the British were engaged in the same maneuver now.[304]

ULTIMATUM

Stalin's regime remained an exceedingly awkward potential partner for the Western powers. Mikhail Bulgakov, who had once again requested permission to leave the country and once again been refused, organized a private reading of his secret manuscript, *The Master and Margarita,* to his close circle of friends. "When he finally finished reading that night, he said: 'Well, tomorrow I am taking the novel to the publisher!' and everyone was silent. . . . Everyone sat paralyzed," Yelena Bulgakova wrote in her diary (May 14, 1939). "Everything scared them."[305] On May 15, in the middle of the night, Isaac Babel was arrested at his dacha in Peredelkino. His most recent short story collection had been published in fall 1936; now the NKVD confiscated some two dozen folders and notebooks of his unpublished manuscripts, translations, and other materials. Babel suffered from his association with Yezhov, who, under interrogation, had named him as a spy. According to the interrogation protocols, Babel implicated Eisenstein ("The organizers of the Soviet film industry were preventing gifted individuals from revealing their talents to the full"), Solomon Mikhoels ("constantly dissatisfied that the Soviet repertoire gave him no chance to demonstrate his talents"), and Ehrenburg ("In Ehrenburg's view, the continued wave of arrests forced all Soviet citizens to break off any relations with foreigners").[306] Babel would also sign a bloodstained protocol confessing to membership in a Trotskyite espionage organization on behalf of France, linked to Malraux.[307]

Babel's association with the Cheka had extended beyond bedding Yezhov's wife, Yevgeniya Gladun, the hostess of a literary salon, whom Babel called a "featherhead," an allusion to Chekhov.[308] "He told us how he spent all his time meeting militiamen and drinking with them," Nadezhda Mandelstam would recall. "The word 'militia' was of course a euphemism. . . . M. asked him why he was so drawn to 'militiamen'; was it a desire to see what it was like in the exclusive store where the merchandise was death? Did he just want to touch it with his fingers?" Babel replied that he just wanted to have a sniff.[309] Now he was in Lubyanka's inner courtyard, for good.

Stalin made some moves to indicate that terror against his own people would not govern all decision making.[310] That spring of 1939, after two years of short-lived acting directors, he had finally named a new chief of Soviet military intelligence: air force commander Ivan Proskurov, a decorated veteran of the Spanish civil war and the son of a railroad worker. Proskurov's first deputy held the lowly rank of major, as did almost all the heads of the departments and sub-departments, and he himself was a mere thirty-two years old. They had to find and reengage the many foreign agents, who remained willing to risk their lives to serve the cause against fascism.[311] NKVD foreign espionage, too, was working to reestablish its networks, straining every nerve to ascertain the intentions of Britain as well as France. Donald Maclean (code-named "Homer"), one of Moscow's Cambridge Five spies, had been promoted to the British foreign office; another Soviet spy in the foreign office, John Herbert King, a walk-in, delivered cipher books to the NKVD. Yet another Soviet spy worked inside the French general staff, and another in the Czechoslovak foreign ministry.[312] All these high-placed clandestine sources provided information that reinforced Stalin's preexisting doubts about the intentions of the Western powers *ever* to align with the Soviets, or stand up to Hitler.

They also detailed Hitler's plans. On May 17, 1939, Proskurov sent Stalin a six-page memorandum, "The Future Plans of Aggression by Fascist Germany," comprising clandestine notes from a briefing fifteen days earlier at the German embassy in Warsaw by Dr. Peter Kleist, the key person for Eastern Europe in Ribbentrop's foreign ministry. "Hitler," Kleist was said to have remarked, based on a conversation between the Führer and Ribbentrop, "has decided to bring Poland to her knees." According to Kleist's account, as reported by a Soviet agent in the Warsaw embassy, German destruction of Poland's army was expected to take a mere eight to fourteen days. Furthermore, any conflict between Germany and Poland was expected to be localized; Britain and France, notwithstanding their public "guarantees" of Poland's territorial integrity, were expected to do essentially nothing if Poland's demise proceeded rapidly. "The whole project arouses in Germany only one fear: the possible reaction of the Soviet Union," Kleist was said to have stated. "In the event of a conflict, we hope, no matter the circumstances, to attain the USSR's neutrality." Poland might yet prove Stalin's opportunity: the despot wrote on his copy of the secret report, "Talk to Proskurov. Who is the 'source.'"[313]

Proskurov was summoned to the Little Corner on May 19, along with Molotov and the Soviet military attaché to Poland. Stalin evidently heard firsthand of Hitler's intention to instigate a pretext for an attack on Poland in the coming summer, then pivot westward against France and Britain, after which it would be the turn of the Soviet Union.[314] So it looked as though a war in the west would come first? The last major war had lasted four years. In such a scenario, Stalin perhaps could wait to see who emerged the likely winner, and reap the gains without the costs—provided, of course, that Britain did not manage to strike another deal with Hitler.

Also on May 19, Beria had executed a confidential task: Radek had his head fatally smashed on the floor of the Verkhne-Uralsk prison, where he was serving a ten-year term. Rumors were loosed that Radek had been killed in a fight with a fellow inmate. In fact, the murder was instigated by a specially dispatched NKVD team—so much for the promise Stalin had made to not execute Radek, in exchange for testimony that Radek had duly delivered against Trotsky and Trotskyites.[315] (Sokolnikov, another defendant in the January 1937 Trotskyite trial who had been spared death in exchange for his testimony, would also be murdered in prison, in Tobolsk on May 21.) The ironies, as ever, were rich: Radek had once been one of Stalin's top advisers on German affairs.

Molotov, too, executed his own confidential task at this time. Stalin, having tried to force the issue with an offer of alliance to Britain and France, now sought to force the issue with Hitler: on May 20, the reliably blunt Molotov summoned Schulenburg and informed him that "economic negotiations with Germany have recently been started more than once but have not led to anything. . . . We have the impression that instead of economic negotiations, the German government is conducting some kind of game." Schulenburg tried to counter Molotov's charges, but the Hammer then struck an even bigger blow: resumption of talks for an economic agreement would now require "a political basis." It was a Soviet invitation, delivered as an ultimatum.[316]

STALEMATE

Soviet economic relations with Britain and France remained dogged by the bitterness over tsarist and Provisional Government debts, but even if the debt issues had somehow been resolved, neither Britain nor France promised nearly as much economically to the Soviets as did Germany.[317] Some sort of a political deal with Nazi Germany also presented the best chance to avoid and perhaps profit from what Stalin saw as the inevitable intracapitalist war.[318] At the same time, however, an iron-clad British-French-Soviet military alliance encircling Germany did hold appeal: it could, at a minimum, prevent an aggression by either of France's formal allies, Poland and Romania.[319] More than that, it could potentially deter Hitler. And even if it failed to prevent him from attacking, a Western alliance, because of geography, promised to shift any fighting from Soviet onto Polish, Romanian, and French soil.

But progress in the formal talks Molotov had opened with the two Western powers in May 1939—a dozen sessions would be held altogether—was halting. Even British officials not adamantly averse to exploring a security deal with the Soviets were hard pressed to overcome the severe practical obstacles. On May 21, Halifax told Maisky again that the Baltic states outright refused a tripartite security guarantee and that the British government "cannot impose guarantees on others by force." The foreign secretary added that "many in Britain think that a tripartite pact may push Hitler to unleash a war straight away, and therefore, rather than preventing war, the pact would hasten it." Maisky countered by evoking "Al Capone as a model," in the sense that "only force will make (Hitler or Mussolini) doff their cap!"[320]

France's ambassador to Berlin, Coulondre, sounded a more alarming note than his British counterparts, warning Paris on May 22 that Ribbentrop was apoplectic over Polish minister Beck's rejection of Hitler's "generous" offer and had come around to favoring a rapprochement with Moscow as "indispensable and inevitable." Among Germany's objectives, Coulondre listed "the possibility of persuading Russia to play the same role in the dismemberment of Poland that the latter country had played with regard to Czechoslovakia. The ultimate object appeared to be to make use of the material resources and manpower of the USSR as a means to destroy the British empire." He noted that "it is possible that up to the present the Führer has resisted these appeals or at any rate hesitated to commit himself to such a policy, for ideological reasons. But, even admitting that such is his present attitude, there is nothing to indicate that he will not change his mind." Coulondre advised that "at this moment, when the Anglo-Franco-Russian negotiations seem to have entered upon a decisive phase, we should . . . bear in mind that the Reich would do its best to take advantage, to the detriment of France and Great Britain, of any failure . . . in the conversations now taking place with Moscow."[321]

Also on May 22, 1939, Stalin addressed a Central Committee plenum on its second day, reiterating his conviction that if it had not been for forced collectivization, "there would be no new major industry, no army and culture," and complaining, apropos of his own concession of small household plots seven years earlier, that "the peasant on his own plot will always scheme to enlarge his interests." He added, "If we are going to lag behind events this way in future instead of leading, then . . . we shall obtain the result of collective farms falling apart and hamlets and new individual farms being formed." A decree followed (May 27) that circumscribed household plots, to combat the "bazaar-ification of collective farm lands," the only document of the plenum made public.[322] Here was an empire of enslavement and political murder, founded on hostility toward private initiative and markets. That same day, the British and the French nominally acceded to Soviet demands and submitted a draft for reciprocal guarantees of security, but their response still excluded the Baltic states. Still more fundamentally, in the event of an attack on the USSR, the French and the British were promising only consultations—and through the League of Nations, to boot—not immediate military action. Molotov would angrily reject their proposal as betraying a lack of seriousness.[323]

ON MAY 22 IN BERLIN, Italy and Germany formally signed their Pact of Steel, which contained an open declaration of cooperation and binding consultation, and a secret protocol of military and economic union, directed against Britain and France.[324] Japan declined to sign but continued negotiating with Germany. To Molotov's blunt maneuver with Schulenburg, Germany offered no immediate response. Some German officials indulged a guarded optimism. "It seems that there still remains fairly wide scope for action in Russo-German relations," observed Weizsäcker, the number two in the foreign ministry, in a memorandum (May 25, 1939). He added, "It should be our aim to prevent Anglo-Franco-Russian relations from assuming a still more binding character."[325] But Schulenburg warned that Soviet-German negotiations could be a mere pretext to assist Moscow in the negotiations with London and Paris. Ribbentrop, unsure of Hitler's thinking, accentuated this caution.[326] For once, though, the Führer seemed ahead of his foreign minister. Secretly, on May 23, Hitler had gathered a small coterie of military men in the Chancellery to convey his resolve for war against Poland, as a step in a looming showdown with Britain. He stressed the imperative to meet the economic challenges of military requirements but indicated that German-Soviet economic relations would be possible only if political relations improved, an unacknowledged reference to Molotov's ultimatum/invitation. Hitler hinted that Moscow would accede to Poland's annihilation.[327]

In parallel, Hitler wanted to use Japan against the Western powers. The Japanese were insisting on firm mutual obligations for a war against the Soviet Union and only loose ones for a war against Britain and France, exactly the opposite of what the Germans sought.[328] Ribbentrop had tried to force the issue by telling Lieutenant General Hiroshi Ōshima, now the Japanese ambassador in Berlin, that if he could not bring about a German-Japanese alliance, Germany would have to conclude a nonaggression pact with the USSR. Ōshima spoke fluent German and had been accorded private audiences with Hitler; he fantasized with Russian émigrés about Stalin's assassination. But the diplomatically inexperienced ultranationalist, a staunch advocate for a German-Japanese military pact, would later claim he had not relayed Ribbentrop's threat to Tokyo.[329] Be that as it may, the Tokyo establishment was divided over whether to take up the German proposal.[330] On May 27, Weizsäcker wrote to Schulenburg that "one link in the whole chain, namely a gradual conciliation between Moscow and Tokyo, was said by the Japanese to be extremely problematical. Rome was also somewhat hesitant, so that eventually the disadvantages of the far-reaching step envisaged were regarded as decisive." He added, "With the approval of the Führer, an approach is nonetheless now to be made to the Russians, though a very much modified one."[331]

Ribbentrop, exasperated, wrote to the German ambassador in Tokyo, Eugen Ott (May 28, 1939), that "we can no longer understand what is actually happening in Tokyo and why the Japanese government, at this advanced stage of the negotiations, are still continuing to avoid making their decision clear." The next day, German foreign ministry officials somehow discerned that the USSR inclined toward signing an accord with Britain.[332] Soviet military intelligence spies, meanwhile, delivered copies of Ribbentrop's internal summary of a conversation with the Polish ambassador in Berlin, supplemented by reports of conversations of the German military attaché in Poland, who expected the Poles to capitulate rather than fight. Stalin's agents supplied him with reports leaked by the British foreign office to the German ambassador in London regarding Soviet negotiations with Britain and France. These leaks contained accurate information and reconfirmed for Stalin where British preferences lay: Berlin, not Moscow.[333]

Round and round the carousel went. German-Japanese, Western-Soviet, Western-German, and German-Italian negotiations all proceeded simultaneously. German officials, far more than British ones, had come to understand the importance of the Japanese question for the Soviet Union, and the difficulty of reconciling Tokyo and Moscow. But nothing was certain, except more intrigue. If diplomacy is the art of managing competing state interests by recognizing other states' vital interests and keeping communication open, then finding one another's bottom line, the principals here could barely comprehend how the other states' systems worked, let alone their aims. Hitler now seemed at logger-heads with Britain, nearing a war over Poland, but his propaganda portrayed history since 1789 as one long march toward "Judeo-Bolshevism," nihilism, and anarchy, which Nazism alone could halt.[334] Hitler claimed a self-assigned burden to fight on behalf of "civilization" against Jews and other purveyors of international-revolutionary inequity—such as Stalin. Could the Führer really be stopped or even deflected?

CHAPTER 11

PACT

In his present mood, PM [Neville Chamberlain] says he
will resign rather than sign alliance with Soviet.

SIR ALEXANDER CADOGAN,
British permanent undersecretary for foreign affairs,
private diary entry, May 20, 1939[1]

HITLER: "The scum of the earth, I believe?"

STALIN: "The bloody assassin of the workers, I presume?"

DAVID LOW, *"Rendezvous,"* Evening Standard,
September 20, 1939

ALMOST THE ENTIRE SUMMER OF 1939, Hitler would be absent from Berlin, ensconced at the Berghof, in the Obersalzberg, with Eva Braun, his longtime companion, leaving little central government to speak of. The Führer made strategic decisions, but their shape and timing depended to an extent on who might, or might not, enjoy access to him. Foreign minister Joachim von Ribbentrop—or his liaison—was contriving to show up at the Berghof to cajole Hitler into taking the plunge of rapprochement with the "Judeo-Bolsheviks." For such a coup de main, the insecure Ribbentrop might seem an unlikely personage. Growing up, he had been middle class, then married the heiress to a champagne fortune, acquired knowledge of French and English, traveled Europe as a wine salesman, and cajoled an aunt into legally adopting him so that he could obtain her (recently acquired) aristocratic title. "Von" Ribbentrop had joined the Nazis late (1932), and, some said, only at his wife's urging.[2] Goebbels said of him, "He bought his name, he married his money, and he swindled his way into office." For Hitler's interpreter, Paul-Otto Schmidt, Ribbentrop called to mind the dog on the label of the gramophone company His Master's Voice. "If Hitler was displeased with him," Schmidt noted, "Ribbentrop went sick and took to his bed like an hysterical woman."[3] Göring mocked Ribbentrop as "Germany's No. 1 parrot" and bad-mouthed him to the Führer. "But," the Führer would respond, Ribbentrop "knows a lot of important people in England." Göring was scathing: "Mein Führer, that may be right, but the bad thing is, they know him."[4]

Ribbentrop was a tool. But he was not only a tool. When serving as ambassador to the Court of St. James's—a posting he had gotten only as a consolation for originally being passed over for state secretary—he had rarely been at his post, for he was courting Hitler or negotiating with Japan and Italy for an alliance against Britain. When in London, he was mocked in British circles as "von Brickendrop," infamous for mistreating all and sundry, including the tailors who served the British aristocracy and related stories of his imperiousness to their clientele. In Ribbentrop's mind, however, the British had maltreated him.[5] Now, for such a staunch Anglophobe, a deal with Moscow could be his revenge, and a stunning feather in his foreign minister's cap.[6] Otto von Bismarck—ostensibly a lodestar for Ribbentrop—had famously established good relations with Russia as a key to Germany's aggrandizement. In truth, Ribbentrop could not even abide working in Bismarck's modest old office at 76 Wilhemstrasse. (Back in the day, the Iron Chancellor had also been his own foreign minister.) Instead, the Nazi foreign minister moved his office to the former presidential palace next door, which was his official residence.[7] But Ribbentrop operated by intuition and strove to be "radical," rarely invoking limits (or consequences), which pleased Hitler no end. And what could be more radical, in its way, than a deal with Communist Moscow?

Molotov, too, was an Anglophobe. He was also a Germanophile, who had publicly differentiated between the "ideologues of National Socialism" and "the German nation, as one of the great nations of our times."[8] He doggedly insisted that a deal could be done with that swine Hitler. This view was, or had become, Stalin's inclination, as Molotov knew. He would seem to be a fitting partner for Ribbentrop, and the two together, in turn, fitting representatives for their respective masters in the complicated game of finding the elusive rapprochement. But Molotov was negotiating with the British and the French; there were no political negotiations per se with Germany, other than the on-again, off-again trade talks. And the Far East seized center stage in the late spring and summer of 1939. There, against Japan, the Soviet Union had not even a whiff of possible "collective security" with the British or the United States (which was a supplier of strategic materials to Japan). On the contrary, with Japan armed in the east and Hitler armed to the teeth in the west, Stalin worried not only about a two-front war against the two powers that had defeated Russia in separate major wars earlier in the century, but about how Britain, opportunistically, might join one or even both.[9]

FAR EASTERN SKIRMISH

Back on May 10–11, 1939, as some twenty Mongol cavalry were grazing horses on the banks of the Halha River (Halhin Gol in Mongolian), near a cluster of huts (the village of Nomonhan, in Japanese), a Manchukuo force drove them off; the next day, the Mongols returned in numbers. Unlike the bloody clash over uninhabited hills at Lake Khasan near the Soviet-Korean-Manchukuo frontier the year before, this one concerned valuable pastures along the river, which served as a boundary.[10] The Tokyo high command's failure to impose unambiguous directives on Japan's Kwantung Army, despite the latter's record of high-handedness, reflected a multicenteredness in the Japanese political system that frustrated the Germans and the Soviets alike. It also allowed hotheads inside Japanese institutions to seize the initiative. The Kwantung Army had devised a new contingency war plan against the Soviet Union involving an all-out offensive toward Chita and Lake Baikal, to cut off the entire Soviet Far East. This bold design to seize a spectacular victory would expose the Kwantung Army to possibly devastating Soviet counterattack from the Mongolian salient, a vulnerability that argued for evicting the Red Army from Mongolia.

The Kwantung command, in this context, had recently issued inflammatory new guidelines, which Tokyo headquarters had rubber-stamped, for border skirmishes. "If the enemy crosses the frontier, . . . annihilate them without delay," the new rules stated. "It is permissible to enter Soviet territory, or to trap or lure Soviet troops into Manchukuoan territory."[11] The new rules even allowed local commanders to establish boundaries "on their own initiative" where ambiguity reigned (in effect, everywhere). When, during a briefing on the new rules of engagement, the latest grazing incident was reported to the Kwantung Army division commander responsible for the border, he decided, on May 13, to implement them.[12] Japanese reconnaissance discovered a pontoon bridge across the Halha to the right bank and decided to cut off this escape, entrap the "intruders," and annihilate them. On May 19, Stalin had Molotov warn Japanese ambassador Tōgō that the Soviets possessed information concerning Japanese and Manchukuo forces violating the Mongolian frontier at the Halha River, and that "there is a limit to all patience, and I ask the ambassador to relay this to the Japanese government: that there will be no more of this."[13]

Voroshilov, meanwhile, was receiving reports of Soviet indecisiveness from the area near the Halha River, and, on the recommendation of chief of staff Shaposh-nikov, summoned a more decisive person. On May 24, in Voroshilov's office, the deputy commander of the Belorussian military district, a cavalry specialist, re-ceived a briefing on developments along Mongolia's borders, to which he was instructed to fly immediately. His mission was to investigate the military situation, then recommend and, if necessary, take corrective measures.[14] That commander was Georgy Zhukov. Like Beria, he would prove to be another missing piece. A peasant's son (b. 1896), he had worked the fields like all the village children (in his case from age seven), attended the local church school for three years, and, at age eleven, departed for Moscow to apprentice in a furrier's shop (where he slept on the floor). Zhukov had been conscripted in the Great War and, despite his lowly ori-gins, awarded two St. George's Crosses before joining the Reds in summer 1918 and fighting in the famed First Cavalry Army. Twenty years later, the NKVD had wiped out almost all the commanders under whom he had served, making him an asso-ciate of "enemies of the people." Zhukov would later claim that his summons by Voroshilov, without explanation, had given him pause, and that his unexpected posting to the Mongolia-Manchukuo frontier had saved his life.[15]

It did not take Zhukov long to see that Soviet forces facing the Japanese were a mess.[16] But, incredibly, Kwantung Army intelligence had failed to notice that the bridgehead on the Halha was held by *Soviet* forces. On the morning of May 28, when 2,500 troops of the Japanese Kwantung Army followed through on the plan to cut off the pontoon escape route of the Mongol cavalry, then launch a frontal assault to drive them backward into waiting Japanese units, they met barrages of Soviet artillery and armor. Japan maintained air superiority, so, over just two days, the Red Air Force lost 15 fighter planes in combat, while the Japanese lost a single plane. (Voroshilov called the front and exploded.)[17] But the Japanese rear unit sent to cut off the Mongol escape route was wiped out nearly to a man, and the battered Japanese troops in the frontal assault retreated.[18] On May 31 at the Supreme Soviet, Molotov, in a speech almost entirely devoted to relations with the Western powers, publicly repeated the patience-running-out warning to Japan, noting that "we will defend the borders of the Mongolian People's Republic as decisively as our own, in line with our mutual assistance pact with them."[19] But the Kwantung Army was not likely to walk away.

GERMAN CUL-DE-SAC

The Germans feared success in the Soviet-British talks, and on May 30, 1939, the German foreign ministry had suddenly been ordered to undertake "definite negotiations" with the Soviets and not to be limited to economic issues—an apparent affirmative response to Molotov's ultimatum, a point conveyed by Weizsäcker to Astakhov, the Soviet chargé d'affaires in Berlin.[20] The next day in Tokyo, however, Ott suddenly became confident about German negotiations with Japan, reporting that the private secretary of Japan's prime minister had told him that "the latter was firmly resolved to put through the [Germany-Japan] alliance," and that the deputy war minister had told him the Japanese army would overcome the opposition of the Japanese navy.[21] If so, this could scuttle any German talks with Moscow. On June 5, the Japanese cabinet approved a compromise vis-à-vis Germany's demands whereby Japan assented to automatic involvement in any German-Soviet conflict and freedom to choose the appropriate moment to enter any other conflicts (such as a German-British one). This compromise represented a major policy victory for the Japanese army. But Japan's unsophisticated representative in Berlin, Lieutenant General Ōshima, seems not to have conveyed the decision to Germany.[22] Stalin, in any case, knew the real Japanese position—policy paralysis—thanks to Sorge, who had high contacts among Japanese ruling circles.

On June 4, further solid information on German plans for an invasion of Poland came from Rudolf von Scheliha, the Soviet spy in the German embassy in Warsaw, via Kleist, Ribbentrop's aide for the east, who had recently visited the Polish capital. The German ambassador there (von Moltke) and the air force attaché had been recalled to Berlin for consultations.[23] The combination of Hitler's designs on Poland and inconclusive German-Japanese talks could potentially push the Führer to cut a deal with the Soviet devil.[24] At long last, it appeared that Stalin's long-standing use of economic talks as a pathway to political talks might bear fruit. But distrust ran deep.[25] And Hitler might be bluffing.

Soviet-German "talks" were not formal and not always direct. On June 14, as the German foreign ministry learned the next day, Astakhov told the Bulgarian envoy in Berlin, Parvan Draganov, that "if Germany would declare that she would not attack the Soviet Union or that she would conclude a nonaggression pact with her, the Soviet Union would probably refrain from concluding a pact with England. However, the Soviet Union did not know what Germany really wanted."[26]

Schulenburg had left Moscow for consultations in Berlin. On June 21, Köstring, also in Berlin for consultations, had an audience with Hitler.[27] Back in Moscow, on June 28, Schulenburg informed the Soviet foreign ministry that Germany sought "not just normalization but improvement in its relations with the USSR," a stance he said had been conveyed to him by Ribbentrop and approved by Hitler.[28] Around this time, Ribbentrop's Italian counterpart and confidant, Ciano, evidently "leaked" to the Soviet chargé in Rome the possibility of a German-Soviet nonaggression pact, economic agreement, joint guarantee of the Baltic states, and mediation in the relations with Japan.[29] But on June 30, Ribbentrop, on Hitler's orders, suddenly directed that the haphazard political contacts be broken off and that any resumption of talks for a trade agreement be delayed.[30]

NO ANSWERS

Soviet-Western talks were formal and direct, but fraught as well. Besides Polish acquiescence in possible Red Army transit, a second major sticking point proved to be Soviet insistence on "guarantees" for the Baltic states' territorial integrity, to prevent Germany from using them as springboards for an attack. But the Western powers—citing the circumstance that these countries themselves were not asking for such guarantees—balked. As the Soviet ambassador would report from Paris, the Western powers viewed such a guarantee as offering Moscow "a free hand in the Baltics."[31] Stalin, for his part, viewed the Balts' professed "strict neutrality" as a pretense.[32] Top political figures in authoritarian Lithuania, Latvia, and Estonia, as well as in democratic Finland, were publicly cozying up to the Nazis. On June 7, 1939, Estonia and Latvia had signed nonaggression pacts with Germany in Berlin; this was soon followed by visits to Estonia by chief of staff Lieutenant General Franz Halder, commander of German land forces, and Admiral Canaris, head of the Abwehr. Molotov demanded that Estonia reverse course and place itself under Soviet protection. But Estonia considered a Soviet "guarantee" of its territorial integrity the worst of both worlds: it would anger Nazi Germany and invite Soviet occupation.[33]

On June 10, Molotov, through Maisky in London, communicated an unambiguous Soviet demand for British assent in preventing the three Baltic states from being used in an aggression against the USSR. *Pravda* (June 13) publicly dismissed possible objections.[34] On June 15, one month into the negotiations with the Western powers, Molotov, in a telegram to the Soviet envoys in London and Paris, wrote that the British and the French "do not want a serious agreement based on the principle of reciprocity and equality of conditions."[35] Some British officials internally urged that London accede to Soviet security demands for "guarantees" for the Baltics, even while conceding that Stalin might then have a pretext to seize them. But Chamberlain—who had handed Hitler Czechoslovakia—refused.

Stalin was stupefied. The British imperialists had seized one quarter of the earth, across oceans, and yet they kept invoking "principle" in a refusal to allow him to protect himself in connection with microscopic territories, contiguous with the Soviet homeland, that until recently had belonged to Russia and that represented a threat? Around this time, at a Grand Kremlin Palace reception, the dancer Igor Moiseyev, whose folk ensemble had become among the most popular acts, was talking to Voroshilov. Stalin cherished their number "Moscow-Region Lyrical," from the dance cycle *Pictures from the Past,* and, as the defense commissar asked what Moiseyev planned to stage next, Stalin approached. Apprised of the conversation, he said, "All the same, they will never stage what Stalin needs." Moiseyev: "Iosif Vissarionovich, do you have a bad opinion of us?" Stalin: "Not at all, but what Stalin needs (he spoke of himself in the third person) you will not stage. . . . For example, will you stage the rout of England and France?" Silence ensued. Faces froze. Stalin moved on.[36]

Domestic political pressures did compel Chamberlain to send someone to Moscow to "accelerate the negotiations." Maisky, the Soviet envoy, had suggested on June 12 that the British send Foreign Secretary Halifax, who seemed favorably disposed to a deal, but nothing had come of it. Nor would Chamberlain consent to sending Anthony Eden, the former foreign secretary, who had met Stalin and offered to go. Instead the PM dispatched William Strang, who, during Eden's Moscow visit, had also met Stalin. "Of all the dictators, Stalin was, in personal intercourse, seemingly most like a normal human being," Strang would write. "In conference as we saw him, . . . his voice was low and even, his manner serene, his delivery unemphatic, his sense of humour quietly playful, his exposition concise in form, conciliatory in tone but unbending in substance. He had a rock-like quality which made him appear to be more securely founded than his rival dictators."[37] But Strang was a mere foreign office functionary, and he was sent not as a special plenipotentiary, but only "to assist" Ambassador Seeds. Zhdanov, on June 29, published an essay in *Pravda* titled "The British and the French Do Not Want an Equal Agreement with the USSR."

Molotov, for his part, referred to his capitalist counterparts as "crooks and cheats" internally, and to their faces he demanded that any obligations be spelled out in detail, telling Seeds that the 1935 Franco-Soviet pact "had turned out to be merely a paper delusion." The Soviet Union's top "diplomat" also made a point of sitting at his desk while raised on a proscenium, forcing his Western interlocutors to remain below in deskless chairs, their notepads uncomfortably perched on their laps. (Neither Molotov nor his deputy Potyomkin, who did the interpreting, took notes, according to the British side, but Molotov seemed to them to be pressing a button on his desk, perhaps to record the conversation.)[38] Seeds and French envoy Naggiar were also unnerved by the door behind Molotov that always seemed to be open, suspecting that Stalin was eavesdropping. (Kremlin logbooks record no meetings in the Little Corner during the time Molotov was negotiating.) Molotov introduced new demands at will, and he failed to perceive the differences in French and British proposals. Such incomprehension of nuance, on top of the disdain for diplomatic convention, might have mattered had the British government been interested in a deal. "I am so skeptical of the value of Russian help," Chamberlain wrote privately to his sister (July 2, 1939), "that I should not feel our position was greatly worsened if we had to do without them."[39]

WAR

Vsevolod Meyerhold, the USSR's most renowned theater director, who had traveled to Leningrad to finalize the choreography of a mass spectacle of physical culture involving 30,000 young athletes moving in unison to glorify the regime, was rewarded by being arrested. At Moscow's infamous Butyrka prison, he would be tortured into confessing to espionage for Britain as well as Japan. "The investigators began to use force on me, a sick, 65-year-old man," he wrote in a letter to Molotov. "I was made to lie facedown and then beaten on the soles of my feet and my spine with a rubber strap. . . . When those parts of my legs were covered with extensive internal hemorrhaging, they again began to beat the red-blue-yellow bruises with the strap, and the pain was so intense that it felt as if boiling hot water was being poured on those sensitive areas. . . . I began to incriminate myself in the hope that this, at least, would lead quickly to the scaffold." Meyerhold's interrogators had urinated into his mouth and smashed his right (writing) hand to bits.[40] Right around the same time, his second wife and lead actress, the Russified ethnic German Zinaida Reich, was brutally stabbed to death, including through the eyes, in their home.[41] None of her valuables were taken.[42] Meyerhold knew nothing of his wife's murder; his colleagues knew nothing of his fate, only that his photographs had been taken down or cut out.

Molotov was stressing to the German ambassador that Berlin's stance toward Soviet-Japanese relations was a key consideration in any possible German-Soviet rapprochement.[43] But Berlin was still looking for a deal with Tokyo, as Sorge had secretly reported on June 27.[44] On July 1, Ott conveyed to Berlin that he had still "not been able to obtain complete clarity regarding Japanese reservations."[45] On July 2, Hitler, in Hamburg for the funeral of a military general, mentioned the possibility of an agreement with the Soviet Union in a speech to Nazi party officials.[46] On July 5, Ott wrote again to Weizsäcker: "As to the negotiations for an alliance, these arguments confirm once again that the Navy has been fighting tenaciously for a policy of waiting and seeing what America would do, and of entering the war only at a later stage." Ribbentrop wrote on the document: "Führer."[47] It had become evident that Germany would not be able to conclude a substantive military alliance with Japan, let alone intercede with Tokyo on behalf of Moscow.[48]

Near Mongolia, as Japan's Kwantung Army readied its counterstrike, Voroshilov was receiving denunciations of Soviet commanders in the Far East, Beria playing his part.[49] Zhukov, with the support of Grigory Stern, head of the Transbaikal military district in Chita (and the victor in the Lake Khasan border skirmish), had sacked the Soviet frontline commander in Mongolia. He also set up a belated intelligence network on the enemy and began massing troops, artillery, tanks, and planes with experienced airmen (many of them Spanish civil war veterans).[50] Colonel Akio Doi, Japanese military attaché in Moscow, who happened to be returning to Japan, warned Kwantung Army headquarters in person on his way home that although the Soviets had often shown passivity during previous border incidents, this time a firm reply could be expected. The Kwantung Army's own intelligence warned that the Soviets had two rifle divisions, not the anticipated small subdivisional unit, poised for action near Nomonhan. Nonetheless, Major Tsuji Masanobu, the author of the new border guidelines at Kwantung Army headquarters, was determined to avenge the earlier failures. The Kwantung Army head ordered an offensive without the approval of his superiors in Tokyo, avoiding sending his directives by telegraph, lest HQ get wind and cancel them.[51]

The Japanese counterattack had commenced on June 26–27, 1939, with a 130-airplane raid deep behind the Soviet-Mongolian positions. Tokyo, which wanted to localize the skirmish, reacted angrily to this "defense" of Manchukuo, but the bombing proved successful. On July 1, at sunrise (4:00 a.m.), the Kwantung Army launched a ground offensive with 15,000 troops. By July 2–3 they had achieved tactical success, crossing the Halha River in force to the western bank, thanks to Tsuji's boldness. By July 4 Zhukov was pounding the Japanese positions with Soviet-made heavy guns as well as German-made 152-millimeter Rheinmetall artillery. The latter, acquired during the cooperation with Germany, had a range (20,000 yards) double that of the Japanese guns. Japanese casualties mounted, and they retreated back across the Halha (the rest of the fighting would take place on the eastern bank). But the Soviets lost huge amounts of armor. Adding to the difficulties, Marshal Kulik, deputy defense commissar and chief of Soviet artillery, had gotten himself posted to the theater and on July 13 ordered Zhukov to withdraw Soviet artillery from the Halha's eastern banks to the western, so as not to lose it. When Shaposhnikov, chief of staff in Moscow, heard of this the next day, he ordered Zhukov to disobey Kulik. Voroshilov, white hot, dressed Kulik down on the high-frequency phone ("Babble less about all kinds of nonsense"). On July 19, the Soviet forces at the frontier were reorganized into a unified First Army Group, to ensure Zhukov's uncontested authority.[52]

SUMMER OF INDETERMINACY

Besides Japan, the Baltic states presented another key to any Nazi-Soviet deal, which Ribbentrop understood, but his deputy, Weizsäcker, opposed any Baltic partition.[53] An internal German decision to renew bilateral economic negotiations with the Soviet Union, offering a 200-million-reichsmark credit for Soviet purchases in Germany, emerged on July 7, 1939, and was conveyed to Mikoyan three days later.[54] On July 9, Proskurov, Soviet military intelligence head, reported to Stalin on the basis of information from the Warsaw-based Soviet spy Kurt Welkisch ("ABC"), who had visited Berlin in June, that Kleist had reconfirmed Nazi plans to annihilate Poland, with a target date of late August or early September (Scheliha's earlier report had it for July). Kleist noted that Hitler was set upon a "radical solution of the Polish question" regardless of the military position of France and Britain. "Neither the Führer nor Ribbentrop," Kleist was quoted as saying, "believe that the Soviet Union would take part in Anglo-French military actions against Germany." That conclusion was based upon the inconclusive state of Western negotiations in Moscow and "the recent behavior of Moscow toward

Berlin. Moscow gave us to understand that it is ready to conduct negotiations with us, that it is utterly uninterested in a conflict with Germany, and that it is also uninterested in fighting for England and France." Kleist added that Germany would keep its hands off the Baltic states, in deference to the Soviet Union, and that "peace-loving relations between Germany and Russia over the next two years, in the Führer's opinion, are the prerequisite for resolving the problems of Western Europe."[55]

But Stalin further learned that, with Chamberlain's approval, on July 18, 1939, Horace Wilson, an adviser to the PM, had met secretly with a "special assistant" to Göring, Dr. Helmuth Wohlthat. The full range of what they discussed cannot be gleaned from Wilson's account.[56] Still, Germany's ambassador to London, Herbert von Dirksen, informed Berlin that Wilson had stated that a nonaggression pact with Germany "would allow England to free itself from its obligations vis-à-vis Poland."[57] On July 19, reinforcing the renewed push to cut a deal with Hitler, Chamberlain and Halifax, at a British cabinet meeting, carried the argument not to accede to Soviet demands to open military talks immediately and earnestly for a full alliance with ironclad commitments. But Britain conveyed its agreement to launch the military talks with Moscow, in parallel with the political ones. Maisky was fooled.[58] On July 20–21, as Stalin took in a physical culture parade on Red Square, the secretary of the British department of overseas trade, Robert Hudson, a scion of a soap king, met with Wohlthat, too, and, as if representing the British government, seems to have offered Hitler not just Danzig and the Polish Corridor but also a large British loan and the settlement of all of Germany's colonial claims—if only the Führer would refrain from taking all of Poland by force.[59]

"The Biggest Bribe in History," ran the scandalous headline in the British *Daily Express* (July 22), which published leaks, evidently from Hudson, of Chamberlain's back-channel efforts to negotiate with Hitler. Forty-eight hours later, *Pravda* carried word of the British offer to Germany, with details that were wildly inaccurate but repeated from the British press.[60]

British intelligence had come to understand that "Germany's future policy is in the keeping of a single man: a visionary, fanatic, and megalomaniac, a being of violent complexes," who aimed for European domination. But they surmised that Hitler's rearmament had resulted in a supposedly fragile German economy starved of resources, as well as a supposedly disaffected German populace. Therefore, British intelligence reasoned, Hitler could fight only short wars, and only in places like Poland and Ukraine, where he could not just expend but also grab resources. Halifax, however, wondered whether the limitations on Germany spotlighted by British intelligence might push "the mad dictator to insane adventures."[61] Chamberlain, for his part, believed that if Britain applied pressure, Germany's strategic weaknesses would compel Hitler to back down from his domination schemes. After all, what government could avoid accommodating social and economic pressures at home? If he became too headstrong, Hitler might even be overthrown by "moderates."[62] "Hitler has concluded that we mean business and the time is not ripe for a major war," the PM wrote to his sister Ida (July 23, 1939). "Unlike some of my critics I go further and say that the longer the war is put off the less likely it is to come at all."[63]

That same day, just as Stalin had learned of Chamberlain's attempts once more to "bribe" Hitler, the despot further learned of Chamberlain's pending acquiescence to Japanese pressure. Britain faced a strategic dilemma in Asia, not just Europe, and it was linked to any British policy options for the USSR. Japanese forces were blockading the British—as well as the French—concession in Tientsin (near Peking). The British Royal Navy was far away, and the United States had no intention of risking war with Japan by coming to the aid of British imperial interests in Asia. With Hitler threatening Poland, for which Britain had issued the "guarantee," London felt constrained to sign the Anglo-Japanese Tientsin Agreement (July 24) to protect its exposed positions. London refused Tokyo's demands to turn over the Chinese silver in British banks, but it handed over four Chinese nationals accused of assassinating Japanese nationals and then hiding out in the British concession. (The four Chinese were soon executed.) Some contemporaries dubbed the Tientsin deal a Far Eastern Munich. For Stalin, Tientsin underscored the absence of serious Western opposition to Japan's aggression in China and its imperial ambitions, including vis-à-vis Soviet territory in the east.[64]

The Japanese war minister had resumed his drive against internal opposition from the navy and the civilian government for a binding alliance with Germany against the USSR; Sorge continued to report on the talks.[65] The Kwantung Army, at the same time, was planning a renewed offensive near Mongolia. In late July, the Red Army began bringing massive reinforcements into the battle zone. Colonel Doi, back in Moscow, warned Tokyo that something very major was afoot.[66]

Also on July 23, 1939, Molotov demanded of Britain and France that, before the conclusion of a political agreement, tripartite military plans against Germany be coordinated in detail. Two days later, the Western ambassadors conveyed their governments' willingness to open military-to-military talks.

BALTIC FLIP

In Berlin, rumors had begun to circulate that Ribbentrop had fallen out of favor, because he had failed to anticipate the British guarantee to Poland and its generally hard-line position after the Nazis' destruction of all of Czechoslovakia.[67] In fact, Ribbentrop had maneuvered himself into the catbird seat. "He asked the liaison man he kept around Hitler to tell him what the Führer had said in the circle of his closest confidants," recalled Gustav Hilger, of the Moscow embassy. "From statements of this kind he drew conclusions about Hitler's intentions and ideas and, at suitable opportunities, would present them to him as his own thoughts."[68] The Wehrmacht's insatiable supply needs, seen against the uncanny complementarity of the Soviet and German economies, and the circumstance that the Soviets could enable Germany to overcome an anticipated British blockade, had provided the foundation for a rapprochement. But the key to everything was Hitler's planning for war against Poland, in the face of the publicly voiced guarantees to Poland by Britain and France.[69] Once Ribbentrop had learned that Hitler wanted to "isolate Poland"—that is, to remove or undercut the Anglo-French "guarantees"—the foreign minister had his opening to encourage Hitler to "seize Russia" from the British and the French.[70]

Suddenly, on July 26, 1939, Schnurre, the trade official in the German foreign ministry, invited Astakhov and a Soviet trade official to a private room at a Berlin restaurant and told them that—in fulfillment of Molotov's prior condition for a commercial treaty—a political agreement was possible, and that the fate of the Baltic states and any other Soviet desiderata would be open for discussion.[71] Astakhov had no instructions for a response. "After the statement of the Russians, I had the impression that Moscow had not decided what they wanted to do," Schnurre observed in a long memorandum the next day. "The Russians were silent about the status and chances of the English pact negotiations. . . . As a further handicap, there is the excessive distrust not only toward us but toward England as well. From our point of view it may be regarded as a noteworthy success that Moscow, after months of negotiations with England, still remains uncertain as to what she ought to do eventually."[72]

On July 29, Nevile Henderson, British ambassador to Germany, drove to Bayreuth to contrive a meeting with Hitler. ("Though absolutely unmusical," Henderson would observe, "I like Wagner.") His car broke down en route. Once finally there, during *Die Walküre,* he managed only to glimpse the Führer from afar. "If he had wanted to speak to me," Henderson noted, "Hitler could have done so; for he must have been informed that I was there."[73] But the envoy did not lose faith. "As I pointed out at the time to His Majesty's Government, the Polish question was not one of Hitler's making," Henderson would write. "The Corridor and Danzig were a real German national grievance, and some equitable settlement had to be found."[74]

Britain had also been consulting in Baltic capitals, posing as the defender of small countries, but the Balts, perceiving fecklessness, more and more looked to Germany as the only realistic counterbalance to the USSR. Germany's position, however, had shifted precipitously. On August 2, Ribbentrop invited in Astakhov and told him that, "from the Baltic to the Black Sea, there was no problem which could not be solved to our mutual satisfaction."[75] The Soviet envoy, in his report to Molotov, surmised that the Germans were declaring their disinterest in the fate of former Russian Poland, the Baltic states (Lithuania excepted), and Bessarabia and repudiating any designs on Ukraine. In exchange, Germany sought Soviet disinterest in the fate of Danzig and the provinces of former German Poland, with former Austrian Poland a matter for further clarification. Germany's ultimate aim, Astakhov concluded, was "to neutralize us in the case of war with Poland," although, he added, any long-term acquiescence by Germany to the above arrangements was doubtful.[76]

Schulenburg enjoyed more frequent access to Molotov than other ambassadors in Moscow, but still he found him largely inscrutable; the pair never developed chemistry. On August 3, Molotov acceded to the German's request for an audience and heard the recent accommodating news from Ribbentrop firsthand. "Molotov abandoned his habitual reserve and appeared unusually open," Schulenburg reported to Berlin the next day, but the Soviet government head nonetheless made a point of condemning the Anti-Comintern Pact and stated that "proofs of a changed attitude of the German Government were for the present still lacking." Schulenburg further noted to Berlin that "my general impression is that the Soviet Government are determined to conclude an agreement with Britain and France, if they fulfill all Soviet wishes." He added that the "negotiations, to be sure, might last a long time, especially since mistrust of England is also great."[77] Hitler had become exceedingly anxious about a British-French-Soviet military convention.[78] Wittingly or unwittingly, Schulenburg was enhancing Stalin's bargaining position.

PLAYED FOR A FOOL

To lead the long-awaited military-to-military talks with the two Western powers, Stalin appointed defense commissar Marshal Voroshilov, assisted by chief of staff Marshal Shaposhnikov, the naval commissar, and the air force head—the highest-level military group the Soviet despot could have assembled.[79] The British, after very long delay, finally indicated that they would send the Honorable Sir Reginald Plunkett-Ernle-Erle-Drax, commandant of Portsmouth. Beria, as per usual, prepared an NKVD dossier, which was unflattering to the unknown "commandant."[80] In London, Maisky noted in his diary, in a tone of considerable optimism about Anglo-Soviet relations, that "a bloc is gradually coming together. . . . The trip of the military missions to Moscow is an historical stage." And yet he also wrote to Moscow, "I think that, judging from the posts they hold, the delegates will not be able to make any decisions on the spot."[81] When the Western ambassadors informed Molotov who would be coming, he evidently launched a tirade, then stormed out of his own office.

Stalin received damning reports about British motives from the spy Guy Burgess, who worked at MI6 and divulged crucial information to Anatoly Gorsky (b. 1907), originally a code clerk who had become acting Soviet intelligence chief in London (since late 1938) after the arrests of two superiors in succession. Gorsky was single-handedly responsible for fourteen field agents, including Burgess, Anthony Blunt, John Cairncross, and Kim Philby. He also had to manage cryptography, photography, translation, typing, and communications.[82] On August 3, Burgess reported to Gorsky that Horace Wilson, Chamberlain's special adviser on foreign affairs, had told him that "the British chiefs of staff are firmly convinced that war with Germany can be won without difficulty and therefore the British government has no need to conclude a defense pact with the Soviet Union. In government circles the opinion expressed is that England never thought about concluding a pact with the USSR. The prime minister's advisers say openly that Great Britain can do without a Russian pact." Gorsky also reported that another source, Montagu "Monty" Chidson, had told him that "it is a fundamental policy to work with Germany whatever happens, and, in the end, against the USSR. But it is impossible to conduct this policy openly." Gorsky added, "Chidson told me that our aim is not to resist German expansion to the east."[83]

Drax and his French counterpart traveled to the USSR by sea. The foreign office explained to the British public that no British or French commercial airline flew to the Soviet Union. Of course, the British had the world's number-one air force. But they had opted not to use their Sunderland "flying boats," because, it was said, at least eight would have been taken up to accommodate all personnel on the mission. Wellington bombers would have been capacious enough, but these were said to be "uncomfortable." Water travel, meanwhile, could have been undertaken on fast naval cruisers, but it was said that such vessels lacked sufficient cabins. And so on. What the British and the French would not say was that they worried about the repercussions of crossing Germany, even in the air; the French in particular wanted to avoid too spectacular a method of travel, in order to avoid embarrassment if the Moscow talks failed.[84] But the Anglo-French decision to travel to Moscow by slow passenger and cargo steamers, and their dubious public explanations, conveyed a stark message to Moscow: this was a charade. On top of everything else, Drax departed the UK only on August 5.

The German foreign ministry official Weizsäcker complained in his diary (August 7) that Berlin was now straining every nerve to achieve a breakthrough, but the Soviets were not responding.[85] Hitler, with his decision to attack Poland despite British and French guarantees, had effectively backed himself into a corner, and time was running out: also on August 7, Soviet intelligence reported to Stalin that Hitler's attack on Poland could commence as soon as August 25.[86] Suddenly, Stalin held all the cards. The despot played it slow. The tension in Berlin reached near hysteria.[87] Chamberlain, too, had played right into Stalin's hands, but, unlike Hitler, the British PM appeared to be taking Stalin for a fool. On August 11, the risible Drax mission finally reached Moscow. It carried nine tons of baggage, but just a single person (an aide) who spoke Russian or had some experience of the Soviet Union.[88] That same day, Stalin convened the politburo and resolved to enter into official talks with Germany.[89]

In the negotiations with the Drax mission, Stalin instructed Voroshilov, mapping out the steps in writing, to take a hard line, but in such a way that the British and the French would be blamed for any failure.[90] At the opening banquet for the late-arriving, low-level Western delegation, Voroshilov, in dress whites, was in top form, exuding his considerable charm as host at the Spiridonovka Palace, the main reception hall for foreign dignitaries.[91] Treated to a fifty-foot-long table of delicacies, rivers of drink, musicians, and acrobats, the British and the French staggered back to their quarters in the wee hours. The next morning, first thing, Voroshilov pointedly requested their credentials. The French had balanced the

British admiral with a general, Joseph Doumenc, who at least had a piece of paper signed by Prime Minister Daladier: it allowed Doumenc to negotiate but not to sign anything. Drax—tall, silver hair, blue eyes—had to admit, as the Soviets already knew, that he had no written authority even to negotiate, let alone sign, a military convention.[92] When Voroshilov pointedly asked whether the Anglo-French mission had secured permission from their Polish ally for Soviet transit across Poland in the event of war with Germany, Drax gave no answer.

The defense commissar insisted on direct confirmation from the Poles and the Romanians. At a break in the talks, Doumenc took it upon himself to send his own envoy to Warsaw to arrange Polish agreement for Soviet passage through its territory.[93] On August 13, with the Nazis openly threatening Danzig, Poland had ordered a partial mobilization of its army. Two days later, the Poles publicly celebrated the nineteenth anniversary of the "miracle on the Vistula," in which they had driven back the Red Army. In response to French inquiries about granting Red Army transit, Warsaw refused again. Soviet "assistance," many Poles felt, would be worse than facing the Nazis. "An intelligent rabbit," Halifax had written of the Poles, "would hardly be expected to welcome the protection of an animal ten times its size, whom it credited with the habits of a boa constrictor."[94] But Halifax, just like the Polish government, failed to grasp that refusing the Soviets would mean facing *both* predators.

Voroshilov initiated a pointed discussion of each side's common-defense contributions to a prospective anti-German military alliance. Shaposhnikov outlined a massive Soviet commitment of up to 120 infantry divisions, as well as 16 cavalry divisions, 5,000 heavy artillery pieces, 9,500 tanks, and as many as 5,500 fighter aircraft and bombers. This amounted to more than a million-man force, to be fielded immediately if necessary. The French claimed to have 110 available combat divisions. The British, reluctant to divulge "military secrets," finally stated that they could commit 16 army divisions. So few? Pressed, the British admitted that the real number was perhaps 5.[95] (In fact, it was probably 2.) The Soviets, as a land power, had difficulty grasping the full measure of British strength, which was in the air and, especially, on the sea.[96] Be that as it may, by forcing such a conversation, one of Voroshilov's interpreters surmised, the defense commissar had deliberately been seeking to humiliate the Anglo-French military men.[97] Fair enough. But could Stalin be faulted? As far as London was concerned, the real action was in Berlin, where the British had even let on that they did not take seriously their own negotiations with Moscow.[98]

THE HITLER CARD

The Soviets, on August 12, 1939, agreed to the German foreign ministry's proposal for political talks, requesting, however, that they take place in Moscow. Hitler contemplated dispatching his personal lawyer and minister without portfolio Hans Frank (who had previously gone to Rome to finalize the Axis accord), but on August 14 he opted to send Ribbentrop, a move that Schulenburg formally proposed to Molotov the next day.[99] That night, at around 8:00 p.m., with Drax in Moscow, Molotov received Schulenburg, who read out a statement received that morning from Ribbentrop. "Germany has no aggressive intentions against the USSR," Schulenburg stated. "The Reich government is of the opinion that there is no question between the Baltic and the Black Sea which cannot be settled to the complete satisfaction of both countries. Among these are such questions as: the Baltic Sea, the Baltic area, Poland, Southeast questions, etc." The ambassador proposed a lightning visit by Ribbentrop to Moscow to "set forth the Führer's views to M. Stalin." Molotov inquired about a possible bilateral nonaggression pact and German mediation of Soviet-Japanese relations, but said that "such a trip required adequate preparation."[100] To increase the pressure on Berlin, the day before (and again two days after), Stalin had the German embassy in London informed that the Anglo-Soviet talks were proceeding smoothly and that the Poles would open staff talks with the Soviets.[101]

On August 16, Rudolf Herrnstadt, a Soviet spy handler in Warsaw, reported to military intelligence HQ in Moscow that the embassy spy Scheliha had revealed that the German invasion of Poland would commence very soon.[102] On August 17, Molotov again received Schulenburg and reported a favorable reaction on the part of "the Soviet government," but insisted first on the signing of an economic agreement, after which the Soviets wanted to see a written proposal for a nonaggression pact, and only then, about a week after the conclusion of an economic agreement, could Ribbentrop's visit take place. The Nazi foreign minister, once apprised, on August 18–19 sent Schulenburg a brief two-article text of a nonaggression pact of twenty-five years' duration, with details to be ironed out in person, promising a special protocol on the Baltic area. "You must keep in mind the decisive fact that an early outbreak of open German-Polish conflict is probable," Ribbentrop instructed Schulenburg, "and that we therefore have the greatest interest in having my visit to Moscow take place immediately."[103]

With *Pravda* (August 19) accusing the British and the French of preparing a "new Munich" with Germany, Stalin received an intelligence report to the effect that Hitler was determined to tackle the Polish question come what may, and that he thought Moscow would "conduct negotiations with us, as she has no interest whatever in a conflict with Germany, nor was she anxious to be defeated for the sake of England and France." Such information dovetailed with the intercepts of Schulenburg's telegrams to Berlin.[104] On the evening of August 19, Schulenburg reported to Berlin that he had been received twice that day by Molotov—at 2:00 p.m., for one hour, and again at 5:00 p.m.—and that the Soviet government had presented him with a Soviet text for a nonaggression pact consisting of five articles and a postscript, to last five years, and had agreed to receive the Nazi foreign minister in Moscow on August 26 or 27.[105] That was the proposed date for Germany's invasion of Poland. A German-Soviet economic agreement had been finalized in Berlin around noon on August 19, but at 4:00 p.m. local time, Soviet negotiators had informed their German counterparts that they could not sign it.

Finally, the Soviets in Berlin consented to sign the economic agreement at 2:00 a.m. on August 20, dating it the previous day. It stipulated that the Reich would export "industrial goods" totaling about 60 million reichsmarks of "current business" (trade covered by earlier clearing agreements) and 180 million reichsmarks of "new business." The Soviets would export the same in raw materials and repay old credits. The Reich, in turn, would finance 200 million reichsmarks' worth of the new Soviet orders. Schnurre, the lead German negotiator, noted that "the framework now set up represents a minimum," and predicted that bilateral trade could leap to nearly 1 billion reichsmarks. The German government agreed to guarantee the loan nearly fully, at a publicly stated interest rate of 5 percent, but with a secret protocol refund of 0.5 percent, reducing the actual interest while allowing a seven-year term of payback, and not requiring an itemized list of goods. The Germans had wanted to grant a larger Soviet credit, 500 million reichsmarks or more, at a higher interest rate, with lower German government loan guarantees, shorter terms of payback (five years maximum), and a specific list of goods to contain Soviet appetites.[106]

Later that afternoon of August 20, 1939, Hitler dispatched a personal telegram to Stalin via the German embassy in Moscow. "The conclusion of a non-aggression pact with the Soviet Union means to me the establishment of a long-range Germany policy," Hitler wrote. "I accept the draft pact that your foreign minister, Herr Molotov, delivered, but consider it urgently necessary to clarify questions connected with it as soon as possible." He referred to "intolerable" tension between Germany and Poland and, noting that Ribbentrop would have full powers to sign a state accord, asked that he be received on August 22, or August 23 latest. Also on August 20, nine days after his arrival in Moscow, Drax finally produced written credentials allowing him to negotiate on behalf of the British government, but Voroshilov adjourned the negotiations indefinitely. Stalin, who was micromanaging the process, sent Voroshilov duck hunting.[107]

Pravda, on the morning of August 21, carried the announcement of the Nazi-Soviet economic agreement, calling it "a serious step in the cause of improving not only economic, but also political relations between the USSR and Germany." Stalin effectively would supply the Germans with grain harvested by his enslaved collective farmers and oil and strategic raw materials extracted partly by his Gulag inmates, for the right to engage in a shopping spree through one of the world's most modern economies for machines and models of modern weaponry.[108] That day at 3:00 p.m., Schulenburg was able to hand Hitler's telegram for Stalin to Molotov.[109] Stalin underlined in blue pencil Hitler's phrase regarding Poland ("A crisis may break out any day"), as well as the Führer's urgent appeal ("I would be pleased to receive your immediate reply").[110] Stalin had Molotov summon Schulenburg back already at 5:00 p.m. Moscow time to reveal that Ribbentrop would be welcome on the 23rd. "The people of our countries," Stalin wrote in his response to Hitler, "need peaceful relations."[111]

Stalin's response, transmitted via the German embassy, arrived in Berlin at 8:30 p.m. local time on August 21. At the Berghof, champagne was ordered. Hitler, a teetotaler, did not imbibe, but he drummed both fists on the wall.[112] Just before midnight, the Nazi regime released the sensational news of its foreign minister's upcoming Moscow visit. In Paris, the government pondered pressing the Poles into "compromise" with Hitler, to buy time. In London, the assembled cabinet sought to appear nonchalant, but MPs were asking about the apparent failure of British intelligence to anticipate such a shocking turn of events.[113] Burgess informed Gorsky of a telegram from Ambassador Henderson, also on August 21: "All measures have been taken for Hermann Göring to arrive under secret cover in London on Wednesday 23rd. This will amount to a historic event and we are just waiting for confirmation of this from the German side."[114]

At the Berghof, very early on the morning of Saturday, August 22, the Führer addressed his top brass. He had summoned them to discuss his plans for Poland even before the news had come from Moscow, with instructions to arrive in civilian attire so as not to give anything away. "It was clear to me that a conflict with Poland had to come sooner or later," he began, according to notes taken by Wilhelm Canaris, the head of military intelligence. "I had already made this decision in the spring, but I thought that I would first turn against the West in a few years, and only after that against the East." But the Polish situation had become "intolerable." His only fear, he said, was "that at the last minute some *Schweinhund* will make a proposal for mediation." He concluded with an injunction about the absolute necessity of taking advantage of his never-to-be-repeated spell over the German people. "Essentially," Hitler said, leaning on a grand piano, "all depends on me, on my existence, because of my political talents." He adjourned them for lunch. To allay worries over his precipitating a new world war, he decided to address them a second time, giving some operational details and asserting that England had no real military. Not a single top general voiced objections. Toward the end of his peroration, Hitler briefly broke off, suddenly recognized Ribbentrop from among those assembled, and, melodramatically, sent his foreign minister with a Nazi salute right from the Berghof to fly to Stalin.[115]

That same Saturday, August 22, following the emergency cabinet meeting, Henderson set out to hand-deliver Chamberlain's latest telegram to Hitler. Received at the Berghof on August 23 at 1:00 p.m., he stated that any German-Soviet pact would not alter Britain's obligations to Poland, but hinted again that Britain could trade Poland away, and suggested again that the very next day, Field Marshal Göring should fly to Britain surreptitiously to meet Chamberlain at Chequers, the prime minister's country residence, to hammer out an Anglo-German accord. Ever the ingrate, Hitler berated Henderson, shouting that London's "blank check" guarantee to Poland had ruled out negotiations. Henderson departed, then was called back, but Hitler, although calmer, blamed Britain for being "determined to destroy and exterminate Germany." The Führer evidently felt that his theatrics, on top of any pact with Stalin, would induce the British and, in their train, the French to back down from their pledges to Poland. After Henderson departed a second time, Hitler slapped his thigh in self-congratulation at his performance. "Chamberlain won't survive this discussion," he said. "His cabinet will fall this evening."[116]

Chamberlain had done more for the Nazi leader than any other foreign politician, and the British PM appeared ready to do even more, in order to avoid war over Poland—but the game was up. In the extended diplomatic three-card monte, after all the dealing and double-dealing, Stalin, not Chamberlain, had turned up the "Hitler" card.

Even as Henderson was en route to the Berghof, Nikita Khrushchev arrived at the Near Dacha, having flown in from Kiev, where he was party boss. Few Moscow party officials, let alone "provincials," enjoyed such access to the despot's residence. Stalin let on that Ribbentrop was flying in to Moscow the next day, then looked at his protégé and smiled. Assuming that Stalin's twisted sense of humor was at work yet again, Khrushchev played along, asking if Ribbentrop was going to defect. Stalin replied that he had gotten a telegram from Hitler.[117]

WINDFALL

The British press phoned Ivan Maisky at home to ask if it was true that Nazi foreign minister Ribbentrop was flying to Moscow; the Soviet ambassador, out of the loop, went with his wife, Agniya, to see Oscar Wilde's *The Importance of Being Earnest*.[118] Göring's proposed secret mission to London was canceled.[119] Ribbentrop, flying on Hitler's personal Condor, landed for a night stopover at Königsberg (August 22) and resumed his flight the next morning. His retinue was large, nearly forty persons, requiring two Focke-Wulf Condors. Genuine drama awaited on the German-Soviet frontier, at Velikie Luki. Markings on aircraft, unless they flew at very low altitudes, were generally not discernible. Stalin, ever hyperconspiratorial, had evidently not informed the Soviet border guard of his diplomatic conspiracy and, as a result, he almost destroyed his foreign policy coup. Soviet antiaircraft units fired on the Führer's personal Condor, swastika on the tail, with Ribbentrop aboard. They missed.[120]

The Nazi foreign minister reached Moscow with alacrity at around 1:00 p.m. on August 23, landing at Moscow's main civilian airfield (near the Dynamo Stadium), a site that had been used for the coronation of Nicholas II, when a stampede over souvenir mugs had resulted in more than 1,000 deaths.[121] There to greet Ribbentrop was deputy foreign affairs commissar Potyomkin, a name historically synonymous with false fronts and Russian deception. Escorted by Stalin's personal bodyguard, General Vlasik, Ribbentrop rode in one of Stalin's personal bulletproof ZIS limousines, outfitted with a Nazi flag. This was his first trip to Moscow and, in the words of German military attaché Köstring, the Nazi foreign minister was "nervous and agitated."[122] Their first destination was the freshly painted neoclassical former Austrian legation, now belonging to Nazi Germany, in the heart of old Moscow. After a short repast, Ribbentrop, accompanied by Schulenburg and Hilger, passed through the gates of the Kremlin, less than three hours after landing. They were greeted by the indispensable, physically unseemly Poskryobyshev, in colonel's uniform, who escorted them upstairs to Molotov's suite. In a surprise for the Germans, Stalin was present, too.[123]

Schulenburg, by now in Moscow almost five years, had never even spoken to Stalin.[124] Schulenburg had previously served in Tehran, and his Moscow residence on Clean (Chisty) Lane "presented a lavish display of marvelous Isfahan carpets covering the walls, old weapons, shields with intricate inlaid designs, sabers, and swords," a Soviet foreign affairs functionary observed, adding that "Persian miniatures hung all over the place, many of them erotic, which was quite shocking in those days."[125] In Molotov's office, Stalin's medium height, military-style tunic, and baggy khaki trousers contrasted vividly with the tall Ribbentrop, in his European-cut suit.[126] A few aides and interpreters were present (neither Stalin nor Molotov could understand German).[127] Shaposhnikov, the elderly Soviet chief of staff, was the only military figure whom Stalin had included in both the diversionary action (the final talks with Drax) and the main battlefield (Ribbentrop). (Shaposhnikov shook in Stalin's presence, not because he had difficulty composing himself but because he suffered from Parkinson's disease.)[128] Ribbentrop brought a document signed by Hitler that accorded him "full power" to sign a state treaty.[129] The Nazi foreign minister's great worry—besides contracting diarrhea from Soviet unsanitariness—was that he would be confronted by the fait accompli of an Anglo-French-Soviet military accord. Ribbentrop further worried that the wily Bolsheviks would drag out negotiations with him.

At the Berghof, having dismissed Henderson, Hitler nervously paced the terrace and sought omens over the majestic Salzburg mountains: the sky was said to go from turquoise to violet to fire red.[130] For weeks, Stalin had known that a German attack on Poland was imminent, from his intelligence sources, his Berlin chargé d'affaires, Astakhov, and even Schulenburg. Hitler's recklessness afforded the despot enormous leverage, and he used it. Ribbentrop had sent a formal proposal on spheres of influence on the eve of the French-British military's arrival in Moscow, but Stalin substituted his own text, which Hitler accepted.[131] The two parties agreed—in the event of an unspecified conflict in Poland—to a mutual demarcation line across the country, right through Warsaw. Germany declared its "disinterest" in Romania's Bessarabia. Stalin's sphere of influence also included Finland, Estonia, and Latvia; Hitler was to get Lithuania. But now Stalin wanted Lithuania's ice-free ports, Liepaja (Libau) and Ventspils (Windau). The talks adjourned so that Ribbentrop could rush to the embassy, where, at 8:05 p.m. Moscow time, he sent a telegram to Hitler, via the German foreign ministry, describing a Soviet request for Libau and Windau as "the decisive point for the final result." The response came back with Hitler's assent, and with such rapidity that it shocked his embassy staff.[132] The Nazi foreign minister had even been authorized, if necessary, to grant a Soviet interest in the Turkish Straits, but Stalin had not thought to make the request.[133]

By 10:00 p.m. Ribbentrop was back at the Kremlin with Hitler's latest concession, on Lithuania. In the one alteration to Stalin's draft that the Führer had been able to introduce, the Pact came into effect immediately upon signing, not ratification. The spheres of influence were written up in a secret protocol: territorially, the Germans got only what they would fight for.

The two sides discussed the Anti-Comintern Pact, which Ribbentrop avowed was not directed against the USSR. He volunteered to bring Berlin's good graces to bear for improved Soviet-Japanese relations. Stalin replied that there were limits to Soviet patience in the face of Tokyo's provocations; that the Soviets were ready to go to war if necessary; and that any German approach to Tokyo should not be made to seem a Soviet initiative. On Italy, Stalin inquired whether it might have aspirations beyond small, thinly populated Albania—perhaps for Greek territory. Ribbentrop answered that Albania was not insignificant, and that Mussolini was a strongman who could not be intimidated and welcomed improved German-Soviet relations.[134] During a break, as the final texts were written up in German and Russian, Stalin, Molotov, and Ribbentrop confirmed their solidarity by trashing the British.[135]

Stalin mentioned that the British foreign office official John Simon, in confidential talks with Germany, had discussed a division of Europe into spheres of influence and had placed Soviet territory into the Nazi sphere. Ribbentrop was taken aback: these conversations were known to only a very narrow circle in Berlin. It was evident that Stalin had spies high up in the German foreign ministry, a problem to be addressed once back home.[136] For now, shared Anglophobia, undergirded by a shared antiliberalism, like a shared *Griff nach der Weltmacht* (at British expense), made for a heady cocktail. To the husband of the heiress to the Henkell champagne fortune, Stalin had lifted a glass of Soviet champagne, stating, "I know how much the German people love their Führer, and that is why I have the pleasure of drinking to his health!"[137] Still, when a giddy Ribbentrop tried to insert an effusive section into the text about German-Soviet friendship, Stalin refused. "Do you not think we should take a little more account of public opinion in both our countries?" he asked Ribbentrop. "For many years now, we have been pouring buckets of shit over each other's head."

Signatures were affixed at around 2:00 a.m. on August 24, a mere thirteen hours after Ribbentrop had landed.[138] He phoned Hitler from Molotov's office with the news. "Convey my congratulations to Herr Stalin, the Führer of the

Soviet people," Hitler responded.[139] Stalin did not request the receiver, and Hitler did not ask to speak directly to him. Stalin toasted Hitler ("To the health of the Führer").[140] Molotov toasted Stalin. "The atmosphere, which had been pleasant, became warmly convivial," according to a German official present. "The ruler of Russia filled his guests' glasses himself, offered them cigarettes and even to light them."[141]

Photographers had been let in to record the moment for history. Hitler had sent his personal photographer so that the Führer could study Stalin's surroundings as well as his physiognomy, for Hitler was anxious to ascertain whether Stalin's earlobes were "ingrown and Jewish, or separate and Aryan"?[142]

Lenin had condemned treaties with secret protocols and spheres of influence as "agreements between robbers behind people's backs." Not a mention of the Pact negotiations, even obliquely, was recorded in politburo minutes.[143] The basic text was published in *Pravda* (August 24, 1939), with stunning photos of Stalin and Molotov alongside the Nazi foreign minister, but without the secret protocol, of course.[144] The Hitler-Stalin Pact lacked a clause of invalidation in the event that one of the signatories attacked a third country. Litvinov had been trumpeting the inclusion of such a provision in Soviet bilateral nonaggression pacts as evidence of moral superiority, thundering that its absence in capitalist nonaggression pacts "means that a state which has secured by such a pact of nonaggression its rear or flank obtains the facility of attacking with impunity third states."[145] On the German side, the fourteen members of the embassy in Moscow signed an oath never to reveal the secret protocol's contents. Hans "Johnnie" Herwarth, the second secretary of the German embassy, on August 24, 1939, divulged to American ambassador Charles Bohlen the full contents of the Secret Additional Protocol signed earlier that morning.[146] On the Soviet side, only Stalin, Molotov, and Shaposhnikov, as well as the twenty-four-year-old interpreter, Pavlov, knew. Molotov, when asked publicly, replied that the imperialists used secret protocols all the time—an evasion that was accurate but placed the Soviets in dubious company from their own point of view.[147]

Hitler had secured his eastern flank for his attack on Poland, preempted a possible broad anti-German coalition, and obtained insurance against the anticipated Western blockade. And then there was the sheer shock value. "That will hit like a bombshell," he remarked to those in the Berghof—for once, an understatement.[148]

Immediately after the signing, Molotov had repaired with Stalin back to the Little Corner between 2:15 and 3:35 a.m.[149] From there, in the wee hours of August

24, the two headed out to the Near Dacha. Voroshilov and the other cronies had returned there with their ducks from the military's exclusive Zavidovo Hunting Preserve, seventy miles outside Moscow. Stalin dropped word that he had signed the Pact with the Nazis, which would allow the Soviets to determine the fate of the Baltic states, Bessarabia, and Finland and to obtain a chunk of Poland, a strategic Soviet sphere of influence and a buffer to protect the socialist homeland. Unlike what had been proposed with the Western powers, moreover, the Pact imposed no obligations on the Soviet Union to fight a war; it was not a military alliance. The treaty also drove a wedge between Germany and Japan: not only had Hitler failed to complete the negotiations with Tokyo to convert the Anti-Comintern Pact into an anti-Soviet military alliance, but he had violated the Anti-Comintern Pact's provision that its signatories would conclude no political agreements with the Soviet Union without first consulting one another. Stalin (as Zhukov later recalled) "was sure that he had twisted Hitler around his finger."[150]

CRUSHING MILITARY DISPLAY

On the Mongolia-Manchukuo border, denouement approached. Grigory Stern, at district headquarters in Chita, Siberia, had drawn up a plan for an offensive involving a double envelopment, encircling the Japanese while pinning them frontally. Zhukov, who would execute the plan on Mongolia's desert steppes, in a salient forty-five miles wide and twelve miles deep, had prepared meticulously. Logistics were nightmarish in the USSR's expansive, underpopulated, physically challenging Asian territory, extending into Mongolia, remote from Soviet industrial centers, but 4,000 trucks had bridged the 400-mile gap from the nearest railhead to support what would be the Soviets' first massive battlefield application of tanks and aircraft. Japan's full-scale invasion of China had altered the strategic calculus to Soviet advantage, a fact that the Kwantung Army, which was not fighting in China, ignored. China absorbed far more of Japan's strength—28 of the 36 Japanese divisions on the Asian mainland—than Spain had of Nazi Germany's (which had supported an indigenous insurgency, not fought a war of conquest).[151] That was one reason the Tokyo high command had blocked the Kwantung Army's plan for a massive offensive, approving operations merely for evicting the Soviets from the Halha, a fact that became known to Soviet military intelligence: Hotsumi Ozaki, the leftist functionary in the Japanese cabinet who belonged to Sorge's spy ring, had learned that Japan's leaders, consumed with China, were adamant that the conflict with the Soviets not escalate. Whether this further emboldened Stalin cannot be established, but the despot, and the Red Army, were already thinking big.

Cloud cover interfered with aerial reconnaissance, hindering Japanese efforts to enumerate Soviet forces. The Kwantung Army resorted to observation balloons, the first of which a Soviet fighter plane shredded with a machine gun a few hours after it went aloft. Zhukov, in any case, had camouflaged his buildup of a huge strike force. He and his team installed artificial noise machines to induce the Japanese to react to ghosts, thereby inuring them to loud sounds and enabling the Soviets to move equipment (which sounded just like the artificial noise). Zhukov also had weapons and men transferred to frontline jumping-off points only at night. Knowing that the Japanese were tapping telephone lines and intercepting radio traffic, Zhukov had disinformation spread, in easily broken code, about the Soviets' purely defensive stance and their preparations for possible military operations in the autumn.[152] The Soviets had detailed intelligence on the location and movement of all Japanese troops in Manchukuo.[153] True, Zhukov, showing Stalin-like suspicion, deemed much of the intelligence forwarded to him speculative. So he organized his own ground combat reconnaissance, as well as fighter plane photography. Finally, learning that the Japanese allowed officers to take leaves on Sundays, Zhukov unleashed the full force of the First Army Group across the Halha on Sunday, August 20, at 5:45 a.m.[154] The Red Army achieved decisive operational surprise.[155]

Japanese intelligence continually, egregiously underestimated Soviet capabilities—because of not only Zhukov's disinformation but also their own prejudices and the reports, a year before, by the defector Lyushkov, whose revelations reinforced the Japanese's condescending racism. The biggest oversights concerned precisely what Lyushkov had downplayed: the scale and firepower of mechanized corps and long-range artillery. Indeed, although the Japanese had numerical superiority on the borderland—perhaps 75,000 troops to Zhukov's 57,000—the Soviets had a colossal advantage in armor: almost 600 tanks, more than 500 artillery pieces, 515 fighter planes.[156] Soviet-built heavy tanks came off assembly lines in numbers, and enjoyed clear superiority to the lighter Japanese models. More prosaically, the Soviets ingeniously used simple piano wires to trap Japanese tanks, immobilizing them long enough that they could be finished off—the kind of resourcefulness used when one does not underestimate one's foe. Mongolia's open grassland and low sandy hills, moreover, proved highly conducive to mechanized warfare (the opposite of the lesson the Soviets had learned in Spain's urbanized areas), and Zhukov managed the feat of coordinating combined tank, motorized infantry, artillery, and aircraft warfare. This sophistication of strategy, tactics, and generalship surprised the Japanese, too. No less extraordinary was Soviet transport of thousands of tons of ammunition, food, and fuel over the primitive roads—more than 1,300 truckloads daily from the Transbaikal military district.[157] The Japanese soldiers, without even water, would take to soaking up the night dew with their towels and chewing.[158]

Japan's cult of fighting "spirit," its piecemeal commitment of forces, pathetic ground support, inferior ordnance, and poor logistics, combined with its no-surrender doctrine, even in the face of superior firepower, to produce catastrophe.[159] Stalin had always gotten lucky in his nemeses—Trotsky-Zinoviev-Kamenev-Bukharin, and now the Kwantung Army. He also got lucky in Zhukov, whom the despot evidently had never even met, but who showed himself a self-assured corps commander whose operational mastery exposed Japan's unsophistication in mobile warfare. To be sure, failure for Zhukov at the Halha River could have meant death in NKVD cellars.[160] But then again, that was true for every Soviet commander. He proved to be willing to assume great responsibility and risk. He was decisive, unsentimental, even ruthless—like Stalin. On the third day of the heavily armored offensive, when the Japanese managed to dig in on a strategic hill, causing enormous Soviet casualties, Stern suggested to Zhukov that he halt for a few days to gather forces. Zhukov rudely rejected the idea.[161]

The very next day, August 24, 1939, as Ribbentrop departed Moscow, the Japanese attempted a desperate broad-daylight frontal assault with no prior scouting or artillery or aerial softening up. This was the beginning of a literal suicide wave. Japanese commanding officers would order their soldiers to take their own lives rather than be captured. Just a week in, on August 28, Zhukov telegrammed Voroshilov: "The Japanese-Manchurian troops that violated the border of the Mongolian People's Republic . . . have been completely surrounded and annihilated."[162]

The Japanese suffered 18,000 casualties (8,000 killed, 8,800 wounded, 1,200 sick), but the Red Army, in victory, lost even more—9,703 killed and 15,952 wounded, nearly 40 percent of its deployment.[163] Still, the entire Halha River had been cleared of Japanese by industrialized brute face, applied with no regard to costs. The thirty-nine-year-old Stern, as the senior-ranking commander and a Central Committee member, headed the list of newly named "Heroes of the Soviet

Union." The forty-three-year-old Zhukov, in his hero citation, was recognized as "a brilliant organizer, a person of unbending willpower and boundless courage."[164] The text could have added a burning desire to clear his name from the scurrilous denunciations during the terror, and win Stalin's favor.[165]

SHOCK WAVES

Zhukov's thrashing of the ineptly led Kwantung Army delivered a trove of captured Japanese operational documents and codes, and a blow to its reputation.[166] "We were quite shocked by the results," the influential *Asahi Shimbun* would concede.[167] The Japanese, as Stalin heard from his ambassador, as well as from the military intelligence spy Sorge, were also shell-shocked by Hitler's Pact with their enemy.[168] The disgraced government in Tokyo fell. The outgoing prime minister, who had misinformed the emperor, called the German-Soviet deal "intricate and baffling."[169]

But the Soviet Pact also produced shock waves right at home. Some proletarians wept at news of the agreement.[170] Thanks in large measure to the civil war in Spain, antifascism (understood globally), not just anticapitalism, had become a pillar of the Communist idea, Soviet identity, and domestic and global loyalties. Veterans of the Spanish civil war wondered why they had fought and left so many fallen comrades behind if the USSR was only going to go on to sign a pact with Nazism. Ehrenburg, who was still in Paris as a correspondent for *Izvestiya*, claimed he had lost his appetite—for eight months.[171] Tukhachevsky and other top Soviet military men and intelligence agents had been shot for alleged links to the German military, while the vivid caricatures of Boris Yefimov had memorably depicted Trotsky as dancing arm in arm with Hitler. "Destroying the party and decapitating the army" as alleged agents of Hitler, Trotsky wrote, "Stalin is now openly advancing his candidacy for the role . . . of Hitler's main agent."[172]

Stalin did not stage a Central Committee plenum to rubber-stamp the Pact or have the press blare the usual mass affirmations at factories and collective farms. The Comintern absorbed yet another moral and psychological blow. "The publication of photographs of Bolsheviks smiling at Nazis and the announcement that Germany and the USSR had signed a pact stupefied us," wrote Jesús Hernández, who had joined the Spanish Communist party in 1922, at age fifteen, and spent more than five years in prison for it.[173] A stunned Georgi Dimitrov had sent

Stalin, Zhdanov, and Molotov a summary of Western Communist reactions, cherry-picking anything supportive of Moscow's position, but pleaded for an audience with Stalin to help him with the "exceptional difficulties" in instructing Communist parties globally.[174] Stalin would receive him in the Little Corner on September 7, in the company of Molotov and Zhdanov. "A war is on between two groups of capitalist countries—(poor and rich as regards colonies, raw materials, and so forth)—for the redivision of the world, for the domination of the world!" the despot gloated. "We see nothing wrong in their having a good fight and weakening each other. It would be fine if at the hands of Germany the position of the richest capitalist countries (especially England) were shaken."[175]

Stalin further stated in the Little Corner that "the division of capitalist states into fascist and democratic no longer makes sense." Such a division had never held much meaning for him even when, in 1935, he had allowed the Comintern to announce a popular front against fascism, which, in the form of Nazi Germany, had become objectively progressive: "Hitler, without understanding it or desiring it, is shaking and undermining the capitalist system."[176]

Soviet propaganda turned on a dime. Nearly half of all expressly antifascist Soviet films (a mere thirteen in total since 1928) had appeared between late 1938 and early 1939, and all of those depicted Germany as the aggressive country— none better than *Alexander Nevsky,* Eisenstein's first completed film in more than a decade.[177] With a score by Prokofyev and USSR People's Artist Nikolai Cherkasov in the main role, the patriotic epic portrayed the Teutonic Knights' thirteenth-century invasion of Great Novgorod, their capture of Pskov (owing to a traitor), and their eventual defeat by Prince Alexander, who rallies the common people in a decisive "Battle on the Ice," set to stirring music. *Nevsky* had premiered on December 1, 1938, and in April 1939 the head of the state cinematography committee reported that 23 million people had seen it.[178] "It came out not bad, it seems," Stalin had written on the screenplay, but after the Pact was signed, he had the film pulled.[179]

Many Communists and foreign fellow travelers who had explained away the monstrous terror, often in the name of antifascism, now broke with the cause. "Everybody else in the world, the Social Democrats, the liberals, the conservatives, had their opinions, but we, the Marxist-Leninists, we had a scientific world outlook," recalled Wolfgang Leonhard, a German Communist studying in Moscow in the second half of the 1930s. "We knew the fundamental answer to the riddle of the past, present, and future, for all nations and for all countries."[180] But a deal with the Nazis crystallized Leonhard's gathering doubts: "The mighty workers' movement in Central Europe was in ruins; Hitler's tanks dominated Europe; Lenin's comrades-in-arms during the Russian Revolution had all been shot as spies; the Spanish Republic had been abandoned by the European democracies, its revolutionary movement stabbed in the back by Soviet agents; and finally Stalin had concluded a pact with Hitler."[181] Even many who wanted to remain loyal struggled to do so. "It was actually shameful, and we weren't able to overcome this feeling of shame for a long time," said the German Communist Ruth von Mayenburg, who traveled in secret from Moscow to Nazi Germany on life-risking missions. "One had to mobilize one's Marxist concept of imperialism, of international struggles, of everything, in order to deceive oneself about this matter of conscience."[182]

Here, again, we see the core of Communism's extraordinary power: its rootedness in beliefs and personal biographies, which, however, also made for its extreme vulnerability. To be sure, for those loyalists less preoccupied with Communist dogma, the Pact spurred elaborate great-power fantasies. "Perhaps we have preserved the last word," Vishnevsky, the playwright who headed the military commission of the writers' union, wrote in his diary after reading the announcement of the Pact in the newspaper. "In the event of war, we'll enter last. And—it is utterly possible—we shall strike that very Germany." Three days later, he wrote, "1) We win time; we shall observe the military prowess of countries in reality; 2) we'll acquire experience, of much greater value than in Spain and China." He went on to suggest the possibility of using the Pact to smash Japan for good and obtain advantageous proposals from France and Britain, and he concluded that "Germany could not be trusted: it has violated many agreements." He foresaw an expansion of Soviet interests in the Carpathians and Balkans and on the Black Sea, in Poland, Czechoslovakia, and Romania. "It is difficult to guess how the game will turn out," he wrote in his diary. "But one thing is clear: the world will be reshaped. . . . This is a new chapter in the history of the party and the country. The USSR has begun an activist global policy."[183]

Beria did his part, imposing a ban on the taunting of Gulag prisoners as "fascists."[184] Molotov, at the USSR Supreme Soviet on August 31, denounced the "short-sighted people in our country" who were "carried away by simplistic antifascist propaganda." Still, publicly, if obliquely, he acknowledged the confusion and consternation. "People ask, with an air of innocence, how could the Soviet Union consent to improve political relations with a state of the fascist type?" he allowed. Nonetheless, he could not help gloating. "If these gentlemen have such an irresistible desire to go to war," Molotov said of the British and the French, "well, then, let them go to war by themselves, without the Soviet Union. (Laughter and cheers.)" He added, "We have never had any equally advantageous economic agreement with Great Britain, France, or any other country."[185] The Supreme Soviet "ratified" the Pact unanimously. German ambassador Schulenburg was right, however, when he reported to Berlin (September 6) that "the distrust expressed toward Germany over many years cannot be eradicated that quickly, despite the effective counter-propaganda [of late] conducted at party and factory meetings."[186]

Among staunch Nazis, the shock and disgust were no less severe than at the Comintern. "A moral loss of respect in the light of our now twenty-year struggle," despaired Alfred Rosenberg, one of Hitler's principal tutors in anti-Bolshevism and anti-Semitism, who blamed Ribbentrop for the betrayal. Hitler assured his photographer, Hoffmann—who relayed word of dismay among the Nazi faithful—that "my party members know and trust me," but the front garden at the Brown House, the national headquarters of the Nazi party in Munich, was littered with badges and insignia thrown away by the disillusioned.[187] By contrast, Ernst Köstring, the German military attaché in Moscow, paid a call on the external relations department of the general staff to congratulate the Red Army on the Pact. He had not been part of the Kremlin negotiations, but now he asserted that he had proposed a Soviet-German Pact already five years earlier, and that Ribbentrop—who was getting all the credit—had doubted the possibility of success right up "until he met personally with the great figure of comrade Stalin."[188]

STRATEGIC CHOICES

In the West, the Pact exploded with concussive force. "All the isms," a British foreign office spokesman soon quipped, "are now wasms." Chamberlain indignantly wrote to his sister Hilda (August 27) of "Russian treachery."[189] Admiral Drax, too, would attribute the failure of his negotiations to Soviet bad faith, accusing Moscow of seeking talks with Britain and France merely to scare up a better deal with Hitler, a rich accusation from the British side. Still, Drax was partly correct: Stalin had effectively organized an auction for a sphere of influence in Eastern Europe. In the event, the British made no offer. Whatever Stalin's preferences, Hitler presented not just the better deal, but the only deal. Daladier, known as the Bull of Vaucluse, had instructed General Doumenc to "bring us back an accord—at any price," but whether a bold French initiative to break with democratic Britain could have produced a binding bilateral military alliance with the undemocratic Soviet Union remains unclear.[190] The French, in any case, remained joined at the hip to the British, and the latter were immovable.[191]

Chamberlain wanted to prevent further Nazi aggression, but, through thick and thin, he had held fast to his policy of conciliation with Hitler. It is not difficult to condemn the vain, overly self-confident, obdurate British PM.[192] But Chamberlain's goals of avoiding war and safeguarding the empire were widely shared.[193] And although Stalin *had* offered a deal, the despot did not exactly inspire trust. Indeed, unlike many of his critics (then and subsequently), Chamberlain understood that the Soviet Union was a terrifying menace, writing to his sister and sounding board, "I distrust [the Soviet Union's] motives which seem to me to have little connection with our ideas of liberty."[194] The PM's worst nightmare was well founded: that if Britain invited the Soviets to help beat back Hitler, Stalin would take advantage, and Communism would end up occupying the heart of Europe.[195]

Of course, had Chamberlain confronted Hitler before the latter's seizure of Austria or of Czechoslovakia, when the Wehrmacht was weak, the PM would have had far less need to rely on the Red Army (as opposed to merely threatening Germany with a British-Soviet united opposition), but before those armed actions, few people understood who Hitler really was. Chamberlain contributed to but did not create what was a genuine dilemma: whether to work with Hitler's professed desire not to dominate all Europe or to facilitate Stalin's suspected desire, if invited, to encroach into Central Europe.

As a traditional conservative, Chamberlain was disgusted by Nazism, and he privately described Hitler as "the blackest devil he had ever met."[196] But because the PM was unwilling to ally with Stalin, the result was not just the Munich debacle, which had severely narrowed his options, but the two-faced guarantee to Poland, the wishful thinking that Hitler might calm down once all the Germans lived under one roof or be removed by Germans worried about the socioeconomic costs of his adventurism, or, barring all that, that Germany might even serve as a bulwark against the dangerous Communists.[197] Such views seem delusional, but Chamberlain was hardly alone in holding them. George Kennan, the American foreign service officer in Moscow, made precisely the same argument regarding Hitler—he merely wanted to unite all Germans—and precisely the same contrast with the supposedly graver threat of Communism.[198] Kennan, too, was wrong, however. Hitler was at least as great a threat as Stalin. Up until 1939, Stalin had been by far the more murderous, and Communism had a clearly stated global ambition as well as party members and fellow travelers in all the main countries, but Stalin was more susceptible to deterrence than Hitler.

Despite Stalin's domestic house of horrors, as well as the Comintern's unscrupulous, albeit often pitiful, machinations abroad, the main armed, expansionist power seeking domination of Europe was Nazi Germany (and in Asia, Japan). Hitler's Versailles revisionism was limitless; Stalin's was limited to opportunities others might present. Chamberlain's final, related error, also self-serving, was his belief that the decapitated Red Army could not really fight anyway.[199] Of course, the Red Army *was* fighting, showing its mettle against Japan all throughout the 1939 Soviet negotiations with Britain and France.

Figuring out a way to both engage and contain Stalin would not have been simple, but it was the strategic choice among two odious options, if only because Hitler's rabid revisionism would be vastly empowered should the Nazi leader reach his own understanding with a spurned Stalin. Here, too, Chamberlain and much of the British establishment had been smug.[200] The defector Krivitsky, a top intelligence operative for the Soviets in Europe, had in 1938 warned MI5 of Stalin's strenuous efforts at a Soviet-German rapprochement. Additionally, General Karl Bodenschatz, for a time the military adjutant to Göring and his liaison to Hitler, relayed the fact of secret Nazi-Soviet talks to London. Foreign Secretary Halifax—no friend of Communism—had warned Chamberlain and the cabinet as early as May 3, 1939, that Stalin and Hitler could cut a deal. But at a cabinet meeting on July 19, according to the minutes, "the Prime Minister said that he could not bring himself to believe that a real alliance between Russia and Germany was possible."[201] Even at this point, there was time for the British government. Hitler did not begin his definitive move to Stalin until late July/early August, when the war to annihilate Poland—the traditional hinge of German-Russian relations—was just weeks away.[202]

MORE SURPRISES

Hitler's decision making appears linear only in retrospect. He was a gambler, but also a vacillator. He seems to have assumed that the Pact with Stalin would force the British and the French to back down over Poland, an assertion that Ribbentrop parroted, as did almost all the ingratiating German reports out of London and Paris. When Dirksen, the German ambassador to London, changed his tune, his communications stopped reaching Hitler.[203] It is not clear whether anyone brought the Führer information that contradicted what he wanted to hear.[204] "The people in the streets," William Shirer, in Berlin, recorded in his diary on August 24, 1939, "are still confident Hitler will pull it off again without war."[205] But after the Pact was made public, the British and French governments publicly reaffirmed their commitments to Poland, hoping, for their part, that these renewed pledges would force Hitler to back down, averting war.[206] In fact, Hitler did now hesitate.

Hitler—still hopeful of averting a pan-European war by scaring or enticing Britain into backing down from defense of Poland—had heeded the advice of Ribbentrop and once more had British ambassador Henderson summoned to the Chancellery. During a meeting on August 25, that commenced at 1:00 p.m. and lasted about an hour, Hitler denounced Chamberlain's recent restatement in Parliament of the guarantee for Poland, but he also divulged that he was still prepared to make "a large comprehensive offer" to guarantee the continued existence of the British empire with German troops *after* he had "solved" the urgent Polish problem. Hitler called this "his last offer." He suggested that Henderson fly immediately to London, putting a plane at his disposal. The Führer had always trained something of a jealous eye on Britain's empire and power, and remained open to some sort of bargain, but only on the basis of full British acquiescence to his domination of the continent.[207] Henderson insisted that any bilateral deal would require that German differences with Poland be settled through negotiations, a concession Hitler refused. "The chancellor," Henderson would report, "spoke with calm and apparent sincerity."[208]

Henderson would fly off to London on the Hitler-supplied plane, carrying his "last offer," but only on the next day (August 26).[209] Already at 3:02 p.m. on August 25, mere minutes after the ambassador's exit from the Chancellery, Hitler issued the final order to proceed with military action against Poland before dawn the next morning.[210] But then, only four and a half hours later, Hitler called the invasion off. Frantic desist orders went out to chief of staff Halder, who was already in his command bunker south of Berlin.[211] German soldiers on the front lines, when told to stand down, remarked that "Hitler got cold feet."[212]

It was the duce—the sole leader who had once stood up to Hitler.

Mussolini, essentially consulting no one in his own government, had signed the Pact of Steel with Germany, so Italy was on the hook for war. Now he pledged support for a war over Poland but wrote that Italy did not command the resources for a war against France and Britain. He also noted that he had been kept in the dark about the deal with Stalin. Hitler had been sure of a favorable reply from Rome. When the Italian ambassador arrived at the Reich Chancellery bearing Mussolini's letter, only an hour or so had elapsed since the Führer had given the order for war.[213] Italy's demurral was inconsequential for the German plan of battle, but it did remove a cudgel to induce France and Britain to back down and, no less consequentially, could damage Hitler's prestige. "The Führer ponders and contemplates," Goebbels recorded in his diary. "That's a serious blow for him."[214] Mussolini's was not the only unpleasant news. The French ambassador, Coulondre, had also been summoned to the Chancellery, and he had stated to Hitler that German reports of Polish atrocities against ethnic Germans were exaggerated and that France would honor its commitments to Poland. Additionally, Ribbentrop had reported word out of London of a new mutual assistance treaty, just signed between Britain and Poland.[215]

When Göring, in the Chancellery that day, asked whether the war had been canceled or just postponed, Hitler vowed to continue to break off the Western powers from Poland, in order to fight only a local war.[216] General Walther von Brauchitsch, Wehrmacht commander in chief, judged that Hitler genuinely did not know what to do.[217] Could the Führer really back down in front of his military inner circle, the German people, and the world? Would he risk a world war over Polish territories that he likely could obtain via negotiations? Chamberlain continued to relay offers of Polish territory to Germany that the Poles had explicitly rejected. Ribbentrop rightly surmised that the British PM was looking for a way out of his commitment.[218] Even if Hitler insisted on fighting a war, would it not have made the most strategic sense to accept British offers regarding Danzig and the Polish Corridor, which would have elicited the Polish government's rejection and thereby given Britain and presumably France a firm pretext to renounce their "guarantees" for Poland's independence and stand aside?

Germany, not Poland, had ended up nearly isolated. On August 26, 1939, Mussolini conveyed another message to Berlin: he would intervene "immediately"—if Germany supplied Italy with 7 million tons of gasoline, 6 million tons of coal, and 2 million tons of steel, among other greedy, impossible desiderata.[219] Hitler could expect nothing from his other formal Anti-Comintern ally, Japan, which remained mired in the war with China and now had allowed itself to become enmeshed in a losing border clash with the USSR, too. With neither Italy nor Japan willing or able to lend support and solidarity, suddenly only Stalin and the "Judeo-Bolsheviks" were on the Führer's side. Grand strategy, stranger than fiction.

At the Pact's signing, Stalin had mischievously proposed a toast to "the new Anti-Cominternist—Stalin" (then apparently winked at Molotov). But upon parting, in utmost earnestness, the despot had told Ribbentrop, "The Soviet Government takes the new Pact very seriously. It can give its word of honor that the Soviet Union will never betray its partner."[220] *Here* was the real "pact of steel."

Hitler reinstated his battle orders. His thought processes remain opaque. "In my life," Hitler told Göring on August 29, "I've always gone for broke."[221] That same day, a resolute Poland wanted to move its troops into their forward positions and declare a general mobilization. Belgium and the Netherlands, which lay in the Nazi path toward France, had already announced general mobilizations on August 23 and 28, respectively, and no one had requested they reconsider, but the British and the French urged Warsaw to withhold an announcement in order to allow for a possible last-ditch Nazi climbdown, with "negotiations" to follow if conducted without menace. But Goebbels recorded in his diary that "the Führer views England as still taking an uncompromising stance. We must not blink."[222] On August 31, Hitler ordered a doubling of production of a new long-range "wonder bomber" (the Ju 88) for use against Britain and its empire.

That same evening, a preplanned Nazi provocation created a casus belli against Poland: SS troops dressed in Polish uniforms attacked a German border post and a German radio station, killing seven people (six prisoners brought from Sachsenhausen concentration camp and one pro-Polish German supplied by the Gestapo) and broadcasting briefly in Polish.[223] On September 1, after an air bombardment before dawn, 62 Wehrmacht divisions—nearly 1.5 million men—ripped into Poland, in Hitler's biggest yet roll of what Bismarck had called the "iron dice."

THE DISTRUST

The Führer arrived at the Kroll Opera House at 10:00 a.m. on September 1 to address the Reichstag (which had only been summoned at 3:00 a.m.). He was treated to standing ovations. British and French diplomatic notes delivered that day in Berlin threatened war—if the German government failed to "agree" to withdraw its forces from Poland and "express readiness" to negotiate. When queried whether their notes of September 1 constituted an ultimatum, the British and the French explicitly stated no.[224] Mussolini, partly to save face, had intervened yet again to float the idea of an international conference, which Chamberlain had already suggested to Hitler (London was communicating with Rome).[225] While the French were seeking time to evacuate Paris and the frontier zones and to puzzle out their prospective moves, the two Western powers were also trying to coordinate their military mobilizations, and a certain chaos ensued in Britain's Parliament. Finally, on September 3, after Hitler had continued to obfuscate on the peace feelers while pressing his military invasion, and the House of Commons exploded in revolt at Chamberlain and Halifax, first Britain and then France (Daladier) declared war on Germany. Hitler was said to be "stunned."[226] In fact, he was aware that the British and the French would have to declare war. But he could not back down at this point.[227] For Germany and its racial destiny, in any case, he had concluded that a war to vanquish the West was inevitable at some point.[228]

Incredibly, the Polish regime had failed to prepare a full-fledged war plan in the event of a German attack, even after the Nazi seizure of Czechoslovakia had made the path to Warsaw that much easier. Poland's contingency planning was focused on a war against the Soviet Union. Most of Poland's military supply bases remained in its western regions, considered the rear.[229] Now, rather than establish a line of defense in depth on the Vistula that could be held, Poland massed its forces forward, in the Poznań salient, troops that were encircled and annihilated. Already on September 3, Wehrmacht units in the north had crossed the entire Corridor and linked up with German East Prussia. On the same day, Ribbentrop cabled Schulenburg in Moscow to gently urge the Soviet Union to occupy its sphere of Poland "at the proper time," as agreed in the Pact, adding that "this would be a relief to us."[230] Of course, his goal was not to gain assistance for the Wehrmacht in its war effort, but to fatally poison relations between the USSR and the Western powers. (Heydrich enthused to his subordinates, "Then Britain would be obliged to declare war on Russia, too.") Molotov was noncommittal. Poland had an army of around 39 divisions and 16 cavalry brigades, plus reserves, while Hitler had mobilized 54 divisions (out of about 80 total at the time). Stalin was waiting to see how well the German offensive went. In the event, the Luftwaffe would end up losing almost as many planes as the small Polish air force; the Luftwaffe would also expend its entire stock of bombs, while fully one quarter of Germany's tank park would be knocked out of commission or outright destroyed.[231]

Stalin, no less than the Polish government, was also waiting to see what concrete military actions Britain and France would undertake. As it happened, those actions proved to be minimal (indicating, perhaps, what the USSR, too, would have received from the Western powers in an alliance against Germany). The British instituted a blockade of Germany but shrank from bombing even Germany's airfields, despite an explicit commitment to Poland to do so. The air attack plans had been quietly abandoned for fear of provoking Luftwaffe retaliation on Britain—but the Poles had not been informed. Similarly, the French government had agreed, in the protocol signed with Poland back on May 19, 1939, to commence military action against Germany within fifteen days of the start of a war, but then, in consultation with Britain, France subsequently decided it would not do so—also without informing Poland. France's 110 divisions did not storm into Germany, which was protected by fewer than 30 divisions, perhaps 12 of them combat ready. The entire sum of French action consisted of a small attack on the Saarland, even though, privately, Wehrmacht chief of staff Halder admitted that he could not have prevented the French from occupying the Ruhr, Germany's industrial heartland, had they moved expeditiously.[232] As France instead hunkered down against an anticipated German attack, the Poles were left to fight alone.[233] The Polish government, in a demoralizing move, abandoned Warsaw beginning on September 5, in a chaotic evacuation southeast, by steps, toward the frontier with Romania—planning, if necessary, to try to travel on to the West and return on the backs of Western military might.

Stalin did not know for sure that the French and the British had effectively written Poland off militarily even before the war had been launched. He was also hypercautious not to walk into a Nazi trap. On September 3, the same day Ribbentrop had tasked Schulenburg, in Moscow, with ascertaining Soviet plans for Poland, Stalin's latest ambassador to Berlin, Alexei Shkvartsev, the former head of the textile institute, was ceremoniously received at the Chancellery. When the envoy presented his credentials to Hitler, in the presence of Göring and Ribbentrop, the Führer remarked, "The German nation is fortunate to have signed the Soviet-German Non-Aggression Pact. This Pact will serve the cause of the commonwealth of these two nations in both the political and economic arenas." Hitler vowed to uphold all the obligations he had undertaken, but he declined to provide any information on the course of his campaign in Poland.[234] Would the Wehrmacht actually halt at the line agreed upon in the just-signed Pact? Would they even stop at the Polish border?[235]

The fact remained that both the Japanese and the German armies—two of the world's biggest, and both bordering on the Soviet Union—were on the move at the same time.

Ribbentrop's requests for the USSR to invade Poland became "urgent," but Stalin needed to be sure of the battlefield and of German intentions, not to mention the need to publicly justify Soviet participation in a new partition.[236] On

September 5, the USSR rejected a request from Poland for military supplies and transit of war matériel, citing a desire not to be dragged into war. Two days later, directives for the initial Red Army mobilization in the Belorussian and Ukrainian military districts, bordering Poland, were issued.[237] On the afternoon of September 9, Stalin had Molotov vaguely inform Schulenburg that the Red Army would be moving into Poland in a matter of days. The next day, a vast Soviet mobilization began. It produced a panicked run on shops, which was not altogether unintended: it let the Germans know the Soviets were moving to a war footing. Also on September 10, Molotov told Schulenburg that the rapidity of the German advance had surprised the Soviets, but that the Red Army had more than 3 million soldiers ready. Molotov's initial draft of a Soviet declaration of a Red Army move into Poland, which he shared with Schulenburg, referred to the supposed disintegration of the Polish state and the resulting urgent need to aid Ukrainian and Belorussian brothers "threatened" by the German advance. Perhaps it was an unintentional slip. Schulenburg reported this calmly (the final joint communiqué would remove the offending implication), but he informed Berlin that the Soviets were in a quandary over the imminent German victory.[238]

On September 11, Voroshilov and Shaposhnikov wrote an order for an invasion to commence on the 14th. But this directive did not go into effect.[239]

That Stalin somehow trusted Hitler was laughable, as Hitler himself noted.[240] Stalin trusted no one (other than perhaps Abram Isayevich Legner, his Jewish tailor and one of the very few people he deferentially addressed by first name and patronymic).[241] The despot had tasked one of his aides, Boris Dvinsky, with assembling a reading packet. Stalin did not travel among adoring masses in an open-top car, as Hitler did, or issue impulsive decisions. When not receiving personnel for sessions in the Little Corner, he sat there alone and read. Like Hitler, he commented or doodled on whatever he was reading. One of his most frequent marginal scribblings was "teacher."[242] With Hitler, however, he had been reduced to pupil, and he had better get the lesson right. Perusing the Dvinsky-assembled dossier on Nazism that summer of 1939, Stalin examined the Russian translation of a book by the Englishwoman Dorothy Woodman, *Hitler Rearms: An Exposure of Germany's War Plans* (London, 1934), which contained a blistering chapter on the sweeping scale of Nazism's "ideological preparation for war." She wrote of Hitler's bathing an entire country in national hysteria and psychological exultation: molding the general will, transcending the individual. The power of those techniques had to be familiar.

Stalin also consulted an internal Russian translation of *Mein Kampf.*[243] The

Soviet population could not read Hitler's book, which by now had sold more than 10 million copies internationally. (The Japanese public could read it, but the translator had censored many passages so that Japanese readers would not know that in Hitler's racial hierarchy, the East Asians were subhumans, too.)[244] Stalin directed his inner circle to read Hitler's text as well.[245] Whether they made it through remains unknown, but some at least grasped the existential threat Nazism posed beyond traditional German imperialism. "I forget how many pages I read, but I was unable, morally, to get through the whole thing," Khrushchev would later recall. "I could not read it because it literally wrenched my gut; I could not look calmly at such delirium; it disgusted me, I did not have the patience, and I put it down without having finished it."[246] Members of the general staff and the foreign affairs commissariat evidently could not manage to finish the text, either, and some did not take Hitler's ravings at face value.[247]

Stalin took one of his thick colored pencils and underlined frothy passages in Hitler's tract about the Nazi *Drang nach Osten* ("drive toward the east"). For example: "And when we speak of new lands in Europe, we can think only of Russia and her borderlands. . . . The future goal of our foreign policy must be . . . acquiring the territory we need for our German nation." Stalin further underlined passages in the Russian translation (1935) of Konrad Heiden's exposé *A History of National Socialism* (Zurich, 1934). To wit: "Hitler, unable to control himself, simply does not know what he promises; his promises cannot be considered the promises of a solid partner. He breaks his promises as soon as it is in his interest to do so, and all the while continues to view himself as an honest person."[248] Heiden's singular point was that Hitler's opponents, as well as his (temporary) allies, dangerously underestimated him. Dvinsky also delivered to Stalin Soviet military intelligence estimates of Nazi German strength: a land army of 3.7 million men, almost half mechanized, 400,000 air force personnel, 60,000 naval personnel, more than 3,000 tanks, 26,000 guns and mortars, 4,000 planes, and 107 warships.[249]

The Wehrmacht, taking advantage of the Polish army's lack of mobility and weak communications and control, reached Warsaw's outskirts in just the second week of fighting. "The operation was carried out like a theatrical performance," recalled Khrushchev. "The Germans had set up movie cameras ahead of time. The battles were filmed from both land and sea, and they sought to distribute this film as widely as possible in all countries of the world." Hitler "proposed that Stalin take this film and have it shown through our network of motion picture theaters, to show our audiences how the Germans dealt with Danzig, with Poland, with all of Europe." Stalin agreed to do so, provided Hitler promised to show an equivalent Soviet film to a mass audience in Germany; Hitler refused. "Nevertheless," Khrushchev concluded, "this film was sent to us by the Germans, and we took a look at it together with Stalin. It really did have a depressing effect."[250] Although *Pravda* (September 11, 1939) contrasted Germany's organizational and technological prowess with the "laughable mouse-like fuss" of Britain and France, scenes of Germany's military romp in Poland were kept out of Soviet newsreels. Stalin got his own firsthand taste. On September 15, an unidentified airplane crossed into Soviet territory above Olevsk, in Ukraine. It was fired upon by Soviet forces and forced to land; it turned out, *Izvestiya* reported, to be a German bomber.[251]

WHO WANTS WAR?

Also on September 15, after intense internal bickering and foot-dragging in Tokyo, the Japanese acceded to a cease-fire in the border war. Signed by the ambassador with Molotov, it took effect at 2:00 a.m. on September 16 and was to be followed by a boundary demarcation commission.[252] Japan's military defeat at Nomonhan village had compounded its severe loss of face over its German ally's nonaggression pact with the USSR.[253] On September 17 at 2:00 a.m., exactly twenty-four hours after the truce had taken effect, Stalin gave German embassy personnel four hours' notice of a Red Army advance into Poland. "In order to avoid incidents, Stalin urgently requested that we see to it that German planes as of today do not fly east of the Białystok-Brest-Litovsk-Lemberg [Lvov] Line," Schulenburg reported to Berlin. "Soviet planes would begin today to bomb the district east of Lemberg. I promised to do my best with regard to informing the German Air Force but asked in view of the little time left that Soviet planes not approach the abovementioned line too closely today." Stalin declined, but he did allow Schulenburg to edit the text of the Soviet statement on Poland for German sensitivities.[254]

There was no Soviet declaration of war. Potyomkin summoned Polish ambassador Grzybowski at 3:15 a.m. and read aloud a note, in the name of Molotov, unilaterally abrogating the Soviet-Polish nonaggression pact; the envoy refused to take the document.[255] Poland's high command had predicted back in June that the Red Army would attack Poland "only in the final period of a war, when disadvantageous developments had turned against us and the Russian government would have concluded that the Poles had lost the campaign."[256] On the radio, Molotov announced a Soviet military action supposedly necessitated by the disappearance of the Polish state and the possible ensuing chaos. "The Soviet government regards as its sacred duty to proffer help to its Ukrainian and Belorussian brothers in Poland," he stated.[257] In fact, the Polish government continued to function, having relocated to Kuty, in the southeast, on the Polish side of the border with Romania. Although Poland's high command had effectively lost contact with its armies, the latter retained about 50 percent of their troop strength, and were still fighting the Wehrmacht in central and southeastern Poland.[258]

Such was the extreme narrowness of the Soviet regime that Nikolai Kuznetsov, the naval commissar, had not been informed beforehand of the Soviet invasion of Poland. He went to Molotov to complain, averring that if he was not trusted, he should not occupy such a high post. "In response, [Molotov] recommended that I read the TASS summaries of foreign news, which he ordered be sent to me from that day," Kuznetsov recalled. "But is that really the way—the naval commissar should learn about major military and (especially important) political events which affect him, from foreign sources?!"[259]

German generals, meanwhile, had crossed the secretly agreed-upon German-Soviet demarcation line (which ran along the Pissa, Narew, Vistula, and San rivers). Schulenburg had warned Molotov, back on September 4, that the Wehrmacht, in hot pursuit of Polish forces, might have to cross over *temporarily* into the Soviet section of Poland. The next day, Molotov had replied in a conciliatory manner, "We understand that as the operations proceed, one of the parties or both parties might be forced temporarily to cross the line of demarcation between the spheres of interest of the two parties; but such cases must not prevent the strict execution of the plan adopted."[260] Whether German generals knew about the Pact's secret protocol on the precise territorial division remained uncertain, however. Stalin had no guarantee the trespass would be temporary, or that the entire Pact had not been a ruse. When had these Nazis kept their word—over the Munich Pact? General Köstring, in the Little Corner with Schulenburg in the wee hours of September 17, had requested a delay in the Red Army offensive so that the Germans would have time to get out of the way. Stalin had declined. As some 600,000 Red Army troops poured into eastern Poland, they encountered few Polish troops, but some German units came under Soviet fire. Hitler himself was in Poland. He had set out on September 3 in his armored train, *Amerika,* trailed by weaponized railcars, and traveled through the front in Pomerania and Upper Silesia, on his way to Danzig, which he would reach on September 19.[261] He billeted, along with

Himmler, Ribbentrop, and a huge entourage, at the Kasino Hotel in Sopot (Zoppot, in German), a Baltic Sea resort adjacent to Danzig.

On September 18, Schulenburg reported that Stalin had told him "that on the Soviet side there were certain doubts as to whether the German high command at the appropriate time would stand by the Moscow agreement and would withdraw to the line that had been agreed upon." In response to assurances, he said that Stalin "replied that he had no doubt at all of the good faith of the German government. His concern was based on the well-known fact that all military men are loath to give up occupied territories."[262] Earlier that day in Berlin, with General Wilhelm Keitel and his chief of operations, Major General Alfred Jodl, away on the eastern campaign, Walter Warlimont, senior operations staff officer, had shown the deputy Soviet military attaché a map indicating that the Lwów/Lviv/Lvov region and its valuable Drohobycz oil fields, as well as a direct train line south from Polish Kołomyja down to Romania, fell within the German sphere. But on the map that Ribbentrop had signed with Molotov in Stalin's presence, these territories were on the Soviet side. Warlimont either had no knowledge of the secret protocol, was deliberately pretending not to know, or was just indicating the location of German forces at that moment. Molotov, on the evening of September 19, summoned Schulenburg and stated that "the Soviet government as well as Stalin personally are surprised at this obvious violation of the Moscow agreement." Schulenburg called it a misunderstanding.[263]

But on September 19–20, 1939, approaching Lwów/Lemberg/Lvov—not far from where the Germans had imposed the diktat of Brest-Litovsk on Soviet Russia in 1918—advancing Red Army troops were greeted by German artillery. Both the Red Army and the Wehrmacht took casualties.[264] Had the Germans mistaken the approaching Soviets for Poles, as some would claim? Or were the attacks deliberate? We shall never know. But the speed and depth of the Soviet military advance into eastern Poland had surprised the condescending German brass.[265]

Hitler, in "liberated" Danzig on September 19, had been soaking in the jubilation. "It was a state built on force and governed by truncheons of the police and the military," the Führer said of Poland, with no hint of irony.[266] The streets of the predominantly ethnic German city—like those of Vienna the year before—were festooned with swastikas, flowers, and admirers. Precisely when, and under what circumstances, the Führer learned of the armed clashes taking place near Lvov is unclear.[267] Ribbentrop instructed Köstring over the phone to attempt to have the accepted demarcation line modified so that Germany could keep this area,

Borisław-Drohobycz, and its oil fields. Köstring phoned the Soviet defense commissariat several times on September 20. "East of Lvov Soviet tanks clashed with German troops," he stated over the phone. "There is a disagreement about who should take Lvov. Our troops cannot withdraw until we have destroyed Polish forces." Köstring proposed, on orders from Berlin, that the Germans and the Soviets storm Lvov together, after which the Germans could hand the city over.[268] The Soviets refused. Schulenburg also conveyed Ribbentrop's request to retain the seized oil fields to Molotov, who rejected it—as well as Schulenburg's fallback position of a temporary German military occupation, pending a final political adjudication.[269]

Somebody would have to back down. On September 20, Köstring got an order directly from Hitler to help negotiate an immediate German withdrawal from Lvov, which was to be abandoned to the Soviets. Voroshilov received Köstring and asked what had caused the military clashes. The German attaché answered that it had been just a small local incident. He joked that Warlimont, who had shown the Soviets the map in Berlin, was an oilman and perhaps had been seduced by the oil fields. Köstring took out his own map, which showed, in black, the line of German advance and, in blue, the agreed-to territorial division, and he again vowed that the German army would withdraw.[270] But even while abandoning the advanced positions in eastern Poland, the Wehrmacht continued to fire on the Red Army.

On September 22, Hitler flew from Sopot to the outskirts of Warsaw to take in the devastation he had wrought.[271] As of that day, after its defenders capitulated, Lvov was in Soviet hands, and by the next day the Red Army had established full operational control over Polish territory up to the Narew, Vistula, and San rivers, a five-day romp facilitated partly by the fact that the Polish command had issued orders not to engage Soviet forces unnecessarily and instead to prepare for evacuation to Hungary or Romania.[272] On the afternoon of September 23, a ceremonial joint military parade was held in Brest-Litovsk to mark the German handover of the town that morning to the Soviets. Presiding over the event, on an improvised low platform, were the respective tank commanders Heinz Guderian, who had been born just 300 miles away in Chełmno (Kulm), and Semyon Krivoshein. The two shook hands. But the Luftwaffe flew aggressively low passes, and the two sides tussled over the city's war booty.[273] Guderian privately observed that relinquishing Brest was "disadvantageous."[274] Germany's commanders had suffered many casualties to seize these Galician territories—needing that oil—and they remained deeply unhappy about the pullback. (Stalin also managed to hold on to the

Volhynian grain fields.) Halder, the man who had planned the Polish campaign, confided in his diary, "A day of disgrace for the German political leadership!"[275]

Hitler, perhaps for the first time, had kept his word in an international agreement. But Stalin gained the impression—fatefully, it would turn out—that German "militarists" wanted war against the Soviets, and that *Hitler* was the restraining influence.

STALIN'S SUDETENLAND

Stalin had managed to undo the Soviet defeat in the 1920 Polish-Soviet War, reclaiming imperial Russian lands at the cost of just 700-odd lives. (Not that he cared about Soviet casualties.) The Germans in Poland, by contrast, had lost between 11,000 and 13,000 killed. At least 70,000 Poles were killed and nearly 700,000 taken prisoner by the aggressors on both sides.[276] Hitler, in improvisational fashion, toyed with leaving a rump independent Poland of some sort, but Poland's state effectively vanished again, partitioned between Germany and the Soviet Union, as well as Lithuania and Slovakia. Members of Poland's government fled into Romania, hoping to proceed to France and set up a government in exile to continue the fight, but they were placed under house arrest.[277] The Polish supreme commander's efforts to have surviving troops evacuated via Romania or Hungary to form a new Polish army in France were interdicted by the NKVD, which sealed the border along the Zbruch River. Many of the Polish army's now 190,000 troops, taken prisoner by the Soviets, were interned in Gulag camps, with the intention of exploiting them as slave laborers. Thousands of Polish officers were separated into special camps.[278]

Poland's immense Jewish population of nearly 3.5 million had experienced trying times under the Polish government. Between 1935 and 1937, 79 Polish Jews had been killed, and significant incidents of anti-Jewish violence had been recorded in 97 towns; quotas introduced in 1937 had halved the number of Jewish university students. Indeed, Jews could be discriminated against within the framework of Polish law, including by exclusion from chartered professional associations. In 1937 alone, 7,000 trials took place of Jews accused of "insulting the Polish nation." When the government suspended the validity of the passports of its citizens who had been living abroad for five years or more consecutively, in an attempt to preempt a mass flow of Jewish immigration from Nazi-annexed Austria (which had ceased to be a refuge), the act precipitated the expulsion of 17,000

Polish Jews from Nazi Germany in October 1938. The Polish regime refused to allow them back into Poland; many were trapped in a no-man's-land, without shelter or food. Several thousand who managed to cross the border at Zbąszyń ended up in a hastily formed restricted camp—with some begging to be let back into Nazi Germany. The head of the Catholic Church in Poland, Cardinal Augustyn Hlond, had accused the Jews of "spreading atheism and revolutionary Bolshevism . . . [and] contributing to the decline of Polish morals."[279] On December 21, 1938, the leader of the politically powerful National Unity Camp had reiterated the oft-stated view that Jews hindered the development of the Polish nation, and urged the government to take energetic action to reduce the number of Jews. Some Polish military leaders called a departure of Jews a matter of national security.[280] But all that turned out to be prelude: with the Nazi occupation, SS Einsatzgruppen (special action groups), as well as militarized regular police—both of which were under Heinrich Himmler—began scouring the land to murder Polish Jews and torch or dynamite synagogues.[281]

The SS also targeted non-Jewish Poles. Nazi terror against the "racial enemy" in these conquered lands far eclipsed what had descended on Germany itself since 1933, and further empowered the SS institutionally. The atrocities would continue long after the main combat was over.[282] More than a million Poles would be forced to work as slaves in Germany. Nazi propaganda portrayed the war as having been imposed on Germany, a necessity for the very survival of the German race—a mutilation of the truth that a majority of Germans appear to have accepted, leavened, as it was, with lurid fables of Polish atrocities and German victimhood.[283]

Soviet terror methods were different, spurring self-destruction of existing social bonds by soliciting anonymous denunciations by aggrieved individuals against their neighbors, a story to be more fully examined below. In the meantime, the occupiers found a cornucopia. "Long trains with Soviet functionaries and their families, mostly from Kiev and Kharkov, began pulling into the station," remarked one observer in what had been Poland's territory. "Streets filled with crowds of shabbily dressed and dirty people frantically eyeing already modest-looking store windows. They bought almost everything available to them, especially watches—the most sought-after commodity." Some Soviet functionaries returned to Kiev with foreign-made cars, provoking volunteerism for service in former Poland. But the Red Army arrived in these regions in torn uniforms and scrounged for food out of obvious hunger, rolling cigarettes with paper picked off the street. When the Poles ridiculed the soldiers for chasing after consumer items even though, according to Soviet propaganda, the USSR enjoyed abundance, the Red Army conscripts shot back that while the Poles had silk stockings and perfumes, the Soviets had tanks, guns, and fighter airplanes. "Frankly," admitted one Pole, "it was a shrewd point, which often cut the discussion off."[284]

Boris Yefimov, the Soviet cartoonist, drew a map of Europe with red arrows showing the Soviet territorial advance westward, with an irate, frightened Neville Chamberlain raising his striped trouser leg to stamp his foot impotently. But the Soviet regime had long trumpeted its policy of "peace," an ideological pillar, and on September 18, 1939, the day after troops had burst into Poland, *Izvestiya* had reiterated that the Soviet Union would maintain "a policy of neutrality" in the European war. Two days later, the British and the French, rather than declare war on the USSR for invading Poland, as they had on Germany, requested an "explanation" of Soviet actions. The Soviets remonstrated in public, as they had in private, that the Polish state had "ceased to exist" and that the "vacuum" threatened the USSR, justifying the dispatch of the Red Army. At the same time, the Soviets portrayed their military action as a class and national rescue operation. The Polish state had, in fact, mistreated not just its Jews but also its large Ukrainian and Belorussian minorities. Molotov privately admitted to the Germans that the Soviet regime had heretofore not bothered much about the Ukrainians and Belorussians living in Poland.[285] But now Soviet propaganda efficaciously cast the invasion and landgrab as Ukrainian-Belorussian "liberation."

Censorship precluded public mention of the fact that perhaps 40 percent of the population in the territories seized by the USSR was ethnic Polish, or that hundreds of thousands of ethnic Poles were being displaced, deported, or pressed into forced labor; that at least 30,000 ethnic Ukrainians sought refuge in the German-occupied zone; that some invading Red Army soldiers had deserted by heading to the German zone; and that even some Jews, who mostly tended to flee toward the Soviet zone, preferred a return to their homes under Nazi occupation to a life under Soviet rule.[286] What the Soviet populace might have made of such information will never be known. What we can say is that many ordinary Soviet inhabitants perceived justice in the fight against Polish "class and national oppression," as well as in a rearranged border that reunited "blood brother" Ukrainians and Belorussians, in repudiation of Piłsudski's "imperialist" Treaty of Riga (1920).[287] The Belorussian Soviet Socialist Republic doubled in size for the second time (the first had been 1924–26, when it was awarded territories carved from the Russian republic). Ukrainian irredentist dreams were fulfilled. "Everyone approves the seizure of (western) Ukraine and Belorussia," wrote the regime critic and geochemist

Vernadsky in his diary that fall of 1939. "The Stalin-Molotov policy is realistic and, it seems to me, correct, a Russian policy of state."[288]

Trotsky deemed Stalin's invasion progressive, despite the Soviet leader's own supposed counterrevolutionary inclinations. "In the regions which must become a component of the USSR, the Moscow government will take measures to expropriate the big property owners and to nationalize the means of production," he explained. "Such action is more likely not because the bureaucracy is true to the socialist program, but because it does not wish to and is unable to share power and the privileges connected with it with the old ruling classes of the occupied regions." Trotsky evoked Napoleon: "The first Bonaparte brought the revolution to a halt with the aid of a military dictatorship. But when French forces invaded Poland, Napoleon signed a decree: 'Serfdom is abolished.' This action was dictated not by Napoleon's sympathies for the peasants, nor by democratic principles, but by the fact that the Bonapartist dictatorship rested not on feudal but on bourgeois property. Since Stalin's Bonapartist dictatorship rests not on private but on state property, the Red Army's invasion of Poland must essentially bring with it the liquidation of private capitalist property, in order thereby to bring the regime of the occupied territories into line with the regime in the USSR."[289]

Soviet dishonesty and spite were epic. Scenes for the film *The First Cavalry Army*, adapted from the play by Vishnevsky about the Polish-Soviet War of 1920, were being shot on location just as the Red Army had smashed across the border into Poland on September 17. It depicted the Poles, not the Ukrainians, as the perpetrators of the civil-war-era pogroms against Jews. On September 21, the film *Burning Years*, directed by Vladimir Korsh-Sablin, which also portrayed the 1920 Polish-Soviet War, premiered to wide acclaim ("not in terms of its artistic merits, but in terms of its political significance," one critic sniffed).[290] The Soviet-Belorussian film *July 11*, by Yuri Tarich, which would premiere October 20, similarly took up the 1919–20 events of that war, showing drunken Polish soldiers forcing Belorussian girls to dance and entertain them, in the ashes of their occupied village, until Soviet partisans fight back and unite with the Red Army to recapture Minsk on July 11, 1920.[291] Polish POWs in Soviet camps were shown *July 11*, rubbing salt in their wounds.[292]

Eastern Poland in a way constituted Stalin's Sudetenland, an analogy that resonated in some quarters of London and Paris, too: the new frontiers, after all, corresponded to the line once proposed by Britain's Lord Curzon. From the despot's point of view, Poland had refused years' worth of probes for bilateral security cooperation. And once the Wehrmacht was on the move, if he had not annexed these eastern Polish regions, Hitler would have seized all of Poland. That would have made possible the creation of a puppet Ukrainian state in eastern Poland, which, in turn, could have been used as a pressure point against Moscow to yield Soviet Ukraine in a "unification." Of course, this was the argument that Poland had used when participating in Hitler's dismemberment of Czechoslovakia (preventing Germany from dominating the entire territory).[293] Now, instead of German troops waltzing right up to the vicinity of Minsk, significantly closer to Moscow, Stalin, as he observed privately, had managed "to extend the socialist system onto new territories and populations."[294] The annexation also delivered a windfall of captured Polish intelligence archives—pleasure reading for the despot, who could sift through what the Poles had made of him and his regime.[295] In the confiscated Polish archives, the NKVD claimed to have discovered 186 secret agents—real ones—who had carried out or were carrying out missions against the USSR, and began to neutralize them.[296]

POLITICAL ECONOMY

During all the foreign policy gamesmanship, Stalin remained in constant private conversation with Lenin, rereading his teacher's texts, inserting strips of paper to mark his place, writing marginal comments. For example, on his copy of the 1939 reissue of *Materialism and Empirio-Criticism* (1909), a philosophical work that had attacked the non-Leninist Bolshevik Alexander Malinovsky, known as Bogdanov, Stalin wrote: "1) Weakness, 2) Idleness, 3) Stupidity. These are the only things that can be called *vices*. Everything else, in the absence of the aforementioned, is undoubtedly *virtue*."[297] But Stalin was experiencing inordinate difficulty executing a Marxist-Leninist textbook on political economy: the labor theory of value, the proper role and significance of money, wage differentiation, trade, prices. In 1939, he received the second version of the text (out of six between 1938 and 1941), which he marked up extensively.[298] In his estimation, the draft did not supersede the old handbook that he continued to consult, *A Course on Political Economy* (1910), last issued in 1925, and written by Bogdanov (1873–1928). The perceived need for an updated treatise on Marxist political economy based on the now twenty-two years of Soviet experience demonstrated again Stalin's fundamental commitment to ideology and putting phenomena in theoretical terms.

Real-world political economy also pressed upon the Little Corner. Economic preparation for war demanded every ounce of labor power, no matter how low its relative productivity. Back on June 10, 1939, Stalin had ended most early releases from the Gulag. Inmates could still be released before term by special boards, but solely on a case-by-case basis. No longer would slave laborers automatically obtain sentence reductions for fulfilling work quotas. The Gulag held around 3 million prisoners, but it probably took more than two camp inmates to perform the labor of one regular worker, which meant forced laborers amounted to just 2 percent of the labor performed in the Soviet economy.[299] But in July 1939, some 160,000 Uzbek and Tajik collective farm "volunteers," watched by NKVD guards, were drafted to build a nearly 200-mile Great Fergana Canal, to move water from the Syr Darya for irrigation of cotton fields. It had been pronounced complete after a mere forty-five days of construction, without mechanization—another propaganda feat.[300] The canal would devastate the inland Aral Sea.

Gulag labor was a Beria responsibility. Since his transfer to Moscow, he had been meeting with Stalin in the Little Corner at least twice weekly and, during some stretches, even every day. By spring 1939, Beria's audiences were lasting two hours or more. He well understood the place of Molotov in the hierarchy, but on August 10, 1939, Stalin had permitted the airing of accusations of "enemy spy elements" in the entourage of Molotov's wife, Zhemchuzhina, one of the few women leading a government agency. As the Red Army was seizing Poland and clashing with the Wehrmacht, her "case" was reviewed at the "politburo." Stalin pronounced the accusations against her "slanderous," but he had her removed as fishing industry commissar "for imprudence in her contacts." After a month of uncertain fate, she was named head of textiles in the light industry commissariat of the RSFSR. The close call, whatever the intrigues behind it, conveyed a message to Molotov and the entire inner circle.[301]

FRIENDSHIP AND THE BORDER

Stalin had second thoughts about Poland. Even before Warsaw had fallen, he had Schulenburg summoned to the Kremlin, on September 25, 1939, to receive a message indicating that the Soviets wanted to trade their share of ethnically Polish Poland for Lithuania, which, except for two ice-free ports, the Pact had assigned to Germany. Stalin's precise motivations remain unrecorded. He had Molotov inform the Germans that the foreign affairs commissar could not reciprocate Ribbentrop's visit to Moscow with one to Berlin, because on the Soviet side the negotiations would require the involvement of "the highest personage," who "could not go abroad."[302] Ribbentrop and his entourage had to fly to Moscow a second time. He arrived on September 27 at around 6:00 p.m.[303] This time, swastika banners, alongside hammer-and-sickle flags, as well as a phalanx of Red Army men and a guard of honor, greeted him.

In Molotov's Kremlin office that same evening, between 10:00 p.m. until 1:00 a.m., Ribbentrop tried to convince Stalin that the Soviet Union was geographically immense compared with little Germany, and that Germany had been the one that annihilated Poland, so the Soviet Union ought to yield not just the ethnic Polish territories Stalin was proposing but also those around the San River, with the oil. Stalin launched a soliloquy about how "the main element of Soviet foreign policy had always been the belief in the possibility of German-Soviet cooperation. At the very beginning, when the Bolsheviks came to power, the world accused the Bolsheviks of being paid agents of Germany. . . . The Soviet Government has now renewed cooperation with Germany with a clear conscience." He observed that "the Soviet government never had sympathy for England. It is only necessary to glance at the works of Lenin and his pupils to understand that the Bolsheviks always cursed and hated England above all." Stalin wanted to hand over Polish territories "with ethnic Polish population," but the oil region was occupied by ethnic Ukrainians, and these lands had already been "promised to Ukraine." Finally, Stalin now wanted Lithuania, too. Overall, he said he was proposing a trade of four million people for two million, "and people are the most important thing one could receive."[304]

Stalin and Molotov, according to the German notetaker, "insisted on their point of view."[305] Ribbentrop indicated that he would send a cable to Hitler regarding the Soviet proposals. He knew the Führer wanted Lithuania, where the Teutonic Knights had settled centuries before, and he was concerned about reports that Stalin was pressuring the Estonians—thought to be racially close to the Germans—for military bases. Soviet ultimatums were issued to the three Baltic states for "mutual assistance pacts," beginning with Estonia, where the Red Army had massed 150,000 troops on the frontier. The next day at 3:00 p.m., the German delegation was back in the Kremlin's Imperial Senate, but there had been no response from the Führer, who was off inspecting U-boats. Ribbentrop nonetheless indicated that he had consulted with Hitler, saying he was in agreement overall but wanted a few small changes. Soviet chief of staff Shaposhnikov unfolded a giant map on the green felt of Molotov's conference table. The two sides discussed their differences, but within the parameters of Stalin's proposal; Stalin offered a few tiny concessions (keeping a railhead here, yielding a forest there), and German and Soviet cartographers set to work on the details. Ribbentrop underscored the expected great value of Soviet economic assistance in the trade negotiations, then asked about the Baltic states. Prematurely, Stalin indicated that Estonia had agreed to his proposals for a pact and a military base.[306] With regard to Bessarabia, he stated that "the Soviet government has no intentions at the current time of touching Romania."[307]

Just before 6:00 p.m., Stalin announced a break for a banquet in Ribbentrop's honor. Rather than the usual venue for foreign dignitaries (Spiridonovka), the festivities took place in the gilded St. Catherine's Hall of the Grand Kremlin Palace.[308] Ascending the majestic sixty-six-step staircase, Ribbentrop was startled to encounter, in the land of Bolshevism, an immense oil painting of Alexander III. Twenty-four courses were served. The drink flowed like the Volga. Stalin sipped his customary wine, but the ex–wine merchant Ribbentrop sampled the pepper vodka ("so potent it took your breath away," he noted). Here, with the amplitude of ancient Russian power on display, Stalin evinced his solicitousness but also his mischievousness. He introduced Ribbentrop to Beria by saying, "Look, this is our Himmler." (SS chief Himmler, a onetime chicken farmer, also happened to wear a pince-nez.) Stalin was not done. As Molotov, the official host, pronounced toasts "in honor of Germany, its Führer, and its minister" and then toasted each member of Ribbentrop's ample delegation, Stalin circumambulated the hall, clinking glasses with them. Suddenly the despot said, "Let's drink to our people's commissar of railways, Lazar Kaganovich!" and walked over and clinked glasses with Kaganovich, a Jew. The Nazi Ribbentrop was compelled to do likewise.[309]

Ribbentrop and entourage were whisked to the imperial box at the Bolshoi to catch an act of *Swan Lake* with one of the great dancers of all time, imported from Leningrad for the occasion, for one of the greatest roles in ballet: Galina Ulanova (b. 1910) as Odette/Odile.[310] This diversion allowed Stalin and Molotov to apply the final screws to the delegation from Estonia. The world might have been divided between capitalism and socialism, but it was also divided between large and small powers. "Poland was a great country," Stalin told the Estonians. "Where is Poland now?"[311] When the Germans returned to complete the negotiations in the Kremlin, at around 1:00 a.m., the browbeaten Estonians were made to glimpse the Nazis in Molotov's suite.

The despot shook down Ribbentrop almost the same way he had the Balts, only affably and, in Ribbentrop's case, not for his own homeland but for a third party's territory. Finally, Hitler surfaced: Ribbentrop spoke to him on a line in Molotov's office. The Führer assented to handing Stalin Lithuania as well as to

Stalin's language for the joint communiqué.[312] Ribbentrop asked the despot about the British. Stalin said there would be talks with them about possible economic cooperation, but that "the Soviet government had no intention of entering into any ties with such states as England, America, and France. Chamberlain is a blabbermouth. Daladier is an even bigger blabbermouth." Stalin further related how Daladier had called in Soviet ambassador Surits to inquire what was going on between Germany and the Soviet Union. "The French government," Stalin noted, "was given to understand that the Soviet Union does not tolerate having its representatives subjected to interrogation."[313] (Unless that was done by the NKVD.) In voicing his dislike, distrust, and dismissiveness of England, Stalin also showed his respect for the United States and its economic prowess, and his glee at having killed so many Japanese in the border war. "This is the only language these Asiatics understand," he told the German diplomats. "After all, I am an Asiatic, too, so I ought to know."[314]

At around 5:00 a.m. on September 29, the state documents were signed (but dated the previous day). They included a full-color map of some three by five feet (scale: 1:1,000,000), which, unlike the Pact, was autographed by Stalin himself, in a ten-inch flourish of blue pencil. The readjusted border was moved 70 to 100 miles east of Warsaw, from the Vistula to the Bug River, placing nearly 5 million more people (Poles and Jews) on the German side and helping to provoke formation of a so-called General Gouvernement for those parts of Poland not directly annexed to the Reich. The Soviet Union, all told, had acquired nearly 13 million inhabitants: 7 million Ukrainian speakers and 3 million Belorussian, as well as just 1 million Poles and 1 million Jews.[315] Ribbentrop, who had arranged for a Mercedes to be given to Molotov's wife as a gift, had been goading Schulenburg into requesting that the Soviets "lease" him hunting grounds in what was now western Ukraine, which was rich in stag, but Molotov demurred. Still, the Nazis did retain a small area on the Polish-Lithuanian frontier, the Suwałki protrusion, which was said to contain prime hunting grounds. Stalin also had Beria extradite 4,000 German political refugees sought by the Nazis. Many were Jewish, and at least 1,000 were Communists. They and their family members would be handed over in ceremonies at the frontier bridge at Brest-Litovsk. Let Hitler expend the bullets.

As Ribbentrop boarded the Condor to depart, the Soviet honor guard raised their right arms in Nazi salute. "The Gauleiter of Danzig, who had accompanied me," Ribbentrop later recalled, "told me on our return flight that at times he had almost imagined himself among old party comrades."[316] Hailed in *Pravda* as "another glorious confirmation of the policy of peace," the September 28 "Treaty of Friendship and the Border" raised eyebrows even among the Communists who had swallowed the nonaggression pact with fascism.[317] "What kind of friendship?" exclaimed the arrested Soviet airplane designer Andrei N. Tupolev (who was working at a so-called prison institute) while crumpling the newspaper. "What's going on with them over there? Have they gone out of their minds!"[318]

A month earlier, Stalin had brushed aside Ribbentrop's desire for a preamble to the Pact on the "friendly" character of Soviet-German relations. In connection with their economic agreement, a Soviet commission of almost fifty members was touring German production facilities and constantly upping its appetites, seeking—and, in many cases, getting—the best that Germany had to offer, from naval cruisers to fighter aircraft.[319] Mikoyan, following Stalin's instructions, was driving a hard bargain, demanding specific machines, ships, and chemical processes, at rock-bottom prices.[320] Many Nazis suspected that the Soviets would not live up to their promises to supply critical raw materials, a suspicion that proved false, while German industrialists whined that they were being forced to give away their secrets, which was true. Equally important, because Stalin had held firm, using armed force, over the Galician oil fields at Drohobycz, he was in effect trading Hitler oil that the Wehrmacht had effectively seized.

KINDRED INTERESTS

In the Little Corner on September 30, 1939, not long after Ribbentrop and the Nazi delegation had departed, Stalin heard a report on lengthening the workday at military factories. To compensate for the extra hours, wages were supposed to be raised. The despot, several times, asked those present about the parameters of the wage hikes; unsatisfied with their answers, he said he would not vote for their proposal until it had been clarified. "Stalin," according to the government notetaker, "turned to Shvernik"—head of the trade unions—"and, jokingly, said, 'What about you, the representative of the workers? You do not defend the interests of workers.' But I, a 'bureaucrat,' defend them, and you are silent!' and he laughed."[321] Of course, the great friend of the workers had just cut a second, even deeper deal with the Nazis. The intelligence defector Krivitsky, who had predicted the Hitler-Stalin Pact, along with Trotsky, went further than the latter and suggested that the agreement had arisen from regime affinity.[322]

Each was a dictatorship with administered mass organizations, an institutionalized ideology, mass state violence against purported enemies, and a leader cult. But salient differences existed, and not just in their irreconcilable worldviews. Nazi party membership stood at 5.3 million by 1939, at a time when the German population was close to 80 million, thus representing approximately 6.5 percent of the population.[323] In 1939, the Soviet Communist party ranks regained some strength, rising to 2.3 million (1.51 million full members and 793,000 candidates), up from 1.9 million the previous year, but, given that the population stood at around 170 million, this represented just 1.3 percent.[324] At the same time, however, Communist party cells were far more ubiquitous. Nazi party "cells" did not exist in every single institution. Hitler abjured a party-state, concerned that an over-empowered Nazi movement could revolt and choose a different leader. German military officers were not allowed to join the party. To be sure, symbolically, the Nazi party spectacularly dominated the German public sphere.[325] But the Nazi party had not victimized itself and the state in enemy hunting.

A second crucial difference consisted in the degree of control over life chances. The Nazi economy was not owned or even managed by the state. Many banks that had been nationalized during the Depression had been reprivatized in 1936–37, and, aside from the Hermann Göring Works (low-quality iron ore), the Nazi regime created few state enterprises. A robust finance ministry opposed state companies as inefficient and expensive. Private companies that refused ministerial directives suffered no consequences. To be sure, plenty of incentives existed for private business to curry favor with the regime, and foreign policy considerations also shaped private investment (one quarter of the labor force worked in industry directly connected with weapons). Still, freedom of contract was preserved as enterprises continued to select their own customers. Private corporate profits had risen 400 percent higher than they had been a decade earlier. Hitler and his regime viewed private property, entrepreneurship, and market incentives as valued instruments for the advance of the German race.[326] Stalin himself explained to the Soviet government notetaker that bourgeois states "have not absorbed the economic organizations, but our state is not only a political organization but an economic one."[327] His point was that the absence of private companies (and legal markets) had created a complex and difficult challenge of management; but it also meant the Soviet state was the only employer, the only source of housing, the only arbiter of schooling for one's children, the only provider—or not—of a host of necessities and amenities. The possibility of self-employment, a private housing market, private religious schools, and private holiday resorts provided for significantly less life control over non-Jews under Nazism.

All that said, the two regimes did share a crucial attribute: personal rule. The Pact had been made possible not by an affinity between the regimes but by the two leaders' unquestioned authority. Hitler and Stalin had no need to worry about parliamentary majorities, genuine ratification votes, a free press, or even independent voices in the inner circle, giving each an absolute freedom to act.[328] They did so because of a temporary confluence of interests against Britain and the Versailles offspring, Poland, engaging in a parallel, if differing, revisionism. In his most revealing comment on the Pact (made later to a British official), Stalin would explain that "the USSR had wanted to change the old equilibrium. . . . England and France had wanted to preserve it. Germany had also wanted to make a change in the equilibrium, and this common desire to get rid of the old equilibrium had created the basis for rapprochement with Germany."[329]

FROM LATE AUGUST through late September 1939, Stalin had the month of a lifetime, convincingly winning a major border war against Japan and obtaining a sweetheart deal with Hitler. Mekhlis, the despot's mouthpiece, had boasted at the 18th Party Congress, in March 1939, that in the event of the outbreak of a "second imperialist war," the Red Army would "carry the battle to the territories of the enemy and fulfill its international duty to increase the number of Soviet republics."[330] In truth, Stalin had lacked the confidence and the external facilitation for such expansionism on his own. Hitler was driving world politics. Stalin presented him a draft pact that greatly favored the Soviet side, and Hitler took it.[331] Stalin was an opportunist, and Hitler had opened the door.[332] Chamberlain, rightly fearing Soviet expansionism in Europe, had nonetheless helped push the Soviet despot through that very door of expansionism by not only rejecting Stalin's offer of a genuine military alliance but playing charades with him. Perhaps Stalin would have agreed to a deal with the Western powers if he had faced a certain imminent British-German agreement at his expense, but Chamberlain would have taken the German deal instead. Hitler, for his part, had done something remarkable: he had scorned Chamberlain's July 1939 feelers to double-cross Poland in a repeat of Munich.[333]

Had the Führer accepted the British PM's entreaties to once again "negotiate" a handover of someone else's territory, it likely would have fatally undermined the talks between Nazi and Soviet intermediaries. Hitler's snubbing of Chamberlain did not signify that the Führer would necessarily cut a deal with Stalin, however. Japan had drawn back from a military alliance with Germany on the latter's terms, influencing Hitler's moves. But the bottom line was that, even if he could obtain a great deal of Polish territory for free, Hitler had thirsted for a war—and Stalin, over many years, had positioned the Soviet Union to reap the rewards of that action.[334] Stalin's Pact with Hitler had not been inevitable, especially the specific content. In the circumstances of the time, the Pact constituted a significant achievement for Soviet state interests. Whereas in the 1938 Munich Pact, Nazi-Western collusion had excluded the Soviets from European affairs, now the Soviet Union had re-emerged as an arbiter of European power politics. In the bargain, the revolutionary expansionist fantasy outlined by Mekhlis had begun to be realized.[335]

Burning with animus toward Britain, Stalin appears to have suspected that the Western "imperialists" would, at some point, declare war on him over Poland.[336] In the meantime, editing the draft of an *Izvestiya* editorial, "Peace or War?" (October 9, 1939), he inserted a remarkable passage about the inadmissibility of any war to "destroy Hitlerism." "Each person is free to express his relation to this or that ideology, and has the right to defend or repudiate it, but it is a senseless and stupid brutality to exterminate people for the fact that someone does not like certain opinions and a certain worldview," Stalin warned of Western opposition to Nazi Germany. He added, "One can respect or hate Hitlerism, as in the case of any system of political views. This is a matter of taste." (So much for the "popular front" against fascism.) Launching a war in opposition to Nazi Germany, Stalin concluded, "returns us to the dark times of the Middle Ages, when devastating religious wars were conducted in the name of eliminating heretics and those who thought differently."[337]

The First Blow, the bestselling novella by Nikolai Shpanov about an easy Red Army victory over Nazi Germany, was quickly withdrawn.[338] But a nonaggression pact founded on mutual state interests would last only as long as those interests did not fundamentally clash. The multisided machinations were in many ways just beginning. Back when the Nazi war machine had been gearing up to launch the assualt on Poland, the German diplomats at the Warsaw embassy had been ordered to evacuate to Germany. This included those secretly working as Soviet agents: Rudolf von Scheliha ("Aryan") and Gerhard Kegel ("X"), as well as the high-placed journalists Ilse Stöbe ("Alta"), Kurt Welkisch ("ABC"), and Margarita Welkisch ("LCL"). Stöbe headed to Berlin, but her husband and handler, Rudolf Herrnstadt ("Arbin"), was Jewish and could not be posted to the Nazi capital; he headed for Moscow. (The couple would never see each other again, their dedication to antifascism trumping their dedication to each other.) Instead, Captain Nikolai Zaitsev (b. 1895), a relatively recent recruit to the bloodied ranks of military intelligence, would become the principal handler of the Soviet spies in Berlin, under the cover of the Soviet trade mission and code name of "Bine." A graduate of an artillery academy, Zaitsev had learned German from Volga Germans he grew up with in his native Saratov; they had since been internally deported. His first boss during an earlier posting in Berlin, Soviet trade representative Kandelaki, had been executed. After familiarizing himself, in Moscow HQ, with the top-secret mission files generated by Herrnstadt, Zaitsev took up residence in Berlin as the new handler for Stöbe in the field. She, in turn, reestablished contact with Kegel, who was hired into the German foreign ministry economics department for the east, and Scheliha, who would be hired into the German foreign ministry press bureau, a prime crossroads of secret information.[339]

Hitler remained volatile. As Warsaw was still burning, in mid-September 1939, the Führer had returned from his triumphal promenade in Danzig and ordered a gathering of his military brass to prepare for an attack against the West at the end of October—that is, within a few weeks. Even Göring was flabbergasted.[340] A handful of old-line German conservatives began to whisper about somehow *stopping* Hitler—the very Chamberlain fantasy of a German palace coup. Halder, the Wehrmacht chief of staff, had taken to carrying a loaded revolver, but, though he saw the Führer often, Halder shrank from using it.[341] Still, a more resolute conspirator, acting alone, was found among Germany's working classes. On November 8, 1939, at around 8:00 p.m., Hitler arrived at the Munich Beer Hall—where he had staged the failed putsch in 1923—to deliver his annual commemorative address to the old fighters and the Bavarian leadership. Goebbels, Heydrich, and Hess were in tow. This was one of the largest beer halls in the city, seating 3,000, and therefore ideal for political gatherings. Munich's upper crust turned out in numbers: party men, military officers, bankers, business owners. The rite usually lasted from around 8:30 p.m. to 10:00 p.m. At 9:20, a time bomb exploded in the high-ceilinged, chandeliered hall, killing eight and wounding more than sixty. Many of the bleeding survivors thought a British warplane had dropped a bomb. In fact, a German cabinetmaker, Georg Elser (b. 1903), had planted the explosive in a pillar right behind the podium.

Elser held Hitler responsible for deceiving the workers and fomenting war. As he would explain, "I considered that the situation in Germany could only be changed by the elimination of the current leadership."[342] During the course of some twelve months, he had planned and stolen explosives and a detonator from his workplace and begun taking his meals at the beer hall. Later, before closing time, he would hide in a storeroom, then come out and set to work by flashlight, creating a secret door in place of the pillar's wood paneling, until the staff returned at 7:30 a.m. and he would sneak out the back. Elser spent more than thirty nights in the beer hall, and carried out cement and other debris, even sawdust, in a suitcase; at least once he was caught on the premises after closing but not turned over to the police. In the daytime he worked on the bomb and the timer. As fortune would have it, on the night of November 8, the fog was too thick to risk flying, and Hitler did not have his own separate train, so he would have to take the regularly scheduled one. This meant he had to begin his speech early, at 8:00 p.m., and end it early, and instead of staying for the usual chitchat, rush out to catch the train back to Berlin, where he was scheduled to finalize the approved battle plans for an offensive in the west. Only the musicians and the cleaning staff remained in the beer hall. The dais was crushed by the collapsed ceiling. The Führer's speech had ended at 9:07 p.m.; he departed the venue no more than ten minutes before the deadly blast.

CHAPTER 12

SMASHED PIG

Voroshilov is a fairy tale. His authority was artificially
created by totalitarian agitation.

TROTSKY, Bulletin of the Opposition, *fall 1939*[1]

It is clear now how Finland was prepared for a major war
against us. They readied every village for that aim.

STALIN, *January 21, 1940, following the annual
commemoration of Lenin's death at the Bolshoi Theater*[2]

THE SOVIET UNION had a longer coastline than any other country—more than
16,000 nautical miles. Stalin, still reliant on imperial Russia's aging fleet, had decided back in late 1935 that the country needed not only a modern navy, but one
larger than any other in the world. He wanted to achieve command of the Gulf of
Finland, the Black Sea, and the Sea of Japan, and, ultimately, attain a substantial
offensive capability to challenge other powers on the oceans. His "big-fleet" program far exceeded in ambition Peter the Great's, and formed part of a global naval
arms race.[3] The despot had established a self-standing naval commissariat during
the terror.[4] Then, between 1938 and 1940, he put to death the chief of Soviet naval
forces, the commanders of the Pacific, Northern, Black Sea, and Baltic fleets, eight
leaders of the central naval administration, five chiefs of staff of fleets, fifteen other
flag officers, and dozens upon dozens of other high-ranking naval officers.[5] In
1939, the navy claimed nearly a fifth of Soviet defense outlays. Nikolai Kuznetsov,
the Serbian immigrants' son who had joined the party at age nineteen in 1924 (the
same year he attended Lenin's funeral on Red Square), was promoted to naval commissar at thirty-four. He recalled that in late 1939, when he perceived Stalin to be
in a good mood, he gently asked how the despot intended to use all the big, expensive ships under construction—the plan now called for 699 total—in light of the
shallowness of the Baltic Sea (which could be readily mined) and the Pact with
Hitler (altering Germany's status as the main enemy). Stalin answered, "We shall
build them even if we have to scramble up the last kopeck!"[6]

A super-dreadnought, the *Soviet Ukraine,* had been laid down at the Nikolayev

Shipyard for the Black Sea Fleet. The keels of two heavy cruisers were laid down for the Pacific Fleet at a new shipyard founded on the Amur River, at remote Komsomolsk, out of range of Japanese fighter planes. About 120,000 slave laborers had started construction on another shipyard for the new Northern Fleet, at Molotovsk, on the delta of the Northern Dvina, above the Arctic Circle. At the Baltic Shipyard, in Leningrad, another super-dreadnought, the *Soviet Union,* had been laid down for the high-priority yet weak Baltic Fleet.[7] By 1940, plans for oceangoing ships would be made larger still, but the number to be built would be reduced in favor of submersibles. (Characteristically, Stalin would order that the revised naval program's details be kept secret from his own fleet commanders.)[8] Blueprints and advanced naval technology had to be purchased abroad. France demurred, and Britain was not even approached, but fascist Italy had proved eager.[9] Still, Nazi Germany was the chief source, and naval equipment formed a centerpiece of Soviet desiderata after the Pact with Hitler—cruisers, coastal and naval guns, battleship blueprints, and at least three samples of the heavy gun turrets fitted on the *Bismarck* and *Tirpitz* battleships.[10]

Stalin's various slave-labor internal canals had not enhanced his navy's room for maneuver. The Black Sea was relatively narrow and hemmed in, while the Arctic Sea was icebound most of the year and the Pacific coast was remote from Soviet industry and population. But the most immediate challenge was the Baltic, where the Soviet shipbuilding program lagged behind the capabilities of both the German and the British navies, and, even worse, the Soviet Fleet depended on the goodwill of Finland and Estonia just to get in and out. Baltic defenses could not block hostile navies from approaching the USSR's shores, as had transpired during the Russian civil war. More broadly, the 1932 Soviet-Finnish treaty recognizing tsarist Finland's independence had settled the land border on the Karelian Isthmus, less than twenty miles from Leningrad, a distance that, by the 1930s, fell well within artillery range. In other words, Leningrad, the only Soviet port on the Baltic and the home to a third of Soviet military industry, could be fired upon without entering Soviet territory. Stalin worried that a hostile great power would make use of Finnish territory as a launch pad to seize the USSR's second capital and set up a Russian "White Guard" regime, with the aim of provoking a new civil war to destroy the Soviet regime.[11]

Finland's trade with Germany, as the Leningrad NKVD noted in a detailed analysis, had doubled since the Nazis came to power and, as with Finnish trade with Britain, exceeded trade with the USSR by a factor of forty.[12] Contacts between the Finnish and German militaries had again come to seem very close. Almost all

Finnish staff officers had trained in Lockstedt, Germany, during the Great War and continued to feel grateful for that opportunity, as well as for the fact that a German military landing—precipitated by Trotsky's antics at Brest-Litovsk—had rescued Finland's independence from Red Guards. In April 1938, on the twentieth anniversary of Germany's anti-Bolshevik intervention—and a few weeks after Hitler's *Anschluss* with Austria—Helsinki had warmly received yet another prominent German military delegation, to the strains of "Alte Kameraden."[13] In summer 1939, Finnish officers paid a visit to Lockstedt to recall their "brotherhood in arms." In mid-June, Beria informed Stalin that the Finns had placed orders for military hardware at the Škoda Works right after it had fallen into Nazi hands.[14] In late June, Lieutenant General Franz Halder had toured Finnish military installations, his first visit abroad as Wehrmacht chief of staff. "I greet you with all my heart, Mr. General, as a representative of the glorious army of Germany," enthused the Finnish foreign minister, Eljas Erkko, according to the NKVD police report. Halder, who flew above the entire length of the Finnish-Soviet border, wrote to Berlin of his trip that the Finnish military "undoubtedly are partisans of Germany."[15]

The Finnish government—a rule-of-law, parliamentary democracy—professed a Nordic orientation and strict neutrality vis-à-vis the great powers. But the fear that smaller nations, if not folded within Russian borders, would fall under the control of a hostile great power and be used against Russia long predated the Soviet regime. After the borderlands, or limitrophes, of Poland, Lithuania, Latvia, and Estonia, as well as Finland, had broken off into independent states, the alarm intensified.[16] Soviet intelligence reported that German specialists were helping the Finns build aerodromes, which exceeded the capacity of the Finnish air force.[17] Even if Stalin had been inclined to take the "White Finns" at their word, which he was not, intentions mattered less to him than capabilities. The despot was not about to wait around while another power forced little Finland into becoming a springboard for attack against him, whether by Germany or Great Britain. In Stalin's mental map, the British were not at the far other end of Europe, but at the gates of Leningrad.[18]

The menacing strategic situation on the northwestern frontier would have exercised the minds of tsarist strategists, too, but the Soviets had a largely untrained naval command as a result of Stalin's mass slaughter, while the despotic regime's bottlenecks were becoming more severe. Even as the relentless barrage of reports had only increased, the regime had continued to narrow, not only to the Little Corner but *within* the Little Corner, where Stalin saw fewer people, despite being responsible for more and more business. He was physically overwhelmed. The despotism, to an extent, was undermining itself, generating colossal quantities of information that neither Stalin nor anyone else could process fully. He and his minions often could not effectively act upon even the information they possessed, because of hypersuspicion and blinkered thinking. And, notwithstanding the semblance of continued camaraderie within the inner sanctums, he was surrounded by men he had broken, or neophytes he had promoted over others' bones, all of whom strained every nerve to divine his thoughts to feed them right back to him. NKVD chief Beria exemplified the dynamic, beginning so many of his memoranda, "In connection with your instructions . . ."[19]

Stalin had shown himself to be more of a gambler than most people understood at the time (or subsequently). He had taken one of the biggest gambles in a millennium of Russian history with forced collectivization-dekulakization, even if to him that course had seemed dictated by iron logic. He had taken a sizable gamble with the mass terror, risking the potentially fatal destabilization of a Soviet state that was involved in wars in Spain and China, and faced Germany on the march in Central Europe. Stalin had also taken a gamble in the Pact with Hitler. True, the despot was not on the hook for anything other than mutually beneficial economic obligations. But the choice to spurn the Western powers and divide the spoils with Hitler constituted a pact of blood. To be sure, in contrast to Hitler's impulsive high-stakes gambling, Stalin usually readied the ground before acting. With Finland, however, he would end up taking a largely unprepared gamble, and without realizing he was doing so. Napoleon is said to have remarked that in war, as in prostitution, amateurs are often superior to professionals. He was wrong. If the Pact with Hitler had involved Stalin's first high-stakes test in the diplomatic arts, Finland, unexpectedly, would entail his first trial by fire in the modern military arts, and the results initially proved disastrous. At the Soviet despot's side during his roll of the "iron dice" in 1939–40 was his civil war crony, the overmatched Voroshilov, who contributed generously to Stalin's own military dilettantism.

DIPLOMACY, OF A SORT

Stalin tried diplomacy, in his own way, with Finland. The NKVD intelligence station chief in Helsinki, Boris Rybkin (b. 1899, code name "Yartsev"), had been doling out bribes to Soviet-friendly Finnish politicians and businessmen; one asked for and received permission to purchase Soviet timber "at an advantageous price."[20] In spring 1938, Yartsev—by then into his third year in-country—had been summoned to Moscow. Massacres of diplomatic and intelligence personnel were in full swing; Yartsev discovered on April 7 that he was not being arrested but would be received, for the first time, by Stalin. The despot tasked him with conducting conspiratorial negotiations with the Finns, reporting only to him, obviating even the head of Soviet intelligence (the operation was code-named "the April 7 Affair"). Yartsev noticed that Stalin manipulated his pipe like a rosary.[21]

On April 14, two days after the departure of a German major general from Finland, Yartsev, nominally a mere second secretary at the Soviet legation, called the Finnish foreign minister and asked to be received, with an urgent message from the Soviet government. The Finns set aside protocol, knowing who the junior embassy official really was. Yartsev informed the Finnish foreign minister that the USSR required "cooperation" in its security, explaining that he had recently been in Moscow and was empowered to conduct "negotiations." He offered the Finns arms at cut-rate prices, in exchange for a "guarantee" not to assist Germany in an anti-Soviet war, and gave assurances that the Soviet Union aimed not to occupy Finland but to protect its own maritime defenses. Yartsev also appears to have indicated that if Germany attacked Soviet territory via Finland, the Red Army did not intend to remain at the Soviet border but would advance to meet the enemy.[22] He flew back to Moscow to report to Stalin on the results.[23] "The approach to the Finnish government had taken place in so strange a fashion," recalled a high Finnish official, "that the members of the government who were aware of it . . . did not at first give it the attention it merited."[24]

The Finnish prime minister, Aimo Cajander, who, as head of the National Progressive Party, led a coalition government with the Social Democrats and the Agrarians, informed the finance minister but not the defense minister or the defense forces commander. The Swedish foreign minister was told, but Finland's ambassador to Sweden was not; Britain's ambassador knew, but not Helsinki's ambassador to London. The Finns, who had been part of Russia until 1917–18, tended to view Russians as gluttonous for territory. But Cajander, a professor of botany, could not discern whether the proposals from Yartsev were genuine. Tsarist experience had shown that one could not always tell if intermediaries spoke for the regime or were engaged in personal intrigues. Stalin, for his part, had employed Radek and Kandelaki, both now dead, as special envoys to spark agreements with Poland and Nazi Germany, respectively. His back-channel warnings and enticements to Finland continued for almost a year, evidently to probe Helsinki's bottom line.[25] Then, having unwittingly deepened Helsinki's already deep distrust of his intentions, he switched to conventional diplomacy.

A Finnish delegation was invited to Moscow and, on March 5, 1939, presented with a formal proposal for a thirty-year lease of the Hanko Cape, which had been used by the tsarist fleet and constituted a choke point where ships from the Baltic Sea could be blocked from entering the Gulf of Finland. The Soviets emphasized that their proposal was not for a full-fledged military base but merely an observation point.[26] The Finns responded negatively within just three days. Beyond the likely public firestorm that would have consumed any Finnish government that consented, the country's constitution called its territory "indivisible" and therefore nonnegotiable by the foreign ministry. A Soviet counterproposal to exchange four Finnish islands in the Gulf of Finland for Soviet territory north of Lake Ladoga was similarly rebuffed, to Moscow's evident disappointment.[27] The more the Soviets doggedly insisted that small states such as Finland were simply unable to prevent third parties from using their territory for aggression against another state, the more the Finns began to see the Soviet Union as that third party.[28]

Diplomatic efforts were also made in Helsinki, but not via the Soviet ambassador, Vladimir Derevyansky; instead, Stalin sent the former envoy to Finland, Boris Stein, who was now stationed in Italy. Stein arrived in Helsinki in March 1939, supposedly to take a holiday in the chilly north. He carried a proposal to exchange Soviet Karelia, a predominantly ethnic Finnish enclave contiguous with Finland, for the Finnish islands the Soviets sought, and to pay for the relocation of Finnish citizens from any territory acquired by the USSR. But he, too, proved unable to convince Foreign Minister Erkko of the ineffectiveness of a policy of neutrality by small states, despite citing recently devoured Czechoslovakia (which, of course, had had mutual assistance pacts with France and the Soviet Union). Stein departed for Moscow empty-handed, albeit not before warning Erkko that "the Soviet government does not accept Finland's answer. We will not give up our demand for the islands in the Gulf of Finland."[29]

NO APPARENT WIGGLE ROOM

Secretly, in the first half of March 1939, Voroshilov had informed the recently appointed commander of the Leningrad military district, Kirill Meretskov, to prepare for a possible military aggression *from* the territory of Finland, by a third party.[30] Stalin called Meretskov "Yaroslavets," according to Molotov, because "the people in Yaroslavl were so shifty there were almost no Jews, and there the Russians themselves perform those functions."[31] (Meretskov actually hailed from a village near Ryazan.) On-site, the ingratiating Meretskov judged that Finnish troops stationed near the border themselves had aggressive intentions to burst through and seize Leningrad.[32] The Soviets launched a massive military construction effort in the region, which the Finns could not help but notice. In June 1939, Meretskov would later claim, Stalin summoned him to discuss the Finnish threat and anti-Soviet moods in the Finnish government. The Leningrad military district's war contingency plans for Finland were defensive. Stalin ordered up operational plans for a "counter-blow."[33]

Soviet interest in Finland would soon be mentioned in the Pact's secret protocol, but the suspicious despot would keep a close eye on the intelligence concerning whether Hitler would keep his word. If Hitler abandoned Finland to its fate, he would be throwing away decades of goodwill toward Germany in this strategically located country. Additionally, as the Soviet ambassador to Berlin would warn the foreign affairs commissariat, Germany had to be careful not to suffer interruption in strategic supplies from Finland of timber, food, copper, and molybdenum for steel alloys.[34] In July 1939, during General Halder's jubilant tour of Finland, Stalin received details, partly from intercepted Japanese military intelligence telegrams sent from Helsinki to Tokyo, about German-Finnish military links.[35] In fact, the Finns were working diplomatic channels to try to exact British protection. On July 4, 1939, a representative of the British war office posted to Helsinki reported to London that the Finns "do not want anything to do with Germany but, rather than accept a Russian guarantee, they would join the Axis."[36]

The August 23 Hitler-Stalin Pact removed that option. After the forced introduction of Soviet military bases onto Estonian soil with the September 28 Treaty of Friendship, the Finns feared being subjected to the same compromise of their neutrality and perhaps even their hard-won independence. Sure enough, on October 5, when the Soviets had forced a treaty and bases on Latvia, too, Molotov "invited" the Finnish foreign minister to Moscow to discuss "concrete political matters."[37] Aiming to show resolve, and perhaps worried about a surprise attack, the Finns soon began calling up the reserves and evacuating their civilian population from frontier zones.[38] But Beria reported to Stalin from a Soviet intelligence source in London on a pessimistic self-assessment by the retired septuagenarian Finnish field marshal Gustaf Mannerheim (b. 1867). As a former lieutenant general in the tsarist army, he had been stationed in Lhasa for a time, where he taught the Dalai Lama pistol shooting, and had learned to speak Finnish only in his fifties while defending Finland's independence. Beria's report had Mannerheim asking a British envoy in Helsinki to inform Whitehall that Finland expected to receive demands analogous to those presented to Estonia, and that "Finland will have to satisfy these demands of the Soviet Union."[39]

Finland got indirect support in an obscure place. "No one feels safe in the Soviet Union," the diplomat-defector Fyodor Raskolnikov wrote in an open letter to Stalin, published posthumously in the émigré press in Paris (October 1, 1939). Raskolnikov condemned the forged trials of victims made to whirl in Stalin's "bloody carousel" and asked, "Where are the big Soviet military theoreticians?" He answered the question himself: "You killed them, comrade Stalin!" Raskolnikov charged the despot with having abandoned the Spanish Republic and predicted that "sooner or later the Soviet people will put you in the dock as traitor to both socialism and revolution, principal wrecker, true enemy of the people, organizer of the famine." Eight days after having first composed the letter, Raskolnikov had tried to jump out a hotel window, but his wife and hotel personnel restrained him. He was committed to a mental hospital in Nice, where he perished anyway, at age forty-seven.[40] In a diary that remained private, he had drawn an incisive psychological portrait of Stalin, naming as the despot's "fundamental psychological trait" a "superhuman strength of will" that "suffocates, destroys the individuality of people who come under his influence." Stalin had broken even the "willful" Kaganovich, Raskolnikov noted, adding that "he demands from his closest aides complete submission, obedience, subjection."[41]

Finland's government was consulting separately with London and Berlin. The Germans bluntly advised acceptance of any Soviet proposal. The British, in talks with the Finns, mostly pooh-poohed the likelihood of a Soviet aggression. Reporting out of Helsinki, a few British foreign office personnel reasoned that a Finnish decision to take up arms against the USSR would be advantageous to the UK, since a war would consume Soviet petroleum, grain, and war materials that otherwise might be shipped to Germany—and could even precipitate that most desirable outcome of all, a Soviet-German clash.[42] This cynicism came with only offers of moral support to the Finns. Winston Churchill, newly appointed first lord of the Admiralty, flat out told Maisky, the Soviet envoy to London, on October 6, 1939, that he understood "well that the Soviet Union must be the master of the eastern coast of the Baltic Sea," and added, "Stalin is now playing the Great Game, and very successfully." This was the same Churchill who, in 1919–20, had schemed with Mannerheim, albeit unsuccessfully, to mount an offensive spearheaded by

Finnish troops to topple the Bolshevik regime. Now, desperately wanting to keep all of Scandinavia out of the clutches of Nazi Germany, Churchill told Maisky that if Estonia and Latvia were to lose their sovereignty, he would be "very glad" if it were to the Soviet, and not the German, sphere.[43]

Soviet military intelligence, on October 9, 1939, reported on Finnish mobilization measures.[44] The next day, Lithuania was compelled to sign a treaty with the Soviet Union, affording military bases and other privileges. In the forced bargain, Lithuania also acquired a gift at the expense of former Poland: the predominantly Polish and Jewish city of Wilno, which became the Lithuanian capital of Vilnius.[45] On October 11, the first Soviet naval ships docked at their new temporary base in Tallinn, Estonia, across from Finland.[46] That same day, Soviet ambassador Derevyansky reported to Moscow that the Finnish general staff, unaware of the Pact's secret protocol, had urgently written to Hitler, requesting that he not grant concessions of Finnish territory to the USSR.[47] Also that same day, the Finnish negotiating team arrived in Moscow.

"MINIMAL" DEMANDS

Despite a specific request from Molotov, Finland did not send foreign minister Erkko or even a plenipotentiary empowered to sign a state accord. Their delegation was led by Juho Kusti Paasikivi (b. 1870), a conservative banker and the Finnish envoy to Sweden, who had negotiated the 1920 Treaty of Tartu with the Soviets, whose border terms Moscow was now trying to overturn. Also included were Colonel Aladár Paasonen (b. 1898), who had been educated at France's elite École Spéciale Militaire de Saint-Cyr and was the foremost expert on the Soviet Union in Finnish military intelligence; the foreign ministry official who handled Soviet affairs; and the Finnish envoy to Moscow. On October 12, with no advance disclosure of the precise agenda, they were summoned to the Kremlin and taken to Molotov's office. Potyomkin and Derevyansky were also present, but so was Stalin—an unmistakable sign of seriousness.[48] Molotov proposed a mutual assistance pact. Paasikivi dismissed this as unthinkable. Molotov dropped his request—apparently astonishing Paasikivi—and proceeded to outline Soviet desiderata for enhancement of its security by way of acquiring a military base on the Finnish coast, mentioning the Hanko Cape. Molotov also indicated a desire to "rectify" both the northern border on the Arctic Sea, near Finnish Petsamo, and the southern border on the Karelian Isthmus, near Leningrad, with territorial compensation from Soviet (eastern) Karelia. Paasikivi responded that Finland's territorial integrity was inviolable.[49] The talks adjourned. Paasikivi wired Helsinki the details of Soviet demands and requested additional instructions.

Stalin was sent eavesdropped conversations among people thought to be privy to Finnish government options. Beria reported that the voluble Swedish military attaché in Moscow, Major Birger Vrang, had expressed regret that the Norwegian and Danish envoys to Moscow had failed to greet Paasikivi at the train station to show Scandinavian solidarity.[50] The Finnish military attaché, Major Kaarlo Somerto, told Vrang that Finland's general staff did not trust British intelligence to the effect that the Soviets had thirty-three divisions on the Finnish border, including just seven between Lake Ladoga and the Arctic Sea, where roads were practically nonexistent. (This looks like Soviet disinformation; the actual figure was almost double that.) Vrang doubted that the Soviets would invade, which would sully their celebrated policy of "peace." Somerto reported this assertion to Helsinki but added, of the Swedes, that "about help, they say nothing." On October 13, Beria reported that the Swedish government had promised Finland's foreign minister "moral support," and that Finland's military intelligence chief had been "very disappointed" by his recent trip to sound out attitudes in Berlin. On October 14, Stalin could read that Vrang had told the military expert on the Finnish negotiating team, Paasonen, that "the Russians are Asiatics: initially they demand a great deal, and later they make concessions to obtain what they need."[51]

That same day in the Kremlin, at the follow-up Soviet-Finnish negotiating session, again with Stalin present, Paasikivi read aloud an analysis by Paasonen rebutting Soviet claims about threats to the Gulf of Finland, but he allowed that the Finns were prepared to discuss a few islands closest to the Soviet shore.[52] In fact, the Red Navy did not even possess enough ships to patrol from all of their newly acquired naval bases in the Baltic states, and the Soviet naval command was most concerned about air attacks from bases situated on Finland's Karelian Isthmus.[53] Whether Stalin shared his navy's assessment of Leningrad's security, however, remains unclear, but at a minimum, a Soviet naval base on Finnish territory could deter the British and the Germans from acquiring such facilities for themselves. Moreover, he looked at the situation in terms of what territory imperial Russia had possessed. Molotov formally requested from the Finns a lease for a naval base on Hanko Cape, as well as the permanent transfer to Soviet possession of Suursaari (Hogland) and other islands in the Gulf of Finland. He further demanded the Finnish portion of the northern Rybachy Peninsula, which guarded the approaches to Petsamo, Finland's only ice-free harbor. And he asked that the border on the Karelian Isthmus be moved westward nearly forty miles, to a location within twenty miles of Viipuri (old Vyborg), a former medieval fortress and Finland's second-largest city.

Stalin offered to compensate the Finns with Soviet Karelia. "We cannot do anything about geography, nor can you," he told Paasikivi, who, like all the Finns present, spoke some Russian. "Since Leningrad cannot be moved, the frontier must be moved farther away. We ask for 1,000 square miles, and we offer more than 2,120 in exchange. Would any other great power do this? No, only we are that stupid."[54]

The Finns kept insisting that they had no intention of allowing Hitler to use their territory; Stalin kept insisting that someone could seize their country as a springboard to attack the USSR.[55] He reminded the Finns that territorial concessions were known to history: Russia had sold Alaska to the United States, Spain had ceded Gibraltar to Britain. He further noted that in Poland, he had annexed only the territories with Belorussian and Ukrainian-speaking majorities. "In Poland we took no foreign territory," he told the Finns, "and now this is a case of exchange."[56] Trying to impart a sense of urgency, Stalin also noted that Finnish soldiers had been mobilized and the nation's frontier cities evacuated, heightening the risk of war and necessitating an agreement. Paasikivi requested a break in the talks to consult in person with Helsinki.[57]

The despot repeatedly underscored how his demands were "minimal," certainly as compared with Hitler's vis-à-vis Czechoslovakia or Poland. But to the leaders of Finland's parliamentary democracy, Stalin was a gangster. Paasikivi was inclined to some sort of deal, but he carried rigid directives: no Soviet military bases to compromise Finnish neutrality, no significant territorial concessions. Back in Finland on October 16, Paasikivi told journalists that Mr. Stalin was a pleasant fellow with a sense of humor.[58] Beria reported that at a meeting with the Social Democratic parliamentary faction in Helsinki on October 17, Väinö Tanner, the finance minister in the coalition government, had stressed the unexpected scope of Soviet demands, without revealing details, but had also noted that "Paasikivi was surprised that he was received so well and that they tried to create a friendly atmosphere. Stalin joked all the time, and when Paasikivi apologized for his poor Russian, Stalin answered that he could not speak Finnish."[59]

Stalin had inside information on the Finnish position. He lacked a spy at the top of the Helsinki government, but Hella Wuolijoki, a Finnish writer and businesswoman and the former mistress of the Soviet intelligence official Meyer Trilisser (her NKVD code name was "the Poet"), hosted a political salon in the capital. She learned details of a Finnish war cabinet meeting on October 16 (perhaps via an intentional leak by Tanner) and concluded that, in terms of Soviet demands, the Finnish defense minister was hostile, the foreign minister passive, and the prime minister wavering. The next day, based upon information from Wuolijoki, the deputy Soviet intelligence chief in Helsinki, Zoya Rybkina (the wife of Boris Rybkin/Yartsev), who posed as the Soviet tourist representative, reported to Moscow that Helsinki might concede some Gulf of Finland islands, but a bilateral military alliance or leases for Soviet bases on Finnish territory had been ruled out. Also on October 17, Soviet intelligence in Helsinki reported that it had gotten word of a secret visit to Berlin by Finland's former security police chief, who, it was reported, had been told by Himmler, "Stand firm if you want to, but we will not help you."[60] Four days later, Stalin received a report from Soviet military intelligence to the effect that the Japanese military attaché in Moscow, Colonel Doi, had complained to his Swedish counterpart, Vrang, that it was incomprehensible how the Germans could afford the Soviets a free hand in Finland.[61]

Beria's rich NKVD reports made plain the narrowness of Finland's options, but the Finns felt uncertain about Stalin's real aims.[62] Right around this time, the Finnish police rounded up 272 known members of the outlawed Finnish Communist party, expecting to uncover a plot on orders from Moscow for domestic subversion. But it turned out that no organized treasonous activities were under way; most of the arrested Finnish Communists were released within three days. Even some who had been trained militarily in the Soviet Union pledged to take up arms for Finland. The interrogations surprised the Finnish authorities.[63]

IMPASSE

Paasikivi, his passage slowed by Finnish troop movements (the reserves had been ordered into training), arrived back in Moscow on October 23 for a second round of talks. He had in tow the Social Democrat Tanner, who it was believed would stand firm against the Communists.[64] In fact, while this representative of the "Finnish working class" evoked mistrust in Moscow, because he came from the Communists' despised rivals on the left, the representative of the big bourgeoisie, Paasikivi, was regarded as a trustworthy partner and proponent of good relations. The intensive consultations in Helsinki had led to the conclusion that Stalin had staked out an absurdly maximalist price, from which he was prepared to come way down to close a deal. The Finnish government, very reluctantly, had come around to the possibility of moving the border westward on the Karelian Isthmus, but only about eight miles from Leningrad. And Helsinki held fast to its condition that no territory could be leased to the USSR for military purposes.[65]

At the next negotiating session, that very evening of October 23, Stalin was again present. The Finns read out a statement on behalf of their government and agreed to offer some islands in the Gulf of Finland that had not been requested by the Soviets, as well as to discuss Suursaari (Hogland). Stalin pointed out to the returning Finnish delegation that his original proposal—the Hanko Cape, the western Rybachy Peninsula near Petsamo in the north, the Karelian Isthmus— had been his indispensable minimum. Still, the despot, who showed himself extremely well versed in the geographical details, did soften his territorial demands, seizing a pencil and drawing a new line across the Karelian Isthmus on a general staff map. It ran slightly south of the border he had first named. That, Stalin concluded, was the best he could do. Two hours of mostly fruitless exchanges ensued, until the Finnish delegation decided to take their leave. "Is it your intention to provoke a conflict?" a surprised Molotov asked. Stalin smiled enigmatically.[66]

The Finns were in the process of preparing to book the next train back to Helsinki when the phone rang, summoning them back to the Kremlin—a sign either of a Soviet ultimatum or, the Finns hoped, of Stalin's climbdown. At 11:00 p.m., Molotov opened by reading a formal memorandum that contained a precise formulation of the new line Stalin had hand drawn. It did, however, contain still more concessions: the strength of a Soviet garrison at Hanko would be not 5,000, but 4,000, and the length of the lease would be altered from thirty years to the date on which the current war in Europe ended.[67] As Stalin knew, the British held Gibraltar, on the Spanish coast at the entrance to the Mediterranean, indefinitely. Again, however, the Finns declared that they needed to consult at home. They departed by train on October 24.[68] By now, Finland's mobilization was complete: all men ages twenty-two to forty for the army, and up to age fifty for the auxiliary Schutz Corps—more than a quarter million total. Beria reported to Stalin that Tanner, on October 26, had told the Social Democratic faction in Helsinki that "the situation is entirely critical" and that further military mobilization would be necessary.[69]

Soviet forces deployed to the new bases in Lithuania, Latvia, and Estonia were issued strict orders not to interfere in domestic affairs.[70] "During the first imperialist war, the Bolsheviks overestimated the situation," Stalin explained to Zhdanov and Dimitrov (October 25), an implicit criticism of Lenin. "The masses must be led to revolution gradually! Slogans must be brought out that will help the masses break with Social D[emocratic] leaders!" He concluded: "We believe that in our pacts of mutual assistance (Estonia, Latvia, Lithuania) we have found the right form to allow us to bring a number of countries into the Soviet Union's sphere of influence. But for that we must wait, strictly observe their internal regimes and independence. We shall not push for their Sovietization. The time will come when they will do that themselves!"[71]

Stalin had not demanded any territory from the Baltic states, perhaps because he had in mind their eventual Sovietization. Perverse as it may seem, his demands for territory from Finland indicated the absence of a plan for eventual wholesale Sovietization—otherwise, why seek pieces? He was having severe difficulty getting this message across, however. The Finnish negotiators, after the second—and, from Stalin's point of view, unusually long—hiatus, boarded a train to return to the Soviet Union on October 31. Almost simultaneously, Molotov, at an extraordinary session of the Supreme Soviet, delivered a speech mocking the Western democracies while also publicly revealing the heretofore secret Soviet negotiating demands made to Finland. Excerpts of the speech were broadcast on Radio Moscow.[72] This public declaration was apparently intended to bring the pressure of world opinion to bear upon Finland. The action also seemed to indicate that Stalin was not bluffing about the "minimalist" quality of his demands, for, once they were made public, they could not be relinquished without loss of prestige.

Molotov's maneuver disoriented the Helsinki government. Just after midnight on October 31–November 1, the Finnish prime minister decided to order Paasikivi and Tanner back to the capital. But at a 3:00 a.m. cabinet meeting, the ministers were divided, with some arguing that recalling the delegation would be interpreted as a unilateral move to terminate negotiations. The cabinet opted to consult by phone with Paasikivi and the negotiating team, effectively putting the onus on them. Reached at Viipuri later that morning, members of the delegation were no less at a loss about how to respond to Molotov's speech, but, not wanting to be responsible for the momentous decision of appearing to break off the talks, they called Helsinki just before Terijoki, the border station on the Finnish side, to report that they had firmly decided to travel on, even though they had no writ to meet the Soviet demands.

Privately, Molotov told Kollontai, whom he had summoned from Stockholm to receive instructions, that "our troops will be in Helsinki in three days, and then the stubborn Finns will be forced to sign an accord that in Moscow they reject."[73] Paasikivi and company arrived in Moscow on November 2 and were invited to the last day of a three-day extraordinary session of the Supreme Soviet, attended by

2,000 people, including 800 invited spectators in the balcony and loges. The day before, part of former eastern Poland had been formally incorporated into the Ukrainian SSR. November 2 was the turn of former eastern Poland's Belorussian-speaking territory to be formally admitted into the Belorussian SSR.[74] On the evening of November 3, the Finnish delegation was again received in Molotov's Kremlin office, for the third round of negotiations; this time Stalin was absent, however. Instead, deputy foreign affairs commissar Potyomkin attended. The session broke up after an hour, with both sides digging in their heels. As the Finns moved to depart, Molotov stated ominously, "We civilians can see no further in the matter; now it is the turn of the military to have their say."[75]

PERSISTENCE

The Finns spent November 4 visiting the Tretyakov Gallery and making the rounds of the Scandinavian representatives. At the Norwegian legation, a call came in from the Finnish legation: it relayed a Kremlin summons for the Finns to yet another bargaining session. This time, Stalin attended. He emphasized how no Russian government had ever tolerated the independence of Finland, but the USSR did. He reiterated the transcendent importance of the Gulf of Finland to Soviet security. He reminded the Finns that they could cede the Hanko Cape in any form they preferred: lease, sale, exchange. The Finnish delegation once more declared Hanko beyond discussion. "Do you need these islands?" Stalin suddenly asked, stabbing his finger toward a wall map, which had little red circles drawn around three small islands (Hermansö, Koö, Hästö-Busö) just east of Hanko. The Soviet Union, he said, would be willing to settle for a leased base on these little islands most Finns had never even heard of.[76]

Again, the Finnish team had no authority to agree, and requested a break to consult Helsinki. November 5 was a Sunday, making it impossible to gather all the members of the Finnish government. On November 6, the Soviets held their customary eve-of-the-anniversary celebration at the Bolshoi.[77] Molotov's holiday address, published the next day in *Pravda,* boasted that with the "liberation campaign" in eastern Poland, the frontiers of socialism were expanding and the capitalist world "getting a bit squeezed and retreating." Voroshilov, in his remarks to the troops on November 7, took note of the Soviet victory over Japan at the Halha River and the reconquest of western Ukraine and western Belorussia, labeled Britain and France "instigators and zealous continuers of war," as well as "aggressors," and celebrated the "mutual interests of the two great countries" that had signed the Hitler-Stalin Pact.[78]

Finland, with a population of 4 million, was defying a great power of 170 million. Stalin nonetheless kept trying to reach a deal.[79] At 10:00 p.m. on November 7, Molotov hosted the foreign commissariat's Revolution Day reception for foreign envoys at the Spiridonovka. Dinner followed a musical program by the country's leading artists. Tanner was seated at Molotov's table. (Paasikivi, complaining of a slight cold, had declined to attend.) Molotov, among more than a dozen toasts, after each of which he drained his glass, proposed one to Finland, wishing for success in the negotiations. Tanner rose to reciprocate. Beria's name card was also at the table, but his place was occupied by his deputy, Merkulov, who sat directly adjacent to Tanner and was uncommunicative. Mikoyan, also at the head table, approached Tanner in private and was evidently astonished to be told that the Soviet demands were excessive; Mikoyan retorted that they were "minimal." The foreign trade commissar, according to Tanner, pointed out that "Stalin is a Georgian, I'm an Armenian, and many of the rest [in our government] are national minorities. We understand the position of a small country well."[80]

Also at the head table was Schulenburg, who, introducing himself to Tanner, said that he had flown in specially from Berlin that day to be present, and that the German foreign ministry expected a Finnish-Soviet deal. (Hitler, after being apprised of the details, had judged Stalin's demands to be moderate.)[81] Not only had Germany declined to help militarily if it came to war, but Britain, France, the United States, and even Sweden had advised Helsinki not to count on military support.[82] As the Soviet joke had it at the time, when the Finns asked the Swedes to send tanks, the Swedes replied, "How many? One or all three?" Stalin, however, took no chances: when having Soviet demands leaked into the stream of intelligence channels, he made sure to emphasize that Moscow would refrain from impinging in any way upon the Ålands, a group of Swedish-populated islands under Finnish suzerainty. Any Soviet presence there would threaten Stockholm. The leaks offered reassurance for Hitler as well: Swedish iron ore exports to Nazi Germany sailed right by that strategic archipelago.[83]

CREDIBILITY GAP

Field Marshal Mannerheim had been urging compromise on his government. Clear-eyed about the imperialist nature of Russia, he nonetheless saw the basis for a deal, and privately explained to the civilians that the Red Army was immensely bigger and better armed than during Finnish resistance, some twenty years earlier—and now the Finns were alone.[84] But Foreign Minister Erkko and Prime Minister Cajander continued to dismiss Stalin's security concerns over Leningrad as a ruse. Other members of the government worried that Stalin would never stop at the acquisition of military bases, suspecting that if Finland conceded any territory, it would face escalating Soviet demands, immediately or in the future, and that Stalin would use territorial encroachments as a pressure point to curtail or even eliminate Finland's sovereign right to independent action. Back on September 22, 1939, Molotov had told the Estonians in the Kremlin—in a message that might also have reached Helsinki—that "the Soviet Union has become a powerful state with a highly developed industry, and in possession of a great military force," so that "the status quo which was established twenty years ago, when the Soviet Union was weakened by civil war, can no longer be considered as adequate to the present situation."[85] But neither Stalin nor even Molotov had said anything like that to the Finnish delegation. On the contrary, they and others in the Soviet regime had repeatedly underscored the Soviets' preferential regard for Finland.

Hitler, from the start, had wanted all of Czechoslovakia—and more—which contemporaries had failed to grasp. They also failed to understand that Stalin was a revolutionary imperialist with limits. He had suppressed not only the genuine, bottom-up collectivization by anarchists in Spain, but also a Communist putsch there, and he pushed back strongly against the revolutionary impulses of the Communists in China. Regarding Finland, too, in his own way, he was showing a sense of limits. Paasikivi, during this latest negotiating pause, telegrammed Helsinki to ask if he could offer the island of Jussarö, in the west, and the fort of Ino (on Cape Inoniemi), in the east (opposite Kronstadt), suggesting that with these concessions, more favorable terms might be reached on Soviet demands for the Karelian Isthmus and near Petsamo, in the far north. But at this decisive phase, the Finnish government took Stalin's last-minute concessions, which aimed to close a deal, as evidence that he would soften still more, and might be bluffing altogether. On the morning of November 8, Helsinki telegrammed instructions—as inflexible as ever. Paasikivi, attempting to acquire *some* authority to cut a deal, wrote back, "Instructions received. If no agreement on this basis, may we let the negotiations be broken off?" Erkko did not take the bait.[86]

That day, the Soviets were still recuperating from the holiday, according to Tanner. On November 9, Molotov had the Soviet chargé d'affaires in Helsinki, the undercover NKVD operative Yelisei Sinitsyn, whose intelligence experience dated back just a few months to Soviet-conquered Lwów/Lvov, call on Erkko. Sinitsyn emphasized the differences between tsarist and Soviet treatment of Finland, but Erkko would not budge.[87] That same evening, the Finns were in Molotov's office, again with Stalin present. Paasikivi read out the Finnish government reply to Stalin's proposal for just the three islands east of Hanko Cape: negative. "The eyes of our opposite numbers opened wide," Tanner later wrote. "It was clear that they had expected us to assent gladly to this suggestion." Paasikivi brought out a chart and proposed to offer the southern part of Suursaari (Hogland) Island. He tried to get Stalin to abandon demands for any territory in western Finland (nearer the entrance to the gulf) and focus solely on eastern Finland (nearer Leningrad). Stalin: "You don't even offer Ino?"[88]

The Finns took their leave. Stalin retreated to the Little Corner with Molotov until 11:05 p.m.[89] No further sessions had been agreed to. Still, that circumstance had occurred twice before, and each time Molotov's office had reinitiated contact. Sure enough, just after midnight, a courier arrived at the Finnish legation. But to the Finns' dismay, the message, from Molotov, contained neither a new proposal nor an invitation, just casuistry about the concept of "territory." Nonetheless, the Soviet side was maintaining communication. Later that morning (November 10), after a bit of sleep, the Finns sent their own letter. But they waited in vain on Saturday and Sunday (November 11–12) for another summons.

Privately, Mekhlis, head of the Red Army political department, told a gathering of the defense commission of the writers' union, regarding Finland (November 10), that "our army is on the border, ready." He added that "Germany was undertaking a useful thing, shattering the British empire. The latter's destruction will lead to a general collapse of imperialism—this is clear." Mekhlis, according to notes by the playwright Vishnevsky, stressed that the USSR's main enemy was, "of course, England."[90] Churchill continued to work to prevent a full-fledged Nazi-Soviet alliance. "I find your demands on Finland completely natural and normal," he told Maisky over lunch (November 13), while reaffirming his view that it would be better for the Soviet Union, rather than Nazi Germany, to dominate the Baltic Sea. "I would like to hope, however, that the USSR will not resort to force to resolve its dispute with Finland. If the USSR did so, then—you yourself understand—it would make a most painful impression here in England and for a long period of time would render the improvement of Anglo-Soviet relations impossible."[91]

Also on November 13, the Finnish delegation was called home from Moscow.[92] No ranking member of the Soviet foreign affairs commissariat saw them off.[93] *Pravda* (November 13) sent them off with accusations that the Helsinki government was allowing Finland to be turned into "an armed camp" targeting the USSR.

Stalin's family had become an afterthought, but his children could suddenly remind him of their existence: that same day, Vasily happened to write a letter to his father. "Little Svetlana got things mixed up telling you that I want to come home for the [winter] holidays and that you authorized me to come," he wrote. "Papa! I'll not come home again until I finish school, even though I miss you very much. There is only a little time to go and I decided to tough it out, because I think that it would be more pleasant for you to see me after I've finished school, and for me too it would be more pleasant. I think you'll understand me and agree with me."[94]

Internationally, Stalin made sure not to appear the aggressor. On November 13, V. I. Chuykov, commander of an army group, had baldly declared from the dais of the Belorussian Supreme Soviet, "If the party says so, we'll follow the lines of the song—first Warsaw, then Berlin." On the ciphered report from the Belorussian party boss, Panteleimon Ponomarenko, Stalin wrote a note for Voroshilov: "Chuykov, it seems, is a fool, if not an enemy element. I suggest you give him a swift kick. This is a minimum."[95]

On November 14, Schulenburg called on Molotov to ascertain the disposition of the Soviet-Finnish negotiations, and he found the foreign affairs commissar "very angry at the Finns" and downright mystified. Molotov voiced suspicions that the Finns' stubbornness "was being bolstered by England."[96]

On November 23, Hitler would summon 200 Wehrmacht officers to urge accelerated preparations for an offensive against the Western powers. "The purpose of this conference is to give you an idea of the world of my thoughts, which governs me in the face of future events, and to tell you my decisions," he began, before reviewing German history and developments under his rule, including the victory over Poland in a war he forced. Germany and he himself had to fight, Hitler insisted. "In fighting I see the fate of all creatures," he noted, encapsulating his worldview. "Nobody can avoid fighting if he does not want to go under." Hitler deemed this "struggle" to be "racial" and material (for oil, rubber, food), and he asserted that "the moment is favorable now; in six months it might not be so anymore." Just weeks before, Hitler had escaped Elser's attempt to assassinate him in Munich. "As a final factor I must, in all modesty, list my own person: irreplaceable," Hitler concluded. "Neither a military nor a civilian personality could take my place. Attempts at assassination may be repeated. . . . The fate of the Reich depends on me alone."[97]

Stalin, as earnestly as he worked for a deal, seems not to have grasped that a Finnish concession of any national territory, in purely procedural terms, required a five-sixths majority in the Finnish parliament, which, the Finns explained, was far from automatic. Accustomed to the Supreme Soviet, he mocked this barrier, proposing that they count his and Molotov's votes, too.[98] Nonetheless, it is beyond doubt that the despot was not *crudely* bullying the Finnish negotiators, as he had the Balts.[99] Why he was treating Finland differently remains unclear. It was not because he feared or even respected the Finnish military. Perhaps it was a dose of sentimentality: it had been in Finland that he first met Lenin, in December 1905, and he himself had found sanctuary there from the tsarist police.[100] Perhaps it reflected realism about the depth of Finnish national pride. Whatever the motive, Stalin was far from being maximalist, and he had reduced his demands multiple times. And yet he could not get the Helsinki government to take him at his word.[101] Stalin's track record and methods—beginning with the approaches by the NKVD station chief in Helsinki—did not inspire confidence. Still, in his own way, he had made plain his sincerity: he had attended six of the seven formal negotiations, on October 12, 14, and 23 (twice) and November 4 and 9. Stalin did not countenance, let alone attend, that many bargaining sessions with anyone else.

WISHFUL THINKING

After the Finns' departure from Moscow, the Soviets had quietly stepped up their massing of troops. The inexperienced NKVD intelligence operative Sinitsyn, on November 12, had sent an ingratiating report to Moscow on the supposedly egregious state of the Finnish army and the discontent of its soldiers, as well as Finland's economic limitations.[102] On November 15, during a seven-hour marathon in the Little Corner, Stalin directed Zhdanov and Meretskov, a member of the Leningrad military district's council as party boss there, to tour the front.[103] The Finnish government announced that citizens who had evacuated from border areas could now avail themselves of free train rides home. Reservists who had been called up were also to be sent home. Schools were reopened. People removed the protective strips on their home windows. These military precautions had been viewed as necessary even before negotiations had commenced; now, after negotiations had failed, they were no longer necessary?[104]

Finnish intelligence, it seems, interpreted the accelerated Soviet military buildup as an exercise in turning up the pressure, to force the Finns back into disadvantageous negotiations. Soviet newspapers had not announced a termination of the negotiations. Finnish intelligence further surmised that the Soviets were hardly likely to attack during harsh winter conditions, or without first issuing an ultimatum, allowing time to respond.[105] Finland, moreover, had a binding nonaggression pact with the USSR. Stalin, however, cynically circumvented that obstacle, borrowing a page out of Hitler's Poland playbook: on the afternoon of November 26, five shells and two grenades were fired on Soviet positions at the border, killing four and wounding nine, manufacturing a casus belli.[106] Already that morning, *Pravda* had likened the Finnish prime minister to a "withering snake," a "circus clown standing on his head," and "a puppet of the imperialist powers." That evening, Molotov summoned the Finnish ambassador, denounced the Finnish "provocation" at the border, and demanded that all Finnish troops be pulled back some twelve to fifteen miles from the frontier.

An investigation by the Finns indicated that the shots had emanated from the Soviet side. They were right. In an operation under Leningrad NKVD chief Goglidze, Soviet forces had deliberately fired at their own lines.[107] (Soviet soldiers were killed; Hitler, in his staging, had had Polish prison inmates killed.) A TASS communiqué in the name of the Leningrad military district, published in *Izvestiya* and *Pravda* on November 27, reported the fatalities and blamed Finland. That evening, Stalin received Sinitsyn, recalled from Helsinki, in the Little Corner. (As it happened, that same evening in Berlin, Soviet military intelligence operative Captain Zaitsev ["Bine"] managed to meet with Ilse Stöbe ["Alta"]: the breathtaking Soviet spy network from Warsaw would now be reconstituted in Berlin.)[108]

Around midnight on November 27–28, after prolonged internal debate in Helsinki, the Finnish embassy delivered its government's response to Molotov's accusatory note about the border incident. The Finns maintained that Soviet troops had not been in range of Finnish batteries, so they could not have been killed by Finnish fire, and suggested a mutual frontier troop withdrawal. On November 28, Molotov announced that, owing to the "aggression" by the Finns, the Soviets had been relieved of their obligations under the bilateral nonaggression pact, even though the accord legally forbade unilateral renunciation.[109] The Finnish envoy was summoned to the Soviet foreign ministry and told by Potyomkin that diplomatic relations had been severed. To maintain operational surprise, a Soviet plant told the Finnish and Swedish military attachés in Moscow that the Soviet stance was actually "neither war nor peace," the old Trotsky line at Brest-Litovsk. Late on November 29, the desperate Finnish government sent instructions for its envoy to convey to Molotov, saying that if the USSR resumed negotiations, Soviet demands could be discussed.[110]

Before dawn on November 30—without a formal declaration of war—Soviet artillery and aerial bombardment commenced, the planes taking off from their new base in Estonia, and a 120,000-troop Red Army force smashed across the frontier. "We go into Finland not as conquerors, but as friends and liberators of the Finnish people from the yoke of the landowners and capitalists," Meretskov and Zhdanov wrote in a proclamation to the troops. "For the security of the USSR's northwestern borders and the glorious city of Lenin! For our beloved Motherland! For the Great Stalin! Forward, sons of the Soviet people, soldiers of the Red Army, to the destruction of the enemy!"[111]

Even as Soviet bombers rained explosives and leaflets on Helsinki, the Finnish cabinet did not comprehend that full-scale war had been unleashed.[112] Somehow, Stalin's open military mobilization had come across as no more credible than his diplomatic concessions.[113] The banker-diplomat Paasikivi, writing in his diary on the day the war began, despaired, "We have allowed our country to slide into war with the giant Soviet Union although . . . 1) Nobody has promised us any help. 2) The Soviet Union has its hands free."[114] On December 1, 1939, Beria ordered Gulag camps to prepare for 26,500 anticipated POWs.[115]

PEOPLE'S FINLAND

Defied by Helsinki, Stalin became determined to get a friendly government. Back on November 10, 1939, he had summoned Otto Kuusinen, the son of a tailor and a top official in the Comintern, to the Little Corner.[116] Kuusinen (b. 1881) had been a participant in the "German October" Communist putsch fiasco in 1923. He had gone on to betray Zinoviev, the nominal Comintern chairman, running to Stalin behind his back. Kuusinen ended up being the only survivor of the Finnish party's Central Committee to reside in the Soviet Union; all the rest had been shot or incarcerated in the Gulag. On November 13—the day the Finnish negotiators departed Moscow—Kuusinen had sent a cryptic summons to Arvo "Poika" (Boy) Tuominen (b. 1894), the general secretary of the Finnish Communist party and the last survivor of Lenin's Comintern presidium, who was in the safety of Swedish exile. Tuominen had sat in Finnish prisons for the better part of a decade, dreaming of the day when "the workers" would come to power in Finland. In 1933, he had been allowed to leave for Moscow. In 1938, he had somehow managed to get himself and his wife out, on assignment to Sweden. "Stalin could be a convivial companion in intimate, friendly circles," he recalled of his occasional audiences, adding that the Soviet leader "undeniably was a highly gifted and above all a highly energetic man."[117] Now Tuominen declined multiple summonses sent via courier to return to Moscow, citing ill health.[118]

Stalin named Kuusinen, without Tuominen, to lead a puppet regime, called the Finnish Democratic Republic or "People's Government," whose existence was announced as having been discovered via a Soviet-intercepted radio broadcast on the day of the outbreak of war, as if the new "government" had formed on its own.[119] "It is necessary," exhorted the "intercepted" proclamation, published in *Pravda* on December 1, 1939, "to establish a broad laboring people's front: the entire working class, the peasantry, artisans, petty traders, and the laboring intelligentsia; to unite the immense majority of our nation in a single united front for the defense of our interests; and to bring to power a government of the laboring nation basing itself on that front—that is, a People's Government."[120] Moscow immediately recognized the People's Government and gave it a "People's Army" corps of up to 13,500 troops, drawing on ethnic Finnish inhabitants of Soviet Karelia, which, it was hoped, would attract rank-and-file soldiers from Finland, thereby splitting the enemy's forces.[121]

Molotov had forewarned German ambassador Schulenburg that "it is not excluded that there will be the formation of a Finnish government friendly to the Soviet Union, as well as to Germany," adding that it would be not a "Soviet government but a democratic republic type. No one will create soviets there."[122] This posture was repeated in the confidential explanation to Communist parties around the world, as well as in Kuusinen's public appeal, which declared his government "provisional," until a newly elected Finnish diet could meet.[123] All in all, it must have seemed like a brilliant strategy: preempt German or British use of Finland for aggression against the USSR; shift international borders to enhance Soviet security; and move to install a pro-Soviet regime, keeping open a future full Sovietization. The ideologue Zhdanov, citing Soviet intelligence, had insisted that the workers and peasants of Finland, who constituted the bulk of the nation's army, were ready to welcome Soviet forces. Even Voroshilov predicted that "the working masses of Finland . . . are threatening to mete out justice on those who pursue a policy hostile to the Soviet Union." After all, had not the Ukrainians and Belorussians of eastern Poland, in early fall 1939, greeted the Red Army as "liberators" in joyous meetings?[124]

Initially, the People's Government was established in Terijoki, the small village resort of summer houses on the Finnish side of the border where the rebel Kronstadt sailors had once obtained refuge.[125] At the outbreak of hostilities, the Finns had abandoned the settlement. Whether Kuusinen even went out to the site of his own government is unclear. He was received in the Little Corner on December 2. That day, *Pravda* carried a front-page story with photographs of Molotov and Kuusinen, along with Stalin, Voroshilov, and Zhdanov, signing a "treaty" between the USSR and the Finnish People's Government, which agreed to all Soviet terms of territorial transfer: shifting the border westward on the Karelian Isthmus, thus granting 1,500 square miles of territory to the USSR; selling five islands in the Gulf of Finland; and selling the western end of the Rybachy Peninsula, in the far north near Petsamo.[126] Military basing rights on the Hanko Cape were granted in a "confidential protocol." In exchange, the puppet government was awarded Soviet Karelia—not 2,120 square miles of its territory, as discussed during the negotiations with Finland, but the entire 27,000. A map of this new "People's Finland" appeared in *Pravda* (December 3, 1939).

Here was one reason Stalin had not issued a formal declaration of war: the Soviet Union was not at war with Finland, but *supporting* that country's "democratic forces" against the "fascist military clique" of the "White" Finnish government in Helsinki.[127] Stalin had Beria collect surviving Finns from the Gulag, including one of Kuusinen's sons (from his first wife), Esa (b. 1906), who had been arrested in Karelia, contracted tuberculosis in Siberian camps, and was now named a government official.[128] Kuusinen "was at bottom a man of immense, rather cynical self-confidence," his estranged second wife, Aino, recalled. "He had no practical knowledge and could never get on terms with ordinary Finnish workers and their families. . . . Throughout his life, the failure of the Communist rising in Finland in 1918 rankled like an open wound. . . . Kuusinen once told me himself that he dreamed of controlling Finland and, eventually, being 'proconsul' for the whole of Scandinavia; then, after the rest of Europe had surrendered to Communism, he would return to Moscow and be the éminence grise of the Soviet empire."[129]

MILITARY DILETTANTE

Hitler had never risen above the rank of corporal in the Great War, but Stalin had never served at all. He had not involved himself in the operational details of the summer 1939 border war at the Halha River (which had been the work of Stern and Zhukov). Nor had he micromanaged the fall 1939 invasion of eastern Poland (commanded by Semyon Timoshenko, of the Kiev military district, and Mikhail Kovalyov, of the Belorussian). The Winter War, as the Soviet invasion of Finland came to be known, proved to be Stalin's first genuine test as a military figure since the Russian civil war. "The scattered episodes in Manchuria, at Lake Khasan or in Mongolia," he later said, "were trifles [*chepukha*], not war, just episodes on a little patch, strictly limited."[130] In fact, the 1939 border war victory against the Japanese, as well as the German-assisted "promenade" through Poland, had induced smugness in Moscow. The Finns, unlike the Poles, did not even have an air force or armor apart from some 1918 vintage tanks. They lacked wireless, too, forcing them to rely on field telephones and, when these inevitably became disrupted, on human runners. But it was the Soviets who turned out to be wholly unprepared for the war Stalin unleashed.

If the negotiations for the pact had been Molotov's star turn, the Winter War should have been Voroshilov's, but the war planning and the war itself were run out of Stalin's office, on the high-frequency phone.[131] Many top officials were kept in the dark, and if they had the naïveté to complain, Stalin would remind them, "When necessary, you, too, will be informed."[132] At a meeting of the Main Military Council, Shaposhnikov had submitted a battle plan calling for a massive invasion force attacking in a narrow-front assault to smash through the formidable Finnish defenses, in a campaign of several months. Stalin respected Boris Mikhailovich, as the despot deferentially addressed his chief of staff, a former tsarist staff officer who had served in that role from 1928 to 1931 and again since 1937. But Stalin dismissed his battle plan as unworthy of a great power. He had shifted the war planning to the Leningrad military district, as if it were a mere local affair of the northwest. The logistics had to be rushed. Worse, Meretskov, the commander there, bent to the despot, as well as to Leningrad party boss Zhdanov, when they insisted that Finnish resistance could be smashed in a mere twelve to fifteen days.[133]

Meretskov's revised battle plan, delivered on October 29, 1939, dutifully slashed the number of Soviet forces necessary, while calling for an attack at widely separated points across the entire 800-mile border—the wide-front approach of the Russian civil war, two decades earlier. Just 12 divisions would strike at an equal number of different points. Stalin chose not to have the Main Military Council discuss the new plan. He had Shaposhnikov sent on holiday to Sochi.[134]

Thanks to Stalin's shift of the economy to wartime production and his personal attention to military factories, the Soviet Union was armed to the teeth. In 1939, the armaments commissariat had been expanded into four, for armaments, ammunition, aircraft, and shipbuilding. The Finns, however, had built a series of defense belts, known as the Mannerheim Line (for their commander in chief), made up of reinforced concrete emplacements two stories high and topped by armor-plated roofs. Although many of the pillboxes and bunkers were too old to withstand modern shell fire, some were sturdy, and there were antitank traps, log barriers, ditches, and minefields. Beyond the line, primitive traps (boulders, barbed wire strung across sticks) were laid. The Finns also glued portraits of Stalin onto structures, making Red Army troops hesitate before firing. Above all, the line was complemented by marshy forest, countless lakes, and other natural obstacles, which constituted a key reason the war had been started in the dead of winter: the frozen watery wastes would presumably allow tanks and wheeled artillery to cross. But in such unsuitable terrain, Soviet mechanized units attempted a German-style war of maneuver.

Without sufficient room to maneuver its heavy forces or bring its superior firepower to bear, the Red Army saw entire divisions sliced to pieces (or frozen to death). Moreover, in trying to race ahead in simple frontal assaults without accompanying infantry, the Red Army exposed its tanks to ad hoc attacks by flammable liquids stuffed in bottles and ignited by hand-lit wicks, first used in the Spanish civil war and now christened "Molotov cocktails." ("I never knew a tank could burn for quite that long," remarked one Finn.) Furthermore, the north's long winter darkness blunted the advantages of Soviet air power. Back on November 19, eleven days before launch, when Meretskov had toured the region to fix deployment problems, his staff car had become stuck in the deep snow, leading him to conclude that "it would be very difficult to conduct military operations in this region."[135] The 1939–40 winter turned out to be especially cold: a site on the Karelian Isthmus recorded a record low of 45 degrees below zero (minus 43 Celsius).[136] The Red Army suffered from pervasive frostbite. Neither the climate nor the terrain should have been a surprise.

Finland showed tactical superiority. Dark silhouettes of Red Army soldiers stood out against the white snow, even if they had not lit fires to try to warm themselves, but the Finns adapted to the subarctic wilderness by donning camouflage whites, using mobile troops on skis, and carrying submachine guns to strike at the Soviet flanks or rear, in asymmetric warfare. The Finns called this tactic *motti*, meaning "firewood battle," or "chopping the enemy off in bits." Especially proficient Finnish snipers became known as "White Death."[137] "The Finns have chosen a special combat tactic in the forests: they climb the pine trees, conceal themselves behind the branches, pull white sheets or camouflage garments over themselves, and become completely invisible," Stalin privately marveled. "As our people approach, they get shot down point-blank from the trees."[138] Even when the Finns yielded some territory, they carried off useful supplies and livestock. They also left behind eye-catching consumer goods—bicycles, gramophones, radios—which were booby-trapped.[139] Some Soviet commanders were observed giving orders to attack and then fleeing the battlefield. Complaints were overheard that, while soldiers got a measly 8 rubles per month, officials in the rear were paid 800 rubles—at safe desk jobs. Reports surfaced in Leningrad that returning soldiers were desperately selling army property.[140]

In the censored Soviet public sphere, the information about the hostilities was miserly and distorted. *Pravda* found it necessary to issue denials that the Red Army was on the verge of defeat. At military hospitals in Leningrad, according to the NKVD, crowds surrounded wounded Red Army soldiers to learn what was really happening in the war.[141]

MISCALCULATION EXPOSED

Vladimir Zenzinov, an émigré, arrived from Paris as a war correspondent on January 20, 1940, and eventually managed to get to the front, where he collected letters from home that were found on dead Red Army soldiers. "Corpses were found everywhere—one, two, whole groups," wrote Zenzinov. "There were places where they lay in piles, one on top of the other, in the most horrific and incomprehensible poses." The letters originated from widely distributed geographical regions, Leningrad to Vladivostok. Written by parents, siblings, sweethearts, wives, children, they were mostly personal, contained playful alliteration, and evinced anxiety about their loved ones' possible wartime injury or death. They frequently ended by invoking God. They mentioned listening to the radio for morsels of information. They overflowed with complaints about red tape over payments to families whose sons had been conscripted, poor pay on collective farms, excessive taxation, and a dearth of available clothing or footwear. Still, they usually referred to the Finns as "fascists, "White Guardists," or "agents of the English bourgeoisie" and urged the conscripts "to rally around our beloved father and friend Comrade Stalin," "defend our sacred borders," and "liberate the Finnish people." Zenzinov concluded that "the whole Soviet population was sincerely convinced that the attacking side was Finland, set against the Soviet Union by the imperialist governments of England and France, and that the Soviet Union was only defending itself."[142]

Zenzinov perhaps underestimated people's desire to ensure their letters got through. (They did not know that while just about every letter from the front was perlustrated and censored, not every letter from the rear was.) Be that as it may, hundreds of these handwritten letters convey a strong sense of inculcated vocabulary ("speaking Bolshevik") and Soviet patriotism.

No such rallying around the flag occurred vis-à-vis the People's Government, which ruled no Finnish people, being located where the country's civilian population had largely been evacuated. With the repulsion of Meretskov's numerous offensives, it acquired no new settlements. Its "personnel" remained in huts at the border village. "In Terijoki there is no government of Finland, and not a single one of Kuusinen's ministers is to be found in Terijoki, nor have they been there," a young reporter for *Signal,* the railroad newspaper, discovered and reported over the telephone to the editorial offices in Moscow. "This government exists on paper only, and our troops suffer immense losses." This reportage never saw the light of day: the NKVD got wind of it.[143] Indeed, about the only operational work in Terijoki was that of the Leningrad branch NKVD, which had moved a field headquarters there and sent back reports about both the emptiness of surrounding villages and attacks by "bandit formations."[144] Although Stalin's People's Government fiasco failed to rally Finns on the basis of supposed class antagonisms, it did stiffen that nation's resolve to fight a war no longer about some islands in the gulf, but about Finland's independent existence.[145]

No foreign country recognized Stalin's stooge regime, and its existence did nothing to alleviate the international perception that Moscow was the aggressor. The arguments that the Soviets had put forth over eastern Poland—that the area was really western Ukraine and western Belorussia, an annexation to "protect" national minorities—did not apply in Finland. The weak League of Nations, with strong British and especially French backing, pronounced the Soviet attack on Finland "illegal" and expelled the USSR on December 14, 1939. Only seven of fifteen Council members voted, violating the League's covenant requiring a majority, and three of those had been added to the Council the day before the vote (South Africa, Bolivia, and Egypt). But the expulsion went through, and it stung. The Soviet Union was the only League member ever to suffer such an indignity.

Stalin had not reckoned with the depth of hostility among the Western powers and the League, failing to consult even the rump experts who had survived his massacres.[146] Nor had he reckoned fully with the negative repercussions of his relationship with Germany. The Soviet invasion of Finland put Hitler in an awkward spot. The German populace had no knowledge of the 1939 Pact's secret protocol granting Finland to a Soviet sphere of influence; what they did know was that fellow "Nordic people" were under attack and that Hitler condoned and aided the aggression. German officials, beginning with the ambassador in Helsinki, tried to change Germany's policy, and some of their complaints reached the Führer, who, in fact, personally sympathized with the Finns. But German diplomats were instructed, more than once, to avoid an anti-Soviet tone even in private conversations on Finland, while arms shipments for Finland from Italy and Hungary were turned back at German ports. In a further outrage, Germany found itself hurriedly evacuating the *Volksdeutsche* (ethnic Germans) from Finland.[147]

The Far East, too, had to be watched. Sorge had reported (November 25, 1939) on discussions among the Japanese general staff about possibly dividing China into three spheres of influence: Japan (northeast, center), the USSR (northwest), and Chiang Kai-shek's Chongqing government (southeast). But in contrast his deal with Hitler over Poland, Stalin never sought to partition China with another power. In any case, as the Chinese Communist party reported to Moscow, the Japanese soon began concentrating additional troops in Manchukuo.[148]

Worst of all, Stalin's Finnish People's Government prevented him from accepting the feelers from the new government in Helsinki. Already on the second day of war, the intransigents in the government who were against a deal had been swept aside, replaced by Finns ready to negotiate many of the concessions that he sought.[149] Finnish politicians, it turned out, had required a show of force in order to agree to a version of Stalin's proposed land-exchange deal and military basing. Wars are won partly with agile responses to unexpected twists and turns but, above all, with political planning in conjunction with military action. "War," as Clausewitz had explained, "should never be thought of as something autonomous but always as an instrument of policy." Had the Soviet attack been cleverly designed as a quick, massive blow, followed by a pause and a demand for immediate return to the political bargaining table, it might have worked after a few days.[150] But such a cunning stratagem would have required a level of subtlety that Stalin, not to mention the broken men around him, lacked. Instead, what transpired was a Soviet catastrophe.[151] "Papa and Mama," a Soviet soldier wrote, in one of the hundreds of letters excerpted in Beria's NKVD reports submitted to the Little Corner, "our army has met enormous resistance. . . . This is a devil's patch, which tanks cannot cross, [instead] sinking in the swamps."[152]

BIRTHDAY BASH

In 1939 and 1940, Stalin authorized 2,000 visits to his office, the peak in his three decades in power. He met foreign officials in Molotov's office as well, and had a hand in additional meetings in Mikoyan's office (to iron out details with German trade representatives).[153] The sessions in the Little Corner frequently stretched to seven hours or more; many ran past midnight, and sometimes until 3:00 a.m. Now, as gallant little Finland attracted the sympathy of the whole world, the Little Corner became even tenser than it had been during the border war with Japan or the high-stakes poker with Hitler and the partition of Poland. Perhaps the stress and long hours took a toll: Stalin had an outbreak of his chronic fevers, streptococ-cus, and staphylococcus, as well as sore throats. Germany's lightning conquest of Poland was fresh in people's minds and made for a devastating contrast to the awkward Soviet thrust into Finland. Adding insult to injury, Schulenburg relayed a German offer to assist the Soviets militarily. "You can imagine it!" recalled Khrushchev. "Hitler was demonstrating our weakness, and he wanted us to admit it by accepting his aid. A feeling of alarm grew in the Soviet leadership."[154]

Serious tensions had arisen in Soviet-German trade and economic relations, too. A Soviet delegation's visit to Germany had begun in October 1939, in con-nection with the new trade agreement, and the Germans had sought to play the consummate hosts, housing the proletarian representatives in the Adlon, Berlin's finest hotel.[155] But the Germans were outraged at a forty-eight-page shopping list presented in late November: not just fighter aircraft, naval cruisers, and artillery, but whole factories, up to 1.5 billion reichsmarks. On December 11, Ribbentrop had to remind Soviet ambassador Shkvartsev that "Germany is at war" and could not go "beyond the humanly possible."[156]

That same day, in a convoy near Suomussalmi, in central Finland, not far from the Soviet border, Mekhlis's car became disabled under fire; several Soviets were wounded. Mekhlis did not reach the Soviet frontier post until thirteen hours later, evidently spending the night in the forest. That same night of December 11–12, after Molotov and Voroshilov had left the Little Corner at almost 1:00 a.m., the despot summoned Beria at 2:30. The unfolding catastrophe had finally been get-ting through via the brutal NKVD reports about the Red Army. On December 15, Stalin ordered Beria to set up seven new NKVD regiments in the rear of Soviet positions, to interdict any soldiers who retreated.[157] But the battlefield situation was not so easily reversed. The despot found himself meeting essentially every night with military men in the Little Corner. On December 15, they were present from 11:00 p.m. until 1:25 a.m.; Voroshilov and Molotov stayed until 5:00 a.m. The brass and the cronies were right back that night. From the evening of December 18 through to the wee hours of December 20, Molotov and Voroshilov were in the Little Corner on and off for nine hours, and then back again the evening of the 20th, until 3:45 a.m. By then, it was officially Stalin's sixtieth birthday (December 21).[158]

Victory in Finland was supposed to have been celebrated as part of the jubilee, and Zhdanov had commissioned a score from Shostakovich to be played in the streets of Helsinki. The *Suite on Finnish Themes* would go unperformed, but the birthday bash went ahead in the St. Catherine's Hall of the Grand Kremlin Palace. The evening called for exactly sixty guests for Stalin's sixty years (some accounts record seventy or eighty); Stalin shook each person's hand individually. After the inevitable toasts to the despot, he answered with toasts to Soviet pilots, artillerymen, tank drivers, sailors, workers, peasants. Everyone got smashed. Molotov, noting that "I do not know a greater leader than Lenin," observed in his toast that "in some ways Stalin has surpassed Lenin. Lenin for many years lived removed from his people, from his country, in emigration, but comrade Stalin the whole time lives and lived among the people, in our country." The despot, entourage in tow, repaired to the adjacent St. George's Hall for a night of entertainment. Molotov danced away, showing off the results of his tango lessons with Voroshilov, while also singing—in key.[159]

Arkady Raikin, a twenty-nine-year-old born in tsarist Russia's Latvian-speaking territory and educated in a Jewish heder, was a master of skits and impersonations, especially of heedless Soviet bureaucrats. That night, he had been summoned to the Kremlin for the first time, but then he was told that the summons was off, so he spent the night performing at a B-list gathering at the House of the Actor. Upon returning to his room at the Hotel Moskva, he was suddenly informed that he had been sought throughout the city—to perform for Stalin—but that now it was too late. Raikin went up to bed. Then the telephone interrupted his slumber at around 5:00 a.m.: he had to be downstairs immediately, whence he was whisked by government vehicle to the Kremlin, next door, and escorted into the St. George's Hall. The entertainment planned by the committee for artistic affairs had long ended, but Stalin and his entourage were still there, so a second "concert" had to be conjured up. (Raikin had discovered upon exiting his hotel that the Bolshoi soprano Natalya Spiller had been bundled into the same waiting car.) The tables in the Grand Kremlin Palace still overflowed with food and drink, and Stalin asked Raikin the purpose of the little netlike string bag he was holding. Raikin said he had brought it for groceries, just in case some became available, the way Soviet inhabitants did when roaming urban streets.

The eating and drinking lasted until 8:00 a.m., in what the Comintern head Dimitrov described as "an unforgettable night."[160] The mischievous Raikin further recalled that when the gathering finally ended, Khrushchev followed Stalin to the exit, clinging to the despot's waist.[161] Alexander Pirogov (b. 1899), the great bass—and the youngest USSR People's Artist ever—also received his summons to the Grand Kremlin Palace birthday bash while celebrations were well under way. He had just finished singing Glinka's *Ivan Susanin* at the Bolshoi and, exhausted, declined the "invitation." His aghast friends and relatives expected his arrest. Pirogov was nonplussed. "It's more difficult to repress me than a people's commissar," he is said to have asserted. "A people's commissar is a political figure, and few are those who could not be replaced in the government. But with a famous actor it's harder."[162]

Sergei Prokofyev had composed a special cantata for Stalin, *Zdravitsa* ("Hail"), using folk melodies; it was performed by Nikolai Golovanov, director of the USSR's Great Symphony Orchestra, which played classical music for Soviet radio.[163] The Red Army chorus gave a series of special performances, and the theme of Stalin as "Leader and Architect of the Red Army" received renewed emphasis. Stalin's image was sewn into Turkmen and Ukrainian carpets, northern bone carvings, miniature Palekh lacquer boxes. The State Tretyakov Gallery mounted *Stalin and the People of the Soviet Land in the Fine Arts,* featuring a mass of oil paintings, busts, engravings, and book illustrations. "The will of millions long ago tasked art with the theme of Stalin as the central theme," wrote one summary.[164] Among the most celebrated works was Alexander Gerasimov's *Stalin and Voroshilov in the Kremlin,* depicting them standing tall, dressed in military overcoats and caps, against a cloudy sky and the Kremlin walls and towers.[165] Most artists had to paint Stalin from retouched photographs, but the despot had sat for Gerasimov.[166] A livelier composition, *An Unforgettable Meeting* (1937) by Vasily Yefanov, depicted Stalin smiling and grasping, with both hands, the hand of a young maiden at a reception for female activists in heavy industry; in a wood-paneled Kremlin room laden with flowers, Orjonikidze, Molotov, Khrushchev, Kaganovich, Voroshilov, Budyonny, Kalinin, and the now deceased Krupskaya are shown applauding.[167]

Stalin received his first Order of Lenin, a decade after the award had been introduced. As bards in each Union republic outdid one another in panegyrics, "Stalin Prizes" were inaugurated for the country's top scientists, military designers, and artists—the top awards ("first class") came with a staggering cash award of 100,000 rubles, at a time when yearly wages averaged perhaps 10,000.[168] More than 4,000 students received Stalin scholarships. The party organized group tours of the buildings in which Stalin had lived, in Solvychegodsk, Tbilisi, and Gori. A new museum of the old Bolshevik underground in Baku was opened.[169] Soviet newsreels depicted how factories all across the country had fulfilled production pledges for the approaching occasion, but also showed pilgrimages to Stalin's birth hovel in Gori, even though Stalin had denied TASS permission to convey the hordes' enthusiasm.[170] "Who won at 'Krivi' [Georgian boxing]? Soso!" recalled Grigory Elisabedashvili, a school chum at both the Gori parish school and Tiflis seminary. "Who could throw the ball the farthest? Soso! At the same time who could read the most books? Soso! . . . Who sings better and more enchantingly than everyone? Soso!" Stalin forbade publication of these recollections, noting that, "apart from everything else, the author shamelessly lied."[171]

The despot did authorize *Pravda* (December 21) to carry a new "short biography," in twelve broadsheet pages (double the usual edition), produced by the Marx-Engels-Lenin Institute; it was also published as an eighty-eight-page book, with an initial print run of more than 1 million. Upon receiving his copy, Stalin told his aides that he had "no time to look at it." In fact, he had changed some wording, made insertions, cut text, and substituted some different photographs.[172] The link to Lenin remained the touchstone. "He thinks about Lenin always; even when his thoughts are deep in problems that require decisions, his hand automatically, machine-like, writes on a sheet of paper, 'Lenin—friend . . . teacher,'" Poskryobyshev and Dvinsky, Stalin's two top aides, wrote in *Pravda*. "Often at the end of the workday we remove papers from his desk with these very words written along and across them."[173]

Pravda's birthday issue also featured some of the congratulations sent from each and every factory and farm, and from around the world. The next day (December 22), the Academy of Sciences made Stalin an "honorary member," despite his lack of a degree. *Pravda* carried a photograph depicting a benevolent Stalin receiving bouquets from women and children of the various Soviet nationalities. Adolf Hitler, too, sent December 1939 birthday greetings—which were printed on *Pravda*'s front page: "On the day of your 60th birthday I ask that you receive my sincerest congratulations. I offer my best wishes, I wish good health to you personally and a happy future to all the peoples of the friendly Soviet Union."

Stalin graciously replied to the Führer: "I ask that you accept my gratitude for the congratulations and my thanks for your kind wishes in connection with the peoples of the Soviet Union."[174] There were no birthday greetings from the leaders of Britain or France. But *Time* magazine named Stalin Man of the Year for 1939, contrasting him favorably with the warmongers Hitler, Mussolini, and Franco, as well as with Roosevelt. (*Time* had named Hitler Man of the Year in 1938.) "Stalin's actions in 1939," the magazine wrote, "were positive, surprising, world-shattering."[175]

COURSE CORRECTION

Back in Finland, as Finnish reservists, often boys barely old enough to shave, starved and froze but fought on against vastly superior Red Army numbers, Soviet corpses piled up. "The Russians," a photographer for America's *Life* magazine observed, "lay lonely and twisted in their heavy trench coats and formless felt boots, their faces yellowed, eyelashes white with a fringe of frost. Across the ice, the forest was strewn with weapons and pictures and letters. . . . Here were the bodies of dead tanks with blown treads, dead carts, dead horses and dead men, blocking the road and defiling the snow."[176] Voroshilov urged that Meretskov and the officers under his command be replaced and court-martialed as "cowards and laggards (there are also swine)."[177] Beria, not to be outdone, recommended arrests, too.[178] Stalin did not indulge them. But he did direct the rabid Mekhlis to travel back to Finland and, on December 29, signed an order, along with Voroshilov and Shaposhnikov, for Soviet armies to adopt a defensive posture and guard against encirclement by the Finns. It admonished commanders—himself, actually—that "the war with Finland is a serious war, distinctly different from our autumn campaign in Poland."[179]

Alarmingly, Soviet military intelligence reported (December 20, 24, 28, 29) that Romania was intensively readying for war against the USSR and preparing concentration camps for people sympathetic to the USSR. Soviet official circles worried that Turkey could be enticed into war against the USSR as well.[180] A piece of uplifting news had been delivered by the Soviet agent Stöbe, who reported from Berlin, based upon information from Scheliha, that Hitler was intending "a major western offensive in 1940. At one meeting, a plan was outlined: first the seizure of France, Belgium, and the Netherlands, then a strike against Britain. Among the military brass, there is opposition on this question." When asked about the USSR's position, Hitler was said to have responded that "the USSR would be occupied by Finland."[181]

On December 28, Stalin finally convoked the Main Military Council, which subjected the failed battle plan of Meretskov to withering criticism. When Stalin asked who among those assembled would be willing to take over, Timoshenko, the ambitious commander of the Kiev military district, volunteered, on the condition that he could alter the battle plan back to what Shaposhnikov and the general staff had proposed. On December 31, 1939, Stalin had Shaposhnikov awarded the Order of Lenin, and seven days later he summoned Zhdanov and Meretskov to the Little Corner. "The whole world is watching us," the despot reproached Meretskov. "The authority of the Red Army is the guarantor of the security of the USSR. If we get stuck in the face of such a weak opponent, that will arouse the anti-Soviet forces of imperialist circles."[182] On January 7, 1940, the despot had Timoshenko formally appointed to "assist" Meretskov, ending the idiotic posture that the war was some local affair of the Leningrad military district.[183]

Timoshenko, born in 1895 to peasants in Bessarabia, near Odessa, had served as a machine gunner in the Great War, joined the Red Army in 1918 and the party in 1919, met Stalin at Tsaritsyn during the civil war, and rose under his patronage, becoming the top commander in the Soviet west. But excavating the country from the Finnish debacle would not be easy. On the night of January 7–8, Stalin, with Voroshilov also on the line, called Stern, recently installed as a frontline commander in Finland, to discuss reports of traffic jams. (Voroshilov had already spoken to Stern that morning.) Stalin warned Stern against transporting troops with trucks on the city roads, as if that were the cause. Stern noted that horse-drawn carts were clogging the roads and turned the conversation to his desperate need for reinforcements and supplies. "It is necessary to mobilize for us all concentrated meat and protein, canned fish, biscuits, and dry spirits, whatever the country can give us, because frequently we are unable to give the troops all the food supplies required," he told Stalin. "It is also necessary not to send troops older than 30 to this severe theater—that's all I have, pardon me for detaining you."[184]

PROTÉGÉS

That January of 1940, in Nazi-occupied Poland (the General Gouvernement), all Jews ten years and older were compelled to wear a white armband with a blue Star of David on the right sleeve of their clothing. In the part of Poland that Germany annexed, Jews were forced to wear yellow patches with the Star of David. Jewish-owned shops or other enterprises were also forced to display a Star of David, which often led to their expropriation. Many Jews in Poland were pressed into forced labor.

Denunciations reached Moscow that Choibalsan, the Mongolian butcher-leader handpicked by Stalin, was helping himself to cash from state vaults. But Stalin knew that he was loyal. Granted an audience in the Little Corner (January 3), Choibalsan brought a wish list: a new railroad, a meatpacking plant, a cement factory. He received the Order of Lenin. Stalin directed that Mongolia's herds should grow from 20-odd million to 200 million head. (They would reach 30 million by the year 2000.) The Soviet despot also chose a new state emblem for Mongolia (a man on horseback) and imposed a new draft constitution and Mongolian People's Party program, which called for extirpation of the remnants of feudalism and, bypassing capitalism, "development along the noncapitalist path in order to prepare for entering socialism." After the puppet Choibalsan's return to Ulan Bator, he would preside over the 10th Congress of the Mongolian People's Party. He would remain concurrently prime minister and war minister, but the Congress would formally confirm the promotions of young people to top positions, including, at Soviet insistence, Yumjaagiin Tsedenbal, a 1938 graduate of the Siberian Finance Institute, in Irkutsk, who became the Mongol party's general secretary, at age twenty-three.[185]

At home, too, Stalin continued his dizzying promotion of new people. On January 8, 1940, Alexander Yakovlev (b. 1906) was sitting at his desk in the design bureau at Moscow Aviation Plant No. 39 when the phone rang. "Are you very busy?" the voice asked. "Might you be able to come over right now?" It was Stalin. Yakovlev was in the Little Corner fifteen minutes later. Stalin told those present that Mikhail Kaganovich, brother of Lazar, was being removed as aviation commissar. "What kind of commissar is he? What does he know of aviation?" Stalin stated to Lazar Kaganovich's face, adding, in an allusion to his Jewish background, "How many years has he lived in Russia and he still hasn't learned how to speak proper Russian." Alexei Shakhurin, party boss of Gorky province (and, before that, Yaroslavl, site of airplane manufacturing), was appointed the new commissar. "And," Stalin continued, turning to Yakovlev, "we decided to make you Shakhurin's deputy." Yakovlev professed his lack of experience, but those present retorted that Shakhurin had no experience, either. "So you don't want to be deputy commissar?" Stalin remarked. "Maybe you want to be commissar?" Smiling, the despot invoked party discipline. "We are not afraid of force, we do not shrink from force when it is necessary. Sometimes force is useful; without force there would have been no revolution. Indeed, force is the midwife of revolution."

Yakovlev recalled wondering: "What would the designers and other figures of our aviation think of me as a deputy commissar—I, the youngest among them?" He got a new apartment in the commissariat's new residential complex, but without a telephone. Stalin called for him. Not wanting to again bother the one neighbor in the building who had a home phone and had received the call, Yakovlev went to the street to return Stalin's call, which prompted the despot to ask what had taken him so long to respond. Yakovlev answered that he had had to use a pay phone. "What, you have no telephone?" Stalin remarked. The next day when Yakovlev got home from work, he found a city phone installed in his apartment. At some point, Stalin called again and began asking questions about a specific airplane, but Yakovlev responded, "It is forbidden to discuss those kinds of questions on a city line." "Yes, right, I forgot," Stalin said, then asked, "What, you don't have a government line in your apartment?" "Of course not," the despot answered his own question. "By rank it is not specified for you." Stalin laughed. The next day, Yakovlev came home to find a second phone installed in his apartment, a Kremlin *vertushka*.[186]

This is how it worked for countless young functionaries: Stalin would summon them to his inner sanctum. Many would learn only then where he worked and the nickname for his inner sanctum—the "Little Corner," magical words they could now whisper to other intimates. Stalin had brought them into his confidence. Invariably, they were startled at his command of detail: the different specifications of the various artillery pieces, the distinguishing characteristics of the various types of steel, even the number of shops in their factory. He had done his homework, he understood technology, he knew the challenges they confronted. Speaking with restraint, he would patiently explain the rightness of a line of action, the necessity of their taking on a certain assignment and of meeting his impossible demands. They came to feel he was watching them, mentoring them. Some would be summoned frequently, others just once in their lifetimes, but even a single visit could last that entire lifetime.

Another young protégé, Vasily Yemelyanov (b. 1901), the deputy commissar for defense industry, was summoned to the Little Corner on January 13. He had studied at Krupp's factories in Germany and been tasked with production of Soviet armored plating. Yemelyanov arrived with a group that included the Izhorsk Factory director and industrial designer, who were supposed to produce a lightweight armored shield for infantry on skis. Poskryobyshev showed them in. They found themselves in the presence of Voroshilov and Molotov, among others, as well as armaments commissar Boris Vannikov, who had brought a new version of an automatic rifle. Stalin was said to have taken the shield prototype and the rifle, hit the floor, and rolled around, adopting various positions while aiming the weapon through the shield's opening. Then he rose and offered suggestions, such as slightly increasing the size of the shield and creating a small shelf on it for spare ammunition. The designer recorded the instructions in a notebook.[187]

Despite Stalin's impromptu floor show, the armored shield prototype—still to be mass-produced—was not going to save the situation in Finland. That would fall to Timoshenko, who arrived in the Little Corner, with Alexander Vasilevsky from the general staff, right after Yemelyanov and the others had departed. Plans were being finalized for an offensive.

SUSPICIONS

Also on January 13, 1940, Soviet intelligence supplied Stalin with Russian translations of the unflattering internal reports on the Soviet-Finnish War sent to Berlin by the German ambassador in Helsinki.[188] At least the intercepted reports showed that Germany was not going to assist Finland. But the British, in January 1940, had begun to discuss possible military assistance to the Finns.[189] Sir Edmund Ironside, chief of the British imperial general staff, had sent an envoy to Mannerheim's field headquarters, and on January 8, in a long conversation, the Finnish supreme commander indicated that he expected a renewed Soviet offensive but maintained that he could hold out until May. He sought British fighter planes, ammunition, artillery, and, crucially, 76.2-millimeter antiaircraft guns—then "maybe the wonder will happen that we should be victorious—we must be." Mannerheim mentioned a 30,000-man foreign legion, but he seemed most intent on the Western powers themselves attacking Soviet oil fields. "Do you think you will make a move in the Caucasus?" he asked. "It should be easy." He asserted that "the capture of Baku would be a deadly blow to Germany, as well as to Russia," and urged a British expedition to seize Murmansk and Arkhangelsk, too. But Ironside took Mannerheim's assertion that the Finns could last until May as a reason not to move expeditiously on his request for weaponry and Western action.[190] Still, Beria sent a report to Stalin (January 13) that Britain would furnish Finland with 12 Bristol Blenheim bombers, to destroy the Leningrad-Murmansk Railway, and conduct demonstration raids over Leningrad and Moscow. Maisky was now reporting that the British were resolute.[191]

Stalin began to wonder whether he had been tricked.[192] British sources, via the

Soviet Union's London station, had been relaying stories of Mannerheim's prewar pessimism—but now those same sources were reporting his confidence. Had British secret services lured Stalin into a trap with disinformation? Intelligence that informed the Soviet battle plan had proved misguided.[193] Churchill had told Maisky how he sympathized with a Soviet seizure of the Gulf of Finland—and now? "Finland—superb, nay, sublime—in the jaws of peril Finland shows what free men can do," he declared in a radio address on January 20, 1940. "The service rendered by Finland to mankind is magnificent. They have exposed, for all the world to see, the military incapacity of the Red Army and of the Red Air Force. Many illusions about Soviet Russia have been dispelled in these few fierce weeks of fighting in the Arctic Circle."[194]

A pig in a poke? Stalin became suspicious that his many agents in Britain—run by Anatoly Gorsky—were too good to be true, a suspicion that cast a shadow over the spectacular Cambridge Five. The despot turned to his spies in Paris, who reported that the French were contemplating air raids on Baku, which supplied 80 percent of Soviet aviation fuel, 90 percent of kerosene, and more than 90 percent of gasoline.[195] The French were also said to be planning attacks on Murmansk and Arkhangelsk in the north, with the goal of eventually seizing Leningrad and installing a White Russian regime. This was the very nightmare scenario whose avoidance had motivated Stalin's launch of the pressure on Finland in the first place. Stalin followed the Western machinations involving Turkey, a possible participant in a Western air assault on Baku. German intelligence began playing up the Western intervention plans, seeking to drive the wedge between France/Britain and the Soviet Union deeper.[196] The Soviet high command issued a general order to open fire, without seeking further permission, on any foreign airplanes that crossed Soviet borders.[197]

On January 17, 1940, Stalin approved a sentencing list containing 457 prominent people; 346 were to be shot, including Yezhov, as well as the writer Isaac Babel, the journalist-propagandist Koltsov, and the dramaturge Meyerhold, three of the country's long-standing brightest lights, each of whom Yezhov had implicated as spies.[198] Four days later, when the regime conducted the annual commemoration of Lenin's passing at the Bolshoi, Stalin made remarks to the inner circle. "Mayakovsky was the finest proletarian poet," he stated. "Ten volumes of verse by Demyan Bedny are not worth that one poem of Mayakovsky's. D. B. could never rise to such a height."

Stalin also stated that night, in the presence of others, that "Voroshilov is a good fellow, but he is no military man." The despot acknowledged that Finland had prepared for a major war, but in a way that went beyond its own military capabilities: "hangars for thousands of aircraft—whereas Finland had [only] several hundred of them." He blustered that, as the Red Army now advanced, "there should be nothing left but the bare bones of a state" in Finland, adding, "We have no desire for Finland's territory. But Finland should be a state that is friendly to the Soviet Union." Then he proposed a toast: "To the fighters of the Red Army, which was untrained, badly clothed, and badly shod, which we are now providing with clothing and boots, which is fighting for its somewhat tarnished honor, fighting for its glory!"

Grigory Kulik arrived at the celebration bearing bad news from the front. Born into a peasant family near Poltava, Kulik had been a staff artillery officer in the tsarist army and became acquainted with Stalin during the civil war; by 1937, the despot had named the notorious bully and blockhead as head of the Red Army's main artillery directorate. "You're lapsing into panic," Stalin now admonished him. "I shall send you [Georgy] Chelpanov's book on the foundation of psychology." Stalin noted that when the pagan Greek priests "would get disturbing reports, they would adjourn to their bathhouses, take baths, wash themselves clean, and only afterward would they assess events and make decisions."[199]

After the Lenin commemoration, between January 23 and February 3, Stalin received people in the Little Corner just once, in the wee small hours of January 29, and only briefly: Molotov (65 minutes), Mikoyan (30 minutes), Kulik (25 minutes), and Shaposhnikov (48 minutes).[200] Later that day, Molotov telegrammed Kollontai in Stockholm, instructing her, to her astonishment, to inform the Swedish government that Soviet peace negotiations with the Finnish government in Helsinki would be possible.[201] Stalin could not have had any intention of conducting actual negotiations, given that planning was well under way for an immense Soviet offensive. Rather, the despot likely wanted to break any momentum, such as it was, in possible Western military assistance to the Finns. In February 1940, Stalin ordered Beria to recall Gorsky and shut down the entire Soviet intelligence station in London, for having served as a conduit of "disinformation."[202]

MASSACRES

On February 10, 1940, in response to an article in *Pravda* summarizing a journal story about his heroic prerevolutionary underground exploits in Baku, Stalin lashed out at inaccuracies (pointing out he had never edited the oil workers' newspaper) and the portrayal of Voroshilov ("Comrade Voroshilov was in Baku for only a few months, and then left Baku without leaving visible traces behind"). In the letter, which he marked "not for publication," Stalin also cast doubt on the reminiscences used in the article, indicating that the memoirs had likely been "dictated" by journalists.[203]

Around this time, death sentences based upon fabricated evidence were implemented for cultural figures, as well as former NKVD first deputy Mikhail Frinovsky, former deputy foreign intelligence chief Spigelglas, former intelligence chief and Comintern operative Trilisser, Yefim Yevdokimov, and Redens, Stalin's ethnic Polish brother-in-law (part of a "Polish diversionary-espionage group"). Frinovsky's wife was executed the day before him; their son, a high school student, was executed not long thereafter. Under interrogation-torture, Redens had admitted his complicity in the annihilation of innocent people while working atop the NKVD in Ukraine, Moscow, and Kazakhstan. His wife Anna—Nadya's sister—and their two boys were not touched, and the family continued to live in the elite House on the Embankment and were allowed to visit Svetlana at Zubalovo (but not the Kremlin).[204]

The principal executioner was usually Vasily Blokhin (b. 1895). The son of a poor peasant from central Russia, he had risen to become the NKVD's head executioner already in the mid-1920s and was known to insiders by his signature brown leather cap, brown leather gauntlets above the elbow, and brown leather apron. He had survived the transition from Yagoda to Yezhov, and then to Beria, although the latter had evidently tried to have him arrested as a Yezhovite, assembling the requisite compromising materials.[205] To Blokhin fell the honor of executing Yezhov.[206] In a last statement to the "court," held in the prison warden's office, Yezhov repudiated the espionage and terrorist charges and requested that his aging mother and adopted daughter not be touched. "I purged 14,000 Chekists," he stated, "but my enormous guilt lies in the fact that I purged so few of them." He was cremated at the Donskoi Monastery Crematorium, his ashes dumped into a mass pit, joining those of Tukhachevsky. Yezhov's very last words were for the despot: "Let Stalin know that I shall die with his name on my lips."[207]

"Yezhov was scum," Stalin told the new deputy aviation commissar, Yakovlev. "A degenerated person. You call him at the commissariat, they say he's left for the Central Committee. You call the Central Committee, they say he left for a job. You send someone to his residence, it turns out he's lying in bed, dead drunk. He destroyed many innocents. We shot him for that."[208]

Massive artillery barrages began to strike Finland, then, on February 11, in frosts reaching 31 degrees below zero (minus 35 Celsius), Timoshenko's onslaught via escalating artillery barrages, known as a Wall of Fire, commenced on the Vii-puri axis. Rather than attempt a war of maneuver through partially frozen swamp with dispersed forces, Timoshenko massed more than 450,000 Soviet troops, against perhaps 150,000 Finns, on a single point, in classic Napoleonic fashion. Within the week, the Red Army finally had pierced the Mannerheim Line, forcing the Finns to retreat. (Voroshilov at first refused to believe Meretskov's phone report that the Red Army had broken through.) Soviet artillery tore the colossal Finnish concrete emplacements right out of the ground, as if trying to make up for their earlier humiliation.[209] On February 15, a much-relieved yet feverish and nauseated Stalin was again examined by his doctor. "In front of Stalin on the table was a map of Finland," the doctor recalled. "Stalin took a large, thick pencil and drew in the course of the war and then, tapping the pencil, said, 'Any day Vyborg will be taken.'"[210]

On the same day that Timoshenko's offensive began in Finland, Stalin deepened his bargain with Hitler, after difficult negotiations, with a new Commercial Agreement (February 11, 1940). The Soviet Union agreed to supply Germany with 650 million reichsmarks' worth of raw materials during the next eighteen months, promising fully two thirds in the first twelve months, while Germany pledged to furnish the same amount of industrial goods, but over twenty-seven months—a significant Soviet concession.[211] The cornucopia for Germany included Soviet feed grain and legumes (1 million tons), oil (900,000 tons), scrap and pig iron (800,000 tons), phosphates (500,000 tons), iron ore (500,000 tons), platinum, chromium ore, asbestos, iridium, and albumin. The earlier vague promises for German "industrial deliveries" were now, at Stalin's insistence, enumerated in four lists covering forty-two pages: a fully equipped Panzer III, five Messerschmitt Bf 109 E and five Bf 100 C fighters, two Junkers 88 bombers, two Dornier 215 light bombers, and one Fa 226 helicopter, as well as extra engines, artillery pieces, armored vehicles, gun sights, and extensive spare parts (piston rings, spark plugs, propellers, submarine periscopes), and the massive naval ship the *Lützow*. The lists also specified turbines, locomotives, excavators, cranes, forges, diesel engines, and steel tubing. There was even a list covering possible future Soviet interests.[212]

In China, the renewed "united front" was coming undone. Under Japan's savage array of air power, artillery, and armored forces, China was losing every engagement on the battlefield, but not the war. First the Nationalist government had abandoned north China, trading space for time, then, after being evicted from ever more territories along the coast, had retreated to the western interior, whence it conducted sabotage and flanking operations designed to outlast Japan and its shoestring logistics.[213] Finally, Chiang Kai-shek launched a multifront counteroffensive. Once again, he confided in his private diary that the threat of the Chinese Communist party to the country, whom he saw as collaborating with Japan, exceeded the threat of the latter.[214] Zhou Enlai, in a long report, claimed a party membership of nearly half a million, and an Eighth Route Army of more than a quarter million (additionally, a New Fourth Army was said to number 30,000). At the same time, the Communists' budget was in severe deficit: about $358,000 per month, a tidy sum Zhou requested from Moscow. His request amounted to more than 40 percent of the Chinese Communists' total military and civilian expenditures. On February 23, Dimitrov sent Stalin a draft letter intended as a response, and two days later he managed to speak with Stalin on the phone. "Cannot see me about Chinese affairs," Dimitrov noted in his diary for that day. "Very busy. Has not read the material he was sent. 'There is a lot of paperwork I am not finding time to read. Decide for yourself.'"[215]

Dimitrov concluded his diary entry: "We shall give the assistance."[216] Zhou Enlai, who had been in Moscow for treatment of a broken arm (he had fallen from a horse), set out for Yan'an, the Red capital, carrying with him a Comintern resolution that afforded the Chinese Communists great leeway in making decisions based upon fluid local circumstances. Mao took advantage by tightening his grip. Dimitrov telegrammed Mao (March 17, 1940) that Zhou "will personally inform you about everything we discussed and agreed upon regarding Chinese affairs. You need to seriously consider everything and take decisive measures completely on your own. In case of disagreement with us on some questions, please inform us promptly and tell us your reasons."[217] Such deference from Moscow to foreign Communists was unheard of. Mao seized upon the Comintern document to appoint his own loyalists and lay plans to set up new Communist bases in China.[218]

Also against the background of Finnish events, in early March 1940, Beria had reported to Stalin that "a large number of former officers of the Polish army, former employees of the Polish police and intelligence services, members of Polish nationalist counterrevolutionary parties, participants in uncovered counterrevolutionary uprising organizations, refugees, and so forth are held in NKVD USSR camps for POWs and in the prisons of the western provinces of Ukraine and Belorussia." He added, on the basis of informants, that they were "sworn enemies of Soviet authority full of hatred for the Soviet system," and that each was "waiting only for his release in order to enter actively into the struggle against Soviet power." Some had had the temerity to write petitions pointing out that if, according to Soviet propaganda, the USSR was *not* at war with Poland, then they could not be held as POWs. To expedite their sentencing, Beria recommended that a troika be formed, made up of himself, Merkulov, and the head of the NKVD's first special department. Stalin, using blue pencil, crossed out Beria's name, underlined Merkulov's, and wrote in "Kobulov."[219] On March 5, in the name of the politburo, Stalin approved a troika and a "special procedure" for executing the 21,857 captured or arrested Polish officers, civil servants, and intellectuals. Voroshilov, who had had to surrender jurisdiction over POWs in the Polish campaign to Beria, also signed the execution order, along with the redoubtable Molotov and Mikoyan. The officers of the Polish army—some of whom were ethnic Ukrainian and Jewish—were murdered at several sites, including near Smolensk, in the Katyn Forest.[220]

Soviet liquidation of the Polish officers in captivity took place around the same time as a similar Nazi action across the border under Hans Frank, who, explaining his operation, stated, "I admit, utterly openly, that this will cause the deaths of thousands of Poles, above all from the leading stratum of the Polish intelligentsia."[221] Soviet preparations for the executions might have commenced as early as January 1940. Through agents in Britain, the Soviets likely picked up on recent French whisperings to employ exiled Polish forces ("volunteers") to attack Soviet positions in northern Finland, around Petsamo, a scenario that eventually could have had Polish army officers inside the USSR playing the role that the Czechoslovak Legion had played in 1918—namely, sparking a civil war.[222] But whatever the anxieties, the massacres ultimately flowed from a bottomless well of Soviet-Polish enmity.[223] Families of the executed, who were deported to Kazakhstan, were told nothing; all too many would not survive their own ordeals. A handful of top Polish officers, such as General Władysław Anders, were kept alive, perhaps for future use; some others survived by offering their services to the NKVD. The Katyn Forest slaughter would prove to be not just another epochal Soviet state crime, but a strategic blunder.

All of this occurred in strictest secrecy. For the Soviet people, fairy tales persisted. *A Member of the Government,* with Gelovani in a cameo as Stalin, premiered on March 8, 1940. The film opens in spring 1930, when a poor peasant, Alexandra Sokolova (played by the radiant theater actress Vera Maretskaya), joins a collective farm and becomes its chairman, courageously coping with all the obstacles to collectivization: other villagers' distrust, false accusations against her, bureaucratism, wrecking. The heroine is seen growing into her position, breaking free of her patriarchal husband in the name of the new life, speaking with authority in the name of the people, and eventually being elected a deputy of the new USSR Supreme Soviet—the strongest female character to emerge in Soviet cinema to date.[224] The Soviet press was preoccupied for several days with celebrating the fiftieth birthday of the head of the actual government, Molotov (March 9, 1940), affording him the designation "very major figure."[225] On March 10, two months shy of his forty-ninth birthday, Mikhail Bulgakov succumbed to nephrosclerosis, an inherited kidney disorder.[226] *The Master and Margarita* and many of his other works remained unpublished.

REVELATION

On March 12, the Finnish government, reeling from Timoshenko's furious Wall of Fire that had reduced Viipuri, now renamed Vyborg, to a bombed-out hulk and opened the road to Helsinki, capitulated. The NKVD reported that Finland appeared to be on the verge of total military collapse. Stalin refrained from trying to overrun the country entirely (which had not been his intention in the first place). He did not deign to participate in the numerous sessions required to hammer out the details of Helsinki's acceptance of defeat. Molotov, reversing the original offer to cede a large part of Soviet Karelia, now claimed a chunk of Finnish Karelia, plus the Karelian Isthmus right through to Vyborg—well beyond prewar proposals. This was more territory than the Finns had lost in the fighting. When they objected, Molotov snapped, "Any other great power in our position would demand war reparations or all of Finland." When the Finns pointed out that in 1721, Peter the Great had paid compensation for the expansion of Russia's Baltic frontier, Molotov barked, "Write a letter to Peter the Great—if he orders it, we will pay compensation."[227]

The consequences of Finland's civilian leaders' prewar refusal to cut a deal struck the country like a punch in the face.[228] "The terms of the peace are onerous for us," stated Tanner, a participant in the failed negotiations, "but the government is happy that the agreement does not limit Finland's sovereignty and independence, and that the program of Kuusinen's government has been abandoned."[229] Flags in Helsinki flew at half-mast, newspapers appeared with black borders, and the radio played funeral dirges.

Two of Stalin's fiercest émigré critics had stood with him regarding Finland. Living in France, Paul Miliukov, the former leader of the Constitutional Democrats (Cadets), observed of the Winter War, "I feel pity for the Finns, but I am for a Vyborg province."[230] Trotsky, too, had supported the USSR in the clash with Finland, imagining, like the ideologue Zhdanov, that the Soviet invasion heralded the onset of a Finnish class-based civil war. Trotsky argued that, just as in Spain, it was right to be on the side of the left, although it was proving difficult for Finland's workers and peasants to rid themselves of landowners and the bourgeoisie. The reality, of course, was that Finnish workers and peasants had staunchly supported the "bourgeois" regime. After the war, Trotsky wrote that Stalin's "authority has been dealt an irreparable blow."[231]

Stalin allowed the Helsinki government to retain the nonaggression pact with the USSR, rather than a mutual assistance pact of the kind imposed on the Balts.[232] He seems to have been keen to avoid, if not further international complications with the Western powers, at least their seizure of a foothold in Scandinavia under the pretext of "aiding" a victimized Finland. It also bears recalling that in tsarist Russia, Finland had had special status (and, for a time, its own constitution). Stalin was perhaps also chastened by the Finns' military resistance. "We knew that Peter I fought for twenty-one years to cut off the whole of Finland from Sweden," he would explain to the Soviet military the next month, perhaps in order to indicate why Finland was not being annexed.[233]

Small countries, in the unforgiving international system, *had* to be smart— and the smaller the country, the smarter it had to be, particularly if its geographical location attracted the close attention and calculations of the great powers.[234] The Finnish government, morally in the right, had been geopolitically in the wrong. Back in 1938, the leaders of Czechoslovakia—diplomatically isolated but possessing an advanced army—had shown themselves unwilling to pay the price of war against Hitler for their independence. In 1939, the diplomatically isolated but under-armed Finns chose to fight, yet it was their neutrality, not their sovereignty, that had been at stake, a fact recognized by the hamstrung Finnish negotiator Paasikivi and Field Marshal Mannerheim and, belatedly, by Tanner and the rest. Hitler's appeal on behalf of ethnic Germans abroad had been revealed as a lie, a mere pretext to swallow the whole Czechoslovak state, but Stalin's security concerns for Leningrad, even if they evoked a history of Russian expansionism, were not a pretext.

Finland paid a heavy price for the avoidable war. Nearly 400,000 Finns (mostly small farmers)—upward of 12 percent of its population—were forced to evacuate the newly annexed Soviet territories for rump Finland, leaving homes and many possessions behind. Finland lost 11 percent of its land and perhaps 30 percent of its prewar economic assets. Beyond the significantly greater territory it was forced to relinquish, compared with what it would have lost in prewar political concessions, Finland suffered at least 26,662 killed and missing, 43,357 wounded, and 847 captured by the Soviets. The Finns had been adamant about not relinquishing the Mannerheim Line of defensive emplacements, but it was now lost. ("Even after it had been blasted and penetrated in many places," observed Alexander Solodovnikov, who traveled by car in spring 1940 from Leningrad to set up a Russian-language theater in newly conquered Vyborg, "the 'line' amazed with its monstrous, agglomerated, ingenious pillboxes, bunkers, concrete blocks, and concealed traps.")[235] The Finns would end up losing their cherished neutrality, too (becoming aligned with Nazi Germany).

Great powers usually can expect to have considerable room to recover from even the most egregious mistakes, but that room, in the late 1930s and into 1940, had vastly narrowed. Thanks to the Finnish resistance, the 105-day Winter War proved even more costly to Stalin than to the Finns. The despot did obtain a more secure border for Leningrad, as well as security for the ocean port Murmansk, while the Red Army, including its command, did get valuable, albeit painful, combat experience.[236] Still, the Soviets lost an astonishing 131,476 dead and missing; at least 264,908 more were wounded or fell to illness, including the frostbitten, who lost fingers, toes, ears. Total Soviet losses neared 400,000 casualties, out of perhaps 1 million men mobilized—almost 4,000 casualties *per day*.[237] (Later, Stalingrad would produce around 3,300 per day.) Another 5,486 Red Army troops were captured, most of whom, upon returning home, would be sent to the Gulag for the crime of falling into enemy hands. Of course, the giant scale of losses was kept secret, but during a discussion of the war's lessons, one Soviet general nonetheless snapped, "We have won enough ground to bury our dead."[238]

The shocking Red Army failures of December 1939 overshadowed not just the impressive corrections of February 1940, but even the fact that, in the end, the Soviets had won the war decisively and exceeded their objectives.[239] Foreign intelligence services had been knocking themselves out trying to gauge the strength of the gigantic Red Army, and now they believed they had the answer: it was impotent. They overlooked the special circumstances of roadless, marshy terrain and deep-winter combat, just as Stalin and his commanders had overlooked them at the outset. The German general staff wrote on New Year's Eve 1939–40 that the Red Army was "in quantity a gigantic military instrument," but "the Russian 'mass' is no match for an army with modern equipment and superior leadership."[240] Even after the Soviets had turned the tide, the Germans, as well as the British and the French, remained confirmed in their prejudice that the Soviet

Union was a colossus of clay. On March 31, 1940, Hitler, in a closed speech in the Chancellery to his commanders, called the USSR a "tenacious adversary" but went on to say that "the Russian is inferior," and the Soviet army "without leadership," undermined by Jewish-Bolshevik lies.[241]

Soviet military doctrine, in its most sophisticated versions, had long stressed aggressive counterattack, decentralized command, and organizational flexibility, but within such a rigidly hierarchical political despotism, only the first principle was realized in practice. In Finland, shocking chaos in the rear services had severely handicapped military operations, and hypercentralization and the inexperience of commanders meant they could not adapt or take initiative on the battlefield. Both the horrific casualty count and the immense expenditure of ordnance testified to the depth of the problems. But Timoshenko had managed to improve both coordination and flexibility, implementing combined attacks of air and armor, as well as continuous vertical and horizontal communications with superiors and neighboring staffs and services. At the same time, Stalin, relying on Mekhlis, had political indoctrination recalibrated to emphasize the discipline and traditions of the Imperial Russian Army. From late 1939 into 1940, the Soviet press published articles on the military genius of Alexander Suvorov, the eighteenth-century generalissimo, as well as Great Russian nationalism, and transformed Finland into a "patriotic war."[242]

The contribution of that notable shift, in the case of Finland, remains hard to gauge. The conscript soldiers—peasants from collectivized villages or workers from factory barracks—on their first trips abroad, with the mission of "liberating" the exploited Finnish people from "White Finns," encountered the well-built, well-equipped homes of ordinary Finnish people. The Soviet lads, and especially their commanders, as in Poland in 1939, madly looted sewing machines, gramophones, bicycles, kitchen utensils, silk stockings, women's dresses, shoes. That said, despite record-breaking frosts, horribly inadequate supplies, and incompetent commanders, Red Army morale had not cracked. Soviet conscripts and reservists often fought on even after having been encircled, entrenching their tanks as makeshift pillboxes.[243] True, NKVD detachments blocked retreat, and even then there were desertions. But the Soviet troops' failure to crush the Finns had aroused a widespread desire to defend their honor. On the front lines, Soviet colonels and captains, themselves conscripts, knew the Red Army could fight.

Among outsiders, only Finland's field marshal Mannerheim—the former tsarist officer—grasped the truth about this contradictory beast. "In the higher ranks there were signs of a kind of inertia," he observed, indicating that the Red Army had reproduced the shortcomings of the army under tsarism. "The Russians based their art of war on the weight of material, and were clumsy, ruthless, and extravagant. There was a striking absence of creative imagination where the fluctuations of the situation demanded quick decisions." With equal perspicacity, again almost uniquely, he comprehended the Red Army's immense brute power, a profligate yet determined fighting machine, one of the hinges of the twentieth century.[244]

FATHERLINESS

Stalin evidently admitted to Shaposhnikov that "concerning Finland you were right."[245] Such an admission of a mistake, even in private, was exceedingly rare for him. It was likely made possible by his respect for Shaposhnikov, a feeling that redounded to a Shaposhnikov protégé, Alexander Vasilevsky (b. 1895), who had graduated from the General Staff Academy in 1937 and joined the party the next year (when admission was reopened). Vasilevsky's father was a priest; his mother, the daughter of a priest. In 1939, he had become a deputy chief of the general staff's operations directorate and had assisted in preparing the Winter War plan of battle that Stalin did not use. In the first half of March 1940, after a long meeting in the Little Corner, Vasilevsky returned to staff headquarters to issue orders based upon the decisions. Suddenly, Poskryobyshev called to say that he was expected at the post-meeting supper at Stalin's Kremlin apartment below the Little Corner. He rushed back and was seated next to Shaposhnikov.

Stalin pronounced one of the many toasts to Vasilevsky's health, then unexpectedly asked why, after graduating from seminary, Vasilevsky had not become a priest. He answered that he had had no such intention. "At that, Stalin smiled through his mustaches and observed, 'I see, I see, you had no such intention. Understandable. But Mikoyan and I did want to become priests, but for some reason they would not take us. Why, I do not understand to this day.'" After this playful gesture of solidarity, Stalin asked Vasilevsky why he did not help his father financially. "As far as I know, one of your brothers is a physician, another is an agronomist, a third is a military commander-aviator and a well-off person," he remarked, underscoring his familiarity with Vasilevsky's personnel file. "I think all of you could be helping your parents, and then the old man could long ago have broken with his church. He would not need the church in order to survive." Vasilevsky had been scrupulously avoiding contact with his father; recently, when he got a letter from home, he had run straight to the party organization at the general staff to confess. Now, Vasilevsky recalled, "Stalin said that I should immediately reestablish contact with my parents and give them systematic assistance and inform the general staff party organization about the authorization to do so."[246]

Vasily Stalin, in the latter half of March 1940, completed his two-year course of study at the military aviation school near Sevastopol with marks of "excellent," according to a report sent to Stalin. He received the rank of air force lieutenant.[247] Later that year, he would marry Galina Burdonskaya, a student of the Moscow Polygraphic Institute, also nineteen years old, who lived in a communal apartment. Stalin would not be informed until after the wedding. "You're married; so be it," he would write to Vasily in red pencil. "I pity her, marrying such a fool."[248]

A RECKONING

A harsh internal Soviet reckoning of the Winter War—which would make no mention of Stalin's errors or his prior murderous rampages—commenced on March 26–28, 1940, at a Central Committee plenum, two weeks after hostilities ended. Molotov reported on the settlement with Finland, prompting Litvinov to criticize the course of foreign policy since his dismissal, while predicting that Germany would attack the Soviet Union. Molotov tried, and failed, to cut Litvinov off; Stalin remained silent.[249] Voroshilov gave an unusually self-critical opening report and offered to resign.[250] Mekhlis was one of those who piled on (hearsay accounts have Mekhlis complaining that "Voroshilov cannot stand Mekhlis," which was true, and likely reflected how every officer in the room felt).[251] But Stalin upbraided his attack dog for "a hysterical speech," called Mekhlis "a good man, a hard worker, but unsuitable for army leadership," and praised Voroshilov for conceding his errors. "It does not happen often around here that a people's commissar speaks so openly about his own shortcomings."[252]

Stalin, in the discussion, brushed off the circumstance that the war had been launched in winter. "We are a northern country," he said, and "if our military leaders had studied the history of the Russian army and followed the fine traditions of the Russian army, then they would know that all of our most impressive victories were won in winter." He mentioned Alexander Nevsky against the Swedes on the ice, Peter the Great against the Swedes and Charles XII on the Baltic, Alexander I's conquest of Finland from Sweden, and Kutuzov's victory over Napoleon.[253] Stalin also criticized the army's use of biscuits instead of dried bread toasts (*sukhari*), stating that in Finnish frosts, the biscuits froze and became ined-ible. "Kutuzov, a real count, visited the soldiers to see what they were eating, but the 'self-made count' Kulik did not do that. (General laughter.)" Despite this dig at Kulik, Stalin praised the artillery. "Now we know the secret of how to smash a fortified defense line. We are the only country that knows this secret. The answer is that first you need to crush the enemy physically and morally with heavy artil-lery, and after that send in the infantry." Stalin added, "The rank and file consti-tute superb material, but the commanders turned out not to be on the heights. . . . The goal is to improve the commanding corps and then our army will be the best in the world."[254]

On the final day of the plenum, Ribbentrop coincidentally instructed Schulen-burg, in Moscow, to revive the invitation of a reciprocal trip by Molotov to Berlin. "It goes without saying that the invitation is not to be confined to Herr Molotov," the Nazi foreign minister telegrammed. "It would suit our own needs better, as well as our really ever closer relations with Russia, if Herr Stalin himself came to Berlin. The Führer would not only be particularly happy to welcome Stalin in Berlin, but he would also see to it that he would get a reception commensurate with his posi-tion and importance, and he would extend to him all the honors that the occasion demanded." Schulenburg replied that he felt confident Molotov would fulfill his obligation to reciprocate, albeit not in the current circumstances, for it would un-dermine the appearance of Soviet neutrality and potentially risk inviting a Western declaration of war against the USSR.[255] Molotov, in a speech to the Supreme Soviet on March 29, 1940, venomously denounced Britain and France, insisting yet again that the Soviet Union would never become a "weapon of the Anglo-French imperi-alists in their struggle for world hegemony." He said that a British buildup in the Near East might entail "objectives antagonistic toward the Soviet Union."[256]

All the while, Soviet merchants were still shopping in Berlin. Also on March 29, Ivan Tevosyan, a German-speaking ethnic Armenian from Karabakh, met Göring. The corpulent Luftwaffe head promised shipments of the contracted Junkers 88 airplane in April and May, noting that "there has never been an in-stance in which I, Göring, did not keep my word," and adding that "the interests of both countries demand that Germany and the Soviet Union are together. This is the Führer's opinion. He has decided this firmly and irreversibly. . . . This wish of Hitler is known to the duce; England and France know about it." Göring fur-ther observed that "he personally had told the Finns repeatedly that it was sense-less for a small state to fight with such a large country and had recommended accepting the USSR's conditions." Tevosyan—who had barely escaped Beria's clutches as an alleged "German spy"—underscored the friendly character of bilateral relations, "reconfirmed in the February 11, 1940, economic agreement," but he pointed out that although the Soviets had shipped everything required of them, "Germany so far has not made a single shipment to the USSR, not one rivet." Göring interrupted to express his regrets at this news of German delays. "I give you my word, I am the guarantee."[257]

On March 31, a Karelo-Finnish Soviet Socialist Republic was established through the merger of Soviet Karelia and territories annexed from Finland (part of the Karelian Isthmus and Ladoga Karelia). The KFSSR became the twelfth Union republic, but the only one whose titular nationality, ethnic Finns, made up a minority of its inhabitants (around one quarter). Stalin soon named Kuusinen the KFSSR's head of state.[258]

Back in Moscow, at a follow-up military conference on the Winter War (April 14–17), Stalin scapegoated his head of military intelligence, Proskurov.[259] In the war's run-up, Soviet military intelligence had produced a photo-and-sketch album of the Mannerheim Line (possibly based on maps delivered by the Germans after the 1939 Pact signing). This album lay on Meretskov's desk.[260] True, there had been subsequent modernization of the defense belt. But Meretskov misunderstood or ignored the implications of the fortifications for his battle plan.[261] That said, extreme hypersecrecy seems to have kept some centrally held intelligence from being shared with the Leningrad military district, to which Stalin had handed the war effort.[262] More broadly, one young military intelligence officer on the front, who later defected, observed, plausibly, that "the maps of Finland supplied to us by military intelligence were extremely poor, an indication of sloppy work. . . . Ironically, we soon found that the maps of that part of the Soviet Union were just as poor."[263] Proskurov, in the discussion at the military conference, pushed back against the criticisms leveled by Stalin, Mekhlis, and Meretskov, whose own head was on the line.[264] Meretskov complained that the army command had no access to foreign newspapers, with their wealth of information about the course of military matters. "An intolerable situation," Stalin interjected. Proskurov pointed out that information from foreign newspapers was translated into Russian, just not circulated. "Why?" Stalin asked. Proskurov: "It contains slander against the Red Army."[265]

Proskurov, a hero aviator, took the fall (and, later, a bullet to the neck).[266] Stalin did criticize himself, too, albeit indirectly. "We expected to bag an easy win," he stated (April 17, 1940). "We were terribly spoiled by the Polish campaign."[267] It was the royal "we." His main theme was that the Russian civil war "had not been a real war, because there was no artillery, aviation, tanks, and mortars used." One more heroic cavalry charge was not going to drive off tanks and artillery. "What hindered our commanding staff from conducting the Finnish war in a new way—not by the civil war style, but in a new way?" Stalin asked rhetorically. "What hindered us, in my view, was a cult of the traditions and experience of the civil war. How did we evaluate commanders: 'Did you take part in the civil war?' 'No, you did not take part—then get lost.' 'That one, did he take part?' 'He took part—let's appoint him.'" Stalin urged everyone—really, himself—"to renounce the cult of the civil war, which only reinforces our backwardness."[268]

Stalin's closest civil war crony, Voroshilov, suffered guilt, anger, and anguish over the regime's massacre of so many innocent officers in the Red Army and his complicity therein. One night at the Near Dacha, during the Finnish events, the despot and his defense commissar went at it. They all must have been even drunker than usual. Stalin "was in a white-hot rage and berated Voroshilov severely," Khrushchev recalled. "He got irate, jumped up, and [verbally] went after Voroshilov. Voroshilov also blew up, got red in the face, rose, and hurled Stalin's accusation back in his face. 'You're to blame in this! You annihilated the military cadres.'" True enough, although Voroshilov had signed 185 extant execution lists—fourth behind Stalin, Molotov, and Kaganovich. After Stalin answered him in kind, "Voroshilov picked up a platter with a roast suckling pig on it and smashed it on the table."[269] That pig, in a way, was plucky little Finland—the "pig rooting around in the Soviet garden," in the dismissive phrase used on the eve of the war—but now it was also Voroshilov's military career and, by association, Stalin's military dilettantism.

LEARNING

With its strong incentives for lying and an absence of institutionalized consultation or corrective mechanisms, despotism is particularly prone to strategic blunders, and yet despotic systems—and despots—can learn. The Winter War launched Stalin's belated military reeducation, which was a long time coming.[270] Prior to the Finnish experience, the Spanish civil war had delivered valuable first-hand experience in sabotage operations behind enemy lines, had battle-tested Soviet weapons systems, and had enabled study of Nazi Germany's arsenal. The initiative to collect this valuable information was taken by Soviet military men whom Stalin then mostly murdered, but the data and analyses remained for their successors. Case studies of individual battles in Spain became available for study at Soviet military schools, in order to assimilate the tactical and operational lessons for artillery, tanks, airplanes, navy, and combined operations, much of which was published in the army newspaper, *Red Star,* for the broadest possible audience. Voroshilov and his aides selected key material on Spain to present to Stalin.[271]

Some key lessons that had been drawn from Spain were blatantly misguided. Kulik, for example, had concluded that the use of large mechanized tank units had turned out to be wrongheaded, for in Spain the infantry had not been able to keep pace with the tanks.[272] He was hardly alone in this misreading, but with Tukhachevsky and others murdered, Kulik's misread had gone largely uncontested, and Stalin had approved the Red Army's dismantling of stand-alone mechanized tank units. Lessons from the border war with Japan were distilled by Zhukov, who was holed up in Ulan Bator. His long report labeled the incompetent commander he had relieved a "criminal" and underlined problems arising from poor battlefield communications and inadequate intelligence, but overall, he called the engagement "a victory which, in our view, should be carefully studied by all commanders." This document was completed only in November 1939, not in time for the Winter War planning.[273] But Zhukov and Stern had improvised back into existence stand-alone mechanized units and demonstrated, in practice, the devastating effectiveness of massive application of tanks and aircraft. Now, after Finland, these units would make a belated comeback. Nonetheless, in front of the full military during discussion of Finland in April 1940, Stalin belittled the brilliant 1939 victory in the border war with Japan.[274]

Development of military technology involves strategic decisions concerning manufacturing capabilities and spare parts availability, cost, ease of use and repair by soldiers, and, of course, effectiveness in combat, all decisions that take time to unfold. In the meantime, the enemy's technology can improve.[275] The consequences of mistakes can be immense. Kulik would soon block the placement of the advanced F-34 guns on the T-34 tank, which would be launched into mass production in fall 1940, largely because the superior gun was not his initiative.[276]

One hard Spanish lesson that the Soviets had learned was the squandering of their initial aviation advantage. The Soviets were winning the quantitative arms race with Nazi Germany, producing 4,270 airplanes in 1936 (to Germany's 5,112), 6,039 in 1937 (to Germany's 5,606), 7,727 in 1938 (to 5,235), and 10,362 in 1939 (to 8,295).[277] But German quality had improved more significantly. Germany had opened a gap with its upgraded Heinkel bomber (He-111), which was capable of carrying 3,000 pounds of bombs, and its Messerschmitt fighter (Me-109), which had a range of 400 miles, a high rate of climb, a bulletproof fuel tank, and a top speed of 350 miles per hour, and had shown its deadliness at Guernica.[278] The belated Soviet responses—Yak-1, Yak-7, MiG-3, and LaGG-3—finally appeared in 1940, but only in experimental production.

The despot summoned the thirty-six-year-old aviation commissar, Shakhurin, and his deputy, the thirty-three-year-old Yakovlev (the designer of the "Yak"), to the Little Corner, and they arrived in the middle of a large gathering. Without asking them to sit, Stalin began to read aloud from a letter written by an airplane designer who complained that he had a brilliant idea for a new killer plane but that the deputy commissar would not brook a rival and was blocking the innovative design, forcing the letter writer to appeal directly to "the Central Committee." Silence ensued. Yakovlev responded that the designer had never actually approached him. (Shakhurin did not know anything about the proposed plane.) "Of course, he should first of all have spoken with both of you," Stalin allowed. "Not speaking with you, and writing a complaint about you, is not the way. I don't know about this proposal—maybe it's a good airplane, maybe it's a bad one—but the promised specs are alluring." Stalin then asked how much it would cost. They answered, "8 to 9 million [rubles]." Stalin ordered it built, adding, "I ask you not to go after this designer for writing the letter. . . . For you it is unpleasant, probably, that such letters are written. But I am pleased. By the way, it is not the first letter." As Yakovlev neared the exit to the Little Corner, Stalin called out. "Do not persecute the designer for writing the complaint; let him build the plane. We shall risk the millions; I shall take the sin on my soul." The plane was duly built. It crashed on its maiden flight, taking with it one of the country's best experimental pilots.[279]

All the while, significant interruptions were occurring in German deliveries of contracted military weapons as called for in the new commercial agreement. Stalin began demanding a new short-term trade agreement with Germany to ensure compliance. Mikoyan, in mid-April 1940, complained to his German interlocutors that he could "no longer afford to make a fool of himself, in practice conducting a bilateral exchange of goods but unilaterally delivering goods to Germany." Stalin had been retaliating for the German shortfall: out of a contractual 1 million tons of grain for Germany, fewer than 150,000 had been delivered.[280] Soviet oil deliveries had barely reached 100,000 tons, just one ninth of the contractual amount and less than 15 percent of German stocks.[281] But Romania was supplying huge multiples of that in oil, while Swedish iron ore shipments dwarfed Soviet supplies to Germany. The major Soviet contribution would come in feed grain and legumes. The original 1 million tons of grain would be raised to 1.5 million, and the Germans soon sought yet another 1 million.[282] In the face of Germany's nearly insatiable demand, Stalin raised prices.

RED ARMY RESURRECTION

At the conclusion of the Finnish war military reckoning, on April 17, 1940, Stalin formalized the appointments of three new deputy heads of the Council of People's Commissars: Mikhail Pervukhin (b. 1904), the chief engineer and then director of the Moscow Energy utility, who had rocketed to first deputy commissar of heavy industry in 1938; Alexei Kosygin, who had been a shop foreman on a factory floor as late as 1937 before becoming textile industry commissar in 1939; and Vyacheslav Malyshev, a locomotive designer and the recently named commissar of heavy machine building. They joined Molotov's six other deputies: Mikoyan, Kaganovich, Nikolai Bulganin (b. 1895, chairman of the state bank), Nikolai Voznesensky (b. 1903, head of state planning), Vyshinsky, and Rozaliya Zemlyachka. The latter was an old revolutionary terrorist (b. 1876), but otherwise these were predominantly economic managers.

Notwithstanding these promotions, the terror continued to cast its shadow. In May 1940, no annual reception took place at the Kremlin for the young graduates of military academies, where arrests and executions during the terror had damaged the level of instruction. On May 4 and 5, Stalin, the immediate retinue, and surviving military elite were gathered in the form of a commission of the Main Military Council to codify the lessons from Finland.[283] No one on that commission, or at the various meetings with Stalin present, blamed the tough going in Finland on the terror, but the thought was on people's minds. At a separate May 1940 meeting on military ideology, Dmitry Pavlov, a Spanish civil war veteran and high-ranking tank commander in the Finnish war, stated, "We had so many enemies of the people that I doubt that all of them could have been enemies." He added, "Here it is necessary to say that the operations of 1937–38, before Beria arrived, so compromised us that, in my opinion, we would [otherwise] have easily had our way with an adversary like the Finns."[284]

Military personnel changes were the most consequential since 1925. On May 7, 1940, Stalin named Timoshenko defense commissar and kicked Voroshilov "upstairs" to the post of deputy chairman of the Council of People's Commissars—making him the tenth.[285] The despot also promoted Timoshenko to the rank of marshal. Stalin had always been taken by Voroshilov's gifted sociability and dog-like loyalty, insurance against a Bonapartist coup, but the price of his military shortcomings had become too high and the despot had hit upon a replacement. The peasant boy Timoshenko had won Stalin's trust in a way that the brilliant aristocrat's son Mikhail Tukhachevsky never could.[286] Returning the number of marshals to five, Stalin also promoted Shaposhnikov and the dense Kulik.[287] Two days before, Stalin had colluded with Beria to have Kulik's beautiful Jewish second wife, Kira Simonich, kidnapped. The despot then pretended he had no idea where she might be, advising Kulik to remarry and forget the "nympho female spy." She was the daughter of the former *okhranka* chief in Helsinki who had been executed by the Cheka in 1919; her first husband had been a NEPman with foreign connections; her two brothers, one of whom had been an officer for the Whites, were arrested for espionage; her mother left for Italy in 1934. Nonetheless, Kulik had refused Voroshilov's entreaties to divorce the fetching Kira.[288] Such compromising associations would have been more than enough to bury any Red Army officer; Kulik, in addition, had been a Socialist Revolutionary, not a Bolshevik, before the October Revolution. He supplied a steady stream of denunciations on the other military men.

Two of the five marshals (Voroshilov and Budyonny) were civil-war-era cavalrymen who defended the role of horse-riding troops deep into the era of tanks and planes. The strategically literate Shaposhnikov—the highest-ranking former tsarist officer still around—had not been able to block the wrongheaded breakup of mechanized divisions, but he had closely advised Stalin on the military operations to recover the old tsarist borders.[289] Nevertheless, the despot soon replaced him as chief of staff with, of all people, the Finnish-war failure Meretskov.[290]

The big story was Timoshenko: the defense of the socialist motherland now rested upon his shoulders. On May 7, 1940, at a celebration of Tchaikovsky's centenary, Timoshenko appeared in the imperial box at the Bolshoi in a threesome with Stalin and Molotov—a Kremlinological signal to the elite, whose whispers could be counted on to spread word of the coronation. With the transfer of the defense portfolio, a chastened Stalin also allowed Timoshenko to conduct a genuine investigation into the state of the Red Army.[291] He sent Timoshenko to inspect key Soviet military districts in person. The despot and his new defense commissar forced through sweeping reforms, including greater discipline and genuine basic training.[292] Military production, already immense, was savagely ramped up, including the mass manufacture of machine guns, which Stalin's idiot cronies had dismissed but the Finns had put to devastating use. Mikoyan negotiated new defense-related trade pacts with more than a dozen countries, which forced still deeper shortages on the Soviet populace in order to free up resources for export.[293] Timoshenko oversaw a hasty expansion of officer training: in 1940, the Soviet Union counted eighteen military academies, plus eight military departments at various civilian universities, as well as 214 schools (*uchilishche*) for the army and six for the navy. Training courses lasted from forty-five to ninety days. The defense commissar also rushed to extend rail lines and build airports—a target of 950 by the end of 1941, meaning more than 300 new ones.[294]

Stalin approved the reintroduction of the ranks of admiral and general on May 7, 1940, as well. Meretskov would be among those promoted to full general, while naval commissar Kuznetsov became a new admiral. "Stalin by that point did not entertain objections," Kuznetsov recalled. "A kind of thick cloud had formed around him of bootlickers and obsequious types who blocked the necessary people from accessing him. For us, young people raised up by the 'unquiet' 1937–38 period and striving out of inexperience to 'develop our own views,' we quickly learned that our part was to listen more and speak less." Still, Kuznetsov noted that "back then I bowed before Stalin's authority, not doubting anything that emerged from him."[295]

There were some 1,000 senior officer promotions altogether. Zhukov, who had remained in Mongolia and missed the Finnish campaign, was among those elevated. Voroshilov recalled him from Ulan Bator, and Stalin summoned him to the Little Corner. "I had never met Stalin before and I went to the meeting very agitated," Zhukov recalled. "Greeting me, Stalin, puffing his pipe, immediately asked, 'How do you assess the Japanese army?'" Zhukov gave a detailed answer, after which Stalin inquired about the performance of Soviet troops and the Soviet commanders Kulik, Dmitry Pavlov, and Nikolai Voronov. Zhukov claimed he had praised the latter two, but not Kulik. After further discussion, Stalin said, "Now you have combat experience. Take over the Kiev military district"—which Timoshenko was relinquishing—"and use your experience in the training of the troops." Zhukov returned to the Hotel Moskva but could not fall asleep. "Stalin's external appearance, his soft voice, his concreteness and depth of thinking, his attentiveness in listening to the report, impressed me greatly."[296]

Stalin also authorized Beria to release more than ten thousand Red Army officers from the Gulag.[297] Colonel Konstanty Rokossowski, who had been arrested as a Polish spy, had been released on March 22, 1940, without explanation, after thirty months in confinement. He had served under Timoshenko back in the Volga military district. Rokossowski, aged forty-four, had refused to sign confessions to crimes he had not committed, but his toes had been smashed to bits with a hammer and nine of his teeth knocked out.[298] He was promoted to general. The regime feared its own returning soldiers who had seen the capitalist world. The Finnish general staff had organized an occasional newspaper for Soviet POWs. Under the rubric "Truth is dearer than everything on earth," the first issue stated, "We consider that your main misfortune and the misfortune of the entire Russian people consists in the fact that you do not at all know the truth about the life that surrounds you. Your authorities kept you isolated from the whole world and told you only what they thought you needed to know. Fate had it that by falling into captivity in a free country, you got the chance to know the truth about how other nations live. . . . You will learn the truth and will be able to compare your life with the life of other countries."[299]

STALIN EMERGED from the war he launched against Finland with both a crushing victory and a severely impaired military reputation, emboldening the country's potential enemies, maybe even more than he had with his executions of his own military. He also undermined further the Soviet Union's international standing as a supposed bulwark of peace. "My anti-Communism, half suppressed by my friendships and the need for Soviet support against the Third Reich, burst forth," noted the French intellectual Raymond Aron of the fall of 1939. "Those who did not denounce Stalin and the German-Soviet pact became unbearable for me."[300] In Philadelphia on November 17, 1939, Professor Carlton Hayes, of Columbia University, noted the convergence of German, Italian, and Soviet "force against Czechs and Albanians, Poles and Finns."[301] Hayes spoke at the first academic conference devoted to the concept of "totalitarianism," which would provide a cudgel for principled opponents of the Soviet regime, both on the right and on the left.[302] On April 25, 1940, Rudolf Hilferding, the Austrian Marxist luminary and author of *Finance Capital* (1910), published an essay in the Menshevik émigré paper in Paris, titled "State Capitalism or Totalitarian State Economy?" He lent his authority among socialists to the view that in the Soviet Union, as in Germany and Italy, politics determined economics, and that the Bolsheviks had "created the first totalitarian state, even before the name was invented."[303]

The Red Army, in 1940, would acquire five times as many weapons as it had as recently as 1935.[304] Stalin also appeared to have caught a stupendous break: on May 10, 1940, Hitler attacked the Low Countries and France. The despot could scarcely have hoped for more.[305] Previously, during what now, in retrospect, became the First World War, the Russian general staff had shuddered at the thought that a quick German rout of the French would lead to a separate peace on the western front, which in turn would give Germany a completely free hand against Russia in the east.[306] But their fears were misplaced: the fighting had lasted four stalemated years. Surely France, assisted again by Britain, even with the Soviet Union on the sidelines, could again stalemate Germany?[307] Like the British, Stalin seemed to have a high opinion of French military capabilities.[308] With a presumed protracted war in the west, he seemed set to gain all the time needed to correct his mistakes, and force-modernize the massive Red Army.

CHAPTER 13

GREED

Stalin takes advantage of the hour. . . . All from our
success. We make victory easy for the others.

JOSEPH GOEBBELS, *diary entry, June 28, 1940*[1]

If the Germans propose a partition of Turkey, then you
can reveal our cards.

STALIN, *instructions to Molotov for meeting with Hitler,*
November 13, 1940[2]

BRITAIN AND FRANCE had supplied weapons to Finland and contemplated attacking a strategic vulnerability—the insatiable thirst for oil—of both the Soviets and their trade partners the Germans, with whom the Western powers were at war. In what was designated Operation Pike, the idea emerged to launch air raids using airfields in Syria, Turkey, and Iran to obliterate the rigs, refineries, and storage tanks in Soviet Baku, Grozny, and Batum. The British put out rumors that the plans were afoot, evidently in part to distract the Soviets from possible Western operations planned to defend Scandinavia, but the Royal Air Force did not undertake reconnaissance flights over the intended Caucasus targets until after Finland had capitulated. Of course, any Western bombing of Baku might have backfired, rendering the perennial British-French accusation—that the USSR and Nazi Germany were in alliance—into a reality. Be that as it may, Pike never occurred.[3] A French threat to intervene militarily on Finland's behalf had never materialized, either: Daladier had once more left the key decision to Chamberlain, and when nothing came of it, the French leader resigned. The upshot was the worst of all worlds: Stalin had escaped without damage, but with his profound distrust of the British and French reinforced.[4]

Hitler, in April 1940, had occupied Norway and Denmark with relative ease, protecting his vital raw material imports from Sweden. On April 9 in Norway, Major Vidkun Quisling seized power in a Nazi-backed coup d'état. Nazi assertions that the Wehrmacht had been compelled to seize these countries to protect them from British-French violations of their neutrality were repeated in the

Soviet press. Molotov voiced Soviet approval of the Nazi occupation of Denmark and Norway to Schulenburg, wishing Germany a complete victory in these "defensive measures." The British, he added, "have gone too far."[5] Similarly, Zhdanov, on April 13, stressed that "from the USSR's point of view," it was "more pleasant, useful, and valuable to have nearby not the anti-Soviet Anglo-French allies who intended to attack either Germany or Leningrad, but a country that is in friendly relations with us."[6] Four days later, at a meeting with the high command, Stalin complained of Britain and France that "they are, you know, fighting a war over there, but it is a weak war; either they are in combat or they are playing cards. They might suddenly make peace."[7]

Stalin and his minions were dead wrong on the latter point. On May 10, 1940, Germany smashed into the Netherlands, Belgium, and Luxembourg, on a path to France. Luxembourg effectively did not oppose the German occupation, while the Netherlands capitulated on May 15; the Belgians did so slightly later (without even consulting their French allies). Such was "the peace" between the Nazis and the Western powers: further conquests by Hitler.[8] A disgraced Chamberlain announced his resignation to the cabinet. His fate had been sealed with the abysmal failed defense of Norway, which had sparked a searing debate in the House of Commons on May 7–8. (One conservative MP had admonished him, "In the name of God, go.") No one had contributed more to Britain's Norway debacle than Winston Churchill, who, as first lord of the Admiralty, was responsible for naval operations. But aided by Conservative rebels, Churchill outmaneuvered his main Tory party rival, foreign secretary Viscount Halifax (a member of the House of Lords, not the Commons), and got himself named the prime minister of a new coalition government with Labour.

Churchill, the scion of a British aristocrat and an American heiress, was lucky to be alive. Back in December 1931, he had been struck by a taxi on Fifth Avenue in New York City, after looking the wrong way while crossing the street. "A man has been killed," a witness had called out erroneously.[9] Churchill was a staunch imperialist, perhaps even more so than Chamberlain, having advocated for using poison gas against rebellious Kurdish tribesmen in Iraq, a British mandate. Also like Chamberlain, Churchill was ready, for the sake of the empire, to bargain with nasty types, but, unlike Chamberlain, he viewed the German national character as dangerous under certain leadership, such as Hitler. Regarding Munich, Churchill had prophetically told the House of Commons that Britain "has been offered a choice between war and shame. She has chosen shame and will get war." In 1940, many British elites were still waffling, urging a "settlement" with the Nazis.

Chamberlain remained in government as lord president of the Privy Council (responsible for much of domestic policy, which did not much interest Churchill) and as formal leader of the Tory party. When Chamberlain entered the House of Commons on May 13, 1940, for the first time since resigning as prime minister, the "MPs lost their heads, they shouted, they cheered, they waved their order papers, and his reception was a regular ovation."[10] Churchill, however, steadfastly refused all entreaties to seek terms with Hitler, a man he would never meet, but whose measure he took.[11]

Born the same decade as Churchill, Stalin missed these important cues. The ideologically blinkered despot tended to be dismissive of all British "imperialists," lumped together, and kept in force the Comintern directive that "not fascist Germany, which entered into an agreement with the USSR, but reactionary anti-Soviet England, with its immense colonial empire, is the bulwark of capitalism."[12]

Stalin had gone in deeper than ever with Nazi Germany. After the signing of the most recent commercial agreement, in 1940, Soviet demands had gone through the roof: they sought the nearly finished "surplus" cruisers *Seydlitz, Prinz Eugen,* and *Lützow,* and the blueprints for the battleship *Bismarck,* 31,000 tons of armor plating, torpedoes, ammunition, artillery, dehydration equipment (for synthetic fuel), steel-hardening technology, and all models of German planes in production (Messerschmitts, Dorniers, Junkers, Heinkels). The Germans were incredulous. Stalin, through Mikoyan, employed pressure tactics, holding up grain and oil deliveries, which induced the Germans to deliver some thirty state-of-the-art warplanes. He also interceded to reduce some Soviet demands. But Molotov and Mikoyan insisted to the Germans that the partially finished heavy cruiser *Lützow* had to be handed over. On May 26, 1940, for a price of 104 million reichsmarks, Germany allowed the ship, renamed *Petropavlovsk,* to be towed to Leningrad for completion, with their help.[13] The Germans were worried that Soviet intelligence would be able to duplicate advanced German construction methods.[14] Soviet counterintelligence would outfit the German team's residence with listening and photographic devices, and promptly set up a honey trap with a young beauty.[15]

Stalin was still obsessing over Trotsky as well. On May 27, word came to the Little Corner that the NKVD had failed, yet again, to assassinate the exile, despite an assault on his villa by some twenty men and the discharge of more than 200 bullets into Trotsky's bedroom. Beria demanded a report from the head of the operations team, Sudoplatov, then whisked him to Stalin's Near Dacha, a half hour's drive from Lubyanka, so that the operative could report in person on the failure—and on new plans to fulfill the assignment. Stalin was said to have asked a single question, then issued instructions: the entire global Trotsky surveillance network should be put on the line to eliminate Trotsky, because once Trotsky was eliminated, the need for surveillance would disappear.[16]

Beyond his greed and distraction, Stalin's inability to pick up on the political changes in London was driven by an abiding antipathy toward the Western powers.[17] But Churchill, too, had trouble perceiving all his options. He reveled in little Finland's fight against the Soviets, publicly declaring that it proved how "Communism rots the soul of a nation."[18] He had ceased his cultivation of Maisky. But the West's war against Germany was going poorly. Even after the first British evacuation of Dunkirk, the new PM had dispatched still more ground troops to France, to prevent that country's fall. In doing so, Churchill almost lost his land army—and the war—right then and there. The commander of British reinforcements in France was soon imploring the PM to evacuate these troops, too. Some 338,000 British as well as French and Belgian soldiers did manage to escape from Dunkirk back across the Channel, thanks only to a blunder by Hitler and his top commander, halting their ground attacks, as well as French sacrifices in a rearguard action. "We shall defend our island, whatever the cost may be," Churchill exhorted on June 4, 1940, as Britain's land army fled in boats. "We shall fight on the beaches, we shall fight on the landing grounds, we shall fight in the fields and in the streets, we shall fight in the hills; we shall never surrender." This ringing oratory elicited a lukewarm domestic reception, a further sign of British precariousness.[19] It did not take a genius to grasp that the only formidable land army remaining on the continent, besides Hitler's, was Stalin's.

NEW REALITIES

On June 5 and 6, *Pravda* printed portraits of Soviet military brass, apparently to reassure the public in the face of the latest triumphal march of the Wehrmacht. By June 14, after a little more than four weeks, the Germans had already entered Paris.[20] The fathers and grandfathers of these troops had fought for more than four years and never seized that prize.[21] On June 17, a new French government sued for peace. "Honor, common sense, and the interests of the country require that all free Frenchmen, wherever they be, should continue the fight as best they may," a general named Charles de Gaulle quixotically broadcast from London to France over BBC radio on June 18.[22] Three days later, the German victory was sealed in the same French forest, inside the very same railway carriage—a rickety old wagon-lit used by Marshal Foch—in which the Germans had surrendered in the First World War. Hitler sat in Foch's former seat.[23] Nazi Germany decided to occupy more than half of France, including the Atlantic and English Channel coasts.[24] A collaborationist rump French state was allowed in the southern city of Vichy.

France's fall came to seem inevitable, especially since it lacked the protection afforded by the Channel, but in the years leading up to 1940, French military industry had created an arsenal roughly equal to the Nazi one.[25] True, the French air force significantly lagged the Luftwaffe, but France fielded more ground soldiers and tanks than did the Wehrmacht. And the German tanks were often inferior.[26] French intelligence operated a remarkable agent network, signals intelligence, and photoreconnaissance, but after France's famed Second Bureau had issued a dozen secret warnings of an imminent German attack—going back to November 1939 and including four in April 1940—and the predicted invasion had failed to materialize, the officers had lost their credibility.[27] French higher-ups, for their part, failed to make proper use of the plentiful information acquired of German plans.[28]

An even deeper problem involved tactics: the French fought a war of position, the Nazis a war of movement.[29] France's plan of battle had two aspects: fixed defensive fortifications, known as the Maginot Line, and a motorized northern army intended to thrust into Belgium and Holland and establish front lines there.[30] Between the two lay a soft spot, the Ardennes, which some French military experts considered traversable even by mechanized forces, despite its forested and mountainous terrain and a substantial river, but the French had done nothing to prepare for such an eventuality, laying no antitank obstacles and only scattered bunkers. This was exactly where the audacious Germans struck.[31] The Wehrmacht could not conceal its massing of troops for an assault through the Ardennes, of course, but Germany conducted a feint, invading the Low Countries through the Gembloux Gap, drawing the bulk of French forces northward to interdict a presumed Wehrmacht advance to the Channel coast. By instead slicing with its main strike *between* the French and British land forces massed in Belgium, to the north, and the Maginot Line, to the south, the German army stormed into a vacuum and achieved the largest encirclement in military history.

This brilliant plan of battle had been serendipitous. The first three versions of the German battle plan had called for an attack via the north, into the teeth of the French deployments, but inclement weather had compelled a delay in Hitler's winter attack scheme, during which two careless German staff officers were shot down over France carrying a portfolio with staff maps. The battle plan could not remain the same. In the meantime, a German intelligence officer playing the part of the French and British commanders in war games had demonstrated to the German general staff that the enemy would position its top forces in Belgium, but only weakly defend the Ardennes, and would be slow to shift forces to counter a German attack there. The late-in-the-day fourth and final battle plan, under Erich von Manstein (b. 1887), a staff officer, hit upon the feint (by 29 divisions through northern Belgium and the Netherlands) and the massive "sickle cut" (by 46 crack divisions through the Ardennes).[32] The plan was beyond audacious, and a nervous high command threw everything into the initial assault, without any reserve panzer divisions, on a very narrow front, in vulnerable columns 250 miles in length, with flammable fuel trucks in front. Yet the much-feared Western bombing raids and counterattacks against exposed German flanks did not materialize until it was too late.

Even then, decisive victory had come only after the German tank specialist Heinz Guderian ignored his orders and, exploiting his Ardennes breakthrough, suddenly raced for the Channel—a bold act of insubordination.[33] He had punched through to the Channel by May 20, a mere ten days into the war (admittedly, over high-quality French roads outside the Ardennes).[34] But neither he nor Hitler had expected this armored blitz to seal the fate of France (Guderian later called it "a miracle"). After all, once caught out by surprise, no foe remains passive. But even after being shown aerial photographs of German traffic jams in the Ardennes woods, the French brass did not manage to redeploy their formidable war machine to seize back the initiative, being, in effect, defeated psychologically.[35] Tactical military failures were compounded by administrative and political ones. Maxime Weygand, an ultrarightist, replaced the initial top French commander, Maurice Gamelin, and undercut the Third Republic's civilian leadership; the lion of the Great War, the eighty-four-year-old Marshal Philippe Pétain, had been brought into government, and immediately plotted against it, too. France's political class folded, opening the way for hard rightists to pursue their long-sought authoritarian regime in rump Vichy. Despite German air superiority, therefore, the defeat of France's Third Republic was contingent—derived from egregious generalship, political treachery, and German audacity.[36]

The myth of a *planned* blitzkrieg—annihilation of the enemy's fighting capacity in a lightning strike—was born. The improvisation notwithstanding, armored warfare had succeeded spectacularly.[37] The French lost 124,000 killed and 200,000 wounded, while 1.5 million Western troops were taken prisoner; German casualties were fewer than 50,000 dead and wounded. (Mussolini had waited until Paris fell to attack southern France; Italy suffered some 4,000 casualties in direct fighting, the French 104.) The Wehrmacht became intoxicated by its swift victory, and bound ever more tightly to Hitler.[38] The Führer, unlike Stalin, had embraced integrated, independently operating armor and panzer divisions, overriding the conservatism of the majority of German generals and standing by Guderian, who had led a minority in the push for the novel formations.[39]

More broadly, Hitler's foreign policy recklessness had once again resulted in exhilarating success. It had taken Stalin 105 days to subdue the Finnish nation; it had taken Hitler less than half that time to subdue a nation ten times the size. "Stalin was very quick-tempered and irritable at that time," recalled Khrushchev. "I had rarely seen him like that. At meetings he hardly ever sat down in his chair but constantly paced. Now he literally ran around the room and cursed like a longshoreman. He cursed the French and he cursed the British, asking how they could have let Hitler smash them like that."[40]

The despot needed to find a mirror. Besides him, there had been a total of thirty-two members and candidate members of the politburo between inception (1919) and 1940. Three of them (Lenin, Dzierżyński, Kuibyshev) had died of natural causes; two (Kirov and one on Stalin's orders) would be assassinated; two (Tomsky, Orjonikidze) had killed themselves. Fourteen had been executed as enemies: Zinoviev, Kamenev, Rykov, Bukharin, Uglanov, Krestinsky, Kosior, Baumanis, Syrtsov, Chubar, Eihe, Postyshev, Rudzutaks, Yezhov. One (Petrovsky) had been expelled but spared. The remaining ten—Molotov, Voroshilov, Kaganovich, Mikoyan, Kalinin, Zhdanov, Andreyev, Shvernik, Khrushchev, Beria—were alive, at his forbearance. Such despotism smothered policy give-and-take. Stalin summoned them when he saw fit; they fed him the information he sought. The conduct of Soviet foreign policy, unlike that of most great powers, was significantly less subject to the usual vagaries of internal regime jockeying among interest groups, but it was utterly hostage to Stalin's misconceptions.[41]

Right after he made the deal with the Nazis, Stalin had privately observed that "the nonaggression pact is to a certain degree helping Germany. Next time we'll urge on the other side."[42] This looks like a blustery lie to soften the political damage of the Pact. Molotov, on June 17, 1940, offered German ambassador Schulenburg his "warmest congratulations . . . on the splendid successes of the German Wehrmacht" (according to the German notetaker), while adding (according to the Soviet notetaker) that "Hitler and the German government could scarcely have expected such rapid successes."[43] It was, of course, Molotov's and Stalin's expectations that had been upended.[44]

Stalin had staked Soviet security on France's fighting capabilities, then contributed mightily to France's defeat: the 1940 economic agreement between the Soviet Union and Germany was four times larger than the 1939 one. Altogether, in 1940, the Soviets would supply 34 percent of German oil, 40 percent of its nickel, 74 percent of phosphates, 55 percent of manganese ore, 65 percent of chromium ore, 67 percent of asbestos, and more than 1 million tons of timber and of grain.[45] True, big new Soviet shipments from the February 1940 agreement did not arrive in time for the offensive against France, but, knowing that Stalin's shipments were coming, German military planners were confidently depleting stocks. "Hitler conducts his military operations, and Stalin acts as his quartermaster," Trotsky had quipped.[46] The Wehrmacht's actual quartermaster general remarked, "The conclusion of this treaty has saved us."[47] Stalin's Pact also allowed Hitler to confidently retain a mere 10 divisions in the east. The Soviet contribution to German logistics was crucial as well. British sea power had once blockaded Napoleon's bid for continental empire, but now, thanks to Stalin, Nazi Germany managed to circumvent a British naval blockade with the transshipment of goods from the Near and Far East through Soviet territory. Thus could a Central European country take on a global empire.[48]

To be sure, Stalin was also making out like a bandit. Berlin dragged its feet over shipments, but he got samples of artillery, tanks (along with the formulas for their armor), chemical warfare equipment, a naval cruiser, the plans to the battleship *Bismarck,* heavy naval guns, locomotives, turbines, generators, diesel engines, machine tools. Stalin evidently was not going to risk that German bounty—and Hitler's wrath—by playing both sides of the conflict. But his overwhelming support of the Nazi war machine, when he was counting on the French land army, smacks of miscalculation and pettiness.

With France's defeat, the strategic ground shifted radically.[49] In the very early morning of June 23, 1940, for the first and only time in his life, an exultant Hitler toured Paris, accompanied by two of his favorites, the architect Albert Speer and sculptor Arno Breker. The Führer was driven first to the neobaroque Opéra, which he examined in light of the architectural plans he had studied as a young man. Later he posed for photographers in front of the Eiffel Tower and took in Napoleon's tomb. "It was the dream of my life to be permitted to see Paris," he remarked. He had been expected to preside over a German victory parade, and in anticipation, some staff inside the British security establishment proposed bombing the reviewing stand, but their suggestion was rejected. In the event, Hitler opted not to stage a parade, evidently because of the danger of a British air raid, and already by 9:00 a.m. on June 23 he was back at the airfield for the return to Berlin. He would tell his entourage, "I am not in the mood for a victory parade. We aren't at the end yet."[50]

As it happened, also on June 23, *Semyon Kotko,* an opera by Sergei Prokofyev, premiered at the Stanislavsky Opera Theater, in Moscow, following many postponements. It was based on a novella by Valentin Katayev, *I Am the Son of the Working People,* and marked Prokofyev's first foray on a quintessential Soviet theme.[51] The score was infused with folk song intonations. "That evening, when I first heard *Semyon Kotko,* I understood that Prokofyev was a great composer," recalled the virtuoso pianist Svyatoslav Richter.[52] When Prokofyev first composed the score, his friend Meyerhold, who also felt a need to demonstrate his allegiance to the regime, begged to be the one to stage it. After Meyerhold had vanished without trace and Sergei Eisenstein claimed to be otherwise occupied, the direction fell to an actress. In the story, Kotko (a tenor) returns, in 1918, from the Romanian front of the Great War to his village in Ukraine, where pillaging foreign interventionists are trying to restore the landlords; an embittered kulak, the father of Kotko's teenage fiancée, Sofia (a soprano), forbids her from marrying a poor peasant. Thanks to heroic partisan warfare and the resolve of this "son of the working people," Semyon and Sofia are reunited as anti-Soviet forces are driven away or executed. Stalin's Pact with Hitler precluded using the novella's portrayal of Germans as the villains, and so in the opera's staging the Germans (as well as Austrians) mostly became Ukrainian nationalists.[53]

A NEW UNION

Molotov had not only congratulated Schulenburg, but also stated—and here the congratulations look like a spoonful of sugar to help the medicine go down—that from June 14, 1940, the Red Army had sent substantial additional forces to Lithuania, Latvia, and Estonia, where "changes of governments" were in process.[54] In the wee hours of June 15–16, Molotov summoned the envoys of Estonia (1:00 a.m.) and Latvia (1:10 a.m.) to inform them that, just as in Lithuania, the Red Army would soon be crossing their borders, and instructed them not to resist militarily but to await the formation of a new government.[55] In other words, the USSR was violating its recent pledges to respect the sovereignty of the three Baltic states. Of the three, Lithuania had the largest Communist party in early 1940—a mere 1,500 members, following Stalin's mass terror.[56] "There are no Communists outside Russia," he had told the Lithuanian foreign minister a few months before. "What you have in Latvia are Trotskyists: if they cause you trouble, shoot them."[57] By summer 1940, Estonia had a mere 150 Communists, out of a country of 1.3 million. Latvia had a similar number.[58] But Stalin's coercive, rapid-fire Sovietization did not rely on indigenous Communist movements. Rather, the operations followed the formula laid down by the Red Army's thrust into eastern Poland in fall 1939.[59]

In eastern Poland, the NKVD had deported more than 1 million of the 13.5 million residents to labor camps. (Interrogators called their truncheons "the Polish Constitution.") Soviet operatives and local collaborators nationalized industry and redistributed some farmland, although an arduous collectivization was put off for the time being. To smoke out locals unreconciled to Soviet rule, the NKVD used provocateurs. The Polish officer in charge of the fledgling Polish underground turned Soviet informant.[60] But even with this formidable apparatus of coercion, the Soviet secret police had lacked the bureaucratic resources to themselves smash all existing institutions and associations. In a cunning type of revolution, however, the NKVD allowed free rein to criminal gangs and vigilante groups, which they glorified as citizen militias, and set up anonymous denunciation boxes and walk-in centers, leveraging the grievances built up in society. Who had been fired from a job and could now seek revenge? Who had lost a court case? Who had sold a cow for a price that in retrospect seemed too low? Who had been cuckolded? By bringing forth these denunciations and then acting upon them without verifying, the NKVD effectively allowed state power to be "privatized" by thousands of people looking for redress, survival, cover-up, or promotion. It was Poles themselves who undermined pre-Soviet social bonds, clearing the way for Communist monopoly.[61] That was the essence of totalitarianism: people's agency was elicited to destroy their own agency.

Despite people's evasions and self-misrepresentations, the NKVD—full of half-educated people—amassed a stunning amount of operational information, seizing local archives and personnel files, and using censuses and tax registers, to enumerate the entire population politically. The NKVD locked factory gates with the workers inside until registrations were complete, and put the onus on urban landlords, who would answer with their heads, to march whole apartment buildings to prearranged sites for "registration." In villages, volunteer or conscripted facilitators were promised rewards for meeting "quotas" of farmers delivered to in-person registrations.[62]

Then, across nearly 80,000 square miles of territory littered with impassable marshes, served by sparse rail or paved roads fit for vehicles, with a mass influx of refugees and other wartime dislocation, functionaries managed to ensure that every adult in former eastern Poland took part in single-candidate "elections" to a "People's Assembly." Posters went up, film screenings were organized, marches staged. The elections provided a legal façade for the transfer of sovereignty, but, more profoundly, they entailed political conditioning in the new regime. The coerced voting took place in full view of others, some of whom were eager or reluctant stool pigeons. Many people nonetheless crossed off the name of the candidate, and some slipped manure into the ballot envelopes. But many of those who spoiled ballots or failed to show were arrested. After the vote, the public displays and slogans remained, and political speeches with mandatory attendance continued. State-sponsored associations were established. State schools replaced private ones, and a new political vocabulary reflecting Communist ideology took over the public sphere and people's identities.[63] In less than two years, western Ukraine and western Belorussia recapitulated much of what had been carried through in the Soviet Union over two decades.

In summer 1940, a similar "revolution from abroad" was enacted in the Baltics. Stalin ordered forced Sovietization of Estonia, to be overseen by Zhdanov; of Latvia, overseen by show-trial prosecutor Vyshinsky; and of Lithuania, overseen by Dekanozov, the Beria protégé and Molotov deputy at foreign affairs. Each commanded gangs of functionaries newly promoted as a result of the terror. But here, too, local inhabitants were incited to orgies of denunciation, such that, in avenging wrongs, assuaging hunger, and satisfying greed, they helped level their societies and pave the way for Communist monopoly. Once again, the local archives were seized for operational purposes.[64] Scores of thousands of local inhabitants would be deported to Siberia, and those not removed were compelled to take part in single-candidate "elections" to People's Assemblies; the installed deputies, in turn, "voted" to form Soviet socialist republics and join the USSR. The economies were confiscated ("nationalized"), including land, although collectivization was held off. Even as underground resistance units formed, substantial numbers of people on the political left in Estonia, Latvia, and Lithuania—including the ethnic Russian and Jewish workers—supported this Sovietization.[65]

All told, between March and June 1940, five new Soviet socialist republics were established (including Karelia, elevated to Union republic status), increasing their total to sixteen and the Soviet population to 200 million. On June 5, 1940, a "Ten-Day" culture festival celebrating the expanded Belorussian SSR, involving 1,200 participants, opened in Moscow.[66] The regime had long since shifted from award ceremonies for milkmaids and cotton pickers, with Stalin and entourage donning national costume, to showcases of the Union's national cultures. The first Ten-Day, in 1936, had celebrated Soviet Ukraine, with some 500 participants, numerous awards bestowed on artistic organizations, and additional funds allocated for the arts in the republic.[67] Similarly extravagant Ten-Days had followed for Kyrgyzstan, Uzbekistan, Azerbaijan, and Armenia, whose troupes and ensembles performed in the top theaters and conservatories of the capital.[68] The USSR committee on artistic affairs took no chances, dispatching composers to republics and lavishing robust sums on them to compose a "national" opera or ballet.[69] Moscow-worthy performances required the addition of singers or musicians from the capital and a large crew comprising everything from choreographers to hairdressers.[70] Each "national" folk dance or "national" opera became recognizably Soviet.[71]

CLASH

Hitler took Stalin's Baltic annexations badly. The secret protocols of the Pact delimited "spheres of influence" but did not specify the actions permitted—or forbidden—within the respective spheres. There was not a word in the Pact about Soviet *occupation* of any countries, let alone implanting clone regimes. Stalin was well aware that Hitler had not authorized him to annex former tsarist possessions. But for a long time the despot had cultivated the idea that a fratricide among the imperialist powers might afford unique opportunities to expand "the revolution" in the resulting chaos and destruction. At the Bolshoi back on January 21, 1940 (the sixteenth anniversary of Lenin's passing), he had boasted, of eastern Poland's Sovietization, that "Red Army activities are also a matter of world revolution."[72] Then, in the face of the lightning German conquest of France, he had decided to unleash his revolutionary opportunism again. In the seemingly endless rows about whether Stalin's Kremlin was pursuing Soviet security, defensively, or revolutionary expansionism, the answer was: both, if someone else provided the opportunity.

On June 26, Molotov conveyed an ultimatum to Romania for former tsarist Bessarabia, which again surprised Germany. German officials pressured the Romanian government not to resist the landgrab and thereby afford Moscow a pretext for a full takeover of the country, whose oil fields thirty-five miles north of Bucharest were a life-or-death resource for the Wehrmacht. The Romanians hastily—and angrily—withdrew as the Red Army occupied Bessarabia. Hitler refrained from public criticism but told his adjutants that this was "the first Russian attack on Western Europe."[73] The Führer became angrier still at the Soviet seizure of northern Bukovina, which had never been tsarist, was not covered by the Pact, and was full of ethnic Germans. Molotov told Schulenburg that "Bukovina constitutes the last part that is still missing from a unified Ukraine."[74] The mass-circulation magazine *Ogonyok* printed photographs of Romanians greeting the Red Army ("the Great Liberator") with flowers and smiles.[75] The Nazi inner circle seethed. The Wehrmacht had smashed Poland on the battlefield while the Soviets had waltzed in and grabbed the Polish territory with the oil. This time, the Wehrmacht had smashed the French land army while the Soviets seized large pieces of Romania, as well as the defenseless Baltic states. "Grave robber!" Goebbels wrote of Stalin in his diary.[76]

Berlin demanded transfer to Germany of the 125,000 *Volksdeutsche* in Bessarabia and Bukovina, receipt of the 100,000 tons of grain from Bessarabia specified in a German contract with Romania, and guarantees for all German property as well as the railroad tracks transporting Romanian oil to the Reich.[77] Stalin began stationing what would increase to 34 divisions on former Romanian soil, linking what was now Soviet Lvov (Lwów, Lemberg) with Soviet Chernovitsy (Cernăuți, Czernowitz), in the Ukrainian SSR, while improving the security of Odessa. The fundamental clash of interests between Moscow and Berlin and the Soviet need to counterbalance Germany's continental aggrandizement could scarcely have been plainer. Just as the Winter War had definitively pushed Finland into the German camp, the seizure of Bessarabia and northern Bukovina consolidated Romania as a staunch German ally.[78]

Stalin also needed to reckon with the circumstance that his own value to Hitler was declining in relative terms. German-annexed Silesia and the Czech lands of Bohemia and Moravia were major industrial centers. (Austria had minimal industry, but it gifted Germany an underemployed labor force.) France, Belgium, Luxembourg, and the Netherlands all possessed significant industries as well, from steel and autos to aircraft and electronics, as well as railway locomotives and freight cars that exceeded the stock of the Reich. France and Norway produced chemicals and aluminum, too. The combined population of Greater Germany and the occupied lands, along with Italy, was now 290 million, and in terms of territory it was almost as large as the United States. This vast potential remained to be consolidated (Denmark refused a move toward a customs-and-currency union), but the direction was clear.[79] And the coup de grâce? Following his self-destructive bloodbath to extirpate phantom enemies, Stalin now acquired an actual fifth column on Soviet territory: resolute anti-Soviet saboteurs in the newly annexed territories of western Ukraine, western Belorussia, and the Baltic republics. In 1940, these regions, which contained a mere 10 percent of the Soviet population, would account for some 60 percent of the arrests by the NKVD. At the same time, thanks to the multiple German economic and trade delegations Stalin was allowing onto Soviet territory and into Soviet factories in 1940, direct German intelligence gathering, which had been almost nonexistent, became significant.[80]

TOYING WITH THE BRITISH

Stalin was presented an opportunity for a strategic shift, thanks to Sir Stafford Cripps, a high-profile, wealthy vegetarian and leftist whose agitation for an anti-fascist united front against Germany had gotten him expelled from the Labour party. The day before the Soviet invasion of eastern Poland, Cripps had urged his friend Foreign Secretary Halifax to send a mission to Moscow to negotiate a non-aggression pact with Moscow, paralleling the Hitler-Stalin Pact. The idea had gone nowhere, but in February 1940, en route to the UK from war-torn China, Cripps had been received by Molotov in Moscow, where he drew the conclusion that the countries could work out a bilateral trade agreement, and possibly more than that. Maisky, in London, had also proposed reviving discussions on trade, but the foreign office had questioned Soviet motives and worried about Soviet re-export of British goods to Britain's enemy Germany. Then, in May 1940, with France about to fall, Churchill, now PM, had acceded to the suggestion by Halifax, perhaps initiated by Maisky, to send Cripps to Moscow as a special envoy to spur trade talks. Molotov refused to accept Cripps under special envoy status. On June 3, 1940, the Soviet spy Gerhard Kegel ("X"), now in the economics section of the German embassy in Moscow, reported to Soviet military intelligence that the Germans were concerned about the pending Cripps visit and a possible Anglo-Soviet trade agreement.[81] At Soviet insistence, London appointed Cripps as a normal ambassador.[82] He arrived in Moscow on June 12.

Britain's imposing embassy, the former residence of a sugar magnate, was located on the embankment directly across the Moscow River from the Kremlin, with a spectacular view. Inside, its condition was appalling: not merely tasteless—sickly looking silk brocade of hideous colors (as Cripps observed)—but dilapidated. The embassy tableware consisted of bits and pieces—no dishes, no glasses, no silver—and the facility lacked a butler or maid, making diplomatic receptions that much more of a challenge. The small staff was unable to keep up with the volume of cipher work, let alone the diplomatic rounds in the complex city. Most British embassy staff were Russians and Soviet ethnic Germans, making German the dominant language.[83] That was British grand strategy: everything on the cheap—you fight my war, you staff my embassy.

Two days after his arrival—the very day Paris fell to Hitler—Cripps saw Molotov in the Kremlin for an hour and expressed a desire to improve relations. That same day, Molotov and his deputies sent birthday cards for the king (George VI) for the first time. But Molotov was not forthcoming with Cripps: also on June 14, the Soviet government head signed off on the Soviet ultimatum to the Lithuanians, a prelude to the occupation of the Baltic states, Bessarabia, and northern Bukovina. These aggressive Soviet actions proved to be an indirect boon to Cripps, though: soon, more than a hundred crates of ill-matched furniture and furnishings were evacuated from shuttered British missions in the three Baltic states and sent to the embassy in Moscow. Still, the moves exacerbated anti-Soviet sentiment in London.

Not everyone in the British establishment was hostile. On June 16, 1940, old David Lloyd George, who had once been an ardent partisan of appeasement, calling Hitler "the George Washington of Germany," told Maisky—during a discussion about a possible evacuation of the British government to Canada, if necessary—that "peace between England and Germany is impossible." When Lloyd George inquired whether the Soviets might finally stand up to Hitler, Maisky demurred. Lloyd George raised his finger: "Watch out that it does not turn out to be too late!"[84]

The British government, for its part, had both minimalist aims—induce the Soviet Union not to *increase* its largesse toward Nazi Germany—and maximalist ones: attain significant Soviet exports to Britain. Cripps believed it was possible to go beyond even the latter and get Britain and the Soviet Union to join forces against Germany, notwithstanding the Hitler-Stalin nonaggression and trade pacts, the dismemberment of Poland, the aggression against Finland, and now the Soviet annexation of the Baltic states.[85] A lawyer rather than a diplomat, Cripps was capable of criticizing Soviet realities, but he had defended Stalin's arrests of British nationals as spies in fabricated trials, as well as the Soviet Union's 1939 seizure of eastern Poland. Unlike Churchill (or Chamberlain), Cripps harbored no anxieties about Soviet penetration of Europe as a catalyst for spreading socialist revolution; he saw Stalin as security-minded and defensive. But Cripps met a wall of skepticism from the British foreign office, whose officials warned against enabling Stalin to exact better terms from Hitler by using "negotiations" with London. Surprisingly, at least to Cripps, the Soviet side was no more receptive.[86] He waited and waited to be received a second time after his first chilly audience with Molotov.

Finally, on July 1, bearing a message from Churchill (dated June 24) on "the prospect of Germany establishing hegemony over the Continent," Cripps was received by none other than Stalin—and in the Little Corner, in the presence of Molotov, between 6:30 and 9:15 p.m.[87] Among the difficult matters aired during what Cripps described as a "severely frank discussion" was that of British sanctions on Soviet imports of nonferrous metals. (The British suspected they would be rerouted by Stalin to Hitler; in fact, Germany needed these raw materials to produce the goods it owed to the Soviet Union.) "I could of course give a promise that not a single pound of metal would go to Germany," Stalin stated acidly, "but that would be dishonest. A promise is of no use which is not fulfilled." He went on to categorize Churchill's message about German expansionism as reactionary. "If the prime minister wants to restore the old equilibrium," he told Cripps, "we cannot agree with him." On the contrary, the despot remarked, "We must change the old balance of power in Europe, for it has acted to the USSR's disadvantage."[88]

Stalin was still preoccupied with British "imperialism" even now. He could not fail to have noticed that Hitler had become uppity following the conquest of France, but seared into the despot's mind was the debacle of the Western-Soviet military talks in summer 1939 and the enmity over the Soviet-Finnish War. Churchill's private communication calling for "harmonious and mutually beneficial" bilateral relations had a concrete aspect—encouraging strong Soviet actions in the Balkans, beyond even Bessarabia, to deny their strategic exploitation by Nazi Germany—but to Stalin this looked like the usual scheming to embroil the USSR in the war, allowing the British to escape. After the session, Cripps soberly wrote, "If anything is to be accomplished here, there is a very difficult past to be got over, and it's going to be slow work at the best."[89]

Cripps's failure to create any momentum toward rapprochement might be blamed on a stubborn Churchill (as well as knaves in the foreign office).[90] Churchill, however, had provided the basis for bilateral cooperation in his resolve. On July 3, 1940, to prevent French warships from falling into German hands, he had scuttled the main part of the French navy, stationed near Algeria, killing 1,297 of his ally's sailors. A French battleship and five destroyers escaped, but Churchill's ruthless action made an impression on Hitler, as well as on Roosevelt. That same day, Churchill received Maisky at 10 Downing Street and told him Britain would never come to terms with Hitler. The next day, when Churchill reported on the naval destruction, the British Parliament rose in ovation; Maisky was present.[91] Stalin kept insisting that Churchill refused to accept how the Versailles order had been shattered, but in truth, the British PM did admit Versailles was kaput.[92] What the Bulldog did not want to admit was that a replacement international order would require a *significant* place for the Communist Soviet Union, in its now expanded borders, including Poland and the Baltics, the same tiny former tsarist possessions causing Stalin trouble with Hitler. The arch-imperialist Churchill, while holding one quarter of the world, took offense at these Soviet annexations of white peoples.[93] He wanted to prevail in the war without empowering the Soviets in Europe in the bargain. Neither he (nor most subsequent scholars) would admit as much, but this was the same sticking point that had inhibited Chamberlain from signing any alliance with Stalin.[94]

The dilemma was stark. "We cannot defeat Germany fully without allies," *The Economist* would editorialize in late July 1940. "Patiently, if need be, but with great persistence, we must work for a Russian alliance."[95] Churchill, however, held to the minimalist British aim of stopping an escalation in Soviet material support of Germany, and he was already fixated on salvation from Roosevelt and the United States, which had the eighteenth-largest land army in the world, with fewer troops than Bulgaria, and no air force to speak of, but had immeasurable potential.[96] Such considerations amounted to formidable obstacles for Stalin to overcome. Perhaps they could not have been overcome. But the despot did not try.

Rumors were swirling in Berlin of a change in the USSR's foreign policy orientation.[97] Back on the eve of Cripps's arrival in Moscow, Soviet military intelligence had warned Stalin that German delays in military deliveries to the USSR stemmed from Berlin's concern that Cripps would be bearing "some gifts."[98] On July 13, Stalin had Molotov send a Soviet record of his conversation with Cripps to the Soviet envoys in London, Berlin, and Rome—and to the German ambassador in Moscow. Stalin aimed not to intimidate Hitler but to demonstrate his continuing loyalty. Stalin, as if speaking not to Cripps but directly to Hitler, was recorded as having replied to the ambassador's suggestion that Britain and the USSR "ought to agree on a common policy of self-protection against Germany and on the re-establishment of the balance of power" by saying that "he did not see any danger of the hegemony of any one country in Europe and still less any danger that Europe might be engulfed by Germany." He added that he "knew several leading German statesmen well" and "had not discovered any desire on their part to engulf European countries. Stalin was not of the opinion that German military successes menaced the Soviet Union and her friendly relations with Germany."[99]

German intelligence was closely following Cripps's activities, thanks to intercepted telegrams sent to Belgrade by the Yugoslav envoy in Moscow, Milan Gavrilović, a Cripps confidant. Hitler was in a position to know the talks were fruitless. But to the Führer, Britain and the USSR were talking. The Wehrmacht, for its part, was monitoring Stalin's troop buildup on the Soviet side of the border throughout southeastern Europe. German military aircraft were violating Soviet airspace but then claiming that these were errors committed by pilots in training.[100] On July 3, 1940, the German army chief of staff, Halder, in a conversation with the head of his operations section, had noted that a "military intervention . . . will compel Russia to recognize Germany's dominant position in Europe."[101]

INCOHERENCE

Other Soviet actions belied this pro-German bluster. That same July of 1940, Shaposhnikov, in his last days as chief of the general staff, signed off on a detailed assessment of what a German attack on the USSR would look like.[102] He never acted without Stalin's approval.[103] Red Army force dislocation also spoke volumes: of its 188 divisions, just 18 were in the Soviet Far East, and 10 in Eastern Siberia. The main concentrations were on the western frontier: the Kiev special military district (27), Western special military district (25), Odessa military district (11), Baltic special military district (18), and Leningrad military district (15).[104] After August 1940, by which time Meretskov had replaced Shaposhnikov, Germany (supported by Italy, Hungary, Romania, and Finland) was being explicitly named as the likely enemy in the Soviet strategic deployment plan; Britain was no longer mentioned. What is more, the Soviet military districts on the frontier had fleshed out detailed contingencies for war against Germany.[105]

At the same time, the economic benefits of the relationship with Germany were still flowing to Moscow. In the second quarter of 1940, the Škoda Works in German-annexed Bohemia would ship orders to the USSR for 393 devices to manufacture machine tools worth billions of rubles.[106] Equally crucial, *Ogonyok* printed dramatic photographs of European war devastation, including the urban bombing, vivid reminders of how the Soviets had remained outside the conflict.[107]

Maisky, according to the British foreign office, said that whereas, according to conventional accounting, in the air war between Britain and Germany, Royal Air Force losses were placed on one side and Luftwaffe losses on another, "he was in the habit of adding them together in one column."[108] Stalin, furthermore, was absolutely convinced that Churchill wanted not to fight Hitler together with him but to deflect the Wehrmacht eastward and conclude a separate peace with Germany.[109]

But Stalin's views on Britain and geopolitics bordered on incoherence. Steeped in Marxism-Leninism, he was given to dismissing the British—the world's number-one arms exporters—as a supposed "nation of shopkeepers" (among the ultimate Marxist insults), yet he was also inclined to regard Britain as the arch-imperialist manipulating all world affairs.[110] Germany, dominating nearly the entire continent, somehow still remained the victim of the Versailles order.

Soviet propaganda banged on about how the British empire constituted the world's principal bloodsucker and threat.[111] The regime called on the full force of its astonishing ideological arsenal: nearly 9,000 newspapers, with a combined daily circulation of 38.4 million, and almost 6 million "radio points" delivering radio by wire (as well as 1 million radio receivers with dials), not to mention countless cinemas showing newsreels, live theater, posters, and publicly displayed slogans. Even if the Soviet masses remained skeptical about this or that regime pronouncement, the population was marinated day and night in Stalin's worldview.

Inside the Little Corner, in the narrow circle that had regular access to the despot, there were no Anglophiles—like Göring, the counterweight to Ribbentrop in the Nazi regime—who could counter Stalin's Germanophilia or the Germanophile influence of Molotov, whose signature was on the Pact and who combined the functions of a Göring (overseeing the economy) and a Ribbentrop (foreign affairs).[112] As for Voroshilov, even had he admired Britain—he did not—he lacked Molotov's strength of character to stand up for any view that contravened Stalin's. Mikoyan, a skilled operative, was too clever to advocate for or against specific policies, knowing Stalin's personality as well as anyone (and having had some clashes with him in the 1920s). The policy views of Beria could best be described as "Yes, comrade Stalin. It shall be done, comrade Stalin." Anyway, it is not even clear whether Stalin informed his minions, besides Molotov, about the details of the new British ambassador's approaches.

In summer 1940, Eugene Lyons published *Stalin: Czar of All the Russians*, reusing the interview he had obtained a decade earlier, only now it was not to humanize the despot but to dehumanize him. He alluded inaccurately to Stalin's "modest apartment of three rooms," a space the journalist never saw, but he wielded the credibility of his rare face-to-face encounter and long service as the Moscow correspondent of the United Press. Disabused dupes had a lot to make up for. Having previously called Stalin a "thoroughly likable person," Lyons (prodigiously borrowing from Souvarine's biography) now cast him as a duplicitous tyrant.[113] According to Lyons, Stalin nursed a youthful humiliation all his life over his lack of any distinction, "the ugly-duckling of Gori, the sulking professional revolutionist of Tiflis and Baku, the shadowy figure among the giants of the overturn of 1917." The author tore into the despot's foreign machinations, from the Spanish civil war to the attack on Finland. "It is not beyond possibility that Stalin may double-cross Hitler at some point, particularly if an Allied victory seems inevitable," Lyons speculated. "There is even more chance that Hitler may double-cross Stalin."[114]

A DESPOT MEETS HIS LIMITS

The Red Army was expanding toward 4 million men (as compared with just 1 million in 1934). Some 11,000 of the 33,000 officers discharged during the terror had been reinstated. Industrial production (in constant prices) had tripled since 1928.[115] That said, 1940 GDP *per capita* in the Soviet Union was not very different from projected trends based on economic performance during the tsarist era. The regime had industrialized in no small part by severely repressing consumption. Consumer shortages had been worsening since 1938.[116] At the same time, alcohol production reached 250 million gallons, up from 96.5 million gallons in 1932. By 1940, the Soviet Union had more shops selling alcohol than selling meat, vegetables, and fruit combined.[117]

None of the wildly ambitious industrial targets in the Five-Year Plans (1928–32, 1933–37, 1938–) had been or would be reached. Output continued to be dogged by input shortages, which managerial black marketeering struggled to overcome through hoarding (which exacerbated the shortages) and bartering. Some enterprising factory officials reopened closed mines and sold the coal on the side, which fetched more than four times the state price; others established commercial exchanges for goods that had vanished from factory books and were in high demand throughout the Union, thereby making markets. But extra-plan entrepreneurialism was illegal.[118] In 1940, a Leningrad military-industrial research institute fulfilled just 14 percent of its plan, and yet the director and the chief engineer, possessing scarce know-how that factories craved, managed to contract with state companies to obtain not just gramophone records and a piano but also vital engineering tools, pneumatic devices, and plastics. Criminal charges resulted, however.[119]

More than one third of all industrial workers were classified as "Stakhanovites," but worker go-slows, also known as Italian strikes, and the constant queuing for food and basic goods continued to depress productivity. So did quitting in search of lower norms and better pay.[120] Back on June 26, 1940, Stalin had had the criminal penalties for absenteeism and unauthorized job changing augmented; additionally, lateness of just twenty minutes was now criminalized. Violations were punishable with "corrective labor," mostly in the form of reduced pay at one's place of employment, but sometimes with several months in a camp.[121] Some 30 million people were now in the Soviet state workforce, and over the next year more than 3 million of them would be investigated for absenteeism and job changing. Of these, nearly half a million would be sentenced to prison for four months; the rest would be sentenced to "forced labor" at their regular place of employment, meaning pay reductions, for six months.[122] And yet the number of such infractions was likely higher. Some people stole goods from work or otherwise violated discipline deliberately to get fired, so that they could leave undesirable jobs.[123] But managers did not investigate many instances of lateness or refrained from sending cases to the procuracy, instead imposing "fines" that were not collected.[124] Stalin's orders to mete out punishments for even minor infractions clashed with his directives to meet production targets at all cost.[125]

STUMPED, WRATHFUL, RESTLESS

Hitler stood at a new zenith of power in July 1940. And yet, despite all his conquests and Britain's manifest inability to dislodge him from the continent, the British government vowed to keep on fighting. He had repaired to his alpine retreat, to confer with his military on the feasibility of a cross-Channel invasion. Germany would need control of the Channel by sea and air, which was not remotely in prospect.[126] Under Chamberlain, the British had built several ships and radar stations and greatly expanded production capacity for fighter airplanes without actually making many of them, thereby controlling peacetime expenses and limiting stockpiles of obsolete weapons. In 1940, when fighting broke out,

Britain quickly managed to outproduce Germany in single-engine fighters, which contributed significantly to the British ability to beat back the Luftwaffe air assault. The British Home Fleet alone—only a part of the Royal Navy—possessed 5 battleships, 11 cruisers, and 30 destroyers.[127] The Norwegian campaign had weakened the German navy, which at this point was down to one heavy cruiser, two light cruisers, and four destroyers. Grand Admiral Raeder, the German naval commander in chief, and others harbored grave doubts about landing on the British Isles without a huge prior buildup. All seemed to depend on the Luftwaffe.[128]

Churchill, under German bombardment, dreamed of escape. "If Hitler fails to beat us here he will probably recoil eastwards," he had written to the prime minister of the Union of South Africa (June 27, 1940). "Indeed, he may do this even without trying invasion [of the UK], to find employment for his Army, and take the edge off the winter strain upon him."[129]

Hitler understood the transcendent value that Britain attached to its global empire and, in his own way, was sincere in his offers to allow that empire to remain intact, certainly in the medium term, in exchange for a free hand on the continent, where raw materials and racial *Lebensraum* awaited him. Churchill, however, genuinely cared about the balance of power on the continent, on which the empire's existence ultimately depended.[130] But Hitler could not fathom Britain's "futile" resistance to an accommodation, except by imagining some hidden encouragement—from the United States, from the USSR.[131] On July 16, he issued Directive No. 16: "Since England, despite her hopeless military situation, still shows no sign of willingness to come to terms, I have decided to prepare, and if necessary to carry out, a landing operation against her. . . . The preparation for the entire operation must be completed by mid-August." The lack of confidence ("if necessary") was evident. On July 19, he gave a much-delayed address to the Reichstag, reviewing German military conquests, current strength, and future strategy, while offering vague "final" peace terms to Britain.[132] The British press and radio were immediately dismissive. Churchill initially greeted the "offer" with cold silence.[133]

At a "Führer conference" with only the highest military men, on July 21, 1940, Hitler stated that "even though Moscow is unenthusiastic about Germany's great success, she will nevertheless make no effort to enter the war against Germany of her own accord." Rumors—duly conveyed to Stalin—were rife that Germany was getting ready to attack the USSR even before France had fallen.[134] The Wehrmacht was transferring back eastern units that had been called to France and Belgium, and Soviet military intelligence was reporting German troop concentrations on the eastern frontier (railroads were under covert surveil-lance).[135] German officers were said to be studying Russian language at courses given in occupied Prague. Ethnic Russians and Ukrainians living in Poland had been organized. Everyone was talking, everywhere: troop exercises, planned dip-lomatic evacuations, imminent war. Was it real? Disinformation? German forti-fications in the east were being greatly expanded; then again, the German state had expanded, so this was to be expected. Germany's military attaché in Mos-cow, Köstring, told his Soviet interlocutors (July 9) that German forces were be-ing "demobilized" from the west and stationed in East Prussia and former Poland, where new garrisons were being formed, "since retaining many troops in the West is no longer necessary."[136]

The "parking" of German troops in the east was accelerating, but bombing raids by the Luftwaffe over Britain continued, as Soviet intelligence also re-ported.[137] Could Hitler really intend to *initiate* a two-front war? At the secret July 21 Führer conference, Hitler called an attack on Britain "not just a river crossing, but the crossing of a sea which is dominated by the enemy."[138] Nonetheless, Raeder was given ten days to work out the parameters of a cross-Channel invasion. At the same time, the Wehrmacht was to make a preliminary study of invading the USSR that very fall of 1940.[139]

Germany endeavored to goad Japan into attacking Singapore, so as to provoke Britain into war in the Far East and perhaps also drag the United States in (and away from European affairs), but Tokyo's ability to commit remained stymied by interest group infighting.[140] At the same time, Major General Alfred Jodl, chief of the operations staff, had raised the possibility of bringing Britain to its knees indi-rectly, by hitting vulnerable spots in the eastern Mediterranean and the Near East, reasoning that as the screws were tightened on Britain's global position, it would surrender, to stem its losses. The Italians, he thought, could occupy the Suez Ca-nal. Spain or another country could grab Gibraltar. The oil terminus in Haifa could just be blown up.[141] This had sparked the notion of a broad anti-British front of Italy, Spain, and maybe the Soviet Union, even as Hitler was contemplating smashing the latter to bits, as a way to get Britain to capitulate. "Crossing of Chan-nel appears very hazardous to the Führer," army chief of staff Halder recorded in his diary (July 22). "Invasion is to be undertaken only if no other way is left to bring terms with England."[142] That same day, Halifax broadcast a definitive British rejection of the German terms for "peace." On July 23, Hitler went on his annual pilgrimage to Bayreuth for the Wagner Festival, taking in *Götterdäm-merung*.[143]

Jodl and Field Marshal Wilhelm Keitel, de facto war minister, managed to convince Hitler that a fall 1940 date for an invasion of the USSR was "hopelessly impractical" (according to a memo written by the former and signed by the latter).[144] On July 29, at another Führer conference at the Berghof, Hitler shifted a Soviet invasion target date out to May 1941, which was both the earliest feasible date and the latest date from the point of view of safe concentration of forces in the east.[145] Jodl informed only a tiny group of war planners, headed by Walter Warlimont, in the strictest secrecy, for Halder and other top Wehrmacht generals saw no basis for a war against the Soviet Union, and plenty of opportunity for rapprochement with Stalin.[146]

On July 31, Hitler convened yet another narrow-circle Führer conference at the Berghof.[147] Raeder and Halder reported. Those present argued that a cross-Channel invasion of Britain could not be carried out until September 1940 (if then). Hitler signed Directive No. 17, on stepping up the air war (which would be called the Battle of Britain) "to prepare the ground for the final crushing of England."[148] He rejected Raeder's postponement of the Channel invasion, Operation Sea Lion, until spring 1941, but postponement is effectively what happened, for Hitler stated that if the results of the air attacks on Britain proved unfavorable, Sea Lion preparations would be stopped.[149] As for the Wehrmacht, despite a plan to reduce its size to lessen the strain on the economy, Hitler ordered a ramp-up from 120 to 180 divisions (a number that would grow) and the launching of a massive logistics program in the east.[150] Göring, when told, would be thrilled.[151] This represented a policy victory for both the peripheral strategy against Britain and the full-scale invasion of the USSR. "Our action must be directed to eliminate all factors that let England hope for a change in the situation," Hitler told the attendees. "Russia is the factor on which Britain is relying the most. . . . With Russia smashed, Britain's last hope will be shattered."[152]

Hitler had effectively conceded that he lacked the resources to defeat the world's leading navy and air force, but he felt he could summon the resources to defeat world's largest land army. This was, in a way, logical, reflecting his own force structure. But several top Wehrmacht officers viewed an unprovoked invasion of the east before securing victory in the west as unsound.

It was, in any case, passing strange. For decades, the Führer had been hammering the necessity of annihilating Bolshevism and following the siren call of *Lebensraum* in the east, in an existential war, but now he was asserting that the way to defeat Britain was to attack the Soviets.[153] Stalin felt secure, because Britain was the one stuck doing the fighting against Nazi Germany, but the more

Britain resisted Hitler, the more Hitler entertained an attack on the Soviet Union. And the more Soviet intelligence warned Stalin about Hitler's aggressive attitudes toward the USSR, the more Stalin suspected British efforts to embroil him in war with Germany.

MISPLACED JOY

On August 10, 1940, Stalin hosted a banquet in the Grand Kremlin Palace to celebrate his newest and expanded Union republics: Lithuania, Latvia, Estonia, and Moldavia (which included Bessarabia and northern Bukovina). He seated their Soviet-installed leaders at his own table, alongside marshals Timoshenko and Voroshilov.[154] Hitler's directives and the accompanying feasibility studies for an attack on the USSR remained supersecret. Soviet military intelligence, on the basis of agent information, reported that, at a conference in Salzburg on August 9, Hitler had proposed to Romania joint regulation of all disputed issues with Hungary and Bulgaria; stated that all territorial changes in Eastern Europe up to that point were temporary; and "declared that current actions were the first stage in preparation for a war against the USSR, which would begin immediately after the end of the war with England."[155] Five days later, Hitler handed out diamond-studded batons to his field marshals in the Reich Chancellery. "Russia has once shown an inclination to overstep the agreements made with us," he remarked privately. "But she remains loyal at present. But should she reveal the intention of conquering Finland or attacking Romania, we shall be forced to strike. Russia should not be allowed to be the sole master of the eastern Baltic. Furthermore, we need Romania's oil."[156]

Mikoyan reported on August 11 that for the first six months of 1940, the Soviets had received goods worth 80 million reichsmarks, while shipping goods worth 190 million.[157] (In the fourth quarter of 1940, Stalin would again shut off the export valves.) Molotov, on August 15, wrote a revealing letter to his wife, Polina, who was away on holiday in Crimea. This was his second letter to her in three days, divulging, in passing, that political negotiations had been launched with Japan ("I hope something serious will result"). He also complained that, "unfortunately, I cannot stay current in economic matters, but I do try not to lose sight of the most important of them, and it seems there is a turn for the better." He broached the idea of holidaying together the next year in Sochi. "I wait impatiently for you in order to hug you tightly-tightly and kiss you all over, my dear, sweet love."[158]

Stalin had not written a letter like that in a decade. He could, at least, rejoice in the fact that Beria's agents, finally, had proved better than Yezhov's: Ramón Mercader managed to smash an alpine pick into the head of Trotsky on August 20, 1940. The exile survived in a coma for twenty-six hours before succumbing.[159] He was sixty years old. "The murder of Leon Trotsky at Mexico City," *The Times* of London editorialized (August 23), "will relieve the Kremlin of not a few anxieties and will draw few tears from the majority of mankind." When the celebrity's open casket was driven through the streets of the Mexican capital, nearly a quarter million people turned out. Stalin edited the *Pravda* report on the "inglorious death of Trotsky" (August 24) and, among many insertions and cross-outs, he altered the conclusion to say, "Trotsky became a victim of his own intrigues, treacheries, and treason. Thus, he ingloriously ended his life, this despicable person, entering the grave with the stamp of an international spy on his skeleton."[160]

The draft was dated August 16, indicating Stalin's sense of anticipation over the operation. The omnipotent despot had maintained a collection of everything written by and about Trotsky in a special cupboard in his study at the Near Dacha: *Stalin School of Falsification, An Open Letter to Members of the Bolshevik Party, The Revolution Betrayed, The Stalinist Thermidor.* These texts, published in dozens of countries, helped shape Stalin's image in world opinion.[161] Trotsky had taken to predicting that war between Hitler and Stalin would sweep away both, in social revolution, and that he (Trotsky) and his Fourth International would replace them. "Under cover of darkness, revolutionary elements in Berlin are putting up posters in the working-class districts saying 'Down with Hitler and Stalin!' and 'Long Live Trotsky!'" he imagined in 1940. "It's lucky Stalin does not have to black out Moscow at night, otherwise the streets of the Soviet capital would also be covered with equally meaningful posters."[162] When the spectral Fourth International, its meager archive pilfered and delivered to Stalin, had finally managed its founding congress, it was attended by a mere twenty-one delegates, who had met in secrecy in a village outside Paris for just a single day, the stateless Trotsky himself had not been able to attend.[163]

Hitler's troop movements and the high tensions in Nazi-Soviet relations were playing out in Eastern Europe.[164] Stalin had begun inciting Hungarian irredentism over their conationals in Romanian-controlled Transylvania; Hitler unilaterally handed northern Transylvania over to Hungary in late August 1940. Stalin had a protest lodged with the German ambassador regarding what he considered to be a violation of their Pact's clause on prior consultation.[165] Romania would also be forced to cede southern Dobruja to Bulgaria, losing the last of the territories it had gained as a result of the Great War and sinking the popularity of the Bucharest government and the monarch. "I was not an enemy of Your Majesty," General Ion Antonescu (b. 1882), the former war minister and the leader of the pro-Nazi Iron Guard, wrote in protest to King Carol II. "I was a fanatic servant of this nation. I was removed through intrigue and calumny by those who have led this country to where it is now."[166] Carol promptly had him arrested. Mass public demonstrations and Iron Guard shock troops known as Legionnaires got Antonescu released. In a quick coup, he would force the beleaguered king to step down in favor of his nineteen-year-old son, Mihai I (a great-great-grandson of Queen Victoria). But most of the monarchy's dictatorial powers would be transferred on September 5 to Antonescu, newly designated as "Conducător" (Führer).[167] He deepened Romania's relationship with Nazi Germany.

ENEMIES RECAST

The writer Vishnevsky had managed to take over the executed Isaac Babel's dacha in Peredelkino, then, in his diary, decried a lack of material incentives ("The stimulation by pay is lacking; we are well cared for, many of us writers fully so, for years to come").[168] He was right only in respect to elite writers. In 1939, when the deputy boss of Central Committee agitprop, Georgy Alexandrov, earned an enormous salary of 27,000 rubles, Nikolai Pogodin, the playwright, had taken in 732,000 in royalties and payments.[169] Vishnevsky went on to lament the lack of attention from Stalin and other top political figures. "After the death of A. M. Gorky we have had fewer possibilities and places where we could speak with big people on big questions of life and our work," he was recorded as stating by the writers' union duty officer in discussion with a colleague. "The last big conversation in the Central Committee was spring 1938. It gave us a lot, but already two years have passed, and writers as a collective, as an 'active,' have not spoken with the Leaders."[170]

As it happened, on the evening of September 9, 1940, party leaders and cultural functionaries assembled to discuss a film, *The Law of Life*, by Alexander Stolper and Boris Ivanov, which had been released in early August. It portrayed a student Communist youth leader as corrupt, yet it had somehow managed to pass all the censorship authorities, from the studio (Mosfilm) through the state committee for cinema affairs (headed by Ivan Bolshakov) right to the Central Committee propaganda department. *Pravda*'s unsigned review, edited by Zhdanov, condemned the film as "insincere," and after ten days, despite being the lead draw of the day, it was withdrawn.[171] Stalin, in the course of extended remarks, reminded those present that workers were not ipso facto trustworthy; Tomsky had been a worker yet fell into conspiracy with Trotsky. Some workers were scum, he added. "It's a law of life."[172]

When Fadeyev, head of the writers' union, praised the ethnic Polish writer Wanda Wasilewska as "a genuine artist," Stalin responded, "I do not know if she's a genuine artist or not, but I do know that she writes truthfully, honestly. I read three of her works: *The Face of the Day,* which depicts the life of a worker correctly, honestly; then *Motherland,* which takes up the life of a farmhand working in bondage for a landlord—wonderfully, nicely, simply conveyed; *Land Under the Yoke,* which depicts the life of an individual poor peasant, middle peasant, and farmhand. Wonderfully well conveyed. But about her, for some reason, there is silence."

At this point, Nikolai Aseyev, the poet and screenwriter, who was attending such a gathering for the first time, committed a remarkable act. "I will speak openly," he stated. "Comrade Stalin said that he likes the writings of Wanda Wasilewska. Very well, I should say, that you liked the works of Wanda Wasilewska. Personally, I read them and they did not touch me deeply. Why am I saying this? Because tomorrow and the day after tomorrow, Wanda Wasilewska will suddenly become the single standard of writerly achievement." Aseyev continued, "I am not afraid of anything; I believe that here everything will be properly taken into account and weighed, but sometimes it happens thusly: 'But comrade Stalin said it!' Of course we must take this into account, but if comrade Stalin likes this or that written work, this or that painting, it does not signify that such works should be repeated, three hundred thousand times repeat the same written work, the same painting." Stalin interjected: "It does not mean that."

Aseyev was dead right: Stalin's tastes were dispositive. The despot offered closing instructions. "I would prefer that we portrayed enemies not as beasts, but as people, harmful to our society, yet not devoid of some human qualities," he advised. "The worst scoundrel has human qualities; he loves someone, he respects someone, he is prepared to sacrifice himself for someone." Then this: "Why not depict Bukharin, no matter what kind of monster he was—he had certain human qualities. Trotsky was an enemy, but he was an able person, indisputably. Portray him as an enemy with negative qualities, but also with positive qualities, because he had them, indisputably."[173]

Who in their right mind might take up Stalin's suggestion to depict Bukharin and Trotsky as having had positive qualities?

Stalin declared that evening that he disliked *The Law of Life*'s depiction of those who unmasked enemies, such as the protagonist Communist Youth League student, as not properly Soviet people. "We had, for example, 25 to 30 million people who starved—there was not enough grain—but now they have started to live well," Stalin suddenly acknowledged. "Our enemies inside the party think as follows: 'We'll give this piece [of land] to the Germans, that to the Japanese; we have plenty of land.' But it has turned out the opposite: we give nothing to anyone. On the contrary, we are expanding the front of socialism. . . . This is beneficial for humanity; indeed, the Lithuanians, western Belorussians, Bessarabians, those we freed from the yoke of the landowners, capitalists, police, and every other kind of scum, consider themselves lucky. From the point of view of the world struggle of forces between socialism and capitalism, this is a big plus, for we are expanding the front of socialism and shrinking the front of capitalism."[174] After midnight, he repaired to the Little Corner with Zhdanov, Molotov, and Beria.[175]

AMBIGUITIES

Thanks to Hitler's secret July 1940 order to expand Germany's already sizable military, shipments to the Soviet Union fell far behind contractual obligations. Beginning in August 1940, in a show of strength, Stalin had his trade representatives convey that the Soviets would be cutting back on all deliveries, including oil.[176] Germany had more options than ever, following the occupation of France, the Low Countries, Denmark, and Norway, to go with strong commercial ties to neutral Sweden and its ally Romania. Continued reliance on the Soviet Union, moreover, was becoming a sore point. Even if Stalin might be ready to resume and perhaps deliver even more, it was better, in the words of the Nazi economics minister, not to be "dependent upon forces and powers over whom we have no influence."[177] By September 1, German divisions in East Prussia, former Poland, Bohemia, Moravia, and Austria climbed to 94 from 27 (as of June 15), according to a report from the new head of Soviet military intelligence, Lieutenant General Filipp Golikov, to Stalin, Molotov, Beria, and the military high command.[178]

On August 31, 1940, Molotov had received Schulenburg and complained that

Germany had violated the Pact by failing to consult the USSR regarding German moves in Hungary and Romania. On September 2, the Soviet envoy in Berlin, Shkvartsev, had an audience with Ribbentrop, who stated of the Pact, "I share your satisfaction and think that the year has brought great benefits to both Germany and Russia. Germany has achieved great victories and will achieve them." That same day, Shkvartsev requested Moscow not to send wives and children to Berlin, "in light of the almost daily systematic bombing" by Britain.[179] On September 3, TASS announced the signing of a clarification agreement in Berlin on regulating the Germany-USSR border, "negotiations for which had proceeded in a benevolent atmosphere."[180]

Ambassador Ott, in Tokyo, had been instructed to inform Germany's ally, as Sorge reported to Moscow, "that the German troops being sent to the eastern borders have no relation whatsoever to the USSR. They were sent there because there is no longer a need for them in France and the time for their dispersal has not arrived."[181] On September 6, Jodl issued a secret order explaining that the concentration of forces in the east would accelerate even more over the following weeks.[182] In parallel, on September 6 and 18, Admiral Raeder submitted detailed plans on the peripheral strategy against Britain.[183] Hitler's Directive No. 18, concerning war in the eastern Mediterranean and the Near East, was drafted that month. Perhaps that was the reason for the massive troop concentrations not only in Nazi-occupied Poland but also in southeastern Europe?

Stalin was sitting on an analysis written in the aftermath of France's fall by Jenő Varga, the director of the Institute of World Economy and International Relations, in Moscow, and a long-standing foreign policy adviser, who argued that the "contradictions" had disappeared between Britain and the United States, such that the latter would enter the war against the Axis. "Comrade Varga!" Stalin answered on September 12. "Your interpretation is completely correct. . . . Matters changed radically after Germany destroyed France and got its hands on all the resources of the European continent, and England lost France. Now the bloc of Germany, Italy, and Japan threatens not only England but also the U.S. In that light, a bloc between England and the U.S. is a natural result of such a turnabout in international affairs. With Communist greetings."[184]

On September 23, 1940, Stalin held a meeting in the Little Corner, summoning, among others, the historian Arkady Yerusalimsky, who had been tasked by the foreign affairs commissariat with preparing the Russian-language reissue, in three volumes, of Otto von Bismarck's *Thoughts and Recollections* (Moscow, 1940–41). Stalin hand-corrected Yerusalimsky's introductory essay, softening its tone where it pointed out the potential consequences of Germany ignoring Bismarck's solicitousness toward Russia.[185] Bismarck had been the lodestar of Stalin's conservative imperial Russian predecessors, Sergei Witte and Pyotr Stolypin. What, if anything, the Soviet despot absorbed from the German's thinking remains unknown. But he seems to have presumed, based on the way things worked inside the Soviet Union, that the Germans would read the introduction to a history book as a statement or signal of Soviet policy.

Stalin gave indications of the economic strain. After the thirty minutes devoted to Bismarck, he received Mikoyan and Khrushchev, followed by the aviation industry commissar (Shakhurin) and a deputy commissar (Vasily Balandin); the heavy machine building commissar (Vyacheslav Malyshev); and the first deputy chairman of the Council of People's Commissars (Nikolai Voznesensky). "When one gives a new task to our people's commissars, they make obligatory the construction of new factories to fulfill it," Stalin complained to them. "But the main thing is that one needs to look at what can be done at the old factories. This is the most reliable and shortest way. One can expand production at old factories more quickly than build new factories."[186]

The tension in the Little Corner was heightened by the arrival at this time of Wehrmacht troops in Finland. Germany had provided no advance warning, in contravention of the consultation clause of the Pact, which, of course, had put Finland in the Soviet sphere.[187] Stalin's war there had brought about the very eventuality it had sought to forestall. His spies passed on details about 1.5 billion reichsmarks in secret military aid from Germany to Finland, deliveries that were supposed to go to the Soviet Union. Stalin suspended all long-term projects for export to Germany, diminishing further any German economic dependency on him.[188] Nothing more starkly demonstrated the deterioration of the Soviet position than Finland, where the Soviet Union had expended so much blood, treasure, and reputation.

TRIPARTITE RELIEF

Japan, Germany, and Italy, on September 27, 1940, signed a Tripartite Pact in the Reich Chancellery. The three Axis signatories delineated spheres of influence and pledged for the next ten years "to assist one another with all political, economic and military means when one of the three contracting powers is attacked."

This represented a turnabout for Japan. Pro-German circles in Tokyo had been systematically removed from influential posts, thanks to Hitler's Pact with Stalin, but with the defeat of France, the Japanese hoped to use German victories in the west to expand southward in French Indochina, which would require deterrence of the United States.[189] "The basic aim of the pact is to avoid war with the United States," Prime Minister Konoe told the cabinet. "However, I think it is necessary for us to display firmness, because if we act humbly, it will only make the United States presumptuous."[190] Perhaps there was also anticipation of some spoils from a British surrender to Germany. Hitler saw Japan's enthusiasm as an attempt "to cash in" on Germany's victories by offering to serve as "harvest helpers."[191] But following the debacle of the air campaign against Britain, the Führer had come around to seeking to deter U.S. support for Britain by wielding the Japanese cudgel.[192]

The agreement still fell short of a binding military alliance. It also specifically excluded the Soviet Union as a target. "Its exclusive purpose," Ribbentrop informed Molotov, two days before the scheduled signing, "is to bring the elements pressing for America's entry into the war to their senses."[193] When Weizsäcker briefed the Soviet ambassador in Berlin on September 28, he underlined the desire on the part of the three signatories for better relations with the USSR.[194] "Exceptional significance," noted Comintern chief Dimitrov in his diary for September 28. "Further expansion of the war to world-war dimensions."[195] An unsigned front-page analysis in *Pravda* (September 30)—written by Molotov—maintained that the new three-country pact signed in Berlin signified formation of two blocs: Germany, Italy, and Japan versus Britain and the United States, the fantasy Stalin had divulged to Varga, with the Soviet Union as happy bystander. Molotov, anonymously, further reassured readers that the Tripartite Pact had been "no surprise" and reemphasized Soviet neutrality and the continuing validity of the bilateral nonaggression pacts with Germany and Italy.[196]

Japanese ruling circles now hoped for improved relations with the USSR, to secure the country's northern flank and increase the pressure on Chiang Kai-shek to capitulate. Secretly, on October 3, 1940, Japanese and Soviet negotiators were working on a draft nonaggression pact and preliminarily agreed that "the USSR will abandon its support for Chiang and will repress the Chinese Communist party's anti-Japanese activities; in exchange, Japan recognizes and accepts that the Chinese Communist party will retain as a base the three northwest provinces (Shaanxi, Gansu, Ningxia)." Negotiators further agreed that the Soviets would acquiesce in any Japanese moves in Indochina, and Japan would not oppose any future Soviet moves in Afghanistan.[197]

The fly in the ointment remained German troops in the east. Golikov had reported (October 2) that the Germans were moving many of the troops from within East Prussia and the General Gouvernement closer to the Soviet border. Stalin's NKVD station chief in Bulgaria secretly reported the shipment of German heavy armaments on barges along the Danube to the Black Sea, right on the Soviet doorstep. But Soviet intelligence adhered to the line that the sharp troop buildup reflected only the unavoidable necessity of moving troops out of France, given the anti-German attitudes prevalent in conquered France. Still, analysts also mentioned Germany's desire to strengthen its influence in Eastern Europe, especially the Balkans.[198]

HITLER'S LATIN FRUSTRATIONS AND BALKAN AMBITIONS

Schulenburg was in Berlin in late September, trying to put relations with Moscow back on track by encouraging a German invitation for a state visit.[199] Ribbentrop had never abandoned his efforts to restore friendly bilateral relations by inviting Molotov, or even Stalin, to Berlin. The Germans, like the British, mistakenly believed that Molotov had never been out of the country (he had visited fascist Italy in 1922), but they nonetheless believed he would reciprocate the German foreign minister's two visits to Moscow.[200] Ribbentrop let the count know that a new invitation to Molotov was in the works. This hoped-for meeting was predicated on a vast European-Asian bloc directed against the British, Ribbentrop's dream castle.[201]

Hitler's failure to subdue Britain was eating at him. Britain's Royal Air Force not only had prevented the Luftwaffe from attaining the air superiority required for a cross-Channel invasion, but was bombing Berlin and other German cities.[202] Between July 10 and October 31, 1940, in the so-called Battle of Britain, Hurricanes and Spitfires shot down 1,733 Luftwaffe aircraft. The British lost 915 planes. ("Never had so many owed so much to so few," Churchill would remark of the air war.) Both Sea Lion and the vague preliminary plans for an invasion of the Soviet Union had been postponed, from fall 1940 to spring 1941. The Wehrmacht was the largest unemployed land army in the world. The Führer, losing the initiative, went into seclusion at the Berghof from October 5 to 8 to contemplate his options.

NKVD intelligence under Beria was reporting that at least 85 infantry divisions—two thirds of the German land army—were deployed in the east, and airfields and other military installations were going up one after another.[203] In October 1940, Beria suddenly became solicitous toward the few hundred Polish officers whom he had not murdered at Katyn and other sites back in spring 1940. He even had the interned Polish lieutenant colonel Zygmunt Berling retrieved from a Soviet labor camp to Moscow in first class. When Merkulov told Berling that there were plans to form a Polish army on Soviet territory, the latter assumed that the more than 20,000 captured Polish officers were in the Soviet Gulag somewhere. "We have no such people now in the Soviet Union," Beria responded, laconically. Merkulov added: "We committed a big mistake with them."[204]

Soon Beria informed Stalin that the NKVD had assembled some two dozen Polish officers as the basis for an anti-German army, just in case. It was a new era. Not a single one of the thirty-five Soviet films produced in 1940 would feature a principal "enemy" of domestic origin.[205] No foreign films would be allowed onto the Soviet screen the entire year. Still, a new breakthrough musical comedy emerged: on October 8, 1940, *The Radiant Path* premiered in Moscow, another smash hit by Grigory Alexandrov, with music by Isaac Dunayevsky, including his "March of the Enthusiasts." *The Radiant Path* would seize honors as the year's top film. It depicted a Cinderella-like illiterate rural housemaid named Tanya (played by the blond-braided, ever radiant Lyubov Orlova), who, thanks to a party organizer, attends literacy classes, becomes a textile factory Stakhanovite weaver, earns the Order of Lenin, flies through the air in an open-top car alongside the Grand Kremlin Palace, and wins love. Tanya easily unmasks the villain, a kulak arsonist, early in the action. "A good film and . . . without a portrait of Comrade Stalin," the despot told Alexandrov, while smiling with his eyes.[206]

Also in October, Marshal Kulik married his third wife (Olga Mikhailovskaya), a friend of his daughter's who was in her final year of high school—he was thirty-two years her senior. Stalin, now in the eighth year of his (second) widowhood, took no such indulgences. He was adjudicating between rival screenplays for a film about a seventeenth-century Georgian military figure, Giorgi Saakadze, who had led an uprising against the Persian shah to liberate and unify Georgia. "The princes and feudalism proved stronger than the [Georgian] tsar and nobles," Stalin explained to film boss Bolshakov in a letter on October 11, 1940, adding that

Saakadze's efforts to compensate for domestic weakness with foreign alliances had failed, for objective reasons.[207]

Hitler emerged from his alpine hideaway with a renewed push to subdue Britain, indirectly. But first, on October 12, Wehrmacht troops occupied Romania to secure the Ploieşti oil fields. "The Germans have raised a barrier," remarked the Italian ambassador to Moscow to his confidant, Schulenburg. "The [Russian] march to the south has been stopped, the oil is at the disposal of the Germans, through Constanza the Germans have reached the Black Sea, the Danube is a German river. This is the first diplomatic defeat of comrade Stalin."[208] In fact, even though TASS issued a denial, Berlin had afforded Moscow forty-eight hours' advance notice of "training troops" to be stationed on the Danube to "instruct" the Romanian army.[209]

Charlie Chaplin's *The Great Dictator* premiered in the United States on October 15, 1940, parodying Hitler (called Adenoid Hynkel) as a megalomaniacal buffoon whose dictatorship threatens a Jewish barber; Chaplin, who was neither German nor Jewish, played both roles. The reviewer in the *New York Times* enthused about "the feeble, affected hand salute, the inclination for striking ludicrous attitudes, the fabulous fits of rage and violent facial contortions," adding of Chaplin's pantomime: "He is at his best in a wild senseless burst of guttural oratory—a compound of German, Yiddish, and Katzenjammer double-talk, and he reaches positively exalted heights in a plaintive dance which he does with a large balloon representing the globe, bouncing it into the air, pirouetting beneath it—and then bursting into tears when the balloon finally pops."[210] In one scene, Hynkel, the dictator of Tomania, meets and bargains with Benzino Napaloni, dictator of Bacteria.[211]

On October 17, Molotov's deputy Vyshinsky received Cripps, who hinted at British movement in its position opposing Soviet incorporation of the Baltic states and claimed to have confidential government information for Molotov personally; when Vyshinsky insisted on a foretaste, according to the Soviet account, Cripps stated, "in connection with events over recent weeks in the Balkans, Near East, and Far East, that British relations with these parts of the world had changed, and accordingly, the relations between Britain and the Soviet Union should also change." Cripps had convinced himself somehow that the USSR did not want Germany to win the war, and he urged de facto British recognition, until the end of the war, of the territories that the USSR had received to entice it to treat Britain and Germany with equal favor.[212] That same day, Molotov bade farewell to the Japanese ambassador, who was returning home after two years in Moscow. Each expressed a desire for continued improved bilateral relations, although they had failed to agree to a neutrality pact. When the Japanese envoy inquired of German-Soviet relations, Molotov called them "solid" and predicted that "they would develop further."[213]

Ribbentrop had dispatched a nineteen-page letter to Stalin inviting Molotov to Berlin, and, also on October 17, Schulenburg managed to hand it to Molotov.[214] The text reviewed German-Soviet bilateral relations, justified German military moves in Eastern Europe, and proposed that four powers—Germany, Italy, and Japan, plus the Soviet Union—divide up the world, at British expense. Ribbentrop ingratiatingly pointed out that both the Soviet Union and Germany "were animated in the same degree by the same desire for a New Order in the world against the congealed plutocratic democracies." What the Nazi foreign minister omitted to mention was that each power had its own "new order," which clashed not just ideologically but physically over the same Eastern European territories. Stalin, angered over the unilateral German move into Romania, nonetheless agreed to send his top deputy to Berlin in the near future and to thank Ribbentrop for "the instructive analysis."[215]

Ribbentrop now felt confident enough to draft a German-Italian-Japanese-Soviet pact, and he mused with Hitler about confronting Britain with the most geographically expansive military coalition in history.[216] At the same time, Hitler was exploring other anti-British chess moves. Heinrich Himmler, the SS chief, was sent on a three-day visit to Spain, beginning on October 20, 1940. He was paraded through Madrid streets bedecked in Nazi swastikas, received by Franco at the Pardo Palace, and shown a special bullfight. Julio Martínez Santa-Olalla, a Spanish ethnoarchaeologist who had studied in Germany, regaled Himmler with tales of Spanish-German racial connections through the Visigoths.[217] But Himmler frowned upon Franco's gratuitous post-civil-war massacres. To the SS chief, it made more sense to incorporate the workers into the new order, not annihilate them. (The German occupation of France had led to many Spanish political refugees being turned over to Franco.) Be that as it may, Himmler's visit was mere preparation. Hitler himself, also on October 20, set out on what would be a journey of nearly 4,000 miles on his special train, *Amerika,* to persuade the French, Spaniards, and Italians to put aside their squabbles in the establishment of a continental bloc against Britain.[218]

On October 23, Hitler met Franco for a one-day summit in France, at Hendaye, a railway station near the Spanish border. The caudillo arrived late, in an aged train once used by King Alfonso XIII, with his foreign minister and brother-in-law

Ramón Serrano Súñer in tow. Franco and Hitler went into the parlor coach of the Führer's train. Admiral Canaris, head of the Abwehr (military intelligence), had warned Hitler that Franco would resemble "not a hero but a little sausage." During the talks and dinner, which lasted some nine hours, Franco made breathtaking territorial claims, mostly at French expense, as his price for entering the war on the Nazis' side. In Hitler's mind, Franco's regime would never have survived had it not been for German military aid back in 1936—and yet the caudillo now saw fit to point out that even if Germany were to defeat Britain on the home isles, the British government would sail with its navy to Canada or the United States and continue the war from there. This cheek provoked a riled Hitler to his feet. "Rather than go through that again," Hitler would tell Mussolini of the meeting, "I would prefer to have three or four teeth taken out."[219]

The next day, Hitler held a one-day summit with Marshal Pétain of Vichy France, also to explore a potential new ally for the anti-British fight. The French leader put forth a relatively more modest territorial wish list as his price to turn against France's erstwhile ally Britain, but Pétain did not appear overly enthusiastic. The elderly marshal kept pretending not to hear Hitler very well. The conversation was vague enough that Hitler could imagine France was going to support his proposal, but nothing concrete was achieved. Only in Romania did the Führer come upon a kindred spirit: General Ion Antonescu. At the general's insistent requests, Hitler had moved German troops into Romania, nominally to help "reorganize" its army.[220] But Mussolini, Hitler's formal ally, bristled at Germany's "fait accompli" in Romania, and viewed inclusion of the Spanish or the French in a bloc as a threat to his own fantastic wish list of spoils. Hitler felt constrained to try to mollify the duce, redirecting his train to Florence for a summit meeting on October 28.[221] That very morning, Mussolini launched an invasion of Greece. "He will learn from the newspapers that I have occupied Greece," the duce privately boasted. "This way, things will be even once again."[222]

Franco, Pétain, and now Mussolini. Greece was already ruled by a pro-Nazi dictator who had studied in Germany, and the gratuitous Italian invasion was launched in the fall rains, on the eve of the winter snows in the Balkan uplands.[223] Moreover, the Balkans were Germany's jumping-off point for attacking British positions in the Near East, in the so-called peripheral strategy. Already on November 4, 1940, the Wehrmacht had been directed to plan its own invasion of Greece, via either Hungary and Romania or Yugoslavia and then Bulgaria.[224] Hitler did not abandon some sort of cooperation with France and Spain against Britain.[225] But Molotov committed to visiting Berlin after the USSR's November 7 holiday.[226] Ribbentrop reminded Molotov of his promise to bring along a portrait of Stalin, and Molotov eagerly agreed to do so.[227] Perhaps the lunatic scheme pushed by the Nazi foreign minister of adding Stalin to the Axis, in a four-power pact, to force Britain into submission, seemed no worse than any of the other (non) options on Hitler's table? If so, it was clear that Hitler would require German dominance of the entire Balkans.[228]

MESSAGE FROM BERLIN

The mass of Soviet inhabitants remained very distant from these machinations, but that was also true of almost all party and state functionaries. They, too, knew little to nothing. Valentin Berezhkov, who was working at the Soviet embassy in Germany, helping to oversee procurement related to the Nazi-Soviet trade agreement, was summoned to Moscow. Previously, he had worked in the tourist bureau in Kiev, where he held the belief that all the foreigners whom he hosted were rich, while "in the Soviet Union we were building a system that would be fair for all." But upon arriving in capitalist Riga in 1940, on his way to Berlin, he had been shocked at the abundance and affordability of food. Berezhkov's father had been arrested in the terror but released, so Berezhkov "came to believe that if a person was truly innocent, no one was going to harm him." Still, having now been recalled to Moscow, he fretted about his own possible arrest. Upon reaching the Soviet Union's side of the border, he experienced a rush of patriotic feeling, but he was subjected to a humiliating search, as if he were a foreign agent. Berezhkov was promoted, becoming one of Molotov's two German interpreters, and instructed to prepare for a state visit to Berlin. Thus, a mere two years after having graduated with a degree in engineering, Berezhkov was set to meet Hitler. "The young people of my generation did not know about Stalin's atrocities," Berezhkov would recall. "We thought he was like a wise, just, and caring, if strict father of the peoples of our country."[229]

Molotov, in response to Ribbentrop's long written tutorial and invitation, had bombarded Schulenburg with accusations that Germany had violated the terms of the 1939 Pact, and with Soviet demands: immediate withdrawal of German forces from Finland; long-term Soviet military bases on the Turkish Straits (the Bosporus and the Dardanelles, promised to tsarist Russia in the Great War by Britain and France); a Soviet security treaty with Bulgaria, another key to controlling the Straits; Japan's revocation of concession rights on Sakhalin; and recognition of a

Soviet sphere south of Batum and Baku, in the direction of the Persian Gulf.[230] In other words, relations with Hitler had gravely deteriorated, and Stalin's ambitions from the relationship had soared.

The Soviet despot was following the same script as he had in August 1939: seeking an advantageous deal. But before Molotov's arrival in Berlin, Hitler did not bother to respond to the soaring demands. NKVD intelligence reported that "in Germany preparations for improved relations with Russia were proceeding apace" and were aimed at showing the whole world, especially Britain, that nothing could come between Berlin and Moscow. The Germans were saying that Britain stood on the verge of total defeat. NKVD intelligence further reported that Germany was ready to propose a Polish-style partition of Turkey with the Soviets, awarding Stalin the Straits, and possibly a partition of the entire Near East, Britain's colonial realm. At the same time, there were warnings of consequences if the Soviets failed to support the "Nazi New Order *in Europe*." The chatter from the Germans seemed to be directed at feeding the Soviets information to the effect that Berlin was going to rewrite the rules, and from a position of strength.[231] Whether Stalin caught this deflating message is unclear.[232]

There were many signals of trouble: Stalin learned from NKVD counterintelligence that Germany was trying to stop Denmark and Sweden from selling machines and equipment to the USSR.[233] Stalin even sent Gorsky back to London, with a handful of young, inexperienced operatives, to restore the USSR's intelligence station. Gorsky arrived in November 1940, and his team set about reestablishing contact with the expansive network of agents who had been abandoned, such as Kim Philby in MI6, Anthony Blunt, nominally an officer of the British general staff but actually in British counterintelligence, and others in the foreign office. They were tasked with digging into British efforts to cut a deal with Germany.

The strain on the despot was hard to miss for the inner circle. In impromptu remarks at the end of the annual intimate banquet for the November 7 holiday, in Voroshilov's Grand Kremlin Palace apartment, Stalin complained that during the major border war with Japan in 1939, he had discovered that "our aircraft can stay aloft for only thirty-five minutes, while German and English aircraft can stay up for several hours!" But when he summoned the aviation specialists for an account, they told him that no one had *specifically tasked them* with designing Soviet planes that would stay aloft longer. "I am busy at this every day now, meeting with designers and other specialists," Stalin lashed out. "But I am the *only* one dealing with all these problems. None of you could be bothered with them. I am out there *by myself. . . .*"

On what was normally a festive occasion, the despot delivered an aggravated-assault speech. Against the background of recent publications reprising the mythology of his defense of Tsaritsyn (Stalingrad) back in 1918, he saw fit to bring up the civil-war-era conflict with Trotsky over tsarist military officers, whom he contrasted with the "people loyal to the revolution, people connected to the masses, by and large noncommissioned officers from the lower ranks." He also asserted that Lenin had supported him in those clashes with the now assassinated Trotsky. It went far beyond defensiveness, however. "You do not like to learn; you are happy just going along the way you are, complacent," Stalin berated the men of his regime. "You are squandering Lenin's legacy." When Kalinin dared interject something, Stalin became especially menacing: "People are thoughtless, do not want to learn and relearn. They will hear me out and then go on just as before. But I will show you, if I ever lose my patience. You know very well how I can do that." The group stood silently. Voroshilov's eyes welled with tears, according to Dimitrov, who observed, "Have never seen and never heard J. V. [Stalin] the way he was that night—a memorable one."[234]

The next night, at the grand banquet in the St. George's Hall of the Grand Kremlin Palace, Stalin—unusually—was absent, provoking rumors among Western diplomats that a struggle for power might be under way.[235] It was nothing of the sort, of course: he was working, likely at the Near Dacha, on his detailed instructions for Molotov's meeting with Hitler. Point 1 would begin as follows: "*To find out* the true intentions of Germany and all the participants of the pact of three (Germany, Italy, and Japan) in the execution of the plan to form the 'New Europe' and similarly the 'Great East-Asian Sphere.'"[236]

SOVIET-BRITISH FEELERS

Litvinov was living under a form of house arrest at a state dacha in the suburbs, making occasional trips to the Lenin Library, in the city center, to research a dictionary of Russian synonyms.[237] Those in the know speculated that Stalin was keeping him as "insurance" against Hitler, for a possible reorientation to the West.[238] But the intuitive, always prepared Beria had his most trusted minions, including the assassin Sudoplatov, prepare scenarios to make Litvinov disappear, in the event of an order to do so.[239] When it came to the West, Stalin seemed unable to forgive and forget. He had observed (back in November 1939) that "in Germany, the petit-bourgeois nationalists are capable of a sharp turn—they are flexible—not tied to capitalist traditions, unlike bourgeois leaders like Chamberlain and his ilk."[240] By 1940 Hitler was at the height of his power, and Chamberlain and his ilk had been sacked. (On the eve of Molotov's Berlin visit, Chamberlain died of bowel cancer.) A new, nontrivial gesture had come from Churchill that seemed to play into Stalin's wheelhouse, but the despot had used an audience with Stafford Cripps to kowtow to Hitler. Not long after Hitler began stationing troops in Romania and making moves to station troops in Turkey, further threatening the British position in the Near East, the foreign office permitted Cripps to submit more formal proposals to Moscow for a British-Soviet pact.[241]

Churchill was not a blind anti-Communist. "I cannot forecast to you the action of Russia," he had remarked in a radio broadcast not long after the Hitler-Stalin Pact and the Treaty of Friendship and the Border. "It is a riddle wrapped in a mystery inside an enigma. But perhaps there is a key. That key is Russian national interest."[242] He did not spell out how Britain, rather than just Germany, could appeal to those interests. Cripps remained deeply convinced that Nazi and Soviet interests were fundamentally inimical, in a way that British and Soviet interests were not. On October 22, 1940, after having been denied a meeting with Molotov, Cripps had handed the latter's deputy Vyshinsky a revised offer from the British government. It vowed to treat the USSR on a par with the United States by consulting with Moscow about a postwar order, and in the meantime not to enter into an alliance against the Soviet Union, provided Moscow also refrained from hostile action (even indirectly through agitation). Cripps further communicated—exceeding his authority—that, pending a final postwar settlement, the British government could recognize de facto Soviet sovereignty in the Baltic states, Bessarabia, northern Bukovina, and "those parts of the former Polish State now under Soviet control."[243]

Cripps relayed that Britain would sign a trade agreement as well, supplying the USSR with goods necessary for its defense. In return, Moscow had to promise to observe the same benevolent neutrality vis-à-vis Britain as the Soviets had adopted toward Germany. Britain was further prepared, if no complications arose with the Axis powers, to proceed to a pact of nonaggression, while asking that if Iran and Turkey became embroiled in war with Germany or its allies, the USSR would assist them in such defense measures as it had adopted toward China (against

Stalin and Voroshilov (dancing), Kalinin (behind Stalin, with goatee and glasses), and Molotov (behind Voroshilov), Orjonikidze (behind Molotov) at an awards ceremony for the fifteenth anniversary of the Sovietization of Georgia, Kremlin Imperial Senate, March 1936. Ceremonial gatherings in the Imperial Senate and especially in the Grand Kremlin Palace became ever more central to Stalin's rule.

Heavy industry commissar shoots himself: Sergo Orjonikidze's bier, February 18, 1937. (Left to right) Molotov, Kaganovich, Jan Gamarnik (bearded), Voroshilov, and Stalin.

Kalinin and Stalin emerging from the Lenin Mausoleum, trailed by the diminutive Nikolai Yezhov (in NKVD uniform), May Day 1937. Stalin relentlessly goaded an already eager-to-please Yezhov to mass arrests.

Physical culture parade, Red Square, July 12, 1937, height of the terror.

Munich Pact fiasco (left to right): Chamberlain, Daladier, Hitler, Mussolini, and the latter's son-in-law and foreign minister, Ciano. The Soviet Union was not invited. Führer House, September 29–30, 1938.

Children and swastikas line the streets to welcome Adolf Hitler in the Sudetenland after the Western powers handed this region of Czechoslovakia to him. Stalin ended his mass terror almost immediately thereafter.

Chiang Kai-shek (right), head of China's ruling Nationalist government, and Zhang Xueliang, a warlord from Manchuria known as the Young Marshal, who later had Chiang kidnapped in collusion with China's Communists. Stalin would intervene to save Chiang.

Choibalsan, Moscow's ruler in the puppet state of Mongolia, during the Soviet-Japanese border war, summer 1939.

The 18th Party Congress. Each delegation was afforded a photograph with Stalin and the leadership (front row). Shown here is the turn of military party members. St. George's Hall of the Grand Kremlin Palace, March 1939.

Revolution Day parade. Red Square, November 7, 1939.

German foreign minister Joachim von Ribbentrop deplaning from Hitler's personal Condor is greeted by German ambassador Werner von der Schulenburg. Soviet antiaircraft battalions at the border—in the dark about Stalin's conspiratorial diplomacy—had attempted to shoot down the plane, but missed. Moscow, August 23, 1939.

Nazi flag on one of Stalin's armored sedans, which he sent to transport Ribbentrop (center, back to the camera).

A study in contrasts, Ribbentrop and Stalin: lightning conclusion of a Hitler-Stalin Pact. Little Corner, August 24, 1939.

Polish foreign minister Józef Beck (in great coat) ascending the steps to meet Hitler at the Nazi leader's mountain retreat. Beck had physically bowed to Hitler as the two shook hands, but refused his territorial demands. To the right is the head of the German protocol department, Alexander "Sandro" von Dörnberg. Berghof, January 5, 1939.

Hitler greets Ribbentrop after the signing of the Pact. Berlin, Reich Chancellery, August 25, 1939.

German engineering: a new bridge over the Vistula erected in two days for the Wehrmacht in Poland, September 1939. The wrecked Fordon Bridge is in the background.

Molotov signing a state treaty with Otto Kuusinen (far right, standing), whom Stalin appointed to head a "People's Government" for Finland, December 1, 1939. Zhdanov and Voroshilov are to Stalin's right. This proved to be one of Stalin's numerous blunders.

Finnish tank traps augmented the concrete emplacements and pillboxes of their Mannerheim Line of defense, Soviet-Finnish Winter War, 1939–40.

This is a rare photograph showing both Stalin and Trotsky (both in white) at Felix Dzierżyński's funeral, 1926. Molotov, at the front, is holding the casket (behind him); Bukharin is between him and Stalin. The bespectacled Trotsky is a ways across from Stalin to the left and next to Genrikh Yagoda (turned toward Trotsky). To Molotov's right is Alexei Rykov (looking up), to whose right is Lev Kamenev (hand on chin). Grigory Zinoviev (bushy, dark hair) is behind the person at the rear of the casket. Stalin executed or imprisoned almost everyone in the photo.

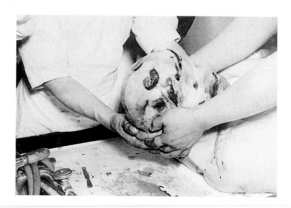

Trotsky's skull.

Molotov's personal photo album from his visit to Berlin, arrival at the Anthalter train station, November 10, 1940. From left (front): Field Marshall Wilhelm Keitel, Foreign Minister Joachim von Ribbentrop, and Molotov. Behind and between Ribbentrop and Molotov is Soviet ambassador Alexei Shkvartsev, a former textile factory manager.

Winston Churchill, trailed by his wife and personal secretary, survey the damage in London from Luftwaffe bombing, 1940. Churchill interrupted the Molotov-Hitler summit with stepped-up Royal Air Force bombing raids.

Confrontation:
Molotov-Hitler,
with Gustav Hilger
interpreting.
Reich Chancellery,
November 12, 1940.

Molotov and Rudolf Hess (right), deputy führer of the Nazi party. Hilger (left) and
Vladimir Pavlov (back to camera) interpreting. Berlin, November 13, 1940.

The arrival of a new
Soviet ambassador
to Berlin, Vladimir
Dekanozov, flanked
by Ernst Woermann
(German foreign
ministry), Gustav
Adolph von Halem
(deputy chief of protocol),
Friedrichstrasse train
station, November 28,
1940. Behind Dekanozov
is Amayak Kobulov,
the head of Soviet
intelligence in Berlin.

Stalin seeing off
Japanese foreign
minister Yōsuke
Matsuoka (wearing
glasses) at Moscow's
Yaroslavl train station,
following the signing
of a bilateral neutrality
pact, April 13, 1941.

Semyon Timoshenko (left) and Georgy Zhukov, the new Red Army leadership, on fall maneuvers, September 1940.

Left:
Filipp Golikov, yet another head of Soviet military intelligence.

Right:
Pavel Fitin, a very young head of NKVD (then NKGB) intelligence.

THE TOP SOVIET SPIES

Rudolf von Scheliha ("Aryan"),
German Foreign Ministry.

Ilse Stöbe ("Alta"),
the contact for "Aryan."

Richard Sorge ("Ramsay"),
German embassy in Tokyo.

Harro Schulze-Boysen ("Elder"),
German aviation ministry.

Arvid Harnack ("Corsican"),
German economics ministry.

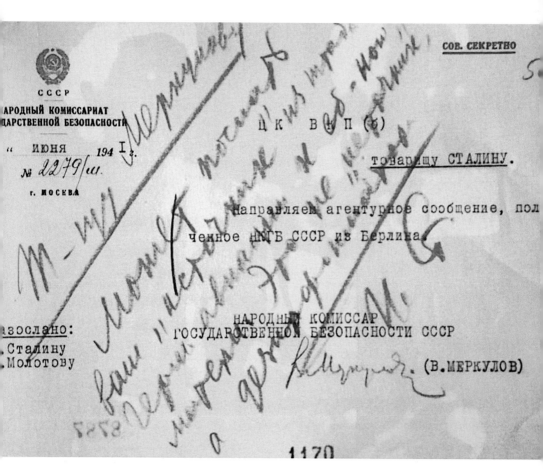

Stalin's markings (in green pencil) on the cover letter accompanying an NKVD intelligence report, June 17, 1941, about the pending German invasion: "To com. Merkulov: You can send your 'source' from German aviation HQ to his fucking mother. This is not a 'source' but a disinformationist. I.S."

Japanese aggression) in the past.[244] A few days later, on October 26, Cripps again saw Vyshinsky, who indicated that the Soviet government regarded the proposals as being of the greatest importance.[245]

Then, silence.

Stalin would appear at a reception on October 30, 1940, to culminate the Ten-Day cultural festival of the Buryat-Mongol autonomous republic, the ninth in the kitschy extravaganzas. "The Ten-Days cemented the friendship of peoples and gave it a deep and concrete concept," enthused Alexander Solodovnikov (b. 1904), a former leather factory worker who had risen to overseeing all theaters for the USSR committee on artistic affairs. "The preparation for the Ten-Days facilitated the development of countless talents, hitherto hidden among the people. Members of Russian theaters actively assisted the establishment of the theaters of brotherly republics. . . . At the same time, they received the richest palette of colors and variety in artistic forms, devices, examples, and cultural traditions lavishly revealed by the peoples of Central Asia, the Caucasus, Ukraine, Belorussia." Solodovnikov had led brigades to Minsk and to Ulan Ude, where he discovered that the local wooden theater had no heat, and that the Ukrainian-born party boss of the Buryat-Mongol republic, Semyon Ignatyev, who had survived the terror, kept a collection of bronze Buddha statues in his office cabinet.[246]

The reason for Soviet silence vis-à-vis Cripps had taken time to emerge: on November 10, Soviet newspapers suddenly announced that Molotov had accepted an invitation from Ribbentrop to visit Berlin. Cripps demanded to see the Soviet foreign affairs commissar but was again fobbed off onto Vyshinsky, with whom he exchanged heated words. When Cripps insisted that Britain's offer could not wait indefinitely and asked whether the Soviet government had a decision to communicate, Vyshinsky told him the answer was still forthcoming.[247]

SPIES AND FOOLS

Because of Stalin's terror rampages and Beria's ascent, the Germans acquired a double agent with ready access to the Soviet embassy in Berlin. Whereas in 1935 the NKVD intelligence station in Berlin had sixteen operatives besides the station chief, by 1939 that number had dropped to two. For nine months after the station chief had died on the operating table with an ulcer in December 1938, he had no replacement, until finally the Beria minion Amayak Kobulov ("Zakhar") arrived, posing as an embassy counselor. Kobulov (b. 1906) was a Tbilisi-born Armenian like his older brother, Bogdan. He had completed five years at the Tiflis Trading School, spoke no German, had no intelligence experience, and had never even been abroad. During the terror, in Gagra, he beat those he arrested himself with a pole, after having them placed on the floor. Most recently he had served as NKVD regional boss for Abkhazia (1938) and then Ukraine (1938–39).[248] In Berlin, Kobulov fooled no one, as confirmed by the Soviet agent in Gestapo counterintelligence, Willy Lehmann ("Breitenbach"), who had fallen completely out of contact but in late June 1940 had taken the risk of throwing a letter into the Soviet embassy mailbox with rendezvous coordinates and password, thereby reestablishing contact.[249] Kobulov was forbidden by Moscow Center to have any contact with the Soviet civilian intelligence spy networks in Germany, which were being reconstituted (see chapter 14). He needed his own.

Kobulov violated basic spycraft, visiting agents at their apartments and bringing them together in a single place. He had been recalled to Moscow HQ to defend his work; Beria complained in writing to Fitin, his underling for foreign intelligence, about the corridor whispers concerning Kobulov's dangerous amateurism.[250] Beria ordered Kobulov to step up the agent recruitment and, in traceable ways, the minion sought spies among the Berlin population who had past Soviet connections. He met Orests Berlings, a twenty-seven-year-old Latvian, the former Berlin correspondent for the Latvian newspaper *Brīvā Zeme,* who claimed to be well disposed to the USSR, well connected to the German foreign ministry press department, and penniless. By August 15, ten days after their initial acquaintance, Kobulov was already reporting directly to Stalin and Beria that Berlings had been "recruited" and put on retainer, calling him "most reliable." Berlings told the Germans, who promptly enrolled him as their agent (code-named "Peter").[251] Kobulov's superiors at the NKVD, belatedly alerted, quickly established that Berlings had opposed the Soviet annexation of Latvia and disseminated pro-Nazi propaganda. But Kobulov bragged in Berlings's presence that his information, bypassing channels, went straight to Stalin.[252]

MOLOTOV-HITLER

While Stalin fantasized about a new pact with Hitler, events on the far eastern flank of the USSR continued to be alarming.[253] In the third Five-Year Plan's investment allocation, the Soviet Far East received fully 10 percent, allowing for construction of strategic railroads to buttress frontiers, a secret tunnel under the Amur River at Khabarovsk, a pipeline under the sea to transport Sakhalin oil to refineries at Komsomolsk, a second port (in addition to Vladivostok) on the Tatar Strait, and roads. Despite mass deportations from the region, a combination of incentives and coercion had boosted the local population to 3.15 million by 1940, up from 2.27 million in 1937.[254] Japan, in a dream come true for Stalin, had become stalemated in its war to conquer all of China. But, contrary to his further wishes, a domestic showdown loomed there, desired by both the Nationalists and the Chinese Communists. Mao had dispatched a coded telegram (November 7, 1940) warning of an imminent Chinese Nationalist attack on the Chinese Communists and seeking Stalin's permission for "a preventive counteroffensive." Mao's telegram was received in Moscow on November 12. Dimitrov convened the Comintern executive committee, then tried to stall, instructing Mao to prepare his forces but not to act. That same day, at around 11:00 a.m., Molotov arrived at Berlin's Anhalter train station, near Potsdamer Platz.[255]

As Molotov stepped off the train in Berlin, there were puddles everywhere. The greeting party included Ribbentrop, Keitel, Robert Ley (German Labor Front), and Himmler, but not the staunch ideologues Goebbels and Rosenberg. Molotov would be in the Nazi capital for forty-eight hours, accompanied by a sixty-five-person entourage, including Dekanozov (foreign affairs), Tevosyan (ferrous metallurgy), Yakovlev (aviation), and Alexei Krutikov (foreign trade), who would remain in-country for industrial and trade matters. Merkulov (NKVD) supervised sixteen "security" guards tasked with maintaining surveillance of the Soviet delegation (and, the Gestapo suspected, leaving agents behind).[256] After an inspection of the honor guard, the Soviets departed the station in a sixty-vehicle convoy. "There was almost no one . . . along the streets," according to an American correspondent.[257] They arrived at the refurbished Schloss Bellevue, a former neoclassical Hohenzollern palace of more than 130 rooms set amid the exotic plants of the Tiergarten. Scented roses filled the opulent rooms and, as at the train station, the hammer-and-sickle flag flew alongside the swastika banner.[258] After breakfast, cigars, and cognac, the Soviets were taken to the foreign ministry. Only Molotov and Dekanozov, with interpreters and notetakers, were received. "A luxurious study, perhaps somewhat smaller than Hitler's own," the Soviet interpreter Berezhkov recalled of Ribbentrop's office, some of whose furnishings might have been trophies looted from the Low Countries and France. "Antique gilded furniture. Tapestry covers the walls from floor to ceiling, pictures hanging in heavy frames, porcelain and bronze statues on high stands placed in the corners."[259]

A genial Ribbentrop pontificated at length about a division of the world, but he refrained from making concrete proposals. "Germany has already won the war," he crowed. "No state in the world could alter the situation created as a result of Germany's victories."[260] Molotov, demanding specifics, managed to get a few words in. Following a white-gloved lunch back at the Bellevue, the foreign affairs commissar was brought to Hitler's grandiose new Chancellery, in an elaborately choreographed entrance designed to awe. The Führer, in a "study" the size of a congress hall, greeted the Soviet representative with the Nazi upturned palm. Invited to sit on a sofa, Molotov, who wore a rimless pince-nez and generally favored gray suits and stiff-necked white collars, was deemed by the Germans to resemble a mathematics professor. Hitler, described by an aide as "surprisingly gracious and friendly," delivered a long monologue from his armchair. He expounded on how Germany had been compelled to "penetrate into territories remote from her," to secure vital raw materials or prevent Britain from establishing a toehold, and acknowledged that "possibly M. Molotov was of the opinion that in one case or another there had been a departure from the conception of spheres of influence which had been agreed." He also asserted that "as soon as atmospheric conditions improved, Germany would be poised for a great and final blow against England." Molotov was not awed. No sooner had the monologue finished, recalled the German interpreter, than "the questions hailed down upon Hitler."[261]

The Hammer made no effort to be ingratiating (not part of his skill set anyway). His top aide had told another member of the delegation, General Alexander Vasilevsky, first deputy chief of the general staff operations directorate (responsible for battle plans), that the aims of the Berlin visit were "to determine the further intentions of Hitler, and as much as possible to delay a German aggression."[262] Whereas Hitler spoke of Soviet interests in British imperial lands (which Britain still controlled), Molotov spoke of Soviet security interests up and down Eastern Europe (which Hitler eyed). Molotov stated that Stalin had given him exact instructions, enumerated the mutual benefits of the Pact, and demanded to know "What was the meaning of the New Order in Europe and in Asia, and what role would the USSR be given in it?"[263] He insisted that "precision is necessary in a delimitation of spheres of influence," and "particular vigilance is needed in the delimitation of spheres of influence between Germany and Russia."[264]

The session lasted two and a half hours before Hitler broke it off. Ribbentrop hosted a lobster dinner, sans Führer, at the Kaiserhof Hotel, near the foreign ministry. The German state secretary, Weizsäcker, thought the Soviets, in their standard-issue dark suits and felt fedoras, resembled extras in a gangster movie.

But then again, Göring sported medals across his corpulent frame, from shoulder to waist, and multiple rings of precious stones on his fat fingers. Based on a report by Berlings, the Gestapo conveyed to Hitler and Ribbentrop that "last night, after the reception in the Kaiserhof, Molotov returned to the Bellevue and gathered a narrow circle of his entourage and embassy personnel. According to our agent, he was in a brilliant mood. The length of the talks he had with the Führer and the Reich foreign minister made a major impression on him. Then he said that he had a wonderful personal impression and that everything was going as he had envisioned and hoped."[265]

Molotov (perhaps suspecting listening devices) understood that his ingratiating words would reach his Nazi hosts.[266] Around midnight at the Bellevue, he wrote a coded telegram for Stalin, his second such cable of the day. "Their answers in conversation are not always clear and require further clarification," he observed of the meetings. "Hitler's great interest in reaching agreement to fortify the friendship with the USSR and spheres of influence is evident." Molotov's statement to Stalin indicates, of course, that this was *Stalin's* great interest. Notwithstanding the nine-page detailed charge (dated November 9, 1940) that Molotov was following to the letter, he took nothing for granted, concluding, "I ask for directives."[267] Molotov was the sole person in the regime to whom Stalin was willing to entrust a one-on-one with Hitler, yet Stalin was micromanaging the talks from Moscow.

Molotov's second day (November 13) included visits to Göring at the air ministry to discuss German military goods, and to Deputy Führer Rudolf Hess at Nazi party HQ, after which Molotov cabled Stalin that "they received me well and it is evident that they want to strengthen relations with the USSR."[268] In the afternoon, Hitler, this time in the company of Goebbels and Ribbentrop, again received Molotov, along with Dekanozov and Merkulov, for breakfast at 2:00 p.m. The menu, spartan as far as the Soviets were concerned, consisted of beef tea, pheasant, and fruit salad. Formal discussions resumed in Hitler's vast ceremonial study, ninety feet long and fifty feet wide, with paneling of rare woods, a massive portrait of Bismarck over the colored marble fireplace, and a white marble statue of Frederick the Great on horseback sitting atop a marble table.[269] The discussion lasted three and a half hours. Hitler was famous as a gifted orator and actor who intuited his audience's moods and aspirations, and adapted accordingly. In the Reichstag he was a wise statesman; at party rallies, a fanatical leader; among industrialists, a reasonable nationalist; to women, a child-friendly father figure; to foreign interlocutors, a theatrical performer, alternating between lordly and warmly intimate.[270] With the impassive Molotov, neither the poses nor the melodrama worked.

Adhering to Stalin's cabled corrections of him, Molotov underscored that the 1939 Pact remained in force, adding that "not without the assistance of the Pact with the USSR had Germany been able to complete its operations in Norway, Denmark, Belgium, Holland, and France so quickly and with such glory."[271] Hitler raised concerns about Bukovina. Molotov accused Hitler of trying to alter the terms of the secret protocol regarding Finland and Romania; Hitler claimed otherwise. Molotov noted that the Soviets merely wanted to protect themselves against an attack through the Gulf of Finland, the Straits, or the Black Sea. The exchange "never became violent," recalled Hitler's interpreter, "but the debate on both sides was conducted with singular tenacity."[272] Goebbels judged that Molotov "made an intelligent, astute impression, very reserved. One gets almost nothing out of him. He listens attentively, but nothing more. Even with the Führer."[273]

Hitler rose. As he escorted Molotov and his entourage to the door, he said he "regretted that he had not yet been able to meet such an immense historical personage as Stalin, especially since he believed he himself might possibly enter history," according to the notetakers. "Molotov agreed with Hitler's statement on the desirability of such a meeting and expressed the hope that such a meeting would take place."[274]

The two sides could not even agree on a follow-up visit by Ribbentrop to Moscow. Amid the inconclusiveness, scores of top Nazis—but not the Führer—attended a farewell banquet given by the Soviet ambassador (the former textile plant manager) at the Unter den Linden Soviet embassy, whose fading tsarist-era splendor was now overseen by a bust of Lenin. The vodka and caviar were prodigious. "No capitalist or plutocratic . . . table could have been more richly spread," recalled the German interpreter. "It was a very good party."[275]

Churchill cut the festivities short: a British bombing squadron appeared over central Berlin at around 8:30 p.m. Ribbentrop conveyed Molotov the short distance to the safety of his bunker beneath the foreign ministry (the Soviet embassy had none). As a result, additional, unplanned talks ensued, from 9:45 p.m. until nearly midnight. The Nazi foreign minister removed from his pocket and read aloud a draft text, three paragraphs in length, on converting the Tripartite Pact into a four-power pact, with secret protocols to be appended later. A four-power pact would have confronted Britain, as well as the United States, with formidable challenges: the likely fall of not just the European continent but the Mediterranean, the Near East, and the Far East into the clutches of authoritarian Germany, Italy, Japan, and the Soviet Union.[276] At the same time, it was doubtful whether the tripartite alliance could counter the combined might of the Anglo-American bloc without the Soviet Union.

Molotov, according to the German record, again insisted that a new understanding of Soviet-German relations was a prerequisite to discussions about the USSR joining a pact of four; the Soviet record indicates that Molotov demanded an explanation of the alliance between Germany, Japan, and Italy and insisted on the importance to the USSR of Bulgaria, Romania, Hungary, Yugoslavia, Swedish neutrality, Finland, and more.[277] Ribbentrop resumed expounding on the pending liquidation of the British empire. "If England is defeated, why are we sitting in this shelter?" Molotov interjected, in a retort Stalin would cherish and retell. "And whose bombs are dropping so close that we can hear the explosions even here?"[278]

THE NONPIVOT

The British press descended into a frenzy over Molotov's visit to Berlin, warning that the Soviet Union was about to join the Axis. Prior to Molotov's return, Stalin had sent suggestions on what the despot assumed would be a joint communiqué issued in Berlin. "The exchange of views took place in an atmosphere of mutual trust," Stalin had written, "and they established mutual understanding on all the most important questions of interest to the USSR and Germany." He had also instructed Molotov that "it would be better if the Germans proposed their draft first." In fact, the Germans proposed nothing, and no joint communiqué was issued. After midnight on November 13–14, Molotov had cabled Stalin and admitted that the Berlin meetings "had not delivered the desired results." The USSR's interests in Eastern Europe were not being acknowledged. "Nothing to boast about, but at a minimum I ascertained the current mood of Hitler, which is something we will have to come to grips with."[279] Molotov departed Berlin later that morning. *Pravda* (November 15) published the proposed joint communiqué unilaterally.[280] But the Soviet press proved unable to name a single concrete achievement of Molotov's visit.[281]

The Germans recorded Amayak Kobulov as having stated that Molotov's visit was a "powerful demonstration," but that "not everything that shines is gold."[282] Some members of the Soviet delegation, while still in Berlin, had voiced suspicions that with the Tripartite Pact, Germany was actually working to "encircle" the Soviet Union, while also embroiling it in conflict with Britain over imperial possessions. Soviet military intelligence would inform Moscow that Scheliha ("Aryan") had heard high officials in the German foreign ministry conclude that, during Molotov's November 1940 visit, "consensus was not reached on a single important question—not on the question of Finland, not on the question of Bulgaria."[283] On the German side, Dr. Otto Meissner, the head of the (ceremonial) presidential chancellery, considered an old-school adherent of the Bismarckian policy of ties with Russia, was given the impression—which, as expected, he repeated so that it reached Soviet ears—that Hitler was "very satisfied with the visit and that Molotov's personality impressed him."[284] This was disinformation that the Nazi regime rightly expected would now spread. Most German insiders judged Molotov's visit a failure. "Two things became clear in the discussions," one of Hitler's interpreters later noted. "Hitler's intention to push the Soviet Union in the direction of the Persian Gulf, and his unwillingness to acknowledge any Soviet interest in Europe."[285]

Molotov reached Moscow on November 15. There is no reliable account of the report he delivered that evening to Stalin and anyone else the despot summoned to the Near Dacha.[286] On orders, Molotov's interpreter (Pavlov) told a pro-Soviet American that Molotov had "thawed" in Berlin and that Hitler had made a big impression. A cable from Molotov to Maisky in London (November 17) soberly noted that the Germans were trying to push the Soviets toward India and wanted Turkey for themselves.[287] But at a reception given by the Italian ambassador, Augusto Rosso, for representatives of "friendly countries," the Bulgarian envoy to Moscow perceived Molotov as "swollen-headed and puffed up."[288] Molotov, just as Stalin instructed, had stood up to Hitler.

Back in 1939, when Stalin had understood, correctly, the emptiness of the British and French negotiating positions vis-à-vis Moscow, he had not hesitated to humiliate them. Of course, at that time, he was assiduously cultivating an alternative: Nazi Germany. In 1940, he had not pursued a genuine alternative to Germany should its negotiating position prove empty. Stalin had not gone to the British of his own accord to create leverage for his demands vis-à-vis a newly triumphant Germany; the British, in the person of Sir Stafford Cripps, had come to him. Stalin only belatedly responded to the sincere British offers of a trade-and-nonaggression pact, and not even through the diplomatic channels in which they had been conveyed. Cripps, to accommodate Stalin's requests, had urged the British government that any talks with Moscow had to be carried out in the utmost secrecy—no small feat for an open society and leak-prone political system like Britain's. But then, on November 16, the confidential British proposals appeared in the English-language press, as Cripps heard over BBC radio in Moscow. Irate, he suspected the British foreign office, but the source was the Soviet embassy in London.[289] In the event, Vyshinsky's initial reaction to the Cripps proposal—deeming it of the greatest importance—had been shamelessly disingenuous. Stalin had used Cripps, again, then hung him out to dry, in a clumsy warning-cum-ingratiation directed at Hitler.

Other British actions unintentionally worked against rapprochement: Molotov's unplanned refuge in the Berlin bomb shelter, a result of British bombing raids, had evidently helped solidify his view that Germany was still deeply mired in a war in the west, a circumstance that he interpreted in light of his conviction that no German leader would willingly launch a two-front war by attacking in the east. "Even after his visit to Berlin in November 1940, Molotov continued to assert that Hitler would not attack," recalled Zhukov, who added that "one must take into account that in Stalin's eyes, in this case, Molotov had the added authority of someone who had personally visited Berlin."[290]

BULGARIAN GAMBIT

The Japanese government, for its part, was disappointed that nothing had emerged from the Hitler-Molotov summit; the Tripartite Pact had been expected to facilitate Japanese-Soviet rapprochement at U.S. and British expense in East Asia (especially the base at Singapore), but these hopes appeared unfulfilled. On November 18, 1940, Molotov received Japan's ambassador, Yoshitsugu Tatekawa, and, referring to his conversation with Ribbentrop, declared that he welcomed Japan's desire to normalize relations with the USSR, but he added that Soviet public opinion could not accept a bilateral nonaggression pact unless Soviet territorial losses in the Far East were "restored." Molotov named Southern Sakhalin and the Kuril Islands, adding that if Japan was not prepared to discuss these claims, then he could recommend only a lesser "neutrality pact," as well as a special protocol stipulating the liquidation of Japanese economic concessions on Soviet-controlled Northern Sakhalin.[291]

That same day, Hitler received Bulgaria's tsar Boris III and his foreign minister at the Berghof, aiming to trump any Soviet entreaties to them. The king, fearing a Soviet backlash, "appeared less inclined than ever" to join the Tripartite Pact, even as he assured Hitler that "down here you have a true small friend, whom you do not have to disown."[292] On November 20, Hungary joined the

Tripartite Pact, followed by Romania (November 23), then Slovakia (November 24), all of them in the Soviet backyard and all agreeing, in effect, to become junior partners in a German-dominated Europe. True, also on November 24, Italy was routed in Albania by Greece. And Soviet intelligence sources passed on word that Bulgaria's king was resisting German pressure. But upon his return to Sofia, Boris did reject Soviet entreaties.

Eisenstein, the Jewish-born convert to Orthodoxy, revived his career with, of all things, a monumental Wagner opera production, which premiered in Moscow on November 21, 1940. The filmmaker's masterpiece, *Alexander Nevsky* (November 1938), which depicted the medieval destruction by invading Teutonic knights, remained on ice, but in spring 1940 he had been commissioned to produce Wagner's *Die Walküre*. The last staging at the Bolshoi had been in 1925, and it had been a revival of the prerevolutionary (1902) production. Eisenstein had not worked in theater since the heady "Proletarian Culture" movement (also 1925). He plunged into the task, reading up on Wagner and mythology, writing in *Ogonyok* that Wagner attracted him by his use of legend and folklore, vital ingredients of art.[293] Eisenstein had found a kindred spirit.[294] His staging, with an ample budget and the Soviet Union's best singers, proved to be original, seeking a Wagnerian synthesis of the spatial, aural, and visual. "People, music, light, landscape . . . color and movement," he explained, "all brought together by a single piercing emotion, a single theme and idea—this is what the filmmaker strives to achieve, and the producer finds the same when he becomes familiar with Wagner's works."[295]

Stalin sent a special envoy, Arkady Sobolev (b. 1903), foreign affairs commissariat secretary general, to Sofia, uninvited, ostensibly on a transit flight to Bucharest. The Bulgarians were informed only a few hours in advance of his arrival. "My impression," the misled Bulgarian envoy to Moscow surmised, "is that they are prepared to do anything if only they could sign a pact with us." On November 25, Sobolev was received by, first, the Bulgarian prime minister, Bogdan Filov—a professor of ancient art and president of the Bulgarian Academy of Sciences—then King Boris, telling them, in elliptical language, that he sought an agreement for transfer of Red Army troops, via Bulgaria, toward the Turkish Straits in case of need, while pledging noninterference in Bulgarian domestic affairs. Sobolev noted that such a bilateral deal did not preclude Bulgaria's also joining the Axis, because a Bulgarian-Soviet pact "might very probably, almost certainly" result in the USSR's own entry into the Axis. Filov was stunned. He obfuscated about "Bulgaria's complicated situation" but shrank from mentioning Nazi Germany by name.[296]

That same day, Dimitrov was summoned to the Little Corner, in the presence of Molotov and first deputy foreign affairs commissar Dekanozov. It was the Comintern head's only audience in the Little Corner in all of 1940, and lasted a half hour.[297] After confirming China policy with Stalin, Dimitrov dispatched an order to Mao not to attack the Nationalists.[298] The main discussion concerned Bulgaria, Dimitrov's homeland. "Historically, this is where the threat has always originated," Stalin told him. "The Crimean War—the taking of Sevastopol, Wrangel's intervention in 1919, and so forth." Stalin added that Sobolev had already been received in Sofia by Filov and that, "in concluding a mutual assistance pact, we not only have no objections to Bulgaria's joining the Tripartite Pact, but we ourselves in that event will also join the pact." Stalin further indicated that he would seek to secure the Straits directly, by pressuring Turkey. "What is Turkey?" he continued. "There are two million Georgians there, one and a half million Armenians, one million Kurds, and so forth. The Turks amount to only six or seven million." Amid the bluster, however, Stalin noted to Dimitrov, "Our relations with Germany are polite on the surface, but there is serious friction between us."[299]

Fifteen minutes after Dimitrov's visit ended, Molotov departed the Little Corner to hand Schulenburg the Soviet Union's formal assent to join a pact of four—by now much expanded in members—but with major conditions: (1) German troops would have to leave Finland; (2) a pact would be signed between the USSR and Bulgaria for Soviet security on the Black Sea; (3) the Soviets would obtain a privileged position on the Turkish Straits and a "center of gravity" south from Batumi and Baku to the Persian Gulf; and (4) Japan would renounce its oil and coal concessions on Northern Sakhalin, with reasonable economic compensation.[300] In other words, facing the threat of ever more German troops arriving on his borders, Stalin sought *everything*: not just Persia, which Hitler was offering, but Finland, the Baltics, the Balkans, and the Straits. ("As I was accompanying Schulenburg out, I was overcome with emotions," recalled the Soviet interpreter. "Soviet bases in the Bosporus and Dardanelles!")[301] Molotov told Schulenburg he hoped for "an early answer" to the Soviet conditions.[302]

Stalin had expressed his readiness to deepen Soviet involvement in German aggression, and to join the aggression of Italy and Japan, which would have been a fateful step for the British empire and the United States. But the despot offered Soviet services to Berlin as if Moscow were, or would be, an equal partner. The depth of his global miscalculation was unintentionally laid bare in little Bulgaria. Evidently Dimitrov was instructed or under the impression that Sobolev's confidential oral proposal to the Bulgarian prime minister and tsar should become known, to increase the pressure, and the next day he wired a written summary to the Bulgarian Communist party, informing Stalin that he had done so. The Bulgarian Communists printed up and distributed the summary as leaflets. The clumsy tactic failed to intimidate the Bulgarian government. Sobolev, the special envoy, had found the government "already committed to Germany to the hilt."[303] Meanwhile, copies of the Soviet demands were whisked to Hitler. "Our people in Sofia have been disseminating leaflets about the Soviet proposal to Bulgaria," Molotov exploded at Dimitrov over the phone on November 28, 1940. "Idiots!"[304]

READING HITLER'S INTENTIONS

Bismarck liked to say that pacts must be observed so long as conditions remain the same (*"Pacta sunt servanda rebus sic stantibus"*), meaning they could be abrogated. His worldview had been predicated upon a sense of limits and international balance. He had refrained from conquering even all German speakers, despite the wherewithal to do so. Hitler possessed the ambition for a total continental conquest, but, unlike Bismarck, he had initially lacked the wherewithal. Over time, Hitler's ambition had delivered the wherewithal, from the Rhineland remilitarization (1936) through the *Anschluss* (1938), the Munich Pact (1938), and, especially, the brazen violation of Munich with his unpunished seizure of all of Czechoslovakia (1939), followed by lightning conquests of Poland (1939) and the Low Countries and France (1940). None of this had been foreordained. Strength deters aggression, as Mussolini had shown with Austria in 1934, while weakness encourages it. By 1940, however, it was not clear that Hitler, given his strength and successes, remained susceptible to conventional deterrence. Britain posed no threat to Germany's continental domination, but the crushing of France had failed to compel Britain's surrender, a snub that the "invincible" Führer could not abide. Equally important, he feared dissipation of Nazism's élan.[305] In other words, Hitler had become both more capable of and more impatient for still greater conquest.

Hitler's calculations are difficult to read even now. "The Führer hopes he can bring Russia into the anti-British front," army chief of staff Halder, after a meeting with the Führer, recorded in his diary (November 1, 1940).[306] Ribbentrop had explained to Mussolini on the eve of Molotov's Berlin visit that the acid test would be Stalin's position vis-à-vis the "dangerous overlapping of interests" in the Balkans: if the Soviets backed down, the Germans could have their way without war. Hitler himself told Mussolini that there would be no accommodation with Stalin beyond Turkey, certainly not regarding Bulgaria or Romania—indicating that some accommodation was possible.[307] Of course, Hitler's sincerity even with his own army, foreign ministry, and principal ally could never be accepted at face value. The Führer's internally stated aim for meeting Molotov—"to entice Russia into participating in a grand coalition against England"—might have been disingenuous. The big play Molotov's visit got in the Nazi press smacks of a transparent effort to drive the wedge still deeper between Britain and the Soviet Union. Hitler had already ordered internal explorations for an invasion of the USSR in fall 1940, a secret idea that remained operative for spring 1941. But then, on the very eve of Molotov's visit to Berlin, Hitler's army adjutant, Major Gerhard Engel, observed that a "visibly depressed" Führer gave the "impression that at the moment he does not know how things should proceed."[308]

On the very day of Molotov's arrival in Berlin, the Führer had signed the secret Directive No. 18, which read like a warning to himself not to fall into temptation to strike a bargain with Moscow again. "Political discussions have been initiated with the aim of clarifying Russia's attitude for the time being," the November 12, 1940, directive explained. "Irrespective of the results of these discussions, all preparations for the East [war] which have already been verbally ordered will be continued."[309] Molotov's ostentatious lack of deference in the Nazi capital afforded the Führer a sense of release. "He is vastly relieved; this won't even have to remain a marriage of convenience," Engel wrote of the Führer's daily noontime military conference on the day of Molotov's departure. "Letting the Russians into Europe would mean the end of central Europe. The Balkans and Finland are also dangerous flanks."[310]

But the question had not been settled. Lingering doubts and possible reversibility in Hitler's momentous decisions, paradoxically, were raised precisely because subsequent directives were issued to reaffirm them. Consider, further, that after the invitation to Molotov had been sent, Hitler had had his utterly fruitless meetings with Franco and Pétain. Could Stalin fill the breach left by the failures of Spain and Vichy France to join Hitler in undercutting Britain's Mediterranean positions? Also on November 12, Hitler signed the order for Germany's "peripheral strategy" to fight Britain, undergirding the quest for allies in an anti-British front. Even after Molotov's abrasive visit, moreover, Jodl, Hitler's closest military adviser, was of the opinion that the Soviets continued to offer important value to Germany, above all in the war against Britain, which had not yet been won.[311] Similar views were expressed by Admiral Raeder and even by Göring.[312] Halder expected the Soviets to join the Axis and, apropos of Molotov's visit, recorded the following in his diary (November 16): "Result: Constructive note; Russia has no intention of breaking with us. . . . As regards the Tripartite Pact it is clear that Russia wants to be a partner, not its object. Pact must be reframed!" Halder judged Hitler inclined to avoid a war with the Soviet Union, provided that Stalin did not demonstrate expansionist tendencies into Europe.[313] On November 18, Halder wrote in his diary that the "Russian operation" had been "pushed into the background."[314]

That same day, Hitler told Italian foreign minister Ciano that "it is necessary to apply strong measures in order to divert Russia from the Balkans and push her southward." Two days later, the Führer made almost the identical statement in a letter to Mussolini.[315] On November 19, when the commander of the Luftwaffe mission in Romania expressly asked for instructions in the event of a German-Soviet war, Hitler had Jodl delay a reply until the arrival of the formal Soviet response to the invitation to join the Tripartite Pact.[316] On November 26, Hitler told the Hungarian prime minister, Count Pál Teleki, that "Russia's conduct is either Bolshevist or Russian nationalist, depending on the situation. . . . Nonetheless we could try to bring her into the great worldwide coalition that stretched from Yokohama to Spain," but "divert them to the south Asiatic continent."[317] Also on November 26, however, Hitler received the Soviet reply to the invitation to join a pact of four, with its over-the-top demands. [318]

SUPREME CUNNING?

In 1940, the USSR had only one third as many tractors as the United States, but twice as many as the whole of Europe. The United States had twenty-eight continuous strip mills for steel, while the Soviet Union possessed five, and all of Europe just three.[319] Stalin had discontinued most new civilian construction and imposed higher assessments on collective farmers (from a calculation based on actual sown acreage to one based on the farm's potentially cultivatable land), while delivering less machinery to farms. Soviet per capita grain production still had not reached pre-1914 levels.[320] At the same time, urbanites were now awarded garden plots en masse to grow their own food. In this tight context, Stalin was nonetheless prepared, in exchange for his demands in joining the Axis, to sweeten his economic contributions, including the delivery (by May 1941) of 2.5 million tons of grain, 1 million above existing Soviet obligations.[321] Stalin feared any interruption in the imports of German military technology, even though he suspected the Germans were deceiving him, and made deputy aviation commissar Yakovlev travel three times to Berlin to verify that the Soviets were getting the best Germany had. ("See to it that our people study the German planes," Stalin told him. "Learn how to smash them.")[322]

Stalin's larger objective remained to keep Hitler focused on the West and avoid entanglement in war himself. But the despot's secret instructions to Molotov regarding a four-power pact indicate more than merely probing Hitler's intentions. If Hitler *had* been willing to meet the despot's key conditions in 1940—conceding Finland, southeastern Europe (the Balkans), and the Straits, so that Stalin could protect his entire western flank—the despot likely would have signed on to the Axis.[323] Territorial annexations and spheres of interest, in Stalin's mind, provided for security. At best, however, the Führer was offering Stalin only a junior partnership in this new world order dominated by a Germanocentric Axis.[324] Ribbentrop had done his best to make the "continental bloc" against Britain attractive to the Soviets, but the Nazi foreign minister felt undercut by Molotov's dogged insistence on expansive Soviet interests in Eastern Europe. Ribbentrop "could only repeat again and again that the decisive question was whether the Soviet Union was prepared and in a position to cooperate with us in the great liquidation of the British empire. On all other questions we would easily reach an understanding."[325] That statement, however, looks delusional. The 1939 Pact had promised a joint division of Eastern Europe, but the November 1940 summit made manifest that Hitler was going to take all of it for himself.[326]

Stalin was game to a new permanent division of Europe that excluded Britain and a vanquished France, provided it made Germany and the Soviet Union equals. He laid out his conditions to Hitler as if from a position of strength—but this was a different Germany now. The despot's unilateral territorial seizures and his further demands had done nothing for those inside the Wehrmacht, the navy, the foreign ministry, or even some top Nazi officials who doubted the wisdom and necessity of war against the Soviet Union. On the contrary, his greed had played right into Hitler's own long-standing anti-Bolshevik, anti-Slav worldview. Stalin's air force, Hitler noted, could turn Romania's Ploiești oil fields, by far Germany's biggest supplier, into "an expanse of smoking ruins," choking the Axis war machine.[327] Stalin had also held up Soviet compensation payments for Baltic property, contracts for oil deliveries (ostensibly over pricing), shipments of rubber from the Far East via the Trans-Siberian, and Afghan cotton. On top of all this came Molotov's refusal inside the Chancellery to be hypnotized or bullied by Hitler. In the event, Stalin's insistence on forceful tactics in the talks not only clarified Hitler's aggressive intentions but seem to have helped solidify them.[328] Ribbentrop later recalled that, in Hitler's mind, Molotov was "pressuring" Germany, and Hitler "was not willing to be taken by surprise once he had recognized a danger."[329]

After Stalin's conditions for joining a four-power pact were conveyed through Molotov, Hitler did not respond. The Soviets would repeat their proposals; again, nothing from Berlin.[330] The silence should have been all Stalin needed to hear. At the same time, the deafening whistles of the British bombs over Berlin during Molotov's visit had offered their own resounding message: namely, that the Kremlin had a possible partner against Nazi aggression. But the bottom line, for Stalin as for Molotov, was that those bombs raining down on Berlin meant that Britain, not the Soviet Union, was at war with Germany.

In the Pact with Hitler, Stalin had been lucky but also shrewd. Now he remained adamant not to let the conniving imperialist Churchill drag him into war with Hitler. Any dramatic chess moves with Britain might provoke Nazi Germany to attack the USSR, while a nonaggression pact and trade agreement with Britain would not have done much for Stalin's principal problem: the massing of scores of German army divisions on the Soviet border. And yet, what if Hitler proved ready to attack the USSR in response to the *very idea* of a British-Soviet rapprochement, even when that option appeared to have been rejected by both parties? This might be the worst possible circumstance: no actual Soviet deal with Britain to deter Hitler, but Hitler acting upon the fact that his enemies were in contact. Stalin had less to lose by giving London a try than he thought. A balancing relationship with Britain might have given pause to the German high command, the wider Nazi elite, and even Hitler.

Stalin erred in not *testing* the real limits of a possible geopolitical pivot toward Britain. At the same time, that was not the only move that he might have tried but did not. He could have instructed Molotov, in Berlin, to say yes to a new deal with Germany, this time entirely on Hitler's terms, conceding most of Eastern Europe, in exchange for a division of the spoils of a dismembered British empire. Acceding to German vassal status would have been an admission of weakness. But Hitler had acceded to Stalin's terms in 1939, when he needed the Pact. What if Stalin had lived up to his reputation for supreme cunning and just accepted the offer of a junior partnership under Nazi Germany (the way Mussolini had done)? Of course, such a surprise embrace would not have removed the German land army from Finland, occupied Poland, or Romania. But might it not have thrown Hitler, his military men, and Nazi propaganda for a loop and, as Stalin wished, refocused them all on Britain?

We shall never know. Stalin confided to Dimitrov that at the end of the day,

Hitler would have no choice but to recognize that the Soviets required a strong position on the Black Sea to make sure the Turkish Straits were not used against Germany.[331] Hitler, however, was not Bismarck; he did not recognize other states' interests as a factor for stability. The combination of German power and Hitler's person was something that neither Stalin nor the rest of the world had faced before. It was, however, most immediately the Soviet despot's problem, given the contiguous geography. His room for maneuver had become ever more circumscribed as the outside world closed in on the Little Corner.

FROM THE START, the Soviet-German rapprochement had been fraught— burdened with tensions and uncertainties. The path from the Munich Pact (September 1938) through the Hitler-Stalin Pact (August 1939), the joint partition of Poland and clashes over the oil fields, with Western declarations of war against Germany (September 1939), the Soviet-German Treaty of Friendship and the Border (September 1939), the Soviet Winter War against Finland (November 1939– February 1940), the German victory over France (June 1940), Soviet annexations of the Baltic states and parts of Romania (June 1940), and Molotov's visit to Berlin (November 1940), had been a roller-coaster ride. Stalin's apprenticeship in high-stakes diplomacy showed him to be cunning, but also opportunistic, avaricious, obdurate. His deal making with Hitler had played out one way in 1939 and altogether differently in 1940. Stalin's strategy remained the same.

Soviet insiders continued to exhibit confidence bordering on arrogance. "The policy of a socialist government consists of using the contradictions between imperialists, in this case the military contradictions, in order to expand the position of socialism whenever the opportunity arises," Zhdanov had crowed at a closed party meeting in Leningrad on November 30, 1940. "Ours is an unusual neutrality: without fighting, we are gaining territory. (Laughter in the hall.)"[332] Stalin's bold seizure and Sovietization of Romanian territory, including Bukovina, as well as the Baltic states, including the strip in southwestern Lithuania that he had promised to Hitler, had ensured that these territories would not fall into Hitler's hands, but the actions had also removed buffers between the Soviet Union and Nazi Germany and risked a clash, right when Berlin's dependence on good relations with Moscow had been reduced. Most fundamentally, Stalin had failed to follow his own advice: even with France kaput, he had not taken the initiative to balance ever-growing German power. Instead, he had allowed the long-standing mistrust in British-Soviet relations to overshadow the escalating imbalance and tensions in German-Soviet relations. Once again, the initiative for a bilateral deal had come from Ribbentrop, and, in response, Stalin had once again revealed his exorbitant appetites, but this time the context was radically different.

One might surmise that Stalin's extravagant demands vis-à-vis Hitler in November 1940 had been diabolically clever, for they managed to expose the irreconcilability of German-Soviet interests and, therefore, the de facto end of his mutually beneficial Pact with Hitler. But Stalin's November 1940 pie-in-the-sky wish list was not a cynical ploy to flush out Hitler. Rather, the despot had instructed Molotov to negotiate a new pact. In doing so, Stalin egregiously overestimated his leverage. His exhorbitant demands for joining the Axis turned out to be his most momentous decision to date. Soviet military intelligence estimated at this time that between 76 and 79 German divisions were in former Poland, and 15 to 17 in Romania. Germany was thought to have 229 to 242 divisions in total (the real number was closer to 185).[333] Even journalists were reporting that Germany was stationing its most mechanized divisions on the Soviet border, and that German construction of roads and infrastructure in the east had become furious. German military exercises for a possible war against the USSR, based on recently completed operational studies by General Friedrich von Paulus, took place in the latter part of November and early December.[334]

Stalin knew he had bungled the Finnish campaign, and he was meeting often with the new top commanders he had promoted in its aftermath, Timoshenko and Zhukov.[335] The USSR now had an army of 4.2 million, triple its size just three years earlier, and the world's largest. The transformation of the country's economic base had been far reaching. Soviet steel production in 1927–28 had been around 4 million tons, and the 1932 plan target had been set at 10.4 million; the actual amount in 1932 was reported as 5.9 million, but by 1940 the regime reported steel production at 18.3 million tons—a huge leap, even allowing for exaggeration.[336] In 1940, industry would produce 243 heavy, 833 medium, and 1,620 light tanks and more than 10,000 aircraft, including 4,657 fighter planes and 3,674 bombers.[337] But the massive military reorganization still had a long way to go.[338] On December 7, 1940, Timoshenko completed his evaluation, which proved to be a brutal indictment of Voroshilov's leadership and a candid enumeration of the weaknesses of the massive war machine, which suffered from a severe lack of experienced commanders, low levels of training for masses of new conscripts, and a glut of now obsolete weaponry. Training was supposed to be year-round, but much army time was lost to working at collective farms during planting and harvesting, and on construction sites.[339]

Nor was it easy for a peasant country to continue supporting such a military. Even officially, the Soviet economic growth rate would drop precipitously, from 10–12 percent per annum in 1928–37 to a mere 2–3 percent per annum in 1937–40, and the key shortfalls occurred in strategic areas: steel, coal, chemical products, crude oil. The terror had exacerbated skilled labor turnover and managerial dearth, while often paralyzing survivors.[340] Mass arrests for "wrecking" struck the highest-priority military factories, too.[341] Military budgets were bloated. Whereas, in 1938, the military had consumed 23.2 billion rubles, or 18.7 percent of the 124 billion in state outlays, in 1940, from a total budget of 174.4 billion rubles, the military would get 56.8 billion, or 32.6 percent.[342] Against GDP, Soviet military spending would rise in 1940 to probably 17 percent (as compared with 2 percent in 1928 and 5 percent in 1913).[343] The Soviet regime's ability to spend that quantity of money efficiently, or indeed to spend it all, was another matter.[344] Moreover, Nazi Germany had been spending 15 percent of a larger national income on its military already since 1937, and that number had grown.[345] Khrushchev, who was in Moscow when Molotov returned from Berlin, would remark, "In Stalin's face and in his manner, one could sense agitation and, I would add, fear."[346]

CHAPTER 14

FEAR

It would be incorrect to say that [Stalin] underestimated
him. He saw that Hitler had organized Germany in a short
period of time. There had been a huge [German]
Communist party and it had disappeared, wiped out!

VYACHESLAV MOLOTOV[1]

Stalin is one of the most extraordinary figures in world
history. He began as a small clerk, and he has never
stopped being a clerk. Stalin owes nothing to rhetoric. He
governs from his office, thanks to a bureaucracy that
obeys his every nod and gesture.

ADOLF HITLER, Table Talk, *1941*[2]

MOLOTOV, BACK FROM BERLIN, sacked the former textile manager serving as
Soviet ambassador there in favor of his own deputy, Vladimir Dekanozov, the
Beria minion who had briefly headed NKVD intelligence. Even Molotov did
not know him well, thinking him an Armenian who pretended to be a Georgian.[3]
He seems to have been of mixed Russian (father) and German Jewish (mother)
heritage, and had been born Ivan Protopopov in Estonia. Blond and blue-eyed,
barely five feet tall, imperious and foul-mouthed with underlings, the forty-one-
year-old was the youngest ambassador in the Nazi capital.[4] He retained his status
as a deputy foreign affairs commissar but could not manage to present his credentials to Hitler. On December 5, 1940, still awaiting an audience, Dekanozov
received an anonymous German-language letter in the mail. "Hitler intends to
attack the USSR next spring," it read. "The Red Army will be destroyed by numerous powerful encirclements." The details of pending bellicose actions impressed the thirty-four-year-old Soviet military intelligence station chief, Nikolai
Skornyakov, and Dekanozov sent the letter to Molotov, who forwarded it: "Comrade Stalin—for your information."[5]

Everyone was talking. They had "heard" that Hitler would attack. It would happen this way. It would happen that way. It would occur on this date. It would occur on that date. The encrypted reports flowed over the wires from Belgrade, Sofia, Prague, Bucharest, Budapest, and Warsaw; London, Paris, Geneva, Stockholm, Helsinki, and Rome; Tokyo, Washington, and Berlin. The noise was shattering. Observers reported rail lines, aerodromes, and weapons depots being laid, troops being massed on the frontier, Russian-language courses being taken. Hitler would seize Ukraine.[6] Or he would demand that Stalin just hand Ukraine over. The Führer was going to invade. Unless he wasn't. Amayak Kobulov, relying on his personal spy, the ethnic Latvian Berlings—code-named "Lycée-ist" by the Soviets, but a plant for the Nazis—reported through NKVD channels (December 14) that Hitler had declared Britain to be Germany's "sole enemy," and that Germany would do everything possible "to avoid a war on two fronts."[7]

The Führer himself had become nearly inaccessible. On the afternoon of December 19, Dekanozov was finally able to present his credentials, in the same Chancellery room where Molotov had been received, but Hitler politely deflected the envoy's effort to discuss Soviet conditions for joining the four-power pact. After a curt half an hour, two giant Nazi protocol officers bundled the diminutive Dekanozov out.[8] Unbeknownst to the Soviet envoy, the previous day Hitler had signed the supersecret Directive No. 21, which ordered that "even before the end of the war with England, the German Armed Forces must be prepared *to annihilate Soviet Russia* in a swift campaign (Operation Barbarossa)." The target date was provisionally set for May 15, 1941.[9]

Nazi Germany was master of the European continent, stalemated with island Britain and economically enmeshed with the Soviet Union. Nazi ideologues railed at the "military buildup" of "Judeo-Bolshevism" on Germany's new borders in the east. Most top Nazis, however, scorned the Red Army's performance against Finland and, more broadly, the inferior Slavic race. SS Chief Heinrich Himmler had told Nazi party functionaries in fall 1940 that the USSR "cannot pose any danger to us at all." Hitler himself had stated that the Soviet Union "will nevertheless make no effort to enter the war against Germany of her own accord" and took its expansive territorial appetites from the Baltic to the Black Sea as indicative of weakness.[10] But in the aftermath of his November 1940 confrontation with Molotov, the Führer had taken to calling the Soviet Union a *gathering* threat that had to be preempted. That view had been Germany's motivation for the Great War in 1914: its giant eastern neighbor had to be attacked *before* it got strong.[11] Hitler added the proposition that now Britain was not capitulating because it was counting on eventual help from the USSR. Thus did it transpire for the second time in the twentieth century that the road to German triumph over the world's greatest power, Britain, was deemed to go through the east.

Hitler's Operation Barbarossa—meaning "Red Beard," the nickname of the Holy Roman emperor Frederick I—consisted of an eight-page typescript dated December 18, 1940, and initialed by Field Marshal Wilhelm Keitel (head of the Wehrmacht high command), General Alfred Jodl (head of the high command's operations staff), Major General Walter Warlimont (Jodl's top aide, who had prepared the document's first draft), and one other person (illegible).[12] Hitler had a mere eight copies prepared, of which four, along with the original, went into the safe. One copy each went to the army commander and the air force commander, and two to the general staff. A mere ten days later, Soviet military intelligence in Berlin delivered word of the existence of the supersecret signed directive.[13]

IDÉES FIXES

On December 23, 1940, Stalin had one of the largest groups ever in his office, more than thirty military-industrial functionaries. "We were all captivated at how simply, amiably, and with such deep knowledge Stalin conducted the meeting," recalled Akaki Mgeladze (b. 1910), who at age twenty-eight, after being released from house arrest, had been named head of Georgia's oil trust. "We were elated and felt such a rush of creative power and energy that we were ready to move mountains."[14] Besides ramping up oil supplies, discussion ensued about the M-105 airplane engine, which had 1,000 horsepower. "If we had a plethora of engines like the M-105," Stalin instructed those gathered in his Little Corner, "we could talk to that scumbag differently."[15]

That same day, the upper ranks of the Soviet army, air force, and navy gathered for a large-scale conference that lasted until December 31. For a modern army, doctrine was as important as size and technological base. A "defense in depth" assumed that the invader would inexorably breach the front lines, so it sacrificed territory, erecting defenses back from the front, aiming to contain the blow by wearing the enemy down. A further option, "mobile defense," involved counterattacks from depth before the enemy's advance had been fully contained, in order to cut off the enemy's frontline tank divisions from its second- and third-line infantry. Such operations required tremendous skill and speed, real-time battlefield intelligence, and sophisticated use of armored divisions to pierce the enemy assault.[16] "Forward defense" meant massing units on the frontier in fortified regions, absorbing and halting the initial blow, then taking the fight to enemy territory.

Soviet military doctrine had long been predicated on forward defense, and assumed that there would be about two weeks between an outbreak of hostilities, characterized by limited skirmishes, and any German ability to engage with the massive force of a full mobilization. During this interval, the Red Army would absorb the charge, then seize the initiative in a quick counteroffensive, inflicting several rapid defeats and thereby disrupting the enemy's mobilization.[17] But the USSR had some 2,500 miles of borders to defend against Germany and its Axis partners from the White Sea to the Black. The Red Army had forward-deployed some of its very best forces—20 of its 29 mechanized corps, almost 80 percent of its newest tanks, and more than half of its most advanced aircraft. This could leave them dangerously exposed if, as had happened to France, the Germans punched through in numbers and carried out an encirclement behind the penetrated lines.[18] The Soviets had ample reserves in the rear that could be brought into battle quickly, but the Germans were preconcentrating truly massive forces on the frontier.

Some sharp critiques of the Soviet military doctrine had been buried in the terror.[19] Stalin forbade consideration of anything other than an attack. Soviet theorists who had warned of the superiority of defense in depth—such as Alexander Verkhovsky, the former war minister in the Provisional Government who had joined the Reds—had exposed themselves to charges of treason for advocating the sacrifice of territory (even Minsk and Kiev).[20] Tukhachevsky had leveled precisely these charges against his intellectual nemesis, the strategist Alexander Svechin, in 1930–31, when Svechin was eventually arrested in the so-called Springtime Operation.[21] The survivor Shaposhnikov, too, firmly, albeit less stridently than Tukhachevsky, advocated for the offensive posture of forward defense.

The December 1940 military conference took place at the defense commissariat's new building, completed two years earlier, which jumbled modernist, neo-classical, and kitsch motifs, including stylized tank bas-reliefs and a central tower topped by a red star. Stalin did not attend. Voroshilov was absent as well. Timoshenko, presiding over his first such meeting as defense commissar, opened with a greeting to the 270 attendees. Next came chief of staff Meretskov's report, which gently took up Red Army shortcomings but reveled in how the imperialists were fighting a war among themselves, and how the USSR had managed to steer clear even as it had been able to "march westward" into new territories. Zhukov, commander of the Kiev military district, got the spotlight for a report accentuating the USSR's commitment to offense. He argued for combining mechanized forces, close air support, and tactical surprise and flanking maneuvers to smash through an enemy's frontline defenses and create havoc in its rear—the old concept of deep operations, a stirring of Tukhachevsky's ashes.[22]

Zhukov's hymn to spirited offense glossed over the critical period right after the launch of the enemy attack. Precisely the period of the onset of hostilities had been analyzed in a penetrating book by the Soviet theorist Georgy Isserson about Spain's civil war and Germany's Polish campaign, *New Forms of Combat* (1940), which argued that enemy forces mobilized and deployed secretly would conduct operations far exceeding mere frontier skirmishes or spoiling attacks, and that these troops would not be vulnerable to a counteroffensive.[23] At the conference, General Pyotr Klenov, commander of the Baltic military district, mentioned having read Isserson's book. "It offers hasty conclusions based upon the war between the Germans and Poland to the effect that there will be no start period for a war, that war today is decided simply—an invasion by readied forces, as was done by the Germans in Poland, deploying a million and a half men," Klenov stated. He dismissed Poland as not analogous to the USSR, calling it a weak country that, moreover, had lost its vigilance, so that it had "absolutely no foreign intelligence as the Germans were undertaking a many-month concentration of forces."

Klenov omitted mention of the German campaign in France. Zhukov did acknowledge Germany's blitz in the west, but he characterized France as a weak state as well, whose experience was therefore supposedly inapplicable to the USSR.[24] Isserson excepted, the Soviets spent less time studying Germany's new style of warfare than they did Anglo-American theories about wars of attrition, in which the USSR feared becoming bogged down.[25]

The deputy general inspector of the air force, Major General Timofei Khryunkin, offered cautionary remarks from his experiences in the trenches of the Soviet-Polish campaign. He noted that air support had arrived too late, when the ground forces had already finished their task (or failed to do so). "We have the experience of the German command in coordinating with armored units," he explained. "I studied it, and it is as follows: After armored units break through to the rear, 70–80 km, and perhaps 100 km, aviation gets its orders not from an aerodrome, but in the air; that is, the commander who directs the tank units that broke through and the aviation commander specify the target to air power by radio. Aviation the whole time is above its troops, and, through radio communication, it destroys pockets of resistance in front of the tanks." Khryunkin added that radio "is the most important thing." Barely thirty years old, not even supposed to have been present (his invited superior could not, or chose not to, attend), Khryunkin, in his incisive remarks—among the briefest of anyone—also managed to underscore the importance of having limited types of planes for efficiency (spare parts, training), which was what the Germans did, as opposed to the French, and the need for higher-caliber guns on Soviet aircraft in order to take out enemy tanks.[26]

Timoshenko closed with a summation. "In terms of the strategic art, the experience of the war in Europe has perhaps brought nothing new," he asserted. "But in the sphere of the operational arts, in the sphere of frontline and army operations, there have been immense changes." He singled out the value of tank armies and motorized divisions coordinated with aviation, noting that whereas offensives in the First World War had been stymied by defense in depth and the employment of reserves, "German tank divisions in 1939–1940 forestalled calling up these reserves." The Germans just "pushed forward," having "rightly taken into account that the force and success of the contemporary offensive consists in its great speed and uninterruptedness." He contrasted the German experience in just bypassing the Maginot Line with the Soviet Winter War, wherein a bypass proved impossible, and accentuated being expert at both wars of maneuver and of heavy concentration, in order to achieve that early breakthrough. He also noted that German success had depended upon preparation, laying railroads, building roads, readying aerodromes, and using agents on enemy territory to sow panic. In conclusion, he said that "the decisive effect of air power is achieved not via long-range raids in an enemy's rear but coordination with infantry in the field of battle, in the location of divisions, the army."[27]

As Timoshenko knew well, however, the Red Army's existing organization, officer skill set, and rank-and-file training did not correspond to this incisive blueprint. How much, if anything, the absent Stalin absorbed of the revelatory discussions of the new German way of war and its implications for Soviet military doctrine remains uncertain. Timoshenko had submitted a draft of his summation to the despot, who inserted several lines: "One organizes defense in order to prepare an offensive." "Defense is especially advantageous only when it is understood as a means to organize an offensive."[28]

SEEKING CLARIFICATION

Also on December 28, Sorge in Tokyo drafted a radio message, the first of many he would send warning of possible war. He had developed a close relationship with the German military attaché Colonel Alfred Kretschmer and was able to meet the many high-level military visitors from Berlin on assignment to Japan. "Every new person arriving in Japan from Germany talks about how the Germans have around 80 divisions on the eastern border, including Romania, with the aim of exerting pressure on the policy of the USSR," his message stated. "In the event that the USSR starts to actively oppose the interests of Germany, as happened in the Baltics, the Germans could occupy territory on a line Kharkov, Moscow, Leningrad. The Germans do not want to do this, but are assembling the means, should they be compelled to do so by the behavior of the USSR." But Sorge added that "the Germans know well that the USSR cannot risk this, because, after the Finnish war debacle, Moscow needs at least twenty years to become a modern army on a par with Germany's."[29]

Sorge's dispatch was characteristic of the mountains of chatter that Stalin would receive. But the December 29 intelligence out of Berlin on the existence of Operation Barbarossa was different. It had been written by Skornyakov ("Meteor"), who worked under the cover of the aviation aide to the Soviet military attaché. "Meteor," in turn, had gotten the information from Captain Nikolai Zaitsev ("Bine"), the intelligence operative in the Soviet trade mission. "Bine," in freezing weather, drove around and took public transportation for up to five hours (to ensure he was not being followed by German counterintelligence) to meet with the German journalist Ilse Stöbe ("Alta"), who ran the field agents in Soviet military intelligence's network in Berlin, including her source for this revelation, Rudolf von Scheliha ("Aryan"). The latter, returning from Warsaw, now worked in the German foreign ministry. Filipp Golikov, the head of Soviet military intelligence, forwarded the information to Stalin, as well as to Molotov, defense commissar Timoshenko, and chief of staff Meretskov (collectively known as List No. 1), writing that "from highly informed military circles, it has become known that Hitler issued an order to prepare a war against the USSR and that the war will be declared in March of the coming year."

From time immemorial, the month of March in the eastern Slavic lands brought the spring thaw, deep mud, and impassable roads, an improbable moment for a military invasion. Still, HQ took the report seriously. On the document, Major General Mikhail Panfilov, deputy head of military intelligence, wrote, "It is necessary to clarify who are the highly informed military circles. To whom, concretely, was the directive issued." On January 4, 1941, "Meteor" reported from Berlin that "'Aryan' confirmed that he obtained this information from a military man known to him, and that this was based not on rumor, but on a special directive of Hitler, which is deeply secret and about which very few people know." "Aryan" had further stipulated that the head of the eastern department of the German foreign ministry had told him that Molotov's visit to Berlin could be compared with Polish foreign minister Beck's—which had been followed by a German invasion. "Aryan" added that "preparations for an offensive against the USSR had begun much earlier, but they had been halted because the Germans had miscalculated the resistance of England. The Germans had reckoned on bringing England to its knees in spring and freeing their hands in the East." He concluded that "Hitler thinks the condition of the Red Army precisely now is so low that in spring he shall have undoubted success."[30]

"Aryan"'s report constituted a stunning achievement—the German officer corps did not yet know of Barbarossa.[31] On the evening of January 7, 1941, Golikov summoned Major General Vasily Tupikov to Znamenka, 19, the three-story Chocolate House that served as military intelligence HQ. An offspring of deep Russia (Kursk province) and a graduate of the Frunze Military Academy, Tupikov (b. 1901) was the chief of staff in the Kharkov military district, though he had served abroad as a military attaché (Estonia, 1935–37). He was now appointed military attaché in Berlin, code-named "Arnold," and tasked with ascertaining the precise location of German forces across multiple theaters. He quickly apprehended that "the sources we have in Germany for the most part do not have serious opportunities to get hold of documentary evidence regarding the armed forces of Germany."[32] Neither "Aryan" nor other Soviet spies secured a physical copy of Barbarossa. No foreign intelligence service did.[33]

WAR GAMES

Following its military conference, the Red Army conducted two war games on charts at general staff headquarters. The Pact had scrambled Soviet war planning. Germany still possessed the greatest destructive potential, and remained the focus of attention, but Poland's disappearance had rendered the entire GP series of plans moot.[34] Annexation of the Baltic states altered the calculation for the northwest as well. Romania remained a likely partner of Germany, to which had been added Finland, Hungary, and Slovakia. There was, however, very considerable internal dispute about whether the principal enemy thrust would come north of the impassable Pripet Marshes, toward Minsk, Smolensk, and Moscow on the central axis and Leningrad on the northernmost axis, or south of the Pripet, toward Kiev and the Caucasus. The January 1941 exercises incorporated both possibilities.[35]

Both iterations of the games glossed over the initial period of war. (Against neither Japan at the Halha River nor Finland had the initial phase been decisive.) The games assumed, in line with Soviet military doctrine, that the enemy ("blues") would initiate hostilities and would not be able to penetrate more than a few score miles before being driven back to prewar frontiers by the Soviet side ("reds"), setting the stage for the onset of the games, which notionally began on the fifteenth day of hostilities. No battles in the games took place on Soviet soil. Almost all the toponyms in the war games documents were Polish and Prussian settlements, rivers, hills. In the first game (January 2–6), Zhukov commanded the blues, attacking north of the Pripet. The reds, led by Pavlov, launched a counterattack into East Prussia, reaching the Neman and Narew rivers, but Zhukov's blues in East Prussia outmaneuvered Pavlov's attempted encirclement and won. The second game (January 8–11) shifted the fighting south of the Pripet into former southern Poland and Silesia, and this time Zhukov commanded the reds and Pavlov the blues. This version pivoted on initial blue penetration in the direction of Lvov and Ternopol and a red reversal, followed by Zhukov's deep operation to punch through and advance beyond the Carpathian passes toward Kraków and Budapest. Pavlov failed to block Zhukov's thrust, but the game was ended before the outcome had been fully decided.[36]

Immediately after being apprised of Zhukov's success in effectively winning from both sides, Stalin would make him the third chief of staff in the past six months.[37] "I have never worked in staffs," Zhukov recalled protesting to the despot. "I have always been a line officer. I cannot be chief of the general staff."[38]

Continuing in his transformation of the military, Stalin also held fast to the view that the economic relationship with Germany served as a deterrent. Many foreign observers, too, surmised that Germany had far more to gain from trade than from a costly attempt at conquest.[39] In December 1940 and January 1941, after the despot had applied pressure (shutting down Soviet exports to Germany in the fourth quarter), German exports to the USSR suddenly ballooned.[40] In Moscow on January 10, the parties signed a new German-Soviet Border and Commercial Agreement, which the trade official Schnurre lauded as "the greatest Germany had ever concluded." The USSR, upping its deliveries, promised to ship 2.5 million tons of grain, some from strategic reserves, and 1 million tons of oil by August 1941, in return for machine tools and arms-manufacturing equipment, whose delivery would *begin* in August.[41] Hitler, however, saw menace. "Stalin is intelligent, clever, and cunning," he stated at a Führer conference of military brass during the two days before the signing of the new trade agreement. "He demands more and more. He's a cold-blooded blackmailer. A German victory has become unbearable for Russia. Therefore: she must be brought to her knees as soon as possible."[42]

Also in January 1941, Wehrmacht troops entered Bulgaria, where the Germans would soon install antiaircraft weapons and shore batteries on the Black Sea.[43] Molotov told Dimitrov that "the Soviet government has declared to the German government that Bulgaria and the Straits belong to the security sphere of the USSR."[44] Major General Alexander Samokhin ("Sophocles"), the Soviet military attaché and military intelligence station chief in Belgrade, reported conversations to the effect that "the Balkans are becoming the decisive center of political events, more so because here is where the direct clash of the interests of Germany and the USSR begins."[45] As late as January 17, Molotov was still pressing Schulenburg about Germany's silence regarding Soviet conditions for joining the Tripartite Pact: "neither an answer nor a hello."[46]

ANXIETIES

In the evening of January 17, Stalin convoked a rare formal meeting of the politburo in the Little Corner to discuss the economic plan for 1941.[47] "For four to five months we have not assembled the politburo," he stated. "All questions are prepared by Zhdanov, Malenkov, and others in the form of smaller gatherings with comrades who have the necessary expertise, and the practice of leadership has gotten not worse but better." He continued, "In the economic sense, our state is not a single entity but consists of a series of pieces. In order to unite these pieces into one whole, we need railroads." Just as France or Britain had connected their empires via ships, the USSR had to expand its railroads, which "would consume a lot of metal." He went on to criticize the economic council inside the Council of People's Commissars. "You are busy with parliamentarism," he charged. "You pronounce big speeches. Issues are often resolved by the principle of who convinces whom, who gives a prettier speech."

After the admonishments, at around 1:00 a.m., they went outside to inspect a new limited-edition automobile, which Stalin deemed "successful." Then the group of about ten repaired to his apartment, one floor below the Little Corner, for supper. They sat until 7:00 a.m. "We sang songs, talked," Malyshev, the commissar of medium machine building and a deputy chairman of the Council of People's Commissars, recorded in his diary. "Comrade Stalin told us at length about his life and proposed a toast 'to the old guys, who are eagerly passing power to the youth, who are eagerly taking this power!'" Stalin was promoting a new team of younger cadres into the government, Molotov's bailiwick, such as Malyshev, who carried responsibility for the automobile industry. When the despot observed Malyshev drinking wine "in limited edition," he grabbed two goblets, hurried over, and poured them both full. The pair drank to the bottom. Stalin then went around the room to pour everyone a full glass, laughing and commenting of Malyshev, with evident zest, "He's a sly type, sly!"[48]

Another interlude of relaxation mixed with menace occurred on February 4: a Kremlin banquet for Voroshilov's sixtieth jubilee. The marshals, some generals, people's commissars, Central Committee apparatchiks, Comintern officials, and others, a few with their wives, toasted one another until 4:00 a.m. "Stalin pronounced a number of toasts," Malyshev noted. "He, in part, again returned to the idea of the old and the young. He said that 'the old should understand that unless the young are admitted to leadership positions, then we will perish. We Bolsheviks are strong in that we boldly promote youth. The old should eagerly yield power to the young.'"[49]

Stalin went on to attribute Soviet successes in foreign affairs to "two means: diplomacy and the army." Dimitrov recorded the despot as stating that "with our foreign policy we have managed to take advantage of the goods of this world and to use those goods (we buy cheap and sell dear!). But the might of our army and navy have helped us conduct a policy of neutrality and keep the country out of war." One of the reasons France fell, Stalin explained, was a failure to promote young cadres. "We have another approach: we promote our young cadres, sometimes even too eagerly. We promote them with pleasure, with joy. Old men cling to the old ways. The young go forward. Replacing the old with the young at the proper time is very essential. The country that fails to do that is doomed to failure." Stalin also toasted Lenin ("We owe him everything") and Soviet might. "We have been lucky. 'God' has helped us. Lots of easy victories. . . . Must not get cocky. . . . We now have an army of 4 million men on their feet and ready for anything. The tsar used to dream of a standing army of 1.2 million men."[50]

HITLER'S GRAND STRATEGY

Hitler's radicalism confounded most contemporaries.[51] Ever since his *Second Book,* written in 1928 but unpublished, he had exhibited envy for the unique vastness of the British empire and, ultimately, for American power. Germany under him had emerged as the world's third-largest economy, but its overall productivity and living standards trailed those of the United States and even Britain. His acute awareness of Germany's limitations relative to Britain's global empire and America's transcontinentality, not just his deeply held racist conceptions, spurred his aggressiveness. The Nazi regime proved to have an astonishing capability to marshal resources and a tremendous depth of domestic political unity, and into 1940 it was overseeing further surges of output and popular acclaim. But shortages of nearly everything, from steel to fodder, held Germany back, undermining the quality of the Wehrmacht's armor and the Luftwaffe's planes. Desperately seeking to break through to world-power status, in his inimical way, Hitler lacked the requisite economic and resource scaffolding.[52] Japan suffered the same predicament: vaulting ambitions and limited raw materials or financial means to import them.[53] For Hitler, this was a matter of the survival of the German race. He held fast to a zero-sum calculus, believing that only one nation could dominate the world.

Hitler could be less impulsive than he seemed. He and his crude propagandists had slandered the United States at every turn for supposedly trying to interfere in European affairs, but once Hitler had precipitated the pan-European war over Poland, he had worked diligently to keep the world's potentially most powerful country out of the hostilities. This was not rocket science: in 1918, on top of the British sea blockade that inhibited vital German imports of food and raw materials, America's 2 million fresh troops and plentiful resources had brought the Germans to defeat. Germany's unrestricted submarine warfare, in turn, had gratuitously provoked America's decision to take up arms, and Hitler ordered the navy not to repeat the mistake this time. Roosevelt, for his part, seemed to want just that: a Nazi-instigated confrontation. Meanwhile, many of Hitler's efforts to bring Japan into the war centered not on opening a two-front war against the USSR but embroiling the United States in a Pacific war such that it would hesitate to get involved on a second front in Europe.[54] But Roosevelt's reelection, by a substantial majority, to a third term on November 5, 1940, and the increasing scale of U.S. aid to Britain gave Hitler grave cause for concern. Even while still fighting Britain, he ordered continued preparations for an anticipated eventual clash with the United States.[55]

In a fireside chat broadcast over the radio on December 29, 1940, Roosevelt had called upon the American people to serve as "the great arsenal of democracy. For us this is an emergency as serious as war itself. We must apply ourselves to our task with the same resolution, the same sense of urgency, the same spirit of patriotism and sacrifice as we would show were we at war." The president explained that "if Great Britain goes down, the Axis powers will control the continents of Europe, Asia, Africa, Australasia, and the high seas—and they will be in a position to bring enormous military and naval resources against this hemisphere." Roosevelt vowed to supply Britain ("the spearhead of resistance to world conquest") with weaponry against Nazi Germany while keeping America out of the fighting.[56] Even at peace, the American colossus was now manufacturing as much weaponry as either Germany or Britain, while also seeing its living standard rise. Germany's many occupied territories could never match the United States or Britain in productivity. In 1941, America would manufacture nearly 20,000 military aircraft, of which more than 5,000 would go to Britain. Germany took deliveries of 78 aircraft from occupied France and the Netherlands.[57]

Hitler was wont to expiate on American degeneracy and contamination by Jewry, but he was well aware of America's productive power and resources, and how the United States, together with Britain, was rich in transport, too. Herein lay the strategic component of his quest for *Lebensraum*. For Hitler, annihilation of the Soviet Union and international Jewry was an end in itself. But he had a further aim, forced upon him, in his view, by necessity: to establish the equivalent of a British empire or U.S. transcontinentality by conquering and racializing Eastern Europe and the Soviet Union. It was his awe and fear of U.S. power, ultimately, that propelled him to take on what he long said needed to be done: eradicate "Judeo-Bolshevism."[58] Hitler was caught in something of a vicious circle: all of his spectacular battlefield victories had only accelerated Anglo-American cooperation, the very phenomenon helping to drive his pursuit of these victories in the first place. To be sure, he could continue to secure crucial resources from Stalin via trade. But whenever Germany ran into difficulty meeting its contractual obligations, Stalin had shown he could turn off the spigot of grain, timber, oil, and alloys. Hitler might end up succumbing to the contemptible fate he foresaw for Britain, running the risk of abject dependency on the United States, but in his case the dependency involved the USSR. How could Germany even supply its own military if the Soviets kept demanding so many advanced machine tools? How long would it be before the USSR became too strong even to take on? How long before Stalin might launch his own war against Germany?

To Hitler, a consolidation of his gains and a defensive stance looked like a losing proposition, for time, he felt, was not on his side. American involvement with Britain would grow; the USSR would just get stronger. Thus, given the military infeasibility of a cross-Channel invasion, his options seemed to be (1) air strikes against peripheral targets of the British empire in the Near East, to raise Britain's costs for refusing his offers of accommodation on his terms, an option that meant continued tolerance of his relationship with "Judeo-Bolshevism" and Stalin's "blackmail"; (2) the continental bloc idea advanced by Ribbentrop, which would confront the Anglo-Americans with equivalent productive and military force but would potentially increase Hitler's dependence on Stalin's good graces; or (3) an unprovoked attack on a country with a massive army of 4 million men and modern weaponry, some of it German supplied. The latter was in many ways the riskiest choice but, given Hitler's worldview, aspirations, and calculations, the one that seemed to make the most sense.[59] Understanding that from the outside required a level of insight no foreign power commanded.

On January 30, 1941, Hitler showed that he understood that the Soviet Union would not launch a preemptive strike, telling his high command behind closed doors, "As long as Stalin lives, the Russians will not attack, for Stalin is cautious and reasonable." Nonetheless, German officialdom and propaganda emphasized the presence of Soviet troops on the common border as a direct threat to Germany. In his speech, the Führer moved the start date of Barbarossa from May 15 to June 2, evidently acknowledging the scale of the operation, and repeated his prophecy, made two years earlier, of a coming annihilation of the Jews.[60]

JUDO

Reconstituted Soviet espionage networks overseas counted some 3,000 different sources, of whom perhaps 70 percent were new since 1938 (such as agents of former Czechoslovak intelligence who agreed to work against Germany).[61] The NKVD also intercepted hundreds of thousands of coded telegrams, but only a small percentage (usually less than 15 percent) could be deciphered and read. Soviet intelligence lacked translators, let alone genuine cryptographers.[62] Still, Stalin could read intercepts of deciphered communications between Japanese military attachés in Moscow and Tokyo as well as U.S. diplomatic communications with the state department from the Soviet Union, France, and Japan.[63] The Soviets did not, however, break British or German codes.[64]

The despot had spies high up in the British establishment. These included the ideologically committed Cambridge Five: Anthony Blunt ("Tony"), in British counterintelligence (MI5); Guy Burgess ("Mädchen"), in the British secret services (MI6); Donald Maclean ("Homer"), for the foreign office in London; Kim Philby ("Söhnchen"), in the saboteur training unit known as the Special Operations Executive; and John Cairncross ("Liszt"), the personal secretary to Sir Maurice Hankey, the former cabinet secretary and now nominally Chancellor of the Duchy of Lancaster, but really minister without portfolio. "Liszt," for example, had evidently provided Moscow the UK's secret September 1940 "Estimate of the Possibilities of War," which had concluded that Hitler could not mount a successful invasion of the British Isles.[65] In 1941, Liszt would pass on 3,349 classified documents, including the telegrams out of Moscow from Ambassador Cripps to Eden at the foreign office, as well as British intelligence reports.[66] "Tony" passed British counterintelligence documents to the restored London station chief Anatoly Gorsky beginning in January 1941. "Söhnchen" informed his handlers that the British were not training any undercover agents for work in the USSR, information that in Moscow was double-underlined in red, reinforcing the suspicions that Philby was a double agent working for the British.[67] Even after he allowed Gorsky to reestablish the London station, Stalin never trusted the Cambridge Five.[68]

In Germany, besides the network of Soviet military intelligence centered on Rudolf von Scheliha, who had delivered word of the existence of Barbarossa (without the name), another network of Soviet civilian intelligence centered on Arvid Harnack (b. 1901), who had studied in the United States, married an American, obtained his Ph.D. in his native Germany, traveled to the USSR on a German-government-sponsored research trip prior to the Nazi regime, passed information to the Americans, become an antifascist spy for the Soviets, and joined the Nazi party and now worked in Nazi Germany's economics ministry. Contact with Harnack ("Corsican") had been reestablished in 1940 by Alexander Korotkov (b. 1909), who had started at Lubyanka as an electrician and elevator operator but, unlike most post-terror recruits, was fluent in German.[69] Korotkov had been appointed deputy head of station under Amayak Kobulov, who initially was kept away from these networks.[70]

Korotkov was one of the many new people posted abroad by the now thirty-three-year-old second-year head of NKVD foreign intelligence, Pavel Fitin, whose directorate had managed to reestablish about forty Soviet intelligence stations abroad.[71] "Corsican" introduced Korotkov to his friend Harro Schulze-Boysen ("Elder"). The Nordic-looking Schulze-Boysen (b. 1909) had campaigned as a youth against the Versailles Treaty imposed on Germany but also against the larger capitalist order; in 1933, SA Brownshirts had smashed his offices and scratched swastikas on his skin. His father was a decorated naval officer (the family was related to Grand Admiral Alfred von Tirpitz) and his mother was friends with Göring; she got him a position in the air ministry (communications).[72, 73] "Corsican" and "Elder," as well as "Aryan" in parallel, cultivated some threescore strategically placed contacts across a variety of ministries, German industry, the Wehrmacht, and German intelligence—a penetration beyond belief in a totalitarian regime.

German counterintelligence had little sense of the true depth and breadth of Soviet intelligence penetration. But a buildup of the scope necessary to launch a monumental war against the USSR—construction of rail lines, roads, aerodromes, barracks; movement and storage of armaments, gasoline, troops—could never be concealed in any case. The tanks and building materials had to be carried on flat cars. The key, however, was not Germany's war preparations—which, as British intelligence noted (January 31), were almost open—but Hitler's intentions.[74] Here, the high command and the SS's intelligence arm, the SD, engaged in a brilliant game of judo, using the power of Communism's nonpareil spy networks against the USSR by pumping them with disinformation.[75] Stalin did not have an agent in Hitler's innermost circle or personal staff who could have exposed the campaign of plausible falsehoods.

The forces being stationed along the Soviet frontier could be used against not just the USSR but also British possessions and clients. Back in July 1940, Hitler had told top generals that the buildup in the east would be passed off as training for a cross-Channel invasion of Britain, a story fed to lower-level German military commanders as well as foreign embassy staff. Plans were drawn up for the rapid movement of these troops westward, with false orders to prepare plans for travel. Detailed maps of Britain were supplied to the eastern units' commanders and intelligence officers. English interpreters were assigned to the German units on the Soviet border. The falsehoods confused Germany's own military at various levels. Once Hitler had postponed Sea Lion, in September 1940, a second rationale was put into play: preparation for an attack on British interests in the Balkans (Greece), the Mediterranean (Cyprus, Malta, Gibraltar), and the Near East (Egypt, Iraq, Palestine). Some top British intelligence officers had interpreted Germany's entry into Romania (October 1940) precisely along these lines. The Germans demonstrably increased their intelligence gathering in the Near East, activity that was duly picked up by the British and made its way to Moscow.[76]

Just such a "peripheral" strategy against Britain, originally invented by Jodl, was actually favored by some members of the Nazi hierarchy, such as Admiral Raeder and Ribbentrop, and by Mussolini, and throughout the spring of 1941 it retained its plausibility.[77] At the same time, a third, even more plausible rationale for the massive German troop concentrations in Eastern Europe was disseminated: that Hitler was going to use the buildup to intimidate Stalin into yielding territory. Stories of German supply shortages—which were real—encouraged the view that the Führer would demand "concessions." Stalin began to get reports that the German troop buildup was prelude to an "ultimatum." The ruse, which appears to have entered the Soviet intelligence bloodstream from Kobulov via "Lycée-ist," soon reached the despot from so many sources, so far and wide, that it came to seem an article of faith. After all, it comported with Hitler's modus operandi. It did seem to explain the buildup on the Soviet border (whose exact dimensions remained a matter of guesswork and dispute).[78] And the idea of an unprovoked war against the colossal Red Army was so preposterous that a giant bluff seemed more likely.[79]

To believe—as Barbarossa secretly stipulated—that the troops were being positioned to launch a surprise attack against the USSR even before Britain had been defeated meant believing that Hitler would voluntarily open a second front. But as we saw, beginning with the December 14 message from "Lycée-ist," Germany's disinformation operation circulated statements attributed to the high command or Hitler himself that a two-front war against Britain and the USSR was impossible, suicidal.[80] In fact, Hitler reasoned that the only way to *escape* a two-front war was to knock out the Soviet Union before the United States joined Britain in a genuine war in the west.[81]

WARNINGS INTENSIFY

In February 1941, Pavlov, commander of the frontline Western military district (Belorussia), asked Stalin for nearly 1 billion rubles for radio work, and another 650 million for rails and for mobilization of high school and college students to replace the republic's dirt roads. Timoshenko answered that Stalin said, "We are not in a position to meet his fantastic proposals." Zhukov, the new chief of staff, had been summoned to Stalin's dacha on a Saturday evening to deliver a brief report, arranged by Timoshenko. In the company of the cronies, Zhukov and Timoshenko dined on thick borscht, stewed meats with buckwheat kasha, fruit, and compote, the kind of simple meal Stalin liked. As the conversation ranged over military needs, the despot relaxed, drinking Khvanchkara, a Georgian wine, joking, and exhibiting the cheerful mood that company often brought him. "Stalin said that we should think and work on the priority issues and bring them to the government for decisions," Zhukov recalled. "But in this connection we need to work from our real possibilities and not fantasize about what we cannot produce in material terms."[82]

Even while constraining the military's limitless demands, Stalin had his secretariat on the special Kremlin phone system, driving factories beyond their limit. Where were the chassis, the motors, the trucks, the tires for the Soviet Union's mechanized divisions? The despot, meanwhile, also summoned aviation industry bosses to the Imperial Senate's Sverdlov Hall, the venue for Central Committee plenums, to hash out the issues with the newest aircraft. He paced, gripping his pipe, listening, waiting for the experts to finish before taking the floor to note that the old planes were easier to fly but easier to knock out. "Then Stalin went through the main military aircraft of the air forces of Germany, England, France, and the United States," aviation commissar Shakhurin recalled. "He spoke about their weaponry, carrying capacities, rate of climb, maximum altitude. He did all this from memory, without any notes, which surprised the specialists and aviators present." Stalin instructed them to "study the new planes. Learn to perfection how to fly them, to use in war their advantages over the old planes in speed and weaponry. That's the only way."[83]

From February 15 to 20, 1941, Stalin convoked the 18th party conference, where he got behind a further force-march of production, especially of MiG-3 aircraft, as well as the T-34 and KV tanks. A party conference involved less rigmarole than a party congress, but it afforded him a semblance of legitimacy to make changes to the Central Committee that only a congress could authorize. He also inserted several army officers into that body, characterizing them as "*modern* military personnel, with an understanding of the nature of modern warfare, not old-fashioned," a reference to Timoshenko and Zhukov, in words recorded by the Comintern's Dimitrov. "Stalin: 'It is a shame we failed to single out such people before. We did not know our cadres well.'" The despot also "said of Golikov that as an intelligence agent, he is inexperienced, naïve. An intelligence officer ought to be like the devil: believing no one, not even himself."[84]

Stalin added three new candidate members to the politburo: Malenkov and two Zhdanov protégés, Nikolai Voznesensky, deputy head of state planning, who had a doctorate in economics, and Alexander Shcherbakov, who, while remaining party boss of Moscow province and city, was promoted to a Central Committee secretary and handed Zhdanov's portfolio as chief of the agitation-and-propaganda directorate.[85] Stalin also removed the state security directorate from the NKVD and made it a self-standing commissariat (NKGB). Beria's literate minion Merkulov remained in charge, now as a full-fledged commissar, and among Merkulov's subordinates were mostly other Beria minions, starting with NKGB deputy commissar Bogdan "Bakhcho" Kobulov, whose brother Amayak remained in Berlin as the NKGB's intelligence chief there.[86]

The intelligence kept pouring in.[87] On February 28, 1941, the Berlin military intelligence station reported that "Alta" had learned from "Aryan," who had spoken to a person in Reich marshal Göring's inner circle, that German military officials were cocksure a war against the USSR would be launched in 1941. "Aryan" had been the one to deliver early word of Barbarossa's existence, and the details he now supplied were as accurate as any that would emerge about the German plan: three army groups for attacks on the axes of Leningrad (under the command of Field Marshal Wilhelm Ritter von Leeb), Minsk-Smolensk-Moscow (Field Marshal Fedor von Bock), and Kiev (Field Marshal Gerd von Rundstedt). Russian-speaking officers had been deployed to the general staff of each group. Armored trains of special gauge, capable of using Soviet rail lines, were under construction. "Hitler intends to export from Russia about 3 million slaves, in order to bring his productivity capacities to full tilt," "Alta" further relayed from "Aryan" and "he supposedly intends to divide the Russian colossus into 20–30 different states, without concern for the retention of all the economic links within the country." The likely invasion date was given as May 20.[88]

That was not the only kind of report Stalin was receiving, however. On March 1, 1941, Nikolai Lyakhterov ("Mars"), in Budapest, reported to Moscow that "everyone considers an attack by the Germans against the USSR at the present time unimaginable before the destruction of England. The military attachés of America, Turkey, and Yugoslavia emphasize that the German army in Romania is in the first instance directed against an English invasion of the Balkans and as a counter-measure, if Turkey or the USSR moves." He added, "After the destruction of England the Germans will attack the USSR."[89] That same evening, Colonel Grigory Yeremin ("Yeshenko"), the peasant-born (1904) military intelligence station chief in Bucharest under cover of embassy third secretary, reported to Moscow about a recent trip to Berlin by the Soviet agent Kurt Welkisch ("ABC"), now serving as press attaché of the German legation in Romania.[90] "In foreign ministry circles and the headquarters of the German command, where he had the opportunity to speak to some people, uncertainty prevails in the political and military position of Germany, just as lack of information does in Germany's future intentions in the political and military spheres," "Yeshenko" noted. "Everyone with whom [ABC] spoke expressed a different view on the plans and future course of developments in the present war."[91]

All serious intelligence work involves sifting through an overwhelming flood of noise; almost never is anything "clean." Rumormongering aims to amplify the cacophony; disinformation, to establish a false certainty. Stalin had no filter to wring out the hearsay and scrutinize the patterns of disinformation. Nor were the voluminous Soviet intelligence reports systematized anywhere. The NKGB did not even have an analytical department; military intelligence had had its department for analysis restored, but Stalin insisted on receiving the intelligence more or less directly, leaving the analytical work to himself.[92] He obviously suspected that his adversaries were engaged in disinformation, but that suspicion, too, failed him. One of the core planks of the German whispering campaign was that Britain was trying to escape the war by provoking an armed German-Soviet clash. Stalin had assumed that for years, but now it colored his perception of all the intelligence suggesting that Hitler would attack.[93]

To be sure, Stalin's intelligence service was playing its own games, exaggerating American preparations for war against Germany and British strength in the Balkans.[94] But whereas Soviet deception efforts reflected Stalin's thinking, not his adversary's, Hitler's disinformation caught Stalin's thinking to a tee. Mostly, however, Soviet intelligence was spreading genuine arguments for Germany to abide by the 1939 bilateral nonaggression pact. Indeed, Stalin had little need for his own disinformation campaign. Just as in the case of Finland, only with infinitely more at stake, he was not trying to deceive. He was not seeking to cut a deal behind Hitler's back with Churchill. He was trying to avoid war and attain a new deal with Hitler. In that context, Germany's instigated chatter stressed that Germany's top leadership was divided over whether to attack the USSR, and that any provocative acts by the Soviets could play into the hands of the "militarists."

On March 6, 1941, the NKGB in Berlin reported that German economic functionaries were calculating the mother lode of raw materials and foodstuffs that could be expected from an occupation of the European part of the USSR, while the Wehrmacht was optimistic about seizing Ukraine in two to three weeks, thanks to the rail network there, and seizing Baku oil quickly as well. "Chief of staff Halder thinks that the Red Army is in no condition to mount the requisite opposition to the German forces' lightning attack."[95] On March 9, Samokhin, of military intelligence, reported out of Belgrade that, based on conversations with the minister of the court and the owner of Yugoslavia's most widely read newspaper, *Politika,* "the German general staff has abandoned an attack on the British Isles, and been given as its next immediate task the seizure of Ukraine and Baku, which it is supposed to carry out in April or May," and that "Hungary, Romania, and Bulgaria are now preparing for this."[96] On March 13, "Yeshenko" reported out of Bucharest that Germany intended to attack the USSR *before* defeating Britain. An SS officer who had arrived in Romania was heard to have boasted, "We'll continue the battle against England with airplanes and submarines. But we have 10 million lads who are itching to fight and are bored. They are thirsting for a serious foe. Our military machine cannot be unoccupied."[97] But on March 14, "Mars" reported, also out of Budapest, that a Hungarian official had summoned him to remonstrate that the rumors of pending war between Germany, Hungary, and Romania against the USSR were lies. "This is English propaganda.... Hungary wants to live in peace with the USSR. Germany has enough with the war with England, and is economically interested in peace with the USSR."[98]

Who had it right—before *or* after defeating Britain?

Hitler, through March 1941, had told only a few hundred people of Barbarossa. Germany's formula for talks with Romania, Hungary, and Finland was not pending invasion but how the "protection of the East" was essential in order to "provide against surprises."[99] Personnel in Göring's air ministry were among the closest to the circles in the know, while Ribbentrop and the foreign ministry had not been directly apprised. But in early March 1941, Scheliha, the foreign ministry official with excellent military contacts, provided further information to "Alta," who reported to Moscow that "there is a basis that speaks to an attack against Russia taking place in the nearest term (dates are named of May 15 to June 15). People are talking about a concentration of 120 divisions in Poland, about the placing of bombers at previously unoccupied aerodromes in East Prussia, intensive establishment of antiaircraft defenses in the eastern cities of Germany, all of which testifies to the preparation of some sort of extraordinary events." She wrote that "Aryan" insisted that "exceptionally well-informed circles of the leading political and military officialdom report unanimously that an attack on the USSR will happen this year, namely before June."

"Aryan" had added the most crucial detail: "the concentration of Soviet forces at the frontiers arouses here a certain disquiet. People are asking, are the

Russians not noticing that something is getting ready against them, and do they not plan to preempt the German strike? Some express satisfaction at this concentration, since they think that the Russian army will not be in a condition to retreat quickly."[100]

RESPONDING TO THE GERMAN BUILDUP

On March 10, amid all the contradictory warnings, Stalin created a new body, the "bureau" of the Council of People's Commissars. It consisted of the chairman, Molotov, and his deputies and could make decisions in the name of the full council (a prerogative Stalin himself had inserted in the decree).[101] The despot also assigned Molotov a new first deputy chairman, Voznesensky, a member of the next generation whom Stalin advanced above Mikoyan and Kaganovich. "What shocked us about the composition of the bureau leadership was that Voznesensky became first deputy," Mikoyan would recall later in life. "Stalin's motives in this leapfrogging were incomprehensible. But Voznesensky in his naïveté was very pleased about his appointment."[102]

The next day, Roosevelt's latest brainstorm to help Britain was signed into American law. Unlike Nazi Germany, the UK was not de facto bankrupt and had been buying American supplies and war matériel under a program known as cash and carry (paying up front and assuming responsibility for transportation). But Britain had begun to run low on cash, and Roosevelt introduced the idea of Lend-Lease ("An Act to Promote the Defense of the United States"), which allowed him to "sell, transfer title to, exchange, lease, lend, or otherwise dispose of, to any such government [whose defense the President deems vital to the defense of the United States] any defense article." The law soon would be applied to China, too. Hitler ordered stronger efforts "to bring Japan into active operations in the Far East as soon as possible," so that "the focal point of the interests of the United States will be diverted to the Pacific."[103]

Also on March 11, 1941, a long-gestating refinement of the Soviet war plan was submitted. A month before, Zhukov, following his replacement of Meretskov as chief of staff, had ordered the chief of the operations directorate, Major General Alexander Vasilevsky, to revise the main mobilization orders (which dated to November 1937) that accompanied the war plan. Known as the Mobilization Plan for 1941 (MP-41), it was based upon a wartime strength of 300 fully equipped divisions, including 60 tank divisions, and 8.7 million troops—a doubling of the already recently doubled Red Army—which were to come into existence by January 1942.[104] Tactically, this mobilization plan for an army that did not yet exist in this size was based upon extreme forward defense and a quick Soviet counteroffensive (approximately two thirds of the divisions were to be stationed in the western military districts). MP-41 reflected Stalin's vision of a possible war: all offense and all in, with wishful-thinking production targets for tanks and aircraft, little allotment for second- and third-echelon strategic reserves for a protracted battle, and the war not commencing this year.

Now, the new war plan itself, occupying some fifteen pages on defense commissariat stationery, in exquisite penmanship, was marked, as per custom, "Top Secret. Very Urgent. Exclusively Personal. The Only Copy." Following the experience of the January war games, it reconfirmed Kiev as the main axis of hostilities, making explicit, unlike previous war plans, that "Germany will most likely deploy its main forces in the southeast, from Siedlce [in eastern Poland] to Hungary, in order to seize the Ukraine by means of a blow to Berdichev and Kiev." This conclusion reflected the accumulating Soviet intelligence reports. But the southern axis was definitively assumed to be the main thrust of the German attack because the anticipated quick Soviet counteroffensive would have a far easier time navigating enemy territory below the Pripet Marshes. It traced the Soviets' long-standing favored strike line, the so-called Lvov protrusion, on the Kraków-Katowice salient, where German defense lines were not as formidable as in East Prussia and where the terrain was conducive to tank armies.[105] Massed in Ukraine, Red Army forces, after blasting through, were to encircle, from behind, the German armies concentrated farther north, while severing links with Germany's Balkan allies, oil, and foodstuffs farther south. The text, however, admitted that "the general staff of the Red Army does not possess documentary data on the plans of likely adversaries either in the West or in the East."[106]

Timoshenko and Zhukov discussed the draft at length in the Little Corner on March 17, with a large number of military and industrial officials, and again on the 18th in a narrower group. They had already beseeched Stalin for authorization to summon Soviet reservists immediately, to fill out the existing divisions in frontier districts. A decree approved the call-up of 975,870 reservists during the course of 1941, in phases, through the fall, but the despot insisted it be done quietly, under the pretext of training exercises. Troops were shipped in trains boarded up with plywood, and even the commanders did not know their points of disembarkation.[107] Beyond wanting to deny warmongers on the German side any excuse to attack, Stalin continued to adhere to the widespread belief that even though, in summer 1914, imperial Russia's mobilization had been defensive and precaution-ary, it had inexorably led the country to war.[108]

INHIBITIONS

Stalin was the only one in the Soviet regime to receive the full gamut of intelli-gence reports, but even he did not see everything. In the first half of 1941, Soviet military intelligence would receive 267 reports from its agents abroad and convey 129 of these to the military and political leadership.[109] (Beria at civilian intelli-gence might have been an even more consequential filter.) Functionaries in des-potic systems often shrink from supplying the despot with information they know he will not welcome.[110] After the terror, it took special courage or naïveté to bring Stalin news he did not want to hear.[111] On March 20, 1941, Golikov sent him one of the first systematic summaries by Soviet intelligence, this one concerning German forces and their dislocation. Tupikov, in Berlin, had produced a 100-page overview of Germany's military.[112] Golikov's summary conveyed Tupikov's anal-ysis of a large concentration of German forces near the frontier and concluded that, "according to the report of our military attaché in Berlin, we can expect the onset of military action against the USSR between May 15 and June 15."

Knowing the despot's beliefs firsthand, Golikov walked a fine line, writing that an attack would likely come "after victory over England or after the conclu-sion with her of an honorable peace for Germany." He also wrote that "the major-ity of the espionage material concerning the possibilities of war with the USSR in the spring of 1941 emanates from Anglo-American sources whose aim today is doubtless to endeavor to worsen relations between the USSR and Germany." Nonetheless, Golikov added, "considering the origins and development of fas-cism, and its aims—implementing the plans of Hitler that were laid out in full and flowery [exposition] in his book *Mein Kampf*—a short outline of all agent material in hand for the period July 1940–March 1941 to a degree deserves serious atten-tion." He sketched a simultaneous assault by three German army groups along three axes: north (Leningrad), center (Moscow), and south (Kiev). Here was the accurate picture of Barbarossa that had been reported by "Aryan."[113]

While Pavel Fitin, of NKGB civilian intelligence, had no access to Stalin, re-porting instead to Beria and Merkulov, Golikov did have to face the despot occa-sionally.[114] All five of Golikov's immediate predecessors had been executed. His March 20, 1941, summary, mangled with caveats, nonetheless constituted a bold step. But then, in his conclusion, Golikov repudiated his report's vital content: "The rumors and documents attesting to the inevitability of war against the USSR this spring need to be assessed as disinformation coming from English and even perhaps German intelligence."[115]

German planes were crossing Soviet frontiers at altitudes of seven miles, out of artillery range but perfect for photographing Soviet military installations and deployments. When confronted about their violations of Soviet airspace, the Germans would point to their military schools near the border and assert that trainee pilots were losing their way. "Elder," in Göring's air ministry, provided unique information, however, which the Berlin NKGB (March 24) reported to Moscow, about intensive compilations of Soviet targets, including bridges to cut the movement of reserves. "Photographs of Soviet cities and other objects are regularly coming into aviation HQ," the report stated, and the German military attaché in Moscow was traveling around by car to verify the locations of Soviet electrical stations for bombing. "Officers at HQ have formed the opinion that military action against the USSR has been set for the end of April or early May. These dates are connected to a German intention to secure the harvest for themselves, calculating that Soviet forces under retreat will not be able to burn the green wheat."[116]

Around this time, a German printer evidently provided the Soviet embassy in Berlin with a book, scheduled for a massive print run, with Latin transliterations of Russian phrases: "Where is the chairman of the collective farm?" "Are you a Communist?" "Hands up!"[117]

On March 28, at 5:00 p.m. Berlin time, Dekanozov's secretary at the embassy received an anonymous tip: "Around May a war will begin against Russia," the caller, speaking in German, stated, then hung up.[118] In Moscow that same day, Stalin sought to squeeze ever more blood from a stone, convening the chemical industry bosses—the commissar, his deputies, factory directors—in the Little Corner. The Soviet Union had still not fully mastered production of tires from synthetic rubber, even though it had invented the latter.[119] Stalin laced into Nikolai Patolichev, a peasant's son (b. 1908) who had been orphaned at twelve, then started working at a factory and, following the terror, in 1939, became party boss of Yaroslavl province, site of the rubber industry. Patolichev, one of Stalin's "new people," had just become a full member of the Central Committee. "Stalin used sharp expressions and I honestly did not know how this conversation was going to end for me," Patolichev would recall. "Stalin paced in silence, thinking. The minutes seemed incredibly long." Finally the despot, smiling, announced the formation of a commission of Patolichev, Khrushchev, and Nikolai Bulganin to get the chemical commissariat to ramp up production.[120]

BALKAN TREACHERY

Under very intense German pressure, Bulgaria had joined the Axis, alongside Hungary, Slovakia, and Romania. This left just two nonaligned states in southeastern Europe: Greece, which was under military assault by Italy, and Yugoslavia. The Yugoslav regent, the Oxford-educated Prince Paul, who ruled for the seventeen-year-old King Petar II, was pressured into signing on to the Axis on March 25. Almost immediately thereafter, at 2:15 a.m. on March 27, 1941, Serbian air force officers overthrew him. Eden telegrammed "provisional authority" to the British envoy in Belgrade "to do what he thought fit to further a change of Government, even at the risk of precipitating a German attack."[121] But although Britain intelligence supported the coup, it was a Yugoslav initiative.[122] A delighted Churchill, content to see the Serbs do the fighting, wrote that "Hitler had been stung to the quick."[123] Golikov sent Stalin, Molotov, Beria, and Timoshenko a detailed report on March 28, 1940, claiming that "German circles were dumbfounded."[124]

Hitler fulminated against the British for pulling the strings, and in his fury, on that very day (March 27), he issued Directive No. 25, "to destroy Yugoslavia militarily and as a state."[125] On March 30, some 250 field marshals, generals, admirals, and staff officers, seated by rank and seniority, secretly gathered for breakfast in the Great Hall of the New Reich Chancellery, where Hitler delivered a two-hour harangue laying out his case for an invasion of the USSR. "The Russian is inferior," he stated. "The army is without leadership," while "armament capacities [are] not very good." Stalin, Hitler allowed, was "clever," but the Soviet leader "had gambled on Germany's bleeding to death in the autumn of 1939." He emphasized that "this is a war of annihilation. If we do not grasp this, we shall still beat the enemy, but thirty years later we shall again have to fight the Communist enemy." Captured commissars were to be "eliminated immediately by the troops." Indeed, "one of the sacrifices which commanders have to make is to overcome any scruples they might have."[126]

German embassy staff in Belgrade were ordered to leave on April 2 (the ambassador had been recalled for consultations) and to warn "friendly" embassies to do likewise.[127] The Yugoslav minister in Moscow, Milan Gavrilović, effectively a

Soviet agent, was instructed by Molotov to have a delegation come to Moscow immediately to conduct secret negotiations for a "military and political pact."[128] Schulenburg, summoned to the Kremlin on April 4, warned Molotov that "the moment chosen by the Soviet Union for negotiation of such a treaty had been very unfortunate." Molotov replied that Yugoslav accession to the Tripartite Pact with Germany could remain in force.[129] On April 4, "Sophocles" reported out of Belgrade on German troops massing on the border with Yugoslavia, and conversations to the effect of "Keep in mind that in May we'll start a war against the USSR, and within seven days we'll be in Moscow; while it is not too late, join us."[130] Stalin knew what was coming: on April 5, "Alta" learned from "Aryan" of Germany's imminent invasion of Yugoslavia and summoned her handler, Zaitsev ("Bine"), to a Berlin cinema; "Bine" hurried to the Soviet embassy to inform Tupikov ("Arnold"), who reported to Moscow that a German invasion of Yugoslavia would take place the next morning, April 6, and that Berlin was reckoning on the destruction of Yugoslavia in fourteen days.[131]

Molotov, Gavrilović, and two other members of the Yugoslav delegation, with Stalin present, signed a "treaty of friendship and non-aggression" (though not an alliance) in Molotov's Kremlin office at around 3:00 a.m. on April 6.[132] At the improvised banquet, which lasted until 7:00 a.m., Molotov promised armaments, munitions, and planes. When Gavrilović asked Stalin if he had heard the rumors of a pending invasion of the USSR, the despot put on a show of confidence. "Let them come," he said. "We have strong nerves."[133]

Soviet radio announced the treaty that morning, and *Izvestiya* published it later that day, with oversized photographs. But before dawn, the Luftwaffe had already begun bombing Yugoslavia (between 3,000 and 4,000 civilians would be incinerated), and Wehrmacht ground forces—retrieved from the border with the Soviet Union—had burst across the Yugoslav frontier. At 4:00 p.m. Moscow time on the 6th, a Sunday, Schulenburg finally was able to read out to Molotov an official note regarding the German military action. "It was extremely deplorable that an expansion of the war turned out to be inevitable after all," Molotov repeated several times, according to the German account.[134] When, a bit later that night, Gavrilović called on the foreign affairs commissar to discuss the promised war matériel—including antitank guns and aircraft—Molotov observed that there "would be a considerable delay in such deliveries as the Soviet Union might agree to make, and that there were serious transport problems."[135]

Stalin had evidently expected that a Balkan war in the rough mountainous terrain, against valiant Serbs, would last several months, bogging the Germans down long enough to render impossible a spring–summer invasion of the USSR and gifting him another year to prepare Soviet defenses.[136] By April 13, however, Wehrmacht troops had already seized Belgrade.[137] The Wehrmacht, while losing fewer than 200 dead, took more than 300,000 Yugoslav soldiers and officers prisoner. The Soviets effectively abandoned Yugoslavia's Communists, the most powerful pro-Soviet movement remaining in Europe, to their own devices.

On April 12, the dramatist Vishnevsky was at the Kremlin in a small group to see Voroshilov for a discussion of a film based on one of his plays. Voroshilov observed that "Stalin said of the war, 'The Germans are seizing the Balkans. They act boldly. The English send forces to the Balkans as if teasing the Yugoslavs and Greeks.'" Vishnevsky recounted, "We moved on to the Hitler theme: the guy turned out to be far smarter and more serious than we supposed. A great mind, strength. Let them fault him: a maniac, a ruffian, expansionist, and so on, but in fact, a genius, strength. We listened attentively. A sober assessment of the potential enemy." Voroshilov continued: "There are rumors, indirect so far, that Hitler will move in the direction of Ukraine and the Caucasus. Either they are trying to intimidate or, perhaps"—here Vishnevsky noted that Voroshilov took a moment to reflect—"it is a fact. But the Red Army will present difficulties for him." Vishnevsky concluded: "Voroshilov does not doubt our strength. But once more he underscored the complete unreliability of the English."[138]

Germany had also declared war on Greece on April 6, to rescue Mussolini's failed invasion (launched back on October 28, 1940). German troops, pouring in via Bulgaria, halted a Greek offensive, and by April 27 the swastika rose over the Acropolis. Mussolini's army had suffered 154,172 dead, wounded, and sick, and the Greek army about 90,000 casualties. German losses for Yugoslavia and Greece combined were 2,559 killed, 5,820 wounded, and 3,169 missing. While Italy occupied the Greek mainland and the Bulgarians hastily went into Thrace, German forces occupied Athens, Thessaloniki, central Macedonia, Crete, and other Aegean islands, taking 218,000 Greek and 9,000 British prisoners.[139] In both Greece and Yugoslavia, Hitler significantly overcommitted the forces needed to secure his right flank, adding to the impression that the German campaigns could be construed as part of a still operative "peripheral strategy" against Britain in the Mediterranean. The British position was certainly further imperiled by the Balkan conquests.[140] But the Soviet Union's was even more so.

CHURCHILL TO STALIN

High frequencies had been introduced for wireless in the mid-1930s, and one result was that more and more ciphered diplomatic and military traffic was intercepted, albeit not always decoded. Remarkably, British intelligence, with valuable
assistance from the Poles, had broken the German code machine, an upgrade in
complexity to the commercially available Enigma system.[141] Without letting on to
his unique source, Churchill, on April 3, 1941, had seen fit to send a telegram to
the British embassy in Moscow, instructing the ambassador, Cripps, to deliver it
to Stalin personally. The context was the German pressure to force Yugoslavia to
join the Axis. "I have sure information from a trusted agent," Churchill wrote,
"that when the Germans thought they had got Yugoslavia in the net, that is to say
after March 20, they began to move three out of five panzer divisions from Romania to southern Poland. The moment they heard of the Serbian revolution this
movement was countermanded. Your excellency will appreciate the significance
of these facts."[142] Churchill, using terseness to maximize impact, meant to imply
that Germany was much weaker than it seemed, as shown by its having to shift
troops around, and that Stalin should take advantage of an opportunity to take on
Germany while it was occupied in Yugoslavia and Greece (conveniently aiding the
British position).[143]

Cripps had long been convinced that the Germans would attack the Soviet
Union, and that a British-Soviet alliance was necessary and possible. At a press
conference for British and American journalists back on March 11, he had warned,
off the record, that "Soviet-German relations are decidedly worsening. . . . A
Soviet-German war is unavoidable."[144] The NKGB, five days later, had reported his
words.[145] Stalin also read the special "Red TASS" translations of the foreign press—
available for the highest echelons of the party-state—and he could see how the
British press openly mused about Ukraine serving as a "training ground" for German tanks, and the "inevitability" of a German-Soviet war.[146] For Stalin, Cripps's
statements, too, were yet another "British provocation" to instigate war. Cripps—
despite his own stumbling—understood that Stalin would also see Churchill's
telegram in the same light, so he had not passed it on, advising London that Stalin
was inundated with warnings and that Churchill's too brief message, for a host of
reasons, would be "not only ineffectual but a serious tactical mistake." Churchill
insisted he proceed.[147] Cripps had not been able to see Stalin since his first audience
after being appointed ambassador; he could not even get to Molotov, so he handed

the cryptic message to Vyshinsky, deputy foreign affairs commissar, on April 19, after Germany had effectively decided the fate of Yugoslavia and Greece.[148]

Neither in the original cryptic text nor in the clumsy way it was communicated did Churchill "warn" Stalin of an impending German attack. On the contrary, the result proved worse than Cripps had feared, and he was the well-intentioned culprit. The day before, on April 18, Cripps, on his own initiative, had handed Vyshinsky a long memorandum addressed to Molotov (the only way he could communicate with him), which outlined the dilemmas facing the USSR, then issued a threat meant as an inducement toward rapprochement, to the effect that it was "not outside the bounds of possibility, if the war were protracted for a long period, that there might be a temptation for Great Britain (and especially for certain circles in Great Britain) to come to some arrangement to end the war."[149]

COUP DE MAIN

Yōsuke Matsuoka had embarked on the first trip outside the empire by a Japanese foreign minister since 1907, a six-week sojourn that brought him to Moscow (twice), Berlin (twice), Rome, and Vichy. Sorge, based on a conversation between Ozaki, Sorge's informant, and Prime Minister Konoe, had delivered the inside story: Matsuoka was to determine whether Hitler intended to invade Britain or not—Konoe feared a German-British deal—and was given wide latitude to conclude a bilateral pact with the USSR.[150] Stalin found Japan's authoritarianism difficult to fathom, with its myriad centers of power, ostensibly rogue military commanders, and a mystifying emperor system (a "god" who reigned but did not exactly rule). What he did know was that the Japanese foreign ministry was now the one offering the USSR a nonaggression pact, hoping to exact a Soviet promise to cease aiding Chiang Kai-shek. But the Soviets would agree to sign only if Japan returned Southern Sakhalin and the Kuril Islands; otherwise, they suggested a neutrality pact, provided Japan would relinquish its oil and coal leases on Soviet-controlled Northern Sakhalin. The Japanese had asked the Soviets to sell them Northern Sakhalin. "Is that a joke?" Molotov responded.

Having ascertained the Soviet bottom line, Matsuoka departed Moscow. In Berlin, Ribbentrop tried to dissuade him from signing any conclusive agreement with the USSR. Matsuoka, for his part, learned definitively that the Nazis would not be invading Britain—Japan would be on its own in taking on the Anglo-Americans—but that an invasion of the USSR was in the cards. He played a double game with the Germans regarding Japan's intentions, payback for the 1939 surprise Hitler-Stalin Pact.[151]

On his way home, Matsuoka returned to Moscow on the day Nazi Germany invaded Yugoslavia and Greece. Soviet negotiators were still demanding territorial concessions. Stalin intervened, receiving the Japanese on April 12 at the Near Dacha—unprecedented for a foreigner. The two evidently shared a rant against Britain and the United States. In the Kremlin the next day, Molotov and Matsuoka signed a neutrality pact vowing "to maintain peaceful and friendly relations" and remain neutral should either of them "become the object of hostilities on the part of one or several third powers."[152] It had taken eighteen months of talks about fishing rights and territories. In a separate declaration, the USSR recognized the territorial integrity of Manchukuo; Japan, of Mongolia.[153] Stalin would continue to aid China militarily.[154] A lubricated feast was laid on. With the Japanese foreign minister scheduled to depart that same day (April 13), the 4:55 p.m. Trans-Siberian was held up.

After Matsuoka had arrived at Moscow's Yaroslavl Station, Stalin, in full view of the diplomatic corps, appeared, striding down the platform in his long military-style overcoat to see him off. An evidently tipsy despot placed his arms around the German ambassador, Schulenburg, telling him, "We should remain friends, and now you need to do everything for that!" When Stalin spotted a six-foot-tall German in full dress uniform (acting military attaché Colonel Hans Krebs), he tapped him on the chest. "German?" he asked. After an affirmative reply, Stalin slapped him on the back, took Krebs's hand in both of his, and said, "We'll remain friends, no matter what." Krebs answered loudly: "I am convinced of that." The schoolmarmish Molotov, staggering a few paces behind Stalin, "kept saluting all the time, shouting the motto of the Soviet scouts: "I am a Pioneer, I am [always] ready." Stalin, escorting Matsuoka to his carriage, was heard to say, "We shall organize Europe and Asia."[155]

MASTER OF CEREMONIES

On April 18, Fitin sent Merkulov a report from "Lycée-ist" out of Berlin, conveying that an inside source had told him that Göring's inner circle "was very worried about the problem of grain reserves in Germany," especially after supplying 2 million tons to Spain and 1.5 million to France. "On its territory Germany cannot gather the quantity of wheat necessary to meet its minimal needs in 1941–1942. . . .

It must seek new sources for wheat. According to German calculations, 'an independent Ukrainian state,' governed by Germans, with German organization and technology, can in the next two years not only meet the needs of Germany but satisfy the needs of the European continent."[156] Did this mean outright seizure of Ukraine, or a demand for a "lease"? On April 20, "Yeshenko" reported from Bucharest on the movement of German troops from Yugoslavia back toward the Soviet frontier in Romania, and Antonescu's increasing war preparations to retrieve Bessarabia.[157]

The next day saw the annual commemoration of Lenin's death at the Bolshoi and the culmination of a Ten-Day festival of Tajik art (April 12–21, 1941) in Moscow, involving some 750 participants.[158] Stalin attended the Tajik ballet *Du Gul* ("Two Roses") and the concert finale at the Bolshoi, lingering after the performance until 2:00 a.m. He hosted the Tajik delegation on April 22 at the Kremlin, regaling attendees with stories about Matsuoka and Lenin. "We are . . . the students of the great Lenin," the despot told the Tajiks. "I, as a Bolshevik, must say it is necessary to remember this man, who trained us, forged us, led us, made us into people, taught us not to know fear in struggle." Stalin continued: "He created a new ideology of humanity, an ideology of friendship and love among peoples, equality among races. An ideology that holds one race above others and calls for other races to be subordinated to that race is a moribund ideology; it cannot last long." After this reference to Nazism, Stalin concluded that "the Tajik people is a distinctive one, with an old, rich culture. It stands higher than the Uzbeks and Kazakhs."[159]

Stalin finished with the Tajiks around midnight and proceeded to host a banquet for the winners of the new Stalin Prize. There were some seventy-five in industrial processes and design, including Alexander Yakovlev and Sergei Ilyushin (aircraft design) and Alexei Favorsky (synthetic rubber), more than forty in science, including Nikolai Burdenko (surgery), Ivan Vinogradov (mathematics), Pyotr Kapitsa (physics), and Trofim Lysenko (agricultural sciences), and more than one hundred in the arts: Grigory Alexandrov, Isaac Dunayevsky, and Lyubov Orlova (for the musicals *Circus* and *Volga-Volga*); Sergei Eisenstein (for *Alexander Nevsky*, which was still not being shown on screens); Mikhail Romm and his collaborators (*Lenin in October*); the composer Aram Khachaturyan (a violin concerto); Mark Reizen, the opera singer; Shostakovich (a piano quintet); novelist Mikhail Sholokhov; Aleksei Tolstoy for *Peter the Great*; Olga Lepeshinskaya, for ballet; Vera Mukhina, the hammer-and-sickle sculptor; Uzeyir Hajibeyov, for the opera *Koroglu*; Alla Tarasova, the theater actress; the crooner Ivan Kozlovsky

("On a Moonlit Night"); Alexander Gerasimov, for the painting *Stalin and Voroshilov in the Kremlin;* and Mikheil Gelovani, the actor who played Stalin. The cash components were enormous (up to 100,000 rubles for Stalin Prize "first class," 50,000 for "second").[160]

The celebration lasted until 7:00 a.m. "The whole time Stalin was unusually animated, cheerful, hospitable," according to the court dramaturge Nikolai Virtá (Karelsky), who won a Stalin Prize for his novel *Solitude.* "No one escaped his attention; he spoke with this one and that, laughing and joking, sharing his cigarettes with the smokers, praising one of the guests who declared he does not smoke." Films were shown, including *Volga-Volga,* which Stalin knew by heart; he sat next to a Tajik actress. Alexandrov, the director, in answer to Stalin's query, revealed that Orlova, his actress wife, had had her voice dubbed for the singing. "She has a remarkable voice; we need to think about how to afford her wide possibilities for the realization of her talent," Stalin said. Virtá wrote that the leader "proposed that everyone dance; he listened to a famous singer and applauded his rumbling bass." Stalin "spoke about *Hamlet* with the actors of the Moscow Art Theater, about politics and literature, about the construction of one factory, about films and songs, about international affairs."[161]

AMERICA'S WARNINGS

The Americans, too, had learned the world's most important secret. A high German economic official from Weimar days, Erwin Respondek, who had been tasked with preparing the currency for the occupied Soviet Union, arranged meetings with the U.S. commercial attaché in a darkened cinema and passed him word of the invasion planning. In early 1941, Respondek had prepared the first of several detailed memoranda for the United States outlining the steps being taken for the destruction of the Soviet Union and "a rigorous liquidation of Bolshevism, all its political and other institutions, and, in particular, the 'extermination' of its leaders by the SS." Respondek, whose key contact was General Halder, had proved a reliable source till now, but officials in Washington were beginning to suspect that he was a plant. After internal debate, Roosevelt had undersecretary of state Sumner Welles tell Konstantin Umansky, the Soviet envoy in Washington, that the United States "has come into possession of information which it regards as authentic, clearly indicating that it is the intention of Germany to attack the Soviet Union." Umansky blanched. He promised to convey the information to

Moscow—and promptly informed the *German* ambassador to Washington (whether under Moscow's instructions or in order to score points by anticipating Kremlin wishes). On March 1, 1941, after further secret reports prepared by Respondek, Welles tried once more to warn Umansky about the coming invasion. His last effort took place on March 20.[162]

U.S. intelligence had been able to confirm Respondek's tips, for they had broken Japanese codes in September 1940 and, after Major General Hiroshi Ōshima, Japan's onetime ambassador to Berlin, had been returned to the Nazi capital, thanks to Matsuoka, the Americans gleaned a mother lode of intelligence: the staunchly pro-German Ōshima, who spoke the language nearly perfectly, was taken into the confidences of Ribbentrop and Hitler. (Ōshima had been able, in February, to present his credentials at the Berghof.) In April 1941, U.S. cryptographers finished decoding long messages sent from Matsuoka's late-March visit with Hitler. "Göring was outlining to Ōshima Germany's plans to attack Russia . . . , giving the number of planes and numbers and types of divisions to be used for this drive and that," recalled one of the cryptographers. "I was too excited for sleep that night." The United States passed additional warnings to Umansky. But he would tell the press that "information presented to the Soviet Union in London and Washington is aimed at provoking a conflict between Germany and the USSR."[163]

ATTEMPTED DETERRENCE

Dekanozov, from Berlin, sent the foreign ministry a special report in April 1941 noting that rumors and information about a pending war between the USSR and Germany "are coming to us every day from various channels" and calling the pressure a deliberate "war of nerves." Listing a dozen or so examples, he stated that the goal of Germany was "an attack on the USSR already during the course of the current war against England."[164] On April 15, in the area of Rovno, in western Ukraine, after one German reconnaissance plane performed a forced landing, the crew was found to possess "a camera, some rolls of used film, and a torn topographical map . . . of the USSR, all of which gives evidence of the crew's aim." The NKGB detained four officers in leather coats lacking insignias; supposedly, they had been unable to destroy their film in time. Once developed, it showed bridges and rail lines along the Kiev axis, while the map turned out to be of Ukraine's Chernigov province. It was as if the Germans *wanted* the Soviets to believe that Ukraine was their main target.[165]

On April 21, the Soviet foreign affairs commissariat protested German violations of its airspace—some eighty incidents over the preceding three weeks alone.
The German chargé d'affaires, Werner von Tippelskirch, who received the diplomatic note, warned Berlin "to expect likely serious incidents if German airplanes
continue to violate Soviet borders."[166] He was dead wrong. Stalin had begun to
unblock shipments to Germany in mid-April—Soviet oil deliveries doubled from
the previous month—signaling that the Germans could get what they needed
without war (or, conversely, that if Hitler attacked, he would lose the valued goods
the Soviets were supplying).[167] Stalin also abruptly ended Soviet objections to the
German position demanding small changes to their common border.[168] To be
sure, the despot understood that too many concessions would be perceived as
weakness. And so, by not interdicting German overflights, he was effectively allowing the Germans to see what they would face.[169]

"We must hope for the best and prepare for the worst," Chamberlain had said
of appeasement, which would have been a good idea, especially if he had done
what he said and pursued both rearmament and diplomacy, but the former remained very partial.[170] Stalin pursued rearmament vigorously. As a result, the
Soviet people stood in queues for hours upon hours to obtain necessities, and
often they could still not meet their minimum needs.[171] Germany had shown the
Soviets their military production facilities, where the Soviets shopped as part of
their bilateral trade agreement. Stalin, under no obligation to reciprocate, since
the Germans were buying raw materials, nonetheless showed them Soviet military factories. He allowed a tour of the chief aviation factories, including the one
building the Petlyakov Pe-8 bombers, which caused a sensation: it had a longer
range than the German Junkers.[172] In April 1941, during a visit to one such factory, the aircraft designer Artyom Mikoyan told Schulenburg—who, as expected,
passed the words on to Berlin that same month—"You saw the awesome technology of the Soviet country. We will bravely repel any strike no matter where it
might emanate from."[173]

Stalin was demonstrating not just his willingness to bargain, but also his possession of a mighty arsenal and weapons-manufacturing capacity.[174] "They let us
see everything," Krebs, the Russian-speaking German deputy military attaché in
Moscow, wrote to Berlin in the middle of a tour of the five biggest Soviet aviation
factories. "Clearly Russia wants to frighten possible aggressors."[175] Schulze-Boysen
("Elder"), the spy in the Nazi air ministry, reported that "the Germans did not
expect to encounter such well-organized and functioning industry. A number of
the objects shown to them proved to be a big surprise. For example, the Germans

did not know about the existence of a 1,200-horsepower plane engine. . . . A big impression was made by the mass of more than 300 I-18 planes. . . . The Germans did not suppose that in the USSR the serial production of such planes in such high numbers had been established." Krebs concluded that the German general staff "was depressed."[176] Stalin's spies also told him that German war games had revealed to the German general staff the logistical problems of waging a prolonged war against the Soviets, and, in parallel, he ordered that Hitler's military attaché be taken deep into the Soviet rear to be shown the mass production of T-34 tanks.[177]

But Hitler, once apprised, was reinforced in his view that the USSR was arming on a massive scale and needed to be attacked before it was too late.[178] At the same time, whereas Germany's military intelligence had had next to no useful information about the Red Army's armaments or troop locations before it ramped up high-altitude reconnaissance flights, in January 1941, now they had it in abundance.[179]

CACOPHONY

In Berlin, fewer and fewer German businessmen were appearing at the Soviet trade mission. The NKVD reported that over the past year and a quarter, it had captured 66 German spy handlers and 1,596 German agents, including 1,338 in western Ukraine, Belarus, and the Baltics, with hundreds of incidents of live fire at the border. Over the first four months of 1941, at least 17,000 trains were reported to have ferried German troops and heavy weapons to Soviet frontiers.[180] Was it certain war? Internally, the British had dismissed the intelligence regarding Hitler's preparations for a war against the Soviet Union, but now, thanks to the Enigma decoding, they had discovered that Hitler was ordering more and more of the Luftwaffe transferred eastward, away from bombing sites for the UK. Still, the British attributed the eastern buildup to a "war of nerves" being waged to force concessions from Stalin.

Stalin knew that the Germans had ceased using the Trans-Siberian to transport their diplomatic pouches to and from Tokyo, and Sorge reported (April 17) that the Germans would also cease to use the Trans-Siberian for the import of critical rubber from Japan. But Sorge undercut this message, noting that "the tension in relations between Germany and the USSR was decreasing," which meant the Germans might not follow through on their intention to cease using the Trans-Siberian. He also wrote of supposed factionalism within Nazi ruling circles and suggested that the "pro-war faction" had not gained ascendancy. Sorge added: "The German embassy [in Tokyo] received a telegram from Ribbentrop stating that Germany would not launch a war against the USSR if the latter did not provoke it. But if the war turned out to be provoked, then it would be short and end with the severe defeat of the USSR. The German general staff has completed all preparations."[181]

On April 22, Sándor Radó ("Dora"), a Hungarian Communist and Soviet military intelligence operative, reported from Geneva a date of June 15 for an attack on Ukraine. On April 23, Stalin and Molotov decreed the formation of large numbers of new artillery and parachute units with forced production of equipment.[182] The next day, Stalin phoned Ilya Ehrenburg to tell him that the second and third parts of his anti-German novel, *The Fall of Paris,* would now be published. Only four days earlier, Ehrenburg had been informed that the censor had rejected it.[183] Rumors spread that the despot had personally approved the antifascist book.[184] On April 25, Golikov estimated the presence of 100 German divisions on the USSR's western frontiers, an increase from the previous month. On April 25–26, some three and a half months into his work, Tupikov sent a long message to Golikov on Germany's buildup in the east, stating plainly that the Soviets were the "next enemy" in German war planning, and that "the timing for the beginning of a conflict could possibly be near and, for sure, during the course of this year."[185]

A worried Schulenburg, in mid-April, had engaged his staff to draft a long memorandum arguing against a titanic war and, with the facilitation of Ribbentrop and Weizsäcker, who also thought the war a mistake, had traveled to Berlin, but Hitler put off seeing him for two weeks. Finally, on April 28, the Führer granted an audience. Schulenburg's memo was sitting on Hitler's desk (he made no mention of it). Schulenburg evidently stated that "Stalin was prepared to make even further concessions to us," including ramping up to 5 million tons of grain the next year. In fact, Mikoyan could barely find, let alone transport, 2.5 million tons of grain, and it was not clear how the Germans could pay for more grain without yielding vital armaments. Hitler, noncommittal and discourteous, said at parting, "Oh, one more thing: I do not intend a war against Russia!"[186]

In London, Maisky was effectively paralyzed by Stalin's position vis-à-vis Britain. On April 30, Churchill's private secretary told the Soviet envoy, "In Conservative circles, one hears the following argument. If Germany attacks the Soviet Union (as many now believe will happen), the USSR will come to us of its own accord. If Germany does not attack the USSR, it will do nothing for us anyway. So is it worth courting the USSR?" Maisky burst out laughing.[187]

That same day, "Elder" reported to Moscow, based on conversations in Göring's air ministry with the liaison to the foreign ministry, that "the question of the German attack against the USSR has been definitively decided and its onset can be expected any day. Ribbentrop, who until now had not been a supporter of an offensive against the USSR, knowing Hitler's firm resolve on this question, has taken the position of support for an attack on the USSR."[188] "Elder" was spot-on: that very day, Hitler settled on a date fifty-three days hence—June 22.

Neither the German invasion of Greece ("Marita") to compensate for Mussolini's failures nor of Yugoslavia (Operation "25") had a material effect on Barbarossa. Many of the divisions earmarked to take part in the Balkans never saw fighting; some were never even sent. Before May was over, all German units that had taken part in the Balkan campaign were back at their positions on the Soviet border.[189] The delay by about five weeks from the original target stemmed mostly from deficits of key equipment in what, after all, was a colossal undertaking. Indeed, "Corsican" had reported (April 28) that Germany was experiencing severe shortages—and therefore would need to expand economic relations with Japan and the Soviet Union, in the latter case "by force." He had heard one top German official state that "the Russians must supply Germany with more raw materials and foodstuffs, without demanding that Germany had to fulfill Soviet orders exactly or by short deadlines."[190] "Elder," too, reported the possibility of Germany engaging in blackmail. The ultimatum canard—which never formed part of Hitler's plans—had contaminated even the best-placed, most reliable Soviet spies.[191]

NO ARMY IS INVINCIBLE

On May 4, Hitler delivered a peroration to the Reichstag detailing how he had smashed Poland, Norway, Belgium, Holland, France, Yugoslavia, and Greece. "The German armed forces have truly surpassed even themselves," he bragged. "Infantry, armored, and mountain divisions, as well as SS formations, battled without rest, in bravery, endurance, and tenacity to achieve their goals. The work of the general staff has been outstanding. The air force has added new heroic deeds to its historic glory. . . . Nothing is impossible for the German soldier!" He concluded: "The German Reich and its allies constitute a power that no coalition in the world can surpass. German armed forces will unremittingly intervene in the course of events whenever and wherever it will be required."[192]

The signals were getting even more confounding.[193] In Tokyo, the day after

Hitler spoke, Japanese foreign minister Matsuoka reassured German ambassador Ott that "no Japanese prime minister or foreign minister could ever be able to maintain Japan neutrality in the event of a conflict between Germany and the Soviet Union. In such an event, Japan, naturally, would be compelled to attack Russia right behind Germany."[194] That would have violated the Soviet-Japanese Neutrality Pact, and it did not comport with Japan's internal deliberations. That same day, a dispatch from "Corsican" in Berlin went to Moscow indicating that a press person from the German economics ministry had told the staff that Germany wanted peace on its eastern frontiers, for it would soon attack the British-controlled Suez Canal. Germany would demand that the USSR attack Britain on the side of the Axis, and, as a guarantee that Moscow would follow through, Germany was going to occupy Ukraine and possibly the Baltics.[195]

Stalin decided to send some signals of his own. Also on May 5, 1941, at 6:00 p.m., Timoshenko opened the graduation ceremony in the Grand Kremlin Palace's combined Andreyev-Alexander hall (the venue for party congresses) for sixteen military academies and nine military departments in civil institutions, with some 1,500 attendees, including professors as well as defense commissariat, government, and Comintern personnel. The graduates had entered the academies in 1937 or 1938. When Timoshenko announced that Stalin would take the dais, the eruption would not die down until the despot glanced at Timoshenko, who quieted the hall. "Comrades, permit me in the name of the Soviet government and the Communist party to congratulate you on the completion of your studies and wish you success in your work," Stalin began, going on to underscore, over the course of forty minutes, the enormous strides in the Red Army's material base. But he criticized the academies' curriculum. "I have an acquaintance who studied at the Artillery Academy," Stalin noted. "I looked over his notes and discovered that a great deal of time is being spent studying cannons that were decommissioned in 1916." This acquaintance was his elder son, Yakov, who was in the audience. "Is it like that, comrade artillerymen?" Shockingly, Lieutenant General Arkady Sivkov, head of the Artillery Academy, shouted from one of the front rows that the school's curriculum was based on modern weaponry. "I ask that you do not interrupt me," Stalin answered. "I know what I am saying. I read the notes of a student of your academy."[196]

Stalin devoted most of his remarks to the Red Army's technological transformation. "Now we have 300 divisions in the army," he asserted. "Of the total number of divisions, a third are mechanized. That is not general knowledge, but you need to know it. Of the 100 [mechanized] divisions, two thirds are tank [divisions]." Someone in the hall shouted, "This is for the removal of Hitler."[197] Stalin's numbers corresponded to the wishful thinking in MP-41 (all supposed to be in place somehow by January 1942).[198] The despot went on to boast that the newest aircraft were faster than ever and that frontline tanks had armor three to four times thicker and could "break through the front." He also addressed the questions on everyone's mind. "Why was France defeated, and Germany victorious?" he asked. "Is Germany really invincible? . . . Why did Germany turn out to have a better army? This is a fact. . . . What explains it?" Germany, he answered, had rearmed with the latest technology, and studied the new methods of war and the lessons of history. "The German army, having been soundly defeated in 1918, studied up," he explained. "The German army's military doctrine advanced. The army rearmed with the newest technology. It studied the newest methods of conducting war." By contrast, he said, the previously victorious French got complacent. Stalin added one revealing observation: "In 1870, the Germans smashed the French. Why? Because they fought on one front. The Germans suffered defeat in 1916–1917. Why? Because they fought on two fronts."[199]

Stalin insisted that the current German army was not invincible. "There are no invincible armies in the world. . . . Germany started the war and initially did so under slogans of liberation from the Versailles peace. These slogans were popular, elicited support and sympathy from all those humiliated by Versailles. . . . Now the German army has . . . altered the slogan of liberation from Versailles to conquest. The German army will not be successful under a slogan of a war of conquest and annexation. . . . While Napoleon conducted a war under slogans of liberation from serfdom, he elicited support, sympathy, had allies, success. When Napoleon switched to wars of conquest, he accumulated many enemies and suffered defeat." Stalin added: "In military terms, there is nothing special about the German army, neither in tanks, artillery, nor aviation." Still, he concluded, "any politician, any political figure, who allows a feeling of self-satisfaction can succumb to surprise, like the catastrophe that befell France."[200]

"It was a fantastic speech," the government notetaker, an attendee, wrote in his diary. "The speech radiated confidence in our military people, in our strength, and dispersed the 'aura' of glory that enveloped the German army."[201]

A banquet followed in the St. George's Hall, with overflow in the Palace of Facets, the St. Vladimir Octagon, and other spaces (where the toasts, broadcast over loudspeakers, were barely audible).[202] Timoshenko triumphantly entered the white-columned St. George's; then, a bit later, came Stalin, followed by his entourage, provoking thunderous hurrahs. Vodka, champagne, fish, game, and myriad delicacies were laid out. The despot assumed his customary place at the Presidium table. Timoshenko proposed a toast to him; everyone downed their glasses standing.[203] Stalin, Dimitrov noted, "was in an exceptionally good mood."[204] The despot offered an extended toast to the graduates and their teachers, again enjoining them to teach the new technology. Those in the St. George's Hall stepped forward to clink glasses with the inner circle and marshals at the Presidium table.[205] Some fifteen minutes later, Timoshenko announced that Stalin would make a second toast. This one turned out to be for those in artillery, which he called "the main force in war. That's how it was earlier, that's how it is today. . . . Artillery is the god of war."[206] Stalin continued, toasting tank drivers, aviators, cavalry, communications specialists, and infantry, whom he called "the lord of the battlefield."

The evening's concert commenced. Some twenty minutes later, Sivkov, evidently hoping to make amends, proposed a toast "to the Stalinist foreign policy of peace." The despot waved his arms; the guard detail blocked Sivkin from moving forward. Then Stalin rose. As recently as the reception for the May Day parade (May 2), Timoshenko, in Stalin's presence, had referred to the Soviet "peace policy," a reference included in the newspaper account.[207] But now, in his third comment of the evening, an agitated Stalin, his Georgian accent more pronounced, interjected, "Allow me to introduce a correction. A peace policy secured peace for our country. A peace policy is a good thing. For a while we conducted a defensive approach—until we rearmed our army, gave it modern means of fighting. But now that we have restructured the army, saturated it with the equipment for modern combat, now that we have become strong, now it is time to go from defense to offense. . . . We need to reconstruct our education, our propaganda, agitation, our press in an offensive spirit. The Red Army is a modern army, and a modern army is an army of offense."[208] Having that night accused Germany (rather than Britain and France) of starting the war, and having declared that Germany's war of conquest would fail, Stalin, according to some witnesses, also stated—in a phrase excised from the informal transcript—that "there's going to be war, and the enemy will be Germany."[209]

EXCHANGE OF LETTERS?

Stalin's last major speech on foreign policy, at the 18th Party Congress (March 1939), had been published in an enormous print run, but this time *Pravda* reported only that he had stressed "the profound changes in the Red Army in the past few years," especially its rearming and reorganization "on the basis of modern war." The brief account fanned rumors. (The German embassy failed to obtain the contents, until fed them by Soviet counterintelligence.)[210] Immediately after the evening, Zhdanov, Malenkov, and Shcherbakov oversaw meetings to introduce slogans of "offensive war" in propaganda. *Red Star,* the army newspaper, was to undermine the myth of German invincibility by publishing articles about German tactical and strategic shortcomings, and French weakness and mistakes.[211] Stalin complemented these continued efforts to deter Nazi Germany, while also boosting Red Army morale, with an even bigger gesture: Soviet newspapers also announced his appointment as head of government.

The despot had recently sent the inner circle an angry note, complaining about a decision that Molotov had signed off on in relation to an oil pipeline for Sakhalin. Suddenly, the long-standing method of approving decisions by polling became "chancellery red tape and bungling." Stalin complained about the absence of meetings in economic decision making, Molotov's bailiwick (previously the despot had complained about an excess of meetings). "I think it is no longer possible to carry on 'running things' like this," he wrote. "I suggest we discuss the matter at the politburo."[212] At the next politburo session, on May 4, Stalin had been unanimously voted to replace Molotov as head of the Council of People's Commissars. He also remained general secretary of the party, with Zhdanov as his formal party deputy, and Molotov remained foreign affairs commissar.[213] But Voznesensky, the Zhdanov protégé, continued as first deputy of the government and, as a result, outranked Molotov (a mere deputy).[214] Beyond his frustrations, Stalin had signaled, in the words of Sudoplatov, that he was "ready for negotiations and that this time he would lead them directly."[215]

But how? The German press (on Goebbels's instruction) carried no mention of the sensational news of Stalin's assumption of the premiership.[216] Dekanozov, who had been unable to engage Hitler, was called back from Berlin to Moscow "for consultations." During the May Day parade, Stalin had placed him front and center on the Lenin Mausoleum, a message to the Germans that Schulenburg picked up.[217] But the despot had been waiting upon Schulenburg's return from his meeting with Hitler, expecting him to bring proposals, and although the count had conspicuously arrived (April 30) on Ribbentrop's personal plane, he did not even call on the Kremlin. In a May 2 coded telegram from Moscow, Schulenburg complained to the German foreign ministry that he could not fulfill his assignment to tamp down the rumors about a pending war between Germany and the Soviet Union. "Everyone coming to Moscow or traveling through Moscow not only is bringing these rumors, but can confirm them by citing facts."[218] More important was the information brought back from Moscow by acting military attaché Hans Krebs (substituting for Köstring, who had contracted severe pneumonia). Krebs, in Berlin on May 5, told chief of staff Halder that "Russia will do anything to avoid war and yield on every issue short of making territorial concessions."[219]

That same day, however, an ostensible breakthrough occurred: Schulenburg hosted Dekanozov at his single-story villa on Clean Lane for breakfast. The deputy foreign affairs commissar was accompanied by Vladimir Pavlov, the interpreter (who was now director of the German desk at the foreign affairs commissariat); also present was the Russian-speaking Hilger. The count told his Soviet interlocutors that relations needed to be improved; too many rumors were circulating about war. He discussed the May 4 speech by Hitler, mentioning that the Führer had found the Soviet-Yugoslav Pact "strange," and noted that Hitler had pointed out that Balkan developments had compelled him to "undertake some precautionary measures on the eastern border of Germany," because his "life experience had taught him to be extremely cautious, and the events of the past few years had made him even more cautious." Schulenburg returned several times to the need to quell the rumors of war, but he offered no ideas about how to stop them; Hilger interceded to suggest they meet again.[220]

On May 7, the Soviet military intelligence agent Gerhard Kegel ("X"), deputy head of the economics section at the German embassy in Moscow, met twice with his handler, Konstantin Leontyev ("Petrov"), reporting that Germany's "high command has given the order to complete readiness of the war theater and concentrate all forces in the East by June 2, 1941." In one of his more than 100 communications about German war preparations, "X" gave the number of German and allied troops as 2 million in East Prussia, 3 million in former Poland, and 2 million in Hungary and the Balkans—7 million total—and insisted that the decision for war had been taken, irreversibly.[221]

On May 9, "Elder" reported that "in the headquarters of German aviation, preparations for an operation against the USSR are being conducted at a reinforced pace. All data testify to the fact that an attack is set for the near future. In conversations among officers of the headquarters, May 20 is often mentioned as a date for the onset of war against the USSR. In these same circles they declare that initially Germany will present the USSR with an ultimatum for more expansive exports to Germany and abandonment of Communist propaganda." To ensure fulfillment, he added, the Germans would station commissars at Ukrainian industrial and agricultural centers, and the German army would occupy some Ukrainian provinces. "The presentation of an ultimatum will be preceded by a 'war of nerves' aiming to demoralize the USSR."[222, 223]

Stalin offered another gesture toward Germany, formally breaking off diplomatic relations and ordering the embassies of the countries that had fallen under Nazi occupation—Belgium, the Netherlands, Greece, Norway, Yugoslavia—shuttered, and their envoys expelled. Dekanozov, meanwhile, reciprocated the breakfast at the Spiridonovka on May 9. Schulenburg urged the Soviets to take the initiative, advising Dekanozov to have Stalin send a personal letter to the Führer. Dekanozov suspected some sort of ploy, and badgered the count about whether Hitler had authorized such an exchange. Schulenburg, having placed himself, his family, and Hilger in danger with his unauthorized suggestion, backed off. Dekanozov brought the discussion back to a possible joint communiqué. Schulenburg said they needed to act with great alacrity and that if they forwarded a draft text for approval, Ribbentrop or Hitler might not be in Berlin, causing delays.[224] The courtly, well-intentioned Prussian nobleman was trying to induce Stalin to launch a bold diplomatic initiative—precisely what Hitler most feared.

Also on May 9, the Council of People's Commissars had its first meeting under the new configuration. "Stalin did not conceal his disapproval of Molotov," according to the notetaker. "He very impatiently listened to Molotov's rather prolix responses to critical remarks from members of the bureau. . . . It seemed as if Stalin was attacking Molotov as an adversary and that he was doing so from a position of strength. . . . Molotov's breathing began to quicken, and at times he would let out a deep sigh. He fidgeted in his chair and murmured something to himself. By the end he could take it no longer. 'Easier said than done,' Molotov stated, sharply but quietly. Stalin heard him. 'It has long been known who fears criticism,' Stalin answered menacingly. Molotov winced but kept quiet. The others silently buried their noses in their papers. . . . At this meeting I once again saw the majesty and strength of Stalin," the notetaker wrote. "Stalin's companions feared him like the devil. They would agree with him on practically anything."[225]

SENSATIONAL MISSION

In May 1941, Germans were hearing rumors that Stalin and Molotov had murdered each other.[226] On May 10, "Alta" relayed to Moscow that the German war ministry had instructed all military attachés abroad to repudiate the rumors of imminent war with the USSR and to explain the troop concentrations in the east by a desire "to be ready to counter actions from the Russian side and exert pressure on Russia."[227] Here, finally, was an insight into the disinformation campaign.[228]

On May 12, a third breakfast took place, again at Schulenburg's residence. Dekanozov immediately told him that Stalin was ready to exchange letters with Hitler and sign a joint German-Soviet communiqué. Schulenburg had tried to give himself some diplomatic cover for his initiative by telegramming Berlin with a suggestion that the German government offer congratulations to Stalin on his appointment to head the government, and a warning that the Soviet regime had likely prepared an evacuation capital farther east that would be difficult to seize (hints of Napoleon, who had captured Moscow yet still failed to win the war). But a reply from Weizsäcker, received just before Dekanozov's arrival, indicated that Schulenburg's proposal had not even been presented to Ribbentrop ("because this would not have been a rewarded matter"). A parallel letter from a contact in the Berlin foreign ministry warned Schulenburg that he was being closely watched. Dekanozov noted that Schulenburg was now "quite emotionless." The count emphasized that he had acted "on his own initiative only and without authority" and implored them "several times not to reveal that he had made these proposals."[229]

Schulenburg nonetheless again tried to impress upon the Soviets the gravity of the situation and the need for them to take proactive measures, urging, according to the Soviet notetaker, that "it would be good if Stalin himself on his own initiative and spontaneously were to approach Hitler with a letter." Then, in a discussion of British bombing of Germany, he made a highly enigmatic observation: "In his opinion, the time is not far off when they (the two warring sides) must reach an agreement and then the calamity and destruction raining down on each of their cities will end."

Stalin received Dekanozov in his office at night on both May 8 and 12, 1941, so he was apprised of the frustrating "talks."[230] Soon the despot came to see why. On May 13, although details were scarce, he learned of a sensation reported out of Berlin the previous night: Rudolf Hess, deputy to the Führer within the Nazi party, had flown to Britain.

Hess had once won an air race around Germany's highest peak, but recently he had been forbidden to fly. Late on May 10, a date chosen on astrological grounds, in a daring, skillful maneuver, he piloted a Messerschmitt Bf-110 bomber across the North Sea toward Britain, some 900 miles, and, in the dark, parachuted into Scotland.[231] His pockets were filled with abundant pills and potions, including opium alkaloids, aspirin, atropine, methamphetamines, barbiturates, caffeine tablets, laxatives, and an elixir from a Tibetan lamasery (passed to him by the explorer Sven Hedin).[232] He was also said to be carrying a flight map, photos of himself with his son, and the business cards of two German acquaintances, but no identification. Initially, he gave a false name to the Scottish plowman on whose territory he had landed; soon, members of the local Home Guard appeared (with whisky on their breath). The British were not expecting Hess; no secure corridor had been set up. Those on the scene, breaching secrecy, brought in a member of the Polish consulate in nearby Glasgow to serve as interpreter; it was he who noticed that the captive was the spitting image of Hess. British air intelligence ignored the first reports of the captive's evident importance.[233]

No one in the Nazi entourage outdid Hess for devotion. He had been in the forefront of the Beer Hall Putsch and had recorded Hitler's prison dictations that became *Mein Kampf,* volunteering his own thoughts, too.[234] Hess was among the small circle in the know about the firmness of Hitler's intentions to invade the USSR.[235] At the Berghof on May 11, Hitler received one of Hess's adjutants, who delivered a sealed letter left by his boss. The Führer raged that he hoped the missing Hess had "crashed into the sea."[236] Germany disclosed his absence over the radio at 8:00 p.m. on May 12, mentioning a letter that exhibited "traces of mental derangement" and speculating that Hess had "crashed en route."[237] Finally, several hours later, the British issued a statement, with precious few details and no photographs but confirmation that Hess had landed in Scotland. The next day, Hitler summoned the sixty or so top Nazi officials to the Obersalzberg. "The Führer," observed Hans Frank, head of the General Gouvernement (Poland), "was more completely shattered than I have ever experienced him to be." Hitler stated that Hess had acted without his knowledge, and called him a "victim of delusions."[238] Ribbentrop was sent to assure Mussolini that there were no Anglo-German peace talks.[239] "What a spectacle for the world," Goebbels confided in his diary of the defection.[240]

Hess jokes proliferated. ("So you're the madman," Churchill says to Hess. "Oh, no," Hess replies, "only his deputy.")[241] He had lost his role in the Nazi regime to his private secretary, Martin Bormann, and seems to have wanted to reingratiate himself with the Führer, intending to land at the hunting lodge owned by the Duke of Hamilton, a commander in the Royal Air Force whom Hess had met at the 1936 Berlin Olympics. (He missed his property by around twelve miles.) Hess imagined that negotiations could take place with pro-German members of the British establishment, who might even overthrow Churchill. The British moved

Hess to a military hospital as a POW and maintained public silence about his motivations or any secret revelations (of which there were none). "He had come without the knowledge of Hitler," the report of Hess's first interrogation established (May 13), "in order to convince responsible persons that since England could not win the war, the wisest course was to make peace now." Hess proffered the old deal, publicly announced by Hitler, of a free hand on the continent in exchange for preservation of the British empire, and denied that Hitler planned to attack the USSR.[242]

Soviet intelligence tasked its entire network with sussing out the real story of Hess's flight, and they duly reported that Hitler had expressly sent his deputy on a peace mission.[243] Stalin needed no confirmation. That a second in command could undertake such a flight without permission was, for him, implausible. Hess had to have been sent to negotiate a separate peace with Britain and a joint attack on the Soviet Union, and in a way that cleverly allowed Hitler to deny it.[244] Molotov had met Hess in Berlin in November 1940: he was not a madman. It all seemed to add up: Schulenburg tells Dekanozov that Stalin should exchange letters with Hitler, then suddenly backs off; Hess flies to the UK. Now, the most sinister interpretation crystallized of Churchill's cryptic message to Stalin and Cripps's written suggestion to Molotov that the British might come to terms with Germany.[245]

On May 13, behind the scenes, Cripps pursued the same tack, writing from Moscow to the foreign office proposing that the Hess windfall be used to disrupt suspected German-Soviet alliance talks and, more ambitiously, to induce Stalin to abandon Germany altogether. The foreign office thought this would drive Stalin deeper into Hitler's arms.[246] But then Eden and Alexander Cadogan, the foreign office permanent undersecretary, who was charged with coordinating the Hess problem across agencies, took up Cripps's prompt. At a press briefing and in conversations with Soviet envoy Maisky, Eden hinted that Hess was bearing peace proposals, and that his flight proved the existence of a split in the Nazi leadership over the course of the war. The whispering campaign achieved the opposite effect of its aim, however, encouraging Stalin's view that, given the divisions in the Nazi leadership, his own negotiations with Hitler to avert war remained possible.[247]

Even Schulenburg's utter failure ended up contributing to that unshakable belief. Foreign couriers transporting diplomatic pouches overnighted at the Metropole Hotel, awaiting their transit out the next day, and the NKGB resorted to trapping couriers in the bathroom or jamming the lift, seizing their pouches, and photographing their contents while those trapped waited to be rescued. Thus was Stalin able to see that Schulenburg, in his secret correspondence with the

German foreign ministry, continued to stress Soviet conciliatory moves and readiness to bargain.[248] Soviet ingenuity combined with Schulenburg's good intentions amplified German intelligence's disinformation campaign about an ultimatum.[249]

PREEMPTION DENIED

May 15, 1941—much mentioned in Stalin's intelligence—passed without a Nazi invasion. That same day, a Junkers 52 transport, either unobserved or unobstructed by Soviet air defenses, traveled more than 650 miles over Białystok/Belostok, Minsk, and Smolensk, landing at Moscow's central aerodrome, Tushino, a few miles from Red Square. The pilot had been able to reconnoiter the entire German path to the Soviet capital. Whispers about the incredible incident spread. The Soviets allowed the German plane to depart, even refueling it.[250] In Berlin that same day, in an internal memorandum, the German trade official Schnurre observed that the Soviets had made concessions to resolve difficult matters in bilateral trade and that, while Germany would have trouble meeting its obligations to the USSR with regard to new armaments, the Soviets were fulfilling the existing agreement punctually, even though it was causing them great difficulties. He pointed out that Germany could advance additional economic demands beyond the existing trade agreement.[251] (A record number of goods would cross the border in both directions that month.) Also on May 15, coincidentally, the Soviet general staff completed a new aggressive offensive war plan, with Stalin's evident involvement.[252]

This was the fifteenth iteration of the main war plan since 1924, although far from all were formally approved. Like its immediate predecessor, it was drafted by Vasilevsky, with cross-outs and additions in the hand of Nikolai Vatutin (b. 1901), a peasant lad (like Timoshenko and Zhukov) who had graduated from the General Staff Academy in 1937 and been vaulted to a top position in the staff. Just as in the 1940 plan, this one envisioned a massive left hook using the full strength of the Red Army to cut off German forces from Romanian oil, then wheeling north, crossing all of German-occupied Poland and capturing East Prussia (a 450-mile thrust), in a colossal encirclement. But now the southwestern strike was to occur *before* a German attack. "Considering that at the present time the German army is mobilized, with its rear deployed, it has the capability to beat us to the punch and deliver a surprise attack," the war plan explained, recommending that the Soviets "not leave the initiative to the German command, but forestall the enemy in deployment and attack the German army while it is still in the deployment stage and has not yet had the time to organize the front and the coordination among the service branches." Timoshenko and Zhukov asked Stalin for authorization for hidden general mobilization and concentration of forces close to the frontier, both under the guise of training, accelerated railway construction and weapons production, and forced erection of new frontier fortifications.[253]

Preemption constituted a logical extension of Soviet military doctrine: if the Red Army was going to launch a counteroffensive immediately after absorbing the enemy's initial attack, why not prevent that attack in the first place with "a sudden blow"?

The volatile Zhukov had formed a tight duo with the ponderous Timoshenko, another veteran of the civil-war-era First Cavalry Army, in whom he could cautiously confide, provided they could get out of earshot of their bodyguards, drivers, cooks, and maids, who closely observed them, on Beria's orders. "The idea to preempt the German attack," Zhukov would tell an interviewer, "came to Timoshenko and me in connection with Stalin's speech of May 5, 1941 . . . in which he spoke of the possibility of an offensive mode of action."[254] Zhukov would also recall that he and Timoshenko did not sign the preemptive strike plan above their printed names, preferring to report on it preliminarily to Stalin. At an hour-long meeting on May 19, as Zhukov reported, Stalin apparently knocked his pipe nervously on the felt-covered table. "When he heard about a preemptive strike against the German troops he just boiled over," Zhukov wrote, adding that Stalin blurted out, "What, have you lost your mind? You want to provoke the Germans?"[255] Molotov, who was present, would recall that Stalin likely feared that a Soviet attack would induce Britain and even the United States to join Germany in a war against the USSR; at a minimum, the despot anticipated that a Soviet attack on Germany would drive London to make peace with Berlin, particularly in light of the Hess mission, clearing the way for attack in the east.[256]

In the meeting, Stalin explained away his May 5 (pre-Hess) speech as an attempt "to encourage the people there, so that they would think about victory and not about the invincibility of the German army, which is what the world's press is blaring on about," Zhukov recalled. "So that's how our idea about a preemptive strike was buried."[257] In fact, the plan did not specify a date for launching a war, and did not motivate an *immediate* preemption: it estimated total German strength at 284 divisions, but only 120 were said to be concentrated near the frontier, a number not appreciably different from prior estimates.[258] The feasibility of the plan, moreover, remained highly dubious. Alexander Zaporozhets, head of the army administration of political propaganda, wrote to Stalin after an inspection tour that "the majority of troops deployed in the fortified districts on our western frontiers are not battle ready."[259] Timoshenko, Zhukov, Vatutin (now Zhukov's top deputy), and Vasilevsky (operations directorate) appear to have believed they could pull off the absurdly ambitious preemptive strike after further intensive preparations, despite their own inexperience with operations of this scale and the Red Army's low level of organizational cohesion and training and its jumble of obsolete and modern (but untested) equipment. And yet massive logistical problems and railway incapacity bedeviled even the Red Army's more gradual deployments.[260]

To achieve anything like the attack posture in the preemptive plan, the Red Army would have needed many months of very intensive preparation from that point forward.[261] In any case, Stalin did not approve the general mobilization or force concentrations necessary for preemption. There was no aerial reconnaissance of German positions to be struck.[262] The despot held fast to the idea of forward defense and counterattack, but in his mind general mobilization made war unavoidable, foreclosing his diplomatic and stalling options. If Hitler was not so mad as to voluntarily open a two-front war—as Stalin said often—then the Führer would have to negotiate a separate peace with Britain to attack the USSR. That was why Stalin desperately wanted to know the details of Hess's "peace proposals." After all, the despot might be able to offer his own terms to Germany, and Hitler, being smart, would want to see what he could obtain from each side before making a choice. Even if the Nazis made the mistake of voluntarily opening a two-front war, Stalin assumed that any German attack would be preceded by demands for far-reaching concessions, negotiations that Stalin could drag out.

Strikingly, though, almost everything in the May 15 war plan except the preemptive strike was being implemented. Stalin had summoned Timoshenko and Zhukov to the Little Corner on May 10 and 12, and on May 13 the general staff had been able to order deployment to the western frontier of interior reserves—four armies (28 rifle divisions) from the Urals, Volga, North Caucasus, and Baikal military districts—by July 10, with more readied for future transfer.[263] Stalin had also allowed Timoshenko and Zhukov to introduce "covering plans" in frontier military districts, which would enable hidden troop concentration.[264] Stalin was enabling implementation of the approved 1940 war plan, the massive left hook below the Pripet Marshes, should the Wehrmacht attack. As a result, the Soviet Union was as vulnerable to a deep German penetration as it was incapable of launching a preemptive attack.

DISINFORMATION, CONFIRMED

On May 14, "Zeus," out of Sofia, reported further on the concentration of German divisions. On May 17, two weeks prior to the onset of Soviet military maneuvers—which were publicly advertised—Stalin terminated the German tours of his weapons factories, and the very next day an exhibit at Moscow's State Historical Museum cataloging Napoleon's defeat, *1812 Fatherland War,* had its grand opening. On May 19, "Dora" reported from Zurich that Nazi attack plans had been finalized. The next day, "Extern" reported from Helsinki on a pending attack. Out of Bucharest, on May 23, "Mars" reported that "the American military attaché in Romania said to the Slovak ambassador that the Germans will attack the USSR no later than June 15."[265]

Talk of secret negotiations was rife. Dekanozov, following his third breakfast with Schulenburg, departed for Berlin (he arrived May 14), but he could not obtain an audience with Ribbentrop to follow up. The envoy appealed to the good graces of Otto Meissner, who had run the office of the president throughout the Weimar Republic, remained in that post when Hitler became head of state, and was viewed as especially close to the Führer, attending to the ceremonial side of the chancellery.[266] The old-school Meissner happened to speak Russian, having spent considerable time in the country, and beginning in mid-May Dekanozov met with him about once a week—four times altogether. They discussed Iraq, Iran, and Turkey, as if the Wehrmacht troops deployed in Eastern Europe would be attacking the British positions in the Near East. "Otto Meissner quickly became his best friend," recalled Berezhkov, who worked under Dekanozov at the Soviet embassy. "Meissner, also short and stocky, regularly joined the ambassador for lunch a few times a month and, slouching in a chair over cognac and coffee, would tell his host 'in confidence' that the chancellery was working on important proposals for the upcoming meeting between Hitler and Stalin."[267]

Rumors spread beginning around May 25 that Germany was manufacturing Soviet flags for a state visit to Berlin. "The rumors we spread about an invasion of England are working," Goebbels wrote in his diary that day. "Extreme nervousness reigns in England. As for Russia, we were able to organize a vast flow of false information. The newspaper 'plants' make it such that those abroad cannot figure out where is the truth, and where is the lie. This is the atmosphere that we need."[268] German intelligence reported to Ribbentrop that many in the diplomatic corps in

Berlin were convinced Germany and the USSR had already reached a secret agreement, putting off the war.[269] *Pravda* (May 25) published a satirical essay on the wild rumors among foreign diplomats.

Also on May 25, Stalin had in his possession an extraordinary report out of Berlin, where Berlings ("Lycée-ist") had told Amayak Kobulov that, although there were 160 to 200 German divisions on the Soviet frontier, "war between the Soviet Union and Germany is unlikely, although it would be very popular in Germany at a time when the present war with England is not approved by the populace. Hitler cannot take such a risk as a war with the USSR, fearing a breach in the unity of the Nazi party." "Lycée-ist" uttered the canard that "Hitler expects Stalin in connection with this to become more accommodating and end all the intrigues against Germany, and above all, to grant him more goods, especially oil." Most remarkable of all, in connection with supposed Soviet plans to relocate the government to the interior, "Lycée-ist" issued a bizarre olive branch inside a threat: "The German war plan has been worked out in the greatest detail. The maximum duration of the war is 6 weeks. During that time Germany would conquer almost the entire European part of the USSR, but the government in Sverdlovsk would not be touched. If after that Stalin would desire to save the socialist system, Hitler would not interfere."[270]

Even the most spectacular feats of Soviet espionage boomeranged. NKGB counterintelligence was headed by Pyotr Fedotov (b. 1900), the son of an orchestra conductor, who had acquired long experience in counterinsurgency in the North Caucasus against Chechen fighters, before transferring to Moscow in late 1937 when terror vacancies had to be filled. He targeted the German embassy, which had perhaps 200 employees, including 20 under military attaché General Ernst Köstring, who spoke nearly perfect Russian and traveled far and wide, proving to be a talented observer of the combat potential of the Red Army, Soviet military industry, and Soviet mobilization status.[271] Köstring resided in a single-story detached house at Bread Lane, 28, and appears to have assumed that it was secure (the NKGB could not employ microphones placed in adjacent apartments, as it usually did). During one of his absences, Fedotov's team managed to tunnel a very considerable distance from a neighboring building, on the pretext of pipe reconstruction, and into the mansion's basement, then entered Köstring's office, opened his safe, photographed its contents, and installed listening devices, while managing to erase all traces of their penetration.[272] Thus could the NKGB eavesdrop on discussions among the Germans and their allies (Italians, Hungarians, Finns,

Japanese, Slovaks), which went straight to Merkulov, and from him to Stalin's desk.[273] On May 31, 1941, Fedotov evidently played a recording for Stalin of Köstring's conversation with the Slovakia ambassador: "Here what we need is to create some kind of provocation. We must arrange for some German or other to be killed and by that means bring on war."[274]

Such chatter offered yet more substantiation for the felt imperative to avoid handing the Germans a casus belli, but despite the military attaché's desire to ingratiate himself, Hitler needed no such provocation to invade. "The transfer of troops according to the mobilization plan is proceeding successfully," General Halder recorded in his diary (May 30). "The Führer decided that the date for starting the operation 'Barbarossa' remains as set—June 22."[275]

STREAM OF VISITORS

Richard Sorge ("Ramsay") passed on to the Germans as well information he picked up from Japanese government circles, in line with long-ago-issued Soviet permission.[276] He so impressed the German ambassador with his knowledge of Japan (based on his secret cabinet source, Ozaki) that Ott gave him the cipher codes for communication with Berlin, allowing Sorge to learn everything known to the embassy about Hitler's plans.[277] But the embassy was receiving information from Berlin late (the pouch was no longer being sent via the Trans-Siberian Railway across Soviet territory) and, even more important, it was not given firsthand information about Barbarossa. On the contrary, Ribbentrop's foreign ministry knowingly disinformed Ott. Sorge's dispatches, meanwhile, were transmitted via smuggled microfilms or, far faster, via wireless to Khabarovsk by the skilled short-wave operator Max Clausen, a German Communist residing in Japan, who built his transmitter from scratch. Clausen did the coding himself, using onetime pads (which worked via a secret, random key), making them effectively unbreakable but requiring a prodigious amount of time. Unbeknownst to Sorge, Clausen appears to have passed on only about half of the dispatches. On top of being busy running his own blueprint machinery and reproduction business, which Clausen made profitable, he had begun to suffer from heart trouble, doubt Marxism-Leninism, and resent Sorge's condescension and personal cluelessness.[278]

Unlike Sorge's reports on Japan, which were based on direct knowledge of government decisions, those on Germany were mostly gossip and speculation.[279] In early May 1941, Clausen had sent a radiogram (coded bursts of data) with three of

Sorge's messages. They noted that "Ott declared that Hitler is full of determination to destroy the USSR and take the European part of the Soviet Union in his hands as a grain and natural resource base for German control over all of Europe." Sorge also wrote, citing the opinions of Ott and the naval attaché, that, "after the conclusion of the sowing campaign, the war against the USSR could begin at any moment, and all the Germans will have to do will be to gather up the harvest." The messages continued: "The possibility of an outbreak of war at any moment is very high because Hitler and his generals are sure that a war with the USSR will not in the least interfere with the conduct of war against England. German generals assess the Red Army's fighting capacity as so low that the Red Army will be destroyed in the course of a few weeks. They consider that the defense system on the German-Soviet border is extraordinarily weak." Much of this information came from Colonel Oskar Ritter von Niedermayer, of the high command, who had been sent to Tokyo to brief Ott, and with whom Sorge also spoke at length. Sorge further wrote that "the decision on the start of the war against the USSR will be taken only by Hitler either already in May or after the war with England."[280]

On May 21, Clausen transmitted another Sorge message from two days earlier, stating that "new German representatives arriving here from Berlin declare that war between Germany and the USSR could begin at the end of May, since they received an order to return to Berlin by that time," and that "Germany has 9 army corps consisting of 150 divisions against the USSR." That was far beyond estimates at HQ, and betokened an invasion. But these visitors also said that "this year the danger might pass." Sorge's report added that "the strategic plan for an attack on the Soviet Union was taken from the experience of the war against Poland."[281]

Stalin continued to view Sorge as a double agent working for Germany.[282] Golikov forwarded the spy's reports to the despot (who showed familiarity with them), while withholding them from his own immediate superiors, Timoshenko and Zhukov.[283] There was considerable bad blood between Golikov and Zhukov, dating from the terror, when Golikov had been sent to destroy Zhukov.[284] But Stalin's skepticism was the key factor.

Two messages from Sorge on May 30 stated flatly that "Berlin has informed Ott that the German offensive against the USSR will begin in the second half of June. Ott 95 percent sure war will start."[285] The next day, a new German military visitor said that 170 to 190 German divisions were massed on the Soviet border and that war was imminent. "The expectation of the start of a German-Soviet war around June 15 is based exclusively on information which Lieutenant Colonel [Erwin] Scholl brought from Berlin," Sorge wrote in a new message, adding, "Ott told me that he could not obtain information on this score directly from Berlin, and that he only has the information of Scholl." Clausen transmitted both sets of dispatches on June 1, without reconciling the different dates. In the second, Sorge noted that he, too, had spoken with Scholl, an old friend, who in early May had departed Berlin to take up the post of German military attaché in Bangkok, and that Scholl told him the Soviets had committed "a great tactical mistake. . . . According to the German point of view, the fact that the USSR defense line is located, fundamentally, against the German line, without major offshoots, constitutes *the greatest mistake*. This will enable the smashing of the Red Army in the first big engagement."[286]

Golikov requested clarifications, but he wrote on the document, "Add to the list of Ramsay's dubious and disinformational communications."[287]

PRESSURE

German intelligence picked up word that on June 1, 1941, Stalin received British and American ambassadors, returned Litvinov to the foreign affairs commissariat, reached an agreement with the United States, and was being pressured by his top brass to oppose Germany militarily. But this was disinformation spread by the Soviets. The Germans had Berlings ("Peter" to the Germans) check on rumors of Soviet-British negotiations, which he verified did not exist.[288]

As German war preparations grew ever more intense, so did the warnings from Soviet intelligence networks. Beria reported to Stalin and Molotov (June 2) that Hitler, accompanied by Göring and Grand Admiral Raeder, had observed maneuvers of the German Fleet in the Baltic Sea, near Gdynia, and traveled to Warsaw and East Prussia.[289] That same day, Goglidze reported from Soviet Moldavia that the commander of Romanian border units had, two full weeks prior, "received an order from General Antonescu immediately to clear mines from bridges, roads, and sectors close to the border with the USSR—mines that had been laid in 1940–41. At present all the bridges have been cleared of mines and they have begun to clear them in the sector along the River Prut." The Romanians, Goglidze concluded, were eagerly expecting to be sent into battle shortly.[290] The next day, Golikov asked frontline NKGB stations for assistance in verifying numbers of German troops, tanks, armored vehicles, combat aircraft, transport aircraft, and explosives, and the locations of German field headquarters in East Prussia, occupied Poland, and Romania. "Try to obtain data on the plans for military operations against the USSR (in any form, documentary or oral etc.)," he wrote to the NKGB station in Berlin, as if they had not been straining every nerve to do this.[291]

Germans were observed taking "samples of [Soviet] oil, motor vehicle and aviation petrol and lubricants," presumably to determine whether they could be used with German equipment.[292] Military intelligence in the Western military district, in an internal memo to commander Dmitry Pavlov (June 4, 1941), noted that reliable sources on the other side of the border had observed immense increases in German artillery, tank, and armored troops, influxes of weaponry through the Warsaw train system and aerodrome, upgrading of railroad stations for nighttime unloading, the takeover by the military of all civilian medical installations, the guarding of bridges by military personnel, and mobilization of bureaucrats to govern occupied territories, and concluded that it was "not excluded" that war would commence in June.[293] On June 5, Golikov reported to Stalin, the entire politburo, Timoshenko, and Zhukov that "the Romanian army is being brought to full combat readiness." Among the details: "In May officers of the Romanian army were given topographical maps of the southern part of the USSR," and schools had their exams early "so that their buildings could be used for military barracks and hospitals."[294] That same day, the NKVD established an affiliate of its central archive in the Siberian city of Omsk to prepare for a possible evacuation of files.[295]

Goebbels, in one of his regular conferences for the Nazi press on June 5, stated, "The Führer has decided that the war cannot be brought to an end without an invasion of Britain. Operations planned in the East have therefore been canceled. He cannot give any detailed dates, but one thing is certain: the invasion of Britain will start in three, or perhaps five weeks."[296] The next day, the British foreign office recalled Cripps to London for "consultations."[297] Berlin was worried that something was up; London, for its part, was still fearing a last-minute new Hitler-Stalin pact against the UK. That day, Stalin signed decrees "on measures for industry's preparedness to switch to the mobilization plan for [producing] ammunition" and for possible wartime mobilization of all industry from July 1.[298] Between June 6 and 10, the Wehrmacht sent its tank and motorized divisions right to the border (until then, the advanced troops were mostly infantry), kicking up prodigious earth and dust and making exceptional noise, a massive, unmistakable change in border concentrations. "Alta," on June 7, 1941, reported, "It is a fact that the date for the start of a campaign against Russia has been moved to after June 20, which is explained by the large material losses in Yugoslavia. No one doubts from informed circles that military action against Russia will be conducted."[299]

Also on June 7, Colonel General Grigory Stern, chief of air defenses, was arrested, one of more than 300 officers incarcerated that month, 22 of whom had earned the highest military decoration, Hero of the Soviet Union.[300] Under torture, Stern admitted to being a German spy since 1931.[301] Stalin had been angry for some time about the loss of two to three planes daily from crashes in training.[302] He also scapegoated air defenses for the border violations by Germany, precipitating a frenzy of mutual denunciation. Others arrested included a deputy chief of the general staff to Zhukov, Lieutenant General Yakov Smushkevich, who was taken into custody (June 8) while in the hospital for a major operation (he was conducted to prison on crutches), and armaments commissar Boris Vannikov (his nemesis, Marshal Kulik, was soon forced to step down but not incarcerated).[303] The former head of the air force, the thirty-year-old Lieutenant General Pavel Rychagov, who had been sacked at Zhukov and Timoshenko's insistence, was also arrested (June 8). Although a flying ace who had won the Hero of the Soviet Union, the Order of Lenin, and three Orders of the Red Banner, Rychagov was not fit for such a top post, but Stalin had murdered all the others. He was beaten with rubber truncheons but refused to confess to treason.[304]

Amid the arrests, Golikov (June 7) advised Stalin that, besides mobilization in Romania and the German right flank, "special attention should be given to the continuing reinforcement of German troops on the territory of Poland."[305] On June 8, the German foreign ministry received word that the Soviet envoy to Romania had said that there would likely be no war but instead negotiations, which could fail if the Germans put forth excessive demands.[306]

Soldiers in full combat kit and completely full fuel tanks saturated the German side of the border, as the NKGB knew.[307] On June 9, Bogdan Kobulov forwarded to Stalin, Molotov, and Beria a memo from Fitin based on communications from "Elder" and "Corsican," noting that the rumors about negotiations and an ultimatum "were being spread systematically by the German ministry of propaganda and the German army high command. The goal is to mask the preparations for an attack on the Soviet Union and maximize the surprise of such an attack." This was correct. But the report also quoted the Soviet section head of the German air force staff that Hitler would present the Soviet Union "with a demand to turn over to Germany economic management of Ukraine, to increase the supplies of grain and oil, and to use the Soviet navy—above all, its submarines—against England."[308]

That same day, Japan's ambassador in Moscow, Lieutenant General Tatekawa, warned Tokyo in a telegram, which the Soviets intercepted and decoded, that

Germany "could not conquer or crush the Soviets in 2 to 3 months," and that "the possibility cannot be excluded that Germany would find itself stuck in a prolonged war."[309] In the Little Corner, also on June 9, Timoshenko and Zhukov unfolded maps of German troop concentrations and a packet of military intelligence reports predicting war, which Stalin leafed through, having already seen them and more. Trying to be droll, the despot, according to recollections by Timoshenko, alluded to a Soviet agent in Japan who was predicting a German attack—"a shit who has set himself up with some small workshops and brothels."[310] This was Sorge, of course, who had indeed cuckolded nearly the entire German community in Tokyo (while finding comfort most often in the bosom of his Japanese consort, Hanako Ishii). But neither Timoshenko nor Zhukov knew of Sorge's existence, let alone his hearsay reports predicting war.

From Berlin on June 9, Ribbentrop telegrammed an order to the embassy in Moscow to secure its archives and organize the "inconspicuous departure of women and children." Two days later, Bogdan Kobulov reported to Stalin, Molotov, and Beria on the evacuation directive and verified that documents were being burned.[311] Also on June 11, Kobulov wrote that, based on information from "Elder," in the air ministry, the decision to invade "has been definitively taken. Whether there will there be any prior demands to the Soviet Union is unknown, and therefore it is necessary to take into account the possibility of a surprise strike." He further noted that "Göring's HQ is moving from Berlin likely to Romania." Germany's battle plan was said to be an invasion from East Prussia in the north and Romania in the south, to create pincers to envelop the Red Army in the center.[312] In fact, Germany's main strike force was in the center.

DESPERATION

On June 10, Germany's high command issued a supersecret order confirming the invasion for June 22, at 3:30 a.m. It stipulated that "June 18 is the latest for a possible delay," and that a signal would be issued on June 21 at 13:00 hours—either "Dortmund" (attack on) or "Alton" (attack delayed).[313] On June 11, NKGB intelligence chief Fitin reported from a source in Helsinki to Merkulov that, at a meeting of the Finnish government two days earlier, Finnish president Risto Ryti had said that Germany was forcing him to order a partial mobilization, but that "the question of whether or not there will be a war between Germany and the USSR would be answered June 24. Maybe there will be no war, since Hitler and Ribbentrop are against a war with the USSR, but the German generals and general staff desire it."[314] On June 12, Tupikov ("Arnold"), in Berlin, based on information from Scheliha ("Aryan"), told Moscow military intelligence that the invasion would occur "June 15–20."[315]

German mapping for the bombing campaign intensified. "Violations of Soviet borders by German planes are not accidental, as confirmed by the direction and depth of the flights above our territory," Beria wrote to Stalin on June 12. "In a few instances they had penetrated 60 miles or more and in the direction of military installations and large troop concentrations."[316] In parallel, the Luftwaffe began moving its attack planes to frontier aerodromes in occupied Poland, a massive concentration of fighters that could not be missed—they were jammed into a very narrow space, right up against the Soviet frontier, which would make them highly vulnerable unless they were about to go into combat.[317] That same day, Berlings ("Peter") reported to the Ribbentrop bureau that Ivan Filippov— nominally the TASS correspondent in Berlin, and the go-between who had introduced Berlings to Amayak Kobulov—had been ordered "to clarify whether or not Germany is actively pursuing peace negotiations with England and whether or not to expect an attempt in the longer term to secure a compromise with the United States." Filippov was also now directed to convey the impression that "we are convinced it is indeed possible to maintain our peace policy. There is still time."[318, 319]

Stalin tried to seize the initiative, composing a TASS bulletin, read out over Moscow radio at 6:00 p.m. on June 13 and published in Soviet newspapers the next morning. The impetus appears to have been the intensified speculation of a German-Soviet war that accompanied Cripps's recall to London. In issuing the bulletin, Stalin was effectively following the suggestion Schulenburg had made to Dekanozov that the Soviet leader write to Hitler, but the despot decided on the form of an open letter. "Germany is also, just as consistently as the USSR, observing the terms of the Soviet-German Non-Aggression Pact," it stated. "In view of this, according to Soviet circles, rumors of Germany's intent to break the Pact and to attack the USSR are utterly groundless." Stalin aimed not only to refute the rumors of war, again blaming them on British provocations to cause that very war, but also to elicit a German denial of any intentions to attack—or, failing that, a German presentation of its anticipated demands, which the rumors said the USSR had already received and rejected, bringing the countries to imminent military confrontation. "Germany," the bulletin noted, "has not presented any demands to the USSR and did not propose any new, even closer agreement, in view of which negotiations on this subject cannot be taking place."[320]

Nazi foreign ministry officials had already instructed the management of the Schloss Bellevue, where Molotov had stayed during his Berlin visit, to prepare for Soviet dignitaries in the near future, while the Anhalter Station had been closed to the public at the beginning of June so it could be outfitted with a large electric red star and Soviet banners. Staff were told not to mention anything, prompting gossip. Rumors absolutely engulfed Berlin that Stalin would arrive at any moment by armored train, or that he and Hitler would meet at the border, or that Hitler was secretly discussing the scope of Germany's imminent demands. One German woman recorded in her diary that her milkman had assured her that hundreds of women were sewing Soviet flags.[321] Some people assumed that the TASS announcement had been published with German agreement.[322]

The foreign affairs commissariat had handed the text to Schulenburg, who relayed it to Berlin.[323] But the German press did not publish it. The press secretary of the German foreign ministry, on June 14, refused to comment on it, despite insistent questioning by foreign journalists.[324]

At the very moment of Stalin's gambit, Hitler was holding a massive war conference (June 14) in the Parliament Chamber of the Old Reich Chancellery, with reports by all commanders of army, naval, and air force groups on their Barbarossa preparations. The number of invited attendees was so large that they were directed to arrive at different times and use different entrances. "After luncheon," General Halder wrote in his diary, "the Führer delivers a lengthy political address, in which he explains the reasons for his intention to attack Russia and evolves his calculation that Russia's collapse would induce England to give in."[325]

The Germans knew, of course, that the Soviets had been calling up reserves, moving forces to the frontier, furiously building border defenses, and stepping up patriotic propaganda.[326] The Wehrmacht's main worry was that, given its absurdly dense concentration of forces and weaponry smack up against the Soviet frontier, the Red Army could inflict great damage by striking preemptively—or, what might be worse, adjust their forward defense posture and move their own extremely vulnerable troops back away from the frontier, removing the danger of being wiped out in a lightning strike and preserving themselves for the counterstrike. Back on June 13, Timoshenko, in Zhukov's presence, had phoned Stalin to request authorization to have frontline Red Army troops brought to a war footing. The despot refused, citing the forthcoming TASS bulletin, but the text baffled many Soviet military men, especially those in the field.[327] Stalin did allow the general staff to order the western military districts to begin moving divisions of the second echelon, under the pretext of military exercises, up to within twelve to fifty miles of the frontier by July 1. This was suicidal.[328]

"The Führer estimates that the operation will take four months. I reckon on fewer," Goebbels wrote in his diary (June 16), after yet another audience. "Bolshevism will collapse like a house of cards. We face victories unequaled in human history. We must act. Moscow intends to keep out of the war until Europe is exhausted and bled white. Then Stalin will move in and Bolshevize Europe and impose his own rule. We shall upset his calculations with one stroke. . . . The alliance with Bolshevism was always a blemish on our honor. Now it will be washed away. . . . The TASS denial, in the Führer's opinion, is little more than a product of Stalin's fear. Stalin is trembling at what is to come."[329]

DOOM CLOSES IN

Golikov, of Soviet military intelligence, reported the accelerated German buildup in April, May, and June, from 70 to an estimated 110-plus divisions.[330] Japanese intelligence refused to believe that Hitler had the temerity to attempt to conquer the Soviet Union, an attempt that the Japanese shrank from after being defeated at the Halha River by superior Soviet weaponry and tactics.[331] British officials had unique, unimpeachable intelligence, yet they were exceedingly slow to understand that Hitler was planning not a campaign of intimidation and blackmail but an all-out invasion.[332] Back on May 31, 1941, the British Code and Cipher School had reviewed the data gleaned from the Enigma intercepts and—finally—concluded that the rail movements eastward involved more than a bluff. But the war office and the foreign office did not rule out a last-second, one-sided deal between Germany and the USSR (the apparent lack of German-Soviet negotiations in Moscow, they speculated, must have meant they were taking place in Berlin, so that Stalin could conceal them from his own officials). On June 7, Enigma delivered the Luftwaffe's order of battle for the USSR: this meant war was certain, and the experts judged that Poland and East Prussia were the principal staging grounds.[333] "From every source at my disposal, including some most trustworthy, it looks as if a vast German onslaught on Russia was imminent," Churchill wrote to Roosevelt (June 14).[334] The NKGB obtained a copy.[335]

British officials, however, did not relinquish the idea of an ultimatum that would allow Hitler to win without fighting, though there was debate about whether Stalin would make the necessary concessions, whatever they might be.[336] The British could afford to be wrong; Stalin could not. June 15, a date for the onset of war mentioned by Scheliha ("Aryan") from Berlin, and Sorge ("Ramsay") from Tokyo, among others, passed without hostilities. That day, Ribbentrop instructed his ambassadors in the capitals of Germany's allies—Rome, Budapest, Tokyo—to inform the governments there that Germany intended "to introduce complete clarity in German-Russian relations at the latest at the beginning of July and in this regard to put forth certain demands." The directive went straight to Stalin.[337] Also that day, Sorge composed a message (transmitted two days later) that "a German courier told the military attaché that he is convinced that the war against the USSR is delayed, probably, until the end of June. The military attaché does not know whether there will be war or not."[338]

From Berlin on June 16, Tupikov ("Arnold"), of military intelligence, transmitted the latest message from the Soviet Union's best spy, "Aryan," reporting that in Germany's high command, people were now talking of "June 22–25."[339, 340] Also on June 16, the NKGB's Amayak Kobulov ("Zakhar"), in Berlin, again reported that "Elder" had relayed that "all military measures by Germany in preparation for an invasion of the USSR have been utterly completed, and that the strike can be expected at any moment." "Elder" did not mention an ultimatum (his report five days earlier had still suggested it as a possibility).

Details on the imminent attack specified that German planes would in the first instance bomb Moscow factories producing parts for airplanes—but these, as Stalin knew, were beyond the range of German aircraft. The report added that "in air ministry circles the TASS communiqué of June 6 [*sic*] was being treated very ironically. They stress that the declaration can have no significance whatsoever." And it stated that "in the economics ministry they say that at a meeting of managers designated for 'occupied territories of the USSR,' [Alfred] Rosenberg also spoke, and declared that 'the concept of the "Soviet Union" should be wiped from the geographical map.'" Fitin sent a summary to Merkulov. "Late on the night of June 16–17 the commissar called me at my office," Fitin would recall, "and said that at 1:00 p.m. he and I had been summoned to see I. V. Stalin."

In the Little Corner, Stalin did not invite them to sit. Fitin noticed a pile of intelligence reports on the felt table, with his latest on top. As he reported, the despot paced the office. Then, complaining intemperately of disinformation in the reports of imminence of war, Stalin ordered that they go back and recheck all the messages from "Corsican" and "Elder."[341] "Despite our deep knowledge and firm intention to defend our point of view on the material received by the intelligence directorate, we were in an agitated state," Fitin would later recall. "This was the Leader of the party and country with unimpeachable authority. And it could happen that something did not please Stalin or he saw an oversight on our part and any one of us could end up in a very unenviable situation."[342] Stalin's displeasure was indeed severe. "To Comrade Merkulov," he wrote in bright green pencil across the commissar's cover note accompanying Fitin's report, "you can send your 'source' from German aviation HQ to his fucking mother. This is not a 'source' but a disinformationist."[343]

WHEN CRIPPS HAD LEFT MOSCOW FOR LONDON, Nazi officials feared the worst: a trip to finalize details of a British-Soviet agreement.[344] Germany's anxieties testify to the potential of this option, which Stalin never pursued. Cripps, for his part, at a June 16 British cabinet meeting, was still expecting the German ultimatum to the USSR, which had never been part of Hitler's intent.[345] Once apprised of the secret Enigma intelligence, however, Cripps changed his mind and lunched with the Soviet envoy. "Hitler cannot embark on the final and decisive attack against Britain before the potential threat to Germany from the East is eliminated," Maisky wrote of their conversation in his diary (June 18). "The Red Army is a powerful force, and by 1942, when all the shortcomings revealed by the Finnish campaign have been eradicated, it will be too late for the Germans to attack the Soviet Union. . . . Cripps is certain that [Hitler] will strike. Moreover, Cripps is in possession of absolutely reliable information that these are Hitler's plans. . . . The members of the British Government with whom Cripps has spoken think that before an attack against the USSR, Hitler would present us with an ultimatum. Cripps does not share these views. Hitler will simply fall on us without warning, because he is not interested in this or that amount of food or raw materials which he can receive from the USSR, but in the complete destruction of the country and the annihilation of the Red Army."[346]

On June 18, General Köstring, knowing Hitler's eagerness to learn of any Soviet general mobilization (which could serve as a convenient pretext), nonetheless reaffirmed to Berlin the truth: the Soviet Union remained calm.[347] Stalin saw the world in the darkest hues, as shaped by unseen sinister forces, with enemies lurking everywhere and no one's motives to be trusted. But in what was by far the grandest challenge of his life, his pathological suspiciousness undermined him. In the machinations during 1941, he perceived two games: a British effort to entangle him in a war with Hitler and a German effort to intimidate and blackmail him.

Neither was the game that was actually on. Ironically, the extensive penetration of Germany by dedicated antifascist agents became another weapon in Nazi hands, thanks to astute German disinformation and Stalin's credulousness. Of course, the despot was far from alone in his misperceptions. But here was the greatest irony of all: even if he had been able to find the signal in the noise, it might not have done him much good. Stalin had allowed the Germans to see firsthand that he had forced into existence an army of colossal size, loaded with modern weaponry. But the Red Army's forward defense posture, the core of Soviet military doctrine, which both Stalin and the high command fully shared, meant that deep German penetration was a foregone conclusion. That deadly vulnerability would have held even in the event of a preemptive Soviet strike.[348] For all that, however, into the third week of June, Stalin had one option left—and it worried Hitler.

CODA: LITTLE CORNER, SATURDAY, JUNE 21, 1941

> The only certain thing is that we face either a battle of global proportions between the Third Reich and the Soviet Empire or the most gigantic case of blackmail in world history.
>
> VILHELM ASSARASSON, *Swedish envoy in Moscow, telegram to Stockholm, June 21, 1941*[1]

> Suddenly addressing me with "thou," he said, "Thou must always keep touch with the Russian emperor; there, no conflict is necessary."
>
> OTTO VON BISMARCK, *recalling the words of a dying Kaiser Wilhelm I*[2]

STALIN PACED AND PACED IN HIS KREMLIN OFFICE, with his usual short steps, gripping a pipe in the hand of his good arm. It was Saturday, June 21, 1941. The night before, he had repaired after midnight to his Near Dacha, in the woods at Kuntsevo, returning to the Kremlin in the afternoon.[3] From his office suite on the bel étage of the tsarist-era Imperial Senate, a person could see the whole world—or, at least, Stalin's world. Over the years, many of the party bosses and industrial managers, military men and secret police, scientists and artists who were granted an audience surmised that he paced to control his explosive emotions or, alternately, to unnerve those in his company. Invariably, he alone was up, trundling back and forth, sidling up to people while they were speaking or just after they had finished, looking them in the eye or the back. Only a few intimates knew that Stalin suffered nearly constant pain in the joints of his legs, which may have been a genetic condition and which the movement partly alleviated.[4] He also strolled the Kremlin grounds, between the Senate and the Arsenal, usually alone, touching the leaves on the trees and shooing away the black ravens. (Afterward, the guards came and massacred the birds.)[5] Stalin's nearly constant motion mimicked his cascading thoughts. For a full year now, essentially since the stunning fall of France to the Germans in June 1940, he had lived in a state of unbearable tension.[6]

Pravda (June 21) reported that Turkmenistan's Central Committee had just concluded a two-day plenum devoted to cotton. The newspaper also rebuked the Stalingrad Tractor Factory for not producing a single ax or frying pan, of the tens of thousands ordered; exhorted a loss-free gathering of the grain harvest; and remained silent about how the German embassy personnel were being evacuated, along with oil paintings, antique rugs, and silver.[7] The NKGB, for its part, reported the mass German exodus and that the Italian embassy, too, had received instructions to evacuate.[8] Intelligence warnings of imminent titanic war were coming from everywhere. The Soviet agent Pavel Shatev ("Costa"), an ethnic Macedonian separatist, reported from Sofia (June 21) that a German emissary had told an official of allied Bulgaria that "a military confrontation is expected on June 21 or 22."[9] Zhou Enlai passed on, through Comintern channels, that Chiang Kai-shek "is declaring insistently that Germany will attack the USSR, and is even giving a date: June 21, 1941!" which prompted Dimitrov to phone Molotov that morning. "The situation is unclear," Molotov told him. "*There is a major game under way.* Not everything depends on us."[10]

Stalin had eliminated private property and made himself responsible for the Soviet equivalents of Washington, Wall Street, and Hollywood all rolled into one, and all rolled into one person, an extreme despotism. He complained of fatigue, especially toward the end of his long workdays, and suffered from insomnia, a condition never acknowledged publicly, but manifest in the now fully nocturnal rhythm of the vast functionary kingdom under him. A tiny group of insiders knew of his infections and multiday fevers. Rumors of various health problems had circulated abroad, and the use of foreign doctors had long ago been discontinued, but a narrow circle of Russian physicians had acquired detailed knowledge of his illnesses and of his bodily deformities, including his barely usable left arm, the thick, discolored toenails on his right foot, and the two webbed toes on his left foot (an omen, in traditional Russia, of Satanic influence). For long periods, Stalin resisted being seen by any doctor, and he had ceased using medicines from the Kremlin apothecary that were issued in his name.[11] The household staff had stopped bringing his meals from the Kremlin canteen, cooking them in his apartment and, in his presence, tasting from the plates. All the same, Stalin's stomach was a wreck. He suffered from regular bouts of diarrhea.[12]

For the fifth consecutive year, since his holiday decision to intervene in Spain, he had no plans to travel to his Sochi getaway. Young Pioneers were departing for summer camps, and a new aquatic center was set to open at Khimki, just outside the capital. Posters advertised the upcoming appearance at Moscow's Hermitage summer theater of Leonid Utyosov and his jazz band, whose magical tunes the entire country could whistle, from the Baltic to the Pacific.[13] Stalin paced and paced in his office inside the Imperial Senate, which had been built by the Teutonic empress of Russia, Catherine the Great, for "the glorification of Russian statehood." A few decades after its opening, in early fall 1812, Napoleon had arrived with his invading forces. The French Grande Armée—full of Western Christian Poles, Italians, and Germans, too—had defecated in the Kremlin's Orthodox churches and taken potshots at the holy icons. After cunning Russian resistance starved the occupiers, a retreating Napoleon had ordered the Kremlin blown to pieces. Heavy rains doused the fuses, limiting the damage, but explosives destroyed parts of the walls and several towers. The Imperial Senate suffered a fire.

Stalin's Kremlin, too, had been violated, albeit not in the way that he long feared. Inside, the long, red-carpeted corridors to and from his Little Corner were attended by an army of sentries. "See how many of them there are?" he once remarked to a military commander. "Each time I take this corridor, I think, which one? If this one, he will shoot me in the back, and if it is the one around the corner, he will shoot me in the front." The commander, Admiral Ivan Isakov, had been born Hovhannes Ter-Isahakyan, an Armenian who shared Caucasus heritage with Stalin but, like everyone else, was dumbfounded by such hypersuspicion.[14] In fact, there had never been a single genuine assassination attempt against Stalin. But the "Man of Steel"—"deeper than the ocean, higher than the Himalayas, brighter than the sun, teacher of the universe," in the words of the Kazakh national poet—was being stalked from afar by a onetime Austrian corporal and former house painter. The pair offered a study in contrasts: Hitler the undisciplined "artist," Stalin the trained seminarian; Hitler the anti-Semite German nationalist, Stalin the Marxist-Leninist imperial Russian nationalist. Not just their different personalities, however, but their countries' very different histories and geographies, and their different systems of rule, had produced clashing geopolitical aims.[15]

Hitler had won the Second World War. He had annexed his native Austria, the Czech lands, much of Poland, and a strip of Lithuania, creating the Greater Germany that in 1871 Otto von Bismarck had deliberately avoided forging during the wars of German unification (deeming Austria-Hungary's existence vital for the balance of power). Hitler's troops had occupied Norway, Denmark, the Low Countries, the Balkans, and northern France. The Führer received obeisance from France's World War I lion, Marshal Philippe Pétain (now the chief of state of rump Vichy), and other vassals, such as the Conducător of Romania (Ion Antonescu), "His Serene Highness" of landlocked Hungary (Admiral Miklós Horthy), the Catholic-priest ruler of Slovakia (Jozef Tiso), the fascist puppet of Croatia (Ante Pavelić), Bulgaria's tsar (Boris III), the president of Finland, and the Italian duce, not to mention the generalissimo of Spain. The Führer essentially controlled all of Europe from the English Channel to the Soviet border, for only Sweden and Switzerland remained neutral, and both cooperated with Nazi Germany economically. True, the defiant Brits still refused to come to terms, but London could never overturn Berlin's continental dominance. And Hitler had the nonaggression pact with Stalin. Would he *really* gamble and risk all his winnings by attacking? Had not Napoleon tried and failed? In 1812, facing the window before Russian winter, Napoleon had invaded on June 24.

JUNE 21 COULD scarcely have been more stifling, and Stalin's top aide, Alexander Poskryobyshev, was sweating profusely, his window open but the leaves on the trees outside utterly still.[16] The son of a cobbler, like the despot whom he served, he occupied the immediate outer office through which all visitors had to pass, and invariably they would spray him with questions—"Why did the Master have me summoned?" "What's his mood?"—to which Poskryobyshev would laconically answer, "You'll find out." He was indispensable, handling all the phone calls and document piles in just the way the despot preferred. But Stalin had allowed Beria to imprison Poskryobyshev's beloved wife as a "Trotskyite" in 1939. (Beria had sent a large basket of fruit to their two baby girls; he then executed their mother.)[17] Now, Poskryobyshev sat at his desk trying to cool down with a bottle of Narzan mineral water, under a photograph of a youthful Stalin wearing a pointy, red-starred civil war cap. On Stalin's instructions, at around 2:00 p.m., he phoned General Ivan Tyulenev, head of the Moscow military district. Soon the general heard Stalin's "muffled voice" asking, "Comrade Tyulenev, what is the situation concerning Moscow's antiaircraft defenses?" After a brief report, Stalin said, "Listen, the situation is unsettled and therefore you should bring the antiaircraft defenses of Moscow up to 75 percent of their readiness state."[18]

Poskryobyshev thumped the latest intelligence, delivered by field courier, onto Stalin's desk. Rather than purloined documents, almost all of it was hearsay. From

London, Ambassador Maisky, despite having been given British intelligence about German force concentrations (gleaned, unbeknownst to him, from Enigma code-breaking), wrote to Moscow (June 21) that he had told Cripps, "As before, I consider a German attack on the USSR unlikely."[19] But from Berlin, Ambassador Dekanozov—who also knew the view in the Kremlin and the consequences of contradicting it—was finally reporting, under the influence of the best spies in the Soviet network, that Germany's actions signaled an imminent invasion.[20] Stalin evidently concluded that his Berlin envoy had been fed disinformation by British agents and stated, "Dekanozov is not such a smart fellow to be able to see that."[21]

From Tokyo, Max Clausen (June 21) radioed yet another message from Sorge, this one composed the day before: "The German ambassador in Tokyo, Ott, told me a war between Germany and the USSR is inevitable."[22] The dispatch gave no start date. For Stalin, the question was not whether war with the Nazi regime was inescapable, but whether it was inescapable *this* year.[23] Scores and scores of invasion warnings had accumulated on his desk, but just about every reported date—including at least fourteen specific ones—had passed. These ranged from the earliest, such as "March 1941" (transmitted on December 29, 1940), "May 20," "April or May," "April 6," "April 20," or "May 15 to June 15," to the more recent: "either in May or after defeating Britain," "not today or tomorrow," "May 18," "May 25," "in late May," "summer 1941 before the harvest gathering," "at the beginning of June," "no later than June 15," "around June 15," "June 15," and "June 15–20." The only remaining possibilities were "June 22–25" (reported on June 16) and "June 21 or 22."[24] The invasion window would soon shut; Stalin was virtually home free for another year.

Never mind the secret intelligence: warnings were splashed across the front pages of the global press. But knowing how he himself used newspapers, Stalin took the screaming headlines to be planted provocations. He reasoned that Britain (and the United States) wanted nothing more than for the USSR and Nazi Germany to become embroiled in war—which was true—but as a result, he dismissed all warnings of a German attack. He knew that Germany was experiencing severe shortages—again true—so he reasoned that it needed even more supplies from him, and that a German invasion would be self-defeating because it would put those supplies at risk. He knew that Germany had lost the First World War because it had fought on two fronts—also true—and so he reasoned that the Germans understood that it would be suicidal for them to attack the USSR before defeating Britain in the west.[25] This logical reasoning had become Stalin's trap, enabling the Germans to spread a seemingly all-encompassing explanation for what they could not conceal: their colossal troop buildup. It was supposedly not for war but for extorting Soviet concessions.[26] When Stalin intemperately damned his intelligence as contaminated by disinformation, he was spot-on.[27] But the despot had no idea which parts were disinformation, and which might be accurate intelligence. He labeled as "disinformation" whatever he chose not to believe.

The Nazis' brilliant disinformation campaign generated reams of Soviet intelligence reports saying both that war was coming and that there would be blackmail—and if the latter was true, the former need not be. The fake ultimatum became for Stalin the ultimate truth, something that, given his lack of confidence in the Red Army's prospects against the Wehrmacht, he desperately needed to be true.

Blackmail certainly fit Hitler's profile. Early on, the British had dismissed the German buildup in the east and the accompanying rumors of a military show-down there as "wishful thinking." Then they latched on to the Hitler-ultimatum theory, which many British officials did not relinquish even after decrypted Enigma intercepts exposed real-time German war orders. While Göring told his high-placed, notoriously indiscreet British contacts that he had personally drawn up a list of demands to be presented to the Soviets so that Germany could continue the fight against Britain, Goebbels's men launched rumors that the Führer would soon demand a ninety-nine-year lease on Ukraine.[28] Stalin found himself in the reverse of the role in which he had placed Finland in 1939. The crucial difference was that, whereas he had issued his demands to the Finns and sought to negotiate, he was still waiting upon Hitler's, and Hitler had no intention to negotiate. In the meantime, Germany had attained the buildup necessary for an invasion.

Colonel Georgy Zakharov, a decorated fighter pilot, had been ordered to conduct a full daylight reconnaissance of the border region on the German side, and he reported that the Wehrmacht was poised to invade.[29] The NKGB had discovered that German saboteurs brazenly crossing into the USSR had been instructed that "in the event German troops cross the frontier before they return to Germany, they must report to any German troop unit located on Soviet territory."[30] Soviet counterintelligence noted vigorous German recruitment of disaffected Belorussians, Balts, and Ukrainians, who were forming underground groups and engaging in terrorism long after Stalin's supposed annihilation of the fifth column in the terror. Overburdened Soviet rail lines that were needed to transport troops westward were swamped with tens of thousands of "anti-Soviet elements" being deported eastward from the annexed territories.[31] On June 21,

Merkulov issued an order to Ukraine for a new wave of preemptive arrests to interdict sabotage: "Immediately telegraph by what deadline the indicated operation could be readied by you, and provide an overall orientation about the number of people who could be removed, with a breakdown by categories."[32]

Stalin paced and paced. Actually, it was more like a waddle as he swung his hips around awkwardly, the result of that childhood collision with a horse-drawn carriage. He wore, as ever, his signature baggy breeches, which he tucked into his well-worn black leather boots, as well as matching khaki tunic, buttoned at the top, simple and functional, and different from the bourgeois suits favored by Lenin. The despot's clothes were martial in look without being an actual military uniform, a style first popularized in Russia by Alexander Kerensky as well as, yes, Trotsky. His former nemesis had survived *sixteen years* beyond Lenin's death—an eternity, burning its way into the Little Corner with his acid pen. But what had Trotsky marshaled—a few thousand dispersed followers?—before Stalin's assassins managed to drive that ice pick through his skull in the run-down Mexican villa?[33] German tanks, warplanes, and pontoon bridges had been advanced into the barbed-wire-protected inner zone of the border, and the barbed wire itself was being removed. The click and whir of German motors resounded across to the Soviet side.

At the centerpiece of the Little Corner, the felt-covered conference table, the despot had held countless sessions devoted to war preparations. "Stalin had an enormous capacity for work," observed Molotov, who, despite his demotion from head of government, had kept his reserved seat at the table. "If the subject was cannons—then cannons; if tanks—then tanks."[34] He had forced into being upward of 9,000 new industrial enterprises during the three Five-Year Plans, and Soviet military production grew even faster than GDP for a decade.[35] He had overseen the formation of 125 new divisions just since 1939, and the Red Army now stood at 5.37 million troops, the largest in the world.[36] It had 25,000 tanks and 18,000 fighter planes, three to four times Germany's stocks. Stalin knew that Germany was underestimating this massive force out of prejudice as well as ignorance, so he had arranged German visits to Soviet aviation and tank factories, and even allowed Göring's planes nearly unimpeded reconnaissance of Soviet troop concentrations, airfields, naval bases, and fuel and ammunition depots.[37] Stalin also had his spies spread rumors that, if attacked, Soviet aircraft would assault Berlin with chemical and biological agents. In Hitler's shoes, Stalin would have been deterred.

Of course, if your own country really was so well armed, why not *let* the foolish enemy underestimate you? Because the Winter War with Finland had exposed Soviet military weaknesses not just to Hitler, but also to Stalin.[38] The Red Army was still in the middle of its gigantic, protracted, contradictory post-Finland rearmament and reorganization.

Stalin's early commitment to mass armament production, amid rapid technological change, meant that more than 10,000 Soviet tanks (T-26s and BT-7s) were now too light, while the more advanced, heavier T-34 (45-millimeter-thick armor) and KV (75-millimeter armor) numbered only around 1,800 units. Similarly, the most advanced warplanes (Yak-1, MiG-3, Pe-2) made up just one quarter of the air force.[39] Stalin's war preparations also bore the mark of his executions of thousands of loyal officers, especially top commanders like Vasily Blyukher, whose eye had been deposited in his hand before he died under torture, and the gifted Mikhail Tukhachevsky, whose blood had been splattered all over his "confession" to being a German agent just before Stalin signed the Pact.[40] Now, 85 percent of the officer corps was thirty-five or under, while those older than forty-five constituted around 1 percent. Fully 620 generals were under forty-five, 393 under fifty-five, and only 63 older than fifty-five. Many had been majors a short time earlier. The Red Army had one officer for every nine soldiers, versus one for every nineteen in Japan and one for twenty-nine in Germany, but Soviet officer ranks were swelled by those in the army's political apparatus. Of the 659,000 Soviet officers, only around half had completed a military school, while one in four had the bare minimum (a few courses), and one in eight had no military education whatsoever.[41]

Lately, the despot's morose side had gotten the upper hand. "Stalin was unnerved and irritated by persistent reports (oral and written) about the deterioration of relations with Germany," Admiral Kuznetsov would recall.[42] Stalin's face gave away stress—even fear—to the point that he sometimes failed to fill his pipe with the Herzegovina Flor cigarette tobacco that had stained his teeth and mustache yellow. "He felt that danger was imminent," recalled Khrushchev, the party boss of Ukraine, who was in Moscow until June 20. "Would our country be able to deal with it? Would our army deal with it?"[43]

SINCE MAY 1941, nighttime use of electric lighting in the Kremlin had been forbidden. But June 21 was the summer solstice, the longest day of the year. At around 5:00 p.m., Stalin ordered Alexander Shcherbakov, party boss of Moscow province and city, and Vasily Pronin, chairman of the Moscow soviet executive committee, to keep all ward party secretaries at their posts.[44] At 6:27 p.m.,

Molotov entered the Little Corner, the first visitor, as usual. At 7:05, in walked Voroshilov, Beria, Voznesensky, Malenkov, Timoshenko, Admiral Kuznetsov, and Grigory Safonov, the young deputy procurator general, who was responsible for the military courts on railroads and in the fleets. The discussion apparently revolved around recent developments pointing toward war, versus Stalin's dread of provocations that might incite it.[45] Germany had achieved the buildup necessary to attack. Filipp Golikov, of Soviet military intelligence, estimated Germany's concentration of forces against the USSR at only 120 to 122 of around 285 total divisions, versus 122 to 126 against Britain (the other 44 to 48 were said to be reserves).[46] In fact, there were around 200 divisions arrayed against the USSR, including 154 German ones—a total of at least 3 million Wehrmacht soldiers and half a million troops from its Axis partners, as well as 3,600 tanks, 2,700 aircraft, and 700,000 field guns and other artillery, 600,000 motor vehicles, and 650,000 horses. The Soviets had massed around 170 divisions, perhaps 2.7 million men in the west, along with 10,400 tanks and 9,500 aircraft.[47] The two largest armies in world history stood cheek by jowl on a border some 2,000 miles long.

Such immense Soviet troop concentrations testify to both Stalin's understanding that Germany represented a monumental danger and his misunderstanding of blitzkrieg. But only one of the two vast armies on the frontier had occupied its firing positions.[48] Stalin had allowed covert strategic redeployments westward and lately had finally yielded to Timoshenko and Zhukov's insistence that the Red Army commence camouflaging of aerodromes, tank parks, warehouses, and military installations (which in many cases would require repainting).[49] But he would not permit assumption of combat positions, which he feared would only play into the hands of German militarist-adventurers, who craved war and schemed to force Hitler's hand, the way they had pushed the Wehrmacht beyond the agreed-upon German-Soviet line in Poland in 1939. Soviet planes were forbidden from flying within six miles of the border. Timoshenko and Zhukov, subject to the despot's admonitions and the watchful eye of Beria and his minions, made sure that frontline commanders did not cause or yield to "provocation."[50] Beria also tasked the assassin Sudoplatov with organizing "an experienced strike force to counter any frontier incident that might be used as an excuse to start a war."[51]

Soviet intelligence was reporting that not just Germany but also Romania, Hungary, Slovakia, and Finland were at full war readiness.[52] But Stalin, having long ago ceded the initiative, was effectively paralyzed. Just about anything he did could be used by Hitler to justify an invasion. On June 20, the head of the Soviet Union's Riga port had telephoned Mikoyan to report that all 25 German ships docked there were preparing to leave en masse on June 21, without having finished loading or unloading, and had asked whether to detain them. When Mikoyan hastened over to the Little Corner with the news, Stalin had ordered him to let the German vessels go, because if the Soviets detained them, Hitler could regard that as a justification for war.[53] While all German vessels departed safely on June 21, a Soviet freighter, the *Magnitogorsk,* hastily sent a panicked radiogram, not even using ciphers, informing the Baltic Commercial Fleet in Leningrad that it was being prevented from departing the German port of Danzig, without explanation. More than forty Soviet merchant ships were immobilized at German ports.[54]

At 7:00 p.m., Gerhard Kegel ("X"), the Soviet spy in the German embassy, had slipped out for the second time that day to tell his Soviet handler, Leontyev ("Petrov"), that German personnel living outside the facility had been ordered to relocate into it immediately, and that "all think that this very night there will be war."[55] At 8:00 p.m., Golikov had a courier dispatched to Stalin, Molotov, and Timoshenko, with this new piece of intelligence in sealed envelopes.[56] In the Little Corner, Timoshenko, Kuznetsov, Safonov, and Voznesensky were dismissed at 8:15. Malenkov was dismissed five minutes later. Nothing significant was decided.[57]

Zhukov phoned in to report that yet another German soldier had defected across the frontier, warning of an invasion within a few hours.[58] This was precisely the kind of "provocation" Stalin feared. He ordered Zhukov to the Kremlin, along with the just-departed Timoshenko. They entered Stalin's office at 8:50, accompanied by the old Stalin crony Marshal Budyonny, a deputy defense commissar.[59] Whereas the two pince-nez minions Molotov and Beria provided an echo chamber for Stalin's denials that Hitler was going to attack, the two peasant commanders could see that Germany was coiled to invade.[60] Still, when Stalin insisted otherwise, they presumed that he possessed superior information and insight. In any case, they knew the costs of losing his trust. "Everyone had in their memory the events of recent years," Zhukov would recall. "And to say out loud that Stalin was wrong, that he is mistaken, to say it plainly, could have meant that without leaving the building, you would be taken to have coffee with Beria."[61]

Nonetheless, the pair evidently used the latest defector to urge a general mobilization—tantamount, in Stalin's mind, to war. "Didn't German generals send that defector across the border in order to provoke a conflict?" Stalin asked. "No," answered Timoshenko. "We think the defector is telling the truth." Stalin: "What do we do now?" Timoshenko allowed the silence to persist. Finally, the defense commissar suggested, "Put the troops on the western border on high alert." He and Zhukov had come prepared with a draft directive.[62]

Where was the ultimatum? Stalin had continued to try to engage Hitler after the TASS bulletin gambit fell flat. "Molotov has asked for permission to visit Berlin, but has been fobbed off," Goebbels wrote in his diary (June 18). "A naïve request."[63] Dekanozov had appeared at the German foreign ministry that same day without an appointment, mentioning nothing of a Molotov visit but inducing terror all the same.[64] "The main political worry here is not to afford Stalin the opportunity for some kind of generous gesture to upend all our cards at the last minute," state secretary Weizsäcker, Ribbentrop's deputy, had written in his diary, but then he noted that the inept Soviet envoy had "merely brought up a few current matters of lesser importance." Weizsäcker had cleverly laid out a map of the Near East, as if Germany's attention was on British positions. "The ambassador took leave of me without anything whatever having been said about German-Soviet relations."[65] On the morning of June 21, Molotov had sent a telegram instructing Dekanozov to hand-deliver an attached diplomatic protest of German border violations to Ribbentrop, and to use it to elicit clarifications.[66] "Several times that day Moscow telephoned, pressing us to carry out our instructions," an embassy duty officer recalled. But Ribbentrop had deliberately vanished from the capital and sent instructions to inform Dekanozov that he would be contacted as soon as the Nazi foreign minister returned, whenever that might be. The Soviet duty officer, remaining behind after other employees had departed at around 7:00 p.m., kept calling the German foreign ministry every thirty minutes.

INSTEAD OF WAITING to see Hitler's ultimatum, Stalin could have peremptorily declared his response to it. This was the last option he had left, and a potentially powerful one. Hitler feared that the wily Soviet despot would somehow seize the initiative and unilaterally, publicly declare dramatic, far-reaching concessions. Stalin appears to have discussed possible Soviet concessions with Molotov, but if he did, no record survives. Evidently he expected Germany to demand Ukraine, the Caucasus oil fields, and unimpeded transit for the Wehrmacht through Soviet territory to engage the British in the Near East and India. In June, *In the Steppes of Ukraine*, the procollectivization farce by the Stalin Prize winner Oleksandr Korniychuk, opened in Moscow, as if to signal that those steppes would not be handed over.[67] The despot used Prague in the Greater Reich and other points to disseminate his own disinformation, which made its way to Berlin, about a supposed split in Soviet ruling circles—Stalin for concessions, military brass for war—and how even if Germany did not attack but proceeded to demand Ukraine, Stalin would be overthrown in a putsch by a "Russian patriotic-imperialist movement" eager to fight, forcing Germany into a two-front war.[68]

Stalin's disinformation campaign, too, was captive to German disinformation. Unlike Germany's, it was not based upon genuine insight into his adversary's thinking.

A cunning despot could have publicly declared his willingness to join the hostilities against Britain, exacting revenge against the great power he most reviled and, crucially, robbing Hitler of his argument that Britain was holding out in anticipation of eventual Soviet assistance. Instead, or in parallel to that, Stalin could have demonstrably begun the withdrawal of Soviet forces back from the entire frontier, which would have struck at the heart of the Nazi leader's public war rationale: a supposed "preventive attack" against the "Soviet buildup."[69]

Instead of acting cunningly, Stalin fooled himself. He clung to the belief that Germany could not attack before defeating the UK, even though Britain did not have an army on the continent and was neither defending territory there nor in a position to invade from there.[70] He assumed that when Hitler finally issued the ultimatum, he could buy time by negotiating: possibly giving in, if the demands were tolerable, thereby averting war, or, more likely, dragging out any talks beyond the date when Hitler could have launched an invasion, gaining one more critical year. Failing that, Stalin further assumed that even if hostilities broke out, the Germans would need at least two more weeks to fully mobilize their main invasion force, allowing him time to mobilize, too. When his spies out of Berlin and elsewhere reported that the Wehrmacht had "completed all war preparations," he did not grasp that this meant that day one would bring full main-force engagement.

WORD FROM THE SOVIET embassy in Berlin was that Ribbentrop was still "out of town." In the Little Corner, while the relatively heated discussion with Timoshenko and Zhukov continued, Molotov stepped out. Stalin had had him summon Schulenburg to the Imperial Senate for 9:30 p.m.[71] The German ambassador arrived promptly, direct from overseeing secret document bonfires at the embassy, on nearby Leontyev Lane. The count had been deeply disappointed that the Hitler-Stalin Pact, in which he had played an important role, had turned out to be an instrument not for a Munich-style territorial deal over Poland to avoid war, but for the onset of the Second World War.[72] Now he feared the much-rumored German-Soviet clash, and he had gone to Berlin to see Hitler himself and come back empty-handed. In desperation, he had recently sent his embassy counselor, Gebhardt von Walther, to Berlin to try one last time to elucidate the suspected war plans and obtain instructions, but this had failed as well.[73] Molotov demanded to know why Germany was evacuating personnel, thereby fanning rumors of war. Why had Germany not responded to the TASS bulletin?

Molotov handed the count the protest detailing systematic German violations of Soviet airspace that had been intended for Ribbentrop, and plaintively told him that "the Soviet government is unable to understand the cause of Germany's dissatisfaction in relation to the USSR, if such dissatisfaction exists." He complained that "there was no reason for the German government to be dissatisfied with Russia." Schulenburg responded that "posing those issues was justified," but he shrugged that "he was not able to answer them, because Berlin utterly refrains from informing him." Molotov had gone toe to toe with Hitler in the gargantuan Nazi Chancellery, inducing the Führer's interpreter to observe, "No foreign visitor had ever spoken to [Hitler] in this way in my presence."[74] But now the foreign affairs commissar could merely express, several times, "his regrets that [Hitler's envoy] was unable to answer the questions raised."[75]

Molotov shuffled back to Stalin's Little Corner, a two- or three-minute walk, descending one floor.[76] Voroshilov, Timoshenko, Zhukov, and Budyonny were still there; Mekhlis arrived. Suddenly, around 10:00 p.m., amid the still suffocating heat, the winds gushed, billowing the curtains at open windows and blowing summer dust on the streets. Then came the thunderclaps. Moscow was struck by a torrential downpour.[77]

Finally, Stalin yielded to his insistent soldiers. Timoshenko and Zhukov rushed out of the Little Corner at 10:20 p.m., armed, at long last, with full-scale war mobilization, Directive No. 1. "A surprise attack by the Germans is possible during 22–23 June 1941," it stated. "The task of our forces is to refrain from any kind of provocative action that might result in serious complications." It ordered that "during the night of June [21–] 22, 1941, the firing positions of the fortified regions on the state border are to be secretly occupied," that "before dawn on June 22, 1941, all aircraft stationed in the field aerodromes are to be dispersed and carefully camouflaged," that "all units are to be put in a state of military preparedness," and that "no further measures are to be carried out without specific instructions." It carried the signatures of Timoshenko and Zhukov. The military men had managed to delete an insertion by the despot that if the Germans attacked, Soviet commanders were to attempt to meet them, to settle any conflict. Still, in Stalin's redaction, the high alert ordered the military to prepare for war but to avoid it.[78]

Molotov, Voroshilov, and Beria remained in Stalin's office, departing at 11:00 p.m.[79] Whether they went together to the Near Dacha for supper, as usual, remains unclear. At some point, Stalin was left alone, and he retired. Timoshenko and Zhukov, meanwhile, had been chauffeured the short distance to the defense commissariat, on the Moscow River embankment. At around 11:00 p.m., Timoshenko summoned Admiral Kuznetsov from the naval commissariat, next door, to hear "very important information." Kuznetsov arrived to find Timoshenko dictating while pacing, and Zhukov at a desk writing, his tunic unbuttoned. They related that they had been to the Kremlin a second time that night and obtained Stalin's permission to raise Soviet armed forces to "readiness No. 1." Timoshenko ordered Kuznetsov's deputy, another admiral, to run back to naval HQ to radiogram the order to the fleet commands.[80]

In Berlin, Ribbentrop's deputy, Weizsäcker, finally agreed to receive Dekanozov. It was 9:30 p.m. in Berlin, 11:30 in Moscow. But this time, too, the Soviet envoy had brought no concrete proposals in the form of last-minute concessions. Dekanozov handed the baron the protest of the border violations that Schulenburg had already received from Molotov. "When Herr Dekanozov tried to prolong the conversation somewhat, I told him that since I had an entirely different opinion from his and had to await the opinion of my government, it would be better not to go into the matter just now," Germany's state secretary noted of the exchange, which he terminated with the comment that "the reply will be forthcoming later."[81]

IT BEING SATURDAY NIGHT, Soviet commanders up and down the frontier were hosting ensemble performances (with the exception of the Baltic military district, where the commander ignored admonitions to adopt a stance of nonchalance).[82] In Minsk, 150 miles east of the border, the Officers' Club put on *The Wedding at Malinovka,* a comic Soviet operetta about a village in the Ukrainian steppes during the civil war. The venue was packed. Attendees included the commander of the critical Western military district, Pavlov, his chief of staff, and his deputies. Six German aircraft had crossed the frontier in Pavlov's region on a recent night. "Never mind. More self-control. I know, it has already been reported! More self-control!" Pavlov was overheard saying on the phone about the reports. As soon as Pavlov put the receiver down and prepared to greet a visitor, the apparatus rang again. "I know; it has been reported," Pavlov was heard to say. "I know. Those at the top know better than us. That's all." He slammed down the phone.[83] During the operetta, Pavlov was interrupted in his box by a new report of unusual activity: the Germans had removed the barbed wire from their side of the border, and the sound of motors had grown louder, even at a distance. As he already knew but could do nothing about, an uninterrupted flow of German mechanized columns was moving forward in East Prussia along the Suwałki protrusion. Pavlov remained at the show.

Around midnight, Mikhail Kirponos, commander of the Kiev military district, called the defense commissariat on the high-frequency phone from his field HQ at Ternopol to report that another German had forded a river and crossed the border near Sokal (Ukraine) and said that Wehrmacht soldiers had taken up their firing positions, with tanks at their start lines. Zhukov called the Near Dacha to inform Stalin.[84] A little after midnight, a train carrying Soviet oil, manganese, and grain crossed the frontier into Greater Germany, its passage observed by waiting German divisions.[85] At around 1:00 a.m., Timoshenko called Pavlov on the high-frequency phone, evidently with word of Directive No. 1 to assume full combat readiness, and a caution not to succumb to provocation.[86]

Some twelve hours earlier, precisely at 13:00 hours, Germany's high command had transmitted the password for war, "Dortmund." That afternoon, Hitler had received Admiral Raeder, Generals Keitel and Jodl, and Albert Speer, then, having already written a few days before to Romania's Antonescu, who was responsible for Germany's critical southern flank in the invasion, he composed explanatory letters for Italy's Mussolini, Finland's Ryti, and Hungary's Horthy.[87] Hitler's adjutant, Nicolaus von Below, noticed that he was "increasingly nervous and restless. The Führer talked a lot, walked up and down; he seemed impatient, waiting for something." In his residence in the Old Reich Chancellery, Hitler did not sleep for the second straight night. He took a meal in the dining room. He listened to *Les Préludes,* the symphonic poem by Franz Liszt. He phoned to summon Goebbels, who had just finished rewatching *Gone with the Wind.* The two walked up and down Hitler's drawing room for quite a while, finalizing the timing and content of the Führer's war proclamation for the next day, about the "salvation of Europe" and the intolerable danger of waiting any longer. Goebbels left at 2:30 a.m., returning to the propaganda ministry, where staff had been told to await him. "Everyone was absolutely astonished," he wrote, "even though most had guessed half of what was going on, and some all of it."[88]

Timoshenko's ciphered radiograms of Directive No. 1 to military districts about advancing to full combat readiness while still avoiding provocations began to go out in the early hours of June 22. Most intended recipients in frontline positions failed to get word. One of Pavlov's subordinates, Major General A. A. Korobkov, of the Fourth Army, who that evening had watched a performance of Johann Strauss II's operetta *The Gypsy Baron* at Korbin, site of his field HQ, was left in the dark: his power and communications lines had been cut. Wehrmacht advance units, many in Red Army uniforms, had already crossed the border and sabotaged Soviet communications.[89] "The beginning of every war is like opening the door into a dark room," Hitler had told one of his private secretaries. "One never knows what is hidden in the darkness."[90]

STALIN'S REGIME HAD REPRODUCED a deep-set pattern in Russian history—a country that considered itself a providential power with a special mission in the world, but that substantially lagged the other great powers to the west, a circumstance that time and again induced Russian rulers to turn to the state for a forced modernization to overcome or at least manage the power asymmetry. This urgent quest for a strong state had culminated, once more, in personal rule. Under Stalin's regime, both the apocalyptic bloodshed and the state's capacity to summon resources and popular involvement intensified, a consequence of the violent mass era that slightly predated but was blown open by the First World War, the heady promises of Marxism-Leninism, and Stalin's personal qualities. His despotic power derived not just from his control over the formidable levers of Leninist dictatorship, which he built, but from the ideology, which he shaped. His regime proved able to define the terms of public thought and individual identity, and he proved able to personify passions and dreams, to realize and represent a socialist modernity and Soviet might. With single-sentence telegrams or brief phone calls, he could spur the clunky Soviet party-state machinery into action, invoking discipline and intimidation, to be sure, but also emotionally galvanizing young functionaries who felt close personal ties to him, and millions more who would never come close to meeting him in person. Stalin was a student of historical forces, and of people, and his rule enabled those who came from nothing to feel world historically significant.

Stalin's regime was not merely a statist modernization, but a purported transcendence of private property and markets, of class antagonisms and existential alienation, a renewal of the social whole rent by the bourgeoisie, a quest for social justice on a global scale. In worldview and practice it was a conspiracy that perceived conspiracy everywhere and in everything, gaslighting itself. In administration it constituted a crusade for planning and control that generated a proliferation of improvised illegalities, a drive for order, and a system in which propaganda and myths about the "system" were the most systematized part. Amid the cultivated opacity and patent falsehoods, even most high officials were reduced to Kremlinology (rumors, parsing of "signals"). The fanatical hypercentralization was often self-defeating as well, but the cult of the party's and especially Stalin's infallibility proved to be the most dangerous flaw of his fallible rule. The superhuman resolve that he had demonstrated in launching and carrying through collectivization was, it turned out, accompanied by a surprising brittleness, which was exposed in his reaction to the criticism that the violent upheaval and famine sparked. Stalin became haunted not by the peasants' horrors under collectivization but by the party criticism of him regarding those horrors, which would become the dark spur of his mass murders in the wanton terror, made possible by Bolshevism but driven by him. The pandemonium of widespread accusations of treason that he fomented reflected not reality or even potential threats, but his own demons. The flip side—his fantasies of a cleansing cadre renewal via promotion of new people—did little to quell his anxieties, partly because of their glaring difficulty assimilating the *Short Course* he produced expressly for them.

By inclination, Stalin was a Russian nationalist in the imperial sense, and anti-Western, the core impulse of long-standing Russian-Eurasian political culture. Initially, the ambitious Soviet version of the quest to match the West in order to preserve Russia's anti-Western identity had increased the country's dependency on the superior West. But after wholesale technology transfer, Stalin's regime went on, at high cost and low efficiency, to develop sophisticated military and related industry to a degree unprecedented for even a military-first country. Geopolitically, however, whereas tsarist Russia had concluded foreign alliances for its security, the Soviet Union sought or could manage only nonaggression pacts. The country's self-isolation became ever more extreme. One flanking power, Japan, had spurred Stalin's no-holds-barred militarization, and after years of timid responses, he had finally decided to rebuff the challenge of this island power by flaunting the USSR's better-armed and better-commanded land forces in a border war. The other flanking power, Germany, presented an incalculably greater challenge, given the geography, Germany's military strength on land, and the special qualities of its ruler. Stalin insisted on calling fascism "reactionary," a supposed way for the bourgeoisie to preserve the old world.[91] But Hitler turned out to be someone neither Marx nor Lenin had prepared Stalin for.

A lifelong Germanophile, Stalin appears to have been mesmerized by the might and daring of Germany's parallel totalitarian regime. For a time, he recovered his personal and political equilibrium in his miraculous Pact with Hitler, which deflected the German war machine, delivered a bounty of German machine tools, enabled the reconquest and Sovietization of tsarist borderlands, and reinserted the USSR into the role of arbitrating world affairs. Hitler had whetted and, reluctantly, abetted Stalin's own appetites. But far earlier than the despot imagined, his ability to extract profit from the immense danger posed by Hitler to Europe and beyond had run its course. This generated unbearable tension in Stalin's life and rule, yet he stubbornly refused to come to grips with the new realities, and not solely out of greed for German technology. Despite his insight into the human psyche, and demonic shrewdness, Stalin was blinkered by ideology and idées fixes. Churchill controlled not a single division on the Soviet frontier, yet Stalin remained absolutely obsessed with British imperialism, railing against the Versailles order long after Hitler had shredded it. He also obsessed over supposed secret British negotiations behind his back with Hitler.[92]

For Hitler, the 1939 Pact with the USSR was nothing more than what the 1918 Brest-Litovsk Treaty with Germany had been for Lenin: a distasteful necessity, which, with luck, would not endure very long. Lenin's luck had been delivered by imperial Germany's idiotic precipitation of American entry into the First World War; Hitler's came from his own audacity and the mistakes of his slow-to-react, divided foreign adversaries. The alliance system had not caused the First World War, but the absence of alliances helped cause the Second. A debate continues over the possibility of a genuine Western-Soviet military alliance to deter and, if necessary, defeat Germany in the 1930s, including the logistical difficulties for any combined military action posed by recalcitrant Poland and Romania. But logistics can always be managed when the will is there. Sir Stafford Cripps, the maladroit, well-intentioned British ambassador, grasped that German-Soviet relations were precarious, but he could bring neither his own government nor the Soviet Union anywhere near a British-Soviet rapprochement. Given the profundity of mutual distrust between London and Moscow, only an unequivocal perception by both of the urgency of state survival could have made a bilateral alliance possible, and even then, only for a time. Of course, survival was precisely what was at stake.

Hitler's racial, Social Darwinist, zero-sum understanding of geopolitics meant that both the USSR and Great Britain would have to be annihilated in order for Germany to realize its master race destiny. To be sure, in the immediate term, he thought in terms of domination of the European continent (*Grossmacht*), which required *Lebensraum* in the east. But in the longer term, he foresaw domination of the world (*Weltmacht*), which would require a blue-water fleet, bases rimming the Atlantic, and a colonial empire in the tropics for raw materials. That was incompatible with the continued existence of the British empire, at least in its present form. Hitler thus put himself in front of a stark choice of either agreeing to deepen the Pact with Stalin, to take on Britain now, which meant conceding at least a partial Soviet sphere in the Balkans and on the Black Sea—on top of the Soviet sphere in the Baltics—or, alternately, freeing himself from the infuriating dependency on Moscow to take on Britain later. In the end, military circumstances helped determine the sequencing: Hitler did not possess the air or naval capabilities or the depth of resources to prevail militarily over island Britain; he did command the land-based wherewithal to attempt to smash the USSR.

A commitment to a prolonged contest for supremacy with Britain, which Hitler expected to be aided more and more by the vast resources of the United States, made quick annihilation of the Soviet Union an absolutely necessary prelude.[93] Moreover, even though Hitler and the German high command knew the Soviet Union was not poised to attack, the invasion amounted to a preventive war all the same in his logic, for the Soviet Union was only getting stronger, and might itself attack at a time it deemed more advantageous. And so, while pushing Japan to attack British positions in East Asia, he had offered the British government a version of the pact he had concluded with Stalin, in order to violate the latter, and he seemed dumbfounded that the British government did not accept.[94] The Nazi leader had grasped his foe's imperial mind-set, and he was sincere when promising that, in exchange for a free hand on the continent, he would keep Britain's empire intact for now (its destruction, in any case, would redound to others besides Germany in the short term). He continued to hold out hope that Britain, patently weak militarily on land and therefore unable to defeat him, would see "reason." But Hitler had failed to grasp Britain's long-standing preference for a balance of power on the continent.[95] He did, however, perceive far more common interest between London and Moscow than either of them saw themselves.

During the all-out preparations for blitzkrieg against the USSR, Hitler continued to order that resources be devoted to preparing for a long naval and air war against the UK and the United States. May–June 1941 was the blackest period yet for Britain: its ships were being sunk and its cities bombed, while its position in the Balkans had been lost to Nazi domination. After German paratroopers had captured Crete, in late May 1941, the British position seemed grievously imperiled. Eleven days before the scheduled launch of the Soviet invasion, Hitler had dictated a draft of Directive No. 32, "Preparations for the Time After Barbarossa." It envisioned subdivision and exploitation of Soviet territories, as well as a pincer movement against the Suez Canal and British Near East positions via Bulgaria-Turkey, the Caucasus, and Iran-Iraq-Syria; the conquest of Gibraltar, northwest Africa, and the Spanish and Portuguese Atlantic islands, to eliminate the British in the Mediterranean; the building of coastal bases in West and possibly East Africa; and the creation of a German base in Afghanistan for seizing British India.[96] Had Hitler thrown all his might into this "peripheral strategy" rather than invading the USSR, Britain might not have survived.[97] The war with the Soviet Union would have gone ahead at some point, but with Britain knocked out of the picture. There would have been no British beachhead to assist an eventual U.S.-led Allied landing in Western Europe.[98]

HITLER, ONE SCHOLAR HAS REMINDED US, cannot be explained in terms of his social origins or his early life and influences, a point that is no less applicable to Stalin.[99] The greatest shaper of Stalin's being was the building and running of a dictatorship, whereby he assumed responsibility for Russia's power in the world. In the name of socialism, Stalin, pacing in his Kremlin office, had grown accustomed to moving millions of peasants, workers—whole nations—across a sixth of the earth, on his own initiative, often consulting no one. But his world had become intensely constricted. Hitler had cornered the Soviet despot in his own Little Corner.

Stalin's dealings with Hitler differed from British appeasement in that he tried significant deterrence as well as accommodation, and he took as much as he gave. But Stalin's policy resembled British appeasement in that he was driven by a blinding desire to avoid war at all costs. He displayed strength of capabilities but not of will. Neither his fearsome resolve nor his supreme cunning—which had enabled him to vanquish his rivals and spiritually crush his inner circle—were in evidence in 1941. He shrank from trying to preempt Hitler militarily and failed to preempt him diplomatically.[100] In the end, however, the question of who most miscalculated is not a simple one. "Of all the men who can lay claim to having paved the way to the new Reich," meaning his Reich, Hitler liked to say, "one figure stands in awe-inspiring solitude: Bismarck."[101] Bismarck, of course, had built his chancellorship on avoiding conflict with Russia. When the bust of Bismarck was transferred from the old German Chancellery to Hitler's new Nazi Chancellery, it had broken off at the neck. A replica was hastily made, aged by soaking in cold tea. The omen of Bismarck's broken neck was kept from the Führer.[102]

SOVIET ADMINISTRATIVE STRUCTURE

Once private property was eliminated, in 1929–30, all institutions in the Soviet Union effectively became statized. At the same time, Communist party organizations expanded inside every institution. The result was an intensification of the party-state dualism, structurally akin to a theocracy, that had been born with the revolution and the civil war. The state, in turn, was variegated, such that one part essentially had no power but another had a great deal.

Party rule comprised periodic gatherings of delegates to a Party Congress (technically the highest body), a party conference (which possessed none of the powers of a congress), the Central Committee (the ruling body between congresses), the politburo (which usurped the Central Committee's policy-making function), the orgburo (which handled personnel decisions), and the secretariat (in which sat the secret department, Stalin's dictatorship within the dictatorship). The secretariat and the orgburo, along with their local equivalents, constituted the "apparatus," which had innumerable departments and whose functionaries were full-time party workers or apparatchiks. All party members, the vast majority of whom did not work in the apparatus, were duty bound to follow party dictates. To investigate party members, the regime had a Central Control Commission (with local affiliates), which until 1934 was joined with a state body known as the workers' and peasants' inspectorate.

Stalin was the general secretary of the Communist party from the inception of the office, in 1922, until 1934, when he became just a "secretary" (but continued to be listed first). He had held a state post (commissar of nationalities) before 1922 but would not hold another until spring 1941.

The weighty component of the state was the executive branch, or Council of People's Commissars, a cabinet-style government. The council's chairman was the equivalent of prime minister (Lenin, then Rykov, then Molotov, and finally Stalin). The various commissariats that made up the council multiplied over time, and included heavy industry, foreign affairs, land, grain collection, finance. The state planning commission worked in parallel with the economic commissariats. The army and eventually the navy (when separated in 1937) were commissariats, too. The commissariat of internal affairs, or NKVD—its infamous Russian acronym—encompassed the regular and the secret police. The latter had originated as the Cheka (secret policemen were often still called Chekists) and then became the OGPU (sometimes rendered as GPU); in 1941 it would split into NKVD and NKGB ("GB" signifying state security). Together, the economic and security commissariats conducted the day-to-day operational management, under the supervision of the party apparatus and Stalin's personal regime.

The lesser part of the state was, ironically, the one that gave the political-administrative structure its name: the Soviet. There were myriad local soviets and a countrywide body, which originally took the form of a periodic Congress of Soviets and in 1938 became a permanent sitting Supreme Soviet, whose members were "elected" in single-candidate elections. This part of the state might be considered the legislative branch, except that it did not have the powers of even a quasi parliament. It also contained its own executive arm between congresses: a central executive committee, which, under the Supreme Soviet, became a presidium. The Soviet's executive powers, in any case, were appropriated by the Council of People's Commissars. Still, the chairman of the central executive committee and then of the presidium was the head of state—Mikhail Kalinin. It was Kalinin, not Stalin, who handed out state medals (which were awarded by the executive arm of the nominal legislature) and who received foreign ambassadors when they presented their credentials. Technically, the Council of People's Commissars served the Soviet, but in reality it served the party. The state also had a judicial component, a procuracy, and courts, also subordinated to the party apparatus, affording a dictatorial rule by law (rather than rule of law).

Workers were enrolled in trade unions, which were part of the state and played a key role in their lives—not by defending their interests but by being the conduits for social welfare. Cultural figures, too, were organized into unions, beginning with writers; Stalin eventually introduced a committee for artistic affairs in the

Council of People's Commissars. Peasants belonged mostly to "collective farms," which were nominally member constituted and self-governing but run by the party-state. "State farms," formed where no villages had existed that could be collectivized, did not bother with even the pretense of being peasant collectives.

The state was constituted as a federation, established in 1922, the Union of Soviet Socialist Republics, whose composition changed over time. Some Union republics were themselves federations. Inside the Union republics, there were autonomous republics and autonomous provinces, also formed on an ethnoterritorial basis. All such units had national Communist parties (the Russian republic excepted), councils of people's commissars (Russia included), and congresses of soviets/supreme soviets, plus procuracies and courts (indeed, there was no USSR legal code, only republic ones). While the state was federal, the party was only nominally so. The council of people's commissars of the Ukrainian Soviet Socialist Republic, for example, had many prerogatives, but the Communist party of Ukraine had only the same standing vis-à-vis Moscow as the Communist party of a province in the Russian republic. The party's pyramidal quality undercut the state's federal nature.

Coordination of the Soviet leviathan, to the extent it took place, was driven by the party apparatus, the invocation of party discipline, and Stalin's personal rule. Stalin also directed the operations of the Communist International (Comintern) for Communist parties around the world, although nominally the body was governed by its infrequent congresses and, in between, by an executive committee (which also held occasional enlarged plenums that resembled minicongresses), and staffed by its own secretariat.

By design, the Soviet regime lacked a central clearinghouse for assembling and analyzing the voluminous espionage reports that its agents generated. The defense commissariat had a directorate for intelligence, known in Russian as the RU but here spelled out as "military intelligence," and the NKVD (and then the NKGB) had its own foreign intelligence directorate, while most foreign correspondents of TASS, the Soviet press agency, engaged in espionage, and the Comintern, too, ran a spy network. Only Stalin knew what was produced by all the parallel intelligence networks.

NOTES

Full citations can be found in the bibliography.

1. *Pravda*, Nov. 7, 1935: 2. This quote would be reprinted later: *Stalin: k shestidesiatiletiiu so dnia rozhdeniia* (Moscow: *Pravda*, 1940), 75.
2. Kumanev, *Riadom so Stalinym*, 387–9 (Yakov Chadayev).
3. RGASPI, f. 558, op. 4, d. 665, l. 361.
4. Murin, *Stalin v ob"iatiakh*, 158 (Svanidze diary: Nov. 4, 1934).
5. Sergeev and Glushik, *Besedy o Staline*, 47.
6. Svechin's conception entailed a war of attrition; Tukhachevsky, among others, would favor attack and preemption. Stone, "Misreading Svechin." About 5,000 of Stalin's books would be kept together (in the Marx-Engels-Lenin Institute). There would be all told 397 books, pamphlets, and articles with his markings, 72 of which are writings by Lenin, another 13 by Marx and Engels in Russian translation, while 25 are works he wrote.
7. Sergeev and Glushik, *Besedy o Staline*, 23–4.
8. Vaiskopf, *Pisatel' Stalin*, 17–22.
9. The drawing was by Valêrijs Mežlauks. Vatlin and Malashenko, *Istoriia VKP (b) v portretakh i karikaturakh ee vozhdei*, 110.
10. Khlevniuk et al., *Stenogrammy zasedanii politbiuro*, III: 551.
11. Sergeev and Glushik, *Besedy o Staline*, 48.
12. Kurliandskii, *Stalin, vlast', religiia*, 67–8.
13. In a 1931 interview with the German writer Emil Ludwig, Stalin would without irony denounce the seminary "fathers" for their "humiliating regime" and "Jesuitical methods" of "surveillance, espionage, penetration of one's soul." *Sochineniia*, XIII: 113–4. The picture of the seminary during Stalin's youth would become more severe in 1930s memoirs. RGASPI, f. 558, op. 4, d. 665, l. 184 (Nikolai Makhatadze, 1936).
14. Iremashvili, *Stalin und die Tragödie Georgiens*, 23. One Gori classmate would imagine in 1932 that Stalin had rejected God because he had decided to be a god himself.
15. Ilizarov, *Tainaia zhizn' Stalina*. In his copy of Lev Kamenev's biography of the iconic Russian writer Chernyshevsky (1933), Stalin underlined a passage about the discipline instilled by observance of religious rites. (Chernyshevsky had also studied in a seminary.) RGASPI, op. 3, d. 84, l. 11; Kamenev, *Chernyshevskii*.
16. Vaiskopf, *Pisatel' Stalin*, 163; Ilizarov, *Tainaia zhizn' Stalina*, 63, 66.
17. Segrè, *Italo Balbo*.
18. Elisabedashvili recalled that Stalin "was given this nickname [Geza] by Ambilarashvili, once a good friend of his, who died in 1911 and was buried in Gori. Apart from us no one knew this name, since otherwise he was called 'Koba.'" RGASPI, f. 558, op. 4, d. 665; the "Geza" reference was cut when these reminiscences were published in *Molodaya Gvardiia*, 1939, no. 12: 86–7.
19. Loginov, *Teni Stalina*, 116. Stalin had contracted smallpox at age seven.
20. Bliskovskii, *M. I. Ul'ianova*, 199–200.
21. Ostrovskii, *Kto stoial*, 191–2 (citing GIAG, f. 153, op. 1, d. 3432, l. 116); Ilizarov, *Taina zhizn' Stalina*, 102; D. Volkogonov, *Stalin*, I/i: 65.
22. Berezhkov, *At Stalin's Side*, 201; Kuznetsov, *Nakanune*, 232.
23. Schmitt, *Die Diktatur*. Lenin had given dictatorship a favorable cast ("bourgeois democracy or proletarian dictatorship!").
24. Maksimovskii, "Ideia diktatury u Ma-

kiavelli," 55–94. See also Rees, *Political Thought from Machiavelli to Stalin*, chapter 8. Maksimovsky had signed the 1923 Trotskyite "Platform of the 46," became a dean at the Agricultural Academy, and would be arrested on July 27, 1937. He is said to have died in internal exile in Nov. 1941.
25. What emerges from the childhood memoirs, such as they are, is evidence not of warmth but of will. Some evidence indicates that he ridiculed weaker classmates, none of which would be noteworthy except for his role as dictator. For example: "Arriving at the sound of a loud scream, I saw Lakerov, who in a state of intense agitation was screaming at Iremashvili and Jughashvili," the seminary deputy inspector recorded in his notebook in 1895. "It turned out that the latter two had been systematically laughing at Lakerov, mercilessly teasing him and ridiculing him, bringing him to distress. They engage in this often, according to the testimony of Lakerov." RGASPI, f. 558, op. 4, d. 13, l. 91.
26. Not long after the scrotum joke, Stalin had Bryukhanov sacked as finance commissar (Oct. 1930), scapegoating him, along with state bank head Pyatakov, for inflation. Kosheleva, *Pis'ma Stalina Molotovu*, 193–6. See also Kuromiya, *Stalin's Industrial Revolution*, 267.
27. The rest of the quote: "Great men are almost always bad men." Lord Acton, letter to Bishop Mandell Creighton, April 5, 1887, in Figgis and Laurence, *Historical Essays and Studies*, 504.
28. "We cannot give a characterization of socialism," Lenin had admitted (March 8, 1918) in reply to Bukharin's demand for a sketch of the future. "What socialism will be like when it reaches its completed form we do not know, we cannot say." *PSS*, XXXVI: 65–6 (8th Party Congress, March 8, 1918). See also Striedter, "Journeys through Utopia," at 36.
29. Already in 1926, Stalin stated, "It would be wrong to think that it is possible to build socialism in white gloves, without getting dirty." RGASPI, f. 558, op. 11, d. 1107, l. 15. See also Von Laue, "Stalin in Focus," and Marwick, "Problems and Consequences of Organizing Society for Total War," 1–22.
30. "Only . . . a revolutionary regime, because it accepts the permanent use of violence, seems capable of attaining perfection," Raymond Aron would write, adding that "violence itself attracts more than it repels." Aron, *Opium of the Intellectuals*, 65.
31. Kołakowski, "Communism as a Cultural Formation."
32. Kenez, *Birth of the Propaganda State*, 186.
33. Zhiromskaia, *Naselenie Rossii v XX veke*, 11–3, 15; Poliakov, *Sovetskaia strana posle okonchaniia grazhdanskoi voiny*, 237. At the first all-Union congress of "shock workers," more than 30 percent of the participants were below the age of twenty-two. *Pervyi vsesoiuznyi s"ezd udarnykh brigad*, 179.
34. Stalin had written to Mikhail Frunze about a document that labeled Trotsky "the Leader [*vozhd'*] of the Red Army," advising, "I think that it would be better if we spoke about a *vozhd* only in terms of the party." Kvashonkin, *Bol'shevistskoe rukovodstvo*, 298–9 (RGASPI, f. 558, op. 1, d. 5254, l. 1: Dec. 10, 1924).
35. Stalin, during a discussion of the coal

industry in 1931, criticized the effusive declarations "for the Leaders," "for the Central Committee," "for the general line" as "nonsense, playing games." Similarly, when delegates to an assembly of state farm bosses offered the customary applause, Stalin thundered, "why are you applauding—you should be ashamed." Davies and Harris, *Stalin's World*, 162–3 (citing RGASPI, f. 558, op. 11, d. 1115, l. 9; d. 1116, l. 34–42); RGASPI, f. 558, op. 11, d. 1116, l. 42 (Oct. 1932); RGASPI, f. 558, op. 11, d. 1118, l. 1–2 (June 1934). See also Davies, "Stalin and the Making of the Leader Cult in the 1930s," 29–46 (at 35). Tucker called Stalin the "master builder" of the cult, but this is too simple. Tucker, "The Rise of Stalin's Personality Cult." Photographs of Stalin in *Pravda* were not frequent into 1933, and usually showed him in the company of other party leaders.
36. Kovaleva et al., *Molotov, Malenkov, Kaganovich, 1957*, 490 (Voroshilov). The following dialogue was recorded on May 13, 1933, between Colonel Robins and Stalin:
   "ROBINS: I consider it a great honor to have an opportunity of paying you a visit.
   STALIN: There is nothing particular in that. You are exaggerating.
   ROBINS (laughs): What is most interesting to me is that throughout Russia I have found the names Lenin-Stalin, Lenin-Stalin, Lenin-Stalin, linked together.
   STALIN: That, too, is an exaggeration. How can I be compared to Lenin?" *Sochineniia*, XIII: 260–73 (at 260).
37. RGASPI, f. 558, op. 11, d. 1187, l. 49–50.
38. Mikoian, *Tak bylo*, 318; Chuev, *Molotov Remembers*, 181; van Ree, *Political Thought*, 161–8.
39. On Stalin's "immodest modesty," see Plamper, *Stalin Cult*, 123–4.
40. Chuev, *Molotov Remembers*, 166.
41. When asked, "To what tribe or clan do you belong?," many Central Asians were said not to understand the question. Zhdanko, "Natsional'no-gosudarstvennoye razmezhevaniye," 23.
42. Stalin publicly affirmed multiple times that ethnic identities would be a part of the Soviet phenomenon for a long time, perhaps disappearing only when a socialist economy encompassed the entire globe. He envisioned the formation of "socialist nations" (also called Soviet nations) free of class contradictions. See his March 1929 long letter on the national question, which would not be published until 1946: *Sochineniia*, XI: 336, 347–9. The basic thrust of the letter had appeared in his discussion with Ukrainian writers on Feb. 12, 1929. RGASPI, f. 558, op. 1, d. 4490. Pipes, *Formation*, 40; d'Encausse, *Great Challenge*, 38; Martin, *Affirmative Action Empire*, 238–48; van Ree, "Stalin and the National Question," at 230.
43. Stalin had never been among those Bolsheviks, such as Lenin, who warned of the dangers of Russian nationalism. What would turn out to be final party congress resolution calling for an end to Great Russian chauvinism would pass in 1930. *Pravda*, June 29, 1930, reprinted in *Sochineniia*, XII: 369.
44. In an incisive portrait published in 1927, Mark Landau, a popular émigré résident novelist known by his pen name of Aldanov, called Stalin "a standout person, inarguably, the most standout in the entire Leninist

guard. Stalin spills blood more freely than any living being, with the exception of Trotsky and Zinoviev. But I cannot deny him, in clear conscience, properties of rare strength of will and courage." He added: "I wait with 'captivating interest' what Stalin will do in this difficult exam in this difficult historical role." "Stalin," *Poslednie novosti*, Dec. 18 and 20, 1927, reprinted in Aldanov, *Sovremenniki*, 111–40 (at 118–9, 137), and in Aldanov, *Bol'shaia Lubianka*, 203–21 (at 207–8, 219–20).

CHAPTER 1. TRIUMPH OF THE WILL

1. "O tak nazyvaemom 'vsesoiuzom trotskistskom tsentre,'" 84.

2. Dubinskaia-Dzhalilova and Chernev, "'Zhmu vashu ruku, dorogoi tovarishch,'" 183 (APRF. F. 45, op. 1, d. 31, l. 10–101ob.).

3. Hindus, *Humanity Uprooted*, 166–7. Hindus, an émigré, had returned as a magazine writer to his native village (Bolshoye Bykovo) in Kherson province. His father had been a better-off peasant. Mugleston, "Hindus."

4. RGASPI, f. 558, op. 3, d. 211, s. 64. See also *Sochinenia*, X: 241. Originally published in 1895, the year of Engels's death, the essay in question had seemed to soften his earlier insistence on revolutionary class struggle, but this was partly the work of an editor. Engels, "The Tactics of Social Democracy"; Tucker, *Marx-Engels Reader*, xxxvi–xxxvii, 556–73. Marx, in a speech (Sept. 8, 1872) in Amsterdam, had allowed for a peaceful road to socialism in the United States and Britain. Tucker, *Marx-Engels Reader*, 522–4.

5. Kingston-Mann, *In Search of the True West.*

6. The Soviet regime was located on four squares and one embankment: Red Square with the triangular Kremlin, inside of which stood the triangular Catherine the Great imperial Senate, where the government or Council of People's Commissars had its main offices; Old Square, north of the Kremlin, where the central party apparatus had its offices in an old merchant emporium; Dzierżyński Square, where the secret police were located in an old insurance building and, not far away, sat the foreign affairs commissariat; Noggin Square (essentially an extension of Old Square), where the heavy industry commissariat stood; and the Frunze embankment, where the defense commissariat and general staff were housed.

7. Stalin's radicalism of 1929 followed peril from the failures of the Communist regime, whose inability to properly regulate the quasi-market of NEP had created a seeming imperative for even greater anti-market measures—which exacerbated the problems, requiring still greater emergency measures. Anticapitalism, the root cause of the problems, was imagined to be the solution. Carr accentuated the "haphazard and impulsive character of the final decision" in late 1929, but failed to elucidate the worldview and governing ideas behind the regime's improvisation. Carr, "Revolution from Above," 327. For an alternative development vision, see Antisferov et al., *Russian Agriculture*, 384. On the scholarly debate, see Harrison, "Why Was NEP Abandoned?"

8. Lenin had written: "Either we must bring the small bourgeoisie under *our* control (which can be done by organizing the poor), or they will overthrow . . . the workers' government just as inevitably and unavoidably as the Napoleons . . . , figures who are bound to develop in a soil permeated with petit-bourgeois mentality." *Sochineniia*, XXII: 515 (pre-1934). See also Valentinov, "Sut' bolshevizma v izobrazhenii Iu. Piatakova"; and Tucker, *Stalin as Revolutionary*, 415–6.

9. Volkogonov, *Stalin: politicheskii portret*, I: 307.

10. Tucker, *Stalin as Revolutionary*, 407–20.

11. Word of the Kamenev-Bukharin meeting had already appeared in the Menshevik *Sotsialisticheskii vestnik* [Berlin], Jan. 20, 1929. Three days later, the leaflet "The Party with Closed Eyes Is Leading the Way to a New Catastrophe" appeared; it was signed "Bolsheviks-Leninists" (the Trotskyite self-designation) and quoted Kamenev's "notes." Danilov and Khlevniuk, *Kak lomali NEP*, IV: 558–63 (RGASPI, f. 84, op. 2, d. 40, l. 2–11: Kamenev's "notes"), 564–5 (l. 12–3: Kamenev to Orjonikidze, Jan. 27), 566–7 (l. 14–5: Sokolnikov to Orjonikidze, Jan. 28), 568–71 (l. 17–24: Tomsky to Orjonikidze, Jan. 14), 572–6 (l. 25–31: Bukharin to Orjonikidze, Jan. 30), 607, 613–5. See also Vaganov, *Pravyi uklon*, 199–202; Tucker, *Stalin as Revolutionary*, 417; and Fel'shtinskii, *Razgovory s Bukharinym*, 30–7. A copy of the "notes" is in the Trotsky Papers at Harvard (T1897); it is presumed to have fallen into Trotsky's hands from F. P. Schwalbe, Kamenev's secretary. The Russian original, from leaflets, was published in *Sotsialistichekii vestnik* (May 4, 1929). Fel'shtinskii, "Dva epizoda iz istorii vnutripartiinoi bor'by."

12. Stalin, "Gruppa Bukharina i pravyi uklon v nashei partii," *Sochineniia*, XI: 318–25; Danilov and Khlevniuk, *Kak lomali NEP*, IV: 577–601. Stalin, ever magnanimous, proposed including Bukharin on the commission to prepare his apology; Bukharin declined, then agreed, but the commission met without him. Danilov and Khlevniuk, *Kak lomali NEP*, IV: 597. See also Daniels, *Conscience of the Revolution*, 352.

13. Danilov and Khlevniuk, *Kak lomali NEP*, 540–8 (resolutions of the joint session Feb. 9, 1929, approved at the April 23, 1929, plenum); *VKP (b) v rezoliutsiiakh* (1933), II: 515; *KPSS v rezoliutsiiakh* (7th ed.), II: 566–7. Bukharin had instigated at least two further meetings with Kamenev, one together with Pyatakov, and a second with Tomsky, and published a pointed reminder of Lenin's Testament in *Pravda* (Jan. 24, 1929). Jules Humbert-Droz, the Swiss Communist who met Bukharin in early 1929, later claimed that Bukharin mentioned getting rid of Stalin. Humbert-Droz, *Mémoirs*, 356, 379–80. "Bukharin," Carr and Davies wrote, "lacked altogether the astuteness and organizing skill of the politician." Carr and Davies, *Foundations of a Planned Economy*, II: 76.

14. Khaustov et al., *Lubianka: Stalin i VChK*, 180 (RGASPI, f. 17, op. 162, d. 7, l. 26: Jan. 10, 1929).

15. Cristian Rakovski, too, managed to carry trunks of official documents with him into internal exile. Fischer, *Men and Politics*, 129.

16. After the *Ilich* had docked at Istanbul, Trotsky was handed $1,500, and put up temporarily in two rooms inside the consulate. Stalin, Trotsky concluded, "was created by the epoch, by the bureaucracy, by the revolution's fall from grace, in order to effect and embody that fall, that degeneration." Trotsky attributed his own defeat to a conspiracy against him. Trotskii, "Kak moglo eto sluchit'sia?" in *Chto i kak proizoshlo*, 25–36.

17. Trotskii, *Dnevnik i pis'ma*, 48–9. On the politeness of the consul staff toward Trotsky, see Serge and Sedova, *Life and Death of Trotsky*, 163.

18. Eastman, *Great Companions*, 117; Deutscher, *Prophet Outcast*, 14 (citing *Manchester Guardian*, March 17, 1931), 16–8. In Jan. 1929, Herbert von Dirksen, the new German ambassador, when asked whether his government could take in Trotsky, was incredulous: Stresemann had no desire to have him explaining to a fellow German politician: "I don't place too high a value on our relations with Soviet Russia. But they are always a trump in our game" of diplomacy with the West. *ADAP*, series b, XI: 74–6 (Dirksen memo, Jan. 29, 1929), 101–2 (Schubert to Dirksen, Feb. 6, 1929), 199 (Stresemann to Paul Loebe, Reichstag president, March 19, 1929).

19. Stalin had the OGPU blackmail or entice Trotsky supporters internally exiled in the USSR to denounce him in the Soviet press. Radek signed a denunciation of Trotsky that was published in *Pravda* (July 13, 1929). See also Broué, "Bolshevik-Leninist Faction," 140; Deutscher, *Prophet Armed*, 390; Volkogonov, *Trotsky*, 281; Yaroslavskii, "Etot son knochen," 2; RGASPI, f. 17, op. 3, d. 782, l. 9. Even Beloborodov and Ivan Smirnov would publicly break with Trotsky. *Pravda*, Nov. 3, 1929. Rakovski, in Astrakhan, nearly alone remained loyal; Trotsky kept a photograph of him on his desk.

20. Trotskii, *Writings (1929)*, 177. See also Kassow, "Trotsky."

21. Volkogonov, *Trotsky*, 325–8.

22. Deutscher, *Prophet Outcast*, 67. At Stalin's behest, the propagandist Miney Gubelman, who went by the name Yemelyan Yaroslavsky, answered with an essay, "Mr. Trotsky at the Service of the Bourgeoisie, or L. Trotsky's First Steps Abroad"—published in Russian in the Soviet press, essentially a salve for Stalin's ego. *Bol'shevik*, 1929, no. 5 and 9.

23. G. G., "Pis'ma iz SSSR." Bukharin was sometimes perceived as a Jew ("Trotsky, Zinoviev, Kamenev, Bukharin . . ."). Borodin, *One Man in His Time*, 59.

24. "O gruppirovokakh v kommunisticheskoi oppozitsii."

25. On March 5, 1929, Mężyński informed the dictator of a supposed thwarted "assassination" plan against him by two Moscow University students and one worker who had tickets to two evening events in the university club in Feb., one of which, it was rumored, Stalin would attend. Under interrogation, one of the students stated he was unsure if he had the fortitude to carry out a terrorist act. In any event, there was no such attempt. Mozokhin and Gladkov, *Menzhinskii*, 325–6 (no citation).

26. Kvashonkin, *Sovetskoe rukovodstvo*, 68 (RGASPI, f. 74, op. 2, d. 39, l. 43, 43ob.).

27. Kvashonkin, *Sovetskoe rukovodstvo*, 73 (RGASPI, f. 74, op. 2, d. 38, l. 42; note, without addressee, in Voroshilov's file, but obviously addressed to Bukharin). Back in Sept. 1926, Stalin had written: "Bukharin is a swine and perhaps worse than a swine because he considers it beneath his dignity to write even two lines about his impressions of Germany. I'll get my revenge for that." This playfulness would look different in retrospect. Kosheleva, *Pis'ma Stalina Molotovu*, 88–93 (Sept. 16, 1926); Lih et al., *Stalin's Letters to Molotov*, 126–9.

28. This was the first plenum of 1929. Stalin invented "joint" plenums with the Central Control Commission as a device to obtain the two-thirds voting majority required by party rules for expulsions from the Central Committee.

29. Danilov and Khlevniuk, *Kak lomali NEP*, IV: 644–84 (RGASPI, f. 558, op, 11, d. 1043, l. 1–131: uncorrected transcript), quote 644; "O pravom uklone v VKP (b)," *Sochineniia*, XII: 1–107 (at 1).

30. *Sochineniia*, XII: 43. See also Abramov, *O pravoi oppozitsii v partii*, 43. Andreyev, North Caucasus party boss, told the plenum: "The GPU was formed to find and expose the very worst and most unfavorable in our country,

and if we build our policy only on the basis of the GPU reports, we will always be in a state of panic, it is perfectly clear, our hair will always stand on end." Danilov and Khlevniuk, *Kak lomali NEP*, IV: 403. Stalin made his own admission of sorts: "Name a single political measure of the party that was not accompanied by these or those excesses?" *Sochineniia*, XII: 92.

31. Stalin even contrasted Bukharin, Tomsky, and Rykov unfavorably to the smashed Trotskyites, asserting that the latter had not used the 1921 Kronstadt or 1926 Georgian rebellions but closed ranks in the face of danger. Danilov and Khlevniuk, *Kak lomali NEP*, IV: 656, 659, 668, 676; *Sochineniia*, XII: 39–40, 69–70.

32. Stalin replaced Bukharin at *Pravda* with an editorial collective of Yaroslavsky, Nikolai Popov, and Harald Krumin.

33. *Sochineniia*, XII: 92–3. Bukharin: "Extraordinary measures is the repeal of NEP, although temporarily, of course. Extraordinary measures as a system exclude the NEP." Orjonikidze interrupted: "You [try to] solve the difficulties this year with grain imports, and next year you do the same?" Bukharin, *Problemy*, 289. A brief mention of the April 29 plenum was published in *Pravda*, April 30, 1930. The plenum's resolutions were first published in 1933: *VKP (b) v rezoliutsiiakh* (1933), II: 515–30.

34. Davies, *Economic Transformation*, 286.

35. *Pravda*, July 20, 1929. The official exchange rate for the ruble—which was not a convertible currency—was set at 1.9415 to the U.S. dollar. Therefore, one gold ruble in foreign trade equaled 51.7 U.S. cents (until early 1933, when the dollar left the gold standard, and the ruble exchange rate was set on the basis of a cross-exchange rate of the currency in question to the French franc, with one ruble equal to 13.1 francs). Gold or foreign trade rubles had no relation to domestic rubles. Dohan, "Soviet Foreign Trade," 701–8. Kaganovich would cite "local demands" for new coercive measures; obviously, he instigated them. Rees, *Iron Lazar*, 94–5 (citing RGASPI, f. 17, op. 2, d. 3188, l. 95; op. 2, d. 417, l. 57–8, 291–3); Taniuchi, *Village Gathering*.

36. Mikhail Sholokhov wrote in letters to an acquaintance (E. G. Lebitskaya) in July 1929 of one peasant, "He told me with a bitter smile, 'They [the Whites] at least took only grain and horses, but our own [Soviet] power takes down to the thread.'" *Znamia*, 1987, no. 10: 181, 183. "See also Chernopitskii, *Na velikom perelome*, 40–1 (citing PARO, f. 7, op. 1, d. 844, l. 202).

37. Mikoyan added, "Of course we would have inevitably come to grips with this task sometime, but it is a question of timing." Mikoian, *Problema snabzheniia strany*, 60.

38. Pavlov, *Anastas Mikoian*, 52 (citing RGASPI, f. 84, op. 3, d. 62, l. 73: Aug. 1929). See also RGASPI, f. 558, op. 11, d. 73, l. 50; and Ivnitskii, *Repressivnaia politika sovetskoi vlasti*, 59–60. Between 1928 and 1935, Mikoyan would undertake more than twenty regional trips in connection with coercive grain collections. Pavlov, *Anastas Mikoian*, 49 (citing RGASPI, f. 84, op. 3, d. 167, l. 411–2).

39. *VKP (b) v rezoliutsiiakh* (1933), II: 531 73. The "plan" was actually in effect as of Oct. 1, 1928. Zaleski, *Planning for Economic Growth*, 70n205, 74; Zaleski, *Stalinist Planning*, 54; Carr and Davies, *Foundations of a Planned Economy*, I/i: 248–52, I/ii: 890–7.

40. Brovkin, *Russia after Lenin*, 122–5 (citing RGASPI, f. 17, op. 69, d. 126, l. 5, 107, 117; f. 1, op. 23, d. 821, l. 22). See also Fischer, *Men and Politics*, 187. Oral exams of university students in 1927 had returned answers that (the

Russian anarchist) Bakunin was a French revolutionary who had led the (British) Chartist movement, and that imperialism was the best path to socialism. One student thought the Communist Youth League was "an international organization of the homeless." Holmes, *Kremlin and the Schoolhouse*, 60–1. Such surveys revealed more than the anxieties of the ambitious revolutionary regime. Gorsuch, *Youth*.

41. *KPSS v rezoliutsiiakh* (7th ed.), II: 450.

42. "People often forget," *Izvestiya* explained (May 23, 1929), "that the Five-Year Plan defines our foreign policy," making it necessary "to delay the war threat and make use of . . . world markets."

43. Haslam, *Russia's Cold War*, 3–5.

44. Jacobson, *When the Soviet Union Entered World Politics*, 86–7.

45. The Bolsheviks had been awarding foreigners concessions (or leases) on Soviet territory to spur technology transfer and revive export industries, but this policy had been deeply fraught with difficulties. (Lenin, as usual, on Dec. 21, 1920, had captured the essence, paraphrasing Clausewitz: "Concessions [leases] do not mean peace with capitalism, but war in a new sphere.") In Feb. 1930, a politburo commission would decide that foreign concessions contradicted socialist industrialization. By 1933, no manufacturing concessions remained. Carr and Davies, *Foundations of a Planned Economy*, III/I (1976): 90–1; Sutton, *Western Technology*, I: 86–91; Fitch, "Harriman Manganese Concession"; Davies, *Soviet Economy in Turmoil*, 109–10 (citing *Za industrialiatsiiu*, May 10, 1930; P. N. Pospelov et al. [eds.], *Leninskii plan sotsialisticheskoi industrializatsii i ego osushchestvlenie* [Moscow: Partizdat, 1969], 186–7; and *DVP SSSR*, XIII: 112 [Litvinov-Dirksen: Feb. 26, 1930]; and Sutton, *Western Technology*, I: 349, II: 17).

46. Davies, *Soviet Economy in Turmoil*, 125–6.

47. Rogachehskaia, *Iz istorii rabochego klassa SSSR*; Oprischenko, *Istoriografiia sotsialisticheskogo sorevnovaniia*; Rogachevskaia, *Sotsialisticheskoe sorevnovanie v SSSR*; Kuromiya, *Stalin's Industrial Revolution*, 128–35.

48. *Pravda*, Jan. 20, 1929; *PSS*, XXVI: 367. See also *Sotsialisticheskii vestnik*, Sept. 27, 1929: 16; and Kravchenko, *I Chose Freedom*, 50.

49. Maksimenkov, *Bol'shaia tsenzura*, 146–53 (RGASPI, f. 558, op. 11, d. 1493, l. 4–13), 153 (d. 1047, l. 48–9); *Na prieme*, 30. On May 4, 1929, Stalin received a delegation of 170 Donbas miners, who promised (in the text he edited) to "fulfill completely the tasks assigned them by Soviet power in the First Five-Year Plan." *Pravda*, May 8, 1929; RGASPI, f. 558, op. 11, d. 1159, l. 93.

50. *Sochineniia*, XII: 108–11; Maksimenkov, *Bol'shaia tsenzura*, 157 (RGASPI, f. 558, op. 11, d. 1047, l. 19).

51. *Sochineniia*, XII: 115–6. Mikulina, who died in 1998, would be asked to recount her audience with Stalin: Maksimenkov, *Bol'shaia tsenzura*, 153n3.

52. Maksimenkov, *Bol'shaia tsenzura*, 162–5 (RGASPI, f. 558, op. 11, d. 1047, l. 51–5: Aleksei Milrud, Sept. 19, 1929).

53. *Sochineniia*, XII: 112–5 (July 9, 1929). See also Maksimenkov, *Bol'shaia tsenzura*, 160 (RGASPI, f. 558, op. 11, d. 1047, l. 62).

54. In Comintern documents, Stalin personally wrote in the epithet "social fascism" for Social Democrats. *Communism and the International Situation*, 6, 16–20; Firsov, "Stalin i Komintern," 7. "Social fascism" became official in 1929, but Stalin's conception was long-standing. "Fascism is the fighting organization of the bourgeoisie, leaning on the

active support of social democracy," he had written in 1924. "Social Democracy is objectively the moderate wing of fascism . . . They are not antipodes but twins. Fascism is an informal political bloc of these two basic political organizations, which arose in the situation of the postwar crisis of imperialism and is intended for the struggle against proletarian revolution." *Sochinennia*, VI: 282; Degras, *Communist International*, 44. See also Degras, *Communist International*, II: 566.

55. Rosenhaft, *Beating the Fascists*, 35–9. The German Social Democrats, who had joined the Weimar Republic government, sought rapprochement with France against the Soviets in a pro-Western orientation.

56. McDermott and Agnew blame SPD policies ("more than any single factor") for "the vitriolic 'social fascist' rhetoric employed by the Comintern in the years 1929–33." McDermott and Agnew, *Comintern*, 100–2.

57. *La correspondance international*, Aug. 17, 1929: 971. This was the first such plenum since Feb. 1928.

58. *Politicheskoe obrazovanie*, 1989, no. 1: 81. *World Situation*, 3–21.

59. Gorelov, *Nikolai Bukharin*, 100–45. Angelo Tasca, after getting out of Moscow in early 1929, had ripped into Stalin in a letter to the Italian Community party, concluding, "The Russian party and all of us will pay dearly for ignoring Lenin's instructions about him." Firsov, "Stalin i Komintern," 5 (citing *Annali Feltrinelli*, VIII, 1968, 670). Before the year was out, Tasca was expelled on Stalin's orders from the Italian Community party, which he had helped establish after having quit the Italian Socialist Party. In exile in France, he would rejoin the Italian Socialists. De Grand, *In Stalin's Shadow*. See also Carr and Davies, *Foundations of a Planned Economy*, III: 554.

60. Bahne et al., *Les Partis communistes*, 165 (March 1929); McDermott and Agnew, *Comintern*, 86. After Hitler would come to power and ban the German Community party, Zetkin would seek asylum in Moscow, where she would die in June 1933.

61. McDermott and Agnew, *Comintern*, 102, citing K. Gottwald, *Spisy* (Prague, 1951), I: 322 (Dec. 1929).

62. Lih et al., *Stalin's Letters to Molotov*, 148–50 (RGASPI, f. 85, op. 1/s., d. 110, l. 1–2ob.). Stalin proposed naming Bukharin commissar of enlightenment, perhaps to tie him down in enervating ideological battles. "Bukharin begged everyone not to name him enlightenment commissar, but proposed, and then insisted on, the Scientific-Technical Administration" of the Supreme Council of the Economy, Voroshilov wrote to Orjonikidze (June 8, 1929). "I supported him in that, a few other comrades supported him and as a majority in one voice (against Koba) we got him so named." Kosheleva, *Pis'ma Stalina Molotovu*, 123; Khlevniuk, *Khoziain*, 30.

63. Vague resolutions to strengthen the military at the 15th Party Congress (Dec. 1927) and the 16th party conference (April 1929) had produced nothing concrete. Voronetskaia, *Industrializatsiia SSSR*, 42; *XVI konferentsiia VKP (b), aprel' 1929 goda*, 240–7, 625. See also Erickson, *Soviet High Command*, 295, 301–7, 322.

64. Kudriashov, *Krasnaia armiia*, 234–40 (APRF, f. 3, op. 50, d. 259, l. 168–80). One of the two classified July 15, 1929, decrees was finally revealed in *KPSS o vooruzhennykh silakh Sovetskogo Soiuza*, 318–21. Contrary to some speculation, the decrees were not related to the launching of military action on the Chinese Eastern Railway. Ken, *Mobilizatsionnoe planirovanie*, 72–3 (RGASPI, f. 17, op. 162, d. 7, l. 12).

65. Stone, *Hammer and Rifle*, 124–9 (citing GARF, f. 5446, op. 55, d. 1966, l. 20–32, 35–43; and RGVA, f. 4, op. 18, d. 15, l. 190: Revvoensovet).

66. Ken, *Mobilizatsionnoe planirovanie*, 74 (RGVA, f. 74, op. 2, d. 101, 105ob.: Litunovsky, July 30, 1929).

67. Gorlov, *Sovershennko sekretno, Moskva-Berlin*; Müller, *Das Tor zur Weltmacht*; Zeidler, *Reichswehr und Rote Armee* (2nd ed.); Erickson, *Soviet High Command*, 247–82.

68. Stalin had received Uborevičius on Nov. 4, 1927. *Na prieme*, 770.

69. In a comprehensive report in 1929, Uborevičius had judged the 4,000-strong German officer corps to be "to the right, far to the right of the Social Democrats. The bulk of them stand for a firm bourgeois dictatorship, even fascism." D'iakov and Bushueva, *Fashistskii mech kovalsia v SSSR*, 255 (RGVA, f. 33987, op. 3, d. 295, l. 141–83).

70. Zdanovich, *Organy*, 423–4 (citing TsA FSB, f. 2, op. 7, d. 61, l. 6). See also Stone, *Hammer and Rifle*, 131 (citing RGVA, f. 33991, op. 1, d. 20, l. 80–92; RGASPI, f. 85, op. 27, d. 93, l. 1; f. 17, op. 162, d. 8, l. 40); and Z., "Sovremennaia artilleriia i modernizatsiia." Stalin had written to Voroshilov (Dec. 31, 1928), who was then livid over budget cuts, that "the point now is our artillery is insufficient, scandalously insufficient." Stone, *Hammer and Rifle*, 102 (RGASPI, f. 74, op. 2, d. 39, l. 19).

71. Tinchenko, *Golgofa*, 106–7; Tichanova, *Rasstrel'nye spiski*, no. 2, 99–101; Smirnov, *Krovavyi marshal*, 337 (I. P. Grave). Grigory Kulik, a Stalin civil-war crony dating to 1918 Tsaritsyn days and the head of the artillery directorate, escaped.

72. Mężyński also appended his name to the explanation as the top responsible official. Vinogradov, *Genrikh Iagoda*, 336–7 (TsA FSB, f.2, op. 2, d. 9, l. 249: Feb. 9, 1929). See the speculations regarding Boris Nicolaevsky's role in Fel'shtinskii, *VChK-GPU*, 271.

73. Yagoda would later testify under pressure that he gave both Rykov and Bukharin, at their requests, "secret OGPU material on the situation in the village." This 1937 testimony, despite the circumstances under which it would be taken, is plausible. Vinogradov, *Genrikh Iagoda*, 112–7 (interrogation April 26, 1937: TsA FSB, f. N-13614, tom 2, l. 57–8). On Trilisser's Comintern intelligence ("communications service")—65 people in Moscow as well as a worldwide system of radio operators, couriers, and safe houses—see Lebedeva and Narinskii, *Komintern i vtoraia mirovaia voina*, 52, 54–5.

74. Dmitrievskii, *Sovetskie portrety*, 218–20.

75. The politburo (Sept. 12, 1929) again ordered him to follow his doctor's regimen. Khaustov et al., *Lubianka: Stalin i VChK*, 190 (RGASPI, f. 17, op. 3, d. 757, l. 9, 15).

76. Kokurin and Petrov, "OGPU, 1929–1934 gg."; Gladkov, *Nagrada*, 345–6. Trilisser maintained that his party meeting report had been approved at the "Central Committee."

77. Kokurin and Petrov, "OGPU, 1929–1934 gg.," 95 (June 27, 1929).

78. Khaustov et al., *Lubianka: Stalin i VChK*, 191 (APRF, f. 45, op. 1, d. 170, l. 42).

79. Khaustov et al., *Lubianka: Stalin i VChK*, 219–20 (APRF, f. 3, op. 50, d. 32, l. 115). Trilisser got kicked over to the workers' and peasants' inspectorate.

80. Tumshis and Papchinskii, *1937, bol'shaia chistka*, 202.

81. Papchinskii and Tumshis, *Shchit, raskolotii mechom*, 208–9.

82. Tumshis and Papchinskii, *1937, bol'shaia chistka*, 202 (citing TsA FSB, arkhivnoe sledvestvennoe delo No. 13144 on Kaul A. I., II: no pagination, words of I. Ia. Ilin; arkhivnoe sledvestvennoe delo N. 14963 on Papashenko

I. P., l. 184: M. A. Listengrut), 203 (l. 240–1). Mikhail Frinovsky was gone by then, out of Yevdokimov's shadow; in Rostov, Frinovsky had had his own gatherings at his house, attended by Yevdokimov.

83. For Stalin's patronage of Yevdokimov in fall 1929, see Khaustov et al., *Lubianka: Stalin i VChK*, 191 (APRF, f. 45, op. 1, d. 170, l. 42). The full membership of the OGPU collegium became: Redens, Prokofyev, Blagonravov, Boki, Balytsky, Messing, and Yevdokimov. Peterrs and Pavlunovsky were taken off.

84. On Oct. 2, 1929, Yagoda wrote apologetically to the dictator that he had spoken to Mężyński and there were no differences between them (contrary to what Yagoda had earlier told Stalin). Vinogradov, *Genrikh Iagoda*, 344–5 (TsA FSB, f. 3, op. 2, d. 9, l. 248).

85. Kokurin and Petrov, *Lubianka*, 42–3. Deribas was pushed out to the Soviet Far East.

86. Kosheleva, *Pis'ma Stalina Molotovu*, 135–8; Lih et al., *Stalin's Letters to Molotov*, 162–3. Stalin included Beso Lominadze among the wayward young functionaries. In early Aug. 1929, Lominadze, demoted to a provincial post, wrote an inflammatory letter about Stalin and party policy to his patron Orjonikidze, who wrote in a protective draft response: "although I keep no party secrets from Stalin, I did not show him your letter." It seems that Orjonikidze did not send the draft and later read Lominadze's letter to Stalin, perhaps when Orjonikidze pushed to promote Lominadze to head the South Caucasus party committee (the appointment took effect May 8, 1930). Khlevniuk, *Stalin i Ordzhonikidze*, 23–5 (citing RGASPI, f. 85, op. 1/s, d. 115, l. 6–10, 1–5); *Kommunist*, 1991, no. 13: 56–7 (RGASPI, f. 17, op. 2, d. 607, l. 267–9: Stalin at the Feb.–March 1937 plenum). Lominadze became a full member of the Central Committee in summer 1930.

87. Kosheleva, *Pis'ma Stalina Molotovu*, 154–8; Lih et al., *Stalin's Letters to Molotov*, 174–6. The main anti-Bukharin essay appeared in *Pravda* on Aug. 24, 1929; Cohen, *Bukharin*, 332.

88. Stalin insisted that re-recognition of the USSR precede any settlement on debts, and that he was not going to rein in Comintern propaganda. Kosheleva, *Pis'ma Stalina Molotovu*, 160–3 (Sept. 9, 1929); Lih et al., *Stalin's Letters to Molotov*, 177–9.

89. Murin, *Stalin v ob"iaitiakh*, 22 (APRF, f. 45, op. 1, d. 1550, l. 5).

90. Gorky had boarded the steamer *Karl Liebknecht* on Aug. 20, and visited Astrakhan and Stalingrad then Rostov and Tiflis. Troyat, *Gorky*, 173. Stalin's doctor Ivan Valedinsky recalled Gorky visiting Stalin in Sochi in 1930. In fact, Gorky visited the USSR in 1928 (May 27–Oct. 12); 1929 (May 31–Oct. 12); and 1931 (May 14–Oct. 18), but not in 1930. Gorky's one and only post-1917 visit to Sochi was in 1929, but Valedinsky wrote that he himself did not see Stalin in 1929. Either Valedinsky "recalled" the Gorky-Stalin encounter based upon stories he was told the next year, or he confused the years he treated Stalin. Valedinskii, "Organizm Stalina vpolne zdorovyi," 69.

91. Murin, *Stalin v ob"iaitiakh*, 22 (APRF, f. 45, op. 1, d. 1550, l. 6–7), 22–3 (l. 8), 23 (l. 9). Rumor had it that that Avel Yenukidze, the godfather, had enlisted Orjonikidze, and together they persuaded Stalin to allow Nadya to go back to school.

92. Murin, *Stalin v ob"iatiakh*, 23–4 (APRF, f. 45, op. 1, d. 1550, l. 10–4).

93. Murin, *Stalin v ob"iatiakh*, 25–7 (APRF, f. 45, op. 1, d. 1550, l. 16–24: between Sept. 16 and 22, 1929), 27 (l. 25: Sept. 23), 41n14 (d. 74, l. 18), 41n15 (d. 778, l. 18–9), 41n16 (d. 778, l. 20–1: Sept. 27). Stalin would thrice receive

Kovalev: Dec. 18 (with Popov and Krumin) and Dec. 30 (alone), 1929, and March 11, 1930 (alone). *Na prieme*, 31–2.

94. Khromov, *Po stranitsam*, 34 (citing RGASPI, f. 558, op. 11, d. 73, l. 98–9, 103–11).

95. Kosheleva, *Pis'ma Stalina Molotovu*, 166–7 (Sept. 30, 1929); Lih et al., *Stalin's Letters to Molotov*, 181–2; Danilov and Khlevniuk, *Kak lomali NEP*, V: 10–1 (RGASPI, f. 558, op. 11, d. 768, l. 91, 92). Rykov, as head of the government, chaired the sessions, just as Lenin had.

96. Murin, *Stalin v ob"iatiakh*, 27–8 (APRF, f. 45, op. 1, d. 1550, l. 27).

97. *DBFP*, 2nd series, VII: 20–38. After the British had effectively agreed on terms, Stalin noted that politburo members Kalinin and Tomsky were not in Sochi to consult, and that he could not speak in the name of the politburo. RGASPI, f. 558, op. 11, d. 73, l. 37; d. 74, l. 25 (Tovstukha, Oct. 3). See also Khromov, *Po stranitsam*, 220 (RGASPI, f. 669, op. 1, d. 8, l. 1a); and RGASPI, f. 558, op. 11, d. 73, l. 12, l. 85.

98. Kosheleva, *Pis'ma Stalina Molotovu*, 166–7, 167–8; Lih et al., *Stalin's Letters to Molotov*, 181, 182.

99. Murin, *Stalin v ob"iatiakh*, 34–5 (APRF, f. 45, op. 1, d. 1550, l. 50–1).

100. Sokolov, "Neizvestnyi G. V. Chicherin," 14 (citing AVP RF, f. 08, op. 12, pap. 74, d. 55, l. 92–3: June 20, 1929).

101. This would be formalized in a politburo directive (Feb. 5, 1930): Khaustov et al., *Lubianka: Stalin i VChK*, 219–20.

102. The reports of a supposed anti-Soviet bloc recorded frustration by the notional members over refusals to share intelligence. Khaustov et al., *Glazami razvedki*, 297 (RGASPI, f. 558, op. 11, d. 184, l. 45–45ob.), 298–9 (TsA FSB, f. 2, op. 9, d. 875, l. 92–4).

103. "We live in very difficult times," the Soviet writer Leonid Leonov, whom Gorky admired, wrote from Moscow to him (Oct. 21, 1929). "All around us everything crumbles . . . There is no way back now . . . The times are dangerous. About many things one cannot write." Semashkina and Evstigneeva, *Perepiska Gor'kogo*, II: 302–3.

104. Danilov et al., *Tragediia sovetskoi derevni*, I: 736 (RGASPI, f. 17, op. 113, d. 789, l. 14: Oct. 22, 1929), 737 (f. 84, op. 2, d. 12, l. 54: Oct. 26).

105. Davies, *Soviet Collective Farm*, 81–2 (citing *Sel'sko-khoziaistvennaia gazeta*, Nov. 28, 1929: Sergei Syrtsov).

106. Theses of the 6th Comintern Congress in 1928 had predicted "the most severe intensification of the capitalist crisis," which, like earthquake forecasts, had suddenly turned correct. At the congress, the Comintern had also welcomed Latin American delegates for the first time, eliciting a boast about its "discovery of America." Manuel, *Latin America and the Comintern*, 65.

107. Coates and Coates, *History of Anglo-Soviet Relations*, II: 332; Izvestiia, Nov. 6, 1929; *DBFP*, 2nd series, VII: doc. 24; *DVP SSSR*, XII: 537–8, 541; Adibekov et al., *Politbiuro TsK RKP (b)–VKP (b) i Evropa*, 182–201 (RGASPI, f. 17, op. 162, d. 7, l. 55, 51, 87, 94, 123, 136, 143, 158–9, 160–3, 178); Izvestiia, July 5, 1929. In the May 30, 1929, general election, Labour had won 287 seats, not enough for a majority (308), while the Tories won 260; Labour was dependent on the votes of Lloyd George's Liberal Party (59 seats) to pass legislation. Three Tories voted for restoration of diplomatic relations with the USSR. Redvaldsen, "'Today Is the Dawn.'"

108. Haslam, *Soviet Foreign Policy*, 21–2. Stalin approved the appointment of Grigory Sokolnikov, the former NEP-era finance commissar and party oppositionist and

current skillful head of the state oil trust, as Soviet envoy. Sir Esmond Ovey became British ambassador in Moscow. Lammers, "Second Labour Government." Ovey would claim that at a banquet given by the foreign affairs commissariat in 1931, the silverware bore the British coat of arms and the motto of the British chivalric Order of the Garter (*Honi soit qui mal y pense*—"May he be shamed who thinks badly of it"). Evidently, the silver had been stolen from the British embassy either during the 1917 revolution or after 1927, when relations had been severed. *Time*, May 11, 1931.

109. Blyumkin had served as Trotsky's adjutant, then was invited to rejoin the secret police, rising to pro-consul in the Soviet satellite of Mongolia and then to undercover OGPU station chief in Istanbul. Yakov Agranov recorded Blyumkin's revealing deposition (Oct. 20, 1929), which Yagoda forwarded to Stalin, and Stalin forwarded to Central Committee members. Khaustov et al., *Lubianka: Stalin i VChK*, 192–212 (TsA FSB, f. 3, op. 24, d. 126, l. 94–124), 213 (RGASPI, f. 17, op. 162, d. 8, l. 2). See also Savchenko, *Avanturisty grazhdanskoi voiny*, 305–36; Mandelstam, *Hope against Hope*, 101ff; Gusterin, *Sovetskaia razvedka*; Agabekov, *G.P.U.*, 221–6; Agabekov, *OGPU*, 214–23; Agabekov, *ChK za rabotoi*, 293–9. Agabekov (Aryutunov), an Armenian OGPU operative sent to Turkey to replace Blyumkin, became the first senior secret police official to defect to the West (1930); he betrayed the Soviet spy network in the Near East. OGPU agents went around whispering that Radek had betrayed Blyumkin, a story that, as intended, reached Trotsky, damaging relations between him and Radek, conveniently for Stalin. Radek would not deny he had informed on Blyumkin. Trotsky is said to have received a letter detailing Radek's betrayal. "Kak i za chto Stalin rasstrelial Bliumkina" *Biulleten' oppozitsi*, no. 9 (Feb.–March 1930): 9–11; Deutscher, *Prophet Outcast*, 85–8; Medvedev, *Let History Judge*, 292–3; Volkogonov, *Trotsky*, 329–30; Orlov, *Secret History*, 194.

110. *Sel'sko-khoziaistvennaia gazeta*, Oct. 15, 1929 (Sergei Syrtsov); *Pravda*, Nov. 10 and Dec. 8, 1929. The slogan became widespread beginning in Feb. 1930: Davies, *Soviet Economy in Turmoil*, 191. A patent-equivalent for a tractor had been issued in tsarist Russia and a tractor prototype had been produced, but it never came into production. Artobolevskii and Blagonravov, *Ocherki*, 215.

111. *Pravda*, Nov. 7, 1929, reprinted with alterations in *Sochineniia*, XII: 118–35; Davies, *Soviet Economy in Turmoil*, 329–45. One of Stalin's post-facto editorial changes was shrinking the anticipated size of Soviet farms to 40,000–50,000 hectares. *Sochineniia*, XII: 129; Davies, "Stalin as Economic Policy-Maker," 123. State farms were being modeled after industry, and, Molotov exhorted the plenum, collective farms should model themselves after state farms. *Bol'shevik*, 1929, no. 22: 20. *Pravda* (Sep. 5, 1929) had declared that all "technically more developed capitalist countries" were organizing agriculture like industry. Davies, *Soviet Collective Farm*, 3.

112. Mikoyan told the plenum (Nov. 11) that in the next year "we will have a significant export of grain," even though key ports lacked large mechanized elevators and the United States, Argentina, and Canada had displaced Russia in European grain markets. Danilov and Khlevniuk, *Kak Iomali NEP*, V: 83 (RGASPI, f. 17, op. 2, d. 441, l. 19–20ob.).

113. *Sdvigi v sel'skom khoziaistve SSSR*, 22–3. See also Ivnitskii, *Kollektivizatsiia i raskulachivanie*, 15; and Davies, *Socialist Offensive*, 116–37, 442.

114. RGASPI, f. 17, op. 3, d. 740, l. 5.

115. Danilov and Khlevniuk, *Kak Iomali NEP*, V: 141 (Syrtsov). Officially, 19.1 percent of households had been collectivized in the North Caucasus by Oct. 1929. Davies, *Socialist Offensive*, 442.

116. *Pravda*, Nov. 26, 1929; Cohen, *Bukharin*, 334–5; Davies, *Socialist Offensive*, 174; Lewin, *Russian Peasants and Soviet Power*, 369.

117. RGASPI, f. 558, op. 11, d. 778, l. 23. Hryhory Petrovsky, a Stalin loyalist, stated at the plenum that "[I] did not belong to the 'rightist baiters' in the way, for example, I fought with the Trotskyites or the new opposition—Kamenev and Zinoviev—when we went wall to wall." 118. *VKP (b) v rezoliutsiiakh* (1933), II; *KPSS v rezoliutsiiakh* (7th ed.), II: 631. During the plenum, Stalin angrily challenged a published account by Volodymyr Zatonsky concerning Lenin's dealings with the Left SRs. RGASPI, f. 558, op. 11, d. 735, l. 11–3, 15–7; Zatonskii, "Otryvki vospominanii," 128–41. See also Zelenov, "Partiinyi kontrol' za izdaniem sochinenii Lenina."

119. Danilov and Ivnitskii, *Dokumenty svidetel'stvuiut*, 23. See also Avtorkhanov, *Stalin and the Soviet Communist Party*, 159–60. 120. Davies, *Socialist Offensive*, 157–74; *KPSS v rezoliutsiiakh* (7th ed.), II: 643.

121. The CER linked the Soviet cities of Chita and Vladivostok as well as the Chinese cities of Manzhouli, Harbin, Tsitsihar, and Suifenho. Tang, *Russian Policy*, 193–241. In the Soviet consulate the Chinese found high-quality imitations of American and Japanese seals, evidently used to reseal letters that had been perlustrated and to mail secret Soviet correspondence under the guise of American or Japanese packages. Lensen, *Damned Inheritance*, 34 (citing *FRUS, 1929*, II: 196–7; FO, 317/13931–F2692, F-2960).

122. Carr and Davies, *Foundations of a Planned Economy*, III/iii: 895–910. Relations were severed on Aug. 16, 1929. Kārlis Baumanis boasted to the Moscow province party conference (Sept. 1929) that the "Chinese aggression had woken up [Soviet] workers," who pledged their readiness to take up arms rather than "surrender to the imperialists." *Pervaia moskovskaia konferentsiia VKP (b): stenpograficheskii otchet*, 39, 42.

123. *Sovetsko-kitaiskii konflikt 1929*, 37, translated in Degras, *Soviet Documents on Foreign Policy*, II: 391; *Krasnoznamenyi Dal'nevostochnyi*, 91; Slavinskii, *Sovetskii Soiuz i Kitai*, 176.

124. Stalin had asked Molotov to think about staging a revolutionary uprising to invade and occupy Harbin "and establish a revolutionary power (massacre the landlords, draw in the peasants, create soviets in the cities and towns)." Kosheleva, *Pis'ma Stalina Molotovu*, 167–8 (Oct. 7, 1929); Lih et al., *Stalin's Letters to Molotov*, 182.

125. Litvinov, *Notes for a Journal*, 113; Stephan, *Russian Far East*, 182. Soviet military intelligence had surmised in spring 1929 in an internal memorandum that "despite the strengthening activeness of anti-Soviet and fascist elements in Japan, Japanese policy regarding the USSR has had a more or less steady character." Zolotarev, *Russkii arkhiv: Velikaia otechestvennaia*, VII/i: 29–31.

126. Krivosheev, *Grif sekretnosti sniat*, 66. 127. Slavinskii, *Sovetskii Soiuz i Kitai*, 178–81; Erickson, *Soviet High Command*, 240–4; Dushen'kin, *Proletarskii marshal*, 98–100; Krasnoznamenyi Dal'nevostochnyi*, 115–24. Blyukher was awarded a Buick automobile and use of the former Chinese consulate in Khabarovsk as his residence. Kondrat'ev, *Marshal Bliukher*, 271–3; Kartunova, *Bliukher v Kitae*, 12; Blyukher, "Vospominania o lichnom," 81, 85.

128. Walker, *War Nobody Knew*, 328 (citing *North China Daily News*, Nov. 28, 1929), 334–5.

129. Degras, *Soviet Documents on Foreign Policy*, II: 434–6; Antonov, "Nekotorye itogi konflikta"; Tang, *Russian Policy*, 242–67; Chuikov, "Konflikt na KVZhD." See also Elleman, *Emergence of Communist Power*, 192–205; and Patrikeef, *Russian Politics*, 85.

130. The Japanese also noted the apparent indifference of the League of Nations to questions of Chinese sovereignty. Lensen, *Damned Inheritance*.

131. Kosheleva, *Pis'ma Stalina Molotovu*, 169–71; Lih et al., *Stalin's Letters to Molotov*, 183–4.

132. *Pravda*, Dec. 11, 1929. See also Davies, *Soviet Economy in Turmoil*, 131, citing Kuibyshev, *Brigady sotsializma: doklad na I Vsesoiuznom s"ezde udarnykh brigad* (1930), 13–4, 17; *Rezoliutsii i postanovlenii*; and *Pervyi vsesoiuznyi s"ezd udarnykh brigad*.

133. Sutton, *Western Technology*, I: 347–8; Davies, *Soviet Economy in Turmoil*, 192, citing *Na agrarnom fronte*, 1930, no. 1: 62–3, and RGAE, f. 7620, op. 1, d. 22, l. 65–1.

134. There would be 124 technical assistance contracts by 1931, compared with 17 contracts in 1927–28. Payments to foreign specialists perhaps consumed one-quarter of Soviet grain export revenues. By 1933, in an effort to save on scarce foreign currency, and with experience and (illegally) replicable blueprints now in hand, just 46 such contracts remained in force. Lewis, "Foreign Economic Relations," 209–10. Foreign technical assistance was codified as the strategy for military industry on Dec. 5, 1929. Simonov, *Voenno-promyshelnnyi kompleks SSSR*, 78.

135. Tsarist gold reserves had been lost in war and revolution, and though the OGPU confiscated precious metals and foreign banknotes in private hands, this amounted to only 10 million rubles a year. But the gold extraction industry would be revived, using prison labor. Aizenberg, *Valiutnaia Sistema SSSR*, 8, 63; Budnitskii, *Den'gi russkoi emigratsii*; Khaustov et al., *Lubianka: Stalin i VChK*, 260 (APRF, f. 4,5 op. 1, d. 170, l. 62: Yagoda, Jan. 7, 1931).

136. Kennan, *Russia and the West*, 195.

137. RGASPI, f. 17, op. 85, d. 531–5; *Stalin: Sbornik statei*; Heizer, "Cult of Stalin," 61, 80.

138. RGASPI, f. 558, op. 11, d. 768, l. 131.

139. *Stalin: sbornik statei*; RGASPI, f. 17, op. 85, d. 531–5 (assembled congratulations). *Stalin: sbornik statei*, 2nd ed. (1930), 10, 44.

140. At this time the censor (Glavlit) laid down strict guidelines for the publication of Stalin photographs. Blium, *Za kulisami*, 128 (RGALI St. Petersburg, f. 31, op. 2, d. 40, l. 3).

141. Stalin, "Vsem organizatsiiam i tovarishcham, prislavshim privetstviia," *Pravda*, Dec. 22, 1929. *Sochineniia*, XII: 140. See also Davies, *Socialist Offensive*, 118–9, 174–5.

142. RGAKFD, ed. khr. 6633, 6 parts. Some of the footage is raw (multiple takes being shot). 143. Volkogonov, *Trotsky*, 125 (citing arkhiv INO OGPU, f. 17548, d. 0292, t. 1, l. 106–7). The letter was among those later stolen with Trotsky's archives by the NKVD. Following not one but two fires, Trotsky would return to his original rented villa on Prinkipo only in Oct. 1932. Cherniavskii, *Lev Trotsky*, 488–9.

144. Voroshilov, "Stalin i krasnaia armiia," *Izvestiia*, Dec. 21, 1929, reprinted in *Stalin: sbornik statei*, and in Voroshilov, *Lenin, Stalin, i krasnaia armiia*, 41–61. Stalin himself crossed out the words that had offended him with red pencil: *Voennye arkhivy Rossii*, 97 (Voroshilov's adjutant Khmelnitsky). Stalin had not been prominent in the press materials on the 9th anniversary of the Red Army's founding (Feb. 23, 1927), but in the

three-volume *Civil War of 1918-1921*, published in 1928-30, A. S. Bubnov wrote a forty-page introduction without mentioning Trotsky's name while celebrating Stalin. Bubnov et al., *Grazhdanskaia voina 1918-1921*, III: 10. Avel Yenukidze, in a private birthday letter to Stalin (Dec. 30, 1929), shrewdly captured Stalin's self-image while managing to quote Pushkin: Kvashonkin, *Sovetskoe rukovodstvo*, 108-10 (RGASPI, f. 667, op. 1, d. 16, l. 4-6).

145. Émigré sources produced a blunter version. "Stalin is the only man we must obey, for fear of getting worse," Pyatakov was said to have remarked privately. "Bukharin and Rykov deceive themselves in thinking that they would govern in Stalin's place; Kaganovich and such would succeed him, and I cannot and will not obey Kaganovich." Whether Pyatkaov actually said that, or Trotsky's supporters reported it so, to please their master, the statement reflected a widespread sense that Stalin stood far above the members of his faction. Souvarine, *Staline*, 450 (no citation); Souvarine, *Stalin*, 489.

146. Popov further distinguished Stalin's leadership by the claim that in difficult situations, he did not succumb to panic. Popov, "Partiia i vozhd'." For a broader discussion, see Aron, *Sociologie des sociétés industrielles*.

147. Graziosi, "Stalin's Anti-Worker 'Workerism' 1924-1931," 253-4; "Iz perepiski A. M. Gor'kogo," 183-8 (Nov. 27, 1929), translated in *Political Archives of the Soviet Union*, 1/2 (1990): 177-80.

148. As Syrtsov had put it, echoing Stalin, "in those places where we broke kulak resistance, a strong flow of grain immediately commenced, as if a cork had been removed." *XVI konferentsiia VKP (b), aprel' 1929 goda*, 322-3.

149. Rationing had emerged haphazardly and varied by locale. By Feb.–March 1930, towns were prioritized based upon size and significance. Local trading agencies welcomed rationing as a better way to obtain supplies they were tasked with getting into workers' hands; factories welcomed rationing, too, lobbying to raise the status of their enterprises for better rations. Davies, *Soviet Economy in Turmoil*, 289-300; Carr and Davies, *Foundations of a Planned Economy*, I: 700-4.

150. Back at a July 4, 1929, politburo meeting, Molotov had proposed the formation of a USSR land commissariat, and Mykola Skrynyk, the enlightenment commissar of Ukraine, immediately understood that this would put the country's land under Union (not republic) ownership and objected, pointing out that such a move would violate the USSR constitution (in terms of republic prerogatives). Stalin, maneuvering, suggested the matter be postponed until a Central Committee plenum, and in the meantime, he prepared a fait accompli. Khlevniuk et al., *Stenogrammy zasedanii politbiuro*, III: 11.

151. *Pravda*, Jan. 27, 1930; *KPSS v rezoliutsiiakh* (9th ed.), V: 39-42, 72-5; RGASPI, f. 17, op. 3, d. 771, l. 3; Danilov et al., *Tragediia sovetskoi derevni*, II: 35-84 (RGASPI, f. 17, op. 3, d. 1876, l. 8; f. 558, op. 11, d. 38, l. 1, 4, 7; RGAE, f. 7486, op. 3, d. 40, l. 5-5ob., 58-53, 174-69, 73-72, 41, 197-87, 211-06, 205, 218, 217-12, 220-220ob.; d. 50, l. 40-39; d. 49, l. 27-24), 85-6; *Spravochnik partiinogo rabotnika*, VII/ii: 114.

152. *Sochineniia*, XII: 141-72. To those who reasoned that given collectivization's universal nature, kulak exclusion would be unnecessary, he replied, "dekulakization represents a component part of the establishment and development of collective farms," adding that "when a head has been cut off, no one cries over the hairs" (170). See also Lewin, *Russian*

Peasants and Soviet Power, 487; *Izvestiia*, Feb. 2, 1930; and *Pravda*, April 3, 1930.

153. Solomon, "Rural Scholars," 148 (quoting S. M. Dubrovsky). Hearsay has Bukharin, Tomsky, and Rykov showing up uninvited on New Year's Eve 1929-30 at Stalin's Kremlin apartment, carrying Georgian wine, with Stalin letting them in. Medvedev, *Let History Judge*, 206 (no citation); Medvedev, *Nikolai Bukharin*, 25 (no citation).

154. This was Nov. 20, 1929. On Nov. 28, Stalin received Kamenev; on Dec. 11, Zinoviev. *Na prieme*, 31. Trotsky soon warned in an article dated Feb. 13, 1930, of the danger of kulaks infiltrating collective farms, which might become "a new form of social and political disguise for the kulaks." But his proposed solution was a vague "industrial and cultural revolution," not mass deportation. *Biulleten' oppozitsii*, 1930, no. 9: 4-5. Tucker, who lacked access to these sources, nonetheless understood that "Stalin placed his own regime before a fait accompli." Tucker, *Stalin in Power*, 145.

155. *Pravda*, Jan. 6, 1930; *Kommunisticheskaia partiia sovetskogo soiuza*, III: 667; Ivnitskii, "Istoriia podgotovki postanovleniia TsK VKP (b)," 265-88; RGASPI, f. 85, op. 27, d. 385, l. 1-5 (letter to Orjonikidze: Jan. 3, 1930); Vyltsan et al., "Nekotorye voprosy," 13. Davies, *Socialist Offensive*, 177-80, 237. For a chronology, see Viola, "Collectivization in the Soviet Union," 71.

156. Danilov et al., *Tragediia sovetskoi derevni*, II: 103-4 (TsA FSB, f. 2, op. 9, d. 21, l. 393-4).

157. Ivnitskii, *Kollektivizatsiia i raskulachivanie*, 108-9.

158. *Sochineniia*, XII: 173-4. Stalin was deferential to Gorky, explaining in a letter in Feb. 1930 to an editor about the republication in Gorky's *Collected Works* of his essay about Lenin from 1925 that "if comrade Gorky expresses doubts or—more than that—does not agree to introduce the changes, . . . then it will be necessary to publish the articles without any changes." Gorky refused to make the changes. Maksimenkov, *Bol'shaia tsenzura*, 173-4 (RGASPI, f. 558, op. 11, d. 822, l. 7, 8-9), 183 (l. 10: Feb. 28, 1930), 183-4 (f. 4, op. 2, d. 474, l. 29-30: A. A. Strunov, 1957).

159. On Feb. 2, 1930, an OGPU secret instruction to the special departments watching over the Red Army instituted a registry of soldiers found to have connections to "kulak elements." Soldiers observed in anti-Soviet activities were to be arrested. Suvenirov, *Tragediia RKKA*, 61; GARF, f. 9414, op. 1, d. 1944, l. 17-25. Stalin also, yet again, dispatched grain plenipotentiaries. Davies, *Socialist Offensive*, 267.

160. He added of the brave new world of anti-market statization: "If we do not put an end to the flood of paperwork, it will drown us. We conquered Denikin and Yudenich, Wrangel and various counterrevolutionary scoundrels, but paper will asphyxiate us." Ikonnikov, *Sozdanie i deiatel'nost'*, 212 (citing RGASPI, f. 85, op. 27, d. 27, l. 9).

161. A politburo decree of Jan. 30, 1930, divided the "kulaks" into three categories: "active counterrevolutionaries," estimated at 60,000 people, were to be "sentenced" extrajudicially either to execution or internment in camps by "troikas" consisting of the local OGPU chief, provincial party boss, and local procurator; those in the second category, around 1.5 million people, were to be dispossessed and deported to uninhabited or sparsely inhabited places; and those in the third, some 2 million, were to be left in place, for now, but expropriated and not allowed to join collective farms. Danliov et al., *Tragediia sovetskoi derevni*, II: 126-30 (RGASPI, f. 17,

op. 162, d. 8, l. 64-9). See also Viola, *Best Sons*, 216. Messing had asked Molotov to explain the party's policy to the OGPU collegium on Jan. 30-31, 1930, but Stalin rejected the request: a Central Committee directive to the OGPU was not a matter of discussion. Mozokhin and Gladkov, *Menzhinskii*, 259-61 (no citation); Danilov et al., *Tragediia sovetskoi derevni*, II: 151-5 (TsA FSB, f. 2os., op. 8, d. 35, l. 2-8).

162. *KPSS v rezoliutsiiakh* (7th ed.), II: 528. A volunteer's employer was supposed to pay for transportation, top off the lower collective-farm wages, and accept the worker back in the future. Many factories resisted releasing their workers. *Pravda*, Dec. 30, 1929; Viola, *Best Sons*, 35, 41, 56-7.

163. In Ukraine, the Caucasus, and Siberia, the regime deployed OGPU border guards as well (both groups inflicted and took casualties). Danilov et al., *Tragediia sovetskoi derevni*, II: 405-9 (TsA FSB, f. 2, op. 8, d. 329, l. 59-65: May 3, 1930). Officials had propagated the notion that collectivization would produce a "sharp improvement in the qualities of the human material available for the army." But soon the army political directorate warned (Sept. 8, 1930) of "sharpening kulak moods in the army" and a flood of peasant letters "asking the soldiers 'to defend the peasantry, to turn their guns against Soviet power.'" Gaevskii, "Kolkhoznoe stroitel'stvo"; Romano and Tarchova, *L'Armata Rossa*, 354-8 (RGVA, f. 9, op. 28, d. 161, l. 80-4). See also Tarkhova, "Krasnaia armiia," 114. The families of soldiers would eventually be exempted from dekulakization. But the Red Army political administration would not pronounce the political atmosphere among the soldiery stable until the end of 1932 (a time of famine). By the end of 1933, discharges would rise to at least 37,000. Tarkhova, *Krasnaia armiia*, 131, 204; Zdanovich, *Organy*, 313-4 (citing TsA FSB, f. 66, op. 1 d. 208, l. 111), 314n134.

164. Fitzpatrick, *Stalin's Peasants*, 52 (citing GASO, f. 1148, op. 148 r/2, d. 65, l. 39).

165. The 23-29 age cohort accounted for just 28.6 percent of the industrial work force. Kuromiya, "Crisis of Proletarian Identity," at 296n101, citing *Politicheskii i trudovoi pod"em rabochego klassa SSSR, 1928-1929 gg.* (Moscow, 1956), 545; Meyer, *Sozialstruktur sowjetischer Industriearbeiter*, 139.

166. Dubbed 25,000ers and "the best sons of the fatherland," they were celebrated in the Vladimir Mayakovsky march "Onward 25!/ Onward 25!" and Mikhail Sholokhov's novel, *Virgin Soil Upturned*. *Rabochaia gazeta*, Jan. 28, 1930; *Litsom k derevne*, 1930, no. 4: 3; Viola, *Best Sons*, 65. A regime official would boast that more than 100,000 factory workers had taken part in forcing through regime policy in the countryside as of June 1930. *XVI s"ezd VKP (b)*, 66; Ivnitskii and Ezerskii, "Dvadtsatipiatitysiachniki i ikh rol'," 462, 489; Selunskaia, *Rabochie-dvadtsatipiatitysiachniki*, 67, 76-7; Davies, *Socialist Offensive*, 168, 208, 210-11; Viola, *Best Sons*, 43. The mobilization officially ended on March 25, 1931: Savel'ev and Poskrebyshev, *Direktivy VKP (b)*, 844.

167. Viola, *Best Sons*, 2 (citing *Trud*, Feb. 2, 1930).

168. Viola, *Best Sons*, 63 (citing GARF, f. 5470, op. 14, d. 204, l. 47).

169. Carr wrote that "policy determined class." Carr, *Socialism in One Country*, I: 99.

170. "O meropriiatiiakh po ukrepleniiu sotsialisticheskogo pereustroistva sel'skogo khoziaistva v raionakh sploshnoi kollektivizatsii i po bor'be s kulachestvom: postanovlenie TsIK i SNK ot 1 fevralia 1930 g.": http://www.defree.ru/publications/p01/p40.htm#0724.

171. Fainsod, *Smolensk under Soviet Rule*, 245. "All properties were seized, including women's cut hair, children's shirts, bowls for syringing, tea cups, spoons, and bed linen," one report in Perm noted. "Confiscated kulak belongings were used as a dowry during some marriages." Suslov, "'Revolution from Above,'" citing PermGANI, f. 2, op. 7, d. 124, l. 112–5: not before March 2, 1930.

172. Hughes, "Capturing the Russian Peasantry," 99, citing GANO corpus 2, f. 2, op. 2–1, d. 3506, l. 2; op. 2, d. 366, l. 189–98.

173. Sevost'ianov et al., "*Sovershenno sekretno*," VIII/i: 746–63 (TsA FSB, f. 2, op. 8, d. 53, l. 31–79: April 29, 1930), 764–71 (d. 655, l. 500–9: May 14, 1930).

174. Viola, *Peasant Rebels*, 117 (citing GARF, f. 5469, op. 9, d. 398, l. 23). In Smolensk province, as elsewhere, party members were warned "to stay away from the windows" at work, and not to walk village streets at night. Fainsod, *Smolensk under Soviet Rule*, 241.

175. One published account has only fifty 25,000ers being killed or seriously wounded, an improbably small number. Selunskaia, *Rabochie-dvadtsatipiatitysiachniki*, 145 (no citation).

176. Fainsod, *Smolensk under Soviet Rule*, 245.

177. Reports also were going to Stalin tracing speculation among European diplomats about a possible Soviet attack against a weak Romania. He wrote on the reports: "to my archive." RGASPI, f. 558, op. 11, d. 184, l. 53–93; Khaustov et al., *Glazami razvedki*, 312–3 (l. 77–8: Feb. 11, 1930), 315–6 (l. 86–7: March 3, 1930).

178. For 1930, the OGPU would register 13,754 "group anti-Soviet protests" and 13,794 "terrorist acts," about half against property. But a mere 176 actions were qualified as full-fledged "uprisings" and another 44 as involving arms. The police recorded around 5,000 cases of leaflets or anonymous declarations. These numbers are likely not comprehensive, but they indicate something less than civil war. Danilov, *Tragediia sovetskoi derevni*, II: 787–808 (TsA FSB, f. 2, op. 8, d. 679, l. 36–72 March 15, 1931). See also Viola, *Peasant Rebels*, 100–31. For the civil war argument, see Graziosi, *Stalinism*, 5–64. The secret police had recorded sixty-three riots and spontaneous localized rebellions over the two years 1926–27. Berelowitch and Danilov, *Sovetskaia derevnia glazami VChK-OGPU-NKVD*, I: 18 (TsA FSB, sekretno-politicheskii otdel OGPU, dokladnaia zapiska 1930: 32).

179. Vasil'ev, "Krest'iane vosstaniia" (quoting declassified local archives without citation); Vasil'ev and Viola, *Kollektivizatsiia i krest'ianskoe soprotivlenie*, 213–5 (TsGAOO Ukrainy, f. 1, op. 20, d. 3154, l. 39–40), 215–6 (l. 42–3), 21620 (l. 48–53); Danilov et al., *Tragediia sovetskoi derevni*, II: 279, 324.

180. *Sochinenii*, XII: 188 (Feb. 9, 1930). On Soviet war fears, see also the telegram from Litvinov to Alexander Arosyev, Feb. 28, 1930: *DVP SSSR*, XIII: 118. Stalin had been cognizant not to aggravate tense relations with Poland (which had once ruled Ukraine), anxious that the Poles might take advantage of Soviet troubles. German-Soviet relations were on a knife's edge as well. Ken and Rusapov, *Zapadnoe prigranich'e*, 173–5 (RGASPI, f. 17, op. 162, d. 8, l. 53: Jan. 25, 1930), 538 43 (op. 162, d. 8, l. 114: March 11, 1930).

181. The article also took to task local officials who had lagged behind in implementing collectivization. *Pravda*, March 2, 1930; *Izvestiia*, March 2, 1930; *Sochineniia*, XII: 191–9. The politburo had voted to have Stalin "publish an article in the newspapers," but it remains unclear whether he had discussed beforehand the specific content of his article

and its self-exculpatory character. The politburo protocol was approved by telephone polling; Stalin's signature on it is from a stamp. A secret report to Orjonikidze from Balytsky, OGPU chief in Ukraine, on Feb. 25, and another the next day from party officials in Kharkov to Molotov, detailed both massive peasant resistance and the idea that local officials provoked dangerous peasant rebellion in key border regions by improperly implementing collectivization, the very language Stalin would use in his article. Adibekov et al., *Politbiuro TsK RKP (b)—VKP (b): povestki dnia zasedanii*, II: 25; Danilov et al., *Tragediia sovetskoi derevni*, II: 270 (RGASPI, f. 17, op. 3, d. 778, l. 5), 832–33n101 (APRF, f. 3, op. 30, d. 145, l. 138–44, 146–7). Syrtsov, who served on the key politburo commission on collective farms, in a speech to the Institute for Red Professors on Feb. 20, 1930, which was only published (March 15) after Stalin's article, foreshadowed many of his themes: *Bol'shevik*, 1930, no. 5: 47, 51.

182. Sevost'ianov et al., "*Sovershenno sekretno*," VIII/ii: 1253–4 (TsA FSB, f. 2, op. 8, d. 257, l. 18), 1257–8 (l. 15–7), 1258–1344 (d. 679, l. 181–319). Yagoda, a mere five days after Stalin's "Dizzy" article, reported to him that many regions were engaged in "conciliatory approaches to the kulak . . . defense of the kulak." Danilov et al., *Tragediia sovetskoi derevni*, II: 292–302 (TsA FSB, f. 2, op. 8, d. 40, l. 6–17). Stalin met with Yagoda that same day. *Na prieme*, 32 (March 7, 1930).

183. In fact, Balytsky was in the field commanding the crackdown; Stalin on the phone had reached Balytsky's deputy, Israel Leplyovsky. Vasil'ev and Viola, *Kollektivizatsiia i krest'ianskoe soprotivlenie*, 221–2 (TsGAOO Ukrainy, f. 1, op. 20, d. 3154, l. 11: March 19, 1930), 233 (RGASPI, f. 85, op. 1/s, d. 125, l. 2–2ob.: no later than March 25, 1930).

184. *Biulleten' oppozitsii*, 10 (April 1930): 2–7.

185. Hindus, *Red Bread*, 147.

186. Davydenko et al., *Put' trudovykh pobed*, 270–5; Viola, *Peasant Rebels*, 171–2 (citing RGAE, f. 7486, op. 37, d. 122, l. 104).

187. Storella and Sokolov, *Voice of the People*, 352 (RGAE, f. 7486s, op. 37, d. 102, l. 77–8). Bukharin, too, was undercut: he had just published yet another essay acknowledging the party was always right, while citing "kulak sabotage," *Pravda*, Feb. 19, 1930. See also Sevost'ianov et al., "*Sovershenno sekretno*," VIII/i: 725, 730 (TsA FSB, f. 2, op. 8, d. 92, l. 1–49).

188. Sevost'ianov et al., "*Sovershenno sekretno*," VIII/i: 722 (TsA FSB, f. 2, op. 8, d. 92, l. 1–49: April 24, 1930). Stalin sent a secret circular (April 2, 1930) to party organizations asserting that had it not been for the tactical retreat—portrayed as fixing the incorrect implementation of the party line—"we would now have had a wave of peasant insurrections, a good half of our 'lower' functionaries would have been killed by the peasants, the spring sowing would have failed, the collective farm construction would have been beaten down, and our internal and external position would have been put under threat." He also depicted his "Dizzy with Success" article as assigned to him by the Central Committee. On April 3, he felt compelled to publish a second article denying that he had written the first on his own initiative, calling it a directive of the Central Committee. Danilov and Ivnitskii, *Dokumenty svidetel'stvuiut*, 387–94. See also Zelenin, "Osushchestvlenie politiki," 47n4.

189. The functionary added: "Our public was so stunned by the unexpectedness of it that they did not know to react." "'Nachalo razgroma profdzvisheniia': dnevnik B. G. Kozeleva, 1927–1930 gg.," 136–7. The diarist Boris Kozelev was accused of right deviationism

and expelled from the party for two years when his diary was found. In Oct. 1930, he was mobilized to Magnitogorsk.

190. On April 21, the Siberian procuracy reported that 328 officials, mostly of rural soviets, had been sentenced to imprisonment or, in eleven cases, execution. One, in a drunken state, had murdered a peasant and raped his wife. Hughes, *Stalinism in a Russian Province*, 187–8 (citing GANO corpus 2, f. 2, op. 2, d. 465, l. 104–9; d. 459, l. 19–20, 32, 40), 190 (d. 460, l. 10, l. 31). In March 1930, the GPU district plenipotentiary in Western Siberia, F. G. Dobygin, had arrested eighty members of the soviet and party active and shot nine of them; he released kulaks from the county jail—they grabbed rifles and led an uprising of four hundred people. Danilov and Krasil'nikov, *Spetspereselentsy v Zapadnoi Sibiri*, 59 (GANO, f. p-1204, op. 1, d. 8, l. 68).

191. Kin's original letter was dated April 2, 1930; Stalin's response to him was returned as undeliverable, and on May 29, Tovstukha inquired of the Kherson party boss whether a Nikolai Kin existed—evidently Kin (whatever his real name) had given a false address. Maksimenkov, *Bol'shaia tsenzura*, 184–6 (RGASPI, f. 558, op. 11, d. 753, l. 114–7), 186 (l. 123), 188 (l. 121).

192. The idea of a rail link between Siberia and Russian Turkestan had first been bruited back in 1886; work had commenced in 1927. Carr and Davies, *Foundations of a Planned Economy*, I: 904–7; Payne, *Stalin's Railroad*.

193. *Izvestiia*, April 27, 1930; Lyons, *Assignment in Utopia*, 304–12 (quote at 304).

194. Another of the main arguments of *Magnetic Mountain* is that authoritarian state power is most effective when it is reproduced in people's everyday lives and identities.

195. Davies, *Soviet Economy in Turmoil*, 249–50.

196. Rassweiler, *Generation of Power*. The local factories slated to use the power supply made less progress. Davies, *Soviet Economy in Turmoil*, 215.

197. The earliest reports of hunger seem to have emerged from the Russian republic in Jan. 1930, in the Volga Valley, Stalingrad county, where half the harvest failed, according to secret police reports. Peasants there formed groups to demand food from the authorities, who took no special actions, as people consumed food surrogates and children stopped going to school. Kondrashin, *Golod v SSSR*, I/i: 146 (TsA FSB, f. 2, op. 8, d. 778, l. 394–8), 177–80 (d. 852, l. 296–302: July 26, 1930), 189–90 (d. 787, l. 992–3), 197–8 (op. 9, d. 546, l. 302–3: June 6, 1930), 198–9 (RGAE, op. 11, d. 17, l. 139–41: July 8, 1930).

198. Kondrashin et al., *Golod v SSSR*, I/i: 228–30 (TsA FSB, f. 2m, op. 8, d. 834, l. 985–6), 230 (RGAE, f. 8043, op. 11, d. 17, l. 208–208ob.), 230–9 (TsA FSB, f. 2, op. 8, d. 834, l. 1072–6).

199. Schoolteachers in Akmolinsk province of Kazakhstan deserted their schools en masse and signed on for work at the railroad, which had some food to distribute. Kondrashin et al., *Golod v SSSR*, I/i: 207–8 (GA Kustanaiskoi obl. Respubliki Kazakhstan, f. 54–p, op. 1, d. 784, l. 14), 220–7 (TSA FSB, f. 2m, op. 8, d. 744, l. 570–6), 227–8 (l. 612). Kazakhstan went from 2 percent collectivization of households as of 1928 to 50 percent as of April 1, 1930, by official statistics. Kozybaev et al., *Kollektivizatsiia v Kazakhstane*, 4.

200. As trade negotiations with Britain continued over Soviet obligations for tsarist and Provisional Government debt, the Soviet envoy to London, Sokolnikov, was receiving wide praise in the British press as one Communist who kept his word. A Russian émigré

periodical edited by Paul Miliukov, the former leader of the Constitutional Democrats, praised Sokolnikov as "the sole Soviet administrator who has demonstrated with deeds that he is capable of learning state affairs." Mischievously, the article posed the question, "Stalin or Sokolnikov?" Miliukov, *Poslednie novosti,* May 16, 1930; see also *Vozrozhdenie,* May 17, 1930; Genis, "Upriamyi narkom s il'inki," 235. Sokolnikov is said to have fretted to his wife, "Stalin will never forgive me this and will necessarily exact revenge." Serebriakova, "Iz vospominanii," at 242. On Sept. 17, 1930, Yaroslavsky wrote a denunciation to Orjonikidze (party Control Commission) of Sokolnikov's alleged expenditure in London of 4,000 gold rubles on sleeping quarters for his mistress. Kvashonkin, *Sovetskoe rukovodstvo,* 134–5 (RGASPI, f. 85, op. 27, d. 267, l. 1–2). Sokolnikov would serve as envoy to Britain through Sept. 14, 1932. He was replaced by Jan Lachowiecki, from a Russified Polish family, who had taken the name Ivan Maisky, a confidant of Litvinov.

201. Ivnitskii, *Kollektivizatsiia i raskulachivanie,* 115 (no citation). "We are facing a combat situation here," one soldier in Bashkiria noted, according to a spring 1930 police report with many such examples. "I see how they are driving the peasants, and my heart is broken. Nothing can be done, I'll have to keep silent." Sevost'ianov et al., *"Sovershenno sekretno,"* VIII/ii: 1219–24 (TsA FSB, f. 2, op. 8, por. 653, l. 305–7).

202. Ivnitskii, *Sud'ba raskulachennykh,* 24. See also Jasny, *Socialized Agriculture,* 308.

203. Davies, *Soviet Collective Farm,* 153.

204. Viola, *Best Sons,* 157–8. Peasants, too, were getting promoted by the hundreds of thousands into positions of rural authority, taking ad hoc study courses. Aruntiunian, *Mekhanizatory sel'skogo khoziaistva SSSR.*

205. Rozenfel'd, *Dvadtsatipiatitysiachniki,* 31, 158–9.

206. Davies, *Soviet Collective Farm,* 292, citing *Sotsialisticheskoe zemleutsroitsvo,* 1930, no. 3–4: 56–9. Individual peasants received the new land allocations last in line and in smaller allotments, which were less conveniently located and often marshy or infested, but they persevered.

207. Davies, *Soviet Collective Farm,* 160, citing *Resheniia partii i pravitel'stva po khoziaistvennym voprosam* (1967), II: 196 (March 14, 1930). No single decree had introduced the NEP, and no single decree would abolish it—in fact, technically, NEP would be "transcended" in the Hegelian, dialectical sense.

208. Decisions on how to distribute income from the 1930 harvest would be made locally. There would be wide variation, but also a basic calculation such that collective farmers would receive compensation out of what remained after expenses and tax payments on a "per eater" basis, meaning farmers would get a portion of the harvest irrespective of how much work they had done, a disincentive to work harder. Davies noted that "perhaps the most remarkable feature of the spring of 1930 is that the sowing took place quite successfully in the *kolkhozy* even though the collective farmers were working on credit for an unknown amount of payment, often not knowing by which system they would be paid." The original compensation idea—that collective farmers would be paid factory-style wages based on a piece rate system (in line with a vision of gigantic farms)—failed, and not only because cash was in short supply: a guaranteed wage promised to shift the financial burden of any crop failures to the state. Davies also shows that only in June 1930, by which time sowing had been completed, did

the regime decide upon remuneration on the basis of "labor days," a system that treated work accomplished as a dividend to be paid from what was left over from the collective farm's income (in kind and money) after state deliveries and taxes. Record keeping remained sporadic, however. Davies, *Soviet Collective Farm,* 140, 140–67; *S"ezdy sovetov Soiuza Sovetskikh SSR,* III: 189.

209. *Partiinoe khoziaistvo,* 1930, no. 7–8: 8 (Wolf).

210. Davies, *Soviet Collective Farm,* 310, citing *Sotsialisticheskoe zemledelie,* June 3, 1930.

211. Murin, *Stalin v ob"iatiakh,* 29 (APRF, f. 45, op. 1, d. 1550, l. 30), 41n17.

212. Trapeznikov, *Kommunisticheskaia partiia,* 38–9; Rigby, *Communist Party Membership,* 178–9; Fainsod, *Smolensk under Soviet Rule,* 211–2, 218. Because some were later rehabilitated, or because incomplete figures were initially reported, sometimes the figure is reported as 130,000, including 14,000 who quit voluntarily: *Partiinoe stroitel'stvo,* 1930, no. 10 (12): 14–9; Schapiro, *Communist Party of the Soviet Union,* 435. Cf. *Pravda,* April 23, 1931. A comprehensive study of rural Communists in the RSFSR in 1929 had shown that one in four owned property worth more than 800 rubles, compared with one in six of the overall peasant population. Communist peasants were also more likely to employ hired labor. Gaister and Levin, "O sostave sel'partorganiztsii."

213. Gill, *Origins,* 137; Rigby, *Communist Party Membership,* 420; Kuromiya, *Stalin's Industrial Revolution,* 48; Carr and Davies, *Foundations of a Planned Economy,* 132. Tsarist-era officials comprised 10 percent of the staff in commissariats, albeit a mere 2 percent had been ministers or high officials. This was after sweeping purges of the state apparatus. *Izvestiia,* Aug. 10, 1930.

214. Stalin also told the congress, "we are in favor of the state dying out, and at the same time we stand for the strengthening of the dictatorship of the proletariat." He acknowledged the contradiction, but called it Marxist dialectics. In 1933, he would reiterate the point. *Sochineniia,* XIII: 211, 350. Engels had written in *Anti-Dühring* (1878) that "the interference of the state power in social relations becomes superfluous in one sphere after another, and then ceases of itself . . . The state is not 'abolished,' it withers away [*es stirbt ab*]." Engels, *Unwälzung der Wissenschaft,* 291–2.

215. *XVI s"ezd VKP (b),* 17–57; *Sochineniia,* XII: 235–373. See also Davies, *Socialist Offensive,* 330–6. Stalin ridiculed "the complete absurdity of chatter about NEP being incompatible with an attack" on capitalist elements. *Sochineniia,* XII: 306–7. Select workers had been invited to deliver personal narratives to the congress, which became the first with no speeches against the leadership. Szamuely, "Elimination of Opposition." Even after the opening of the archives, Szamuely's article remains the most incisive on the problem of opposition to Stalin.

216. Shitts, *Dnevnik,* 195; Pavlova, *Stalinizm,* 68–9 (citing GARF, f. 1235, op. 133, d. 11, l. 28, 30). Shitts, born (1874) in Tambov, studied history with the medievalist P. Vinogradov at Moscow University, where he eventually got a position teaching Latin. In 1928 he became the editor of the *Great Soviet Encyclopedia.* He would be arrested in 1933.

217. These words were omitted from *Sochineniia,* XII: 233, 234.

218. Davies, *Soviet Economy in Turmoil,* 250–1, 372–5; *Za industrializatsiiu,* June 19, July 5, Oct. 8, 1930. On June 16, 1930, in his recognition of the newly opened Rostov Agricultural

Engineering Works, Stalin also thanked "all those foreign specialists—engineers and technicians—who have helped." Stikh, *Zavod griadushchikh urozhaev,* 22; *Pravda,* June 17, 1930.

219. Glan, *Iakov Il'in,* 235. See also Il'in, *Bol'sheviki dolzhny ovladet' tekhnikoi;* Il'in, *Liudi stalingradskogo traktornogo;* and his incomplete posthumous novel *Bol'shoi konveier* (Moscow: Molodaia gvardiia, 1934). Il'in (b. 1905) died in Dec. 1932. Margaret Bourke-White, the photographer, observed at the Stalingrad Tractor Factory how "one Russian is screwing in a tiny bolt and twenty other Russians are standing around watching him, talking it over, smoking cigarettes, arguing . . . They are like children marveling over new toys. More than that, they are religious fanatics worshipping before a new shrine." Bourke-White, *Eyes on Russia,* 118–9.

220. Boris Sheboldayev remarked at the congress (June 29): "In many party organizations we have witnessed demonstrations, both of the most straightforward right-wing opportunist and of the 'leftist' Trotskyite type, that for sheer boldness and effrontery surpass anything seen even at the height of our struggle with the rights." *XVI s"ezd VKP (b),* 135–6.

221. While Mikoyan ripped into the "right deviation," Rudzutaks told the delegates the rightists had engaged in "direct slander of the party, direct slander of comrade Stalin." *XVI s"ezd VKP (b),* 39–44. The exiled Trotsky wrote that "the plebiscite regime has been established conclusively," without acknowledging the root cause. Trotsky, "Preliminary Comments on the Sixteenth Congress" [July 25, 1930], II: 335–6.

222. Bukharin had known Larina since she was four. She had grown up in her stepfather Yuri Larin's apartment in the Metropole, which was visited by top party officials, including Stalin. Bukharin lived one floor below. On the Black Sea he was still involved with Alexandra Travina—a lover planted on him (it seems she had miraculously appeared in the same coupé on the overnight train from Moscow to Leningrad). Larina and Bukharin would marry in 1934. " 'No ia to znaiu, chto ty prav': pis'mo N. I. Bukharina I. V. Stalinu iz vnutrennei tiur'my NKVD," 49 (APRF, f. 3, op. 24, d. 301, l. 129–33). Gregory, *Politics, Murder, and Love,* 57–60, 67–9, 72–4; Larina, *This I Cannot Forget,* 107–12.

223. *XVI s"ezd VKP (b),* 142–8. Rykov was no coward: when criticized in person at a Urals party gathering in June 1930, he had responded forcefully and received an ovation.

224. Murin, *Stalin v ob"iatiakh,* 29–30 (APRF, f. 45, op. 1, d. 1550, l. 31–2).

225. *XVI s"ezd VKP (b),* 63; *XVI s"ezd VKP (b), 26 iiunia–13 iiulia 1930 g.,* I: 122. Tomsky was eventually replaced by the Stalin favorite Nikolai Shvernik (b. 1888), whom the dictator had promoted from Leningrad in 1926 to the central apparatus, then assigned to the Urals. When Shvernik had reported in 1929 that his Urals party organization had failed to fulfill assigned targets, Stalin wrote back, "There are no grounds to complain, you did all you could." Davies and Harris, *Stalin's World,* 42 (citing RGASPI, op. 11, d. 36, l. 103); Kosheleva, *Pis'ma Stalina Molotovu,* 141–44.

226. Kirov, *Izbrannye stat'i rechi,* 539.

227. Kvashonkin, *Sovetskoe rukovodstvo,* 117–29 (RGASPI, f. 85, op. 27, d. 397, l. 2–7). Pyatakov had been inspired to set out his thoughts in writing by a conversation with Orjonikidze, as noted in a letter to the latter (129n4: l. 1, July 20). See also Lih et al., *Stalin's Letters to Molotov,* 187–9.

228. *Vechernyi klub,* Dec. 22, 1992 (interview with Poskryobyshev from 1964). The

secretariat had a "bureau, which in March 1926 was replaced by a 'secret department.'" RGASPI, f. 17, op. 84, 85, 86. See also Rosenfeldt, *"Special" World*. Stalin had posted his former top aide, the Marxist scholar Ivan Tovstukha (b. 1889), who had only one lung and tuberculosis, to the Lenin Institute; another long-standing top aide, the high-strung Lev Mekhlis, who hankered after Tovstukha's intellectual authority, browbeat Stalin into allowing him, finally, to take leave to bootstrap a Marxist education at the Institute of Red Professors. This opened the way for Poskryobyshev, who eventually became Stalin's top aide. His wife was the sister of the wife of Trotsky's son Lev Sedov. See also Bazhanov, *Damnation of Stalin*, 34–40.

229. Already by the next day he was said to be feeling fine. The drivers of the two vehicles went unpunished. *Gosudarstvennaia okhrana Rossii*, 47 (citing TsA FSB, f. 2, op. 8, d. 107).

230. RGASPI, f. 558, op. 11, d. 700, l. 4. OR l. 47.

231. Chigirin, *Stalin*, 79–83 (RGASPI, f. 558, op. 11, d. 1482, l. 44–51).

232. Valedinskii, "Organizm Stalina vpolne zdorovyi," 69. Kaganovich, too, got a new apartment, and was said to be "very satisfied" and "touched by Stalin's attention." Murin, *Stalin v ob"iatiakh*, 33 (APRF, f. 45, op. 1, d. 1550, l. 46–7). Kaganovich's apartment was in the so-called children's wing of the Grand Kremlin Palace, also known as the tsarevich's quarters.

233. Kosheleva, *Pis'ma Stalina Molotovu*, 196–7; Lih et al., *Stalin's Letters to Molotov*, 207–8.

234. The regime had rechristened the peasant commune, whose origins went back deep into the mists of ancient Russia, a "land society." But in the RSFSR, a decree of July 30, 1930, stipulated that land societies were to be liquidated wherever 75 percent of households belonged to the new collective farms. (Unlike collective farms, the commune entailed working land individually while holding it in common.) Davies, *Soviet Collective Farm*, 34–5; Davies, *Socialist Offensive*, 227–8; Atkinson, *End of the Russian Land Commune*, 369–70. In Ukraine, where communes did not predominate, they had been abolished by decree already in Jan. 1930.

235. Khaustov et al., *Lubianka: Stalin i VChK*, 250 (RGASPI, f. 17, op. 162, d. 9, l. 16, 20). As of Oct. 1, 1930, the OGPU apparatus consisted of 22,180 employees. That included around 2,000 in the central apparatus, 5,067 on transport, 1,425 at the OGPU central school, 612 at the transport school, 97 at the Lubyanka inner prison, and 270 at the Butyrka prison; more than 10,000 were deployed in localities. Yagoda complained in a directive, however, that operatives preferred to remain in provincial towns and administrative centers, refusing to be deployed in counties or villages. Petrov and Skorkin, *Kto rukovodil NKVD*, 34–5 (TsA FSB, f. 2, op. 9, d. 183), 36n1 (Nov. 12, 1930).

236. Most other crops also did well. Davies, *Socialist Offensive*, 337–8, 419 (table 1).

237. Procurements were 6 million more than in 1929–30 (and double the total of 1928–29). The MTS were entrusted with scarce heavy equipment, which they leased to collective farms in exchange for part of the crop. Miller, *One Hundred Thousand Tractors*. At the end of 1930, the 158 machine tractor stations controlled more than 31,000 tractors but only about 200 trucks and 17 cars. Davies, *Soviet Collective Farm*, 31, citing *Sotsialistichekoe zemledelie*, Dec. 20, 1930.

238. Rakovski gave a similar incisive analysis from exile that was also published abroad. Braginskaia, "Pobeda plana i rekord besplan-

novosti"; Rakovski, "Na s"ezde i v strane"; Filtzer, *Soviet Workers*, 39–41. See also Lewin, "Disappearance of Planning."

239. Filtzer, *Soviet Workers*, 37, citing *Severenyi rabochii*, April 15, 1930, and *Za industrializatsiiu*, July 20, 1930.

240. Filtzer, *Soviet Workers*, 38, 43.

241. He instructed Molotov (Aug. 6, 1930) to "pay attention to the Stalingrad and Leningrad [Putilov] tractor factories. Things are bad there." Lih et al., *Stalin's Letters to Molotov*, 200–1, 201n8 (RGASPI, f. 17, op. 3, d. 793, l. 3).

242. Stalin singled out by name Ivan Klimenko. Lih et al., *Stalin's Letters to Molotov*, 202, 203n2 (RGASPI, f. 17, op. 3, d. 793, l. 21–3, 7).

243. In Stalin's absence the politburo had twice examined the South Caucasus party infighting; he demanded that a damning politburo decree be published in full. Lih et al., *Stalin's Letters to Molotov*, 202, 203n3 (RGASPI, f. 17, op. 3, d. 790, l. l. 8; d. 791, l. 23, 24: July 20, Aug. 3, 1930).

244. In 1929 and the first half of 1930, Kalinin's central executive committee had received an astonishing 172,500 petitions of wrongful dekulakization (337,563 households would be dekulakized in 1930); Kalinin's secretariat managed to adjudicate just 785 of them (ruling in the plaintiff's favor 519 times). "Rol' OGPU v raskulachivanii krest'ianskih khoziaistv": http://helion-ltd.ru/ogpu-role.

245. Khlevniuk, *Master of the House*, 7 (RGASPI, f. 85, recent acquisitions, d. 2, l. 1–11, 28–30); Khlevniuk, *Khoziain*, 31.

246. In a follow-up letter of Sept. 2, Stalin put Kalinin on the same plane as Rykov. Kosheleva, *Pis'ma Stalina Molotovu*, 198–202, 211–3; Lih et al., *Stalin's Letters to Molotov*, 210–1.

247. Kosheleva, *Pis'ma Stalina Molotovu*, 198–202; Lih et al., *Stalin's Letters to Molotov*, 203–4. The next day, on the basis of Mikoyan's reports on successful procurements, Stalin demanded still more exports, writing to Molotov, "Otherwise we risk being left without our new iron and steel and machine-building factories (Nizhny Novgorod auto factory, Chelyabinsk Tractor Plant, etc.)." Lih et al., *Stalin's Letters to Molotov*, 200–1, 201n8 (RGASPI, f. 17, op. 3, d. 793, l. 3: Aug. 6, 1930).

248. Dohan, "Economic Origins of Soviet Autarky," 615–6; Tracy, *Agriculture in Western Europe*, 127; Davies, *Socialist Offensive*, 107. See also *Course and Phases of the World Economic Depression*, 167ff.

249. Stalin also felt that Mikoyan was not coping as trade commissar ("a job that is difficult, if not impossible, for one person to handle"), and proposed he be removed or given an outstanding deputy, suggesting Arkady Rozenholz, a member of the Central Control Commission. The politburo formally appointed Rozengolts deputy trade commissar for foreign trade on Sept. 10. On Nov. 15, 1930, trade was redivided into two commissariats, and Rozenholz became commissar for foreign trade. Kosheleva, *Pis'ma Stalina Molotovu*, 202–6; Lih et al., *Stalin's Letters to Molotov*, 204–6, 206n7 (RGASPI, f. 17, op. 3, d. 796, l. 9; d. 804, l. 6). Prices for other Soviet exports fell by 20 percent.

250. *Vneshniaia torgovlia SSSR, 1918–1966*, 20.

251. Timber exports, which had only resumed in 1927, would attain 18 percent of the world market in 1931; imperial Russia had had 15 percent of the world timber market in 1913. The USSR targeted the United States, Italy, Germany, and Britain; the British market for Soviet raw materials opened in April 1930.

252. Potocki, *Polityka państwa polskiego*, 262–72; Snyder, *Sketches from a Secret War*, 102 (citing CAW I/303/4/6982).

253. To pay for this new expense, he instructed Molotov to "raise the money through an increase in the production of vodka." Kosheleva, *Pis'ma Stalina Molotovu*, 209–10; Lih et al., *Stalin's Letters to Molotov*, 208–10; RGASPI, f. 17, op. 162, d. 9, l. 31. In short order, the politburo enacted his will. RGASPI, f. 17, op. 3, d. 796, l. 7 (Sept. 25, 1930).

254. An estimated 3,000 engineers had been arrested in the Donbass in 1928–29. "Over the last several years we liquidated counterrevolutionary organizations almost in every sphere of the economy," the OGPU reported in May 1930. Sevost'ianov et al., "*Sovershenno sekretno*," VIII/ii: 1140 (TsA FSB, f. 2, op. 8, por. 435, l. 169–241).

255. Kosheleva, *Pis'ma Stalina Molotovu*, 178–9 (Aug. 2, 1930); Lih et al., *Stalin's Letters to Molotov*, 199–200; *Kommunist*, no. 11 (1990): 96 (RGASPI, f. 558, op. 1, d. 5275, l. 1). In Oct., after Stalin returned from holiday, he sacked Pyatakov from the state bank.

256. Stalin singled out the tsarist-era economists Vladimir Groman and Nikolai Kondratiev (of "long wave" fame), insisted they were linked to Bukharin, Tomsky, and Rykov, and wrote that "Kondratiev, Groman and a few other scoundrels must definitely be shot." Kosheleva, *Pis'ma Stalina Molotovu*, 193–6; Lih et al., *Stalin's Letters to Molotov*, 200–1 (Aug. 6), 201n8 (RGASPI, f. 17, op. 3, d. 793, l. 3).

257. Kosheleva, *Pis'ma Stalina Molotovu*, 211–3 (Sept. 2, 1930); Lih et al., *Stalin's Letters to Molotov*, 210–1. Stalin worried whether the trial would come off as scripted ("Are we ready for this? Do we consider it necessary to take the 'case' to trial?"). Finally, in March 1931, fourteen members of a supposed Menshevik party were publicly tried and convicted of attempting to restore their party and overthrow the Soviet regime. Litvin, *Men'shevistskii protsess 1931 goda*; *Menshevik Trial*. See also Evdoshenko, "Delo neftianikov-'vreditelei' 1929–1931 gg.," 331–89.

258. Kosheleva, *Pis'ma Stalina Molotovu*, 216–8 (Sept. 13, 1930), 218, n2 (RGASPI, f. 17, op. 3, d. 798, l. 12); Lih et al., *Stalin's Letters to Molotov*, 213–5.

259. *Pravda*, Sept. 25, 1930; Sevost'ianov et al., "*Sovershenno sekretno*," VIII/ii: 1184–5 (TsA FSB, f. 2, op. 8, d. 658, l. 106–12: Sept. 28, 1930).

260. RGANI, f. 89, op. 48, d. 1, Hoover Institution Archives; Prystaiko and Shapoval, *Sprava "Spilky Vzvolennaia Ukrainy*," 236; Sevost'ianov et al., "*Sovershenno sekretno*," VIII/ii: 1148 (TsA FSB, f. 2, op. 8, por. 435, l. 169–241: late May 1930).

261. 'voeno-fashistskii zagovor,' 103–4; Lebedev, "M. N. Tukhachevskii i voenno-fashistskii zagovor," at 247–8.

262. Minakov, *Voennaia elita*, 114–5.

263. Isserson, "Sud'ba polkovodtsa," 189 (Todorovsky, head of Red Army training). The book in question was Triandafillov, *Kharakter operatsii sovremennoi armii*. Triandafillov, an ethnic Greek who had been born (1894) in tsarist Kars province (later ceded to Turkey), would die in a military plane crash in a fog on July 12, 1931. The politburo forbade the regime's highest officials from flying. Stalin would not get on an airplane until 1943.

264. Aptekar' and Uspenskii, *Marshal M.N. Tukhachevskii* (RGVA, f. 7, op. 10, d. 1047, l. 2–8ob., Jan. 11, 1930); Ken, *Mobilizatsionnoe planirovanie*, 91–3 (l. 10ob.–140b, 22–3: Shaposhnikov analysis, Feb. 15). See also Biriuzov, "Predislovie," 12; Erickson, *Soviet High Command* (3rd ed.), 326–30, 349–57; and Ken, *Mobilizatsionnoe planirivanie*, 83.

265. Ken, *Mobilizatsionnoe planirovanie*, 97 n7, 8 (RGVA, f. 4, op. 19, d. 10, l. 125: Voroshilov to Stalin, March 5, 1930).

266. Samuelson, *Soviet Defence Industry Planning*, 126 (RGVA, f. 33987, op. 3, d. 155: March 5, 1930). Voroshilov was angling for greater military expenditures. *Pravda*, Feb. 23, 1930.

267. Ken, "'Moia otsenka byla slyshkom rezkoi,'" 150–1 (RGASPI, f. 74, op. 2, d. 38, l. 58: March 23, 1930); Kvashonkin, *Sovetskoe rukovodstvo*, 113. See also Stone, "Tukhachevskii in Leningrad," 1379; Samuelson, *Plans for Stalin's War Machine*, 99–112. RGASPI, f. 558, op. 11, d. 446, l. 13–18.

268. On Aug. 14, the OGPU arrested a former tsarist colonel, Ivan Troitsky, who taught at the Frunze Military Academy and called himself "the agitator for Tukhachevsky's achievements," and, on Aug. 19, Nikolai Kakurin, a former tsarist staff officer who had served in various White armies but gone over to the Reds, taught at the military academy, too, and fought under Tukhachevsky's command. Olga Zajonczkowska-Popova—the daughter of the former tsarist general and nobleman Andrzej Zajonchkowski, who had died in 1926 and had served as a secret-police informant—was herself a secret police informant, making use of her famous father's name to mix in the highest military circles, and she had denounced Kakurin, who was her first cousin. Tinchenko, *Golgofa*, 114–5 (citing GA SBU, fl. D. 67093, t. 54, delo Kakurina N. E.: 40).

269. *Voennye arkhivy Rossii*, 103–4. By Oct. 5, OGPU interrogators had Kakurin imagining that Tukhachevsky had indirectly revealed he was contemplating Stalin's assassination. *Voennye arkhivy Rossii*, 104; Lebedev, "M. N. Tukhachevskii i 'voenno-fashistskii zagovor,' 248.

270. Zdanovich, *Organy*, 395–6 (citing TsA FSB, f. 2, op. 8, d. 258, l. 248).

271. Chuev, *Tak govoril Kaganovich*, 60.

272. Kosheleva, *Pis'ma Stalina Molotovu*, 216–8, 220–2, 222–3; Lih et al., *Stalin's Letters to Molotov*, 213–5, 216–7, 217–9. This frustration extended well beyond Stalin. Gregory and Markevich, "Creating Soviet Industry," 802, citing RGAE, f. 7297, op. 38, d. 104, l. 2; Khlevniuk, *Politbiuro*, 42; Davies, *Soviet Economy in Turmoil*, 439.

273. Syrtsov made some critical remarks at the 16th Party Congress in July 1930, but Stalin had permitted him to be reelected as candidate member of the politburo. Still, the dictator continued to grumble. Kosheleva, *Pis'ma Stalina Molotovu*, 214–6; Lih et al., *Stalin's Letters to Molotov*, 212. On Sept. 25, the politburo dispatched Syrtsov to the Mid-Volga territory to expedite grain procurements. RGASPI, f. 17, op. 3, d. 798, l. 4.

274. RGASPI, f. 558, op. 11, d. 769, l. 37–8; Khlevniuk, "Stalin, Syrtsov, Lominadze," 90–1 (citing RGASPI, f. 17, op. 3, d. 797, l. 1–2). Mężyński and Olsky, for their part, kept sounding alarms about planned "terrorist acts," including against Stalin. Sevost'ianov et al., "*Sovershenno sekretno*," VIII/ii: 1451–2 (TsA FSB, f. 2, op. 8, d. 258, l. 236: Sept. 19, 1930).

275. Khlevniuk, *Politbiuro*, 40–52; Watson, *Molotov*, 99–104. On Rykov, see *Aleksei Ivanovich Rykov*; Oppenheim, *Practical Bolshevik*; Shelestov, *Vremia Alekseia Rykova*; and Senin, *A. I. Rykov*.

276. *Voennye arkhivy Rossii*, 103–4.

277. Khaustov et al., *Lubianka: Stalin i VChK*, 256–7 (TsA FSB, f. 2, op. 9, d. 388, l. 270–1: Oct. 1930); *Kommunist*, 1990, no. 11: 99–100 (RGASPI, f. 558, op. 1, d. 5276); Kosheleva, *Pis'ma Stalina Molotovu*, 187–8; Lih et al., *Stalin's Letters to Molotov*, 195–6.

278. Murin, *Stalin v ob"iatiakh*, 30 (l. 34–5: Sept. 5), 31 (36–7: Sept. 8). Fifteen and sixteen

years earlier, Stalin had written to fellow revolutionaries asking for something to read in English or French while he was in remote Siberian exile. Ostrovskii, *Kto stoial*, 399–401, 409, 413.

279. Murin, *Stalin v ob"iatiakh*, 31 (APRF, f. 45, op. 1, d. 1550, l. 36, 37), 32 (l. 41–2), 32–3 (l. 43–5), 33 (l. 38–40), 34 (l. 48–9). Stalin responded on Oct. 8: "You hint at some kind of excursions by me. I inform you that I have not traveled anywhere (anywhere at all!) and I have no intention of traveling." Murin, *Stalin v ob"iatiakh*, 34–5 (l. 50–1).

280. RGASPI, f. 558, op. 11, d. 738, l. 110.

281. Kvashonkin, *Sovetskoe rukovodstvo*, 144–6 (RGASPI, f. 558, op. 11, d. 765, l. 68a); Enker, "Struggling for Stalin's Soul," 172–5.

282. Khlevniuk, *Politbiuro*, 42–3.

283. Khlevniuk, *Master of the House*, 30–3 (citing RGASPI, f. 558, op. 11, d. 769, l. 68a; d. 765, l. 55–58; d. 738, l. 110–1; d. 778, l. 43); Khlevniuk, *Politbiuro*, 42–3. Kaganovich later in life recalled that he had supported Molotov, in the event Stalin declined to head the government. Chuev, *Tak govoroil Kaganovich*, 60.

284. Stalin is listed as meeting (with Nikolai Popov of *Pravda*) on Oct. 13, his first meeting since July 22. *Na prieme*, 34–5.

285. Stalin to Bukharin, Oct. 14, and Bukharin's second letter of Oct. 14: Kvashonkin, *Sovetskoe rukovodstvo*, 146–7 (RGASPI, f. 329, op. 2, d. 6, l. 78); 147–8 (l. 77).

286. Iakovlev et al., *Reabilitatsiia: politicheskie protsessy*, 242, 244. The politburo meeting also censured a pamphlet Syrtsov had published based on a presentation he had made on control figures for output in physical units for 1930–31, supposedly "among those series of questions that are not to be made public and disseminated." Khlevniuk et al., *Stalinskoe politbiuro*, 95 (RGASPI, f. 17, op. 2, d. 446, l. 2–4), 106n4 (RGASPI, f. 17, op. 3, d. 800, l. 7); Khlevniuk, *Politbiuro*, 44. Syrtsov's pamphlet is reprinted in Khlevniuk et al., *Stenogrammy zasedanii politbiuro*, 323–46 (RGASPI, f. 82, op. 2, d. 53, l. 92–108).

287. The Soviets decided to reduce trade with the United States: it would fall during the period from Oct. 1930 to March 1931 by nearly half, compared with the same period the year before. This reflected a surmise that increased trade had diminished the argument for diplomatic recognition. Haslam, *Soviet Foreign Policy*, 38, 53–4; *Ekonomicheksia zhizn'*, Oct. 12, 1930.

288. Also present was Pavel Postyshev, a Central Committee secretary. *Na prieme*, 35. Lominadze, in Stalin's mind, enjoyed the inexplicable protection of Orjonikidze, a source of friction between them. Lih et al., *Stalin's Letters to Molotov*, 162–3 (July 29, 1929); Khromov, *Po stranitsam*, 201–3 (RGASPI, f. 558, op. 11, d. 23, l. 81–8); Khlevniuk, *In Stalin's Shadow*, 32.

289. RGASPI, f. 17, op. 3, d. 801, l. 9. Complaining officials in Western Siberia were dismissed. Lih et al., *Stalin's Letters to Molotov*, 202n2 RGASPI, f. 17, op. 3, d. 793, l. 7). Lih gives the date of the politburo session as Oct. 19.

290. Lebedev, "fraviashchaia portiia," 94; Khlevniuk et al., *Stenogrammy zasedanii politbiuro*, 353n93 (RGASPI, f. 17, op. 162, d. 9, l. 54); Khaustov et al., *Lubianka: Stalin i VChK*, 255–6. The politburo resolutions were approved by telephone poll (dated Oct. 25). At the session, Stalin evidently had ordered the windows closed, even though they were high up on the top floor of Old Square. Khlevniuk et al., *Stalinskoe politbiuro*, 98n2 (RGASPI, f. 17, op. 3, d. 800, l. 7; d. 801, l. 12); Iakovlev et al., *Reabilitatsiia: politicheskie protsessy*, 242, 244.

291. Khlevniuk, *Politbiuro*, 39 (RGASPI, f. 17, op. 3, d. 801, l. 12; f. 589, op. 3, d. 9333, t. 2, l. 135).

292. Khlevniuk et al., *Stenogrammy zasedanii politbiuro*, III: 205–9. Stalin passed it to Orjonikidze (party Control Commission) and Postyshev (CC secretary); Molotov and Kaganovich were away on holiday. Reznikov would soon be hired by Mekhlis.

293. Reznikov asserted that Syrtsov had called the Oct. 22 meeting. Other attendees were Vladimir Kavraisky, in whose apartment the meeting took place, I. Nusinov, and A. Halperin. Khlevniuk et al., *Stenogrammy zasedanii politbiuro*, III: 209 (Reznikov), 272 (Kavraisky, according to the OGPU), 280 (Nusinov), 285 (Halperin).

294. Stalin received Syrtsov on Old Square on Oct. 22 at 2:40 p.m. Postyshev was present. *Na prieme*, 35.

295. Khlevniuk et al., *Stenogrammy zasedanii politbiuro*, III: 121, 347n4 (RGASPI, f. 613, op. 1, d. 142, l. 105, 109).

296. Khlevniuk et al., *Stalinskoe politbiuro*, 96–7 (RGASPI, f. 589, op. 3, d. 9333, t. 2, l. 134–5); Khlevniuk et al., *Stenogrammy zasedanii politbiuro*, III: 209–13, 25. See also Khlevniuk, "Stalin, Syrtsov, Lominadze," 78–96; and Davies, "The Syrtsov-Lominadze Affair."

297. Kosheleva, *Pis'ma Stalina Molotovu*, 231–2; Lih et al., *Stalin's Letters to Molotov*, 223–4. Around this time, Stalin heard Mark Reizen (b. 1895), a lush, voluminous basso cantante, sing the role of Mephistopheles in a production of Charles Gounod's *Faust* at the Bolshoi, and had the Leningrad-based artist relocated to Moscow. Reizen, *Mark Reizen, Avtobiograficheskie zapiski*, 135–53; Marshkova, *Bol'shoi teatr*, 824–38.

298. The episode would be revealed only in 1937: *Voennye arkhivy Rossii*, 104–5; Lebedev, "M. N. Tukhachevskii i 'voenno-fashistskii zagovor," 248–9. Not everyone vouched for Tukhachevsky: Shchadenko supported his arrest. Ken, *Mobilizatsionnoe planirovanie*, 131n25 (RGASPI, f. 17, op. 165, d. 59, l. 102–3: uncorrected stenogram of the June 2, 1937, Main Military Council). Troitsky was sentenced to three years and became an OGPU secret informant; Kakurin, who had been released, would be rearrested in 1932 and given a death sentence, which was commuted to ten years.

299. Kosheleva, *Pis'ma Stalina Molotovu*, 231–2; Lih et al., *Stalin's Letters to Molotov*, 223. Voroshilov did not desist, however: in Jan. 1931 he sent "Dear Koba" a letter with two compromising documents on Tukhachevsky (letters from Verkhovsky and Bergavinov). Ken, *Mobilizatsionnoe planirovanie*, 131–2 n27 (RGASPI, f. 74, op. 2, d. 37, l. 24).

300. Khlevniuk, *Stalin i Ordzhonikidze*, 27–8 (citing RGASPI, f. 17, op. 2, d. 607, l. 270–1). Syrtsov was replaced on Nov. 3, 1930, as head of the RSFSR Council of People's Commissars by D. E. Sulimov: RGASPI, f. 17, op. 3, d. 803, l. 13.

301. Khlevniuk et al., *Stenogrammy zasedanii politbiuro*, III: 119–93 (at 119: RGASPI, f. 17, op. 163, l. 1–218: corrected transcript). See also Khlevniuk et al., *Stalinskoe politbiuro*, 99–100 (RGASPI, f. 589, op. 3, d. 9333, t. 2, l. 121).

302. Khlevniuk et al., *Stenogrammy zasedanii politbiuro*, III: 123–4, 163–4.

303. Khlevniuk et al., *Stenogrammy zasedanii politbiuro*, III: 178, 316 (RGASPI, f. 17, op. 163, d. 1001, l. 182–208: the uncorrected transcript, which has Kalinin, Mikoyan, Molotov, and Orjonikidze interjecting some of the statements that would be incorporated as Stalin's words).

304. Khlevniuk et al., *Stenogrammy zasedanii politbiuro*, III: 125.

305. Kuromiya, "Stalin in the Politburo Transcripts," 48.

306. Khlevniuk et al., *Stenogrammy zasedanii politbiuro*, III: 193–4 (RGASPI, f. 17, op. 163, d. 1003, l. 22–5). At one point, when Postyshev had admonished Syrtsov that he should have talked to Orjonikidze, Stalin interjected, "That's all he does, talk to people." Stalin removed this sneer from the transcript. But his frustration with Orjonikidze in the role of party disciplinarian was manifest. Khlevniuk et al., *Stenogrammy zasedanii politbiuro*, III: 176.

307. He added that the mass violence in the Soviet Union was "the brutality of the self-defense of the people, surrounded by secret and open traitors, uncompromising enemies. This brutality is provoked and—by that—justified." Of course, the brutality was being directed *against* the people by the Soviet state.

308. *Pravda*, Nov. 26, 1930; *Za industrializtasiiu*, Nov. 27, 1930; Shitts, *Dnevnik*, 250–1. When the marching workers reached the trial venue, their chants were said to be audible inside—"Death! Death! Death!" Lyons, *Assignment in Utopia*, 370–80.

309. Khaustov et al., *Lubianka: Stalin i VChK*, 258–9 (RGASPI, f. 17, op. 162, d. 9, l. 81–2: Nov. 25, 1930).

310. Copies were sent to Poskryobyshev for Stalin, as well as to Molotov, Kaganovich, Postyshev, and Orjonikidze, but to no one else in the politburo or political leadership. Sevost'ianov et al., "*Sovershenno sekretno*," VIII/i: 591–6 (TsA FSB, f. 2, op. 8, d. 658, l. 268–73).

311. Khaustov et al., *Lubianka: Stalin i VChK*, 804.

312. This was Pyotr Palchinsky: *Ramzin et al., Protsess "Prompartii*," 9, 13–4. See also Rothstein, *Wreckers on Trial*.

313. Sergei Kirov's credulous notes on the supposed specific plans of the foreign intervention have survived: Golubev et al., *Rossiia i zapad*, 154 (citing RGASPI, f. 80, op. 14, d. 16, l. 4).

314. Degras, *Soviet Documents on Foreign Policy*, II: 444–5 (June 26, 1930). France hosted a large anti-Soviet émigré community that got under Stalin's skin.

315. Haslam, *Soviet Foreign Policy*, 43–5 (Oct. 3). Litvinov telegrammed Valerian Dovgalevsky in Paris to make an oral protest, which he did: *DVP SSSR*, XIII: 821 (Oct. 11), 566–9 (Oct. 14); Adibekov et al., *Politbiuro TsK RKP (b)—VKP (b) i Evropa*, 231 (RGASPI, f. 17, op. 162, d. 9, l. 48), 232–3 (l. 54, 56).

316. Ramzin et al., *Protsess "Prompartii*," 531–7. "Among the ordinary public, especially among workers and the Communist herd, there prevails a conviction that there was a plot, there was a 'party,' others 'believe' even in the participation of Poincaré himself," Shitts recorded in his diary. He deemed workers ready to "tear to shreds the entire intelligentsia," in a kind of "dekulakization." Shitts, *Dnevnik*, 254.

317. Haslam, *Soviet Foreign Policy*, 3–4; *DBFP*, 2nd series, VII: 153–5 (Strang to Henderson, referring to briefing by Arens, Aug. 30, 1930). "World imperialism is carrying on a policy of never-ending provocation for war," *Pravda* had succinctly editorialized (Aug. 28, 1930).

318. RGASPI, f. 558, op. 11, d. 184, l. 117 (Oct. 20, 1930).

319. *DVP SSSR*, XIII: 484–6 (Arosyev to Moscow: Sept. 4, 1930), 497 (Stomonyakov's response to Arosyev: Sept. 6). Stalin refrained from public comment on the Industrial Trial until the summer of 1931. *Sochinenia*, XIII: 70–2.

320. Ramzin et al., *Protsess "Prompartii*," 517–26 (Dec. 7, 1930), 527 (Dec. 8).

321. Samygin, "Prompartiia."

322. In a prison institute, Ramzin conducted research on construction of boilers. Five years after the trial, he would be freed and awarded the Order of Lenin. Medvedev, *Let History Judge*, 263–72.

323. Sevost'ianov et al., "*Sovershenno sekretno*," VIII/ii: 1210 (TsA FSB, f. 2, op. 8, d. 658, l. 398–408: Dec. 20, 1930).

324. An anonymous letter from the USSR printed in Trotsky's *Bulletin of the Opposition* quoted workers' dissatisfaction with the light sentences: "now for small infractions they punish all of us severely, but here, for a gigantic crime, their sentences are lightened." *Biulleten' oppozitsii*, no. 19 (March 1931): 18. Ciliga, who was in prison at the time the verdicts were announced, recalled that "this unexpected clemency did . . . strike a very suspicious note," given that people were being shot for lesser crimes. Ciliga, *Russian Enigma*, 222.

325. *Sotsialisticheskii vestnik* [Paris], Dec. 20, 1930: 14. "The anger and indignation of the workers condemning the traitors' acts have remained in my memory for life," one worker at Moscow's Red Proletarian factory recalled. Ermilov, *Schast'e trudnykh dorog*, 133.

326. Yaroslavsky, despite his proximity to Stalin, revealed his own naïveté during Syrtsov's interrogation, dismissively stating that "Trotsky is a dead cat." Khlevniuk et al., *Stenogrammy zasedanii politbiuro*, III: 224 (Oct. 23, 1930).

327. Yezhov was received during a meeting on foreign trade, and in the company of Postyshev. He was back again on Nov. 29, one-on-one. *Na prieme*, 37. Yezhov's early biography can be found in Pavliukov, *Ezhov*, 6–100; and in Petrov and Jansen, *Stalinskii pitomets*, 10–33.

328. Lyons, "Stalin Urges U.S. Trade"; Lyons, "Stalin Laughs!"; *Na prieme*, 37. Lyons had worked at TASS offices in New York and might have been picked for the exclusive because of Stanisław Czacki, a former OGPU undercover intelligence operative in the United States and now head of the Anglo-American desk of OGPU foreign intelligence, who arrived in Stalin's office twenty minutes beforehand and remained during the interview. Stalin's office logbook does not specify which office; Lyons fixes it as Old Square (not the Kremlin). Lyons claimed that in media res Voroshilov entered; Voroshilov is quoted in the reportage, but his name does not appear in Stalin's office logbook that day, showing that it can be incomplete.

329. Lyons, *Assignment in Utopia*, 384–5, 387, 390; "Eugene Lyon Papers, 1929–1964," Knight Library, Special Collections, University of Oregon, box 2, typescript; Lyons, *Stalin*, 197. Compare the leftist journalist Paul Sheffer's dismissive characterization from around the same time (Sheffer never met Stalin, and relied on the writings of Trotsky). Sheffer, "Stalin's Power."

330. Duranty, "Stalin Sees Capitalists." See also Taylor, *Stalin's Apologist*, 169 (citing interview with Henry Shapiro, March 15, 1979). Duranty became one of the prime sources for the view that Stalin had become a revolutionary because of the "Jesuitic repression" at the Orthodox seminary. Duranty, "Stalin."

331. RGASPI, f. 558, op. 11, d. 726, l. 161–5; *Na prieme*, 37 (in the company of Yakov Pudolsky, head of the foreign affairs commissariat press department).

332. Keke was quoted as saying that Stalin had visited her in 1921 and "three years ago" (1926), and that she had stayed with him once in the Kremlin in Moscow ("I didn't like it"). Knickerbocker, "Stalin Mystery Man," in Hoover Institution Archives, Edward Ellis Smith papers, box 2. See also Smith, *Young Stalin*, 54.

333. "According to news from the West (which is conveyed secondhand from people who have been there or 'from above'), over there they laugh at the nervousness of the Bolsheviks, and are not planning to fight," Shitts, the encyclopedia editor, recorded in his diary in Nov. 1930. "But here people are sure of war." Shitts, *Dnevnik*, 248–9. See also Anon., *An Impression of Russia*, 10.

334. Stalin struck this revealing outburst when editing the transcript. RGASPI, f. 17, op. 3, d. 1011.

335. Khlevniuk, *Politbiuro*, 36–7, 39; van Ree, *Political Thought*, 118–9.

336. *Pravda*, Dec. 2, 1930. The poll was recorded as a one-day "meeting" of the plenum.

337. RGASPI, f. 17, op. 2, d. 735, l. 9–10, 12–3, 14–5. Stalin tasked Andreyev with reporting to the politburo—not to a Central Committee plenum—on Nov. 25 on collectivization in the North Caucasus and had the session, which emphasized success, transcribed to circulate it to party functionaries. Khlevniuk et al., *Stenogrammy zasedanii politbiuro*, III: 357–82 (RGASPI, f. 17, op. 163, d. 1004, l. 1–64: uncorrected, l. 67–127: corrected, l. 128–45: printed; op. 3, d. 805, l. 3; d. 809, l. 40–5).

338. Dubinskaia-Dzhalilova and Chernev, "'Zhmu vashu ruku, dorogoi tovarishch,'" 183 (APRF, f. 45, op. 1, d. 32, l. 100–1ob.).

339. RGASPI, f. 558, op. 11, d. 729, l. 36. On Nov. 20, 1930, *Pravda* had published a statement by Bukharin, edited by Kaganovich, again admitting his mistakes, condemning the Syrtsov-Lomoindze "right-left bloc," and calling for unity. Kvashonkin, *Sovetskoe rukovodstvo*, 147n1 (RGASPI, f. 17, op. 3, d. 805, l. 6).

340. The repeated delays of the plenum sparked rumors: the Menshevik *Socialist Herald* speculated about a rift between Stalin and other members of the politburo over the right deviation; Trotsky's *Bulletin of the Opposition* imagined a break between Stalin and Molotov, with Stalin blaming Molotov for the failures in industry. Khlevniuk, *Politbiuro*, 21–2 (citing *Biulleten' oppozitsii*, 1930, no. 17–18: 3, and *Sotsialisticheskii vestnik*, 1930, no. 24: 15); Artizov and Naumov, *Vlast'*, 134–7 (RGASPI, f. 558, op. 11, d. 2939, l. 1–6); *Socbineniia*, XIII: 23–7 (excerpts). The last such joint plenum had been April 1929, for the assault on Bukharin. Rykov's fate, formally, was not included on the agenda.

341. RGASPI, f. 17, op. 2, d. 735, l. 81–3, 87. See also Khlevniuk, *Master of the House*, 28–37. Molotov's appointment took effect that day. His two deputies were Kuibyshev and Nikolai Voznesensky. Platon Kerzhentsev (Lebedev) became business manager of the Council of People's Commissars, moving over from agitprop in the party apparatus and succeeding Nikolai Gorbunov.

342. Molotov, *V bor'be za sotsializm*, 76.

343. Getty and Naumov, *Road to Terror*, 45–50 (RGASPI, f. 17, op. 2, d. 453, l. 53–61, 70–4, 77–8, 87–92).

344. Shepilov, *Kremlin's Scholar*, 9.

345. Besedovskii, *Na putiakh k terimodru*, 294. The memoir of Besedovsky, a Soviet diplomat who defected, contained fanciful nonsense (for example, that Stalin used Lenin's old dacha at Gorki and Lenin's Rolls-Royce), but also correctly explained the crucial roles of Molotov and Kaganovich. Besedovskii, *Im Dienste der Sowjets*, 219. Besedovsky had defected in Paris on Oct. 2, 1929. The next month, Kaganovich told a Central Committee plenum, "Besedovskys are not few, unfortunately." In fact, by then seventy-two Soviet officials had refused to return from abroad since late 1928. RGASPI, f. 17, op. 2, d. 441, l. 110, 113.

346. At the time of Lenin's fatal illness, the politburo had had seven members and six candidates, but now only four of those remained: Stalin, Molotov, Kalinin, and Rudzutaks (now a full member). The new full members besides Orjonikidze were Kaganovich, Voroshilov, Kuibyshev, Kirov, and Kosior; the new candidate members were Mikoyan, Vlas Chubar, and Petrovsky. All were Stalin loyalists. *VKP (b) v rezoliutsiiakh* (1933), II: 669–73.

347. "Blizhaishee okruzhenie diktatora," *Sotsialisticheskii vestnik*, Nov. 10, 1933: 3–10. "If we have used the word ruthless for Kaganovich," Robert Conquest wrote, "it must be taken quite literally—there was no ruth, no pity, at all in his make-up." Conquest, *Reassessment*, 13. "There was no question about his devotion to the party and to the cause," Kaganovich's protégé Khrushchev would recall. "He never flagged in strength or energy. He was as stubborn as he was devoted." Khrushchev, *Khrushchev Remembers*, 65.

348. Rees, "Stalin as Leader, 1924–1937." Rees, *Iron Lazar*, 123–43.

349. Chuev, *Tak govoril Kaganovicha*, 53.

350. Stalin entrusted the party's Central Control Commission and the workers' and peasants' inspectorate to his young protégé Andreyev. By party rules, the chairman of the Central Control Commission could no longer be a member of the politburo. On Oct. 2, 1931, however, Stalin would name Andreyev transport commissar; Rudzutaks got the Central Control Commission. On Feb. 4, 1932, Andreyev became a full member of the politburo, replacing Rudzutaks.

351. Fitzpatrick, "Ordzhonikidze's Takeover." Trotsky misjudged Orjonikidze, too. Trotsky, *Stalin*, 348.

352. Orjonikidze added that the Magnitorgorsk Iron and Steel Works, Nizhny Novgorod Auto Plant, and other well-under-way highest-priority constructions projects *still* "lacked blueprints." RGASPI, f. 558, op. 11, d. 145, l. 43–54.

353. Another example: In Dec. 1931, Amayak Nazaretyan, Stalin's first top aide in the party secretariat, proposed publishing the impressions of the foreign workers who had participated in the socialist construction. "Correct. To the politburo," Stalin wrote on the memo. On the fifteenth anniversary in Nov. 1932, a 700-plus-page book, *Through the Eyes of Foreigners*, with testimonies of more than 100 people, would be published. *Glazami inostrantsev; Maksimenkov, Bol'shaia tsenzura*, 210 (RGASPI, f. 17, op. 163, d. 920, l. 126).

354. Kvashonkin, *Sovetskoe rukovodstvo*, 144–5 (RGASPI, f. 558, op. 11, d. 765, l. 68a); Enker, "Struggling for Stalin's Soul," 172–5.

355. Stalin's personal secretariat appears to have moved from party HQ on Old Square to Government HQ in the Kremlin at the beginning of the 1930s. Rosenfeldt, "'The Consistory of the Communist Church,'" 318n31, citing Robert Tucker, personal communication. The move displaced some offices of the central executive committee from the Kremlin to the GUM department store across Red Square. Kvashonkin, *Sovetskoe rukovodstvo*, 136–7 (RGASPI, f. 667, op. 1, d. 17, l. 25–6), 141 (f. 78, op. 1, d. 376, l. 107). See also Balashov and Markhashov, "Staraia ploshchad', 4 (20-e gody)," 183.

356. RGASPI, f. 558, op. 11, d. 851, l. 15.

357. RGASPI, f. 558, op. 4, d. 667. See also Kolesnik, *Khronika zhizni sem'i Stalina*, 58–62.

358. Ilizarov, *Tainaia zhizn' Stalina*, 310. Stalin departed Kureika in late 1916 (when summoned to the draft board), more than nine months before the boy's birth was officially registered (Nov. 6, 1917); the registration could have been delayed by remoteness or falsely reported. Pereprygina (b. 1900/1) went on to marry Yakov Davydov and become a hairdresser in Igarka (100 miles north of Kureika); she would die around 1964. In 1956, Ivan Serov of the KGB would send a report to Khrushchev based on an interview with Pereprygina-Davydova, attributing paternity to Stalin; it contains obvious errors and reflects lazy police work. *Izvestiia*, Dec. 8, 2000; RGASPI, f. 558, op. 11, d. 1288; Gelii Kleimenov, *O lichnoi zhizni Iosifa Stalina*, chast' 2, glava 9 (2013): http://www.proza.ru/2013/05/11/894. The boy, Alexander, later fought in WWII, lived in Siberia, and died in 1987. In 1934 the log cabin in Kureika became a Stalin museum.

359. "Chto dal'she," *Biulleten' oppozitsii*, no. 17–18 (Nov.–Dec. 1930): 22.

360. In another private letter of March 1930, Bakhmeteff foresaw the consequences as well ("agricultural catastrophe . . . famine on a great scale"). Bakhmeteff also understood that Stalin would succeed in asserting state control over the countryside, whatever the human and economic costs ("that is second order from the point of view of Communist political goals"). He concluded: "A regime that forms in such conditions can only be compared with a military occupation by an armed external enemy." Budnitskii, "Sovershenno lichno i doveritel'no!," III: 420–1 (Feb. 12, 1929), 433 (April 19, 1929), 466 (Feb. 1930), 468–73 (March 4, 1930).

361. Trotsky would later write in his diary that back in 1926, Kamenev had warned him that his life was in danger, and that Zinoviev had told him, "Do you think that Stalin has

not discussed the question of your physical removal?" Trotsky did not record these alleged conversations at the time, and neither Kamenev nor Zinoviev ever stated as much publicly. Trotskii, *Dnevniki i pis'ma*, 72–74 (Feb. 18, 1935).

362. Khlevniuk rightly pointed out that Stalin's victory over Rykov, Bukharin, and Tomsky required significant effort, but he did not specify whether another outcome was possible.

363. Mikoian, *Tak bylo*, 289. "The Right Opposition was more a state of mind than an organization," observed Victor Serge. Serge, *Memoirs of a Revolutionary*, 253.

364. Tomsky conceded to the 16th Party Congress: "Any opposition, any struggle against the party line under the dictatorship of the proletariat . . . will inevitably find a response outside the party. And whatever the opposition's platform may be . . . it will become the organizational nucleus for a third force, for the enemies of the proletarian dictatorship." Rykov told the delegates: "Any utilization of our difficulties for criticism of the party general line must automatically include an appeal for the support of the petit bourgeois elements against the socialist elements of the countryside." *XVI s"ezd VKP (b)*, 145 (Tomsky), 152 (Rykov). The Russian-speaking American journalist William Reswick, who met with Rykov in his Kremlin apartment, has him stating: "Only a year back, we still had the situation in hand. Even six months ago we still could have forced a showdown and won. But there was always a haunting fear of an interparty fight turning into a civil war and now it is too late." The conversation is undated, but from the context it seems this was Nov. 1929. Reswick, *I Dreamt Revolution*, 253–4.

365. Cohen, *Bukharin*, 315, 60–106; von Hagen, *Soldiers in the Proletarian Dictatorship*, 335. Bukharin, according to his biographer, perceived that Voroshilov wavered, at least in 1930. But if so, that passed. Cohen, *Bukharin*, 287, 289. Voroshilov, at the 16th Party Congress, on July 2, 1930, found it necessary to deny that any wavering had taken place inside the Red Army ("not one, not one case"). *XVI s"ezd VKP (b)*, 504–16, reprinted in Voroshilov, *Stat'i i rechi*, 434–50 (at 444). According to Reese, many lower-level Red Army party cells sympathized with the right's program of voluntary collectivization and higher state prices for grain, though it is unclear whether they also supported individual household farming. Reese, "Red Army Opposition," esp. 37. On rumors about the army, see Haslam, *Soviet Foreign Policy*, 121–2.

CHAPTER 2. APOCALYPSE

1. Starkov, *Martem'ian Ryutin*, 259. "O dele tak nazyvaemogo 'Soiuza Marksistov-Lenintsev,'" 103–15; "Platforma 'Soiuza Marksistov-Lenintsev' ('Gruppa Riutina'): 'Stalin i krzis proletarskoi diktatury.'" There are some hints that the texts underwent changes as they were circulated from hand to hand (105). The party archives contain no originals of either document. The version that is extant is purported to be a copy of the original "certified" and signed by "First Operational Commissar of the Special Political Department (SPO) of the OGPU, Bogan." Whether the police made insertions cannot be established.

2. Bix, *Hirohito*, 209–10 (citing Bonner F. Fellers Collection, Hoover Institution Archives: Answer to Japan, Southwest Pacific Area, July 1, 1944: 9).

3. On July 25, 1930, the politburo had decreed that by late Sept. 1931, collectivization would

reach 65–70 percent in the chief grain growing areas, and 35–40 percent elsewhere, but just 15–20 percent in the grain deficit territories. The regime significantly raised taxes on individual family farms and curtailed the land available to them. Officials also engaged in arbitrary confiscations of seed grain, implements, and other property "for the good of the collectives." Many peasants just gave up and headed for the factory construction sites. Davies and Wheatcroft, *Years of Hunger*, 1 (citing RGASPI, f. 17, op. 3, d. 790, l. 13), 14 (RGAE, f. 7486, op. 37, d. 193, l. 99).

4. *Pravda*, Dec. 22, 1930; *VKP (b) v rezoliutsiiakh* (1933), II: 675–92; Davies, *Socialist Offensive*, 380–1. On the plenum's eve, Kaganovich had exhorted the Moscow party organization to "struggle against excesses, but in that lies the whole trick, the whole art of the Bolshevik leadership's Marxism-Lenin-

ism, to be able, without excesses, to double and triple collectivization." Kir'ianov, "Kollektivizatsiia tsentra Rossii," 79 (citing RGASPI, f. 81, op. 3, d. 139, l. 74: Dec. 1930).

5. Ivnitskii, *Kollektivizatsiia i raskulachivanie*, 167 (citing former politburo archive, without details).

6. *VKP (b) v rezoliutsiiakh* (1933), II: 677–8; Kuromiya, *Stalin's Industrial Revolution*, 263. The 1931 plan itself was printed in just 1,200 copies, for internal circulation only: *Narodno-khoziaistvennyi plan na 1931 god: kontrol'nye tsifry* (Moscow: 1931).

7. Kuromiya, *Stalin's Industrial Revolution*, 109–13. Benito Mussolini, in 1912, then a member of the Italian Socialist Party, had written: "We want to believe in [socialism], we must believe in it, humanity needs a credo. It is faith which moves mountains because it gives the illusion that mountains move.

Illusion is perhaps the only reality in life." Falasca-Zamponi, *Fascist Spectacle*, 43 (citing *Avanti!* June 18, 1912, reprinted in Mussolini, *Opera Omnia*, IV: 173-4).

8. Lyons was most impressed with the pithy slogans, such as "Five-in-Four," which he noted was instantly understood to refer to the Five-Year Plan and its early attainment, and judged "as effective as our 4-out-of-5 for toothpaste." Lyons, *Moscow Carrousel*, 209. See also Mikhutina, "SSSR glazami pol'skikh diplomatov," 46; and Sukhanov, *Zapiski*, III: 214.

9. Following Mekhlis's graduation in May 1930 from the Institute of Red Professors, Stalin had appointed him head of the Central Committee press department and, concurrently, to *Pravda*'s editorial collective; he took over as editor-in-chief in 1931, and would help boost *Pravda*'s circulation to 1.8 million, but Stalin worried about his ability to handle the load. Khlevniuk et al., *Stalin i Kaganovic*, 37 (RGASPI, f. 81, op. 3, d. 100, l. 115-8: earlier than Aug. 6, 1931). See also Avtorkhanov, *Tekhnologiia vlasti*, 109-10, 116; and Rubtsov, *Teni vozhdia*, 81-2.

10. Stalin had stopped bothering to attend formal meetings of the party secretariat or orgburo. The latter functioned as a kind of permanently empowered commission of the politburo, while the former, from 1931, did not even refer questions to the politburo. Detached from even nominal politburo oversight, the central apparatchiks all reported to Stalin. Rosenfeldt, *"Special" World*. By 1933, secret department salaries were 30-40 percent higher than in the rest of apparatus. Khlevniuk, *Master of the House*, 53. At the government (Council of People's Commissars), procedures stipulated "only in matters of special importance to refer them to the politburo," but Molotov sought approval for all "sensitive" issues at the politburo. Rees, "Stalin as Leader, 1924-1937," 33-5; RGASPI, f. 17, op. 3, d. 823, l. 9.

11. The melding of zeal ("You will be masters of the whole world!") and opportunism was often intense. But some speakers at the Communist Youth League Congress in Jan. 1931 mentioned a "desertion rate" of nearly half among Communist Youth assigned to the Donbass coal mines. Davies, *Crisis and Progress*, 10 (citing *Ekonomicheskaia zhizn'*, Jan. 22, 1931); Fisher, *Pattern for Soviet Youth*, 162, 257; *IX Vsesoiuznyi s"ezd VLKSM*.

12. Viola, "Peasant Nightmare," 762; Davydenko et al., *Put' trudovykh pobed*, 270-5.

13. Globally, learning how to mechanize production in concrete cases was easier said than done, and mass production was not readily achieved in some industries, or even in some countries. Kinch, "Road from Dreams," 107-36. Soviet mass production, even more than that in Germany, would be associated with producer (or capital) goods. There were fierce internal debates in the USSR about proper industrial organization, with references to American and German production experiences. Shearer, *Industry, State, and Society*.

14. *Istoriia industrializatsii SSSR, 1926-1941*. Stalin had offered a threefold justification for the crash Five-Year Plan the month after it launched: to catch and overtake capitalist countries; to ensure the Soviet Union's ability to remain independent in the international system; and to furnish agriculture with machines because industry could not move forward without agriculture being modernized. Stalin, "Ob industrializatsii strany i o pravom uklone v VKP," *Sochineniia*, XI: 245-90 (at 247-53).

15. Sutton, *Western Technology*, II. On Feb. 14, 1931, Mężyński reported to Stalin that at the Chelyabinsk Tractor Plant "extensive housing construction is being done completely unconnected to when the factory goes into production," and that "not a single factory shop will be completed during the year." Such a state of affairs was typical. Khaustov et al., *Lubianka: Stalin i VChK*, 261 (TsA FSB, f. 2, op. 9, d. 18, l. 162-3).

16. Lewis, "Technology and the Transformation of the Soviet Economy," 196.

17. Davies et al., *Years of Progress*, xiv.

18. During the first Five-Year Plan, the urban labor force would rise from around 11.9 million to 22.9 million. Heavy industry would count more than 6 million employees in 1932, as against perhaps 3 million in 1928. Most newcomers came from villages. By 1932-33, between 45 and 60 percent of industrial workers had begun factory work in 1926 or later. Drobizhev, *Industrializatsiia i izmeneniia*, 4-5.

19. The first decree forbidding free movement of labor (Oct. 1930) was followed by one forbidding factory directors from hiring workers who had quit their previous employ without authorization. Davies, *Soviet Economy in Turmoil*, 419-30; Davies, *Crisis and Progress*, 26-7; Rees, *Stalinism and Soviet Rail Transport*, 44; Friedman, *Russia in Transition*, 218; *Izvestiia*, Jan. 14, 1931; *Za industrializatsiiu*, Feb. 14 and 16, 1931.

20. The number of peasant households would plunge from 25-26 million to 19 million by 1937. Many of those who left the village were young males, those most in favor of the regime's social transformation, including early stalwarts of the collective farms. Fitzpatrick, *Stalin's Peasants*, 81; Wheatcroft and Davies, "Population," 69.

21. Kotkin, *Magnetic Mountain*, 72-105.

22. The regime used "taxation" against private traders. NEPmen were also being systematically evicted from their apartments. Davies, *Development of the Soviet Budgetary System*,112; Davies, *Soviet Economy in Turmoil*, 97-101, citing *Kontrol'nye tsifry narodnogo khoziaistva SSSR 1929/30* (1930), 188; *Pravda*, Oct. 12, 1929; and *Ekonomicheskaia zhizn'*, Feb. 14, 1930; Ball, *Russia's Last Capitalists*, 78. On Feb. 9, 1930 Stalin would criticize those "trying to 'supplement' the slogan of the liquidation of the kulaks as a class with the slogan of the liquidation of the urban bourgeoisie," a mistake given that the latter, unlike the kulaks, had no control over the means of production. But the "dekulakization" of the NEP-era "bourgeoisie"—the majority of whom were petty traders—proceeded apace, and would further unhinge the supply of food and other goods in cities. *Sochineniia*, XII: 186; *Ianvarskii ob"edinennyi plenum MK i MKK*, 31 (Bauman); Rukeyser, *Working for the Soviets*, 217.

23. Tikhomirov, *Promyslovaia kooperatsiia*, 15-7. On June 28, 1931, the Council of People's Commissars issued a directive to shore up enforced artisan "cooperatives." Kiselev and Shchagin, *Khrestomatiia po otechestvennoi istorii*, 401-5 (RGAE, f. 3429, op. 1, d. 5249-6, l. 42-6).

24. Fitzpatrick, "After NEP." NEPmen and other "non laboring elements" were denied access to state-owned housing and to rationing—but not if they reinvented themselves.

25. Lih et al., *Stalin's Letters to Molotov*, 207-8; Rubinstein, *Razvitie vnutrennei torgovli*, 290; Randall, *Soviet Dream World*, 19-21, 24-6; Hessler, *Social History of Soviet Trade*, 177-82.

26. Kotkin, *Magnetic Mountain*, 225.

27. Of perhaps 2 million functionaries, around 160,000 were subjected to investigation as of mid-1931 and at least 5,000 in the central economic administration and 4,500 on the railways were arrested, mostly for "sabotage." Davies, *Soviet Economy in Turmoil*, 117-8, 134-5, 533; *XVI s"ezd VKP (b)* (2nd ed.), 316; *Chistka sovetskogo apparata*, 22.

28. Werth, "Stalin's System," 50 n25 (no citation).

29. *Sotsialisticheskoe stroitel'stvo SSSR*, 344-5; Davies, *Soviet Economy in Turmoil*, 126-7. As a side effect, the number of students in secondary schools plummeted from around 1 million in 1928-30 to a mere 4,234 in 1931-32. Before the end of 1932, secondary students would shoot up again, to 1.2 million, although their preparation left much to be desired. Nove, *Economic History of the USSR* (1992), 199. On March 15, 1931, the politburo decreed an end to worker advancement into administration and ordered those recently advanced to be returned to where they were actually needed: as skilled workers in factories. *Spravochnik partiinogo rabotnika*, VIII: 386.

30. In 1929-30, only 3,166 people graduated from engineering and technical schools, but that was compared with just 1,282 in 1928-29; the education of the graduates was not comprehensive. Soviet engineers-in-training learned mostly on the job, including while working alongside European and American specialists employed in the USSR. Davies, *Socialist Offensive*, 123 (citing *Pravda*, May 11, 1930), 124-5; Hoover Institution, AER, box 4, R. W. Stuck ms., 29.

31. Ordzhonikidze, *Stat'i i rechi*, II: 284-301. There were 728 attendees. *Pervaia vsesoiuznaia konferentsiia rabotnikov sotsialisticheskoi promyshlennosti*. Stalin crossed out or softened barbed references to bourgeois specialists from the original draft of his speech to the conference of industrialists on Feb. 4, 1931; a politburo resolution of Feb. 20 would indicate concern about the number of engineers arrested and their disposition. RGASPI, f. 558, op. 1, d. 22960, l. 7, 9, 23; f. 17, op. 162, d. 9, l. 139. On April 10, the politburo would allow industrial specialists convicted of wrecking to work in prison institutes, which would play a significant part in Soviet industrial design. Viktorov, *Bez grifa "sekretno*," 169; Westwood, *Soviet Locomotive Technology*, 88-9, 163. On June 23, 1931, in a speech to industrialists ("New Conditions, New Tasks"), Stalin would belatedly absolve bourgeois specialists as a class, though not specific individuals, a turnabout echoed by *Pravda* (June 25). *Sochineniia*, XIII: 51-7; Kuromiya, *Stalin's Industrial Revolution*, 263-86; *Sochineniia*, XIII: 72-3. A note to Stalin (Nov. 26, 1931) would list 1,087 imprisoned specialists who had been handed over to economic agencies; industry had placed requests for another 700. Khaustov et al., *Lubianka: Stalin i VChK*, 287-8 (APRF, f. 3, op. 58, d. 143, l. 15-6: Akulov). By fall 1931, many "bourgeois" specialists were amnestied, and the police began to restore specialists who had not been executed to work. Dzanovich, *Organy*, 438.

32. "O zadachakh khoziaistvennikov," *Pravda*, Feb. 5, 1931, reprinted, with changes, in *Sochineniia*, XIII: 38-9. "The country ought to know its heroes," *Pravda* wrote (March 6, 1931). "The outstanding shock worker, the inventor, the rationalizer who has mastered production technology—this is the hero of the land of socialism under construction."

33. Il'in, *Bolshoi konveier*, 143-50; *1933 god*, 104-9.

34. In *Sochineniia*, XIII: 41. In Sept. 1929, culminating a year-long campaign, unified management (*edinonachalie*) had been formally introduced for industrial enterprises: the manager was supreme, not the party cell or the technical director, who was usually a "bourgeois" specialist. Kuromiya, "Edinonachalie and the Soviet Industrial Manager, 1928–1937"; Gregory, *Restructuring the Soviet Economic Bureaucracy*, 57–9. On Aug. 23, 1931, the regime would award sole decision-making powers for both military and political issues to the military commanders over the political commissars. "Letopis' stroitel'stva sovetskikh vooruzhennykh sil 1931 god (maiiul')," 122–3.

35. Directives from above tasked local communists and Communist Youth League organizers with drawing up lists, usually in a few frantic days, and the police placed special boxes in rural soviets, schools, or streets to solicit denunciations. Fainsod, *Smolensk under Soviet Rule*, 241.

36. Peasant letter writers called for establishing collective farms without haste on a voluntary basis, and respecting churches. Zelenin, *Stalinskaia 'revoliutsiia sverkhu,'* 17 (RGAE, f. 7486, op. 37, d. 194, l. 252); Fainsod, *Smolensk under Soviet Rule*, 252. Officials more often took notice of the village solidarity: "in many villages the kulaks were seen off by the whole population, in tears of sympathy," the party boss of the Tatar autonomous province reported to Stalin. RGASPI, f. 558, op. 11, d. 822, l. 43.

37. Although category I "kulaks"—those subject to exile to remote regions or execution—had been envisioned at around 60,000, the actual number turned out to be 283,717 for the period from Jan. 1 to Oct. 1, 1930, half of them following the tactical retreat of "Dizzy with Success." Danilov et al., *Tragediia sovetskoi derevni*, II: 704 (TsA FSB, f. 2, op. 8, d. 329, l. 198–212: Nov. 17, 1930); Viola, "Role of the OGPU," 21, 43n82. In the Urals, the typical dekulakized household had one cow, one horse, three sheep, a modest family residence and stable, a bath-house, a storehouse, and between six and eight acres of sown land. Bedel' and Slavko, "Iz istorii raskulachennykh spetspereselentsev," 12. See also Scott, *Behind the Urals*, 17–8.

38. Yagoda ordered this situation corrected, informing operatives that it was "not obligatory to seize by the quota." But there was no state medal for trailing the overachievers. Berelowitch and Danilov, *Sovetskaia derevnia glazami VChK-OGPU-NKVD*, III/i: 107–9 (TsA FSB, f. 2, op. 8, d. 41, l. 38–41).

39. Suslov, "'Revolution from Above.'" Better-off peasants rushed to sell their implements, kill off their livestock, and flee, prompting the regime to issue strongly worded orders to prevent self-dekulakization.

40. Popov, "Gosudarstvennyi terror," 28–9; Davies and Wheatcroft, *Years of Hunger*, 492; Davies et al., *Economic Transformation*, 68, *Unknown Gulag*, 2, 6, 29–32 (GARF, f. 9479, op. 1, d. 89, l. 205; RGASPI, f. 17, op. 120, d. 56, l. 59). Timing varied: Uzbekistan's dekulakization took place mostly in Aug. and Sept. Pokrovskii, *Politbiuro i krest'ianstvo*, I: 439–41 (APRF, f. 3, op. 30, d. 195, l. 157–8: Oct. 10, 1931). The state "planned" losses of 5 percent of the special settlers, but mortality was far higher thanks to the state's unpreparedness for its own policy. Danilov and Krasil'nikov, *Spetspereselentsy v Zapadnoi Sibiri*, III: 10.

41. Between 1928 and 1931, on the territory of the former Moscow gymnasium no. 3, behind Lubyanka, 2, a new Constructivist edifice was built for the OGPU (Lubyanka, 12), with a distinctive façade and round windows on the top (seventh) floor. It contained 65,000

square feet of office space, a three-story department store, 120 residential apartments, a club, cafeteria, and 1,500-seat cinema. Pogonii, *Lubianka*, 68. As of July 1934, the OGPU would count 200,125 border guards and internal troops, another 18,000 convoy troops, nearly 200,000 in the regular police or militia, 18,951 in Gulag administration, and 20,125 field couriers, and others, for a total of 514,838—not even including state security (GUGB). Khaustov, "Deiatel'nost' organov," 477–8 (TsA FSB, f. 3, op. 32, d. 8, l. 346–7). "Comrades, leave us in peace and don't interfere with our work," one exasperated professor at Tomsk University pleaded. Another professor at a technical school in Kiev remarked, "I do not intend ever to drive across a bridge built by an engineer from the workers." Sevost'ianov et al., *"Sovershenno sekretno,"* VIII/ii: 1136–75 (TsA FSB, f. 2, op. 8, por. 435, l. 169–241: late May 1930).

42. RGASPI, f. 17, op. 162, d. 9, l. 138. On Feb. 25, 1931, the politburo resolved by telephone poll to recommend that during the course of six months the OGPU "prepare" kulak settlements for 200,000–300,000 families near Karaganda in northern Kazakhstan. Khaustov et al., *Lubianka: Stalin i VChK,* 263 (APRF, f. 3, op. 30, d. 149, l. 51). For a time, urgent requests for cheap "kulak" laborers skyrocketed, but sites that had large numbers of the deported often begged not to be sent any more: the ones they had were just dying. RGASPI, f. 17, op. 120, d. 26, l. 37 (Kuznetskstroi); Viola, *Unknown Gulag*, 4.

43. Solzhenitsyn, *Gulag Archipelago*, I: 56. See also Khlevniuk, *History of the Gulag*, 10–12, 16–7.

44. Of the 2 million slated for exile within their own region, a large number of these also fled to the construction sites after their property was confiscated for the collective farms. Zemskov, "'Kulaktskaia ssylka,'" 3; Danilov and Ivnitskii, *Dokumenty svidetel'stvuiut*, 46–7. Actual criminals flourished in the tumult, a public order challenge. Shearer, *Policing Stalin's Socialism*, 289.

45. Zelenin, *Stalinskaia 'revoliutsiia sverkhu,'* 52–3 (RGASPI, f. 17, op. 120, f. d. 26, l. 77–85: June 26, 1931). On Oct. 12, 1931, Yagoda would report to Stalin on the completion of kulak operations in regions of wholesale collectivization. As of Jan. 1, 1932, the OGPU reported that 1.3 million people were in special settlements. Berelowitch and Danilov, *Sovetskaia derevnia glazami VChK-OGPU-NKVD,* III/i: 774 (TsA FSB, f. 2, op. 10, d. 379, l. 93); Khaustov et al., *Lubianka: Stalin i VChK,* 267 (APRF, f. 3, op. 30, d. 195, l. 163); Pokrovskii, *Politbiuro i krest'ianstvo,* I: 442; Davies and Wheatcroft, *Years of Hunger,* 47 (GARF, f. 9479, op. 1, d. 89, l. 206); Viola, *Unknown Gulag,* 6 (GARF, f. 9479, op. 1, d. 89, l. 205; d. 949, l. 75–9).

46. A Central Committee circular of Jan. 20, 1931, had directed local party organizations to conduct mass agitation to prepare for the spring sowing campaign, expedite the flow of households into collective farms via creation of initiative groups, dispatch workers who could repair tools and equipment, and prevent distribution of the harvest according to the number of souls, as in the previous year, but instead according to the amount of work accomplished. *Partiinoe stroitel'stvo,* 1931, no. 2: 61–2; *Kollektivizatsiia sel'skogo khoziaistva,* 354–6.

47. *Piatiletnyi plan,* II/i: 328–9, 330–1; *Kollektivizatsiia sel'skogo khoziaistva,* 350. These harvest numbers reflected multiplication of planned sown area by planned yields, neither of which was based on actual data. Davies and Wheatcroft, *Years of Hunger,* 65–6. Yields had been declining since the

mid-1920s, a trend whose causes were not well understood. Nove, *Economic History of the USSR* (1992), 176.

48. Drought, in different ways, affected other world regions around this time. In the United States the "great southern drought" of 1930–31, which coincided with a price collapse and banking failures, inflicted hardship across twenty-three states from West Virginia to Texas; President Herbert Hoover sought to have the Red Cross, a private agency, be wholly responsible for relief, opposing federal drought relief (seeing it as opening the door to general federal relief). French West Africa suffered drought, locusts, and its worst famine ever; the French authorities did not relent on tax demands. Mortality in French West Africa was disproportionately higher (in an immensely smaller area and overall population) than in the Soviet Union. China in 1931–32 suffered the opposite problem: large snowmelt and tremendous rainfall that inundated an area equivalent in size to England and half of Scotland, flooding some 52 million people, and killing as many as 2 million from drowning and especially starvation. Tauger, "Natural Disaster," 8, citing Woodruff, *Rare as Rain: Report of the National Flood Relief Commission, 1931–32* (Shanghai, 1933); Fuglestad, "La grande famine." See also Buck, *1931 Flood.*

49. A secret OGPU report addressed to Stalin in early June 1931 complained that that machinery and buildings were unready for the harvest. On June 5, the politburo belatedly approved purchase of 2,500–3,000 additional trucks in the United States and Europe, beyond the 4,000 already ordered. Davies and Wheatcroft, *Years of Hunger,* 68–9 (RGASPI, f. 17, op. 3, d. 883, l. 3: June 30, 1931; op. 162, d. 10, l. 66; RGAE, f. 7486, op. 37, d. 194, l. 273–253: June 10, 1931). On June 8, 1931, the regime felt constrained to redirect 30,000 tons of wheat and rye from export to consumption in Moscow and Leningrad. Davies and Wheatcroft, *Years of Hunger,* 85–6 (RGASPI, f. 17, op. 162, d. 10, l. 80).

50. Kvashonkin, *Sovetskoe rukovodstvo,* 153 (RGASPI, f. 667, op. 1, d. 17, l. 28–9).

51. Wheatcroft and Davies, "Agriculture," 125.

52. "Settlement is the liquidation of the *bai* semi-feudals, . . . the destruction of tribal attitudes," intoned Isay Goloshchokin, known as Filipp, the Jewish-born party boss of the autonomous republic. Zveriakov, *Ot kochev'ia k sotsializmu,* 53; *Iz istorii Kazakhskoi SSR,* II: 255; Aldazhumanov et al., *Nasil'stvennaia kollektivizatsiia,* 28, 34–9 (APRK, f. 141, op. 1, d. 2968, l. 141–8); Tursunbaev, "Torzhestvo kolkhoznogo stroia," 259–308 (at 266, citing APRK, f. 141, op. 1, d. 2404, l. 23).

53. While the overall share of grain procurement from grain surplus regions declined between 1928 and 1932 from 67.5 to 50 percent, the share from grain-deficit regions grew from 9.4 to 16.9 percent. Davies and Wheatcroft, *Years of Hunger,* 329 (citing RGAE, f. 4372, op. 30, d. 881, l. 82: Aug. 4, 1932).

54. Pianciola, "Famine in the Steppe." In the Kazakh autonomous republic, significant numbers of deaths from starvation began in spring and summer 1930. That year an estimated 35,000 Kazakh households, more than 150,000 people with 900,000 head of livestock, fled for China, Iran, and Afghanistan. The USSR land commissariat resolved that even southern Kazakhstan—an area of nomads and semi-nomads—should see "reinforced state farm and collective farm construction," partly in order to "narrow the basis for nomadic and semi-nomadic land utilization." Davies and Wheatcroft, *Years of Hunger,* 3–4 (RGAE, f. 7486, op. 19, d. 130, l. 6–7: on Feb. 1, 1931); Kondrashin et al., *Golod*

v SSSR, I/i: 207–8 (GA Kustanaiskoi obl. Respubliki Kazakhstan, f. 54–p, op. 1, d. 784, l. 14), 220–7 (TsA FSB, f. 2m, op. 8, d. 744, l. 570–6), 227–8 (l. 612); Aldazhumanov et al., *Nasil'stvennaia kollektivizatsiia*, 72–3 (APRK, f. 141, op. 1, d. 3336, l. 97). Turar Ryskulov reported to Stalin that between Feb. 1931 and Feb. 1932, private Kazakh herds had shrunk by more than 4 million head, but only 1.5 million livestock had been delivered to the state. Ryskulov blamed "excesses in collectivization," "alongside the evil murder of livestock by kulak-herders [*bai*]." Danilov et al., *Tragediia sovetskoi derevni*, III: 503–9 (RGASPI, f. 82, op. 2, d. 670, l. 1–14ob.); *Partiinaia zhizn' Kazakhstana*, 1990, no. 10: 76–84; Ryskulov, *Sobranie sochinenii*, III: 304–16 (APRK, f. 141, op. 1, d. 6403, l. 13–6).
55. Aldazhumanov, "Krest'ianskoe dvizhenie soprotivleniia," 66–93. One district of Dagestan reported 10,000 people on the verge of starvation already in Dec. 1930: Kondrashin et al., *Golod v SSSR*, I/1: 321 (RGAE, f. 8043, op. 1, d. 20, l. 128). A Central Committee plenum (June 11–15, 1931) discussed the completed sowing campaign and upcoming harvest, but was largely preoccupied with Moscow city reconstruction and Union-wide rail transport bottlenecks, which Stalin addressed in his usual way: forcing personnel changes, including an influx of OGPU personnel into the railroad commissariat. *Pravda*, June 17, 1931; *VKP (b) v rezoliutsiiakh* (1933), II: 693–720; Khlevniuk et al., *Stalin i Kaganovich*, 109–10 (RGASPI, f. 81, op. 3, d. 99, l. 35–6: Sept. 19, 1931), 123–4 (f. 558, op. 11, d. 76, l. 85–85ob.: Oct. 1), 127–8 (l. 88ob.: Oct. 5); Rees, *Stalinism and Soviet Rail Transport*, 51–2; RGASPI, f. 17, op. 3, d. 854, l. 7.
56. Discussion ensued of some heretical ideas, such as allowing state companies independence and disposal of their own profits, to create incentives, but the transcript was not published. RGASPI, f. 17, op. 162, d, 11, l. 119 (July 15, 1931).
57. RGASPI, f. 85, op. 28, d. 7, I: 176–82. This text, as delivered, differs from the text published two weeks later and reprinted in *Sochineniia*, XIII: 51–80.
58. When hostile governments fed the Soviets information aimed at compromising Red Army officers, much of it had actually originated with the OGPU's schemes. The defector Bazhanov colorfully told French intelligence that "I often heard politburo members and major OGPU functionaries say that émigré organizations were so saturated with agents that at times it was difficult to make out where émigré activities began and provocational ones ended." Gutinov, "'Unichtozhit' vragov, predvaritel'no ikh obmanuv," 38. See also Bazhanov, *Organy*, 92 (citing TsA FSB, f. PF, d. 6159, t. 1, l. 228ob.).
59. "At the beginning of Soviet power I was neither sympathetic nor certain it would endure," Colonel Vasily Svechin testified, according to his interrogation protocols. "Although I participated in the civil war, it was not in my heart. I fought eagerly when the war took on the character of an external war (the Caucasus front). I fought for the territorial integrity and preservation of Russia, although it was called the RSFSR" (i.e., Russian Soviet Federated Socialist Republic). Tynchenko, *Golgofa*, 146 (citing GA SBU, fp., d. 67093, t. 189 [251], delo Afanas'eva A. V.: 56). See also Suvenirov, *Tragediia RKKA*, 46–47 (citing AVKVS RF, op. 55, d. 8651, l. 52; RGVA, f. 9, op. 29, d. 10, l. 214: Gamarnik report, May 1931; AVKVS RF, op. 66, d. 2552, l. 1–13).
60. Snesarev had voiced the latter fear after his arrest in late 1930. Zdanovich, *Organy*, 376 (citing TsA FSB, f. 2, op. 4, d. 774, l. 4).

61. Voroshilov had boasted to a Central Committee plenum in April 1928 that "the commanders we received from the tsarist army at the present time have become completely reliable, ours, if not 100 percent, then 99 percent, we assimilated them and melded them in with the young red cadres." Danilov and Khlevniuk, *Kak lomali NEP*, I: 280. The defense commissar kept a vigilant eye on rivals, and had once denounced Budyonny to Stalin as "too much a peasant, excessively popular and very cunning," adding that "in the imagination of our enemies, Budyonny will play the role of some sort of savior [a peasant Leader], heading a 'people's' movement." "'Cherkni . . . desiatoic slov," 408 (Feb. 1, 1923). Voroshilov also complained about negative reports generated by the Red Army's political administration. Khlevniuk, *Politburo*, 37; Zdanovich, *Organy*, 158 (citing TsA FSB, f. 2, op. 1, d. 5, l. 21ob.–22), 114 (op. 5, d. 478, l. 168). Voroshilov's aide-de-camp was Rafail Khmelnitsky (b. 1898).
62. According to the *Lesser Soviet Encyclopedia* (1931): "Officers constituted a closed caste, access to which was open predominantly to those of the ruling class . . . they were a true bulwark of the autocracy in the struggle against the revolutionary movement." *Malaia Sovetskaia entsiklopediia* (Moscow, 1931), VI: 208. Much the same would be stated, even more colorfully, eight years later: *Bol'shaia Sovetskaia entsiklopediia* (Moscow, 1939), XLIII: 674. See also Denikin, *Ocherki russkoi smuti*, III: 144–5.
63. "According to OGPU data," Mężyński reported to Stalin, "all counterrevolutionary organizations and groups are striving to penetrate the Red Army . . . Recently we have uncovered numerous such rebel groups tied to the Red Army, about which we will offer a special report. I consider it necessary to convey to you a communication about one such organization discovered by the Ukraine GPU that presents the greatest interest." Stalin had received Mężyński on Oct. 14 and 26, 1930. Ukraine GPU chief Balytsky was summoned to Moscow. Zdanovich, *Organy*, 388–9 (citing TsA FSB, f. 2, op. 8, d. 247, l. 292; d. 15, l. 451–2).
64. Khaustov and Samuelson, *Stalin, NKVD*, 122; Zdanovich, *Organy*, 390 (citing TsA FSB, f. 2, op. 8, d. 237, l. 144, 136). Evidently, when the central OGPU in Moscow sent a brigade to the Ukrainian capital of Kharkov, it found anti-Soviet moods among former tsarist officers but no organization. Zdanovich, *Organy*, 391–2 (citing TsA FSB, delo R-4807, t. 1, l. 39, 44: May 8, 1938), 433. A Russian All-Military Union (ROVS) had been founded in Belgrade in 1924 by General Wrangel, Lieutenant General Alexander Kutepov, and the Romanov pretender, Grand Duke Nikolai Niloaevich, and was run out of Paris by Kutepov. His deputy, Major General Nikolai Skoblin, was an OGPU agent. The general staffs of Poland and Finland allowed their diplomatic pouches to carry ROVS materials to and from Moscow. Kutepov had concluded that only terrorist acts could shake the entrenched Soviet regime (or as Kutepov is said to have remarked, "detonate" the country), precisely the reasoning of the underground leftist terrorists during the tsarist days. On Jan. 26, 1930, Kutepov was kidnapped by an OGPU team coordinated by Yakov Serebryansky (the "Yasha team" for special tasks). Voitsekhovskii, *Trest*, 10–11; Sudoplatov, *Special Tasks*, 58; Barmine, *One Who Survived*, 186; Pipes, *Struve*, 379–87; Haslam, *Soviet Foreign Policy*, 23; *Krasnaia zvezda*, Sept. 22, 1965.
65. Khaustov et al., *Lubianka: Stalin i VChK*, 262 (APRF, f. 45, op. 1, d. 171, l. 4–5); Zdanovich, *Organy*, 390 (citing TsA FSB, f.

2, op. 8, d. 63, l. 50: Feb. 16, 1931). The Moscow "center" was said to consist of Mikhail Bonch-Bruevich, Alexander Verkhovsky, Sergei Kamenev, Alexander Svechin, Kakurin, and Snesarev—several with ties to Tukhachevsky.
66. Artizov et al., *Reabilitatsiia: kak eto bylo*, II: 671–788; *Z arkhiviv VUChK, GPU, NKVD, KGB*, no. 1, issue 18 (2002): 209; Khaustov, *Lubianka: Stalin i VChK*, 212–3 (RGASPI, f. 17, op. 162, d. 7, l. 188, 192); Zdanovich, *Organy*, 423–31. The main scholarly authority, who provides a list of names while admitting the impossibility of establishing exact figures, writes that as many as 10,000 officers might have been arrested and sentenced. Tynchenko, *Golgofa*, 242, 248–311. See also Berkhin, *Voennaia reforma*, 261.
67. "Letopis' stroitel'stva sovetskikh vooruzhennykh sil 1931 goda (ianvar'-aprel')," 114–5 (March 13, 1931). The accuser, Sergei Bezhanov (Sakvorelidze), would be executed (Balytsky had recommended a ten-year sentence, based upon his cooperation). *Voennye arkhivy Rossii*, 106; Tynchenko, *Golgofa*, 209–12 (GA SBU, fp., d. 67093, t. 21, delo Bzhanova S. G.: 102–3; t. 23: 578; t. 2, protokoly troika NKVD USSR: 89). Shaposhnikov had been placed at the head of non-party senior military men who approved industrialization and condemned the right deviation at the 16th Party Congress in 1930, when Stalin had allowed him to join the party expeditiously. In June 1931, Alexander Yegorov, whom Stalin knew from the civil war, was named chief of the staff.
68. Tynchenko, *Golgofa*, 124 (citing TsA FSB, f. R-40164, d. 4–b, delo Snesareva A. E.: 250); Snesarev, *Filosofiia voiny*, 33 (no citation). Mikhail Bonch-Bruevich, a former chief of staff, was arrested (Feb. 1931) but then released (May); Sergei Kamenev, the former supreme commander of the Red Army, was untouched despite compromising material gathered on him. Alexander Svechin was re-arrested in Feb. 1931 and got five years but would be released early in Feb. 1932; Verkhovsky was also arrested in Feb. 1931 and, in July, sentenced to execution, but this was commuted to ten years; Kakurin was sentenced in Feb. 1932 extrajudicially to execution, which was commuted immediately to ten years of solitary confinement (he would die in prison in summer 1936). Snesarev ended up at Solovki. In Sept. 1934 he would be granted early release because of ill health; he would die in a Moscow hospital on Dec. 4, 1937, and be buried at the Vaganskoye cemetery. Dudnik and Smirnov, "Vsia zhizn'-nauke," (no. 2), (no. 8); *Bol'shaia Sovetskaia entsiklopediia* (1976), XXIII: 635; Medvedev, *Let History Judge*, 287; Khrushchev, *Memoirs*, II: 141–3, 143n2.
69. Rölling and Rüter, *Tokyo Judgment*, I: chap. 6; Haslam, *Soviet Foreign Policy*, 73, 86–9; Andrew and Gordievsky, *KGB*, 178–80.
70. Tukhachevsky took part in the May 13, 24, and 25, 1931, sessions of the Revolutionary Military Council in Moscow. RGASPI, f. 17, op. 3, d. 816, 818, 824, d. 829, l. 4 (June 10, 1931); RGASPI, f. 17, op. 162, d. 9, l. 162; d. 10, l. 2, 7, 33; Nikulin, *Tukhachevskii*, 169. Orjonikidze might have played a role in Tukhachevsky's promotion. Dubinskii-Mukhadze, *Ordzhonikidze*, 277. Tukhachevsky had been working hard to demonstrate his loyalty to Voroshilov, sending an especially sycophantic fiftieth birthday greeting (Feb. 4, 1931). Voroshilov, *Stat'i i materialy k 50-letiiu*, 250–1.
71. *Voennye arkhivy Rossii*, 100–13. The same key informant, Olga Zajonczkowska-Popova, continued her work.
72. Next up was the R-5, and Stalin was told it had a transmitter and receiver, which he

could test. "And you are not deceiving us? Show me the radio station . . ." Turzhanskii, "Vo glave Sovetskoi aviatsii," 183–9. Turzhansky would be arrested on July 23, 1938, accused of taking part in a military-fascist plot against the USSR and tortured; he would refuse to confess and be deported to the Kolyma camps; he would be released on Feb. 29, 1940, and, on June 4, named a major general of the air force.

73. Tumshis and Papchinskii, *1937, bol'shaia chistka,* 213 (citing ORAF UFSB po Stavorpol'skomy kraiu, arkhivnoe sledstvennoe delo no. 13144 on Kaul A. I. t. 2).

74. Kokurin and Petrov, "OGPU, 1929–1934 gg.," 104; Khaustov et al., *Lubianka: Stalin i VChK,* 226–9 (APRF, f. 3, op. 20, d. 193, l. 129–31: March 7, 1930); Zdanovich, *Organy,* 415 (Sept. 1930); Whitewood, *Red Army,* 130 (citing RGVA, f. 33987, op. 3, d. 293, l. 220). Yevdokimov had used his authority to send commissions to Sverdlovsk and Alma-Ata to gather compromising material on forced confessions and other abuses to use against Yagoda. Tumshis and Papchinskii, *1937, bol'shaia chistka,* 213, (citing ORAF UFSB po Stavorpol'skomy kraiu, arkhivnoe sledstvennoe delo no. 13144 on Kaul A. I. t. 2: 37).

75. He had taken a long holiday in 1930, and spent the entire winter 1930–31 at his dacha outside Moscow, but his health worsened again in Feb.–March 1931. *Meditsinskaia gazeta,* June 29, 1988.

76. See Seyed-Gohrab, *Great Umar Khayyam.*

77. He would suffer severe flu in Sept. and Oct. 1931.

78. Akulov had a storied past as the organizer before the 1917 revolution of a 60,000-strong worker demonstration in St. Petersburg, and had assisted Stalin's machinations in the removal of Rykov as head of the government several months before. Blinov, *Ivan Akulov.*

79. Belsky was kicked over to the lowly supply commissariat, Messing to the foreign trade commissariat, and Olsky to the trust overseeing Moscow cafeterias. Stalin took the opportunity to insert Lavrenti Beria into the OGPU collegium as well. Artuzov, after a phone conversation with Mężyński, wrote him a letter (Dec. 3, 1931), upset that his loyalty had come under question, professed never to have collected material against Yagoda, and asked to be assigned different work. Vinogradov, *Genrikh Iagoda,* 354–8 (TsA FSB, d. R-4489, t. 3, l. 12–4). See also Kokurin and Petrov, "OGPU, 1929–1934 gg.," 104; Gladkov, *Nagrada,* 375–7.

80. Khaustov et al., *Lubianka: Stalin i VChK,* 275 (RGASPI, f. 17, op. 162, d. 10, l. 127), 276 (RGASPI, f. 17, op. 3, d. 840, l. 1, 2), 805–6n87 (RGASPI, f. 17, op. 3, d. 842, l. 5, 14); Il'inskii, *Narkom Iagoda,* 211. In the 1960s, Medved's brother-in-law (D. B. Sorokin) would claim that Kirov had blocked Medved's transfer out of Leningrad. RGANI, f. 6, op. 13, d. 67, l. 7–14 (Sorokin to Khrushchev, March 5, 1962). There is a garbled version in Orlov, *Secret History,* 14–15.

81. Yevdokimov would take with a vengeance to his new assignment to bring rebels, known as "Basmachi," to heel in the Tajikistan mountains bordering Afghanistan and the Turkmenistan desert bordering Iran. Tumshis and Papchinskii, *1937, bol'shaia chistka,* 221 (citing TsA FSB, arkhivnoe sledvestvennoe delo no. 14963 on Papashenko I. P., l. 120, quoting Iu. K. Ivanov-Borodin).

82. Naumov, *Bor'ba v rukovodstve NKVD,* 31–2. Balytsky, for example, brought a substantial number of Chekists to Moscow from Ukraine, while also leaving many loyalists behind to watch over Ukraine for him. Sever, *Volkodav Stalina,* 69–70. Molchanov, of Ivanovo province, would be moved to Moscow as

head of the secret-political department on Nov. 20, 1931: Khaustov et al., *Lubianka: Stalin i VChK,* 287 (RGASPI, f. 17, op. 3, d. 861, l. 9).

83. Parker, *Chamberlain and Appeasement,* 16 (citing Bodleian Library, Simon MS70, fols 86, 132). "France—at the head of our enemies," was the title of a section of a 1931 Soviet pamphlet. *Mezhdunarodnoe polozhenie,* 12. On July 18, 1931, for the first time since the war, a German chancellor, Brüning, went to Paris. Soon, Brüning, backed by Britain, would announce that Germany would seek the cancellation of all reparations.

84. The incident, involving Artashes Khalatyants, known as Artyom Khalatov, a Baku-born (1894) ethnic Armenian and the director of the state publishing house (since 1927), is related by Ivan Gronsky, then the editor of *Izvestiya.* Gronskii, *Iz proshlogo,* 153. Stalin wrote a note to Khalatov, along with Kaganovich and Kalinin, on Sept. 12, 1931, indicating he had not been excommunicated, but he would be sacked from the state publishing house on April 15, 1932; the disgraced Tomsky was named in his stead. Adibekov et al., *Politbiuro TsK RKP (b)—VKP (b): povestki dnia zasedanii,* II: 201, 205, 296 (RGASPI, f. 17, op. 3, d. 840, 842, 880); Khlevniuk et al., *Stalin i Kaganovich,* 100 (RGASPI, f. 558, op. 11, d. 76, l. 61), 110 (l. 73), 112 (l. 73–73ob.). Khalatov would be arrested on Sept. 26, 1937, and executed in Oct. 1938.

85. Khaustov et al., *Lubianka: Stalin i VChK,* 275–6 (RGASPI, f. 17, op. 162, d. 10, l. 127; op. 3, d. 840, l. 1–2), 280 (d. 841, l. 5, 9: Aug. 10 circular); 280 (d. 841, l. 5, 9: Aug. 6, 1931); *Na prieme,* 48. After Stalin had departed the capital, Kaganovich asked who ought to announce the personnel changes to the OGPU itself; Stalin insisted it had to be a party secretary, so that "the report is not assessed as revenge by one part of the OGPU against another." Khlevniuk et al., *Stalin i Kaganovich,* 48 (f. 558, op. 11, d. 76, l. 9–9ob.: Aug. 15, 1931), 48n1 (f. 17, op. 162, d. 10, l. 127), 49 (RGASPI, f. 558, op. 11, d. 76, l. 10–10ob.: Aug. 15). On July 10, the politburo had decreed that "no Communists, working in the organs of the GPU or outside the organs, either in the center or in locales, should be arrested without the consent of the Central Committee," and that "no specialists (engineering technical personnel, military, agronomists, physicians, and so on) should be arrested without the consent of the corresponding people's commissar." *Voennye arkhivy Rossii,* 107; Khlevniuk et al., *Stalinskoe politbiuro,* 60 (RGASPI, f. 17, op. 3, d. 840, l. 9). Later, this need to obtain a higher-up's permission for arrests of subordinates would have the effect of making complicit people's commissars and others in the annihilation of loyal cadres.

86. Shreider has a version of the internal OGPU struggle: Shreider, *NKVD iznutri,* 10, 13, 14–15.

87. Yagoda concluded: "There is not a single blot on the glorious banner of the OGPU. Ahead are still many years of struggle and glorious victories. We shall close Chekist ranks still more tightly!" Khaustov et al., *Lubianka: Stalin i VChK,* 277–9 (APRF, f. 45, op. 1, d. 171, l. 6–9); *Istoriia sovetskikh organov gosudarstvennoi bezopasnosti (Moscow: Vysshaia krasnoznamennaia shkola KGB, 1977),* 234–5. Slyly, Yagoda gave the Yevdokimov protégé Yakov Weinstok the assignment of evicting Yevdokimov's family from their Moscow apartment, ensuring everlasting bad blood between patron and protégé. Zhukovskii, *Lubianskaia imperiia NKVD,* 211.

88. Kvashonkin, *Sovetskoe rukovodstvo,* 161 (RGASPI, f. 74, op. 2, d. 38, l. 46: Sept. 24, 1931).

89. RGASPI, f. 558, op. 11, d. 728, l. 29. See also Valedinskii, "Organizm Stalina vpolne zdorovyi," 69. Stalin wrote a similar letter (undated) to Molotov. Kosheleva, *Pis'ma Stalina Molotovu,* 255; Lih et al., *Stalin's Letters to Molotov,* 239. Stalin was traveling through Mingrelia and Abkhazia in mid-Aug. 1931, on his way to Sochi.

90. Khromov, *Po stranitsam,* 12–5.

91. Davies, "Stalin as Economic Policy-Maker," 126–9.

92. The letters to Stalin brought to his attention were enumerated in lists in late 1930 and for Jan.–July 1931; no other such lists survive until 1945. Khlevniuk, "Letters to Stalin," citing RGASPI, f. 558, op. 11, d. 849-82.

93. Functionaries left Stalin to decide whether the people really knew him, or whether the proposed inventions should be considered. RGASPI, f. 558, op. 11, d. 861, l. 100.

94. RGASPI, f. 558, op. 11, d. 856, l. 138. Stalin occasionally replied to letters in the press, when he perceived an issue of general interest. Stalin, "Reply to Comrade Kolkhozniks," *Pravda* (April 3, 1930), reprinted in *Sochineniia,* XII: 202.

95. Khlevniuk, "Letters to Stalin," 331 (citing RGASPI, f. 558, op. 11, d. 850, l. 34–55).

96. Khlevniuk et al., *Stalin i Kaganovich,* 50–1 (RGASPI, f. 81, op. 3, d. 100, l. 101–2).

97. Two days later he told Kaganovich to circulate to politburo members a telegram accusing Mikoyan of lying about the silos there for tea and tobacco, based on other reports the dictator received ("Who is right and who is deceiving the Central Committee?"). Mikoyan replied that he had reported the truth, not conflated grain silos with other kinds; Stalin went back at him, prompting an irate Mikoyan to tender his resignation ("Dear Stalin!"). Stalin resolved the incident by denigrating supply personnel for their red tape, and instructing Kaganovich to have the workers' and peasants' inspectorate, as well as Caucasus OGPU boss Beria, oversee the silos in western Georgia. Khlevniuk et al., *Stalin i Kaganovich,* 51–2 (RGASPI, f. 558, op. 11, d. 76, l. 14–8); Khromov, *Po stranitsam,* 35–6 (citing RGASPI, f. 558, op. 11, d. 76, l. 8–8ob,14–5); Pavlov, *Anastas Mikoian,* 83–4 (citing RGASPI, f. 84, op. 1, d. 134, l. 2, 5: Sept. 12, 1931); RGASPI, f. 558, op. 11, d. 76, l. 72–3.

98. Andrei F. Andreyev, a Red Army veteran in Zdorovets village of the Central Black Earth province, somehow got a letter through to Stalin on Feb. 2, 1931, in which he claimed that he had fought the Whites in the civil war and been wounded, returned to his poor family in his native village, and become a rural correspondent, continuing the struggle, but had been hindered by local officials, who evicted him from the collective farm. "Now all these criminals, whose work I exposed in the press, have managed to have me arrested without even presenting a cause for my arrest," he wrote of fruitless petitions to the county procurator and OGPU. "I led companies, regiments, and battalions into battle against the Whites not in order that I would now sit under arrest by these same White Guards." Stalin wrote on the letter: "To comrade Yagoda. Request: immediately assign one of your people (someone completely reliable) to sort this out in Bolshevik fashion—honestly, quickly, and impartially and 'no matter who.'" Vinogradov, *Genrikh Iagoda,* 351–3 (TsA FSB, f. 2, op. 9, d. 11, l. 138–40); Khaustov et al., *Lubianka: Stalin i VChK,* 260–1 (APRF, f. 45, op. 1, d. 171, l. 2–3). Andreyev (b. 1894) was vindicated and readmitted to a collective farm. (He would be arrested in 1942 and sentenced to ten years in a labor camp.)

99. See the case of the head of the Artyom Coal Trust in the Donbass, Konstantin Rumyantsev, in which Stalin expressed distrust of the motives of his brother-in-law Redens (Ukraine OGPU boss): RGASPI, f. 558, op. 11, d. 42, l. 104. Rumyantsev (b. 1891), who won an Order of Lenin in 1931, died in a plane crash the next year.

100. Khaustov et al., *Lubianka: Stalin i VChK*, 284 (RGASPI, f. 558, op. 11, d. 76, l. 70: Sept. 19, 1931).

101. Khlevniuk, *Politbiuro*, 84 (citing RGASPI, f. 81, op. 3, d. 100, l. 101). Besides Orjonikidze, Stalin was concerned about Kuibyshev, who, he knew, was an alcoholic and clashed with Molotov as well.

102. Khlevniuk, *Master of the House*, 73–4 (citing RGASPI, f. 558, op. 11, d. 779, l. 21–3: Sept. 11, 1931; l. 32–33: Oct. 4, 1931). "Sergo did not love Molotov very much," Mikoyan recalled. But disputes were generally not over first principles but bureaucratic interests. Mikoian, *Tak bylo*, 324, 520; Rees, *Decision-making in the Stalinist Command Economy*, 262–74.

103. Murin, *Stalin v ob"iatiakh*, 35 (APRF, f. 45, op. 1, d. 1550, l. 52), 35–6 (l. 53–8), 37 (l. 59), 44 (APRF, f. 45, op. 1, d. 1552, l. 1), 37 (l. 60), 39 (l. 65–6: Sept. 26). The openly pro-fascist Dmitrievsky expressed a positive view of Stalin, imagining him to represent "the national-socialist imperialism that aspires to destroy the West in its strongholds." *Stalin* (Stockholm: Bonnier, 1931), in Swedish and in Russian (Stockholm: Strela, 1931). See also the review by Kuskova: *Sovremennye zapiski*, 1931, no. 47: 518. See also the gossip about Stalin and Alliluyeva that circulated in the secret police: Orlov, *Secret History*, 318–9.

104. The tracks would be fully repaired before 6:00 a.m. the next morning. Yoshihashi, *Conspiracy at Mukden*; Ogata, *Defiance in Manchuria*; Crowley, *Japan's Quest for Autonomy*; *Istoriia voiny na Tikhom okeane*, I: 187. See also Iriye, *After Imperialism*.

105. Crowley, *Japan's Quest for Autonomy*, 114–21.

106. Patrikeef, *Russian Politics*, 101–3. The early 1920s Soviet thrust into Manchuria, as in the case of Mongolia, had been defensive, to secure Siberia's flanks against anti-Soviet White armies abroad, but then Manchuria became a largely commercial venture, subject to material cost-benefit rather than revolutionary calculations.

107. The League, founded in 1920 following the Versailles treaty negotiations with forty-two members, was the first international organization dedicated to world peace, aiming to prevent wars with what it called "collective security," disarmament, and arbitration. Headquartered in Geneva it had a general assembly of all members and a secretariat, but lacked its own military and depended on the great powers comprising its executive council to enforce its resolutions. Japan was one of five permanent members of the League's executive council (along with Great Britain, France, Italy, and Germany, which had been added later). The United States, one of the originators, had failed to join. American economic power could be converted into military power—such as in the decision to build a two-ocean navy in 1916—but American geopolitical power remained constrained by limits set by Congress and public opinion. The Soviet Union was not a member of the League either. Kennedy, "Move to Institutions." Membership would peak at fifty-eight in late 1934 and early 1935.

108. Lensen, *Japanese Recognition*; Lensen, *Damned Inheritance*, 223–6; Dallin, *Rise of Russia in Asia*, 244–8; Beloff, *Foreign Policy of Soviet Russia*, I: 76–7.

109. Under Nicholas II, the Pacific had come to seem the theater of gravest threat, but in Soviet military thinking the Vistula commanded center stage. Contradictions stemming from strategic anxiety and pessimism were endemic to imperial Russian strategy. Fuller, *Strategy and Power*, 430.

110. Menning, "Soviet Strategy," I: 215–6; Daines, "Voennaia strategiia," 247–8.

111. Between 1932 and 1936, the Soviet Far Eastern Army would increase from six to fourteen divisions. Coox, *Nomonhan*, 76–8.

112. The USSR's sparsely populated, exposed Far Eastern territory was not even administered by the local party machine, but by the army (Vasily Blyukher) and secret police (Terenty Deribas), in vicious rivalry. Rumors of Blyukher's pending arrest, in connection with Operation "Springtime," had circulated in late 1930 and resurfaced in May and June 1931, although on Aug. 6, the second anniversary of the Far Eastern Army, Voroshilov, on an extended inspection tour, locally announced Blyukher's award of the Order of Lenin. Haslam, *Soviet Foreign Policy*, 72 (citing *Times*, Nov. 20, 22, 25, 1930); *Izvestiia*, Aug. 18, 1931; Dushen'kin, *Proletarskii marshal*, 111.

113. Toshihio, "Extension of Hostilities," 241–33; Slavinskii, *Sovetskii Soiuz i Kitai*, 219–20 (citing AVP RF, fond Litvinova, op. 12, pap. 85, d. 45, 8–9); Coox, *Nomonhan*, 23; Stephan, *Russian Far East*, 183–5; Steiner, *Lights that Failed*, 719–20. On Oct. 28, 1931, the Japanese ambassador conveyed an ultimatum warning against a military response; TASS published it and the Soviet reply (a policy of "strict noninterference") two days later. The Japanese suspected the Soviets were supplying the Chinese resistance. *DVP SSSR*, XIV: 820.

114. Khlevniuk et al., *Stalin i Kaganovich*, 116–7 (RGASPI, f. 558, op. 11, d. 76, l. 76–76ob.). Stalin called for toning down the boasts in the press about ongoing Red Army military maneuvers in the Western military district. Khlevniuk et al., *Stalin i Kaganovich*, 121–2 (RGASPI, f. 558, op. 11, d. 76, l. 81: Sept. 27, 1931).

115. Davies, *Crisis and Progress*, 113 (citing RGAE, f. 4372, op. 91, d. 871, l. 98–9), 115 (GARF, f. 4372, op. 57, d. 16, l. 30: art. 223ss).

116. Kondrashin and Penner, *Golod*, 114. Later, Kondrashin republished this book excising Penner's co-authorship (Moscow: Rosspen, 2008).

117. The official 1931 harvest estimate had been lowered several times, to 69.5 million tons, which still ended up to be a massive overestimate. Davies and Wheatcroft, *Years of Hunger*, 76, 446; Davies et al., *Economic Transformation*, 286–8 (table 19).

118. Khlevniuk et al., *Stenogrammy zasedanii politbiuro*, 14–5 (citing RGASPI, f. 17, op. 2, d. 732, l. 18; d. 484, l. 42, 48). For different figures (38 million as of early 1932), see Carr and Davies, *Foundations of a Planned Economy*, I: 700–4; Davies, *Soviet Economy in Turmoil*, 289–300; Davies, *Crisis and Progress*, 177. A newly established grain reserve fund had stood at 2 million tons, but it soon vanished through export and a massive increase in internal consumption.

119. "There are few Englishmen who do not rejoice at the breaking of our golden fetters," John Maynard Keynes wrote. Eichengreen, *Golden Fetters*, 21.

120. France by itself was too weak to stabilize the global monetary system, and the United States, which had its own economic and financial challenges, refused to do so. Steiner, *Lights that Failed*, 698–9; more broadly, see Tooze, *Deluge*.

121. "The End of an Epoch," *Economist*, Sept. 26, 1931: 547; Steiner, *Lights that Failed*, 663–8; Eichengreen, *Golden Fetters*, 298–9.

122. Eichengreen, *Golden Fetters*. Politicians, with the post–Great War widening of the suffrage and the spread of trade unions and leftist parties, proved skittish about imposing economic adjustment on their electorates for the sake of the stability of financial markets, a lack of credible commitment that undid global finance and trade. Simmons, *Who Adjusts?* Of course, "international cooperation" might not have been an issue at all if the United States had undertaken expansionary policies, generating the capital outflow that could have supplied much-needed liquidity and therefore the security sought by the governments in Europe that lacked confidence. (Given that the consumers' expenditure average value index dropped close to 30 percent between 1929 and 1933, moderately expansionary policies would not have threatened inflation.) Britain would launch monetary expansion in 1932, and endure a relatively milder crisis; Japan would emulate the British and enjoy a robust recovery. Franklin Roosevelt would rescue the banks with public money, in 1933. Many people at the time, and subsequently, viewed his actions as opening a path to recovery. But that recovery would be halting, at best, and full of policy mistakes. Kindleberger, *World in Depression*; Friedman and Schwartz, *Monetary History*; Eichengreen, *Golden Fetters*.

123. Steiner, *Lights that Failed*, 668–70.

124. Soviet foreign trade, despite the dislocation in the capitalist world from 1929, had initially expanded more rapidly than envisioned in the Five-Year Plan, but even though the USSR had exported more than twice as much grain in 1930 as in 1927–28, it had earned only about the same revenues because of lower prices. Revenues in 1931 were worse. Catastrophic livestock losses, moreover, destroyed the animal-products export plan, and even mechanization of agriculture brought costs (tractors consumed fuel, reducing petroleum-product exports). *Sel'skoe khoziaistvo SSSR*, 222; *Vneshniaia torgovlia SSSR za 20 let, 1918–1937 gg.*, 35. Grain exports officially rose to about 4.8 million tons in 1930 and 5.06 million tons in 1931, accounting for just under one-fifth of total exports (others included timber, oil, flax, animal products, even medicinal herbs). Dohan, "Economic Origins of Soviet Autarky," 612–3. One gold ruble in foreign trade equaled $0.52 until early 1933.

125. Dmytro Manuilsky, at a Comintern enlarged plenum in March 1931, stated: "Can the perspective of the people's revolution in Germany be viewed outside of the whole complicated international tangle and especially outside the question of the USSR?" A German revolution might provoke British and French intervention, forcing the Soviet Union to send in the Red Army, or allow "the imperialists" to annihilate the German Communists. Manuilsky, *Communist Parties*, 99; Carr, *Twilight of the Comintern*, 32–3, 37. The German trade delegation was in Moscow from Feb. 26 to March 11, 1931. Hilger and Meyer, *Incompatible Allies*, 239–42; von Dirksen, *Moscow, Tokyo, London*, 89–96. Stalin had received an analysis of the credit disposition toward the USSR of German banks on Nov. 19, 1930. The OGPU worried about the opposition inside the newly created Bank of International Settlements (1930) in Basel to German bank co-operation with the USSR. *Glazami razvedki*, 322–3 (TsA FSB, f. 2, op. 9, d. 861, l. 14–5), 328–9 (l. 7–8: May 7, 1931).

126. The agreement had been signed on April 14, 1931. Dyck, *Weimar Germany*, 223–4; Haslam, *Soviet Foreign Policy*, 55; *Izvestiia*, March 10, April 21 and 24, 1931; *DVP SSSR*, XIV: 116–9 (Krestinsky to Khinchuk in

Berlin: March 10, 1931), 172 (Tass communiqué, March 10), 246–8 (Russian text of the agreement). On June 24, the two sides agreed on a protocol extending the April 1926 Treaty of Berlin, a treaty of neutrality and nonaggression, with a two-year moratorium for either side to denounce it, but the German side did not ratify it. It had been set to expire on June 29. *DVP SSSR*, XIV: 395–6. Dyck, *Weimar Germany*, 229–36.
127. By 1932, Germany would account for nearly half of Soviet imports. Dyck, *Weimar Germany*, 216; Ericson, *Feeding the German Eagle*, 14. The USSR had already gone from eleventh to fourth place in German exports between 1930 and 1931. *DVP SSSR*, XIV: 118, 247, 749–50.
128. The pound was devalued by some 30 percent after Britain withdrew from the gold standard, and because much of Soviet debt was payable in sterling Moscow might have gotten debt relief, but just about all Soviet gold payments in the years 1931–34 went to Germany, and the Soviets had to purchase marks (with gold) at the official parity rate of the reichsmark (the German government refused to devalue the mark). The Soviets covered their debt to Britain with commodity exports, whose prices were falling, so that the Soviets failed to achieve the full windfall in paying off debt that was denominated in devalued sterling. In 1933, when the United States would leave the gold standard and the dollar would be devalued, the Soviets would reap about 300 million gold rubles' worth of debt relief. Dohan, "Soviet Foreign Trade," 607–10. The exchange rate for sterling, which had been 9.46 rubles to £1, fell to 6.58–6.42 rubles by late 1931. Aizenberg, *Valiutnaia Sistema SSSR*, 104.
129. Germany, Greece, and Hungary would default in 1932. Reinhart and Rogoff, *This Time Is Different*, 96 (table 6.4). The real value of the ruble would drop by perhaps 60 percent during the Five-Year Plan. Mozokhin, *VChK-OGPU*, 213.
130. Dohan, "Economic Origins of Soviet Autarky," 606–7; *DBFP*, 2nd series, VII: 222 (Strang to Marquess of Reading); Davies, *Crisis and Progress*, 121n80. Strang surmised that a stable capitalism was a sine qua non for the success of socialism in the USSR. See also *New York Times*, Dec. 6, 1931, and Jan. 10, 1932. Some foreigners knew better: *Le Temps*, Nov. 23, 1931 (L. Vitin). The British came to understand that the Germans would not let the Soviets default: *British Documents on Foreign Affairs*, part II, series A, X: 377, XVI: 4–5.
131. The year 1931 would mark a peak for Soviet industrial imports, when the USSR accounted for 27.5 percent of U.S. industrial exports and 80 percent of German engineering exports. Dohan, "Economic Origins of Soviet Autarky." Cloth imports fell from more than 10 million meters to under 1 million. See, "Foreign Economic Relations," 208. The year 1932 would turn out to be the worst in the history of Soviet foreign trade because of higher tariffs abroad and decreased credit availability.
132. Dohan, "Economic Origins of Soviet Autarky," 626–7. See also Tauger, "1932 Harvest," 88n52.
133. Davies and Wheatcroft, *Years of Hunger*, 86 (RGASPI, f. 17, op. 162, d. 10, l. 119). On Sept. 4, Stalin complained to Kaganovich that "you are putting every kind of pressure for the export of grain when they pay pennies for grain," suggesting instead they export butter; Kaganovich recommended no changes for now. Khlevniuk et al., *Stalin i Kaganovich*, 80–1 (RGASPI, f. 81, op. 3, d. 99, l. 16–9), 83–6 (f. 558, op. 11, d. 739, l. 76–87: Sept. 6).

134. Kurliandskii, *Stalin, vlast', religiia*, 233–463, 610–28.
135. Khlevniuk et al., *Stalin i Kaganovich*, 54–7 (RGASPI, f. 558, op. 11, d. 739, l. 28–39), 60 (d. 76, l. 30–1); Davies and Wheatcroft, *Years of Hunger*, 85 (RGASPI, f. 17, op. 162, d. 10, l. 128, 153), 88–91 (RGASPI, f. 17, op. 2, d. 479, l. 267; d. 484, l. 43, 47ob., 45, 53, 53ob., 54, 55, 55ob., 61; d. 481, l. 123); Kondrashin and Penner, *Golod*, 116 (RGAE, f. 7496, op. 37 d. 159, l. 98).
136. Davies and Wheatcroft, *Years of Hunger*, 69 (RGASPI, f. 17, op. 3, d. 484, l. 60).
137. Davies and Wheatcroft, *Years of Hunger*, 75 (RGASPI, f. 17, op. 2, d. 484, l. 53–5: Stalin mocking V. V. Ptukha). *Pravda*'s coverage of the plenum did not mention the discussion of grain procurement, in which regional party bosses condemned incompetence in harvest gathering and mass theft of the grain. Mikoyan interjected that collective farmers needed to be told: "first, satisfy the state plan, then satisfy your own plan." Oskolkov, *Golod 1932/1933*, 17–9 (RGASPI, f. 17, op. 2, d. 484, l. 119).
138. Davies and Wheatcroft, *Years of Hunger*, 88, 90–1 (RGASPI, f. 17, op. 162, d. 481, l. 123, 55ob., 61), 96–7.
139. In 1926–27 the average market price per centner for rye had been 7.53 rubles while the state price had been 4.31. Davies and Wheatcroft, *Years of Hunger*, 93 (citing *Tovaroob-orot*, 1932: 140–45).
140. Kondrashin and Penner, *Golod*, 121 (citing RGAE, osobaia papka Kolkhoztsentra). No date is given.
141. Khaustov et al., *Lubianka: Stalin i VChK*, 255–6 (RGASPI, f. 17, op. 162, d. 9, l. 54). Stalin received twenty people that day, an unusually large number; the last departed at 5:10 p.m. He was back in the office the next day. *Na prieme*, 79–80.
142. The incident occurred near Ilinka 5/2 across from the Old Gostinny Dvor. Ogarev's real name was said to be Platonov-Petin, and he was identified as an aide to the British intelligence station chief responsible for the border states that used to be part of imperial Russia. On the OGPU report, Molotov wrote: "To the members of the politburo: comrade Stalin needs to cease walking on foot in Moscow." Kaganovich, Kalinin, Kuibyshev, and Rykov affixed their signatures. This might have helped accelerate Stalin's own move permanently into the Kremlin. "Agent angliiskoi razvedki sluchayno vstretil Vas . . . ," 161–2 (APRF, f. 3, op. 58, d. 226, l. 18, 19: Nov. 18, 1931); Khaustov et al., *Lubianka: Stalin i VChK*, 286. APRF, f. 3, op. 58, d. 200, l. 147.
143. Japanese patriots extolled their country as a liberating conqueror, while the army leadership and many civilian supporters cast Manchuria's takeover as a matter of national survival. Duara, *Sovereignty and Authenticity*. It took "more than ministers and generals to make an empire." Young, *Total Empire*, 8. Japanese casualties occurred mostly in a diversionary action over Shanghai.
144. Kvashonkin, *Sovetskoe rukovodstvo*, 161–3 (RGASPI, f. 74, op. 2, d. 38, l. 48–51). See also Stone, *Hammer and Rifle*, 185 (citing l. 52–3). Japan's military was effectively dictating the country's foreign policy with an aggressive strategy that asserted a need to "protect" investments in China from China's protracted civil war and from perceived Soviet encroachment, while actually forcing into being a self-sufficient empire in Asia. Paine, *Wars for Asia*.
145. Soviet anxiety about appearing either belligerent or too weak was evident in a speech by Molotov on Dec. 22, 1931, at the central executive committee (repeating Stalin's words of June 1930): "We need no one

else's land, but not one inch of our land will we cede to anyone else." Molotov, "O vypolnenie pervoi pitaitletki: doklad na vtoroi sessii IsIK SSSR o narodno-khoziaistvennom plane na 1932 god," *Pravda*, Dec. 25, 1931, reprinted in *DVP SSSR*, XIV: 725–8, and in Molotov, *V bor'be za sotsializm* (1935), 236–76 (at 262–3); *Sochineniia*, XII: 269. Molotov's speech might have been the regime's first public statement on Japan's action in Manchuria. Haslam, *Soviet Foreign Policy*, 79, 81; Thorne, *Limits of Foreign Policy*, 133.
146. Ken, *Moskva i pakt*. The Soviets interpreted France's diplomatic efforts to manage its predicament vis-à-vis Germany as directed against the USSR. Kun, *Kommunisticheskii internatsional v dokumentakh*, 966–72; Eudin and Slusser, *Soviet Foreign Policy*, I: 324–31. In the eyes of Paris, a nonaggression pact with Moscow promised to loosen Soviet-German ties and secure genuine Soviet neutrality in the event of any Franco-German conflict, but after initialing a draft agreement the French had backed off signing it, preferring instead to try to get Germany to freeze frontiers and forswear rearming in exchange for aid. (The Weimar Republic chancellor would decline.) After the Nazi party electoral success in Sept. 1930 and a German government announcement (March 1931) of a pending customs union with Austria, Paris conveyed to Moscow a willingness for exploratory talks on both a nonaggression pact and credits for trade, but mutual suspicion continued to undermine efforts. *DVP SSSR*, XIV: 452–6 (Dovgalevsky to Moscow, Aug. 8, 1931), 573–581 (V. L. Mezhlauk to Moscow: Oct. 16, 1931); Coulondre, *De Staline à Hitler*, 12; Herriot, *Jadis*, II: 312–3; Scott, *Alliance against Hitler*, 24–5; Wheeler-Bennett, *Documents on International Affairs, 1931*, 3–6; Scott, *Alliance against Hitler*, 8–9; Steiner, *Lights that Failed*, 553; Carley, "Five Kopecks," at 36. France would turn out to be the only country in the world that increased its imports from the USSR in 1931–32. Williams, *Trading with the Bolsheviks*, 142. In 1932, the Nazis would win 230 seats, the most by any party during the entire Weimar period. That same year, 90 percent of German reparation payments would be canceled.
147. Kvashonkin, *Sovetskoe rukovodstvo*, 163n6 (RGASPI, f. 17, op. 162, d. 11, l. 64); *Dokumenty i materialy po istorii sovetski-kh-pol'skikh otnoshenii*, V: 502–5 (AVP RF, f. 05, op. 11, d. 5, l. 157–62: Nov. 14, 1931); *Izvestiia*, Nov. 22, 1931; Lechik, "'Vo frantsuzsko-pol'sko-rossiiskom treugol'nike," 120–3; Haslam, *Soviet Foreign Policy*, 98.
148. *Izvestiia*, July 26, 1930 (Litvinov interview). Stalin had hesitated to promote the rightist-leaning Litvinov, telling Chicherin, "You should be the commissar, even if you work only two hours a day," but Litvinov had filled the vacuum anyway. Cherniavskii, "Fenomenon Litvinova"; "'Diktatura iazyko-cheshyshchikh nad rabotaiushchimi': poslednaia sluzhebnaia zapiska Chicherina," 112n7; Farnsworth, "Conversing with Stalin," 958 (citing RGASPI, f. 558, op. 11, d. 749, l. 80–3); Carley, *Silent Conflict*, 410–1 (citing AVP RF, f. 05, op. 9, pap. 43, d. 1, l. 130–2: Sept. 7, 1929); Adibekov et al., *Politbiuro TsK RKP (b)–VKP (b) i Evropa*, (Dec. 3, 1929); Kvashonkin, *Sovetskoe rukovodstvo*, 100; Besedovskii, *Na putiakh*, 385–6. See also Kennan on Chicherin, *Russia and the West*, 205–6. Mikoyan would recall that "the arguments between Chicherin and Litvinov at politburo meetings . . . helped us figure out the most difficult issues of world politics." Those who worked with both judged them equivalent in quality of mind and breadth of horizons.

Sheinis, *Maksim Maksimovich Litvinov*, 4; Sheinis, "Polpred B. E. Shtein," 108. Rumors in Moscow on Chicherin's likely replacement had run the gamut (Chicherin's farewell memo seems to have had Kuibyshev in mind). See also Haslam, *Soviet Foreign Policy*, 14–5; Ken and Rupasov, *Zapadnoe iogranich'e*, 562–3; and O'Connor, *Diplomacy and Revolution*, 157–64.

149. Chicherin added: "The OGPU leaders have blind faith in the words of every idiot and cretin they make their agent." 'Diktatura iazykocheshyshchikh nad rabotaiushchimi': posledniaia sluzhebnaia zapiska G.V. Chicherina," 108–10. Chicherin had effectively failed in his Stalin-supported quest to forge a genuine alliance with Germany, but had prevented an anti-Soviet coalition, a version of Soviet strategy he had enunciated in a note to Stalin in 1929: "Any sharpening of the antagonisms between Germany and the Entente, France and Italy, Italy and Yugoslavia, England and America means a strengthening of our position, a lessening of the various threats to us." V. V. Sokolov, "Neizvestnyi G. V. Chicherin: iz rassekrechennykh arkhivov MID RF," 12 (citing AVP RF, f. 08, op. 12, pap. 74, d. 55, l. 86). The Germans suspected that because of his British wife, Litvinov was secretly pro-British-French. Von Dirksen, *Moscow, Tokyo, London*, 81.

150. Stalin both criticized and praised Litvinov. Kosheleva, *Pis'ma Stalina-Molotovu*, 167–8 (Oct. 7, 1929), 169–71 (Dec. 5, 1929); Ken and Rupasov, *Zapadnoe prigranich'e*, 568 (RGASPI, f. 17, op. 162, d. 10, l. 62: March 1931). Litvinov, according to his daughter, had preferred Stalin to Trotsky. Phillips, *Between the Revolution and the West*, 109 (citing Tatyana Litvinova).

151. Stalin expanded the number of the commissariat's departments responsible for the West and promoted strong officials to lead them, to curb Litvinov's powers. The foreign affairs collegium now consisted of Litvinov and his three deputies: Krestinsky (first deputy), Boris Stomonyakov (an ethnic Bulgarian), and Lev Karakhan (a Chicherin protégé). Eventually, however, Stalin would grant abolition of the collegium and a reduction in deputy commissars, strengthening Litvinov's grip over that body. Dullin, *Men of Influence*, 58–9; Sokolov, "Zamestitel' narkoma inostrannykh del B. Stomoniakov," 120.

152. Officials who had joined the foreign affairs commissariat in the early NEP years occupied about one-third of the senior posts dealing with Europe, but an influx during the Great Break, under Litvinov, brought people with fewer than five years of service, some filling entirely new posts, many replacing defectors or those purged. Of diplomats who joined before 1925, around 48 percent were Russian; 33 percent were Jewish; another 4.5 percent were Balts. Of those who joined after 1929, 56 percent were Russian, nearly 30 percent were Jewish, and 6 percent were Ukrainian. At the very top, few were ethnic Russians. Litvinov, Sokolnikov, Surits, Khinchuk, Dovgalevsky were all Jewish. Some of the Russians were the wrong class (of noble descent): Kollontai, Alexandrovsky. Old-line diplomats, with foreign-language and -country expertise, were hostile to the "neophytes" mobilized into the corps by the Central Committee. The arrivistes looked askance at the "bourgeois" habits and mentality of the old guard. Dullin, *Men of Influence*, 52–3 (comparing the diplomatic yearbooks of 1925 and 1933–6); *Sostav rukovodiashchikh rabotnikov i spetsialistov Soiuza SSR*, 296–303.

153. Ken, *Moskva i pakt*, 44–6; Khlevniuk et al., *Stalin i Kaganovich*, 71–3 (RGASPI, f. 81, op. 3, d. 99, l. 12–4: Aug. 30, 1931), 88–9 (l.

21–3: Sept. 7). To ensure timely exchange of information and control over decision making, Stalin created a standing politburo commission for foreign affairs (Nov. 22, 1931) consisting of himself, Molotov, and Kaganovich (Orjonikidze would be added a month later). Litvinov helped initiate the establishment (Nov. 26) of a lesser, separate commission just for Poland. Khlevniuk, *Politbiuro*, 84–5; Watson, "The Politburo and Foreign Policy," 134–67 (RGASPI, f. 17, op. 162, d. 11, l. 68, 98, 99, 111); Ken and Rupasov, *Zapadnoe prigranich'e*, 589–90 (l. 73; AVP RF, f. 010, op. 4, pap. 21, d. 63, l. 635–6).

154. It was not just Stalin who voiced this view. Chicherin, speaking to the Afghan king Amanullah Khan in May 1928, had noted "whether England is preparing a war for us, we shall see later. England is always striving to push others instead of itself into military actions against us. She could push Poland against us." *DVP SSSR*, XI: 301–7 (at 303). Stalin also knew that Piłsudski had offered his services to the Japanese as early as 1905, promising to lead an uprising in Russian Poland.

155. Kaganovich exploded at the foreign affairs commissariat to Stalin, writing that "they have no serious materials" in support of their opposition. To Kaganovich's mind, Litvinov showed himself given to Germanophilia, seeking to build Soviet security one-sidedly on the relationship with Germany while dismissing Poland; Kaganovich also complained of Litvinov's self-satisfied smugness. But the entire foreign affairs commissariat was united in opposition to a Soviet pact with Poland, even Litvinov's enemy Karakhan, suspecting that Warsaw's probes with Moscow were mere ploys to frighten Berlin into deals with Poland and France. Khlevniuk et al., *Stalin i Kaganovich*, 76–7 (RGASPI, f. 558, op. 11, d. 739, l. 65–7: Sept. 3, 1931), 105–8 (l. 14–22: Sept. 16), 114n1 (f. 17, op. 162, d. 10, l. 177–8; op. 162, d. 11, l. 1, 9); *Dokumenty i materialy po istorii sovetsko-pol'skikh otnoshenii*, V: 490–2 (Karakhan, Aug. 4, 1931); *DVP SSSR*, XIV: 488–9 (Aug. 6, 1931); *Izvestiia*, Aug. 30, 1931, Jan. 26, 1932; Tisminets, *Vneshniaia politika SSSR*, III: 517–9, III: 519–20, 556–8; Dyck, *Weimar Germany*, 240; Adibekov et al., *Politbiuro Tsk RKP (b)—VKP (b) i Evropa*, 259 (RGASPI, f. 17, op. 162, d. 11, l. 9: Sept. 20, 1931), 261–2 (l. 17: Sept. 30, 1931); Haslam, *Soviet Foreign Policy*, 69. On Nov. 22, 1931, TASS published a communiqué on the resumption of Polish-Soviet negotiations. *DVP SSSR*, XIV: 647–50, 675; RGASPI, f. 17, op. 162, d. 11, l. 64. See also Budurowycz, *Polish-Soviet Relations*, 8–9.

156. Dyck, *Weimar Germany*, 242–9 (citing 9187/H249372–8: Dirksen memo, Nov. 10, 1931); RGASPI, f. 558, op. 11, d. 76, l. 75–75ob. German ambassador Herbert von Dirksen wrote in a report on a meeting with Voroshilov (Dec. 12, 1931)—which was intercepted by Soviet intelligence and passed to Voroshilov (Dec. 21)—that "Voroshilov said that, of course, under no circumstances can one speak about any guarantees of the Polish western border; the Soviet government is a principled opponent of the Versailles Treaty; it will never undertake anything that would somehow contribute to strengthening the Danzig corridor or Memel border." Duraczyński and Sakharov, *Sovetsko-Pol'skie otnosheniia*, 64 (RGVA, f. 33987, op. 3, d. 70, l. 264–5); Zeidler, *Reichswehr und Rote Armee*, 262; D'iakov and Bushueva, *Fashistskii mech kovalsia v SSSR*, 128–9 (RGVA, f. 33987, op. 3, d. 70, l. 253–8).

157. A declaration by Litvinov, after he had met with Kōki Hirota, was published in

the Soviet press: the USSR "affords great significance to the maintenance and strengthening of existing relations with Japan. The Soviet government observes a policy of strict noninterference in the conflicts among various countries." *DVP SSSR*, XIV: 668–72; *Izvestiia*, Nov. 21, 1931. On Nov. 23 the two countries signed a long-completed convention on postal exchange. *DVP SSSR*, XIV: 675–6. On Nov. 26, Karakhan in Tokyo began negotiations with Hirota on a fisheries agreement. *DVP SSSR*, XIV: 680–3.

158. Khaustov et al., *Lubianka: Stalin i VChK*, 291–5 (RGASPI, f. 558, op. 11, d. 185, l. 1–9). Soviet military intelligence also obtained a copy of a secret Japanese brochure for their officer corps, *The Red Army and the Methods of Struggle With It*, whose sixteen points included: "at the outset of a war it is necessary to inflict a decisive strike," because the Red Army was weak in the face of strength; "the goal should be not to seize territory but to destroy the functioning field army"; "the most advantageous area of the front is where there are units of different nationalities"; "it is necessary to use anti-Soviet Russians." Zolotarev, *Russkii arkhiv: Velikaia otechestvennaia*, VII/i: 47–9 (RGVA, f. 33987, op. 3, d. 1233, l. 339–45).

159. Khaustov et al., *Lubianka: Stalin i VChK*, 291–5 (RGASPI, f. 558, op. 11, d. 185, l. 1–9: Dec. 19, 1931). In a second intercepted memo sent to Stalin on Feb. 28, 1932, Kasahara again emphasized that "the military might of the Soviet Union" would reach great heights "in ten years." Stalin underlined this passage, too. Khaustov et al., *Lubianka: Stalin i VChK*, 298–308 (RGASPI, f. 558, op. 11, d. 185, l. 15–36).

160. Stalin added: "Those comrades who remained in Russia, who did not go abroad, of course, are far more numerous in our party and its leadership than former émigrés, and they, of course, had greater opportunities to contribute to the revolution than those who were located in the foreign emigration." Leushin, "'Schitaiv nizhe svoego dostoinstua': fragment zapisi besedy U. V. Stalina s E. Liudvigom," 216–17 (RGASPI, f. 558, op. 1, d. 2989, l.17–8).

161. Stalin added: "'Fate' is something that is not part of the laws of history, something mystical. I do not believe in mysticism." On Feb. 8, 1932, he had a transcript circulated to members and candidate members of the politburo and Central Committee ("for your information"). In April 1932 the party journal *Bolshevik* published a version he edited. RGASPI, f. 558, op. 1, d. 2989, l. 1. Stalin would authorize its publication as a standalone pamphlet in 1938, and allowed it to be included in *Collected Works* in 1951. "Beseda s nemetskim pisatelem Emilen Liudvigom," *Bol'shevik*, 1932, no. 8: 33–42 (at 41); *Sochineniia*, XIII: 104–23 (at 114–5, 120–1); Degras, *Soviet Documents on Foreign Policy*, II: 517–8.

162. Kenkichi Yoshizawa, Japan's newly named foreign minister, returning home from his ambassadorial post in Paris via the Trans-Siberian, received a "princely welcome" in Moscow on Dec. 30–31, 1931, according to British observers. Two days after Yoshizawa reached Tokyo, Moscow forced the issue by having *Izvestiya* (Jan. 16, 1932) publish news that a nonaggression pact had again been proffered. Both Yoshizawa and Ambassador Hirota claimed to be surprised. *DVP SSSR*, XIV: 746–8 (Litivinov-Yoshizawa conversation); Lensen, *Damned Inheritance*, 337–41; Sokolov, *Na boevykh postakh*, 157; Grechko et al., *Istoriia vtoroi mirovoi voiny*, I: 277.

163. Voroshilov was especially skeptical of rumors about the ranks of White Guard émigrés ready to enlist for Japan. Kvashonkin, *Sovetskoe rukovodstvo*, 167–8 (RGASPI, f. 74, op. 2, d. 44, l. 53–5). Japanese officials continued to engage in open talk about annexing Northern Sakhalin, the Soviet Far Eastern coastline and Kamchatka. Haslam, *Soviet Foreign Policy*, 79–80.

164. Artuzov judged the French general staff to be against a Franco-Soviet nonaggression pact, but noted that French military intelligence "is of the opinion that the USSR at the present time will avoid a conflict with Europe and Japan and not react to provocations." Khaustov et al., *Lubianka: Stalin i VChK*, 296–8 (RGASPI, f. 558, op. 11, d. 185, l. 11–4). The French general staff was focused on Germany, not the USSR. Vidal, *Une alliance improbable*.

165. Haslam, *Soviet Foreign Policy*, 98. The OGPU were also reporting delight among peasants, angry at collectivization, at rumors Japan would seize Siberia, and Poland or Germany would take advantage in the West. Golubev, *"Esli mir obrushitsia na nashu Respubliku,"* 141–5; Vernadskii, *Dnevnik, 1926–1934*, 240, 256, 271, 275; Davies and Wheatcroft, *Years of Hunger*, 15–16 (citing RGAE, f. 7486, op. 37, d. 235, l. 12–10: Jan. 19, 1932).

166. Johnston, *New Mecca*, 122, citing *Vozrozhdenie*, March 5, 1932. See also Besedovskii, *Na putiakh k termidoru*, 286.

167. *XVII konferentsiia VKP (b)*, 156.

168. According to the same hostile witness, when Stalin appeared at the Bolshoi on Feb. 23, 1932, at a celebration of the Red Army's fourteenth anniversary, he was met with "cold silence." *Biulleten' oppozitsii*, 28 (July 1932): 3–5. Davies surmises that the letter writer was Ivan Smirnov: Davies, *Crisis and Progress*, 133 n1, 136, 145. On the conference resolutions, see: *VKP (b) v rezoliutsiiakh* (1933), II: 728–46.

169. The regime also mandated mobilization plans for each major factory. Ken, *Mobilizatsionnoe planirovanie*, 175. Still, even now, Tukhachevsky failed once more to force the creation of a separate army industrial research and development empire. Samuelson, *Plans for Stalin's War Machine*, 42–7, 55–9, 162 (RGVA, f. 33987, op. 2, d. 280, l. 7–8); Harrison and Simonov, "Voenpriemka," 230.

170. Drobizhev, *Glavnyi shtab*, 171–2; Davies, *Crisis and Progress*, 90; GARF, f. 5446, op. 15, d. 15, l. 13; Stone, *Hammer and Rifle*, 192 (RGAE, f. 7297, op. 41: intro); Davies, *Soviet Economy in Turmoil*, 241, 243; Seiranian, *Nadezhneishii voennyi rabotnik*, 138. On Jan. 12, 1932, the politburo appointed party organizers in military factories who were responsible to the Central Committee. Poltaev, *Industrializatsiia SSSR*, 608.

171. The wildly ambitious 10,000 number included 2,000 BTs (Christie chassis), 3,000 T-26s (Vickers six-ton), and 5,000 machine-gun carrier T-27s (Carden Loyd tankette). Stone, *Hammer and Rifle*, 193 (citing RGVA, f. 4, op. 17, d. 76, l. 10). Voroshilov, at a Jan. 1933 party plenum, would claim that Stalin had ordered to "take all measures, spend the money, even large amounts of money, run people to all corners of Europe and America, but get models, plans, bring in people, do everything possible and impossible in order to set up tank production here." RGASPI, f. 17, op. 2, d. 514, part 1, l. 125; Stone, *Hammer and Rifle*, 193 (citing RGASPI, f. 17, op. 162, d. 8, l. 13, 18–9: Dec. 5, 1929); RGVA, f. 31811, op. 1, d. 1, l. 52–3 (Pavlunovsky).

172. The Soviet delegation chose the Vickers medium tank prototype from a commercial catalogue. Vickers refused to sell its heavy tanks, but a clever member of the Soviet delegation managed to outsmart the British and obtain specifications (which would eventually go into the T-28). Svirin, *Bronia krepka*, 136–7, 253. The French firm Citroën refused to sell the Soviets tanks with blueprints. Vereshchak, "Rol' inostrannogo tekhnicheskoi pomoshchi," 234, 236 (citing RGASPI, f. 85, op. 27, d. 65: Jan. 11, 1930).

173. Milson, *Russian Tanks*; Cooper, "Defence Production," 13; Tupper, "Red Army and the Defence Industry," 13–5, 359–60; Hofman, "United States' Contribution"; Mukhin, "Amtorg," no. 3: 34–41, no. 4: 37–53. See also Sutton, *Western Technology*, 240–2. In Nov. 1931, the Kharkov Locomotive Factory was designated a "super shock" plant, granting access to raw materials, transport, and daily life necessities. Christie reasoned that tanks should be light and move quickly to penetrate enemy lines, and his suspension system, a sprung bogie instead of a rigid system, afforded tanks a low center of gravity and a low silhouette, as well as an ability to move at high speeds. His original model-1928 or M-1928 had little firepower; it was the improved M-1931 that interested the Soviets. The M-1931 weighed 12 tons, had a 338-horsepower engine, room for a crew of three and a 37mm gun as well as a machine gun, and a speed of 50 mph without tracks (which were removable for travel on paved roads). (Later, the Soviets would thicken the armor and enlarge the guns without losing the mobility.) The Soviets bought the rights to the production, sale, and use of tanks inside the borders of the Soviet Union for ten years. Pavlov et al., *Tanki BT chast' I*. The Christie contract (signed on April 28, 1930) cost $164,000. Kolomiets, *Legkie tanki BT*, 10. In 1931, the Poles also agreed to buy the M-1931, but then Christie reneged (the deal was illegal without U.S. government permission); he returned the Polish government's money. Christie's advanced tank designs never went into mass production in the United States; he would die nearly penniless in 1944. The Soviets also worked on a tank from the experimental designs of German engineer Edward Grotte, of Rheinmetal, who was employed on a technical assistance contract at the Bolshevik Factory in Leningrad. "Do not by any means allow Grotte to go back to Germany," Stalin told Poskryobyshev to inform Kirov (Aug. 25, 1931). "Take all measures up to arrest and compel him to prepare the tank for serial mass production. Do not allow him go to Germany after the tank enters serial production, because he might give away secrets. Establish thorough surveillance on him making [Filipp] Medved responsible. Do not let him out of sight for even an hour." RGASPI, f. 558, op. 11, d. 76, l. 42–3. Grotte's tank design never entered mass production, and in 1933 he was allowed to leave, but his work fed into other Soviet tank design efforts.

174. Stalin, in a letter to Voroshilov, singled out armor-plating as the most difficult aspect. Some 60 percent of armor plates that would be produced at the Red October factory in 1933 for the T-26 were unusable. Vereshchak, "Rol' inostrannogo tekhnicheskoi pomoshchi," 241 (citing RGASPI, f. 74, op. 2, d. 37, l. 49; RGAE, f. 7719, op. 4, d. 76, l. 228).

175. The final tank tally in 1932 would be 2,585 instead of 10,000; 800 of them had no turrets, 290 lacked treads, and even the "finished" T-26s had no turrets for mounting a 45mm gun (they carried only machine guns). By 1933 the number of tanks would leap to 4,700. Similar exponential growth would occur in military aircraft and artillery. And the

BT—soon the fastest moving tank in the world—was world class. Stone, *Hammer and Rifle*, 192–202 (citing RGVA, f. 4, op. 14, d. 717, l. 11–2: Pavlunovsky to Voroshilov, Jan. 2, 1933; d. 896, l. 7: Yegorov, Jan. 26; d. 717, l. 9–10: Voroshilov to Molotov); Maiolo, *Cry Havoc*, 18–9.

176. Davies, "Soviet Military Expenditures," 580–1, 594 (table 3); Davies, *Crisis and Progress*, 165. Already between Oct. and Dec. 1931, Soviet armaments production shot up by 75 percent, to claim more than one of four workers in machine building. Then, in the first weeks of 1932, the military procurement budget nearly doubled. The capacity to absorb that funding influx efficiently was another matter. Davies, *Crisis and Progress*, 111–8; Stone, *Hammer and Rifle*, 190–1 (citing RGVA, f. 4, op. 417, l l. 29, 31ff; op. 14, d. 603, l. 31).The Soviet Far Eastern Army had doubled in size between May and Feb. 1932, and would reach 152,000 by the end of that year, with more than 300 tanks, 300 armored vehicles, and 250 planes. Ken, *Mobilizatsionnoe planirovanie*, 207 (RGVA, f. 4, op. d. 39, l. 63ob.: Blyukher, Oct. 25, 1932; op. 14, d. 754, l. 26: Dec. 1932–Jan. 1933).

177. Soviet propagandists huffed that Tokyo presented itself as "the apostle of peace" and asserted that China had "insulted" Japan and threatened it with "chaos." Conversely, an Osaka newspaper fumed (March 3, 1932), "Why is the American annexation of the Philippines justified, while the Japanese seizure of Formosa [Taiwan] is not?" Tanin and Kogan, *Voenno-fashistskoe dvizhenie v Iaponii*, 251–62; Paine, *Wars for Asia*, 24.

178. Kasahara and his Polish contacts were clearly trying to spur Tokyo. Stalin underlined passages in the text suggesting a need to study the technical development of the Red Army, and wrote on the document: "From hand to hand. To the members of the politburo (to each individually). With the obligation to return to the politburo." Khaustov et al., *Lubianka: Stalin i glavnoe upravlenie*, 298–308 (RGASPI, f. 558, op. 11, d. 185, l. 15–36), 807.

179. Blyukher had given orders to fire at the overflights, and Stalin vented his anger when he found out. RGASPI, f. 558, op. 11, d. 43, l. 116. Voroshilov had instructed Blyukher in a secret order (Feb. 28, 1932) to annihilate anyone who violated the Soviet border. Stone, *Hammer and Rifle*, 187 (citing RGASPI, f. 74, op. 2, d. 88, l. 9–10).

180. The regime also created a special collective farm corps "to reinforce Soviet Far Eastern frontiers," and directed seven tank battalions with infantry escorts, armored trains, antiaircraft machine guns, and antitank weapons to the Soviet Far East. Stone, *Hammer and Rifle*, 187–8 (RGASPI, f. 17, op. 162, d. 11, l. 196–7); Grechko et al., *Istoriia vtoroi mirovoi voiny*, I: 110 (March 16, 1932); Dmitriev, *Sovetskoe podvodnoe korablestroenie*, 71, 240–55; Isaev, "Meropriiatie KPSS po ukrepleniiu dal'nevostochnykh rubezhei"; Zakharov, "Krasnoznamennomu Tikhookeanskomu flotu"; Dmitriev, "Stroitel'stvo sovetskogo podvodnogo flota."

181. For monitoring and subverting the USSR, the Kwantung Army had already deployed a vast intelligence apparatus through Manchuria (Harbin, Manchouli, Mukden, Jilin), which they expanded (to Qiqihar, Hailar, Heihe) after the formation of Manchukuo. Japanese intelligence personnel were also deployed at their consulates in Vladivostok, Khabarovsk, and Novosibirsk, and at the Manchukuo consulate in Chita (and soon, a Manchukuo consulate in Blagoveshchensk). The Japanese legation in Tehran was also used

against the Soviet Union. Kuromiya and Pepłoński, "The Great Terror," citing, among other works, Tsutao Ariga, *Nihon riku kai gun no jōhōkikō to sono katsudō* (Tokyo: Kindai Bungeisha, 1994), 84–100. Japanese police in Manchuria enlisted local bandits for assassinations and kidnappings, set up rings for prostitution and drug trafficking, and concocted subterfuges to fool a League of Nations fact-finding mission. Vespa, *Secret Agent of Japan.*

182. The original plan dated to 1927, and had been reworked (to Stalin's approval) in summer 1930: RGVA, f. 33987, op. 3, d. 490, l. 19–23.

183. Puyi was converted to "emperor" in 1934. Most of Japan's conquests, beginning with Taiwan (1895) and followed by Korea (1905), had not been driven primarily by economic concerns—trade between China and Japan, for example, dwarfed that between Korea and Japan—but Manchukuo was seen as a vast settler colony, a solution to Japan's rural poverty.

184. Lensen, *Damned Inheritance*, 210–1; *Izvestiia*, March 22, 1932.

185. Lensen, *Damned Inheritance*, 225–6; RGASPI, f. 17, op. 162, d. 12, l. 36, 68 (March 26, 1932), 94 (April 6), 107–8 (April 17). Into summer 1932, international observers noted Moscow's "extreme forbearance" toward Japan bordering on "pusillanimity" (in the words of the British consul in Harbin). Lensen, *Damned Inheritance*, 373 (citing FO 371/16173–665: Garstin to Ingram, Harbin, June 11, 1932); Haslam, *Soviet Foreign Policy*, 81.

186. It was Romania, not the Soviet Union, that refused to sign the bilateral pact. Lungu, "Nicolae Titulescu." The Soviets refused to recognize Bessarabia's annexation by Romania. According to Louis Fischer, however, Litvinov was long ready to relinquish Soviet claims to Bessarabia to normalize relations with Romania. Elleman, "Secret Soviet-Japanese Agreement"; Fischer, *Men and Politics*, 135. When Tukhachevsky had reported on the 1932 Poland war plan to Voroshilov, he had noted that "a similar operation would be very easy to prepare against Bessarabia." D'iakov and Bushueva, *Fashistskii mech kovalsia v SSSR*, 131–2 (RGVA, f. 33987, op. 3, d. 342, l. 179–80), 132n2 (d. 400, l. 14–29). See also Ken, *Mobilizatsionnoe planirovanie*, 127–8.

187. *Le Temps*, Nov. 30, 1932; Haslam, *Soviet Foreign Policy*, 98.

188. The OGPU's Balytsky and Artuzov reported to Stalin (March 19, 1932) on new intelligence from an informant in Warsaw regarding the French general staff's preparation for a military intervention against the USSR that relied on Poland and Japan while attempting to draw in Britain. The report was filled with misspellings of the principal actors (Polish general staff chief Janusz Gąsiorowski listed as Gonsiarowski, French Marshal Pétain as Lecien). Khaustov et al., *Glazami razvedki*, 329–32 (RGASPI, f. 558, op. 11, d. 185, l. 65–70).

189. Ken, *Moskva i pakt*, 113–4; *Dokumenty i materialy po istorii sovetsko-pol'skikh otnoshenii*, V: 492–4 (AVP RF, f. 08, op. 14, d. 137, l. 31–3), 494–6 (l. 13–5), 496–7, 497–8, 498–500, 501; Budurowych, *Polish-Soviet Relations*, 16–7; Karski, *Great Powers*, 109. See also *Izvestiia*, Aug. 27, 28, 30, 1931; *DVP SSSR*, XIV: 562–4 (Dovgalevsky to Karakhan, Oct. 6, 1931), 566 (Dovgalevsky to Moscow, Oct. 9), 570–2 (Litvinov and Zelezynski: Oct. 14); and Biegański et al., *Documents on Polish-Soviet Relations*, I: 14–6.

190. D'iakov and Bushueva, *Fashistskii mech kovalsia v SSSR*, 131–2 (RGVA, f. 33987, op. 3,

d. 342, l. 179–80 to Khinchuk). As late as Dec. 1932, the politburo approved the dispatch of four officers to German military academies. Stone, *Hammer and Rifle*, 198 (citing RGASPI, f. 17, op. 162, d. 14, l. 39: Dec. 16, 1932).

191. Kochan, *Russia and the Weimar Republic*, 159. German diplomats interpreted the Franco-Soviet and Polish-Soviet nonaggression pacts as "a complete change in the course of Soviet foreign policy." Sluch, "Germano-sovetskie otnosheniia," 103 (citing AVP RF, f. 082, op. 14, pap. 62, d. 2, l. 365).

192. On April 13, 1932, Piłsudski arrived in Romania, with plans to travel on to Japan, trips that the Soviets viewed as setting the stage for a long-anticipated military pact against USSR; in fact, the Polish president was trying (and failing) to induce his Romanian allies into ratcheting down tensions with Moscow and become part of the broad regional nonaggression commitments. Haslam, *Soviet Foreign Policy*, 104–5. On April 22, 1932, with Piłsudski in Tokyo, deputy foreign affairs commissar Stomonyakov speculated in a letter to Antonov-Ovseyenko that "in all likelihood he is holding specific military negotiations related to Far Eastern complications for the event of a war between Poland and Romania against the USSR." Revyakin, "Poland and the Soviet Union," 79–101 84 (no citation).

193. Stalin might have felt dissatisfied with the information at his disposal, for he had recently received Radek one-on-one for an hour and a half and then ordered creation of an "information bureau" on international affairs inside his secretariat (formalized on April 1, 1932). Effectively an extension of the foreign bureaus of *Izvestiia*, Radek's bureau, in theory, had the right to make use of "all existing institutions concerned with economic, political, and military matters in the capitalist countries." *Na prieme*, 64 (March 27, 1932); Ken and Rupaov, *Politbiuro TsK VKP (b) i otnosheniia SSSR*, chast' 1: 196, 553–4, 574–5; Rupasov, *Zapadnoe zagranich'e*, 590–2 (RGASPI, f. 17, op. 3, d. 878, l. 5), 592–6 (op. 162, d. 11, l. 135, 143: May 16, 1932); Ken, "Karl Radek i Biuro." On Radek's value to Stalin, see Duda, *Jenő Varga*, 113–4. See also Gronskii, *Iz proshlogo*, 147. Radek managed to cast the Soviet Union as a champion of peace in *Foreign Affairs*, the journal of the American establishment, and in May 1932 he would work with Voroshilov on contacts with the American military over a possible common policy toward Japan—which, however, would prove fruitless. Radek, "War in the Far East"; RGASPI, f. 17, op. 162, d. 12, l. 113; 173–4; Safronov, *SSSR*, 369. Stalin counseled Voroshilov on the proper way to engage with the U.S. military. Kvashonkin, *Sovetskoe rukovodstvo*, 173–4 (RGASPI, f. 74, op. 2, d. 37, l. 46–8: Voroshilov to Stalin, June 6, 1932), 175–6 (RGASPI, f. 74, op. 2, d. 38, l. 66: June 12), 176n3 (f. 17, op. 162, d. 12, l. 194–5: June 20).

194. Danilov et al., *Tragediia sovetskoi derevni*, III: 277–82 (RGASPI, f. 631, op. 5, d. 52, l. 48–53: Feb. 10, 1932).

195. Some foods for those still on lists were derationed (no longer promised). Davies and Wheatcroft, *Years of Hunger*, 406–7 (March 23, 1932).

196. Davies, *Crisis and Progress*, 147–54.

197. Danilov et al., *Tragediia sovetskoi derevni*, III: 312–5 (RGAE, f. 7486, op. 37, d. 236, l. 4–13); Zelenin, *Stalinskaia 'revoliutsiia sverkhu,'* 22–4.

198. "Otkrytoe pis'mo Prezidiumu Ts.I.K'a Soiuza SSR," *Biulleten' oppozitsii*, no. 27 (March 1932): 1–6 (at 5).

199. Davies and Wheatcroft, *Years of Hunger*, 311 (RGASPI, f. 17, op. 2, d. 877, l. 9); *Sovetskaia iustitsiia*, no. 12 (1932): 29; Zelenin, "Byl li 'kolkhoznyi neonep'?" 108–9 (citing GARF, f. 7486, op. 3, d. 237, l. 225–6); Davies et al., *Years of Progress*, 14. Stalin had crossed out a section in the draft of the decree that would have guaranteed feed to collective farmers for their personal animals. RGASPI, f. 558, op. 1, d. 3016, l. 1. Another decree, a fortnight later, publicized the decision. Davies stresses that although Stalin did not initiate the relaxation on livestock, he would grab credit. Davies, "Stalin as Economic Policy-Maker," 136–7. One scholar argues that Yakovlev and "bourgeois" specialists working under him had initiated a shift from extensive to intensive growth already in late 1931–early 1932. Tauger, "People's Commissariat of Agriculture," 157–9.

200. *Sochineniia*, XIII: 134. Stalin permitted a foreigner, James Abbé, to photograph him in the Little Corner on April 13, 1932, resulting in a sensational portrait on the *New York Times* front page. Abbé, *I Photograph Russia*; von Dewitz and Johnson, *Shooting Stalin*. Stalin attended the politburo meetings throughout April and May 1932: RGASPI, f. 17, op. 3, d. 874–885. The same day Abbé got twenty minutes in the Kremlin, an infirm Mężyński wrote to Stalin pleading to be relieved of his position. Stalin refused. Molotov concurred. Kuibyshev wrote on the resignation request, "read it and understand nothing." Mężyński had suffered a heart attack on Dec. 13, 1931, returning to work on Jan. 25, 1932.

201. Rudich, *Holod 1932–33 rokiv*, 148–50. Stalin received an OGPU report enumerating the mass flight out of villages region by region, and naming "food difficulties" as a prime motivator. Zelenin, *Stalinskaia 'revoliutsiia sverkhu,'* 25–6 (no citation).

202. Khlevniuk, *Master of the House*, 43 (citing RGASPI, f. 17, op. 42, d. 26, l. 1–6).

203. The areas affected were better supplied than villages, but a low priority among industrial regions. Rossman, *Worker Resistance under Stalin*. On strikes, see also Gromtseva, *Teni izchezaiut v smol'nom*, 28–9.

204. Werth and Moullec, *Rapports secrets soviétiques*, 209–16 (at 214).

205. Davies, *Crisis and Progress*, 188–91 (citing APRF, f. 3, op. 2, d. 39, l. 6–7).

206. Rossman, *Worker Resistance under Stalin*, 231 (citing RGASPI, f. 81, op. 3, d. 213, l. 90); Danilov et al., *Tragediia Sovetskoi derevni*, III: 318–54 (TsA FSB, f. 2, op. 10, d. 53, l. 1–64: April 1932).

207. Kotkin, *Magnetic Mountain*. In Ivanovo in 1937, there would be a mere three work stoppages involving a very small number of people protesting rising norms and food shortages. Rittersporn, *Anguish*, 233 (citing RGASPI, f. 81, op. 3, d. 230, l. 87).

208. Later, while reading back issues of *Pravda*, Stalin would erupt at the loyalist Yaroslavsky over an article (May 31, 1932) admitting the fact of strikes in Ivanovo—even though the article blamed the already sacked local party leadership—because he felt that any admission handed ammunition to enemies to speak of "a 'new Kronstadt.'" Khlevniuk et al., *Stalin i Kaganovich*, 120–2 (RGASPI, f. 558, op. 11, d. 77, l. 11, 12–12ob.: June 5, 1932), 139n1 (f. 17, op. 3, d. 887, l. 9); Khromov, *Po stranitsam*, 34–5. The politburo condemned Yaroslavsky's article and removed him from the editorial position at *Pravda*.

209. Berson, *Sowieckie zbrojenia moralne*, 7. Berson, under the pseudonym Otmar, served as Moscow correspondent for the Polish

Telegraph Agency and *Gazeta Polska*, until his expulsion in 1935.
210. Rassweiler, *Generation of Power*; Goriaeva, "*Velikaia kniga dnia*," 256–7.
211. On May 3, Stalin received the *International Herald Tribune* correspondent to reiterate Soviet interest in expanded trade with the United States and told him that in the forthcoming second Five-Year Plan, "yes, light industry will develop to a much greater extent than before." *Sochineniia*, XIII: 258 (Ralph Barnes). More broadly, see Mahoney, *Dispatches and Dictators*. Stalin played little role in drawing up the second Five-Year Plan, which was overseen by Molotov, Kuibyshev, and Orjonikidze, yet it could not go forward until he approved.
212. The Soviets also planned to import 10,000 breeding cattle from South America, Germany, and Britain. Davies and Wheatcroft, *Years of Hunger*, 138; Kondrashin et al., *Golod v SSSR*, I/ii: 290–1 (RGASPI, f. 17, op. 162, d. 12, l. 114, 124). That same day, the politburo decreed the expulsion of 38,300 "kulak" households, but ten days later, this would be circumscribed to individual arrests of "evil elements in the village." Danilov et al., *Tragediia sovetskoi derevni*, III: 367 (RGASPI, f. 17, op. 162, d. 12, l. 134). May 5, 1932, was the 30th birthday of *Pravda*, which was celebrated without mention of Bukharin, its editor for twelve years. Medvedev, *Nikolai Bukharin*, 49.
213. Soon, the regime clarified that such trade would be "carried out at prices formed on the market." Davies and Wheatcroft, *Years of Hunger*, 138 (RGASPI, f. 17, op. 3, d. 883, l. 9), 140; *Sobranie zakonov*, 1932, no. 1: article 190; *Sobranie zakonov*, 1932, no. 33: article 195; *Partiinoe stroitel'stvo*, 1932, no. 11–2: 50; *Kollektivizatsiia sel'skogo khoziaistva*, 411–3, 416–7; Khlevniuk, *Politbiuro*, 58–9 (no citation). An Oct. 1931 decree had legalized peasant trade of grain at "cooperative prices." Additional decrees after May 6, 1932, reduced procurement targets for other agricultural products. Gorelik and Malkis, *Sovetskaia torgovlia*, 125; Whitman, "Kolkhoz Market," 387. From Jan. 15, 1933, the regime would concede free trade in meat, too.
214. RGASPI, f. 17, op. 2, d. 484, l. 36–46. "We still have bazaars that are not Soviet but purely private, in almost every village, almost every town," North Caucasus party boss Sheboldayev complained at the 17th party conference. "Not only do these bazaars fail to make the individual peasant into a socialist, they sometimes prevent him from becoming a collective farmer." *XVII konferentsiia VKP (b)*, 210.
215. Davies, *Crisis and Progress*, 187–90. Whereas (black) market prices for grain in 1929 had been double the state procurement prices, in 1932 the multiple reached 28 times. Ellman, "Did the Agricultural Surplus Provide the Resources for Increased Investment in the USSR during the First Five-Year Plan?" *Economic Journal* 85 (1975): 844–63 (table 6); James R. Millar, "Mass Collectivization and the Contribution of Soviet Agriculture to the First Five-Year Plan: A Review Article," *Slavic Review* 33/4 (1974): 750–66.
216. Davies, *Crisis and Progress*, xv.
217. Davies, *Crisis and Progress*, 51 (citing *Za industrializatsiiu*, March 15, 1931: Dukarevich). "You cry that you do not have this or that but you never say what is necessary to correct the situation," Orjonikidze complained at a heavy industry commissariat meeting on June 6, 1932. "You are placing the blame on others when you yourself are to blame." Gregory and Markevich, "Creating Soviet Industry," 798 (citing RGAE, f. 7297, op. 38, d. 10, l. 4).

218. Kvashonkin, *Sovetskoe rukovodstvo*, 171–2 (RGASPI, f. 74, op. 2, d. 38, l. 56–7). See also Samuelson, *Plans for Stalin's War Machine*, 108–12, 141–3; Ken, "'Moia otsenka byla slishkom rezkoi': I. V. Stalin rekonstrucktsiia RKKA," 150–2 (RGASPI, f. 74, d. 38, l.58, 56–7); and *Voennye arkhivy Rossii*, 79–80. Tukhachevsky was in Stalin's office on April 7 and 14, 1932. In Aug. 1932, Stalin would even invite him over to his dacha in Sochi. *Na prieme*, 65–6; Ken, *Mobilizatsionnoe planirovanie*, 198n90 (RGASPI, f. 74, op. 2, d. 105, l. 56–7: Tukhachevsky to Voroshilov, Aug. 27, 1932). During Voroshilov's summary speech at the June 1–4, 1937, meeting of the Main Military Council, a revealing exchange would occur when he labeled Tukhachevsky's Jan. 1930 proposals "idiocies." Stalin interjected: "It would have been good to have such a force, but it was necessary to rebuff it at that time." Voroshilov persisted: "This was a wrecking proposal." Ken, *Mobilizatsionnoe planirovanie*, 319n43 (citing RGASPI, f. 17, op. 165, d. 61, l. 130: uncorrected transcript).
219. On May 8, Stalin approved a commission, headed by Kaganovich, to check the production and distribution of consumer goods. Rees, *Iron Lazar*, 107 (citing RGASPI, f. 17, op. 3, d. 883, l. 1).
220. Danilov et al., *Tragediia sovetskoi derevni*, III: 365 (RGASPI, f. 558, op. 11, d. 43, l. 60).
221. A decree of May 20, 1932, that lowered taxes on the legalized collective-farmers' trade urged local officials to disallow "the opening of shops and kiosks by private traders," adding that "middlemen and speculators trying to live off the workers and peasants must be extirpated everywhere." Ball, *Russia's Last Capitalists*, 81, citing *Resheniia partii i pravitel'stva po khoziaistvennym voprosam*, 16 vols. (Moscow: Politicheskaia literatura, 1967–), II: 388–9.
222. Soviet officials had been discussing the market following the launch of "wholesale" collectivization, but the discussions could be deceiving. At the 17th party conference (Jan.–Feb. 1932), for example, the ideologue Alexei Stetsky had mentioned the imperative to "develop Soviet trade, the Soviet market," but he meant state-controlled trade and markets. *XVII konferentsiia VKP (b)*, 193. At the Jan. 1933 plenum, when Stalin would underscore the place of trade in a socialist economy, he would insist that "this is not a return to NEP." Bordiugov and Kozlov, "Dialektika teorii i praktiki stsialisticheskogo stroitel'stva," 14 (citing unspecified party archives).
223. Davies, *Stalin-Kaganovich Correspondence*, 11–2.
224. Sandag and Kendall, *Poisoned Arrows*, 72–3. On Mongolia's collectivization, see Zelenin, *Stalinskaia 'revoliutsiia sverkhu*,' 11 (RGASPI, f. 17, op. 162, d. 9, l. 73).
225. Bawden, *Modern History of Mongolia*, 290–327. A list of Mongol rebellions against Soviet domination can be found in Misshima and Goto, *Japanese View of Outer Mongolia*, 16–24. A purge would reduce the Mongol People's Party from around 40,000 to 11,000. Lkhamsuren, *Ocherki istorii Mongol'skoi narodno-revoliutsionnoi partii*, 147.
226. At the same time as ordering dispatch of the goods, on March 16, 1932, the regime established a standing politburo commission for Mongolia headed by Postyshev, with Voroshilov, Karakhan, and Eliava as members. Instructions for the Soviet proconsul Okhtin were approved on April 23. RGASPI, f. 17, op. 162, d. 12, l. 18–20, 31, 92, 111–2; Baabar, *Twentieth-Century Mongolia*, 282–325 (esp. 317).
227. RGASPI, f. 17, op. 162, d. 12, l. 113; Terayama, "Soviet Policies toward Mongolia," I:

37–66. Stalin emerges in the documents as trying to impose order amid conflicting reports, while venting his fury.
228. Kondrashin et al., *Golod v SSSR*, I/ii: 152–5 (GA Minskoi obl., f. 164p, op. 1, d. 132, l. 546–9).
229. Davies et al., "Stalin, Grain Stocks, and the Famine of 1932–33," 650–1 (citing RGASPI, f. 79, op. 1, d. 375, l. 1–3; f. 17, op. 162, d. 12, l. 153–4; GARF, f. 5446, op. 27, d. 33, l. 127).
230. Davies and Wheatcroft, *Years of Hunger*, 114–5 (RGASPI, f. 17, op. 162, d. 12, l. 153; f. 82, op. 2, d. 138, l. 150–3: Redens to Molotov, May 28 and 29, 1932).
231. Davies and Wheatcroft, *Years of Hunger*, 115–6.
232. Kosheleva, *Pis'ma Stalina Molotovu*, 243; Lih et al., *Stalin's Letters to Molotov*, 231 (before June 1932). During his summer 1932 holiday, Stalin received 91 registered documents, many lengthy. He did not answer all of them. A politburo commission (Kaganovich, Postyshev, Yenukidze) on fixing resorts recommended forming an all-Union agency; Stalin abstained from weighing in. The body was approved on June 23, 1932. Khlevniuk, et al., *Stalin i Kaganovich*, 201 (RGASPI, f. 558, op. 11, d. 77, l. 114), 201n (f. 17, op. 3, d. 881, l. 12, 29–31; d. 889, l. 9, 29; d. 895, l. 15).
233. Stalin added that only if the situation was truly beyond internal rescue, which he doubted, could Soviet troops be dispatched, and then only ethnic Buryats. Kvashonkin, *Sovetskoe rukovodstvo*, 173–4 (RGASPI, f. 74, op. 2, d. 37, l. 46–8: June 6, 1932), 174n3 (f. 17, op. 162, d. 12, l. 133; f. 81, op. 3, d. 99, l. 49–52), 174n5 (f. 17, op. 162, d. 12, l. 175); Khlevniuk et al., *Stalin i Kaganovich*, 136 (RGASPI, f. 81, op. 3, d. 99, l. 49–52: June 4, 1932), 143, 156–7, 182 (f. 558, op. 11, d. 77, l. 76: June 19, 1932).
234. In a June 10 telegram, Stalin reiterated his opposition to overt military intervention in Mongolia to Molotov, Voroshilov, and Kaganovich. "A hurried and insufficiently prepared decision could provoke a conflict with Japan and give a basis for a united front of Japan, China, Mongolia against the USSR," he warned. "We will be portrayed as occupiers . . . and the Japanese and Chinese as liberators . . ." Khlevniuk et al., *Stalin i Kaganovich*, 157–8 (RGASPI, f. 558, op. 11, d. 77, l. 42–5).
235. RGASPI, f. 558, op. 11, d. 779, l. 47. The policy shift ("New Turn") was confirmed at a Mongolia People's party extraordinary plenum June 29–30, 1932, with Soviet advisers present. Genden attacked the leftists and pronounced the noncapitalist path a failure in Mongol conditions. By Sept. 1, Stalin would add himself to the politburo's Mongolian commission. (He had named Voroshilov to replace Karakhan as chairman.) On Nov. 10, the politburo would approve a telegram from Eliava to the Mongols (copy to Okhtin) instructing the Mongolian Central Committee to remove all "leftists," amnesty rank and file rebels who turned in their weapons, and call out the leaders of the uprising as Chinese agents and Japanese imperialists seeking to end Mongolia's independence. Soon the Soviets were asking about Mongolia's mobilization possibilities in the event of war with Japan. RGANI, f. 89, op. 63, d. 1, 2, 3, 4, 5, 6, 7, 8, 9; Roshchin, *Politicheskaia istoriia Mongolii*, 254–65.
236. Kvashonkin, *Sovetskoe rukovodstvo*, 175 (RGASPI, f. 74, op. 2, d. 38, l. 60). Without irony Stalin advised Kaganovich (June 7, 1932) that "the bureaucrats at *Pravda* have replaced letters from workers and collective farmers with letters from professional correspondents and 'plenipotentiaries'. But the bureaucrats have to be reined in. Otherwise, *Pravda* risks falling utterly out of touch with

live human beings at factories and collective farms." Khlevniuk et al., *Stalin i Kaganovich*, 149 (RGASPI, f. 81, op. 3, d. 99, l. 58–60). Kaganovich had the new rubric created, "Letters from workers and collective farmers" (164: f. 558, op. 11, d. 740, l. 37–43; f. 17, op. 114, d. 302, l. 13. 166: f. 558, op. 11, d. 740, l. 43–52). 237. Khlevniuk et al., *Stalin i Kaganovich*, 180–1 (RGASPI, f. 81, op. 3, d. 100, l. 152).

238. Pyrih et al., *Holodomor*, 33–6 (RGASPI, f. 82, op. 2, d. 139, l. 162–5). "Do you realize what is happening in the lands around Belaia Tserkov, Uman, and Kiev?" G. I. Tkachenko, a twenty-year-old Ukrainian student, wrote to Ukrainian party boss Kosior on June 18, 1932. "There are vast areas of land not sown . . . In collective farms in which there were 100–150 horses, there are now only 40–50, and these are dying off. The population is terribly hungry." Rudich, *Holod 1932–1933 rokiv*, 183–5. In March 1932, Kosior had managed to procure a seed loan for Ukraine of 110,000 tons from storehouses in better-off regions outside Ukraine (RGASPI, f. 17, op. 162, d. 12, l. 30). On April 29, 1932, the politburo advanced a further seed loan to collective farms in Ukraine (l. 115–6).

239. Khaustov, "Deiatel'nost' organov," 335.

240. The politburo (June 21) formally resolved to summon them, but in the meantime refused additional emergency aid to Ukraine. Khlevniuk, *Stalin i Kaganovich*, 163–5 (RGASPI, f. 558, op. 11, d. 740, l. 37–42: June 12, 1932), 169 (f. 81, op. 3, d. 99, l. 62–3: June 15, 1932), 168–9n5. That day, a telegram in the names of Stalin and Molotov admonished the Ukrainian hierarchy that "no manner of deviation—regarding either amounts or deadlines set for grain deliveries—can be permitted from the plan established for your region for collecting grain from collective and private [family] farms or for delivering grain to state farms." Kosheleva, *Pis'ma Stalina Molotovu*, 242n3; Lih et al., *Stalin's Letters to Molotov*, 230n3; Rudich, *Holod 1932–1933 rokiv*, 190.

241. Khlevniuk et al., *Stalin i Kaganovich*, 187 (RGASPI, f. 558, op. 11, d. 77, l. 83–5).

242. The politburo (in July 1932) would formally approve slight reductions. Khlevniuk et al., *Stalin i Kaganovich*, 197–8 (RGASPI, f. 81, op. 3, d. 99, l. 81–7), 198n3 (f. 17 op. 162, d. 13, l. 11, 30, 133). Stalin was showing a bit of uncharacteristic flexibility, writing to Kaganovich and Molotov (June 26, 1932) that Sheboldayev might be right in suggesting that rural consumer cooperatives be freed from enacting state grain procurements, while their role as distributors of industrial goods to the countryside should be enhanced and their taxes reduced. Khlevniuk et al., *Stalin i Kaganovich*, 197–8 (RGASPI, f. 81, op. 3, d. 99, l. 81–7). On June 25, 1932, the decree "On Revolutionary Legality" stipulated criminal prosecution of officials who violated the law in dealings with peasants and protected judges from dismissal. Enforcement of the decree was another matter. Solomon, *Reforming Justice*, 193.

243. The Soviet Union was by no means alone in its emphasis on heavy over light bombers at this time. Bailes, "Technology and Legitimacy," 381–406.

244. They agreed on better supervision of air force missions and more quality control in industry. Khlevniuk et al., *Stalin i Kaganovich*, 203–4 (RGASPI, f. 84, op. 2, d. 37, l. 49–50; d. 38, l. 69, 70; f. 558, op. 11, d. 77, l. 121; d. 78, l. 8). Aircraft losses were a long-standing problem. Sevost'ianov et al., "*Sovershenno sekretno*," VIII/ii: 1225–6 (TsA FSB, f. 2, op. 8, d. 16, l. 492–4: July 18, 1930). After perusing a copy of the German-language book by Major Helders (Robert Knauss), *Air War 1936: The*

Destruction of Paris (Berlin, 1932), which imagined a future war between Britain and France decided by the "flying fortress," Stalin wrote to Voroshilov (June 12, 1932) that the "wonderful book" should be published in Russian translation to teach and inspire aviators. Kvashonkin, *Sovetskoe rukovodstvo*, 175 (RGASPI, f. 74, op. 2, d. 38, l. 64–5). Robert Knauss, *Luftkrieg 1936: die Zertrümmerung von Paris* (Berlin: Wilhelm Rolf, 1932) was translated: *Vozdushnaia voina 1936: razrushenie Parizha*, 2nd ed. (Moscow: Voenizdat, 1934); RGASPI, f. 558, op. 3, d. 52.

245. "We made a lot of noise but did not blow up the bridge," the OGPU's Terenty Deribas would admit. The politburo (July 16, 1932) reprimanded the OGPU for "poor organization." The captured Soviet agent confessed. Karakhan denied any involvement to the Japanese ambassador. Khlevniuk et al., *Stalin i Kaganovich*, 208 (RGASPI, f. 81, op. 3, d. 100, l. 147), 213n13 (f. 17, op. 162, d. 13, l. 12, 33), 227 (f. 558, op. 11, d. 78, l. 43–4, l. 73, 72); *DVP SSSR*, XVI: 814n44 (July 26, 1932); Khaustov et al., *Lubianka: Stalin i VChK*, 315 (RGASPI, f. 17, op. 162, d. 13, l. 33), 807n99. The operative transferred was Nikolai Zagvozdin (b. 1898), who would rise to head of the NKVD in Uzbekistan and then Tajikistan—until his arrest (Feb. 9, 1939) and execution (Jan. 19, 1940). In summer 1932, Heinz Neumann (b. 1902), the leader of the German Communist party's paramilitary wing, which conducted assassinations, was evidently invited to Sochi. An elderly man of Caucasus extraction, according to the memoirs of Neumann's lover, was among the many guests. "This is comrade X, my assassin," Stalin supposedly remarked, before explaining, affably, that the old man's plot to kill him had been foiled by the OGPU. Neumann's lover recounted: "The assassin had been condemned to death. But he, Stalin, deemed it proper to pardon this old man, who had, after all, simply acted out of nationalist infatuation, and in order for him to feel like the hatchet had been buried once and for all, had invited him to Matsesta as his guest . . . During this lengthy exposition the old man stood before the gaggle of guests with a downcast gaze." Such anecdotes about Stalin's perverse sense of humor abound, usually with a single witness. Buber-Neumann, *Von Potsdam nach Moskau*, 274–5. Heinz Neumann would be executed in Moscow on Nov. 26, 1937.

246. Khlevniuk et al., *Stalin i Kaganovich*, 179–80 (RGASPI, f. 558, op. 11, d. 740, l. 69–72; f. 81, op. 3, d. 99, l. 65–8); RGASPI, f. 17, op. 3, d. 890, l. 8; Molotov, *O pod'eme sel'skogo khoziaistva*.

247. Stalin had used the word "famine" when characterizing what enemies predicted would happen as a result of Soviet policies, for example, in reference to bourgeois specialists in the original version of his "six conditions" speech in June 1931: RGASPI, f. 85, op. 28, d. 7, II: l. 189–91. In summer 1932, Molotov told the politburo upon return from Ukraine, "We are indeed faced with the spectre of famine, and in rich grain districts to boot." Ivnitskii, *Kollektivizatsiia i razkulachivanie*, 203. See also Kuromiya, *Freedom and Terror*, 167.

248. Davies and Wheatcroft, *Years of Hunger*, 90, 476.

249. He also reminded Kaganovich and Molotov that the conference was to have led to "obligatory 100 percent fulfillment of the grain procurements." The next day Stalin instructed them to "concentrate the most serious attention on Ukraine," and "take all the measures to break the current mood of officials, isolate the whiners and rotten diplomats (no matter who!) and ensure genuinely Bolshevik decisions." Khlevniuk et al., *Stalin i*

Kaganaovich, 205 (RGASPI, f. 558, op. 11, d. 77, l. 129–30), 210 (RGASPI, f. 81, op. 3, d. 99, l. 45–7; f. 558, op. 11, d. 740, l. 1), 210–3 (l. 2–9).

250. Kostiuk, *Stalinist Rule in Ukraine*, 19 (citing *Visti*, July 17, 1932). Kaganovich wrote to Stalin that Kosior held a firm line on fulfilling the plan at the conference, thereby protecting him.

251. Khlevniuk et al., *Stalin i Kaganaovich*, 219 (RGASPI, f. 558, op. 11, d. 78, l. 16).

252. The politburo resolved "to accept the recommendation of comrade Stalin on a reduction of the planned grain procurement in Ukraine by 722,000 tons as an exception for those regions of Ukraine particularly suffering." (That was from 5.8 million.) The politburo also resolved to summon Kosior to Moscow and to direct him, along with Kuibyshev and Kaganovich, to determine which regions in Ukraine to assign the reduced targets. Antipova et al., *Golod v SSSR*, 183 (RGASPI, f. 17, op. 162, d. 13, l. 75, 76: signed by Kaganovich, in Stalin's absence); Khlevniuk et al., *Stalin i Kaganovich*, 241–2 (RGASPI, f. 558, op. 11, d. 78, l. 79–81: July 24, 1932). Stalin denied the Sept. 10, 1932, request from Ivan Kabakov, party boss in the Urals, for lower grain procurement targets. Then, on Sept. 22, he approved the distribution of 39,000 tons of grain to the Urals, instead of the previous 37,000. Antipova et al., *Golod v SSSR*, 184 (APRF, f. 3, op. 40, d. 81, l. 148), 185 (l. 149), 186 (RGASPI, f. 17, op. 162, d. 13, l. 131, 133, 134).

253. Khlevniuk et al., *Stalin i Kaganovich*, 244–5 (RGASPI, f. 81, op. 3, d. 99, l. 115–9); Davies and Wheatcroft, *Years of Hunger*, 182–3 (f. 17, op. 162, d. 13, l. 76: Aug. 17, 1932; l. 85: Sept. 1, 1932).

254. Peasants could not distinguish between rust and other diseases, a Soviet agronomist reported. But as Tauger has demonstrated, local officials, too, did not understand plant disease and, at harvest time, when they would discover that the crop had been rotted out, would wrongly blame social causes. Tauger, "Natural Disaster," 15 (citing *Na zaschitu urozhaia*, 1933, no. 10: 14–6; S. E. Grushevoi; and RGAE, f. 7486, op. 37, d. 237, l. 388), 40–5.

255. A major contributing factor to the famine was the extreme deterioration in party-village relations. Penner, "Stalin and the Ital'ianka." Whereas in 1928 there had been 1 horsepower for every 3.63 hectares of land sown to grain, in 1932 the number was 1 for every 6.02 hectares. A. A. Barsov, *Balans stoimostnykh obmenov*, 85.

256. Kvashonkin, *Sovetskoe rukovodstvo*, 176–80 (RGASPI, f. 74, op. 2, d. 37, l. 49–51), 180–1 (RGASPI, f. 74, op. 2, d. 38, l. 68–71), 181–5 (d. 37, l. 54–9); f. 17, op. 162, d. 13, l. 6. According to Polish intelligence, between Oct. 1, 1932, and June 20, 1933, 20 Soviet soldiers sought asylum in Poland. Zdanovich, *Organy*, 507 (citing RGVA, f. 308, op. 3, d. 303, l. 2).

257. Kvashonkin, *Sovetskoe rukovodstvo*, 185–6 (RGASPI, f. 74, op. 2, d. 38, l. 76–7).

258. Zdanovich, *Organy*, 435–6 (citing TsA FSB, f. 2, op. 10, d. 94, l. 1, 3, 7: L. Ivanov). See also Ken, *Mobilizatsionnoe planirovanie*, 162–3.

259. Rees, *Decision-making in the Stalinist Command Economy*, 43–4 (citing RGASPI, f. 17, op. 3, d. 894, l. 12; f. 79, op. 1, d. 376, l. 1–2: Kuibyshev's memo; and RGASPI, f. 85, op. 29, d. 433, l. 1); Khlevniuk et al., *Stalinskoe politburo*, 125–6.

260. Lensen, *Damned Inheritance*, 365; *DVP SSSR*, XV: 465–8 (Spilvanek and Japanese journalist Fuse: Aug. 12, 1932), 479–81 (Troyanovsky-Karakhan, Aug. 19), 614–8, 798. Between Dec. 4 and 6, 1932, more than 4,000

Chinese, including 2,400 soldiers (11 generals among them), were taken into Soviet custody. After Japanese demands for their surrender, the Soviets decided to send them to Xinjiang, announcing that they were being sent out of USSR territory. Sladkovskii, *Znakomomstvo s Kitaem i kitaitsami*, 186 (citing Tsentral'nyi arkhiv porgrannichnykh voisk, f. 160, op. 2, d. 1, l. 7); Barmin, *Sovetskii Soiuz i Sintszian*, 124 (citing RGASPI, f. 17, op. 162, d. 15, l. 117); *DVP SSSR*, XV: 677; *Izvestiia*, Dec. 21, 1932.

261. From Jan. 1 through July 1, 1932, 1.37 million households quit collective farms in the RSFSR; 200,000 households quit in Ukraine. Zelenin, "By li 'kolkhoznyi Neonep'?" 106 (citing RGAE, f. 7446, op. 14, d. 108, l. 34; op. 3, d. 364, l. 2; d. 378, l. 2; op. 2, d. 338, l. 57). The number collectivized by the end of 1932 (completion of the Five-Year Plan) was officially 14.9 million households, or 61.5 percent, rather than the target of 17.9 million.

262. Cairns added that "what surprised me most in Kiev was not what the people said (although conditions there seemed to be worse than in any place I visited in the next five weeks), but that they should all—young, middleaged and old alike—be unanimous and that none of them seemed to care what they said or who heard them, even the police and GPU." Carynnyk et al., *Foreign Office*, 13, 51, 42, 105, 111. See also Cairns, *Soviet Famine*. "There's no bread, no meat, no fats—nothing," a senior OGPU official in Leningrad is said to have told the British ambassador. Haslam, "Political Opposition," 396 (citing FO 371/16322: Strang to Simon in London, Aug. 14, 1932).

263. Khlevniuk et al., *Stalin i Kaganovich*, 235–6 (RGASPI, f. 81, op. 3, d. 99, l. 106–13: July 20, 1932), 240–1 (d. 100, l. 137–40: before July 24, 1932). The methods of theft could be ingenious. Kondrashin and Penner, *Golod*, 135–7. Stalin was keen to institutionalize the importance of socialist property in social consciousness. Solomon, *Soviet Criminal Justice*, 119, 222–3. "State socialist property" was theorized as synonymous with "people's patrimony." Stuchka, *Kurs Sovetskogo grazhdanskogo prava*, III: 29.

264. RGAPSI, f. 17, op. 3, d. 895, l. 14 (politburo Aug. 2/8); *Sobranie zakonov*, 1932, article 360; *Kollektivizatsiia sel'skogo khoziaistva*, 423–4; Davies, *Crisis and Progress*, 242–56. See also Shearer, *Policing Stalin's Socialism*, 21.

265. Khlevniuk et al., *Stalin i Kaganovich*, 273–5 (RGASPI, f. 81, op. 3, d. 99, l. 144–51). A second decree, "On the struggle with speculation," stipulating sentences of five to ten years, followed on Aug. 22: RGASPI, f. 17, op. 3, d. 896, l. 13; *Sobranie zakonov*, 1932, article 375. This, too, had come from Stalin's instructions on holiday. Khlevniuk et al., *Stalin i Kaganovich*, 243–4 (RGASPI, f. 558, op. 11, d. 740, l. 104–11); Khaustov et al., *Lubianka: Stalin i VChK*, 316 (RGASPI, f. 17, op. 162, d. 13, l. 52); RGASPI, f. 17, op. 3, d. 896, l. 13.

266. *Pravda*, Aug. 9, 1932. See also *Izvestiia TsIK SSSR i VTsIK*, Aug. 8, 1932. Already, places of confinement were far over capacity.

267. Zelenin et al., *Istoriia sovetskogo krest'iantsva*, II: 428–9n137 (citing RGAE, f. 1562, op. 152, d. 29, l. 58, 29). In the RSFSR alone, more than 160,000 people were convicted under the law in the first year alone. Werth and Mironenko, *Istoriia stalinskogo gulaga*, I: 135–8.

268. The names are crossed out from the record of the meeting. Khlevniuk et al., *Stalin i Kaganovich*, 256–8 (personal archive of Kaganovich); Danilov et al., *Tragediia sovetskoi derevni*, III: 418–9 (RGASPI, f. 81, op. 3, d. 99,

l. 106–13, 117, 121–3, 144–5, 151; d. 100, l. 1–7).

269. Khlevniuk et al., *Stalin i Kaganovich*, 273–5 (RGASPI, f. 81, op. 3, d. 99, l. 144–5).

270. Polish intelligence was still sending ethnic Ukrainian agents across the border on espionage missions, but almost all were being caught, as Stalin knew from intercepted Japanese correspondence out of Warsaw. Mikulicz, *Prometeizm w polityce II Rzeczypospolitej*, 110–5; Kuromiya, *The Voices of the Dead*, 220–1. Japan cooperated with Poland to support Ukrainian anti-Communist nationalists, but Soviet intelligence knew this, too, having penetrated Ukrainian groups abroad. Sotskov, *Neizvestnyi separatizm*, 75–81. On Soviet-Polish prisoner exchanges, including spies, see Pepłoński, *Wywiad Polski na ZSSR*, 122–3. See also Gronskii, *Iz proshlogo*, 147–8.

271. Stanisław Patek, the Polish envoy to the USSR, and Krestinsky had signed the pact in Moscow on July 25, 1932; it went into effect on Dec. 23, when ratifications were exchanged in Warsaw between Beck and Antononv-Ovseyenko. Ken and Rupasov, *Politbiuro TsK VKP (b) i otnosheniia SSSR*, 514–9; Ken, *Moskva i pakt*, 104.

272. Khlevniuk et al., *Stalin i Kaganovich*, 283–5 (RGASPI, f. 558, op. 11, d. 740, l. 153–60: Aug. 16). Balytsky would not arrive in Ukraine as a special plenipotentiary until Nov. 1932; he would be promoted to republic OGPU chief in Feb. 1933. Khaustov et al., *Lubianka: Stalin i VChK*, 340 (RGASPI, f. 17, op. 3, d. 907, l. 20: Nov. 25, 1932); Shapoval et al., *ChK-GPU-NKVD*, 47–8, 436. But Stalin directed Kaganovich to bring the Red Army into the harvest campaign in Ukraine. Danilov et al., *Tragediia sovetskoi derevni*, III: 460 (RGASPI, f. 558, op. 11, d. 79, l. 21).

273. Khlevniuk et al., *Stalin i Kaganovich*, 232 (RGASPI, f. 81, op. 3, d. 99, l. 91–104), 285–6 (RGASPI, f. 85, op. 3, d. 99, l. 157–60). This overturned the recent politburo decision on sown area expansion that Stalin had mandated (f. 17, op. 3, d. 895, l. 14: Aug. 7, 1932). Total sown area for the 1933 harvest would be 4.7 million hectares fewer than for 1932. Still, crop rotation would not be restored even by 1935, when it was practiced on just 50 percent of the sown area. Davies, "Stalin as Economic Policy-Maker," 133–4.

274. Antipova et al., *Golod v SSSR*, 180–1 (APRF, f. 3, op. 40, d. 81, l. 107–10), 182 (l. 105).

275. RGASPI, f. 558, op. 11, d. 728, l. 38 (Aug. 16, 1932).

276. Also present were Dmitry Maretsky, editor-in-chief of *Leningrad Pravda*; Pyotr Petrovsky, first deputy editor of *Pravda* and former editor of *Red Star*; and Alexander Sleptsov, a founding editor of *Communist Youth League Pravda*. Petrovskii, "Poslednii rot front," 179–98.

277. Merridale, "Reluctant Opposition," it 392; Merridale, *Moscow Politics*, 231–3; Starkov, *Martem'ian Ryutin*, 176; Cohen, *Bukharin*, 234. Ryutin had been born in Eastern Siberia, joined the Menshevik wing of the Russian Social Democrats in 1914, and, after the seizure of power, managed to get elected a delegate to the 10th Party Congress, while participating in the regime crackdown against the Kronstadt sailors. He had once been admonished for alluding to Lenin's Testament at a ward party bureau session ("We know that Comrade Stalin has his faults, about which Comrade Lenin spoke"). "O dele tak nazyvaemogo 'Soiuza Marksistov-Leninstev,'" 108; Zagoria, *Power and the Soviet Elite*, 11; Iakovlev et al., *Reabilitatsiia: politicheskie protsessy*, 92–104. Around the time of the 16th Party Congress (June 1930), Stalin evidently offered him an opportunity to remain in the

Central Committee in exchange for publicly denouncing the right; Ryutin demurred. "M. N. Riutin," 156. Stalin wrote to Molotov of Ryutin (Sept. 13), "This counterrevolutionary scum must be completely disarmed." Lih et al., *Stalin's Letters to Molotov*, 215. Eight days later, as if on cue, a denunciation came forward from a former official in the Krasnaya Presnya ward party committee who claimed that in Aug. 1930 Ryutin had called Stalin "a trickster and political intriguer who will lead the party to ruin." Radzinsky, *Stalin*, 273 (quoting A. Nemov, without a reference). Hauled before the Central Control Commission, Ryutin denied the accusations ("99 percent of it is the most vile lie") but did admit that back in 1928 "Comrade Stalin defamed me needlessly and had me thrown out of party work with a clever maneuver. I consider that dishonesty toward me on his part." On Oct. 5, 1930, Ryutin was expelled from the party for "double-dealing" and right opportunism. On Nov. 13, the OGPU imprisoned Ryutin at Butyrka for counterrevolutionary agitation, but interrogators were unable to break him: Mężyński wrote to Stalin that Ryutin "poses as an innocent wronged." Stalin, for reasons that remain obscure, ordered Ryutin's release, which took place on Jan. 17, 1931. "O tak nazyvaemom 'vsesoiuzom trotskistskom tsentre,'" 110–1; Starkov, "Delo Riutina," 166–7); Starkov, *Martem'ian Ryutin*, 22–25; Anfert'ev, "Osobennosti preodoleniia I. V. Stalinym krizisnoi situatsii," 2 (citing RGASPI, f. 558, op. 1, d. 5282, l. 1). Radzinsky speculates that Ryutin was meant to be used to entrap other oppositionists. Radzinsky, *Stalin*, 273. See also Tel'man, "Riutin protiv Stalina" (purporting to quote additional instructions from Stalin to Mężyński). Ryutin got hired as an economist at an electrical production unit.

278. "Platforma 'Soiuza Marksistov-Lenintsev' ('Gruppa Riutina'): 'Stalin i krzis proletarskoi diktatury'" (1990, no. 8), 201–6, (no. 9), 172.

279. Ryutin had said back at the 12th Party Congress in 1923, when Trotsky attacked the leadership, that "a party cannot exist without its leaders. . . . A party that discredits its leaders is unavoidably weakened, disorganized. Parties are always led by leaders." *XII s"ezd RKP (b)*, 165. See also Getty and Naumov, *Yezhov*, 74; Starkov, "Trotsky and Ryutin," 71. See also Joffe, *Back in Time*, 45; *Sotsialisticheskii vestnik*, 1928, no. 1; *Poslednie novosti*, Dec. 4, 1927; Starkov, *Martem'ian Ryutin*, 13; Pavlov [pseudonym], *1920-e: revoliutsiia i biurokratiia*, 86–7: a manuscript in the Hoover Institution archives ("Pavlov file"); the identity of the author, a student at Moscow University in the 1920s, remains unclear.

280. Medvedev, *Let History Judge*, 296. Getty and Naumov, *Road to Terror*, 53. Besides Ryutin, Ivanov, and the two Kayurovs, the attendees were Natalia Kayurova (wife of Vasilii Kayurov), Vasily Demidov, Professor Pavel Fyodorov, Pavel Galkin, Viktor Gorelov, Nikolai Kolokolov, Boris Ptashny, Grigory Rokhkin, Semyon V. Tokarev, Nikolai Vasileyev, Pyotr Zamyatin. The home was Pyotr Silchenko's. He was absent.

281. Getty and Naumov, *Road to Terror*, 54–8. In 1932, Stalin learned from Anna Ulyanova, Lenin's sister, that their mother was the daughter of a baptized Jew, Alexander Blank, born Srul Moissevich Blank, who had become a landowner and physician. Ulyanova stressed how beneficial it would be to reveal Lenin's one-quarter Jewish ancestry. Stalin made it a state secret. Volkogonov, *Lenin*, 9. Lenin had Russian, Qalmyk, German, and Swedish along with Jewish ancestry.

282. "Platforma 'Soiuza Marksistov-Lenint-sev' ('Gruppa Riutina'): 'Stalin i krzis prole-tarskoi diktatury'," (1990, no. 12), 198–9.

283. "Platforma 'Soiuza marksistov-lenintsev' ('Gruppa Riutina'): 'Stalin i krzis proletarskoi diktatury'," (1990, no. 11), 162–3, (no. 12), 190, (no. 8), 201.

284. "Platforma 'Soiuza Marksistov-Lenint-sev' ('Gruppa Riutina'): 'Stalin i krzis prole-tarskoi diktatury'" (1990, no. 12), 193; Starkov, Martem'ian Riutin, 237–8.

285. Ryutin proposed no alternative leader (he had in mind a collective leadership). Starkov, "Trotsky and Ryutin," 73. On Oct. 15, 1932, OGPU raided Silchenko's home, where they found the original 167-page handwritten "Stalin and the Crisis of Proletarian Dictatorship," which they then typed up, the only extant copy.

286. Notwithstanding Ryutin's bravery, the only way out was not to seize the party but to dissolve it, deliberately or accidentally, by introducing democracy—competitive elections, secret ballot, alternative parties, private property, market relations. There was no salvation from tyranny in Bolshevism.

287. "O dele tak nazyvaemogo 'Soiuza Marksistov-Lenintsev,'" 106 (N. K. Kuz'min and N. A. Storozhenko, who claimed to have received the appeal from Alexander Kayurov).

288. Getty and Naumov, Road to Terror, 54. According to a Molotov speech that was published, Zinoviev in testimony had stated "as far as I can judge, recently a fairly significant section of party members were seized by the idea of a retreat, that it is necessary to retreat somewhere. This conception comes from my impressions, what I read and hear." Pravda, Jan. 12, 1933.

289. Biulleten' oppozitsii, 29–30 (Sept. 1932): 1–5. Davies, Crisis and Progress, 298–9.

290. Biulleten' oppozitsii, 31 (Nov. 1932): 18–20. Trotsky's prescriptions, dated Oct. 22, 1932, presaged Soviet policy in 1933: lowering capital investment and concentrating resources on bringing existing construction to completion. Davies, Crisis and Progress, 298–9.

291. Trotsky received the letter on Oct. 4, 1932: Trotsky archive, Harvard, T 4782; Davies, Crisis and Progress, 246–7, citing conversations with Pierre Broué, editor of Trotsky's notebooks in French. In late Sept. 1932, the well-informed Menshevik émigré paper Socialist Herald carried word from Moscow of a "letter of the eighteen Bolsheviks" who united "former right and left oppositionists" around the imperative "to remove Stalin." Sotsialisticheskii vestnik, Sept. 26, 1932 (report dated Sept. 7). In the Bulletin, Trotsky elaborated: "If the bureaucratic equilibrium in the USSR were to be upset at present, this would almost certainly benefit the forces of counterrevolution." Prophet Outcast, 175.

292. Davies and Wheatcroft, Years of Hunger, 167–8 (RGASPI, f. 17, op. 3, d. 900, l. 33–4; op. 162, d. 13, l. 99–100); Khaustov et al., Lubianka: Stalin i VChK, 319 (APRF, f. 3, op. 57, d. 60, l. 10), 321–4 (l. 13–9). See also Solomon, Soviet Criminal Justice, 463. Stalin's first meeting back in Moscow was on Aug. 27, 1932. Na prieme, 70. Insider theft would remain an obsession for Stalin. On Nov. 15, 1932, he sent politburo members the interrogation record of a collective farm bookkeeper, with a cover letter deeming it "one of many documents demonstrating the organized embezzlement of collective farm property." Khaustov et al., Lubianka: Stalin i VChK, 336–7 (APRF, f. 3, op. 57, d. 60, l. 29–34).

293. Tauger, who stresses the natural causes of the famine, carefully showed that the annual reports from the collective farms for 1932 implied an extremely low harvest, and that not only the official figure for the 1932 harvest but revised figures given by Davies and Wheatcroft were likely too high. Ultimately, the size of the 1932 harvest remains uncertain, but the annual report data from 40 percent of the collective farms—which are the only actual harvest data so far discovered—imply a harvest on the order of 50 million tons. Tauger, "1932 Harvest." Davies and Wheatcroft estimate the 1932 harvest at 58–60 million, but that is based on pre-harvest forecasts. It should be noted, however, that Wheatcroft, who has rejected Tauger's views, often stridently, subsequently allowed 50 million as the lower band of the estimate without then citing Tauger. Davies, Economic Transformation, 286 (56 million tons plus or minus 10 percent). The Five-Year Plan had originally envisioned a harvest by 1932 of 100–106 million tons; as late as July 1932, the harvest had been estimated at 76–78 million tons, better than in 1931, but in Sept. 1932 the estimates were reduced to 67–71 million. Revised estimates conducted in early 1933 would put the figure between 60 and 65 million; the final official figure, from politburo decision in Sept. 1933, was 69.87 million. Davies and Wheatcroft, Years of Hunger, 443–6; Piatiletnyi plan, II/i: 298; Kosheleva, Pis'ma Stalina Molotovu, 248–9 (Sept. 12, 1933); Lih et al., Stalin's Letters to Molotov, 234–5.

294. Tauger, "Natural Disaster," 40–5.

295. Molot, Jan. 23, 1934; VIII Vsekazakh-stanskaia kraevaia konferentsiia VKP (b), 159. "The Ukrainian village was leading a nomad life," in one official's description of starving refugees, while the Kazakh steppe nomads were being forced into a sedentary life—which also spurred mass flight. Swianiewicz, Forced Labor, 121 (citing a statement to the author in 1933 from an unnamed Central European Communist who had just escaped the USSR). In Aug. 1932, the head of the Kazakhstan Council of People's Commissars wrote that "the administrative transformation of semi-desert livestock districts into 'agricultural' districts had had a ruinous effect on livestock farming." Aldazhumanov et al., Na-sil'stvennaia kollektivizatsiia, 155.

296. Uraz Isaev (b. 1899), an ethnic Kazakh and chair of the autonomous republic's Council of People's Commissars, estimated 10,000 to 15,000 human deaths in spring 1932. Äb-diraiymūly et al., Golod v kazakhskoi stepi, 140–51 (APRK, f. 141, op. 17, d. 607, l. 1–14); Aldazhumanov et al., Nasil'stvennaia kollektivizatsiia, 153–162; Partiinaia zhizn' Kazakhstana, 1990, no. 6: 83–9.

297. Kuramysov, Na putiakh sotsialisticheskogo pereustroitastva kazakskogo aula, 3–4; Davies and Wheatcroft, Years of Hunger, 324 (citing RGASPI, f. 17, op. 162, d. 13, l. 113–7). Turar Ryskulov, a vice chairman of the Council of People's Commissars of the RSFSR, to protest courageously but vainly to Stalin (Sept. 29) that the settlement mania exhibited "ignorance of the interests of livestock in districts that were mainly livestock districts." Danilov et al., Tragediia sovetskoi derevni, III: 503–9 (RGASPI, f. 82, op. 2, d. 670, l. 11–14ob.); Partiinaia zhizn' Kazakhstana, no. 10 (1990): 76–84; Ryskulov, Sobranie sochinenii, III: 304–16 (APRK, f. 141, op. 1, d. 6403, l. 13–6). Kazakh nomads were driven into farming partly by impoverishment, not solely by the regime's organized sedentarization. Of course, coercive collective farming was not the only farming option those people would have wanted.

298. Pianciola, "Famine in the Steppe," 184 (citing GARF, f. 6985, op. 1, d. 9, l. 2). Livestock allowances would be increased on Dec. 19, 1934. Pianciola, "Collectivization Famine," at 244 (citing Kazakhstanskaia pravda,

Dec. 20, 1934; GARF, f. 6985, op. 1, d. 9, l. 133); Davies and Wheatcroft, Years of Hunger, 183–4 (RGASPI, f. 17, op. 162, d. 13, l. 113–7, 118).

299. Khatayevich wrote on Sept. 22, 1932; he had been in Stalin's office on Sept. 1, 2, and 14. Na prieme, 70–1. On Oct. 23, Kosior wrote to Stalin that Khatayevich "acted incorrectly, doing all this without an agreement with me" (again, the letter is underlined through and through in red pencil), and assured the dictator that the grain still might be procured, and that "the weather right now in the south of Ukraine, even in the Right Bank, is exceptionally fine," and "the mood of the mass of collective farms is also not bad." Antipova et al., Golod v SSSR, 187–91 (APRF, f. 3, op. 40, d. 82, l. 136–40), 192–5 (l. 132–5). Khatayevich wrote to Stalin again, at length (Dec. 27, 1932), declaring how hard he was working for the cause, and requesting new party personnel for localities in Ukraine immediately. Antipova et al., Golod v SSSR, 224 (APRF, f. 3, op. 40, d. 85, l. 88–94).

300. In normal times, Ukraine and the North Caucasus produced perhaps one-third of the country's harvest and half its marketable grain. Conquest, Harvest of Sorrow, 221 (no citation).

301. Davies et al., Economic Transformation, 316 (table 48). See also Lewin, Making of the Soviet System (1985), 166–7. The 1932 grain procurement plan had been based upon an assumed harvest of 90 million tons, with planned collection of 29.5 million tons—5 million more than the previous year—and export of 6.235 million.

302. VKP (b) v rezoliutsiiakh (1933), II: 747–61; VKP (b) v rezoliutsiiakh (1936), II: 669. Pravda (Oct. 11, 1932) published the expulsion resolution and a list of the Ryutin group. Twenty Communists were expelled without recourse, and four others for a year, after which they could appeal for reinstatement.

303. Anfert'ev, "'Delo M. N. Riutina' v sud'be G. E. Zinovieva i L. B. Kameneva, oktiabr' 1932 g.," Istoricheskii arkhiv, 2006, no. 1: 73, 80; "O dele tak nazyvaemogo 'Soiuza Marksistov-Lenintsev,'" 107. All during the summer of 1932, the politburo had been mulling over proposals by the light industry commissar (I. E. Lyubimov) to allow state industrial enterprises to sell their above-plan output on the open market, but now, after Stalin's return to the capital from holiday, the idea was turned aside. Khlevniuk et al., Stalin i Kaganovich, 188–90 (RGASPI, f. 558, op. 11, d. 740, l. 76–81), 190n6 (f. 17, op. 3, d. 887, l. 7; d. 891, l. 4; d. 895, l. 3; d. 903, l. 15: Oct. 16, 1932). Stalin did not seek Ryutin's execution. Rees, "Stalin as Leader, 1924–1937," 45. On Dec. 14, 1933, both Zinoviev and Kamenev would be reinstated in the party.

304. Serge, Portrait de Staline, 95; Basseches, Stalin, 188. See also Letter of an Old Bolshevik; Krivitsky, I Was Stalin's Agent, 203; and Serge, Memoirs of a Revolutionary, 259.

305. Pravda, Oct. 14, 1932. "Ryutin in prison!" recalled Ante Ciliga (b. 1898), a Yugoslav-born inmate and fervent Trotsky supporter. "The prison received Ryutin coldly but calmly." (Ryutin was soon transferred.) Ciliga noted that it had been arduous trying to follow political events in the Soviet Union while at liberty, "but to be among two hundred prisoners representing . . . all the shades of opinion that are to be found in the immense country that is Russia—that was a precious privilege which allowed me to acquire a full knowledge of Russian political life in all its aspects." He called the prison groupings "truly an illegal parliament." Ciliga, Russian Enigma, 228, 209–10. Ciliga would become an ardent supporter of the Croatian Ustaše

fascist regime, criticizing Ante Pavlević as too soft.

306. Radzinsky, *Stalin*, 274 (no citation). See also Vinogradov, *Genrikh Iagoda*, 361–3 (TsA FSB, f. 2, op. 11, d. 1264, l. 1–3).

307. Alliluyeva, *Twenty Letters*, 223.

308. "My dear child Ioseb, first of all I greet you with great love and wish you a long life and good health together with your family. Child, I ask nature to give you complete victory and annihilation of the enemy. . . . Be victorious!" Rayfield, *Stalin and His Hangmen*, 7 (citing RGASPI, f. 558, op. 11, d. 721, l. 68). This letter is absent from Murin.

309. Murin, *Stalin v ob"iatiiakh*, 1–19 (APRF, f. 45, op. 1, d. 1549, l. 1–2, 13–4, 15–6, 19–20, 21–2, 23–4, 36–7, 38–9, 41–2, 43–4, 45–6, 51–2, 53–4, 55–6, 59–60, 72–3, 61–3, 64–5).

310. Murin, *Stalin v ob"iatiakh sem'i*, 16 (Dec. 22, 1931).

311. Alliluyeva, *Dvadtsat' pisem*, 71; Mac-Neal, "Stalin's Family." Nadya might have visited her sister Anna in Kharkov, in famine-stricken Ukraine, that fall.

312. Sergeev and Glushik, *Besedy o Staline*, 41. Zubalovo consisted of different buildings, the largest was divided between Mikoyan's large family and others; Stalin got the smaller (still ample) dacha. Also there were two servants' buildings (Sergei Alliluyev built a machine shop in the servants' block).

313. "Kirov and Molotov danced a Russian handkerchief dance with their partners," Yekaterina Voroshilova would later recall. "Mikoyan hovered around Nadezhda Sergeyevna [Alliluyeva] and asked her to dance the lezginka with him. Mikoyan danced very quickly and with great energy . . . Nadezhda Sergeyevna was timid and shy, just as she always was. She covered her face with her hand." Voroshilova's husband danced the Ukrainian hopak and then a polka ("he was particularly good at it"). Kun, *Stalin*, 226 (citing RGASPI, f. 74, op. 2, d. 42: diary written 1950s).

314. RGASPI, f. 558, op. 11, d. 786, l. 123–4 (July 10, 1932). At the same time, Galina Serebryakova (the third and final wife of Sokolnikov) saw Nadya in 1932 waiting at a bus stop jammed with people at the corner of Vozdvizhenka and Mokhovaya. Serebriakova, "Smerch," 253–4. According to Kamenev's daughter-in-law Galina Kravchenko, Nadya went to church; no other source confirms this. Vasil'eva, *Kremlevskie zheny*, 156.

315. Deviatov et al., *Blizhniaia*, 48 (citing family archive of A. N. Shefov).

316. One fellow student recalled her as full of life and sparkle that Nov. 1932; his account portrays her marriage to Stalin as widely known. Tokaev, *Betrayal of an Ideal*, 160–1. Tokaev, an Ossetian born (1909) Gokhi Tokati, studied at a Moscow military academy and would seize a chance to defect on a trip to Germany in 1947.

317. "In Moscow I determinedly try not to have anything to do with anyone," she had written to Maria Svanidze ("Auntie Marusya"), back in 1926. "Sometimes it is strange: so many years not to have acquaintances, close friends. But that obviously depends on character." Nadya added that she felt closer to the non-party people. "The many new prejudices are terrible. If you don't work, you're a 'hussy' ['baba']." She insisted: "It's absolutely necessary to have a profession, so that you don't have to be a gopher for anybody, as normally happens in secretarial work." RGASPI, f. 44, op. 1, d. 1, l. 417; Montefiore, *Court of the Red Tsar*, 7; Radzinskii, *Stalin*, 297–8. Maria Svanidze (née Korona) had been born in Tiflis in 1899 of Jewish extraction, divorced in 1918, and three years

later married Nadya's brother Alexander "Alyosha" Svanidze. She studied at the conservatory in Georgia and in the 1920s sang in the Tiflis opera. See also RGASPI, f. 558, op. 4, d. 666.

318. Cherviakova, "Pesochnye chasy," no. 5: 83. "In Iosif's presence," Gogua would later claim, "Nadya resembled the pitiful type [fakir] who in the circus walks barefoot on broken glass smiling at the public. . . . She never knew what would happen next, the next explosion. He was an utter boor. The only creature that softened him was Svetlana . . . Vaska always annoyed him." Gogua, "Semeinye istorii." "Nadya repeatedly told me with a sigh," wrote the defector Boris Bazhanov, who knew her in the 1920s. "'He's been silent for three days now. He speaks to no one, he does not respond when someone addressed him. He is a particularly difficult person.'" Bazhanov, *Vospominaniia*, 154.

319. Svetlana claimed she had received only one letter from her mother, and it was a scolding. Alliluyeva, *Twenty Letters*, 96. See also Sullivan, *Stalin's Daughter*, 21 (citing interview with Chrese Evans, formerly Olga Peters), 27 (interview with Svetlana, London, 1994, Meryle Secrest Collection, audio recording, group 2, tape 28, HIA).

320. Kun, *Stalin*, 201 (citing interviews from the 1960s–70s with László Pollacsek). See also the hearsay in the secret police: Orlov, *Secret History*, 315, 318; Orlov, *Tainaia istoriia*, 303–4.

321. Vladimir Alliluyev (son of Anna Alliluyeva and Redens) wrote that she suffered "ossification of the cranial sutures. The disease began to progress, accompanied by bouts of depression and headaches . . . She traveled to Germany for consultations with the leading German neuropathologists . . . Nadezhda threatened to commit suicide more than once." Alliluev, *Khronika odnoi sem'i*, 30. Svetlana thought it was schizophrenia. There is hearsay that Nadya had an abortion at one point, causing gynecological complications. Montefiore, *Court of the Red Tsar*, 12.

322. Alliluev, *Khronika odnoi sem'i*, 33. See also Shatunovskaia, *Zhizn' v Kremle*, 188.

323. Murin, *Iosif Stalin v ob"iatiakh*, 15–6 (APRF, f. 45, op. 1, d. 1549, l. 40–40ob.: March 12, 1931).

324. Kun, *Stalin*, 204 (citing RGASPI, f. 668, op. 1, d. 15).

325. Khrushchev, *Vremia, liudi, vlast': vospominaniia*, 4 vols. (Moscow: Novosti, 1999), I: 291–3. The defector Alexander Barmine claimed he saw her on Red Square the day before her death: he recalled her as looking exhausted. But others said she looked in good spirits. Barmine, *One Who Survived*, 63; Vasil'eva, *Kremlevskie zheny*, 197.

326. *Na prieme*, 78; RGASPI, f. 558, op. 11, d. 45, l. 23; Aldazhumanov et al., *Nasil'stvennaia kollektivizatsiia*, 193–4 (APRK, f. 141, op. 1, d. 5235, l. 139–40). On Oct. 22, Stalin had sent commissions headed by Molotov to Ukraine and by Kaganovich to the North Caucasus for ten days, to break "the kulak sabotage." Oskolkov, *Golod 1932/1933*, 26–8 (citing RGASPI, f. 17, op. 3, d. 904, l. 11); Sheboldaev, *Doklad*, 11; *Na prieme*, 77.

327. Vladimir Alliluyev recalled that Stalin and Nadya had gone to the Bolshoi together and fought there, but Stalin's office logbook seems to preclude theater attendance that particular night before the banquet. Alliluev, *Khronika odnoi sem'i*, 25.

328. Radzinsky, *Stalin*, 287 (quoting an interview with Nadezhda Stalin, daughter of Vasily Stalin and Galina Burdonskaya).

329. Rybin, *Stalin v Oktiabre*, 20; Vasilieva, *Kremlin Wives*, 103–11. *Druzhba narodov*,

1997, no. 5: 83 (Lyola Treshtsalina, of the protocol department). Vlasik later told Khrushchev (who was not present at the banquet) that Stalin left for a tryst with Feodosiya Drabkina-Guseva, a woman of Jewish extraction and the wife of the commander Yakov Drabkin (known as Sergei Gusev).

330. Orange peel as the item: Alliluev, *Khronika odnoi sem'i*, 25 (based on the hearsay of his grandmother Olga Evgeneevna). A piece of bread as the item, according to Molotov: "Stalin made a tiny ball of bread and, in front of everyone, threw it at Yegorov's wife." That act, Molotov claims, triggered Nadya's departure from the banquet. Chuev, *Sto sorok*, 250. Svetlana's version largely adheres to Molotov's, but also has Stalin proposing a toast to "the destruction of enemies of state," and rudely reprimanding Nadya for not drinking. Polina observed that Nadya was "perfectly calm" at their parting back at her own apartment. Alliluyeva, *Twenty Letters*, 108–10. Most scholars follow this account: Radzinskii, *Stalin*, 287–9; Montefiore, *Court of the Red Tsar*, 3–22; Service, *Stalin*, 292–3.

331. Chuev, *Molotov Remembers*, 173–4. Stalin supposedly said, "Let her go." Shatunovskaia, *Zhizn' v Kremle*, 196–7.

332. Svetlana's account—that Til ran to fetch Bychkova and the two hoisted Nadya's body onto the bed—is an obvious impossibility because Svetlana, and hence Bychkova, were at the Sokolovka dacha that night. Alliluyeva, *Twenty Letters*, 109 (citing much later discussions with Bychkova). Alliluyeva, *Twenty Letters*, 117; Vaslieva, *Kremlin Wives*, 67.

333. Secret report of Dr. Kushner: "There is a five millimeter hole over the heart—an open hole. Conclusion: Death was immediate from an open wound to the heart." GARF, f. 7523, op. 149, d. 2, l. 1–6. Montefiore, *Court of the Red Tsar*, 16.

334. At her seventh birthday, following her mother's death, Svetlana was said to have asked what present her mother had sent from Germany. If so, this implies she had not seen the open coffin, as she later claimed. Sergeev and Glushik, *Besedy o Staline*, 37; "Priemysh vozhdia," *Moskovskii komsomolets*, Aug. 3, 2004; Alliluyeva, *Twenty Letters*, 111–3. See also Sullivan, *Stalin's Daughter*, citing Artyom Sergeyev in Kreml'-9 writers, *Svetlana Stalina: Escape from the Family*).

335. Sergeev and Glushik, *Besedy o Staline*, 39.

336. Chuev, *Molotov Remembers*, 173–4.

337. For eight days running, *Pravda* published obituaries attributed to Voroshilov's wife, Molotov's wife, Orjonikidze's wife, Postyshev's wife, as well as Mikoyan, Kagananovich, and others. The obituary published in *Pravda* (Nov. 10, 1932) was signed by Yekaterina Voroshilova, Polina Zhemchuzhina, Zinaida Orjonikidze, Dora Khazan, Maria Kaganovich, Tatyana Postysheva, and Aikhen Mikoyan. *Izvestiya* (Nov. 11) published Demyan Bedny's poem "Death Has Its Severe Guile." On Nov. 16, *Pravda* published a letter of grief from Krupskaya to Stalin.

338. No suicide note has turned up. Alliluyeva, *Twenty Letters*, 112–3. See also Sullivan, *Stalin's Daughter*, 50–1 (citing interview with Alexander Alliyuev). The funeral commission consisted of Yenukize (chairman), Pauker, Dora Khazan, Kaganovich, Peterson, and Ruben. GARF, f.7523c, op. 149a, d. 2, l. 10–1.

339. *Pravda*, Nov. 10, 1932; RGASPI, f. 558, op. 4, d. 666 (Alisa Radchenko). Radzinsky quotes Nadya's medical file, without citation, from Aug. 1932: "acute pains in the abdominal region—return for further examination in 2–3 weeks' time". Another entry, the last: "August 31, 1932. Examination to consider operation in 3–4 weeks." Radzinsky, *Stalin*,

292. The medical file is RGASPI, f. 558, op. 11, d. 1551. Dr. Boris Zbarsky prepared the body for the lying in state (he had mummified Lenin in 1924) and, many years later, is said to have told a friend he covered over a temple wound (rather than a shot to the heart). Kanel, "Vstrecha na lubianke," 495. Khrushchev recalled that Kaganovich summoned the Moscow party apparatchiks the day after the parade and informed them that Nadya had died suddenly, offering no explanation. Kaganovich summoned the same officials a day or two later, according to Khrushchev, and said, "Stalin has ordered me to tell you that Alliluyeva did not just die; she shot herself." The implication: it was a traitorous act. Khrushchev, *Vospominaniia*, I: 52–3.

340. Kuusinen, *Rings of Destiny*, 91–3. The author, the wife of a Comintern official, worked in the organization from 1924 through 1933.

341. Kozlov, *Neizvestnaia Rossiia*, IV: 172 (Solovyov); Medvedev, "Smert' Nadezhdy Alliluevoi"; Alliluyeva, *Tol'ko odin god*, 127. By some accounts, Stalin had his trusted minion Mekhlis "investigate" the circumstances of Nadya's death to clear him of rumored responsibility for shooting her. Seleznev, *Tainy rossiiskoi politiki XX veka*.

342. Kaganovich, *One Who Survived*, 264. Kaganovich had a sister named Rachel; she died in 1926; he had a niece named Rosa (born 1919).

343. Mironenko, *Moskovskii kreml'*, 184, 210; Larina, *This I Cannot Forget*, 141; Medvedev, *Nikolai Bukharin*, 39. "An almost indistinguishable door in the wall separated the dining room from Stalin's bedroom," one functionary noted. "A bed; two small armoires for underwear, coats, and a jacket; a sink." Shepilov, *Kremlin's Scholar*, 2. Stalin first moved to a two-story building (no. 6) closer to the Trinity Gate, the so-called cornered extension of the Amusement Palace, his fourth Kremlin apartment; he moved into the Imperial Senate after its refurbishment.

344. *Sochineniia*, XIII: 411 ("November 11, 1932, Stalin accompanied the casket with the body of N. S. Alliluyeva-Stalina to the Novodevichy cemetery"). According to Orlov, Stalin followed for only a few minutes, as far as the Manège (right outside the Kremlin), then got into a car with Pauker. Orlov, *Secret History*, 319–21. Rumors circulated that Stalin's brother-in-law and fellow Georgian Alexander Svanidze, who was around his height and had a mustache, substituted for him. Kolsenik, *Khronika zhizni sem'i Stalina*, 21.

345. *Pravda*, Nov. 13, 1932. "Everyone knows that some beings are as tender and delicate as flowers—she was one of them," Alexandra Kollontai, the daughter of a tsarist general and the erstwhile wife of another (before she left him), who served as Soviet envoy to Sweden, wrote ingratiatingly to Stalin of Nadya. "Those who knew her will treasure the beauties of her soul in their memories . . . Please remember that the Cause has need of you. Take care of yourself!" Kun, *Stalin*, 210 (citing RGASPI, f. 134, op. 3, d. 35).

346. Sergeev and Glushik, *Besedy o Staline*, 39.

347. Kaganovich would recall that Stalin "was terribly down." Chuev, *Kaganovich, Shepilov*, 94. Svetlana recalled: "He said that he did not want to go on living. . . . [Stalin] was in such a state that they were afraid to leave him alone. He had sporadic fits of rage." Alliluyeva, *Twenty Letters*, 112; Richardson, *Long Shadow*, 129–30. "The children forgot her in a few days, but me she crippled for life," Stalin was later to have complained, according to Maria Svanidze, who blamed her. Murin, *Iosif Stalin v ob"iatialkh*, 177 (May 9, 1935).

348. One of his bodyguards recalled late in life that Stalin would sit for long periods at Nadya's grave at Moscow's Novodevichy Cemetery. Svetlana asserted that her father never visited the grave. *Stalin* (film by Thames Television, London, 1990); Alliluyeva, *Twenty Letters*, 113. Some writers have asserted that a copy of Ryutin's appeal denouncing her husband was found in Nadya's room. Radzinsky, *Stalin*, 296 (quoting a Vlasik interview with N. Antipenko); Rayfield, *Stalin and his Hangmen*, 239–40.

349. Fridberg, "Gosudarstvennye zagotovki," 350.

350. Ken, "'Moia ostenka byla slishkom rezkoi': I. V. Stalin i rekunstruktsiia RKKA," 152n3 (RGVA, f. 4, op. 14, d. 754, l. 43–5: Jan. 1933).

351. Kuibyshev, back on Aug. 2, 1932, in a speech not covered by the press but published in 200,000 copies, had told Moscow party officials that peasants lacked incentives—so he knew the score. Kuibyshev, *Uborka, khlebozagotovki, i ukrelplenie kolkhovov: rech' na sobranii dokladchikov Moskovskoi partiinoi organziatsii* (Moscow, 1932), reprinted in Kuibyshev, *Stat'i i rechi*, V: 294–322; Davies, *Crisis and Progress*, 242. Ivnitsky points out that Stalin had denied he was forcing collectivization to solve the procurement problem; rather, Stalin claimed he was building socialism in the countryside. Ivnitskii, *Kollektivizatsiia i raskulachivanie*, 205.

352. Rees, *Iron Lazar*, 110, citing O *kolkhoznom stroitel'stve* (Moscow, 1932), 218; Danilov et al., *Tragediia sovetskoi derevni*, III: 520–1 (RGASPI, f. 17, op. 21, d. 3377, l. 83), 575–7 (op. 3, d. 2025, l. 42–42ob.: Dec. 14, 1932); Graziosi, *Soviet Peasant War*, 67–8. "If one were to sack them one would have to sack half," Kaganovich wrote to Stalin (Nov. 5) about the state farm directors. "We will have to remove some, and work on others. . . . Judges passed sentences, but no one carried them out. Clearly, in such a situation, they are mocking us." Khlevniuk et al., *Stalin i Kaganaovich*, 298–9 (RGASPI, f. 558, op. 11, d. 740, l. 177–80). About 26,000 of the 120,000 rural Communists in the North Caucasus would be purged; another 30,000 would quit rather than submit to the procedure. Shimotomai, "Note on the Kuban Affair"; O *kolkhoznom stroitel'stve* (Rostov, 1932), 281–3, 286–90.

353. RGASPI, f. 558, op. 11, d. 769, l. 108. In the wake of the North Caucasus purge, party organizations in Kazakhstan and Ukraine requested permission to purge their ranks. RGASPI, f. 17, op. 26, d. 54, l. 265; Tauger, "People's Commisariat of Agriculture," 298n99 (RGASPI, f. 17, op. 3, d. 907, l. 73/49–74/50).

354. Stalin also sent a secret telegram to OGPU plenipotentiaries to forward interrogation protocols on sabotage of grain procurement and embezzlement of collective farm property to "the Central Committee." Antipova et al., *Golod v SSSR*, 201 (APRF, f. 3, op. 40, d. 84, l. 84: Nov. 29, 1932). Goloshchiokin replied immediately that severe repression was already under way, apologizing for not having informed Stalin earlier. Antipova et al., *Golod v SSSR*, 197 (APRF, f. 3, op. 40, d. 83, l. 137), 198–9 (l. 138–138ob.).

355. Fitzpatrick, *Stalin's Peasants*, 74 (citing *Sotsialisticheskoe zemledelie*, Nov. 12, 16, 28, and Dec. 17, 1932).

356. Maximilien Savelev wrote the letter to Stalin (Nov. 19), indicating he had heard of the meeting from someone else (I. V. Nikolsky), a colleague of Eismont's. Savelev and Nikolsky co-signed a second letter to Stalin (Nov. 22) with new details. They quoted the drunk Eismont as stating, "What is to be done! Either comrade Stalin, or peasant uprisings." According to the informant, "Smirnov said that one speech by Stalin at the congress of Agrarians Marxists in a few days brought to nothing the results of his [Smirnov's] three-year work to restore the herds." Kozlov, *Neizvestnaia Rossiia*, I: 56–128 (at 66); Vatlin, *Stenogrammy zasedanii politburo*, III: 551–676 (at 642: RGASPI, f. 17, op. 3, d. 1011).

357. Mikoyan as well as Kirov, among others, inserted more fervid condemnations into the transcript when offered a chance to edit their remarks. Wynn, "'Right Opposition,'" 97–117. Stalin removed his heckling of Smirnov. The crisis atmosphere was well summarized by the émigré press: *Sotsialisticheski vestnik*, Nov. 26, 1932.

358. Serge, *Portrait de Staline*, 94–5. Serge gives no date for the rumored resignation, vaguely referring to a time after Nadya's suicide and before the 17th Party Congress. Serge was in Moscow then. Deutscher has Stalin asking to resign in late 1932. Deutsher, *Stalin*, 333–4.

359. He underscored the many nonaggression pacts as evidence of his success, asserting that capitalists do not sign such pacts with the weak, and once again blamed food difficulties on kulak saboteurs, their silent middle-peasant supporters, and soft (or worse) rural party officials. RGASPI, f. 558, op. 11, d. 1116, l. 141–2. See also Davies and Harris, *Stalin's World*, 52. Stalin's gloss on the countryside was fed back to him in the secret police reports. Danilov et al., *Tragediia sovetskoi derevni*, 446–52 (RGASPI, f. 81, op. 3, d. 43, l. 75–95), 472–6 (TsA FSB, f. 2, op. 10, d. 520, l. 699–708), and 488–9 (d. 514, l. 145–7).

360. Stalin demanded a "knockout blow" to any internal opposition. Vatlin, *Stenogrammy zasedanii politburo*, 581 (RGASPI, f. 17, op. 163, d. 1010); Danilov et al., *Tragediia sovetskoi derevni*, III: 557–561 (d. 1011, l. 9ob.-15). See also Davies and Wheatcroft, *Years of Hunger*, 187–8.

361. A Central Committee plenum (Jan. 1933) rubber-stamped the expulsions, and the reprimands to Tomsky, Rykov, and V. V. Schmidt (a Rykov associate) for encouraging anti-party work. *KPSS v rezoliutsiiakh* (9th ed.), VI: 32–3.

362. Koenker et al., *Revelations*, 405–6 (RGASPI, f. 17, op. 85, d. 379, l. 1, 1ob, 2); Antipova et al., *Golod v SSSR*, 202 (APRF, f. 3, op. 40, d. 84, l. 139). On Dec. 15, 1932, Stalin set up a separate agricultural department in the Central Committee apparatus and named Kaganovich responsible.

363. Haslam, *Threat from the East*, 8; Bridges, "Yoshizawa Kenkichi." Alexander Troyanovsky (b. 1882) was the scion of lesser gentry, educated at the Mikhailov artillery school, and originally a Menshevik; during the NEP, he worked in trade before being appointed envoy to Japan in late 1927.

364. *Izvestiia*, Jan. 17, 1933; Tisminets, *Vneshniaia politika SSSR*, III: 574–5.

365. RGASPI, f. 17, op. 3, d. 910, l. 2. At this time the regime also tightened the screws by introducing political departments into the machine tractor stations and state farms. These would be announced at the Jan. plenum, when Stalin would blame failures of county party committees for forcing his hand. Zelenin, "Politotdely MTS," 45; Shimotomai, "Springtime for the Polkitotdel," 1034; Thorniley, *Rise and Fall*, 124–40.

366. Stalin received the OGPU's Yagoda and Prokofyev that day. *Na prieme*, 83. Kirov at the OGPU jubilee stated, "It is necessary to say openly that the Cheka-GPU is an organ called to punish, and to simplify the matter,

not just to punish but to punish in real fashion, so that population growth in the 'other world' will be duly noticed." Pogonii, *Lubianka*, 200 (no citation).

367. Campbell, *Russia*, 13–8; Stalin, "Gospodin Kembell priviraet," *Bolshevik*, 1932, no. 22: 1–16 (dated Dec. 23, 1932; published in the Nov. 30 issue). "He was very erect and alert, dressed in Russian costume, consisting of boots, breeches, and a white Russian shirt worn outside the trousers with a black belt," Campbell wrote of Stalin, while recalling the presence of American-made typewriters and filing cabinets. Campbell claimed the audience with Stalin (Jan. 28, 1929) had taken place in the Kremlin but then wrote about ascending to the sixth floor (i.e., at Old Square). Campbell appears in Stalin's office logbook as "Kellbell." *Na prieme*, 30. In response to the condemnation, Campbell told a reporter, "I have a very high regard for Mr. Stalin," adding, "I consider him a real leader and perhaps the only man who can bring that country out of its duress and turmoil." *Spokesman Review*, Dec. 31, 1932. Trotsky seized upon the Campbell book: *Biulleten' oppozitsii*, no. 32 (Dec. 1932).

368. Khaustov et al., *Lubianka: Stalin i VChK*, 339–40 (APRF, f. 3, op. 58, d. 175, l. 9: Nov. 25, 1932); *Sobranie zakonov*, 1932, no. 84: article 516; Hoffman, *Peasant Metropolis Social Identities*, 52; Kessler, "Passport System." From Jan. through April 1933, the state issued 6.6 million passports while denying 265,000 applications. Violations were rampant; the passports had no photographs.

369. Collective farmers living within 60 miles (100 km) of Moscow and Leningrad would be given passports, as an exception.

370. Zelenin, "O nekotorykh 'belykh piatnakh,'" 14 (citing RGASPI, f. 17, op. 26, d. 68, l. 1–9, 32, 35).

371. Davies, *Crisis and Progress*, 270.

372. Khlevniuk, *Politbiuro*, 134–5 (citing RGASPI, f. 17, op. 2, d. 750, l. 52, 54–6; op. 3, d. 913, l. 9); *KPSS v rezoliutsiiakh* (9th ed.), VI: 18; *Pravda*, Jan. 13, 1933; *VKP (b) v rezoliutsiiakh* (1933), II: 762–83.

373. "Itogi pervoi piatiletki: doklad 7 ianvaria 1933 g.," *Sochineniia*, XII: 161–215. See also Kontorovich, "Military Origins." On class struggle, Stalin had remarked in July 1928 that "as we move forward, the resistance of capitalist elements will grow, the class struggle will become sharper, and Soviet power, whose forces will grow even more, will carry out . . . a policy of suppression of the exploiter's resistance." *Sochineniia*, XI: 170–1. Trotsky in April 1918 had observed, "The further and the more the revolutionary movement develops, here and abroad, the more tightly the bourgeoisie of all lands will close ranks." Volkogonov, *Trotsky*, 121–2 (citing *Sochineniia*, XVII/i: 205).

374. He added: "They are for the procurements, but they insist on creating all sorts of unnecessary reserves for animal husbandry, insurance," which enabled them to steal socialist property. *Sochineniia*, XIII: 216–33 (at 229–30, 207–8); Kaganovich, "Tseli i zadachi," 17, citing Stalin; *Materialy ob"edinennogo plenuma TsK i TsKK VKP (b)*, 144. Nikolai Krylenko reported to the plenum that 54,645 people in the RSFSR had been convicted under the law on theft of socialist property, leading to 2,100 executions. He complained of resistance to implementing the law: "One people's judge straight-out said to me: 'My hand will not rise to punish a person with ten years for stealing wisps of grain.'" Zelenin, *Stalinskaia 'revoliutsiia sverkhu,'* 73–4, 126–7 (RGASPI, f. 17, op. 2, d. 514, l. 15–21). A Jan. 30, 1933, decree would extend application of the law to accounting fraud as well as wrecking or sabotage. Volin, "Agrarian Collectivism," 622. In a series of decrees, including on Jan. 19, 1933, the regime attempted to incentivize sowing and attain larger yields by shifting from confiscatory "grain procurement" to "compulsory delivery" in the form of a tax, which was to be levied not on harvest estimates but "from the land actually under cultivation." All surpluses above the obligations were supposed to remain at the disposal of the collective farmers, but the legalized peasant markets were supposed to be shut down until state taxes had been met. *Kollektivizatsiia sel'skogo khoziaistva*, 441–5.

375. RGASPI, f. 17, op. 2, d. 514, vyp. 1, l. 55. Stalin had had Trotsky stripped of his citizenship on Feb. 20, 1932.

376. Getty and Naumov, *Road to Terror*, 91–4 (RGASPI, f. 17, op. 2, d. 511, l. 12–22: typescript with Rudzutaks's corrections), 95–7 (l. 215–20: typescript with Bukharin's corrections), 76–7 (l. 17–9: typescript with Smirnov's corrections). The plenum confirmed Smirnov's expulsion from the Central Committee, the expulsions from the party of Eismont and Tolmachev, and the reprimands for Tomsky and Rykov.

377. Davies and Wheatcroft, *Years of Hunger*, 200 (RGAE, f. 8040, op. 8, d. 20, l. 25–25ob.); RGASPI, f. 17, op. 3, d. 913, l. 15. The Ukrainian hierarchs, mimicking Stalin from the spring, decided the latest reduction had to be kept secret, lest grain procurement officials get demoralized.

378. Stalin had Levon Mirzoyan, an ethnic Armenian serving as second secretary of the Urals province, replace Goloshchyokin, who was sacked Jan. 21, 1933. RGASPI, f. 17, op. 3, d. 914, l. 9. At the Jan. 1933 Central Committee plenum, Goloshchyokin had trumpeted Kazakhstan's supposed successes in collectivization in the face of unmitigated catastrophe. Danilov et al., *Tragediia sovetskoi derevni*, III: 625–31 (RGASPI, f. 17, op. 2, d. 514, vyp. l, l. 19ob.–21ob., 43ob.–44ob.); Aldazhumanov et al., *Nasil'stvennaia kollektivizatsiia*, 202–4; Ryskulov, *Sobranie sochenenii*, III: 316–8, (APRK, f. 141, op. 1, d. 6403, l. 17).

379. One "Trotskyite," during his arrest, was pointedly noted to have been on the phone with Radek. Khaustov et al., *Lubianka: Stalin i VChK*, 388–9 (APRF, f. 3, op. 24, d. 139, l. 173–6).

380. From Jan. 1933, even formal politburo meetings would decline. Detailed politburo protocols were still compiled, as if Stalin's decisions and the ad hoc gatherings in his office constituted an official meeting. Adibekov et al., *Politbiuro TsK RKP (b)—VKP (b): povestki dnia zasedanii*, II: 386 ff.

381. Khromov, *Po stranitsam*, 23–4.

382. Special settlements in Kazakhstan and Western Siberia were ordered to prepare to receive up to 500,000 each: In the event, 133,000 were deported to Siberia during 1933, and a similar number to other remote destinations, for a total of 270,000 by year's end. Khaustov et al., *Lubianka: Stalin i VChk*, 418 (RGASPI, f. 17, op. 162, d. 14, l. 96: March 20, 1933); Ellman, "Role of Leadership Perceptions," 831; Krasil'nikov, *Serp i molokh*, 95, 106, 110–26; Khlevniuk, *History of the Gulag*, 55–6, 63.

383. "Information has reached the Central Committee and the Council of People's Commissars about a mass exodus of peasants from the Kuban and Ukraine 'for grain' into the Central Black-Earth province, Volga, Moscow province, the Western province, Belorussia," the decree stated. "The Central Committee and Council of People's Commissars do not doubt that this peasant exodus, just as in the previous year from Ukraine, is organized by the enemies of Soviet power, the SRs and agents of Poland, with the aim of agitating 'through the peasants' in the northern regions of the USSR against collective farms and generally against Soviet power." The decree was composed in Stalin's hand; Molotov's signature on the original was absent. Danilov et al., *Tragediia sovetskoi derevni*, III: 634–5 (RGASPI, f. 558, op. 11, d. 45, l. 109–109ob.), 635–6 (f. 17, op. 42, d. 80, l. 9–11), 636–8 (d. 72, l. 109–11), 638 (l. 113); Oskolkov, *Golod 1932/1933*, 19 (citing PARO, f. 79, d. 74, l. 40). Yevdokimov, in his report on implementation, tied peasant flight to rebellion, and noted how the heavy secret police pressure was curbing the exodus. Stalin underlined these passages. By contrast, Balytsky, who gave exact numbers (31,963 people), observed that "in the majority of cases exodus is motivated by a search for earnings," that "only part of those leaving villages are bringing their families," and that "the exodus of collective farmers is of significantly less scope than that of individual farmers." Stalin did not underline any of these revealing passages. Khaustov et al., *Lubianka: Stalin i VChK*, 392–4 (APRF, f. 3, op. 30, d. 189, l. 3–10). On Feb. 16, 1933, a politburo decree ordered the OGPU to apply the Jan. 22 interdiction decree to the Lower Volga. Ivnitskii, *Golod 1932–1933 godov*, 269–70 (RGASPI, f. 558, op. 11, d. 45, l. 109).

384. The regime proved better able to block emigration to Poland and Romania than into China, Iran, and Afghanistan. Conquest, *Harvest of Sorrow*, 237, 246–47. On March 1, the politburo granted extrajudicial troikas in Belorussia powers of execution in "cases of counterrevolutionary organizations and groupings consisting of kulaks and White Guard elements." Khlevniuk et al., *Stalinskoe politbiuro*, 63 (APRF, f. 3, op. 58, d. 212, l. 1–2).

385. On Feb. 17, Yagoda reported the interdiction of 150,391 people across eight republics or regions, of whom 114,579 had been returned. Khaustov et al., *Lubianka: Stalin i VChk*, 397–8 (RGASPI, f. 17, op. 3, d. 914, l. 1; op. 162, d. 14, l. 48, 51), 398–9 (APRF, f. 3, op. 30, d. 189, l. 26–7), 399–406 (d. 196, l. 127–38), 406–7 (d. 189, l. 36–6).

386. *Pravda*, Jan. 24, 1933.

387. Kosheleva, *Pis'ma Stalina Molotovu*, 245; Lih et al., *Stalin's Letters to Molotov*, 232.

388. In July 1932, the Nazi party had received 13.7 million votes, 37 percent, and 230 seats, vs. 133 seats for the Social Democrats. (The July 1932 turnout was Weimar's largest, 84.1 percent.) In Nov. 1932, the Nazis dropped to 196 seats.

389. Orlow, *History of the Nazi Party*, II: 18–9. Nazi party membership, 25,000 in 1925 and around 2 million in 1933 when Hitler was made chancellor, would grow to 4.4 million by 1936, when membership requirements would be tightened. Over time, the Nazi party would become more proletarian; the Soviet party, less so. At the same time, Nazism enjoyed far stronger appeal in rural locales than the Soviet Community party did.

390. Jones, "Establishment of the Third Reich"; Jones, "Hindenburg and the Conservative Dilemma." See also Turner, *Hitler's Thirty Days to Power*, 83–4.

391. Winkler, *Weimar*, 509. "I solemnly prophesy to you that this damnable man will plunge our Reich into the abyss and bring inconceivable misery down upon our nation," General Ludendorff wrote to Hindenburg. "Coming generations will curse you on your grave because of this action." Fest, *Hitler*, 411. Ludendorff had collaborated with Hitler in the lunatic Beer Hall putsch of 1923.

392. Turner, *Hitler's Thirty Days to Power*. The cabinet led by Hitler lacked a majority in the Reichstag, a fact von Papen concealed from

Hindenburg. This was the third "presidential" cabinet in a row. See also Bracher, *Die Auflösung der Weimarer Republik*, 443–80; and Kershaw, *Hitler: 1889–1936*, 374–5, 413–25.

393. Beckles, "Hitler, the Clown."

394. Fröhlich, *Tagebücher von Joseph Goebbels*, II/iii: 120–1 (Jan. 31, 1933).

395. Hoffmann, *Hitler Was My Friend*, 69; *DBFP*, 2nd series, IV: 402; Francois-Poncet, *Souvenirs*, 70.

396. Fritzsche, *Germans into Nazis*.

397. Bessel, *Political Violence*, 76–7; Broszat, *Der Staat Hitlers*, 44.

398. The Center Party and the Bavarian People's Party had entertained the possibility of coalition government with the Nazis, whereas the Social Democrats, the only consistently unequivocal defenders of Weimar democracy, remained fixated on the letter of the law even though they had been victims of extra-constitutional maneuvers. The SPD opposed as demagogy popular job-creation measures such as public works, which the Nazis strongly supported. Gates, "German Socialism."

399. Geyer, "Etudes in Political History," 101–23; Deist, *Wehrmacht and German Rearmament*.

400. Winkler, *Der Weg*, 444–5, 754. Even after the Nazis had come to power and decimated the German labor movement, the Comintern executive committee would continue to single out Social Democrats as "the main prop of the bourgeoisie also in the countries of open dictatorship." McDermott and Agnew, *Comintern*, 112. See also Fischer, *Stalin and German Communism*; and Bahne, *Die K.P.D.*

401. Thälmann wrote to the Comintern (Jan. 27, 1933) that the Nov. 1932 election showed a crisis had overtaken the Nazi party, and some "petit-bourgeoisie" were moving to the antifascist camp, joining the working masses. (Not long thereafter, Thälmann, who had consistently called Nazism and Social Democracy "twins," was arrested by the Nazis. He would spend eleven years in solitary confinement before being executed at Buchenwald.) Shirinia, *Komintern v 1933 godu*, 119 (citing RGASPI, f. 495, op. 19, d. 248, l. 17–8). By contrast, the Comintern's Georgi Dimitrov was urging unification of Communists with Social Democrats in "antifascist actions." Sobolev, *Georgii Dimitrov*, 102–3; Leibzon and Shirinia, *Povorot v politike kominterna*, 50–7. See also von Rauch, "Stalin und die Machtergreifung Hitlers," 117–40.

402. This is the surmise of Tucker, *Stalin in Power*, 232.

403. A Nov. 1933 document, advanced at the next Comintern enlarged plenum, which could not be put forward without Stalin's approval, defined "fascism as the open terrorist dictatorship of the more reactionary, more chauvinistic and more imperialist elements of finance capital." Shirinia, *Komintern v 1933 godu*, 469–70 (citing RGASPI, f. 495, op. 171, d. 38, l. 212; d. 299, l. 103; d. 301, l. 4; op. 19, d. 248, l. 222); Ferarra and Ferarra, *Conversando con Togliatti*.

404. *DGFP*, series C, I: 464; G. Castellan, "Reichswehr et Armée Rouge," in *La Relation Germano-Soviétiques de 1933 a 1939*, 248; F. L. Carsten, *The Reichswehr and Politics*, 360; A. E. Ioffe, *Vneshniaia politika Sovetskogo Soiuza, 1928–1932*, 267.

405. Sluch, "Germano-sovetskie otnosheniia," 105 (citing AVP RF, f. 05, op. 13, pap. 91, d. 28, l. 189). On Jan. 23, 1933, days before Hitler's formal ascension, in his speech on foreign affairs, Molotov declared that "of all the countries that have diplomatic relations with us, with Germany we have had and have the strongest economic relations." The many Jewish diplomats in Soviet service distinguished between the fascist Mussolini—with whom the Soviets enjoyed amicable relations—and Nazism. *DVP SSSR*, XVI: 50–6; *III sessiia TsIK SSSR 6-ogo sozyva: stenograficheskii otchet, 23–3o invaria 1933 g., biulleten' no.1*, 37–43; Dullin, *Men of Influence*, 93 (citing internal Soviet diplomatic correspondence referring to *Mein Kampf*).

406. Sluch, "Germano-sovetskie otnosheniia," 105 (citing AVP RF, f. 05, op. 13, pap. 91, d. 28, l. 90–1). Foreign Minister Neurath was not a Nazi. Neither was Germany's ambassador to Moscow, Dirksen, who assured the foreign affairs commissariat that Hitler's and Rosenberg's public statements "contain no real political significance" and that "real state policy will quickly compel the Nazis to forget about their previous plans." Sluch, "Germano-sovetskie otnosheniia," 105 (citing AVP RF, f. 05, op. 13, pap. 91, d. 28, l. 206).

407. Goebbels convinced Hitler to make May 1, 1933, a paid holiday ("Germany honors labor"). As workers marched from factories through the capital to the parade grounds at Tempelhof, airplanes flew in formation overhead, and radio loudspeakers broadcast songs about miners, farmers, and soldiers. In the evening, Hitler addressed workers as patriots responsible for Germany's industrial might. "The biggest demonstration of all times," noted the *Berliner Morgenpost*, a leftist newspaper. The grandiose Nazi initiative had elicited the support of the socialist Free Trade Unions, but on May 2 Nazi storm troopers assaulted them. Fritzsche, *Life and Death*, 46–7. A decade later Goebbels would reminisce that "only then was the National Socialist state on stable foundations." Fröhlich, *Die Tagebücher von Joseph Goebbels*, teil II, VIII: 197 (May 2, 1943).

408. Davies and Wheatcroft, *Years of Hunger*, 207–9.

409. *Pravda*, Feb. 18, 1933; Danilov et al., *Tragediia sovetskoi derevni*, III: 21. Rees, *Iron Lazar*, 113. At the gathering land commissar Yakovlev painted a more truthful, grim picture of collective farm operation from observations in Odessa province. *Pravda*, Feb. 19, 1933. Kaganovich had returned to the North Caucasus in late Jan. 1933, and reported cases of cannibalism but also of feigned starvation and "vicious terror" against the regime. He would go to his grave without acknowledging the tragedy. Danilov et al., *Tragediia sovetskoi derevni*, III: 639 (RGASPI, f. 81, op. 3, d. 215, l. 74); "Dve besedy s L. M. Kaganovichem."

410. *Pervyi vsesoiuznyi s"ezd kolkhoznikov-udarnikov*, 66–7.

411. *Pravda*, Feb. 23, 1933, *Sochineniia*, XIII: 236–56 (at 251–2).

412. *Sochineniia*, XIII: 246–7. Oja, "From Krestianka to Udarnitsa." Officially, only 15.25 million households were collectivized as late as mid-1933. *Kolkhozy vo vtoroi*, 1.

413. The arsonist confessed and claimed to have acted alone. German Communists alleged the Nazis had set him to the task to justify a premeditated anti-Communist repression. In fact, Nazi higher-ups appear to have been panicked the night of the fire. Mommsen, "Reichstag Fire," 129–222; Kershaw, *Hitler: 1889–1936*, 456–8, 731–2. There is one eyewitness account, by a journalist of the *London Daily Express*: Delmer, "Reichstag Fire."

414. Kershaw, "Hitler Myth," 52–3. The Communists, despite the terror, still won 12.3 percent, but Hitler now banned the party by decree. The Social Democrats won 18.3 percent. Turnout was a record 88.8 percent.

415. Germany's constitutional court accepted the validity of the Enabling Act. Bracher, *German Dictatorship*, 224. See also Broszat, *Der Staat Hitlers*, 117.

416. Mommsen, "Der Reichstagbrand." See also Kershaw, "Hitler Myth," 54–6.

417. The consul had just seen the body of a man flayed alive. Larson, *In the Garden of Beasts*, 5 (citing the Messersmith Papers).

418. "Germany," he had warned in *Mein Kampf*, in his typical inversion, "is the next great objective of Bolshevism." Hitler, *Mein Kampf*, 750–1. See also Thies, *Architekt der Weltherrschaft*.

419. Hitler had not tried to block a special bridge credit of 140 million reichsmarks by Dresdner and Deutsche banks (Feb. 23, 1933). The refinancing alleviated pressure on the Soviets, who owed Germany 1.2 billion marks, of which 700 million was due. (By Dec. 1934, the debt would amount to 250 million.) Hilger and Meyer, *Incompatible Allies*, 283–7. Hitler also submitted the 1931 protocol extending the 1926 Berlin Treaty to the Reichstag for ratification on May 5, 1933. *DGFP*, series C, I: 91–3n7, 355–8 (April 28), 385–9 (May 5); von Dirksen, *Moscow, Tokyo, London*, 122; Niclauss, *Die Sowjetunion*, 87–8.

420. Between April 30 and May 4, 1933, the editor of the semiofficial *Gazeta Polska*, Bogusław Miedziński, visited Moscow as a back channel contact; Radek reciprocated to Warsaw, July 6–22, under the pretext of visiting his mother. Radek's report: "Polish-Soviet Rapprochement" (July 26, 1933): AVP RF, f. 010, op. 7, d. 12, l. 71–81. The Nazi ideologue Alfred Rosenberg traveled to Britain in May 1933 to gin up support against the Communist menace, *Kommunisticheskii Internatsional*, 1933, no. 12: 14–20.

421. Shirinia, *Komintern v 1933 godu*, 141–2 (citing RGASPI, f. 495, op. 25, d. 237, l. 69, 79–80; d. 233, l. 69–80). German Communist party turnover was high: Up to three-quarters of the members were unemployed and therefore unconnected to factories. Bahne, "Die Kommunistitche Partei Deutschlands," 662; Grebing, *Geschichte der deutschen Arbeiterbewegung*, 310.

422. Firsov, "Stalin i Komintern," 10; Shirinia, *Komintern v 1933 godu*, 169–77 (citing RGASPI, f. 495, op. 18, d. 963, l. 134–5, 182). By late 1933, the number of legal Communist parties would dwindle to sixteen, from a peak of seventy-two; another seven were semilegal.

423. Robert Tucker held Stalin "chiefly responsible" for the failure of the German Communists and Social Democrats to work together in a united front of the left against Hitler, but did not explain how the two leftist parties would have reconciled in Stalin's absence. Winkler argued that "the gulf between the two workers' parties became so deep . . . that a common unified front was no longer imaginable." Tucker, *Stalin in Power*, 225–32; Winkler, *Der Weg*, 864.

424. Ivnitskii, "Gold 1932-1933 gg.: kto vinovat?," 36. Davies and Wheatcroft estimate perhaps as many as 70 million lived in regions affected by famine, even excluding the Urals, Siberia, and the Far East. Davies and Wheatcroft, *Years of Hunger*, 411.

425. Khlevniuk, *Master of the House*, 47.

426. Ivnitskii, "Gold 1932-1933 godov: kto vinovat?," 61 (citing the politburo archive without details). Peasants from "surplus" population regions were being forcibly resettled to ghost villages of the North Caucasus and elsewhere as well. Davies and Wheatcroft, *Years of Hunger*, 428 (citing RGASPI, f. 17, op. 3, d. 929, l. 133, op. 162 d. 15, l. 100–1; GARF, f. 5446, op. 1, d. 470, l. 179–80). On March 17, 1933, the regime sought to restrict seasonal labor migration, requiring collective farm permission for exit and threatening food

denial to "flitters who leave before the sowing and return for the harvest." *Pravda*, March 20, 1933.

427. Antipova et al., *Golod v SSSR*, 254–65 (TsA FSB, f. 2, op. 11, d. 960, l. 1–12).

428. Maksudov, "Geografiia goloda 1933 goda"; Maksudov, "Ukraine's Demographic Losses," 27–43.

429. On March 15, Kosior sent a long report to Stalin from Ukraine begging for more tractors and food aid of not less than 36,000 tons. Antipova et al., *Golod v SSSR*, 304–17 (APRF, f. 3, op. 61, d. 794, l. 73–86). Ryskulov noted, correctly, that "the situation that has taken shape right now in Kazakhstan . . . cannot be found in any other territory or republic." He even wrote that because of the previous local party leadership group, "it was forbidden officially to say (even in Alma-Ata, where Kazakh corpses were collected from the streets), that there was famine and deaths therefrom. More than that, local functionaries were not bold enough to admit that livestock had declined." Kvashonkin, *Sovetskoe rukovodstvo*, 204–25 (GARF, f. R-5446, op. 27, d. 23, l. 245–53); Ryskulov, *Sobranie sochinenii*, III: 320–48 (APRK, f. 141, op. 1, d. 6403, l. 138–46). See also Aldazhumanov et al., *Nasil'stvennaia kollektivizatsiia*, 220–3 (APRK, f. 141, op. 1, d. 5287, l. 33–8); Äbdīraīymūly et al., *Golod v kazakhskoi stepi*, 166–7 (APRK, f. 141, op. 1, d. 6403, l. 37), 196–200; Werth, "La famine au Kazakhstan"; and Danilov et al., *Tragediia sovetskoi derevni*, III: 687–91 (RGASPI, f. 112, op. 47, d. 7, l. 26, 269–83: Dec. 23, 1933).

430. Stragglers were congregating near factories, according to Molchanov, and knocking on the doors of workers begging ("'Help me, I was fired without cause.' 'Help me, I am a starving unemployed'"). Antipova et al., *Golod v SSSR*, 298–303 (TsA FSB, f. 2, op. 11, d. 56, l. 11–6). Khatayevich, in Dnepropetrovsk, reported (March 15, 1933) that "in reality there are no bazaars," meaning no way to supplement rations. *Golod 1932–33 rokiv na Ukraini*, 465–7.

431. Rudich, *Holod 1932–1933 rokiv na Ukraini*, 409 (March 5, 1933), 433–7 (March 12), 480–1 (April 1); Davies and Wheatcroft, *Years of Hunger*, 420 (RGAE, f. 8040, op. 8, d. 25, l. 32–5: March 22, 1933). "Citizenness Gerasimenko ate the corpse of her dead sister," noted a March 1933 report from the North Caucasus for the OGPU higher-ups. "Citizen Doroshenko, after the death of his father and mother, was left with infant sisters and brothers, ate the flesh of his brothers and sisters when they died of hunger." OGPU operatives appended many names of hardworking farmers who had died of starvation. Danilov et al., *Tragediia sovetskoi derevni*, III: 648–9 (TsA FSB, f. 4, op. 11, d. 42, l. 62–4: March 7, 1933), 662–5 (f. 2, op. 11, d. 42 l. 113–6: April 3, 1933).

432. Antipova et al., *Golod v SSSR*, 363–64 (TsA FSB, f. 2, op. 11, d. 42, l. 149–50: North Caucasus, March 21, 1933), 422–4 (d. 551, l. 36–8: March 31, 1933).

433. Danilov et al., *Tragediia sovetskoi derevni*, III: 527–8 (TsA FSB, f. 2, op. 10, d. 514, l. 234–6: Nov. 5, 1932), 661–2 (op. 11, d. 42, l. 101–3: April 1, 1933).

434. Danilov et al., *Tragediia sovetskoi derevni*, III: 644–5 (RGASPI, f. 558, op. 11, d. 741, l. 3). That March of 1933, Trotsky, from Turkey, sought to reconcile himself with Stalin, pledging readiness to "enter into preliminary negotiations without any publicity." Stalin might have played along, trying to lure him back to Moscow, but, whether from distraction or other causes, appears not to have tried. In summer 1933, Trotsky would accept an offer of asylum in France, although he would not be allowed to settle in Paris. Petrement, *Simone Weil: A Life*, 189–91.

435. Davies and Wheatcroft, *Years of Hunger*, 206, 420 (RGAE, f. 8040, op. 8, d. 25, l. 32–5: March 22, 1933).

436. Antipova et al., *Golod v SSSR*, 330–1 (RGASPI, f. 17, op. 3, d. 918, l. 1, 18–19, 23–4).

437. This was part of a re-registration of weapons Union-wide. Khaustov et al., *Lubianka: Stalin i VChk*, 419 (RGASPI, f. 17, op. 162, d. 14, l. 96–7).

438. Kvashonkin, *Sovetskoe rukovodstvo*, 192–4 (RGASPI, f. 74, op. 2, d. 907, l. 58–60: Voroshilov to Gamarnik, from Sochi, Dec. 7, 1932), 196–7 (d. 38, l. 80: Dec. 17, 1932), 213 (d. 43, l. 60–3).

439. The year before, Kopelev had fallen in love with the daughter of a specialist accused of being a Polish spy in the Shakhty case (Iu. N. Matov), who was sentenced to death but received a reprieve. Kopelev, *I sotvoril sebe kumira*, 234.

440. Kopelev, "Last Grain Collections (1933)," 224–86. The official was Roman Terekhov. He would survive and, after Stalin's death, recall the following rebuke in late 1932: "We've been told that you, Comrade Terekhov, are a good speaker. It seems that you are a good storyteller—you have made up quite a good fable about famine, thinking to frighten us, but it won't work! Wouldn't it be better for you to quit the post of provincial party secretary and the Ukrainian Central Committee and join the Writers' Union? Then you can write your fables, and fools will read them." Medvedev, *Let History Judge*, 241 (citing *Pravda*, May 26, 1964); Zelenin, "O nekotorykh 'belykh piatnakh,'" 15–6.

441. Kotkin, *Magnetic Mountain*, 198–237.

442. One contemporary described Postyshev as "tall and thin as a lath, with a grating bass voice. No fool . . . but careless of others' feelings." Tokaev, *Betrayal of an Ideal*, 166. Conspicuously, Postyshev had told the Jan. 1933 Central Committee plenum that "it is not good hiding behind the back of the kulak, even more so when his back is not as wide as before," warning "we will not change the situation like that" and urging plenum attendees to get better at administration of the large-scale, complex economy. Zelenin, "Politotdely MTS," 53. In March 1933, two months after Postyshev's arrival and one month after the appointment of Balytsky as NKVD plenipotentiary in Ukraine, Mykola Skrypnyk had been sacked as the republic's education commissar. On July 7, 1933, vilified as the Ukrainian politburo by Postyshev for "counterrevolutionary nationalism," Skrypnyk would go home to his apartment in Kharkov and take his own life rather than politically recant. Corbett, "Rehabilitation of Mykola Skrypnyk."

443. Kopelev managed to transfer to Moscow University, where he did German studies. He would be expelled from the Communist Youth League for ties to Trotskyites.

444. Kopelev, *Education of a True Believer*, 11–2. See also Crossman, *God That Failed*, 43, 53 (Koestler). Kopelev's father, an agronomist, raged at him, the "editor-philosopher," who had seized starving peasants' grain. Their argument dissolved in drunken tears. Kopelev regarded his father as "a conscientious specialist, but a limited, vacillating philistine, weighed down with old Socialist Revolutionary prejudices."

445. Davies and Wheatcroft, *Years of Hunger*, 423 (citing TsDAGOU, f. 1, op. 20, d. 6275, l. 225: Kharkov, May 30, 1933).

446. Sholokhov largely blamed regional officialdom, but he also called what he saw "not individual instances of excesses," but "the 'method' of carrying out grain procurements." On July 4, 1933, the politburo would hear Shkiryatov's report on "excesses" in

Veshensk county, after which the second secretary, the plenipotentiary for grain collections, and others were transferred elsewhere, but not arrested. Danilov et al., *Tragediia sovetskoi derevni*, III: 717 (RGASPI, f. 17, op. 3, d. 2035, l. 4), 717–20 (RGASPI, f. 558, op. 11, d. 827, l. 1–22), 720–1 (f. 17, op. 3, d. 2040, l. 5–6); "Sholokhov i Stalin: perepiska nachala 30-x godov"; *Pravda*, March 10, 1964; Murin, *Pisatel' i vozhd'*, 28–58, 68, 145–7.

447. Khaustov et al., *Lubianka: Stalin i VChK*, 429–35 (APRF, f. 45, op. 1, d. 171, l. 91–101). Whereas in 1932, 3,889 "socially alien elements" were removed from the ranks, the number jumped to 22,308 in 1933. There would be more than 20,000 arrests in 1933 in the army of spies and wreckers. Suvenirov, *Tragediia RKKA*, 49–51. Stalin had told the Central Committee (May 2, 1933) that "the Russian nation is the most talented nation in the world," a long-standing theme of his, but also that "the peasant [muzhik]" had to be taught "not to oppose his interests to the state," not to live in the past, for "the old must die out." Stalin's approach to the village rested largely on his view of the Russian peasant (*muzhik*), rather than the Ukrainian peasant or Kazakh nomad. RGASPI, f. 558, op. 11, d. 1117, l. 10, 11, 14, 23.

448. On April 24, 1933, the Japanese ambassador to Moscow (Ota) inquired of Karakhan about purchasing the Chinese Eastern Railway, and on May 2 the Soviets agreed to negotiations quickly, but the Kwantung Army had no intention of buying what they could seize, the NKVD reported to Stalin. *DVP SSSR*, XVI: 831–2 n114; RGASPI, f. 558, op. 11, d. 83, l. 39. Litvinov favored a sale, to take the wind out of the sails of the pro-war party in Tokyo, while Karakhan viewed such an act as an invitation to Japanese aggressors to increase their demands; Stalin backed Litvinov. *Izvestiya*, May 1 and 12, 1933; *DVP SSSR*, XIII: 736–42, XIV: 320 (May 7, 1931), 786–9n76, 533–5, 544–8; XV: 790–1n229, 794n245; XVI: 831–2n114, 115.

449. Japanese Interior Minister Goto Shinpei had characterized the United States as "a great hypocritical monster clothed in justice and humanity." Tooze, *Deluge*, 143. Japan formally quit the League on March 27, 1933. Burkman, *Japan and the League of Nations*. Eight days before Japan withdrew, Mussolini announced a desire to create a "four-power pact" between Britain, France, Italy, and Germany to arbitrate European and world affairs in place of the League. It was classic nineteenth-century balance of power, imagining Italy as one of the powers. A diluted version amounting to nothing was signed in Rome on July 15, 1933. Jaurusch, *Four Power Pact*.

450. *International Military Tribunal for the Far East* (Tokyo: 1946–48), exhibit 193; Crowley, *Japan's Quest for Autonomy*, 185.

451. Harris, "Encircled by Enemies," 534 (citing RGVA, f. 9, op. 39/5c, l. 2–21, 76–82, 109–116).

452. RGASPI, f. 558, op. 11, d. 185, l. 97–102.

453. RGASPI, f. 558, op. 11, d. 791, l. 33–8; Kvashonkin, *Sovetskoe rukovodstvo*, 235–6 (RGASPI, f. 667, op. 1, d. 17, l. 38–9: Karakhan to Yenukidze, June 4, 1933); *DVP SSSR*, XVI: 837–8.

454. Kuznetskii [pseudonym], "Kakov smysl tokiiskikh peregovorov o prodazhe KVZhD," *Bol'shevik*, 1933, no. 14: 65–71.

455. The pair wrote disapprovingly that collective farm chairmen and county and district plenipotentiaries were being arrested "according to the rule: 'first arrest, then figure it out.'" Their directive also set an upper limit of inmates for the Union, excluding labor camps and colonies, of 400,000—half the number then imprisoned. (Another 500,000

were in camps.) Afanas'ev et al., *Istoria stalinskogo Gulaga*, I: 609. Krylenko reported (July 19, 1933) the prison population to Stalin and Molotov as 397,284, so *on paper* the objective was met, in very short order. Khlevniuk, *Master of the House*, 87 (citing GARF, f. R-5446, op. 15a, d. 1073, l. 35).

456. Goliakov, *Sbornik dokumentov po istorii ugolovnogo zakonodatel'stva SSSR*, 335–6 (May 8, 1933); Danilov et al., *Tragediia sovetskoi derevni*, III: 746–50 (RGASPI, f. 17, op. 163, d. 981, l. 229–38); Khlevniuk et al., *Stalinskoe politbiuro*, 63; Fainsod, *Smolensk under Soviet Rule*, 185–8; Krasil'nikov, *Serp i molokh*, 94–107; Khlevniuk, *History of the Gulag*, 54–82. In the military, too, arrests were being made by anyone. Suvenirov, *Tragediia RKKA*, 62. Stalin wrote in notes to himself (May 13, 1933): "(1) Who can arrest? (2) What to do about the former White military people in our economic organs? (3) decrease the prison population in a lawful way (by accelerating cassation) (what to do about quarantine) (accelerate the work of courts). (4) What to do about different groups of arrested people? (5) allow expulsion, deportation?" RGASPI, f. 558, op. 11, d. 27, l. 69. See also Béládi and Krausz, *Stalin*, 169–70.

457. RGASPI, f. 558, op. 11, d. 46, 140. "It is a small thing to win power, it is no small thing to drive out the capitalists," Kaganovich told Moscow party activists on May 22, 1933, contrasting 1917 with the Stalin revolution. "What is necessary is to destroy the root from which capitalism grows." Rees, *Iron Lazar*, 115 (citing *Partiinoe stroitel'stvo*, 1933, no. 11: 10).

458. Dolot, *Execution by Hunger*, 155.

459. A similar fate sometimes met adult interlopers: one man had his ear cut off, then his fingers put in a door and smashed; he was still alive when the farmers threw him down a well, into which they dumped dirt. Danilov et al., *Tragediia sovetskoi derevni*, III: 774 (TsA FSB, f. 2, op. 11, d. 1047, l. 212–8: July 15, 1933).

460. The politburo discontinued grain exports in April 1933, after Mikoyan, among others, lobbied Stalin to reduce them. Pavlov, *Anastas Mikoian*, 68 (citing RGASPI, f. 84, op. 2, d. 8, l. 5). Forestry exports (logs, lumber, plywood, cellulite, paper) in 1933 brought in nearly four times as much (119 million gold rubles), oil and petroleum products almost twice as much (60.4 million), and furs nearly as much (30.2 million) as grain. Total export revenues in 1933 were 388.7 million, versus 812.7 million in 1930. Even the 1933 level represented a high-water mark compared with what would follow (239.7 million in 1940). *Vneshniaia torgovlia SSSR, 1918–1966*, 18–22.

461. Davies, "Soviet Military Expenditures," 586–9, 593, 598.

462. *Pravda*, April 29, 1933; *KPSS v rezoliutsiiakh* (9th ed.), VI: 46–7; Fainsod, *Smolensk under Soviet Rule*, 221–2; Rigby, *Communist Party Membership*, 201–4; Thorniley, *Rise and Fall*, 141. Stalin had Kaganovich chair the all-Union purge commission. RGASPI, f. 17, op. 3, d. 910, l. 2. Initially, the purge targeted the provinces of Moscow, Leningrad, Urals, Donetsk, Odessa, Kiev, and Vinnitsa, as well as Belorussia and Eastern Siberia and Far Eastern regions. From May 15, 1934, it would be extended to the provinces of Gorky, Western Siberia, Azov-Black Sea, the North Caucasus, Crimea, Kharkov, Dnepropetrovsk, Chernigov, and Uzbekistan. *Partiinoe stroitel'stvo*, 1934, no. 14: 2. The seventeen remaining provinces or republics would undergo a purge during a Union-wide party card verification campaign in 1935. Iaroslavskii, "K chistke partii," 18; and Iaroslavskii, "o chistke partii"; Rigby, *Communist*

Party Membership, 52; Gill, *Origins*, 201–218; Getty, *Origins of the Great Purges*, 22, 38–48. Two previous "general" party purges had taken place (1921 and 1929).

463. Thorniley, *Rise and Fall*, 145–7; Armstrong, *Politics of Totalitarianism*, 9–10. As of Jan. 1934, the party would number 1.826 million members and 874,000 candidates, or 2.7 million total. Rigby, *Communist Party Membership*, 52.

464. Kolpakidi and Seriakov, *Shchit i mech*, 357–61 (Sept. 9, 1933). Back on Nov. 5, 1924, the politburo had formed a commission for political crimes; the commission forbade local organs from issuing sentences without Central Committee authorization. Mozokhin, *VChK-OGPU*, 130–31 (citing APRF, f. 3, op. 57, d. 73, l. 9, 23, 37, 112, 123–4, 128–9; d. 60, l. 11).

465. Katzenellenbaum, *Russian Currency and Banking*, 9.

466. Robbins, *Famine in Russia*; Simms, "Crop Failure of 1891"; Simms, "Economic Impact of the Russian Famine"; Miller, *Economic Development*, 49; Figes, *A People's Tragedy*, 158.

467. Davies and Wheatcroft, *Years of Hunger*, 412–5; Davies et al., *Economic Transformation*, 67–77.

468. At least half a million Kazakhs resettled permanently outside the republic, including 200,000 beyond Soviet frontiers. Ohayon, *La sedentarisation des Kazakhs*, 264–8; Maksudov, "Migratsii v SSSR"; Pianciola, *Stalinismo di frontiera*, 463–6; Davies and Wheatcroft, *Years of Hunger*, 408 (citing RGAE, f. 1562, op. 329, d. 143: Jan. 14, 1937); Danilov et al., *Tragediia sovetskoi derevni*, III: 420–7 (TsA FSB, f. 2, op. 11, d. 1449, l. 106–18: July 20, 1932); Cameron, "Hungry Steppe." See also Jasny, *Socialized Agriculture*, 323. The Soviet census of 1926 gave a Kazakh ASSR population of 6.2 million, of whom 3.6 million were ethnic Kazakh, some 2 million were Slavs, some 230,000 Uzbeks and 62,000 Uighurs. The 1939 census gave a figure of 1.321 million fewer ethnic Kazakhs. On this basis, one scholar estimated the catastrophe at 2 million lives lost. The local ethnic Ukrainian population in Kazakhstan declined from 859,000 to 658,000. Tatimov, *Sotsial'naia obuslovlennost' demograficheskikh protsessov*, 122–4; Abylkhozhin et al., "Kazakhstanskaia tragediia," 67. In the neighboring Kyrgyz autonomous republic, the catastrophe was less pronounced. Pianciola, *Stalinismo di frontiera*, 377–81.

469. *Sel'skoe khoiziastvo SSSR*, 517; Davies and Wheatcroft, *Years of Hunger*, 321–2; Davies et al., *Economic Transformation*, 69. Even the data supplied to Kazakh party bosses severely underestimated the losses of human and animal life, partly because of fear of reporting the truth, and partly from logistical difficulties of surveying such a vast and sparsely populated territory. Pianciola, *Stalinismo di frontiera*, 468.

470. The regime managed to begin to rebuild Kazkah herds by allowing (in Sept. 1932) *artel* collective farms to be replaced by so-called TOZ ("association for the joint cultivation of land"), in which only some land was worked in common, and most implements and all animals, including even draft animals, were held by households. Aitiev and Ishmukhamedov, *Torzhestvo leninskogo kooperativnogo plana*, 36–7. On March 29, 1933, Mirzoyan asked Stalin to purchase more livestock from western China and release more food aid (16,500 tons) for the region, to allow him to sell significant nationalized livestock back to the Kazakh herders, and to stop Uzbekistan, Siberia, and the Volga from returning Kazakhs who fled. Aldazhumanov et al.,

Nasil'stvennaia kollektivizatsiia, 220–3 (APRK, f. 141, op. 1, d. 5287, l. 33–8); Ábdiraïymŭly et al., *Golod v kazakhskoi stepi*, 196–200 (at 199). The livestock losses were still hurting agricultural productivity in 1940. In the USSR as a whole, the cattle and sheep population did not recover to the 1914 level until the late 1950s. Hunter, "Soviet Agriculture"; Millar and Nove, "Debate on Collectivization."

471. *Investigation of the Ukrainian Famine*, 424; Chamberlain, *Russia's Iron Age*, 88–9; Muggeridge, *Chronicles of Wasted Time*, 257. See also Bright-Holmes, *Like It Was*; Kravchenko, *I Chose Freedom*, 118. Thomas Walker, in a series of five articles in 1935, asserted that not crop failure but "*a planned process of extermination by Moscow*, is what caused the terrific loss of life in this district in the past year." Walker, "Children Starve." Walker offered no evidence; he purported to be an eyewitness, but visited in 1934, after the mass famine had subsided. Fischer, "Heart's Russian 'Famine'"; Tottle, *Fraud, Famine, and Fascism*, 9. See also Mace, "Man-made Famine," 86–90.

472. Ellman, "Role of Leadership Perceptions," 824. P. Blonskii, a doctor from Kiev province, wrote in a letter to the health commissar of Ukraine, which the police intercepted and excerpted, that "the politically harmful 'theory' that the starving people themselves are responsible for the famine is prevalent among leaders and rank-and-file workers; it is claimed that they did not want to work, so in that case, let them die—no pity there." Antipova et al., *Golod v SSSR*, 384–6 (TsA FSB, f. 2, op. 11, d. 56, l. 203–5).

473. Fitzpatrick, *Stalin's Peasants*, 75 (citing *Molot*, March 10, 1933); Zelenin, "Kolkhoznoe stroitel'stvo v SSSR," 28–9 (citing GARP, f. 3316, d. 815, l. 4; RGASPI, f. 17, op. 21, d. 2415, l. 1181ob.); "Kollektivizatsiia: istoki, suchnost', posledtsviia," 46–56.

474. Davies and Wheatcroft persuasively refute Ellman's assertions that Stalin intentionally starved peasants, concluding: "We regard the policy of rapid industrialisation as an underlying cause of the agricultural troubles of the early 1930s, and we do not believe that the Chinese or NEP versions of industrialisation were viable in Soviet national and international circumstances." Davies and Wheatcroft, "Reply to Ellman," 626. Robert Conquest wrote the principal book on the supposedly intentional famine—*Harvest of Sorrow* (1986)—but in a letter to Davies (Sept. 7, 2003), he acknowledged that Stalin did not intentionally cause the famine. Davies and Wheatcroft, *Years of Hunger*, 441n145. Kuromiya noted there was no evidence to support intentionality. "Stalin does not appear to have anticipated the deaths of millions of people," he concluded. "The millions of deaths de-stabilised the country politically and generated political doubt about his leadership even within the party (most famously the Ryutin Platform)." Kuromiya, "The Soviet Famine of 1932–1933 Reconsidered," 667.

475. Merl, "Entfachte Stalin die Hungersnot?"

476. For Ukraine, the initial procurement target had been 5.83 million tons (May 6, 1932), which was lowered to 5.17 million (Aug. 17, 1932), then to 4.22 million (Oct. 30, 1932), and finally to 3.77 million tons (Jan. 12, 1933); actual collections amounted to 3.59 million. Davies and Wheatcroft, *Years of Hunger*, 123, 137 (RGASPI, f. 17, op. 162, d. 11, l. 131–5), 478. For the North Caucasus, the quota was reduced overall from 2.52 to 1.59 million tons. Davies and Wheatcroft, *Years of Hunger*, 478; Davies et al., *Economic Transformation*, 290 (table 22). See also Lewin, *Making of the Soviet System* (1985), 151.

478. Tauger, "1932 Harvest," 74 (table 2).

479. Davies and Wheatcroft, "Reply to Ellman," 627–8; Gintsburg, "Massovyi golod," 124, 126.

480. One Ukrainian scholar correctly conceded that in Ukraine, ethnic Russians and Jews died in lesser proportion than ethnic Ukrainians partly because the former lived in greater proportion in cities. Kul'chyts'kyi, "Skil'ky nas zahynulo pid holodomoru 1933 roku?," 15. A decree of Dec. 14, 1932, enjoined the authorities in Soviet Ukraine "to direct serious attention to the correct implementation of Ukrainianization, eliminate a mechanical implementation, chase out Petlyura-ites and other bourgeois-nationalists elements from party and soviet organizations, thoroughly select and rear Ukrainian Bolshevik cadres, furnish systematic party leadership and control over the implementation of Ukrainianization." A follow-up decree of Dec. 26 ended Ukrainianization in the neighboring Kuban region of the RSFSR. Brian Boeck has demonstrated that Ukrainianization in the Kuban was opposed by the populace, who preferred a Cossack or Kuban identity, and by local officials. He also shows that Kaganovich seized upon, and twisted, a single report by a local official about a single Cossack settlement (Poltavskaya) that blamed supposedly successful Ukrainianization as a cause of resistance. "Thus," Boeck concludes, "there is no compelling evidence that the success of Ukrainianization, or the Central Committee's perceptions of the success of Ukrainianization, led to the decree of 14 December." Boeck, "Complicating the National Interpretation," 31–48; Pyrih et al., Holod, 291–4 (Tsentral'nyi gos. Arkhiv obshchestvennykh obedeinenii Ukrainy, f. 39, op. 4, d. 1, l. 8–10); Trapeznikov, Istoricheskii opyt KPSS, 262. A related decree was issued for Belorussia: RGASPI, f. 17, op. 3, d. 917, l. 7 (Dec. 19, 1932).

481. "In the archives of Russia, in the archives of the republics of the former USSR, millions of documents have been preserved [of] the famine in the USSR at the beginning of the 1930s of the last century in various regions of the large country," wrote V. P. Kozlov, the head of the Russian archival service, in the preface to a collection of declassified materials. "Not a single document has been found confirming the conception of a 'Holodomor-genocide' in Ukraine or even a hint in the documents about ethnic motives of what occurred, including in Ukraine." Antipova, Golod v SSSR, 6–7 (the collection consists entirely of facsimiles of original documents). Klid and Motyl define the Holodomor (or Ukrainian Holocaust) as "the murder by hunger of millions in the 1932–33 famine in Soviet Ukraine and the Kuban region of the North Caucasus, where Ukrainians formed a large percentage of the population." This becomes "genocide" when the authors include the executions of Ukrainian intellectuals, writers, poets, musicians, artists, church officials. They offer no

evidence of intentional starvation or of ethnic targeting. They do not dwell on the ethnic Ukrainian agency in the alleged genocide against Ukrainians (in regions where lots of Russians lived and died). They do not include the Volga Valley, Kazakhstan, the Urals, Western Siberia, and other famine-wracked regions where Ukrainians did not form a large percentage of the population. Klid and Motyl, Holodomor Reader, xxix–xxx.

482. Rudich, Holod 1932–1933 rokiv, 441–4 (at 443: March 15, 1933).

483. Davies and Wheatcroft, Years of Hunger, 238 (GARF, f. 5446, op. 82, d. 19, l. 66–8: Feigin, April 12, 1933).

484. RGASPI, f. 558, op. 11, d. 799, l. 24–5, 30–1; Kurliandskii, Stalin, vlast', religiia, 88–9. Stalin did not refer to "enemies" or "wreckers" in his explanations to Robins. The conversation was severely edited when originally published: Sochineniia, XIII: 260–73. See also Salzman, Reform and Revolution, 355–6. See also Postyshev's public comments about "teaching" the peasants: Izvestiia, June 22, 1933.

485. Davies et al., "Stalin, Grain Stocks, and the Famine of 1932–33," 653.

486. The threat of attack by Japan, the need for grain stockpiling, and the fact that an overwhelmed transport network had had to carry military and industrial equipment, troops, and deported kulaks to Siberia and the Soviet Far East, would be another way the regime would explain the severe domestic hardships to the party. Duranty, USSR, 190–2; Dalrymple, "Soviet Famine of 1932–1934," at 273; Stone, Hammer and Rifle, 206 (citing RGAE, op. 41, d. 33, l. 23–4: directive sent by Stalin and Molotov: March 31, 1932). RGASPI, f. 17, op. 2, d. 514, part 1, l. 9 (Stalin to CC plenum, Jan. 7, 1933); Sochineniia, XIII: 182–3. But Davies, rightly, discounts militarization and instead blames absurd plan targets. Davies, Crisis and Progress, 176ff; Davies, "Soviet Defence Industries," 266.

487. Barmine, One Who Survived, 101–2.

488. Trotskii, "Nuzhno chestnoe vnutripartiinoe soglashenie." See also Deutscher, Stalin, 352.

489. When Kaganovich demonstrated a bit of leniency toward procurements in Ukraine in Sept. 1933, Stalin rebuked him. Khlevniuk et al., Stalin i Kaganovich, 479 (RGASPI, f. 558, op. 11, d. 85, l. 44–5), 479–80 (f. 81, op. 3, d. 100, l. 76–82).

490. Additional arrests were carried out by the various grain procurement plenipotentiaries and the regular police. In Ukraine, OGPU arrests totaled 124,463 in 1933 (compared with 74,859 people in 1932); OGPU arrests in Ukraine would fall to 30,322 in 1934. Vasil'ev, "Tsena golodnogo khleba," 144. When Kaganovich demonstrated a bit of leniency toward procurements in Ukraine in Sept. 1933, Stalin rebuked him. Khlevniuk, Stalin i Kaganovich: perepiska, 479 (RGASPI, f. 558, op. 11, d. 85, l. 44–45), 479–80 (f. 81, op. 3, d. 100, l. 76–82).

491. Zelenin, "O nekotorykh 'belykh piatnakh,'" 15. The regime issued numerous decrees to provide food aid to orphaned children in the tens of thousands in Ukraine, Kazakhstan, and elsewhere. Antipova et al., Golod v SSSR, 428 (RGAE, f. 8043, op. 11, d. 74, l. 97: June 13, 1932), 487 (d. 75, l. 255; d. 61, l. 155: Aug. 20, 1933).

492. Penner, "Stalin and the Ital'ianka," 45–7 (citing RGASPI, f. 166, op. 1. d. 12, l. 4 and "Golod 1932–1933 godov na Ukraine: svidetel'stvuiut arkhivnye dokumenty," 79. See also Kondrashin and Penner, Golod, 214–5.

493. Stalin would later boast in a discussion of five historical turning points—1905, 1917, the Brest-Litovsk peace of 1918, the Russian civil war, "and especially collectivization"—that the latter entailed "a completely novel, historically unprecedented event." Banac, Diary of Georgi Dimitrov, 69 (Nov. 11, 1937).

494. The figure officially reported was 89.8 million tons (as of Oct. 1933), 20 million more than the wildly inflated 1932 official figure of 69.8 million. Davies and Wheatcroft, Years of Hunger, 446. The degree to which the regime contributed to the bumper harvest, by the distribution of tractors, seed aid, and food relief, remains a matter of intense controversy. Some of it was improvisation by local officials. Kravchenko, I Chose Freedom, 117–30. Tauger, seeking to place the Soviet story in a broader one of agricultural modernization, emphasizes how the collective farm system facilitated Soviet relief efforts and the peasants' ability to generate the harvest that saved them and the country. Tauger, "Soviet Peasants"; Tauger, "Stalin, Soviet Agriculture, and Collectivization," 109–42.

495. Famine conditions persisted into late fall 1933 and, in some places, would last through summer 1934. Ammende, Human Life in Russia, 80–4. In fall 1933, the regime was pressing for workers to cultivate gardens to grow their own food, on the example of Ukraine's Donetsk region. Pavlov, Anastas Mikoian, 71 (citing RGASPI, f. 84, op. 2, d. 19, l. 125–6). Kazakhstan would be given 18,000 tons of food aid by decree on Nov. 28, 1933. Antipova et al., Golod v SSSR, 507 (RGASPI, f. 17, op. 162, d. 15, l. 142, 145, 148).

496. Kvashonkin, Sovetskoe rukovodstvo, 240–1 (RGASPI, f. 667, op. 1, d. 16, l. 7–9); Khromov, Po stranitsam, 158. Voroshilov, too, sent a letter to Yenukidze that month, doubtless aware the OGPU perlustrated his correspondence and the contents could get to Stalin. "A remarkable man, our Koba," he wrote. "It is simply incomprehensible how he can combine the great mind of the proletarian strategist, the will of a statesman and revolutionary activist, and the soul of a completely ordinary kind comrade who bears in mind every detail and cares for everything that concerns the people he knows, loves, and values." Kvashonkin, Sovetstskoe rukovodstvo, 241–2 (RGASPI, f. 667, op. 1, d. 17, l. 5–7: Voroshilov to Yenukidze, June 29, 1933). See also Rayfield, Stalin and His Hangmen, 186.

CHAPTER 3. VICTORY

1. Lunacharskii, "Puti i zadachi sovetskoi ramaturgii," Literaturnaia gazeta, Feb. 28, 1933, retitled (and not abridged) as "Sotsialisticheskii realism," Sovetskii teatr, 1933, no. 2-3; reprinted in Lunacharskii, Sobranie sochinenii, VIII: 491–523 (at 497). Lunacharskii, in a draft text from around the same time, explained: "The socialist realist . . . may resort to all manner of hyperbole, caricature and utterly improbable comparisons, not to conceal reality but, via stylization, to reveal it." Or, as he put it, "A Communist who cannot dream is a bad

Communist," Lunacharskii, Sobranie sochinenii, VIII: 615–6: RGASPI, f. 142, op. 1, d. 318, l. 15–21, Feb. 10, 1933. See also Louis Fisher, in Crossman, God that Failed, 205–6.

2. Hunter, "Optimal Tautness in Development Planning"; Hunter, "First Soviet Five-Year Plan"; Cheremukhin et al., "Was Stalin Really Necessary?"

3. Instead of an anticipated 5.426 billion gold rubles of revenue from all exports (grain, timber, oil) over the course of the Five-Year Plan, the Soviets managed to bring in 3.283 billion. Industry was short 1.873 million rubles,

including 832 million just in 1932. The Soviets ran out of convertible currency even for purchases of foreign military technology. Kondrashin et al., Golod v SSSR, I/i: 46 (citing RGAE, f. 1562, op. 329, d. 4, l. 2–4). A key source of foreign currency revenue were the shops designed for "trade with foreigners" (Torgsin), which in fact placed no restrictions on who could enter and buy and sell: around 80 percent of their trade involved Soviet inhabitants. In 1933, during the worst of the famine, Torgsin stores had their best year, expanding deeply across the countryside to

sell flour, cooking oil, and sugar for the population's valuables. That year, family-heirloom revenue exceeded foreign grain sale revenues. After 1933, with the population's closets tapped out, Torgsin revenues declined. Still, sales from 1932 until the shops were closed in early 1936 totaled 287.2 million, which paid for imports for Magnitorgorsk worth 44 million rubles; Gorky Auto Plant, 42.3 million; Stalingrad Tractor, 25 million rubles; Stalin Auto factory, 27.9 million rubles; Cheliabinsk Tractor, 23 million; Kharkov Tractor, 15.3 million; and Uralmash, 15 million. Aizenberg, *Valiutnaia sistema SSSR*, 65; Osokina, *Zoloto dlia industrializatsii.*
4. Robert Allen argues that per capita consumption, after falling in the early 1930s, increased significantly, being perhaps a fifth higher in 1937 than a decade earlier, but he has rightly been taken to task separately by Davies and Ellman. Allen, *Farm to Factory*, 147–50, 185–6; R. W. Davies (http://eh.net /book_reviews/farm-to-factory-a-reinterpretation-of-the-soviet-industrial-revolution); Ellman, "Soviet Industrialization."
5. Millar, "Mass Collectivization"; Barsov, *Baslans stoimostnykh obmenov*; Ellman, "Agricultural Surplus"; Davies et al., *Economic Transformation*, 11–3. See also Barsov, "NEP i vyravnivanie ekonomicheskikh otnoshenii," 93–102. Even a Stalinist publication, with exaggerated figures, admitted that industrial exports constituted the primary source of export revenues during the Five-Year Plan (2 billion of 3.5 billion gold rubles total). From 1932, all Soviet exports declined in physical terms, not just in revenue, but agricultural exports declined faster than industrial ones. Ginzburg, *Vneshniaia torgovlia SSSR*, 67, 72. Prices changed favorably toward agriculture, when one takes into consideration more than grain and the legalized markets for selling "surpluses."
6. E. H. Carr, writing in the wake of the Soviet Union's World War II victory, concluded that Stalin's collectivization and industrialization "were imposed by the objective situation which Soviet Russia in the later 1920s had to face." Well, yes, *if* Bolshevik monopoly and anticapitalism were to be retained. There are multiple ways to modernize, but not multiple ways to modernize *without* the rule of law, political pluralism, private property, and the market. Carr, "Stalin Victorious." In later years, Carr's position shifted slightly. Davies, Introduction to *Russian Revolution*, xxxiv–xxxv; Nove, "The Peasants," at 389. See also Gnedin, *Vykhod iz labirinta*, 54.
7. As Alec Nove pointed out, something is a necessity, although not inevitable, if it follows logically from the objective circumstances *and the values* of the decision maker(s). Nove, "Was Stalin Really Necessary?" reprinted in Nove, *Was Stalin Really Necessary?*, 17–39; Grossman, *Review*. See also Millar and Nove, "Debate on Collectivization"; and Brown and Cairncross, "Alec Nove." The otherwise trenchant Millar incorrectly averred that collectivization was "an unmitigated policy disaster," failing to distinguish between economic and political outcome. See Swianiewicz, *Forced Labor*, 91.
8. Maksimenkov, *Sumbur*, 52. Another scholar has asserted that Stalin spent as much time on culture as foreign policy and military affairs. Gromov, *Stalin*, 6. On formalization of Stalin's role in culture, see Khlevniuk, *Stalinskoe politbiuro*, 112–3 (RGASPI, f. 17, op. 113 d. 818, l. 10), 141, 143; Khlevniuk, *Politbiuro*, 67, 112.
9. Trotsky, *Literature and Revolution*, 218.
10. Trotsky supported establishment of a nonparty literary journal to focus and multiply their efforts in favorable directions, and

proposed that the censorship organ, Glavlit, compile a register of artists, in order to track them. Artizov and Naumov, *Vlast'*, 36–7 (APRF, f. 3, op. 34, d. 185, l. 8–10: June 30, 1922).
11. *Pravda*, July 1, 1925; RGASPI, f. 17, op. 3, d. 506, l. 4, 31–7: June 18, 125; Kemp-Welch, *Stalin and the Literary Intelligentsia*, 21–67 (esp. 34); *Literaturnoe nasledstvo*, vol. 74 (Moscow: Nauka, 1965): 29–37; Ermakov, 376–7.
12. RGASPI, f. 17, op. 3, d. 633, l. 3–4: May 5, 1927; Artizov and Naumov, *Vlast'*, 84 (RGASPI, f. 17, op. 3, d. 697, l. 10). Non-party though it might have been, the weekly *Literaturnaya gazeta* was going to be overseen by the apparatus.
13. See also Fitzpatrick, *Cultural Front*, 145.
14. One scholar observed that "writers embroiled in controversy sought to use Stalin against their adversaries and were therefore themselves to some extent responsible for establishing the pattern of authoritarian control." Brown, "Year of Acquiescence," 57.
15. Krivenko, "Solovetskii ITL OGPU." In April 1930, the OGPU system was organized under a "Main Administration of Camps"—in Russian "Gulag," a bureaucratic moniker that soon changed but would stick in popular reference. Carr and Davies, *Foundations of a Planned Economy*, II: 359–60, 373; Wheatcroft, "Assessing the Size," at 287; Ivanova, *Gulag*; Upadyshev, "Ot Solovkov k GULAGu," 93; Kokurin and Petrov, "OGPU, 1929–1934 gg.," 100. The Main Administration of Construction of the Far North, centered in Magadan, lasted from 1931 to 1957; and the Karaganda Camp Complex, which at its height would reach 80 camps, lasted from 1931 to 1959. Kokurin and Petrov, *Gulag*; Krivenko, "Karagandinskii ITL"; Sigachev, "Glavnoe upravlenie stroitel'stva Dal'nego Severa"; Krivenko, "Belomoro-Baltiiskii ITL."
16. Solzhenitsyn would dub Dalstroi "the greatest and most famous island, the pole of ferocity of that amazing country of Gulag." Solzhenitsyn, *Gulag Archipelago*, I: ix. See also Kokurin and Petrov, *Gulag*, 72 (RGASPI, f. 17, op. 162, d. 11, l. 57, 63).
17. That year 9,928 of the approximately 16,000 prisoners reached Magadan alive; in 1933, 27,390 would survive the journey. Subsequently, 32,304 would survive the journey in 1934; 44,601 in 1935; and 62,703 in 1936—a labor force. About 20 percent of the workers were not prisoners. Stephan, *Russian Far East*, 225–32. Reported gold extraction rose from 511 kilograms of pure gold in 1932 to 5,515 kilograms in 1934; 14,458 kg in 1935; and 33,360 kg in 1936. Total gold mining across the entire Soviet Union had been 13,215 kg in 1928. Nordlander, "Economic History of Dalstroi," 105–25.
18. Aizenberg, *Valiutnaia sistema SSSR*, 64; Davies, *Crisis and Progress*, 162–3 (citing GARF, f. 5446, op. 57, d. 18, l. 85–95: art. 234/45s, 138–9: art. 372/79ss). Roy Medvedev wrote that "there existed a system of examinations which allowed ten-year sentences to be reduced to two or three years, excellent food and clothing, a workday of four to six hours in winter and ten in summer, and good pay, which enabled prisoners to help their families and to return home with funds." Medvedev, *Let History Judge*, 508. See also Shalamov, *Kolyma Tales*, 368–9.
19. Swianiewicz, *Forced Labor*. There were instances when Gulag labor was more productive than "free" labor.
20. Vinogradov, *Genrikh Iagoda*, 363–4 (TsA FSB, f. 2, op. 11, d. 4, l. 58: Yagoda to Mężyński, June 27, 1933). See also *Izvestiia*, June 26, 1933; *Pravda*, June 29, 1933; and *Leningradskaia pravda*, June 23, 27, and 29, 1933.

Stalin had rescued the canal from Rykov's cost-cutting. Lih et al., *Stalin's Letters to Molotov*, 212. The Suez Canal, 117 miles long, was built in 15 years, without locks; the Panama Canal, 48 miles long, was built in 33 years, with locks.
21. Pazi, *Nash Mironych*, 447. Kirov first took a test drive to Moscow, with a single guard, to see if the route was safe, then did the trip again, to pick up the passengers. Lenoe, *Kirov Murder*, 406 (citing RGANI, f. 6, op. 13, d. 73, l. 96–132: Sveshnikov, 1966).
22. Stalin and Kirov likely first met in Oct. 1917, at the 2nd Congress of Soviets that had proclaimed a seizure of power (Kirov was a delegate of the Vladikavkaz-Kabardinya soviet). Their relationship is documented from May 29, 1918, when Stalin recommended Kirov as worthy of "complete trust." Plimak and Antonov, "1 dekabria 1934–go," 35.
23. RGASPI, f. 558, op. 11, d. 149, l. 70 (March 6, 1929).
24. RGASPI, f. 558, op. 1, d. 4554; *Sochineniia*, VI: 422.
25. In late 1929, during the party purge, several targeted Leningrad officials fought back, demanding Kirov be sacked for prerevolutionary work on behalf of what they called a "Cadet" (bourgeois-liberal) newspaper: Kirov's signed articles—which his attackers dug up in the public library—had welcomed the Provisional Government. Orjonikidze defended Kirov, divulging that Stalin himself, at *Pravda*, had not been anti-Provisional Government in early 1917. Kirov's denouncers were removed, but Stalin had Kirov's prerevolutionary political "error" recorded in his party file. Khlevniuk, *Politbiuro*, 120 (citing RGASPI, f. 17, op. 162, d. 8, l. 24–5: Dec. 11, 1929); Khlevniuk, *Stalin i Orzhonikidze*, 19–20; Khlevniuk, *In Stalin's Shadow*, 26–9; Rosliakov, *Ubiistvo*, 108–10; Lenoe, *Kirov Murder*, 93–106. See also Ciliga, *Russian Enigma*, 120–1; and Tokaev, *Betrayal of an Ideal*, 109, 241.
26. Vladimir Loginov, *Teni Stalina*, 97. Artyom concurred: "Kirov after Nadezhda Sergeevna was the closest person to Stalin." Sergeev and Glushik, *Besedy o Staline*, 59–60.
27. Molotov also noted of Kirov: "He was a weak organizer. He was a good mass agitator." He dismissed the notions that Stalin could have killed Kirov ("odiousness") or that Kirov could have taken Stalin's place. ("Absurd! . . . look, pretty speeches of a secondary character. That was not enough.") Chuev, *Molotov*, 377.
28. Kirov won the Order of Lenin (March 31, 1931) for helping fulfill the oil industry five-year plan in 2.5 years.
29. Sergeev and Glushik, *Besedy o Staline*, 71–3.
30. Chukhin, *Kanaloarmeitsy*, 18 (no citation).
31. The canal laborers gave their name ("zek" or *zakliuchennyi kanalstroia*) to all Gulag prisoners. Chukhin, *Kanaloarmeitsy*, 189–209. Yagoda built a large number of critical objects, from the country's first-ever stadium (Dynamo) in Moscow to new administrative buildings for the NKVD itself.
32. Murin, *Stalin v ob"iatiiakh*, 44 (RGASPI, f. 558, op. 11, d. 1552, l. 19).
33. Aug. 27, 1933.
34. Chigirin, *Stalin*, 84–5 (RGASPI, f. 558, op. 11, d. 1482, l. 53: Aug. 25 to Sept. 2, 1933).
35. Kvashonkin, *Sovetskoe rukovodstvo*, 249–52 (RGASPI, f. 667, op. 1, d. 16, l. 8–12: Aug. 27, 1933), 252–3 (f. 74, op. 2, d. 41, l. 63–71: Aug. 30), 253–4 (l. 72–3: Sept. 7). See also Kvashonkin, *Sovetskoe rukovodstvo*, 255 n1 (RGASPI, f. 74, op. 2, d. 41, l. 74; GARF, f. R-3316, op. 1, 3d. 18, l. 168).
36. RGASPI, f. 558, op. 11, d. 80, l. 68.

37. In summer 1931, the first high-frequency phone lines were installed between Moscow and Leningrad and Moscow and Kharkov. The scramblers and encrypters were purchased in Germany from Siemens and Halske AG and AEG, copied and adapted. Moscow would soon be connected to Smolensk and Minsk (1932), Gorky and Rostov (1933), Kiev (1934). Other systems grew in parallel: the Kremlin self-dialing ATC ("vertushka"); the NKVD state security first directorate (bodyguard) telephone station; etc.

38. *Na prieme*, 107–12.

39. Khlevniuk et al., *Stalin i Kaganovich*, 330 (RGASPI, f. 558, op. 11, d. 80, l. 87).

40. Khlevniuk et al., *Stalin i Kaganovich*, 315 (RGASPI, f. 558, op. 11, d. 741, l. 7–12: Aug. 26, 1933), 319 (f. 81, op. 3, d. 100, l. 107–8: Aug. 29), 323 (f. 558, op. 11, d. 80, l. 66: Sept. 1), 325–7 (d. 741, l. 20–6: Sept. 2); Rees, *Iron Lazar*, 119 (citing RGASPI, f. 54, op. 1, d. 100, l. 107–8); Kosheleva, *Pis'ma Stalina Molotovu*, 248–9 (Sept. 12, 1933), 247–8n2 (RGASPI, f. 17, op. 3, d. 929, l. 21; d. 930, l. 13); Lih et al., *Stalin's Letters to Molotov*, 234–5, 233n2; Kvashonkin, *Sovetskoe rukovodstvo*, 261–3 (RGASPI, f. 85, op. 27, d. 214, l. 25–30: Sept. 30); Khlevniuk et al., *Stalinskoe politbiuro*, 133; Davies et al., "The Politburo and Economic Decision Making," 110.

41. The dacha had been constructed in 1932–33 in a mad rush (the construction director, from the central executive committee of Abkhazia, begged for more labor power). Lakoba Papers, Hoover Institution Archives, 1–65. Lakoba, Yenukidze, his deputy N. I. Pakhomov, and Pauker conducted a final inspection in early July 1933.

42. Imperial Russia had annexed the Black Sea territory from Istanbul in 1864, which provoked a mass exodus to the Ottoman empire and a mass influx of settlers, especially Mingrelians from adjacent western Georgia, ethnic Georgians, Russians, and Armenians. The Abkhaz language belongs to a North Caucasus language group unrelated to Georgian or Russian, and the differences were strongly felt. Ethnic Abkhaz became concentrated in three districts: Gudauta, Kodor, and Samurzakan, while non-Abkhaz made up 90 percent of Abkhazia's other districts. Voronov, *Abkhazia*." See also Tardy, "Caucasus Peoples."

43. Dzidzariia et al., *Revoliutsionnye komitety Abkhazii*, 253. See also Pritsker, *Istoriia kurortov Abkhazskoi SSR*; Orynianskii, *Sovetskaia Abkhaziia*; Grigoliia, *Kurortnye bogatsva Abkhazii*; Abkhazia had perhaps 150 available beds for patients and holiday-makers in 1922, which jumped to 3,680 by 1935, under Lakoba's construction. Around 300 people took advantage in 1922, and 16,755 by 1935.

44. Tulumdzhian, *S'ezdy Sovetov Abkhazii*.

45. A party commission went after Lakoba, citing "the presence in the Abkhazia organization of elements of factionalism, degeneration, 'private property-ism,' nepotism and group cohesion reaching toadyism." Stalin, vacationing on the Black Sea, got dragged into the intrigues and, in a letter co-signed by Orjonikidze (Oct. 19, 1929), faulted Lakoba for "sometimes not subordinating himself to the decisions of the provincial party committee." The mild rebuke protected Lakoba from worse. Hoover Institution Archives, Lakoba Papers, box 1, folder 55, 56; Blauvelt, "Abkhazia Patronage," 214 (citing Partarkhiv TsK KPG, f. 14, op. 7, d. 3516, l. 1–3).

46. Rikhter, *Kavkaz nashikh dnei*, 98; Blauvelt, "'From Words to Action!,'" 243–4 (citing sakartvelos shss arkivi [II], f. 14, op. 2, d. 485, 49–56).

47. "When Stalin and I were there," Orjonikidze had noted, "Comrade Lakoba made the best impressions of all the comrades present." Lakoba, "'Ia Koba, a ty Lakoba,'" 58 (1925). See also Hoover Archives, Lakoba papers, 1–25, 1–26; and Kvashonkin, *Bolshevistskoe rukovodstvo*, 338–41.

48. Trotskii, "Yenukidze" [Jan. 8, 1938], in *Portrety*, 251–72 (at 264–6). "My ears hold me back, but so what," Lakoba had written to Orjonikidze (March 12, 1922). Kvashonkin, *Bolshevistskoe rukovodstvo*, 237–8.

49. Khrushchev, *Memoirs*, I: 188–9. Lakoba has only a single recorded listing in Stalin's office logbook, Nov. 20, 1933, and for just twenty minutes. *Na prieme*, 114.

50. Sergeev and Glushik, *Besedy o Staline*, 76–7. In 1929, a Lakoba confidant wrote to the Abkhaz leader that "being in Sochi I saw Stalin at the central executive committee rest house, and he asked the whole time, where are you, are you coming, Long Live Abkhazia and sang Abkhaz songs." Lakoba, "'Ia Koba, a ty Lakoba,'" 59–60 (Ladariya).

51. "Autobiography, December 12, 1936," Hoover Archives, Lakoba papers, box 1, item 2; Bgazhba, *Nestor Lakoba*; Argun, *Stalin i Lakoba*; Lakoba, "History: 1917–1989," 89–101.

52. Whereas Georgia was undergoing vigorous Georgification, the ratio of ethnic Abkhaz in the enclave's population of 146,000 had fallen, to under 30 percent in 1926 (from 55 percent as late as 1897). By 1939, the Abkhaz share would shrink to 18 percent. By comparison, the Ajarians, a Muslim people in Georgia, accounted for around 70 percent in Ajaristan, an autonomous republic in Georgia. The penurious Abkhaz administration issued circulars in three languages (Abkhaz, Georgian, Russian). Sagariia, *Natsional'noe stroitel'stvo v Abkhazii*, 115; Agrba, *Abkhazskaia oblastnaia organizatsiia kompartii Gruzii v tsifrakh*; Partarkhiv Abkhazskogo obkoma KP Gruzii, f. 1, op. 1, d. 180, l. 95–6: Lakoba at 7th province party conference. Abkhaz were almost never accepted at Georgia's institutions of higher learning (where the instruction was solely in Georgian). Hoover Archives, Lakoba papers, 2–42.

53. A few days after the letter to Lenin and Stalin (dated March 26, 1921), Lakoba was one of three people to sign a telegram addressed to Lenin, Stalin, Chicherin, Kirov, all Soviet republics, the whole world, proclaiming the new Abkhaz Soviet Socialist Republic, which Lenin approved, and on May 21, 1921, the Georgian SSR signed an agreement recognizing the separate Abkhaz SSR. But on Dec. 16, 1921, under pressure, the Abkhaz signed a treaty with Georgia providing for a confederal structure. Sagariia, "K istorii obrazovaniia Abkhazskoi avtonomnoi respubliki"; *Bor'ba za uprochenie Sovetskoi vlasti v Gruzii*, 58–9 (Gosarkhiv Abkhazskoi SSR, f. 38, d. 74, l. 176). *Golos trudovoi Abkhazii*, 1921, no. 134, reprinted in *Bor'ba za uprochenie Sovetskoi vlasti v Gruzii*, 80; Sagariia, *Natsional'noe stroitel'stvo v Abkhazii*, 142–6.

54. A partial census in 1920 had listed 55 nations, but the 1926 census allowed for 190; in the 1930s, the number would fall to around three score, then climb to 106 (1937 census). Hirsch, *Empire of Nations*, 284, 327–30.

55. If a nation got a Union republic, members of that nation who lived outside it—Russians in Ukraine, Tajiks in Uzbekistan—did not receive an autonomous republic there. In an exception, there was a predominantly ethnic Armenian autonomous republic in Azerbaijan, Karabakh ("Black Mountain"). Armenians there had sought inclusion in Armenia. RGASPI, f. 558, op. 11, d. 133, l. 28–31.

56. Haugen, *Establishment*, 195–7 (citing RGASPI, f. 82, op. 2, d. 87, l. 73–6; d. 101,

68–9, 76; d. 107, 29, 55, d. 104, l. 165; GARF, f. 1235, op. 26, d. 28, l. 4). See also Aworth, *Modern Uzbeks*; Haugen, *Establishment*, 206–10. Uzbekistan also got Tashkent, which the Kazakhs had wanted despite its population of 96,000 Uzbeks and 172 Kazakhs, because they insisted it was surrounded by Kazakh nomads who needed a city to rise out of backwardness. Fedtke, "How Bukharans Turned into Uzbeks and Tajiks," 19–50; Slezkine, "USSR as a Communal Apartment," 428; Fainsod, *Smolensk under Soviet Rule*, 452; RGASPI, f. 17, op. 3, d. 776, l. 1.

57. Soviet Uzbekistan accounted for 60 percent of Central Asia's arable lands and perhaps 70 percent of its GDP. But in carving out Tajikistan, Stalin perhaps wanted to blunt a too strong Uzbek entity, stabilize the border with Afghanistan, and curry favor with Iran. Berge, *Birth of Tajikistan*; Hirsch, *Empire of Nations*, 174–86. The Tajiks were shunted into the Pamirs: some 90 percent of Tajikistan's landmass consisted of high mountains, and its "capital" was the village of Dushanbe, which was renamed Stalinabad. Perhaps 60 percent of Soviet Tajiks ended up outside the Tajik republic. Iurkevich, *U vorot Indostana*, 16. See also Teichman, "Red Man's Burden," 177 (citing RGASPI, f. 62, op. 2, d. 2542, l. 155–7); and Teichman, "Canals, Cotton." On the occasion of Tajikistan's inaugural party congress, in June 1930, the Tajik party boss, Mirza Davud Huseynov, an ethnic Azeri, proposed sending greetings to the toilers of India, but Stalin objected, evidently concerned not to raise outcries of interference in British India. RGASPI, f. 558, op. 11, d. 63, l. 58. See also Baberowski, *Der Feind*, 230–5, 279–82, 620; Kangas, "Faizulla Khodzhaev"; and Norling, "Myth and Reality," 114 (citing RGASPI, f. 82, op. 2, d. 154, l. 79–92: Jan. 25, 1931).

58. There had been more than 26,000 mosques in Turkestan in 1912 under the tsarist regime, but there would be a mere 1,300 by 1942. The remnants of the Islamic legal and educational systems would be closed down, as were most of the places where mullahs were trained. Between 1927 and 1930 local alphabets were changed from Arabic script to Latin (as was done in Turkey), which cut future generations from the past and the Quran. The pilgrimage to Mecca would be prohibited from 1935. Later the regime would shift the languages to Cyrillic. Gatagova et al., *TsK RKP (b)—VKP (b) i natsional'nyi vopros*, II: 128–9 (RGASPI, f. 17, op. 114, d. 588, l. 3, 4), 191–6 (d. 751, l. 38–47; d. 607, l. 4–5).

59. Wohlforth, "Russian-Soviet Empire," 225. The success of the coercive Soviet project is all the more remarkable when one examines the depth of the challenges faced by national activists in mixed-language regions. Judson, *Guardians of the Nation*.

60. This was where the peasantry in Abkhazia had been most receptive to original Bolshevik revolutionary demands for radical land reform against local nobles. Dzidzariia, *Ocherki istorii Abkhazii*, 62–6, 108–9.

61. The status change was formally approved at the 6th Congress of Soviets of Abkhazia on Feb. 11, 1931, although it had not been included on the agenda. Dzhonua et al., *Sovety Abkhazii*, 227–8; Sagariia, *Natsional'noe stroitel'stvo v Abkhazii*, 142–6.

62. Blauvelt, "Abkhazia Patronage," 227–8 (citing Arkhiv TsK KPG, f. 14, op. 6, d. 267: "Informsvodki Abkhaz. GPU: dokladnaia zapiska raikoma o rukovodstve obkoma vo antosovetskikh vystupleniakh krest'ian v Gudautskom raione, 177–9).

63. Mamiya Orakhelashvili and Beria arrived, but peasant delegations insisted on speaking to Lakoba. They wanted permission to emigrate to Turkey, like many of their

nineteenth-century forebears. Blauvelt, "Abkhazia Patronage," 227 (citing secret police reports). Danilov, "Tragediia Abkhazskogo naroda."

64. Ethnic Russians, who constituted just 10 percent of Abkhazia's population in the early 1930s, accounted for more than 40 percent of the local apparatus, versus around 9 percent ethnic Abkhaz. Lakoba also got the apparatus in Moscow to renew calls for indigenization of Abkhazia's apparatus. But the ongoing party purges pushed in the opposite direction. Sagariia, *Natsional'noe stroitel'stvo v Abkhazii*, 132 (citing TsGAA f. 1, op. 2, d. 300, l. 3-4).

65. Beria denounced the Feb. 1931 Abkhaz "demonstration" to Stalin, suggesting that Lakoba had encouraged the peasants to rebel and that Lakoba's mother had stood in the front, so the secret police troops could not shoot. Lakoba, "'Ia Koba, a ty Lakoba,'" 58.

66. Beria's mother, Marta Jakeli, and her second husband, Pavel Beria, had two other children: Lavrenti's elder brother died at age two of smallpox; his sister Akesha, or Anna (b. 1905), was rendered a deaf mute by childhood measles. His father died when Lavrenti was school age and, like Stalin, Beria was raised by his mother, who, like Keke, had ambitions for her boy. (She would later marry a Georgian Jew, Levan Loladze.) At age sixteen, Beria left for the oil boomtown Baku and enrolled in its high school for mechanical-building studies, spending a summer working for Alfred Nobel's concern. Reliable material on Beria's biography is scant. See Danilov, "K biografii L. Beriia"; Popov and Oppokov, "Berievshchina" (1989, no. 5), 39n1 (citing Chekryzhev), (1990, no. 1), 70-2. See also Popov and Oppokov, "Berievshchina"(1990, no. 3): 81-2; ("Berievshchina" was reprinted in Nekrasov, *Beria*, 300-80); "O sud'be chlenov i kandidatov v chleny TsK VKP (b), izbrannogo XVII s"ezdom partii," 82-113: 88. See also Popov and Oppokov, "Berievshchina," no. 3 (1990): 81-2; RGASPI, f. 5, op. 15, d. 448, l. 246-8.

67. Beria's arrests, releases, and rearrests remain murky. Popov and Oppokov, "Berievshchina," no. 1 (1990): 77-8; Toptygin, *Lavrentii Beriia*, 11; Kazarmzadeh, *Struggle for Transcaucasia*, 307-9; Mlechin, *KGB*, 176; Sokolov, *Beriia*, 31-2.

68. RGASPI, f. 85, op. 29, d. 414, l. 3 (Beria letter to Orjonikidze); "Ochen' vysoko tsenit t. Beria," 163-5 (APRF, f. 45, op. 1, d. 788, l. 114-50b; RGASPI, f. 558, op. 11, d. 788, l. 114-16ob, Pavlunovsky to Stalin, June 25, 1937); *Zaria vostoka*, Nov. 15, 1931. Ruhulla Akhundov, a former Left SR and a Baku Communist party official, attended the late-1920 discussion of Beria's Musavat past. "He has outstanding abilities, as demonstrated in various apparatuses of the state mechanism," Akhundov wrote of Beria in 1923, calling the results-oriented functionary "so necessary at this moment of Soviet construction." Zen'kovich, *Marshaly i genseki*, 161.

69. That same month, April 1921, Beria married the sixteen-year-old upper-class Georgian Nino Gegechkori, whose uncle had been a member of the tsarist State Duma and foreign minister in the overturned Georgian Menshevik government. The pair may have met in prison, when Nino and her mother came to visit her Bolshevik father, Alexander Gegechkori, who had been arrested and held along with Beria in the Kutaisi prison. Nino went on to graduate university in economics. Sokolov, *Beriia*, 40-2. See also Dumbadze, *Na sluzhbe cheka i kominterna*, 93 Beria's patron Bagirov was expelled from the party for torture, oppressing national minorities (Armenians, Russians), and bribe-taking. He was sacked from the secret police in May 1927 for "exceeding his authority, intrigues, and using

the organs against the party." But Stalin, writing to Molotov in 1929, decided that "Bagirov (despite his past sins) will have to be confirmed as chairman of the Cheka in Azerbaijan: he is now the only person who can cope with the Musavatists and Ittikhadists who have reared their heads in the Azerbaijan countryside. This is serious business, and there should be no fooling around." Lih et al., *Stalin's Letters to Molotov*, 168. See also "Iz otchetov komiteta partiinogo kontrolia pri TsK KPSS o partiinoi reabilitatsii kommunistov v 50-kh-nachale 60-kh gg.," 47; and RGASPI, f. 613, op. 1, d. 90, l. 47. In 1930, Bagirov would be brought to Moscow to study Marxism-Leninism for twenty-four months. *Zaria vostoka*, Dec. 15, 1933; Knight, *Beria*, 39. In Oct. 1932, Bagirov was returned to Azerbaijan as chairman of the republic's Council of People's Commissars, and in Dec. 1933 he became party boss of Azerbaijan. Khlevniuk et al., *Stalin i Kaganovich*, 396n2; RGASPI, f. 17, op. 3, d. 935, l. 2, 32-4. Bagirov occupied the mansion of the former Baku agent of the Rothschilds.

70. Iusif-Zade, *Chekisty Azerbaidzhana*, 26, 31-57. Mikhail Kedrov, head of a traveling commission on secret police abuses, relayed a damning report on Beria to Dzierżyński, who in Dec. 1921 issued an arrest order. Beria desperately appealed to the local top man, Orjonikidze, arguing that Kedrov did not understand Baku's rough conditions. Orjonikidze supposedly later told a secretary that upon learning of Beria's service in Musavat counterintelligence, Dzierżyński wanted to execute him, but that Orjonikidze interceded to save Beria's life. In another version, the son of the arresting officer claimed Stalin telephoned Dzierżyński and vouched for Beria, citing the word of Mikoyan. Whatever the cause, Dzierżyński countermanded the warrant. Berezin, "Istoriia ordera na arrest Berii," 195-6 (recollections of the son of Yan Berezin); Agabekov, *G.P.U.*, 170; Leggett, *Cheka*, 270-1. Khaustov and Samuelson, *Stalin, NKVD*, 134 (citing TsA FSB, ASD P-771, l. 5, testimony of Orjonikidze's secretary). All the paperwork would later disappear from Dzierżyński's files except a document indicating that there had been paperwork. Plekhanov, *VChK-OGPU*, 168-9. On June 27, 1922, Kirov, then party boss in Azerbaijan, directed him to cease police surveillance on Bolshevik officials. (Beria wrote back denying any involvement.) Popov and Oppokov, "Berievshchina" (1990, no. 1): 68. A denunciation of Beria in the later 1920s accused him of surrounding himself with dubious types. Plekhanov, *VChK-OGPU*, 236 (TsA FSB, f. 2, op. 8, d. 9, l. 78-85).

71. In Sept. 1929, after a torrent of complaints, Orjonikidze had sent in a Central Control Commission team. Beria once again begged to be relieved of his post and allowed to resume his studies. "Time passes, all around people are growing, developing, and those who yesterday were far behind me today moved ahead," Beria noted. "My backwardness is painful and humiliating, the more so when one knows that the country now needs people with expertise . . . Dear Sergo, I implore you to take me from the Caucasus and, if I cannot be sent to study, then transfer me to different work in one of the regions of the USSR . . . After all, I cannot argue with everyone for my lifetime, it will ruin my nerves." But Orjonikidze blocked the Georgian push for disciplinary action against Beria in spring 1930. Toptygin, *Nezivestnyi Beriia*, 27-8; Knight, *Beria*, 39-40 (citing RGASPI, f. 85, op. 27, d. 71, l. 1-6); Plekhanov, *VChK-OGPU*, 236 (TsA FSB, f. 2, op. 8, d. 9, l. 78-85).

72. In 1925, a Junkers airplane en route to Sukhum had caught fire and crashed near the

Tiflis aerodrome, killing the chairman of the South Caucasus Council of People's Commissars and another high government official as well as Mogilevsky. *Trudovaia Abkhazia*, March 25, 1925; *Biulleten' oppozitsii* (Jan. 1939): 2-15. Beria transformed an obituary for Mogilevsky into a self-tribute. Antonov-Ovseenko, *Beriia*, 31.

73. Popov and Popokov, "Berievshchina," 1989, no. 5: 40. Orjonikidze had told Pavlunovsky that "he rated the work of Beria as a growing functionary very highly, and that Comrade Beria would develop into a big-time functionary." "Ochen' vysoko tsenit t. Beria," 163-5 (APRF, f. 45, op. 1, d. 788, l. 114-50b; RGASPI, f. 558, op. 11, d. 788, l. 114-16ob, June 25, 1937).

74. Rubin, *Lavrentii Beriia*, 57-8.

75. Whether Beria set Redens up remains unknown (Redens had a well-known weakness for the bottle and women). Tumshis, *VChK: voina klanov*, 207-8; Knight, *Beria*, 43-4 (citing Merkulov: RGANI, f. 5, op. 30, d. 4, l. 86). "In the GPU apparat whole legends circulated about [Beria]," the operative Agabekov wrote at the time. Traveling with Beria for three days in a train in 1928, he found Beria "more interested in Tiflis street happenings than events of all-Union significance." Agabekov, *G.P.U.*, 169-70; Agabekov, *OGPU*, 159.

76. Popov and Oppokov, "Berievshchina," 1990, no. 5: 86-7; Nekrasov, *Beria*, 354; Rubin, *Lavrentii Beriia*, 63-4. Beria or someone on his behalf spread rumors he was destined for promotion to a big job in Moscow. Popov and Oppokov, "Berievshchina" (1989, no. 7), 85; Tumshis, *VChK: voina klanov*, 204-5. See also Smyr, *Islam v Abkhazii*, 148-51.

77. Beria had been cultivating Lakoba for some time, sending him gifts, but at the same time, filth spread about Lakoba—his halfbrother Mikhail received a horse ("bribe") when he brokered peace between families after a murder; his mother got 7,000 bricks for a two-story house ("palace")—which bore the mark of Beria's minions. Hoover Archives, Lakoba papers, 1-392-35. Lakoba's compound in Sukhum—a two-story brick villa, with two balconies, built by an Armenian magnate—took up a full city block in the finest neighborhood. Everyone had a room, including the governess, like prerevolutionary nobility.

78. "A few days ago members of the South Caucasus regional committee, secretaries of the Georgian central committee, and several Azerbaijani functionaries . . . visited me," Stalin wrote to Kaganovich. "They are embroiled in unbelievable infighting, and it seems to me a long way from over." He directed Kaganovich to schedule an orgburo meeting. On Sept. 10, Kaganovich acceded to the Caucasus comrades who wanted Samson Mamuliya removed as Georgian party boss and replaced by Kartvelishvili (who would last only until Nov. 14). On Oct. 31, the politburo, following an orgburo meeting, passed a resolution on the "unprincipled struggle of certain individuals for influence (elements of 'ataman-ism')." Khlevniuk et al., *Stalin i Kaganovich*, 68-9 (RGASPI, f. 81, op. 3, d. 99, l. 7-11: Aug. 26, 1931), 104-5n6; RGASPI, f. 17, op. 3, d. 847, l. 4; Kvashonkin, *Sovetskoe rukovodstvo*, 188n1 (RGASPI, f. 17, op. 114, d. 265, l. 75-137; op. 3, d. 857, l. 9. 12-19)

79. Lakoba wrote: "Koba: Will Beria do for South Caucasus? Me: The only person who works properly is Beria." Hoover Archives, Lakoba papers, notes (1931) of a conversation with Stalin and Orjonikidze. Stalin rejected Polonsky as inappropriate to run the South Caucasus party because "he does not speak any of the local languages." Khlevniuk, *Stalin i Kaganovich*, 276 (RGASPI, f. 82, op. 3, d. 99, l. 153-5).

80. Makarova, "Stalin i 'blizhnyi krug,'" 302. "Dear Comrade Nestor!" Beria wrote (Sept. 27, 1931). "I send my greetings and best wishes. Thank you for the letter. I'd very much like to meet with Koba before he leaves. It'd be good if you could remind him about this if the opportunity arises . . . Regards. Your Lavrenti Beria." Lakoba, "'Ia Koba, a ty Lakoba,'" 60. Some believe Stalin first met Beria on Nov. 6, 1920, when Stalin addressed a crowd at the Baku Soviet and Beria, fresh out of a Georgian Menshevik prison, worked as business-manager of the Azerbaijan Central Committee. Some say it took place in summer 1923, in Moscow at Stalin's Zubalovo dacha, or in fall 1923 at a resort in Abkhazia. Whenever the pair first met, Beria got to know Stalin up close thanks to Lakoba. Iskenderov, Iz istorii bor'by kommunisticheskoi partii Azerbaidzhana, 527–8; Knight, Beria, 33 (citing interview with Devi Sturua, son of Georgi Sturua).

81. Zaria vostoka, Nov. 15, 1931; Esaiashvili, Ocherki istorii Kommunisticheskoi partii Gruzii, II: 115–6. "I will not work with that charlatan," Kartvelishvili supposedly objected when Stalin had told him he was going to get Beria as his deputy (second secretary of South Caucasus regional party committee). Medvedev, Let History Judge, 462–3 (citing A. V. Snegov, former member of the South Caucasus party committee bureau); Khrushchev, "O kul'te lichnosti," 155–6; Deviatyi v sesoiuznysi s"ezd professional'nyk soiuzov SSSR, 205, 253. Using the Russified name Lavrentyev, Kartvelishvili would serve as party boss of the Soviet Far East territory from 1933 through Dec. 1936.

82. Beria wrote to Kaganovich (July 13, 1932) in a familiar tone, outlining his work so far and requesting a reduction in grain delivery quotas—a touchy subject with Stalin. Beria mentioned grave difficulties arising from massive livestock destruction—under his predecessor—an absence of cash, different options for locating a coke-chemical plant, the critical need to improve rail transport, overseen by Papuliya Orjonikidze (Sergo Orjonikidze's elder brother). Beria added pointedly: "I was twice at Koba's and had the chance to inform him in detail about our affairs. The materials concerning the matters addressed in this letter were also conveyed to comrade Koba." Sokolov, Beriia, 83–4; RGAPSI, f. 17, op. 120, d. 75, l. 15.

83. On June 21, 1932, Orakhelashvili was disciplined for "groupism [gruppovshchina]," and his wife, Maria, was removed for supposedly inciting the Georgian Communist party against the South Caucasus regional party committee with "false rumors," particularly against "comrade Beria." Blauvelt, "Abkhazia Patronage" (citing RGAPSI, f. 17, op. 120, d. 82, l. 88). Stalin wrote to Kaganovich: "My opinion: for all the angularity of Beria's 'actions,' it is Orakhelashvili who's wrong in this. . . . Everyone says that the positive work is going very well in Georgia [under Beria], and the mood of the peasants has improved." Kaganovich wrote to Stalin (June 23) supporting Beria. When Orakhelashvili asked for the grain quota to be lowered, Stalin lost all patience (July 24). Khlevniuk et al., Stalin i Kaganovich, 185, 189.

84. Orakhelashvili wrote to Orjonikidze of Beria (Aug. 1, 1932): "Our relations are worse and worse and unbearable. Comrade Beria does not come to see me, and we don't even have telephone conversations . . . He behaves like some kind of League of Nations commissar appointed to a mandate country." Orhakhelashvili added that he had written to Stalin a month ago asking to be relieved of his duties as first secretary of the South Caucasus,

but had received no response. Kvashonkin, Sovetskoe rukovodstvo, 186–9 (RGASPI, f. 85, op. 92, d. 472, l. 1–2). See also Mlechin, KGB, 195; and Gazarian, "O Berii i sude nad Berievtsami v Gruzii," 113–4.

85. Stalin added: "Sergo insisted on the candidacy of Mamuliya for secretary of the Georgian party, but now it is obvious that Mamuliya is not worth even Beria's left foot." Khlevniuk et al., Stalin i Kaganovich, 276 (RGASPI, f. 81, op. 3, d. 99, l. 153–5), 283–5 (f. 558, op. 11, d. 740, l. 153–60).

86. Khlevniuk et al., Stalin i Kaganovich, 276n3 (RGASPI, f. 17, op. 3, d. 903, l. 8); RGASPI, f. 17, op. 120, d. 75, l. 15: Oct. 9, 1932); RGASPI, f. 17, op. 3, d. 903, l. 8. Konstantin "Tite" Lordkipanidze, not a close associate of Beria, was given the Georgian OGPU.

87. Thereafter, Beria would be recorded in Stalin's office in 1933 (twice), 1935 (twice), 1936 (twice), 1937 (twice), and several times in 1938. Na prieme, 569.

88. In Dec. 1932, Lakoba wrote to Beria, with copies to Stalin and Kaganovich, protesting the reprimand given to himself and Ladariya for approaching the USSR Council of People's Commissars without the authorization of the Georgian Central Committee on the question of again lowering the Abkhaz tobacco procurement target. Hoover Archives, Lakoba papers, 1–42. Bagirov, who had been in Moscow, had returned and told Beria that Lakoba had gossiped to Orjonikidze that Beria had been slandering Orjonikidze, supposedly saying that, back when the Menshevik uprising was crushed, "Sergo would have shot all Georgians if it hadn't been for me." Enraged, Beria wrote to Orjonikidze (Dec. 18, 1932), "I know there are many big-mouths among those who left the South Caucasus, and it is impossible to prohibit big-mouths from gossiping idiocies, I know that many rumors circulate about me and our work in the South Caucasus, but I cannot for the life of me understand what led comrade Lakoba, what goals he followed, when he informed you about false matters . . . Dear Sergo, you know me more than ten years. You know all my shortcomings, you know what I am capable of . . . I admire you too much and value your relations too much. I ask you only one thing—don't believe anyone." Kvashonkin, Sovetskoe rukovodstvo, 197–8 (RGASPI, f. 85, op. 29, d. 413, 1–3). See also Knight, Beria, 50–1. In a March 2, 1933, letter to Orjonikidze, Beria complained that according to Lakoba, Levan Gogoberidze, on holiday in Sukhum, was spreading disinformation about Beria's involvement in Musavat counterintelligence. Beria reviewed how the matter had been adjudicated in his favor in 1920 in the presence of Orjonikidze and others, and how Beria sent Orjonikidze an official decision of the Azerbaijan Central Committee in 1925. Kvashonkin, Sovetskoe rukovodstvo, 202–4 (RGASPI, f. 85, op. 29, d. 414, 1–4). See also Mlechin, KGB, 193–4.

89. Artamonov, Spetsob"ekty Stalina, 137–8. A stone stairway of 870 steps to the beach below would be built.

90. Gosudarstvennaia okhrana Rossii, 47–9 (no citation). The regime had laid a road to Pitsunda in 1930. See also Sergei Deviatov et al., Garazh osobogo naznacheniia: 90 let na sluzhbe Otechestvu, 1921–2011 (Moscow: MediaPress), 157; and Rosenfeldt, "Special" World, 168–70.

91. Zhukov, "Tak, byl li 'zagovor' Tukhachevskogo?" (Gagra and Sochi incidents). After Stalin's death, Chechulin would testify (Oct. 14, 1953): "In order to avoid being shot at again, this time from closer range, I leapt from the glass cabin and told the drivers that the launch should take only a straight course, to the open sea. . . . Comrade Stalin

initially attributed the shooting at the launch, after a three-hour stay on the shore in the Pitsunda area, to Abkhaz customs, saying that among the Abkhaz it was customary to greet guests by firing shots. But when the rifle shots rang out so severely, comrade Stalin, it seems, changed his mind about such firing, so that by the time we returned to Cold Spring in order to ascertain the cause of the shots, that very night, as soon as we disembarked, he sent Bogdanov to Pitsunda. . . . Five days after the shooting of the launch, a letter came to Cold Spring from one of the border guards, whose name I do not recall. In that letter he asked comrade Stalin to forgive him for firing at the launch, and explained that he had taken the launch to be not ours (foreign). That launch did in fact appear in the Pitsunda area for the first time. . . . I reported the content of this letter to comrade Stalin. He heard me out and took the letter."

92. Popov and Oppokov, "Berievshchina" (1991, no. 1), 47.

93. The fired OGPU chief was A. N. Mikeladze. In 1937, the incident was reclassified as a terrorist act; Lavrov as well as Mikeladze would be shot. Lakoba, "'Ia Koba, a ty Lakoba,'" 61–3.

94. Popov and Oppokov, "Berievshchina" (1991, no. 1), 46–7; Zen'kovich, Marshaly i genseki, 196–8. Vlasik late in life erroneously dated the incident to 1935, and perceived an interconnected conspiracy: this attempt on Stalin's life, the Kirov murder, the death of Kuibyshev, etc., all the work of a "fifth column." Loginov, Teni Stalina, 98–9.

95. Dimitrov's words and a broad counternarrative to Nazi propaganda were propagated in the global press by the Comintern and its media wizard Willi Münzenberg, who had created the Münzenberg Trust (encompassing newspapers, magazines, and film production companies), the fourth-largest media organization in the Weimar Republic. When Nazi newspaper accounts tied Münzenberg to the Reichstag fire, he fled into exile. Gross, Willi Münzenberg.

96. Kaganovich had opposed Koltsov's request to travel to Paris for the reportage, but Stalin had approved it. The trial would end on Dec. 23, 1933, and the Dutch Communist Marinus van der Lubbe would be guillotined in Jan. 1934. Litvinov wrote to Stalin, regarding Soviet personnel in Berlin, "In the opinion of the foreign affairs commissariat, given the current political situation in Germany, it would be inconvenient to have a single-race composition of the upper stratum of the embassy." In 1934, Khinchuk would be replaced by Jacob Surits, who, however, was also Jewish (he had a law degree from the University of Berlin and had been a member of the Jewish Bund). Sluch, "Germano-sovetskie otnosheniia," 106 (AVP RF, f. 05, op. 13, pap. 94, d. 78, l. 46).

97. DGFP, series C, I: 848–51 (Thomsen, Sept. 26, 1933), 851–3 (Bernhard von Bülow, Sept. 26). German government actions against Soviet citizens and property effectively provoked the Soviet cancellation. Weinberg, Foreign Policy, I: 81; Niclauss, Die Sowjetunion, 134–41. Going back to the nineteenth century, "the German and Russian economies were basically complementary so that there existed a broad basis for economic cooperation . . . in the absence of offsetting political factors." For the Germans, the goal has always been to increase foreign trade, while for the Russians, it was to advance domestic industrialization. Shoemaker, "Russo-German Economic Relations," 336.

98. In 1931, Hitler had proposed an Anglo-German partnership to British journalists invited to the Brown House in Munich,

offering a free hand at sea in exchange for a free hand on the continent in the East. This was the beginning of a long bilateral courtship. Hildebrand, *Foreign Policy*, 25. See also Wagener, *Memoirs of a Confidant*, 173–4. (Wagener worked closely with Hitler 1929–32 and wrote these recollections in 1946 in British captivity.) Hitler turned to Joachim von Ribbentrop, who visited London in Nov. 1933 as a special envoy to forge an entente against the Bolshevik menace. Hoover Institution Archives, Louis P. Lorchner Collection, Ribbentrop to Hitler original files, 1933–38: Nov. 20 and 26, 1933; Bloch, *Ribbentrop*, 41–4; Waddington, *Hitler's Crusade*, 69 (citing House of Lords, Davidson papers, memo Nov. 20, 1933); Winterbotham, *Nazi Connection*, 53–4; Ernest William Dalrymple Tennant, *True Account* (London: M. Parish, 1957), 164–9; Davidson, *Memoirs of a Conservative*, 399–401; *von Ribbentrop, Memoirs*, 36–7.

99. *Le Matin* (Nov. 23, 1933).

100. Stalin's fixation on Polish spies in Ukraine revealed his and the wider regime's fears about Soviet vulnerabilities. See the tortured case of the head of the Polish section of the Chernigov province party committee, Bolesław Skarbek, executed for leading a fictive clandestine "Polish military organization" on Soviet soil. Khaustov et al., *Lubianka: Stalin i VChK*, 460 (APRF, f. 3, op. 58, d. 240, l. 105–6), 467–8 (d. 243, l. 86–8), 525–6 (d. 245, l. 59–60), 530 (RGASPI, f. 17, op. 162, d. 16, l. 86); Snyder, *Sketches from a Secret War*, 116–7; Rubl'ov and Reprintsev, "Repressii protiv poliakiv," 121; Mitzner, "Widmo POW," 22.

101. Negotiations had opened on June 26, 1933. Stalin, in the fall, instructed Kaganovich and Molotov to conduct a campaign against Japan in *Pravda* and to a lesser extent *Izvestiya* and to republish an internal-use anti-Japanese brochure for wide circulation. Lensen, *Damned Inheritance*, 237–334; Haslam, *Threat from the East*, 22–4; *DVP SSSR*, XVI: 573–5 (Sokolnikov to Yurenev in Tokyo: Oct. 17, 1933); Khlevniuk et al., *Stalin i Kaganovich*, 396–7 (RGASPI, f. 81, op. 3, d. 100, l. 131–4: Oct. 21, 1933), 401 (f. 558, op. 11, d. 741, l. 112–5: Oct. 24); *Na prieme*, 111–2. Roosevelt had promised Litvinov "100 percent moral and diplomatic support" against Japan, and even ordered Bullitt to study the possibility of a nonaggression pact. The U.S. State Department had no interest. Stalin, meanwhile, had used Sokolnikov to undercut Karakhan, a hawk on Japan: on May 25, 1933, the politburo had named Sokolnikov deputy foreign affairs commissar for Far Eastern Affairs (Japan, China, Mongolia); Karakhan was reduced to oversight of just the Near East. Genis, "Upriamyi narkom s il'inki," 238. Ken and Rusapov, *Zapadnoe zagranich'e*, 596–7 (RGASPI, f. 17, op. 3, d. 923, l. 18). Sokolnikov was also placed on the politburo's Mongolia commission (soon becoming deputy to Voroshilov on that body).

102. Niclauss, *Die Sowjetunion*, 134–6. Yenukidze, who oversaw many sensitive government affairs, had gone on holiday to Germany in summer 1933; back in the Soviet Union, he invited German ambassador Dirksen and his aide Twardowski to his dacha in Aug. 1933; Krestinsky and Karakhan, deputy commissars, the former a former Soviet envoy to Berlin, also attended. Yenukidze, described by Dirksen as "a fair-haired, blue-eyed, kindly Georgian with definite pro-German leanings," ventured that the statists would triumph over the agitators in National Socialism; Dirksen and Twardowski agreed that a modus vivendi could be found with Moscow.

103. When Twardowski explained to Litvinov the reasons for German abandonment of the

League, "Mr. Litvinov demonstrated such understanding of our position that I expressed regrets that such a stance of the leader of Soviet foreign policy did not find expression in the Soviet press." *DGFP*, series C, II: 14–9 (Oct. 17, 1933). See also Bennett, *German Rearmament*. On Nov. 12, 1933, 93 percent of German voters had approved the German government's decision to withdraw from the League and 92 percent voted for Nazi candidates (the only party allowed to stand).

104. Bloch, *Ribbentrop*, 40–1.

105. RGASPI, f. 558, op. 11, d. 81, l. 141–144–144ob.

106. Krestinsky returned via Vienna. *DGFP*, series C, I: 862–4 (Bülow, Sept. 27), 901–4 (Twardowski with Stern, Oct. 10). Stalin opened a back channel through his foreign-policy fixer Radek, who helped arrange a meeting between Dirksen and Molotov. Dirksen, due to depart the Moscow posting (to be replaced by Rudolf Nadolny), returned to Moscow from Berlin on Oct. 28 and was afforded a lavish farewell dinner and gifts. Von Dirksen, *Moscow, Tokyo, London*, 116–8; Hilger and Meyer, *Incompatible Allies*, 260–1; Gnedin, *Iz istorii otnoshenii*, 13, 22–3; Tucker, *Stalin in Power*, 235–6.

107. Back in Sept. 1930, Stalin, accompanied by Nadya, Svetlana, and Orjonikidze, had stayed for the first time at the Sinop villa in Sukhum's outskirts, where Trotsky used to stay. (In late 1931 Sinop was transferred from Abkhazia's agriculture commissariat to the USSR central executive committee.) Lakoba, Stalin's host in 1930, whisked the group the next day to reconnoiter Myussera, where Lakoba suggested creating a new dacha for Stalin. Stalin tweaked proposed secret passages between the buildings, three from his bedroom, including one directly to the hillside. Stalin asked for 50 mandarin trees; Lakoba had 100 planted of the Satsuma variety. Already in 1932, the main structure was pronounced usable, though far from finished, and in Sept. 1932 Stalin arrived to go hunting with Lakoba, Goglidze, Pauker, and Vlasik. Stalin demanded changes and Myussera, like Cold Spring, underwent much further construction. Lakoba Papers, Hoover Institution Archives, 2–28. Myussera ended up being used more by Molotov and Mikoyan (Stalin would stay a mere eight times through the end of his life). 108. The magnate was Stepan Lianosyan, known as Lianozov (whom John Reed had labeled "the Russian Rockefeller"). One more dacha was being built at Abkhazia's stunning Lake Ritsa. By one account, in summer 1932, while visiting Cold Spring, in Abkhazia, with Nadya, Stalin was persuaded by Lakoba to travel by horseback up to Lake Ritsa, which formed part of the Bzyb River basin, and lay in a deep mountain hollow reached by a steep trail of sheer cliffs and landslides. The lake was cool in summers and warm in winters. Here, at the point where the Yupshara River flowed out of Ritsa, Lakoba oversaw construction on another dacha for Stalin. No mean feat: one of the trucks carrying construction materials collapsed a bridge and plunged. Dzhikhashvili, "Kavkaskie safari Stalina"; *XX let Sovetskoi Abkhazii*, 110. There were dachas for Stalin's use on the Black Sea seashore in the area of Green Cape, about five miles north of Batum in Ajaria, at Borjomi (the former retreat of Georgian kings), in Crimea (Mukhalatka) and Valdai (between Moscow and Leningrad). The number would grow to eighteen total, including five in Abkhazia.

109. Khlevniuk et al., *Stalin i Kaganovich*, 385–6 (RGASPI, f. 558, op. 11, d. 81, l. 134, 138), 386 (l. 134), 391–3 (d. 82, l. 6–7, 8, 9, 10; f.

17, op. 162, d. 15, l. 112, 124), 393 (f. 558, op. 11, d. 82, l. 5), 393–4 (l. 21–2), 394–5 (d. 741, l. 108–11); Cherniavskii, "Fenomenon Litvinova."

110. Khlevniuk et al., *Stalin i Kaganovich*, 408 (RGASPI, f. 558, op. 11, d. 741, l. 117–8); *Na prieme*, 112.

111. According to Molchanov, the "organization" aimed to overturn Soviet power and restore monarchism, and was led by Anna Abrikosova (b. 1882), the daughter of a former Moscow factory owner, and Anna Brilliantova (b. 1906), daughter of a former Menshevik, and financed with Catholic church money. They would be sentenced on Feb. 19, 1934, to either eight or ten years in Gulag. Abrikosova would die in the camp in 1936; the other would be rearrested while in confinement and executed in Oct. 1937. Vinogradov, *Genrikh Iagoda*, 369–71 (TsA FSB, f. 2, op. 11, d. 1271, l. 1–3: Nov. 20, 1933).

112. In 1934, there would be at least four more. Hoffmann, *Hitler's Personal Security*, 24.

113. Bilateral talks had been spurred by U.S. efforts to stabilize world wheat prices in summer 1933. Bowers, "American Diplomacy." Recognition became official on Nov. 16, 1933. *FRUS, 1933*, II: 778–840; *DVP SSSR*, XVI: 609–10 (Litvinov telegrams, Nov. 8, 1933), 621–2 (Nov. 10), 639 (Nov. 15), 640 (joint communique, Nov. 15), 641–55 (exchange of notes and letters, Nov. 16), 655–8 (Litvinov press conference, Nov. 17), 658–60 (Litvinov telegram, Nov. 19), 662–3 (Litvinov telegram, Nov. 18), 655–6 (Kalinin radio address to America, Nov. 20), 666–7 (Litvinov telegrams, Nov. 20), 675 (Litvinov to Roosevelt, Nov. 22), 675–6 (Litvinov telegram, Nov. 22); *Izvestiia*, Nov. 20 and 23, 1933; http://nsarchive.gwu.edu/coldwar/documents/episode-1/fdr-ml.htm; http://www.presidency.ucsb.edu/ws/?pid=14563; http://www.fdrlibrary.marist.edu/daybyday/daylog/november-17th-1933. See also Bishop, *Roosevelt-Litvinov Agreements*; Maddux, *Years of Estrangement*, 1–26; and Browder, *Origins of Soviet-American Diplomacy*, 37, 45, 72, 85–6, 95, 99–152.

114. "This success for Soviet diplomacy," Molotov stated at the central executive committee on Dec. 28, 1933, of the various Soviet bilateral agreements, "is inseparably linked with the name of Comrade Litvinov, whose services are widely recognized, but here we should especially underscore them." Litvinov was given the floor the next day. *DVP SSSR*, XVI: 778–81 (at 779), 781–97. Litvinov would take to complaining about his "security" detail. "Ne chuvstvovat' za soboiu topota,'" 123–4 (APRF, f. 57, op 1, d. 18, l. 99–100; Litvinov to Yezhov, Sept. 9, 1935).

115. Lensen, *Damned Inheritance*, 361–445.

116. Crowley, *Japan's Quest for Autonomy*, 190–6.

117. Stalin received considerable intelligence pointing to a Japanese desire for war against the USSR. In late Nov. 1933, after Hirota became Japan's foreign minister, Stalin received an intercepted letter from the U.S. ambassador in Japan to Washington indicating Hirota's promotion heralded a more aggressive Japanese posture. That same month, the OGPU sent Stalin intelligence obtained in Paris in the circles of the former prime minister Kokovtsov, who had a document from Japan concerning "the manifest threat to the main Japanese islands over which Soviet squadrons could appear in a few hours . . ." Stalin underscored this passage and wrote, "for Klim." On Jan. 14, 1934, Artuzov and Agranov sent Stalin a Russian translation of an article published back in April 1933 in a closed journal of the Japanese general staff bruiting war with the Soviet Union. On Feb.

26, Yagoda sent Stalin materials from the Japanese military attaché (Kawabe) assessing the technical level of the Red Army, and stating, "in defense industry the USSR has freed itself of foreign dependence." Stalin underlined the passage. On March 11, Yagoda sent Stalin materials dispatched by the Japanese military attaché in Turkey to Tokyo (dated Feb. 15) on mobilizing Muslim peoples against the USSR through propaganda, and asking for finances to set it up. The document asserted that "the interests of England and the USSR [are] in irreconcilable contradiction"—a passage Stalin underlined. RGASPI, f. 558, op. 11, d. 185, l. 126–32; d. 186, l. 1, 37–53, 91–5, 118–26; Crowley, *Japan's Quest for Autonomy*, 206; Haslam, *Threat from the East*, 38–9. Germany learned that Litvinov had expressed fears of a Japanese attack as well as a German-Polish reconciliation, and thus of a triple alliance against the USSR, on a visit to Rome: *DGFP*, series C, II: 183 (Hassell, Dec. 7, 1933).

118. *Moscow Daily News*, Dec. 30, 1933. Marx spent eight weeks on tour. Litvinov did the knives routine himself, to Harpo's surprise, at the final performance. Harpo evidently served as a secret courier, smuggling letters for Ambassador Bullitt by taping sealed envelopes to his leg under his pants. Marx, *Harpo Speaks!*, 299–337; Fromkin, *In the Time of the Americans*; Harlow, "Secrets in His Socks."

119. *FRUS, The Soviet Union, 1933–1939*, 53–4 (Bullitt, Dec. 24, 1933), 60–1 (Jan. 4).

120. Costiliogla, *Roosevelt's Lost Alliances*, 268.

121. Bullitt returned the kiss. Bullitt, *For the President*, 68–9 (Jan. 1, 1934); *FRUS, The Soviet Union, 1933–1939*, 59–61 (Bullitt to Phillips, Jan. 4, 1934); Farnsworth, *Bullitt and the Soviet Union*, 109–14; and Tucker, *Stalin in Power*, 224. Soviet counterintelligence used the ballerina Irena Charnodskaya, who made the rounds of Bullitt and his bachelor aides, Chip Bohlen and Charles Thayer. "We simply cannot keep our hands off her," Thayer wrote. "She has become an acquisition of the Embassy and . . . sleep[s] in some vacant room which the three of us carefully lock together and then fight violently as to who will keep the key . . . What an embassy!" The exuberance would end quickly for all. Costiliogla, *Roosevelt's Lost Alliances*, 263–70 (citing Thayer diary, April 14–May 20, 1934, box 6, Thayer papers; Bohlen to Mother, April 15–May 15, 1934, box 36, Bohlen papers); George F. Kennan, *Memoirs, 1950–1963*, 126; "Fair Day, Adieu!," p. 18, box 240, Kennan papers; Kennan, *Memoirs, 1925–1950*, 190; Kennan, "Flashbacks," in *At a Century's Ending*, 31.

122. The text also noted that the situation in the United States "is most favorable for the establishment of socialism." Eudin and Slusser, *Soviet Foreign Policy*, II: 577–85; *Theses and Decisions*, 20–47.

123. "Stalin to Duranty," *Time*, Jan. 8, 1934: 26. See also *Sochineniia*, XIII: 276–81, and the slightly longer Soviet transcript: RGASPI, f. 558, op. 11, d. 374, l. 1–6; *Na prieme*, 118. Duranty had been allowed to accompany Litvinov to Washington in Nov., and returned to Moscow with Bullitt in Dec. See also Duranty, *I Write as I Please*, 166–7; and Taylor, *Stalin's Apologist*, 190–2. Thayer, the U.S. embassy official, wrote of Duranty, "Always witty, always ready to take any side in an argument, he usually kept every party he was at in an uproar of argument and vituperation." Thayer, *Bears in the Caviar*, 60.

124. *DVP SSSR*, XVI: 772–4 (Dovgalevsky, Dec. 29, 1933), 876–7n321. The politburo had resolved (Dec. 19, 1933) to join the League and enter a regional pact in the framework of the League, in the face of Nazi aggression, under certain conditions. Adibekov et al., *Politbiuro TsK RKP (b)—VKP (b) i Evropa*, 305–6

(RGASPI, f. 17, op. 162, d. 15, l. 154–5: Dec. 19, 1933). A possible new "collective security" policy was also discussed by the Central Committee (Dec. 29, 1933), among the last prewar instances when the Central Committee was tasked with discussing Soviet foreign policy. On Dovgalevsky (who had become ambassador to France in Jan. 1928), see Barmine, *One Who Survived*, 178.

125. At a Dec. 9, 1933, Kremlin meeting Stalin gave the go-ahead for formal negotiations with France. "We have adopted a firm course of closer relations with France," Litvinov overly enthused in a telegram to Dovgalevsky. Soviet proposals did go far beyond the original French idea, insisting that holdout League members had to extend diplomatic recognition to the USSR, colonial mandates had to be revised (a major plank of Soviet propaganda), and a regional pact had to include not only Poland but also the Baltic states, Finland, and Czechoslovakia, as well as security assistance if Japan attacked the USSR in Asia. Borisov, *Sovetsko-frantsuzskie otnosheniia*, 202 (AVP RF, f. 0136, op. 17, pap. 159, d. 778, l. 79), 204; *DVP SSSR*, XVI: 576–8 (Oct. 20, 1933), 773, 735–6 (Dec. 11, 1933); 876–7 n321; *DDF*, 1e série, IV: 160–1, 165; RGASPI, f. 17, op. 162, d. 15; Paul-Boncour, *Entre deux guerres*, I: 363–4; Dullin, "La rôle de l'Allemagne," 245–62. Litvinov also urged the signing of a trade pact, however modest. *DVP SSSR*, XVIII: 752. Even if the Soviet Union represented an important market, the two countries could not get beyond the Soviets' repudiation of tsarist-era debt. French elite circles also remained embittered at the confiscation without compensation of some 13 billion gold rubles in investments from tsarist times. Some private French arms dealers refused to sell to the Communists for fear of reverse engineering or because the orders were too small for the bother. Dullin, *Men of Influence*, 100.

126. The visit took place Aug. 26–Sept. 9, 1933. *Pravda* underscored that Herriot "categorically contradicted the lies of the bourgeoisie press in connection with a famine in the USSR." *Pravda*, Sept. 13, 1934; Werth et al., *Black Book of Communism*, 159–60; Khlevniuk et al., *Stalin i Kaganovich*, 311 (RGASPI, f. 558, op. 1, d. 80, l. 24), 317 (l. 41). Laval's fellow Radical Party member Pierre Cot, air minister in the government, followed Herriot, arriving in Moscow with an air squadron on Sept. 15, and becoming the first foreign delegation afforded Soviet military honors. *Izvestiia*, Sept. 15, 24, and 25, 1933. Cot was allowed to observe aviation maneuvers and the secret bomber factory in Fili outside Moscow—the Germans had just evacuated their secret air training station at Lipetsk three days before—and became the object of intense attention by Soviet intelligence. Khaustov et al., *Lubianka: Stalin i VChK*, 598–9 (APRF, f. 3, op. 58, d. 203, l. 19–21). Cot, based on the WWII intercepts, would later be tagged as a Soviet "agent." Romerstein and Breindel, *Venona Secrets*, 56–7. Draitser, *Stalin's Romeo Spy*, 191. See also Baker, *Rezident*; and Stavinskii, *Zarubiny*.

127. Kvashonkin, *Sovetskoe rukovodstvo*, 198–9 (RGASPI, f. 74, op. 2, d. 45, l. 70–70ob.).

128. Eldev-Ochir, a leftist and scourge of the lamas, had been Mongolian People's Party leader for a year in 1929–30, during the catastrophe that had compelled the new course correction. In July 1932, he served a second term (for one month), giving way to Lhumbe (b. 1902). On Oct. 8, 1933, the politburo Mongolia commission discussed "the matter of a spy organization," and Eliava received instructions to root out pro-Japanese elements

and prepare for possible war and evacuation. Between July 1933 and June 1934, there would be perhaps 2,000 arrests in a campaign against "left deviationists" and a so-called Lhumbe group accused of spying for the Japanese. At least fifty-six Mongols would be executed, including Lhumbe. On May 23, 1934, the politburo directed Artuzov to "make a complete list of Mongolians who had come to the Soviet Union at various times." RGASPI, f. 17, op. 162, d. 15, l. 100, 125–7; d. 16, l. 63. M. Chibisov, a Soviet proconsul who helped fabricate the Lhumbe Affair, would remark upon departure from Mongolia for Moscow in July 1934: "Stalin has already said that all lamas are counterrevolutionaries. They must be convicted as traitors before the people." Sandag and Kendall, *Poisoned Arrows*, 76. See also Baabar, *Twentieth-Century Mongolia*, 327–33. Karakhan would tell American ambassador Bullitt about the discovery of a Japanese plot to replace the Mongolian government with a pro-Japanese government, and, in a further fabrication, how the Mongols had again asked to be admitted into the USSR as a Union republic but the Soviets declined, demonstrating they were not imperialists. *FRUS*, 1934, III: 232–3.

129. Stalin suggested cutting by half the 4,000 Soviet personnel in country. He asked the Mongols (in terms of language), "Can you understand Buryats (yes), Qalmyks (somewhat), Tuvins (no)?" The conversation between Dobchin (b. 1896), a deputy prime minister, and Eldev-Ochir (b. 1905), a Central Committee secretary and presidium member, and Sokolnikov/Voroshilov was written down from memory. RGANI, f. 89, op. 63, d. 10, l. 1–7.

130. RGANI, f. 89, op. 63, d. 11, l. 1: Jan. 16, 1935. The politburo had allocated 100,000 rubles for Genden's delegation: RGASPI, f. 17, op. 3, d. 953, l. 58 (Oct. 19, 1934).

131. "'Zhmu vashemu ruku, dorogoi tovarishch': perepiska Maksima Gorkogo i Iosifa Stalina" *Novy Mir*, 1997, no. 9: 169; Artizov and Naumov, *Vlast'*, 124–5 (IMLI, arkhiv Gor'kogo: Jan. 8, 1930); *Sochineniia*, XII: 177. "I am not an expert in literature and, of course, not a critic," Stalin wrote, also in 1930, while intervening to support a leftist playwright and poet, Alexander Bezymenskii (Stalin did fault Bezymenskii for "some holdovers of Communist Youth League avant-gardism"). *Sochineniia*, XII: 200–1; Maksimenkov, *Bol'shaia tsenzura*, 180–1. Back in 1925, Stalin had responded to an inquiry from enlightenment commissar Lunacharsky about the Bolshoi Theater's centenary, "I am not strong in artistic matters, as you yourself know, and I do not dare say anything decisive in this area." RGASPI, f. 558, op. 11, d. 760, 146–8.

132. Artizov and Naumov, *Vlast'*, 157–9 (RGALI, f. 2750, op. 1, d. 140, 141: Oct. 29 and Nov. 9, 1931); RGASPI, f. 17, op. 3, d. 858, l. 6. Initially permitted as an experiment, the play was terminated during rehearsals in spring 1932.

133. At a deeper level, the novel took up myth-making, salvation through a woman, eternity versus the cut and thrust of the moment, an atheist turned into a believer, the urban environment as a character, and estrangement of the physical world—all hallmarks of Bulgakov's work. Proffer, *Bulgakov*, 146. "I love this novel more than all my other writings," Bulgakov observed in Oct. 1924 of *White Guard*. Brainina and Dmitrieva, *Sovetskie pisateli*, III: 86.

134. *Rossiia*, 1926, no. 4 and 5. A pirated Russian edition of the full novel appeared in Riga in 1927. A complete Russian version, corrected by Bulgakov, was published in Paris under the revised title: *Dni Turbinykh (Belaia*

gvardiia), 2 vols. (Paris: Concorde, 1927). Proffer, *Bulgakov*, 137–9; Agursky, *Third Rome*, 305–17; Bulgakov, *Early Plays*, 86–8. The publisher of the journal *Russia*, Isai Altshuler, known as Lezhnev, emigrated to Estonia in 1926 and soon declared himself the official representative to sell the rights abroad of Bulgakov's works, prompting the writer to issue a denial through TASS of any such right. Lyandres, "Russkii pisatel" (Jan. 9, 1928); "Teatral'nyi roman," in Bulgakov, *Izbrannaia proza*, 518–41; Chudakova, "Arkhiv Bulgakova."

135. Boris Vershilov, head of the Moscow Art Theater's second studio, had sent Bulgakov a penciled note after reading *White Guard* asking him to render it into a play, which the writer did in four months. Curtis, *Manuscripts Don't Burn*, 62. It had premiered on Oct. 5, 1926. Gorchakov, *Istoriia Sovetskogo teatra*, 132–5; Gorchakov, *Theater in Soviet Russia*. How the play had gotten approved stumped Moscow cultural circles. Lunacharsky was ordered to open it in a private phone call from Stalin, a fact kept secret. Lunacharsky *Moskovskie novosti*, April 25, 1993; APRF, f. 3, op. 34, d. 240, l. 2; d. 239, l. 23; Sarnov, *Stalin i pisateli*, II: 421–2; Krylov, *Puti razvitiia teatra*, 232;" Lunacharskii, "Pervye novinki sezona," *Izvestiia*, Oct. 1926, reprinted in Lunacharskii, *Sobranie sochinenii*, III: 325–31; Gorchakov, *Istoriia Sovetskogo teatra*, 133. Gorchakov, *Theater in Soviet Russia*, 185–7.

136. Artizov and Naumov, *Vlast'*, 68, 82, 86–8, 742n2. See also *Pravda*, Feb. 9, 1930 (Kerzhentsev).

137. "'Polozhenie ego deistvitel'no bezyskhodnoe': 110–4 (APRF, f. 3, op. 1, d. 241, l. 69–80; Kerzhentsev, Jan. 6, 1929), 114 (l. 83: Voroshilov to Stalin, Jan. 29), 115 (RGASPI, f. 17, op. 3, d. 724, l. 5: Jan. 30); Artizov and Naumov, *Vlast'*, 91–6, 99, 100; Proffer, *Bulgakov*, 275–87.

138. On Feb. 2, 1929, Stalin had written an open reply to the proletarian playwright Vladimir Bill-Belotserkovsky that *Turbins* "is not such a bad play, because it does more good than harm. Do not forget that the chief impression it leaves with the spectator is one that is favorable to the Bolsheviks: 'if even such people as the Turbins are compelled to lay down their arms and submit to the will of the people, admit their cause as definitely lost, then the Bolsheviks must be invincible, and there is nothing to be done about it.' *Days of the Turbins* is a demonstration of the all-conquering power of Bolshevism. Of course, the author is 'not guilty' of this demonstration, but what is that to us?" *Sochineniia*, XI: 326–9. See also Kemp-Welch, *Stalin and the Literary Intelligentsia*, 53–5. See also Lunacharsky's letter to Stalin on *Turbins*: Artizov and Naumov, *Vlast'*, 108–9 (RGASPI, f. 142, op. 1, d. 461, l. 8–80b.: Feb. 12, 1929); Smeliansky, "Destroyers"; and L. M. Leonidov, in *Sovetskoe iskusstvo*, Dec. 21, 1939.

139. Artizov and Naumov, *Vlast'*, 102–7 (RGASPI, f. 558, op. 1, d. 4490, l. 3–17: Feb. 12, 1929). See also Shapoval, "'Oni chuvstvuiut sebia, kak gosti . . . ,'" 120–6. The "brotherly" visit of the Ukrainian writers' delegation was accompanied by exhibitions and performances as part of a Ukrainian week, punctuated by the audience with Stalin. *Pravda*, Feb. 9, 12, 13, 14, 1929.

140. Curtis, *Manuscripts Don't Burn*, 92–4 (July 1929). Bulgakov had just had a chapter of a new novel rejected for publication. On July 30, 1929, A. Svidersky, a former agricultural commissar overseeing arts in the enlightenment commissariat, reported sympathetically to Alexander Smirnov, a Central Committee secretary, about a long conversation with

Bulgakov, whom he characterized as "a person hounded and doomed. I am not even sure his nerves are healthy. His situation is genuinely hopeless." Svidersky supported Bulgakov's request to go abroad. Smirnov agreed in a note to Molotov (Aug. 3, 1929). "'Polozhenie ego deistvitel'no bezyskhodnoe,'" 116 (APRF, f. 3, op. 34, d. 239, l. 6); Artizov and Naumov, *Vlast'*, 115. Bulgakov was not allowed to leave.

141. Stalin had the letter circulated to the upper party and state ranks. *Oktiabr'*, 1987, no. 6: 176–80; Milne, *Mikhail Bulgakov*, 268–74.

142. Bulgakova, *Dnevnik*, 299–300; Bulgakov and Bulgakova, *Dnevnik Mastera i Margarity*, 497; *Bulgakov, Vospominaniia*, 394 (L. E. Belozerskaya); "'Polozhenie ego deistvitel'no bezyskhodnoe'": 116 (APRF, f. 3, op. 34, d. 239, l. 6); Fleishman, "O gibeli maiakovskovo kak 'literaturnom fakte,'" 128; Artizov and Naumov, *Vlast'*, 127 (RGASPI, f. 17, op. 3, d. 783, l. 11). See also Gromov, *Stalin*, 114–6.

143. Woroszylski, *Life of Mayakovsky*, 514–30 (esp. 526); Sundaram, "Manufacturing Culture," 75–87. Trotsky wrote an obituary (*Biulleten' oppozitsii*, May 11, 1930), but Stalin stayed publicly silent. More than 100,000 mourners, with no prompting from the state, had turned out for Mayakovsky's burial in the Novodevichy Cemetery, a number surpassed only at Lenin's Red Square funeral. Boyrn, "Death of the Revolutionary Poet," 158.

Mayakovsky was involved in a recent romance with a very young married woman, the actress Veronika Polonskaya, who refused to leave her husband. On April 14, when he shot himself in the heart, Polonskaya had just left his apartment to attend a rehearsal against his protestations. Rumors spread that the bullet removed from Mayakovsky did not match the revolver he owned (a prop in a play), and that neighbors had heard two shots. Ten days after the poet's death, the investigating police officer was killed. The handwritten suicide note, however, was unquestionably Mayakovsky's. "The idea of suicide was like a chronic disease inside him," his former lover and muse Lily Brik would write, "and like any chronic disease it worsened under circumstances that, for him, were undesirable." The official report of his death stated that "the suicide was caused by reasons of a purely personal order, having nothing in general to do with the public and literary activity of the poet, the suicide was preceded by an illness from which the poet still had not completely recovered." *Pravda*, April 15, 1930. The suicide spurred the removal of the poet's works from children and youth libraries. *Literaturnaia gazeta*, July 10, 1930. See also Brown, *Mayakovsky*; and Terras, *Vladimir Mayakovsky*.

144. On May 30, 1931, Bulgakov wrote a long letter to Stalin, quoting Gogol, vainly requesting a long rest holiday in Europe, stating he had never been abroad, contrary to published accounts, and pledging his loyalty ("I do not know if the Soviet theater needs me, but I need the Soviet theater like oxygen"). Artizov and Naumov, *Vlast'*, 147–50 (otdel rukopisi GPB, f. 562, k. 19, d. 30). In 1931, Stalin allowed both Pilnyak and Zamyatin to travel to Western Europe, and in 1932 Babel would be permitted to travel to Paris, where his wife was undergoing an operation. Artizov and Naumov, *Vlast'*, 180 (APRF, f. 3, op. 34, d. 206, l. 21).

145. Paustovsky, *Story of a Life*, 63–5. Bulgakov persisted in his supplications to be permitted to travel to France and Italy, writing to Stalin (June 11, 1934) that functionaries must be afraid he would defect. Artizov and Naumov, *Vlast'*, 210–3 (APRF, f. 3, op. 34, d. 206, l. 37–380b.). Bulgakov would write one more letter to Stalin (Feb. 1938) about the fate of his friend Nikolai Erdman.

146. During the civil war, Red Army soldiers at the front recited Bedny's colloquial verses (they were also dropped by airplanes behind White lines). Bedny had received an Order of the Red Banner on the occasion of an infirm Lenin's last birthday, the first such award for literary efforts in Soviet history. Trotsky had pushed for the prize: Bedny had ridden his civil war train and helped him inspire the troops. But during the intraparty struggle Bedny slashed at Trotsky ("a spent politician"). Bedny suffered high sugar levels and was overweight, and Stalin allocated scarce foreign currency for his diabetes treatment in Germany. Bedny wrote a report for Stalin about his trip, jokingly noting that his wife had gone crazy over the cleanliness, order, and abundance of consumer goods in the dying capitalist world ("She stands in front of any store window and dies, dies. You drag her away, and she stares at the next window"). Maksimenkov, *Bol'shaia tsenzura*, 129 (RGASPI, f. 17, op. 163, d. 739, l. 39–40: July 19, 1928), 129–33 (d. 701, l. 43–5: Sept. 20; Artizov and Naumov, *Vlast'*, 114 (RGASPI, f. 17, op. 162, d. 7, l. 96); Volkogonov papers, Hoover Archives, container 18; Trotskii, *Literatura i revoliutsiia*, 166–7. "Nobody ever worked so wholeheartedly for the Soviet regime," Nadezhda Mandelstam bitingly wrote about Bedny. Mandelstam, *Hope Against Hope*, 26.

147. "Receiving your assignment, I turned for advice to a very well-informed, authoritative comrade, to whom I usually approach in similar or delicate or, I would say, shock-work tasks," Bedny wrote to Blyukher, commander of the Soviet Far East who had asked for a poem. The poet alluded to how his unnamed "adviser," "grinning and removing his immutable pipe from his mouth," had suggested a folk rhyme. Bedny, in *Polnoe sobranie sochinenii*, XVII: 76 (1929).

148. Artizov and Naumov, *Vlast'*, 131 (APRF, f. 45, op. 1, d. 718, l. 82–820b.: Nov. 2, 1930),131–2 (RGASPI, f. 17, op. 114, d. 201, l. 13: Dec. 6).

149. Artizov and Naumov, *Vlast'*, 132–3 (RGASPI, f. 558, op. 1, d.939, l. 7–9), 134–7 (l. 1–6. Stalin would include the rebuke in his collected works: *Sochineniia*, XIII: 23–6. Bedny continued to step on the wrong toes. Kaganovich asked Stalin to read Bedny's poem ("What Next?"), which *Izvestiya* had published (Sept. 23, 1931), and which seemed potentially provocative to Japan. Kaganovich indicated Litvinov had approved and possibly commissioned the poem. "I did not read and have no intention of reading Demyan's verses, since I am sure they are not worth it," Stalin wrote back (Sept. 29). Khlevniuk et al., *Stalin i Kaganovich*, 119–20 (RGASPI, f. 558, op. 11, d. 739, l. 129–35), 122 (f. 81, op. 3, d. 99, l. 40; f. 17, op. 114, d. 264, l. 11). See also Tucker, *Stalin as Revolutionary*, 470–1; Dubrovsky, "Chronicle of a Poet's Downfall," 188–90; and Chuev, *Sto sorok*, 269.

150. Bedny's apartment served as a salon of artistic life. It was here that Fyodor Chaliapin met Stalin. "Stalin spoke little, and when he did it was with a fairly strong Caucasus accent," the singer would recall. "Yet everything he said had a weighty ring to it, perhaps because he spoke briefly. From his short sentences, which were not always clear in meaning but energetic in tone, I went away with the impression that this was a man who did not fool around. If necessary he could easily—as easily as his light lezginka step-in soft boots—do a dance or blow up the cathedral of Christ the Savior." Medvedev, *Let History Judge*, 65 (citing *Izvestiia* 1962, no. 249).

151. Maksimenkov, *Bol'shaia tsenzura*, 246–7 (RGASPI, f. 558, op. 11, d. 702, l. 68), 248 (l.

68, 70), 269 (f. 667, op. 1, d. 18, l. 6: Nov, 19, 1932).

152. Stalin evidently showed the *Izvestiia* editor Gronsky a journal full of Bedny's unflattering remarks about the denizens of the Kremlin, which, Stalin explained, had been written by a "journalist." (Gronsky has the story slightly garbled, because Bedny got the Order of Lenin, and it was before the writers' congress.) Gronskii, *Iz proshlogo*, 155. Bedny appears to have made the same complaint to Fyodor Raskolnikov, according to memoirs of Raskolnikov's wife. Kanivez, "Moia zhizn' s Raskol'nikovom," 95. See also Gromov, *Stalin*, 166.

153. Adibekov et al., *Politbiuro TsK RKP (b)– VKP (b): povesti dnia zasedanii, II:* 416 (April 13, 1933). Stalin did not have an Order of Lenin; he had two Orders of the Red Banner (Nov. 1919; Feb. 1930).

154. Stalin had the letter circulated to the politburo for information. Maksimenkov, *Bol'shaia tsenzura*, 283–6 (RGASPI, f. 558, op. 11, d. 702, l. 79–84: April 5, 1933).

155. Chukovskii, *Dnevnik*, 68 (Aug. 18, 1932).

156. Stalin edited the draft decree. *Partiinoe stroitel'stvo*, 1932, no. 9: 62; Artizov and Naumov, *Vlast'*, 168 (RGASPI, f. 17, op. 3, d. 875, l. 11: March 8, 1932), 172–3 (d. 881, l. 6, 22; op. 163, d. 938, l. 37–8: April 23, 1932). The theater director Vsevolod Meyerhold is said to have hung a framed copy of the decree on the wall in his expansive double apartment on Bryusov Lane, a few blocks up from Red Square. Kirpotin, *Rovesnik zheleznogo veka*, 156–7.

157. Artizov and Naumov, *Vlast'*, 176–7 (RGASPI, f. 17, op. 163, d. 941, l. 68–9). An architects' union was also formed in 1932, but it would not hold its inaugural congress until 1937. The politbuto formed a commission led by Stalin that concluded (June 7, 1932): "It is considered inexpedient to establish an organizational committee for musical organizations." There were associations below the Union level, in Moscow and Leningrad, that did not have jurisdiction over each other. Maksimenkov, *Sumbur*, 29–32 (RGASPI, f. 17, op. 114, d. 300, l. 144). A decision to form a Composers' Union would be made on May 3, 1939, but it would not be formed until 1948. Iakovlev, "Soiuz kompozitorov SSSR," V: 232–3; Maksimenkov, *Sumbur*, 32 (RGASPI, f. 17, op. 163, d. 1124, l. 81; d, 1509, l. 4–5).

158. *Na prieme*, 68 (literary critic Leopold Averbakh, writer Vladimir Kirshon, Gronsky, and Stetsky), 70 (Gronsky, Stetsky, and Mekhlis).

159. Gronskii, *Iz proshlogo*, 334–6 (letter to Alexsander Ovcharenko, Oct. 22, 1972). See also arkhiv A. M. Gor'kogo MoG-3-25-7 (Gronsky reminiscences with Gorky archive staff, Nov. 30, 1963); and Kemp-Welch, *Stalin and the Literary Intelligentsia*, 132.

160. Gronsky was the proposed union's working head, and leader of its party faction. Artizov and Naumov, *Vlast'*, 175–6 (RGASPI, f. 17, op. 14, d. 295, l. 1–3; APRF, f. 3, op. 35, d. 32, l. 24–24ob.: May 7, 1932); "Perepiska A. M. Gor'kogo s G. G. Iagodoi," in Keldysh, *Neizvestnyi Gor'kii*, 168–206.

161. Gronskii, *Iz proshlogo*, 151–2. Gorky played a hand in getting Lev Kamenev appointed the first director of the Institute, but on Dec. 16, 1932, Kamenev was arrested. At that evening in the Bolshoi, Stalin had Henri Barbusse come to the stage from the audience and yielded him his seat. *Izvestiia*, Sept. 25 and 26, 1932. Andrei Bubnov, RSFSR commissar of enlightenment, on holiday in Gagra, had written to Stalin asking to be excused; Stalin ordered him to appear. RGASPI, f. 558, op. 11, d. 44, l. 115.

162. In the play (1931), an old professor makes the accusation that Soviet society is built

solely upon fear. Lyons, *Six Soviet Plays*, 585–9; Lih, "Melodrama and the Myth," 178–207. On April 2, 1933, Afinogenov asked Stalin to read his new play called *The Lie*, which depicted how low-level party apparatchiks had to lie, and how their lies worked their way up the system, with consequences. Stalin made voluminous marginal comments, and wrote to Afinogenov that "the idea of the play is rich, the formulation of the idea came out not rich." The Communists all seemed ugly, physically, morally, politically, Stalin noted, prohibiting its staging in that form. Afinogenov reworked his draft but, strangely, did not follow Stalin's instructions. Artizov and Naumov, *Vlast'*, 758n37 (RGASPI, f. 558, op. 1, d. 5088, l. 1), 758n38 (d. 4591, l. 4), 192 (d. 5088, l. 118–118ob.); Hindus, *Crisis in the Kremlin*, 249.

163. Maksimenkov, *Bol'shaia tsenzura*, 261–8 (RGASPI, f. 558, op. 11, d. 1116, l. 20–7). Feoktist Berezovsky made notes of the Oct. 20 meeting (but would send the text to Stalin only on April 29, 1933). "It is easy to alienate a sympathizer," Stalin pointed out, "and much harder to win him over." He also stated: "Poems are good. Novels are even better. But at the moment more than anything we need plays." RGASPI, f. 558, op. 11, d. 1116, l. 29–31.

164. Zelinskii, "Odna vtrecha," 156–7 (RGALI, f. 1604, op. 1, d. 21, l. 112–46). There would be no press coverage or official transcript of the meeting. Zelinskiy was observing Stalin up close for the first time. See also Maksimenkov, "Ocherki nomenklaturnoi istorii," 221–4; Maksimenkov, *Bol'shaia tsenzura*, 521; RGASPI, f. 558, op. 11, d. 1116, l. 28. The recollections in old age of Nikolai Nakoryakov (1881–1970), director in the 1930s of the state publishing for *belles lettres*, of another such meeting in Sept. 1933 are actually of the Oct. 1932 meeting. "Iz vospominanii: vstrecha Stalina s sovetskimi pisateliami v 1933 godu" (arkhiv A. M. Gor'kogo, MoG-10-13–3: Feb. 3, 1966).

165. Kemp-Welch, *Stalin and the Literary Intelligentsia*, 131 (citing "vstrecha pisatelei s I. V. Stalinym," arkhiv A. M. Gor'kogo, Oct. 26, 1932). The phrase resonated for some. "I immediately liked the permanently repeated aphorism: 'writers are the engineers of human souls,'" Valentin Katayev noted, attributing it, however, to the writer Yuri Olyesha. Kataev, "Sobytie nebyvaloe," 216.

166. Zelinskii, "Odna vtrecha," 157, 160–1, 168.

167. "A Russian writer," Gorky had written in a private letter back in 1902, "should never live in friendship with a Russian government." Gorky, *Letters of Gorky and Andreev*, 41.

168. Vinogradov, *Genrikh Iagoda*, 367 (TsA FSB, f. 2, op. 11, d. 510, l. 60); Antipina, *Povsednevnaia zhizn'*, 107–10. At the entrance to one prisoner barrack, a "menu" had been hung, surrounded by flowers, with the saying "Eat, and build the way you eat." The lunch was listed as cabbage soup, porridge with meat, fish cutlets with sauce, and pirohzki with cabbage. ("I with the pen, you with the shovel—together we built the canal," wrote the prisoner Vladimir Kavshchyn.) Draskoczy, *Belomor*, 11 (citing RGALI, f. 1885, op. 3, d. 34, l. 100). "From the minute we became guests of the Chekists, complete Communism began for us," recalled the then fledgling writer Alexander Avdeyenko, during this time of famine. "We ate and drank as we wanted, and paid for nothing. Smoked sausages. Cheeses. Caviar. Fruit. Chocolate. Wines. Brandy." Avdeenko, "Otluchenie" (no. 3), 11, (no. 4), 80–133. A group of satirists wrote to Yagoda that "they were thrilled by

the grandiose work of the OGPU!" Vinogradov, *Genrikh Iagoda*, 365 (TsA FSB, f. 2, op. 11, d. 510, l. 27: signed Kupriyanov, Krylov, Sokolov), 366 (l. 24, l. 68). The trip culminated in a copiously illustrated 400-page compilation published in early 1934 under Gorky's name. Gor'kii et al., *Belomorsko-Baltiiskii kanal imeni Stalina*. Gorky et al., *Belomor*; Gorky et al., *The White Sea Canal* (London: National Centre for Marxist and 'Left' Literature, 1935). See also Solzhenitsyn, *Gulag Archipelago*, III: 78–101; and Ruder, *Making History for Stalin*, 47–52, 213–4.

169. *XVII s"ezd*, 620.

170. Back in 1929, in connection with Stalin's official fiftieth birthday, Tovstukha's *Short Biography* (1927), shorter than a newspaper article, had been slightly enlarged and reissued in *Pravda* (Dec. 21, 1929). Tovstukha promised more, but there the matter had stood.

171. RGASPI, f. 558, op. 11 [4?], d. 1493, l. 50. Orjonikidze did not consider Koltsov's draft a success, stating of Stalin "he will beat you and thrash me." Koltsov nonetheless sent his text to the censor, which in turn forwarded it to Stalin, who supposedly read the manuscript, phoned Koltsov, told him "you praise me too much." True or not, the book never saw the light of day. Chukovskii, *Dnevnik*, 38–9. Koltsov's the "Riddle of Stalin," published in connection with the official fiftieth birthday, had used the conceit that Stalin might be a riddle to the world bourgeoisie—"Stalin the enigma," "the Communist sphinx," "the incomprehensible personality"—but not to the Soviet worker. *Pravda*, Dec. 21, 1929.

172. *Days*, the émigré paper in Paris edited by Alexander Kerensky, had alleged in Oct. 1929 that members of the so-called right opposition had compromising documents on Stalin's pre-1917 revolutionary past. They did not. The fabricated Yeremin "document" (a tsarist police official) appeared in the mid-1930s. (It would be published in *Life* on April 23, 1956.) Valdlen S. Izmozik, *Zhendarmy Rossii* (St. Petersburg: Neva, 2002), 466–8. The collection *Batumskaia demonstratsiia 1902 goda* (Moscow: Partizdat, 1937) contained recollections that Stalin had escaped from Eastern Siberian exile and traveled back to the Caucasus using a fabricated police I.D. in his name.

173. The memoirist Iosif "Soso" Iremashvili also claimed Stalin had emerged with "a grim and bitter hatred against the seminary administration, the bourgeoisie, and all that existed in the country and represented tsarism." Iremashvili, *Stalin und die Tragödie Georgiens*, 6, 11–2, 24; Tucker, *Stalin as Revolutionary*, 73.

174. The Comintern operative (Münzenberg) also mentioned Boris Bazhanov, the defector from Stalin's secretariat, who published a damning exposé in 1930 (and German 1931). Kun, *Stalin*, 69–70; RGASPI, f. 155, op. 1, d. 85, l. 1, 3.

175. Bey, *Career of a Fanatic*; and Bey, *Stalin*. A Russian translation of *Stalin* was published in Riga (Filin, 1932). Bey elaborated his stories of Stalin's criminal expropriations, amid exotic pageantry, in parallel volumes: *Blood and Oil in The Orient* (1931) and *Twelve Secrets of the Caucasus* (1931). See also Rieber, "Fun with my Buddy." When Lev was six years old, his mother, Berta Slutzkin (née Ratner), from the Russian empire's Pale of Settlement, had committed suicide (possibly by drinking acid); Nussimbaum's father, Abraham, also an Ashkenazi Jew but born in Tiflis, profited from the fin-de-siècle Caspian oil boom, and cashed in his wells to the Nobels in 1913, with exquisite timing. In 1917, when revolution struck, father and son fled by ship to Kizil-Su

(Red Water), in Turkestan, where they allegedly lived in a cinema. Then they fled to Persia by camel caravan, briefly returning to the Caucasus (by then under Ottoman occupation), and in 1921 they boarded a refugee ship (the *Kleopatra*) from Batum to Istanbul. In 1932, Bey married an heiress, Erika Loewendahl (who did not know his real origins), and resettled in Vienna. Following the Anschluss with Austria, Nussimbaum-Bey would relocate in March 1938 to Italy, but then went to Los Angeles. That same year, his wife publicly denounced him as a Jew and they divorced. "He told me he was of princely Arabian heritage," she wrote. "I learned after our marriage . . . that he was just plain Leo Nussinbaum!" Erika was herself a Jew, the daughter of a shoe magnate from Leipzig who built up the successful Berlin franchise of the Czech company Bata. In Hollywood, while Lev was developing a script for Clark Gable, Erika started an affair with an older married man, a Viennese-born Hungarian visionary named René Fülöp-Miller, who wrote in German and was an acquaintance and rival of Nussimbaum-Bey. Nussimbaum would die in Sept. 1942 of Raynaud's syndrome, having written some sixteen books in German, most of them translated into numerous languages, on Islam, desert escapades, the global oil industry, love in the Caucasus, Judaism's "oriental" roots, Muhammad, Nicholas II, Lenin, and Stalin. Reiss, *Orientalist*.

176. Beria also had his party organization publish Stalin's 1909 "Letter from the Caucasus," and mandated its study in educational circles. Sukharev, "Litsedeistvo," 105 (citing Partiinyi arkhiv Institutta istorii partii pri TsK KP gruzii, f. 13, op. 10, d. 11, l. 45–6); f. 14, op. 7, d. 34, l. 10; *Sbornik materialov v sviazi*.

177. Tovstukha and his assistants gathered an immense volume of materials: RGASPI, f. 71, op. 10, d. 192–218, 364–73.

178. Tucker, *Stalin in Power*, 335n.109; Brandenberger, "Stalin as Symbol," 249–70 (at 256).

179. Maksimenkov, *Bol'shaia tsenzura*, 270 (RGASPI, f. 558, op. 11, d. 699, l. 61: Dec. 8. 1932), 271 (l. 62). Barbusse had written two books about his travels inside the Soviet Union, and both had flattered Stalin.

180. Van Ree, *Political Thought*, 164; Maksimenkov, "Kul't"; RGASPI, f. 558, op. 1, d. 3087. When Ukrainian Communists wanted to publish a pamphlet on his life in connection with the 1933 fifteenth anniversary of the founding of the Communist Youth League, Stalin balked. That same year, he crossed out references to his contributions from the theses of the Institute of Marxism-Leninism on the Bolshevik party's thirtieth anniversary. The next year he deleted the second part of the phrases "Lenin-Stalin party" and "teachings of Lenin and Stalin" from a publication. Davies and Harris, *Stalin's World*, 149–50 (citing RGASPI, f. 558, op. 11, d. 3087, l. 30; d. 3118). A 1934 *Pravda* essay on Turukhansk, including an image of Stalin's exile hut, elicited his disdain ("rubbish"). RGASPI, f. 558, op. 11, d. 1494, l. 6–10. When the Youth League journal *Young Guard* prepared a writer's travelogue across the USSR for publication, Stalin expunged mentions of visits to his places of exile. El'-Registan, "Neobychainoe puteshestvie"; RGASPI, op. 11, 1494, l. 121–5. Trotsky had underlined in the manuscript of one of his writings: "If personalities do not make history, then history makes itself by means of personalities." Volkogonov, *Trotsky*, xxxii–xxxiii.

181. RGASPI, f. 558, op. 11, d. 4572, l. 1 (July 1933); Sukharev, "Litsedeistvo," 104; Gromov, *Stalin*, 143–4.

182. Radek's encomium was reissued as a pamphlet in 225,000 copies (and multiple

languages): *Zodchii sotsialisticheskogo obshchestva* (Moscow: Partizdat, 1934); *The Architect of a Socialist Society* (Moscow-Leningrad: Co-operative Publishing Society of Foreign Workers in the U.S.S.R., 1934); *Der Baumeister der sozialistischen Gesellschaft* (Moscow-Leningrad: Verlagsgenossenschaft ausländischer arbeiter in der UdSSR, 1934). See also Petrov and Petrov, *Empire of Fear*, 69; and Tucker, *Stalin in Power*, 244–6.

183. The congress amended the statutes to stipulate a gathering every three years. *XVII s"ezd*, 525–66. Even half the collective farms now contained at least one Communist. Party members of peasant social origin had risen to 28.5 percent, from 20.4 percent in 1930, but the still ongoing purge would wipe out these gains.

184. Kamenev had published an essay in *Pravda* (May 25, 1933) enjoining the opposition to desist (they were in prison or exile). The politburo had approved the reinstatement of Zinoviev and Kamenev on Dec. 12, 1933 (RGASPI, f. 17, op. 3, d. 936, l. 5). After the Congress, Kamenev would be installed as head of Academia, the country's highest prestige press for scholarship, which in 1934 would publish the first volume of a Russian translation of Machiavelli's collected works containing *The Prince*, whose publication had already been scheduled, but now Kamenev was able to write the preface, and he offered Soviet readers a Machiavelli who was an unmasker of despots, and repeatedly called him "secretary" of the Florentine republic—Stalin's title. Kamenev characterized the Florentine "secretary" as having "no gift for profound philosophical inquiry" and his society as "an oppressive class of masters struggling among themselves for power over the laboring masses." Kamenev, "Predislovie," I: 7–15.

185. *XVII s"ezd*, 124–9 (Bukharin), 209–12 (Rykov), 492–7 (Zinoviev), 516–21 (Kamenev). Stalin allowed Zinoviev to be named an editor of *Bolshevik*, the party journal. At a politburo session on Feb. 20, 1934, on Stalin's initiative, Bukharin was named editor of *Izvestiya* (replacing Gronsky, who was moved to the editorship of the journal *Novy Mir*). RGASPI, f. 17, op. 3, d. 939, l. 2. Even the diehard Trotsky supporter Rakovski would publicly recant and be allowed back from internal exile, though not into the party. *Pravda*, April 18, 1934; Khaustov et al., *Lubianka: Stalin i VChK*, 326–34 (APRF, f. 3, op. 24, d. 139, l. 35–52: Oct. 11, 1932); Bukharin's appointment had implications for Kalinin, since *Izvestiya* was the organ of his own Soviet central executive committee. Brontman, *Dnevniki*. Brontman (b. 1905), who published under the name Ognev, wrote many of *Pravda's* unsigned editorials.

186. Chernobaev, *Vvikhre veka*, 178 (Alexander Arosyev diary, Jan. 26, 1934).

187. *Sochineniia*, XIII: 282–379 (at 366–70).

188. *Sochineniia*, XIII: 371.

189. *Sochineniia*, XIII: 294.

190. *XVII s"ezd*, 8–36; *Sochineniia*, XIII: 283. Stalin would repeat the idea that imperialist war could generate new revolutions at the next congress in 1939. *Sochineniia*, XIV: 338; van Ree, *Political Thought*, 212. See also Rieber, "Stalin as Foreign Policy Maker," 142–3. There were close parallels between Varga's *New Phenomena in the World Economic Crisis* (1934) and Stalin's report to the 17th Party Congress. Varga, "Vskryt' cherez 25 let," 155–6; Duda, *Jenő Varga*, 89, 109–10, 115. One émigré who claimed to have worked in Varga's Institute claimed that its staff had no reason to fear reprisals for what in their mind were realistic portrayals of the capitalist world. Rosenfeldt, *Stalin's Special*

Departments, 71–3 (citing unpublished manuscript "Organizatisia i funktsiia Osobogo sektora TsK VKP (b)" held at the Library of Congress). On German fears of a Soviet policy shift dating to 1933, Von Riekhoff, *German-Polish Relations*, 385. See also Sluch, "Germano-sovetskie otnosheniia," 153 (citing AVP RF, f. 082, op. 14, pap. 62, d. 2, l. 365).

191. *DGFP*, series C, II: 421–2; *Reichgesetzblatt*, 1934, II: 118–9 (German and Polish originals); Ahmann, *Nichtangriffspakte*, 310–25, 255–342; Niclauss, *Die Sowjetunion*, 151–63; Wandycz, *Twilight of French Eastern Alliances*, 300–35; Cienciala, "Declaration of Non-Aggression"; Ken and Rusapov, *Politbiuro Tsk VKP (b) i otnosheniia SSSR*, 62–3; Haslam, *Struggle for Collective Security*, 14, 20–1; Beck, *Final Report*, 31–2. For the public Soviet reaction: *Izvestiia* and *Pravda*, Jan. 29, 1934.

192. Cienciala, "Polish Foreign Policy," 44–59; Cienciala, "Foreign Policy of Józef Piłsudski."

193. Wandycz, "Polish Foreign Policy: Some Observations," citing Louis Eisenmann, "La Question de Teschen." *La Vie des peuples*, I, 1920: 837. While Piłsudski had tried to diminish the Russian menace by carving out a quasi-federation of states in the east centered on an independent Ukraine, his nemesis Dmowski had pushed for annexations. Both had failed.

194. The French embassy in Warsaw seems to have submitted nothing to Paris between Dec. 21 and Jan. 26: *DDF*, 1e série, VII: 907–10.

195. Laroche, *La Pologne de Pilsudski*, 18–45; Weinberg, *Foreign Policy*, I: 169–72; Steiner, *Triumph of the Dark*, 63.

196. Gasiorowski, "German-Polish Nonaggression Pact of 1934," 27; Cienciala, review of *La Décadence*, 539; Pohle, *Der Rundfunk*, 397–8. The perceptive French ambassador in Washington ventured to the Americans that Germany wanted a short period of peace to strengthen itself for eventual European domination. Weinberg, *Foreign Policy*, I: 73 (citing State 760c.6212/10: undersecretary Phillips on conversation with de Laboulaye, Jan. 27, 1934).

197. Radek had argued to Stalin that while France was seeking to align with Germany, France's ally Poland could be wooed away and promised a Soviet-Polish pact against Germany founded on Polish desires for a free hand in independent Lithuania and perhaps Danzig. Alarmingly for Moscow, however, in mid-Nov. 1933, Hitler and the new Polish ambassador Józef Lipski issued an odd public joint communiqué, vaguely implying (or maybe not) the possibility of a nonaggression pact. On Nov. 27, Piłsudski secretly received a concrete German proposal, which he sat on for some time.

198. This occurred on Dec. 20, 1933, at the sixteenth anniversary commemoration of the Cheka's founding. Gorbunov, "Voennaia razvedka v 1934–1939 godakh" (no. 2), 103. Artuzov was said to have recruited Polish agents as double agents as far back as 1920, including the Riga-born, Moscow University–educated Ignay Sosnowski (Dobrzynski), who worked for the intelligence department of the Polish general staff. Pogonii, *Lubianka 2*, 175–9. See also Tumshis and Papchinskii, *1937*, 445–51 (citing Artuzov's letter to Yezhov, March 22, 1937); and Kolpakidi and Prokhorov, *Imperiia GRU*, I: 205–7. Vladimir Antonov-Ovseyenko, Soviet envoy in Warsaw, had written shrewdly to Stomonyakov in Moscow that the Polish government had never believed an alliance with France or the Little Entente would guarantee its security against Germany. "You will be in all the combinations," one Polish contact told him, "but we?" Still,

Antonov-Ovseyenko had been taken in by Polish assurances that there were no negotiations under way with Germany. *Dokumenty o materialy po istorii sovetsko-pol'skikh otnoshenii*, VI: 112–6 (Nov. 29, 1933).

199. Yegorov, chief of the general staff, was urging Twardowski, "Change your policy and everything will be all right again." *DGFP*, series C, II: 338–9 (Jan. 11, 1934), 352–3 (Jan. 13), 376–9 (Jan. 17). See also Hilger and Meyer, *Incompatible Allies*, 271; and Tucker, *Stalin in Power*, 256–60. Nadolny, in reference to Stalin's Jan. 26 speech, noted its "calm tone and matter-of-factness," especially compared with Litvinov, and suggested the Germans make an acknowledgment. Hitler mentioned Stalin's speech in his own speech to the Reichstag (Jan. 30). *DGFP*, series C, II: 435–6 (Jan. 29, 1934); Baynes, *Speeches of Adolf Hitler*, II: 1151–71; *Völkischer Beobachter*, Jan. 31, 1934. Nadolny, after arguing with Hitler, who blocked his efforts to attain a rapprochement, would resign on June 16, 1934. He would be succeeded by Count Friedrich Werner von der Schulenburg. "The German Foreign Office," in Craig and Gilbert, *Diplomats*, 417–8; Weinberg, *Foreign Policy*, I: 180–3.

200. Shore, "Hitler's Opening Gambit."

201. On the eve of the Polish-German coup de main, the USSR had signed a modest, provisional trade agreement with France. Adibekov et al., *Politbiuro TsK RKP (b)–VKP (b) i Evropa*, 307 (RGASPI, f. 17, op. 162, d. 15, l. 166: Jan. 11, 1934); *DDF*, 1e série, V: 436–7. See also Carley, "Five Kopecks." In early 1934, France and the USSR also exchanged aviation attachés, as Cot's mission bore delayed fruit, and in Aug. 1934 the Soviets reciprocated Cot's visit with an aviation squadron that landed in France. Scott, *Alliance Against Hitler*, 119–21.

202. Piłsudski received the interlocutor in question, Hermann Rauschning, head of state in Danzig, in Warsaw on Dec. 11, 1933. Weinberg, *Foreign Policy*, I: 72 (citing German foreign ministry memo IV Po 9133, T-120, 3024/6601/E 495072-77: Dec. 14, 1933). On Nov. 23, 1934, Rauschning would resign his Nazi party membership and later emigrate.

203. Ken, *Mobilizatsionnoe planirovanie*, 269; Ken, *Collective Security or Isolation*, 121–2, 146–7; Morozov, *Pol'sko-Chekhoslovatskie otnosheniia*, 9, 27, 504; *DVP SSSR*, XVII: 133–4; *Izvestiia*, April 20, 1934.

204. *Dokumenty i materialy po istorii sovetsko-pol'skikh otnoshenii*, VI: 167–73; *DDF*, 1e série, V: 783–5. Beck admitted that Piłsudski convened discussions of possible preemptive war against Germany, but claimed the idea was put to rest in spring 1934. Beck, *Final Report*, 51–3.

205. *Sochineniia*, XIII: 321–2, 329–30. Stalin also conceded that "it must be said of state farms that they have failed to achieve what is required of them." He deemed them too specialized and too cumbersome to administer properly, without admitting this had been his vision. *XVII s"ezd*, 23. In 1933, state farms had supplied only a few million of the 20 million tons of grain procured by the state. Davies and Wheatcroft, *Years of Hunger*, 332–47.

206. Davies et al., *Years of Progress*, 11–4; *XVII s"ezd*, 435–6, 439–41, 443–55, 668; Zaleski, *Stalinist Planning*, 132. A politburo decree of Jan. 20, 1934, committed state supplies of seeds and equipment for workers to garden on household plots in their free time, legally and without being taxed. Antipova et al., *Golod v SSSR*, 509–11 (RGASPI, f. 17, op. 3, d. 937, l. 1, 8, 52, 68–9).

207. *XVII s"ezd*, 525. The views of actual farmers were far from the discussion. "Under the current regime it is necessary to tie a noose around one's neck, or to cheat the state," I. Gribanov told a group of collective farmers in 1934, according to a police summary. Kedrov, *Lapti Stalinizma*, 151 (citing GAAO, otdel DSPI, f. 290, op. 2, d. 337, l. 16–8).

208. *XVII s"ezd*, 236–9.

209. *XVII s"ezd*, 251–9; RGASPI, f. 671, op. 1, d. 271, l. 529–33 (Chagin). Kirov, exhausted, had been compelled to spend Nov. 23 to Dec. 29, 1933, at a sanatorium in Tolmachevo, outside Leningrad, but insisted on a direct telephone line to Smolny and daily postal deliveries, with his wife serving as his secretary. He complained to his physician (G. F. Lang) of heart palpitations, pains, insomnia, and occasional trouble walking, and submitted to a regimen of saltwater baths. Pazi, *Nash Mironych*, 412–8, 448; Sinel'nikov, *Kirov*, 357–8; Krasnikov, *Kirov v Leningrade*, 179–83; Knight, *Who Killed Kirov?*, 167–8.

210. *XVII s"ezd*, 269. "Whereas at the 15th Congress it was still necessary to prove the correctness of the party line and to fight certain anti-Leninist groupings, and at the 16th Congress to finish off the last supporters of these groupings," Stalin had noted in his congress report, "at the present congress there is nothing to prove and, it seems, nobody to beat." *XVII s"ezd*, 28. Manuilsky also made no reply to the discussion of his report on the Comintern.

211. At the 15th Congress (1927), forty-three did not. At the 1939 congress vote, forty-four bulletins would go unused. RGASPI, f. 56, op. 1, d. 61, l. 39; op. 2, d. 36, l. 23; f. 58, op. 1, d. 37, l. 31–3; op. 2 d. 46, l. 9; Pavliukov, *Ezhov*, 99–106 (citing f. 477, op. 1, d. 41, l. 4). Delegates had to insert their folded ballots into urns specifically for their delegation.

212. Mikhailov and Naumov, "Skol'ko delegatov XVII s"ezda partii golosovalo protiv Stalina?"; Lenoe, *Kirov Murder*, 613 (RGANI, f. 6, op. 13, d. 23, l. 43–43ob.: Napoleon V. Andreosyan [sic] deposition). According to Mikoyan, Andreasyan told him that his delegation alone recorded twenty-five votes against Stalin. Mikoian, *Tak Bylo*, 592–3.

213. *Sotsialisticheskii vestnik*, Feb. 25, 1934; Medvedev, *Let History Judge*, 331–4.

214. *Pravda*, Feb. 7, 1964. V. Verkhovykh would later claim that "in conversation with Kosior the latter told me: 'Some of us spoke with Kirov in order to get him to agree to become general secretary.' Kirov refused, saying: 'It's necessary to wait, all will settle down.'" Mikhailov and Naumov, "Skol'ko delegatov XVII s"ezda partii golosovalo protiv Stalina?" 114. Khrushchev, who at the time of the 17th Congress was close to Stalin, would recall (or imagine) that Sheboldayev had approached Kirov on behalf of a group of colluding provincial bosses, but that Kirov went straight to Stalin, which implanted permanent suspicions of Kirov in Stalin's mind. (Khrushchev acknowledged that he "personally did not have direct interaction with" Kirov.) Mikoyan claims that, in Stalin's office on the evening of Dec. 2 (the meeting was actually the 3rd), when he questioned why Yagoda was not being held accountable, Stalin defended him—raising suspicions that Stalin had organized the assassination through Yagoda. Mikoyan has the events taking place at the Winter Palace, not Tauride, and has Medved, not Zaporozhets, absent from Leningrad. Khrushchev, *Vospominaniia*, I: 97–9; Khrushchev, *Memoirs*, I: 91–3; Mikoian, "V pervyi raz bez Lenina," 6; Mikoian, *Tak bylo*, 316–8. It has also been asserted that the Caucasus delegations lobbied Mikoyan and Orjonikidze to have Kirov (an honorary Caucasus figure) replace Stalin as general secretary, with Stalin moving over to head the government in place of Molotov. Bondarenko and Efimov, *Utaennye stranitsy sovetskoi istorii*, 70.

215. Kirilina, *Rikoshet*, 76–80; Benvenuti, "Kirov in Soviet Politics." Kirov's public profile paled in comparison to those of Kaganovich, Orjonikidze, or Molotov, let alone Stalin. Kirov rarely attended politburo meetings, which took place in Moscow, and sometimes did not even vote on politburo matters by telephone poll. See also Khlevniuk, *Politbiuro*, 122; Khlevniuk, *Khoziain*, 215–6.

216. Khrushchev, *Vospominaniia*, I: 93; Khrushchev, *Memoirs*, I: 86.

217. Rosliakov, *Ubiistvo*, 122–3.

218. *XVII s"ezd*, 303. See also Tucker, *Stalin in Power*, 247.

219. *XVII s"ezd*, 573–6; Furer, *Novaia Gorlovka*. In response to disarray in Ukraine's strategic coal industry, Kaganovich had visited the mining town of Gorlovka, then the Donbass capital, in spring 1933. Among the many measures forced through, Furer became Gorlovka party boss and worked like a demon to lift the miners out of mud huts and barracks, paving streets, building housing, sidewalks, tram lines, a hospital, schools, and a stadium with lights for night matches, a first for the USSR (it opened in Sept. 1933 and was named for living Ukraine OGPU chief Balytsky). Furer would last in Gorlovka until Dec. 1934, when Kaganovich would summon him to head the agitation and propaganda department in the Moscow province-city party committee. Kuromiya, "The Commander and the Rank and File," 154–5; *XVII s"ezd*, 162–3; www .gorlovka360.dn.ua/sport-i-zdorovie/ stadion-shahter-virtualnyiy-tur.

220. Chuev, *Sto sorok*, 307–8, 478; Chuev, *Molotov*, 375–6; Krasnikov, *Kirov v Leningrade*, 187–8; Rosliakov, *Ubiistvo*, 28–9. There is some ambiguity as to whether the Kirov incident took place in a narrow circle or at the Central Committee plenum.

221. Khlevniuk, *Politbiuro*, 121–2. Kirov would end up spending more time in Moscow: he would be recorded in Stalin's office for 63 hours in 1934, compared with 10 in 1933, 28 in 1932, and 23 in 1931. *Na prieme*.

222. Zhdanov replaced the now Ukraine-based Postyshev, whom Stalin promoted to candidate member of the politburo even as he relieved him of the Central Committee secretary position. Kaganovich remained Stalin's top deputy in the party, receiving all the documentation concerning party affairs, economic management, and foreign affairs. On Jan. 17, 1934, Stalin had required that all hiring and firing in the Central Committee apparatus have either his own or Kaganovich's authorization. Khlevniuk et al., *Stalin i Kaganovich*, 5; Khlevniuk, *Khoziain*, 195–6; RGASPI, f. 558, op. 11, d. 77, l. 3.

223. Zhdanov, born in Mariupol, had grown up mostly in Tver, where in Aug. 1914 he joined a Marxist group led by A. I. Krinitsky. In Jan. 1918, Zhdanov, a veteran of the Great War, was part of a group of Red Guards who seized the small town of Shadrinsk in the Urals (near Perm); by 1919, however, he was said to be exhausted and allowed to go home to Tver to recuperate; his comrades abandoned Shadrinsk. Zhdanov served for a decade as party boss of Nizhny Novgorod, 1924–1934. He would go after Krinitsky in 1935 and help destroy him in 1938. Mikoian, *Tak bylo*, 562; *Andrei Aleksandrovich Zhdanov, 1896–1948*; Glotova, "Andrei Aleksandrovich Zhdanov"; Borisov, *Andrei Aleksandrovich Zhdanov*.

224. "Vospominaniia: memurary Nikity Sergeevicha Khrushcheva," 62–3. The scien-

tist and Leningrad-resident Vladimir Vernadsky, in his diary, would deem Zhdanov a "petty, talentless figure, especially after Kirov." Vernadskii, "Dnevnik 1940 goda."

225. Kaganovich, in Feb. 1932, had needed a six-week respite, bedridden for headaches and dizziness. He would have a tonsillitis operation in July 1934. Rees, *Iron Lazar*, 217. Zhdanov was given the agriculture portfolio on March 3, which Kaganovich had managed, but Zhadanov held it for a mere thirty-eight days (it went to Yakovlev) and instead got planning, finance, and trade; Yezhov got industry, which he would hold for a year; Kaganovich, transport (the next area for a trouble-shooter, after agriculture's stabilization); Stetsky, culture and propaganda. Posokryobyshev remained head of the special sector; that is, Stalin's office. Zhdanov, although not a member of the politburo, would attend more than half the meetings in Stalin's office in 1934. E. K. Pramnek, appointed hastily to replace Zhdanov in Nizhny Novgorod, was awkwardly promoted to Central Committee candidate member after the Congress.

226. Khlevniuk, *Master of the House*, 102. See also Chuev, *Sto sorok*, 468. Whereas in 1923, 88 percent of all decisions were taken at a formal meeting, by 1933 that was down to 13 percent (by 1937, it would be 0.6 percent). In 1933, there were twenty-four formal politburo sessions for the year, two a month, usually on the first and fifteenth; from Sept. 1934, formal meetings would drop to one per month, with additional meetings as necessary. In 1936, there were no politburo meetings in Jan., Aug., and Nov. Rees, "Stalin as Leader, 1924–1937," 25–7. See also Khlevniuk, *Politburo*, 289. Formal politburo meetings could be attended by sixty people or more at any one time: non-members were invited for specific agenda items or the whole meeting. Wheatcroft, "From Team-Stalin to Degenerate Tyranny," 88–9.

227. *XVII s"ezd*, 680–1. Stalin allowed the former Trotsky supporter Pyatakov into the Central Committee, and Bukharin, Rykov, Tomsky, and Sokolnikov to return as candidate members.

228. Stalin also formally pared back the powers of his own workers' and peasants' inspectorate–party Control Commission (he had already entrusted the 1933 party purge to a special commission), slashing its size in a push for greater efficiency and less local collusion. "What we need now," he had told the congress, "is not inspection but check-up on fulfillment of the center's decisions." Many of the commission's powers, in any case, had already been taken by the OGPU. *XVII s'ezd*, 35; Turkan, *Ian Rudzutak*, 91–2; Rees, *State Control in Soviet Russia*, 219–23. "From now on," Stalin added, "nine-tenths of the responsibility for the failures and defects in our work rest not on 'objective' circumstances but on ourselves and on ourselves alone." *Sochineniia*, XIII: 367–70. See also Markevich, "Monitoring and Interventions."

229. *Pravda*, Feb. 7 and 8, 1934. Stalin had been signing documents for some time simply as "secretary of the CC." From 1931, he was being listed as just "secretary," not general secretary. Rosenfeldt, *Stalin's Special Departments*, 9. Politburo members as of Feb. 1934 were: Stalin, Molotov, Kaganovich, Voroshilov, Kalinin, Orjonikidze, Kuibyshev, Kirov, Andreyev, and Kosior. Candidate members were: Mikoyan, Chubar, Petrovsky, Postoyshev, and Rudzutaks. Secretariat members were: Stalin, Kaganovich, Kirov, and Zhdanov.

230. Inside the street entrance used by visitors to Stalin's Kremlin office, there was a small, dark waiting room and an elaborate staircase. Upstairs, a broad corridor led to a massive double door, behind which was Stalin's spacious anteroom. A table there was usually piled with newspapers and other reading materials, paper, and pencils. Another door led to the office of his top aide, Alexander Poskryobyshev, where two or three guards in uniform sat, and whence there was access to Stalin's office. Stalin's expansive wing, formally the "special sector" of the Communist party apparatus, had a special door separating it from the offices for the Council of People's Commissars and the Soviet central executive committee, on the same floor and one floor above. "I had a pass to all areas [of the Kremlin], except to the corridor leading to Stalin's wing of the building," wrote Valentin Berezhkov, an interpreter. "A special pass was made out for each trip" to Stalin's office. Berezhkov, *At Stalin's Side*, 203–4. See also Deviatov et al., *Blizhniaia dacha Stalina*, 57; Shepilov, *Kremlin's Scholar*, 16; Iakovlev, *Tsel' zhizni* (2nd ed.), 184–5; Yakov Chadaev, in Kumanev, *Riadom so Stalinym*, 383; and Chuev, *Sto sorok*, 292.

231. Before the Near Dacha was built, Soviet higher-ups had used a small pensione on the steep banks of the Setun River in the Volynskoe Wood, which was on the ninth kilometer of the Mozhaisk Road (Zubalovo was on the 32nd km). Dmitry Donskoi had once awarded the land as a gift to one of the victors in the Battle of Kulikovo Field, Voevoda Bobrok-Volynsky. In the sixteenth century, the land was claimed by the sovereign; after that it went to the courtier who had conducted the inquiry into the death of Ivan the Terrible's son, then to the Dolgorukys, the Loanov-Rostovskys. Rudomino, *Legendarnaia Barvikha*, 44: Deviatov et al., *Blizhniaia*, 28.

232. Merzhanov had been named central executive committee chief architect in June 1931. In 1929, he had won an open competition to design a resort for the Red Army in Sochi. It was built into a hillside (with a funicular), a triumph of constructivism in harmony with the landscape, completed on July 1, 1934, and named in honor of Voroshilov. (It would win a grand prize at the 1937 Paris Exhibition.) The architect and defense commissar struck up a friendship, and the Soviet press spotlighted his Sochi sanatorium. Merzhanov got many commissions, including the NKVD sanatorium in Kislovodsk.

233. Murin, *Stalin v ob"iatiaiakh*, 160; Sergeev and Glushik, *Besedy o Staline*, 41–2; Shepilov, *Kremlin's Scholar*, 2. In the nineteenth century, Kuntsevo had become a summer resort for Muscovites (Ivan Turgenev stayed there). It was recognized as a town in 1925–6 and by the mid-1930s counted perhaps 40,000 inhabitants. There was a sewing needle factory, and a dacha that served as the Comintern's department for international communications (known as facility No. 1). Davydkovo, less than a mile from the territory of Stalin's dacha complex, became a dacha complex for others in the elite at Stalin's directive. Trembitskii, *Po Zapadnomu okrugu*.

234. Zubalovo-4 stood on the left bank of the Medvenka River. Nadya had soured on it and found another spot much farther out on an old estate, Lipki, at the 200km mark on the Dimitrov Highway, where she initiated construction on a new single-family dacha, perhaps to avoid the relatives—both the Alliluyevs and Savnidzes had accommodations at Zubalovo—but Lipki had been finished only after her death. The building of a new Far Dacha, Semenovskoe, would begin in 1937, according to the Near Dacha design, but with bricks from the start. Murin, *Stalin v o"iatiakh*, 23–4; Alliluyeva, *Dvadtsat' pisem*, 30–1, 36. The regime established other elite dacha settlements in the dense forests of largely unsettled rural Barvikha county, along the Moscow River and several tributaries, where there had been estates of the Romanovs (Ilinskoe, Usovo, Znamenskoe) or other grandees: Prince Yusupov (Arkhangelskoe), Prince Golitsyn (Petrovskoe), Baron Meyendorf (Podkushino). The Chekists took a shine to Zhukovka: on the high right bank of the Moscow River, between Barvikha village and Usovo. Rudomino, *Legendarnaia Barvikha*.

235. Hitler had initially rented the alpine hideaway, known as the Haus Wachenfeld, a modest, rustic lodge, during a 1926 holiday (the rent was paid by an admirer), and by 1933, using monies he earned from the sale of *Mein Kampf*, he had purchased the property. "This place is mine," Hitler had proudly told a writer for the British *Homes and Gardens* in 1938. "I built it with money that I earned." The breathless magazine article, featuring photographs, called Hitler "his own decorator, designer, and furnisher, as well as architect." It would acquire a remodeled study, a film screening room, and a great room with a marble fireplace, chandeliers, Persian rugs, paintings, and wall tapestries. The furniture was Teutonic-style.

236. Stratigakos, *Hitler at Home*. See also Schuster-Winkelhof, *Adolf Hitlers Wahlheimat*; and Hoffmann, *Hitler in seinem Bergen*.

237. Pauker had a personal Cadillac, a gift from Stalin. Yezhov would ride in a gold-colored Chrysler airflow sedan, one of two in the USSR. Lakoba got a Lincoln. Beria would obtain a coveted Packard. Zhukovskii, *Lubianskaia imperiia NKVD*, 31; Orlov, *Tainaia istoriia*, 309; Orlov, *Secret History*, 346.

238. "There are others like Leshchenko," Stalin was said to have told Artyom and Vasya, "but there's only one Vertinsky." Sergeev and Glushik, *Besedy o Staline*, 42.

239. Mikoian, *Tak bylo*, 352–3.

240. Their treehouse ("Robinson Crusoe") was removed, perhaps for security reasons, even though Stalin did not go there much anymore. Alliluyeva, *Twenty Letters*, 122. Zubalovo would be renamed Gorky-4.

241. Pauker had ended up in Russia in April 1915 as an Austro-Hungarian POW, and was sent to work on a railroad in Turkestan; where in March 1917 he was released and stayed on and joined the Cheka (Dec. 1918), and, around 1920, relocated to Moscow. Petrov and Skorkin, *Kto rukovodil NKVD*, 102, 335; Naumov, *Stalin i NKVD*, 80. Orlov is the source of numerous fairy tales about Pauker, which have been repeated in the secondary literature. Orlov, *Taina istoriia*, 305–17.

242. Svetlana began first grade in fall 1933; Vasily entered fifth. After completing the eighth grade, Vasily in 1937 would be transferred to special School No. 2; the next year he would be sent to the Kachinsk Military Aviation School in Sevastopol. Svetlana would complete all ten grades at No. 25 and graduate in 1943. Holmes, *Stalin's School*, 165–8. Pauker's men would drop the children off in a car at Pushkin Square, after which they walked the short rest of the way.

243. The unofficially adopted Artyom, after Nadya's suicide, had gone back to live with his mother full-time in her Moscow apartment, though he continued to visit the Stalin family. He recalled how once at a meal Stalin discovered ashes in the soup and demanded to know the culprit. Artyom admitted responsibility. Stalin told him to eat the soup and if he liked

it to ask Karolina Til to put ashes in it every day, but if he did not like it, to desist from doing so ever again. Sergeev and Glushik, *Besedy o Staline,* 89–96, 123. In 1937, Artyom's mother would obtain a dacha in the elite settlement of Zhukova.

244. Loginov, *Teni Stalina,* 97.

245. "She and her father are great friends," Nadya had written to Keke, back on March 12, 1931, when Svetlana was five. Murin, *Stalin v ob"iatiakh,* 15–6 (APRF, f. 45, op. 1, d. 1549, l. 40–40ob.).

246. After her mother's death Svetlana got a new governess, Lidiya, with whom she clashed. Alliluyeva, *Twenty Letters,* 132.

247. Charkviani, *Napriki da naazrevi,* 503. Khrushchev claimed he observed such scenes and pitied Svetlana "as I would feel for an orphan. Stalin himself was brutal and inattentive. . . . [Stalin] loved her, but . . . his was the tenderness of a cat for a mouse." Krushchev, *Khrushchev Remembers,* 310–1.

248. Alliluyeva, *Twenty Letters,* 30, 144. Stalin usually had his afternoon meal in his Kremlin apartment, around 7:00 p.m., often in company, and that was when he saw the children. The conversation was often just between the adults, but eventually he would get around to asking Svetlana and Vasily about school. "His time for seeing me and Vasily was during dinner at the apartment," Svetlana recalled. "He'd ask me about my lessons, look at the [day]book my marks were entered in and sometimes ask me to show him my exercise books. He used to sign my books, as parents were supposed to do." Vasily often left his daybooks at home, and refused to carry out his assignments, or did them in ways that violated school regulations, prompting his homeroom teacher to phone his governess. Alliluyeva, *Twenty Letters,* 122–3, 133; Holmes, *Stalin's School,* 71–2, 166–7. Stalin in 1937 ordered the keeping of a secret second daybook to track Vasily's academic work. Murin, *Stalin v ob"iatiiakh,* 56.

249. Murin, *Stalin v ob"iatiakh,* 177 (Svanidze diary: May 9, 1935). Svetlana sometimes visited grandma Olga Alliluyeva and grandpa Sergei Alliluyev, who had a homey Kremlin apartment. Alliluyeva, *Twenty Letters,* 43.

250. Alliluyeva, *Twenty Letters,* 145–6.

251. The first article, "Stalin the Terrible," appeared April 8, but the note from Doletsky (TASS) in London was dated April 7, so the Soviets had a heads-up. Maksimenkov, *Bol'shaia tsenzura,* 313 (RGASPI, f. 558, op. 1, d. 1540, l. 33), 313–4 (l. 34–5), 315 (l. 36), 315–6 (l. 51), 316 (l. 37), 316–7 (l. 52: Astakhov in London), 317 (l. 53: Soviet ambassador), 317–8 (l. 54: German press). The newspaper was owned by Lord Beaverbrook.

252. Maksimenkov, *Bol'shaia tsenzura,* 318 (RGASPI, f. 558, op. 11, d. 49, l. 30, 31–31ob.).

253. Slavinskii, *Sovetskii soiuz i kitai,* 275–6.

254. Barmin, *Sovetskii Soiuz i Sin'tszian,* 146–7.

255. Chiang had been ready to send his own expeditionary force to back the Muslim rebels against the warlord. Forbes, *Warlords and Muslims;* Gritsenko, "Chto eto bylo?"; *Pravda,* June 22, 1934; Hedin, *History of the Expedition in Asia,* III: 84, 112–5; Goldman, *Red Road through Asia,* 132. On Dec. 15, 1934, the politburo resolved to have a commission look into whether some Uzbek and Kazakh school textbooks could be adapted for Xinjiang. Gatagova, *Sovetskaia etnopolitika 1930–1940-e gody,* 33–4 (RGASPI, f. 17, op. 166, d. 533, l. 14). Molotov would publicly deny, at the 7th Congress of Soviets in Jan. 1935, "the slanderous rumors of the Sovietization of Xinjiang." Not long thereafter, Soviet forces were fully withdrawn from Xinjiang. *DVP SSSR,* XVIII: 45; Barmin, *Sovetskii Soiuz i Sintszian,* 77–9

(citing AVP RF, f. 8/08, op. 14, pap. 130, d. 146, l. 12; d. 147, l. 17, 31; RGASPI, f. 62, op. 2, d. 2798, l. 27), 107–8 (citing RGASPI, f. 495, op. 154, d. 457, l. 31–8, 9), 111–2 (AVP RF, f. 8/08, op. 15, pap. 162, d. 117, l. 3, 9), 116, 129–30 (RGASPI, f. 17, op. 162, d. 16, l. 32), 132 (l. 113).

256. Bullitt, *For the President,* 83.

257. Litvinov wrote to Maisky (April 19) that "the negotiations with America have for now ground to a halt. The Johnson Act has as good as halted our trade with America . . . We have firmly stated that we will not give in to pressure and that we can exist without American trade." Haslam, *Threat from the East,* 40; *DVP SSSR,* XVII: 274–5.

258. Radek and Bukharin told Bullitt, in wishful thinking, "If war can be delayed for a few years a social upheaval in Japan may not be out of the question." Haslam, *Threat from the East,* 41, citing *FRUS,* 109–10 (Bullitt to Hull, April 16, 1934).

259. Litvinov had proposed to German ambassador Nadolny a joint "guarantee" of the independence and territorial inviolability of the Baltic states. On April 14, Germany declined the proposal, observing that the Baltic states might view such a guarantee as tantamount to a German-Soviet protectorate over them. "This fascist concern for the national sentiment of our Baltic neighbors sounds truly touching on fascist lips," *Pravda* (April 27, 1934). See also *DGFP,* series C, II: 686 (Nadolny report, March 29, 1934).

260. Stalin wrote: "my archive." RGASPI, f. 558, op. 11, d. 196, l. 54–62 (received at the foreign office on Feb. 5). RGASPI, f. 558, op. 11, d. 196, l. 131–7. In May 1934, Stalin received Phipps's account of his meeting with Hitler and Neurath in Dec. 1933. RGASPI, f. 558, op. 11, d. 196, l. 17–23. Stalin had told the 17th Party Congress that the termination of parliamentarism in Germany was a sign of "the bourgeoisie's" weakness, its inability to maintain its rule by so-called respectable methods. *Sochineniia,* XIII: 283, 293. "Lots of foolishness, but still interesting," he had written, without specifics, in green pencil on a report from a Soviet agent in Berlin forwarded by the OGPU (April 11, 1934).

261. Stalin also underlined another passage: "The single great achievement is the rather paradoxical success in the sphere of foreign policy . . . Inside the country, there is none of the socialism that he promised to impose . . ." Phipps also noted "empty theaters, bankrupt bookstores, starving writers, artists, and composers all remind one that the cultural life of Berlin is threatened with disappearance under the National Socialist regime." RGASPI, f. 558, op. 11, d. 186, l. 68–9, 76–8 (sent to London Feb. 7, 1934).

262. These Nazi consulates, Balytsky claimed, also aimed to use German specialists working in the USSR to sabotage Soviet military industry. Khaustov et al., *Lubianka: Stalin i VChK,* 494–500 (APRF, f. 45, op. 1, d. 172, l. 11–23: March 5, 1934). Throughout 1934, the OGPU had been secretly gathering information on all ethnic Germans employed in industry in the Soviet Union. Fleischhauer and Pinkus, *Soviet Germans,* 89–91 (citing Evgeniia Evelson, who had taken part in drawing up the lists of Germans before emigrating). On Nov. 5, 1934, the party apparatus sent a ciphered telegram to "all Central Committees of national communist parties, krai committees and oblast committees," including Western Siberia (home to many Soviet ethnic Germans), warning that Soviet ethnic Germans "openly conduct counterrevolutionary work." Hundreds of arrests followed. Shishkin, "Sovetskie nemtsy."

263. *Pravda,* May 6, 1934; Biegański et al., *Documents on Polish-Soviet Relations,* I: 21–2

(extension until Dec. 31, 1945); Demski, "Pol'sko-sovetskie otnosheniia," 191–218; Soviet intelligence had reported that Piłsudski was prepared to strengthen his nonaggression declaration with Germany in the event of a Franco-Soviet alliance, though he would be cautious not to stray too far from France. Soviet intelligence would note to Stalin that Poland was trying to mount two horses at once and would fail. RGASPI, f. 558, op. 11, d. 187, l. 18 (May 9, 1934).

264. Germany was a disarmed state, yet a resentful and prideful one that British operatives knew would endeavor to create a military befitting its self-conception. An ad hoc committee of British intelligence designated Nazi Germany the "ultimate potential enemy" in a series of meetings across late 1933 and mid-1934. Undersecretary Vansittart's April 7, 1934, memorandum for the cabinet on *Mein Kampf* and recent propaganda, added, as one Foreign Office contemporary noted of his essays generally, "the forlorn beauty of hopelessness to all their other beauties." *DBFP,* 2nd series, VI: 975 ff; Lawford, *Bound for Diplomacy,* 270.

265. Britain had been cast as the main driver of a new imperialist war in a 1933 trial in Moscow of engineers of the British company Metropolitan-Vickers ("a frame-up," as one of the arrested British citizens stated, "based on evidence of terrorized prisoners"). Mozokhin, *VChK-OGPU,* 284–90 (citing APRF, f. 3, op. 58, d. 363, l. 119; d. 364, l. 176–77; d. 368, l. 18, 62, 70–72, 87, 93; d. 367, l. 1–2, 9–10, 58–64; TsA FSB, no. PF-6740, t. 17, l. 175, 177; t. 12, l. 203); Khaustov et al., *Lubianka: Stalin i VChk,* 415–6 (APRF, f. 45, op. 1, d. 171, l. 84–5: interrogation of MacDonald, March 16, 1933). See also Morrell, *Britain Confronts the Stalin Revolution.* On April 2, 1933, Rozengolts, foreign trade commissar, had reported to Stalin and Molotov that of the 33 turbines supplied between 1925 and 1933, 24 experienced breakdowns, some multiple times. The contract with Metropolitan Vickers had been annulled. Litvinov negotiated the release and deportation of the engineers in exchange for termination of the embargo the British had imposed following their arrests.

266. *DBFP,* 2nd series, VII: 558 (June 4, 1933); Palme-Dutt, "Britanskii imperialism"; *Pravda,* Aug. 19, 1933.

267. *XVII s"ezd,* 305–22 (at 307–8); Ken, *Mobilizatsionnoe planirovanie,* 267–8. See also *Pravda,* June 1, 1934 (Mayorsky); and *VII Kongress Kommunisticheskogo internatsionala,* 383–4.

268. Kokoshin, *Armiia i politika,* 95, 96–9.

269. Ken, *Mobilizatsionnoe planirovanie,* 243–7 (citing RGVA, f. 40442, op. 2, d. 32, l. 103: draft of Voroshilov report, not earlier than Dec. 13, 1933). Lithuania secretly cooperated militarily with the USSR on the basis of shared antagonism toward Poland. Tukhachevsky visited the United Kingdom in April 1934 and returned with a description of the Royal Air Force new Hampden bomber with a sketch of its weaponry, obtained by Soviet military intelligence. Hastings, *Secret War,* 2–3 (no citation).

270. Stone, *Hammer and Rifle,* 23, 237n33; Tukhachevskii, *Voprosy sovremennoi strategii* (Moscow: Voennyi vestnik, 1926), reprinted in Tukhachevskii, *Izbrannye proizvedeniia,* I: 244–61 (at 254–5).

271. "Europe remains in equal doubt both as to our policy and to our capacity," Vansittart, the dominant official in the foreign office, observed in an internal memorandum (June 2, 1934). "The results are already—or perhaps I should say at last—becoming manifest. Italy, Poland, Yugoslavia, Romania, are all at varying degrees tending to be drawn into the

German orbit; and on Italy's inconstancies now largely depend Austria, Hungary and Bulgaria. The political map of Europe is, in fact, altering under our eyes and to our disadvantage, if we must look upon Germany as the eventual enemy." McKercher, "Deterrence," 98 (citing "Minute by Sir R. Vansittart" [DQMX32] 117], PRO, CAB 27/510). On British intelligence and Germany, see also Winterbotham, *Ultra Secret*, 4–5; Winterbotham, *Nazi Connection*; West, *MI6*, 45–7.

272. Anon., "Zametki o peresechenii biografii," 316.

273. Shentalinsky, *Arrested Voices*, 168–96 (citing the case file). See also Bykov, *Boris Pasternak*, 472–7.

274. *Literaturnaia gazeta*, May 14 and 16, 1934.

275. Pridvorov, "Ob otse," 219.

276. Fleishman, *Pasternak v tridtsatye gody*, 153–96; Mandelstam, *Hope against Hope*, 25–6); Akhmatova, "Mandelshtam (Listki iz dnevnika)," 182; Anon., "Zametki o peresechenii biografii," 316–7; "Impressions of Boris Pasternak," 88. Neither the generally unforgiving Nadezhda nor Osip ever blamed Pasternak.

277. Ivinskaya, *Captive of Time*, 61–3. It remains unknown which of the narrow circle of people informed on Mandelstam. Shentalinsky, *Arrested Voices*, 172, 178–80.

278. Mandelstam, *Hope against Hope*, 84–5.

279. Stalin wrote in blue pencil on the letter: "And who gave them authorization to arrest Mandelstam? An outrage." RGASPI, f. 558, op. 11, d. 709, l. 167–167ob. See also Maksimenkov, "Ocherki nomenklaturnoi istorii."

280. Bykov, *Boris Pasternak*, 495–504. Stalin might have been bothered by the circumstance that Pasternak had run to Bukharin, who at *Izvestiya* was attempting to act as patron and protector of the great writers, rather than directly to the dictator. Trapping Pasternak into failing to admit friendship with Mandelstam, if that is what Stalin did, could have been like psychological payback for an offense Pasternak did not knowingly commit.

281. In the 1950s Pasternak would tell two British academics, Isaiah Berlin and D. P. Costello. Fleishman, *Pasternak v tridtsatye gody*, 185–7. Pasternak's friend and German studies specialist Nikolai William-Wilmont was present, and Pasternak's second wife, Zinaida Neuhaus, was sitting on a couch in the adjacent room during the call.

282. Koltsov, who had helped make Dimitrov famous, was in the airport greeting party. *Pravda*, Feb. 28 and March 1, 1934. In 1932, in Berlin, the married Koltsov had started a romance with his interpreter, the blond beauty Maria Gresshöner (b. 1908), who accompanied him back to Moscow and took the surname Osten ("East"). He installed her at a German-language periodical in Moscow, and took her on his foreign trips.

283. Banac, *Diary of Georgi Dimitrov*, 8 (Feb. 27, 1934). B. Popov and V. Tanev arrived with Dimitrov in Moscow.

284. Borkenau, *Communist International*, 405; Cockburn, *Crossing the Line*, 54.

285. In 1933, the original four stories of the Lux were expanded to six, bringing the hotel to 300 rooms. Visiting Soviet inhabitants had to leave their identification cards at the desk and fill out questionnaires in order to enter the Lux; at midnight, all were supposed to be out. Kennel, "New Innocents Abroad," 15; von Mayenburg, *Hotel Lux*; Vaksberg, *Hôtel Lux*.

286. The sprawling twelve-floor structure had some 550 rental apartments, which were centrally allocated and equipped with oak wood floors, gas stoves, constructivist furniture, telephones, radio receivers, gramophones, and frescoes on the ceilings. The complex had schools and nurseries, shops, a laundry, a medical facility, a savings bank branch, a post office, a performance space, and the "Shock Worker" cinema (the country's first sound-equipped cinema), with 1,500 seats. Prepared food could be delivered to one's door. Each family had access to a maid, and there were elevator operators and building staff who kept the keys. It was assumed that early service personnel worked for or reported to the OGPU.

287. After nearly an hour, Molotov and others joined. *Na prieme*, 126. The central Comintern apparatus numbered about 500 staff (more than 800 with inclusion of technical personnel).

288. Jackson, *Popular Front*, 17–51.

289. Banac, *Diary of Georgi Dimitrov*, 11 (April 3, 1934), 12–5 (April 7, 1934). Hundreds of Austrian socialist "Schutzbundists" escaped the crackdown, fleeing to Czechoslovakia, whence they were invited to the USSR. Banac, *Diary of Georgi Dimitrov*, 19n16; Fischer, *Le grande rêve socialiste*, 280–1."

290. Banac, *Diary of Georgi Dimitrov*, 19 (May 2, 1934).

291. Dobry, "February 1934," 129–50; Jenkins and Millington, *France and Fascism*.

292. Chase, *Enemies within the Gates?*, 15 (citing Community party archives, Sofia, f. 146, op. 2, a.e. 317, l. 11); Leibzon and Shirina, *Povorot v politike Kominterna*, 93 (citing Tsentralen partien arkhiv pri TsK na VKP [Sofia], f. 146, op. 2, d. 317, l. 11). See also Carr, *Twilight of the Comintern*, 127, 191. In Austria, in Feb. 1934, street thugs, police, and army forces loyal to Chancellor Engelbert Dollfuss (who had suspended parliamentary rule) assaulted banned yet still powerful socialist organizations—and Social Democrat-led workers fought back.

293. Artuzov was in the Little Corner on April 19, May 16 and 25, 1934. *Na prieme*, 127, 562–3. In May 1934, Stalin also cut off the ability of Radek's bureau to request secret information from Soviet intelligence or diplomatic agencies. Ken, "'Rabota po istorii,'" 108–16.

294. The exposures occurred in Vienna, Riga, Hamburg, Helsinki, and Paris between 1931 and 1933, and led to the loss of dozens of agents. A politburo injunction against recruitment of agents among foreign Communists (Dec. 8, 1926) came up against the fact that individuals who were ready to serve the Soviet cause, held foreign passports, and spoke accentless foreign languages were in very short supply outside foreign Communist circles. Kolpakidi and Prokhorov, *Imperiia GRU*, I: 196; Lurie and Kochik, *GRU*, 477; Khaustov, "Deiatel'nost' organov," 185–6; Gorbunov, *Stalin i GRU*, 248–9; Damaskin, *Stalin i razvedka*, 164. One key figure in the Soviet spy network in Paris, Léopold Trepper (b. 1904), the son of a failed Jewish shopkeeper in Habsburg Galicia, escaped via Nazi Germany to the Soviet Union; he would eventually be posted to Brussels.

295. Gorbunov, "Voennaia razvedka v 1934–1939 godakh" (no. 2), 99 (citing RGVA, f. 33987, op. 3, d. 599); Kolpakidi and Prokhorov, *Imperiia GRU*, I: 201; Adibekov et al., *Politbiuro TsK RKP (b)—VKP (b) i Evropa*, 311 (RGASPI, f. 17, op. 162, d. 16, l. 25). TASS denied the Soviets in France had been engaged in espionage. *Pravda*, March 30, 1934. See also Primakov, *Ocherki*, III: 62.

296. On May 25, 1934, Stalin received Artuzov without Berzin. *Na prieme*, 127, 130. The politburo decree insisted on better cooperation between military and civilian intelligence, better compartmentalization in operations, paying attention in hiring not only to social origins but nationality, and quickly establishing a school to train large numbers of new spies in small groups. Khaustov et al., *Lubianka: Stalin i VChK*, 522–3 (RGASPI, f. 17, op. 162, d. 16, l. 64–6).

297. Khaustov, "Deiatel'nost' organov," 208–9. Artuzov was supposed to spend two-thirds of his time in military intelligence. At civilian intelligence, his deputies, Abram Slutsky and Boris Berman, were to bear the load.

298. In June 1934, the civil war–era Revolutionary Military Council was abolished, and a more modest advisory Main Military Council was created. Erickson, *Soviet High Command*, 371–2.

299. Khaustov et al., *Lubianka: Stalin i VChK*, 526 (APRF, f. 45, op. 1, d. 172, l. 105: Igor Sitnikov). Back on March 15, 1934, Artuzov had reported that Captain Makoto Tanaka of the Japanese army had reconnoitered parts of the Chinese Eastern Railway, possibly for sabotaging tunnels. Stalin underlined passages and wrote: "Comrade Artuzov, what should be the measures to counter explosions and in general diversionary activity? Who is working them out, who is implementing them?" Khaustov, *Lubianka: Stalin i VChK*, 505–6 (RGASPI, f. 558, op. 11, d. 186, l. 115–6).

300. Khaustov, "Deiatel'nost' organov," 202–3 (Vaizer). See also, Khaustov, *Lubianka: Stalin i VChK*, 526 (APRF, f. 45, op. 1, d. 172, l. 105: Igor Sitnikov).

301. Yagoda wrote to Stalin (Feb. 17, 1934) recommending removal of Smagin (b. 1894) as head of Red Army external relations. Smagin had served as an aide to the deputy head of military intelligence (1924–26) and then through May 1930 as an aide to the Soviet military attaché in Japan, Primakov, who had reported that a Japanese officer in a drunken state had uttered the secret code used for the head of Soviet military intelligence Berzin ("Crow") and had referred to content in a classified report by Primakov. Only Primakov and Smagin knew that code name. Primakov's report of the incident had not been properly investigated at the time. Smagin returned to Soviet military intelligence in Moscow, then, in July 1933, was appointed to his current post. Yagoda recommended against trying to turn Smagin against the Japanese. Stalin made a note to himself: "Speak with Klim." Maybe Stalin decided, contrary to Yagoda, to try to "double" Smagin. But Smagin was removed in June 1934 and left unemployed. In Jan. 1935, he would be appointed to the Frunze Military Academy. Khaustov et al., *Lubianka: Stalin i VChK*, 482–5 (RGASPI, f. 558, op. 11, d. 186, l. 79–87); Lurie and Kochik, *GRU*, 303; RGVA, f. 37837, op. 1, d. 1300, l. 19ob.–27. In 1934, Kawabe would be named chief of intelligence to the Kwantung Army. Smagin would be arrested Dec. 16, 1937, and executed Aug. 26, 1938.

302. Paul-Boncour, *Entre deux guerres*, II: 364. "The mystique of the League," notwithstanding its failures, "remained the essential element of our foreign policy as well as our domestic policy," General Maurice Gamelin would later claim. Gamelin, *Servir*, II: 56; *DDF*, 1e série, IV: 258–62 (April 16, 1934).

303. Dullin, *Men of Influence*, 2, citing Leon Trotsky, *Oeuvres* (Paris: EDI, 1985), XII: 107–9. Karakhan was banished as envoy to Ankara, and Sokolnikov by May 1934 to the timber commissariat. Their departures enhanced Litvinov's position. But the party cell inside the commissariat kept a watchful, envious eye on Litvinov and his associates. Total foreign affairs personnel in the 1930s hovered around 1,000, including the central

commissariat and the roughly 30 embassies and 40 to 50 consulates. Roshchin, "V narkomindele v predvoennye gody," 41–9; Crowley, *Soviet Diplomat Corps.*

304. Bernard Attolico, the Italian envoy in Moscow, explained to Twardowski that the Soviets pursued "the policy of the free hand," but "if there is no other way out, they would swallow the bitter pill, join the League of Nations and make an alliance with France, . . . unless German policy succeeded in meeting the Russian 'pact mania' in a form acceptable to them." *DGFP*, series C, III: 150–1 (Twardowski, July 9, 1934).

305. Hochman, *Failure of Collective Security*, 37–44. Litvinov latched onto a renewed offer on April 20, 1934, by a new French foreign minister, the conservative nationalist Louis Barthou, to renew the talks begun under his predecessor for a regional alliance. In private talks with Germany, however, the Soviets distanced themselves from the "French idea." AVP RF, f. 5, op. 14, pap. 103, d. 117; *Na prieme*, 128; *DDF*, 1e série, VI: 496–502.

306. *Pravda*, June 10, 1934; Wheeler-Bennet, *Documents on International Affairs*, I: 253ff. The thorny issue of Bessarabia was left unresolved. *DVP SSSR*, XVII: 379–81; *Pravda*, June 11, 1934; Adibekov et al., *Politbiuro TsK RKP (b)—VKP (b) i Evropa*, 312 (RGASPI, f. 17, op. 162, d. 16, l. 59, 87, 89). *DDF*, 1e série, VI: 664–6. Diplomatic relations had been normalized with Hungary (Feb. 1934). "The Russians do not understand what dogs they could have against Europe in the form of Central European small states," the Czechoslovak diplomat Jaroslav Papoušek had told the Soviet envoy in Prague, Alexandrovsky, on March 24, 1934, claiming to be citing President Masaryk. Ken and Rupasov, *Zapadnoe prigranich'e*, 123 (AVP RF, f. 0138, op. 15, pap. 122, d. 2, l. 226).

307. Stalin forwarded the report to Molotov, Voroshilov, Kuibyshev, and Orjonikidze for discussion. The report asserted that Poland and Germany, in parallel, were negotiating a military alliance with Japan and that Romania would join and perhaps even Italy, Austria, and Hungary. "War against the Soviet Union," the alarmist report concluded, "was never as realistic a possibility as now." Khaustov et al., *Lubianka: Stalin i VChK*, 533–41 (RGASPI, f. 558, op. 11, d. 187, l. 28–44). See also Harris, "Encircled by Enemies," 536. In July 1934, the head of the Polish foreign ministry's Eastern Department (Colonel Tadeusz Schaetzel) told the Bulgarian chargé d'affaires in Warsaw that Poland "was counting on the circumstance that if a war broke out in the Far East, Russia would be crushed, and then Poland would include in its borders Kiev and part of Ukraine." Jurkiewicz, *Pakt wschodni*, 66 (citing Bulgarian foreign ministry archives).

308. Banac, *Diary of Georgi Dimitrov*, 24–5 (June 18, 1934). From late 1934, Dimitrov and Fleischmann would start a household in Moscow as she became his second wife.

309. It met from June 29 through July 1, 1934. *KPSS v rezoliutsiiakh* (9th ed.), VI: 166.

310. Longerich, *Die braunen Battallione*, 223; Bessel, *Political Violence*; Frei, *National Socialist Rule in Germany.*

311. In April 1934, Hindenburg became terminally ill, meaning a presidential succession loomed. On June 11, the *Evening Standard* in London implied that the German military could take over. On June 17, Vice Chancellor Franz von Papen publicly called for restoration of some freedoms and an end to the SA's lawlessness. He had failed to coordinate his speech (written for him) with the Reichswehr or the Reich president, but its remarkable content made it seem that he had. Evans, *Third Reich in Power*, 26–41; Kershaw: *Hitler:*

1889–1936, 499–525, 744n57. See also Höhne, *Mordasche Röhm*, 218–24.

312. Longerich, *Die braunen Bataillione*, 215–6; von Bedrow, *Hitler rast*; von Papen, *Memoirs*, 310–1; Wheeler-Bennett, *Nemesis of Power*, 319–20; von Fallois, *Kalkül und Illusion*. See also Hancock, "Purge of the SA Reconsidered." When the SA leader in the Rhineland had received information in late June about an impending crisis, he rightly assumed this meant Göring was preparing a putsch against Röhm. Hüttenberger, *Die Gauleiter*, 86.

313. Domarus, *Hitler: Reden*, I: 418 (July 13, 1934). Domarus commented that Hitler projected onto the SA the failings of the Nazi party (400n138, 414n155).

314. The British ambassador dubbed the episode Hitler's "Sicilian vespers." Wark, *Ultimate Enemy*, 82 (citing MI3 summary, July 18, 1934, WO 190/263; Phipps dispatch, Nov. 14, 1934, C7703/20/18, FO 371/17696); Steiner, *Triumph of the Dark*, 74 (no citation).

315. Carr, *Twilight of the Comintern*, 123 (citing *Rundschau*, July 5, 1934: 1541–3). See also Radek in *Pravda* (July 3, 1934).

316. Nekrich, *1941*, 19 (citing a personal conversation in the 1950s with Surits, the envoy in question). Krivitsky, an NKVD operative in Europe at the time (who later defected), would claim from hearsay that Stalin summoned Jan Berzin, head of military intelligence, the very night of the long knives. But Berzin was recorded in Stalin's office on April 19, 1934, and then not again until 1937. Krivitsky would also assert that "Stalin was profoundly impressed by the manner in which Hitler exterminated his opposition, and studied minutely every secret report from our agents in Germany relating to the events of that night." Krivitsky, *In Stalin's Secret Service*, 1–2, 183; *Na prieme*, 569.

317. *Izvestiia*, July 16, 1934.

318. Mikoian, *Tak bylo*, 534.

319. Kershaw, *Nazi Dictatorship*, 73.

320. Those killed included the immediate previous chancellor Kurt von Schleicher, the Catholic Action leader, aides to von Papen, and other conservatives. Höhne, *Mordasche Röhm*, 319–21. Another scholar gives a figure of ninety killed: Gritschneder, *"Der Führer hat Sie zum Tode verurteilt . . . ,"* 60–2.

321. German National Socialism tipped even more decisively away from its internal factions pushing for full-scale nationalization of banks and industry and for closer ties with the Soviet Union, while the SS felt even less encumbered. Pringle, *Master Plan*, 41. Von Hindenburg died on Aug. 2, 1934; von Papen resigned as vice chancellor five days later. On Aug. 19, in a 90 percent vote, Hitler became head of state ("Führer and chancellor").

322. Dallin and Firsov, *Dimitrov and Stalin*, 13–6 (RGASPI, f. 495, op. 73, d. 1, l. 1–3); Firsov, "Stalin i komintern," 12 (citing TsPA na TsK na BKP, f. 146, op. 6, a.e. 754, l. 1); Komolova, *Komintern protiv fashizma*, 326–9; Borkenau, *European Communism*, 110–1. On July 4, Dimitrov was again received one-on-one by Stalin ("thorough discussion!"), but in late July Stalin was still defending his "social fascist" theory. Banac, *Diary of Georgi Dimitrov*, 24 (July 4, 1934); *Na prieme*, 135–6; McDermott and Agnew, *Comintern*, 92.

323. RGASPI, f. 17, op. 162, d. 15, l. 114–4: July 5, 1934. The Soviet envoy in Rome told Mussolini if Germany ceased its hostility, "nothing would prevent the Soviet government from continuing the friendly collaboration with Germany in the spirit of the Rappallo and Berlin agreements." *DVP SSSR*, XVII: 471 (July 13, 1934). Negotiations with Germany for the proffered credit would drag on. RGASPI, f. 17, op. 162, d. 17, l. 88–9: Dec. 5.

324. *Izvestiia*, July 11, 1934.

325. Khaustov et al., *Lubianka: Stalin i VChK*, 801 n70 (Feb. 6, 1934). He had abandoned his small Kremlin apartment in the Cavalry Building for good, unable any longer to climb to the second floor, and stayed at his state dacha in Gorki-6 (Arkhangelskoe). Mozokhin and Gladkov, *Menzhinskii*, 346–9, 354–5 (no citation). After the death of his second wife, Maria Rostovtsa, in 1925 he was said to have become a recluse. But he married a third time, and had another child, his fifth.

326. An intentionally provocative obituary in a prominent surviving liberal German newspaper alleged a falling-out between Yagoda and Stalin over forced collectivization. Paul Scheffer, in *Berliner Tageblatt*, May 11, 1934, translated in Vinogradov, *Genrikh Iagoda*, 377–81 (TsA FSB, f. 3, op. 1, d. 12, l. 2–5).

327. Shreider, *NKVD iznutri*, 25.

328. Stalin had initiated the change, introducing a politburo resolution Feb. 20, 1934, to place the OGPU inside an all-Union NKVD, and forming a commission. Khaustov et al., *Lubianka: Stalin i VChK*, 486 (RGASPI, f. 17, op. 3, d. 939, l. 2), 487–9 (APRF, f. 3, op. 58, d. 4, l. 14–5), 509 (l. 20), 514–5 (l. 124–6), 515 (RGASPI, f. 17, op. 3, d. 943, l. 10) 543–4 (d. 948, l. 33, 92–3); Yezhov had sent suggestions on personnel for the NKVD on April 8, 1934: Khaustov et al., *Lubianka: Stalin i VChK*, 514–5.

329. The expansion occurred on June 8, 1934. On June 6, 1937, the regime would add subarticle 14: "counterrevolutionary sabotage." Zaitsev, *Sbornik zakonodatel'nykh i normativnykh aktov*. "In all truth, there is no step, thought, action, or lack of action under the heavens which could not be punished by the heavy hand of Article 58," Solzhenitsyn would write. Solzhenitsyn, *Gulag Archipelago*, 60. Criminal codes were by republic, and in Ukraine, it was article 54.

330. Adibekov et al., *Politbiuro TsK RKP (b)—VKP (b): povestki dnia zasedanii*, II: 511 (RGASPI, f. 17, op. 3, d. 941: March 20, 1934); Karnitskii, *Ugolovnyi kodeks RSFSR*. See also RGASPI, f. 558, op. 11, d. 730, l. 22 (Oct. 7, 1934).

331. Yagoda had already issued a circular on the imperative for labor camp bosses to better organize their work, properly employ machinery, and fulfill the plan with attention to quality and cost, citing cases of failures to meet plan targets. Vinogradov, *Genrikh Iagoda*, 375 (TsA FSB, f. 3, op. 1, d. 594, l. 20: June 22, 1934), 382–90 (d. 7, l. 4–14). In Nov. 1934, the USSR NKVD would assume control over the prisons previously under the commissariats of justice in the Union republics, and thereby unite them with the corrective labor camps and colonies and special settlements. Jakobson, *Origins of the Gulag.*

332. Solomon, *Soviet Criminal Justice*, 166–7 (citing RGASPI, f. 17, op. 3, 948, d. l. 95–100); *Pravda*, July 26, 1934.

333. Solomon, *Soviet Criminal Justice*, 166 (citing RGASPI, f. 17, op. 165, d. 47, l. 3). USSR procurator general Ivan Akulov had followed up a petition by Aleksei Selyavkin (b. 1896), the former head of anti-aircraft defense, who was serving a ten-year sentence in Gulag from 1933 for the alleged sale of secret military documents. Selyavkin's petition, which Akulov forwarded to Stalin, stated that he had falsely admitted his guilt under the threat of execution. Stalin decided to use this as an example. On June 5, 1934, the politburo freed him and admonished the OGPU leadership and even the procuracy for ignoring Selyavkin's earlier petitions. Khaustov and Samuelson, *Stalin, NKVD*, 106 (no citation); APRF, f. 3, op. 58, d. 71, l. 11–31; RGASPI, f. 17, op. 162, d. 16, l. 88–9. On July 9, Voroshilov

had written to Stalin in Sochi about granting early release to the Provisional Government war minister General Alexander Verkhovsky from his ten-year sentence ("considering that the situation has now sharply changed, I think that we could free him without special risk, using him in scholarly-research work"). Stalin accepted the recommendation, further evidence he had decided to rein in indiscriminate repression. Khlevniuk, *Khoziain*, 222 (RGASPI, f. 17, op. 163, d. 1015, l. 61–2).

334. The secret-police central apparatus in Moscow alone now numbered more than 8,200, and the chaotic expansion had come at the expense of educational levels, competence, and probity. Police bookkeeping, as the rival procuracy's investigations showed, entailed all manner of "black" accounts enabling self-dealing, while contraband running and other abuses of office were pervasive. OGPU archives were spread around many buildings of Moscow's Lubyanka quarter. Yakov Genkin, head of the OGPU records and statistics department, wrote to the hierarchs (Feb. 15, 1934) that the archives then contained almost 825,000 folders (dela), and more than 100,000 folders were not enumerated. Investigation records were merely "a mountain of paper which presents itself for reading with difficulty," often handwritten, in pencil, and sewn in such a way that trying to read them led to ripping the pages; they were also filthy, overwhelmed with stamps on the cover. Of his predecessors Genkin wrote, "They looked upon the archive like a warehouse, where they could dump paper, if there was no room to hold it or send it some place." In May 1934, the OGPU archives got a new facility, in the basement of one of the Lubyanka quarter's buildings, and a staff increase to five, as well as folders for redoing files and metal cupboards for securing secret materials. Vinogradov, "Istoriia formirovaniia arkhiva VChK," 15 (citing TsA FSB, f. 3, op. 3, d. 1607, l. 1).

335. Yagoda cited Stalin's speech of Jan. 1933 about enemies ("This of course is not frightening. But we have to keep it in mind if we want to terminate these elements quickly and without especially numerous victims"). Vinogradov, *Genrikh Iagoda*, 407, 410 (TsA FSB, f. 3, op. 1, d. 4, l. 1–35).

336. Molchanov would later testify that "in 1934 Yagoda many times pointed out to me the need to conduct a more liberal course in our punishment policy. I recall, for example, a conversation in the summer of 1934 at the Water Station Dynamo. In this conversation Yagoda openly said that it is time perhaps to stop shooting people." RGASPI, f. 558, op. 11, d. 174, l. 137.

337. Solomon, *Soviet Criminal Justice*, 168–70; Sharlet and Beirne, "In Search of Vyshinsky." See also Goliakov, *Sbornik dokumentov po istorii ugolovnogo zakonodatel'stva SSSR*, 333–4.

338. "Autocracy," as one scholar observed of the tsarist regime, had "maneuvered between arbitrariness and legality, between the principle of unlimited personal power and the imperative to strive for a more rational organization of the state." Taranovsky, "Osobennosti rossiiskoi samoderzhavnoi monarkhii," 166.

339. Max Eastman, who had created a sensation in the 1920s by defending Trotsky and publishing Lenin's Testament, did so again with *Artists in Uniform* (1934), which equated the Soviet and the Hitler-Mussolini enlistment and regimentation of cultural figures. Eastman had belatedly come to understand that the problem was not Stalin alone but "the bigotry of Marxist metaphysics." Radek wrote a rebuttal that highlighted Nazi book

burnings and concentration camps in *Izvestiya* (July 18, 1934), bringing Eastman's book greater attention. (The newspaper's circulation was 1.5 million.) Eastman, *Artists in Uniform*, 133–4. See also Eastman, "Artists in Uniform." "All Moscow writers seem to have been promoted in rank: they've all acquired high-style apartments, fur coats, and mistresses and fallen in love with the luxurious life," Korney Chukovsky had written in his diary as early as Nov. 24, 1931. (Chukovsky moved to Peredelkino, the leafy writers' colony.) Chukovskii, *Dnevnik*, 34. The émigré Vladimir Nabokov wrote that "in Russia before Soviet rule there did exist restrictions, but no orders were given to artists." Nabokov, "Russian Writers, Censors, Readers," 3.

340. Artizov and Naumov, *Vlast'*, 370–2 (RGASPI, f. 17, op. 120, d. 304, l. 171–5: May 3, 1937).

341. Several years earlier, a group of nearly one hundred cultural figures had established a cooperative to build dachas in Peredlkino, just twelve miles from Moscow. Gorky had written to Stalin "skeptical" about such a writers' village, and Stalin had agreed ("a far-fetched business that could also remove writers from the real world and develop their conceit"). But the regime approved it anyway. (APRF, f. 45, op. 1, d. 719, l. 104: Feb. 28, 1933; l. 112: March 1, 1933). The original cooperative was abolished, and the money returned.

342. Khodasevich, *Portrety slovami*, 280.

343. Shentalinsky, *Arrested Voices*, 262–78. For speculation on possible murder, see Baranov, *Gorky bez grima*. Yagoda was in love with Maxim Peshkov's wife, Timosha. Gel'man, "Zalozhnik OGPU," 8. Maxim had joined the party in April 1917, served in the Cheka 1918–1919, but emigrated in 1922 to join his father in Italy, where he married and had two daughters; he returned, bringing his family, with his father, in 1932. Maxim had no job, lived the life of a sybarite, and clashed with Gorky's secretary, Pyotr Kryuchkov.

344. Khlevniuk et al., *Stalin i Kaganovich*, 430–2 (RGASPI, f. 558, op. 11, d. 742, l. 21–7: Aug. 12, 1934), 437–8 (d. 83, l. 67–9: Aug. 15); Artizov and Naumov, *Vlast'*, 220–3 (IMLI, Arkhiv Gor'kogo: Aug. 2, 1934).

345. Artizov and Naumov, *Vlast'*, 219–20 (RGASPI, f. 17, op. 3, d. 949, l. 29, 95); Antipina, *Povsednevnaia zhizn'*, 63–4 (citing RGALI, f. 631, op. 1, d. 40, l. 18: Sept. 5, 1934).

346. In 1935, the average monthly salary in industry was 194 rubles; in state administration, 212; in management of the economy, 293; but 750 for the Literary Fund director; 500 for his deputy; and 300 for a secretary of the directorate. In time, when bona fide writers were unable to work, the Literary Fund awarded them significant monthly sums (200 to 600 rubles, to a total of 3,000 to 6,000 per year). The USSR also established an administration for the protection of authors' rights, for writers and composers, covering the live stage, cinema, clubs, traveling and restaurant performances. But these were done at the public level, and sometimes the author of a work in the RSFSR found that work re-used without compensation in a different Union republic. Tolstoi and Vishnevskii, "Ob avtorskom prave," 3.

347. Babichenko, *Literaturnyi front*, 16–20 at 18: RGASPI, f. 17, op. 120, d. 257, l. 14–9: Aug. 29, 1936), 23–5 (at 24: d. 304, l. 171–5). The Literary Fund lobbied to build at least eighty dachas at state expense, and got permission for thirty. Writers watched over the construction, often a full-time job because of insider theft of scarce construction materials, not to mention shoddy workmanship. Sartakova, "Nash pisatel'skii les," 24.

348. Wells was under the spell of Roosevelt's New Deal and now envisioned a collectivist world-state, with the United States and the USSR converging—if only Stalin would give up Marx. Stalin dismissed Wells's technocratic enthusiasms, insisting that only classes could make history and that the technical intelligentsia was a mere stratum. For Stalin, any New Deal–Five-Year Plan convergence was a non-starter, and so was the concept of general humanity ("I do not believe in the goodness of the bourgeoisie"). But Stalin also denied capitalism was in its death throes. "It seems to me that I am more to the Left than you, Mr. Stalin," Wells, twelve years Stalin's senior, interjected. *New Statesman and Nation*, Oct. 27, 1934. Wells received a copy of the transcript Stalin had already edited. Wells, as president of the PEN club, added a delicate reference as to whether freedom of thought was possible in the USSR, to which Stalin replied it already existed: Bolshevik "self-criticism." RGASPI, f. 558, op. 11, d. 3151, l. 1–23; Khlevniuk et al., *Stalin i Kaganovich*, 495 (RGASPI, f. 558, op. 11, d. 742, l. 99–104 Sept. 24, 1934), 496n5 (RGASPI, f. 558, op. 11, d. 3151, l. 2–3). Stalin had the edited interview published in the party journal, but not in a mass circulation newspaper. *Bol'shevik*, 1934, no. 17: 8–18. In the United Kingdom, two prominent public figures jumped on Wells for the interview, George Bernard Shaw (not enough praise of Stalin) and John Maynard Keynes (too much praise of a demagogue): *Stalin-Wells Talk: Verbatim Record and Discussion* (London: The New Statesman and Nation, 1934). See also Wells, *Experiment in Autobiography*, 684–702; Cowley, "Interview with Stalin"; Taunton, "Russia and the British Intellectuals," 209–24; and Lel'chuk, "Beseda I. V. Stalina s angliiskim pisatelem G. Uellsom," 326–52. Wells correctly recalled his interpreter as Konstantin Umansky; Stalin's logbook has N. M. Goloded (a government official in Soviet Belorussia). *Na prieme*, 138.

349. RGASPI, f. 558, op. 11, d. 792, l. 121–46 (at 121: Nov. 9, 1934).

350. "I accompanied Stalin on his trips to the south, I spent a lot of time with him, we always ate meals together, and practically all his free time he spent with us," Vlasik would recall. "I mean myself and my secretary Poskryobyshev. In Moscow I saw him far less. I accompanied him on his trips around the city, to the theater, the cinema." Loginov, *Teni Stalina*, 106.

351. "O nekotorych voprosakh istorii bol'-shevizma," *Proletarskaia revoliutsiia*, 1931, no. 6: 3–21 (Oct. 26, 1931); Pikhoia, *I. V. Stalin*, 128–37 (RGASPI, f. 558, op. 1, d. 2983, l. 1–15). *Sochineniia*, XII: 84–102. See also Slutskii, "Bol'sheviki o germanskoi sotsi-al-demokratii"; Dunaevskii, "Bol'sheviki i germanskie levye na mezhdunarodnoi arene," 504–6 (citing a letter from Slutsky, June 9, 1964); Barber, "Stalin's Letter to the Editors of *Proletarskaya Revolyutsiya*," 39–41; and Tucker, "The Rise of Stalin's Personality Cult," 355–8.

352. Enteen, "Marxist Historians During the Cultural Revolution"; Kvashonkin, *Sovetskoe rukovodstvo*, 189–91 (RGASPI, f. 81, op. 3, d. 255, l. 179–82). Popov, *Ocherk istorii*.

353. "History at long last has been restored" to schools, Andrei Bubnov, the enlightenment commissar, had remarked at the Communist Academy (March 13, 1934). "Peter was Peter, Catherine was Catherine . . . We must give an impression of the epoch, about the events that took place at that time, who ruled, what sort of government there was, what sort of policies were carried out, and how events transpired." Brandenberger and Dubrovsky, "'The People Need a Tsar,'" 874 (citing Arkhiv RAN, f. 350,

op. 1, d. 905, l. 1–3ob.); Brandenberger, *National Bolshevism*, 32–3. See also Pikhoia, *I. V. Stalin*, 186 (RGASPI, f. 17, op. 163, d. 1013, l. 4: March 3, 1934). History education was reintroduced as a separate subject in schools, and meant to displace the study of Engels's *Anti-Dühring* or *Dialectics of Nature*. Scott, *Behind the Urals*, 45.

354. The meeting took place March 20, 1934. Litvin, *Bez pravo na mysl'*, 55–7 (quoting the unpublished diary of Sergei A. Piontkovsky). D. Osipov in *Pravda* (April 5, 1934), lambasted schemata without facts as "skeletons in the schools." See also *Pravda* and *Izvestiya*, May 16, 1934: 1; *Spravochnik partiinogo rabotnika*, IX: 137; Suny, *Structure of Soviet History*, 229.

355. For example: Banac, *Diary of Georgi Dimitrov*, 12–5 (April 7, 1934).

356. Farnsworth, "Conversing with Stalin," 961 (Kollontai diary, summer 1934: RGASPI, f. 558, op. 11, d. 749, l. 105).

357. "Iurii Zhdanov, vtoroi muzh docheri 'otsa narodov': ia znal Stalina s 15 let," *Komsmol'skaia pravda*, Jan. 10, 2007.

358. Rybin, *Stalin v oktiabre*, 9. Kirov had been in Stalin's office July 25, 26, and 27: *Na prieme*, 138.

359. Similarly, Kirov complained in a letter to a minion in Leningrad, "By the whim of fate I've ended up in Sochi, and I'm unhappy about it. The heat here is not tropical but hellish." Kirilina, *Neizvestnyi Kirov*, 141 (citing Kirov Museum, f. III-414), 324–8 (TsPA, f. 80, op. 26, d. 68, l. 1, 4–6, ob. 7).

360. Andreev, *Vospominaniia, pis'ma*, 294.

361. Stalin also noted that foreign currency had to be conserved. Khlevniuk et al., *Stalin i Kaganovich*, 462 (RGASPI, f. 558, op. 11, d. 84, l. 20–20ob.).

362. Khlevniuk et al., *Stalin i Kaganovich*, 455 (RGASPI, f. 81, op. 3, d. 100, l. 61–6), 465 (f. 558, op. 11, d. 84, l. 23–23ob.), 473–6 (d. 742, l. 75–84). Stalin demanded additional grain levies from the harvest, in the form of purchases (*zakupki*) at low prices, beyond the obligatory quotas. But grain exports in 1934 were a mere 800,000 tons, less than half the much reduced 1933 amount. Baykov, *Soviet Foreign Trade*, appendix, table IV. The NKVD was ordered to take charge of grain elevators and grain collection points as of July 27, 1934.

363. RGASPI, f. 558 op. 1, d. 3155; Kvashonkin, *Sovetskoe rukovodstvo*, 245–9 (RGASPI, f. 81, op. 3, d. 419, l. 55–7: Goloshchokin, Aug. 4, 1933); Kirilina, *Neizvestny Kirov*, 328 (LPA, f. 24, op. 2–v, d. 936, l. 94: Sveshnikov to Agranov, Dec. 16, 1934), 331–2 (RGASPI, f. 80, op. 18, d. 67, l. 67–9; d. 137, l. 1–2). Kirov was in Kazkahstan Sept. 6–29. Pazi, *Nash Mironych*, 449.

364. Khlevniuk et al., *Stalin i Kaganovich*, 479 (RGASPI, f. 558, op. 11, d. 85, l. 44–5: Sept. 12, 1934), 479–80 (f. 81, op. 3, d. 100, l. 76–82: to Kaganovich, Zhdanov, Molotov, Kuibyshev—but not Kirov, Sept. 13).

365. *Pervyi vsesoiuznyi s"ezd sovetskikh pisatelei*, 687–96. See also Struve, "Pan-Soviet Literary Congress." Garrard, *Inside the Soviet Writers' Union*.

366. Antipina, *Povsednevnaia zhizn'*, 27.

367. Maksimenkov, "Ocherki nomenklaturnoi istorii sovetskoi literatury," 247 (Pavel Yudin, Aug. 15, 1934).

368. "K 40-letiiu Pervogo vsesoiuznogo s"ezda," *Voprosy literatury*, 1974, no. 8: at 14 (Valery Kirpotin).

369. *Pervyi vsesoiuznyi s"ezd sovetskikh pisatelei*, 1, 5–18. One bitter witness would recall that Gorky just stopped reading his own text partway through. Kochin, *Spelye kolos'ia*, 299. See also Baranov, "'Nado prekoslovit!'"

370. *Pervyi vsesoiuznyi s"ezd sovetskikh pisatelei*, 20–38, 291–318, 416–20.

371. Kuz'min, *Dnevnik 1934 g.*, 95 (Aug. 30, 1934).

372. Zhdanov thought that party-member writers spoke less brightly than the nonparty, and noted to Stalin that Gorky thought the party-member writers had no authority whatsoever in the writers' milieu. Artizov and Naumov, *Vlast'*, 230–1 (RGASPI, f. 77, op. 3, d. 112, l. 2–8).

373. Babel added: "Since everything is done artificially, under the stick, the congress is proceeding deathlike, like a tsar's parade, and no one abroad will believe in this tsar's parade." Artizov and Naumov, *Vlast'*, 232–4 (TsA FSB, f. 3, op. 1, d. 56, l. 185–89). The nonparty loyalist Ilya Ehrenburg would later deem the gathering "a great and marvelous festival." Ehrenburg, *Men, Years—Life*, IV: 40. Rozhkov, who was not a delegate to the congress, published an essay collection on the value of romanticism right at this time: *Nuzhna li nam romantika?* (Moscow: Sovetskaia literatura, 1934). Stalin evidently took an interest in Rozhkov's ideas. Maksimenkov, *Bol'shaia tsenzura*, 412–3 (RGASPI, f. 558, op. 11, d. 793, l. 95: Radek to Poskryobyshev, April 10, 1936).

374. *Pervyi vsesoiuznyi s"ezd sovetskikh pisatelei*, 74–103; Zhgenti, "S"ezd velikogo edineniia," 53; Fleishman, *Pasternak v tridtsatye gody*, 201–2. Toroshelidze's report was published in the press the next day with a front-page photograph of the Georgian delegation accompanied by Pasternak (known for his translations from Georgian). *Literaturnaia gazeta*, Aug. 21, 1934. One scholar has asserted that, as a minority, "Ukrainian writers lost more than their Russian colleagues." Luckyj, *Literary Politics*, 203.

375. *Pervyi vsesoiuznyi s"ezd sovetskikh pisatelei*, 286–7 (as translated by Olyesha).

376. Artizov and Naumov, *Vlast'*, 232–4 (TsA FSB, f. 3, op. 1, d. 56, l. 185–89). Kirilenko served as the secretary to Petrovsky, head of the central executive committee in Soviet Ukraine.

377. Artizov and Naumov, *Vlast'*, 223–6 (TsA FSB, f. 3, op. 1, d. 56, l. 125–32), 226 (l. 150), 227–8 (l. 160–3), 229 (RGASPI, f. 17, op. 3, d. 950, l. 40).

378. Khlevniuk et al., *Stalin i Kaganovich*, 447 (RGASPI, f. 558, op. 11, d. 83, l. 122–122ob.). Attendees' national composition was registered as follows: 201 Russians, 113 Jews, 28 Georgians, 25 Ukrainians, 19 Armenians, 19 Tatars, 17 Belorussians, and 12 Uzbeks (43 other nationalities were represented by fewer than 10 and in some cases just one person). The politburo strongly criticized the party organizations in Bashkiria, Buryat-Mongolia, Yakutia, and the German region in the Volga for sending ill-chosen delegates and not overseeing the speeches. Gatagova et al., *TsK RKP (b)—VKP (b) i natsional'nyi vopros*, II: 795 (RGASPI, f. 17, op. 3, d. 951, l. 8: Aug. 28, 1934).

379. RGASPI, f. 558, op. 11, d. 83, l. 156–7.

380. Antipina, *Pvsednevnaia zhizn'*, 43–4; Osokina, *Za fasadom*, 113.

381. "Many members of our government attended," recalled Valentina Khodasevich, principal designer of the storied Leningrad (formerly Mariinsky) Theater of Opera and Ballet. "Supper, served in the dining room, was very lively and interesting. People made speeches. Aleksei Maximovich asked that I sit next to Malraux, since I speak French, to entertain him and translate . . . [Louis] Aragon, Elsa Triolet, the Spanish writer Mara-Teresa Léon and many others spoke very well." Khodasevich, *Portrety slovami*, 280–1.

382. *Pravda*, June 19, 1934; Katsman, "Cheliuskin"; Groza and Dubenskii, *Slavnym zavoevateliam Artiki*.

383. Radio was still mostly live at this time, and arrests followed "accidental" announcements (e.g., mentioning that there had been a famine in 1933), but sometimes the utterances were deliberate: the announcer of the ceremony on Red Square for the *Chelyuskin* rescuers signed off, "The comedy is over." (He turned out to have noble descent and a relative arrested by the OGPU.) Goriaeva, *Radio Rossii*, 158. See also Bollinger, *Stalin's Slave Ships*, 65–71; McCannon, *Red Arctic*, 61–8; *The Cheliuskin Odyssey* (1934).

384. *Pervyi vsesoiuznyi s"ezd sovetskikh pisatelei*, 4–5. Pavel Yudin and Alexander Fadeyev authored "On Socialist Realism," which had been approved by the Central Committee and published in *Pravda* (May 8), on what was thought to be the eve of the congress. See also Kemp-Welch, *Stalin and the Literary Intelligentsia*, 177. The literary section of the institute of philosophy, at the Communist Academy, would mount what ended up to be a debate about socialist realism on Dec. 20 and 28, 1934, and Jan. 3, 1935, prompted by a draft encyclopedia article on the novel by a Hungarian-born Germanophone intellectual, György Lukács (b. 1885), a Hegel devotee who had once been expelled from the Hungarian Communist party for the heresy of advocating alliances with non-proletarian forces in democratic settings, and lived in Moscow, for a time editing Marx's German-language notebooks and manuscripts at the Institute of Marx-Engels-Lenin. Lukács cast the novel as both pure avatar of bourgeois culture and capitalist modernity and as temporary displacement of the grand epic tradition, but the proletariat's rise forced the creation of a "positive hero," the "conscious worker," who overcame the "degradation of man" and forced the novel back into the arms of the epic. Socialist realism—thanks to this class analysis contortion—became an instrument for a supposedly genuine world literature. "Problemy teorii romana: doklad G. Lukacha," *Literaturnyi kritik*, 1935, no. 2: 214–49, and "Pravlennaia stenogramma diskusii po dokladu G. Lukacha," *Literaturnyi kritik*, 1935, no. 3: 231–54; Clark, *Moscow*, 163–5; Tikhanov, *Master and the Slave*, 112–28; Lukach, "Roman kak burzhuaznaia eopopeia," IX: 795–832; Szikalai, *After the Revolution*; Gurvich, "Vtoroe rozhdenie," 347–8.

385. *Pervyi vsesoiuznyi s"ezd sovetskikh pisatelei*, 464–6 (Aug. 28). Zarkhi (b. 1900) died July 17, 1935.

386. Katerina Clark presents "Soviet socialist realism as a canonical doctrine defined by its patristic texts," and offers an "official short list of model novels." For Boris Groys, socialist realism just signifies "the art of the Stalin period." Evgeny Dobrenko calls socialist realism "the USSR's most successful industry . . . a machine for distilling Soviet reality into socialism." Clark, *Soviet Novel*, 3, appendix B; Groys, *Total Art of Stalinism*, 72; Dobrenko, *Political Economy of Socialist Realism*, 5–6.

387. Jelagin, *Taming of the Arts*, 42–3. Jelagin was himself class enemy, like his stand-partner, "Count" Sheremetyev. See also Smrž, *Symphonic Stalinism*.

388. Matthew Cullerne Bown, *Socialist Realist Painting* (New Haven: Yale University Press, 1998), 87, 109. As Bown notes, there is scant information on Stalin's views on painting (184). Bown rehabilitates socialist realist visual art by arguing that avant-garde artists changed their style voluntarily in order to make their work widely accessible, a goal they passionately wanted to achieve. Margarita Tupitsyn's work on photography—which the authorities did not consider an art form, and therefore for which no union was established—also argues that the Soviet version of

the avant-garde aesthetic project was about mass media, such as the photograph in a mass-produced journal, and mass culture. Christina Kiaer, in her work on Alexaander Deneika, attempts to show how socialist realism was avant-garde. These works follow from Boris Groys's provocation. Tupitsyn, *Soviet Photograph*; Kiaer, "Was Socialist Realism Forced Labor?," 45; Kiaer, *Imagine No Possessions*. See also Susan Reid, "Socialist Realism in the Stalinist Terror"; Reid, "In the Name of the People," 716; and Johnson, "Alternative Histories of Soviet Visual Culture." Stalin had become the subject of oil paintings in 1928, 1931, and 1932 by the Leningrad-based artist Isaac Brodsky (b. 1883), who depicted him in exaggerated size, with an iconic copy of *Pravda* on the desk. In 1934, Brodsky became the first painter to receive the Order of Lenin. That same year Alexander Gerasimov (b. 1881), a traditional realist before the revolution (when he opposed the avant-garde) and a Red Army veteran of the civil war, completed his *Stalin Gives His Report to the 17th Party Congress*. Gersaimov, too, favored a larger-than-life heroic realism. *Pravda*, April 10, 1934, and Feb. 6, 1935. Mikhail Avilov painted *The Arrival of Comrade Stalin at the First Cavalry in 1919* for the 1933 exhibition "15 Years of the Red Army." *Pravda*, Aug. 13, 1933. Yevgeny Katsman recorded Stalin's reaction to the exhibition: "Next to Nikonov's picture, Stalin said, when looking at Kolchak with a revolver in his hand, 'he wants to shoot himself.' . . . When we got to Avilov, Stalin saw himself painted, laughed and immediately turned his eyes to other works. Then back to Avilov, and he examined himself longer." Plamper, *Stalin Cult*, 136-7 (citing RGALI, f. 2368, op. 2, d. 36, l. 12-3).
389. The sales were carried out by the foreign trade commissariat, which had no expertise in art treasures and formed a state company, Antiquariat. Some of the paintings that were

sold, along with icons, furniture, jewelry, and antiquarian books, came from museum collections, but many were looted from the public or churches. The first paintings sold were bartered for oil (in 1930). Andrew Mellon, the U.S. secretary of the treasury, purchased twenty-one of the paintings in 1931, for $6.65 million; one painting alone sold for $1.166 million, then the largest amount ever paid. "'Nuzhen li nam ermitazh'," 106-10 (APRF, f. 3, op. 42, d. 141, l Ill.89-90, 94-95ob.); Stetsky to Kaganovich; 94-95ob.: Lergan to Stalina); Artizov and Naumov, *Vlast'*, 179 (RGASPI, f. 17, op. 162, d. 12, l. 183); Odom and Salmond, *Treasures into Tractors*. Mellon would donate the art in 1937 to the U.S. government in Washington, where they would form the basis of the National Gallery. The Metropolitan Museum of Art bought some. Stetsky wrote to Kaganovich (Oct. 23, 1933) that the secretive process had resulted in rumors of a firesale, lowering prices, and that the Hermitage Museum had sunk from third-ranked in the world to perhaps seventeenth. The politburo resolved to terminate the sales on Nov. 15, 1933. Ilin and Semenova, *Prodannye Sokrovisha Rossii*. Hermitage deputy director Iosif Orbeli soon replaced his boss (Legran) who had complied with the sales as mandated by the regime. Megrelidze, *Iosif Orbeli*; Iubashian, *Akademik Iosif Orbeli*.
390. Bown, *Socialist Realist Painting*, 87, 109.
391. Mindlin, *Neobyknovennye sobesedniki*, 429.
392. Conformism was rampant but with a culture this vast, various tendencies inevitably vied with each other. Schlögel, *Terror und Traum*, 30-1.
393. Stalin commented that he had liked Radek's speech but not Gorky's. Khlevniuk et al., *Stalin i Kaganovich*, 461-2 (RGASPI, f. 558, op. 11, d. 84, l. 53; d. 50, l. 49), 465-6 (RGASPI, f. 558, op. 11, d. 84, l. 42-42ob.), 466n3 (f. 17, op. 3, d. 951, l. 28: Sept. 1, 1934).

394. Ponomarev, *Aleksandr Shcherbakov*, 18.
395. Maksimenkov, *Bol'shaia tsenzura*, 329-32 (RGASPI, f. 558, op. 11, d. 1494, l. 13ob.–18ob.).
396. Chukovskii, *Dnevnik*, 140 (April 10, 1936).
397. Jelagin, *Taming of the Arts*, 114.
398. Mirskii, *Istoriia russkoi literatury*, 794.
399. Maksimenkov, *Bol'shaia tsenzura*, 340-1 (RGASPI, f. 558, op. 11, d. 730, l. 18-20, 17: Sept. 6, 1934). An abridged version of Bukharin's speech to the congress was published in *Pravda* (Aug. 30, 1934); his closing speech was also published (Sept. 3). Gorky's closing speech was likewise published in *Pravda* (Sept. 2). Zhdanov had written another report to Stalin on the Writers Congress, Sept. 3, 1934. Maksimenkov, *Bol'shaia tsenzura*, 332-8 (RGASPI, f. 558, op. 11, d. 730, l. 2-16).
400. Artizov and Naumov, *Vlast'*, 236-8 (RGASPI, f. 17, op. 3, d. 951, l. 28-30).
401. Artizov and Naumov, *Vlast'*, 238-50 (TsA FSB, f. 3, op. 1, d. 56, l. 70-93).
402. Ivanov-Razumnik, *Neizdannyi Shchedrin*; RGASPI, f. 558, op. 3, d. 231, s. 301-2; Gromov, *Stalin*, 161-2.
403. Artizov and Naumov, *Vlast'*, 170-1 (APRF, f. 3, op. 34, d. 186, l. 213-5: March 1932).
404. Jelagin, *Taming of the Arts*, 73.
405. Bykov, *Boris Pasternak*, 491.
406. For an analysis of the reader under the Stalin dictatorship, see Dobrenko, *Formovka Sovetskogo chitatelia*.
407. Maksimenkov, *Bol'shaia tsenzura*, 338-40 (RGASPI, f. 58, op. 11, d. 729, l. 52-65: Sept. 5, 1934). The Sukharyov Tower in Moscow had also been demolished, despite vehement opposition from scholars. "We cannot deal with a single decrepit little church without a protest being delivered," Kaganovich complained. "K istorii snosa Sukharevskoi bashni," 109-16.

CHAPTER 4. TERRORISM

1. The other task: "The mood of the masses regarding the revolutionary movement in Spain." Kozlova, *Sovetskie liudi*, 232 (citing the Memorial archive, TsDNA, f. 30, d. 12, l. 64-5: Stepan Polubny, b. 1914).
2. Zolotarev et al., *Velikaia Otechestvennaia voina 1941-1945 gg.*, I: 9; Grechko et al., *Istoriia Vtoroi mirovoi voiny*, I: 214; Kirshner and Novikov, *Kanun i nachalo voiny*, 29; Mel'tiukhov, *Upushchennyi shans Stalina*, 358.
3. Włodarkiewicz, *Przed 17 września 1939 roku*, 132; Habeck, *Storm of Steel*, 214-5 (citing RGVA, f. 4, op. 18, d. 51: "Stenograficheskii otchet zasedanie Voennogo Soveta pri NKO Soiuza SSR 10-12 dekabria 1934 g.: ob itogakh boevoi podgotovki 1934 i zadachakh na 1935 g.").
4. E.g.: Khlevniuk et al., *Stalin i Kaganovich*, 477 (RGASPI, f. 81, op. 3, d. 100, l. 72-5: Sept. 6), 479 (f. 558, op. 11, d. 85, l. 44-5: Sept. 12), 479-80 (f. 81, op. 3, d. 100, l. 76-82: Sept. 13), 483-4 (f. 558, op. 11, d. 742, l. 85-9: Sept. 16).
5. By late July 1934, Stalin had shaved the list of Soviet conditions for joining the League of Nations down to a mere seat on its Council. Adibekov et al., *Politbiuro TsK RKP (b)—VKP (b) i Evropa*, 313 (RGASPI, f. 17, op. 162, d. 16, l. 119); *DVP SSSR*, XVII: 479 (Litvinov to Rosenberg, July 14, 1934); *DDF, 1e série*, VII: 5 (Barthou to Payart, July 27, 1934).
6. Haslam, *Struggle for Collective Security*, 59.
7. Adibekov et al., *Politbiuro TsK RKP (b)— VKP (b) i Evropa*, 315-6 (RGASPI, f. 17, op. 162, d. 17, l. 49); RGASPI, f. 558, op. 11, d. 85, l. 26, 31-32ob.
8. The invitation was portrayed as coming from France, just as the Soviets had insisted.

Poland demanded that Moscow declare that all bilateral agreements with Warsaw remained inviolable. *Dokumenty i materialy po istorii sovetsko-pol'skikh otnoshenii*, VI: 220-1, 225; *DDF, 1e série*, VII: 406-7; Beck, *Final Report*, 65; Khlevniuk et al., *Stalin i Kaganovich*, 483 (RGASPI, f. 558, p. 11, d. 85, l. 48, 61: Sept. 16). Thirty-nine member countries voted yes, three voted no (Netherlands, Portugal, Switzerland), and seven abstained.
9. Haslam, "Soviet-German Relations," 789, citing *Sotsialistichekii vestnik*, Jan. 25, 1934, and *Kommunisticheskaia revoliutsiia*, 1934, no. 8: 43-4.
10. Back on Nov. 5, 1927, Stalin had told a delegation of foreign workers that "the Soviet Union is not prepared to become a part of that camouflage for imperialist machinations represented by the League of Nations. The League is a 'house of assignations' for the imperialists who arrange their business there behind the scenes." *Sochineniia*, X: 206-7 Carr, *Twilight of the Comintern*, 104-16; *Izvestiia*, Jan. 4, 1934.
11. *Pravda*, Sept. 17 and 20, 1934; *DVP SSSR*, XVII: 589; *DDF, 1e série*, VI: 683-4. Left unsaid was that Geneva would be a gold mine of information: more than 600 people worked at the League, of varied nationalities, and many were willing to talk to the builders of a new socialist world. Zhukovskaia, "SSSR i liga natsii."
12. *DVP SSSR*, XVII: 606 (Litvinov on Beck, Sept. 22, 1934), 608 (Litvinov on Bartou, Sept. 25); Adibekov et al., *Politbiuro TsK RKP (b)— VKP (b) i Evropa*, 318 (RGASPI, f. 17, op. 162, d. 17, l. 17: Sept. 23), 318-9 (l. 75-6: Nov. 2, 1934); *DDF, 1e série*, VII: 254-5.

13. Milićević, *King Dies in Marseilles*; Paul-Boncour, *Entre deux guerres*, II: 21-7. On the supposed involvement of Nazi Germany, see Thorndike et al., *Unternehmen Teutonenschwert*, 21-43; Volkov, *Operatsiia "Tevtonskii mech"*; and Volkov, *Germano-iugoslavskie otnosheniia*, 64.
14. RGASPI, f. 558, op. 11, d. 86, l. 89, 26. Voroshilov received a secret intelligence brief (Oct. 23, 1934) remarking on the increasing closeness of Japan, Poland, Finland, and Latvia to Nazi Germany. "War," the analysts wrote, "might not happen for several years and at the same time it could break out quickly and unexpectedly." P. N. Bobylev et al., *Voennyi sovet pri narodnom komissare oborony SSSR, dekabr' 1934 g.*, 5 (RGVA, f. 4, op. 14, d. 1136, l. 90-5).
15. Dallin and Firsov, *Dimitrov and Stalin*, 18-22 (RGASPI, f. 495, op. 73, d. 1, l. 4-7; f. 558, op. 1, d. 3162, l. 1-2: Oct. 25, 1934); Leibzon and Shirina, *Povorot v politike Kominterna*, 97 (TsPA pri TsK na VKP [Sofia], f. 146, op. 4, d. 639, l. 7-8).
16. Multiday discussions took place (Dec. 9-19, 1934) in the Comintern. Carr, *Twilight of the Comintern*, 144-5, citing Thorez, *Fils du peuple* (Paris: Éditions sociales, 1960), 102.
17. Khaustov et al., *Lubianka: Stalin i VChK*, 566 (APRF, f. 3, op. 58, d. 246, l. 1: Sept. 2, 1934); Khaustov and Samuelson, *Stalin, NKVD*, 70; RGASPI, f. 17, op. 162, d. 17, l. 31; Khlevniuk et al., *Stalinskoe politbiuro*, 19, 58-66.
18. Khlevniuk, *Khoziain*, 229-30 (citing RGASPI, f. 17, op. 162, d. 17, l. 74, 80, 82, 86; GARF, f. R-5446, op. 27, d. 73, l. 3); Khlevniuk

et al., *Stalin i Kaganovich*, 511 (f. 558, op. 11, d. 86, l. 41: Oct. 9, 1934; l. 23: Oct. 9), 512 (l. 55: Oct. 10).

19. Khlevniuk, *Khoziain*, 226–8 (citing APRF, f. 3, op. 58, d. 72, l. 180–7, 253–4; RGASPI, f. 671, op. 1, d. 80, l. 4, 33–40, 91; f. 17, op. 162, d. 17, l. 2–3, 42, 57, op. 163, d. 1046, l. 21–3; GARF, f. R-5446, op. 27, d. 81, l. 428–9); Viktorov, *Bez grifa "sekretno,"* 139–40; Khlevniuk, *Politbiuro*, 130–4. With the kulak crushed, Kaganovich had explained to the Moscow party organization (Sept. 21, 1934), it was necessary "to conduct our measures, repressions, the struggle with enemies within the law . . . educating our population within the frame of socialist legal consciousness." Khlevniuk, *Khoziain*, 222 (RGASPI, f. 87, op. 3, d. 164, l. 39).

20. "Reconciliation inside the party could not have appealed to him," Tucker surmised of Stalin at this time. Tucker, *Stalin in Power*, 243.

21. Whereas the OGPU had made 505,000 arrests in 1933, including 283,000 for counterrevolution, in 1934 the OGPU-NKVD would make 205,000, including 90,000 for counterrevolution. Khlevniuk, *Khoziain*, 229 (GARF, f. R-9401, op. 1, d. 4157, l. 202); Werth and Mironenko, *Istoriia stalinskogo gulaga*, I: 609; Khlevniuk, *Master of the House*, 123.

22. As an overstated U.S. headline, which was translated for the internally circulated regime summaries of the foreign press, had it, "Red Russia was becoming pink." Khlevniuk, *Politbiuro*, 106 (*Baltimore Sun*). Utyosov (who had been born Lazar Weisbein) discovered jazz on a trip to Paris.

23. Stalin's first post-holiday meeting is recorded as Oct. 31. *Na prieme*, 139.

24. Khlevniuk, *Politbiuro*, 288–9.

25. Dullin, *Men of Influence*, 97 (citing AVP RF, f. 05, op. 14, d. 103, l. 117); Adibekov et al., *Politbiuro TsK RKP (b)–VKP (b) i Evropa*, 318–9 (RGASPI, f. 17, op. 162, d. 17, l. 75–6). In Nov. 1934, the regime belatedly created a training institute inside the foreign affairs commissariat.

26. Medvedev, *Let History Judge*, 587.

27. On Nov. 3, 1934, Stalin repaired to his Kremlin apartment after meetings in his office until 8:30 p.m. On Nov. 4, he had late supper at his Kremlin apartment with Kaganovich and Zhdanov. Murin, *Stalin v ob"iatiakh*, 158–9 (Svanidze diary: Nov. 4, 1934); *Na prieme*, 139–40. Rybin, *Stalin v oktiabre*, 9; See also Barmine, *One Who Survived*, 268.

28. Sergeev and Glushik, *Besedy o Staline*, 108.

29. Stalin would also be rumored to be having Kremlin rendezvous with the Bolshoi soprano Valeria Barsova [Vladimirova] and the mezzo-soprano Vera Davidova, who many years later would assert that Stalin had wanted her to be his "housekeeper." Kun, *Stalin*, 222.

30. Gromov, *Stalin*, 63.

31. Shumyatsky had replaced the Stalin critic Ryutin, who had been shunted over to the then backwater film industry for a time. Kepley Jr., "The First Perestroika." Shumyatsky compiled notes of his notes on his film showings at the Kremlin from May 1934 through Jan. 26, 1937. In summer 1935, in Shumyatsky's absence, Ia. Chuzin, his deputy, made notes. Anderson et al., *Kremlevskii kinoteatr*, 919–1053. The first Soviet sound film, *Putevka v zhizn'*, by N. V. Ekka, had premiered in June 1931. Shumiatskii, *Kinematografiia millionov*, 121; RGASPI, f. 558, op. 11, d. 892, l. 93; Christie, "Making Sense of Early Soviet Sound," 176–92; *Kul'turnaia zhizn' v SSSR, 1928–1941*, 184, 199, 255.

32. Mar'iamov, *Kremlevskii tsenzor*, 9.

33. Alliluyeva, *Twenty Letters*, 144–5.

34. Late into the 1930s, all Soviet sound films were released in silent versions, too, for many movie projectors still lacked audio equipment. Bulgakova, *Sovetskii slukhoglaz*, 98.

35. Stalin first saw *Chapayev* on Nov. 4, 1934; an anxious Shumyatsky had asked Stalin's permission to summon the directors, the brothers Sergei and Georgy Vasilyev, to help answer questions. Stalin would watch *Chapayev* again and again that month (the viewing on Nov. 8–9 lasted until 3:51 a.m.). Anderson et al., *Kremlevskii kinoteatr*, 949–51 (RGASPI, f. 558, op. 11, d. 828, l. 56). On the arguments between the Vasilyev brothers and the actor who played Chapayev, Boris Babochkin (b. 1904) of the Leningrad Drama Theater, see Babochkin, *Litso Sovetskogo kinoaktera*.

36. Anderson et al., *Kremlevskii kinoteatr*, 959–61 (RGASPI, f. 558, op. 11, d. 828, l. 63–63ob.). Stalin invited Budu Mdvinai, with whom he had clashed in the 1920s over Georgian affairs, to the screening that evening.

37. *Pravda*, Nov. 3, 1934 (S. S. Dinamov); *Izvestiia*, Nov. 10 (Kh. N. Khersonsky). Stalin directed Shumyatsky to work more closely with Mekhlis; on Nov. 20, the dictator again phoned Mekhlis directly from a screening, which resulted in "The Whole Country Is Watching Chapayev" (*Pravda*, Nov. 21, 1934). Anderson et al., *Kremlevskii kinoteatr*, 969–70 (RGASPI, f. 558, op. 11, d. 828, l. 69–69ob.: Nov. 20, 1934). See also Brooks, "Thank You, Comrade Stalin!," 59–60.

38. Anderson et al., *Kremlevskii kinoteatr*, 961–7 (RGASPI, f. 558, op. 11, d. 828, l. 64–6).

39. Murin, *Stalin v ob"iatiakh*, 160–2 (Nov. 14 and 26). See also Alliluyeva, *Twenty Letters*, 138.

40. Bullard and Bullard, *Inside Stalin's Russia*, 243; Rosliakov, *Ubiistvo*, 68–70.

41. Rosliakov, *Ubiistvo*, 70–1; Kokurin and Petrov, *Lubianka*, 49. Medved had served as OGPU boss in the Soviet Far East (1926–1929) before his transfer to Leningrad in Jan. 1930. Petrov and Skorkin, *Kto rukovodil NKVD*, 295.

42. Viktorov, *Bez grifa "Sekretnosti,"* 140 (Stalin to Kuibyshev and Zhdanov). At the May 2, 1934, Kremlin reception, when Voroshilov observed "from the Chekists no one has come. Neither Yagoda nor anyone else," Stalin responded, "Yesterday I somewhat offended them. They arrested people for nothing." Banac, *Diary of Georgi Dimitrov*, 18 (May 2, 1934).

43. In Medved's case, Yagoda singled out lapses in reconnoitering the Finnish frontier (permitting spies and saboteurs to cross), grain procurements, and the struggle against factory sabotage. Viznogradov, *Genrikh Iagoda*, 372–4 (TsA FSB, f. 3, op. 2, d. 9, l. 243–5); Khaustov et al., *Lubianka: Stalin i VChK*, 569–71.

44. Rosliakov, *Ubiistvo*, 68. On Aug. 16, 1934, Stalin had Zinoviev sacked from the journal *Bolshevik*, as a scapegoat for controversy related to writings of Engels. Khlevniuk et al., *Stalin i Kaganovich*, 716–7 (RGASPI, f. 17, op. 3, d. 950, l. 87–9), 419 (f. 81, op. 3, d. 100, l. 43–6), 428–9 (f. 558, op. 1, d. 742, l. 15–20), 439–40 (f. 81, op. 3, d. 100, l. 154–60); Tucker, "The Emergence of Stalin's Foreign Policy," 564–5. Zinoviev's sacking spurred an NKVD move to arrest fourteen ex-Zinovievites in Leningrad, but Kirov, according to Medved, overruled the operation as counter to Stalin's recent stress on "socialist legality." Sedov et al., "Spravka," 473; Lenoe, *Kirov Murder*, 146 (citing RGANI, f. 6, op. 13, d. 62, l. 62–76: Fomin deposition, 1956). On Kirov's continuing confidence in Medved in 1934, see Rosliakov, *Ubiistvo*, 71. Sveshnikov, interviewed in 1960

and 1964, recalled tensions in 1934 between Kirov and Medved. Lenoe, *Kirov Murder*, 146–7 (citing RGANI, f. 6, op. 13, d. 73, l. 102); V. K. Zavalishin, "Vokrug ubiistva Kirova," Boris I. Nicolaevsky Collection, Hoover Institution Archives, series 236, box 411, file I: 1–55.

45. Markus had taken charge of a clinic (Bolshaya Podyacheskaya, no. 30) for patients with syphilis, mostly prostitutes, whom she strove to reeducate by forcing them to attend political meetings and read about exemplary Bolsheviks. She took the tram to work, dressed simply, and wore no makeup, but two students she had recruited pimped the prostitutes at a nearby bar, causing a scandal. The difficult hospital environment was thought to have exacerbated her health problems and she resigned. Chudov arranged for one of Markus's sisters, a doctor, to come stay with her in Tolmachevo. Lebina, *Povsedevnaia zhizn'*, 95–6; Lebina and Shkarovskii, *Prostitutsiia v Peterburge*, 148–9; Kirilina, *Neizvestny Kirov*, 324, 405–6 (recollections of Danil Shamko, Feb. 11, 1965). Markus was officially listed as born 1885—Kirov was born in 1886—but she seems to have been at least three to four years older than him. Zen'kovich, *Samye sekretnye rodsvtvenniki*, 184–5.

46. Tumshis and Papchinskii, *1937, bol'shaia chistka*, 37–8.

47. Kirov's office had been on the long part of the L-shaped corridor, closer to the main stairway, but was moved to the short part. Deviatov et al., "Gibel' Kirova," 59; Lenoe, *Kirov Murder*, 125–6, 403–9 (RGANI, f. 6, op. 13, d. 80, l. 137–9: Gubin to Mironov, Jan. 7, 1935; d. 13, l. 1–18: Pelshe report). Lenoe gives a figure of fifteen guards, citing Pelshe; Deviatov gives a figure of twelve (through Feb. 1934). While in Leningrad, Stalin chose not to stay at Kirov's place—a building with some 250 apartments—but in a detached house, which prompted Medved to have subordinates scope out a possible detached house as a more secure residence for Kirov. Kirov resisted any move. Rosliakov, *Ubiistvo*, 37; Lenoe, *Kirov Murder*, 407–8 (RGANI, f. 6, op. 13, d. 13, l. 279–81, 288–95ob.).

48. Sept. 28–Oct. 8, 1934, the Mongol party had held its first congress since the New Course. Batbayar, "Stalin's Strategy in Mongolia."

49. RGANI, f. 89, op. 63, d. 13, l. 1–24. Stalin noted that when property was collective, enrichment signified raising the general well-being; under private property, enrichment meant exploitation by some of others. But Mongolia was a "bourgeois-democratic republic," even if "of a new type," so there would be exploitation. "Allowing exploitation, you do not sympathize with it and support it but circumscribe it by means of taxes." He advised that the better-off should be kept out of the party. Stalin edited the transcript of the conversation. See also "Sovety I. Stalina mongol'skomu premer'u," *Azia i Afrika segodnia*, no. 6 (1991): 63–5.

50. Choibalsan belonged to the arrested Lhumbe's circle, and was evidently incarcerated with the "Japanese spy group," but soon he himself was torturing the other arrested Mongols on Moscow's behalf. Okhtin, Moscow's former envoy to Mongolia, wrote to Choibalsan absolving him of the Lhumbe association yet emphasizing that a lesson had been imparted. Roshchin, *Politicheskaia istoriia Mongolii*, 285–6, citing L. Bat-Ochir, *Choibalsan: namtryn n' balarkhaig togruulakhui* (Ulan Bator: [n.p.], 1996), 105–7. Choibalsan studied for long periods in the USSR (April–Sept. 1933; Feb.–autumn 1934).

51. Khaustov, *Lubianka: Stalin i VChK*, 594–7 (RGASPI, f. 558, op. 11, d. 188, l. 1–7: Jan. 5, 1935). On April 17, 1935, Stalin received a secret report via an agent in New York about a possible U.S.-Japan pact of nonaggression (661–2: l. 71–3).

52. RGANI, f. 89, op. 63, d. 14, l. 1–8. The Mongols were in the Soviet Union Oct. 21–Dec. 2, 1934. On Nov. 24, 1934, Molotov hosted a diplomatic luncheon for them: Stalin, Voroshilov, and, Mikoyan attended. Gol'man and Slesarchuk ; RGASPI, f. 558, op. 11, d. 351, l. 66.

53. Baabar, *Twentieth-Century Mongolia*, 342–3.

54. A letter from the Mongol leadership in Ulan Bator (Dec. 20, 1934) to Stalin reported unanimous formal approval of the negotiations with the USSR (RGANI, f. 89, op. 63, d. 15, l. 1–4).

55. Stalin had decided unilaterally to abolish rationing for bread in the new year while in Sochi in Oct. 1934. On Dec. 8 the regime finally published the much-rumored forthcoming decree. Malenkov wrote to Kaganovich (Dec. 21) about large numbers of workers at factories condemning the move, amid anger over wage arrears as well. Khlevniuk et al., *Stalin i Kaganovich*, 513 (RGASPI, f. 81, op. 3, d. 100, l. 83–7); Davies and Khlevniuk, "Otmena kartochnoi sistemy v SSSR"; Khlevniuk and Davies, "The End of Rationing in the Soviet Union, 1934–1935"; Kvashonkin, *Sovetstskoe rukovodstvo*, 302–3 (RGASPI, f. 81, op. 3, d. 255, l. 1).

56. Stalin added: "Money will circulate, money will become fashionable, which has not been the case here for a long time, and the money economy will strengthen." RGASPI, f. 17, op. 2, d. 530, l. 79–98.

57. On Nov. 6, at dinner with Bagirov, Orjonikidze fell ill with high fever and chills. He returned to Tiflis to take part in the Revolution Day parade, but that night, at Beria's apartment, he suffered stomach pains and intestinal bleeding. Four days later, he had heart palpitations. Several photos of Orjonikidze with Beria were published in the newspaper Beria controlled: *Zaria Vostoka*, Nov. 4, 18, and 27, 1934.

58. Rybin, *Riadom so Stalinym*, 10.

59. Kirilina, *Rikochet*, 38–9.

60. They lived at Bateinin St. 9/39, Vyborg Side. According to her party autobiography (June 1933), Draule was born in St. Petersburg gubernia of peasant parents; her supposedly landless father had moved there from the ethnic Latvian province, and Milda supposedly began tending the gentry family's pigs and cows at age nine. Secret police files indicate her father managed an estate in Luga province and was well-off, making her a class enemy. Deviatov et al., "Gibel' Kirova," 60–1 (TsGA IPD St.P, f. 1051, op. 2, d. 6, l. 93; f. 1728, d. 698355, l. 10–12ob.: Olga Draule); Sukharnikova, "My nagnli takoi."

61. Deviatov et al., "Gibel', Kirova" 62.

62. Sedov et al., "Spravka," 465; Kirilina, "Vstrely v Smol'nom," 72; Lenoe, *Kirov Murder*, 200–5 (RGANI, f. 6, op. 13, d. 25, l. 39–43).

63. Kirilina, *Neizvestnyi Kirov*, 247; Sedov et al., "Spravka," 464; RGASPI, f. 671, op. 1, d. 112, l. 5; Lenoe, *Kirov Murder*, 215–6 (RGANI, f. 6, op. 13, d. 1, l. 10–53). Also in Aug. 1934, borrowing money, Milda had rented a dacha on the Gulf of Finland at Sestroretsk with the two children. Deviatov et al. have Kirov on holiday there at the same time, but Kirov was in Sochi with Stalin for all of Aug. Deviatov et al., "Gibel' Kirova," 62 (TsGA IPD ST.P, f. 1957, op. 2, d. 3754, l. 161).

64. Kirilina, *Neizvestnyi Kirov*, 257; Lenoe, *Kirov Murder*, 220–2 (RGANI, f. 6, op. 13, d. 1, l. 65–74).

65. Lenoe, *Kirov Murder*, 398–9 (RGANI, f. 6, op. 13, d. 13, l. 7–45: Klimov report on Nikolayev detentions, 1961). See also Tumshis and Papchinskii, *1937, bol'shaia chistka*, 43; and Barmine, *One Who Survived*, 252.

66. Deviatov et al., "Gibel' Kirova" 57–8; Lenoe, *Kirov Murder*, 183, 185, 191, 647, 664, 685. Nikolayev purchased bullets and practiced shooting at the city's Dynamo sport society, run by the NKVD (perhaps the only place to get ammunition legally).

67. According to Draule's testimony: Zhukov, "Sledstvie," 40 (citing Yezhov archive materials).

68. Lenoe, *Kirov Murder*, 209, 227 (TsA FSB, a.u.d. N-Sh44, t. 12, l. 401–10: May 13, 1934); Zhukov, "Sledstvie," 40; Kirilina, *Neizvestny Kirov*, 253.

69. *Sotsialisticheskaia zakonnost'*, 1991, no. 2: 70–1; Sedov et al., "Spravka," 466–7; Kirilina, *Neizvestnyi Kirov*, 262; Lenoe, *Kirov Murder*, 229–35 (RGANI, f. 6, op. 13, d. 24, l. 24–32; d. 1, l. 65–74). "Dear Wife and School Brothers!" he wrote again, probably in late Oct. "I am dying for political convictions, on the basis of historical reality, without even a dollop of fear, or an iota of consolation . . . I must die since there is no freedom of agitation, the press, or voting, in life." Zhukov, "Sledstvie," 38; Lenoe, *Kirov Murder*, 228 (RGANI, f. 6, op. 13, d. 24, l. 24–32).

70. Kirilina, *Neizvestnyi Kirov*, 258–9, 997; Lenoe, *Kirov Murder*, 237–8, 242–3 (TsA FSB, a.u.d. N-Sh44, t. 12, l. 401–10).

71. Petukhov and Khomchik, "Delo o 'Leningradskom tsentre,'" 17–8; Lenoe, *Kirov Murder*, 245–6 (RGANI, f. 6, op. 13, d. 1, l. 85). Leonid's half-brother Pyotr had deserted from the Red Army and would be captured in a gunfight. Lenoe, *Kirov Murder*, 217–8, 247–8.

72. Deviatov et al., "Gibel' Kirova," 59 (citing TsGA IPD, f. 24, op. 2a, d. 30, l. 16–7: report by Alekhin, head of the NKVD operative department, to Zakovsky on Dec. 12, 1934). Smolny had had no pass system whatsoever through 1932; in 1933, its security was taken over by the secret police.

73. Kirilina, *Neizvestnyi Kirov*, 408–9 (Nikolayev interrogation, Dec. 3, 1934).

74. Kirilina, *Neizvestnyi Kirov*, 211–4; Rosliakov, *Ubiistvo Kirova*, 40; Lenoe, *Kirov Murder*, 150–1 (citing RGANI, f. 6, op. 13, d. 73, l. 114–5: Sveshnikov interview). On rationing anxiety: Rimmel, "Another Kind of Fear"; Khlevniuk, *Politbiuro*, 125–6.

75. Deviatov et al., "Gibel' Kirova," 60; Lenoe, *Kirov Murder*, 162 (RGANI, f. 6, op. 13, d. 80, l. 137–9: Gubin testimony, Jan. 7, 1935), 408–9 (RGANI, f. 6, op. 13, d. 13, l. 252–62, 263–74, 279–81, 289–95pb.: Baskakov and Mikhalchenko, 1960–1); Sedov et al., "Spravka," 494. Deviatov et al. have Borisov as head of Kirov's bodyguards from Feb. 1, 1934.

76. Sedov et al., "Spravka," 494. Borisov initially testified that he was twenty steps behind, but later that it was twenty to thirty. RGASPI, f. 671, op. 1, d. 113, l. 22 (Dec. 1, 1934); Kirilina, *Neizvestnyi Kirov*, 209. Deviatov et al. write that Kirov's traveling detail did not go inside the building, in violation of regulations. Vinogradov, *Genrikh Iagoda*, 390–1 (TsA FSB, f. 3, op. 2, d. 60, l. 47); Deviatov et al., "Gibel' Kirova."

77. Lebina, *Povsednevnaia zhizn'*, 216–8.

78. Kirilina, *Neizvestnyi Kirov*, 408; RGASPI, f. 671, op. 1, d. 114, l. 81, 7.

79. Bravy, the commandant duty officer, on the basis of having heard the shot, placed two calls to NKVD headquarters. According to A. L. Molochnikov, chief of economic security in the Leningrad NKVD, who was at Liteiny, the first call was merely a summons of

Medved; the second, seconds later, mentioned Kirov being shot. He judged that Fomin had also received a call, evidently placed by Mikhalchenko, Bravy's superior as deputy commander of the Smolny guard. Zhukov, "Sledstvie," 36; Lenoe, *Kirov Murder*, 159–60 (RGANI, f. 6. Op. 13, d. 71, l. 15–7: Molochnikov, Dec. 9), 164–6 (TsA FSB, a.u.d. N-Sh44, t. 24, l. 99–104: Mikalchenko, Dec.), 762–3n28 (RGASPI, f. 671, op. 1, d. 113, l. 72–3: Bravy).

80. *Reabilitatsiia, kak eto bylo* 490.

81. Bogen, chief of the Leningrad health department, who was on the third floor, arrived early to the scene, and found Kirov without a pulse. Dr. Maria Galperina, of the Smolny clinic, found Kirov already dead when she arrived (nonetheless she applied artificial respiration). Professors began arriving around 5:00 p.m.; Professor of Surgery Yustin Janelidze arrived last at 5:40 p.m., not long after which Kirov was finally pronounced dead. Rosliakov, *Ubiistvo*, 41–2; Kirilina, *Neizvestny Kirov*, 221–8; Koenker et al., *Revelations*, 74–5 (Sept. 9, 1965); Lenoe, *Kirov Murder*, 168–9.

82. Zhukov, "Sledstvie," 36; Deviatov et al., "Gibel' Kirova," 58. Deviatov has the Draule interrogation taking place at Smolny; Zhukov, at NKVD HQ. The location is not specified on the protocol, which lists 16:45 as the start and 19:10 as the conclusion. The otherwise scrupulous Lenoe surmises that the interrogation commenced at 18:45, and a mix-up of 6 and 8 occurred in the record. He bases this unnecessary speculation on the brevity of the protocol, arguing that its length corresponds to a twenty-five-minute conversation. Of course, the NKVD interrogators included in "protocols" what they deemed important. A short text could have resulted from a conversation lasting 2 hours and 25 minutes. Lenoe, *Kirov Murder*, 176 (RGASPI, f. 671, op. 1, d. 114, l. 1–2).

83. Kirilina, *Neizvestnyi Kirov*, 218; Lenoe, *Kirov Murder*, 157. The witness accounts are supported by the post-Stalin memoirs of Rosliakov (first put to paper around 1959–60, and published in 1991), who was the deputy director of Leningrad regional planning (for finances), and was in Chudov's office and one of the first to the scene. (Rosliakov believed Stalin organized the assassination.) Silverest Platoch, an electrician, was fixing the light fixtures on the third floor; Grigory G. Vasilyev, a stockman, was also there, to carry a typewriter from the secret department to the former Tauride Palace for the speech.

84. "It seems to be the most likely that at the moment Kirov was wounded he was not in a vertical position." Deviatov et al., "Gibel' Kirova," 64; author interview with Devyatov in Moscow (Dec. 23, 2014). Kirov's body was cremated at the Donskoi Monastery; his clothing was preserved at a museum dedicated to him in Leningrad.

85. RGANI, f. 6, op. 13, d. 117, l. 1–18 (Pelshe commission report, 1966); Petukhov and Khomchik, "Delo o 'Leningradskom tsentre,'" 15–8; Rosliakov, *Ubiistvo Kirova*, 43–4; Lenoe, *Kirov Murder*, 763n30 (RGANI, f. 6, op. 13, d. 13, l. 314–6: Kulesh, 1960).

86. The person closest to Kirov at the time of the shot, Platoch, who upon seeing an approaching Kirov had turned his back to lock the glass door (it had been opened to use the elevator to transport the typewriter), claims when he heard the shot he turned again and saw Kirov on the floor in the corridor alongside another male, whom he punched in the face. Another witness, Mikhail Lioninok, a city party functionary, claimed he came into the hall after hearing

the first shot and saw Nikolayev standing, screaming, waving the gun, and then firing the second shot. Lenoe, *Kirov Murder*, 153–4 (RGANI, f. 6, op. 13, d. 44, l. 22: Platoch testimony, Dec. 1, l. 15–7: Molochnikov testimony, Dec. 9; RGASPI, f. 671, op. 1, d. 113, l. 18–20: Platoch testimony, Dec. 2), 154 (TsA FSB, a.u.d. N-Sh44, t. 24, l. 81: Dec. 1), 167 (TsA FSB a.u.d. N-Sh44, t. 12, l. 15–6: Nikolayev testimony, Dec. 3). On the bullets, see RGANI, f. 6, op. 13, d. 117, l. 1–18 (Pelshe commission report, 1966); Petukhov and Khomchik, "Delo o 'Leningradskom tsentre,'" 15–8; Rosliakov, *Ubiistvo*, 43–4; Lenoe, *Kirov Murder*, 763n30 (RGANI, f. 6, op. 13, d, 13, l. 314–6: Kulesh, 1960).

87. Lenoe, *Kirov Murder*, 170, 671–2, 764n32. The autopsy, performed on Dec. 2, determined that the bullet from the Nagant had entered Kirov's cerebellum from behind, near his left ear, passed through the cerebellum and part of the left side of the temporal lobe, then bounced backward off the front of the skull slightly above the left eye; Kirov fell face forward with the left side of his forehead hitting the floor, and the combined bullet ricochet and floor impact cracked his skull, causing massive bleeding and bruising. He died instantly. Kirilina, *Neizvestny Kirov*, 223–5 (Kirov Museum, f. III-293, l. 1–4).

88. Deviatov et al., "Gibel' Kirova," 64 (TsA IPD StP, f. 25, op. 5, d. 52, l. 3–4, 119; d. 54, l. 53, 56).

89. Kirilina, *Neizvestnyi Kirov*, 211–4; Rosliakov, *Ubiistvo*, 40; Lenoe, *Kirov Murder*, 150 (citing RGANI, f. 6. op. 13, d. 73, l. 114–5: testimony of NKVD courier M. F. Fyodorova).

90. Rimmel, "Kirov Murder and Soviet Society," 59, 62–4. Pavel Sudoplatov, whose wife (Emma Kaganova) was said to have helped compile a list in the central NKVD of Kirov's mistresses and possible mistresses, wrote that Draule and Kirov were intimate, but that party leaders refused to acknowledge their hero had died because of adultery. Sudoplatov also asserted that Draule was a waitress in the Smolny cafeteria, and had considered filing for divorce. Sudoplatov, *Razvedka i kreml'*, 60–1; Sudoplatov, *Special Tasks*, 50–1.

91. Kirilina, "Vystrely v Smol'nom," 33, 70–8 (interview with interrogator Leonid Raikhman, recounting his Dec. 2, 1934, interrogation of Draule).

92. Tatyana Sukharnikova, director of the Kirov Museum in St. Petersburg, with the aid of Marx Dunda, was able to read through all eighty-five volumes of the Kirov investigation in secret police archives, and reported that the notebook-diary in Nikolayev's hand and that there is no mention of an affair between Draule and Kirov. Sukharnikova, "My nagnali takoi"; Lenoe, *Kirov Murder*, 691–2.

93. Lenoe, *Kirov Murder*, 171–2 (RGANI, f. 6, op. 13, d. 62, l. 62–76: Fomin testimony, March 1, 1956; TsA FSB, a.u.d. N-Sh44, t. 24, l. 332–3: clinic examination, Dec. 1); Sedov et al., "Spravka," 465; Petukhov and Khomchik, "Delo o 'Leningradskom tsentre,'" 18 (Isakov, March 15, 1961); Kirilina, *Neizvestnyi Kirov*, 251.

94. The interrogator noted that, upon reading the written record, Nikolayev "categorically refused to sign the present protocol of his testimony, and attempted to rip it up." Zhukov, "Sledstvie," 37; Petukhov and Khomchik, "Delo o 'Leningradskom tsentre,'" 18; Kirilina, *Neizvestnyi Kirov*, 250, 406–7; Lenoe, *Kirov Murder*, 256–9 (RGANI, f. 6, op. 13, d. 1, l. 92–9).

95. Vinogradov, *Genrikh Iagoda*, 390–1 (TsA FSB, f. 3, op. 2, d. 60, l. 47); Lenoe, *Kirov Murder*, 151 (RGANI, f. 6, op. 13, d. 71, l. 14). Why Medved's telegram was sent so late—well

after Kirov was dead and Draule had been arrested—remains puzzling.

96. Sedov et al.," Spravka," 491; Deviatov et al., "Gibel' Kirova," 58; Koenker et al., *Revelations*, 73–4 (Poskryobyshev's written recollections, 1961). Poskryobyshev recalled Stalin not being in; this could be faulty memory, or a reflection of the fact that Poskryobyshev's office was in the Kremlin's Imperial Senate, while that day Stalin was at Old Square.

97. Chuev, *Tak govoril Kaganovich*, 71–2.

98. Lenoe, *Kirov Murder*, 259 (citing RGANI, f. 6, op. 13, d. 62, l. 62–76: Fomin, 1956).

99. Molotov has Stalin saying "shliapy," but he could have used saltier language. Chuev, *Molotov*, 376.

100. *Pravda*, Dec. 2 and 4, 1934; Lenoe, *Kirov Murder*, 488 (APRF, f. 3, op. 62, d. 95, l. 14–15ob.).

101. *Na prieme*, 142. This was Suslov's first recorded visit to Stalin's office.

102. *Pravda*, Dec. 4, 1934. A draft terrorist law had been prepared after an earlier assassination (Voikov, the Soviet envoy in Warsaw, in 1927). Now, this one would be approved by telephone poll of politburo members by Dec. 3, but dated the day of the assassination. *Pravda*, Dec. 4, 1934; RGASPI, f. 17, op. 162, d. 17, l. 87; Getty and Naumov, *Road to Terror*, 795n55, 796n60; Khaustov et al., *Lubianka: Stalin i VChK*, 137–8 (APRF, f. 3, op. 58, d. 3, l. 113–113ob.); Lenoe, *Kirov Murder*, 252 (APRF, f. 3, op. 62, d. 95, l. 1); Khlevniuk, *Khoziain*, 233. Both the decree and the order for the special train were issued after the assassination. Rayfield, *Stalin and His Hangmen*, 240–5. The Dec. 1 decree scuttled the work of the commission and its draft politburo resolution on "rooting out illegal methods of investigation." Khlevniuk, *Politbiuro*, 132–3.

103. Local newspapers for the next morning, as well as some late-night extra editions, carried the announcement. *Leningradskaia pravda*, Dec. 2, 1934; Kirilina, *Rikoshet*, 30–1; Rimmel, "Kirov Murder and Soviet Society," 21, 27–8; Boris I. Nicolaevsky Collection, Hoover Institution Archives, series 212, box 249, file 3 (V. I. Rudolf-Iurasov memoir). Ehrenburg's name along with that of Pasternak and other writers was affixed to a note that appeared in *Izvestiya* (Dec. 2). *Liudi, gody, zhizn'*, in Ehrenburg, *Sobranie sochinenii*, IX: 53.

104. Lenoe, *Kirov Murder*, 173–5 (TsA FSB, a.u.d. N-Sh44, t. 24, l. 1–2), 177–8 (l. 3–4). The consulate was actually at 43; the phone number was correct. *Ves' Leningrad na 1933 g.* (Leningrad: Lenoblispolkom i Lensovet, 1934), 19.

105. Taubman, *Khrushchev*, 69, 71 (quoting Gostinskaya); Khrushchev, *Vospominaniia*, l: 39, 92.

106. Kirilina, *Neizvestnyi Kirov*, 232 (A. Tammi).

107. Agranov took possession of the case materials at 11:00 a.m., and put the local army garrison, local NKVD troops, and regular police, as well as Fomin, at Pauker's disposal. Lenoe, *Kirov Murder*, 263 (RGANI, f. 6, op. 13, d. 62, l. 62–76). Stalin, according to Fomin, demanded all operational documents concerning anti-Soviet groups and individuals, and, after looking over the list said, "Your record-keeping is poor." Petukhov and Khomchik, "Delo o 'Leningradskom tsentre,'" 19 (Fomin recollections).

108. Lenoe, *Kirov Murder*, 152–3 (RGANI, f. 6, op. 13, d. 71, l. 14: Borisov's Dec. 1 interrogation), 159 (l. 15–7: Molochnikov, Dec. 9), 263 (d. 92, l. 169–72: Zavilovich, Dec. 4).

109. Lenoe, *Kirov Murder*, 414–27 (TsA FSB, a.u.d., N-Sh44, t. 24, l. 253–4: Maly, 255–6: Vinogradov, 259–62: Kuzin, twice; 242–44: expert commission report, 291–2:

Chopovsky; RGANI, f. 6, op. 13, d. 1, l. 10–53: Khvuiizov; d. 2, l. 78–107: Aug. 1956 commission report; RGASPI, f. 671, op. 1, d. 271, l. 539–40), 686 (Lyushkov, 1939); Sedov et al., "Spravka," 494–8; "O kul'te lichnosti," 138; Kirilina, *Neizvestny Kirov*, 343–54.

110. The bodyguard responsible for the entire third floor, Nikolai Dureiko, had been even farther behind Kirov than Borisov on Dec. 1, and he was not killed in a vehicle accident. In fact, no other operative was killed.

111. Fomin and others, seeking a foreign link, had again interrogated Nikolayev in the wee hours on Dec. 2. After Stalin's arrival, the Leningrad NKVD interrogated Nikolayev again, on Dec. 3. Lenoe, *Kirov Murder*, 260–1 (TsA FSB, a.u.d. N-Sh44, t. 12, l. 12–4), 157, 249–50 (TsA FSB, a.u.d. N-Sh44, t. 12, l. 15–6: Nikolaev interrogation, Dec. 3).

112. See Stalin's response to the incident (Aug. 5, 1934) involving Artyom Nakhayev, who brought unarmed cadets to an infantry barracks in Moscow and told them to start a new revolution: "He is, of course (*of course!*), not alone . . . He is probably a Polish-German (or Japanese) agent." Khlevniuk et al., *Stalin i Kaganovich*, 411–2, 421, 425, 429, 431–2, 437, 459–60; RGASPI, f. 17, op. 162, d. 17, l. 87; Khaustov et al., *Lubianka: Stalin i VChK*, 565 (RGASPI, f. 558, op. 11, d. 84, l. 15: Agranov to Stalin, Aug. 26, 1934), 818–9n147; Khromov, *Po stranitsam*, 154–5. Nakhayev had been expelled from the party and the Red Army for supporting the Trotskyite opposition in 1926–28. Zdanovich, *Organy*, 326 (citing TsA FSB, delo R-45677, l. 1).

113. Molotov added: "I don't think any woman was involved." Chuev, *Sto sorok*, 310–1; Chuev, *Molotov*, 376.

114. Lenoe, *Kirov Murder*, 264–7 (RGANI, f. 6, op. 13, d. 21, l. 86–93: A. I. Katsafa, who retook custody of Nikolayev after the interrogation); Rosliakov, *Ubiistvo*, 36; Artizov, *Reabilitatsiia: kak eto bylo*, I: 296 (Molotov, Dec. 31, 1955).

115. Lenoe, *Kirov Murder*, 271–3 (RGANI, f. 6, op. 13, d. 79, l. 1).

116. The NKVD pursued not the German but the Latvian consul connection. Nikolayev proved able to pick the Latvian consul (Georgs Bissenieks) out of eighteen photographs, and to describe the facility's interior. Bissenieks was expelled from the Soviet Union on Dec. 30, 1934. (The Soviets would capture and execute him in 1940–1.)

117. Sedov et al., "Spravka," 482. Mikoyan is among the many sources who falsely assert that from the first minutes Stalin fingered the Zinovievites. Mikoian, *Tak bylo*, 311.

118. RGASPI, f. 17, op. 3, d. 955, l. 20. A former Socialist Revolutionary who had joined the Bolsheviks in 1919, Kandelaki had served as commissar of enlightenment in Georgia (1925–30) and Soviet trade representative in Sweden. He would make twenty visits to Stalin's office, according to the logbooks. *Na prieme*, 627.

119. Gnedin, *Iz istorii otnoshenii*, 34–5; Gnedin, *Katastrofa i votoroe rozhdenie*, 237–9. See also Raymond, "Witness and Chronicler."

120. Rybin, *Riadom so Stalinym*, 10.

121. Anderson et al., *Kremlevskii kinoteatr*, 970–2 (RGASPI. f. 558, op. 11, d. 828, l. 70–3). See also Mikoian, *Tak bylo*, 115, 148–50. The filmed Kirov speeches were to the second Leningrad province congress of collective farmers (July 17, 1933) and the Leningrad party plenum (Oct. 10, 1934). The documentary would open Jan. 14, 1935. Bliokh was awarded the Order of Lenin.

122. According to the heavy industry staffer Semyon Ginzburg, for days after Kirov's death Orjonikidze would not appear at the commissariat. Upon his return, the staff "did

not recognize the typically enthusiastic and vivacious Sergo. He had turned gray and aged noticeably. He often seemed lost in thought, with a face heavy from grief." Ginzburg, "O gibeli Sergo Ordzhonikidze," 89. Zinoviev and his former supporter Grigory Yevdokimov evidently sent an obituary to *Pravda*, which refused to publish it. *Pravda*, Aug. 15, 1936.

123. Stalin also liked "The Varangian" ("Tell the whole word, seagulls, the sad news: they did not surrender to the enemy, they fell for Russian honor"). Sergeev and Glushik, *Besedy o Staline*, 22–3, 78.

124. Stalin added: "Moreover, in the hands of talented masters, it is the most powerful art. We, the leaders, need to get directly involved in the work of cinema to help this extremely important cause. Those working in film need to take a great deal of care to ensure that films should be varied, that, together with serious works there should also be jolly ones, as in theatre, so that the viewer, depending on his mood and his level, might choose where he'd rather go today." Anderson et al., *Kremlevskii kinoteatr*, 973–42 (RGASPI. f. 558, op. 11, d. 828, l. 74–5).

125. Taranova, *Golos Stalina*, 69–70. Levitan had been designated to break the news of Kirov's assassination for the Soviet public, but he had been out sick. His voice ("Moscow speaking!") was now heard across the USSR multiple times a day, in a broadcast known as "The Latest News," from a studio at the Central Telegraph Station. (Natalya Tolstova was the second-most-heard voice.) Legend also has it that Stalin, in his office working on Jan. 25, 1934, on his speech for the 17th Party Congress, had turned up the dial on the radio and heard Levitan, who after a three-year training period, had finally gotten a chance to be assigned to read the next morning's edition of *Pravda* over the radio; Stalin called the head of Soviet radio, Konstantin Maltsev, and directed that his congress report the next day—a five-hour performance—be read over the radio in its entirety by the same announcer. Taranova, *Golos Stalina*, 55–6. See also Tolstova, *Vnimanie, vkliuchaiu mikrofon!*; Liachenko, "Tak proletelo sorok let . . . ," 47–51; and Goriaeva, "*Veilkaia kniga dnia,*" 77 (GARF, f. R-6903, op. 1 l/s, d. 25, l. 24).

126. Murin, *Stalin v ob"iatiaikh*, 168 (Svanidze diary: Dec. 5, 1934).

127. Lenoe, *Kirov Murder*, 281–3 (TsA FSB, u.a.d., N-Sh44, t. 12, l. 95–6: Nikolayev interrogation, Dec. 4). Agranov reported to Stalin and Yagoda (Dec. 5) over the phone that, according to Draule's interrogation, "until August she participated in the compilation of her husband's diary. She confirmed that she read several of his entries that carried a counterrevolutionary character." He added that Draule's relatives, in Latvia, were "traders" (i.e., class enemies) and that her brother in Leningrad had been sentenced to a three-year term in a labor colony for embezzlement. Vinogradov, *Genrikh Iagoda*, 393 (TsA FSB, f. 3, op. 2, d. 60, l. 1–6).

128. Vinogradov, *Genrikh Iagoda*, 391–6 (TsA FSB, f. 3, op. 2, d. 60, l. 1–6); Lenoe, *Kirov Murder*, 285–7 (RGANI, f. 6, op. 13, d. 71, l. 23–6). Nikolayev, in an interrogation protocol (Dec. 13) delivered to Stalin, "confessed" that he belonged to a "group" of former oppositionists (Shatsky and Kotolynov), which adhered to Trotskyite-Zinovievite views and "considered it necessary to change the existing party leadership by all possible means." This passage was underlined in pencil. The protocol further stated that they had directed Nikolayev to make it appear he acted alone "to hide the participation of the Zinovievite group."

This passage was also highlighted with pencil. Agranov called the threesome "best friends." He tried to get Nikolayev to confess that his visits to the German and Latvian consulates in summer and fall 1934 constituted attempts by his "group" to contact Trotsky abroad. Khaustov et al., *Lubianka: Stalin i VChK*, 578–9 (APRF, f. 3, op. 24, d. 198, l. 2); Zhukov, "Sledstvie."

129. Khlevniuk, *Stalin: zhizn'*, 187 (no citation).

130. *Na prieme*, 144; Mikoian, *Tak bylo*, 316. Agranov was relieved of his post as acting director of the Leningrad NKVD to focus on the investigation; Zakovsky was appointed in his place (Dec. 10).

131. Lenoe, *Kirov Murder*, 304 (RGANI, f. 6, op. 13, d. 138, l. 4–9; RGASPI, f. 671, op. 1, d. 271, l. 542); Kotolynov had been expelled in 1927 and reinstated in 1928. Kirilina, *Neizvestnyi Kirov*, 411.

132. Khaustov and Samuelson, *Stalin, NKVD*, 49–50 (APRF, f. 3, op. 58, d. 130, l. 161), 51 (d. 131, l. 34). From Dec. 1934, Polish-language instruction at schools and institutes was curtailed or eliminated. Kuromiya, *Freedom and Terror*, 208 (citing TsDAHO, f. 1, op. 16, spr. 12, ark. 278, 304, 313).

133. Murin, *Stalin v ob'iatiakh*, 167; *Na prieme*, 144.

134. Zhukov, "Sledstvie," 42.

135. Kotolynov claimed he heard the following from Zinoviev: "It would be better if he [Stalin] did not exist." Kirilina, *Neizvestnyi Kirov*, 416.

136. Khaustov et al., *Lubianka: Stalin i VChK*, 577–8 (APRF, f. 3, op. 24, d. 198, l. 8, 9).

137. When they came for Zinoviev at night, he hastily composed a note to Stalin: "In no way, no way, am I guilty before the party, before the Central Committee or before you personally. I swear to you all by everything that is holy to a Bolshevik, I swear to you by Lenin's memory. I cannot even imagine who could have raised suspicion against me. I beg you to believe this, my word of honor. I am shaken to the depth of my soul." Stalin did not answer. He had Zinoviev, along with Kamenev, expelled from the party again on Dec. 20. The first draft of the indictment (Jan. 13) would note that Zinoviev and Kamenev pleaded innocent; the indictment soon changed. "O dele tak nazyvaeomom 'Moskovskom tsentre.'"

138. "O dele tak nazyvaeomom 'Moskovskom tsentre,'" 80; Iakovlev et al., *Reabilitatsiia: politicheskie portsessy*, 154.

139. RGASPI, f. 17, op. 3, d. 955, l. 42 (Dec. 19, 1934). "We lived and live under an unflagging regime of terror and force," the Nobel Laureate Ivan Pavlov wrote to the Council of People's Commissars (Dec. 21, 1934). "I more and more see the parallel between our life and the life of ancient Asiatic despotisms . . . Remember that humans, descended from animals, can fall easily, but elevating them is difficult . . . Take pity on the motherland and on us." *Sovetskaia kul'tura*, Jan. 14, 1989.

140. *Na prieme*, 144. Akulov, frozen out by the clans at the OGPU, had been removed as first deputy there in Oct. 1932; he had been named USSR procurator general with the position's creation on June 20, 1933. Golunskii, *Istoriia zakonodatel'stva SSSR*, 510–1; Kolpakidi and Seriakov, *Shchit i mech*. 343. In Feb. 1936, Akulov would fall off a horse, cracking his skull. "Bolezn' tov. Akulova," *Pravda*, Feb. 28, 1936: 6. Akulov would be arrested (July 1937) and executed.

141. Svetlana developed a high temperature (from scarlet fever). Sergeev and Glushik, *Besedy o Staline*, 144, 147.

142. Murin, *Stalin v ob"iatiakh*, 169–71 (Maria Svanidze diary: Dec. 23 and 28, 1934). Svanidze effectively confessed to her diary

that she was in love with Stalin, and vied with many women for the now twice-widowed Stalin's attention: Sashiko and Mariko Svanidze, the sisters of Stalin's deceased first wife; Anna Alliluyeva; Yevgeniya "Zhenya" Alliluyeva (Stalin's sister-in-law, married to Pavel Alliluyev, Nadya's elder brother)—all of whom hoped to become indispensable to "poor Iosif," as Maria described him. Svanidze imagined that Stalin was having an affair with Zhenya (b. 1898), since he was attentive to her and the two were often missing at the same time. Murin, *Stalin v ob"iatiakh*, 157–8.

143. On Dec. 25 at 9:15, Stalin convened a meeting in his office to discuss and edit the indictment; the sentence of execution for all fourteen defendants was printed before the trial commenced. Lenoe, *Kirov Murder*, 344–52 (RGANI, f. 6, op. 13, d. 34, l. 36; TsA FSB, a.u.d. N-Sh44, t. 1, l. 1–16).

144. Vinogradov, *Genrikh Iagoda*, 396–404 (TsA FSB, f. 3, op. 2, d. 60, l. 48–56, 33); Lenoe, *Kirov Murder*, 358–77. Others have Nikolayev supposedly falling to the ground and shouting, "You cannot shoot me. Comrade Stalin promised . . ." Kirilina, *Rikoshet*, 67.

145. Kirilina, *Neizvestnyi Kirov*, 303 (Matveyev).

146. Sedov et al., "Spravka"; Kirilina, *Neizvestnyi Kirov*, 302–3; Lenoe, *Kirov Murder*, 370–1 (RGANI, f. 6, p. 13, d. 24, l. 51–68).

147. Maslov and Chistiakov, "Stalinskie repressii i sovetskaia iutsitsiia," 105.

148. Lugovskaia, *Diary of a Soviet Schoolgirl*, 140.

149. Stalin had the politburo in May 1934 decree the Stalin Institute, in Tiflis, subordinated as an affiliate to the central Marx-Engels-Lenin Institute. Still, whether he was fully aware of the enormous pile of documents concerning his youth that was being accumulated remains unclear. Kun, *Stalin*, 3–4.

150. Hoover Archives, Lakoba papers, 1–57.

151. Lakoba, *Stalin i Khashim*, 5, 32–5.

152. Hoover Archives, Lakoba papers, 2–22. Sebastian Kirakozov made a painting of Stalin and Hashim. Kravchenko, *Stalin v izobrazitel'nom iskusstve*, opposite 26.

153. See also the intrigue surrounding Baron Bibineishvili's biographical celebration of *Kamo* (1934), the revolutionary bandit: Sukharev, "Litsedeistvo," 107, citing PA IIP pri TsK KP Gruzii, f. 8, op. 1, d. 22, l. 5; f. 14, op. 9, d. 18, l. 239. Bibineishvili, *Kamo*.

154. Enukidze, *Nashi podpol'nye tipografii Kavkaza*.

155. Shaumian, "Stoikii bol'shevik."

156. Yenukidze wrote a response (Jan. 8, 1935) claiming the mistakes were not his; Stalin marked up and had Yenukidze's response circulated. Maksimenkov, *Bol'shaia tsenzura*, 351–5 (RGASPI, f. 558, op. 11, d. 206, l. 111), 355–61 (d. 728, l. 108–24); Enukidze, *Bol'shevistskie nelegal'nye tipografii*.

157. Stalin had ordered a film crew out of the 16th party conference in April 1929 for creating a ruckus ("turning the conference into a bazaar"). Anderson et al., *Kremlevskii kinoteatr*, 100 (RGASPI, f. 558, op. 1, d. 132, l. 77).

158. Anderson et al., *Kremlevskii kinoteatr*, 227 (RGASPI, f. 17, op. 114, d. 379, l. 163–4), 229–30 (d. 661, l. 97–9: Jan. 17, 1934). "Newsreels are an interesting type of art, they have notably done well here, they are pleasant and edifying to watch," Stalin remarked after watching the May Day 1934 newsreel. Typically, he wanted them shortened and sharpened. Anderson et al., *Kremlevskii kinoteatr*, 919–23 (RGASPI, f. 558, op. 11, d. 828, l. 27–30).

159. Bulgakova, *Eisenstein*, 137 (citing Eisenstein archive, 1923–2–1116); Anderson et al.,

Kremlevskii kinoteatr, 139 (PARf, f. 3, op. 35, d. 87, l. 13). Geduld and Gottesman, *Sergei Eisenstein and Upton Sinclair*. On Dec. 1, 1931, Eisenstein's colleagues in Moscow pronounced the AWOL director a "deserter." Anderson et al., *Kremlevskii kinoteatr*, 150 (APRF, f. 3, op. 35, d. 87, l. 27: Yukov, Dec. 1, 191), 151 (l. 32: Shumiatsky, Dec. 1). On May 20, 1932, eleven days after Eisenstein and his assistant Grigory Alexandrov had finally arrived back from their three-year sojourn, they asked for an audience with Stalin, who wrote on the request, "I cannot receive them, no time."

160. Anderson et al., *Kremlevskii kinoteatr*, 184 (APRF, f. 3, op. 35, d. 87, l. 81: June 8, 1932). See also Pyr'ev, *Izbrannye proizvedeniia*, I: 64; Anderson et al., *Kremlevskii kinoteatr*, 176–7 (APRF, f. 3, op. 35, d. 87, l. 77–8), 180 (RGASPI, f. 17, op. 114, d. 403, l. 62); and *Pravda*, Jan. 23, 1973. *Thunder over Mexico*, attributed to Eisenstein, was screened in Los Angeles on May 10, 1933. In July 1933, he entered a hospital in Kislovodsk with depression. Anderson et al., *Kremlevskii kinoteatr*, 195–200 (RGASPI, f. 142, op. 1, d. 586, l.11–22).

161. Shumiatsky had only been able to show parts of the film at the first screening; a week later he showed it in its entirety. Anderson et al., *Kremlevskii kinoteatr*, 940–5 (RGASPI, f. 558, op. 11, d. 828, l. 46–60: July 14, 1934), 945–7 (l. 51–2), 947n3 (d. 27, l. 88). One of the film's numbers, "Such a lot of nice girls!," would be immortalized as the tango "Heart" by Pyotr Leshchenko. Stalin tended to like thoughtful songs, even those a bit sad (such as "Suliko") but he was captivated by the dance numbers. Stalin's thirst for relaxation was immense. Anderson et al., *Kremlevskii kinoteatr*, 947–9 (RGASPI, f. 558, op. 11, d. 828, l. 53–4).

162. Aleksandrov, *Epokha i kino*, 159; Kushnirov, *Svetlyi put'*, 96–7; Shumiatskii, *Kinematografiia millionov*, 236. On the resistance of some musicians to the acting tricks under Utyosov, and the changeover in his band's personnel, see Batashev, *Sovetskii dzhaz*, 40–3; and Chernov and Bialik, *O legkoi muzyke*, 120. Igor Savchenko, the Ukrainian filmmaker, had actually made the first Soviet musical comedy, *The Accordion* (June 1934), about a youth who stops playing the supposedly frivolous instrument after he becomes a village Communist Youth league secretary. Aleksandrov, *Epokha i kino*, 196; Zel'dovich, *Liubov' Orlova*, 17. Stites, *Russian Popular Culture*, 90–2.

163. "A film and its success are directly linked to the degree of entertainment in the plot," Shumiatsky had noted in Dec. 1933. But that year, of the eight Soviet films released, a mere three were comedies. Shumiatskii, "Tvorcheskie zadachi templana"; Taylor, "Ideology as Mass Entertainment," 193.

164. At the orgburo cinema commission, *Jolly Fellows* came in for severe criticism as "counterrevolutionary" and "muck, hooliganism, false throughout." Sidorov, "'Veselye rebiata'—komediia kontrrevoliutsionnaia," 73–4; (RGASPI, f. 74, op. 1, d. 293, l. 18–20: July 28, 1934), 75 (l. 21: July 29). Iurii Saakov, "Secha v kommunal'noi kvartire," *Iskusstvo kino*, 1995, no. 2: 134-44; Salys, *Films of Grigorii Aleksandrov*, 34. Stalin had the orgburo cinema commission dissolved. Anderson et al., *Kremlevskii kinoteatr*, 246–7, 248, 252 (f. 17, op. 163, d. 1048, l. 156: Dec. 17, 1934), 252n3 (op. 3, d. 955, l. 57). Shumiatsky showed Stalin a screed in *Literarturna gazeta* accusing *Jolly Fellows* of being "great talent wasted." Stalin erupted and tasked Zhdanov with setting things right. Anderson et al., *Kremlevskii kinoteatr*, 969–70 (RGASPI, f. 558, op. 11, d. 828, l. 69: Nov. 20, 1934); *Literaturnaia*

gazeta, Nov. 18, 1934. On Dec. 11, 1934, when Stalin asked Shumiatsky how things were going he got an earful; the dictator phoned Molotov on the vertushka and inquired about the reserve budget fund and how much extra could be given for cinema. Anderson et al., *Kremlevskii kinoteatr*, 976–8 (RGASPI, f. 558, op. 11, d. 828, l. 77–80).

165. Douglas, *Inventing American Broadcasting*.

166. In Britain, the number of radios would jump from 3 million in 1930 to 9 million by the end of the decade—three of four British households—while the number of listeners would increase from an estimated 12 million in the 1920s to 34 million by 1939. By the second half of the 1930s, Germany would have more than 9 million radio receivers. Goebbels had noted (Aug. 1933), "What the press was to the 19th century, radio will be to the 20th." Bowden and Offen, "Revolution that Never Was," 244–74; Williams, *Communications*; Bergmeier and Lorz, *Hitler's Airwave*, 6, 9.

167. The USSR would have 7 million by decade's close, including 1.6 million in rural areas. It had planned for far more, but Soviet industry could not manufacture sufficient quantities of vacuum tubes. Inkeles, *Public Opinion in Soviet Russia*, 243–4, 274–5; Gurevich and Ruzhnikov, *Sovetskoe radioveshchanie*, chap. 5.

168. Lovell, *Russia in the Microphone Age*, 101. Small local stations had proliferated, but they were soon obliged to rebroadcast set amounts of Moscow material. Initially, live material predominated, although by 1933 texts for live broadcasts had to be submitted in advance, and programs were monitored for compliance. Goriaeva, *Radio Rossii*, 157; Goriaeva, "Veilkaia kniga dnia," 91–2 (RGASPI, f. 17, op. 114, d. 558, l. 9–10: July 9, 1935), 93 (GARF, f. A-2306, op. 60, d. 79, 84: Dec. 27, 1935); Goriaeva, "Zhurnalistika i tsenzura."

169. Taylor, "Ideology as Mass Entertainment," 198.

170. Letters to the party propaganda department asked that radio lectures be read more slowly, to allow for notetaking. Lovell, *Russia in the Microphone Age*, 67 (citing Mikhail Angarskii and Voiacheslav Knushev, "Slovo slushatelei o peredachakh: obzor pisem radioslushatelei," *Govorit SSSR*, 1933, no. 12–13: 33–4; GANO, f. 3630, op. 5, d. 54, l. 15–6; GARF, f. 6903, op. 1, d. 49, l. 2, 4, 9). Nazi-era radio featured popular music and comedy as well as anti-Semitic speeches. "Disney, Dietrich and Benny Goodman," Anson Rabinbach observed, "shared radio time with Goebbels, Göring and the Führer." Rabinbach, "Imperative to Participate," 7.

171. Nikolaevich, "Poslednii seans," at 22.

172. Ivanov, *Ocherki istorii rossiisko (sovetsko)-pol'skikh otnoshenii*, 195; Dolinskii, *Sovetskaia kinokomediia tridtsatykh godov*, I: 11.

173. Zil'ver, *Za bol'shoe*, 22–49, 58–80 (quote at 72).

174. *Sovetskoe Kino*, 1935, no. 1: 9; Taylor and Christie, *Film Factory*, 348–55 (Leonid Trauberg). See also Shumiatskii, *Kinematografiia millionov*, 7.

175. Maksimenkov, *Kremlevskii kinoteater*, 257–61 (RGASPI, f. 17, op. 3, d. 958, l. 15, 45–7; op. 163, d. 1051, l. 90–4); *Pravda*, Jan. 12, 1935; *Sovetskoe kino*, 1935, no. 1: 11–2; Fomin and Deriabin, *Letopis' Rossiiskogo kino*, II: 315–6. See also Miller, *Soviet Cinema*, 22–3.

176. Eisenstein's closing remarks were published (*Kino*, Jan. 17, 1935: 4), and Shumyatsky sent a withering complaint about them. Fomin and Deriabin, *Letopis' rossiiskogo kino*, II: 317 (RGALI, f. 2456, op. 4, d. 23, l. 17–8). When the film industry completed an

apartment house in 1934 in central Moscow (between Malaya Nikitskaya and Povarskaya streets, behind the House of Cinema), Eisenstein put in for two apartments (for himself and his mother); he got nothing. Bulgakowa, *Eisenstein*, 159–60.

177. Leyda, *Kino*, 319–20. Leyda attended the evening at the Bolshoi.

178. Shumiatskii, *Kinematografiia millionov*, 249, 8.

179. Evans, *Third Reich in Power*, 623–7; Domarus, *Hitler: Reden*, II: 643–8 (at 644); Kershaw, *Hitler: 1889–1936*, 546–8. "The French have definitely missed the opportunity for a preventive war," Hitler remarked internally once the plebiscite arrangements had been finalized. *DGFP*, series C, III: 704–6 (Dec. 4, 1934).

180. Bud, "Fil'm o Kirove."

181. Iakovlev et al., *Reabilitatsiia: politicheskie protsessy*, 162, 166

182. *Pravda*, Jan. 16, 1935. See also Haslam, "Political Opposition," 409–10.

183. A third trial, with another 77 defendants, including Zinoviev's wife, Zlata Radić, and various relatives of Nikolayev, would result in sentences of two to five years.

184. Stalin authored the letter. The day before he sent the text to other politburo members. "O tak nazyvaemom 'Antisovetskom ob"edinennom tsentre Trotskistko-Zinov'evskom tsentre,'" 95–100; Iakovlev et al., *Reabilitatsiia: politicheskie protsessy*, 191–5; Getty and Naumov, *Road to Terror*, 147–50; Lenoe, *Kirov Murder*, 381 (RGANI, f. 6, op. 13, d. 13, l. 18).

185. Lenoe, *Kirov Murder*, 446–7 (APRF, f. 3, op. 24, d. 201, l. 106–8, 114), 447–50 (RGANI, f. 6, op. 13, d. 92, l. 173–7: draft), 450 (169–72: draft). A draft is also in Khaustov et al., *Lubianka: Stalin i VChK*, 592–3 (TsAFSB, f. 3, op. 2, d. 7, l. 1–2).

186. Brontman, *Dnevniki*. See also *Kommunisticheskaia revoliutsiia*, 1935, no. 1: 23–4.

187. Stalin offered both praise and complaints about parts that were missing despite his instructions. Anderson et al., *Kremlevskii kinoteatr*, 989–90 (RGASPI, f. 558, op. 11, d. 828, l. 111); *Pravda*, Jan. 21 and 22, 1935. I. P. Kopalin and I. F. Setkina made the Lenin documentary.

188. Lenoe, *Kirov Murder*, 436–52 (RGANI, f. 6, op. 13, d. 79, l. 99–104; 82, l. 15–132).

189. See also Gronsky to Stalin in 1933 on Kuibyshev's drinking: RGASPI, f. 558, op. 11, d. 725, l. 49–58.

190. Recently, on his trip to Central Asia to pressure the cotton harvest, he had undergone an emergency operation, but then returned to Moscow to work, refusing to lie in hospital. One evening, after countless meetings, he told his staff that before giving a speech that night he was going across the courtyard to his nearby apartment (on the third floor) to lie down. His aides and the apartment staff woman wanted to call a doctor. He refused. By the time a doctor arrived, he was dead. Kabytov, "Valerian Kuibyshev"; *Sochineniia*, XI: 220.

191. Lota, "*Alta*" protiv "*Barbarossy*," 143–191, 248–55; Lota, *Sekretnyi front*, 75–94; Lurie and Kochik, *GRU*, 504, 511–2, 531, 532.

192. Sorge had been born in the Baku oil fields (1895)—his father was an oil technician—and grew up in Germany, where he fought in the Great War, then became a Communist in 1919, before moving to Moscow. In late 1929, military intelligence poached him from Comintern intelligence and sent him to China; he arrived in Tokyo in 1933. He joined the Nazi party, to aid his spy work, and criticized Nazi officials and actions, which, however, enhanced his credibility. He chased women and drank. Colonel Ott, the German military attaché in Tokyo, invited Sorge to

travel with him to Manchuria in Oct. 1934; Sorge wrote the trip's report. Soon, Sorge bedded Ott's wife, Helma. When Ott learned of the affair, he surmised it would not endure and did nothing, keeping the valuable Sorge, whom he called "the Irresistible" and "the man who knew everything." Whymant, *Stalin's Spy*, 145–94 (at 153, 184, no citation).

193. Primakov, *Ocherki*, III: 20, 26–39, 41; Costello and Tsarev, *Deadly Illusions*, 448n50, 449n65; Tsarev and West, *KGB v Anglii*, 44–7; Poretsky, *Our Own People*, 72–85; Peake, *Private Life of Kim Philby*, 220–1; Gazur, *Secret Assignment*, 15. See also Borovik, *Philby Files*; and Koch, *Double Lives*.

194. Golubev, "Nash tovarisch"; Costello and Tsarev, *Deadly Illusions*, 445n3. Maclean would deliver his first purloined secret file in Jan. 1936 (about secret negotiations between Britain and Nazi Germany over an airforce agreement). The Soviets soon were able to discern that the British had an agent in the foreign affairs commissariat and in Willi Münzenberg's circle. Maclean would also discover, through correspondence, the home address of Vernon Kell, the head of the secret MI5, allowing the Soviets to establish surveillance on the residence. See Primakov, *Ocherki*, III: 40–9. An alleged Polish agent who worked in Molotov's secretariat, who passed on evaluations of Soviet brass, was never discovered. Dzanovich, *Organy*, 723n54, citing TsA FSB, f. 1, op. 9, d. 19, l. 339–400.

195. Shearer, *Policing Stalin's Socialism*, 136–7. The special departments were particularly busy hauling in soldiers for counterrevolutionary utterances in relation to the Kirov murder. Suvenirov, *Tragediia*, 27; Whitewood, *Red Army and the Great Terror*, 170 (citing RGVA, f. 37837, op. 10, d. 26, l. 289, 194–6). In March 1935, the NKVD instructed an agent in Germany to investigate the links between Tukhachevsky and the Wehrmacht high command. "M. N. Tukachevskii i 'voenno-fashistskii zagovor'," 11.

196. Artizov et al., *Reabilitatsiia: kak eto bylo*, II: 735: Dec. 13, 1934); Gamarnik had managed, during the push for socialist legality, to obtain a ruling whereby the OGPU could summon army personnel for interrogation only with the agreement of the unit's commissar. Khaustov et al., *Lubianka: Stalin i VChK*, 524 (RGASPI, f. 17, op. 162, d. 16, l. 66: May 26, 1934).

197. *Dokumenty i materialy po istorii sovetsko-pol'skikh otnoshenii*, VI: 249–250 (AAN, d. AMSZ, Poselstwo RP, Berlin); Roos, *Polen und Europa*, 208–12; Weinberg, *Foreign Policy*, I: 193 (citing Bundesarchiv, Papers of General Beck, H 08–28/1, f. 54: Schindler to Blomberg, Feb. 22, 1935); Mikhutina, *Sovetsko-pol'skie otnosheniia*, 239–41, citing *Diariusz i teki Jana Szembeka, 1935–1945*, 2 vols. (London: Polish Research Centre/Orbis, 1964–6), I: 217–25, 230; Wojciechowski, *Stosunki polsko-niemieckie*, 243–4; and Beck, *Final Report*, 27–31. See also Weinberg, *Foreign Policy*, I: 204.

198. "General Goering to Visit Poland," "General Goering's Secret Visit to Warsaw," and "Conscription in Germany," *Manchester Guardian*, Jan. 25, 28, and 29, 1935, respectively; "General Goering in Warsaw," *The Times*, Jan. 28, 1935; *Izvestiia*, Feb. 14, 1935. See also Harris, "Encircled by Enemies," 539 (citing AVP RF f. 05, op. 15, pap. 109, d. 67, l. 5: Göring with Bek).

199. Bobylev et al., *Sovetskie Vooruzhennye Sily*, 143 (no citation). In 1933, the actual figure for military expenditures had been 4.299 billion, versus the published 1.421 billion rubles (hence Tukhachevsky's claims of fourfold increase in one year). Harrison and

Davies, "Soviet Military-Economic Effort," 369–70.

200. Barmine, *One Who Survived*, 221 (confirmed in the *Pravda* account).

201. Erickson, *Soviet High Command*, 381; Berson, *Kreml na białą*, 49. On Feb. 23, 1935, *Red Star* published a photomontage of five military portraits: Tukhachevsky occupied third position, after Voroshilov and Gamarnik, ahead of Yakir and Uborevičius.

202. Iurii Domobrovskii, in *Literaturnaia gazeta*, Aug. 22, 1990: 6; Larina, *Nezabyvaemoe*, 270.

203. Zhavaronkov, "I snitsia noch'iu den'," 52; Pavliukov, *Ezhov*, 335–6 (citing Aleksander Fadeev, "Nikolai Ivanovich Ezhov").

204. Encountering Yezhov in spring 1930 at a government resort in Sukhum on the Black Sea coast, Nadezhda Mandelstam, wife of the poet Osip, found him "a modest and rather agreeable person." Mandelstam, *Hope against Hope*, 321–5.

205. Razgon, *Plen v svoem otechestve*, 50–1.

206. On Yezhov's remarkable workload, see Pavliukov, *Ezhov*, 96 (citing RGASPI, f. 17m, op. 114, d. 298, l. 1–5; d. 300, l. 8–11).

207. "Blizhaishee okruzhene diktatora," *Sotsialisticheskii vestnik*, 1933, no. 23: 8–9. Yezhov suspected the essay's source was Pyatakov, first deputy commissar of heavy industry, who had traveled to Berlin in late 1932. Pyatakov was Yezhov's old drinking buddy. (Once, after Pyatakov, inebriated, had pricked him with a pin, Yezhov had punched in the face.) Pavliukov, *Ezhov*, 99–100; Petrov and Jansen, *Stalinskii pitomets*, 29–30.

208. They would adopt a daughter (Natasha) from a children's home. Yevgeniya ran a literary salon, while pursuing extramarital affairs. Yezhov, for his part, bedded subordinates' wives, household and cleaning personnel, prostitutes, and various male lovers; he drank and became pugnacious, beating her.

209. Chubar, whom Stalin met during the October days of 1917, had a reputation as an expert, and Stalin promoted him to deputy chairman of the Council of People's Commissars and finance commissar and invited him to inner-circle meals. Khlevniuk, *Politbiuro*, 228–9; Murin, *Stalin v ob"iatiakh sem'i*, 167.

210. This resolution appears to have been dictated by Stalin to Poskryobyshev; other members of the politburo signed it in the same red pencil on Stalin's desk (Kalinin's was evidently a telephone approval). The logbook for Stalin's office records no meeting that day. Khlevniuk, *Master of the House*, 139 (citing RGASPI, f. 17, op. 163, d. 1056, l. 35–6); Khlevniuk et al., *Stalinskoe politbiuro*, 142 (RGASPI, f. 17, op. 3, d. 960, l. 7; op. 2, d. 538, l. 3), 143 (op. 3, d. 961, l. 16); *Na prieme*, 152.

211. Khaustov and Samuelson, *Stalin, NKVD*, 141.

212. Mironenko, *Moskovskii kreml'*, 187, 210, 241.

213. On Sept. 23, 1934, Barbusse had requested an audience with Stalin, which was granted. Maksimenkov, *Bol'shaia tsenzura*, 341–2 (RGASPI, f. 558, op. 11, d. 699, l. 81). On the Sept. 16, 1937, audience, see RGASPI, f. 558, op. 11, d. 699, l. 2–10; "'U nas malo rasstrelivaiut': beseda I. V. Stalina s A. Babiusom" (APRF, f. 45, op. 1, d. 699, l. 2–10); and Barbusse, *Voici ce qu'on a fait de la Géorgie* (Paris: E. Flammarion, 1929). On the Oct. 5, 1932, meeting: Maksimenkov, *Bol'shaia tsenzura*, 251–8 (RGASPI, f. 558, op. 1, d. 699, l. 35–42, 43–51), 259 (l. 53–4).

214. Stetsky, who was assigned to edit Barbusse, mostly raised issues about the portrayal of Trotsky and the Stalin-Trotsky clash. Maksimenkov, *Bol'shaia tsenzura*, 341–6 (RGASPI, f. 558, op. 11, d. 699, l. 124–5: Sept. 29, 1934).

215. Barbusse described the Amusement Palace apartment, where Stalin no longer lived by the time the book came out. Barbusse, *Stalin*, vii–viii, 7, 277, 278. Louis Fischer would write that in Moscow, Barbusse had talked mostly about Jesus Christ. Margarete Buber-Neumann, who had encountered Barbusse in Moscow in 1932, would write that "I was very surprised my idol Barbusse displayed such traits of the bourgeois and the prima donna" by complaining about the hotel. Fischer, *Men and Politics*, 193; Buber-Neumann, *Von Potsdam nach Moskau*, 326.

216. Davies et al., *Years of Progress*, 153–6; *Pravda*, Jan. 30 and Feb. 16, 1935; *Vtoroi vsesoiuznyi s"ezd kolkhoznikov-udarnikov*, 186–7 (Yezhov), 247–97; Vyltsan, *Zavershchaiushchii etap*, 25–40.

217. *Pravda*, Feb. 10, 1935; *Vtoroi vsesoiuznyi s"ezd kolkhoznikov-udarnikov*, 144. See also *Kolkhoznitsa*, 1935, no. 11–12: 14–5; "Priem kolkhoznits-udarnits sveklovichnykh polei rukovoditeliami partii i pravitel'stva," *Sotsialisticheskaia rekonstruktsiia sel'skogo khoziaistva*, no. 11 (1935): 15–8; Kataev, "Mariia Demchenko," 295–300 (dated 1938).

218. Buckley, *Mobilizing Soviet Peasants*, 235–6, citing Sergei K. Korotkov et al., *My predsedatel'stvuem na Vsesoiuznom s"ezde* (Moscow: Sel'khozgiz, 1935), 12–3, 39. See also *Kazakhstanskaia pravda*, Feb. 18, 1935. All congress delegates received a copy of the bound published record. Stoletov, "Zamechatel'nye knigi."

219. *Pravda*, Feb. 15, 1935. A model statute had been drafted in late 1929 and published in revised form on March 2, 1930, but it had contained no specifics on organization, forms of payment, and so on. Ivnitskii, *Kollektivizatsiia i raskulachivanie*, 78–80. As one scholar has demonstrated, enduring regulations governing the collective farm system were not in place until 1933, when the concessions of 1932 were acknowledged as permanent. Merl, *Bauern unter Stalin*.

220. Danilov et al., *Tragediia sovetskoi derevni*, IV: 390–402 (RGASPI, f. 17, op. 120, d. 138, l. 68–91). Yakov Yakovlev, head of the CC agriculture department, gave the report on the new model statute the first day; Mikhail Chernov, the new USSR land commissar and chairman of the commission, reported on Feb. 17 with the Stalin-corrected version. *II vsesoiuznyi s"ezd kolkhoznikov-udarnikov*, 225–32. The 1935 statute defined "land as state property owned by the whole people, and assigned to *artels* for permanent use." Land was "not subject to either purchase-sale or leasing." Nomad households in Kazakhstan were allowed 8–10 cows and their calves, 100–150 sheep/goats, 10 horses, and 5–8 camels. *Izvestiia*, Feb. 18, 1935; *Sobranie zakonov*, 1935, art. 82; "Soviet Legislation (XIII): Selection of Decrees and Documents," *Slavonic and East European Review* 14, no. 40 (1935): 188–99.

221. Women made up 30.5 percent of the delegates (more than double the number at the first congress in 1933). *Pravda*, Feb. 16, 1935. According to the Soviet press, more than 7,000 women served as collective farm chairmen (up from just 1,290 in 1931), 8.1 percent of the total. Women made up 49.2 percent of managers of livestock units. *Sotsialisticheskoe zemledelie*, March 7, 1935; *II vsesoiuznyi s"ezd kolkhoznikov-udarnikov*, 247–97.

222. Yakovlev, in a report to party activists, summarized Stalin's remarks: *Pravda*, March 13, 1935; *Sotsialisticheskie zemledelie*, March 13, 1935; *Sotsialisticheskaia rekonstruktsiia sel'skogo khoziaistva*, no. 2–3: 8–30. See also Fitzpatrick, *Stalin's Peasants*, 122 (quoting *Krestian'skaia pravda*, Feb. 27, 1935: 2).

223. Whitman, "Kolkhoz Market," 393. Rural laborers' market sales fed regime coffers in

the form of taxes, but the household plots and the direct marketing absorbed time from collective farm duties, and the opportunities for marketing further reinforced rural laborers' deep commitment to the plots.

224. Maslov, *Kolkhoznaia Rossiia*, 198, 227-8.

225. Remuneration was calculated by a system known as the "labor day" (time plus skill, so that the chairman's work time was worth more than the field hand's). But only about 10 percent of the collective farmers' cash income came from collective farm work; more than half came from sales at market or to state contractors. Seasonal labor at factories and construction sites provided significant cash income as well. Vyltsan, *Zavershchaiushchii etap*, 101 (citing GRAE, f. 4372, op. 36, d. 356, l. 18), 203-4; *Kolkhozy vo vtoroi*, 37; *20 let sovetskoi vlasti*, 48.

226. *Pravda*, March 13, 1935 (Yakovlev). New members were to be admitted even if they had no animals or implements to contribute, a bitter pill for those who had had to yield up their property. Fitzpatrick, *Stalin's Peasants*, 124-7, citing *Krest'ainskaia pravda*, Feb. 28, 1935; *II vsesoiuznyi s"ezd kolkhoznikov-udarnikov*, 17-8, 85.

227. Fitzpatrick, *Stalin's Peasants*, 139-42. Collective farmers "could shout, fume, curse," wrote the eyewitness Hindus, "but they could not dodge the challenge the kolkhoz had thrust upon them." Hindus, *Red Bread*, 210.

228. Peterson (b. 1897), an ethnic Latvian who had commanded Trotsky's civil war train in 1919, since 1920 served as a punctilious Kremlin commandant, earning high praise and two Orders of the Red Banner and the Order of Lenin. Suvenirov, *Tragediia RKKA*, 158 (citing AVKVS RF, op. 64, d. 776, l. 1-4); Zhukov, *Inoi Stalin*, 141-3.

229. "We were sitting together, Avdeyeva, Zhalybina-Bykova, and I on the first floor of the government building in a small room drinking tea," one woman, E. S. Mishakova, testified. "Avdeyeva started to talk about how we lived badly, how our bosses drank, ate well, and we eat poorly. And I said to her that I live better now than before." Then Avdeyeva supposedly started to say that Stalin was not a Russian, divorced his first wife [sic], and the second had shot herself. "I said that this is not true, we do not know. On this note the conversation ended and we returned to work." For her part, A. E. Avdeyeva, a twenty-two-year-old cleaning lady in the central executive committee school, claimed "all that was said by [M. S.] Zhalybina." Khaustov et al., *Lubianka: Stalin i VChK*, 599-600 (APRF, f. 3, op. 58, d. 231, l. 1, 14).

230. Khaustov and Samuelson, *Stalin, NKVD*, 84-5 (TsA FSB, f. 3, op. 2, d. 8, l. 3). This was not Stalin's first such appearance at a secret police meeting, sessions that were followed by generous tables of food and drink. Shreider, *NKVD iznutri*, 22, 27.

231. "O tak-nazyvaemom dele 'Moskovskogo tsentra,'" 70; Iakovlev et al., *Reabilitatsiia: politicheskie protsessy*, 155; Sedov et al., "Spravka," 465.

232. Vasily Doroshin, a forty-year-old aide to the Kremlin commandant, was said to have testified that "the commandant of the Grand Kremlin Palace Lukyanov Ivan Petrovich told me on the second day after the death of N. A. Alliluyeva that the Kremlin commandant Peterson had gathered a group of comrades and announced that Alliluyeva had died an unnatural death." Khaustov et al., *Lubianka: Stalin i VChK*, 602-3 (APRF, f. 3, op. 58, d. 231, l. 22-6).

233. Khaustov et al., *Lubianka: Stalin i VChK*, 606-10 (APRF, f. 3, op. 58, d. 230, l. 67-75: E. K. Mukhanova testimony, Feb. 10). Another

librarian, P. I. Gordeyeva, daughter of workers and herself a Communist Youth League member, testified (March 1) that after the official news about Kirov's death, Kremlin library employees discussed how "the murder of Kirov was not political, but a result of personal revenge" (618-9: d. 232, l. 31-4).

234. Khaustov et al., *Lubianka: Stalin i VChK*, 604-12 (APRF, f. 3, op. 58, d. 231, l. 54-9: Feb. 10, 1935). See also Khlevniuk, *Khoziain*, 253.

235. Khaustov et al., *Lubianka: Stalin i VChK*, 604-6 (APRF, f. 3, op. 58, d. 231, l. 32-6: Feb. 7), 230 (d. 230, l. 67-75: Feb. 10).

236. *Gosudarstvennaia okhrana Rossii*, 49 (no citation).

237. Khaustov et al., *Lubianka: Stalin i VChK*, 617 (APRF, f. 3, op. 58, d. 231, l. 88).

238. "O tak nazyvaemon 'Kremlevskom dele,'" 90-1.

239. RGASPI, f. 17, op. 3, d. 961, l. 58 (March 31, 1935). See also Hoover Institution Archives, Nicoalevsky Collection, box 233, folder 9 ("Iz zapisonoi knizhki Boris Ivanovicha Nikolaevskogo [rasskazy A. F. Almazova]), 1-2.

240. Ivanov, "Operatsiia 'Byvshie liudi,'" 118-9; 121, 129; Vinogradov, *Genrikh Iagoda*, 465-6.

241. Of the 11,095 he listed, 5,044 were said to be former "big" merchants and rentiers, 2,360 aristocrats, and nearly 1,000 family members of executed terrorists, spies, and saboteurs. Khaustov et al., *Lubianka: Stalin i VChK*, 613-6 (APRF, f. 3, op. 58, d. 174, l. 42-9: Feb. 16, 1935), 617 (l. 41).

242. Khaustov et al., *Lubianka: Stalin i VChK*, 613-6 (APRF, f. 3, op. 58, d. 174, l. 42-49: Zakovsky to Yagoda, Feb. 16, 1935), 617 (l. 41: Yagoda to Stalin, Feb. 26, 1935).

243. Various officials in Karelia, too, were arrested as "spies," and at least 5,000 "kulak" families within a fifteen-mile radius of the Finnish border were evicted, and their livestock and possessions confiscated. Dmitriev, *Pominal'nye spiski Karelii*, 17. In Oct. 1935, Zakovsky opened an NKVD training school in Leningrad desperately seeking more personnel. Tumshis and Papchinskii, *1937, bol'shaia chistka*, 51.

244. Dubinskaia-Dzhalilova and Chernev, "Zhmu vashu ruku, dorogoi tovarishch,'" 188-9. *Turbins* had been approved for staging in Leningrad in 1933. In 1936, it would be permitted in Kiev. Milne, *Mikhail Bulgakov*, 168.

245. On Stalin's fifteen visits, see V. Lakshin, preface to Bulgakov, *Izbrannaia proza*, 30. See also Jelagin, *Taming of the Arts*, 102-3; Shapoval, "'Oni chuvstvuiut sebia, kak gosti . . . ,'" 107-8, 121; Smeliansky, *Is Comrade Bulgakov Dead?* 170-3; Shentalinskii, *Raby svobody*, 120. Between 1926 and 1941, the Moscow Art Theater would stage *Turbins* 987 times. Bulgakov, *Dramy i komedii*, 583.

246. Sergeev and Glushik, *Besedy o Stalin*, 247. Bulgakova, *Eisenstein*, 168-72. Sixty-five films were submitted and twenty-six accepted. *Kino*, Feb. 2 and Feb. 21, 1935; *Pravda*, Feb. 22, 1935: 4. On Feb. 22, the state medals for cinema that had been announced in Jan. were presented by Kalinin in the Kremlin, with Stalin in attendance.

248. *Pravda*, Nov. 29, 1935.

249. Iasenskii, "O dvukh neudachnykh popytkakh."

250. Mekhlis summoned the editors to Old Square (March 11), reading them the riot act; the next day's editorial in *Pravda* was unchanged. Anderson et al., *Kremlevskii kinoteatr*, 996-7 (RGASPI, f. 558, op. 1, d. 829, l. 9-10: March 11, 1935); Fomin and Deriabin, *Letopis' Rossiiskogo kino*, II: 325; *Pravda*, March 12, 1935.

251. *Izvestiia*, March 3, 1935; *Kino*, March 5, 1935; "K itogam pervogo sovetskogo

kinofestivalia," *Sovetskoe kino*, no. 3 (1935): 3-5. By now, *Chapayev* was being shown in New York on Broadway. "Sovetskie fil'my v N'iu-Iorke," *Pravda*, March 2, 1935.

252. The Soviets produced almost no expressly antifascist movies, beyond Pyryev's *Assembly Line of Death* (Nov. 7, 1933), set in an unspecified European country, which portrayed fascism as a movement aiming to restore capitalism in the Soviet Union.

253. Friedberg, *Literary Translation in Russia*, 115. See also Baer, "Literary Translation." "The Style of Soviet Culture," a *Pravda* article by a literary critic, put forth Balzac, Goethe, Shakespeare, and Lev Tolstoy for emulation. *Pravda*, April 29, 1935 (Dinamov, pen name of Sergei Ogladkov). ("Mayakovsky shot himself while I translate," Pasternak supposedly remarked of his means of livelihood.)

254. "Bol'she' shekspirovat'!" *Literaturnaia gazeta*, April 23, 1933. Translations included Rabelais's *Gargantua and Pantagruel* (1929), Virgil's *Aeneid* (1933), Homer's *Iliad* (1935), and Homer's *Odyssey* (1935).

255. Litovskii, "Korol' Lir"; Harshav, *Moscow Yiddish Theater*, 90; Clark, *Moscow*, 189 (citing GARF, f. 5283, op. 8, d. 242). See also Fowler, "Yiddish Theater in Soviet Ukraine."

256. Mikhoels, "Moia rabota nad 'Korolem Lirom,'" 94-123. A Shakespeare conference (Nov. 25-27, 1935) sparked controversy about how best to translate and interpret the playwright. *Pravda*, Nov. 29, 1935; O. Litovskii, "Zhivoi Shekspir," 7-8; Clark, *Moscow*, 184-5.

257. Lang, *Modern History of Soviet Georgia*, 253.

258. Lakoba, *Ot VI k VII s"ezdu sovetov ASSR Abkhazia*; Lakoba, "Sel'skoe khoziaistvo Abkhazii—baza Sovetskoi pishchevoi promyshlennosti," Hoover Archives, Lakoba papers, 2-32. See also Kolt'sov and Lezhava, *Sovetskie subtropiki*.

259. Lakoba, "'Ia Koba, a ty Lakoba,'" 58 (March 15, 1935).

260. Khaustov et al., *Lubianka: Stalin i VChK*, 610-2 (APRF, f. 3, op. 58, d. 231, l. 54-9: Feb. 10).

261. It seems that in 1932, Kamenev had stopped by Yenukidze's Kremlin office after being sentenced to exile in Minusinsk, asking that he be allowed to keep his Moscow apartment and that Yenukidze later passed on to Stalin a letter Kamenev intended to write from exile asking to be allowed to return to Moscow. Vinogradov, *Genrikh Iagoda*, 508-17 (TsA FSB, f. 13614, tom 2, l. 308-10, 314-22: May 30, 1937).

262. "Irina Gogua: semeinye istorii," *Ogonek*, April 1997: http://kommersant.ru/doc/2284891; Cherviakova, "Pesochnye chasy." Maria Svanidze took a more sinister view, writing in her diary about Yenukidze's deceit, abuse of the perquisites of his office, and involvement with girls as young as nine to eleven, corrupting them morally if not physically." Murin, *Stalin v ob"iatiakh*, 182 (Svanidze diary: June 28, 1935).

263. *Zaria vostoka*, March 5, 1935. Peterson was dismissed in April 1935 but not arrested (Yakir brought him to the Kiev military district as an aide in June).

264. Lenoe, *Kirov Murder*, 287-8 (RGANI, f. 6, op. 13, d. 33, l. 49-50: Ulrich to Stalin, March 11, 1934).

265. Kokurin and Petrov, *Lubianka*, 548-52; RGASPI, f. 671, op. 1, d. 271, l. 565-65ob.: Yezhov notes for presentation to Stalin, Dec. 1934 or Jan. 1935.

266. Khaustov et al., *Lubianka: Stalin i VChK*, 628-31 (APRF, f. 3, op. 58, d. 232, l. 168-76: March 11, 1935). A June 17, 1935, joint Central Committee and Council of People's Commissars decree, "On the procedure for

conducting arrests," superseded the May 8, 1933, instruction, and stipulated that the NKVD could make arrests only with the sanction of the procuracy; arrests of personnel who reported to commissariats could be made only with the sanction of that particular commissar, including in the defense commissariat. Arrests of members and candidates of the Central Committee only with CC approval. A further directive would be issued Dec. 1, 1938, to take into account institutional changes, but arrests still required the authorization of the governing institution's leadership. Suvenirov, *Tragediia RKKA*, 63 (citing RGVA, f. 9, op. 36, d. 1339, l. 191–2ob.).

267. Khaustov et al., *Lubianka: Stalin i VChK*, 648–50 (APRF, f. 3, op. 58, d. 234, l. 1–6: March 21, 1935). Zakovsky would report from Leningrad that more than 11,000 "former people" had already been sentenced and 22,000 inhabitants of border zones deported. Khaustov and Samuelson, *Stalin, NKVD*, 64; Vinogradov, *Genrikh Iagoda*, 465–76 (March 31, 1935); Khaustov et al., *Lubianka: Stalin i VChK*, 654–7. Yezhov presented Stalin a list (April 4, 1935) of the recipients of the various dachas that Yenukidze had doled out. Maksimenkov, *Lubianka: Stalin i VChK*, 371n4 (RGASPI, f. 671, op. 1, d. 52, l. 32: Yezhov to Stalin, April 4, 1935). The politburo ordered the purchase—rather than the confiscation—of some valuable literary archives by people being deported from Leningrad in the wake of the Kirov murder. Artizov and Naumov, *Vlast'*, 255 (RGASPI, f. 17, op. 3, d. 962, l. 48: April 23, 1935), 763n92 (APRF, f. 3, op. 58, d. 174, l. 78–9).

268. The document was worked out by Stalin, Molotov, Kaganovich, and Yezhov, but not Voroshilov or Orjonikidze, and would be dated April 3, 1935. Stalin was in his office with those three only on March 15, 1935. Khaustov et al., *Lubianka: Stalin i VChK*, 658–60 (APRF, f. 3, op. 58, d. 234, l. 47–53); *Na prieme*, 156–7.

269. "'Zamenit' Vas nekem': pis'ma M. Gor'kogo I. V. Stalinu," 116–7 (APRF, f. 3, op. 58, d. 284, l. 127–127ob, 124).

270. *Izvestiia*, March 24, 1935; *DVP SSSR*, XVIII: 204–13; Lensen, *Damned Inheritance*, 457–9; Slavinskii, *Vneshniaia politika*, 53. See also RGASPI, f. 558, op. 11, d. 83, l. 73–83, 104–6.

271. Davies et al., *Years of Progress*, 91n5 (citing RGASPI, f. 17, op. 162, d. 17, l. 157–8). Stalin would inspect the first ZIS-101 luxury limousine on April 29, 1936.

272. Paine, *Wars for Asia*, 92.

273. Crowley, *Japan's Quest for National Autonomy*, 214–7; Safronov, *SSSR, SShA, i iaponskaia*, 145.

274. *DVP SSSR*, XVIII: 626 (Spil'vanek in Nanking to Moscow, Jan. 28, 1935).

275. Khlevniuk, *Stalin: zhizn'*, 195.

276. Murin, *Stalin v ob"iatiakh*, 173–6 (Svanidze diary: April 29, 1935), 178 (May 9); *Na prieme*, 161. See also Medvedev, *K sudu istorii*, 628; Brandenberger and Dubrovsky, "'The People head a Tsar,'" 873, 884n4. When a common person, Petrushenko, was asked in

a study circle that same year who Stalin was and answered, "someone like the tsar used to be," the secret police reported the remark. RGASPI, f. 17, op. 120, d. 176, l. 45; Davies, *Popular Opinion*, 168–9. The metro opened with two lines: from Sokolniki to the Park of Culture through Hunters Row station; and from the latter to Smolensk Square. Medvedev, *All Stalin's Men*, 124–5.

277. Tucker, *Stalin in Power*, 223–37. Ulam observed that "it is unlikely that Stalin would have wanted to establish the precedent of a successful assassination attempt against a high Soviet official." Ulam, *Stalin*, 385. "One thing is certain," wrote the émigré Nicolaevsky, "the only man who profited by the Kirov assassination was Stalin." Nicolaevsky, "Kirov Assassination."

278. Medved evidently discussed with other NKVD officials and his closest relatives his suspicion that Stalin and Yagoda were responsible for Kirov's death. Shreider, *NKVD iznutri*, 26–9. In 1935, Yefim Yevdokimov evidently asked Frinovsky if he had any information about the hand of Yagoda in the murder of Kirov (insinuating Stalin's involvement). Protocol of Frinovsky interrogation, Beria to Stalin, April 11, 1939 (APRF, f. 3, op. 24, d. 373, l. 3–44), http://www.hrono.ru/dokum/193_dok/19390413beria.php.

279. All six 1956–57 commissions formed under Khrushchev concluded that no underground Zinoviev-Trotskyite terrorist group existed; the thirteen people executed with Nikolayev would be rehabilitated in 1989.

280. Lenoe rightly assesses the evidence provided by Genrikh Lyushkov, who worked alongside Agranov and interrogated Draule, Zinoviev, Kamenev, and others, as the most important. Lysuhkov would write in 1939: "I can confirm that Kirov's murder was the individual deed of Nikolayev. Nikolayev was a psychologically unbalanced person who suffered many anxieties and was unhappy with life. He believed that he had the abilities to accomplish anything and he imagined himself as a man of intrigue. In reality, he was a constant complainer who could not get along with people. Confronted at every turn by the horrifying inertia of the state apparatus, he nonetheless fought to maintain the right and battle corruption. Society's indifference aroused in him hatred and an intense desire for revenge . . . And so Nikolayev's disenchantment with the party apparatus drove him to make plans for the assassination of one of the party leaders." Lenoe, *Kirov Murder*, 681–6 (*Kaizo*, April 1939).

281. Rimmel, "Another Kind of Fear," 484, citing TsGAIPD, f. 25, op. 5, d. 47, l. 1, 2, 492, citing TsGAIPD, f. 25, op. 5, d. 46, l. 3ob.

282. A group of workers from the Kirov plant in a letter to new Leningrad party boss Zhdanov condemned "deceivers," "scoundrels," and the regime's "soap-bubble comedy," and called the end of rationing "Molotov's vile deception," given how workers continued to live in squalor. Davies, *Popular Opinion*, 137 (citing TsGAIPD, f. 24, op.

2v, d. 1518, l. 184–8). By contrast, Tokayev, a young military engineer, noted that "the public . . . felt a cloud lifted . . . There was a new sense of freedom in domestic life; not that food became more plentiful, but it was not hard to draw the conclusion that, if the Government could take this step, 'things could not be so bad after all.'" Tokaev, *Betrayal of an Ideal*, 278–9.

283. Davies, *Popular Opinion*, 115–6 (citing TsGAIPD St.P f. 25, op. 5, d. 35, l. 7, 90; d. 54, l. 99; f. 24, op. 5, d. 240, l. 22; TsKhDMO, f. 1, op. 23, d. 1102, l. 167); Rimmel, "Another Kind of Fear," 484. See also Kedrov, *Lapti Stalinizma*, 152 (citing GAAO, otdel DSPI, f. 290, op. 2, d. 312, l. 107–10; d. 462, l. 56–60); Fainsod, *Smolensk under Soviet Rule*, 422; and Kuromiya, *Freedom and Terror*, 210 (citing DAHO, f. 326p, op. 1, spr. 304, ark. 34).

284. As we shall see, all of Orjonikidze's relatives would suffer from the dictator's falling out with his former intimate, while none of Kirov's relatives suffered.

285. "Comrade Stalin, as I now recall, summoned me and Kosaryov and said: 'Look for the murderers among the Zinovievites,'" Yezhov would state three years later. "I must say the Chekists did not believe in that and as insurance for themselves they were developing a second scenario, involving foreigners, on the off chance something would leap out." Yezhov was discrediting Yagoda and added that in Yezhov's presence, Stalin phoned Yagoda and said, "Look, we'll smash your face." L. P. Kosheleva et al., "Materialy fevral'-martovskogo plenuma TsK VKP (b) 1937 goda," (1995, no. 2): 16–7; Sedov et al., "Spravka," 482–3.

286. The bodyguard detail lacked even written operational instructions. Sedov et al., "Spravka," 494.

287. Shubin, *Vozhdi i zagovorshchiki*, 273.

288. A wealth of documents demonstrates this, which Yezhov would stress at the Feb.–March 1937 plenum: "Materialy martofevral'skogo plenuma TsK VKP (b) 1937 goda" (1995, no. 2), 17.

289. See the incisive memorandum by the American diplomat George Kennan (March 1935) about how "all the resources of the Soviet state have been applied to the construction of a vast military machine . . . A generation has been reared whose patriotic arrogance and whose ignorance of the outside world rival the formidable traditions which the history of Tsardom can offer in this respect." Kennan noted further that the Soviet willingness to sign pacts and enter the League of Nations derived from a belief that the next war would be fought by others, so that the Kremlin was interested not in collective security but in continuing to throw wrenches in efforts to achieve any sort of peaceful settlement among the Western powers. George Kennan, "The War Problem of the Soviet Union," in George F. Kennan Papers, Box 1, Mudd Library, Princeton University, reprinted in Hochman, *Failure of Collective Security*, 176–83 (at 178).

CHAPTER 5. A GREAT POWER

1. The correspondent added that pure Communist types had been set on edge by French Foreign Minister Laval's pending arrival. *Sotsialisticheskii vestnik*, May 25, 1935: 24.

2. About a quarter million copies of *Mein Kampf*, first published in 1925–26, had sold before he became chancellor, when sales really took off. In 1933, he earned more than 1 million marks in royalties, when schoolteachers averaged under 5,000 marks in annual salary. See also Lukacs, *Hitler of History*, 3.

3. Hitler, *My Struggle* (London: Hurst and Blackett, 1933); Hitler, *Mon combat* (Paris:

Nouvelles éditions latines, 1934). Horace Rumbold, British ambassador in Berlin, made a 5,000 word report (April 23, 1933) about *Mein Kampf* ("blood and thunder book") of Hitler's vow to restore German power "by force of arms." The memo was read by the cabinet and prime minister, and internally called "our Bible" on Germany. *DBFP*, 2nd series, V: 47–55 (Rumbold to Simon, April 26, 1933); Medlicott, *Britain and Germany*, 6n1; Steiner, *Triumph of the Dark*, 22–3; Durocelle, *La décadence*, 61. But see also Vansittart, *Mist Procession*, 305, 500; Glibert, *Roots of Appeasement*, 132.

4. Gitler, *Moia bor'ba* (Shanghai: Gong, 1935).

5. Hitler, *Mein Kampf*, 553. Radek would pointedly tell a German official in Moscow that there had been no changes to chapter 14 (treating of expansion to the east) in the recent reissue of Hitler's book—evidently the argument being used against Radek by foreign affairs commissariat personnel. *DGFP*, series C, II: 296–8 (unsigned memorandum, likely Twardowski, Jan. 1, 1934).

6. Pipes, *Russian Revolution*, 586; Ludendorff, *Kriegsführung und Politik*, 51.

7. *Krasnaia zvezda*, 1935, no. 57; see also no. 10, no. 31, no. 40, and no. 59.

8. Harris, "Encircled by Enemies," 513–4 (citing RGASPI, f. 558, op. 11, d. 188, l. 31–51).

9. Wandycz, "Polish Foreign Policy: an Overview," 65–73.

10. *Na prieme*, 152 (Feb. 28, 1935), 154–5 (March 8).

11. Ken, *Mobilizatsionnoe planirovanie*, 280 (citing AVP RF, f. 82, op. 18, pap. 80, d. 3, l. 35: Stern to Bessonov, March 17, 1935).

12. In Feb. 1935, Tukhachevsky and Jeronimas Uborevičius, commander of the Belorussian military district, had separately submitted secret memoranda arguing for war plan revisions. For Tukhachevsky, defeat of Poland remained a primary objective, but he foresaw Germany as "the chief agent of anti-Soviet intervention." Uborevičius also named Germany and Poland as the main enemies, and deemed this new coalition more formidable because it could quickly get assistance from Finland and the Baltic states, and perhaps Britain, while still, as before, drawing in Japan in a two-front war. He argued that a quick defeat of Poland would prevent Germany from being able to mobilize fully. Aptekar' and Uspenskii, *Marshal M.N. Tukhachevskii*, 2–11; Samuelson, *Soviet Defence Industry Planning*, 193–4; Samuelson, "Wartime Perspectives," 187–214, at 207 (citing RGVA, f. 33987, op. 3, d. 400, l. 226–36: Tukhachevsky, Feb. 5, 1935; and d. 279, l. 124–49: Uborevičius, Feb. 19, 1935); Roberts, "Planning for War," 1304–5; Dullin, *Men of Influence*, 97–8; Bruce Menning, personal communication.

13. Adibekov et al., *Politbiuro TsK RKP (b)–VKP (b) i Evropa*, 300 (RGASPI, f. 17, op. 162, d. 15, l. 5–6).

14. Hochman, *Failure of Collective Security*, 50–1.

15. Seraphim, *Das politische Tagebuch Rosenbergs*, 74–5.

16. Kershaw, *Hitler, 1889–1936*, 549–53; Shirer, *Berlin Diary*, 34; Weinberg, *Foreign Policy*, I: 204; *Pravda*, March 17 and 18, 1935.

17. *New York Times*, March 17 and 18, 1935; *Washington Post*, March 18, 1935.

18. Bullock, *Hitler*, 333; Weinberg, *Foreign Policy*, I: 203–6.

19. He added: "The only unusual thing about him was the length at which he spoke." Schmidt, *Hitler's Interpreter*, 17–26. This was Schmidt's first encounter with Hitler.

20. *DBFP*, 2nd series, XII: 703–46; *DGFP*, series C, III: 1043–80 (Schmidt). A few days later, Hitler told Luftwaffe officers: "I don't know how many aeroplanes Göring really has got, but that seemed about what there ought to be." Kershaw, *Making Friends with Hitler*, 99–102 (citing PRO FO 800/290, fol. 200: April 2, 1935). See also Simon, *Retrospect*, 200–3; Strang, *At Home and Abroad*, 66–7; and Dodd and Dodd, *Ambassador Dodd's Diary*, 228 (April 4, 1935).

21. Andrew and Elkner, "Stalin and Foreign Intelligence," 76–7; West and Tsarev, *Crown Jewels*, 81–2.

22. Primakov, *Ocherki*, III: 461–7.

23. Khaustov et al., *Lubianka: Stalin i VChK*, 651–3 (RGASPI, f. 558, op. 11, d. 188, l. 74–8: Slutsky); Khaustov, "Deiatel'nost' organov," 234 (APRF, f. 45, op. 1, d. 188, l. 74–6).

24. *DBFP*, 2nd series, XII: 793–5 (Sargent: April 1, 1935), 795 (Simon to G. Clerk in Paris, April 1). "Laval," one shrewd observer noted, "was very intelligent but he was also more cunning than competent. He wasn't a man of clear-cut decisions but rather 'everybody's friend.'" Duroselle, *France and the Nazi Threat*, 87. In general, the French got caught up in "pactomania," then sought loopholes in them.

25. A joint intelligence committee would be established in July 1936, but only at deputy director level; it would remain peripheral until summer 1939. In the 1930s, major military ies switched from medium to high frequencies for wireless, which, paradoxically, allowed more signals to be intercepted, but these still had to be decrypted. (Britain, after the end of the Great War, had not even tried to intercept German traffic again until 1934.) By 1935, Britain's specialists had broken Japan's main army and naval ciphers and some of Italy's, but German, as well as Soviet, ciphers remained inaccessible. Hinsley et al., *British Intelligence*, I: 36–43, 52–3, 57, 61, 199–200; Wark, *Ultimate Enemy*, 158–60; West, *MI6*, 45, 48–9; Strong, *Intelligence at the Top*, 24.

26. Benjamin Disraeli, at the time Britain's Tory party opposition leader, had admonished his fellow conservatives in 1872 that the choice was "whether you will be content to be a comfortable England, modelled and molded upon continental principles and meeting in due course an inevitable fate, or whether you will be a great country—an imperial country—a country where your sons, when they rise, rise to paramount positions, and obtain not merely the esteem of their countrymen, but command the respect of the world." Kebbel, *Selected Speeches*, 529–34 (at 534).

27. Holman, "Air Panic of 1935"; Levy, *Appeasement and Rearmament*; Neville, "Prophet Scorned?" British intelligence knew the claim of air parity to be false. Wark, *Ultimate Enemy*, 44 (citing CP 100[35], May 13, 1935, Cab 24/255; and AA Berlin to Director, AI, April 3, 1935, Air 2/1356); Vansittart, *Mist Procession*, 499; Winterbotham, *Nazi Connection*, 127–33.

28. *DVP SSSR*, XVIII: 228–39 (at 232–3, 235–6); *DBFP*, 2nd series, XII: 771–84 (Chilston to Simon, April 1).

29. Eden rose to answer that his mission aimed for an exchange of views in the quest for peace and toasted Litvinov's health. The festivities ended at 1:30 a.m. *Pravda*, March 29, 1935; *DVP SSSR*, XVIII: 226–8; Eden, *Facing the Dictators*, 144–63.

30. Eden, *Facing the Dictators*, 164.

31. When Eden and Chilston broached the issue of expanding bilateral trade, Litvinov, according to the British notetaker, replied positively ("why not?"), but, according to the Soviet notetaker, stated that no negotiations were possible because of the British position on tsarist debts. *DVP SSSR*, XVIII: 240–5 (at 242–3); *DBFP*, 2nd series, XII: 784–91.

32. Eden found the exchange enigmatic. Eden, *Facing the Dictators*, 156.

33. *DVP SSSR*, XVIII: 246–251; Naumov, *1941 god*, II: 521; Maiskii, *Dnevnik diplomata*, I: 98–101.

34. On the evening of March 29, Eden was taken to *Swan Lake* at the Bolshoi, where the orchestra played "God Save the King," the British anthem. He was also afforded a ride on the new Moscow metro and a visit to the aircraft factory at Fili, just outside Moscow, which produced the TB-3 heavy bomber. Eden, *Facing the Dictators*, 155–60. The British omitted their full record of the Eden-Stalin conversation from the published document collection. See also *DBFP*, 2nd series, XII: 803–10 (Eden and Beck in Warsaw, April 2–3, 1935), 812–7 (Eden and Beneš in Czechoslovakia, April 4). By early 1936, after Eden would become foreign secretary, he would no longer doubt German aggressiveness, according to Maisky. *DVP SSSR*, XIX: 77 (conversation Feb. 11, 1936).

35. The idea had grown out of the recent cooperation with Germany, but "deep operations" offered a more comprehensive vision. Triandafillov, *Kharakter operatsii sovremennykh armii*; Isserson, *Evolution of Operational Art*, 43–76; Savushkin, *Razvitie sovetskikh vooruzhennykh sil*, 59–62; Iakov, *V. K. Triandafillov*; Harrison, *Russian Way of War*, 194–217; Habeck, *Storm of Steel*, 206–28.

36. Of three main Red Army groups, a Northwestern (Leningrad military district), Western (Belorussian military district), and Southwestern (Kiev military district), the first was primarily to deter aggression from enemy use of Finland and the Baltic states, while the second and third would launch operations on enemy territory (north and south of the swampy Pripet Marshes) by means of mobile ground and air forces prepositioned and concealed in fortified frontier regions. Menning, "Soviet Strategy," I: 218–9; Gorkov, "Gotovil li," 30–1.

37. Reprinted (abridged) in Tukhachevskii, *Izbrannye proizvedeniia*, II: 233–9.

38. "Nakanune voiny (Dokumenty 1935–1940 gg.)," 168–9 (RGVA, f. 33987, op. 3, d. 400, l. 238ff.). Tukhachevsky's argument resembled what Svechin had suggested back in 1926–27. Svechin, *Strategiia*, 184. Tukhachevsky had savaged Svechin as "a conduit for the influence of bourgeois ideology" in the introduction to the Russian edition of Hans Delbrück's *History of the Military Art*, "Predislovie k knige G. Del'briuka," in Tukhachevskii, *Izbrannye proizvedeniia*, II: 144. See also Kokoshin, "A. A. Svechin," 134. Soviet war planning envisioned only enemies, no allies: *Budushchaia voina*, 35–6; Plekhanov, *VChK-OGPU*, 102; Stoecker, *Forging Stalin's Army*, 148–9; Samuelson, *Soviet Defence Industry Planning*, 46–52.

39. *DGFP*, series C, IV: 1–2 (Schulenburg, April 1, 1935), 7 (state secretary, April 2); *DVP SSSR*, XVIII: 262 (April 4); "Nakanune voiny (Dokumenty 1935–1940 gg.)," 171–2 (Gekker for Berzin, April 4).

40. *DBFP*, 2nd series, XII: 766–7 (Chilston to Simon quoting Eden, sent March 30, 1935), 768–9 (March 31).

41. Eden deemed Stalin "the quietest dictator I have ever known, with the exception of [Portugal's] Dr. Salazar." Eden, *Facing the Dictators*, 153.

42. An "economic agreement" had been signed March 20, 1935, but the more critical loan terms were signed on April 9. *DGFP*, series C, III: 1028–31, IV: 28–38, 38–43; *DVP SSSR*, XVIII: 270–4. Schacht (now acting economics minister), who had sought to sabotage the credit negotiations, emerged as the lead proponent. Ericson, *Feeding the German Eagle*, 17–9; *DGFP*, series C, III: 367–9 (Aug. 29, 1934), 682–5 (Nov. 27, 1934), 930–3 (Feb. 14, 1935), 935–6 (Feb. 15), 960–1 (Feb. 25), 1002. See also Doering, *Deutsche Aussenwirtschaftspolitik*, 169–75; von Strandmann, "Grossindustrie und Rapallopolitik," at 337.

43. Abramov, "Osobaia missiia Davida Kandelaki," 147 (citing AVP RF, f. 082, op. 18, pap. 81, d. 7, l. 150–1: April 12, 1935). Kandelaki returned from Berlin and Stalin received him on April 13, May 4 and 5, July 5 and 7, 1935. Kandelaki appears to have imagined that opposition to Hitler existed and could be galvanized via improved relations, a view dismissed by Litvinov and Surits. *Na prieme*, 160, 162, 169; Roberts, "Soviet Bid for Coexistence."

44. Laval had been stalling Moscow over the deadlocked negotiations with Germany for a multilateral Eastern Pact, but on March 30, 1935, fearful that events would outrun him, he had handed Potyomkin a text for a bilateral pact solely between France and the Soviet Union, and possibly one also with Czechoslovakia, and with Italy, all within the framework of the League. *DDF*, 1e série, X: 75–83; *DVP SSSR*, XVIII: 253–4. The politburo

instructions for Litvinov specified that the Soviet government preferred a Franco-Soviet pact that included Germany, or if not, then Poland, or if not, then France, Czechoslovakia, and the Baltic states. The French stuck to two bilateral pacts, France-USSR, Czechoslovakia-USSR. *DVP SSSR*, XVIII: 158–60 (Litvinov to Potyomkin: March 4, 1935), 174 (Potyomkin, April 9, 1935), 174 (April 10); Borisov, *Sovetsko-fratsuzskie otnosheniia*, 248–9; Herriot, *Jadis*, II: 530. It seems that both Edvard Beneš (Czechoslovak foreign minister) and Nicolae Titulescu (Romanian foreign minister) were at the French foreign ministry and helped draft the public announcement of France's decision. Hochman, *Failure of Collective Security*, 51 (citing AMZV Prague, incoming 1935, Osuský from Paris, April 9). During three meetings in the Little Corner (April 22, 23, 28, 1935), Litvinov pressed for France's much-reduced incarnation (no Germany, Poland, or even Baltic states); Stalin agreed. *DVP SSSR*, XVII: 280–6 (at 281: April 21, 1935), 292–3 (April 18, 1935), 295, 296; Adibekov et al., *Politbiuro TsK RKP (b)—VKP (b) i Evropa*, 322–3 (RGASPI, f. 17, op. 162, d. 18, l. 2), 323–4 (l. 5: April 19, 1935); *DDF*, 1e série, X: 322–5, 334–5; *Na prieme*, 160–1.

45. *Pravda*, May 4, 1935. Stalin was seen to leave early, but it is unclear why. Ken, *Mobilizatsionnoe planirovanie*, 293 (N. Charles to John Simon, May 7, 1935: PRO FP 371/19450/N2376).

46. Voroshilov had initiated these celebratory "breakfasts" (as well as a separate annual May graduation ceremony for the military academies). At the May 2, 1933, reception, during the famine, 1,800 pounds of meat, poultry, fish, and sausage were served. Nevezhin, *Zastol'ia*, 66; Osokina, *Ierarkhia potrebleniia*, 79n21; Nevezhin, *Zastol'nye*, 41–5 (RGASPI, f. 558, op. 11, d. 1117, l. 9–10); Borev, *Staliniada*, 90.

47. The immense interior encompassed more than seven hundred rooms. Deviatov and Zhuravleva, *Dvortsy Kremlia*; V. Bogomolova et al., *Moskovskii kreml'*; Chuev, *Molotov*, 96; Kabanov, *Stal'nye peregony*, 53. Two ancient monasteries (the Chudov and Voznesensky) were demolished. So was Moscow's onion-domed Savior in the Wood, originally consecrated in the thirteenth century, to make way for a five-story service facility, while the magnificent Red Porch leading to the Palace of Facets was destroyed for a two-story canteen. Vinogradov, *Genrikh Iagoda*, 435–6 (TsA FSB, f. 3, op. 3, d. 883, l. 1–2, June 2, 1936).

48. "Stalin slowly gets up from his chair" amid deafening applause, noted a record of the 1933 banquet. "The hall quiets. 'I am not inclined to speak, but I am being obliged. The first toast is for Lenin, the second for technology.'" Warming to the room, Stalin continued: "Lenin did not die, he lives together with the party he created, together with the Soviet power he created. Who are we, Soviet power and the party of Bolsheviks? We are considered great people. No, we are little people in comparison with Lenin. Lenin organized the party and the proletarian revolution on one-sixth of the earth, which astounded the whole world . . . To the dictatorship of the proletariat, to the great teacher Lenin!" Stalin then toasted "the Russian nation—the most talented nation in the world," and raised a glass to "our military technology! To our air industry personnel! To aviators! To our tank drivers! . . . To the leaders and *vozhds* of the Red Army! To the best student of Lenin, Klim Voroshilov! Hurrah!' (stormy applause)." Nevezhin, *Zastol'nye*, 43–5 (RGASPI, f. 558,

op. 11, d. 1117, l. 9–10). See also *Pravda*, May 2 and May 4, 1934; Nevezhin, *Zastol'nye*, 46–55 (RGASPI, f. 74, op. 1, d. 164, l. 165–8, 162–4; d. 160, l. 23–5). The Soviet brand of champagne had been developed on the basis of tsarist foundations in Crimea and blossomed after 1934, when a former aristocrat and chemist, Anton Mikhailovich Frolov-Bagreev, perfected a process of fermenting sparkling wine in large reservoirs, rather than in bottles, facilitating mass production.

49. *Izvestiia*, May 2, 1935. See also Nevezhin, "Bol'shie Kremlevskie priemy Stalina" (no. 3), 56–70, (no. 4), 123–39. Stalin would approve replacement of the tsarist double-headed eagles atop the Kremlin's main gates—the Savior (Spassky), Nikolsky, Trinity, and Pinewood (Borovitsky)—with metal red stars in 1935 (two years later, the metal would give way to glass).

50. Nevezhin, *Zastol'ia*, 280.

51. Shmidt, "Priemy v Kremle," at 274; Nevezhin, *Zastol'nye*, 192.

52. *Izvestiia*, May 4, 1935. The account in *Pravda* (May 4, 1935) by Mekhlis was less exuberant. In Feb. 1935, Bukharin had written to Stalin begging for approval, "in order that I could say, 'all the same. comrade Stalin thinks that the newspaper is not such a bad one.'" Adibekov and Anderson, "'U menia odna nadezhda na tebia,'" 50. Security at the banquets would tighten considerably. Moiseev, *Ia vospominaiu*, 47.

53. Krenkel', *RAEM*, 492–3. One scholar has asserted (without presenting the evidence) that Soviet military academies began teaching ballroom dancing and manners in the 1930s. Tumkina-Perfil'eva, *Russkii etiket*, 148.

54. RGASPI, f. 558, op. 4, d. 657, l. 236.

55. Back on May 2, 1932, at the close of the evening's concert, Stalin had remarked that the artists "were dressed not the way artists of a great country should be" (part apology for Soviet material life, part directive). Barsova, "Nash veilikii drug," 59.

56. *Pravda*, May 4, 1935; *Le Temps*, May 5, 1935.

57. Beloff, *Foreign Policy of Soviet Russia*, I: 152–4; Scott, *Alliance against Hitler*, 247. "One must remember that there was never an alliance between the tsarist government and France," Maisky wrote to Litvinov on May 3, 1935, of the 1892 military convention that was activated by the Great War, "only an exchange of notes and an agreement between the two high commands." Dullin, *Men of Influence*, 112, citing AVP RF, f. 10, op. 10, pap. 48, d. 7.

58. Hilger, a German embassy counsellor, reported goodwill toward Germany in Ukraine in late spring 1935. "Germany was only trying to liberate itself from the oppressive fetters of the Versailles Treaty," the chairman of the provincial soviet told him as a consul reception in Kiev. "But instead of aiding her to do so, the Soviet government was making a pact with Germany's oppressors." The Ukrainians blamed Litvinov. Hilger and Meyer, *Incompatible Allies*, 269.

59. *Pravda* and *Izvestiia*, May 16, 1935; *Humanité*, May 17, 1935.

60. Some Polish officials understood better than others. In Nov. 1934, the Polish envoy to Germany, Lipski, had told his American counterpart that "Germany intends to re annex part of our country, the maps posted all over Germany show this clearly." Lipski predicted Hitler would also annex Alsace-Lorraine, Austria, and Czechoslovakia, too. Dodd and Dodd, *Ambassador Dodd's Diary*, 192 (Nov. 17, 1934).

61. Nevezhin, *Zastol'nye*, 71–5 (RGASPI, f. 74, op. 1, d. 160, l. 42–9). A German periodical would observe in late 1935, in a comment

reprinted in the Red Army newspaper, that "alongside his great organizational talent, the people's commissar Voroshilov possesses a surpassing gift for speaking, thanks to which he takes listeners prisoners of war." *Krasnaia zvezda*, Jan. 5, 1936.

62. Stalin was said to have directed the bygones quote at Bukharin and to have proposed a toast to him, which elicited applause, but if so, this was not recorded in the raw transcript. Larina, *Nezabyvaemoe*, 33.

63. Back on Dec. 27, 1934, at a Kremlin reception for the metal industry, Stalin, speaking about the first Five-Year Plan slogan, "Technology Decides Everything," had stated that the people operating the technology were more important, and "must be carefully and attentively cultivated the way a gardener tends a beloved fruit tree." "Metallurgi u tovarishcha Stalina, Molotova, i Ordzhonikidze," *Pravda*, Dec. 29, 1934: 1, reprinted in *Sochineniia*, XIV: 49–50.

64. Stalin loved gardening metaphors. Jochen Hellbeck, "Laboratories of the Soviet Self: Diaries of the Stalin Era," PhD dissertation, Columbia University, 1998, 64–6. One scholar noted a shift in novels in the 1930s from machine to gardening metaphors. Clark, *Soviet Novel*, 99, 105.

65. Nevezhin, *Zastol'nye*, 76–84 (RGASPI, f. 558, op. 11, d. 1077, l. 43–9).

66. See also Arsenidze, "Iz vospominaniia o Staline," 235. One scholar has argued that "consumption . . . was one of the most frequent items on the politburo's agenda" and, in Stalin's words, one of "the most contested issues." Gregory, *Political Economy of Stalinism*, 94.

67. The original had been: "Now we have reached the stage of development when cadres decide everything, not mares and machines." *Pravda*, May 6, 1935. See also Rees, *Political Thought from Machiavelli to Stalin*, 227. The newspaper account contained an insertion after Stalin's mention that he had had a hand in smashing some people along the way: "stormy applause." Nevezhin, *Zastol'nye*, 69, 84–91 (RGASPI, f. 558, op. 11, d. 1077, l. 31–42); *Pravda*, May 6, 1935, reprinted in *Sochineniia*, XIV: 56–64 (at 61–4). See also Oleinikov, "Chetvertoe maia." In his speech on May 4, 1934, for Soviet military academy graduates, Stalin had also struck a note of populism. "I do not deny that leaders [*vozhdi*] have significance, they organize and lead the masses," he allowed. "But leaders without the mass are nothing. Such people as Hannibal, Napoleon, perished as soon as they lost the masses." Nevezhin, *Zastol'nye*, 55 (RGASPI, f. 74, op. 1, d. 160, l. 23–5).

68. Svanidze noted of Stalin's May 4, 1935, speech: "Iosif said that he had forgotten to add 'our leaders came to power as landless peasants and have remained that way to the end, that they are driven by ideas, not acquisitiveness,' as we can observe in capitalist countries. Over there, being in power means getting rich. I don't remember exactly, but something to that effect." A mixed message: soulless functionaries yet selfless leader(s). Murin, *Stalin v ob"iatiakh*, 177–8 (Svanidze diary: May 9, 1935).

69. *DDF*, 1e série, X: 575–7, 630–1. The Soviets did not publish the record of the conversation, only a speech by Litvinov at the May 13 banquet for Laval: *DVP SSSR*, XVIII: 328–30. See also *DVP SSSR*, XVIII: 337 (TASS); *Pravda*, May 14, 1935.

70. Harrison and Davies, "Soviet Military-Economic Effort," 391 (citing RGASPI, f. 17, op. 162, d. 18, l. 123: Aug. 28, 1935).

71. "'Osnovnaia tsel' ego priezda,'" 139. On May 14, 1935, a grand ceremony was held in

the Columned Hall of the House of Trade Unions for the Moscow metro. Lazar Brontman and another *Pravda* colleague were assigned to the event. Kaganovich opened the proceedings for his beloved project ("his most memorable, temperamental speech," Brontman decided). But Stalin walked in during the speech, with Voroshilov and others in tow, provoking an ovation. The dictator took the podium, to delirium. In the din, Brontman and a colleague had a difficult time transcribing the speech (the journalists stopped to applaud as well). They rushed to *Pravda*'s offices, typed it up and had the text run over to Poskryobyshev for approval—Brontman crowed in his diary that only *Pravda* had the speech the next day. *Pravda*, May 15. This was Brontman's second encounter with Stalin: "The first time it happened during the 5th Congress of Soviets at the Bolshoi . . . Stalin looked at my astonished face, laughed and continued to his box." Brontman, *Dnevniki* (Aug. 10, 1936): http://mathscinet.ru/files/Dnevniki_1932_1947.pdf.

72. "I listened without comment," Schulenburg reported. *DGFP*, series C, IV: 138 (May 8, 1935). On the immediate public distancing from the pact in France, see Borisov, *Sovetsko-frantsuzskie otnosheniia*, 230–95; and Haslam, *Struggle for Collective Security*, 83–5.

73. Laval, according to Litvinov, was shocked at Stalin's bluntness. Maiskii, *Dnevnik diplomata*, I: 110–1 (June 19, 1935); Gorodetsky, *Maisky Diaries*, 51–2. On June 7, 1935, Laval took the reins of the French government for the second time.

74. Scott, *Alliance against Hitler*, 253–4. Trotsky, then living in Grenoble, noted: "Even though I am sufficiently familiar with the political cynicism of Stalin, his contempt for principles . . . , I still could not believe my eyes when I read those lines." *Trotsky's Diary in Exile, 1935*, 120 (May 17, 1935).

75. M. Mourin, *Les Relations Franco-Sovietiques (1917—1967)* (Paris, 1967), 208; Scott, *Alliance against Hitler*, 254–5, 266; *Les événements survenues en France de 1933 à 1945*, I: 142–3 (Laval to Flandin, May 16, 1935).

76. "The obligations of mutual assistance will take effect only under the condition, as stipulated in this agreement, of assistance being extended on the part of France to the side that is the victim of aggression." *DVP SSSR*, XVIII: 336–7; *DDF*, 1e série, X: 575–7, 630–1; Adibekov et al., *Politbiuro TsK RKP (b)—VKP (b) i Evropa*, 326–7 (RGASPI, f. 17, op. 162, d. 18, l. 49: June 1, 1935). The Soviets would undertake no efforts to establish a transit right for the Red Army through Poland or Romania to defend Czechoslovakia in the event of a German attack. Both bilateral pacts, as per French insistence, were limited to Europe. Still, Czechoslovakia pledged not to supply Japan with arms. Hochman, *Failure of Collective Security*, 53, citing *Zahraniční politika* (Prague, 1935), 324–6. For a time, the Soviets took credit for the clause that provided for taking action only if France did so. Potemkin, *Istoriia diplomatii*, III: 387–9.

77. Potocki, *Master of Lancut*, 207; Szemberg, *Journal*, 85.

78. Roos, *Polen und Europa*, 218–9; Weinberg, *Foreign Policy*, I: 209. Göring was in Poland May 17–24, 1935: *DGFP*, series C, IV: 184–5 (May 21), 223–5 (May 28).

79. Domarus, *Hitler: Reden*, I: 505–14; Kershaw, "*Hitler Myth*," 125–6.

80. Stalin had Berzin, after eleven years heading military intelligence, reassigned to the Soviet Far Eastern Army. Moisei Uritsky, the nephew of the celebrated Chekist who had been assassinated in 1918, brought over his own deputy, Alexander Nikonov, who was appointed alongside Artuzov. Primakov, *Ocherki*, III: 11; Kolpakidi and Prokhorov, *Imperiia GRU*, I: 121–2, 196, 219–20; Gorbunov, "Voennaia razvedka v 1934–1939 godakh" (no. 2); Lota, "*Alta"protiv "Barabrossy*," 51; *Na prieme*, 161–2. The Danes shared their findings with other European intelligence services, which produced still more revelations on Soviet agents. See G. Solonitsyn, "Nachal'nik sovetskoi razvedki."

81. Yagoda had reported to Stalin (May 2, 1935) that the NKVD had completed interrogations of the librarian Nina Rozenfeld, establishing that the Mukhanova "terrorist group" in the library, to which Rozenfeld was said to belong, had "links" to the Kremlin commandant office and a group of Trotskyite youth and White Guards. "Lev Kamenev," Yagoda wrote of Nina's brother, "is not only the inspiration, but the organizer of the terror." Vinogradov, *Genrikh Iagoda*, 427–8 (TsA FSB, f. 3, op. 2, d. 9, l. 241–42). See also Khaustov, "Deiatel'nost' organov," 380 (TsA FSB, f. 3, op. 2, d. 900, l. 137). As of summer 1935, the Kremlin housed just 374 inhabitants (102 households), not including bodyguards, soldiers, and service personnel.

82. Yagoda had proposed nine death sentences (for "Trotskyites"), eighteen sentences of ten years in camps for key figures, and for the rest, three to five years in camps or exile; three were to be released. Stalin wrote in ten years instead of five for Irina Gogua, and freed three more of the hundred and twelve. Khaustov et al., *Lubianka: Stalin i VChK*, 663–9 (APRF, F, 3, op. 58, d. 237, l. 37–49), 681 (d. 238, l. 1: July 17).

83. RGASPI, f. 17, op. 3, d. 963, l. 37.

84. The circular threatened local party bosses with expulsions for failures to restore order, giving a deadline of two to three months. Adibekov et al., *Politbiuro TsK RKP (b): povestki dnia zasedanii*, II: 645; Khlevniuk et al., *Stalinskoe politbiuro*, 240; Pavlov, *Kommunistichskaia partiia*, 51. In Oct. 1934—before Kirov was murdered by a holder of a party card—the regime had decided on a universal re-registration of party members in 1935. RGASPI, f. 17, op. 3, d. 963, l. 3.

85. Getty, *Origins of the Great Purges*, 60–1 (citing *Partiinoe stroitel'stvo*, 1935, no. 4: 32–6); *Pravda*, May 16, 1935. Another 340,000 Communists had been expelled in the 1934 purge, which mostly targeted those who had recently joined. Total membership as of January 1, 1935, was 2.35 million. Fainsod, *How Russia Is Ruled*, 212, 224; *Bol'shevik*, 1934, no. 15: 9.

86. "We have a lot of Americans," Yezhov stated during a meeting connected to the party document verification. "Traditionally our people take the view that these are wonderful people. Relations with Germany have worsened, so you need to keep an eye on them, Poles as well, and you need to watch the English . . . Keep in mind, that Americans, as a rule, are almost all spies." Pavliukov, *Ezhov*, 159–60 (RGASPI, f. 671, op. 1, d. 32, l. 20–1: July 1, 1935).

87. Khaustov and Samuelson, *Stalin, NKVD*, 86 (RGASPI, f. 671, op. 1, d. 273, l. 700).

88. Iakovlev et al., *Reabilitatsiia: politicheskie protsessy*, 175.

89. *Biulleten' oppozitsiia*, no. 1–2 (July 1929): 2; Trotsky, *Writings of Leon Trotsky, 1929*, 61–2. When Radek asked Stalin (June 4, 1935) whether he should be republishing Trotsky's writings in the regime's internal *Bulletin of the Foreign Press* for high officials, the dictator told him "to liquidate" the publication. Khaustov and Samuelson, *Stalin, NKVD*, 86 (RGASPI, f. 558, op. 11, d. 420, l. 4ob.). By contrast, when

Tal (head of the Central Committee press and publications department) queried the politburo about which émigré subscriptions he should take for the next year, Stalin commanded: "Order the lot!" Volkogonov, *Stalin: Triumph and Tragedy*, 228 (citing RGVA, f. 33987, op. 3, d, 273, l. 36: Dec. 1935).

90. Getty and Naumov, *Road to Terror*, 161–6 (RGASPI, f. 17, op. 2, d. 542, l. 55–86), 177–71 (l. 125–41), 172–3 (l. 175–8).

91. The usual chorus had followed the dictator's lead and remained reticent. Getty and Naumov, *Road to Terror*, 161–7 (RGASPI, f. 17, op. 2, d. 542, l. 55–86).

92. Getty and Naumov, *Road to Terror*, 176 (RGASPI, f. 17, op. 2, d. 547, l. 69), 177 (d. 544, l. 22, l. 70); *Pravda*, June 8, 1935. The regime abolished the Society of Old Bolsheviks (which had its own publishing house) on May 25, 1935, and the Society of Political Prisoners on June 25.

93. No new charges were brought in the Kirov case, despite Yezhov's ominous speech, which Stalin alone could have authorized. *Pravda* (June 16 and 19, 1935) issued follow-up fulminations, by Zhdanov and Khrushchev, over "former princes, ministers, courtiers, Trotskyites, etc. . . . a counterrevolutionary nest."

94. *DBFP*, 2nd series, XIII: 364–71 (June 5, 1935), 477–84 (E. Drummond in Rome to Samuel Hoare, June 25); XIV: 329–33 (Drummond in Rome to Hoare); *DGFP*, series C, IV: 253–62 (June 4), 262–6 (June 4), 269–71 (June 5), 271 (June 5), 272–3 (June 5); Weinberg, *Foreign Policy*, I: 213. Germany's Admiral Raeder had caught British attention in April 1935 when he had announced, in an obvious negotiating ploy, that Germany had begun to build twelve submarines. To London, it appeared to be a choice between a deal to get the Germans to proceed more slowly, as Hitler claimed he was inclined to do, or to build up the British fleet even more rapidly. But even beyond financial straits, the British admiralty rightly anticipated that between 1936 and 1941 their ship building capacity would be sufficient to replace the existing fleet but not to expand it. The British also reasoned, conveniently, that resistance to approving German rearmament of any kind (the French position) would only elicit a far stronger German action. And British naval intelligence concluded that Hitler needed a fleet for use against the Soviet Union in the Baltic Sea, not against Britain. Wark, *Ultimate Enemy*, 134–9, 141–2.

95. The battleship plans originally dated to Nov. 1934. Dülffer, *Weimar, Hitler und die Marine*, 570. In May 1936, Germany laid the keels for five instead of the agreed two A-cruisers. Hildebrand, *Foreign Policy*, 43. The *Bismarck* would be laid down in July 1936 (and finished in Sept. 1940), while the *Tirpitz* would be laid down in Oct. 1936 (and finished in Feb. 1941). The Germans reported the *Bismarck* to Britain as 35,000 tons displacement; in reality, the design was for 41,000. See also R. Ingrim, *Hitlers Glücklichster Tag: London, den 18 Juni* (Stuttgart: Seewald, 1962).

96. Aubrey Kennedy, the journalist, replied that Baldwin was more the kind of man to hear political proposals than expositions of ideas. Martel, *Times and Appeasement*, 180. Kennedy had written a book calling early for Versailles treaty revision. Kennedy, *Old Diplomacy and New*.

97. Most of the rest of the seats had to be purchased. Many of the attendees were political émigrés, such as Bertolt Brecht, Heinrich and Klaus Mann, Anna Seghers, and Robert Musil. Stalin evidently wanted to prevent an anti-German eruption, for though Shcherbakov

had been dispatched to keep a watchful party eye on the proceedings, the dictator sent him a telegram to "harmonize all reports and speeches with our envoy Potyomkin." Maksimenkov, *Bol'shaia tsenzura*, 386n7 (RGASPI, f. 558, op. 11, d. 52, l. 114: June 20, 1935). Shcherbakov wrote privately in his diary, "there is not one tractor or motorcar on the roads of Poland . . . And Vienna loses its past greatness, and withers, and is dying." Golubev et al., *Rossiia i zapad*, 145 (citing RGASPI, f. 88, op. 1, d. 467, l. 1, 3–4); Golubev, "*Esli mir obrushitsia na nashu Respubliku,*" 13 (citing RGASPI, f. 88, op. 1, d. 467, l. 1).

98. Maksimenkov, *Bol'shaia tsenzura*, 384–6, n1 (RGASPI, f. 329, op. 2, d. 4, l. 160–161ob.), n2 (f. 17, op. 163, d. 1059, l. 186), n3 (d. 1063, l. 131; f. 558, op. 11, d. 52, l. 108), n5, n7; Artizov and Naumov, *Vlast'*, 256–7 (RGASPI, f. 88, op. 1, d. 472, l. 1–2: Shcherbakov to Stalin, May 27), 264–5 (f. 17, op. 3, d. 965, l. 42: June 19). A giant Gorky likeness was set up in the hall. Ehrenburg, living in Paris with a Soviet passport, had written worriedly to Bukharin (editor of *Izvestiia*, which published Ehrenburg) that "there will be few stars and many Bohemian wretches of the Trotskyite-anarchist type. Our delegation is peculiar: none speak foreign languages, and out of eighteen souls just five are even a bit known in the West as writers." Voroshilov voted against Babel's inclusion.

99. Ehrenburg's denunciation: *Literaturnaia gazeta*, June 17, 1933, published in French translation in his essay collection *Dumael, Gide, Malraux, Mauriac*.

100. *Mezhdunarodnyi kongress pisatelei*; Klein, *Paris 1935*; Teroni and Klein, *Pour le défense de la culture*. A joint report to Stalin by Shcherbakov and Koltsov deemed this "the biggest event in the sphere of the consolidation of antifascist forces," but added that "not a little difficulty in our work was caused by the ambiguous behavior of Ehrenburg," whom they accused of wanting to "appear neutral," rather than influencing the French or defending Soviet interests. Ehrenburg in a report that reached Stalin called Koltsov a journalist rather than a writer. Stalin, for his part, advised Kaganovich not to allow Soviet Communists to "finish off" Ehrenburg. Maksimenkov, *Bol'shaia tsenzura*, 382–6 (RGASPI, f. 558, op. 11, d. 710, l. 25–9: July 20, 1935), 387–9 (RGASPI, f. 558, op. 11, d. 710, l. 30–4: July 21).

101. Artizov and Naumov, *Vlast'*, 255 (RGASPI, f. 17, op. 3, d. 964, l. 14: May 19, 1935). The timing with the congress in Paris might have been a coincidence; Rolland had delayed the trip for reasons of health.

102. Remark dating to 1928, as cited in Drabovitch, *Les Intellectuels français et le bolchévisme*, 151–2. An internal Soviet evaluation (1934) of Rolland cited his "individualistic humanism" and pacifism as detriments. David-Fox, *Showcasing the Great Experiment*, 243 (citing RGALI, f. 631, op. 14, d. 716).

103. Yagoda had commissioned a twenty-volume Russian translation of Rolland's collected works and assigned oversight of the task to the Russian-French Maria Kudryashova; Rolland had married her, and she accompanied him as interpreter. "Stalin did not look anything like his portraits," Rolland wrote in his diary. "He is neither large nor stocky, as he is imagined . . . His characteristic coarse dark hair is beginning to turn gray and lighten . . . But as before he has a direct and vigorous visage and enigmatic smile, which is (or can be) cordial, impenetrable, indifferent, good-natured, implacable, amused and mocking. In all situations, a perfect self-control. He speaks

without raising his voice, with a timber a bit nasal and guttural at times (a Georgian accent, I'm told), with long pauses, to think things through. He listens still better than he talks, noting the principal points of what I said, scribbling with blue and red pencil on a piece of paper while I spoke. (I greatly regret not having asked him for that sheet.)" Rolland, *Voyage à Moscou*, 126–34; "Moskovskii dnevnik Romena Rollanda," 217.

104. Stalin did not let on that he had personally edited the draft of the law. "Moskovskii dnevnik Romena Rollanda," 221–2. That night, after returning to the Savoy hotel with his wife, Rolland was approached by Antonio Gramsci's two sons, aged nine and eleven, who thanked him for all he had done for their father (imprisoned in Mussolini's Italy). On the law, see *Izvestiia*, April 8, 1935; RGASPI, f. 17, op. 3, d. 962, l. 32, 57; Khlevniuk, *Politbiuro*, 145–6 (citing RGASPI, f. 17, op. 163, d. 1059, l. 23–4, 27); Khlevniuk et al., *Stalinskoe politbiuro*, 144–5 RGASPI, f. 78, op. 1, d. 550, l. 7, 7a: (Voroshilov, March 18, 1935). See also Suvenirov, *Tragediia RKKA*, 325.

105. Besides a certain hero-worship, Rolland's purpose had included inquiring about the fate of the writer Viktor Kibalchich, known as Viktor Serge, who had been born in Brussels to Russian Jewish political émigrés from tsarism, emigrated after the revolution to the Soviet Union, and had been arrested in Leningrad (March 9, 1933) and internally exiled for "Trotskyite" propaganda. (Rolland would leave without being satisfied.) Serge's case had been forced into the discussion at the international gathering in Paris. Vinogradov, *Genrikh Iagoda*, 428–31 (TsA FSB, f. N-13614, tom 2); Mikhailov, *M. Gor'kii i R Rollan*, 313–5; Bialik, *Gor'kii i ego epokha*, III: 190–2 (Gorky to Yagoda, July 29, 1935), 191–2 (Gorky to Yagoda, March 7, 1936), 206; *Comédie*, August 30, 1933; Flores, *L'immaginare dell'URSS*, 235–42; Stern, *Western Intellectuals*, 27–8; Serge, *Memoirs of a Revolutionary*, 317–8.

106. RGASPI, f. 558, op. 11, d. 775, l. 1–16 (unedited). Both Stalin and Rolland edited the text. Rolland, *Voyage à Moscou*, 237–47. Rolland recorded the session in his diary immediately, and noted that it lasted from 4:10 to 5:50 p.m. *Pravda* (June 29, 1935) also reported a duration of one hour and forty minutes, while the logbook for Stalin's office has two hours. "Moskovskii dnevnik Romena Rollanda," 215–6; *Na prieme*, 168. Alexander Arosyev, the head of all-Union society for cultural ties with foreigners, who was present (and made the transcript), reported to Stalin that Rolland "repeated several times to me that he had not expected anything like that and that he had never in his life imagined Stalin that way." Stalin wrote: "into my archive." Maksimenkov, *Bol'shaia tsenzura*, 377–8 (RGASPI, f. 558, op. 11, d. 795, l. 60–1). Rolland would also pepper Gorky with queries about Soviet repression.

107. "Moskovskii dnevnik Romena Rollanda," 226–8 (July 9, 1935). Rolland read out a greeting on Soviet radio that July. "It's a wonderful thing, to laugh . . . Genuine joy is . . . in us, comrades, in a well dispositioned spirit, in a proud consciousness, in any beloved labor, joy is in the work in the cornfield of all humanity." Goriaeva, "*Veilkaia kniga dnia,*" 300–1 (GARF, f. 6953, op. 15, d. 53).

108. Rolland, *Voyage à Moscou*, 149–54 (July 4, 1935); "Moskovskii dnevnik Romena Rollanda," 238–40. Stalin's pipe, by now, had become a significant part of his iconography. *Pravda* (April 17, 1935), for ex., had run a caricature by Viktor Deni called "peace pipes"

contrasting Stalin's with that of a fat bulldog-faced bourgeois.

109. Hitler received Beck again in the afternoon, with Göring, Neurath, and Ribbentrop, but skipped Beck's third and final conversation on July 4, when the Polish foreign minister summoned the courage to mention Germany's freight arrears and the currency exchange problems Germany caused in Danzig. *DGFP*, series C, IV: 398–407 (July 3), 410 (July 4); Wojciechowski, *Stosunki polsko-niemieckie*, 205; Beck, *Przemówienia*, 164–5; Beck, *Final Report*, 92–9. A British Foreign Office summary mentioned deep Soviet fears of becoming simultaneously the object of Western and Japanese ambitions, as well as smaller countries' opportunism. Lensen, *Damned Inheritance*, 465 (FO 371/19460-881, Colonel Ismay to Collier, July 8, 1935). The NKVD's Prokofyev wrote to Stalin (July 11, 1935) about the arrest of a saboteur parachuted in by Japan; two of three were killed, one fled but was captured, and the politburo resolved to stage a public trial in Irkutsk. Khaustov et al., *Lubianka: Stalin i VChK*, 679–81 (APRF, f. 3, op. 58, d. 247, l. 105–7), 681 (l. 104), 683 (l. 157).

110. It is not clear the German foreign ministry even knew of Schacht's proposal. Kandelaki wanted the offer in writing. Litvinov warned against it as a German "maneuver." Weinberg, *Foreign Policy*, I: 221; *DVP SSSR*, XVIII: 646–7 (Litvinov to Potyomkin, June 26, 1935), 647 (Litvinov to Surits, June 27); Haslam, *Struggle for Collective Security*, 85–6, 127; *Na prieme*, 169.

111. On the unexpected twists and turns concerning finance and cash in a "planned" economy, see Arnold, *Banks, Credit and Money*; Nakamura, "Did the Soviet Command Economy Command Money?"; and Gregory, *Political Economy*, 213–42.

112. Stalin had played a key role in the moderation of investment targets in 1932-4, which proved important for stabilization. Davies et al., "The Politburo and Economic Decision Making," 113–4. The state planning commission did have a few line-management functions, but mostly it served in an advisory capacity, and tried to counter the systemic prevarication of commissariats and factories. Gregory and Harrison, "Allocation under Dictatorship."

113. *Na prieme*, 170.

114. The 22 billion included 6.5–6.7 billion for Orjonikidze's heavy industry (vs. the proposed 6, and a requested 9), and 3.5 billion for Kaganovich's railroad commissariat (vs. the proposed 3, and a requested 4.5).

115. Khlevniuk et al., *Stalinskoe politbiuro*, 241–2; Adibekov et al., *Politbiuro TsK RKP (b)–VKP (b): povestki dnia zasedanii*, II: 673.

116. Davies et al., *Years of Progress*, 264 (citing GARF, f. 5446, op. 26, d. 66, l. 266, 264–6), 266 (RGASPI, f. 558, op. 11, d. 769, l. 159–60, 162–3); RGASPI, f. 17, op. 3, d. 969, l. 1, 31–8; Kosheleva, *Pis'ma Stalina Molotovu*, 249–50 (Aug. 2, 1935); Davies, "Making Economic Policy," 64–80.

117. *Narodno-khoziaistvennyi plan 1936*, 269, 280. In July 1936, the investment plan introduced for 1937 would, again, be relatively moderate. Davies and Khlevnyuk, "Stakhanovism."

118. Following much back-and-forth, the agreed amount was 112.75 billion in July, but the battles were refought and the numbers rose again to 133 billion. Khlevniuk, *Politbiuro: mekhanizmy*, 136–7 (RGAE, f. 4372, op. 92, d. 17, l. 366; d. 18, l. 76–8); Davies, *Crisis and Progress*, 292–301. Stalin wrote to Molotov (Sept. 12, 1933), "I agree that capital investment should not be fixed at more than 21 billion rubles for '34, and that the growth of

industrial output should not be more than 15 percent. That will be better." Kosheleva, *Pis'ma Stalina Molotovu*, 248–9.

119. *DVP SSSR*, XVIII: 646–7n157 (Litvinov to Potyomkin, June 26, 1935); Abramov, "Osobaia missiia Davida Kandelaki," 147 (citing AVP RF, f. 010, op. 10, nap. 51, d. 45, l. 136). Schacht advised Kandelaki to have the Soviet ambassador approach the foreign ministry. *DGFP*, series D, IV: 453–4. Kandelaki was received by Stalin on July 5 and July 7, 1935. *Na prieme*, 169.

120. *Kommunisticheskii Internatsional pered VII Vsemirnym kongressom: materialy* (Moscow: Partizdat, 1935), 116.

121. Dimitrov, "Nastuplenie fashizma," 12–1; Dimitroff, *Against Fascism and War*, 14. Manuilsky spoke of the victories of socialist construction in the USSR, Thorez about how the USSR's very existence had radicalized capitalism's crisis and contradictions, and Togliatti about Soviet foreign policy ("Can one imagine a more remarkable achievement than a great capitalist country having to sign a mutual assistance pact with the Soviet Union, involving defense against an aggressor and a willingness to defend peace and the borders of the homeland of the dictatorship of the proletariat?"). This was the only Comintern Congress for which a complete stenographic record was not published. Carr, *Twilight of the Comintern*, 403–27. See also Haslam, *Struggle for Collective Security*, 52–9.

122. There was speculation that the photograph in *Pravda* of Stalin and the delegates was faked. Peschanski, *Marcel Cachin*, IV: 111 (July 26, 1935).

123. Clark, "Germanophone Exiles." At a meeting with the scholars at the Institute of World Economics and World Politics, Yezhov "said that he does not trust political émigrés and those who have been abroad." By Sept. 1935, he would come to the (inevitable) conclusion that spies were rampant among the political émigrés. Solov'ev, "Tetradi krasnogo professora 1912–1941 gg.," IV: 178. See also Zhuravlev and Tiazhel'nikova, "Inostrannye kolonii," 181. On Feb. 28, 1936, a politburo decree would restrict the movement and further arrivals of political émigrés. RGASPI, f. 17, op. 162, d. 79, l. 98–100; Khaustov et al., *Lubianka: Stalin i VChK*, 738–41 (APRF, f. 3, op. 58, d. 248, l. 115–8: March 9), 823n171. In 1935–6, of the 9,965 arrests for espionage, 7,100 were accused of espionage on behalf of Germany (1,322), Japan (2,275), or Poland (3,528). Khaustov and Samuelson, *Stalin, NKVD*, 46 (TsA FSB, f. 8 os, op. 1, d. 79). 317).

124. One person died before sentencing. "O tak nazyvaeomom 'Kremlevskom dele'"; RGASPI, f. 17, op. 163, d. 1062, l. 167–9; Zhukov, *Inoi Stalin*, 133–72. Abroad, a Ukrainian-language newspaper published in the then Romania-controlled city of Cernăuți (Chernivtsi/Czernowitz) imagined with the Kremlin Affair that Soviet elites could not be bought off with a return to bourgeois private property or reinvigorated with an influx of youth. "Dictatorship in Soviet Russia is seriously reeling," the article fantasized. "Stalin already is no longer master of the secret police . . . Stalin—whose name makes 160 million quake with fear—is already staggering." "Propast' radianskogo soiuzu i nezaleshna Ukraina!" *Chas*, July 6, 1935, courtesy of Cristina Florea.

125. Bediya did not write the text; he oversaw the working group (P. Butyrina, G. Khachapuridze, V. Mertskhulava), whose draft Merkulov edited. Sukharev, "Litsedeistvo," 112 (citing PA IIP pri TsK KPSS, f. 8, op. 1, d. 39, l. 1; f. 8, op. 2, chast' 1, d. 32, l. 117; f. 8, op. 1, d. 39., l. 3, 11–12). See also Beria's remarks

(Jan. 1934): *VII s"ezd Kommunisticheskikh organizatsii Zakavkaz'ia*, 29–30. *Dawn of the East* also published "responses" confirming the narrative. Bediya would be arrested on Oct. 20, 1937; Beria would have him admit Beria's authorship in his presence. Popov and Oppokov, "Berievshchina" (1989, no. 7), 82–7; "Plenum TsK KPSS, iiul' 1953 goda: stenograficheskii otchet," 181.

126. *Pravda*, July 29 to August 5, 1935. *Pravda* then praised it in a separate editorial (Aug. 10, 1935). See also RGASPI, f. 558, op. 11, d. 704–5; op. 4, d. 662, l. 428.

127. Beria, *K voprosu ob istorii bol'shevistskikh organizatsii na Zakavkaz'e* (Moscow: Partizdat, 1935); Maslov, "'Kratkii kurs istorii VKP (b),'" 53n15.

128. *Zaria vostoka*, Sept. 2, 1935. The Soviet envoy to Hungary, Alexander Bekzadyan, an ethnic Armenian, while giving a mandatory report about the Central Committee plenum to embassy party members, was said to have remarked, "They took down Yenukidze wrongly, he's a big-time revolutionary of the Caucasus, and they swallowed him on the basis of settling personal scores." He said in reference to Beria, "I know him." APRF, f. 3, op. 24, d. 324, l. 84–8 (a denunciation by I. D. Ovsiannikov later sent by Yezhov to Stalin: http://www.alexanderyakovlev.org/fond/issues-doc/61210).

129. Nevezhin, *Zastol'nye*, 94–100 (RGASPI, f. 558, op. 11, d. 1077, l. 62–5), 100–7 (l. 67–73), 108–10; *Pravda*, Aug. 2, 1935.

130. Menning has noted that in Dec. 1935, "a special group of the party Control Commission would report to Stalin that an investigation had revealed that railroads along the Baltic, western, and southwestern strategic directions 'were unprepared in a full sense for a mobilization period.'" Voroshilov pointed out that on the right bank of the Dnieper, Poland's throughput capacity exceeded the Soviet Union's, 195 trains against 156, and he requested massive construction, and special appropriation of 387 million rubles. Bruce W. Menning, "Soviet Railroads and War Planning," unpublished ms., 19–20 (citing RGVA, f. 4, op. 14, d. 1452, l. 27, 30–33, 2–3).

131. Nevezhin, *Zastol'nye*, 94–100 (RGASPI, f. 558, op. 11, d. 1077, l. 62–5), 100–7 (67–73—a second variant). Stalin removed from the transcript Kaganovich's phrase "for the victory of the world revolution." It became just "toward victory."

132. Leibzon and Shirina, *Povorot v istorii Kominterna*, 93–102.

133. Rosenfeldt, *Knowledge and Power*, 181. On Sept. 29, 1935, the Central Committee decreed the founding of the Central Museum of Lenin in Moscow. All documents and other materials were ordered sent to Moscow (local museums were supposed to make do with photo duplications, even if the original had been generated in their locale). RGASPI, f. 17, op. 3, d. 971, l. 72; Shul'gina, "Teoretiko-metodoligicheskie osnovy deiatel'nosti museev." In 1936, the Lenin Museum would be given the building of the old Moscow city Duma.

134. RGASPI, f. 558, op. 1, d. 5089, l. 1; Brandenberger, "Stalin as Symbol," at 257–8. Tovstukha, rebuffing Yarosvalsky's request for assistance, had rudely stated: "It will not turn out as a biography of Stalin—it will just be another history of the party and Stalin's role therein." Sukharev, "Litsedeistvo," 105–7, 110–1, 116; RGASPI, f. 89, op. 8, d. 1001, l. 7, 23–4; f. 155, op. 1, d. 88, l. 1; d. 90, l. 1–1ob. On Aug. 19, on the dictator's instructions from Sochi, the politburo forbade Beria to republish Stalin's writings from 1905–10 without his express authorization. Beria responded that there had never been a plan to republish without authorization. The politburo also

resolved to publish Stalin's collected works, projected at eight volumes. Khlevniuk et al., *Stalin i Kaganovich*, 526 (RGASPI, f. 558, op. 11, d. 88, l. 21–2, 23; f. 17, op. 3, d. 970, l. 50); Maksimenkov, *Bol'shaia tsenzura*, 394 (RGASPI, f. 558, op. 11, d. 905, l. 6, 10; d. 1164, l. 113); Artizov and Naumov, *Vlast'*, 745n17. Ilizarov, *Tainaia zhizn' Stalina*, 138; Maksimenkov, *Bol'shaia tsenzura*, 405–6 (RGASPI, f. 558, op. 11, d. 905, l. 11–3: Nov. 13, 1935). The second edition of Lenin's *Collected Works* was being completed in thirty volumes: *Sochineniia*, 30 vols. (Moscow-Leningrad: Gosizdat, 1926–35).

135. Despite the secrecy and lies of the regime surrounding Stalin's life, Souvarine managed thorough, judicious research in published sources. He wrote a classic political history of the regime rather than a biography per se, but attained an insight into Stalin's character. Souvarine, *Stalin*, with a new chapter added to the 1937 French re-edition. See also Lyons, "Stalin, Autocrat of all the Russias." In France, Gallimard had rejected the manuscript. Panné, *Souvarine*, 222–6. Adam Ulam, and many others, would largely follow Souvarine's template. Ulam, *Stalin*.

136. The breakout to the Long March occurred on Oct. 16, 1934. Radio contact with the Comintern had already been lost the month before. Wilson, *Long March*; Yang, *From Revolution to Politics*; Shuyun, *Long March*; Braun, *Kitaiskie zapiski*. The Japanese had demolished Chinese Communist organizations in Manchuria by 1934. Lee, *Revolutionary Struggle in Manchuria*, 231; in Krymov, "Istoricheskie portrety," 65–6.

137. Kosheleva, *Pis'ma Stalina Molotovu*, 252–3 (Aug. 5, 1935). Trotsky predicted from exile that the gathering would "pass into history as the liquidation congress." *Biulleten' oppozitsii*, no. 46 (Dec. 1935): 12.

138. RGASPI, f. 17, op. 162, d. 18, l. 110. Kaganovich and Yezhov telegrammed from Moscow that they had spoken to Pyatnitsky and Knorin, both of whom were being moved out of the Comintern. Khlevniuk et al., *Stalin i Kaganovich*, 523 (RGASPI, f. 558, op. 11, d. 88, l. 9: Aug. 14, 1935), 523 (l. 9: Aug. 15), 523 n1 (f. 17, op. 3, d. 970, l. 42: Aug. 16).

139. Khaustov and Samuelson, *Stalin, NKVD*, 141–3 (TsA FSB, ASD P-4497, t. 1, s. 24, ASD p-4574, t. 1, l. 31: Baumanis). Kaganovich's profile had risen higher still thanks to the successful metro construction. He would receive a thunderous ovation at the Central Committee plenum in Dec. 1935. After a Dec. 1936 banquet for the wives of engineers, Galina Shtange would write in her diary that Kaganovich was "simple, expressive, and handsome, with "above all, enormous serenity and intelligence, then firmness of purpose and an unyielding will; but when he smiles, his basic goodness shows through." Garros et al., *Intimacy and Terror*, 184.

140. *Pravda*, Aug. 21, 1935.

141. Bullitt had conveyed the same warning to Litvinov. FRUS, *The Soviet Union, 1933–1939*, 111, 131, 156–7, 221–3. U.S. complaints were already frequent about Soviet violations of the no-domestic-interference clause. The Nov. 16, 1933, agreement on noninterference in internal affairs did not specifically mention the Comintern, but the Soviet government had promised "not to permit the formation or residence on its territory of any organization or group—and to prevent the activity on its territory of any organization or group, or of representatives of any organization or group—which has as an aim the overthrow or the preparation for an overthrow of, or the bringing about by force of a change in, the political or social order of the whole or any part of the United States." FRUS, *The Soviet*

Union, 1933–1939, 29. Louis Fischer, who on July 2, 1935, had passed to Bullitt the probable dates of the Comintern Congress, lobbied him not to protest, given the spread of fascism in Europe and the Comintern's intention to take up the question of how to stop it. Fischer, Autobiography, 305; Bennett, Search for Security, 63.

142. VII Congress of the Communist International, 83–8, 245–8; Maddux, Years of Estrangement, 41 (citing Bullitt to Washington, Aug. 21, 1935).

143. From Washington, Troyanovsky wrote that the Aug. 25 note could be seen as a threat of war. On Aug. 27, Krestinsky handed Bullitt a response (approved by Stalin) maintaining that the Americans had not cited one fact of the supposed interference in their domestic affairs. In a new telegram to Washington, Bullitt additionally recommended expulsion of the Soviet military navy and air attachés. FRUS, The Soviet Union, 1933–1939, 242–3, 249, 250 (Bullitt to Hull); DVP SSSR, XVIII: 474, 476–7; Sevost'ianov, "Obostreniie sovetsko-amerikanskikh otnoshenii," 27 (citing APRF, f. 05, op. 15, pap. 113, d. 126, l. 85, l, 11); Maddux, Years of Estrangement, 149 (citing National Archives, 711.61/541: Bullitt to Hull, Aug. 29, 1935); Bishop, Roosevelt-Litvinov Agreements, 50; Hull, Memoirs, I: 305.

144. DVP SSSR, XVIII: 507 (letter to Warsaw, B. G. Podolsky, Sept. 8, 1935).

145. Khlevniuk et al., Stalin i Kaganovich, 532–3 (RGASPI, f. 558, op. 11, d. 88, l. 87, 88–91: Aug. 25, 1935), 534–5 (l. 81–3: Aug. 26), 535 (l. 81: Aug. 27), 536–7 (l. 110–110ob.: Aug. 27), 546 (d. 89, l. 4, 5–8: Sept. 2); Khromov, Po stranitsam, 205. Soviet press accounts were restrained: Pravda and Izvestiia, Aug. 28 and Sept. 3, 1935.

146. G.N. Sevost'ianov, "Sud'ba soglasheniia Ruzvel't—Litvinov o dolgakh i kreditakh"; Maddux, Years of Estrangement, 27–43; Browder, Origins of Soviet-American Diplomacy, 204–13.

147. Dodd and Dodd, Ambassador Dodd's Diary, 277–8 (Nov. 19, 1935). Bullitt would return to Moscow in Feb. 1936, but leave for good in April 1936 without informing Soviet officials that he was not coming back.

148. No meetings are recorded in Stalin's office from Aug. 10, 1935, through Nov. 2, 1935. Na prieme, 171.

149. Khlevniuk et al., Stalin i Kaganovich, 527 (RGASPI, f. 81, op. 3, d. 100, l. 89–90: Aug. 19, 1935).

150. Kaganovich and others sent a telegram to Sochi with a recommendation to make the funeral broader than just a Comintern event, and to send the ashes to Paris. Stalin agreed, pending the wishes of Barbusse's relatives. RGASPI, f. 558, op. 11, d. 83, l. 139.

151. Barbusse, Stalin. Barbusse's book contained numerous names of people who would turn out to be enemies of the people, and within two years, all copies would be pulled. Medvedev, Let History Judge, 817–8.

152. The regime would claim a harvest of 90 million tons, based on inflated yield estimates. Davies et al., Years of Progress, 254–5 (citing RGASPI, f. 17, op. 3, d. 977: April 29, 1936; RGAE, f. 4372, op. 35, d. 467, l. 85–6), 258; Danilov et al., Tragediia sovetskoi derevni, IV: 615 (Oct. 18, 1935); Sochinenlla, XIV: 93–9.

153. Kaganovich added that "the smartest of the foreign correspondents, Duranty, had written: 'in America they make noise about the Comintern Congress and do not see the most decisive main thing that was published yesterday in the newspapers—the report of the Azov–Black Sea territory about the completion of grain procurements.'" Khlevniuk et al., Stalinskoe politbiuro, 145–6 (RGASPI, f.

85, op. 27, d. 93, l. 1–11). See also Khlevniuk et al., Stalin i Kaganovich, 553–5 (RGASPI, f. 558, op. 11, d. 743, l. 29–36: Sept. 5).

154. Khlevniuk et al., Stalin i Kaganovich, 553–5 (RGASPI, f. 558, op. 11, d. 743, l. 29–36), 558 (f. 81, op. 3, d. 100, l. 91–4: Sept. 8, 1935), 558n3 (APRF, f. 3, op. 64, d. 663, l. 128–9: Kandelaki to Stalin, Sept. 3).

155. "Since Yenukidze does not admit his fall, and does not suffer from humility, he is trying to control the local organizations, assigning them tasks, distributing holidaying comrades among the sanatoriums, giving them their residences," Stalin explained, adding that this had spurred talk Yenukidze had not been sent to Kislovodsk "as punishment but on holiday." Stalin also noted that local comrades Yevdokimov and Sheboldayev had objected to Yenukidze's appointment in Kislovodsk, and that Kalinin and Shkiryatov (head of party control), holidaying in Sochi, agreed. Khlevniuk et al., Stalin i kaganovich, 557–8 (RGASPI, f. 558, op. 11, d. 89, l. 71–76). Agranov (Sept. 5, 1935) wrote to Stalin about an anonymous letter sent early in the summer to "the Moscow party organization, Khrushchev personally," which stated of the Kremlin Affair that "the whole plan consists in removing that odious figure who now blocks even the sun." Stalin wrote in "Stalin" next to the words "odious figure." In another passage, which referred to "that cook," he also wrote in "Stalin." The letter blamed Lominadze's suicide (still not publicly announced) on "the new tyrant" and expressed concern that Yenukidze would commit suicide, too. The NKVD checked hundreds of people via handwriting analysis and arrested B. I. Shilikhin, who until 1930 had worked in Kalinin's reception office and in 1935 was a jurist in the metal import office. Khaustov et al., Lubianka: Stalin i VChk, 683–6 (APRF, f. 3, op. 58, d. 238, l. 86–93), 821n163. The letter to Khrushchev was dated June 4, 1935.

156. The decree was dated Sept. 10–11, 1935, but Yenukidze stalled his relocation from Kislovodsk. Khlevniuk et al., Stalin i Kaganovich, 557–8 (RGASPI, f. 558, op. 11, d. 89, l. 71–76), 558 (RGASPI, f. 81, op. 3, d. 100, l. 91–4: Sept. 8, 1935), 560 (f. 558, op. 11, d. 89, l. 89; f. 17, op. 3, d. 971, l. 30), 580 (f. 558, op. 11, d. 743, l. 37–9; d. 755, l. 39; d. f. 17, op. 163, d. 1079, l. 63; op. 3, d. 971, l. 57).

157. Yezhov sought permission to conspire behind Yagoda's back with Yagoda's first deputy Agranov to get to the bottom of things. Agranov, it seems, fell ill, so Yezhov schemed with others in the NKVD. Pavliukov, Ezhov, 162–3, 170–1 (citing RGASPI, f. 671, op. 1, d. 28, l. 177–81); Pavliukov, Ezhov, 172; Khaustov and Samuelson, Stalin, NKVD, 91.

158. The politburo decreed that Yezhov take a two-month holiday, and approved hard currency worth 3,000 rubles for him to go abroad for medical treatment with his wife. Khlevniuk et al., Stalin i Kaganovich, 572n5 (RGASPI, f. 558, op. 11, d. 743, l. 37–9; d. 755, l. 39; d. f. 17, op. 163, d. 1079, l. 63; op. 3, d. 971, l. 57).

159. Chigirin, Stalin, 83 (RGASPI, f. 558, op. 11, d. 1482, l. 51ob.).

160. Valedinskii, "Organizm Stalina vpolne zdorovyi," 72. The incident is not dated; Shneiderovich saw Stalin in 1934–6.

161. RGASPI, f. 558, op. 11, d. 1479, l. 14–8.

162. Soviet diplomats noted cold, distant attitudes of the French officials with whom they interacted, while in Sept. 1935, a Soviet military mission to France received a favorable reception and were shown the Maginot Line (which was to be operational the next year) but came away unimpressed. Gamelin evaded being drawn into political discussions. Alexander Sedyakin (b. 1893), deputy head of the general staff responsible for Red Army training, concluded that the Soviets had next to nothing to learn from the French. DVP SSSR, XVIII: 505–6 (Potyomkin, Sept. 11, 1935), 659n212 (Hirschfeld to Krestinsky, Sept. 11); Castellan, "Reichswehr et armée rouge," at 254–5; Orlov, "V poiskakh soiuznikov." France had sharply curtailed military spending beginning in 1932. Jackson, "French Strategy," 63.

163. Kievskii Krasnoznamenyi, 101–6 (citing RGVA, f. 25580, op. 74, d. 25, l. 12; d. 29, l. 332–3, 373–6); Dubynskii, "Bol'shie kievskie manevry," 157–69; Eremenko, V nachale voiny, 7–13 (esp. 9 and 13, illustrations); Orlov, "V poiskakh soiuznikov," 48; Sovetskaia voennaia entsiklopediia, V: 121–2; Grechko et al., Istoriia Vtoroi mirovoi voiny, I: 299; Kokoshin, Armiia i politika, 95, 192–6; Ziemke, Red Army, 194; Erickson and Simpkin, Deep Battle.

164. Kvashonkin, Sovetstskoe rukovodstvo, 311–2 (RGASPI, f. 74, op. 2, d. 37, l. 94–6). Voroshilov studied the assembled foreign reactions. Samuelson, Plans for Stalin's War Machine, 242n43 (citing RGVA, f. 33987, op. 3, d. 740, l. 193–208). On the Red Army's internal assessment and subsequent extended discussion: RGVA, f. 4, op. 15, d. 5, l. 419–23 (Sept. 22, 1935); op. 18, d. 52 (Dec. 8–14, 1935). General Ludvík Krejčí, head of the general staff, led the Czechoslovak delegation.

165. Loizeau's observations were reported in Le Temps, Sept. 20, 1935. See Loizeau's meeting with Tukhachevsky: DVP SSSR, XVIII: 518–21 (Sept. 25, 1935); Samuelson, Plans for Stalin's War Machine, 242n44 (citing RGVA, f. 33987, op. 3, d. 687, l. 64–74: Sept. 25); Izvestiia, Sept. 27, 1935.

166. Dreifort, "French Popular Front," 219, citing General Lucien Loizeau, "Une Mission militaire en U.R.S.S.," Revue des Deux Mondes, Sept. 15, 1935: 275.

167. Habeck, Storm of Steel, 231 (citing RGVA, f. 4, op. 15, d. 5, l. 419–23: Sept. 22; l. 163, 165–6: Dec. 28, 1935).

168. Habeck, Storm of Steel, 231 (citing PA-AA, R31683K, pp. 134–39: report from Hagemeier, German Consulate in Kiev, "Inhalt: Herbstmanover der Roten Armee bei Kiew," Oct. 2, 1935).

169. In his final remarks Hitler repudiated those who said, "The Führer, yes—but the party, that's a different matter." "No, gentlemen! The Führer is the party, and the party is the Führer." Der Parteitag der Freiheit vom 10.-16. September 1935, 287.

170. It also forbade employment of German females under forty-five in Jewish households. Pätzold, Verfolgung, Vertreibung, Vernichtung, 113–4.

171. Kershaw, Hitler: 1889–1936, 569–71; Domarus, Hitler: Reden, I: 536–7.

172. Goebbels, Kommunismus ohne Maske, 5, 7. See also Bamsted, Goebbels and National Socialist Propaganda.

173. Khlevniuk et al., Stalin i Kaganovich, 567 (RGASPI, f. 558, op. 11, d. 89, l. 122: Sept. 15, 1935), 569 (l. 114–7: Sept. 15). In response to Kaganovich's and Molotov's proposed list of Soviet journalists to be sent to Prague at the invitation of Czechoslovakia, Stalin wrote, "It is necessary to include . . . one or two female journalists, one more Ukrainian writer, one or two Belorussian writers; in that

connection, it's not required to send editors of newspapers, it's possible to send just popular writers." Khlevniuk et al., *Stalin i Kaganovich*, 567 (RGASPI, f. 558, op. 11, d. 89, l. 110–110ob.), 571 (l. 152: Sept. 17), 571 (l. 154: Sept. 17).

174. Holmes, *Stalin's School*, 167 (citing interview of Krasnogliadova, who referred to conversations with Belogorskaya).

175. Murin, *Stalin v ob"iatiakh*, 53–4 (APRF, f. 45, op. 1, d. 1553, l. 7–8).

176. Murin, *Stalin v ob"iatiakh*, 183–4 (Svanidze diary: Nov. 17, 1935), 185 (Dec. 4).

177. Leushin, "Staliniada," 105 (RGASPI, f. 558, op. 11, d. 754, l. 112–3).

178. The upshot was a drop between 1927 and 1935 in the ratio of dependents to earners from 2.5 to 1.6. Goldman, *Women, the State and Revolution*, 103. "I like good clothes," Sophie Kienya, a technician at Shaft 82, Metro Construction, was quoted as telling a foreign resident. "At work underground I wear rubber waders, breeches, and tie up my hair in a handkerchief. But at home and on free days I want my dresses to be fashionable and pretty and to fit well. All our girls like pretty clothes. At the theater or at parties when you meet girls from the Metro you would never think that they spent their days working underground . . . Our shoes are now excellent, but our factories should pay more attention to producing elegant buttons, trimmings, bags, gloves." Malnick, *Everyday Life*, 221.

179. Kaganovich assured Stalin that "many workers made a calculation and themselves pointed out that, since previously they were buying supplementary meat and butter at markets, now they were gaining. Now, it seems, we will need to pay attention to shops and organizing sales." Davies et al., *Years of Progress*, 174–6; Khlevniuk et al., *Stalin i Kaganovich*, 589–90 (RGASPI, f. 558, op. 11, d. 743, l. 40–4: Sept. 26, 1935). See also Davies and Khlevniuk, "Otmena kartochnoi sistemy v SSSR," 127.

180. Suvenirov, *Tragediia RKKA*, 34.

181. Osokina, *Ierarkhiia potrebleniia*; Osokina, *Za fasadom*; Hessler, *Social History of Soviet Trade*; Randall, *Soviet Dream World*.

182. "Moscow restaurants left nothing to be desired," wrote Juri Jelagin, a violinist at the Vakhtangov Theater, of an evening meal that, with entertainment, could easily cost two weeks of a worker's salary. "Magnificent, live Volga sturgeons swam in a pool in the center of the dining room at the Metropol on Theater Square. The patrons could select the fish they wanted in the clear water." Ziegler's Czech jazz band at the Metropol and Tsafman's and Utyosov's bands at the National, while gypsies sang at the Prague on the Arbat. Jelagin, *Taming of the Arts*, 136–8. Charles Thayer, the U.S. embassy official, recalled, "a good dinner at the Metropol or the Medved Restaurant was cheap enough." Thayer, *Bears in the Caviar*, 106.

183. Martelli, *Italy Against the World*; Hardie, *Abyssinian Crisis*; Robertson, *Mussolini as Empire Builder*; Strang, *Collision of Empires*. See also Durand, *Crazy Campaign*.

184. Khlevniuk et al., *Stalin i Kaganovich*, 545 (RGASPI, f. 558, op. 11, d. 89, l. 2–2ob.: Sept. 2, 1935). The Abyssinian invasion also did not inhibit Soviet participation in Milan's first international air show (Oct. 12–28, 1935), where the Soviets exhibited their well-designed Il-15 biplane, which impressed as best in show. Their Il-16, a low-wing cantilever monoplane, was then the fastest fighter in the world, but the international audience dismissed its performance data as too good to be true. *1 Salone Internazionale Aeronautico*; Ziemke, *Red Army*, 193. The story would make the rounds that Stalin mischievously

ordered one of his NKVD attendants to get Ras Kasa—a tribal leader in the resistance to Italian forces—on the phone, and when the operative returned distraught, unable to connect to the mountain Ethiopian, Stalin was said to have replied, "And you are still working in security?" Gromyko, *Memoirs*, 103 (no citation).

185. The USSR had lost to Mexico by a single vote. Stalin added that "now you couldn't chase Litvinov from the assembly presidium with a broom." Khlevniuk et al., *Stalin i Kaganovich*, 561–2 (RGASPI, f. 558, op. 11, d. 89, l. 92–3: Sept. 11, 1935), 562–3 (l. 93: Sept. 11), 563 (l. 103: Sept. 12), 563–4 (l. 99–102: Sept. 12). See also *DVP SSSR*, XVIII: 523–4 (telegram to Litvinov, Oct. 4, 1935), 525–6 (Potyomkin speech Oct. 10), 661 (Potomykin telegram, Oct. 11); Adibekov et al., *Politbiuro TsK RKP (b)—VKP (b) i Evropa*, 329–30 (RGASPI, f. 17, op. 162, d. 18, l. 173), 330 (l. 175), 330–1 (l. 178), 332 (l. 187), 333 (op. 162, d. 19, l. 14), 334 (l. 32), 337–8 (d. 20, l. 4, 8); and Walters, *History of the League of Nations*, I: 358–9. Stalin allowed Litvinov to support sanctions against Italy, but the politburo instructed him to "follow an independent Soviet line . . . and avoid anything that could be interpreted as a subordination of our line to the position of Britain." Adibekov et al., *Politbiuro TsK RKP (b)—VKP (b) i Evropa*, 331 (RGASPI, f. 17, op. 162, d. 18, l. 178: Oct. 15, 1935).

186. *DGFP*, series C, IV: 778–9 (Oct. 29, 1935).

187. Murin, *Stalin v ob"iatiakh*, 183 (Svanidze diary: Nov. 17, 1935).

188. She was either 75 or 77 (Keke's birth year remains uncertain because of a possible effort to increase her age at marriage). Stalin had visited her, briefly, in 1921 and in 1927.

189. Murin, *Stalin v ob"iatiakh*, 16–7 (l. 45–6: March 24, 1934). "I. V. profoundly suffered from the loss of his wife and friend," Vlasik would recall. Loginov, *Teni Stalina*, 97. Artyom recalled an incident when Vasily told his father that he and his buddies had seen old women crossing themselves and praying, and how they threw a firecracker at their feet. Stalin erupted: "Why, why did you do that?!" Vasily: "Why were they praying?!" Stalin: "Do you respect grandmother? Do you love her? She prays. Because she knows something that you do not know!" Sergeev and Glushik, *Besedy o Staline*, 89–96; *Moskovskii komsomolets*, Aug. 3, 2004.

190. Sukharev, "Litsedeistvo," 106 (citing PA IIP pri TsK KP Gruzii, f. 8, op. 1, d. 17, l. 20, 24: G. V. Khachapuridze, 54).

191. A visiting Moscow inspector had just approved the plans. Sokolov, *Beriia*, 97–8 (Sept. 1935).

192. Stalin, in a letter to his mother (June 11, 1935), mentioned she was ill ("Do not be afraid of illness, get strong, it shall pass"). Murin, *Stalin v ob"iatiakh*, 18 (APRF, f. 45, op. 1, d. 1549, l. 55–6). Beria had had a journalist transcribe and edit what were purported to be Keke's "memoirs," which he evidently intended to use to flatter Stalin. (Instead, they were buried in the Georgian party archive.) The interviews took place on Aug. 23, 25, and 27, 1935. Dzhugashvili, *Moi syn Iosif Stalin*. See also the hearsay about Stalin in Georgia at this time: Blagoveshchenskii, "V gostiakh u P. A. Sharii," 472n28.

193. The same source has Stalin saying, "Mama, do you remember our tsar? Well, I'm something like the tsar." "You'd have done better to become a priest," Keke is said to have replied. Radzinsky, *Stalin*, 24 (recollections of N. Kipshidze, a doctor who treated Keke, quoted without citation).

194. On the supposed lingering influence of Georgian literary styles on Stalin, see Vaiskopf, *Pistael' Stalin*, 130–1, 181–98.

195. RGASPI, f. 558, op. 11, d. 92, l. 22–3.

196. Dorofeev, "Mat." One observer in the same issue reminisced that "whoever has met comrade Stalin even just once, will never forget his modesty, wisdom, and ability to size up events quickly and offer correct, clear directives, will never forget his sagacity, his ability to cultivate in a person a lifelong selfless dedication to the cause of the working class, implacability against all enemies of the revolution." Here was a self-portrait in another's words.

197. "Beseda s mater'iu tovarishcha Stalina," *Pravda*, Oct. 27, 1935; *Zaria vostoka* (Oct. 28).

198. RGASPI, f. 558, op. 11, d. 92, l.82.

199. *DGFP*, series C, IV: 482–3 (July 26, 1935), 493–6 (July 27, 507–10 (July 30), 596–8 (Aug. 29), 618–20 (Sept. 5), 825–9 (Nov. 18), 833–5 (Nov. 19), 835–7 (Nov. 19), 841–2 (Nov. 20), 847–9 (Nov. 22), 849–51 (Nov. 23), 859–62 (Nov. 27), 866–8 (Nov. 30), 872–4 (Dec. 8), 925–6 (Dec. 18). The French Assembly would ratify the pact with the USSR on Feb. 27, 1936 (353 votes to 164); the Congress of Soviets would do so on March 8, 1936.

200. *DGFP*, series C, IV: 778–9 (Oct. 28, 1935), 783–4 (Nov. 1), 811–3 (Nov. 11, 1935); *Na prieme*, 171; Weinberg, *Foreign Policy*, I: 221–2. Schacht and Kandelaki haggled over how much of existing debts the Soviets needed to pay in gold and hard currency.

201. Functionaries had dug out the old tsarist emblems and made sketches for Soviet versions. Stalin also allowed the "staff" to become once again the "general staff." Solov'ev, "Tetrady krasnogo professor, 1912–1941 gg.," IV: 183; Erickson, *Soviet High Command*, 366–403, 445–6; Zaloga, "Soviet Tank Operations," note 2.

202. The decree creating the marshal rank was issued on Sept. 22, 1935, and the rank was ceremoniously conferred on Nov. 20; *Pravda's* account (the next day) sought to smother the whiff of tsarism: "Kliment Voroshilov is a proletarian to the marrow, a Bolshevik in every movement, a theoretician and practitioner of the military art, a cavalryman, a sharpshooter, one of the best orators in the party, a thoughtful and hardworking organizer of the immense defense machine."

203. Suvenirov, *Tragediia RKKA*, 51–4.

204. Khaustov et al., *Lubianka: Stalin i VChK*, 822n166.

205. By fall 1935, 16,000 people had received a USSR state medal, such as the Order of Lenin or Order of the Red Banner. Khlevniuk et al., *Stalin i Kaganovich*, 81n6 (citing GARF, f. R-3316, op. 65, d. 144, l. 5). The regime would introduce a "director's fund" in 1936 for payment of "bonuses."

206. Murin, *Stalin v ob"iatiakh*, 183 (Svanidze diary: Nov. 17, 1935).

207. Yevgeny was born Jan. 10, 1936. At some point Yakov acknowledged him and his last name was changed from Golyshev to Jughashvili. Golysheva received money from the Jughashvili household for the boy.

208. Murin, *Stalin v ob"iatiakh*, 183–4 (Svanidze diary: Nov. 17, 1935).

209. Norm-busters appeared in automobiles (Alexander Busygin), machine tools (I. I. Gudov), textiles (Yevdokiya and Maria Vinogradov), and the Gulag, but it was Stakhanov's name that got affixed to the "movement." Siegelbaum, *Stakhanovism*; Benvenuti, "Stakhanovism and Stalinism"; Davies and Khlevniuk, "Stakhanovism"; Davies et al., *Years of Progress*, 164–9; Kvashonkin, *Sovetskoe rukovodstvo*, 310–1 (RGASPI, f. 85, op. 29, d. 460, l. 2–3: Orjonikidze to Sarkisov, Sept. 6, 1935); Goriaeva, "Veilkaia kniga

dnia," 301 (RGAKFD, no. Sh-192, Vr. Zv. 02:00).

210. Soldatenkov, *Politicheskie i nravstvennye posledstviia*, 82–8 (citing TsGAIPD StP., f. 24, op. 2, d. 1190, l. 6: Zhdanov, April 5, 1936).

211. In 1937, the mine's party organizer, Konstantin Petrov (b. 1908), would replace the mine boss, Iosif Zaplavsky, who ended up in Norilsk, a Gulag site.

212. Mikoyan advised that "if one is to study by the capitalists, then in the first instance it is necessary to study by the Americans." *Pervoe soveshchanie rabochikh;* Mikoian, *V polose velikogo pod"ema*, 15.

213. *Pravda*, Nov. 22, 1935; *Sochineniia*, XIV: 79–102 (at 89–91).

214. Stakhanov made the cover of *Time* on Dec. 16, 1935. Stalin also pushed through a campaign against managers' "sabotage" in late 1935, which, like Stakhanovism, he largely abandoned by spring 1936. See also Stakhanov, *Rasskaz o moei zhizni.*

215. Raskol'nikov, *O vremeni i o sebe*, 476–86. Raskolnikov's acquaintances were phoning with congratulations, having somehow heard news of Stalin's treatment of him. He and Molotov had once studied together at the St. Petersburg Polytechnic and worked together at *Pravda* before the revolution. Bulgaria was Raskolnikov's fourth ambassadorship. In between, he had chaired the state repertory committee, which oversaw live theater, and himself tried his hand at writing plays.

216. Raskolnikov mentions that he encountered Mikhail Koltsov in the reception area; in fact, Koltsov was received by Stalin just before RaskolniIov. Raskol'nikov, *O vremeni i o sebe*, 486–8; *Na prieme*, 174–5.

217. Roediger (deputy head of the German foreign ministry's Eastern Department) told Bessonov that "except for the ideological hostility between Germany and the USSR there are no differences and we certainly welcome expansion of economic relations." On Dec. 12, Hermann Göring told Bessonov that War Minister Blomberg and Schacht had "agreed a readiness to supply the USSR with any military equipment, including the most advanced," under a new credit, which Bessonov continued to view as the key to unlocking political rapprochement, rather than as entirely separate, the way the Germans treated it. Abramov, "Osobaia missiia Davida Kandelaki," 147 (citing AVP RF, f. 082, op. 18, pap. 81, d. 7, l. 360–5); *DGFP*, series C, IV: 870–2 (Dec. 4, 1935), 897–9 (Dec. 10), 931–3 (Dec. 21). See also Nekrich, *1941*, 23; and Fischer, *Russia's Road*, 240. Litvinov wrote to Surits (Dec. 19, 1935) that he was skeptical of any movement on the German side, while Krestinsky wrote to Surits (Jan. 11, 1936), "it seems to me we shall reach agreement with the Germans on this 500-million credit. As for the question of the Germans changing their political position in relation to us, there has been no indication of any changes in this direction neither in Berlin nor in Moscow nor any other points on the planet. *DVP SSSR*, XVIII: 595–7, XIX: 25–6.

218. *DGFP*, series C, III: 306–9 (Aug. 10, 1934), 556–8 (Nov. 1); *DBFP*, 2nd series, VI: 883 (July 31). The British were still waiting for a German response to the Feb. 1935 Anglo-French proposals; Hitler claimed he had already responded. Orme Sargent and Wigram had written a long memorandum (Nov. 21, 1935) rejecting both inaction toward and encirclement of Germany, and concluding that "a policy of coming to terms with Germany in Western Europe might enable Britain and France to moderate the development of German aims in the Centre and East." Medlicott, *Britain and Germany*, 19 (citing C7752/55/18 FO 371/18851).

219. The German notetaker has Hitler characterizing Phipps's suggestion for engagement as analogous to "having plague germs shut up in a cupboard and then believing that one could make them less dangerous by opening the door and letting the germs loose on mankind." *DBFP*, 2nd series, XV: 488–93 (Phipps to Hoare, Dec. 16, 1935). *DGFP*, series C, IV: 917–9 (Neurath account, Dec. 14). Hitler told a ministerial conference after meeting Phipps that he could not agree to arms limitations with Britain and France so long as the Soviet Union freely armed, or take part in any Western European treaty system in which the Soviet Union took part. *DGFP*, series C, IV: 913–4.

220. The renaming was official on Dec. 17, 1935. A writers' union plenum dedicated to poetry had been planned for Dec. 1935 in Minsk but was postponed to February 1936, likely in connection with Stalin's sudden elevation of Mayakovsky. Fleishman, *Boris Pasternak*, 293.

221. Stalin added: "I am ready if my help is needed." Artizov and Naumov, *Vlast'*, 270–2 (APRF, f. 45, op. 1, d. 729). Back at the writers' congress the previous year, Stetsky had said, "I also don't know of any decisions of the party and government about the canonization of Mayakovsky." *Pervyi vsesoiuznyi s"ezd sovetskikh pisatelei*, 614.

222. V. A. Katanian would recall that Mekhlis, editor of *Pravda*, "did not evince any particular enthusiasm" on the literary page of *Pravda*, dedicated to Mayakovsky, which appeared a few days later (Dec. 5), two sentences from that resolution, which soon gained worldwide fame, were printed with a mistake. Instead of 'the best and most talented' it read 'the best and talented.'" *Pravda* issued a correction, however (Dec. 17). Katanian, "Ne tol'ko vospominaniia," 224–5.

223. Artizov and Naumov, *Vlast'*, 275 (APRF, f. [4]5, op. 1, d. 788, l. 107–110ob.). An affirmation of Stalin's praise was hastily arranged in the form of a letter, in the name of several Soviet poets then on a trip to Paris, and published in Moscow (it was written by Aragon, whose name was left off). "Sovetskie poety v Parizhe," *Literaturnaia gazeta*, Dec. 9, 1935; Maksimenkov, *Sumbur*, 17–8 (RGASPI, f. 88, op. 1, d. 512, l. 1).

224. Seishirō Itagaki, who as Kwantung Army intelligence chief had helped stage the Mukden incident to seize Manchuria and was promoted to Kwantung vice chief of staff, "urged Japanese predominance in Inner Mongolia, to deny the USSR a platform (like it enjoyed in Xinjiang) and to serve as a springboard for conquest of Outer Mongolia, which would allow takeover of the Soviet Far East almost without fighting." Haslam, *Threat from the East*, 48–9 (citing Hoover Institution Archives, *International Military Tribunal, the Far East Documents*, 7830–33: prosecution document no. 1466, exhibit no. 761–A). Stalin decided to support Sheng, and NKVD operatives brought the leader of the anti-Sheng Muslim rebellion, General Ma Zhingying, to the Soviet Union, both to deflate the rebellion and for insurance. Primakov, *Ocherki*, III: 216–8; Khlevniuk et al., *Stalin i Kaganovich*, 594–5 (RGASPI, f. 558, op. 11, d. 90, l. 119, Oct. 1, 1935). On further developments, see Milward, *Eurasian Crossroads*, 200ff; and Ledovskii, *SSSR i Stalin v sud'ba Kitaia*, 190–1.

225. Baabar, *Twentieth-Century Mongolia*, 338–9. The Soviet Union continued to fudge the recognition question, so as not to anger Chiang Kai-shek's government (which claimed "Outer" Mongolia as part of China), but Japan quietly hinted at recognizing Mongolia's independence. In late Nov. 1935, the

Mongols, following Soviet orders, had broken off a months-long Mongolia-Manchukuo conference to regulate their disputed border, citing Manchukuo's demands for diplomatic recognition. *DVP SSSR*, XVIII: 649–50n172; *Pravda*, Nov. 21, 1935.

226. Chang and Halliday, *Mao*,139.

227. Haslam, *Threat from the East*, 61–5; *DVP SSSR*, XVIII: 587–8 (Dec. 9, 1935), 601–3 (Dec. 28). In Jan. 1936, the Soviet Union and Xinjiang signed an agreement on military and economic aid that excluded access to "third powers." Hasiotis, *Soviet Political, Economic, and Military Involvement*, 100.

228. Haslam, *Threat from the East*, 50 (citing *FRUS*, 489–90: Henderson in Moscow to Hull in Washington, Dec. 14, 1935). The follow-up border incident took place on Dec. 19.

229. The Soviet foreign trade commissariat had sent Choibalsan 20 Gorky Factory (GAZ) automobiles, which the Moscow loyalist awarded as patronage to other Mongol ministers. Genden had felt constrained to send a lengthy report to Stalin, Molotov, and Voroshilov on implementation of Stalin's recommendations, but also noted that 96.4 percent of Mongolia's 731,686 people were illiterate, and expressed concern about Japanese war provocations. RGANI, f. 89, op. 63, d. 16, l. 1–33 (Oct. 14, 1935).

230. Baabar, *Twentieth-Century Mongolia*, 344–6.

231. Murin, *Stalin v ob"iatiakh*, 185–6 (Svanidze diary: Dec. 26, 1935), 189. Kun, *Stalin*, 227. The polar explorer Belyakov witnessed an evening of dancing at Stalin's Black Sea dacha: "He played many records, mostly Georgian folk songs. He explained to us that Georgians sing on their way to the market." RGASPI, f. 558, op. 4, d. 668.

232. As of July 1935, the party had 1.66 million full members and 681,245 candidates. By the time the exchange process was all done, about a quarter million party cards would be confiscated. RGASPI, f. 17, op. 2, d. 561, l. 127–64; Khlevniuk, *1937–i*, 56–7. Yezhov's report was published: *Pravda*, Dec. 26, 1935; *Partiinoe stroitel'stvo*, 1936, no. 2: 9–23. According to the NKVD date, as of Oct. 20, 1935, 255 "spies" had been expelled from the party, but the NKVD of Eastern Siberia and the Soviet Far East—the front line with Japan—together had found only one spy in the party ranks. Khaustov et al., *Lubianka: Stalin i VChK*, 822–3n169 (TsA FSB, f. 3, op. 2, d. 3, l. 131–4), 724–31 (op. 3, d. 62, l. 129–44).

233. Beria followed him to the dais, boasted that the South Caucasus NKVD had arrested 1,020 enemies through this month, and congratulated himself. RGASPI, f. 17, op. 2, d. 561, l. 143, 146, 162.

234. Damage of machinery while operating it as well as the production or supply of poor quality goods became crimes of sabotage too. Andreyev gave the main report, for which he had been copiously supplied with NKVD materials on "sabotage" of the Stakhanovite movement. Other speakers cited cases of anti-Stakhanovite "sabotage" in their regions. Davies et al., *Years of Progress*, 171–2 (citing RGASPI, f. 73, op. 1, d. 141, l. 205; f. 17, op. 2, d. 561, l. 32: Ryndin); *Pravda*, December 29, 1935.

235. *Pravda*, Dec. 27, 1935. Yagoda reported an expansion in Polish agents crossing Soviet borders in pursuit of information on weapons depots and other secrets. Khaustov et al., *Lubianka: Stalin i VChK*, 712–4 (APRF, f. 3, op. 58, d. 248, l. 80–4: Dec. 27, 1935).

236. Harrison and Davies, "Soviet Military-Economic Effort," 370, citing RGASPI, f. 17, op. 162, d. 19, l. 16: Dec. 15, 1935; GARF, f. 5446, op. 57, d. 38: Dec. 16, 372; Cooper, "Defence Production," 35.

237. The Mongols complained that it was very difficult to struggle against the lamas "when some officials believe in and pray to god." RGANI, f. 89, op. 63, d. 17, l. 1–5.

238. RGANI, f. 89, op. 63, d. 17, l. 6–8.

239. Baabar, *Twentieth-Century Mongolia*, 347–8 (citing the eyewitness Luvsansharev, a secretary of the Mongolian Central Committee, speaking at the 2nd plenum [March 11–20, 1936], in connection with Genden's removal). See also Dashpürev and Soni, *Reign of Terror*, 34. Another version has Genden chasing Stalin around the table, yanking his pipe out of his mouth, and dashing it to the floor. Sandag and Kendall, *Poisoned Arrows*, 77.

240. Murin, *Stalin v ob"iatiakh*, 186 (Svanidze diary: Dec. 7, 1936: erroneous dating, more likely Jan. 7).

241. Molotov himself said it was "up to the German government to draw practical conclusions." *Izvestiia*, Jan. 12, 1936.

242. DGFP, series C, IV: 967–72 (Jan. 6, 1936).

243. The foreign office forwarded the report to Chilston in Moscow for comment. The British in Moscow were skeptical. Hochman, *Failure of Collective Security*, 110 (citing DBFP/Russia Correspondence, F.P. 371/19460, 142–8: Dec. 7, 1935; F.P. 371/20346, 150–2: Jan. 29, 1936).

244. Bezymenskii, *Gitler i Stalin*, 98, 100–1; Brügel, *Stalin und Hitler*, 38. Hitler soon forbade new sales of military technology to the Soviets. DGFP, series C, IV: 1033 (Jan. 24, 1936). Schacht omitted any mention of Kandelaki or the negotiations in his memoir. Schacht, *My First Seventy-Six Years*.

245. It is not out of the question that the NKVD tasked the Swiss-born Olberg, who had been expelled from the German Communist party in 1932 for Trotskyism, with infiltrating Trotskyite circles in Europe, then decided he needed to serve another purpose. On Olberg, see Chase, *Enemies within the Gates?*, 134 (citing RGASPI, f., 495, op. 175, d. 105, l. 9). Vyshinsky wrote to Stalin and Molotov (Jan. 8) of a separate case of a "Trotskyite group" just turned over to the courts with supposed plans for a "terrorist" act against the dictator Stalin on Red Square back during the Revolution Day parade, while Yagoda and Vyshinsky together wrote to him (Jan. 11, 1936) about the liquidation of a Zinovievite organization of thirty-four people, asking how should they be tried. Khaustov et al., *Lubianka: Stalin i VChK*, 715–6 (APRF, f. 3, op. 58, d. 230, l. 65–65ob.), 716–20 (l. 68–76), 723 (l. 64).

246. Jansen and Petrov, *Stalin's Loyal Executioner*, 46–8.

247. Baabar, *Twentieth-Century Mongolia*, 346–7. On the evening of Jan. 7, 1936, Stalin had received the Mongols again in Molotov's office, and repeated his demands. Stomonyakov summarized the discussion about the lamas to the Soviet envoy in Mongolia (Tairov), noting, "comrade Stalin said that in a difficult moment one does not liberate criminals but punishes them or holds them under lock and key, like a hostage." RGANI, f. 89, op. 63, d. 18, l. 1–9; d. 19, l. 1–8: Jan. 10. On Jan. 29, a Manchukuo border company killed its Japanese officers and successfully defected to the Soviet Union. The next day, two Japanese companies crossed the Soviet border in belated pursuit, killing three Soviet border guards and suffering dozens of casualties in a gun battle. They retreated. Shishov, *Rossiia i Iaponiia*, 424–68; Erickson, *Soviet High Command*, 414. In Jan. and Feb. 1936, the politburo authorized the building of new roads, petrol stations, aircraft and artillery repair installations, shipbuilding plants, oil storage facilities, and a refinery capable of

making airplane fuel in the Soviet Far East. Davies et al., *Years of Progress*, 278 (citing RGASPI, f. 17, op. 162, d. 19, l. 27–9: Jan. 11, 1936, 73–5, 93–7: Feb. 18, 81–2).

248. Dawson, "Convenient Medical Death," 1445; Rose, *King George V*.

249. Castellan, "Reichswehr et Armée Rouge," 244. Göring would tell the Poles in February that "Marshal Tukhachevsky, when on his way through Germany, had not been received, although he had clearly wanted to get in touch with military circles." DGFP, series C, IV: 1201–2 (Feb. 26, 1936).

250. In late Jan., Uborevičius traveled via Warsaw to Paris, ostensibly to link up with Tukhachevsky, and met an aide to the German military attaché in Poland, from whom he requested a meeting on his return from Paris with an authoritative German military official such as War Minister Blomberg. McMurry, *Deutschland und die Sowjetunion*, 320–1.

251. Tukhachevsky had never accepted German officers' professions of friendship at face value. "I spoke especially long with Tukhachevsky," Ambassador Dirksen had written to a friend (Oct. 17, 1931). "He is far from the direct and sympathetic person who speaks openly in support of a German orientation, as does Uborevičius." In 1933, Tukhachevsky did profess profound friendship, to rescue the relationship. D'iakov and Bushueva, *Fashistskii mech kovalsia v SSSR*, 121; Bushueva and D'iakov, "Reikhsver i sovety, tainyi soiuz," 183 (no citation).

252. Castellan, "Reichswehr et armée rouge," 217–8 (citing Köstring); Gamelin, *Servir*, II: 196; Erickson, *Soviet High Command*, 412. The strongly anti-German French journalist Geneviève Tabouis, who was present at a farewell banquet at the Soviet embassy, would later allege that Tukhachevsky, while entertaining Édouard Herriot, the French foreign minister Joseph Paul-Boncour, and the Romanian foreign minister Nicolae Titulescu, among others, had rhapsodized about Nazi Germany ("They are already invincible, Madame Tabouis!"). Ambassador Potyomkin was present but appears to have reported nothing of the kind to Litvinov. Neither did French diplomatic sources. Tabouis, *They Called Me Cassandra*, 257; Erickson, *Soviet High Command*, 413. Tukhachevsky, seeking rubber-stamp approval for the military budget at the Central Executive Committee (Jan. 15, 1936), had stressed that Germany could attack the USSR even without a common border, as it had attacked France—smashing through Belgium—in 1914. Tukhachevskii, *Zadachi oborony SSSR*, 6, 14–5.

253. Sipols, "SSSR i problema mira," 50–1 (citing PRO 418/81: 55, 78–79: Jan. 11, 1936). Maisky did not desist: DVP SSSR, XIX: 62–4 (Feb. 5, 1936), 206–11 (April 2).

254. Buryat-Mongol households individually held between twenty and seventy cattle. "The collective farmers' relation to labor has changed fundamentally," the leaders' report boasted, praising the expansion of skilled personnel, schools, and theaters. Gatagova et al., *TsK RKP (b)–VKP (b) i natsional'nyi vopros*, II: 164–6 (RGASPI, f. 78, op. 1, d. 585, l. 25–8: D. Dorzhiev, Council of People's Commissars, M. Yerbanov, party secretary).

255. The Mongol-Buryat pageant had been preceded by collective farmers of Uzbekistan, Kazakhstan, and Kara-Kalpak, when Stalin, Molotov, and Kaganovich were photographed in the national costumes, including head covering, for the first time. At a Dec. 4, 1935, Kremlin reception for forty-three Tajik and thirty-three Turkmen collective farmers in national dress, honored for the cotton

harvest, a ten-year-old girl, Mamlakat Nakhangova, presented Stalin with the Tajik translation of his *Questions of Leninism*, and a photograph was taken of her in her head shawl, her arm around a seated Stalin's shoulder. *Pravda*, Dec. 6, 1935; Kun, *Stalin*, 220–1. See also Levushin, "Dokumenty VKP (b) kak istochnik po istorii istoricheskoi nauki," 386–9; Nevezhin, *Zastol'nye*, 247–72; and RGASPI, f. 558, op. 1, d. 4314, l. 2–4. Whereas in *Pravda*'s coverage of the First All-Union Congress of Collective Farm Shock Workers, one-third of the photographs were of non-Russians, by the second gathering two years later in 1935, the ratio was reversed: Central Asians, Ukrainians, and Belorussians accounted for two-thirds of the photographs and illustrations. Brooks, "Thank You, Comrade Stalin!" 75.

256. "Comrades, there is one thing more valuable than cotton—that is the friendship of the peoples of our country," Stalin was quoted as remarking during the Tajik-Turkmen reception. The tsarist legacy, "a savage, wolf-like policy," had been overcome. "While this friendship lives and flourishes, we are afraid of no one, neither internal nor external enemies. You can have no doubt about this, comrades. (Stormy applause, all present stand and shout, 'Stalin, Hurrah')." "Rech' tovarishcha Stalina na soveshchanii peredovykh kolkhoznikov i kolkhoznits Tadzhikistana i Turkmenistana," *Pravda*, Dec. 5, 1935; *Sochineniia* (Hoover), XIV: 113–5. Molotov's speeches at the many Kremlin national receptions were published as a pamphlet: *Velikaia druzhba narodov SSSR* (Moscow: Partizdat, 1936).

257. *Pravda*, Dec. 21 and 31, 1935; Jan. 24 and 30, 1936.

258. This was not his first photograph with children, a shift first visible in schoolbooks for children, which had rendered Stalin overtly fatherly. *Rasskazy o Staline*. Unlike the fatherly tsars, Stalin was called *otets*, not *batushka*.

259. *Pravda*, Aug. 3, 1935 (credited to Vlasik). Stalin visited a children's home in Moscow as well. Heizer, "Cult of Stalin," 169; Plamper, *Stalin Cult*, 44; Plamper, "Georgian Koba or Soviet 'Father of Peoples,'" 131. Maria Osten wrote to Stalin requesting permission to republish the photograph in her book *Hubert in Wonderland*, about adopting a son in the Saarland under the Nazis and bringing him to the USSR. "This would be such a pleasure for all little grown-up readers of my book in the USSR and the entire world!" she wrote. Stalin acceded ("I agree"). RGASPI, f. 558, op. 11, d. 781, l. 126.

260. Kun, *Stalin*, 316.

261. During the first Five-Year Plan images of modernity in the borderlands—railroads, factories, workers—had predominated, but in the 1920s, even the most modern architects, who generally eschewed any hint of ornamentation, when outside Russia proper had chosen to incorporate folkloric "national" flourishes in public buildings, such as Moisei Ginzburg's administrative center in Alma-Ata or others in Baku. Bliznakov, "International Modernism," 112–30. Ginzburg had lived in Crimea and studied Tatar art there. On female and backwardness, as well as nurturing, see Stites, *Russian Popular Culture*, 83–4; and Iğmen, *Speaking Soviet*, 66.

262. The RSFSR was the only union republic without its own Communist party, and although it had state institutions, they often overlapped with those of the USSR (Kalinin was the head of both the RSFSR and the USSR central executive committees of the Soviet). Although there had been some institutions for ethnic Ukrainians and ethnic Belorussians in the RSFSR, these were abolished or

allowed to lapse, which seems to have further spurred some ethnic Ukrainians and Belorussians in the RSFSR to identify as ethnic Russians. Martin, *Affirmative Action Empire*, 403–6.

263. Back on Dec. 15, 1925, at a central Committee plenum, Stalin had lauded the Russians as "the most industrial, the most active, and the most Soviet of all nations in our country," a statement partly in response to unexpected resistance to the alteration of the party's name from all-Russian to all-Union, but also reflecting deep conviction. RGASPI, f. 558, op. 11, d. 205, l. 5. In his furious letter (Dec. 12, 1930) to Bedny over the latter's mocking Russians warming themselves on stoves, Stalin had called the Russian working class "the advanced guard of Soviet workers, its acknowledged leaders, having conducted a more revolutionary policy and activist politics than any other proletariat of the world could dream of." On July 6, 1933, at one of his Moscow dachas, in the presence of the portraitists Yevgeny Katsman and Isaak Brodsky, Stalin had toasted Russians as "the boldest Soviet nation, which achieved the socialist revolution before others." Nevezhin, *Zastol'nye*, 42 (RGALI, f. 2368, op. 2, d. 36, l. 16). For the impressions of one of the artists ("What a colossal man! To me he seems as immense and beautiful as nature"), see Plamper, *Stalin Cult*, 92 (RGASPI, f. 74, op. 1, d. 292, l. 92–92ob.: July 15, 1933).

264. Ryutin had derided Stalin's regime as "national Bolshevism," a designation originated in a positive sense by the anti-Marxist nationalist émigré Nikolai Ustryalov (b. 1890). "Platforma 'Soiuza marksistov-lenintsev' ('Gruppa Riutina')," (1990, no. 9), 76.

265. The demolition had taken place on Dec. 5, 1931. Conceived in the wake of the defeat of Napoleon by Alexander I, it had been consecrated in 1883 on the day Alexander III had been crowned. Its valuable gold (half a ton from the cupola alone) was removed before demolition, whereas its marble went into the Moscow metro construction. Once the rubble was cleared, the crater was supposed to see erection of a grandiose Palace of Soviets designed by Boris Yofan, who sketched a neoclassical stepped colossus of porphyry, marble, and jasper, which aimed to be taller than the Eiffel Tower, at more than 1,300 feet, topped by a 260-foot statue of Lenin, making it resemble a pedestal. Construction of even the foundation was delayed by the grandiosity, and would finally commence in 1937, with the foundation completed in 1939, but nothing else after that. RGASPI, f. 17, op. 3, d. 827, l. 9 (May 25, 1931); d. 828, l. 17 (June 5); Kvashonkin, *Sovetskoe rukovodstvo*, 158 (RGASPI, f. 667, op. 1, d. 17, l. 95–7: Molotov to Yenukidze, Aug. 24, 1931); Lebedeva, "O snose khrama Khrista Spasitelia," 14; Iofan, "Dvorets s"ezdov SSSR." See also Tarkhanov and Kavtaradze, *Architecture of the Stalin Era*; Paperny, *Architecture in the Age of Stalin*. Before the revolution, Moscow counted 460 Orthodox churches; already by Jan. 1, 1933, this stood at fewer than 100.

266. Arfon Rees correctly noted that "the significant aspect of Stalinist ideology was not the extent to which it adjusted to a nationalist perspective . . . but the extent to which . . . a Marxist-Leninist perspective, modified over time, remained the dominant ideology." Rees, "Stalin and Russian Nationalism," 102–3. Carr wrongly called Russian nationalism "the only political creed which moved [Stalin] at all deeply." Carr, *Russian Revolution*, 170.

267. "'Neizmennyi drug'—eto obiazyvaet . . . : pis'ma O. I. Sobalevoi-Mikhal'tsevoi," 113 (APRF, f. 345, op. 34 1, d. 2731118, l. 7149:

Dec. 10, 1935); Artizov and Naumov, *Vlast'*, 279–80. The writers' union was a trade union and its members wrote to management seeking all manner of material help. Even some of the published writers said they could not make a living and requested additional employment (as editors or reviewers). Osip Mandelstam wrote from internal exile in 1936 to the poet and union management official Nikolai Tikhonov, "I am seriously ill, abandoned by everyone and destitute . . . I cannot translate either, because I have become very weak, and even the worry about my verse, which I cannot lay aside, is costing me palpitations." Antipina, *Povsednevnaia zhizn'*, 12–3 (citing RGALI, f. 631, op. 15, d. 637, l. 136), 13–21.

268. Golubev, *"Esli mir obrushitsia na nashu Respubliku,"* 64 (citing TsAODM, f. 3, op. 50, d. 75, l. 38).

269. The censor organ was organized into four sectors: political-economic, artistic, agricultural, and regional (or provincial). In late 1935, according to a party commission probe, the political-economic sector did not have even a single economist, and the artistic sector lacked anyone with specialized arts training. "And if the situation with the censor in the center is blatantly unsatisfactory," the commission report concluded, "in locales, and especially in the counties, it is utterly catastrophic." Zhuravlev, *Obshchestvo i vlast'*, 114–6. Locally, almost every member of the censor staff had to work other jobs concurrently.

270. Shcherbakov composed a long analysis of the situation in literature (Jan. 2, 1936), professing optimism about recent and forthcoming literary works, but complaining that his deputy Stavsky was going behind his back (something Stalin encouraged). Artizov and Naumov, *Vlast'*, 284–8 (RGASPI, f. 88, op. 1, d. 474, l. 1–8). Shcherbakov had sent two memoranda to Stalin, Kaganovich, and Yezhov about a struggle to the death of "two camps" inside the underperforming Moscow Art Theater, "'Priniat' srochnnye mery k ozdorovleniiu': 122–3 (APRF, f. 3, op. 35, d. 24, l. 10–1: Aug. 3, 1935), 125–6 (l. 18–21: Sept. 17), 131–2 (l. 33–4); Artizov and Naumov, *Vlast'*, 265–6, 267–9, 288–9, 327–31 (APRF, f. 3, op. 35, d. 24, l. 45–51: Oct. 11, 1936).

271. The committee was approved on Dec. 16, 1935, and Kerzhentsev named on Jan. 17, 1936. Artizov and Naumov, *Vlast'*, 281 (RGASPI, f. 17, op. 3, d. 973, l. 3); *Pravda*, Jan. 18, 1936. See also Maksimenkov, *Sumbur*, 69 (RGASPI, f. 77, op. 1, d. 557, l. 1). Kerzhentsev must have been glad to escape radio, where the NKVD had turned up "anti-Soviet class alien elements, climbers, and hacks." Goraeva, *Radio Rossii*, 158–9 (APRF, f. 3, op. 35, d. 14, l. 44–60, 70–1: May 9, 1935); RGASPI, f. 17, op. 114, d. 588, l. 9–10. In 1937, Stalin would subordinate the Bolshoi, Maly, Moscow Art Theater, Vakhtangov State Theater, Kirov ballet, and others to the committee. RGASPI, f. 17, op. 114, d. 588, l. 12.

272. Maksimenkov, *Sumbur*, 77–9 (RGALI, f. 962, op. 10, d. 13, l. 12–3). Gorky had reached his wit's end with Shcherbakov ("Literature for him is alien, a secondary matter") and the bureaucratic machinations in the writers' union. Artizov and Naumov, *Vlast'*, 276–8 (RGASPI, f. 73, op. 2, d. 44, l. 17–20: Dec. 8, 1935); Maksimenkov, *Bol'shaia tsenzura*, 413–5 (RGASPI, f. 558, op. 11, d. 720, l. 101–6). In Sept. 1936, Shcherbakov would be sent back to Leningrad as second secretary. He was replaced at the writers' union by Stavsky.

273. Maksimenkov, *Sumbur*, 88–112. Samosud's production of Shostakovich's *Lady*

MacBeth had premiered in Moscow at the Bolshoi affiliate on Dec. 26, 1935, but Stalin had not attended. Soviet press accounts had been ecstatic. A third festival production, *Bright Stream*, also elicited superlatives; Stalin did not see that one either before it had closed. On Jan. 16, 1936—the same day as the government decree appointing Kerzhentsev to the new committee—Stalin, in the company of Kerzhentsev, Molotov, and others, returned for the final performance of *Quiet Flows the Don*. Again he showed himself applauding in the imperial box. Stravinsky would deem the opera *Lady MacBeth* "lamentably provincial." *Pravda* criticized its sympathetic portrait of the murderess. Taruskin, "Opera and the Dictator," 34–40.

274. Artizov and Naumov, *Vlast'*, 307–8 (RGASPI, f. 17, op. 3, d. 976, l. 56). Of the Bolshoi dancers, only Igor Moiseyev (then 30 years old) remained, but the Leningraders commenced intrigues against him. Kerzhentsev enabled him to establish what would become a celebrated folk dance ensemble. Moiseev, *Ia vospominaiu*, 292–4.

275. RGASPI, f. 558, op. 11, d. 829, l. 69–72. *Pravda* (Feb. 29, 1936) celebrated the achievements of Soviet film music.

276. RGALI, f. 962, op. 6, d. 42, l. 6. The NKVD's Molchanov reported that most cultural figures properly understood the *Pravda* article, but named and quoted a number who had reacted with "anti-Soviet" remarks. Artizov and Naumov, *Vlast'*, 290–5 (TsA FSB, f. 3 op. 3, d. 121, l. 31–8: Feb. 11, 1936). Gorky wrote to Stalin (March 1936) complaining of the vicious campaign against Shostakovich. Gorky also complained that the theater of "the genius Meyerhold" semed to exist solely for his lover, the actress Raikh, while the theater of "the genius Tairov" seemed to exist solely for the actress Koonen. Artizov and Naumov, *Vlast'*, 300–2; *Literaturnaia gazeta*, March 10, 1993.

277. Artizov and Naumov, *Vlast'*, 289–90 (APRF, f. 3, op. 35, d. 32, l. 42). See also Maksimenkov, *Sumbur*, 110–2. The day before Shostakovich was received, another attack had appeared in *Pravda* (Feb. 6, 1936) titled "Balletic Falsity" (about *Bright Stream*). See also Glikman, *Pis'ma k drugu*, 317.

278. Artizov and Naumov, *Vlast'*, 308–9 (RGASPI, f. 17, op. 163, d. 1108, l. 125–6: May 19, 1936); Maksimenkov, *Sumbur*, 227–8.

279. On Feb. 18, Bulgakov met with the new Moscow Art Theater director Mikhail Arkadyev, who asked about his next project. Bulgakov, according to his wife, "answered that the sole subject that interested him at the moment was Stalin." This referred to a planned play, *Batum*, likely inspired by recent publications about Stalin's days in the underground. Losev and Ivanovskaia, *Dnevnik Eleny Bulgakovoi*, 112, 114. The critic Osaf Litovsky had mercilessly attacked previews of *Molière* in the journal *Sovetskoe iskusstvo* (Feb. 11, 1936). Other vicious denunciations followed in lesser periodicals by Bulgakov rivals (Alexander Afinogenov, Yuri Olyesha, Vsevolod Ivanov).

280. "'Polozhenie ego deistvitel'noe bezyskhodnoe,'" 117–9 (RGASPI, f. 17, op. 163, d. 1099,l. 96–8: Feb. 29, 1936); Artizov and Naumov, *Vlast'*, 298–300 (otdel rukopisi GPB, f. 562, k. 19, d. 33). See also Sakharov, *Mikhail Bulgakov*, 439. In 1933, Bulgakov had authored a life of Molière in the series *Lives of Remarkable People*, a popular prerevolutionary staple which Gorky and Koltsov had revived, but the manuscript was rejected.

281. *Pravda*, March 9, 1936. (Yelena wrote in her diary: "When we read it, M. A. said, 'the end of *Molière* is the end of *Ivan Vasilevich*.'")

Literaturnai gazeta followed suit (March 10). Kerzhentsev summoned Bulgakov on March 16, an encounter that lasted ninety minutes inside the just opened grandiose new Council of People's Commissars building, on Hunters Row. Elena deemed it a "senseless meeting." Losev and Ivanovskaia, *Dnvenik Eleny Bulgakovy*, 116, 118.

282. Losev and Ivanovskaia, *Dnevnik Eleny Bulgakovoi*, 72, 120–1. Whether the Bulgakovs knew that Kerzhentsev had been the author of the anonymous article against Bulgakov and the ban on his works is unclear. Maksimenkov, *Sumbur*, 184, 187–90. In Sept. 1936, Bulgakov would resign from the Moscow Art Theater and take a nominal position at the Bolshoi as a consultant-librettist, rewriting the illiterate works submitted by Soviet librettists who retained the credit for them.

283. Stalin inserted "in connection with the 20th anniversary of the October Revolution." Artizov and Naumov, *Vlast'*, 295–6 (RGASPI, f. 17, op. 163, d. 1101, l. 65–6).

284. Miller, *Soviet Cinema*, 26–9.

285. *Pravda*, July 3, Aug. 20, 21, and 25, 1935; *Doklad komissii B. Z. Shumiatskogo*, 150; Anderson et al., *Kremlevskii kinoteatr*, 1026–7 (RGASPI, f. 558, op. 11, d. 828, l. 55–56ob.). After Shumyatsky had returned, he wrote to the Council of People's Commissars, on Sept. 29, 1935, requesting hard currency to purchase copies of Charlie Chaplin's *Modern Times*. Molotov indicated it was for the politburo to decide. (Kaganovich wrote on the document: "I do not object, though we should know its content.") It turned out to be a smash hit in the USSR. Anderson et al., *Kremlevskii kinoteatr*, 286–7 (RGASPI, f. 17, op. 163, d. 1082, l. 114–5; op. 3, d. 972, l. 14: Oct. 7, 1935); *Pravda*, Dec. 2, 1935.

286. Stalin, with Svetlana and Vasily present, watched *Girlfriends*, written and directed by Leningrad's Lev Arnstham, with music by Shostakovich. Anderson et al., *Kremlevskii kinoteatr*, 1031–3 (RGASPI, f. 558, op. 11, d. 829, l. 64–6).

287. Shumyatsky explained the enormous efficiencies of having producers for each film and centralized studios—a single Hollywood studio was outproducing all Soviet cinema—and argued that a single location would enable economies of scale and eliminate the costly trips around the USSR in search of sites for each film. Just 45 Soviet films had been completed in 1935, against a plan of 130, and 46 would be made in 1936, against a plan for 165. For its Hollywood, the government settled on the Lapsi valley near Foros in Crimea, with an initial budget of 400 million rubles. Anderson et al., *Kremlevskii kinoteatr*, 312–14 (APRF, f. 3, op. 35, d. 63, l. 23–6: Shumyatsky to Stalin, March 26, 1936), 327 (RGASPI, f. 82, op. 2, d. 958, l. 15, 16: Shumyatsky to Molotov, July 15, 1936); Taylor, "Ideology as Mass Entertainment," 215–6; *Kino*, July 4, 1936: 4.

288. In their letter to Stalin, which he forwarded to Shumyatsky and the politburo, the satirists pointed out that in Hollywood directors did not use natural light anyway, shooting their works on indoor sets. Stalin dismissed their letter as blowing hot air. But Shumyatsky found himself on the receiving end of Kerzhentsev's denunciations for insubordination. Anderson et al., *Kremlevskii kinoteatr*, 302–5 (APRF, f. 3, op. 35, d. 63, l. 23–7: Ilf and Petrov to Stalin, Feb. 26, 1936), 1050–1 (RGASPI, f. 558, op. 11, d. 829, l. 94–6); Deriabin, *Letopis' rossiiskogo kino, 1930–1945*, 399, 408, 419. Hearsay has Beria learning of the proposed construction in Sukhum of a cinema city, and instigating the Ilf and Petrov opposition letter. On Dec. 26, 1935, Chiaureli had screened *The*

Last Masquerade for Stalin, Beria, Svetlana, and Vasily. Anderson et al., *Kremlevskii kinoteatr*, 1033–4 (RGASPI, f. 558, op. 11, d. 828, l. 67–8); Fomin and Deriabin, *Letopis' rossiiskogo kino*, II: 391–2; Minchënok, *Isaak Dunaevskii*, 302–19 (no citations).

289. Ilf and Petrov were in the United States Sept. 19, 1935, to Jan. 22, 1936, and accredited as correspondents of *Pravda*. Ilf, with his Leica, took a wealth of photographs, which he and Petrov published along with eleven light, satirical installments about their travels in the illustrated mass magazine *Ogonyok*. They found ordinary America provincial and ignorant of the outside world. Ilf and Petrov, *Odnoetazhnaia Amerika*; Wolf, *Ilf and Petrov's Road Trip*, 136 (quotation); Ilf and Petrov, "Amerikanskie fotografii"; Rodchenko, "Amerikanskie fotograiia Il'ia Il'fa."; Anderson et al., *Kremlevskii kinoteatr*, 1050–1 (RGASPI, f. 558, op. 11, d. 829, l. 94–6).

290. These data were for Jan. 1, 1937. Zemskov, "GULAG," 11 (GARF, f. 9401, op. 1, d. 4157, l. 201–5), reproduced in Davies et al., *Years of Progress*, 432. Mikoyan had pushed for the construction of large meat factories in Moscow, Leningrad, Orsk, and Semipalatinsk, on the model of Chicago slaughterhouses, and Stalin backed him. The machinery was to be imported from Germany, the labor to come from the Gulag. Pavlov, *Anastas Mikoian*, 73 (citing RGASPI, f. 84, op. 1, d. 135, l. 1–2).

291. Yagoda sent a directive (April 2, 1936) to all camp commandants demanding they combat insect infestation, wash barrack floors and clothes, reduce the interminable queues and food poisonings at mess halls, and ensure that forced laborers, especially skilled ones, were employed properly. Kokurin and Petrov, "Gulag," 113–7. The regime was cutting costs and mortality statistics with mass releases of invalids and the chronically ill, and incentivizing productivity with early release of inmates who earned the designation "shock worker."

292. From inception in 1932 through 1941, Dalstroi would produce 430 tons of pure gold. Shirokov, *Dal'stro*, 141 (citing GAMO, f. R-23ss, op. 1, d. 5, l. 14–5); Khlusov, *Ekonomika Gulaga*, 74–7 (GARF, f. 5446, op. 20a, d. 9496, l. 2–3, 6, 58: Oct. 30, 1937). The steep rise in gold production enabled the USSR to export 411 gold rubles' worth of precious metals between 1932 and 1936. Dohan, "Economic Origins of Soviet Autarky," 610.

293. Khaustov, "Deiatel'nost' organov," 67 (TsA FSB, f. 8os, op. 1, d. 80, l. 39, 51). Yagoda also noted that the ranks of the regular police in 1935 were still only half the total in 1913 (albeit for a somewhat smaller country: no Poland, Baltic states, or Bessarabia). Shearer, "Social Disorder, Mass Repression," 518 (citing GARF, f. 5446, op. 18a, d. 904, l. 2–14).

294. *Paris Midi*, Feb. 28, 1936. This was only Hitler's second interview for the French press, and the first since fall 1933. For a detailed chronology of Nazi foreign policy through 1938, see Jacobsen, *Nationalsozialistische Aussenpolitik*, 765–841.

295. *DBFP*, 2nd series, XVI: 73–7 (Feb. 28, 1936); Toynbee, *Acquaintances*, 279–82; Medlicott, *Britain and Germany*, 24 (C1814/4/18 FO 371/19891). Toynbee was director of studies at Chatham House, at Balliol College, Oxford University, from 1924. McNeill, *Arnold J. Toynbee*. Surits, the Soviet envoy, desperately scoured the German press for any lessening of hostility and wrote to Moscow (late Feb. 1936) that it was widely believed in the diplomatic corps "that German military circles continue to follow a special line in German policy toward the Soviet Union." Abramov, "Osobaia missiia Davida

Kandelaki," 149, (citing AVP RF, f. 082, op. 19, pap. 83, d. 4, l. 36).

296. Ambassador von Moltke reported that Göring's "declaration was received with obvious satisfaction." *DGFP*, series C, IV: 1201–2 (Feb. 26, 1936).

297. Shillony, *Revolt in Japan*; Crowley, *Japan's Quest for Autonomy*, 244–300.

298. Trotsky would seize upon the Roy Howard interview ("the export of revolution is nonsense") to reassert his "gravedigger" portrait of Stalin. *Revolution Betrayed*, 186.

299. *New York World Telegram*, March 4, 1936; *Pravda*, March 5, 1936, reprinted in *Sochineniia*, XIV: 116–31. In mid-March 1936, returning from a trip through Western Europe, Uborevičius held a gathering of the Communist Youth League in the Western province that he expected war in the Far East "at any moment" and that "in this year or the next, or in two to three years, it's unavoidable that we will have an encounter with German fascism. . . . The fascists cannot not unleash war. Without war they cannot long exist." "Dva ochaga opasnosti: vystupeniie komanduiushchego Belorusskim voennym okrugom komandarma 1 ranga I. P. Uborevicha na soveshchanii v Zapadnom obkome VLKSM v 1936 g." See also Erickson, *Soviet High Command*, 397–400.

300. War minister Blomberg and the German brass were apprehensive and instituted extensive air-raid precautions, spreading the anxiety. Hossbach, *Zwischen Weltkrieg und Hitler*, 97–8; Weinberg, *Foreign Policy*, I: 262.

301. Fröhlich, *Tagebücher von Joseph Goebbels*, III/ii: 30 (March 2, 1936).

302. Medlicott, *Britain and Germany*, 24–5 (citing CP73[36], CAB24, 261, extract in FO 371/19889); *DBFP*, 2nd series, XV: 713–36.

303. The German ambassador reported that the war minister, Duff Cooper, had told him "that though the British people were prepared to fight for France in the event of a German incursion into French territory, they would not resort to arms on account of the recent occupation of the German Rhineland." *DGFP*, series C, V: 57–8 (Hoesch, March 9, 1936); *The Times*, March 13, 1936. "With two lunatics like Mussolini and Hitler you can never be sure of anything," Prime Minister Baldwin would observe. "But I am determined to keep the country out of war." Jones, *Diary with Letters*, 191 (April 30, 1936).

304. *DBFP*, 2nd series, XVI: 45–226; Braubach, *Der Einmarch deutscher Truppen*, 26–8; Emmerson, *Rhineland Crisis*, 97–8; Gunsburg, *Divided and Conquered*, 301–1; Bell, *France and Britain*, 205–6; Adamthwaite, *France*, 37–9; Höhne, *Zeit der Illusionen*, 325. "The need, and yet the difficulty, for Britain and France to work in tandem was the dominant feature of Anglo-French relations," one scholar aptly noted of the interwar period. Davis, *Anglo-French Relations*, 189.

305. Kershaw, *Hitler: 1889–1936*, 581–9. The United States did not bother to register a protest.

306. Shirer, *Berlin Diary*, 49–51. The ambassadors of Britain, France, the Soviet Union, and Poland chose not to attend. Dodd and Dodd, *Ambassador Dodd's Diary*, 318 (March 7, 1936). Hitler, at the opera house, had proposed "negotiations" to demilitarize both sides of the Rhine, and yet again offered nonaggression pacts to all and sundry. Then, he dissolved the Reichstag and called for new elections (the Nazis would win a publicly announced 98.7 percent of the vote). Litvinov wrote to Maisky (March 9) castigating the British for rewarding aggressors by intending to enter negotiations with Germany now, pronounced "collective security" and the League of Nations in grave danger, and noted (March 10)

Hitler's finesse in driving a wedge between Britain and France. *DVP SSSR*, XIX: 130, 134.
307. *DDF*, 2e série, II: 15–6 (April 1, 1936).
308. The treaty specified "military aid" in the event of a third-party attack on either country. Article 3 stipulated that troops "will be withdrawn from that territory as soon as the danger is passed, just as took place in 1925 with respect to the withdrawal of Soviet troops." The Soviets published the treaty with a delay, following a major border clash near Tamsagbulag that involved tanks and aircraft. *Izvestiia*, April 8, 1936; Tisminets, *Vneshniaia politika SSSR*, IV: 99–104. The Soviet-Mongolia treaty did not mention Chinese sovereignty over Mongolia (recognized in a 1924 Sino-Soviet agreement) and Chiang Kai-shek's government sent two diplomatic notes of objection. Stalin played it both ways. "No other country except us recognizes Mongolia," Stalin had told Genden. "You are still a part of China. We have no obligation to help you at all." Friters, *Outer Mongolia*, 203–4 (citing *Chinese Year Book*, 1938, 321–2); *China Weekly Review*, April 7, 1936: 227; April 25: 270; Baabar, *Twentieth-Century Mongolia*, 347–8. The treaty was signed by Amar (head of state) and Genden (prime minister), but not long after the signing, Amar displaced Genden, whom the Mongol leadership resolved to send to Moscow as ambassador. Genden, upon arrival, would refuse to take up the post and would be sent to Crimea on "medical leave," effectively taken hostage. RGANI, f. 89, op. 63, d. 21, l. 1–3, and d. 25, l. 1; Dashpürev and Soni, *Reign of Terror in Mongolia*.
309. Stalin's informal adviser Varga had been propagating the thinking that "the imperialists" might go after each other. Varga, "Konets Locarno." Mistakenly, George Kennan surmised that Stalin had decided upon a great purge of the upper ranks (his potential opposition) following the March 1936 German reoccupation of the Rhineland, in order to gain a free hand to deal with Germany. But in foreign policy he already had a free hand, and the terror was not a single decision. Kennan, *Russia and the West*, 286–90. Kennan's argument was repeated by Ulam, *Stalin*, 404–7.
310. *DDF*, 2e série, II: 15–6 (April 1, 1936).
311. Costello and Tsarev, *Deadly Illusions*, 78 (citing FSB archives). See also Sibley, "Soviet Industrial Espionage."
312. *Le Temps*, March 19, 1936; *Izvestiia* (March 24, 1936), reprinted in Molotov, *Stat'i rechi*, 231–3, and *DVP SSSR*, XIX: 166–72. See also Watson, *Molotov*, 133–4. Also in 1936, Eliava, deputy commissar for foreign trade, let on to the Soviet embassy staff in Berlin that in Moscow, "at the top," they evaluate Hitlerism "differently." Gnedin, *Iz istoriia otnoshenii*, 37; Nekrich, *1941*, 23. See also Hilger and Meyer, *Incompatible Allies*, 267–8.
313. Molotov reverted to Georgian at the end: "Gaumardzhos saakartvelos mshromel khakhs!" "Long live the toilers of Georgia!" *Pravda*, March 21, 1936; Molotov, *Velikaia druzhba*, 55–60.
314. Paustovsky, *Story of a Life*, 133–4.
315. Chukovsky, who spoke at the congress, had spotted Pasternak, whom he fetched to take an open seat next to him. Chukovskii, *Dnevnik*, 141 (April 16 and April 22, 1936). See also Baruzdin, "U Kornee Chukovskom," 111–21; Bode, "Humor in the Lyrical Stories"; Luk'ianova, *Kornei Chukovskii*, 624–6. Also in April 1936, Stalin allowed the imprisoned Victor Serge to leave the USSR for the West, despite understanding that Serge would campaign against the Stalinist line, with the credibility of a firsthand observer. His release testified to the importance Stalin attached to the fellow-travelers, especially Rolland. So improbable did Serge's release seem that

Krivitsky, the Soviet spy in the Hague, suspected Serge of being an NKVD plant sent to infiltrate the Trotskyites. But Stalin did not need to pay the cost of international defamation by Serge to infiltrate the Trotskyists; he had already done so. Krivitsky, *MI5 Debriefing*, 40–9 (letter to Boris Nicolaveksy, Paris, Oct. 25, 1938). Like Trotsky, Serge would die in a Mexican villa (in Serge's case, in 1947, of a heart attack, just short of fifty-seven years old).
316. *Pravda's* account omitted Voroshilov's improvisational references to Bolshevik vigilance in the context of filling glasses. Stalin altered the wording for the newspaper of his toast for Voroshilov, eliminating "to the Supreme Leader [*vozhd*'] of the Red Army." There was only one Supreme Leader of the army as well as the country. Nevezhin, "Bol'shie Kremlevskie priemy Stalina" (no. 3), 134–6 (citing RGASPI, f. 74, op. 1, d. 164, l. 206–13); *Pravda*, May 4, 1936; *Krasnaia zvezda*, May 4, 1936.
317. *Voennye arkhivy Rossii*, 62; Isserson, "Zapiski sovremennika o M. N. Tukhachevskom," 73–5; Vinogradov, "1937: pokazaniia marshala Tukhachevskogo," (no. 9), 63. "The neutrality of the Baltic states plays a very dangerous role for us," Tukhachevsky would explain at length in prison in 1937, and underscore the need for a proper base far better than Kronstadt on the Baltic. He would add that "war against Finland presents a completely independent problem, difficult to a sufficient degree for us." Vinogradov, "1937: pokazaniia marshala Tukhachevskogo" (no. 8) 48 (no. 9), 62.
318. Tukhachevsky replaced Alexander Sedyakin, who had been the subject of relentless criticism, not least from Tukhachevsky himself. Ken, *Mobilizatsionnoe planirovanie*, 350. More broadly, see Gareev, "Ob opyte boevoi podgotovki voisk."
319. Vinogradov, "1937: pokazaniia marshala Tukhachevskogo," (no. 8), 48 (between May 26 and June 10, 1937). If, in 1914, the tsarist army foresaw 360 train cars per day for its mobilization goals in the West (the number would reach 560 per day by 1917), the USSR in the mid-1930s in the western theater could perhaps count on 436 per day. Menning, "Sovetskie zheleznye dorogi," 363.
320. Simonov, *Voenno-promyshlennyi kompleks SSSR*, 91–2; Reese, *Stalin's Reluctant Soldiers*; Mawdsley, review of Roger Reese, *War in History*, 7/3 (2000): 375–7. Despite the vast buildup, some exhibited a startling lack of confidence. "Of course, the USSR is not prepared to fight a war, neither politically nor economically, we need to gain at least three to five years," Ivan Kutyakov, deputy commander of the Volga military district, had written in his diary (Jan. 9, 1936). Viktorov, *Bez grifa "sekretno,"* 258–9.
321. Stalin had met with Tukhachevsky six times in 1931, eight times in 1932, seven times in 1933, twice in 1934, and three times in 1935. Stalin again received him on July 21, 1935, with Voroshilov and Yegorov, among others. *Na prieme*, 154, 718. In April 1936, *Banner of Russia*, a Russian-language monthly published by the emigration in Prague, concluded a sensational four-part series about "Kraskomov," said to be a clandestine organization of Red Army commanders plotting a putsch. The April issue offered responses to letters received doubting Kraskomov's existence and wondering, if it did exist, why *Banner of Russia* would expose it. A military coup to save Russia from Communism was a long-standing fantasy of the emigration, which was penetrated by the Soviet secret police. Lukes, *Czechoslovakia between Stalin and Hitler*, 92–4; *Znamia Rossii*, Dec. 1935, Feb., March,

and April 1936. In parallel, Voroshilov had received a convoluted secret report that insinuated a "secret connection" between Red Army and Nazi military circles which would enable the Germans to bring forth a "friendly" regime in Moscow. The report, said to be by a White Russian officer for the French General Staff, had been shared with the Czechoslovak staff, which, in turn, passed it to Moscow. Samuelson, *Plans for Stalin's War Machine*, 185–6 (RGVA, f. 33987, op. 3, d. 740, l. 170–5: Dec. 6–7, 1935).
322. The trade protocol was signed on April 29, 1936. *DGFP*, series C, V: 488–94. See also Ericson, *Feeding the German Eagle*, 35–6; and *DGFP*, series C, IV: 1009–10 (Jan. 18, 1936). On April 19, Litvinov had fretted to Surits in Berlin that any new large trade deal with Germany would alienate France and "play into Hitler's hands." Abramov, "Osobaia missiia Davida Kandelaki," 149 (citing AVP RF, f. 010, op. 11, pap. 68, d. 34, l. 85 –7).
323. Bessonov's offer included walking back criticism (made by Litvinov in Geneva) of the Rhineland militarization. *DGFP*, series C, V: 512 (Andor Hencke: May 6, 1936). Bessonov was accompanied by Yevgeny Gnedin, who would later falsely deny the involvement of himself or the foreign affairs commissariat in efforts to win over Nazi Germany. Gnedin, *Katastrofa i votrooe rozhdenie*, 34–5. Andor Hencke had been German consul in Kiev, and witnessed the famine.
324. Schacht, who was trying to rein in expenditures and inflation, miscalculated in suggesting Göring's appointment. Overy, *Göring*, 40. Stalin had received Kandelaki without foreign affairs commissariat personnel on March 16, 1936; again, five days later, with a slew of police, intelligence, and military men; and finally, with Litvinov and Stomonyakov on April 4. *Na prieme*, 181, 183.
325. *DGFP*, series C, V: 571–3 (May 20, 1936).
326. Niclauss, *Die Sowjetunion*, 192 (citing Dirksen report, May 19, 1936).
327. *DGFP*, series C, V: 572.
328. Dembski, "Pol'sko-Sovetskie otnosheniia," 196–7 (citing *Akten zur Deutschen Auswärtigen Politik [ADAP]*, series C, VI/1: doc. 341); and Archiwum Akt Nowych, Warszawa, MSZ, Kabinet Ministra, 108, A.T. II, k. 47–8). Germany remained in arrears on paying transit costs for freight through the Polish Corridor, owing to hard currency shortages. On May 22, 1935, during a monologue with Polish ambassador Lipski, Hitler alluded to the need to build a railroad through the Polish Corridor, according to the Polish record—information Stalin received. Morozov, *Pol'sko-Chekhoslovatskie otnosheniia*, 242 (citing AVP RF, f. 02, op. 1, d. 35, l. 162–9: Lipski from Berlin, May 27, 1935). Von Moltke had broached the railroad idea to Beck back on May 26, 1934. Wojciechowski, *Stosunki polsko-niemieckie*, 200–1, 232.
329. Golubev et al., *Rossiia i zapad*, 157 (citing RGASPI, f. 78, op. 1, d. 636, l. 73). Leopold Trepper, the military intelligence operative, recalled Berzin saying that "here we talk the whole time about the Nazi threat, but it is envisioned as something very far off." Trepper, *Bol'shaia igra*, 79.
330. Robertson, "Hitler and Sanctions." Mussolini had given approval for Hitler's Rhineland remilitarization in advance.
331. The British, despite everything, were still trying to restart negotiations for an air-force arms limitation agreement with Germany. The Italians had mobilized half a million men and lost just 3,000 killed. On May 5 Italian troops took Addis Adaba. Bosworth, *Mussolini's Italy*, 396–7. Ethiopia never officially surrendered. On June 18, 1936, Britain would end the limited economic sanctions imposed

in 1935. The Soviet Union, along with China, the United States, and three others, would not recognize Italy's annexation. Italy would use far more aerial bombing and chemical weapons in Ethiopia *after* the nine-month war of conquest, during the period of "rule."

332. Medlicott, *Britain and Germany*, 26–7 (citing C3662–3/4/18 FO 371/19905). The remark is absent from the German record: *DGFP*, series C, V: 547–9 (May 14).

333. Weinberg, *Foreign Policy*, I: 363 (citing U.S., 1936, I: 300–1).

334. Sats, *Sketches from My Life*, 210–27. Attendance at opening night "was poor," the composer lamented to himself, and it "failed to attract much attention"—a problem of venue. Prokofiev, *Autobiography*, 89.

335. Morrison, *People's Artist*, 29–49. See also Morrison, *Sergey Prokofiev and His World*. Prokofyev would compose a series of "mass songs" (op. 66, 79, 89), adapting the lyrics of poets who were in favor, and in 1939 the oratorio *Zdravitsa* or Hail to Stalin (op. 85).

336. The orchestra portrayed the decadent world that the woman leaves behind, a trope borrowed from Chaplin's *Modern Times*. A black doll was used for the infant son. During the filming of Marion Dixon's escape from the American troupe, Orlova tripped on the slag under the railroad tracks, ripping her stockings and skirt and bloodying her knees. She got up and shouted, "Is the baby alive?" The film's long-gestating appearance coincided with the opening of an outdoor cinema in Moscow's Gorky Park called "Giant," which had a three-story screen and a 400-watt imported sound system (instead of the usual Soviet-made 8–10 watts), and which could hold up to 20,000 people on wooden benches. Salys, *Films of Grigorii Aleksandrov*, 5, 123–200; Taylor, "Illusion of Happiness"; Kushnirov, *Svetlyi put'*, 145–6; Malkov, "Charlie Chaplin i Dunaevskii."

337. Kuromiya, *Freedom and Terror*, 184–200.

338. RGASPI, f. 558, op. 11, d. 829, l. 84–5; Pyr'ev, *Izbrannye proizvedeniia*, I: 74–5. Stalin, after previewing the film (Feb. 28), had introduced a new denouement whereby Anna learns of the villain's dark past and turns a gun on him, at which point the local party chief tells us the villain had killed the Communist Youth League activist and is a foreign spy, and the NKVD escort him away. The film would be shown in the United States beginning in July. After the film, Pyryev was suspended by Mosfilm, for reasons that are unclear, but managed to relocate to Ukraine. Iurenev, introduction to *Ivan Pyr'ev v zhizni i na ekrane*, at 32.

339. RGASPI, f. 17, op. 162, d. 19, l. 78 (Feb. 27, 1936); "O tak nazyvaemom 'antissovetskom ob'edinennomm Trotskistsko-Zinov'evskom tsentre," 83 (Léopold, March 25, 1936); no. 9: 35 (Vyshinsky's comment to Stalin on Yagoda's letter, March 31).

340. Khaustov et al., *Lubianka: Stalin i VChK*, 753 (APRF, f. 3, op. 24, d. 223, l. 1–2: April 29, 1936). The ones found with Trotsky's *Bulletin* were Eduard Goltsman and A. N. Safonova.

341. Khaustov et al., *Lubianka: Stalin i VChK*, 756 (APRF, f. 3, op. 24, d. 224, l. 130); RGASPI, f. 17, op. 162, d. 19, l. 172.

342. Khaustov et al., *Lubianka: Stalin i VChK*, 757–63 (APRF, f. 3, op. 24, d. 225, l. 71–86).

343. RGASPI, f. 17, op. 2, d. 572, l. 34ob.–35; APRF, f. 3, op. 22, d. 150, l. 129; Davies et al., *Years of Progress*, 301–2.

344. *Pravda*, June 5, 1936.

345. Getty and Naumov, *Road to Terror*, 231–5 (RGASPI, f. 17, op. 2, d. 572, l. 67–73).

346. Gorky visited his son's grave on May 27, 1936. Stalin managed to see Gorky on June 8 and June 12. Maksimenkov, *Bol'shaia*

tsenzura, 420 (RGASPI, f. 558, op. 11, d. 720, l. 121); *Rossiiskaia gazeta*, June 17, 2011. Mekhlis had written to Stalin (May 27) that Gorky had submitted an article for *Pravda*, "The History of the Young Person in the 19th Century," which he judged full of philosophical issues that "raise doubts." Stalin ordered Mekhlis to publish the essay without changes. Maksimenkov, *Bol'shaia tsenzura*, 418 (citing RGASPI, f. 558, op. 11, d. 720, l. 119).

347. *Pravda*, June 21, 1936; Artizov and Naumov, *Vlast'*, 310 (RGASPI, f. 17, op. 3, d. 978, l. 55); Yedlin, *Maxim Gorky*, 214.

348. Artizov and Naumov, *Vlast'*, 310 (RGASPI, f. 17, op. 3, d. 978, l. 55); *Letopis' zhizni i tvorchestva A. M. Gor'kogo*, IV: 599. Gorky had requested in his will to be buried next to his son. Shentalinsky, *Arrested Voices*, 276.

349. MacNeal, *Stalin*, 206; Tucker, *Stalin in Power*, 364.

350. Shentalinsky, *Arrested Voices*, 274.

351. The most authoritative study of Gorky's death, by the then head of IMLI, inclined towards natural causes, without ruling out foul play: Barakhov, "M. Gor'kii," 191. Gorky had returned to Moscow from his dacha in Tesseli, Crimea, on May 26, 1936. Malraux had visited Gorky at Tesseli March 7–10, in the company of Koltsov, who wrote of Gorky: "He was not well." Babel, also present, found Gorky alone and depressed. *Letopis' zhizni i tvorchestva A. M. Gor'kogo*, IV: 575–6, 586–93, 600–1; Shentalinsky, *Arrested Voices*, 269. Koltsov had conveyed a request from Malraux to see Stalin; Stalin chose not to grant an audience. Maksimenkov, *Bol'shaia tsenzura*, 411–2 (RGASPI, f. 558, op. 11, d. 754, l. 77–77ob.).

352. Kuskova, "Na rubezhe dvukh epoch." Carr, in an obituary in the *Spectator* (June 26, 1936), wrote that "posterity will not place Gorky with Dostoevsky, Chekhov and Tolstoy." See also Schroeder, *Mit der Menschheit auf Du und Du*, 83–5; and Trotsky, *Portraits*, 160–3 (July 9, 1936). That same day, Gide lunched with Babel and Eisenstein in Babel's Moscow apartment. Gide praised the USSR to the skies, but after he left, according to an informant for the NKVD, Babel said, "Do not believe the rapture. He is cunning, like the devil . . . Upon return to France he could conjure up some devilish piece." Artizov and Naumov, *Vlast'*, 316–8 (TsA FSB, f. 3, op. 3, d. 65, l. 225–8: July 5, 1936). Mikhail Apletin, the head of all-Union society of foreign cultural ties, noted of Gide, "he's not a simple writer like Rolland." Clark, *Moscow*, 140 (RGALI, f. 631, op. 14, d. 5, l. 18).

353. Kotkin, "Modern Times."

354. Vastly increased organization of society by the state under Stalin was one of the main reasons for the marked increase in his state's capacity. Kotkin, *Magnetic Mountain*. Hannah Arendt's characterization of the Nazi and Soviet regimes as almost condemned "to organize everyone and everything within its framework and to set and keep them in motion" was apt. Arendt, *Origins of Totalitarianism*, 361, 326. Barrington Moore noted the coincidence in Soviet politics of heavy coercion and grass-roots activism. Moore, *Soviet Politics*, 403. See also Gelb, "Mass Politics under Stalin."

355. Kasza, *Conscription Society*. See also Straus, *Factory and Community*. Generally, in U.S. social science, the effective organization of society has been viewed in terms of self-organization (nonstate), for example in the influential work of Robert Putnam, but as Sheri Berman points out, civic organizations served as an important vehicle for the spread and institutionalization of the Nazi movement, and did not cease to exist under the Nazis. Putnam, *Bowling Alone*; Sheri Berman, "Civil Society."

In his critique of the state's utopian aspirations in so-called "high modernism," which effectively places forced collectivization on the same plane as surveys of land use, James Scott writes about the failure of society to resist, rather than its thorough organization in state-led crusades. Scott, *Seeing Like a State*, 89.

356. Pre-1914 France had managed to get tsarist Russia to build strategic railroads to the border with imperial Germany in exchange for rolling over massive economic development loans. Rieber, "Persistent Factors," 328.

357. Arnason, "Communism and Modernity."

358. Tsarism's executive branch was in theory autocratic but was moved—or not—by the operation of patronage networks. Only a strong-willed person at or near the top could impose direction and energy, and usually only for limited periods. Many tsarist loyalists had objected in principle to a strong government, detesting Witte and Stolypin; they wanted firm rule led only by the autocrat himself. But Nicholas II went into audiences with his ministers without seeking to be briefed beforehand, and, suspecting them of sabotage, worked to divide them. The tsar, one scholar has noted, "had his own interest in preserving the very confusion in government that was to be remedied." Even an audience did not translate into effective action. Orlovsky, *Limits of Reform*, 125; Kuropatkin, *Dnevnik A. N. Kuropatkina*, 53 (conversation with Plehve); Yaney, "Some Aspects of the Imperial Russian Government," 88–9; Khristoforov, *Aristokraticheskaia oppozitsiia Veilkim reformam*, 300.

359. The tsarist department of police had no more than 10,000 informants across its entire history, a scale the Soviets would dwarf. Lauchlan, *Russian Hide and Seek*, 133, 203. For perceptive comments on the Leninist revolutionary disposition and social engineering, see Massell, *Surrogate Proletariat*, 39–40.

360. Kotkin, *Magnetic Mountain*, 198–237.

361. Pokrovsky in his 1927 *Essays on the History of the October Revolution* wrote that the revolution had been the only way to avoid "the colonization of Russia by Anglo-American capital." *Ocherki po istorii oktiabr'skoi revoliutsii*, II, 447–8. See also Agursky, "The Bolshevik Revolution as a Revolution of National Liberation."

362. Baynes, *Speeches of Adolf Hitler*, II: 1312–3 (March 20, 1936); Bullock, *Hitler*, 404.

363. Stalin also said to Howard that "public [obshchestvennye] organizations, which we have created, may be called Soviet, socialist organizations even though they are not yet completed, but they are the root of the socialist organization of the public." *Pravda*, March 5, 1936. De Tocqueville had dismissed the authoritarians who, hiding behind constitutional facades, cherished "the illusion that they can combine the prerogatives of absolute power with the moral authority that comes from popular assent." De Tocqueville, *Old Regime and the French Revolution*, 45. Mobilization of the masses lay behind the claim of Giovanni Gentile, the fascist ideologue, for the superiority of Italian fascism over a parliamentary liberal order. Gentile, "Philosophical Basis of Fascism." In Lenin's vision of the party, the militant vanguard became meaningful if linked to a militant people. Miliukov, in emigration, would pay Stalin a backhanded compliment: "If, contrary to the American saying, Stalin succeeded in cheating the whole people the whole time, it was because people wished to be deceived." Tucker, *Political Culture and Leadership in Soviet Russia*, 39; P. N. Miliukov, "From Nicholas II to Stalin: Half a Century of Foreign Politics," typescript (n.d.), 334, Hoover Institution Archives.

364. George Mosse argued that the massification of politics threatened anarchy, but that the masses were shaped into a manageable political body by nationalist symbols and liturgy, a key challenge for liberal orders, too. He went too far in asserting that "parliamentary republics were naturally unable to construct effective representations of themselves, just as they failed to create national festivals.'" Mosse, *Nationalization of the Masses*, 72.

365. A March 30, 1936, secret report for Maurice Gamelin warned bleakly of low morale and high Communist subversion among the French troops. Gamelin sent it to Daladier with a warning that France was coming to resemble Spain. Jackson, "French Strategy" (citing SHAT, 7N 4034–1, "Eta d'esprit de l'armée, April 1, 1936).

366. Rieber, "Persistent Factors," 336–7.

367. Khaustov and Samuelson, *Stalin, NKVD*, 93. In Odessa in 1934, a single Trotskyite "group" was unmasked; in 1935, suddenly, thirty-one such groups were found.

PART II. TERROR AS STATECRAFT

1. Kollontai added: "If I don't fall 'underneath the wheel,' it will be almost a miracle." Vaksberg, *Alexandra Kollontai*, 393; Farnsworth, "Conversing with Stalin," 944 (citing RGASPI, f. 134, op. 3, d. 62, l. 6).

2. "A hero ventures forth from the world of common day into a region of supernatural wonder," Campbell wrote. "Fabulous forces are there encountered and a decisive victory is won: the hero comes back from this mysterious adventure with the power to bestow boons on his fellow man." Campbell, *Hero with a Thousand Faces*, 30.

3. One of Bukharin's works, "Toward a Theory of the Imperialist State" [1916], which influenced Lenin, had argued that a "militaristic state capitalism" would produce a "new Leviathan, in comparison with which the fantasy of Thomas Hobbes seems like child's play." He denied socialism could lead to this result because "socialism is the regulation of production directed by *society*, not by the state." Needless to say, his new Leviathan ("absorbing within the domain of state management everyone and everything") had turned out to fit the Soviet state. Bukharin, "K teorii imprialisticheskogo gosudarstva," 5–32. See also Harding, "Authority, Power and the State," 32–56. Daniels, "The State and Revolution"; and Cohen, *Bukharin*, 39–40.

4. A typical absolution of Marx from the Soviet catechism is Dalrymple, "Marx and Agriculture." The distance between Stalin and Marx was one of time period and context. "Everyone who contradicted him, he treated with abject contempt," one of Marx's fellow radicals, Carl Schurz, a student radical from Bonn (later a U.S. senator), wrote of their first meeting in Cologne in 1848. "Every argument that he did not like he answered either with biting scorn at the unfathomable ignorance that had prompted it, or with opprobrious aspersions upon the motives of him who had advanced it." McLellan, *Karl Marx*, 15 (1909 memoir).

5. Self-styled socialists in the nineteenth century, initially, had employed other terms—"the anti-social system," "the system of bourgeois property"—but then hit upon this single all-encompassing notion whose essence (property relations, a mode of production), if replaced, would supposedly alter not merely the economy but the entire world, delivering abundance, social justice, and peace. The invention of "capitalism" was a stunning achievement for the socialists, in a way, but a tragedy for humanity, and ultimately, for the entire left, too. Unlike Leninists, Social Democrats were never sure whether this "capitalism" would implode on its own, could be peacefully overcome inside parliaments by large worker-majority parties, or in the end required revolutionary intervention, but it had to go. Those Social Democrats who came to believe that "capitalism" was amenable to becoming more humane—capitalism with a human face—opened themselves up to accusations of being accomplices to exploitation and imperialism.

6. Hegel stated in a series of lectures published posthumously (1837): "But even regarding History as the slaughter-bench [*Schlachtbank*] at which the happiness of peoples, the wisdom of States, and the virtue of individuals have been victimized—the question involuntarily arises—to what principle, to what final aim these enormous sacrifices have been offered." The answer was not Hegel's Reason or World Spirit but misbegotten ideas. Hegel, *Lectures on the Philosophy of History*. Hegel's lectures were published in Russian translation in 1932 as vols. IX and X of his *Works* by Partizdat.

7. In Marxism-Leninism, only one set of interests can be legitimate, the "proletariat's," the rest are ipso facto expressions of the "wrong" class interests, a stricture that effectively excludes lawful politics. But politics is how different groups, interests, and opinions are represented and allowed to compete via peaceful means, and with institutional restraint. Crick, *In Defence of Politics*, 28. More broadly, the idea that a self-appointed elite has the right, even the duty, to coerce a population for the latter's benefit is beyond pernicious. That the destruction of whole "classes" can somehow produce freedom is beyond folly. Systemic prevarication and political murder in the name of some supposed higher humanity get institutionalized. Chamberlin, *Evolution of a Conservative*, 13.

8. Carr defended Stalin's bloody revolution from above because it was the only way to build socialism (a system not based on private property and markets), which was true, but also because it enabled the socialist state to defend itself in the rapacious international order. A self-styled realist, Carr understood he was defending a morally repugnant system, but in his eyes capitalism had failed, while state planning and collectivization had appeared to succeed, against expectations. It also helped that socialism's extreme violence and waste could be attributed to inevitable birth pangs that would pass, while capitalism's crisis was seen as permanent. Wohlforth, "Russian-Soviet Empire," at 226. See also Jonathan Haslam, "We Need a Faith," 37.

9. Robert Caro has argued that Lyndon Johnson had a "hunger for power not to improve the lives of others but to manipulate and dominate them, to bend them to his will in a hunger so fierce and consuming that no consideration of morality or ethics, no cost to himself—or to anyone else—could stand before it." Of course, Johnson was head of the Senate and then president in a constitutional order. Caro, *Path to Power*, xix.

10. Much escaped Stalin's attention, obviously. And yet, nothing was too trivial to be brought to him by someone, or for him to involve himself. "People say that the square on the Arbat (where there used to be a church, in front of the cinema) has not yet been paved with blocks (or asphalt)," he wrote to Kaganovich (September 24, 1931) from Sochi. "Shameful! One of the busiest squares and it is full of potholes! Pressure them and make them finish up the square." Khlevniuk et al., *Stalin i Kaganovich*, 117 (RGASPI, f. 81, op. 3, d. 99, l. 38).

11. Sometimes the underlining in documents was done by an aide. Sometimes the underlining. Much is not underlined. Volkognov, *Triumf i tragediia*, I/i: 221, I/ii: 141, II/ii: 153; Khlevniuk, *Stalin; Zhizn'*, 144–5.

12. "He wrote everything himself," Molotov would recall. "The staff never wrote for him.

This was a Leninist tradition. Zinoviev wrote for himself, Kamenev, too, not to mention Trotsky." Chuev, *Molotov Remembers*, 168. Stalin's style borrowed from the catechism approach of his seminary training, and was well suited for agitation among the lower orders, including non-native speakers, where he had cut his teeth.

13. Brooks, "Thank You, Comrade Stalin!," 83–105. "What more is there to ask when there is Soviet power; when exploitation, oppression, lack of rights, and slavery have been abolished forever; when there is the party of Lenin-Stalin, a worker-peasant government, which exists only to make an abundant, joyful, and happy life for millions of working people—the men and women of the new socialist society," a group of female shock workers were quoted in *Pravda* (March 11, 1936). "We are obliged to you, our own dear Iosif Vissarionovich." *Pravda*, March 11, 1936. "Our republic," the writer Mikhail Prishvin had written in his diary in mid-1929, "resembles a photographic dark room, in which not a single ray of light is admitted from the outside, but inside everything is illuminated by a red lantern." Prishvin, *Dnevniki*, VI: 432 (July 22, 1929).

14. Simonov, *Glazami cheloveka moego pokoleniia*, 65 (Feb. 27, 1979).

15. Rees, "Leader Cults," at 22.

16. Goebbels intuited that "genius" was fine, but a leader needed to be in touch with the pulse of the people. Kershaw, "Hitler Myth," 59. See also Volkognov, *Triumf i tragediia*, I/ii: 308.

17. Lewin, *Making of the Soviet System* (1985, 1994).

18. In 1935 the regime had stepped up the deportations of certain ethnics and convicted criminals, increased the size of the NKVD border guards, and erected forbidden zones along the western border, sometimes more than ten miles wide, removing people and installing barbed wire, watch towers, and strips of raked land in which footprints could be spotted. Dullin, *La frontière épaisse*, 206. See also Erickson, *Soviet High Command*, 406–7; and Chandler, *Institutions of Isolation*, 55–66; and *XVII s"ezd*, 71–3.

19. "The Bolsheviks can satisfy the characteristic human striving for a purposeful and significant life, man's natural craving to transcend the humdrum routine of daily life, to give his activities a purpose more than personal." Gurian, *Bolshevism*. See also Stern, "National Socialism as Temptation," 151.

20. Garros et al., *Intimacy and Terror*, 206 (Galina Shtange). See also Overy, *Dictators*, 54–5.

21. Jasny, *Soviet Industrialization*.

22. Vagts, "Capitalist Encirclement," 506. See also *Izvestiia*, March 21, 1937: 2 (Zhdanov).

23. An entry on the "Inquisition" in the *Great Soviet Encyclopedia* that happened to appear in 1937 noted that "during just eighteen years under the principal Spanish Inquisitor Torquemada, more than 10,000 people were burned alive." *Bol'shaia Sovetskaia entsiklopediia* (1937), XXVIII: 510–2.

24. Soviet terror statistics are suspect, of course, but still indicate orders of magnitude. We will never know how many of those beaten to death during interrogations were recorded

as dying from heart attacks, for example. Officially, executions were almost evenly distributed between the horrific years of 1937 (353,074) and 1938 (328,618). The number included both political and common crimes. These two years accounted for 91 percent of all the death sentences for political crimes handed down between 1921 and 1940. GARF, f. 9041, op. 1, d. 4517, l. 201–5 (report of late 1953); Vinogradov, *Genrikh Iagoda*, 26; Lukianov, "Massovye represii opravdany byt' ne mogut," 120 (data presented by a commission in 1962–3); Popov, "Gosudarstvennyi terror"; Ellman, "Soviet Repression Statistics"; Khaustov, "Deiatel'nost' organov," 477–8 (TsA FSB, f. 8, op. 1, d. 80, l. 57–8, 61–2). The number 1.575 million does not include arrests by the regular police (militia).
25. Davies, "Soviet Economy," 11–37.
26. Davies, *Popular Opinion*, 35.
27. Many Soviet collective farmers preferred bribing the capitalists, with grain or whatever it took, to avoid war, and some were reportedly even ready to pay double tax if that meant war could be avoided for sure. *'Esli mir obrushitsia na nashu Respubliku,'* 125 (citing TsDOOSO, f. 4, op. 5, d. 87, l. 111).
28. Conquest, *Stalin's Purge*. "The nature of the whole purge depends in the last analysis on the personal and political drives of Stalin." Conquest, *Reassessment*, 33. "The Soviet Union one sees in the archives is perfectly recognizable to people who have tried to understand it from the open sources alone," wrote Joseph Berliner. Gregory, *Behind the Façade*, 6.
29. Gerschenkron, "On Dictatorship."
30. Rees, "Stalin as Leader, 1937–1953," 202–3.
31. Medvedev, *Let History Judge*, 585. Volkgonov largely echoed Medvedev. Lars Lih argued that Stalin pursued an "anti-bureaucratic scenario," but also that Stalin recognized the necessity of the state, an unresolved paradox. Lih, Introduction to *Stalin's Letters to Molotov*, 1–63.

32. Trotsky, *Stalin*; Tucker, *Stalin in Power*; Lewin, "Stalin in the Mirror of the Other," 120. This represents a considerable improvement on the traditional Trotskyite formulation, whereby, in the misguided words of Deutscher, Stalin's "own behaviour was now dictated by the moods, needs, and pressures of the vast political machine." Deutscher, *Stalin*, 226–7.
33. Kuromiya, *Stalin*; Kuromiya, "Stalin in the Politburo Transcripts," 41–56; Kuromiya, *Freedom and Terror*; van Ree, *Political Thought*; Rees, *Political Thought from Machiavelli to Stalin*. Harris depicted Stalin as a consummate misperceiver who never adequately understood that his own central policies were driving the phenomena he hated and struggled against—and so he murdered everyone. Harris, "Encircled by Enemies." This misperception differs markedly from Harris's earlier assertion that the terror arose "not because of the opposition to collectivization, high-tempo industrialization, or the leadership of Stalin," but because regional officials, struggling to cope, had engaged in deception, blame-shifting, and scapegoating, which Stalin suddenly discovered—as if he had not known about inflated production reports before, and as if he needed such a pretext to attack. Harris, *Great Urals*, 189–90.
34. Ulam, "Price of Sanity," 133.
35. Without embarrassment, Yuri Zhukov has asserted that the terror was forced upon a reluctant Stalin by regional officials, making Stalin a victim (meanwhile, all those who allegedly forced his hand were cremated). Zhukov, *Inoi Stalin*. J. Arch Getty has even suggested that the terror was provoked by "tensions" between the center and periphery, and fallout from genuine efforts to introduce democracy, a crackpot assertion he shares with Zhukov. "[I]t was a purely domestic event (the 1937 electoral campaign) that sparked the terror," argued Getty, who added that the terror operations were "unplanned,

ad hoc reactions to a perceived immediate political threat." Getty, "'Excesses are not permitted.'" See also Manning, "Government in the Soviet Countryside"; Getty, "State and Society."
36. Kotkin, "Conspiracy So Immense."
37. Kotkin, *Magnetic Mountain*, 286.
38. According to the recollections of S. Yakubovsky, the phrase "Stalin is the Lenin of our day" arose at an editorial meeting of *Pravda*. Lel'chuk, "Beseda I. V. Stalina s angliiskim pisatelem G. Uellsom," 345.
39. Scholars have identified a "dictator's dilemma": the more power the dictator has, the less sure he can be of the loyalty of subordinates. Wintrobe, *Political Economy of Dictatorship*, 20. In all authoritarian regimes, the ruler perceives the only path to securing his rule is an expansion of his power at the expense of elites (who, in theory, can remove him). That said, elite palace coups are hard, whereas the ruler enjoys greater opportunity to behave opportunistically, or cut back the degree of power-sharing or collective decision making, and, once his power passes a certain point, rebellion becomes near impossible and participation in decision making shrinks or even vanishes. Svolik, *Politics of Authoritarian Rule*. Machiavelli had argued that those who lead a country have more to fear from the scheming elites than from the populace, and therefore he advised a leader to form an alliance with the people against the aristocracy.
40. "The frenzy with which [Stalin] pursued the feud, making it the paramount preoccupation of international communism as well as of the Soviet Union and subordinating to it all political, tactical, intellectual, and other interests, beggars description," Deutscher would write. "There is in the whole of history hardly another case in which such immense resources of power and propaganda were employed against a single individual." Deutscher, *Prophet Outcast*, 125–6. See also Szamuely, "Elimination of Opposition," 323.

CHAPTER 6. ON A BLUFF

1. Trotsky, *Fourth International* 2, no. 5 (1941): 150–4, reprinted in Trotsky, *Writings of Leon Trotsky, 1936–1937*.
2. Payne, *Collapse of the Spanish Republic*, 175–7. There would be some runoffs, reruns, and shifts in coalition allegiance, altering the totals.
3. On the problems of Spain's democracy, some of them analogous to the situation in late Weimar Germany, see Payne, *Spain's First Democracy*; and Preston, "Explosive Experiment." Stalin might have received an intelligence warning about the Spanish generals' plotting in April 1936. Mereshcheriakov, "SSSR i grazhdanskaia voina v Ispanii," 84, no citation. Spanish conspirators had informed the British foreign office, in late May 1936, of an intention "to restore law and order," that is, overthrow the Popular Front in favor of "a civilian, right-wing government." The British cabinet, discussing Spain on July 6, knew a coup was imminent. Volodarsky, *Stalin's Agent*, 143 (citing PRO FO 371, file 20522, documents W4919 and W5693; records of the cabinet office, minutes, file 85); Coverdale, *Italian Intervention*, 60.
4. Thomas, *Spanish Civil War*, 900; Preston, *Spanish Holocaust*.
5. This argument has been advanced by Khlevniuk and reinforced by Kuromiya, but rightly rejected by Rees. Khlevniuk, "Objectives of the Great Terror"; Khlevniuk, *Master of the House*, 173 (citing APRF, f. 3, op. 65, d. 223, l. 90, 141–2, 146); Khlevniuk, "Reasons for the 'Great Terror'"; Kuromiya,

"Accounting for the Great Terror"; Rees, "Stalin as Leader, 1937–1953."
6. Khaustov et al., *Lubianka: Stalin i VChK*, 764–5 (APRF, f. 3, op. 24, d. 226, l. 159–61). The innermost circle—Kaganovich, Voroshilov—privately expressed their support to Stalin, at his prompting, for the annihilation of "low-lifes" such as Dreitser and Pikel. Khlevniuk et al., *Stalin i Kaganovich*, 627 (RGASPI, f. 558, op. 11, d. 743, l. 53: Kaganovich to Stalin, July 6, 1936); Kvashonkin, *Sovetskoe rukovodstvo*, 333–4 (RGASPI, f. 74, op. 2, d. 37, l. 104–6: Voroshilov to Stalin, July 9, 1936).
7. Volodarsky, *Stalin's Agent*, 216. Publicly, Stalin did not comment much on Spain. Many military intelligence reports from Spain were addressed to Voroshilov. Radosh et al., *Spain Betrayed*, 58–63 (Sept. 25, 1936), 63–5 (Oct. 16, 1936), 66–70 (Oct. 16, 1936). A mass of documents regarding Spain in the so-called Politburo or Presidential Archive were addressed to Kaganovich (and sometimes Molotov) in Stalin's absence, but Stalin's voluminous holiday correspondence with Kaganovich does not elucidate his motives on Spain. Crucially, there is no Dimitrov diary from Jan. 31, 1935, to Aug. 19, 1936, or Sept. 21 to Nov. 22, 1936, when Dimitrov and his wife were on holiday.
8. Some scholars have asserted that Stalin followed all events in Spain closely and read every single document on the country. Mereshcheriakov, "SSSR i grazhdanskaia voina v Ispanii," 87 (no citation); Novikov, *SSSR, Komintern*, II: 7; Sarin and Dvoretsky, *Alien Wars*, 3. In fact, as the Russian analyst

Rybalkin noted, "Stalin's position in relation to the Spanish Republic was unpredictable and changed depending on his mood and the situation on the fronts of the Iberian Peninsula and in the international arena." He continued: "Gradually Stalin's interest in country X [Spain] fell—on the contrary, hostility arose. From mid-1937 at politburo meetings it became more frequent to discuss aid not to Spain but to Mongolia and China (country Z), as well as the struggle against anti-state elements inside the country." Rybalkin, *Operatsiia "X,"* 45. Another scholar refers to "improvisations and adaptations." Roberts, "Soviet Foreign Policy and the Spanish Civil War." Yet another noted that "a historian looking back over events encounters the danger of reading into facts future motives of which the participants were not yet aware." Cattell, *Soviet Diplomacy and the Spanish Civil War*, 120.
9. Stalin had many decisions on Spain approved by the politburo, but almost always via "telephone poll," so it is not clear whether any discussions took place. (No transcripts were made of politburo meetings between the end of 1932 and late 1938.) Many of the decisions regarding Spain—"Operation X"—were left out of the politburo protocols entirely, not even with oblique reference. These were recorded as OOP, which could have connoted "separate special file" [*otdelnaia osobaia papka*], and are found in the Presidential Archive. Kudriashov, *SSSR i grazhdanskaia voina v Ispanii*, 23. Compare Adibekov et al., *Politbiuro TsK RKP (b)—VKP (b) i Evropa*.

10. No politburo member, and no other people's commissar except for Litvinov, had traveled across the ocean. In Jan. 1936, Mikoyan had been awarded the Order of Lenin for the food industry commissariat's overfulfillment of the 1935 plan and introduction of machinery. Pavlov, *Anastas Mikoian*, 75–6 (citing RGASPI, f. 84, op. 3, d. 164, l. 603), 76–7 (l. 590). See also Mikoian, *Pishchevaia promyshlennost Sovertskogo Soiuza*, 9–10. In the United States during the course of two months, he visited more than 100 enterprises: bread and biscuits, canned meats, non-alcoholic drinks, refrigerators, as well as slaughterhouses. He saw the mass production of hamburger patties at Macy's and bought machines for manufacturing meat cutlets. "We traveled across America from east to west and back, and nowhere did the police create any difficulties for us," Mikoyan would later remember. Pavlov, "Iz zapisok narkoma," 107. See also Medvedev, *Blizhnyi krug Stalina*, 173.
11. Orjonikidze found out about the Soviet military intervention in Spain either by voting (via polling) for the politburo resolution on Sept. 29, 1936, or from Kaganovich's letter to him the next day. Khlevniuk et al., *Stalinskoe politbiuro*, 149 (Sept. 30, 1936). See also Maisky, *Spanish Notebooks*, 20–1.
12. "Stalin's position" in Spain, Daniel Kowalsky summarized, "was never one of strength, but rather one of weakness, incompetence, inexperience, and indecisiveness." Kowalsky largely omits the Soviet domination of the Spanish Communist party. Kowalsky, *Stalin*, paragraphs 792–5.
13. Firsov, "Stalin i Komintern," 8 (no citation); Volkogonov, *Trotskii*, II: 295–7. See also Preston, *We Saw Spain Die*, 3.
14. Preston, *Franco*, 16; Fusi, *Franco*, 18. The statement dates to Dec. 31, 1938.
15. In 1934, when leftists in Spain had seized power in the mining province of Asturias—thanks to solidarity among normally uncooperative Socialists, Communists, and anarchists—it had been Franco who was summoned to suppress the strikers; more than 1,000 people died. Ferran and Amago, *Unearthing Franco's Legacy*, 61.
16. Preston, *Franco*, 114.
17. Thomas, *Spanish Civil War*, 243. See also Jackson, *Spanish Republic*; Preston, *Concise History*; Broué, *Civil War in Spain*; Carr, *Spanish Tragedy*; Payne, *Spanish Civil War*; and Linz and Stepan, *Breakdown of Democratic Regimes*, 142–215.
18. Preston, *Franco*, 129–30, 134.
19. De Madariaga, "Intervention of Moroccan Troops," 77.
20. "We have to create the impression of mastery, eliminating without scruples or hesitation those who do not think as we do," General Mola boasted. Preston, *Spanish Holocaust*, 179.
21. Malefakis, "La revolución social," 319–54.
22. Payne, *Franco Regime*, 176; Novikov, *SSSR, Komintern*, II: 73 (citing RGASPI, f. 495, op. 120, d. 245, l. 7, 11); *Mezhdunarodnaia vstrecha*, 201; Pertsov, *Voina i revoliutsiia v Ispanii*, I: 63. On July 6, 1936, the Popular Front government had imprisoned the Falange leader, Antonio Primo de Rivera. He would be sentenced to death on Nov. 20, 1936. Franco would not try to free him.
23. Edwards, *British Government and the Spanish Civil War*, 77; Kowalsky, *Stalin*, paragraph 791.
24. Spain had finally recognized the USSR in July 1933, but Madrid's efforts to name an envoy were stymied by changes of government, while Moscow's appointed representative, Anatoly Lunacharsky, had fallen ill in Paris en route to Madrid and died on the Cote d'Azur at age fifty-eight (Dec. 26, 1933), never taking up his post. Lunacharskaia-Rozenel', *Pamiat'*

serdtsa, 15–6. Lunacharsky had written the play *Don Quixote Liberated* (1922), one of the few interesting books in Russian on Spanish culture.
25. Haslam, *Struggle for Collective Security*, 107–8; Alpert, *New International History*, 19–24.
26. British intelligence had been warning about Comintern "financing" and "overt and subterranean activities in Spain," while advising its French counterparts that "the establishment of a Soviet regime in the Iberian Peninsula is hardly a happening which anyone can view with equanimity for military, political or economic reasons." The British ambassador to Madrid, Sir Henry Chilton, had bluntly warned that "if the military coup d'état, which it is generally believed is being planned, does not succeed, things will turn pretty awful." Jeffrey, *MI6*, 22; Little, *Malevolent Neutrality*, 196; Steiner, *Triumph of the Dark*, 202–3. On July 26, Baldwin instructed foreign secretary Eden "that on no account, French or other, must he bring us into the fight on the side of the Russians." Jones, *Diary with Letters*, 213.
27. Churchill, *Step by Step*, 76; Moradiellos, "Origins of British Non-Intervention."
28. "Non-Intervention," Blum's chef de cabinet would later assert, "was essentially an attempt to prevent others from doing what we were incapable of achieving." Lacouture, *Léon Blum*, 370.
29. Abendroth, *Hitler in der spanischen Arena*.
30. Göring had objected to Franco's request. Leitz, "Nazi Germany Intervention," 53–85; Kershaw, *Hitler: 1889–1936*, 13–7; von Ribbentrop, *Memoirs*, 59; Preston, *Franco*, 158–60.
31. Fröhlich, *Tagebücher von Joseph Goebbels*, III/ii: 140 (July 27, 1936).
32. Mussolini added: "to found a parliamentary republic today [1931] means using an oil lamp in the era of electric lights." Bosworth, *Mussolini*, 315; Coverdale, *Italian Intervention*.
33. Bosworth, *Mussolini*, 316–7.
34. Jackson, "French Strategy," 55–80.
35. Coulondre, *De Staline à Hitler*, 20–2. See Ford and Schorske, "Voice in the Wilderness," 556–61; and Jordan, *Popular Front*, 228.
36. "O tak nazyvaemom 'antisovetskom ob"edinennom trotskistsko-zinov'ievskom tsentre,'" 94.
37. Il'inskii, *Narkom Iagoda*, 709–16; Khaustov and Samuelson, *Stalin, NKVD*, 89.
38. "My soul burns with one desire: to prove to you that I am no longer an enemy," Zinoviev wrote to Stalin in 1935. "I am at the point where I sit for long periods and stare at your portrait in the newspapers and those of other members of the Politburo thinking: my dear ones, look into my heart and surely you will see that I'm no longer your enemy . . ." Iakovlev et al., *Reabilitatsiia: politicheskie protsessy*, 184–5. "There has been a distinct cooling in my relations with Zinoviev," Kamenev told his interrogator. "I think it necessary to mention that living in one dacha in the summer of 1934 we led completely separate lives and met rarely. . . . At the time of the inner-party struggle, I never regarded Zinoviev as fit to run the party; the recent years have confirmed my conviction that he possesses no leadership qualities." Volkogonov, *Lenin*, 286, citing Arkhiv Ministerstvo Bezzaposnosti Rossiisskoi Federatsii no. R-33 834, t. 1, l. 107. See also *Izvestiia*, March 21, 1990 (Kamenev to his wife, T. Glebova, Nov. 12, 1935).
39. Profound insight into a despot's psychology can be found in Canetti, *Crowds and Power*, esp. 231–4. Rogovin, *1937*, 5–9.

40. Orlov, *Tainaia istoriia*, 135–6. Kaganovich confirmed the fact that Stalin and Voroshilov received Zinoviev and Kamenev: Chuev, *Tak govoril Kaganovich*, 140.
41. Trotskii, *Prestuplenia Stalina*, 72.
42. Yagoda was said to have written across the interrogation testimony of a link to Trotsky: "untrue," "rubbish." Iakovlev et al., *Reabilitatsiia: politicheskie protsessy*, 179; "Materialy marto-fevral'skogo plenuma TsK VKP (b) 1937 goda" (1994, no. 12), 18.
43. On July 21, 1936, for example, Manuilsky relayed to Stalin a note with a citation from a document received from the head of the Spanish Communist party to the effect that "the military uprising has been put down." Kudriashov, *SSSR i grazhdanskaia voina v Ispanii*, 28 (APRF, f. 3, op. 65, d. 221, l. 33). The British intercepted and decrypted the Spanish Communist party ciphered telegrams. Roberts, "Soviet Foreign Policy and the Spanish Civil War," 100n11 (citing PRO HW/17/27).
44. Kudriashov, *SSSR i grazhdanskaia voina v Ispanii*, 28 (APRF, f. 3, op. 65, d. 221, l. 34).
45. RGASPI, f. 495, op. 18, d. 1101, l. 15, 21–3 (ECCI Protocol No. 60, July 23, 1936); Dallin and Firsov, *Dimitrov and Stalin*, 46–8 (RGASPI, f. 495, op. 74, d. 210, l. 2–3).
46. Meshcheriakov, "SSSR i grazhdanskaia voina v Ispanii," 85 (citing AVP RF, f. 048 z, op. 14–6, d. 4, pap. 7, l. 69–106).
47. Steiner, *Triumph of the Dark*, 187. Stalin's Kremlin office logbook shows few or no visitors July 25–27, 1936. *Na prieme*, 190.
48. *Na prieme*, 190–1.
49. *VII Kongress Kommunisticheskogo Internatsionala*, 10–1, 28–33.
50. Titarenko, *VKP (b), komintern i kitai: dokumenty*, IV/ii: 1055–60 (RGASPI, f. 495, op. 74, d. 249, l. 8–17: Dimitrov to Stalin, early July 1936); Dallin and Firsov, *Dimitrov and Stalin*, 96–100.
51. Titarenko, *VKP (b), komintern i kitai: dokumenty*, IV/ii: 1060–4 (RGASPI, f. 495, op. 18, d. 1101, l. 17–20: edited transcript). See also Braun, *Comintern Agent in China*; and Garver, "Origins of the Second United Front."
52. Borkenau, who went to Spain in Sept. 1936, was describing the scene in Barcelona, and added: "Practically all the factory-owners, we were told, had either fled or been killed, and their factories taken over by the workers." Borkenau, *Spanish Cockpit*, 70–1. In a 1936 biography of Vilfredo Pareto, Borkenau employed the latter's "circulation of elites" theory to try to explain the rise of and affinities among Italian fascism, Nazism, and Soviet communism. Jones, "Toward a Theory of Totalitarianism," 457.
53. Kudriashov, *SSSR i grazhdanskaia voina v Ispanii*, 29–31 (APRF, f. 3, op. 65, d. 221, l. 38–40).
54. Primakov, *Ocherki*, III: 84–5. Primakov names two Soviet agents in Trotsky's inner circle, one code-named "Tomas," the other "Tyulpan," which is known to be Zborowski. Primakov, *Ocherki*, III: 82.
55. Høidal, *Trotsky in Norway*.
56. Zipperstein, "Underground Man."
57. Volkogonov, *Trotskii*, II: 134–5 (citing Arkhiv INO OGPU, f. 31660, d. 9067, t. 1, l. 24–5). See also Antonov, "Kaznen i opravdan."
58. In 1934, Stalin had quoted Trotsky's *Bulletin of the Opposition* from the dais of the 17th Party Congress: *XVII s"ezd*, 32. In 1935, Yezhov quoted from Trotsky's *Bulletin* at length at a Central Committee meeting. RGASPI, f. 17, op. 2, d. 542, l. 73–6. In March 1937, Yezhov's staff in the NKVD would give Stalin a very detailed compilation of all Trotskyite publications on every continent, with their contents outlined. Volkogonov, *Trotskii*, II: 141–2 (citing Arkhiv INO OGPU-NKVD, f.

17548, d. 0292, l. 17); Volkogonov, *Trotsky*, 347. At least one concrete example of draft articles forwarded before publication to Stalin (and Molotov), by Yezhov, has come to light. Volkogonov, *Trotskii*, II: 141 (citing Arkhiv INO OGPU-NKVD, f. 17548, d. 0292, t. 2, l. 160). See also Poretsky, *Our Own People*, 272–3.

59. Trotsky, "Lesson of Spain."

60. Pozharskaia and Saplin, *Komintern i grazhdanskaia voina v Ispanii*, 9; Payne, *Spanish Civil War*, 124.

61. The official post-Soviet history of intelligence justifies Stalin's assassination of Trotsky by referring to the latter's responsibility for the fever pitch of anti-Sovietism abroad, the supposed role of Trotskyites in destabilizing the Spanish Republic, and the threat of the Fourth International. Primakov, *Ocherki*, III: 90. The forged Litvinov "diaries" that were handed to Carr and published in 1955 observed of Spain: "There was some confusion there. The Trotskyites have started a strong propaganda campaign against Iosif Vissarionovich calling him liquidator and traitor to the Spanish revolution, abettor of Hitler and Mussolini." Litvinov, *Notes for a Journal*, 208, 211. The forger appears to have been Besedovsky, who figures prominently in them. Wolfe, "Adventures in Forged Sovietica"; Wolfe, "Case of the Litvinov Diary"; Wolfe, *Strange Communists*, 207–22. See also Agursky, "Soviet Disinformation," 21. Litvinov's actual diary is thought to have been destroyed by his American wife, Ivy's, closest confidant, Joseph Freeman. Danielson, "Elusive Litvinov Memoirs."

62. *Pravda's* editorial (June 7, 1936) echoing Postyshev's stance decried blanket accusations against the "majority of engineering and technical personnel." Postyshev himself was criticized at the June 1936 plenum for a "high-handed" approach to the expulsions of rank and file party members.

63. *Sovet pri narodnom komissare tiazheloi promyshlennosti SSSR, 25–29 iuniia 1936 g.: stenograficheskii otchet* (Moscow, 1936), 390; Khlevniuk, *1937-i*, 116–20, 122; Khlevniuk, *Stalin i Ordzhonikidze*, 60–3; Benvenuti, "Stakhanovism and Stalinism," 42–9; Davies, "Soviet Economy," 20–1; *Pravda*, July 5, 1936. Zhdanov noted in a speech (July 16, 1936) that "it is not possible to declare that all engineers and technicians who do not lead the Stakhanovite movement are saboteurs." Priestland, *Politics of Mobilization*, 347 (citing RGASPI, f. 77, op. 1, d. 600, l. 19).

64. Rybin, *Kto otravil Stalina?*, 23–4 (citing conversations with V. Tukov, one of Orjonikidze's guards, responsible for his train carriage when he visited factories around the country).

65. *Za industrializatsiiu*, Feb. 20, 1937: 5 (S. Birman); Ordzhonikidze, *O Sergo Ordzhonikidze*, 259 (quoting I. I. Gudov); RGASPI, f. 17, op. 3, d. 978, l. 75.

66. Khlevniuk et al., *Stalin i Kaganovich*, 627 (RGASPI, f. 558, op. 11, d. 743, l. 53).

67. "Zakrytoe pis'mo Tsk VKP (b)," 100–15; Getty and Naumov, *Road to Terror*, 250–7. Stalin's motives have been a matter of guesswork: Khlevniuk, *Politbiuro*, 203–6. Getty and Naumov speculate that the secret circular was actually Yezhov's initiative, in a careerist move. Getty and Naumov, *Road to Terror*, 578. Agranov divulged to a meeting of the NKVD "active" that the original trial of Zinovievites, in 1935, had resulted not from operational work, but from a command from the country's leadership. Khaustov and Samuelson, *Stalin, NKVD*, 90 (March 1937).

68. Harris, *Great Urals*, 178–9.

69. Rees, *Stalinism and Soviet Rail Transport*, 144–8 (citing *Sotsialisticheskii transport*,

1936, no. 5: 8, 150, 158–9); *Pravda*, July 31 and Aug. 2, 1936.

70. *Izvestiia*, Aug. 26, 27, 1936; Rees, *Stalinism and Soviet Rail Transport*, 150.

71. *Izvestiia*, Feb. 20, 1937.

72. Radek, "Dikhanie voiny."

73. Vostryshev, *Moskva Stalinskaia*, 348.

74. "I am full of doubts," Gide said in Pasternak's oral account. "What I have seen in your country is not at all what I anticipated. Here state power is unbelievable. . . . While I was in France, it seemed that here there was personal freedom, but in reality I do not see it. This concerns me greatly, and I want to write about it in an essay and I came here to consult with you about it." RGASPI, f. 57, op., 1, d. 64, l. 58–61 (Report to Molchanov). Christopher J. Barnes, *Boris Pasternak: A Literary Biography*, vol. 2 (New York: Cambridge University, 1998), 127–32. Gide took off for Soviet Georgia and Crimea, and would depart the USSR almost without notice.

75. Mikhail Kol'tsov, "Ispanskii dnevnik: kniga pervaia," *Novyi mir*, 1938, no. 4: 5–125 (at 5), reprinted in Kol'tsov, *Ispanskii dnevnik*, 11–2.

76. Kirschenbaum, "Exile, Gender, and Communist Self-Fashioning," 572. When *We of Kronstadt* (1936), Yefim Dzigan's tale of an anarchist band's transformation into disciplined Red Army men during Russia's civil war, premiered in Spain, the entire Spanish Republic cabinet attended. Kowalsky, "Soviet Cinematic Offensive"; Kudriashov, *SSSR i grazhdanskaia voina v Ispanii*, 51 (APRF, f. 3, op. 65, d. 221, l. 86).

77. Kudriashov, *SSSR i grazhdanskaia voina v Ispanii*, 32 (APRF, f. 3, op. 65, d. 221, l. 44); *Pravda*, Aug. 4 and 5, 1936; *Izvestiia*, Aug. 4 and 5, 1936; *Trud*, Aug. 4 and 5, 1936.

78. RGASPI, f. 495, op. 18, d. 1105, l. 1.

79. By the end of Oct., nearly 48 million rubles would be deducted from the pay of Soviet factory workers in solidarity with Spain. That was equivalent to £2 million sterling. *Izvestiia*, Oct. 27, 1936.

80. *Pravda*, Aug. 3, 1936; Kowalsky, *Stalin*, paragraphs 187–8. "The German and Italian fascists are preparing to intervene against the Spanish revolution to place in their hands the important trump cards for preparation of a world war and a new territorial distribution of the world," Radek argued, outlining the case in *Izvestiia* (Aug. 4, 1936) for "humanitarian" aid by the USSR.

81. Haslam, *Struggle for Collective Security*, 111, citing *FRUS, 1936*, II: 461 (Henderson to Hull).

82. Pons, *Stalin and the Inevitable War*, 43.

83. *DDF*, 1e série, III: 97–8, 100–1.

84. Adibekov et al., *Politbiuro TsK RKP (b)—VKP (b) i Evropa*, 339n2 (RGASPI, f. 71, op. 25, d. 3663); *DVP SSSR*, XIX: 392–3 (Veinberg, head of the Western department, report on conversation with Payart); 393–4 (Krestinsky to Maisky); Degras, *Soviet Documents on Foreign Policy*, III: 203; Haslam, *Struggle for Collective Security*, 112; *Izvestiia*, Aug. 6, 1936.

85. Volkogonov, *Trotsky*, 370 (citing Arkhiv INO OGPU-NKVD, f. 17548, d. 0292, t. 2, l. 130–2).

86. Volkogonov, who has little to say about Spain, noted that "Stalin's determination to get rid of Trotsky stiffened when he learned in late 1936 that Trotsky was writing *The Revolution Betrayed* and continuing his biography of Stalin himself." Volkogonov, *Trotsky*, 444.

87. See also MacNeal, "Trotskyist Interpretations of Stalinism."

88. Pavliukov, *Ezhov*, 189 (RGASPI, f. 671, op. 1, d. 168, l. 202: testimony attributed to Pikel');

Orlov, *Tainaia istoriia*, 81; *Pravda*, Aug. 20, 1936 (Reingold).

89. Haslam, "Spanish Problem," 70–85 (citing PRO, HW17/26: British decryptions of Comintern telegrams). "Madrid's not receiving substantial external assistance could have heavy consequences for the course of the struggle," Soviet military intelligence concluded in Aug. 1936. Rybalkin, *Operatsiia "X*," 20 (citing RGVA, f. 33987, op. 3, d. 845, l. 9). On Aug. 7, 1936, the politburo approved Krestinsky's proposal to invite Blum of France's Popular Front government to Moscow. No visit materialized. Adibekov et al., *Politbiuro TsK RKP (b)—VKP (b) i Evropa*, 338–9 (RGASPI, f. 17, op. 162, d. 20, l. 38); *DVP SSSR*, XXII: 49.

90. *DVP SSSR*, XIX: 394–6 (Stein); Haslam, *Struggle for Collective Security*, 112–3. See also Adibekov et al., *Politbiuro TsK RKP (b)—VKP (b) i Evropa*, 340 (RGASPI, f. 17, op. 162, d. 20, l. 58).

91. Moradiellos, "British Government and General Franco," 44 (citing PRO FO371/20475, W11340, Sir Maurice Hankey, *The Future of the League of Nations*).

92. Krestinsky had written to Surits (Aug. 11) that "we recently discussed the so-called 500-million credit. It was rejected." Abramov, "Osobaia missiia David Kandelaki," 149 (citing AVP RF, f. 010, op. 11, pap. 68, d. 34, l. 130, 131).

93. Tooze, *Wages of Destruction*, 205 (citing Institut für Konjunkturforschung, *Weekly Report*, May 6, 1936).

94. *DGFP*, series C, V: 853–62 (unsigned; Hitler's authorship established in a note by Speer, Aug. 1936).

95. According to an official then working in the Western military district: Samsonov, "Smysl ego znizhi," 217.

96. Tooze, *Wages of Destruction*, 219–24.

97. Titarenko, *VKP (b), kommintern i kitai: dokumenty*, IV/ii: 1067 (RGASPI, f. 495, op. 74, d. 275, l. 1: Dimitrov to Stalin, July 27, 1936), 1067–71 (l. 5–9); Titarenko, *Kommiunisticheskii internatsional*, 262–6, 266–9; Dallin and Firsov, *Dimitrov and Stalin*, 101 (RGASPI, f. 495, op. 73, d. 48, l. 54), 102–5.

98. Schram, *Mao's Road to Power*, V: 232–32.

99. Meshcheriakov, "SSSR i grazhdanskaia voina v Ispanii," 83–4 (citing AVP RF, f. 048 z, op. 14–6, pap. 4, d. 7, l. 194–5).

100. Kudriashov, *SSSR i grazhdanskaia voina v Ispanii*, 42 (APRF, f. 3, op. 65, d. 221, l. 66); Zuehilke, *Gallant Cause*, 35. See also Karmen, *No Pasaran!*; and Makaseev, "Iz khroniki geroicheskoi respubliki," 158–64. Karmen would make the film *Ispaniia* (1939).

101. Litvinov instructed the Soviet chargé d'affaires in Paris to inform the Spanish ambassador that "the Soviet leadership does not consider it possible to comply with requests to supply arms on the grounds that Spain is far away from Russia, such deliveries are expensive, arms cargo can be intercepted, and because the USSR is bound by its declaration of nonintervention and cannot violate it." *DVP SSSR*, XIX: 402–3; Degras, *Soviet Documents on Foreign Policy*, III: 203–4.

102. Iakovlev et al., *Reabilitatsiia: politicheskie protsessy*, 219; "O tak nazyvaemom 'parallel'nom antisovetskom trotskistom tsentre,'" 37. Pyatakov's ex-wife Zina had been arrested in Dec. 1927 as a Trotskyite and internally exiled. See also Getty and Naumov, *Road to Terror*, 311. After Pyatakov, in bilateral negotiations, had unwittingly demonstrated too detailed knowledge of German metal industry, a Soviet undercover agent in Germany was arrested. Khaustov, "Deiatel'nost' organov," 157 (referencing uncited recollections of Spiegelglass).

103. *Pravda*, Aug. 15, 1936.

104. For Stalin's role micromanaging the trial, see "O tak nazyvaemom 'antisovetskom ob"edinennom trotskistsko-zinov'evskom tsentre'," 92. See also "O tak nazyvaemom 'parallel'nom antisovetskom trotskistskom tsentre'," 42. The trial transcript was made available in foreign translations, including in English: *The Case of the Trotskyite-Zinovievite Center* (New York, 1936). For a multisided analysis of how contemporaries saw the trial, including Trotsky's misapprehensions, see Schrader, *Der Moskauer Prozess 1936*.

105. Kamenev's Machiavelli volume was quoted against him at his trial in 1936. "You, Kamenev, transmitted the rules of Machiavelli and developed them to the height of unprincipled-ness and immorality," thundered Vyshinsky, who deemed Machiavelli the "spiritual teacher" of the Trotskyites. Yet Vyshinsky also called the Italian "a bumpkin" and amateur compared with the Trotskyites. Vyshinskii, *Sudebnye rechi*, 403–4.

106. Testimony about a 1932 meeting that had allegedly taken place with Trotsky in Copenhagen's Hotel Bristol ignored that the building had been torn down in 1917 (the NKVD fabricators confused two sites). Orlov, *Tainaia istoriia*, 70.

107. Iakovlev et al., *Reabilitatsiia: politicheskie protsessy*, 187–8.

108. *Izvestiia*, Aug. 21, 1936.

109. Dem'ian Bednyi, "Poshchady net!" *Pravda*, Aug. 21, 1936, reprinted in *Literaturnaia gazeta*, Aug. 27, and in Bednyi, *Sobranie sochinenii*, IV: 288–90. See also Horvath, "Poet of the Terror"; Artizov and Naumov, *Vlast'*, 415–6 (Sept. 9, 1938). On Aug. 13, 1936, in the presence of Molotov, Voroshilov, Orjonikidze, and Yezhov, Bedny spent an hour in the Little Corner, his one and only recorded visit to Stalin's Kremlin office. Bedny's abandoned wife, Vera Rufovna [Pridvorova], had written to Stalin indicating that she wanted to ask him for material help for her four children, possibly reminding the dictator of the poet's existence. Maksimenkov, *Bol'shaia tsenzura*, 421–2 (RGASPI, f. 558, op. 11, d. 702, l. 109, 110–1); *Na prieme*, 191. Before the year was out, Bedny would be fearing arrest. He would somehow survive. Pridvorov, "Ob otse," 219.

110. Whereas since 1931 more than 40 percent of the correspondence had concerned economic matters (internal and external), especially grain collections, in 1936 these nearly vanished—despite the fact that a spring-summer drought in the Volga heartland and other difficulties resulted in a poor harvest in fall 1936. Davies, "Soviet Economy," 22–3.

111. Stalin had afforded Bukharin an opportunity to defect: in Feb. 1936, he had appointed Bukharin to lead a commission to purchase a Marx-Engels archive in France, leaving the trip's duration up to Bukharin and permitting the pregnant Larina to join him. But his father, brother, first wife, second wife, and daughter lived in Moscow, and the trip to France had taken place before Zinoviev and Kamenev had been executed. Cohen, *Bukharin*, 472; Liebich, "I Am the Last." See also Dan, "Bukharin o Staline," 181–2; and Nicolaevsky, *Power and the Soviet Elite*.

112. Trotsky, *Writings of Leon Trotsky, 1935–1936*, 389; Høidal, *Trotsky in Norway*, 133–4. In Dec. Trotsky would be expelled from Norway, and placed on a Norwegian oil tanker to Mexico; en route he would write in his journal that Zinoviev and Kamenev "lacked sufficient character." Trotsky, "Zinoviev and Kamenev [Dec. 31, 1936]," in Trotsky, *Writings of Leon Trotsky, 1936–1937*, 48–55 (at 49).

113. "Samoubiistvo ne opravdanie: predsmertnoe pis'mo Tomskogo Stalinu," *Rodina*, 1996, no. 2: 90–3; Gorelov, *Tsugtsvang Mikhaila Tomskogo*, 234.

114. *Pravda*, Aug. 23, 1936. The Menshevik émigré newspaper eulogized Tomsky as a "most colorful and splendid figure among the Bolshevik leaders." *Sotsialisticheskii vestnik*, Aug. 30, 1936: 11.

115. Molchanov, dispatched to Tomsky's dacha to investigate the scene, retrieved the note, which stated: "If you want to know who it was that pushed me onto the path of right deviation in May 1928, ask my wife personally. Only she will name them." Tomsky's widow told Yezhov that the person who had recruited Tomsky to the path of opposition was none other than NKVD chief Yagoda. Yezhov's report to Stalin defended Yagoda. Iakovlev et al., *Reabilitatsiia: politcheskie protsessy*, 244–5; "O partiinosti lits, prokhodivshikh po delu tak nazyvaemogo 'antisovetskogo pravotrotskistskogo bloka,'" 71. Khlevniuk, *Politbiuro*, 204–6 (no citation).

116. Kvashonkin, *Bol'shevistskoe rukovodstvo*, 16 (RGASPI, f. 558, op. 1, d. 5391, l. 3).

117. Khlevniuk et al., *Stalin i Kaganovich*, 642–3 (RGASPI, f. 558, op. 11, d. 93, l. 77–80).

118. Stalin forbade mention of the fact that there would be no appeal ("these words are superfluous and would give a bad impression"). Khlevniuk et al., *Stalin i Kaganovich*, 642 (RGASPI, f. 558, op. 11, d. 93, l. 62–4).

119. Vostryshev, *Moskva stalinskaia*, 349 (Alexander G. Solovyov).

120. Eduard Gol'tsman wrote a note that he would not seek clemency. Volkogonov, *Lenin*, 276 (citing AMBRF, archive no. R-33833, t. 41, l. 256).

121. Conquest, *Great Terror: Reassessment*, 71–108; Getty and Naumov, *Road to Terror*, 247–57.

122. Kudriashov, *SSSR i grazhdanskaia voina v Ispanii*, 44 (APRF, f. 3, op. 65, d. 217, l. 21); *Izvestiia*, Aug. 28, 1936.

123. Kudriashov, *SSSR i grazhdanskaia voina v Ispanii*, 43 (APRF, f. 3, op. 65, d. 217, l. 21), 44 (l. 20).

124. Antonov-Ovseyenko would take to the Spanish assignment energetically, writing pleading notes to Kaganovich suggesting resolute measures for organizing serious military resistance even before he had reached Barcelona (Oct. 1). Kudriashov, *SSSR i grazhdanskaia voina v Ispanii*, 67 (APRF, f. 3, op. 65, d. 217, l. 23), 70 (d. 221, l. 141), 81–2 (l. 184–5); RGASPI, f. 17, op. 3, d. 981, l. 213; *Izvestiia*, Oct. 3, 1936; Ehrenburg, *Sobranie sochinenii*, IX: 114–9. Antonov-Ovseyenko wrote to Rosenberg (Oct. 6): "Our view of anarchism in Catalonia is a mistaken one . . . The government is genuinely willing to organize a defense and it is doing a lot in that direction." Ehrenburg, who arrived in Spain from Paris in the latter part of August 1936 as a special correspondent for *Izvestiya*, had already written to Rosenberg, in letters sent on to Stalin, accusing the anarchists of not understanding the critical importance of heavy industry and discipline, being infiltrated by German agents and, under the guise of pressing for "revolution," aiming to demoralize and defeat the Republic. RGASPI, f. 17, op. 120, d. 259, l. 73–4; Radosh et al., *Spain Betrayed*, 23–32; Kudriashov, *SSSR i grazhdanskaia voina v Ispanii*, 39 (APRF, f. 3, op. 65, d. 217, l. 19), 43 (l. 17), 110 (d. 222, l. 88), 113–14 (l. 87); Adibekov et al., *Politbiuro TsK RKP (b)—VKP (b) i Evropa*, 342–3 (RGASPI, f. 17, op. 162, d. 20, l. 162); Ehrenburg, *Sobranie sochinenii*, IX: 100. By Nov. 1936, Antonov-Ovseyenko was complaining of the anarchy caused by the anarchists: Kudriashov, *SSSR i grazhdanskaia voina v Ispanii*, 142–3 (APRF, f. 3, op. 65, d. 222, l. 145–46ob.).

125. Kudriashov, *SSSR i grazhdanskaia voina v Ispanii*, 39 (APRF, f. 3, op. 65, d. 217, l. 11). See also Efimov, "Vernost' prizvaniiu," 29.

126. Koltsov had also composed profiles of Lenin (1920, 1923, 1924), Dzierżyński (1928), Gorky (1932, 1936), and Stakhanov (1935), and captured the boorishness of the new epoch in his short story "Ivan Vadimovich, A Person of a Certain Level." Kol'tsov, *Khochu letat'*; Kol'tsov, *Izbrannye proizvedeniia v trekh tomakh*; Kol'tsov, *Pisatel' v gazete*.

127. Cockburn, *In Time of Trouble*, 245.

128. Skorokhodov, *Mikhail Kol'tsov*, 158–9. On Koltsov's links to Soviet military intelligence in Spain, see Volodarsky, *Stalin's Agent*, 219, citing Paulina Abramson and Adelina Abramson, *Mosaico Roto* (Madrid: Compañía Literara, 1994), 64 (Emma Wolf, Vladimir Gorev's interpreter and perhaps mistress). Ehrenburg would later call his rival Koltsov "the most important" Soviet representative in Spain, "more important than the official adviser." *Literaturnaia gazeta*, June 15, 1988. A recommendation by Berzin and Gorev (Jan. 4, 1937) to award Koltsov the Order of Lenin would be downgraded by Stalin to an Order of the Red Banner. Kudriashov, *SSSR i grazhdanskaia voina v Ispanii*, 170 (APRF, f. 3, op. 53, d. 470, l. 124). On May 23, 1937, Koltsov would send a telegram directly to Stalin from Paris about preparations for an antifascist congress in Spain; it included a number of political observations about Largo Caballero and Negrín, as well as about Ehrenburg and Gide. Maksimenkov, *Bol'shaia tsenzura*, 468 (RGASPI, f. 558, op. 11, d. 214, l. 67–8). Koltsov's archive seems not to have survived. Rubashkin, *Mikhail Kol'tsov*.

129. Trotsky, "The Treachery of the POUM," *New Militant*, Feb. 15, 1936, and Trotsky, "The Tasks of the Fourth International in Spain," *New Militant*, May 2, 1936, reprinted in Trotsky, *Spanish Revolution*, 207–11, 211–4. Trotsky similarly condemned Spain's anarchists.

130. Rogovin, *1937*, 341 (citing Trotsky archives, document no. 5020); Thomas, *Spanish Civil War*, 631; *Biulleten' oppozitsii*, no. 56–7 (1937): 14–5. See also Trotsky, "Lessons of Spain," 322.

131. Kennan, *Russia and the West*, 238.

132. Rogovin, *1937*, 40–5, 8.

133. Khlevnuik et al., *Stalin i Kaganovich*, 664–5 (RGASPI, f. 558, op. 11, d. 94, l. 32–9).

134. Petrov and Jansen, *Stalinskii pitomets*, 249–52 (RGASPI, f. 558, op. 11, d. 729, l. 83–4). On Aug. 22, 1936, in connection with the Moscow trial, Budyonny had sent a letter to Voroshilov noting that the Trotskyite network had penetrated the army, which needed to be thoroughly checked; Voroshilov forwarded the letter to Stalin, Yezhov, and Andreyev (Sept. 1). Whitewood, *Red Army*, 202 (citing RGVA, f. 4, op. 19, d. 16, l. 262, 265).

135. Volkogonov, *Lenin*, 298 (Sept. 1, 1936).

136. Jansen and Petrov, *Stalin's Loyal Executioner*, 58 (citing APRF, f. 57, op. 1, d. 176; RGASPI, f. 671, op. 1, d. 176, l. 66–74).

137. Davies et al., *Stalin-Kaganovich Correspondence*, 357.

138. RGASPI, f. 558, op. 11, d. 710, l. 164–5.

139. RGASPI, f. 558, op. 11, d. 779, l. 99–107; Khlevniuk, *Master of the House*, 154.

140. Arkhiv MB r-3383, d. 3257, Volkogonov papers, Hoover Institution Archives, container 4.

141. RGASPI, f. 558, op. 11, d. 779, l. 106. On Sept. 11, when Stalin had Pyatakov's arrest submitted for post-facto politburo approval, Orjonikidze wrote: "I vote 'Yes.'" RGASPI, f. 558, op. 11, d. 94, l. 75, 84; Getty and Naumov, *Road to Terror*, 290–1 (RGASPI, f. 17, op. 2, d. 573, l. 33). The NKVD arrested Radek on Sept. 16. Radek's mouth was a security risk: Lerner,

Karl Radek, 163–4 (citing memo from Bullitt to Hull, Decimal Files, U.S. Department of State Archives, file no. 7600.61/692); Ken, "Karl Radek i Biuro," 173–4.
142. Adibekov et al., *Politbiuro TsK RKP (b)— VKP (b) i Evropa,* 340 (RGASPI, f. 17, op. 162, d. 20, l. 62); *DVP SSSR,* XIX: 418 (to S. B. Kagan). Litvinov had written to Rosenberg (Aug. 30, 1936) in Madrid that "the question of assisting the Spanish government has been discussed by us several times, but we have come to the conclusion that it will be impossible to send anything from here." Meshcheriakov, "SSSR i grazhdanskaia voina v Ispanii," 85, citing AVP RF, f. 048 z, op. 14–16, pap. 4, d. 7, l. 88, 105–6. See also Pons, *Stalin and the Inevitable War,* 46 (citing AVP RF, f. 05, op. 16, pap. 114, d. 1, l. 195–8; Sept. 7).
143. Kowalsky, *Stalin,* paragraph 434, 441; *Pravda,* Sept. 4, 1936.
144. These developments were reported by Diaz, the Spanish Communist party head, via Comintern channels to Kaganovich as symptomatic of Popular Front internal tension. Kudriashov, *SSSR i grazhdanskaia voina v Ispanii,* 44–5 (APRF, f. 3, op. 65, d. 221, l. 74), 45 (l. 78).
145. Khlevniuk et al., *Stalin i Kaganovich,* 666 (RGASPI, f. 558, op. 11, d. 94, l. 53–4). Precisely when Stalin ordered and approved contingency planning for Soviet military assistance to Spain remains uncertain. On Aug. 13, he had received Vladimir Gorev and Semyon Uritsky together for twenty minutes. *Na prieme,* 191. Around the time of the Sept. 6 telegram, Stalin was also exchanging instructions with Kaganovich about Soviet protests to the Norwegian government about Trotsky's political activities.
146. Meshcheriakov, "SSSR i grazhdanskaia voina v Ispanii," 85.
147. Banac, *Diary of Gerogi Dimitrov,* 27 (Aug. 28, 1936); Richardson, *Comintern Army,* 30–46; Thomas, *Spanish Civil War,* 439–50; Eby, *Comrades and Commissars;* Kudriashov, *SSSR i grazhdanskaia voina v Ispanii,* 115, 162 (APRF, f. 3, op. 65, d. 222, l. 90–1, 187). An international brigade training base was set up near Albacete, where the first 500 volunteers commenced their service on Oct. 14, 1936, and as many as 35,000 foreigners would be trained. Novikov, *SSSR, Komintern,* II: 100 (citing RGASPI, f. 495, op. 76, l. 33, l. 18).
148. Krivitsky, *In Stalin's Secret Service,* 95.
149. On Aug. 21–22, 1936, with the trial in Moscow climaxing, the politburo had formally approved the dispatch of a group of military and intelligence personnel, as well as the diplomats, to Spain. Kowalsky, *Stalin,* chap. 2, note 21 (citing RGASPI, f. 17, op. 3, d. 980, l. 308; d. 981, l. 213), 65, d. 217, l. 20, 22).
150. Kuznetsov, *Na dalekom meridian,* 8–15. Kuznetsov got to Spain Sept. 5.
151. On Gorev in the United States, see Ulanovskaia and Ulanovskaia, *Istoriia odnoi sem'i,* 101.
152. Krivitsky, *In Stalin's Secret Service,* 96–9.
153. Pospelov, *Istoriia Velikoi Otechestvennoi voiny,* I: 113; Rybalkin, *Operatsiia "X,"* 11n6.
154. Primakov, *Ocherki,* III: 132; Kowalsky, *Stalin,* paragraph 462, citing Aleksandr Orlov, "Answers to the Questionnaire of Prof. S. G. Payne" (unpublished, 1968), 1–3.
155. Fischer, *Men and Politics,* 361.
156. Sudoplatov, *Special Tasks,* 45; Costello and Tsarev, *Deadly Illusions,* 349; Volodarsky, *Stalin's Agent,* 129. The assistant was Galina Voitova.
157. Volodarsky, *Stalin's Agent,* 153 (citing stamp in Orlov's diplomatic passport, a copy of which is at LSE's Cañada Blanch Centre).
158. Kudriashov, *SSSR i grazhdanskaia voina v Ispanii,* 48–50 (APRF, f. 3, op. 65, d. 221, l. 103–6).

159. Steiner, *Triumph of the Dark,* 215–6; Girard de Charbonnières, *La plus evitable de toutes les guerres,* 114–22; Gromyko and Ponomarev, *Istoriia vneshnei politiki SSSR,* I: 321.
160. Edwards, *British Government and the Spanish Civil War,* 137.
161. Isserson, "Zapiski sovremennika o M. N. Tukhachevskom," 73–5.
162. Ovchinnikov et al., *Krasnoznamennyi Belorusskii voennyi okrug,* 119–20; *Sovetskaia voennaia entsiklopediia,* V: 121.
163. Martel, *Russian Outlook,* 21–4; Erickson, *Soviet High Command,* 436–7. See also Lukes, *Czechoslovakia Between Stalin and Hitler,* 91. Major General Archibald P. Wavell, head of the British delegation, spoke Russian.
164. *DDF,* 2e série, IV: 510–4 (Daladier to Delbos, Oct. 13, 1936, reference to Schweisguth report Oct. 5). Schweisguth had traveled to Czechoslovakia (Aug. 15–Sept. 1) on his way to the USSR (Sept. 5–23).
165. Colton, *Leon Blum,* 211; Young, *In Command of France,* 147–8, 288n50.
166. *DDF,* 2e série, III: 511–4 ("Rapport du General Schweisguth, Chef de la Mission française," included in note from Daladier to foreign minister Delbos, Oct. 13, 1936); Dreifort, "French Popular Front," 218–9; Young, *In Command of France,* 145. See also Ragsdale, *Coming of World War II,* 32–3.
167. Yakir had visited France (August 19–September 2, 1936) accompanied by the Soviet military and aviation attachés and the air force officer Khripin, flattered his hosts, but back in the USSR quietly offered a negative assessment. *Le Temps,* Aug. 21, 26, 29, and Sept. 4, 1936; *Pravda,* Aug. 21 and Sept. 9, 1936; Orlov, "V poiskakh osiuznikov," 51.
168. Moravec added that soon enough the Soviets "made careful note of our experience with provincial newspapers, published in the smaller German towns, in which numerous indiscretions about military matters could still be found despite the severe Nazi censorship." Moravec, *Master of Spies,* 48–57.
169. Even British intelligence, by fall 1936, conceded German rearmament might be unlimited and aiming for domination of the continent. Wark, *Ultimate Enemy,* 228–31.
170. "No army," he wrote, "can manage without modern, well-organized and well-taught infantry." Habeck, *Storm of Steel,* 242–3 (citing RGVA, f. 33987, op. 3, d. 838, l. 2–5: Uborevičius to Voroshilov and Yegorov, Sept. 7–10, 1936; f. 4, op. 18, d. 53, l. 23–25, 712–7: Oct. 13–19, 1936). Voroshilov, in 1934, had called the tank corps "a very far-fetched idea and therefore we should have nothing to do with it." Erickson, *Road to Stalingrad,* 15.
171. At the invitation of General Fritzsch, Uborevičius attended German maneuvers in fall 1936; Hitler became angry at German generals who "get drunk and go around with Communist generals." Görlitz, *German General Staff,* 308; Hegner, *Die Reichskanzlei,* 255–6. Voroshilov tried to move Uborevičius to Moscow, out of his power base in the Belorussian military district. *Fakel,* II: 237–8 (RGASPI, f. 85, op. 1/s, d. 151, l. 2–4); Minakov, *1937,* 236–7. Yakir, who ran the Ukraine (then Kiev) military district for twelve years, for his part declined a promotion to head the general staff, also preferring a command in the field. Iakir, *Komandarm Iakir,* 226–7; *Istoriia Kommunisticheskoi partii Sovetskogo Soiuza,* IV/ii: 301.
172. Banac, *Diary of Georgi Dimitrov,* 32; Kudriashov, *SSSR i grazhdanskaia voina v Ispanii,* 57–8 (APRF, f. 3, op. 65, d. 221, l. 109–11). On Sept. 13, 1936, Yagoda submitted a memorandum to Kaganovich and Molotov in reference to an unspecified decision in the name of the politburo six days earlier about

the clandestine purchase through third parties in Europe of rifles and fighter planes for Spain, which had been occasioned by a letter from Stalin in Sochi. Kudriashov, *SSSR i grazhdanskaia voina v Ispanii,* 52–3 (APRF, f. 3, op. 65, d. 221, l. 92–6). The politburo had met on Sept. 11 in Stalin's absence and, in part, discussed Spain, but what decision was reached or confirmed remains unclear. Khlevniuk et al., *Stalin i Kaganovich,* 666; Kudriashov, *SSSR i grazhdanskaia voina v Ispanii,* 50–1 (APRF, f. 3, op. 65, 221, l. 85).
173. Kudriashov, *SSSR i grazhdanskaia voina v Ispanii,* 54–6 (APRF, f. 3, op. 65, d. 221, l. 97–101). See also Kowalsky, *Stalin,* paragraphs 458–62 (citing Iurii E. Rybalkin, "Voennaia pomoshch' Sovetskogo Soiuza ispanskomu narodu v natsional'no-revoliutsionnoi voine 1936–1939," PhD diss, Institute of Military History [Moscow], 1992, 79). See also Novikov, *SSSR, Komintern,* II: 44.
174. Gorkii et al., *Krakh germanskoi okkupatsii na Ukraine,* 16.
175. Domarus, *Hitler: Reden,* II: 645 (editor's note). See also Kerrl, *Nürnberg 1936: Der Parteitag der Ehre.*
176. Waddington, *Hitler's Crusade,* 109 (citing National Archives, State Department decimal file, 761.62/395: Dodd to Hull, Sept. 11). The British embassy in Berlin reported that "the extent of the attacks and their violent and pointed, and in fact provocative, nature exceeded all expectations." *DBFP,* 2nd series, XVII: 319–26 (Newton, Sept. 23, 1936).
177. Fröhlich, *Tagebücher von Joseph Goebbels,* III/ii: 178 (Sept. 9, 1936).
178. Pons, *Stalin and the Inevitable War,* 46–7 (citing AVP RF, f. 05, op. 16, papka, 114, d. 1, l. 213); RGASPI, f. 558, op. 11, d. 743, l. 56; *DVP SSSR,* XIX: 423, 762 n160; Adibekov et al., *Politbiuro TsK RKP (b)—VKP (b) i Evropa,* 341 (RGASPI, f. 17, op. 162, d. 20, l. 78).
179. Howson, *Arms for Spain,* 126.
180. Rybalkin, *Operatsiia "X,"* 26 (citing RGASPI, f. 17, op. 120, d. 266, l. 24; RGVA, f. 33987, op. 3, d. 845, l. 14, 17–18, 40; d. 848, l. 109).
181. Haslam, *Struggle for Collective Security,* 115 (citing German intelligence reports). For Spain, 274 million rubles would be spent from 1936–39. Komshukov, "Natsional'no-revoliutsionnaia voina ispanskogo naroda," 179. On aid, see also Novikov, *SSSR, Komintern,* I: 152–63; and RGASPI, f. 17, op. 120, d. 274, l. 1–2, 4–5.
182. *Vechernyi Cheliabinsk,* Aug. 9, 2001.
183. *DVP SSSR,* XIX: 762; Sipols, "SSSR i problema mira," 51.
184. Dimitrov, "Zashchishchat' podlykh terroristov" (no. 14), 3–6, (no. 15), 17–8. In the same issue, Palmiro Togliatti presented Stalin's retrospective criminalization of long-ago factional activity as "an act to defend democracy, peace, socialism, and the revolution." Ercoli, "Uroki protsessa," 37, 43. "The Moscow trial has had a catastrophic effect and has dreadfully compromised the policy of the Popular Front," the Austrian Marxist Rudolf Hilferding had lamented in Aug. 1936. McDermott and Agnew, *Comintern,* 156.
185. Pavliukov, *Ezhov,* 209 (citing author's archive); Petrov and Jansen, *Stalinskii pitomets,* 53 (citing APRF, f. 57, op. 1, d. 27, l. 1–26; f. 045, op. 1, d. 729, l. 86–9).
186. Petrov and Jansen, *Stalinskii pitomets,* 66–7; Jansen and Petrov, *Stalin's Loyal Executioner,* 54.
187. Vinogradov, *Genrikh Iagoda,* 147.
188. Orjonikidze was also summoned to Sochi from Kislovodsk, a distance of 200 miles over the mountains. Khlevniuk, *In Stalin's Shadow,* 104 (citing Kaganovich to Orjonikidze, Sept. 30, 1936: RGASPI, f. 85, op. 1/s. d. 136, l. 46).

189. Khlevniuk et al., *Stalin i Kaganovich*, 682–3 (RGASPI, f. 558, op. 11, d. 94, l. 124–7).

190. Tumshis and Papchinskii, *1937, bol'shaia chistka*, 241–2.

191. RGVA, f. 33987, op. 3, d. 852, l. 138–41; RGASPI, f. 17, op. 3, d. 981, l. 50. Agranov was retained as deputy NKVD commissar under Yezhov.

192. Starkov, "Narkom Ezhov," 27.

193. Khlevniuk et al., *Stalin i Kaganovich*, 683n1 (RGASPI, f. 558, op. 11, d. 94, l. 131); Vinogradov, *Genrikh Iagoda*, 437–8 (TsA FSB, f. 3, op. 2, d. 9, l. 239–40: Vlasik).

194. Petrov and Jansen, *Stalinskii pitomets*, 66.

195. Khlevniuk et al., *Stalinskoe politbiuro*, 148; RGASPI, f. 85, op. 27, d. 93, l. 12–23.

196. Shreider, *NKVD iznutri*, 35. Shreider recalled a conversation in which a colleague "began to extol [Yezhov's] democratism and simplicity, explaining that he visited the offices of all the investigators, personally acquainting himself how the work was going" (37). Those visits often entailed Yezhov's demonstrations of how to extract testimony by beating the accused to a pulp.

197. "O tak nazyvaemom 'parallel'nom antisovetskom trotskistom tsentre,'" 39; APRF, f. 3, op. 24, d. 241, l. 213. Also on Sept. 29, 1936, the politburo formally approved Operation X, which was well under way. Kudriashov, *SSSR i grazhdanskaia voina v Ispanii*, 75–7 (APRF, f. 3, op. 65, d. 221, 178–82), 78 (l. 173–7); Rybalkin, *Operatsiia "X,"* 28–9 (citing APRF, f. 3, op. 74, d. 20, l. 87); RGASPI, f. 17, op. 162, d. 20, l. 87.

198. Rybalkin, *Operatsiia "X,"* 42; Kowalsky, *Stalin*, paragraph 472 (citing RGAVMF, f. 1529, op. 1, d. 147, l. 56).

199. Grechko et al., *Istoriia vtoroi mirovoi voiny*, I: 54. Cf. Kowalsky, *Stalin*, paragraphs 491–2.

200. Rybalkin, *Operatsiia "X,"* 37 (RGVA, f. 33987, op. 3, d. 853, l. 45); Howson, *Arms for Spain*, 125–6.

201. Rybalkin, *Operatsiia "X,"* 42 (RGVA, f. 33987, op. 3, d. 870, l. 341–3).

202. Khlevniuk et al., *Stalin i Kaganovich*, 700 (RGASPi, f. 558, op. 11, d. 95, l. 97), 700 n2 (l. 96). Kaganovich told Stalin that the Spanish ambassador, Pascua, feared the fall of Madrid and was "not a genuine revolutionary-Bolshevik, but a Menshevik" (701–2: d. 743, op. 64–71: Oct. 11, 1936).

203. Rybalkin, *Operatsiia "X,"* 42 (RGVA, f. 33987, op. 3, d. 870, l. 341–3).

204. Gorev appended an eyewitness account: "the greatest impression, sometimes impossible to convey, was made by the tanks." Kudriashov, *SSSR i grazhdanskaia voina v Ispanii*, 105 (APRF, f. 3, op. 65, d. 222, l. 66–7: Oct. 16, 1936).

205. Rybalkin, *Operatsiia "X,"* 36–7, 43–5 (RGVA, f. 33987, op. 3, d. 870, l. 278–9); Grechko, *Istoriia votori mirovoi voiny*, I: 53; Howson, *Arms for Spain*, 138–42; Kowalsky, *Stalin*, paragraph 502.

206. Kowalsky, *Stalin*, paragraphs 503–14. When Kaganovich and Molotov reported (Sept. 5, 1936) on a proposed deal to sell England and Sweden petroleum products at a 5 percent discount to the world price, Stalin wrote back from Sochi, "Why . . . do we have so much oil? Stalin." They informed him that that was standard international practice. RGASPI, f. 558, op. 11, d. 94, l. 65–6. Stalin had just recommended selling oil to Republican Spain at well below world prices (d. 9, l. 28–30). The Nationalists got their oil from Standard Oil of New Jersey and the Texas Oil Company.

207. The regime discharged 22,000 soldiers for various reasons (including political ones) in 1936, worsening the housing shortage. RGVA, f. 33 987, op. 3, d. 1045, Volkogonov papers, Hoover, container 17.

208. The Soviets also unloaded on Spain some 280 British-, French-, and Japanese-made artillery pieces. Rybalkin, *Operatsiia "X,"* 30 (citing TsAMO, f. 119, op. 663, d. 1, l. 22: Nov. 2, 1936).

209. Kowalsky, *Stalin*, paragraph 604 (citing RGVA, f. 33987, op. 3, d. 961, l. 158).

210. Meshcheriakov, "Sovetskii Soiuz i antifashistskaia voina ispanskogo naroda," 29; Radosh et al., *Spain Betrayed*, 147 (RGVA, f. 33987, op. 3, d. 1010, l. 295: Krivoshein to Voroshilov, undated, probably early 1937); Rybalkin, *Operatisiia "X,"* 25.

211. Costello and Tsarev, *Deadly Illusions*, 255–6 (citing ASVRR, file 17679, operational correspondence, Spain, I: 20). On the mixed performance of Soviet military advisers, see Payne, *Spanish Civil War*, 166–72.

212. Pons, *Global Revolution*, 81 (citing RGASPI, f. 495, op. 18, d. 1135).

213. *Pravda*, Oct. 16, 1936; Degras, *Soviet Documents on Foreign Policy*, III: 212.

214. De Mayo, *Last Optimist*, 281, 285–6. It is possible other Soviet officials knew of the secret gold stash earlier than Rosenberg. The Spanish government made the request official on Oct. 15. Four days later, Krestinsky telegrammed Soviet assent and conditions to Rosenberg. Kudriashov, *SSSR i grazhdanskaia voina v Ispanii*, 89 (APRF, f. 3, op. 65, d. 234, l. 1), 99 (APRF, f. 3, op. 65, d. 234, l. 2: Krestinsky to Rosenberg, Oct. 13, 1936), 102 (l.3), 106 (l. 5), 107–9 (l. 9–10, 6, 11); Rybalkin, *Operatsiia "X,"* 92–3 (citing APRF, f. 3, op. 74, d. 20, l. 104).

215. Kuznetsov worked with the Spanish navy, which had arrived at Cartagena around Oct. 18, to provide a secure escort. Possibly because of an enemy air raid, departure was delayed until the next night. Rybalkin, *Operatsiia "X,"* 93 (APRF, f. 3, op. 74, d. 20, l. 104–5; RGVA f. 33987, op. 3, d. 912, l. 84); Bolloten, *Spanish Civil War*, 150; Kuznetsov, "S ispanskimi moriakami," 241–4.

216. Rybalkin, *Operatisia "X,"* 31 (citing AVP RF, f. 010, op. 11, d. 53, pap. 71, l. 141: early Nov. 1936). See also Haslam, *Struggle for Collective Security*, 115; Pons, "Papers on Foreign and International Policy." Litvinov wrote on a report by the Soviet delegate Stein from the League of Nations in Geneva that "France has given striking evidence of her weakness and indecision." Dullin, *Men of Influence*, 127 (citing AVP RF, f. 5, op. 17, d. 128, pap. 15).

217. *DVP SSSR*, XIX: 463–4, 513–4.

218. *DBFP*, 2nd series, XVII: 475–6.

219. That Oct. 1936, a new French ambassador, Robert Coulondre, assumed his duties in Moscow and conveyed that French participation in any "preventive" war was unthinkable and instructed his hosts that Soviet interference in French domestic affairs was impermissible. Coulondre, *De Staline a Hitler*, 30–46.

220. *DGFP*, series C, V: 1066–8 (Oct. 12, 1936).

221. The memo by Schnurre called for trade to be "rendered completely non-political." *DGFP*, series C, V: 1115–8; Hilger and Meyer, *Incompatible Allies*, 284.

222. Surits wrote to Litvinov (Oct. 27, 1936) that "the initiative for revitalizing and strengthening economic relations in recent years has come from Göring and his entourage." Abramov, "Osobaia missiia Davida Kandelaki," 149 (citing AVP RF, f. 082, op. 19, pap. 83, d. 4, l. 110). In late Oct. 1936, Göring received Kandelaki (accompanied by Friedrichson), but would then push further contact into the hands of his cousin Herbert, who lacked the authority to make the decisions. Kandelaki would go back to Schacht, whose power had waned. Göring would pull together aluminum plants, oil refineries, ironworks, and manufacturing of synthetic oil and rubber (made from coal) and synthetic textiles (made from pulped wood). He also requisitioned foreign currency from the populace. Tooze, *Wages of Destruction*, 214 (citing BAI R2501 6446, 13–9), 219–24.

223. Khlevniuk, *Stalin i Ordzhonikidze*, 88–9; RGASPI, f. 17, op. 71, d. 43, l. 3, 26, 28–9, 31–2.

224. *Izvestiia*, Nov. 22, 1963.

225. Knight, *Beria*, 73–4; Vaksberg, *Neraskrytye tainy*, 123.

226. RGASPI, f. 17, op. 3, d. 981, l. 384. His arrest was publicly announced on Nov. 14, 1936.

227. Ordzhonikidze, *O Sergo Ordzhonikidze*, 272 (Zinaida). Beria was preparing a volume of reminiscences on the occasion of Orjonikidze's fiftieth birthday. Kvashonkin, *Sovetskoe rukovodstvo*, 336 (RGASPI, f. 85, op. 29, d. 418, l. 1).

228. Khlevniuk, *Politbiuro*, 173 (citation without specifics).

229. Leushin, "Ia davno uzhe ostavil sei greshnyi mir': pis'ma Stalina s togo sveta," *Istochnik*, 2003, no. 2: 33–5 (RGASPI, f. 558, op. 11. d, 1160, l. 102–3, 98, 105, 107, 106). The AP bureau chief was Charles P. Nutter.

230. Rybalkin, *Operatsiia "X,"* 94–5; Kudriashov, *SSSR i grazhdanskaia voina v Ispanii*, 126 (APRF, f. 3, op. 65, d. 234, l. 34), 134–5 (l. 52–4). See also Kudriashov, *SSSR i grazhdanskaia voina v Ispanii*, 124–5 (APRF, f. 3, op. 65, d. 234, l. 23–24), 126–7 (l. 36–7). Orlov received the Order of Lenin for the gold transfer, though his award was announced in *Pravda* under his former pseudonym (Nikolsky).

231. Karmen, *No Pasarán!*, 261; Volodarsky, *Stalin's Agent*, 172 and photographic plates (crediting Adelina Abramson-Kondraytyeva, one of the attendees, LSE Cañada Blanch Centre).

232. Larina, *This I Cannot Forget*, 299; Cohen, *Bukharin*, 369; Volobuev and Kuleshov, *Ochishchenie*, 155. Rykov was evicted at this time from his Kremlin apartment and moved to the House on the Embankment.

233. Khaustov and Samuelson, *Stalin, NKVD*, 108 (APRF, f. 3, op. 24, d. 252, l. 99); Whitewood, *Red Army*, 206–10 (citing RGVA, f. 9, op. 29, d. 285, l. 22, 232–42); Cherushev, *1937 god*, 70, 97. Arrests in the Red Army for Jan.–March 1937 kept the same pace: 125, including 43 officers. Whitewood, *Red Army*, 209 (f. 33837, op. 21, d. 107, l. 14).

234. The longer-term goal was to turn Spain into an economic colony. Harper, *German Economic Policy*; Leitz, *Economic Relations*; Barbieri, *Hitler's Shadow Empire*.

235. Ernest Hemingway, a war correspondent for the North American Newspaper Alliance living in Madrid's Florida Hotel, would complete *Fifth Column*, his first and only play, the next year. Kale, "Fifth Column."

236. Soviet personnel viewed foreign embassy compounds and residences as storehouses for weapons to be used by fifth columnists, justifying raids and sweeping roundups. Primakov, *Ocherki*, III: 152–3; Kol'tsov, *Ispaniia v ogne*, I/ii: 227.

237. Kol'tsov, *Ispanskii dnevnik*, 233–45.
238. Preston, *Last Ukraine*, 70–88.
239. Bollinger, "Fifth Column Marches On."
240. V. A. Suiazin, "V boi vstupaiut istrebiteli," in *My internatsionalisty: vospominaniia sovetskikh dobrovol'tsev-uchatsnikov natsional'noirevoliutsionnoi voiny v Ispanii* (Moscow: Politizdat, 1975), 52. Airplane losses from accidents were high: 147 for the Republic, versus a mere 13 for the putschists. Kowalsky, *Stalin*, paragraph 677.
241. Kowalsky, *Stalin*, paragraph 724.
242. Medvedev, *Nikolai Bukharin*, 130; Conquest, *Reassessment*, 143–4, citing Solzhenitsyn, *Gulag Arkhipelago*, I: 415.
243. Preston, *Franco*, 205–6.
244. "Our great friend and parent," Kaganovich wrote to Orjonikidze, "does not want to facilitate the nasty work of smothering the Spanish Republic, on the contrary he wants to help the Spanish Republic smother the fascists." Khlevniuk et al., *Stalinskoe politbiuro*, 151 (RGASPI, f. 85, op. 29, d. 435, l. 1–12; Oct. 12, 1936). Stalin told Spain's ambassador in Jan. 1937 that "in opposing the triumph of Italy and Germany, they are trying to prevent any weakening in France's power or military situation." Smyth, "Soviet Policy," 99.
245. *DBFP*, 2nd series, XVII: 30.
246. *Pravda*, Nov. 26, 1936; Chukovskii, *Dnevnik*, 149.
247. At the 7th Congress of Soviets, *Pravda* had announced a possible constitutional revision, including the prospect of direct, secret elections. *Pravda*, Feb. 7 and 8, 1935.
248. Bukharin and Radek, commission members, undertook analyses of the constitutions of Germany and of France; the commission also examined the Provisional Government's 1917 electoral law. On holiday in fall 1935, Stalin, working on a draft, asked Kaganovich for a copy of Switzerland's constitution (Kaganovich had it translated by Radek). RGASPI, f. 558, op. 11, d. 83, l. 92; d. 90, l. 121, 126; d. 53, l. 122; *Pravda*, July 8, 1935. An editorial subcommittee—Akulov, Krylenko, Vyshinsky, Stalin—drafted the text of the constitution.
249. Trotsky, "New Constitution." Whether Trotsky's article influenced Stalin is unknown. Before it was published (May 9), but not necessarily before Stalin read it (it was finished April 16), Yakov Yakovlev, Stetsky, and Tal were summoned to the Little Corner (April 17, 18, 19, and 22, 1936) to go over the draft text of the constitution with Stalin. On May 15, the draft was discussed and further revised at a meeting.
250. Siegelbaum and Sokolov, *Stalinism as a Way of Life*, 158–206 (at 159–60).
251. Schapiro, *Communist Party of the Soviet Union* (2nd ed.), 410–1.
252. Translated in Field, *Three French Writers*, 29. See also Unger, *Constitutional Development in the USSR*.
253. For example: Petr Garvi, "Novaia Sovetskaia konstituttsiia," *Sotsialisticheskii vetsnik*, July 10, 1936. See also Liebich, *From the Other Shore*, 249–51.
254. Kozlov, *Neizvestnaia Rossiia*, II: 270–80. "Everybody thanks Soviet rule for the fact that the government took all the enterprises away from the landowners, and everybody thanks it for saying that there should be no war," stated a letter from Voronezh province to *Peasant Newspaper*. "But people on the collective farm are not happy and everybody is hungry and are quietly saying, but obviously afraid to say, that because the whole enterprise belongs to the state, the peasant does all this work and has to give a certain amount from each hectare to the state, so that there will be no war." She added that farmers

wanted to quit the collectives, but newspapers made no mention of this. Siegelbaum and Sokolov, *Stalinism as a Way of Life*, 175 (RGASPI, f. 17, op. 120, d. 232, l. 83); 176 (l. 80–2).
255. In a few cases leaflets were printed and posted. Vasil'ev, "30-e gody na Ukraine."
256. Many comments entailed demands to guarantee pensions, social insurance, and access to sanatoriums for collective farmers (the benefits accorded to workers). Siegelbaum and Sokolov, *Stalinism as a Way of Life*, 158–206; Petrone, *Life Has Become More Joyous*, 184–202. See also intelligentsia speculation about Stalin not trusting the party and instead wanting to be a president or emperor: Davies, *Popular Opinion*, 172 (citing Ts-GAIPD SPb, f. 24, op. 2b, d. 185, l. 50-2).
257. Trotsky, *Revolution Betrayed*, chap. 10 ("The Soviet Union in the Mirror of the New Constitution"). See also Hoffmann, *Stalinist Values*.
258. Chuev, *Sto sorok*, 289. Stalin had once said that "the dictatorship of the proletariat is the sharpest form of class struggle." Danilov and Khlevniuk, *Kak lomali NEP*, IV: 654 (politburo meeting, uncorrected transcript, April 22, 1929).
259. *Pravda*, Nov. 26, 1936.
260. *Krasnaia zvezda*, Nov. 28, 1936. The order to print Stalin's speech in 20 million brochure copies also ordered 5 million phonographic records. Petrone, *Life Has Become More Joyous*, 178 (citing RGALI, f. 962, op. 3, d. 293, l. 35, *SSSR na ekrane*, 1936, no. 10); 181–2 (TsMAM, f. 528, op. 1, d. 409, l. 7; f. 150, op. 5, d. 26. L. 163; TsAODM, f. 63, op. 1, d. 716, l. 4), 184–5. For the film of the speech: RGAKFD, 1–3470. Between 1921 and 1935, Stalin's publications amounted to 160 separate items, in 75 languages, and nearly 116 million copies.
261. *International Military Tribunal*, X: 239–41. The negotiations had been conducted with Lieutenant-Colonel Hiroshi Ōshima, the military attaché to Berlin. Tokushirō, "Anti-Comintern Pact."
262. Wheeler-Bennett, *Documents on International Affairs*, 299–300; Shirer, *Berlin Diary*, 69–70; *DVP SSSR*, XIX: 779 (Surits in Berlin to Moscow, Nov. 27, 1936). See also Beloff, *Foreign Policy of Soviet Russia*, I: 593.
263. Quoted in Chamberlain, *Japan over Asia*, 163–4. See also Presseisen, *Germany and Japan*, 115–6.
264. Presseisen, *Germany and Japan*, 190, citing *International Military Tribunal for the Far East, Documents Presented in Evidence*, exhibits 487, 3508; Jones, *Japan's New Order*, 99n2.
265. Muggeridge, *Ciano's Diplomatic Papers*, 58 (October 24, 1936). Alfred Rosenberg, the ideologue, had stated at a Nuremberg rally, "We acknowledge the destiny of the Yellow race and wish it in its own Lebensraum the development of its culture which originated from its racial soul." Presseisen, *Germany and Japan*, 90; Baynes, *Speeches of Adolf Hitler*, II: 1258–9; Toynbee, *Survey of International Affairs*, 384–5n3; Rosenberg, *Blut und Ehre*, 347.
266. The Soviets undercut their own accusations that the pact was directed at the USSR by their long-standing pretense that the Comintern was an independent organization not controlled from Moscow.
267. "Well informed people refuse to believe that for the drawing up of the two scantly published articles of the German-Japanese agreement it was necessary to conduct negotiations for fifteen months, and that on the Japanese side it was necessary to entrust these negotiations to an Army general, and on the German side to an important diplomat,"

Litvinov huffed to the Congress of Soviets (Nov. 28, 1936). Wheeler-Bennett, *Documents on International Affairs*, 1936, 302. The Soviet Union suspended the agreed but not yet signed bilateral fisheries convention with Japan. Grew, *Ten Years in Japan*, 196; Iklé, *German-Japanese Relations*, 41–2 (citing U.S. Govt., Dept. of State, Files 762.94/108: U.S. embassy in France to secretary of state).
268. Khaustov, "Deiatel'nost' organov," 240; Volkov, "Legendy i desitvitel'nost' o Rikharde Zorge," 100; Korol'kov, *Chelovek, dlia kotorogo ne bylo tain*, 108; *DGFP*, series C, VI: 208 (Dirksen in Tokyo to Berlin, Dec. 23, 1936).
269. *Peace and War—United States Foreign Policy*, 340–2; *Documents on International Affairs*, I: 4–5. A Soviet diplomat in Tokyo would even inform his German counterparts that they had read the actual text. *FRUS, Japan, 1931–1941*, II, 153.
270. *Chrezvychainyi VIII Vsesoiuznyi s"ezd Sovetov*.
271. Waddington, *Hitler's Crusade*, 110 (citing BK, ZSg. 101/14, Presseanweisung, Nov. 28, 1931). Following a discussion with Hitler, Goebbels had recently written in his diary: "The showdown with Bolshevism is coming . . . The army is completely won over by us. Führer untouchable . . . Dominance in Europe is as good as certain." Fröhlich, *Tagebücher von Joseph Goebbels*, III/ii: 251–2 (Nov. 15, 1936). In fact, German planning was directed at a war in the West, an aim for which the Hitler regime anticipated subordinating Poland and Hungary. Weinberg, *Hitler's Foreign Policy*, 13–4.
272. Fröhlich, *Tagebücher von Joseph Goebbels*, II: 272–3 (Dec. 2, 1936).
273. Moradiellos, "British Government and General Franco," 44 (citing PRO FO371/20470, W15925, minute by Gladwyn Jebb: Nov. 25, 1936).
274. Dullin, *Men of Influence*, 124–5 (citing RGVA, f. 33987, op. 3, d. 1027, l. 148: Potyomkin to Krestinsky, Nov. 12, 1936; AVP RF, f. 010, op. 11, d. 77, l. 113: Litvinov to Potyomkin, Nov. 19).
275. Litvinov had made the same point. Pons, *Stalin and the Inevitable War*, 60, 68. See also Haslam, *Struggle for Collective Security*, 122, citing *Pravda*, Nov. 29, 1936 (Litvinov speech to the Congress of Soviets).
276. Petrov and Jansen, *Stalinskii pitomets*, 254–89 (at 269, citing TsA FSB, f. 3–os, op. 4, d. 6, l. 1–61).
277. Getty and Naumov, *Road to Terror*, 304–8 (RGASPI, f. 17, op. 2, d. 575, l. 11–9, 40–5, 49–53, 57–60, 66–7); "Fragmenty stenogrammy dekabr'skogo plenuma TsK VKP (b) 1936 goda," 6; APRF, f. 3, op. 24, d. 256, l. 12.
278. Kaganovich differentiated party guilt from juridical guilt. Getty and Naumov, *Road to Terror*, 309–12 (RGASPI, f. 17, op. 2, d. 575, l. 69–74, 82–6).
279. Mikoyan chimed in with other names (Skrypnyk, Khanjyan). RGASPI, f. 558, op. 11, d. 1119, l. 63.
280. How many attendees (besides the stool pigeon Khrushchev) understood this targeting of Kaganovich remains unclear. Khrushchev, *Vospominaniia*, I: 156–8; Khrushchev, *Memoirs*, I: 150–3; http://www.gorlovka360.dn.ua/sport-i-zdorovie/stadion-shahter-virtualnyiy-tur; http://www.memo.ru/history/1937/dec_1936/VI9501.htm; Getty and Naumov, *Road to Terror*, 312 (RGASPI, f. 17, op. 2, d. 576, l. 67–70); Rogovin, *Stalin's Terror*, 143. Shortly thereafter, Andreyev condemned Furer at a party meeting in Rostov. Khlevniuk, *In Stalin's Shadow*, 161.
281. RGASPI, f. 558, op. 11, d. 132, l. 132; Khlevniuk, *Khoziain*, 277.

282. Jansen and Petrov, *Stalin's Loyal Executioner*, 58 (citing RGASPI, f. 17, op. 2, d. 575, l. 6–68); "Fragmenty stenogrammy dekabr'skogo plenuma TsK KPSS (b) 1936 goda," 4 (APRF, op. 76, d. 20, l. 129 -133); Getty and Naumov, *Road to Terror*, 303–22 (RGASPI, f. 17, op. 2, d. 575, l. 69–74, 82–6, 94–7, 100–4, 122–6, 134–7, 1159–62, 165–7, 169–72; d. 576, 67–70); "O partiinosti lits, prokhodivshikh po delu tak nazyvaemogo 'antisovetskogo pravotrotskistskogo bloka,'" 75–6; Banac, *Diary of Georgi Dimitrov*, 38–9. No transcript appears to exist of Stalin's full speech to the plenum, just excerpts.
283. Rogovin, *1937*, 179–80. Bukharin ceased to be listed as editor from Jan. 16, 1937.
284. Banac, *Diary of Georgi Dimitrov*, 40 (Dec. 9, 1936). See also the entry for Nov. 26, 1936 (37).
285. Dmitri Bogomolov, the Soviet consul in China, told Dimitrov in Moscow (Dec. 9) that "Chiang Kai-shek will decide on an agreement with the Communists only on the brink of war with Japan and in connection with an agreement with the Soviet Union." Banac, *Diary of Georgi Dimitrov*, 40.
286. Wai Chor, "Making of the Guomindang's Japan Policy."
287. Bertram, *Crisis in China*, 108.
288. Titarenko, *VKP (b), komintern i kitai: dokumenty*, IV/ii: 1068 (RGASPI, f. 495, op. 74, d. 275, l. 5–9).
289. Taylor, *Generalissimo*, 122, 124–5 (Zhang Xueliang, Columbia Interviews, XXXVII: 25–189).
290. Taylor, *Generalissimo*, 124 (Chiang Diaries, Hoover Institution Archives, box 39, folder 4: Nov. 24, 1936).
291. Zhang may have divulged to Mao's secret liaison in Xi'an that he intended to "stage a coup d'état." Guotao, *Rise of the Chinese Communist Party*, II: 478–9; Chang and Halliday, *Mao*, 181–2.
292. On Dec. 9, 1936, as a light snow fell, students marked the one-year anniversary of a nationwide anti-Japanese protest and headed out to confront Chiang; upon reaching Lintong they were fired upon; there were casualties. Taylor, *Generalissimo*, 126–7 (Zhang Xueliang, Columbia Interviews, XXXVII: 25–1901).
293. Li-fu, *Storm Clouds*, 119–20; Kai-shek, *Soviet Russia in China*, 73. Chinese Communists had repeatedly tried to solicit the help of the Young Marshal and, despite Moscow's warnings about his unreliability, preferred Zhang to the Nationalists. Many Chinese Communists were champing at the bit to eliminate Chiang by any means. See also Snow, *Random Notes*, 1–3.
294. Pantsov and Levine, *Mao*, 299, citing Ye Zilong, *Ye Zilong huiyilu* (Beijing: Zhongyang wenxian chbanshe, 2000), 38–9; Chang and Halliday, *Mao*, 183. See also Guotao, *Rise of the Chinese Communist Party*, II: 480.
295. Kai-shek, "A Fortnight," 58–63.
296. Peter H. L. and Edith Chang Papers, 1930s–2001, Columbia University, box 7.
297. Selle, *Donald of China*, 324. William Henry Donald, a journalist and assistant to Chiang, arrived in Xi'an on Dec. 14, sent by the wife, Soong Mayling, and brother T. V. Soong. Donald, once an adviser to Zhang (until 1933), was allowed to see Chiang, and pleaded with him to compromise on a united front and turn against the Japanese. Mayling, *Sian*.
298. Banac, *Diary of Georgi Dimitrov*, 41 (Dec. 13, 1936); RGASPI, f. 146, op. 2, d. 3, l. 29.
299. Krymov, *Istoriko-memuarnye zapiski*, 288–90.
300. Wu, *Sian Incident*, 101. Otto Braun, a Comintern official, recalled that word of the arrest "produced a genuine rapture, for Chiang

Kai-shek was the most hated man in the CCP and the Chinese Red Army." At an open air meeting, Mao declared it time to settle accounts with the traitor and "bring him before a people's court." Those assembled adopted a resolution for a "mass trial" of Chiang Kai-shek. Braun, *Comintern Agent in China*, 183; Snow, *Random Notes*, 1; Short, *Mao*, 347; Guotao, *Rise of the Chinese Communist Party*, II: 481. Another account has Mao urging Zhou Enlai to make haste to Xi'an, several days away by horseback, to persuade Zhang "to carry out the final measure." Chang and Halliday, *Mao*, 184, citing Central Archive, 1997, 213, and *Zhang Xueliang nianpo* (Beijing, 1996), 1124.
301. Guotao, *Rise of the Chinese Communist Party*, II: 479–82; Taylor, *Generalissimo*, 128–9, citing *Zhongguo gongchandang guanyu Xi'an shibian dangan shiliao xuanbian* (Peking: Zhunguo dangan chubanshe, 1997), 213.
302. Dallin and Firsov, *Dimitrov and Stalin*, 106 (RGASPI, f. 495, op. 74, d. 294, l. 6); Titarenko, *VKP (b), komintern i kitai: dokumenty*, IV/ii: 1084–5.
303. Banac, *Diary of Georgi Dimitrov*, 42; RGASPI, f. 146, op. 2, d. 3, l. 30.
304. Banac, *Diary of Georgi Dimitrov*, 41–2; RGASPI, f. 146, op. 2, d. 3, l. 29–30.
305. *Na prieme*, 195.
306. Titarenko, *VKP (b), komintern i kitai: dokumenty*, IV/ii: 1085–7 (RGASPI, f. 495, op. 74, d. 281, l. 11); Titarenko, *Kommunisticheskii internatsional*, 270 (abridged).
307. Shai, *Zhang Xueliang*, 77.
308. Gibson, "Chiang Kai-shek's Central Army," 333–4. See also van Slyke, *Enemies and Friends*, chapter 4; Wu, *Sian Incident*; Braun, *Comintern Agent in China*, 182–90; Sheng and Garver, "New Light on the Second United Front"; Garver, "Soviet Union and the Xi'an Incident."
309. Banac, *Diary of Georgi Dimitrov*, 42–3.
310. Banac, *Diary of Georgi Dimitrov*, 44 (Dec. 18, 1936); Radzinsky, *Stalin*, 352 (citing D. Karavkina, employee of VOKS, Dec. 19, 1936).
311. Snow, *Random Notes*, 1–3. Mao supposedly kept the telegram secret from Zhou, who was en route to persuade Zhang to execute Chiang; in any case Zhang had not moved to eliminate Chiang.
312. Pantsov and Levine, *Mao*, 302, citing Jin, *Mao Zedong zhuan (1893–1949)* (Beijing: Zhongyang Wenxian Chubanshe, 2003), 431–2.
313. Zhang had sent his personal Boeing for Zhou. Leonard, *I Flew for China*, 99. On Dec. 20, Zhang greeted T. V. Soong at the Xi'an airport and took him to Chiang; upon seeing his brother, a surprised Chiang wept. Chiang's wife, Mayling, arrived in Xi'an, too. Taylor, *Generalissimo*, 132 (T. V. Soong papers, box 60, folder 3), 133 (citing interview in 1995 with Wang Chi, who cited a conversation with Zhang; and T. V. Soong Papers, box 60, folder 3, pp. 6–7); Kai-shek, "Fortnight," 97; Mayling, *Sian*, 54–5.
314. Taylor, *Generalissimo*, 130 (citing Zhang Xueliang Interviews, Columbia University, XXIX: 25–1928); Suyin, *Eldest Son*, 153–4; Guotao, *Rise of the Chinese Communist Party*, II: 479–87.
315. Germany had its own naval technology (which the Soviets also sought). Maiolo, "Anglo-Soviet Naval Armaments Diplomacy." See also Adibekov et al., *Politbiuro TsK RKP (b)—VKP (b) i Evropa*, 336 (RGASPI, f. 17, op. 162, d. 19, l. 185: May 27, 1936), 337 (l. 202: June 27); *DVP SSSR*, XIX: 272, 376. In London on July 17, 1937, Anglo-Soviet and Anglo-German naval treaties were signed, but Stalin's large fleet construction appetites had only grown by then.
316. Banac, *Diary of Georgi Dimitrov*, 38–40; Volodarsky, *Stalin's Agent*, 209 (citing PRO

HW 17/27, mask traffic Moscow-Madrid-Moscow); Haslam, *Struggle for Collective Security*, 116; *Communist International* 142 (Feb. 1937): 136–8.
317. Kol'tsov, "Podlye manevry ispanskikh trotskistov," 5; "Gnusnye manevry trotskistov v Katalonii," *Pravda*, Dec. 17, 1936.
318. Also on December 17, an article appeared in the émigré press based on an interview with Noe Jordania, the exiled elder statesman of Georgian Marxism. "For him unacceptable methods do not exist . . . He is vindictive, ruthless, relentless. He is capable of any actions for the sake of power. The spirit of despotism of old times lives in him." Vakar, "Stalin," 2.
319. Kol'tsov, "Agentura trotskistov v Ispanii." See also "Ispanskii dnevnik," *Novyi mir*, no. 4 (1938): 5 (Jan. 21, 1937).
320. Valedinskii, "Organizm Stalina vpolne zdorovyi."
321. Murin, *Stalin v ob"iatiakh*, 190–1. "Stalin's children not there," observed Dimitrov. "Till 5:30 in the morning!" Banac, *Diary of Georgi Dimitrov*, 47 (Dec. 21, 1936).
322. Kudriashov, *SSSR i grazhdanskaia voina v Ispanii*, 156–7 (APRF, f. 3, op. 65, d. 222, l. 172–5); Pertsov, *Voina i revoliutsiia v Ispanii*, I: 419–21; Carr, *Comintern and the Spanish Civil War*, 86–8. See also *VII kongress Kommunisticheskogo Internatsionala*, 452 (Dec. 27, 1936, Comintern decree). Stalin would reiterate to Pascua in person on Feb. 3, 1937, that there would be no Soviet model for Spain, which was called "a democratic republic of a new type."
323. Ercoli, "Ob osobennostiakh ispanskoi revoliutsii." "Kautsky" was also the code name used for Diaz, the leader of the Spanish Communist party.
324. Göring had extended the invitation on Dec. 6; Litvinov had telegrammed permission to accept. Abramov, "Osobaia missiia Davida Kandelaki," 150 (citing AVP RF, f. 05, op. 16, pap. 118, d. 46, l. 157–9; op. 17, pap. 130, d. 42, l. 7: Surits to Krestinsky: Jan. 27, 1937); Adibekov et al., *Politbiuro TsK RKP (b)—VKP (b) i Evropa*, 346–7n1 (RGASPI, f. 71, op. 25, d. 3646).
325. RGANI, f. 89, op. 63, d. 22, l. 1–5 (Stomonyakov, Nov. 10, 1936); RGANI, f. 89, op. 63, d. 23, l. 1–9 (Dec. 24). Stalin and entourage received the Mongols again on Jan. 4, 1937, this time with trade and economics officials. The meeting ended with supper and toasts. Stalin told the story of his escape from Buryat Novaya Uda in 1903. RGANI, f. 89, op. 63, d. 24, l. 1–12.
326. Taylor, *Generalissimo*, 134–6.
327. Zhang was kept in indefinite house arrest. Taylor, *Generalissimo*, 135 (citing T. V. Soong Papers, box 60, folder 3, p. 15); Gibson, "Chiang Kai-shek's Central Army," 336.
328. "Chiang had left for Xian a popular leader," his biographer writes, "but returned a national hero." Taylor, *Generalissimo*, 135–6.
329. "The terrific personal shock Chiang had suffered might have embittered and unbalanced a man less gifted with foresight and hastened him into precipitate actions of revenge—which, in fact, Chiang's angry followers in Nanking demanded," wrote Edgar Snow. *Red Star over China*, 465.
330. Chiang Ching-kuo would return via Vladivostok to China on April 19, 1937.
331. In Dec. 1936, Wang Jingwei had an audience with Hitler, discussing China's entry into the Pact and Germany's reciprocation with greatly expanded aid. (The German foreign ministry dismissed reports of the meeting as "hearsay.") Taylor, *Generalissimo*, 622n142. See also Wai Chor, "Making of the Guomindang's Japan Policy," 244. In late 1938, Wang would depart Chongqing for Hanoi, French Indochina, and announce his support for a negotiated settlement with the Japanese; he would fly to Shanghai and enter into

negotiations with Japan, defecting to the Japanese side.

332. Larina, *This I Cannot Forget*, 324, 304.

333. Valedinskii, "Organizm Stalina vpolne zdorovyi."

334. *Kommunisticheskii Internatsional*, 1937, no. 1: 8-9.

335. AVP RF, f. 05, op. 17, d. 49, p. 131, l. 59-60 (*La Batalla*, Jan. 21, 1937). Orlov seems to have pushed in Jan. 1937 for approval for an armed uprising in the Nationalist rear, in Spanish Morocco, but the Spanish Republican government did not support the idea, wary of overly antagonizing France given the proximity to French Morocco. Costello and Tsarev, *Deadly Illusions*, 274, 467n21 (citing ASVRR file 17679, l: 54). Orlov finally became official NKVD station chief in Spain in late Feb. 1937.

336. It seems that in Nov. 1936, one POUM activist who traveled to Mexico as head of a sports delegation transmitted a request from the POUM leadership to the Mexican president to grant Trotsky political asylum there. The next year, this same man, Bartolome Costa-Amik, met three times with Trotsky. The two men argued over the desirability and feasibility of POUM carrying out a socialist revolution in Spain, as in Russia. Rogovin, *1937*, 355 (citing *Trud*, Feb. 22, 1994).

337. L. Trotskii, "V Meksike," Hoover Institution Archives, Nicolaevsky Collection, box 354, folder 37, pp. 124-5. Trotsky was under surveillance by the Mexican police, the Mexican Communist party (on behalf of Moscow), the NKVD, and the U.S. Government. Hoover Institution Archives, Joseph Hansen Papers, box 70, folder 8, pp. 1-15.

338. RGASPI, f. 558, op. 11, d. 1120, l. 1-20. On Jan. 6, 1937, the USSR conducted a population census (it had been delayed twice), the first since 1926. The enumeration encompassed Gulag camps, too, but it returned only 162 million people, versus an expectation of more than 170 million. The census further showed that 57 percent of inhabitants above the age of sixteen identified themselves as religious. That was more than 55 million people. The census results were suppressed. Zhiromskaia et al., *Polveka pod grifom "sekretno,"* 98, 100. See also Merridale, "1937 Census."

339. RGASPI, f. 558, op. 11, d. 1120, l. 7-8, 11-12.

340. RGASPI, f. 558, op. 11, d. 1120, l. 8-10. Stalin had supposedly said much the same, more colorfully, to the Soviet writer Mikhail Sholokhov ("What can you do? People need a little god"). Gromov, *Stalin*, 160, citing M. M. Sholokhov, "Razgovor o otsom," *Literaturnaia gazeta*, May 23, 1990. See also Feuchtwanger, *Moskva 1937 goda*, 65. Kolakowski asserted that "Stalin as a despot was much more the party's creation than its creator," but he got right that Stalin "was the personification of a system which irresistibly sought to be personified." Kolakowski, *Main Currents of Marxism*, III: 2, 5. See also Ennker, "'Struggling for Stalin's Soul.'"

341. RGASPI, f. 558, op. 11, d. 1120, l. 14-7. What Stalin did not divulge was that while the number of people arrested for terrorist acts and statements had dropped in 1936, to 3,388 people (from 8,988 in 1935 and 6,504 in 1934), the number of those rounded up for belonging to an opposition had jumped to 23,279 (from 3,447 in 1935 and 631 in 1934). Khaustov and Samuelson, *Stalin, NKVD*, 93 (citing TsA FSB, f. 8os., op. 1, d. 79).

342. RGASPI, f. 558, op. 11, d. 1120, l. 7-8, 11-12.

343. Stalin could be ingratiating in these circumstances, but this statement about fascism was not at all what the antifascist crusader Feuchtwanger wanted to hear. RGASPI, f. 558, op. 11, d. 1120, l. 18-9.

344. RGASPI, f. 17, op. 3, d. 983, l.14-15, 110-1. On Jan. 16, 1937, Postyshev was removed as Kiev province party secretary for having allowed "an extraordinarily great level of contamination by Trotskyites." RGASPI, f. 558, op. 1, d. 5023, l. 1-17 (Jan. 13, 1937); Getty and Naumov, *Road to Terror*, 353-7; Na prieme, 198-9; Khlevniuk, *1937-i*, 90-114.

345. Larina, *This I Cannot Forget*, 312.

346. Titarenko, *VKP (b), komintern i kitai: dokumenty*, IV/ii: 1090-1 (RGASPI, f. 495, op. 74, d. 281, l. 17-18); Titarenko, *Kommunisticheskii internatsional*, 271-2.

347. Titarenko, *VKP (b), komintern i kitai: dokumenty*, IV/ii: 1098 (RGASPI, f. 495, op. 74, d. 281, l. 28: March 2, 1937).

348. Khaustov et al., *Lubianka: Stalin i glavnoe upravlneie*, 9-19 (APRF, f. 3, op. 24, d. 269, l. 38-58, 80).

349. Khlevniuk, *Stalin i Ordzhonkidze*, 88-97.

350. *Report of Court Proceedings*, 54; "O tak nazyvaemom 'parallel'nom antisovetskom trotskistom tsentre'": 30-50.

351. Yagoda belatedly lost this rank. Khaustov et al., *Lubianka: Stalin i glavnoe upravlenie*, 60 (RGASPI, f. 17, op. 3, d. 983, l. 50); Kokurin and Petrov, *Lubianka, 1917-1960*, 14. In 1937, chief of the Gorky [Nizhny Novgorod] NKVD Lavrushin wrote a note to Moscow about Yagoda's supposed past as an *okhranka* agent, with testimony from a witness about the removal on July 15, 1935, by former local NKVD boss Matvei Pogrebinsky of Yagoda's tsarist police file from the local archives. Il'inskii, *Narkom Iagoda*, 51-2; Vinogradov, *Genrikh Iagoda*, 83-4 (testimony of Alexander Yevstifeyev, 1937). See also Orlov, *Tainaia istoriia*, 209-10. Yagoda's supposed *okhranka* past would not be used against him at trial, perhaps because it was too evocative of whispers about Stalin. Pogrebinsky would commit suicide on April 4, 1937.

352. Lyons, *Assignment in Utopia*, 585. Some years earlier a German count had likened Radek to "something between Puck and Wolf, a bit of a street Arab, a cheeky, amusing, and terrifying Mephisto physiognomy." Kessler, *Tagebücher*, 354 (1922).

353. Banac, *Diary of Georgi Dimitrov*, 51 (Feb. 2, 1937). The émigré Miliukov fantasized that Russia was being reborn, on the analogy of the French Revolution's counterrevolution. *Poslednie novosti*, Jan. 23, 1937: 1. See also Nielsen, *Miliukov i Stalin*.

354. Broué, "Trotsky"; Broué, "Party Opposition to Stalin," 166; Rogovin, *1937*, 60-6.

355. In public, Smirnov alone retracted his confession. Rogovin, *1937*, 23.

356. Trotskii, "Otkrytoe pis'ma."

357. Ingratiatingly, the NKVD agent Zborowski managed to report that, on Jan. 22, Trotsky's son Lev Sedov had told him apropos of the accusations, "now there is no longer vacillation, Stalin should be killed." Volkogonov, *Trotskii*, II: 197 (citing Arkhiv INO OGPU-NKVD, f. 31660, d. 9067, t. 1, l. 98). Although, in an article (Oct. 1933), Trotsky had written that "the only way to compel the bureaucracy to hand over power to the proletariat is *by force*," in a subsequent article on the Kirov murder he wrote that assassinating

Stalin would accomplish nothing, because he would just be replaced by "one of those Kaganoviches." "Klassovaia priroda sovetskogo gosudarstva (problemy chetvertogo internatsionala)," *Biulleten' oppozitsii*, no. 36-7 (October 1933): 1-12 (at 9-10); Trotskii, "Stalinskaia biurokratiia i ubiistvo Kirova"; Volkogonov, *Triumf i tragediia*, II/i: 270.

358. Maksimenkov, *Kremlevskii kinoteatr*, 366 (RGASPI, f. 558, op. 11, d. 1082, l. 1-2), 1051-3 (d. 829, l. 107-8).

359. Artizov and Naumov, *Vlast'*, 350-1 (RGASPI, f. 71, op. 10, d. 127, l. 188-9; f. 558, op. 1, d. 5324, l. 33). Arrests at Lenfilm continued throughout the film's shooting. Mar'iamov, *Kremlevskii tsenzor*, 35. See also Latyshev, "Stalin i kino," 495-6.

360. Artizov and Naumov, *Vlast'*, 350-1 (RGASPI, f. 71, op. 10, d. 127, l. 188-9); Latyshev, "Stalin i kino," 494-6; Milovidov, "Velikii grazhdanin," 6.

361. Titarenko, *VKP (b), komintern i kitai: dokumenty*, IV/ii: 1094-6 (RGASPI, f. 495, op. 74, d. 281, l. 22-3).

362. Yezhov's pretrial instructions to Ulrich specified execution for all defendants, so Stalin had changed his mind and rewarded Radek. "'Vse, chto govorit Radek—eto' absoliutno zlostnaia kleveta . . .'"

363. *Pravda*, Jan. 31, 1937.

364. Dullin, *Men of Influence*, 138, citing AVP RF, f. 5, op. 17, pap. 126, d. 1 (Jan. 8, 1937, draft). Soviet-German efforts at contact were convoluted. Abramov, "Osobaia missiia Davida Kandelaki," 150 (citing AVP RF, f. 05, op. 17, pap. 126, d. 1, l. 17), 150-1 (citing AVP RF, f. 17, pap. 130, d. 41, l. 3), 151 (citing AVP RF, f. 011, op. 1a, pap. 1, d. 2, l. 5; f. 059, op. 1, pap. 244, d. 1717, l. 10), 151 (citing AVP RF, f. 05, op. 17, pap. 130, d. 42, l. 6, 17); Fischer, *Russia's Road*, 241.

365. Krivitsky, *In Stalin's Secret Service*. Maisky (in London), writing to Litvinov, surmised that "Hitler is not yet ready for a large-scale war and it is unlikely that Mussolini ever will be." *DVP SSSR*, XIX: 673 (Dec. 17, 1936).

366. Radosh et al., *Spain Betrayed*. Stalin's refusal to permit a Spanish Communist takeover was manifest well before access to Soviet archives. Cattell, *Communism and the Spanish Civil War*. See also Schauff, *Der verspielte Sieg*.

367. Kowalsky, *Stalin*.

368. On Soviet motivations as given in the contemporary Soviet press, see Allen, "Soviet Union and the Spanish Civil War."

369. *DBFP*, 2nd series, XVII: 754-6 (Jan. 2, 1937); "The Anglo-American Agreement," *Bulletin of International News* 15/8 (1938): 11-3.

370. *Izvestiia*, Jan. 5, 1937. Hitler sent Göring to Italy to shore up relations; Mussolini received him on January 15. When Göring brought up Germany's desire to annex Austria, a development he insisted Italy had no choice but to accept, Mussolini became visibly displeased. Kershaw, *Hitler: 1936-1945*, 68.

371. Khaustov, "Deiatel'nost' organov," 235 (APRF, f. 45, op. 1, d. 188 l. 100).

372. Andrew and Elkner, "Stalin and Foreign Intelligence," 85.

373. "The Communists have got into the habit of denouncing as a Trotskyist everybody who disagrees with them about anything," the Austrian Borkenau would note. "For in Communist mentality, every disagreement in political matters is a major crime, and every political criminal is a Trotskyist." Borkenau, *Spanish Cockpit*, 240.

CHAPTER 7. ENEMIES HUNTING ENEMIES

1. Boris Yefimov, in Beliaev, *Mikhail Koltsov*, 71 (1989 ed.), 103.

2. Arrests in the NKVD included incarcerations of border guards and regular police (the

militia), who accounted for the overwhelming majority of NKVD personnel (around 400,000), as well as of Gulag camp guards and administrators and fire brigades, who were

not directly involved in the mass arrests. Khaustov and Samuelson, *Stalin, NKVD*, 258; Khaustov, "Deiatel'nost' organov," 150 (TsA FSB, f. 3, op. 5, d. 996, l. 187-9); Petrov and

Skorkin, *Kto rukovodil NKVD*, 501. Different figures are given in Luk'ianov, "Massovye repressii opravdany byt' ne mogut," 121.

3. Lebedev, "M. N. Tukhachevskii i 'voenno-fashistskii zagovor,'" 7–20, 255; *Voennye arkhivy Rossii*, 111; Khaustov, "Deiatel'nost' organov," 188–9.

4. Mlechin, *KGB*, 162–3.

5. Radek at his public trial on Jan. 24, 1937, had mentioned Tukhachevsky's name as a co-conspirator. Radek then tried to retract, but the deed had been done. *Report of Court Proceedings*, 105, 146. After the first Moscow trial, Werner von Tippelskirch, a German military attaché in Moscow, had reported to Berlin (Sept. 28, 1936) the speculation about a pending trial of Red Army commanders. Erickson, *Soviet High Command*, 427 (citing Serial 6487/E486016–120: Report A/2037).

6. Wollenberg, *Red Army*, 224; Erickson, *Soviet High Command*, 465; Conquest, *Great Terror: Reassessment*, 201–35; Ulam, *Stalin*, 457–8; Tucker, *Stalin in Power*; Volkogonov, *Stalin: Triumph and Tragedy*. Assertions of a real plot go back to the time and have persisted: Duranty, *USSR*, 222; Davies, *Mission to Moscow*, I: 111. The claptrap persists: Prudnikova and Kolpakidi, *Dvoinoi zagovor*.

7. Whitewood, *Red Army*. This is a variant on Harris, "Encircled by Enemies."

8. Khrushchev had blamed German intelligence for inciting Stalin's suspicious personality. For the fables, see Höttl, *Secret Front*, 77–85 (Höttl was an Austrian intelligence officer swept into the German S.D. in 1938); Reitlinger, *SS*, 93–6. See also Krivitsky, *In Stalin's Secret Service*, 213–43, and Erickson, *Soviet High Command*, 433–6. No such Tukhachevsky dossier obtained from abroad was ever mentioned by Stalin in the many discussions he held that have been transcribed; no reference to such a dossier appears in Tukhachevsky's secret case files.

9. Spalcke, "Der Fall Tuchatschewski"; Sluch, "'Delo Tukhachevskogo.'" The archive fire took place on the night of March 1–2, 1937. Volkogonov, *Triumf i tragediia*, I/ii: 258 (quoting a Yezhov report to Stalin, no citation). The Gestapo had long been trying to set up the talented Red Marshal Tukhachevsky, echoing the Russian emigration's fantasies about a Russian Bonaparte. RGVA, f. 33 987, op. 3, d. 864, l. 60–7, Volkogonov papers, Hoover, container 17; Golubev et al., *Rossiia i zapad*, 186 (citing GARF, f. 5853, op. 1, d. 8, l. 126; d. 9, l. 125; d. 14, l. 85); *Voennye arkhivy Rossii*, 99; Il'in, "Zapiski."

10. *Pravda*'s Berlin correspondent wrote home that Wehrmacht circles were abuzz about their secret links to the Red Army, especially to Tukhachevsky. Mekhlis excerpted the letter for Stalin (Jan. 16, 1937). Lebedev, "M. N. Tukhachevskii i 'voenno-fashistskii zagovor,'" 15.

11. Uritsky discounted the possibility of such clandestine collaboration, but reported the rumors anyway. Volkogonov, *Triumf i tragediia*, I/ii: 255, citing TsGASA, f. 33987, op. 3, d. 1036, l. 270–4 (April 9, 1937).

12. Lebedev, "M. N. Tukhachevskii i 'voenno-fashistskii zagovor,'" 20–2 (Daladier warning, Potyomkin to Moscow, March 16, 1937); Artizov et al., *Reabilitatsiia: kak eto bylo*, II: 601. Czechoslovak president Edvard Beneš supposedly was informed of secret negotiations between Berlin and Moscow for a rapprochement, as well as of a military coup to topple the Soviet regime, and passed word or documents to the Soviet regime, but there is no such information in records of conversations by Alexandrovsky in Prague. No documents from Heydrich via Beneš have ever been found in Soviet or German archives, either. Nor were the alleged documents ever

mentioned in the innumerable internal interrogation protocols or at the trial. Stalin had no need for such documents: if they had existed and he had used them, the Gestapo could have crowed about its handiwork, fooling Stalin into executing one of his best military men. Polišenská and Kvaček, *Archivní dokumenty hovoří*," 29; TsRGVA, f. 33987, op. 3, d. 1028, l. 107–14; Lebedev, "M. N. Tukhachevskii i 'voenno-fashistskii zagovor,'" 5–6, 23–9; Lukes, *Czechoslovakia Between Stalin and Hitler*, 91–112. See also Watt, "Who Plotted against Whom?," 49 (citing PRO, FO 371/21104, N 3287/461/38, Newton, June 21, 1937); *Les Événements Survenues en France de 1933 à 1945*, I: 129. There is a grievous mistake in the annotations to Stalin's office logbooks connected to the myth of the Beneš role in passing on a Nazi file implicating Tukhachevsky: on May 21, Stalin received Mikhail K. Alexandrovsky, *not* the Soviet representative to Czechoslovakia (Sergei S. Alexandrovsky). Gorbunov, "Voennaia razvedka v 1934–1939 godakh" (no. 8), 93; Plimak and Antonov, "Nakanune strashnoi daty," 151; Khaustov and Samuelson, *Stalin, NKVD*, 120–1 (citing RGASPI, f. 558, op. 11, d. 175, l. 82); *Na prieme*, 208; Naumov, *Stalin i NKVD*, 344.

13. Lebedev, "M. N. Tukhachevskii i 'voenno-fashistskii zagovor,'" 10–1 (citing the interrogation of I. M. Kedrov, May 25, 1939).

14. Reese, *Stalin's Reluctant Soldiers*, 134–46. From 1937 to 1938, 34,501 Red Army officers, air force officers, and military political personnel were discharged, either because of expulsion from the party or arrest; 11,596 would be reinstated by 1940. As Voroshilov noted, some 47,000 officers had been discharged in the years following the civil war, almost half of them (22,000) in the years 1934–36; around 10,000 of these discharged were arrested. Few were higher-ups, however. Confusingly, sometimes the totals include the Red Air Force, and sometimes not. "Nakanune voiny (dokumenty 1935–1940 gg.)," 188; Suvenirov, *Tragediia RKKA*, 137. In 1939, when Stalin turned off the pandemonium, 73 Red Army personnel would be arrested.

15. Alliluyeva, *Tol'ko odin god*, 334.

16. *Pravda*, Feb. 11, 1937: 3 (N. Tikhonov). See also the satire by Mikhail Zoshchenko, "V pushkinskie dni," originally in *Krokodil*, 1937, nos. 3 and 5, reprinted in Zoshchenko, *Sobranie sochinenii*, II: 416–21. In the restored apartment at Moika, 12, in Leningrad, busts of Pushkin and Stalin appeared side by side. Mastenitsa, "Iz istroii muzeinoi pushkiniany," 116; Tkhorzhevskii, "Cherez sto let," 9–10. See also Sandler, *Commemorating Pushkin*, 107–16; and Molok, *Pushkin v 1937 g.*

17. Snow, *Red Star over China*, 474.

18. Taylor, *Generalissimo*, 143 (citing Chiang Diaries, Hoover Institution Archives, box 39, folder 8: Feb. 18, 1937). An analysis by Varga (April 20, 1937) began with the premise that "recent years in China, undoubtedly, are characterized by the process of the transition to a bourgeois social system," but he called the conditions of transition unique (a combination of pre-capitalist agrarian relations, partial colonialism, and strong revolutionary forces). And although he noted an imperative to transcend feudalism, for the creation of a bourgeois economic and military superstructure on the feudally exploited peasantry would only worsen their exploitation, he cautioned that if a Japanese aggression was coming soon against China and/or the USSR, the Soviet Union would have to work to delay China's agrarian revolution. Titarenko, *VKP (b), komintern i kitai: dokumenty*, IV/ii: 1105–13 (RGASPI, f. 514, op. 1, d. 868, l. 20–32).

19. Adzhubei, *Te desiat' let*, 194–5. Similarly, Nikolai Leonov, the future chief analyst of the KGB, nine years old in 1937, would later choose to study the Spanish language under the lingering influence of the Spanish civil war. Leonov, *Likholet'e*, 7–13, 18–21. "Moscow lived Spain," wrote Louis Fischer. Fischer, *Men and Politics*, 403. For typical Soviet press accounts, see *International Solidarity with the Spanish Republic*. But see also Davies, *Popular Opinion*, 96.

20. Kowalsky, *Stalin*, paragraph 224; Fitzpatrick, *Everyday Stalinism*, 171. Helen Grant, a British woman traveling in Catalonia in 1937, noted that at a film screening, there were "great cheers from the gallery when Stalin's photo appeared on the screen, but *only* from the gallery [her emphasis]." Among the higher-paying middle class part of the audience (where she sat) "people kept quiet." Jackson, *British Women*, 117.

21. Radosh et al., *Spain Betrayed*, 129–33 (RGVA, f. 33987, op. 3, d. 960, l. 251–77: Nikonov, Feb. 20, 1937).

22. Kowalsky, *Stalin*, paragraph 591.

23. He added that Soviet advisers "often led Spanish brigades in combat, especially in their first combat operations to show the officers how to command their units." Meretskov, *Serving the People*, 147–8.

24. Altogether, 204 interpreters, mostly women, served in Spain. On the White Guard émigrés in Spain, see Yezhov's note to Stalin (Jan. 19, 1937): Kudriashov, *SSSR i grazhdanskaia voina v Ispanii*, 179–81 (APRF, f. 3, op. 65, d. 223, l. 33–39).

25. RGASPI, f. 17, op. 120, d. 263, l. 32; Kudriashov, *SSSR i grazhdanskaia voina v Ispanii*, 163–4 (APRF, f. 3, op. 65, d. 223, l. 3–4: Gaikis, Dec. 31, 1936), 165 (l. 2: Litvinov to Stalin, Jan. 2, 1937), 166 (l. 1: politburo decision).

26. Kowalsky, *Stalin*, paragraph 742, citing a memorandum of Colonel Sverchevskii, undated [1938], in RGVA, f. 33987, op. 3, d. 1149, l. 237, 233.

27. Fischer, *Men and Politics*, 361.

28. Broué, *Staline et la révolution*, 102–3 (citing Luis Araquistain); Bolloten, *Spanish Civil War*, 319. Writing to Voroshilov in mid-October 1936, the military attaché Gorev reported that the Soviet ambassador possessed an "unhealthy self-esteem. He is terribly afraid for his authority." Radosh et al., *Spain Betrayed*, 94 (RGVA, f. 33987, op. 3, d. 832, l. 239).

29. Kudriashov, *SSSR i grazhdanskaia voina v Ispanii*, 157–8 (APRF, f. 3, op. 65, d. 222, l. 164–64ob.: Dec. 21, 1936).

30. Thomas, *Spanish Civil War*, 517. Largo Caballero had tried to tamp down any tensions: "we are all satisfied with his [Rosenberg's] behavior and activities with us. Here everyone loves him." Kudriashov, *SSSR i grazhdanskaia voina v Ispanii*, 173–4 (APRF, f. 3, op. 65, d. 223, l. 17–19: Jan. 12, 1937).

31. The request to be received, relayed by Krestinsky to Stalin, was dated the same day as the audience was granted (Feb. 3). Kudriashov, *SSSR i grazhdanskaia voina v Ispanii*, 189–90 (APRF, f. 3, op. 65, d. 223, l. 80), 190 (l. 87); *Na prieme*, 201. On Feb. 4, Krestinsky had Gaikis summoned to Moscow: Kudriashov, *SSSR i grazhdanskaia voina v Ispanii*, 190 (APRF, f. 3, op. 65, d. 223, l. 80), 190 (l. 88).

32. Kowalsky, *Stalin*, paragraph 64 (reconstruction from Pascua's notes of the meeting: AHN-Madrid. Diversos. M. Pascua, leg. 2, exp. 6, 12), paragraph 99.

33. Kudriashov, *SSSR i grazhdanskaia voina v Ispanii*, 191 (APRF, f. 3, op. 65, d. 223, l. 86: letter to Largo Caballero, Feb. 4, 1937).

34. Kudriashov, *SSSR i grazhdanskaia voina v Ispanii*, 191–5 (APRF, f. 3, op. 65, d. 223, l. 81,

82, 85). Stalin seems to have discussed them in the Little Corner on Feb. 5, 1937: *Na prieme*, 201.

35. Kudriashov, *SSSR i grazhdanskaia voina v Ispanii*, 197 (APRF, f. 3, op. 65, d. 217, l.54).

36. Kowalsky, *Stalin*, paragraphs 145, 789. Rosenberg's replacement was Gaikis.

37. Costello and Tsarev, *Deadly Illusions*, 265-6 (citing file 17697, I: 28).

38. Radosh et al., *Spain Betrayed*, 456-8 (Gorev report, March 23, 1937, secret archive 15), 69 (Gorev, code-named Sancho, Oct. 16, 1936). On the unreliability of communications, see Rees, "The Highpoint of Comintern Influence? The Communist Party and the Civil War in Spain," 150.

39. Kowalsky, *Stalin*, paragraph 582, citing RGVA, f. 33987, op. 3, d. 961, l. 171.

40. Voroshilov sent telegrams white-hot with accusations about "not putting into practice" his directives and threatening "severe penalties for all of you." Rybalkin, "Voennaia pomoshch,'" 108 (citing TsAMO, f. 132, op. 2642, d. 173, l. 23-24; d. 192, l. 1-3); Rybalkin, *Operatsiia "X*," 56 (citing TsAMO, f. 132, op. 2642, d. 192, l. 32), 56 (d. 182, l. 22-3: Dec. 4, 1936).

41. Rybalkin, *Operatsiia "X*," 82-83 (citing RGVA, f. 33987, op. 3, d. 1082, l. 206: A. Agaltsov). Dimitrov wrote to Stalin that "the foe has the advantage that he has many spies in the Government camp." Khlevniuk, *Khoziain*, 293 (APRF, f. 3, op. 65, d. 221, l. 38-40, Dec. 14, 1936); Sharapov, *Naum Eitingon*, 53.

42. Khlevniuk, "Prichiny 'bol'shogo terrora,'" 10.

43. Khaustov et al., *Lubianka: Stalin i glavnoe upravlenie*, 83 (RGASPI, f. 17, op. 3, d. 983, l. 64). Two days later Blyukher and Deribas sent a telegram from Khabarovsk asking to be excused from having to travel to the plenum, a request Stalin approved. Khaustov et al., *Lubianka: Stalin i glavnoe upravlenie*, 83 (citing RGASPI, f. 558, op. 11, d. 65, l. 25).

44. Khaustov, "Razvitie sovetskikh organov gosudarstvennoi bezopasnosti"; RGASPI, f. 17, op. 71, d. 43, 44, 45, 46. Malenkov's lists further specified that a mere 15.7 percent of provincial party bosses had any higher education, and that 70.4 percent had just elementary education. Similar percentages obtained for the next rungs down, county and city party bosses.

45. RGASPI, f. 17, op. 2, d. 773, l. 115.

46. RGASPI, f. 17, op. 114, d. 622, l. 13; Getty and Naumov, *Road to Terror*, 421. See also Conquest, *Reassessment*, 33; and Kvashonkin, *Sovetskoe rukovodstvo*, 364-5, 393-7.

47. Only a draft resolution in Orjonikidze's hand survives: RGASPI, f. 558, op. 1, d. 3350, l. 1; *Kommunist*, 1991, no. 13: 59-60.

48. Khlevniuk, *Master of the House*, 165.

49. Khlevniuk, *In Stalin's Shadow*, 128-31 (citing RGASPI, f. 85, op. 29, d. 156, l. 12, 14); Kuromiya, *Freedom and Terror*, 221 (d. 156, l. 10-2). S. Z. Ginzburg, head of the construction industry, investigated the Ural Train Carriage Construction Factory in Nizhny Tagil, returned to Moscow February 18, 1936—the same day the Popular Front won its electoral victory in Spain—and Poskryobyshev called him that same day to relay that Stalin had requested a copy of his report. Ginzburg, *O proshlom*, 195.

50. *Za industrializatsiiu*, Feb. 21, 1937: 6 (A. P. Zaveniagin); Orjonikidze bumped into Bukharin's wife, Anna, on Kremlin grounds returning to his apartment. Larina, *Nezabyvaemoe*, 333.

51. Dubinskii-Mukharadze, *Ordzhonikidze*, 6. Orjonikidze had lived in the so-called children's section of the Grand Kremlin Palace (Krestinsky lived here, too, as did Sverdlov's widow Klavdiya and her son Andrei, an

NKVD operative), but when the palace was being reconstructed, Orjonikidze and others moved into the Amusement Palace, near the Trinity Gate, where Stalin had lived until the 1932 suicide of Nadya and where Bukharin lived.

52. *Izvestiia*, Nov. 22, 1963; Dubinskii-Mukhadze, *Ordzhonikidze*, 6. The evening before, Yezhov was received alone in the Little Corner. *Na prieme*, 202. Alternately, the apartment search may have occurred on Feb. 16, prompting Orjonikidze's tête-à-tête with Stalin on the morning of Feb. 17.

53. Khlevniuk, *In Stalin's Shadow*, 143-9; Medvedev, *Let History Judge*, 402-3. Around midnight, Orjonikidze had met with his deputy for the chemical industry to discuss Donbass coke plant sabotage. After leaving the commissariat, Orjonikidze might have spoken again with Stalin. Dubinskii-Mukhadze, *Ordzhonikidze*, 6.

54. Chubar, Mekhlis, Andreev, and Kalinin joined at that point. Levin was called back at 9:55 p.m. for another five minutes; he was among the four people who signed the official medical bulletin. (Levin would be tried and executed the next year.) *Pravda*, Feb. 19, 1937; *Na prieme*, 202-3.

55. Murin, *Stalin v ob"iatiakh*, 154-96 (at 191). Amayak Nazaretyan wrote on the back of a photograph of his close friend Orjonikidze: "Every one of us who sees with his own eyes the enormous achievements of the Soviet regime in the field of socialist construction cannot and must not forget the people who gave their lives that we might build the world's first socialist state, marching toward communism." *Pravda*, Nov. 17, 1964: 4.

56. *Pravda*, Feb. 22, 1937. Molotov, later in life, would make Orjonikidze out to be the villain, harming Stalin with his suicide. Chuev, *Sto sorok*, 191-2. Khrushchev blamed Pyatakov already: *Pravda*, Feb. 19, 1937.

57. *Sotsialisticheskii vetsnik*, 1937, no. 5: 16; Pil'niak, *Rasplesnutoe vremia*, 582 (quoting the Georgian poet Titian Tabidze); Conquest, *Reassessment*, 170.

58. Khlevniuk, *Khoziain*, 284-5.

59. Lenin, *PSS*, XLV: 361.

60. Tucker, *Stalin in Power*, 418.

61. Mikoian, *Tak bylo*, 327-33.

62. Mikoyan was in Stalin's office on Nov. 2 and 14, 1937, both times with Yezhov. Mikoian, *Tak bylo*, 318-9; *Na prieme*, 224.

63. As one scholar explained, "Up to 1936, the leading group was held together by shared convictions in a shared project, but after 1937 the nature of the group changed." Rees, "Stalin as Leader, 1937-1953," 207. Mikoyan and Beria, assigned to comb through Orjonikidze's personal archive, discovered two sealed folders (received back when he headed the Central Control Commission), which held compromising tsarist police materials on politburo members Kalinin and Rudzutaks. Orjonikidze had marked the folders "Do not open without me." Kvashonkin, *Sovetskoe rukovodstvo*, 9-10 (RGASPI, f. 85, d. 2, l. 1-30).

64. The Feb.-March 1937 plenum is one of the few in the 1930s whose materials have been published in detail. Another was June 1935: *Plenum Tsentral'nogo Komiteta VKP (b) 5-7 iiunia 1935 g.* (Moscow: Partizdat, 1935).

65. Kosheleva et al., "Materialy fevral'-martovskogo plenuma TsK VKP (b) 1937 goda," (1995, no. 3): 8, 14; Getty and Naumov, *Road to Terror*, 470. This was an old theme of his. Back on Sept. 19, 1931, for example, expressing disapproval of then transport commissar Moisei Rukhimovich, Stalin had vented to Kaganovich, "New people who believe in our cause and who can successfully replace the bureaucracy can always be found in our party,

if one searches seriously." Khlevniuk et al., *Stalin i Kaganovich*, 109-10 (RGASPI, f. 81, op. 3, d. 99, l. 35-6). See also Fitzpatrick, *Cultural Front*, 180, and Khlevniuk, *Master of the House*, 172.

66. Kosheleva et al., "Materialy fevral'-martovskogo plenuma TsK VKP (b) 1937 goda," (1992, nos. 4-5): 36.

67. RGASPI, f. 558, op. 11, d. 710, l. 180-1.

68. Khaustov and Samuelson, *Stalin, NKVD*, 143.

69. Rogovin, *1937*, 221-2.

70. "Materialy marto-fevral'skogo plenuma TsK VKP (b) 1937 goda" (no. 2), 13, 17, 18, 20, 26, 27 (1994, no. 1), 12-3; Getty and Naumov, *Road to Terror*, 412-5.

71. Kosheleva et al., "Materialy fevral'-martovskogo plenuma TsK VKP (b) 1937 goda," (1994, no. 1): 12-3. Stalin's recommendation was fixed in a formal plenum resolution on March 3: RGASPI, f. 17, op. 2, d. 577, l. 4 (l. 30-3 draft with corrections).

72. "O partiinosti lits, prokhodivshikh po delu tak nazyvaemogo 'antisovetskogo pravotrotskitskogo bloka,'" 82-3; *Stranitsy istorii* (Leningrad: Lenizdat, 1990), 18; Galumov, *Neizvestnye "Izvestiia*," 185.

73. Kosheleva et al., "Materialy fevral'-martovskogo plenuma TsK VKP (b) 1937 goda," (1992, no. 11-12), 10.

74. Kosheleva et al., "Materialy fevral'-martovskogo plenuma TsK VKP (b) 1937 goda," (1993, no. 5: 3-5, 6, no. 7: 3, A. S. Kalygina).

75. Schlögel, *Terror und Traum*, 250-3.

76. Kosheleva et al., "Materialy fevral'-martovskogo plenuma TsK VKP (b) 1937 goda," (1993, no. 8): 3-26 (Molotov), (no. 9): 3-32 (Kaganovich). Stalin marked up the draft of Molotov's plenum speech. Where Molotov wrote that Trotsky had instructed his supporters inside the Soviet Union "to save their strength for a more important moment—for the beginning of the war—and at that moment strike decisively at the most sensitive areas of our economy"—Stalin underlined it. In the margin beside Molotov's words about the party having been deserted by those who did not have the stomach to fight and "cast their lots with the bourgeoisie, and not with the working class," Stalin wrote: "This is good. It would be worse if they had left during wartime." RGASPI, f. 558, op. 11, d. 772, l. 14, 88.

77. Svanidze surmised that Stalin did not come to Svetlana's party "on purpose." Murin, *Stalin v ob"iatiakh sem'i*, 191-2. Svanidze would be arrested December 29, 1939, and sentenced to eight years for "concealing the anti-Soviet actions of her husband" (Alexander Svanidze, the brother of Stalin's first wife). She would be executed in March 1942.

78. Yakov met Meltzer when she was married to Nikolai Bessarab, an aide to the head of the Moscow province NKVD, Stanisław Redens, Stalin's brother-in-law. She gave her birth year as 1911, but was likely born in 1906. She and Yakov would legalize their marriage on Feb. 18, 1938 (the day before she would give birth to a daughter, whom they named Galina, the same as Yakov's first child, who had died in infancy in 1929). The family lived in a four-room apartment on elite Granovsky Street while keeping the Zubalovo dacha. Meltzer had a child from her first marriage. Alliluev, *Khronika odnoi sem'i*, 118; Zen'kovich, *Samye sekretnye rodsvtvenniki*, 372-3.

79. Kosheleva et al., "Materialy fevral'-martovskogo plenuma TsK VKP (b) 1937 goda" (1994, no. 3), 4.

80. Kosheleva et al., "Materialy fevral'-martovskogo plenuma TsK VKP (b) 1937 goda" (1995, no. 2), 7. Molchanov had been arrested Feb. 2-3, 1937.

81. Kosheleva et al., "Materialy fevral'-martovskogo plenuma TsK VKP (b) 1937 goda" (1995, no. 2), 21 (Ivan Zhukov).
82. Kosheleva et al., "Materialy fevral'-martovskogo plenuma TsK VKP (b) 1937 goda" (1995, no. 3), 13–4. The theory went back to Lenin: "O diktature proletariata," *PSS*, XXXIX: 261–3.
83. *Sochineniia*, XIV: 207–8.
84. Kosheleva et al., "Materialy fevral'-martovskogo plenuma TsK VKP (b) 1937 goda" (1995, no. 7), 11–3; *Pravda*, March 4, 1937.
85. Kosheleva et al., "Materialy fevral'-martovskogo plenuma TsK VKP (b) 1937 goda" (1995, no. 11–12), 13, 14, 16. Stalin's March 5 concluding speech was belatedly published in *Pravda* (April 1, 1937) and as a pamphlet (Moscow: OGIZ, 1938) with translations into foreign languages. See also *Sochineniia*, XIV: 225–47, and Zhukov, *Inoi Stalin*, 360–1. None of the references to Orjonikidze's sheltering of enemies appeared in *Pravda*'s version of Stalin's speech, but plenum attendees once back home could orally convey Stalin's remarks.
86. Banac, *Diary of Georgi Dimitrov*, 56 (March 4, 1937: misdated, should be March 5).
87. "O Partiinosti lits, prokhodivshikh po delu tak nazyvaemogo 'antisovetskogo pravotrotskistskogo bloka,'" 74. One operative stated that the oppositionists in prison were able to hold debates, read newspapers and books, meet with friends and relatives, and drink brandy, and that during their volleyball games in the yard, if the ball were knocked far, NKVD personnel would run and retrieve it. Vinogradov, *Genrikh iagoda*, 6–7.
88. Kosheleva et al., "Materialy fevral'-martovskogo plenuma TsK VKP (b) 1937 goda" (1995, no. 11–12), 21; RGASPI, f. 17, op. 2, d. 773, l. 115; Khlevniuk, *Kohoziain*, 309–10.
89. Pavliukov, *Ezhov*, 266–8. At a plenum of the Spanish Communist party, also on March 5, 1937, José Diaz asked, "Who are the enemies of the people? The enemies of the people are the fascists, Trotskyites and uncontrolled elements." Diaz called Trotsky "a direct agent of the Gestapo." Novikov, *SSSR, Komintern*, II: 95. At a Nov. 1937 plenum of the Spanish Communist party, Diaz said of "Trotskyites" in Spain: "You need to eliminate them with the same mercilessness with which we eliminate fascists." *Bolshevik*, 1937, no. 23–24 (1937): 86–7.
90. Khaustov et al., *Lubianka: Stalin i glavnoe upravlenie*, 639–40n18 (TsA FSB, f. 3, op. 4, d. 13, l. 54–67: Lev Mironov).
91. Afanas'ev, *Oni ne molchali*, 217; Starkov, "Narkon Ezhov"; Ivanova, *Gulag*, 152; Jansen and Petrov, *Stalin's Loyal Executioner*, 61–2; Petrov and Jansen, *Stalinskii pitomets*, 73–4; Conquest, *Reassessment*, 39–40. Krivitsky refers to a Yezhov speech on March 18 to the NKVD party active, and Pavliukov a Yezhov speech on March 19 to the NKVD higher-ups. Krivitsky, *In Stalin's Secret Service*, 167; Pavliukov, *Ezhov*, 264–5 (citing TsA FSB stenogram of a Yezhov speech of March 19).
92. Il'inskii, *Narkom Iagoda*, 17–18. See also Shreider, *NKVD iznutri*, 39.
93. On March 31, 1937, Central Committee members were informed that "in view of the danger of leaving Yagoda at liberty for even a single day," he had been arrested, a formulation by which Stalin could justify violating the regulation of having the Central Committee vote to expel him first. The 65 remaining full members of the Central Committee, down from 71, then "voted" in writing to expel Yagoda post-facto. RGASPI, f. 17, op. 2, d. 614, l. 94–105; op. 3, d. 985, l. 34; Khaustov et al., *Lubianka: Stalin i glavnoe upravlenie*, 124–5 (APRF, f. 3, op. 24, d. 299, l. 188–9), 126; *Pravda*, April 4, 1937.

94. Agabekov, *ChK za rabotoi*, 134, 178.
95. Shreider, *NKVD iznutri*, 17, 36.
96. Koenker et al., *Revelations*, 77 (Vlasik interviewed in 1965).
97. Kaganovich had written to Stalin that "some of the apparatus, even though it has quieted down, will not be loyal to him [Yezhov] . . . There is talk that Yagoda remains general commissar [of state security], while Yezhov, they say, will not be given that rank and so on." Khlevniuk et al., *Stalin i Kaganovich*, 683 (RGASPI, f. 558, op. 11, d. 95, l. 132), 701–2 (Oct. 12, 1936).
98. Conquest, *Inside Stalin's Secret Police*, 13.
99. In April 1937, Yezhov and the new chief of the NKVD Special Department monitoring the army, Israel Leplyovsky, pressured Balytsky (his former superior) in Ukraine to uncover a gigantic military conspiracy there; Balytsky evidently complained to military district chief Iona Yakir on the telephone about this directive, an implicit warning to Yakir about the gathering danger. Leplyovsky, who had been chased from Ukraine in 1933, was returned to Ukraine, now as republic NKVD chief, on June 14, 1937, and carried out a pogrom against the republic NKVD. Tumshis, *VChK: voina klanov*, 391. Leplyovsky would be arrested on April 26, 1938, and shot in July.
100. One NKVD operative acknowledged Yagoda as a gifted organizer, but vainglorious. Shreider, *NKVD iznutri*, 17, 36. Another who had defected abroad judged Yagoda "an adventurist, murderer, and sadist." Agabekov, *ChK za rabotoi*, 134, 178. "He was a pragmatic type, a do-er, lacking any foundation in ideas," recalled Boris Gudz, an NKVD foreign intelligence station chief in Tokyo (who would survive the terror). "In his relations with subordinates, he sought the negative moments, in order to use these moments to pressure this or that subordinate." http://www.fsb.ru/fsb/history/author/single.ht m!id%3D10318010@fsbPublication.html. Gudz was expelled from the party and kicked out of the secret police in April 1937, after the arrest of his sister. He got a job as a bus driver and worked his way up to director of the bus company. He would retire in 1962 and die in 2006, at age 104. His sister was married to Varlam Shalamov, who claimed that Gudz wrote the denunciation that got the writer arrested in Jan. 1937. http://shalamov.ru /library/27/#t10.
101. Vinogradov, *Genrikh Iagoda*, 89–93 (TsA FSB, f. N-13614, t.2, l. 15–20).
102. On Yagoda's relations with other NKVD personnel: http://tortuga.angarsk.su/fb2 /abramv02/Evrei_v_KGB.fb2_4.html.
103. Il'inskii, *Narkom Iagoda*, 96.
104. Stefan Zweig's German-language biography *Joseph Fouché* (1929) was translated into Russian in 1932 (Leningrad: Vremia). Vyshinsky would quote from the Zweig biography at Yagoda's trial, equating the Soviet secret chief with "the old, treacherous, double-dealing school of the political careerist and dishonest scoundrel . . . Joseph Fouché." *Protsess pravo-trotskistskogo bloka* (Moscow: Iuridicheskoe izdatel'stvo, 1938), 610.
105. Khaustov et al., *Lubianka: Stalin i glavnoe upravlenie*, 135–44 (APRF, f. 3, op. 24, d. 302, l. 125–44).
106. Petrov and Skorkin, *Kto rukovodil NKVD*, 139–40; Artizov et al., *Reabilitatsiia: kak eto bylo*, II: 674 (Ans Zalpeter); Khaustov et al., *Lubianka: Stalin i glavnoe upravlenie*, 135–44 (at 136: APRF, f. 3, op. 24, d. 302, l. 125–44).
107. Yezhov even went so far as to attack the sacred founder of the Cheka ("Yes, comrades, everyone must grasp that Felix Edmundovich Dzierżyński vacillated in 1925–1926"). Afanas'ev, *Oni ne Molchali*, 217 (this speech

appears to have taken place in April). Mark Gai (Stokland) was arrested on April 1, and Pauker on April 19. Between April 22 and 25, Georgy Prokofyev and Gai, under torture, linked Yagoda to Tukhachevsky in the plot for a military palace coup. Vinogradov, *Genrikh Iagoda*, 522.
108. Jansen and Petrov, *Stalin's Loyal Executioner*, 60 (citing TsA FSB, f. 3, op. 4, d, 147, l. 34).
109. Agranov would be arrested on July 20, 1937, a fact not publicized. Khaustov and Samuelson, *Stalin, NKVD*, 232 (APRF, f. 3, op. 24, d. 313, l. 37); Pavliukov, *Ezhov*, 271–3.
110. Kosheleva et al., "Materialy fevral'-martovskogo plenuma TsK VKP (b) 1937 goda" (1994, no. 8), 25 (Molotov).
111. When *Pravda* (Jan. 8, 1936) had reported on an assembly of so-called leading workers of machine tractor stations and agricultural agencies, Stalin had added Voroshilov's name to the conclusion of the text as an object, along with himself and Molotov, of the panegyrics. RGASPI, f. 558, op. 11, d. 1479, l. 34–5.
112. "'Cherkni . . . desiatok slov,'" 406.
113. Orlov, *Tainaia istoriia*, 325 (according to NKVD functionary L. L. Nikolsky).
114. Montefiore, *Court of the Red Tsar*, 9–10.
115. Lebedev, "M. N. Tukhachevskii i 'voenno-fashistskii zagovor,'" 228 (Kutyakov diary entry for March 15, 1937; he was arrested May 15).
116. Khaustov, "Deiatel'nost' organov," 348 (TsA FSB, f. 3, op. 4, d. 87, l. 292); Khaustov and Samuelson, *Stalin, NKVD*, 106.
117. Kosheleva et al., "Materialy fevral'-martovskogo plenuma TsK VKP (b) 1937 goda," (1994, no. 8): 15; Lebedev, "M. N. Tukhachevskii i 'voenno-fashistskii zagovor,'" 1: 164–5. In notes for his remarks made prior to the plenum, Voroshilov had written, "It is not excluded, on the contrary it is likely, that in the Red Army ranks there are not a few unrevealed, not unmasked Japanese-German, Trotskyite-Zinovievite spies, diversionaries, and terrorists"—a point he omitted at the plenum. Suvenirov, "Narkomat oborony," at 28, citing TsGASA, f. 33987, op. 3, d. 1022, l. 267, 281. Voroshilov made only grammatical corrections to the plenum stenogram (film 2.2726, reel 78).
118. "Delo o tak nazyvaemoi 'antisovetskoi trotskistskoi organizatsii' v Krasnoi Armii," 45; Suvenirov, "Narkomat oborony," 28 (citing RGVA, f. 9, op. 36, d. 2376, l. 28). On March 29, 1937, Stalin had all party expellees in Red Army commanding ranks discharged and redirected to economic commissariats—where the grim reaper would come for them. Khaustov and Samuelson, *Stalin, NKVD*, 189–227.
119. Suvenirov, *Tragediia RKKA*, 57. On Tukhachevsky's holiday, see Bourne and Watt, *British Documents on Foreign Affairs*, XIV: 52–4. (Chilston report Feb. 23, 1937, PRO, FO 371/21099, N 1082/250/3); DDF, 2e série, IV: 42 (Coulondre, Feb. 10, 1937).
120. Voroshilov's formal report, stretching to eighty pages, stated: "I repeat, we have arrested [in the army] 15 or 20 so far, but that does not mean, comrades, that we have cleansed all the enemies. . . . We need to cleanse completely. We in the Worker Peasant Red Army have no right to tolerate even one enemy." Suvenirov, *Tragediia RKKA*, 58 (citing RGVA, f. 4, op. 14, d. 1820, l. 58). Voroshilov's report to the party active in the Red Army, in mid-March, was far sharper about Trotskyite-fascist penetration and the need for a complete cleansing, indicating his succumbing to Stalin's pressure. Budyonny and Gamarnik at the same gathering reinforced the pressure. Whitewood, *Red Army*, 226–7 (citing RGASPI, f. 74, op. 2, d. 117, l. 42, 47, 51, 51–3, 58, 95–7).

121. Rybalkin, *Operatsiia "X,"* 85 (citing RGVA, f. 33987, op. 3, d. 961, l. 123). Kulik appeared in the Little Corner, for the first time, on May 23, 1937, along with Molotov, Voroshilov, Kaganovich, and Yezhov, arriving after them, and departing before. *Na prieme,* 210. See also "Beria protiv Kulika," in Bobrenev and Riazantsev, *Palachi i zhertvy,* 197–264 (esp. 203–4).

122. Suvenirov, *Tragediia RKKA,* 56 (citing RGVA, f. 9., op. 39, d. 69, l. 13).

123. Khaustov, "Razvitie sovetskikh organov gosudarstvennoi bezopasnosti," 362 (citing TsA FSB, f. 3, op. 45, d. 29, l. 246). Peterson would be shot on Aug. 21, 1937.

124. Volkogonov, *Triumf i tragediia,* I/ii: 261 (citing TsGASA, f. 33987, op. 3, d. 400, l. 137–9).

125. Eden, *Foreign Affairs,* 182–3 (Jan. 12, 1937).

126. Evidently, it was not until Feb. 16, 1937, that Largo Caballero would issue the first order to convert some gold ($51 million worth) to pay off the Spanish debt to the Soviets for the military supplies. Kowalsky, *Stalin,* paragraph 539. Some of Spain's gold reserves would be drawn upon in convertible currency via the Spanish Republic's Eurobank account in Paris ($256 million of expenditures in 1937 alone) to pay for purchases of weapons and military supplies. Kudriashov, *SSSR i grazhdanskaia voina v Ispanii,* 137 (APRF, f. 3, op. 65, d. 234, l. 56).

127. Kowalsky, *Stalin,* paragraphs 532–48; Howson, *Arms for Spain,* 151. On gold see also Viñas, "Financing the Spanish Civil War," 266–83. In summer 1938, Stalin would receive a denunciation that some of the gold had been embezzled before shipment to the Soviet Union, and he had Beria investigate. Sudoplatov, *Special Tasks,* 42–3. The total mobilization of Soviet war matériel was something on the order of 600,000 tons. Grechko et al., *Istoriia vtoroi mirovoi voiny,* II: 54, 137.

128. Payne, *Fascism in Spain,* 262–3; Bosworth, *Mussolini,* 319; Preston, *Franco,* 228.

129. Payne, *Falange,* 212.

130. Preston, *Franco,* 242.

131. By the time Franco would finally advance on the Catalan front, in spring 1938, the Republic's defenders would melt away, rendering his move more a military parade than an offensive. Thomas, *Spanish Civil War,* 852.

132. In Portugal and Greece, too, traditional authoritarian conservatism blunted indigenous fascist movements. Blinkhorn, *Fascists and Conservatives.*

133. Preston, *Franco,* 175–87; Orwell, *Homage to Catalonia,* chapter 5.

134. Thomas, *Spanish Civil War,* 905–6.

135. The Carlists supported the claim to the throne of Alfonso Carlos I de Borbón y Austria, but after he died in late Sept. 1936 without an heir, they had splintered, with some supporting Alfonso Carlos's appointed regent (Prince Xavier of Bourbon-Parma) and others supporting Alfonso XIII (in exile at Rome's Grand Hotel).

136. Thomas, *Spanish Civil War,* 907.

137. Bolloten, *Spanish Revolution.*

138. Before the putsch, on May 20, 1936, Dimitrov had informed Manuilsky that he had a discussion with Stalin about the Spanish question, and that Stalin had approved the Comintern line: support for the Spanish Republic government rather than the Spanish Communist party or revolution. Meshcheriakov, "SSSR i grazhdanskaia voina v Ispanii," 88 (citing RGASPI, f. 495, op. 74, d. 208, l. 31; f. 17, op. 120, d. 439, l. 266). After the putsch, Stalin would still not support a Communist takeover or putsch, despite being urged to do so by Soviet military men who craved political unity in Spain. Sadly, some scholars continue to

insist—against a wealth of evidence—that the "moderate" policies of the Comintern as well as the Spanish Communist party in the civil war were mere "temporary tactical adjustments." Payne, *Spanish Civil War,* 293. Payne's book is dedicated to Bolloten, his mentor, who called the Popular Front a "grand camouflage" for Communist penetration. Bolloten, *Grand Camouflage.* This is the same Bolloten mentioned in Soviet intelligence documents from the Spanish civil war as "our source." Costello and Tsraev, *Deadly Illusions,* 237 (citing ASVRR, file 17679, I: 15 [or 161]; Volodarsky, *Stalin's Agent,* 237.

139. The Soviet Union had interest groups—regional, institutional, personal—that formed over struggles for resources and influence, but they competed for Stalin's favor, trying to anticipate his preferences and to destroy their rivals—jockeying that made them ultimately dependent upon him.

140. Solomon Dridzo, known as Lozovsky, the general secretary of the Red Trade Union International, was just as incredulous: "And so, Hitler does not express the interests of finance capital in Germany?" Manuilsky felt compelled to inquire: "Comrade Varga, it is clear to the [Comintern] secretariat that Germany is ruled by finance capital. Comrade Pieck is not denying that fact." Komolova, *Komintern protiv fashizma: dokumenty,* 445–8 (RGASPI, f. 495, op. 18, d. 1171, l. 24–9)

141. Fischer, *Russia's Road,* 242 (Feb. 11, 1937); Abramov, "Osobaia missiia Davida Kandelaki," 151–2 (citing AVP RF f. 05, op. 17, pap. 126, d. 1, l. 22; f. 059, op. 1, pap. 244, d. 1717, l. 15), 152 (pap. 244, d. 1715 (Surits to Litvinov, March 21, 1937).

142. Abramov, "Osobaia missiia Davida Kandelaki," 152 (citing AVP RF, f. 05, op. 17, pap. 130, d. 42, l. 28, 29, 34; f. 059, op. 1, pap. 244, d. 1715, l. 28–9, 45: March 21, 1937).

143. RGASPI, f. 558, op. 11, d. 56, l. 29.

144. *Izvestiia,* April 2, 1937. Rosenholz would be removed as foreign trade commissar on July 14, 1937, and replaced by Yevgeny Chvyalev.

145. Abramov, "Osobaia missiia Davida Kandelaki," 152 (citing AVP RF, f. 5, op. 17, pap. 1304, d. 42, l. 77).

146. *DVP SSSR,* XX: 174–5.

147. Khaustov, "Deiatel'nost' organov," 299–300 (TsA FSB, f. 3, op. 58, d. 249, l. 158); Khaustov and Samuelson, *Stalin, NKVD,* 45–6 (APRF, f. 3, op. 58, d. 249, l. 142–3; RGASPI, f. 17, op. 162, d. 21, l. 29), 286 (APRF, f. 3, op. 58, d. 254a, l. 82).

148. Khlevniuk et al., *Stalinskoe politbiuro,* 55; Khlevniuk, *Politbiuro,* 229–30.

149. Well described by Buber-Neumann, *Under Two Dictators,* 3–25. Her husband, Heinz, was arrested in April 1937; she was arrested the next year and sent to a camp in Karaganda as "the wife of an enemy of the people."

150. Thurston, *Life and Terror.*

151. Medvedev, *On Stalin,* 102. See also Beck and Gordin, *Russian Purge,* 146 ("He's not a party member and he's not a Jew, so why has he been arrested?").

152. *Pravda,* April 17 and Aug. 12, 1938. See also *Vlast' sovetov,* 1938, no. 10: 52–3.

153. *Pravda,* April 29, May 11, June 24, Aug. 14 and 25, 1937.

154. Mandelstam, *Hope against Hope,* 336.

155. Muza, "Tragedy of a Russian Woman," 495; "Iz stenogrammy repetitsii spektaklia 'Anna Karenina,'" in V. I. *Nemirovich-Danchenko, o tvorchestve aktera: khrestomatiia* (Moscow: Iskusstvo, 1984), 338. The play was featured at the Paris Exposition of 1937.

156. The coronation was scheduled for May 12, 1937. Between April 1 and June 10, 1937,

4,370 people would be discharged from the Red Army for political reasons, compared with 577 during the first three months of that year. Suvenirov, "Narkomat oborony," 29 (citing, RGVA, f. 9, op. 29, d. 340).

157. *Izvestiia,* April 23, 1937; *Pravda,* April 23, 1937.

158. *Sovetskoe foto,* 1973, no. 9; *Ogonek,* 1937, no. 16–7; Lopatin, *Volga idet v Moskvu;* Shein, *Kanal Moskva-Volga;* Fedenko, *Kanal Moskva-Volga.* Stalin had visited sections of the canal on June 4, 1934, June 14, 1936, and April 22, 1937: http://moskva-volga.ru/trete-prishestvie-stalina.

159. Davies et al., *Economic Transformation,* 127.

160. Osokina, "Economic Disobedience," 180.

161. Ellman, *Socialist Planning,* 107; Harrison, "National Income," 52–3.

162. "What is there to say about the success of Soviet power," one worker complained. "It is lies. The newspapers cover up the real state of things. I am a worker, wear torn clothes, my four children go to school half-starving, in rags. I, an honest worker, am a visible example of what Soviet power has given the workers in the last twenty years." Davies, *Popular Opinion,* 135 (citing TsGAIPD, f. 24, op. 2v, d. 2282, l. 109).

163. Thurston, *Life and Terror,* 166–8.

164. Danilov et al., *Tragediia sovetskoi derevni,* V/i: docs. 71, 76, 81, 93, 94, 98, 106, 125, 127; Berelowitch and Danilov, *Sovetskaia derevnia glazami VChK-OGPU-NKVD,* IV: 273–450.

165. Khlevniuk, *Stalin: Zhizn',* 221 (citing RGASPI, f. 82, op. 2, d. 887, l. 17, 32, 41–2: March 2, 1937, and April 14 and 21, 1937).

166. Semyon Firin-Pupko later alleged that in 1937 Stalin raised the question of a canal from Moscow to Vladivostok, cutting a westeast waterway across the entire continent to link the northern flowing Siberian rivers, a gargantuan task unprecedented in recorded history. Sokolov, *Obshchestvo i vlast',* 163–4.

167. Kosheleva et al., "Materialy fevral'-martovskogo plenuma TsK VKP (b) 1937 goda" (1994, no. 8), 18; Davies, "Soviet Economy," 26–7.

168. Khlevniuk, "Economic Officials in the Great Terror," 58. Semyon Lobov (b. 1888), a former steelworker and forestry industry commissar until Oct. 1936 (when he was shifted to the food industry), had stated, "is it really normal that if I, the commissar, need to obtain a pair of traincars with sheet steel or equipment for papermaking, I need to get the authorization of the Central Committee." Khaustov and Samuelson, *Stalin, NKVD,* 144 (TsA FSB, ASD P-4879, t. 2, s. 109). Lobov would be arrested June 21, 1937, and executed Oct. 30 of that year.

169. Khaustov and Samuelson, *Stalin, NKVD,* 128 (APRF, f. 3, op. 58, d. 405, l. 64–5).

170. Radosh et al., *Spain Betrayed,* 146–8 (RGVA, f. 33987, op. 3, d. 1010, l. 295–300). Krivoshein appears to have returned from Spain at this time.

171. Banac, *Diary of Georgi Dimitrov,* 43 (Dec. 16, 1936), 58 (March 14, 1937).

172. Kudriashov, *SSSR i grazhdanskaia voina v Ispanii,* 212 (APRF, f. 3, op. 65, d. 223, l. 141–2), 213 (l. 146). "We are well aware of the scale of Soviet assistance, the steamships with Russian weapons all the while are passing by our shores," Leonardo Vitetti, director of European Affairs in the Italian foreign ministry, told the Soviet embassy in Rome in April 1937. "We have not touched them, not wanting to complicate the already extremely sharp and awful Italo-Soviet relations." Meshcheriakov, "SSSR i grazhdanskaia voina v Ispanii," 86 (citing AVP RF, f. 048 z, op. 14–16,

pap. 4, d. 8, l. 195); and Tournier, *Les archives secretes de la Wilhelmstrasse III*, 88, 91–2. On March 24, 1937, Mekhlis wrote to Stalin that "according to the information we have, comrade M. E. Koltsov is severely exhausted and completely physically worn down," and was requesting permission to recall him to Moscow, a request Stalin approved. On Nov. 22, 1937, Mekhlis would write to Stalin that "Koltsov is in a bad mood now and, it seems, he has lost his bearings and could commit mistakes. He has been away from Moscow and party influence for a long time." Mekhlis would again propose his recall, which Stalin would approve. Kudriashov, *SSSR i grazhdanskaia voina v Ispanii*, 215 (APRF [transferred to RGANI), f. 3, op. 34, d. 127, l. 27), 312 (l. 33–4). Mekhlis appears to have been angry that Koltsov wrote to him complaining he had been left out of the candidates approved for the Dec. 12, 1937, elections to the Supreme Soviet.
173. Banac, *Diary of Georgi Dimitrov*, 59 (March 16, 1937). Four days later, in the presence of Dimitrov, Stalin told the Spanish writers Rafael Alberti and María-Teresa Léonon that "the people and the whole world must be told the truth—the Spanish people are in no condition now to bring about a proletarian revolution—the internal and especially the international situation do not favor it." Stalin added that "victory in Spain will loosen fascism's hold in Italy and Germany. Communist and socialist forces must join forces—they now share the same basic aims—a democratic republic." Banac, *Diary of Georgi Dimitrov*, 60–1 (March 20, 1937). Dimitrov did not relent: On March 23, he provided Stalin with a report by a Bulgarian Comintern official who had spent two months in Spain. "The ability of the government to govern is very limited . . . Everyone, the broad popular masses, feels the need for a strong government, a government capable of ruling . . . The fundamental source of weakness of the government is that it lacks . . . a state apparatus." Stalin may well have agreed with this assessment, but he still refrained from having the Communists in Spain seize power. Dallin and Firsov, *Dimitrov and Stalin*, 51–8.
174. Kaganovich to Orjonikidze, Sept. 30, 1936; Khlevniuk et al., *Stalinskoe politburo*, 149.
175. Spain's Communist party is alleged to have grown to 400,000 at its peak. Thomas, *Spanish Civil War*, 506–7.
176. Communist agents could not fail to learn of these probes. Payne, *Spanish Revolution*, 271–2. On April 15, 1937, a Comintern representative in the Republican camp wrote to Stalin urging him to break completely with Largo Caballero. Radosh et al., *Spain Betrayed*, 184–95.
177. Banac, *Diary of Georgi Dimitrov*, 58 (March 14, 1937).
178. Kudriashov, *SSSR i grazhdanskaia voina v Ispanii*, 221 (APRF, f. 3, op. 65, d. 223, l. 151), versus Berzin's report: 219 (l. 152). Berzin blamed the weak artillery support and weak offensive capabilities of the blue infantry, and the recent strengthening of the whites as well as the advantageous geography seized by them.
179. Southworth, *Guernica, Guernica*. Preston, *Franco*, 243–7. The article was by George Steer, South African born, who had written authoritatively about the Italian atrocities in the Abyssinian War. Steer would be killed in Burma in 1945. A Pablo Picasso canvas, an 11 x 25 foot mural commissioned by the Republican government for the Spanish pavilion at the 1937 Paris International Exposition, was completed already by mid-June and exhibited in July; it depicts the intense suffering of

people, animals, and buildings subjected to violence.
180. Lebedev, "M. N. Tukhachevskii i 'voenno-fashistskii zagovor,'" 30–3. Stalin could have had the "information" delivered into the hands of the Japanese in Warsaw, in order to have it "leaked" back through foreign channels, perhaps to persuade Voroshilov.
181. Maclean, *Escape to Adventure*, 15; Krivitsky, *In Stalin's Secret Service*, 227–8; Conquest, *Reassessment*, 214. Unusually, on April 28, 1937, *Izvestiya* issued a correction to a photo caption published the previous day: "Comrade Stalin the organizer of the strike of Tiflis railroad workers in 1902." The newspaper had to admit that at the time Stalin was imprisoned in Batum. It seems Stalin himself, or his aide, conveyed to the newspaper editor that the caption was "an utter misunderstanding from the point of view of historical truth." *Izvestiia*, April 27 and April 28, 1937.
182. Lebedev, "M. N. Tukhachevskii i 'voenno-fashistskii zagovor,'" 178; "Delo on tak nazyvaemoi 'antisovetskoi trotskistskoi organizatsii' v Krasno armii," 46–7 (S. P. Uritsky); Cristiani and Mikhaleva, *Le repressioni*, 254, 256 (RGVA, f. 33987, op. 3, d. 1047, l. 70). Stalin canceled the annual reception at the Kremlin Grand Palace for graduates of military academies.
183. Sharapov, *Naum Eitingon*, 57.
184. Thomas, *Spanish Civil War*, 628–45.
185. Tatiana Tess, in Efimov, *Mikhail Koltsov*, 325.
186. S. Prokofeva and N. Godon, in Efimov, *Mikhail Kol'tsov*, 285, 384. The Embankment was officially known as Bersenevskaya. Koltsov previously lived on Bolshaya Dmitrovka. Of the fifty-six or so Central Committee members and candidates who had apartments in the House on the Embankment, forty-five would be arrested. Many residents, like Koltsov, were not Central Committee members.
187. Efimov, *Mikhail Koltsov*, 26–135 (at 103, 94–5). Koltsov had been in the Little Corner on Dec. 9, 1935, for twenty minutes, one-on-one. *Na prieme*, 174.
188. The Kremlin audience took place on April 15, after which Koltsov received a coveted invitation to the 1937 May Day reception at the St. George's Hall of the Grand Kremlin Place, where he was toasted by Voroshilov. On May 14, Stalin again received Koltsov in the Little Corner for one hour, alone. Kudriashov, *SSSR i grazhdanskaia voina v Ispanii*, 215 (APRF, f. 3, op. 34, d. 127, l. 27); *Na prieme*, 207, 209. Koltsov's Spanish Diary picks up again on May 23, on a train from Italy to Bilbao.
189. Orlov, the Soviet station chief in Spain, who was close to Koltsov, would comment, "The NKVD is like a gigantic mailbox into which any irresponsible person may drop an irresponsible invention." Orlov, *Tainaia istoriia*, 187–8; Orlov, *Secret History*, 187–8.
190. Kudriashov, *SSSR i grazhdanskaia voina v Ispanii*, 233 (APRF, f. 3, op. 53, d. 471, l. 73–4), 241 (op. 65, d. 224, l. 32), 242 (l. 30), 268, 276 (l. 115, 117–9), 249–52 (op. 53, d. 471, l. 3–4, 5–7, 55), 298–9 (d. 472, l. 3–4).
191. Volodarsky, *Stalin's Agent*, 205.
192. Costello and Tsarev, *Deadly Illusions*, 165–8, 454n73, 454n75 (citing ASVRR, file 5581, I: 38, 45). See also Philby's obfuscatory memoir: *Silent War*, 17.
193. Andrew and Mitrokhin, *Mitrokhin Archive*, 114. (Later Grigulevich would be one of many tapped to assassinate Trotsky in Mexico.) Sudoplatov, *Special Tasks*, 193; "V Madride ia rukovodil gruppoi" (Grigulevich interview); Primakov, *Ocherki*, III: 148–54.
194. Primakov, *Ocherki*, III: 153. With Orlov, Girgulevich participated in the kidnapping and murder of Nin.

195. Kol'tsov, "Fashistsko-shpionskaia rabota ispanskikh trotskistov." On the forgery: *Izvestiia*, Nov. 26, 1992.
196. Sharapov, *Naum Eitingon*, 53. See also Costello and Tsarev, *Deadly Illusions*, 291–2.
197. "It was a successful piece of disinformation reported directly to Stalin by Yezhov." Sudoplatov, *Special Tasks*, 44–5.
198. A Soviet military intelligence report had concluded that the "Trotskyite" and anarchist strongholds in Spain had to be broken. Radosh et al., *Spain Betrayed*, 129–33 (RGVA, f. 33987, op. 3, d. 960, l. 251–77: Nikonov, Feb. 20, 1937).
199. Orwell, *Homage to Catalonia*, 9. Orwell would complete his *Homage to Catalonia* in Jan. 1938, but his publisher, Victor Gollancz, who controlled the Left Book Club, would reject it—unseen. (The Left Book Club instead published pro-Soviet material on Spain.) But Frederic Warburg published *Homage to Catalonia* in a print run of 1,500, and managed to sell 800. Warburg also published Souvarine's *Stalin* and Gide's *Back from the USSR*. Arthur Koestler, who went to Spain in 1936 as a correspondent for Münzenberg, recalls how the latter shouted at him concerning his manuscript about Spain, "Too weak. Too objective. Hit them! Tell the world how they run over their prisoners with tanks, how they pour petrol over them and burn them alive. Make the world gasp with horror. Hammer it into their heads. Make them wake up." Koestler wrote in the published book: "If those who have at their command printing machines and printer's ink for the expression of their opinions, remain neutral and objective in the face of such bestiality, then Europe is lost." Koestler, *Spanish Testament*, 177; Koestler, *Invisible Writing*, 333.
200. Herbert, *Paris 1937*. Both Speer and Yofan won gold medals; Kaplan, *Red City, Blue Period*, 179–87.
201. Petrov, *Stroitel'stvo politorganov*, 224, 237–8; Petrov, *Partiinoe stroitel'stvo*, 298; Erickson, *Soviet High Command* (3rd ed.), 460.
202. "Delo o tak nazyvaemoi 'antisovetskoi trotskistskoi organizatsii' v Krasnoi armii," 47–8; Artizov et al., *Reabilitatsiia: kak eto bylo*, II: 678 (Aleksandr Avseevich, 1962); *Pravda*, April 29, 1988 (B. Viktorov). Primakov (a Bolshevik since 1914) had served as military attaché in Afghanistan (1927–29) and then Japan (1930); in 1928 he had been forced to declare a break with the Trotskyites. Zdanovich, *Organy*, 320 (citing TsA FSB, delo R-9000, t. 4, l. 53).
203. "Delo o tak nazyvaemoi 'antisovetskoi trotskistskoi organizatsii' v Krasnoi armii," 46; Zolotarev, *Russkii arkhiv: Velikaia Otechestvennaia*, XIII (2–1): 12. Also on May 10, 1937, the office of political commissar was reinstated (it had been abolished in 1934).
204. *Voennye arkhivy Rossii*, 41; Lebedev, "M. N. Tukhachevskii i 'voenno-fashistskii zagovor,'" 182; *Na prieme*, 209; Viktor A. Aleksandrov, *Delo Tukhachevskogo*.
205. Khaustov and Samuelson, *Stalin, NKVD*, 115–6 (TsA FSB, ASD P-4615, l. 258–61; ASD N. 15301, tom 2: 37–8); Khaustov et al., *Lubianka: Stalin i VChk*, 170–6.
206. Tukhachevsky managed to clash not only with the partisan-war types of the civil war (Voroshilov, Budyonny, Kulik), but also old-line professionals, such as Shaposhnikov, whom Tukhachevsky derided as "cautious" and "an office Napoleon." Koritskii et al., *Tukhachevskii*, 17. That said, Shaposhnikov's earlier appointment to the general staff might have been on Tukhachevsky's recommendation. Ken, *Mobilizatsionnoe planirovanie*, 198–9 (RGASPI, f. 134, op. 3, d. 17, l. 65: Kollontai diary); Nord, "Marshal Tukhachevskii," 114.

207. Zdanovich, *Organy*, 282–4 (citing TsA FSB, delo R-9000, t. 24, l. 1, l. 210, l. 48ob, l. 72.).

208. Sudoplatov, *Special Tasks*, 89–90.

209. German intelligence purportedly sought to exploit these appetites, too, sending the blond, blue-eyed singer Josephine Heinze Tukhachevsky's way. Leskov, *Stalin i zagovor Tukhachevskogo*, 222–47.

210. Kantor, *Zakliataia druzhba*, 295. German general Blomberg had described Tukhachevsky as "youthfully fresh, sociable, sympatisch . . . He withheld himself from conversations about any political themes, but was a talkative and purposeful conversationalist when touching upon the operational and tactical areas. A very winning persona." Kantor, *Voina i mir*, 296–7, 300 (citing Blomberg's private archive, "Reise des Chefs des Truppenamts nach Russland," Aug.–Sept. 1928, 2–3, 14–16, 46).

211. Not long after Stalin had absolved Tukhachevsky, back in fall 1930, of plotting a seizure of power with the rightists, Voroshilov had forwarded two letters incriminating him, commenting that one "gave a brilliant and damning characterization." The letters to Voroshilov were from Verkhovsky and Bergavinov, and forwarded to Stalin in Jan. 1931. Ken, *Mobilizatsionnoe planirovanie*, 132. For hearsay about Tukhachevsky's criticisms of Voroshilov for incompetence, including in front of others, see Nevzorov, *Marshal Tukhachevsky*, 102; and Simonov, *Glazami chloveka moeogo pokoleniia*, 383 (Zhukov).

212. Uborevičius, known for his tactical and operational insight, mentored an extraordinary group of officers, including Semyon Timoshenko (b. 1895), Alexander Vasilevsky (b. 1895), Georgy Zhukov (b. 1896), Kirill Meretskov (b. 1897), Dmitry Pavlov (b. 1897), Ivan Konev (b. 1897), and Matvei Zakharov (b. 1898).

213. Svetlanin, *Dal'nevostochnyi zagovor*, 101 (the deputy was I. F. Fedko). In Sept. and Dec. 1936, the NKVD had received information that Blyukher was planning a military putsch. "M. N. Tukhachevskii i 'voenno-fashistkii zagovor,'" 10.

214. This went far down the chain of command. "I feel that my every step is under observation," remarked K. I. Sokolov-Strakhov, editor of the *Military-Historical Bulletin*, in comments that helped provoke his arrest. "It is hard and even frightening now to work on the literary-historical front." (Sokolov-Strakhov was married to the niece of a former chief of the gendarmes.) Suvenirov, "Narkomat oborny," 33, 56 (citing RGVA, f. 9, op. 39, d. 29, l. 5).

215. "The causes behind why I came to military intelligence are known to all," Uritsky told the group's "party active" on May 19, 1937. "The causes were a breach . . . I arrived here and there were people who did not help me much. You and I are bad intelligence agents." Gorbunov, "Voennaia razvedka v 1934–1939 godakh" (no. 3), 57 (citing RGVA, f. 9, op. 30, d. 54, l. 26).

216. *Rodina*, 1995, no. 2: 87; Pogonii, *Lubianka, 2*, 203; Tumshis and Papchinskii, *1937, bol'shaia chistka*, 404–6, 445–51. Artuzov would be executed on Aug. 21, 1937.

217. Khaustov and Samuelson, *Stalin, NKVD*, 299, 304, 307–10. Frinovsky had helped supervise Stalin's visit to the Moscow-Volga Canal on April 22, 1937, before being arrested on May 9 as a German spy. Kokurin and Petrov, "Gulag," 114.

218. Sever and Kolpakidi, *GRU*, 358.

219. Stalin also underscored the need to portray Soviet spies as "genuine patriots, heroes, of their country," in order "to attract youth, talented people, girls, scientists" to intelligence work, but warned that "the enemy's strong intelligence and our weakness are a provocation to war." Petrov and Jansen, *Stalinskii pitomets*, 290–3 (TsA FSB, f. 6, op. 5, d, 25, l. 208–10). See also Vinogradov, "Tret'ia reform organov bezopasnosti," II: 76–96, esp. 93. One account has Stalin going in person, on May 22, 1937, to military intelligence HQ: Gorbunov, "Voennaia razvedka v 1934–1939 godakh" (no 3.), 57. On the consequences, see also Alekseev et al., *Entsiklopediia voennoi razvedki*, 508–9.

220. *Voennye arkhivy Rossii*, 44; Lebedev, "M. N. Tukhachevskii i 'voenno-fashistskii zagovor,'" 188. See also Pankov, *Komkor Eideman*, 103. Voroshilov had recommended promoting Eideman to head of antiaircraft, arguing that it needed someone of "major authority." Whitewood, *Red Army*, 212 (citing RGVA, f. 4, op. 19, d. 18, l. 176).

221. Some say the arrest occurred in the office of the provincial party secretary, others in his train coach (he had not yet moved into an apartment). Nikulin, *Tukhachevskii*, 190; Sokolov, *Tukhachevskii*, 310–1, (citing P. A. Ermolin); Kantor, *Voina i mir*, 370 (citing letter of N. I. Shishikin, in the personal archives of Iu. V. Khitrovo); Koritskii et al., *Tukhachevskii*, 128–9; Zen'kovich, *Marshaly i genseki*, 488.

222. Pechenkin, "1937 god," 43, citing RGASPI, f. 17, op. 2, d, 615, l. 8, 10, 14.

223. Kantor, *Voina i mir*, 386–7; Svetlana Tukhachevsky's statement in Yuliya Kantor, Mikhail Nikolaevich Tukhachevsky: www .pseudology.org/colonels/Tukhachevsky.htm. The Central Committee, without a plenum, expelled Tukhachevsky as well as Rudzutaks from the party and handed them over to the NKVD. Khaustov et al., *Lubianka: Stalin i glavnoe upravlenie*, 190 (APRF, f. 3, op. 24, d. 304, l. 112); Getty and Naumov, *Road to Terror*, 448. Ushakov would be executed in Jan. 1940.

224. *Na prieme*, 210. Kandelaki would be arrested Sept. 11, 1937.

225. Krivitsky, *In Stalin's Secret Service*, 234.

226. Volkogonov, *Triumf i tragediia*, I/ii: 263; *Krasnaia zvezda*, June 4, Aug. 13, 1964. *Pravda* announced his suicide on June 1, 1937. There were nearly 800 suicides in the Red Army in 1937, and more than 800 the next year. Khlevniuk, *1937–i*, 207. Gamarnik had been parroting the Stalin line, telling a party meeting in the military (March 13, 1937), for ex.: "Comrades, the Japanese-German Trotskyist agents, spies, and wreckers are in a full range of our army organization, in the staffs, the institutions, the academies, the military-training institutions." He repeated this in more speeches before his arrest for being the phenomenon he was warning against. Whitewood, "Purge of the Red Army," 296, citing RGVA, f. 9, op. 29, d. 319, l. 2.

227. Minakov, *Za otvorotom marshal'skoi shineli*, 249–358.

228. Davies et al., *Stalin-Kaganovich Correspondence*, 556–7. The Azov–Black Sea Territory was divided in Sept. 1937; Yevdokimov became party chief of the new Rostov province.

229. Rumors circulated that when a preeminent sadist (Anatoly Yesaulov) had failed to beat a confession out of Yagoda for espionage, Stalin had assigned the task to Yevdokimov. The rumor was false yet indicative. Vinogradov, *Genrikh Iagoda*, 95–243.

230. Pavliukov, *Ezhov*, 270–1.

231. Pavliukov, *Ezhov*, 274–5; Petrov and Jansen, *Stalinskii pitomets*, 67–8. See also Wheatcroft, "Agency and Terror." Kursky shot himself on July 8, 1937.

232. Petrov and Skorkin, *Kto rukovodil NKVD*; Naumov, *Stalin i NKVD*, 173–88.

233. http://www.hrono.ru/dokum/193_ dok/19390413beria.php (APRF, f. 3, op. 24, d. 373, l. 3–44: protocol of Frinovsky interrogation, Beria to Stalin April 11, 1939). Frinovsky and Yezhov were not close. "I had multiple clashes at work with him," Yezhov would later observe of Frinovsky. "I cursed him out, and called him a fool to his face, because no sooner would he arrest someone among the NKVD operatives then he would run to me and shout that it was all fabrication [*lipa*], that the person was wrongly arrested." "Poslednee slovo Nikolai Ezhova."

234. http://www.hrono.ru/dokum/193_ dok/19390413beria.php (APRF, f. 3, op. 24, d. 373, l. 3–44: protocol of Frinovsky interrogation, sent by Beria to Stalin April 11, 1939); Afanas'ev, *Oni ne molchali*, 218.

235. "Poslednee slovo Nikolai Ezhova"; Petrov and Jansen, *Stalinskii pitomets*, 536 (citing TsA FSB, sledstvennoe delo No. N-15302, t. 1, l. 184–6); Getty and Naumov, *Road to Terror*, 560–2.

236. Gide, *Vozvrashchenie iz SSSR* (Moscow: Moskovskii rabochii, 1990), 80. On the Soviet response to the Gide book, see Fleishman, *Pasternak v tridtsatye gody*, 378–83.

237. RGASPI, f. 77, op. 3–e, d. 117, l. 33.

238. Koltsov, who was cohabitating with Feuchtwanger's wife, Maria Osten, had lobbied for Feuchtwanger to be received in the Soviet Union. RGASPI, f. 17, op., 114, d. 952, l. 48 (Angarov to Ezhov, Nov. 2, 1936; note from Mikhail Apletin, deputy head of the writers' union foreign commission, to Angarov).

239. Feuchtwanger, *Moskva 1937*, 68. See also Volkogonov, *Stalin: Triumph and Tragedy*, 238.

240. Feuchtwanger, *Moskva 1937*, 64–5, 91. See also Feuchtwanger, *Moscow 1937*, 93–5. Feuchtwanger visited Moscow Dec. 1, 1936, to Feb. 5, 1937. Stalin received him on Jan. 8. RGASPI, f. 558, op. 11, d. 820, l. 3–22; Feuchtwanger, *Moscow 1937*, 152–3. Feuchtwanger's book would be withdrawn from Soviet libraries in 1938. One scholar noted that he "was the last in the line of the celebrated fellow-travelers of the interwar period to turn his journey into an eyewitness' public endorsement of Stalinism; he was the last European intellectual sympathizer to be received on the grand scale of Rolland and Gide." David-Fox, *Showcasing the Great Experiment*, 270. Orwell conceded that he would support Communism over fascism if forced to choose. Davison, *George Orwell*.

241. Vishnevskii, *Sobranie sochinenii*, VI: 410–1.

242. Anderson, *Voennyi sovet*, 40–1, 57; "Delo o tak nazyvaemoi 'antisovetskoi trotskistskoi voennoi organizatsii' v krasnoi armii," *Izvestiia TsK KPSS*, 1989, no. 4: 52.

243. Meretskov, *Na sluzhbe narodu*, 166–7.

244. *Na prieme*, 211; Pechenkin, "1937 god," 51.

245. Polishchuk, "Zasedanie RVS 1–3 iuinia 1937 goda." Polishchuk was then the head of the Military Electrical-Technology Academy. He is listed as having received the interrogation protocols to read: Anderson, *Voennyi sovet*, 41.

246. Anderson, *Voennyi sovet*, 66–70, 74–5. See also Sokolov, *Mikhail Tukhachevskii*, 378.

247. "'Nevol'niki v rukakh germanskogo reiskhvera,'" 74 (RGASPI, f. 558, op. 11, d. 1120, l. 28–57 at 31–2). See also "Sovetskaia razvedka i russkaia voennaia emigratsiia 20–40x gg.," 119. On Nov. 14, 1932, Mężyński sent a letter to Stalin proposing Dzierżyński for a medal; Stalin wrote on it "Opposed." He had still not forgiven Dzierżyński's brief wavering. But Stalin had authorized a Dzierżyński statue to be erected in front of the NKVD headquarters, on Dzierżyński Square, on the

tenth anniversary of his death, in July 1936. RGASPI, f. 558, op. 1, d. 5284, l. 1–3; Plekhanov and Plekhanov, *F. E. Dzerzhinskii,* 671 (RGASPI, f. 17, op. 3, d. 279, l. 41).

248. Anderson, *Voennyi sovet,* 128–43 (esp. 128, 131, 134–5); "'Nevol'niki v rukakh germanskogo reikhsvera,'" 74 (RGASPI, f. 558, op. 11, d. 1120, l. 28–57 at 31–2). See also Gorbatov, *Gody i voiny,* 122–3. In Jan. 1938, Stalin would take to arguing, unpersuasively, that skill in the military arts was not so crucial for military success and that what mattered were the social origins of military leaders and the overall correct government policy of the workers-peasants state. RGASPI, f. 558, op. 11, d. 1120, l. 104–5, 109.

249. RGASPI, f. 558, op. 11, d. 1120, l. 28–57 (at 46–7).

250. Pechenkin, "1937 god." The 1961 commission on Stalin's military repressions was published in two places: *Voennye arkhivy Rossii,* 29–113 (incomplete); and *Voenno-istoricheskii arkhiv,* 1997, no. 1: 173–255, no. 2: 3–81. See also the illuminating testimony about opposition to collectivization extracted from or written for Pavel Bulanov about Yagoda. Il'inskii, *Narkom Iagoda,* 500–8 (at 500: TsA FSB, N-13614, tom 2: 211–21: April 30, 1937).

251. Pechenkin, "1937 god," 50–1.

252. "'Nevol'niki v rukakh germanskogo reikhsvera,'" 75–6.

253. The ten were Voroshilov, Budyonny, Shaposhnikov, Timoshenko, Kulik, Apanasenko, Gorodovikov, Shchadenko, Khrulyov, and Meretskov (arrested but released). The majority had been members of the First Cavalry Army in the civil war. Pavliukov, *Ezhov,* 288. Pechenkin gives eight not arrested. Pechenkin, "1937 god," 52.

254. Anderson, *Voennyi sovet,* 250–6, 243–5.

255. Preston, *Franco,* 278–9.

256. Anderson, *Voennyi sovet,* 340–1. Already on May 10, 1937, in a detailed report to Stalin and Molotov, Voroshilov had parroted the new Stalin line. The mass arrests of the highest commanders had followed almost immediately. Whitewood, "Purge of the Red Army," 300, citing RGVA, f. 33987, op. 3, d. 965, l. 65.

257. Ulam, *Stalin,* 18 (attributing the line to Budu Mdivani).

258. RGASPI, f. 558, op. 11, d. 1549. Keke had taken ill on May 13, 1937.

259. The inventory of her belongings: RGASPI, f. 558, op. 11, d. 1549; Ilizarov, *Tainaia zhizn' Stalina,* 281–2. The effects went to Maria Kvinkadze.

260. *Memuary freiliny imperatritsy,* 204–5 (Tatuli Gviniashvili).

261. Elagin, *Ukroshchenie iskusstv,* 55; Jelagin, *Taming of the Arts,* 51–2.

262. "You're wrong to talk about famine and penury abroad, because they write to me that everything here is cheaper than here and they send money," one woman in Vologda, Stalin's former place of internal exile, observed in 1937 in response to party agitation. Golubev, *"Esli mir obrushitsia na nashu Respubliku,"* 68–9 (citing BOANPI, f. 1858, op. 2, d. 940, l. 56). A Sept. 1938 secret directive confirmed the institutions that could receive foreign literature, dividing them into three categories. Only those in the first category—the secretariat of the Council of People's Commissars, the Central Committee, the Supreme Soviet, *Pravda* and *Izvestiya* editorial boards, the foreign affairs commissariat, the NKVD foreign department, TASS, the Institute of Marxism-Leninism, leading members of foreign Communist parties, and foreign embassies—enjoyed unlimited privileges. Blium, *Tsenzura v Sovetskom Soiuze,* 279–80. Despite the tight control, the censor still ended up pulping 10 percent of the purchased foreign periodicals (which cost the state a

quarter million gold rubles). In 1939, the USSR would import 2.36 million individual foreign publications (books, pamphlets, issues of periodicals); the censorship examined about one-quarter of the total, and 10 percent were again destroyed. Goriaeva, *Istoriia sovetskoi politicheskoi tsenzury,* 311, 326.

263. "The window to the world can be covered by a newspaper," in the ironic words of Stanisław Jerzy Lec, Polish poet and aphorist, who had been born de Tusch-Letz in Habsburg Lemberg (Lwów) in 1909. Lec, *Unkempt Thoughts.*

264. Meerovich, "V narkomindele, 1922–1939: interv'iu s E. A. Gnedinym," *Pamiat': istoricheskii sbornik* [Paris], 1981, vyp. 5: 381.

265. Rittersporn, "Omnipresent Conspiracy," 101–20; also found in Getty and Manning, *Stalinist Terror,* 99–115. See also Rittersporn, *Anguish.*

266. He added that "we junior officers knew that personally we ran no hazards." Akhmedov, *In and Out of Stalin's GRU,* 104.

267. For a detailed account of how the NKVD fabricated the case, see Cherushev, *1937 god.* Stalin edited the copy, drafted by Mekhlis, following sessions in the Little Corner. *Na prieme,* 211–2; Khaustov et al., *Lubianka: Stalin i glavnoe upravlenie,* 217–19 (APRF, f. 3. op. 24. d. 308. l. 78–83). Józef Unszlicht, although long out of the military, was arrested that day but not included in the military trial. He would be executed on July 28, 1938.

268. *Pravda,* June 9–13, 1937. An abridged Soviet version appeared as *Razvedka i kontrrazvedka* (Moscow: Voenizdat, 1938).

269. *Voennye arkhivy Rossii,* 50; Lebedev, "M. N. Tukhachevskii i 'voenno-fashistskii zagovor,'" 194; Artizov et al., *Reabilitatsiia: kak eto bylo,* II: 688.

270. Suvenirov, *Tragediia RKKA,* 103 (citing RGVA, f. 33987, op. 3, d 1038, l. 188–9: letter, June 5).

271. Gorchakov, *Ian Berzin,* 113. Berzin would only last until Aug. 1, 1937.

272. One author has alleged that there was a "plot" by these military men, not to seize power, but to have Voroshilov removed, which provoked Stalin's actions. Minakov, *1937.* There is no evidence whatsoever for such a "plot" (as opposed to a wish). Khaustov and Samuelson, *Stalin, NKVD,* 17.

273. Volkogonov, *Triumf i tragediia,* I/ii: 264–5. A facsimile of Tukhachevsky's "confession" and a copy of the "plan of defeat" are in: "Pokazaniia marshala Tukhachevskogo."

274. Trotsky had condemned Tukhachevsky's idea of a Red-Army-led "revolution from abroad" (which the latter had applied unsuccessfully to Poland in 1920). See also Tukhachevsky's militant contribution to *Der bewaffnete Aufstand,* 21, 23.

275. Rapoport and Alexeev, *High Treason,* 5–8. The street where Tukhachevsky met his death, formerly known as Nikolskaya, had been the location of his original Moscow apartment.

276. Jansen and Petrov, "Mass Terror and the Court."

277. Lebedev, "M. N. Tukhachevskii i 'voenno-fashistskii zagovor,'" 199.

278. Verevkin-Rakhal'skii, *Moi 90 let,* 193. Voroshilov's diary for June 7 indicates that Stalin went back and forth on precisely who of those already arrested would be put on trial, and who would sit in the panel of judges. Deputy Commander of the Far Eastern Army Mikhail Sangursky, who was arrested June 1–2, 1937, appeared in Voroshilov's June 7 order on the trial, but before June 11 was removed. Voroshilov had Berzin and Smirnov originally listed as judges but crossed them off. Kun, *Stalin,* 400–1 (facsimiles of pages from Voroshilkov's diary); "Prikaz

narodnogo komissara oborony Soiuza SSR no. 072 (7 iiunia 1937 g.)," 46; Suvenirov, *Tragediia RKKA,* 91, 379.

279. Zen'kovich, *Marshaly i genseki,* 510–1 (citing the eleven-page trial transcript). Five of the seven military men sitting as judges with Ulrich would soon be executed themselves, except for Budyonny and Shaposhnikov.

280. RGVA, f. 33 987, op. 3s, d. 828, Volkogonov papers, Hoover, container 17. In his account for Stalin (June 26), Budyonny noted that although Tukhachevsky had shaken his head "no" during the reading of the charges and testimony, and denied passing any classified documents to the Germans, in the end he pronounced himself guilty. *Voennye arkhivy Rossii,* 55–6; Lebedev, "M. N. Tukhachevskii i 'voenno-fashistskii zagovor,'" 199–200; APRF, f. 3, op. 24, d. 310, l. 170–83. See also the report of another "judge," I. P. Belov, in Cristiani and Mikhaleva, *Le repressioni,* 192–8.

281. "Delo o tak nazyvaemoi 'antisovetskoi trotskistskoi organizatsii' v Krasnoi Armii," 57.

282. Blokhin was assisted by Ignatev. Lebedev, "M. N. Tukhachevskii i 'voenno-fashistskii zagovor,'" 199. Just after Ulrich had pronounced sentences, Stalin received Timoshenko, alone, for half an hour (June 12). He would be posted to Ukraine, to replace Yakir as commander of the Kiev military district. *Na prieme,* 212.

283. "World fascism this time, too, has discovered that its loyal agents, the Garmarniks and the Tukhachevskys, the Yakirs and the Uboreviches, as well as similar treasonous offal, lackeys serving capitalism, have been wiped from the face of the earth," wrote Voroshilov, in a directive to all Red Army servicemen printed in *Pravda* (June 13). "Their memory will be cursed and forgotten." Tukhachevsky was equated with "playing the same role as Franco."

284. *Pravda,* June 13, 1937 (Krupskaya). See also *Komsomol'skaia pravda,* Jan. 18, 2013.

285. Vostryshev, *Moskva stalinskaia,* 361–2; *Kommersant vlast',* July 9, 2012.

286. Bailes, *Technology and Society,* 387; Egorov and Kliucharev, *Grazhdanskaia aviatsiia SSSR,* 98–9, 101; Karpov, *Aviatsiia strany sotsializma,* 60–2. Stalin sometimes summoned these flight crews to the Little Corner before their flights, going over their plans, and occasionally saw them off at the airfield. Chkalov (with Baidukov) was recorded in the Little Corner twice: July 14, 1936, and May 25, 1937 (before the Pacific Coast flight). *Na prieme,* 189, 210.

287. *Velikii letchik nashego vremeni,* 315.

288. Bailes, *Technology and Society,* 381–406.

289. Volkogonov, *Stalin: Triumph and Tragedy,* 332.

290. Kumanev, *Riadom so Stalinym,* 435–6 (Chadaev). See also Rubtsov, *Alter ego Stalina;* Rubtsov, *Iz-za spiny vozhdia.*

291. Volkogonov papers, Hoover, container 4, telegrams to and from the military districts from TsAMO; Khrushchev, *Khrushchev Remembers,* 160–4. Mekhlis soon replaced Gamarnik as chief of the political department in the military (from Dec. 1937), a post he would hold until Sept. 1940. "The more 'enemies of the people' Stalin exterminates, rising upward on their corpses," Trotsky acidly wrote of Mekhlis after his promotion to deputy defense commissar, "the greater the void that forms around him." "Voroshilov Is Next in Line," *Biulleten' oppozitsii,* no. 62–3 (1938): 23.

292. A contemporary Soviet diplomat, who defected and survived, well understood the impossibility, physically and psychologically,

of a Red Army plot in cahoots with Nazism. Barmine, *One Who Survived*, 223.

293. Volkogonov, "Marshal Voroshilov," 163.

294. Khaustov and Samuelson, *Stalin, NKVD*, 321 (TsA FSB, f. 3, op. 5, d. 343, l. 84); Khaustov, "Razvitie sovetskikh organov gosudarstvennoi bezopasnosti," 362. Khrulyov was demoted to the Kiev military district in 1938, but Stalin would bring him back to Moscow in Sept. 1939. Voroshilov evidently also managed to save Mikhail Lukin, who became a lieutenant general. Muratov and Gorodetskaia, *Komandarm Lukin*, 262. See also Voroshilov's appeal to Stalin (July 11, 1937) for a member of the military council of the Ural Military District. (The file contains no answer.) Volkogonov papers, Hoover, container 17.

295. Suvenirov, *Tragediia RKKA*, 64; Volkogonov papers, Hoover, container 4, telegrams to and from the military districts from TsAMO (this one dated Oct. 2, 1937). See also Cristiani and Mikhaleva, *Le repressioni*, 66.

296. Memo of Govorukhin, chief of PUR in Leningrad Military District, June 12, 1937, RGVA, f. 33 987, op. 3, d. 993, l. 159ss, Volkogonov papers, Hoover, container 17. Similar mood reports that month to Voroshilov contained the following: "Now, no one except the politburo can be believed." "Only Comrade Stalin can be believed now, and no one else." RGVA, f. 33 987, op. 3, d. 993, l. 157-8, Volkogonov papers, Hoover, container 17 (Kruglov, temporarily implementing duties of chief of PUR.)

297. Khaustov and Samuelson, *Stalin, NKVD*, 194 (citing APRF, f. 3, op. 24, d. 312, l. 162, June 29, 1937). "Over there, over here, they started to arrest commanders, about whom we had never heard a bad word before," recalled a division commander in the Kiev military district. "From mouth to mouth rumors were whispered, one more absurd than the next, about plots and espionage malefaction." Gorbatov, "Shkola Iakira," 176. See also Khaustov and Samuelson, *Stalin, NKVD*, 199 (APRF, f. 3, op. 24, d. 308, l. 212-3).

298. Afanas'ev, *Oni ne molchali*, 380.

299. The defense commissariat received more than 200,000 letters in 1938 (and would receive more than 350,000 in 1939). No small number were petitions sent from prisons. *Kommunist*, 1990, no. 17: 70.

300. Volkogonov, *Triumf i tragediia*, I: 438; Suvenirov, "Za chest' i dostoinstvo voinov RKKA," 372-87 (at 377).

301. Kuznetsov, *Krutye povoroty*, 59, 76-9.

302. Just one of many examples: between May 7 and 10, Voroshilov issued a plan for liquidating wrecking—check all warehouses, all construction sites, all secret information storage holdings, all military units—but he did so without naming a single example of actual wrecking in the army. Khaustov and Samuelson, *Stalin, NKVD*, 75 (APRF, f. 3, f. 401, l. 107-9).

303. Suvenirov, "Narkomat oborony," 29 (citing RGVA, f. 33987, op. 3, d. 1023, l. 22, 24, 26: June 1937). Notes to himself for his Nov. 1938 speech to the Main Military Council show how far Voroshilov had come. Suvenirov, *Tragediia RKKA*, 74-5 (citing RGVA, f. 33987, op. 3, d. 1137, l. 3, 5, 6).

304. A few days after the June 1937 military soviet gathering, Voroshilov told an assembly of party members at the defense commissariat that the army was "the last place" in terms of "revealed" enemies, but that during the previous three months the situation had "sharply changed." Whitewood, *Red Army*, 249 (citing RGASPI, f. 74, op. 2, d. 118, l. 3).

305. Kollontai, *Diplomaticheskie dnevniki*, II: 369-70. Voroshilov's despair would also be evident in a draft outline of his speech to the

June 1937 Central Committee plenum, in which he had written that the unmasking of the military-fascist plot "means that our method of work, our whole system for running the army, and my work as people's commissar, have utterly collapsed." This line was evidently not uttered. Brandenberger, *Propaganda State in Crisis*, 190.

306. Dubinskii, *Osobyi schet*, 212. Dubinsky was slandered and arrested back in Kazan.

307. Trotskii, *Stalin*, II: 276.

308. Machiavelli, *Discourses*, 181-2, 184-5.

309. Chuev, *Sto sorok*, 37.

310. Kosheleva et al., "Materialy fevral'-martovskogo plenuma TsK VKP (b) 1937 goda" (1995, no. 3), 6.

311. Kosheleva et al., "Materialy fevral'-martovskogo plenuma TsK VKP (b) 1937 goda" (1994, no. 2), 21.

312. Chuev, *Sto sorok*, 416. Or again: "We owe the fact that we did not have a fifth column during the war to '37." (Of course, the Soviet Union *did* have an immense Fifth Column during WWII.) Chuev, *Molotov*, 464. One scholar, who correctly cautioned against accepting the fifth column argument to explain Stalin's motivations, hypothesized that Molotov's and Kaganovich's resort to the fifth column rationale might have assuaged their consciences. Rees, "Stalin as Leader, 1937-1953," 210.

313. RGASPI, f. 17, op. 2, d. 575, l. 69. Kaganovich, in June 1938, addressing the Donbass party organization, would state that if the enemies, spies, and kulaks had not been annihilated, "perhaps we would be at war already." Kuromiya, "Accounting for the Great Terror," 96 (citing RGASPI, f. 81, op. 3, d. 231, ll. 73, 79). G. K. Dashevskii [Donskoi], a Latin Americanist at the Soviet Union's Institute of World Economics and World Politics, published a pamphlet in 1938 drawing the parallels: *Fashistskaia piataia kolonna v Ispanii* (Moscow: Voenizdat, 1938). See also Kublanov, "Razgrom fashistskoi trotskistsko-bukharinskoi 'piatoi kolonii' v SSSR."

314. The perceptive American John Scott cited four factors to explain the terror, two of which involved the presence of many "former" people, which he called "potentially good material for clever foreign agents to work with," as well as the circumstance that Japan, Italy, and Germany "sent fifth-columnists of all kinds into Russia, *as they did into every country*" (italics added). The other two factors Scott cited were the long history of a secret police in Russia and Bolshevik intolerance toward opposition. Scott, *Behind the Urals*, 188-9. See also Davies, *Mission to Moscow*. See also the fellow traveler Strong, *Stalin Era*, 68; and Deutscher, *Stalin*, 376-7.

315. Stepanov, *Rasstrel po limitu*, 13-4. Sholokhov mentioned a fifth column in a letter to Stalin (Feb. 1938). Getty and Naumov, *Road to Terror*, 309; Murin, "'Prosti menia, Koba . . .': neizvestnoe pis'mo N. Bukharina," 23 (APRF, f. 3, op. 24, d. 427, l. 13-8); "'Vokrug menia vse eshche pletut chernuiu Pautinu . . . ,'" 18 (f. 45, op. 1, d. 827, l. 41-61, Feb. 16, 1938).

316. The influential Khlevniuk has asserted that, based upon the intelligence he was being fed, Stalin became convinced the Republican side in Spain was being defeated because of traitors in its midst and that he feared the same could happen in the Soviet Union, goading him to undertake the domestic terror. Kuromiya, another top scholar, sought to refine the point, arguing that Stalin feared not latent internal opposition per se but internal opposition transformed by a war launched from without. Khlevniuk, "Objectives of the Great Terror," 158-76; Khlevniuk, *Master of*

the House, 173 (citing APRF, f. 3, op. 65, d. 223, l. 90, 141-2, 146); Kuromiya, "Accounting for the Great Terror."

317. Border guards were gathering the harvest. Solov'ev and Chugnuov, *Pogranichnye voiska SSSR*, 9-10.

318. *Voennye arkhivy Rossii*, 104; Lebedev, "M. N. Tukhachevskii i 'voenno-fashistskii zagovor,'" 247-8.

319. Suvenirov, *Tragediia RKKA*, 296 (citing RGVA, f. 33987, op. 3, d. 1049, l. 260-1, 265, July 14, 1937), 297; Suvenirov, "Klim, Koba skazal," 57-8.

320. During the nine days after the in-camera trial, nearly 1,000 more Soviet commanders and military intelligence operatives were arrested, a number now continuously rising. Khaustov and Samuelson, *Stalin, NKVD*, 190-1 (TsA FSB, f. 3, op. 4, d. 30, l. 250-1; APRF, f. 3, op. 46, d. 807, l. 62); "Delo o tak nazyvaemoi 'antisovetskoi trotskistskoi organizatsii' v Krasnoi Armii," 57; Suvenirov, *Tragediia RKKA*, 160-1.

321. Rybalkin, *Operatisia "X,"* 64 (RGVA, f. 33987, op. 3, d. 852, l. 115); Wheatley, *Hitler and Spain*, 102-3; Proctor, *Hitler's Luftwaffe*. It has been estimated that barring its losses in Spain, Italy could have gone to war in June 1940 with 50 full strength divisions, instead of the 19 full and 34 partial strength it mounted. Sullivan, "Fascist Italy's Military Involvement," 703, 718.

322. Some 100 Soviet military advisers served in Spain in 1936, 50 in 1937, 250 in 1938, and 95 in 1939, for a total of 495. Rybalkin, *Operatsiia "X,"* 57 (citing RGVA, f. 33987, op. 3, d. 870, l. 344; f. 35082, op. 1, d. 15, l. 47-9); Tolmachaev, "Sovetskii Soiuz i Ispaniia," 150 (citing RGVA, f. 33987, op. 3, d. 1143, l. 127). See also Kowalsky, *Stalin*, paragraph 768 (citing RGVA, f. 33987, op. 3, d. 912, l. 158; d. 961, l. 170-1).

323. Kowalsky, *Stalin*, paragraph 577. See also Krivitsky, *In Stalin's Secret Service*, 95.

324. Mallett, *Mussolini*, 92.

325. Leitz, *Economic Relations*. Spain enabled Göring to increase his role in German economic planning at home. Franco was uneasy but had to accept Germany's economic aggrandizement inside Spain. Germany was able to obtain militarily significant raw materials—pyrites, copper, mercury, zinc (some 80 percent of Spanish exports of key materials were going to Germany by 1939), while Spain went into debt to Berlin. Wheatley, *Hitler and Spain*, 85.

326. Stalin was told on July 26, 1937, that the USSR had dispatched 460,000 tons of goods to Spain since Aug. 1936, from food, oil, and timber to trucks, tractors, ammonium sulfate, cotton, and cigarettes. Kudriashov, *SSSR i grazhdanskaia voina v Ispanii*, 260-4 (APRF, f. 3, op. 65, d. 224, l. 95-102). By Feb.–March 1938, the Spanish gold had been spent; Moscow extended a credit of $70 million to the Republic for further purchases. The loans, which might have reached $155 million, were never repaid. Kowalsky reasoned that "even if we subtract Howson's $51 million in overcharges, acknowledge only the unpaid loan of $70 million, (rather than the potential $155 million), and subtract the cost of three DC-3s (roughly $360,000), the total value of the Soviet assistance provided to the Republic comes to approximately $525 million, or $7 million more than their gold should have bought." Kowalsky, *Stalin*, paragraph 548. Politburo agenda items on Spain more and more took up resettling Spanish orphans in the USSR, as well as prisoner exchanges with Italy and Germany.

327. Antonov-Ovseyenko would be summoned to Moscow "for a short period to report" on

July 24, 1937. Three days later he would write to Stalin asking to be received. Stalin would grant an audience only on Sept. 14 (first alone, then in the company of Yezhov and Molotov), when Antonov-Ovseyenko would be appointed justice commissar for the RSFSR. Kudriashov, *SSSR i grazhdanskaia voina v Ispanii*, 265 (APRF, f. 3, op. 65, d. 224, l. 106); *Na prieme*, 220. In Spain, management of Soviet diplomacy would fall to Tateos Mandalyan (b. 1901), an ethnic Armenian who went by the name Sergei Marchenko. Kudriashov, *SSSR i grazhdanskaia voina v Ispanii*, 418–9 (APRF, f. 3, op. 65, d. 228, l. 1–3).

328. On May 20, 1937, Pascua asked to see Stalin regarding the fall of Largo Caballero and the formation of a new Spanish coalition government. Pascua was worried (as he told Potyomkin) that he had committed errors that put him in Stalin's bad graces; Stalin assented to

an audience—on Aug. 2, after Potyomkin reminded Stalin of Pascua's request on July 27. Kudriashov, *SSSR i grazhdanskaia voina v Ispanii*, 239 (APRF, f. 3, op. 65, d. 224, l. 18), 265 (105); *Na prieme*, 217.

329. Through summer 1938, Dimitrov and the Comintern continued to be preoccupied with Spain, sending many long reports to Stalin, but the dictator's engagement with Spain was essentially finished. Already in Sept.–Oct. 1937, the majority of Soviet advisers were withdrawn from Spain; the Comintern group there was disbanded. Novikov, *SSSR, Komintern*, II: 78. By Sept. 1938, the Soviets issued an order to withdraw the International brigades (Franco did not reciprocate by sending the Germans and Italians home).

330. The transfer east was formalized on May 11. Already on June 19, Yezhov ordered Balytsky to report to Moscow. Balytsky had to

understand this meant his own arrest. Still, perhaps Balytsky imagined he could persuade the dictator of his loyalty, claiming, for example, that even though he and the enemy Yakir had worked together in Ukraine, he had not known of Yakir's plotting. Khaustov and Samuelson, *Stalin, NKVD*, 127, citing APRF, f. 3, op. 58, d. 33, l. 81–5. At one time thought to be a candidate to replace Yagoda, Balytsky was executed on Nov. 21, 1937, at Kommunarka, Yagoda's former dacha. "O sud'be chlenov i kandidatov v chleny TsK VKP (b), izbrannogo XVII s"ezdom partii," 88.

331. Fröhlich, *Tagebücher von Joseph Goebbels*, IV: 214 (July 10, 1937). Erich Wollenberg, a German Communist who served fifteen years in the Red Army (1921–36), noted, "One cannot deny that as a result of the executions the Red Army is leaderless." Hitler, too, would use this phrase. Wollenberg, *Red Army*.

CHAPTER 8. "WHAT WENT ON IN NO. 1'S BRAIN?"

1. "Secret Speech" [1956], in Khrushchev, *Khrushchev Remembers*, 616.

2. Chuev, *Molotov Remembers*, 263.

3. Solzhenitsyn, without access to regime archives, got this right, writing that "old prisoners claim to remember that the first blow allegedly took the form of mass arrests" in Aug. 1937. Solzhenitsyn, *Gulag Archipelago*, I: 68. See also Weissberg-Cybulski, *Accused*, 7–10.

4. Yezhov's report was followed by four days of discussion. No transcript was made of the plenum through June 26 (RGASPI, f. 17, op. 2, d. 614, l. 1), and no complete text of Yezhov's speech has been adduced. We do, however, have his outline: Petrov and Jansen, *Stalinskii pitomets*, 293–312 (TsA FSB, f. 3, op. 4, d. 20, l. 117–22, 163–83); Khaustov and Samuelson, *Stalin, NKVD*, 321–2; Danilov et al., *Tragediia sovetskoi derevni*, V/i: 306–8 (d. 29, l. 200–7). On June 27–29, the plenum discussed the Supreme Soviet election laws, grain seeds, crop rotation, and machine tractor stations, which is what the *Pravda* post-plenum summary (June 30) mentioned, leaving out Yezhov's report.

5. Stalin had Voroshilov, Molotov, Mikoyan, and Zhdanov affix their assent. L. B., "Tain Kremlia' bol'she ne budet?," 37.

6. The creative intelligentsia might have suffered fewer arrests per capita than other groups. Getty and Manning, *Stalinist Terror*, 243.

7. Koestler, *Darkness at Noon*, 15–6.

8. Payne, *Life and Death of Adolf Hitler*, 350; Conquest, *Breaker of Nations*, 317. Bullock asserted that both Hitler and Stalin "owed a great deal of their success as politicians to their ability to disguise from allies as well as opponents, their thoughts and their intentions." Bullock, *Hitler and Stalin*, 367.

9. Enteen, "Intellektual'nye predposylki."

10. Conquest, *Reassessment*, 14 (no citation).

11. Tichanova, *Rasstrel'nye spiski*, 202, 211; *Moskovskie novosti*, 1994, no. 5.

12. The "politburo" ordered Yezhov to go on holiday on Dec. 7, 1937, outside Moscow, and directed Stalin to make sure Yezhov did not appear at work. RGASPI, f. 17 op. 3, d. 993, l. 74.

13. Pavliukov, *Ezhov*, 399–405. Savoleinen, the accused mercury poisoner, was executed in Aug. 1937.

14. Orlov, *Secret History*, 221–2. Yezhov's office as of Oct. 1936 was on the fourth floor (410). Petrov and Jansen, *Stalinskii pitomets*, 67, citing GARF, f. 9401, op. 1a, d. 15, l. 242.

15. Those who had long minimized Stalin's role now admit that his "name is all over the horrible documents authorizing the terror."

(Getty and Naumov, *Road to Terror*, 451.) And if it were not? If Stalin had kept his name off the documents, while making others sign them, would we be wondering if he were an instrument in their hands, or a neutral figure caught between factions, or an opponent of terror who went along with it? If all the documents on the terror had been destroyed during a wartime bombing or a botched evacuation, or by a fire, or on his command, would it still be unclear that the mass arrests and executions did not somehow begin and wind down of their own accord, but were carried out on Stalin's orders?

16. Khaustov et al., *Lubianka: Stalin i glavnoe upravlenie*, 348–51 (APRF, f. 3, op. 58, d. 254, l. 165–72). Many examples have been gathered in Kurliandskii, *Stalin, vlast', religiia*, 41–3.

17. Mlechin, *KGB*, 176.

18. Yezhov was instructed to "spend ninetenths of his time on NKVD business": RGASPI, f. 17, op. 3, d. 981, l. 50.

19. Fadeev, "Nikolai Ivanovich Ezhov," cited in Pavliukov, *Ezhov*, 335–6, RGASPI, f. 671, op. 1, d. 270, l. 69–86 (at 80–1); excerpts are also in Petrov and Jansen, *Stalinskii pitomets*, 13. This was part of a commissioned biography of Yezhov, whose arrest took place before the biography could be published.

20. Khlevniuk, *Politbiuro*, 207; Pavliukov, *Ezhov*, 536.

21. Kosheleva et al., "Materialy fevral'-martovskogo plenuma TsK VKP (b) 1937 goda" (1995, no. 1), 10.

22. In this case, by Poluvedko et al., *Mech i tryzub*, 122. See also Sudoplatov, *Special Tasks*, 12–29.

23. TsA FSB, p-23634, t. 1, l. 195. Spiegelglass handled multiple key double agents, controlled Zborowski's virtuoso work with Sedov, and would oversee several more priority assassinations abroad—until his own regime executed him.

24. Rees has argued that the Great Terror "was the central and decisive event" in the history of Stalin's regime, a view I do not share, but I do share his contention that "in the experience of modern states [the terror] is without precedent." Rees, "Stalin as Leader, 1937–1953," 200–39.

25. Khlevniuk, *Khoziain*, 299–300. As of Nov. 30, 1937, Stalin started receiving not the lengthy raw interrogation protocols but summaries, and only of the most important cases. Khaustov and Samuelson, *Stalin, NKVD*, 319–20.

26. Khaustov and Samuelson, *Stalin, NKVD*, 322 (TsA FSB, f. 3os, op. 6, d. 11, l. 384).

27. Conquest, *Great Terror: Reassessment*, 268–9; Krivitsky, *In Stalin's Secret Service*, 143–4.

28. Sukhanovka had been retrofitted as a prison in 1931, and in late 1938 into early 1939 would be expanded for "especially dangerous enemies of the people." Golovkova, *Sukhanovskaia tiur'ma*; GARF. f. 5446, op. 22a, d. 125, l. 5.

29. Papkov, *Stalinskii terror v Sibiri*, 230–1. In 1938, for example, the party boss of Karelia would tell Yezhov that because local prisons were already overflowing, he was unable to arrest more than a thousand "enemies." Takala, "Natsional'nye operatsii," 196–7. See also Joyce, "Soviet Penal System," 90–115.

30. Gur'ianov, *Repressii protiv poliakov*, 30. As Frinovsky traveled by train in July 1938 through regions that had sent arrest albums to Moscow, he and his aides, having brought the overdue paperwork, rendered decisions on the train and dropped them off as they passed through. Khaustov and Samuelson, *Stalin, NKVD*, 323.

31. The anti-terrorist machinery that had been introduced on the day of the Kirov murder in the form of a USSR Central Executive Committee decree (Dec. 1, 1934), had been formally approved nine days later by the RSFSR Central Executive Committee and the RSFSR Council of People's Commissars, but the anti-terrorism laws were not finalized until Feb. 1936, entered into the RSFSR criminal code via an added 18th chapter ("On the investigation and hearing of cases of terrorist organizations and terrorist acts against Soviet power"). *Istoriia zakonodatel'stva SSSR i RSFSR po ugolovnomu protsessu*, 53. These procedures were extended to wrecking and diversionary acts on Sept. 14, 1937. On the confusion, see Scott, *Behind the Urals*, 194.

32. Mironov, "Vosstanovlenie i razvitie leninskikh printsipov," 19. In Yerevan in Sept. 1937, Malenkov, Mikoyan, and Beria, overseeing a regional party plenum, turned the sitting party bosses over to the NKVD and decided upon the new first, second, and third party secretaries for Armenia, sending a proposal to Stalin and Molotov in Moscow. Stalin approved "if the plenum of the Central Committee of Armenia does not have any doubts regarding these candidates." RGASPI, f. 17, op. 19, d. 62, l. 2, 4; RGASPI, f. 558, op. 11, d. 135, l. 65–65ob. Although this could have been a pose of false party democracy, he could hardly know or remember everyone even in the *nomenklatura*. On Yevdokimov's telegrammed request to arrest Amatouni Amatouni [Vardapetyan] Stalin had written, "Who is this Amatouni? Where does he work?" (Amatouni was the party boss in Armenia and among the gaggle of high officials arrested there on Sept. 23.) Khaustov et al., *Lubianka: Stalin i glavnoe upravlneie*, 68 (RGASPI, f. 558, op. 11, d. 65, l.

24), 379–80 (APRF, f. 3, op. 24, d. 332, l. 43). Amatouni was executed on July 28, 1938, from a long list of names approved by Stalin. N. P. Mironov, "Vosstanovlenie i razvitie leninskikh printsipov sotsialisticheskoi zakonnosti (1953–1963 gg.)," 19.

33. Some 43,000 people are on the lists; the USSR military collegium handed down 14,732 sentences in 1937 and 24,435 in 1938, a little more than 39,000 people total. An example of someone who survived is Ya. Yelkovich of the Altai, who was on two lists. Tepliakov, *Mashina terrora*, 296. Iakushev, *Stalinskie rasstrel'nye spiski.*

34. As of June 1941, 1,500 telegrams and 33,000 thousand letters were being sent abroad from the Soviet Union and 1,000 telegrams and 31,000 letters were arriving from abroad every day. Most of that was likely official business, but not all. The censors were requesting a vast increase in personnel. Goriaeva, *Istoriia sovetskoi politicheskoi tsenzury*, 85–6 (GARF, f. R-9425, op. 1, d. 19, l. 153–4).

35. Kotkin, *Magnetic Mountain*, 280–354.

36. Chegodaev, "Iz vospominanii."

37. Many of the Soviet institutions and instruments of state power had been invented in expropriations of property and physical elimination of class enemies, and then reinvented or vastly expanded in the forced collectivization of the peasantry. Barrington Moore offered a general theory of the state as a reflection of its handling of the peasantry, but without adequately addressing the specifics of the Soviet case. Moore, *Social Origins of Dictatorship and Democracy*. See also van Atta, "USSR as a 'Weak State.'" Von Atta, like others, missed how Stalin's regime created its own *society*, which contributed immensely to state capacity.

38. Ellman rightly noted that "having destroyed independent social organizations, established total media censorship, and created a socioeconomic system in which organizations at all levels had an incentive to understate their possibilities and overstate their needs, getting accurate information became very difficult." Ellman, "Political Economy of Stalinism," 116.

39. Davies et al., "The Politburo and Economic Decision Making," 126–7.

40. Markevich, "Monitoring and Interventions," 1466.

41. Khlevniuk, *Politbiuro*, 288–91.

42. Stalin was the decisive actor, although "not immune to pressure and persuasion from politburo members, or from society at large." Davies, "Making Economic Policy," 69. See also Gregory, *Political Economy*, 68. A few functionaries cultivated clients across agencies. Khlevniuk, *Politbiuro*, 262–3.

43. Chuev, *Sto sorok*, 258–9, 263.

44. Rosenfeldt, *"Special" World*, I: 55–8.

45. "The essence of party leadership," Stalin had remarked in July 1924, "lies precisely in the implementation of resolutions and directives." "O kompartii Pol'shi" [July 3, 1924], *Bol'shevik*, Sept. 20, 1924, reprinted in *Sochineniia*, VI: 264–72 (at 269–70). How this was to come about was another matter entirely. "To raise the quality of the party official with a wave of the hand is not so simple," Stalin had told Sverdlov university students. "It is still common for officials to apply the old habits of hasty administrative-izing . . . so-called party leadership sometimes degenerates into a sorry amalgam of useless directives, into empty and glib 'leadership' that accomplishes nothing." *Sochineniia*, V: 197–222, VII: 171–2, VII: 349–50; Davies and Harris, *Stalin's World*, 24.

46. Khlevniuk et al., *Stalin i Kaganovich*, 19.

47. Lih et al., *Stalin's Letters to Molotov*, 217–9 (Sept. 22, 1930).

48. Lih et al., *Stalin's Letters to Molotov*, 210–1.

49. Kosheleva, *Pis'ma Stalina Molotovu*, 88–93 (Sept. 16, 1926); Lih et al., *Stalin's Letters to Molotov*, 126–9. See also Markevich, "Monitoring and Enforcement." One scholar has argued that Stalin's own policies made the country nearly impossible to govern, which infuriated and haunted him. Harris, "Was Stalin a Weak Dictator?," 377, echoing Lewin, *Making of the Soviet System* (1985).

50. For the rubbish about Stalin's terror as a reaction to regional party bosses' failure to obey central authority, see Getty and Naumov, *Road to Terror*, 12–14, 16, 22. For the refutation that Stalin was not motivated by fear of elite resistance, see Tucker, *Stalin in Power*, 264–8; and Khlevniuk, "Stalinist 'Party Generals,'" 195–6.

51. Soviet functionaries experienced inordinate mobility compared with their tsarist predecessors. In the tsarist state, those who started careers in the provinces remained there, destined never to reach the heights and perquisites of the capital. Pinter, "Social Characteristics."

52. This statement occurred during forced collectivization and dekulakization, and Gorky helpfully pointed out that "if the enemy does not surrender, he is to be exterminated." Hosking, *First Socialist Society*, 163.

53. Rigby, *Communist Party Membership*, 212–3.

54. The rise of the politburo had undercut the Central Committee's authority, but, in turn, Stalin's informal caucusing undermined the politburo; it met just fifteen times in 1935 and nine times in 1936. Daniels, "Office Holding and Elite Status," 77–95; Gill, *Origins*, 65.

55. Hearsay recollections by people not at the plenum have claimed Osip Pyatnitsky stood up to Stalin and Yezhov. Afanas'ev, *Oni ne molchali*, 219–20; Vilenskii, *Dodnes' tiagoteet*, 265–6. For a debunking, see Pavliukov, *Ezhov*, 300–5.

56. These totals do not include other functionaries who attended but were not members: for example, Nazaretyan, Stalin's first top aide, was arrested on his way to the Kremlin to attend the plenum. (He would be executed Nov. 30, 1937.) *Pravda*, Nov. 17, 1964. "During the breaks in the sessions," one person later poetically claimed, "Deputy NKVD Head Frinovsky walked through the corridors smoking, and used his cigarette to point, take this one, take that one." Afanas'ev, *Oni ne molchali*, 209 (Afanasy Krymov).

57. Syrtsov was serving as director of a factory in Moscow province when the NKVD came for him on April, 19, 1937. He would be executed on Sept. 10, 1937, and cremated at the Donskoe crematorium.

58. Conquest, *Reassessment*, 214–34; Gill, "Stalinism and Industrialization," 131–2. Already by late Oct. 1937, of the 139 members and candidates of the Central Committee, more than half had been arrested and seven shot; another 23 were now scheduled to be executed. The next month Yezhov submitted to Stalin a list for execution of all 45 incarcerated Central Committee personnel who were still alive. Stalin crossed out half the names, perhaps because they had yet to "testify" fully, but many of them were executed some months later. Pavliukov, *Ezhov*, 339.

59. See the example in Dagestan in 1937: *Pravda* (Sept. 25, 1937): *Dagestanskaia pravda*, Oct. 23, 2013; Akhmedabiev, "I opiat' o mifakh."

60. Khaustov and Samuelson, *Stalin, NKVD*, 101–2 (citing APRF, f. 3, op. 58, d. 6, l. 28: Feb. 13, 1937).

61. Khrushchev, *Vospominaniia*, I: 121; Khrushchev, *Memoirs*, I: 115.

62. Kaganovich telegrammed Stalin that "acquaintance with the situation shows that the right-Trotskyite wrecking here has taken broad dimensions—in industry, agriculture, supply, trade, medicine, education and political work." *XXII s"ezd Kommunisticheskoi partii Sovetskogo soiuza*, III: 153.

63. Shreider, *NKVD iznutri*, 68–70.

64. Hlevnjuk, "Les mécanismes de la 'Grande Terreur'"; Thurston, *Life and Terror*, 62 (citing GARF, f. 8131, op. 27, d. 145, l. 49–57: Sept. 1939 report).

65. Gill, *Origins of the Stalinist Political System*, 273.

66. Scott, *Behind the Urals*, 195–6. Scott added: "Whereas most of the workers in the mills were fairly well trained by 1935, had acquired the knacks of electric welding, pipe-fitting, or what not, most of the administrators were far from having mastered their jobs" (175).

67. Khlevniuk, "Economic Officials in the Great Terror," 39 (citing GARF, f. 5446, f. 1, d. 122a, 26–8).

68. More than 2,000 personnel in the various commissariats were arrested just between Oct. 1936 and March 1937, and that did not even include the NKVD, foreign affairs commissariat, and defense commissariat, which did not fall under the jurisdiction of the Council of People's Commissars. Lukianov, "Massovye represii opravdany byt' ne mogut," 120 (data presented by a commission in 1962–3). Veitser was arrested on Oct. 17, 1937, and would be shot (May 7, 1938) at Kommunarka.

69. Kuromiya, "Stalinist Terror in the Donbas."

70. Vasiliev, "Great Terror in the Ukraine," 144–5 (citing TsGAOO Ukraini, f. 1, op. 20, d. 7115, l. 67, 86, 90, 167; d. 7177, l. 43–5, 47); *Pravda*, May 29, 1937; Kuromiya, *Freedom and Terror*, 219 (citing RGASPI, f. 17, op. 2, d. 574, l. 74; f. 589, op. 3, d. 2042); Likholobova, *Totalitarnyi rezhym ta politychni represii*, 72n.

71. Likholobova, *Stalins'kii totalitarnyi rezhym*, 76–8.

72. Avdeenko, *Nakazanie bez prestupleniia*, 182–3.

73. Vasiliev, "Great Terror in the Ukraine," 145; Shapoval, *Lazar Kaganovich*, 35.

74. Kuromiya, *Freedom and Terror*, 224n141 (RGASPI, f. 558, op. 1, d. 3215, l. 3).

75. Kvashonkin, *Sovetskoe rukovodstvo*, 361–62 (RGASPI, f. 17, op. 114, d. 953, l. 212–3, Manuilsky letter to Yezhov, Andreev, and Shkiryatov, May 21, 1937).

76. Banac, *Diary of Georgi Dimitrov*, 52 (Feb. 11, 1937); Latyshev, "Riadom so Stalinym," 19.

77. Chase, *Enemies within the Gates?*, 275–6; Banac, *Diary of Georgi Dimitrov*, 69 (Nov. 11, 1937). On May 26, 1937, Dimitrov had cryptically recorded in his diary: "At Yezhov's (1 o'clock in the morning). The major spies worked in the Comintern." The next day: "Examination of the apparatus" of the Comintern Executive Committee. (61: May 26, 1937.)

78. Weber, "Weisse Flecken," 19–20, 24. By some accounts, the Nazis killed six German politburo members. Overall, of the 1,400 leading German Communists, a total of 178 were killed in Stalin's terror, nearly all of them residents of Hotel Lux. The Nazis killed 222 of them. Fritz Platten, the Swiss Communist who had organized Germany's help for Lenin's sealed-train return in 1917, and who lived at the Hotel Lux since 1924, was caught in the sweeps (he would die in Gulag).

79. The resolution was written in Nov. 1937, but it is not clear when the disbandment went into effect. The resolution was formally passed by the Comintern presidium on Aug. 16, 1938. *Voprosii istorii KPSS*, 1988, no. 12:

52; Chase, *Enemies within the Gates?*, 287–9; Lazitch, "Stalin's Massacre," 139–74; McDermott, "Stalinist Terror."

80. Naszkowski, *Nespokoinye dni*, 209–10.

81. Wladyslaw Stein, known as Anton Krajewski, a leading official in the Comintern cadres department, had presented a report on Oct. 25, 1934, accusing émigrés of acting as foreign agents. Yezhov, in a September 1935 speech to party secretaries, had voiced suspicion of political émigrés, especially from Germany and Poland, calling them foreign agents. "I'd like to discuss the question of verification measures of the Polish Communist party, which, as you know, in recent years has been the main supplier of spies and provocative elements in the USSR," Manuilsky (an ethnic Ukrainian) had written ingratiatingly to Yezhov on Jan. 19, 1936, knowing this was Stalin's view. Chase, *Enemies within the Gates?*, 48 (citing RGASPI, f. 495, op. 21, d. 23, l. 6, 9, 23); 105–7 (op. 18, d. 1147a, l. 1–3); Khaustov, "Deiatel'nost' organov gosudarstvennoi bezopasnosti," 210 (APRF, f. 57, op. 1., d. 73, l. 3).

82. In April 1938, Pyatnitsky evidently named Mao among the "Bukharin group" in the Comintern as a spy for Japan. Boris Melnikov, a former Soviet agent in China who had been accused of having gone over to the Japanese, was accused of being involved in the Comintern "conspiracy" of Osip Pyatnitsky, and his "testimony" supposedly denounced Mao as "the leader of Trotskyism in the inmost depths of the CCP." Piatnitskii, *Zagovor protiv Stalina*, 120–5 (citing a July 1987 interview with Mikhail Menndeleyev, a former cellmate of Melnikov); Vaksberg, *Hôtel Lux*, 218–21, 235. See also Chang and Halliday, *Mao*, 208–9. In 1935, Pyatnitsky had been moved out of the Comintern to the central party apparatus.

83. Starkov, "Ar'ergardnye boi staroi partiinoi gvardii," 220–1. As of July 1938, a year after his arrest, Pyatnitsky was still not broken and Yezhov's power was waning. (Béla Kun and Wilhelm Knorin, said to have been in league with Pyatnitsky, were broken.) Pyatnitsky was tried in camera and, on July 29, 1938, executed. Starkov, "The Trial that Was Not Held." See also Dmitrievskii, *Piatnitskii. ogists.*

84. Murray, *I Spied for Stalin*, 83.

85. Stalin's letters to Karakhan in the 1920s—an epoch ago—had burst with affection, but subsequent mentions were venomous. As late as April 14, 1937, he had asked Karakhan, then Soviet envoy to Turkey, if he would agree to a big promotion to ambassador to the United States. On May 3, he had Karakhan recalled to Moscow and arrested. RGASPI, f. 558, op. 11, d. 56, l. 68 (ciphered telegram to Karakhan in Ankara). Yezhov, whether on Stalin's direct order or to please him, had Karakhan implicated in the case against Tukhachevsky; Stalin wrote "important" on the first page of Karakhan's June 2, 1937, interrogation protocols (which the dictator received on June 19). Karakhan was sentenced and executed on Sept. 20, 1937. Khaustov et al., *Lubianka: Stalin i glavnoe upravlenie*, 222–5 (APRF, f. 3, op. 24, d. 309, l. 123–30).

86. Khaustov and Samuelson, *Stalin, NKVD*, 180 (citing TsA FSB, f. 3, op. 4, d. 469, l. 167).

87. At the Feb.–March 1937 plenum, when Voroshilov asserted that Rykov had several times been trembling—a supposed admission of his guilt—Litvinov interjected, "When was this?" Deeper into the terror, Litvinov would complain to Andreyev that arresting journalists at the Soviet *Journal de Moscou* for having contacts with foreigners was tantamount to arresting them for doing their job. Dullin, *Men of Influence*, 217, citing AVP RF, f. 5, op. 17, pap. 126, d. 1, letter Oct. 26, 1937. The journal's editor (Rayevsky) had been arrested in Oct. 1936; his successor, a bona fide proletarian, Viktor Kin (Surovikin), would be arrested in Jan. 1938. *Journal de Moscou* was soon shuttered. Babichenko, "'Esli aresty budut prodolzhatsiia, to . . . ne ostanetsiia ni odnogo nemtsa-chlena partii,'" 119 (RGASPI, f. 495, op. 292. d. 101, l. 13–8).

88. Uldricks, "Impact of the Great Purges" 192 (citing National Archives decimal file 861.00/11705: Henderson to secretary of state, June 10, 1937); Barmine, *One Who Survived*, 3.

89. The next greatest of executions would be 1942—23,000. Popov, "Gosudarstvennyi terror," 20–31 (using the 1963-4 Shvernik commission report). See also Wheatcroft, "Victims of Stalinism"; and Khlevniuk, "Les mécanismes de la Grande Terreur."

90. Beck and Godin, *Russian Purge*, 75; Avtorkhanov, *Stalin and the Soviet Communist Party*, 219–21; Junge and Binner, *Kak terror stal "bol'shym"*; Gregory, *Terror by Quota*.

91. Shreider, *NKVD iznutri*, 85.

92. Shapoval and Zolotar'ov, *Vsevolod*, 337; Iakovenko, *Agnessa*, 65.

93. Tepliakov, *Mashina terrora*, 571.

94. Iakovenko, *Agnessa*, 86–92.

95. According to Otto Shmidt, Stalin, in the course of conversation at the Presidium table, mentioned the names of high officials who had been arrested. Shmidt, "Priemy v kremle," 273–4; Shevelev, 86.

96. *Nezavisimaia gazeta*, July 6, 1991.

97. Tepliakov, *Mashina terrora*, 477–8, 538; Gos. arkhiv Novosibirskoi oblasti (GANO), f. 4, op. 34, d. 26, l. 2; Khaustov and Samuelson, *Stalin, NKVD*, 262, 332–3. Yezhov and Frinovsky may have been concerned about Western Siberian party boss Eihe getting out ahead of them in gaining credit for the reinstituting of troikas. On the establishment of a Western Siberian troika as supposedly an initiative of Eihe, see Zhukov, *Inoi Stalin*, 433–4; Getty and Naumov, *Road to Terror*, 469; Kosheleva et al., "Materialy fevral'-martovskogo plenuma TsK VKP (b) 1937 goda" (1993, no. 6), 5; Khlevniuk, *Politbiuro*, 134, 228). Mironov was made chairman of the troika. When his arrest quotas were immediately increased, he tried to have them returned to the originally agreed levels. Danilov et al., *Tragediia sovetskoi derevni*, V/i: 430 (telegram Aug. 9, 1937). See also Khaustov et al., *Lubianka: Stalin i glavnoe upravlenie*, 296 (RGASPI, f. 558, op. 11, d. 65, l. 58), 335 (d. 57, l. 68).

98. RGASPI, f. 17, op. 166, d. 575, l. 19–22. The typed version was first brought forth in "Rasstrel po raznariadke, ili kak eto delali bol'sheviki," *Trud*, June 4, 1992. See also Danilov et al., *Tragediia Sovetskoi derevni*, V/i: 258 (RGASPI, f. 17, op. 162, d. 21, l. 89). The troikas instituted as a result of Mironov's "request" would account for more than 90 percent of the mass sentences for execution in 1937 and 1938. Getty and Naumov, *Road to Terror*, 470. One available factoid indicates that in the Mordovia autonomous republic (Russian Federation), 96 percent of those who passed through the sentencing troika refused to admit they were wreckers, but it remains unclear if this represented resistance or laziness (or incompetence) on the part of the local NKVD. Khaustov and Samuelson, *Stalin, NKVD*, 286 (TsA FSB, f. 3, op. 5, d. 43, l. 113).

99. That day, Stalin had received twelve people in the Little Corner, a mere two of whom were politburo members (Voroshilov and Molotov); the draft decree is in Kaganovich's handwriting, but he was not recorded in the Little Corner that day. Eight politburo members eventually signed the resolution. Junge et al., *Vertikal bol'shogo terrora*, 114–6; Adibekov et al., *Politbiuro TsK RKP (b)—VKB (b): povestki dnia zasedanii*, II: 876, 887. There would be no politburo meetings from June 19, 1937, to Feb. 23, 1938. Only two additional gatherings were held in 1938 (April 25 and Oct. 10–12), and only two more in 1939 (Jan. 29 and Dec. 17). "Politburo" decisions were taken in the Little Corner by Stalin alone or in limited company, written up by Poskryobyshev and "approved" by telephone vote or with signatures affixed the next time the cronies were summoned to appear. Khlevniuk et al., *Stalinskoe politbiuro*, 248–9. Stalin occasionally dropped all pretense and merely sent directives as his personal instructions: Khaustov et al., *Lub'ianka: Stalin i glavnoe upravlenie*, 329; Khlevniuk, *Khoziain*, 340.

100. Junge and Binner, *Kak terror stal "bol'shim,"* 79.

101. Khaustov et al., *Lubianka: Stalin i glavnoe upravlenie*, 238–9 (APRF, f. 3, op. 58, d. 174, l. 107). See also Ilič, "Forgotten Five Percent," 116–39.

102. RGASPI, f. 17, op. 162, d. 21, l. 95–9; Petrov and Jansen, *Stalinskii pitomets*, 265; Tepliakov, *Mashina terrora*, 348.

103. To ensure everyone got the message, on July 16 Yezhov convened the regional NKVD chiefs from the Russian Federation, Ukraine, and Belorussia in Moscow. Petrov and Jansen, *Stalinskii pitomets*, 98–101; *Leningradskii martirolog*, I: 39; Junge et al., *Vertikal' Bol'shogo terrora*, 32–3. See also Shreider, *NKVD iznutri*, 41–3. A separate NKVD conference took place with the NKD chiefs of the Central Asian republics, eastern Siberia, and the Soviet Far East.

104. Iakovenko, *Agnessa*, 59; Khaustov, "Deiatel'nost' organov gosudarstvennoi bezopasnosti," 142–3 (TsA FSB, N-15301, t. 15, l. 387). The chief in Chelyabinsk was Yos-Gersh Blat; in Tataria, Pyotr Rud.

105. Khaustov et al., *Lubianka: Stalin i glavnoe upravlenie*, 249 (RGASPI, f. 17, op. 3, d. 989, l. 57, 60). "The greatest revolutionary vigilance and iron will, a sharp Bolshevik eye and organizing talent, an exceptional mind and the subtlest proletarian sense—these are the qualities shown by comrade Yezhov," *Pravda* wrote, adding that he was assisted by "millions of eyes, millions of hands of workers . . . Such a force is invincible." *Pravda*, July 18, 1937. On July 18, Alexander Barmine, a Soviet diplomat in Greece, defected, obtaining asylum in France. Rogovin, *Partiia rasstreliannykh*, 353–5.

106. Tepliakov, *Mashina terrora*, 528–32.

107. "I can testify that my father's apartment did not resemble in the least the shop of a poor junk-dealer described in the document," wrote Anton Antonov-Ovseyenko of his arrested father, Vladimir. The NKVD inventory of his family residence, the son claimed, had omitted "original engravings by famous artists, a typewriter, a radio phonograph player with eight albums of records, his wife's jewelry, her squirrel coat, expensive French perfume . . . and much, much more." Antonov-Ovseienko, *Portet Tirana*, 187. V. Antonov-Ovseyenko had been arrested Oct. 12, 1937 (he would be executed on Feb. 10, 1938), and had lived at the famed Finance Commissariat House (Novinsky Boulevard, 25), built in 1930 by Moisei Ginzburg.

108. Uimanov and Petrukhin, *Bol' liudskaia*, V: 102 11; Junge and Binner, *Kak terror stal "bol'shim,"* 81–3; Tepliakov, "Personal i povsednevnost' Novosibirskogo UNKVD," 254.

109. The jazzmen's rendition prompted the aviators to rise, applauding, and shout for an encore. Chkalov, *Nash transpoliarnyi reis*, 59; Vodop'ianov, *Letchik Valerii Chkalov*, 195; Skorokhodov, *V poiskakh utrachennogo*, 21–3. Utyosov claimed, in his recollections, that he was never invited back to a Kremlin

reception, but the program for May 2, 1938, contradicts him. Nevezhin (*Zastol'ia*, 298–9) misdates the reception to Aug. 13, 1936, after a nonstop flight to the Soviet Far East, but Utyosov dates the performance to "summer 1937"—that would be July 26, 1937—when Baiduk, Chkalov, and Belyakov flew nonstop from Moscow to Vancouver; Chkalov also makes clear that the evening took place after their return from the United States.
110. *Trud*, June 4, 1992; Khaustov et al., *Lubianka: Stalin i glavnoe upravlenie*, 273–81 (APRF, f. 3, op. 58, d. 212, l. 59–78), 281–2 (l. 52–4); Danilov et al., *Tragediia sovetskoi derevni*, V/i: 328–37; Werth and Mironenko, *Istoriia Stalinskogo gulaga*, I: 277–80; Junge and Binner, *Kak terror stal "bol'shim*," 84–93, 94–6. This was followed by further related directives: Werth and Mironenko, *Istoriia Stalinskogo gulaga*, I: 363–5. Frinovsky had three audiences with Stalin in July 1937: July 7 (fifteen minutes), July 26 (five minutes), July 29 (fifty-five minutes). *Na prieme*, 216.
111. Korneev and Kopylova, "Arkhivy na sluzhbe totalitarnogo gosudarstva." The order specified that the mass operations were to last four months (instead they would last fifteen): on Jan. 31, 1938, the regime would extend the deadline and nearly double the country-wide quota to 500,000. Even the "final" quotas would be exceeded: in Georgia and Uzbekistan by 50 percent, in the USSR as a whole by 100 percent, in Western Siberia by 200 percent. The mass operations ended in different places at different times. Junge and Binner, *Kak terror stal "bol'shim*," 83–103.
112. Mironov worked alongside another member of the local troika, Western Siberian party boss Eihe, and Mironov complained to Yezhov that the latter "interferes in the affairs of the NKVD," showing up to participate in interrogations and arrests of party members. Yezhov advised Mironov not to conflict with Eihe. Petrov and Jansen, *Stalinskii pitomets*, 107 (citing TsA FSB ASD Frinovskogo, N-15301, t. 7: 36–7). Provincial practice varied. According to the NKVD operative Mikhail Shreider, Ivanovo province NKVD chief Israel Radzivilovsky rendered the "troika" decisions himself, just sending the paperwork to the two other troika members, the local party boss and the procurator, to sign. Shreider, *NKVD iznutri*, 76.
113. Khlevniuk, *History of the Gulag*, 157–61 (GARF, f. 8131, op. 37, d. 145, l. 49–84); Leibovich, "*Vkliuchen v operatsiiu*," 302–3.
114. Artizov et al., *Reabilitatsiia: kak eto bylo*, I: 320; Kuz'micheva, "Resheniia osobykh troek privodit' v ispolnenii nemedlenno," 85.
115. Leibovich et al. "*Vkliuchen v operatsiiu*," 314–7 (based on former KGB archives in Perm). Some former kulaks, after their terms of exile ended, managed to return to their former places of habitation and sometimes even to reclaim their lands, which the regime deemed "sabotage." Fitzpatrick, *Stalin's Peasants*, 238–54. Recidivism was also a focus. "The main contingent committing disruptive offenses (robbery, brigandage, murder, aggravated theft) are people who have been convicted before, in most cases recently released from camps or places of detention," Yezhov wrote in a memorandum to Stalin, a passage the despot marked in pencil. Petrov and Jansen, *Stalinskii pitomets*, 96 (citing APRF, f. 3, op. 58, d. 166, l. 151–4); Rittersporn, "'Vrednye element,'" 103; Hagenloh, "'Socially Harmful Elements,'" 300.
116. Ellman, "Regional Influences."
117. Frinovsky sent out a ciphered directive that "anti-Soviet elements" whom local officials assigned to category 1 ("especially socially dangerous") were not even to be presented with charges, just executed in cold blood. Stepanov, *Rasstrel po limitu*, 30 (Aug.

8, 1937); Junge and Binner, *Kak terror stal "bol'shim*," 99. See also Rabishchev, "Gnilaia i opasnaia teoriia," esp. 55.
118. National operations would claim approximately 350,000 victims, 247,157 of whom would be shot.
119. In April 1936, the regime had decided to deport the ethnic Poles and Germans in Ukraine near the western border (more than 10,000 families) to Kazakhstan; then it deported Soviet Finns from the border areas with Finland as well as Iranians near the border with Afghanistan (some 2,000 families). Stalin authorized a request to arrest all Afghan nationals in Merva, Turkmenistan (where there was an Afghan consulate). RGANI, f. 89, op. 48, d. 8, l. 1–2 (ciphered telegram from Anna Mukhamedov, acting party boss of Turkmenistan, to Stalin, July 23, 1937, with Stalin's handwriting). Mukhamedov was arrested Oct. 5, 1937.
120. RGASPI, f. 17, op. 162, d. 22, l. 16; d. 21, l. 157; Gelb, "Early Soviet Ethnic Deportation"; Bugai, "Vysylenie sovetskikh koreitsev," 144; Pohl, *Ethnic Cleansing*, 9–20; Khaustov et al., *Lubianka: Stalin i glavnoe upravlenie*, 352 (APRF, f. 3, op. 58, d. 139, l. 23). The Soviet Pacific Fleet had been put on alert to prevent the Koreans from fleeing by sea, but several hundred boats from Korea showed up, just off Soviet waters, to rescue these people; Soviet border guards detained many of the boats. Khaustov and Samuelson, *Stalin, NKVD*, 300. See also Polian, *Against Their Will*, 99–101. About 25,000 ethnic Koreans not near the border were not deported, at least not immediately. *Belaia kniga*, 68, 82. Khaustov and Samuelson claim around 180,000 Koreans were deported: Stalin, *NKVD*, 300 (TsA FSB, f. 3, op. 5, d. 14). The population of ethnic Koreans in the Soviet Far East had tripled, to 170,000, between 1917 and 1926; a secret plan had been adopted (Dec. 6, 1926) but not implemented to relocate 88,000 of them from frontier zones. In 1928, 1930, and 1933, a few thousand Koreans had been shifted to the interior. Khisamutdinov, 119–21; Boldyrev, "Iaponiia i Sovetskii Dal'nyi Vostok," 187–94, 193–4; Stephan, *Russian Far East*, 212; Petrov, *Ukrepim sovety DVK*, 97. *Sibirskaia Sovetskaia Entsiklopediia*, II: 95.
121. Petrov and Roginskii, "'Pol'skaia operatsiia' NKVD," 22–43.
122. About 70 percent of Soviet ethnic Poles were in Ukraine, and until 1937 Poland maintained consulates in Moscow, Leningrad, Kharkov, Kiev, Minsk, and Tiflis, where they ran intelligence operations. But Stalin's clampdown led the Polish embassies and consulates to desist from recruiting agents among Soviet ethnic Poles. Khaustov, "Deiatel'nost' organov," 48; Pepłoński, *Wywiad Polski na ZSSR*, 126–7. Conversely, when a Polish citizen showed up at the Lubyanka front door to betray his masters, he was tortured and forced to confess to having been sent to penetrate the NKVD for Poland. Stalin also demanded to know what border point he had crossed. Khaustov and Samuelson, *Stalin, NKVD*, 229–30 (APRF, f. 3, op. 58, d. 254, l. 92-3, 203).
123. Khaustov et al., *Lubianka: Stalin i glavnoe upravlenie*, 352–9 (APRF, f. 3, op. 58, d. 254, l. 173–88: September 14, 1937); Khaustov and Samuelson, *Stalin, NKVD*, 291; Sudoplatov, *Tainaia zhizn'*, I: 366–93; Gur'ianov, *Repressii protiv poliakov*, 16–20. Stalin's vindictiveness against "foreigners" was not unique. "Stop playing internationalism, all these Poles, Koreans, Latvians, Germans, etc. should be beaten, these are all mercenary nations, subject to termination," one provincial party boss stated at a local NKVD conference. "All nationals should be caught, forced to their knees, and exterminated like mad dogs." Petrov and

Jansen, *Stalinskii pitomets*, 114 (quoting Sergei Sobolev, Krasnoyarsk). On Sept. 15, 1938, the regime ended the "album procedure" and allowed troikas for the national operation; two months later, it ended the troikas.
124. Okhotin and Roginskii, "Iz istorii 'nemetskoi operatisii' NKVD," 66. Mass operations were also ordered against the returning Harbin émigrés (Sept. 20, 1937), among others. Zaitsev, *Sbornik zakonodatel'nykh i normativnykh aktov*, 430–7.
125. "All Germans working on our military, semimilitary and chemical factories, on electric stations and building sites, in *all* regions are all *to be arrested*," Stalin instructed (July 20, 1937). Yezhov, five days later, issued this as an operational order (no. 00439). Perhaps 4,000 German citizens were resident in the Soviet Union; around 800 were arrested and deported to Germany. APRF, f. 3, op. 58, d. 254a, l. 82; Okhotin and Roginskii, "Iz istorii 'nemetskoi operatisii' NKVD," 35–7; Khlevniuk, *History of the Gulag*, 144–5.
126. Khaustov et al., *Lubianka: Stalin i glavnoe upravlenie*, 251 (APRF, f. 3, op. 58, d. 253, l. 141). The author of the report, Alexander Minayev, was arrested on Nov. 6, 1938, and executed on February 25, 1939. Petrov and Skorkin, *Kto rukovodil NKVD*, 298–9.
127. Khaustov et al., *Lubianka: Stalin i glavnoe upravlenie*, 662 n86; Khlevniuk et al., *Stalinskoe politbiuro*, 156 (RGASPI, f. 17, op. 3, d. 987, l. 79). Rudzutaks, even under severe torture, refused to admit any guilt. Chuev, *Sto sorok*, 410–2. According to Irina Gogua, the arrested Kremlin librarian, Rudzutaks kept the issue of the Menshevik *Socialist Herald* with Martov's obituary behind books on his home bookshelf.
128. Pavliukov, *Ezhov*, 333–4 (citing GARf, f. 8131, op. 37, d. 86, l. 138–48). Nasedkin is listed in the Little Corner on Nov. 23, 1937. *Na prieme*, 225. Often, NKVD interrogators began by asking why the prisoner had been arrested, as if it were up to the prisoner to establish his or her own guilt.
129. Alliluyeva, *Only One Year*, 388.
130. Chuev, *Sto sorok*, 409.
131. Primakov, *Ocherki*, III: 65 (no citation). The attaché's country is not identified.
132. Khaustov et al., *Lubianka: Stalin i glavnoe upravlenie*, 60 (RGASPI, f. 17, op. 3, d. 983, l. 46: Jan. 9, 1937), 66; Maksimenkov, *Bol'shaia tsenzura*, 509n2 (f. 17, op. 163, d. 1143, l. 73).
133. The sole German-speaking operative in the Soviet intelligence station in Paris was recalled to Moscow in 1937. Primakov, *Ocherki*, III: 66 (no citation). The person is not identified.
134. Yezhov informed Stalin that a housekeeper reported that Berzin had been close to Trotsky, who had promised him a future post. The housekeeper also supposedly said that Berzin had a great deal of White Guard literature in his personal library, in Russian and foreign languages, including works by Trotsky. (Berzin was head of military intelligence.) Stalin tasked Yezhov with going after military intelligence in the military districts as well, especially Ukraine, Belorussia, and Leningrad ("Did they not link the Trotskyites with Poland, like our Far Eastern intelligence linked the Trotskyites to Japan?"). Khaustov and Samuelson, *Stalin, NKVD*, 221 (APRF, f. 3, op. 24, d. 316, l. 86). Berzin was removed Aug. 1, 1937, and soon arrested for Trotskyism; he would be executed on July 29, 1938, at Kommunarka. In the meantime, on Sept. 8, 1937, Yezhov implanted a counterintelligence NKVD man as acting military intelligence chief, Semyon G. Gendin, telling his staff that he himself would run military intelligence.

135. Instead, the regime examined trunks, which had been lying around for some time, and found writings of Trotsky, Zinoviev, and other such former politburo officials. Kochik, "Sovetskaia voennaia razvedka" (no. 9–12), 101–2.

136. RGASPI, f. 17, op. 162, d. 21, l. 133 (Semyon Gendin).

137. Lota, "Alta" protiv "Barbaraossy," 56 (no citation). Several dozen more were sacked but not arrested.

138. Polyakova added that "these comrades became my first pupils and later some became my bosses." Kochik, "Sovetskaia voennaia razvedka" (no. 9–12), 98.

139. In an earlier part of the discussion, a mid-level commander stated his uncertainty about whether he could speak about enemies of the people "in full voice." Stalin: "To the whole world?" The commander: "No, internally." Stalin: "You are obliged to do so." Suvenirov, Tragediia RKKA, 93 (citing RGVA, f. 9, op. 29, d. 318, l. 173, 174, 64).

140. Solov'ev and Chugnuov, Pogranichnye voiska SSSR, 538–58, 574–7.

141. Beloff, Foreign Policy of Soviet Russia, II: 179–80; Ikuhiko, "Japanese-Soviet Confrontation," 137–40.

142. Goldman, Nomonhan, 1939, 28–34 (quote on 31).

143. Coox, Nomonhan, 102–19 (quote at 116).

144. Taylor, Generalissimo (citing Chiang's Diaries, Hoover Institution Archives, box 39, folder 13: July 12, 1937).

145. Jansen, Japan and China, 394–5.

146. The month before (June 1937), the Japanese completed the multiyear standardization of the railway gauge in northern China, converting from the wide gauge that the Russians had originally installed—just in time to move around their troops. Paine, Wars for Asia, 28.

147. Barnhart, "Japanese Intelligence," 435.

148. Izvestiia, Aug. 30, 1937; DVP SSSR, XX: 466–8; Kurdiukov et al., Sovetsko-Kitaiskie otnosheniia, 161–2; Ledovskii et al., Russko-kitaiskie otnosheniia v XX veke, IV/i: 88–9 (APRF, f. 3–a, op. 1, d. 52, l. 1–3); Slavinskii, Sovetskii soiuz i kitai, 314–20. Dmitri Bogomolov, the Soviet envoy to China (since 1933), who signed the nonaggression pact, had been predicting there would be no full-scale Japanese attack on China. In July 1937, Litvinov rebuked him for supposedly implying to the Chinese that the Soviet Union might agree to a full alliance (a mutual assistance pact). In Sept., Stalin had Bogomolov recalled; he returned to Moscow on Oct. 7 and vanished. DVP SSSR, XX: 737–8 (July 19 and July 22, 1937); Ledovskii, "Zapiski diplomata," 114; Sokolov, "Zabytyi diplomat"; Haslam, Struggle for Collective Security, 149.

149. RGASPI, f. 17, op. 162, d. 21, l. 157; Bugai, "Vyselenie sovetskikh koreetsev," 144.

150. FRUS, 1937, III: 636 (Bullitt to Washington, Oct. 23, 1937).

151. Chang and Halliday, Mao, 200–3.

152. The Soviets would extend $250 million in 1938–39; by mid-1939 there would be 3,665 Soviet advisers in China. Ageenko, Voennaia pomoshch' SSSR, 49.

153. Whiting and Shih-ts'aicai, Sinkiang, 51 (citing memoirs of the general who ruled Xinjiang with Soviet backing).

154. Garver, "Chiang Kai-shek's Quest." Bogomolov called Chiang Kai-shek's hopes for a direct Soviet-Japanese war his "idée fixe." DVP SSSR, XX: 389. Chiang did not submit the nonaggression pact for formal ratification until April 26, 1938, indicating he wanted either a formal alliance or was waiting on the Western powers to change their minds.

155. Ledovskii et al., Russko-kitaiskie otnosheniia v XX veke, IV/i: 105–8 (APRF, f. 3, op. 1, d. 321, l. 10–15).

156. Stalin's views on China in 1937 after the Japanese attack were recorded by Dimitrov: Banac, Diary of Georgi Dimitrov, 67–9 (Nov. 11, 1937). Far more Soviet advisers and pilots would serve in China—3,665—than had served in Spain.

157. Barmin, Sovetskii Soiuz i Sin'tszian, 157–8.

158. Kolt'sov, Ispanskii dnevnik, 519–20 (July 7, 1937).

159. The other wife was Elizaveta Koltsova, who had been sacked in Madrid from her job. Kudriashov, SSSR i grazhdanskaia voina v Ispanii, 268 (APRF, f. 3, op. 65, d. 217, l. 68).

160. Codovilla was replaced in Spain by Togliatti. Kudriashov, SSSR i grazhdanskaia voina v Ispanii, 283–8 (APRF, f. 3, op. 65, d. 225, l. 2–10). See also Payne, Spanish Civil War, 32. In 1938, Stalin would twice come to the conclusion that the Communists should quit the Popular Front government and form a new government of just Communists and Socialists; both times, Dimitrov—of all people—appears to have talked Stalin out of it. Meshcheriakov, "SSSR i grazhdanskaia voina v Ispanii," 93 (citing RGASPI, f. 495, op. 74, d. 216, l. 2; TsPA VS BSP, f. 146, op. 2, d. 42, l. 1). In February–March 1938, Pascua tried to impress upon Potyomkin the dire military and economic situation of the Spanish Republic; the upshot was a Soviet $70 million loan to Spain, which had spent down its gold reserves. Kudriashov, SSSR i grazhdanskaia voina v Ispanii, 325–37 (APRF, f. 3, op. 65, d. 226, l. 28–31, 33–5, 37–8, 39; d. 232, l. 46, d. 234, l. 165–6, d. 226, l. 57–8, 42–4, 45, 46–460b., 59–60). By April 1938, Pascua had been transferred to Paris. He wrote yet another artful letter to Stalin, offering his gratitude on behalf of Spain. Kudriashov, SSSR i grazhdanskaia voina v Ispanii, 338 (citing APRF, f. 3, op. 65, d. 226, l. 64–64ob.). In Aug. 1938 Pascua came to Moscow from Paris, with a letter to Stalin from Negrín. But by Aug. 29, 1938, Dimitrov and Manuilsky were writing to Stalin about the evacuation of the international brigades from Spain. Kudriashov, SSSR i grazhdanskaia voina v Ispanii, 344 (APRF, f. 3, op. 65, d. 226, l. 83), 346–7 (l. 85), 354–5 (l. 109), 358 (l. 119–20).

161. Roshchin, Politicheskaia istoriia Mongolii.

162. They reconvened the next day, too. Na prieme, 218.

163. Iakovenko, Agnessa, 95. The Soviet envoy, Vladimir Tairov (Teryan), an Armenian, arrested on Aug. 5, 1937, was evidently being convoyed in the other direction (to Moscow) along the same route.

164. Papkov, Stalinskii terror v Sibiri, 269; Iakovenko, Agnessa, 97–8.

165. Pavliukov, Ezhov, 382–7; Pravda, Aug. 29, 1937; Kolarz, Peoples of the Soviet Far East, 138–9. The secret autopsy cited death "as a result of . . . external poison." Luzianin, "Rossiia-Mongoliia-Kitai," 323.

166. Dashpürev and Soni, Reign of Terror in Mongolia, 33–5. Captain Bimba, who defected to the Japanese, told them about a pro-Japanese conspiracy among the Mongol elite to which Demid supposedly belonged. But Bimba's account is highly inconsistent and often blatantly wrong about dates and verifiable facts. Coox, Nomonhan, 161–3 (who largely accepts the testimony of defector Captain Bimba); Dashpürev and Soni, Reign of Terror in Mongolia, 2–3 (who point out that the testimony is unreliable).

167. RGANI, f. 89, op. 63, d. 26, l. 1.

168. Choibalsan had denounced Demid to Voroshilov in Oct. 1936. Baabar, Twentieth-Century Mongolia, 355–6, 360.

169. When Frinovsky returned from Mongolia, his possible transfer to the defense commissariat, as deputy commissar, was evidently

bruited. Protocol of Frinovsky interrogation, sent by Beria to Stalin April 11, 1939: http://www.hrono.ru/dokum/193_dok/19390413beria.php (APRF, f. 3, op. 24, d. 373, l. 3–44: protocol of Frinovsky interrogation, Beria to Stalin, April 11, 1939).

170. Dashpürev and Soni, Reign of Terror in Mongolia; Sandag and Kendall, Poisoned Arrows.

171. Genden was never repatriated and was executed in Moscow in Nov. Pavliukov, Ezhov, 388; Kaplonski, "Prelude to Violence"; Baabar, Twentieth-Century Mongolia, 361–2.

172. Khlevniuk, "Economic Officials in the Great Terror," 61 (citing RGASPI, f. 17, op. 3, d. 997, l. 79–82; op. 120, d. 339, l. 42; op. 3, d. 992, l. 28: Feb. 1938; op. 120, d. 339, l. 57).

173. At the Feb.–March 1937 plenum, Stalin had referred to the top 3,000–4,000 officials as the "general staff of the party." Kosheleva et al., "Materialy fevral'-martovskogo plenuma TsK VKP (b) 1937 goda" (1995, no. 3), 14. In one ward of Smolensk city for which we have data, forty-one people born in the nineteenth century were promoted in 1937–38—not exactly new people. Thurston, Life and Terror, 133 (citing the Smolensk archive).

174. The budget for 1938 envisioned 160,400; the actual number would be 180,500. Khlevniuk, "Economic Officials in the Great Terror," 60 (citing GARF, f. 5446, op. 22, d. 1065, l. 19–20; d. 1060, l. 89).

175. Without CC approval young specialists were forbidden from beginning work. Khlevniuk, "Economic Officials in the Great Terror," 60 (RGASPI, f. 17, op. 3, d. 992, l. 97). In 1938, after the name of Arseny Zverev (b. 1900) was presented on a list of party members who had completed the Moscow Institute of Finance and Economics, he was named finance commissar. Chuev, Sto sorok, 291.

176. "Machiavellian duplicity" is the interpretation offered by Robert Tucker, Stalin in Power, 320. Cf. Fitzpatrick, "Making of a New Elite."

177. Pravda, Oct. 31, 1937; Nevezhin, Zastol'nye, 117–33; RGASPI, f. 81, op. 3, d. 96, l. 148; Bardin, "Ispolin-mudrets," 54–5. See also Khlevniuk, 1937–i, 104–5.

178. Svetlana Alliluyeva, quoted in Richardson, Long Shadow, 211.

179. Farcically, Getty and Naumov have asserted that "it is not an exaggeration to say that the Riutin Platform began the process that would lead to terror, precisely by terrifying the ruling nomenklatura." Getty and Naumov, Road to Terror, 54.

180. Stalin might have wanted to clear a path for the rising new generation, but what kind of path? Confessions to crimes people did not commit and mass executions? Khlevniuk, "The Stalinist 'Party Generals,'" esp. 59–60. See also Rees, "The Great Purges and the XVIII Party Congress of 1939," 191–211.

181. Artizov, "V ugodu vzgliadam vozhdia," (on the 1936 competition); Dubrovskii, "A. A. Zhdanov v rabote nad shkol'nym uchebnikom istorii," 128–43. Mikhail Pokrovsky, before his death in 1932, had entrenched a Marxist orthodoxy based upon Engels deeming tsarist Russia the most reactionary power, the "gendarme of Europe." Stalin countered that in the nineteenth century all the great powers were gendarmes. Even though almost all members of Pokrovsky's School would be physically annihilated, the summons to incorporate imperial Russian legacies in a patriotic history of the Soviet Union proved no easy task. The Pokrovsky School had destroyed the careers of most other historians, leaving a wasteland. Shestakov was one of the few Pokrovsky students to endure.

182. Dubrovskii, Istorik i vlast', 274–5.

183. Kutskii, "A. V. Shestakov." Shestakov would be elected a corresponding member of the Academy of Sciences in 1939. For commentary on Shestakov as of 1929, see Iurganov, *Russkoe natsional'noe gosudarstvo*, 26n3.

184. Shestakov, *Kratkii kurs istorii SSSR*; Shestakov, *Short History of the USSR*, 8.

185. Brandenberger, *National Bolshevism*, 260. Another 5.7 million copies would be printed in 1938 and 3 million in 1939.

186. Brandenberger, *National Bolshevism*, 67 (citing GARF, f. 2306, op. 69, d. 2640, l. 1).

187. The book mentioned Stanisław Kosior and others who were soon arrested as enemies, but rather than recall and pulp the long-awaited, highly sought textbook, the censors dispatched directives to paste over the offending names and illustrations. Mekhlis would cross out a photograph of Marshal Blyukher in his own copy: RGASPI, f. 17, op. 120, d. 373, l. 99–99ob., 103ob., 108.

188. A. K., "Kratkii kurs istorii SSSR," 85–6. The journal of the historical profession called the book "a great victory on the historical front." "Bol'shaia pobeda na istoricheskom fronte," *Istoricheskii zhurnal*, 1937, no. 8: 6. "He who understands history," a Communist Youth League mass pamphlet of fall 1938 written by Shestakov would advise, "will better understand contemporary life and struggle more effectively with the enemies of our country and strengthen socialism." Shestakov, "Ob izuchenii istorii SSSR," 39 (quoting his own *Short Course History of the USSR*).

189. Brandenberger and Dubrovsky, "'The People Need a Tsar'" 879 (citing RGASPI, f. 77, op. 1, d. 847, l. 3–4). Zatonsky was arrested in a cinema (where he was with his family) on Nov. 3, 1937. He would be executed July 29, 1938.

190. Harold Denny, the Moscow correspondent for the *New York Times*, caught the trend with the observation that "there is a legend in Moscow—and the writer does not know whether or not it is true—that Stalin questioned his own son on English history and found that while his son could talk glibly about economic periods he had never heard of Cromwell." Denny, "No 'Formalism.'" Denny served in Moscow 1934–39, having replaced Walter Duranty, and he proved no less mendacious regarding Stalin's crimes. Heilbrunn, "*New York Times* and the Moscow Show Trials."

191. Shestakov, *Short History of the USSR*, 76.

192. Shestakov, *Short History of the USSR*, 49–50. See also Tucker, *Stalin in Power*, 282.

193. The film, applauded *Izvestiya* (Sept. 2), "answers like nothing else the cultural demands of our country's populace. The masses are showing an interest of interest in history . . . They want to see the paths that have brought them to glory."

194. Tolstoi, in *Polnoe sobranie sochinenii*, XIII: 355. See also Petrone, *Life Has Become More Joyous*, 159 (citing RGALI, f. 962, op. 3, d. 287, l. 34); and Tucker, *Stalin in Power*, 114–8.

195. Garros et al., *Intimacy and Terror*, 209 (Galina Shtange). The depiction of Peter was so over-the-top positive that the American worker John Scott, who saw the film in Magnitogorsk, guessed that *Peter the First* had been imported. Scott, *Behind the Urals*, 236. See also Siegelbaum and Sokolov, *Stalinism as a Way of Life*, 211 (I. K. Karniush to *Krest'ianskaia Gazeta*, Oct. 30, 1938).

196. Back in April 1926, Stalin had ridiculed comrades who imagined Ivan the Terrible or even Peter as Russia's industrializers ("not all industrial development constitutes industrialization. The heart of industrialization, its

basis, consists in the development of heavy industry, . . . the production of the means of production, in the development of its own machine-building"). At a Central Committee plenum in Nov. 1928, Stalin had said, "when Peter the Great, having dealings with the more developed countries of the West, feverishly built factories for the supply of the army and strengthening the country's defenses, this was the original attempt to leap out from the limits of backwardness. It is fully understood, however, that not one of the old classes, neither the feudal aristocracy nor the bourgeoisie, could resolve the task of liquidating our country's backwardness." In 1931, speaking to Emil Ludwig, Stalin had again brushed off the parallel with Peter, because Soviet modernization efforts were not on behalf of the landowners or merchants but the working class. *Sochineniia*, VIII: 120–1, XI: 248–9, XIII: 104–5.

197. There is an anecdote that has Stalin rebuking Vasily when he caught his son attempting to trade on his name: "You're not Stalin and I'm not Stalin. Stalin is Soviet power. Stalin is what he is in the newspapers and the portraits, not you, no, not even me!" Montefiore, *Court of the Red Tsar*, 6 (citing only "Artyom Sergeev").

198. As Giuseppe Boffa observed, "no matter how numerous its ties with Russia's past (and certainly it does have many), Stalinism is still a modern phenomenon, well rooted in our century." Boffa, *Stalin Phenomenon*, 58. See also Rees, "Stalin and Russian Nationalism," 77–106 (esp. 93–5).

199. Koliazin and Goncharov, "*Vernite mne svobodu!*," 78–95 (Pyotr Tyurkin). Union and autonomous republics lobbied against too much time devoted to teaching Russian (time devoted to native languages would increase in 1938–39). Many locales lacked trained instructors to teach the Russian language. Russian was taught in fewer than half of Turkmenistan's 728 schools, one-third of Kyrgyzstan's 667, and one-seventh of Kazakhstan's 330, and even when taught the quality of instruction was low. Blitstein, "Nation-Building or Russification?," 256 (citing RGASPI, f. 17, op. 114, d. 840, l. 76–7).

200. RGASPI, f. 17, op. 2, d. 628, l. 121–2. The decree rendering Russian obligatory in schools would not be issued until March 13, 1938 (evidently delayed by the terror and bureaucratic complexities). Never published, it stipulated that "in the conditions of a multinational state such as the USSR, knowledge of the Russian language should be a powerful means for communication and contact among the peoples of the USSR, enabling further economic and cultural growth." RGASPI, f. 17, op. 3, d. 997, l. 103. Local versions of the decree were published. *Kul'turnaia zhizn' v SSSR, 1928–1941*, 606n6. In the meantime, on Oct. 30, 1937, Mekhlis complained to Stalin and the other Central Committee secretaries, as well as Yezhov, about the absence of Russian-language newspapers in Ukraine. Georgia, Azerbaijan, and Kazakhstan all had republic-level Russian newspapers, while of the eleven republic and provincial newspapers published in Kiev, all the main ones were in Ukrainian. Of Ukraine's twelve regions, only the Donbas had even a province-level Russian newspaper. Even Odessa lacked a local Russian-language newspaper. Kiev had German, Polish, Yiddish, and Bulgarian papers, but none in Russian. Maksimenkov, *Bol'shaia tsenzura*, 481–2 (RGASPI, f. 17, op. 114, d. 829, l. 135–6). Other changes included beginning instruction with seven-year-olds (one year earlier than previously), replacing Latin with Cyrillic for many languages of Soviet peoples, and abolishing all remaining

national units in the Red Army. RGASPI, f. 17, op. 3, d. 997, l. 95–6 (March 7, 1938).

201. During the viewing, the film snapped fifteen times. Schlögel, *Moscow, 1937*, 372–3; Petrone, *Life Has Become More Joyous*, 163–4; *Literaturnaia gazeta*, Dec. 12, 1937.

202. Massing, *This Deception*, 248–9.

203. Banac, *Diary of Georgi Dimitrov*, 65; van Ree, "Stalin as Marxist," 175. Stalin had rendered still more severe the draft directives for spouses (including those divorced), children, siblings, brothers and sisters-in-law. And when relatives of the arrested wrote to him begging for help because of their indigence, he often ordered their arrests. Kurliandskii, *Stalin, vlast', religiia*, 44–5.

204. Khrushchev, in his ever-ingratiating way, sought to reconcile the moment: "What we have is a felicitous combination—both the great leader and the middle cadres!" Banac, *Diary of Georgi Dimitrov*, 65–7 (Nov. 7, 1937). Tucker imagined that in the speech in Voroshilov's apartment, Stalin self-consciously emulated Ivan the Terrible. Tucker, *Stalin in Power*, 482–6.

205. Such was Dimitrov's account; a longer version was recorded by Voroshilov's adjutant: "Trotsky was known, he was not a Bolshevik, he joined the Bolsheviks with his program of permanent revolution. Many said that the Republic was Lenin and Trotsky, he was an orator. Major figures joined together: Trotsky, Bukharin, Rykov, Tomsky, Zinoviev, Pyatakov (God only knows what kind of a figure); add to that Nadezhda Konstantinova [Krupskaya], who always supported these 'leftist' Communists. Me, Stalin, I was known, but not like Trotsky. Be brave and don't invent what was not the case." Nevezhin, *Zastol'nye*, 158 (citing RGAPSI, f. 558, op. 11, d. 1122, l. 158–65; 167–74: Khmelnitsky notes).

207. Nevezhin, *Zastol'nye*, 62–4, RGAPSI, f. 558, op. 11, d. 1122, l. 158–65, 167–74).

208. No figure acquired more place-names than the deceased Kirov. Murray, *Politics and Place Names*, 51.

209. Wang Ming had requested an audience with Stalin on Oct. 21, 1937. Moscow also sent an envoy to Yan'an, V. A. Adrianov, from the general staff, with $3 million, to build up the forces to fight the Japanese. Titarenko, *VKP (b), kominern i kitai*, V: 73 (RGASPI, f. 495, op. 74, d. 281, l. 48); Banac, *Diary of Georgi Dimitrov*, 67–9; III: 124, 197–200, 229–33.

210. Banac, *Diary of Georgi Dimitrov*, 67–9.

211. *Zaria vostoka*, Oct. 29, 1937. See also Wilson, "Stalin as Ikon," 271–3 (Wilson attended a physical culture parade on Red Square that glorified Stalin). Also on Nov. 15, 1937, two nervous functionaries in the party's culture-enlightenment department wrote to Kaganovich and Yezhov about perceived shortcomings in *Man with a Gun*, the play by Nikolai Pogodin (Stukalov) on the October Revolution, which had premiered at Moscow's Vakhtangov Theater. Kerzhentsev had inserted the character of Stalin, played by Ruben Simonov (b. 1899), days before the opening. "Simonov was given this important part [young Stalin] because he was Armenian and looked somewhat like a Georgian, and because next to Shchukin Simonov was the best actor in our company," the letter writers complained. "But all this was not enough to transform the charming, spruce, somewhat eccentric Ruben Simonov into a future father of the people." Kerzhentsev had dressed down Shchukin for his portrayal of Lenin ("Shchukin turned white and we stood frozen in amazement"), but Molotov told the actor that Kerzhentsev would regret his criticism. Maksimenkov, *Bol'shaia tsenzura*, 487–8 (RGASPI, f. 17, op. 120, d. 256, l. 161–3:

F. Shablovsky and K. Yukov); Jelagin, *Taming of the Arts*, 107-9. Molotov had witnessed Stalin's positive reaction to Shchukin's portrayal of Lenin in Romm's film. See also Shchukin, *Boris Vasil'evich Shchukin*.

212. Stalin had instructed a visiting Chinese Nationalist delegation (Nov. 18, 1937) to build their own weapons and aviation factories, in the rear, because capitalists tended to sell mostly substandard arms, and might stop selling to China altogether. Ledovskii et al., *Russko-kitaiskie otnosheniia v XX veke*, IV/i: 151-7 (November 18, APRF, f. 45, op. 1, d. 321, l. 20-8). See also Ledovskii et al., *Russko-kitaiskie otnosheniia v XX veke*, IV/i: 136-8 (APRF, f. 45, op. 1, d. 321, l. 16-9: Voroshilov, Nov. 1).

213. Taylor, *Generalissimo*, 161.

214. MacKinnon, *Wuhan*. Membership would reach 800,000 by 1940.

215. Ledovskii et al., *Russko-kitaiskie otnosheniia v XX veke*, IV/i: 180 (APRF, f. 45, op. 1, d. 324, l. 21, Dec. 24, 1937).

216. The Soviet of Nationalities was to be filled by representatives of the union and the autonomous republics without regard to their size or population.

217. Pavlova, "1937." As one soldier in the Soviet Far East aptly commented, according to an NKVD report, "So Stalin says that's the way it will be and then everything is democratic." Merritt, "Great Purges," 168.

218. *Pravda*, Dec. 7, 1937; Getty, "State and Society."

219. Fitzpatrick, *Everyday Stalinism*, 179-82. See also Golubev, "Esli mir obrushitsia na nashu Respubliku," 68 (citing TsAODM, f. 3, op. 50, d. 16, l. 117-9).

220. RGASPI, f. 558, op. 1, d. 5011, l. 1-2. At factories and collective farms, Cheka anniversary lectures were staged.

221. Khaustov et al., *Lubianka: Stalin i glavnoe upravlenie*, 459 (RGASPI, f. 17, op. 3, d. 994, l. 17: Dec. 9, 1937).

222. *Pravda*, Dec. 21, 1937; *Izvestiia*, Dec. 21, 1937; Sultanbekov, "Nikolai Ezhov," 28; Mlechin, *KGB*, 176-7.

223. Conquest, *Inside Stalin's Secret Police*, 50-1.

224. *Vecherniaia Moskva*, Dec. 21, 1937: 1.

225. Jelagin, *Taming of the Arts*, 167. *Pravda* (Dec., 17, 1937) had denounced Meyerhold in a broadside titled "A Foreign Theater."

226. *Na prieme*, 227.

227. Khaustov et al., *Lubianka: Stalin i glavnoe upravlenie*, 268 (APRF, f. 3, op. 24, d. 316, l. 50-61; July 23, 1937).

228. Bowing to practical demands, Molotov had to acquiesce in the promotion of non-party specialists to factory and administrative positions. "We have to admit at the present time, it is not simply a question of the selection of cadres," Molotov said of a draft decree on Dec. 29, 1937. "What we are doing is a broad-front promotion of new cadres. We need to select new cadres who can work better than the old ones, who have not turned sour or gone over to the enemy camp." Khlevniuk, "Economic Officials in the Great Terror," 60 (citing GARF, f. 5446, op. 22, d. 1065, l. 10-7, 19-20).

229. This was evidently a meeting of the politburo, which commenced at 6:05 p.m. The logbook lists Molotov, Kaganovich, Kalinin, Chubar, Mikoyan, Voroshilov, Andreyev, Yezhov, and Zhdanov (candidate members), and Voznesensky (not a member). It does not list Kosior (full member) or Postyshev, Eihe, or Petrovsky (candidate members). *Na prieme*, 227-8.

230. Chigirin, *Stalin*, 88-114 (RGASPI, f. 558, op. 11, d. 1482, l. 60-99). Yezhov would have the medical record forwarded to Vlasik on Dec. 12, 1938.

231. Bobylev et al., *Voennyi sovet pri narodnom komissare oborony SSSR, noiabr' 1937 g.*,

73-4; Iakulov, "Stalin i Krasnaia Armiia," 172. The gathering took place Nov. 21-27, 1937. Kuibyshev would be arrested on Feb. 2, 1938, and executed on August 1. The Soviet officer corps would total 179,000 in 1939.

232. Rapoport and Geller, *Izmena rodine*, 283-8.

233. Reese, *Stalin's Reluctant Soldiers*.

234. *DGFP, 1918-1945*, series D, I: 29-39 ("Hossbach Memorandum").

235. Kershaw, *Hitler: 1936-1945*, 46-60; Fest, *Hitler*, 539-43. Whereas Kershaw renders the ascent of Hitler to the top of the military command as almost an accident, Fest makes it overly preplanned.

236. Fröhlich, *Tagebücher von Joseph Goebbels*, V: 117 (Jan. 27, 1938). Read, *The Disciples*, 450. The bride was Eva Gruhn.

237. Hitler assembled all the generals to deliver the news in person on the afternoon of Feb. 5, 1938. No one objected. That evening he addressed the cabinet (it was the last formal cabinet meeting of the Reich) and sought to dispel rumors of rifts between the Nazi party and the Wehrmacht. The sensational news of the momentous changes in the Wehrmacht took up the press and radio airtime for days—both Blomberg and Fritsch were said to have retired "on health grounds"—spurring rumors of a plot on Hitler's life. McDonogh, *Hitler's Gamble*, 7-19.

238. RGASPI, f. 17, op. 3, d, 994, l. 51.

239. Kostrychenko, *Tainaia politika Stalina*, 160, 207-8. Postyshev, acting party boss in Kuibyshev (since March 18, 1937), was specially reprimanded for excesses.

240. Khlevniuk et al., *Stalinskoe politbiuro*, 159-67; Khlevniuk, "Party and NKVD," 26-7; Petrov and Jansen, *Stalinskii pitomets*, 140-3; Getty and Naumov, *Road to Terror*, 501. See also Rigby, *Communist Party Membership*, 214-8.

241. Khaustov et al., *Lubianka: Stalin i glavnoe upravlenie*, 463 (RGASPI, f. 558, op. 11, d. 729, l. 94-5). Individual reprieves were often short-lived. On Sept. 25, 1937, following the arrest of his brother Aleksei Simochkin in the Western province, Vasily Simochkin, party boss of Ivan-Voznesensk province, wrote to Stalin to disown his brother. "You cannot answer for your brother," Stalin answered. "Continue your work." RGASPI, f. 558, op. 11, d. 57, l. 93. But Vasily Simochkin was arrested on Nov. 26, 1938, and executed on March 10, 1939.

242. Starkov, "Kak Moskva chut' ne stala Stalinodarom," 126-7.

243. *Pravda*, Jan. 18, 1938; *Pervaia sessia Verkhovnogo Soveta SSSR*, 135-41; Maksimenkov, *Sumbur*, 238-9; RGASPI, f. 77, op. 1, d. 672 (Zhdanov's notes). On Jan. 4, 1938, Shumyatsky reported to Molotov on the need to install permanent filming and sound equipment in the Great Kremlin Palace hall used for party congresses; the equipment had already been purchased in the United States. That same day Malenkov signed an order for Kerzhentsev's removal. Three days later, the politburo replaced Shumyatsky with Dukelsky (who would last two months). This spurred Gr. Zeldovich, an editor at Mosfilm, to denounce artists for drunken debaucheries at the Metropole and their "immense love for 'the West'. Many dream about foreign trips . . . I heard that G[rigory] Alexandrov has often been inside certain foreign embassies." Zeldovich had one uncle living in Poland and another in Riga, while relatives on his mother's side lived in America, perhaps accounting for his going on the offensive. Maksimenkov, *Kremlevskii kinoteatr*, 455-6 (RGASPI, f. 82, op. 2, d. 958, l. 66), 455-6n1 (l. 67), 457 (f. 17, op. 3, d. 994, l. 46), 462-77 (op. 120, d. 349, l. 47-60), 477n3 (f. 82, op. 2, d.

958, l. 38). In 1938, Kerzhentsev was replaced (by Aleksei Nazarov) but would die a natural death (heart failure on June 2, 1940). Maksimenkov, *Sumbur*, 288-90. Nazarov would last until April 1, 1939, giving way to his deputy, the enduring Mikhail Khrapchenko (b. 1904).

244. Nevezhin, *Zastol'nye rechi*, 170-83. Stalin allowed Zhdanov to give the speech commemorating Lenin at the Bolshoi.

245. Jelagin, *Taming of the Arts*, 109, 287-8; Elagin, *Ukroshchenie iskusstv*, 322-3.

246. Milovidov, "Velikii grazhdanin," 6; Dobrenko, *Stalinist Cinema*, 229-50.

247. In Feb. 1938, the NKVD received a report from Mark Zborowski out of Paris that had Trotsky's son Sedov once more stating, while reading a newspaper, that "'the whole regime in the USSR rests upon Stalin and it would be enough to kill him so that it would come crashing down.' He returned to and underscored many times the necessity of killing comrade Stalin." Volkogonov, *Trotskii*, II: 198 (citing Arkhiv INO OGPU-NKVD, f. 31660, d. 9067, t. 1, l.140a-140v). See also Volkogonov, *Trotsky*, 378-80. See also Sudoplatov, *Special Tasks*, 82-3; Serge, "Leon Sedov," 203-7; Costello and Tsarev, *Deadly Illusions*, 469-70 (quoting Spiegelglass interrogation). Supposedly in 1937, the NKVD's Yakov Serebryansky had been tasked with kidnapping Lev Sedov without commotion on a Paris street and transferring him alive to Moscow, leaving no trace of the operation (and not informing the Paris intelligence station). Instead, Sedov suddenly died. This story appears to be given in an effort to deny Soviet intelligence's involvement in Sedov's death. Primakov, *Ocherki*, III: 83-4.

248. Banac, *Diary of Georgi Dimitrov*, 73 (Feb. 18, 1938). A Communist Youth League member appears to have written Stalin seeking redress after having been fired for failing to affirm that socialism in the Soviet Union had won "final victory" (preserving the country against repeat foreign intervention to restore capitalism). Stalin wrote back, agreeing with the fired petitioner, in a lengthy letter he had printed in *Pravda* (Feb. 14, 1938): "Since we do not live on an island but in a 'system of states,' a considerable number of which are hostile to the land of socialism, creating a danger of intervention and restoration, we say openly and honestly that the victory of socialism in our country is not yet final." Tucker, "The Emergence of Stalin's Foreign Policy," 570.

249. Kowalsky, *Stalin*, paragraph 608 (citing Pascua's personal notes of Kremlin meeting of Feb. 26, 1938. AHN-Madrid. Diversos. M. Pascua, Leg. 2, Exp. 6).

250. Danilov et al., *Tragediia Sovetskoi derevni*, V/i: 452, 486; Ellman, "Soviet 1937 Provincial Show Trials" (the order dated to Aug. 3, 1937, right as the "kulak" operation was unfolding); Ellman, "Soviet 1937-1938 Provincial Show Trials Revisited." See also RGASPI, 558, op. 11, d. 57, l. 57; *Izvestiia*, June 10, 1992: 7.

251. Gupta, *Ryutin Platform*. On the difficulties involved in staging fabricated trials, see Lih, "Melodrama and the Myth," 178-207 (esp. 202).

252. "O dele tak nazyvaemogo 'soiuza marksistov-lenintsev'," 112-5 (Nuv. 1, 1936).

253. Conquest, *Great Terror: Reassessment*, 23; and Tucker and Cohen, *Great Purge Trial*, 348. Vyshinsky, claiming to be quoting the defendant Sokolnikov, noted on Jan. 28, 1937, in his statement to the court that "as for the lines of the program, as far back as 1932 the Trotskyites, the Zinovievites and the Rightists all agreed in the main on a program, which was characterized as the program of the Rightists. This was the so-called Ryutin

Platform; to a large extent, as far back as 1932, it expressed the program policy common to all three groups." *Report of Court Proceedings*, 489.

254. Bukharin, *Tiuremnye rukopisi*. Four letters are dated between April 15, 1937, and Dec. 10, 1937. In the latter, Bukharin wrote: "I thought about what was taking place, and came up with the following conception: There is some kind of grand, bold political idea of a general purge a) in connection with a prewar time; b) in connection with a transition to democracy. This purge encompasses a) the guilty b) the suspicious and c) the potential-suspicious." Bukharin also wrote that he had dreamt Nadya Alliluyeva—in whose room he had been living—was still alive and had promised to get Stalin to release him. Stalin circulated the letters to the other politburo members, who wrote across them, "The letter of a criminal," "A criminal farce," "A typical Bukharin lie." Murin, "Prosti menia, Koba . . .': neizvestnoe pis'mo N. Bukharina," 23 (APRF, f. 3, op. 24, d. 427, l. 13–8); "'No ia to znaia, chtoty prov': pis'mo N. I. Bukharina I. V. Staliny iz vnutrennei t'iurmy NKVD," 56 (d. 301, l. 127, 128); 56–8; Getty and Naumov, *Road to Terror*, 556–62. See also Pons, *Stalin and the Inevitable War*, 78–9; and Fel'shtinskii, *Razgovory s Bukharinym*, 114–5. In late Feb. 1938, on the eve of the trial, Yezhov lied to Bukharin that his life would be spared: Khaustov, "Deiatel'nost' organov," 365 (TsA FSB, f. 3, op. 5, d. 589, l. 108). Bukharin's last communication with Stalin came March 13, 1938 (a futile appeal of his death sentence). Larina was arrested and sent to the Tomsk camp for wives of traitors and enemies (she would survive).

255. The indictment was presented for an international audience by Yaroslavsky, *Meaning of the Soviet Trials*. The defendants' biographies had been rewritten to make them descendants of capitalists and priests.

256. On Yagoda's attempt to negotiate for his life, see the prison snitch's report: Vinogradov, *Genrikh Iagoda*, 233–5 (TsA FSB, f. 3, op. 5, d. 318, l. 113–4: V. Kirshon).

257. Conquest, *Reassessment*, 341–98; Maclean, *Escape to Adventure*, 59–83; Hedeler, "Ezhov's Scenario," 34–55.

258. Sokolov, "N. N. Krestinskii," 120–42; *Trud*, May 26, 1988.

259. Conquest, *Reassessment*, 352; Popov, "Byl i ostaius' kommunistom," 244–51.

260. *Trial of the Anti-Soviet "Bloc of Rights and Trotskyites*," 675.

261. Khaustov and Samuelson, *Stalin, NKVD*, 173–6 (TsA FSB, f. 3, op. 5, d. 42, l. 29–33; d. 40, l. 128, 347; d. 41, l. 51–70; APRF, f. 3, op. 24, d. 338, l. 59).

262. Avdeenko, "Otluchenie" (no. 4), 90–1. Avdeenko did not get in to the trial.

263. *New York Times*, March 1, 1938.

264. Besides Bukharin, Rykov, Yagoda, Krestinsky, and Ravovsky (former ambassador to Great Britain and France), the defendants were: Arkady Rosenholtz, Vladimir Ivanov (former People's Commissar for Timber Industry), Mikhail Chernov (former People's Commissar for Agriculture), Grigori Grinko (former People's Commissar for Finance), Isaac Zelensky (former Central Committee Secretary), Akmal Ikramov and Fayzulla Khodzhayev (Uzbek leaders), Vasily Sharangovich (former party boss in Belorussia), Prokopy Zubarev, Pavel Bulanov (NKVD operative), Venyamin Maximov-Dikovsky, Pyotr Kryuchkov (Gorky's secretary), Sergei Bessonov (a trade representative), and three Kremlin doctors: Lev Levin, Dmitry Pletnev, and Ignaty Kazakov. Levin and Kazakov were sentenced to execution; Pletnev, like Rakovsky and Bessonov, was given a long

sentence, but, after being remanded to Orlov prison, he would be shot without retrial in 1941. Borodulin and Topolianskii, "Dmitrii Dmitrievich Pletnev," 51. On the NKVD's toxicology lab, see Sudoplatov, *Spetsoperatsii*, 441. The executioner was Pyotr Maggo.

265. http://www.memo.ru/memory/communarka/index.htm; Golovkova, *Butovksii Poligon*. Among those whose cremated remains were dumped at Kommunarka were Bukharin, Rykov, Béla Kun, Abram Belenky (Lenin's former bodyguard), Peters of the Cheka, Yakov Agranov, Trilliser, Leonid Zakovsky, Grigory Kaminsky, Krestinsky, Pyatnitsky, Postyshev, and Pauker.

266. Khaustov and Samuelson, *Stalin, NKVD*, 238 (TsA FSB, ASD H-13706, l. 55–6: Grigory Vyatkin). Plestsov would survive and prosper; Vyatkin, already infamous in 1934 in Novosibirsk for having knocked out someone's teeth with a whip, would be arrested in Nov. 1938, charged with having destroyed more than 4,000 people in Ukraine, and executed in 1939. Tepliakov, *Mashina terrora*, 252, 263, 478, 516.

267. Orlov, *Tainaia istoriia*, 188; Orlov, *Secret History*, 188. "If the purges were bewildering to a person in my privileged position in Moscow," a secret police defector observed, "they must have been absolutely incomprehensible to the toiling officials and loyal party workers in remote provinces, who suddenly found themselves denounced as secret enemies of the cause they served." Petrov and Petrov, *Empire of Fear*, 78.

268. Iakir and Geller, *Komandarm Iakir*, 211.

269. Petrov and Petrov, *Empire of Fear*, 78.

270. Khaustov and Samuelson, *Stalin, NKVD*, 138–9 (citing TsA FSB, f. 3, op. 5, d. 591, l. 31–3). Rosenholtz (b. 1889) had met with Stalin often over many years as the Soviet representative to the secret negotiations for cooperation with the German military in 1922, a member of the central control commission from 1927, and foreign trade commissar. *Na prieme*, 694.

271. "Agoniia kapitalizma i zadachi Chetvertogo Internatsionala," *Biulleten' oppozitsii*, no. 66 (May–June 1938): 19.

272. Bohlen, *Witness to History*, 51.

273. Ullman, "Davies Mission," 265.

274. Simonov, *Glazami cheloveka*, 54–5.

275. Maria Joffe, the widow of the Soviet diplomat, recounted a story, said to have been told to her by the inventive Radek, about how at the beginning of the 1920s Stalin, in a relaxed state, supposedly said, "The sweetest thing is to devise a plan, then, being on alert, waiting in ambush for a good long time, finding out where the person is hiding. Then catch the person and take revenge!" Another version of this story appears in the memoirs of the widow of Grigory Sokolnikov Joffe, *Odna noch'*, 33–4; Serebriakova, "Iz vospominanii," 241–2.

276. Not just those who had worked with Lenin and knew of his 1922–23 Testament were targeted, such as Trotsky, Kamenev, Zinoviev, Rykov, and Bukharin, but also those who were entirely creatures of Stalin (Kosior, Postyshev, Chubar, Eihe, and Rudzutaks, the loyalist whom Stalin had elevated to replace Zinoviev in the politburo). For a list of Central Committee members and candidate members not destroyed in the terror, see Mawdsley, "An Elite within an Elite," 63.

277. The original end of the antikulak "mass operations" was to have been the second week of Dec.—the precise time of the elections—and in the meantime, functionaries who suddenly would have to stand against competition were writing to the Central Committee apparatus complaining that former "kulaks" might get their names on the ballot. Petrov and

Jansen, *Stalinskii pitomets*, 123; "Demokratiia . . . pod nadzorom NKVD," *Nesizvestnaia Rossiia*, II: 272–81; Khlevniuk, *Politbiuro*, 195. Wendy Goldman asserts that Stalin's speech back at the Feb.–March 1937 plenum "aimed for a ruthless yet limited attack on former oppositionists," but that (pseudo)democratic procedures involving criticism from below wildly expanded the modestly set targets. Goldman, *Terror and Democracy*, 129.

278. Ehrenburg, *Sobranie sochinenii*, IX: 189; Medvedev, "O lichnoi otvestvennosti Stalina za terror," 289–330 (at 289–90). Sholokhov wrote to Stalin (Feb. 6, 1938) requesting that the arrests be checked, for "they are removing not only White Guardists, émigrés, torturers—in a word, those deserving of removal—but genuinely Soviet people." The NKVD evidently arrived to arrest Sholokhov at his home in the village of Veshenskaya. He had fled north to Moscow; Stalin decided to spare him. "'Vokrug menia vse eshche pletut chernuiu Pautinu . . . ': pis'ma M. A. Sholokhova I. V. Stalinu (1937–1950)," 18. See also Murin, "'Prosti, menia, Koba . . . ': neizvestnoe pis'mo N. Bukharina."

279. Shreider, *NKVD iznutri*, 106, 154–7. The case of Shreider (b. 1902) is particularly illuminating, and involves Stanisław Redens, Stalin's brother-in-law and by now the NKVD boss in Kazakhstan, then Beria. Shreider would refuse to confess but get ten years and be dispatched to the Northern Railway construction camps (SveZhelDorlag), where, because he was employed in administrative work, he would survive. Shreider, *NKVD iznutri*, 85–95, 252. Redens was arrested in Nov. 1938 and executed in Jan. 1940.

280. Vernadsky showed considerably more understanding of Soviet realities than most contemporaries: "Millions of prisoners—forced labor, playing a very significant and huge role in the state's economy," he recorded on Jan. 5, 1938. *Sovershenno sekretno*, no. 8 (1990): 10–3; Khlevniuk, *1937–i*, 214–5. See also Prychodko, *One of Fifteen Million*, 21.

281. Fyodor Stebenev, the commissar, speaking to Andrei Vedenin, continued: "I would bet my head that Iosif Vissarionovich [Stalin] does not know. Signals, complaints, protests are being intercepted and not reaching him. We need to get Stalin to know about this. Otherwise ruin. Tomorrow they'll take you, and after you me. We cannot keep quiet." Vedenin, *Gody i liudi*, 55.

282. For the gamut of contemporary (and ongoing) speculations, see Medvedev, *Let History Judge*, 523–601. Then there is the "theory" of a Russian "tradition" of violence. Courtois, "Conclusion: Why?," 728–31.

283. On April 3, 1938, Mironov reported to Frinovsky that 10,728 "conspirators" had been incarcerated. Pavliukov, *Ezhov*, 390; Petrov and Jansen, *Stalinskii pitomets*, 118.

284. Mironov appeared at the Kremlin on New Year's; he would be arrested on Jan. 6, 1939, at the foreign affairs commissariat and executed on the night of Feb. 21–2, 1940.

285. Misshima and Goto, *Japanese View of Outer Mongolia*, 21–2.

286. Coox, *Nomonhan*, 164–5.

287. *Pravda*, March 29, 1937; Getty, *Origins of the Great Purges*, 140. In 1935, the Soviet authorities recorded 340 aircraft "incidents" as well as 54 crashes (in which 88 people died); of these 394 events, fewer than half (163) were investigated as involving possible wrecking, but in 1937–8 everything became wrecking. Khaustov, "Deiatel'nost' organov," 330 (TsA FSB, f. 3, op. 3, d. 1411, l. 255).

288. Zhukov, *Inoi Stalin*, 293. Stalin's Nov. 1936 dismissal of the notion that all former kulaks and White Guardists were enemies

would be republished in the 1939 edition of his *Questions of Leninism*. Stalin, *Voprosy Leninizma*, 531–2.

289. Artizov et al., *Reabilitatsiia: kak eto bylo*, II: 586 (Aug. 1937). Similarly, arrests under article 58-10 (anti-Soviet agitation) had numbered 100,000 in 1931, during peasant rebellion, then fell to 17,000 in 1934, climbed to 230,000 in 1937, and fell to 18,000 in 1940. Davies, "Crime of 'Anti-Soviet Agitation.'"

290. Chuev, *Tak govoril Kaganovich*, 138–9.

291. Kuromiya, *Stalin*, 136. This was a long-standing, self-serving view of Stalin: viz. Nov. 25, 1932, politburo session, RGASPI, f. 17, op. 3, d. 11012.

292. Getty and Naumov, *Road to Terror*, 306.

293. Stalin, polemicizing with Uglanov and the rightists at the politburo (April 22, 1929), continued: "Don't you know what class struggle is, don't you know what class are?" Danilov and Khlevniuk, *Kak Iomali NEP*, IV: 654, 674 (uncorrected transcript); Kuromiya, "Stalin in the Politburo Transcripts," 52.

294. *Pravda*, Oct. 20, 1937.

295. Khaustov, "Deiatel'nost' organov," 48, 52 (APRF, f. 45, op. 1, d. 187, l. 24), 55, 55–6.

296. Baker, "Surveillance of Subversion," 497.

297. Khaustov and Samuelson, *Stalin, NKVD*, 93; Rittersporn, *Anguish*, 39.

298. Khlevniuk, *Master of the House*, 175; RGASPI, f. 558, op. 11, d. 203, l. 62, 77–8. On April 26, 1937, Uritsky, head of military intelligence, had reported to Stalin that "according to your directive a collective of military intelligence operatives wrote a number of articles concerning the organization and methods of work of foreign espionage." (Stalin underlined this passage in pencil.) Seven such articles had already been published; five more were enclosed for final approval; six others awaited completion. Stalin was waiting upon the big article that would be published in *Pravda* on May 4. Khaustov et al., *Lubianka: Stalin i glavnoe upravlenie*, 134–5 (RGASPI, f. 558, op. 11, d. 1594, l. 1). See also "Spy International," *Pravda*, Aug. 21, 1937; RGASPI, f. 558, op. 11, d. 203, l. 62–88, 93–100; Davies and Harris, *Stalin's World*, 60.

299. RGASPI, f. 558, op. 11, d. 203, l. 62, 77–8. When the Soviet press launched saturation coverage of public charges about Soviet inhabitants serving as espionage agents on behalf of Japan, the Japanese embassy conducted thorough checks, verifying that the "confessions" contained lies and were contradicted by the whereabouts on the days in question of those Japanese officials said to be involved. These facts were internally acknowledged by the NKVD, at least early on: on April 2, 1937, NKVD document, for example, admitted that "evidence of the guilt of the arrested is lacking." Khaustov and Samuelson, *Stalin, NKVD*, 47, 48 (TsA FSB, f. 66–1t., op. 30, d. 17, l. 185).

300. Khaustov, "Deiatel'nost' organov," 316 (TsA FSB, f. 8os, op. 1, d. 57–65); Khaustov et al., *Liubianka: Stalin i glavnoe upravlenie*, 659–60 n78 (TsA FSB, 8os, op. 1, d. 80); Plotnikova, "Organy," 160.

301. In March 1938, all Soviet stamp collectors who engaged in correspondence with foreigners were registered. Khaustov, "Deiatel'nost' organov," 305 (TsA FSB, f. 3, op. 4, d. 13, l. 81–4; f. 66, op. 1, d. 460, l. 261). When Yezhov sent Stalin (April 5) an intercepted Japanese ciphered telegram noting that the number of Finnish tourists arriving via Intourist had increased and that their geographical possibilities of travel once inside the USSR had expanded, Stalin had Intourist placed under the NKVD. The decree was not made public. After a Dec. 1938 court case would be opened against Intourist in the United States for espionage activity—it

belonged to the NKVD—Beria would get Stalin's approval to transfer Intourist from the NKVD to the foreign trade commissariat in Jan. 1939. RGASPI, f. 16, op. 163, d. 1207, l. 69–72; Khaustov, "Deiatel'nost' organov," 223–5; Kokurin and Petrov, *Lubianka*, 20. A total of only 100,000 foreigners visited the USSR in the 1920s and 1930s, around 5,000 per year, and their interactions with Soviet inhabitants had become increasingly circumscribed to the point of prohibiting nearly all contact. At peak, between 20,000 and 30,000 foreign-born workers and specialists as returning émigrés were working alongside Soviets in factories and offices in the early 1930s, but by the mid-1930s they would be gone. Lel'chuk and Pivovar, "Mentalitet sovetskogo obshchestva," at 29.

302. Khaustov, "Deiatel'nost' organov," 46 (citing TsA FSB, f. 3, os, op. 6, d. 9, l. 209, 216).

303. Khaustov and Samuelson, *Stalin, NKVD*, 45.

304. When in fall 1937 the USSR had proposed opening two more consulates in Germany (Breslau and Munich), and to bring the total in each country to four by closing three of the seven German consulates, the Germans refused; Stalin ordered the number of German consulates brought down to two. In 1938, all consulates of both countries were shuttered. Adibekov et al., *Politbiuro TsK RKP (b)–VKP (b) i Evropa*, 355, 355n1, n2 (RGASPI, f. 17, op. 162, d. 22, l. 50, 56, 142); DGFP, series D, I: 903–4 (Schulenburg to foreign ministry, Jan. 13, 1938), 904–9 (Schulenburg to foreign ministry, Jan. 17). See also Haslam, *Struggle for Collective Security*, 155; Hilger and Meyer, *Incompatible Allies*, 279.

305. Rittersporn, *Anguish*, 41–2 (citing Plotnikova, "Organy," 70–1), 43 (citing PA AA, MOSKAU I 394: Gestapo to foreign ministry, July 27, 1939; I 393: 275, I 394: foreign ministry to Moscow embassy, May 14, 1939, R 101388: Rosette Eimeke to foreign ministry, March 27, 1940, Abwehr to chief of chancery, Aug. 29, 1940; I 419: Dec. 16, 1937 notes; I 421: July 2, 1938 note); Plotnikova, "Organy," 25.

306. Rittersporn, *Anguish*, 51 (citing BA-MA, RW, 67, 48: 55).

307. Pepłoński, *Wywiad Polski na ZSSR*, 126–7. Stalin was aware that the Polish government sent spies posing as Communist refugees to the USSR, which served to further discredit Moscow-resident foreign Communists in his eyes. The Poles, in turn, were aware that the NKVD recruited Soviet agents among émigrés in Poland, and managed thereby to infiltrate Soviet espionage efforts.

308. Khaustov, "Deiatel'nost' organov," 48.

309. Kozlov, "Pokozatel'i po trudu" (a secret GPU-NKVD file from the Magadan archives). Back in 1936, Japan's Kwantung Army had set up a school to train Koreans for political agitation and espionage assignments on the Soviet side of the border. Nair, *Indian Freedom Fighter*, 141–6.

310. Solov'ev and Chugnuov, *Pogranichnye voiska SSSR*, 8–36.

311. Kuromiya, *Freedom and Terror*, 283–4. See also the story of the Polish agent who crossed the frontier at Baranovichi, was caught by the NKVD, confessed to being a Polish agent, but was beaten to confess to fantastic accusations that were untrue: Cybulski, *Accused*, 455–9.

312. Khaustov, "Deiatel'nost' organov," 316 (TsA FSB, f. 8os, op. 1, d. 57–65); Khaustov et al., *Lubianka: Stalin i glavnoe upravlenie*, 659–60n78 (d. 80).

313. "*All foreign bourgeois specialists are or may be intelligence agents*," Stalin had written to Kaganovich (Aug. 7, 1932). The next year, he had exploded at Kaganovich when he learned that American journalists were

traveling to the famine-stricken Kuban region, noting "there already are many spies in the USSR." Davies et al., *Stalin-Kaganovich Correspondence*, 177; Khlevniuk et al., *Stalin i Kaganovich*, 307.

314. Rzheshevskii and Vehviläinen, *Zimniaia voina*, II: 207. For Stalin's connect-the-dots theory, see also Broide, *Vreditel'stvo*.

315. A Soviet writer has speculated that Stalin simultaneously believed and disbelieved his inventions of plots. Sinyavsky, *Soviet Civilization*, 99, 94.

316. Volkogonov, *Stalin: Politicheskii portret*, I: 263 (on Stalin's notes kept in the Presidential Archive). See also Tucker, *Stalin in Power*, 474 ff; and van Ree, *Political Thought*, 117–25. A fire at Kaganovich's residence spurred Stalin to issue a resolution (April 1937) to the effect that the politburo "considers this fire not an accidental occurrence but one organized by enemies." RGASPI, f. 17, op. 162, d. 21, l. 30.

317. "Fragmenty stenogrammy dekabrskogo plenuma TsK VKP (b) 1936 goda," 6.

318. The year 1937 did not begin on Dec. 1, 1934, contrary to Yevgeniya Ginzburg's famous *bon mot*. Ginzburg, *Into the Whirlwind*, 11.

319. See the letter (Sept. 2, 1936) from Moiseyev (Yershisty), on which Molotov wrote: "To comrade Yezhov: Moiseyev-Yershisty could hardly be troublesome to anybody in Leningrad. I doubt he was justifiably expelled from the VKP (b)." Getty and Naumov, *Road to Terror*, 294–7 (RGASPI, f. 17, op. 120, d. 272, l. 54–5).

320. Chuev, *Sto sorok*, 463.

321. As Conquest wrote, "The nature of the whole purge depends in the last analysis on the personal and political drives of Stalin." Conquest, *Reassessment*, 33.

322. Khlevniuk, *Politbiuro*, 291.

323. Countless examples could be adduced. For ex., when Yezhov sent Stalin a list of people "who were being checked for possible arrest," Stalin wrote on it: "Don't check, arrest." Mironov, "Vosstanovlenie i razvitie Leninskikh printsipov," 19. One scholar has noted that "to attribute events that cost tens of millions of lives to the agency of a few individuals violates historians' sense of proportion, not to speak of theoretical commitments." Pomper, "Historians and Individual Agency." This issue is readily resolved, however, by the distinction between causative agency and collaborative agency. Kotkin, *Magnetic Mountain*.

324. Cherushev, "*Dorogoi nash tovarishch Stalin!*"

325. Suvenirov, *Tragediia RKKA*, 31 (citing RGVA, f. 9, op. 29, d. 318, l. 103: Prokofyev).

326. Mikoian, "V pervyi raz bez Lenina," 6; Chuev, *Tak govoril Kaganovich*, 154; Chuev, *Kaganovich, Shepilov*, 211; Khrushchev, *Vospominaniia*, I: 85–6; Khrushchev, *Memoirs*, I: 79. Although Bukharin grasped that Stalin was evil, he, too, failed to take the full measure of Stalin's enigmatic character. Dan, "Bukharin o Staline," 181–2. See also Nicolaevsky, *Power and the Soviet Elite*, 3–7.

327. *Stalin* (film by Thames Television, London, 1990); Alliluyeva, *Twenty Letters*, 113.

328. Robert Tucker offered the most detailed and thought-through portrait of Stalin as psychopath, which he attributed, among other factors, to Stalin's childhood years. But many of the observations (in memoirs) of Stalin's early years are dubious, while Tucker's clever additional arguments—e.g., that Stalin had a "Lenin complex" and craved the feat of a "second October"—border on reducing to matters of psychology colossal events of geopolitics, Russian historical legacies, and Bolshevik ideas. In less capable hands than Tucker's, the psychologizing gets absurd. A

bastardization of his argument portrays Stalin as a deformed product of his abusive father and overly devoted mother, motivated by unconscious urges, a need to alleviate anxieties arising out of an impaired narcissism (his "core"), and thus fundamentally irrational. Stalin, we are told, identified with "aggressors," and his favorite was Hitler, to whom he was homosexually attracted, and turned his "inner conflict" outward, with murderous results. Rancour-Lafferiere, *Mind of Stalin*.

329. These came not just from the secret police but from such sources as *Pravda* correspondents, forwarded to him by Mekhlis, which presented highly tendentious characterizations of the situation in localities or institutions. Khaustov and Samuelson, *Stalin, NKVD*, 153.

330. "We knew exactly by whom and where anti-Soviet conversations were conducted, badmouthing Stalin," recalled one NKVD operative of those years. "We opened dossiers [*formuliary*] on everyone." Kirillina, "Vystrely v Smol'nom," 73 (Popov).

331. Rudzutaks, for example, an erstwhile deputy chairman of the Council of People's Commissars, regaled cellmates with how during the early civil war Lenin had informed him he was being assigned to the Southern Front, where he would be working with Stalin. Rudzutaks had quickly affirmed his readiness to carry out the assignment, but Lenin, according to Rudzutaks, warned him it would be difficult: Stalin was an unscrupulous intriguer. Vladimir Khaustov, personal communication (Dec. 2012), referring to material in the APRF. Khlevniuk speculates that Stalin knew he was not held in high regard by those who knew earlier times. Khlevniuk, *Khoziain*, 303–4.

332. Alliluyeva, *Twenty Letters*, 78. As an illustration, see the summer 1938 incident involving the Communist Youth League chief Alexander Kosaryov, as described by his widow, when Stalin clinked glasses with and kissed Kosaryov, then is said to have whispered in his ear, "If you're a traitor, I'll kill you." Kosaryov was arrested. Medvedev, *Let History Judge*, 595 (citing an unpublished memoir).

333. Volkogonov, *Stalin: Triumph and Tragedy*, 318. One scholar has elaborated a so-called dictator's dilemma: the more powerful, the less he can trust his minions who claim to be loyal. Wintrobe, *Political Economy of Dictatorship*, 335–7. See also Harrison, *Guns and Rubles*, 7.

334. The Kremlin physicians Dmitry Pletnev and Lev Levin (executed in 1938) were said to have arrived at the diagnosis of paranoia, but Levin was an internist and Pletnev a heart specialist, and they appear to have diagnosed Stalin with a heart condition and gall bladder ailment. Valedinskii, "Organizm Stalina vpolne zdorovyi." For the hearsay, see Volski and Souvarine, "Un Caligula à Moscou," 16; Souvarine, *Staline* (1977), 582. Superficial psychologizing about dictators is rampant: Glad, "Why Tyrants Go Too Far." Rees, writing of Stalin, sought to distinguish between "criminal psychopaths," who tend to be impulsive, reckless, and "Machiavellian psychopaths," who are calculating, organized, determined, untroubled by self-doubt, audacious and often rise to the top of organizations. Rees, *Iron Lazar*, 218–22. See also

Kovalevskii, *Psikhiatricheskie eskizy iz istorii*, III: 65–75 (on Ivan the Terrible). Stalin's self-control was duly noted by Conquest, Roy Medvedev, and many others. See Bullock, *Hitler and Stalin*, 494. One scholar has rightly observed that "the precise proportions of political calculation and psychological derangement that drove Stalin to these extreme measures will always be a matter of speculation." Rieber, "Stalin as Foreign Policy Maker," 142–3.

335. Rybin, *Riadom so Stalinym*, 76.

336. Molotov later admitted that he and Stalin knew the secret police exaggerated the supposed threat, but Molotov did not admit that Stalin relentlessly pressured the police to do so. Chuev, *Molotov*, 466, 473–5.

337. Rees, *Political Thought from Machiavelli to Stalin*, 237–47.

338. Machiavelli, *Gosudar'*; Tucker, *Stalin as Revolutionary*, 315; Tucker, *Stalin in Power*, 282. Others denied Machiavelli's influence on Stalin: Souvarine, *Stalin*, 563, 583. Volkogonov claims he saw Stalin's copy of Machiavelli: Volkogonov, *Triumf i tragediia*, II/1: 107. Nikolai Ryzhkov, Soviet prime minister under Gorbachev, claims he read Stalin's underlined copy of Machiavelli: "To tell the truth, the book with its markings gave me a thousand times greater understanding of the personality of Stalin than all the biographies, all the films, about him, all the recollections of his friends and enemies." Ryzhkov made off with it. Ryzhkov, *Perestroika*, 354–6. The underlinings, in Russian, are: "Neestestvenno, chtoby vooruzhenyi stal okhotno pokoriat'sia nevooruzhenomu"; "Bez boiazni mogut byt' Gosudari zhestokimi v voennoe vremia."

339. Volubuev and Kuleshov, *Ochishchenie*, 146.

340. Volkogonov, *Stalin: Triumph and Tragedy*, 267.

341. In the discussion of Augustus Octavian in Samuil Lozinskii's *History of the Ancient World: Greece and Rome* (Petrograd, 1923), Stalin underlined "first citizen, prince . . . supreme ruler." Volubuev and Kulsheov, "Istoriia ne terpit polupravdy."

342. Van Ree, *Political Thought*, 258–61.

343. Discussion of statecraft was almost entirely absent from Marx's voluminous writings. He had begun from the premise that the state did not possess interests of its own but incarnated class interests; those class interests were, therefore, the main object of analysis. Marx saw no need to subject the state's institutions and procedures—which differ significantly from country to country—to careful analysis. True, the phenomenon of Napoleon III in France provoked a change of heart in Marx, but not a full-fledged rethinking. Marx, *Eighteenth Brumaire*, 130–1; *Civil War in France*, 42. Engels had famously added the idea that after the proletarian revolution, as class contradictions were overcome, the state would "wither away." Lenin, initially, had also concurred that the state was an instrument of class oppression and would wither away (*State and Revolution* [1903]), but then changed his mind, albeit without managing to fill the theoretical gap.

344. van Ree, *Political Thought*, 135–8, 258.

345. RGASPI, f. 558, op. 3, d. 143, l. 372, 382, 424, 438.

346. RGASPI, f. 558, op. 3, d. 202, l. 21.

347. Medvedev, *Let History Judge*, 551–3; Brzezinski, *Permanent Purge*, 168.

348. Isaac Deutscher would imagine that Stalin ordered the purges to prevent "the managerial groups from consolidating as a social stratum," which could indeed have been part of Stalin's thinking. But Deutscher remained under the spell of Stalin's supposed special targeting of the Old Bolsheviks. Deutscher, *Prophet Outcast*, 306–7. It has been asserted with no evidence that young, aggressive new administrative cadres themselves pushed for the terror, being envious of the old guard Leninists. Voslensky, *Nomenklatura* (1984), 53–5, (1980), 82–6.

349. *Stalinskie rasstrel'nye spiski*.

350. Khlevniuk, "Economic Officials in the Great Terror," 39.

351. Chuev, *Molotov Remembers*, 167.

352. Chalaia, *Oboronnaia dramaturgiia*, 3. See also Kuleshova, "'Bol'shoi den'"; Kuznetsova, "Esli zavtra voina"; and Scott, *Behind the Urals*, 197–203 (about the play "Witness Confrontation"). Iu. Olesha and A. Macheret would adapt *Confrontation* for the big screen as *The Mistakes of Engineer Kochin*, which would premiere on Dec. 14, 1939 (Mosfilm).

353. Uldricks, "Impact of the Great Purges," 188–92; Haslam, *Struggle for Collective Security*, 130.

354. Khaustov and Samuelson, *Stalin, NKVD*, 184. Several of the agents who had been assigned to Sedov were diverted to hunt down Soviet NKVD personnel abroad.

355. Mekhlis's response was to denounce Voroshilov to Stalin for impeding the destruction of additional "enemies." Rubtsov, *Marshaly Stalina*, 50–1 (Ivan Ilichev report to Mekhlis; Mekhlis letter to Stalin, Nov. 20, 1938).

356. Primakov, *Ocherki*, III: 17.

357. Pavel Alliluyev (Stalin's brother-in-law), Georgy Savchenko, Dmitry Pavlov, Kirill Meretskov, and Grigory Kulik supposedly sent a petition to Voroshilov that further arrests threatened the Red Army with disintegration. No such letter has been seen, only Pavlov's testimony, under torture, in July 1941 before he was shot. The letter seems to have been written in summer 1938. (Alliluyev died Nov. 2, 1938, in his Moscow office, unexpectedly, the day after returning from a holiday down south.) "Kulik was the main author of the text," Pavlov was recorded as testifying. "We sent it to Voroshilov but his secretariat informed us that the people's commissar would not even read our letter and requested us to withdraw it. At this Kulik called us together on a Sunday. We made some changes to the letter and sent it to the General Secretary of the Central Committee with a copy to Voroshilov. The letter argued that the main forces of the counterrevolution had already been liquidated within the army yet the arrest of its commanders continued. Indeed, to such an extent that the army might start to disintegrate . . . We believed that the Government would reduce the arrests." Bobrenev and Riazantsev, *Palachi i zhertvi*, 182–3, 186–91.

358. "The whole period of the purges was one of disillusionment and revulsion, the intensity of which, I suppose, accounted for my previous enthusiasm," confessed E. H. Carr. Cox, *E. H. Carr*, xviii.

CHAPTER 9. MISSING PIECE

1. Ehrenburg, *Memoirs*, 421; Ehrenburg, *Sobranie sochinenii*, IX: 183.

2. Khrushchev, *Khrushchev Remembers*, 314.

3. Yezhov also ordered the NKVD secretariat to reduce the number of "workers" and "collective farmers" in reported arrest statistics.

Khaustov and Samuelson, *Stalin, NKVD*, 279. This is hardly the only falsification in arrest statistics.

4. Pavliukov, *Ezhov*, 416 (citing RGASPI, f. 671, op. 1, d. 271, l. 708).

5. He sometimes also got drunk at a safe house, on Gogol Boulevard, before heading

out for "exercise" at Lefortovo. Petrov and Jansen, *Stalinskii pitomets*, 139.

6. Rees, "The People's Commissariat of Water Transport," 235–61.

7. In March 1938, Malenkov ordered all leading party organs urgently, not later than the fifteenth of that month, to prepare lists of

their members and candidate members who were "Poles, Germans, Latvians, Estonians, Finns, Lithuanians, Bulgarians, Greeks, Koreans, Chinese, Japanese, Turks, Iranians, English, French, Italian, Hungarians," and to indicate their place of employment as well as nationality and citizenship. Golubev, "*Esli mir obrushitsia na nashu Respubliku,*" 82 (citing TsAODM, f. 3, op. 50, d. 74, l. 7).

8. Pavliukov, *Ezhov*, 348–9.

9. Conquest, *Reassessment*, 57.

10. Zakovsky was a drinker, and Yezhov's notes on him refer to conversations about Stalin. Pavliukov, *Ezhov*, 441.

11. Petrov and Jansen, *Stalinskii pitomets*, 151 (TsA FSB, f. 3–os, op. 6, d. 3, l. 6: testimony of Frinovsky's son).

12. Shreider, *NKVD iznutri*, 43. Karutsky shot himself on May 13, 1938. Zakovsky, demoted to the Kuibyshev hydroelectric station, an NKVD object, and arrested there, was executed on Aug. 29, 1938, as an "agent of Polish and German counter-espionage." Stalin had Zakovsky blamed for arrests that supposedly ruined the naval shipbuilding program, an unwitting admission of the deadly effect of the terror on war preparation. Khaustov and Samuelson, *Stalin, NKVD*, 242–3 (APRF, f. 3, op. 58, d. 254a, l. 1).

13. Pavliukov, *Ezhov*, 412.

14. Pavliukov, *Ezhov*, 411–3; Petrov and Jansen, *Stalinskii pitomets*, 170 (TsA FSB, f. 3os, op. 6, d. 3, l. 83). Yezhov would later claim, "I have known Yevdokimov, it seems, since 1934. I considered him a party man, verified. I visited him at his apartment, he visited me at my dacha." But "by my own denunciation to the Central Committee he was removed from his post" in the NKVD. "Poslednee slovo N.I. Ezhova na sudebnom protsesse, 3 fevralia 1940 goda": http://www.perpetrator2004.narod.ru/documents/Yezhov/Yezhov.htm

15. Khaustov and Samuelson, *Stalin, NKVD*, 311 (TsA FSB, ASD p-4000, t. 7, l. 83–6).

16. Khaustov and Samuelson, *Stalin, NKVD*, 319.

17. Khlevniuk, *1937-i*, 67; Starkov, "Narkom Ezhov," 21–39 (at 37–8).

18. Popov and Oppokov, "Berievshchina" (1990, no. 1), 69.

19. According to his son, Beria speculated that Stalin had Persian blood and compared him to Shah Abbas I [1571–1629], the ruler of Persia's Safavid dynasty. (In 1587, a teenage Abbas had shoved aside his weak father, taking over a divided, nearly failed state, then went on to break the power and confiscate the wealth of the provincial chiefs, and fashion an imperial power that stretched from the Caucasus to the Tigris to the Indus and was distinguished by robust diplomatic relations and flourishing arts and architecture.) This might have been a Beria self-image. Beria, *My Father*, 21, 284.

20. Mikoian, *S liubov'iu i pechal'iu*, 27–8, 31–3; Mikoian, *Svoimi glazami*, 33–4, 36–40.

21. Khaustov and Samuelson, *Stalin, NKVD*, 57–8. Nami Mikoyan's father would soon be arrested.

22. In Armenia, his replacement had been Khachik Moughdousi [Astvatsaturov], a Beria loyalist.

23. Popov and Oppokov, "Berievshchina" (1990, no. 1), 69. Tsaturov was arrested in Oct. 1937 but would survive.

24. Stepanyan also wrote about the absence of Leninist party democracy under Stalin. Aganian, *Nersik Stepanian*, 40, 49–50 (citing Arianskii filial IML, f. 4033, op. 6, d. 312, l. 1–6); Matossian, *Impact of Soviet Policies*, 129; *Revoliutsionnyi vostok*, 1936, no. 4: 50. In April 1936 and again in Sept., Lyudmila Yanushevskaya, the wife of Semyon Sef, head of the party's culture-propaganda department in

Tblisi, told people that Sef, not Beria, was the author of the work. Word reached Yezhov, who launched an investigation with interviews of witnesses. On Aug. 16, 1936, Yezhov wrote on the resolution: "Give me the material." Another report from a participant, written Oct. 22, 1936, after Yezhov had been named head of the NKVD, was less categorical, as if Yezhov had merely wanted to gather and hold the compromising material on Beria. (Sef and his wife were expelled from the party.) Sokolov, *Beriia*, 98–105.

25. Aganian, *Nersik Stepanian*, 52 (citing Arianskii filial IML, f. 1, d. 35, l. 98–9).

26. The bodyguards were detained but released after a month and a half. Sokolov, *Beriia*, 108–20.

27. Antonov-Ovseenko, *Beriia*, 92–6; Artsuni, "Samoubiistvo A. G. Khandzhiana"; Gazarian, "Etno ne dolzhno povtorit'sia" (no. 2), 65. After Beria's destruction in 1953, witnesses came forward to charge him with shooting Khanjyan in his (Beria's) office, then having the body somehow delivered past the bodyguards to Khanjyan's room. The Armenian head of the typist pool of the South Caucasus secretariat (Sushannik Safaryan) would testify that she was carrying the bureau-meeting typescript to Beria, gently pushed open his office door a bit, caught a glimpse of a man lying on the carpet, and quickly retreated. In 1961, KGB chief Shelepin concluded that Beria had killed Khanjyan in his (Beria's) office. The idea that the experienced operative Beria—with members of the Moscow Central Control Commission in the next room—would shoot Khanjyan in his own office raises more questions than it answers. "Sovetskie praviteli Armenii"(Jan. 2009): http://www.noev-kovcheg.ru/mag/2009–01/1499.html; *Izvestiia*, Oct. 28, 1961; Medvedev, *Let History Judge*, 413, 624–5.

28. http://www.noev-kovcheg.ru/mag/2009–01/1499.html#ixzz23qnzhqky. See also Aganian, *Nersik Stepanian*, 52–3.

29. *Zaria vostoka*, July 11, 1936; *Pravda* [Armenia], July 12, 1936.

30. Tzitzernak, "Aghassi Khanjian."

31. *Zaria vostoka*, July 20, 1936.

32. In Georgia between 1932 and 1936, the combined print run of all writings by Marx—in both Russian and Georgian—had totaled 20,000; those of Lenin, 200,000; those of Stalin, 696,000; those of Beria, 430,000. Toptygin, *Neizvestnyi Beriia*, 41. Beria's *Lado Ketskhoveli* (1937), which celebrated Stalin's martyred mentor in Marxism, was evidently plagiarized from the manuscript of L. Shengelaya, a copy of which had entered the Tiflis Affiliate of the Marxism-Leninism Institute in Sept. 1935. Here, too, Beria emulated the master. Sukharev, "Litsedeistvo," 112 (citing PA IIP pri TsK KPSS, f. 8, op. 1, d. 39, l. 23).

33. After Papuliya's arrest, Orjonikidze summoned the Azerbaijan party boss Bagirov to Kislovodsk. "Orjonikidze drilled me about Beria, and spoke of him very negatively," Bagirov would later testify. "In particular, Orjonikidze said that he couldn't believe in the guilt of his brother Papuliya . . . Beria learned through his own people that Orjonikidze had summoned me to Kislovodsk, and he asked me the reasons for it over the telephone." Shariya would testify: "I knew that on the surface Beria thought well of Orjonikidze, but in fact he said all manner of despicable things about him to his circle of confidants." Goglidze would testify: "Beria in my presence and that of others made sharp, deprecatory comments about Sergo Orjonikidze . . . I formed the impression that Beria said that as a result of some personal grudge against Orjonikidze and set others against him."

Nekrasov, *Beria*, 360; Popov and Oppokov, "Berievshchina," 1991, no. 1: 50.

34. Hoover Archives, Lakoba papers, 2–26 (speech to Sukhum city soviet, Jan. 1, 1936). *Pravda* on March 4, 1936, celebrated fifteen years of Soviet power in Abkhazia with a front-page photo of Lakoba, alongside Stalin, Orjonikidze, and Mikoyan, from 1927, which was said to have come from Stalin's private collection. No functionary—especially Beria—could miss a Kremlinological signal so immense, and for a place so small, a mere autonomous republic. Lakoba did not get to claim an article himself; instead, an article ("Itogi bor'ba i pobed") was printed under the byline of Agrba, Abkhaz party secretary (*Pravda* was a party paper). In 1935 or 1936 Beria moved from an apartment building to a mansion at Machabeli St. 11. He also used a white stucco villa in Gagra, near Stalin's villa. Harriman and Abel, *Special Envoy*, 511–2 .

35. An opportunity for Beria's pressure came with the suicide, in 1935 or 1936, of the daughter of the foreign trade commissar Rosenholtz at Lakoba's dacha in Gagra. At the time Beria was at his own dacha in Gagra, and there was a suspicion he had had sexual intercourse with her. In fact, she had sexual relations that day, but earlier, in the city, at the hotel where she was staying. In Gagra by invitation, she had supper with the host and others, then retired for the night and shot herself with one of Lakoba's guns. Beria either could not manage or chose not to mount a case against Lakoba. Popov and Oppokov, "Berievshchina" (1991, no. 1), 47–8.

36. Abbas-ogly, *Ne mogu zabyt'*; Abbas-ogly, *Moia Abkhaziia, moia sud'ba*.

37. Musto, "Pistolet ili iad?": http://www.hrono.ru/statii/2004/musto_yad.html. Once, it was said, in 1935, when Beria had used foul language in the presence of women, Mikhail Lakoba, Nestor's half-brother, had put a Brauning to Beria's temple. Rayfield, *Stalin and His Hangmen*, 294 (no citation).

38. Lakoba, "'Ia Koba, a ty Lakoba,'" 74.

39. Lakoba, "'Ia Koba, a ty Lakoba,'" 67. See also the hearsay in reminiscences by Musto Dkhikhasvili, "Konkurenty" (http://www.hrono.ru/statii/2004/musto_konkur.html). Musto writes that he did not attend the funeral in protest; photos show him as a pallbearer. Dimitrov's diary notes (Dec. 12, 1936) "with Lakoba and his wife." Banac, *Diary of Georgi Dimitrov*, 41.

40. Lakoba had to obtain formal permission from the local party bureau to travel to Tiflis at Beria's summons; permission was granted by telephone poll to him and M. Gobechiya on Dec. 25, 1936. Marykhuba, *Moskovskie arkhivnye*, 8 (citing RGASPI, f. 17, op. 8, d. 97, l. 217–8).

41. By some accounts, Anastas Engelov, the Abkhaz plenipotentiary in Tblisi, assisted Lakoba in the walk to the hotel because Lakoba's driver, as instructed, was waiting back at the hotel. Engelov would be executed in connection with the Nov. 1937 trial of Lakoba-ites.

42. Minchenok, "Nestor i ten'." Beria arrived at the hotel with South Caucasus NKVD chief Goglidze and, evidently, German Mgaloblishvili, chairman of the Georgian Council of People's Commissars. (Mgaloblishvili might have attended the theater with Lakoba and been at the hotel already.) Two Georgian NKVD operatives were already on the scene (including Kobulov), where the deceased Lakoba lay on the bed.

43. On April 26, 1935, the politburo in Moscow had discussed Lakoba's health, and directed him to observe physicians' instructions and enter the Kremlin hospital. The Kremlin doctors had recommended that Lakoba cut his workday down to four hours for a few

weeks, observe a proper diet (including reducing meat consumption), refrain from smoking and drinking alcohol, engage in physical therapy, and apply cream and ointments. Marykhuba, *Moskovskie arkhivnye*, 23–4 (citing RGASPI, f. 17, op. 3, d. 971, l. 12); Hoover Archives, Lakoba papers, 1–7, Sept. 16, 1935.

44. Marykhuba, *Moskovskie arkhivnye*, 8 (citing RGASPI, f. 17, op. 8, d. 97, l. 215: Dec. 29, 1936).

45. *Pravda* reported the death that day (Dec. 29).

46. Medvedev, *Let History Judge*, 624.

47. This started with Mgaloblishvili, whom Beria had chosen to lead the honor guard accompanying Lakoba's casket home from Tblisi and who was arrested for "ties." Popov and Oppokov, "Berievshchina" (1991, no. 1), 48–9. The story goes that Beria's men beat Sarie to testify that Lakoba had wanted to sell Abkhazia to Turkey; she evidently refused, even when they beat her fourteen-year-old son Rauf in front of her. She was said to have died of torture in her cell. Medvedev, *Let History Judge*, 495–6.

48. Coincidentally or not, after Lakoba's demise, Stalin would not return to the Caucasus on a holiday for nine years. In 1937, the alphabet for writing the Abkhaz language would be changed to Georgian. On Dec. 16, 1936, the Abkhaz party bureau discussed an order to switch from the Latin to the Georgian alphabet (when elsewhere in the Union the Latin alphabet was being replaced by Cyrillic); all-new printing presses and typewriters would be required. Georgian peasants received land grants to settle on the Abkhaz coast, and Abkhaz language radio broadcasts were discontinued. Marykhuba, *Moskovskie arkhivnye*, 9 (citing RGASPI, f. 17, op. 8, d. 105, l. 16–7); *Abkhazia*, 4. (The Abkhaz would switch to Cyrillic in 1954.)

49. Guruli and Tushurashvili, *Correspondence*, 64 (Aug. 4, 1937), 67–8 (Aug. 16, 1937), 69–70 (Aug. 16, 1937).

50. Beria promised documentation if necessary to testify to the supervision of lower level party organizations. Guruli and Tushurashvili, *Correspondence*, 29–30.

51. Mlechin, *KGB*, 199 (diary of Alexander G. Solovyov).

52. Popov and Oppokov, "Berievshchina" (1990, no. 5), 85 (testimony of Malik Dotsenko, citing Litvin).

53. Popov and Oppokov, "Berievshchina" (1990, no. 5), 86–7. (Yezhov's holiday was 1931–2.) Khrushchev recalled going out with Malenkov to Yezhov's Meshcherino dacha and finding Beria there. Khrushchev, *Vospominaniia*, I: 180.

54. Beria raised his own status by noting that "Georgia, Armenia, and Azerbaijan are objects of especially heightened work of the imperialist powers"—a self-award of carte blanche to go after his enemies. Kosheleva et al., "Materialy fevral'-martovskogo plenuma TsK VKP (b) 1937 goda" (1995, no. 5–6): 8–13.

55. Popov and Oppokov, "Berievshchina" (1989, no. 7), 86 (Goglidze).

56. Nekrasov, *Beria*, 367.

57. In Sept. 1937, Orakhelashvili was said to have testified: "In my presence, in Sergo Orjonikidze's apartment, Beso Lominadze, after a number of counterrevolutionary slurs aimed at the party leadership, made an exceptionally insulting and hooliganistic slur against comrade Stalin. To my surprise, in response to this counterrevolutionary audacity by Lominadze, Orjonikidze, smiling, turned to me and said, 'Have a look at him!' And continued to conduct the conversation with Lominadze in a calm tone . . . In general I have to say that the parlor in Sergo Orjonikidze's

apartment and, on days off, at his dacha (first in Volynskoe, then in Sosnovka) was a frequent meeting place for members of our counterrevolutionary organization, which, while waiting for Seergo Orjonikidze to arrive, conducted the most candid counterrevolutionary conversations, which continued right on after Orjonikidze himself showed up." Nekrasov, *Beria*, 78. See also Knight, *Beria*, 83. As her husband had his eyes gouged out and eardrums perforated, Orakhelashvili's wife, Maria, Georgia's commissar of enlightenment, was compelled to watch.

58. Ginzburg, "O gibeli Sergo Ordzhonikidze," 91–2. Beria's minion Goglidze would later admit the obvious: such "testimony" compromising Orjonikidze had been intended to please Stalin. Nekrasov, *Beria*, 360; Popov and Oppokov, "Berievshchina" (1991, no. 1), 55; Nekrasov, *Beria*, 378–9.

59. At the Pyatakov trial Mdivani was accused of plotting to kill Yezhov and Beria. *Report of Court Proceedings*, 74. Toroshelidze, former head of the Georgian Affiliate of the Institute of Marx-Engels-Lenin, was also arrested in Oct. 1936.

60. Khaustov and Samuelson, *Stalin, NKVD*, 113. Nadezhda Lukina, Bukharin's first wife, had written to Stalin on Aug. 23, 1936, the day of the verdict against Kamenev and Zinoviev, claiming that during Kirov's Red Square funeral Kamenev had smiled at Mdivani ("I simply could not keep myself from writing you"). RGASPI, f. 558, op. 11, d. 710, l. 135–6.

61. *Zaria vostoka*, May 27, 1937; *Pravda*, June 5, 1937.

62. Guruli and Tushurashvili, *Correspondence*, 53–5. On police-reported gossip in Georgia, see Junge and Bonwetsch, *Bolshevistskii poriadok*, II: 69–72 (Arkhiv MVD Gruzii, 2–I otdel, f. 14, op. 11, d. 244, l. 19–22).

63. Beria's telegram to Stalin noted that Mezenin's superior in Moscow, Alexander Nikitin, had sent a telegram tasking the correspondent with delivering sharply critical information, and that Nikitin had twice phoned Meznin to render his reportage still sharper. Nikitin (b. 1901) would be named editor of *Komsomolskaya Pravda* in Aug. 1937 and head of the Central Committee press department in Jan. 1938, arrested on Sept. 3, 1939 (under Beria), and executed in July 1941.

64. Avalishvili, "'Great Terror.'" May 29, 1937, would be Ilya Chavchavadze's 100th jubilee, and Beria telegrammed Stalin eight days prior to request permission to re-publish Stalin's poetry from 1896 (some of which Chavchavadze's journal had published). Stalin refused. Guruli and Tushurashvili, *Correspondence*, 46.

65. Nekrasov, *Beria*, 242–3. Mikoyan would recall that Beria's role in Musavat was discussed at a Central Committee plenum in 1937. Naumov, *Lavrentii Beriia, 1953*, 165–6; Antonov-Ovseenko, *Beriia*, 19.

66. Khrushchev, *Vospominaniia*, I: 253–4. See also Kvashonkin, *Sovetskoe rukovodstvo*, 374 (RGASPI, f. 73, op. 2, d. 19, l. 49–50, Kaganovich to Stalin, Sept. 20, 1937).

67. Kaminskii, *Grigorii Kaminsky*; "Grigorii Naumovich Kaminskii."

68. Pavliukhhov, *Ezhov*, 296–7. Kaminsky supposedly told his wife on the morning of June 25 that he might not return home from the plenum; he is said to have already removed all documents from his safe and desk at the commissariat, prompting his assistant to ask if he was being transferred. Zhavaronkov and Pariiskii, "Skazavshii budet uslyshan," 200–3 (quoting the recollections of Karmanova, his deputy in the health commissariat, and the writer Aleksandra Bentsianova, neither of whom attended the plenum), 209 (quoting I. I. Mukhovoz).

69. *Afanas'ev, Oni ne molchali*, 204 (Svetlana Kaminskaya). Kaminsky had been perhaps the sole Soviet journalist on the ground in Germany in fall 1923 reporting objectively that the Comintern efforts to instigate a seizure of power were disastrous. Lozhechko, *Grigorii Kaminskii*.

70. *Afanas'ev, Oni ne molchali*, 210–1 (Kaminskaya).

71. The sentence was carried out Feb. 10, 1938, at Yagoda's former dacha (Kommunarka).

72. "Ochen' vysoko tsenit t. Beria," 163–5 (APRF, f. 45, op. 1, d. 788, l. 114–5ob; RGASPI, f. 558, op. 11, d. 788, l. 114–16ob, June 25, 1937). Tite Lordkipanidze, a former head of the South Caucasus secret police, was arrested on June 22, 1937, along with several subordinates, in the Crimea autonomous republic; he was sentenced to execution on Sept. 14, 1937, and shot fifteen days later.

73. Already back on Oct. 21, 1933, Stalin had written to Kaganovich: "Pavlunovsky destroyed the artillery. Orjonikidze has been given a scolding for having trusted two or three of his favorites. He was ready to give state benefits to these imbeciles." Stalin to Kaganovich, RGASPI, f. 81, op. 3, d. 100, l. 38–9. Pavlunovsky would be shot on Oct. 30, 1937.

74. Already during his 1920s police work rooting out Menshevik sympathies, Beria had begun collecting dossiers on literary figures, musicians, and university personnel. Rayfield, *Stalin and His Hangmen*, 299.

75. *Pravda*, Jan. 15, 1937; *Literaturnaia gazeta*, Jan. 5 and 10, 1937. The central regime awarded 3 million additional rubles for new apartments for artists of the Georgian National Opera and Ballet Theater, 700,000 for the theater's refurbishment, 1 million to build a concert hall in the Tblisi conservatory, and half a million to refurbish its building. Gatagova et al., *TsK RKP (b)—VKP (b) i natsional'nyi vopros*, II: 212–3 (RGASPI, f. 17, op. 3, d. 983, l. 28: Jan. 14, 1937).

76. Akhmeteli was executed on June 27, 1937. Urushadze, *Sandro Akhmeteli*, 250–1, 266–70. On Akhmeteli's theater, see also Rayfield, *Literature of Georgia*, 213–4.

77. Rayfield, "Death of Paolo Iashvili," 635–6.

78. Akhmeteli had been scathing toward fellow Georgian writers, whom he accused of giving in to political pressure; they now shrank from defending his name. Rayfield, "Death of Paolo Iashvili," 655n23.

79. Zelinskii, "V iune 1954 goda," 82–3.

80. According to the recollections of Semyon Chikovani, who carefully listed all the people who had been present. (Interview with Lasha Bakradze, director of the Georgian Literary Museum, who read out Chikovani's Georgian-language memoir to me.) By other accounts, after Yashvili shot himself, Javakhishvili muttered, "He was a real man, he was a real man." Be that as it may, four days later, the writers voted approval of a resolution condemning "Javakhishvili as an enemy of the people, spy and diversant [who] is to be expelled . . . and physically annihilated." One friend, Geronti Kikodze, had the courage to walk out (and he would survive). Rayfield, "Death of Paolo Iashvili," 660; Rayfield, *Stalin and His Hangmen*, 344; Rayfield, *Literature of Georgia*, 269.

81. Pasternak, *Essay in Autobiography*, 110; Rayfield, "Pasternak and the Georgians"; Rayfield, *Literature of Georgia*, 247. Beria also stripped Tblisi University of its professors, including the papyrologist and classical scholar Grigol Tsereteli.

82. Rayfield, "Death of Paolo Iashvili," 636, 647; Rayfield, *Literature of Georgia*, 247. Countless others were executed, including Dimitri Shevardnadze, a painter who had established the country's national gallery in

1920 (and had co-designed the emblem of Georgia's Mensevik-dominated republic of 1918–1921); he had led opposition to a proposal by Beria to tear down Tbilisi's ancient Metekhi Church (which would survive).

83. Guruli and Tushurashvili, *Correspondence*, 16–9, 20 (Mikoyan and Beria to Stalin Jan. 5, 1937). These are documents from the former Communist Party Archive, Georgian Affiliate of the Institute of Marxism-Leninism, Tbilisi (f. 14, op. 11, korobka 18, d. 152: telegrammy, poslannye na imia sekretaria TsK VKP [b] tov. Stalina).

84. Beria had asked Molotov for 33,000 more tons, and received an answer from Molotov's aid (Antipov) that Georgia would have to make do within its existing allocation. Guruli and Tushurashvili, *Correspondence*, 31 (Feb. 4, 1937), 40 (May 5, 1937), 47–8 (May 22, 1937).

85. Guruli and Tushurashvili, *Correspondence*, 41–5 (May 9, 1937).

86. Guruli and Tushurashvili, *Correspondence*, 61–3 (Beria to Stalin and Molotov, July 31, 1937).

87. Guruli and Tushurashvili, *Correspondence*, 58–9, 66, 73–5 (Sept. 1, 1937). In Sept. 1937 Beria wrote to Stalin asking for additional kerosene, complaining of severe shortages and queues because of central cutbacks in supplies to the republic. Demand, he wrote, was increasing as a result of the return of students to Tbilisi and provincial capitals for the academic year. In Oct. 1937, he wrote to Stalin and Molotov about failures to deliver planned supplies of gasoline, complaining that the Azerbaijan oil distribution company was sending Georgia's allotments to Moscow. Guruli and Tushurashvili, *Correspondence*, 76–7, 88–9.

88. Zen'kovich, *Marshaly i genseki*, 194–5. See also Kremlev, *Beriia*, 84–5.

89. Khaustov et al., *Lubianka: Stalin i glavnoe upravlenie*, 252–5 (APRF, f. 3, op. 24, d. 315, l. 24–42).

90. *Zaria vostoka*, July 11, 1937; Conquest, *Reassessment*, 225. There is a story that Mdivani told his interrogators at Metekhi: "Being shot is not enough punishment for me; I need to be quartered! It was me who brought the 11th Army here. I betrayed my people and helped Stalin and Beria, these degenerates, enslave Georgia and bring Lenin's party to its knees." Antonov-Ovseenko, *Beriia*, 27.

91. The trial was staged Sept. 24, 1937, in Batum's House of the Red Army. Junge and Bonwetsch, *Bol'shevistskii poriadok*, II: 293–9 (Arkhiv MVD Gruzii, 2–i otdel, f. 14, op. 11, d. 106, l. 61–6).

92. The trial took place on Nov. 3, 1937, in the Drama Theater. RGANI, f. 89, op. 48, d. 5; APRF, Volkogonov papers, Hoover, container 27; *Abkhazia*, 433–40. See also Delba, "Besposhchadno borot'sia s vragami naroda," 427–30. See also *Sovetskaia Abkhazia*, Nov. 3, 1937; Marykhuba, *Moskovskie arkhivnye*, 12–5, 26–7 (RGASPI, f. 17, op. 18, d. 104, l. 15–7; op. 3, d. 993, l. 3).

93. Guruli and Tushurashvili, *Correspondence*, 71–2. See also *Zaria vostoka*, Aug. 26, 1937.

94. *Ocherki istorii Kommunisticheskoi partii Armenii*, 387; Artizov et al., *Reabilitatsiia: kak eto bylo*, II: 586. On Aug. 19, 1937, Sahak Ter-Gabrielyan, former head of the Armenian Council of People's Commissars, died, apparently throwing himself out the fourth floor window of the Lubyanka. For another version, see Matossian, *Impact of Soviet Policies*, 158.

95. Agrba would be executed April 21, 1938. Zakhar Suleimanovich Agrba, the director of the Abkhaz theater, was also arrested and executed.

96. Mikoian, *Tak bylo*, 583.

97. *Ocherki istorii Kommunisticheskoi partii Armenii*, 387; Tucker, *Stalin in Power*, 488–9.

98. Blauvelt, "March of the Chekists." Beria wrote to Stalin to request authorization to strengthen defenses on the border with Turkey, reacting quickly after a central decree had ordered such strengthening in Central Asia on the borders with Iran and Afghanistan. Beria understood not to push too far: in one draft telegram to Stalin, he changed the phrase "the Georgia Central Committee proposes" to "requests" when seeking to escape a new decree by the railroad commissariat. Beria also reported to Stalin that Artyomi Geurkov, the former party boss of Ajaria, had shot himself in his apartment, leaving a letter to Beria (which he forwarded) admitting his guilt, perhaps to try to protect family members ("I should be punished, I am doing this myself, perhaps in excess"). Guruli and Tushurashvili, *Correspondence*, 78–9 (Sept. 26, 1937), 80–1 (Sept. 1937), 82–4 (Oct. 1, 1937).

99. Rayfield, *Literature of Georgia*, 270; Rayfield, "Death of Paolo Iashvili," 663. Back on Oct. 30, 1937, Beria had written to Stalin that of the 12,000-plus people arrested, only 7,374 had had their cases decided, leaving some 5,000 in overcrowded prisons, because the traveling military collegium from Moscow was busy going around to various locations; Beria requested permission for a special collegium of the Georgian court to determine sentences. Khaustov et al., *Lubianka: Stalin i glavnoe upravlenie*, 415–6 (APRF, f. 3, op. 58, d. 212, l. 137–9); Junge and Bonwetsch, *Bol'shevistskii poriadok*, II: 23–4 (Arkhiv MVD Gruzii, 2–I otdel, f. 14, op. 11, d. 152, l. 171–3). Beria staged what would turn out to be his final show trial in Tbilisi, which resulted in executions for "wreckers" at the Georgian Animal Husbandry Institute. *Zaria vostoka*, Jan. 25, 1938.

100. Beria had sought Stalin's permission to hold a plenum of the Soviet writers' union in Tbilisi in honor of the Rustaveli celebrations: Guruli and Tushurashvili, *Correspondence*, 56–7 (Beria to Stalin, May 31, 1937). Vsevolod Vishnevsky did a radio broadcast from Gori on Dec. 26, 1937, briefly narrating its thirteen centuries of history and describing a visit to Stalin's birth hovel. Goriaeva, "Veilkaia kniga dnia," 317–21 (RGALI, f. 1038, op. 1, d. 1181, l. 8–15).

101. In absolute terms, this was third highest, after the Russian and Ukrainian republics. Avalishvili, "'Great Terror'"; http://stalin.memo.ru/images/note1957.htm.

102. Georgia's list for the proposed mass operations (NKVD 00447), sent to Yezhov and Frinovsky in Moscow on July 8, 1937, contained 1,419 names in first category (execution) and 1,562 in second (Gulag). An additional 2,000 people were said to be members of former political parties in the republic. RGASPI, f. 17, op. 166, d. 588, l. 36. The NKVD quotas for Georgia were set at 2,000 (first) and 3,000 (second). APRF, f. 3, op. 58, d. 212, l. 55–78. The Georgia troika would assemble in Goglidze's office, usually around midnight until 4:00 a.m., and work through 100 to 150 "cases" in a session, spending two minutes or so on each. Junge and Bonwetsch, *Bol'shevistskii poriadok*, II: 411–28 (Arkhiv MVD Gruzii, 1–i otdel, f. vosstanovlennykh del G. Mamuliya: I. Takahadze, Jan. 8, 1957).

103. Junge and Bonwetsch, *Bol'shevistskii poriadok*, I: 68, 71, 75, 81, 95, 200.

104. Esaiashvili, *Ocherki istorii Kommunisticheskoi partii Gruzii*, II: 160 (partarkhiv GF IML, f. 14, op. 40, d. 35, l. 13–4), 163.

105. "Beria as a literary critic," quipped Rayfield, "had been successful beyond the dreams of most critics: every writer he had disapproved of had ceased to write." Rayfield, *Literature of Georgia*, 262–3.

106. Already by this date, Beria reported to Stalin that more than 12,000 people had been arrested, of which 7,374 had been convicted, 5,236 extrajudicially (by troika). Guruli and Tushurashvili, *Correspondence*, 95–7 (Oct. 30–31, 1937).

107. Overall in Georgia, nearly 20,000 new members would join the party between Nov. 1936 and March 1939. Almost half were children of functionaries. *XVIII s"ezd Vsesoiuznoi Kommunsticheskoi partii (b)*, 577.

108. Among the targets were immigrants to Armenia: more than 40,000 ethnic Armenians had returned from Asia and Europe in the period 1921–1936, and many now met a grim fate. Melkonian, "Repressions in 1930s Soviet Armenia." The decapitation at the top was roughly similar in Azerbaijan, under Bagirov: 22 people's commissars, 49 county party secretaries, 29 chairmen of local soviet executive committees, 57 directors of factories, 95 engineers, 110 military men, 207 trade unionists, and 8 professors were arrested and, in the majority of cases, executed. And that was just in 1937. Ismailov, "1937." See also *Ocherki istorii Kommunisticheskoi partii Azerbaidzhana*.

109. Tepliakov, *Mashina terrora*, 599.

110. Stephan, "'Cleansing' the Soviet Far East," 51–3. The Soviet Far East was the fastest-growing region in terms of population in the Russian republic, doubling between 1926 and 1939. Stephan, *Russian Far East*, 185.

111. In 1938, 98 percent of the troika sentences in Ukraine were death; in Georgia, 68 percent. Georgia was not a land of exile or giant Gulag camps with which to pad or exceed quotas. It was, however, rich in members of former non-Bolshevik parties. Junge and Bonwetsch, *Bolshevistskii poriadok*, II: 55, 77.

112. Beria wrote to Stalin and Molotov seeking authorization to shut down the prestigious Sukhum Subtropical Institute and instead to transform a department at Georgia's Agricultural Institute into the new de facto all-Union institution for training subtropical agronomists. Guruli and Tushurashvili, *Correspondence*, 36–7 (April 21, 1937). The Abkhazia Subtropical institute, as it had originally been known, had been opened in 1926 and six years later was designated an all-Union Institute. Anchbadze et al., *Istoriia Abkhazskoi ASSR*, 155; Blauvelt, "'From Words to Action!,'" 252.

113. *Abkhazskaia oblastnaia organizatsiia*, 25–56.

114. Grdzelidze, *Mezhnatsional'noe obshchenie*, 102–3. Ethnic Abkhaz in the Communist party of Abkhazia fell from 28.3 to 18.5 percent over a single year (1929–30); the high water mark thereafter was 21.8 percent in 1936. In 1939, Abkhaz were down to just over 15 percent in their own party.

115. Ajarians had been designated "Muslim Georgians" under the tsars. Guruli and Tushurashvili, *Correspondence*, 104–5; Junge and Bonwetsch, *Bolshevistskii poriadok*, II: 67–8 (Arkhiv MVD Gruzii, 2–I otdel, f. 14, op. 11, d. 152, l. 169, 188: Jan. 5, 1937). Beria would sacrifice the boss of the Abkhaz NKVD, Grigory Pauchiliya (b. 1904), an ethnic Georgian whom he had promoted from the NKVD sports team Dynamo.

116. Iskanderov, *Ocherki*, 540–3. Bagirov initially had sought to impose limits. "Some people are not against demonstrating their 'orthodoxy' by firing from work the wives of those arrested, sisters-in-law, relatives," he told a congress of soviets in Azerbaijan in March 1937. "Pardon me, please, this is not correct. This means arousing greater dissatisfaction, greater anger. This means increasing the number of enemies of Soviet power."

Where are they supposed to go? We cannot leave them to starve." Ismailov, *Istoria "bol'shogo terora,"* 72–3 (citing APD UDP AR, f. l, op. 88, d. 137, l. 1), 73–4 (l. 8–9; RGASPI, f. 17, op. 162, d. 20, l. 131–2), 92–3 (citing APD UDP AR, f. l, op. 77, d. 101, l. 98).

117. Khaustov et al., *Lubianka: Stalin i glavnoe upravlenie,* 380 (RGASPI, f. 558, op. 11, d. 57, l. 99).

118. Ismailov, *Istoria "bol'shogo terora,"* 145–8 (citing APD UDP AR, f. 1, op. 88, d. 137, l. 1), 73–4 (l. 8–9; RGASPI, f. 17, op. 162, d. 20, l. 131–2).

119. For some, Khrushchev's rise presented a mystery. "I took part in the Moscow city party committee meeting, at which we were given instructions . . . Khrushchev's speech was confused and chaotic," Aleksandr Solovyov had recorded in his diary (Dec. 14, 1931). "It is incomprehensible how he got to that position, obtuse and narrow minded as he is." On Jan. 28, 1932, Solovyov privately added following Khrushchev's promotion: "I am, like many others, astonished at Khrushchev's rapid rise. He did very badly in his studies at the Industrial Academy. But he has won the sympathy of his classmates . . . He is an incredibly obtuse man. And a frightful bootlicker." Kozlov, *Neizvestnaia Rossiia,* IV: 170–1.

120. Kolman, *My ne dolzhny byli tak zhit',* 192. A reporter for *Vechernaia Moskva,* A. V. Khrabovitsky, would recall: "I always saw Khrushchev together with Kaganovich. Kaganovich was the active, powerful one, whereas all I ever heard Khrushchev saying was, 'Yes, Lazar Moiseyevich,' 'Right, Lazar Moiseyevich.'" Medvedev, *All Stalin's Men,* 124–5.

121. Dmitrii Shepilov, in Vostryshev, *Moskva stalinskaia,* 365.

122. Khrushchev, *Vospominaniia,* I: 112–5 (reference to D. Rabinovich and I. Finkel).

123. Khrushchev, *Vospominaniia,* 1: 132–4, 145–7; Khrushchev, *Memoirs,* I: 127–9, 138–40; Chuev, *Tak govoril Kaganovich,* 99; Taubman, *Khrushchev,* 103–4, 114–7; *Na prieme,* 227–9. See also Borys, "Who Ruled the Soviet Ukraine in Stalin's Time?" A blithe absence of genuine concern from Stalin was evident in another favorite, the peasant-born Andreyev, who as a young man back in 1920–22 had voted for Trotsky's platform in the trade union debate. During the June 1937 sessions of the Main Military Council, Stalin was seated next to Andreyev, pointed to him, and stated that "he had been a very active Trotskyite in 1921." "Which Andreyev?" a voice interjected. "Andrei Andreyevich Andreyev, Central Committee Secretary," Stalin answered, adding that Andreyev had "disarmed" and "is fighting the Trotskyites very well." *Istochnik,* 1994, no. 3: 74.

124. That included both Moscow and Ukraine. Makarova, "Stalin i 'blizhnyi krug,'" 301.

125. RGASPI, f. 17, op. 3, d. 995, l. 5.

126. Borys, "Who Ruled the Soviet Ukraine in Stalin's Time?," 230.

127. Khrushchev, *Vospominaniia,* I: 139–40.

128. Khrushchev, *Vospominaniia,* I: 184; Khrushchev, *Memoirs,* I: 178–80.

129. Mikoyan later wrote that "Khrushchev made a career for himself in Moscow literally within a couple of years. As for how and why—it was because almost everybody else had been put in prison in the meantime. Besides, Khrushchev had Alliluyeva as his patron. They met at the Industrial Academy where Khrushchev was active in fighting against the opposition. It was then that he became secretary of the district party committee. He finally got onto the Central Committee over others' dead bodies, as it were." Mikoian, *Tak bylo,* 614.

130. This was formalized in a politburo decree on Feb. 17, 1938: RGASPI, f. 17, op., 162, d. 22, l. 127.

131. Yezhov's orders were dated Feb. 26 and March 3, 1938. Uspensky, for his part, told one of the newly appointed provincial NKVD chiefs under him, "all Germans and Poles living in Ukraine are spies and saboteurs." Kuromiya and Pepłoński, "The Great Terror," 650 (citing Z arkhiviv VUChK-HPU-NKVD-KHB, 1998, no. 1-2: 215).

132. Leplyovsky was transferred to NKVD transport; he would be arrested on April 26, 1938, and "confessed" that he had been a plotter since 1930, when he had helped mount the Springtime case against former tsarist officers. Naumov, *Stalin i NKVD,* 515–21. The last person connected with the Tukhachevsky trial, Marshal Blyukher, would be arrested on Oct. 22, 1938.

133. *Na prieme,* 220 (Sept. 21, 1937).

134. Getty and Naumov, *Road to Terror,* 418–9. At a Jan. 24–25, 1938, gathering of NKVD central and regional bosses, several requested extensions for the mass operations. Yezhov goaded them on, indirectly invoking Stalin. Frinovsky interrupted the speech of Grigory Gorbach, Mironov's successor as NKVD chief in Western Siberia, "Have you heard? Fifty-five thousand arrested! Bravo Gorbach! There's a star [molodets]!" Both Yezhov and Frinovsky ominously warned that additional enemies were lurking in NKVD ranks. "We have provinces where the local GB apparatus has not been touched at all." Danilov et al., *Tragediia Sovetskoi derevni,* V/ii: 548; Khaustov and Samuelson, *Stalin, NKVD,* 241–2 (TsA FSB, f. 3, op. 5, d. 13, l. 358–9, 280); Pavliukov, *Ezhov,* 348–55.

135. Of the 204 special reports from the locales during the second half of July 1938 concerning the "struggle against counterrevolutionary elements," Uspensky was responsible for more than thirty. Khaustov and Samuelson, *Stalin, NKVD,* 243–5 (TSA FSB, f. 3 os, op. 6, d. 4, l. 31–4; op. 5, d. 63); Shapoval et al., *ChK-GPU-NKVD,* 173–4.

136. Petrov and Jansen, *Stalinskii pitomets,* 364–5 (TsA FSB, H-15301, t. 9, l. 100–2).

137. Pavliukov, *Ezhov,* 359–62; RGASPI, f. 560, op. 1, d. 10, l. 38 (Zhabokritsky).

138. Vasilev et al., *Politicheskoe rukovodstvo Ukrainy,* 35–47 (TsDAGOU, f . 1, d. 548, l. 1–105: June 13, 1938).

139. Slutsky was in the Little Corner once in 1935, three times in 1936, and twice in 1937 (the last time on July 5, for twenty minutes). *Na prieme,* 705.

140. Galina would later deny that this was her half-brother: V. Nechaev, "Vnuchka Stalina 'o belykh piatniakh v istorii svoei sem'i," *Argumenty i fakty,* Nov. 3, 1999.

141. Orlov, *Secret History,* 231–2, 237–8.

142. Pavliukov, *Ezhov,* 362–71 (citing TsA FSB, sledstvennoe delo No. N-15302, III: 100, N2: 184, Frinovsky testimony, Uspensky testimony); Petrov and Jansen, *Stalinskii pitomets,* 81–2 (citing TsA FSB, sledstvennoe delo No. N-15301, t. 3, l. 117–23). Also in April 1938, an NKVD passport decree denied individuals the ability to determine their nationality and thus, from the regime's point of view, to hide behind a false front: rather, the determination would be derived from the nationality of one's parents. If mother and father were of different nations, both were inscribed in the passport. The decree aimed to "unmask" people, particularly in border regions, who had co-nationals abroad and were concealing their true nationality. Hirsch, *Empire of Nations,* 275, 294 (GARF, f. 7523, op. 65, d. 304, l. 1).

143. For example, the June 16, 1937, reception given by Latvia for its foreign minister would be attended by Molotov, Litvinov, Mikoyan,

Budyonny and Yegorov, and Kerzhentsev. *Pravda,* June 18, 1937. On July 10, 1937, a breakfast given by the Swedish foreign minister would be attended by Voroshilov, Kaganovich, Chubar, Rukhimovich, and Bulganin. *Pravda,* July 11, 1937.

144. RGASPI, f. 558, op. 11, d. 773, l. 1 (December 8, 1932); Murin, *Stalin v ob"iatiakh sem'i,* 159–60 (Nov. 4, 1934); Deviatov et al., *Blizhniaia,* 88.

145. Duggan, *Fascist Voices,* 319–24.

146. "Recently I have been dreaming about you a lot, perhaps, I don't know, that is what stimulated me to write to you," wrote Rakhil Dizik, a pedagogue of the Moscow region, in an undated letter, evidently from the 1930s, that mentioned her Communist Youth League membership and desire to get to know him better. Stalin returned her letter and accompanying photo with a note: "Comrade Unknown! I ask you to believe me that I have no desire to insult you . . . But all the same I must say that I am without the opportunity [no time!] to satisfy your wish. I wish you all the best." "'Tovarishch neznakomaia': iz perepiski I. V. Stalina."

147. Another service woman, who would be rumored to be Stalin's mistress, the housekeeper Varvara Istomina [née Zhbychkina, b. 1917], would be assigned to the Near Dacha only in 1946. Deviatov et al., *Blizhniaia,* 384. The top service position at the Nearby Dacha was held by Matryona "Motya" Butuzova.

148. The occasion, Aug. 18, 1938, was Aviation Day, one of the country's most important holidays. Rybin, *Stalin v oktiabre,* 18–9; Rybin, *Stalin na fronte,* 41; Turchenko, "Zhenschiny diktatora." Rybin gives her name as Rusudan Jordaniya (Rybin, *Stalin v oktiabre*) and as Ruzadan Pachkoriya (Rybin, *Stalin na fronte*).

149. Vlasik had served in the tsarist army in the Great War, then in the Red Army, soon joining the Cheka, and worked under Pauker from 1926 in the operative department as part of the elite bodyguard corps. On Nov. 19, 1938 (in an appointment signed by both Yezhov and Beria), Vlasik took command of the First Department (bodyguards) in the Main Directorate of State Security (GUGB) (the Kremlin Commandantura of State Security went to N. K. Spiridonov). GARF, f. R-9401, op. 1, d. 1623, l. 157. On Dec. 27, 1938, Vlasik was promoted from senior major to commissar of state security, third level: GARF, f. R-9401, op. 57, d. 1625, l. 273, 76. Like his nemesis Beria, Vlasik would move into a private mansion on Moscow's innermost ring road.

150. Elagin, *Ukroshchenie isskustv,* 328.

151. Khaustov, "Deiatel'nost' organov," 289 (TsA FSb, f. 3, op. 5, d. 82, l. 51), 304 (TsA FSB, f. 66, op. 1, d. 391, l. 55).

152. Kuromiya and Pepłoński, "The Great Terror," 665 (citing RGVA, f. 308k, op. 3, d. 456, l. 37, and Archiwum akt nowych Warsaw, Sztab Główny, 616/249: Dec. 10–13, 1937).

153. Japanese consulates remained at Vladivostok, Petrovavlovsk, Okha, and Aleksandrovsk; Manchukuo, Japan's puppet state, maintained consulates in Chita and Blagoveshchensk.

154. Stephan, *Russian Far East,* 207.

155. *Na prieme,* 216 (July 28, 1937); Coox, "Lesser of Two Hells, Part 1," 151.

156. Shreider, *NKVD iznutri,* 16.

157. Tumshis and Papchinskii, *1937, bol'shaia chistka,* 254.

158. Petrov and Petrov, *Empire of Fear,* 74–5. Petrov wrongly gives the date for Lyushkov in Rostov as 1938, instead of 1937.

159. On July 17, 1938, Balytsky wrote a confession to Yezhov of his involvement in a conspiracy, which Frinovsky forwarded to Stalin on July 21; Stalin underlined several passages

and wrote: "discuss with Yezhov." Balytsky had refused to confess only three days earlier. Khaustov et al., *Lubianka: Stalin i glavnoe upravlenie*, 257–8 (APRF, f. 3, op. 24, d. 316, l. 8–12).

160. *Na prieme*, 216. Lyushkov was received in the company of Yezhov, Molotov, and Voroshilov. It was Lyushkov's one recorded visit to the Little Corner.

161. Khaustov and Samuelson, *Stalin, NKVD*, 234–5 (APRF, f. 3, op. 24, d. 321, l. 11; op. 58, d. 405, l. 175).

162. *Pravda*, Dec. 20, 1937; Khaustov et al., *Lubianka: Stalin i glavnoe upravlenie*, 368–73 (APRF, f. 3, op. 58, d. 254, l. 203–15).

163. Tumshis and Papchinskii, *1937, bol'shaia chistka*, 79.

164. Ethnic Chinese had comprised 13 percent of the Russian Far East population in 1911, but would fall to under 1 percent as of 1939. Stephan, *Russian Far East*, 213; Coox, "L'Affaire Lyushkov," 416. In 1938, the NKVD took inventory of all Chinese in the Soviet Far East with the idea of forcing anyone remaining to emigrate to Xinjiang or resettle in Kazakhstan. But on June 10, 1938, only those who wanted to relocate had to do so, and many Chinese under arrest were released and allowed to go to China. Yezhov informed the NKVD in the Soviet Far East that the USSR was following "friendly relations with China." Pobol' and Polian, *Stalinskie deportatsii*, 103–4.

165. Merritt, "Great Purges," 456–7.

166. Not including Yagoda, who was general commissar (equivalent to marshal), there were three levels of commissar of state security: first rank, second rank, third rank. Frinovsky held a military rank [*komkor*]. Two of these state security commissars would survive to 1941. Naumov, *Stalin i NKVD* (2010), 74–5; Pavliukov, *Ezhov*, 426.

167. Yezhov supposedly directed Frinovsky to instruct Lyushkov to commit suicide if he were to be recalled to Moscow. Petrov and Jansen, *Stalinskii pitomets*, 160 (citing TsA FSB, ASD Frinovskogo, N-15301, t. 2: 173).

168. The second Order of Lenin came on Feb. 23, 1938, Red Army Day. Conquest, *Inside Stalin's Secret Police*, 90.

169. Svetlanin, *Dal'nevostochnyi zagovor*, 92 (referring to a conversation with Blyukher's political adjutant Semyon Kladko, whom the author ran into in Moscow in mid-Aug. 1938). On July 10, 1937, Stalin received a letter from Blyukher addressed to Voroshilov, in which the Far Eastern marshal rebuked those who had organized his meeting in July 1936 with visiting communications commissar Rykov, blaming the arrested former Far Eastern party boss Kartvelishvili-Lavrentyev. But Blyukher also attacked Vareikis for passing on different information to the Center. Stalin kept Blyukher's self-justification in his personal archive. Khaustov and Samuelson, *Stalin, NKVD*, 205–6 (APRF, d. 313, l. 146–8).

170. Blyukher, "S. Vasiliem Konstantinovichem Bliukherom," 80.

171. Coox, "Lesser of Two Hells, Part 1," 158.

172. Pavliukov, *Ezhov*, 422–4 (citing TsA FSB, seldstvennoe delo N-15302, t. 10, l. 169, 175), 428.

173. Haslam, *Threat from the East*, 94 (citing *DDF*, 2e série, IX: 613–5, May 3, 1938).

174. The despot elaborated "that it was the ultimate objective of the Japanese to capture the whole of Siberia as far as Lake Baikal," yet he made clear that "the Soviet Union would not, however, intervene in the war." U.S. ambassador William Bullitt, relating a conversation with Sun Fo (the envoy who spoke to Stalin): *FRUS, 1938*, III: 165.

175. RGASPI, f. 558, op. 11, d. 58, l. 21–4, 33–4 (May 14, 1938).

176. Soviet Naval Commissar Pyotr Smirnov, who co-signed the warning, was sent to the Soviet Far East at this time. Coox, "Lesser of Two Hells, Part 2," 87.

177. Svetlanin, *Dal'nevostochnyi zagovor*, 105. Between May 28 and June 8, 1938, the Main Military Council in Moscow, with Stalin in attendance, resolved, among multiple agenda items in connection with the Far Eastern Army, "to purge the command-political cadres of enemies of the people, doubtful and morally debased elements." All ethnic Germans, Poles, Latvians, Estonians, Koreans, Lithuanians, Romanians, Turks, Hungarians, and Bulgarians in the Far Eastern Army's ranks were to be immediately discharged. *Glavnyi voennyi sovet RKKA*, 84–5.

178. Pavliukov, *Ezhov*, 427 (according to the then head of bodyguards, Dagin).

179. Petrov and Jansen, *Stalinskii pitomets*, 160–1 (citing TsA FSB, ASD Frinovskogo, N-15301, t. 2: 179).

180. It was said that Lyushkov had dispatched his twenty-seven-year-old wife, Nina, and their eleven-year-old adopted daughter, who needed a medical operation, to Moscow, with a secret plan for them to escape to Poland by train; to signal this plan was working, Nina was to send her regards by telegram. The telegram supposedly arrived. Whether this actually happened or was an invention by Lyushkov to put himself in a better light for having tried to save rather than abandon his family is unclear. It was also said that the Japanese used their "sources" to try to trace the fate of wife and daughter but without success; Lyushkov never saw or heard from his wife and daughter again. (His mother and sister were also arrested.) Nina was sentenced to eight years and incarcerated in a camp in Karaganda (Akmolinsk), survived, and was released in summer 1946. Coox, "L'Affaire Lyushkov," 410; Tumshis and Papchinskii, *1937, bol'shaia chistka*, 129.

181. *Na prieme*, 237; Petrov and Jansen, *Stalinskii pitomets*, 161; *Glavnyi voennyi sovet RKKA*, 110n1.

182. RGANI, f. 6, op. 13, d. 102, l. 54–6 (Soviet intelligence translation of Lyushkov's remarks); Pavliukov, *Ezhov*, 429–31; Iakovlev et al., *Reabilitatsiia: politicheskie protsessy*, 183.

183. Coox, "Lesser of Two Hells, Part 2," 83.

184. Coox, "Lesser of Two Hells, Part 1," 176.

185. Coox, "Lesser of Two Hells, Part 1," 153.

186. Coox, "Lesser of Two Hells, Part 2," 79–80, 86–8. According to Lyushkov, in March 1938, Stalin had even dispatched an envoy—known under the code name Major Yartsev—to investigate the possibility of repositioning the Pacific Fleet and bringing Sakhalin, where Japanese companies managed economic concessions, to a state of full military readiness, including the building of new air strips, which would be conspicuous. It seems that Japanese sea, air, and ground forces were to be lured to defending Southern Sakhalin. Yartsev was Boris Rybkin (see chap. 12, below).

187. Kahn, *Codebreakers*, 637; Goldman, "Spy Who Saved the Soviets."

188. According to Coox, for strictly military matters the Japanese preferred the information of artillery officer Major Frontyarmar Frantsevich, of the 36th Motorized Infantry Division, who had defected to the Japanese by motor car from Outer Mongolia two weeks before Lyushkov, on May 29, 1938. Coox, "L'Affaire Lyushkov," 418.

189. "I did not want to leave my country any more than a fish wants to leave water, but the delinquent activity of criminal people has cast me up like a fish on ice," Orlov wrote in a letter for Yezhov and Stalin hand-delivered to the Soviet embassy in Paris after he was safely gone. Costello and Tsarev, *Deadly Illusions*, 308–12 (letter to Yezhov from NKVD file).

190. In 1938, a book in Spanish, *Espionage in Spain* (Barcelona: Ediciones Unidad), was published under the name Max Rieger, a member of Spain's Socialist party, which brought together vast incriminating materials on the POUM; it was quietly translated into Russian with a different title: *Spanish Trotskyites in Franco's Service*. The secret materials had not been assembled by the rank and file leftist, but under the direction of the NKVD's Orlov, who had assigned a journalist to write the text. POUM members were said to have been discovered in Franco's intelligence service after the capture of a top Franco agent. Primakov, *Ocherki*, III: 140–1, 144.

191. According to the official historical essays on Soviet intelligence, Orlov never divulged to the West the secrets he knew. Primakov, *Ocherki*, III: 146n1.

192. Merritt, "Great Purges," 500 (citing "Statistika antirmeiskogo terrora," *Voenno-istoricheskii arkhiv*, 1997, no. 2: 105–12). Lyushkov told his interrogators that between July 1937 and May 1938, more than 4,000 Far Eastern Army personnel—1,200 officers and political commissars and 3,000 junior officers—were arrested, including almost all of Blyukher's immediate subordinates. Stephan, *Russian Far East*, 220 (citing U.S. Army Department, "The Interrogation of Lyushkov," frame 0982).

193. Stephan, *Russian Far East*, 234.

194. Kubeev, "Obrechennyi na kazn'," 93–4; Tumshis and Papchinskii, *1937, bol'shaia chistka*, 133–4; Coox, "L'Affaire Lyushkov," 412.

195. A large-scale operation at Lake Khasan appeared in the Japanese army's plan for 1938. Savin, "O podgotovke Iaponii k napadeniiu na SSSR."

196. Coox, *Anatomy of a Small War*, 3–9; Coox, *Nomonhan*, 124; Ikuhiko, "Japanese-Soviet Confrontation," 140–57.

197. Solov'ev and Chugnuov, *Pogranichnye voiska SSSR*, doc. 623 (Colonel Fedotov).

198. This would be Lyushkov's one and only intentional public appearance. He would publish an "open letter to Stalin" in the Japanese periodical *Kaizo* (April 1939). *Kaizo*, April 1939: 106–25, excerpted in Lenoe, *Kirov Murder*, 681–6. For a detailed Japanese report on the July 13 public appearance, see Zolotarev, *Russkii arkhiv: Velikaia otechestvennaia*, VII/i: 148–51 (TsKhIDK, f. 1, op. 3,4 d. 4601, l. 210–6).

199. Solov'ev and Chugunov, *Pogranichnye voiska SSSR*, 591–3; "Prikaz narodnogo komissara oborony Soiuza SSR no. 0040 (4 sentiabria 1938)."

200. Petrov and Jansen, *Stalinskii pitomets*, 161–2. See also Svetlanin, *Dal'nevostochnyi zagovor*, 124–6.

201. *Far Eastern Affairs*, 1990, no. 3: 176–84 (Ivan Minka); Merritt, "Great Purges," 513–5 (citing RGVA, f. 35083, op. 1, d. 3, l. 35, 67; f. 33987, op. 3, d. 1084, l. 37–8; RGASPI, f. 71, op. 25, d. 359, l. 1–2), 526 (citing RGVA, f. 33987, op. 3, d. 1136, l. 10; f. 35083, op. 1, d. 28, ll. 113–4).

202. On July 20, 1938, the Japanese ambassador, Mamoru Shigemitsu, paid a call on Litvinov and the two clashed sharply over maps; Litvinov also complained of penetration of Soviet embassy territory in Tokyo by a person who then flung leaflets: Tisminets, *Vneshniaia politika SSSR*, IV: 369–71 (July 22, 1938).

203. A published Soviet assessment noted Japanese strength in traditional infantry, a low level of mechanization, rendering them unable to mount breakthrough operations, and a domestic Japanese aircraft industry that, despite access to foreign prototypes, was

relatively weak by top international standards. The Soviets had a high opinion of Japanese prowess on the sea. Japanese cruisers were state of the art in speed and firepower; they even carried more torpedo tubes than their American counterparts. New Japanese battleships, moreover, were coming off the stocks. Shvede, *Voennyi flot Iaponii*, 31–2. This assessment would be maintained in the next edition: *Voenno-morskoi flot Iaponii* (1939).

204. Khaustov, "Deiatel'nost' organov," 252 (TsA FSB, f. 3, op. 5, d. 67, l. 28).

205. Coox, *Nomonhan*, 123–4; Haslam, *Threat from the East*, 113–4.

206. Coox, *Anatomy of a Small War*, 57–70; Coox, *Nomonhan*, 134–5. Sorge would report that "this incident will not lead to a war between the Soviet Union and Japan." Volkov, "Legendy i deistvitel'nost o Rikharde Zorge," 100, referring to Toshito Obi, *Zoruge jiken*, 4 vols. (Tokyo: Misuzu Shobō, 1962–71), I: no page number.

207. Grebennik, *Khasanskii dnevnik*, 54–7.

208. Coox, *Anatomy of a Small War*.

209. Zolotarev, *Russkii arkhiv: Velikaia otechestvennaia*, VII/i: 146–7 (TsAMO, f. 23, op. 22383, d. 3, l. 185–6).

210. Fesiun, *Delo Rikharda Zorge*, 87–9

211. Back on July 20, 1936, the then head of Soviet military intelligence (Uritsky) had written to Voroshilov about Sorge concerning a review of intelligence, which had indicated that German-Japanese negotiations for a military alliance were bogged down because of Germany's desire not to force the issue. Stalin had written on it: "In my view, this is a disorientation emanating from German circles." Uritsky explained to Voroshilov that the inside knowledge had come primarily from Sorge, who "usually produced good quality information and not infrequently genuine secret documentary material. For example, we have now received from this intelligence operative a report of the German military attaché in Tokyo (sent to you separately). We were able to verify the genuineness of this report, having received analogous documents directly from the German general staff." On the basis of additional materials, including decoded telegraph traffic between Berlin and Tokyo, Uritsky concluded firmly that Sorge was correct. "In presenting these interpretations and materials to you, I request your instructions about their further forwarding to comrade Stalin." Voroshilov's response is unknown. (Uritsky, of course, was later executed as a foreign spy.) Zolotarev, *Russkii arkhiv: Velikaia otechestvennai*, VII/i: 141–2 (TsAMO, f. 23, op. 3108, d. 3, l. 239–41).

212. Volkogonov, *Triumf i tragediia*, II/1: 273 (citing TsGASA, f. 33987, op. 3, d. 1140, l. 18–22); Volkogonov, *Stalin: Triumph and Tragedy*, 327–8; Kortunova, "1938–I," 175.

213. Shigemitsu made the suggestion to Litvinov in person on the evening of Aug. 4, 1938: Tisminets, *Vneshniaia politika SSSR*, IV: 373–5. The next day Soviet intelligence reported to Moscow that Kung Hsianghsi of the Chinese secret service, a stogie-smoking seventy-fifth generation descendant of Confucius, had pledged China's unconditional support to the USSR in the conflict with Japan. Ganin, who met Kung and wrote the report, inquired whether he should convey the information he had received to the Soviet foreign affairs commissariat. Zolotarev, *Russkii arkhiv: Velikaia otechestvennai*, VII/i: 97–9 (RGVA, f. 33987, op. 3, d. 1114, l. 324–8).

214. Sorge repeated that appraisal on Aug. 10: Fesiun, *Delo Rikharda Zorge*, 91–2; Zolotarev, *Russkii arkhiv: Velikaia otechestvennaia*, VII/i: 147–8 (TsAMO, f. 23, op. 22383, d. 3, l. 198–9).

215. *DVP SSSR*, XXI: 433–4 (Aug. 11, 1938).

216. Coox, *Nomonhan*, 138 (quoting Inada), 140–1.

217. MacKinnon, "Tragedy of Wuhan"; MacKinnon, *Wuhan*.

218. *DGFP*, series C, VI: 337–8, 396–7; von Weizsäcker, *Memoirs*, 126–7; Presseisen, *Germany and Japan*, 126–7.

219. Cherepanov, *Zapiski voenno sovetnika*, 323–3; Kaliagin, *Po neznakomym dorogam*, 92n, 282.

220. "Problems of War Strategy" (Nov. 6, 1938), reprinted in Tse-tung, *Selected Military Writings*, 269–85 (at 269, 273).

221. Goldman, *Nomonhan, 1939*, 76–7.

222. Krivosheev, *Soviet Casualties*, 47–51; Coox, *Nomonhan*, 132.

223. Blyukher, "S Vasiliem Konstantinovichem Bliukherom," 84–7. See also Erickson, *Soviet High Command*, 498–9.

224. Konev, when queried after World War II, would judge Blyukher a man of the past unsuited to modern warfare. "Besedy s marshalom Sovetskogo Soiuza I. S. Konevym," in Simonov, *Glazami cheloveka moego pokoleniia*, 304–5.

225. One example was Mikhail Viktorov (Novoselov), newly named as NKVD chief in Sverdlovsk, who turned up a shocking state of affairs, even by standards of the terror, in the work of his predecessor (Dmitriev). Viktorov freed a large number of prisoners and sent Lubyanka a long analysis of local falsifications of cases. Pavliukov, *Ezhov*, 444–5 (citing TsA FSB, sledstvennoe delo no. R-24334, t. 1, l. 67–8). Viktorov would be arrested on Jan. 22, 1939, and sentenced to fifteen years; he died in a camp in 1950.

226. RGVA, f. 33987, op. 3, d. 1075, l. 57–63.

227. Khlevniuk, *Politbiuro*, 229.

228. Khaustov and Samuelson, *Stalin, NKVD*, 86 (APRF, f. 3, op. 24, d. 364, l. 155). Chubar would be arrested on July 4, 1938, and executed on Feb. 26, 1939; Beria would get his dacha.

229. Getty and Naumov, *Road to Terror*, 538–41.

230. According to the memoirs of D. N. Sukhanov (b. 1904), an aide to Malenkov, dated March 6, 1993, Stalin had asked Malenkov for files on people who could be appointed to replace Yezhov as commissar of state security. Sukhanov claims he looked through the nomenklatura lists and selected as the finalists Beria, Kruglov, Pegov, Kuznetsov, and Gusarov. Malenkov's son said seven names were submitted to Stalin, who chose Beria. Hoover Archives, Volkogonov papers, container 13, excerpted Sukhanov memoirs (dated March 6, 1993); Malenkov, *O moem otse*, 34. Pavliukov has Malenkov asking his aide V. A. Donskoi to compile the list, not Sukhanov.

231. Another report (July 21, 1938) outlined the dubious leadership style and methods of Beria and Dekanozov. Petrov and Jansen, *Stalinskii pitomets*, 164–5, citing APRF, f. 57, op. 1, d. 264; f. 3, op. 24, d. 463, l. 236–7. Rumors circulated that Yezhov ordered Beria's arrest in July 1938, and that Beria was tipped off and flew to Moscow to see Stalin. The rumors were bunk. Jansen and Petrov, *Stalin's Loyal Executioner*, 149. See also Gol'dshtein, *Tochka opory*, II: 34–5 and Knight, *Beria*, 87–8.

232. Petrov and Jansen, *Stalinskii pitomets*, 355–9 (RGASPI, f. 671, op. 1, d. 265, l. 16–26ob.).

233. Pavliukov, *Ezhov*, 452, citing TsA FSB, sledstvennoe delo, N-15302, t. 7, l. 180.

234. Pavliukov, *Ezhov*, 451, citing TsA FSB, sledstvennoe delo, N-15302, t. 10, l. 163; Petrov and Jansen, *Stalinskii pitomets*, 163, citing TsA FSB, f. 3–os, op. 6, d. 3, l. 316–7.

235. Khrushchev, *Vospominaniia*, I: 179–80. Beria might have told Khrushchev

afterward; Khrushchev might have been invited to the meal afterward at the dacha and heard there.

236. According to Malenkov's son, Stalin phoned Malenkov: "You wrote this yourself?" "Yes, I wrote it." "This is what you think?" "Yes, I think this." Malenkov, *O moem otse*, 33.

237. Khrushchev, *Vospominaniia*, I: 179–80.

238. RGANI, f. 5, op. 30, d. 4, l. 94–5; Knight, *Beria*, 88.

239. Petrov and Jansen, *Stalinskii pitomets*, 165, citing TsA FSB, f. 3, op. 5, d. 92, l. 23.

240. Of course, by letting good slave laborers go, the camps would be left with the worst, rendering them unable to fulfill their assigned economic tasks. Vostryshev, *Moskva stalinskaia*, 376; the politburo decree would be issued on June 10, 1939 (RGASPI, f. 17, op. 162, d. 25, l. 54–5), and formalized by the Supreme Soviet presidium on June 15.

241. Petrov and Jansen, *Stalinskii pitomets*, 167 (no citation). Frinovsky's advice was for Yezhov to stop moping and prevent Beria from implanting all his people in the NKVD. Pavliukov, *Ezhov*, 457–8, TsA FSB, sledstvennoe delo, no. N-15302, t. 1. 10, l. 59; RGASPI, f. 671, op. 1, d. 265, l. 24.

242. Frinovsky testified that on Aug. 27–28, 1938, Yevdokimov, Yezhov's deputy in water transport, called and asked him to come to his apartment. "Verify whether Zakovsky has been shot and whether all the Yagoda people have been shot, because with Beria's arrival the investigations of these cases could be resumed and these cases could be turned against us." Zakovsky, Lev Mironov, and others had been shot on Aug. 26–27. http://www.hrono.ru/dokum/193_dok/19390413beria.php (APRF, f. 3, op. 24, d. 373, l. 3–44: protocol of Frinovsky interrogation, Beria to Stalin, April 11, 1939:); Khaustov and Samuelson, *Stalin, NKVD*, 247 (TsA FSB, ASD p-4406). Yevdokimov would be arrested Nov. 9, 1938.

243. Rybin, *Riadom so Stalinym*, 73. See also Medvedev, *Let History Judge*, 587.

244. "People have completely stopped trusting each other," Mikhail Prishvin, the writer, noted in his diary in Oct. 1937. "They go about their work and do not even whisper to one another. There is a huge mass of people raised up from poor social backgrounds who have nothing to whisper about: they just think 'That's how it should be.' Others isolate themselves to whisper, or study the art of silence." Prishvin, *Dnevniki*, IX: 762–3.

245. The incident took place in summer 1937. Zaporozhets, "Iz vospominaniia," 532–8 (the old friend, Zaporozhets' stepfather, was Pavel Dorofeyev).

246. Mandelstam, *Hope against Hope*, 108.

247. Pis'mennyi, "Ia iskrenne veril Stalinu . . . ," 10.

248. Scott, *Behind the Urals*, 195. See also Rittersporn, "Omnipresent Conspiracy," 112 (citing Smolensk party archives).

249. Davies, *Popular Opinion*, 124.

250. RGASPI, f. 17, op. 3, d. 995, l. 17 (Feb. 3, 1938). "As a rule, not one operational meeting, which were called often in Rostov, took place without a grandiose drinking bout, a total debauch, lasting sometimes twenty-four hours or more," complained one subordinate of the North Caucasus boss Yevdokimov. "There were cases when we found some operatives only on the third or fourth day somewhere in a tavern or with a prostitute." In Kazakhstan, the predecessor of NKVD chief Vasily Karutsky had actually been removed for corruption; Karutsky, a heavy drinker, maintained a harem (his wife committed suicide). Balytsky in Ukraine cohabitated with the wives of subordinates, emulating tsarist-era lords of the manor who slept with the

wives of house serfs and field hands. Tumshis, "Eshche raz o kadrakh chekistov," 190–1 (I. Ia. Ilin); Shapoval and Zolotar'ov, *Vsevolod*, 268, 337; Iakovenko, *Agnessa*, 55. Prime objects for liaisons were the wives of those arrested who sought information about their husbands or other favors, and were given false promises.
251. Shreider, *NKVD iznutri*, 22–4. Shreider claims he and his wife were frequent guests at Ostrovsky's dacha.
252. Afinogenov, *Dnevniki*, 481. Afinogenov had been criticized for excessively complex characters lacking obvious heroism, and in April 1937 he was expelled from the writers' union. Despite his reprieve in 1938, his plays were mothballed. *Literaturnaia gazeta*, May 1, 1937; Hellbeck, "Writing the Self in the Time of Terror," 69–93.
253. Stalin never cared for the popular front, but long-standing popular-frontists such as Dimitrov, Manuilsky, and Kuusinen survived, while anti-Popular Frontists, such as Kun, Knorin, and Pyatnitsky, were destroyed. Stalin badmouthed Manuilsky ("strictly a lightweight") to Dimitrov, while using him to maintain surveillance on Dimitrov. Banac, *Diary of Georgi Dimitrov*, 105 (April 26, 1939).
254. "Muzhestvo protiv bezzakoniia," *Problemy mira i sotsializma*, 1989, no. 7: 89–91 (RGASPI, f. 495, op. 73, d. 60, l. 1–5). Varga was Jewish (at a time when Jews were being targeted), not a youth (at a time when long-time functionaries were targeted), and had once associated with the "renegade" Kautsky. See also Duda, *Jenő Varga*; Mommen, *Stalin's Economist*.
255. Yegorov had been removed as deputy defense commissar on Jan. 25, 1938. That same day, Pavel Dybenko was removed as commander of the Leningrad military district, soon transferred to the forestry commissariat, then, on Feb. 26, 1938, arrested. He was accused not only of the customary espionage but of using state funds for alcohol-fueled orgies, and, on July 29, 1938, was executed. By contrast, on March 2, 1938, at a confrontation with the arrested Belov, Graynov, Grinko, and Sedyakin, Yegorov was said to have performed well. Still, his wife was pronounced a Polish spy and he was expelled from the Central Committee although not arrested. Khaustov et al., *Lubianka: Stalin i glavnoe upravlenie*, 465–6 (APRF, f. 3, op. 24, d. 330, l. 112–3), 456–7 (l. 113), 490 (d. 338, l. 4). Every officer acquired a damning dossier as a traitor, including Shaposhnikov, Timoshenko, Zhukov, and Vasilevsky, but they were not touched. Cherushev, "*Nevinovnykh ne byvaet . . . ,*"382–3.
256. *Inostrannaia literatura*, 1988, no. 4: 172.
257. Ehrenburg, *Memoirs*, 429. Ehrenburg, in 1939, was listed as politically suspect, along with Babel and Pasternak. Babichenko, *Literaturnyi front*, 29–30 (RGASPI, f. 17, op. 121, d. 1, l. 39–40: July 1939), 38 (l. 38: July 26, 1939). "Koltsov along with his boon companion Malraux made contact with the local Trotskyite organization POUM," Marti (commissar of the international brigades in Spain) wrote to Stalin. "If one takes into account Koltsov's long-time sympathy for Trotsky, these contacts do not carry an accidental character." Marti added that the "so-called civil wife of Koltsov Maria Osten . . . is, I personally have no doubt whatsoever, a secret agent of German intelligence." Gromov, *Stalin*, 319. On Koltsov's recall, see also Kudriashov, *SSSR i grazhdanskaia voina v Ispanii*, 215 (APRF, f. 3, op. 34, d. 127, l. 27), 312 (APRF, f. 3, op. 34, d. 127, l. 33–4: Mekhlis to Stalin Nov. 12, 1937); Maksimenkov, *Bol'shaia tsenzura*, 486–7 (RGASPI, f. 558, op. 11, d.

754, l. 82: Nov. 6), 487n1 (RGASPI, f. 17, op. 71, d. 46, l. 52); Efimov, *Mikhail Kol'tsov*, 114.
258. TsA FSB, f. 3, op. 5, d. 262, l. 57–60. Stalin had had a sarcastic note about Bedny's long antifascist poem, "Struggle or Die," read to the poet in July 1937. Bedny kept trying, sending Mekhlis a poem for *Pravda* about the anniversary of the Kirov murder, which Mekhlis forwarded to Stalin and Molotov with a recommendation of rejection, and another about beating enemies, which Stalin called "weak." Maksimenkov, *Bol'shaia tsenzura*, 476–9 (RGASPI, f. 558, op. 11, d. 702, l. 112; d. 130, l. 100; d. 702, l. 133; l. 113–21), 481 (f. 82, op. 2, d. 984, l. 50: Oct. 20, 1937; 496–7: f. 558, op. 11, d. 702, l. 134–6: Jan. 26, 1938). Without a paid job, Bedny was forced to sell his spectacular private library, which he had been assembling since his university days; Vladimir Bonch-Bruevich found out and bought it for the State Literary Museum. Bonch-Bruevich, *Vospominaniia*, 184. In Aug. 1938, Bedny was expelled from the party and the Union of Soviet Writers. Gronsky claimed that Stalin confidentially "took an exercise book out of his safe. Written in it were some rather unflattering remarks about the denizens of the Kremlin. I said that the handwriting was not Demyan's. Stalin replied that these were the sentiments of the slightly tipsy poet, taken down by a certain journalist." Gronskii, *Iz proshlogo*, 155. See also Gromov, *Stalin*, 165–6. The "journalist" may have been Mikhail Prezent, who was arrested and had kept a diary, writing in it that the literati joked, "Trotsky decided to commit suicide, so Trotsky sent Stalin a letter challenging him to a socialist competition." Stalin underlined the passage. RGASPI, f. 558, op. 11, d. 69 (diary); excerpts in Sokolov, *Narkomy strakha*, 24–37. Prezent died in prison from a lack of insulin.
259. Tolstoy, *Tolstoys*.
260. Litvin, "'Chto izhe znam delat'?,'" I: 505–27 (at 509, 521–3).
261. Poretsky, *Our Own People*, 214–6.
262. Duff, *Time for Spies*; West and Tsarev, *Crown Jewels*, 103–26.
263. Lewin, "Grappling with Stalinism," 308–9; Khlevniuk, "Stalinist 'Party Generals,'" 60.
264. Bagirov remained party boss in Azerbaijan and Grigor Arutyunov in Armenia. Tsay, *Making of the Georgian Nation*, 278; Knight, *Beria*, 89.
265. *Glavnyi voennyi sovet RKKA*, 135–41 (RGVA, f. 4, op. 18, d. 46, l. 183–90).
266. Blyukher, "S. Vasiliem Konstantinovichem Bliukherom," 82–3. The same "take a holiday in Sochi" approach had been ominously suggested to Nikolai Kuznetsov when he returned from Spain in Sept. 1937; Kuznetsov survived to get a new assignment.
267. Zolotarev, *Russkii arkhiv: Velikaia otechestvennaia*, VII/i: 103–8 (TsAMO, f. 2, op. 795437, d. 1, l. 35–44). Gorbach, who replaced Lyushkov as NKVD chief for the Soviet Far East, wrote a report to Beria (dated Sept. 15, 1938), which was forwarded to Stalin and Voroshilov, that echoed the blame for Blyukher. Khaustov, "Deiatel'nost organov," 332 (TsA FSB, f. 3, op. 5, d. 883, l. 100–3).
268. *Na prieme*, 239. Molotov and Zhdanov had left at midnight (Sept. 12) and were called back.
269. Goldbstab complained to Stalin: "I am ready to yield this high honor if the artist Gelovani captures this genius of humanity better than I," adding the names of many people who "openly told me that I convey your image more truthfully, sincerely, and softly." Markova, "Litso vraga," 98 (citing RGALI, f. 2456, op. 1, d. 345, l. 88).
270. Bernshtein, Mikhail Gelovani, no pagination; Bernshtein, "V roli Stalina." See also

Kenez, *Cinema and Soviet Society from the Revolution to the Death of Stalin*, 208.
271. Khrushchev, *Vospominaniia*, I: 73, 181.
272. Petrov, "Rodos."
273. Rodos, *Ia syn palacha*.
274. Mozokhin, *Pravo na represii*, 217.
275. Tepliakov, "Sibir'" (citing testimony of L. F. Bashtakov, Jan. 1954); Sanina, "R. I. Eikhe." Eihe had been transferred from Western Siberia to USSR commissar of agriculture in Oct. 1937 (replacing the arrested Mikhail Chernov) and was arrested April 29, 1938.
276. Gazarian, "Etno ne dolzhno povtorit'sia" (1989, no. 2), 63.
277. "I know him from 1923, when he was deputy chairman of the Cheka of Georgia," Merkulov would write of Beria. "He was then all of twenty-four years old but that post already at that time did not satisfy him. He aimed higher. In general he considered all people beneath himself, especially those to whom he was subordinated." Merkulov pointed out that Beria had studiously compiled a record of shortcomings everywhere in his domain, which he used to discredit officials who stood in his way around, and that he badmouthed other officials to his tight circle of subordinates, but when someone was powerful, Beria became obsequious. The second anyone fell under a cloud, however, Beria became rude. "'Khochetsia prokliast' den' i chas moego znakomstva s Beriia,'" 101 (APRF, f. 3, op. 24, d. 465, l. 2–28); Merkulov to Khrushchev, re-sent to Malenkov, July 21, 1953), 96–104 (APRF, f. 3, op. 24, d. 465, l. 2–28: Merkulov to Malenkov, July 23).
278. Loginov, *Teni Stalina*, 31 (Georgii A. Egnatashvili).
279. Also on Oct. 22, 1938, the Far Eastern territory was subdivided into two provinces, and Stalin had Nikolai Pegov, a student at the Moscow Industrial Academy, sent as the new party boss of the chunk whose capital remained Khabarovsk. Pegov, whom Malenkov had placed on the shortlist of candidates to take over as first deputy USSR NKVD chief, was instructed to gather five hundred Communists from the Moscow party organization to bring with him; he barely managed to round up a few dozen, including his brother. "Our whole life then was illuminated by sunshine, joy, and happiness," Pegov would recall. He became a member of the local troika responsible for the still ongoing conveyor-belt mass arrests. Pegov, *Dalekoe-blizkoe*, 7; Stephan, *Russian Far East*, 216.
280. Blyukher died on Nov. 9, 1938. He would be convicted and sentenced to death posthumously, on March 10, 1939. Dushen'kin, *Ot soldata do marshala*. His wife received eight years in the Karaganda camp complex.
281. At the Sverdlovsk transit prison, Galina Serebryakova, whose husband, Sokolnikov, had been executed in the 1936 Trotskyite trial, was looking out upon a gaggle of fellow prisoners arrested for being "a member of the family of a traitor to the motherland," when a companion nudged her and asked if she knew the identity of a tall, thinning woman a short distance away sitting on a sack of her belongings. She did not. "What? That's Yekaterina Ivanovna Kalinina[-Lorberg], the wife of Mikhail Ivanovich Kalinin . . . Yes, she herself. Her husband is our president." Although married to Kalinina Lorberg since 1906, Kalinin, since 1924, had essentially been living with his nanny-housekeeper, Alexandra Gorchakova. Serebryakova approached and told Kalinina to remain firm, for Stalin had been duped but would figure things out and release them all. Serebriakova, "Smerch," 335. Serebryakova, arrested while in exile, would be sentenced to eight years but serve eleven. In 1939 Kalinina would be sentenced to fifteen years; she would be released in 1945.

282. From Irkutsk, Shcherbakov had written to Zhadnov (June 18, 1937), his former superior, that "all leaders of the province soviet departments, the heads of provincial party departments and their deputies (with the exception of two so far), and the lower level province party officials, a number of party secretaries of the district party, the leaders of economic organizations, the directors of factories, [and so on] have been arrested. Thus, there are no functionaries in the party or the soviet apparatuses. It is difficult to imagine something like this. Now they have begun to dig into the NKVD." Shcherbakov begged Zhdanov for cadres from Leningrad. Kvashonkin, *Sovetskoe rukovodstvo,* 363 (RGASPi, f. 88, op. 1, d. 1045, l. 1–5); *Na prieme,* 212.

283. Khrushchev, *Vospominaniia,* I: 78–80; Ponomarev, *Aleksandr Shcherbakov,* 47–50; *Pravda,* March 12, 1991 (Aleksandr Aleksandrovich Shcherbakov, the son); *Na prieme,* 212, 234 (April 4, 1938), 244 (Nov. 4, 1938). The Shcherbakov family lived in the same building—Granovsky, 3—as Stalin's son Yakov; occasionally, Yakov and his wife, Yulia, paid visits to Shcherbakov and his wife, Vera. Ugarov had been the other person besides Shcherbakov whom Stalin had favored for the writers' union secretary in 1934. Stavsky, at the Soviet Union of Writers, sent denunciation after denunciation of various writers; finally, Andreyev wrote to Stalin in 1938 that Stavsky had to be removed. The NKVD listened in on the phone conversations of Fadeyev, Pavel Yudin, and F. Panferov to assess their reactions to the move. Artizov and Naumov, *Vlast',* 412–3 (RGASPI, f. 73, op. 2, d. 17, l. 105), 775–6n12 (TsA FSB, f. 3, op, 5, d. 262, l. 19–35).

284. Kennan wrote that Stalin was "a man of incredible criminality . . . without pity or mercy: a man who . . . was most dangerous of all to those who were his closest collaborators in crime, because he liked to be the sole custodian of his own secrets." Conversely, Rigby argued that Stalin was not "a disloyal patron." Of the ten voting members of the politburo as of 1934, one was assassinated (Kirov), one committed suicide (Orjonikidze), and one died of a heart attack (Kuibyshev), but only one was executed—Kosior. Three candidate members from 1934 through 1937 were executed (Chubar [promoted to full member in 1935], Eihe, and Yezhov), while Mikoyan and Petrovsky survived. Kennan, *Russia and the West,* 254–5; Rigby, "Was Stalin a Disloyal Patron?"

285. The Zhdanov-Malenkov rivalry would perform a similar function of each holding the other in check. Harris, "Origins of the Conflict."

286. Beria's son Sergo recalled that his father noticed he was being spied upon by subordinates, who, he said, reported directly to Zhdanov in Moscow. Beria, *Moi otets,* 56. In Moscow who was watching Beria for Stalin remains unclear—those sources remain classified, if they survived.

287. Nabokov, for the English translation, later explicitly called his fictional dictator a composite. Nabokov, *Tyrants Destroyed,* 2.

288. Davies and Harris, *Stalin's World,* 4.

289. Graziosi, "New Soviet Archival Sources," 34. See also Priestland, *Politics of Mobilization.* Some scholars see this as calculated manipulation of war scares and threats. Rieber, *Struggle for Supremacy,* 92, 98–9. Others assert that Stalin could not help himself. Davies and Harris, *Stalin's World.*

290. Without explaining where Stalin acquired the wherewithal to destroy the political machines with ease, Getty continues to insist not on a hypercentralized but a decentralized Soviet system whereby the central apparatus detested its supposed dependence on the backward clan dynamics of local party machines. Getty and Naumov, *Road to Terror.* See also Rittersporn, *Stalinist Simplifications,* which holds up 1938 as evidence of Stalin's defeat.

291. Cherushev, *Udar po svoim,* 109–10.

292. Overall, between May 1935 and May 1941, Stalin would convoke twelve Central Committee plenums, a single party congress, and one party conference, but more than forty major state banquets. That compares, in the ten-year period from 1924–34, with four party congresses, five party conferences, and forty-three plenums. Nevezhin, *Zastol'ia,* 382, 429–32. See also Nevezhin, *Zastol'nye,* 201–11.

293. "Vospominaia Velikuiu otechestvennuiu," 54; Emel'ianov, *Na poroge voiny,* 85; Nevezhin, *Zastol'ia Iosifa Stalina,* 424–5 (Brontman diary); *Pravda,* Oct. 28, 1938. On other occasions of use of the Facets, see *Pravda,* April 18 and Oct. 28, 1938, and June 5 and Nov. 5, 1939.

294. Gromov, *Stalin,* 147; *SSSR na stroike,* 1938, no. 9.

295. Rees, "Stalin as Leader, 1937–1953," 209. In Feb. 1938, when Detizdat wanted to publish Smirnova's *Tales of Stalin's Childhood,* he told them to burn it and not indulge a "cult of the personality, vozhdi, infallible heroes," which he condemned once again as an "SR theory." RGASPI, f. 558, op. 11, d. 1121, l. 24.

296. Stalin's best biographers and analysts have well understood that he combined Marxism-Leninism with imperial Russian traditions. Tucker characterized Stalin's approach as "imperial-communist"; Erik van Ree, as "revolutionary patriotism"; Arfon Rees, as "revolutionary Machiavellism." Tucker, "Stalin and Stalinism," 1–16; van Ree, *Political Thought;* Rees, *Political Thought from Machiavelli to Stalin.*

297. For Shakespeare on the medieval Scottish tyrant Macbeth, see Frye, "Hitler, Stalin, and Shakespeare's Macbeth."

298. Khaustov et al., *Lubianka: Stalin i glavnoe upravlenie,* 499 (APRF, f. 3, op. 24, d. 339, l. 199: March 13, 1938).

299. "I cannot not inform you about the abuses and nightmares in the activities of the NKVD organs in Abkhazia that I personally saw and, in truth, in writing about them, I risk my life, but I write in honor of justice and love of humanity," Mikhail Saliya (b. 1908) wrote to Stalin (Aug. 3, 1938). "A citizen is arrested following a denunciation, supposedly as a counterrevolutionary and is charged as such, and when he begins to protest his innocence, then he is subjected to 'repression.' First, he is stripped naked and placed on the floor, 'fighters' arrive with knouts in hand, about four of them, and begin to beat him, the combat lasts until the victim loses consciousness, he gets a breather of about forty-five minutes, for the 'fighters' too get tired from the combat, he is given ammonia under the nose, to revive him, then his whole body is soaked in water, and the four people begin to beat him again with all their might, the person gives off inhuman sounds, begs, that he is not guilty, but they are immovable. The person loses consciousness again, collapsed without memory, 'the fighters' among themselves say, 'oh, the scoundrel, he is simulating.' They tie paper or a rag in his mouth and continue beating him until he confesses that he is a counterrevolutionary." The rest of the description details rotting flesh ripped off by the blows and covered with flies. Saliya noted that this was not personal (none of his relatives had been arrested), and gave his address. His letter would serve as the pretext for an investigation, after Beria had been transferred to Moscow, which would reveal that a livestock pen water storage bin had been converted into a solitary confinement cell in early 1938 in the Sukhum internal prison and kept filled several inches high with water for interrogations. Stalin notified Georgian party officials (Nov. 14, 1938) of a Central Committee decision to investigate all top NKVD operatives in Georgia during the next three months, and demanded to be informed of all results and actions. Pauchiliya was arrested in Oct. 1938, fired from the NKVD in May 1939, and returned to the Dynamo sports club. Junge and Bonwetsch, *Bolshevistskii poriadok,* II: 355–58 (Arkhiv MVD Gruzii, 1–i otdel, f. 6, d.5520, tom 1, l. 28–30), 361–73 (Arkhiv MVD Gruzii, 1–i otdel, f. 6, d.5520, tom 1, l. 15–24: Oct. 10, 1938), 375–8 (2–i otdel, f. 14, op. 12, d. 256, l. 142–5), 378 (d. 363, l. 146: Nov. 15), 403–9 (1–i otdel, f. 6, d. 5520, tom 3, l. 73–6); Khaustov et al., *Lubianka: Stalin i glavnoe,* 604–6 (APRF, f. 3, op. 58, d. 6, l. 80–3: Nov. 14, 1938).

300. Volkogonov, *Stalin: Triumph and Tragedy,* 339.

PART III. THREE-CARD MONTE

1. "Prime Minister on the Issues," *The Times,* Sept. 28, 1938: 10. See also Chamberlain, *Struggle for Peace.*

2. *DDF,* 2e série, XI: 685 (Delmas to Daladier, Sept. 28, 1938).

3. Corvaja, *Hitler and Mussolini.* The duce would pass his own anti-Semitic laws and boast to his mistress (Aug. 5, 1938), "I've been a racist since '21. I don't know why people think I am imitating Hitler, he wasn't even born. It makes me laugh." Incensed at reports of the illegal miscegenation in Italy's Africa colonies, he added, "I need to teach these Italians about race, so that they don't create half castes and don't ruin what is beautiful in us." Petacci, *Mussolini segreto,* 391: 2.

4. Corvaja, *Hitler and Mussolini,* 27–41. Stalin had an undercover agent report via Poland on the Hitler-Mussolini meeting, and underlined passages related to their reported joint plans for an aggression against the USSR. Khaustov et al., *Lubianka: Stalin i VChK,* 533–41 (RGASPI, f. 558, op. 11, d. 187, l. 28–44).

5. The duce had once told the British ambassador in Rome that Hitler was "a dreamer" and suffered "from an inferiority complex and a bitter sense of injustice." Robertson, *Mussolini as Empire Builder,* 57 (citing *DBFP,* 2nd series, V: 674–5: R. Graham to V. Wellesley, Oct. 11, 1933). Back in July 1934, British foreign secretary Simon wrote to the PM (MacDonald), "We must keep out of trouble in central Europe at all costs . . . There are circumstances in which Italy might move troops into Austria. There are no circumstances in which we would ever dream of doing so." Aldcroft, "Versailles Legacy."

6. Mallett, "Fascist Foreign Policy."

7. Low, *Years of Wrath,* no pagination.

8. Speer, *Spandauer Tagebücher,* 199.

9. "That politics is an art there is no doubt," Mussolini had observed in a speech in 1926 at an art exhibit. "'Political,' like artistic, creation is a slow elaboration and a sudden divination. At a certain moment the artist creates with inspiration, the politician with decision." Falasca-Zamponi, *Fascist Spectacle,* 15, citing Mussolini, *Scritti e discorsi,* V: 279.

10. Dilks makes the further point that the full depravity of Hitler and his regime was neither understood nor evident in 1938. Dilks, "'We Must Hope for the Best,'" 318, 347.

11. Honig, "Totalitarianism and Realism."

12. Litvinov, too, rejected a Soviet solo defense of the Versailles order. Haslam, *Struggle for Collective Security*, 153–4.

13. By March 18, 1938, Churchill was writing, in an article entitled "The Austrian Eye-Opener," that "the scales of illusion have fallen from many eyes." "Friendship with Germany" (Sept. 17, 1937), reprinted in Churchill, *Step by Step*, 141–4 (at 143–4), 192–5.

14. Weinberg, *Hitler's Foreign Policy*, 13.

15. "Three bluffers united are much more powerful than three bluffers playing each for his own hand," wrote Freda Utley. "Germany, Japan, and Italy stand together, possessing neither the necessary economic strength nor political stability for a real war, yet able to blackmail the democratic powers which possess such strength." Utley, "Germany and Japan." Stalin, on Stomonyakov's recommendation, decided to notify Italy that the Anti-Comintern Pact was not an act of friendship toward the USSR. Sevost'ianov, *Moskva-Rim*, 436–8 (APRF, f. 3, op. 64, d. 692, l. 78, 80), 438 (l. 37). See also *DVP SSSR*, XVI: 494–6.

16. Eberhardt, *Ethnic Groups and Population Changes*, 111–36; Glassheim, *Noble Nationalists*; Heimann, *Czechoslovakia*.

17. RGVA, f. 33 987, op. 3, d. 1144, l. 39–41. Prague was sharing intelligence with Moscow; Stalin had his own spy in the Czechoslovak general staff. Khaustov, "Deiatel'nost' organov," 277 (TsA FSB, f. 3, op. 1, d. 210, l. 257; op. 5, d. 63, l. 123; APRF, f. 3, op. 50, d. 32, l. 139).

18. Brook-Shepherd, *Anschluss*; Gehl, *Austria, Germany, and the Anschluss*; von Schuschnigg, *Brutal Takeover*; Low, *Anschluss Movement*.

19. Hitler privately judged Halifax "a clever politician who fully supported Germany's claims." After Eden resigned in a huff in Feb. 1938, Halifax became foreign secretary. Roberts, *Holy Fox*, 71 (citing A4 410 33); Eberle and Uhl, *Hitler Book*, 24–5. On Hitler and Britain, see also von Schuschnigg, *Austrian Requiem*, 20–32.

20. "His Majesty's Government," stated the torturous wording for Henderson to convey to the German government, "could not guarantee that they would not be forced by circumstance to become involved also." *DBFP*, 3rd series, I: 331–2 (Halifax to Henderson, May 21, 1938, also referencing a Chamberlain warning in Parliament in March); *DDF*, 2e série, VIII: 772–4 (March 15); Haslam, *Struggle for Collective Security*, 174.

21. Steiner, *Triumph of the Dark*, 565–6.

22. Taylor, *Sword and Swastika*, 182. See also Waldenegg, "Hitler, Göring, Mussolini."

23. Price, *Year of Reckoning*, 91–117; von Schuschnigg, *Austrian Requiem*, 20–32; Gehl, *Austria, Germany, and the Anschluss*; Churchill, *Second World War*, I: 270.

24. Lassner, "Invasion of Austria," 447–86. See also *French Yellow Book*, 2–3 (François-Poncet to Paris, March 12, 1938). The French military had its eyes on Spain. "The defeat of Franco would open the door to communism in Spain," French military intelligence had noted on March 10, 1938. "Will [the communists] be able to retain power? No. But it would take only a few months for such a regime to precipitate a general European war." Jackson, "French Strategy," 68 (citing SHAT, 7N 2762–2, "L'influence soviétique en Espagne").

25. Tooze, *Wages of Destruction*, 246.

26. *Pravda*, March 13 and 14, 1938.

27. Bukharin's doctored final statement appeared in the press (*Izvestiia* and *Pravda*, March 13, 1938), and in the 700–page court record, which went to the printer on March 28. Murin, "Kak fal'sifitsirovalos' 'delo Bukharina,'" 69: APRF, f. 3, op. 24, d. 401, l. 03; "'Moe poslednee slovo na sude, veroiatno, budet moim poslednim solovom voobshche': kto i kak pravil rech' N. I. Bukahrina." From March 1938, whether by coincidence or instruction, the NKVD political mood summaries mentioned "wrecking" less in reports on the actual problems of Soviet defense industry. Khaustov and Samuelson, *Stalin, NKVD*, 173–6 (TsA FSB, f. 3, op. 5, d. 42, l. 29–33; d. 40, l. 128, 347; d. 41, l. 51–70; APRF, f. 3, op. 24, d. 338, l. 59). Litvinov finally expressed an official Soviet reaction to the "aggression" at a press conference on March 17, 1938, proposing an international conference, but the Soviets followed with no concrete measures. *Izvestiia*, March 18, 1938; Tisminets, *Vneshniaia politika SSSR*, IV: 342–4; *DVP SSSR*, XXI: 138; Dullin, *Men of Influence*, 253.

28. *DVP SSSR*, XVIII: 309–12 (pact with France), 333–6 (pact with Czechoslovakia); *Dokumenty i materialy po istorii sovetsko-chekhoslovatskikh otnoshenii*, III: 106–7 (Beneš and Alexandrovsky, May 2–3, 1935), 111 (Beneš to Czechoslovak missions abroad, May 9), 112 (Litvinov to Alexandrovsky, May 11). Hochman argues that the condition of Soviet obligations (obliged to act only if France did so) had been insisted upon by Moscow. Hochman, *Failure of Collective Security*, 52–3. Cf. Haslam, *Struggle for Collective Security*, 51.

29. *DVP SSSR*, XXI: 125–6 (Potyomkin, March 15, 1938).

30. *DVP SSSR*, XXI: 142–7 (Alexandrovsky with Krofta, March 21); Spáčil and Mal'tsev, *Dokumenty po istorii miunkhenskogo sgovora*, 49–52 (Shaprov, March 15); *Dokumenty po istorii sovetsko-chekhoslovatskikh otnoshenii*, III: 382 (Fierlinger from Moscow, March 15).

31. Sluch, "Pol'sha v politike Sovetskogo Soiuza," 160 (citing AVPRF, f. 0138, op. 19, pap. 128, d. 1, l. 19); *Na prieme*, 233.

32. RGVA, f. 33 987, op. 3, d. 1144, l. 86–7 (Kashuba from Prague, April 9, 1938), Volkogonov papers, Hoover, container 16.

33. *Pravda*, March 29, 1938.

34. Young, "French Intelligence," 274, 278: April 6, 1938.

35. *Na prieme*, 235–6; *Dokumenty i materialy po istorii sovetsko-chekhoslovatskikh otnoshenii*, III: 402 (Fierlinger to Krofta, April 23, 1938). "We come to the aid of Czechoslovakia in the event France comes to its aid and, conversely, Czechoslovakia comes to our aid in the event that France comes to our aid," Kalinin explained to a gathering of propagandists on April 26. He added that the Soviet-Czechoslovak pact "does not prohibit either party rendering assistance to the other without waiting for France"—a statement not reproduced in the press account. Zemskov, *Novye dokumenty iz istorii Miunkhena*, 27–8; *Dokumenty i materialy po istorii sovetsko-chekhoslovatskikh otnoshenii*, III: 402–3 (April 26). On May 8, Kalinin informed a visiting Czechoslovak delegation that the Soviet Union would honor its treaty obligations "to the last letter." Lukes, *Czechoslovakia between Hitler and Stalin*, 143.

36. Bandinelli, *Hitler e Mussolini*; Baxa, "Capturing the Fascist Moment"; Corvaja, *Hitler and Mussolini*, 59–74.

37. *DVP SSSR*, XXI: 276 (Alexandrovsky, May 18, 1938).

38. Henke, *England in Hitlers politischem Kalkül*, 150–62. Sir Horace Wilson, at a luncheon on May 10, 1938, told Soviet ambassador Maisky that "Germany's expansionary

ambitions to create a Mitteleuropa would undermine it by its conglomerate of nationalities, state organizations, and economic regions, producing internal frictions and weaknesses." Gorodetsky, *Maisky Diaries*, 114.

39. Lukes, "Czechoslovak Partial Mobilization." František Moravec, then head of Czechoslovak military intelligence, later insisted that the German attack plans (intercepted and decoded) were real, and that the Czechoslovaks had no choice except to mobilize in response. Moravec, *Master of Spies*, 110–1.

40. Weinberg, *Hitler's Foreign Policy*, II: 691–4; *DGFP*, series D, II: 473–7 (June 18, 1938); Grechko et al., *Istoriia vtoroi mirovoi voiny*, I: 104; Haslam, *Struggle for Collective Security*, 176. The British government tried to restrain the domestic press from crowing about Hitler's apparent climbdown. Parker, *Chamberlain and Appeasement*, 149.

41. Weinberg, *Foreign Policy*, II: 335, 465–6.

42. RGVA, f. 33 987, op. 3, d. 1144, l. 325.

43. *Glavnyi voennyi sovet RKKA*, 135–42 (RGVA, f. 4, op. 18, d. 46, l. 183–90). On Lake Khasan, see also *Voennyi sovet pri narodnom kommissare oborony SSSR*, 206–18 (RGVA, f. 4, op. 14, d. 2030, l. 108–23; op. 18, d. 47, l. 92–5: Nov. 26, 1938). On Aug. 4, 1938, in the middle of the Lake Khasan border war, the Soviet envoy to Czechoslovakia would assure Beneš that the Soviet Union would live up to its European military obligations regardless of the situation in the Far East.

44. Sakwa, "Polish Ultimatum"; *DGFP*, series D, V: 434, 442–3; *DVP SSSR*, XXI: 153–5 (Potyomkin, March 26, 1938). On March 24, Shaposhnikov, chief of the general staff, sent a draft war plan to Voroshilov stating that "the most likely enemies in the West were Germany and Poland." Naumov, *1941 god*, II: 557–60.

45. Gal'ianov, "Kuda idet Pol'sha." Already in Feb. 1938, Potyomkin had told the Bulgarian envoy to Moscow that there might well be a new partition of Poland. Lipinsky, *Das geheime Zusatzprotokoll*, 24. See also Sluch, "Pol'sha v politike Sovetskogo Soiuza," 162–3 (citing AVPRF, f. 05, op. 18, pap. 148, d. 158, l. 30: April 4, 1938); and Raack, "His Question Asked and Answered."

46. Ragsdale, *Coming of World War II*, 81–2, 112–126, 166–7, 185.

47. The Romanian military did not oppose granting transit rights to the Red Army, but King Carol vetoed the idea. Ragsdale, "Soviet Position at Munich," 35–72; Ragsdale, *Coming of World War II*, 81–2, 90–1; Hochman, *Failure of Collective Security*, 56–77, 144–69. No airlift of troops of the necessary magnitude for aiding Czechoslovakia took place even during World War II. See also Ragsdale, in "Munich Crisis," who demolishes the assertions in Pfaff, *Die Sowjetunion und die Verteidigung der Tschechoslowakei*, 392–7.

48. RGVA, f. 33 987, op. 3, d. 1144, l. 150–5, 160, 183; 158–94; Seaton, *Russo-German War*, 56n16.

49. Ulam, *Expansion and Coexistence*, 254; Jackson, *France and the Nazi Menace*, 291; Jackson, "French Military Intelligence," 88–9. Churchill (March 23, 1938) had put the question squarely to Maisky about the Red Army's self-annihilation. Maisky suggested to Litvinov that Churchill be permitted to observe Red Army maneuvers to put to rest the impression derived from the terror. No such visit took place. *DVP SSSR*, XXI: 151–3; Gorodetsky, *Maisky Diaries*, 107; Steiner, "Soviet Commissariat of Foreign Affairs," 755.

50. Primakov, *Ocherki*, III: 65 (no citation). Successive French military attachés had been reprimanded by superiors in Paris for "exaggerating" the USSR's military capacity.

Young, *In Command of France*, 145–49; Coulondre, *De Staline à Hitler*, 129.

51. On Sept. 2, 1938, Jean Payart, long-serving French chargé d'affaires in Moscow, asked Litvinov what assistance the USSR could render to Czechoslovakia, given the reluctance of Poland and Romania to allow Soviet troops and aircraft to pass through; Litvinov reminded him that it was France that was under treaty obligation in the first instance, and that if France came to Czechoslovakia's aid, the Soviet Union would fulfil its obligations "utilizing every means at our disposal." Litvinov repeated the Soviet proposal for an immediate conference of Great Britain, France, and the USSR with military representatives, but Payart left the last part out of his report to the French foreign ministry, and instead managed to incite the idea that the Soviet answer had been "evasive." Steiner, "Soviet Commissariat of Foreign Affairs," 763–5. Litvinov repeatedly warned Alexandrovsky in Prague to make sure the Czechoslovaks did not expect unilateral Soviet assistance.

52. Weinberg, *Hitler's Foreign Policy*, 398; *DDF*, 2e série, IX: 394–5 (July 16, 1938), 402–4 (July 17), 437–8 (July 20), 487n2; Adamthwaite, *France*, 197–9.

53. Young, "French Military Intelligence," 271–309 (at 287).

54. Tooze, *Wages of Destruction*, 246, 255–6, 271–2.

55. *Das Deutsche Reich und der Zweite Weltkrieg*, IX/i: 751–6; Mueller, *Das Heer und Hitler*, 361.

56. Moorhouse, *Killing Hitler*, 79–104, at 99, citing Helmuth Groscuth, *Tagebücher eines Abwehroffiziers 1938–1940* (Stuttgart, 1970), 35.

57. See, for ex., the characteristic letter of Viscount Halifax to Sir Neville Henderson, July 28, 1938, in *DBFP*, 3rd series, II: 17.

58. Parker, *Chamberlain and Appeasement*, 174–81.

59. Weinberg, "Germany, Munich, and Appeasement," 115–6.

60. Young, *Diaries of Sir Robert Bruce Lockhart*, I: 402.

61. Dilks,"'We Must Hope for the Best," 329 (Sept. 11, 1938).

62. Haslam, *Struggle for Collective Security*, 185.

63. Sorge had reported (Sept. 3, 1938) Tokyo's preference for an alliance with Germany directed solely against the USSR. Eleven days later Sorge's radio man transmitted another of his dispatches about Japanese commitment to planning war against the Soviet Union. Gromyko et al., *SSSR v bor'be za mir nakanune*, 650n8.

64. *Glavnyi voennyi sovet RKKA*, 142–52 (RGVA, f. 4, op. 18, d. 46, l. 191–4), 145–8 (l. 195–200), 149–51 (l. 201–5).

65. Zemskov, *Novye dokumenty iz istorii Miunkhena*, 98–100; *Dokumenty i materialy kanuna vtoroi mirovoi voiny*, I: 240; *DVP SSSR*, XXI: 498–9, 500; Adibekov et al., *Politbiuro TsK RKP (b)–VKP (b) i Evropa*, 363–4 (RGASPI, f. 17, op. 162, d. 24, l. 5–6); *DVP SSSR*, XIX: 498–9, 500.

66. Ragsdale, *Coming of World War II*, 121–2; *Dokumenty i materialy po istorii sovetsko-chekhoslovatskikh otnoshenii*, III: 515–17 (Voroshilov's mobilization order, Sept. 21, 1938), 518 (implementation, Sept. 22, 1938); Spáčil and Mal'tsev, *Dokumenty po istorii Miunkhenskogo sgovora*, 254–6. See also Grylev, "Nakanune i v dni Miunkhena," 220–7; Grechko et al., *Istoriia Vtoroi mirovoi voiny*, II: 104–7; Zakharov, *General'nyi shtab*, 112–5; Jukes, "Red Army."

67. See Litvinov's appeal to Stalin from Geneva to seize the moment: *DVP SSSR*, XXI:

520 (Sept. 23, 1938). In Geneva since early Sept., Litvinov repeatedly urged Stalin toward a more activist policy over Czechoslovakia while vowing that his recommended actions would not increase the USSR's obligations, an implied reading of Stalin's concerns. Steiner, "Soviet Commissariat of Foreign Affairs."

68. Dullin, *Men of Influence*, 261 (citing SHAT, 7N3123: report of attaché, Oct. 18, 1938).

69. "Prime Minister on the Issues," *The Times*, Sept. 28, 1938: 10. See also Chamberlain, *In Search of Peace*, 393.

70. Weinberg, *Foreign Policy*, II: 378–464. See also Wendt, *Grossdeutschland*, 150–2.

71. The Soviets, Churchill later wrote of the Munich Pact, "were not brought into the scale against Hitler, and were treated with an indifference—not to say disdain—which left a mark in Stalin's mind." He added: "Events took their course as if Soviet Russia did not exist. For this we afterward paid dearly." Churchill, *Second World War*, I: 305. See also Eberle and Uhl, *Hitler Book*, 30–4.

72. Overy, "Germany and the Munich Crisis"; Kershaw, *Hitler: 1936–1945*, 113–25. On Aug. 2, 1938, British ambassador to Germany Neville Henderson had envisioned exclusion of the Soviet Union from a Four Power Conference supposedly for want of time. *DBFP*, 3rd series, III: 35–6 (Henderson to Strang).

73. Chamberlain had written (Sept. 13) to King George VI about the pending trip to meet Hitler. Haslam, *Struggle for Collective Security*, 188. See also Crozier, *Causes of the Second World War*, 144.

74. Fry, "Agents and Structures."

75. Gunsburg, *Divided and Conquered*, 66–7.

76. Girard de Charbonnières, *La plus évitable de toutes les guerres*, 159–63; Thomas, "France and the Czechoslovak Crisis." Daladier told American ambassador Bullitt (Oct. 2) that Munich had been an "immense defeat for France and England." Haight, *American Aid to France*, 13 (citing Bullitt Papers).

77. Lukes, *Czechoslovakia between Hitler and Stalin*, 237.

78. Murray, *Change in the European Balance of Power*; Hauner, "Czechoslovakia as a Military Factor." Wilhelm Keitel, head of the High Command in 1938, when interrogated at Nuremberg in 1946 about whether Germany would have attacked Czechoslovakia in 1938 if the Western powers had come to Prague's aid militarily, would reply, "Certainly not. We were not strong enough militarily." Fritz Erich von Manstein, another general, would state under interrogation, "had Czechoslovakia defended itself, we would have been held up by her fortifications, for we did not have the means to break through." Similarly, Alfred Jodl would say that, after an invasion of Czechoslovakia, it would have been "militarily impossible" to hold out against a French move from the West. *International Military Tribunal*, X: 572, 600, 772. See also Churchill, *Second World War*, I: 392.

79. Deutsch, *Hitler and His Generals*; Steiner, *Triumph of the Dark*, 575–9.

80. Parssinen, *Oster Conspiracy*, 162.

81. Khaustov, "Deiatel'nost' organov," 247 (TsA FSB, f. 3, op. 4, d. 297, l. 50).

82. Volkogonov, *Triumf i tragediia*, II/i: 17 (citing TsAMO, f. 5, op. 176703, d. 7, l. 431).

83. Herwarth, *Against Two Evils*, 123. The German invasion plan (Fall Grünn) excluded Soviet intervention because of the upheaval in the Red Army. Hochman, *Failure of Collective Security*, 140.

84. Hochman, *Failure of Collective Security*, 162–3, 166–7.

85. Because Stalin did not take his southern holiday, there are none of the instructional

letters to Moscow that are revealing of his thinking. In addition, Comintern General Secretary Georgi Dimtrov, who kept a diary on Stalin's thinking, *was* away on holiday (in Kislovodsk and Crimea) through Oct. 19, 1938.

86. Lukes, *Czechoslovakia between Hitler and Stalin*, 224.

87. Alexandrovsky wrote in his diary: "I confess that I felt uncomfortable, as I could say nothing." "Miunkhen," *Mezhdunarodnaia zhizn'*, 1998, no. 11: 138–40.

88. Lukes, "Stalin and Beneš," 41. Stalin had to think about Japan's obligation in the Anti-Comintern Pact to assist Germany if the USSR and Germany clashed militarily over Czechoslovakia, as pointedly noted in *Izvestiia* (Sept. 30, 1938) in a TASS report on speculation in London newspapers. Koltsov had been dispatched to Czechoslovakia, whence he filed many evocative stories on the crisis—"Alarming Days of Prague," "Czechoslovakia on the Eve of New Tribulations," "Aggressors Mangle Czechoslovakia"—illuminating the Stalinist line.

89. *DVP SSSR*, XXI: 516–7 (Potyomkin, Sept. 23, 1938), 523 (conversation of Jankovski and Potyomkin, Sept. 23).

90. Cienciala, "Foreign Policy of Józef Piłsudski," 143, citing *Polskie dokumenty dyplomatyczne 1938* (Warsaw: Polski Instytut Spraw Micdzynarodowych, 2007), docs. 297, 317.

91. Coulondre, *De Staline à Hitler*, 165. On Sept. 26, the Soviet military attaché in Paris had claimed that thirty infantry and cavalry divisions, along with tanks and airplanes, had been positioned along the frontier with Poland. Gamelin, *Servir*, II: 356.

92. Landau and Tomaszewski, *Monachium 1938*, 462 (Beck to Lipski, Sept. 28, 1939).

93. For indirect evidence of Stalin's designs on Poland's eastern territories, see Raack, "His Question Asked and Answered."

94. Pons, *Stalin and the Inevitable War*, 134–5 (citing RGASPI, f. 495, op. 73, d. 61a, l. 1); *DVP SSSR*, XXI: 738.

95. On Sept. 28, Potyomkin was in the Little Corner from 3:15 a.m. to 3:25 a.m., in the presence of Molotov, Voroshilov, Kaganovich, Zhdanov, and Yezhov, all of whom were there from 2:00 a.m. to 4:15 a.m. *Na prieme*, 241.

96. Banac, *Diary of Georgi Dimitrov*, 77–8. On Sept. 30, Timoshenko and Poliakov gave an overview of Poland's military posture on the Soviet border to Voroshilov. Duraczyński and Sakharov, *Sovetsko-Pol'skie otnosheniia*, 82–3 (RGVA, f. 33797, op. 5, d. 479, l. 199–200).

97. Maslov, "I. V. Stalin o 'Kratkom kurse istorii VKP (b)'"; APRF, f. 45, op. 1, d. 1122, l. 28–11; RGASPI, f. 558, op. 11, d. 1122, l. 54ff.

98. In the early and mid-1930s, the regime had tried but failed to publish an official four-volume and then a two-volume history of the party. Yaroslavsky and Pyotr Pospelov (b. 1898), a graduate of the Institute of Red Professors, began work on a new text. In the meantime, Yaroslavsky's wife, Kirsanova, was expelled from the party, and his son-in-law, Marcel Rosenberg, was arrested. Finally, on April 3, Yaroslavsky and Pospelov presented Stalin with a text. RGASPI, f. 558, op. 11, d. 1217, l. 2–24; Khrushchev, *Vospominaniia*, I: 252; Petrov and Jansen, *Stalinskii pitomets*, 193; Zelenov and Brandenberger, "*Kratkii kurs*," I: 213–8 (d. 1219, l. 1–6). Stalin had the draft circulated among the retinue and, with Zhdanov in tow, received Pospelov (without Yaroslavsky) in the Little Corner on March 4 and 5, 1938, during the Bukharin trial. Stalin made many changes: he transformed all leftist parties other than the Communists into counterrevolutionaries already *before* Oct. 1917, and all oppositionists (left and right) into foreign

agents. From late May 1938, he was engaged in proofreading the revision, then decided to rewrite the text himself. On the author page, he replaced the names of Yaroslavsky and Pospelov with "party commission." "Of the twelve chapters," Stalin reported on Aug. 16, 1938, to the inner circle and the authors, "it turned out to be necessary to revise eleven." (Chapter 5 had been deemed acceptable.) RGASPI, f. 558, op. 11, d. 1219, l. 36–7.

99. In his summary speech at the Feb.–March 1937 plenum, too, Stalin had included a reference to Antaeus and how Hercules defeated him. *Pravda*, April 1, 1937. See also Krivitsky, *In Stalin's Secret Service*, 121.

100. *Istoriia Vsesoiuznoi Kommunisticheskoi partii*, 291–2. See also Deutscher, *Stalin*, 540; and Tucker, "Stalinism as Revolution from Above," 77–110. The expression "revolution from above" had first appeared as a characterization of Germany's unification in the "Bismarck" entry in the *Great Soviet Encyclopedia* published in 1927, a fact now forgotten.

101. Zelenov, "I. V. Stalin v rabote," 6. A collective farmer would write asking for more biographical detail on Stalin to be inserted in the book. Brandenberger, *Propaganda State in Crisis*, 210 (citing RGASPI, f. 17, op. 125, d. 1, l. 5: I. Shabarov, collective farmer from Rostov). Tucker wrote that if Stalin had written memoirs, they would have amounted to nothing more than a second edition of the *Short Course of the History of the Communist Party*. Tucker, *Stalin in Power*, 533, 539.

102. Zelenov, "I. V. Stalin v rabote," 3, 6, 10–1, 25–7. Stalin deleted extended passages, including on his supposed leading party work in the South Caucasus before 1917.

103. Shestakov, *Kratkii kurs*, 291. See also Lih, "Melodrama and the Myth."

104. RGASPI, f. 558, op. 11, d. 1122, l. 3–4. Stalin would elaborate this core axiom two weeks later at the politburo. Khlevniuk et al., *Stenogrammy zasedanii politbiuro*, III: 693; "I. V. Stalin v rabote nad 'Kratkim kursom,'" 19.

105. *Na prieme*, 239–40; Zelenov and Brandenberger, "Kratkii kurs," I: 373–4 (RGASPI, f. 558, op. 11, d. 1219, l. 37); Zelenov, *I. V. Stalin, Istoricheskaia ideologiiia*, I: 312–91. See also Medvedev, "How the Short Course Was Created"; and Avrich, "Short Course and Soviet Historiography."

106. Zelenov and Brandenberger, "Kratkii kurs," I: 375–81 (RGASPI, f. 77, op. 3, d. 159, l. 338–78).

107. Zelenov and Brandenberger, "Kratkii kurs," I: 425 (RGASPI, f. 17, op. 3, d. 1002, l. 12: Sept. 19, 1938). It would be translated into the languages of Union and autonomous republics the next year and, eventually, reach 42.8 million copies in 67 languages. "Izdanie proizvedenii I. V. Stalina v Sovetskom Soiuze c 7 noiabria 1917 goda na 5 marta 1953: statisticheskie tablitsii," *Sovetskaia bibliografiia: sbornik statei i materialov*, vyp. 1 (Moscow: Vsesoiuznaia knizhnaia palata, 1953), and Maslov, "'Kratkii kurs istorii VKP (b)'—Entsiklopediia kul'ta lichnosti," 51. In 1937-38, the censor withdrew from circulation 16,435 titles, amounting to 24 million volumes. This was a partial accounting (the main censor lacked jurisdiction over military publications). Brandenberger, *Propaganda State in Crisis*, 222 (citing GARF. F. 9425, op. 1, d. 5, l. 66; d. 11, l. 61).

108. RGASPI, f. 558, op. 11, d. 1122, l. 1–18, 28–111. Stalin's speeches at the meeting can also be found in Zelenov, *I. V. Stalin, Istoricheskaia ideologiiia*, I: 394–9 (Sept. 27, 1938), 401–24 (Oct. 1).

109. RGASPI, f. 558, op. 11, d. 1122, l. 58–9.

110. During *Pravda*'s publication of the *Short Course*, Stalin phoned the editors, according

to the journalist Brontman, and reiterated, over and over, the need to publish more material on the "white collar." Brontman noted: "It's a new matter." Brontman, *Dnevniki* (entry for Sept. 20, 1938).

111. Back when battling the Georgian Mensheviks before 1917, Stalin had advocated for working-class party members, but in power he offered ambiguous views. Chuev, *Tak govoril Kaganovich*, 31; Graziosi, "Stalin's Anti-worker Workerism, 1924–1931"; Lih et al., *Stalin's Letters to Molotov*, 219. The secret circular he had dispatched after Kirov's assassination warned that Bolsheviks with worker origins sometimes turned out to be provocateurs (citing Roman Malinowski, whose secret spying for the *okhranka* had put Stalin back in prison before the revolution). Yezhov, in 1935, had complained, "look, this veneration for the worker is completely un-Bolshevik and un-Marxist." Davies and Harris, *Stalin's World*, 198 (citing RGASPI, f. 558, op. 11, d. 1118, l. 56–60); "Zakrytoe pis'mo Tsk VKP (b)," 97; Getty and Naumov, *Road to Terror*, 201.

112. RGASPI, f. 558, op. 11, d. 1122, l. 10.

113. RGASPI, f. 17, op. 120, d. 307, l. 7–11, 68–72, 80–5, 113–4.

114. RGASPI, f. 558, op. 11, d. 1122, l. 3–4. "I am not a theoretician [*teoretik*], but a practitioner [*praktik*] who knows theory," Stalin explained, adding, "such are the kind of people we want to have: practitioners with knowledge of theory." See the prompt from Yaroslavsky: Zelenov and Brandenberger, "Kratkii kurs," I: 419–20 (RGASPI, f. 558, op. 11, d. 1219, l. 101).

115. Hochman, *Failure of Collective Security*, 166.

116. Telegrams had to be sent directly from the telegram office; there were also phonegrams transmitted by special telephone. Moscow received the first message around 5:00 p.m., and the second at 5:15; each had to be decoded. *DVP SSSR*, XXI: 549–50 (Potyomkin, Sept. 30, 1938); Lukes, "Stalin and Beneš," 37–9. Beneš's moods vacillated, according to Alexandrovsky (one of the few envoys to see the Czechoslovak president regularly). Alexandrovskii, "Munich Witness's Account," 129, 132. See also Steiner, "The Soviet Commissariat of Foreign Affairs," 772–3 (citing AVP RF, f. 0138, op. 19, pap. 128, d. 6, l. 161–75: Alexandrovsky's diary, written Oct. 1938).

117. *DVP SSSR*, XXI: 548–9 (Alexandrovsky, Sept. 30, 1938), 549 (Sept. 30, 1938), 549–50 (Potyomkin, Sept. 30, 1938), 552–3 (Alexandrovsky, Oct. 1, 1938).

118. Lukes, *Czechoslovakia between Hitler and Stalin*, 262; Lukes, "Stalin and Czechoslovakia," 14–6.

119. Soon he would add "cultural-educational" organization to the list of the state's functions. *Pravda*, March 11, 1939, reprinted in *Sochineniia*, XIV: 394.

120. Zelenov and Brandenberger, "Kratkii kurs," I: 452–66 (RGASPI, f. 558, op. 11, d. 1122, l. 28–9, 34–42, 44–9, 51, 53–61, 63, 65–70, 77–88).

121. Wandycz, *Twilight of French Eastern Alliances*, 452, 478; Prażmowska, *Eastern Europe*, 144.

122. Gromyko et al., *SSSR v bor'be za mir nakanune*, 25–28, at 28 (Lipski to Beck, Oct. 1, 1938).

123. Khaustov and Samuelson, *Stalin, NKVD*, 28. Churchill would famously call interwar Poland a "hyena" for its actions over Těšín (Cieszyn), Churchill, *Second World War*, I: 311. Soviet intelligence evidently reported rumors from Riga (Oct. 10, 1938) that Poland had also demanded Latvia's ethnic Polish regions (such

as Daugavpils/Dźwińsk-Dyneburg). Sotskov, *Pribaltika i geopolitika*, 56 (no citation).

124. *DVP SSSR*, XXI: 599. Stalin possessed a manuscript on German-Polish relations by the émigré Alexander Guchkov, one of the two Duma representatives in 1917 who had been sent to obtain Tsar Nicholas II's abdication. Pilfered in Paris, the text discussed the possibility of Poland handing Danzig over to Germany, with the thinking that this would satiate German claims and redirect German aggression against Stalin's Soviet Union. Khaustov, "Deiatel'nost' organov," 234. See also Tokarev, "'Kará panam! Kará.'"

125. On Oct. 2, Soviet ambassador to London Ivan Maisky telegrammed Moscow reporting that, on Sept. 30, he had gone to see Tomáš Masaryk, the Czechoslovak representative in Britain, to express condolences. "They sold me into slavery to the Germans," Masaryk was reported to have told Maisky through tears, "the way that once the Negroes were sold into slavery in America!" Gromyko et al., *SSSR v bor'be za mir nakanune*, 29–31 (AVP RF, f. 059, op. 1, pap. 278, d. 1931, l. 53–6: Oct. 2, 1938); *God krizisa*, I: 41–3. On Oct. 5, 1938, Beneš would resign under German pressure and, seventeen days later, go into exile in London.

126. Craigie, *Behind the Japanese Mask*, 67–8. Craigie served as Britain's ambassador to Tokyo.

127. Von Hassel, *Die Hasseltagebücher*, 51; Genoud, *Testament of Adolf Hitler*, 84–5; Fest, *Hitler*, 742. Not for Hitler the ancient Sun Tzu's wisdom: "the greatest victory is that which requires no battle."

128. Jackson, "End of Appeasement," 237 (citing SHAT, 7N 2515 [Oct. 10–16, 1938] and 2605 [Oct. 11, 1938], 2602–1 [Nov. 9, 1938]). Hitler and his minions even felt that Munich had somehow reconfirmed the Western powers' objections to Germany's assumption of its rightful place, which justified Germany's forcing through even greater expenditures on the military, railways, highways, and other infrastructure. Tooze, *Wages of Destruction*, 288.

129. *The Times*, Oct. 1, 1938. The Soviets were in difficult trade negotiations with Italy at this time. The Italians were demanding additional oil deliveries; Litvinov recommended offering grain. Sevost'ianov, *Moskva-Rim*, 454 (APRF, f. 3, op. 65, d. 246, l. 128: Litvinov to Stalin, Oct. 15, 1938), 455 (l. 127: Oct. 22, 1938, politburo decree).

130. *DGFP*, series D, IV: 602–4 (Tippelskirch, Oct. 3, 1938).

131. *Sochineniia*, XVI: 118.

132. *Pravda*, Sept. 18, 1938. See also *Pravda*, Nov. 4, 1938 (Zhdanov) and *Izvestiia*, Nov. 10, 1938 (Molotov).

133. Khaustov, "Deiatel'nost' organov," 235 (TsA FSB, f. 3, op. 5, d. 81, l. 140); Khaustov and Samuelson, *Stalin, NKVD*, 305. Surits, in Paris, wrote to the foreign affairs commissariat in Moscow that "any Frenchman" could see that for France the Munich Pact constituted "a most terrible defeat" equivalent to a "second Sedan" (when Germany crushed France in Bismarck's wars of unification). Gromyko et al., *SSSR v bor'be za mir nakanune*, 35–6 ("excerpted": Oct. 12, 1938). Following the Munich Pact, the British agent in Salamanca, Robert Hodgson, told Eberhard von Stohrer, the German ambassador to Franco's regime, that Britain intended to mediate the conflict in Spain. Franco, at dinner with Stohrer on Oct. 1, rhapsodized over Hitler's triumph at Munich. *DGFP*, series D, III: 754–60; Thomas, *Spanish Civil War*, 555–6, 827–8.

134. Passov, appointed on March 28, 1938, had remained head of civilian intelligence with the

formation of the NKGB in Sept. 1938, but would be arrested on Oct. 23 for anti-Soviet conspiracy. Sudoplatov served as acting chief of NKGB espionage until Dec. 2, 1938, when Vladimir Dekanozov would be appointed. Passov would be executed on Feb. 14, 1940. Abramov, *Evrei v KGB*, 260–1; Khaustov et al., *Lubianka: Stalin i glavnoe upravlenie*, 7; Khaustov, "Deiatel'nost' organov," 252 (TsA FSB, f. H-15014, t. 2, l. 90); Kolpakidi and Prokhorov, *Vneshniaia razvedka Rossii*, 106–7.
135. Khlevniuk et al., *Stenogrammy zasedanii politbiuro*, III: 694–6; RGASPI, f. 17, op. 163, d. 1217, l. 51–2. Only after publication of the *Short Course* would Stalin relinquish formal control over ideology in the Central Committee secretariat, giving the portfolio to Zhdanov on Nov. 27, 1938. Khlevniuk et al., *Stalinskoe politbiuro*, 171.
136. Zelenov and Brandenberger, "*Kratkii kurs*," I: 494–5. Stalin added: "Comrade Khrushchev thinks that to this day he remains a worker, when in fact he is an intelligent."
137. Eugene Lyons would write that "only another war, and a catastrophically losing one, could effectively challenge Stalin's ascendancy." Lyons, *Stalin*, 290. See also Kuromiya, "Accounting for the Great Terror."
138. Pons, *Stalin and the Inevitable War*; Gorodetsky, *Grand Delusion*, 4. Yefim Dzigan's feature film *If War Comes Tomorrow*, which had premiered earlier in the year, had made the Red Army seem invincible, mixing documentary footage of paratroopers during maneuvers with a catchy, reassuring song with words by Vasily Lebedev-Kumach: "If war comes tomorrow, if tomorrow it's into battle, be prepared today!"

139. *Dokumenty i materialy po istorii sovetsko-pol'skikh otnoshenii*, VI: 366 (Grzibowski telegram to Warsaw, Oct. 9, 1938). Following a secret gathering of German military brass on Aug. 19, 1938, at the special SS complex in Yuteborg, Soviet intelligence reported on Nazi Germany's aggressive designs on the Soviet Union, noting that a major general on Göring's chief of staff had said that "the main goal of the Führer is a struggle with our real enemies, the Soviets, who have paralyzed Japan in the East and could defend Ukraine only with weak forces. The Führer's goal is to avoid conflicts with England and France and attain a European pact of the four. Germany needs colonies, not in Africa, but in Eastern Europe, she needs a breadbasket—Ukraine." A Soviet military intelligence analysis of Germany in Jan. 1939 would conclude that, whereas "Czechoslovakia had served as a barrier to German expansion toward the southeast, now, on the contrary, it serves as a trampoline." But the report would also quote the *Manchester Guardian* to the effect that "a shortage of oil might turn out to be the fateful weakness of the German war machine." Gavrilov, *Voennaia razvedka informiruet*, 21–2 (RGVA, f. 25888, op. 11, d. 86, l. 15), 25–6.
140. On Oct. 31, Litvinov told the Polish ambassador their nonaggression pact remained in force. This would be confirmed bilaterally on Nov. 26, 1938, and announced by TASS the next day.
141. Khaustov and Samuelson, *Stalin, NKVD*, 253, 309–10 (TsA FSB, f. 3 os, op. 6, d. 8, l. 13).
142. "Vospominaniia Nikity Sergeevicha Khrushcheva," 87; Pavliukov, *Ezhov*, 470; Petrov and Jansen, *Stalinskii pitomets*,

179–80; Khlevniuk, *Khoziain*, 344. It seems that at Stalin's direction, Yezhov had called Uspensky and summoned him to Moscow—Uspensky drew his own dubious conclusions.
143. RGASPI, f. 17, op. 162, d. 24, l. 62.
144. Kostrychenko and Khazanov, "Konets Kar' ery Ezhova," 125–8 (RGASPI, f. 17, op. 3, d. 1003, l. 85–86); Khaustov et al., *Lubianka: Stalin i glavnoe upravlenie*, 607–11 (APRF, f. 3, op. 58, d. 6, l. 85–7); Getty and Naumov, *Road to Terror*, 532–7. On Yezhov's anger at being accused of lawlessness, when he was following Stalin's instructions, with which Vyshinsky had colluded, see Ushakov and Stukalov, *Front voennykh prokurorov*, 70–2.
145. "The fear of war had spawned mass terror," wrote Ulam. "But terror in its turn increased Stalin's fear of war." This appears to be exactly backward: Stalin's fear of war seems to have *ended* the mass terror. Ulam, *Stalin*, 491–2. On Oct. 16, 1938, the politburo resolved to demobilize and return the forces called to the western borders: 330,000 troops, 27,500 horses, and 5,000 vehicles. RGASPI, f. 17, op. 162, d. 24, l. 172.
146. Kissinger, *Diplomacy*, 333. E. H. Carr also portrayed Stalin as the embodiment of Russian realpolitik in his forced industrialization and foreign policy. The Carr student Gabriel Gorodetsky has asserted that "Machiavelli rather than Lenin was Stalin's idol," a dubious claim that does not diminish the value of the treasure trove of evidence that Gorodetsky brought to the fore. Gorodetsky, *Grand Delusion*, 317; Haslam, "Stalin and the German Invasion of Russia," 134. See also, on Carr, D'Agostino, "Stalin Old and New."

CHAPTER 10. HAMMER

1. Chuev, *Sto sorok*, 414–5. Stalin, in the name of the politburo, had removed A. M. Mogilny, head of Molotov's secretariat, on Aug. 17, 1937; he removed M. Khlusser, another top Molotov aide, eleven days later. RGASPI, f. 17, op. 3, d. 990, l. 54, 72.
2. Shpanov, *Pervyi udar*; Shpanov, "Pervyi udar." The fantasy novella had been completed back in 1937, under the title *Twelve Hours of War*, and slated for publication by the Union of Soviet Writers publishing house, but the main censor had blocked it on the grounds that it was aesthetically "hopeless." "Dokladnaia zapiska agitpropa TsK M. A. Suslovu po povodu izdaniia knigi 'podzhigateli' N. N, Shapnova" (April 20, 1949): http://alexanderyakovlev.org/fond/is sues-doc/69631. It would be republished with other stories in summer 1939 by *Sovetskii pisatel'*. See also Ulam, *Stalin*, 492.
3. Vishnevskii, "Kniga o budushchei voine."
4. Yezhov had tried to take Litvinov down. Khaustov and Samuelson, *Stalin, NKVD*, 184–5. On Jan. 1, 1939, in verification of 22,000 people with access to classified materials in people's commissariats and current agencies of USSR and RSFSR, more than 3,000 were fired. Khaustov, "Deiatel'nost' organov," 361–2.
5. *DVP SSSR*, XX: 579 (Litvinov to Maisky, Oct. 29, 1937).
6. The perspicacious British envoy Chilston observed "bitter disappointment" in Moscow over Munich, noting that the Kremlin "would like more than ever to pursue a policy of isolation if they could safely do so, [but] realize that, after Munich, they can afford to risk isolation even less than they could before." Neilson, *Britain, Soviet Russia*, 257 (citing Chilston to FO, disp. 442 Oct. 18, 1938, FO 371/22289/N5164/97/38: minute, Collier, Oct. 28, 1938).

7. Edwards, *British Government and the Spanish Civil War*, 130 (July 5, 1938).
8. George Kennan, "The War Problem of the Soviet Union" (March 1935), George F. Kennan Papers, Box 1, Mudd Library, Princeton University, reprinted in Hochman, *Failure of Collective Security*, 176–83 (at 176).
9. One group of analysts has argued that he began with a genuine commitment to achieve "collective security" with the West, only to sour on this option as a result of Anglo-French behavior. Haslam, *Struggle for Collective Security*. Diametrically opposed, another group of analysts has insisted Stalin was bent all along on a deal with Hitler. Hochman, *Failure of Collective Security*. Stalin pursued both options. What neither group fully appreciated was the extent to which he was not the driver of events.
10. The British especially had looked to non-Nazi members of the German cabinet such as Baron von Neurath (foreign minister), General von Blomberg (war minister), and Hjalmar Schacht (economics minister), all of whom were gone by 1938. Then the British elevated Göring to the role of presumed restraining influence on the Nazi "wild" men around Hitler. Watt, "British Intelligence," 249.
11. Bond, *Chief of Staff*, I: 155–6 (Aug. 8, 1938).
12. Hinsley et al., *British Intelligence*, I: 47, 68, 80.
13. Hitler, because of its association with Bolshevism, had rejected the term "dictator" and preferred to be known as the Führer of the German race, viewing democracy, dictatorship, and Judentum as of a piece. Nolte, "Diktatur," I: 922; Schmitt, *Die Diktatur*; Cobban, *Dictatorship*. Baehr, "Dictatorship."
14. Krivitskii, "Iz vospominaniia sovetskogo kommunista."

15. In 1933, Hitler had arranged that all private documents concerning his childhood and youth were confiscated. These would be destroyed in April 1945. Ullrich, *Hitler: Ascent*, 17.
16. Ryback, *Hitler's Private Library*. Some 1,200 volumes of Hitler's 16,000-volume library are in the Library of Congress.
17. Hitler had met Mari Reiter, a pretty blonde, in Berchtesgaden in fall 1926; he was thirty-seven, she was sixteen. Her father was a founding member of the local Social Democrat Party and she ran a clothing shop. He called her "my dear child"; she called him Wolf. Their intimacy was episodic. Hitler met Eva Braun in Hoffmann's Munich studio. He was then forty; she was seventeen, middle-class, pretty. He took her for sausages and beer under a false name (Herr Wolf), but initially she rebuffed him. Hitler's main affections were directed at his niece, Geli Raubal, a girl with dark, wavy brown hair who resided in his Munich apartment, but in Sept. 1931 she was found dead there, shot with a revolver, and scandal rocked Munich. But Hitler was absent from the city that day. Geli's demise proved Eva's opening: in fall 1932, still living in Munich but despairing over her infrequent access to Hitler, she shot herself with her father's pistol, but survived. She tried and failed to kill herself again in 1935. By early 1936, she and Hitler had become a regular, if non-public unmarried couple. At the Reich Chancellery in Berlin, the company was almost all male, but at the Berghof alpine sanctuary, Hitler had afforded Eva a private apartment, next to his bedroom, and she presided as mistress of the retreat, present at meals (seated to his left) and at his ramblings on race and global conquest. Kershaw, *Hitler: 1889–1936*, 353; Görtemaker, *Eva Braun*.
18. Speer, *Erinnerungen*, 116.

19. Ullrich, *Hitler: Ascent*, 380–411; Hanfstaengl, *Zwischen Weissem und Braunem Haus*, 165; Speer, *Spandauer Tagebücher*, 523; Joachimsthaler, *Hitlers Liste*, 362; Ribbentrop, *Zwischen London und Moskau*, 48.

20. Speer, *Inside the Third Reich*, 140, 154. When films were shown, bodyguards and some of the female staff were admitted.

21. Fröhlich, *Tagebücher von Joseph Goebbels*, II/ii: 251 (March 29, 1932).

22. Neumann, *Behemoth*; Hayes, "Polycracy and Policy," 190–210; Broszat, *Hitler State*; Broszat, *Der Staat Hitlers*. See also Trevor-Roper, *Last Days of Hitler*, 54; and Overy, *Göring*, 4.

23. On Oct. 28, 1938, the Head of the Reich Chancellery (Lammers)—the link between Hitler and state ministers—had written to Hitler's adjutant begging to report on urgent state matters, adding that he had not spoken with the Führer for more than six weeks. Noakes and Pridham, *Nazism*, II: 245.

24. Speer, *Inside the Third Reich*, 145.

25. Wiedemann, *Der Mann*, 69; also available, translated, in Noakes and Pridham, *Nazism*, II: 207–8. After 1933, Hitler almost never wrote anything either. The important exception was perhaps his "Four Year Memorandum" (1936), written in anger and frustration at the 1935–6 economic crisis; Hitler passed copies of the memorandum only to two people, both in the military: Göring and Blomberg. (Much later, a third copy went to Speer.) The Economics Minister did not get a copy. Kershaw, "Working towards the Führer," 90.

26. Stalin "enjoyed settling . . . trivial issues," one biographer has noted. He "got used to the idea that people couldn't manage without him, that he must do everything." Volkogonov, *Stalin: Triumph and Tragedy*, 147.

27. Kershaw, *Nazi Dictatorship*, 70.

28. Ullrich, *Hitler: Ascent*, 397 (citing BA Koblenz N 1340/384); Speer, *Erinnerungen*, corrected ms. (2nd version), chapter 1; and Schroeder, *Er War Mein Chef*, 78–81.

29. Shirer, *Rise and Fall*, 275–6. As Bracher noted, "among the men closest to the Führer, all joined long before the big wave of newcomers in March 1933." They were distinguished by "the right of immediate access." Bracher, *German Dictatorship*, 277; Bracher, *Die nationalsozialistische Machtergreifung*, 607.

30. Kershaw, "Nature of the Hitler Dictatorship," 117; Kershaw, *Hitler: 1889–1936*, 527–91; Noakes and Pridham, *Nazism*, II: 207. Adolf Eichmann would testify that, "No sooner had Hitler made a speech—and he invariably touched on the Jewish question—then every party or government department felt that it was up to them to do something." When it came to specific incidents—such as the pogrom known as Kristallnacht (Night of Broken Glass), on Nov. 8–9, 1938, which would leave around 100 Jews dead and 7,500 Jewish businesses vandalized—Hitler explicitly approved the action. On Dec. 6, 1938, Göring warned the Gauleiters against initiatives predicated upon the Führer's presumed wishes. Von Lang, *Eichman Interrogated*, 59; Fröhlich, *Tagebücher von Joseph Goebbels*, VI: 179–81 (Nov. 10, 1938); Friedlander, "Path that Led into the Abyss." See also Rebentisch, *Führerstaat und Verwaltung*. Kershaw presented the concept very broadly—a small businessman besting a competitor by questioning his Aryan credentials; ordinary people perniciously denouncing neighbors to the Gestapo to settle private scores—and in that guise, it could be tantamount to just living under Nazi rule. Kershaw himself writes, moreover, that "there was never any suggestion that Hitler might be bypassed or ignored, that anyone but he could make a key decision. And, once he finally decided to act, he did so . . . with ruthlessness." Kershaw, *Hitler: 1889–1936*, 328. See also Kershaw, "Uniqueness of Nazism"; and Mommsen, "Hitler's Position," 163–88; Kershaw, *Nazi Dictatorship* (4th ed.), 59–79. The basic idea that minions were in competition to gain the favor of the Führer, creating a dynamic that radicalized policy, appears in Hannah Arendt. Seweryn Bialer had called this phenomenon "preemptive obedience." Bialer, *Stalin's Successors*.

31. Zhuravlyov's denunciation followed the formation of the commission on the NKVD. Beria had passed the letter to Stalin on Oct. 13, 1938. Khaustov and Samuelson, *Stalin, NKVD*, 249–50; *Na prieme*, 245–6. See also Shreider, *NKVD iznutri*, 237. Zhuravlyov briefly got a promotion to Moscow, but Beria would send him to run the Karaganda camps. Yezhov's response—accepting guilt, claiming poor health, confessing he "had taken badly the appointment of Beria as my deputy. I see in this an element of lack of trust towards me," and requesting to resign—is misdated as Sept. (rather than Nov.) 23, 1938. Kostrychenko and Khazanov, "Konets Kar'ery Ezhova," 129–30 (RGASPI, f. 17, op. 3, d. 1003, l. 82–4); Khaustov et al., *Lubianka: Stalin i glavnoie upravlenie*, 552–4 (RGASPI, f. 17, op. 3, d. 1003, l. 82–4); Petrov and Jansen, *Stalinskii pitomets*, 355–9 (RGASPI, f. 671, op. 1, d. 265, l. 16–26ob.). See also Sudoplatov and Sudoplatov, *Memoirs of an Unwanted Witness*, 59. This is another example where Sudoplatov's memoir comports with archival materials.

32. Petrov and Jansen, *Stalinskii pitomets*, 355–9, at 357 (from APRF, f. 57, op. 1, d. 265, l. 16–26ob.).

33. Kostrychenko and Khazanov, "Konets Kar'ery Ezhova," 131 (RGASPI, f. 17, op. 3, d. 1003, l. 34–5); Khaustov et al., *Lubianka: Stalin i glavnoie upravlenie*, 611 (RGASPI, f. 17, op. 3, d. 1003, l. 34–5).

34. Petrov and Jansen, *Stalinski pitomets*, 354–5 (RGASPI, f. 558, op. 11, d. 58, l. 61–2); Khaustov et al., *Lubianka: Stalin i glavnoie upravlenie*, 611–2; RGASPI, f. 17, op. 3, d. 1003, l. 35 (appointment of Beria). The last of the infamous execution lists for 1938 was dated Sept. 29: APRF, f. 3, op. 24, d. 409–19: http://stalin.memo.ru/images/intro.htm. But Volkgonov, citing military archives, claimed that Stalin, having received some 383 extended lists of names for execution in 1937–38, received yet another on Dec. 12, 1938, containing 3,167 names, albeit without even the charges or the results of any "investigation." Volkogonov, *Triumf i tragediia*, I/ii: 301 (citing TsAMO, f. 32, op. 701323, d. 38, l. 14–6).

35. Khaustov and Samuelson, *Stalin, NKVD*, 255–6. Of the 14,500 new NKVD employees in 1939, around 11,000 came from the party apparatus or Communist Youth League. Of the 3,460 newcomers in the central NKVD, 3,242 were party apparatchiks and Komsomol. Petrov and Skorkin, *Kto rukovodil NKVD*, 491–502. There was no hint of societal rebellion. In early 1939, the police discovered a self-styled "fascist organization" in Moscow. Evidently, its handful of youthful members had fashioned a flag and put up seventy posters on the eve of Red Army Day, drew some graffiti, and wrote poems. They also seem to have discussed Nazism, anti-Semitism, and Russian nationalism. Four arrests were made; three of them turned out to have been nineteen years old when they joined the group, and the organizer was seventeen. The NKVD produced five volumes on the case.

Rittersporn, *Anguish*, 174 (citing GARF, f. 5446, op. 81a, d. 335, l. 109–14).

36. Suvenirov, *Tragediia RKKA*, 332 (citing RGVA, f. 9, op. 39, d. 54, l. 114, 119, 154).

37. Khaustov, "Deiatel'nost' organov," 146 (TsA FSB, f. 3os, op. 6, d. 11, l. 185). Khaustov et al., *Lubianka: Stalin i glavnoe upravlenie*, 629–30 (RGASPI, f. 17, op. 3, d. 1004, l. 22). See also Knight, *Beria*, 91. Another 1,960 operatives in the NKVD would be arrested in 1939, including border guards and Gulag. Khaustov, "Deiatel'nost' organov," 151; Khaustov and Samuelson, *Stalin, NKVD*, 259. Some 7,372 NKVD personnel were let go in 1939, not all of whom were arrested. Petrov and Skorkin, *Kto rukovodil NKVD*, 501; all told, some 60 percent of NKVD personnel would turn over between Oct. 1936 and the end of 1939, while 21,088 new people were promoted to operative positions in 1939. Khaustov and Samuelson, *Stalin, NKVD*, 259.

38. Petrov and Skorkin, *Kto rukovodil NKVD*, 495.

39. As of Oct. 1, 1936, of the 110 most senior operatives in state security, 43 had been Jews (declared), and 42 had been eastern Slavs (Russians, Ukrainians, Belorussians), along with 9 Latvians, 5 Poles, and 2 ethnic Germans; by Sept. 1938, of the 150 most senior ranks, 98 were ethnic Russians and 32 Jews, with no Latvians and 1 Pole. By 1939, there would be 122 Russians, 6 Jews, and 12 Georgians. Petrov and Skorkin, *Kto rukovodil NKVD*, 492–500.

40. Simonov, *Glazami cheloveka moego pokoleniia*, 58 (dated Feb. 27, 1979).

41. The Georgia NKVD was given to Avksenti Rapava, Beria's minion who had helped pulverize Abkhazia. Guruli and Tushurashvili, *Correspondence*, 89 (Beria to Stalin, Oct. 21, 1937).

42. The transfer took place in Aug. 1938, with Beria's promotion. Merkulov: RGANI, f. 5, op. 30, d. 4, l. 76–7: letter, to Malenkov, July 23, 1953; "'Khochetsia prokliast' den' i chas moego znakomstva s Beriia,'" 101 (APRF, f. 3, op. 24, d. 465, l. 2–28); Tumshis, *VChK*, 211.

43. Kuromiya and Pepłoński, "Stalin und die Spionage," 29. Amid Stalin's self-inflicted chaos, NKVD operatives placed one foreign ambassador's perlustrated letter into the envelope of another. Plotnikova, "Organy," 77, 79.

44. Khaustov, "Deiatel'nost' organov," 162–3 (TsA FSB, f. 3os, op. 7, d. 4, l. 14).

45. Kochik, "Sovetskaia voennaia razvedka," (Dec. 15, 1938). Khaustov writes that "by the results of the special reports that came to Stalin during the second half of the 1930s, one can judge that we did not succeed in recruiting valuable sources of information in European representative offices." Khaustov, "Deiatel'nost' organov," 292.

46. Jacobsen, *Nationalsozialistische Aussenpolitik*; Maser, *Hitlers Mein Kampf*; Hildebrand, "Hitlers *Mein Kampf*, Propaganda oder Programm?"

47. Jackel, *Hitler's Worldview*, 47–66. Hitler did not use anti-Semitism as a vote-gathering or scapegoating ploy to come to power, but was using power to realize a deeply held anti-Semitic agenda. Kershaw, *Nazi Dictatorship* (4th ed.), 93–132.

48. Heiden had been the correspondent for the liberal *Frankfürter Zeitung* in his hometown in the 1920s, watching Hitler's rabble-rousing, then in 1933 had gone into exile in the Saarland, before moving to Switzerland and eventually France. "The 'hero' of this book is neither a superman nor a puppet," he wrote in the preface (dated 1935). "He is a very interesting contemporary and, viewed quantitatively, a man who has stirred up the masses more

than anyone else in human history." He depicted Hitler as both the reflection of and the antithesis to Europe, which, he argued, was a community of shared interests and of democracy that provided for freedom and peace. He called for a new "people's parliament, constituted by freely elected representatives of all nations," to replace "the conference of diplomats and bureaucrats in Geneva." Heiden, *Hitler*, I: 6, 330; Heiden, *Hitler*, II: 267, 369. Volume 1 was translated as *Hitler: A Biography* (New York: A. A. Knopf, 1936).

49. Yaney, "War and the Evolution of Russian Government," 302-3.

50. Khaustov and Samuelson, *Stalin, NKVD*, 30-2.

51. "If there is any fighting in Europe to be done," British Prime Minister Stanley Baldwin had told a group of parliamentarians in 1936, "I should like to see the Bolsheviks and the Nazis doing it." He also remarked: "If he [Hitler] moves East, I shall not break my heart." Middlemas and Barnes, *Baldwin*, 947; Carley, "Soviet Foreign Policy."

52. Bullard also complained of his colleague, the British ambassador to Moscow, that "the dishonesty of the Soviet leaders does not disgust him." Bullard and Bullard, *Inside Stalin's Russia*, 144, 151.

53. Carley, *1939*.

54. "We are in the remarkable position of not wanting to quarrel with anybody because we have got most of the world already, or the best parts of it, and we only want to keep what we have got and prevent others from taking it away from us," Admiral Sir A. E. Chatfield had observed privately in mid-1934. "We are a very rich and very vulnerable Empire and there are plenty of poor adventurers who are not far away who look on us with hungry eyes," Chamberlain had written in a private letter (Jan. 16, 1938). Thorne, *Limits of Foreign Policy*, 397-8 (letter to Warren Fisher, June 4, 1934); Freiling, *Life of Neville Chamberlain*, 323 (Chamberlain to Mrs. Morton Prince).

55. Haas, *Ideological Origins of Great Power Politics*, 105-45. See also Neilson, *Britain, Soviet Russia*.

56. Overy, *Twilight Years*.

57. Gibbs, *Ordeal in England*, 409-10.

58. Schroeder, "Munich and the British Tradition."

59. Caputi, *Neville Chamberlain and Appeasement*; McDonough, *Neville Chamberlain*; Mills, "Chamberlain-Grandi Conversations"; Parker, *Chamberlain and Appeasement*.

60. Layne, "Security Studies"; Peden, *Arms, Economics*, 127, 138; and Reynolds, *In Command of History*, 99.

61. McKercher, "Deterrence," 119.

62. Kennedy, "Tradition of Appeasement," 195.

63. Carley, *1939*, 108; Haslam, "Soviet-German Relations," 792 (citing a 1982 lecture by Lord Home, an eyewitness to the Munich Pact).

64. Tooze, *Deluge*.

65. Indigenous enmities in Eastern Europe would eventually prove enabling to Hitler, creating a kind of competition for his favor. Not for nothing did Czeslaw Milosz recoil at the region's "acute national hatreds." Milosz, *Native Realm*, 23.

66. Wolfer, *Britain and France*.

67. Dullin, *Men of Influence*, 265, citing AVP RF, f. 136, op. 22, pap. 172, d. 865 (Litvinov to Surits, Oct. 17, 1938); *DVP SSSR*, XXI: 618-9 (Litvinov to Surits, Nov. 4, 1938); Pons, *Stalin and the Inevitable War*, 136. Stalin had Potyomkin reaffirm to Paris that their 1935 treaty remained in force. *DVP SSSR*, XXII/i: 79-80 (Jan. 27, 1939).

68. Adibekov et al., *Politbiuro TsK RKP (b)—VKP (b) i Evropa*, 301 (RGASPI, f. 71, op. 25,

d. 3695); Laney, "Military Implementation of the Franco-Russian Alliance." *Pravda* and *Izvestiya* voiced disappointment on the second anniversary of the signing of the May 2, 1935, Franco-Soviet Pact. By late 1937, even Litvinov had broached the possibility to a French correspondent of Soviet rapprochement with Nazi Germany, an attempted warning to Paris. Dreifort, "French Popular Front," 222, citing Bullitt (Paris) to Sec. of State, June 17, 1937, State Department, no. 851.00/1684; Cot, *Triumph of Treason*, 362-3; Haslam, *Struggle for Collective Security*, 153-4.

69. *DDF*, 2e série, V: 311-2 (March 30, 1937), 363-5 (April 8), 507-9 (April 21), 510-1 (April 21), 613-4 (April 29), 614-5 (April 29), 615-8 (April 29); Coulondre, *De Staline à Hitler*, 44; Ford and Schorske, "Voice in the Wilderness," 556-61.

70. Dreifort, "French Popular Front." An internal French analysis—"Reflections on the Possible Consequences of Franco-Soviet military contacts" (May 1937)—had underscored how any deepening military ties with Moscow would risk alienating not just "Germany, Poland, Romania, Yugoslavia," but Great Britain. "French security rests above all on a close entente with England," the analysis noted, and "a Franco-Soviet military agreement risks putting in jeopardy the warmth and candor of Franco-English relations." Haslam, *Struggle for Collective Security*, 140-1, citing *DDF*, 2e série, V: 647-8 (May 1, 1937); Bell, *France and Britain*, 224-5; Adamthwaite, *France*, 49-50.

71. Jackson, *France and the Nazi Menace*, 237.

72. Haslam, *Struggle for Collective Security*, 140. Litvinov had informed Coulondre that he could do nothing "to suppress the French Communist party," but that he "did not care in the least what the French government did to them. All that interested Russia was the military alliance with France." Carley, "Five Kopecks," 48-9 (citing PRO FO 371 20702, C362O/532/62: note of E. Rowe-Dutton, British embassy, Paris, June 17, 1937, MAE RC, Russie/2057, dos. 3: André-Charles Corbin, French ambassador in London, April 17, 1937); PRO FO 371 20702, C362O/532/62: (Note by R. Vansittart, May 13, 1937), and C3685/532/62: "Extract from a record of conversation at a lunch given by the Secretary of State to M. Delbos & Léger on May 15, 1937"); *DVP SSSR*, XX: 43-6 (Potyomkin with Chautemps, Jan. 19, 1937), 227-8 (Potyomkin to Surits in Berlin, May 4, 1937).

73. Kaiser, *Economic Diplomacy*, 239. In Jan. 1939, Léon Blum (Daladier's recent predecessor as prime minister) implored Litvinov for an invitation to Moscow to negotiate directly with Stalin for a "broad antifascist bloc." Blum also mentioned possibly merging the socialist and communist parties in France. The Soviet politburo formally approved the meeting request, but the trip never happened. Adibekov et al., *Politbiuro TsK RKP (b)—VKP (b) i Evropa*, 368 (RGASPI, f. 17, op. 162, d. 24, l. 85); *DVP SSSR*, XXII/ii: 49 (AVP RF, f. 06, op. 1, pap. 2, d. 11, l. 39).

74. "Stalin considered vocal music as the finest form of music," Jelagin thought. Jelagin, *Taming of the Arts*, 297-9.

75. Jelagin, *Taming of the Arts*, 268-75; Elagin, *Ukroshchenie iskusstv*, 302-9. Nazarov would be demoted to deputy chief of the state publishing house on April 1, 1939, and replaced by his deputy Mikhail Khrapchenko (b. 1904).

76. Novikova, "Obruchennyi s bogom," 427-8. Novikova, a journalist, was only born in 1938, and evidently heard the story from Kozlovsky. Concerning Stalin's views toward Kozlovsky, see also Gromyko, *Pamiatnoe*, 203.

77. Ivanov, *Aleksei Ivanov*, 159; Elagin, *Ukroshchenie iskusstv*, 332-3.

78. Jelagin, *Taming of the Arts*, 296-7.

79. Khaustov et al., *Lubianka: Stalin i NKVD*, 9 (APRF, f. 3, op. 57, d. 96, l. 110).

80. Petrov and Jansen, *Stalinski pitomets*, 359-63 (TsA FSB, f. 3-os, op. 6, d. 1, l. 1-6); APRF, f. 3, op. 58, d. 409, l. 3-9). The commission concluded its work on Jan. 10, 1939; the report was dated Jan. 29.

81. Maksimenkov, *Bol'shaia tsenzura*, 502 (RGASPI, f. 558, op. 11, d. 5086, l. 1-2). In June 1939, Duklesky would insert twenty-six line-item corrections in Vishnevsky's screenplay for *First Cavalry Army*—a copy of the document made its way into Stalin's files (510-2: d. 165, l. 199-201).

82. Volkogonov papers, Hoover Institution Archives, container 10, dated 26/27 Dec. 1938. Stalin had edited the proposal by Beria, composed at Stalin's wish, to restrict NKVD surveillance and arrests of *nomenklatura*. Khaustov, "Razvitie sovetskikh organov gosudarstvennoi bezopasnosti," 364. An additional decree was issued reiterating the requirement for the NKVD to obtain army permission for arrests of officers and soldiers. Suvenirov, "Narkomat oborony i NKVD v predvoennye gody," 34 (citing RGVA f. 4, op. 15, d. 21, l. 3ob.).

83. APRF, f. 3, op. 22, d. 91, l. 168-70.

84. Khaustov et al., *Lubianka: Stalin i NKVD*, 14-5 (APRF, f. 3, op. 58, d. 6, l. 145-6); Volkogonov papers, Hoover Institution Archives, container 27; Iakovlov et al., *Reabilitatsiia: Politicheskie protsessy*, 40-1 (a copy of the telegram found in the Dagestan regional party committee: all such documents had to be returned to the Central Committee, so this one evidently survived thanks to negligence); *Sluzhba bezopasnosti*, 1993, no. 6: 2; Afanas'ev, *Inogo ne dano*, 561-2n2 (wrong date of Jan. 20, 1939). Kaganovich later testified (in 1957) that Stalin had written out the decree by hand. Kovaleva et al., "Posledniaia 'antipartiinaia' gruppa," 86-9.

85. Prażmowska, *Eastern Europe*, 228.

86. *DGFP*, series D, *DAP*, V: 167-8 (Ribbentrop and Beck, Jan. 26, 1939); Gromyko et al., *SSSR v bor'be za mir nakanune*, 171-3 (AVP RF, f. 059, op. 1, pap. 300, d. 2075, l. 46-9: Surits, Jan. 27, 1939); *God krizisa*, I: 194-6; Mel'tiukhov, *Sovetsko-pol'skie voiny* (2001); Haslam, *Struggle for Collective Security*, 160-4. Citing hearsay from Hans-Adolf von Moltke, Luftwaffe Lieutenant-General Alfred Gerstenberg, the German air force attaché in Poland in 1938 (who would fall into Soviet captivity and be interrogated on Aug. 17, 1945) would assert that Hermann Göring, while traveling to Poland on the pretext of hunting, bribed Beck to work on behalf of Nazi Germany. Gerstenberg knew how much the Soviets despised Beck. *Tainy diplomatii Tret'ego Reikka*, 581 (TsA FSB, d. N-21147, t. 1, l. 35-53).

87. *DGFP*, series D, V: 159-61; Cienciala, "Poland in British and French Policy," at 202, citing *DDF*, 2e série, XVI: 196 (May 17, 1939), and *DBFP*, 3rd series, VI: appendix II (foreign office on Danzig, May 5, 1939). Beck had also pursued "Third Europe," a bloc to be led by Poland with Romania, Hungary, Italy, and Yugoslavia, but that had failed amid mutual hostilities. Roberts, "Diplomacy of Colonel Beck," 579-614; Kornat, "Polish Idea of 'The Third Europe.'" On the intense dislike for Beck even inside Polish circles, see Lukes, *Czechoslovakia between Hitler and Stalin*, 165n124.

88. Gavrilov, *Voennaia razvedka informiruet*, 26-7 (TsAMO, f. 23, op. 9717, d. 2, l. 93-5: Feb. 10, 1939). Retrospectively, a Polish journalist argues that, given the distasteful

options, Beck should have yielded to Hitler's demands for Danzig and an extra-territorial highway through the Corridor and joined him in an attack against the Soviet Union. Zychowicz, *Pakt Ribbentrop-Beck*. For Beck's contemplation of possible concessions and his worries over the loss of international prestige and domestic political earthquake, see Weinberg, "Proposed Compromise"; Weinberg, "German Foreign Policy."

89. Gromyko et al., *SSSR v bor'be za mir nakanenu*, 198–9; *God krizisa*, I: 228; Gavrilov, *Voennaia razvedka informiruet*, 28.

90. Gromyko et al., *SSSR v bor'be za mir nakanune*, 169–70.

91. From 1938, the regime had begun a crash radio construction program. Khaustov, "Deiatel'nost' organov," 369–70 (TsA FSB, f. 3, op. 2, d. 160, l. 4).

92. Baynes, *Speeches of Adolf Hitler*, I: 737–41; Hitler, untitled speech; Mommsen, "Hitler's Reichstag Speech"; Kershaw, "*Hitler Myth*," 240–1.

93. In a Jan. 25, 1939, circular, the Nazi foreign ministry identified the United States as the "headquarters of world Jewry." *DGFP*, series D, V: 926–33.

94. Gerwarth, *Bismarck Myth*, 151 (citing "Wegbereiter des nueun Reiches," *Völkischer Beobachter*, Feb. 15, 1939).

95. At the first meeting of the Reich Defense Council, on Nov. 18, 1938, Göring had told those assembled, "Gentlemen, the financial situation looks critical." Goebbels wrote in his diary: "The financial situation of the Reich is catastrophic. We must look for new ways. It cannot go on like this. Otherwise we will be faced with inflation." Mason, *Arbeitsklasse*, 925; Fröhlich, *Tagebücher von Joseph Goebbels*, VI: 219 (Dec. 13, 1938). In early Jan. 1939, the Reichsbank Directorate sent Hitler a collective petition urging "financial restraint" to avoid the "threatening danger of inflation." Hitler, upon seeing eight signatures, responded, "That is mutiny." Twelve days later he fired Schacht as Reichsbank president. But that (and a mass of resignations from the bank's board) did nothing to alleviate the circumstance. Schacht, *My First Seventy-Six Years*, 392–4. Nazi Germany also canceled at the last minute a planned visit to Moscow in Feb. 1939 by Karl Schnurre, humiliating the Soviets.

96. Kershaw, *Hitler: 1936–1945*, 161–2.

97. Given the labor shortages—estimated to be at least 1 million as of Jan. 1939—foreign laborers looked necessary for factories and farms. Mason, *Arbeiterklasse*, 847–55; Mason, *Nazism*, 106–113.

98. Bezymenskii, *Stalin und Hitler*, 183–209. Politburo approval came on Jan. 21, 1939.

99. Lisovskii, *SSSR i kapitalisticheskoe okruzhenie*. See also Barghoorn, *Soviet Image of the United States*, 18.

100. Zemskov, "Zakliuchennye," 55–6; Joyce, "Soviet Penal System," 104. A Nov. 17, 1938, report by the party cell in the Gulag finance department stated that the Gulag had attained just 71.6 percent of its assigned plan targets, including just 62.7 percent of railway construction. The report stated that costs were high, labor productivity low, and mismanagement so rampant it could not all be attributed to deliberate wrecking. Pliner, the Gulag head, was soon sacked and arrested. Afanas'ev et al., *Istoriia stalinskogo gulaga*, III: 148–56 (Chugunikhin); Joyce, "Soviet Penal System," 103. Beria, in April 1939, wrote to Molotov claiming that he lacked slave laborers to complete his assigned tasks—a shortage across Gulag of some 400,000 prisoners. Beria wanted a freeze on new projects assigned to Gulag and a recall of those prisoners loaned out on contracts to non-Gulag enterprises,

and he sought measures to improve slave laborers' diet and health. Afanas'ev et al., *Istoriia stalinskogo gulaga*, III: 162–3; Khlevniuk, *History of the Gulag*, 203–5.

101. Nordlander, "Evolution of the Dal'stroi Bosses"; Kozlov, "Pervyi direktor"; Ginzburg, *Within the Whirlwind*, 290–304. Stalin had congratulated and rewarded Berzin on a number of occasions. RGASPI, f. 558, op. 11, d. 56, l. 13 (Feb. 8, 1937).

102. Dalstroi had grown from 62,703 recorded prisoners in late 1936 to 93,978 by the end of 1938. Conquest, *Inside Stalin's Secret Police*, 106; Afanas'ev et al., *Istoriia Stalinskogo Gulaga*, II: 153–4 (RGASPI, f. 558, op. 11, d. 58, l. 77, 80); Nordlander, "Evolution of the Dal'stroi Bosses." Stalin received A. A. Khodyrev, deputy chief of Dalstroi, twice (Jan. 24 and Feb. 7, 1939). *Na prieme*, 251, 253. Some of the ships used by the Soviets to transport prisoners were British and American built. Bollinger, *Stalin's Slave Ships*.

103. *Sovietland*, 1939, no. 4: 10.

104. Dallin and Nicolaevsky, *Forced Labor*, 133–34; Nikolaevskii, "Dal'stroi," 256–7; Conquest, *Kolyma*.

105. Rittersporn, *Anguish*, 174 (citing GARF, f. 5446, op. 81a, d. 335, l. 109–14).

106. Stalin had instructed the teacher to be firmer. In fact, the teacher and school director were fired. Murin, *Stalin v ob"iatiakh sem'i*, 60–2 (APRF, f. 45, op. 1, d. 1553, l. 9: June 8, 1938).

107. Murin, *Stalin v ob"iatiakh sem'i*, 58–9 (l. 20–22: Dec. 8, 1938); Polianskii, *10 let s Vasiliem Stalinym*, 17–8; Sokolov, *Vasilii Stalin*, 76–8; Tokaev, *Stalin Means War*, 120.

108. Murin, *Stalin v ob"iatiakh sem'i*, 60–2 (APRF, f. 45, op. 1, d. 1553, l. 26–8).

109. Vasily also "was a good athlete, rode a horse with aplomb, and was fond of motorcycles and cars." Polianskii, *10 let s Vasiliem Stalinym*, 20.

110. Alliluyeva, *Twenty Letters*, 145–6. She recalled that "by 1937 or 1938, except for my nurse, there was no one left of the people my mother had found." Even the long-standing head of the household staff, Karolina Til, "in spite of the fact that she'd been with us for ten years and was practically a member of the family," was replaced by a young Georgian woman from Beria's NKVD. "The whole staff at Zubalovo was changed, and new people whom none of us knew appeared at my father's house in Kunstevo as well." Alliluyeva, *Twenty Letters*, 143–4, 123–4.

111. Waltz, *Theory of International Politics*, 161–76 (esp. 3, 168); Posen, *Sources of Military Doctrine*, 61–3; Mearsheimer, *Tragedy of Great Power Politics*, 13, 129; Posen, "Competing Images." See also Christensen and Snyder, "Chain Gangs and Passed Bucks."

112. *Partiinoe stroitel'stvo*, Oct. 1936: 3–5, July 1937: 42–44. In Aug. 1938, the apparatus streamlined recruitment procedures. *Partiinoe stroitel'stvo*, Aug. 1938: 63–4, Oct. 1938: 79–80.

113. RGAKFD, ed. khr. 3049, 3050, 3051.

114. *XVIII s"ezd Vsesoiuznoi Kommunisticheskoi partii (b)*, 149.

115. Kumanev and Kulikova, *Protivostoianie*, 224–44; *Pravda*, Feb. 27, 1939; Drizdo, *Nadezhda Konstantinovna Krupskaia*.

116. Krupskaia became deathly ill the night of a pre-birthday celebration outside Moscow in Arkhangelskoe, in a narrow circle with her longtime secretary Vera Dridzo, as well as Gleb and Zinaida Kryżanowski, Dmitry Ulyanov, Felix Kon, and Mężyński's sister Ludmila. Stalin had restrained himself from arresting Krupskaya, despite their mutual enmity, or Maria Ulyanova, both of whom continued to live in the apartment they had shared with Lenin. Lenin's former secretaries

Lidia Fotiyeva and Maria Volodicheva also went untouched. Fotiyeva (b. 1881) from 1938 was posted to the Central Lenin Museum. *Pravda*, Aug. 28, 1975.

117. *Rodnoi Lenin (Vladimir Il'ich) i ego sem'ia:* http://leninism.su/private/4131–rod noj-lenin.html?showall=&start=1.

118. *Pravda*, Feb. 28, 1939 (A. E. Badaev). See also *Pravda*, March 3, 1939; and *Izvestiia*, Feb. 28 and March 1, 1939.

119. Trotsky imagined that "Stalin always lived in fear of a protest on her part. She knew far too much." *New International*, 5/4 (April 1939): 117. In 1937–38, at the commissariat of enlightenment, Krupskaya had received upward of 400 letters *per day*, mostly asking for her intercession, which she was powerless to give.

120. Zhukov, *Vsesoiuznoe soveshchanie*, 260.

121. Kumanev and Kulikova, *Protivostoianie*, 243 (citing GARF, f. upravdelami SNK SSR, otdel sekretariata, d. 4, l. 12). Nonetheless, Stalin would permit remembrance of the first anniversary of Krupskaya's death: see the news chronicle, RGAFKFD film 1-3163.

122. *XVIII s"ezd VKP (b), 10-21 marta 1939 goda: stenograficheski otchet*, 175, 561; Medvedev, *Let History Judge*, 529. "It was the fault of the Comintern workers that they allowed themselves to be deceived by the class enemy, failed to detect his maneuvers in time, and were late in taking measures against the contamination of the Communist parties by enemy elements," Manuilsky, a survivor, told the 18th Party Congress. *Land of Socialism Today and Tomorrow*, 89. In May 1939, Proskryobyshev moved to create a new department—staffed by twenty-nine people—in the special sector to handle correspondence of ordinary Soviet inhabitants with Stalin. Khlevniuk, "Letters to Stalin," 329 (citing APRF, f. 3, op. 22, d. 65, l. 37).

123. Khlevniuk, "Economic Officials in the Great Terror," 57.

124. Volkogonov, *Triumf i tragediia*, II/ii: 52–3; Khlevniuk, *Khoziain*, 351 (RGASPI, f. 477, op. 1, d. 41, l. 62–83, 143–4; f. 17, op. 2, d. 773, l. 128); Khlevniuk, "Objectives of the Great Terror," 170; Davies, "Soviet Economy," 11–38 (at 31).

125. Whereas between 1918 and 1928 the USSR had graduated an average of just 46,000 new specialists per year, the number would climb to 335,000 per annum in the period 1938–41, which would give the Soviet Union nearly 1 million specialists with (some form of) higher education as of Dec. 31, 1940. Unger, "Stalin's Renewal."

126. *Pravda-5*, 1995, no. 1: 8 (Chuev via Mgeladze).

127. Whereas in 1928 the country counted about 4 million white-collar employees; by 1939, that number reached nearly 14 million. Lewin, "Bureaucracy and the Stalinist State," 63. The proportion of working-class party members, even by official statistics (which inflated worker social origins), would drop from 8 percent (1933) to 3 percent (1941). Rittersporn, "From Working Class," 187.

128. This was true from 1932 onward. DeWitt, *Soviet Professional Manpower*, 179.

129. "The enormous and unjustified growth, cost, proliferation, inefficiency, nepotism, narrow-mindedness, false reporting, inflexibility and arbitrariness," the leading historian of the Soviet state summarized, "defied all party and other controls." Lewin, "Bureaucracy and the Stalinist State," 65.

130. Lewin, *Russia/USSR/Russia*, 204–6. An extraordinary seven of eight applicants for candidate membership in the party would be accepted between April and Oct. 1939; over the year, the party would grow by a record 1.1 million new full members.

131. An editorial in the Menshevik émigré newspaper duly noted the transition, commenting, "this is . . . the Congress of a new party which should be called Stalinist." "Pered s"ezdom," *Sotsialisticheskii vestnik*, March 15, 1939. See also Vishnevskii, "Stalin na XVIII s"ezde partii," 73–83.

132. *Pravda*, March 11, 1939, reprinted in *Sochineniia*, XIV: 380–1.

133. Petrovsky was officially removed as a deputy chairman of the USSR Supreme Soviet presidium on May 31, 1939. He remained without employment for half a year, but then became deputy director of the Museum of the Revolution under Fyodor Samoilov, who knew him from the days in the Bolshevik Duma faction. Medvedev, *Let History Judge*, 407.

134. *XVIII s"ezd VKP (b)*, 510–9; *Pravda*, March 20, 1939.

135. Chuev, *Molotov Remembers*, 221–2. Behind the scenes Zhdanov was said to have wisecracked about the terror. "Stalin complains that his pipe has disappeared," Zhdanov supposedly joked. "'I would give a lot to find it,' Stalin states. Within three days Beria has already unmasked ten thieves, each of whom confesses to being the one who stole Stalin's pipe. A day later Stalin finds his pipe, which had fallen behind the couch." Zhdanov, his interlocutor recalled, "laughed merrily at this terrible joke." Iakovlev, *Tsel' zhizni* (2nd ed.), 509.

136. Shvernik and one of his aides were trying to solve a difficult problem, and when the aide made a suggestion, Shvernik pointed out that it contradicted a Central Committee decree, to which the aide replied that this body could err. "It is difficult to describe what transpired with Nikolai Mikhailovich at these words. Reddening, he shouted, 'Hands on the trouser seams, comrade Pogrebnoi, when you speak about the Central Committee, hands on the trouser seams!!!'" Guseinov, "Ves'ma neodnoznachnyi N. M. Shvernik," 102.

137. The Beria household census form for 1939 listed their Moscow address as Malaya Nikitskaya, 28, apt. 1. Beria himself is not listed for some reason; the five listed were his wife, Nina [Nino] (34 years old), his mother, Marta (66 years old), his sister Akesha (32), his son Sergei [Sergo] (14), and the German nanny Ellia Almeshtigler (38), who was a student at the Moscow Institute of Economics and Finances. Koenker et al., *Revelations*, 344 (GARF, f. 9430, op. 1S, d. 166, l. 1–2). Kuropatkin died in 1925. Knox, "General Kuropatkin."

138. At the dacha, the Berias' neighbors were the Kaganoviches. Beria, *My Father*, 34–5. Svetlana recalls it as Chubar's dacha, not Postyshev's. Alliluyeva, *Only One Year*, 412–3. It is possible that Chubar had it after Postyshev. Postyshev and Chubar, arrested at different times, were shot the same day (Feb. 26, 1939).

139. "'Khochetsia prokliast' den' i chas moego znakomstva s Beriia,'" 100–101 (APRF, f. 3, op. 24, d. 465, l. 2–28: Merkulov to Malenkov, July 23, 1933). Merkulov claimed that Beria never opened up to him.

140. *Traktory i sel'khozmashiny*, 1967, no. 6: 2, no. 7: 41. On harvest exaggerations for 1937–40, see Davies et al., *Economic Transformation*, 288nf. Tractors held by the regional MTS would rise from 7,100 in 1930 to 356,800 by 1937; harvester combines from 10,400 in 1933 to 96,300 by 1937.

141. Davies et al., *Economic Transformation*, 288nf; Zelenin, *Stalinskaia 'revoliutsiia sverkhu,'* 262–7; Borisov, *Proizvodstvennye kadry derevni*, 200–1. Whereas about 3.3 million tons of grain had been exported in 1937–38, only 2 million tons would be exported in 1940 and the first half of 1941.

142. Osokina, *Za fasadom*, 201; Danilov et al., *Tragediia sovetskoi derevni*, IV: 794–5 (RGASPI, f. 17, op. 3, d. 978, l. 62), 831–2 (f. 558, op. 11, d. 94, l. 17), 839 (d. 95, l. 3), 843–4 (l. 40–1), 862–4 (GANO, f. P-3, op. 2, d. 1063, l. 34–7), 868–74 (TsA FSB, f. 3, op. 3, d. 1292, l. 8–19), 886–90 (l. 247–57), 900–4 (l. 320–30), 913–4 (RGASPI, f. 17, op. 3, d. 982, l. 31–2). In 1936, Stalin had not objected to requests to mention in the regional press the assistance extended to regions suffering hunger (885–6: RGASPI, f. 558, op. 11, d. 55, l. 109).

143. Zelenin, *Stalinskaia 'revoliutsiia sverkhu,'* 241–2 (RGASPI, f. 477, op. 1, d. 4, l. 114–5); *Kolkhozy vo vtoroi*, 24.

144. The first subdivision had taken place in Aug. 1937, when a separate machine building commissariat was formed. By 1941, there would be twenty-two separate industrial commissariats, one for each branch. Rees and Watson, "Politburo and Sovnarkom," 24.

145. Davies, "Soviet Economy," 32 (RGASPI, f. 17, op. 120, d. 336, l. 9–12). The author was Pakhomov, but this was not N. I. Pakhomov, the water transport commissar (who been shot in Aug. 1938). Stalin had Poskryobyshev forward the letter to Zhdanov.

146. *Krokodil*, 1939, no. 7; Chegodaeva, *Dva lika vremeni*, 50.

147. RGAKFD, ed. khr. 1–3050 (year 1939).

148. Reid, "Socialist Realism"; Bown, *Socialist Realist Painting*, 145–55, 180.

149. *XVIII s"ezd VKP (b)*, 16.

150. "If I had said it right," Molotov later explained, "Stalin would have felt that I was correcting him." Pavlov, "Dve poslednie vstrechi"; Tucker, *Stalin in Power*, 586.

151. *XVIII s"ezd VKP (b)*, 34, 26; Volkogonov, *Triumf i tragediia*, II/1: 10–1.

152. *Pravda*, March 11, 1939; *XVIII s"ezd VKP(b)*, 15; *Sochineniia*, XIV: 337–8. For British reactions, see *DBFP*, 3rd series, IV: 210–7 (Henderson to Halifax, March 9, 1939), 260 (Henderson to Halifax, March 15), 266–9/8 (Halifax to Phipps, March 15), 278–9 (Henderson to Halifax, March 16). Ivan Maisky had written to Stalin in late 1937 on how to handle appeasement: "Let 'Western democracies' reveal their hand in the matter of the aggressors. What is the point of us pulling their chestnuts out of the fire for them? To fight together—by all means. To serve as cannon fodder for them—never!" Gorodetsky, *Maisky Diaries*, xxv (no citation).

153. Haslam, *Struggle for Collective Security*, 205. *Izvestiya*'s foreign department did internally discuss the possibility of a change in foreign policy orientation, and the newspaper did suddenly discontinue its antifascist writings from Paris by "Paul Jocelyn" (a pseudonym of Ehrenburg's). When Ehrenburg sought an explanation from Surits, the latter was said to have snapped, "Nothing is asked of you, and you are worried!" Ehrenburg, *Sobranie sochinenii*, IX: 228.

154. Sluch, "Germano-sovetskie otnosheniia," 109 (citing Bundesarkhiv Koblenz, Zsg. 101/12: 72).

155. From 1907 through 1914, Schulenburg had been a German consul in tsarist Russia. Sommer, *Botschafter Graf Schulenburg*. See also Chuev, *Molotov Remembers*, 19.

156. Schorske, "Two German Diplomats." At the German embassy on Leontyev Lane, on March 5, 1932, five shots had been fired at Dirksen's car, but he was not inside (one of the bullets struck an embassy counselor in the hand). A hasty trial linked the episode to the Polish embassy (a transparent Soviet effort to poison German-Polish relations). Dirksen, a parvenu aristocrat (from a long line of bourgeois civil servants), had been moved to Japan (1933–8), where he belatedly joined the Nazi

Party (1936), and then to Britain (1938–9), where he succeeded Ribbentrop as ambassador and recognized that Chamberlain's government was among Germany's greatest political assets. Hilger, *Incompatible Allies*, 247–8. In 1938, Leontyev Lane would be renamed Stanislavsky Street, for the celebrated Russian theater director.

157. Maisky wrote from London to Litvinov (Feb. 10, 1939) to the effect that war between the Axis and the "so-called" Western democracies was not imminent, though "one could not completely exclude such a possibility, especially in 1939," because "matters depended on Hitler and Mussolini." Maisky also wrote that Hitler "is little inclined to go full bore against Poland, let alone the USSR." AVP RF, f. 06, op. 1, pap. 3, d. 35, l. 51–3 (Volkogonov papers, Hoover Institution Archives, container 1). Five days after the March 15 occupation of Czechoslovakia, Litvinov wrote to Stalin, latching on to Chamberlain's dispatch to Moscow of a trade negotiator, Robert Hudson, but the Soviets put the onus on the British. "Since our many previous proposals have failed to yield results," Litvinov wrote to Hudson, "we do not now intend to advance any new proposals and are awaiting an initiative from those who must in some way indicate that they are ready to take measures to enter collective security." *DVP SSSR*, XXII/i: 209–11 (AVP RF, f. 06, op. 1, pap. 2, d. 11, l. 154–8). *DVP SSSR*, XXII/i: 209–11 (AVP RF, f. 06, op. 1, p. 2, d. 11, l. 154–8: March 20, 1939). The visit by Hudson would yield nothing, as Litvinov complained.

158. Watt, *How War Came*, 154.

159. Nowak, "Von der Karpatenukraine zum Karpatenland"; Winch, *Republic for a Day*; Kennan, *From Prague after Munich*, 58–75; Stercho, *Diplomacy of Double Morality*. Soon Mussolini, whom the Führer had not informed about his march into Czechoslovakia, responded by invading Albania, which would be incorporated into the Italian "empire."

160. *Dokumenty i materialy kanuna vtoroi mirovoi voiny*, II: 47.

161. A. Gerasimov, "O zakhvate Chechoslavakii Germaniei," RGVA, f. 33 987, op. 3, d. 1237, l. 162–7. Litvinov had written to Maisky that the Western democracies were in essence saying to Hitler, "Go east, or we will unite with them [the Soviets] against you. I would not be surprised if Hitler undertakes the same gestures towards us." AVP RF, f. 06, op. 1, pap. 4, d. 34, l. 39–41 (Volkogonov papers, Hoover Institution Archives, container 1).

162. Volkogonov, *Trotsky*, 343–5; *The Founding Conference of the Fourth International: Program and Resolutions* (New York: The Socialist Workers Party, 1939).

163. On the eve of the Munich Pact, Trotsky had dismissed Stalin's policy of "collective security" against Nazi Germany as a "lifeless fiction" and predicted that "we may now expect with certainty Soviet diplomacy to attempt a rapprochement with Hitler." On the eve of Czechoslovakia's destruction, Trotsky wickedly observed that Hitler went from triumph to triumph, whereas "Stalin met only defeat and humiliation (China, Czechoslovakia, Spain)." Trotsky, *Writings of Leon Trotsky, 1938–39*, 29–30 (Sept. 22, 1938), 216–9 (March 11, 1939).

164. A plan would be presented to him in July 1939 and be approved in Aug. Soviet intelligence's documents on the Trotsky assassination efforts are said to be largely missing, except for the period Aug. 1940 to the end of 1941. Primakov, *Ocherki*, III: 91, 93, 109n1.

165. One of the abandoned field agents, codenamed Felipe, would manage to get back to Moscow in Jan. 1940 and report details on

Trotsky's security system and the comings and goings from his villa in Mexico, all of which he had undertaken to ascertain on his own; he would be sent back to Mexico to be part of the operations. Primakov, *Ocherki*, III: 94–5.

166. Eitingon had helped direct sabotage of rail lines and airfields, as a deputy to Orlov. Sudoplatov, *Special Tasks*, 29–36.

167. "This is not just an act of revenge, although Konovalets is an agent of German fascism," Stalin had supposedly explained to Sudoplatov. "Our goal is to behead the movement of Ukrainian fascism on the eve of war and force these gangsters to annihilate each other in a struggle for power." Sudoplatov, *Special Tasks*, 23–4.

168. Sudoplatov, *Special Tasks*, 103.

169. Sudoplatov, *Special Tasks*, 64–7; Volkogonov, *Trotsky*, 441–54. Sudoplatov's visits to the Little Corner are not recorded in Stalin's Kremlin logbooks; Volkgonov's work and the documents he brought to bear strongly support Sudoplatov's overall veracity.

170. Eitingon was denounced by Peterss and Karakhan. Sharapov, *Naum Eitingon*, 70.

171. Schroeder, "Alliances 1815–1945," 195–222. More broadly, see Posen, *Sources of Military Doctrine*.

172. Posen, *Sources of Military Doctrine*.

173. On Nov. 10, 1938, Hitler told four hundred invited German journalists: "It was only out of necessity that for years I talked of peace. But it was now necessary gradually to re-educate the German people psychologically and make it clear that there are things which *must* be achieved by force." Noakes and Pridham, *Nazism*, III: 721–4.

174. Britain lost its Czechoslovakia intelligence station. Earlier, the Austrian station chief for British intelligence had been arrested in 1938 when the Nazis marched in. Hinsley et al., *British Intelligence*, I: 57.

175. Gavrilov, *Voennaia razvedka informiruet*, 29–33 (RGVA, f. 33987, op. 3, d. 1237, l. 162ss–167ss.).

176. Parker, *Chamberlain and Appeasement*, 204–5; Salter, *Personality in Politics*, 85.

177. Iampol'skii et al., *Organy*, I/i: 9–12.

178. *DGFP*, series D, VI: 91–6; *DVP SSSR*, XXII/ii: 537–8n86. A Romanian-German timber agreement followed on May 13, 1939.

179. Khaustov and Samuelson, *Stalin, NKVD*, 286 (TsA FSB, f. 3, op. 4, d. 105, l. 96–107).

180. *DGFP*, series D, VI: 121–4; *Trial of the Major War Criminals*, IV: 404 (Brauchitsch), III: 217. In March 1939, Lieutenant Colonel Stefan Mossor of the general inspectorate of the Polish armed forces wrote a memorandum urging the general staff "to prepare for Soviet air bases in the region of Brest and anticipate the march of Soviet forces primarily through northern Poland to attack East Prussia." He was removed from his position.

181. *DVP SSSR*, XXII/i: 230 (AVP RF, f. 06, op. 1, pap. 2, d. 11, l. 172), 231 (pap. 20, d. 228, l. 1–2), 232 (pap. 1, d. 5, l. 117–8), 233 (l. 121).

182. Andrew, *Defense of the Realm*, 205.

183. *French Yellow Book*, 104 (George Bonnet to Léon Noel, French ambassador to Warsaw, March 31, 1939).

184. Gromyko et al., *SSSR v bor'be za mir nakanune*, 290–1 (Maisky, 31, 1939); Falin, *Soviet Peace Efforts*, I: 300.

185. Gibbs, *Grand Strategy*, I: xxi–xxii, 689ff.

186. Interview in London, March 18, 1939: *Fourth International* (New York) 3/1 (1942): 117. Confronting Hitler would indeed cost the empire.

187. "As Prime Minister," explained Strang, an adviser, "Chamberlain took increasingly into his own hands the conduct of foreign policy, or rather of that branch of foreign policy which might involve issues of peace or war, namely relations with the two European dictatorships"—meaning Germany and Italy. Strang, *Home and Abroad*, 124.

188. Aster, *1939*, 14–16, 359–60. See also Bond, *British Military Policy*, 306; and Parker, *Chamberlain and Appeasement*, 214.

189. Chamberlain had assured the Cabinet that "it would, of course, be for us to determine what action threatened Polish independence. This would prevent us from becoming embroiled as the result of a frontier incident." Newman, *March 1939*, 202 (citing CAB/98: Cabinet Minutes, March 31, 1939).

190. Strang, "Once More unto the Breach"; Newman, *March 1939*.

191. "It was in Spain that men learnt that one can be right and still be beaten, that force can vanquish spirit, and that there are times when courage is not its own reward," Albert Camus would write. "It is this which explains why so many men throughout the world regard the Spanish drama as a personal tragedy." Camus, "préface," in Georges Bataille (ed.), *L'Espagne libre*.

192. Parker, *Churchill and Appeasement*, 156.

193. Thompson, *Anti-Appeasers*.

194. The gold was on deposit with the Bank for International Settlements, founded in 1930 in Switzerland, which used the Bank of England; still, the latter honored the request for transfer of the reserves. Blaazer, "Finance and the End of Appeasement."

195. Watt, *How War Came*, 162–87; Cienciala, "Poland in British and French Policy," reprinted in Finney, *Origins of the Second World War*, 413–33. On long-standing British sympathy for Germany's claims to Danzig and the Corridor, see Cienciala, "German Propaganda."

196. Steiner, *Triumph of the Dark*, 737–8.

197. Because Hitler could not attack the Soviet Union without bringing Poland into play, the French ambassador to the Soviet Union believed that, in effect, the "guarantee" to Poland brought about, indirectly, what Chamberlain had said he would never do: put Britain on the line to defend the USSR. Coulondre, *De Staline à Hitler*, 263.

198. Gorodetsky, *Maisky Diaries*, 170.

199. *DBFP*, 3rd series, V: 104.

200. Gorodetsky, *Grand Delusion*, 4–5.

201. On March 13, 1939, Frinovsky had written to Stalin recalling a conversation he had had in Molotov's office in Jan. 1938 when, in front of Kaganovich and Mikoyan, Stalin had informed Frinovsky that a number of others had testified against him. Stalin had asked Frinovsky whether he was "honest before the party." Frinovsky had answered affirmatively. "You will not let us down, then?" Stalin had said. "No," Frinovsky had answered. What was this? A psychological game, theater, self-amusement, a moment of indecision? Toptygin, *Neizvestnyi Beriia*, 50.

202. "'Druzhba narodov': pervaia polveka (1939–1989)": http://magazines.russ.ru/druzhba/site/history/i39.html.

203. E. V. Tarle, *Taleiran* (Moscow: Molodaia gvardiia, 1939).

204. Khaustov, "Deiatel'nost' organov," 237 (APRF, f. 45, op. 1, d. 180, l. 30). The Polish ambassador to Tokyo had been told by the Japanese foreign minister that the fisheries negotiations with the USSR were a matter not merely of economics but of national prestige, and that if a new agreement were not reached the Japanese "would undertake decisive steps, as I understand, of a military nature." The Japanese foreign minister also said that "the Japanese government had not yet definitively decided the issue of deepening the Anti-Comintern Pact." Gromyko et al., *SSSR v bor'be za mir nakanune*, 230 (March 10, 1939).

205. Anderson et al., *Kremlevskii kinoteatr*, 529 (RGASPI, f. 558, op. 11, d. 163, l. 2–2ob.). On April 9, Eisenstein wrote to Stalin requesting permission to travel to London for the premiere there of *Alexander Nevsky*. Stalin wrote to Molotov that "this matter does not concern me," but Molotov knew Stalin's views and forbid Eisenstein to travel. Anderson et al., *Kremlevskii kinoteatr*, 538 (APRF, f. 3, op. 35, d. 86, l. 45–6). Andro Kobaladze would play Stalin in *Yakov Sverdlov* (1940).

206. Trauberg, "Rasskaz o velikom vozhde," 7–15; Trauberg, "Proizvedenie mysli i strasti," 32–8. See also Tsimbal, "Obraz Lenina v kino," 13–7; and Lebedev, *Shchukin—akter kino; Sovetskie khudozhestvennye fil'my*, 4 vols. (Moscow: Iskusstvo, 1961–77), II: 197.

207. Toward the film's end, Dzierżyński divulges that an agent-provocateur has "penetrated" the Cheka. Kataev, "Lenin v 1918 godu"; Sadovskii, "Lenin v 1918 godu"; Dobrenko, *Stalinist Cinema*, 220–9.

208. Vernadskii, *Dnevniki, 1935–1941*, II: 52.

209. Khaustov et al., *Lubianka: Stalin i NKVD*, 33–50 (APRF, f. 3, op. 24, d. 373, l. 3–44); Petrov and Jansen, *Stalinskii pitomets*, 204 (citing APRF, f. 3, op. 24, d. 374, l. 3–47); Stepanov, "O masshtabakh repressii" (no. 5), 61–2.

210. D. N. Sukhanov, an aide to Malenkov, claimed he witnessed Yezhov's arrest by Beria in Malenkov's office: Hoover Institution Archives, Volkogonov papers, container 13, excerpted memoirs (dated March 6, 1993); Khrushchev, *Vospominaniia*, I: 179–81; Briukhanov and Shoshkov, *Opravdaniiu ne podlezhit*, 132; Sudoplatov, *Spetsoperatsii*, 100; Petrov and Jansen, *Stalinskii pitomets*, 200–1; Pavliukov, *Ezhov*, 512–3; Polianskii, *Ezhov*, 205–6, 219.

211. Kostrychenko and Khazanov, "Konets Kar'ery Ezhova," 129–30 (RGASPI, f. 17, op. 3, d. 1003, l. 82–4).

212. Khaustov, "Razvitie sovetskikh organov gosudarstvennoi bezopasnosti," 362 (citing TsA FSB, f. 3, op. 45, d. 29, l. 246).

213. Khrushchev, *Vospominaniia*, I: 182.

214. Nikolai P. Afanasev, USSR deputy general procurator, recalls this as taking place at Lefortovo, but all other sources indicate Yezhov was held in Sukahnovka. Ushakov and Stukalov, *Front voennykh prokurorov*, 69.

215. Viktorov, *Bez grafa "sekretnosti,"* 326.

216. "Vospominaniia: memurary Nikity Sergeevicha Khrushcheva," 87; Piliatskin, "'Vrag naroda'," *Ezhov*, 513; Polianskii, *Ezhov*, 216–7. Others suggest these documents—which disappeared—need not have been compromising, but could have been flattering material Yezhov collected for a Stalin museum. Petrov and Jansen, *Stalinskii pitomets*, 228.

217. Briukhanov and Shoshkov, *Opravdaniiu ne podlezhit*, 132–3. Malenkov's son would assert that when his father had Yezhov's safe opened, they discovered dossiers on Malenkov as well as Stalin; the latter included the recollections of an old Bolshevik that Stalin had prerevolutionary links to the tsarist okhranka. Malenkov, *O moem otse Georgii Malenkove*, 34.

218. Khlevniuk, *Khoziain*, 423–5. It is said that when Malenkov finally saw a transcript of this interrogation, in Feb. 1955, he destroyed it. Kovaleva et al., *Molotov, Malenkov, Kaganovich*, 44; Kovaleva et al., "Posledniaia 'antipartiinaia' gruppa," 23. For Khrushchev's defense of Malenkov in 1937 in Moscow, see Ponomarev, "Nikita Khrushchev," 135.

219. Artizov et al., *Reabilitatsiia, kak eto bylo,* 330.

220. Tumshis and Papchinskii, *1937,* 68. The former colleague was Sergei Schwarz.

221. Pavliukov, *Ezhov,* 470; Khrushchev, *Vremia, liudi, vlast',* I: 172; Petrov and Skorkin, *Kto rukovodil NKVD,* 417.

222. Petrov and Jansen, *Stalinskii pitomets,* 365–6 (TsA FSB, f. 3–os, op. 6, d. 3, l. 42–3). For Yezhov's interrogation on April 26 (by Kobulov and others), see Khaustov et al., *Lubianka: Stalin i NKVD,* 52–72 (APRF, f. 3, op. 24, d. 375, l. 122–64).

223. Sontag, "Last Months of Peace."

224. Gromyko et al., *SSSR v bor'be za mir nakanune,* 332–3 (April 15, 1939); Falin, *Soviet Peace Efforts,* I: 342.

225. Stalin wrote on the TASS summary: "Expel the representative of this newspaper from Moscow." (In Feb. 1939, the politburo had approved the foreign affairs commissariat request to grant Howard an entry visa, while warning him not to expect another audience with Stalin.) Maksimenkov, *Bol'shaia tsenzura,* 506–9 (RGASPI, f. 558, op. 11, d. 207, l. 36–41; f. 17, op. 162, d. 24, l. 105). Howard also published a dispatch from Paris at this time pointing out that anti-Jewish actions in Nazi Germany were underestimated, not exaggerated.

226. *God krizisa,* I: 386–7 (AVP RF, f. 06, op. 1a, p. 25, d. 4, l. 27–8); *DVP SSSR,* XXII/i: 283–4, 284–5 (AVP RF f. 059, op. 1, p. 303, d. 2093, l. 27–8); Gromyko et al., *SSSR v bor'be za mir nakanune,* 335–7 (April 17, 1939); Falin, *Soviet Peace Efforts,* I: 346–7.

227. Gromyko et al., *SSSR v bor'be za mir nakanune,* 332–3 (April 17, 1939); Falin, *Soviet Peace Efforts,* I: 345–6; Aster, *1939,* 163; Neilson, *Britain, Soviet Russia,* 283, 287–9; *God krizisa,* I: 386 (AVP RF, f. 06, op. 1a, pap. 25, d. 4, l. 27–8); *FRUS, 1939,* I: 240; *DDF, 2e série,* XV: 789–90; *Na prieme,* 256. See also Carley, *1939,* 126–34; and Pons, *Stalin and the Inevitable War,* 159.

228. *DVP SSSR,* XXII/i: 291–3 (Astakhov record: AVP RF, f. 06, op. 1, p. 7, d. 65, l. 69–71); *DGFP,* series C, IV: 783 (Bräutigam memo, Nov. 1, 1935); Sontag and Beddie, *Nazi-Soviet Relations,* 1–2; Roberts, "Infamous Encounter?"; Roberts, *Origins of the Second World War,* 69–71; Haslam, *Struggle for Collective Security,* 202–15.

229. Gafencu, *Last Days of Europe,* 78.

230. Neilson, *Britain, Soviet Russia,* 283 (citing FP [36], minutes of 43rd meeting, April 19, 1939, Cab 27/624); *DVP SSSR,* XXII/ii: 541–2n101 (citing PRO, Cab. 27/624: 300–3, 309–12); Dilks, *Diaries of Sir Alexander Cadogan,* 175. Halifax told a British cabinet meeting (April 26) that the "time was not ripe for so comprehensive a proposal, and we were proposed to ask the Russian government to give further consideration to our plan." Gromyko et al., *SSSR v bor'be za mir nakanune,* 341 (April 21), 684n103 (citing PRO, CAB 23/39: 58); Falin, *Soviet Peace Efforts,* I: 340, II: 308n103.

231. Overy, "Strategic Intelligence," 474, citing *DGFP,* series D, VI: 289–90 (chargé d'affaires in London Kordt to foreign ministry, April 19, 1939), 336 (Kordt to foreign ministry, April 26, 1939), 472–3 (Dirksen to foreign ministry, May 11); Andrew and Gordievsky, *KGB,* 197–8.

232. *DVP SSSR,* XXII/i: 252–3 (AVP RF, f. 06, op. 1, pap. 7, d. 63, l. 14–5: Litvinov to Merekalov, April 4, 1939), 268–9 (f. 011, op. 4, pap. 27, d. 61, l. 77–8: Merekalov's reply, April 12, 1939). See also Bartel, "Aleksej Fedorovič Merekalov." Litvinov's Anglophilia has been exaggerated. It was always a means to an end—Soviet security—which he saw as solely possible with a collective security agreement

against fascism. Phillips, *Between the Revolution and the West,* 21–2, 52–3.

233. In early April, Potyomkin sent two notes, both handwritten, to Surits warning of "the very hard line" being adopted in Moscow vis-à-vis cadres. "The slightest lapse is not only recorded but also provokes a swift and violent reaction." He had Surits send his subordinate to Moscow. Dullin, *Men of Influence,* 216 (citing AVP RF, f. 11, op. 4, pap. 32, d. 179: April 4 and 19, 1939). Surits was represented by Krapivintsev, who worked under him as embassy counselor in Paris. *Na prieme,* 257–8. This was only Maisky's second visit to Stalin's office, the first having been June 1, 1938, with Litvinov.

234. For the grim documentary trail of Litvinov's memorandums to Stalin, see *DVP SSSR,* XXII/i: 208–9 (AVP RF, f. 06, op. 1, pap. 2, d. 11, l. 159: March 20, 1939), 209–11 (l.154–8: March 20), 220–1 (l. 167–8: March 23), 230 (l. 172: March 27), 246 (l. 186: April 3), 269–70 (l. 209: April 13), 275–7 (l. 213–7: April 15), 277–8 (l. 218–9: April 15), 283 (l. 220–1: April 17); Resis, "Fall of Litvinov."

235. Sheinis, *Maksim Maksimovich Litvinov,* 360–3; Dullin, *Des hommes d'influence,* 310–3; Dullin, *Men of Influence,* 230–1. Sheinis suggests that the meeting described by Maisky took place on April 27, but Litvinov does not appear in the Kremlin office logbook that day. *Na prieme,* 257–8.

236. Mel'tiukhov, *17 September 1939,* 232; Neilson, *Britain, Soviet Russia,* 284.

237. The July 29, 1936, secret circular to the entire provincial party and state apparatus had omitted Molotov's name on the list of the assassination targets of the Zinoviev-Trotskyite Center, and at the public trial that Aug., the defendants never mentioned him as a target, possibly a show of Stalin's displeasure. But if so, Molotov's purgatory had not lasted long: on Sept. 21, 1936, a two-year-old attempt on Molotov's life had been included in the "testimony" taken in preparation for the second Moscow trial. And from the day of Stalin's return to Moscow (Oct. 25), Molotov was regularly in the Little Corner again. "The thought alone that it was possible," *Pravda* (Nov. 23, 1936) would intone of an assassination of Molotov, "is capable of making every citizen of the Soviet Union shudder." Stalin's decision to ratchet up the psychological pressure on Ordjonikidze might have been a factor in Molotov's abrupt return to favor. See also Iakovlev et al., *Reabilitatsiia: Politicheskie protsessy,* 231–2; Orlov, *Tainaia istoriia,* 154–9; Conquest, *Reassessment,* 90–1; *Pravda,* Oct. 26, 1961; Watson, *Molotov,* 130. The incident in question had occurred on a visit to the Siberian coal town of Prokopevsk when Molotov's local driver had veered off an inclined road and came to a stop in a ditch (called "a ravine"). At the time, the driver had received merely a party reprimand, which Molotov had interceded to get rescinded. But in 1936, the driver was retrospectively charged with terrorism, and confessed. Molotov and Chuev wrongly recalled the incident as having occurred in 1932. Chuev, *Sto sorok,* 302.

238. *Biulleten' oppozitsii,* no. 50 (1936): 15, no. 52–53 (1936): 47, no. 58–59 (1936): 18–19; Chuev, *Sto sorok,* 302. For Lev Sedov's response to the Novosibirsk trial, see *Biulleten' oppozitsii,* no. 54–55 (1937): 4. Molotov was included as a target in the Jan. 1937 trial, alongside Stalin, Kaganovich, Voroshilov, Orjonikidze, Yezhov, Zhdanov, and four provincial party bosses, one of whom was Beria.

239. Rudzutaks, a deputy chairman of the Council of People's Commissars under Molotov, told the latter to his face that he had been tortured. "I think that he was not a conscious participant" in a conspiracy, Molotov

admitted later in life. "A former [tsarist] prisoner, he had been at hard labor for four years . . . I formed the impression when he was my deputy, he had begun to self-indulge a bit . . . He enjoyed the life of a philistine—he would sit around, dine with friends, spend time with companions . . . It is difficult to say what brought about his downfall, but I think he shared the type of company where non-party elements were present, or god knows what other kinds." Another close Molotov comrade, Alexander Arosyev, the hack writer and head of the all-Union Society for Cultural Ties Abroad, was also executed. "The most devoted person," Molotov recalled. "It seems he was not discriminating in his acquaintances. It was impossible to mix him up in anti-Soviet affairs. But he had ties . . ." Chuev, *Sto sorok,* 410–1, 422–3. See also David-Fox, "Stalinist Westernizer?"

240. Chadaev in Kumanev, *Riadom so Stalinym,* 421–2. Molotov's Poskryobyshev was I. I. Lapshov.

241. *XVIII s"ezd VKP (b),* 493.

242. Watson, "Politburo and Foreign Policy," 141; Watson, *Molotov,* 147.

243. Dullin, *Men of Influence,* 233–6. Already by late 1937, fourteen of the foreign consulates in Leningrad had been forced to close—including those of Germany, Japan, Italy, and Poland. Magerovsky, "The People's Commissariat," II: 337–8.

244. Foreign policy had already been delegated to a permanent commission of the politburo back on April 14, 1937. Khlevniuk et al., *Stalinskoe politbiuro,* 55, RGASPI, f. 17, op. 3, d. 986 (protocol for April 16, 1937).

245. In 1938, Litvinov had not traveled for his annual rest at Karlsbad, and had to summon his children home from England. Litvinov's talkative British wife, Ivy, had already been sent to the isolation of the Urals some years before. Carswell, *Exile,* 165–8.

246. Ulricks, "Impact of the Great Purges," 188–92; Haslam, *Struggle for Collective Security,* 130. Personnel arrested in the second wave included deputy commissar Stomanyakov (who tried to commit suicide but failed), as well as Litvinov's personal secretary (Nazarov) and others. After the March 1938 Bukharin trial, rumors had circulated in Moscow of a public trial of diplomatic personnel, but as in the case of the Comintern, no public process took place. Conquest, *Reassessment,* 423.

247. Kennan, *Russia and the West,* 231, 336; Watson, *Molotov,* 153–6; Gnedin, *Katastrofa i vtoroe rozhdenie,* 105–15; Meerovich, "V narkomindele 1922–1939"; Chuev, *Sto sorok,* 332–3.

248. Voroshilov's annual May Day holiday declaration to the troops for 1939 observed that "the capitalist world has entered the plane of new powerful shocks. The economic crisis threatens to become prolonged and more difficult than previous crises. Fascist aggressors, reshaping the world's map by force, have dragged humanity into a Second Imperialist War. . . . Unbridled fascist military aggression, intoxicated by easy victories, does not cease to threaten new attacks against weak and intimidated countries." *Krasnaia zvezda,* May 1, 1939, reprinted in Zolotarev, *Russkii arkhiv: Velikaia otechestvennaia,* XIII (II/i): 100–2 (RGVA, f. 4, op. 15, d. 25, l. 227–29).

249. Maiskii, *Dnevnik diplomata,* I: 385–6; Gorodetsky, *Maisky Diaries,* 182–3.

250. Gnedin, *Katastrofa i votoroe rozhdenie,* 108–10.

251. *DBFP,* 3rd series, V: 400 (Seeds to Halifax, May 3), 410 (Seeds to Halifax, May 4), 542 (Seeds to Halifax, May 19); Haslam, *Struggle for Collective Security,* 213–4.

252. Litvinov evidently did refer to Molotov as "fool" (*durak*), including over the phone,

which he knew was eavesdropped, according to Litvinov's daughter Tatiana, cited in Phillips, *Between the Revolution and the West*, 166. Litvinov is listed for a mere thirty-five minutes in the Little Corner on May 3, 1939: *Na prieme*, 258.

253. Stalin's telegram on Molotov's replacement of Litvinov mentioned "the serious conflict between the chairman of the People's Council of Commissars, Comrade Molotov, and the People's Commissar for Foreign Affairs, Comrade Litvinov," and blamed Litvinov's "disloyalty." APRF, f. 3, op. 63, d. 29, l. 71; *DVP SSSR*, XXII/i: 327 (AVP RF, f. 059, op. 1, pap. 313, dl. 2154, l. 45); *Sochineniia*, XVIII: 174.

254. On Molotov's influence on Stalin, see Volkogonov, *Triumf i tragediia*, II/i: 11–16. See also Gromyko, *Memories*, 30, 33, 404.

255. Watson, "Molotov's Apprenticeship."

256. Sudoplatov, *Special Tasks*, 98–102. Sudoplatov was then deputy director of NKVD intelligence and in charge of the German desk.

257. Khrushchev, "Vospominaniia," 18.

258. Zhukov added that "it was another matter later, when all the calculations turned out to be incorrect and collapsed; more than once in my presence Stalin berated Molotov for this." Simonov, "Zametki k biografii G. K. Zhukova," 49, reprinted in Mirkina and Iarovikov, *Marshal Zhukov*, II: 201–2.

259. Sheinis, *Maksim Maksimovich Litvinov*, 363. The dacha may have belonged to Stalin, who had awarded it to Litvinov.

260. Gnedin, *Katastrofa i votoroe rozhdenie*, 128–52. Gnedin would be the only one to survive to old age from the Soviet embassy or trade mission to Berlin.

261. "Sometimes he would stop for a few minutes and he would play his mouth organ and play arias from operas on it," Korzhenko's daughter Nora wrote of Nikolai, aged twenty-eight. "He was a brilliant player and if I closed my eyes I could imagine I was listening to an organ." She added: "All the time we were living in the beautiful wooden house at Klyazma life was perilous and uncertain. Nearly every day men and women were being arrested, shot or sent into exile. You could never escape from the atmosphere of intrigue, misery and sudden death. It was a strange and sinister atmosphere for a young girl to live in, but somehow one just accepted these things as part of life." Murray, *I Spied for Stalin*, 83–9, 112–3.126; Barmine, *Memoirs of a Soviet Diplomat*, 17. Nora, who had studied foreign languages and mingled with foreigners, would become an informant in that milieu for the organization that wrecked her family and the families of nearly everyone she knew—the NKVD.

262. Conquest, *Reassessment*, 423.

263. "Vospominaniia nachal'nika vneshnei razvedki P. M. Fitina," in Primakov, *Ocherki*, IV: 19; Bondarenko, *Fitin*, 41–7. Of the six hundred or so students admitted to the NKVD Central School in Moscow (Bolshoi Kiselny Pereulok) in those years, just fifty were chosen for the separate spy school in Balashikha, just outside Moscow. Sinitsyn, *Rezident svidetlet'stvuet*, 5; Sergutov, "Organizatsionnye aspejty deiatel'nosti vneshnei razvedki," III: 237. See also Pavlov, *Tragediia Sovetskoi razvedki*, 349.

264. Sudoplatov, *Special Tasks*, 66–8.

265. Trotsky speculated that Stalin was titillated by Kollontai's love life. Trotsky, *Stalin*, 243–4.

266. In late 1938, Litvnov had written several times to Boris Stein in Rome, forbidding him to return to Moscow because he was "needed" abroad. Sheinis, "Sud'ba diplomata," 301. Stalin would dispatch Stein to Finland, after which, in Feb. 1939, he did return to Moscow.

He would be spared, demoted to the editorial board of the periodical *Trud*, along with Troyanovsky, who had been ambassador to Tokyo and Washington.

267. *DVP SSSR*, XXII/i: 10–12 (AVP RF f. 06, op. 1, p. 2, d. 11, l. 4–7: Jan. 3, 1939).

268. Molotov claims he was specifically tasked with removing the preponderance of Jews. Chuev, *Sto sorok*, 274.

269. "Avtobiograficheskie zametki" V. N. Pavlova—perevodchika I. V. Stalina." Pavlov turned over this unpublished short memoir to the Foreign Ministry in 1987, and was interviewed in 1989 to clarify certain points.

270. Bohlen, *Witness to History*, 65.

271. Chuev, *Molotov Remembers*, 68–9.

272. Seabury, *Wilhelmstrasse*, 31, citing Picker, *Hitlers Tischgespräche*, 106. By 1940, 71 of the 120 highest officials in the German foreign ministry would belong to the Nazi party. Davidson, *Trial of the Germans*, 152.

273. Serge, "Litvinov," 419. Litvinov's inner circle included young people, such as Eduard Hershelman (head of his secretariat from age thirty), who was nevertheless arrested.

274. Even before the massacre-induced vacancies, half of the 1,500 personnel in the Soviet diplomatic corps at home and abroad were recruited right out of school at the beginning of the 1930s. Still, some 85 percent of Soviet diplomatic personnel active from 1940 to 1946 had begun a diplomatic career after 1936. Magerovsky, "The People's Commissariat," II: 345. "It happened that one made an appointment with a colleague but could not find him on the fixed day—he had been arrested," recalled one high-level official in the commissariat. "Exchange of opinions and conversations were reduced to a minimum." Roshchin, "People's Commissariat of Foreign Affairs," 110–11. The commissariat's private apartments at Blacksmith Bridge were sealed in wax after the arrest of their occupants, and the new residents often witnessed the unsealing by the NKVD. Dullin, *Men of Influence*, 238.

275. Kordt, *Wahn und Wirklichkeit*, 153.

276. Gafencu, *Last Days of Europe*, 83. On June 13, 1939, Nazi Party organizations would be forbidden to use "Third" when referring to the Reich—a repudiation of the Holy Roman empire (800–1806) as the first Reich (Bismarck's having then been the second). Wilson, *Heart of Europe*.

277. Butler, *Mason-Mac*, 74–5. Mason-Macfarlane's drawing-room window overlooked the Charlottenburg Chausee, which ran from the Siegesäule gilded column commemorating the 1870–71 war of reunification eastward to the Brandenburg Gate.

278. Moorehouse, *Killing Hitler*, 190–1, citing *DBFP*, 3rd series, IV, appendix V, Mason-Macfarlane Memorandum, 626; Imperial War Museum Archive, Mason-Macfarlane papers, ref. MM40.

279. Kershaw, *Hitler: 1936–1945*, 183–5.

280. McKee, *Tomorrow the World*, 27.

281. Domarus, *Hitler: Reden*, III: 1148–79; Domarus, *Hitler: Speeches*, III: 1561–96; Below, *Als Hitlers Adjutant*, 161–2; Muggeridge, *Ciano's Diary*, 78; Shirer, *Berlin Diary*, 133.

282. Haffner, *Meaning of Hitler*, 32–4.

283. *DGFP*, series D, VI: 460 (Braun von Stumm, May 9, 1939). The order ("Immediately cease polemics against the Soviet Union and Bolshevism") was issued on May 5, 1939. Sluch, "Germano-sovetskie otnosheniia," 110 (citing Politisches Archiv des Auswärtiges Amt, Bonn, Zsg. 101/13: 5).

284. Stehlin, *Témoignage pour l'histoire*, 147–53; and *French Yellow Book*, 132–6 (Coulondre to Bonnet, May 7, 1939); Andrew, *Secret Service*, 423–4. On June 16, Bodenschatz would tell Coulondre that "Germany was

making great efforts for an agreement with Russia."

285. Borev, *Staliniada*, 182–3. Dunayevsky, the songwriter, would get the Order of Lenin after *Volga-Volga*. Turovskaia, "*Volga-Volga* i ego vremia." On May 7, the annual Kremlin banquet for military academy graduates was held, after a two-year hiatus.

286. Nekrich, *Pariahs*, 154 (citing RGAE, f. 413, op. 13, d, 2856, l. 5–6).

287. Sontag and Beddie, *Nazi-Soviet Relations*, 3.

288. *DVP SSSR*, XXII/i: 339–41 (AVP RF, f. 06, op. 1, pap. 7 d. 66, l. 21–4: Astakhov to Molotov, May 6, 1939); *God krizisa*, I: 457–8 (AVP RF, f. 082, op. 22, pap. 93, d. 7, l. 214–5: Astakhov to Potyomkin, May 12, 1939).

289. On the Germany embassy's favorable report concerning Litvinov's dismissal, see *DGFP*, series D, VI: 419–20 (Tippelskirch, May 4).

290. Ericson, *Feeding the German Eagle*, 45; Sipols, *Tainy*, 323–40.

291. Watt, "Initiation of the Negotiations," 164–5. Alfred Rosenberg, following a conversation with Göring in spring 1939, had noted a willingness to go along with a temporary deal with Moscow out of expediency. United States Holocaust Museum, Alfred Rosenberg's Diary, 269.

292. Medvedev, *Let History Judge*, 308–9; Fischer, *Life and Death of Stalin*, 56. Ehrenburg, along with everyone else, puzzled over why Litvinov had not been arrested. Ehrenburg, *Post-War Years*, 276–8.

293. Lev Helfand, the Soviet ambassador to Rome, who would defect in July 1940, surmised that Stalin was willing to reach agreement with the British at least through June 1939. Haslam, *Russia's Cold War*, 8 (citing a report of Helfand's Sept. 12, 1940, interview with Neville Butler, Washington, D.C.: FO 371/24845).

294. Gromyko et al., *SSSR v bor'be za mir nakanune*, 375–6 (May 5, 1939). See also Gavrilov, *Voennaia razvedka informiruet*, 153–4 (TsAMO, f. 23, op. 22407, d. 2, l. 183: April 14, 1939, l. 192, 210: April 17 and 26, 1939); and Fesiun, *Delo Rikharda Zorge*, 98–9.

295. Muggeridge, *Ciano's Diplomatic Papers*, 283, 286; Gibson, *Ciano Diaries*, 78–9, 82, 84–5 (May 7, 14, and 21, 1939).

296. *DVP SSSR*, XXII/i: 342 (AVP RF, f. 059, op. 1, pap. 303, d. 2093, l. 60–1: Molotov to Surits, May 8, 1939), XXII: 546n113 (pap. 294, d. 2036, l. 75: Molotov to Maisky, May 8), XXII/i: 356 (AVP RF, f. 059, op. 1, pap. 300, d. 2076, l. 189–90: Maisky to Molotov, May 10); Gromyko et al., *SSSR v bor'be za mir nakanune*, 380–2 (May 8, 1939), 383–4 (May 8), 388–6 (May 10, 1939), 687n113; Falin, *Soviet Peace Efforts*, II: 25–6, 28, 311n113; *DBFP*, 3rd series, V: 487 (May 8).

297. Sluch, "Germano-sovetskie otnosheniia," 110 (citing Politisches Archiv des Auswärtiges Amt, Bonn, Schnurre, "Aus einem bewegten Leben," ms., 74–5). Hilger's family's property had been expropriated by the October revolution, yet he had taken part in the reestablishment of diplomatic relations between Germany and the Soviet Union and had joined the German embassy staff in 1923. Herwarth, *Against Two Evils*, 76–7.

298. Teske, *General Ernst Köstring*, 133–6.

299. *DGFP*, series D, VI: 494–6 (Ribbentrop to Tokyo, May 15, 1939).

300. Cienciala, "Foreign Policy of Józef Piłsudski"; Meysztowicz, *Czas przeszły dokonany*, 216; Beck, *Final Report*, 183–9; Mackiewicz, *Colonel Beck and His Policy*, 135; Overy, *Road to War*, 1–23; Von Riekhoff, *German-Polish Relations*, 329.

301. Potyomkin concluded his report by maintaining that he had summarized the

conversation before departing and Beck had confirmed his statement. *DVP SSSR*, XXII/i: 352 (AVP RF, f. 059, op. 1, pap. 296, d. 2047, l. 92: May 10, 1939), 352–4 (d. 2046, l. 122–5: May 10); Gromyko et al., *SSSR v bor'be za mir nakanune*, 389.

302. *God krizisa*, I: 448–9 (AVP RF, f. 06, op. 1a, pap. 26, d. 18, l. 110: May 11, 1939); *DVP SSSR*, XXII/i: 356–7; Gromyko et al., *SSSR v bor'be za mir nakanune*, 393–4.

303. Still, Romania, like Turkey, viewed a Western-Soviet agreement as effectively inevitable. Watt, *How War Came*, 284–5.

304. Gorodetsky, *Maisky's Diaries*, 202 (no citation).

305. Bulgakova, *Dnevnik*, 256–9. Mikhail Bulgakov's play *Batum* (1939), which depicted a young Stalin, in the revolutionary underground, as a decisive personality—incisive, flexible, cunning, even deceitful, above all able to do whatever it took to lead people through difficult challenges, while lusting for power—had been banned before rehearsals. Bulgakov, *Sobranie sochinenii*, V (*Master and Margarita*), VII: 305–76 (*Batum*).

306. Shentalinsky, *KGB's Literary Archive*, 42, 47. See also Povarov, *Prichina smerti rasstrel*; Pirozhkova, *At His Side*, 115.

307. Shentalinskii, "Proshu menia vyslushat'," 430–43.

308. Shentalinsky, *KGB's Literary Archive*, 44.

309. Mandelstam, *Hope against Hope*, 321. Mandelstam records Babel's brazenness in associating with foreigners as well.

310. Stalin could reveal limits to his hyper-suspiciousness. From Dec. 1938—when Valery Chkalov died in a crash during the maiden flight of an experimental fighter plane—through May 15, 1939, the country suffered thirty-four aviation crashes in which seventy people were killed. On May 16, at a meeting of the Main Military Council, Stalin raised the possibility of sabotage ("technicians can do this deliberately, and the aviators trust the aircraft") but added of Chkalov and four other heroes of the Soviet Union, "The aviator does not want to recognize the laws of physics and meteorology." *Glavnyi voennyi sovet RKKA*, 237. Nearly two hundred defects had been found on the rushed airplane earlier in the month that Chkalov flew it; the temperature was 25 below zero Celsius the day of the test flight. Maslov, *Rokovoi istrebitel' Chkalova*; Ivanov, *Neizvestnyi Polikarpov*; Bergman, "Valerii Chkalov."

311. Gorbunov, "Voennaia razvedka v 1934–1939 godakh" (no. 3), 60–1.

312. Khaustov, "Deiatel'nost' organov," 233.

313. Gavrilov, *Voennaia razvedka informiruet*, 81–4 (TsAMO, f. 23, op. 9157, d. 2, l. 173–9). The source might have been Kurt Welkisch ("ABC"), a German journalist and diplomat in Warsaw (1935–39). Soviet intelligence had reported that Kleist, following the destruction of Czechoslovakia in March 1939, had privately averred that "war against the Soviet Union remains the last and decisive task of German policy." Gavrilov, *Voennaia razvedka informiruet*, 60–4 (TsAMO, f. 23, op. 9197, d. 2, l. 245–54).

314. "Soobshchenie I. I. Proskurova I. V. Stalinu," 216–9; *Na prieme*, 259.

315. APRF, f. 3, op. 24, d. 455, l. 33–5 (June 1956 note from KGB chief Serov to the Central Committee); d. 448, l. 184, 189 (testimony by operatives Fedotov and Matusov). See also Petrov and Petrov, *Empire of Fear*, 69.

316. Ribbentrop inserted suggestions, in the German foreign ministry transcripts of the talks with the Soviets, to make it look as if Stalin was beseeching the great Hitler. Dębski, *Między Berlinem a Moskwą*, 84–91.

317. Dullin, *Men of Influence*, 30. "If one can speak of a pro-German in the Kremlin," Krivitsky asserted, "Stalin has been that figure all along." Krivitsky, *In Stalin's Secret Service*, 3, 10.

318. Pons, *Stalin and the Inevitable War*.

319. Savushkin, "K voprosu o zarozhdenii teorii," 78–82.

320. Maiskii, *Denevnik diplomata*, I: 398–400; Gorodetsky, *Maisky Diaries*, 192.

321. *French Yellow Book*, 147–9. "Russia is a good card, it is perhaps not necessary to play it," Beneš had told the French envoy in Prague back in April 1937, "but it is necessary not to abandon it from fear that Germany pick it up." Dreifort, "French Popular Front," 229 (citing *DDF*, 2e série, V: 513–4: April 21, 1937).

322. *Pravda*, May 28, 1939; *KPSS v rezoliutsiiakh* (8th ed.), V: 398–404 (May 27, 1939). Stalin also complained about labor shortages and called for extracting additional labor power from collective farms, claiming that much of it was idle. Zelenin, *Stalinskaia "revoliutsiia sverkhu,"* 246–7, 285; RGASPI, f. 558, op. 11, d. 1123, l. 1–30: uncorrected transcript; Danilov et al., *Tragediia sovetskoi derevni*, v/ii: 416–24. The transcript of the plenum, which met May 21–24 and 27, was never printed or distributed to regional party committees. There would not be another plenum until March 26–28, 1940.

323. Gromyko et al., *SSSR v bor'be za mir nakanune*, 395 (May 14, 1939), 417–21 (May 27, 1939); Falin, *Soviet Peace Efforts*, II: 39–40, 61–4; *DBFP*, 3rd series, V: 679–80.

324. *Nazi Conspiracy and Aggression*, V: 453 (*Völkischer Beobachter*, May 23, 1939); Toscano, *Origins of the Pact of Steel*.

325. *DGFP*, series D, VI: 586 (Weizsäcker, May 25, 1939). That same day, Japanese ambassador Shigenori Tōgō told Molotov that, according to the 1924 Soviet-Chinese Agreement, the USSR recognized Chinese suzerainty over Outer Mongolia, and therefore the Japanese government did not recognize the Soviet-Mongolian Pact. Tōgō also remonstrated that not Manchukuo but Outer Mongolia had violated the border. Zolotarev, *Russkii arkhiv: Velikaia otechestvennaia*, XVIII (VII/i): VII/i: 115–6 (RGVA, f. 33987, op. 3, d. 1233, l. 165–6).

326. Sontag and Beddie, *Nazi-Soviet Relations*, 8–9; *DVP SSSR*, XXII/i: 386–7 (AVP RF, f. 06, op. 1, p. 1, d. 2, l. 24–26: May 20, 1939), also in *God krizisa*, I: 482–3; Stronski, "Soviet Russia's Common Cause." Schulenburg was evidently not allowed to bring an interpreter and had to speak French for the Russian interpreter.

327. Below, *Als Hitlers Adjutant*, 163–4; *Der Prozess gegen die Hauptkriegsverbrecher*, XXXVII: 546–56; *DGFP*, series D, VI: 574–80; Weinberg, *Foreign Policy*, II: 576, 579–83; Kershaw, *Hitler: 1936–1945*, 191–3.

328. Presseisen, *Germany and Japan*, 221–2; Sommer, *Deutschland und Japan*, 238–42, 248–56; Morley, *Deterrent Diplomacy*, 105–11.

329. Iklé, *German-Japanese Relations*, 101 (April 28, 1939, citing *International Military Tribunal for the Far East, Documents Presented in Evidence*, exhibit 497: Ōshima's interrogation).

330. On May 27, 1939, the German ambassador in Tokyo, Eugen Ott, reported to Berlin that "I hear from another source that the Emperor, during a report by [chief of the general staff] Prince Kanin, who put forward the Army's demands on the alliance, made his consent dependent on the Army and Navy coming to an agreement. In view of the stubborn resistance by opponents of the alliance, rumors have cropped up about terrorist plans by radical groups." *DGFP*, series D, VI: 594–5.

331. *DGFP*, series D, VI: 597–8 (received at Moscow embassy on June 2).

332. *DGFP*, series D, VI: 599–600, 603–4 (unsigned, May 29, 1939).

333. Gavrilov, *Voennaia razvedka informiruet*, 88–99 (TsAMO, f. 23, op. 9157, d. 2, l. 101–17, 120–4), 740n40; *God krizisa*, I: 379–87, 405.

334. Mehringer, *Die NSDAP*, 5; Overy, *Dictators*, 639–40.

CHAPTER 11. PACT

1. Cadogan also wrote that he himself was "in favor of it [a Soviet alliance]. So, I think, is H. [Halifax]." Dilks, *Diaries of Sir Alexander Cadogan*, 182.

2. Michalka, *Ribbentrop und die deutsche Weltpolitik*; Bloch, *Ribbentrop*. "I honestly hated him," the long-serving state secretary in Ribbentrop's foreign ministry Baron von Weizsäcker would later claim. No one had a good word for him. Ribbentrop "was a man who occupied a responsible position for which he had neither talent, knowledge, nor experience, and he himself knew or sensed this very well," surmised the Moscow embassy official Gustav Hilger. "He sought to hide his feelings of inferiority by an arrogance that often seemed unbearable." Hilger and Meyer, *Incompatible Allies*, 293. The old-line conservative Franz von Papen—who had midwifed the invitation to Hitler to assume the Chancellorship at Ribbentrop's villa—deemed Ribbentrop "a husk with no kernel." 3. Schmidt, *Statist*, 312, 317. On the aspects of Schmidt's memoirs requiring scholarly

caution, see Namier, *In the Nazi Era*, 104–8. The best account of Ribbentrop in London is Spitzy, *So haben wir das Reich verspielt*, 92–122. Ribbentrop actually spent limited time in London: Jacobsen, *Nationalsozialistische Aussenpolitik*, 706.

4. Rees, *Nazis*, 93–5 (citing Spitzy); Snyder, *Encyclopedia of the Third Reich*, 295. Prince Otto von Bismarck, grandson of the Iron Chancellor and Counselor at the German embassy in Rome, told Ciano of Ribbentrop "he is such an imbecile, he is a freak of nature." Ciano, *Ciano's Hidden Diary*, 151.

5. Ribbentrop had ended up in London almost by accident. On April 18, 1936, the German ambassador to the Court of St. James's, Leopold von Hoesch, died; initially, no one was aware he had taken his place. Then, when von Bülow died on June 21, Ribbentrop expected to get his position as state secretary (number two) under Neurath, but the latter objected, and Ribbentrop was posted to London as consolation. Ribbentrop spent most of 1936 and 1937 not in the United Kingdom, but

negotiating with Japan and Italy for an alliance against the UK. On Dec. 28, 1937, he wrote to Hitler that Britain was Germany's "most dangerous enemy." Heineman, *Hitler's First Foreign Minister*, 140–44; Seabury, *Wilhelmstrasse*, 54–6; Weinberg, "Hitler and England," 87–8; Waddington, "Ribbentrop and the Soviet Union"; *Ciano's Diary 1937–1938*, 24.

6. Almost alone, von Ribbentrop had interpreted the Munich Pact as a blow against Britain, commenting that Chamberlain "has signed a death sentence for the British empire and invited us to fix the date of implementation of this sentence." Dalton, *Fateful Years*, 195.

7. Ribbentrop later wrote that he constantly reminded Hitler of Bismarck's Russia policy. Ribbentrop, *Memoirs*, 151. Wilhelmstrasse, 76, was a two-story former private home constructed in the eighteenth century; Bismarck had had his medium-sized office as well as family quarters on the upper floor. Pflanze, *Bismarck*, II: 35.

8. Molotov, *Stati'i i rechi, 1935–1936*, 12, 20–1 (Jan. 28, 1935); Haslam, *Struggle for Collective Security*, 46. On a document sent to him by Molotov, Zhdanov wrote that "entering into agreement with England and France against Germany, even concluding a military alliance with them, we should not forget for one minute that in this alliance, England and France will conduct a policy of insincerity, provocation, and betrayal with respect to us." Nekrich, *Pariahs*, 105 (undated reference, letter by V. P. Zolotov).

9. Recall Stalin's statement to Eden that the world situation was worse than it had been on the eve of the Great War, "because in 1913 there was only one source of the threat of war—Germany—and presently there are two such sources, Germany and Japan" (both of which bordered the Soviet Union). *DVP SSSR*, XVIII: 246–251 (at 249–50: March 29, 1935); RGVA, f. 33 987, op. 3, d. 1144, l. 325.

10. Efimenko et al., *Vooruzhennyi konflikt*, 32–6 (RGVA, f. 32113, op. 1, d. 203, l. 6–11: May 16, 1939), 36–40 (d. 202, l. 6–10: May 16), 41–3 (f. 33797, op. 1, d. 37, l. 17–21), 43–4 (op. 3, d. 1225, l. 5–6), 44–5 (op. 1, d. 38, l. 6), 45–6 (d. 36, l. 39–40, 48), 46–8 (l. 51), 48–50 (d. 35, l. 26–35), 51–2 (op. 3, d. 1225, l. 12–4), 52–3 (f. 32113, op. 1, d. 204, l. 33), 53–4 (f. 7977, op. 1, d. 37, l. 55); Coox, "Introduction," 122.

11. Coox, *Nomonhan*, 186–9 (April 25, 1939); Goldman, *Nomonhan, 1939*, 1 (citing U.S. Department of the Army, Forces in the Far East, *Japanese Special Studies on Manchuria*, 13 vols. [Tokyo, 1954–6], XI/1: 99–102), 83–8.

12. Coox, *Nomonhan*, 188–95.

13. Gromyko et al., *SSSR v bor'be za mir nakanune*, 406; Efimenko et al., *Vooruzhennyi konflikt*, 54–6: RGASPI, f. 82, op. 2, d. 1386, l. 8–12; AVP RF, f. 06, op. 1, pap. 1, d. 2, l. 22–3.

14. Krasnov, *Neizvestnyi Zhukov*, 90–9; Zhukov, *Vospominaniia*, II: 249–87(at 250–3). Zhukov's memoir dates the meeting with Voroshilov to June 2, but a letter to his wife and other documents indicate May 24. See also Roberts, *Stalin's General*, 48–9.

15. Sokolov, *Neizvestnyi Zhukov*, 115–8. June 1938, when Zhukov had been promoted to deputy commander of the Belorussian military district, he denied in writing any ties to enemies of the people. Daines, *Zhukov*, 81.

16. Krasnov, *Neizvestnyi Zhukov*, 100–1 (Zhukov to Voroshilov, May 30, 1939).

17. Zolotarev, *Russkii arkhiv: Velikaia otechestvennaia*, XVIII (VII/1): 116–8 (RGVA, f. 33987, op. 1, d. 38, l. 102–6). See also Efimenko et al., *Vooruzhennyi konflikt*, 77–8 (RGVA, f. 37977, op. 1, d. 38, l. 110–2: Shaposhnikov, May 28, 1939).

18. Coox, *Nomonhan*, 200–65; Efimenko et al., *Vooruzhennyi konflikt*, 82–4 (RGVA, f. 37977, op. 1, d. 37, l. 109–15), 88 (RGVA, f. 37977, op. 1, d. 82, l. 74: May 31, 1939).

19. Tret'ia sessiia Verkhovnogo Soveta SSSR, 25–31 maia 1939 g., 467–76 (at 476); *God Krizisa*, I: 523–30.

20. *God krizisa*, I: 520–2 (AVP RF, f. 011, op. 4, pap. 27, d. 59, l. 105–10). Astakhov informed Moscow of Germany's evident wish to throw a wrench into Soviet-British talks. Weizsäcker sensed Soviet suspicions of German motives. *DVP SSSR*, XXII/i: 406; Hill, *Weizsäcker Papiere*, 154. Ribbentrop had informed Weizsäcker and Friedrich Gaus (director of the foreign ministry legal department) on May 25 that Hitler for some time had been thinking about improving relations with the USSR; the two officials drafted instructions for the embassy in Moscow, to convey to Molotov, but then these instructions were not sent, either because Ribbentrop was still hopeful of a formal military alliance with Japan, which a deal with Moscow would scuttle, or Hitler found them excessive. *DGFP*, series

D, VI: 589–93 (Ribbentrop instructions, May [26], 1939); Fleischhauer, *Der Pakt*, 202–7.

21. *DGFP*, series D, VI: 614–5.

22. The freedom to choose the moment implied Japan might not even carry out military actions. Iklé, *German-Japanese Relations*, 117–8 (citing *International Military Tribunal for the Far East, Documents Presented in Evidence*, exhibit 614: Ott telegram to foreign ministry, June 5, 1939); Presseisen, *Germany and Japan*, 212–3 (citing exhibit 614); Tokushirō, "The Anti-Comintern Pact," 103–5.

23. Gavrilov, *Voennaia razvedka informiruet*, 99–105 (TsAMO, f. 23, op. 9157, d. 2, l. 350–60); *DVP SSSR*, XXII/ii: 583 n169.

24. Iklé, *German-Japanese Relations*, 87–118; Nolte, *Der europäische Bürgerkrieg*, 308.

25. Sontag and Beddie, *Nazi-Soviet Relations*, 18–20 (Schulenburg to Berlin, June 5, 1939), 21–2 (Tippelskirch, June 18, on Mikoyan's distrust). The Germans had gotten Stalin's point: in May 1939, the anti-Nazi Herwarth of the German embassy secretly conveyed it to U.S. ambassador Bohlen. Bohlen, *Witness to History*, 69–82 (at 71).

26. Sontag and Beddie, *Nazi-Soviet Relations*, 20–1 (Woermann foreign ministry memo, June 15, 1939).

27. Weinberg, *Foreign Policy*, II: 603. The German foreign ministry expert Nadolny was of the opinion that the Treaty of Berlin was still valid. *DGFP*, series D, VI: 686–7 (June 9, 1939), 687 (June 9, 1939), 741–2 (June 17, 1939), 843–5 (July 4, 1939).

28. On June 17, Schulenburg, in Berlin, requested a meeting with Astakhov, and told him the German foreign ministry awaited a response to Weizsäcker's prompt of May 30, underscoring its sincerity and seriousness. *God krizisa*, II: 40 (AVP RF, f. 059, op. 1, pap. 294, d. 2036, l. 115–6), 65–7 (f. 06, op. 1a, pap. 26, d. 1, l. 4–6: Molotov and Schulenburg, June 28).

29. Schulenburg brought up this incident to Molotov as a way of broaching touchy issues. Sontag and Beddie, *Nazi-Soviet Relations*, 53–6 (at 54: Schulenburg to the foreign ministry, Aug. 16, 1939).

30. Sontag and Beddie, *Nazi-Soviet Relations*, 25–6 (Hewel, June 29, 1939), 27–8 (Weizsäcker to Schulenburg, June 30). See also *DGFP*, series D, VI: 820–1 (Schnurre, June 30).

31. *God krizisa*, II: 105–6 (AVP RF, f. 059, op. 1, pap. 302, d. 2090, l. 171–2: Surits, July 19, 1939); Gromyko et al., *SSSR v bor'be za mir nakanune*, 496–7.

32. Duhanovs et al., *1939*, 46–85.

33. Gromyko et al., *SSSR v bor'be za mir nakanune*, DK266.A3 S2 1971; Gromyko et al. (eds.), *Soviet Peace Efforts on the Eve of World War II* (Moscow: Progress, 1973), 363. Lithuania further feared that Poland would immediately announce its own acceptance of a Soviet guarantee if Lithuania did so and that Hitler would blame Poland's action on Lithuania and take revenge. *DVP SSSR*, XXII/i: 545–6 (AVP RF, f. 06, op. 1, pap. 12, d. 126, l. 1–2: Pozdnyakov report to Molotov, July 19, 1939).

34. *DVP SSSR*, XXII/i: 449 (AVP RF, f. 059, op. 1, pap. 301, d. 2079, l. 186–7); *Pravda*, June 13, 1939.

35. *God krizisa*, II: 34–5 (AVP RF, f. 059, op. 1, pap. 313, d. 2154, l. 107 8); Gromyko et al., *SSSR v bor'be za mir nakanune*, 453.

36. Moiseev, *Ia vospominaiu*, 45–7. Moiseev provides no date for the incident, except that it took place before the Pact (Aug. 1939). His troupe's first appearance at a Kremlin reception was May 17, 1938 (banquet for school-teachers); they appeared again on New Year's Eve 1938–9, May 5 and 7, 1939, July 5 and 20, 1939. Shamina, "Igor Moiseev." On Nov. 8, 1939, Moiseyev would write to Stalin,

complaining of a lack of facility and resources; Stalin would turn the letter over to Shcherbakov, who gave them rehearsal space in the Tchaikovsky Concert Hall and apartments to some of the dancers. "My peremenili 16 mest raboty," *Izvestiia*, 2002, no. 3: 11–2; Ponomarev, *Aleksandr Shcherbakov*, 60.

37. Strang, *Home and Abroad*, 68. "Halifax invited me over and started complaining bitterly: we were creating unnecessary difficulties, we were absolutely unyielding, we were reusing the German method of negotiating (announcing our price and demanding 100% acceptance)," Maisky confided in his diary (June 23). "He admitted that, despite the large quantity of telegrams from Seeds and Strang, he still could not grasp what the problem was." Maiskii, *Dnevnik diplomata*, I: 415–6; Gorodetsky, *Maisky Diaries*, 201.

38. Strang, *Home and Abroad*, 175.

39. Aster, *1939*, 273 (citing letter to Hilda Chamberlain, Chamberlain Papers). Chamberlain, one British insider who hosted him in an intimate setting noted, "is not genuine in his desire for an agreement." Neilson, *Britain, Soviet Russia*, 300–1 (citing FO 371/23068/ C8370/3356/18: Peake to Cadogan, June 9, 1939; Harvey Papers, ADD, MSS 5639).

40. Koliazin, "Vernite mne svobodu!," 220–40.

41. Medvedeva, "'Chornoye leto' 1939 goda," 318–66; Braun, "Vsevolod Meyerhold," 145–62; Morrison, People's Artist, 99–100 (citing RGALI f. 1929, op. 1, ed. khr. 655, l. 26ob.: Lina Prokofyeva); "Zagadka smerti Zinaidi Raikha," *Komsomol'skaia pravda*, Nov. 14, 2005.

42. Beria evidently awarded the larger part of Meyerhold's spacious, now vacant apartment in the heart of Moscow (just off Gorky St.) to one of his mistresses, Vardo Mataradze, officially a typist, whom he had brought from Georgia and, it is said, arranged to marry one of his NKVD drivers. The smaller half went to the driver, who found it too small and moved out. Sudoplatov, *Special Tasks*, 103–4. See also Radzinsky, *Stalin*, 434.

43. *DGFP*, series D, VI: 1059–62, VII: 67–9; Goldman, *Nomonhan, 1939*, 161–2.

44. Gavrilov, *Voennaia razvedka informiruet*, 108–9 (TsAMO, f. 23, op. 22407, d. 2, l. 359–60); *DGFP*, series D, VI: 737–40, 750–1.

45. *DGFP*, series D, VI: 821–2.

46. Domarus, *Hitler: Reden*, III: 1216; Vauhnik, *Memoiren eines Militärattachés*, 29.

47. *DGFP*, series D, VI: 858–60.

48. Weinberg, *Foreign Policy*, II: 601–27.

49. On June 9, 1939, Beria provided a denunciation from the local special department ("A powerful fist to destroy the enemy has not been formed. Troops are being thrown into battle without coordination and mutual support, suffering heavy losses"). Daines, *Zhukov*, 95–6 (RGVA, f. 33987, op. 3, d. 1181, l. 126–7).

50. Sevos'tianov, "Voennoe i diplomaticheskoe porazhenie iaponii," 70–1.

51. Barnhart, "Japanese Intelligence," 436–7. The Kwantung chief was Ueda Kenkichi.

52. Efimenko et al., *Vooruzhennyi konflikt*, 133–4 (RGVA, f. 37977, op. 1, d. 86, l. 10–3: June 27, 1939), 192–3 (op. 3, d. 1225, l. 155–6: July 14, 1939), 164–5 (op. 1, d. 83, l. 166–71), 195 (d. 54, l. 121), 196–7 (d. 55, l. 92–6: Kulik), 219 (f. 4, op. 11, d. 54, l. 276); Zolotarev, *Russkii arkhiv: Velikaia otechestvennaia*, XVIII (VII/i): 124 (RGVA, f. 33977, op. 1, d. 54, l. 121), 124–5 (l. 129); Krasnov, *Neizvestnyi Zhukov*, 118–21. On July 10, 1939, Beria sent Voroshilov a copy of an intercepted letter from the Germany embassy in Moscow to Berlin concerning events at the Halha River. Military attaché Köstring reported the rumors that the Soviets had staged the border

incident either to push the Japanese army back or to re-confirm to the British and French that the Japanese were a threat in the Far East, but he deemed these possibilities "unlikely." Instead, he adhered to the view in the Japanese press that the borders were not clear and that the Mongol nomads migrated with their horses. He discounted the possibility of a full-scale Soviet-Japanese war in this remote border region. Zolotarev, *Russkii arkhiv: Velikaia otechestvennaia*, XVIII (VII/i): 121–2 (RGVA, f. 33987, op. 3, d. 1181, l. 166–9).

53. Hill, *Weizsäcker Papiere*, 157, 181.

54. *DGFP*, series D, VI: 870–1 (July 7), 889 (July 10).

55. Gavrilov, *Voennaia razvedka informiruet*, 112–5 (TsAMO, f. 23, op. 9157, d. 2, l. 418–31).

56. *DBFP*, 3rd series, VI: 389–91 (Wilson and Wohltat, July 19, 1939). See Metzmacher, "Deutsch-englische Ausgleichbemühengen."

57. Gromyko et al., *SSSR v bor'be za mir nakanune*, 499–502 (July 21, 1939); Schorske, "Two German Diplomats," 505–6.

58. Maiskii, *Dnevnik diplomata*, I: 426–7; Gorodetsky, *Maisky Diaries*, 208; *DVP SSSR*, XXII/ii: 574n158.

59. Aster, *1939*, 243–51. On the parade: *Pravda*, July 21, 1939.

60. Dirksen, *Moscow, Tokyo, London*, 242; Read and Fisher, *Deadly Embrace*, 113.

61. Hinsley et al., *British Intelligence*, I: 67–9; Gladwyn, *Memoirs*, 86–7. *Pravda* happened to announce on July 22, 1939, the resumption of Soviet-German trade and credit negotiations in Berlin. That same day, the German foreign ministry instructed the embassy in Moscow to try to restart political talks as well. *DGFP*, series D, VI: 955–6.

62. Overy, "Strategic Intelligence," 465–6 (citing PRO WO 190/745: "Note on Germany's Present Position and Future Aims," Jan. 17, 1939). See also MacDonald, "Economic Appeasement." On May 23, 1939, Hitler had told his upper military that "it is not Danzig that is at stake. For us it is a matter of expanding our living space in the East and making food supplies secure and also solving the problem of the Baltic States. . . . No other openings can be seen in Europe." *DGFP*, series D, VI: 574–80.

63. Neilson, *Britain, Soviet Russia*, 316 (citing Chamberlain Papers, NC 18/1/1108).

64. *DBFP*, 3rd series, IX: 323 (Halifax to Sir Robert Craigie in Tokyo, July 24, 1939); Neilson, *Britain, Soviet Russia*, 301–10 (citing Halifax Papers, FO 800/315: Henderson to Halifax, June 17, 1939; FO 371/23527/F7395/6457/10: Halifax interview with Maisky, July 25, 1939; Shai, "Was There a Far Eastern Munich?"; Parker, *Chamberlain and Appeasement*, 246–71; Watt, *How War Came*, 356–9.

65. Iklé, *German-Japanese Relations*, 182; Tokushirō, "The Anti-Comintern Pact," 107–11. On June 24, 1939, Sorge reported by telegram that he had learned from Ott that the Japanese had allowed that "in the event of a war between Germany and the USSR, Japan will automatically enter into a war against the USSR." Gromyko et al., *SSSR v bor'be za mir nakanune*, 463 (June 24, 1939); See also Tokushirō, "The Anti-Comintern Pact," 9–111.

66. Barnhart, "Japanese Intelligence," 436–7.

67. Coulondre reported hearsay out of Berlin to Bonnet on July 11, 1939, that Ribbentrop had fallen out of favor with Hitler for failing to anticipate the strong British resistance to Germany's plans to reclaim Danzig. *French Yellow Book*, 186–8.

68. Hilger and Meyer, *Incompatible Allies*, 294.

69. Ericson, *Feeding the German Eagle*, 54. On Aug. 10, 1939, Hitler had summoned Carl

Burckhardt, the conservative Swiss high commissioner of the League of Nations in Danzig, who had been working to avert a British-German war and generally blamed Polish intransigence. "Everything I undertake is aimed at Russia," Hitler told him at the Berghof the next day, according to Burckhardt. "If the West is too stupid and too blind to see this, I shall be forced to come to an understanding with the Russians, defeat the West, and then marshal my forces against the Soviet Union. I need the Ukraine so that they cannot starve us out, as they did in the last war." Hitler aimed to neutralize the British and sow distrust between London and Warsaw. Burckhardt, *Meine Danziger Mission*, 347–8; Levine, "Mediator." On Sept. 1, 1939, the Nazi Gauleiter in Danzig, Forster, would order Burckhardt out of the "former" free city.

70. As Gaus testified at Nuremberg, "in the early Summer of 1939 . . . von Ribbentrop asked . . . von Weizsäcker and myself to come to his estate, Sonnenburg, near Freienwalde-an-der-Oder, and informed us that Adolf Hitler had for some time been considering an attempt to establish better relations between Germany and the Soviet Union." This was Ribbentrop talking, not Hitler. Lasky, "Hitler-Stalin Pact," 9, 15. Ribbentrop would seize upon any reports that Jews were being purged by Stalin to inform Hitler that the Soviet system appeared to be evolving toward a Russian fascism.

71. *DGFP*, series D, VI: 755–6, 1006–9, 1015–6, 1047–8; Hill, *Weizsäcker Papiere*, 157 (July 30, 1939); Weinberg, *Foreign Policy*, II: 604–5; Sipols, *Tainy*, 79–80.

72. Sontag and Beddie, *Nazi-Soviet Relations*, 33–7.

73. Henderson, *Failure of a Mission*, 252–3. Henderson had written to Horace Wilson in May 1939: "The responsibility of my small job in Berlin is greater than my capacity and I cannot feel otherwise than profoundly pessimistic." Overy, *1939: Countdown*, 57 (citing NA, PREM 1/331a).

74. Henderson, *Failure of a Mission*, 234. See also Cienciala, "German Propaganda."

75. Sontag and Beddie, *Nazi-Soviet Relations*, 38; *DGFP*, series D, VI: 1006–9 (July 27, 1939), 1059–62 (Aug. 4); *DVP SSSR*, XXII/i: 566–9 (AVP RF, f. 0745, op. 14, pap. 32, d. 3, l. 27–30: Aug. 2, 1939); AVP RF, f. 06, op. 1a, p. 26, d. 1, l. 7–12; f. 059, op. 1, pap. 294, d. 2036, l. 162–5, in Volkogonov papers, Hoover Institution Archives, container 1. In Aug. 1939, Astakhov was recalled to Moscow; the Germans asked for him to be named ambassador to Berlin. Instead, Astakhov was demoted to a position in the Museum of the Peoples of the USSR. He seems to have died of muscular dystrophy in 1941.

76. *DVP SSSR*, XXII/i: 585–7 (AVP RF, f. 011, op. 4, pap. 27, d. 61, 126–9: Astakhov to Molotov, Aug. 8, 1939); *God krizisa*, II: 179–80.

77. *DGFP*, series D, VI: 1059–62 (Schulenburg to Berlin, Aug. 3–4, just after midnight); Sontag and Beddie, *Nazi-Soviet Relations*, 41.

78. Halder, who looked with trepidation on any pact between Britain and the Soviet Union, was said to have called the prospect "the only thing that could stop Hitler now" in a private conversation. Kordt, *Nicht aus Akten*, 313–19; Mosley, *On Borrowed Time*, 252.

79. Voroshilov appeared on nineteen of the twenty-seven days in August for which audiences were recorded in Stalin's office logbook. For the instructions to Voroshilov (Aug. 4, 1939), see Volkogonov, *Triumf i tragediia*, II/i: 20 (citing AVP RF, f. 06, op. 1b, p. 27, d. 5, l. 22–32). Voroshilov would report to Stalin immediately after the conclusion of a session, and Kuznetsov writes that on occasion, he

and Shaposhnikov attended, too. Kuznetsov appears in the office logbook only on Aug. 20 (without Voroshilov or Shaposhnikov); Shaposhnikov appears on Aug. 13, 14, and 25. There could also have been meetings at the dacha. *Na prieme*, 268–71; Kuznetsov, *Nakanune*, 249.

80. Volkogonov, *Triumf i tragediia*, II/i: 19 (RGVA, f. 33987, op. 3, d. 1235, l. 66–72). Beria continued to keep Voroshilov well informed of French, German, Italian, British, and other actors through eavesdropped conversations and agent reports, in the European capitals and in Moscow. RGVA, f. 33 987, op. 3, d. 1235, l. 9/cc (Sept. 23, 1939: Volkogonov papers, Hoover Institution Archives, container 16).

81. Maiskii, *Dnevnik diplomata*, I: 434–5 (Aug. 5, 1939); Pankrashova and Sipols, "Soviet-British-French Talks"; Roberts, *Unholy Alliance*, 140–1.

82. Primakov, *Ocherki*, IV: 261–2.

83. Primakov, *Ocherki*, III: 55.

84. Neilson, *Britain, Soviet Russia*, 310–1.

85. Hill, *Weizsäcker Papiere*, 157–8. Molotov (July 28) praised Astakhov's detailed reporting of Schnurre's proposals and non-response. *God krizisa*, II: 145 (AVP RF, f. 059, op. 1, pap. 295, d. 2038, l. 93); Fleischhauer, *Der Pakt*, 273–4.

86. Primakov, *Ocherki*, III: 290.

87. The intense impatience in Berlin was conveyed by Schnurre to Schulenburg in a telegram sent on Aug. 2 and received two days later: "Secret: Politically, the problem of Russia is being dealt with here with extreme urgency. During the last ten days I have daily had at least one direct or telephone conversation with the foreign minister and know that he is also constantly exchanging views with the Führer on this. The foreign minister is concerned to obtain some result on the Russian question as soon as possible, not only on the negative side (disturbing the British negotiations) but also on the positive side (an understanding with us) . . . You can imagine how eagerly talks with Molotov are awaited here." *DGFP*, series D, VI: 1047–8.

88. *DBFP*, 3rd series, VI: 762–89 ("Instructions to the British Military Mission to Moscow, Aug. 1939"); *Izvestiia*, Aug. 12, 1939; Tisminets, *Vneshniaia politika partii*, IV: 439.

89. Sipols, *Tainy*, 89; *Pravda*, Dec. 24, 1989. Haslam maintained that "given the lack of serious intent in London it was inevitable that the Russians would turn to the Germans." Haslam, *Struggle for Collective Security*, 216.

90. *DVP SSSR*, XXII/i: 584 (AVP RF, f. 06, op. 16, pap. 27, d. 5, l. 38: Aug. 7, 1939); Sluch, "Germano-sovetskie otnosheniia," 111.

91. Spiridonovka St. became Alexei Tolstoy St.; Litvinov resided on this street when he was people's commissar for foreign affairs.

92. *Dokumenty i materialy kanuna vtoroi mirovoi voiny*, II: 212–8 (AVP RF, f. 06, op. 1a, pap. 25, d. 12, l. 3–12); *God krizisa*, II: 191–6.

93. Drax suggested that if the negotiations were switched to London, he would be able to produce the desired confirmation of his plenipotentiary powers. Someone remarked, to general laughter, that it would be simpler to have the documents sent to Moscow than to bring all the delegations to London. Kuznetsov, *Nakanune*, 247.

93. Young, *In Command of France*, 239.

94. Overy, *1939: Countdown*, 13 (Borthwick Archive, University of York, Halifax Papers, A4.410.12/1).

95. *Dokumenty i materialy kanuna vtoroi mirovoi voiny*, II: 218–23 (AVP RF, f. 06, op. 1a, pap. 25, d. 12, l. 13–22, Aug. 13, 1939), II: 239–47 (AVP RF, f. 06, op. 1a, pap. 25, d. 12, l. 48–59, Aug. 15, 1939); *God krizisa*, II: 196–202, 202–7, 220–8.

96. "He that commands the sea," Sir Francis Bacon had explained of British strategy already in the seventeenth century, "is at great liberty, and may take as much and as little of the war as he will." Bacon, "Of the True Greatness of Kingdoms and Estates" [1612, enlarged 1625], as cited in Corbett, *Some Principles of Maritime Strategy*, 55.

97. Ponomarev, *Pokoriteli neba*, 68–75.

98. Schorske, "Two German Diplomats," 508. On Aug. 11, 1939, firm intelligence that Germany's attack on Poland was imminent reached the war office in London, effectively rendering further British moves toward Berlin a show to ensure that responsibility for the outbreak of war fell on Germany. Hinsley et al., *British Intelligence*, I: 83n.

99. Schnurre summoned Astakhov on Aug. 13 (a Sunday) to convey agreement to conduct talks in Moscow. *God krizisa*, II: 185 (AVP RF, f. 06, op. 1, pap. 7, d. 70, l. 1–2); *DVP SSSR*, XXII/i: 603, 606–7; *DGFP*, series D, VII: 62–4 (Ribbentrop to Schulenburg, Aug. 14), 68–9 (Weizsäcker to Schulenburg, Aug. 15). Interactions with Astakhov in Berlin had indicated to the Germans that an agreement was likely. *DGFP*, series D, VII: 17–20 (Schnurre to Berlin, Aug. 10, 1939), 20–1 (Schnurre to Schulenburg in Berlin, Aug. 10), 58–9 (Schnurre to Moscow embassy, Aug. 14).

100. Sontag and Beddie, *Nazi-Soviet Relations*, 50–2 (Ribbentrop to Schulenburg), 52–3 (Schulenburg to German foreign ministry), 53–7 (Schulenburg), 57 (Schulenburg); *Die Beziehungen*, 55–7 (Ribbentrop's original instructions and Schulenburg's amendments); *God krizisa*, II: 229–31 (AVP RF, f. 0745, op. 14, pap. 32, d. 3, l. 33–6), 232–3 (l. 37–9); Volkogonov, *Stalin: Triumph and Tragedy*, 353 (citing AVP RF, f. 0745, op. 15, pap. 38, d. 8, l. 126–8).

101. Also on Aug. 15, the Soviet military attaché in Tokyo reported that Japanese ruling circles remained gridlocked over a military alliance with Germany and Italy: the key players wanted the alliance to be directed solely against the USSR, while Berlin and Rome wanted to add Japan to their alliance against the Western powers. Gromyko et al., *SSSR v bor'be za mir nakanune*, 583; The attaché was L. A. Mishin.

102. Lota, *"Alta" protiv "Barbarossy"*, 70, 72 (no citation).

103. Sontag and Beddie, *Nazi-Soviet Relations*, 61–3 (Ribbentrop to Schulenburg, received in Moscow at 5:45 a.m. on Aug. 19).

104. Gorodetsky, *Grand Delusion*, 7 (citing RGVA, f. [unspecified], op. 9157, d. 2, l. 418–31, 447, 453–4).

105. Sontag and Beddie, *Nazi-Soviet Relations*, 64–5 (Schulenburg to foreign ministry, Aug. 19, 1939), 65–6; *God krizisa*, II: 269–71 (AVP RF, f. 0745, op. 14, pap. 32, d. 3, l. 40–3), 271–3 (l. 44, 45–6), 274–6 (l. 47–51), 277–8 (l. 52–3), 280–91 (AVP RF, f. 03a, d. 05 Germaniia); *DGFP*, series D, VII: 134 (Schulenburg to Berlin, Aug. 19, 1939); Read and Fisher, *Deadly Embrace*, 214. Britain knew as well: Group Captain Malcom Christie, a former British air attaché who had excellent contacts among senior German officers and others hostile to Hitler, reported secret leaks to Sir Robert Vansittart (the retired undersecretary of the foreign office), who relayed the reports to the government. On June 27, 1939, Christie conveyed that the German mobilization for Poland would begin from Aug. 1 and be completed by the 27th. On Aug. 17, Christie reported that the war would commence between Aug. 25 and 28. Overy, *1939: Countdown*, 23 (citing Churchill College, Cambridge, Christie Papers, CHRS I/29B); Andrew, *Secret Service*, 429.

106. Ericson, *Feeding the German Eagle*, 57–61; *Trial of the Major War Criminals*, XXXI:

233; *DGFP*, series D, VIII: 310–3 (Ritter and Schulenburg to the foreign ministry, Oct. 18, 1939); Sontag and Beddie, *Nazi-Soviet Relations*, 83–5.

107. As late as Aug. 20, Drax had written to Voroshilov that he had not yet received an answer from his government: Volkogonov, *Triumf I tragediia*, II/1: 21–2 (RGVA, f. 33987, op. 3, d. 1235, l. 73); Volkogonov, *Stalin: Triumph and Tragedy*, 351.

108. The agreement, at Soviet insistence, mentioned German "industrial goods," but had not specified what the term encompassed. In Oct. 1939, both Schnurre and Karl Ritter would deny this included armaments, perhaps as a way of bargaining for better terms of exchange. Wish lists the Soviets had passed on made abundantly clear industrial goods meant weaponry. Schwendemann, *Die Wirtschaftliche Zussamenarbeit*, 90–7.

109. Sontag and Beddie, *Nazi-Soviet Relations*, 66–7; *Akten zur deutschen auswärtigen Politik*, VII: 131 (Russian translation, Volkogonov, Hoover Institution Archives, container 1); *DGFP*, series D, VII: 156–7 (Ribbentrop to the Moscow embassy, Aug. 20, 1939); *God krizisa*, II: 302 (AVP RF, f. 0745, op. 14, pap. 32, d. 3, l. 63–4); *DVP SSSR*, XXII/ii: 585 n172; Volkogonov, *Triumf I tragediia*, II/1: 28–9.

110. Fleischhauer, *Diplomatischer Widerstand*, 14–28. Stalin preserved the exchange with Hitler in his personal archive: RGASPI, f. 558, op. 11, d. 296, l. 1–3.

111. *God krizisa*, II: 303 (AVP RF, f. 0745, op. 14, pap. 32, d. 3, l. 65); *DVP SSSR*, XXII/i: 624.

112. Hilger and Meyer, *Incompatible Allies*, 300; Hoffman, *Hitler Was My Friend*, 102; Speer, *Erinnerungen*, 176; Domarus, *Hitler: Reden*, III: 1233; *Das deutsche Reich und der Zweite Weltkrieg*, IV: 142.

113. Watt, *How War Came*, 466–70; Meehan, *Unnecessary War*, 233–4; Maser, *Der Wortbruch*, 59–60.

114. Antonov, "Anatolii Gorskii."

115. Kershaw, *Hitler: 1936–1945*, 207; Baumgart, "Zur Ansprache Hitlers" (no. 2), esp. 126, 132–3 n53 and n55, 149n113; Below, *Als Hitlers Adjutant*, 180; Albrecht, "'Wer redet heute noch von der Vernichtung der Armenier?'"

116. Kershaw, *Hitler: 1936–1945*, 212–3; Maiskii, *Dnevnik diplomata*, I: 439–40 (Aug. 22, 1939). "Of all the big Nazi leaders, Hermann Göring was for me by far the most sympathetic," Henderson would write in 1940. He had certain attractive qualities; and I must say that I had a real personal liking for him." Henderson, *Failure of a Mission*, 76. Prażmowska concluded that Britain's "guarantee to Poland had more to do with obtaining leverage with Poland in order to force her to the negotiating table, than with the defence of Poland from aggression." Prażmowska, *Britain, Poland*, 190.

117. Khrushchev, *Vospominaniia*, I: 225–6. On Aug. 22, 1939, with the TASS announcement of Ribbentrop's pending arrival, the Comintern executive (Gottwald, Dimitrov, Kuusinen, Manuilsky, Marti, and Florin) assembled to map out a position defending against attacks by the "bourgeois" press in Britain and France. Lebedeva and Narinskii, *Komintern i Vtoraia mirovaia voina*, 69–71 (RGASPI, f. 495, op. 18, d. 1291, l. 141–3).

118. Gorodetsky, *Maisky Diaries*, 220.

119. Dilks, *Diaries of Sir Alexander Cadogan*, 199n. Sydney Cotton, an Australian pilot and aerial photography specialist who worked for British Air Intelligence, had been sent to Berlin to pick up Göring. *DGFP*, series D, VII: 235–6 (Woermann note, Aug. 23, 1939).

120. Volkogonov, *Triumf i tragediia*, II/i: 110. For an earlier such incident involving Lord

Beaverbrook in 1933, see Thayer, *Bears in the Caviar*, 33–4.

121. Memoir accounts claim that the airfield was festooned with Nazi flags, retrieved from the anti-Nazi productions at Mosfilm studios, and that a Soviet military band struck up "Deutschland über Alles," but the detailed Soviet newsreels show neither the flags nor the band. RGAKFD, ed. khr. 16332. The German planes were "locked up" in a hangar under NKVD guard, no doubt so that they could be thoroughly examined. Baur, *Hitler's Pilot*, 95.

122. Teske, *General Ernst Köstring*, 142.

123. Stalin had gathered Molotov, Mikoyan, Zhdanov, Voroshilov, Beria, and Kaganovich in the Little Corner until 3:30 p.m. *Na prieme*, 270–1. Also, on Aug. 23, 1939, the Moscow city soviet resolved to award land around the main NKVD HQ at Lubyanka, 2, for the building's expansion; several residential structures housing 440 people were slated for demolition. (The residents received a mere 2,500 rubles' compensation and free moving costs, and had to find or build their own new housing on plots granted outside Moscow.) Construction would begin almost immediately even as plans were still being drawn up by the architect, Alexei Shchusev, who went through various designs. The war would interrupt construction, which would be completed in 1948. A lack of resources inhibited the blending of the facades of the existing building and the addition until later (1979–82). Pogonii, *Lubianka, 2*, 70–9.

124. Kalinin had told Schulenburg upon his appointment, "Don't pay too much attention to the shoutings in the press. The peoples of Germany and the Soviet Union are linked by many different lines and to a great extent are dependent on each other." Nekrich, *1941*, 21 (citing German archives).

125. Berezhkov, *At Stalin's Side*, 49–50.

126. "It was a move," Hilger guessed, "that was calculated to put the [German] foreign minister off balance." In fact, Stalin sought to demonstrate Moscow's commitment to the new pact. Hilger and Meyer, *Incompatible Allies*, 301. On Aug. 23, 1939, the logbook for Stalin's office shows Molotov, Mikoyan, Zhdanov, Voroshilov, Beria, and Kaganovich (listed from 1:12 p.m. or so to 3:30 p.m., before the negotiations), then Molotov from 2:15 a.m. to 3:35 a.m. *Na prieme*, 270–1.

127. Chuev, *Sto sorok*, 257.

128. Shaposhnikov, *Vospominaniia*.

129. Sontag and Beddie, *Nazi-Soviet Relations*, 69.

130. Kershaw, *Hitler: 1936–1945*, 210.

131. Hilger and Meyer, *Incompatible Allies*, 303. Sontag and Beddie, *Nazi-Soviet Relations*, using only German documents, attributed the Pact to Soviet initiative. This collection was immediately translated into Russian for Stalin and provoked his involvement in countervailing efforts, originally entitled "Answer to the Slanderers," which in Stalin's hands became *Falsifiers of History*, a work that would be published in Russian and English translation in 1948: RGASPI, f. 558, op. 2, d. 239–45. See also Nekrich, "Soviet German Treaty," 9–13.

132. *DGFP*, series D, VII: 220 (Ribbentrop to the foreign ministry, Aug. 23, 1939), 223 (Kordt to Moscow embassy, Aug. 23, 1939); Herwarth, *Against Two Evils*, 165.

133. Van Creveld, *Hitler's Strategy*, 186n8; Read and Fisher, *Deadly Embrace*, 488–9 (no citation).

134. Sontag and Beddie, *Nazi-Soviet Relations*, 72–3.

135. "Mr. Stalin and Molotov commented in a hostile way on the behavior of the British military mission in Moscow which had not told the Soviet government what it actually

wanted." Naumov, *1941 god*, II: 580 (German record). See also Sontag and Beddie, *Nazi-Soviet Relations*, 72–6.

136. Antonov, "Anatolii Gorskii."

137. Naumov, *1941 god*, II: 581 (Politisches Archiv des Auswärtiges Amtes. Bonn, Bestand Büro RAM F/110019–30); Chuev, *Sto sorok*, 19. An alert SS adjutant, Lieutenant Richard Schulze, claims he managed to have his glass refilled from Stalin's personal flask, and that it contained not vodka but water. Read and Fisher, *Deadly Embrace*, 256. Schulze appears in the Pact photos.

138. For the text of the Pact, and the secret protocol, see *DVP SSSR*, XXII/i: 630–2 (AVP RF, f. 3a, d. 243; APRF, f. 3, op. 64, d. 675a, l. 3–4). *Izvestiya* carried the announcement of the Pact later that same day (Aug. 24, 1939).

139. Volkogonov, *Triumf i tragediia*, II/ii: 107 (no citation). Berezhkov writes that the cocktail party went on until dawn and that only after that was Ribbentrop able to inform Hitler. Berezhkov, *At Stalin's Side*, 40.

140. "'Avtobiograficheskie zametki' V. N. Pavlova—perevodchika I. V. Stalina," 99.

141. This was Andor Hencke, the under state secretary, who added: "The cordial and yet at the same time dignified manner in which Stalin, without losing face, attended to each one of us, left a strong impression on us all." Rees, *World War II behind Closed Doors*, 18 (citing Hencke's 1950 interrogation, *DGFP*, series D, VII: 225–9).

142. Bullock, *Hitler and Stalin*, 676. See also Hoffmann, *Hitler Was My Friend*, 102–14. Two German photographers were present, Hoffmann and Helmut Laux. Hoffmann, *Hitler Was My Friend*, 109.

143. Stalin's logbook of visitors for Aug. 22 and 23 contains six names (aides were never logged in). On Aug. 24, Molotov alone is logged in (2:15 a.m. to 3:35 a.m.). *Na prieme*, 270–1. See also Sudoplatov, *Special Tasks*, 96–7.

144. For the full Pact, see Sontag and Beddie, *Nazi-Soviet Relations*, 76–8; and Naumov, *1941 god*, II: 576–8, 585–93. Gaus appeared in the photos.

145. Degras, *Soviet Documents on Foreign Policy*, III: 145 (Sept. 1935).

146. "Johnnie" Herwarth and his Bavarian wife, Pussi, spent time at Bohlen's dacha, as Soviet intelligence and Stalin knew, but, officially, Herwarth was the chief contact at the German embassy in Moscow to Britain, the United States, and France. At the dacha they rode horses, played tennis, and sipped tea. Herwarth was one quarter Jewish. Bohlen, *Witness to History*, 69–83; Herwarth, *Against Two Evils*, 167.

147. Bezymenskii, "Secret Protocols of 1939," 76; Bezymenskii, "Sovetsko-Germanskie dogovory," 3, 20–1. Molotov would hold on to the Soviet original of the secret protocol until Oct. 1952, when it was belatedly placed in the "osobaia papka" of the party archives. Other 1930s agreements that contained secret protocols included the German-Polish nonaggression declaration of 1934, Franco-Italian and Anglo-Italian agreements of 1935 regarding Africa, the 1938 Munich Pact, the 1939 Anglo-Japanese Agreement on China, and so on.

148. Below, *Als Hitlers Adjutant*, 181–4; Ribbentrop, *Memoirs*, 109–15 (composed in prison while waiting to be hanged after the Nuremberg trial in 1946); Schmidt, *Statist*, 452–4; Bloch, *Ribbentrop*, 249. Stalin rewrote the text of the communiqué regarding Poland, and Hitler judged it superior to the text drafted in Berlin. Hilger recalled: "'The old Romans,' Stalin said, turning to me, 'did not

go into battle naked but with shields. Today correctly worded political communiqués play the role of such shields.'" Hilger and Meyer, *Incompatible Allies*, 302. Ribbentrop, who had conceded everything, later claimed to have been impressed by Stalin: "his sober, almost dry and yet so apt way of expressing himself, the hardness and yet generosity of his bargaining." Ribbentrop, *Memoirs*, 113.

149. *Na prieme*, 271.

150. Simonov, "Zametki k biogfraii G. K. Zhukova," 49. Khrushchev, who was at the Near Dacha on Aug. 23, 1939, recalled that Stalin said, "This is a game, who can outsmart and deceive whom." Khrushchev, *Vospominaniia*, I: 225-8. Stalin well understood that the Pact helped Hitler, too. Banac, *Diary of Georgi Dimitrov*, 115. Gaus claimed he overheard Stalin mutter "deception." It is unclear if Gaus understood what could have been the Russian word (*obman*), though Stalin did know some words in German and might have uttered *Täuschung*; or Gaus could have misheard.

151. At the same time, complicating Japan's attempt to conquer China, many Japanese forces were tied down in Manchukuo to deter the Soviet Union. Goldman, *Nomonhan, 1939*, 35 (citing U.S. Department of the Army, Forces in the Far East, *Japanese Special Studies on Manchuria*, 13 vols. [Tokyo, 1954–6], XI/3: 193).

152. Krasnov, *Neizvestnyi Zhukov*, 118–20.

153. Khaustov, "Deiatel'nost' organov," 252.

154. Efimenko et al., *Vooruzhennyi konflikt*, 319–20 (RGVA, f. 32113, op. 1, d. 670, l. 57–9). Zhukov would claim that he acted on Aug. 20 also because he learned that the Japanese planned an offensive beginning Aug. 24, but there is no such plan in the Japanese documentation record. Coox, *Nomonhan*, 578–9.

155. Coox, *Nomonhan*, 582. The Japanese espionage network in Mongolia, which had never amounted to much, evidently missed this massive buildup.

156. Grechko et al., *Istoriia vtoroi mirovoi voiny*, II: 217; Zhilin, *Pobeda na reke Khalkhin-gol*, 18; *Khalkhin Gol*, 71.

157. Vorozheikin, *Istrebiteli*, 224.

158. Mongol troops had been pressed into fighting by both belligerents, but, supposedly, many on the Japanese side refused to fight or defected to the Soviets. Dylykov, *Demoktraicheskoe dvizhenie mongol'skogo naroda*, 39–40. Coox, *Nomonhan*. See also the blistering critique of Japanese strategy: Wilson, *When Tigers Fight*.

160. Erickson, *Soviet High Command*, 522.

161. Krasnov, *Neizvestnyi Zhukov*, 136–7.

162. Voroshilov forwarded the Zhukov telegram to Stalin, with a note: "As one could have anticipated, no divisions turned out to be surrounded, the enemy having either managed to remove the main forces in time or, more likely, no major forces were in this region for a long time, instead there was a specially prepared garrison, which now is completely destroyed." A concentration camp for two thousand Japanese POWs had been prepared in Verkhne-Udinsk, but only around one hundred soldiers had been captured and they were sent to the Chita prison. Zolotarev, *Russkii arkhiv: Velikaia otechestevennaia*, XVIII (VII/i): 127 (RGVA, f. 33987, op. 3, d. 1225, l. 162), 139 (TsKhIK, f. 1t/p, op. 1, d. 5, l. 93–4). See also Krasnov, *Neizvestnyi Zhukov*, 137.

163. Coox, *Nomonhan*, 914; *Rossiia i SSSR v voinakh XX veka*, 177, 179; Goldman, *Nomonhan, 1939*, 101–53. For other numbers, see Krivosheev, *Grif sekretnosti sniat'*, 77–85. Mongolia suffered 556 casualties.

164. "Muzhestvo i geroizm," *Krasnaia zvezda*, Aug. 30, 1939; Sokolov, *Georgii Zhukov*, 143.

165. Simonov, "Zmetki k biografii G. K. Zhukova," 54.

166. Gavrilov, *Voennaia razvedka informiruet*, 163–4 (RGVA, f. 37977, op. 1, d. 91, l. 32–3: Sept. 1, 1939). Zhou En-Lai supplied some of the captured Japanese army codes to Moscow in Sept. to Dimitrov, who passed them to Beria. Lebedeva and Narinskii, *Komintern i Vtoraia mirovaia voina*, 99 (RGASPi, f. 495, op. 74, d. 316, l. 12: note by Stern, Aug. 15); Sergutov, "Organizatsionnye aspekty deiatel'nosti vneshnei razvedki," III: 241. "For the Japanese army, Nomonhan was the graveyard of reputations." Coox, *Nomonhan*, 952; Ikuhiko, "Japanese-Soviet Confrontation," 157–78.

167. Coox, *Nomonhan*, 1002 (Oct. 4, 1939); Coox, "The Lesser of Two Hells, Part 2," 108.

168. Fesiun, *Delo Rikharda Zorge*, 100–3; Gavrilov, *Voennaia razvedka informiruet*, 123 (TsAMO, f. 23, op. 22407, d. 2, l. 417).

169. Weizsäcker, *Memoirs*, 210; Craigie, *Behind the Japanese Mask*, 71; *DBFP*, 3rd series, IX: 495–7; Iklé, *German-Japanese Relations*, 135 (citing *International Military Tribunal for the Far East, Documents Presented in Evidence*, exhibit 486: Ott to Weizsäcker, Aug. 25, 1939); Presseisen, *Germany and Japan*, 218 (citing exhibit 2735–A, 225, exhibit 3587); *DGFP*, series D, VII: 259–60 (Ott to foreign ministry, Aug. 24, 1939). The Soviet military attaché's aide in Tokyo sent a quick report to Moscow on Aug. 26: Zolotarev, *Russkii arkhiv: Velikaia oteechestvennaia*, XVIII (VII/i): 159 (TsAMO, f. 23, op. 22410, d. 2, l. 131–2).

170. Robinson, *Black on Red*, 137. "It left us all stunned, bewildered, and groggy with disbelief," recalled one loyal party member (who later defected). "Hatred of Nazism had been drummed into our minds year after year." Kravchenko, *I Chose Freedom*, 332–5. Kravchenko, thirty-four years old in 1939, directed a factory in the industrial district of western Siberia.

171. Ehrenburg, *Liudi, gody, zhizn'*, II; 202. Vsevolod Vishnevsky, then in the Soviet Far East, also heard about the Pact over the radio and was similarly shocked. The Far East received central newspapers with delay, and after the Aug. 23 treaty he received the August 15–17 newspapers, which had continued to rage about "cannibals" (Nazis). "What about the general ideational-philosophical and political evaluation of fascism, the bloc of aggressors?" he wrote in his diary. Golubev et al., *Rossiia i zapad*, 200 (citing RGALI, f. 1038, op. 1, d. 2077, l. 39ob., 41).

172. *Biulleten' oppozitsii*, no. 74 (1939): 4 (Trotsky, "Stalin's Capitulation," March 11, 1939), reprinted in Trotskii, *Portrety revoliutsionerov*, 147–9. Trotsky also asserted that Stalin was afraid. "The main source of the policy of Stalin himself is now fear in the face of the fear that he himself has begotten," he wrote, apropos of Afinogenov's old play *Fear*. "Stalin never trusted the masses; now he fears them." Trotskii, "Iosif Stalin: opyt kharakteristiki (Sept. 22, 1939)," in *Portrety revoliutsionerov*, 46–60 (at 58).

173. Manuilsky tried to explain to Hernandez at the Comintern villa in Kuntsevo, "Everything has been taken care of. We can't lose! ... If the capitalists want to slit each other's throats, so much the better. When the time is right, when they begin to get weary, we will undoubtedly be solicited by both sides and can chose the one which suits us best. Don't worry, our army won't pull the chestnuts out of the fire for any capitalist country." Hernández, *La grande trahison*, 206–7.

174. Lebedeva and Narinskii, *Komintern i Vtoraia mirovaia voina*, 71–85 (RGASPI, f. 495, op. 73, d. 67, l. 44–59), 88 (op. 74, d. 517, l. 43); Dallin and Firsov, *Dimitrov and Stalin*, 150; "Komintern i sovetsko-germanskii dogovor o nenapedenii," 206; Firsov, "Arkhivy Kominterna"; Firsov, "Komintern," 21–2. Daniil Kraminov (b. 1910), assigned to draft the first editorial for *Izvestiya* about the Pact, had no idea what to write. The editor, Yakov Selikh, approached Voroshilov, who compared the Pact to the 1918 Brest-Litovsk treaty with Germany for providing a breathing space. Already on Aug. 24, Selikh knew that Ribbentrop had proposed to insert words about German-Soviet friendship into the text, but Stalin had refused to do so. Seilkh also knew the subjects of the toasts and the jokes exchanged. None of this information had been recorded in the Soviet documents. Kraminov, *V orbite voiny*, 55.

175. Banac, *Diary of Georgi Dimitrov*, 115–6 (Sept. 7, 1939). For the resultant new Comintern directive, dispatched abroad, see Banac, *Diary of Georgi Dimitrov*, 117 (Sept. 8, 1939); Lebedeva and Narinskii, *Komintern i Vtoraia mirovaia voina*, 88–90 (RGASPI, f. 495, op. 18, d. 1292, l. 47–8); and King and Matthews, *About Turn*, 69–70. More broadly, see also Dallin and Firsov, *Dimitrov and Stalin*, 154–63.

176. Banac, *Diary of Georgi Dimitrov*, 115–6 (Sept. 7, 1939).

177. An antifascist documentary, *Ispaniya* (Spain), by Esther Shub, had premiered on July 20, 1939. Short and Taylor, "Soviet Cinema."

178. Anderson et al., *Kremlevskii kinoteatr*, 539. See also Luk'ianov, "'Aleksandr Nevskii': na s"emakh filma"; S. M. Eisenstein, "Zametkie rezhissera," *Ogonek*, 1938, no. 22: 19, 20–1; and *Izvestiia*, Nov. 11, 1938. On Eisenstein's self-critique of the film, whose commercial success puzzled him, see Eisenstein, *Film Sense*, 123–68. Five other recently made anti-German films were also pulled.

179. RGASPI, f. 558, op. 11, d. 160, l. 1 (note to Dukelsky). The Comintern's Dimitrov sent a long telegram admonishing Earl Browder, leader of the American Communists, that "now the issue is not just fascism, but the existence of the entire capitalist system," and insisted there would be no more juxtaposing "democratic" capitalist countries to fascist ones. "This war is a continuation of the struggle between the rich great powers (England, France, the United States), which are the spine of the whole capitalist system, and the disadvantaged states (Germany, Italy, Japan), which in their struggle for a new division of the world are deepening and sharpening the crisis of the capitalist system." Lebedeva, *Komintern i Vtoraia mirovaia voina*, 132–6 (RGASPI, f. 495, op. 74, d. 469, l. 108–12).

180. Quoted in Hosking, *First Socialist Society*, 218–9.

181. Leonhard, *Betrayal*, 90.

182. Uttitz, *Zeugen der Revolution*, 134.

183. Vishnevskii, "'Sami peredem v napadenie,'" 104–5: Aug. 28, 31, and Sept. 1, 1939.

184. The Anti-Komintern agency inside Goebbels's propaganda ministry, whose purpose was "a world anti-Bolshevik movement under German leadership," was wound down with the signing of the Pact, but the Nazi regime's identity remained founded upon German racial superiority and a crusade against "Judeo-Bolshevism." Waddington, "Anti-Komintern," 576, citing NA, GFM34/1265: Goebbels circular, Dec. 8, 1936. See also Waddington, *Hitler's Crusade*.

185. *Pravda*, Sept. 1, 1939; Naumov, *1941 god*, II: 581–3 (at 582); *Mirovoe khoziaistvo i miroavaia politika*, no. 9 (1939): 3; Degras,

Soviet Documents on Foreign Policy, III: 363–71. In connection with the Pact, the Soviets talked out of both sides of their mouths, allowing subsequent scholars on opposite sides to find quotes supporting their arguments about whether or not Stalin ever wanted a deal with the West. For example, Voroshilov said, via the Soviet press, that "military negotiations with England and France were not broken off because the Soviet Union concluded a nonaggression pact with Germany. On the contrary, the Soviet Union concluded a nonaggression pact with Germany because, among other reasons, the military negotiations with France and England had run into a blind alley because of insuperable differences." (Those differences, he said, came down to a failure to guarantee western transit rights to Germany for the USSR in the event of an aggression.) But to the Germans, Stalin said that "the Soviet government"—i.e., himself—"never had sympathies toward England." Stalin told Dimtrov, "We preferred agreements with the so-called democratic countries and therefore conducted negotiations. But the English and the French wanted us for farmhands and at no cost! We, of course, would not go for being farmhands, still less for getting nothing in return." Of course, these words on the Pact were precisely what the staunch antifascist Dimitrov would have wanted to hear. *Izvestiia*, Aug. 27, 1939, and *Pravda*, Aug. 27, 1939, in Tisminets, *Vneshniaia politika SSSR*, IV: 444–5; Degras, *Soviet Documents on Foreign Policy*, III: 361–2; *DVP SSSR*, XXII/ii: 606–17 (at 609, Schulenburg's papers); Banac, *Diary of Georgi Dimitrov*, 115–6 (Sept. 7, 1939). See also Nekrich, *Pariahs*, 137; Roberts, "Pact with Nazi Germany," 94–5; and Fischer, *Life and Death of Stalin*, 162.

186. Fel'shtinskii, *Oglasheniiu podlezhit*, 92.

187. Seraphim, *Das politische Tagebuch Rosenbergs*, 89–90 (Aug. 22, 1939); *Deutschland-Berichte der Sozialdemokratischen Partei Deutschlands*, VI: 985–8; Hoffman, *Hitler Was My Friend*, 103.

188. D'iakov and Bushueva, *Fashistskii mech kovalsia v SSSR*, 364–5 (RGVA, f. 33987, op. 3, d. 1237, l. 413). Maisky fell into shock upon word of the Pact: "Our policy is clearly making a sharp turnabout, the sense and consequences of which are so far not entirely clear to me" (Aug. 24, 1939). *DVP SSSR*, XXII/i: 647 (AVP RF, f. 017a, op. 1, pap. 1, d. 6, l. 223: Aug. 24, 1939); Maiskii, *Dnevnik diplomata*, I: 441.

189. Neilson, *Britain, Soviet Russia*, 314 (citing Chamberlain Papers, NC 18/1/1115).

190. Read and Fisher, *Deadly Embrace*, 147.

191. Bell, *France and Britain*, 224–5; Adamthwaite, *France*, 49–50. Toward the end of 1939, a falsified "transcript" of a supposed politburo meeting would be published in France depicting a devious Stalin, in an effort to discredit him in Hitler's eyes, and depicting the French Communist party as treasonous. Sluch, "Rech' Stalina," 113–39.

192. Just such a one-sided view of Chamberlain can be found in the once pro-appeasement foreign office official turned scholar E. H. Carr: *German-Soviet Relations*, 135–6. Carr's influential history of international relations since 1919 mocked "the notion that the maintenance of British supremacy is the performance of a duty to mankind." He sent his completed manuscript to the press in July 1939, and the book came out that Sept., when Nazism and Communism were together annihilating Poland. Carr, *Twenty Years' Crisis*, 72.

193. This priority on Chamberlain's part, however self-serving, had a strategic dimension: British success in maintaining the

Commonwealth and empire in the interwar period would prove to be of considerable significance in the Allied victory over the Axis. Clayton, *British Empire as Superpower*, 517.

194. Neville Chamberlain Papers, University of Birmingham Library, 18/1/1091 (Chamberlain to Ida, March 26, 1939).

195. Chamberlain, according to Eden, had feared that "Communism would get its clutches into Western Europe" via the Spanish civil war. Smyth, "Soviet Policy," 105. It has been asserted that Chamberlain should have accepted Soviet expansionism into Central Europe if that could have avoided a war on the scale of World War II. Shaw, *British Political Elite*.

196. Overy, *1939: Countdown*, 15 (citing Magdalene College, Cambridge, Inge papers, vol. 36, diary 1938–9, March 16, 1939).

197. Other Brits went even further in the Hitler apologetics than did Chamberlain, at the time and after. A. J. P. Taylor infamously wrote that Hitler "aimed to make Germany the dominant Power in Europe and maybe, more remotely, in the world. Other Powers have pursued similar aims, and still do. . . . In international affairs there was nothing wrong with Hitler except that he was a German." Taylor, *Origins*, 293.

198. Kennan in 1935 deemed the idea that Hitler intended to expand into the Soviet Union "the wildest stretch of the imagination." George Kennan, "The War Problem of the Soviet Union," in George F. Kennan Papers, Box 1, Mudd Library, Princeton University, in Hochman, *Failure of Collective Security*, 178. Looking back, Kennan would admit that he misread Hitler and the Nazi threat. Kennan, *Memoirs, 1925–1950*, 70–3.

199. Haslam, *Struggle for Collective Security*, 206–7 (the letter is dated March 26, 1939).

200. Conversely, the British ambassador to Germany had written in his annual report for 1935, a document read by Stalin, that "demanding a guarantee from Hitler vis-à-vis the Soviet Union is equivalent to demanding from the Church obligations to the devil." Khaustov, "Deiatel'nost' organov," 234–5 (TsA FSB, f. 3, op. 2, d. 315, l. 136).

201. Aster, *1939*, 281.

202. Roberts, *Holy Fox*, 157.

203. *Documents and Materials Relating to the Eve of the Second World War*, 190–1 (von Dirksen memo, Sept. 1939).

204. Overy, "Strategic Intelligence," 455.

205. Shirer, *Berlin Diary*, 148.

206. Overy, *1939: Countdown*, 11, 34.

207. Below, *At Hitler's Side*, 29; Hill, *Die Weizsäcker-Papiere*, 160 (Aug. 25, 1939).

208. Henderson, *Failure of a Mission*, 259.

209. *Documents Concerning German-Polish Relations*, 122–3; *DBFP*, 3rd series, VII: 230, 235, 239; Fröhlich, *Tagebücher von Joseph Goebbels*, VII: 77 (Aug. 26, 1939); Domarus, *Hitler: Reden*, III: 1257.

210. Hofer, *Die Entstehung des Zwieiten Weltkriegs*, 234; Weinberg, *Foreign Policy*, II: 633–4; *Das Deutsche Reich unde der Zweite Weltkrieg*, II: 101–2.

211. Hartmann, *Halder*, 137.

212. Engelmann, *In Hitler's Germany*, 150. Not all German units received the new order to stand down, which meant fighting erupted in a few places, notably in the Jablonka Pass on the Slovak-Polish border.

213. *I documenti diplomatici Italiani*, 8th ser., 13 vols. (Rome: Libreria dello Sstato, 1952–), XIII: 164–5. *DGFP*, series D, VII: 285–6 (Mussolini to Hitler, Aug. 25, 1939); Hill, *Die Weizsäcker-Papiere*, 160–1 (Aug. 25, 1939); Gibson, *Ciano Diaries*, 128–9 (Aug. 25, 1939); Ciano, *Diary*, 264–5.

214. Kershaw, *Hitler: 1936–1945*, 215. Italy had already informed Germany, in general terms, on May 31, 1939, that it would not be ready for war before 1943. In June 1939, Chamberlain told the committee of imperial defence that "the Italians would be on the lookout for any excuse to keep out of the war." DGFP, series D, VI: 617–20; Overy, "Strategic Intelligence," 470 (citing PRO CAB 2/8: Minutes of CID meeting, June 22, 1939, 6).

215. Overy, *1939: Countdown*, 36 (citing NA, PREM 1/331a: Strang to Cadogan, Aug. 26, 1939, 1; Halifax Papers, A4.4103/10 (i): Birger Dahlerus, 11; and *Le Livre jaune francais: documents diplmatiques 1938–1939* [Paris, 1939]), 312 (Coulondre to Bonnet, Aug. 25, 1939).

216. Kershaw, *Hitler: 1936–1945*, 215; Hofer, *Die Entstehung des Zwieiten Weltkriegs*, 276.

217. Engel, *Heeresadjutant bei Hitler*, 60 (Aug. 27 and 29, 1939).

218. Cienciala, "Poland in British and French Policy," 215–6; DGFP, series D, VII: 405–7 (Ribbentrop to Bernardo Attolico, Aug. 29, 1939). Joseph Kennedy, the U.S. ambassador to London, reported that Chamberlain was concerned that the Poles be "reasonable" vis-à-vis Hitler's demands. FRUS, *1939*, I: 392 (Kennedy telegram, Aug. 30, 1939).

219. De Felice, *Mussolini*, II: 670.

220. Naumov, *1941 god*, II: 581 (German account); Chuev, *Molotov Remembers*, 12. Ribbentrop had first told Stalin of the joke making the rounds in Berlin that "Stalin will join the Anti-Comintern Pact." Sontag and Beddie, *Nazi-Soviet Relations*, 75.

221. Hillgruber, *Die Zerstörung Europas*, 212. The expression to play *"va banque"* (translated here as "go for broke"), from baccarat, connotes wagering an amount equal to that held by the banker of the game.

222. Fröhlich, *Tagebücher von Joseph Goebbels*, VII: 85–6 (Aug. 31, 1939). On Sept. 1, Hitler launched a tirade at Dahlerus to the effect that he was prepared to fight Britain for a decade if forced to do so. Dahlerus, *Der letze Versuch*, 130–1. On Aug. 28, 1939, Clare Hollingworth, a British correspondent traveling by car from Katowice to Gleiwitz, had glimpsed the vast German arsenal in the valley poised to attack and broken the news. *Daily Telegraph*, Aug. 29, 1939.

223. Dederichs, *Heydrich*, 89; Schellenberg, *Schellenberg Memoirs*, 68–70. On the bomber: Homze, *Arming the Luftwaffe*, 231; Weinberg, *Foreign Policy*, II: 513–4.

224. DBFP, 3rd series, VII: 501 (Halifax to Phipps, Sept. 1, 1939), doc. 504 (Henderson Sept. 2, 1939).

225. *French Yellow Book*, 307 (François-Poncet in Rome to Bonnet, Aug. 31, 1939).

226. Dietrich, *The Hitler I Knew*, 47; Schmidt, *Statist*, 464; Eberle and Uhl, *Hitler Book*, 47–8.

227. Back on Aug. 22, 1929, in a secret speech to his military brass, Hitler had restated his original grand strategy preference for attacking the Western powers first, explained his reversal of that sequence, declared his intention to strike Poland even if the Western Powers upheld their vows to act, and concluded that his sole concern was that the *Schweinhund* Chamberlain would find a way to cheat him out of war, just as the PM had at Munich. Weinberg, *Foreign Policy*, II: 610–1, 643n80. See also Baumgart, "Zur Ansprache Hitlers"; and Meyer, *Generalfeldmarschall Wilhelm Ritter von Leeb*, 184.

228. The prospect of Poland's destruction and the "emancipation" of the ethnic German minority there beguiled the Wehrmacht brass as well, despite the latter's concern about preparedness for a general conflict. Weinberg, *Foreign Policy*, II: 654; Tooze, *Wages of*

Destruction, 321–2; Maiolo, "Armaments Competition," 286–307.

229. Poland possessed only a provisional study for a western front, conducted in 1936. Prażmowska, *Britain, Poland*, 90–2, citing *Polskie Siły Zbrojne w drugiej wajnie światowej*, 3 vols. (London: Instytut Historyczny im. gen. Sikorskiego, 1951–86), I/i: 117–22, 209 (General Stachiewicz); Kirchmayer, *1939 i 1944 Kilka Zagadnień Polskich*, 46–9; Colonel Jaklicz, typescript at the Polish Institute and the Sikorski Museum, London, 33, 121–2.

230. DGFP, series D, VII: 540–1; DVP SSSR, XXII/ii: 600; Sontag and Biddie, *Nazi-Soviet Relations*, 86, 90.

231. Zaloga and Madej, *Polish Campaign*, 145–9; Tooze, *Wages of Destruction*, 304–29.

232. Cienciala, "Poland in British and French Policy in 1939"; May, *Strange Victory*, 93; Frieser, *Blitzkrieg Legend*, 18. On Sept. 5, Halder recorded in his diary of Poland: "enemy practically beaten." (*Halder Diaries*, I: 53.) In fact, Polish forces emerged victorious in a major engagement with Wehrmacht forces in southeastern Poland.

233. Bédarida, *La Strategic sécrete*, 95.

234. AVP RF, f. 06, op. 1, pap. 7, d. 68, l. 3–4, 5–6; *God krizisa*, II: 359–60; DVP SSSR, XXII/ii: 6–7; *Na prieme*, 270–1. Accompanying Shkvartsev to Berlin was Vladimir Pavlov, sent as the new first secretary of the embassy; a new NKVD station chief, Amayak Kobulov; and a new military attaché, Maxim Purkayev ("Marble"). Shkvartsev had been received in the Little Corner on Aug. 19 (only with Molotov), and on Sept. 1 (again with Molotov, Voroshilov, Mikoyan, Pavlov, Purkayev, Kobulov, and Dekanozov). Shkvartsev would be present in the Molotov's office on Sept. 28 during Ribbentrop's second visit. In late December 1940, Pavlov would be transferred to Moscow as head of the Central European desk at the foreign affairs commissariat—at age twenty-five—overseeing Germany, Hungary, and former Czechoslovakia (under German occupation).

235. Weinberg, *Germany and the Soviet Union*, 55.

236. Konstantin Simonov, then a writer at *Red Star*, would recall viewing the German invasion as an attack of the strong against the weak and not wanting to see a German victory. Simonov, *Glazami cheloveka moego pokoleniia*, 309. See also Prishvin, *Dnevniki*, X: 276.

237. Semiriaga, "17 sentiabria 1939 g."; DVP SSSR, XXII/ii: 25–6 (AVP RF, f. 011, op. 4, pap. 24, d. 5, l. 29: Molotov-Grzybowski, Sept. 5, 1939).

238. Sontag and Beddie, *Nazi-Soviet Relations*, 91, 100.

239. Shaposhnikov had crossed out the order's date in red pen and written in Sept. 14. Pikhoia and Gieysztor, *Katyn': plenniki*, 59–63 (TsAMO, f. 148a, op. 3763, d. 69, l. 1–3, 4–6); Mel'tiukhov, *Sovetsko-pol'skie voiny* (2004), 435–47.

240. "The distrust on my side toward Stalin," Hitler would observe to Mussolini on Oct. 28, 1940, "is matched by Stalin's distrust toward me." Langer, *Undeclared War*, 136 (no citation). According to Zhukov, Zhdanov, too, said it was impossible to trust Hitler. Simonov, "Zametki k biogfraii G. K. Zhukova," 49.

241. Legner held an NKVD officer's rank. Rybin, *Stalin v oktiabre*, 65–6. In Legner's workshop, Nina Matveevna Gupalo sewed the clothes for politburo and other high-placed spouses. Back in 1938, after half the government guard detail had been arrested in a single night, Alexei Rybin (b. 1908), a member of the construction team for the Nearby Dacha and once a bodyguard for Kaganovich, then Orjonikidze, became military commandant

of the Bolshoi Theater. Radzinskii, *Stalin*, 401; Rybin, *Kto otravil Stalina?*, 59.

242. Sharapov, "Piat'sot stranits v den'"; Shefov, "Dve vstrechi," 154; Ilizarov, *Tainaia zhizn' Stalina*, passim; Medvedev and Medvedev, *Neizvestnyi Stalin*; Shepilov, *Kremlin's Scholar*.

243. By some accounts, Radek had translated *Mein Kampf* for politburo members already in the early 1930s, before Hitler had come to power. The internal Russian translation of *Mein Kampf* would be published only after the fall of the Soviet Union: Adol'f Gitler, *Moia bor'ba* (Moscow: T-Oko, 1992).

244. Asada, *From Mahan to Pearl Harbor*, 168.

245. Kalinin's copy has been preserved with marginalia about "a prolix, contentless" book "for petty shop owners": RGASPI, f. 78, op. 8, d. 140; Ilizarov, *Tainaia zhizn' Stalina*, 137; Ilizarov, "Stalin" (no. 4) 190–1.

246. Khrushchev, *Vospominaniia*, I: 219; Khrushchev, *Memoirs*, I: 216.

247. Gareev, *Neodnoznachnye stranitsy*, 20. Makhmut Gareyev (b. 1923) would rise to army general.

248. Heiden, *Die Geschichte des Nationalsozialismus*; Geiden, *Istoriia germanskogo fashizma*, 60. Volkogonov, *Stalin: Triumf i tragediia*, II/i: 23–26; Volkogonov, *Stalin: Triumph and Tragedy*, 352–3. Heiden also produced the valuable *Hitler: eine Biographie*, 2 vols. (Zurich: Europa, 1936–7).

249. Volkogonov, *Triumf i tragediia*, II/1: 25 (no citation); Volkogonov, *Stalin: Triumph and Tragedy*, 352.

250. Khrushchev, *Memoirs*, I: 274–5.

251. *Izvestiia*, Sept. 16, 1939; Tisminets, *Vneshniaia politika SSSR*, IV: 446.

252. On the military orders, see Zolotarev, *Russkii arkhiv: Velikaia otechestvennaia*, XVIII (VII/i): 133 (RGVA, f. 33977, op. 1, d. 28, l. 36); and Efimenko et al., *Vooruzhennyi konflikt*, 409 (RGVA, f. 33977, op. 1, d. 28, l. 38). On July 18, 1940, Japan would effectively recognize the boundaries as claimed by the USSR. Ikuhiko, "Japanese-Soviet Confrontation," 174–5.

253. Ikuhiko, "Japanese-Soviet Confrontation." See also Sorge's report of Sept. 10, 1939: Zolotarev, *Russkii arkhiv: Velikaia oteechestvennaia*, XVIII (VII/i): 159 (TsAMO, f. 23, op. 22407, d. 2, l. 455–6).

254. DGFP, series D, VIII: 79–80 (Schulenburg, Sept. 17, 1939)

255. Biegański et al., *Documents on Polish-Soviet Relations*, I: doc. 69; DVP SSSR, XXII/ii: 94–96 (AVP RF, f. 011, op. 4, pap. 24, d. 7, l. 176–9: Potyomkin-Grzybowski, Sept. 17, 1939), 96 (f. 059, op. 1, pap. 313, d. 2155, l. 49–51: diplomatic note); *Izvestiia*, Sept. 18, 1939; Pikhoia and Gieysztor (eds.), *Katyn': plenniki*, 65–7 (APRF, f. 3, op. 50, d. 410, l. 35–9: Potyomkin diary, Sept. 17, 1939); Cienciala et al., *Katyn*, 44–7; *Official Documents Concerning Polish-German and Polish-Soviet Relations*, 211–12. Schulenburg had been shown the note and allowed to suggest changes. Sontag and Beddie, *Nazi-Soviet Relations*, 96.

256. Liszewski, *Polsko-sowiecka wojna*, 24 (citing the prophetic words of Marshal Rydz-Smilga).

257. *Pravda*, Sept. 18, 1939; *Izvestiia*, Sept. 18, 1939, in Tisminets, *Vneshniaia politika SSSR*, IV: 446–8; *New York Times*, Sept. 18, 1939: 5. Zhdanov had written in *Pravda* (Sept. 14, 1939) that the Polish state was collapsing because of its repression of Ukrainian and Belorussian national minorities, which he blamed on the Polish bourgeoisie, capitalists, and landowners.

258. Zaloga and Madej, *Polish Campaign*, 131–8.

259. Kuznetsov, *Krutye povoroty*, 47.

260. Sontag and Beddie, *Nazi-Soviet Relations*, 86–7.

261. "Itinerar Hitlers vom 1.9.1939–31.12.1941," in Hillgruber, *Hitlers Strategie*, 659–98 (at 660–1); Below, *Als Hitlers Adjutant*, 205.

262. *DGFP*, series D, VIII: 92.

263. *DGFP*, series D, VIII: 104–5; Weinberg, *Germany and the Soviet Union*, 55. On Sept. 20, having received assurances from Berlin, both Schulenburg and Köstring separately offered assurances to Soviet officials.

264. RGVA, f. 4, op. 19, d. 22, l. 62. Soon, rumors would spread of additional clashes. "In town there is more and more talk about the Russians returning and about battles between German and Soviet troops somewhere along the Bug River and other locations," Dr. Zygmunt Klukowski recorded in his diary (Oct. 15, 1939). "Sorry to say, but some citizens are as equally brutal as the Germans toward the Jews." Klukowski, *Diary from the Years of Occupation*, 41–2.

265. Wheeler-Bennett, "From Brest-Litovsk to Brest-Litovsk."

266. Domarus, *Hitler: Reden*, III: 1354–66 (Hitler's Danzig speech).

267. *DVP SSSR*, XXII/ii: 28–9 (AVP RF, f. 059, op. 1, pap. 924, d. 2027, l. 19–20: Shkvartsev to Molotov, Sept. 5, 1939).

268. RGVA, f. 4, op. 19, d. 22, l. 60–3.

269. Molotov did allow that Germany might claim the Suwałki triangle (between East Prussia and Lithuania), except for Augustovo. Rossi, *Deux ans*, 75n1, 75–6n1 (Schulenburg to Ribbentrop, Sept. 20, 1939); Rossi, *Russo-German Alliance*, 62–3 (citing a telephone message from Ribbentrop to Köstring and a telegram from Schulenburg to Berlin, neither published in Sontag and Beddie, *Nazi-Soviet Relations*).

270. Mel'tiukhov, *Sovetsko-pol'skie voiny* (2004), 496–7 (RGVA, f. 4, op. 19, d. 22, l. 60–1); Teske, *General Ernst Köstring*, 176ff.

271. "Itinerar Hitlers vom 1.9.1939–31.12.1941," in Hillgruber, *Hitlers Strategie*, 661.

272. Mel'tiukhov, *Sovetsko-pol'skie voiny*, (2001), 303–350, (2004), 463–92; Erickson, "Red Army's March," 18–20; Włodarkiewicz, *Lwów*. Fifteen thousand Lvov defenders (1,000 of them officers) were taken prisoner; many would not survive captivity.

273. Krivoshein, *Mezhdubur'e*, 234–9; Schmidt-Scheeder, *Reporter der Hölle*, 101; *Deutscher Allgemeine Zeitung*, Sept. 25, 1939.

274. Guderian, *Vospominaniia soldata*, 105.

275. Halder, *Halder Diaries*, I: 85–6 (Sept. 20, 1939); Mel'tiukhov, *Sovetsko-pol'skie voiny* (2001), 319–23, 326–33 (citing RGVA, f. 4, op. 19, d. 22, l. 60–5); Nekrich, *Pariahs*, 130–2.

276. Back in 1934, Stalin's ambassador to Poland (Yakov Davtyan) had confided in the American ambassador his "doubt concerning the capacity of Poland to exist as an independent nation"—a widely held Soviet prejudice. The next year, Piłsudski, dictator of Poland, had died. "Piłsudski is the entire Poland," Radek claimed he had heard Stalin say. Kuromiya, "Stalin's Great Terror," 8 (citing Centralne Archiwum Wojskowe, I.303.4.3158, 235).

277. Wańkowicz, *Po klęsce*, 612.

278. Pikhoia and Gieysztor, *Katyn': plenniki*, 77 (RGVA, f. 35084, op. 1, d. 8, l. 168), 78–83 (Tsentr khraneniia istoriko-dokumental'nykh kollektsii, f. 1/p, op. 1a, d. 1, l. 1–9), 89–92 (l. 63–7), 92–5 (op. 1e, d. 1, l. 17–18), 114–8 (APRF, f. 3 op. 5, d. 614, l. 228–30), and 118–9 (APRF, f. 3, op. 50, d. 410, l. 148–9).

279. Freidländer, *Nazi Germany and the Jews*, I: 267–8; Polonsky, *Politics in Independent Poland*, 467–9; Melzer, *No Way Out*, 22, 43, 91; Milton, "Expulsion of Polish Jews from Germany"; Heller, *On the Edge of Destruction*.

280. Buell, *Poland*, 307 (General Stanisław Skwarczyński).

281. Westermann, *Hitler's Police Battalions*, 124–8; Madajczyk, *Die Okkupationspolitik Nazi-Deutschlands*, 19–20.

282. Broszat, *Nationalsozialistische Polenpolitik*, 41ff.

283. Fritzsche, *Life and Death*.

284. Gross, *Revolution from Abroad*, 48.

285. *DGFP*, series D, VIII: 77 (Schulenburg, Sept. 16, 1939). Stalin in Aug. 1923 had predicted the need for "a war against Poland, and possibly the other *limitrofa* states," in connection with revolution in Germany. ("Naznachit' revolutsiia v Germanii na 9 noiabria," 133.) Tukhachevsky shared this view and his close friend, the Polish Communist Tomasz Dąbal, deputy general secretary of the fledgling Peasant International, in May 1925 had spoken openly in *Red Star*, the Red Army newspaper, of "a right to separate [the Ukrainians and Belorussians] from Poland and join them to the Soviet republics." *Krasnaia zvezda*, May 7, 1925. According to French military intelligence, basing itself on a Polish source, the Soviet military commander Uborevičius, an ethnic Lithuania, had stated ingratiatingly at a banquet in Berlin with the German military brass on Feb. 1, 1930, "Have we not moved far enough in the past two years to be able to pose the question of a revision of the borders and a drubbing of the Poles? In fact, we ought to partition Poland again." Castellan, *Le réarmement clandestin du Reich*, 185 (citing letter att. mil., Berlin, no. 152: 295, March 28, 1930).

286. Gross, *Revolution from Abroad*, chap. 1, 206. Sukiennicki, "Establishment of the Soviet Regime"; Vakar, *Byelorussia*, 164–5, 168–9. Perhaps ten thousand more Ukrainians were repatriated westward as labor power by Nazi intelligence under falsified German racial origin designations.

287. Simonov, *Glazami cheloveka moego pokoleniia*, 80–1.

288. Vernadsky also pointed out a lack of white bread even for those with the money to pay, a decline in the quality of black bread, queues for vodka, and general dissatisfaction and hardship. Vernadskii, *Dnevniki, 1935–1941*, II: 56. See also Nevehzin, "Pol'sha v sovetskoi propagande," 69–88. *Bolshevik*, the party journal, in its Sept. 1939 issue called the Red Army's crossing into eastern Poland "a liberation" of ethnic Ukrainians and Belorussians, while making no mention of the Pact. The same issue described the first anniversary of the *Short Course* and the country's pending progress in Marxist-Leninist training. *Bol'shevik*, 1939, no. 17: 6–11, 12–21. Identical treatment appeared in *Ogonyok* (no. 24 [1939]: 1–7), which had a thrice-monthly circulation of 300,000. On a poster by Viktor Korecki, printed in four languages and 800,000 copies, Stalin was quoted as declaring, "Our army is an army of liberators."

289. "SSSR v voine," *Biulleten' oppozitsii*, no. 79–80 (1939): 8.

290. *Iskusstvo kino*, 1940, no. 1-2: 44. "In the heat of our work the radio brought news of the historic decision of the Soviet Government," enthused the director Yefim Dzigan of *First Cavalry Army*. Kino, Nov. 7, 1939. Semyon Goldstab [b. 1906], who had debuted the Stalin role in *Lenin in October*, played him again. The real Stalin hand-corrected the screenplay. RGASPI, f. 558, op. 11, d. 165, l. 1. See also Chernova and Tokarev, "Pervaia Konnaia'"; Vishnevskii, "Pervaia konnaia." During the Nov. 7, 1939, commemoration of the October Revolution, *Burning Years* would be screened outdoors on Moscow's Sverdlov Square, across from the Bolshoi Theater.

291. *Krasnaia zvezda*, Oct. 17, 1938.

292. Tokarev, "'Kará panam! Kará,'" 49 (citing RGVA, f. 9, op. 36, d. 3792, l. 221), and Lebedeva, *Katyn': prestuplenie*, 112.

293. Cienciala, "The Foreign Policy of Józef Piłsudski and Józef Beck," 130–43; Kornat "Anna Maria Cienciala," 37.

294. Stalin told the staunch antifascist Georgi Dimitrov, "Now [Poland is] a fascist state, oppressing Ukrainians, Belarussians, and so forth. The annihilation of that state under current conditions would mean one fewer bourgeois fascist state to contend with!" Banac, *Diary of Georgi Dimitrov*, 116 (Sept. 7, 1939).

295. For example, Duraczyński and Sakharov, *Sovetsko-Pol'skie otnosheniia*, 67–70.

296. Primakov, *Ocherki*, III: 291.

297. Volobuev and Kuleshov, *Ochishchenie*, 157; Rayfield, *Stalin and His Hangmen*, 22 (citing *Pravda*, Dec. 21, 1994). Before the revolution, of Bogdanov's critique of Lenin (which continued to circulate underground into the 1930s), Stalin had written privately in a letter, "How do you like Bogdanov's new book? In my opinion *some* of Ilich's blunders are very tellingly and correctly noted. It is also correctly pointed out that Ilich's materialism differs in many ways from that of Plekhanov, which in spite of the demands of logic (and for the sake of diplomacy?) Ilich tries to cover over." Dubinskii-Mukhadze, *Ordzhonikidze*, 92–3, n1. Stalin also wrote something similar in a letter to Mikho Tskhkaya: *Istoriia KPSS*, 6 vols. (Moscow: Politizdat, 1967), II: 272.

298. RGASPI, f. 558, op. 3, d. 257–63. Van Ree, *Political Thought*, 107–8.

299. Jasny, *Soviet Economy*, 418; Allen, *Farm to Factory*, 107–8. Some 77 percent of Soviet camp inmates at this time were ethnic Russians or Ukrainians.

300. Afanas'ev et al., *Istoriia Stalinskogo Gulaga*, 158 (RGANI f. 89, op. 73, d. 3, l. 1–2). A "labor day" was worth *nothing* in 15,700 out of 240,000 collective farms. Hosking, *First Socialist Society*, 169.

301. Khlevniuk et al., *Stalinskoe politbiuro*, 171–2 (RGASPI, f. 17, op. 162, d. 25, l. 156; f. 17, op. 3, d. 1015, l. 30; f. 17, op. 3, d. 1016, l. 33; f. 17, 163, d. 1237, l. 223–4); Khlevniuk, *Politbiuro*, 242–4.

302. Fel'shtinskii, *SSSR-Germaniia*, I: 103–4; Sontag and Beddie, *Nazi-Soviet Relations*, 102; Ulam, *Stalin*, 515. Warsaw fell on Sept. 26.

303. "Upon his arrival in Moscow, von Ribbentrop was welcomed by a group of Soviet officials and by Count Schulenburg," wrote Herwarth. "I was standing next to Gebhardt von Walther," who "seized my arm and pointed to a group of Gestapo agents who warmly greeted their counterparts from the NKVD." Herwarth, *Against Two Evils*, 165.

304. *DVP SSSR*, XXII/ii: 606–17n226 (translation of Hilger's official record, discovered in Schulenburg's papers in 1990); in German in Fleischhauer, "Der Deutsch-sowjetische Grenz- und Freundschaftsvertrag vom 28 September 1939."

305. *DVP SSSR*, XXII/ii: 611, 614–5.

306. The pact with Estonia was printed the day after next (*Izvestiia*, Sept. 29, 1939), without the confidential protocol: *Polpredy soobshchaiut*, 62–4 (AVP RF, f. 03a Estoniia, d. 010).

307. *DVP SSSR*, XXII/ii: 614.

308. Nevezhin, *Zastol'nye*, 223–7.

309. Fleischhauer, "Molotov-Ribbentrop Pact"; Chuev, *Kaganovich, Shepilov*, 118; Chuev, *Sto sorok*, 19, 24; Chuev, *Tak govoril Kaganovich*, 90; Hilger and Meyer, *Incompatible Allies*, 313–4.

310. Davlekamov, *Galina Ulanova*.

311. Mel'tiukhov, *Upushchennyi shans Stalina*, 179–80; Ilmjärv, *Silent Submission*, 365; Kuromiya, *Stalin*, 143; *Izvestiia*, Sept. 29,

1939. Already on Sept. 27, before seeing Ribbentrop inside the Kremlin, the Estonians had noticed a big airplane with a swastika at the Soviet aerodrome at Velikie luki. Rei, *Drama of the Baltic Peoples*, 264.

312. Bezymenskii, *Gitler i Stalin*, 309; Sommer, *Das Memorandum*; Sontag and Beddie, *Nazi-Soviet Relations*, 103–7; Fleischhauer, "Molotov-Ribbentrop Pact"; Kaslas, "Lithuanian Strip."

313. *DVP SSSR*, XXII/ii: 616–7.

314. Hilger and Meyer, *Incompatible Allies*, 304–5. Apparently, Stalin promised to come to Germany's aid if it fell into difficulties, a remark that appears to have stunned Ribbentrop. Stalin: "The fact is that for the time being Germany does not need foreign help, and it is possible that in the future they will not need foreign help either. But if, against all expectations, Germany finds itself in a difficult situation, then she can be sure that the Soviet people will come to Germany's aid and will not allow Germany to be suppressed." Zhilin, *O voine*, 185; Fleischhauer, "Der deutsch-sowjetisch Grenz- und Freundschaftsvertrag," 457–64.

315. Sontag and Beddie, *Nazi-Soviet Relations*, 267–8; *DGFP*, series D, VII: 92, 105, 109, 130. The "General Gouvernement for the occupied Polish territories" was proclaimed on Oct. 8, 1939.

316. Ribbentrop, *Memoirs*, 129–32 (at 132). Ribbentrop would call the Soviets old party comrades to Mussolini on March 10, 1941. *DGFP*, series D, VIII: 886. See also Dallin, *Soviet Russia's Foreign Policy*, 76–7.

317. *Pravda*, Sept. 29, 1939. For the text and secret protocol, see: *DVP SSSR*, XXII/ii: 134–5 (AVP RF, f. 3a Germaniia, d. 246), 135–6 (APRF, f. 3, op. 64, d. 675a, l. 20). Facsimiles of the document in German and Russian can be found in Hass, *23 August 1939*, 246–51; facsimiles of the maps, with Stalin's signature, can be found in Pikhoia and Gieysztor, *Katyn': plenniki*, 98–9. See also *Izvestiia*, Sept. 29, 1939.

318. Golovanov, "1,367 dnei iz zhizni Andreia Tupoleva."

319. Ericson, *Feeding the German Eagle*, 90, 92.

320. Supposedly, Stalin, good-cop style, puffing his pipe, took to appearing from behind a curtain in Mikoyan's office and offering "compromises" to the Germans.

321. The regime's notetaker, Vyacheslav Malyshev, paid tribute to the effectiveness of the faux-populism, recording that "this was a characteristic trait of Stalin's: to drill down to the smallest details, especially when those small details affected people." Malyshev, "Dnevnik narkoma," 109; *Na prieme*, 275. This appears to have been a secret (non-published) decree. No such decree appears in late 1939 or 1940 in the account offered by Barber and Harrison, *Soviet Home Front*, chapter 9.

322. The "affinity thesis"—despite the profound ideological enmity—was subsequently re-presented by Tucker and Nekrich. Tucker, *Stalin in Power*; Nekrich, *Pariahs*.

323. More than four of every five Nazi Party members were male. A National Socialist Women's League counted approximately 2 million members; it offered classes for schoolgirls and brides and promoted consumption of German-made products. Payne, *History of Fascism*, 184.

324. Rigby, *Communist Party Membership*, 52. Communist Youth League membership, for those from age fourteen (to maximum twenty-eight), shrank to just 400,000 in 1938. Hitler Youth membership, which was compulsory from age fourteen for Aryans and closed to others, exceeded 7 million by then.

325. The best overview remains Orlow, *History of the Nazi Party*, II.

326. To be sure, German state demand for goods and services had gone through the roof since 1932, as the state share of GDP more than doubled to 30.5 percent. The state also influenced foreign exchange, set some wages, and froze some prices, but it only rarely nationalized property. Jewish property was confiscated by forced sale, but usually to Aryan private owners. Buchheim and Scherner, "Role of Private Property."

327. Malyshev, "Dnevnik narkoma," 111 (May 26, 1940).

328. Herwarth would tell U.S. ambassador Charles Bohlen after WWII that "We were able to make a deal with the Soviets because we were able without any problems with German opinion to deliver the Baltic states and eastern Poland to Russia. This the British and the French, with their public opinions, were unable to do." Bohlen, *Witness to History*, 86.

329. Weinberg, "Nazi-Soviet Pacts," 185 (citing PRO, FO 371/24846, f. 10, N 6526/30/38, Cripps to the Foreign Office, July 16, 1940). For the mostly matching Soviet transcript: "Priem angliiskogo posla S. Krippsa," in *Sochineniia*, XVIII: 190–7 (at 191). Versailles revision was something Chamberlain, too, pursued in his own way, albeit only with regard to Germany—not the Soviet Union.

330. *XVIII s'ezd VKP (b)*, 27.

331. Nevile Henderson, in an unintentional self-indictment, would correctly note that "though Hitler was constantly talking of the hand which he had held out to England and complaining that England had rejected it, whenever definite advances were made to him, he always found some way of withdrawing and of refusing to meet us half-way." Henderson, *Failure of a Mission*, 110.

332. Bullock wrote that from "1934 through 1939 Hitler's priorities were the reverse of Stalin's: foreign policy and rearmament, not domestic issues. If Stalin had to pay increasing attention to foreign policy and defense in 1938 and 1939, it was not because of expansionist ambitions of his own but because Hitler's successes threatened the security of Stalin's achievement within the Soviet Union." This misses Stalin's opportunism and intense resentment at British power. Bullock, *Hitler and Stalin* (New York: Knopf, 1991), 639.

333. Hitler had told his military commanders on May 23, 1939, "for us it is a matter of expanding our Lebensraum in the East and of making food supplies secure," not merely the city of Danzig. Overy, *1939: Countdown*, 2 (citing *ADAP*, VI: 479).

334. "I am certain that even if the Germans were given more than they ask for they would attack just the same, because they are possessed by the demon of destruction," Ciano recorded in his diary after meetings with Ribbentrop and Hitler on Aug. 11–12. Ciano, *Diary*, 118–20 (Aug. 11–13, 1939).

335. See the cryptic notes on Sept. 1939 by Orlova, *Vospominaniia*, 101. This passage was omitted from the translation: Orlova, *Memoirs*, 90–1.

336. Pons, *Stalin and the Inevitable War*, 178.

337. RGASPI, f. 558, op. 11, d. 451, l. 37–40, 57. On Oct. 7, 1939, the actor Boris Shchukin died suddenly, at age forty-five; he had been in the company of the Vakhtangov since 1920, where he played more than one hundred roles, including Lenin, and been named a USSR People's Artist in 1936. But he had suffered some sort of nervous breakdown, after which he had developed a heart condition.

338. Trying to take advantage of the Pact, Boris Pasternak approached the journal *Znamia* in early Nov. 1939 to try to publish his three-year-old translation of the German writer Heinrich von Kleist's *Prince of Homburg* (1809–10). The play, about the necessity of unquestioning obedience to orders, was enjoying good runs in theaters in Nazi Germany. But *Znamia* (under Vishnevsky) rebuffed Pasternak. Still, the play was published in a collection of translations: Pasternak, *Izbrannye perevody*; Tarasenkov, "Pasternak."

339. "Thus begins a politics resembling a fight between two wild animals," the antifascist Vishnevsky recorded in his diary on Oct. 5, 1939. "Uncommon cunning, but diplomatic, military, and hunting tricks—a common phenomenon between wild animals. This is what our Russian person fears, when he hears about 'friendship' with fascism." Vishnevskii, *Sobranie sochinenii*, VI: 298.

340. Warlimont, *Inside Hitler's Headquarters*, 37.

341. Kershaw, *Hitler: 1936–1945*, 262–71. In Nov. 1939, Halder did engage acquaintances in the officers corps, civil service, and counterintelligence in conversation about possibly arresting Hitler and putting Göring in power (who was known to oppose war with Britain and France), but the plotters panicked and abandoned their talks.

342. Moorhouse, *Killing Hitler*, 49 (citing Bundesarchiv, Elser interrogation file, BA R30001/310/106).

CHAPTER 12. SMASHED PIG

1. *Biulleten' oppozitsii*, no. 79–80 (Aug.–Oct. 1939), 14–6.

2. Banac, *Diary of Georgi Dimitrov*, 124–5 (Jan. 21, 1940).

3. Monakov, "Zachem Stalin stroil okeanskii flot?"; Rohwer and Monakov, *Stalin's Ocean-Going Fleet*. A key motivation had been the Anglo-German Naval Agreement that had abandoned Versailles Treaty restrictions on the size of the German fleet. Ivanov, *Morskoe sopernichestvo imperialisticheskikh derzhav*; *Morskoi sbornik*, 1937, no. 9: 114–25. Contrary to some analyses, the key prompt was not the Spanish Civil War. Voroshilov, as early as the 17th Party Congress, in Jan. 1934, had promised that, as a result of industrialization, "we shall be able to create our shipbuilding industry and soon produce our fleets." Herrick, *Soviet Naval Strategy*, 38–45; *XVII s'ezd*, 230. Naval commander Vladimir Orlov had presented the initial draft of a big-fleet program in early Feb. 1936 and later detailed it publicly in a speech to the Congress of Soviets (Nov. 28, 1936). Gromov, *Tri veka Rossiiskogo Flota*, *Pravda*, Nov. 29, 1936; Orlov, "Rech' tov V. M. Orlova."

4. The naval commissariat was approved Dec. 30, 1937. *Pravda*, January 17, 1938. Between May 1937 and Sept. 1938, more than 3,000 naval officers were executed. During the second Five-Year Plan (1933–37) Soviet naval academies graduated about the same number of green officers. Gromov, *Tri veka Rossiiskogo flota*, III: 358. Admiral ranks would be restored on May 7, 1940; Kuznetsov, Galler, and Isaakov became admirals.

5. Rohwer and Monakov, "Soviet Union's Ocean-Going Fleet," 855.

6. "Thus ended the conversation about battleships," Kuznetsov commented, "whose construction was already going full speed ahead, while I as a Navy commissar was still not

quite clear in my head why they were being built at all!" Kiselev, *Admiral Kuznetsov*, 105. As Hauner explains of the impossible fleet plans, in 1939 "the Soviets lacked much basic industrial infrastructure: their gun factories could not yet produce or test guns of sixteen-inch caliber; boilers for the powerful steam turbines could not have been manufactured until after the war; there was no sophisticated optical equipment for fire control." Hauner, "Stalin's Big-Fleet Program," 106. In 1939, the Soviets remained a one-ocean power—i.e., the Arctic, frozen much of the year.

7. Aselius, *Rise and Fall of the Soviet Navy*; Philbin, *Lure of Neptune*.

8. Kuznetsov signed off on the new plan on July 27, 1940. Kuznetsov, "Voenno-Morskoi flot nakanune Velikoi Otechestvennoi voiny"; Rohwer and Monakov, *Stalin's Ocean-Going Fleet*, 71–106 (citing RGA VMF, f. 2, d. 39526, l. 1–33). Of the 25 billion rubles that would be earmarked for weapons systems in 1940, almost one quarter would go to the navy. The Soviets never completed the colossal battleships, but by the middle of 1941 they would have 267 submarines, more than any other country.

9. Stalin dispatched deputy commissar Admiral Ivan Isakov in May 1939 to the United States, but he proved unable to achieve a breakthrough in the negotiations (asking for the moon), and the attack on Finland ended them. *FRUS, The Soviet Union, 1933–1939*, 457–91, 670–707, 869–903; Davies, *Mission to Moscow*, 208. See also Maddux, *Years of Estrangement*, 86–8, 96–8. Stalin had unexpectedly appeared at negotiations with then U.S. Ambassador Davies in 1938, offering to settle repudiated tsarist-era debts in return for access to naval technology. The disadvantage of the Komsomolsk shipyard was the Amur's lack of depth, forcing larger ships to be towed downstream after launch to be fitted out at Pacific Coast shipyards.

10. On Oct. 26, 1939, a sixty-person Soviet delegation led by shipbuilding commissar Ivan Tevosyan arrived in Berlin with a breathtaking wish list: complete materials for building four light cruisers; two hulls of heavy cruisers (*Admiral Hipper* class); ship and coastal guns (all calibers); torpedoes and mines; optical range finders, fire control directors, and hydro-acoustical devices; and entire blueprints for the battleship *Bismarck*, the *Hipper*-class heavy cruisers, *Scharnhorst*-class battle cruiser, and aircraft carrier *Graf Zeppelin*. Hauner, "Stalin's Big-Fleet Program." Bezymensky, "Sovetsko-Germanskie dogovory." Thanks to Göring's intercession, Tevosyan managed to inspect the Krupp plants in Essen twice in Nov. 1939. Von Strandmann, "Appeasement and Counter-Appeasement," 167 (citing HA Krupp, WA 7, F 1044, Sept. 7 and Nov., 1114–5, 1939).

11. See Stalin's self-justifying remarks on April 17, 1940, analyzing the Finnish campaign, in Chubarian and Shukman, *Stalin and the Soviet-Finnish War*, 263–75 (at 263). Stalin repeated this point a year later: Naumov, *1941 god*, II: 599–608 (RGASPI, f. 17, op. 165, d. 77, l. 178–211).

12. Bernev and Rupasov, *Zimniaia voina*, 85–112 (at 85–6: July 13, 1939). In 1932, Helsinki signed a nonaggression pact with Moscow, initially for just three years at Finnish insistence, but reaffirmed in 1934 for ten years. After the Nazis came to power, moreover, German-Finnish relations cooled for a time. But anti-Soviet agitation persisted on the part of Finnish nationalist pressure groups, whose activists the NKVD assessed as mere cover for

the Finnish government. Stover, "Finnish Military Politics"; Rintala, *Three Generations*; Bernev and Rupasov, *Zimniaia voina*, 17–55 (1934), 58–82 (April 12, 1936); Backlund, "Nazi Germany and Finland." The treaty and its subsequent modifications can be found in *Development of Finnish-Soviet Relations*, 23–37.

13. It was led by Major General von der Golz. Jakobson, *Diplomacy of the Winter War*, 27. Jakobson based his account on unpublished Finnish foreign ministry sources, but did not cite them. He was a sixteen-year-old schoolboy in Helsinki when the war broke out.

14. Khristoforov et al., *Zimniaia voina*, 147 (TsA FSB, f. 3, op. 6, d. 18, l. 32: June 19, 1939).

15. Bernev and Rupasov, *Zimniaia voina*, 97; Manninen and Baryshnikov, "Peregovory osen'iu 1939 goda," I: 114 (citing Bundesarchiv-Militätrarchiv, N 220/19; AVP RF, f. 0135, op. 22, d. 7, l. 8–9, 12–4); Haslam, *Struggle for Collective Security*, 221 (citing Falin, *Soviet Peace Efforts*, doc. 352: Derevyansky, June 28, 1939; and FO 371/23648: Snow to Halifax, July 3, 1939).

16. Before the signing of the Nazi-Soviet Pact, the Finnish military attaché in Moscow had managed to obtain information about the secret consultations from the wife of a high-level Soviet figure, an indication of Finland's obvious concern for its security, but, for Stalin, of something more sinister. Khaustov, "Deiatel'nost' organov," 47 (TsA FSB, f. 3, op. 5, d. 172, l. 2). One of the Soviet sources in Finland was the former Kronstadt rebel leader Stepan Petrichenko, who had escaped into exile. V. P. Naumov and A. A. Kosakovskii (eds.), *Kronshtadt, 1921* (Moscow: Mezhdunarodnyi fond Demokratiia, 1997), 402; APRF, f. 3, op. 58, d. 283, l. 27, Volkogonov papers, Hoover Institution Archives, container 27 (Yagodato Stalin).

17. Volkovskii, *Tainy i uroki*, 4.

18. Dullin, "Understanding Russian and Soviet Foreign Policy," 179. Secret planning through May 1940 in the Black Sea fleet specified the "likely enemy" as "England, France, Romania, Turkey." The fleet's aviation staff were studying the routes to India, while war contingency plans included Iran, Afghanistan, Iraq, Syria, Palestine, and Egypt as well as India—all colonies or allies of Britain.

19. Kumanev, *Riadom so Stalinym*, 26 (Mikoyan on Molotov); Volkogonov, *Stalin: Triumph and Tragedy*, 390–1; Khrushchev, *Memoirs*, I: 288.

20. Khaustov, "Deiatel'nost' organov," 282 (APRF, f. 45, op., 1, d. 178, l. 35, 37). "Yartsev" also donated funds to the Finnish Small Farmers Party, which agitated for "peace" with the Soviet Union.

21. Primakov, *Ocherki*, III: 296–309; *Na prieme*, 234. Zoia Voskresenskaya (b. 1907) had been sent to Finland in 1936 as an intelligence operative, operating under Intourist cover; Rybkin, the new station chief, arrived six to seven months later, without his family, and she became his deputy. Half a year later, they asked NKVD intelligence in Moscow for permission to marry, which was granted. Her account has the correct Kremlin meeting date and the fact that Molotov and Voroshilov were also there, and gives a description of his impressions of the visit, as relayed via a conversation Rybkin had with Kollontai. Voskresenskaia, *Pod psevdonym Irina*, 150–5.

22. Jakobson, *Diplomacy of the Winter War*, 7–11; Peshcherskii, "Kak I. V. Stalina pytalsia predotvarit' voinu s Finliandiei." Gerrard, *Foreign Office and Finland*, 88–9 (quoting Lascelles's and Lawrence Collier's minutes on

a report from Helsinki, Oct. 8, 1939), 28 (citing FO 371/22270/N2338: Snow to Halifax, April 26, 1938).

23. Primakov, *Ocherki*, III: 301. Rybkin-Yartsev does not appear again in Stalin's office logbook, but he could have been received at the dacha.

24. Tanner, *Winter War*, 5; Sharapov, *Dve zhizni*, 345–51; Primakov, *Ocherki*, III: 302.

25. Sudoplatov, the assassin who had leapt into the leadership rung of Soviet intelligence, surmised that Yartsev's work was also a device to sow dissension in the Finnish leadership. Sudoplatov and Sudoplatov, *Special Tasks*, 94, 266. Sudoplatov is off by one day on the meeting: *Na prieme*, 234.

26. *DVP SSSR*, XXII/i: 163 (AVP RF, f. 059, op. 1, pap. 297, d. 2054, l. 33: Litvinov to Derevyansky).

27. Litvinov, on March 11, told the Finnish representative that the "Soviet government did not expect such an answer." Dongarov, "Voina, kotoryi moglo ne byt'," 34 (citing AVP RF, f. 06, op. 1, pap. 17, d. 183, l. 80–2; pap. 18, d. 198, l. 6); "The Winter War (Documents on Soviet-Finnish Relations in 1939–1940)," 53–61.

28. Semiriaga, *Tainy stalinskoi diplomatii*, 143. Litvinov complained to the Swedish envoy to Moscow that "we cannot be sure that Germany, embarking on some sort of adventurism, might not demand from Finland even temporarily the transfer of its islands, and that Finland, either voluntarily, or involuntarily would, under threat, perhaps earlier agree to accede to such a demand." Dongarov, "Voina, kotoryi moglo ne byt'," 34 (citing AVP RF, f. 06, op. 1, pap. 18, d. 198, l. 8: March 11, 1939).

29. Jakobson, *Diplomacy of the Winter War*, 63–5; Dongarov, "Voina, kotoryi moglo ne byt'," 34 (citing AVP RF, f. 06, op. 1, pap. 17, d. 183, l. 61–5). The politburo designated Stein an envoy of Litvinov (RGASPI, f. 17, op. 162, d. 24, l. 120). Stein left Helsinki on April 6. On April 19—the same day Litvinov was received in the Little Corner to discuss the failure of collective security negotiations—Stein wrote a memo to Stalin arguing that Helsinki could not respond positively to Soviet proposals prior to the upcoming Finnish elections, but predicted that afterward there would be some chance of success. He was also received that day (in the company of Litvinov and Potyomkin, as well as inner regime cronies). *DVP SSSR*, XXII/i: 297–9 (AVP RF, f. 06, op. 1, pap. 2, d. 11, l. 224–8), XXII/ii: 526n65; *Na prieme*, 257. Very soon, of course, Litvinov was removed. Stein would be transferred out of Italy on Oct. 7, 1939; he would get a teaching post at the USSR higher diplomatic school.

30. The Soviets had a plan of attack against Finland (and Estonia) already by March–April 1939, but that is what all militaries do: they plan wars, just in case. Aptekar', *Sovetsko-finskie voiny*.

31. Chuev, *Sto sorok*, 34; Chuev, *Molotov Remembers*, 24.

32. Meretskov, *Na sluzhbe*, 177. Voroshilov visited the Karelian Isthmus sometime in April and ordered that combat readiness be raised and plans be developed for evacuation of women and children should war break out. Semiriaga, *Tainy stalinskoi diplomatii*, 146 (citing RGVA, f. 33987, op. 4, d. 366, l. 134). Also in April 1939, the NKVD transport directorate produced an internal assessment of all the ports and military bases of all countries on or near the Baltic Sea. Khaustov, "Deiatel'nost' organov," 250.

33. Meretskov, *Na sluzhbe*, 177–80. Meretskov (*Na sluzhbe*, 178) claims that he was present

during a conversation between Kuusinen and Stalin in late June 1939, and that Stalin expressed alarm over the situation with Finland. Neither appears in the logbooks for summer 1939. *Na prieme*, 646, 661. In summer 1939, the Finnish-Soviet border was largely quiet. Chugunov, *Granitsa nakanune voiny*, 10.

34. Fel'shtinskii, *SSSR-Germaniia*, II: 17 (Oct. 10, 1939).

35. Bernev and Rupasov, *Zimniaia voina*, 85–112 (Leningrad-province state security, July 13, 1939); Khristoforov et al., *Zimniaia voina*, 150–1 (TsA FSB, f. 3, op. 6, d. 405, l. 200: Beria, no earlier than July 10, 1939).

36. Van Dyke, *Soviet Invasion*, 7 (citing PRO FO 371 23648, N3199). The British general might have been trying to induce London to help the Finns.

37. *Development of Finnish-Soviet Relations*, 42; Baryshnikov, *Ot prokhladnogo mira*, 229. On Latvia, see Dr. Alfred Bilmanis: *Latvian Russian Relations*, 192–8; *Polpredy soobshchaiut*, 75–86 (AVP RF, f. 06, op. 1, pap. 12, d. 119a, l. 3–8, 9–17); Mel'tiukhov, *Upushchennyi shans Stalina*, 184; *Izvestiia*, Oct. 6, 1939.

38. Gavrilov, *Voennaia razvedka informiruet*, 201–3; Manninen and Baryshnikov, "Peregovory osen'iu 1939 goda," I: 116–7.

39. Volkogonov, *Triumf i tragediia*, II/i (citing RGVA, f. 33987, op. 3, d. 1235, l. 99); Khristoforov et al., *Zimniaia voina*, 160–1 (TsA FSB, f. 3, op. 6, d. 30, l. 225–6). On the formulation of Soviet demands, see Manninen and Baryshnikov, "Peregovory osen'iu 1939 goda," I: 119–21.

40. Raskol'nikov, "Otkrytoe pis'mo Stalinu" (Aug. 17, 1939). He died Sept. 12. See also Artizov et al., *Reabilitatsiia: kak eto bylo*, II: 420–53; and Magerovsky, "The People's Commissariat," II: 342–3. Speculation on the cause of Raskolnikov's death—poisoning, nervous breakdown—is inconclusive. Konstantinov, *F. F. Ilin-Raskol'nikov*, 153; "Smert' Raskol'nikov," *Vorozhdenie*, September, 29, 1939; Barmine, *One Who Survived*, 21; Ehrenburg, *Memoirs*, 469. Raskolnikov evidently did lose his mind. N. P. V., "Sumashestvie Raskol'nikova: beseda s A.G. Barminym," *Poslednie novosti*, Aug. 28, 1939; I. M., "Raskol'nikov soshel s uma," *Vorozhdenie*, Sept. 1, 1939.

41. Raskolnikov added: "He does not like people who have their own opinion, and with his usual nastiness drives them away." Medvedev, *Let History Judge*, 592.

42. Gerrard, *Foreign Office and Finland*, 88–9 (quoting Lascelles's and Lawrence Collier's minutes on a report from Helsinki, Oct. 8, 1939). For the argument about Finland being a pawn in British strategy, see Pritt, *Must the War Spread?* (Pritt was expelled from the Labour Party, partly as a result of his pro-Soviet views in the Soviet-Finnish War.) On Britain's possible lack of inside information concerning the Helsinki government, see Sotskov, *Pribaltika i geopolitika*, 64–5 (Oct. 16, 1939).

43. *DVP SSSR*, XXII/i: 167–9 (Maisky, Oct. 7, 1939); Maisky, *Dnevnik diplomata*, II/i: 28–31 (Oct. 6, 1939); Gorodetsky, *Maisky Diaries*, 232. Churchill continued this line in further discussions with Maisky: *DVP SSSR*, XXII/ii: 2 (Nov. 13, 1939). See also Gerrard, *Foreign Office and Finland*, 95 (citing FO 371/23683/N6384: British War cabinet, Nov. 16, 1939). Back in the Russian civil war, the lengthy Helsinki-London plotting had come to naught, opposed by the British cabinet, the Finnish parliament, and newly independent border states wary of collaboration with the Russian nationalist Whites. Ruotsila, "Churchill-Mannerheim Collaboration."

44. Gavrilov, *Voennaia razvedka informiruet*, 196 (RGVA, f. 25888, op. 11, d. 76, l. 12).

Mobilization was complete by a second report, on Oct. 13 (199: l. 16).

45. *Izvestiia*, Oct. 11, 1939; *SSSR i Litva*, I: 205–46; *Polpredy soobshchaiut*, 94–144; Mel'tiukhov, *Upushchennyi shans Stalina*, 193.

46. Zonin, *Admiral L. M. Galler*, 309.

47. *DPV SSSR*, XXII/ii: 178 (AVP RF, f. 059, op. 1, pap. 297, d. 2053, l. 197).

48. Stalin had received Molotov and Derevyansky that afternoon, just prior to meeting the Finns: *Na prieme*, 276.

49. Dongarov, "Voina, kotoryi moglo ne byt'," 35 (citing AVP RF, f. 06, op. 1, pap. 18, d. 193, l. 4); Tanner, *Winter War*, 25 (who claims his account of Stalin's presentation is based on the Finnish interpreter's notes). Paasikivi had been born Johan Gustaf Hellsten and Finnicized his name at age fifteen, in 1885, after he had been orphaned.

50. The Beria report was dated Oct. 12, 1939. Vrang had become a celebrity in Moscow diplomatic circles as a result of the circumstance that in a Soviet espionage film, the actor who played the role of the main bad guy, a foreign military attaché, happened to be a dead ringer for the Swede. Rentola, "Intelligence and Stalin's Two Crucial Decisions," 1091, citing U. A. Käkönen, *Sotilasasiamiehenä Moskovassa 1939* (Helsinki, 1966), 62; Norberg, "Det militära hotet."

51. Khristoforov et al., *Zimniaia voina*, 162–3 (TsA FSB, f. 3, op. 7, d. 393, l. 122–4: Oct. 12, 1939), 163–4 (op. 6, d. 31, l. 117–9, Oct. 12), 164–5 (d. 31, l. 122–4: Oct. 13), 165–6 (TsA FSB, f. 3, op. 7, d. 393, l. 122–4), 166–7 (l. 147–9: Oct. 14, 1939); Volkogonov Papers, Hoover Institution Archives, box 1. See also Rentola, "Intelligence and Stalin's Two Crucial Decisions," 1091–2. One clandestine Soviet source in Helsinki, Cay Sundström, a pro-Communist Social Democrat in the Finnish parliament (his NKVD code name was "the Count"), complained to the NKVD that when the parliamentary foreign-affairs committee discussed Soviet demands in his presence, other members told the rapporteur to stop speaking. He informed Moscow that Erkko had stated there was no need for any concessions to the Soviet Union because Finland could count on the support of Britain, the United States, and Sweden. Rentola, "Intelligence and Stalin's Two Crucial Decisions"; Khristoforov et al., *Zimniaia voina*, 163–4 (TsA FSB, f. 3, op. 6, d. 31, l. 117–9: Oct. 12); Volkogonov Collection, Hoover Institution Archives, box 1 (identifying the source as Sundström); Sinitsyn, *Rezident svidel'stvuet*, 21. See also Manninen and Baryshnikov, "Peregovory osen'iu 1939 goda," 119.

52. Stalin received Molotov for fifteen minutes prior to meeting the Finns: *Na prieme*, 276.

53. Erickson, *Soviet High Command*, 474.

54. Upton, *Finland*, 29–30 (quoting J. K. Paasikivi, *Toimintani Moskovassa ja Suomessa 1939–1941* [Porvoo: Werner Söderström, 1959], I: 45–6); Jakobson, *Diplomacy of the Winter War*, 114–8; Tanner, *Winter War*, 27–8; Dongarov, "Voina, kotoryi moglo ne byt'," 35 (citing AVP RF, f. 06, op. 1, pap. 18, d. 193, l. 1–2). Apparently, the Soviet side made no formal record of the talks: Baryshnikov, *Ot prokhladnogo mira*, 237–8.

55. Stalin also suspected that a coup could bring an avowedly fascist regime to power in Helsinki. The NKVD in Leningrad characterized the Cayander-Tanner government in Helsinki as proto-fascist. Bernev and Rupasov, *Zimniaia voina*, 85–112 (July 13, 1939).

56. Tanner, *Winter War*, 30.

57. A Soviet military intelligence on Finnish civilian evacuations from frontline areas was

dated Oct. 14, 1939; the evacuations would be pronounced complete seven days later. Gavrilov, *Voennaia razvedka informiruet*, 199–200 (RGVA, f. 25888, op. 11, d. 76, l. 17), 200 (l. 20).

58. Jakobson, *Diplomacy of the Winter War*, 120.

59. Khristoforov et al., *Zimniaia voina*, 170–1 (TsA FSB, f. 3, op. 6, d. 31, l. 282–4: Oct. 19, 1939).

60. Khristoforov et al., *Zimniaia voina*, 169–70 (TsA FSB, f. 3, op. 6, d. 31, l. 216–8: Beria, Oct. 17, 1939), 170–1 (l. 282–4: Oct. 19); Rentola, "Intelligence and Stalin's Two Crucial Decisions," 1093. See also Voskresenskaia, *Pod psevdonym Irina*, 112–8. On German policy toward Finland, see Jonas, *Wipert von Blücher*, 105–58. Stalin prohibited engaging ethnic Finns in espionage work, reminding Proskurov (head of Soviet military intelligence) that a radio operator working for them in Mongolia (under the name of Voroshilov, no less) had been exposed as a Finn. Khaustov et al., *Lubianka: Stalin i NKVD*, 123 (Aug. 25, 1939).

61. Khristoforov et al., *Zimniaia voina*, 172–3 (TsA FSB, f. 3, op. 6, d. 31, l. 341–3: from Colonel Doi).

62. Stalin's ultimate aims are not spelled out in internal Soviet documents. We are left, like the Finns, to deduce his aims from his statements in the negotiations, and, above all, from his actions.

63. Rentola, "Finnish Communists and the Winter War," 596.

64. Upton, *Finland*, 35.

65. Dongarov, "Voina, kotoryi moglo ne byt'," 35 (citing AVP RF, f. 06, op. 1, pap. 18, d. 193, l. 3–6).

66. Tanner, *Winter War*, 42.

67. Jakobson, *Diplomacy of the Winter War*, 125.

68. Tanner, *Winter War*, 40–56. Stalin had been warned the Finns would drag out the talks. *DVP SSSR*, XXII/ii: 184.

69. Khristoforov et al., *Zimniaia voina*, 173 (TsA FSB, f. 3, op. 6, d. 31, l. 145–6: Oct. 27, 1939).

70. Roberts, "Soviet Policy and the Baltic States." On pogroms against Jews by Poles in Wilno, following the arrival of Soviet and Lithuanian troops, see Senn, *Lithuania*, 55–67.

71. Banac, *Diary of Georgi Dimitrov*, 119–20. Dimitrov does not appear in Stalin's office logbook for Oct. 25 (no one does): *Na prieme*, 277. Dimitrov published his article "The War and the Working Class in the Capitalist Countries," in *Communist International*, 1939, no. 8–9.

72. *Izvestiia*, Oct. 31, 1939; Kabanen, "Dvoinaia igra."

73. Kollontai, *Diplomaticheskie dnevniki*, II: 466. Molotov instructed Kollontai to ensure the neutrality of Sweden in a Soviet-Finnish War. In the scholarly publication of her diplomatic notebooks, the Nov. visit to Moscow occurs without a meeting with Stalin. Kollontai is not recorded in the office logbooks after 1934. Kollontai, *Diplomaticheskie dnevniki*, II: 467. Another version has her meeting Stalin: "Beseda Stalina s A. M. Kollontai," in *Sochineniia*, XVIII: 606–11 (originally published in *Dialog*, 1998, no. 8: 92–4). Kollontai knew she was closely watched by the NKVD. Vaksberg, *Alexandra Kollontai*, 414–21.

74. *Pravda* (Nov. 3) stated defiantly in an editorial, "we will defend the security of the Soviet Union regardless, breaking down all obstacles of whatever character, in order to attain our goal."

75. Jakobson, *Diplomacy of the Winter War*, 135; Tanner, *Winter War*, 67. Khrushchev recalled that at a dinner sometime in Nov. 1939,

Stalin, along with Molotov and Otto Kuusinen, agreed "the Finns should be given a last chance to accept the territorial demands," otherwise "we would take military action." Khrushchev, *Khrushchev Remembers*, 177–8.

76. It is not clear that Paasikivi and Tanner were familiar with theses islands. Rzheshevskii et al., *Zimniaia voina*, I: 127; Tanner, *Winter War*, 67–8; Jakobson, *Diplomacy of the Winter War*, 136.

77. Molotov delivered a speech from the stage, followed by music and dancing. Stalin sat in the tsar's box, obscured. At intermission, as the guests took advantage of the buffet, Derevyansky, the Soviet envoy to Helsinki, approached Tanner, who claims to have told him the negotiations were going poorly. Tanner, *Winter War*, 69.

78. Zolotarev, *Russkii arkhiv: Velikaia otechestvennaia*, XIII (II/i): 100–2 (RGVA, f. 4, op. 15, d. 25, l. 636–38). *Pravda*, in articles and cartoons (Oct. 6, 25, and 26, Nov. 12 and 20), relentlessly pounded home the view that the imperialist powers (Britain and France) were inciting war to garner profit and suppress freedoms at home, while scheming to drag "neutral powers" such as the Soviet Union into their bloody game—meaning a Soviet-German war.

79. "There can be no doubt that Stalin was genuinely anxious to reach a settlement," concluded the scholar Max Jakobson: *Diplomacy of the Winter War*, 144. Stalin watched the morning Revolution Day parade on Nov. 7 atop the Mausoleum, as massive columns of Red Army soldiers and armor passed, followed by columns of workers bearing aloft portraits of him, then attended the late-afternoon luncheon with the retinue at Voroshilov's apartment. "I believe that the slogan of turning the imperialist war into a civil war (during the first imperialist war) was appropriate only for Russia, where the workers were tied to the peasants and under tsarist conditions could engage in an assault on the bourgeoisie," he told those assembled. "For the European countries that slogan was inappropriate, for there the workers had received a few democratic reforms from the bourgeoisie and were clinging to them, and they were not willing to engage in a civil war (revolution) against the bourgeoisie." Banac, *Diary of Georgi Dimitrov*, 120–1.

80. Tanner, *Winter War*, 71–2.

81. *DGFP*, series D, VIII: 293 (Hitler to Sven Hedin); Tanner, *Winter War*, 82–3.

82. Upton, *Finland*, 43–44; Tanner, *Winter War*, 82; Jakobson, *Diplomacy of the Winter War*, 142; Bernev and Rupasov, *Zimniaia voina*, 172; Ken et al., *Shvetsiia v politike Moskvy*.

83. Rentola, "Intelligence and Stalin's Two Crucial Decisions," 1091 (citing report by the Swedish military attaché to Moscow, Major Vrang, no. 44, Oct. 4, 1939, KrA, FST/Und, E I: 15).

84. Mannerheim, *Memoirs*, 300–3, 315; Jakobson, *Diplomacy of the Winter War*, 64, 150–1; Virmarita, "Karl Gustaf Emil' Mannergeim," 65–6.

85. Rei, *Drama of the Baltic Peoples*, 259–60. Rei was the notetaker for Estonian foreign minister K. Selter with Molotov. "Soviet Russia's period of weakness was over," Paasikivi observed of the Pact. Paasikivi, *Meine Moskauer Mission*, 56.

86. Tanner, *Winter War*, 73.

87. Van Dyke, *Soviet Invasion*, 21 (citing AVP RF, f. 0135, op. 22, pap. 145, d. 1, l. 22–3: Yeliseyev to Dekanozov, Nov. 12, 1939). Sinitsyn captured the rivalry between Beria and Molotov firsthand. He also had an audience with Stalin, evidently on Nov. 27, 1939, which is not

recorded in the office logbooks. He noted that "Mikoyan, Zhdanov, Kaganonovich and even Voroshilov behaved like bad pupils in front of a strict teacher, or, more accurately, like mannequins." Sinitsyn, *Rezident svidetel'stvuet*, 20–56 (quote at 40).

88. Tanner, *Winter War*, 75–6.

89. *Na prieme*, 279.

90. Golubev et al., *Rossiia i zapad*, 221 (citing RGALI, f. 1038, op. 1, d. 2076, l. 31ob.), 225–6 (l. 68). The very same day, the all-Union Society of Cultural Ties Abroad demonstratively assembled novelists, film directors, composers, painters, journalists, and more to affirm friendship with Nazi Germany, according to the head of the import agency International Book (A. Solovyev). The next day, Vishnevsky told a meeting of screenwriters that "the question of the British empire, the destruction of this gigantic colonial empire, has been sharply posed, and here, paradoxically, . . . Germany is doing a progressive thing." Solov'ev, "Tretrady krasnogo professor, 1912–1941 gg.," IV: 205; Golubev et al., *Rossiia i zapad*, 221–2, citing RGALI, f. 2456, op. 1, d. 445, l. 23).

91. Maiskii, *Dnevnik diplomata*, II/i: 55–8; Gorodetsky, *Maisky Diaries*, 184. Isolationist sentiment in Britain had not receded despite the guarantees to Poland. "What concerns me is the fate of the British empire!" Lord Beaverbrook, the conservative press baron, told Maisky in London on Nov. 15, 1939. "I want the empire to remain intact, but I don't understand why for the sake of this we must wage a three-year war to crush 'Hitlerism.' To hell with that man Hitler! If the Germans want him, I happily concede them this treasure and make my bow. Poland? Czechoslovakia? What are they to us?" Maiskii, *Dnevnik diplomata*, II/i: 60–1; Gorodetsky, *Maisky Diaries*, 239.

92. Upton, *Finland*, 25–50; Tanner, *Winter War*, 80–1; Spring, "Soviet Decision for War."

93. A Soviet protocol official improbably reported that he found the departing Finns in high spirits. Baryshnikov, *Ot prokhaldnogo mira*, 259 (citing AVPRF, f. 06, op. 1, p. 1, d. 7, l. 64 [B. Pontikov]).

94. Murin, *Stalin v ob"iatiakh sem'i*, 63 (APRF, f. 45, op. 1, d. 1552, l.15–6).

95. RGASPI, f. 558, op. 11, d. 66, l. 13.

96. *DGFP*, series D, VIII: 427–8. Molotov would blame the "Social Democrat" Tanner, rather than the prime minister and foreign minister back in Helsinki. See also Kollontai, "'Seven Shots'"; and Kollontai, *Diplomaticheskie dnevniki*, II: 466–7. Paasikivi would make telling criticisms of Tanner in his memoirs.

97. Domarus, *Hitler: Reden*, II: 1422–4; Domarus, *Hitler: Speeches*, III: 1882–91; *DGFP*, series D, VIII: 439–46.

98. Khristoforov et al., *Zimniaia voina*, 171 (TsA FSB, f. 3, op. 6, d. 31, l. 282–4). Tanner recorded a different version of Stalin's flippancy ("You are sure to get 99 percent support"). Tanner, *Winter War*, 30.

99. Paasikivi later recalled, "The proposals Stalin made to us in the fall of 1939 were completely different from those to the Baltic countries . . . Stalin from the very beginning backed off discussing with us a mutual assistance pact." Baryshnikov, *Ot prokhladnogo mira*, 238.

100. Tuominen, *Bells of the Kremlin*, 154–5.

101. Upton, *Finland*, 30–2.

102. Rentola, "Intelligence and Stalin's Two Crucial Decisions," 1094, citing V. Vladimirov, *Kohti talvisotaa* (Helsinki, 1995), 163–4; Rentola, "Finnish Communists and the Winter War," 598n27; Kolpakidi, *Entsiklopediia sekretnykh sluzhb Rossii*, 711–2. Unexpectedly, a report by the general staff for

the Leningrad military district (Nov. 10, 1939) praised Finnish military training and judged "the morale of the Finnish army, despite the class difference between the officers and soldiers," as "sufficiently steadfast." Gavrilov, *Voennaia razvedka informiruet*, 205–7 (RGVA, f. 25888, op. 11, d. 17, l. 194–200). Stalin finally posted a new military intelligence officer to Helsinki, Colonel Ivan Smirnov, who replaced the man executed in the terror. Sinitsyn, in his posthumously published memoir, would claim he had conveyed the opposite of what he had actually reported.

103. They took along Nikolai Voronov, the artillery specialist. Voronov, *Na sluzhbe voennoi*, 134; *Na prieme*, 279–80. The Main Military Council in Moscow, with Stalin in attendance (Nov. 21), approved a plan for an expansion to a peacetime army of 2.3 million. *Glavnyi voennyi sovet RKKA*, 269–86 (RGVA, f. 4, op. 18, d. 49, l. 1–26), 440–53 (RGVA, f. 40442, op. 2, d. 128, l. 120–39: Smorodinov and Gusev).

104. Jakobson, *Diplomacy of the Winter War*, 140.

105. Rentola, "Intelligence and Stalin's Two Crucial Decisions," 1090.

106. Meretskov reported to Stalin that the deadly attack had originated from the Finnish side. Meretskov, *Na sluzhbe*, 182; Dvoynikh and Eliseeva, *Konflikt*, doc. 8 (RGVA. F. 33987, op. 3, d. 1240, l. 115).

107. Manninen, "Vystreli byli" (citing the recollections of a Soviet officer who took part). See also Zhdanov's cryptic but suggestive notes: Baryshnikov and Manninen, "V kanun zimnei voiny," I: 137 (RGASPI, f. 77, op. 3, d. 163, l. 3120). Khrushchev recalled that "Kuusinen and I . . . found out when we were at Stalin's apartment that the first shots had been fired from our side. There's no getting around that fact." Khrushchev, *Memoirs*, I: 254.

108. *Na prieme*, 282; Lota, *"Alta" protiv "Bararossy,"* 200–3.

109. Balashov, *Prinimai nas*, 23; *Pravda*, Nov. 29, 1939.

110. Rentola, "Intelligence and Stalin's Two Crucial Decisions," 1096 (citing KrA, FST/Und E II: 15); Dongarov, "Voina, kotoryi moglo ne byt'," 37 (citing AVP RF, f. 06, op. 1, pap. 18, d. 188, l. 22–3, 26).

111. Dvoynikh and Eliseeva, *Konflikt*, doc. 16 (RGVA, f. 34980, op. 1, d. 794, l. 1). See also Azarov, *Osazhdennaia Odessa*, 5.

112. Vehviläinen, "Trudnaia doroga k miru," I: 228. See also Jakobson, *Diplomacy of the Winter War*, 142.

113. For a top-secret Finnish intelligence assessment (Nov. 25, 1939) translated into Russian, see Khristoforov et al., *Zimniaia voina*, 195–200.

114. Upton, *Finland*, 50 (citing J. K. Paasikivi, *Toimintani Moskovassa ja Suomessa 1939–1941* [Porvoo: Werner Söderström, 1959], I: 116); *Development of Finnish-Soviet Relations*, 72–3; Baryshnikov and Manninen, "V kanun zimnei voiny," 135 (citing Finnish officials).

115. Pikhoia and Gieysztor, *Katyn': plenniki*, 227–9 (GARF, f. 9401, op. 1, d. 528, l. 228–30: Dec. 1, 1939).

116. *Na prieme*, 279. On Stalin' s corrections of Kuusinen dating back to Aug. 1928, see Adibekov et al., *Politbiuro TsK RKP (b)—VKP (b) i Komintern*, 545–6 (RGASPI, f. 558, op. 11, d. 755, l. 116–7); RGASPI, f. 558, op. 11, d. 755, l. 164.

117. Tuominen judged Stalin's humor offbeat (mostly from stories he heard from Kuusinen, with whom he had shared a flat in the House on the Embankment). Tuominen, *Bells of the Kremlin*, 158, 166, 173.

118. A few days after Tuominen's initial summons by Kuusinen, the Soviet embassy in Stockholm followed up; again he refused. On Nov. 21, he claimed, he received a third order, this one delivered by a courier; Tuominen still refused. He also claimed that he decided not to inform the Finnish regime in Helsinki of the sensational news of a pending Soviet attack. Tuominen, *Bells of the Kremlin*, 315–8; Jakobson, *Diplomacy of the Winter War*, 147. After seeing the Finnish resistance, Tuominen would issue feelers to Finland's Social Democrats and publicly break with Moscow in spring 1940.

119. Dongarov, "Voina, kotoryi moglo ne byt'," 38 (citing AVP RF, f. 06, op. 1, pap. 18, d. 192). More broadly, see Vehviläinen, *Finland in the Second Word War*, 30–73; and Kirby, *Concise History of Finland*, 197–216.

120. *Pravda*, Dec. 1, 1939.

121. Dongarov, "Voina, kotoryi moglo ne byt'," 39 (citing RGVA, f. 33987, op. 3, d. 1380, l. 3; f. 25888, op. 13, d. 76, l. 1).

122. *DVP SSSR*, XXII/ii: 351–2 (AVP RF, f. 06, op. 1, pap. 1, d. 4, l. 75–8: Molotov to Schulenburg, Nov. 30, 1939).

123. *Bor'ba Finnskoogo naroda*, 11. The protocols of the first official meeting of the "government" were recorded in Russian by Kuusinen's son. RGASPI, f. 522, op. 1, d. 46, l. 1, as cited in Baryshnikov and Baryshnikov, "Pravitel'stvo v Teriioki," 179.

124. Baryshnikov, *Ot prokhladnogo mira*, 261 (citing RGVA, f. 25888, op. 1, d. 17, l. 199: report of the Leningrad general staff); Volkogonov, "Kliment Efremovich Voroshilov," 316. *Krasnaia zvezda*, Nov. 30, 1989 (A. M. Noskov); Volkogonov, "Drama of the Decisions," 32; Mel'tiukhov, "'Narodnyi front' dlia Finliandii?" 100n2 (citing RGASPI, f. 77, op. 1, d. 889, l. 1–10, 15–6; d. 891, l. 1–3). See also Mel'tiukhov, "'Narodnyi front' dlia Finliandii?," 100n2 (citing RGASPI, f. 77, op. 1, d. 889, l. 18–25: Dec. 26, 1939).

125. Jakobson, *Diplomacy of the Winter War*, 144–8; Spring, "Soviet Decision for War," 217; Balashov, *Prinimai nas*, 43.

126. Dongarov, "Pravitel'stvo Kuusinena," 74–5, 76–9 (facsimile).

127. A Feb. 1, 1940, "Appeal to the soldiers of the Finnish army," issued in the name of the "People's Government" and written by Zhdanov, initially declared that "the Soviet Union does not want anything other than a government in Finland that would not fashion intrigues with the imperialist powers threatening the security of Leningrad." Zhdanov excised this passage in the final draft. Mel'tiukhov, "'Narodnyi front' dlia Finliandii?," 100 (citing RGASPI, f. 77, op. 1, d. 891, l. 14–5).

128. Rentola, "Finnish Communists and the Winter War," 600 (citing RGASPI, f. 495, op. 269, d. 134, l. 36: autobiography of Esa Kuusinen, Aug. 1, 1940). See also Rayfield, *Stalin and His Hangmen*, 316.

129. Kuusinen, *Rings of Destiny*, 225, 230, 231. Aino last saw Otto in 1935.

130. RGASPI, f. 17, op. 165, d. 77, l. 178–212, in Rzeshevskii et al., *Zimniaia voina*, II: 272–83; Chubarian and Shukman, *Stalin and the Soviet-Finnish War*, 268; Roberts, *Stalin's Wars*, 46.

131. *Na prieme*, 282–94; Meretskov, *Na sluzhbe*, 179.

132. Kuznetsov, *Nakanune*, 309, 328.

133. Zakharov et al., *50 let Vooruzhenykh Sil SSSR*, 230; Baryshnikov, "Sovetsko-Finliandskaia voina," 33 (citing RGVA, f. 25888, op. 14, d. 2, l. 1). Mekhlis and Kulik, both deputy defense commissars, mocked Voronov, the artillery specialist, in the presence of Meretskov when Voronov said the Soviets would be fortunate to achieve their combat

aims in two to three months; they told him the war plan was for ten to twelve days. Voronov, *Na sluzhbe voennoi*, 136. Meretskov later admitted that the forces under his command were not ready to attack. Meretskov, *Na sluzhbe*, 171, 173–4, 179, 181–2.

134. Shaposhnikov would learn of the outbreak of hostilities from the press. Simonov, *Glazami cheloveka moeogo pokoleniia*, 442–3; Simonov, "Glazami cheloveka moego pokoleniia," 79.

135. Baryshnikov and Manninen, "V kanun zimnei voiny," I: 133 (RGVA, f. 37977, op. 1, d. 233, l. 4: telegram to Shaposhnikov, Nov. 19, 1939); Meretskov, *Serving the People*, 100–1.

136. Mannerheim, *Memoirs*, 366. See also Tillotson, *Finland at Peace and War*, 121–75. During only 10 of the 105 days of the campaign was the temperature above freezing. The record low was on Jan. 16, 1940.

137. Chew, *White Death*; Trotter, *Frozen Hell*.

138. Khrushchev, *Memoirs*, I: 252.

139. Akhmedov, *In and Out of Stalin's GRU*, 112.

140. Rittersporn, *Anguish*, 235 (citing GARF, f. 9415, op. 5, d. 87, l. 17).

141. Davies, *Popular Opinion*, 100 (citing TsGAIPD SPb, f. 24, op. 2v, d. 3723, l. 62, 50).

142. Zenzinov, *Vstrecha s Rossiei*, 37, 138. Zenzinov's book includes the full text of 277 out of the 376 surviving letters.

143. Khristoforov et al., *Zimniaia voina*, 253–61 (TsA FSB, f. 3, op. 6, d. 185, l. 454–71: Dec. 7, 1939).

144. Bernev and Rupasov, *Zimniaia voina*, 115–266.

145. "The pessimist Mannerheim raised his marshal's baton, the would-be appeaser Tanner emerged as the most resolute political leader, and workers and peasants, who had voted the Centre-Left government into power, fulfilled their duty as soldiers," as one historian aptly remarked. Rentola, "Intelligence and Stalin's Two Crucial Decisions," 1096.

146. Maisky recorded in his diary (Dec. 1): "The British reaction is rabid. The press, the radio, the cinema, Parliament—all have been mobilized." Maiskii, *Dnevnik diplomata*, II/i: 75; Gorodetsky, *Maisky Diaries*, 243. See also Maisky, *Memoirs of a Soviet Ambassador*, 40; Carley, "'Situation of Delicacy,'" 195–6; and Stalin's comments to the chief of the Estonian armed forces, Dec. 11–12, 1939, as recorded by Rei, in *Sotsialisticheskie revoliutsii v Estonii*, 109. In Dec. 1939, Kollontai wrote from Stockholm to Molotov (a copy went to Voroshilov), calling the working situation "difficult and serious" and concluding, "I cannot fail to point out I still have no aide, and no one even to consult with, since everyone is new and they all need to be taught." Gavrilov, *Voennaia razvedka informiruet*, 218–20 (RGVA, f. 33987, op. 3, d. 1202, l. 99–101ss). On the lack of experienced staff in Moscow, see Kraminov, *V orbite voiny*, 79.

147. Ericson, *Feeding the German Eagle*, 134; Philbin, *Lure of Neptune*, 61, 129.

148. Gavrilov, *Voennaia razvedka informiruet*, 361 (TsAMO, f. 23, op. 22407, d. 2, l. 586), 363 (op. 22410, d. 2, l. 196: Dec. 8, 1939), 372–3 (RGASPI. F. 495, op. 74, d. 618, l. 12, 13–4, 16). See also Zolotarev, *Russkii arkhiv: Velikaia otechestvennaia*, XVIII (VII/i): 162.

149. Rentola, "Intelligence and Stalin's Two Crucial Decisions," 1096, citing Paasikivi's notes from the Government of Finland foreign affairs committee, Dec. 2 and 3, 1939, in O. Manninen and K. Rumpunen (eds.), *Murhenäytelmän vuorosanat: Talvisodan hallituksen keskustelut* (Helsinki, 2003).

150. Khristoforov et al., *Zimniaia voina*, 230–3. Molotov refused to meet with the Swedish mediator to hear the Helsinki government's

proposed concessions; Molotov told the American mediator that the Soviets would have no dealings with the Finnish government in Helsinki, especially since Tanner (the Social Democrat) had become foreign minister. *FRUS, 1939, I*: 1008–9, 1014–5.

151. The NKVD leadership demanded and received an accurate picture of the Red Army. Khristoforov et al., *Zimniaia voina*, 406–7 (Dec. 31, 1939).

152. Khristoforov et al., *Zimniaia voina*, 324 (TsA FSB, f. 3, op. f, d. 351, l. 212-6).

153. *DVP SSSR*, XXIII/i: 57–61, 77–78. These German officials do not appear in the logs for Stalin's office.

154. Khrushchev, *Memoirs*, I: 251-2.

155. At the Johannisthal airfield outside Berlin Göring had paraded before them "twin-engine Junkers 88 and Dornier 215 bombers, single-engine Henkel-100 and Messerschmitt-110 fighters, Focke-Wulf-187 and Henschel reconnaissance planes, a twin-engine Messerschmitt-110 fighter, a Junkers 87 dive bomber, and other types of aircraft," as Alexander Yakovlev described the scene. General Ernst Udet, Göring's deputy, took Hovhannes "Ivan" Tevosyan, head of the Soviet delegation, up in a Fiesler Storch reconnaissance plane, then executed a "splendid landing, stopping exactly where it had started from." Tevosyan was impressed. Later, Göring made him a gift of the aircraft. The delegation, according to Yakovlev, "returned to the Adlon strongly impressed." Tarpaulins and ropes curtained off whole areas of the sites the Soviets visited—Messerschmitt in Augsburg, Focke-Wulf in Bremen, Junkers in Dessau, BMW in Munich, Henschel and Siemens in Berlin. Bialer, *Stalin and His Generals*, 117–8; Berezhkov, *At Stalin's Side*, 81–2.

156. *DGFP*, series D, VIII: 472–5 (shopping list), 513 (Ribbentrop, Dec. 11, 1939), 516–7 (Ritter to Schulenburg, Dec. 11, 1939).

157. Khristoforov et al., *Zimniaia voina*, 289–91 (TsA FSB, f. 3, op. 6, d. 35, l. 154–60: Dec. 12), 292 (d. 540, l. 266: Dec. 12), 312–4 (l. 225–9: Dec. 14), 319–21 (l. 276–9), 321–2 (l. 280–3), 326 (l. 290).

158. *Na prieme*, 9, 279, 284–5.

159. Malyshev, "Dnevnik narkoma," 109–10.

160. Banac, *Diary of Georgi Dimitrov*, 122–3 (Dec. 21, 1939). Some guests at the banquets were known to carry home candies, nuts, fruit, and other portables for their families.

161. Raikin, *Vospominaniia*, 195–7.

162. Pirogov, *S otsom*, 133–4. Pirogov was not again invited to perform at Kremlin banquets, but escaped arrest.

163. Vladimir Orlov, "Prokofiev."

164. I. S. Rabinovich, in *Stalin i liudi sovetskoi strany*, 3. See also Rabinovich, "Obraz vozhdia"; Grabar', "Stalin i liudi sovetskoi strane"; and Kravchenko, *Stalin v izobrazitel'nom iskusstve*.

165. *Pravda*, March 18, 1939. The painting had first been exhibited at the show "Twenty Years of the Red Army."

166. Stalin had also supposedly sat for the painter Dmitry Sharapov in the 1930s, but did not like the result; in any case, Sharapov was arrested. Medvedev, "O Staline i stalinzme."

167. Chegodaeva, *Dva lika vremeni*, 152–8. Perhaps the most striking image of all appeared in *USSR in Construction*, a Stalin profile portrait formed from a vast abundance of tiny multihued flecks of millet, alfalfa, and poppy. *USSR in Construction*, 1939, no. 11–2; Margolin, "Stalin and Wheat."

168. *Pravda*, Dec. 20 and 21, 1939; Heizer, "Cult of Stalin." The thousands of congratulations in *Pravda* ran with Dec. 2, 1940.

169. *Komsol'skaia pravda*, Dec. 22, 1939.

170. For example: RGAKFD, ed. khr. 1–3553 (year 1939). A model of the hovel was on

display in the Georgia pavilion at the all-Union Agricultural Exhibition in Moscow.

171. RGASPI, f. 558, op. 11, d. 1499, l. 39–54. Yaroslavsky incorporated many "reminiscences" in his book, *O tovarishche Staline* (Moscow: Gospolitizdat, 1939), in English, *Landmarks in the Life of Stalin* (Moscow: Foreign Languages Publishing House, 1940), printed in some 200,000 copies, which, unusually, included a chapter on Stalin's childhood. The work was based on a long speech on Stalin's life that Yaroslavsky had delivered at a conference of agitprop cadres on Sept. 17, 1939, which had been published in two parts in the agitprop journal: "Vazhneishie vekhi zhizni i deiatel'nosti tovarishcha Stalina," *V pomoshch' marksistsko-leninsokomu obrazovaniiu*, 1939, no. 10: 33–61, no. 13–4: 22–92. Also, some of the "reminiscences" Beria's minions had gathered and published in Tbilisi about Stalin's youth were republished in the mass-circulation youth periodical *Molodaya Gvardiya* (1939, no. 12). In Sept. 1940, Stalin forbade publication in Russian of the Georgian-language book *Childhood of the Leader*, by the famed children's writer Konstantin Gamsakhurdia, issued the previous year in connection with Stalin's sixtieth birthday. Galleys had been readied. Maksimenkov, *Bol'shaia tsenzura*, 524–5 (RGASPI, f. 558, op. 11, d. 730, l. 190); d. 787, l. 1–2. See also Davies and Harris, *Stalin's World*, 159.

172. RGASPI, f. 558, op. 11, d. 3226, l. 1; d. 1281; Koniuskaia, "Iz vosponinanii," 3; RGASPI, f. 629, op. 11, d. 55, l. 52.

173. *K shestidesiatiletiiu*, 177. See also Barmine, *One Who Survived*, 258. The regime published recommended readings for Stalin's jubilee: Markovich, *O Staline*. See also *O Staline: ukazatel' literatury*. Yaroslavky described the three earliest meetings between Stalin and Lenin: Dec. 1905 in Tampere, Finland at the 3rd Party Congress; April 1906 in Stockholm, at the 4th Party Congress; and in May 1907 in London, at the 5th Party Congress (the numbers were disputed by non-Bolshevik members of the Russian Social Democrat Workers Party). Iaroslavskii, "Tri vstrechi."

174. *Pravda*, Dec. 23 and 25, 1939, reprinted in Iu. Fel'shtinskii, *Oglasheniiu podlezhit*, 170–1. Stalin's name, one author wrote in a biographical note, "glows like a torch of freedom, like a battle flag of the toilers of the whole world." Badaev, "O Staline."

175. *Time*, Jan. 1, 1940.

176. Mydans, *More than Meets the Eye*, 119.

177. Van Dyke, *Soviet Invasion*, 77 (citing an unpublished essay by G. A. Kumanev).

178. Khaustov, "Deiatel'nost' organov," 332, 357.

179. Volkogonov, Hoover Institution Archive, box 1 (Voroshilov, Stalin, and Shaposhnikov order to frontline commanders); van Dyke, *Soviet Invasion*, 103, citing N. F. Kuz'min, *Na strazhe mirovogo truda, 1921–1941 gg.* (Moscow: Voenizdat, 1959), 238.

180. Gavrilov, *Voennaia razvedka informiruet*, 210–2 (RGVA, f. 33988, op. 4, d. 13, l. 197ss–200ss), 212–4 (l. 247ss–249ss), 215–16 (l. 244ss–246ss), 216–8 (239ss–243ss).

181. Lota, *"Alta" protiv "Barbarossy,"* 203. She sent the message on Dec. 8, 1939. When and in what form Stalin received this information remains unclear. On German troop positioning in the West, see Gavrilov, *Voennaia razvedka informiruet*, 257–63 (Jan. 1940).

182. Semiriaga, *Tainy stalinskoi diplomatii*, 163–4; Meretskov, *Na sluzhbe*, 185–7; *Na prieme*, 288.

183. Stalin also permitted selection of quality troops from various military districts for Finland. Van Dyke, *Soviet Invasion*, 104 (citing RGASPI, f. 71, op. 25, d. 59).

184. RGVA, f. 33 987, op. 3, d. 1386, l. 169–71; Volkogonov papers, Hoover Institution Archives, container 17; RGASPI, f. 71, op. 25, d. 6861, l. 411–4. On Jan. 13, 1940, Beria reported that Soviet military communication codes had been carelessly distributed on the battlefield and fallen into enemy hands. Khristoforov et al., *Zimniaia voina*, 428–9 (TsA FSB, f. 3, op. 7, d. 280, l. 18-20).

185. In Moscow Choibalsan also met with Voroshilov and Beria, who "helped" the Mongol leader reinforce his personal security detail, which increased Soviet surveillance. Baabar, *Twentieth-Century Mongolia*, 366–78 (citing sources with Mongol archives). After victory at the Halha River over the Japanese, Choibalsan had traveled again to the Soviet capital, arriving in Dec. 1939. He had last been there from Sept. 1938 through Jan. 1939, when Kremlin doctors diagnosed him with "physical and intellectual fatigue" and prescribed treatment at the Matsesta baths, after which, upon returning to Mongolia, he had Prime Minister Amar publicly tried and extradited to the NKVD in Siberia for execution.

186. Iakovlev, *Tsel' zhizni* (6th ed.), 157–61. Yakovlev indicates he met Stalin twice, in late Dec. 1939 and on Jan. 9, but the logbooks give dates of late Oct. 1939 and Jan. 8, 1940. *Na prieme*, 277, 288. Yakovlev's father had worked for Alfred Nobel's oil concern. Mikhail Kaganovich was removed on Jan. 10, and demoted to the directorship of a military aviation factory (no. 124) in Kazan. In Feb. 1941, after being told by his brother Lazar that Stalin had criticized him, Mikhail would shoot himself.

187. Emel'ianov, *Na poroge voiny*, 154–8; "Vospominaia Velikuiu Otechestvennuiu," 56; Malyshev, "Dnevnik narkoma," 109. Yemelyanov recalls the meeting as taking place sometime in Dec. 1939, but the office logbooks indicate the Jan. date. *Na prieme*, 289.

188. Khristoforov et al., *Zimniaia voina*, 431–2 (TsA FSB, f. 3, op. 7, d. 189, l. 69–71: Beria, Jan. 13, 1940).

189. Finnish intelligence passed to the British a Soviet codebook that "bore the marks of a bullet." Jeffrey, *MI6*, 371–2 (no citation).

190. Rentola, "Intelligence and Stalin's Two Crucial Decisions," 1098 (citing Brig Ling notes on Interview with Mannerheim on Jan. 8, 1940; Mannerheim to Ironside, Jan. 9: TNA War Office 208/3966; and Memo by Gen. Ironside, "Operations in Scandinavia," Jan. 12: TNA, WO 208/3966).

191. Khristoforov et al., *Zimniaia voina*, 431–2 (TsA FSB, f. 3, op. 7, d. 189, l. 69–71: Jan. 13, 1940), 409 (TsA FSB, f. 3, op. 6: Jan. 1940); *DVP SSSR*, XXIII/i: 53–6 (Maisky to Molotov, Jan. 26, 1940); Pons, *Stalin and the Inevitable War*, 195. Maisky feared British-Soviet diplomatic relations again would be severed and he himself deported. In the event, he remained in London but as a pariah. The British intended to publish a book of documents on the failed negotiations with Moscow, exculpating themselves, which would have exposed Maisky's initiatives beyond his instructions. Maisky procured a microfilm of the never-published text, which would turn up in a search of his possessions and figure in his trial in 1955.

192. Rentola, "Intelligence and Stalin's Two Crucial Decisions," 1098–9.

193. Stalin had learned back on Oct. 13, 1939, that Paasonen, the Finnish military intelligence officer, had told Major Vrang, the Swedish military attaché, that, just as during the historic battle in 1808 against the invading Imperial Russian Army, the Finns would slowly withdraw toward the north and Sweden. Stalin had had the Soviet battle plan adjusted to include the goal of cutting Finland

in two at Oulu (Oleaborg) on the Finnish far coast, to interdict Helsinki's land contact with Sweden. The thought had sunk in so deeply that Stalin had reiterated the need to pay attention to the 1808 battle in a directive as late as Dec. 29, 1939. But by Jan. 8 the Finns had won what became known as the Battle of Suomussalmi, which protected the axis toward Oulu. The objective of slicing Finland in half appeared plausible on a map, but the territory was mostly forested marshland with only logging trails for roads. Nor had the Finns withdrawn the way Soviet intelligence had reported they would. The Soviets lost huge stores of war material and men. (It was in the drive toward the Oulu where Mekhlis had almost been killed.) Volkogonov Papers, Hoover Institution Archives, box 1 (Leningrad military district cipher telegram to the general staff, Nov. 29, 1939; order, Voroshilov to Shaposhnikov, Dec. 2).

194. Hastings, *Inferno*, 36–7 (no citation).

195. Pospelov, *Istoriia Velikoi otechestvennoi voiny*, I: 275; Richardson, "French Plans."

196. RGVA, f. 33988, op. 4, d. 35, l. 35ss, in Gavrilov, *Voennaia razvedka informiruet*, 227.

197. Rentola, "Intelligence and Stalin's Two Crucial Decisions," 1100 (Jan. 20, 1940).

198. APRF, f. 3, op. 24, d. 177, l. 116–36.

199. Banac, *Diary of Georgi Dimitrov*, 124–5, 144–5. In a lecture on June 26, 1940, at the Frunze Military Academy concerning the lessons of the Finnish war, Meretskov would claim that the Finns had built 150 airfields to receive foreign aircraft. Van Dyke, *Soviet Invasion*, 31n55 (citing RGVA, f. 34980, op. 14, d. 6, l. 1).

200. *Na prieme*, 290.

201. Khristoforov et al., *Zimniaia voina*, 481 (TsA FSB, f. 3, op. 6, d. 12, l. 59). See also Tanner, *Winter War*, 125–63.

202. West and Tsarev, *Crown Jewels*, 144 (citing an inaccessible secret *History of the London Rezidentura*, in Russian, file no. 89113, I: 434).

203. RGASPI, f. 558, op. 11, d. 1509, l. 82. Stalin was responding to E. Gorodetsky's article in *Pravda* (Feb. 4, 1940), which was a summary of M. Moskalev's article in *Istorik-Marksist* (Jan. 1940). Later, on April 27, 1940, when Yaroslavsky sought to rebut Stalin by citing many sources, Stalin again exploded ("sycophancy is incompatible with scientific history"). RGASPI, f. 558, op. 11, d. 842, l. 35–44.

204. Zhukovskii, *Lubianskaia imperiia NKVD*, 214–5.

205. http://alya-aleksej.narod.ru/index/0-181; Voronov, "Palach v kozhanom fartuke"; Nikita Petrov, "Chelovek v kozhanom fartuke lichno rasstrelial bolee desiati tysiach chelovek" http://discussiya.com/2010/08/26/blokhinexecutioner. Stalin signed the list, containing 457 names, including Yezhov's, on Jan. 17, 1940: APRF, f. 3, op. 24, d. 177, l. 116–36. Another principal executioner was the Latvian Pēteris Mago, Russified as Pyotr Maggo (1879–1941), who would soon die of cirrhosis of the liver.

206. Ushakov and Stukalov, *Front voennykh prokurorov*, 75 (USSR deputy military procurator Nikolai Afanasev, who was present). Among the many rumors that would circulate inside the NKVD about Yezhov's execution, one had Beria ordering that Yezhov undress and be beaten before being shot, just as Yezhov had done to humiliate his predecessor Yagoda. Kamov, "Smert' Nikolai Ezhova."

207. "Poslednee slovo Nikolai Ezhova," *Moskovskie novosti*, Jan. 30–Feb. 6, 1994; Petrov and Jansen, *Stalinskii pitomets*, 536 (citing TsA FSB, sledstvennoe delo No. N-15302, t. 1, l. 184–6); Getty and Naumov, *Road to Terror*, 560–2.

208. Iakovlev, *Tsel' zhizni* (6th ed.), 212.

209. Voronov, *Na sluzhbe voennoi*, 153; Solovev, *My Nine Lives*, 119; Erickson, *Road to Stalingrad*, 13; Baryshnikov et al., *Istoriia ordena Lenina*, 137.

210. Valedinskii, "Vospominaniia," 124. Vyborg fell roughly three weeks later. On Stalin's illness and treatment in mid-February 1940, see also Chigirin, *Stalin*, 115–20 (RGASPI, f. 558, op. 11, d. 1482, l. 101–5ob.).

211. In Nov. 1939, thanks to Gerhard Kegel, the Soviet agent, the NKVD managed to photograph a long document on the German negotiating strategy in the talks, including the maximum prices the Germans would pay for various Soviet goods. "The negotiations were difficult and lengthy," the German trade negotiator Karl Schnurre wrote in an internal memorandum, adding that, because "the Soviet Union does not import any consumer goods whatsoever, their wishes concerned exclusively manufactured goods and war materiel. Thus, in numerous cases, Soviet bottlenecks coincide with German bottlenecks, such as machine tools for the manufacture of artillery ammunition." On top of that, "psychologically the ever-present distrust of the Russians was of importance as well as the fear of any responsibility. And people's commissar Mikoyan had to refer numerous questions to Stalin personally, since his authority was not sufficient." *DGFP*, series D, VIII: 752–9 (economic agreement), 814–7 (Schnurre memorandum); Sontag and Beddie, *Nazi-Soviet Relations*, 131–4; Ericson, *Feeding the German Eagle*, 97–106; Read and Fisher, *Deadly Embrace*, 439.

212. *Pravda* did not crow in its announcement. *Pravda*, Feb. 18, 1940. See also Werth, *Russia at War*, 62–71.

213. After his Dec. 1939 offensive quickly petered out, Chiang, in Feb. 1940, had convened a military conference in Liuzhou (Guangxi). He attributed Japan's strength to its surprise attacks (on poorly defended places), stout defense of occupied positions, and disguise of movements. He saw its weakness in a failure to deploy sufficient forces, sustain its operations for sufficient time, and prepare sufficient reserves. Ryōichi, "Japanese Eleventh Army," 227–8, citing *Dai Tōa Sensō* (Tokyo: Sankei Shuppan, 1977), in the series *Shō Kaiseki Hiroku*, XIII: 47–8.

214. Taylor, *Generalissimo*, 171 (citing Chiang Diaries, Hoover Institution archives, box 40, folder 15: Dec. 30, 1939).

215. The Chinese Communists were receiving $110,000 to support their armed forces from the Nationalist government and themselves collected some $200,000 in local currency via local governments under Communist control in northern regions, likely through traditional land taxes. Party dues amounted to another $40,000. But they were spending around $700,000 per month. Dallin and Firsov, *Dimitrov and Stalin*, 123–5 (RGASPI, f. 495, op. 74, d. 317. l. 53–5).

216. Banac, *Diary of Georgi Dimitrov*, 126 (Feb. 23 and 25, 1940). On Feb. 25, 1940, Yan Xishan, the warlord ruler of small, poor, remote Shanxi region, who had an off-again, on-again collaboration with the Communists against the Japanese, halted his offensive against the Communists. The Eighth Route Army was based there.

217. A memo from the Comintern's personnel department to Dimitrov denigrated Wang Ming, Mao's rival, as possessing "no authority among the old cadres of the party," and recommended that he not be given "leading positions," while proposing promotion of a long list of Mao loyalists (including a young military leader in the Eighth Route Army named Deng Xiaoping). "Mao Zedong is certainly the most important political figure in the Chinese Communist party. He knows China better than the other CCP leaders, knows the people, understands politics and generally frames issues correctly." Pantsov and Levine, *Mao*, 333–4 (citing RGASPI, f. 495, op. 225, d. 71, t. 3: l. 186–9).

218. Taylor, *Generalissimo*, 172; Suyin, *Eldest Son*, 170.

219. Pikhoia and Gieysztor, *Katyn': plenniki*, 384–90 (APRF, f. 3, zakrytyi paket no. 1, with facsimile). Between late Sept. 1939 and March 1940, the Soviets and the Nazis had held a series of meetings (apparently four in total) to discuss anticipated Polish resistance, coordination of the respective occupations, POWs, and refugees. Contrary to some claims, the Feb. 20, 1940, meeting (at the Pan Tadeusz villa of the Zakopane spa, in the Tatra Mountains) did not coordinate or precipitate the Soviet Katyn massacre. Vishlëv, *Nakanune*, 119–23; Bór-Komorowski, *Secret Army*. Beria's March 1940 report and recommendation to Stalin is in Sudoplatov, *Special Tasks*, 476–8.

220. Pikhoia and Gieysztor, *Katyn': plenniki*, 390–2 (APRF, f. 3, zakrytyi paket no. 1); Cienciala et al., *Katyn*, 118–20; *Ubyty v Katyni*; Kozlov et al., *Katyn' mart 1940–sentiabr'2000 g.* The total includes approximately 14,500 POWs held in NKVD camps in Kozelsky, Ostaskhovsky, and Starobelsky, and more than 7,300 in remand prisons in the western regions of the Ukrainian and Belorussian republics. The execution sites included Smolensk city, Kalinin, Kharkov, and other places, as well as Katyn forest. Documents establishing the fact of Soviet culpability survived, but the full story will never be known because the files were purged. Pikhoia and Gieysztor, *Katyn': plenniki*, 42n21.

221. Pikhoia and Gieysztor, *Katyn': plenniki*, 16. See also Sudoplatov, *Special Tasks*, 276–7, 295.

222. Osborn, *Operation Pike*, 92–6. Overflowing camps and prisons placed a strain on NKVD resources in the western regions. Of course, the inmates could have been deported eastward to labor camps rather than executed without trial.

223. In Nov. 1939, Mekhlis, as head of the army's political administration, had told a gathering of Soviet writers that Polish officers held as prisoners of war could form the leadership of Polish legions of up to 100,000 men, which were being constituted in France, and therefore that they should not be released. Jasiewicz, *Zagłada polskich Kresów*, 175 (Vishnevsky diary, Nov. 11, 1939). This passage was not included in Vishnevskii, *Stat'i, dnevniki, pis'ma*, 372.

224. Boiadzhiev, *Maretskaia*, 100; Kalashnikov, *Ocherki istorii sovetskogo kino*, II: 169–84.

225. *Izvestiia*, March 8, 9, 10, and 11, 1940; *Pravda*, March 9, 1940. That month, a "short biography" of Molotov, barely ten pages, went to press in a print run of half a million. It recounted his days in the underground, the 1917 revolution, and the civil war, and stressed his orthodox Leninism, organizing prowess, and close association with "the Supreme Leader of peoples comrade Stalin." Tikhomirov, *Viacheslav Mikhailovich Molotov*, 15.

226. Shvarts, "Zhizn' i smert' Mikhaila Bulgakova," 126. Pasternak, having learned Bulgakova was terminally ill, had paid a last visit.

227. Upton, *Finland*, 140 (citing J. K. Paasikivi, *Toimintani Moskovassa ja Suomessa 1939–1941* [Porvoo: Werner Söderström, 1959], I: 187, 191); Tanner, *Winter War*, 235. For brief excerpts of the Finnish record of the March 12 discussions, in Russian translation, see Khristoforov et al., *Zimniaia voina*, 497–503.

228. For a Finnish police summary (March 15, 1940) of the domestic shock from the peace terms, see Khristoforov et al., *Zimniaia voina*, 519–22.

229. Dallin, *Soviet Russia's Foreign Policy*, 190.

230. Vakar, "Milukov v izgnan'e'," 377.

231. "The USSR, to be sure, received strategic gains in the northwest, but at what price?" Trotsky wrote in March 1940. "The prestige of the Red Army is undermined. The trust of the toiling masses and exploited peoples of the whole world has been lost. As a result the international position of the USSR has not been strengthened but weakened." He added that Stalin "personally has emerged from this operation completely smashed." Trotskii, "Stalin posle finliandskogo opyta [March 13, 1940]," in *Portrety revoliutsionerov*, 162–66 (at 166). Trotsky later clarified that "it does not follow from this that the USSR must be surrendered to the imperialists but only that the USSR must be torn out of the hands of the bureaucracy." Trotsky, "Balance Sheet of the Finnish Events." See also Trotsky, "A Petty-Bourgeois Opposition in the Socialist Workers' Party" (Dec. 15, 1939), published posthumously in *In Defense of Marxism*, 44–62 (at 56–9).

232. This concession appears to have been connected to Finland's efforts to sign a defensive alliance with Sweden and Norway, which Molotov warned Helsinki would be considered a violation of the Soviet-Finnish peace treaty. Dallin, *Soviet Russia's Foreign Policy*, 196; van Dyke, *Soviet Invasion*, 190.

233. Chubarian and Shukman, *Stalin and the Soviet-Finnish War*, 263–75.

234. Waltz, *Theory of International Relations*, 194–5; Keohane, "Lilliputians' Dilemmas."

235. Solodovnikov,"My byli molodye togda," 210.

236. Timoshenko told the Finnish military attaché in Moscow, "the Russians have learnt much in this hard war in which the Finns fought with heroism." Mannerheim, *Memoirs*, 371. Altogether, from Sept. 1939 through March 12, 1940, Red Army call-ups had amounted to 3.16 million. About half were demobilized, leaving an army of 1.547 million. Mikhail Mel'tiukhov, *Upushchennyi shans Stalina*, 360 (citing RGVA, f. 40443, op. 3, d. 297, l. 128).

237. Krivosheev, *Grif sekretnosti sniat'*, 93–126 (esp. 125); RGVA, f. 34980, op. 15, d. 200, 203, 204, 206, 208, 211, 213, 215, 217, 219; f. 33987, op. 3, d. 1301, l. 165–8; Rossiiskaia Federatsiiia, *Kniga pamiati*; Manninen, "Moshchnoe Sovetskoe nastuplenie," I: 324–35; "O nakoplenii nachal'stvuiushchego sostava Raboche-Krest'ianskoi Krasnoi Armii," 181; Balashov, *Prinimai nas*, 182, 186. Neither Hanko nor the islands would prove to be any protection for Leningrad, since the future Nazi onslaught against the city would not come from the Baltic Sea/Gulf of Finland but from overland.

238. Bialer, *Stalin and His Generals*, 130. In early spring 1940, right after the end of the Soviet-Finnish War, the Soviet ambassador to Paris, Surits, would be declared persona non grata by the French, in which he referred to the French and British as warmongers. It was payback.

239. The German ambassador to Finland (Wipert von Blücher) sent a report to Berlin in Jan. noting that "the Red Army has such shortcomings that it cannot even dispose of a small country and the Comintern does not even gain

ground in a population that is more than forty percent socialist." Read and Fisher, *Deadly Embrace*, 411; Semiryaga, *Winter War*, 63–4 (no citation). German circles were said by a Swedish Soviet agent to be stunned by the dismal Soviet effort, and wondered about the necessity of abiding by the Hitler-Stalin Pact. Gavrilov, *Voennaia razvedka informiruet*, 220–1, 224–8.
240. *Nazi Conspiracy and Aggression*, VI: 981–2 (Dec. 31, 1939).
241. Förster and Mawdsley, "Hitler and Stalin in Perspective," 68. See also Förster, "German Military's Image of Russia," 123–4.
242. Van Dyke, *Soviet Invasion*, xii–xiii, 103–27, 189–193.
243. Reese, "Lessons of the Winter War."
244. Mannerheim, *Memoirs*, 367. See also Liddell-Hart, *Expanding War*, 72. One Soviet political commissar observed, "Regiments and divisions were sometimes given to incompetent, inexperienced, and poorly trained people who failed at the slightest difficulty in battle." Rzheshevskii et al., *Zimniaia voina*, II: 21–2. The inadequacy of the Soviet officer corps was a long-standing point of critique. Zaitsev, "Krasnaia armiia," 12.
245. This testimony is second-hand, from Vasilevsky, Shaposhnikov's top subordinate at the general staff. Vasilievskii, *Delo vsei zhizni*, I: 102; Bialer, *Stalin and his Generals*, 132.
246. Vasilevsky, *Lifelong Cause*, 108–9. Vasilevsky was in the Little Corner between March 2 and 17, 1940, on all the days Stalin received visitors except one—thirteen visits total. *Na prieme*, 293–5.
247. Murin, *Stalin v ob"iatiakh sem'i*, 64–5 (APRF, f. 45, op. 1, d. 1553, l. 38–9).
248. They would marry on New Year's Eve 1940–1, just before Vasily would be scheduled to return to his officers' study courses in Lipetsk, where they would live together in the dormitory. In May 1941, they would return to Moscow; Stalin would order that they move into his Kremlin apartment, which would be subdivided for them. Mamaeva, "Vasily Stalin."
249. Sheinis, *Maksim Maksimovich Litvinov*, 367–8; Haslam, "Soviet Foreign Policy," 116–7; Watson, *Molotov*, 180.
250. Voroshilov, "Uroki voiny s Finliandiei." Much of the lively discussion of operations and strategy, prominent through 1936, had been killed off by the terror, but the disastrous Finnish war experience forced its revival. Naumov, *1941 god*, II: 500–7.
251. Supposedly, Stalin privately fumed of Voroshilov, "He boasted, assured us, reassured us, that any strike would be answered by a triple strike, that everything is good, everything is in order, everything is ready, Comrade Stalin." Simonov, "Zametki k biografrii G. K. Zhukova," 50. This conversation evidently transpired when Timoshenko was sent to Finland and after Zhukov was put in charge of the Kiev military district.
252. Banac, *Diary of Georgi Dimitrov*, 128 (March 28, 1940); Rubtsov, *Alter ego Stalina*, 135 (quoting, without citation, recollections of General Khrulev); Voroshilov, "Uroki voiny s Finliandiei" (APRF, f. 3, op. 50, d. 261, l. 114–58); Volkovskii, *Tainy i uroki*, 426–49 (RGASPI, f. 74, op. 2, d. 121, l. 1–35: Voroshilov report).
253. Banac, *Diary of Georgi Dimitrov*, 128. See also Gorodetsky, *Grand Illusion*, 117–8.
254. Malyshev, "Dnevnik narkoma," 110.
255. Stalin, Schulenburg added, could at most be expected to meet Hitler in a border town. Sontag and Beddie, *Nazi-Soviet Relations*, 134–6.
256. *Pravda*, March 30, 1940.
257. Duraczyński and Sakharov, *Sovetsko-Pol'skie otnosheniia*, 153–4 (RGVA, f.

33987, op. 3, d. 1305, l. 210–1). Tevosyan's sister (Yuliya) was married to Levon Mirzoyan, the Armenian party official, who fell afoul of Beria. She was arrested. "Stal'noi narkom" (Jan. 15–31, 2011): http://noev-kovcheg.ru /mag/2011-02/2363.html.
258. The first issue of the KFSSR newspaper *Pravda* in Finnish came out on April 10, 1940. *Bol'shevistskaia pechat'*, 1940, no. 8: 71.
259. For the complete proceedings, see Rzheshevskii et al., *Zimniaia voina*, II (excerpts in Volkovskii, *Tainy i uroki*, 450–516, and Gavrilov, *Voennaia razvedka informiruet*, 235–48); Chubarian and Shukman, *Stalin and the Soviet-Finnish War*.
260. Volkovskii, *Tainy i uroki*, 450–5, 464–5. See also Meretskov, *Na sluzhbe*, 182. Later, Khrushchev, citing a conversation with Timoshenko, said that "every pillbox the Finns had built on the Mannerheim line—all that was well known and even mapped out." Khrushchev, *Memoirs*, I: 253.
261. Baryshnikov and Manninen, "V kanun zimnei voiny," I: 133 (RGVA, f. 37977, op. 1, d. 722, l. 410–1); Elliston, *Finland Fights*, 142 (citing German military attaché in Finland, General Arniké).
262. Baryshnikov, *Ot prokhladnogo mira*, 264 (citing RGVA, f. 37977, op. 1, d. 722, l. 411). Meretskov claimed he asked but could not get the necessary information on what to expect in the war. Meretskov, "Ukreplenie severo-zapadnykh granits SSSR," 123.
263. Akhmedov, *In and Out of Stalin's GRU*, 109.
264. Novobranets, "Nakanune voiny," 170.
265. Proskurov added that "If on the paper it is written 'secret,' then people will read it, but if it is just a simple publication, they'll say it's rubbish. (Laughter). I am convinced that big bosses treat materials thusly." Volkovskii, *Tainy i uroki*, 464–5, 492–504.
266. Stalin received Proskurov, alone, on July 7, 1940, for an hour. Four days later came the announcement that he had been replaced by Golikov. Proskurov was transferred to command of the Far East military district.
267. Naumov, *1941 god*, II: 602 (RGASPI, f. 17, op. 165, d. 77, l. 178–211).
268. Chubarian and Shukman, *Stalin and the Soviet-Finnish War*, 267, 268; "*Zimniaia voina*": *rabota nad oshibkami*, 36. See also Volkogonov, *Triumf i tragediia*, II/1: 47; Volkognov, *Stalin: Triumph and Tragedy*, 365–6 (citing TsAMO, f. 132, op. 264 211, d. 73, l. 67–110). Stalin would also criticize army political work. "It is not enough that the political worker in the army will repeat 'the party of Lenin-Stalin,' it is no more than repeating 'Hallelujah, Hallelujah,'" he complained of the Finnish war campaign. RGASPI, f. 558, op. 11, d. 1124, l. 27.
269. Khrushchev added, "It was the only time I have ever witnessed such an outburst." Khrushchev, *Vospominaniia*, I: 257; Khrushchev, *Memoirs*, I: 256. Khrushchev is the only source for this incident. He gives no date, though it seems likely to have occurred in 1940 after the Finnish war debacle.
270. "Military history—especially Russian—is being studied poorly," Mekhlis, head of the army's political directorate, complained in a speech to the Main Military Council (May 10, 1940). "We have a lot of unfair ridiculing of the old army despite the fact that we had such notable tsarist army generals as Suvorov, Kutuzov, and Bagration . . . All of this leads to the ignoring of concrete historical experience despite the fact that history is the best teacher." Brandenberger and Dubrovsky, "The People Need a Tsar," 881 (citing "O Voennoi ideologii," RGVA, f. 9, op. 376a, d. 4252, l. 121, 138–40). In 1940, the war of 1812

against Napoleon once again became known as the Fatherland War: Nechkina, *Istoriia SSSR*, II: 76.
271. More than twenty top officials received copies of these top-secret documents. Rybalkin, *Operatisia "X,"* 105–6. Stalin had received a long analysis, forwarded by Orlov and dated Dec. 31, 1938, on the performance of Soviet aviation in Spain. The analysis was written by F. A. Agaltsov (b. 1900), a commissar of the Red Air Force in the Spanish Republic army. Stalin wrote on the cover letter, questioning why Orlov and not Loktionov was sending him materials on aviation. Kudriashov, *SSSR i grazhdanskaia voina v Ispanii*, 433–53 (APRF, f. 3, op. 65, d. 228, l. 38, 39–84), 532n585.
272. Helmuth Klotz, an émigré German writer living in France, argued of Spain that the tank had been overtaken by the new German anti-tank guns. Klotz, *Les leçons militaires de la guerre civile en Espagne* (Paris, Édité par l'auteur, 1937); *Militärische Lehren des Bürgerkrieges in Spanien* (Paris, Selbstverlag des Verfassers 1938); *Uroki grazhdanski voiny v Ispanii* (Moscow: Voenizdat, 1938). In the preface to the Russian translation, Soviet editors took Klotz to task for wrongly minimizing the role of the air force in Spain.
273. Roberts, *Stalin's General*, 64 (citing RGVA, f. 32113, op. 1, d. 2). Stern wrote up a report, too. "In many ways, this operation resembles Hannibal's campaign at Cannae," he would boast, comparing Khalkin-Gol to Carthage's battle against the Romans (216 B.C.). "I think it will become the second perfect battle of encirclement in all history." Vorozheikin, *Istrebiteli*. Stern would later complain officially that Zhukov and his men were gossiping that Stern had had nothing to do with drawing up the battle plan. Krasnov, *Neizvestnyi Zhukov*, 121–2.
274. Rzheshevskii et al., *Zimniaia voina*, II: 276.
275. For example, Russian observers of the Crimean War (1853–6) had come to see the necessity of replacing the .70-caliber smoothbore musket, in use since Peter the Great. In 1857, Russia decisively opted for the .60-caliber muzzle-loader (manufactured abroad) and, by 1862, had acquired more than a quarter million of these shoulder rifles, nicknamed the *vintovka*. But in a head-snapping turnabout, the 1866 Austro-Prussian War demonstrated the inferiority of muzzle-loaders to breechloaders. Here was a very expensive decision for Russia: junk its huge stock of rifles, or try, somehow, to adapt them. After emotional debate, experiment, and testing, Russian strategists could not make up their minds and pursued both replacement and adaptation, which were at cross-purposes. Menning, *Bayonets before Bullets*, 30–3.
276. Despite failing to obtain approval, Gorky Factory No. 92 began producing the superior 76.2-mm F-34 guns, and they ended up being available for inclusion on the tank. Zaloga and Grandsen, *Soviet Tanks*, 130.
277. Mel'tiukhov, *Upushchennyi shans Stalina*, 600.
278. Thomas, *Spanish Civil War*, 606, 658–59; Kowalsky, *Stalin*, paragraphs 670, 784; Rybalkin, *Operatisia "X,"* 118. In 1937, Italian aviation also stalled (industry could not build reliable motors above 1,000 horsepower). Maiolo, *Cry Havoc*, 199. The Soviets had captured a Messerschmidt Bf 109, which they discovered was superior to the Soviet Il-16. This would prompt a scramble to upgrade the latter with fourteen-cylinder, two-row radial engines, but that would take time.

279. Iakovlev, *Tsel' zhizni* (6th ed.), 166–7. The meeting in the Little Corner may have been Aug. 5, 1940: *Na prieme*, 308.
280. Gorodetsky, *Grand Delusion*, 24, citing APRF, f. 56, op. 1, d. 298, l. 29–32 (Stalin-Ritter, Feb. 8, 1940) and AVP RF, f. 059, op. 1, pap. 315, d. 2174, l. 153–4 (Shkvartsev, March 5, 1940); APRF, f. 3, op. 64, d. 688, l. 58–64 (Mikoyan Schulenburg, April 5, 1940), l. 72–8 (Mikoyan meeting Hilger, April 21, 1940); Sipols, "Torgovo-ekonomicheskie otnosheniia mezhdu SSSR." See also Hilger and Meyer, *Incompatible Allies*, 317.
281. Ericson, *Feeding the German Eagle*, 202: table 3.2; Musial, *Stalins Beutezug*, 28–9.
282. Ericson, *Feeding the German Eagle*, 205: (table 3.5, 210: table 5.1.
283. "Zimniaia voina": rabota nad oshibkami, 215–43.
284. Suvenirov, *Tragediia RKKA*, 296 (citing RGVA, f. 9, op. 36, d. 4252, l. 160); van Dyke, "Legko otdelalis'," 115.
285. Suvenirov, *Tragediia RKKA*, 317–24.
286. Erickson, *Soviet High Command*, 555. Timoshenko got an apartment in the turn-of-the-century building on the former Romanov Way, renamed Granovsky Street, which was the most prestigious address for those living outside the Kremlin; this is where Mikhail Frunze had lived when he became defense commissar. Budyonny had his apartment here as did the functionaries Yaroslavsky, Malyshev, and Khrushchev. This is where Trotsky was exiled from.
287. See also Mikoian, *Tak bylo*, 386.
288. Kira was evidently seized on May 5, 1940, by a squad overseen by Merkulov; she was executed by Blokhin without indictment or trial. "Beria protiv Kulika," in Bobrenev and Riazantsev, *Palachi i zhertvy*, 197–264 (esp. 195–201, 211–3); Sokolov, *Istreblennye marshaly*, 300–1; Leskov, *Stalin i zagovor Tukhachevskogo*, 53–5; Montefiore, *Court of the Red Tsar*, 293–4.

289. *DGFP*, series D, VIII: 942; Erickson, *Soviet High Command*, 508, 553.
290. One scholar gives the reason as Stalin's desire to show the world that the lessons of the Finnish War had been absorbed by replacing both the defense commissar and chief of staff, even though Stalin acknowledged that Shaposhnikov had gotten the war right. Balandin, *Marshal Shaposhnikov*, 317–23.
291. Gavrilov, *Voennaia razvedka informiruet*, 717.
292. *Komandnyi i nachal'stvuiushchii sostav Krasnoi Armii*, 4–14; Kirshin, *Dukhovnaia gotovnost' Sovetskogo naroda k voine*, 379; van Dyke, *Soviet Invasion*, 198–9; Volkogonov, *Triumf i tragediia*, II/i: 63–4.
293. Osokina, *Za fasadom*, 206–18; Khanin, *Ekonomicheskaia istoriia Rossii*, I: 29.
294. Erickson, *Road to Stalingrad*, 13–49.
295. Kuznetsov, *Krutye povoroty*, 37.
296. Zhukov, *Vospominaniia*, II: 283–7. Zhukov recalls Kalinin being present. The logbook lists Zhukov on June 2, 1939, only in the presence of Molotov and Stalin, and on June 3 in the presence of twenty-five people, almost all military men, but not Kalinin. Kalinin and Zhukov both appear on June 13, but not at overlapping times. *Na prieme*, 300–1, 302–3.
297. Already by May 1940, 12,000 repressed Red Army officers and troops had been reinstated (not including the air force or navy). "O nakoplenii nachal'stvuiushchego sostava Raboche-Krest'ianskoi Krasnoi Armii," 182, 187, 188–9.
298. Konstantinov, *Rokossovskii*, 42. See also Gorbatov, *Gody i voiny*, 162–72.
299. *Drug plennykh*, Jan. 27, 1940: 1.
300. Aron, *Mémoires*, 158.
301. Dullin, "How to Wage Warfare," 224. See also Borkenau, *Totalitarian Enemy*, published in March 1939.
302. Schapiro, *Totalitarianism*; Gleason, *Totalitarianism*; Jones, *Lost Debate*. Stalin was

likely unaware of these adverse currents. For May Day 1940, he altered the draft slogan for the Young Pioneers from "the cause of communism" to the "cause of Lenin-Stalin." RGASPI, f. 17, op. 163, d. 1257, l. 137.
303. Hilferding, "Gosudarstvennyi kapitalizm ili totalitarnoe gosudarstvennoe khoziaistvo?" The Mensheviks, just before the Nazis would occupy Paris, would relocate to New York, while Hilferding would stay behind and fall into the clutches of the Gestapo. Liebich, *From the Other Shore*, 240–3.
304. Harrison and Davies, "Soviet Military-Economic Effort," 373–93.
305. Adamthwaite, *France*, 269–79. There is little solid evidence on German intelligence assessments of Soviet capabilities. Germany used Iran, which in 1939 had declared its neutrality, as a platform for reconnaissance and covert action against the Soviet Union (the Shah shared with Hitler fear of the spread of Bolshevism; nearly half of Iranian trade was with Nazi Germany, mostly raw materials and oil for German weapons). Richard August, who went by the name Franz Meyer, an SS officer and spy working undercover as a representative of the Reichsgroup for Industry in the USSR from Sept. 1939 through Feb. 1940, was among those based in Tehran. He evidently reported that the Red Army was strong and the Russian émigré predictions of a pending anti-Bolshevik uprising fantastical. Dolgopolov, *Vartanian*, 16–7.
306. Emets, "O roli russkoi armii," 64.
307. Adamthwaite, *France*, 232–4; Gates, *End of the Affair*, 57–8; Ulam, *Expansion and Coexistence*, 295.
308. Erickson, *Soviet High Command*, 513. For British views, see Murray, *Change in the European Balance of Power*, 274; and Adamthwaite, *France*, 51. On Stalin's respect for the French army ("worthy of consideration"), expressed to Ribbentrop on Aug. 23, 1939, see *DGFP*, series D, VII: 227.

1. Fröhlich, *Tagebücher von Joseph Goebbels*, VIII: 196–7 (June 28, 1940).
2. Naumov, *1941 god*, I: 374–5 (AVP RF, f. 059, op. 1, pap. 339, d. 2315, l. 35, 34, a, 36, 38, 39).
3. Osborn, *Operation Pike*. See also Richardson, "French Plans"; Millman, "Toward War with Russia."
4. Gorodetsky, *Grand Delusion*, 317–8.
5. Fel'shtinskii, *Oglasheniiu podlezhit*, 180.
6. Golubev et al., *Rossiia i zapad*, 223 (citing RGASPI, f. 77, op. 1, d. 745, l. 34).
7. Solonin, "Tri plana tovarishcha Stalina," 44.
8. On May 10, 1940, the same day Hitler attacked France, Moscow was invaded by Leningrad culture. After so many Ten-Day festivals for the various Union republics—beginning with Ukraine in 1936 and most recently with Armenia in Oct. 1939—now came the star turn of the Union's second capital, with performances by the latter's principal theaters, symphony orchestras, choral group, and the fabled Leningrad choreography school, cradle of the country's ballet dancers. Altogether, 2,765 cultural figures from Leningrad would take part (by one press account, closer to 4,000). On May 29, Stalin hosted a banquet for them in the Grand Kremlin Palace. *Izvestiia*, May 10, 26, and 28, 1940; *Kul'turnaia zhizn' v SSSR, 1928–1941*, 732; Nevezhin, *Zastol'ia*, 120–1. Also in May 1940, the Nazis sealed off the Jews of German-occupied Łódź into a ghetto behind barbed wire.
9. Gilbert, *Churchill and America*, 131–3.
10. Self, *Neville Chamberlain*, 432–3; Lukacs, *Five Days in London*.
11. In a May 24–28, 1940, Cabinet debate, Churchill prevailed. Reynolds, "British 'Decision' to Fight," 147–67.

CHAPTER 13. GREED

12. Firsov, "Arkhivy Kominterna," 22 (RGASPI, f. 495, op. 184, d. 4, l. 53: Sept. 29, 1939). Stalin evidently harbored a certain admiration for the new British PM, Haslam, *Soviet Foreign Policy*, 152n1.
13. Von Strandmann, "Appeasement and Counter-Appeasement," 168. Germany sent a team under retired Rear Admiral Otto Feige (b. 1882) to fit out the 690-foot battleship's superstructure above the first deck. Philbin, *Lure of Neptune*, 121–2.
14. Ericson, *Feeding the German Eagle*, 117, 121n101 (citing PA, R 106232, E0418717 and PA/Schnurre, *Leben*, 97).
15. While dancing the ancient dance with her, Feige was said to have heard a clicking noise, started probing, and found a hidden camera in a large wall painting (it had a small hole cut out). Feige remained impassive to Beria's clumsy blackmail recruitment effort, while Hitler became indignant about the Soviet entrapment effort. According to Khrushchev, Stalin laced into Beria. Khrushchev, *Memoirs*, I: 258.
16. Just before midnight, Stalin evidently invited Beria and Sudoplatov to stay for supper. Volkogonov, *Trotsky*, 454; Primakov, *Ocherki*, III: 98–9; Sudoplatov, *Special Tasks*, 76–7.
17. Ribbentrop in fall 1939 had wanted to make a public declaration to counter British press assertions that while in Moscow he had requested Soviet military assistance but been rebuffed. Stalin rewrote the German foreign ministry's draft of his words to read, "The attitude of Germany in declining military aid commands respect. However, a strong Germany is the absolute prerequisite for peace in Europe, where it follows that the Soviet Union

is interested in the existence of a strong Germany. Therefore, the Soviet Union cannot give its approval to the Western powers creating conditions which would weaken Germany and place her in a difficult position. Therein lay the community of interests between the Soviet Union and Germany." Sontag and Beddie, *Nazi-Soviet Relations*, 124–27; Fel'shtinskii, *SSSR-Germaniia*, II: 18.
18. British policy-makers had discussed a possible seizure of Sweden and Norway, which were also major German suppliers, as well as the deployment of British naval squadrons to the Baltic Sea, in order to cut off Germany and confront the Soviets militarily. Such offensive operations remained largely in the realm of fantasy, however, their costs higher than the Western publics or even Western leaders were willing to incur. In any case, Hitler had beaten Britain and France to the punch, invading Norway.
19. Shirer, *Rise and Fall*, 731–8 (citing Halder letter, July 19, 1957). Hastings, *Finest Years: Churchill as Warlord* (London: Harper, 2009), 1–59; Lukacs, *Duel*, 97–103.
20. The June 10 issue of *Poslednie novosti*, the émigré newspaper of Paul Miliukov, announcing the Nazi triumph over France, would be its last in Paris; the next day it was shut down.
21. Kershaw, *Hitler: 1936-1945*, 297.
22. http://www.bbc.co.uk/news/10339678.
23. Shirer, *Berlin Diary*, 419–25. The Germans removed the railway carriage to Berlin.
24. On June 21, 1940, Köstring, the German military attaché, met his Soviet liaison officer, Colonel Grigory Osetrov, who asked about the terms imposed on France. Köstring

stated, "I do not know the intentions of our command staff, but I think that there will still be something with Britain." Gavrilov, *Voennaia razvedka informiruet*, 333–4 (RGVA, f. 33988, op. 4, d. 36, l. 69s); Gorodetsky, *Grand Delusion*, 33 (citing APRF, f. 3, op. 64, d. 674, l. 128).

25. France's military budget had jumped from 12.8 billion FF in 1935 to 93.7 billion FF by 1939; it was investing 2.6 times as much on weapons production as it had on the eve of the Great War. Doise and Vaïsse, *Diplomatie et outil militaire*, 402; Frankenstein, *Le prix du réarmement français*, 34–35.

26. Of Germany's 93 combat-ready divisions, only 9 were panzer divisions, with a total of 2,439 tanks; France had 3,254 tanks (4,200 with Belgian, Dutch, and British ones included). Stolfi, "Equipment for Victory"; Tooze, *Wages of Destruction*, 371–2.

27. Forcade, "Le Renseignement face à l'Allemagne," 126–55.

28. French intelligence (the Second Bureau of the General Staff) had monitored the transfer of German divisions westward following completion of the Polish campaign, and by early May 1940, despite Germany's minimizing the use of radio communications, the Second Bureau nailed the number of German divisions almost exactly (estimating 137 for an actual 136). The Germans had altered their compromised codes on May 1, cutting off French signals intelligence for a time, making the already skeptical decision makers at the top that much more so when it came to intelligence, however. Schuker, "Seeking a Scapegoat," 81–127, citing Col. Ulrich Liss, "Die Tätigkeit des französischen 2. Bureau im Westfeldzug 1939/40," *Wehrwissenschaftliche Rundschau*, 10 (1960): 267–78.

29. Bloch, *Strange Defeat*, 36, 52.

30. France's Maginot Line, mocked by subsequent analysts, proved difficult to overcome even when the Germans attacked it from the rear, toward war's end; not one of its major fortresses was captured in the fighting. Doughty, *Breaking Point*, 69–70.

31. Förster, "Dynamics of Volksgemeinschaft," III: 204. In 1939, French intelligence had taken note of Guderian's new, controversial strategy of using combined tank and air power to smash through and get behind enemy artillery and wreak havoc, but very few German generals, even in 1940, expected an armored blitzkrieg to succeed in delivering a knockout blow (based on the experience of World War I). Young, "French Military Intelligence," 288–90.

32. Jacobsen, *Dokumente zum Wesfeldzug 1940*; Jacobsen, *Fall Gelb" der Kampf*; Frieser, *Blitzkrieg-Legende*, 66–116; Goutard, *Battle of France*; May, *Strange Victory*, 215–26; Geyer, "Restorative Elites," 139–44.

33. "The great western offensive was a one-shot affair," one historian aptly explained. "Success, and Germany would acquire the economic base to fight a long war; failure, and the war would be over." Murray, *Change in the European Balance of Power*, 361.

34. Frieser, *Blitzkrieg-Legende*, 3. The same day—May 20, 1940—the Nazis opened a concentration camp at Oświęcim/Auschwitz for Polish political prisoners. It would later be expanded and specialize in gassing Jews.

35. Hooten, *Luftwaffe at War*, II: 61; Schuker, "Seeking a Scapegoat," 114, citing Villelume, *Journal*, 333 (May 12, 1940). As the historian May has observed of France, "When Germany opened its offensive against the Low Countries and France in 1940, not a single general expected victory as a result." May, *Strange Victory*, 7.

36. Nord, *France 1940*. See also Gunsburg, *Divided and Conquered*.

37. Deutscher, *Stalin*, 437–41; Erickson, *Soviet High Command*, 537. In France, the advocates of armor, such as de Gaulle, lacking a patron, had been stymied by traditionalists.

38. Hillgruber, "Das Russlandbild," 296–310; Kershaw, *Hitler: 1936–1945*, 297–300.

39. Haffner, *Meaning of Hitler*, 31.

40. Khrushchev, *Vospominaniia*, I: 267; Khrushchev, *Memoirs*, I: 266.

41. Jervis, "Hypotheses on Misconceptions," esp. 475–6. "The vozhd," the contemporary Konstantin Simonov would later observe, "had created for himself a situation in the party and the state such that if he decided something firmly, no one contemplated the possibility of direct resistance. Stalin did not have to defend his correctness before anyone, he was by definition correct if he had taken the decision." Simonov, *Glazami cheloveka moego pokoleniia*, 82.

42. Banac, *Diary of Georgi Dimitrov*, 115–6 (Sept. 7, 1939). "Hitler without knowing it leads to shattering [of the] bourgeoisie," explained a secret cipher in early Oct. 1939, from the Dimitrov to Earl Browder of the American Communist party, in reference to the Pact. Jaffe, *Rise and Fall of American Communism*, 46–7.

43. *DGFP*, series D, IX: 585–6 (June 18, 1940); Naumov, *1941 god*, I: 40–2 (AVPRF, f. 06, op. 2, pap. 14, d. 155, l. 206–8).

44. Lemin, "Novyi etap voiny v Evrope," 28; Zhukov, *Vospominaniia*, I: 373–4; Ulam, *Expansion and Coexistence*, 296–7. Halifax, British foreign secretary, wrote in his diary on May 25, 1940: "the mystery of what looks like the French failure is as great as ever. The one firm rock on which everybody had been willing to build for the last two years was the French Army, and the Germans walked through it like they did through the Poles." Colville, *Footprints in Time*, 92; Reynolds, "1940," 329 (citing Halifax diary: Hickleton papers, A 7.8.4, Borthwick Institute, York).

45. Schwendemann, *Die wirtschaftliche Zusammenarbeit*, 373. The German air attaché in Moscow, Lieutenant Colonel Heinrich Aschenbrenner, called upon the international liaison department of the defense commissariat back on May 21, 1940, and in a jolly mood attributed German successes in the West to Soviet support. "Before my departure for your country," he told his Soviet interlocutor, "I was received by Hitler, who said to me: 'Remember, Stalin did a great thing for us, about which you should never forget, under any circumstances. Remember this, and do not turn yourself into a merchant, but be a worthy representative of our army in a country friendly to us.'" Later that same day, Köstring, the German army attaché, visited the international liaison department and passed on photographs from the war with France. (The package was marked solely for Stalin.) When asked how events would now unfold, Aschenbrenner had made ostensibly definitive statements; the shrewder Köstring had answered, "only Hitler and a very narrow circle of people close to him know. I am given very limited information." Aschenbrenner asked that his conversation not be reported to Köstring, for the latter "is jealous, like a girl, and might be offended that I got here before him." Gavrilov, *Voenaia razvedka informiruet*, 315–375 (RGVA, f. 33987, op. 3, d. 1305, l. 374s–375s; report of Colonel Grigory I. Osetrov [b. 1901]).

46. Trotsky, "Stalin—Intendant Gitlera." *Biulleten' oppozitsii*, 79–80 (Aug.–Oct. 1939).

47. Wager, *Der Generalquartiermeister*, 106. "All in all," Karl Schnurre, the German economic official, had crowed on May 10, 1940, the day Germany struck France, "trade with Eastern Europe, as a result of the Economic

Agreement with the Soviet Union, has attained a volume that it never reached in previous years." *Der Deutsche Volkswirt* (May 10, 1940), in RGAE, f. 413, op. 13, d., 2856, l. 5–6, cited in Nekrich, *Pariahs*, 154; Ericson, *Feeding the German Eagle*, 116–7. Hitler had written (March 8, 1940) to mollify Mussolini that "the trade agreement which we have concluded with Russia, duce, means a great deal in our situation!" *DGFP*, series D, VIII: 876 (March 8, 1940); Ericson, *Feeding the German Eagle*, 111.

48. In addition, the Soviets lent Germany a submarine base near Murmansk for refueling and maintenance, as well as launching raids on British shipping. An oil tanker with Soviet oil arrived to refuel Nazi warships and landing craft during the attack on Norway in April 1940.

49. "Friendship with Germany, the Pact, and so on is all a temporary move, tactical devices," wrote Vishnevsky in his diary in May 1940. "Will we win? Or will we only give the Germans time, a breathing space, supplies?" Golubev et al., *Rossiia i zapad*, 228–9 (RGALI, f. 1038, op. 1, d. 2077, l. 63, 64ob.).

50. Speer, *Inside the Third Reich*, 172. Speer gets the date wrong. See also Reynolds, "1940."

51. He had settled upon the novella after a long search for a vehicle, as he had once explained, to explore "the heroism of construction, the new [Soviet] man, struggle and the overcoming of obstacles." Morrison, *People's Artist*, 88 (citing RGALI, f. 1929, op. 3, ed. khr. 30, l. 1); *Vecherniaia Moskva*, Dec. 6, 1932.

52. Richter, "On Prokofiev," 187–8.

53. Final approval had come only after Vyshinsky, deputy commissar for foreign affairs, saw it and the film's depiction of the German occupation of Ukraine was toned down. Morrison, *People's Artist*, 102–4 (citing RGASPI f. 82, op. 2, d. 950, l. 99); Perkhin, *Deiateli russkogo iskusstva*, 607–8n4. See also Shlifshtein, "Semyon Kotko," 3.

54. Zubkova, *Pribaltika i Kreml*. A Greek diplomat speculated, in an intercepted and deciphered communication, that "Moscow would like above all to drag out the war [in the West], from which it is trying to extract advantages—which, by the way, it is achieving, as evidenced by the example of the new impositions on the Baltic states." Khaustov, "Deiatel'nost' organov," 256 (TsA FSB, f. 3, op. 7, d. 22, l. 106: June 1940).

55. *DVP SSSR*, XXIII/1: 350–2 (AVP RF, f. 06, op. 2, pap. 2, d. 13, l. 103–4, 127).

56. Sabaliunas, *Lithuania in Crisis*, 54.

57. Kirby, "Baltic States," 27 (citing *Third Interim Report of the Select Committee to Investigate Aggression and the Forced Incorporation of the Baltic States into the USSR* [Washington, 1954], 315–6; File N 4794/803/59: Preston to Order, April 19, 1940).

58. *Ocherki istorii kommunisticheskoi partii Latvii*, II: 429. Stalin had murdered the entire Estonia Central Committee. Many of them had spent fourteen years in Estonian prisons following the 1924 failed coup, before being released in an amnesty in 1938 and emigrating to the USSR.

59. Gross, *Revolution from Abroad*. See also Kotkin, "The State." Lithuania had emerged from Stalin's gratuitous massacres with just 1,220 Communists.

60. Gross observes that "the Polish Military underground organization, the ZWZ, which thrived under the Nazi occupation in spite of persistent Gestapo efforts to destroy it, never had a chance under the NKVD." Gross, *Revolution from Abroad*, 148.

61. Gross, "Nature of Soviet Totalitarianism." Because Poland underwent Nazi and Soviet occupations simultaneously, it would seem

the ideal (if that is the word) place to make the case for "totalitarianism" as a concept encompassing both regimes, yet Gross, a proponent of the term, also noted significant differences between the nature and consequences of Nazi and Soviet rule. Gross, *Revolution from Abroad*, 230–1. After a trip to newly acquired western Ukraine and western Belorussia as a *Pravda* correspondent, the writer Avdeyenko returned with a new Buick. (On Sept. 9, 1940, he would be taken to task for being a "serial goods pursuer.") Babichenko, *Pisateli i tsenzory*, 22–31. The writer Vishnevsky, afforded a visit to the front in Finland, had written in his diary (Jan. 2, 1940), "I am ashamed to the point of horror to see how our people soiled many homes in Finland, how they carried off everything." Golubev et al., *Rossiia i zapad*, 226–7 (citing RGALI, f. 1038, op. 1, d. 2076, l. 2).

62. Khabarovsk OGPU materials of the early 1930s (to which I was given access in 1993) contain extremely specific, comprehensive characterizations for the population, right down to dwellings drawn to scale, in the émigré settlements across the border in Manchuria, even as the Soviet authorities could not feed or clothe the population in Khabarovsk region.

63. In the 1940 *Explanatory Dictionary of the Russian Language*, the word *sovetizirovat'* (to Sovietize) was defined as "To implant Soviet ideology, worldview, and understanding of the practical tasks of Soviet power." Amar, "Sovietization as a Civilizing Mission in the West," 31.

64. Beria wrote to Stalin that in the summer of 1940, the police archive in Kishinëv, seized from Romania, had been burned before the NKVD could seize it. Khaustov, "Deiatel'nost' organov," 308 (TsA FSB, f. 3, op. 7, d. 22, l. 301).

65. "The capitalists succeeded for a time in playing on the national distrust of Latvian, Estonian, and Finnish peasants, as well as shopkeepers, toward the Great Russians," Shcherbakov would admit after the annexations to the Supreme Soviet (Aug. 1, 1940), in connection with the failures in 1918–20 to reconquer these lands. When the transcript was getting ready for publication, he crossed out "national distrust" and inserted a passage about "bourgeois politicians" in cahoots with the "imperialist bourgeoisie," "deceiving" these peoples. Golubev et al., *Rossiia i zapad*, 86 (citing RGASPI, f. 88, op. 1, d. 1015, l. 5).

66. *Kul'turnaia zhizn' v SSSR, 1928–1941*, 734.

67. The Taras Shevchenko Theater of Ballet and Opera performed *Natalka-Poltavka*, *The Zaporozhets beyond the Danube*, and other folk favorites. *Literaturnaia gazeta*, March 27, 1936; *Sovetskaia kul'tura v rekonstruktivnyi period*, 517. *Pravda*, March 24, 1936; Nevezhin, *Zastol'ia*, 115 (citing RGALI, f. 962, op. 21, d. 1, l. 10); Cherushev, *Komendanty Kremlia*, 477–8. A Kazakh Ten-Day followed (May 17–26), with 350 participants, including the Kazakh Musical Theater, which performed the first Kazakh opera, a form that was a Soviet implant but, in this case, with a story based on the sixteenth-century oral epic *Kyz Zhibek*. The sensation proved to be the traditional improviser-troubadours (*akyns*), who sang tales accompanied by a dombra. *Literaturnaia gazeta*, May 10 and 15, 1936; Nevezhin, *Zastol'ia*, 115–6 (citing RGALI, f. 962, op. 21, d. 1, l. 10). See also Ubiria, *Soviet Nation-Building*, 169–70. Maya Plisteskaya, the ballerina, condescendingly observed that "Soviet Leaders positively loved these showy-imitation Ten-Days," then admitted that "these parades mobilized creative people to an extreme. Everyone worked to the limits (otherwise, you look up, and you don't get the

little medal, and they don't summon you to the final banquet). So you forget all the negatives. . . . These Ten-Days gathered the best forces." Plisetskaia, *Chitaia zhizn' svoiu*, 93.

68. Uzbekistan's Ten-Day had taken place May 21–30, 1937, with some 600 participants; they performed *Farkhad and Shirin* by V. A. Uspensky and *Giulsara* by R. M. Glier and T. D. Jalilov, with a Kremlin reception on May 31, 1937. *Literaturnaia gazeta*, May 30, 1937; Nevezhin, *Zastol'ia*, 116–7 (citing RGALI, f. 962, op. 21, d. 1, l. 11). Azerbaijan's took place on April 5–15, 1938, with more than 600 participants and a banquet on April 17 in the St. George's Hall and the Palace of Facets. Fadeev, *Vstrechi s tovarishem Stalinym*, 168. Armenia's would take place Oct. 20–29, 1939, with 550 participants. The Spendiarov Opera and Ballet Theater performed Spendiarov's opera *Almast*, A. T. Tigranyan's opera *Anush*, and Khachaturyan's ballet *Happiness*. Nevezhin, *Zastol'ia*, 119–20 (citing RGALI, f. 962, op. 21, d. 20, l. 70; d. 1, l. 11); Chegodaeva, *Dva lika vremeni*, 301.

69. The committee had sent the conductor Vasily Tselikovsky (b. 1900) of the Bolshoi to Frunze, the Kyrgyz capital, already in 1936 for the Ten-Day in Moscow (planned for 1938). Ballet master L. I. Lukin, also sent to Frunze, would be imprisoned there as an enemy of the people, but released five days before the much-delayed Ten-Day opened in Moscow on May 25, 1939, with more than 500 participants. Bakhtarov, *Zapiski aktera*, 85–86. A Kyrgyz ensemble performed *Altyn Kys* as well as *Aichurek* (Moon Beauty), the first Kyrgyz opera, co-written by Vladimir Vlasov and Vladimir Feré from Moscow. Ivanov, *Dnevniki*, 28. Nevezhin, *Zastol'ia*, 113–4. Bakhtarov, *Zapiski aktera*, 82. Brusilovsky wrote the Kazakh operas, Bogatryev, the Tajik ones. "The resourceful officials of the committee on Artistic Matters," Jelagin wrote, "even managed to conjure up a Buryat-Mongol opera." Elagin, *Ukroshchenie iskusstv*, 262, 263.

70. Jelagin, *Taming of the Arts*, 232–3.

71. Latyshev, "I eshche odin tost 'vozhdia narodov,'" 141–2; *Sovetskaia kul'tura v rekonstruktivnyi period*, 517–20. Gromov, *Stalin*, 330.

72. Banac, *Diary of Georgi Dimitrov*, 120. See also Sudoplatov, *Special Tasks*, 98–102.

73. Sontag and Beddie, *Nazi-Soviet Relations*, 163 (Ribbentrop to Fabricius, June 27, 1940); Halder, *Halder Diaries*, I: 483–4 (June 25, 1940); Halder, *Kriegstagebuch*, I: 371–3; Gafencu, *Last Days of Europe*, 387–91. Gafencu resigned as foreign minister; Read and Fisher, *Deadly Embrace*, 489 (no citation).

74. Novikov, *Vospominaniia diplomata*, 41; Read and Fisher, *Deadly Embrace*, 488–9 (no citation). The secret protocol (clause 3) of the Pact was ambiguous: "With regard to Southeastern Europe attention is called by the Soviet side to its interest in Bessarabia. The German side declares its complete political disinterestedness in these areas." Sontag and Beddie, *Nazi-Soviet Relations*, 78n34.

75. *Izvestiia* (June 29, 1940) trumpeted "the new victory of the USSR's politics of peace," and called the northern part of Bukovina "a typically Ukrainian province."

76. Fröhlich, *Tagebücher von Joseph Goebbels*, VIII: 196–7 (June 28, 1940). Stalin had even obtained approval for this action from Mussolini, Hitler's ostensible ally, in exchange for recognition of Italian primacy in the Mediterranean. Gorodetsky, *Grand Delusion*, 29 (citing AVP RF, f. 06, op. 2, pap. 20, d. 229, l. 1–6: Molotov-Rosso, June 20, 1940; f. 059, op. 1, pap. 330, d. 2269, l. 84–5: Molotov to Gorelkin, June 27, 1940); Schramm-von Thadden, *Griechenland*, 27. See also Dima, *Bessarabia and Bukovina*, 26.

77. Sontag and Beddie, *Nazi-Soviet Relations*, 158–9 (Ribbentrop to Schulenburg, June 25, 1940), 159–60 (Schulenburg to Ribbentrop, June 25, 1940); 161–2 (Schulenburg to Ribbentrop, June 26, 1940), 163; Rossi, *Deux ans*, 153 n2 (Schulenburg to Ribbentrop, July 17, 1940). Romanian oil production had begun to decline after 1936. Pearton, *Oil and the Romanian State*, 201–3. On July 4, 1940, Moscow asked Tokyo, which had long agreed not to recognize Romania's annexation of Bessarabia, to recognize the Soviet annexation. Elleman, "Secret Soviet-Japanese Agreement," 294 (citing Gaimushō, B100–JR/1).

78. Gafencu, *Last Days of Europe*, 390–2.

79. German occupation authorities in Belgium sought to shutter the Soviet trade mission. Mikoyan urged Stalin and Molotov not to allow that to happen, for "we have unfulfilled orders from Belgium and the Belgian Congo totaling 8,578,000 rubles." Pavlov, *Anastas Mikoian*, 125 (citing RGASPI, f. 84, op. 2, d. 62, l. 39: July 20, 1940).

80. Soviet counterintelligence personnel did not trust even the Communists installed in power there by Moscow, especially in Estonia. Khaustov, "Deiatel'nost' organov," 306–7 (TsA FSB, f. 8os, op. 1, d. 81, l. 2; f. 14os, op. 1, d. 15, l. 201–2). On July 27, 1940, Stalin's "big fleet" program was reined in: ten instead of fifteen battleships, eight instead of sixteen battle cruisers, even as two small aircraft carriers for the Pacific Fleet were added. Hauner, "Stalin's Big-Fleet Program"; Rohwer and Monakov, *Stalin's Ocean-Going Fleet*, 113.

81. The report reached Stalin the very next day. Naumov, *1941 god*, I: 20–6 (APRF, f. 45, op. 1, d. 435, l. 39–51).

82. Of Chamberlain and the Tories, Cripps had publicly written, "I am convinced that our reactionaries have no genuine desire to enter into a reciprocal agreement with Russia, but rather wish to use Russia for our own purposes so that by embroiling Russia with Germany they may save their own skins." *Tribune*, March 24, 1939.

83. Gorodetsky, *Mission to Moscow*, 42–3.

84. Maiskii, *Dnevnik diplomata*, II/i: 197–99; Jones, *Lloyd George*, 247–8; Rudman, *Lloyd George*. Lloyd George had met Hitler in Sept. 1936, gushing that the Nazi desired friendship with the British people, had "achieved a marvelous transformation in the spirit of the [German] people, and was the greatest German of the age, the George Washington of Germany—the man who won for his country independence from all her oppressors." He even concluded that "the establishment of a German hegemony in Europe, which was the aim and dream of the old pre-war militarism, is not even on the horizon of Nazism." "I Talked to Hitler," *Daily Express* [London], Nov. 17, 1936; Jones, *Diary with Letters*, 269.

85. Hanak, "Sir Stafford Cripps"; Gorodetsky, *Mission to Moscow*; Clarke, *Cripps Version*, 183–241.

86. "I am sorry for Sir S. Cripps, who is now entering the humiliating phase which all British negotiators in Moscow have to go through when they are simply kept waiting on the doormat until such time as the Soviet Government considers it desirable, as part of their policy of playing off one Power against the other to take notice," a perceptive foreign office official in London observed on June 23, 1940. "Stalin hopes to be able to counter any German browbeating and nagging by pointing to Sir S. Cripps on the doormat, threatening to have him in and start talking with him instead of the German Ambassador." Hanak, "Sir Stafford Cripps," 59 (citing TNA, FO 371/24844 5853: Sir Orme Sargent).

87. The logbooks for Stalin's office for July 1 list only Molotov, 5:35 p.m. until 6:25 p.m.,

but also note "last ones departed at 9:40 p.m." It is likely that Molotov left to retrieve Cripps, who noted that the meeting commenced at 6:30 p.m., and returned with Cripps, but neither was recorded in the logbooks. *Na prieme*, 305. Cripps had handed Molotov the letter from Churchill at 5:00 p.m., according to the Soviet translator-notetaker Pavlov: *DVP SSSR*, XXIII/i: 399 (AVP RF, f. 06, op. 2, pap. 10, d. 100, l. 1–2).

88. For the Soviet transcript of Cripps's July 1, 1940, conversation with Stalin, see "Priem angliiskogo posla S. Krippsa," *Diplomaticheskii vestnik* (Moscow, 1993), 74–7, reprinted in *Sochineniia*, XVIII: 190–7, and in *DVP SSSR*, XXXIII/i: 394–9 (APRF, f. 45, op. 1, d. 278, l. 4–11). For the British version, see Gorodetsky, *Mission to Moscow*, 52 (citing PRO, FO 371/24846, f. 10, N 6526/30/38: Cripps to the Foreign Office, July 16, 1940); and Clarke, *Cripps Version*, 192.

89. Gorodetsky, *Grand Delusion*, 19–22; Gorodetsky, *Stafford Cripps in Moscow*, 5–5; Gorodetsky, *Mission to Moscow*, 60. For Churchill's message to Stalin: Woodward, *British Foreign Policy*, I: 466–7. British embassy staff concluded that "nothing of importance emerged from this interview" with Stalin. Clarke, *Cripps Version*, 192 (citing FO 371/29464, f. 128).

90. Gorodetsky, *Grand Delusion*, 19–22. Maisky was convinced the foreign office was sabotaging Cripps. Maiskii, *Dnevnik diplomata*, II/i: 211–3 (July 1, 1940). Churchill later sought to scapegoat Cripps, but Gorodetsky, *Mission to Moscow*, 116–22. Still, there was some truth to Churchill's remark concerning the Labourite Cripps that "we did not at that time realise that Soviet Communists [read: Stalin] hate extreme Left Wing politicians even more than they do Tories and Liberals." Churchill, *Second World War*, II: 118.

91. Paxton, *Vichy France*, 43; Lukacs, *Duel*, 160–5. Maisky also claimed to have been received by Churchill at 10 Downing Street on July 3. Maisky, *Memoirs of a Soviet Ambassador*, 96–100.

92. "The 'Vienna to Versailles' period has run its course," wrote the Polish-born British historian Lewis Namier in Feb. 1940. "The first task is to save Europe from the Nazi onslaught—a difficult task; but even greater will be the work of resetting a morally and materially bankrupt world on a new basis." Namier, "From Vienna to Versailles," 17–8.

93. On the Baltics as a sticking point for Britain, see Henderson, *Failure of a Mission*, 251.

94. A corrective, in domestic political terms, to those who see a gulf between the two Conservatives, Churchill and Chamberlain, can be found in Lawlor, *Churchill and the Politics of War*, 88–111.

95. "Russia and the West," *The Economist*, July 27, 1940: 113.

96. Lukacs, *Duel*, 72–7, 184–6, 207–10; Maiskii, *Dnevnik diplomata*, II/i (Dec. 29, 1940: Lloyd George surmise).

97. Amid rumors of a Soviet-British rapprochement, Schulenburg reported that Stalin remained loyal to Berlin and only wanted some tin and rubber from Britain. Sontag and Beddie, *Nazi-Soviet Relations*, 142–3.

98. Gorodetsky, *Grand Delusion*, 38 (citing APRF, f. 45, op. 1, d. 435, l. 39–51: Proskurov to Stalin, June 4, 1940).

99. *DVP SSSR*, XXIII/i: 399 (AVP RF, f. 059, op. 1, pap. 326, d. 2238, l. 149–51: July 13, 1940); *DGFP*, series D, X: 207–8 (Schulenburg to Ribbentrop, July 13,1940); Sontag and Beddie, *Nazi-Soviet Relations*, 166–8; Teske, *General Ernst Köstring*, 258–60.

100. Back in Feb. 1940, German violations of Soviet airspace had drawn fire, and the

intruders turned tail. On March 17, thirty-two German fighters and bombers entered Soviet airspace on the path to Moscow, and again Soviet border guards opened fire; one German plane was hit and crashed. On March 29, Beria, following Stalin's instructions, sent a directive to the border guards: no opening fire; airspace violations were merely to be registered. On April 5, 1940, came a further prohibition against the use of firearms anywhere on the frontier (with the inflow of diversionists, the order was sometimes ignored). A June 10, 1940, border convention specified that any plane crossing the border *accidentally* was to be returned. *Pogranichnye voiska SSSR, 1939–iiun' 1941*, 292; Sechkin, *Granitsa i voina*, 53–5 (citing TsAPV, f. 14, op. 224, d. 110, l. 1, 17, 21).

101. Halder, *Halder Diaries*, I: 490 (July 3, 1940); Halder, *Kriegstagebuch*, II: 6-7.

102. This was before, it turned out, secret feasibility studies had even been completed by the Wehrmacht. Alt, "Die Wehrmacht im Kalkül Stalins," 107–9; Glantz, *Stumbling Colossus*, 90–2.

103. Golovanov, *Zapiski komanduiushchego ADD*, 299. In the 1920s, Shaposhnikov, along with the Voroshilovs and Mikoyans, had used the dacha Zubalovo-2 when Stalin and his wife Nadzezhda used the dacha Zubalovo-4 next door. Alliluyeva, *Twenty Letters*, 27.

104. Zolotarev, *Russkii arkhiv: Velikaia otechestvennaia*, XVIII (VII/i): 86 (RGVA, f. 40442, op. 2, d. 170, l. 112).

105. A. M. Vasilevskii, "Nakanune voiny," 5–8 (citing TsAMO, f. 16, op. 2951, d. 239, l. 1–37, l. 197–244: Sept. 18, 1940), (d. 242, l. 84–90: Oct. 5), d. 239, l. 245–77 (not later than Dec.).

106. Pavlov, *Anastas Mikoian*, 125 (citing RGASPI, f. 84, op. 1, d. 15, l. 82).

107. *Ogonek*, Sept. 1940, Jan. 1941.

108. Woodward, *British Foreign Policy*, I: 487–500. See also Weinberg, *World at Arms*, 164. "Cripps argues that we must give everything—recognition, gold, ships and trust to the Russians," Cadogan wrote in his diary (Aug. 17, 1940): "This is simply silly . . . Extraordinary how we go on kidding ourselves. Russian policy will change exactly when and if they think it will suit them. And if they do think that, it won't matter whether we've kicked Maisky in the stomach. Contrariwise, we could give Maisky the Garter and it wouldn't make a penn'orth of difference." Dilks, *Diaries of Sir Alexander Cadogan*, 321.

109. On July 9, 1940, Pavel Fitin, head of NKVD intelligence, reported that "the former King Edward together with his wife, Simpson, are currently in Madrid, whence they maintain contacts with Hitler. Edward is conducting negotiations with Hitler on the question of forming a new English government and the conclusion of a peace with Germany on the condition of a military alliance against the USSR." This could well have been disinformation from MI6 to push Moscow into talks with London. Shirokorad, *Velikii antrakt*, 99. See also Varga, "Mezhdunarodnoe polozhenie," 15–6.

110. "Vansittart spoke eloquently and at length about the misunderstanding and underestimation of the English character abroad," Maisky would record in his diary (Dec. 12, 1940). "It has been so ever since time immemorial. Napoleon, Bismarck, the Kaiser, and now Hitler, Ribbentrop and Mussolini—they were all grossly mistaken in fancying the English to be a 'nation of shopkeepers,' 'degenerate gentlemen,' 'depraved plutocrats,' etc., who cannot and will not fight whatever the circumstances. A profound mistake." Maiskii, *Dnevnik diplomata*, II/I: 305–6; Gorodetsky, *Maisky Diaries*, 324. On British arms exports, see Edgerton, *Britain's War Machine*.

111. Golubev, "*Esli mir obrushitsia na nashu Respubliku*," 174–5. All propaganda outlets, from TASS on down, continued to trumpet the Soviet pursuit of "peace." Golubev et al., *Rossiia i zapad*, 76 (citing RGASPI, f. 17, op. 125, d. 57, l. 59–74).

112. Zhukov later stated that "the only one in Stalin's inner circle, in my memory and in my presence, who voiced another point of view about the possibility of a German attack was Zhdanov. He consistently spoke very sharply about the Germans and insisted that Hitler could not be trusted in anything." But Zhdanov distrusted the British no less. Simonov, "Zametki," 49. A table of Stalin's inner circle visitors appears in Khlevniuk, *Politbiuro*, 290. Zhdanov had observed to the Leningrad party in spring 1940 that for the USSR, "it is more pleasant, useful, and valuable to have alongside us not anti-Soviet Anglo-French allies, who harbor the intention of attacking either Germany or Leningrad . . . [but] a country that is in friendly relations with us"—i.e., Germany. Nevezhin, "Sovetskaia politika," 26.

113. "'He's a thoroughly likeable person,' I remember thinking as we sat there, and thinking it in astonishment," Lyons had recalled of the conversation in 1930. "'Are you a dictator?' Stalin smiled, implying that the question was on the preposterous side. 'No,' he said slowly, 'I am no dictator.'" Lyons, *Stalin*, 196, 200, 203; Lyons, *Assignment in Utopia*, 387. Waldemar Gurian rightly noted of Lyons's book that "the most valuable parts are based upon Souvarine's monumental study of Stalin." *Review of Politics* 2/4 (1940): 506–8. Souvarine's work had been translated into English the year before.

114. Lyons, *Stalin*, 278, 291–2.

115. Gregory and Harrison, "Allocation under Dictatorship."

116. Osokina, *Za fasadom*, 206–18; Khanin, *Ekonomicheskaia istoriia Rossii*, I: 29. Harvests had stabilized (at overreported levels), and state procurements were high, but grain exports and their revenues had declined. In 1940 the Soviet state procured 33.8 million tons of grain and exported 1.2 million, earning the hard currency equivalent of 51.2 million rubles, compared with 26 million tons and exports of 2.1 million, earning 48.8 million gold rubles, in 1937. *Vneshniaia torgovlia SSSR, 1918–1966*, 20–1.

117. Pykhov, *Ekononomika*, 12. Annual per capita consumption of *absolute* alcohol was estimated at 0.6 gallon (2.24 liters) in 1940, and that was excluding brandy, champagne, fruit and berry wines, and imports. Prot'ko, *V bor'be za trezvost'*, 129.

118. The police labeled them "black commodity exchanges" and noted their shadowy existence in nineteen cities, but also that some instituted an arbitration panel to resolve disputes, and bribed investigative officials to avert their cases. Those involved often legally worked as plenipotentiaries tasked with pushing along fulfillment of the official orders for state companies. Rittersporn, *Anguish*, 225 (citing GARF, f. 9415, op. 5, d. 87, l. 8–14, 18, 20ob.).

119. Rittersporn, *Anguish*, 220 (citing GARF, f. 8131, op. 37, d. 242, l. 103–4).

120. Siegelbaum, *Stakhanovism and the Politics of Productivity*, 280; Filtzer, *Soviet Workers*.

121. *Pravda*, June 26, 1940; Filtzer, *Soviet Workers*, 233–53. Back at a meeting on June 19, 1940, Stalin had explained that workers in capitalist countries worked ten to twelve hours, and that the Bolsheviks had "understood the economy poorly" when introducing the seven-hour workday in 1927. The new labor law restored the eight-hour workday (without additional pay). He partly blamed

indiscipline and turnover on Soviet trade unions ("not a school of communism, but a school of self-seekers"). Malyshev, "Dnevnik narkoma," 112 (June 19, 1940); Khlevniuk, "26 iiunia 1940 goda," 89.

122. "Vot gde Pravda, Nikita Sergeevich!,"17.

123. Solomon, Soviet Criminal Justice, 300–1, 327; Rittersporn, Anguish, 233 (citing RGASPI, f. 17, op. 88, d. 550, l. 922–3, 101–3; GARF, f. 8131, op. 37, d. 137, l. 53–4; f. 9415, op. 5, d. 205, l. 5).

124. Filtzer, Soviet Workers, 239. Some managers were demoted or demonstratively arrested for failing to apply the draconian law, but job turnover and absenteeism persisted. "O kontrole nad provedeniem v zhizn' ukaza presidiuma verkhovnogo soveta SSSR ot 26 iiunia 1940," RGASPI, f. 17, op. 2, d. 676, l. 41–42ob.

125. Khlevniuk, "26 iiunia 1940 goda." See also Markevich and Sokolov, "Magnitka bliz Sadovogo kol'tsa." "We cannot be indifferent to who is joining the working class," Stalin would lament later. "If this goes on in spontaneous fashion, the composition of the working class may be ruined. And correspondingly, the regime as a dictatorship of the working class may be ruined. But at present they latch on to anyone who turns up for a job." Malyshev, "Dnevnik narkoma," 113 (Sept. 26, 1940).

126. Davies and Harris, Stalin's World, 225 (citing RGASPI, f. 558, op. 11, d. 1124, l. 46–7).

127. Das deutsche Reich und der Zweite Weltkrieg, II: 368–74.

128. Hillgruber, Hitlers Strategie, 168.

129. Trial of the Major War Criminals, XXXIV: 277 (Raeder for Assmann, Jan. 30, 1944).

130. Churchill, Second World War, II: 200 (letter to Smuts).

131. Hillgruber, Hitlers Strategie; Martin, Friedensinitiativen und Machtpolitik.

132. Raeder explained on July 11 that "in her weakened state, Britain will seek the support of the United States, in whose interests it is to preserve England as a powerful European state. This will automatically make the United States Germany's enemy. The two Anglo-Saxon powers will retain or rebuild their maritime resources in order to defend their empire and will thus become the next natural enemies of Germany to be dealt with." The next day Hitler ordered redirection of armaments investment to the Luftwaffe and the navy, with highest priority to U-boats. None of that would be achieved quickly. On July 13, Hitler convened a military conference at the Berghof. "He sees the answer (as we do) in Britain's hopes on Russia," General Halder wrote in his diary. Hillgruber, Hitlers Strategie, 147 (citing Kriegstagebuch der Seekriegsleitung, Teil A, July 11, 1940); Tooze, Wages of Destruction, 394 (citing BAMA RW19/164; and IWM EDS al 1492, Chef Wi Rue Amt, Aug. 20, 1940, Aktennotiz); Halder, Halder Diaries, I: 504–6 (July 13, 1940); Halder, Kriegstagebuch, II: 19–22.

133. Shirer, Berlin Diary, 355–6.

134. Churchill, Second World War, II: 230–1. Ciano, who met with Ribbentrop that day before the speech, recorded it as "a last appeal to Great Britain." The next day, he met with Hitler and recorded: "He would like an understanding with Great Britain. He knows that war with the English will be hard and bloody, and knows also that people everywhere today are averse to blood." Gibson, Ciano Diaries, 277 (July 19, 20, 1940).

135. "Telegramma I. F. Dergacheva I. I. Proskurovu," 220 (June 6, 1940).

136. Dietrich, The Hitler I Knew, 124–5; Kershaw, Hitler: 1936–1945, 306–7; Weinberg,

Germany and the Soviet Union, 107–8; Naumov, 1941 god, I: 91 (TsAMO, f. 23, op. 22434, d. 4, l. 261: "Meteor," July 9, 1940).

137. Gavrilov, Voennaia razvedka informiruet, 440–1 (RGVA, f. 33987, op. 3, d. 1305, l. 438s), 443–5 (TsAMO, f. 23, op. 9171, d. 4, l. 61–9: July 20, 1940).

138. Gavrilov, Voennaia razvedka informiruet, 442 (RGVA, f. 29, op. 35, d. 98, l. 11ss–12ss: July 16, 1940).

139. Fuehrer Conferences, 1940, I: 81; Wheatley, Operation Sea Lion, 43 (quoting naval staff diary, July 21, 1940).

140. Halder, as a result of hearing from Brauchitsch about the July 21 meeting, noted in his diary: "reasons for continuance of war by Britain: 1) Hope for a change in America . . . 2) Puts hope in Russia." He added that "crossing the channel appears very hazardous to the Führer. On that account, invasion is to be undertaken only if no other means is left to come to terms with Britain. . . . Stalin is flirting with Britain to keep her in the war and tie us down, with a view to gain time and take what he wants. . . . Our attention must be turned to tackling the Russian problem and prepare planning." Halder, Halder Diaries, I: 515–8 (July 22, 1940), I: 519 (July 24, 1940); Halder, Kriegstagebuch, II: 30–4, 35–6.

141. By fall 1940, this would take the form of Germany declaring Japan's "preeminence" in East Asia. Gavrilov, Voennaia razvedka informiruet, 396 (TsAMO, f. 23, op. 22425, d. 3, l. 668).

142. Van Crefeld, Hitler's Strategy, 28; DGFP, series D, VIII: 631–3. Jodl's original memorandum on the peripheral strategy dated to Jan. 1940. By the end of June, with France defeated, he fleshed it out. "England's will must be broken," he wrote, via "a) Warfare against the British isles. b) Extension of the war to the periphery." Trial of the Major War Criminals, XXVII: 301. See also Warlimont, Inside Hitler's Headquarters, 109–10.

143. Halder, Kriegstagebuch, II: 30–4.

144. Kershaw, Hitler: 1936–1945, 294–337 (at 306).

145. Warlimont, Inside Hitler's Headquarters, 112.

146. Leach, German Strategy, 63.

147. Halder noted in his diary: "Russia's aspirations to the Straits and in the direction of the Persian Gulf need not bother us. On the Balkans, which falls within our economic sphere of interest, we could keep out of each other's way. . . . We could deliver the British a decisive blow in the Mediterranean, shoulder them away from Asia, help the Italians in building their Mediterranean empire and, with the aid of Russia, consolidate the Reich which we have created in Western and Northern Europe. That much accomplished, we could confidently face war with Britain for years." Brauchitsch agreed. Halder, Halder Diaries, I: 527–30 (July 30, 1940); Halder, Kriegstagebuch, II: 46 (July 30, 1940); Leach, German Strategy, 60–71). Halder as well as Jodl could see that the navy was proposing a force inadequate to an invasion of Britain. Halder, Halder Diaries, I: 523–4 (July 28), I: 527–30 (July 30); Halder, Kriegstagebuch, II: 39–40, 43–6.

148. Attendees were Hitler, Keitel, Jodl, Raeder, Brauchitsch, Halder, and Puttkamer (naval adjutant at Hitler's headquarters). The Luftwaffe was not represented.

149. This represented a change: from "prepare a landing" (July 16) to "prepare the ground" for a landing. Weinberg, Germany and the Soviet Union, 106–7; Halder, Halder Diaries, I: 510–2 (July 19, 1940); Halder, Kriegstagebuch, II: 26–8.

150. Halder, Kriegstagebuch, II: 47–8 (July 31, 1940); Halder, Halder Diaries, I: 530–4. Fabry

quotes a letter (Oct. 5, 1954) from Halder to the historian Hillgruber stating that neither Halder nor Brauchitsch had understood the July 31, 1940, conference as an "irrevocable decision" to invade the USSR, only as the "start gun for foreseeable possibilities." Fabry, Der Hitler-Stalin Pakt, 498n272.

151. Keitel ordered planning for production of armaments for 180 divisions on Aug. 17; within four days planning was under way for 200 divisions. Weinberg, Germany and the Soviet Union, 119.

152. Weinberg, Germany and the Soviet Union, 120.

153. Weinberg, Germany and the Soviet Union, 109–17; Warlimont, Inside Hitler's Headquarters, 111–4; DGFP, series D, X: 321; Vishlev, Nakanune, 11.

154. Kershaw, Hitler: 1936–1945, 305–6.

155. Pravda, Aug. 11, 1940; Paletskis, V dvukh mirakh, 346.

156. Gavrilov, Voennaia razvedka informiruet, 451–4 (RGVA, f. 33988, op. 4, d. 35, l. 134ss–135ss, 138ss–141ss).

157. Leach, German Strategy, 80 (citing Bundesarchiv/Militärarchiv N 22/7, Fedor von Bock, "Tagebuchnotizen," Aug. 18, 1940). The Germans also now had confiscated French oil stocks.

158. Pavlov, Anastas Mikoian, 121–2 (citing RGASPI, f. 84, op. 1, d. 150, l. 1–5).

159. RGASPI, f. 82, op. 2, d. 1592, l. 4–7. In July 1940, after the two sides had hashed out a new demarcation of the Mongolia-Manchukuo frontier, the Japanese had proposed a neutrality pact, but Molotov told Ambassador Tōgō that "the Japanese had committed serious violations, and as a result we cannot consider the [1905] Portsmouth Treaty to be valid in its entirety." Molotov sought to terminate Japanese oil and coal concessions on Soviet-controlled Northern Sakhalin, and reclaim Southern Sakhalin and the Kuril Islands, restoring Russia's pre-1905 position in the Far East. After Nov. 1940, the Japanese would propose a bilateral nonaggression pact, but Molotov remained adamant. Another five months of negotiations would ensue. Presseisen, Germany and Japan, 273–7.

160. Volkogonov, Trotsky, 454–69.

161. Khaustov et al., Lubianka: Stalin i VChK, 182–4. Stalin further inserted into the Pravda report of Trotsky's demise a hint of the biblical Cain and a reference to the old saw of Trotsky as Judas, making him not just a supposed murderer (à la Cain) but a traitor. Maksimenkov, Bol'shaia tsenzura, 521–4 (RGASPI, f. 558, op. 11, d. 1124, l. 63–6). Stalin had also edited the Pravda editorial about the Soviet-Finnish Friendship Agreement (Dec. 4, 1939) and the Izvestiia editorial (Oct. 9, 1939) about a Reichstag speech by Hitler. Maksimenkov, Bol'shaia tsenzura, 516–21 (citing RGASPI, f. 558, op. 11, d. 1123, l. 41–51), 53– (d. 1124, l. 32–7).

162. Volkogonov, Stalin: Triumph and Tragedy, 254–9.

163. Biulleten' oppozitsii, no. 81 (1940): 5; Volkogonov, Trotsky, 342–4. "Whatever the circumstances of my death," Trotsky had written in his will, "I will die with unshakeable faith in a Communist future." Trotskii, Dnevniki i pis'ma, 167–8. On July 17, 1940, just weeks before his murder, Trotsky's personal archive was shipped to the United States by train, arriving at Harvard University. Trotsky, Stalin, rev. ed., 863.

164. Deutscher, Prophet Outcast, 419–21.

165. Langer, Undeclared War, 129–46.

166. Degras, Soviet Documents on Foreign Policy, III: 470–4 (Sept. 26, 1940); McMurry, Deutschland und die Sowjetunion, 214.

167. Watts, Romanian Cassandra, 217.

168. Deletant, Hitler's Forgotten Ally, 48–55.

169. Golubev et al., *Rossiia i zapad*, 198 (citing RGALI, f. 1038, op. 1, d. 2077, l. 56: May 7, 1940). Other coveted dachas also changed hands, sometimes in unorthodox fashion. Sartakova, "Nash pisatel'skii les," 25; Antipina, *Povsednevnaia zhizn'*, 156–7 (citing RGALI, f. 631, op. 15, d. 457, l. 19).

170. Babichenko, *Pisateli i tsenzory*, 41. Many writers worked at factory clubs or publishing houses and were paid bureaucratic salaries, which in some cases exceeded their honoraria (royalties). Not many could count on reissues of their works, which paid 60 percent of the normal honorarium. Alexei Tolstoy, who had become chairman of the administration for protection of authors' rights, got the latter organization's staff to award him an advance of 83,000 rubles—an act that precipitated a special meeting in Sept. 1940. "His receipt of such an advance cannot in any way be justified," stated Lev Nikulin, a member of the writers' union apparatus. "This is when his average monthly earnings are 9,745 rubles." Tolstoy answered that he had no savings, and that the theatrical season had ended. "I think there is nothing to be surprised about here," he asserted. "Every month I pay 6,000 rubles to my first family." The writers' union decided to sack the functionary who had signed off on the advance. Antipina, *Povsednevnaia zhizn'*, 72–3 (RGALI, f. 631, op. 15, d. 451, l. 80, 85, 99, 4).

171. Antipina, *Povsednevnaia zhizn'*, 20 (citing RGALI, f. 631, op. 15, d. 501, l. 61: July 3, 1940).

172. *Pravda*, Aug. 15, 1940 (unsigned); RGASPI, f. 77, op. 1, d. 907, l. 1–5; Miller, *Soviet Cinema*, 67. The film was based upon a screenplay by Avdeyenko, who was subjected to withering criticism at the meeting. He was expelled from the writers' union and the party, but not arrested.

173. Anderson et al., *Kremlevskii kinoteatr*, 573–604 (RGASPI, f. 558, op. 11, d. 1124, l. 134–45; f. 77, op. 1, d. 907, l. 12–82); Artizov and Naumov, *Vlast'*, 450–5.

174. Anderson et al., *Kremlevskii kinoteatr*, 587–9, 597.

175. Anderson et al., *Kremlevskii kinoteatr*, 599–600 (RGASPI, f. 71, op. 10, d. 127, l. 391, 396).

176. *Na prieme*, 311.

177. Ericson, *Feeding the German Eagle*, 123–6, 134–6.

178. Kershaw, *Fateful Choices*, 69; Ericson, *Feeding the German Eagle*, 143. At the time, the journalist William Shirer remarked upon Hitler's dependency on Stalin: *Berlin Diary*, 173–4.

179. Gavrilov, *Voennaia razvedka informiruet*, 459–62 (TsAMO, f. 23, op. 9181, d. 7, l. 17–23). See also Weinberg, *Germany and the Soviet Union*, 107–8, 119; *Trial of the Major War Criminals*, VII: 263 (Brauchitsch); Deitrich, *The Hitler I Knew*, 124–5; and Kershaw, *Hitler: 1936–1945*, 306–7. Altogether, between 1937 and 1940, five military intelligence chiefs had been arrested: Uritsky, Berzin, Nikonov, Gendin, and Alexander G. Orlov; Proskurov would be arrested in 1941. Golikov (b. 1900), a former member of the flying "Red Eagles" of the civil war, had been a commander in the 1939 Polish campaign and Finnish Winter War; in summer 1940 he commanded the Sixth Army, based in Lvov. He had never worked in military intelligence before; no one had spoken with him prior to the announcement of his appointment on July 11, 1940. Gavrilov, *Voennaia razvedka informiruet*, 718 (RGVA, f. 4, op. 19, d. 71, l. 278–9), 719 (op. 15a, d. 496, l. 7: July 26, 1940). Military intelligence—officially the fifth department of the Red Army—was formally transferred to the army general staff, but Stalin had Golikov

report directly to him. In 1939–1940, 326 new people were hired, the majority of whom did not know foreign languages and had little or no experience of the outside world. Lota, *"Alta" protiv "Barbarossy,"* 57.

180. *DVP SSSR*, XXIII/i: 546–7 (AVP RF, f. 06, op. 2, pap. 15, d. 156, l. 96–8), 552–3 (AVP RF, f. 059, op. 1, pap. 316, d. 2176, l. 180), 553–4 (l. 185–7).

181. *Izvestiia*, Sept. 3, 1940.

182. Fesiun, *Delo Rikharda Zorge*, 109 (Aug. 17, 1940); Lota, *Sekretnyi front*, 155–6. See also Gavrilov, *Voennaia razvedka informiruet*, 443–5 (TsAMO, f. 23, op. 9171, d. 4, l. 61–9: July 20, 1940).

183. Naumov, *1941 god*, I: 216–7; Schramm, *Kriegstagebuch des Oberkommando*, I: 973.

184. *Fuehrer Conferences*, 1940, II: 17–21, 22–3.

185. Cherkasov, *IMEMO*, 31–3 (RGASPI, f. 558, op. 11, d. 716, l. 26: facsimile of Stalin's letter). Stalin was encouraging designs for bombers with payloads weighing a ton that could travel 2,000 miles, even 3,000, while the distance from Minsk to Berlin was all of 600 miles, and Vladivostok to Tokyo, 750. These weapons made sense only in terms of attacking far-off British colonies, and possibly the United States.

186. Bismarck, *Mysli i vospominaniia*. Mikhail Gefter, a professional historian who came upon Stalin's pencil edits, deemed them "reasonable editing, pointing to quite a good taste and an understanding of history." Gefter, *Iz etikh i tekh let*, 261–2. The Central Committee propaganda department was raised at this time to a directorate.

187. Malyshev, "Dnevnik narkoma," 113; *Na prieme*, 312 (Malyshev wrongly dates it to Sept. 21).

188. Sontag and Beddie, *Nazi-Soviet Relations*, 188–9 (Ribbentrop to Schulenburg, Sept. 16, 1940), 198–9 (Tippelskirch to Ribbentrop, Sept. 26, 1940), 202 (text of German-Finnish diplomatic agreement on transit of German troops and equipment: Sept. 22, 1940), 201–2 (Ribbentrop to Tippelskirch, Oct. 2), 203–4 (Tippelskirch to Ribbentrop, Oct. 4).

189. Khaustov, "Deiatel'nost' organov," 247 (TsA FSB, f. 3, op. 5, d. 67, l. 28).

190. Iklé, *German-Japanese Relations*, 181–2 (citing *International Military Tribunal for the Far East, Documents Presented in Evidence*, exhibit 1215: privy council, Sept. 26, 1940); Chihiro, "Tripartite Pact 1939–1940," and Ikuhiko, "Japanese-Soviet Confrontation," 191–257.

191. Hosoya Chihiro, "The Tripartite Pact 1939–1940," "Japanese-Soviet Confrontation," 256 (citing Japanese Foreign Ministry archives, "Nichi-Doku-I sangoku jōyaku," 228). In 1940, Japan celebrated the 2,600th anniversary of its empire, traced to mythical origins. Ruoff, *Imperial Japan*.

192. Trefousse, *Germany and American Neutrality*, 69.

193. Langer and Gleason, *Challenge to Isolation*, 24–5. "There is one common element in the ideology of Germany, Italy and the Soviet Union: opposition to the capitalist democracies of the West." Fest, *Hitler*, 589–90.

194. Sontag and Beddie, *Nazi-Soviet Relations*, 197–9 (Tippelskirch to Ribbentrop, Sept. 26, 1940).

195. Weinberg, *Germany and the Soviet Union*, 136, citing NG–3074: 1–2 (memorandum).

196. Banac, *Diary of Georgi Dimitrov*, 129. Moscow did not know but on that very day—the two-year anniversary of the German-Soviet Treaty of Friendship and the Border—Hitler issued a directive to ramp up military outlays. Thomas, *Geschichte*, 432; Leach, *German Strategy*, 72. Stalin had begun

to talk about disbanding the Comintern as early as spring or summer 1940, when the Soviet Union annexed the Baltic states; he would raise the issue again in April 1941. Dallin and Firsov, *Dimitrov and Stalin*. The Comintern would be dissolved in May 1943.

197. Bezymenskii, "Vizit V. M. Molotova v Berlin," 126–7 (citing APRF, f. 56, op. 1, d. 1161, l. 3). Molotov also received a clarification on Sept. 26, 1940, from Tippelskirch. *DVP SSSR*, XXIII/i: 627–30 (AVP RF, f. 059, op. 1, p. 328, d. 2253, l. 144).

198. Elleman, *International Competition*, 131 (citing Gaimushō, file B100–JR/1, 2.1.00–23).

199. Gavrilov, *Voennaia razvedka informiruet*, 466–70 (Sept. 1940), 474–5 (RGVA, f. 29, op. 35, d. 98, l. 149ss–152ss: Oct. 2, 1940); Iampol'skii et al., *Organy*, I/i: 245–6 (TsA FSK). See also van Crefeld, *Hitler's Strategy*, 69–72; Gorodetsky, *Grand Delusion*, 41. Germany was also moving its troops through Finland to other locations, such as Norway.

200. Gafencu, *Last Days of Europe*, 133–6.

201. *DGFP*, series D, IX: 40–1 (Ribbentrop to embassy in Moscow, March 28, 1940), VIII: 53–4 (Schulenburg reply, March 30). Fabry, *Die Sowjetunion und das Dritte Reich*, 227; *DBFP*, 3rd series, V: 544 (Seeds to Halifax, May 19, 1938); Chuev, *Molotov Remembers*, 145. Ribbentrop sincerely strove to bring about a Hitler-Stalin meeting, "but this came to nothing because Hitler said that Stalin could not leave Russia and he could not leave Germany." Ribbentrop, *Memoirs*, 148; Davidson, *Trial of the Germans*, 162.

202. Muggeridge, *Ciano's Diplomatic Papers*, 402. On May 31, 1940, in light of the German successes in the West against France and Britain, Sorge had offered views on the basis of conversations with Germans in Tokyo, including some who had had contact with Ribbentrop. One group, according to Sorge, consisted of "young fascists" who wanted to follow a victory in the West with an immediate settling of scores with the USSR. Another group ("more important people") sought continued peaceful relations with the USSR, given its political, economic, and military superiority over Germany. Of course, Hitler was the decider. Gavrilov, *Voennaia razvedka informiruet*, 433–4 (TsAMO, f. 23, op. 22425, d. 3, l. 359, 357).

203. Below, *Als Hitlers Adjutant*, 244.

204. "Iz istorii Velikoi Otechestvennoi voiny," 200.

205. Berling, *Wspomnienia*, I: 103–13, 168–76; *The Katyń Forest Massacre: Hearings*, 82nd Cong., 2nd Sess., March–April 1952, Part 3: 431–3, 488–90 (Henryk Szymanski), Part 4: 1233–4 (Józef Czapski). There is some discrepancy over the date of the meeting concerning the list; Berling gives Jan. 1941, Czapski and Szymanski, who heard about it, give fall 1940.

206. Kenez, "Picture of the Enemy," 104. Other indications of war preparation included a secret inventory of films compiled in Oct. 1940, which listed some 200 titles, including the "particularly recommended" *Circus* (1936)—seen by more than 40 million Soviet inhabitants—*Chapayev* (1934), and *Lenin in October* (1938), to be relied upon for shoring up morale. Fomin, *Kino na voine*, 60–3. See also Salys, *Films of Grigorii Aleksandrov*, 295 (citing RGASPI, f. 77, op. 1, d. 908: Zhdanov complaints, Sept. 1940).

207. Saraeva-Bondr', *Siluety vremeni*, 199; Aleksandrov, *Epokha i kino*, 220. See the review by Grigory Roshal, "Melodiia i dissonans," *Kino*, 1940, no. 44: 1–3. Alexandrov had seen a Soviet version of the Cinderella story, *Zolushka*, by Viktor Ardov, at the Moscow Satire Theater in 1938. Salys, *Films of Grigorii Aleksandrov*, 281–340.

208. *Pravda,* June 18 and Oct. 31, 1940; RGASPI, f. 558, op. 11, d. 1124, l. 147–8 (letter to Bolshakov, Oct. 11, 1940), reprinted in *Sochineniia,* XVIII: 199–204, 205. See also Artizov and Naumov, *Vlast',* 460–1 (RGASPI, f. 71, op. 10, d. 127, l. 399–400).

209. Gorodetsky, *Grand Delusion,* 57 (citing Gafencu, *Misiune la Moscova,* raport 2384, 69–78: Gafencu to Sturdza, Sept. 21, 1940); Gibson, *Ciano Diaries,* 299–303 (Oct. 8, 12, 14, and 22, 1940).

210. *Pravda,* Oct. 16, 1940.

211. *New York Times,* Oct. 16, 1940.

212. It is said that Stalin disliked *The Great Dictator.* In any case, it was never released in the USSR. Konchalovsky, *Inner Circle,* 27.

213. *DVP SSSR,* XXIII/i: 674–6 (APRF, f. 3, op. 64, d. 341, l. 80–4: Vyshinsky); Dilks, *Diaries of Sir Alexander Cadogan,* 331 (brackets).

214. *DVP SSSR,* XXIII/i: 677–9 (AVP RF, f. 06, op. 2, pap. 3, d. 17, l. 50–5).

215. *DGFP,* series D, XI: 291–7; Halder, *Kriegstagebuch,* II: 148 (Oct. 15, 1940); Halder, *Halder Diaries,* I: 622–6; Fabry, *Der Hitler-Stalin Pakt,* 343–5.

216. *DGFP,* series D, XI: 291–7 (Ribbentrop to Stalin, Oct. 13, 1940); Sontag and Beddie, *Nazi-Soviet Relations,* 207–16; Naumov, *1941 god,* I: 302–5 (AVP RF, f. 06, op. 2, pap. 15, d. 157, l. 47–51), 305–10 (Russian version, APRF, f. 45, op. 1., d. 296, l. 9–20), 317–8 (Stalin's reply, APRF, f. 3, op. 64, d. 675, l. 1); "'Ia pochtu za udovol'stvie vnov' priekhat' v Moskvu': obmen poslaniiami mezhdu I. Ribbentropom i I. V. Staliym v oktiabre 1940 g." 21), 141–5 (APRF, f. 45, op. 1, d. 296, l. 31–3: Ribbentrop, Oct. 21); *DVP SSSR,* XXIII/i: 680–2 (AVP RF, f. 06, op. 2, pap. 15, d. 1576, l. 47–51: Schulenburg-Molotov conversation); Degras, *Soviet Documents on Foreign Policy,* III: 474–5; Hilger and Mayer, *Incompatible Allies,* 321; Carr, *Poland to Pearl Harbor,* 120.

217. *DGFP,* series D, XI: 508–10. Ribbentrop later quoted Hitler to the effect that "Ribbentrop, we have achieved many things together; perhaps we shall also pull this one off together." Ribbentrop, *Memoirs,* 151.

218. Santa Olalla, at Himmler's invitation, would lay plans for joint study of Visigoth tombs in Spain. Treglown, *Franco's Crypt,* 246–7.

219. Van Crefeld, *Hitler's Strategy,* 41. See also Halder, *Kriegstagebuch,* II: 124 (Aug. 3, 1940); Halder, *Halder Diaries,* I: 538.

220. Preston, *Franco,* 392–400; *DGFP,* series D, IX: 311. The account of Hendaye by Paul Schmidt, Hitler's interpreter, is fraudulent: Schmidt was not there. Pike, "Franco and the Axis Stigma," 377–9.

221. The Germans were put off by the Guardists' indiscipline. Deletant, *Hitler's Forgotten Ally,* 59–63. Germany had inserted economic (not military) advisers into the Romanian state in spring 1939.

222. Halder, *Kriegstagebuch,* II: 154 (Oct. 29, 1940), 158 (Nov. 1, 1940); Halder, *Halder Diaries,* I: 641–2, 669–71; *Fuehrer Conferences,* 1940, II: 32–6; Schmidt, *Hitler's Interpreter,* 185–8, 193–9; van Crefeld, *Hitler's Strategy,* 47 (citing German Foreign Ministry 1247/337515: H. von Etzdorf note, Oct. 28); Corvaja, *Hitler and Mussolini,* 131–41; Pons, *Stalin and the Inevitable War,* 199.

223. Corvaja, *Hitler and Mussolini,* 137 (citing Ciano).

224. Schmidt, *Statist,* 516–7.

225. Schramm, *Kriegstagebuch der Oberkommando,* I: 148–9 (Nov. 1, 1940), 150–1 (Nov. 4, 1941), 152, 157, 158 (Nov. 7, 1940), 160 (Nov. 8, 1940), 182 (Nov. 19, 1940); Trevor-Roper, *Hitler's War Directives,* 39–43.

226. Halder, *Kriegstagebuch,* II: 163–4 (Nov. 4, 1940); Halder, *Halder Diaries,* I: 672–5.

227. Seidl, *Die Beziehungen,* 239 (Schulenburg to Ribbentrop, Oct. 19, 1940), 243 (Schulenburg to Dörnberg, Oct. 30), 243–4 (Ribbentrop to Schulenburg, Oct. 31), 244–5 (Schulenburg to Ribbentrop, Nov. 1).

228. Rossi, *Deux ans,* 173n3; Rossi [Tasca], *Russo-German Alliance,* 163.

229. Van Crefeld, *Hitler's Strategy,* 62–5. Germany had become the number-one trading partner with southeastern Europe, accounting for between 30 and 60 percent of each country's trade, paying above world market prices for agricultural goods, preferring the stable, long-term market access, which also did not require hard currency (they used clearing accounts). The Yugoslav and Romanian prime ministers understood this dependence on German markets, and refused to listen to French or British political pitches. Despite their racial condescension, the Germans did not view the Balkans through a Lebensraum prism. Gross, *Export Empire.* On Oct. 25, 1940, NKVD transport secretly reported the construction of border fortifications and a concentration of pontoon bridges on the frontier with Ukraine. Naumov, *1941 god,* I: 324–6.

230. Berezhkov would meet Stalin in 1941. He would claim that in Berlin he observed "the same idolization of the 'leader,' the same mass rallies and parades . . . Very similar, ostentatious architecture, heroic themes depicted in art much like our socialist realism . . . massive ideological brainwashing," but that he did not recognize this at the time (1940). Berezhkov, *At Stalin's Side,* 7, 72.

231. Naumov, *1941 god,* I: 311–4 (AVPRF, f. 06, op. 2, pap. 15, d. 157, l. 55–60), 316–7 (l. 61–2), 326–7 (APRF, f. 3, op. 64, d. 686, l. 120–4). Gorodetsky stresses the Balkan dimension: *Grand Illusion,* 67–75.

232. Bezymenskii, "Vizit V. M. Molotova v Berlin," 125. Stalin, in the company of Molotov, had spent five full hours with the Turkish foreign minister, Şükrü Saraçoğlu, on Oct. 1, 1940, discussing a mutual assistance pact, which Turkey wanted, but only if Ankara was not obliged to act in the event of a Soviet conflict with Britain and France. *DVP SSSR,* XXII/i: 12, 49–51.

233. All this information emanated from the Latvian journalist Berlings. Internally, Nazi circles had discussed how Hitler would try to push Moscow out of Europe and toward a clash with British interests in India. Sipols, *Tainy,* 273–4 (citing *ADAP,* XII/i: 255, XI/i: 212–3).

234. Khaustov, "Deiatel'nost' organov," 248 (TsA FSB, f. 3, op. 7, d. 342, l. 21).

235. Stalin also stated, "We are not prepared for the sort of air war being waged between Germany and England." Banac, *Diary of Georgi Dimitrov,* 131–4 (italics and ellipsis in the original). On Stalin feeling alone, especially with the weight of military matters, see also Khrushchev, *Memoirs,* I: 273. See also Genkina, *Bor'ba za Tsaritsyn;* and Melikov, *Geroicheskaia oborona Tsaritsyna,* which was reissued in 1940.

236. Nevezhin, *Zastol'ia,* 291 (no citation); Nevezhin personal communication.

237. Naumov, *1941 god,* I: 349–51 (APRF, f. 36, op. 1, d. 1161, l. 147–55); Bezymenskii, "Direktivy I. V. Stalina V. M. Molotovu pered poezdkoi." See also "Poezdka Molotova v Berlin v noiabre 1940 g."

238. Ehrenburg, *Post-War Years,* 276–8; Fischer, *Life and Death of Stalin,* 56; Phillips, *Between the Revolution and the West,* 166–7.

239. The rumor had been that Litvinov would be tried as a British-U.S. spy. Vaksberg, *Alexandra Kollontai,* 407; Gnedin, *Katastrofa i votoroe rozhdenie,* 148–51; Vaksberg, *Hôtel Lux,* 154–7.

240. Artizov et al., *Reabilitatsiia: kak eto bylo,* II: 499 (Beria's Aug. 1953 interrogation).

241. Banac, *Diary of Georgi Dimitrov,* 121 (Nov. 7, 1939).

242. Cripps had continued to try to see Molotov and had finally done so on Aug. 7, 1940. But when Cripps had broached the possibility of a British-Soviet nonaggression pact, Molotov made no direct reply. Internally, Cripps continued to urge his own government to each recognize Soviet annexations of the Baltic states. Gorodetsky, *Stafford Cripps in Moscow,* 74–90.

243. Churchill, *Second World War,* I: 353 (Oct. 1, 1939).

244. Halifax wrote to A. V. Alexander, the First Sea Lord at this time: "If there were reason to think that immediate recognition would cause an appreciable change in Soviet policy towards us, I might have felt inclined to recommend a derogation in this case from the general principle that political changes produced during this war and as a consequence of the war situation should not be recognized pending the final peace settlement." Hanak, "Sir Stafford Cripps," 65.

245. Hanak, "Sir Stafford Cripps," 66 (citing TNA, FO 371/29464 1604: Oct. 22, 1940). "I think we have managed to avoid losing this war," confided Harold Nicolson in a private letter of Nov. 8, 1940. "But when I think how on earth we are going to win it, my imagination quails." Overy, *Battle of Britain,* 113, citing Nicolson, *Diaries and Letters,* 126 (to Vita Sackville).

246. Woodward, *British Foreign Policy,* I: 492–4.

247. Solodovnikov, "My byli molodye togda," 209. Solodovnikov deemed the Bolshoi's Yakov Leontyev, who served as impresario at the banquets in the St. George's Hall for the Ten-Days, "a person of tremendous charm, with vast experience, deeply cultured" (207–8).

248. Osborn, *Operation Pike,* 210 (citing Cripps to Distribution B, nos. 985 and 986, Nov. 12, 1940, N7165/40/38 and N7166/40/38, FO 371/24848); Woodward, *British Foreign Policy,* I: 495–6; Hanak, "Sir Stafford Cripps," 66.

249. Primakov, *Ocherki,* III: 329. Berezhkov recalled Amayak Kobulov as "the exact opposite of Bogdan, a repulsive, short, fat, and creepy character. Amayak—a tall, slim, handsome Caucasian, sprouting a well-trimmed little mustache and a shock of black hair, urbane, even charming—was the life of any party." Berezhkov, *At Stalin's Side,* 196.

250. Primakov, *Ocherki,* III: 338–9, 420–1.

251. Beria wrote: "I heard that the leadership of intelligence is dissatisfied with Zakhar's work and has wished its hands of him. Perhaps one should not pay attention to this chatter, but when it concerns responsible comrades with whom I personally maintain contact, such corridor conversations must not take place." Primakov, *Ocherki,* III: 444.

252. Berlings first appeared in Soviet files in Aug. 1940, when Kobulov reported that through the Soviet intelligence operative posing as the TASS correspondent, Ivan Filippov ("the Philosopher"), he had met a young journalist for a Latvian newspaper and proposed paying him a retainer in German marks for secret information. Fitin warned Kobulov that because Berlings had yet to be verified, "we suggest you show reasonable caution in working with him and on no account put him into contact with any operatives of the station." But Kobulov could bypass Fitin and report straight to Merkulov. Vishlev, "Pochemu zhe," 74 (citing Bundesarchiv, Abt. Potsdam: Film 14467, Bl. 25091 ff.); Vishlev, *Nakanune,* 49 (PA AA Bonn: Dienstelle Ribbentrop. UdSSSR-RC, 7/1 (R27168, Bl. 25899–25902),

132. The SS officer Rudolf Likus, who was detailed to the Ribbentrop bureau, recruited and handled Berlings. In 1947, the Soviets would discover as a result of interrogations of the Gestapo officer Siegfried Müller that Berlings had been a plant, passing information that had been reviewed and approved by Hitler personally. Primakov, *Ocherki*, III: 441–51. See also Roewer, *Die Rote Kapelle*, 62.

253. Zamoiskii and Nezhnikov, "U rokovoi cherty."

254. Barros and Gregor, *Double Deception*, 9 (citing German Foreign Ministry Archives, Rudolf Likus, Confidential Report, November 22, 1940, microfilm T120, serial 36, frames 25933, 25938–9).

255. Stephan, *Soviet Far East*, 235.

256. Filippov, *Zapiski*, 142.

257. Schellenberg, *Labyrinth*, 137–8. Schellenberg—Heinrich Himmler's personal aide (1939–1942)—was responsible for security and total surveillance over Molotov's entourage during the Berlin visit.

258. Flannery, *Assignment to Berlin*, 37.

259. Schmidt, *Statist*, chapter 21.

260. Berezhkov, *At Stalin's Side*, 45.

261. Naumov, *1941 god*, I: 356–61 at 357 (APRF, f. 3, op. 64, d. 675, l. 21–30); *DGFP*, series D, XI: 533–41.

262. *DGFP*, series D, XI: 541–9; Schmidt, *Hitler's Interpreter*, 210–1. Schmidt did not speak Russian; he served as notetaker. Before meeting Molotov, recalled another confidant of the Führer, "Hitler totally underestimated him, declaring that he was a cipher, a typical bureaucrat." Baur, *Hitler's Pilot*, 122. The Germans had offered to send Hitler's Condor to pick up Molotov, but the Soviets said their delegation was too large; they took the train.

263. Vasilevskii, *Delo vsei zhizni*, 108–9 (citing Molotov aide I. I. Lapshov).

264. Sontag and Beddie, *Nazi-Soviet Relations*, 226–34 (at 232), and *DVP SSSR*, XXIII/ii: 30–2 (APRF f. 56, op. 1, d. 1161, l. 147–55); Naumov, *1941 god*, I: 361–6 (at 365) (APRF, f. 3, op. 64, d. 675, l. 31–41). See also Schmidt, *Statist*, 520–1.

265. Sontag and Beddie, *Nazi-Soviet Relations*, 224–5; Naumov, *1941 god*, I: 356–61 (APRF, f. 3, op. 64, d. 675, l. 21–30); the German record has also been translated into Russian: Fel'shtinskii, *Oglasheniiu podlezhit*, 251–301. See also Schmidt, *Statist*, 517–26; Chuev, *Molotov Remembers*, 15.

266. Naumov, *1941 god*, I: 384–5 (Politisches Archiv des Auswärtiges Amtes. Bonn, Bestand Dienstelle Ribbentrop, R 27168, bl. 25933, 25934, 25940); Lota, *"Alta" protiv "Barbarossy,"* 235 (no citation).

267. Berlings would pass on a supposed internal German assessment of Molotov's visit to Berlin as marking the onset of "a new era." Primakov, *Ocherki*, IV: 447–8 (interrogation of Müller).

268. Naumov, *1941 god*, I: 369 (AVPRF, f. 59, op. 1, p. 338, d. 2314, l. 11–8). See also Hilger and Meyer, *Incompatible Allies*, 323. On Nov. 12, Molotov had sent Stalin a brief cable after his first meeting with Ribbentrop, a two-hour-plus affair. Stalin replied with a correction of one of Molotov's formulations. Naumov, *1941 god*, I: 366–7 (AVPRF, f. 59, op. 1, p. 338, d. 2314, l. 5–6, 7–9).

269. Naumov, *1941 god*, I: 384 (AVPRF, f. 059, op. 1, p. 338, d. 2314, l. 36). Molotov's talks with Göring: Naumov, *1941 god*, I: 370–3 (APRF, f. 3, op. 64, d. 675, l. 84–92). Ribbentrop and Himmler were present when Göring received Molotov.

270. Eberle and Uhl, *Hitler Book*, 36–7.

271. Ullrich, *Hitler: Ascent*, 386. "I was expecting a thundering Jove in his castle and what I got was a simple, gentle, possibly shy man in his country home," French ambassador Coulondre wrote of Hitler. "I had heard the rough, screaming, threatening, and demanding voice

of the Führer on the radio. Now I became acquainted with a Hitler who had a warm, calm, friendly and understanding voice. Which one is the true Hitler? Or are they both true?"

272. In response to Molotov's cable after the first meeting with Ribbentrop, Vyshinsky had called the Berlin embassy to read a message for Molotov correcting him—eliciting a Molotov apology—for having implied that the 1939 Pact had ceased to be in force ["ischerpan"]. Naumov, *1941 god*, I: 367 (AVP RF, f. 059, op. 1, p. 339, D. 2315, l. 16–7).

273. Schmidt, *Hitler's Interpreter*, 217.

274. Fröhlich, *Tagebücher von Joseph Goebbels*, VIII: 417–8 (Nov. 14, 1940).

275. Sontag and Beddie, *Nazi-Soviet Relations*, 234–47; Naumov, *1941 god*, I: 375–83 (APRF, f. 3, op. 64, d. 675, l. 49–57); *DGFP*, series D, XI: 550–62. Berezhkov writes: "Perhaps more important—and Molotov informed Stalin about this—Hitler was prepared to meet this face-to-face." Berezhkov, *At Stalin's Side*, 48.

276. Schmidt, *Hitler's Interpreter*, 219; *Time*, Nov. 20, 1940; TASS (Nov. 13, 1940), printed in *Izvestiia*, Nov. 14, 1940, and reprinted in Naumov, *1941 god*, I: 392–3.

277. Waddington, "Ribbentrop and the Soviet Union," 21–2.

278. *DGFP*, series D, XI: 533–41; Sontag and Beddie, *Nazi-Soviet Relations*, 247–54.

279. Berezhkov, *S diplomaticheskoi missiei*, 48; Berezhkov, *At Stalin's Side*, 44–9. The line does not appear in the official record made by Pavlov: Naumov, *1941 god*, I: 385–92 (APRF, f. 3, op. 64, d. 675, l. 68–83, 92–3). British air raids deliberately coincided with Molotov's visit to Berlin. Churchill, *Second World War*, II: 586. "How did he put up with you telling him all this?" Molotov recalled Stalin asking of his dealings with Hitler. Chuev, *Molotov Remembers*, 17.

280. Naumov, *1941 god*, I: 394 (AVPRF, f. 059, op. 1, pap. 339, d. 2315, l. 38–9), 393–4 (pap. 33, d. 2314, l. 41–4).

281. *Pravda*, Nov. 15, 1940; Degras, *Soviet Documents on Foreign Policy*, III: 476–7.

282. *Pravda*, Nov. 13, 14, 15, and 16, 1939. See also Werth, *Russia at War*, 106–9.

283. Naumov, *1941 god*, I: 384–5 (Politisches Archiv des Auswärtiges Amtes. Bonn, Bestand Dienstelle Ribbentrop, R 27168, bl. 25933, 25934, 25940); Lota, *"Alta" protiv "Barbarossy,"* 235.

284. Naumov, *1941 god*, I: 508 (TsAMO, f. 23, op. 24119, d. 3, l. 6–7: Jan. 4, 1941); Gorodetsky, *Grand Delusion*, 125.

285. Naumov, *1941 god*, I: 398 (AVPRF, f. 82, op. 23, p. 95, d. 6, l. 141–2).

286. Hilger and Meyer, *Incompatible Allies*, 324. Hitler's interpreter would note that "just as the march into Prague on March 15, 1939, signified the decisive turn in the break with the West, so the outbreak of the fateful clash with the East . . . had its prelude in the November 1940 encounter between Hitler and Molotov in Berlin." Schmidt, *Statist*, 515; Schmidt, *Hitler's Interpreter*, 209.

287. The 1982 recollections of Yakov Chadayev have Molotov reporting on his Berlin trip at a meeting of the politburo on Nov. 14—but Molotov had not yet arrived back in Moscow. Chadayev's recollections, moreover, have Stalin understanding at this point that the Pact had become worthless, a conclusion that does not comport in the least with Stalin's actions. Kumanev, *Riadom so Stalinym*, 399–406 (Chadayev); Sipols, *Tainy*, 274–5. Molotov first appears again in Stalin's office logbook on Nov. 18, alone, for a mere thirty minutes. *Na prieme*, 317–8.

288. Naumov, *1941 god*, I: 395–6 (AVP RF, f. 059, op. 1, p. 326, d. 2239, l. 113–4). Molotov also denied any agreement had been signed in Berlin.

289. Gorodetsky, *Grand Delusion*, 76 (citing AMVnR, p. 42, op. 1sh, pop. 315, l. 34: Stamenov, Nov. 16, 1940).

290. *News Chronicle*, Nov. 16, 1940; *The Times*, Nov. 18, 1940; Hanak, "Sir Stafford Cripps," 67n3; Gorodetsky, *Mission to Moscow*, 83.

291. Simonov, "Zametki k biografii G. K. Zhukova," 49. See also Volkogonov, *Triumf i tragediia*, II/i: 64, 67.

292. Gavrilov, *Voennaia razvedka informiruet*, 357–8 .

293. Gorodetsky, *Grand Delusion*, 77–8, citing *DGFP*, XI: 606–10, 652n2 (Nov. 19, 1940), 653–4 (Nov. 18); Filov, *Dnevnik*, 199.

294. Bartlett, "Embodiment of Myth"; Bartlett, *Wagner and Russia*, 227, 259–57, 271–2, 288–9. "Even now I can still hear the bewilderment with which Sergei Mikhailovich responded to my telephone call when, without any diplomatic 'approaches,' I asked him to stage Wagner's 'Walküre' at the Bolshoi Theatre," recalled the head of the Bolshoi (Samuil Samosud). "Wagner?!" Eisenstein told him. "But I've never put on any opera before . . . let alone Wagner." Iurenev, *Eizenshtein v vospominaniiakh sovremennikov*, 310; Eizenshtein, "Tvorcheskaia vstrecha s Vagnerom," 8. During the Wagner rehearsals, in Oct. 1940, Eisenstein had been appointed director of Mosfilm, the country's leading studio.

295. It would, however, enjoy a mere six performances. For contrasting assessments, see Kuznetsov, "'Val'kiriia' Vagnera v Bol'shom Teatre SSSR," 76–9; and Iurenev, *Eizenshtein v vospominaniiakh sovremennikov*, 311 (Sergei Prokofyev).

296. Eizenshtein, "Pered prem'eroi 'Val'kirii,'" 3.3. On Wagner, see also "Voploshchenie mifa" [Oct. 1940], in Eizenshtein, *Izbrannye proizvedeniia*, Iskusstvo, 1964–71, IV: 23–4.

297. Gorodetsky, *Grand Delusion*, 80–1 (citing AVP RF, f. 059, op. 1, pap. 331, d. 2272, l. 167–8: Sobolev to Molotov, Nov. 25, 1940).

298. *Na prieme*, 319.

299. Dallin and Firsov, *Dimitrov and Stalin*, 126–34.

300. Banac, *Diary of Georgi Dimitrov*, 136; Lebedeva and Narinskii, *Komintern i vtoraia mirovaia voina*, 454; Gorodetsky, *Grand Delusion*, 81–2 (citing AMVnR, PREII/i/3 pap. 1, op. 2sh, pop. 1, l. 19: anonymous pamphlet, Nov. 27, 1940).

301. *DVP SSSR*, XXXIII/ii: 135–7.

302. Berezhkov, *At Stalin's Side*, 50–1.

303. Naumov, *1941 god*, I: 415–8 (APRF, f. 3, op. 64, d. 675, l. 108–14); Sontag and Beddie, *Nazi-Soviet Relations*, 217–59; *DGFP*, XI: 714–5, 1124–5; *DVP SSSR*, XXIII/ii: 136–7 (APRF, f. 3, op. 64, d. 675, l. 108–16); McMurry, *Deutschland und die Sowjetunion*, 296; Degras, *Soviet Documents on Foreign Policy*, III: 477–8.

304. Gorodetsky, *Grand Delusion*, 79–81 (citing AMVnR, d. 40, p. 34, op. 1sh, pop. 272, l. 246, 248: Stamenov. Nov. 26, 1940; l. 246: AVP RF, f. 059, op. 1, pap. 331, d. 2272, l. 167–8: Sobolev to Molotov, Nov. 25, 1940).

305. Banac, *Diary of Georgi Dimitrov*, 139. "Consul General in Prague Kulikov came to see me," Dimitrov also wrote in his diary (Nov. 27). "The Bat'a, Škoda, and other plants are working at full capacity for the German army. In the environs of Prague an enormous aviation factory is being built, which is to produce up to a thousand aircraft a month." Banac, *Diary of Georgi Dimitrov*, 138.

306. Kershaw, *Hitler: 1936–1945*, 342.

307. Halder, *Halder Diaries*, I: 669–71 (Nov. 1, 1940); Halder, *Kriegstagebuch*, II: 157–9.

308. Gorodetsky, *Grand Delusion*, 69–72.

309. Engel, *Heeresadjutant bei Hitler*, 91 (Nov. 15, 1940), 89–90 (Nov. 4, 1940).

310. *Nazi Conspiracy and Aggression*, III: 442.

311. Engel, *Heeresadjutant bei Hitler*, 91 (November 15, 1940).
312. Fabry, *Die Sowjetunion und das Dritte Reich*, 243.
313. For Göring's objections to an attack on the Soviet Union (at least in Nov. 1940) on economic grounds, see Irving, *Hitler's War*, 181–2; Irving, *Göring*, 307–9. "The Führer is still inclined towards a showdown with Russia. The Commander in Chief, Navy, recommends postponing this until after victory over Britain, since demands on German forces would be too great, and an end to hostilities could not be foreseen." *Fuehrer Conferences*, 11: 41 (Nov. 14, 1940). "There are serious doubts as to the advisability of operation 'Barbarossa' before the overthrow of Britain" [the Navy's responsibility]. *Fuehrer Conferences*, II: 70–1 (Dec. 27, 1940).
314. Halder, *Halder Diaries*, I: 691–3 (Nov. 16, 1940); Halder, *Kriegstagebuch*, II: 182–3. Similar sentiments remained in the foreign ministry (Weizsäcker noted to himself on Nov. 28, "War against Russia is impossible as long as we are busy with England, and afterward it will be unnecessary"). Hill, *Die Weizsäcker-Papiere*, 227. See also ibid., 226 (Nov. 17, 1940).
315. Halder, *Kriegstagebuch*, II: 184–8 (Nov. 18, 1940).
316. *DGFP*, series D, XI: 606–10 (Nov. 19, 1940), 63–43 (Nov. 20). Ciano would observe that "I will immediately state that after Molotov's visit we speak very little of Russia, and in a somewhat different tone than that used by Ribbentrop during my recent visit. . . . Russia is once again a country not to be trusted." Van Crefeld, *Hitler's Strategy*, 213n74 (citing Ciano, *L'Europa verso la catastrofe*, 616).
317. Schramm, *Kriegstagebuch der Oberkommando*, I: 179.
318. *DGFP*, series D, XI: 632–6 (Nov. 26, 1940).
319. Van Crefeld, *Hitler's Strategy*, 82. Martin Bormann would later state that, in Feb. 1945, Hitler had told him, "my decision was made immediately after the departure of Molotov . . . I decided . . . to settle accounts with the Russians." Trevor-Roper, *Le Testament politique de Hitler*, 95–6.
320. The Soviet Union's modern technology was highly concentrated in just a few sectors. The railways remained steam-powered, not incorporating electricity on a mass scale, and the construction industry still used bricks and timber, not reinforced concrete. Above all, Soviet factories had far more workers, and lower productivity per worker, than their American or German prototypes, suffering from gigantomania and the lack of legal market mechanisms. The Soviets failed to exercise their option to purchase the Ford Co.'s V-8 engine, and Soviet trucks (the GAZ model) remained relatively primitive. Lewis, "Technology and the Transformation of the Soviet Economy," 190. The number of women working outside the home between 1928 and 1940 increased from 2.8 million to 13.2 million and constituted 39 percent of the labor force in 1940. Drobizhev, *Industrializatsiia i izmeneniia*, 4–5. Nearly 20 million peasants had relocated to towns and industrial construction sites over the past decade.
321. Ganson, "Food Supply, Rationing and Living Standards," 70.
322. Nekrich, *Pariahs*, 203; Weinberg, *World at Worms*, 201. Stalin again was privy to the German strategy in bilateral economic negotiations, thanks to Gerhard Kegel ("X"). Naumov, *1941 god*, I: 334–9 (APRF, f. 45, op. 1, d. 437, l. 1–12: Nov. 2, 1940).

323. Iakovlev, *Tsel' zhizni* (6th ed.), 179, 188; Berezhkov, *At Stalin's Side*, 75–106. See also Sobolev and Khazanov, *Nemetskii sled*. Goring had again interceded to get Krupp to treat contracts with the Soviet Union as equivalent to those with the German military and to accelerate a Soviet deal for six battleship turrets and 38-cm guns, giving the impression that the overall bilateral relationship could be salvaged. Von Strandmann, "Appeasement and Counter-Appeasement," 168–9 (citing HA Krupp, WA 40, B 381, October 4, 1940; WA 4, 2925, Oct. 8, 1940, Nov. 31, 1940).
324. Naumov, *1941 god*, I: 374–5 (AVP RF, f. 059, op. 1, p. 339, d. 2315, l. 35, 35 a, 36, 38, 39).
325. This was a far cry from Ribbentrop's statement in the Pact negotiations that Germany was "politically disinterested" in southeastern Europe. Sontag and Beddie, *Nazi-Soviet Relations*, 155–63. See also Ulam, *Expansion and Coexistence*, 298–9. It must be said that by 1940, some in the Nazi regime feared that the Soviets could not be contained in the role of junior partner because of their leverage in being the key repository of raw materials. Halder, *Kriegstagebuch*, II: 20–14.
326. Sontag and Beddie, *Nazi-Soviet Relations*, 252–4; *DGFP*, series D, XI: 562–70. Hitler appears not to have informed Ribbentrop about his intentions at this point. Ribbentrop, *Memoirs*, 151–2; Waddington, "Ribbentrop and the Soviet Union," 25–6.
327. "Two things became clear in the discussions: Hitler's intention to push the Soviet Union in the direction of the Persian Gulf, and his unwillingness to acknowledge any Soviet interest in Europe." Hilger and Meyer, *Incompatible Allies*, 324.
328. *Der Prozess gegen die Hauptkriegsverbrecher*, XXXIV: 469 (Hitler. Jan. 20, 1941); Kershaw, *Hitler: 1936–1945*, 343. In 1940, Greater Germany produced only a quarter of the oil it consumed. By mid-1941, Germany's oil resources would total 10 million tons; of these, 500,000 were produced by Germany proper, 800,000 by countries occupied by Germany, and 8.7 million tons by Germany's allies, primarily Romania.
329. Kershaw, *Hitler: 1936–1945*, 332. Jold evidently told Wehrmacht High Command planners on Dec. 5, 1940, following a "Führer Conference": "The Führer is determined to carry through this operation in the East even the Army will never again be as strong as it is at this moment and Soviet Russia has recently given one more proof that she will always, whenever possible, stand in Germany's path." Warlimont, *Inside Hitler's Headquarters*, 137.
330. Ribbentrop, *Memoirs*, 152.
331. *Trial of the Major War Criminals*, X: 291, 314–5 (Ribbentrop).
332. Gorodetsky, *Grand Delusion*, 80–1.
333. Nekrich, *Pariahs*, 229–30 (citing RGASPI, f. 77, op. 1, d. 913, l. 62, 65–6, l. 119). See also Nekrich, "Dynamism of the Past," 232–3.
334. Mueller-Hildebrand, *Sukhoputnaia armiia Germanii*, 596 (Nov. 15, 1940). Reports of heavy German troop concentrations in Romania as of Nov. 1940 turned out to be fictitious, possibly part of a disinformation campaign. The actual stationing order was issued only on Dec. 13, 1940. Gavrilov, *Voennaia razvedka informiruet*, 492–4 (TsAMO, f. 23, op. 9181, d. 6, l. 17–9).
335. *Trial of the Major War Criminals*, VII: 254 (Paulus); Weinberg, *Germany and the Soviet Union*, 137. Between May 1939 and Dec. 1940, Soviet military intelligence received

more than two dozen warnings from its agents of German invasion planning; during the same period, military intelligence prepared more than one dozen summaries for the top brass and political leadership (Stalin and Molotov). Lota, *Sekretnyi front*, 129.
336. Gor'kov, *Kreml'*, 30–5.
337. Similarly, electricity consumption in 1932 badly missed its target—13.4 instead of 22 billion kilowatt-hours—but by 1940 was reported at 48.6 billion. Coal extraction, which had been 35.4 million tons in 1927–28, rose to a reported 140.5 million in 1940. Nove, *Economic History of the USSR* (1989), 183, 217; *Narodnoe khoziaistvo SSSR za 70 let*, 161, 163–4; Stone, *Hammer and Rifle*, 108–9.
338. Mass production of the famed T-34 began in June 1940, but that year the Soviet Union managed to turn out just 115 T-34s, as well as 243 KV tanks.
339. Banac, *Diary of Georgi Dimitrov*, 137 (Nov. 25, 1940).
340. Iampol'skii et al., *Organy*, I/I: 286–96 (TsA FSK). See also Simonov, *Voenno-promyshlennyi kompleks SSSR*, 100; Ken, *Mobilizatsionnoe planirovanie*, 335. Conscripts' food was irregular, and bathing and laundry infrequent, to put it mildly; housing was the sorest point of all.
341. Staff who had been gathering the statistics went to prison or into unmarked graves. Katz, "Purges and Production." See also Khlevniuk, "Economic Officials in the Great Terror," 38–67. Problems in the Great War, such as severe shortages of artillery shells that had undermined the tsarist war effort, were common knowledge in Stalin's time. Manikovskii, *Boevoe snabzhenie russkoi armii*, 161; Barsukov, *Russkaia artilleriia*, 161.
342. Sokolov, *Ot voenproma k VPK*, 361–78.
343. In 1940, military outlays represented more than the entire 1934 state budget. Plotnikov, *Ocherki istorii biudzheta Sovetskogo gosudarstva*, 260–1. The Soviet Union had 218 military factories when the defense industry commissariat was established in 1939 (versus 45 in the late 1920s). Harrison and Davies, "Soviet Military-Economic Effort," 372, 377 (citing RGAE, f. 2097, op. 1, d. 1051, l. 17–8: Nov. 15, 1929); Simonov, *Voennyo-promyshlennyi kompleks SSSR*, 38–41. See also Werner, *Military Strength of the Powers*. The Soviets had also built in extra capacity for rapid switch in wartime. Davies and Harrison, "Defence Spending," 90; Harrison, *Accounting for War*, 110. An earlier scholar calculated the peacetime share of Soviet military spending as 2 percent in 1928, 6 percent in 1937, and 15 percent in 1940. Bergson, *Real National Income*, 46; Gregory, *Russian National Income*, 57.
344. Bruce Menning, private communication. See Khaustov and Samuelson, *Stalin, NKVD*, 160 (TsA FSB, ASD P-4574, t. 1, l. 53).
345. Abelshauser, "Germany," 138.
346. Khrushchev, *Memoirs*, I: 271. "Stalin is afraid of Hitler—and not for nothing," Trotsky had thundered in 1939. Other perspicacious observers, such as Hilger, also recognized that "there is not the slightest doubt that a deep fear of Hitler's Germany was the essential guide to all Soviet foreign policy in the 1930s." But Hilger, unlike Trotsky, grasped that this fear "made the Kremlin bend every effort and strain every muscle to render the country strong politically, economically, ideologically, and militarily." *Biulleten' oppozitsii*, no. 79–80, Aug.–Oct. 1939, 14–6. Hilger and Meyer, *Incompatible Allies*, 276.

CHAPTER 14. FEAR

1. Molotov continued: "Stalin, as a cold-blooded person, took this matter very seriously when discussing grand strategy." Chuev, *Sto sorork*, 45–6; Chuev, *Molotov Remembers*, 34.
2. Weinberg, *Hitler's Table Talk*, 9.

3. Chuev, *Sto sorok*, 28–9.
4. Barros and Gregor, *Double Deception*, 49 (citing Liudas Dovydenas and J. Edgar

Hoover: OSS Papers, RG 266 NA, file 10532: Hoover to Donovan, Jan. 27, 1942); Naumov, *1941 god*, I: 455–7 (AVPRF, f. 082, op. 23, pap. 95, d. 6, l. 268–72).

5. Molotov would pass Dekanozov's Dec. 7 report to Stalin only on Dec. 24. Naumov, *1941 god*, I: 440–1 (AVFRF, f. 06, op. 3 (dop.), pap. 36, d. 467, l. 1–4); "Nakanune voiny (1936–1940 g.): doklady i zapiski v TsK VKP (b)," 220–2; Voiushin and Gorlov, "Fashistskaia agressiia," 15–6.

6. Soviet intelligence reports about Hitler's intention to seize Ukraine ("the bread-basket of Europe") had become more or less regular from early 1939, and continued after the signing of the Pact. Gavrilov, *Voennaia razvedka informiruet*, 25–6.

7. Naumov, *1941 god*, I: 449 (TsA FSB: Dec. 14, 1940). Varga sent Stalin a report from his Institute of World Economics and Politics, with detailed tables of the "resources Germany is receiving from its occupied territories," information that "might be interesting for you." Cherkasov, *IMEMO*, 33 (RGASPI, f. 558, op. 11, d. 716, l. 28: Dec. 16, 1940).

8. Naumov, *1941 god*, I: 455–7; Chuev, *Molotov Remembers*, 20; Berezhkov, *At Stalin's Side*, 211–2. Pavlov, not Berezhkov, accompanied Dekanozov on the visit to Hitler. On Dec. 13, 1940, *The Siberians*, a children's film by Lev Kuleshov, premiered in Moscow. It featured a Buryat hunter who, on New Year's Eve, tells two boys the story of how a hunter had once helped Stalin escape from Siberian exile, and how Stalin had given him his pipe as a memento, but the hunter had died in the civil war and left the pipe to another hunter/red partisan. The two boys decide to try to track down the pipe and return it to Stalin (played by Gelovani).

9. The directive stated that it was "of decisive importance that the intention to attack should not become known." Hubatsch, *Hitlers Weisungen*, 84–92; Naumov, *1941 god*, I: 452–5; Butler, *Grand Strategy*, III/i: 540.

10. Fabry, *Der Hitler-Stalin Pakt*, 365–7.

11. Berghahn, *Germany and the Approach of War*, 191–2. "Backward Russia constituted a vulnerable yet provocative target for its European competitors," one scholar argued. "Huge and lumbering, Russia always seemed an immense threat, but one that could be neutralized by a bold stroke aimed at one of its innumerable weak points . . . At the same time, the sharp fluctuations in Russian power, linked to the stop-and-go nature of its efforts to catch up to the West, created strong incentives for preventive war initiated by Russia's foes." Snyder, "Russian Backwardness."

12. Photostat: http://ww2db.com/photo.php?source=all&color=all&list=search&for eigntype=D&foreigntype_id=168. "One of the more remarkable facts in the history of the German Supreme Headquarters is that from the end of June to the beginning of December 1940 the highest-level staff of the Wehrmacht and its Supreme Commander played only a very small part in the preparations for the greatest campaign in the Second World War," wrote Warlimont. "There was no carefully thought-out plan as a basis for action against Russia such as would have been made in the old days by the Prussian-German General Staff." Warlimont, *Inside Hitler's Headquarters*, 135, 138–9. In Dec. 1940, Beria's NKVD drafted a decree to get all code and decoding departments—foreign affairs commissariat, foreign trade, defense, and fleet—moved into NKVD state security; Stalin approved. Khaustov, "Deiatel'nost' organov," 359–60.

13. "Nakanune voiny (1940–1941 gg.)," 219; Gavrilov, *Voennaia razvedka informiruet*, 498–9 (TsAMO, f. 23, op. 22424, d. 4, l. 537); Naumov, *1941 god*, I: 466; Lota, *"Alta" protiv*

"Barbarossy," 451 (facsimile). Scholars have access only to what Soviet intelligence archives themselves have published. Frederick Barbarossa, who led the third crusade through Asia Minor, drowned on June 10, 1190, a failure. His corpse was never found.

14. "A large portrait of Marx hung in the office, and in a glass case there was a bust of Lenin," recalled Mgeladze. "The simplicity and modesty caught one's eye, and, looking around, we could not help but think that the offices of some commissars in the republic had more lavish appointments." Stalin stood next to the long felt-covered table smoking a cigarette, which surprised Mgeladze (all the portraits had him with a pipe). In front of Stalin sat a glass of tea and a lemon, which during the discussion he squeezed into his tea. Mgeladze recalled the meeting as taking place in Jan. He also remembered the presence of Molotov, Beria, and Voznesensky, all of whom appear in the logbook for the one day that Mgeladze appears (Dec. 23, 1940). Mgeladze, *Stalin, kaki a ego znal*, 25–9; *Na prieme*, 321.

15. Shakhurin, *Krylia pobedy*, 186–7; *Na prieme*, 321. See also Patolichev, *Vospominaniia*, 105–7.

16. Mearsheimer, *Conventional Deterrence*, 46–52.

17. The 1939 field service regulations had stated: "The Red Army will be the most offensive-minded of all the attacking armies that ever existed." Stalin had told a Central Committee plenum on Jan. 19, 1925: "Our banner remains the banner of peace. But if war breaks out, we will not be able to sit with folded arms—we will have to take action, but we will be the last to do so. And we will do so in order to throw the decisive weight into the scales." Meltiukhov, almost alone, correctly has the arrows moving west on maps illustrating Soviet war plans. Mel'tiukov, *Upushchennyi shans*, 256–7.

18. One Soviet agent reported that France had expected a number of tactical engagements with Germany, not a surprise knockout blow with massed German forces, and that France compounded this error by forward deployment at the Belgian-German border, rendering those units unable to respond quickly to German flanking maneuvers. Roberts, "Planning for War" (citing RGVA, f. 33987, op. 3, d. 1302, l. 180, 185–6); RGVA, f. 33988. op. 4, d. 35, l. 287–292: June 3, 1940; Simonov, "Zametki k biografii G. K Zhukova," 53; Zhukov, *Vospominaniia*, I: 324. A book published in early 1940 argued that the German experience in Poland had reconfirmed that the only way to defend against a surprise attack by secretly massed, highly mobile mechanized forces was to preempt the enemy by achieving one's strategic deployment first. Krasil'nikov, "Nastupatel'naia armeiskaia operatsiya," 487–96.

19. On May 14, 1938, Yezhov sent Stalin a report laying out an analysis by the incarcerated Vasily Lavrov, who noted that in early 1937, during war games, Tukhachevsky, playing the southern attack variant of the blues (Germany, Poland, Finland, and Balts) on the Lvov-Donetsk axis, had proven that the Germans could deliver a deadly strike against Soviet military industry. The precondition for this outcome was a German occupation of Czechoslovakia (with its military industry) as well as of Romania (with its oil and food). Lavrov put together charts and maps showing the extent of the possible catastrophe. On July 29, 1938, he was executed. Khaustov and Samuelson, *Stalin, NKVD*, 205 (TsA FSB, f. 3, op. 5, d. 343, l. 28–48); Suvenirov, *Tragediia RKKA*, 378. In Dec. 1937, when Stalin received "testimony" from Lavrov implicating Lieutenant General Yakov Smushkevich, the

aide for aviation to the chief of the general staff, the despot wrote on it, "He lies, the swine," a rare instance in which he appears to have rejected an interrogation protocol. Khaustov and Samuelson, *Stalin, NKVD*, 208 (APRF, f. 3, op. 24, d. 329, l. 59). See also the call by General Jan Strumis, known as Zhigur, in a denunciation of Alexander Yegorov (July 20, 1937), for reexamination of all war plans to take account of recent war games. He was arrested in Dec. and executed on July 22, 1938. RGVA, f. 33987, f. 3, op. 10, d. 1046, l. 209–29; Samuelson, *Plans for Stalin's War Machine*, 188; Zakharov, *General'nyi shtab*, 125–33.

20. Verkhovskii, *Ogon', manevr, i maskirovka*, 131.

21. Tukhachevskii, "O strategicheskikh vzgliadakh Prof. Svechina," 3–16.

22. Timoshenko asked twenty-eight generals to sketch their views on the future war, and he chose five to report at the meeting, including Zhukov, commander of Kiev military district, on offensive operations; Ivan Tyulenev, head of Moscow military district, on defense; and Dmitri Pavlov, commander of the Western military district, on mechanized warfare. See also Zolotarev, *Russkii arkhiv: Velikaia Otechestvenaia*, XII (I): 13–29 (Meretskov), 129–51 (Zhukov); Golubev et al., *Rossiia i zapad*, 99 (citing RGASPI, f. 77, op. 116, d. 97, l. 12: Zhdanov, Nov. 20, 1940).

23. Cynthia Roberts notes that Isserson was not alone. Colonel A. I. Starunin published an article in early 1941 explaining that Germany's victories had undone the theory that the initial period of war would see "armies of incursion" attempting to seize various objectives as the main forces completed mobilization in the rear. Starunin, however, blunted the force of his argument, proposing that the Red Army could attain air superiority and disrupt German rail lines to inhibit the enemy's mobilization, after proving that no such mobilization would be necessary. Starunin, "Operativnaia vnezapnost'."

24. Isserson's text, dated June–July 1940, had not taken up the German campaign in France, but had concluded with an oblique reference: "Only six months later in the West, events transpired that further showed the development of the new military art to a higher level of large-scale modern European war." Isserson, *Novye formy bor'by*, 28; Anfilov, *Doroga k tragedii*, 74; Zolotarev, *Russkii arkhiv: Velikaia Otechestvenaia*, XII (I): 15 (Meretskov), 152–4, 247–9 (Klyonov); Volkogonov, *Triumf i tragediia*, II/i: 56. See also Harrison, *Architect of Victory*, 228–34. Isserson (b. 1898) had been shown up by the Finnish War (during which he headed the staff of the Seventh Army). He would be arrested on June 7, 1941, and condemned to death, but reprieved to ten years in a camp in northern Kazakhstan.

25. As early as 1936, Soviet military analysts argued that a frontal assault-style war would not work in the East. Erickson, "Threat Identification," 396–8 (citing *Krasnaia zvezda*, May and June 1936).

26. Zolotarev, *Russkii arkhiv: Velikaia Otechestvennaia*, XII (I): 204–5 (RGVA, f. 4, op. 18, d. 57, l. 70–3). Khrunkin had led a bomber squadron that had sunk a Japanese aircraft carrier, been given China's highest military award, and went on to complete the General Staff Academy and lead an army in the Winter War. Timoshenko, in his concluding summary, which was published as a brochure for internal use, giving it the character of a general directive, acknowledged that the leaders of the air force disagreed on the best ways to employ air power and urged them to think more about achieving air supremacy.

Zolotarev, *Russkii arkhiv: Velikaia Otechestvennaia*, XII (I): 173–82 (RGVA, f. 4, op. 18, d. 57, l. 1–24), 164–7 (d. 56, l. 85–92), 338–72 (op. 15, d. 27, l. 575–607).

27. Zolotarev, *Russkii arkhiv: Velikaia Otechestvennaia*, XII (I): 339–40.

28. Naumov, *1941 god*, I: 498n2 (citing APRF, f. 45, op. 1, d. 437); Lota, *"Alta" protiv "Barbarossy*," 262. "I read your 'In the steppes of Ukraine,'" the document-centric despot wrote to Korneychuk (Dec. 28, 1940). "It came out brilliantly—artistic and complete, cheery and joyous. . . . By the way: I also added some words on page 68. That was for greater clarity." The words he inserted specified that, despite some changes, the collective farm tax would essentially stay the same. RGASPI, f. 558, op. 1, d. 4674, l. 1–2; Gromov, *Stalin*, 223–4; *Sochineniia*, XVIII: 209. In the book *Subversive Activity of Foreign Intelligence in the USSR*, published in Dec. 1940, the author wrote that "as the main method of masking they chose hypocritical-sham 'devotion' to the cause of proletarian revolution and socialist construction." Loyalty, in other words, was a sign of disloyalty. Minaev, *Podryvnaia deiatel'nost' inostrannykh razvedok v SSSR*.

29. Fesiun, *Delo Rikharda Zorge*, 111. On Dec. 27, 1940, at a meeting of the high command, Raeder once again insisted on concentrating all forces against Britain, the main enemy, and "expressed the most serious doubts in the possibility of a war against Russia before England was destroyed." *Trial of the Major War Criminals*, XXXIV: 714.

30. Golikov circulated this message to List no. 1. Gavrilov, *Voennaia razvedka informiruet*, 527 (TsAMO, f. 23, op. 24119, d. 3, l. 6–7); Lota, *"Alta" protiv "Barbarossy*," 449–50 (facsimile). In early 1941, the NKVD, military intelligence, and naval intelligence were ordered to submit their reports to the ambassador, who would coordinate them and inhibit rivalries. Neither the coordination nor the tamping down of rivalries happened.

31. SD chief of counterintelligence Schellenberger was not officially informed of Barbarossa until late Jan. 1941. Senior German field commanders would only be told that the deployments were a precaution against Soviet massing of forces. Both the high command and the foreign ministry would issue documents with false information. Hitler would oversee three major war conferences between Jan. and March 1941, the first two in Berchtesgaden, the third in Berlin. Warlimont, who had had a hand in drawing up Barbarossa, claims that on Jan. 18, at the Berchtesgaden, he had to ask General Jodl, the principal military adviser in Hitler's entourage, whether Barbarossa was even still on. Jodl replied affirmatively, adding, "The Russian colossus will prove to be a pig's bladder; prick it and it will burst." Warlimont, *Inside Hitler's Headquarters*, 140. See also Whaley, *Codeword*, 133. By the March 30 conference, 250 commanders were in the know. The Wehrmacht had 320,000 officers, including at least 3,000 generals.

32. Lota, *"Alta" protiv "Barbarossy*," 275–6; Lota, *Sekretnyi front*, 42. Tupikov arrived in Berlin on Jan. 8. His appointment reflected the recent report out of Berlin on Dec. 29 (and its follow-up on Jan. 4) about a supersecret war directive against the Soviet Union signed by Hitler. Before Tupikov, Maxim Purkayev ("Marble"), a village-born (1894) ethnic Mordvin on his first assignment abroad, had been in over his head, a circumstance Hitler himself had noticed at their initial meeting (Sept. 1939). On Feb. 14, 1940, German military counterintelligence had made an effort to compromise Purkayev to get him to work for them. He was replaced in Berlin by his deputy for aviation, Skornyakov, until Tupikov's

arrival. Lota, *"Alta protiv "Barbarossy*," 210–25; *Na prieme*, 292–3.

33. Sipols, *Tainy*, 395.

34. Erickson, *Road to Stalingrad*, 1–9; Erickson, "Threat Identification," 375–423. The immediate pre-Pact war plan, drawn up by Shaposhnikov in March 1938 and approved in Nov. of that year, had assumed a combined German-Polish assault, with Minsk-Smolensk-Moscow as the main axis, although a variant assumed a less likely thrust farther south, toward Kiev. Naumov, *1941 god*, II: 557–71; Zakharov, *General 'nyi Shtab*, 1.

35. An Aug. 1940 revised war plan under Shaposhnikov's supervision, authored by Vasilevsky, who had become deputy chief of the operations department in April 1940, had anticipated that a German attack would most likely come north of the Pripet. It did not rule out enemy targeting of Ukraine (the southern axis), but proposed concentrating 70 percent of the 237 Red Army divisions on the Western frontiers north of the Pripet. Shaposhnikov dutifully wrote of "inflicting defeat on German forces" on their own soil (East Prussia and the Warsaw region), yet indicated that the Red Army would not finish mobilization until thirty days in. He implied that only surpassing intelligence on Germany and prewar covert Soviet mobilization could enable the Red Army to halt a deep German penetration that would preempt any Soviet counterattack and push the fighting entirely onto Soviet territory. Naumov, *1941 god*, I: 181–93; Mikhalev, *Voennaia strategiia*, 309–11; Alt, "Die Wehrmacht im Kalkül Stalins," 107–9. Shaposhnikov was removed before the plan was approved; an update (again authored by Vasilevsky) was submitted by Timoshenko and Meretskov on Sept. 18, 1940. Stalin evidently rejected their supposition, carried over from the previous plan, that the main German thrust would be north of the Pripet, insisting instead that the main German strike would occur to the south, because "Ukrainian grain and Donbass coal have special importance for the Germans." Stalin had the politburo approve this plan on Oct. 14, 1940. Naumov, *1941 god*, I: 236–53; Volkogonov, *Triumf i tragediia*, II/1: 132–5 (citing TsAMO, f. 16, op. 2951, d. 242, l. 84–90); Roberts, "Planning for War," 1315–6 (citing TsAMO, f. 16. op. 2951, d. 239, l. 197–244); excerpts published in *Voenno-istoricheskii zhurnal*, 1992, no. 1: 24–8; Vasilevskii, *Delo vsei zhizni*, 102–5. Zakharov unpersuasively attempts to blame Meretskov and not Stalin for the shift toward the southern axis. Zakharov, *General'nyi shtab*, 219–25. Vasilevsky would recall that Georgy Anisimov had twice in 1940 brought the top secret operational plan (in its only copy) to the Little Corner for discussion. Both times, according to Vasilevsky, the plan was returned without any markings, changes, or an official stamp. The staff officers of the Leningrad, Baltic, Western, and Kiev military districts in the second half of 1940 and first half of 1941 were summoned to Moscow to work on the detailed operational plans for their theaters. Murin, "Nakanune," 8–9 (memoirs of Vasilevsky).

36. Roberts, "Planning for War," 1313–4 (citing RGVA, f. 37977, op. 5, d. 563, 564, 565, 568, 569, 570, 577); Bobylev, "Repetitsiia katastrofy"; Bobylev, "K kakoi voine gotovilsia General'nyi shtab RKKA,"; Bobylev, "Tochky v diskussii stavit' rano,"; Menning, "Soviet Strategy," I: 224–5.

37. Zhukov was named chief of staff on Jan. 14, 1941. The day before, Stalin and the Main Military Council heard the results of the war games. Meretskov gave the main report, but the date had been moved up a day and the written materials had not been finished, so he

extemporized, badly. Stalin rebuked him. Kulik held forth about infantry divisions of 18,000 troops supported only by horses, ignoring mechanization, which infuriated Stalin still more. Shaposhnikov, one witness recalled, "sat there gloomily, glancing from time to time at the people next to him or toward the members of the politburo." "Nakanune voiny: iz postanovlenii vysshikh partiinykh i gosudarstvennykh organov (Mai 1940 g.—21 Iiunia 1941 g.)," 197–8; Bialer, *Stalin and His Generals*, 141–5 (M. I. Kazakov), 146–51 (A. I. Eremenko). On Jan. 23 at the Bolshoi, Stalin, spotting Meretskov, said to him in front of others, "You are courageous, capable, but without principles, spineless. You want to be nice, but you should have a plan instead and adhere to it strictly, despite the fact that someone or other is going to be resentful." Stalin also said: "Voroshilov is a fine fellow, but he is no military man." Banac, *Diary of Georgi Dimitrov*, 145.

38. Zhukov, *Vospominaniia*, I: 296. See also Sokolov, *Georgii Zhukov*, 20 (citing a 1930 assessment).

39. In 1941, Soviet counterintelligence reported that many foreign diplomats in Moscow concluded that the Nazi regime's need for imports from the Soviet Union excluded a military confrontation. Khaustov, "Deiatel'nost' organov," 256 (TsA FSB, f. 3os, op. 8, d. 5, l. 169).

40. Sipols, "Torgovo-ekonomicheskie otnosheniia mezhdu SSSR," 37.

41. Ericson, *Feeding the German Eagle*, 150–3, 160; Ziedler, "German-Soviet Economic Relations," 108. Stalin also settled a border dispute in Lithuania with Germany on German terms, paying RM 31 million ($7.5 million) for the sparsely inhabited Lithuania strip abutting East Prussia that the Red Army had unilaterally occupied. The border was formally set between the Igorka River and the Baltic Sea. *DGFP*, series D, XII: 560–1; Sipols, *Tainy*, 387; Read and Fisher, *Deadly Embrace*, 608; Kaslas, "Lithuanian Strip." See also McSherry, *Stalin, Hitler, and Europe*, II: 50–66; and Weinberg, *Germany and the Soviet Union*, 159–63. In Feb. 1941, German paid 22 million marks in gold for cereals from now Soviet Bessarabia.

42. Halder, *Halder Diaries*, I: 751 (Jan. 16, 1941); Halder, *Kriegstagebuch*, II: 243–6; Erickson, *Road to Stalingrad*, 59–8 (German Naval Conference, Jan. 8, 1941); *Fuehrer Conferences, 1941*, I: 1–4 See also Lota, *"Alta" protiv "Barbarossy*," 259 (no citation).

43. Kuznetsov, "Voenno-morskoi flot nakanune Velikoi Otechestvennoi voiny," 68; "Iz istorii Velikoi otechestvennoi voiny," 202.

44. Banac, *Diary of Georgi Dimitrov*, 144 (Jan. 21, 1939).

45. On Feb. 14, 1941, Samokhin reported Yugoslav general staff estimates of 250 German divisions total, while specifying their locations. Gavrilov, *Voennaia razvedka informiruet*, 528–9 (TsAMO, f. 23, op. 24119, d. 4, l. 65–6), 532 (l. 106–7). One scholar has argued that revolutionary states end up in war because the revolution exacerbates existing security dilemmas with neighbors, so that one side or the other comes to view offense as a form of self-defense. Walt, "Revolution and War." This was a case of two revolutionary states heightening each other's security dilemma.

46. *DVP SSSR*, XXIII/ii, 343–5 (AVPRF, f. 06, op. 3, p. 1, d. 4, l. 37–41). On Jan. 21, 1941, the Iron Guard in Romania rebelled against its own government, and lashed out at Jews. "The stunning thing about the Bucharest bloodbath," one observer noted, "is the quite bestial ferocity of it." Ninety-three persons were killed. Friedlander, *Years of Extermination*, 166.

47. Attendees, besides Zhdanov, Molotov, Beria, Voroshilov, and Kaganovich, included Mikoyan, Voznesensky, Bulganin, Pervukhin, Kosygin, and Malyshev—effectively, the economic group. *Na prieme,* 323.

48. Malyshev, "Dnevnik narkoma," 114 (APRF, f. 3, op. 62, d. 131, l. 2-91).

49. Malyshev, "Dnevnik narkoma," 114-5 (APRF, f. 3, op. 62, d. 131, l. 2-91).

50. Banac, *Diary of Georgi Dimitrov,* 146. "The Soviet Union," boasted a Red Army political instruction pamphlet of 1941, "has been transformed into a heavy-duty socialist great power exerting enormous influence on the entire course of international development." Airapetian, *Etapy vneshnei politiki SSSR,* 93.

51. "My program was to abolish the Treaty of Versailles," Hitler stated in Berlin (Jan. 31, 1941). "It is nonsense for the rest of the world to pretend that I did not reveal this program until 1933, or 1935, or 1937 . . . No human being has declared or recorded what he wanted more often than I." Prange, *Hitler's Words,* 216.

52. Tooze, *Wages of Destruction.*

53. Miller, *Bankrupting the Enemy.*

54. "You are expressly instructed to treat all questions concerning the United States with even more caution than hitherto," Goebbels instructed the press in 1939. "Even statements made by Mrs. Roosevelt are not to be mentioned." Friedlander, *Prelude,* 50.

55. Gallup polls accurately forecast the outcome, and indicated that without a war in Europe, voters would have preferred the Republican candidate, Wendell Willkie. Katz, "Public Opinion Polls." General Georg Thomas of Germany's high command received directives to prepare for a long war mere days after Roosevelt won re-election. Friedlander, *Prelude,* 158.

56. Public Papers and Addresses of Franklin D. Roosevelt, IX: 633-44; Sweeting, "Building the Arsenal of Democracy."

57. Tooze, *Wages of Destruction,* 407, 410, 420. The Soviets noted that the British aviation industry had the capacity to mass produce 60,000 planes annually. Erickson, "Threat Identification," 397, 399. By 1941, some 40 percent of German steel production came from outside the Reich's 1937 borders. Murray, *Change in the European Balance of Power,* 13.

58. Hillgruber, *Hitlers Stategie,* 192-397.

59. The "peripheral" strategy in the Mediterranean was never fundamental, and never a substitute for the invasion of the Soviet Union. Leach, *German Strategy,* 72-3. See also *Feuhrer Conferences,* 1941, I: 1-4.

60. Domarus, *Hitler: Reden,* II: 1663; Förster and Mawdsley, "Hitler and Stalin in Perspective," 65n8a: Bundesarchiv-Militärarchiv, N 664/2 (Captain Karl Wilhelm Thilo diary).

61. Khaustov, "Deiatel'nost' organov," 169 (TsA FSB, f. 3, op. 1, d. 3, l. 14). See also Sudoplatov, *Special Tasks,* 112-3.

62. Khaustov, "Deiatel'nost' organov," 181.

63. An excerpted summary report of NKGB foreign intelligence for 1939 through April 1941 appears in Iampol'skii et al., *Organy,* I/ii: 130-2 (TsA FSK).

64. Khaustov, "Deiatel'nost' organov," 278 (f. 3, op. 7, d. 1732, l. 156). The Soviets had the Italian cipher codes since 1936. Khaustov, "Deiatel'nost' organov," 276.

65. Murphy, *What Stalin Knew,* 102 (no citation); Naylor, *Man and an Institution;* Cairncross, *Enigma Spy,* 85-93. On Stalin's knowledge of the German inability to mount "Sea Lion," see Vishlev, *Nakanune,* 37 (citing Spravka KGB SSSR, 219); and Chuev, *Sto sorok,* 32.

66. West and Tsarev, *Crown Jewels,* 214. As Andrew observes, their recruiter, Arnold Deutsch, offered a siren call of liberation that

had both sexual and political appeal: "Burgess and Blunt were gay and Maclean bisexual at a time when homosexual relations, even between consenting adults, were illegal. Cairncross, like Philby a committed heterosexual, later wrote a history of polygamy." Andrew, *Defence of the Realm,* 35. See also Knightley, *Master Spy,* 35. In 1940, Krivitsky, the Soviet defector, was invited in by Jane Archer of MI5 and claimed there were sixty-one Soviet agents in Britain, and gave descriptions that fitted Philby and Maclean, but his revelations were not followed up. Blunt gave Gorsky a secret copy of Krivitsky's debriefing in Jan. 1941. Krivitsky died in mysterious circumstances in a Washington, D.C., hotel on Feb. 9, 1941. Kern, *Death in Washington,* 264-5; Costello, *Mask of Treachery,* 351; West and Tsarev, *Crown Jewels,* 145 (quoting KGB archives, without citation). John King, the cipher clerk in the foreign office, had been exposed as a Soviet spy in fall 1939.

67. Borovik, *Philby Files,* 167 (quoting KGB archives, without citation). German disinformation (about not attacking the USSR until after Britain's fall) appears to have started early. Pavlov, "Sovetskaia voennaia razvedka," 54 (no citation), Jan. 16, 1941.

68. Voskresenskaia, *Pod psevdonimom Irina,* 48-9.

69. Korotkov was evidently recommended to move up from the maintenance department by Venyamin Gerson, Yagoda's personal secretary, who had met him in the exercise room at the Dynamo sports club. In 1939 Korotkov was discharged for ties to Gerson, among others, but he fought back and got reinstated. For a time he was returned to Moscow over fears that his cover had been blown. He handled Lehman as well as Schulze-Boysen and Harnack. Petrov and Skorkin, *Kto rukovodil NKVD,* 491; Pavlov, *Tragediia sovetskoi razvedki,* 364; Gladkov, *Korotkov.* Korotkov might have been involved in assassinations abroad. Sudoplatov, *Special Tasks,* 48. The NKVD foreign department had 81 people; in 1940, 225. But central Soviet intelligence lost most of its Latvians, Poles, Jews, and other nationalities, who were replaced in almost every instance by Russians and Russified Ukrainians, with the usual notation "from the peasantry," "from workers," but often without foreign languages. Khaustov et al., *Lubianka: Stalin i VChK,* 24; Khaustov, "Deiatel'nost' organov," 156-7.

70. "If Zakhar [Kobulov] is ever mentioned Sudoplatov and Zhuravlyov simply wave their hands," read a note in Kobulov's personnel file. Costello and Tsarev, *Deadly Illusions,* 441n30 (TsA SVR, delo "Zakhar," no. 15952, t. 1., l 41); *Izvestiia,* May 5, 1990.

71. Pavlov, *Tragediia Sovetskoi razvedki,* 353.

72. Höhne, *Kennwort;* Primakov, *Ocherki,* III: 414-32; Costello and Tsarev, *Deadly Illusions,* 77-80. Another member of the Soviet spy circle was Martha Dodd, daughter of the U.S. ambassador in Berlin.

73. Lehmann, head of Gestapo counterintelligence for Soviet espionage, was said to have transmitted to his Soviet handler the contents of a report by Himmler (June 10, 1941) that revealed that the Germans did not know the depth and breadth of Soviet spying. This report has not been published. Primakov, *Ocherki,* III: 340. Hitler supposedly intuited that Soviet intelligence services were "much more thorough and probably much more successful" than those of other states, such as the British. Walter Schellenberg, *Labyrinth,* 321.

74. The British also noted that Russian speakers were being recruited into the German army and Russian émigrés into German intelligence units. Hinsley, "British Intelligence and Barbarossa," 52.

75. Read and Fisher, *Deadly Embrace,* 593-601; Ivanov, *Nachal'nyi period voiny,* 191-96, 206, 209-13. In 1938, Goebbels's wife, Magda, kicked up a fuss about his affair with the Czech actress Lida Baarova, and Hitler told Goebbels he would have to choose loyalty to the cause over his mistress. Hitler esteemed Goebbels's propaganda wizardry, but not his political advice—a sore point for Goebbels, but also a spur for him to prove himself to the Führer. Hitler encouraged the rivalry between Goebbels and Ribbentrop. Longerich, *Goebbels.*

76. Hinsley et al., *British Intelligence,* I: 437-8, 446-7.

77. Kuznetsov, *Nakanune,* 288; Tippelskirch, *Geschichte des Zweiten Weltkriegs,* 165; Vishlev, *Nakanune,* 38-40. The Soviets considered as possible the deployment of German troops to Turkey, Iraq, Iran, and a strike at the USSR from the south. Meretskov, *Na sluzhbe,* 207; Shtemenko, *General'nyi shtab,* 20. On May 9, TASS denied foreign news reports that the Soviet fleet was being fortified on the Black and Caspian Seas.

78. Vinogradov et al., *Sekrety Gitlera,* 15.

79. Guderian, brought into confidence already in Nov. 1940, shortly after Molotov's visit to Berlin, would recall surmising that the plan, which he deemed militarily inappropriate, could only be part of a bluff. Guderian, *Panzer Leader,* 142.

80. Sipols, *Tainy,* 393-4. Fitin, commenting on yet another report from Philby about a possible German attack, would write: "German planes are daily bombing London and other cities of Great Britain. Is a German invasion of the Soviet Union possible in these conditions or have England's secret services deliberately chosen to deceive Moscow through Philby?" Antonov, "Na pol'skom napravlenii."

81. The German High Command spelled out the disinformation themes in directives of Feb. 15, 1941, and May 12, 1941. Naumov, *1941 god,* I: 661-4 (Deutsches Militärarchiv, Potsdam, W. 31.00/5, Bl. 114-7); II: 195-6 (Bl. 256-7); Whaley, *Codeword,* 247-51. See also Ribbentrop, *Memoirs,* 152-3.

82. Zhukov, *Vospominaniia,* I: 313-16, 342-3, 367, 377. See also Zakharov, *Nakanune velikikh ispytanii,* originally a limited circulation secret work, reprinted in Zakharov, *General'nyi shtab,* 420. "Recalling how we military men made demands of industry in the last months before the war," Zhukov would admit, "I see that at times we did not take into account all the real economic possibilities of the country." He would further note that in Feb. 1941, General Pavlov (head of the Western military district) sent a report to Stalin requesting many defense actions and that Timoshenko was told by Stalin that "notwithstanding the justice of his [Pavlov's] demands we do not have the possibility today to satisfy his 'fantastical' suggestions." Zhukov, *Vospominaniia,* I: 331-2.

83. Shakhurin, *Krylia pobedy,* 98-100.

84. Banac, *Diary of Georgi Dimitrov,* 149 (Feb. 20, 1941). Stalin had dressed down Golikov's predecessor, Proskurov, exactly the same way, warning that a spy "should not believe in anyone." Rzhevskii and Vehviläinen, *Zimnaia voina,* II: 206. German counterintelligence was well aware of the tensions between Soviet civilian and military intelligence. Schellenberg, *Labyrinth,* 143-4. The 18th party conference also sought to impart renewed impetus to the publishing of Stalin's *Collected Works.* Maksimenkov, *Bol'shaia tsenzura,* 526 (RGASPI, f. 558, op. 11, d. 905, l. 18-9: Mitin, Feb. 20, 1941).

85. Varga would recall Shcherbakov as "one of the worst representatives of the uncurbed

bureaucracy." Varga, "Vskryt' cherez 25 let," 157.

86. Beria was named a deputy chairman of the Council of People's Commissars, with oversight for the NKVD, NKGB, and the commissariats of timber, nonferrous metals, oil, and river fleet. Merkulov's new first deputy was Ivan Serov; another deputy was M. V. Gribov (for personnel). Fitin headed the new NKGB First Directorate (foreign intelligence), and Fedotov headed the Second (counterintelligence). The guards department (Vlasik) fell under the NKGB. Beria's new first deputy at the NKVD was Sergei Kruglov; other deputies were Abakumov, Chernyshov, Maslennikov, and B. P. Obruchnikov. The NKVD retained control of the border guards and the Gulag.

87. According to Sándor Radó ("Dora"), a Hungarian Communist and Soviet military intelligence officer in Geneva who posed as the owner of a cartographic enterprise and led an intelligence network encompassing 97 agents, the Swiss general staff estimated the number of German divisions in the East at an astonishing 150. Naumov, 1941 god, I: 676 (TsAMO, f. 23, op. 24122, d. 1, l. 49). See also Radó, Pod psevdonim "Dora."

88. The document is only excerpted, and in the form presented shows Soviet military intelligence in a very good light. Naumov, 1941 god, I: 683 (TsAMO, op. 7279, d. 4, l. 30–1); Gavrilov, Voennaia razvedka informiruet, 536–7. Stöbe ("Alta") handed "Aryan" 30,000 German marks. She evidently disliked the aristocratic "Aryan," because of his laments over his still unrealized grandiose diplomatic career and his thirst for money (she lived exceedingly frugally). "Aryan" informed "Alta" that he would also supply information to the British and the French. Around this time, she became ill and requested re-posting to a German spa town to undergo treatment; her request was denied (she was too valuable in Berlin). But as of Jan. 1941, she had lost her plum job in the German foreign ministry (press bureau), though she kept her six agents there. Lota, "Alta" protiv "Barbarossy," 277–9, 305 (no citation).

89. Naumov, 1941 god, I: 704 (TsAMO, f. 23, op. 24119, d. 4, l. 160–1).

90. Welkisch had joined the German Communist party in 1930, worked at the Breslauer Zeitung from 1934, and been recruited into Soviet military intelligence by Herrnstadt in Warsaw. He married Margarita Welkisch, a photographer, in 1937; she had already been recruited into Soviet military intelligence by Herrnstadt.

91. Naumov, 1941 god, I: 706–8 (TsAMO, f. 23, op. 24119, d. 1, l. 296–303). The Geneva Convention legally allowed military attachés to gather information about the armed forces of the country in which they were accredited. Many other Soviet military intelligence representatives, such as Major General Ivan Susloparov ("Maro") in Paris, Nikolai Nikitushev ("Akasto") in Stockholm, and I. A. Sklyarov ("Brion") in London. Their reports are omitted here.

92. Iampol'skii et al., Organy, I/i: viii. "Annihilating his own intelligence apparatus, Stalin cut down a bough, on which he sat, and became a victim of the disinformation of German intelligence," Golikov's deputy later wrote. Novobranets, "Nakanune voiny," 171.

93. Vishlev, "Pochemu zhe," 70–2; Warlimont, Im Hauptquartier der deutschen Wehrmacht, 164;

94. Between Feb. and June 1941, the Soviets fed disinformation to Ivar Lissner, a Baltic German journalist, in Harbin, Manchuria, which purported to be from Russian consulates and embassies, and were designed to

impress upon the Germans the costs of deeper involvement in the Balkans. Barros and Gregor, Double Deception, 52–60.

95. Iampol'skii et al., Organy, I/ii: 44–5 (TsA FSK); Primakov, Ocherki, III: 472 (TsA FSB).

96. Golikov requested clarification from "Sophocles." Gavrilov, Voennaia razvedka informiruet, 548 (TsAMO, f. 23, op. 24119, d. 4, l. 199); "Nakanune voiny (1940–1941 gg.)," at 219. On March 9, "Corsican," who had seen the German air reconnaissance photos of the USSR, including of Kronstadt, conveyed that he had been told the "military attack on the USSR is an already decided issue." Bondarenko, Fitin, 195–6 (citing FSB archives). On March 11, "Ramsay" reported out of Tokyo that Germany was still urging Japan to attack British Singapore. Gavrilov, Voennaia razvedka informiruet, 563–4 (TsAMO, f. 23, op. 24127, d. 2, l. 195–6); Fesiun, Delo Rikharda Zorge, 113 (March 10, 1941), 114–5 (March 15).

97. Gavrilov, Voennaia razvedka informiruet, 564–5 (TsAMO, f. 23, op. 24119, d. 1, l. 394–5). On March 26, 1941, "Yeshenko" reported that "a German attack against Ukraine will occur in two to three months." Lota, Sekretnyi front, 40.

98. Naumov, 1941 god, I: 770.

99. Halder, Halder Diaries, II: 91 (April 30, 1941); Halder, Kriegstagebuch, II: 386–8. On April 2, 1941, Hitler informed Rosenberg of the coming invasion, without specifying the date; Rosenberg immediately formed an office that would become the Ministry for the East.

100. Lota, "Alta" protiv "Barbarossy," 303 (no citation); Gavrilov, Voennaia razvedka informiruet, 577 (no archival citation). At the end of March 1941, Germany had about forty divisions on the frontier. Gavrilov, Voennaia razvedka informiruet, 515.

101. RGASPI, f. 17, op. 163, d. 1304, l. 150–1.

102. Mikoian, Tak bylo, 346. Evidently, complaints against Molotov were reaching Stalin, many a result of Beria intrigues.

103. Friedlander, Prelude, 199.

104. Naumov, 1941 god, I: 607–40, 641–50. See also Zakharov, General'nyi shtab, 226–30. The Red Army had been expanded by creating new divisions, which, by design, were partially manned, rather than by filling out the many existing partially manned divisions. After the onset of a war, all divisions were to be brought to full strength by summoning 5,000 or so reservists for each. But this approach, which had failed under the tsars, did not foresee the constraints that would prevent reservists from reaching their assigned units in time, did not foster unit cohesion in the meantime, and increased the number of required experienced officers, who were in insufficient supply. Reese, Stalin's Reluctant Soldiers, 36–9.

105. Mawdsley, "Crossing the Rubicon," 822–3, 831, 863. This was the southern variant of the approved fall 1940 war plan.

106. V. N. Kiselev, "Upriamye fakty nachala voiny," 18–22; Iampol'skii et al., Organy, I/ii: 50–2 (excerpted); Gor'kov, "Gotovil li," 35; Gor'kov, Kreml', 61. The plan has not been published in full. See also Vasilevskii, Delo vsei zhizni (6th ed.), Politizdat, 112. See also Gareev, Neodnoznachnye stranitsy, 93, 99.

107. Naumov, 1941 god, I: 731–2 (RGASPI, f. 17, op. 3, d. 273, l. 27–8: March 8, 1941); Nakanune voiny (1941 g.)," 198: April 26, 1941); Zhukov, Vospominaniia, I: 307; Gor'kov and Semin, "O kharaktere voenno-operativnykh planov," 109; Na prieme, 328.

108. MP-41 specified two kinds of mobilization, regular or open and "hidden" under the guise of training. "Mobilization is war, and we cannot understand it in any other way," Shaposhnikov had written in the 1920s.

Shaposhnikov, Vospominaniia, 558. "There were reasons enough to try to delay the USSR's entry into the war, and Stalin's tough line not to permit what Germany might be able to use as a pretext for unleashing war was justified by the historic interests of the socialist motherland," Vasilevsky would state. "His guilt consists in not seeing, in not catching, the limit beyond which such a policy became not only unnecessary but also dangerous." Volkogonov, Triumf i tragediia, II/ii: 242.

109. Lota, Sekretnyi front, 129.

110. Jervis, "Strategic Intelligence and Effective Policy," 165–81.

111. Volkogonov, Triumf i tragediia, II/i: 125–48. This would be Khrushchev's self-defense in the secret speech.

112. TsAMO, f. 23, op. 7272, d. 1, l. 693–793 (March 15, 1941); Gavrilov, Voennaia razvedka informiruet, 591–6 (TsAMO, f. 23, op. 7277, d. 1, l. 140–52); Lota, "Alta protiv "Barbarossy," 285–93. According to a top defector's memoir, Tupikov came to the conclusion that about 180 German divisions were being concentrated on the frontier, but Dekanozov dismissed "it airily as a figment of someone's imagination." Akhmedov, In and Out of Stalin's GRU, 145. In fact, Dekanozov reported to Moscow (March 16), 1941: "every day trains are heading east with weaponry (equipment, shells, vehicles and construction materials)." "Kanun voiny: preduprezhdeniia diplomatov," 71.

113. Golikov noted that the main German thrust would supposedly not be for Moscow but Kiev and the riches of Ukraine. Naumov, 1941 god, I: 776–80 (TsAMO, op. 14750, d. 1, l. 12–21); Pavlov, "Sovetskaia voennaia razvedka," 56; Sipols, Tainy, 395.

114. One account claims Golikov met with the despot only twice following his appointment in July 1940. Lota, Sekretnyi front, 6, 46–7. Stalin's office logbook lists five meetings, the last on April 11, 1941. Na prieme, 595. "It is quite true that Golikov was a misinformer—but that is not the point," Gnedich, who delivered Golikov's reports to Stalin, would recall. "All the 'reliable' parts of Golikov's regular reports appeared in one form or another in the official press. Stalin, however, on principle, was interested in anything deemed by Golikov as 'doubtful.'" Erickson, "Threat Identification," 377 (citing a photostatic copy of the transcript of the discussion in the Institute of Marxism-Leninism, 1966, with Gnedich's reminiscences); Petrov, "June 22, 1941," 257; "Sovetskie organy gosudarstvennoi bezopasnosti v gody Velikoi otechestvennoi voiny," 27. In 1965, the historian Viktor Anfilov asked Golikov in the archives about his March 20, 1941, report. Golikov responded: "Did you know Stalin?" Anfilov: "I saw him up on the mausoleum when I stood in the parade columns." Golikov: "Well, I was subordinated to him, I reported to him and was afraid of him. He had formed the opinion that as long as Germany had not finished its war with England it would not attack us. Knowing his character, we constructed our conclusions to conform to his point of view." Anfilov, Doroga k tragedii, 193; Naumov, 1941 god, I: 42–3. According to Novobranets, Golikov issued imprecise orders; then later, if something went wrong, he would say, "I did not give such a directive," or "You misunderstood me." "We did not respect him." Novobranets, "Nakanune voiny," 172.

115. Naumov, 1941 god, I: 776–80 (TsAMO, op. 14750, d. 1, l. 12–21: March 20, 1941); Gavrilov, Voennaia razvedka informiruet, 568–71; Lota, Sekretnyi front, 178–84 (citing TsAMO, op. 14750, d. 1, l. 12–21). "ABC" reported (March 26, 1941) that he had spoken with an adviser in the German embassy in

Romania, who claimed Mihai "Antonsecu told me that his grandfather—the head of state, [Ion] Antonescu—already in January had a meeting with Hitler supposedly devoted by Hitler himself to plans for a war between Germany and the USSR, and that a detailed conversation about this subject also took place during a meeting between Antonescu and Göring in Vienna." Mihai considered the month of May to be "critical." Gavrilov, *Voennaia razvedka informiruet*, 573–4 (TsAMO, f. 23, op. 24119, d. 1, l. 468–9).

116. Iampol'skii et al., *Organy*, I/ii: 61–2 (TsA FSK); "Iz istorii Velikoi otechestvennoi voiny," 207. Also on March 24, "Yeshenko" reported further information from "ABC" about a meeting in Vienna where Göring supposedly told Antonescu to coordinate mobilization of the Romanian army with the German army. Naumov, *1941 god*, 788–9 (TsAMO, f. 23, op. 24119, d. 1, l. 452–5). That same day Stalin received Japanese foreign minister Matsuoka (791–3: APRF, f. 45, op. 1, pap. 404, l. 83–8), and Vysheinsky received Schulenburg (793–6: AVP, f. 07, op. 2, pap. 9, d. 22, l. 44–7).

117. Berezhkov, *S diplomaticheskoi missiei*, 79.

118. Naumov, *1941 god*, I: 804 (AVFRF, f. 082, op. 24, pap. 106, d. 8, l. 307). According to a Moscow NKGB summary of a report from Berlin sent by Kobulov on April 2, 1941, "El'der" met with "Corsican," telling him "about the complete preparation and working out of a plan for an attack on the Soviet Union by his agency." "Elder" was conveyed numerous details of German targets, German discussions concerning the involvement of Romania and Finland, and the opinion of German air ministry officers that an attack would take place. "'Elder' himself is not completely sure that the action will take place." Kobulov's report also included conversations with "Lycée-ist." Naumov, *1941 god*, 13–5 (TsA SVR, d. 23078, t. 1, l. 236–41). On March 31, the NKGB reported that "from December 1940 to the present time the movement of German troops to our borders has strengthened." "Nakanune voiny (1940–1941 gg.)," 208.

119. Sergeienko, *Sinteticheskii kauchuk*; Lewis, "Innovation in the USSR"; Sutton, *Western Technology*, II: vii.

120. The upshot would be a commissariat for rubber. Patolichev, *Isptytanie na zrelost'*, 84–5; *Na prieme*, 329. Patolichev had studied at a rabfak, and in 1937 graduated from the newly established Military Academy of Chemical Defense (one of his classmates was Sorge). By Jan. 1939, still only thirty years old, he was named party boss of Yaroslavl province (replacing Shakhurin) and that year earned the Order of Lenin. In 1940, General Khrulyov introduced Patolichev to Stalin—the name clicked: Patolichev's father, Semyon, had been a friend of Stalin's and died in the Polish-Soviet War in 1920. The son declined Stalin's invitation to assume leadership of the Communist Youth League. Patolichev did manage to get a protégé appointed as first secretary of the Communist Youth League in the Karelo-Finish Soviet Socialist Republic formed in March 1940—a young enthusiast by the name of Yuri Andropov (b. 1914), a graduate of the Rybinsk Water Transport School and, like his mentor in Yaroslavl, an orphan.

121. Hinsley et al., *British Intelligence*, I: 369–70.

122. Stafford, "SOE and British Involvement." The Soviet role in the coup remains murky. Soviet intelligence had dispatched an NKVD operations group to Belgrade headed by Solomon Milstein and including the ace Vasily Zarubin; they arrived on March 11, 1941. Sudoplatov, *Razvedka i kreml'*, 136–7. German

military intelligence suspected Soviet collusion with Britain in the coup. Vishlev, *Nakanune*, 25 (PA AA Boon: I. M. Akten betr. Abwehr allgemein, Bd. 12 [R 101997], Bl. Ohne Nummer [April 15, 1941]. Geheim. Aus vertraulicher Quelle. Betr.: Russland-Juogoslavien; betr. Balkan: Politischer Stimmungsbericht; Büro RAM, betr.: Schreiben des V.A.A. beim OKH vom 28.4.41).

123. Churchill, *Second World War*, III: 144. As in the case of Norway, Britain had helped embroil a neutral country in the war. Unlike Norway, Yugoslavia would be dismembered and descend into civil war. Catherwood, *Balkans in World War Two*, 157.

124. Naumov, *1941 god*, I: 804–5 (TsAMO, op. 7237, d. 2, l. 79–81).

125. This was accompanied by an admission that Barbarossa would be delayed by up to four weeks, which might have happened anyway. *DGFP*, series D, XII: 372–3; Halder, *Kriegstagebuch*, II: 248. See alsao Dedijer, "Sur l'armistice." Erwin Rommel, head of Germany's Afrika Corps, independently launched a desert offensive on March 31, 1941, unaware of Hitler's Yugoslavia directive, the pending invasion of Greece, or Barbarossa, from which his successful actions drained resources. Higgins, *Hitler and Russia*, 104, 108–9; Goerlitz, *Paulus and Stalingrad*, 30–3; Rommel, *Rommel Papers*, 119.

126. Germany, Hitler added, could not count on its allies: the Finns were too few, the Romanians "cowardly, corrupt, depraved." Förster and Mawdsley, "Hitler and Stalin in Perspective," 72–8; Halder, *Kriegstagebuch*, II: 335–8 (March 30, 1941); Warlimont, *Inside Hitler's Headquarters*, 160–1.

127. Tomasevich, *War and Revolution in Yugoslavia*, 50–1.

128. The discussions, in which Colonel Dragutin Savić and Bozin Simić, of the air force, also took part, had begun on April 2, with Vyshinsky. On April 3, Vyshinsky denied that the Soviets had ever mentioned a political and military pact. Stalin played the role of meliorator to obtain the signing. Barros and Gregor, *Double Deception*, 68–9 (citing Bakhmeteff Archive, Columbia University, Prince Regent Paul papers, box 14: Gavrilović to the foreign ministry, April 4, 1941). Soviet-Yugoslav relations dated from June 24, 1940.

129. Clissold, *Yugoslavia and the Soviet Union*, 121–2.

130. Gavrilov, *Voennana razvedka informiruet*, 578–9 (TsAMO, f. 23, op. 24119, d. 4, l. 279–80).

131. Lota, *"Alta" protiv "Barbarossy*," 304; Gavrilov, *Voennaia razvedka informiruet*, 581 (no archival citation). "Yeshenko" out of Bucharest also confirmed the pending German invasion of Yugoslavia (581–2: TsAMO, f. 23, op. 24119, d. 1, l. 521–4).

132. Clissold, *Yugoslavia and the Soviet Union*, 122–3. Hilger speculated: "Nothing the Russians did between 1939 and 1941 made Hitler more genuinely angry than the treaty with Yugoslavia; nothing contributed more directly to the final break." Hilger and Meyer, *Incompatible Allies*, 326–7.

133. Gavrilović conveyed the gist of the meetings to Cripps and the American envoy Laurence Steinhardt. Gorodetsky, *Stafford Cripps in Moscow*, 120 (citing FO 371 29544 N1401/1392/38, Cripps's telegram April 6, cabinet min. April 7); Gorodetsky, *Grand Delusion*, 149–51; *FRUS, 1941*, I: 302 (Steinhardt to Hull, April 6), 311.

134. Sontag and Beddie, *Nazi-Soviet Relations*, 316–20; Fel'shtinskii, *SSSR-Germaniia*, II: 156; Clissold, *Yugoslavia and the Soviet Union*, 123–4.

135. Barros and Gregor, *Double Deception*, 71 (citing European War 1939/9712, RG 59, NA,

file 740.0011: Steinhardt to Sec. of State, no. 703, April 7, 1941; and FO/371/29544: Cripps to Foreign Office, April 6, 1941).

136. This is what Krebs reported from Moscow to Berlin. Teske, *General Ernst Köstring*, 296. See also Barros and Gregor, *Double Deception*, 75 (citing National Archives, German foreign ministry archives, microfilm T120, serial 36, frame 26013–14: Rudolf Likus, April 8, 1941; and Dept. of State Special Interrogation Mission, RG 59: interrogation of Gustav Hilger); Erickson, *Road to Stalingrad*, 74–7 (quoting Gavrilović, no citation); and Narochnitskii, "Sovetsko-iugoslavskii dogovor." The defensive possibilities of the mountains were mentioned in the *Pravda* editorial (April 6, 1941). Churchill, too, vastly overestimated the Serbs' fighting capacity. Hinsley et al., *British Intelligence*, 369.

137. The NKGB operative Sudoplatov recalled: "We didn't expect such total and rapid military defeat of Yugoslavia. We were shocked." Sudoplatov added that Gavrilović, presumed by all and sundry to be a Soviet agent, was not fully trusted by the Soviets; he was seen to be meeting with the British every week. Sudoplatov, *Special Tasks*, 119. Parts of Yugoslavia were annexed by Italy, Bulgaria (Macedonia), Hungary (the Banat), and Germany, which set up a puppet government in Croatia. King Petar fled into exile, making his way to Britain.

138. Vishnevskii, "'Sami peredem v napadenie,'" 105, 107–8; Nevezhin, "Sobiralsia li Stalin nastupat'," 81; Volkogonov, *Triumf i tragediia*, II/i: 127–8. Samuilovich pleaded with Dimitrov (April 12) for instructions on how to characterize the German-Yugoslav war. Dimitrov approached Stalin, who allowed that it was a just war against German aggressors, but at the same time the larger "imperialist" nature of the war held. Lebedeva and Narinskii, *Komintern i Vtoraia mirovaia voina*, 524–6 (RGASPI, f. 495, op. 73, d. 99, l. 23).

139. Mazower, *Inside Hitler's Greece*, 132–3. The Nazi invasion of Greece had been planned for April 1, but was briefly delayed because of the coup in Yugoslavia. Disastrously, Britain sent a force to rescue the Greeks in Feb. 1941: the political authorities in London were moved by what they thought Britain's Near East military commanders desired, while the latter proffered the advice that they thought the politicians in London wanted. Britain's Balkan commitment of 1941 would become a commitment, in 1945, to defend Greece, while in parallel Britain would abandon Poland, the country for which it had gone to war in the first place. Lawlor, *Churchill and the Politics of War*, 165–256, 259.

140. Van Creveld, *Hitler's Strategy*. On the limited, essentially defensive nature of German aims in Greece, see also Schramm-von Thadden, *Griechenland*, 143–4. Göring was among those who wanted to finish off Britain by continued bombing and or seizure of Gibraltar and the Suez. Overy, *Göring*, x.

141. Through most of the 1930s, German and Soviet ciphers remained essentially impregnable to British cryptanalysts, except for what was sent using only low-grade codes (instructions during training exercises, for ex.). The German-manufactured Enigma machine was a system of electro-mechanical rotor ciphers invented by a German engineer, which had been put on the commercial market in the 1920s, but which the German military had progressively made more secure, including going from three to five wheels, making decryption very labor- and resource-consuming. But the Poles reverse-engineered and reconstituted the Enigma, passing a replica to the British. By Aug. 1939, Britain's code and

cipher school had moved to Bletchley Park, to a secluded country house some fifty miles north of London, which was where the Enigma was brought. Finally, in spring 1940, the British broke German naval Enigma communications. The decryption was called "Ultra Secret" or "Ultra." Hinsley et al., *British Intelligence*, I: 53–4, 487–95; Hinsley, *British Intelligence, Abridged Version*, 14–5; Bertrand, *Enigma*. See also Winterbotham, *Ultra Secret*, 10–1.

142. Woodward, *British Foreign Policy*, I: 604; Churchill, *Second World War*, III: 320–1. On March 30, the JIC concluded that the Enigma evidence indicated a large-scale operation against the Soviet Union "either for intimidation or for actual attack." Hinsley et al., *British Intelligence*, I: 451–2 (citing CX/JQ/S/7).

143. Gorodetsky, "Churchill's Warning"; Gorodetsky, *Mission to Moscow*, 118–9.

144. "Nakanune voiny (1940–1941 gg.)," 206–7. On March 24, Cripps advised indirect disclosure to Moscow of the coming German-Soviet war via the Turkish or Chinese ambassadors to the Soviet ambassador in London, Maisky, but his proposal was not immediately acted upon.

145. According to the Soviet report, Cripps also stated that if faced with possible U.S. entry into the war on Britain's side, Germany might seek a peace deal with London involving the restoration of France, Belgium, and the Netherlands, in exchange for German capture of the USSR. Primakov, *Ocherki*, III: 472–3 (TsA FSB).

146. Gorodetsky, *Grand Delusion*, 155–78. Soviet self-isolation was severe: whereas in 1937, Intourist, the Soviet state travel agency, had handled just 13,000 foreign passport holders who came to the USSR and in 1938, 5,000; in 1939–41 it had 3,000 customers, the majority of them from Germany. Dvornichenko, *Nekotorye aspekty funktsionirovaniia industrii turizma*, 23; Orlov and Kressova, "Inostrannyi turizm v SSSR," 163. Zhdanov noted at a meeting at Intourist that wherever foreigners could be expected to congregate, such as hotels and restaurants, "the general course of the Central Committee is not to allow Soviet inhabitants [*grazhdan*] into these places." Golubev, *"Esli mir obrushitsia na nashu Respubliku,"* 80 (citing RGASPI, f. 17, op. 125, d. 11, l. 1).

147. Gorodetsky, *Mission to Moscow*, 123 (citing FO 371 29479 N1573/78/38 Cripps to London, April 12, 1941).

148. Cripps was informed by Vyshinsky on April 23 that the message had been passed to Stalin. Gorodetsky, *Mission to Moscow*, 124 (citing FO 371 29480 N1725/78/38 Cipps to London, April 22, 1941); Gorodetsky, *Grand Delusion*, 155–78; Churchill, *Second World War*, III: 316, 319–23; Woodward, *British Foreign Policy*, I: 606–7; Zhilin, *Kak fashistskaia Germaniia gotovila napadenie*, 219.

149. Cripps did write that "at the moment there is no question whatever if the possibility of such a negotiated peace as far as His Majesty's Government are concerned." Still, his frustration-filled unauthorized memo contradicted government policy. Woodward, *British Foreign Policy*, I: 607–9; Gorodetsky, *Mission to Moscow*, 126–7 (citing FO 371 29465 N1828/3/38); Naumov, *1941 god*, II: 91–6 (AVP RF, f. 07, op. 2, pap. 9, d. 20, l. 34–6); Miner, *Between Churchill and Stalin*, 119–22. The Soviets, by April 26, had a copy of Eden's telegram to Cripps (sent April 17, received at the British embassy in Moscow the 18th): Primakov, *Ocherki*, III: 473–5 (TsA FSB, f. 3 os, op. 8, d. 56, l. 903–6). On May 5, the NKGB sent to Stalin, Molotov, and Beria the April 30, 1941, telegrams from Cripps to the foreign office (obtained in London) in which Cripps alluded to Hitler's likely forthcoming demands on the Soviet Union.

150. Gavrilov, *Voennaia razvedka informiruet*, 416–7 (TsAMO, f. 23, op. 24127, d. 2, l. 198–9: March 11, 1941). Matsuoka's rivals would have seen his trip as reckless grandstanding at a dangerous moment. Such a trip was facilitated by the Trans-Siberian (otherwise a trip by boat, via the Suez, would have lasted many months).

151. Presseisen, *Germany and Japan*, 291, citing *International Military Tribunal*, XXIX: 292–3. Hitler did not inform Japan of the timing of Barbarossa and did not consider Japan's assistance necessary. He would learn from Ott's reports, partly based on Sorge's information, that Japan would not fulfill his wishes of attacking Singapore. Menzel, "German-Japanese Relations," 57; *DGFP*, series D, XII: 931–2 (May 18, 1941, 967–70 (June 6).

152. *Izvestiia*, April 15, 1941; Tisminets, *Vneshniaia politika SSSR*, IV: 549–51; Chihiro, "Japanese-Soviet Neutrality Pact"; *DVP SSSR*, XXX/i: 403, XXX/ii: 111–2, 118. Tikhvinskii, "Zakliuchenie sovetsko-iaponskogo pakta o neitralitete"; Slavinskii, *Pakt o neitralitete mezdu SSSR i Iaponiei*, 91–5; Slavinskii, *Japanese-Soviet Neutrality Pact*. In the Sino-Soviet nonaggression pact, Moscow had promised not to sign a nonaggression pact with Japan until Sino-Japanese relations were normalized. Ledovskii et al., *Russko-kitaiskie otnosheniia*, IV: 583 (AVP RF, f. 3, op. 65, d. 355, l. 42).

153. Japan and the USSR had signed a protocol again extending the 1928 fisheries agreement on Jan. 20, 1941, through year's end, after Japan had made concessions. *Izvestiia*, Jan. 21, 1941; Tisminets, *Vneshniaia politika SSSR* IV: 539–42.

154. Matsuoka, according to information Sorge gleaned from German ambassador Ott, sent a telegram to U.S. secretary of state Hull inquiring about improved bilateral relations. He hoped the United States could be persuaded to cease its support for Chiang Kai-shek, and not be drawn into trade to assist Nazi Germany. The same Soviet intelligence report observed that the new German military attaché in Tokyo "is extremely pessimistic and expects open Japanese treachery, and asked to be released from his post." Gavrilov, *Voennaia razvedka informiruet*, 425 (TsAMO, f. 23, op. 5840, d. 7, l. 87). On April 22, 1941, Soviet military intelligence reported to Moscow that the chief of staff of the Kwantung Army (Takahashi) told a group of journalists that "the USSR, acknowledging the might of Japan, concluded a neutrality pact in order to concentrate its forces in the West." He added that "now Japan's fundamental task is to conclude the Chinese war." Gavrilov, *Voennaia razvedka informiruet*, 423 (TsAMO, f. 23, op. 24127, d. 2, l. 321: April 26, 1941).

155. The diminutive Japanese ambassador to Moscow, Lieutenant General Yoshitsugu Tatekawa, the former head of Japanese military intelligence for the USSR, waved his handkerchief and was heard to say in Russian, "Spasibo, Spasibo (Thank you, thank you)." *DGFP*, series D, XII: 537; Teske, *General Ernst Köstring*, 300–1; Sipols, *Tainy*, 389; Scott, *Duel for Europe*, 234–7 (an eyewitness); Herwarth, *Against Two Evils*, 190; Gorodetsky, *Grand Delusion*, 198. See also Simonov, *Glazami cheloveka moego pokoleniia*, 350–1.

156. Vinogradov et al., *Sekrety Gitlera*, 31–2 (TsA FSB, f. 3o, op. 8, d. 56, l. 789–91). The full report from Kobulov also stated, based on another source, that Matsuoka had signed the Neutrality Pact on German orders, to win the later time. He concluded that this showed that "not only was Germany intending a march against the USSR, but also is taking all necessary diplomatic measures for it." Naumov, *1941 god*, 82–4 (TsA SVR, d. 23078, t. 1, l. 236–301: April 16).

157. "Yeshenko" wrote of Welkisch: "'ABC' reports: 'people are speaking openly and without the least doubt about the pending German military actions against the USSR, Antonescu's meetings more and more concretely concern military preparations against the USSR.'" Gavrilov, *Voennaia razvedka informiruet*, 586–7 (TsAMO, f. 23, op. 24119, d. 1, l. 606–9).

158. RGASPI, f. 17, op. 163, d. 1305, l. 79; *Pravda* followed the activities on its front page (April 19 and 21).

159. Nevezhin, *Zastol'nye*, 259–61 (RGASPI, f. 558, op. 11, d. 1124, l. 17–18); Banac, *Diary of Georgi Dimitrov*, 155–7. *Pravda* (April 23) published a short notice about the Kremlin reception and a long essay (April 24), "One Thousand Years of Tajik Literature," by Iosif Braginsky, the Persian language specialist, stressing that the Tajiks were an Iranian people and culture.

160. *Izvestiia*, March 15, 1941; *Vestnik AN SSSR*, no. 4 (1941): 15–6; "Prazdnik sotsialisticheskoi kul'tury," *Iskusstvo*, 1941, no. 6: 3–10.

161. Nevezhin, *Zastol'nye*, 266–70 (RGASPI, f. 558, op. 11, d. 1124, l. 15–20). The following day (April 23), in the Little Corner, at 7:10 p.m. for fifty minutes, Stalin received the Tajik party boss (Dmitri Protopopov) and government head (M. Kurbanov), as well as Khrapchenko, the head of USSR committee for artistic affairs, evidently to finalize the state wards for the artists. Kalinin, handing out the state awards to the Tajik participants in the Kremlin, quoted Stalin on Tajik culture: "ancient, with a grand reserve among the people, this culture is distinguished by special subtlety." *Pravda*, April 26, 1941; *Na prieme*, 331.

162. Barros and Gregor, *Double Deception*, 38–9 (citing War Department, Military Intelligence Division, General Staff, report 17,875: Jan. 17, 1941, by Colonel B. R. Peyton, MID file 2016–1326/7, MID, correspondence, 1917–1941, box 634, RG 165, NA), 40–4; Laquer and Breitman, *Breaking the Silence*, 282n; Long, *War Diary of Breckinridge Long*, 182–4; Hull, *Memoirs*, II: 967–9; Welles, *Time for Decision*, 170–1; *FRUS, 1941*, I: 712, 714 (Hull to Steinhardt, March 4, 1941), 723; Damaskin, *Stalin i razvedka*, 262–3. Whaley has the timing and source a bit crossed. Whaley, *Codeword*, 37–40, 45, 227–8, 277–8. The U.S. commercial attaché, the Texan Sam Woods (b. 1892), mischaracterized as "a genial extrovert whose grasp of world politics and history was not striking," fooled everyone. Shirer, *Rise and Fall*, 843n; Dippel, *Two Against Hitler*.

163. Boyd, *Hitler's Japanese Confidant*, 21 (citing NSA, RG 457, SRH-252: 30); Damaskin, *Stalin i razvedka*, 262–3. See also Shirer, *Rise and Fall*, chapter 23. Ōshima had been recalled from Berlin in Sept. 1939, after the unpleasant surprise of the Nazi-Soviet Pact. When Laurence Steinhardt, U.S. ambassador, "very confidentially" told foreign affairs commissariat deputy head Lozovsky (April 15) that "according to trustworthy information received from the embassy in Berlin Germany's position is getting worse and worse and it is preparing an attack on Ukraine," Lozovsky said, "I do not think that Germany will attack the USSR . . . In any case the USSR will always be ready and will not allow itself to be captured by enemies." Lozovsky reported that Steinhardt "pledged that in the event of a German attack on the USSR the USA would provide aid to the USSR." Naumov, *1941 god*, 80–1 (AVP RF, f. 06, op. 3,

pap. 4, d. 35, l. 173–7); "Kanun voiny: preduprezhdeniia diplomatov," 80. Welles leaked to Umansky, whose government had him leak to the German ambassador in Washington, that the United States had broken the Japanese codes, and were deciphering Ōshima's communications, on April 28, 1941. DGFP, series D, XII: 661 (Hans Thomsen from D.C. to Berlin). The Americans intercepted and decoded this message.

164. "Kanun voiny: preduprezhdeniia diplomatov," 71–2.

165. The Germans were still demanding the plane's return as of May 15. Fel'shtinskii, Oglasheniiu podlezhit, 330–1 (Ritter to Schulenburg); Iampol'skii et al., Organy, I/ii: 342; Rokossovskii, Soldatskii dolg, 31–2; Bezymenskii, Osobaia papka "Barbarossa," 276.

166. Fel'shtinskii, Oglasheniiu podlezhit, 344–5 (April 22, 1941).

167. Stalin suddenly began overfulfilling his trade obligations, even though the Germans had fallen way behind in reciprocal deliveries. May 1941 would be the peak month for two-way trade. DGFP, series D, XII: 282–3 (March 12, 1941), 826 (May 15); Sontag and Beddie, Nazi-Soviet Relations, 318–9 (report of Schnurre, April 5, 1941); Hilger and Meyer, Incompatible Allies, 326. See also Von Strandmann, "Appeasement and Counter-Appeasement," 164. Stalin also made gestures to Hungary, returning banners and flags from the 1848 revolution (which tsarist troops had put down), and to Romania, with which he settled one border dispute.

168. DVP SSSR, XXIII/ii: 572 (April 15, 1941), 661–3, 714. But Stalin had also jacked up the freight rates for the transhipment of goods to Germany across Soviet territory, pocketing the windfall. Sipols, Tainy, 387; Barros and Gregor, Double Deception, 47 (citing Ministry of Economic Warfare, Trans-Siberian Railway: Freight Rates, April 3, 1941, FO/371/29497). See also Read and Fisher, Deadly Embrace, 608.

169. Soviet capabilities should not be exaggerated. Its advance warning system (VNOS) did not always warn of approaching German aircraft, and Soviet interceptors could not follow them across the frontier so well, while the Red Army lacked sufficient antiaircraft artillery to shoot them out of the sky.

170. Dilks, "'We Must Hope for the Best'"; DBFP, 3rd series, II: 686 (Chamberlain to Halifax, Aug. 19, 1938); Parker, Chamberlain and Appeasement, 291, 347.

171. Osokina, Za fasadom, 272–7.

172. Sipols, Tainy, 389–90. Between March 21 and April 17, a German delegation was shown the major Soviet aviation factories (Moscow, Rybinsk, Molotov). The Germans had let the Soviets see the Heinkel and Junkers aircraft production facilities in Nov.–Dec. 1940, following Molotov's trip to Berlin.

173. Schwendemann, Die Wirtschaftliche Zusammenarbeit, 329; Sudoplatov, Razvedka i Kreml', 135; Vishlev, Nakanune, 30–1.

174. Too many scholars have wrongly interpreted Stalin's behavior in spring 1941 as abject appeasement, without acknowledging the attempted deterrence. Lisann, "Stalin the Appeaser."

175. Teske, General Ernst Köstring, 297.

176. Naumov, 1941 god, II: 131 2; Iampol'skii et al., Organy, I/ii: 122, 128. See also Herwarth, Against Two Evils, 187–8.

177. Sudoplatov, Special Tasks, 117.

178. Below, At Hitler's Side, 92.

179. Rittersporn, Anguish, 56 (citing RGVA, f. 501k, op. 3, d. 534, l. 7ob.–15); Buchheit, Der deutsche Geheimdienst, 253; Plotnikova, "Organy," 31. The existence of a major Luftwaffe air reconnaissance program had been confirmed out of Berlin by "Elder" as early as Dec.

1940. Naumov, 1941 god, I: 550 (TsA SVR, d. 23078, t. 1, l. 199–201), I: 769–70 (TsA SVR), II: 89–91 (TsA SVR, d. 23078, t. 1, l. 269–74), II: 179–80 (TsAMO, f. 23, op. 24119, d. 1, l. 762–3). Stalin was also sending reconnaissance flights over German lines, with German knowledge. Whaley, Codeword, 32; DGFP, series D, XII: 602–3, 1061–3; Weinberg, Germany and the Soviet Union, appendix 3; Sontag and Beddie, Nazi-Soviet Relations, 329.

180. Halder, Halder Diaries, II: 104 (May 7, 1941); Halder, Kriegstagebuch, II: 400–2.

181. Sorge noted: "in Himmler's circles and the general staff there is a strong tendency for launching a war against the USSR, but this tendency is not yet predominant." Gavrilov, Voennaia razvedka informiruet, 585–6 (TsAMO, f. 23, op. 24127, d. 2, l. 300). On April 29, Kegel ("X"), deputy head of the economics section of the German embassy in Moscow, correctly reported that Germany intended to have transferred all the necessary synthetic rubber from Asia by May 15. Gavrilov, Voennaia razvedka informiruet, 710; Lota, Sekretnyi front, 230–4. In April 1941, Korotkov, having returned from Moscow, discussed with Kobulov setting up ciphered radio communications for "Elder" and "Corsican" in the event of war; the effort got bogged down. Costello and Tsarev, Deadly Illusions, 394–6.

182. Naumov, 1941 god, II: 100 (TsAMO, op. 24122/1, l. 178), 105–4 (APRF, f. 93: April 23, 1941), 506; Mel'tiukhov, Upushchennyi shans Stalina, 330, 362–3; Gareev, Neodnoznachnye stranitsy, 115.

183. Ehrenburg, Liudi, gody, zhizn', II: 228.

184. Baranov, Goluboi razliv, 86–7.

185. In fact, from April 1941, the German deployments shifted to a qualitatively new level. Van Creveld, Hitler's Strategy, 150. Tupikov added: "If it happens that, in laying out these conclusions, I am pushing at an open door, this will in no way discourage me. If it happens that I am mistaken, you will correct me—and I shall be grateful." Naumov, 1941 god, II: 113–8 (TsAMO, op. 7272, d. 1, l. 140–52); Lota, Sekretnyi front, 44, 189–97. Only on June 3, 1941, did Golikov instruct his subordinate Kuznetsov that it was necessary to answer Tupikov.

186. Schulenburg and his embassy secretary were back at the Hotel Adlon in less than an hour. Sontag and Beddie, Nazi-Soviet Relations, 330–2. It seems that Hans "Johnnie" Herwath, the anti-Nazi who had divulged the Pact's secret protocols to the American ambassador in Moscow, had quit Germany's Moscow embassy to join the Wehrmacht and through contacts had evidently gotten wind of the firm decision for an attack on the USSR. During a military leave in Berlin, he claims to have used the pretext of visiting his wife, Pussi, who was still working in Moscow, to travel back and inform ambassador Schulenburg that plans for an attack on the USSR were well under way. Herwarth, Against Two Evils, 182–4, 191; Hilger and Meyer, Incompatible Allies, 328; Gorodetsky, Grand Delusion, 203–17; Hinsley, British Intelligence, Abridged Version, 27–8. Stalin would get word of Schulenburg's cold reception by the Führer from (Kegel) "X," who pointed out that in 1939 Hitler had similarly lied to his ambassador to Poland, Hans-Adolf von Moltke.

187. Gorodetsky, Maisky Diaries, 349 (Bernard Bracken). In March 1941, Moscow had ordered a secret police operative, Kyrill Novikov, to accompany Maisky to all official meetings. A telegram from Eden to Cripps (April 18, 1941) obtained by Soviet intelligence in London, inquired whether rapprochement with Moscow was still possible,

but Soviet annexation of the Baltic states remained a stumbling block. Primakov, Ocherki, III: 474–5 (TsA FSB, f. 3, op. 8, d. 56, l. 903–6).

188. Stalin was sent the report the next day. Naumov, 1941 god, II: 130 (TsA SVR, d. 23078, t. 1, l. 349–51). "Elder" had asserted (April 17) that two groups existed, one, led by Göring, champing at the bit to attack the USSR, the other, led by Ribbentrop, dead-set against. This was likely true at the time. Naumov, 1941 god, II: 90 (TsA SVR RF, d. 23078, t. 1, l. 269–74). Hitler seems to have taken Ribbentrop into full confidence on Barbarossa only in April 1941. Weizsäcker would claim that he finally got Ribbentrop to admit it to him on April 21, in Vienna. Nonetheless, the foreign minister gave Weizsäcker approval to compose a memorandum, on April 28, stating that delivering a death blow to the Communist system was not in itself a necessary goal. "Only one thing is decisive: whether this undertaking would hasten the fall of England." The memo further asserted that Britain was already close to collapse. "A German attack on Russia would only give a lift to English morale," the memo predicted. "It would be evaluated there as German doubt of the success of our war against England. We would in this fashion not only admit that the war would still last a long time, but we could in this way actually lengthen instead of shorten it." Weizsäcker, Memoirs, 246–7; Davidson, Trial of the Germans, 154–5.

189. Van Creveld, Hitler's Strategy. Hitler would also shift the main thrust, ordering that following the seizure of Belorussia, Army Group Center was to pause to take the Baltics, resuming the advance on Moscow only after Leningrad and Kronstadt had been captured. He argued that it was necessary to cut the Russians off from the Baltic Sea, to deny them imports, but he envisioned the creation of a Greater Finland as well. Warlimont, Inside Hitler's Headquarters, 138.

190. Naumov, 1941 god, II: 129–30 (TsA SVR, d. 23078, t. 1, l. 352–5).

191. Gavrilov, Voennaia razvedka informiruet, 518.

192. Völkishcher Beobachter, May 5, 1941. A Russian translation of Hitler's May 4 Reichstag speech was conveyed to Soviet front line military districts on June 10, 1941. TsAMO, f. 32, op. 11 306, d. 5 (Volkogonov papers, Hoover, container 7). Colonel Kuznetsov writes that when he reported to the deputy head of the tank forces in the general staff (Panfilov) on German force concentration, "Panfilov said to me that we are being subject to disinformation, adding that only a few minutes ago Comrade Stalin had phoned and said, 'the Germans want to frighten us, at the current time they will not move against us, they themselves are afraid of the USSR.'" Naumov, 1941 god, II: 476 (note to CC department head Silin, Aug. 15, 1941).

193. "Mars" reported out of Budapest (May 1) that German forces were leaving Belgrade for Poland, and that German troops were talking about "the inevitability of war against the USSR in the nearest term." Naumov, 1941 god, II: 150 (TsAMO, f. 23, op. 24119, d. 4, l. 381); Gavrilov, Voennaia razvedka informiruet, 613 On May 5, "Yeshenko" from Bucharest reported on conversations by "ABC" that German forces were being relocated from the Balkans to Romania and the Soviet frontier, as well as many other signs of impending war. Gavrilov, Voennaia razvedka informiruet, 612–4 (TsAMO, f. 23, op. 24119, d. 1, l. 737–40, 744–5).

194. DGFP, series D, 723–5 (Ott, May 6). See also Sipols, Tainy, 392. On May 17, Weizsäcker misinformed Japanese ambassador Ōshima

that "German-Russian relations were unchanged," and that it was wrong to characterize them as "in a state of tension." Sontag and Biddie, *Nazi-Soviet Relations*, 342. See also *Trial of the Major War Criminals*, XII: 165 ("The Ministries' Case").

195. In the same dispatch, forwarded by Merkulov to Stalin and Molotov, "Elder" reported that German officers had told him that Hitler had given a speech some days earlier at the Sports Palace during which he said "in the near future events will take place that will seem inexplicable to many. But the measures, which we will launch, are a state necessity, since the Red Menace has reared its ugly head over 'Europe.'" Naumov, *1941 god*, II: 152 (TsA SVR RF); Iampol'skii et al., *Organy*, I/ii: 292-3 (TsA FSK); Vinogradov et al., *Sekrety Gitlera*, 65-6 (TsA FSB, f. 3os, op. 8, d. 56, l. 1157-8). On May 6, Admiral Kuznetsov wrote to Stalin that the Soviet naval attaché in Berlin (Vorontsov) reported that a Soviet inhabitant named Bozer (a Jew from Lithuania) told the naval attaché's aide that according to one officer in Hitler's HQ, the Germans were preparing to invade on May 14 through Finland, the Baltics, and Romania, but Kuznetsov added: "I suggest that this information is false and specially directed in this fashion to reach our government in order to test how the USSR would react." Volkogonov papers, Hoover Institution Archives, container 18.

196. Pechenkin, "'Sovremennaia armiia,'" 31n9 (no citation); Muratov, "Shest' chasov," 283; Nevezhin, *Sindrom*, 169-70; Nevezhin, *Zastol'ia*, 278-9. Sivkov was sacked from the military academy directorship. Nevezhin, *Sindrom*, 180 (citing RGASPI, f. 17, op. 3, d. 1039, l. 32).

197. Kuztesova, "Nachalo voiny."

198. Further, Stalin claimed that each division numbered 15,000 troops (twice the actual number in many cases). Pechenkin, "'Sovremennaia armiia,'" 26. Zhukov would remind Stalin on June 15, 1941, that "even 8,000-men divisions are practically twice weaker than German ones." Bezymenskii, *Gitler i Stalin*, 427-33.

199. Naumov, *1941 god*, II: 160 (RGASPI, f. 558, op. 1, d. 3808, l. 1-12); Pechenkin, "Sovremennaia armiia,'" 27-8; Nevezhin, *Sindrom*, 170 (citing RGALI, f. 1038, op. 1, d. 2079, l. 31). Over the first six months of 1941, the Soviet Union would produce more than 1,100 T-34 medium tanks and 393 KV heavy tanks, not nearly enough to meet the general staff's professed needs against a German adversary being supplied by all of Europe. In March 1941, Stalin was informed that industry had only enough parts to supply 30 percent of all the army's tank and armored units. New aircraft models were running at 10 to 20 percent of the military's needs. Volkogonov, *Stalin: Triumph*, 375-6 (citing TsAMO, f. 15a, op. 2154, d. 4, l. 224-33).

200. Pechenkin, "'Sovremennaia armiia,'" 28-9); Banac, *Diary of Gerogi Dimitrov*, 159-60; Muratov, "Shest' chasov," 282.

201. Malyshev, "Dnevnik narkoma," 116. See also Anfilov, "'Razgovor zakonchilsia ugrozoi Stalina,'" 41.

202. Bezymenskii, *Gitler i Stalin*, 437.

203. Muratov, "Shest' chasov"; Nevezhin, *Zastol'nye*, 291-3. There is no stenographic account of the May 5, 1941, speech and no written notes by Stalin found in his personal papers. Naumov, *1941 god*, II: 294n2. Malyshev and Dimtrov wrote accounts for their diaries. Nevezhin, *Zastol'nye*, 273-93. Pechenkin, "'Sovremennaia armiia.'" This is the so-called "brief record" made by K. V. Semenov, a staff person at the defense commissariat.

204. Banac, *Diary of Georgi Dimitrov*, 160.

205. Pechenkin, "'Sovremennaia armiia,'" 29; Naumov, *1941 god*, II; 161-2; Vainrub, *Eti stal'nye parnii*, 19; Nevezhin, *Zastol'nye*, 287-8, 290-1.

206. Malyshev, "Dnevnik narkoma," 115, 116-7; Muratov, "Shest' chasov," 284-5; Pechenkin, "'Sovremennaia armiia,'" 29-30; Nevezhin, *Zastol'nye*, 279-80.

207. *Pravda*, May 3, 1941.

208. Pechenkin, "'Sovremennaia armiia,'" 29-30; Naumov, *1941 god*, II; 161-2; Nevezhin, *Zastol'nye*, 287-9 (at 289); Muratov, "Shest' chasov," 285; Nevezhin, *Sindrom*, 174-6.

209. Muratov, "Shest' chasov," 287; Zhipin, *Kak fashistskaia Germaniia gotovila napadenie*, 224; Liashchenko, "S ognem i krov'iu popolam"; Radzinskii, *Stalin*, 485 (quoting Chadayev, unpublished ms., "V groznye vremena," GARF, without detailed citation). Sivkov was sacked a few days later. Nevezhin, *Sindrom*, 180 (RGASPI, f. 17, op. 3, d. 1049, l. 32). Both of Sivkov's brothers, Alexander and Pyotr, also military men, had been executed in 1938.

210. Schulenburg would send an account of the speech to Berlin only a month later, suggesting that Stalin seemed "anxious to prepare his followers for a new 'compromise' with Germany." *DGFP*, series D, XII: 964-5 (June 4, 1941).

211. Golubev et al., *Rossiia i zapad*, 111 (citing RGASPI, f. 17, op. 125, d. 60, l. 58-9). The party apparatus held conferences on May 8 and 9, 1941, with editors of the major newspapers and journals and those responsible for the TASS news agency. Zhdanov, addressing a special gathering of fifty-four invited film industry personnel, directors, cameramen, actors, and studio heads, as well as twenty-seven top propaganda functionaries and newspaper editors, on May 14-15, blustered about the Baltics, Western Ukraine, Western Belorussia, and Bessarabia, and how "if circumstances permit, we shall widen the front of socialism still more." Alexander Zaporozhets, head of propaganda for the army's political directorate, was ordered to revise propaganda for the troops. But draft decrees were not readied until late May or in the case of the military, June, and would not be approved prior to June 22. Nevezhin, *Sindrom*, 186-251; Nevezhin, "Dve direktivy 1941 g.," 191-207; Golubev et al., *Rossiia i zapad*, 105-7 (citing RGASPI, f. 17, op. 121, d. 115, l. 3-7, 124, 162). Kalinin gave a provocative closed speech (May 20, 1941) to a party and Communist Youth League meeting of the Supreme Soviet presidium staff, in which he castigated Britain and France for fighting poorly, noting "if the same thing were happening here, it would be judged a criminal unpreparedness for war." Kalinin suggested that "the army should think: the sooner the fight starts, the better." He received a rousing ovation. Nekrich, *Pariahs*, 231-3 (citing RGASPI, f. 78, op. 1, d. 84, l. 6-7, 20-1, 35-6). In May, Soviet radio broadcasts directed at German soldiers took on an antagonistic tone. Hoffman, "Podgotovka Sovetskogo Soiuza," 247.

212. RGASPI f. 558, op. 11, d. 769, l. 176-176 ob.: April 28, 1941.

213. Stalin had the Central Committee approve the politburo recommendation by voice vote. "'Naznachit' tov. Stalina I. V.' postanovelnie politbiuro TsK VKP (b) Mai 1941 g."; RGASPI, f. 17, op. 3, d. 1039, l. 13; Naumov, *1941 god*, II: 155-7 (RGASPI, f. 2, op. 1, d. 1a, l. 1, 3-4); *Pravda*, May 7, 1939; *Izvestiia*, May 7, 1939. The decree stated that Molotov was removed "in light of numerous declarations that he has difficulty fulfilling his duties

alongside the duties of a people's commissar." Zhdanov arrived from Leningrad, and was the sole person Stalin received on May 5, for twenty-five minutes. A May 7 meeting in Stalin's office evidently hashed out how a new Council of People's Commissars would operate: present were Voznesensky, Molotov, Bulganin, Kaganovich, Mikoyan, Beria, and Shakhurin. *Na prieme*, 332.

214. Khlevniuk et al., *Stalinskoe Politburo*, 34-5 (citing APRF f. 3, op. 52, d. 251, l. 58-60); "'Naznachit' tov. Stalina I. V.'," 222.

215. Sudoplatov, *Special Tasks*, 121. See also Petrov, "June 22, 1941," 257 (Gnedich).

216. Boelcke, *Secret Conferences*, 158-9 (May 7). Alexander Kerensky told the *New York Times* that the formalization of Stalin's power signified his active participation in the war on the Nazi side. *New York Times*, May 7, 1941.

217. *DGFP*, series D, XII: 791. See also Akhmedov, *In and Out of Stalin's GRU*, 139-40.

218. Naumov, *1941 god*, II: 151.

219. Halder, *Halder Diaries*, II: 100 (May 5, 1941); Halder, *Kriegstagebuch*, II: 400-2. Halder also recorded Krebs's opinion that the Russian upper officer corps was "decidedly bad" and that "compared with 1933, picture is strikingly depressing. It will take twenty years to reach her old level." Krebs was also dubious about Soviet pilots.

220. Naumov, *1941 god*, II: 167-9 (APRF, f. 3, op. 4, d. 675, l. 158-62). Pavlov composed his record of the breakfast that same day. Voiushin and Gorlov, "Fashistskaia agressiia," 22- (citing AVP RF, f. 082, op. 23, pap. 96, d. 16a, l. 120-4).

221. Lota, *Sekretnyi front*, 59. Also in May 1941, the Germans sent a group of Berlin opera soloists to perform in Moscow, and the NKGB operative Zoya Rybkina (b. 1907), posing as a representative of the Society for Cultural Ties Abroad, attended the reception at the German embassy, where she discovered a pile of suitcases, and walls emptied of paintings. Voskresenskaia, *Teper' ia mogu skazat' pravdu*, 10-16; Voskresenskaia, *Pod psevdonimom Irina*, 38-44; Sudoplatov, *Special Tasks*, 123. Vinogradov et al., *Sekrety Gitlera*, 166-8, 97-8 (d. 57, l. 1287-8: May 14). ("Rybkina" became a children's writer under the name Voskresenskaya.) Also on May 7, Tito ("Walter") sent two coded telegrams to Dimitrov reporting intensive German preparations for an attack. Lebedeva and Narinskii, *Komintern i Vtoraia mirovaia voina*, 536 (RGASPI, f. 495, op. 184, d. 7 no. 412, l. 112), 537 (no. 423, l. 116).

222. This was forwarded by Merkulov to Stalin, Molotov, and Beria on May 14, and included additional detail about Romania's preparations for war. Naumov, *1941 god*, II; 181-4 (APRF, f. 3, op. 64, d. 675, l. 162-8). See also Sipols, *Tainy*, 403.

223. Hilger speculated that Hitler perceived Soviet weakness, fear. Hilger and Mayer, *Incompatible Allies*, 327.

224. Naumov, *1941 god*, II; 181-4 (APRF, f. 3, op. 64, d. 675, l. 162-8). See also Sipols, *Tainy*, 403.

225. Khlevniuk, *Master of the House*, 243-4 (no citation); Khlevniuk, *Stalin: Zhizn'*, 251-2 (citing GARF, vospominaniia Ia. E. Chadaeva). On May 8, Stalin received Khrushchev, alone, for thirty minutes; nearly four hours later, he received Beria, alone, for five minutes. Those were the only people he saw that day. *Na prieme*, 333. As of May 10, Molotov was back in the customary position, entering the Little Corner before any other visitors. *Na prieme*, 333.

226. Boberach, *Meldungen aus dem Reich*, VII: 3374, 2380, 2394.

227. Lota, *"Alta" protiv "Barbarossy,"* 305.

228. Whether it was noticed in Moscow remains uncertain.

229. *DVP SSSR*, XXIII/ii: 654–7, 664–7, 675–9; Naumov, *1941 god*, II: 193 (APRF, f. 3, op. 64, d. 675, l. 174: Molotov instructions to Dekanozov, May 12), II: 193–5 (l. 169–73: Dekanozov notes); *DGFP*, series D, XII: 734–5 (May 7, 1941); Gorodetsky, *Grand Delusion*, 218–21 (citing APRF, f. 3, op. 64, d. 675, l. 169–73: Dekanozov notes on May 12 breakfast); Hilger and Meyer, *Incompatible Allies*, 351. There is nonsense, from Mikoyan and Kumanev, that Schulenburg had warned Dekanozov, in the presence of Hilger and Pavlov, of the forthcoming invasion. Kumanev, "'22ogo' na rassvete," 3. "He didn't warn," Molotov stated of Schulenburg, "he just hinted at it." Chuev, *Molotov Remembers*, 29.

230. *Na prieme*, 332–3.

231. Hess's flight likely was unassisted by German electronic systems. Deighton, "Hess the Aviator," 121–38. One of the Luftwaffe's best pilots would claim, after the war, that on May 10, 1941, Göring had called and ordered him to intercept Hess, who was already in the air. Adolph Galland, the pilot, would also claim that he implemented the order only perfunctorily, having no idea how to find Hess's Messcherschmitt Bf 110 amid all the others in the sky at that time. Tolliver and Constable, *Fighter General*.

232. Fox, "Propaganda," 88 (citing FO 1093/10: Medical Research Council report); Rees et al., *Case of Rudolf Hess*, 16; Pick, *Pursuit of the Nazi Mind*, 42. See also Hess, *Prisoner of Peace*, 31–8.

233. Gorodetsky, *Grand Delusion*, 246–9 (citing WO 199/3288/A: May 11, 1941, and FO 1093/11 fols. 152–5).

234. Heiden, "Hitler's Better Half."

235. Schellenberg, *Schellenberg Memoirs*, 201. Churchill would later assert that Hess denied Germany was planning an invasion and asserted that Germany had certain demands the USSR would have to satisfy—i.e., the ultimatum. Churchill, *Second World War*, II: 46.

236. Engel, *Heeresadjutant bei Hitler*, 103 (May 11, 1941); Schmidt, *Statist*, 549; Kershaw, *Hitler: 1936–1945*, 372, citing Heinz Linge, "Kronzuege Linge: der kammerdiener des 'Führers,'" *Revue, Munich*, Nov. 1955–March 1956, 60; Halder, *Halder Diaries*, II: 117–8 (May 15, 1941); Halder, *Kriegstagebuch*, II: 412–5. Hess left four letters: the others were for his wife, Ilse, Willy Messerschmitt (whose plane he took), and Helmut Kaden (whose flight suit he took).

237. Kershaw, *Hitler: 1936–1945*, 372–3.

238. Fest, *Face*, 292; Kershaw, *Hitler: 1936–1945*, 375–6.

239. Kershaw, *Hitler: 1936–1945*, 372. When Hitler summoned Mussolini on June 2, 1941, to the Brenner Pass they talked, among other matters, about Hess. The Führer was said to have had tears in his eyes. Corvaja, *Hitler and Mussolini*, 174.

240. Fröhlich, *Tagebücher von Joseph Goebbels*, IX: 309–10 (May 13, 1941). See also Below, *Als Hitlers Adjutant*, 274. The next day the Germans issued a fuller statement, calling Hess's mission a result of "mental confusion" that would change nothing in German-British relations. Goebbels had objected, to no avail ("It's rightly being asked how such an idiot could be the second man after the Führer"). Domarus, *Hitler: Reden*, IV: 1716; Fröhlich, *Tagebücher von Joseph Goebbels*, IX: 311 (May 14). See also Noakes and Pridham, *Nazism*, IV: 532 (Leipzig SD report, May 17, 1941).

241. Kershaw, *Hitler: 1936–1945*, 375; Gamm, *Der Flüsterwitz*, 36; Vassiltchikov, *Berlin Diaries*, 51 (May 18, 1941).

242. The British interrogator (Ivone Kirkpatrick) concluded: "Hess does not seem . . . to be in the near counsels of the German government as regards operations; and he is not likely to possess more secret information that he could glean in the course of his conversations with Hitler and others." See also Schmidt, "Der Hess-Flug," 14. Goebbels (May 15) intuited that the British had chosen to "let the lies run free" and became gleeful that the British had failed to play this trump card properly, and said the German people were comparing the incident to "a razor cut on the face" that would heal quickly and be forgotten. Fröhlich, *Tagebücher von Joseph Goebbels*, IX: 317–9 (May 17, 1941); Boelcke, *Secret Conferences*, 165 (May 19).

243. Tsarev, "Poslednii polet," III: 433–40. On May 18, Philby, after a conversation with a foreign office press department contact, reported that Hess had not given away any valuable information, remained loyal to Hitler, and called the German-British war a crime. Tsarev, "Poslednii polet," III: 435–7; Naumov, *1941 god*, II: 200–1 (May 14, 1941).

244. Khrushchev, *Memoirs*, I: 272; Khrushchev, *Khrushchev Remembers*, 116. The Soviets also believed the British secret services had been involved in luring Hess. Andrew and Mitrokhin, *Mitrokhin Archive*, 157; and Erickson, "Rudolf Hess." Roosevelt doubted the official British story as well, and feared there was substance to the rumors of a substantive peace mission. Kimball, "Hess Distraction"; Kimball, *Churchill and Roosevelt*, I: 184–6; Pick, *Pursuit of the Nazi Mind*, 45 (citing PPF3716, letters from John Coar and Ambassador William Dodd). Dekanozov sent Molotov a comprehensive analysis (May 21, 1941) of the Hess mission, based on the German press and hearsay in Berlin, asserting that it proved the existence of divisions within the German leadership and a tendency toward an agreement with Britain. It was forwarded to Stalin on May 26. Nauomv, *1941 god*, II: 261–6 (APRF, f. 3, op. 64, d. 689, l. 64–74).

245. Cripps, in some desperation back on April 23, 1941, had telegrammed London about Soviet-German negotiations (which did not exist), speculating that Hitler could get what he wanted from Moscow by blackmail without war, and that the Soviets feared a separate deal between Britain and Germany, which could be used by London to prevent a Soviet-German deal. He stressed that only the fear of a separate peace would bring the Soviets around to the British side. This had been intercepted and decrypted, and forwarded by Fitin on May 5 to Stalin, Molotov, and Beria. Naumov, *1941 god*, II: 152–3 (TsA FSB, f. Zos, op. 8, d. 56, l. 1160–3). Cadogan noted in his diary (May 30, 1941), effectively repudiating Cripps, that because of British military weakness, its diplomacy was "completely hamstrung. For instance—Russia. You can't do anything nowadays with any country unless you can a) threaten b) bribe it. Russia has a) no fear of us *whatever* and b) we have *nothing* to offer her." Dilks, *Diaries of Sir Alexander Cadogan*, 382.

246. Woodward, *British Foreign Policy*, I: 614–5; Gorodetsky, *Mission to Moscow*, 134–5.

247. Gorodetsky, *Grand Delusion*, 262–7 (citing AVP RF, f. 059, op. 1, pap. 352, d. 2402, l. 174, and *The Times*, May 27, 1941). See also Görtemaker, "Bizarre Mission," 75–101; Kettenacker, "Mishandling a Spectacular Event,"

19–38; and Fox, "Propaganda." On June 5, Maisky insisted to Eden that no German-Soviet negotiations were under way; Eden replied that he knew they were. Gorodetsky, *Grand Delusion*, 273 (citing AVP RF, f. 059, op. 1, pap. 352, d. 2402, l. 149–52: Maisky to Moscow); Gorodetsky, *Maisky Diaries*, 359. Woodward gives the date of this encounter as June 10: *British Foreign Policy*, I: 620.

248. Sudoplatov, *Special Tasks*, 123. See also Gorodetsky, *Grand Delusion*, 221–2. The Japanese ambassador to Moscow complained to Tokyo that Soviet counterintelligence was smothering, adding that "they steal suitcases from military attachés." Khaustov, "Deiatel'nost' organov," 289 (TsA FSb, f. 3, op. 5, d. 82, l. 51), 304 (TsA FSB, f. 66, op. 1, d. 391, l. 55). Schulenburg reported to Berlin (May 24, 1941) that he had been received by Molotov with the familiar degree of confidence and in the same office as previously, albeit with the nameplate altered (to deputy chairman), but that Molotov effectively held the same position of power as previously—Stalin's top deputy. The ambassador added that Soviet policy remained "directed at avoidance of a conflict with Germany," which was "proved by the attitude taken by the Soviet government in the last few weeks, the tone of the Soviet press, . . . and the observance of the trade agreements concluded with Germany." Nonetheless, he began to resign himself to having failed in his larger mission. He had finally acquired his dream castle, the Burg Falkenberg in the Upper Palatinate, in the late 1930s, and, after Molotov's disastrous Nov. 1940 visit to Berlin, Hitler had ordered that the count be given a humongous bribe, 200,000 reichsmarks, which the count had used to renovate it. Herwarth, *Against Two Evils*, 95–6; Sontag and Biddie, *Nazi-Soviet Relations*, 344–5; Fleischhauer, *Diplomatischer Widerstand*, 312, 404n; *DVP SSSR*, XXIII/ii: 521 (Soviet assessment of Schulenburg, from the former KGB archive).

249. Fleischhauer, *Diplomatischer Widerstand*, 194.

250. Some have speculated that the aircraft delivered a letter from Hitler to Stalin, supposedly a response to an earlier Stalin letter requesting an explanation for the German troop build-up. Zhukov, in interviews in 1966, said: "Sometime in early June I decided that I should again try to convince Stalin of the accuracy of the intelligence reports on the approaching danger. . . . Together with Defense Commissar Semyon Konstantinovich Timoshenko we brought along general staff maps with the locations of enemy troops. I reported. Stalin listened attentively but silently. After my report he sent us away without giving us his opinion . . . A few days passed and Stalin called for me. When I entered he was seated at his desk. I approached. Then he opened the middle drawer and took out several pieces of paper. 'Read,' said Stalin. I began to read. It was a letter from Stalin to Hitler in which he briefly outlined his concern over the German deployments, about which I had reported a few days earlier." Bezymenskii, *Gitler i Stalin*, 472. Zhukov told Simonov around the same time (1965–6) that at a Jan. 1941 meeting Stalin had he "turned to Hitler in a personal letter advising him that this was known to us, that it surprised us, and that it created the impression among us that Hitler intended to go to war with us." Hitler's supposed reply: Yes, there are large military formations on the frontier, but they "are not directed against the Soviet Union." Simonov, "Zametki k biografii G. K. Zhukova," 50–1 (published twenty-one years after the conversation). No such documents have emerged

from Soviet or German archives. Hitler did have a secret archive, but in the bunker on April 22, 1945, he would order his adjutant to liquidate the contents of two safes; other such safes were found in Berghof and in his Munich apartment; their contents would be destroyed, including Hitler's correspondence with heads of state. But even so, copies would be expected to be in Soviet archives.

251. Sontag and Biddie, *Nazi-Soviet Relations*, 339–41; Fel'shtinskii, *SSSR-Germaniia*, II: 164–5. That same evening, Schulenburg received instructions from Berlin to inform the Soviets that the alleged seventy-one border violations by Germans were "being investigated," and that the investigation would "require some time." Sontag and Biddie, *Nazi-Soviet Relations*, 341–42. According to Zhukov, sometime in May 1941 Stalin told him and Timoshenko that German ambassador Schulenburg had requested that German officers be allowed to reconnoiter the Soviet border in what they presented as a search for the graves of German soldiers who went missing in World War I. Zhukov, *Vospominaniia*, I: 346–7; Ivanov, *Shtab armeiskii*, 98–9.

252. Mawdsley, "Crossing the Rubicon," 849–53. See also Lota, *"Alta" protiv "Barbarsossy,"* 309–10.

253. The proposed surprise attack of 152 divisions and 3,000–4,000 aircraft against German positions in former southern Poland carried timetables and maps of the theater (one map carried a date, the lone one on the document). Gor'kov, "Gotovil li," 40–5; Gor'kov, *Kreml'*, 303–9; Naumov, *1941 god*, II: 215–20 (TsAMO, f. 16, op. 2951, d. 237, l. 1–15); Bobylev, "Tochku v diskussii stavit' rano"; Zakharov, *General'nyi shtab*, 219–21. A partial, misleading version of the Vasilevsky plan was published: Kiselev, "Upriamye fakty nachala voiny," 18–22. There has also been misleading commentary: Volkogonov, *Triumf i tragediia*, II/i: 136. For an analysis, see Bezymenskii, "O 'Plane Zhukova.'" Bezymensky was Zhukov's interpreter during the war. He reproduced a facsimile of some pages of the May 15 war plan (showing the quality penmanship): Bezymenskii, *Gitler i Stalin*, 478–9. The April 1941 local version of the war plan stated: "The USSR does not contemplate attacking Germany and Italy. These states are probably also not contemplating attacking the USSR in the near future." Solonin, "Tri plana tovarischa Stalina," 45–49.

254. Anfilov, "'Razgovor zakonchilsia ugrozoi Stalina,'" 40–1; Forster and Mawdsley, "Hitler and Stalin in Perspective," 86. There is a third-hand account of a blow-up between Stalin and Zhukov and Timoshenko. Bezymenskii, "O 'Plane Zhukova,'" 61–2, 62n27 (citing General Nikolai Liashchenko, a major in 1941, who recorded conversations with Timoshenko in the 1960s); Gorodetsky, *Grand Delusion*, 299 (citing the same source). A less dramatic version appears in Svetlishin, *Krutye stupeni*, 57–8 (interviews with Zhukov).

255. Anfilov, "'Razgovor zakonchilsia ugrozoi Stalina,'" 41. Stalin also met with Timoshenko and Zhukov, but not Vatutin, on May 23, for two hours and fifty-five minutes. *Na prieme*, 333–4.

256. Molotov cautioned in connection to those such as Vasilevsky who claimed to know Stalin's thinking: "'Stalin believed this, Stalin thought that.' As if anyone knew what Stalin thought about the war." Chuev, *Sto sorok*, 42, 45.

257. Anfilov, "'Razgovor zakonchilsia ugrozoi Stalina,'" 41; Anfilov, *Doroga k tragedii*, 166; Svetlishin, *Krutye stupeni*, 57–8. The document's authenticity is beyond question, but in addition to the lack of signatures, there are no

markings by Stalin on it. The document was apparently locked in the personal safe of Vasilevsky until 1948, and not kept in Stalin's archive or Zhukov's. From Vasilevsky's safe it went to the military archives (TsAMO RF, f. 16a, op. 2951, d. 237). Danilov, "Stalinskaia strategiia nachala voiny."

258. Gor'kov, "Gotovil li," 40–1. A May 15 special communication by Golikov on the dislocation of German forces estimated 114–19 divisions in the frontier zone, and concluded: "The strengthening of German forces on the border with the USSR continues. The main territories of concentration are the southern part of the General-Gouvernement, Slovakia, and the northern part of Moldavia." Lota, *Sekretnyi front*, 205–9 (citing TsAMO, op. 7237, d. 2, l. 109–13); Gavrilov, *Voennaia razvedka informiruet*, 518. Vasilevsky would later show hindsight appreciation of German force concentrations, which had not been reflected in the May 15 war plan text. Kumanev, *Riadom so Stalinym*, 232–3. See also Anfilov and Golikov, *Zagadka 1941 goda*, 251; Vasilevskii, *Delo vsei zhizni*, 310.

259. A special inspection (May 23–June 5, 1941) of western military districts found their combat readiness unsatisfactory. Volkogonov, "German Attack," 80.

260. Gareev, *Neodnoznachnye stranitsy*, 96. Only at the end of May 1941 had the general staff organized a war game to test the viability of covering plans under conditions of surprise attack. Nothing is known of the game's results. Denisova and Tumash, *Nakanune*, 391. See also Murin, "Nakanune," 9 (Arkhiv politbiuro TsK KPSS, f. 73, op. 2, d. 3, l. 30–44).

261. Mawdsley, "Crossing the Rubicon," 836–44. Mawdsley, whose analysis is the best in print, notes that the late amendations by Vatutin were defensive, not preemptive, suggesting confusion or compromise even in the drafting, although these changes might have been written in Stalin's presence. The assertion that Hitler's invasion preempted an imminent Soviet attack, a baldfaced German lie circulated to justify their invasion, was shredded by Gabriel Gorodetsky, *Mif "Ledokola."*

262. Preemption bordered on the preposterous. The May 15 war plan envisioned 196 Soviet divisions concentrated in the West; as of June 22, first and second strategic echelons numbered 56 rifle and cavalry divisions on the western frontier and 52 at a distance of 60–250 miles from the frontier. Many of these divisions were under-strength in personnel and equipment. Moreover, whereas MP-41 stipulated 6.5 million troops in the west, on June 22 there were 3 million. In the Western special military district—"special" meant the district was supposed to be able to battle without added reserves—a significant number of Pavlov's divisions were made up of reservists, who had almost no training; the district had only a single mechanized corps. It relied on the civilian communications network. It was expected to complete its combat preparations in the first half of 1942. Mawdsley, "Crossing the Rubicon," 855; Zolotarev, *Russkii arkhiv: Velikaia otechestvennaia*, XII (I): 339–40 (RGVA, f. 4, op. 15, d. 27, l. 575–607); Gareev, *Neodnoznachnaye stranitsy*, 12; Murin, "Nakanune," 10 (Vasilevsky); "GKO postanovliaet . . . ," 20–1; Nekrich, *Pariahs*, 242–3. See also Nikulin, *Tukhachevskii*, 194. Soviet military districts were converted to "fronts" for war. This had happened on Sept. 11, 1939, for Poland (six days in advance); on Jan. 7, 1940, for Finland (in media res, reflecting the change in the war strategy); on June 9, 1940, for Bessarabia (nine days in advance); and in March 1941: northwest, west (central), and southwest. On May 27, Timoshenko would

order that field command points be set up for the "fronts." Vishlev, *Nakanune*, 29, 42–3; Vasilevskii, *Delo vsei zhizni*, 119.

263. One goal was to create a second strategic echelon along the Dnieper and Western Dvina Rivers but beyond the range of Luftwaffe aerial reconnaissance. (The first strategic echelon was already deployed within the boundaries of the frontier military districts at sixty or fewer miles from the border.) Gorkov, "Gotovil li," 40–5; Zhukov, *Vospominaniia*, I: 345–6; Ivanov, *Nachal'nyi period voiny*, 211–2; Vasilevskii, *Delo vsei zhizni*, 114.

264. On the night and early morning of May 14–15, Stalin met with Timoshenko and Zhukov yet again, along with Kaganovich, railways commissar, a crucial aspect of mobilization. *Na prieme*, 333. Soviet railway capacity limits on mobilization were a long-standing subject of Soviet analysis. Naumov, *1941, god*, I: 545–8 (RGAE, f. 1884, op. 49, d. 1247, l. 1–6: Jan. 17, 1941). On these problems in the Imperial Russian Army, see Fuller, *Strategy and Power*, 303–6. On May 24, Stalin gathered more than twenty military men and other officials in the Little Corner from around 6:00 p.m., for three and a half hours. *Na prieme*, 334. Almost no information on this meeting has been adduced by Soviet military historians with access to the archives. Even the politburo special files contain no information on what was discussed or decided. RGASPI, f. 17, op. 162, d. 34–5. Stalin next saw Timoshenko and Zhukov in the Little Corner on June 3, and again on June 6, 7, 9, 11, 18, and 21. The regime sought to get this stance across in the provincial press and the Red Army's army political-propaganda directorate. Golubev et al., *Rossiia i zapad*, 110 (citing RGASPI, f. 17, op. 121, d. 128, l. 36). Vishnevsky had attended Stalin's May 5 speech and the closed door sessions of the army political-propaganda directorate. He wrote in his diary (May 13, 1941): "the struggle against Germany," . . . "against fascism, against the most dangerous military neighbor, in the name of revolutionizing Europe and, of course, Asia." Vishnevsky also mentioned Stalin's words at the Tajik banquet (April 22): "about Lenin, about a new ideology, about the brotherhood of peoples, about the ruinous and dead ideology of racism." Golubev et al., *Rossiia i zapad*, 118 (citing RGALI, f. 1038, op. 1, d. 2079, l. 31).

265. Gavrilov, *Voennaia razvedka informiruet*, 628–9 (TsAMO, f. 23, op. 24119, d. 4, l. 435).

266. Meissner, *Staatssekretär unter Ebert, Hindenburg, Hitler*.

267. Berezhkov, *S diplomaticheskoi missiei*, 73; Berezhkov, *At Stalin's Side*, 53; AVPRF, f. 082, op. 23, p. 95, d. 6, l. 141–2 (Nov. 19, 1940); Barros and Gregor, *Double Deception*, 150–9.

268. Fröhlich, *Tagebücher von Joseph Goebbels*, IX: 333–5. Werner Wächter, chief of staff in Goebbels propaganda ministry, would later call this "the age of whispering propaganda," and boast about the flood of rumors, "all of which were equally credible, so that in the end there wasn't a bugger left who had any idea what was really up." Boelcke, *Secret Conferences*, 174 (1942).

269. Naumov, *1941 god*, II: 270–1 (PA AA Bonn. Dienstelle Ribbentrop. UdSSR-RC, 7/1 R 27168, B126041–26043); Vishlev, *Nakanune*, 153–4. Hilger would later write that "we thought the stories were being circulated deliberately, to exert pressure upon the Soviet Union" for extortion. Hilger and Mayer, *Incompatible Allies*, 328–9. See also Barros and Gregor, *Double Deception*, 198, 225.

270. Vinogradov et al., *Sekrety Gitlera*, 124–7 (TsA FSB, f. 03os, op. 8, d. 57, l. 1500–4);

Naumov, *1941 god*, II: 259–60; Primakov, *Ocherki*, III: 483–5. On May 27, British forces approached the outskirts of Baghdad, and German personnel prepared to evacuate. That same day the British sank the battleship *Bismarck*. In East Africa, Italy had capitulated to British forces (on May 18); Rommel, in North Africa, was faring poorly; Germany was suffering high casualties in efforts to seize Crete. (Of course, Germany had vast unused forces coiled to attack the USSR that were not being used against Britain.) All this could be considered to have put a definitive end to the concept of a German "peripheral strategy" attack in the Near East.

271. A Soviet counterintelligence profile (June 1940) noted: "Köstring has perfect command of Russian . . . an experienced and cunning person . . . commands an enormous tactical horizon, undergirded by rich practical experience." The profile added: "At every occasion Köstring uses personal observations, conversations with the local population to compose wide-ranging overviews, reports and so on about the situation of the population, new construction sites etc." Pogonii, *Lubianka, 2*, 225. Hitler had briefed Köstring about his intention to attack the USSR already on Sept. 3, 1940, in the company of Halder, but the specifics of Barbarossa do not appear to have been known to him. Halder, *Kriegstagebuch*, II: 86.

272. This account comes from Vasily Ryasnoi, a Samarkand-born (1904) ethnic Ukrainian and the head of the German department in Soviet counterintelligence (abruptly inducted in 1937 from party work). Pogonii, *Lubianka, 2*, 224.

273. Several examples of purported transcripts of eavesdropping in April and May 1941 have been published: *Istoriia Sovetskikh organov gosudarstvennoi bezopasnosti*, 313 (internal use only); Pronin, "Nevol'nye informatory Stalina," 1–2 (citing unspecified FSB archives); Naumov, *1941 god*, I: 598; Vinogradov et al., *Sekrety Gitlera*, 52–5 (TsA FSB, f. 3os, op. 8, d. 56, l. 1011–5: April 30), 109–12 (d. 57, l. 1346–51: May 18; a slightly different version with names omitted). NKGB counterintelligence did not know the extent to which Stalin read or extracted useful information from the bugged conversations. Pogonii, *Lubianka, 2*, 225. erik, op. 45, d. 29, l. 246.

274. Matveev and Mezhliakov, "Akademik kontrarazvedki," 7; Karpov, "Vo glave komiteta informatsii," 53.

275. Moritz, *Fall Barbarossa*, 160; Halder, *Halder Diaries*, II: 943 (May 30, 1941); Halder, *Kriegstagebuch*, II: 435–6.

276. Military intelligence HQ supposedly responded to Sorge: "We doubt the veracity of your information." Andrew and Gordievsky, *KGB*, 224 (no citation).

277. Whymant, *Stalin's Spy*, 184. Soviet military intelligence had evidently sent a military attaché to Tokyo to check into his behavior and work, which exposed Sorge to risk. The young operative who checked him became quickly and utterly convinced of Sorge's reliability. Fesiun, *Delo Rikharda Zorge*, 173–5 (Kh. D. Mamsurov).

278. Clausen began to lose faith in Communism, as he would tell Japanese interrogators after his arrest on Oct. 18, 1941. Whymant, *Stalin's Spy*, 119–22, 292; Fesiun, *Delo Rikharda Zorge*, 18. Clausen's radio had no outside aerial, for security purposes, but at night he could still broadcast more than 2,000 miles. (Although Japanese counterintelligence picked up the unauthorized signals, it could not pinpoint their source or decrypt the code.) Normally, the radio operator was not allowed to encrypt or decrypt the messages. But Sorge had had a motorcycle

accident on May 13, 1938, and he had had to teach Clausen the cipher code and delegate to him the task of putting the material into code before sending it. Once Clausen (b. 1899) could read the content of Sorge's messages, he was in a position to decide what to transmit (or not).

279. Sipols, *Tainy*, 397.

280. Gavrilov, *Voennaia razvedka informiruet*, 617–8 (TsAMO, f. 23, op. 24127, d. 2, l. 340–1); Naumov, *1941 god*, II: 175; Fesiun, *Delo Rikharda Zorge*, 116; Whymant, *Stalin's Spy*, 146–7, citing Obi, *Zoruge jiken*, I: 248, 274. See also "Tiuremnye zapiski Rikharda Zorge." Sorge's messages via Clausen had not only to be decoded but translated from the German. Evidently, Sorge's raw material, after being received at HQ in Moscow, was not always promptly processed and forwarded to the information (analytical) department.

281. Gavrilov, *Voennaia razvedka informiruet*, 627 (TsAMO, f. 23, op. 24127, d. 2, l. 381); Fesiun, *Delo Rikharda Zorge*, 117–8; Naumov, *1941 god*, II: 252. Golikov wrote on the document: "ask 'Ramsay,' corps or armies?"

282. Fesiun, *Delo Rikharda Zorge*, 137–9 (Sudoplatov); Zhukov, "Iz neopublikovannykh vospominanii"; Zhukov, *Vospominaniia*, I: 380. At the time, Zhukov recalls, Stalin did not name the suspected double agent to him, but later Zhukov concluded it must have been Sorge. "Sorge's tragedy," Sudoplatov later surmised, "was that with the authorization of Artuzov, Uritsky, Berzin, Karin, and Borovich (his communications officer) he cooperated with German intelligence in Japan. This put him a position of less than full trust." Fesiun, *Delo Rikharda Zorge*, 137.

283. Zhukov would later claim he was not informed by Stalin about the intelligence the regime was receiving. This was only partially true. Naumov, *1941 god*, I: 378, 380. There is a story that during a showing to senior Soviet officers of a Franco-German film, *Who Are You, Dr. Sorge?* (1961), a retired Zhukov lost his composure, stood up in the cinema, and shouted out in the dark to Golikov, "Why did you at that time, Filipp Ivanovich, hide everything from me? Not report about such a document [Sorge's report on an imminent German attack] to the chief of the general staff?" Golikov was said to have replied, "And what, should I have reported to you if this Sorge was a double, ours and theirs?" Vorob'ev, "Kazhdaia piad' zemli," 165–6. After Khrushchev saw the foreign film about Sorge, the story goes, he asked Mikoyan and then Soviet intelligence whether the USSR had had such an agent. A commission was formed under Kosygin and, posthumously, Sorge was awarded the Hero of the Soviet Union on Nov. 5, 1964; his paramour/wife in Japan, Hanako Ishii, began receiving a Soviet pension.

284. Back in 1937, when Zhukov had been stationed in the Belorussian military district, Golikov had been sent there as a member of its military council, evidently on assignment for Mekhlis to help annihilate the local military elite. Golikov accused Zhukov, among others, of friendship with enemies of the people, interrogated Zhukov over his associations, and built a dossier on him (his wife had had his daughter christened in a church, he treated his subordinates rudely). But one of Zhukov's accusers, it seems, was arrested ("he dug a pit for another, but fell into it himself," in the popular saying, Zhukov wrote). *Tragediia RKKA*, 109; Spahr, *Zhukov*, 22–3.

285. This was partly based on having learned that transport of Far Eastern rubber to Germany via the Trans-Siberian Railroad was to be minimized. Gavrilov, *Voennaia razvedka informiruet*, 657–8 (TsAMO, f. 23, op. 24127,

d. 2, l. 422); Fesiun, *Delo Rikharda Zorge*, 119–20; Naumov, *1941 god*, II: 303–4.

286. Whymant, citing Sorge's testimony to his Japanese captors, surmises that some or all of the messages were not transmitted to Moscow. For ex., Sorge claims to have told Moscow: "Lieutenant General Scholl conveyed clearly to Ambassador Ott, in total secrecy, that Germany and the USSR were finally to go to war and he should take the necessary measures; and he told me various details about it." Whymant, *Stalin's Spy*, 164–5, citing Obi, *Zoruge jiken*, III: 183.

287. Sorge added: "Scholl avers that the most powerful strike will be struck by the left flank of the German army." Gavrilov, *Voennaia razvedka informiruet*, 658 (TsAMO, f. 23, op. 24127, d. 2, l. 424); Fesiun, *Delo Rikharda Zorge*, 119–20; *Novoe vremia*, 1990, no. 26: 32 (photocopy of the radiogram). Golikov asked for clarification on the nature of the "tactical mistake" and on Scholl's revelation about a left flank strike. By the time Sorge would able to reply, it was July 3, 1941. Gavrilov, *Voennaia razvedka informiruet*, 714 (TsAMO, f. 23, op. 24127, d. 2, l. 527–9). Scholl had been a deputy military attaché in Tokyo (1938–1940).

288. Vishlev, *Nakanune*, 53–5 (PA AA Bonn: Büro des Staatssekretar. Aufzeichunungen uber Diplomatenbesuche. Bd. 8 [R 29833], Bl. Ohne Nummer; Russland, Bd. 5 [R 29716], Bl. 035 [113439], 091 [113495], Bl. 087 [113491]).

289. Beria wrote: "In many places along the border the Germans have concentrated pontoons, wooden and inflatable boats. The greatest number of them can be found on the Brest-Lvov salient. Work continues on the mounting of defensive installations near the borders, mostly at night. Leaves for soldiers of German army units have been forbidden. Moreover, information has been received about the relocation of German troops from Budapest and Bucharest on an axis toward the borders of the USSR." Iampol'skii et al., *Organy*, I/ii: 202–3 (TsA FSK).

290. "Nakanune voiny (1941 g.)," 206; Iampol'skii et al., *Organy*, I/ii: 200–1. Romania had accumulated excellent intelligence on Soviet forces in the south of the USSR, material that was passed to the head of German military intelligence Admiral Canaris during his visit in May.

291. Iampol'skii et al., *Organy*, I/ii: 206–7 (TsA FSK).

292. Iampol'skii et al., *Organy*, I/ii: 208–9 (TsA FSK: June 3, 1941).

293. Volkogonov papers, Hoover Institution Archives, container 6 (Blokhin and Samoilovich). Kuznetsov requested more funding in connection with shifting the navy to combat footing from July 1. Solonin, "Tri plana tovarishcha Stalina," 57 (citing GARF, f. R-8418, op. 25, d. 481, l. 32–33: June 4). Further, on June 4, Kaiser Wilhelm II died peacefully in Dutch exile at age eighty-two; the Reich Commissioner for the Occupied Netherlands laid a wreath in Hitler's name. "There is no doubt that the Kaiser had the best intentions," Goebbels instructed the Nazi press, "but . . . the decisive factor in history is not goodwill but great ability." Boelcke, *Secret Conferences*, 172.

294. Naumov, *1941 god*, II: 324–5. Beria (June 5) reported that "between June 1 and 5, the Romanian general staff had ordered all military personnel who are on leave as well as all reservists up to forty years of age on farming duty to report to their units." Vinogradov et al., *Sekrety Gitlera*, 138–9 (TsA FSB, f. 3os, op. 8, d. 9, l. 68–9).

295. Omsk would not get equipment or shelving until late 1944 (around the time some materials would begin to be returned to

Moscow). Vinogradov, "Istoriia formirovaniia arkhiva VChK," 37. Large numbers of files are still there.

296. Boelcke, *Secret Conferences*, 174 (June 5, 1941).

297. Cripps arrived in London on June 11, by way of Stockholm, where the general director of the Swedish foreign ministry, taken aback at Cripps's insistence on secret German-Soviet negotiations, shared details of Swedish intercepts of Wehrmacht orders to troops in Norway for an invasion of the USSR. The Swedish official stressed a coming attack in the week of June 20–25. Gorodetsky, *Grand Delusion*, 304 (citing FO 371 29482 N2680/78/38, Mallet: June 8, and CAB 65/22/59 (41)2: June 12); Boheman, *Pä Vakt*, 154–5.

298. Samuelson, *Plans for Stalin's War Machine*, 197–8. Also on June 6, Stalin received a report that the USSR had 5.7 million wired radio receiver points, more than 80 percent of all its radio equipment, but that the wires were in disrepair, subject to interruption and breakdown. The other 20 percent, wireless radios, were deemed below international standard. Altogether, whereas the United States had 343 receivers (wireless and wired) for every 1,000 people, and Nazi Germany 159, the Soviet Union had just 36. Lovell, *Russia in the Microphone Age*, 41 (citing GARF, f. 6093, op. 1, d. 56, l. 10–2, 13–4, 19).

299. Lota, *"Alta" protiv "Barbarossy,"* 308. This was her last meeting with Zaitsev ("Bine"), who was recalled to Moscow; she was assigned a new handler, Anatoly Staritsky ("Tal"), a radio specialist, who was to teach her cipher codes and met with her on June 12.

300. Pavlov, "Ot 'Iunkersa' 1941 k Tsessne 1987"; Kuznetsov, "Krutye povoroty," esp. no. 6 (1993): 79; Stepanov, "O masshtabakh repressii," no. 5: 62; Medvedev, *Let History Judge*, 473.

301. Stalin arrested the family members of the military men he executed, but when one of his behind-the-lines saboteurs was killed in the line of duty, the despot awarded a 25,000-ruble cash award to the family and a pension to the widow of 500 rubles per month (the salary of the deceased). Khaustov, "Deiatel'nost' organov," 261–2 (TsA FSB, f. 3, op. 4, d. 105, l. 205).

302. Timoshenko and Zhukov reported that in the first quarter of 1941, there had been 156 crashes killing 141 crew and destroying 138 aircraft. Volkogonov, *Stalin: Triumph*, 375 (citing TsAMO, f. 75284, op. 1, d. 119, l. 18). From Sept. 1, 1939, through June 22, 1941, the Luftwaffe, in training at flight schools, lost 1,924 killed and another 1,439 injured. Additionally, units in combat in the same period, in accidents and disasters, lost 1,609 killed and 485 injured. On average, this was 248 people a month. Solonin, "Delo aviatorov."

303. Suvenirov, *Tragediia RKKA*, 135, 383. Kulik had sidetracked the Soviets' own superior F-34 tank gun, whose production had been initiated by others, and even got Stalin to cut production of the versatile 76-mm anti-tank gun. "Disorganized but with a high opinion of himself, Kulik thought all his actions infallible," recalled his first deputy. "Holding his subordinates in a state of fear was what he considered to be the best way of working." Voronov, *Na sluzhbe voennoi*, 163. See also Pospelov, *Istoriia Velikoi Otechestvennoi voiny*, I: 414–6, 475–6; Zakharov, *Nakanune velikikh ispytanii*, reprinted in idem., *General'nyi shtab*, 391; "Nakanune voiny: iz postanovlenii vysshikh partiinykh i gosudarstvennykh organov (Mai 1940 g.–21 iiunia 1941 g.)," 201–3; Zhukov, *Vospominaniia*,

I: 367; Vannikov, "Iz zapisok narkoma vooruzheniia"; Erickson, *Road to Stalingrad*, 62–3. When Khrushchev overstepped his writ and questioned Kulik's competence, Stalin exploded: "You don't even know Kulik! I know him from the civil war when he commanded the artillery in Tsaritsyn. He knows artillery!" Khrushchev, *Vospominaniia*, I: 283–4.

304. Kuznetsov and Dzhoga, *Pervye geroi Sovetskogo Soiuza*, 54. Rychagov was succeeded by his deputy, the forty-one-year-old Pavel Zhigaryov. Rychagov had proven his mettle in Spain in 1936 and at Lake Khasan in 1938. During the Finnish War, his forces, the 8th Army, had been surrounded and practically annihilated. See also "Beseda s admiralom flota Sovetskogo Soiuza I. S. Isakovym [May 21, 1962]," in Simonov, *Glazami cheloveka moego pokoleniia*, 372–9.

305. Gavrilov, *Voennaia razvedka informiruet*, 671–2 (TsAMO, f. 23, op. 7237, d. 2, l. 120–1). The Germans were issuing knowingly false military radio reports, overheard by Soviet signals intelligence agents, about the movement of their troops into Romania and Hungary, as if they were preparing to strike Ukraine. Mel'tiukhov, *Upushchennyi shans Stalina*, 252, 296–7. See also Andrew and Gordievsky, *KGB*, 174, 178–82, 225–6.

306. The envoy was Anatoly Lavrentyev (b. 1904), who until 1939 had worked in the heavy industry commissariat. Vishlev, "Pochemu zhe" (no. 2), 75: PA AA Bonn: Büro des Staatssekretär, Russland, Bd. 5 (R 29716), Bl. 081 (113485); Vishlev, *Nakanune*, 50. The Slovak envoy in Moscow, according to the Germans, surmised that Stalin would satisfy German demands for whatever goods its war economy needed, but would not consent to placing Soviet territories under German rule. Nekrich, *Pariahs*, 229 (citing Bundesarchiv-Militärarchiv. RMII/34: 238: German naval attaché to Berlin, May 21, 1941).

307. An NKGB agent traveled the border on the German side, finding it saturated with troops in full combat gear hiding in the forests, with special weapons depots and oil tanks stuffed, and bridges fortified and heavily guarded. Gorodetsky, *Grand Delusion*, 276–7 (citing TsA SVR, d. 21616, t. 2, l. 372–5: Kobulov to Timoshenko, June 9, 1941).

308. Vinogradov et al., *Sekrety Gitlera*, 148–50 (TsA FSB, f. 3os, op. 8, d. 58, l. 1841–5: June 9, 1941). See also Bezymenskii, *Gitler i Stalin*, 474.

309. Iampol'skii et al., *Organy*, I/ii: 212 (TsA FSK: June 9, 1941). A note with the published document states that "the Japanese shared intelligence about the USSR with the Swedish, Turkish, Bulgarian and other embassies."

310. Kumanev, "'22ogo' na rassvete," 3 (citing Timoshenko recollections, at the Institute of History, Feb. 19, 1967); Gorodetsky, *Grand Delusion*, 296–7; Whymant, *Stalin's Spy*, 184 (no citation). Timoshenko's recollections came after the Moscow showing of the film about Sorge. The Kremlin meeting could have happened on June 6, 1941. Vatutin evidently was also present. Gordetsky gives the date as June 18.

311. Vinogradov et al., *Sekrety Gitlera*, 151 (TsA FSB, f. 3os, op. 8, d. 58, l. 1846: June 11, 1941); "Sovetskie organy gosudarstvennoi bezopasnosti v gody Veliki otechestvennoi voiny." See also Hilger and Mayer, *Incompatible Allies*, 334–6.

312. Iampol'skii et al., *Organy*, I/ii: 219–20 (TsA FSK); Primakov, *Ocherki*, III: 486 (TsA FSB, f. 3 os, op. 8, d. 58, l. 1853–55); "Nakanune voiny (1940–1941 gg.)," 216. The NKGB First Directorate summary of Kobulov's report for the leadership altered the paragraph

structure slightly, emphasizing the sentence: "Whether there will initially be some kind of demands presented to the Soviet Union is unknown." Naumov, *1941 god*, II: 342–3. Kobulov stressed that the recommendation of "Elder" to preempt the Germans was "straight from the heart," not a "provocation." Gorodetsky, *Grand Delusion*, 296 (citing TsA SVR, d. 23078, t. 1, l. 430–1). On June 9, 1941, border intelligence reported that as of May 28 the concentration of all troops against the USSR, including on the territory of the former Austria, the Protectorate of Bohemia and Moravia, Greece, Romania, and Germany east of Berlin, reached approximately 4.5 million. "Furthermore, Major Wendel [the source at German HQ] said that this army is fully ready for war with the USSR." Gavrilov, *Voennaia razvedka informiruet*, 676–80 (TsAMO, f. 127, op. 12915, d. 16, l. 362–8).

313. Moritz, *Fall Barbarossa*, 192. All the German war updates for the USSR can be found in Whaley, *Codeword*, 251–6. Hitler had returned from the Berghof to Munich on June 11, 1941, and late the next day left for Berlin, arriving by train near noon on June 13. The next day, he delivered a final all-day briefing to his forty-five most senior commanders at the Reich chancellery. Warlimont, *Inside Hitler's Headquarters*, 605–6; Halder, *Kriegstagebuch*, II: 455 (June 14, 1941), 456 (June 14). On June 17 Hitler and then the High Command confirmed the timetable. *Nazi Conspiracy and Aggression*, VI: 1001; Hillgruber, *Hitlers Strategie*, 508.

314. Vinogradov et al., *Sekrety Gitlera*, 151–3 (TsA FSB, f. 3os, op. 8, d. 58, l. 1857-50). See also Sinitsyn, *Rezident svidetel'stvuet*, 117–8 (referring to the agent "Monk," who does not appear in the published intelligence materials); and Bezhanov, *Leningradskaia oborona*, 28. The Soviet London station had reported on how Finland would join a German invasion of the USSR. TsA FSB, f. 3os, op. 8, d. 57, l. 1178–9 (May 4), l. 1220–1 (May 7), l. 1373–4 (May 16); Naumov, *1941 god*, II: 177 (TsA SVR, f. 23078, t. 1, l. 366: May 7). The NKGB reported a partial Finnish mobilization on June 13. Vinogradov et al., *Sekrety Gitlera*, 156–7 (TsA FSB, f. 3os, op. 8, d. 58, l. 1861–2).

315. Lota, *"Alta" protiv "Barbarossy,"* 309.

316. Beria added that from Oct. 1940 through June 10, the NKVD recorded 185 planes violating Soviet air space. He further reported that from Jan. 1 through June 10, more than 2,000 border violators from the German side had been detained. Many had grenades and portable radio stations. There were worries of biological warfare terror (vials with epidemic-inducing diseases). Iampol'skii et al., *Organy*, I/ii: 220–1 (TsA FSK: June 12, 1941), 228 (TsA FSK).

317. On June 13, Dekanozov telegrammed Molotov about Soviet agents having observed a massive transport of troops and equipment toward the Soviet frontier: heavy artillery, tanks, trucks, planes. "Kanun voiny: preduprezhdeniia diplomatov," 76. On June 14, Dekanozov added that the Swedish and Danish military attachés in Berlin no longer believed troop concentrations constituted a tactic to force concessions but instead amounted to "genuine preparation for a war against the Soviet Union." Sipols, *Tainy*, 398–9. Dekanozov had met "Elder" and "Corsican" and was evidently persuaded by them that this was war, not an ultimatum. Sokolov, "Novye dannye."

318. Vishlev, *Nakanune*, 163 (PA AA Bonn: Dienstelle Ribbentrop. Vertrauliche Berichte über Russland [Peter], 2/3 [R 27113], Bl.

462591–462594); Vishlev, "Pochemu zhe," 94–5. Hitler did not trust Berlings, and on June 18 ordered "close surveillance" on him and, after the onset of hostilities, his arrest. In fact, he would be sent to Sweden. Vishlev, "Pochemu zhe," 74 (citing ADAP, XII/ii: doc. 639, 645). The Russian press frequently cites a report by Yankel "Jan" Chernyak ("Jean") on June 12 that the attack would commence on June 22 at 3:30 a.m. This warning, if it occurred, has not been published in the various collections of intelligence documents.

319. "These rumors," the bulletin stated, "are the clumsy product of the propaganda of forces inimical to the USSR and Germany, forces interested in the extension of the war." Also, the Soviet embassy on June 10 had reported word that Simon had begun secret negotiations with Hess on June 10. Rozanov, Stalin-Gitler, 203–4.

320. Izvestiia, June 14, 1941; Tisminets, Vneshniaia politika SSSR, IV: 555–6. See also Werth, Russia at War, 125–6; Gafencu, Prelude to the Russian Campaign, 207–8. "The affairs of the TASS communique was a last resort," recalled Molotov late in life. "If we had been successful in delaying the war beyond the summer it would have been very difficult to start it in the autumn. So far, diplomacy had been very successful in delaying war, but no one could predict when it would fail." Chuev, Sto sorok, 42–3.

321. Andreas-Friedrich, Berlin Underground, 67–8. Other rumors, however, indicated an impending attack that very month. Boberach, Meldungen aus dem Reich, VII: 3374, 2380, 2394.

322. Herwarth, Against Two Evils, 195.

323. Sontag and Biddie, Nazi-Soviet Relations, 345–46.

324. Vishlev, "Pochemu zhe," 78 (citing PA AA Bonn: Dienstelle Ribbentrop, Vertaruliche Berichte über Russland [Peter], 2/3 [R 27113], Bl. 462597).

325. Halder, Kriegstagebuch, II: 455–6 (June 14); Warlimont, Inside Hitler's Headquarters, 147.

326. Vishlev, "Pochemu zhe," 76 (citing PA AA Bonn: Büro des Staatssekretär, Russland, Bd. 5 [R 29716], Bl. 051–054 [113455–113457], 066 [113470], 104–6 [113508–114510], 130–31 [113534–113535]; Jacobsen, Kriegestagebuch, I: 404.

327. Zhukov offers a colorful treatment of the call. Zhukov, Vospominaniia, I: 383; Zhukov, Vospominaniia, I: 367. For restrictions on measures to improve military readiness, see also Anfilov, Krushenie pokhoda Gitlera, 98ff. Some Soviet commanders viewed the TASS communique as an indication that war, somehow, was averting war, despite the colossal buildup. But the general staff was told the TASS bulletin bore no relation to ongoing Soviet military preparations. Ivanov, Shtab armeiskii, 40; Vasilevskii, Delo vsei zhizni, 108.

328. Vasilevskii, Delo vsei zhizni, 43. The western military districts were also ordered to field headquarters. Mobilized units from Eastern Siberia and Mongolia, ordered west on May 22, were due to arrive in Ukraine (Berdichev, Proskurov, Shepetovka) between June 17 and July 10.

329. Fröhlich, Tagebucher von Joseph Goebbels, IX: 376–81; Taylor, Goebbels Diaries, 414–6. See also Vishlev, Nakanune, 26–9, 151. Concerning Hitler's "silence" after the TASS bulletin, the Romanian envoy, telegrammed Bucharest (June 16) that "the war of nerves is at full blast, worsened by the news from Finland and Romania about more and more significant military preparations."

Gorodetsky, Grand Delusion, 307. Köstring wrote to Berlin (June 18) that "gossip and rumors here have reached unfathomable magnitude. To transmit them would take whole volumes." Teske, General Ernst Köstring, 320.

330. Golikov's warnings were more balanced than many critics have asserted. Naumov, 1941 god, II: 87–9 (April 16, 1941), II: 119–20 (April 25, 1941), II: 213–5 (May 15, 1941), II: 324–5 (June 5, 1941), II: 333 (June 7, 1941); "Nakanune voiny (1940–1941 gg.)," 219–20; Iampol'skii et al., Organy, I/ii: 136–7 (May 5, 1941). But Golikov clashed over assessments of German troop concentrations with Novobranets, acting head of the information (analytical) bureau of military intelligence. Golikov was said to have used a derogatory name for the Ukrainian Novobranets (khokhol). Novobranets quotes a document from Beria, supposedly prepared on June 21, 1941: "Lt.-General F. I. Golikov, the head of military intelligence (where the Berzin band recently reigned), complains about his Colonel Novobranets, who also lies, claiming that Hitler has concentrated 170 divisions against us on our western border. But I and my people, Iosif Vissarionovich, firmly remember your wise forecast: Hitler will not attack us in 1941!" Novobranets, "Nakanune voiny," 176–8, 165; Krasnaia zvezda, Feb. 2 1991; Naumov, 1941 god, II: 46–7 (TsAMO, op. 7237, d. 2, l. 84–6: April 4, 1941).

331. Erickson, Road to Stalingrad, 88–9; Coox, "Japanese Foreknowledge," 225; McNeal, Stalin, 237.

332. On May 20 Churchill told General Sikorski that a German attack on the USSR "does not seem to enter into consideration." On May 23, a British Joint Intelligence Committee report, which the Soviets obtained, noted: "With her usual thoroughness Germany is making all preparations for an attack so as to make the threat convincing." Antonov, "Anatolii Gorskii."

333. On June 13, the British Joint Intelligence Committee concluded that Stalin would make the concessions necessary to escape war. That day, Eden summoned Maisky, telling him to come alone; Maisky had no choice but to bring his minder, Novikov, which irritated Eden. The British foreign secretary explained the intensity of the German buildup, indicating the information came from extremely reliable sources, and pledged British assistance if the USSR were attacked. Gorodetsky, Maisky Diaries, 361; Haslam, Near and Distant Neighbors, 115 (citing JIC [41] 251 [Final]: FO 371/29484). By June 10, Enigma intercepts made clear that attack would not commence until after June 15. Hinsley et al., British Intelligence, I: 472 (citing FO 371/29481, N 2498/78/38), 474 (citing CX/JQ/ S11), 477, 479; Woodward, British Foreign Policy, 617, 619–20.

334. Barros and Gregor, Double Deception, 194–6 (citing PRO, PREM3/230/1).

335. Gorchakov, "Nakanune, ili tragediia Kassandry," 21.

336. Gorodetsky, Grand Delusion, 282–3, 305. Churchill wrote to his counterpart Smuts in South Africa (June 18), "According to all the information I have, Hitler is going to take what he wants from Russia, and the only question is whether Stalin will attempt a vain resistance."

337. DGFP, series D, XII: 1030; Frölich, Tagebücher von Joseph Goebbels, IX: 373–76; Vishlev, Nakanune, 58; Hilger and Meyer, Incompatible Allies, 328, 330, 334; Fel'shtinskii, Oglasheniiu podlezhit, 359.

338. Sorge added: "I saw a message to Germany that in the event a war arises between

Germany and the Soviet Union, Japan will demand around six weeks before beginning an attack on the Soviet Far East, but the Germans think the Japanese will need more time, because that will be a war on land and sea . . ." Gavrilov, Voennaia razvedka informiruet, 692 (TsAMO f. 23, op. 24127, d. 2, l. 454); Naumov, 1941 god, II: 380; Fesiun, Delo Rikhard Zorge, 120–1; Gorodetsky, Grand Delusion, 161 (photocopy of the original telegram). In a second message transmitted on June 17, Sorge clarified that his earlier message was indeed about nine full armies (150 divisions), not nine army corps. Gavrilov, Voennaia razvedka informiruet, 692 (TsAMO f. 23, op. 5840, d. 7, l. 88).

339. Lota, "Alta" protiv "Barbarossy," 349; Gavrilov, Voennaia razvedka informiruet, 691. Military intelligence reported on June 15, that as of June 1 Germany had 286 to 296 total divisions, and had concentrated 120 to 122 of them on the Soviet frontier with Germany and Romania, and that this movement continued. Gavrilov, Voennaia razvedka informiruet, 686–90 (June 15, 1941).

340. On June 16, "Corsican" informed Korotkov ("Stepanov") about Rosenberg's speech. Peshcherskii, "Krasnaia kapella," 145.

341. Sinitsyn, Rezident svidetel'stvuet, 132–3; "Vospominaniia nachal'nika razvedki P.M. Fitina," 18, 20–1; Sharapov, "Za sto chasov do voiny"; Lota, Sekretnyi front, 35–6; Chudodeev, "Chelovek iz 'gruppy Ya,'" 18–24. See also Sudoplatov, Special Tasks, 122–3. Fitin does not appear in Stalin's office logbook; neither does the GB personnel Sinitsyn, Sudoplatov, or Rybkin-Yartsev. Bondarenko, Fitin, 222–3. On June 17 Merkulov and his two deputies, Bogdan Kobulov and Mikhail Gribov, were summoned to Stalin's office (Molotov was also present) for some forty minutes (8:20–9:00 p.m.). Kobulov was back on June 18 for five minutes, in the company of Molotov, Timoshenko, Zhukov, and Malenkov. Na prieme, 336–7.

342. Primakov, Ocherki, IV: 17–25 (Fitin's remembrances, evidently composed in 1970). Another version of Fitin's recollections appeared in Pravda, May 8, 1989 (A. Baidakov, citing conversations with Fitin). This episode provoked the one systematization of NKGB intelligence: back at HQ, Fitin's team would produce a "Calendar of Information Obtained through Corsican and Elder," a chronological summary from the first report (Sept. 6, 1940) through the latest (June 16, 1941), running to eleven typed pages. "We were given all the material from every espionage station," Rybkina recalled. "We got to work. Zhuravlyov and I did not leave the office. We looked at individual files, we looked at how much a source could be trusted, how their previously supplied information had been confirmed and so on. We did everything to make sure that the information was thoroughly tested and checked." The Calendar conveyed that there would be a German invasion; only the details and timing were uncertain. Still, the compilers wondered whether Stalin's skepticism could somehow be right, since he had not just their NKGB reports but also those of military intelligence, embassies, trade representatives, journalists, and who knew what else. Merkulov was in the Little Corner on the evening of June 20 for an hour, but, if the document was completed by then, he evidently shrank from presenting it to the despot. Nor did he sign it. Fitin was said to have returned it to Zhuravlyov with a notation: "You keep this. P[avel] F[itin]. June 22." Iampol'skii et al., Organy, I/ii: 286–96; Naumov, 1941 god, II: 400–7 (TsA FSB); Primakov, Ocherki, III:

431–2, 452, 493n33. Gorodetsky asserts (without citation) that the finalized document only got to Merkulov hours after the German attack, then made its way to the archives. Gorodetsky, *Grand Delusion*, 297. In parallel to the Calendar [*kalendar'*] compiled by the NKGB, military intelligence put together a List [*perechen'*], which is undated. The list, which was not comprehensive, contained 56 reports of Germany's war preparations, 54 of them received since Jan. 1941. Fully 20 came from one source—Kegel ("X")—and 10 from another: Yeremin ("Yeshenko"). Thirty-seven offered a date for a German attack; some of the dates overlapped, but they varied and several were imprecise. Of the sixteen reports that indicated the principal thrust for a German attack, ten specified Ukraine. There is a high likelihood that the list was compiled after the invasion, in late June, perhaps in connection with Stalin's summons of Golikov, Timoshenko, and Zhukov on June 28, 1941 or shortly thereafter. Gavrilov, *Voennaia razvedka informiruet*, 701–13; Lota, *Sekretnyi front*, 220–34 (citing TsAMO, op. 7272, d. 1, l. 87–98).

343. The report also said the Germans would target Svir-3 power station, which could be judged to have little military significance. Vinogradov et al., *Sekrety Gitlera*, 161–3 (TsA FSB, f. 3os, op. 8, d. 58, l. 1914–6); "Nakanune voiny (1940–1941 gg.)," 221; Naumov, *1941 god*, II: 382–3 (APRF, f. 3, op. 50, d. 415, l. 50–2); Iampol'skii et al., *Organy*, I/ii: 236–7

(TsA FSK), 237–8; Primakov, *Ocherki*, III: 487–8 (TsA FSB, f. 3 os, op. 8, d. 58, l. 1914–6). Gorodetsky speculates that Stalin was rattled. Gorodetsky, *Grand Delusion*, 296–7.

344. The Germans assumed that any British-Soviet negotiations would be leaked, and there were no such leaks (the British press was besotted with predictions of Hitler's blackmail of the USSR). Vishlev, "Pochemu zhe," 76–7 (citing PA AA Bonn: Büro des Staatssekretär, Russland, Bd. 5 [R 29716], Bl. 087 [113491], 146 [113540]; Dienstelle Ribbentrop UdSSSR-RC 7/1 [R 27168], Bl. 26071).

345. Hinsley et al., *British Intelligence*, I: 480–1 (CAB 65/22, WM [41] 60 CA, June 16).

346. "We argued for a long time, but Cripps clung to his views," Maisky added. Cripps, for his part, noticed that Maisky "seemed much less confident that there would be not be a war" and "now seemed very depressed." The editor of the *Times* (Geoffrey Dawson) also found Maisky suddenly persuaded that a German invasion was coming. Gorodetsky, *Stafford Cripps in Moscow*, 111–2; Gorodetsky, *Grand Delusion*, 305–6 (citing AVP RF, f. 059, op. 1, pap. 352, d. 2402, l. 235–6: Maisky to Molotov; and f. 0171: Maisky's diary, June 18; and FO 371 29466 N3099/3/38: Cripps memo, June 19); *Times* archives, Dawson to Halifax, June 22. After Eden had failed to persuade Maisky that Britain had definitive intelligence showing a coming German invasion, Churchill and the British cabinet had taken the remarkable decision to share the Enigma

intelligence. Cadogan had summoned Maisky and on June 16 recited German war preparations, then showed him a map of German troop concentrations on the border, in minute detail. Maisky's dispatch reporting the stages and numbers of Germany's buildup arrived in Moscow amid the silence in Berlin over the TASS bulletin, but the reaction, if any, remains unclear. "Kanun voiny: preduprezhdeniia diplomatov," 77–8; Naumov, *1941 god*, II: 374; Gorodetsky, *Grand Delusion*, 303 (citing AVP RF, f. 059, op. 1, pap. 352, d. 2402, l. 214–5: Maisky to Molotov, June 16); Gorodetsky, *Maisky Diaries*, 361–3. The NKGB reported (June 17) on the movement of some German divisions, based on sources inside Britain, mentioning either "an undertaking of great scale, as the Germans maintain, or possibly . . . maximum pressure on the USSR." Naumov, *1941 god*, II: 381–2 (TsA SVR, d. 21616, t. 2, l. 411).

347. Nekrich, *Pariahs*, 229 (citing Bundesarchiw-Militärarchiw. RMII/34: 320: Köstring to Matzky).

348. Roberts, "Planning for War," 1320–1. Even Gorodetsky, who writes of "Stalin's failure to prepare for the German onslaught," admits that "even with hindsight, it is hard to devise alternatives which Stalin could have safely pursued. If he had made a preemptive strike, the blow would at best have softened but definitely not averted." Gorodetsky, *Grand Delusion*, 323.

CODA. LITTLE CORNER, SATURDAY, JUNE 21, 1941

1. Gorodetsky, *Grand Delusion*, 306 (citing UD:s Arkhiv 1920 ARS, HP/1557/LVIII, June 21, 1941). The citation contains a typo, indicating the Swedish ambassador in Berlin, but this was from Moscow.

2. Bismarck, *Bismarck, The Man and the Statesman*, II: 301.

3. Stalin might have taken a meal in his apartment in the company of the inner circle that afternoon; alternately, he could have done so later in the evening. Mikoyan would recall many years later that "we, politburo members, gathered in Stalin's Kremlin apartment. . . . We left around 3:00 a.m." The timing of Mikoyan's account does not jibe with the Kremlin office logbook, in which, moreover, Mikoyan does not figure on June 21. Molotov late in life remembered that "on June 21, we stayed until 11 or 12 p.m. at Stalin's dacha. Maybe we had even watched a movie. We used to do this often, watch a movie." These times, too, are contradicted by the office logbook. Kumanev, *Riadom so Stalinym*, 24; Mikoian, *Tak Bylo*, 388; Chuev, *Molotov Remembers*, 36; *Na prieme*, 337.

4. Anna Alliluyeva, Stalin's sister-in-law, is the main source for the theory that an infected childhood bruise on his left arm had resulted in a chronically stiff elbow. Alliluyeva, *Vospominaniia*, 167.

5. Dokuchaev, *Moskva, Kreml, Okhrana*, 113–6. Stalin hated the black ravens, who shat on the monuments, so the Kremlin commandant fought an all-out war against them, trapping at least 35,000 birds, which were given as feed to the zoo.

6. Molotov recalled: "The tension was palpable in 1939 and 1940. Tensions ran very high." Chuev, *Molotov Remembers*, 25.

7. German embassy personnel in Moscow did not know the precise date of the invasion. "I am personally very pessimistic, and although I do not know anything concrete, I think Hitler will launch a war against the USSR," Schulenburg said at Köstring's mansion (June 16) in a conversation the NKGB

eavesdropped. "At the end of April I saw [Hitler] personally and completely openly I said to him that his plans for a war against the USSR are utter folly, that now is not the time to talk about war with the USSR. Believe me, for my candor I fell out with him and I'm risking my career and, perhaps, soon I'll be in a concentration camp." Vinogradov et al., *Sekrety Gitlera*, 169–70 (TsA FSB, f. 3os, op. 8, d. 58, l. 1978–80: June 20, 1941).

8. "From June 10 to 17," Merkulov wrote (June 18), "thirty-four people left the German embassy to return to Germany; the upper ranks were sending home their families and belongings." Naumov, *1941 god*, II: 384–5 (TsA FSB, f. 3os, op. 8, d. 58, l. 1945–8). That same day, Augusto Rosso, the Italian ambassador, went to see Schulenburg at his residence (the NKGB eavesdropped the conversation). The German ambassador admitted to receiving his own instructions to evacuate embassy staff families and non-essential employees. Rosso telegrammed Rome asking for instructions in the event of war, especially about what to do with documents. Altogether, NKGB counterintelligence, in Moscow and Rome, secured three versions, independent of one another, of the Rosso-Schulenburg exchange, reporting that Rosso noted Schulenburg's lack of information, but wrote "in strict confidence he [Schulenburg] added that in his personal opinion . . . a military conflict was unavoidable and that it could break out in two or three days, possibly on Sunday [June 22]." Pronin, "Nevol'nye informatory Stalina," 1–2 (citing FSB archives); Naumov, *1941 god*, II: 389 (TsA FS); Iampol'skii et al., *Organy*, I/ii: 267–8. Sudoplatov commented on the June 19 report from the NKGB Rome station chief, "It appears we are being robustly disinformed." In other words, a privileged conversation between allies—Germany and Italy—was intended to trick the Soviets into preparing for war and thereby provoke war. Under such reasoning, anything and everything the Germans did could be dismissed. The

extraordinary achievement and exertions of total surveillance were in vain. Sharapov, "Za sto chasov do voiny."

9. Gavrilov, *Voennaia razvedka informiruet*, 693–4 (TsAMO, f. 23, op. 24119, d. 2, l. 83).

10. Molotov added: "I will have a talk with I.V. [Stalin]. If anything particular comes of it, I will give a call!" Banac, *Diary of Georgi Dimitrov*, 165–6 (June 21, 1941); Naumov, *1941 god*, II: 416. Molotov late in life, to a question about anticipated blackmail, replied, "And why not think so? Hitler was an extortionist, to be sure. He could have been extorting concessions. . . . Around each issue there could have been extortion and deception and duplicity and flattery and . . . it's hard to say really." Chuev, *Molotov Remembers*, 30.

11. "Iz perepiska N. V. Valentinova-Vol'skogo s B. I. Nikolaevskim," in Valentinov, *Nasledniki Lenina*, 214.

12. Valedinskii, "Organizm Stalina vpolne zdorovyi." See also, among other important sources, RGASPI, f. 558, op. 11, d. 1289, l. 6, 6 ob., 22–3; d. 1482, l. 7 ob., 23.; Ilizarov, *Tainaia zhizn' Stalina*, 113.

13. Tiulenev, *Cherez tri voiny* (2007), 224; Utesov, *Spasibo, Serdtse!*, 249–50.

14. Simonov, *Glazami cheloveka moego pokoleniia*, 422–3 (quoting an interview with Isakov in 1962).

15. Bullock understood that Hitler and Stalin possessed dissimilar personalities, but he portrayed them as two similar lower-class malcontents, ambitious yet resentful of the political regimes and social orders they lived under. Still, in his telling, neither represented a mere expression of supposed impersonal forces. On the contrary, he portrays each as uniquely decisive in the creation of their respective regimes and policies. In Overy's follow-up, the infrastructure of rule and systems of domination, rather than the persons, drive the respective systems, which emerged from the destruction of the Great War, sought to realize alternatives to the perceived failures of parliamentary order, and drew upon popular

support. Overy understands that the two systems represented very different utopias. Still, he, too, overdoes the similarities. Bullock, *Hitler and Stalin,* 349, 977; Overy, *Dictators.*

16. Kumanev, *Riadom so Stalinym,* 409–10 (Chadayev); Kuznetsov, *Nakanune,* 355, 370.

17. Recollections of one of Poskryobyshev's two daughters, Natalya: http://sloblib.narod .ru/slob/poskreb.htm. Poskrebyshev's first wife, Jadwiga, a Pole, had died in 1929 of tuberculosis.

18. Tyulenev wrote that he saw Timoshenko and Zhukov that evening at the defense commissariat, evidently before their audience with Stalin, and that he departed the city for his dacha in Serebryannyi Bor, where his family was staying. Tiulenev, *Cherez tri voiny* (2007), 224, 226. This version of his memoirs—purportedly restoring censored parts—does not differ in essence from the earlier version regarding this episode: Tiulenev, *Cherez tri voiny* (1972), 123–4; Bialer, *Stalin and His Generals,* 200–3. Admiral Kuznetsov recalled that Tyulenev, when giving a lecture, reminisced that he had been phoned by Stalin at 2:00 p.m. Kuznetsov, *Nakanune,* 357, which also appears in the first edition (1966), 329.

19. That day Cripps had visited Maisky on his own initiative, and sought to ensure cooperation following the German invasion that Cripps knew was coming. Maisky's detailed summary of the conversation was received in Moscow on June 22 at 11:00 a.m. "Iz neopublikovannykh dokumentov (Beseda I. Maiskogo) S. Krippson 21 iiunia 1941g.), 39. See also Vishlev, *Nakanune,* 54. Gorodetsky (personal communication) notes that Maisky had decided to spend the weekend at the country house of his old friend, Negrín, the last Spanish Republican prime minister, and that the envoy would be genuinely surprised when he heard the news of war. Beyond his fear of crossing Stalin, he could not get out of his head that all the warnings might just be a self-serving British provocation. Supposedly, Major General Susloparov ("Maro"), the military attaché and intelligence chief in Vichy, sent a message on June 21 that the invasion would begin the next morning, and Stalin wrote on it: "This information is an English provocation. Clarify who is the author of this provocation and punish him." This document has not been published. Ivashutin, "Dokladyvala tochno," 57; *Krasnaia zvezda,* Feb. 2, 1991 (Ivashutin interview). Susloparov had told his French interlocutors (June 18) that Germany would not attack the USSR, that the rumors, being spread out of Germany (not Britain, as he formerly believed), formed part of the "pressure which the German government is expected to exert on Moscow to increase considerably the delivery of grain, oil products, and other raw materials, indispensable for continuing the war." Gorodetsky, *Grand Delusion,* 307–8 (citing Quai d'Orsay Archives, 835/Z312/2: 261–4). See also Trepper, *Great Game,* 127.

20. Later, Dekanozov would be accused of having edited reports to Moscow to downplay the attack warnings, at least through late May, but in June he began to try to reduce Soviet personnel (arrivals kept coming, however, including children and pregnant wives). On June 15, he summoned the courage to telegram Molotov: "The news is that now people do not speak about the concentration as German demonstration to compel concessions from the USSR. Now they affirm that this is for genuine preparation for war against the Soviet Union." Berezhkov, *History in the Making,* 72; "Kanun voiny: preduprezhdeniia diplomatov," *Vestnik Ministerstva inostrannykh del SSSR,* 76–7. Lehmann ("Breitenbach"), in Gestapo counterintelligence, a Soviet source since 1929, evidently told his handler (now the young, inexperienced Boris Zhuravlyov) at a meeting in the outskirts of Berlin on the evening of June 19 that his Gestapo unit had received an order that Germany would invade the USSR on June 22 at 3:00 a.m. But no such communication has been published. Primakov, *Ocherki,* III: 348; Kolpakidi and Prokhorov, *Vneshniaia razvedka Rossii,* 454; Damaskin, *Stalin i razvedka,* 263–4. Beria supposedly erupted at Dekanozov (his former minion who now reported to Molotov and who sent the Lehmann message), writing to Stalin: "I again insist on the recall and punishment of our ambassador in Berlin, Dekanozov, who keeps on bombarding me with *deza* about a supposed Hitler attack on the USSR. . . . He reported that the attack commences tomorrow." But this document has not been published. Ivashutin, "Dokladyvala tochno," 57; *Krasnaia zvezda,* Feb. 2, 1991:5 (Ivashutin interview); Lota, *"Alta" protiv "Barbarossy,"* 283–4; Lota, *Sekretnyi front,* 46. See also *Krasnaia zvezda,* June 16 and 21, 2001; and *Nezavisimoe voennoe obozrenie,* 2001, no. 22: 7.

21. Mikoian, *Tak bylo,* 377.

22. Gavrilov, *Voennaia razvedka informiruet,* 694 (TsAMO f. 23, op. 24127, d. 2, l. 463); Naumov, *1941 god,* II: 383; Primakov, *Ocherki,* III: 366; Grechko et al., *Istoriia vtoroi mirovoi voiny,* III: 254, 335–8.

23. On June 21, Berlings ("Peter") reported to his German handlers that Filippov, the TASS journalist-intelligence operative, told him: "We are firmly convinced that Hitler has ventured a colossal bluff. We do not believe that the war could begin tomorrow . . . It is clear that the Germans intend to exert pressure on us in the hope of attaining advantages, which Hitler needs for continuation of the war." Vishlev, *Nakanune,* 61 (PA SS Bonn: Dienstelle Ribbentrop. Vertarauliche Berichte über Russland 23/3 [R 27113], Bl. 462604–62605), 164; Vishlev, "Pochemu zhe," 96.

24. Hitler had shifted the date of attack (something that could have been expected). There were many contradictions among the reports. Vinogradov et al., *Sekrety Gitlera,* 11–2, 17; "Predislovie," in Gavrilov, *Voennaia razvedka informiruet,* 6. Molotov complained that as 1941 progressed, he "spent half a day every day reading intelligence reports. What was not in them! What dates did they not name!" He added: "I think you cannot rely on the intelligence officers. You have to listen to them, but you have to check up on them. Intelligence operatives can push you into such a dangerous position that you do not know where you are." Chuev, *Sto sorok,* 31–2; Chuev, *Molotov Remembers,* 22. Hitler, according to an interview with Halder on June 19, 1958, had told him in Aug. 1938, "You will never learn what I am thinking. And those who boast most loudly that they know my thoughts, to such people I lie even more." Deutsch, *Conspiracy Against Hitler,* 32.

25. Zhukov stated in 1965, "I well remember the words of Stalin, when we reported the suspicious actions of German forces: 'Hitler and his generals are not such fools that they would fight simultaneously on two fronts, which broke their necks in World War I. . . . Hitler does not have the strength to fight on two fronts, and Hitler would not embark on a crazy escapade.'" Zhukov continued: "Who at that time could doubt Stalin, his political prognoses? . . . We all were accustomed to viewing Stalin as a farseeing and cautious state leader, the wise Supreme Leader of the party and Soviet people." Anfilov, "'Razgovor zakonchilsia ugrozoi Stalina'," 39–46; Lota, *Sekretnyi front,* 15 (citing RGVA, f. 41107, op. 1, d. 48, l. 1–58).

26. Hilger got it right: "Everything indicated that he [Stalin] thought that Hitler was preparing for a game of extortion in which threatening military moves would be followed by sudden demands for an economic or even territorial concessions. He seems to have believed that he would be able to negotiate with Hitler over such demands when they were presented." Hilger and Meyer, *Incompatible Allies,* 330.

27. It is a half-truth that Soviet intelligence performed its function and warned of the attack. No document has come forward analyzing the likelihood, let alone the contents, of Germany's systemic campaign of deception while it was taking place.

28. Dahlerus, *Last Attempt.*

29. Iampol'skii et al., *Organy,* I/ii: 266–7; Naumov, *1941 god,* II: 383; Primakov, *Ocherki,* III: 366; Grechko et al., *Istoriia vtoroi mirovoi voiny,* III: 254, 335–8.

30. NKVD transport had reported on German movements from summer 1940 and, in May and June 1941, produced memos of more than twenty numbered paragraphs. Naumov, *1941 god,* I: 135–6, 157, 174–6, 268–9, 324–6, 426–7, 462–5, 541–2, 545–9, 656–8, 681–3, 800–3, II: 279–82, 306–7; Iampol'skii et al., *Organy,* I/i: 299, I/ii: 19–21, 56–60, 62–4, 79–80, 82–5, 85–7, 96–7, 108–10.

31. On May 17, 1941, Merkulov had reported to Stalin, Molotov, and Beria on mass arrests and deportations of anti-Soviet elements in the Baltic republics (some 40,000). On June 21, Merkulov reported 24,000 arrests and deportations in western Belarus. GARF, f. 9475, op. 1, d. 87, l. 121, in Volkogonov papers, Hoover Institution Archives, container 21. See also container 15.

32. Iampol'skii et al., *Organy,* I/ii: 297.

33. Gefter, *Iz etikh i tekh let,* 262–3.

34. Chuev, *Molotov Remembers,* 179.

35. The notion of Stalin's willful blindness to coming war retains the stature of folklore. The accusation, engagingly delivered in Nekrich, *1941, 22 iuinia,* gained weight when Nekrich was persecuted and his book removed from Soviet libraries. But already by 1939, the Soviets counted more than 10,000 aircraft (versus less than 1,000 in 1931), and nearly 3,000 armored vehicles (from a mere 740 in 1931). From the signing of the Pact through mid-1941, another 18,000 fighter planes and 7,000 armored vehicles and tanks had come off assembly lines. In 1941, the defense share of the state budget was set to exceed 40 percent. Davies et al., *Economic Transformation of the Soviet Union,* 299; Volkogonov, *Triumf i tragediia,* II/i: 65–80.

36. Anfilov, *Doroga k tragedii,* 104.

37. To evaluate Soviet strength, the Nazi regime relied partly on Germans who had been born in the Soviet Union or lived there but were then expelled, and, "like émigrés everywhere, they underestimated the strengths of their former place of residence and overestimated the animosity of the people against their own government." Herwarth, *Against Two Evils,* 187.

38. "Stalin was not a cowardly person," wrote Zhukov, "but he well understood that the country's leadership, which he headed, had been manifestly tardy with the fundamental preparations for the country's defense in such a big war against such a powerful and experienced enemy as Germany." Admiral Kuznetsov noted—in a passage excised from the book version of his memoirs—that Stalin's "mistake was in miscalculating the date of the conflict. Stalin directed war preparations—extensive and many-sided preparations—on

the basis of very distant dates. Hitler disrupted his calculations." Zhukov, *Vospominaniia*, I: 368; Bialer, *Stalin and His Generals*, 198 (Kuznetsov). See also Pospelov, *Istoriia Velikoi Otechestvennoi voiny*, I: 479. "We of course cannot manage to avoid war before 1943," Stalin was said to have told Meretskov in Jan. 1941. "We are being dragged in against our will. But it is not out of the question that we can stay out of the war until 1942." Meretskov, *Na sluzhbe narodu* (1984), 197–8.

39. The Red Army had perhaps 13,000 tanks in western border regions, of which 469 were KV-1s and 832 were T-34s (they had begun to arrive in May–June). The Red Army had a large edge in combat aircraft. Morukov, *Velikaia Otechestvennaia*, I: 6; Pospelov, *Istoriia Velikoi Otechestvennoi voiny*, I: 415, 475–6.

40. Stepanov, "O masshtabakh repressii."

41. Only one in fourteen had higher military education. All these percentages were lower than they had been in 1937 for the far smaller officer corps. Another 1 million officers were in the reserves, perhaps a third of whom had some training. The officer corps had grown by more 2.5 times from 1937 to 1940, through the purges. Reese, *Stalin's Reluctant Soldiers*; Cherushev, "Nevinovnykh ne byvaet . . . "; Kalashnikov et al., *Krasnaia Armiia*, 10–1.

42. Kuznetsov added of Stalin: "He brushed facts and arguments aside more and more abruptly." Kuznetsov, however, has been disingenuous. In his telling, on June 21 he met Rear Admiral Mikhail Vorontsov, the Soviet naval attaché in Berlin, whom he had recalled to report in person and who had managed to travel by train from Berlin to Moscow. Vorontsov was full of details about the deployed German war machine, and Kuznetsov claimed he reportedly this immediately to Stalin. In fact, the naval commissar conveyed it as an example of a likely provocation. Kuznetsov writes in his memoirs that the last time he saw Stalin before the war was "June 13 or 14," but he is in the logbook for June 21. Kuznetsov, *Nakanune*, 348–9, 355; Shustov, "No Other Ambassador," 167; Bialer, *Stalin and His Generals*, 579n5 (citing *Der Spiegel*, March 20, 1967: 135).

43. Khrushchev, *Memoirs*, I: 269, 273–4, 287–91. Soviet military journals in 1940–1 presented a frightening picture of German capabilities. Glantz, *Stumbling Colossus*, 258–9; Konenenko, "Germano-pol'skaia voina 1939 g."; Konenenko, "Boi v Finlandii"; Konenenko, "Kratkii obzor voennykh desitvii na zapade"; Khorseev, "VVS v germane-pol'skoi voine"; Desiatov, "Operatsii v Norvegii"; Ratner, "Pororyv na Maase"; Belianovskii, "Desitviia tnkovykh." Zhukov would later state: "When I asked him [Stalin] to allow bringing the troops of the western frontier districts to full combat readiness . . . he brought me to the map and, pointing to the Near East, said 'that's where they [the Germans] will go.'" This could have been perhaps Stalin's way of blunting Zhukov's pressure without discussing with him the anticipated ultimatum. In any case, the despot had long abandoned any credence to an attack on British positions in the Near East. Anfilov, *Doroga k tragedii*, 195.

44. Kuznetsov, *Nakanune*, 357 (citing a conversation with Pronin) and in the first edition (1966), 329. See also Erickson, *Road to Stalingrad*, 108. The Moscow province party committee was holding a plenum (June 20–1). *Pravda*, June 22, 1941. Yakov Chadayev, the government notary, was quoted as stating that Stalin "summoned them." Neither Shcherbakov nor Pronin appear in the office logbook; they could have been received in the apartment, which seems unlikely given their low

stature. The prohibition on use of electric lighting applied to residences as well. As of 1941, only 68 families, 239 people, still resided in the Kremlin, most of them widows and pensioners (such as the widows of Sverdlov and Orjonikidze); this was down from 374 people in 1935 (not including service personnel and guards) and 2,100 in 1925.

45. Voronov, *Na sluzhbe voennoi*, 175; Tiulenev, *Cherez tri voiny* (1960), 138. As Zhukov wrote, "The Soviet Government did everything possible so as not to give any justification for Germany to start a war. This determined everything." Zhukov, *Vospominaniia*, I: 340.

46. As of June 1, 1941, Golikov estimated German divisions arrayed near the joint frontier at 120–2, along with 122–6 arrayed against Britain in the West, Norway, Italy, Crete, and Africa, plus 44–48 of reserves. He noted that in "transferring significant forces from Yugoslavia, Greece, and Bulgaria to Romania, the Germans are to a great degree strengthening their right flank"—in the direction of Ukraine. Gavrilov, *Voennaia razvedka informiruet*, 520, 646–7 (TsAMO, f. 23, op. 7237, d. 2, l. 114–6).

47. These Soviet divisions, to reach full strength, needed more than 1 million reservists to join them. Zolotarev et al., *Russkii arkhiv: Velikaia otechestvennaia*, XIII (II/i): 7–8, 11, 77, 581; Zhukov, *Vospominaniia*, I: 359. Another source gives a figure of 3,900 German aircraft, 60 percent of their air force, plus 1,000 planes of Romania and Finland. Pospelov, *Istoriia Velikoi Otechestvennoi voiny*, II: 9.

48. The totalitarian Soviet state, with its vast armed forces, was the only one not fully mobilized, "an absolutely impossible, improbable situation," as one analyst noted. Mark Solonin, "Tri plana tovarishcha Stalina," 71. On June 18, the Soviet Union observed the fifth anniversary of Gorky's death. *Pravda*, June 18, 1941; Artizov and Naumov, *Vlast' i khudozhestvennaia intelligentsiia*, 474 (RGASPI, f. 17, op. 3, d. 1041, l. 8). At the defense commissariat on June 19, Major General Mikhail Kazakov, commander of the staff of the Central Asian military district, who had been summoned to Moscow, and others were shown a German film of the Wehrmacht being greeted warmly in the Balkans by Slavic females bearing wine and flowers. Kazakov would recall that Vasilevsky told him, "We'll be lucky if it doesn't begin in the next fifteen to twenty days." Kazakov, *Nad kartoi bylykh srazhenii*, 69–70; Bialer, *Stalin and His Generals*, 188–9.

49. The work was supposed to be completed by July 15, 1941. Zolotarev et al., *Russkii arkhiv: Velikaia otechestvennaia*, XIII (II/i): 280–2 (RGVA, f. 4, op. 11, d. 62, l. 201–3, 204–5).

50. On the many local measures undertaken to bring Soviet forces to combat readiness, especially the initiatives in the Baltic region, and their countermanding under threat, see *Sbornik boevykh dokumentov Velikoi Otechestvennoi voiny*, XXXIV: 7–11 (f. 344, op. 2459ss, d. 11, l. 30–6), 21–4 (f. 221, op. 7833ss, d. 3, l. 17–21); Bialer, *Stalin and His Generals*, 199–200 (Colonel General Kuznetsov); Kuznetsov, "Voenno-Morskoi flot nakanune Velikoi Otechestvennoi voiny," 72–3; Kuznetsov, *Nakanune*, 343–4; Voronov, *Na sluzhbe voennoi*, 175–8; Zhukov, *Vospominaniia*, I: 386–7; Erickson, *Road to Stalingrad*, 82–3; Anfilov, "'Razgovor zakonchilsia ugrozoi Stalina'," 42. Zhdanov conspicuously departed Leningrad for holiday in Sochi on June 19; this had to be approved by the politburo.

51. Sudoplatov was not to allow "German provocateurs to stage actions like those against Poland in 1939." He recalled that, at the office on the night of June 21, "I sensed the danger of military provocation or conflict but not the magnitude of the full-scale invasion that followed." Sudoplatov, *Special Tasks*, 123–5. See also Possony, "Hitlers Unternehmen 'Barbarossa.'" Soviet intelligence was reporting that Ukrainian schools in German-occupied Poland were teaching the geography of a forthcoming independent Ukraine and that many Ukrainian nationalists, and even some Poles with eyes on Ukraine's territory, were keen to stage provocations to provoke a German attack on the Soviet Union. Naumov, *1941 god*, I: 135–6, 157, 174–6, 268–9, 324–6, 426–7, 462–5, 545–8, 656–8, 681–3; Iampol'skii et al., *Organy*, I/ii: 172–87 (May 31, 1941).

52. Iampol'skii et al., *Organy*, I/ii: 266–7; Naumov, *1941 god*, II: 383; Primakov, *Ocherki*, III: 366; Grechko et al., *Istoriia vtoroi mirovoi voiny*, III: 254, 335–8.

53. Kumanev, *Riadom so Stalinym*, 23–4 (Mikoyan); *Na prieme*, 337 (Mikoyan is listed as arriving at 8:15 p.m. and leaving four hours later). The Soviet navy reported that German engineers and specialists working in Leningrad on a battleship acquired from Germany had left, but in response, Molotov told Admiral Kuznetsov, "Only a fool would attack us!" Zhdanov similarly assured Kuznetsov that the Germans were concentrating forces as a means of exerting psychological pressure and would never open a two-front war. Kuznetsov, "Voenno-Morskoi flot nakanune Velikoi Otechestvennoi voiny," 73; Bialer, *Stalin and His Generals*, 190–1 (Kuznetsov); Watson, *Molotov*, 187. Beria is not listed in the logbook for Stalin's Kremlin office between appearances on June 10 and June 20.

54. They would be confiscated as war booty. Panteleev, *Morskoi front*, 36. By June 1941, Nazi Germany was heavily in debt to the Soviet Union.

55. This was the second time that day that Kegel had risked an in-person meeting with his handler. In June 1941 alone, he met his military intelligence handler Leontyev nine times in person. Separately, Beria was reporting to Stalin from his agents that the smoke from burning documents in German embassy inner courtyard could be seen from great distance; some thought it was a fire. *Krasnaia zvezda*, June 16 and 21, 2001; *Nezavisimoe voennoe obozrenie*, 2001, no. 22: 7. Leontyev (b. 1911) had not thought to arrange for contacts with Kegel after the predicted war broke out. Lota, *"Alta" protiv "Barbarossy,"* 443 (V. V. Bochkarev).

56. How Stalin reacted to Kegel's information remains unknown. Gavrilov, *Voennaia razvedka informiruet*, 711–3; Lota, *Sekretnyi front*, 58–60; Kegel, *V buriakh nashego veka* (the German original was published in 1983). Kegel had spoken directly with Walter Schellenberg, the head of political intelligence for the SS, who had evidently visited the USSR under the cover of a chemical industry representative. Kiknadze, "Gerkhard Kegel," 124; Vasil'evich and Sgibnev, "Podvig v teni eshafota," 106.

57. "The Master in an agitated state just talked to Timoshenko . . . Apparently something is expected . . . you yourself could guess . . . the German attack," Poskryobyshev supposedly said to Chadayev. "A German attack is possible." Kumanev, *Riadom so Stalinym*, 410. In a draft decree, written in pencil by Malenkov with many crossouts, dated, in someone else's hand, June 21, and not entered into the

approved protocols, Tyulenev was to be appointed commander of the "southern front" with two armies. Meretskov was to be named commander of the northwestern front; Zhukov, of the southwestern front, where the main German attack was expected. Zaporozhets was to become his deputy, and in the latter's place Mekhlis would be restored to head of the Red Army political directorate. "Nakanune voiny: iz postanovlenii vysshikh partiinykh i gosudarstvennykh organov (Mai 1940 g.–21 iiunia 1941 g.)," 209–10 (with facsimile); APRF, f. 3, op. 50, d. 125, l. 75–6.

58. Zhukov does not name the defector, and more than one crossed that night into Soviet territory (perhaps as many as four). Zhukov, *Vospominania*, I: 386–9. See also Erickson, *Road to Stalingrad*, 105–6; and Khrushchev, *Vospominania*, I: 299–301. See also Fediuninskii, *Podniatye po trevoge*, 10–2; Bialer, *Stalin and His Generals*, 241–2 (Fediunsky). Sevastianov, *Neman-Volga-Dunai*, 5; and Naumov, *1941 god*, II: 279–82 (TsA SVR RF, d. 21616, t. 2, l. 389–97: May 30, 1941).

59. *Na prieme*, 337. Budyonny had not been in Stalin's office for two months, according to the logbook.

60. On the evening of June 21, Meretskov would later recall, Timoshenko told him, "Gain whatever time we can! A month, a month and a half, another week. It is possible the war will start tomorrow." Meretskov, *Na sluzhbe narodu* (1984), 205; Meretskov, *Na sluzhbe narodu*, 209–10.

61. Simonov, "K biografii G. K. Zhukova," 106.

62. Zhukov, *Vospominaniia*, I: 387. Zhukov recalls that his deputy Vatutin accompanied them. Vatutin does not appear in Stalin's logbook. Timoshenko and Zhukov were in Stalin's office at least nineteen times in the last three months, including six in June, but the despot did not receive them between June 11 and 18. In that interval only Vatutin was in the Little Corner, on June 17 for half an hour (Molotov and Kagnovich were there), on June 18 Stalin received the military men for four hours and thirty-five minutes. *Na prieme*, 336–7.

63. Goebbels continued: "Should have been made six months ago." (In fact, seven months ago Molotov had been in Berlin.) Goebbels added: "I read a comprehensive report on Russian-Bolshevik radio propaganda. It will give us some real problems, because it is not so stupid as the English material. Probably written by Jews." Fröhlich, *Tagebücher von Joseph Goebbels*, 1, IX: 391–93 (June 21); Taylor, *Goebbels Diaries*, 420. A request for Molotov to meet Hitler on June 18 was also recorded by Halder, *Kriegstagebuch*, II: 458–9 (June 20); Halder, *Halder Diaries*, II: 960.

64. Dekanozov appeared at 6:00 p.m. on June 18, but despite an audience of fifty minutes, managed only to complain about German delays in issuing exit visas for a Soviet consular official in Königsberg, ships at Baltic ports, and the costs of building a bomb shelter. Naumov, *1941 god*, II: 386–7 (AVP RF, f. 082, op. 24, pap. 106, d. 7, l. 94–7).

65. Hill, *Die Weizsäcker-Papiere*, 260 (June 18); DGFP, series D, XII: 1050; Weizsäcker, *Erinnerungen*, 317.

66. The protest listed 260 flight violations between March 27 and June 19. On June 20, the NKVD border guard had reported that just since June 10, there had been 86 more unauthorized reconnaissance flights from Greater Germany, Finland, Hungary, and Romania. Solov'ev and Chugunova, *Pogranichnye voiska SSSR*, 755–6.

67. The play was a production of the Franko Ukrainian Academic Theater on tour in Moscow. *Pravda*, June 22, 1941. See also Dallin, *Soviet Russia's Foreign Policy*, 375. Whether Stalin might have been ready to offer far-reaching concessions remains a matter of speculation. Mastny, *Russia's Road to the Cold War*, 34.

68. Vishlev, *Nakanune*, 64–72 (citing Politisches Archiv des Auswärtigen Amts Bonn: Büro des Staatssekretär, Russland, BD. 5 [R 29716], Bl. 049 [113453]–053 [113457], 100 [113504], 103 [113507]–105 [113509], 112 [113516], 125 [113529]–126 [113530], 130 [113653]; Dienstelle Ribbentrop, Vertrauliche Berichte, 2/2 Teil 2 [R 27097], Bl. 30853; Dienstelle Ribbentrop, UdSSR-RC, 7/1 [R 27168], Bl. 26051, 26097–8; Dienstelle Ribbentrop, Vertrauliche Berichte über Russland [Peter], 2/3 [R 27113], Bl. 462607). Some of the information being spread was true: that the Soviet Union was making plans for population, industrial, and government evacuations eastward; that the USSR had refrained from forced collectivization in the Baltic states; that the regime was undertaking measures to stimulate Soviet patriotism. These whisperings about Stalin being Nazi Germany's best hope, and under internal threat for that reason, were advanced "in strictest confidence" by Amayak Kobulov and Ivan Filippov to their German interlocutors in Berlin, by a Soviet intelligence operative in Stockholm, and others elsewhere.

69. Simonov, "Zametki," 53. According to Zhukov, Stalin was aware of and to a degree accepted the argument of German propaganda that Wehrmacht forces were stationed on the border partly because Soviet forces were there and Germany had no ultimate guarantee that Stalin would not attack preemptively.

70. Zhukov later wrote that Stalin said: "Germany is up to its neck in war in the West, I believe Hitler would never risk creating a second front for himself by attacking the Soviet Union. Hitler is not such a fool that he fails to understand the Soviet Union is not Poland, not France and that it is not even England and all these taken together." Timoshenko supposedly asked, "What if it does happen?" and requested bringing the frontier troops to a war footing and sending more westward, but Stalin refused, designating their proposal tantamount to "launching a war." Zhukov, *Vospominaniia* (1995), I: 383–4; Naumov, *1941 god*, II: 500 (RGVA, f. 41107, op. 1, d. 48, l. 1–58).

71. Sontag and Beddie, *Nazi-Soviet Relations*, 353–4; DGFP, series D, XII: 1059; Taylor, *Goebbels Diaries*, 423; Berezhkov, *S diplomaticheskoi missiei*, 78–106; Bialer, *Stalin and His Generals*, 215–6 (Berezhkov).

72. Schulenburg was said to have observed of the Pact: "I gave my all in order to work toward good relations between Germany and the Soviet Union, and in some ways I have achieved my aim. But you know yourself that in reality I have achieved nothing. This treaty will lead us into the second world war and bring ruin upon Germany . . . This war will last for a long, long time, just as did the First World War." Wegner-Korfes, "Ambassador Count Schulenburg," 187–204; Fleischhauer, *Der Pakt*, 400.

73. Gorodetsky, *Grand Delusion*, 307 (citing UD:s Arkhiv 1920 ARS, HP/1557/LVII, Swedish ambassador in Moscow, June 16). According to the unpublished memoir of his daughter, American ambassador Steinhardt observed at the Moscow airport how von Walther, in tears, had had to part with his beloved boxer, which was being shipped back to Berlin. Lukes, *On the Edge of the Cold War*, 75–6

(citing Steinhardt Sherlock, "R.S.V.P.," 65; interview with Laurene Sherlock and Peter Rosenblatt, Oct. 27, 2007).

74. Schmidt, *Statist auf diplomatische Bühne*, 214.

75. Naumov, *1941 god*, II: 414–5 (AVP RF, f. 06, op. 3, pap. 1, d. 5, l. 8–11), 416 (l. 1: text of the protest); Iampol'skii et al., *Organy*, 1/ii: 370–1; DGFP, XII: 1070–1; Sontag and Beddie, *Nazi-Soviet Relations*, 355–6 (Schulenburg account); DVP SSSR, XXIII/ii: 751–2; Hilger and Meyer, *Incompatible Allies*, 335–6; Gorodetsky, *Grand Delusion*, 310 (citing AVP RF, f. 06, op. 3, pap. 1, d. 5, l. 6–7). Schulenburg's summary reached the foreign ministry in Berlin at 2:30 a.m. on June 22. See also Vishlev, "Pochemu zhe," 80; and Fel'shtinskii, *Oglasheniiu podlezhit*, 371–6.

76. Molotov's departure to receive Schulenburg was not recorded. *Na prieme*, 337.

77. Kumanev, *Riadom so Stalinym*, 409–10 (Chadayev); Kuznetsov, *Nakanune*, 355.

78. Zolotarev et al., *Russkii arkhiv: Velikaia otechestvennaia*, XIII (II/i), 282 (TsAMO, f. 48–A, op. 1554, d. 90, l. 257–9); Naumov, *1941 god*, II: 423; Pospelov, *Istoriia Velikoi Otechestvennoi voiny*, II: 11; Zakharov, *General'nyi shtab*, 224–5; Zhukov, *Vospominaniia* (1971), 233–4; Zhukov, *Vospomininia* (1995), I: 387. See also Erickson, *Road to Stalingrad*, 110; and Gorodetsky, *Grand Delusion*, 311.

79. Beria at some point left and came back, but only his re-arrival was recorded in the logbook. Others present might have come and gone without their movements having been recorded.

80. Erickson, *Road to Stalingrad*, 114–5; Bialer, *Stalin and His Generals*, 193 (Kuznetsov).

81. DGFP, series D, XII: 1061–3; Sontag and Beddie, *Nazi-Soviet Relations*, 353–4; Vishlev, "Pochemu zhe," 80; Taylor, *Goebbels Diaries*, 423. Precisely when Dekanozov informed Moscow of his failure remains unclear. Berezhkov, the Soviet embassy employee who claimed he had been tasked with phoning the German foreign ministry to obtain the meeting with Ribbentrop, wrongly implied that no meeting had been arranged until the German foreign ministry itself called back at 3:00 a.m. Berlin time (5:00 a.m. Moscow time) with a summons for Dekanozov. Bialer, *Stalin and His Generals*, 215–6 (Berezhkov).

82. "Stalin sought by the condition and behavior of troops in the border military districts to make it clear to Hitler that we had a quiet atmosphere, bordering on carelessness," recalled army general Semyon Ivanov. He characterized this as a form of criminal self-demobilization. Ivanov, *Shtab armeiskii*, 104–6.

83. Lieutenant General Nikolai Klich, head of artillery in the Western several military district, told Colonel Ilya Starinov of Pavlov's phone calls to Moscow about every ominous development: "Always the same reply—'Don't panic! Keep calm! "The Boss" knows everything.'" Bialer, *Stalin and His Generals*, 222–3 (Starinov).

84. The defector was Alfred Liskow. (Nekrich writes that he crossed the border around 11:00 p.m.) The NKGB established that he was a lance corporal, thirty years old, a furniture joiner and Communist (before Hitler's rise), who said that his unit had been told they would cross the Bug River on boats and pontoons in a few hours. Liskow was still being held by the NKGB when the German attack commenced. Naumov, *1941 god*, II: 422; "Nakanune voiny (1940–1941 gg.)," 218; Nekrich, *1941, 22 iuinia*, 197.

85. Germany continued to send military equipment to the Soviets in June, with Göring

and others reasoning that the Soviets would never be able to make full use in time of the advanced technology that was delivered. Von Strandmann, "Appeasement and Counter-Appeasement," 171 (citing HA Krupp, WA 40, B, C 381); Schwendemann, *Wirtschaftliche Zusammenarbeit*, 265–79.

86. Pavlov, in testimony after his arrest, would not mention Timoshenko mentioning Directive No. 1, but he would note that when he hung up the phone, he (Pavlov) had ordered all units to combat readiness. http:// liewar.ru/tragediya-22-iyunya/178-protoko ly-doprosa-d-g-pavlova.html (Pavlov testimony, July 7, 1941, with commentary). Pavlov might have spoken with Timoshenko earlier, from the theater, by a special telephone brought in for just such a contingency.

87. "Itinerar Hitlers vom 1.9.1939–31.12.1941," 691. Hitler had written to Antonescu on June 14. Supposedly, already on June 12 Antonescu was let in on the closely guarded secret of the precise date of attack. Schmidt, *Statist auf diplomatische Bühne*, 233.

88. Goebbels added: "Feverish activity begins." Fröhlich, *Tagebücher von Joseph Goebbels*, IX: 393–7 (June 22).

89. Pospelov, *Istoriia velikoi otechestvennoi voiny*, I: 478–9; Sechkin, *Granitsa i voina*, 54.

90. Zoller, *Hitler Privat*, 142–3 (Frau Christa Schroeder). Hitler was said to have told Below before retiring: "This will be the hardest struggle that our soldiers have to endure this war." Below, *Als Hitlers Adjutant*, 279.

91. Mertsalov and Mertsalova, *Stalinizm i voina*, 164–7.

92. Gorodetsky, whose account of Stalin's approach to foreign policy stands above all others in English, overreacted to attributions of Soviet expansionism to ideology. "Stalin was little affected by sentiment or ideology in the pursuit of foreign policy," Gorodetsky wrongly imagined. "His statesmanship was rooted in Russia's tsarist legacy, and responded to imperatives deep within its history . . . Stalin's policy appears to have been rational and level-headed." Obviously, Sovietization of the Baltic states, eastern Poland, Bessarabia, and Bukovina, or Stalin's obsession with Trotsky and his terror, had nothing to do with realpolitik or level-headedness. Indeed, Gorodetsky himself writes, two pages on, of the "paranoiac atmosphere in the Kremlin." Gorodetsky, *Grand Delusion*, 316, 318.

93. Hillgruber, *Hitlers Strategie*.

94. Hitler had expected Britain, as he told one of his top military men already back on June 23, 1940, to "knuckle under," conceding Germany's free hand on the continent. Förster, "Hitler Turns East," 117 (citing Notizen des Wehrmachtsführungsamtes, BA-MA, RW 4/v. 581).

95. Hitler had also misunderstood British anti-Communism. The phlegmatic British had always been interested only in containment, not an anti-Bolshevik crusade, since the latter, even if successful, would just bring Nazi domination of the continent, so London took a similar approach to Moscow as to Berlin: engagement to try to "moderate" the regime. Waddington, "Idyllis and Unruffled Atmosphere."

96. Hubatsch, *Hitlers Weisungen*, 129–39. See also *DGFP*, series D, XII: 1012–6.

97. Overy, *Why the Allies Won*, 1–24.

98. To carry the consequences to their conclusion: Hitler would have either gone on to conquer the USSR, or been vanquished by the latter, which could have enveloped all of Europe. Catherwood, *Balkans in World War Two*, 170.

99. Schramm, *Hitler*, 125.

100. "The analyst can choose which problem he wishes to study, whereas the statesman's problems are imposed on him," Kissinger wrote. "The analyst can allot whatever time is necessary to come to a clear conclusion; the overwhelming challenge to the statesman is the pressure of time. The analyst runs no risk. If his conclusions prove wrong, he can write another treatise. The statesman is permitted only one guess; his mistakes are irretrievable." Kissinger, *Diplomacy*, 27.

101. Gerwarth, *Bismarck Myth*, 128.

102. Speer, *Inside the Third Reich*, 135–9.

BIBLIOGRAPHY

ADAP: Akten zu Deutschen Austwärtigen Politik, 1918–45, serie B, 1925–1933, 18 vols. (Göttingen: Vandenhueck und Ruprecht.)

APRF: Russian Presidential Archive (former politburo archive)

AVPRF: Foreign Policy Archive of the Russian Federation

DBFP: Documents on British Foreign Policy, 1919–1939. 62 vols. London: H. M. Stationery Office, 1946–

DDF: Documents diplomatiques français, 1932–1939. 1ère Série: 1932–1935. 13 vols. 2ème Série: 1936–1939. 19 vols. Paris: Imprimerie nationale, 1964–81

DGFP: Documents on German Foreign Policy, 1918–1945, series C, series D. 13 vols. Washington, D.C.: Government Printing Office, 1949

DVP SSSR: Dokumenty vneshnei politiki SSSR. 24 vols. Moscow: Politcheskaia literatura, 1957–92

FRUS: Foreign Relations of the United States Diplomatic Papers. Volumes I–III. Washington, D.C.: U.S. Government Printing Office, 1949–1950

GANO: State Archive of Novosibirsk

GARF: State Archive of the Russian Federation

GF IML: Georgian Affiliate of the Communist Party Archive

GIAG: Georgia State Historical Archive

Hoover Institution Archives, Stanford University

RGAE: Russian State Economic Archive

RGAKFD: Russian State Archive of Photographs and Film

RGALI: Russian State Archive of Literature and Art

RGASPI: Russian State Archive of Social and Political History (former central party archive)

RGVA: Russian Military Archive

TsAMO: Central Archive of the Ministry of Defense

TsA FSB: Central Archive of the Federal Security Service (former KGB)

Abbas-ogly, Adile. *Moia Abkhaziia, moia sud'ba*. Moscow: AST, 2009.

——. *Ne mogu zabyt'*. Moscow: AST, 2005.

Abbé, James E. *I Photograph Russia*. New York: R. M. McBride & Co., 1934.

Äbdiraīymŭly, Serik, et al., eds. *Golod v kazakhskoi stepi: pis'ma trevogi i boli*. Alma-Ata: Qazaq Universiteti, 1991.

Abelshauser, Werner. "Germany: Guns, Butter, and Economic Miracles." In *The Economics of World War II: Six Great Powers in International Comparison*, edited by Mark Harrison. New York: Cambridge University, 1988, 122–76.

Abendroth, Hans-Henning. *Hitler in der spanischen Arena: die deutsch-spanischen Beziehungen im Spannungsfeld der europäischen Interessenpolitik vom Ausbruch des Bürgerkrieges bis zum Ausbruch des Weltkrieges 1936–1939*. Paderborn: F. Schöningh, 1973.

Abkhazia: dokumenty svidetel'stvuiut, 1937–1953. Sukhumi: Alashara, 1992.

Abkhazskaia oblastnaia organizatsiia kommunisticheskoi partii Gruzii v tsifrakh, 1921–1980. Sukhumi: Alashara, 1980.

Abramov, Ark. *O pravoi oppozitsii v partii*. Moscow: Molodaia gvardiia, 1929.

Abramov, N. A. "Osobaia missiia Davida Kandelaki," *Voprosy istorii*, 1991, no. 4–5: 144–56.

Abramov, Vadim. *Evrei v KGB: palachi i zhertvy*. Moscow: Iauza/EKSMO, 2005.

Abylkhozhin, Zhulduzbek B., Manash K. Kozybaev, and Maqash B. Tatimov. "Kazakhstanskaia tragediia," *Voprosy istorii*, 1989, no. 7: 53–71.

Adamthwaite, Anthony. *France and the Coming of the Second World War, 1936–1939*. London: Frank Cass, 1997.

——. *Grandeur and Misery: France's Bid for Power in Europe, 1914–1940*. London: Arnold, 1995.

Adibekov, G. M., and K. M. Anderson. "'U menia odna nadezhda na tebia': poslednie pis'ma N. I. Ivanovicha I. V. Stalinu," *Istoricheskii arkhiv*, 2001, no. 3: 47–85

——, et al., eds. *Politbiuro TsK RKP (b)–VKP (b) i Evropa: resheniia 'osoboi papki', 1923–1939*. Moscow: Rosspen, 2001.

——, eds. *Politbiuro TsK RKP (b)–VKP (b): povestki dnia zasedanii 1919–1952*. 3 vols. Moscow: Rosspen, 2001.

——, eds. *Politbiuro TsK RKP (b)–VKP (b) i Komintern, 1919–1943: dokumenty*. Moscow: Rosspen, 2004.

Adzhubei, Aleksei. *Te desiat' let*. Moscow: Sovetskaia Rossiia, 1989.

Afanas'ev, A. V., ed. *Oni ne molchali*. Moscow: Politizdat, 1991.

Afanas'ev, Iu. N. *Inogo ne dano: perestroika—glasnost', demokratiia, sotsializm*. Moscow: Progress, 1988.

——, et al., eds. *Istoriia stalinskogo Gulaga, konets 1920-x—pervaia polvina 1950-x godov: sbornik dokumentov*. 7 vols. Moscow: Rosspen, 2004–5.

Afinogenov, Aleksandr. *Dnevniki i zapisnye knigi*. Moscow: Sovetskii pisatel, 1960.

——. *Izbrannoe*. 2 vols. Moscow: Iskusstvo, 1977.

Agabekov, G. S. *ChK za rabotoi*. Berlin: Strela, 1931.

——. *G.P.U.: zapiski chekista*. Berlin: Strela, 1930.

——. *OGPU: The Russian Secret Terror*. New York: Brentano's, 1931.

Aganian, Tsatur P. *Nersik Stepanian*. Yerevan: Aistan, 1967.

Ageenko, K. P., et al., eds. *Voennaia pomoshch' SSSR v osvoboditelnnoi bor'be kitaiskogo naroda*. Moscow: Voenizdat, 1975.

"'Agent angliiskoi razvedki sluchayno vstretil Vas . . . ,'" *Istochnik*, 1996, no. 3: 161–2.

Agrba, R. K., ed. *Abkhazskaia oblastnaia organizatsiia kompartii Gruzii v tsifrakh, 1921–1980 gg*. Sukhumi: Alashara, 1980.

Agursky, Mikhail. "The Bolshevik Revolution as a Revolution of National Liberation," *Journal of Communist Studies*, 3/2 (1987): 177–84.

——. "Soviet Disinformation and Forgeries," *International Journal on World Peace*, 6/1 (1989): 13–30.

——. *The Third Rome: National Bolshevism in the USSR*. Boulder, CO: Westview, 1987.

Ahmann, Rolf. *Nichtangriffspakte: Entwicklung und operative Nutzung in Europa, 1922–1939*. Baden-Baden: Nomos, 1988.

Airapetian, M. E. *Etapy vneshnei politiki SSSR, 1917–1941*. Moscow: Voenizdat, 1941.

Aitiev, T. A., and B. M. Ishmukhamedov. *Torzhestvo leninskogo kooperativnogo plana v Kazakhstane*. Alma-Ata: Nauka, 1969.

Aizenberg, Isaac P. *Valiutnaia Sistema SSSR*. Moscow: Sotsial'no-ekonomicheskaia literatura, 1962.

A. K. "Kratkii kurs istorii SSSR," *Bol'shevik*, 1937, no. 17: 84–96.

Akhmatova, Anna. "Mandelshtam (Listki iz dnevnika)." In *Sochineniia*. 2 vols. Washington, D.C.: Inter-Language Literary Associates, 1967–8, II: 166–87.

Akhmedabiev, Aleksandr. "I opiat' o mifakh," *Chernovik*, March 11, 2015. Available at http://chernovik.net/content/hronograf/i-opyat-o-mifah.

Akhmedov, Ismail. *In and Out of Stalin's GRU: A Tatar's Escape from Red Army Intelligence*. Frederick, MD: University Publications of America, 1984.

Albrecht, Richard. "'Wer redet heute noch von der Vernichtung der Armenier?' Kommentierte Wiederveröffentlichung der Erstpublikation von Adolf Hitlers Geheimrede am 22. August 1939," *Zeitschrift für Weltgeschichte*, 9/2 (2008): 115–32.

Aldanov, Mark. *Bol'shaia Lubianka*. Moscow: Olma, 2002.

——. *Sovremenniki*. 2nd ed. Berlin: Slovo, 1932.

Aldazhumanov, Kaidar. "Krest'ianskoe dvizhenie soprotivleniia." In *Deportirovannye v Kazakhstan narody: vremia, sud'by*, edited by A. K. Kekilbaev. Almaty: Arys, 1998, 66–93.

——, et al., eds. *Nasil'stvennaia kollektivizatsiia i golod v Kazakhstane, 1931–1933 gg.: dokumenty i materialy*. Almaty: XXI vek, 1998.

Aldcroft, Derek. "The Versailles Legacy," *History Review*, no. 29 (1997): 8–13.

Aleksandrov, Grigorii. *Epokha i kino*. Moscow: Politcheskaia literatura, 1976.

Aleksandrov, Viktor A. *Delo Tukhachevskogo*. Rostov-na-Donu: Rostovskii universitet, 1990, 163–4.

Alekseev, M. A., et al. *Entsiklopediia voennoi razvedki*. Moscow: Kuchkovo pole, 2012.

Aleksei Ivanovich Rykov: kratkaia biografiia. Moscow: Gosizdat, 1927.

Alexandrovskii, Sergei. "Munich Witness's Account," *International Affairs [Moscow]*, 1988, no. 12: 119–32.

Alexopoulos, Golfo. "Exposing Illegality and Oneself: Complaint and Risk in Stalin's Russia." In *Reforming Justice in Russia, 1864–1996: Power Culture, and the Limits of Legal Order*, edited by Peter H. Solomon, Jr. Armonk, NY: M. E. Sharpe, 1997, 167–89.

Allen, Jr., David E. "The Soviet Union and the Spanish Civil War." PhD diss. Stanford University, 1952.

Allen, Robert C. *Farm to Factory: A Reinterpretation of the Soviet Industrial Revolution.* Princeton, NJ: Princeton University, 2003.

Alliluev, Vladimir. *Khronika odnoi sem'i: Alliluevy-Stalin.* Moscow: Molodaia gvardiia, 1995.

Alliluyeva, Svetlana. *Dvadtsat' pisem k drugu.* New York: Harper & Row, 1967.

——. *Only One Year.* New York: Harper & Row, 1969.

——. *Tol'ko odin god.* Moscow: Kniga, 1990.

——. *Twenty Letters to a Friend.* New York: Harper & Row, 1967.

——. *Vospominaniia.* Moscow: Sovetskii pisatel', 1946.

Alliueva, Anna S. *Vospominaniia.* Moscow: Sovetskii pisatel, 1946.

Allworth, Edward. *The Modern Uzbeks: From the Fourteenth Century to the Present, A Cultural History.* Stanford, CA: Hoover Institution, 1990.

Alpert, Michael. *A New International History of the Spanish Civil War.* 2nd ed. New York: Palgrave Macmillan, 2004.

Alt, K. "Die Wehrmacht im Kalkül Stalins." In *Die Wehrmacht: Mythos und Realität,* edited by R. D. Müller and H. E. Volkmann. Munich: Oldenbourg, 1999, 105–22.

Amar, Tarik. "Sovietization as a Civilizing Mission in the West." In *The Sovietization of Eastern Europe: New Perspectives on the Postwar Period,* edited by Balázs Apor et al. Washington, D.C.: New Academia, 2008, 29–45.

Ammende, Ewald. *Human Life in Russia.* London: George Allen and Unwin, 1936.

Anchbadze, Z. V., et al., eds. *Istoriia Abkhazskoi ASSR 1917–1937.* Sukhumi: Alashara, 1983.

Anderson, Kirill M, ed. *Voennyi sovet pri narodnom komissarie oborony SSSR, 1–4 iunia 1937 g.: dokumenty i materialy.* Moscow: Rosspen, 2008.

——, ed. *Kremlevskii kinoteatr, 1928–1953: dokumenty.* Moscow: Rosspen, 2005.

Andreas-Friedrich, Ruth. *Berlin Underground, 1938–1945.* New York: Henry Holt, 1947.

Andreev, A. A. *Vospominaniia, pis'ma.* Moscow: Politicheskaia literatura, 1985.

Andrei Aleksandrovich Zhdanov, 1896–1948. Moscow: Gosizdat, 1948.

Andrew, Christopher. *The Defense of the Realm: The Authorized History of MI5.* New York: Knopf, 2009.

——. *Secret Service: The Making of the British Intelligence Community.* London: Heinemann, 1985.

——, and Julie Elkner. "Stalin and Foreign Intelligence," *Totalitarian Movements and Political Religions,* 4/1 (2003): 69–94.

——, and Mitrokhin, Vasily. *The Mitrokhin Archive: The KGB in Europe and the West.* London: Allen Lane, 1999.

——, and Oleg Gordievsky. *KGB: The Inside Story.* New York: HarperCollins, 1990.

Anfert'ev, Ivan A. "Osobennosti preodoleniia I. V. Stalinym krizisnoi situatsii v SSSR v nachale 1930-X gg.," *Rossiiskie i slavianskie issledovaniia; nauchnyi sb ornik* 2010 vyp.: 177–82.

——. "'Delo M. N. Riutina' v sud'be G. E. Zinov'eva i L. B. Kameneva, oktiabr' 1932 g.," *Istoricheskii arkhiv,* 2006, no. 1: 64–94.

——, ed. *Smerch.* Moscow: DOSAAF SSSR, 1988.

Anfilov, Viktor A. *Doroga k tragedii sorok pervogo.* Moscow: Voenizdat, 1965.

——. *Krushenie pokhoda Gitlera na Moskvu 1941.* Moscow: Nauka, 1989.

——. "'Razgovor zakonchilsia ugrozoi Stalina': desiat' besed s marshalom G. K. Zhukovym v mae-iune 1965 goda," *Voenno-Istoricheskii zhurnal,* 1995, no. 3: 39–46.

——, and F. I. Golikov, *Zagadka 1941 goda: o voine pod raznymi resursami.* Moscow: Veche, 2005.

Angelo Rossi [Tasca]. *Deux ans d'alliance Germano-Soviétique.* Paris: A Fayard, 1949.

——. *The Russo-German Alliance: August 1939–June 1941.* Boston: Beacon, 1951.

Anon. "Zametki o peresechenii biografii Osipa Mandel'shtama i Boris Pasternaka," *Pamiat': istoricheskii sbornik (Paris),* no. 4 (1981).

Antipina, Valentina. *Povsednevnaia zhizn' sovetskikh pisatelei 1930–1950-e gody.* Moscow: Molodaia gvardiia, 2005.

Antipova, O. A., et al., eds. *Golod v SSSR, 1930–1934 gg.* Moscow: Federal'noe arkhivnoe agentstvo, 2009.

Antsiferov, Alexis N., et al. *Russian Agriculture During the War: Rural Economy.* New Haven, CT: Yale University, for the Carnegie Endowment for International Peace, 1930.

Antonov, K. V. "Nekotorye itogi konflikta na KVZhD," *Sovetskoe gosudarstvo i revoliutsiia prava,* 1930, no. 2: 122–38.

Antonov, Vladimir. "Anatolii Gorskii na peredovoi vneshnei razvedki," *Nezavisimoe voennoe obozrenie,* Dec. 16, 2011.

——. "Kaznen i opravdan," *Nezavisimoe voennoe obozrenie,* Aug. 31, 2007.

——. "Na pol'skom napravlenii pered' 22 iiunia," *Nezaivismoe voennoe obozrenie,* June 3, 2011.

Antonov-Ovseenko, Anton. *Beriia.* Moscow: AST, 1999.

——. *Portet Tirana.* Moscow: Grègori Pèjdž, 1994.

Applebaum, Anne. *Gulag: A History.* New York: Doubleday, 2003.

Aptekar', Pavel. *Sovetsko-finskie voiny.* Moscow: Yauza-EKPSO, 2004.

——, and I. V. Uspenskii, eds. *Marshal M. N. Tukhachevskii (1893–1937): komplekt dokumentov iz fondov RGVA.* Moscow, 1994.

Arendt, Hannah. *The Origins of Totalitarianism.* New York: Harcourt, Brace, Jovanovich, 1973.

Argun, Aleksei. *Stalin i Lakoba.* Sukhumi: Alashara, 2002.

Armstrong, John A. *The Politics of Totalitarianism: The Communist Party of the Soviet Union from 1934 to the Present.* New York: Random House, 1961.

——. *The Soviet Bureaucratic Elite: A Case Study of the Ukrainian Apparatus.* New York: Praeger, 1959.

Arnason, Johann P. "Communism and Modernity," *Daedalus,* 129/1 (2000): 61–90.

Arnold, Arthur. *Banks, Credit and Money in Soviet Russia.* New York: Columbia University, 1937.

Aron, Raymond. *Mémoires.* Paris: Julliard, 1983.

——. *The Opium of the Intellectuals.* New Brunswick, NJ: Transaction Publishers, 2001 (originally 1955).

——. *Sociologie des sociétés industrielles: esquisse d'une théorie des régimes politiques.* Paris: Centre de documentation universitaire, 1958. Translated as *Democracy and Totalitarianism.* New York: Praeger, 1968.

Arsenidze, Rajden. "Iz vospominaniia o Staline," *Novy zhurnal,* 72 (1963): 218–36.

Artamonov, Andrei. *Spetsob"ekty Stalina: ekskursiia pod grifom "sekretno."* Moscow: Algoritm, 2013.

Artizov, Andrei N. "V ugodu vzgliadam vozhdia (Konkurs 1936 g. na uchebnik po istorii SSSR)," *Kentavr,* 1991, no. 1: 125–35.

——, and Oleg Naumov, eds. *Vlast' i khudozhestvennaia intelligentsiia.* Moscow: Mezhdunarodnyi fond Demokratiia, 1999.

——, et al., eds. *Reabilitatsiia: kak eto bylo: dokumenty Prezidiuma TsK KPSS i drugie materialy.* 3 vols. Moscow: Mezhdunarodnyi fond Demokratiia, 2000–4.

Artobolevskii, E. E., and A. A. Blagonravov. *Ocherki istorii tekhniki v Rossii (1861–1917).* Moscow: Nauka, 1975.

Artsuni, Ashot. "Samoubiistvo A. G. Khandzhiana," *Kavkaz,* 1936, no. 8 (32): 29–31.

Aruntiunian, Iurii V. *Mekhanizatory sel'skogo khoziaistva SSSR v 1929–1957 gg.: formirovanie kadrov massovykh kvalifikatsii.* Moscow: AN SSSR, 1960.

Asada, Sadao. *From Mahan to Pearl Harbor: The Imperial Japanese Navy and the United States.* Annapolis, MD: Naval Institute, 2006.

Aselius, Gunnar. *The Rise and Fall of the Soviet Navy in the Baltic, 1921–1941.* New York: Frank Cass, 2005.

Aster, Sidney. *1939: The Making of the Second World War.* New York: Simon & Schuster, 1972.

Atkinson, Dorothy. *The End of the Russian Land Commune, 1905–1930.* Stanford, CA: Stanford University, 1983.

Avalishvili, Levan. "The 'Great Terror' of 1937–1938 in Georgia: Between the Two Reports of Lavrentiy Beria," *Caucasus Analytical Digest,* 22 (2010): 2–6.

Avdeenko, Aleksandr O. *Nakazanie bez prestupleniia.* Moscow: Sovetskaia Rossiia, 1991.

——. "Otluchenie," *Znamia,* 1989, no. 3: 5–73, no. 4 : 78–133.

Averbakh, I. L. *Ot prestupleniia k trudu.* Moscow: Sovetskoe zakonodatel'stvo, 1936.

Avrich, Paul. "The Short Course and Soviet Historiography," *Political Science Quarterly,* 75/4 (1960): 539–63.

"Avtobiograficheskie zametki" V. N. Pavlova—perevodchika I. V. Stalina," *Novaia i noveishaia istoriia,* 2000, no. 4: 94–111.

Avtorkhanov, Abdurakhman. *Stalin and the Soviet Communist Party: A Study in the Technology of Power.* New York: Praeger, 1959.

——. *Tekhnologiia vlasti.* Moscow: Slovo, 1991.

Azarov, I. I. *Osazhdennaia Odessa.* Moscow: Voenizdat, 1962.

Baabar. *Twentieth-Century Mongolia.* Cambridge, UK: White Horse, 1999.

Baberowski, Jörg. *Der Feind ist überall: Stalinismus im Kaukasus.* Munich: Deutsche Verlags-Anstalt, 2003.

Babichenko, D. L. *Pisateli i tsenzory: sovetskaia literatura 1940–x godov po politicheskim kontrolem TsK.* Moscow: Rossiia Molodaia, 1994.

——. "'Esli aresty budut prodolzhatsia ni odnogo nemtsachlena partii': stalinskie 'chistki' nemetskoi politemigratsii v 1937–1938 godach," *Istorisheskii arkhiv,* 1992, no 1 : 117–23.

——, ed. *Literaturnyi front, istoriia politicheskoi tsenzury 1932–1936 gg.: sbornik dokumentov.* Moscow: Entsiklopediia rossiiskikh derevn', 1994.

Babochkin, Boris. *Litso sovetskogo kinoaktera.* Moscow: Kinofotoizdat, 1935.

Backlund, Lawrence Sigmund. "Nazi Germany and Finland, 1933–1939: A Waning Relationship," PhD diss. University of Pennsylvania, 1983.

Badaev, A. E. "O Staline," *Pravda,* Dec. 19, 1939.

Baehr, Peter. "Dictatorship." In *The Blackwell Dictionary of Modern Social Thought,* edited by William Outhwaite and Tom Bottomore. 2nd ed. Malden, MA: Blackwell, 2002.

Baer, Brian. "Literary Translation and the Construction of the Soviet Intelligentsia," *Massachusetts Review,* 47/3 (2006): 437–60.

Bahne, Siegfried. "Die Kommunistitche Partei Deutschlands." In *Das Ende der Parteien, 1933*, edited by Erich Matthias and Rudolf Morsey. Königstein: Droste, 1979, 655–739.

———. *Die K.P.D. und das Ende von Weimar: das Scheitern einer Politik, 1932–1935*. Frankfurt am Main: Campus, 1976.

———, et al., eds. *Les Partis communistes et l'Internationale communiste dans les années 1928–1932*. Dordrecht, Holland, and Boston, MA: Kluwer, 1988.

Bailes, Kendall E. *Technology and Society under Lenin and Stalin: Origins of the Soviet Technical Intelligentsia, 1917–1941*. Princeton, NJ: Princeton University, 1978.

Baker, Donald N. "The Surveillance of Subversion in Interwar France: The Carnet B in the Seine, 1922–1940," *French Historical Studies*, 10/3 (1978): 486–512.

Baker, Robert K. *Rezident: The Espionage Odyssey of Soviet General Vasily Zarubin*. Bloomington, IN: iUniverse, 2015.

Bakhtarov, G. Iu. *Zapiski aktera: genii i podletsy*. Moscow: Olma, 2002.

Balandin, R. K. *Marshal Shaposhnikov*. Moscow: Veche, 2005.

Balashov, A. P., and Iu. S. Markhashov. "Staraia ploshchad', 4 (20-e gody)," *Polis*, 1991, no. 4: 182–8.

Balashov, Evgenii A., ed. *Prinimai nas, suomi-krasavitsa! "Osvoboditel'nyi" pokhod v Finliandiiu 1939–1940 gg*. 2nd ed. St. Petersburg: Ostrov, 2004.

Balashov, Evgenii M. *Shkola v rossiiskom obshchestve 1917–1927 gg.: stanovlenie "novogo cheloveka."* St. Petersburg: D. Bulanin, 2003.

Ball, Alan. *Russia's Last Capitalists: The NEPmen, 1921–1929*. Berkeley: University of California, 1987.

Bamsted, Ernest K. *Goebbels and National Socialist Propaganda, 1925–1945*. East Lansing: Michigan State University, 1965.

Banac, Ivo, ed. *The Diary of Georgi Dimitrov, 1933–1949*. New Haven, CT: Yale University, 2003.

Bandinelli, Renuccio Bianchi. *Hitler e Mussolini 1938: Il viaggio del Führer in Italia*. Rome: Edizioni E/O, 1995.

Barakhov, V. S. "M. Gor'kii: posledniaia stranitsa zhizni," *Voprosy literatury*, 1990, no. 6: 182–206.

Baranov, Iurii. *Goluboi razliv: dnevniki, pis'ma, stikhotvoreniia*. Yaroslavl: Verkhne-Volzhskoe knizhnoe izd-vo, 1988.

Baranov, Vadim. *Gorky bez grima, taina smerti: roman-issledovanie*. 2nd ed. Moscow: Agraf, 2001.

———. "'Nado prekoslovit'!' M. Gorkii i sozdanie Soiuza pisatelei," *Voprosy literatury*, 2003, no. 5: 34–56.

Barber, John. "Stalin's Letter to the Editors of *Proletarskaya Revolyutsiya*," *Soviet Studies*, 38/1 (1976): 21–41.

Barber, John, and Mark Harrison. *The Soviet Home Front, 1941–1945*. London: Longman, 1991.

Barbieri, Pierpaolo. *Hitler's Shadow Empire: Nazi Economics and the Spanish Civil War*. Cambridge, MA: Harvard University, 2015.

Barbusse, Henri. *Stalin: chelovek, cherez kotorogo rasskryvaetsia novyi mir*. Moscow: Khudozhestvennaia literatura, 1936.

———. *Stalin: A New World Seen through One Man*. New York: Macmillan, 1935.

Bardin, I. "Ispolin-mudrets." In *Vstrechi s tovarishem Stalinym*, edited by A. A. Fadeev. Moscow: Gospolitizdat, 1939.

Barghoorn, Frederick C. *The Soviet Image of the United States: A Study in Distortion*. New York: Harcourt, Brace and Company, 1950.

Barmin, V. A. *Sovetskii Soiuz i Sintszian, 1918–1941 gg.: regional'nyi faktor vo vneshnei politike Sovetskogo Soiuza*. Barnaul: Barnaul'skii gosudarstvennyi pedagogicheskii universitet, 1999.

Barmine, Alexander. *Memoirs of a Soviet Diplomat: Twenty Years in the Service of the USSR*. London: Dickson, 1938.

———. *One Who Survived: The Life Story of a Russian Under the Soviets*. New York: G. P. Putnam's Sons, 1945.

Barnhart, Michael A. "Japanese Intelligence before the Second World War: 'Best Case' Analysis." In *Knowing One's Enemies: Intelligence Assessments before the Two World Wars*, edited by Ernest R. May. Princeton, NJ: Princeton University, 1984, 424–55.

Barros, James, and Richard Gregor. *Double Deception: Stalin, Hitler, and the Invasion of Russia*. DeKalb: Northern Illinois University, 1995.

Barsov, A. A. *Balans stoimostnykh obmenov mezhdu gorodom i derevnei*. Moscow: Nauka, 1969.

———. "NEP i vyravnivanie ekonomicheskikh otnoshenii mezhdu gorodom i derevnei." In *Novaia ekonomicheskaia politika: voprosy teorii i istorii*, edited by Maksim P. Kim. Moscow: Nauka, 1974, 93–102.

Barsova, V. "Nash veilikii drug." In *Vstrechi s tovarishchem Stalinym*, edited by Aleksandr Fadeev. Moscow: Ogiz, 1939, 57–9.

Barsukov, Evgenii A. *Russkaia artilleriia v mirovuiu voinu*. Moscow: Gos. voennoe izd-vo narkomata oborony Soiuza SSSR, 1938.

Bartel, Heinrich. "Aleksej Fedorovič Merekalov: Fragmente zur historischen Biographes Sowjetdiplomaten in Berlin 1938/39," *Jahrbücher für Geschichte Osteuropas*, 33/4 (1985): 518–45.

Bartlett, Rosamund. "The Embodiment of Myth: Eizenshtein's Production of 'Die Walküre,'" *Slavonic and East European Review*, 70/1 (1992): 53–76.

———. *Wagner and Russia*. New York: Cambridge University, 1995.

Baruzdin, Sergei A. "O Kornee Chukovskom: zametki Baruzdin," In *Zametki o detskoi literature*. Moscow: Detskaia literatura, 1975.

Baryshnikov, N. I. "Sovetsko-Finliandskaia voina 1939–1940 gg.," *Novaia i noveishaia istoriia*, 1989, no. 4 : 28–41.

———, and B. N. Baryshnikov. "Pravitel'stvo v Teriioki." In *Zimniaia voina 1939–1940*, edited by Oleg A. Rzhevskii and Olli Vehviläinen. 2 vols. Moscow: Nauka, 1998, I: 176–91.

———, and O. Manninen, "V kanun zimnei voiny." In *Zimniaia voina 1939–1940*, edited by Oleg A. Rzhevskii and Olli Vehviläinen. 2 vols. Moscow: Nauka, 1998, I: 131–41.

———, et al., *Istoriia ordena Lenina Leningradskogo voennogo okruga*. 3rd ed. Moscow: Voenizdat, 1988.

Baryshnikov, V. N. *Ot prokhladnogo mira k zimnei voine: vostochnaia politika Finlandii v 1930-e gody*. St. Petersburg: Izdatel'stvo Sankt Peterburgskogo universiteta, 1997.

Basseches, Nikolaus. *Stalin*. London: Staples Press, 1952.

Batashev, Aleksei. *Sovetskii dzhaz: istoricheskii ocherk*. Moscow: Muzyka, 1972.

Batbayar, Tsedendambyn. "Stalin's Strategy in Mongolia, 1932–1936," *Mongolian Studies*, 22 (1999): 1–17.

Baumgart, Winfried. "Zur Ansprache Hitlers von den Führen der Wehrmacht am 22. August 1939," *Vierteljahrshefte für Zeitgeschichte* 16/2 (1968): 120–49; 19/3 (1971): 294–304.

Baur, Hans. *Hitler's Pilot*. London: Frederick Muller, 1958.

Bawden, C. R. *The Modern History of Mongolia*. 2nd ed. New York: Kegan Paul International, 1989.

Baxa, Paul. "Capturing the Fascist Moment: Hitler's Visit to Italy in 1938 and the Radicalization of Fascist Italy," *Journal of Contemporary History*, 42/4 (2007): 227–42.

Baykov, Alexander. *Soviet Foreign Trade*. Princeton, NJ: Princeton University, 1946.

Baynes, N. H., ed. *The Speeches of Adolf Hitler*. 2 vols. London: Oxford University, 1942.

Bazhanov, Boris. *Bazhanov and the Damnation of Stalin*, edited by David W. Doyle. Columbus: Ohio State University, 1990.

———. *Vospominaniia byvshego sekretaria Stalina*. 2nd ed. Paris and New York: Tret'ia vol'na, 1983.

Beck, F., and W. Godin, *Russian Purge and the Extraction of Confession*. New York: Viking, 1951.

Beck, Józef *Przemówienia, deklaracje, wywiady 1931–1939*. Warsaw: Nakład Gebethnera i Wolffa, 1938.

———. *Final Report*. New York: Robert Speller & Sons, 1957.

Beckles, Gordon. "Hitler, the Clown Who Wants to Play Statesman," *Daily Herald*, January 31, 1931.

Bédarida, François. *La Strategie sécrete de la drôle de guerre: le conseil suprême interallié, Septembre 1939–Avril 1940*. Paris: CNRS, 1979.

Bedel', Aleksandr E., and Tatiana. I. Slavko. "Iz istorii raskulachennykh spetspereselentsev na Urale v pervoi polovine 30-kh godov." In *Raskulachennye spetspereselentsy na Urale (1930–1936): sbornik dokumentov*, edited by V. V. Alekseev, et al. Yekaterinburg: UIF "Nauka", 1993, 10–27.

Bednyi, Dem'ian. "Shtrikhi," *Pravda*, December 21, 1929.

———. *Sobranie sochinenii*. 5 vols. Moscow: Khudozhestvennaia literatura, 1953–4.

Béládi, László, and Tamás Krausz. *Stalin*. Moscow: Politicheskaia literatura, 1989.

Belaia kniga o deportatsii koreiskogo naseleniia Rossii v 30–40-x godakh. Vol. 1. Moscow: Interparx, 1992.

Beliaev, N., ed. *Mikhail Koltsov, kakim on byl*. Moscow: Sovetskii pisatel', 1965.

Belianovskii, B. S. "Deistviia tankovykh i motorizirovannykh voisk v Pol'she, Bel'gii i Frantsii," *Voennaia mysl'*, 1940, no. 8: 39–58.

Bell, P. M. H. *France and Britain, 1900–1940: Entente and Estrangement*. London and New York: Longman, 1996.

Beloff, Max. *The Foreign Policy of Soviet Russia, 1929–1941*. 2 vols. London: Oxford University, 1947–49.

Below, Nicolaus von. *Als Hitlers Adjutant 1937–1945*. Mainz: Hase & Koehler, 1980.

———. *At Hitler's Side: The Memoirs of Hitler's Luftwaffe Adjutant, 1937–1945*. Translated by Geoffrey Brooks. London: Greenhill Books, 2001.

Bennett, E. M. *Franklin Roosevelt and the Search for Security: American-Soviet Relations 1933–1939*. Wilmington, DE: Scholarly Resources, 1985.

Bennett, Edward W. *German Rearmament and the West, 1932–1933*. Princeton, NJ: Princeton University, 1969.

Benvenuti, Francesco. "Kirov in Soviet Politics, 1933–1934." Soviet Industrialisation Project Series no. 8, University of Birmingham, 1977.

———. "Stakhanovism and Stalinism, 1934–1938." Discussion paper no. 30, Centre for Russian and East European Studies, University of Birmingham, 1989.

Berelowitch, Alexis, and Viktor Danilov, eds. *Sovetskaia derevnia glazami VChK-OG-PU-NKVD, 1919–1939: dokumenty i materialy.* 4 vols. Moscow: Rosspen, 2003.

Berezhkov, Valentin. *S diplomaticheski missiei v Berlin, 1940–1941.* Moscow: Izdat. Agentstva Pechati Novosti, 1966.

———. *History in the Making: Memoirs of World War II Diplomacy.* Moscow: Progress, 1983.

———. *At Stalin's Side: His Interpreter's Memoirs from the October Revolution to the Fall of the Dictator's Empire.* New York: Birch and Lane, 1994.

Berezin, F. Ia. "Istoriia ordera na arest Berii." In *Beria: konets kar'ery,* edited by V. F. Nekrasov. Moscow: Politizdat, 1991, 195–201.

Bergan, Ronald. *Sergei Eisenstein: A Life.* Woodstock, NY: Overlook, 1997.

Berge, Paul. *The Birth of Tajikistan: National Identity and the Origins of the Republic.* London and New York: I. B. Tauris, 2007.

Berghahn, Volker R. *Germany and the Approach of War in 1914.* New York: St. Martin's, 1973.

Bergman, Jay. "Valerii Chkalov: Soviet Pilot as New Soviet Man," *Journal of Contemporary History,* 33/1 (1998): 135–52.

Bergmeier, Horst J. P., and Rainer E. Lorz. *Hitler's Airwave: The Inside Story of Nazi Radio Broadcasting and Propaganda Swing.* New Haven, CT: Yale University, 1997.

Bergson, Abram. *The Real National Income of Soviet Russia since 1928.* Cambridge, MA: Harvard University, 1961.

Beria, Sergo. *My Father.* London: Duckworth, 2001.

Beriia, Sergo. *Moi otets—Lavrentii Beriia.* Moscow: Sovremennik, 1994.

Berkhin, I. B. *Voennaia reforma v SSSR, 1924–1925.* Moscow: Voenizdat, 1958.

Berling, Zygmunt. *Wspomnienia.* 3 vols. Warsaw: Polski Dom Wydawniczy, 1990–91.

Berman, Sheri. "Civil Society and the Collapse of the Weimar Republic," *World Politics,* 49/3 (1997): 401–29.

Bernev, S. K., and A. I. Rupasov, eds. *Zimniaia voina 1939–1940 gg.: v dokumentakh NKVD.* St. Petersburg: Lik, 2010.

Bernshtein, Aron. *Mikhail Gelovani.* Moscow: Kinotsentr, 1991.

———. "V roli Stalina," *Ogonek,* 1989, no. 50: 18–9.

Berson, Jan. *Kreml na biało.* Warsaw: Rój, 1936.

———. *Sowieckie zbrojenia moralne.* Warsaw: Główna Księgarnia Wojskowa, 1937.

Bertram, James. *Crisis in China: The Story of the Sian Mutiny.* London: Macmillan, 1937.

Bertrand, Gustave. *Enigma ou la plus grand énigme de la guerre 1939–1945.* Paris: Plon, 1973.

Besedovskii, Grigorii Z. *Na putiakh k termidoru: iz vospominanii byvshego sovetskogo diplomata.* 1st ed. 2 vols. Paris: Mishen, 1930–1; Moscow: Sovremennik, 1997.

———. *Im Dienste der Sowjets: Erinnerungen.* Leipzig, Zürich, Grethlein & Co., 1930. Translated as *Revelations of a Soviet Diplomat.* London: Williams & Norgate, 1931.

Beshanov, Vladimir V. *Leningradskaia oborona.* Minsk: Kharvest, 2006.

———. *"Po svoim artilleriia b'et": slepye bogi voiny.* Moscow: Iauza, 2013.

Bessel, Richard. *Political Violence and the Rise of Nazism: The Stormtroopers in Eastern Germany, 1925–1934.* New Haven, CT: Yale University, 1984.

Bey, Essad [Lev Nussimbaum]. *Stalin.* Berlin: G. Kiepenheuer, 1931. Translated as *Stalin: Career of a Fanatic.* New York: Viking, 1932; London: John Lane, 1932.

Bezymenskii, Lev A. "Direktivy I. V. Stalina V. M. Molotovu pered poezdkoi v Berlin v noiabre 1940 g.," *Novaia i noveishaia istoriia,* 1995, no 4: 76–9.

———. "O 'Plane Zhukova' ot 15 maia 1941 g.," *Novaia i noveishaia istoriia,* 2000, no. 3: 58–67.

———. "Sovetsko-Germanskie dogovory 1939 g.: novye dokumenty i starye problem," *Novaia i noveishaia istoriia,* 1998, no. 3: 3–26.

———. "The Secret Protocols of 1939 as a Problem of Soviet Historiography." In *Soviet Foreign Policy, 1917–1991: A Retrospective,* edited by Gabriel Gorodetsky. London: Frank Cass, 1994, 75–85.

———. "Vizit V. M. Molotova v Berlin v noiabre 1940 g. v svete novykh dokumentov," *Novaia i noveishaia istoriia,* 1995, no 6: 121–44.

———. *Gitler i Stalin pered skhvatkoi.* Moscow: Veche, 2000.

———. *Osobaia papka "Barbarossa": dokumental'naia povest'.* Moscow: Novosti, 1972.

———. *Stalin und Hitler: das Pokerspiel der Diktatoren.* Berlin: Aufbau, 2002.

Bgazhba, Mikhail. *Nestor Lakoba.* Tbilisi: Sabchota sakartvelo, 1965.

Bialer, Seweryn, ed. *Stalin and His Generals: Soviet Military Memoirs of World War II.* London: Souvenir Press, 1970.

———. *Stalin's Successors: Leadership, Stability, and Change in the Soviet Union.* New York: Cambridge University, 1980.

Bialik, B. A., ed. *Gor'kii i ego epokha: issledovaniia i materialy,* 6 vols. Moscow: Nauka, 1989–94.

Bibineishvili, B. *Kamo.* Moscow: Staryi Bol'shevik, 1934.

Biegański, Stanisław, et al., eds. *Documents on Polish-Soviet Relations, 1939–1945.* 2 vols. London: Heinemann, 1961–7.

Bilmanis, Alfred, ed. *Latvian Russian Relations: Documents.* Washington, D.C.: Latvian Legation, 1944.

Biriuzov, S. S. "Predislovie." In *Izbrannoe proizvedeniia,* by M. N. Tukhachevskii. Vol. 1. Moscow: Voennoe Izdatel'stvo Ministerstva Oborony SSSR, 1964.

———. *Kogda gremeli pushki.* Moscow: Voenizdat, 1961.

Bishop, Donald. *The Roosevelt-Litvinov Agreements: The American View.* Syracuse, NY: Syracuse University, 1965.

Bismarck, Otto von. *Bismarck, the Man and the Statesman, Being the Reflections and Reminiscences of Otto Prince von Bismarck.* 2 vols. London: Smith, Elder, 1898.

———. *Mysli i vospominaniia.* 3 vols. Moscow: Ogiz, 1940–1.

Bix, Herbert P. *Hirohito and the Making of Modern Japan.* New York: HarperCollins, 2000.

Blaazer, David. "Finance and the End of Appeasement: The National Government, the Bank of England, and the Czech Gold," *Journal of Contemporary History,* 40/1 (2005): 25–39.

Blagoveshchenskii, F. "V gostiakh u P.A. Sharii," *Minuvshee,* no. 7 (1989): 451–72.

Blauvelt, Timothy K. "'From Words to Action!' Nationality Policy in Soviet Abkhazia (1921–38)." In *The Making of Modern Georgia, 1918–2012: The First Georgian Republic and Its Successors,* edited by Stephen F. Jones. London and New York: Routledge, 2014, 232–62.

———. "Abkhazia Patronage and Power in the Stalin Era," *Nationalities Papers,* 35/2 (2007): 203–32.

———. "March of the Chekists: Beria's Secret Police Patronage Network and Soviet Crypto-Politics," *Communist and Post-Communist Studies,* 44/1 (2011): 1–16.

Blinkhorn, Martin, ed. *Fascists and Conservatives: The Radical Right and the Establishment in Twentieth-Century Europe.* London: Unwin Hyman, 1990.

Blinov, A. S. *Ivan Akulov.* Moscow: Politizdat, 1967.

Bliskovskii, Z. D., et al., eds. *M.I. Ul'ianova: sekretar' Pravdy.* Moscow: Pravda, 1965.

Blitstein, Peter A. "Nation-Building or Russification? Obligatory Russian Instruction in the Soviet Non-Russian School, 1938–1953." In *A State of Nations: Empire and Nation-State in the Age of Lenin and Stalin,* edited by Ronald Grigor Suny and Terry Martin. New York: Oxford University, 2001, 253–74.

Blium, Arlen V. *Za kulisami "ministerstva pravdy": tainaia istoriia sovetskoi tsenzury 1917–1929.* St. Petersburg: Akademicheski proekt, 1994.

———, ed. *Tsenzura v Sovetskom Soiuze, 1917–1991 gg.: dokumenty.* Moscow: Rosspen, 2004.

Bliznakov, Milka. "International Modernism or Socialist Realism: Soviet Architecture in the Eastern Republics." In *New Perspectives on Russian and Soviet Artistic Culture,* edited by John O. Norman. New York: St. Martin's, 1993, 112–30.

Bloch, Marc. *Strange Defeat: A Statement of Evidence Written in 1940.* London: Oxford University, 1949.

Bloch, Michael. *Ribbentrop.* New York: Crown, 1992.

Blyukher, Glafira. "S Vasiliem Konstantinovichem Bliukherom—shest' let," *Voenno-istoricheskii zhurnal,* 1990, no. 1: 79–83.

———. "Vospominania o lichnom," *Voenno-istoricheskii zhurnal,* 1989, no 4: 79–87.

Boberach, Heinz, ed. *Meldungen aus dem Reich: die geheimen Lageberichte des Sicherheitsdientes des SS 1938–1945.* 7 vols. Herrsching: Pawlak, 1984.

Bobrenev, V. A., and V. Ia. Riazantsev. *Palachi i zhertvy.* Moscow: Voenizdat, 1993.

Bobylev, Pavel N. "K kakoi voine gotovilsia General'nyi shtab RKKA v 1941 godu," *Otechestvennaia istoriia,* 1995, no. 5: 3–20.

———. "Repetitsiia katastrofy," *Voenno-istoricheski zhurnal,* 1993, no. 7: 14–21, no. 8: 28–35.

———. "Tochky v diskussii stavit' rano: k voprosu o planirovanii v General'nom shtabe RKKA vozmozhnoi voiny s Germaniei v 1940–1941 godakh," *Otechestvennaia istoriia,* 2000, no. 1: 47–54.

———, et al., eds. *Sovetskie Vooruzhennye Sily: voprosy i otvety, 1918–1988.* Moscow: Politicheskaia literatura, 1987.

———, *Voennyi sovet pri narodnom komissare oborony SSSR, noiabr' 1937 g.: dokumenty i materialy.* Moscow: Rosspen, 2006.

———, *Voennyi sovet pri narodnom komissare oborony SSSR, 1938, 1940: dokumenty i materialy.* Moscow: Rosspen, 2006.

Bochever, A. M., ed. *O Staline: ukazatel' literatury, izdannoi k 60-letiiu I. V. Stalina.* Moscow: Vsesoiuznaia knizhnaia palata, 1940.

Bode, Andreas. "Humor in the Lyrical Stories for Children of Samuel Marshak and Korney Chukovsky," *The Lion and the Unicorn,* 13/2 (1989): 34–53.

Boeck, Brian J. "Complicating the National Interpretation of the Famine: Reexamining the Case of Kuban." In *After the Holodomor: The Enduring Impact of the Great Famine on Ukraine,* edited by Andrea Graziosi et al. Cambridge, MA: Harvard University Press for the Ukrainian Research Institute, 2013, 31–48.

Boelcke, Willi A., ed. *The Secret Conferences of Dr. Goebbels: The Nazi Propaganda War, 1939–43.* New York: E. P. Dutton, 1970.

Boffa, Giuseppe. *The Stalin Phenomenon.* Ithaca, NY: Cornell University, 1992.

Bohlen, Charles E. *Witness to History, 1929–1969.* New York: W. W. Norton, 1973.

Boiadzhiev, G. *Maretskaia.* Moscow: Iskusstvo, 1954.

Boiko, N. V., et al., eds. *Ivan Mikhailovich Maiskii: izbrannaia perepiska c inostrannymi korrespondentami, 1916–1975.* 2 vols. Moscow: Nauka, 2011.

Boldyrev, Vasilii G. "Iaponiia i Sovetskii Dal'nii Vostok," *Sibirskie ogni,* 1925, no. 1: 187–94.

Bollinger, Dwight L. "Fifth Column Marches On," *American Speech,* 19/1 (1944): 47–9.

Bollinger, Martin J. *Stalin's Slave Ships: Kolyma, the Gulag Fleet, and the Role of the West.* Westport, CT: Praeger, 2003.

Bolloten, Burnett. *The Grand Camouflage: The Communist Conspiracy in the Spanish Civil War.* New York: Frederick A. Praeger, 1961.

——. *The Spanish Civil War: Revolution and Counterrevolution.* Chapel Hill: University of North Carolina, 1991.

——. *The Spanish Revolution: The Left and the Struggle for Power during the Civil War.* Chapel Hill: University of North Carolina, 1979.

Bonch-Bruevich, V. D. *Vospominaniia.* Moscow: Khudozhestvennaia literatura, 1968.

Bond, Brian. *British Military Policy between the Two World Wars.* Oxford: Clarendon, 1980.

——, ed. *Chief of Staff: The Diaries of Lieutenant General Sir Henry Pownall.* 2 vols. London: Leo Cooper, 1972–74.

Bondarenko, Aleksandr. *Fitin.* Moscow: Molodaia gvardiia, 2015.

——, and N. N. Efimov. *Utaennye stranitsy sovetskoi istorii.* Moscow: Kuchkovo Pole, 2007.

Bor'ba za uprochenie sovetskoi vlasti v Gruzii: sbornik dokumentov i materialov 1921–1925 gg. Tbilisi: Sabchota Sakartvelo, 1959.

Bordiugov, Gennadii A., and V. A. Kozlov. "Dialektika teorii i praktiki stsialisticheskogo stroitel'stva: k voprosu o deformatsiiakh sotsializma," *Istoriia SSSR,* 1989, no. 6: 3–21.

Borev, Iurii. "Staliniada," *Pod"em,* 1990, no. 1: 42–3.

——. *Staliniada: memuary po chuzhim vospominaniiam s istoricheskimi anekdotami i razmyshleniiami avtora.* Moscow: Sovetskii pisatel', 1990.

Borisov, Aleksandr V. *Politsiia i militsiia Rossii: stranitsy istorii.* Moscow: Nauka, 1995.

Borisov, Iu. S. *Proizvodstvennye kadry derevni, 1917–1941.* Moscow: Nauka, 1991.

Borisov, Iurii V. *Sovetsko-frantsuzskie otnosheniia (1924–1945 gg.).* Moscow: Mezhdunarodnye otnosheniia, 1964.

Borisov, S. B. *Andrei Aleksandrovich Zhdanov: opyt politicheskoi biografii.* Shadrinsk: Poset, 1998.

Borisova, Tatiana. "The Digest of Laws of the Russian Empire: The Phenomenon of Autocratic Legality," *Law and History Review,* 30/3 (2012): 901–25.

Borkenau, Franz. *European Communism.* New York: Harper Brothers Publishers, 1953.

——. *The Communist International.* London: Faber & Faber, 1938.

——. *The Spanish Cockpit: An Eyewitness Account of the Political and Social Conflicts of the Spanish Civil War.* London: Faber and Faber, 1937.

——. *The Totalitarian Enemy.* London: Faber and Faber, 1939.

Bór-Komorowski, Tadeusz. *The Secret Army.* New York: Macmillan, 1951.

Borodin, N. M. *One Man in His Time: An Autobiography.* London: Constable, 1955.

Borodkin, Leonid, et al. *Gulag: ekonomika prinuditel'nogo truda.* Moscow: Rosspen, 2005.

Borodulin, V. I., and V. D. Topolianskii. "Dmitrii Dmitrievich Pletnev," *Voprosy istorii,* 1989, no. 9: 36–54.

Borovik, Genrikh. *The Philby Files: The Secret Life of Master Spy Kim Philby.* Boston: Little, Brown, 1994.

Borys, Juriy. "Who Ruled the Soviet Ukraine in Stalin's Time? (1917–1939)," *Canadian Slavonic Papers,* 14/2 (1972): 213–33.

Bosworth Goldman, *Red Road through Asia: A Journey by the Arctic Ocean to Siberia, Central Asia, and Armenia.* 2nd ed. London: Methuen, 1934.

Bosworth, R. J. W. *Mussolini.* New York: Oxford University, 2002.

——. *Mussolini's Italy: Life under the Dictatorship.* London: Allen Lane, 2005.

Bourke-White, Margaret. *Eyes on Russia.* New York: Simon & Schuster, 1931.

Bourne, Kenneth, and David Cameron Watt, eds. *British Documents on Foreign Affairs: Reports and Papers from the Foreign Office Confidential Print: Part II, Series A, The Soviet Union, 1917–1939.* 3 vols. University Publications of America, 1984.

Bowden, Sue, and Avner Offen. "The Technological Revolution that Never Was: Gender, Class, and the Diffusion of Household Appliances in Interwar England." In *The Sex of Things,* edited by Victoria de Grazia. Berkeley: University of California, 1996, 244–74.

Bowers, Robert E. "American Diplomacy, the 1933 Wheat Conference, and Recognition of the Soviet Union," *Agricultural History,* 40/1 (1966): 39–52.

Bown, Matthew Cullerne. *Socialist Realist Painting.* New Haven, CT: Yale University, 1998.

Boyd, Carl. *Hitler's Japanese Confidant: General Hiroshi Ōshima and MAGIC Intelligence, 1941–1945.* Lawrence: University Press of Kansas, 1993.

Boyrn, Svetlana. "The Death of the Revolutionary Poet" In *Death in Quotation Marks: Cultural Myths of the Modern Poet.* Cambridge, MA: Harvard University, 1991.

Bracher, Karl Dietrich. *Die Auflösung der Weimarer Republik: eine Studie zum Problem des Machtverfalls in der Demokratie.* 3rd ed. Berlin: Villingen/Schwarzwald, 1960.

——. *The German Dictatorship: The Origins, Structure, and Effects of National Socialism.* New York: Holt, Rinehart, Winston, 1970.

Braginskaia, Iu. "Pobeda plana i rekord besplannovosti," *Sotsialisticheskii vestnik,* Sept. 27, 1930.

Brainina, B., and A. Dmitrieva, eds. *Sovetskie pisateli avtobiografii.* 4 vols. Moscow: Khudozhestvennaia literatura, 1959–1988.

Brandenberger, David. "Stalin as Symbol: A Case Study in the Personality Cult and its Construction." In *Stalin: A New History,* edited by Sarah Davies and James Harris. New York: Cambridge University, 2005, 249–70.

——. *National Bolshevism: Stalinist Mass Culture and the Formation of Modern Russian National Identity, 1931–1956.* Cambridge, MA: Harvard University, 2002.

——. *Propaganda State in Crisis: Soviet Ideology, Indoctrination, and Terror under Stalin, 1927–1941.* New Haven, CT: Yale University, 2012.

Brandenberger, D. L., and A. M. Dubrovsky. "'The People Need a Tsar': The Emergence of National Bolshevism as Stalinist Ideology," *Europe-Asia Studies,* 50/5 (1998): 873–92.

Braubach, Max. *Der Einmarch deutscher Truppen in die entmilitarisierte Zone am Rhein in März 1936.* Cologne: Westdeutscher Verlag, 1956.

Braun, Edward. "Vsevolod Meyerhold: the Final Act." In *Enemies of the People: The Destruction of the Soviet Literary, Theater, and Film Arts in the 1930s,* edited by Katherine Bliss Eaton. Evanston, IL: Northwestern University, 2002, 145–62.

Braun, Otto. *A Comintern Agent in China, 1932–1939.* Stanford, CA: Stanford University, 1982.

——. *Kitaiskie zapiski: 1932–1939.* Moscow: Politizdat, 1974.

Brenan, Gerald. *The Spanish Labyrinth: An Account of the Social and Political Background of the Civil War.* New York: Macmillan, 1943.

Bridges, Brian. "A Note on the British Monitoring of Soviet Radio, 1930," *Historical Journal of Film, Radio, and Television,* 5/2 (1985): 183–9.

——. "Yoshizawa Kenkichi and the Soviet-Japanese Non-Aggression Pact Proposal," *Modern Asian Studies,* 14/1 (1980): 111–27.

Bright-Holmes, John, ed. *Like it Was: The Diaries of Malcolm Muggeridge.* London: Collins, 1981.

Briukhanov, B. B., and E. N. Shoshkov. *Opravdaniiu ne podlezhit: Ezhov i ezhovshchina 1936–1938.* St. Petersburg: Petrovskii Fond, 1998.

Broide, S. O. *Vreditel'stvo, shpionazh i belyi terror.* Moscow: Gosiurizdat, 1930.

Brontman, Lazar K. *Dnevniki, 1932–1947.* Moscow: Zhurnal 'Samizdat', 2004.

Brooke, Caroline. "Soviet Musicians and the Great Terror," *Europe-Asia Studies,* 54/3 (2002): 397–413.

Brooks, Jeffrey. *"Thank You, Comrade Stalin!" Soviet Public Culture from Revolution to Cold War.* Princeton, NJ: Princeton University, 2000.

Brook-Shepherd, Gordon. *Anschluss: The Rape of Austria.* Philadelphia: Lippincott, 1963.

Broszat, Martin. *Der Staat Hitlers.* Munich: DTV, 1989.

——. *Nationalsozialistische Polenpolitik 1939–1945.* Stuttgart: Deutsche Verlags-Anstalt, 1961.

——. *The Hitler State: The Foundation and Development of the Internal Structure of the Third Reich.* London and New York: Longman, 1981.

Broué, Pierre. "Party Opposition to Stalin (1930–32) and the First Moscow Trial." In *Essays on Revolutionary Culture and Stalinism: Selected Papers from the Third World Congress for Soviet and East European Studies,* edited by John W. Strong. Columbus, OH: Slavica Publishers, 1990, 98–111.

——. "The Bolshevik-Leninist Faction," *Revolutionary History,* 9/4 (2008): 137–60.

——. "Trotsky et la Bloc des oppositions de 1932," *Cahiers Léon Trotsky,* no. 5 (Paris, 1980): 5–37.

——. *Staline et la révolution: le cas espagnol.* Paris: Fayard, 1993.

——. *The Revolution and the Civil War in Spain.* Chicago: Haymarket, 1988.

Brovkin, Vladimir N. *Russia after Lenin: Politics, Culture, and Society, 1921–1929.* London and New York: Routledge, 1998.

Browder, Robert Paul. *Origins of Soviet-American Diplomacy.* Princeton, NJ: Princeton University, 1953.

Brown, Archie, and Alec Cairncross. "Alec Nove, 1915–1994: An Appreciation," *Europe-Asia Studies,* 49/3 (1997): 627–41.

Brown, E. J. "The Year of Acquiescence." In *Literature and Revolution in Soviet Russia,*

1917–62, edited by Max Hayward and Leo Labedz. London: Oxford University, 1963, 44–61.

———. *Mayakovsky: A Poet in the Revolution*. Princeton, NJ: Princeton University, 1973.

Brügel, J. W., ed. *Stalin und Hitler: Pakt gegen Europa*. Vienna: Europa Verlag, 1973.

Bruski, Jan Jacek, ed. *Hołodomor 1932–1933: Wielki głód na Ukrainie w dokumentach polskiej dyplomacji i wywiadu*. Warsaw: Polski Instytut Spraw Międzynarodowych, 2008.

Brzezinski, Zbigniew. *The Permanent Purge: Politics in Soviet Totalitarianism*. Cambridge, MA: Harvard University, 1956.

Buber-Neumann, Margarete. *Under Two Dictators*. New York: Dodd, Mead, 1949.

———. *Von Potsdam nach Moskau: Station eines Irrweges*. Stuttgart: Deutsche Verlags-Anstalt, 1957.

Bubnov, Andrei, et al., eds. *Grazhdanskaia voina 1918–21*. 3 vols. Moscow: Voennyi vestnik, 1928–30.

Buchanan, Tom. *Britain and the Spanish Civil War*. New York: Cambridge University, 1997.

Buchheim, Christoph, and Jonas Scherner. "The Role of Private Property in the Nazi Economy: The Case of Industry," *Journal of Economic History*, 66/2 (2002): 390–416.

Buchheit, Gert. *Der deutsche Geheimdienst: Geschichte der militärischen Abwehr*. Munich: List, 1966.

Buck, John Lossing, ed. *The 1931 Flood in China: An Economic Survey*. Nanking: University of Nanking, 1932.

Buckley, Mary. *Mobilizing Soviet Peasants: Heroines and Heroes of Stalin's Fields*. Latham, MD: Roman and Littlefield, 2006.

Bud, R. "Fil'm o Kirove," *Sovetskoe kino*, 1935, no. 1: 16–9.

Budnitskii, Oleg, ed. *"Sovershenno lichno i doveritel'no!" B. A. Bakhmetev–V. A. Maklakov: perepiska 1919–1951*. 3 vols. Moscow and Stanford: Rosspen and the Hoover Institution Press, 2001–2.

———. *Den'gi russkoi emigratsii: kolchakovskoe zoloto 1918–1957*. Moscow: Novoe literaturnoe obozrenie, 2008.

Budurowych, Bohdan B. *Polish-Soviet Relations, 1932–1939*. New York: Columbia University, 1963.

Buell, Raymond L. *Poland: Key to Europe*. New York: Knopf, 1939.

Bugai, N. F. "Vysylenie sovetskikh koreitsev s Dal'nego Vostoka," *Voprosy istorii*, 1994, no. 5: 141–8.

Bukharin, N. K. "K teorii imperialisticheskogo gosudarstva." In *Revoliutsiia prava: sbornik pervyi*. Moscow: Kommunisticheskaia akademiia, 1925.

———. *Problemy teorii i praktiki sotsializma*. Moscow: Politizdat, 1989.

———. *Tiuremnye rukopisi*. 2 vols. Moscow: Airo-XX, 1996.

Bulgakov, Mikhail, and Elena Bulgakova. *Dnevnik Mastera i Margarity*. Moscow: Vagrius, 2001.

Bulgakov, Mikhail A. *Dramy i komedii*. Moscow: Iskusstvo, 1965.

———. *Izbrannaia proza*. Moscow: Khudozhestvennaia literatura, 1966.

———. *The Early Plays of Mikhail Bulgakov*, edited by Ellendea Proffer. Bloomington: Indiana University, 1972.

———. *Sobranie sochinenii*. 8 vols. St. Petersburg: Azbuka-klassika, 2002.

Bulgakova, Elena S. *Dnevnik Eleny Bulgakovoi*. Moscow: Knizhnaia palata, 1990.

———. *Vospominaniia o Mikhaile Bulgakove*. Moscow: Astrel, 2006.

Bulgakova, Oksana. *Sovetskii slukhoglaz: kino i ego organy chuvstv*. Moscow: Novoe literaturnoe obozrenie, 2010.

Bulgakowa, Oksana. *Sergei Eisenstein: A Biography*. Berlin and San Francisco: Potemkin, 2001.

Bullard, Julian, and Margaret Bullard, eds. *Inside Stalin's Russia: The Diaries of Reader Bullard, 1930–1934*. Chadbury, Oxfordshire: Day Books, 2000.

Bullitt, Orville H., ed. *For the President, Personal and Secret: Correspondence between Franklin D. Roosevelt and William Bullitt*. Boston: Hougton Mifflin, 1972.

Bullock, Alan. *Hitler and Stalin: Parallel Lives*. New York: Knopf, 1991.

———. *Hitler: A Study in Tyranny*. 2nd ed. New York: Harper & Row, 1962.

Bunich, Igor. *Piatistoletnaia voina v Rossii*. 3 vols. St. Petersburg: Oblik, 1996–7.

Burckhardt, Carl J. *Meine Danziger Mission 1937–39*. Munich: George D. W. Caliwey, 1960.

Burkman, Thomas W. *Japan and the League of Nations: Empire and World Order, 1914–1938*. Honolulu: University of Hawaii, 2008.

Bury, J. B. *The Ancient Greek Historians*. New York: Dover, 1958.

Busheva, T. S., and Iu. L. D'iakov. "Reikhsver i sovety, tainyi soiuz: neizvestnye dokumenty sovetskikh arkhivov," *Oktiabr'*, 1991, no. 12: 182–201.

Butler, Ewan. *Mason-Mac, the Life of Lieutenant-General Sir Noel Mason-Macfarlane: A Biography*. London: Macmillan, 1972.

Butler, J. R. M. *Grand Strategy*. 6 vols. London: H. M. Stationery Off., 1956–76.

Bykov, Dmitrii. *Boris Pasternak*. Moscow: Molodaia gvardiia, 2005.

Cairncross, John. *The Enigma Spy: The Story of the Man Who Changed the Course of World War Two*. London: Century, 1997.

Cairns, Andrew. *The Soviet Famine of 1932–33: An Eyewitness Account of Conditions in the Spring and Summer of 1932*. Edmonton: Canadian Institute of Ukrainian Studies, 1989.

Cameron, Sarah I. "The Hungry Steppe: Soviet Kazakhstan and the Kazakh Famine, 1921–1934," PhD diss. Yale University, 2010.

Campbell, Joseph. *Hero of a Thousand Faces*. New York: Pantheon, 1949.

Campbell, Thomas D. *Russia: Market or Menace?* New York: Longmans, Green, 1932.

Camus, Albert. *L'Espagne Libre*. Paris: Calmann-Lévy, 1945.

Canetti, Elias. *Crowds and Power*. London: Victor Gollancz, 1960.

Caputi, R. J. *Neville Chamberlain and Appeasement*. Selinsgrove, PA: Susquehanna University, 2000.

Carley, Michael J. "'A Situation of Delicacy and Danger': Anglo-Soviet, August 1939–March 1940," *Contemporary European History Review*, 8/2 (1999): 175–208.

———. "Five Kopecks for Five Kopecks: Franco-Soviet Trade Relations, 1928–1939," *Cahiers du monde russe et soviétique*, 33/1 (1992): 23–58.

———. "Soviet Foreign Policy in the West, 1936–1941: A Review Article," *Europe-Asia Studies*, 56/7 (2004): 1081–90.

———. *1939: The Alliance that Never Was and the Coming of World War II*. Chicago: I. R. Dee, 1999.

———. *Silent Conflict: A Hidden History of Early Soviet-Western Relations*. Lanham, MD: Rowman & Littlefield, 2014.

Caro, Robert A. *The Path to Power: The Years of Lyndon Johnson*. New York: Knopf, 1982.

Carr, Edward Hallett, and R. W. Davies. *Foundations of a Planned Economy, 1926–1929*. 3 vols. London and Basingstoke: Macmillan, 1969–1978.

———. "Revolution from Above: Some Notes on the Decision to Collectivize Soviet Agriculture." In *The Critical Spirit: Essays in Honor of Herbert Marcuse*, edited by K. H. Wolff and Barrington Moore, Jr. Boston: Beacon, 1967, 313–27.

———. "Stalin Victorious," *Times Literary Supplement*, June 10, 1949.

———. *German-Soviet Relations between the Two World Wars, 1919–1939*. Westport, CT: Greenwood Press, 1983.

———. *Socialism in One Country: 1924–1926*. 3 vols. New York: Macmillan, 1958.

———. *The Comintern and the Spanish Civil War*. New York: Pantheon, 1984.

———. *The Russian Revolution from Lenin to Stalin, 1917–1929*. New York: Macmillan, 1979.

———. *The Twenty Years' Crisis, 1919–1939: An Introduction to the Study of International Relations*. London: Macmillan, 1939.

———. *The Twilight of the Comintern, 1930–1935*. New York: Pantheon Books, 1983.

Carr, Raymond. *The Spanish Tragedy: The Civil War in Perspective*. London: Phoenix Press, 2001.

Carr, William. *Poland to Pearl Harbor: The Making of the Second World War*. London: E. Arnold, 1985.

Carsten, F. L. *The Reichswehr and Politics: 1918–1933*. Berkeley, CA: University of California, 1973.

Carswell, John. *The Exile: A Life of Ivy Litvinov*. London and Boston: Faber and Faber, 1983.

Carynnyk, Marco, et al., eds. *The Foreign Office and the Famine*. Kingston, Ontario, and Vestal, NY: Limestone Press, 1988.

Castellan, Georges. "Reichswehr et Armée Rouge." In *Les relations germano-soviétiques du 1933 à 1939*, edited by Jean-Baptiste Duroselle. Paris: Librairie A. Colin, 1954, 137–260.

———. *Le réarmement clandestin du Reich, 1930–1935, vu par le 2. Bureau de l'État-major français*. Paris: Plon, 1954.

Catherwood, Christopher. *The Balkans in World War Two*. Houndmills, Basingstoke: Palgrave Macmillan, 2003.

Cattell, David T. *Communism and the Spanish Civil War*. Berkeley: University of California, 1955.

———. *Soviet Diplomacy and the Spanish Civil War*. Berkeley: University of California, 1957.

Chalaia, Zinaida. *Oboronnaia dramaturgiia: opyt issledovanii nashei tvorcheskoi raboty v svete zadach sovremennosti*. Moscow-Leningrad: Gosizdat Iskusstvo, 1938.

Chamberlain, Neville. *In Search of Peace*. London: Hutchinson, 1939.

———. *The Struggle for Peace*. London: Hutchinson, 1939.

Chamberlain, William Henry. *Japan over Asia*. Boston: Little, Brown, 1937.

———. *Russia's Iron Age*. Boston: Little, Brown, 1934.

———. *The Evolution of a Conservative*. Chicago: Henry Regnery, 1959.

Chandler, Andrea. *Institutions of Isolation: Border Controls in the Soviet Union and its Successor States, 1917–1993*. Montreal: McGill Queen's University, 1998.

Chang, Jung, and Jon Halliday. *Mao: The Unknown Story*. New York: Knopf, 2005.

Charkviani, Kandid. *Napriki da naazrevi*. Tbilisi: Merani, 2004.

Chase, William J. "Microhistory and Mass Repression: Politics, Personalities, and Revenge in the Fall of Béla Kun," *Russian Review*, 67/3 (2008): 459–83.

———. *Enemies within the Gates? The Comintern and the Stalinist Repression, 1934–1939*. New Haven, CT: Yale University, 2001.

Chegodaev, A. "Iz vospominanii," *Detskaia literatura*, 1993, no. 10–11: 8–16.

Chegodaeva, Mariia. *Dva lika vremeni: 1939 odin god stalinskoi epokhi*. Moscow: Agraf, 2001.

Cheliuskin Odyssey, The (1934), video, available at Seventeen Moments in Soviet History: An On-line Archive of Primary Sources. http://soviethistory.msu.edu/1936-2/pilots-and-explorers/pilots-and-explorers-video/the-cheliuskin-odyssey-1934/. Accessed April 3, 2017.

Cheremukhin, Anton, et al., "Was Stalin Really Necessary for Russia's Economic Development?" Working Paper 19425, National Bureau of Economic Research, Cambridge, MA, 2013. http://www.nber.org/papers/w19425.pdf.

Cherepanov, A. I. *Zapiski voennogo sovetnika v Kitae*. 2nd ed. Moscow: Nauka, 1976.

Cherkasov, Petr P. *IMEMO, Institut mirovoi ekonomiki i mezhdunarodnykh otnoshenii: portret na fone epokhi*. Moscow: Ves' mir, 2004.

"'Cherkni . . . desiatok slov,'" *Voenye archivy Rossii*, 1993, vyp. 1: 404–11.

Cherniavskii, Georgii. "Fenomenon Litvinova," *XX Vek: istoriia Rossii i SSSR*, Feb. 4, 2004, http://kackad.com/kackad/?p=5428.

———. *Lev Trotsky*. Moscow: Molodaia gvardiia, 2010.

Chernobaev, Anatolii A. *V vikhre veka*. Moscow: Moskovskii rabochii, 1987.

Chernopitskii, Pavel G. *Na velikom perelome: sel'skie sovety Dona v perioda podgotovki i provedeniia massovoi kollektivizatsii, 1928–1931 gg*. Rostov: Rostovskii universitet, 1965.

Chernov, A. A., and M. G. Bialik. *O legkoi muzyke, o dzhaze, o khorosem vkuse*. Moscow-Leningrad: Muzyka, 1965.

Chernov, Viktor. "Sotsializatsiia zemli s iuridicheskoi tochki zrenia." In *Zemlia i Pravo*. Petrograd: Tipografia Soikina, 1917; first published 1906.

Chernova, Nina V., and Vasilii Tokarev. "'Pervaia Konnaia,' kinematograficheskii reid v zabven'e: istoricheskie komentarii k sovetskomu kinoprotsessu 1938–1941 gg.," *Kinovedcheskie zapiski*, 65 (2003): 280–313.

Cherushev, Nikolai S. *"Nevinovnykh ne byvaet . . .": chekisty protiv voennykh, 1918–1953*. Moscow: Veche, 2004.

———. *1937 god: elita Krasnoi Armii na Golgofe*. Moscow: Veche, 2003.

———. *Komendanty Kremlia v labirintakh vlasti*. Moscow: Veche, 2005.

———. *Udar po svoim: Krasnaia Armiia, 1938–1941*. Moscow: Veche, 2003.

———, ed. *"Dorogoi nash tovarishch Stalin!"—i drugie tovarishchi: obrashcheniia rodstvennikov repressirovannykh komandirov Krasnoi Armii k rukovoditeliam strany*. Moscow: Zvenia, 2001.

Cherviakova, I. "Pesochnye chasy: istoriia zhizni Iriny Gogua v vos'mi kassetakh, pis'makh i kommentariiakh," *Druzhba narodov*, 1997, no. 4: 59–104, no. 5: 75–119.

Chew, Allen F. *The White Death: The Epic of the Soviet-Finnish Winter War*. East Lansing: Michigan State University, 1971.

Chigirin, I. I. *Stalin, bolezni i smert': dokumenty*. Moscow: Dostointsvo, 2016.

Chihiro, Hosoya. "The Japanese-Soviet Neutrality Pact." In *Deterrent Diplomacy: Japan, Germany, and the USSR 1935–1940*, edited by James W. Morley. New York: Columbia University, 1976, 129–78.

———. "The Tripartite Pact 1939–1940." In *Deterrent Diplomacy: Japan, Germany, and the USSR 1935–1940*, edited by James W. Morley. New York: Columbia University, 1976, 191–257.

Chistiakov, B. "Narkomvoenmor nomer tri," *Smena*, Feb. 19, 1989.

Chistka sovetskogo apparata k XVI s"ezdu VKP (b). Moscow: Tekhnika upravleniia, 1930.

Chkalov, V. P. *Nash transpoliarnyi reis: Moskva-Severnyi polius-Severnaia Amerika*. Moscow: OGIZ-politicheskaia literatura, 1938.

Chrezvychainyi VIII Vsesoiuznyi s"ezd Sovetov: stenograficheskii otchet. Moscow, 1936.

Christensen, Thomas J., and Jack Snyder. "Chain Gangs and Passed Bucks: Predicting Alliance Patterns in Multipolarity," *International Organization*, 44/2 (1990): 137–68.

Christie, Ian. "Making Sense of Early Soviet Sound." In *Inside the Film Factory: New Approaches to Russian and Soviet Cinema*, edited by Richard Taylor and Ian Christie. London: Routledge, 1991, 208–15.

Chubarian, A. O., and H. Shukman, eds. *Stalin and the Soviet-Finnish War, 1939–1940*. London and Portland, OR: Frank Cass, 2002.

Chudakova, M. "Arkhiv Bulgakova," *Gosudartsvennaia biblioteka imeni Lenina: zapiski otdela rukopisei*, no. 37 (1976): 52–5.

Chudodeev, Aleksandr. "Chelovek iz 'gruppy Ya'," *Itogi*, July 5, 2001.

Chuev, Feliks. *Kaganovich, Shepilov*. Moscow: Olma, 2001.

———. *Molotov Remembers: Inside Kremlin Politics*. Chicago: I. R. Dee, 1993.

———. *Molotov: Poluderzhavnyi vlastelin*. Moscow: Olma, 1999.

———. *Sto sorok besed s Molotovym*. Moscow: Terra, 1991.

———. *Tak govoril Kaganovich: ispoved' stalinskogo apostola*. Moscow: Otechestvo, 1992.

Chugunov, A. I. *Granitsa nakanune voiny: iz istorii pogranichnykh voisk 1939–22 iuinia 1941*. Moscow: Voenizdat, 1985.

Chuikov, V. "Konflikt na KVZhD," *Voennoistoricheskii zhurnal*, 1976, no. 7: 49–57.

Chukhin, Ivan. *Kanaloarmeitsy: istoriia stroitel'stva Belomorkanala v dokumentakh, tsifrakh, faktakh, fotografiiakh, svidetel'stvakh uchastnikov i ochevidtsev*. Petrozavodsk: Kareliia, 1990.

Chukovskii, Kornei. *Dnevnik: 1930–1969*. Moscow: Sovremennyi pisatel, 1995.

Chukovsky, Kornei. *Diary, 1901–1969*. New Haven, CT: Yale University, 2005.

Churchill, Winston. *Step by Step, 1936–39*. London: T. Butterworth, 1939.

———. *The Second World War*. 6 vols. Boston: Houghton Mifflin, 1948–1953.

Ciano, Count Galleazzo. *Ciano's Hidden Diary 1937–1938*. New York: Dutton, 1953.

———. *Diary, 1937–1943*. New York: Enigma, 2002.

———. *L'Europa verso la catastrofe: 184 colloqui*. Verona: A. Mondadori, 1948.

———. *The Ciano Diaries 1939–1943: The Complete, Unabridged Diaries of Count Galeazzo Ciano Italian Minister for Foreign Affairs, 1936–1943*. New York: Doubleday, 1946.

Cienciala, Anna M. "German Propaganda for the Revision of the Polish-German Frontier in Danzig and the Corridor: its Effects on British Opinion and the British Policy-Making Elite in the Years 1919–1933," *Antemurale*, 20 (1976): 77–129.

———. "Poland in British and French Policy in 1939: Determination to Fight—or Avoid War?" *The Polish Review*, 34/3 (1989): 199–226.

———. "Polish Foreign Policy, 1926–1939, 'Equilibrium': Stereotype and Reality." In *Poland Between Germany and Russia 1926–1939: The Theory of Two Enemies*,

edited by Alexander Korczyński and Tadeusz Świętochowski. New York: Pilsudski Institute of America, 1975, 44–59.

———. "The Declaration of Non-Aggression of January 26, 1934 in Polish-German and International Relations: A Reappraisal," *East European Quarterly*, 1/1 (1967): 1–30.

———. "The Foreign Policy of Józef Piłsudski and Józef Beck, 1926–1939: Misconceptions and Interpretations," *Polish Review*, 56/1–2 (2011): 111–51.

———. Review of *La Décadence, 1932–1939*, by Jean Baptiste Duroselle. Paris: Paris Imprimerie Nationale, 1979, *Kwartalnik Historyczny*, 88/2 (1981).

———, et al., eds. *Katyn: A Crime Without Punishment*. New Haven, CT: Yale University, 2008.

Ciliga, Ante. *The Russian Enigma*. London: Scribner's, 1940.

Citrine, Walter McLennan. *A Trade Unionist Looks at Russia*. London: Trades Union Congress General Council, 1936.

Clark, Katerina. "Germanophone Exiles in Stalin's Russia: Diaspora and Cultural Identity in the 1930s," *Kritika*, 2/3 (2001): 529–51.

———. *Moscow: The Fourth Rome: Stalinism, Cosmopolitanism, and the Evolution of Soviet Culture, 1931–1941*. Cambridge, MA: Harvard University, 2011.

———. *The Soviet Novel: History as Ritual*. 3rd ed. Bloomington: Indiana University, 2000.

Clarke, Peter. *The Cripps Version: The Life of Sir Stafford Cripps, 1889–1952*. London: Allen Lane, 2002.

Clayton, Anthony. *The British Empire as Superpower, 1919–1939*. London: Macmillan, 1986.

Clissold, Stephen, ed. *Yugoslavia and the Soviet Union, 1939–1973: A Documentary Survey*. New York: Oxford University, 1975.

Coates, William P., and Zelda K. Coates. *A History of Anglo-Soviet Relations*. 2 vols. London: Lawrence & Wishart, 1944, 1958.

Cobban, Alfred. *Dictatorship: Its Theory and History*. New York: Haskell House, 1939.

Cockburn, Claud. *Crossing the Line*. London: MacGibbon & Kee, 1958.

———. *In Time of Trouble*. London: Rupert Hart-Davis, 1957.

Cohen, Stephen F. *Bukharin and the Bolshevik Revolution: A Political Biography, 1888–1938*. New York: Oxford University, 1971.

Colton, Joel. *Léon Blum: Humanist in Politics*. New York: Knopf, 1966.

Colville, John. *Footprints in Time*. London: Collins, 1976.

Communism and the International Situation: Thesis . . . Adopted at the Sixth World Congress of the Communist International, 1928. London: Modern Books, 1929.

Conquest, Robert. *Harvest of Sorrow: Soviet Collectivization and the Terror-Famine*. New York: Oxford University, 1986.

———. *Inside Stalin's Secret Police: NKVD Politics 1936–1939*. Stanford, CA: Hoover Institution, 1985.

———. *Kolyma: The Arctic Death Camps*. New York: Viking, 1978.

———. *Stalin and the Kirov Murder*. New York: Oxford University, 1989.

———. *Stalin: Breaker of Nations*. New York: Viking, 1991.

———. *The Great Terror: A Reassessment*. New York: Oxford University, 1990.

———. *The Great Terror: Stalin's Purge of the Thirties*. New York: Macmillan, 1968.

Cooper, Julian. "Defence Production and the Soviet Economy, 1929–1941," University of Birmingham, UK, Centre for Russian and East European Studies, discussion papers, 1976.

Coox, Alvin D. "Introduction: The Japanese-Soviet Confrontation, 1935–1939." In *Deterrent Diplomacy: Japan, Germany, and the USSR 1935–1940*, edited by James W. Morley. New York: Columbia University, 1976, 115–27.

———. "Japanese Foreknowledge of the Soviet-German War, 1941," *Soviet Studies*, 23/4 (1971).

———. "L'Affaire Lyushkov: Anatomy of a Defector," *Soviet Studies*, 19/3 (1966): 405–20.

———. "The Lesser of Two Hells: NKVD General G.S. Liushkov's Defection to Japan, 1938–1945, Part 1," and "Part II," *Journal of Slavic Military Studies*, 11/3 (1998): 145–86, 11/4 (1998): 72–110.

———. *Nomonhan: Japan against Russia, 1939.* Stanford, CA: Stanford University, 1985.

———. *The Anatomy of a Small War: The Soviet-Japanese Struggle for Changkufeng/Khasan, 1938.* Westport, CT: Greenwood, 1977.

Corbett, D. M. "The Rehabilitation of Mykola Skrypnyk," *Slavic Review*, 22/2 (1963): 304–13.

Corbett, Julian S. *Some Principles of Maritime Strategy.* New York: Longman, Green, 1911.

Corvaja, Santi. *Hitler and Mussolini: The Secret Meetings.* New York: Enigma, 2008.

Costello, John. *Mask of Treachery.* New York: William Morrow, 1988.

———, and Oleg Tsarev. *Deadly Illusions: The KGB Orlov Dossier Reveals Stalin's Master Spy.* New York: Crown, 1993.

Costiliogla, Frank. *Roosevelt's Lost Alliances.* Princeton, NJ: Princeton University, 2011.

Cot, Pierre. *Triumph of Treason.* Chicago: Ziff-Davis Publishing Co., 1944.

Coulondre, Robert. *De Staline à Hitler: souvenirs de deux ambassades, 1936–1939.* Paris: Hachette, 1950.

Course and Phases of the World Economic Depression, The. Geneva: League of Nations, 1931.

Courtois, Stéphane. "Conclusion: Why?" In *The Black Book of Communism: Crimes, Terror, Repression.* Cambridge, MA: Harvard University, 2015.

Coverdale, John F. *Italian Intervention in the Spanish Civil War.* Princeton, NJ: Princeton University, 1975.

Cowley, Malcolm. "H. G. Wells' Interview with Stalin Helped Change the Fundamental Principles of Liberalism," *New Republic*, April 23, 1935.

Cox, M., ed. *E. H. Carr: A Critical Appraisal.* Basingstoke and New York: Macmillan, 2000.

Craig, Gordon Alexander, and Felix Gilbert, eds. *The Diplomats, 1919–1939.* Princeton, NJ: Princeton University, 1994.

Craigie, Sir Robert. *Behind the Japanese Mask.* London: Hutchinson, 1946.

Creveld, Martin L. van. *Hitler's Strategy, 1940–1941: The Balkan Clue.* New York: Cambridge University, 1973.

Crick, Bernard. *In Defence of Politics.* Chicago: University of Chicago, 1962.

Cristiani, Antonella, and Vera M. Mikhaleva, eds. *Le repressioni degli anni trenta nell'Armata rossa: racconta di documenti dai Fondi dell'Archivio militare di Stato russo.* Naples: Istituto universitario orientale, 1996.

———, et al., eds. *Repressii v Krasnoi Armii (30-e gody): sbornik dokumentov.* Naples: Istituto universitario orientale, 1996.

Crossman, Richard, ed. *The God that Failed.* New York: Columbia University, 1949.

Crowley, Edward L., ed. *The Soviet Diplomat Corps, 1917–1967.* Metuchen, NJ: Scarecrow, 1970.

Crowley, James B. *Japan's Quest for Autonomy: National Security and Foreign Policy*

1930–1938. Princeton, NJ: Princeton University, 1966.

Crozier, Andrew J. *The Causes of the Second World War.* Oxford, UK, and Malden, MA: Blackwell Publishers, 1997.

Curtis, J. A. E. *Manuscripts Don't Burn: Mikhail Bulgakovv, a Life in Letters and Diaries.* London: Bloomsbury, 1991.

D'Agostino, Anthony. "Stalin Old and New," *Russian Review*, 54/3 (1995): 447–51.

Dahlerus, Birger. *Der letze Versuch.* Munich: Nymphenburger Verlagshandlung, 1948.

———. *The Last Attempt.* London: Hutchinson, 1948.

Daines, Vladimir O. "Voennaia strategiia mezhdu grazhdanskoi i Velikoi Otechestvennoi voinami." In *Istoriia voennoi strategii Rossii*, edited by V. A. Zolotarev Moscow: Kuchkovo pole, 2000, 125–90.

———. *Zhukov.* Moscow: Molodaia gvardiia, 2005.

Dallin, Alexander, and F. I. Firsov, eds. *Dimitrov and Stalin, 1934–1943: Letters from the Soviet Archives.* New Haven, CT: Yale University, 2000.

Dallin, David J. *Soviet Russia's Foreign Policy, 1939–1942.* New Haven, CT: Yale University, 1942.

———. *The Rise of Russia in Asia.* New Haven, CT: Yale University, 1949.

———, and Boris I. Nicolaevsky. *Forced Labor in Soviet Russia.* New Haven, CT: Yale University, 1947.

Dalrymple, Dana G. "Marx and Agriculture: The Soviet Experience," mimeograph, Department of Agricultural Economics, Michigan State University, East Lansing, November 1961.

———. "The Soviet Famine of 1932–1934," *Soviet Studies*, 15/3 (1964): 250–84.

Dalton, H. *The Fateful Years: Memoirs, 1931–1935.* London: Muller, 1957.

Damaskin, Igor A. *Stalin i razvedka.* Moscow: Veche, 2004.

Dan, Lidiia. "Bukharin o Staline," *Novy zhurnal*, no. 75 (1964): 176–84.

Daniels, Robert V. "Office Holding and Elite Status: The Central Committee of the CPSU." In *The Dynamics of Soviet Politics*, edited by Paul Cocks et al. Cambridge, MA: Harvard University, 1976, 77–95.

———. "The State and Revolution: A Case Study in the Genesis and Transformation of Communist Ideology," *American Slavic and East European Review*, 12/1 (1953): 22–43.

———. *Conscience of the Revolution: Communist Opposition in Soviet Russia.* Cambridge, MA: Harvard University, 1960.

Danielson, Elena S. "The Elusive Litvinov Memoirs," *Slavic Review*, 48/3 (1989): 477–83.

Danilov, S. "K biografii L. Beriia," *Na rubezhe* [Paris], 1952, no. 3–4: 31–2.

———. "Tragediia Abkhazskogo naroda," *Vestnik instituta po izucheniii istorii i kul'tury SSSR* [Munich], no. 1 (1951): 2–12.

Danilov, V. D. "Stalinskaia strategiia nachala voiny: plany i realnost'," *Otechestvennaia istoriia*, 1995, no. 3: 33–8.

Danilov, Viktor P. "Organizovannyi golod: K 70-letiiu obshchekrest'ianskoi tragedii," *Otechestvennaia istoriia*, 2004, no. 5: 97–110.

———, and N. A. Ivnitskii, eds. *Dokumenty svidetel'stvuiut: iz istorii derevni nakanune i v khode kollektivizatsii, 1927–1932 gg.* Moscow: Politizdat, 1989.

———, and Oleg Khlevniuk, eds. *Kak lomali NEP: stenogrammy plenumov TsK VKP(b) 1928–1929 gg.* 5 vols. Moscow: Demokratiia, 2000.

———, Lynne Viola, and Robert T. Manning, eds. *Tragediia sovetskoii derevni:*

kollektivizatsiia i raskulachivanie. Dokumenty i materialy, 1927–1939. 5 vols. Moscow: Rosspen, 1999–2006.

———, and Sergei Krasil'nikov. *Spetspereselentsy v Zapadnoi Sibiri: 1930-vesna 1931 g.* Novosibirsk: Nauka, 1992.

Das Deutsche Reich und der Zweite Weltkrieg. 9 vols. Stuttgart: Deutsche Verlags-Anstalt, 1979–.

Dashpürev, D., and S. K. Soni. *Reign of Terror in Mongolia, 1920–1990.* New Delhi: South Asian Publishers, 1992.

David-Fox, Michael. "Stalinist Westernizer? Aleksandr Arosev's Literary and Political Depictions of Europe," *Slavic Review*, 62/4 (2003): 733–59.

———. *Showcasing the Great Experiment: Cultural Diplomacy and Western Visitors to the Soviet Union, 1921–1941.* Oxford & New York: Oxford University, 2014.

Davidson Eugene. *The Trial of the Germans: An Account of the Twenty-two Defendants before the International Military Tribunal at Nuremberg.* New York: Macmillan, 1967.

Davidson, J. C. C. *Memoirs of a Conservative.* London: Weidenfeld and Nicolson, 1969.

Davies, Joseph E. *Mission to Moscow.* New York: Simon & Schuster, 1941.

Davies, Robert W. "Making Economic Policy." In *Behind the Façade of Stalin's Command Economy*, edited by Paul R. Gregory. Stanford, CA: Hoover Institutions, 2013, 64–80.

———. "Soviet Defence Industries during the First Five-Year Plan." Unpublished *Discussion Papers*, SIPS no. 27. CREES, University of Birmingham, 1987.

———. "Soviet Military Expenditures and the Armaments Industry, 1929–1933: A Reconsideration," *Europe-Asia Studies*, 45/4 (1993): 577–608.

———. "Stalin as Economic Policy-Maker: Soviet Agriculture, 1931–1936." In *Stalin: A New History*, edited by Sarah Davies and James Harris. New York: Cambridge University, 2005, 121–39.

———. "The Soviet Economy and the Launching of the Great Terror." In *Stalin's Terror Revisited*, edited by Melanie Ilič. Basingstoke: Palgrave Macmillan, 2006, 1–37.

———. "The Syrtsov-Lominadze Affair," *Soviet Studies*, 33/1 (1981): 29–50.

———. Introduction to *The Russian Revolution from Lenin to Stalin, 1917–1929.* Edited by E. H. Carr. London: Palgrave Macmillan, 2004.

———. *The Development of the Soviet Budgetary System.* Cambridge, UK: Cambridge University, 1958.

———. *The Industrialisation of Soviet Russia, Volume 1: The Socialist Offensive: The Collectivization of Soviet Agriculture, 1929–1930.* Cambridge, MA: Harvard University, 1980.

———. *The Industrialisation of Soviet Russia, Volume 2: The Soviet Collective Farm, 1929–1930.* Houndmills, Basingstoke: Macmillan, 1980.

———. *The Industrialisation of Soviet Russia, Volume 3: The Soviet Economy in Turmoil, 1929–1930.* Houndmills, Basingstoke: Macmillan, 1989.

———. *The Industrialisation of Soviet Russia, Volume 4: Crisis and Progress in the Soviet Economy, 1931–1933.* Houndmills, Basingstoke: Macmillan, 1996.

———. *The Industrialisation of Soviet Russia, Volume 5: The Years of Hunger: Soviet Agriculture, 1931–1933.* New York: Palgrave Macmillan, 1994.

———, and Mark Harrison. "Defence Spending and Defence Industry in the 1930s." In *The Soviet Defence-Industry Complex from Stalin to Khrushchev*, edited by John

Barber and Mark Harrison. London and Basingstoke: Macmillan, 2000, 70–98.

——, and O. V. Khlevniuk. "Otmena kartochnoi sistemy v SSSR, 1934–1935 gody," *Otechestvennaia istoriia*, 1999, no. 5: 87–107.

——, and O. V. Khlevniuk. "Stakhanovism and the Soviet Economy," *Europe-Asia Studies*, 54/6 (2002): 867–903.

——, and Stephen G. Wheatcroft. "Stalin and the Soviet Famine of 1932–33: A Reply to Ellman," *Europe-Asia Studies*, 58/4 (2006): 625–33.

——, et al., eds. *The Stalin-Kaganovich Correspondence, 1931–36*. New Haven, CT, and London: Yale University, 2003.

——, Mark Harrison, and Stephen G. Wheatcroft, eds. *The Economic Transformation of the Soviet Union, 1913–1945*. New York: Cambridge University, 1994.

——, Melanie Ilič, and Oleg Khlevniuk, "The Politburo and Economic Decision Making." In *The Nature of Stalin's Dictatorship: The Politburo, 1924–1953*, edited by E. A. Rees. Houndmills, Basingstoke: Palgrave Macmillan, 2004, 108–33.

——, Oleg Khlevnyuk, and Stephen G. Wheatcroft. *The Industrialisation of Soviet Russia, Volume 6: The Years of Progress, 1934–1936*. Houndmills, Basingstoke: Palgrave Macmillan, 2014.

——, Stephen G. Wheatcroft, and M. B. Tauger, "Stalin, Grain Stocks, and the Famine of 1932–33," *Slavic Review*, 54/3 (1995): 642–57.

Davies, Sarah. "Stalin and the Making of the Leader Cult in the 1930s." In *The Leader Cult in Communist Dictatorships: Stalin and the Eastern Bloc*, edited by Balász Apor et al. New York: Palgrave Macmillan, 2004, 29–46.

——. *Popular Opinion in Stalin's Russia: Terror, Propaganda and Dissent, 1934–1941*. Cambridge, UK: Cambridge University, 2001.

——. "The Crime of 'Anti-Soviet Agitation' in the Soviet Union in the 1930s," *Cahiers du monde russe*, 39/1–2 (1998): 149–68.

——, and James Harris. *Stalin's World: Dictating the Soviet Order*. New Haven, CT, and London: Yale University, 2014.

Davis, Richard. *Anglo-French Relations before the Second World War: Appeasement and Crisis*. New York: Palgrave, 2001.

Davison, Peter, ed. *George Orwell: A Life in Letters*. New York: Liveright, 2013.

Davlekamova, Saniia. *Galina Ulanova: Ia ne khotela tansevat'*. Moscow: AST Pess SKD, 2005.

Davydenko, S. S., et al., eds. *Put' trudovykh pobed: sbornik dokumentov i materialov*. Volgograd: Nizhne-Volzhskoe knizhnoe izd-vo, 1967.

Dawson, J. H. R. "A King, a Doctor, and a Convenient Medical Death," *British Medical Journal*, no. 308 (1994).

d'Encausse, Hélène Carrère. *The Great Challenge: Nationalities and the Bolshevik State, 1917–1930*. New York: Holmes & Meier, 1992.

Deborin, A., ed. *Na boevom postu: sbornik k shestidesiatiletiiu D. B. Riazanova*. Moscow: Gosizdat, 1930.

Dębski, Sławomir. *Między Berlinem a Moskwą. Stosunki niemiecko-sowieckie 1939–1941*. Warsaw: Polski Instytut Spraw Międzynarodowych, 2003.

Dederichs, Mario. *Heydrich: The Face of Evil*. London: Greenhill Books, 2006.

Dedijer, Vladimir. "Sur l'armistice 'germano-yougoslave' (7 avril 1941): Peut-on dire qu'il y eut réellement un armistice?" *Revue d'histoire de la Deuxième Guerre mondiale*, 23 (1956): 1–10.

De Grand, Alexander J. *In Stalin's Shadow: Angelo Tasca and the Crisis of the Left in Italy and France, 1910–1945*. Dekalb: Northern Illinois University, 1986.

Degras, Jane, ed. *Soviet Documents on Foreign Policy, 1917–1941*. 3 vols. London and New York: Oxford University, 1951–53.

——, ed. *The Communist International, 1919–1943: Documents*. 3 vols. London: Frank Cass, 1971.

Deighton, Len. "Hess the Aviator." In *Flight from Reality: Rudolf Hess and His Mission to Scotland, 1941*, edited by David Stafford. London: Pimlico, 2002, 121–38.

Deist, Wilelm. *The Wehrmacht and German Rearmament*. London: Macmillan, 1981.

Delba, Mikhail. "Besposhchadno borot'sia s vragami naroda," *Sovetskaia abkhazia*, Aug. 15, 1937, in *Abkhazia: dokumenty svidetel'stvuiut, 1937–1953*. Sukhumi: Alashara, 1992.

Deletant, Dennis. *Hitler's Forgotten Ally: Ion Antonescu and His Regime in Romania, 1940–1944*. Houndmills, Basingstoke and New York: Palgrave Macmillan, 2006.

Delmar, D. Sefton. "The Reichstag Fire." In *The Mammoth Book of EyeWitness History 2000*, edited by Jon E. Lewis. New York: Carroll and Graf, 2000.

"Delo o tak nazyvaemoi 'antisovetskoi trotskistskoi voennoi organizatsii' v Krasnoi armii," *Izvestiia TsK KPSS*, 1989, no. 4: 41–62.

de Madariaga, Maria Rosa. "The Intervention of Moroccan Troops in the Spanish Civil War," *European History Quarterly*, 22/1 (1992): 67–97.

de Mayo, Julio Álvarez. *The Last Optimist*. London: Putnam, 1950.

Dembski, S. "Pol'sko-Sovetskoi otnosheniia v otsenkakh Berlina v 30-e gody: nekotorye voprosy." In *Sovetsko-Pol'skie otnosheniia v politicheskikh usloviakh Evropy 30-x godov XX stoletiia: sbornik statei*, edited by E. Duraczyński and A. N. Sakharov. Moscow: Nauka, 2001, 191–218.

Demski, S. "Pol'sko-sovetskie otnosheniia v otsenkakh Berlina v 30-e gody: nekotorye voprosy." In *Sovetsko-pol'skie otnosheniia, 1918–1945: sbornik statei*, edited by I. I. Kostiushko et al. Moscow: Nauka, 1974, 191–218.

Denikin, A. I. *Ocherki russkoi smuty: krushenie vlasti i armii*. 5 vols. Paris and Berlin: J. Povolozky & Cie, 1921–26.

Denisova, N. A., and M. E. Tumash, eds. *Nakanune: zapadnyi osobyi voennyi okrug (konets 1939 g.—1941 g.)*. Minsk: NABR, 2007.

Denny, Harold, "No 'Formalism' for Soviet," *New York Times*, Oct. 23, 1938.

Der bewaffnete Aufstand: Versuch einer theoretischen Darstellung. Zürich: Meyer, 1928. Translated as *Armed Insurrection*, by A. Neuberg [false name]. London: NLB,1970.

Deriabin, Aleksandr, ed. *Letopis' rossiiskogo kino, 1930–1945*. Moscow: Materik, 2007.

Der Parteitag der Freiheit vom 10.-16. September 1935: offizieller Bericht über den Verlauf des Reichsparteitags mit samtlichen Kongressreden. Munich: Zentralverlag der NSDAP, F. Eher Nachf., 1935.

Der Prozess gegen die Hauptkriegsverbrecher vor dem Internationalen Militärgerichtshof, Nürnberg, 14. November 1945–1. Oktober 1946. 42 vols. Cologne: Reichenbach, 1994.

Desiatov, L. "Operatsii v Norvegii (aprel'–iiun' 1940 g.)," *Voenno-istoricheskii zhurnal*, 1940, no. 4: 3–12.

Deutsch, Harold C. *Hitler and His Generals: The Hidden Crisis, January-June 1938*. Minneapolis: University of Minnesota, 1974.

——. *The Conspiracy against Hitler in the Twilight War*. Minneapolis: University of Minnesota, 1968.

Deutscher, Isaac. *Stalin: A Political Biography*. 2nd ed. New York: Oxford University, 1966.

——. *The Prophet Armed: Trotsky, 1879–1921*. New York: Oxford University, 1954.

——. *The Prophet Outcast: Trotsky, 1929–1940*. New York: Oxford University, 1963.

Deutschland-Berichte der Sozialdemokratischen Partei Deutschlands, 1934–1940. 7 vols. Frankfurt am Main: Zweitausendeins, 1980.

Development of Finnish-Soviet Relations during the Autumn of 1939, The. Helsinki: Suomen kirja, 1940.

Deviatov, Sergei V., and Elena Zhuraveva. *Dvortsy Kremlia*. Moscow: Slovo, 2001.

——. *Kremlevskii senat*. Moscow: Ivan i tovarishchestvo, 1999.

Deviatov, Sergei V., et al. "Gibel' Kirova: fakty i versii," *Rodina*, 2005, no. 3: 57–65.

——. *Bliznaia dacha Stalina: opyt istoricheskogo putevoditeli*. Moscow: Kremlin Multimedia, 2011.

——. *Garazh osobogo naznacheniia: 90 let na sluzhbe Otechestvu, 1921–2011*. Moscow: MediaPress, 157.

Deviatyi vsesoiuznyi s"ezd professional'nyk soiuzov SSSR: stenograficheskii otchet. Moscow, 1933.

DeWitt, N. *Soviet Professional Manpower: Its Education, Training and Supply*. Washington, D.C.: U.S. Government Printing Office, 1955.

D'iakov, Iu. L., and T. S. Bushueva, eds. *Fashistskii mech kovalsia v SSSR, Krasnaia Armiia i Reikhsver, tainoe sotrudnichestvo 1922–1933: neizvestnye dokumenty*. Moscow: Sovetskaia Rossiia, 1992.

Die Schulze-Boysen-Harnack Organizations in Antifascistischen Kampf. East Berlin: Dietz, 1975.

Dietrich, Otto. *The Hitler I Knew*. London: Methuen, 1955.

"'Diktatura iazykocheshyshchikh nad rabotaiushchimi': posledniaia sluzhebnaia zapiska Chicherina," *Istochnik*, 1995, no. 6: 99–116.

Dilks, David, ed. *The Diaries of Sir Alexander Cadogan, O.M., 1938–1945*. London: Cassell, 1971.

——. "'We Must Hope for the Best and Prepare for the Worst': the Prime Minister, the Cabinet, and Hitler's Germany," *Proceedings of the British Academy*, 73 (1987): 309–52.

Dima, Nicholas. *Bessarabia and Bukovina: The Soviet-Romanian Territorial Dispute*. Boulder, CO: East European Monographs, 1982.

Dimitrov, Georgi. "Nastuplenie fashizma i zadachi Komunnisticheskogo internatsionala v bor'be za edinstvo rabochego klassa protiv fashizma," In *Sed'moi congress i bor'ba protiv fashizma i voiny: sbornik dokumentov*, edited by Kirill K. Shirinia. Moscow: Politicheskaia literatura, 1975.

——. "Zashchishchat' podlykh terroristov—znachit pomogat' fashizmu," *Kommunisticheskii Internatsional*, 1936, no. 14, no. 15.

——. *Against Fascism and War. Report before the Seventh World Congress of the Communist International, 1935*. Sofia: Sofia Press, 1982.

Dippel, John V. H. *Two Against Hitler: Stealing the Nazis' Best-Kept Secrets*. New York: Praeger, 1992.

Djilas, Milovan, ed. *Besedy so Stalinym*. Moscow: Tsentrpoligraph, 2002.

Dmitriev, Vladimir I. "Stroitel'stvo sovetsk-ogo podvodnogo flota v mezhvoennyi pe-riod," *Voenno-istoricheskii zhurnal*, 1974, no. 10: 82–3.

———. *Sovetskoe podvodnoe korablestroenie*. Moscow: Voenizdat, 1990.

Dmitriev, Yurii, ed. *Pominal'nye spiski Karelii, 1937–1938*. Petrozavodsk: [s.n.], 2002.

Dmitrievskii, Sergei V. *Sovetskie portrety*. Berlin: Strela, 1932.

———. *Stalin*. Stockholm: Bonnier and Strela, 1931.

Dmitrievskii, V. *Piatnitskii*. Moscow: Molo-daia gvardiia, 1971.

Dobrenko, Evgeny. *Formovka Sovetskogo chi-tatelia: sotsial'nye i esteticheskie predpo-sylki retseptsii sovetskoi literatury*. St. Petersburg: Akademicheskii proekt, 1997. Translated as *The Making of the State Reader: Social and Aesthetic Contexts of the Reception of Soviet Literature*. Stanford, CA: Stanford University, 1997.

———. *Political Economy of Socialist Realism*. New Haven, CT: Yale University, 2007.

———. *Stalinist Cinema and the Production of History: Museum of the Revolution*. New Haven, CT, and London: Yale University, 2008.

Dobry, Michel. "February 1934 and the Dis-covery of French Society's Allergy to the 'Fascist Revolution.'" In *France in the Era of Fascism: Essays on the French Authori-tarian Right*, edited by Brian Jenkins. Ox-ford: Berghahn, 2005.

Documents Concerning German-Polish Rela-tions and the Outbreak of Hostilities be-tween Great Britain and Germany on September 3, 1939. London: HMSO, 1939.

Documents of the Fourth International. New York: Pathfinder Press, 1973.

Documents on International Affairs, 1939–1946. 2 vols. London: Oxford University, 1951–54.

Documents and Materials Relating to the Eve of the Second World War: The Dirksen Pa-pers (1938–1939). Moscow: Foreign Lan-guages Publishing House, 1948.

Dodd, Jr., William E., and Mary Dodd, eds. *Ambassador Dodd's Diary, 1933–1938*. New York: Harcourt, Brace, 1941.

Doering, Dötre. *Deutsche Aussenwirtschafts-politik 1933–5: die Gleichschaltung der Aussenwirtschaft in der Früh die deutsche Wirtschafts- und Rüstungspolitik zwischen den Weltkrieg*. Berlin: [s.n.], 1969.

Dohan, Michael R. "Soviet Foreign Trade in the NEP Economy and Soviet Industrial-ization Strategy." PhD diss. Massachusetts Institute of Technology, 1969.

———. "The Economic Origins of Soviet Au-tarky, 1927/8–1934," *Slavic Review*, 35/4 (1976): 603–35.

Doise, Jean, and Maurice Vaïsse. *Diplomatie et outil militaire, 1871–1969*. Paris: Impr. nationale, 1987.

Doklad komissii B. Z. Shumiatskogo po izucheniiu tekhniki i organiatsii ameri-kanskoi i evropeiskoi kinematografii. Mos-cow, 1935.

Dokuchaev, Mikhail. *Moskva, kreml', okhrana*. Moscow: Bizness-Press, 1995.

Dokumenty i materialy kanuna vtoroi mirovoi voiny: 1937–39. 2 vols. Moscow: Gos-politizdat, 1948.

Dokumenty i materialy po istorii sovets-ko-chekhoslovatskikh otnoshenii. 5 vols. Moscow: Nauka, 1973–88.

Dokumenty i materialy po istorii sovets-ko-pol'skikh otnoshenii. 12 vols. Moscow: Akademiia nauk SSSR, 1963–1986.

Dolgopolov, Nikolai. *Vartanian*. Moscow: Molodaia gvardiia, 2014.

Dolonskii, L. L. *Sovetskaia kinokomediia tri-dtsatykh godov*. 2 vols. Moscow: Vsesoiu-znyi gos. institut kinematografii, 1957.

Dolot, Miron. *Execution by Hunger: A Survi-vor's Account of the Famine of 1932–1933 in Ukraine in which Over Seven Million People Were Deliberately Starved to Death*. New York: W. W. Norton, 1985.

Domarus, Max, ed. *Hitler: Reden und Proklo-mationen 1932–1945*. 2 vols. Munich: Sud-deutscher Verlag, 1965.

———, ed. *Hitler: Speeches and Proclamations 1932–1945: The Chronicle of a Dictator-ship*. 4 vols. Wauconda, IL: Bolcha-zy-Carducci, 1990–2004.

Dongarov, A. G. "Pravitel'stvo Kuusinena—epizod sovetsko-finliandskoi voiny 1939–1940 godov," *Vestnik Ministerstva inostrannykh del SSSR*, 1989, no. 22.

———. "Voina, kotoryi moglo ne byt'," *Vo-prosy istorii*, 1990, no. 5: 28–45.

Dongarov, Aleksandr. "Mezhdu reinom i vol-goi," *Rodina*, 1991, no. 5: 39–40.

Dorofeev, Boris. "Mat'," *Pravda*, Oct. 23, 1935.

Doughty, Robert Allan. *The Breaking Point: Sedan and the Fall of France, 1940*. Ham-den, CT: Archon, 1990.

Douglas, Susan. *Inventing American Broad-casting, 1899–1922*. Baltimore: Johns Hopkins University, 1987.

Drabovitch, Wladimir. *Les Intellectuels français et le bolchévisme: La Ligue des droits de l'homme; le néo-marxisme uni-versitaire; quelques grands intellectuels: André Gide-Romain Rolland, et certains autres*. Paris: Les Libertés françaises, 1938.

Draitser, Emil. *Stalin's Romeo Spy: The Re-markable Rise and Fall of the KGB's Most Daring Operative, the True Life of Dmitri Bystrolyotov*. Evanston, IL: Northwestern University, 2010.

Draskoczy, Julie. *Belomor: Criminality and Creativity in Stalin's Gulag*. Boston: Aca-demic Studies, 2014.

Dreifort, John E. "The French Popular Front and the Franco-Soviet Pact, 1936–1937: A Dilemma in Foreign Policy," *Journal of Contemporary History*, 11/2–3 (1976): 217–36.

Drizdo, Vera. *Nadezhda Konstantinovna Krupskaia*. Moscow: Gosizdat, 1958.

Drobizhev, V. B. *Industrializatsiia i izme-neniia v sotsial'noi structure sovetskogo obshchestva*. Moscow: Nauka, 1970.

Drobizhev, V. Z. *Glavnyi shtab sotsialistich-eskoi promyshlennosti*. Moscow: Mysl', 1966.

Druzhnikov, Iurii. *Informer 001: The Myth of Pavlik Morozov*. New Brunswick, NJ: Transaction Publishers, 1997.

Duara, Prasenjit. *Sovereignty and Authentic-ity: Manchukuo and the East Asian Mod-ern*. Lanham, MD: Rowman and Littlefield, 2003.

Dubinskaia-Dzhalilova, T., and A. Chernev. "'Zhmu vashu ruku, dorogoi tovarishch': perepiska Maksima Gor'kogo i Iosifa Sta-lina," *Novyi mir*, 1997, no. 9: 167–92.

Dubinskii, I. V. *Osobyi schet*. Moscow: Voe-nizdat, 1989.

Dubinskii-Mukhadze, Il'ia M. *Ordzhoni-kidze*. Moscow: Molodaia gvardiia, 1963.

Dubrovskii, Aleksandr M. "A. A. Zhdanov v rabote nad shkol'nym uchebnikom isto-rii." In *Otechestvennaia kul'tura i istorich-eskaia nauka XVIII-XX vekov: sbornik statei*. Briansk: BGPU, 1996, 128–43.

———. *Istorik i vlast': istoricheskaia nauka v SSSR i kontseptsiia istorii feodal'noi Rossii v kontekste politiki i ideologii (1930-1950-e gg.)*. Briansk: BGPU, 2005.

Dubrovskii, S. M. *Krest'ianskoe dvizhenie v revoliutsii 1905–1907 g.g*. Moscow: Aka-demiia nauk SSSR, 1956.

Dubrovsky, Alexander M. "Chronicle of a Po-et's Downfall: Dem'ian Bednyi, Russian History, and *The Bogatyri*." In *Epic Revi-sionism: Russian History and Literature as Stalinist Propaganda*, edited by Kevin Platt and David Brandenberger. Madison: University of Wisconsin, 2006, 77–114.

Dubynskii, I. I. "Bol'shie kievskie manevry," *Moskva*, 1967, no. 4.

Duda, Gerhard. *Jenő Varga und die Geschichte des Instituts für Weltwirtschaft und Wel-politik in Moskau 1921-1970: Zu den Möglichkeiten und Grenzen wissenschaft-licher Auslandanalyse in der Sowjetunion*. Berlin: Akademie-Verlag, 1994.

Dudnik, V., and D. Smirnov. "Vsia zhizn'—nauke," *Voenno-istoricheskii zhurnal*, 1965, no. 2: 47–57, no. 8: 118–24.

Duff, William E. *A Time for Spies: Theodore Stepanovich Mally and the Era of the Great Illegals*. Nashville: Vanderbilt University, 1999.

Duggan, Christopher. *Fascist Voices: An Inti-mate History of Mussolini's Italy*. New York: Oxford University, 2013.

Duhanovs, M., I. Feldmanis, and A. Stranga. *1939: Latvia and the Year of Fateful Deci-sions*. Riga: Latvian University, 1994.

Dülffer, Jost. *Weimar, Hitler und die Marine: Reichspolitik und Flottenbau 1920 bis 1939*. Düsseldorf: Droste, 1973.

Dullin, Sabine. "How to Wage Warfare with-out Going to War? Stalin's 1939 War in the Light of other Contemporary Aggres-sions," *Cahiers du monde russe*, 53/2–3 (2012): 221–43.

———. "La rôle de l'Allemagne dans le rap-prochement franco-soviétique, 1932–1935." In *Deutschland-Frankreich-Russland*, ed-ited by Ilya Mieck and Pierre Guillen. Mu-nich: R. Oldenbourg, 2000, 245–62.

———. "Understanding Russian and Soviet Foreign Policy from a Geocultural Per-spective," *Kritika*, 12/1 (2011): 161–81.

———. *Des hommes d'influence: Les ambassa-deurs de Stalin en Europe 1930–1939*. Paris: Payot, 2001.

———. *La frontière épaisse: aux origines des politiques soviétiques 1920-1940*. Paris: Éditions de l'École des hautes études en sciences sociales, 2014.

———. *Men of Influence: Stalin's Diplomats in Europe, 1930–1939*. Edinburgh: Edin-burgh University, 2008.

Dumbadze, Evgenii. *Na sluzhbe cheka i ko-minterna: lichnye vospominaniia*. Paris: Mishen, 1930.

Dunaevskii, V. A. "Bol'sheviki i germanskie levye na mezhdunarodnoi arene v dorev-liutsionnyi period." In *Evropa v novoe i noveishee vremia: sbornik statei*. Moscow: Nauka, 1966, 491–513.

Dunsterville, L. C. *The Adventures of Dun-sterforce*. London: Edwin Arnold, 1920.

Duraczyński, E., and A. N. Sakharov, eds. *Sovetsko-Pol'skie otnosheniia v politich-eskikh usloviakh Evropy 30-x godov XX stoletiia: sbornik statei*. Moscow: Nauka, 2001.

Durand, Mortimer. *Crazy Campaign: A Per-sonal Narrative of the Italo-Abyssinian*. London: Routledge, 1936.

Duranty, Walter. "Stalin Sees Capitalists Drifting Surely to War: Puzzled by Our Attitude," *New York Times*, Dec. 1, 1930.

———. "Stalin: Man, Mouthpiece, Machine," *New York Times*, Jan. 18, 1931.

———. *I Write as I Please*. New York: Simon & Schuster, 1935.

———. *USSR, The Story of Russia*. New York: J. B. Lippincott, 1944.

Duroselle, Jean Baptiste. *La décadence, 1932–1939*. 2nd ed. Paris: Imprimerie nationale, 1979.

———. *France and the Nazi Threat: The Collapse of French Diplomacy, 1932–1939*. New York: Enigma, 2004.

Dushen'kin, Vasilii V. *Ot soldata do marshala*. 3rd ed. Moscow: Politizdat, 1966.

———. *Proletarskii marshal: (o V. K. Bliukhere)*. Moscow: Politicheskaia literatura, 1973.

20 let sovetskoi vlasti: statisticheskii sbornik. Moscow: Partizdat, 1937.

"Dva ochaga opasnosti: vystupeniie komanduiushchego Belorusskim voennym okrugom komandarma 1 ranga I. P. Uborevicha na soveshchanii v Zapadnom obkome VLKSM v 1936 g.," *Voenno-istoricheskii zhurnal*, 1998, no. 10: 38–43."

"Dve besedy s L. M. Kaganovichem," *Novaia i noveishaia istoriia*, 1999, no. 2: 101–22.

Dvornichenko, V. V. *Nekotorye aspekty funktsionirovaniia industrii turizma*. Moscow: Vestnik, 1998.

Dvoynikh, L. V., and N. E. Elisseva, eds. *Konflikt: komplekt dokumentov o sovetskoi-finlandskoi voine (1939–1940 gg.) iz fonda Tsentral'nogo gosudartsvennogo arkhiva sovetskoi armii*. Minneapolis, MN: Eastview, 1992.

Dyck, Harvey L. *Weimar Germany and Soviet Russia, 1926–1933: A Study in Diplomatic Instability*. New York: Columbia University, 1966.

Dylykov, S. D. *Demokraticheskoe dvizhenie mongol'skogo naroda v Kitae*. Moscow: Akademiia nauk, 1953.

Dzanovich, A. A. *Organy gousdarstvennoi bezopasnosti i Krasnaia armiia*. Moscow: Kuckovo pole/Iks-Khistorii, 2008.

Dzhikhashvili, Musto. "Kavkaskie safari Stalina (Vospominaniia rodstvennika Nestora Lakoby)," Batum-Moscow, 2003. http://www.apsuara.ru/lib_d/musto_yad.php.

Dzhonua, A. N., et al., eds. *Sovety Abkhazii, 1922–1937: sbornik dokumentov i materialov*. Sukhumi: Alashara, 1976.

Dzhugashvili, Ekaterina Gavrilovna. *Moi syn Iosif Stalin*. Moscow: Algoritm, 2013.

Dzidzariia, G. A., et al., eds. *Revoliutsionnye komitety Abkhazii: Sbornik dokumentov i materialov*. Sukhumi: Abgosizdat, 1961.

———. *Efrem Eshba: biograficheskii ocherk*. Sukhumi: Alashara, 1967.

———. *Ocherki istorii Abkhazii, 1910–1921*. Tbilisi: Gosizdat sabchota sakartvelo, 1963.

Eastman, Max. "Artists in Uniform," *The Modern Monthly*, 7 (August 1933), 397–404.

———. *Artists in Uniform: A Study of Literature and Bureaucratism*. New York: Knopf, 1934.

Eberhardt, Piotr. *Ethnic Groups and Population Changes in Twentieth-Century Central-Eastern Europe: History, Data, and Analysis*. Armonk, NY: M. E. Sharpe, 2003.

Eberle, Henrik, and Matthias Uhl, eds. *The Hitler Book: The Secret Dossier Prepared for Stalin from the Interrogations of Hitler's Personal Aides*. New York: Public Affairs, 2005.

Eby, Cecil. *Comrades and Commissars: The Lincoln Battalion in the Spanish Civil War*. University Park: Pennsylvania State University, 2007.

Eden, Anthony. *Facing the Dictators: The Memoirs of Anthony Eden, Earl of Avon*. Boston: Houghton Mifflin, 1962.

———. *Foreign Affairs*. London: Faber and Faber, 1939.

Edgerton, David. *Britain's War Machine: Weapons, Resources and Experts in the Second World War*. London: Allen Lane, 2011.

Edwards, Jill. *The British Government and the Spanish Civil War, 1936–1939*. London: Macmillan, 1979.

Efimenko, A. R., et al., eds. *Vooruzhennyi konflikt v raione reki Khalkhin-Gol, mai—sentiabr' 1939 g.: dokumenty i materialy*. Moscow: Novalis, 2014.

Efimov, Boris. "Vernost' prizvaniiu." In *Bol' i pamiat'*, edited by B. S. Burkov and V. A. Miakushkov. Moscow: Respublika, 1993, 17–37.

———. *Mikhail Koltsov, kakim on byl: sbornik vosmpominanii*. 2nd ed. Moscow: Sovetskii pisatel', 1989.

Egorov, A. Ia., and V. P. Kliucharev. *Grazhdanskaia aviatsiia SSSR*. Moscow: [s.n.], 1937.

Ehrenburg, Ilya. *Memoirs: 1921–1941*. Cleveland and New York: World, 1963.

———. *Men, Years—Life*. 6 vols. London: MacGibbon and Kee, 1962–66.

———. *Post-War Years, 1945–1954*. London: MacGibbon and Kee, 1966.

Eichengreen, Barry J. *Golden Fetters: The Gold Standard and the Great Depression, 1919–1939*. New York: Oxford University, 1992.

Eideman, R. P. "K voprosu o kharaktere nachaln'nogo perioda voiny (v poriadke obsuzhdenii)," *Voina i revoliutsiia*, 1931, no. 8: 111–7.

Eisenstein, S. M. *The Film Sense*. New York: Meridian, 1958.

Eizenshtin, Sergei M. "Pered prem'eroi 'Val'kirii,'" *Vecherniaia Moskva*, Sept. 21, 1940.

———. "Samoe vazhnoe," *Izvestiia*, January 6, 1935.

———. "Tvorcheskaia vstrecha s Vagnerom," *Ogonek*, 1940, no. 29.

———. *Izbrannye proizvedeniia*. 6 vols. Moscow: Iskusstvo, 1964–1971.

Elagin, Iurii. *Ukroshchenie iskusstv*. Moscow: Russkii put, 2002.

Elleman, Bruce A. "The 1925 Secret Soviet-Japanese Agreement on Bessarabia," *Diplomacy and Statecraft*, 5/2 (1994): 287–95.

———. *International Competition in China, 1899–1991: The Rise, Fall, and Restoration of the Open Door Policy*. New York: Routledge, 2015.

———. *Moscow and the Emergence of Communist Power in China 1925–1930: The Nanchang Rising and the Birth of the Red Army*. New York: Routledge, 2009.

Elliston, H. *Finland Fights*. Boston: Little, Brown, 1940.

Ellman, Michael. "Did the Agricultural Surplus Provide Resources for the Increase in Investment during the First Five Year Plan?" *Economic Journal*, 85 (1975): 844–63.

———. "Regional Influences on the Formulation and Implementation of NKVD Order 00447," *Europe-Asia Studies*, 62/6 (2010): 915–31.

———. "Soviet Industrialization: A Remarkable Success?" *Slavic Review*, 63/4 (2004): 841–9.

———. "Soviet Repression Statistics: Some Comments," *Europe-Asia Studies*, 54/7 (2002): 1151–72.

———. "The Political Economy of Stalinism in the Light of the Archival Revolution," *Journal of Institutional Economics*, 4/1 (2008): 99–125.

———. "The Role of Leadership Perceptions and of Intent in the Soviet Famine of 1931–1934," *Europe-Asia Studies*, 57/6 (2005): 823–41.

———. "The Soviet 1937 Provincial Show Trials: Carnival or Terror," *Europe-Asia Studies*, 53/8 (2001): 1221–33.

———. "The Soviet 1937–1938 Provincial Show Trials Revisited," *Europe-Asia Studies*, 55/8 (2003): 1305–21.

———. *Socialist Planning*. 2nd ed. Cambridge, UK: Cambridge University, 1989.

El'-Registan, G. "Neobychainoe puteshestvie," *Molodaia gvardiia*, 1935, no. 10–12.

Emel'ianov, V. S. *Na porose voiny*. Moscow: Sovetskaia Rossiia, 1971.

Emets, Valentin A. "O roli russkoi armii v pervyi period mirovoi voiny, 1914–1918 gg.," *Istoricheskie zapiski*, 77 (1965): 57–84.

Emmerson, James T. *The Rhineland Crisis, 7 March 1936: A Study in Multicultural Diplomacy*. London: Maurice Temple Smith, 1977.

Engel, Gerhard. *Heeresadjutant bei Hitler 1938–1943*. Stuttgart: Deutsche Verlags-Anstalt, 1974.

Engelmann, Bernt. *In Hitler's Germany: Daily Life in the Third Reich*. New York: Pantheon Books, 1986.

Engels, Friedrich. "The Tactics of Social Democracy." In *The Marx-Engles Reader*, 2nd ed., edited by Robert C. Tucker. New York: W. W. Norton, 1978, 556–73.

———. *Herrn Eugen Dührings Unwälzung der Wissenschaft*. Moscow, 1935.

Ennker, Benno. "Struggling for Stalin's Soul: The Leader Cult and the Balance of Social Power in Stalin's Inner Circle." In *Personality Cults in Stalinism*, edited by Klaus Heller and Jan Plamper. Göttingen: V&R Unipress, 2004, 161–95.

Enteen, George. "Intellektual'nye predposylki utverzhdeniia stalinizma v sovetskoi istoriografii," *Voprosy istorii*, 1995, no. 5–6: 149–55.

———. "Marxist Historians During the Cultural Revolution: A Case Study in Professional Infighting," in *Cultural Revolution in Russia*, Sheila Fitzpatrick, ed. Bloomington: Indiana University, 1978, 154–79.

Enukidze, A. S. "Istoriia organizatsii i raboty nelegal'noi tipografii R.S.D.R.P. na Kavkaze za vremia 1900–1906 gg.," *Proletarskaia revoliutsiia*, 1923, no. 14: 152–66.

———. *Bol'shevistskie nelegal'nye tipografii*, 3rd ed. Moscow: Molodaia gvardiia, 1934.

———. *Bol'shevistskie podpo'lnye tipografii*. 2nd ed. Moscow-Leningrad: Molodaia gvardiia, 1930.

———. *Nashi podpol'nye tipografii Kavkaza*. Moscow: Novaia Moskva, 1925.

Ercoli [Togliatti], M. "Ob osobennostiakh ispanskoi revoliutsii," *Kommunisticheskii Internatsional*, 1936, no. 16: 15–22.

———. "Uroki protsessa trotskistsko-zinov'evskogo terroristicheskogo tsentra," *Kommunisticheskii Internatsional*, 1936, no. 15.

Eremenko, A. I. *V nachale voiny*. Moscow: Nauka, 1964.

Erenburg, Il'ia. "Iz literaturnogo proshlogo," *Oktiabr'*, 1988, no. 7.

———. "O moem Parizhe: iz vyskazayvanii Il'i Erenburga," *Sovetskoe foto*, 1934, no. 4–5.

———. *Dumael, Gide, Malraux, Mauriac, Morand, Romains, Unamuno: vus par un écrivain d'U.R.S.S.* Paris: Gallimard, 1934.

———. *Liudi, gody, zhizn': vospominaniia*. 2nd ed. 6 vols. Moscow: Sovetskii pisatel', 1990.

———. *Moi Parizh*. Moscow: Izogiz, 1933.

———. *No pasarán! Grazhdanskaia voina ii-ul'-dekabr' 1936 goda.* Moscow: OGIZ-IZOGIZ, 1937.

———. *Sobranie sochinenii.* 9 vols. Moscow: Khudozhestvennaia literatura, 1962–7.

Erickson, John, and Richard E. Simpkin. *Deep Battle: The Brainchild of Marshal Tukhachevskii.* London: Brassey's Defence, 1986.

———. "Rudolf Hess: A Post-Soviet Postscript." In *Flight from Reality: Rudolf Hess and His Mission to Scotland, 1941,* edited by David Stafford. London: Pimlico, 2002, 38–60.

———. "The Red Army's March into Poland, September 1939." In *The Soviet Takeover of the Polish Eastern Provinces, 1939–1941,* edited by Keith Sword. New York: Macmillan, 1991, 1–27.

———. "Threat Identification and Strategic Appraisal by the Soviet Union 1930–1941." In *Knowing One's Enemies: Intelligence Assessment before the Two World Wars,* edited by Ernest R. May. Princeton, NJ: Princeton University, 1984, 375–423.

———. *The Road to Stalingrad.* London: Weidenfeld and Nicolson, 1975.

———. *The Soviet High Command: A Military-Political History, 1918–1941.* London: Macmillan, 1962. Note: all references are to this edition unless otherwise indicated.

———. *The Soviet High Command: A Military-Political History, 1918–1941.* 3rd ed. New York: Frank Cass, 2001.

Ericson, Edward E., III. *Feeding the German Eagle: Soviet Economic Aid to Nazi Germany, 1933–1941.* Westport, CT: Praeger, 1999.

Ermakov, A. F. "A. V. Luncharskii i politika partii v oblasti iskusstva, 1917–1925 gg." In *Obogashchenie metoda sotsialisticheskogo realizma i problema mnogoobraziia sovetskogo iskusstva,* edited by Mikhal N. Parkhomenko. Moscow: Mysl', 1967, 340–83.

Ermilov, Viktor V. *Schast'e trudnykh dorog.* Moscow: Moskovskii rabochii, 1972.

Erofeev, V. I. *Diplomat: kniga vospominanii.* Moscow: Zebra E., 2005.

Esaiashvili, V. G., ed. *Ocherki istorii Kommunisticheskoi partii Gruzii.* 2 vols. Tbilisi, Izd-vo TsK KP Gruzii, 1957, 1963.

Esakov, V. D., ed. *Akademiia Nauk v resheniiakh Politbiuro TsK RKP (b)-VKP (b), 1922–1952.* Moscow: Rosspen, 2000.

Eudin, Xenia Joukoff, and Robert M. Slusser, eds. *Soviet Foreign Policy, 1928–1934: Documents and Materials.* 2 vols. University Park: Pennsylvania State University, 1966–7.

Evans, Richard J. *The Third Reich in Power, 1933–1939.* New York: Penguin, 2005.

Evdoshenko, Iu. V. "Delo neftianikov-'vreditelei' 1929–1931 gg. i sud'by nobelevskikh sluzhashchikh v SSSR: k voprosu o genezise 'ekonomicheskoi kontrrevoliutsii.'" In *Ekonomicheskaia istoriia: ezhegodnik 2013,* edited by L. I. Borodkin and Iu. A. Petrov. Moscow: Rosspen, 2014.

Fabry, Philipp W. *Der Hitler-Stalin Pakt, 1939–1941: ein Beitrag zur Methode sowjetischer Aussenpolitik.* Darmstadt: Fundus, 1966.

———. *Die Sowjetunion und das Dritte Reich: eine dokumentierte Geschichte der deutsch-sowjetischen Beziehungen von 1933 bis 1941.* Stuttgart: Seewald, 1971.

Fainsod, Merle. *How Russia Is Ruled.* Cambridge, MA: Harvard University, 1959.

———. *Smolensk under Soviet Rule.* Cambridge, MA: Harvard University, 1958.

Fakel. 2 vols. Moscow: Politicheskaia literatura, 1989–90.

Falasca-Zamponi, Simonetta. *Fascist Spectacle: The Aesthetics of Power in Mussolini's Italy.* Berkeley: University of California, 1997.

Falin, V. M., ed. *Soviet Peace Efforts on the Eve of World War II, September 1938–August 1939: Documents and Records.* 2 vols. Moscow: Novosti, 1971–73.

Farnsworth, Beatrice. "Conversing with Stalin, Surviving the Terror: The Diaries of Aleksandra Kollontai and the Internal Life of Politics," *Slavic Review,* 694 (2010): 944–70.

———. *William C. Bullitt and the Soviet Union.* Bloomington: Indiana University, 1967.

Fedenko, I. I., ed. *Kanal Moskva-Volga: spravochnik-putevoditel'.* Moscow: Vodnyi transport, 1938.

Fediuninskii, I. I., *Podniatye po trevoge.* Moscow, Voenizdat, 1961.

Fedotoff-White, D. *The Growth of the Red Army.* Princeton, NJ: Princeton University, 1944.

Fedtke, G. "How Bukharans Turned into Uzbeks and Tajiks: Soviet Nationalities Policy in the Light of a Personal Rivalry." In *Patterns of Transformation in and around Uzbekistan,* edited by P. Sartori and T. Trevisani. Reggio Emilia: Diabasis, 2007, 19–50.

Felice, Renzo de. *Mussolini.* 4 vols. Turin: Einaudi, 1965–97.

Fel'shtinskii, Iurii G. "Dva epizoda iz istorii vnutripartiinoi bor'by: konfidentsial'nye besedy Bukharina," *Voprosy istorii,* 1991, no. 2–3: 182–203.

———. *Oglasheniiu podlezhit: SSSR-Germaniia, 1939–1941.* Moscow: Terra-Knizhny klub, 2004.

———. *Razgovory s Bukharinym.* New York: Telex: 1991.

———, ed. *SSSR-Germaniia, 1939–1941 gg.: sbornik dokumentov.* 2 vols. Vilnius: Mokslas, 1989.

———, ed. *VChK-GPU: dokumenty i materialy.* Moscow: Izdatel'stvo Gumanitarnoi Literatury, 1995.

Ferarra, Marcello, and Maurizio Ferarra. *Conversando con Togliatti: Note Biografiche.* Rome: Edizioni di cultura sociale, 1953.

Ferran, Carlos Jerez, and Samuel Amago. *Unearthing Franco's Legacy: Mass Graves and the Recovery of Historical Legacy in Spain.* Notre Dame, IN: University of Notre Dame, 2010.

Fesiun, A. G., ed. *Delo Rikharda Zorge: neizvestnye dokumenty.* Moscow: Letnii sad, 2000.

Fest, Joachim C. *Hitler.* New York: Harcourt Brace Jovanovich, 1974.

———. *The Face of the Third Reich: Portraits of the Nazi Leadership.* New York: Ace Books, 1963.

Feuchtwanger, Lion. *Moscow 1937: My Visit Described for My Friends.* London: V. Gollancz, 1937.

———. *Moskva 1937: otchet o poezdke dlia moikh druzei.* Moscow: Khudozhestvennaia literatura, 1937.

Field, Frank. *Three French Writers and the Great War.* New York: Cambridge University, 1975.

Figes, Orlando. *A People's Tragedy: The Russian Revolution, 1891–1924.* London: Jonathan Cape, 1996.

Figgis, J. N., and R. V. Laurence, eds. *Historical Essays and Studies.* London: Macmillan, 1907.

Filippov, I. F. *Zapiski o "tret'em reikhe."* Moscow: Mezhdunarodnye otnosheniia, 1966.

Filov, Bogdan. *Dnevnik.* Sofia: Izdatelstvo na OF, 1986.

Filtzer, Donald. *Soviet Workers and Stalinist Industrialization: The Formation of Modern Soviet Production Relations, 1928–1941.* Armonk, NY: M. E. Sharpe, 1986.

Finney, Patrick, ed. *The Origins of the Second World War.* London: Arnold, 1997.

Firsov, F. I. "Arkhivy Kominterna i vneshniaia politika SSSR v 1939–1941 gg.," *Novaia i noveishaia istoriia,* 1992, no. 6: 12–35.

———. "Komintern: opyt, traditsii, uroki—nereshenye zadachi issledovaniia." In *Komintern: opyt, traditsii, uroki.* Moscow, 1989.

———. "Stalin i Komintern," *Voprosii istorii,* 1989, no. 8: 3–23, no. 9: 3–19.

Fischer, Ernst. *Le grande rêve socialiste: Souvenirs et réflexions.* Paris: Denoël, 1974.

Fischer, Louis. "Heart's Russian 'Famine,'" *The Nation,* March 19, 1935.

———. *Men and Politics: An Autobiography.* New York: Duell, Sloan, and Pearce, 1941.

———. *Russia's Road from Peace to War: Soviet Foreign Relations, 1917–1941.* New York: Harper & Row, 1969.

———. *The Life and Death of Stalin.* New York: Harper & Row, 1952.

———. *The Nation,* Aug. 9, 1933: 154.

Fischer, Ruth. *Stalin and German Communism: A Study in the Origins of the State Party.* Cambridge, MA: Harvard University, 1948.

Fisher, Ralph Talcott. *Pattern for Soviet Youth: A Study of the Congresses of the Komsomol, 1918–1954.* New York: Columbia University, 1959.

Fitch, Stephen D. "The Harriman Manganese Concession in the Soviet Union: Lessons for Today," *International Tax and Business Law,* 9/1 (1991).

Fitzpatrick, Sheila. "After NEP: The Fate of NEP Entrepreneurs, Small Traders, and Artisans in the 'Socialist Russia' of the 1930s," *Russian History/Histoire Russe,* 13/2–3 (1986): 187–234.

———. "Ordzhonikidze's Takeover of VSNKh: A Study of Soviet Bureaucratic Politics," *Soviet Studies,* 37/2 (1985): 153–72.

———. "Stalin and the Making of a New Elite, 1928–1939," *Slavic Review,* 38/3 (1979): 377–402.

———. *Everyday Stalinism: Ordinary Life in Extraordinary Times: Soviet Russia in the 1930s.* New York: Oxford University, 1999.

———. *Stalin's Peasants: Resistance and Survival in the Russian Village after Collectivization.* New York: Oxford University, 1996.

———. *The Cultural Front: Power and Culture in Revolutionary Russia.* Ithaca, NY: Cornell University, 1992.

Flannery, Henry W. *Assignment to Berlin.* New York: Knopf, 1942.

Fleischhauer, Ingeborg. "Der deutsch-sowjetische Grenz- und Freundschaftsvertrag vom 28. September 1939. Die deutschen Aufzeichnungen über die Verhandlungen zwischen Stalin, Molotov und Ribbentrop in Moskau," *Vierteljahreshefte für Zeitgeschichte,* 39/3 (1991): 447–70.

———. "The Molotov-Ribbentrop Pact: The German Version," *International Affairs* (August 1991): 114–29.

———, and Benajmin Pinkus. *The Soviet Germans: Past and Present.* London: C. Hurst & Co., 1986.

———. *Der Pakt: Hitler, Stalin und die Initiative der Deutsche Diplomatie, 1938–1939.* Berlin: Ullstein, 1990.

———. *Diplomatischer Widerstand gegen "Unternehmen Barbarossa": die Friedensbemühungen der Deutschen Botschaft Moskau 1939–1941.* Berlin: Ullstein, 1991.

Fleishman, L Lazar'. "O gibeli maiakovskogo kak 'literaturnom fakte': postskriptum k stat'e B. M. Gasparova," *Slavica Hierosoly-mitana,* 1979, no. 4: 126–30.

———. *Boris Pasternak v tridtsatye gody.* Jerusalem: Magnes Press, 1984.

Flores, Marcello. *L'immaginare dell'URSS.* Milan: Mondadori, 1990.

Fomin, Valerii, and Aleksandr Deriabin, eds. *Letopis' rossiiskogo kino.* 4 vols. Moscow: Materik, 2004–2015.

———. *Kino na voine: dokumenty i svidetel'stva.* Moscow: Materik, 2005.

Forbes, Andrew D. W. *Warlords and Muslims in Chinese Central Asia: A Political History of Republican Sinkiang 1911–1949.* New York: Cambridge University, 1986.

Forcade, Olivier. "Le Renseignement face à l'Allemagne au printemps 1940 et au début de la champagne de France." In *La champagne de 1940: Actes du colloque, 16 au 18 novembre 2000,* edited by Christine Levisse-Touzé. Paris: Tallandier, 2001, 126–55.

Ford, Franklin L., and Carl E. Schorske. "The Voice in the Wilderness: Robert Coulondre." In *The Diplomats, 1919–1939,* edited by Gordon A. Craig and Felix Gilbert. Princeton, NJ: Princeton University, 1953, 555–78.

Förster, Jürgen, and Ewan Mawdsley. "Hitler and Stalin in Perspective: Secret Speeches on the Eve of Barbarossa," *War in History,* 11/1 (2004): 61–103.

———. "Hitler Turns East: German War Policy in 1940 and 1941." In *From Peace to War: Germany, Soviet Russia, and the World, 1939–1941,* edited by Bernd Wegner. Providence, RI, and Oxford, UK: Berghahn, 1997, 115–33.

———. "The Dynamics of Volksgemeinschaft: The Effectiveness of the German Military Establishment in the Second World War." In *Military Effectiveness,* edited by Allan R. Millett and Williamson Murray. 3 vols. Boston: Allen, Unwin, 1988, III: 180–220.

———. "The German Military's Image of Russia." In *Russia: War, Peace and Diplomacy: Essays in Honour of John Erickson,* edited by L. Erikson and M. Erickson. London: Weidenfeld & Nicolson, 2004, 117–29.

Fowler, Mayhill. "Yiddish Theater in Soviet Ukraine: Reevaluating Ukrainian-Jewish Relations in the Arts," *Ab Imperio,* 3 (2011): 167–88.

Fox, Jo. "Propaganda and the Flight of Rudolf Hess, 1941–1945," *Journal of Modern History,* 83/1 (2011): 78–110.

"Fragmenty stenogrammy dekabr'skogo plenuma TsK VKP (b) 1936 goda," *Voprosy istorii,* 1995, no. 1: 3–22.

François-Poncet, André. *Souvenirs d'une ambassade à Berlin, Septembre 1931—Octobre 1938.* Paris: Flammarion, 1946.

Frankenstein, Robert. *Le prix du réarmement français, 1935–1939.* Paris: Publications de la Sorbonne, 1982.

Frei, Norbert. *National Socialist Rule in Germany: The Führer State 1933–1945.* Oxford: Blackwell, 1993.

Freiling, Keith. *Life of Neville Chamberlain.* London: Macmillan, 1946.

French Yellow Book: Diplomatic Documents (1938–1939). London: Hutchinson, 1940.

Freud, Sigmund. *Why War? The Correspondence between Albert Einstein and Sigmund Freud.* Chicago: Chicago Institute for Psychoanalysis, 1933.

Fridberg, I. Ia. "Gosudarstvennye zagotovki i obrazovanie khlebnykh fondov v SSSR (1920–1940-e gg.)." PhD diss. Moscow Financial Institute, 1973.

Fridenson, Patrick. "The Coming of the Assembly Line to Europe." In *The Dynamics of Science and Technology: Social Values, Technical Norms, and Scientific Criteria in the Development of Knowledge,* edited by W. Krohn et al. Dordrecht, Holland and Boston: D. Reidel, 1978.

Friedberg, Maurice. *Literary Translation in Russia: A Cultural History.* University Park: Pennsylvania State University, 1997.

Friedlander, Saul. "The Path that Led into the Abyss," *TLS,* Oct. 2, 1998.

———. *Prelude to Downfall: Hitler and the United States, 1939–41.* New York: Knopf, 1967.

Friedman, Elisha M. *Russia in Transition: A Business Man's Appraisal.* New York: Viking, 1933.

Friedman, Milton, and Anna Schwartz. *A Monetary History of the United States, 1867–1960.* Princeton, NJ: Princeton University, 1963.

Frieser, Karl-Heinz, with John T. Greenwood. *The Blitzkrieg Legend: the 1940 Campaign in the West.* Annapolis, MD: Naval Institute, 2005.

———. *Blitzkrieg-Legende: der Westfeldzug 1940.* Munich: Oldenbourg, 1996.

Friters, Gerard M. *Outer Mongolia and Its International Position.* Baltimore: Johns Hopkins University, 1949.

Fritzsche, Peter. *Germans into Nazis.* Cambridge, MA: Harvard University, 1998.

———. *Life and Death in the Third Reich.* Cambridge, MA: Belknap Press of Harvard University, 2008.

Fröhlich, Elke, ed. *Die Tagebücher von Joseph Goebbels, Teil I: Aufzeichnungen 1923–1941.* 9 vols. Munich: K. G. Saur, 1998–2005.

———. *Teil 2: Diktate.* 15 vols. Munich: K. G. Saur, 1993–96.

Fromkin, David. *In the Time of the Americans: FDR, Truman, Eisenhower, Marshall, MacArthur—The Generation that Changed America's Role in the World.* New York: Knopf, 1995.

FRUS, 1934. Volume III: The Far East, 1950.

FRUS, 1937. Volume III: The Far East, 1954.

FRUS, 1938. Volume III: The Far East, 1955.

FRUS, 1939. General, Volume I, 1956.

FRUS, 1933. Volume II: The British Commonwealth, Europe, Near East and Africa, 1949.

FRUS, 1941. Volume I: General, The Soviet Union, 1959.

FRUS, The Soviet Union, 1933–1939, 1952.

FRUS, Japan, 1931–1941: Volume II, 1943.

Fry, Michael Graham. "Agents and Structures: The British Dominions and the Munich Crisis, September 1938," *Diplomacy and Statecraft,* 10/2–3 (1999): 293–341.

Frye, Roland Mushat. "Hitler, Stalin, and Shakespeare's Macbeth: Modern Totalitarianism and Ancient Tyranny," *Proceedings of the American Philosophical Society,* 142/1 (1998): 81–109.

Fuehrer Conferences on Matters Dealing with the German Navy, 1939 to 1945. 9 vols. Washington, D.C.: U.S. Navy Department, 1946–7.

Fuglestad, Finn. "La grande famine de 1931 dans l'Ouest Nigériene," *Revue francaise d'Outre Mer,* no. 61 (1974): 18–33.

Fuller, William C., Jr. *Strategy and Power in Russia 1600–1914.* New York: Free Press, 1992.

Furer, Veniamin. *Novaia Gorlovka: zapiski partrabotnika.* Moscow: Partizdat, 1935.

Fusi, Juan Pablo. *Franco: A Biography.* New York: Harper & Row, 1987.

Gaevskii, D. "Kolkhoznoe stroitel'stvo v sisteme oborony SSSR," *Voina i revoliutsiia,* 1930, no. 3: 38–39.

Gafencu, Grigore. *Prelude to the Russian Campaign.* London: Frederick Muller, 1945.

———. *The Last Days of Europe: A Diplomatic Journey in 1939.* New Haven, CT: Yale University, 1948.

Gaister, A., and A. Levin. "O sostave sel'part-organiztsii," *Bol'shevik,* 1930, no. 9–10: 75–90.

Gal'ianov, V. N. [V. Potemkin]. "Kuda idet Pol'sha," *Bol'shevik,* 1938, no. 8: 61–8.

Galumov, Erast. *Neizvestnye "Izvestiia."* Moscow: Izvestiia, 2009.

Gamelin, Maurice. *Servir.* 3 vols. Paris: Plon, 1946–47.

Gamm, Hans-Joachim. *Der Flüsterwitz im Dritten Reich.* Munich: List, 1972.

Ganson, Nicholas. "Food Supply, Rationing and Living Standards." In *The Soviet Union at War, 1941–1945,* edited by David R. Stone. Barnsley: Pen and Sword, 2010, 69–92.

Ganzha, I. F., et al. "Ukrainskoe selo na puti k sotsializmu." In *Ocherki istorii kollektivizatsii v soiuznykh respublikakh,* edited by Viktor P. Danilov. Moscow: Gospolitizdat, 1963, 151–223.

Gareev, Makhmut A. "Ob opyte boevoi podgotovki voisk," *Voenno-istoricheskii zhurnal,* 1983, no. 4: 11–20.

———. *Neodnoznachnye stranitsy voiny: ocherki problemnykh voprosakh istorii Velikoi Otechestvennoi voiny.* Moscow: RFM, 1995.

Garrard, John Gordon. *Inside the Soviet Writers' Union.* New York: Free Press, 1990.

Garros, Veronique, et al., eds. *Intimacy and Terror: Soviet Diaries of the 1930s.* New York: Free Press, 1998.

Garver, John W. "Chiang Kai-shek's Quest for Soviet Entry into the Sino-Japanese War," *Political Science Quarterly,* 102/2 (1987): 295–316.

———. "The Origins of the Second United Front: The Comintern and the Chinese Communist Party," *China Quarterly,* 123 (1988): 29–59.

———. "The Soviet Union and the Xi'an Incident," *Australian Journal of Chinese Affairs,* 26 (1991): 145–75.

Gasiorowski, Zygmunt J. "The German-Polish Nonaggression Pact of 1934," *Journal of Central European Affairs,* 15/1 (1955): 3–29.

Gatagova, Liudmila S., ed. *Sovetskaia etnopolitika 1930–1940-e gody: sbornik dokumentov.* Moscow: Institut rossiiskoi istorii RAN, 2012.

———, et al., eds. *TsK RKP(b)—VKP(b) i natsional'nyi vopros.* 2 vols. Moscow: Rosspen, 2005.

Gates, Eleanor M. *End of the Affair: The Collapse of the Anglo-French Alliance, 1939–1940.* Berkeley: University of California, 1981.

Gates, Robert A. "German Socialism and the Crisis of 1929–33," *Central European History,* 7/4 (1974): 332–59.

Gavrilov, V. A., ed. *Voennaia razvedka informiruet: dokumenty' razvedupravleniia Krasnoi Armii, ianvar' 1939—iun' 1941 g.* Moscow: Mezhdunarodnyi fond Demokratiia, 2008.

Gazarian, Suren. "Etno ne dolzhno povtorit'sia," *Zvezda,* 1989, no. 1: 3–79, no. 2: 7–77.

———. "O Berii i sude nad Berievtsami v Gruzii," *SSSR: vnutrennye protivorechiia,* no. 6 (1982): 109–46.

Gazur, E. *Secret Assignment: The FBI's KGB General.* London: St. Ermin's, 2001.

Geduld, Harry M., and Ronald Gottesman. *Sergei Eisenstein and Upton Sinclair: The Making and Unmaking of Que Viva Mexico!* Bloomington: Indiana University, 1970.

Gefter, Mikhail A. *Iz etikh i tekh let.* Moscow: Progress, 1991.

Gehl, Jürgen. *Austria, Germany, and the Anschluss, 1931–1938.* New York: Oxford University, 1963.

Gelb, Michael. "An Early Soviet Ethnic Deportation: the Far Eastern Koreans," *Russian Review*, 54/3 (1995): 389–412.

———. "Mass Politics under Stalin: Party Purges and Labor Productivity Campaigns in Leningrad, 1928–1941," PhD diss. University of California, Los Angeles, 1987.

Gel'man, S. "Zalozhnik OGPU: snokha Maksima Gor'kogo, posledniaia liubov' Genrikha Iagody," *Nezaisimaia gazeta*, January 17, 1997.

Genis, V. L. "G. Ia. Sokol'nikov," *Voprosy istorii*, 1988, no. 12: 59–86.

———. "Upriamyi narkom s Il'inki." In *Otkryvaia novye stranitsy, Mezhdunarodnye voprosy: sobytiia i liudi*, edited by A. A. Iskenderov. Moscow: Politizdat, 1989, 213–43.

Genkina, Esfir' B. *Bor'ba za Tsaritsyn v 1918 godu*. Moscow: Politizdat pri TsK VKP (b), 1940.

Genoud, Francois, ed. *The Testament of Adolf Hitler: The Hitler-Bormann Documents, February-April 1945*. London: Cassell, 1961.

Gentile, Giovanni. "The Philosophic Basis of Fascism," *Foreign Affairs*, 6/1 (1928): 290–304.

Geoffrey Roberts, *Stalin's Wars: From World War to Cold War, 1939–1953*. New Haven, CT: Yale University, 2006.

Gerrard, Craig. *The Foreign Office and Finland: Diplomatic Sideshow*. London: Frank Cass, 2005.

Gerschenkron, Alexander. "On Dictatorship," *New York Review of Books*, June 19, 1969.

Gert Meyer, *Sozialstruktur sowjetischer Industriearbeiter Ende der zwanziger Jahre: Ergebnisse der Gewerkschaftsumfrage unter Metall-, Textil- und Bergarbeitern 1929*. Marburg: Verl. Arbeiterbewegung u. Gesellschaftswiss, 1981.

Gerwarth, Robert. *The Bismarck Myth: Weimar Germany and the Legacy of the Iron Chancellor*. Oxford: Clarendon, 2005.

Getty, J. Arch. " 'Excesses are not permitted': Mass Terror and Stalinist Governance in the Late 1930s," *Russian Review*, 61/1 (2002): 113–38.

———. "Stalin as Prime Minister." In *Stalin: A New History*, edited by Sarah Davies and James Harris. New York: Cambridge University, 2005, 83–107.

———. "State and Society under Stalin: Constitutions and Elections in the 1930s," *Slavic Review*, 50/1 (1991): 18–35.

———. *Origins of the Great Purges: The Soviet Communist Party Reconsidered, 1933–1938*. Cambridge, UK: Cambridge University, 1985.

———, and Oleg V. Naumov. *The Road to Terror: Stalin and the Self-Destruction of the Bolsheviks, 1932–1939*. New Haven, CT: Yale University, 1999.

———. *Yezhov: The Rise of Stalin's 'Iron Fist.'* New Haven, CT: Yale University, 2008.

———, and Roberta T. Manning, eds. *Stalinist Terror: New Perspectives*. New York: Cambridge University, 1993.

Geyer, Michael. "Etudes in Political History: Reichswehr, NSDAP and the Seizure of Power." In *The Nazi Machtergreifung*, edited by Peter D. Stachura. London: Allen & Unwin, 1983, 101–23.

———. "Restorative Elites, German Society, and the Nazi Pursuit of War." In *Fascist Italy and Nazi Germany: Comparisons and Contrasts*, edited by Richard Bessel. Cambridge, UK: Cambridge University, 1996, 134–64.

G. G. "Pis'ma iz SSSR: vnutri pravo-tsentristskogo bloka [March 20, 1929]," *Biulleten' oppozitsii*, no. 1–2 (1929): 15–7.

Gibbs, N. H. *Grand Strategy*. 6 vols. London: HMSO, 1956–76.

Gibbs, Philip. *Ordeal in England*. London: Heinemann, 1938.

Gibson, Hugh, ed. *The Ciano Diaries*. New York: Doubleday, 1946.

Gibson, Michael. "Chiang Kai-shek's Central Army, 1924–1938." PhD diss. George Washington University, 1985.

Gilbert, Martin. *Churchill and America*. New York: Free Press, 2005.

Gill, Graeme J. "Stalinism and Industrialization: The Nature of Stalin's Regional Support." In *Essays on Revolutionary Culture and Stalinism*, edited by John W. Strong. Columbus, OH: Slavica, 1990.

———. *The Origins of the Stalinist Political System*. New York: Cambridge University, 1990.

Gintsburg, L. I. "Massovyi golod v sochetanii s eksportom khleba v nachale 30-kh godov: po materialam 'osobykh papok' politbiuro TsK VKP(b)," *Voprosy istorii*, 1999, no. 10: 119–26.

Ginzburg, Evgeniia. *Into the Whirlwind*. London: Collins, Harvill, 1967.

———. *Within the Whirlwind*. New York: Harcourt, Brace, Jovanovich, 1981.

Ginzburg, I. S. *Vneshniaia torgovlia SSSR*. Moscow: Gos. sotsial'no-ekonomicheskoe izdatel'stvo, 1937.

Ginzburg, S. Z. "O gibeli Sergo Ordzhonikidze," *Voprosy istorii KPSS*, 1991, no. 3: 88–98.

———. *O proshlom—dlia budushchego*. Moscow: Politizdat, 1984.

Girard de Charbonnières, Guy de. *La plus evitable de toutes les guerres*. Paris: Albatros, 1985.

Girgor'ev, A. "Pavel Mif (1901–1938)," *Vidnye sovetskie kommunisty-uchastniki kitaiskoi revoliutsii*, edited by G. V. Astaf'ev. Moscow: Nauka, 1970.

"GKO postanovliaet . . . ," *Voenno-istoricheskii zhurnal*, 1992, no. 4–5: 19–23.

Glad, Betty. "Why Tyrants Go Too Far: Malignant Narcissism and Absolute Power," *Political Psychology*, 23/1 (2002): 1–37.

Gladkov, Teodor K. *Korotkov*. Moscow: Molodaia gvardiia, 2005.

———. *Kuznetsov: legenda sovetskoi razvedki*. Moscow: Veche, 2004.

———. *Nagrada za vernost'—kazn'*. Moscow: Tsentrpoligraf, 2000.

———, and Mikhail A. Smirnov. *Menzhinskii*. Moscow: Molodaia gvardiia, 1969.

Gladwyn, Lord [Gladwyn Jebb]. *The Memoirs of Lord Gladwyn*. London: Weidenfeld and Nicolson, 1972.

Glan, B. N. *Iakov Il'in: vospominaniia sovremennikov*. Moscow: Sovetskii pisatel', 1967.

Glantz, David M. *Stumbling Colossus: The Red Army on the Eve of World War*. Lawrence: University Press of Kansas, 1998.

Glassheim, Eagle. *Noble Nationalists: The Transformation of the Bohemian Aristocracy*. Cambridge, MA: Harvard University, 2005.

Glavnyi voennyi sovet RKKA, 1 marta 1938 g.–20 iiuni 1941 g.: dokumenty i materialy. Moscow: Rosspen, 2004.

Glazami inostrantsev, 1917–1932. Moscow: Gosizdat, 1932.

Gleason, Abbott. *Totalitarianism: The Inner History of the Cold War*. New York: Oxford University, 1995.

Glibert, Martin. *The Roots of Appeasement*. London: Weidenfeld and Nicolson, 1966.

Glikman, Isaak D. *Pis'ma k drugu: Dmitrii Shostakovich-Isaaku Glikmanu*. Moscow: DSCH, Kompozitor, 1993.

Glotova, Olesia A. "Andrei Aleksandrovich Zhdanov: ideologicheskaia deiatel'nost' v 1920–1940-e gg." PhD diss. Rossiiskaia akademiia gosudarstvennoi sluzhby pri prezidente RF, 2004.

Gnedin, Evgenii. *Iz istorii otnoshenii mezhdu SSSR i fashistkoi Germanii*. New York: Khronika Press, 1977.

———. *Katastrofa i vtoroe rozhdenie: Memuarnye zapiski*. Amsterdam: Fond im. Gertsena, 1977.

———. *Vykhod iz labirinta*. New York: Chalidze, 1982.

God krizisa, 1938–1939: dokumenty i materialy, 2 vols. Moscow: Politizdat, 1990.

Goebbels, Joseph. *Kommunismus ohne Maske*. Munich: Eher, 1935.

Goerlitz, Walter. *Paulus and Stalingrad: A Life of Field Marshal Friedrich Paulus*. New York: Citadel, 1963.

Gogua, Irina. "Semeinye istorii: otryvok iz dokumental'noi povesti 'Pesochnye chasy'," *Ogonek*, April 13, 1997.

Goldman, Stuart D. "The Spy Who Saved the Soviets," *HistoryNet*, July 30, 2010. http://www.historynet.com/the-spy-who-saved-the-soviets.htm.

———. *Nomonhan, 1939: The Red Army's Victory that Shaped World War II*. Annapolis, MD: Naval Institute Press, 2012.

Goldman, Wendy Z. *Terror and Democracy in the Age of Stalin: The Social Dynamics of Repression*. New York: Cambridge University, 2007.

———. *Women, the State and Revolution: Soviet Family Policy and Social Life, 1917–1930*. Cambridge, UK: Cambridge University, 1993.

Gol'dshtein, Pavel. *Tochka opory*. 2 vols. Jerusalem: Graff-Press, 1978, 1982.

Goliakov, I. T., ed. *Sbornik dokumentov po istorii ugolovnogo zakonodatel'stva SSSR i RSFSR 1917–1952 gg*. Moscow: Iuridicheskaia literatura, 1953.

Gol'man, M. I., and G. I. Slesarchuk, eds. *Sovetsko-mongol'skie otnosheniia: sbornik dokumentov, 1921–1966*. Moscow: Nauka, 1966, doc. 46–47.

"Golod 1932–1933 godov na Ukraine: svidetel'stvuiut arkhivnye dokumenty," *Pod znamenem leninizma*, 1990, no. 8: 64–86.

Golovanov, A. E. *Svoimi glazami: Zapiski komanduiushchego* Moscow: Voenizdat, 1994

Golovanov, I. "1,367 dnei iz zhizni Andreia Tupoleva," *Literaturna gazeta*, November 9, 1988.

Golovkova, Lidiia, ed. *Butovskii Poligon, 1937–1938: kniga pamiati zhertv politicheskikh repressii*. 8 vols. Moscow: Alzo, 1997–2004.

———. *Sukhanosvakia tiur'ma: spetsobekt 110*. Moscow: Vozrashchenie, 2009.

Gol'tsman, A. Z. *Upravlenie promyshlennost'iu v Germanii i v SSSR*. Moscow-Leningrad: Gosizdat, 1930.

Golubev, A. V. *"Esli mir obrushitsia na nashu Respubliku": sovetskoe obshchestvo i vneshniaia ugroza*. Moscow: Kuchkovo pole, 2008.

———, et al. *Rossiia i zapad: formirovanie vneshnepoliticheskikh stereotipov v soznanii rossiiskogo obshchestva pervoi poloviny XX veka*. Moscow: RAN, Institut Rossiiskoi Istorii, 1998.

Golubev, Sergei. "Nash tovarisch: Kim Filbi," *Krasnaia zvezda*, Aug. 9–11, 2006.

Golunskii, A. S., ed. *Istoriia zakonodatel'stva SSSR i RSFSR po ugolovnomu protsessu i organizatsii suda*. Moscow: Gosizdat, 1955.

Gorbatov, A. V. "Shkola Iakira." In *Komandarm Iakir: vospominaniia druzei i soratnikov*, edited by Petr I. Iakir. Moscow: Voenizdat, 1963.

———. *Gody i voiny*. Moscow: Voenizdat, 1965.

Gorbunov, Evgenii. "Voennaia razvedka v 1934–1939 godakh," *Svobodnaia mysl'*, 1998, no. 2: 98–109, no. 3: 54–61, no 8: 93.

———. *Stalin i GRU.* Moscow: Yauza/Eksmo, 2010.

Gorchakov, N. A. *Istoriia sovetskogo teatra.* New York: Chekhov Publishing House, 1956.

———. *Theater in Soviet Russia,* translated by E. Lehrman. New York: Columbia University, 1957.

Gorchakov, Ovidii A. "Nakanune, ili tragediia Kassandry: povest' v dokumentakh," *Nedelia,* 1998, no. 42–44.

———. *Ian Berzin—kommandarm GRU.* St. Petersburg: Neva, 2004.

Gorelik, S. M., and A. I. Malkis. *Sovetskaia torgovlia: ocherki teorii i praktiki torgovlii v SSSR.* Moscow and Leningrad: Gos. Sots.-ekonomicheskoe izdatel'stvo, 1933.

Gorelov, Ignat E. *Nikolai Bukharin.* Moscow: Moskovskii rabochii, 1988.

Gorelov, O. I. *Tsugtsvang Mikhail Tomskogo.* Moscow: Rosspen, 2001.

Goriaeva, T. M. "Zhurnalistika i tsenzura, po materialam sovetskogo radioveshchaniia 20–30-kh godov: istochnikovedcheskii aspect," *Istoriia SSSR,* 1990, no. 4: 113–23.

———. *Istoriia sovetskoi politicheskoi tsenzury: dokumenty i kommentarii.* Moscow: Rosspen, 1997.

———. *Radio Rossii: politicheskii kontrol' sovetskogo radioveshchaniia v 1920–1930-x goakh: dokumentirovannia istoriia.* Moscow: Rosspen, 2000.

———, ed. "*Velikaia kniga dnia*": *radio v SSSR, dokumenty i materialy.* Moscow: Rosspen, 2007.

Gorkii, Maxim, et al., eds. *Krakh germanskoi okkupatsii na Ukraine (po dokumentam okkupantov).* Moscow: Ogiz, Gos. Izd-vo Istoriia grazhdanskoi voiny, 1936.

Gor'kii, M., L. L. Averbakh, and S. G. Firin. *Belomorsko-Baltiiskii kanal imeni Stalina: istoriia stroitel'stva.* Moscow: Istoriia fabric i zavodov, 1934.

Gorkov, Iu. A. "Gotovil li Stalin uprezhdaiushchii udar protiv Gitlera v 1941 g.," *Novaia i noveishaia istoriia,* 1993, no. 3: 29–45.

———. *Kreml', genshtab, stavka.* Tver: TOO TK ANTEK, 1995.

———, and Iu. N. Semin. "O kharaktere voenno-operativnykh planov SSSR nakanune Velikoi Otechestvennoi voiny: novye arkhivnye dokumenty," *Novaia i noveishaia istoriia,* 1997, no. 5: 108–25.

Gorky, Maksim, et al. *Belomor: An Account of the Construction of the New Canal between the White Sea and the Baltic Sea.* New York: H. Smith and R. Haas, 1935.

———. *The White Sea Canal: Being an Account of the Construction of the New Canal between the White Seat and the Baltic Sea.* London: The National Centre for Marxist and "Left" Literature, 1935.

———. *Letters of Gorky and Andreev, 1899–1912.* New York: Columbia University, 1958.

Görlitz, Walter. *History of the German General Staff, 1657–1945.* New York: Praeger, 1953.

Gorlov, Sergei A. *Sovershenno sekretno, Moskva-Berlin 1920–1933: voenno-politicheskiie otnosheniia mezhdu SSSR i Germaniei.* Moscow: IVI RAN, 1999.

Gorodetsky, Gabriel, ed. *Stafford Cripps in Moscow 1940–1942: Diaries and Papers.* London and Portland, OR: Valentine Mitchell, 2007.

———, ed. *The Maisky Diaries: Red Ambassador to the Court of St James's 1932–1943.* New Haven, CT: Yale University, 2015.

———. "Churchill's Warning to Stalin: a Reappraisal," *Historical Journal,* 29/4 (1986): 979–90.

———. *Grand Delusion: Stalin and the German Invasion of Russia.* New Haven, CT: Yale University, 1999.

———. *Mif "Ledokola": nakanune voiny.* Moscow: Progress-Akademiia, 1995.

———. *Stafford Cripps' Mission to Moscow, 1940–42.* New York: Cambridge University, 1984.

Gorsuch, Anne. *Youth in Revolutionary Russia: Enthusiasts, Bohemians, Delinquents.* Bloomington: Indiana University, 2000.

Görtemaker, Heike B. *Eva Braun: Life with Hitler.* New York: Knopf, 2011.

Görtemaker, Manfred. "The Bizarre Mission: Rudolf Hess in Britain." In *Britain and Germany in the 20th Century,* edited by Görtemaker. New York: Berg, 2006, 75–100.

Gosudarstvennaia okhrana Rossii, 1881–2006: katalog vystavki. Moscow: Petronius, 2006.

Goutard, Adolphe. *The Battle of France, 1940.* New York: I. Washburn, 1959.

Grabar', I. "Stalin i liudi sovetskoi strane v izobrazitel'nom iskusstve," *Pravda,* Dec. 26, 1939.

Graham, Loren. *The Soviet Academy of Sciences and the Communist Party, 1927–1932.* Princeton, NJ: Princeton University, 1967.

Graziosi, Andrea. "Stalin's Anti-Worker 'Workerism' 1924–1931," *International Review of Social History,* 40/2 (1995): 223–58.

———. "The New Soviet Archival Sources: Hypotheses for a Critical Assessment," *Cahiers du monde russe,* 40/1–2 (1999): 13–64.

———. *Stalinism, Collectivization, and the Great Famine.* Cambridge, MA: Ukrainian Studies Fund, 2009.

———. *The Great Soviet Peasant War: Bolsheviks and Peasants 1917–1933.* Cambridge, MA: Harvard University, 1996.

Grdzelidze, R. K. *Mezhnatsional'noe obshchenie v razvitom sotsialisticheskom obshchestve.* Tbilisi: Izdatel'stvo Tbiliskogo gosudarstvennogo universiteta, 1980.

Grebennik, K. E. *Khasanskii dnevnik.* Vladivostok: Dal'nevost. kn. izd-vo, 1978.

Grebing, Helga. *Geschichte der deutschen Arbeiterbewegung: eine Überblick.* Munich: Nymphenburger Verlags, 1966.

Grechko, Andrei A., et al., eds. *Istoriia mirovoi voiny 1939–1945.* 12 vols. Moscow: Voenizdat, 1973–82.

Gregory, Paul R., ed. *Behind the Façade of Stalin's Command Economy: Evidence from Soviet State and Party Archives.* Stanford, CA: Hoover Institution, 2001.

———. *Politics, Murder, and Love in Stalin's Kremlin: The Story of Nikolai Bukharin and Anna Larina.* Stanford, CA: Hoover Institution, 2010.

———. *Restructuring the Soviet Economic Bureaucracy.* Cambridge, UK: Cambridge University, 1990.

———. *Russian National Income, 1885–1913.* New York: Cambridge University, 1982.

———. *Terror by Quota: State Security from Lenin to Stalin, an Archival Study.* New Haven, CT, and Stanford, CA: Yale University and Hoover Institution, 2009.

———. *The Political Economy of Stalinism.* New York: Cambridge University, 2004.

———, and Andrei Markevich. "Creating Soviet Industry: The House that Stalin Built," *Slavic Review* 61/4 (2002): 787–814.

———, and Mark Harrison. "Allocation under Dictatorship: Research in Stalin's Archives," *Journal of Economic Literature,* 43/3 (2005): 721–61.

Grew, Joseph C. *Ten Years in Japan: A Contemporary Record Drawn from the Diaries and Private and Official Papers of Joseph C. Grew, United States Ambassador to Japan, 1932–1942.* New York: Simon & Schuster, 1944.

Grigoliia, A. L. "Kratkaia istoriia kurortov Abkhazii, sovremennoe ikh sostoianie k 15–letiiu sovetizatsii Abkhazii." Unpublished manuscript, 1937.

———. *Kurortnye bogatsva Abkhazii.* Leningrad, 1934.

Grigorian, Vladimir. "Neubitie liudi." http://www.rusvera.mrezha.ru/708/l0.htm.

Grigorii Kaminskii: sbornik vospominanii. Tula: Priokskoe knizhnoe izd-vo, 1965."

"Grigorii Naumovich Kaminskii," *Voprosy istorii KPSS,* 1965, no. 11: 124–8.

Grin'ko, G. F. *The Five-Year Plan of the Soviet Union: A Political Interpretation.* London: Martin Lawrence, 1930.

Gritschneder, Otto. *"Der Führer hat Sie zum Tode verurteilt . . ." Hitlers "Röhm-Putsch": Morde vor Gericht.* Munich: C. H. Beck, 1993.

Gritsenko, Iakov I. "Chto eto bylo? K sobytiiam v Sin'tsziane v 1933–1934 gg.," *Problemy Dal'nego Vostoka,* 1990, no. 5: 79–84.

Gromov, Evgenii S. *Stalin: Iskusstvo i vlast'.* Moscow: Eksmo Algoritm, 2003.

Gromov, F. N., ed. *Tri veka Rossiiskogo Flota 1696–1996.* 3 vols. St. Petersburg: Logos, 1996.

Gromtseva, Ol'ga. *Teni izchezaiut v smol'nom: ubiistvo Kirova.* St. Petersburg: Evropeiskii dom, 2001.

Gromyko, Andrei A., and B. N. Ponomarev, eds. *Istoriia vneshnei politiki SSSR, 1917–1985.* 5th ed. 2 vols. Moscow: Nauka, 1986.

———. *Memories: From Stalin to Gorbachev.* London: Hutchinson, 1989.

———. *Pamiatnoe.* Moscow: Politizdat, 1988.

———, et al., eds. *SSSR v bor'be za mir nakanune vtoroi mirovoi voiny (sentiabr' 1938—avgust 1939 g.): dokumenty i materialy.* Moscow: Politizdat, 1971.

Gronskii, Ivan. *Iz proshlogo. Vospominaniia.* Moscow: Izvestiia, 1991.

Gross, Babette. *Willi Münzenberg: A Political Biography.* East Lansing: Michigan State University, 1974.

Gross, Jan T. "A Note on the Nature of Soviet Totalitarianism," *Soviet Studies,* 34/3 (1982): 367–76.

———. *Revolution from Abroad: The Soviet Conquest of Poland's Western Ukraine and Western Belorussia.* Princeton, NJ: Princeton University, 1988.

Gross, Stephen G. *Export Empire: German Soft Power in Southeastern Europe, 1890–1945.* New York: Cambridge University, 2015.

Grossman, Gregory. Review of *Was Stalin Really Necessary? Some Problems of Soviet Political Economy,* by Alec Nove. *Europe-Asia Studies,* 17/2 (1965): 256–60.

Groys, Boris. *The Total Art of Stalinism: Avant-Garde, Aesthetic Dictatorship, and Beyond.* Princeton, NJ: Princeton University, 1992.

Groza, I. R., and P. S. Dubenskii, eds. *Slavnym zavoevateliam Artiki.* Moscow: Sotssekgiz, 1934.

Grylev, A. N. "Nakanune i v dni Miunkhena." In *Sovetsko-chekhoslovatskie otnosheniia mezhdu dvumia voinami, 1918–1939: iz istorii gosudarstvennykh, diplomaticheskykh, ekonomicheskykh i kul'turnykh sviazei,* edited by S. I. Prasolov and P. I. Rezonov. Moscow: Nauka, 1968, 220–7.

Guderian, Heinz. *Panzer Leader.* New York: E. P. Dutton, 1952.

———. *Vospominaniia soldata.* Rostov-na-Donu: Feniks, 1998.

Guliev, Dzhamil, ed. *Azerbaidzhanskaia respublika: dokumenty i materialy 1918–1920 gg.* Baku: Elm, 1998.

Gunsburg, Jeffrey A. *Divided and Conquered: The French High Command and the Defeat of the West.* Westport, CT: Greenwood Press, 1979.

Guotao, Zhang. *Rise of the Chinese Communist Party.* 2 vols. Lawrence: University Press of Kansas, 1971–72.

Gupta, Sobhanlal Datta, ed. *The Ryutin Platform: Stalin and the Crisis of Proletarian Dictatorship: Platform of the "Union of Marxists-Leninists."* Parganas, India: Seribaan, 2010.

Gurian, Waldemar. *Bolshevism: Theory and Practice.* New York: Macmillan, 1932.

Gur'ianov, Aleksandr E., ed. *Repressii protiv poliakov i pol'skikh grazhdan.* Moscow: Zvenia, 1997.

———. *Ubity v Katyni.* Moscow: Zvenia, 2015.

Guruli, Vakhtang, and Omar Tushurashvili, eds. *Correspondence between Lavrenty Beria and Joseph Stalin (1937).* Appendix to *The Archival Bulletin* (Tbilisi), 2008, no. 3.

Gurvich, Abram S. "Vtoroe rozhdenie." In *V poiskakh geroia: literaturno-kriticheskie stat'i.* Moscow-Leningrad: Iskusstvo, 1938: 310–49.

Guseinov, E. "Ves'ma neodnoznachnyi N.M. Shvernik," *Sovetskie profsoiuzy,* 1990, no. 13–4.

Gusterin, P. V. *Sovetskaia razvedka na Blizhnem Vostoke v 1920-30-x godakh.* Saarbrücken: Lap Lambert Academic Publishing, 2014.

Gutinov, Dmitrii. "'Unichtozhit' vragov, predvaritel'no ikh obmanuv': materialy doprosa byvshego pomoshchnika General'nogo Sekretaria TsK VKP (b) Borisa Bazhanova frantzuskimi spetssluzhbami," *Istochnik,* 2001, no. 6: 31–41.

Haas, Mark L. *The Ideological Origins of Great Power Politics, 1789–1989.* Ithaca, NY: Cornell University, 2005.

Habeck, Mary R. *Storm of Steel: The Development of Armor Doctrine in Germany and the Soviet Union, 1919–1939.* Ithaca, NY: Cornell University, 2003.

Haffner, Sebastian. *The Meaning of Hitler.* Cambridge, MA: Harvard University, 1979.

Hagenloh, Paul. "'Socially Harmful Elements' and the Great Terror." In *Stalinism: New Directions,* edited by Sheila Fitzpatrick. London: Routledge, 2000, 286–308.

Haight, J. McVickar. *American Aid to France.* New York: Atheneum, 1970.

Halder, Generalobst. *Kriegstagebuch.* 3 vols. Stuttgart: W. Kohlhammer Verlag, 1961–64.

———. *The Halder Diaries: The Private War Journals of Colonel General Franz Halder,* edited by Hans-Adolf Jacobsen. 2 vols. Boulder, CO: Westview, 1976.

Hanak, H. "Sir Stafford Cripps as British Ambassador in Moscow May 1940 to June 1941," *English Historical Review,* 94/1 (1979): 48–70.

Hancock, Eleanor. "The Purge of the SA Reconsidered: 'An Old Putschist Trick'?" *Central European History,* 44/4 (2011): 669–83.

Hanfstaengl, Ernst. *Zwischen Weissem und Braunem Haus: Memoiren eines politischen Aussenseiters.* Munich: Piper Verlag, 1970.

Hardie, Frank. *The Abyssinian Crisis.* London: Batsford, 1974.

Harding, Neil. "Authority, Power and the State, 1916–1920," In *Authority, Power and Policy in the USSR: Essays Dedicated to Leonard Schapiro,* edited by T. H. Rigby et al. New York: St. Martin's, 1980, 32–56.

Harlow, John. "Harpo Marx Smuggled Stalin's Secrets in His Socks," *Sunday Times* (UK), December 22, 2001.

Harper, Glenn. *German Economic Policy in the Spanish Civil War, 1936–1939.* Paris: Mouton, 1967.

Harriman, Averell W., and Elie Abel. *Special Envoy to Churchill and Stalin.* New York: Random House, 1975.

Harris, James. "Encircled by Enemies, Stalin's Perceptions of the Capitalist World, 1918–1941," *Journal of Strategic Studies,* 30/3 (2007): 513–45.

———. "Was Stalin a Weak Dictator?" *Europe-Asia Studies,* 75/2 (2003): 375–86.

———. *The Great Urals: Regionalism and the Evolution of the Soviet System.* Ithaca, NY, and London: Cornell University, 1999.

Harris, Jonathan. "The Origins of the Conflict between Malenkov and Zhdanov, 1939–1941," *Slavic Review,* 35/2 (1976): 287–303.

Harrison, Mark, ed. *Guns and Rubles: The Defense Industry in the Stalinist State.* New Haven, CT: Yale University, 2008.

———. "National Income." In *The Economic Transformation of the Soviet Union, 1913–1945,* edited by Robert W. Davies et al. New York: Cambridge University, 1994, 38–56.

———. "Why Was NEP Abandoned?" In *The Soviet Rural Economy,* edited by Robert C. Stuart. Totowa, NJ: Rowman & Allanheld, 1984, 63–78.

———. *Accounting for War: Soviet Production, Employment, and the Defence Burden, 1940–1945.* New York: Cambridge University, 1996.

———, and N. S. Simonov. "Voenpriemka: Prices, Costs, and Quality Assurance in Defence industry." In *The Soviet Defence-Industry Complex from Stalin to Khrushchev,* edited by John Barber and Mark Harrison. London and Basingstoke: Macmillan, 2000, 223–45.

———, and Robert W. Davies, "The Soviet Military-Economic Effort during the Second Five Year Plan (1933–1937)," *Europe-Asia Studies* 49/3 (1997): 369–406.

Harrison, Richard W. *Architect of Victory: The Life and Theories of G. S. Isserson.* Jefferson, NC: McFarland, 2010.

———. *The Russian Way of War: Operational Art, 1904–1940.* Lawrence: University Press of Kansas, 2001.

Harshav, Benjamin. *The Moscow Yiddish Theater: Art on Stage in a Time of Revolution.* New Haven, CT: Yale University, 2008.

Hartmann, Christian. *Halder: Generalstabschef Hitlers 1939–1942.* Paderborn: F. Schöningh, 1991.

Hasiotis, Jr., Arthur C. *Soviet Political, Economic, and Military Involvement in Sinkiang from 1928 to 1949.* New York: Garland, 1987.

Haslam, Jonathan, *Russia's Cold War: From the October Revolution to the Fall of the Wall.* New Haven, CT: Yale University, 2011.

———. "Political Opposition to Stalin and the Origins of the Terror in Russia, 1932–1936," *Historical Journal,* 29/2 (1986).

———. "Soviet Foreign Policy, 1939–1941: Isolation and Expansion," *Soviet Union/Union Soviétique,* 18/1–3 (1991): 103–21.

———. "Soviet Russia and the Spanish Problem." In *The Origins of World War Two: The Debate Continues,* edited by Robert Boyce and Joseph A. Maiolo. New York: Palgrave Macmillan, 2003, 70–85.

———. "Soviet-German Relations and the Origin of the Second World War: The Jury Is Still Out," *Journal of Modern History,* 69/4 (December 1997): 785–97.

———. "Stalin and the German Invasion of Russia 1941: A Failure of Reasons of

State?" *International Journal,* 76/1 (2000): 133–9.

———. "We Need a Faith: E. H. Carr, 1892–1982," *History Today,* 33/8 (1983): 36–9.

———. *Soviet Foreign Policy, 1930–33: The Impact of the Depression.* New York: St. Martin's Press, 1983.

———. *The Soviet Union and the Struggle for Collective Security in Europe, 1933–1939.* New York: St. Martin's Press, 1984.

———. *The Soviet Union and the Threat from the East, 1933–41: Moscow, Tokyo, and the Prelude of the Pacific War.* Houndmills, Basingstoke: Macmillan, 1992.

Hass, Gerhart. *23 August 1939, der Hitler-Stalin Pakt: Dokumentation.* Berlin: Dietz, 1990.

Hassel, U. von. *Die Hasseltagebücher 1938–1944: Aufzeichnungen vom andern Deutschlands.* Berlin: Siedler, 1989.

Hastings, Max. *Inferno: The World at War, 1939–1945.* New York: Knopf, 2011.

———. *The Secret War: Spies, Codes and Guerrillas, 1939–45.* New York: HarperCollins, 2015.

———. *Winston's War: Churchill, 1940–1945.* New York: Knopf, 2010.

Haugen, Arne. *The Establishment of National Republics in Soviet Central Asia.* Houndmills, Basingstoke: Palgrave Macmillan, 2003.

Hauner, Milan L. "Czechoslovakia as a Military Factor in British Considerations of 1938," *Journal of Strategic Studies,* 1/2 (1978): 194–223.

———. "Stalin's Big-Fleet Program," *Naval War College Review,* 57/2 (2004): 97–120.

Hayes, Peter. "Polycracy and Policy in the Third Reich: The Case of the Economy." In *Reevaluating the Third Reich,* edited by Thomas Childers and Jane Caplan. New York: Holmes and Meier, 1993, 190–210.

Hedeler, Wladislaw. "Ezhov's Scenario for the Great Terror and the Falsified Record of the Third Moscow Show Trial." In *Stalin's Terror,* edited by Barry McLoughlin and Kevin McDermott. Houndmills, Basingstoke: Palgrave Macmillan, 2002, 34–55.

Hedin, Sven Anders. *History of the Expedition in Asia, 1917–1935.* 3 vols. Stockholm: [s.n.], 1943–45.

Hegel, Georg Wilhelm Friedrich. *Lectures on the Philosophy of History.* London: H. G. Bohn, 1857.

Hegner, H. S. *Die Reichskanzlei, 1933–1945: Anfang und Ende des Dritten Reiches.* Frankfurt am Main: Societas, 1959.

Heiden, Konrad. "Hitler's Better Half," *Foreign Affairs,* 20/1 (1941): 73–86.

———. *Adolf Hitler: eine Biographie. Das Zeitalter der Verantwortungslosigkeit.* Vol. 1. Zurich: Europaverlag, 1936.

———. *Adolf Hitler: eine Biographie. Ein Mann gegen Europa.* Vol. 2. Zurich: Europaverlag, 1937.

———. *Die Geschichte des Nationalsozialismus bis Hebst 1933: Geburt des dritten Reiches.* Zurich: Europa, 1934.

Heilbrunn, Jacob. "The New York Times and the Moscow Show Trials," *World Affairs,* 153/3 (1991): 87–101.

Heimann, Mary. *Czechoslovakia: The State that Failed.* New Haven, CT: Yale University, 2009.

Heineman, John L. *Hitler's First Foreign Minister: Constantin Freiherr von Neurath.* Berkeley: University of California, 1979.

Heizer, James L. "The Cult of Stalin, 1929–1939." PhD diss. University of Kentucky, 1977.

Hellbeck, Jochen. "Laboratories of the Soviet Self: Diaries of the Stalin Era," PhD diss. Columbia University, 1998.

———. "Writing the Self in the Time of Terror: Alexander Afinogenov's Diary of 1937." In *Self and Story in Russian History*, edited by Laura Engelstein and Stephanie Sandler. Ithaca, NY: Cornell University, 2000, 69–93.

Heller, Celia Stopnicka. *On the Edge of Destruction: Jews of Poland Between the Two World Wars*. Detroit, MI: Wayne State University, 1993.

Henderson, Nevile. *Failure of a Mission: Berlin 1937–1939*. New York: G. P. Putnam's Sons, 1940.

Henke, Josef. *England in Hitlers politischem Kalkül, 1935–1939*. Boppard am Rhein: H. Boldt, 1973.

Herbert, James D. *Paris 1937, Worlds on Exhibition*. Ithaca, NY: Cornell University, 1998.

Hernández, Jesus. *La grande trahison*. Paris: Fasquelle, 1953.

Herrick, R. V. *Soviet Naval Strategy: 50 Years of Theory and Practice*. Annapolis, MD: Naval Institute Press, 1968.

Herriot, Édouard. *Jadis*. 2 vols. Paris: Flammarion, 1948–52.

Herwarth, Hans von. *Against Two Evils*. New York: Rawson and Wade, 1981.

Hess, Ilse. *Prisoner of Peace*. London: Britons Publishing Co., 1954.

Hessler, Julie. *A Social History of Soviet Trade*. Princeton, NJ: Princeton University, 2004.

Higgins, Trumbull. *Hitler and Russia: The Third Reich in a Two-Front War, 1937–1943*. New York: Macmillan, 1960.

Hildebrand, Klaus. "Hitlers *Mein Kampf*, Propaganda oder Programm? zur Frühgeschichte der nationalsozialistischen Bewegung," *Neue Politische Literatur*, 14/1 (1969): 72–82.

———. *The Foreign Policy of the Third Reich*. Berkeley: University of California, 1973.

Hilferding, Rudolf. "Gosudarstvennyi kapitalizm ili totalitarnoe gosudarstvennoe khoziaistvo?" *Sotsialisticheskii vestnik*, April 25, 1940.

Hilger, Gustav, and Meyer, A. G. *The Incompatible Allies: A Memoir-History of German-Soviet Relations, 1918–1941*. New York: Macmillan, 1953.

Hill, Leonidas E., ed. *Die Weizsäcker-Papiere, 1933–1950*. Frankfurt am Main and Berlin: Propyläen, 1974.

Hillgruber, Andreas. "Das Russlandbild der führenden deutschen Militärs vor Beginn des Angriffs auf die Sowjetunion." In *Russland, Deutschland, Amerika*, edited by Alexander Fischer et al. Wiesbaden: Steiner, 1978, 296–310.

———. *Die Zerstörung Europas: Beiträge zur Weltkriegsepoche, 1914 bis 1945*. Frankfurt am Main and Berlin: Propyläen, 1988.

———. *Hitlers Strategie under Kriegsführung, 1940–1941*. Frankfurt am Main: Bernard and Graefe Verlag für Wehrwesen, 1965.

Hindus, Maurice. *Crisis in the Kremlin*. Garden City, NY: Doubleday, 1953.

———. *Humanity Uprooted*. New York: Jonathan Cape and Harrison Smith, 1930.

———. *Red Bread*. London: Jonathan Cape, 1931.

Hinsley, F. H., et al. *British Intelligence in the Second World War: its Influence on Strategy and Operations*. 5 vols. New York: Cambridge University, 1979–90.

———. "British Intelligence and Barbarossa." In *Barbarossa: the Axis and the Allies*, edited by John Erickson and David Dilks. Edinburgh: Edinburgh University, 1994, 43–75.

———. *British Intelligence in the Second World War: Abridged Version*. New York: Cambridge University, 1993.

Hirsch, Francine. *Empire of Nations: Ethnographic Knowledge and the Making of the Soviet Union*. Ithaca, NY: Cornell University, 2005.

History of the Communist Party of the Soviet Union (Bolsheviks), Short Course. Toronto: Francis White, 1939.

Hitler, Adolf. Untitled speech. Berlin. January 30, 1939, http://www.ushmm.org/wlc/en/media_fi.php?ModuleId=10005175&MediaId=3108.

———. *Mein Kampf*. Munich: Zentralverlag der NSDAP, 1938.

Hlevnjuk, Oleg. "Les mécanismes de la 'Grande Terreur' des années 1937–1938 au Turkménistan," *Cahiers du monde russe*, 39/1–2 (1998): 197–208.

Hochman, Jiři. *The Soviet Union and the Failure of Collective Security, 1934–1938*. Ithaca, NY: Cornell University, 1984.

Hofer, Walter. *Die Entstehung des Zweiten Weltkriegs: eine Studie über die internationalen Beziehungen im Sommer 1939*. 3rd ed. Frankfurt am Main: Fischer, 1964.

Hoffman, I. "Podgotovka Sovetskogo Soiuza k nastupatel'noi voine," *Otechestvennaia istoriia*, 1993, no. 4 : 19–31.

Hoffmann, David L. *Peasant Metropolis Social Identities in Moscow, 1929–1941*. Ithaca, NY: Cornell University, 1994.

———.*Stalinist Values : The Cultural Norms of Soviet Modernity, 1917–1941*. Ithaca, NY: Cornell University, 2003.

Hoffmann, Heinrich, ed. *Hitler in seinem Bergen*. Berlin: Zeitgeschicte, 1935.

———. *Hitler Was My Friend*. London: Burke, 1955.

Hoffmann, Peter. *Hitler's Personal Security*. New York: Da Capo Press, 2000.

Hofman, George F. "The United States' Contribution to Soviet Tank Technology," *Journal of the Royal United Services Institute for Defence Studies*, 125/1 (1980): 63–8.

Höhne, Heinz. *Die Zeit der Illusionen: Hitler und die Anfänge des Dritten Reiches, 1933–1936*. Düsseldorf: ECON Verlag, 1991.

———. *Kennwort: Direktor: die Geschichte der Roten Kapelle*. Frankfurt am Main: S. Fischer, 1970.

———. *Mordsache Röhm: Hitlers Durchbruch zur Alleinherrschaft 1933–1934*. Reinbek: Rowohlt, 1984.

Høidal, Oddvar K. *Trotsky in Norway: Exile, 1935–1937*. Dekalb: Northern Illinois University, 2013.

Holloway, David. "Barbarossa and the Bomb: Two Cases of Soviet Intelligence in World War II." In *Secret Intelligence in the European States System, 1918–1989*, edited by Jonathan A. Haslam and Karina Urbach. Stanford, CA: Stanford University, 2014, 36–80.

Holman, Brett. "The Air Panic of 1935: British Press Opinion between Disarmament and Rearmament," *Journal of Contemporary History*, 46/2 (2011): 288–307.

Holmes, Larry. *Stalin's School: Model School No. 25, 1931–1937*. Pittsburgh, PA: University of Pittsburgh, 1999.

———. *The Kremlin and the Schoolhouse: Reforming Education in Soviet Russia, 1917–1931*. Bloomington: Indiana University, 1991.

Homze, Edward L. *Arming the Luftwaffe: the Reich Air Ministry and the German Aircraft Industry, 1919–1939*. Lincoln: University of Nebraska, 1976.

Honig, Jan Willem. "Totalitarianism and Realism: Hans Morgenthau's German

Years," *Security Studies*, 5/2 (1995): 283–313.

Hooten, Edward R. *Luftwaffe at War: Blitzkrieg in the West, 1939–1940*. Vol. 2. Hersham, Surrey: Midland, 2007.

Horvath, Robert. "The Poet of the Terror: Dem'ian Bedny and Stalinist Culture," *Russian Review*, 65/1 (2006): 53–71.

Hosking, Geoffrey. *The First Socialist Society: A History of the Soviet Union from Within*. 2nd ed. Cambridge, MA: Harvard University, 1992.

Hossbach, Friedrich. *Zwischen Wehrmacht und Hitler, 1934–1938*. Wolfenbüttel: Wolfenbütteler Verlagsanstalt, 1949.

Höttl, Wilhelm. *The Secret Front: The Story of Nazi Political Espionage*. New York: Praeger, 1954.

Hounshell, D. H. *From the American System to Mass Production 1800–1932*. Baltimore: Johns Hopkins University, 1984.

Howson, Gerald. *Arms for Spain: The Untold Story of the Spanish Civil War*. London and New York: John Murray, 1998.

Hubatsch, Walther, ed. *Hitlers Weisungen für die Kriegsführung*. Frankfurt: Bernard und Graefe, 1962.

Hughes, James. "Capturing the Russian Peasantry: Stalinist Grain Procurement Policy and the Ural-Siberian Method," *Slavic Review*, 53/1 (1994): 76–103.

———. *Stalinism in a Russian Province: A Study of Collectivization and Dekulakization in Siberia*. London: Macmillan, 1996.

Hull, Cordell. *The Memoirs of Cordell Hull*. 2 vols. New York: Macmillan, 1948.

Humbert-Droz, Jules. *De Lénine à Stalin: dis ans au service de l'internationale communiste, 1921–1931*. Neuchâtel: La Baconnière, 1971.

Hunter, Holland. "Optimal Tautness in Development Planning," *Economic Development and Cultural Change*, 9/4 (1961): 561–72.

———. "Soviet Agriculture with and without Collectivization, 1928–1940," *Slavic Review*, 47/2 (1988): 203–26.

———. "The Over-Ambitious First Soviet Five-Year Plan," *Slavic Review*, 32/2 (1973): 237–57.

Hüttenberger, Peter. *Die Gauleiter: Studie zum Wandel des Machtgefüges in der NSDAP*. Stuttgart: Deutsche Verlags-Anstalt, 1969.

Iablonovskaia, Dina, and Mikhail Shul'man. *"Odesa-Tel-Aviv" i "Radio—liubov' moia."* Tel-Aviv: [s.n.], 1985.

Iakir, Petr I., and I. A. Geller, eds. *Komandarm Iakir: vospominaniia druzei i soratnikov*. Moscow: Voenizdat, 1963.

Iakov, Sergei V. *V. K. Triandafillov i voenno-politicheskoe myshlenie 1920-kh godov*. St. Petersburgh: Institut material'noi kul'tur RAN, 1992.

Iakovenko, Mira M. *Agnessa: Ustnye rasskazy Agnessy Ivanovny Mironovoi-Korol'*. Moscow: Zvenia, 1997.

Iakovlev, A. N., et al., eds. *Reabilitatsiia: politicheskie protsessy 30–50-x godov*. Moscow: Politizdat, 1991.

Iakovlev, A. S. *Tsel' zhizni: zapiski aviakonstruktora*. 2nd ed. Moscow: Politizdat, 1969.

———. *Tsel' zhizni. zapiski aviakonstruktora*. 6th ed. Moscow: Respublika, 2000.

Iakovlev, Georgii N. *Nikita Izotov*. Moscow: Molodaia gvardiia, 1989.

Iakovlev, M. M. "Soviuz kompozitorov SSSR." In *Muzykal'naia entsiklopediia*, edited by Iu. V. Keldysh. 6 vols. Moscow: Sovetskaia entsiklopediia, 1973–82. V: 232–3.

Iakupov, N. M. "Stalin i Krasnaia Armiia," *Istoriia SSSR*, 1991, no. 5, 170–5.

Iakushev, V. N. et al., eds. *Stalinskie rasstrel'nye spiski*. Moscow: Zvenia, 2002.

Iampol'skii, V. P., et al., eds. *Organy gosudarstvennoi bezopasnosti SSSR v Velikoi Otechestvennoi voine: sbornik dokumentov*. 5 vols. Moscow: Kngia i biznes, 1995–2003.

Ianvarskii o"bediennyi plenum MK i MKK, 6–10 invaria 1930 g. Moscow, 1930.

"Ia pochtu za udovol'stvie vnov' priekhat' v Moskvu': obmen poslaniiami mezhdu I. Ribbnetropom i I. V. Staliym v oktiabre 1940 g." 21), *Istochnik*, 1999, no. 1: 140–6.

Iaroslavskii, E. M. *Chego trebuet ot kommunista*. Moscow: Partizdat, 1935.

——. "K chistke partii," *Bol'shevik*, 1933, no. 7–8: 13–31.

——. "O chistke partii," *Bol'shevik*, 1933, no. 9: 1–8.

——. "Tri vstrechi," *Pravda*, Dec. 23, 1939.

Iasenskii, B. "O dvukh neudachnykh popytkakh," *Literaturnaia gazeta*, March 6, 1935.

Ierusalimskii, A. "Anglo-Germanskie protivorechiia nakanune voiny 1914–1918 godov," *Bol'shevik*, 1938, no. 15: 18–30.

Iğmen, Ali. *Speaking Soviet with an Accent: Culture and Power in Kyrgyzstan*. Pittsburgh, PA: University of Pittsburgh, 2012.

Iklé, Frank William. *German-Japanese Relations, 1935–1940: A Study of Totalitarian Diplomacy*. New York: Bookman Associates, 1956.

Ikonnikov, Sergei N. *Sozdanie i deiatel'nost' ob"edinennykh organov TSKK-RKI v 1923–1934 gg.* Moscow: Gosizdat, 1971.

Ikuhiko, Hata. "The Japanese-Soviet Confrontation, 1935–1939." In *Deterrent Diplomacy: Japan, Germany, and the USSR 1935–1940*, edited by James W. Morley. New York: Columbia University, 1976, 129–78.

Il'f, Il'ia, and Evgenii Petrov. *Odnoetazhnaia Amerika*. Moscow: Gospolitizdat, 1937.

——. "Amerikanskie fotografii," *Ogonek*, 1936, no. 11–17, no. 19–23.

——. "Slavnyi gorod Gollivud," *Pravda*, Sept. 5, 1936.

Ilič, Melanie. "The Forgotten Five Percent: Women, Political Repressions, and the Purges." In *Stalin's Terror Revisited*. Basingstoke: Palgrave Macmillan, 2006, 116–39.

——. *Women Workers in the Soviet Interwar Economy: From "Protection" to "Equality."* New York: St. Martin's Press, 1999.

Il'in, I. A. "Zapiski o politicheskom polozhenii: oktiabr' 1923 g. adresovana P. Vrangeliu," *Russkoe proshloe: istoriko-doukmental'nyi al'manakh*. St. Petersburg, 1996, vyp. 6.

Il'in, Iakov N. *Bol'sheviki dolzhny ovladet' tekhnikoi (chemu uchit' opyt stalingradskogo traktornogo)*. Moscow, 1931.

——. *Bolshoi konveier*. Moscow: Molodaia gvardiia, 1934.

——. *Liudi stalingradskogo traktornogo*. Moscow: Molodaia gvardiia, 1932.

Il'in, Nikolas, and Natal'ia Semenova. *Prodannye sokrovishcha Rossii*. Moscow: Trilistnik, 2000.

Il'inskii, Mikhail. *Narkom Iagoda*. Moscow: Veche, 2002.

Ilizarov, Boris S. "Stalin, Strikhi k portretu na fone ego biblioteki i arkhiva," *Novaia i noveishaia istoriia*, 2000, no. 3: 182–205, no. 4: 152–66.

——. *Tainaia zhizn' Stalina: po materialam ego biblioteki i arkhiva. K istoriosofii Stalinizma*. Moscow: Veche, 2003.

Ilmjärv, M. *Silent Submission: Formation of Foreign Policy of Estonia, Latvia and Lithuania: Period from Mid-1920s to Annexation in 1940*. Stockholm: Almqvist & Wicksell International 2004.

Impression of Russia, An. London: The Economist, 1930.

"Impressions of Boris Pasternak," *New Reasoner*, 4 (1958): 86–90.

Inkeles, Alex. *Public Opinion in Soviet Russia: A Study in Mass Persuasion*. Cambridge, MA: Harvard University, 1950.

Insnarov, A. S. *Baltiisko-Belomorskii vodnyi put'*. Moscow: Gostranzitizdat, 1934.

International Military Tribunal for the Far East (Tokyo: 1946–48), exhibit 193.

International Solidarity with the Spanish Republic, 1936–1939. Academy of Sciences of the USSR, 1972.

Investigation of the Ukrainian Famine 1932–1933: Report to Congress. Washington, D.C.: U.S. Government Printing Office, 1988.

Iofan, Boris. "Dvorets s"ezdov SSSR," *Planovoe khoziaistvo*, 1933, no. 7–9: 169–76.

Ioffe, A. E. *Vneshniaia politika Sovetskogo Soiuza, 1928–1932*. Moscow: Nauka, 1968.

Ioffe, Mariia. *Odna noch': povest' o pravde.* New York: Khronika, 1978.

Iremashvili, Joseph. *Stalin und die Tragödie Georgiens: Erinnerungen*. Berlin: Verfasser, 1932.

Iriye, Akira. *After Imperialism: The Search for a New Order in the Far East, 1921–1931.* Cambridge, MA: Harvard University, 1965.

Irving, David. *Göring: A Biography.* New York: Morrow, 1989.

——. *Hitler's War.* New York: Viking, 1977.

Isaev, S. "Meropriiatie KPSS po ukrepleniiiu dal'nevostochnykh rubezhei v 9131–1941," *Voenno-istoricheskii zhurnal*, 1981, no. 9: 64–9.

Iskanderov, M. S. *Ocherki istorii kommunisticheskoi partii Azerbaidzhana.* Baku: Azerbaidzhanskoe gosizdat, 1963.

——. *Iz istorii bor'by kommunisticheskoi partii Azerbaidzhana za pobedu sovetskoi vlasti.* Baku: Azerbaijanskii gosizdat, 1958.

Ismailov, Eldar. "1937: 'Great Terror' in Azerbaijan," *Caucasus Analytical Digest*, no. 22 (2010): 9–12.

——. *Istoria "bol'shogo terora" v Azerbaidzhane.* Moscow: Rosspen, 2015.

Isserson, Georgii S. "Sud'ba polkovodtsa," *Druzhba narodov*, 1988, no. 5: 179–92.

——. "Zapiski sovremennika o M. N. Tukhachevskom," *Voenno-istoricheskii zhurnal*, 1963, no. 4: 64–78.

——. *Novye formy bor'by: opyt issledovaniia sovremennykh voin.* Moscow: Voenizdat, 1940.

——. *The Evolution of Operational Art.* Fort Leavenworth, KS: Combat Studies Institute, 2013.

Istoriia industrializatsii SSSR, 1926–1941 gg.: dokumenty i materialy. Moscow: Nauka, 1969.

Istoriia Kazakhskoi SSR, 2 vols. Alma-Ata: Akademiia nauk KSSR, 1957–1959.

Istoriia Kommunisticheskoi partii Sovetskogo Soiuza. 4 vols. Moscow: Politizdat, 1971.

Istorii Sovetskikh organov gosudarstvennoi bezopasnosti. Moscow: Vysshia krasnoznamennaia shkola KGB, 1977, 234–5.

Istoriia voiny na Tikhom okeane. 5 vols. Moscow: Inostrannaia literatura, 1957–8.

Istoriia Vsesoiuznoi Kommunisticheskoi partii (bol'shevikov): kratkii kurs. Moscow: Pravda, 1938.

Istoriia zakonodatel'stva SSSR i RSFSR po ugolovnomu protsessu i organizatsii suda i porkuratury: sbornik dokumentov. Moscow: [s.n.], 1955.

Iubashian, K. N. *Akademik Iosif Orbeli, 1887–1961.* 2nd ed. Moscow: Nauka, 1986.

Iurenev, Rostislav N. Introduction to *Ivan Pyr'ev v zhizni i na ekrane: stranitsy vospominanii*, edited by G. B. Mar'iamov. Moscow: Kinotsentr, 1994.

——, ed. *Eizenshtein v vospominaniiakh sovremennikov*. Moscow: Iskusstvo, 1974.

Iurganov, Andrei. *Russkoe natsional'noe gosudarstvo: zhiznennyi mir istorikov epokhi stalinizma.* Moscow: RGGU, 2011.

Iurkevich, Lev. *U vorot Indostana.* Moscow: Federatsiia, 1932.

Iusif-Zade, Z. M., ed. *Chekisty Azerbaidzhana: dokumenty, ocherki, rasskazy.* Naku: Azerneshr, 1981.

Ivanov, Aleksei. *Aleksei Ivanov—bogatyr' opernoi stseny: dnevniki, zapisi, vospominaniia*, edited by Zoi N. Shliakhova and G. N. Gorbenko. Moscow: Golos-Press, 2004.

Ivanov, Iu. V. *Ocherki istorii rossiisko (sovetsko)-pol'skikh otnoshenii v dokumentakh 1914–1945.* Moscow: Mezhdunarodnye otnosheniia, 2014.

Ivanov, L. *Morskoe sopernichestvo imperialisticheskikh derzhav.* Moscow: Gossotsekiz, 1936.

Ivanov, S. P. *Shtab armeiskii, shtab frontovoi.* Moscow: Voenizdat, 1990.

——, ed. *Nachal'nyi period voiny.* Moscow: Voeinizdat, 1974.

Ivanov, V. A. "Operatsiia 'Byvshie liudi' v Leningrade (fevral'-mart 1935 g.)," *Novyi chasovoi* [St. Petersburg], 1997, no. 6–7: 118–20.

Ivanov, V. V. *Dnevniki.* Moscow: IMLI RAN, Nasledie, 2001.

Ivanov, Vladimir. *Neizvestnyi Polikarpov.* Moscow: Iauza-EKSMO, 2009.

Ivanova, G. M. *Gulag v sisteme totalitarnogo gosudarstva.* Moscow: Moskovskii obshchestvennyi nauchnyi fond, 1997.

Ivanov-Razumnik, R. V. *Memoirs.* New York: Oxford University, 1965.

——. *Neizdannyi Shchedrin.* Leningrad: Izd-vo pisatelei v Lenugrade, 1931.

Ivashutin, Petr I. "Dokladyvala tochno (Vospominaniia o minuvshei voine)," *Voenno-istoricheskii zhurnal*, 1990, no. 5: 55–59.

Ivinskaia, Olga. *A Captive of Time: My Years with Pasternak.* New York: Doubleday, 1978.

Ivkin, V. I., ed. *Gosudarstvennaia vlast' SSSR: vysshie organy vlasti upravleniia ikh rukovoditeli, 1923–1991 gg., Istoriko-biograficheskii spravochnik.* Moscow: Rosspen, 1999.

Ivnitskii, N. A. "Golod 1932–1933 gg.: kto vinovat? (po dokumentam 'Kremlevskogo arkhiva')." In *Holodomor 1932–1933 rr. v Ukrainy: prychyny i naslidky*, edited by Stanislav V. Kul'chyts'kyi. Kiev: Instytut istorii Ukraïny NAN Ukraïny, 1995, 43–66.

——. "Golod 1932–1933 godov: kto vinovat?" In *Golod 1932–1933 godov*, edited by Iu. N. Afanas'ev. Moscow: RGGU, 1995, 35–44.

——. "Istoriia podgotovki postanovleniia TsK VKP(b) o tempakh kollektivizatsii sel'skogo khoziaistva ot 5 ianvaria 1930 g," *Istochnikovedenie istorii sovetskogo obshchestva*, vyp. 1. Moscow: Nauka, 1964, 265–88.

——. *Golod 1932–1933 godov v SSSR: Ukraina, Kazakhstan, Severnyi Kavkaz, Povolzh'e, Tsentral'no-Chernozemnaia oblast', Zapadnaia Sibir', Ural.* Moscow: Sobranie, 2009.

——. *Kollektivizatsiia i raskulachivanie (nachalo 30-x godov).* Moscow: Magistr, 1996.

———. *Repressivanaia politika sovetskoi vlasti v derevne, 1928–1933 gg.* Moscow: Institut rossiiskoi istorii RAN, 2000.

———, and D. M. Ezerskii, eds. "Dvadtsatipiatitysiachniki i ikh rol' v kollektivizatsii sel'skogo khoziaistva v 1930 g.," *Materialy po istorii SSSR: dokumenty po istorii sovetskogo obshchestva*, vyp. 1. istorii RAN, Moscow: AN SSSR, 1955.

———. *Sud'ba raskulachennykh v SSSR.* Moscow: Sobranie, 2004.

IX Vsesoiuznyi s"ezd VLKSM: stenograficheskii otchet. Moscow, 1931.

"Izdanie proizvedenii I. V. Stalina v Sovetskom Soiuze c 7 noiabria 1917 goda na 5 marta 1953: statisticheskie tablitsii," *Sovetskaia bibliografiia:sbornik statei i materialov*, vyp. 1. Moscow: Vsesoiuznaia knizhnaia palata, 1953.

Izmozik, Valdlen S. *Zhendarmy Rosii.* St. Petersburg: Neva, 2002, 466–8.

Izotov, Nikita. *Moia zhizn', moia rabota.* Kharkov: Ukrainiskii rabochii, 1934.

"Iz neopublikovannykh dokumentov (Beseda I. Maiskogo s S. Krippsom 21 iunia 1941 g.)," *Rossiiskaia assotsiatsiia istorikov vtoroi mirovoi voiny: informatsionnyi biulleten'*, 1993, no. 1: 38–40.

"Iz vospominani: vstrecha Stalina s sovetskimi pisateliami v 1933 godu," *Istochnik*, 2003, no. 5: 55–62.

Jackel, Eberhard. *Hitler's Worldview: A Blueprint for Power.* Cambridge, MA: Harvard University, 1981.

Jackson, Angela. *British Women and the Spanish Civil War.* London: Routledge, 2002.

Jackson, Gabriel. *The Spanish Republic and the Civil War, 1931–1939.* Princeton, NJ: Princeton University, 1965.

Jackson, Julian. *The Popular Front in France: Defending Democracy, 1934–38.* New York: Cambridge University, 1988.

Jackson, Peter. "French Intelligence and Hitler's Rise to Power," *Historical Journal*, 41/3 (1998): 795–824.

———. "French Military Intelligence and Czechoslovakia, 1938," *Diplomacy and Statecraft*, 5/1 (1994): 81–106.

———. "French Strategy and the Spanish Civil War." In *Spain in an International Context*, edited by Christian Leitz and David J. Dunthorn. New York: Berghahn, 1999, 55–80.

———. "Intelligence and the End of Appeasement." In *French Foreign and Defence Policy, 1918–1940: The Decline and Fall of a Great Power*, edited by Robert Boyce. New York: Routledge, 1998, 234–60.

———. *France and the Nazi Menace: Intelligence and Policy Making, 1933–1939.* New York: Oxford University, 2000.

Jacobsen, Hans-Adolf, ed. *Dokumente zum Westfeldzug 1940.* Goettingen: Musterschmidt, 1960.

———. *Fall Gelb: Der Kampf um den deutschen Operationsplan zur Westoffensive 1940.* Wiesbaden: Franz Steiner, 1957.

———. *Nationalsozialistische Aussenpolitik, 1933–1938.* Frankfurt am Main: Alfred Metzner, 1968.

Jacobson, Jon. *When the Soviet Union Entered World Politics.* Berkeley: University of California, 1994.

Jaffe, Philipp J. *The Rise and Fall of American Communism.* New York: Horizon, 1975.

Jakobson, Max. *The Diplomacy of the Winter War: An Account of the Russo-Finnish War, 1939–1940.* Cambridge, MA: Harvard University, 1961.

Jakobson, Michael. *Origins of the Gulag: The Soviet Prison Camp System, 1917–1934.* Lexington: University of Kentucky, 1993.

Jansen, Marc, and Nikita Petrov. "Mass Terror and the Court: The Military Collegium of the USSR," *Europe-Asia Studies*, 58/4 (2006): 589–602.

———. *Stalin's Loyal Executioner: People's Commissar Nikolai Ezhov, 1893–1940.* Stanford, CA: Hoover Institution, 2002.

Jansen, Marius. *Japan and China: From War to Peace, 1894–1972.* Chicago: Rand McNally, 1975.

———. *The Making of Modern Japan.* Cambridge, MA: Belknap, 2000.

Jasiewicz, Krzysztof. *Zagłada polskich Kresów: ziemiaństwo polskie na Kresach Północno-Wschodnich Rzeczypospolitej pod okupacją sowiecką 1939–1941: studium z dziejów zagłady dawnego narodu politycznego.* Warsaw: Volumen, 1998.

Jasny, Naum. *Soviet Industrialization, 1928–1952.* Chicago: University of Chicago, 1961.

———. *The Socialized Agriculture of the USSR.* Stanford, CA: Stanford University, 1949.

———. *The Soviet Economy during the Plan Era.* Stanford, CA: Stanford University, 1951.

Jaurusch, Konrad. *The Four Power Pact, 1933.* Madison: State Historical Society of Wisconsin, 1966.

Jędrzejewicz, Wacław, ed. *Diplomat in Berlin, 1933–1939: Papers and Memoirs of Józef Lipski, Ambassador of Poland.* New York: Columbia University, 1968.

Jeffrey, Keith. *MI6: The History of the Secret Intelligence Service 1909–1949.* London: Bloomsbury, 2010.

Jelagin, Juri. *The Taming of the Arts.* New York: E. P. Dutton, 1951.

Jenkins, Brian, and Chris Millington. *France and Fascism: February 1934 and the Dynamics of Political Crisis.* London: Routledge, 2015.

Jervis, Robert. "Hypotheses on Misconceptions," *World Politics*, 20/3 (1968): 454–79.

———. "Strategic Intelligence and Effective Policy." In *Security and Intelligence: New Perspectives for the 1990s*, edited by Stuart Farson et al. London: Frank Cass, 1991, 165–81.

Joachimsthaler, Anton. *Hitlers Liste: ein Dokument persönlicher Beziehungen.* Munich: Herbig Verlag, 2003.

Joffe, Nadezhda. *Back in Time: My Life, My Fate, My Epoch.* Oak Park, MI: Labor Publications, 1995.

Johnson, Oliver. "Alternative Histories of Soviet Visual Culture," *Kritika*, 11/3 (2010), 581–608.

Johnston, Robert Harold. *New Mecca, New Babylon: Paris and the Russian Exiles, 1920–1945.* Kingston, Ontario: McGill-Queen's University, 1988.

Jonas, Michael. *Wipert von Blücher und Finnland: Alternativpolitik und Diplomatie im 'Dritten Reich.'* Dissertation. Helsinki, 2009.

Jones, David William. *The Lost Debate: German Socialist Intellectuals and Totalitarianism.* Champaign, IL: University of Chicago, 1999.

Jones, F. C. *Japan's New Order in East Asia, 1937–1945.* London: Oxford University, 1954.

Jones, Larry Eugene. "Hindenburg and the Conservative Dilemma in the 1932 Presidential Elections," *German Studies Review*, 20/2 (1997): 235–59.

———. "Nazis, Conservatives, and the Establishment of the Third Reich," *Tel Aviver Jahrbuch für Deutsche Geschichte*, 23 (1994): 41–64.

Jones, Thomas. *Lloyd George.* Cambridge, MA: Harvard University, 1951.

———. *A Diary with Letters, 1931–1950.* New York: Oxford University, 1954.

Jones, William David. "Toward a Theory of Totalitarianism: Franz Borkenau's Pareto," *Journal of the History of Ideas*, 53/3 (1992): 455–66.

Jordan, Nicole. *The Popular Front and Central Europe: The Dilemmas of French Impotence, 1918–1940.* New York: Cambridge University, 1992.

Joyce, Christopher. "The Soviet Penal System and the Great Terror." In *Stalin's Terror Revisited*, edited by Melanie Ilič. Basingstoke: Palgrave Macmillan, 2006.

Judson, Pieter. *Guardians of the Nation: Activists on the Language Frontiers of Imperial Austria.* Cambridge, MA: Harvard University, 2006.

Jukes, Geoffrey. "The Red Army and the Munich Crisis," *Journal of Contemporary History*, 26/2 (1991): 195–214.

Junge, Marc, and Rolf Binner. *Kak terror stal "bol'shym": sekretnyi prikaz No. 00447 i tekhnologiia ego ispol'neniia.* Moscow: AIRO-XX, 2003.

Junge, Mark, and Bernd Bonwetsch, eds. *Bolshevistskii poriadok v Gruzii.* 2 vols. Moscow: AIRO-XXI, 2015.

———, et al. "Operativnyi prikaz no. 00447: vyplonenie v provintsii." In *Stalinizm v sovetskoi provintsii: 1937–1938 gg.: massovaia operatistiia na osnove prikaza no. 00447*, edited by Mark Junge et al. Moscow: Rosspen, 2009.

———, Gennadii Bordiugov, and Rolf Binner. *Vertikal' bol'shogo terrora: isoiia operatsii po prikazu NKVD no. 00447.* Moscow: Novyi khronograf, 2008.

Jurkiewicz, Jarosław. *Pakt wschodni: z historii stosunków międzynarodowych w latach 1934–1935.* Warsaw: Mnisterstwo Oborony Narodowej, 1963.

Kabanen, P. "Dvoinaia igra: Sovetsko-Finliandskie peregovory 1938–1939 gg." *Rodina*, 1995, no. 12: 44–8.

Kabanov, P. A. *Stal'nye peregony.* Moscow: Voenizdat, 1973.

Kabytov, P. S. "Valerian Kuibyshev: mify i real'nost," In *Golos zemli Samarskoi: literaturno-publitsistischeskie stat'i, Andrei Kuchma.* Kuybyshev: Kuĭbyshevskoe knizhnoe izd-vo, 1990.

Kaganovich, L. M. "Tseli i zadachi politicheskikh otdelov MTS i sovkhozov," *Bol'shevik*, 1933, no. 1–2: 12–35.

Kahn, David. *The Codebreakers.* Rev. ed. New York: Scribner, 1996.

Kaiser, David E. *Economic Diplomacy and the Origins of the Second World War: Germany, Britain, France, and Eastern Europe, 1930–1939.* Princeton, NJ: Princeton University, 1980.

Kai-shek, Chiang. "A Fortnight." In *Sian: Extracts from a Diary.* Shanghai: China Publishing Company, 1937, 58–63.

———. *Soviet Russia in China: A Summing Up at Seventy.* New York: Farrar, Straus & Giroux, 1965.

Kalashnikov, Iu. S., ed. *Ocherki istorii sovetskogo kino.* 3 vols. Moscow: Iskusstvo, 1956–61.

Kalashnikov, K. A., et al., eds. *Krasnaia Armiia v iiune 1941 goda: statisticheskii sbornik.* Novosibirsk: Sibirskii khronograf, 2003.

Kale, Verna. "The Fifth Column: A Play by Ernest Hemingway," *The Hemingway Review*, 27/2 (2008): 131–4.

Kaliagin, A. Ia. *Po neznakomym dorogam: zapiski voennogo sovetnika v Kitae.* 2nd ed. Moscow: Nauka, 1979.

Kalinin, M. I. *Sotsialisticheskaia rekonstruktsiia sel'skogo khoziaistva.* Moscow: Partizdat, 1934.

Kamenev, Lev B. "Predislovie." In *Sochineniia*, edited by N. Makiavelli. Moscow-Leningrad: Academia, 1934.

——. *Chernyshevskii.* Moscow: Zhurnal'no-gazetnoe ob"edinenie, 1933.

Kamov, Boris. "Smert' Nikolaia Ezhova," *Iunost'*, 1993, no. 8: 41–3.

Kanel', Nadezhda V. "Vstrecha na lubianke," In *Dodnes' tiagoteet*, edited by S. S. Vilenskii. Vyp. 1. Moscow: Sovetskii pisatel', 1989, 495–9.

Kangas, Roger. "Faizulla Khodzhaev: National Communism in Bukhara and Soviet Uzbekistan, 1896–1938," PhD diss. Indiana University, 1991.

Kanivez, Muza V. "Moia zhizn' s Raskol'nikovym," *Minuvshee*, vyp. 7, 1992, 58–111.

Kantor, Iulia. *Voina i mir Mikhaila Tukhachevskogo.* Moscow: Vremia, 2005.

——. *Zakliataia drzuhba: sekretnoe sotrudnichestvo SSSR i Germanii v 1920–1930-e gody.* Moscow: Piter, 2009.

Kaplan, Temma. *Red City, Blue Period: Social Movements in Picasso's Barcelona.* Berkeley: University of California, 1992.

Kaplonski, Christopher. "Prelude to Violence: Show Trials and State Power in 1930s Mongolia," *American Ethnologist*, 35/2 (2008): 321–37.

Karaev, Ali G. *Iz nedavnego proshlogo: materialy k istorii Azerbaidzhanskoi kommunisticheskoi partii (b).* Baku: Bakinskii rabochii, 1926.

Karmen, Roman. *No Pasaran!* Moscow: Sovetskaia Rossiia, 1972.

Karnitskii, Dmitrii A. *Ugolovnyi kodeks RSFSR.* Moscow: Sovetskoe zakonodatel'stvo, 1934.

Karpov, I. *Aviatsiia strany sotsializma.* Leningrad: Gazetno-zhurnal'noe i knizhnoe izd-vo Leningradskogo Soveta PK i KD, 1939.

Karpov, V. "Vo glave komiteta informatsii," *Voiskoe bratstvo*, special edition, 2005.

Karski, Jan. *The Great Powers and Poland: From Versailles to Yalta.* Lanham, MD: Rowman and Littlefield, 2014.

Kartunova, Anastasia I. *V. K. Bliukher v Kitae, 1924–1927: dokumentirovannyi ocherk, dokumenty.* Moscow: Nauka, 1979.

Kaslas, B. J. "The Lithuanian Strip in Soviet-German Secret Diplomacy, 1939–1941," *Journal of Baltic Studies*, 4/3 (1973): 204–19.

Kassow, Samuel. "Trotsky and the Bulletin of the Opposition," *Studies in Comparative Communism*, 10/1–2 (1977): 184–97.

Kassymbekova, and Christian Teichman, "The Red Man's Burden: Soviet European Officials in Central Asia in the 1920s and 30s." In *Helpless Imperialists: Imperial Failure, Fear, and Radicalization*, edited by Maurus Reinkowski and Gregor Thum. Gottingen: Vandenhoeck & Ruprecht, 2013.

Kasza, Gregory. *The Conscription Society: Administered Mass Organizations.* New Haven, CT: Yale University, 1995.

Kataev, Valentin. "Lenin v 1918 godu," *Pravda*, March 3, 1939.

——. "Mariia Demchenko." In *V budniakh velikikh stroek: zhenshchiny-kommunistki geroini pervykh piatiletok*, edited by L. I. Stishova. Moscow: Politicheskaia literatura, 1986.

——. "Sobytie nebyvaloe," *Novyi mir*, 1984, no. 5.

Katanian, V. A. "Ne tol'ko vospominaniia: k istorii izdaniia Maiakovskogo," *Druzhba narodov*, 1989, no. 3: 220–7.

Katsman, R. "Cheliuskin," *Sovetskoe kino*, 1935, no. 8–9: 35–46.

Katz, Barbara G. "Purges and Production: Soviet Economic Growth, 1928–1940," *Journal of Economic History*, 35/3 (1975): 567–90.

Katz, Daniel. "The Public Opinion Polls and the 1940 Election," *Public Opinion Quarterly*, 5/1 (1941): 52–78.

Katzenellenbaum, S. S. *Russian Currency and Banking, 1914–1924.* London: P. S. King, 1925.

Kaufman, Peter B. "Soviet Attitudes towards Collective Security in Europe, 1936–38," *Russian History*, 15/2–4 (1988): 427–44.

Kazakov, M. I. *Nad kartoi bylykh srazhenii.* 2nd ed. Moscow: Voenizdat, 1971.

Kazemzadeh, Firuz. *The Struggle for Transcaucasia, 1917–1921.* New York: Philosophical Library, 1951.

Kebbel, T. E., ed. *Selected Speeches of the Late Right Honorable the Earl of Beaconsfield.* London: Longmans, Green and Co., 1889.

Kedrov, Nikolai. *Lapti Stalinizma: politicheskoe soznanie krest'ianstva russkogo Severa v 1930-e gody.* Moscow: Rosspen, 2013.

Kegel, Gerhard. *V buriakh nashego veka: zapiski razvedchika-antifashista.* Moscow: Politicheskaia literatura, 1987.

Keldysh, V. A., ed. *Neizvestnyi Gor'kii (k 125-letiiu so dnia rozhdeniia).* Moscow: Naslede, 1994.

Kelly, Catriona. *Comrade Pavlik: The Rise and Fall of a Soviet Boy Hero.* London: Granta Books, 2005.

Kemp-Welch, A. *Stalin and the Literary Intelligentsia, 1918–1939.* Houndmills, Basingstoke: Macmillan, 1991.

Ken, Oleg. " 'Moia otsenka byla slyshkom rezkoi'. I. V. Stalin i rekonstruktsii RKKA, 1930–1932 gg.," *Istoricheskii arkhiv*, 1998, no. 5–6: 147–52.

——. " 'Rabota po istorii' i strategiia avtoritarizma, 1935–1937 gg." In *Lichnost' i vlast v istorii Rossii v XIX-XX vv.*, edited by A. N. Tsamutali. St. Petersburg: Nestor, 1997, 108–16.

——. "Karl Radek i Biuro Mezhdunarodnoi Informatsii TsK VKP(b), 1932–1934 gg.," *Cahiers du monde russe*, 44/1 (2003): 135–78.

——. *Collective Security or Isolation: Soviet Foreign Policy and Poland, 1930–1935.* St. Petersburg: Evropeiskii dom, 1996.

——. *Mobilizatsionnoe planirovanie i politicheskie resheniia: konets 1920-serdina 1930-x gg.* St. Petersburg: Evropeiskii universitet, 2002.

——. *Moskva i pakt o nenapadenii s Pol'shei, 1930–1932 gg.* St. Petersburg: PIIAF RAN, 2003.

——, and Aleksandr Rusapov. *Politbiuro TsK VKP (b) i otnosheniia SSSR s zapadnymi sosednimi gosudasrtvami (konets 1920–1930-kh gg.): problemy, dokumenty, opyt kommentariia.* St. Petersburg: Evropeiskii dom, 2000.

——. *Zapadnoe priganich'e: politbiuro TsK VKP (b) i otnosheniii SSSSR s zapadnymi sosednimi gosudarstvami, 1928–1934.* Moscow: Algoritm, 2014.

——, et al. *Shvetsiia v politike Moskvy 1930–1950e gody.* Moscow: Rosspen, 2005.

Kenez, Peter. "The Picture of the Enemy in Stalinist Films." In *Insiders and Outsiders in Russian Cinema*, edited by Stephen M. Norris and Zara M. Torlone. Bloomington: Indiana University, 2008, 96–112.

——. *Cinema and Soviet Society from the Revolution to the Death of the Stalin.* London and New York: I. B. Tauris, 2001.

——. *The Birth of the Propaganda State: Social Methods of Mass Mobilization,* 1917–1929. New York: Cambridge University, 1985.

Kennan, George F. *At a Century's Ending: Reflections, 1982–1995.* New York: W. W. Norton, 1996.

——. "The War Problem of the Soviet Union" (1935), in *The Soviet Union and the Failure of Collective Security, 1934–1938*, by Jiři Hochman, 176–83.

——. *From Prague after Munich: Diplomatic Papers, 1938–1940.* Princeton, NJ: Princeton University, 1968.

——. *Memoirs, 1925–1950.* Boston: Little, Brown, 1967.

——. *Memoirs, 1950–1963.* Boston: Little, Brown, 1972.

——. *Russia and the West under Lenin and Stalin.* Boston: Little, Brown, 1961.

Kennedy, A. L. *Old Diplomacy and New, 1876–1922, From Salisbury to Lloyd George.* London: John Murray, 1922.

Kennedy, David. "The Move to Institutions," *Cardozo Law Review*, 8/5 (1987): 841–988.

Kennedy, Paul M. "The Tradition of Appeasement in British Foreign Policy, 1865–1939," *British Journal of International Studies*, 2/3 (1976): 195–215.

Kennel, Ruth. "The New Innocents Abroad," *American Mercury*, XVII (May 1929): 10–8.

Keohane, R. O. "Lilliputians' Dilemmas: Small States in International Politics," *International Organization*, 23/2 (1969): 291–310.

Kepley, Jr., Vance. "The First Perestroika: Soviet Cinema under the First Five-Year Plan," *Cinema Journal*, no. 35 (1996): 31–53.

Kern, Gary. *A Death in Washington: Walter G. Krivitsky and the Stalin Terror.* New York: Enigma Books, 2004.

Kerrl, Hanss, ed. *Nürnberg 1936: Der Parteitag der Ehre.* Berlin: C. A. Weller, 1936.

Kershaw, Ian. " 'Working Toward the Führer': Reflections on the Nature of the Hitler Dictatorship," *Contemporary European History*, 2/2 (1993): 103–18.

——. "Hitler and the Uniqueness of Nazism," *Journal of Contemporary History*, 39/2 (2004): 239–54.

——. *Fateful Choices: Ten Decisions that Changed the World, 1940–1941.* London: Allen Lane, 2007.

——. *Hitler: 1889–1936: Hubris.* New York: Longman, 1998.

——. *Hitler: 1936–1945: Nemesis.* New York: W. W. Norton, 2001.

——. *Making Friends with Hitler: Lord Londonderry, the Nazis, and the Road to War.* London: Allen Lane, 2004.

——. *The "Hitler Myth": Image and Reality in the Third Reich.* New York: Oxford University, 1987.

——. *The Nazi Dictatorship: Problems and Perspectives of Interpretation.* 4th ed. New York: Oxford University, 2000.

——. *The Nazi Dictatorship: Problems and Perspectives.* London and Baltimore, MD: Edward Arnold, 1985.

——. "Working towards the Führer." In *Stalinism and Nazism: Dictatorships in Comparison*, edited by Ian Kershaw and Moshe Lewin. New York: Cambridge University, 1997, 88–106.

Kessler, Gijs. "The Passport System and State Controls over Population Flows in the Soviet Union, 1932–1940," *Cahiers du monde russe*, 42/2–4 (2001): 477–504.

Kessler, Harry Graf. *Tagebücher, 1918–1937.* Frankfurt: Insel-Verlag, 1961.

Kettenacker, Lothar. "Mishandling a Spectacular Event: the Rudolf Hess Affair." In *Flight from Reality: Rudolf Hess and His*

Mission to Scotland, 1941, edited by David Stafford. London: Pimlico, 2002, 19–38.

Khalkhin Gol: piat'desiat let spustia (Materialy 'kruglogo stola' istorikov Sovetskogo Soiuza, Mongolii i Iaponii). Moscow: Institut voennoi istorii Ministerstva oborony SSSR, 1989.

Khanin, G. I. *Ekonomicheskaia istoriia Rossii v novesishee vremia.* 2 vols. Novosibirsk: NGTU, 2003.

Khaustov, Vladimir N. "Deiatel'nost' organov gosudarstvennoi bezopasnosti NKVD SSSR, 1934–1941 gg." PhD diss. Akademiia federal'noi sluzhby bezopasnosti, 1997.

———. "Razvitie sovetskikh organov gosudarstvennoi bezopasnosti: 1917–1953 gg.," *Cahiers du monde russe,* 42/2–4 (2001): 357–74.

———, et al., eds. *Glazami razvedki, SSSR i Evropa 1919–1938: sbornik dokumentov.* Moscow: Istoricheskaia literatura, 2015.

———, eds. *Lubianka: Stalin i glavnoe upravlenie gosudarstvennoi bezopasnosti NKVD, 1937–1938.* Moscow: Materik, 2004.

———, eds. *Lubianka: Stalin i NKVD–NKGB–GUKR 'Smersh', 1939—mart 1946.* Moscow: Materik, 2006.

———, eds. *Lubianka: Stalin i VChK-GPU-OGPU-NKVD, ianvar' 1922–dekabr' 1936.* Moscow: Mezhdunarodnyi fond Demokratiia, 2003.

———, and Lennart Samuelson. *Stalin, NKVD i repressii 1936–1938 gg.* Moscow: Rosspen, 2009.

Khisamutdinov, Amir. *The Russian Far East: Historical Essays.* Honolulu: Center for Russia in Asia, 1993.

Khlevniuk, Oleg V. "26 iiunia 1940 goda: Illiuzii i real'nosti administriovaniia," *Kommunist,* 1989, no. 9: 86–96.

———. "Economic Officials in the Great Terror, 1939–1938." In *Stalin's Terror Revisited,* edited by Melanie Ilič. Basingstoke: Palgrave Macmillan, 2006, 38–67.

———. "Les mécanismes de la Grande Terreur au Turkmenistan," *Cahiers du monde russe,* 39/1–2 (1998): 197–208.

———. "Letters to Stalin: Practices of Selection and Reaction," *Cahiers du monde russe,* 56/2–3 (2015): 327–44.

———. "Party and NKVD: Power Relationships in the Years of the Great Terror." In *Stalin's Terror,* edited by Barry McLoughlin and Kevin McDermott. Basingstoke: Palgrave Macmillan, 2002, 21–33.

———. "Prichiny 'bol'shogo terrora': Vneshnepolitcheskii aspekt." Unpublished manuscript delivered at a conference at Cortona, Italy, 1997.

———. "Stalin as Dictator: The Personalization of Power." In *Stalin: A New History,* edited by Sarah Davies and James Harris. New York: Cambridge University, 2005.

———. "Stalin, Syrtsov, Lominadze: Preparations for the 'Second Great Breakthrough'." In *The Lost Politburo Transcripts: From Collective Rule to Stalin's Dictatorship,* edited by Paul R. Gregory and Norman Naimark. New Haven, CT: Yale University, 2008, 78–96.

———. "The Objectives of the Great Terror, 1937–1938." In *Soviet History, 1917–1953: Essays in Honour of R. W. Davies,* edited by Julian Cooper et al. New York: St. Martin's Press, 1995, 158–76.

———. "The Reasons for the 'Great Terror': The Foreign Policy Aspect." In *Russia in the Age of Wars, 1914–1945,* edited by Silvio Pons and A. Romano. Milan: Feltrinelli, 2000, 159–69.

———. "The Stalinist 'Party Generals'." In *Centre-Local Relations in the Stalinist State, 1928–1941,* edited by E. A. Rees.

New York: Palgrave Macmillan, 2002, 37–64.

———. *1937–i: Stalin, NKVD, i sovetskoe obshchestvo.* Moscow: Respublika, 1992.

———. *In Stalin's Shadow: The Career of "Sergo" Ordzhonikidze.* Armonk, NY: M. E. Sharpe, 1995.

———. *Khoziain: Stalin i utverzhdenie stalinskoi diktatury.* Moscow: Rosspen, 2010.

———. *Master of the House: Stalin and His Inner Circle.* New Haven, CT, and Stanford, CA: Yale University and the Hoover Institution, 2009.

———. *Politbiuro: mekhanizmy politcheskoi vlasti v 30-e gody.* Moscow: Rosspen, 1996.

———. *Stalin i Ordzhonikidze: konflikty v politbiuro v 30-e gody.* Moscow: Izdatel'skii tsentr Rossia molodaia, 1993.

———. *Stalin: zhizn' ondogo vozhdia: biografiia.* Moscow: Corpus, 2015.

———. *The History of the Gulag: From Collectivization to the Great Terror.* New Haven, CT: Yale University, 2004.

———, et al., eds. *Stalin i Kaganovich: perepiska, 1931–1936.* Moscow: Rosspen, 2001.

———, eds. *Stalinskoe politbiuro v 30-e gody: sbornik dokumentov.* Moscow: AIRO-XX, 1995.

———, Paul Gregory, and Aleksandr Vatlin, eds. *Stenogrammy zasedanii politbiuro TsK RKP (b), 1923–1938.* 3 vols. Moscow: Rosspen, 2007.

———, and R. W. Davies, "The End of Rationing in the Soviet Union, 1934–1935," *Europe-Asia Studies,* 51/4 (1999): 557–609.

Khlusov, M. I., ed. *Ekonomika gulaga i ee rol' v razvitii strany, 1930-e gody: sbornik dokumentov.* Moscow: Institut rossiiskoi istorii RAN, 1998.

"'Khochetsia prokliast' den' i chas moego znakomstva s Beriia,'" *Istochnik,* 2002, no. 4: 90–109.

Khodasevich, Valentina. *Portrety slovami: ocherki.* Moscow: Galart, 1995.

Khodorov, I. "Natsional'noe razmezhevanie Srednei Azii," *Novyi Vostok,* 1926, no. 8–9.

Khorseev, K. I. "VVS v germane-pol'skoi voine," *Voennaia mysl',* 1940, no. 7: 28–44.

Khristoforov, Igor A. *Aristokraticheskaia oppozitsiia Veilkim reformam (konets 1850—serdenia 1870-kh gg.* Moscow: Russkoe slovo, 2002.

Khristoforov, V. S., et al., eds. *Zimniaia voina 1939–1940 gg. issledovaniia, dokumenty, kommentarii.* Moscow: Akademkniga, 2009.

Khromov, S. S. *Po stranitsam lichnogo arkhiva Stalina.* Moscow: Moskovskii gos. Universitet, 2009.

Khrushchev, Nikita. "O kul'te lichnosti i ego posledstviiakh," *Izvestiia TsK KPSS,* 1989, no. 3: 128–70.

———. "Vospominaniia," *Ogonek,* 1989, no. 36.

———. *Khrushchev Remembers.* Boston: Little, Brown, 1970.

———. *Memoirs of Nikita Khrushchev.* 4 vols. University Park: Pennsylvania State University, 2004–7.

———. *Vospominaniia: izbrannye fragmenti.* Moscow: Vagrius, 1997.

———. *Vremia, liudi, vlast': vosponinaniia.* 4 vols. Moscow: Novosti, 1999.

Kiaer, Christina. "Was Socialist Realism Forced Labor? The Case of Aleksandr Deneika in the 1930s," *Oxford Art Journal,* 28/3 (2005): 321–45.

———. *Imagine No Possessions: The Socialist Objects of Russian Constructivism.* Cambridge, MA: MIT, 2005.

Kievskii Krasnoznamenyi: istoriia Krasnoznamenskogo kievskogo voennogo

okruga, 1991–1972. Moscow: Voenizdat, 1974.

Kiknadze, A. "Gerkhard Kegel'." In *Liudi molchalivogo podviga: Sbornik ocherkov.* Vol 2. Moscow: Politizdat, 1987, 111–27.

Kimball, Warren E. "The Hess Distraction: A Footnote from America." In *Flight From Reality: Rudolf Hess and His Mission to Scotland, 1941,* edited by David Stafford. London: Pimlico, 2002, 61–77.

———, ed. *Churchill and Roosevelt: The Complete Correspondence.* 3 vols. Princeton, NJ: Princeton University, 1984.

Kinch, Nils. "The Road from Dreams of Mass Production to Flexible Specialization: American Influences on the Development of the Swedish Automobile Industry, 1920–1939." In *Fordism Transformed: The Development of Production Methods in the Automobile Industry,* edited by Haruhito Shiomi and Kazuo Wada. Oxford: Oxford University, 1995, 107–36.

Kindleberger, Charles P. *The World in Depression, 1929–1939.* Berkeley and Los Angeles: University of California, 1973.

King, F., and G. Matthews, eds. *About Turn: The British Communist Party and the Second World War.* London: Lawrence Wishart, 1990.

Kingston-Mann, Esther. *In Search of the True West: Culture, Economics, and Problems of Russian Development.* Princeton, NJ: Princeton University, 1999.

Kirby, David. "The Baltic States, 1940–1950." In *Communist Power in Europe, 1944–1949,* edited by Martin McCauley. London: Macmillan, 1977, 22–35.

———. *A Concise History of Finland.* Cambridge, UK: Cambridge University, 2006.

Kirchmayer, Jerzy. *1939 i 1944 Kilka Zagadnień Polskich.* Warsaw: Książka i Wiedza, 1956.

Kir'ianov, E. A. "Kollektivizatsiia tsentra Rossii (1929–1937 gg.)," *Otechestvennaia istoriia,* 2006, no. 5: 74–85.

Kirilina, Alla A. "Vstrely v Smol'nom," *Rodina,* 1989, no. 1.

———. *Neizvestnyi Kirov.* Moscow: Olma, 2001.

———. *Rikoshet, ili, Skol'ko chelovek bylo ubito vystrelom v Smol'nom.* St. Petersburg: Ob-vo "Znanie" Rossii, Sankt-Peterburgskaia organizatsiia, 1993.

Kirov, Sergei M. *Izbrannye stat'i rechi, 1912–1934.* Moscow: Politicheskaia literatura, 1957.

Kirpichenko, V. A. *Razvedka: litsa i lichnosti.* Moscow: Geiia, 1998.

Kirpotin, V. Ia. *Rovesnik zheleznogo veka: memuarnaia kniga.* Moscow: Zakharov, 2006.

Kirschenbaum, Lisa A. "Exile, Gender, and Communist Self-Fashioning: Dolores Ibárruri (La Pasionaria) in the Soviet Union," *Slavic Review,* 71/3 (2012): 566–89.

Kirsher, L. A., and N. K. Novikov. *Kanun i nachalo voiny: dokumenty i materialy.* Leningrad: Lenizdat, 1991.

Kiselev, A. F., and E. M. Shchagin, eds. *Khrestomatiia po otechestvennoi istorii, 1914–1945 gg.* Moscow: Gumanitarnyi izdatel'skii tsentr VLADOS, 1996.

Kiselev, A. S., ed. *Admiral Kuznetsov: Moskva v zhizni i sud'be flotovodtsa.* Moscow: Mosgorarkhiv, 2000.

Kiselev, V. N. "Upriamye fakty nachala voiny," *Voenno-istoricheskii zhurnal,* 1992, no. 2: 14–22.

Kissinger, Henry. *Diplomacy.* New York: Touchstone, 1994.

Klebanov, I. I., et al., eds. *Istoriia sozdaniia oboronno-promyshlennogo kompleksa Rossii i SSSR, 1900–1963: dokumenty i materialy*. Moscow: Novyi kronograf, 2004.

Klein, Wolfgang, ed. *Paris 1935: erster Internationaler Schriftstellerkongreß zur Verteidigung der Kultur, Reden und Dokumente*. Berlin: Akademie, 1982.

Klid, Bohdan, and Alexander J. Motyl, eds. *The Holodomor Reader: A Sourcebook on the Famine of 1932–1933 in Ukraine*. Edmonton and Toronto: Canadian Institute of Ukrainian Studies, 2012.

Klukowski, Zygmunt. *Diary from the Years of Occupation, 1939–1944*. Urbana and Chicago: University of Illinois, 1993.

Kniaz'kov, A. S., et al., eds. *Voennyi sovet pri narodnom komissare oborony SSSR, dekabr' 1934 g.: dokumenty i materialy*. Moscow: Rosspen, 2007.

Knickerbocker, H. R. "Stalin Mystery Man Even to His Mother," *New York Evening Post*, Dec. 1, 1930.

Knight, Amy. *Beria: Stalin's First Lieutenant*. Princeton, NJ: Princeton University, 1993.

——. *Who Killed Kirov? The Kremlin's Greatest Mystery*. New York: Hill and Wang, 1999.

Knightley, Phillip. *The Master Spy: The Story of Kim Philby*. New York: Knopf, 1988.

Knox, Alfred. "General Kuropatkin," *Slavonic Review*, 4/1 (1925): 164–8.

Koch, Stephen. *Double Lives: Stalin, Willi Muenzenberg and the Seduction of the Intellectuals*. Rev. ed. New York: Enigma, 2004.

Kochan, Lionel. *Russia and the Weimar Republic*. Cambridge, UK: Bowes and Bowes, 1954.

Kochik, Valerii. "Sovetskaia voennaia razvedka: struktura i kadry," *Svobodnaia mysl'*, 1998, no. 5: 94–104, no. 6: 88–103, no. 7: 97–109, no. 8: 68–94, no. 9–12: 98–117.

Kochin, Nikolai. *Spelye kolos'ia: nizhegorodskie byli*. Nizhny Novgorod: Knigi, 2001.

Koenker, Diane, and Ronald D. Bachman. *Revelations from the Russian Archives*. Washington, D.C.: Library of Congress, 1997.

——, et al., eds. *Revelations from the Russian Archives: Documents in English Translation*. Washington, D.C.: Library of Congress, 1997.

Koestler, Arthur. *Darkness at Noon*. New York: Macmillan, 1941.

——. *Spanish Testament*. London: Viktor Gollancz, 1937.

—— *The Invisible Writing*. New York: Macmillan, 1954.

Kokoshin, Andrei A. "A. A. Svechin: o voine i politike," *Mezhdunarodnaia zhizn'*, 1988, no. 10: 133–42.

——. *Armiia i politika: sovetskaia voenno-politicheskaia i voenno-stratigicheskaia mysl', 1918–1991*. Moscow: Mezhdunarodnye otnosheniia, 1995.

Kokurin, Aleksandr I., and Nikita V. Petrov. *Lubianka, 1917–1960: spravochnik*. Moscow: Demokratiia, 1997.

——, eds. *GULAG: glavnoe upravlenie lagerei, 1918–1960*. Moscow: Materik, 2000.

——. "Gulag: struktura i kadry," *Svobodnaia mysl'*, 2000, no. 2: 110–25.

——. "OGPU, 1929–1934 gg.," *Svobodnaia mysl'*, 1998, no. 8: 95–114.

——. *Lubianka, organy VChK-OGPU-NKVD-NKGB-MGB-MVD-KGB, 1917–1991: spravochnik*. Moscow: Mezhdunarodnyi fond Demokratiia, 2003.

Kołakowski, Leszek. "Communism as a Cultural Formation," *Survey*, 29/2 (1985): 136–48.

——. *Main Currents of Marxism: The Founders, the Golden Age, the Breakdown*.

3 vols., in 1 ed. New York: W. W. Norton, 2005.

Kolarz, Walter. *The Peoples of the Soviet Far East*. New York: Prager, 1954.

Kolesnik, Aleksandr. *Khronika zhizni sem'i Stalina*. Moscow: IKRA, 1990.

Koliazin, Vladimir F., and Vladimir Goncharov, eds. *"Vernite mne svobodu!" deiateli literatury i iskusstv Rossii i Germanii, zhertvy stalinskogo terrora*. Moscow: Medium, 1997.

Kolkhozy vo vtoroi stalinskoi piatiletki: statisticheskii sbornik. Moscow-Leningrad: Gosplanizdat, 1939.

"Kollektivizatsiia: istoki, suchnost', posledstviia," *Istoriia SSSR*, 1989, no. 3: 3–62.

Kollektivizatsiia sel'skogo khoziaistva: vazhneishie postanovleniia Kommunisticheskoi partii Sovetskogo Soiuza, 1927–1935. Moscow: Akademiia nauk, 1957.

Kollontai, A. M. "'Seven Shots' in the Winter War of 1939," *International Affairs*, 1990, no. 1: 185–6.

——. *Diplomaticheskie dnevniki, 1922–40*. 2 vols. Moscow: Academia, 2001.

Kolman, Ernst. *My ne dolzhny byli tak zhit'*. New York: Chalidze, 1982.

Kolomiets, Maksim. *Legkie tanki BT: "letaiushchii tank" 1930-kh*. Moscow: Eksmo, 2007.

Kolpakidi, A. I., ed. *Entsiklopediia sekretnykh sluzhb Rossii*. Moscow: Tranzitkniga, 2004.

——, and M. L. Seriakov. *Shchit i mech*. Moscow: Olma, 2002.

——, and D. Prokhorov. *Imperiia GRU: Ocherki istorii rossiiskoi voennoi razvedki*. Moscow: Olma, 2000.

——. *Vneshniaia razvedka Rossii*. Olma, 2001.

Kol'tsov, Mikhail. "Agentura trotskistov v Ispanii," *Pravda*, January 22, 1937.

——. "Fashistsko-shpionskaia rabota ispanskikh trotskistov," *Pravda*, June 19, 1937.

——. "Podlye manevry ispanskikh trotskistov," *Pravda*, December 14, 1936.

——. *Ispaniia v ogne*. 2 vols. Moscow: Politizdat, 1987.

——. *Ispanskii dnevnik*. Moscow: Sovetskii pisatel', 1958.

——. *Izbrannye proizvedeniia v trekh tomakh*. Moscow: Gospolitizdat, 1957.

——. *Khochu letat'*. Moscow: Voenizdat, 1931.

——. *Pisatel' v gazete: vstupleniia, stat'i, zametki*. Moscow: Sovetskii pisatel', 1961.

——, and Andrei Lezhava. *Sovetskie subtropiki*. Moscow: Zhurnal'no-gazetnoe ob"edninenie, 1934.

Komandnyi i nachal'stvuiushchii sostav Krasnoi Armii v 1940–1941 gg. Struktura i kadry tsentral'nogo apparat NKO SSSR, voennykh okrugov i obshchevoiskovykh armii: dokumenty i materialy. Moscow-St. Petersburg: Letnii sad, 2005.

Komolova, N. P., ed. *Komintern protiv fashizma: dokumenty*. Moscow: Nauka, 1999.

Komshukov, Afanasii Arsen'evich. "Natsional'no-revoliutsionnaia voina ispanskogo naroda 1936–1939 gg. i sovetskaia obshchestvennost'." PhD diss. Kharkov, 1979.

Konchalovsky, Andrei. *The Inner Circle: An Inside View of Soviet Life Under Stalin*. New York: Newmarket Press, 1991.

Kondrashin, Viktor V., et al., eds. *Golod v SSSR 1929–1934: dokumenty*. 3 vols. Moscow: Mezhdunarodnyi fond Demokratiia, 2011.

——, and D'Ann Penner. *Golod 1932–1933 gody v sovetskoi derevne (na materialakh Povolzh'ia, Dona i Kubani)*. Samara-Penza: Samarskii gos. Universitet, Penzenskii gos. universitet, 2002.

Kondrat'ev, Nikolai D. *Marshal Bliukher*. Moscow: Voenizdat, 1965.

Konenenko, A. "Germano-pol'skaia voina 1939 g.," *Voenno-istoricheskii zhurnal*, 1940, no. 11: 49–67.

——. "Kratkii obzor voennykh desitvii na zapade," *Voennaia mysl'*, 1940, no. 7: 3–12.

——. Boi v Finlandii (mai 1940 g.)," *Voenno-istoricheskii zhurnal*, 1941, no. 3: 3–25.

Koniuskaia, R. "Iz vospoininanii ob izdanii sochinenii I.V. Stalina i ego kratkoi biografii," *Edinstvo*, January 19, 1995.

Kononenko, V. P. "Ubit, no esche opasen," *Sovetskaia kul'tura*, October 4, 2003.

——. "Pavlik Morozov: pravda i vymysel," *Komsomolskaia pravda*, April 5, 1989.

Konstantinov, Aleksandr P. *F. F. Ilin-Raskol'nikov*. Leningrad: Lenizdat, 1964.

Konstantinov, Kirill. *Rokossovskii: pobeda ne liuboi tsenoi*. Moscow: Yauza-Eksmo, 2006.

Kontorovich, Vladimir. "The Military Origins of Soviet Industrialization," *Comparative Economic Studies*, 57/4 (2015): 1–24.

Kopelev, Lev. "Last Grain Collections (1933)." In *Education of a True Believer*. New York: Harper & Row, 1980, 224–86.

——. *Education of a True Believer*. New York: Harper & Row, 1980.

——. *I sotvoril sebe kumira*. Ann Arbor, MI: Ardis, 1978.

Kordt, Erich. *Nicht aus Akten: die Wilhelmstrasse in Frieden und Krieg, 1928–1945*. Stuttgart: Deutsche Verlags-Anstadt, 1950.

——. *Wahn und Wirklichkeit*. Stuttgart: Union deutsche Verlagsgesellschaft, 1948.

Korets, L. B. *Kurorty Abkhazii—Sukhum—Gagry*. Moscow: Glavnoe kurortnoe upravlenie, 1925.

Koritskii, N. I., et al., eds. *Marshal Tukhachevskii: vospominaniia druzei i soratnikov*. Moscow: Voenizdat, 1965.

Kornat, Marek. "Anna Maria Cienciala as a Historian of Polish Diplomacy," *Polish Review*, 61/1 (2016): 29–45.

——. "The Polish Idea of 'The Third Europe' (1937–1938): A Realistic Concept or an Ex-Post Vision?" *Acta Poloniae Historica*, 103 (2011): 101–26.

Korneev, V. E., and O. N. Kopylova. "Arkhivy na sluzhbe totalitarnogo gosudarstva," *Otechestvennye arkhivy*, 1992, no. 1: 13–24.

Korol'kov, Iu. *Chelovek, dlia kotorogo ne bylo tain (Rikhard Zorge)*. Moscow: Politizdat, 1965.

Kortunova, A. I. "1938–i: poslednii god zhizni i deiatel'nosti marshala V.K. Bliukhera," *Novaia i noveishaia istoriia*, 2004, no. 1: 164–83.

Kosheleva, L. P., et al. *Pis'ma I. V. Stalina V. M. Molotovu, 1925–1936 gg.: sbornik dokumentov*. Moscow: Rossiia molodaia, 1995.

Kostiuk, Hryhory. *Stalinist Rule in Ukraine: A Study of the Decade of Mass Terror (1929–1939)*. New York: Praeger, 1960.

Kostrychenko, G. V. *Tainaia politika Stalina: vlast' i antisemitizm*. Moscow: Mezhdunarodnye otnosheniia, 2001.

Kostrychenko, G. V., and B. Ia. Khazanov. "Konets kar'ery N. I. Ezhova," *Istoricheskii arkhiv* 1992, no. 1: 123–31.

Kotkin, Stephen. "A Conspiracy So Immense," *The New Republic* (February 13, 2006).

——. "Modern Times: The Soviet Union and the Interwar Conjuncture," *Kritika*, 2/1 (2001): 111–65.

——. "The State—Is It Us? Memoirs, Archives, and Kremlinology," *Russian Review*, 61/1 (2002), 35–51.

——. *Magnetic Mountain: Stalinism as a Civilization*. Berkeley: University of California, 1995.

Kotliar, E. "'Faust v ITL." In *Teatr Gulaga: vospominaniia, ocherki*, edited by M. M. Korallov. Moscow: Memorial, 1995.

Kovaleva, N. V., et al., eds. *Molotov, Malenkov, Kaganovich, 1957: stenogramma iiun'skogo plenuma TsK KPSS i drugie dokumenty.* Moscow: Mezhdunarodnyi fond demokratiia, 1998.

———. "Posledniaia 'antipartiinaia' gruppa: stenograficheskii otchet iiunskogo (1957 g.) plenuma TsK KPSS," *Istoricheskii arkhiv*, 1993, no. 3: 4–94.

Kovalevskii, Pavel I. *Psikhiatricheskie eskizy iz istorii.* 3 vols. Kharkov: Zil'berberg, 1893.

Kowalsky, Daniel. "The Soviet Cinematic Offensive in the Spanish Civil War," *Film History*, 19/1 (2007): 7–19.

———. *Stalin and the Spanish Civil War.* New York: Columbia University, 2008.

Koyré, Alexandre. *La philosophie et le problème enational en Russie au début du XIX siècle.* Paris: Vrin, 1929.

Kozlov, A. G. "Pervyi direktor: perechityvaia stranitsy istorii," *Politicheskaia agitatsiia [Magadan]*, 1988, no. 17: 28–31, no. 18: 27–32.

Kozlov, Aleksandr. "Pokazateli po trudu, 1932–1942," *Magadanskaia pravda*, March 26, 1992.

Kozlov, V. A., ed. *Neizvestnaia Rossiia: XX vek.* 4 vols. Moscow: Istoricheskoe nasledie, 1992–1993.

Kozlov, V. P., et al., eds. *Katyn' mart 1940–sentiabr'2000 g.: dokumenty.* Moscow: Ves mir, 2001.

Kozlova, N. N. *Sovetskie liudi: stseny iz istorii.* Moscow: Evropa, 2005.

Kozybaev, M. K., et al. *Kollektivizatsiia v Kazakhstane: tragediia krest'iantsva.* Alma-Ata, 1992.

KPSS v rezoliutsiiakh i resheniiakh s"ezdov, konferentsii i plenumov TsK. 7th ed. 4 vols. Moscow: Politicheskaia literatura, 1954–60.

———. 8th ed. 8 vols. Moscow: Politicheskaia literatura, 1970–1982.

KPSS v rezoliutsiiakh i resheniiakh s"ezdov, konferentsii i plenumov TsK. 9th ed. 15 vols. Moscow: Politicheskaia literatura, 1983–1989.

KPSS o vooruzhennykh silakh Sovetskogo Soiuza: sbornik dokumentov. Moscow: Voenizdat, 1958.

Kraminov, D. F. *V orbite voiny: zapiski sovetskogo korrespondenta za rubezhom, 1939–1945 gody.* Moscow: Sovetskaia Rossiia, 1980.

Krasil'nikov, Sergei A. *Serp i molokh: krest'ianskaia ssylka v Zapadnoi Sibiri v 1930-e gody.* Moscow: Rosspen, 2003.

Krasil'nikov, S. N. "Nastupatel'naia armeiskaia operatsiia." In *Voprosy strategii: i operativnogo iskusstva v sovetskikh voennykh trudakh: 1917–1940 gg.*, edited by A. B. Kadishev et al. Moscow: Voenizdat, 1965, 487–96.

Krasnikov, Stepan. *S. M. Kirov v Leningrade.* Leningrad: Lenizdat, 1966.

Krasnov, Valerii. *Neizvestnyi Zhukov: lavry i ternii polkovodtsa. Dokumenty, mneniia, razmyshleniia.* Moscow: Olma, 2000.

Krasnoznamennyi Dal'nevostochnyi: istoriia Krasnoznamennogo dal'nevostochnogo voennogo okruga. Moscow: Ministerstva oborony SSSR, 1971.

Kravchenko, Ksenia S. *Stalin v izobrazitel'nom iskusstve.* Moscow: Gosizdat Iskusstvo, 1939.

Kravchenko, Victor. *I Chose Freedom: The Personal and Political Life of a Soviet Official.* New York: Scribner's, 1947.

Kremlev, Sergei. *Beriia: luchshii menedzher XX veka.* Moscow: Iauza, 2011.

Krenkel', Ernst T. *RAEM—moi pozyvnye.* Moscow: Sovetskaia Rossiia, 1973.

Krivenko, S. "Belomoro-Baltiiskii ITL (Belomorsko-Baltiiskii ITL, Belbaltlag, BBL)." In *Sistema ispravitel'no-trudovykh lagerei*

v SSSR, edited by N. G. Okhotin and A. B. Roginskii. Moscow: Zvenia, 1998.

———. "Karagandinskii ITL." In *Sistema ispravitel'no-trudovykh lagerei v SSSR*, edited by N. G. Okhotin and A. B. Roginskii. Moscow: Zvenia, 1998.

———. "Solovetskii ITL OGPU (Solovetskie lageria osobogo naznacheniia, Solovestkii lager' prinuditel'nykh rabot osobogo naznacheniia OGPU, SLON, CLAG, Solovetskie i Karelo-Murmanskie lageria, SKMITL)." In *Sistema ispravitel'no-trudovykh lagerei v SSSR*, edited by N. G. Okhotin and A. B. Roginskii. Moscow: Zvenia, 1998.

Krivitskii, Valter. "Iz vospominanii sovetskogo kommunista," *Sotsialisticheskii vestnik*, April 15, 1938.

Krivitsky, Walter G. *I Was Stalin's Agent.* London: Hamish Hamilton, 1940.

———. *In Stalin's Secret Service: An Exposé of Russia's Secret Policies by the Former Chief of the Soviet Intelligence in Western Europe.* 2nd ed. New York: Harper & Brothers, 1939.

———. *MI5 Debriefing and other Documents on Soviet Intelligence.* Riverside, CA: Xenos Books, 2004.

Krivosheev, G. F. *Soviet Casualties and Combat Losses in the Twentieth Century.* London: Greenhill Book, 1997.

———, ed. *Grif sekretnosti sniat: poteri Vooruzhennykh Sil SSSR v voinakh, boevykh deistviiakh i voennykh konfliktakh: statisticheskoe issledovanie.* Moscow: Voenizdat, 1993.

———. *Kniga pamiati.* 10 vols. Moscow: Patriot, 1998.

Krivoshein, Semen. *Mezhdubur'e.* 2nd ed. Voronezh: Tsentral'noe chernozemnoe, 1968.

Krylov, S. M., ed. *Puti razvitiia teatra: stenograficheskii otchet i resheniia partiinogo soveshchaniia po voprosam teatra pri agitprope TsK VKP(b) v mae 1927 g.* Moscow: Kinopechat', 1927.

Krymov, A. "Istoricheskie portrety: Manfred Shtern—General Kleber," *Narody Azii i Afriki*, 1978, no. 1.

Krymov, A. G. [Kuo Shao-tang], *Istoriko-memuarnye zapiski kitaiskogo revoliutsionera.* Moscow: Nauka, 1990.

K shestidesiatiletiiu so dnia rozhdeniia I.V. Stalina. Moscow: Pravda, 1940.

Kubeev, M. "Obrechennyi na kazn': dokumental'nyi rasskaz o Rikharde Zorge i ego sosaratnikakh," *Dal'nii Vostok*, 1990, no. 2.

Kublanov, A. "Razgrom fashistskoi trotskistko-bukharinskoi 'piatoi kolonii' v SSSR." PhD diss. Leningrad, 1946.

Kudriachenko, A. I., ed. *Holodomor v Ukraini 1932–1933 rokiv za dokumentamy politychnoho arkhivu Ministerstva zakordonnykh sprav Federatyvnoi Respubliky Nimechchyna.* Kiev: Natsional'nyi instytut stratehichykh doslidzhen', 2008.

Kudriashov, Sergei, ed. *Krasnaia armiia v 1920-e gody.* Moscow: Vetsnik arkhiza prezidenta Rossiiskoi Federatsii, 2007.

———, ed. *SSSR i grazhdanskaia voina v Ispanii: 1936–1939 gody.* Moscow: Vestnik arkhiva prezidenta RF, 2013.

Kuibyshev, Valerian V. *Stat'i i rechi.* Moscow: Partizdat, 1937.

Kul'chyts'kyi, Stanislav V "Skil'ky nas zahynulo pid holodomoru 1933 roku?" *Dzerkalo tyzhnya*, November 23, 2002.

Kuleshova, N. Iu. "'Bol'shoi den': griadushchaia voina v literature 1930-x godov," *Otechestvennaia istoriia*, 2002, no. 1: 181–91.

Kul'turnaia zhizn' v SSSR, 1928–1941 gg.: khronika. Moscow: Nauka, 1976.

Kumanev, Georgii A. "'22ogo' na rassvete," *Pravda*, June 22, 1989.

———. *Riadom so Stalinym: Otkrovennye svidetel'stva. Vstrechi, besedy, interv'iu, dokumenty.* Moscow: Bylina, 1999.

Kumanev, Viktor, and I. S. Kulikova. *Protivostoianie: Krupskaia-Stalin.* Moscow: Nauka, 1994.

Kun, Béla, ed. *Kommunisticheskii internatsional v dokumentakh: resheniia, tezisy i vozzvaniia kongressa Kominterna i plenumov IKKI, 1918–1932.* Moscow: Partizdat, 1933.

Kun, Miklos. *Bukharin: ego druz'ia i vragi.* Moscow: Respublika, 1992.

———. *Stalin: An Unknown Portrait.* Budapest: Central European University, 2003.

Kuramysov, I. *Na putiakh sotsialisticheskogo pereustroitstva kazakskogo aula.* Moscow: Alma-Ata, 1932.

Kurdiukov, I. F., et al., eds. *Sovetsko-kitaiskie otnosheniia: sbornik dokumentov 1917–1957.* Moscow: Izd-vo vostochnoi literatury, 1959.

Kuritsyn, V. M. *Istoriia gosudarstva i prava Rossii, 1929–1940 gg.* Moscow: Mezhdunarodnye otnosheniia, 1998.

Kurliandskii, Igor A. *Stalin, vlast', religiia.* Moscow: Kuchkovo pole, 2011.

Kuromiya, Hiroaki. "Accounting for the Great Terror," *Jahrbücher für Geschichte Osteuropas*, 53/1 (2005): 86–101.

———. "Edinonachalie and the Soviet Industrial Manager, 1928–1937," *Europe-Asia Studies*, 36/2 (1984): 185–204.

———. "Stalin in the Politburo Transcripts." In *The Lost Politburo Transcripts: From Collective Rule to Stalin's Dictatorships*, edited by Paul R. Gregory and Norman Naimark. Stanford, CA, and New Haven, CT: Hoover Institution and Yale University, 2008, 41–56.

———. "Stalin's Great Terror and Espionage," NCEEER paper, September 2009.

———. "The Commander and the Rank and File: Managing the Soviet Coal-Mining Industry, 1928–1933." In *Social Dimensions of Soviet Industrialization*, edited by William G. Rosenberg and Lewis H. Siegelbaum. Bloomington: Indiana University, 1993.

———. "The Crisis of Proletarian Identity in the Soviet Factory, 1928–1929," *Slavic Review*, 44/2 (1985): 280–97.

———. "The Soviet Famine of 1932–1933 Reconsidered," *Europe-Asia Studies*, 60/4 (2008): 663–75.

———. *Freedom and Terror in the Donbas: A Ukrainian-Russian Borderland, 1870–1990s.* New York: Cambridge University, 1998.

———. *Stalin.* New York: Pearson/Longman, 2005.

———. *Stalin's Industrial Revolution: Politics and Workers, 1928–1932.* New York: Cambridge University, 1988.

———. *The Voices of the Dead: Stalin's Great Terror in the 1930s.* New Haven, CT, and London: Yale University, 2007.

———, and Andrzej Pepłoński, "Stalin und die Spionage," *Transit*, 2009, no. 38.

———. "The Great Terror: Polish-Japanese Connections," *Cahiers du monde russe*, 50/4 (2009): 647–70.

Kuropatkin, A. N. *Dnevnik A. N. Kuropatkina.* Nizhny Novgorod: Nizhpoligraf, 1924.

Kushnirov, Mark. *Svetlyi put'. ili Charli i Spenser.* Moscow: Terra-knizhnyi klub, 1998.

Kuskova, E. "Na rubezhe dvuh epoch: pamiat A.M. Gor'kogo," *Poslednie novosti [Paris]*, June 26, 1936.

Kutskii, E. A. "A. V. Shestakov," *Istoriia SSSR*, 1967, no. 3: 134–41.

Kuusinen, Aino. *The Rings of Destiny: Inside Soviet Russia from Lenin to Brezhnev.* New York: William Morrow, 1974.

Kuz'micheva, T. M. "Resheniia osobykh troek privodit' nemedlenno," *Istochnik*, 1999, no. 5: 81–5.

Kuz'min, Mikhail A. *Dnevnik 1934 g.* St. Petersburg: Ivan Limbakh, 1998.

Kuznetskii metallurgicheski kombinat: ocherki po istorii. Novokuznetsk: Kuznetskaia krepost', 1997.

Kuznetsov, I. I., and I. M. Dhzoga. *Pervye geroi Sovetskogo Soiuza.* Irkutsk: Irkutsk University, 1983.

Kuznetsov, K. "'Val'kiriia' Vagnera v Bol'shom Teatre SSSR," *Sovetskaia muzyka*, 1941, no. 2: 76–79.

Kuznetsov, Nikolai G. "Krutye povoroty: iz zapisok Admirala Kuznetsova," *Voenno-istoricheskii zhurnal*, 1992, no. 12, 1993, no. 1, no. 3, no. 4, no. 6, no. 7, no. 10.

———. "S ispanskimi moriakami v natsional'no-revoliutsionnoi voine." In *Pod znamenem ispanskoi respubliki: vospominaniia sovetskikh dobrovol'tsev-uchastnikov.* Moscow: Nauka, 1965.

———. "Voenno-morskoi flot nakanune Velikoi Otechestvennoi voiny," *Voenno-istoricheskii zhurnal*, 1965, no. 9: 59–76.

———. *Krutye povoroty: iz zapisok admiral.* Moscow: Molodaia gvardiia, 1995.

———. *Na dalekom meridiane: vospominaniia uchastnika natsional'no-revoliutsionnoi voiny v Ispanii.* Moscow: Nauka, 1988.

———. *Nakanune: kursom k pobede.* Moscow: Voenizdat, 1991.

———. *Nakanune.* Moscow: Voenizdat, 1966, 1969.

Kuznetsova, M. V. "Esli zavtra voina: oboronnye fil'my 1930-x godov," *Istorik i khudozhnik*, 2005, no. 2: 17–26.

Kuztesova, P. "Nachalo voiny he bylo 'gromoi s iasnogo neba': iz zapisok Admirala flota Sovetskogo Soiuza Kuznetsova N. G.," *Pravda*, July 20, 1991.

Kvashonkin, A. V., ed. *Bol'shevistskoe rukovodstvo: perepiska, 1912–1927.* Moscow: Rosspen, 1996.

———. *Sovetskoe rukovodstvo: perepiska, 1928–1941.* Moscow: Rosspen, 1999.

Lacouture, Jean. *Léon Blum.* Paris: Seuil, 1977.

Lakoba, Nestor A. *Stalin i Khashim.* Sukhum: Abpartizdat, 1934.

——— *Ot VI k VII s"ezdu sovetov ASSR Abkhazia.* Sukhum: Abpartizdat, 1935.

Lakoba, Stanislav "History: 1917–1989." In *The Abkhazians*, edited by George Hewitt. Richmond, UK: Curzon, 1999.

———. "'Ia Koba, a ty Lakoba.'" In *Moe serdtse v gorakh: ocherki o sovremennoi Abkhazii*, edited by Fasil Iskander. Ypshkar Ola: Izd-vo Mariiskogo poligrafkombinata, 2001, 50–78.

Lammers, Donald N. "The Second Labour Government and the Decision and the Restoration of Relations with Soviet Russia (1929)," *Bulletin of the Institute of Historical Research*, 37 (1964): 60–72.

Landau, Zbigniew, and Jerzy Tomaszewski, eds. *Monachium 1938: polskie dokumenty dyplomatyczne.* Warsaw: Państwowe Wydawn. Naukowe, 1985.

Land of Socialism Today and Tomorrow: Reports and Speeches at the Eighteenth Congress . . . March 10–21, 1939, The. Moscow: Foreign Language Publishing House, 1939.

Laney, Frank M. "The Military Implementation of the Franco-Russian Alliance, 1890–1914." PhD diss. University of Virginia, 1954.

Lang, David Marshall. *A Modern History of Soviet Georgia.* New York: Grove Press, 1962.

Lang, Lucy Roberts. *Tomorrow Is Beautiful.* New York: Macmillan, 1948.

Langer, William L. *The Undeclared War, 1940–1941.* New York: Harper & Brothers, 1953.

———, and S. Everett Gleason. *The Challenge to Isolation, 1937–1940.* New York: Harper & Brothers, 1953.

Laquer, Walter, and Richard Breitman. *Breaking the Silence.* New York: Simon & Schuster, 1986.

Larina, Anna. *Nezabyvaemoe.* Moscow: APN, 1989.

———. *This I Cannot Forget: The Memoirs of Nikolai Bukharin's Widow.* New York: W. W. Norton, 1993.

Laroche, Jules. *La Pologne de Pilsudski: Soovernirs d'un ambassade 1926–1935.* Paris: Flammarion, 1953.

Larson, Erik. *In the Garden of Beasts: Love, Terror, and an American Family in Hitler's Berlin.* New York: Crown, 2011.

Lasky, Melvin. "The Hitler-Stalin Pact: Secret Documents from Nuremberg Give New Light on Agreement," *New Leader*, Nov. 30, 1946.

Lassner, Alexander N. "The Invasion of Austria in March 1938: Blitzkrieg or Pfusch?" In *Contemporary Austrian Studies*, vol. 8, edited by Günter Bischof et al. New Brunswick, NJ: Transaction, 2000, 447–86.

Latyshev, Anatolii G. "I eshche odin tost 'vozhdia narodov,'" *Iskusstvo kino*, 1991, no. 5: 141–2.

———. "Riadom so Stalinym," *Sovershenno sekretno*, 1990, no. 12.

———. "Stalin i kino." In *Surovaia drama narodov: uchenye i publitsisty o prirode stalinizma*, edited by Iu. P. Senokosov. Moscow: Politizdat, 1989.

Lauchlan, Iain. *Russian Hide-and-Seek: The Tsarist Secret Police in St. Petersburg, 1906–1914.* Helsinki: Suomalaisen Kirjallisuuden Seura/Finnish Literature Society, 2002.

Lawford, Valentine. *Bound for Diplomacy.* London: John Murray, 1963.

Lawlor, Sheila. *Churchill and the Politics of War 1940–1941.* New York: Cambridge University, 1994.

Layne, Christopher. "Security Studies and the Use of History: Neville Chamberlain's Grand Strategy Revisited," *Security Studies*, 17/3 (2008): 397–437.

Lazitch, Branko. "Stalin's Massacre of the Foreign Communist Leaders." In *The Comintern, Historical Highlights: Essays, Recollections, Historical Documents*, edited by M. N. Drachkovitch and Branko Lazitch. Stanford, CA: Hoover Institution, 1996, 139–74.

L. B., "'Tain kremlia' bol'she ne budet?" *Novoe vremia*, 1994, no. 50.

Leach, Barry A. *German Strategy against Russia, 1939–1941.* Oxford: Clarendon, 1973.

Lebedev, N. A. *Shchukin—akter kino.* Moscow: Goskinoizdat, 1944.

Lebedev, V. "Praviashchaia partiia ostavalas' podpol'noi," *Istochnik*, 1993, no. 5–6: 88–95.

Lebedev, V. A. "M. N. Tukhachevski i 'voenno-fashistskii zagovor,'" *Voenno-istoricheskii arkhiv*, 1997, vyp. 1: 149–55, 1998, vyp. 2: 3–81.

Lebedeva, Natalia S., and M. M. Narinskii, eds. *Komintern i vtoraia mirovaia voina.* Moscow: Pamiatniki istoricheskoi mysli, 1994.

———, et al., eds. *Katyn': plenniki neob"iavlennoi voiny.* Moscow: Mezhdunarodnyi fond Demokratiia, 1997.

Lebedeva, Natal'ia S. *Katyn': prestuplenie protiv chelovechestva.* Moscow: Progress/Kul'tura, 1994.

Lebedeva, V. "O snose khrama Khrista Spasitelia," *Literaturnaia Rossiia*, Nov. 27, 1932.

Lebina, Natalia B. *Povsedvenaia zhizn' sovetskogo goroda: normy i anomalii*

1920–1930 gody. St. Petersburg: Letnyi sad, 1999.

———, and M. V. Shkarovskii. *Prostitutsiia v Peterburge.* Moscow: Progress-Akademiia, 1994.

Lec, Stanisław Jerzy. *Unkempt Thoughts.* New York: St. Martin's, 1962.

Lechin, M. "'Vo frantsuzsko-pol'sko-rossiiskom treugol'nike, 1922–1934." In *Sovetsko-pol'skie otnosheniia v politicheskikh usloviiakh 30-kh godov XX stoletiia*, edited by E. Durachinskii and A. N. Sakharov. Moscow: Nauka, 2001, 120–33.

Ledovskii, Andrei. M. *SSSR i Stalin v sud'bakh Kitaia: dokumenty i svidetel'stva uchastnika sobytii, 1937–1952.* Moscow: Pamiatniki istoricheskoi mysli, 1999.

———. "Zapiski diplomata," *Problemy Dal'nego Vostoka*, 1991, no. 1: 108–18.

———, R. Mirovitskaia, and V. Miasnikov, eds. *Russko-kitaiskie otnosheniia v XX veke.* 5 vols. Moscow: Rossiiskaia akademiia nauk, 2000.

Lee, Chong-Sik. *Revolutionary Struggle in Manchuria.* Berkeley: University of California, 1983.

Leggett, George. *Cheka, Lenin's Secret Police: The All-Russian Extraordinary Commission for Combating Counter-Revolution and Sabotage, December 1917 to February 1922.* Oxford: Clarendon, 1981.

Leibovich, O. L., ed. *"Vkliuchen v operatsiiu": Massovyi terror v prikam'e 1937–38 gg.* Perm': Permskii gosudarstvennyi tekhnicheskii universitet, 2006.

Leibovich, Oleg, et al. *"Vkliuchen v operatsiiu": massovyi terror v Prikam'e v 1937–1938 gg.*, 2nd ed. Moscow: Rosspen, 2009.

Leibzon, Boris M., and Kirill K. Shirinia. *Povorot v politike kominterna: istoricheskoe znachenie VII kongressa Kominterna.* 2nd ed. Moscow: Mysl', 1975.

Leitz, Christian. "Nazi Germany Intervention in the Spanish Civil War and the Foundation of HISMA/ROWAK." In *The Republic Besieged: Civil War in Spain, 1936–1939*, edited by Paul Preston and Ann L. Mackenzie. Edinburgh: Edinburgh University, 1996, 53–85.

———. *Economic Relations between Nazi Germany and Franco's Spain 1936–1945.* Oxford: Oxford University, 1996.

Leksin, Iu. "Khochetsia dumat', chto ia ne obryval sviaz' vremen'," *Znanie-sila*, Feb. 1988.

Lel'chuk, Vitalii S. "Beseda I. V. Stalina s angliiskim pisatelem G. Uellsom: dokumenty, interpretatsii, razmyshleniia." In *Istoricheskaia nauka na rubezhe vekov*, edited by A. A. Fursenko. Moscow: Nauka, 2001, 326–52.

———, and Efim I. Pivovar. "Mentalitet sovetskogo obshchestva i 'kholodnaia voina,'" *Otechestvennaia istoriia*, 1993, no. 6: 63–78.

Lemin, I. "Novyi etap voiny v Evrope," *Mirovoe khoziaistvo i mirovaia politika*, 1940, no. 4–5.

Lenin, V. I. *Pol'noe sobranie sochinenii [PSS].* 5th ed. 55 vols. Moscow: Politicheskaia literatura, 1958–65. Cited as *PSS* (author understood).

———. *Polnoe sobranie sochinenii.* 19 vols. Moscow-Leningrad, 1925–1933.

Leningradskii martirolog, 1937–1938. 5 vols. St. Petersburg: Rossiiskaia natsional'naia biblioteka, 1995–.

Lenoe, Matthew E. *The Kirov Murder and Soviet History.* New Haven, CT: Yale University, 2010.

Lensen, George A. *Japanese Recognition of the USSR: Japanese Recognition of the USSR 1921–1930.* Tallahassee, FL: Diplomatic Press, 1970.

———. *The Damned Inheritance: The Soviet Union and the Manchurian Crises, 1924–1935*. Tallahassee, FL: Diplomatic Press, 1974.

Leonard, Royal. *I Flew for China: Chiang Kai-shek's Personal Pilot*. Garden City, NY: Doubleday, 1942.

Leonhard, Wolfgang. *Betrayal: The Hitler-Stalin Pact of 1939*. New York: St. Martin's, 1989.

Leonov, Nikolai S. *Likholet'e*. Moscow: Mezhdunarodnye otnosheniia, 1995.

Lerner, Warren. *Karl Radek: The Last Internationalist*. Stanford, CA: Stanford University, 1970.

Les Événements survenus en France de 1933 à 1945: Témoignages et documents. 9 vols. Paris: Presses Universitaires de France, 1951–2.

Leskov, Valentin. *Stalin i zagovor Tukhachevskogo*. Moscow: Veche, 2003.

"Letopis' stroitel'stva sovetskikh vooruzhennykh sil 1931 god (mai-iiul')," *Voenno-istoricheskii zhurnal*, 1977, no. 4: 122–3.

Letopis' zhizni i tvorchestva A. M. Gor'kogo. 4 vols. Moscow: Izdatel'stvo Akademii Nauk SSSR, 1958–60.

Letter of an Old Bolshevik. New York: Rand School, 1937.

Leushin, Maksim E. "Staliniada," *Istochnik*, 2002, no. 1: 103–6.

———. "'Ia davno uzhe ostavil sei greshnyi mir': pis'ma Stalina s togo sveta," *Istochnik*, 2003, no. 2: 33–5.

———. "'Schitaiu nizhe svoego dostoinstva . . .': fragment zapisi besedy I. V. Stalina s E. Liudigom, *Istoricheskii arkhiv*, 1998, no. 3: 216–17.

Levgur, M. *Obiazannosti komsomoltsa*. Moscow: Novaia Moskva, 1924.

Levine, Herbert S. "The Mediator: Carl J. Burckhardt's Efforts to Avert a Second World War," *Journal of Modern History*, 45/3 (1973): 439–55.

Levushin, M. A. "Dokumenty VKP (b) kak istochnik po istorii istoricheskoi nauki v SSSR: 1945–1955 gg." PhD diss. Moscow, 2000.

Levy, James P. *Appeasement and Rearmament: Britain, 1936–1939*. Lanham, MD: Rowman & Littlefield, 2006.

Lewin, Moshe. "Bureaucracy and the Stalinist State." In *Stalinism and Nazism: Dictatorships in Comparison*, edited by Ian Kershaw and Moshe Lewin. Cambridge, UK: Cambridge University, 1997, 53–74.

———. "Grappling with Stalinism." In *The Making of the Soviet System: Essays in the Social History of Interwar Russia*. New York: Pantheon/New Press, 1985, 1994, 286–314.

———. "Stalin in the Mirror of the Other." In *Stalinism and Nazism: Dictatorships in Comparison*, edited by Ian Kershaw and Lewin. Cambridge, UK: Cambridge University, 1997, 107–34.

———. "The Disappearance of Planning in the Plan," *Slavic Review*, 32/3 (1973): 271–87.

———. *Russia/USSR/Russia: The Drive and Drift of a Super State*. New York: The New Press, 1995.

———. *Russian Peasants and Soviet Power: A Study of Collectivization*. New York: W. W. Norton, 1968.

———. *The Making of the Soviet System: Essays in the Social History of Interwar Russia*. New York: Pantheon/New Press, 1985, 1994.

Lewis, R. A. "Innovation in the USSR: The Case of Synthetic Rubber," *Slavic Review*, 38/1 (1979): 48–59.

Lewis, Robert. "Foreign Economic Relations." In *The Economic Transformation of the Soviet Union, 1913–1945*, edited by Robert

W. Davies et al. New York: Cambridge University, 1994, 198–215.

———. "Technology and the Transformation of the Soviet Economy." In *The Economic Transformation of the Soviet Union, 1913–1945*, edited by Robert W. Davies et al. New York: Cambridge University, 1994, 182–97.

Leyda, Jay. *Kino: A History of the Russian and Soviet Film*. London and New York: Macmillan, 1960.

———, and Zina Voynow. *Eisenstein at Work*. New York: Pantheon, 1982.

Liachenko, B. P. "Tak proletelo sorok let . . ." In *Iurii Levitan: 50 let u mikrofona*, edited by V. M. Vozchikov. Moscow: Iskusstvo, 1987.

Liashchenko, P. N. "S ognem i krov'iu popolam," *Voenno-istoricheskii zhurnal*, 1995, no. 2: 22–8.

Liddell-Hart, B. *This Expanding War*. London: Faber and Faber, 1942.

Liebich, André. "I Am the Last—Memories of Bukharin in Paris," *Slavic Review*, 51/4 (1992): 767–81.

———. *From the Other Shore: Russian Social Democracy after 1921*. Cambridge, MA: Harvard University, 1997.

Li-fu, Chen. *The Storm Clouds Clear Over China: The Memoir of Ch'en Li-fu, 1900–1992*. Stanford, CA: Hoover Institution, 1994.

Lih, Lars T. "Melodrama and the Myth of the Soviet Union." In *Imitations of Life: Two Centuries of Melodrama in Russia*, edited by Louise McReynolds and Joan Neuberger. Durham, NC: Duke University, 2002, 178–207.

———, Oleg V. Maumov, and Oleg V. Khlevniuk, eds. *Stalin's Letters to Molotov, 1925–1936*. New Haven, CT, and London: Yale University, 1995.

Likhachev, D. S. *Reflections on the Russian Soul: A Memoir*. Budapest and New York: Central European University, 2000.

Likholobova, Z. G. *Stalins'kii totalitarnyi rezhym ta politychni represiï kintsia 30-kh rokiv v Ukraïni: perevazhno na materialakh Donbasu*. Donetsk: DonDU, 1996.

———. *Totalitarnyi rezhym ta politychni represii v Ukraïni u druhii polovyni 1930-kh rokiv: perevazhno na materialakh Donets'koho rehionu*. Donetsk: Donets'kyï natsional'nyï universytet, 2006.

Linz, Juan, and Alfred Stepan, eds. *The Breakdown of Democratic Regimes*. Baltimore: Johns Hopkins University, 1978.

Lipinsky, Jan. *Das geheime Zusatzprotokoll zum deutsch-sowjetischen Nichtangriffsvertrag von 23. August 1939 und seine Entstehungs- und Rezeptionsgeschichte von 1939 bis 1989*. Frankfurt am Main and New York: Lang, 2004.

Lisann, Maury. "Stalin the Appeaser," *Survey*, 76 (1970): 57–60.

Lisovskii, P. A. *SSSR i kapitalisticheskoe okruzhenie*. Moscow: Politcheskaia literatura, 1936.

Liszewski, K. *Polsko-sowiecka wojna 1939 g*. London: Polski fundusz kultury, 1986.

Litovskii, O. "Korol' Lir," *Pravda*, Feb. 27, 1935.

———. "Zhivoi Shekspir," *Sovetskii teatr*, 1935, no. 4.

Little, Douglas. *Malevolent Neutrality: The United States, Great Britain, and the Origins of the Spanish Civil War*. Ithaca, NY: Cornell University, 1985.

Litvin, Alter L. *Bez prava na mysl': istorik v epokhu bol'shogo terrora—ocherk sudeb*. Kazan: Tatarskoe knizhnoe Izdatel'stvo, 1994.

———, ed. *Men'shevistskii protsess 1931 goda: sbornik dokumentov*. 2 vols. Moscow: Rosspen, 1999.

Litvin, E. Iu. "'Chto zhe nam delat'?' (Pis'ma k A.N. Tol'stomu—deputatu Verkhovnomu Sovetu SSSR)." In *Zvenia: Istoricheskii al'manakh*. 2 vols. Moscow: Progress/Feniks/Atheneum, 1991, 505–27.

Litvinov, Maxim M. *Notes for a Journal*. New York: William Morrow, 1955.

Livi-Bacci, Massimo. "On the Human Costs of Collectivization in the Soviet Union," *Population and Development Review*, 19/4 (1993): 743–66.

Lkhamsuren, B., ed. *Ocherki istorii Mongol'skoi narodno-revoliutsionnoi partii*, 3rd ed. Moscow: Politizdat, 1971.

Loginov, Vladimir. *Teni Stalina: General Vlasik i ego soratniki*. Moscow: Sovremennik, 2000.

Long, Breckinridge. *The War Diary of Breckinridge Long: Selections from the Years 1939–1944*. Lincoln: University of Nebraska, 1966.

Longerich, Peter. *Die braunen Battalione: die Geschichte der SA*. Munich: C. H. Beck, 1989.

———. *Goebbels: A Biography*. New York: Random House, 2015.

Lopatin, P. I. *Volga idet v Moskvu*. Moscow: Partizdat, 1937.

Lordkipanidze, V. "Ubiistvo Kirova," *Argumenty i fakty*, 1989, no. 6: 5–6.

Losev, Viktor, and Lidiia Ianovskaia, eds. *Dnevnik Eleny Bulgakovoi*. Moscow: Knizhnaia palata, 1990.

Lota, Vladimir. *"Alta" protiv "Barbarossy": kak byli dobyty svedeniia o podgotovke Germanii k napadeniiu na SSSR*. Moscow: Molodaia gvardiia, 2004.

———. *Sekretnyi front General'nogo shtaba: kniga o voennoi razvedke, 1940–1942*. Moscow: Molodaia Gvardiia, 2005.

Lovell, Stephen. *Russia in the Microphone Age: A History of Soviet Radio 1919–1970*. New York: Oxford University, 2015.

———. *Summerfolk*. Ithaca, NY: Cornell University, 2003.

Low, Alfred D. *The Anschluss Movement, 1931–1938, and the Great Powers*. Boulder, CO: East European Monographs, 1985.

Low, David. *Years of Wrath*. New York: Simon & Schuster, 1946.

Lozhechko, A. B. *Grigorii Kaminskii*. Moscow: Politizdat, 1966.

Luckyj, George S. N. *Literary Politics in the Soviet Ukraine, 1917–1934*. Durham, NC: Duke University, 1990.

Ludendorff, Erich. *Kriegsführung und Politik*. Berlin: Mittler und Sohn, 1922.

Lugovskaia, Nina. *The Diary of a Soviet Schoolgirl, 1932–1937*. Moscow: Glas, 2003.

Lukács, Gyorgy. "Roman kak burzhuaznaia epopeia." In *Literaturnaia entsiklopediia*, edited by A. V. Lunacharskii. 11 vols. Moscow: Kommunisticheskaia akademiia, 1929–91.

Lukacs, John. *Five Days in London, May 1940*. New Haven, CT: Yale University, 1999.

———. *The Duel, 10 May–31 July 1940: The Eighty-Day Struggle between Churchill and Hitler*. New York: Ticknor & Fields, 1991.

———. *The Hitler of History*. New York: Knopf, 1997.

Lukes, Igor. "Stalin and Beneš at the End of September 1938: New Evidence from the Prague Archives," *Slavic Review*, 52/1 (1993): 28–48.

———. "Stalin and Czechoslovakia in 1938–39: an Autopsy of a Myth," *Diplomacy and Statecraft*, 10/2–3 (1999): 13–47.

———. "The Czechoslovak Partial Mobilization in May 1938: a Mystery (almost) Solved," *Journal of Contemporary History*, 31/4 (1996): 699–720.

———. *Czechoslovakia between Hitler and Stalin: The Diplomacy of Edvard Beneš in the 1930s*. New York: Oxford University, 1996.

———. *On the Edge of the Cold War: American Diplomats and Spies in Postwar Prague*. New York: Oxford University, 2012.

Luk'ianov, A., ed. "Massovye repressii opravdany byt' ne mogut," *Istochnik*, 1995, no. 1: 117–32.

Luk'ianova, Irina. *Kornei Chukovskii*. Moscow: Molodaia gvardiia, 2006.

Lunacharskaia-Rozenel', Natal'ia. *Pamiat' serdtsa*. Moscow: Iskusstvo, 1962, 1965, 1975.

Lunacharskii, Anatolii V. *Osvobozhdenyi Don Kikhot*. Moscow: Gosizdat, 1922.

———. *Sobranie sochinenii: literaturavedenie, kritika, estetika*. 8 vols. Moscow: Khudozhestvennaia literatura, 1963–67.

Lungu, Dov B. "Nicolae Titulescu and the 1932 Crisis Concerning the Soviet-Romanian Pact of Non-Aggression," *East European Quarterly*, 18/2 (1984): 185–213.

Lurie, V. M., and V. Ia. Kochik. *GRU: dela i liudi*. Moscow: Olma, 2003.

Luzianin, S. G. "Rossiia-Mongoliia-Kitai: vneshnepoliticheskie otnosheniia v 1911–1946 gg.," PhD diss. Moscow, 1997.

Lyandres, S. "Russkii pisatel' ne mozhet zhit' bez rodiny," *Voprosy literatury*, 1966, no. 9: 134–9.

Lyons, Eugene, ed. *Six Soviet Plays*. London: V. Gollancz, 1935.

———. "Stalin Laughs!" *Time*, December 1, 1930.

———. "Stalin Urges U.S. Trade with Soviet in His Only Interview in Four Years," *New York Herald Tribune*, Nov. 24, 1930.

———. "Stalin, Autocrat of all the Russias," *American Mercury*, 48 (Oct. 1939): 238–43.

———. *Assignment in Utopia*. New York: Harcourt, Brace, 1937.

———. *Moscow Carrousel*. New York: Knopf, 1935.

———. *Stalin: Czar of All the Russias*. Philadelphia: J. B. Lippincott, 1940.

MacDonald, C. A. "Economic Appeasement and the German 'Moderates,' 1937–1939: an Introductory Essay," *Past and Present*, 56 (1972): 105–31.

Mace, James E. "The Man-made Famine of 1933 in the Soviet Ukraine: What Happened and Why?" In *Famine in Ukraine, 1932–1933*, edited by Roman Serbyn and Bohdan Krawchenko. Edmonton: Canadian Institute of Ukranian Studies, 1986, 67–83.

Machiavelli, Niccolò. *Gosudar'*. St. Petersburg: Tiblen, 1869.

———. *The Discourses of Niccolò Machiavelli*. London and New York: Routledge, 1975.

Mackiewicz, Stanisław. *Colonel Beck and His Policy*. London: Eyre and Spottiswoode, 1944.

MacKinnon, Stephen R. "The Tragedy of Wuhan, 1938," *Modern Asian Studies*, 30/4 (1996): 931–43.

———. *Wuhan, 1938: War, Refugees, and the Making of Modern China*. Berkeley: University of California, 2008.

Maclean, Fitzroy. *Escape to Adventure*. Boston: Little, Brown, 1950.

MacNeal, Robert H. "Stalin's Family: A Commentary on Svetlana Alliluyeva's Memoirs," *Russian Review*, 27/1 (1968), 78–86.

———. "Trotskyist Interpretations of Stalinism." In *Stalinism: Essays in Historical Interpretation*, edited by Robert C. Tucker. New York: W. W. Norton, 1977, 30–52.

———. *Stalin: Man and Ruler*. Basingstoke: Macmillan, 1988.

Madajczyk, Czesław. *Die Okkupationspolitik Nazi-Deutschlands in Polen, 1939–1945*. Cologne: Pahl-Rugenstein Verlag, 1989.

Maddux, Thomas R. *Years of Estrangement: American Relations with the Soviet Union,*

1933–1941. Tallahassee: University Presses of Florida, 1980.

Magerovsky, Eugene. "The People's Commissariat of Foreign Affairs, 1917–1946." 2 vols. PhD diss. New York: Columbia University, 1975.

Mahoney, Barbara S. *Dispatches and Dictators: Ralph Barnes for the Herald Tribune*. Corvallis: Oregon State University, 2002.

Main, Steven. *The Red Army and the Future War in Europe, 1925–1940*. Camberley, Surrey: Conflict Studies Research Centre, 1997.

Maiolo, Joseph A. "Anglo-Soviet Naval Armaments Diplomacy before the Second World War," *English Historical Review*, 123/501 (2008): 351–78.

———. "Armaments Competition." In *The Origins of World War Two: The Debate Continues*, edited by R. Boyce and Maiolo. Basingstoke: Palgrave Macmillan, 2003, 286–307.

———. *Cry Havoc: How the Arms Race Drove the World to War, 1931–1941*. New York: Basic Books, 2010.

———. *The Royal Navy and Nazi Germany, 1933–39: A Study in Appeasement and the Origins of the Second World War*. New York: St. Martin's, 1998.

Maiskii, Ivan M. *Bernard Shou i drugie: vospominaniia*. Moscow: Isskustvo, 1967.

———. *Dnevnik diplomata: London, 1934–1943*. 2 vols. Moscow: Nauka, 2006–9.

———. *Iz vospominanii o Bernarde Shou i Gerberte Uellse*. Moscow: Idz-vo "Pravda," 1973.

———. *Vospominaniia sovetskogo diplomata 1925–1945*. Moscow: Mezhdunarodnye otnosheniia, 1971.

Maisky, Ivan M. *Memoirs of a Soviet Ambassador: The War, 1939–43*. New York: Scribner, 1967.

———. *Spanish Notebooks*. London: Hutchinson, 1966.

Makarova, N. N. "Stalin i 'blizhnyi krug': printsipy rotatsii erzats-elity (1934–1939)." In *Problemy Rossiiskoi istorii*, Moscow-Magnitogorsk, 2007, 294–314.

Makaseev, Boris. "Iz khroniki geroicheskoi respubliki." In *My internatsionalisty: vospominaniia sovetskikh dobrovol'tsev-uchastnikov natsional'no-revoliutsionnoi voiny v Ispanii*. 2nd ed. Moscow: Politicheskaia literatura, 1986, 158–64.

Maksimenkov, Leonid. "Kul't: zametki o slovakh v sovetskoi politicheskoi kul'ture," *Svobodnaia mysl'*, 1993, no. 11: 28–9.

———, ed. *Bol'shaia tsenzura: pisateli i zhurnalisty v Strane Sovetov 1917–1956*. Moscow: Mezhdunarodnyi fond Demokratiia-Materik, 2005.

———. "Ocherki nomenklaturnoi istorii sovetskoi literatury, 1932–1946: Stalin, Bukharin, Zhdanov, Shcherbakov i drugie," *Voprosy literatury*, 2003, no. 4: 212–58.

———. *Sumbur vmesto muzyki: stalinskaia kul'turnaia revoliutsiia, 1936–1938*. Moscow: Iuridicheskaia kniga, 1997.

Maksimovskii, V. N. "Ideia diktatury u Makiavelli," *Istorik Marksist*, 1929, no. 13: 55–94.

Maksudov, M. "Geografiia goloda 1933 goda," in *SSSR: vnutrennie protivorechiia*. 22 vols. New York and Benson, VT: Chalidze, 1981–8, VII: 5–17.

———. "Ukraine's Demographic Losses, 1927–1938." In *Famine in Ukraine, 1932–1933*, edited by Roman Serbyn and Bohdan Krawchenko. Edmonton: Canadian Institute of Ukrainian Studies, 1986, 27–43.

Maksudov, Sergei. "Migratsii v SSSR v 1926–1939 godakh," *Cahiers du monde russe*, 40/4 (1999): 770–96.

Malefakis, E. E. "La revolución social." In *La guerra de España, 1936–1939*. Madrid: Taurus, 1996.

Malenkov, Andrei G. *O moem otse Georgii Malenkove*. Moscow: Technoekos, 1992.

Malkov, N. "Charlie Chaplin i Dunaevskii," *Rabochii i teatr*, 1936, no. 16: 18–29.

Mallett, Robert. "Fascist Foreign Policy and Official Italian Views of Anthony Eden in the 1930s," *The Historical Journal*, 43/1 (2000): 157–87.

———. *Mussolini and the Origins of the Second World War*. Houndmills, Basingstoke: Macmillan, 2003.

Malnick, Bertha. *Everyday Life in Russia*. London: George G. Harrap, 1938.

Malyshev, V. A. "Dnevnk narkoma. 'Proidet desiatok let, i eti vstrechi ne vosstanovish' uzhe v pamiati,'" *Istochnik*, 1997, no. 5: 103–47.

Mamaeva, Tat'iana. "Vasily Stalin, 'ia zhiv, poka zhiv otets',," *Bizness online*, Oct. 29, 2013.

Mandelstam, Nadezhda. *Hope against Hope: A Memoir*. New York: Atheneum, 1970.

Manfred Zeidler, "German-Soviet Economic Relations during the Hitler-Stalin Pact." In *From Peace to War*, edited by Bernd Wegner. Oxford, UK: Berghahn, 1997.

Manikovskii, Aleksei A. *Boevoe snabzhenie russkoi armii v mirovuiu voinu*. Moscow: Gos. voennoe izd-vo narkomata oborony Soiuza SSSR, 1937.

Mannerheim, Carl G. *The Memoirs of Marshal Mannerheim*. London: Cassell, 1953.

Manninen, O. "Moshchnoe sovetskoe nastuplenie." In *Zimnaia voina 1939–1940*, edited by Oleg A. Rzhevskii and Olli Vehviläinen. 2 vols. Moscow: Nauka, 1998, I: 324–35.

———. "Vystreli byli," *Rodina*, 1995, no. 12: 56–7.

———, and N. I. Baryshnikov, "Peregovory osen'iu 1939 goda." In *Zimnaia voina 1939–1940*, edited by Oleg A. Rzhevskii and Olli Vehviläinen. 2 vols. Moscow: Nauka, 1998, I: 113–30.

Manning, Roberta T. "Government in the Soviet Countryside in the Stalinist Thirties: The Case of Belyi Raion in 1937," Carl Beck Papers, University of Pittsburgh, Center for Russian and East European Studies, no. 301 (1984).

———. "The Rise and Fall of the 'Extraordinary Measures,' January-June 1928: Towards a Reexamination of the Onset of the Stalin Revolution." Carl Beck Papers, University of Pittsburgh, Center for Russian and East European Studies, no. 1504 (2001).

Manuel, Caballero. *Latin America and the Comintern, 1919–1943*. New York: Cambridge University, 1986.

Manuilsky, D. Z. *The Communist Parties and the Crisis of Capitalism*. London: Modern Books, 1931.

Margolin, Victor. "Stalin and Wheat: Collective Farms and Composite Portraits," *Gastronomica: the Journal of Food and Culture*, 3/2 (2003): 14–6.

Mar'iamov, Grigorii B. *Kremlevskii tsenzor: Stalin smotrit kino*. Moscow: Kinoteatr, 1992.

Markevich, Andrei. "How Much Control is Enough? Monitoring and Interventions in the Stalinist Command Economy," *Europe-Asia Studies*, 63/8 (2011): 1449–68.

———, and Andrei Sokolov. "Magnitka bliz Sadovogo kol'tsa": stimuli k rabote na moskomskom zavode 'Serp i Molot,' 1883–2001. Moscow: Rosspen, 2005.

Markova, Liliana. "Litso vraga." In *Kino: politika i liudi, 30-e gody*, edited by L. Mamatova. Moscow: Materik, 1995, 79–99.

Markovich, R. M. *O Staline: kratkii ukazatel' literatury.* Moscow, 1939.

Marshkova, Tat'iana. *Bol'shoi teatr: zolotye golosa.* Moscow: Algoritm, 2011.

Martel, Giffard. *The Russian Outlook.* London: M. Joseph, 1947.

Martel, Gordon, ed. *The Times and Appeasement: The Journals of A. L. Kennedy, 1932–1939.* Cambridge, UK: Cambridge University, 2000.

Martelli, George. *Italy Against the World.* New York: Harcourt, Brace and Co., 1938.

Martin, Bemd. *Friedensinitiativen und Machtpolitik im Zweiten Weltkrieg, 1939–42.* Dusseldorf: Droste, 1974.

Martin, Terry. *The Affirmative Action Empire: Nations and Nationalism in the Soviet Union, 1923–1939.* Ithaca, NY: Cornell University, 2001.

Marwick, Arthur. "Problems and Consequences of Organizing Society for Total War." In *Mobilization for Total War: the Canadian, American, and British Experience, 1914–1918, 1939–1945,* edited by Nándor F. Dreisziger. Waterloo, Ontario: Wilfrid Laurier University, 1981.

Marx, Harpo, with Rowland Barber. *Harpo Speaks!* New York: B. Geis Associates, 1961.

Marx, Karl, and Friedrich Engels. *The Russian Menace to Europe.* Glencoe, IL: The Free Press, 1952.

———. *The Civil War in France.* Chicago: Kerr, 1998. Originally published London: E. Trulove, 1871.

———. *The Eighteenth Brumaire of Louis Napoleon.* New York: International Publishers, 1926.

Marykhuba, Igor', ed. *Moskovskie arkhivnye dokumenty ob Abkhazii XX veka.* Sukhumi: Akua, 2008.

Maser, Werner. *Der Wortbruch: Hitler, Stalin und der Zweite Weltkrieg.* 4th ed. Munich: Heyne, 1997.

———. *Hitlers Mein Kampf: Entstehung, Aufbau, Stil, Änderungen, Quellen, Quellenwert, kommentiterte Auszüge.* Munich, Bechtle, 1966.

Maslov, M. A. *Rokovoi istrebitel' Chkalova: samaia strashnaia aviakatastrofa Stalinskoi epokhi.* Moscow: Iauza-EKSMO, 2010.

Maslov, N. N. "'Kratkii kurs istorii VKP (b)'—Entsiklopediia kul'ta lichnosti," *Voprosy istorii KPSS,* 1988, no. 11: 51–67.

———. "I. V. Stalin o 'Kratkom kurse istorii VKP (b),'" *Istoricheskii arkhiv,* 1994, no. 5: 4–32.

Maslov, Sergei. *Kolkhoznaia Rossiia.* Berlin: Krestianskaia Rossiia, 1937.

Maslov, Vasilii, and Nikolai Chistiakov. "Stalinskie repressii i sovetskaia iutitsiia," *Kommunist,* 1990, no. 10: 102–12.

Mason, Timothy W. *Arbeiterklasse und Volksgemeinschaft: Dokumente und Materialien zur deutschen Arbeiterpolitik, 1936–1939.* Opladen: Westdeutscher Verlag, 1975.

———. *Nazism, Fascism, and the Working Class: Essays by Tim Mason.* Cambridge, UK: Cambridge University, 1995.

Massell, Gregory J. *The Surrogate Proletariat: Moslem Women and Revolutionary Strategies in Soviet Central Asia, 1919–1929.* Princeton, NJ: Princeton University, 1974.

Massing, Hede. *This Deception.* New York: Duell, Sloan and Pearce, 1951.

Mastenitsa, E. N. "Iz istroii muzeinoi pushkiniany, 1937 g." In *Peterburgskaia pushkiniana,* edited by Pavel A. Podbolotov. St. Petersburg: SpbGUKI, 2000, 113–20.

Mastny, Vojtech. *Russia's Road to the Cold War: Diplomacy, Warfare, and the Politics of Communism, 1941–1945.* New York: Columbia University, 1979.

"Materialy marto-fevral'skogo plenuma TsK VKP (b) 1937 goda," *Voprosy istorii,* 1992,

no. 2–3: 3–44, no. 4–5: 3–36, no. 6–7: 3–29, 8–9: 3–29, no. 3–36, 11–12: 3–19; 1993, no. 2: 3–33, no. 5: 3–23, no. 6: 3–30, no. 7: 3–24, no. 8: 3–26, no. 9: 3–32, no. 10: 3–27; 1994, no. 1: 12–28, no. 2: 3–29, no. 6: 3–23, no. 8: 3–29, no. 10: 3–27, no. 12: 3–29; 1995, no. 1: 3–22 , no. 2: 3–26, no. 3: 3–15, no. 4: 3–18, no. 5–6: 3–24, no. 7: 3–25, no. 8: 3–25, no. 10: 3–28, no. 11–12: 3–23; in slightly fuller form, on the Internet: www .memo.ru/history/1937/feb_mart_1937 /index.html.

Materialy ob"edinennogo plenuma TsK i TsKK VKP (b), 7–12 ianvaria, 1933 g. Moscow: Partizdat, 1933.

Matossian, Mary Kilbourne. *The Impact of Soviet Policies on Armenia.* Leiden, Netherlands: E. J. Brill, 1962.

Matveev, Oleg, and Vladimir Merzhliakov. "Akademik kontrarazvedki," *Nezavisimoe voennoe obozrenie,* 2001, no. 15.

Mawdsley, Evan. "An Elite within an Elite: Politburo/Presidium Membership under Stalin, 1927–1953." In *The Nature of Stalin's Dictatorship: The Politburo, 1924–1953,* edited by E. A. Rees. Houndmills, Basingstoke: Palgrave Macmillan, 2004.

———. "Crossing the Rubicon: Soviet Plans for Offensive War, 1940–41," *International History Review,* 25/4 (2003): 818–65.

May, Ernest R. *Strange Victory: Hitler's Conquest of France.* New York: Hill and Wang, 2001.

Mayling, Soong. *Sian: A Coup D'etat.* Shanghai: Chine Publishing Company, 1937.

Mazower, Mark. *Inside Hitler's Greece: The Experience of Occupation, 1941–44.* New Haven, CT: Yale University, 2001.

McCannon, John. *Red Arctic: Polar Exploration and the Myth of the North in the Soviet Union, 1932–1939.* New York: Oxford University, 1998.

McDermott, Kevin. "Stalinist Terror in the Comintern: New Perspectives," *Journal of Contemporary History,* 30/1 (1995): 111–30.

———. *Stalin: Revolutionary in an Era of War.* New York: Palgrave Macmillan, 2006.

———, and Jeremy Agnew. *The Comintern: A History of International Communism from Lenin to Stalin.* Houndmills, Basingstoke: Macmillan, 1996.

McDonogh, Giles. *1938: Hitler's Gamble.* New York: Basic, 2009.

McDonough, Frank. *Neville Chamberlain, Appeasement and the British Road to War.* New York: Manchester University, 1998.

McKee, Ilse. *Tomorrow the World.* London: Dent, 1960.

McKercher, B. J. C. "Deterrence and the European Balance of Power: The Field Force and British Grand Strategy, 1934–1938," *English Historical Review,* 123/500 (2008): 98–131.

McLellan, David, ed. *Karl Marx: Interviews and Recollections.* New York: Macmillan, 1981.

McMurry, Dean Scott. *Deutschland und die Sowjetunion, 1933–1936: Ideologie, Machtpolitik und Wirtschaftsbeziehungen.* Cologne-Vienna: Böhlau, 1979.

McNeal, Robert H. *Stalin: Man and Ruler.* New York: New York University, 1988.

McNeill, William H. *Arnold J. Toynbee: A Life.* New York: Oxford University, 1989.

McSherry, James E. *Stalin, Hitler, and Europe.* 2 vols. Cleveland, OH: World Publishing Co., 1968–70.

McSmith, Andy. *Fear and the Muse Kept Watch.* New York: New Press, 2015.

Mearsheimer, John J. *Conventional Deterrence.* Ithaca, NY: Cornell University, 1983.

———. *The Tragedy of Great Power Politics.* New York: W. W. Norton, 2001.

Medlicott, W. N. *Britain and Germany: The Search for Agreement 1930–1937.* London: Athlone, 1969.

Medvedev, Roi, and Zhores Medvedev. *Neizvestnyi Stalin.* Moscow: Vremia, 2007.

———. "O lichnoi otvetvennosti Stalina za terror 1937–1938 gg." In *Vozhd', khoziain, diktator,* edited by A. M. Razumikhin. Moscow: Patriot, 1990, 289–330.

———. "O Staline i stalinizme," *Znamia,* 1989, no. 1: 159–209, no. 2: 174–222, no. 3: 144–92, no. 4: 166–2024.

———. "Smert' Nadezhdy Alliluevoi," *Leninskoe znamia,* June 28, 1991.

———. *Blizhnyi krug Stalina: soratniki vozhdia.* Moscow: Eskmo, 2005.

———. *K sudu istorii: Genezis i posledstviia stalinizma.* New York: Knopf, 1974.

Medvedev, Roy. "How the Short Course Was Created," *Russian Politics and Law,* 43/3 (2005): 69–95.

———. *All Stalin's Men.* Oxford: Blackwell, 1986.

———. *Let History Judge: The Origins and Consequences of Stalinism.* New York: Columbia University, 1989.

———. *Nikolai Bukharin: The Last Years.* New York: W. W. Norton, 1980.

———. *On Stalin and Stalinism.* Oxford and New York: Oxford University, 1979.

Medvedeva, Irina. "'Chornoye leto' 1939 goda." In *Sergei Prokof'ev: vospominaniia, pis'ma, stat'i,* edited by M. P. Rakhmanova. Moscow: Deka-VS, 2004, 318–66.

Meehan, Patricia. *The Unnecessary War: Whitehall and the German Resistance to Hitler.* London: Sinclair-Stevenson, 1992.

Meerovich, A. "V narkomindele, 1922–1939: interv'iu s E. A. Gnedinym," *Pamiat': istoricheskii sbornik,* 1981–82, vyp. 5: 357–93.

Megrelidze, I. V. *Iosif Orbeli,* 2nd ed. Tbilisi: Metsniereba, 1987.

Mehringer, Hans. *Die NSDAP als politische Auslese Organisation.* Munich: Deutscher Volksverlag, 1938.

Meissner, Otto. *Staatssekretär unter Ebert, Hindenburg, Hitler: der Schicksalsweg des deutschen Volkes von 1918–1945, wie ich ihn erlebte.* Hamburg: Hiffman und Kampe, 1950.

Melikov, Vladimir A. *Geroicheskaia oborona Tsaritsyna.* Moscow: Voenizdat, 1938.

Melkonian, Eduard. "Repressions in 1930s Soviet Armenia," *Caucasus Analytical Digest,* no. 22 (2010): 6–9.

Mel'tiukhov, Mikhail I. "'Narodnyi front' dlia Finliandii? K voprosu o tseliakh sovetskogo rukovodstva v voine s Finliandiei 1939–1940 gg.," *Otechestvennaia istoriia,* 1993, no. 3: 95–101.

———. *17 September 1939: Sovetsko-pol'skie konflikty, 1918–1939.* Moscow: Veche, 2009.

———. *Sovetsko-pol'skie voiny: voenno-politicheskoe protivostoianie 1918–1939 gg.* Moscow: Veche, 2001, and Moscow: Eksmo, 2004.

———. *Upushchennyi shans Stalina: Sovetskii Soiuz i bor'ba za Evropu, 1939–1941: dokumenty, fakty, suzhdeniia.* Moscow: Veche, 2000.

Melzer, Emanuel. *No Way Out: The Politics of Polish Jewry, 1935–1939.* Cincinnati, OH: Hebrew Union College, 1997.

Memuary freiliny imperatritsy: tsarskaia sem'ia, Stalin, Beriia, Cherchill' i drugie v semeinykh dnevnikakh trekh pokolenii. Moscow: Artel', 2013.

Menning, Bruce W. "Sovetskie zheleznye dorogi i planirovanie voennykh desitvii: 1941 god." In *Voina i politika, 1939–1941,* edited by A. O. Chubar'ian. Moscow: Nauka, 1999.

——. "Soviet Railroads and War Planning," unpublished manuscript.

——. "Soviet Strategy," In *The Cambridge History of the Second World War*, edited by Ewan Mawdsley et al. 3 vols. Cambridge, UK: Cambridge University, 2015, I: 213–44.

——. *Bayonets before Bullets: The Imperial Russian Army, 1861–1914*. Bloomington: Indiana University, 1992.

Menshevik Trial: The Text of the Indictment of the Counter-Revolutionary Menshevik Organization: The Trial of the All-Union Bureau of the Central Committee of the Counter-Revolutionary Menshevik Party, The. Workers Library Publishers, 1931.

Menzel, J. M. "German-Japanese Relations during the War, 1939–1945." PhD diss. University of Chicago, 1957.

Meretskov, Kirill A. "Ukreplenie severo-zapadnykh granits SSSR," *Voprosy istorii*, 1968, no. 9: 120–9.

——. *Na sluzhbe narodu: stranitsy vospominanii*. 4th ed. Moscow: Vysshaya shkola, 1984.

——. *Na sluzhbe narodu: stranitsy vospominanii*. Moscow: Politizdat, 1968.

——. *Serving the People: A Memoir*. Moscow: Progress, 1971.

Merl, Stephan. "Entfachte Stalin die Hungersnot von 1932–1933 zur Auslöschung des ukrainischen Natsionalismus?" *Jahrbücher für Geschichte Osteuropas*, 37/4 (1989): 569–90.

——. *Bauern unter Stalin: die Formierung des sowjetischen Kolchossystems 1930–1941*. Berlin: Duncker und Humblot, 1990.

Merridale, Catherine. "The 1937 Census and the Limits of Stalinist Rule," *Historical Journal*, 39/1 (1996): 225–40.

——. "The Reluctant Opposition: The Right 'Deviation' in Moscow, 1928," *Soviet Studies*, 41/3 (1989): 382–400.

——. *Moscow Politics and the Rise of Stalin: The Communist Party in the Capital, 1925–32*. New York: St. Martin's, 1990.

Merritt, Steven Edward. "The Great Purges in the Soviet Far East, 1937–1938." PhD diss. University of California, Riverside, 2000.

Mertsalov, A. N., and L. A. Mertsalova. *Stalinizm i voina: iz neprochitannykh stranits istorii (1930–1990–e)*. Moscow: Rodnik, 1994.

Meshcheriakov, M. T. "Sovetskii Soiuz i antifashistskaia voina ispanskogo naroda 1936–1939," *Istoriia SSSR*, 1988, no. 1: 22–40.

——. "SSSR i grazhdanskaia voina v Ispanii," *Otechestvennaia istoriia*, 1993, no. 3: 83–95.

Metzmacher, Helmuth. "Deutsch-Englische Ausgleichbemühengen in Sommer 1939," *Verteljahrshefte für Zeitsgeschichte*, 14/4 (1956): 369–412.

Meyer, Georg, ed. *Generalfeldmarschall Wilhelm Ritter von Leeb: Tagebuchaufzeichnungen und Lagebeurteilungen aus zwei Weltkriegen*. Stuttgart: Deutsche Verlags-Anstalt, 1976.

Meysztowicz, Jan. *Czas przeszły dokonany: wspomnienia ze służby w Ministerstwie Spraw Zagranicznych w latach 1932–1939*. Warsaw: Instytut Prasy i Wydawn Novum, 1989.

Mezhdunarodnaia vstrecha, posviashchenaia 30-letiiu VIII kongressa Koninterna, Praga, 21–23 oktiabria 1965 g. Moscow: Mir i sotsializm, 1966.

Mezhdunarodnoe polozhenie i ugroza novoi voiny. Rostov-na-Donu: Literatura, 1931.

Mezhdunarodnyi kongress pisatelei v zaschitu kul'tury, Parizh, 1935. Moscow: Khudozhestvennaia literatura, 1936.

Mgeladze, Akaki. *Stalin, kakim ia ego znal: stranitsy nedavnogo proshlogo*. Tbilisi: [s.n.], 2001.

Michalka, Wolfgang. *Ribbentrop und die deutsche Weltpolitik, 1933–1940: Aussenpolitische Konzeptionen und Entscheidungsprozesse im Dritten Reich*. Munich: W. Fink, 1980.

Middlemas, Keith, and John Barnes. *Baldwin: A Biography*. New York: Macmillan, 1969.

Mif, Pavel. "Tol'ko Sovety moguy spasti Kitai," *Bol'shevik*, 1934, no. 7: 56–69.

Mikhailov, A. D. *M. Gor'kii i R. Rollan: perepiska 1916–1936*. Moscow: Nasledie, 1995.

Mikhailov, N., and Vladimir Naumov, "Skol'ko delegatov XVII s"ezda partii golosovalo protiv Stalina?" *Izvestiia TsK KPSS*, 1989, no. 7: 114–21.

Mikhalev, S. N. *Voennaia strategiia: podgotovka i vedenie voin novogo i noveishego vremeni*. Moscow: Kuchkovo pole, 2003.

Mikhoels, Solomon. "Moia rabota nad 'Korolem Lirom.'" In *Mikhoels: stat'i, besedy, rechi*. Moscow: Iskusstvo, 1964, 94–123.

Mikhutina, Irina V. "SSSR glazami pol'skikh diplomatov, 1926–1931 gg.," *Voprosy istorii*, 1993, no. 9: 45–58.

——. *Sovetsko-pol'skie otnosheniia, 1931–1935*. Moscow: Nauka, 1977.

Mikoian, A. I. "V pervyi raz bez Lenina," *Ogonek*, Dec. 12–9, 1989.

——. *Feliks Dzerzhinskii*. Moscow: Partizdat, 1936.

——. *Pishchevaia promyshlennost' Sovetskogo Soiuza: vtoraia sessia TsIK Soiuza SSSR, VII sozyva*. Moscow: TsIK, 1936.

——. *Problema snabzheniia strany i rekonstruktsiia narodnogo khoziaistva: rech' na III plenume MK VKP (b)*. Moscow: Moskovskii rabochii, 1929.

——. *Tak bylo: razmyshleniia o minuvshem*. Moscow: Vargrius, 1999.

——. *V polose velikogo pod"ema: rech' na pervom Vsesoiuznogo soveshchanii rabochikh i rabotnits stakhanovtsev*. Voronezh, 1935.

Mikoian, Nami. *S liubov'iu i pechal'iu: vospominaniia*. Moscow: Terra, 1998.

——. *Svoimi glazami*. Moscow: Kukushka, 2003.

Mikulicz, Sergiusz. *Prometeizm w polityce II Rzeczypospolitej*. Warsaw: Książka i Wiedza, 1971.

Milićević, Vladeta. *A King Dies in Marseilles: The Crime and Its Background*. Bad Godesberg, Germany: Hohwacht, 1959.

Millar, James R. "Mass Collectivization and the Contribution of Agriculture to the First Five Year Plan," *Slavic Review*, 33/4 (1974): 750–66.

——, and Alec Nove. "A Debate on Collectivization: Was Stalin Really Necessary?" *Problems of Communism*, 25/4 (1976): 49–62.

Miller, Edward S. *Bankrupting the Enemy: The U.S. Financial Siege of Japan before Pearl Harbor*. Annapolis, MD: Naval Institute, 2007.

Miller, Jamie. *Soviet Cinema: Politics and Persuasion under Stalin*. London: I. B. Tauris, 2010.

Miller, Margaret S. *The Economic Development of Russia, 1905–1914*. London: P. S. King and Son, 1926.

Miller, Robert F. *One Hundred Thousand Tractors: The MTS and the Development of Controls in Soviet Agriculture*. Cambridge, MA: Harvard University, 1970.

Millman, Brock. "Toward War with Russia: British Naval and Air Planning for Conflict in the Near East, 1939–1940," *Journal of Contemporary History*, 29/2 (1994): 261–84.

Mills, W. C. "The Chamberlain-Grandi Conversations of July–August 1937 and the Appeasement of Italy," *International History Review*, 19/3 (1997): 594–619.

Millward, James A. *Eurasian Crossroads: A History of Xinjiang*. New York: Columbia University, 2007.

Milne, Leslie. *Mikhail Bulgakov: A Critical Biography*. New York: Cambridge University, 1990.

Milosz, Czeslaw. *Native Realm: A Search for Self-Definition*. Garden City, NY: Doubleday, 1968.

Milovidov, A. "Velikii grazhdanin," *Pravda*, Feb. 17, 1938.

Milson, John. *Russian Tanks, 1900–1970: The Complete Illustrated History of Soviet Armoured Theory and Design*. Harrisburg, PA: Stackpole, 1971.

Milton, Sybil. "The Expulsion of Polish Jews from Germany, October 1938 to July 1939: a Documentation," *Leo Baeck Institute Yearbook*, 29 (1984): 169–99.

Minaev, V. *Podryvnaia deiatel'nost' inostrannykh razvedok v SSSR*. Moscow: Voenizdat, 1940.

Minakov, S. T. *1937: zagovor byl!* Moscow: Iauza-Press, 2012.

——. *Sovetskaia voennaia elita 20-kh godov: sostav, evoliutsiia, sotsoikul'turnye, osobennosti i politicheskaia rol'*. Orel: Orelizdat, 2000.

——. *Voennaia elita 20–30–kh godov XX veka*. Moscow: Russkoe slovo, 2004.

——. *Za otvorotom marshal'skoi shineli*. Orel: Orelizdat, 1999.

Minchenok, Dimitri. *Isaak Dunaevskii: bol'shoi kontsert*. Moscow: Olimp, 1998.

——. "Nestor i ten'," *Ogonek*, November 23, 2003.

Mindlin, Emilii L. *Neobyknovennye sobesedniki: kniga vospominanii*. Moscow: Sovetskii pisatel', 1968.

Miner, Steven Merritt. *Between Churchill and Stalin: The Soviet Union, Great Britain, and the Origins of the Grand Alliance*. Chapel Hill: University of North Carolina, 1998.

Mirkina, A. D., and V. S. Iarovikov, eds. *Marshal Zhukov: polkovodets i chelovek*. 2 vols. Moscow: APN, 1988.

Mironenko, S. V., et al., eds. *Moskovskii Kreml': tsitadel' Rossii*. Moscow: VVP, 2008.

Mironov, N. P. "Vosstanovlenie i razvitie Leninskikh printsipov sotsialisticheskoi zakonnosti (1953–1963 gg.)," *Voprosy istorii KPSS*, 1964, no. 2: 17–41.

Mirskii, D. S. *Istoriia russkoi literatury s drevneishikh vremen po 1925 god*. London: Overseas Publications Interchange Ltd., 1992.

Misshima, Yasuo, and Tomio Goto. *A Japanese View of Outer Mongolia*. New York: Institute of Pacific Relations, 1942.

Mitzner, Piotr. "Widmo POW," *Karta*, 1993, no. 11: 21–3.

Mlechin, Leonid. *KGB, predsedateli organov bezopasnosti: rassekrechenye sud'by*. 3rd ed. Moscow: Tsentrpoligraf, 2005.

"'Moe poslednee slovo na sude, veroiatno, budet moim poslednim solovom voobshche': kto i kak pravil rech' N. I. Bukahrina," *Istochnik*, 1996, no. 4: 78–92.

Moiseev, Igor' A. *Ia vospominaiu: gastrol' dlinnoiu v zhizn'*. 2nd ed. Moscow: Soglasie, 1996.

Molok, Iu. A. *Pushkin v 1937 g.: materialy i issledovaniia po ikonografii*. Moscow: NLO, 2000.

Molotov, V. M. *O pod'eme selskogo khoziaistva i kolkhoznom stroitelstve: rech' na III Vseukrainskoi konferentsii K.P.(b)U, 8 iiulia 1932 g.* Moscow: Partizdat, 1932

——. *Stat'i rechi, 1935–1936*. Moscow: Partizdat, 1937.

———. *V bor'be za sotsializm: rechi i stat'i.* Moscow: Partizdat, 1934, 2nd ed, 1935.

———. *Velikaia druzhba narodov SSSR.* Moscow: Partizdat, 1936.

Mommen, André. *Stalin's Economist: The Economic Contributions of Jenö Varga.* London and New York: Routledge, 2011.

Mommsen, Hans. "Der Reichstagbrand und sein politischen Folgen," *Vierteljahreshefte für Zeitgeschichte,* 12/4 (1964): 350–413.

———. "Hitler's Position in the Nazi System." In *From Weimar to Auschwitz.* New York: Oxford University, 1991, 163–88.

———. "Hitler's Reichstag Speech of 30 January 1939," *History and Memory,* 9/1–2 (1997): 147–61.

———. "The Reichstag Fire and Its Political Consequences." In *Republic to Reich: The Making of the Nazi Revolution,* edited by Hajo Holborn. New York: Pantheon, 1972, 129–222.

Monakov, Mikhail. "Zachem Stalin stroil okeanskii flot?" *Morskoi sbornik,* 1998, no. 12: 74–9.

Montefiore, Simon Sebag. *Stalin: Court of the Red Tsar.* London: Weidenfeld, 2003.

Moore, Barrington. *Social Origins of Dictatorship and Democracy: Lord and Peasant in the Making of the Modern World.* Boston: Beacon Press, 1966.

———. *Soviet Politics—the Dilemma of Power: The Role of Ideas in Social Change.* Cambridge, MA: Harvard University, 1950.

Moorhouse, Roger. *Killing Hitler: The Plots, The Assassins, and the Dictator Who Cheated Death.* New York: Bantam, 2006.

Moradiellos, Enrique. "The British Government and General Franco during the Spanish Civil War." In *Spain in an International Context,* edited by Christian Leitz and David J. Dunthorn. New York: Berghahn, 1999, 41–53.

———. "The Origins of British Non-Intervention in the Spanish Civil War: Anglo-Spanish Relations in Early 1936," *European History Quarterly,* 21/3 (1991): 339–64.

Moravec, František. *Master of Spies: The Memoirs of General František Moravec.* Garden City, NY: Doubleday, 1975.

Moritz, Erhard, ed. *Fall Barbarossa: Dokumente zur Vorbereitung der faschistischen Wehrmacht auf die Aggression gegen die Sowjetunion (1940/41).* Berlin: Deutscher Militärverlag, 1970.

Morley, James W., ed. *Deterrent Diplomacy: Japan, Germany, and the USSR 1935–1940.* New York: Columbia University, 1976.

Morozov, Stanislav V. *Pol'sko-Chekhoslovatskie otnosheniia, 1933–1939: chto skryvalos' za politikoi "ravnoudalennosti" ministra Iu. Beka.* Moscow: Moskovskii universitet, 2004.

Morrell, Gordon W. *Britain Confronts the Stalin Revolution: Anglo-Soviet Relations and the Metro-Vickers Crisis.* Waterloo: Wilfrid Laurier University, 1995.

Morrison, Simon, ed. *Sergey Prokofiev and His World.* Princeton, NJ: Princeton University, 2008.

———. *The People's Artist: Prokofiev's Soviet Years.* New York: Oxford University, 2009.

Morukov, Iu. N., ed. *Velikaia Otechestvennaia voina 1941–1945 gg. kampanii i strategicheskie operatsii v tsifrakh.* 2 vols. Moscow: Obedinennaia redaktsiia MVD Rossii, 2010.

"Moskovskii dnevnik Romena Rollanda," *Voprosy literatury,* 1989, no. 3: 190–246.

Mosley, Leonard. *On Borrowed Time: How World War II Began.* New York: Random House, 1969.

Mosse, George L. *The Nationalization of the Masses: Political Symbolism and Mass*

Movements in Germany from the Napoleonic Wars through the Third Reich. New York: New American Library, 1975.

Mozokhin, O. B. *Pravo na repressi.* Moscow: Kuchkovo pole, 2006.

Mozokhin, Oleg. *VChK-OGPU: na zashchite ekonomicheskoi bezopasnosti gosudarstva i v bor'be s terrorizmom.* Moscow: Eksmo, 2004.

———, and Teodor Gladkov. *Menzhinskii: intelligent s Lubianki.* Moscow: Iauza, 2005.

Mueller, K. J. *Das Heer und Hitler: Armee und nationalsozitialistiches Regime 1933–1940.* Stuttgart: Deutsche Verlags-Anstalt, 1969.

Mueller-Hildebrand, Burkhart. *Sukhoputnaia armiia Germanii 1933–1945 gg.* Moscow: Eksmo, 2002.

Muggeridge, Malcolm, ed. *Ciano's Diplomatic Papers.* London: Odhams Press, 1948.

———. *Chronicles of Wasted Time.* London: Collins, 1972.

———. *Ciano's Diary: 1939–1943.* London: Heinemann, 1947.

Mugleston, W. F. "Hindus, Maurice Gerschon (1891–1969)," *Dictionary of American Biography,* supplement 8, edited by John A. Garraty. New York: Scribner's, 1988, 260–1.

Mukhin, Iurii. "Amtorg: amerikanskii sled v sovetskoi oboronke," *Poligon,* 2000, no. 3: 34–41, no. 4: 37–53.

Müller, Rolf-Dieter. *Das Tor zur Weltmacht: die Bedeutung der Sowjetunion für die deutsche Wirtschafts- und Rüstungspolitik zwischen den Weltkriegen.* Boppard am Rhein: Harald Boldt, 1984.

Muratov, V. "Shest' chasov s I.V. Stalinym v Kremle," *Neva,* 1993, no. 7: 280–8.

———, and Iu. Gorodetskaia. *Komandarm Lukin: povest'.* Moscow: Voenizdat, 1990.

Murin, Iurii G. "Kak fal'sifitsirovalos' 'delo Bukharina,'" *Novaia i noveishaia istoriia,* 1995, no. 1: 61–70.

———. "'Prosti, menia, Koba . . . ': neizvestnoe pis'mo N. Bukharina," *Istochnik,* 1993, no. 0: 23–5.

———. "Nakanune 22 iiunia 1941 g.: neopublikovannoe interv'iu marshala Sovetskogo Soiuza A. M. Vasilevskogo" [Dec. 6, 1965], *Novaia i noveishaia istoriia,* 1992, no. 6: 3–11.

———. *Iosif Stalin v ob"iatiakh sem'i: iz lichnogo arkhiva.* Moscow: Rodina, 1993.

———, ed. *Pisatel' i vozhd', perepiska M.A. Sholokhova s I.V. Stalinym: sbornik dokumentov iz lichnogo arkhiva I.V. Stalina.* Moscow: Raritet, 1997.

Murphy, David E. *What Stalin Knew: The Enigma of Barbarossa.* New Haven, CT: Yale University, 2005.

Murray, John. *Politics and Place Names: Changing Names in the Late Soviet Period.* Birmingham, UK: Department of Russian University of Birmingham, 2000.

Murray, Nora. *I Spied for Stalin.* New York: W. Funk, 1951.

Murray, Williamson. *The Change in the European Balance of Power, 1938–1939.* Princeton, NJ: Princeton University, 1984.

Musial, Bogdan. *Stalins Beutezug: die Plünderung Deutschlands und der Aufstieg der Sowjetunion zur Weltmacht.* Berlin: Propyläen, 2010.

Mussolini, Benito. *Opera Omnia.* 35 vols. Edited by Edoardo Susmel and Duilio Susmel. Florence: La Fenice, 1951–1962.

———. *Scritti e discorsi.* 12 vols. Milan: Hoepli, 1934–1939.

Muza, Anna. "The Tragedy of a Russian Woman: Anna Karenina in the Moscow Art Theater, 1937," *Russian Literature,* 65/4 (2009): 467–506.

Mydans, Carl. *More than Meets the Eye.* New York: Harper, 1959.

Nabokov, Vladimir. "Russian Writers, Censors, Readers." In *Nabokov: Lectures on Russian Literature,* edited by Fredson Bowers. New York: HBJ, 1981, 12–8.

———. *Tyrants Destroyed and Other Stories.* New York: McGraw Hill, 1975.

"'Nachalo razgroma profdvizheniia': dnevnik B. G. Kozeleva, 1927–1930 gg.," *Istoricheskii arkhiv,* 1997, no. 1: 115–51.

Naida, Sergei F. *Bor'ba finskogo naroda za svoe osvobozhdenie.* Moscow-Leningrad: Voenno-morskoe izdatel'stvo, 1939.

Nair, A. M. *An Indian Freedom Fighter in Japan.* New Delhi: Vikas, 1985.

Nakamura, Yasushi. "Did the Soviet Command Economy Command Money? A Quantitative Analysis," *Europe-Asia Studies,* 63/7 (2011): 1133–56.

Namier, Lewis. "From Vienna to Versailles." In *Conflicts: Studies in Contemporary History.* London: Macmillan, 1942, 1–18.

———. *In the Nazi Era.* London: Macmillan, 1952.

Naporko, Aleksandr G., et al., eds. *Zheleznodorozhnyi transport v gody industrializatsii SSSR, 1926–1941.* Moscow: Transport, 1970.

Na prieme u Stalina: tetradi (zhurnaly) zapisei lits, priniatykh I.V. Stalinym: 1924–1953 gg. Moscow: Novyi khronograf, 2008.

Narkiewicz, Olga A. *The Making of the Soviet State Apparatus.* Manchester: Manchester University, 1970.

Narochnitskii, A. L. "Sovetsko-iugoslavskii dogovor 5 aprelia 1941 g. o druzhbe i nenapadenii (po arkhivnym materialam)," *Novaia i noveishaia istoriia,* 1989, no. 1: 3–19.

Narodnoe khoziaistvo SSSR za 70 let. Moscow: Finansy i statistika, 1987.

Narodno-khoziaistvennyi plan 1936: chetvertyi god vtoroi piatiletki. 2nd ed. Moscow: Gosplan SSSR, 1936.

Naszkowski, Marian. *Nespokoinye dni: vospominaniia o tridsatykh godakh.* Moscow: Inostrannaia literatura, 1962.

Naumov, Leonid A. *Bor'ba v rukovodstve NKVD, 1936–1938 gg.: oprichnyi dvor Iosifa Groznogo.* Moscow: Sputnik, 2004.

———. *Stalin i NKVD.* Moscow: Yauza-Eksmo, 2007.

Naumov, V. P. *Lavrentii Beriia, 1953: dokumenty.* Moscow: Mezhdunarodnyi fond Demokratiia, 1999.

———. *1941 god: uroki i vyvody.* 2 vols. Moscow: Mezhdunarodnyi fond Demokratiia, 1998.

———, et al., eds. *Georgii Zhukov: stenogramma oktiabr'skogo (1957 g.) plenuma TsK KPSS i drugie dokumenty.* Moscow: Mezhdunarodnyi fond Demokratiia, 2001.

Naylor, John F. *A Man and an Institution: Sir Maurice Hankey, the Cabinet Secretariat and the Custody of Cabinet Secrecy.* New York: Cambridge University, 2009.

Nazi Conspiracy and Aggression. 8 vols., with 2 suppl. Washington, D.C.: U.S. Government Printing Office, 1946–48.

"'Naznachit' revoliutsiiu v Germanii na 9 noiabria'," *Istochnik,* 1995, no. 5: 115–39.

Nechkina, M. V., ed. *Istoriia SSSR.* 2 vols. Moscow: Gosudarstvennoe sotsial'no-Economicheskoe izdatel'stvo, 1940.

"'Ne chuvstvovat' za soboiu topoto': M. M. Litvinov o svoei okhrane," *Istochnik,* 1996, no. 5: 123–4.

Neilson, Keith. *Britain and the Last Tsar: British Policy towards Russia, 1894–1917.* Oxford: Clarendon, 1995.

———. *Britain, Soviet Russia, and the Collapse of the Versailles Order, 1919–1939.* New York: Cambridge University, 2006.

"'Neizmennyi drug'—eto obiazyvaet . . . : pis'ma O. I. Sobalevoi-Mikhal'tsevoi," *Istochnik,* 1998, no. 3: 113–8.

Nekrasov, V. F., ed. *Beria: konets kar'ery.* Moscow: Politizdat, 1991.

Nekrich, Alexander M. "The Dynamism of the Past." In *Operation Barbarossa,* edited by Joseph L. Wieczynski. Salt Lake City: Charles Schlacks Jr., 1993, 228–40.

———. "The Soviet German Treaty of August 1939," Russian Research Center, Harvard University, May 18, 1977.

———. *1941, 22 iuinia.* 2nd ed. Moscow: Pamyatniki istoricheskoi mysli, 1995.

———. *"June 22, 1941": Soviet Historians and the German Invasion.* Columbia: University of South Carolina, 1968.

———. *Pariahs, Partners, Predators: German-Soviet Relations 1922–1941.* New York: Columbia University, 1997.

Neumann, Franz L. *Behemoth: The Structure and Practice of National Socialism.* London: Victor Gollancz, 1942.

Nevakivi, Jukka. "The Soviet Union and Finland after the War, 1944–1953." In *The Soviet Union and Europe in the Cold War, 1943–1953,* edited by Francesca Gori and Silvio Pons. London: Macmillan, 1996, 89–105.

Nevezhin, Vladimir A. "Bol'shie Kremlevskie priemy Stalina (1930-e—nachalo 1940-x gg.)," *Otechestvennaia istoriia,* 2005, no. 3: 56–70, no. 4: 123–39.

———. "Dve direktivy 1941 g.: o propagandistskoi podgotovke SSSR k voine." In *Arkheograficheskii ezhegodnik za 1995 god.* Moscow: Nauka, 1997, 191–207.

———. "Pol'sha v sovetskoi propagande 19389–1945 gg." In *Rossiia i vneshnyi mir: dialog kul'tur,* edited by Iurii S. Borisov et al. Moscow: Akademiia nauk SSSR, 1997, 69–88.

———. "Sobiralsia li Stalin nastupat' v 1941 g. (Zametki na poliakh 'Ledokola' V. Suvorova)," *Kentavr,* 1995, no. 1: 76–85.

———. "Sovetskaia politika i kul'turnye sviazi s Germaniei, 1939–1941 gg.," *Otechestvennaia istoriia,* no. 1 (1993): 18–34.

———. *Sindrom nastupatel'noi voiny: sovetskakia propaganda v preddverii 'sviashchennykh boev', 1939–1941 gg.* Moscow: AIRO-XX, 1997.

———. *Zastol'ia iosifa Stalina: bol'shie kremlevskie priemy 1930–1940-x gg.* Moscow: Novyi khronograf, 2011.

———. *Zastol'nye rechi Stalina: dokumenty i materialy.* Moscow: AIRO-XX, 2003.

Neville, Peter. "A Prophet Scorned? Ralph Wigram, the Foreign Office and the German Threat, 1933–36," *Journal of Contemporary History,* 40/1 (2005): 41–54.

"'Nevol'niki v rukakh germanskogo reiskhvera': rech' I. V. Stalina v Narkomate oborony," *Istochnik,* 1994, no. 3: 72–88.

Newman, Simon. *March 1939: The British Guarantee to Poland.* Oxford: Clarendon, 1976.

Niclauss, Karlheinz. *Die Sowjetunion und Hitlers Machtergreifung: eine Studie über die deutsch-russischen Beziehungen der Jahre 1929 bis 1935.* Bonn: Röhrscheid, 1966.

Nicolaevsky, Boris. "The Kirov Assassination," *The New Leader,* August 23, 1941.

———. *Power and the Soviet Elite.* New York: Praeger, 1965.

Nielsen, Jens Petter. *Miliukov i Stalin: o politicheskoi evoliutsii P.V. Miliukova v emigratsii (1918–1943).* Oslo: Universitetet i Oslo, Slavisk-Baltisk Institutt, 1983.

Nikolaevich, S. "Poslednii seans, ili sud'ba beloizhenshchinyvSSSR," *Ogonek,* 1992, no. 4.

Nikolaevskii, Boris. "Dal'stroi: sovetskaia katorga v Kolymskom krae," *Sotsialisticheskii vestnik,* Dec. 10, 1945.

———. *Tainye stranitsy istorii.* Moscow: Izdatel'stvo gumanitarnoi literatury, 1995.

Nikulin, Lev. *Tukhachevskii: biograficheskii ocherk.* Moscow: Voenizdat, 1963.

———. *Tukhachevskii: biograficheskii ocherk.* Moscow: Voenizdat, 1964.

Noakes, Jeremy, and Jeffrey Pridham, eds. *Nazism, 1919–1945: A Documentary Reader.* 4 vols. Exeter: University of Exeter, 1983–98.

"'No ia to znaiu, chto ty prav': pis'mo N. I. Bukharina I. V. Stalinu iz vnutrennei tiur'my NKVD," *Istochnik,* 2000, no. 3: 46–58.

Nolte, Ernst. "Diktatur." In *Geschichtliche Grundbegriffe: historisches Lexikon zur politisch-sozialen Sprache in Deutschland,* edited by Otto Brunner et al. 8 vols. Stuttgart: E. Klett, 1972–97.

———. *Der europäische Bürgerkrieg 1917–1945: Nationalsozialismus und Bolschewismus.* Frankfurt-am-Main: Ullstein, 1987.

Nord, Lidiia A. "Marshal Tukhachevskii," *Vozrozhdenie,* 66 (1957).

———. *Marshal Tukhachevsky.* Paris: Lef, 1978.

Nord, Philip G. *France 1940.* New Haven, CT: Yale University, 2015.

Nordlander, David J. "Magadan and the Evolution of the Dal'stroi Bosses in the 1930s," *Cahiers du monde russe,* 42/2–3–4 (2001): 649–65.

———. "Magadan and the Economic History of Dalstroi in the 1930s." In *The Economics of Forced Labor: The Soviet Gulag,* edited by Paul R. Gregory and Valery Lazerev. Stanford, CA: Hoover Institution, 2003.

Norling, Nicklas. "Myth and Reality: Politics in Soviet Uzbekistan." PhD diss. Johns Hopkins University, 2014.

Novak, George, ed. *The Case of Leon Trotsky: Reports of Hearings on the Charges Made against Him in the Moscow Trials.* New York: Merit, 1968.

Nove, Alec. "The Peasants, Collectivization, and Mr. Carr," *Soviet Studies,* 10/4 (1958–9): 384–9.

———. "Was Stalin Really Necessary?" *Encounter,* April 1962: 86–92.

———. *An Economic History of the USSR, 1917–1991.* 3rd ed. London and New York: Penguin Books, 1992.

———. *An Economic History of the USSR.* 2nd ed. London: Penguin Books, 1989.

———. *An Economic History of the USSR.* London: Allen Lane, 1969.

———. *Stalinism and After: The Road to Gorbachev.* 3rd ed. London: Allen, Unwin, 1989.

———. *Was Stalin Really Necessary? Some Problems of Soviet Political Economy.* New York: Praeger, 1964.

Novikov, M. V. *SSSR, Komintern i grazhdanskaia voina v Ispanii: 1936—1939 gg.* 2 vols. Iaroslavl: Iaroslavskii pedagogicheskii universiteta, 1997.

Novikov, Nikolai V. *Vospominaniia diplomata: zapiski 1938-1947.* Moscow: Politizdat, 1989.

Novikova, Lidiia. "Obruchennyi s bogom." In *Ivan Kozlovskii: vospominaniia, stat'i.* Moscow: Natalis, Ripol Klassik, 2005.

Novobranets, Vasily Andreevich. "Nakanune voiny," *Znamia,* 1990, no. 6: 165–92.

Nowak, Robert. "Von der Karpatenukraine zum Karpatenland," *Zeitschrift für Geopolitik,* 16/5 (1939): 313–32.

"'Nuzhen li nam ermitazh'," *Istochnik,* 1999, no. 1: 106–10.

Obi, Toshito. *Zoruge jiken.* 4 vols. Tokyo: Misuzu shobō, 1962–71.

"'Ochen' vysoko tsenit t. Beria,'" *Istochnik,* 1996, no. 3: 163–5.

Ocherki istorii kommunisticheskoi partii Armenii. Yerevan: Aiastan, 1967.

Ocherki istorii kommunisticheskoi partii Azerbaidzhana. Baku: Azerbaidzhanskoe gosizdat, 1963.

Ocherki istorii kommunisticheskoi partii Latvii. 2 vols. Riga: Latviiskoe gosizdat, 1965.

O'Connor, Timothy E. *Diplomacy and Revolution: G. V. Chicherin and Soviet Foreign Affairs 1918–1930.* Ames: Iowa University, 1988.

"O dele tak nazyvaeomom 'Moskovskom tsentre,'" *Izvestiia TsK KPSS,* 1989, no. 7: 65–85

Odom, Anne, and Wendy Salmond, eds. *Treasures into Tractors: The Selling of Russia's Cultural Heritage, 1918–1938.* Washington, D.C.: Hillwood Estate, 2009.

Official Documents Concerning Polish-German and Polish-Soviet Relations, 1933–1939. London: Hutchinson, 1940.

Ogata, Sadako N. *Defiance in Manchuria: The Making of Japanese Foreign Policy, 1931–1932.* Berkeley: University of California, 1964.

Ohayon, Isabelle. *La sedentarisation des Kazakhs dans l'URSS de Staline.* Paris: Maisonneuve et Larose, 2006.

Oja, Matt F. "From Krestianka to Udarnitsa: Rural Women and the Vydvizhenie Campaign, 1933–1941," Carl Beck Papers, University of Pittsburgh, Center for Russian and East European Studies, no. 1203 (1996).

Okhotin, N. G., and A. Roginskii. "Iz istorii 'nemetskoi operatisii' NKVD 1937–1938 gg." In *Nakazannyi narod: repressii protiv rossiiskikh nemtsev,* edited by I. L. Shcherbakova. Moscow: Zvenia, 1999, 35–75.

Oleinikov, S. "Chetvertoe maia," *Pravda,* November 7, 1935.

"O nakoplenii nachal'stvuiushchego sostava Raboche-Krest'ianskoi Krasnoi Armii," *Izvestiia TsK KPSS,* 1990, no. 1: 177–89.

Oppenheim, Samuel A. *The Practical Bolshevik: A. I. Rykov and Russian Communism, 1881–1938.* Stanford, CA: Hoover Institution, 1979.

Oprischenko, A. L. *Istoriografiia sotsialisticheskogo sorevnovaniia rabochego klassa SSSR.* Kharkov: Vishcha shkola, 1975.

Ordzhonikidze, G. K. *Stat'i i rechi.* 2 vols. Moscow: Politicheskaia literatura, 1956–7.

Ordzhonikidze, Z. G. *O Sergo Ordzhonikidze: vospominaniia, ocherki, stat'i sovremennikov.* Moscow: Politizdat, 1981.

Orlov, Alexander. *Tainaia istoriia stalinskikh prestuplenii.* New York: Vremia i my, 1983.

———. *The Secret History of Stalin's Crimes.* New York: Random House, 1953.

Orlov, B. M. "V poiskakh soiuznikov: komandovanie Krasnoi Armii i problemy vneshnei politiki SSSR v 30-x goadkh," *Voprosy istorii,* 1990, no. 4: 40–53.

Orlov, I. B., and M. D. Kressova. "Inostrannyi turizm v SSSR v kontse 1920–x-nachale 1930–x godov: problemy stanovleniia 'Freemen Industry.'" In *Problemy istorii servisa: zdravookhranenie, kul'tura, dosug,* edited by Iu. A. Poliakov. Moscow: Moskovskii universitet servisa, 2004, 159–69.

Orlov, V. M. "Rech' tov V. M. Orlova na Chrezvychainom VIII Vsesiuznom S"ezde Sovetov (28 noiabria 1936 g.)," *Morskoi sbornik,* 1936, no. 12: 8–9.

Orlov, Vladimir. "Prokofiev and the Myth of the Father of Nations: The Cantata Zdravitsa," *Journal of Musicology,* 30/4 (2013): 577–620.

Orlova, Raisa D. *Memoirs.* New York: Random House, 1983.

———. *Vospominaniia o neproshedshem vremeni.* Moscow: Slovo, 1993.

Orlovsky, Daniel T. *The Limits of Reform: The Ministry of Internal Affairs in Imperial Russia, 1802–1881.* Cambridge, MA: Harvard University, 1981.

Orlow, Dietrich. *The History of the Nazi Party.* 2 vols. Pittsburgh: University of Pittsburgh, 1969, 1973.

Orwell, George. *Homage to Catalonia.* Reprint ed. London: Martin Secker & Warburg, 1984.

Orynianskii, A. A. *Sovetskaia Abkhaziia: putevoditel' po Abkhazii.* Sukhumi: Izdanie ekskursionnogo biuro pri glavpolitprosvete A.S.S.R. Abkhazii, 1930, 1932, 1935.

Osborn, Patrick R. *Operation Pike: Britain versus the Soviet Union, 1939–1941.* Westport, CT: Greenwood Press, 2000.

Oskolkov, Evgenii N. *Golod 1932/1933: khlebozagotovki i golod 932/1933 g. v Severo-Kavkavskom krae.* Rostov-na-Donu: Rostovskii universitet, 1991.

"'Osnovnaia tsel' ego priezda': otchety sotrudnikov VOKSa o prebyvanii v SSSR deiateli nauk i kultury Velikobritanii, 1934–1936 gg.," *Istoricheskii arkhiv,* 1996, no. 3: 134–35.

Osnovnoi zakon (konstitutsiia) Sovetskoi Sotsialisticheskoi Respubliki Gruzii. Tiflis: NKIU SSRG, 1926.

Osokina, Elena A. "Economic Disobedience under Stalin." In *Contending with Stalinism,* edited by Lynne Viola. Ithaca, NY: Cornell University, 2002, 170–200.

———. *Ierarkhiia potrebleniia: o zhizni liudei v usloviakh stalinskogo snabzheniia, 1928–1935 gg.* Moscow: Izdatel'stvo MGU, 1993.

———. *Za fasadom "stalinskogo izobiliia": raspredelenie i rynok v snabzhenii naseleniia v gody industrializatsii 1927–1941.* Moscow: Rosspen, 1997.

———. *Zoloto dlia industrializatsii: Torgsin.* Moscow: Rosspen, 2009.

Ostrovskii, Aleksandr V. *Kto stoial za spinoi Stalina?* Moscow: Tsentropoligraf-Mim Delta, 2004.

"O tak nazyvaemom 'antisovetskom ob"edinennom trotskistsko-zinov'evskom tsentre'," *Izvestiia Tsk KPSS,* 1989, no. 8: 78–115.

"O tak nazyvaemom 'parallel'nom antisovetskom trotskistskom tsentre'," *Izvestiia Tsk KPSS,* 1989, no. 9: 30–50.

Ovchinnikov, A. G., et al., eds. *Krasnoznamennyi belorusskii voennyi okrug.* Minsk: Belarus, 1973.

Overy, Richard J. "Germany and the Munich Crisis: A Mutilated Victory?" *Diplomacy and Statecraft,* 10/2–3 (1999): 191–215.

———. "Strategic Intelligence and the Outbreak of the Second World War," *War in History,* 5/4 (1998): 451–80.

———. *1939: Countdown to War.* London: Allen Lane, 2009.

———. *Göring: Hitler's Iron Knight.* London and New York: I. B. Tauris, 2012.

———. *The Battle of Britain: the Myth and the Reality.* New York: W. W. Norton, 2001.

———. *The Dictators: Hitler's Germany, Stalin's Russia.* New York: W. W. Norton, 2004.

———. *The Road to War: The Origins of World War II.* rev. ed. New York: Penguin, 1999.

———. *The Twilight Years: The Paradox of Britain between the Wars.* New York: Viking, 2009.

———. *Why the Allies Won.* New York: W. W. Norton 1996.

Paasikivi, Juho K. *Meine Moskauer Mission 1939–1941.* Hamburg: Holsten, 1966.

Paine, S. C. M. *The Wars for Asia, 1911–1949.* New York: Cambridge University, 2012.

Paletskis, Iustas. *V dvukh mirakh.* Moscow: Politizdat, 1974.

Palme-Dutt, Rajani. "Britanskii imperializm, fashizm i antisovetskaia kompaniia,"

Kommunisticheskii internatsional, July 20, 1933: 46–54.

Pankov, D. V. *Komkor Eideman.* Moscow: Voenizdat, 1965.

Pankrashova, M., and Vilnos Ia. Sipols, eds. "Soviet-British-French Talks in Moscow in 1939: A Documentary Survey," *International Affairs,* 1969, no. 7: 74–83, no. 8: 87–95, no. 9: 62–6, no. 10 : 61–8.

Panné, Jean-Louis. *Souvarine: le premier désenchanté du communisme.* Paris: R. Laffont, 1993.

Panteleev, Iu. A. *Morskoi front.* Moscow: Voenizdat, 1965.

Pantsov, Aleksandr, and Steven Levine. *Mao: The Real Story.* New York: Simon & Schuster, 2012.

Papchinskii, Aleksander, and Mikhail Tumshis. *Shchit, raskolotyi mechom: NKVD protiv VChK.* Moscow: Sovremennik, 2001.

Paperny, Vladimir. *Architecture in the Age of Stalin: Culture Two.* New York: Cambridge University, 2002.

Papkov, S. A. *Stalinskii terror v Sibiri, 1928–1941.* Novosibirsk: Sibirskoe otdeleniie RAN, 1997.

Parker, Robert A. C. *Chamberlain and Appeasement: British Policy and the Coming of the Second World War.* New York: St. Martin's, 1993.

———. *Churchill and Appeasement: Could Churchill Have Prevented the Second World War?* New York: Macmillan, 2000.

Parnov, Eremei. *Skelety v seife.* 2 vols. Moscow: Terra, 2000.

Parssinen, Terry. *The Oster Conspiracy of 1938: The Unknown Story of the Military Plot to Kill Hitler and Avert World War II.* New York: HarperCollins, 2003.

Pasternak, Boris. *An Essay in Autobiography.* Translated by Manya Harari. London: Collins & Harvill, 1959.

———. *Izbrannye perevody.* Moscow: Sovetskii pisatel', 1940.

Patolichev, Nikolai S. *Isptytanie na zrelost'.* Moscow: Politizdat, 1977.

———. *Vospominaniia.* Moscow: Ob-vo sokhraneniia literaturnogo naslediia, 2008.

Patrikeef, Felix. *Russian Politics in Exile: The Northeast Asian Balance of Power, 1924–1931.* New York: Palgrave Macmillan, 2002.

Pätzold, Kurt, ed. *Verfolgung, Vertreibung, Vernichtung: Dokumente des faschistischen Antisemitismus 1933 bis 1942.* Leipzig: Reclam, 1983.

Paul-Boncour, Joseph. *Entre deux guerres: souvenirs sur la IIIe république.* 3 vols. Paris: Plon, 1945–46.

Paustovsky, Konstantin. *Story of a Life, VI: The Restless Years.* London: Harvill, 1974.

Pavliukov, A. *Ezhov: Biografia.* Moscow: Zaharov, 2007.

Pavlov, A. G. "Sovetskaia voennaia razvedka nakanun Velikoi Otechestvennoi voiny," *Novaia i noveishaia istoriia,* 1995, no. 1: 49–60.

Pavlov, A. P. *Kommunisticheskaia partiia v bor'be za zavershenie sotsialistichskoi rekonstrukstii narodnogo khoziaistva: pobeda sotsializma v SSSR (1933–1937 gg.).* Moscow: VPSh, 1959.

Pavlov, Dmitrii. "Dve poslednie vstrechi s V.M. Molotovym," *Literaturnaia gazeta,* April 18, 1990.

———. "Iz zapisok narkoma," *Novaia i noveishaia istoriia,* 1988, no. 6: 106–27.

Pavlov, Ivan. *1920-e: revoliutsiia i biurokratiia: zapiski oppozitsionera.* St. Petersburg: Peterburg—XXI vek, 2001.

Pavlov, L. G. "Ot 'Iunkersa' 1941 k Tsessne 1987," *Voenno-istoricheskii zhurnal,* 1990, no. 6: 43–6.

Pavlov, M. Iu. *Anastas Mikoian: politicheskii portret na fone sovetskoi epokhi.* Moscow: Mezhdunarodnye otnosheniia, 2010.

Pavlov, M. V., et al. *Sovetskie srednie tanki dovoennogo perioda (1924–1941).* Moscow, 2000.

———. *Tanki BT Chast' 1.* Moscow: Armada, 1999.

Pavlov, Vitalii. *Tragediia sovetskoi razvedki.* Moscow: Tsentropoligraf, 2000.

Pavlova, Irina V. "1937: Vybory kak mistifikatsiia, terror kak real'nost," *Voprosy Istorii,* 2003, no. 10: 19–37.

———. *Stalinizm: Stanovlenie mekhanizma vlasti.* Novosibirsk: Sibirskii khronograf, 1993.

Paxton, Robert O. *Vichy France: Old Guard and New Order, 1940–1944.* New York: Knopf, 1972.

Payne, Matthew J. *Stalin's Railroad: Turksib and the Building of Socialism.* Pittsburgh, PA: University of Pittsburgh, 2001.

Payne, Robert. *The Life and Death of Adolf Hitler.* New York: Praeger, 1973.

Payne, Stanley G. *A History of Fascism, 1914–1945.* Madison: University of Wisconsin, 1995.

———. *Falange: A History of Spanish Fascism.* Stanford, CA: Stanford University, 1961.

———. *Fascism in Spain, 1923–1977.* Madison: University of Wisconsin, 1999.

———. *Spain's First Democracy: The Second Republic, 1931–1936.* Madison: University of Wisconsin, 1993.

———. *The Collapse of the Spanish Republic, 1933–1936: Origins of the Civil War.* New Haven, CT: Yale University, 2006.

———. *The Franco Regime, 1936–1975.* Madison: University of Wisconsin, 1987.

———. *The Spanish Civil War, the Soviet Union, and Communism.* New Haven, CT, and London: Yale University, 2004.

———. *The Spanish Revolution.* New York: W. W. Norton, 1970.

Pazi, A. N. *Nash Mironych: vospominania o zhizni i deiatel'nosti S.M. Kirova v Leningrade.* Leningrad: Lenizdat, 1969.

Peace and War—United States Foreign Policy, 1931–1941. Washington, D.C.: U.S. Government Printing Office, 1943.

Peake, Hayden. *The Private Life of Kim Philby: The Moscow Years.* London: Fromm International, 1999.

Pearton, Maurice. *Oil and the Romanian State.* Oxford: Clarendon, 1971.

Pechenkin, A. A. "'Sovremennaia armiia— armiia nastupatel'naia'," *Istoricheskii arkhiv,* 1995, no. 2: 23–31.

———. "1937 god: Stalin i voennyi sovet," *Otechestvennaia istoriia,* 2003, no. 1: 35–53.

Peden, G. C. *Arms, Economics, and British Strategy: from Dreadnoughts to Hydrogen Bombs.* New York: Cambridge University, 2007.

Pegov, N. M. *Dalekoe-blizkoe: vospominaniia.* Moscow: Politizdat, 1982.

Penner, D'Ann R. "Stalin and the Ital'ianka of 1932–1933 in the Don Region," *Cahiers du monde russe,* 39/1–2 (1998): 27–67.

Pepłoński, Andrzej. *Wywiad Polski na ZSSR, 1921–1939.* Warsaw: Gryf, 1996.

Peris, Daniel. *Storming the Heavens: The Soviet League of the Militant Godless.* Ithaca, NY: Cornell University, 1998.

Perkhin, V. V., ed. *Deiateli russkogo iskusstva i M.B. Khrapchenko, predsedatel' Vsesiuznogo komiteta po delam iskusstv, aprel' 1939—ianvar' 1948: svod pisem.* Moscow: Nauka, 2007.

Pertsov, V., et al. *Voina i revoliutsiia v Ispanii, 1936–1939.* 4 vols. Moscow: Progress, 1968.

Pervaia moskovskaia konferentsiia VKP (b): stenpograficheskii otchet. Moscow:

Moskovskii oblastnoi komitet VKP b, 1929.

Pervaia sessia Verkhovnogo Soveta SSSR, 12–19 ianvaria 1938 g. (sozyv I): stenografocheskii otchet. Moscow: Verkhovnyi Sovet SSSR, 1938.

Pervaia vsesoiuznaia konferentsiia rabotnikov sotsialisticheskoi promyshlennosti: stenograficheskii otchet s 30 ianvaria po 5 fevralia 1931. Moscow: Gos. sots-ekonomicheskoe izdatel'stvo, 1931.

Pervoe soveshchanie rabochikh i rabotnits—stakhanovtsev 1935. Moscow: Partizdat, 1935.

Pervyi vsesoiuznyi s"ezd kolkhoznikov-udarnikov, 15–19 fevralia 1933 g.: stenograficheskii otchet. Moscow, Leningrad: Selkhozgiz, 1933.

Pervyi vsesoiuznyi s"ezd sovetskikh pisatelei: stenograficheskii otchet. Moscow: Khudozhestvennaia literatura, 1934.

Pervyi vsesoiuznyi s"ezd udarnykh brigad: sbornik dokumentov i materialov. Moscow: Profizdat, 1959.

Peschanski, Denis, ed. *Marcel Cachin: Carnets 1906–1947.* 4 vols. Paris: CNRS Editions, 1993–8.

Peshcherskii, V. L. *"Krasnaia kapella": sovetskaia razvedka protiv gestapo.* Moscow: Tsentropoligraf, 2000.

———. "Kak I. V. Stalina pytalsia predotvarit' voinu s Finliandiei," *Voenno-istoricheskii zhurnal,* 1998, no. 1: 54–63.

Peshekhonov, Alexei. *Pravo na zemliu (natsionalizatsia i sotsializatsia).* Petrograd: Zadruga, 1917.

Petacci, Claretta. *Mussolini segreto: Diari 1932–1938.* Milan: Rizzoli, 2009.

Petrement, Simone. *Simone Weil: A Life.* New York: Schocken, 1988.

Petrone, Karen. *Life Has Become More Joyous, Comrades: Celebrations in the Time of Stalin.* Bloomington: Indiana University, 2000.

Petrov, G. E., ed. *Ukrepim sovety DVK.* Khabarovsk: Dalgiza, 1934.

Petrov, Iurii P. *Partiinoe stroitel'stvo v sovetskoi armii i flote: deiatel'nost' KPSS po sozdaniiu i ukrepleniiu politorganov, partiinykh i komsomolskikh organizatsii v vooruzhennykh silakh, 1918–1961 gg.* Moscow: Voenizdat, 1964.

———. *Stroitel'stvo politorganov, partiinykh i komsomol'skikh organizatisii armii i flota.* Moscow: Voenizdat, 1968.

Petrov, Nikita. "Rodos: ostrov arkhipelaga Gulaga," *Novaia gazeta,* September 22, 2010.

———, and Marc Jansen. *Stalinskii pitomets—Nikolai Ezhov.* Moscow: Rosspen 2008.

Petrov, N. V., and A. B. Roginskii. "'Pol'skaia operatsiia' NKVD, 1937–1938 gg." In *Repressi protiv poliakov i pol'skikh grazhdan,* edited by A. E. Gur'ianov. Moscow: Zvenia, 1997, 22–43.

———, and K. V. Skorkin, eds. *Kto rukovodil NKVD, 1934–1941: spravochnik.* Moscow: Zvenia, 1999.

Petrov, Vladimir, and Evdokia Petrov. *Empire of Fear.* London: Andre Deutsch, 1956.

Petrovskii, L. P. "Poslednii rot front." In *Oni ne molchali,* edited by A. V. Afanas'ev. Moscow: Politizdat, 1991, 179–91.

Petukhov, N., and V. Khomchik, "Delo o 'Leningradskom tsentre,'" *Vestnik Verkhovnogo suda SSSR,* 1991, no. 5: 15–18, no. 6: 19–21.

Pfaff, Ivan. *Die Sowjetunion und die Verteidigung der Tschechoslowakei: Versuch einer revision einer Legende.* Cologne: Böhlau, 1996.

Pflanze, Otto. *Bismarck and the Development of Germany.* 2nd ed. 3 vols. Princeton, NJ: Princeton University, 1990.

Philbin, III, Tobias R. *The Lure of Neptune: German-Soviet Naval Collaboration and Ambitions, 1919–1941.* Columbia: University of South Carolina, 1994.

Phillips, Hugh D. *Between the Revolution and the West: A Political Biography of Maxim M. Litvinov.* Boulder, CO: Westview Press, 1992.

Pianciola, Niccolò. "Famine in the Steppe: The Collectivization of Agriculture and the Kazak Herdsmen, 1928–1934," *Cahiers du monde russe,* 45/1–2 (2004): 137–92.

———. "The Collectivization Famine in Kazakhstan, 1931–1933," *Harvard Ukrainian Studies,* 25/3–4 (2001): 237–51.

———. *Stalinismo di frontiera: Colonizzazione agricola, sterminio dei nomadi e costruzione statale in Asia centrale (1905–1936).* Rome: Viella, 2009.

Piatiletnyi plan narodnokhoziaistvennogo stroitel'stva SSSR. 2nd ed. 2 vols. Moscow, 1929.

Piatnitskii, Vladimir. *Zagovor protiv Stalina.* Moscow: Sovremennik, 1998.

Pick, Daniel. *The Pursuit of the Nazi Mind: Hitler, Hess, and the Analysts.* New York: Oxford University, 2012.

Picker, Henry, ed. *Hitlers Tischgespräche im Führerhauptquartier, 1941–1942.* Bonn: Atheneum, 1951.

Pike, David Wingeate. "Franco and the Axis Stigma," *Journal of Contemporary History,* 17/3 (1982): 369–407.

Pikhoia, Rudol'f G., ed. *I. V. Stalin: istoricheskaia ideologiia v SSSR v 1920–1950-e gody.* St. Petersburg: Nauka, 2006.

———, and Aleksander Gieysztor, eds. *Katyn': plenniki neob"iavlennoi voiny.* Moscow: Mezhdunarodnyi fond Demokratiia, 1997.

Piliatskin, B. "'Vrag naroda': Ezhov ostaetsia vragom naroda," *Izvestiia,* June 4, 5, 1998.

Pil'niak, Boris. *Rasplesnutoe vremia: rasskazy, povesti, romany.* Moscow: Sovetskii pisatel', 1990.

Pinter, Walter M. "The Social Characteristics of the Early Nineteenth-Century Russian Bureaucracy," *Slavic Review,* 29/3 (1970): 429–43.

Pipes, Richard. *Struve, Liberal on the Right, 1905–1944.* Cambridge, MA: Harvard University, 1980.

———. *The Formation of the Soviet Union: Communism and Nationalism, 1917–1923.* Cambridge, MA: Harvard University, 1953.

———. *The Russian Revolution.* New York: Knopf, 1990.

Pirogov, O. A. *S otsom: vospominaniia o A. S. Pirogove.* Riazan: Uzorch'e, 2004.

Pirozhkova, Antonina N. *At His Side: The Last Years of Isaac Babel.* South Royalton, VT: Steerforth Press, 1998.

Pis'mennyi, A. "Ia iskrenne veril Stalinu . . . ," *Knizhnoe obozrenie,* October 6, 1989.

Plamper, Jan. "Georgian Koba or Soviet 'Father of Peoples'," in *The Leader Cult in Communist Dictatorships: Stalin and the Eastern Bloc,* edited by Balász Apor, et al. New York: Palgrave Macmillan, 2004, 123–40.

———. *The Stalin Cult.* New Haven, CT: Yale University, 2012.

Plekhanov, A. A., and A. M. Plekhanov, eds. *F. E. Dzerzhinskii—predsetael' VChK-OGPU: sbornik dokumentov, 1917–1926.* Moscow: Mezhdunarodnyi fond Demokratiia, 2007.

Plekhanov, A. M. *VChK-OGPU v gody novoi ekonomicheskoi politiku 1921–1928.* Moscow: Kuchkovo pole, 2006.

Plimak, E Evgenii G., and V Vadim S. Antonov. "1 dekabria 1934-go: tragediia Kirova i tragediia sovetskoi Rossii," *Otechestvennaia istoriia,* 2004, no. 6: 31–45.

———. "Nakanune strashnoi daty," *Oktiabr',* 1997, no. 2: 149–60.

Plisetskaia, Maya. *Chitaia zhizn' svoiu.* Moscow: AST-Astrel', 2010.

Plotnikov, K. N. *Ocherki istorii biudzheta Sovetskogo gosudarstva.* Moscow: Gosfinizdat, 1954.

Plotnikova, Nadezhda S. "Organy OGPU-NKVD-NKGB SSSR v bor'be so spetssluzhbami Germanii, 1933–1941 gg." PhD diss. Moscow: Akademiia FSB, 2002.

Pobol', N. L., and P. M. Polian, eds. *Stalinskie deportatsii, 1928–1953.* Moscow: Mezhdunarodnyi fond Demokratiia—Materik, 2005.

Pod znamenem Leninizma, 1990, no. 8.

Pogonii, Iakov F., et al., *Lubianka, 2: iz istorii otechestvennoi kontrrazvedki.* Moscow: Mosarkhiv, 1999.

Pogranichnye voiska SSSR, 1939–iuin' 1941: sbornik dokumentov i materialov. Moscow: Nauka, 1970.

Pohl, Otto. *Ethnic Cleansing in the USSR, 1937–1949.* Westport, CT: Greenwood Press, 1999.

Pohle, Heinz. *Der Rundfunk als Instrument der Politik.* Hamburg: Hans Bredow-Institut, 1955.

"Pokazaniia marshala Tukhachevskogo," *Voenno-istoricheskii zhurnal,* 1989, no. 8: 44–54, no. 9: 55–63.

Pokrovskii, M. N. *Ocherki po istorii oktiabr'skoi revoliutsii.* 2 vols. Moscow and Leningrad: Gosizdat, 1927.

———, ed. *Politbiuro i krest'ianstvo: vysylka, spetspereselenie 1930–1940.* 2 vols. Moscow: Rosspen, 2005.

Poletaev, Vladimir E., ed. *Industrializatsiia SSSR, 1929–1932.* Moscow: Nauka, 1970.

Poliakov, Iu. A. *Sovetskaia strana posle okonchaniia grazhdanskoi voiny: territoriia i naseleniie.* Moscow: Nauka, 1986.

Polian, Pavel. *Against Their Will: the History and Georgtraphy of Forced Migration in the USSR.* Budapest: CEU, 2004.

Polianskii, Aleksei. *Ezhov: istoriia 'zheleznogo' stalinskogo narkoma.* Moscow: Veche, 2001.

Polianskii, Viktor V. *10 let s Vasiliem Stalinym.* Tver: IPP Vikant, 1995.

Polišenská, Milada, and Robert Kvaček. "Archivní dokumenty hovoří: Beneš a 'případ Tuchačevskij,'" *Mezinárodní politika,* 1991, no. 8: 28–30.

Polishchuk, K. E. "Zasedanie RVS 1–3 iuinia 1937 goda: svidetel'stvo ochevidtsa," *Znanie-sila,* 1990, no. 5 : 26–32.

Polonsky, Antony. *Politics in Independent Poland 1921–1939.* London: Oxford University, 1972.

"'Polozhenie ego deistvitel'no bezyskhodnoe': dokumenty o pes'akh M. A. Bulgakova," *Istochnik,* 1996, no. 5: 108–22.

Polpredy soobshchaiut: sbornik dokumentov ob otnosheniakh SSSR s Latviei, Litvoi i Estoniei, avgust 1939–avgust 1940. Moscow: Mezhdunarodnye otnosheniia, 1990.

Poluvedko, K., D. V. Viedenieiev, and H. S. Bystrukhin, *Mech i tryzub: rozvidka i kontrrozvidka rukhu ukrains'kykh natsionalistiv ta UPA (1920–1945).* Kiev: Heneza, 2006.

Pomper, Philip. "Historians and Individual Agency," *History and Theory,* 35/3 (1996): 281–308.

Ponomarev, Aleksandr N. *Aleksandr Shcherbakov: stranitsy biografii.* Moscow: Glavarkhiv, 2004.

———. "Nikita Khrushchev: nachalo kar'ery." In *Neizvestnaia Rossiia XX vek,* edited by V. A. Kozlov. Moscow: Istoricheskoe nasledie, 1993, III: 119–42.

———. *Pokoriteli neba.* Moscow: Voenizdat, 1980.

Pons, Silvio. "The Papers on Foreign and International Policy in the Russian Archives," *Cahiers du monde russe*, 40/1–2 (1999): 235–49.

——. *Stalin e la guerra inevitabile: 1936–1941.* Turin: G. Einaudi, 1995. Translated as *Stalin and the Inevitable War, 1936–1941.* London and Portland, OR: Frank Cass, 2002.

——. *The Global Revolution: A History of International Communism, 1917–1991.* Oxford: Oxford University, 2014.

Popov, B. S., and V. G. Oppokov. "Berievshchina," *Voenno-istoricheskii zhurnal*, 1989, no. 5: 38–41, no. 7: 82–7; 1990, no. 1: 68–78, no. 3: 81–90, no. 5: 85–9; 1991, no. 1: 44–57.

Popov, K. "Partiia i vozhd'," *Partiinoe stroitel'stvo*, 1930, no. 1(3)/2: 5–9.

Popov, N. N. *Ocherk istorii Vsesoiuznoi kommunisticheskoi partii (bol'shevikov).* 15th ed. Moscow: Partizdat, 1932.

Popov, N. V. "Byl i ostaius' kommunistom (O.N.N. Krestinskom)." In *Otkryvaia novye stranitsy—mezhdunarodnye voprosy: sobytiia i liudi*, edited by Akhmed A. Iskenderov. Moscow: Politcheskaia literatura, 1989, 244–51.

Popov, V. P. "Gosudarstvennyi terror v Sovetskoi Rossii, 1923–1953 gg.: istochniki i ikh interpretatsiia," *Otechestvennye arkhivy*, 1992, no. 2: 20–32.

Porecky, Elizabeth K. *Our Own People: A Memoir of 'Ignace Reiss' and His Friends.* London: Oxford University, 1969.

Posen, Barry R. "Competing Images of the Soviet Union," *World Politics*, 39/4 (1987): 579–97.

——. *Sources of Military Doctrine: France, Britain, and Germany between the World Wars.* Ithaca, NY: Cornell University, 1984.

"Poslednee slovo Nikolai Ezhova," *Moskovskie novosti*, Jan.–Feb. 6, 1994.

Pospelov, P. N. *Istoriia Velikoi Otechestvennoi voiny Sovetskogo Soiuza, 1941–1945 gg.* 6 vols. Moscow: Voenizdat, 1960–65.

Possony, Stefan T. "Hitlers Unternehmen 'Barbarossa' und die Rolle der sowjetischen Geheimdienstchefs Berija," *Beiträge zur Konfliktforschung*, 5/3 (1975): 99–114.

Potemkin, V. P., ed. *Istoriia diplomatii.* 3 vols. Moscow: Gossotsekiz, 1941–5.

Potocki, Alfred. *Master of Lancut.* London: W. H. Allen, 1959.

Potocki, Robert. *Polityka państwa polskiego wobec zagadnienia ukraińskiego w latach 1930–1939.* Lublin: IEŚW, 2003.

Povarov, S. N. *Prichina smerti rasstrel: khrinika poslednikh dnei I. Babelia.* Moscow: Terra, 1996.

Pozharskaia, S. P., and A. I. Saplin, eds. *Komintern i grazhdanskaia voina v Ispanii: dokumenty.* Moscow: Nauka, 2001.

Prange, Gordon W. *Hitler's Words.* Washington, D.C.: American Council on Public Affairs, 1944.

Prażmowska, Anita J. *Britain, Poland, and the Eastern Front, 1939.* New York: Cambridge University, 1987.

——. *Eastern Europe and the Origins of the Second World War.* New York: St. Martin's, 2000.

Presseisen, Ernst Leopold. *Germany and Japan: A Study in Totalitarian Diplomacy, 1933–1941.* The Hague: Martinus Nijhoff, 1958.

Preston, Paul. "Explosive Experiment," *TLS*, Dec. 17, 1993.

——. *A Concise History of the Spanish Civil War.* London: Fontana, 1986, 1996.

——. *Franco: A Biography.* London: HarperCollins, 1993.

——. *The Coming of the Spanish Civil War: Reform, Reaction, and Revolution in the Second Republic.* 2nd ed. New York: Routledge, 1994.

——. *The Last Stalinist: The Life of Santiago Carillo.* London: William Collins, 2014.

——. *The Spanish Holocaust: Inquisition and Extermination in Twentieth-Century Spain.* New York: W. W. Norton, 2012.

——. *We Saw Spain Die: Foreign Correspondents in the Spanish Civil War.* London: Constable, 2008.

Price, G. Ward. *Year of Reckoning.* London: Cassell, 1939.

Pridvorov, Dmitrii. "Ob otse." In *Vospominaniia o Dem'iane Bednom.* Moscow: Sovetskaii pisatel', 1966.

Priestland, David. *Stalinism and the Politics of Mobilization: Ideas, Power and Terror in Inter-War Russia.* New York: Oxford University, 2007.

"Prikaz narodnogo komissara oborony Soiuza SSR no. 0040 (4 sentiabria 1938)," *Voenno-istoricheskii zhurnal*, 1990, no. 1: 84–7.

"Prikaz narodnogo komissara oborony Soiuza SSR no. 072 (7 iiunia 1937 g.)," *Voenno-istoricheskii zhurnal*, 1990, no. 5: 45–6.

Primakov, E. M., ed. *Ocherki istorii rossiiskoi vneshnei razvedki.* 6 vols. Moscow: Mezhdunarodnye otnosheniia, 1996–2007.

1 Salone Internazionale Aeronautico: catalogo ufficiale. Milano: Fiera di Milano, 1935.

Pringle, Heather. *The Master Plan: Himmler's Scholars and the Holocaust.* New York: Hyperion, 2006.

"'Priniat' srochnnye mery k ozdorovleniiu': o krizisnoi situatsii vo MKhATe," *Istochnik*, 1997, no. 6: 122–36.

Prishvin, Mikhail M. *Dnevniki.* 11 vols. Moscow: Moskovskii rabochii, 1991–2012.

Pritsker, Lazar M. *Istoriia kurortov Abkhazskoi SSR, 1921–1945 gg.* Tbilisi: Metsniereba, 1987.

Pritt, Denis N. *Must the War Spread?* Harmondsworth: Penguin, 1940.

Proctor, Raymond L. *Hitler's Luftwaffe in the Spanish Civil War.* Westport, CT: Greenwood Press, 1983.

Proffer, Ellendea. *Bulgakov: Life and Work.* Ann Arbor, MI: Ardis, 1984.

Prokofiev, Sergey. *Autobiography, Articles, Reminiscences.* Moscow: Foreign Languages Publishing House, 1959.

Pronin, Aleksandr. "Nevol'nye informatory Stalina," *Nezavisimoe voennoe obozrenie*, 2001, no. 45: 1–2.

Prot'ko, V. S. *V bor'be za trezvost': stranitsy istorii.* Minsk: Nauka i tekhnika, 1988.

Protsess kontrrevoliutsionnoi organizatsii men'shevikov (1 marta–9 marta 1931): stenograzramma sudebnogo protsessa. Moscow: Sovetskoe zakonodatel'stvo, 1931.

Prudnikova, Elena, and A. Kolpakidi. *Dvoinoi zagovor: tainy stalinskikh repressii.* Moscow: Olma, 2006.

Prychodko, Nicholas. *One of Fifteen Million.* Boston: Little, Brown, 1952.

Prystaiko, Volodomyr, and Iurii Shapoval, eds. *Sprava "Spilky Vzvolennaia Ukrainy": nevidomi dokumenty i fakty.* Kiev: INTEL, 1995.

Psurtsev, N. D. ed., *Razvitie sviazi v SSSR.* Moscow: Sviaz', 1967.

Public Papers and Addresses of Franklin D. Roosevelt. 13 vols. Random House/Harper & Brothers, 1938–50.

Putnam, Robert D. *Bowling Alone: The Collapse and Revival of Community in America.* New York: Simon & Schuster, 2000.

Pykhov, V. G. *Ekonononika, organizatsiia i planirovanie spirtnogo proizvodstva.* Moscow: Pishchevaia promyshlennost', 1966.

Pyr'ev, Ivan. *Izbrannye proizvedeniia.* 2 vols. Moscow: Iskusstvo, 1978.

Pyrih, Ruslan Ia., et al., eds. *Holodomor 1932–1933 in Ukraine: Documents and Materials.* Kiev: Kyiv Mohyla Academy, 2008.

Raack, R. C. "His Question Asked and Answered: Stalin on 'Whither Poland?'" *Polish Review*, 55/2 (2010): 195–216.

Rabinbach, Anson. "The Reader, the Popular Novel and the Imperative to Participate: Reflections on Public and Private Experience in the Third Reich," *History and Memory*, 3/2 (1991): 5–44.

Rabinovich, I. S. "Obraz vozhdia v proizvedeniiakh zhivopisi i kul'tury," *Arkhitektura SSSR*, 1939, no. 12: 11–21.

Rabishchev, N. "Gnilaia i opasnaia teoriia prevrashcheniia klassovykh vragov v ruchnykh," *Bol'shevik*, 1937, no. 7 .

Radek, Karl. "Dikhanie voiny," *Izvestiia*, Aug. 1, 1936.

——. "The War in the Far East: A Soviet View," *Foreign Affairs*, 10/4 (July 1932): 541–57.

Radó, Sándor. *Pod psevdonim "Dora."* Moscow: Voenizdat, 1973.

Radosh, Ronald, Mary Habeck, and Grigory Sevostianov, eds. *Spain Betrayed: The Soviet Union in the Spanish Civil War.* New Haven, CT: Yale University, 2001.

Radzinskii, Edvard. *Stalin.* Moscow: Vagrius, 1997.

Ragsdale, Hugh. "The Munich Crisis and the Issue of Red Army Transit across Romania," *Russian Review*, 57/4 (1998): 614–7.

——. "The Soviet Position at Munich Appraised: the Romanian Enigma." In *Extending the Borders of Russian History*, edited by Marsha Seifert. Budapest: CEU, 2003.

——. *The Soviet Union, the Munich Crisis, and the Coming of World War II.* New York: Cambridge University, 2004.

Raikin, Arkadii. *Vospominaniia.* St. Petersburg: Kul't-Inform, 1993.

Rakovski, Cristian. "Na s"ezde i v strane [July 27–Aug. 7, 1930]," *Biulleten' oppozitsii*, no. 25–26 (Nov.–Dec. 1931): 9–32.

Ramzin, Leonid K., et al., eds. *Protsess "Prompartii," 25 noiabria–7 dekabria 1930 g.: stenogramma sudebnogo protsessa i materialy, priobshchennye k delu.* Moscow: Sovetskoi zakonodatel'stvo, 1931.

Rancour-Lafferiere, Daniel. *The Mind of Stalin: A Psychoanalytic Study.* Ann Arbor, MI: Ardis, 1988.

Randall, Amy E. *The Soviet Dream World of Retail Trade and Consumption in the 1930s.* New York: Palgrave Macmillan, 2008.

Rapoport, Vitalii, and Iurii Geller. *Izmena rodine.* Moscow: Strelets, 1995.

Rapoport, Vitaly, and Yuri Alexeev. *High Treason: Essays on the History of the Red Army, 1918–1938.* Durham, NC: Duke University, 1985.

Raskol'nikov, Fedor. "Otkrytoe pis'mo Stalinu," *Novaia Rossiia* [Paris], October 1, 1939.

——. *O vremeni i o sebe: vospominaniia, pis'ma, dokumenty.* Leningrad: Lenizdat, 1989.

Rasskazy o Staline. Moscow: Detskaia literatura, 1939.

Rassweiler, Anne D. *The Generation of Power: The History of Dneprostroi.* New York: Oxford University, 1988.

Ratner, I. "Proryv na Maase (na uchastke Divan-Sedan, mai 1940 g.)," *Voenno-istoricheskii zhurnal*, 1940, no. 5: 3–22.

Rayfield, Donald. "Pasternak and the Georgians," *Irish Slavonic Studies*, 3 (1982): 39–46.

———. "The Death of Paolo Iashvili," *Slavonic and East European Review*, 68/4 (1990): 631–64.

———. *Literature of Georgia: A History*. 2nd ed. Richmond, Surrey: Curzon, 2000.

———. *Stalin and His Hangmen: An Authoritative Portrait of a Tyrant and Those Who Served Him*. New York: Viking, 2004.

Raymond, P. D. "Witness and Chronicler of Nazi-Soviet Relations: The Testimony of Evgeny Gnedin (Parvus)," *Russian Review* 44/4 (1985): 379–95.

Razgon, Lev. *Plen v svoem otechestve*. Moscow: Knizhnyi Sad, 1994.

Read, Anthony. *The Devil's Disciples: The Lives and Times of Hitler's Inner Circle*. London: Jonathan Cape, 2003.

———, and David Fisher. *The Deadly Embrace: Hitler, Stalin, and the Nazi-Soviet Pact, 1939–1941*. London: Michael Joseph, 1988.

Rebentisch, Dieter. *Führerstaat und Verwaltung im zweiten Weltkrieg*. Stuttgart: Franz Steiner, 1989.

Redvaldsen, David. "'Today is the Dawn': The Labour Party and the 1929 General Election," *Parliamentary History*, 29/3 (2010): 395–415.

Rees, E. A. *"Iron Lazar": A Political Biography of Lazar Kaganovich*. London and New York: Anthem Press, 2012.

———. "Leader Cults: Varieties, Preconditions and Functions." In *The Leader Cult in Communist Dictatorships: Stalin and the Eastern Bloc*, edited by Balász Apor et al. Houndmills, Basingstoke: Palgrave Macmillan, 2004, 3–25.

———. "Stalin and Russian Nationalism." In *Russian Nationalism Past and Present*, edited by Geoffrey Hosking and Robert Service. New York: St. Martin's, 1998, 77–106.

———. "Stalin as Leader, 1924–1937: From Oligarch to Dictator." In *The Nature of Stalin's Dictatorship: The Politburo 1924–1953*, edited by E. A. Rees. Houndmills, Basingstoke: Palgrave Macmillan, 2004, 19–57.

———. "Stalin as Leader, 1937–1953: From Dictator to Despot." In *The Nature of Stalin's Dictatorship: The Politburo 1924–1953*, edited by E. A. Rees. Houndmills, Basingstoke: Palgrave Macmillan, 2004, 200–39.

———. "The Great Purges and the XVIII Party Congress of 1939." In *Centre-Local Relations in the Stalinist State, 1928–1941*, edited by E. A. Rees. New York: Palgrave Macmillan, 2002, 191–211.

———. "The People's Commissariat of Water Transport." In *Decision-making in the Stalinist Command Economy, 1932–37*, edited by E. A. Rees. New York: St. Martin's, 1997, 235–61.

———, ed. *Centre-Local Relations in the Stalinist State, 1928–1941*. New York: Palgrave Macmillan, 2002.

———, ed. *Decision-making in the Stalinist Command Economy, 1932–37*. Houndmills, Basingstoke: Palgrave Macmillan, 1997.

———. *Political Thought from Machiavelli to Stalin: Revolutionary Machiavellism*. Houndmills, Basingstoke: Palgrave Macmillan, 2004.

———. *Stalinism and Soviet Rail Transport, 1928–41*. Houndmills, Basingstoke: Palgrave Macmillan, 1995.

———. *State Control in Soviet Russia: The Rise and Fall of the Workers' and Peasants' Inspectorate, 1920–34*. Houndmills, Basingstoke: Palgrave Macmillan, 1987.

———, and D. Watson. "Politburo and Sovnarkom." In *Decision-making in the Stalinist Command Economy, 1932–37*, edited by E. A. Rees. New York: St. Martin's, 1997, 9–32.

Rees, John Rawlings, et al. *The Case of Rudolf Hess: A Problem in Diagnosis and Forensic Psychiatry*. London: Heinemann, 1947.

Rees, Laurence. *The Nazis: A Warning from History*. London: BBC Books, 1997.

———. *World War II behind Closed Doors: Stalin, the Nazis and the West*. New York: Pantheon, 2008.

Rees, Tim. "The Highpoint of Comintern Influence? The Communist Party and the Civil War in Spain." In *International Communism and the Communist International, 1919–1943*, edited by Tim Rees and Andrew Thorpe. Manchester, England: University of Manchester, 1998, 143–68.

Reese, Roger R. "Lessons of the Winter War: A Study in the Military Effectiveness of the Red Army, 1939–1940," *Journal of Military History*, 72/3 (2008): 825–52.

———. "Red Army Opposition to Forced Collectivization, 1929–1930: The Army Wavers," *Slavic Review*, 55/1 (1996): 24–45.

———. *Stalin's Reluctant Soldiers: A Social History of the Red Army, 1925–1941*. Lawrence: University Press of Kansas, 1996.

Rei, August. *Sotsialisticheskie revoliutsii v Estonii 1917–1940 i ego vkhozhdeniie v sostav SSSR: dokuemnty i materialy*. Tallinn: Periodika, 1987.

———. *The Drama of the Baltic Peoples*. Stockholm: Kirjaustus Vaba Eesti, 1970.

Reid, Susan. "In the Name of the People: The Manege Affair Revisited," *Kritika*, 6/4 (2005), 673–716.

———. "Socialist Realism in the Stalinist Terror: The Industry of Socialism Art Exhibition, 1935–41," *Russian Review*, 60/2 (2001), 153–84.

Reinhart, Carmen M., and Kenneth S. Rogoff. *This Time Is Different: Eight Centuries of Financial Folly*. Princeton, NJ: Princeton University, 2009.

Reiss, Tom. *The Orientalist: Solving the Mystery of as a Strange and Dangerous Life*. New York: Random House, 2005.

Reitlinger, Gerald. *The SS: Alibi of a Nation*. New York: Viking, 1957.

Reizen, Mark, et al. *Mark Reizen, Avtobiograficheskie zapiski: stat'i i vospominaniia*. 2nd ed. Moscow: Sov. kompozitor, 1986.

Rentola, Kimmo. "Intelligence and Stalin's Two Crucial Decisions in the Winter War, 1939–40," *International History Review*, 35/5 (2013): 1089–1112.

———. "The Finnish Communists and the Winter War," *Journal of Contemporary History*, 33/4 (1998): 591–607.

Report of Court Proceedings, Case of the Anti-Soviet Trotskyite Center, January 23–30, Moscow, 1937. Moscow: People's Commissariat of Justice of the U.S.S.R., 1937.

Resis, A. "The Fall of Litvinov: Harbinger of the German-Soviet Non-Aggression Pact," *Europe-Asia Studies*, 52/1 (2000): 36–47.

Reswick, William. *I Dreamt Revolution*. Chicago: Henry Regnery, 1952.

Revyakin, Aleksandr R. "Poland and the Soviet Union in the Late 1920s and Early 1930s." In *White Spots, Black Spots: Difficult Matters in Polish-Russian Relations, 1918–2008*, edited by Adam Daniel Rotfeld and Anatoly V. Torkunov. Pittsburgh: University of Pittsburgh, 2015, 79–101.

Reynolds, David. "1940: Fulcrum of the Twentieth Century?" *International Affairs*, 66/2 (1990): 325–50.

———. "Churchill and the British 'Decision' to Fight in 1940: Right Policy, Wrong Reasons." In *Diplomacy and Intelligence during the Second World War*, edited by R. Langhorne. Cambridge, UK: Cambridge University, 1985, 147–67.

———. *In Command of History: Churchill Fighting and Writing the Second World War*. New York: Random House, 2005.

Rezoliutsii i postanovlenii pervogo Vsesoiuznogo s"ezda udarnykh brigad. Moscow, 1930.

Ribbentrop, Joachim von. *The Ribbentrop Memoirs*. London: Weidenfeld and Nicholson, 1954.

———. *Zwischen London und Moskau: Erinnerungen und letzte Aufzeichnungen*. Leoni: Druffel-Verlag, 1953.

Richardson, Charles O. "French Plans for Allied Attacks on the Caucasian Oil Fields, January-April 1940," *French Historical Studies*, 8/1 (1973): 130–56.

Richardson, R. Dan. *Comintern Army: The International Brigades and the Spanish Civil War*. Lexington: University of Kentucky, 1982.

Richardson, Rosamond. *The Long Shadow: Inside Stalin's Family*. New York: St. Martin's, 1993.

Richter, Stanislav. "On Prokofiev." In *Sergei Prokofiev: Materials, Articles, Interviews*, edited by Vladimir Blok. Moscow: Progress, 1978.

Rieber, Alfred J. "Fun with My Buddy," *TLS*, August 17, 2007.

———. "Persistent Factors in Russian Foreign Policy: An Interpretive Essay." In *Imperial Russian Foreign Policy*, edited by Hugh Ragsdale. Washington, D.C.: Wilson Center Press, 1993, 315–59.

———. "Stalin as Foreign Policy Maker." In *Stalin: A New History*, edited by Sarah Davies and James Harris. New York: Cambridge University, 2005, 140–58.

———. *Stalin and the Struggle for Supremacy in Eurasia*. New York: Cambridge University, 2015.

Riekhoff, Harald von. *German-Polish Relations, 1918–1933*. Baltimore: Johns Hopkins University, 1971.

Rigby, T. H. "Was Stalin a Disloyal Patron?" *Soviet Studies*, 38/3 (1986): 311–24.

———. *Communist Party Membership in the USSR, 1917–1967*, Princeton, NJ: Princeton University, 1968.

———. *The Stalin Dictatorship*. Sydney: Sydney University, 1968.

Rikhter, Zinaida. *Kavkaz nashikh dnei, 1923–1924*. Moscow: Zhizn' i znanie, 1924.

Rimmel, Leslie Ann. "Another Kind of Fear: The Kirov Murder and the End of Bread Rationing in Leningrad," *Slavic Review*, 56/3 (1997): 481–99.

———. "The Kirov Murder and Soviet Society: Propaganda and Popular Opinion in Leningrad, 1934–1935." PhD diss. University of Pennsylvania, 1995.

Rintala, Marvin. *Three Generations: The Extreme Right Wing in Finnish Politics*. Bloomington: Indiana University, 1962.

Rittersporn, Gábor Tamás. "'Vrednye element,' 'opasnye menshinstva' i bol'shevistskie trevogi: massovye operatsii 1937–1938 gg. i etnicheskii vopros v SSSR." In *V sem'e edinoi: national'naia politika partii bol'shevikov i ee osuchestvlenie na Severeo-Zapadne Rossii v 1920–1950e gody*, edited by Timo Vikhavainen and Irina Takala. Petrozavodsk: Izdatel'srvo Petrozavodskogo universiteta, 1998, 99–122.

———. "From Working Class to Urban Laboring Mass." In *Making Workers Soviet: Power, Class, and Identity*, edited by Lewis H. Siegelbaum and Ronald G. Suny. Ithaca, NY: Cornell University, 1994, 253–73.

———. "The Omnipresent Conspiracy: On Soviet Imagery of Politics and Social Relations in the 1930s." In *Stalinism: Its*

Nature and Aftermath, edited by Nick Lampert and Gábor Rittersporn. Armonk, NY: M. E. Sharpe, 1992, 101–20.

——. *Anguish, Anger, Folkways in Soviet Russia*. Pittsburgh, PA: University of Pittsburgh, 2014.

——. *Stalinist Simplifications and Soviet Complications: Social Tensions and Political Conflicts in the USSR 1933–1953*. Philadelphia: Harwood, 1991.

Robbins, Richard G. *Famine in Russia, 1891–1892*. New York: Columbia University, 1975.

Roberts, Andrew. *The Holy Fox: A Biography of Lord Halifax*. London: Weidenfeld and Nicholson, 1991.

Roberts, Cynthia. "Planning for War: The Red Army and the Catastrophe of 1941," *Europe-Asia Studies*, 47/8 (1995): 1293–1326.

Roberts, Geoffrey. "A Soviet Bid for Coexistence with Nazi Germany, 1935–1937: The Kandelaki Affair," *International History Review*, 16/3 (1994): 466–90.

——. "Soviet Foreign Policy and the Spanish Civil War, 1936–1939." In *Spain in an International Context*, edited by Christian Leitz and David J. Dunthorn. New York: Berghahn, 1999, 81–103.

——. "Soviet Policy and the Baltic States, 1939 and 1940: A Reappraisal," *Diplomacy & Statecraft*,6/3 (1995), 672–700,

——. "Stalin, the Pact with Nazi Germany, and the Origins of Postwar Soviet Diplomatic Historiography," *Journal of Cold War Studies*, 4/4 (1995): 93–103.

——. "The Infamous Encounter? The Merekalov-Weizsäcker Meeting of 17 April 1939," *Historical Journal*, 35/4 (1992): 921–4.

——. *Stalin's General: The Life of Georgy Zhukov*. New York: Random House, 2012.

——. *The Soviet Union and the Origins of the Second World War: Russo-German Relations and the Road to War, 1933–1941*. New York: St. Martin's, 1995.

——. *Unholy Alliance: Stalin's Pact with Hitler*. London: Tauris, 1989.

Roberts, Henry L. "The Diplomacy of Colonel Beck." In *The Diplomats, 1919–1939*, edited by Gordon A. Craig and Felix Gilbert. Princeton, NJ: Princeton University, 1953, 578–614.

Robertson, Esmonde M. "Hitler and Sanctions: Mussolini and the Rhineland," *European Studies Review*, 7/2 (1977): 409–35.

——. *Mussolini as Empire Builder: Europe and Africa 1932–1936*. London: Macmillan, 1977.

Robertson, Jake A. "Captive Audiences." Senior thesis. Princeton University, 2015.

Robinson, Robert, with Jonathan Slavin. *Black on Red: My 44 Years Inside the Soviet Union*. Washington, D.C.: Acropolis Books, 1988.

Rodchenko, Aleksandr. "Amerikanskie fotograiia Il'ia Il'fa," *Sovetskoe foto*, 1936, no. 8: 26–7.

Rodos, Valerii. *Ia syn palacha: vospominaniia*. Moscow: OGI, 2008.

Roeder, Philip G. *Red Sunset: The Failure of Soviet Politics*. Princeton, NJ: Princeton University, 1993.

Roewer, Helmut. *Die Rote Kapelle und andere Geheimdienst Mythen: Spionage zwischen Deutschland und Russland im Zweiten Weltkrieg 1941–1945*. Graz: Ares, 2010.

Rogachevskaia, Liudmila S. *Iz istorii rabochego klassa SSSR v pervye gody industrializatsii, 1926–1927*. Moscow: Akademii nauk SSSR, 1959.

——. *Rabochii klass SSSR, 1926–1929 gg.* Moscow: Znanie, 1960.

——. *Sotsialisticheskoe sorevnovanie v SSSR: istoricheskie ocherki 1917–1930 gg.* Moscow: Nauka, 1977.

Rogovin, Vadim Z. *1937: Stalin's Year of Terror*. Oak Park, MI: Mehring, 1998.

——. *Partiia rasstreliannykh*. Moscow: Rogovin, 1997.

——. *Stalin's Terror of 1937–1938: Political Genocide in the USSR*. Oak Park, MI: Mehring, 2009.

Rohwer, Jürgen, and Mikhail S. Monakov. "The Soviet Union's Ocean-Going Fleet," *International History Review*, 18/4 (1996): 837–68.

——. *Stalin's Ocean-Going Fleet: Soviet Naval Strategy and Shipbuilding Programmes 1935–1953*. London: Frank Cass, 2001.

Rokossovskii, K. K. *Soldatskii dolg.* Moscow: Voenizdat, 1997.

Rolland, Romain. *Voyage à Moscou (juin-julliet 1935)*. Paris: Albin Michel, 1992.

Rölling, B. V. A., and C. F. Rüter, eds. *The Tokyo Judgment: The International Military Tribunal for the Far East*. Amsterdam: APA University, 1977.

Romano, Andrea, and Nonna S. Tarchova, eds. *L'Armata Rossa e la collettivizzazione delle campagne nell'URSS, 1928–1933: raccolta di documenti dai Fondi dell'Archivio militare di Stato Russo*. Naples: Istituto universitario orientale, 1996.

Romerstein, Herbert, and Eric Breindel. *The Venona Secrets: Exposing Soviet Espionage and America's Traitors*. Washington, D.C.: Regnery, 2001.

Rommel, Erwin. *The Rommel Papers*. Edited by B. H. Liddell Hart. New York: Da Capo Press, 1953.

Roos, Hans. *Polen und Europa: Studien zur politischen Aussenpolitik, 1931–1939*. Tübingen: Moor, 1957.

Rose, Kenneth. *King George V*. London: Weidenfeld and Nicolson, 1983.

Rosenberg, Alfred. *Blut und Ehre*. Munich: Zentralverlag der NSDAP, 1938.

Rosenfeldt, Niels Erik. "'The Consistory of the Communist Church': The Origins and Development of Stalin's Secret Chancellery," *Russian History*, 9/2–3 (1982): 308–24.

——. *Knowledge and Power: The Role of the Secret Chancellery in Stalin's System of Government*. Copenhagen: Rosenkilder and Bagger, 1978.

——. *Stalin's Secret Chancellery and the Comintern: Evidence about the Organizational Patterns*. Copenhagen: Reitzel, 1991.

——. *Stalin's Special Departments: A Comparative Analysis of Key Sources*. Copenhagen: University of Copenhagen, 1989.

——. *The "Special" World: Stalin's Power Apparatus and the Soviet System's Secret Structures of Communication*. 2 vols. Copenhagen: Museum Tusculanums, 2008.

Rosenhaft, Eve. *Beating the Fascists? The German Communists and Political Violence, 1929–1933*. New York: Cambridge University, 1983.

Roshchin, Aleksei A. "V narkomindele v predvoennye gody," *Otkryvaia novye stranitsy, mezhdunarodnye voprosy: sobytiia i liudi*. Moscow: Politicheskaia literatura, 1989, 41–9.

——. "People's Commissariat of Foreign Affairs before World War II," *International Affairs* (May 1988), 108–14.

Roshchin, Sergei K. *Politicheskaia istoriia Mongolii, 1921–1940 gg.* Moscow: Institut Vostokovedeniia RAN, 1999.

Rosliakov, Mikhail V. *Ubiistvo Kirova: politicheskie i ugolovnye prestupleniia v 30-kh godakh*. Leningrad: Lenizdat, 1991.

Rossiia i SSSR v voinakh XX veka: statisiocheskoe issledovanie. Moscow: Olma, 2001.

Rossman, Jeffrey J. *Worker Resistance under Stalin: Class and Revolution on the Shop Floor*. Cambridge, MA: Harvard University, 2005.

Rote Kapelle: The CIA's History of Soviet Intelligence and Espionage Networks in Western Europe, 1936–1945, The. Washington, D.C.: University Publications of America, 1979.

Rothstein, Andrew, ed. *Wreckers on Trial: A Record of the Trial of the Industrial Party Held in Moscow, November–December, 1930*. New York: Workers' Library, 1931.

Rozanov, German L. *Stalin-Gitler: dokumental'nyi ocherk sovetsko-germanskikh diplomaticheskikh otnoshenii, 1939–1941 gg.* Moscow: Mezhdunarodnye otnosheniia, 1991.

Rozenfel'd, V. Ia. *Dvadtsatipiatitysiachniki*. Moscow: Selk'khozgiz, 1957.

Rubashkin, Aleksandr. *Mikhail Kol'tsov: kritiko-biograficheskii ocherk*. Leningrad: Khudozhestvennaia literatura, 1971.

Rubenstein, Joshua. *Tangled Loyalties: The Life and Times of Ilya Ehrenburg*. New York: Basic Books, 1996.

Rubin, Nikolai *Lavrentii Beriia: mif i real'nost'*. Moscow: Olimp, 1998.

Rubinstein, Grigorii L. *Razvitie vnutrennei torgovli v SSSR*. Leningrad: Leningradskii universitet, 1964.

Rubl'ov, Oleksandr, and Vladimir Reprtinstev. "Repressii protiv poliakiv v Ukraiini u 30-ti roki," *Z arkhiviv VUChK-HPU-NKVD-KHB*, I, 1995, no. 2.

Rubtsov, Iurii. *Alter ego Stalina: stranitsy politicheskoi biografii L.V. Mekhlisa*. Moscow: Zvonnitsa-MG, 1999.

——. *Iz-za spiny vozhdia: politicheskaia i voennaia deiatel'nost' L. V. Mekhlisa*. Moscow: Kompaniia Ritm Esteit, 2003.

——. *Marshaly Stalina*. Moscow: Feniks, 2002.

——. *Teni vozhdia*. Moscow: Yauza-EKSMO, 2007, 81–2.

Ruder, Cynthia A. *Making History for Stalin: The Story of the Belomor Canal*. Gainesville: University of Florida, 1998.

Rudich, Feliks M., and Ruslan Ia. Pyrih, eds. *Holod 1932–33 rokiv na Ukraini: ochima istorykiv, movuiu dokumentiv*. Kiev: Vyd-vo politychnoi literatury Ukraïny, 1990.

Rudman, Stella. *Lloyd George and the Appeasement of Germany, 1919–1945*. Newcastle upon Tyne, UK: Cambridge Scholars Publishing, 2011.

Rudomino, Adrian V. *Legendarnaia Barvikha*. Moscow: Tonchu, 2009.

Rukeyser, Walter A. *Working for the Soviets: An American Engineer in Russia*. New York: Covisi-Friede, 1932.

Ruoff, Kenneth J. *Imperial Japan at its Zenith: The Wartime Celebration of the Empire's 2600th*. Ithaca, NY: Cornell University, 2010.

Ruotsila, Markku. "The Churchill-Mannerheim Collaboration in the Russian Intervention, 1919–1920," *Slavonic and East European Review*, 80/1 (2002): 1–20.

Ryback, Timothy W. *Hitler's Private Library: The Books that Shaped His Life*. New York: Knopf, 2008.

Rybalkin, Iurii E. "Voennaia pomoshch' Sovetskogo Soiuza ispanskomu narodu v natsional'no-revoliutsionnoi voine 1936–1939," PhD diss. Institute of Military History, Moscow, 1992.

——. *Operatsiia "X": Sovetskaia voennaia pomoshch' respublikanskoi Ispanii (1936–1939)*. Moscow: AIRO-XX, 2000.

Rybin, A. T. *Kto otravil Stalina? Zapiski telokhranitelia.* Moscow: Izdatel'stvo Veteran, 1995.

———. *Next to Stalin: Notes of a Bodyguard.* Toronto: Northstar Compass Journal, 1996.

———. *Riadom so Stalinym v Bol'shom teatre: zapiski voennogo komendanta.* Moscow: [s.n.], 1995.

———. *Stalin na fronte: zapiski telokhranitelia.* Moscow: [s.n.], 1995.

———. *Stalin v oktiabre 1941 g.: zapiski telokhranitelia.* Moscow: [s.n.], 1995.

Ryōichi, Tobe. "The Japanese Eleventh Army in Central China, 1938–1941." In *The Battle for China: Essays on the Military History of the Sino-Japanese War of 1937–1945*, edited by Mark Peattie et al. Stanford, CA: Stanford University, 2011, 207–36.

Ryskulov, Turar R. *Sobranie sochinenii v trekh tomakh.* 3 vols. Almata: Kazakhstan, 1997–8.

Ryzhkov, Nikolai. *Perestroika: istoriia predatel'svt.* Moscow: Novosti, 1992.

Rzheshevskii, Oleg A., and Olli Vehviläinen, eds. *Zimnaia voina 1939–1940: I. V. Stalin i finskaia kampaniia. Stenogramma soveshchaniia pri TsK VKP (b).* 2 vols. Moscow: Nauka, 1998.

Rzeshevsky, Oleg A., ed. *War and Diplomacy: The Making of the Grand Alliance. Documents from Stalin's Archives.* Amsterdam: Harwood Academic, 1996.

S"ezdy sovetov Soiuza SSR, soiuznykh i avtonomnykh sovetskikh sosialisticheskikh respublik: sbornik dokumentov. 7 vols. Moscow: Institut prava, Akademiia nauk SSSR, 1960.

Sabaliunas, Leonas. *Lithuania in Crisis: Nationalism to Communism, 1939–1940.* Bloomington: Indiana University, 1972.

Sadovskii, A. "Lenin v 1918 godu," *Leningradskaia Pravda*, April 2, 1939.

Safronov, V. P. *SSSR, SShA i iaponskaia agressiia na Dal'nem Vostoke i Tikhom okeane, 1931–1945 gg.* Moscow: Institut istorii RAN, 2001.

———. *SSSR, SShA i iaponskaia agressiia na Dal'nem Vostoke i Tikhom okeane, 1931–1945 gg.* Moscow: Institut istorii RAN, 2001.

Sagariia, Badzhgur E. *Natsional'noe stroitel'stvo v Abkhazii, 1921–1931 gg.* Sukhumi: Alashara, 1970.

Sagariia, V. "K istorii obrazovaniia Abkhazskoi avtonomnoi respubliki." In *Trudy Sukhumskogo gosudarstvennogo pedinstituta im. A. M. Gor'kogo.* Sukhumi: Alashara, 1962.

Sakharov, A. N. *Zimniaia voina 1939–1940 gg. v rassekrechennykh dokumentakh.* Moscow: Akademkniga, 2009.

Sakharov, Valentin A. *"Politicheskoe zaveshchanie" Lenina: real'nost' istorii i mify politiki.* Moscow: Moskovskii universitet, 2003.

Sakharov, Vsevolod. *Mikhail Bulgakov: pisatel' i vlast'.* Moscow: Olma, 2000.

Sakwa, George. "The Polish Ultimatum to Lithuania in March 1938," *Slavonic and East European Review*, 55/2 (1977): 204–26.

Salter, Arthur. *Personality in Politics: Studies of Contemporary Statesmen.* London: Faber and Faber, 1947.

Salys, Rimgaila. *The Musical Comedy Films of Grigorii Aleksandrov: Laughing Matters.* Chicago: University of Chicago, 2009.

Salzman, Neil V. *Reform and Revolution: The Life and Times of Raymond Robins.* Kent, OH: Kent State University, 1991.

Samsonov, F. P. "Smysl ego zhizhi." In *Komandarm Uborevich: vospominaniia druzei i soratnikov.* Moscow: Voenizdat, 1964, 207–23.

Samuelson, Lennart. "Wartime Perspectives and Economic Planning: Tukhachevsky and the Military-Industrial Complex, 1925–1937." In *Russia in the Age of Wars, 1914–1945*, edited by Silvio Pons and Andrea Romano. Milan: Feltrinelli, 2000, 187–214.

———. *Plans for Stalin's War Machine: Tukhachevskii and Military Planning, 1925–1941.* London and Basingstoke: Macmillan, 2000.

———. *Soviet Defense Industry Planning: Tukhachevskii and Military-Industrial Mobilization, 1926–1937.* Stockholm: Institute of East European Economies, 1996.

Samygin, M. M. "Prompartiia," n.d., Columbia University Archive of Russian History and Culture.

Sandag, Shagdariin, and Harry H. Kendall. *Poisoned Arrows: The Stalin-Choibalsan Mongolian Massacres, 1921–1941.* Boulder, CO: Westview Press, 2000.

Sandler, Stephanie. *Commemorating Pushkin: Russia's Myth of a National Poet.* Stanford, CA: Stanford University, 2004.

Sanina, I. I. "R. I. Eikhe," *Voprosy istorii KPSS*, 1965, no. 7: 92–7.

Saraeva-Bondar', Avgusta Mikhailovna. *Siluety vremeni.* St. Petersburg: Istoricheskaia illustratsiia, 1993.

Sarin, Oleg, and Lev Dvoretsky. *Alien Wars: The Soviet Union's Aggressions against the World, 1919 to 1989.* Novato, CA: Presidio, 1996.

Sarnov, Benedikt. *Stalin i pisateli.* 4 vols. Moscow: Eksmo: 2008–2001.

Sartakova, T. "Nash pisatel'skii les," *Chitaiushchaia Rossiia*, 1994, no. 2.

Sats, Natalia. *Sketches from My Life.* Moscow: Raduga Publishers, 1985.

Saul Friedlander, *Nazi Germany and the Jews.* 2 vols. New York: HarperCollins, 1997.

Savchenko, Viktor A. *Avantiuristy grazhdanskoi voiny: istoricheskoe rassledovanie.* Moscow: AST, 2000.

Savel'ev, Maximilian, and Aleksandr Poskrebyshev, eds. *Direktivy VKP (b) po khoziaistvennym voprosam.* Moscow-Leningrad: Gos. sotsial'no-eknomicheskooe izd-vo, 1931.

Savin, A. S. "O podgotovke Iaponii k napadeniiu na SSSR: iaponskie istoriki svidetel'stvuiut," *Voenno-istoricheskii zhurnal*, 1991, no. 7: 88–9.

Savushkin, R. A. "K voprosu o zarozhdenii teorii posledovatel'nykh nastupatel'nykh operatsii," *Voenno-istoricheskii zhurnal*, 1983, no. 5: 77–83.

———. *Razvitie sovetskikh vooruzhennykh sil i voennogo iskusstva v mezhvoennyi period (1921–1941 gg.).* Moscow: Voenno-Politicheskaia Akademiia, 1989.

Sbornik boevykh dokumentov Velikoi Otechestvennoi voiny. 43 vols. Moscow: Voenizdat, 1947–1953.

Sbornik materialov v sviazi s "Pis'mom c Kavkaza" tov. Stalina. Baku: Azerneshp, 1932.

Scammell, Michael. *Koestler: The Literary and Political Odyssey of a Twentieth-Century Skeptic.* New York: Random House, 2009.

Schacht, Hjalmar. *My First Seventy-Six Years.* London: Wingate, 1955.

Schäfer, Hans Dieter. *Das gespaltene Bewusstsein: deutsche Kultur und Lebenswirklichkeit 1933–1945.* Munich: Carl Hanser Verlag, 1981.

Schapiro, Leonard *Totalitarianism.* New York: Praeger, 1972.

———. *The Communist Party of the Soviet Union.* New York: Random House, 1960; 2nd ed., 1971.

Schauff, Frank. *Der verspielte Sieg: Sowjetunion, Kommunistische Internationale und Spanischer Bürgerkrieg 1936–1939.* Frankfurt: Campus, 2004.

Schellenberg, Walter. *The Labyrinth.* New York: Harper, 1956.

———. *The Schellenberg Memoirs: A Record of the Nazi Secret Service.* London: Andre Deutsch, 1956.

Schlögel, Karl. *Terror und Traum: Moskau 1937.* Munich: Karl Hanser, 2008. Translated as *Moscow, 1937.* Cambridge, UK: Polity, 2012.

Schmidt, Paul Otto. *Hitler's Interpreter.* New York: Macmillan, 1951.

———. *Statist auf diplomatischer Bühne: Erlebnisse des Chefdolmetschers im Auswärtigen Amt mit den Staatsmännern Europas.* Bonn: Athenäum, 1949.

Schmidt, Rainer F. "Der Hess-Flug und das Kabinet Churchill," *Vierteljahreshefte für Zeitgeschichte*, 42/1 (1994): 1–38.

Schmidt-Scheeder, Georg. *Reporter der Hölle: deutscher Propaganda-Kompanien im 2. Weltkrieg, Erlebnis und Dokumentation.* Stuttgart: Motorbuch Verlag, 1977.

Schmitt, Carl. *Die Diktatur: von den Anfängen des modernen Souveränitätsgedankens bis zum proletarischen Klassenkampf.* Munich and Leipzig: Duncker & Humblot, 1921; 2nd ed., 1928.

Schorske, Carl. "Two German Diplomats: Dirksen and Schulenburg." In *The Diplomats, 1919–1939*, edited by Gordon A. Craig and Felix Gilbert. Princeton, NJ: Princeton University, 1953, 477–511.

Schrader, Fred E. *Der Moskauer Prozess 1936: zur Sozialgeschichte eines politische Feindbilder.* Frankfurt and New York: Campus Verlag, 1995.

———, ed. *Kriegstagebuch der Oberkommando der Wehrmacht (Wehrmachtführungsstab) 1940–1945.* 4 vols. Frankfurt am Main: Bernard & Graefe, 1961–5.

Schram, Stuart R., ed. *Mao's Road to Power: Revolutionary Writings 1912–1949.* 5 vols. Armonk, NY: M. E. Sharpe, 1989–1997.

Schramm-von Thadden, Ehrengard. *Griechenland und die Grossmächte im zweiten Weltkrieg.* Wiesbaden: F. Steiner, 1955.

Schroeder, Christa. *Er War Mein Chef: aus dem Nachlass der Sekretärin von Adolf Hitler.* Munich: Langen Müller, 1985.

Schroeder, Paul W. "Alliances 1815–1945: Weapons of Power or Tools of Management." In *Systems, Stability, and Statecraft: Essays in the International History of Modern Europe.* New York: Palgrave, 2004, 195–222.

———. "Munich and the British Tradition," *Historical Journal*, 19/1 (1976): 223–43.

Schroeder, Ralf, ed. *Mit der Menschheit auf Du und Du: Schriftsteller der Welt über Gorkij.* Berlin: Verlag Kultur und Fortschritt, 1969.

Schuker, Stephen A. "Seeking a Scapegoat: Intelligence and Grand Strategy in France, 1919–1940." In *Secret Intelligence in the European States System, 1918–1989*, edited by Jonathan A. Haslam and Karina Urbach. Stanford, CA: Stanford University, 2014, 81–127.

Schuschnigg, Kurt von. *Austrian Requiem.* London: Victor Gollancz, 1947.

———. *The Brutal Takeover: The Austrian ex-Chancellor's Account of the Anschluss of Austria by Hitler.* New York: Atheneum, 1971.

Schuster-Winkelhof, Karl. *Adolf Hitlers Wahlheimat.* Munich: Münchener, 1933.

Schwendemann, Heinrich. *Die Wirtschaftliche Zussamenarbeit zwischen dem Deutschen Reich under der Sowjetunion von 1939 bis 1941: Alternative zu Hitlers Otsprogramm?* Berlin: Akademie, 1993.

Scott, James. *Seeing Like a State: How Certain Schemes to Improve the Human Condition Have Failed.* New Haven, CT: Yale University, 1998.

Scott, John. *Behind the Urals: An American Worker in Russia's City of Steel.* Bloomington: Indiana University, 1989.

———. *Duel for Europe: Stalin versus Hitler.* Boston: Houghton Mifflin Co., 1942.

Scott, William Evans. *Alliance against Hitler: The Origins of the Franco-Soviet Pact.* Durham, NC: Duke University, 1962.

Sdvigi v sel'skom khoziaistve SSSR mezhdu XV i XVI partiinymi s"ezdami: statisticheskie svedeniia po sel'skomu khoziaistvu za 1927–1930 gg. 2nd ed. Moscow-Leningrad: Gos. sotsial'no-ekonomicheskoe izd-vo, 1931.

Seabury, Paul. *The Wilhelmstrasse: A Study of German Diplomats under the Nazi Regime.* Berkeley and Los Angeles: University of California, 1955.

Seaton, Albert. *The Russo-German War 1914–1945.* New York: Praeger, 1970.

Sechkin, Georgy. *Granitsa i voina: pogranichnye voiska v Velikoi Otechestvennoi voine sovetskogo naroda, 1941–1945.* Moscow: Granitsa, 1993.

Sedov, I., N. V. Kulish, and A. Ia. Valetov. "Spravka rabotnikov prokuratury SSSR i sledstvennogo otdela KGB SSSR po povodu zapiski A. N. Iakovleva 'Nekotorye soobrazheniia po itogam izucheniia obstoiatel'stv ubiistva S. M. Kirova,'" (June 14, 1990), 459–507. In *Reabilitatsiia: kak eto bylo: dokumenty Prezidiuma TsK KPSS i drugie materialy,* vol. 3, edited by Andrei N. Artizov et al. Moscow: Mezhdunarodnyi fond Demokratiia, 2003.

Segrè, Claudio G. *Italo Balbo: A Fascist Life.* Berkeley: University of California, 1987.

Seidl, Alfred, ed. *Die Beziehungen zwischen Deutschland under der Sowjetunion, 1939–1941: Dokumente des Auswärtigen Amtes.* Tübingen: H. Laupp'sche, 1949.

Seiranian, F. G. *Nadezhneishii voennyi rabotnik: ocherk o voenno-organizatorskoi deiatel'nosti G. K. Ordzhonikidze.* Moscow: Voenizdat, 1989.

Seleznev, Ivan A. *Tainy rossiiskoi politiki XX veka.* Krasnodar: Sovetskaia kuban', 1997.

Self, Robert. *Neville Chamberlain: A Biography.* Aldershot: Ashgate, 2006.

Selle, Earl Albert. *Donald of China.* New York: Harpers, 1948.

Sel'skoe khoziaistvo SSSR: ezhegodnik 1935. Moscow: Sel'khozgiz, 1936.

Selunskaia, V. M. *Rabochie-dvadtsatipiatity-siachniki.* Moscow: Moskovskii universitet, 1964.

Semashkina, M. A., and L. A. Evstigneeva, eds. *Perepiska Gor'kogo.* 2 vols. Moscow: Khudozhestvennaia literatura, 1986.

Semiriaga, Mikhail I. "17 sentiabria 1939 g.," *Sovetskoe slavianovedenie,* 1990, no. 5: 3–18.

———. *Tainy stalinskoi diplomatii, 1939–1941,* Moscow: Vysshaia shkola, 1992.

Semiryaga, Mikhail. *The Winter War: Looking Back after Fifty Years.* Moscow: Novosti, 1990.

Senin, A. S. *A. I. Rykov: stranitsy zhizni.* Moscow: Rosvuznauka, 1993.

Senn, Alfred Erich. *Lithuania 1940: Revolution from Above.* Amsterdam and New York: Rodopi, 2007.

Seraphim, Hans-Guenther. *Das politische Tagebuch Alfred Rosenbergs 1934–35 und 1939–40.* Goettingen: Musterschmidt-Verlag, 1956.

Serebriakova, Galina. "Iz vospominanii." In *Smerch,* edited by Ivan A. Anfert'ev. Moscow: DOSAAF SSSR, 1988, 230–49.

———. "Smerch." In *Smerch,* edited by Ivan A. Anfert'ev. Moscow: DOSAAF SSSR, 1988, 250–338.

Serge, Victor. "Leon Sedov," *La Révolution prolétarienne,* February 21, 1938. Translated in *The Serge-Trotsky Papers,* edited by David Coterrill. London: Pluto Press, 1994.

———. "Litvinov," *Esprit,* June 1939.

———. *Memoirs of a Revolutionary, 1901–1941.* New York: Oxford University, 1963.

———. *Portrait de Staline.* Paris: Bernard Grasset, 1940.

———, and Natalya Sedova Trotsky. *The Life and Death of Leon Trotsky.* New York: Basic Books, 1975.

Sergeev, F. "Istoriia odnogo politicheskogo podloga: o 'dele' Tukhachevskogo," *Politicheskoe obrazovanie,* 1989, no. 5: 48–56.

Sergeev, A. F., and E. F. Glushik. *Besedy o Staline.* Moscow: Krymskii most, 2006.

Sergeienko, S. P. *Sinteticheskii kauchuk: istoricheskii ocherk.* Moscow: Gos. nauchno-tekhnicheskoe izd-vo khimicheskoi lit-ry, 1940.

Sergutov, S. V. "Organizatsionnye aspekty deiatel'nosti vneshnei razvedki NKVD-NKGB SSSR v 1934–1941 gg." In *Trudy Obshchestva izucheniia istorii otechestvennykh spestsluzhb,* vol. 3. Moscow: Kuchkovo pole, 2007, 234–53.

Service, Robert. *Stalin: A Biography.* Cambridge, MA: Harvard Belknap, 2005.

Sevast'ianov, Petr V. *Neman-Volga-Dunai.* Moscow: Voenizdat, 1961.

Sever, Aleksandr, and Aleksandr Kolpakidi. *GRU: unikal'naia entsiklopediia.* Moscow: Eksmo, 2009.

———. *Volkodav Stalina: Pravdivaia istoriia Pavla Sudoplatova.* Moscow: Algoritm, 2015.

Sevost'ianov, Grigorii N. "Obostreniie sovetsko-amerikanskikh otnoshenii letom 1935 g.: prichiny i posledstviia," *Novaia i noveishaia istoriia,* 1998, no. 6: 19–35.

———. "Sud'ba soglasheniia Ruzvel't—Litvinov o dolgakh i kreditakh, 1934–1935 gg: novye dolumenty," *Novaia i noveishaia istoriia,* 1995, no. 2: 115–34, no. 3: 118–44.

———. "Voennoe i diplomaticheskoe porazhenie iaponii v periode sobytyi u reki Khalkhin-Gol," *Voprosy istorii,* 1957, no. 8: 63–84.

———, ed. *Moskva-Rim, politika i diplomatiia Kremlia 1920–1939: sbornik dokumentov.* Moscow: Nauka, 2002.

———, et al., eds. *"Sovershenno sekretno": Lubianka—Stalinu o polozhenii v strane (1922–1934 gg.).* 10 vols. Moscow: Institut rossiiskoi istorii RAN, 2001–13.

Seyed-Gohrab, A. A. *The Great Umar Khayyam: A Global Reception of the Rubaiyat.* Leiden: Leiden University, 2012.

Shai, Aron. "Was There a Far Eastern Munich?" *Journal of Contemporary History,* 9/3 (1974): 161–9.

———. *Zhang Xueliang: The General Who Never Fought.* Basingstoke: Palgrave Macmillan, 2010.

Shakhurin, A. I. *Krylia pobedy.* Moscow: Politizdat, 1985.

Shalamov, Varlan. *Kolyma Tales.* New York: Penguin, 1994.

Shamina, Lidiia. "Igor Moiseev: Nachalo puti, dnevniki khoreografa," *Kul'tura,* 2008, no. 9.

Shaposhnikov, Boris M. *Vospominaniia: voenno-nauchnye trudy.* Moscow: Voenizdat, 1974.

Shapoval, Iurii I. "'Oni chuvstvuiut sebia, kak gosti . . .' (nad storinkamy stenohramy zustrichi Stalina z ukrains'kymy pys'mennykamy 12 liutoho 1929 roku)." In *Ukraina XX stolittia: osoby ta podii v*

konteksti vazhkoi istorii. Kiev: Heneza, 2001, 93–130.

———. *Lazar Kaganovich.* Kiev: Znannia, 1994.

———, and Vadim Zolotar'ov. *Vsevolod Balyt'skyi: osoba, chas, otochennia.* Kiev: Stylos, 2002.

———, et al. *ChK-GPU-NKVD v Ukraini: osoby, fakty, dokumenty.* Kiev: Abrys, 1997.

Sharapov, Eduard. "Za sto chasov do voiny," *Krasnaia zvezda,* June 22, 1994.

———. *Dve zhizni.* In *Taina Zoi Voskresenskoi,* edited by Z. I. Voskresenskaia. Moscow: Olma, 1998, 345–51.

Sharapov, Iu. "Piat'sot stranits v den'," *Moskovskie novosti,* Sept. 18, 1988.

Sharapov, Z. P. *Naum Eitingon—karaiushchii mech Stalina.* St. Petersburg: Neva, 2003.

Sharlet, Robert, and Piers Beirne. "In Search of Vyshinsky: the Paradox of Law and Terror," *International Journal of the Sociology of Law,* 12/2 (1984): 153–77.

Shatunovskaia, Lidiia. *Zhizn' v kremle.* New York: Chalidze Publications, 1982.

Shaumian, Lev. "Stoikii bol'shevik," *Pravda,* May 19, 1962.

Shaw, Louise Grace. *The British Political Elite and the Soviet Union, 1937–1939.* Portland, OR: Frank Cass, 2003.

Shchelokov, Nikolai A. *Istoriia sovetskoi militsii.* 2 vols. Moscow: Akademiia nauk SSSR, 1977.

Shchukin, Boris. *Boris Vasil'evich Shchukin: stat'i, vospominaniia, materialy.* Moscow: Iskusstvo, 1965.

Shearer, David. "Crime and Social Disorder in Stalin's Russia: A Reassessment of the Great Retreat and the Origins of Mass Repression," *Cahiers du monde russe,* 39/1–2 (1998): 119–48.

———. "Social Disorder, Mass Repression and the NKVD during the 1930s," *Cahiers du monde russe,* 42/2–4 (2001): 505–34.

———. *Industry, State, and Society in Stalin's Russia, 1926–1934.* Ithaca, NY: Cornell University, 1997.

———. *Policing Stalin's Socialism: Repression and Social Order in the Soviet Union, 1924–1953.* New Haven, CT: Yale University, 2009.

Sheboldaev, B. P. *Doklad na pervoi kraevoi Azovo-Chernomorskoi part-konferentsii, 19 ianvaria 1934 g.* Roston-na-Donu, 1934.

Sheffer, Paul. "Stalin's Power," *Foreign Affairs,* (July 1930): 549–67.

Shefov, Aleksandr N. "Dve vstrechi." In *I k nim primknuvshii Shepilov: pravda o cheloveke, uchenom, voine, politike,* edited by Tamara Tolchanova and Mikhail Lozhnikov. Moscow: Zvonittsa-MG, 1998.

Shein, K. I., ed. *Kanal Moskva-Volga: spravochnik-putevoditel'.* Moscow: Narkomvod, 1937.

Sheinis, Zinovii S. "Polpred B. E. Shtein: strikhi k biografii," *Novaia i noveishaia istoriia,* 1991, no. 1: 101–16.

———. "Sud'ba diplomata: strikhi k portretu Borisa Shteina." In *Arkhivy nakryvaiut tainy . . . Mezhdunarodnye voprosy: sobytiia i liudi,* edited by V. N. Popov. Moscow: Politizdat, 1991, 286–311.

———. *Maksim Maksimovich Litvinov: revoliutsioner, diplomat, chleovek.* Moscow: Politizdat, 1989.

Shelestov, Dmitrii. *Vremia Alekseia Rykova.* Moscow: Progress, 1990.

Sheng, Michael M., and John W. Garver. "New Light on the Second United Front: An Exchange," *China Quarterly,* 129 (1992): 148–93.

Shentalinskii, Vitalii. "Proshu menia vyslushat'. . . (poslednie dni Babelia)." *Vozvrashchenie,* 1991, no. 1.

———. *Raby svobody v literaturnykh arkhivakh KGB.* Moscow: Parus, 1995, 430–43.

Shentalinsky, Vitaly. *Arrested Voices: Resurrecting the Disappeared Writers of the Soviet Regime.* New York: Martin Kessler, 1996.

———. *The KGB's Literary Archive.* Translated by John Crowfoot. London: Harvill, 1995.

Shepilov, Dmitrii. *The Kremlin's Scholar: A Memoir of Soviet Politics under Stalin and Krushchev.* New Haven, CT: Yale University, 2007.

Shestakov, Andrei V. "Ob izuchenii istorii SSSR." In *Ob izuchenii istorii SSSR.* Moscow: Molodaia gvardiia, 1938, 22–39.

———. *Kratkii kurs istorii SSSR: uchebnik dlia 3–go i 4–go klassov.* Moscow: Gosudarstvennoe uchebno-pedagogicheskoe iizd-vo, 1937.

———, ed. *A Short History of the USSR: Textbook for 3rd and 4th classes.* Moscow: Cooperative Publishing Society of Foreign Workers in the USSR, 1938.

Shevelev, M. I. *Arktika—sud'ba moia: vospominaniia pervogo nachal'nika poliarnoi aviatsii.* Voronezh: Modek, 1999.

Shikshin, V. "Sovetskie nemtsy: U istokov tragedii," *Nauka v Sibiri,* 1992, no. 28: 5–6.

Shilony, Ben-Ami. *Revolt in Japan: The Young Officers and the February 26, 1936, Incident.* Princeton, NJ: Princeton University, 1973.

Shimotomai, Nabuo. "Springtime for the Politotdel: Local Party Organizations in Crisis," *Acta Slavica Iaponica,* 4 (1986): 1–34.

———. "A Note on the Kuban Affair (1932–1933): The Crisis of Kolkhoz Agriculture in the North Caucasus," *Acta Slavica Iaponica,* 1 (1983): 39–56.

Shirer, William. *Berlin Diary: The Journal of a Foreign Correspondent, 1934–1941.* New York: Knopf, 1941.

———. *The Rise and Fall of the Third Reich.* New York: Simon & Schuster, 1960.

Shirinia, Kirill K. *Komintern v 1933 godu.* Moscow: Eks libris, 2006.

Shirokorad, Aleksandr B. *Velikii antrakt.* Moscow: AST, 2009.

Shirokov, Anatolii. *Dal'stro v sotsial'no-ekonomicheskoe razvitii severo-vostoka SSSR (1930–1950-e gg.).* Moscow: Rosspen, 2014.

Shishov, Aleksei V. *Rossiia i Iaponiia: istoriia voennykh konfliktov.* Moscow: Veche, 2001.

Shitts, Ivan I. *Dnevnik "velikogo perloma" mart 1928–avust 1931.* Paris: YMCA-Press, 1991.

Shlifshtein, Semen. "Semyon Kotko," *Sovetskoe iskusstvo,* June 29, 1940.

Shmidt, Sigurd O. "Priemy v Kremle v chest' poliarnikov." In *Istoriia Moskvy i problemy moskvovedeniia.* Moscow: Russkii put', 2004, 272–82.

Shoemaker, Merle Wesley. "Russo-German Economic Relations, 1850–1914," PhD diss. Syracuse University, 1979.

"Sholokhov i Stalin: perepiska nachala 30-x godov," *Voprosy istorii,* 1994, no. 3: 3–25.

Shore, Zachary. "Hitler's Opening Gambit: Intelligence, Encirclement, and the Decision to Ally with Poland," *Intelligence and National Security,* 14/3 (1999): 103–22.

———. *What Hitler Knew: The Battle for Information in Nazi Foreign Policy.* New York: Oxford University, 2003.

Short, Ken R. M., and Richard Taylor. "Soviet Cinema and the International Menace, 1928–1939," *Historical Journal of Film, Radio, and Television,* 6/2 (1986): 131–59.

Short, Philip. *Mao: A Life.* New York: Henry Holt, 2000.

Shpanov, Nikolai. "Pervyi udar: povest' o budushchei voine," *Znamia,* 1939, no. 1: 36–119.

———. *Pervyi udar: povest' o budushchei voine.* Moscow: Voenizdat, 1939.

Shreider, Mikhail *NKVD iznutri: zapiski cheskista.* Moscow: Vozvrashchenie, 1995.

Shtemenko, S. M. *General'nyi shtab v gody voiny.* Moscow: Voenizdat, 1968.

Shubin, A. V. *Vozhdi i zagovorshchiki.* Moscow: Veche, 2004.

Shul'gina, N. I. "Teoretiko-metodoligicheskie osnovy deiatel'nosti museev V. I. Lenina," PhD diss. Moscow, 1989.

Shumiatskii, Boris Z. "Tvorcheskie zadachi templana," *Sovetskoe kino,* 1933, no. 12: 1–15.

———. *Kinematografiia millionov: opyt analiza.* Moscow: Kinofotoizdat, 1935.

Shustov, V. "No Other Ambassador Served in So Many Countries," *International Affairs,* 51/1 (2005): 166–74.

Shuyun, Sun. *The Long March: The True History of Communist China's Founding Myth.* New York: Anchor, 2008.

Shvarts, Anatolii. "Zhizn' i smert' Mikhaila Bulgakova," *Kontinent,* no. 53 (1987): 10–97, no. 54 (1987): 60–142.

Shvede, E. E. *Voennyi flot Iaponii.* Leningrad: ONTI NKTP SSSR, 1936.

Sibirskaia Sovetskaia Entsiklopediia. 3 vols. Novosibirsk: Sibirskoe kraevoe izd-vo, 1929–32.

Sibley, Katherine. "Soviet Industrial Espionage against American Military Technology and the US Response, 1930–1945," *Intelligence and National Security,* 14/2 (Curzon) 94–123.

Sidorov, Nikolai. "'Veselye rebiata'—komediia kontrrevoliutsionnaia," *Istochnik,* 1995, no. 3: 72–8.

Siegelbaum, Lewis, and Andrei Sokolov. *Stalinism as a Way of Life.* New Haven, CT: Yale University, 2009.

———. *Stakhanovism and the Politics of Productivity in the USSR, 1935–1941.* Cambridge, UK: Cambridge University, 1988.

Sigachev, S. "Glavnoe upravlenie stroitel'stva Dal'nego Severa." In *Sistema ispravitel'no-trudovykh lagerei v SSSR,* edited by N. G. Okhotin and A. B. Roginskii. Moscow: Zvenia, 1998.

Simmons, Beth A. *Who Adjusts? Domestic Sources of Foreign Economic Policy during the Interwar Years.* Princeton, NJ: Princeton University, 1994.

Simms, J. Y. "Economic Impact of the Russian Famine of 1891–92," *Slavonic and East European Review,* 60/1 (1982): 63–74.

———. "The Crop Failure of 1891: Soil Exhaustion, Technological Backwardness, and Russia's 'Agrarian Crisis,'" *Slavic Review,* 41/2 (1982): 236–50.

Simon, John Allsebrook, Viscount. *Retrospect: The Memoirs of the Rt Hon. Viscount Simon.* London: Hutchinson, 1952.

Simonov, Konstantin M. "Glazami cheloveka moego pokoleniia: besedy s marshalom Sovetskogo Soiuza A.M. Vasilevskim," *Znamia,* 1998, no. 5.

———. "K biografii G. K. Zhukova." In *Marshal Zhukov: Kakim my ego pomnim.* Moscow: Politicheskaia literatura, 1988.

———. "Zametki k biogfraii G.K. Zhukova," *Voenno-Istoricheskii zhurnal,* 1987, no. 9: 48–56.

———. *Glazami cheloveka moego pokoleniia.* Moscow: Novosti, 1989.

Simonov, N. S. *Voenno-promyshlennyi kompleks SSSR v 1920–1950-e gody: tempy ekonomicheskogo rosta, struktura, organizatsiia proizvodstva i upravlenie.* Moscow: Rosspen, 1996.

Sinel'nikov, A. *Kirov.* Moscow: Molodaia gvardiia, 1964.

Sinitsyn, Elisei T. *Rezident svidetel'stvuet.* Moscow: Geia, 1996.

Sinyavsky, Andrei. *Soviet Civilization: A Cultural History.* New York: Arcade, 1990.

Sipols, Vilnos Ia. "SSSR i problema mira i bezopasnosti v vostochnoi Evrope (1931–1938 gg.)." In *SSSR v bor'be protiv fashistskoi agressii 1933–1945 gg.,* edited by A. L. Narochnitskii et al. Moscow: Nauka, 1976, 8–72.

———. "Torgovo-ekonomicheskie otnosheniia mezhdu SSSR i Germanii v 1939–1941 gg. v sevete novykh arkhivnikh dokunmentov," *Novaia i noveishaia istoriia,* 1997, no. 2: 29–41.

———. *Tainy diplomaticheskie: kanun velikoi otechestvennoi voiny, 1939–1941.* Moscow: Institut Rossiiskoi istorii, RAN, 1997.

Skorokhodov, Gleb A. *Mikhail Kol'tsov: kritiko-istoricheskii ocherk.* Moscow: Sovetskii pisatel', 1959.

———. *V poiskakh utrachennogo.* Moscow: Rutena, 2000.

Sladkovskii, M. I. *Znakomomstvo s Kitaem i kitaitsami.* Moscow: Mysl', 1984.

Slavinskii, Boris N. *Pakt o neitralitete mezdu SSSR i Iaponiei: diplomaticheskaia istoriia 1941–1945 gg.* Moscow: Novina, 1995.

———. *Vneshniaia politika na Dal'nem vostoke.* Moscow: Mezhdunarodnye otnosheniia, 1988.

Slavinskii, Dmitrii B. *Sovetskii Soiuz i Kitai: istoriia diplomaticheskikh otnoshenii, 1917–1937 gg.* Moscow: Iaponiia segodnia, 2003.

Slavinsky, Boris N. *The Japanese-Soviet Neutrality Pact: A Diplomatic History 1941–1945.* London: RoutledgeCurzon, 2004.

Slezkine, Yuri. "The USSR as a Communal Apartment, or How a Socialist State Promoted Ethnic Particularism," *Slavic Review,* 53/2 (1994): 414–52.

Sluch, Sergei Z. "'Delo Tukhachevskogo': Veilka li zasluga SD? (po povodu novoi knigi nemetskogo istorika)," *Sovetskoe slavianovedenie,* 1992, no. 1: 27–9.

———. "Germano-sovetskie otnosheniia v 1918–1941 gg.: motivy i posledstviia vneshnepoliticheskikh reshenii," *Slavianovedenie,* 1996, no. 3: 101–13.

———. "Pol'sha v politike Sovetskogo Soiuza 1938–1939." In *Sovetsko-Pol'skie otnosheniia v politicheskikh usloviiakh Evropy 30–kh godov XX stoletiia: sbornik statei,* edited by E. Duraczyński and A. N. Sakharov. Moscow: Nauka, 2001, 156–90.

———. "Rech' Stalina, kotoroi ne bylo," *Otechestvennaia istoriia,* 2004, no. 1: 113–39.

Slutskii, A. G. "Bol'sheviki o germanskoi sotsial-demokratii v period ee predvoennogo kriziza," *Proletarskaia revoliutsiia,* 1930, no. 6: 38–73.

Smeliansky, Anatoly. "The Destroyers: Lunacharsky's Letter to Stalin on Censorship at the Moscow Art Theater," *Comparative Criticism,* 16 (1994): 33–7.

———. *Is Comrade Bulgakov Dead? Mikhail Bulgakov at the Moscow Art Theater.* New York: Routledge, 1993.

Smirnov, German V., ed. *Krovavyi marshal: Mikhail Tukhachevskii.* St. Petersburg: Korona print, 1997.

Smith, Edward Ellis. *The Young Stalin: The Early Years of an Elusive Revolutionary.* New York: Farrar, Straus & Giroux, 1967.

Smrž, Jiří. *Symphonic Stalinism: Claiming Russian Musical Classics for the New Soviet Listener, 1932–1953.* Berlin: Lit, 2011.

Smyr, G. V. *Islam v Abkhazii i puti preodoleniia ego perezhitkov v sovremennykh usloviiakh.* Tbilisi: Metsniereba, 1972.

Smyth, Denis. "Soviet Policy towards Republican Spain: 1936–1939." In *The Republic Besieged: The Civil War in Spain, 1936–1939,* edited by Paul Preston and Ann L. Mackenzie. Edinburgh: University of Glasgow, 1996, 87–105.

Snesarev, A. E. *Filosofiia voiny*. Moscow: Lomonosov, 2013.

Snow, Edgar. *Random Notes on China (1936–1945)*. Cambridge, MA: Harvard University, 1957.

———. *Red Star over China*. London: Victor Gollancz, 1937.

Snyder, Jack. "Russian Backwardness and the Future of Europe," *Daedalus*, 123/2 (1994): 179–201.

Snyder, Louis. *Encyclopedia of the Third Reich*. New York: McGraw-Hill, 1976.

Snyder, Timothy. *Sketches from a Secret War: A Polish Artist's Mission to Liberate Soviet Ukraine*. New Haven, CT: Yale University, 2005.

Sobolev, A. I., ed. *Georgii Dimitrov—vydaiushchiisia deiatel' kommunisticheskogo dvizheniia*. Moscow: Politizdat, 1972.

Sobolev, D. A., and D. B. Khazanov. *Nemetskii sled v istorii otechestvennoi aviatsii*. Moscow: Rusavia, 2000.

Sobranie zakonov i rasporiazhenii SSSR. Moscow: Upravlenie delami Soveta Narodnykh Komissarov SSSR, 1924–1950.

Sochineniia. See Stalin, I. V., Sochineniia.

Sokolov, A. K. *Obshchestvo i vlast' v 1930-e gody: povestvovanie v dokumentakh*. Moscow: Rosspen, 1998.

———. *Ot voenproma k VPK: sovetskaia voennaia promyshlennost' 1917–1941 gg*. Moscow: Novyi khronograf, 2012.

Sokolov, Boris V. *Beriia: sud'ba vsesil'nogo narkoma*. Moscow: AST, 2008.

———. *Georgii Zhukov*. Moscow: AST, 2003.

———. *Istreblennye marshaly*. Smolensk: Rusich, 2000.

———. *Mikhail Tukhachevskii: zhizn' i smert' "Krasnogo marshala."* Smolensk: Rusich, 1999.

———. *Narkomy strakha: Iagoda, Ezhov, Beriia, Abakumov*. Moscow: AST, 2001.

———. *Neizvestnyi Zhukov: portret bez retushi v zerkale epokhi*. Minsk: Rodiola-plius, 2000.

———. *Tukhachevskii: zhizn' i smert' krasnogo marshala*. Moscow: Veche, 2003.

———. *Vasilii Stalin*. Smolensk: Rusich, 2000.

Sokolov, V. V. "N. N. Krestinskii—revoliutsioner, diplomat," *Novaia i noveishaia istoriia*, 1989, no. 5: 120–42.

———. "Neizvestnyi G. V. Chicherin: iz rassekrechennykh arkhivov MID RF," *Novaia i noveishaia istoriia*, 1994, no. 2: 3–18.

———. "Novye dannye o podgotovke Germanskogo vtorzheniii v SSSR," *Voenno-istoricheskii zhurnal*, 2000, no. 1: 86–9.

———. "Zabytyi diplomat: D. V. Bogomolov (1890–1938)," *Novaia i noveishaia istoriia*, 2004, no. 3: 165–95.

———. "Zamestitel' narkoma inostrannykh del B. Stomoniakov." In *Otkryvaia novye stranitsy . . . Mezhdunarodnye voprosy: sobytiia i liudi*, edited by N. V. Popov. Moscow: Politizdat, 1989, 257–93.

———. *Na boevykh postakh diplomaticheskogo fronta: zhizn' i deiatel'nost' L.M. Karakhana*. Moscow: Politizdat, 1983.

Soldatenkov, L. D. *Politicheskie i nravstvennye posledstviia usileniia vlasti VKP (b), 1928–1941*. St. Petersburg: Otd-nie izdatel'stva Prosveshchenie, 1994.

Solodovnikov, A. V. "My byli molodye togda: vospominaniia." In *Teatral'nye stranitsy: sbornik statei*. Moscow: Iskusstvo, 1979, 186–223.

Solomon, Jr., Peter H. *Soviet Criminal Justice under Stalin*. Cambridge, UK: Cambridge University, 1996.

———. *Soviet Criminologists and Criminal Policy: Specialists in Policy-Making*. New York: Columbia University, 1978.

———, ed. *Reforming Justice in Russia, 1864–1996: Power, Culture, and the Limits of Legal Order*. Armonk, NY, and London: M. E. Sharpe, 1997.

Solomon, Susan Gross. "Rural Scholars and the Cultural Revolution." In *Cultural Revolution in Russia, 1928–1931*, edited by Sheila Fitzpatrick. Bloomington: Indiana University, 1978, 129–53.

Solonin, Mark. "Delo aviatorov," *Voenno-promyshlennyi kur'er*, June 9, 2010.

———. "Tri plana tovarishcha Stalina." In *Pravda Viktora Suvorova: okonchatel'noe reshenie*, edited by D. S. Khmlenitsii. Moscow: Iauza, 2009, 31–89.

Solonitsyn, G. "Nachal'nik sovetskoi razvedki," *Voenno-istoricheskii zhurnal*, 1979, no. 11: 92–4.

Solovev, Mikhail. *My Nine Lives in the Red Army*. New York: D. McKay, 1955.

Solov'ev, A. G. "Tetradi krasnogo professora, 1912–1941 gg." In *Neizvestnaia Rossiia, XX vek*, edited by V. A. Kozlov, 4 vols. Moscow: Istoricheskoe nasledie, 1992–3, IV: 140–228.

Solov'ev, D. E., and A. I. Chugunov, eds. *Pogranichnye voiska SSSR, 1929–1938: sbornik dokumentov i materialov*. Moscow: Nauka, 1973.

Solzhenitsyn, Aleksandr. *The Gulag Archipelago, 1918–1956: An Experiment in Literary Investigation*. 3 vols. New York: Harper & Row, 1974–79.

Sommer, Erich F. *Botschafter Graf Schulenburg: der letzte Vertreter des Deutschen Reiches in Moskau*. Asendorf: MUT-Verlag, 1987.

———. *Das Memorandum: Wie der Sowjetunion der Krieg erklärt wurde*. Munich: Herbig, 1981.

Sommer, Theo. *Deutschland und Japan zwischen den Mächten 1935–1940*. Tübingen: Mohr, 1962.

Sontag, Raymond J. "The Last Months of Peace, 1939," *Foreign Affairs*, 35/3 (1957): 507–24.

———, and James S. Beddie, eds. *Nazi-Soviet Relations, 1939–1941: Documents from the Archives of the German Foreign Office*. Washington, D.C.: Department of State, 1948.

Sorel, Georges. *Réflexions sur la violence*. Paris: Librarie de pages libres, 1908.

Sostav rukovodiashchikh rabotnikov i spetsialistov Soiuza SSR. Moscow: Soiuzorguchet, 1936.

Sotsialisticheskoe stroitel'stvo v SSSR: statisticheskii ezhegodnik. Moscow: Soiuzorguchet, 1934.

Sotskov, Lev F. *Neizvestnyi separatizm: na sluzhbe SD i Abvera (Iz sekretnykh dos'e razvedki)*. Moscow: Ripol klassik, 2003.

———, ed. *Pribaltika i geopolitika: sbornik dokumentov*. Moscow: SVR, 2006.

Southworth, Herbert Rutledge. *Guernica, Guernica: A Study of Journalism, Diplomacy, Propaganda, and History*. Berkeley: University of California, 1997.

Souvarine, Boris. *Staline: Aperçu historique de bolchévisme*. Paris: Plon, 1935. Reissued Paris: Editions Champ Libre, 1977. Translated as *Stalin: A Critical Survey of Bolshevism*. London: Secker and Warburg, 1939.

Sovetskaia kul'tura v rekonstruktivnyi period, 1928–1941. Moscow: Institut istorii SSSR, 1988.

"Sovetskaia razvedka i russkaia voennaia emigratsiia 20–40x gg.: interv'iu s polkovnikom V. N. Karpovym," *Novaia i noveishaia istoriia*, 1998, no. 3: 119–24.

Sovetskaia voennaia entsiklopediia. 8 vols. Moscow: Voenizdat, 1976–80.

Sovetsko-kitaiskii konflikt 1929: sbornik dokumentov. Moscow: Litizdat NKID, 1930.

So Wai Chor. "The Making of the Guomindang's Japan Policy, 1932–1937: the Roles of Chiang Kai-Shek and Wang Jing-wei," *Modern China*, 28/2 (2002): 213–51.

Spáčil, D., and V. F. Mal'tsev, eds. *Dokumenty po istorii miunhkenskogo sgovora 1937–1939*. Moscow: Politizdat, 1979.

Spahr, William J. *Zhukov: The Rise and Fall of a Great Captain*. Novato, CA: Presidio, 1993.

Spalcke, Karl. "Der Fall Tuchatschewski: die Wehrmacht, die rote Armee under 'die grosse Säuberung,'" *Die Gegenwart*, 13 (1958): 45–8.

Spaso, Liudmil Iordanovich. *Bulgariia i SSSR 1917–1944: politiko-diplomaticheskii otnosheniia*. Veliko Turnovo: Faber, 2008.

Speer, Albert. *Erinnerungen*. Berlin: Propyläen, 1969.

———. *Inside the Third Reich: Memoirs*. New York: Macmillan, 1970.

———. *Spandauer Tagebücher*. Franklin am Main: Propyläen, 1975.

Spitzy, Reinhard. *So haben wir das Reich verspielt: Bekenntnisse eines Illegalen*. 4th ed. Munich: Langen Müller, 1994.

Spravochnik partiinogo rabotnika. 9 vols. Moscow: Partizdat, 1921–1935.

Spring, D. W. "The Soviet Decision for War against Finland, 30 November 1939," *Soviet Studies*, 38/2 (1986): 207–26.

SSSR i Litva v gody vtoroi mirovoi voiny: sbornik dokumentov. 2 vols. Vilnius: Institut istorii Litvy, 2006.

Stafford, David A. T. "SOE and British Involvement in the Belgrade Coup d'État of March 1941," *Slavic Review*, 36/3 (1977): 399–419.

Stakhanov, Aleksei G. *Rasskaz o moei zhizni*. Moscow: Gossotsizd, 1937.

Stalin, I. V. *Sochineniia*, 13 vols. Moscow: Politicheskaia literatura, 1946–51. Vols. 14–16, Robert H. MacNeal, ed. Stanford, CA: Hoover Institution, 1967. Cited as *Sochineniia* (author understood).

———. *Voprosy Leninizma*. Moscow: Gosizdat, 1939.

Stalin, Joseph. *Leninism*. Moscow: Cooperative Publishing Society of Foreign Workers in the USSR, 1933.

Stalin: k shestidesiatiletiiu so dnia rozhdeniia. Moscow: Pravda, 1940.

Stalin: sbornik statei k piatidesitiletiu so dnia rozhdeniia. Moscow-Leningrad: Gosizdat, 1929.

Stalin i liudi sovetskoi strany v izobrazitel'nom iskusstve: katalog vystavki. Moscow: Tret'iakovskaia galeriia, 1939.

Starinov, I. T. *Miny zhdut svoego chasa*. Moscow: Voenizdat, 1964.

Starkov, Boris A. "Ar'ergardnye boi staroi partiinoi gvardii." In *Oni ne molchali*, edited by A. V. Afanas'ev. Moskva: Politizdat, 1991, 215–25.

———. "Delo Riutina." In *Oni ne molchali*, edited by A. V. Afanas'ev. Moskva: Politizdat, 1991, 145–78.

———. "Kak Moskva chut' ne stala Stalinodarom," *Izvestiia TsK KPSS*, 1990, no. 12: 126–7.

———. "Narkom Ezhov." In *Stalinist Terror: New Perspectives*, edited by J. Arch Getty and Roberta T. Manning. New York: Cambridge University, 1993, 21–39.

———. "The Trial that Was Not Held," *Europe-Asia Studies*, 46/8 (1994): 1297–1315.

———. "Trotsky and Ryutin: From the History of the Anti-Stalin Resistance in the 1930s." In *The Trotsky Reappraisal*, edited by Terry Brotherstone and Paul Dukes. Edinburgh: Edinburgh University, 1992, 70–83.

———, ed. *Martem'ian Riutin: na koleni ne vstanu*. Moscow: Politizdat, 1992.

Starunin, A. I. "Operativnaya vnezapnost'," *Voennaia mysl'*, 1941, no. 3: 7–35.

Stavinskii, Ervin. *Zarubiny: semeinaia rezidenty.* Moscow: Olma, 2003.

Stehlin, Paul. *Témoignage pour l'histoire.* Paris: Robert Laffant, 1966.

Steiner, Zara S. "The Soviet Commissariat of Foreign Affairs and the Czechoslovakian Crisis in 1938: New Material from the Soviet Archives," *Historical Journal*, 42/3 (1999): 751–9.

———. *The Lights that Failed: European International History 1919–1933.* Oxford: Oxford University, 2005.

———. *The Triumph of the Dark: European International History, 1933–1939.* New York: Oxford University, 2011.

Stepanov, A. F. *Rasstrel po limitu: iz istorii politicheskikh repressa v TASSR v gody "ezhovshchiny."* Kazan: Novoe znanie, 1999.

Stepanov, A. S. "O masshtabakh repressii v Krasnoi Armii v predvoennye gody," *Voenno-istoricheskii zhurnal*, 1993, no. 1: 56–63, no. 2: 71–80, no. 3: 25–34, no. 5: 59–67.

Stepanov, I. *Parizhskaia kommuna 1871 goda i voprosy taktiki proletarskoi revoliutsii.* 6th ed. Moscow: Partizdat, 1937.

Stephan, John J. "'Cleansing' the Soviet Far East, 1937–1938," *Acta Slavica Iaponica*, 10 (1992): 43–64.

———. *The Russian Far East: A History.* Stanford, CA: Stanford University, 1994.

Stercho, Peter G. *Diplomacy of Double Morality: Europe's Crossroads in Carpatho-Ukraine, 1919–1939.* New York: Carpathian Research Center, 1971.

Stern, Fritz. "National Socialism as Temptation." In *Dreams and Delusions: The Drama of German History.* New York: Knopf, 1987, 147–91.

Stern, Ludmila. *Western Intellectuals and the Soviet Union, 1920–40: From Red Square to the Left Bank.* New York: Routledge, 2007.

Stikh, M. *Zavod griadushchikh urozhaev: rostovskii krasnoznamenskii sel'mash.* Moscow: Gos. nauchno-tekhnicheskoe izd-vo, 1931.

Stites, Richard. *Russian Popular Culture: Entertainment and Society since 1900.* New York: Cambridge University, 1992.

Stoecker, Sally. *Forging Stalin's Army: Marshal Tukhachevsky and the Politics of Military Innovation.* Boulder, CO: Westview, 1998.

Stoletov, V. "Zamechatel'nye knigi o velikikh pobedakh kolkhozov," *Sotsialisticheskaia rekonstruktsiia sel'skogo khoziaistva*, 1935, no. 6: 180–3.

Stolfi, R. H. "Equipment for Victory in France in 1940," *History*, 55/183 (1970): 1–20.

Stone, David R. "Misreading Svechin: Attrition, Annihilation, and Historicism," *Journal of Military History*, 76/3 (2012): 673–93.

———. "Tukhachevskii in Leningrad: Military Politics and Exile, 1928–1931," *Europe-Asia Studies*, 48/8 (1996): 1365–86.

———. *Hammer and Rifle: The Militarization of the Soviet Union, 1926–1933.* Lawrence: University Press of Kansas, 2000.

Storella, Carmine J., and A. K. Sokolov, eds. *The Voice of the People: Letters from the Soviet Village, 1918–1932.* New Haven, CT: Yale University, 2013.

Stover, William J. "Finnish Military Politics between the Two World Wars," *Journal of Contemporary History*, 12/4 (1977): 741–5.

Strang, G. Bruce, ed. *Collision of Empires: Italy's invasion of Ethiopia and its International Impact.* Burlington, VT: Ashgate, 2013.

———. "Once More unto the Breach: Britain's Guarantee to Poland, March 1939," *Journal of Contemporary History*, 31/4 (1996): 721–52.

Strang, William. *Home and Abroad.* London: Andre Deutsch, 1956.

Stratigakos, Despina. *Hitler at Home.* New Haven, CT: Yale University, 2015.

Straus, Kenneth M. *Factory and Community in Stalin's Russia: The Making of an Industrial Working Class.* Pittsburgh, PA: University of Pittsburgh, 1997.

Striedter, Jurij. "Journeys through Utopia: Introductory Remarks to the Post-Revolutionary Russian Utopian Novel," *Poetics Today*, 3/1 (1982): 33–60.

Strong, Anna Louise. *The Stalin Era.* New York: Mainstream Publishers, 1956.

Strong, Kenneth, Major General. *Intelligence at the Top: The Recollections of an Intelligence Officer.* London: Cassell, 1968.

Stronski, Stanislaw. "Soviet Russia's Common Cause with Nazi Germany, 1939," *Eastern Quarterly*, 2/2 (1949): 28–37.

Struve, Gleb. "The Pan-Soviet Literary Congress," *Slavonic and East European Review*, 13/39 (1935): 641–3.

Stuchka, Petr. *Kurs Sovetskogo grazhdanskogo prava.* 3 vols. Moscow-Leningrad: Gosudarsvtennoe sotsialno-ekonomicheskoe izdatelstvo, 1931.

Sudoplatov, A. P. *Tainaia zhizn' generala Sudoplatova: pravda i vymysel o moem otse.* 2 vols. Moscow: Soveremennik, Olma, 1998.

Sudoplatov, Pavel. *Razvedka i kreml': zapiski nezhelatel'nogo svidetelia.* Moscow: Geja, 1996.

———. *Spetsoperatsii: Lubianka i kreml', 1930–1950 gody.* Moscow: Olma, 1997.

———, et al. *Special Tasks: The Memoirs of an Unwanted Witness, a Soviet Spymaster.* Boston: Little, Brown, 1994.

Sukhanov, Nikolai. *Zapiski.* 7 vols. Berlin: Z. I. Grzhebin, 1922–23.

Sukharev, S. V. "Litsedeistvo na poprishche istorii (Beriia—apologet kul'ta lichnosti Stalina)," *Voprosy istorii KPSS*, 1990, no. 3: 102–18.

Sukharnikova, Tat'iana. "My nagnali takoi velichaishii, podobaiushchii strakh revoliutsii." Interviewed by Iuliia Kantor. *Vremia*, Nov. 29, 2007.

Sukiennicki, Wiktor. "The Establishment of the Soviet Regime in Eastern Poland in 1939," *Journal of Central European Affairs*, 23/2 (1963): 191–218.

Sullivan, Brian R. "Fascist Italy's Military Involvement in the Spanish Civil War," *Journal of Military History*, 59/4 (1995): 697–727.

Sullivan, Rosemary. *Stalin's Daughter: The Extraordinary and Tumultuous Life of Svetlana Alliluyeva.* New York: Harper-Collins, 2015.

Sultanbekov, Bulat. "Nikolai Ezhov: Palach i zhertva," *Tatarstan*, 1992, no. 2.

Sundaram, Chantal. "Manufacturing Culture: The Soviet State and the Mayakovsky Legend 1930–1993." PhD diss. University of Toronto, 2000.

Suny, Ronald Grigor, ed. *The Structure of Soviet History: Essays and Documents.* Oxford: Oxford University, 2003.

———. *The Making of the Georgian Nation.* 2nd ed. Bloomington: Indiana University, 1994.

Suslov, Andrei B. "'Revolution from Above': 'Dekulakization' as a Part of Stalin's Social Revolution (The Case of the Perm Region)." Unpublished manuscript.

Sutton, Anthony C. *Western Technology and Soviet Economic Development 1930–1945.* 3 vols. Stanford, CA: Hoover Institution, 1968–73.

Suvenirov, Oleg F. "Klim, Koba skazal," *Voenno-istoricheskii zhurnal*, 1988, no. 12: 51–60.

———. "Narkomat oborony i NKVD v predvoennye gody," *Voprosy istorii*, 1991, no. 6: 26–35.

———. "Za chest' i dostoinstvo voinov RKKA." In *Oni ne molchali*, edited by A. V. Afanas'ev. Moscow: Politizdat, 1991, 372–87.

———. *Tragediia RKKA 1937–1938.* Moscow: Terra, 1998.

Suyin, Han. *Eldest Son: Zhou Enlai and the Making of Modern China.* New York: Hill and Wang, 1994.

Svechin, A. A. *Strategiia.* Moscow: Voenizdat, 1927.

Svetlanin, Andrei [Nikolai Likhachev]. *Dal'nevostochnyi zagovor.* Frankfurt am Main: Posev, 1953.

Svetlishin, N. A. *Krutye stupeni sud'by: zhizn' i ratnye podvigi marshala G. K Zhukova.* Khabarovsk: Khabarovskoe knizhnoe izd-vo, 1992.

Svirin, M. N. *Bronia krepka: istoriia sovetskogo tanka 1919–1937.* Moscow: Eksmo, 2006.

Svolik, Milan W. *The Politics of Authoritarian Rule.* New York: Cambridge University, 2012.

Sweeting, George Vincent. "Building the Arsenal of Democracy: The Government's Role in Expansion of Industrial Capacity, 1940 to 1945." PhD diss. Columbia University, 1994.

Swianiewicz, Stanislaw. *Forced Labor and Economic Development: An Enquiry into the Experience of Soviet Industrialization.* New York: Oxford University, 1965.

Syrtsov, Sergei. *O nashikh uspekhakh, nedostatkakh i zadachakh.* Moscow: Gosizdat, 1930.

Szamuely, Tibor. "The Elimination of Opposition between the Sixteenth and Seventeenth Congresses of the CPSU," *Soviet Studies*, 17/3 (1966): 318–38.

Szikalai, Laszlo. *After the Revolution: Georg Lukac's Marxist Development, 1930–1945.* Budapest: Akademia Kiado, 1992.

Tabouis, Geneviève. *They Called Me Cassandra.* New York: Scribner, 1942.

Tainy diplomatii Tret'ego Reikka: germanskie diplomaty, rukovoditeli zarubezhnykh voennykh misii, voennye i politseiskie attaché v sovetskom plenu. Dokumenty iz sledstvennykh del. Moscow: Mezhdunarodnyi fond Demokratiia, 2011.

Takala, I. "Natsional'nye operatsii OGPU/ NKVD v Karelii." In *V sem'e edinoi: natsional'naia politika partii bol'shevikov i ee osushchestvlenie na Severo-Zapade Rossii v 1920–1950-e gody*, edited by V. Vikavainen and Takala. Petrozavosk: Izd-vo petrozavodskogo universiteta, 1998, 161–206.

Tang, Peter S. H. *Russian Policy in Manchuria and Outer Mongolia, 1911–1931.* Durham, NC: Duke University, 1959.

Tanin, O., and E. Kogan. *Voenno-fashistskoe dvizhenie v Iaponii.* Moscow: Partizdat, 1933.

Taniuchi, Yuzuru. *The Village Gathering in Russia in the Mid-1920s.* Birmingham, UK: University of Birmingham, 1968.

Tanner, Väinö. *The Winter War: Finland against Russia, 1939–1940.* Stanford, CA: Stanford University, 1957.

Taranova, Alla. *Golos Stalina.* St. Petersburg: Partner SPb, 2010.

Taranovsky, Theodore K. "Osobennosti rossiiskoi samoderzhavnoi monarkhii v XIX stoletii." In *Rossiiskaia monarkhiia: voprosy istorii i teorii*, edited by M. D. Karpachev. Voronezh: Istoki, 1998, 157–71.

Tarasenkov, A. "Pasternak: chernovye zapisi 1934–1939," *Voprosy literatury*, 1990, no. 4: 96–101.

Tardy, L. "The Caucasus Peoples and their Neighbours in 1404." In *Acta Orientalia Academiae Scientarium Hung*, XXXII/1 (1978): 83–111.

Tarkhanov, Alexei, and Sergeo Kavtaradze. *Architecture of the Stalin Era*. New York: Rizzoli, 1992.

Tarkhova, N. S. "Krasnaia armiia i kollektiviizatsiia sovetskoi derevni, 1928–1933: avtoreferat dissertatsii doktora istoricheskikh nauk," Saratov, 2006.

———. *Krasnaia armiia i stalinskaia kollektivizatsiia, 1928–1933 gg*. Moscow: Rosspen, 2010.

———, et al., eds. *"Zimniaia voina": Rabota nad oshibkami, aprel'–mai 1940 g. Materialy komissii Glavnogo voennogo soveta Krasnoi Armii po obobshcheniiu opyta Finskoi kampanii*. Moscow: Letnii sad, 2004.

Taruskin, Richard. "The Opera and the Dictator: the Peculiar Martyrdom of Dmitri Shostakovich," *New Republic*, March 20, 1989.

Tatimov, Maqash B. *Sotsial'naia obuslovlennost' demograficheskikh protsessov*. Al-ma-Ata: Nauka Kazakhskoi SSR, 1989.

Taubman, William. *Nikita Khrushchev*. New Haven, CT: Yale University, 2000.

Tauger, Mark B. "Natural Disaster and Human Actions, 1931–1933," Carl Beck Papers, University of Pittsburgh, Center for Russian and East European Studies, no. 1506 (2001).

———. "Soviet Peasants and Collectivization: Resistance and Adaptation," *Journal of Peasant Studies*, 31/3–4 (2004): 427–56.

———. "Stalin, Soviet Agriculture, and Collectivization." In *Food and Conflict in Europe in the Age of the Two World Wars*, edited by Frank Trentmann and Flemming Just. New York: Palgrave Macmillan, 2006, 109–42.

———. "The 1932 Harvest and the Famine of 1933," *Slavic Review*, 50/1 (1991): 70–89.

———. "The People's Commissariat of Agriculture." In *Decision-making in the Stalinist Command Economy, 1932–37*, edited by E. A. Rees. Houndmills, Basingstoke: Palgrave Macmillan, 1997, 150–75.

Taunton, Matthew. "Russia and the British Intellectuals: The Significance of the Stalin-Wells Talk." In *Russia in Britain: Melodrama to Modernism*, edited by Rebecca Beasley and Philip Bullock. New York: Oxford University, 2013, 209–24.

Taylor, A. J. P. *The Origins of the Second World War*. 2nd ed. Greenwich, CT: Fawcett, 1965.

Taylor, Frederick, ed. *The Goebbels Diaries 1939–1941*. New York: G. P. Putnam's Sons, 1983.

Taylor, Jay. *The Generalissimo: Chiang Kai-shek and the Struggle for Modern China*. Cambridge, MA: Belknap Press of Harvard University, 2009.

Taylor, Richard, and Ian Christie, eds. *The Film Factory: Russian and Soviet Cinema in Documents, 1896–1939*. London: Routledge & Kegan Paul, 1988.

———. "Ideology as Mass Entertainment: Boris Shumyatsky and Soviet Cinema in the 1930s." In *Inside the Film Factory: New Approaches to Russian and Soviet Cinema*, edited by Richard Taylor and Ian Christie. London: Routledge, 1991, 193–216.

———. "Singing on the Steppes for Stalin: Ivan Pyr'ev and the Kolkhoz Musical in Soviet Cinema," *Slavic Review*, 58/1 (1999): 143–59.

———. "The Illusion of Happiness and the Happiness of Illusion: Grigorii Aleksandrov's *The Circus*," *Slavonic and East European Review*, 74/4 (1996): 601–20.

Taylor, Sally J. *Stalin's Apologist: Walter Duranty, the New York Times Man in Moscow*. New York: Oxford University, 1990.

Taylor, Telford. *Sword and Swastika: Generals and Nazis in the Third Reich*. New York: Simon & Schuster, 1952.

Teichman, Christian. "Canals, Cotton, and the Limits of De-Colonization in Soviet Uzbekistan, 1924–1941," *Central Asia Survey*, 26/4 (2007): 499–519.

"Telegramma I. F. Dergacheva I. I. Proskurovu," *Izvestiia TsK KPSS*, 1990, no. 3: 220.

Telitsyn, V. L., et al., eds. *Stalin: diktator v "zerkale" inostrannoi pressy*. Moscow: Olma, 2006.

Tel'man, Iosef. "Riutin protiv Stalina," *Sekret*, Jan. 15, 2012.

Teodor, Gladkov. *Nagrada za vernost'—kazn'*. Moscow: Tsentrpoligraf, 2000.

Tepliakov, Aleksei G. "Personal i povsednevnost' Novosibirskogo UNKVD v 1936–1946," *Minuvshee: istoricheskii al'manakh*, no. 21 (1997): 240–93.

———. "Sibir': protsedura ispolneniia smertnykh prigovorov 1920–1930-x godov," *Golos Sibiri*, 2004.

———. *Mashina Terrora: OGPU-NKVD Sihiri v 1929–1941 gg*. Moskva: Novyi Khronograf; AIRO-XXI, 2008.

Terayama, Kyosuke. "Soviet Policies toward Mongolia after the Manchurian Incident, 1931–34." In *Facets of Transformation of the Northeast Asian Countries*, edited by Yoshida Tadashi and Hiroki Oka. 2 vols. Sendai, Japan: CNEAS Tohoku University, 1998, 37–66.

Teroni, Sandra, and Wolfgang Klein, eds. *Pour le défense de la culture: les textes du Congrès international des écrivains, Paris, juin 1935*. Dijon: Éditions universitaire du Dijon, 2005.

Terras, Victor. *Vladimir Mayakovsky*. Boston: Twayne, 1983.

Teske, Hermann, ed. *General Ernst Köstring: Der militärische Mittler zwischen dem Deutschen Reich und der Sowjeunion 1921–1941*. Frankfurt am Main: E. S. Mittler & Sohn, 1965.

Thayer, Charles W. *Bears in the Caviar*. Philadelphia: J. B. Lippincott, 1951.

Theses and Decisions, Thirteenth Plenum of the ECCI. Moscow: Co-operative Publishing Society of Foreign Workers in the USSR, 1934.

Thies, Jochen. *Architekt der Weltherrschaft: die "Endziele" Hitlers*. Düsseldorf: Droste, 1976.

Thomas, Georg. *Geschichte der deutschen Wehr- und Rüstungswirtschaft (1918–1943/45)*. Boppard am Rhein: Harald Boldt Verlag, 1966.

Thomas, Hugh. *The Spanish Civil War*. New York: Modern Library, 2001.

Thomas, Martin. "France and the Czechoslovak Crisis," *Diplomacy and Statecraft*, 10/2–3 (1999): 122–59.

Thompson, Neville. *The Anti-Appeasers: Conservative Opposition to Appeasement in the 1930s*. Oxford: Clarendon, 1971.

Thorndike, Anneli, Andrew Thorndike, and Karl Raddatz. *Unternehmen Teutonenschwert: die grosse Karriere eines kleines Spions*. Berlin: Ministerium für Nationale Verteidigung, 1959. Translated as *Operatsiia "Tevtonskii mech": bol'shaia kar'era melkogo shpiona*. Moscow: Voenizdat, 1960.

Thorne, Christopher. *The Limits of Foreign Policy: The West, the League, and the Far Eastern Crisis of 1931–1933*. London: Hamish Hamilton, 1972.

Thorniley, Daniel. *The Rise and Fall of the Soviet Rural Communist Party, 1927–1939*. New York: Macmillan, 1988.

Thurston, Robert W. *Life and Terror in Stalin's Russia, 1934–1941*. New Haven, CT, and London: Yale University, 1996.

Tichanova, Valentina. *Rasstrel'nye spiski, no. 2: Vaganskoe kladbishche, 1926–1936*. Moscow: Tekst, 1995.

Tien-Wei Wu. *The Sian Incident: A Pivotal Point in Modern Chinese History*. Ann Arbor: Center for Chinese Studies, University of Michigan, 1976.

Tikhanov, Galin. *The Master and the Slave: Lukács, Bakhtin, and the Ideas of their Time*. Oxford: Clarendon, 2000.

Tikhomirov, G. A. *Viacheslav Mikhailovich Molotov: kratkaia biografiia*. Moscow: politcheskaia literatura, 1940.

Tikhomirov, V. A. *Promyslovaia kooperatsiia na sovremennom etape*. Moscow: [s.n.], 1931.

Tikhvinskii, S. L. "Zakliuchenie sovetsko-iaponskogo pakta o neitralitete 1941 g.," *Novaia i noveishaia istoriia*, 1990, no. 1: 21–4.

Tillotson, H. M. *Finland at Peace and War, 1918–1993*. Rev. ed. Welby, Norwich: Michael Russell, 1996.

Tinchenko, Iaroslav. *Golgofa russkogo ofitsertva v SSSR: 1930–1931 gody*. Moscow: Moskovskii obshchestvennyi nauch. fond, 2000.

Tippelskirch, Kurt von. *Geschichte des Zweiten Weltkriegs*. 2nd ed. Bonn: Athenäum, 1956.

Tisminets, A. S., ed. *Vneshniaia politika SSSR, 1917–1946 gg.: sbornik dokumentov*. 4 vols. Moscow: OGIZ, 1944–46.

Titarenko, Mikhail L. *Kommiunisticheskii internatsional i kitaiskaia revoliutsii: dokumenty i materialy*. Moscow: Nauka, 1986.

———. *VKP (b), Komintern i Kitai, 1920–1943: dokumenty*. 8 vols. Moscow: Rosspen, 1996–2007.

Tiulenev, I. V. *Cherez tri voiny: vosmponianiia komanduiushchego iuzhnym i zakavkazskim frontami*. Moscow: Tsentropoligraf, 2007. Previously published by Voenizdat, 1960, 1972.

"Tiuremnye zapiski Rikharda Zorge," *Novaia i noveishaia istoriia*, 1994, no. 4, 5: 141–76, no. 6: 91–116, 1995, no. 2: 79–100.

Tkhorzhevskii, Iv. "Cherez sto let," *Vozrozhdenie*, February 6, 1937.

Tocqueville, Alexis de. *The Old Regime and the French Revolution*. Garden City, NY: Doubleday, 1955.

Tokaev, Grigory A. *Betrayal of an Ideal*. Bloomington: Indiana University, 1955.

———. *Stalin Means War*. London: Weidenfeld and Nicolson, 1951.

Tokarev, V. A. "'Kará panam! Kará': Pol'skaia tema v predvoennom kino (1939–1941 gg.)," *Otechestvennaia istoriia*, 2003, no. 6: 47–59.

Tokushirō, Ōhata. "The Anti-Comintern Pact, 1935–1939." In *Deterrent Diplomacy: Japan, Germany, and the USSR 1935–1940*, edited by James W. Morley. New York: Columbia University, 1976, 9–111.

Tolliver, Col. Raymond F., and Trever J. Constable. *Fighter General: The Life of Adolph Galland*. Atglen, PA: Schiffer Publishing, 1999.

Tolmachaev, V. A. "Sovetskii Soiuz i Ispaniia: opyt i uroki internatsional'noi pomoshchi (1936–1939)." PhD diss. Leningrad, 1991.

Tolstoi, Aleksei, and Vsevolod Vishnevskii. "Ob avtorskom prave," *Pravda*, June 26, 1937.

Tolstova, Natalya A. *Vnimanie, vkliuchaiu mikrofon!* Moscow: Iskusstvo, 1972.

Tolstoy, Leo. *The Kingdom of God Is within You: Christianity not as a Mystic Religion but as a New Theory of Life*. New York: Castell, 1894.

Tolstoy, Nikolai. *The Tolstoys: Twenty-Four Generations of Russian History*. London: Hamish Hamilton, 1983.

Tomasevich, Jozo. *War and Revolution in Yugoslavia, 1941–1945: Occupation and Collaboration*. Stanford, CA: Stanford University, 1975.

Tooze, J. Adam. *The Deluge: The Great War and the Remaking of the Global Order, 1916–1931*. New York: Viking, 2014.

———. *Wages of Destruction: The Making and Breaking of the Nazi Economy*. New York: Viking, 2006.

Toptygin, Aleksei. *Lavrentii Beriia: Neizvestnyi marshal gosbezopasnosti*. Moscow: Iauza-EKSMO, 2005.

———. *Neizvestnyi Beriia*. Moscow: Olma, 2002.

Toscano, Mario. *Origins of the Pact of Steel*. Baltimore, MD: Johns Hopkins University, 1964.

Toshihiko, Shimada. "The Extension of Hostilities, 1931–1932." In *Japan Erupts: The London Naval Conference and the Manchurian Incident, 1928–1932*, edited by James William Morley. New York: Columbia University, 1984: 241–335.

Tottle, Douglas. *Fraud, Famine and Fascism: The Ukrainian Genocide Myth from Hitler to Harvard*. Toronto: Progress Press, 1987.

Tournier, Michael, ed. *Les archives secrètes de la Wilhelmstrasse*, 6 vols. Vol. III. Paris: Librairie Plon, 1950.

"'Tovarishch neznakomaia': iz perepiski I. V. Stalina," *Istochnik*, 2001, no. 2: 51–2.

Toynbee, A. J. *Acquaintances*. London: Oxford University, 1967.

———, ed. *Survey of International Affairs, 1936*. Oxford: Oxford University, 1937.

Tracy, Michael. *Agriculture in Western Europe: Challenge and Response, 1880–1980*. 2nd ed. New York: Granada, 1982.

Transchel, Kate. *Under the Influence: Working-class Drinking, Temperance, and Cultural Revolution in Russia, 1895–1932*. Pittsburgh, PA: University of Pittsburgh, 2006.

Trapeznikov, Sergei P. *Istoricheskii opyt KPSS v sotsialisticheskom preobrazovanii sel'skogo khoziaistva*. Moscow: Politicheskaia literatura, 1959.

———. *Kommunisticheskaia partiia v period nastupleniia sotsializma po vsemu frontu: pobeda kol'khoznogo stroia v derevne, 1929–1932 gg.* Moscow: VPSH, 1961.

Trauberg, Il. "Proizvedenie mysli i strasti: Lenin v 1918 godu," *Iskusstvo kino*, 1939, no. 3.

———. "Rasskaz o velikom vozhde: o stsenarii 'Lenin,'" *Iskusstvo kino*, 1939, no. 1.

Trefousse, H. L. *Germany and American Neutrality, 1939–1941: An Analysis of Axis Diplomacy*. New York: Bookman Associates, 1951.

Treglown, Jeremy. *Franco's Crypt: Spanish Culture and Memory since 1936*. New York: Farrar, Straus & Giroux, 2013.

Trembitskii, A. A. *Po zapadnomu okrugu: Fili, Kuntsevo, opisanie zhizni rodnoi zemli*. Moscow: Sputnik, 1999.

Trepper, Léopold. *Bol'shaia igra: gody ucheniia "Krasnyi orkestr" vozvrashchenie, vospominaniia sovetskogo razvedchika*. Moscow: Politicheskaia literatura, 1990.

———. *The Great Game: Memoirs of the Spy Hitler Couldn't Silence*. New York: McGraw-Hill, 1977.

Tret'ia sessiia Verkhovnogo Soveta SSSR, 25–31 maia 1939 g: stenograficheskii otchet. Moscow: Verkhovnyi Sovet SSSR, 1939.

Trevor-Roper, Hugh, ed. *Le Testament politique de Hitler: Notes recueilles part Martin Bormann*. Paris: Hachette, 1959.

———. *Hitler's War Directives, 1939–1945*. London: Sidgwick & Jackson, 1964.

———. *Last Days of Hitler*. 2nd ed. London: Macmillan, 1962.

Trial of the Anti-Soviet "Bloc of Rights and Trotskyites." Moscow: Moscow News, 1938.

Trial of the Major War Criminals before the International Military Tribunal. 42 vols. Nuremberg, Germany: International Military Tribunal, 1947–49.

Triandafillov, Vladimir. *Kharakter operatsii sovremennoi armii*. Moscow: Gosizdat, otdel voennoi literatury, 1929. 2nd ed. Moscow: Voenizdat, 1937.

Trotskii, Leon. "Nuzhno chestnoe vnutripartiinoe soglashenie [March 30, 1933]," *Biulleten' oppozitsii*, no. 34 (May 1933): 29–30.

———. "Otkrytoe pis'ma prezidiumu TsIKa Soiuza SSR," *Biulleten' oppozitsii*, no. 27 (March 1932): 1–6.

———. "Stalinskaia biurokratiia i ubiistvo Kirova: otvet amerikanskim druz'iam," *Biulleten' oppozitsii*, no. 41 (1935): 1–10.

———. *Chto i kak proizoshlo: shest' statei dlia mirovoi burzhuaznoi pechati*. Paris: Navarre, 1929.

———. *Dnevniki i pis'ma*. Tenafly, NJ: Ermit-age, 1986, 1990.

———. *Literatura i revoliutsiia*. Moscow: Krasnaia nov', 1923.

———. *Moia zhizn': opyt avtobiografii*. 2 vols. Berlin: Granit, 1930.

———. *Portrety revoliutsionerov*, edited by Iu. Fel'shtinskii. Benson, VT: Chalidze, 1984.

———. *Sochineniia*. 21 vols. Moscow: Gosizdat, 1920–27.

———. "Stalin—Intendant Gitlera," *Biulleten' Oppozitsii*, 79–80 (August–October, 1939).

Trotsky, Leon. *Stalin: An Appraisal of the Man and His Influence*. New York: Grosset & Dunlap, 1941.

———. *Stalin: An Appraisal of the Man and His Influence*. Revised edition. London: Wellred, 2016.

———. *Stalins Verbrechen*. Zürich: Jean Christophe-Verlag, 1937. Translated as *Prestupleniia Stalina*. Moscow: Gumanitarnaia literatura, 1994.

———. "Balance Sheet of the Finnish Events" [April 25, 1940], *The Fourth International*, 1/2 (1940): 41–4.

———. "Preliminary Comments on the Sixteenth Congress." In *Writings of Leon Trotsky (1930–1931)*, edited by George Breitman and Sarah Lovell. New York: Pathfinder, 1973.

———. "The Lesson of Spain," *Socialist Appeal* [Chicago] 2/8 (Sept. 1936).

———. "The Lessons of Spain: The Last Warning," *Socialist Appeal* [New York], Jan. 8 and Jan. 15, 1938.

———. "The New Constitution of the USSR," *The New Militant* [New York], May 9, 1936.

———. *In Defense of Marxism (against the petty-bourgeois opposition)*. New York: Pioneer, 1942.

———. *Literature and Revolution*. Translated by Rose Strunsky. New York: International Publishers, 1925.

———. *Portraits: Political and Personal*. New York: Pathfinder, 1977.

———. *The Revolution Betrayed: What Is the Soviet Union and Where Is It Going?* London: Faber, 1937.

———. *The Spanish Revolution, 1931–1939*. New York: Pathfinder Press, 1973.

———. *The Writings of Leon Trotsky, 1929*. New York: Pathfinder Press, 1975.

———. *The Writings of Leon Trotsky, 1935–1936*. New York: Pathfinder Press, 1977.

———. *The Writings of Leon Trotsky, 1936–1937*. 2nd ed. New York: Pathfinder Press, 1978.

———. *The Writings of Leon Trotsky, 1938–1939*. New York: Pathfinder Press, 1974.

Trotter, William F. *A Frozen Hell: The Russo-Finnish War of 1939–1940*. Chapel Hill, NC: Algonquin Books, 1992.

Troyat, Henri. *Gorky*. New York: Crown, 1989.

Tsarev, Oleg. "Poslednii polet 'Chernoi Berty.'" In *Ocherki istorii rossiiskoi vneshnei razvedki*, edited by E. M. Primakov. 6 vols. Moscow: Mezhdunarodnye otnosheniia, 1996–2007, III: 433–40.

———, and Nigel West. *KGB v Anglii*. Moscow: Zentrpoligraf, 1999.

Tsimbal, S. "Obraz Lenina v kino," *Iskusstvo kino*, 1938, no. 1, 13–17

Tucker, Robert C. "Stalin and Stalinism: Sources and Outcomes," in *Stalinismus vor dem zweiten Weltkrieg: neue Wege der Forschung*, edited by Manfred Hildermeier and E. Müller-Luckner. Munich: R. Oldenbourg Verlag, 1998.

———. "Stalinism as Revolution from Above." In *Stalinism: Essays in Historical Interpretation*, edited by Robert C. Tucker. New York: W. W. Norton, 1977, 77–110.

———. "The Emergence of Stalin's Foreign Policy," *Slavic Review*, 36/4 (1977): 563–89.

———. "The Rise of Stalin's Personality Cult," *American Historical Review*, 84/2 (1979): 347–46.

———. *Political Culture and Leadership in Soviet Russia*. New York: W. W. Norton, 1987.

———. *Stalin as Revolutionary, 1879–1929: A Study in History and Personality*. New York: W. W. Norton, 1973.

———. *Stalin in Power: The Revolution from Above, 1929–1941*. New York: W. W. Norton, 1990.

———. *The Marx-Engles Reader*. 2nd ed. New York: W. W. Norton, 1978.

———, and Stephen F. Cohen, eds. *The Great Purge Trial*. New York: Grosset & Dunlap, 1965.

Tukhachevskii, Mikhail N. "O strategicheskikh vzgliadakh Prof. Svechina." In *Protiv reaktsionnykh teorii na voennonauchnom fronte*. Moscow: Gosvoenizdat, 1931, 3–16.

———. *Budushchaia voina*. Moscow: Klub realisty, 1928.

———. *Izbrannye proizvedeniia*. 2 vols. Moscow: Voenizdat, 1964.

———. *Zadachi oborony SSSR: rech' 15 ianvaria 1936 g*. Moscow: Partizdat, 1936.

Tulumdzhian, A. O., ed. *S'ezdy sovetov Abkhazii: sbornik dokumentov i materialov (1922–1923)*. Sukhumi: Abgosizdat, 1959.

Tumkina-Perfil'eva, L. M. *Russkii etiket ot Vladimira Monomakha do nashikh dnei*. Moscow: Russkie idei, 2010.

Tumshis, Mikhail A. "Eshche raz o kadrakh chekistov 30-x godov," *Voprosy istorii*, 1993, no. 6: 190–1.

———. *VChK, voina klanov: Lubianka bez retushi*. Moscow: Eksmo, 2004.

———, and Aleksander Papchinskii. *1937, bol'shaia chistka: NKVD protiv ChK*. Moscow: Yauza-EKSMO, 2009.

Tuominen, Arvo. *The Bells of the Kremlin: An Experience of Communism*. Hanover: University of New England, 1983.

Tupitsyn, Margarita. *The Soviet Photograph, 1924–1937*. New Haven, CT: Yale University, 1996.

Tupper, S. M. "The Red Army and the Defence Industry, 1934–1941." PhD diss. University of Birmingham, UK, 1982.

Turchenko, Sergei. "Zhenschiny diktatora," *Trud*, October 2, 1999.

Turkan, G. A. *Ian Rudzutak*. Moscow: Academy of Sciences, 1963.

Turner, Henry Ashby, Jr. *Hitler's Thirty Days to Power*. Reading, MA: Addison-Wesley, 1996.

Turovskaia, Maia. "I. A. Pyr'ev i ego musikal'nye komedii: k problem zhanra," *Kionvedcheskie zapiski*, 1988, no. 1: 111–46.

——. "*Volga-Volga* i ego vremia," *Iskusstvo kino*, 1998, no. 3: 59–64.

Tursunbaev, A. B. "Torzhestvo kolkhoznogo stroia v Kazakhstane." In *Ocherki istorii kollektivizatsii*, edited by Victor P. Danilov. Moscow: Gosizdat, 1963, 259–308.

Turzhanskii, A. A. "Vo glave Sovetskoi aviatsii." In *Revvoensovet nas v boi zovet*, edited by N. V. Ivushkin. Moscow: Voenizdat, 1967, 183–9.

Tynchenko, Iaroslav. *Golgofa russkogo ofitserstva v SSSR, 1930–1931 gody*. Moscow: Moskovskii obshchestvennyi nauchnyi fond, 2000.

1933 god: sbornik ocherkov i statei. Moscow: Sovetskaia literatura, 1934.

Tzitzernak, K. "Aghassi Khanjian," *Armenian Review*, 3/2 (1950): 58–9.

Ubiria, Grigol. *Soviet Nation-Building in Central Asia: The Making of the Kazakh and Uzbek Nations*. London and New York: Routledge, 2016.

Uimanov, V. N., and Iu. A. Petrukhin, eds. *Bol' liudskaia: kniga pamiati tomichei, repressiovannykh v 30–40-e i nachale 50-x*. 5 vols. Tomsk: Upr. KGB SSSR po Tomskoĭ oblasti, 1991–5, V: 102–11.

Ulam, Adam B. "The Price of Sanity." In *Stalinism: Its Impact on Russia and the World*, edited by G. R. Urban. London: Maurice Temple Smith, 1982.

——. *Expansion and Coexistence: Soviet Foreign Policy, 1917–1973*. New York: Praeger, 1974.

——. *Stalin: The Man and His Era*. New York: Viking, 1973.

Ulanovskaia, Nadezhda, and Maia Ulanovskaia. *Istoriia odnoi sem'i*. New York: Chalidze, 1982.

Uldricks, Teddy J. "The Impact of the Great Purges on the People's Commissariat of Foreign Affairs," *Slavic Review*, 36/2 (1977): 187–204.

Ullman, Richard. "The Davies Mission and United States-Soviet Relations, 1937–1941," *World Politics*, 9/2 (1957): 220–39.

Ullrich, Volker. *Hitler: Ascent 1889–1939*. New York: Knopf, 2016.

"'U nas malo rasstrelivaiut': beseda I. V. Stalina s A. Babiusom," *Istochnik*, 1999, no. 1: 101–5.

Unger, Aryeh L. "Stalin's Renewal of the Leading Cadres: A Note on the Great Purge," *Soviet Studies*, 20/3 (1969): 321–30.

——. *Constitutional Development in the USSR: A Guide to the Soviet Constitutions*. London: Methuen, 1981.

Upadyshev, N. V. "Ot Solovkov k Gulagu: zarochdenie sovetskoi lagernoi sistemy," *Otechestvennaia istoriia*, 2006, no. 6: 85–94.

Upton, A. F. *Finland, 1939–40*. Newark: University of Delaware, 1974.

Uralov, Alexander [A. Avtorkhnov]. *The Reign of Stalin*. Westport, CT: Hyperion Press, 1953.

Urushadze, N. *Sandro Akhmeteli*. Moscow: Iskusstvo, 1990.

Ushakov, S. Iu., and A. A. Stukalov. *Front voennykh prokurorov*. Moscow: Vyatka, 2000.

Ustinov, D. F. *Vo imia pobedy*. Moscow: Voenizdat, 1988.

Utesov, Leonid. *Spasibo, Serdtse!* Moscow: Vagrius, 1999.

Utley, Freda. "Germany and Japan," *Political Quarterly*, 8/1 (1937): 51–65.

Uttitz, Friedrich. *Zeugen der Revolution: Mitkämpfer Lenins und Stalins berihcten*. Cologne: Bund-Verlag, 1984.

Vaganov, F. M. *Pravyi uklon v VKP (b) i ego razgrom, 1928–1930*. Moscow: Politicheskaia literatura, 1970.

Vagts, Alfred. "Capitalist Encirclement: a Russian Obsession—Genuine or Feigned?" *Journal of Politics*, 18/3 (1956): 499–519.

Vainrub, M. G. *Eti stal'nye parnii: povest' o perezhitom*. Kiev: Modol', 1972.

Vaiskopf, Mikhail Ia. *Pisatel' Stalin*. Moscow: Novoe literaturnoe obozrenie, 2001.

Vakar, Nicholas. *Byelorussia: The Making of a Nation*. Cambridge, MA: Harvard University, 1956.

Vakar, Nikolai. "Stalin: po vospominaniiam N.N. Zhordaniia," *Posledni novosti*, Dec. 16, 1936.

——. "P. N. Milukov v iznzan'e,'" *Novyi zhurnal*, no. 6 (1943): 369–78.

Vaksberg, Arkadi. *Alexandra Kollontai*. Paris: Fayard, 1996.

——. *Hôtel Lux: les partis frères au service de l'Internationale communiste*. Paris: Fayard, 1993.

——. *Neraskrytye tainy*. Moscow: Novosti, 1993.

Valedinskii, Ivan Aleksandrovich. "Organizm Stalina vpolne zdorovyi," *Istochnik*, 1998, no. 2: 68–73.

Valentinov, N. V. "Sut' bolshevizma v izobrazhenii Iu. Piatakova," *Novy Zhurnal*, no. 52 (1958): 146–9.

——. *Nasledniki Lenina*. Benson, VT: Chalidze, 1990.

van Atta, Don. "The USSR as a 'Weak State': Agrarian Origins of Resistance to Perestroika," *World Politics*, 42/1 (1989): 129–49.

van Dyke, Carl. "Legko otdelalis'," *Rodina*, 1995, no. 12: 113–6.

——. *The Soviet Invasion of Finland, 1939–40*. London and Portland, OR: Frank Cass, 1997.

van Ree, Erik. "Stalin and the National Question," *Revolutionary Russia*, 7/2 (1994): 214–38.

——. "Stalin as Marxist: the Western Roots of Stalin's Russification of Marxism." *In Stalin: A New History*, edited by Sarah Davies and James Harris. New York: Cambridge University, 2005, 159–80.

——. *The Political Thought of Joseph Stalin: A Study in Twentieth-Century Revolutionary Patriotism*. New York: RoutledgeCurzon, 2002.

van Slyke, Lyman. *Enemies and Friends*. Stanford, CA: Stanford: University, 1964.

Vannikov, Boris L. "Iz zapisok narkoma vooruzheniia," *Voenno-Istoricheskii zhurnal*, 1962, no. 2: 78–86.

Vansittart, Lord Robert. *The Mist Procession*. London: Hutchinson, 1958.

——. "Vskryt' cherez 25 let," *Polis*, 1991, no. 3: 148–63.

Varga, Jenő. "Mezhdunarodnoe polozhenie (na konets iiunia)," *Mirovoe khoziaistvo i mirovaia politika*, 1940, no. 6: 15–6.

——. "Konets Locarno," *Mirovoe khoziaistvo i mirovaia politika*, 1936, no. 4: 5–15.

Vasil'ev, Valerii. "30-e gody na Ukraine," *Kommunist*, 1990, no. 17: 77–82.

——. "Krest'iane vosstaniia na Ukraine, 1929–1930 gg.," *Svobodnaia mysl'*, 1992, no. 9: 70–8.

——. "Tsena golodnogo khleba: politika rukovodstva SSSR i USSSR v 1932–1933 gg." In *Komandiri velikogo golodu: poizdki V. Molotova i L. Kaganovicha v Ukrainu na Pivnichnii Kavkaz, 1932–1933 rr*, edited by Valerii Vasil'ev and Iu. Shapoval. Kiev: Heneza, 2001.

——, and Lynne Viola, eds. *Kollektivizatsiia i krest'ianskoe soprotivlenie na Ukraine, noiabr' 1929–mart 1930 gg*. Vinnitsa: Lohos, 1997.

Vasileva, Larisa. *Kremlin Wives*. New York: Arcade, 1994.

Vasil'eva, Larisa. *Kremlevskie zheny*. Moscow: Vagrius, 2001.

Vasil'evich, I., and A. Sgibnev. "Podvig v teni eshafota," *Pogranichnik*, 1988, no. 11.

Vasilevskii, A. M. *Delo vsei zhizni*. 7th ed. 2 vols. Moscow: Politicheskaia literatura, 1990.

——. *A Lifelong Cause*. Moscow: Progress Publishers, 1981. Originally published in Russian as *Delo vsei zhizni*. Moscow: Politizdat, 1974.

Vasiliev, Valerii. "The Great Terror in the Ukraine, 1936–38." In *Stalin's Terror Revisited*, edited by Melanie Ilič. Basingstoke: Palgrave Macmillan, 2006.

Vassiltchikov, Marie. *The Berlin Diaries of Marie "Misie" Vassiltchikov*. London: Methuen, 1985.

Vatlin, A. Iu., and L. N. Malashenko, eds. *Istoriia VKP (b) v portretakh i karikaturakh ee vozhdei*. Moscow: Rosspen, 2007.

Vauhnik, Vladimir. *Memoiren eines Militärattachés*. Buenos Aires: Editorial Palabra Elsovena, 1967.

Vedenin, A. Ia. *Gody i liudi: vospominaniia*. Moscow: Politicheskaia literatura, 1964.

Vehviläinen, Olli. "Trudnaia doroga k miru." In *Zimnaia voina 1939–1940*, edited by Oleg A. Rzhevskii and Olli Vehviläinen. 2 vols. Moscow: Nauka, 1998, 228–59.

——. *Finland in the Second World War: Between Germany and Russia*. Houndmills, Basingstoke: Palgrave Macmillan, 2002.

Velikii letchik nashego vremeni. Moscow: OGIZ, politicheskaia literatura, 1939.

Vereshchak, Maksim I. "Rol' inostrannogo tekhnicheskoi pomoshchi v sozdanii i razvitii sovetskoi bronetankovoi promyshlennosti (1925–1935)." in *Ekonomicheskaia istoriia: ezhegodnik 2013*, edited by Leonid I. Borodkin and Iurii A. Petrov. Moscow: Rosspen, 2014, 226–50.

Verevkin-Rakhal'skii, N. A. *Moi 90 let: vospominaniia*. Moscow: Triada, 2000.

Verkhovskii, A. I. *Ogon', manevr, i maskirovka*. Moscow: Voennyi vestnik, 1928.

Vernadskii, V. I. "Dnevnik 1940 goda," *Druzhba narodov*, 1993, no. 9: 173–94.

——. *Dnevniki, 1926–1934*. Moscow: Nauka, 2001.

——. *Dnevniki, 1935–1941*. Moscow: Nauka, 2008.

Vespa, Amleto. *Sceret Agent of Japan: A Handbook of Japanese Imperialism*. Boston: Little, Brown, 1938.

Vidal, Georges. *Une alliance improbable: l'armée française et la Russie soviétique, 1917–1939*. Rennes: Presses universitaires de Rennes, 2015.

VII Congress of the Communist International: Abridged Stenographic Report of the Proceedings. Moscow: Foreign Languages Publishing House, 1939.

VII Kongress Kommunisticheskogo internatsionala i bor'ba protiv fashizma i voiny: sbornik dokumentov. Moscow: Politizdat, 1975.

VII s"ezd Kommunisticheskikh organizatsii Zakavkaz'ia: stenograficheskii otchet. Tiflis, 1934.

VIII Vsekazakhstanskaia kraevaia konferentsiia VKP (b), 8–16 ianvaria 1934 g.: stenograficheskii otchet. Alma-Ata: Kazkraikom VKP (b) 1935.

Viktorov, Boris A. *Bez grifa "sekretno": zapiski voennogo prokurora*. Moscow: Iuridicheskaia literatura, 1990.

Viktorov, Ivan V. *Popol'shchik, voin, chekist.* Moscow: Politizdat, 1963.

Vilenskii, Semen S., ed. *Dodnes' tiagoteet.* Moscow: Sovetskii pisatel', 1989.

Viñas, Oro. "Financing the Spanish Civil War." In *Revolution and War in Spain, 1931–1939,* edited by Paul Preston. London: Methuen, 1984, 266–83.

Vinogradov, V. K. "1937: pokazaniia marshala Tukhachevskogo," *Voenno-istoricheskii zhurnal,* 1991, no. 8: 44–53, no. 9: 55–63.

———. "Istoriia formirovaniia arkhiva VChK." In *Arkhiv VChK: Sbornik dokumentov.* Moscow: Kuchkovo Pole, 2007.

———. "Tret'ia reforma organov bezopasnosti (1934–1941)." In *Trudy obshchestva izucheniia istorii otechestvennykh spetssluzhb.* Moscow: Kuchkovo pole, 2006, 76–96.

———, ed. *Genrikh Iagoda, narkom vnutrennykh del SSSR, General'nyi kommissar gosudarstvennoi bezopasnosti: sbornik dokumentov.* Kazan: [no publisher listed], 1997.

———, et al., eds. *Sekrety Gitlera na stole u Stalina: razvedka i kontrrazvedka o podgotovke germanskoi agressii protiv SSSR, mart-iiun' 1941 g., dokumenty iz Tsentral'nogo arkhiva FSB Rossii.* Moscow: Mosgosarkhiv, 1995.

Viola, Lynne. "Collectivization in the Soviet Union: Specificities and Modalities." In *The Collectivization of Agriculture in Communist Eastern Europe,* edited by Constantin Iordachi and Arnd Bauerkämper. Budapest: CEU, 2014, 49–77.

———. "The Peasant Nightmare: Visions of Apocalypse in the Soviet Countryside," *Journal of Modern History,* 62/4 (1990): 747–70.

———. "The Role of the OGPU in Dekulakization, Mass Deportations, and Special Resettlement in 1930." *Carl Beck Papers,* University of Pittsburgh, Center for Russian and East European Studies, no. 1406 (2000).

———. *Peasant Rebels under Stalin: Collectivization and the Culture of Peasant Resistance.* New York: Oxford University, 1996.

———. *The Best Sons of the Fatherland: Workers in the Vanguard of Soviet Collectivization.* New York: Oxford University, 1989.

———. *The Unknown Gulag: The Lost World of Stalin's Special Settlements.* New York: Oxford University, 2007.

Virmarita, J. "Karl Gustaf Emil' Mannergeim," *Voprosy istorii,* 1994, no. 1: 56–74.

Vishlev, Oleg V. "Pochemu zhe medlil Stalin v 1941 g.? (iz germanskikh arkhivov)," *Novaia i noveishaia istoriia,* 1992, no. 1: 86–100, no. 2: 70–96.

———. *Nakanune 22 iiunia 1941 goda: Dokumental'nye ocherki.* Moscow: Nauka, 2001.

Vishnevskii, Vsevolod. " 'Sami peredem v napadenie': za dnevnikov 1939–1941 godov," *Moskva,* 1995, no. 5: 103–10.

———. "Kniga o budushchei voine," *Bol'shevik,* 1939, no. 11–12: 119–23.

———. "Pervaia konnaia," *Iskusstvo kino,* 1970, no. 12.

———. "Stalin na XVIII s"ezde partii." In *Vstrechi s tovarishchem Stalinym,* edited by Aleksandr Fadeev. Moscow: OGIZ, 1939, 73–83.

———. *Sobranie sochinenii.* 6 vols. Moscow: Politicheskaia literatura, 1961.

———. *Stat'i, dnevniki, pis'ma.* Moscow: Sovetskii pisatel', 1961.

VKP (b) v rezoliutsiiakh i resheniiakh. 4th ed. Moscow: Partizdat, 1933. 5th ed. Moscow: Partizdat, 1936.

"V Madride ia rukovodil gruppoi ktoroi polzovalsia dlia samykh vaznykh del'," *Latinskaia Amerika,* 1993, no. 3: 63–9.

Vneshniaia torgovlia SSSR za 20 let, 1918–1937 gg.: statisticheskii spravochnik. Moscow: Mezhdunarodnaia kniga, 1939.

Vneshniaia torgovlia SSSR za 1918–1940 gg.: statisticheskii obzor. Moscow: Vneshtorgizdat, 1960.

Vneshniaia torgovlia SSSR, 1918–1966: statisticheskii sbornik. Moscow: Mezhdunarodnye otnosheniia, 1967.

Voennye arkhivy Rossii, 1993, vyp. 1.

Voennyi sovet pri narodnom kosmmissare oborony SSSR, 1938, 1940: dokumenty i materialy. Moscow: Rosspen, 2006.

Voitsekhovskii, Sergei L. *Trest: vospominaniia i dokumenty.* Ontario, Canada: Zaria: 1974.

Voiushin, V. A., and S. A. Gorlov, "Fashistskaia agressiia: o chem soobshchali diplomaty," *Voenno-istoricheskii zhurnal,* 1991, no. 6: 13–23.

" 'Vokrug Menia vse eshche pletut chernuiu Pautinu . . . ': pis'ma M. A. Sholokhova I. V. Stalinu (1937–1950)," *Istochnik,* 1993, no. 4: 4–19.

Volin, Lazar. "Agrarian Collectivism in the Soviet Union: I," *Journal of Political Economy,* 45/5 (1937): 606–33.

Volkogonov, Dmitrii. "Kliment Efremovich Voroshilov." In *Stalin's Generals,* edited by Harold Shukman. London: Weidenfeld and Nicholson, 1993, 313–24.

———. "Marshal Voroshilov," *Oktiabr',* 1996, no. 4: 158–67.

———. "The Drama of the Decisions of 1939," *Soviet Studies in History,* 29 (1990–91): 10–42.

———. "The German Attack, the Soviet Response, Sunday 22 June 1941." In *Barbarossa: The Axis and the Allies,* edited by John Erickson and David Dilks. Edinburgh: Edinburgh University, 1994.

———. *Lenin: Life and Legacy.* London: HarperCollins, 1994.

———. *Stalin: politicheskii portret.* 4th ed. 2 vols. Moscow: Novosti, 1996.

———. *Stalin: Triumph and Tragedy.* New York: Grove Weidenfeld, 1991.

———. *Triumf i tragediia: politicheskii portret I. V. Stalina.* 2 vols. Moscow: Novosti, 1989.

———. *Trotskii: politcheskii portret.* 2 vols. Moscow: Novosti, 1992.

———. *Trotsky: The Eternal Revolutionary.* New York: The Free Press, 1996.

Volkov, F. D. "Legendy i deistvitel'nost' o Rikharde Zorge," *Voenno-istoricheskii zhurnal,* 1996, no. 12: 96–102.

———. *Podvig Rikharda Zorge.* Moscow: Znanie, 1976.

Volkov, V. K. *Germano-iugoslavskie otnosheniia i razval Maloi Antenty, 1933–1938.* Moscow: Nauka, 1966.

———. *Operatsiia "Tevtonskii mech."* Moscow: Mysl', 1966.

Volkovskii, N. L., ed. *Tainy i uroki zimnei voiny, 1939–1940: po dokumentam rassekrechennykh arkhivov.* St. Petersburg: Poligon, 2000.

Volobuev, O., and S. Kuleshov. *Ochishchenie: Istoriia i perestroika.* Moscow: Novosti, 1989.

———. "Istoriia ne terpit polupravdy," *Sotsialisticheskaia industriia,* June 25, 1988.

Volodarsky, Boris. "Soviet Intelligence Services in the Spanish Civil War, 1936–1939." PhD diss. London School of Economics, 2010.

———. *Stalin's Agent: the Life and Death of Alexander Orlov.* Oxford: Clarendon, 2015.

———. *The KGB Orlov File: The Greatest Deception of All Time.* New York: Enigma, 2009.

Voloshin, S. D., et al. *Spravochnik po khlebnomu delu.* 2nd ed. Leningrad: Snabkoopgiz, 1932.

Volski [Valentinov], Nicholas, and Boris Souvarine, "Un Caligula à Moscou: Le cas pathologique de Staline," *Bulletin de l'Association d'études et d'informations politiques internationales,* 98 suppl. (1953): 1–24.

Volubuev, Oleg V., and Sergei V. Kuleshov. *Ochishchenie, istoria i perestroika: publitsistskie zametki.* Moscow: Izd-vo Agentstva pechati Novosti, 1989.

von Bedrow, Klaus. *Hitler rast: der 30. Juni, Ablauf, Vorgeschichte under Hintergründe.* Saarbrücken: [s.n.], 1934.

von Dewitz, Bodo, and Brooks Johnson, eds. *Shooting Stalin: The "Wonderful" Years of Photographer James Abbé (1883–1973).* Göttingen: Steidl, 2004.

von Dirksen, Herbert. *Moscow, Tokyo, London: Twenty Years of German Foreign Policy.* Norman: University of Oklahoma, 1952.

von Fallois, Immo. *Kalkül und Illusion: der Machtkampf zwischen Reichswehr und SA während der Röhm-Krise 1934.* Berlin: Duncker & Humblot, 1994.

von Hagen, Mark. *Soldiers in the Proletarian Dictatorship: The Red Army and the Soviet Socialist State, 1917–1930.* Ithaca, NY: Cornell University, 1990.

von Lang, Joseph. *Eichmann Interrogated: Transcripts from the Archives of the Israeli Police.* Toronto: Lester and Orpen Denny, 1983.

von Laue, Theodore H. "Stalin in Focus," *Slavic Review,* 42/3 (1983): 373–89.

von Mayenburg, Ruth. *Hotel Lux: Mit Dimitroff, Ernst Fischer, Ho Tschi Minh, Pieck, Rakosi, Slansky, Dr. Sorge, Tito, Togliatti, Tschou En-lai, Ulbricht und Wehner im Moskauer Quartier der Kommunistischen Internationale.* Munich: Bertelsmann, 1978.

von Papen, Franz. *Memoirs.* New York: E. P. Dutton & Co., Inc., 1953.

von Rauch, Georg. "Stalin und die Machtergreifung Hitlers." In *Deutsch-russische Beziehungen von Bismarck bis zur Gegenwart,* edited by Werner Markert. Stuttgart: W. Kohlhammer, 1964, 117–40.

von Riekhoff, Harald. *German-Polish Relations, 1918–1933.* Baltimore: Johns Hopkins, 1971.

von Strandmann, H. Pogge. "Appeasement and Counter-Appeasement: Nazi-Soviet Collaboration 1939–1941." In *Conflict, Catastrophe, and Continuity: Essays on Modern German History,* edited by Frank Biess et al. New York: Berghahn, 2007, 157–76.

———. "Grossindustrie und Rapallopolitik: deutsch-sowjetishche Handelsbeziehungen in der Weimaer Republik," *Historische Zeitschrift,* no. 222/2 (1976): 265–341.

Vorob'ev, Evgenii. "Kazhdaia piad' zemli." In *Marshal Zhukov: kakim my ego pomnim.* Moscow: Politicheskaia literatura, 1988, 157–75.

Voronetskaia, A. A., ed. *Industrializatsiia SSSR 1926–1928 gg.: dokumenty i materialy.* Moscow: Nauka, 1969.

Voronov, L. *Abkhazia—ne Gruziia.* Moscow: [s.n.], 1907.

Voronov, N. N. *Na sluzhbe voennoi.* Moscow: Voenizdat, 1963.

Voronov, Vladimir. "Palach v kozhanom fartuke," *Sovershenno sekretno,* March 1, 2010.

Voroshilov, Kliment E. "Uroki voiny s Finliandiei: neopublikovannyi doklad narkoma oborony SSSR K. E. Voroshilova na plenume TsK VKP (b) 28 marta 1940 goda," *Novaia i noveishaia istoriia,* 1993, no. 4: 104–22.

———. *Lenin, Stalin, i krasnaia armiia: stat'i i rechi.* Moscow: Partizdat, 1934.

———. *Stat'i i materialy k 50-letiiu.* Moscow: Voenizdat, 1931.

———. *Stat'i i rechi.* Moscow: Voenizdat, 1936.

Vorozheikin, Arsenii V. *Istrebiteli.* Moscow: Voenizdat, 1961.

Voskresenskaia, Zoia. *Pod psevdonym Irina.* Moscow: Sovremennik, 1997.

———. *Teper' ia mogu skazat' pravdu: iz vospominanii razvedchitsy.* Moscow: Respublika, 1993.

Voslensky, Michael. *Nomenklatura: The Soviet Ruling Class.* New York: Doubleday, 1984. Originally published as *La nomenklatura, les privilégiés en URSS.* Paris: Pierre Belfond, 1980.

"Vospominaia Velikuiu Otechestvennuiu," *Otechestvennaia istoriia,* 2003, no. 3: 49–70.

"Vospominaniia: memurary Nikity Sergeevicha Khrushcheva," *Voprosy istorii,* 1990, no. 4: 62–82; 1992, no: 2: 75–102.

Vostryshev, Mikhail. *Moskva Stalinskaia: bol'shaia illustrirovannia letopis'.* Moscow: Algoritm, 2008.

"Vot gde Pravda, Nikita Sergeevich!" *Voenno-istoricheskii zhurnal,* 1990, no. 1: 9–18.

"'Vse, chto govoroit Radek—eto absoliutno zlostnaia kleveta . . .': ochnaia stavka K. Radeka i N. Bukharina v TsK VKP (b) 13 ianvaria 1937 g.," *Istochnik,* 2001, no. 1: 63–77.

Vtoroi vsesoiuznyi s"ezd kolkhoznikovudarnikov, 11–17 fevralia 1935 g.: stenograficheskii otchet. Moscow: Sel'khozgiz, 1935.

Vyltsan, Mikhail A. *Zavershchaiushchii etap sozdaniia kolkholznogo stroia, 1935–1937 gg.* Moscow: Nauka, 1978.

———, et al. "Nekotorye voprosy istorii kollektivizatsii v SSSR," *Voprosy istorii,* 1965, no. 3: 3–25.

Vyshinskii, Andrey. *Sudebnye rechi.* 4th ed. Moscow: Gosizdat, 1955.

Waddington, Geoffrey T. "An Idyllic and Unruffled Atmosphere of Complete Anglo-German Misunderstanding: Aspects of the Operations of the Dienststelle Ribbentrop in Great Britain, 1934–1938," *History,* 82 (1997): 44–72.

———. "Ribbentrop and the Soviet Union, 1937–1941" In *Barbarossa: The Axis and the Allies,* edited by John Erickson and David Dilks. Edinburgh: Edinburgh University, 1994, 7–32.

Waddington, Lorna L. "The Anti-Kominkern and Nazi Anti-Bolshevik Propaganda in the 1930s," *Journal of Contemporary History,* 42/4 (2007): 573–94.

———. *Hitler's Crusade: Bolshevism and the Myth of the International Jewish Conspiracy.* London and New York: I. B. Tauris, 2007.

Wagener, Otto. *Memoirs of a Confidant.* New Haven, CT: Yale University, 1985.

Wager, Elisabeth, ed. *Der Generalquartiermeister: Briefe under Tagebuchaufzeichnungen des Generalquartiermeisters des Heeres der Artillerie Eduard Wagner.* Munich: Günter Olzog, 1963.

Waldenegg, Georg Christoph Berger. "Hitler, Göring, Mussolini und der 'Anschluss' Österreichs an das Deutsche Reich," *Vierteljahreshefte für Zeitgeschichte,* 51/2 (2003): 147–82.

Walker, Michael W. *The War Nobody Knew: Chinese Nationalism and the 1929 Sino-Soviet Conflict.* Lawrence: University Press of Kansas, 2016.

Walker, Thomas. "Children Starve among the Soviet Dead," *New York Evening Journal,* Feb. 19, 1935.

Walt, Stephen. "Revolution and War," *World Politics,* 44/3 (1992): 321–68.

Walters, F. P. *A History of the League of Nations.* 2 vols. New York: Oxford University, 1952.

Waltz, Kenneth N. *Theory of International Relations.* Reading, MA: Addison-Wesley, 1979.

Wandycz, Piotr S. "Polish Foreign Policy: An Overview," In *Poland between the Wars: 1918–1939,* edited by Timothy Wiles. Bloomington: Indiana University Polish Studies Centre, 1989, 65–73.

———. "Polish Foreign Policy: Some Observations," *Polish Review,* 20/1 (1975): 58–63.

———. *The Twilight of French Eastern Alliances, 1926–1936: French-Czechoslovak-Polish Relations from Locarno to the Remilitarization of the Rhineland.* Princeton, NJ: Princeton University, 1988.

Wańkowicz, Melchior. *Po klęsce: Prószyński i Spółka.* Warsaw, 2009.

Wark, Wesley K. *The Ultimate Enemy: British Intelligence and Nazi Germany, 1933–1939.* Ithaca, NY: Cornell University, 1985.

Warlimont, Walter. *Im Hauptquartier der deutschen Wehrmacht 1939–1945.* Frankfurt am Main: Bernard & Graefe, 1962.

———. *Inside Hitler's Headquarters, 1939–45.* London: Weidenfeld and Nicholson, 1964.

Watson, Derek. "Molotov's Apprenticeship in Foreign Policy: The Triple Alliance Negotiations in 1939," *Europe-Asia Studies* 52/4 (2000): 695–722.

———. *Molotov: A Biography.* Houndmills, Basingstoke: Palgrave Macmillan, 2005.

———. "The Politburo and Foreign Policy in the 1930s." In *The Nature of Stalin's Dictatorship: The Politburo, 1924–1953,* edited by E. A. Rees. Houndmills, Basingstoke: Palgrave Macmillan, 2004, 134–67.

Watt, Donald Cameron. "British Intelligence and the Coming of the Second World War in Europe." In *Knowing One's Enemies: Intelligence Assessment before the Two World Wars,* edited by Ernest R. May. Princeton, NJ: Princeton University, 1984, 237–70.

———. "The Initiation of the Negotiations Leading to the Nazi-Soviet Pact: a Historical Problem." In *Essays in Honour of E. H. Carr,* edited by C. Abramsky. London: Archer, 1974, 152–70.

———. "Who Plotted against Whom? Stalin's Purge of the Soviet High Command," *Journal of Soviet Military Studies,* 3/1 (1990): 46–65.

———. *How War Came: The Immediate Origins of the Second World War, 1938–1939.* London: Heinemann, 1989.

Watts, Larry. *Romanian Cassandra: Ion Antonescu and the Struggle for Reform, 1916–1941.* Boulder, CO: East European Monographs, 1993.

Weber, H. *"Weisse Flecken" in der Geschichte: Die KPD—Opfer der Stalinschen Säuberungen und ihre Rehabilitierung.* Frankfurt am Main: Isp-Verlag, 1989.

Wegner-Korfes, Siegfried. "Ambassador Count Schulenburg and the Preparations for 'Barbarossa.'" In *From Peace to War: Germany, Soviet Russia, and the World, 1939–1941,* edited by Bernd Wegner. Providence, RI, and Oxford, UK: Berghahn, 1997, 187–204.

Weinberg, Gerhard L. "A Proposed Compromise over Danzig in 1939?" *Journal of Central European Affairs,* 14/4 (1955): 334–8.

———. "German Foreign Policy and Poland, 1937–38," *Polish Review,* 20/1 (1975): 5–23.

———. "Germany, Munich, and Appeasement." In *Germany, Hitler, and World War II: Essays in Modern Germany and World History.* New York: Cambridge University, 1995, 109–20.

———. "Hitler and England, 1933–1945." In *Germany, Hitler, and World War II: Essays in Modern Germany and World History.* New York: Cambridge University, 1995, 85–94.

———. "The Nazi-Soviet Pacts: A Half-Century Later," *Foreign Affairs,* 68/4 (1989): 175–89.

———. *A World at Arms: A Global History of World War II.* Cambridge, UK: Cambridge University, 1995.

———. *Germany and the Soviet Union, 1939–1941.* Leiden: E. J. Brill, 1954.

———. *Hitler's Foreign Policy: The Road to World War II, 1933–1939.* New York: Enigma, 2005.

———. *The Foreign Policy of Hitler's Germany,* 2 vols. Chicago: University of Chicago, 1970, 1980.

———, ed. *Hitler's Table Talk, 1941–1944: His Private Conversations.* New York: Enigma, 1951.

Weissberg-Cybulski, Alexander. *The Accused.* New York: Simon & Schuster, 1951.

Weissman, Susan. *Victor Serge: The Course Is Set on Hope.* New York: Verso, 2001.

Weizsäcker, Ernst von. *Erinnerungen.* Munich: List, 1950.

———. *Memoirs.* London: Victor Gallancz, 1951.

Welles, Sumner. *The Time for Decision.* New York: Harper, 1944.

Wells, H. G. *Experiment in Autobiography: Discoveries and Conclusions of a Very Ordinary Brain (Since 1866).* London: Viktor Gollancz, 1934.

Wendt, B. J. *Grossdeutschland: Aussenpolitik und Kriegsvorbereitung des Hitlers Regime.* Munich: Deutscher Taschenbuch Verlag, 1987.

Werner, Max. *The Military Strength of the Powers: A Soldier's Forecast for Citizens.* New York: Modern Age, 1939.

Werth, Alexander. *Russia at War, 1941–1945.* London: Barrie and Rockliff, 1964.

Werth, Nicolas. "La famine au Kazakhstan 1931–1933. Le rapport à Staline du 9 mars 1933," *Communisme,* 74–5 (2003): 9–41.

———. "Stalin's System during the 1930s." In *Stalinism and Nazism: History and Memory Compared,* edited by Henry Rousso. Lincoln: University of Nebraska, 1999, 29–55.

———, and Gaël Moullec. *Rapports secrets soviétiques: la société russe dans les rapports confidentiels, 1921–1991.* Paris: Gallimard, 1995.

———, and Sergei Mironenko, eds. *Istoriia stalinskogo gulaga: konets 20-x-pervaia polovina 50-kh godov.* 7 vols. Moscow: Rosspen, 2004.

———, et al., eds. *The Black Book of Communism: Crimes, Terror, Repression.* Cambridge, MA: Harvard University, 1999.

West, Nigel. *MI6: British Secret Intelligence Operations, 1909–1945.* London: Weidenfeld and Nicolson, 1983.

———, and Oleg Tsarev. *The Crown Jewels: The British Secrets at the Heart of the KGB Archives.* New Haven, CT: Yale University, 1999.

Westermann, Edward B. *Hitler's Police Battalions: Enforcing Racial War in the East.* Lawrence: University Press of Kansas, 2005.

Westwood, J. N. *Soviet Locomotive Technology during Industrialization, 1928–1952.* London: Macmillan, 1982.

Whaley, Barton. *Codeword Barbarossa.* Cambridge, MA: MIT, 1973.

Wheatcroft, Stephen G. "Agency and Terror: Evdokimov and Mass Killing in Stalin's Great Terror," *Australian Journal of Politics and History,* 53/1 (2007): 20–44.

———. "From Team-Stalin to Degenerate Tyranny." In *The Nature of Stalin's*

Dictatorship: The Politburo, 1924–1953, edited by E. A. Rees. Houndmills, Basingstoke: Palgrave Macmillan, 2004, 79–107.

——. "On Assessing the Size of Forced Concentration Camp Forced Labour in the Soviet Union, 1929–1956," *Soviet Studies*, 33/2 (1982): 265–95.

——. "Victims of Stalinism and the Soviet Secret Police: The Comparability and Reliability of Archival Data," *Europe-Asia Studies* 51, no. 2 (1999): 315–45.

——, and R. W. Davies. "Agriculture." In *The Economic Transformation of the Soviet Union, 1913–1945*, edited by Robert W. Davies, et al. New York: Cambridge University, 1994, 106–30.

——. "Population." In *The Economic Transformation of the Soviet Union, 1913–1945*, edited by Robert W. Davies, et al. New York: Cambridge University, 1994, 57–80.

Wheatley, Robert H. *Hitler and Spain: The Nazi Role in the Spanish Civil War, 1936–1939*. Lexington: University Press of Kentucky, 2015.

Wheatley, Ronald. *Operation Sea Lion: German Plans for the Invasion of England 1939–1942*. Oxford: Clarendon, 1958.

Wheeler-Bennet, John W. *The Nemesis of Power: The German Army in Politics, 1918–1945*. New York: St. Martin's, 1953.

——. "From Brest-Litovsk to Brest-Litovsk." *Foreign Affairs*, 18/2 (1940): 196–210.

——, ed. *Documents on International Affairs, 1931*. London: Milford, 1932.

——, ed. *Documents on International Affairs, 1935*. London: Royal Institute of International Affairs, 1936.

Whitewood, Peter. "The Purge of the Red Army and the Soviet Mass Operations, 1937–38," *Slavonic and East European Review*, 93/2 (2015): 286–314.

——. *The Red Army and the Great Terror: Stalin's Purge of the Soviet Military*. Lawrence: University Press of Kansas, 2015.

Whiting, Allen S., and General Sheng Shih-ts'aicai. *Sinkiang: Pawn or Pivot?* East Lansing: Michigan State University, 1958.

Whitman, John T. "The Kolkhoz Market," *Soviet Studies*, 7/4 (1956): 384–408.

Whymant, Robert. *Stalin's Spy: Richard Sorge and the Tokyo Espionage Ring*. London and New York: I. B. Tauris, 1996.

Wiedemann, Fritz. *Der Mann, der Feldherr werden wollte*. Vellbert/Kettwig, 1964.

Williams, Andrew J. *Trading with the Bolsheviks: The Politics of East-West Trade 1920–1939*. Manchester, UK: Manchester University, 1992.

Williams, Karel, Colin Haslam, and John Williams, "Ford versus 'Fordism': The Beginning of Mass Production?" *Work, Employment and Society*, 6/4 (1992): 517–55.

Williams, Raymond. *Communications*. 2nd ed. New York: Barnes and Noble, 1967.

Wilson, Dick. *The Long March, 1935: The Epic of Chinese Communism's Survival*. New York: Penguin Press, 1971.

——. *When Tigers Fight: The Story of the Sino-Japanese War, 1937–1945*. New York: Viking, 1982.

Wilson, Edmund. "Stalin as Ikon," *New Republic*, April 15, 1936.

Wilson, Peter H. *Heart of Europe*. Cambridge, MA: Belknap Press of Harvard University, 2016.

Winch, Michael. *Republic for a Day: An Eye-Witness Account of the Carpatho-Ukraine Incident*. London: R. Hale, 1939.

Winkler, Heinrich August. *Der Weg in die Katastrophe: Arbeiter und Arbeitsbewegung in der Weimarer Republic, 1930 bis 1933*. Berlin: J. H. W. Weitz, 1987.

——. *Weimar, 1918–1933: die Geschichte der ersten Deutschen Demokratie*. Munich: Beck, 1993.

Winterbotham, Frederick W. *The Nazi Connection*. New York: Harper & Row, 1978.

——. *The Ultra Secret*. New York: Harper & Row, 1974.

Wintrobe, Ronald. *The Political Economy of Dictatorship*. New York: Cambridge University, 1998.

Włodarkiewicz, Wojciech. *Lwów*. Warsaw: Bellona, 2003.

——. *Przed 17 września 1939 roku: Radzieckie zagrożenie Rzeczypospolitej wocenach polskich naczelnych władz wojskowych 1921–1939*. Warsaw: Wydawn Neriton, 2002.

Wohlforth, William C. "The Russian-Soviet Empire: A Test of Neorealism," *Review of International Studies*, 27/5 (2001): 213–35.

Wojciechowski, Marian. *Stosunki polsko-niemieckie, 1933–1938*. Poznan: Instytut Zachodni, 1965.

Wolf, Erika, ed. *Ilf and Petrov's Road Trip*. New York: Architectural Press, 2007.

Wolfe, Bertram. "Adventures in Forged Sovietica," *New Leader*, Aug. 11, 1955.

——. "The Case of the Litvinov Diary," *Encounter*, 6/1 (1956): 339–47.

——. *Strange Communists I Have Known*. New York: Stein and Day, 1965.

Wolfer, Arnold. *Britain and France between the Two Wars: Conflicting Strategies of Peace since Versailles*. New York: Harcourt Brace, 1940.

Wollenberg, Erich. *The Red Army*. London: Secker & Warburg, 1938.

Womack, J. P., D. I. Jones, and D. Roos. *The Machine that Changed the World*. New York: Rawson Associates, 1990.

Woodruff, Nan Elizabeth. *As Rare as Rain: Federal Relief in the Great Southern Drought of 1930–31*. Urbana: University of Illinois, 1985.

Woodward, E. L. *British Foreign Policy in the Second World War*. 5 vols. London: H.M.S.O., 1970.

——, and Rohan Butler, eds. *Documents on British Foreign Policy, 1919–1939*, 62 vols. Second series. London: H. M. Stationery Office, 1947–1984. Cited as *DBFP*, 2nd series.

——, eds. *Documents on British Foreign Policy, 1919–1939*, 62 vols. Third series. London: H. M. Stationery Office, 1947–1984. Cited as *DBFP*, 3rd series.

World Situation and Economic Struggle: Theses of the Tenth Plenum E.C.C.I., The. London: CPGB, 1929.

Woroszylski, Wiktor. *The Life of Mayakovsky*. New York: Orion, 1970.

Wynn, Charters. "The 'Right Opposition' and the 'Smirnov-Eismont-Tolmachev Affair.'" In *The Lost Politburo Transcripts: From Collective Rule to Stalin's Dictatorship*, edited by Paul R. Gregory and Norman Naimark. New Haven: Yale University, 2008, 97–117.

XII s"ezd RKP (b): stenograficheskii otchet. Moscow: Krasnaia nov', 1923.

XVI konferentsiia VKP (b), aprel' 1929 goda: stenograficheskii otchet. Moscow: Politicheskaia literatura, 1962.

XVI s"ezd VKP (b), 26 iiunia–13 iiulia 1930 g.: stenograficheskii otchet. 2 vols. Moscow: Partizdat, 1935.

XVI s"ezd VKP (b): stenograficheskii otchet. 2nd ed. Moscow and Leningrad: Gosizdat, 1931.

XVI s"ezd VKP (b): stenograficheskii otchet. Moscow and Leningrad: Gosizdat, 1930. All citations refer to this edition unless otherwise indicated.

XVII konferentsiia VKP (b): stenograficheskii otchet, 30 ianvaria–4 fevralia 1932. Moscow, 1932.

XVII s"ezd VKP (b), 26 ianvaria–10 fevralia 1934 g.: stenograficheskii otchet. Moscow: Partizdat, 1934.

XVIII s"ezd VKP (b), 10–21 marta 1939 goda: stenograficheskioi otchet. Moscow: Politcheskaia literatura 1939.

XX let Sovetskoi Abkhazii: politiko-ekonomicheskii ocherk. Sukhumi, 1941.

XXII s"ezd KPSS: stenograficheskii otchet. 2 vols. Moscow: Politizdat, 1961.

Yaney, George L. "Some Aspects of the Imperial Russian Government on the Eve of the First World War," *Slavonic and East European Review*, 43/1 (1964): 68–90.

——. "War and the Evolution of Russian Government," *South Atlantic Quarterly*, 66/2 (1967): 291–306.

——. *The Systematization of Russian Government: Social Evolution in the Domestic Administration of Imperial Russia 1711–1905*. Urbana: University of Illinois, 1973.

Yang, Benjamin. *From Revolution to Politics: Chinese Communists on the Long March*. Boulder, CO: Westview, 1990.

Yaroslavskii, E. M. "Etot son knochen," *Izvestiia*, May 30, 1929.

Yaroslavsky, Yemelyan. *The Meaning of the Soviet Trials*. New York: Workers Library, 1938.

Yedlin, Tovah. *Maxim Gorky: A Political Biography*. Westport, CT: Praeger, 1999.

Yoshihashi, Takehiko. *Conspiracy at Mukden: The Rise of the Japanese Military*. New Haven, CT: Yale University, 1963.

Young, Kenneth, ed. *The Diaries of Sir Robert Bruce Lockhart, 1915–1938*. 2 vols. London: Macmillan, 1973.

Young, Louise. *Total Empire: Manchuria and the Culture of Wartime Imperialism*. Berkeley: University of California, 1998.

Young, Robert J. "French Military Intelligence and Nazi Germany, 1938–1939." In *Knowing One's Enemies: Intelligence Assessment before the Two World Wars*, edited by Ernest F. May. Princeton, NJ: Princeton University, 1984, 271–309.

——. *In Command of France: France's Foreign Policy and Military Planning, 1933–1940*. Cambridge, MA: Harvard University, 1978.

Z. "Sovremennaia artilleriia i modernizatsiia," *Voina i tekhnika*, 1929, no. 4: 9–14.

Zagoria, Janet D., ed. *Power and the Soviet Elite: "The Letter of an Old Bolshevik" and Other Essays by Boris I. Nicolaevsky*. Ann Arbor: University of Michigan, 1975.

Zaitsev, A. "Krasnaia armiia," *Chasovoi*, 1931, no. 54.

Zaitsev, E. A. *Sbornik zakonodatel'nykh i normativnykh aktov o repressiakh i reabilitatsii zhertv politichcheskikh repressii*. Moscow: Respublika, 1993.

Zakharov, M. V. *General'nyi shtab v predvoennye gody*. Moscow: Voenizdat, 1989.

——. *Nakanune velikikh ispytanii*. Moscow: Voenizdat, 1968.

——, et al. *50 let Vooruzhenykh Sil SSSR*. Moscow: Voenizdat, 1968.

Zakharov, S. "Krasnoznamennomu Tikhookeanskomu flotu—50 let," *Voenno-istoricheskii zhurnal*, 1982, no. 4: 93–6.

Zaleski, Eugene. *Planning for Economic Growth in the Soviet Union, 1918–1932*. Chapel Hill: University of North Carolina, 1971.

——. *Stalinist Planning for Economic Growth, 1933–1952*. London: MacMillan, 1980.

Zaloga, Steven J. "Soviet Tank Operations in the Spanish Civil War," *Journal of Slavic Military Studies*, 123 (1999).

——, and James Grandsen. *Soviet Tanks and Combat Vehicles of World War Two*. London: Arms and Armour Press, 1984.

——, and Victor Madej. *The Polish Campaign, 1939*. New York: Hippocrene, 1985.

"'Zamenit' Vas nekem': pis'ma M. Gor'kogo I. V. Stalinu," *Istochnik*, 1999, no. 5: 115–7.

Zamoiskii, L., and Iu. Nezhnikov. "U u rokovoi cherty: sovetskaia razvedka nakanune voiny," *Izvestiia*, May 5, 1990.

Zaporozhets, Natal'ia. "Iz vospominaniia." In *Dodnes' tiagoteet*, edited by Semen S. Vilenskii. Moscow: Sovetskii pisatel', 1989, 532–8.

Zatonskii, V. P. "Otryvki vospominanii ob Ukrainskoi revoliutsii," *Letopis' revoliutsii*, 1929, no. 5–6: 128–41.

Zdanovich, A. A. *Organy gosudarstvennoi bezopasnosti i Krasnaia armiia: deiatel'nost' organov VChK-OGPU po obespecheniiu bezopasnosti RKKA, 1921–1934*. Moscow: Kuchkovo pole/Iks-Khistori, 2008.

Zdanovich, Semen F. *Karl Bauman*. Moscow: Politizdat, 1967.

Zeidler, Manfred. *Reichswehr und Rote Armee, 1920–1933: Wege und Stationen einer ungewöhnlichen Zusammenarbeit*. 2nd ed. Munich: Oldenbourg, 1994. Originally published 1993.

Zel'dovich, G. *Liubov' Orlova*. Moscow: Goskinoizdat, 1939.

Zelenin, Il'ia E. "Byl li 'kolkhoznyi neonep'?" *Otechestvennaia istoriia*, 1994, no. 2: 105–21.

——. "Kolkhoznoe stroitel'stvo v SSSR v 1931–1932 gg.: k itogam sploshnoi kollektivizatsii sel'skoogo khoziaistva," *Istoriia SSSR*, 1990, no. 6: 19–39.

——. "O nekotorykh 'belykh piatnakh' zavershaiushchego etapa sploshnoi kollektivizatsii," *Istoriia SSSR*, 1989, no. 2: 3–19.

——. "Osushchestvlenie politiki 'likvidatsii kulachestva kak klassa' (osen' 1930–1932 gg.)," *Istoriia SSSR*, 1990, no. 6: 31–49.

——. "Politotdely MTS (1933–1934 gg.)," *Istoricheskie zapiski*, no. 76 (1965): 2–56.

——. *Stalinskaia 'revoliutsiia sverkhu' posle 'velikogo pereloma,' 1930–1939: politika, osushchestvlenie, rezultaty*. Moscow: Nauka, 2006.

——, et al., eds. *Istoriia sovetskogo krest'iantsva*. 4 vols. Moscow: Nauka, 1986–8.

Zelenov, M. V. "Partiinyi kontrol' za izdaniem sochinenii Lenina i literature o nem v 1924–1937," *Voprosy istorii*, 2004, no 11: 3–28.

——. "I. V. Stalin v rabote nad 'Kratkim kursom istorii VKP (b),'" *Voprosy istorii*, 2001, no. 11: 3–29.

——, ed. *I. V. Stalin, Istoricheskaia ideologiia v SSSR v 1920–1950-e gody: perepiska s istorikami, stat'i i zametki po istorii, stenogrammy vystuplenii. Sbornik dokumentov i materialov*. St. Petersburg: Nauka-Piter, 2006.

——, and David Brandenberger. *"Kratkii kurs istorii VKP (b)": tekst i ego istoriia*. 2 vols. Moscow: Rosspen, 2014–.

Zelinskii, Kornelii. "Odna vtrecha u A. M. Go'kogo," *Voprosy literatury*, 1991, no. 5: 144–70.

——. "V iune 1954 goda," *Minuvshee*, no. 5 (1988): 54–103.

Zemskov, I. N., ed. *Novye dokumenty iz istorii Miunkhena*. Moscow: Politicheskaia literatura, 1958.

Zemskov, V. N. "'Kulaktskaia ssylka' v 30-e gody." In *Naselenie Rossii v XX veke: istoricheskie ocherki*, edited by Iuri A. Poliakov. 3 vols. Moscow: Rosspen, 2000–12, I: 277–310.

——. "GULAG: isoriko-sotsiologicheskii aspect," *Sotsiologicheskie issledovania*, 1991, no. 6: 10–27, no. 7: 3–16.

——. "Zakliuchennye v 1930-e gody: sotsial'no-demograficheskie problemy," *Otechestvennaia istoriia*, 1997, no. 4: 54–79.

Zen'kovich, Nikolai A. *Marshaly i genseki: intrigi, vrazhda, zagovory*. Moscow: Olma, 2000.

——. *Samye sekretnye rodsvtvenniki: entsiklopediia biografii*. Moscow: Olma, 2005.

Zenzinov, Vladimir M. *Vstrecha s Rossiei, kak i chem zhivut v Sovetskom Soiuze: pis'ma v Krasnuiu armiiu, 1939–1940*. New York: [s.n.], 1944.

Zhavaronkov, G. N. "I snitsia noch'iu den'," *Sintaksis*, 1992, no. 32: 46–65.

——, and V. I. Pariiskii, "Skazvashii budet uslyshan." In *Oni ne molchali*, edited by A. V. Afanas'ev. Moscow: Politizdat, 1991, 199–215.

Zhdanko, T. "Natsional'no-gosudarstvennoye razmezhevaniye i protsessy etnicheskogo razvitiya u narodov Srednei Azii," *Sovetskaia etnografiia*, 1972, no. 5: 13–29.

Zhgenti, Beso. "S"ezd velikogo edineniia," *Literaturnaia Gruziia*, 1974, no. 9.

Zhilin, P. A. *Kak fashistskaia Germaniia gotovila napadenie na Sovetskii Soiuz*. Moscow: Mysl', 1965.

——. *Kak fashistskaia Germaniia gotovila napadenie na Sovetskii Soiuz*. 2nd ed. Moscow: Mysl', 1966.

——. *O voine i voennoi istorii*. Moscow: Nauka, 1984.

——, ed. *Pobeda na reke Khalkhin-gol*. Moscow: Nauka, 1981.

Zhirnov, Evgenii. "NKVD pod kolpakom u Miullera," *Kommersant vlast'*, June 20, 1940.

Zhiromskaia, V. B., ed. *Naselenie Rossii v XX veke: istoricheskie ocherki v 3-kh t.* Vol. 1, *1900–1939*. Moscow: Rosspen, 2000.

——, I. N. Kisleva, and Iu. A. Poliakov. *Polveka pod grifom "sekretno": vsesoiuznaia perepis' naseleniia 1937 goda*. Moscow: Nauka, 1996.

Zhukov, E. M., ed. *Vsesoiuznoe soveshchanie o merakh uluchsheniia podgotovki nauchno-pedagogicheskikh kadrov po istoricheskim naukam, 18–21 dekabria 1962 g.* Moscow: Nauka, 1964.

Zhukov, G. K. "Iz neopublikovannykh vospominanii," *Kommunist*, 1988, no. 14: 97–9.

——. *Vospominaniia i razmyshleniia*. 3 vols. 13th ed. Moscow: Olma, 2002.

——. *Vospominaniia i razmyshleniia*. 3 vols. 12th ed. Moscow: Novosti, 1995.

——. *Vospominaniia i razmyshleniia*. 3 vols. Moscow: Novosti, 1969.

Zhukov, Iurii N. "Sledstvie i sudebnye protsessy po delu ob ubiistve Kirova," *Voprosy istorii*, 2000, no. 2: 33–51.

——. "Tak, byl li 'zagovor' Tukhachevskogo?" *Otechestvennaia istoriia*, 1999, no. 1: 176–81.

——. *Inoi Stalin: Politicheskie reform v SSSR v 1933–1937 gg.* Moscow: Vagrius, 2003.

Zhukovskaia, Tat'iana Iu. "SSSR i liga natsii." PhD diss. Rostov-na-Donu, 2005.

Zhukovskii, V. S. *Lubianskaia imperiia NKVD, 1937–1939 gg.* Moscow: Veche, 2001.

Zhukunov, E. V., ed. *1941g.—Uroki i vyvody*. Moscow: Voenizdat, 1992.

Zhuravlev, S. V., ed. *Obshchestvo i vlast', 1930-e gody: povestvovanie v dokumentakh*. Moscow: Rosspen, 1998.

——, and V. S. Tiazhel'nikova, "Inostrannye kolonii i sovetskoi Rossii v 1920–1930 gody," *Istoricheskie zapiski*, 1994, no. 1: 179–89.

Ziemke, Earl F. *The Red Army, 1918–1941: From Vanguard of World Revolution to US Ally*. London: Frank Cass, 2004.

Zil'ver, E. *Za bol'shoe kinoiskusstvo*. Moscow: Kinofotoizdat, 1935.

Zipperstein, Steven J. "Underground Man: The Curious Case of Mark Zborowski and the Writing of a Modern Jewish Classic," *Jewish Review of Books*, 2 (2010): 38–42.

Zoller, Albert, ed. *Hitler Privat: Erlebnissbericht seiner Geheimsek- retuerin*. Dusseldorf: Droste Verlag, 1949.

Zolotarev, Vladimir A., ed. *Istoriia voennoi strategii Rossii*. Moscow: Kuchkovo Pole, 2000.

——, ed. *Russkii arkhiv: Velikaia otechestvennaia. Prikazy narodnogo kommissar oborony SSSR*. 14 vols. Moscow: Terra, 1993–2002.

——, et al., eds. *Velikaia Otechestvennaia voina 1941–1945 gg.: voenno-istoricheskie ocherki*. 4 vols. Moscow: Nauka, 1998–9.

Zonin, S. A. *Admiral L.M. Galler*. Moscow: Voenizdat, 1991.

Zoshchenko, Mikhail. *Sobranie sochinenii*. 2 vols. Leningrad: khudozhestvennaia literatura, 1986.

Zubkova, E. Iu. *Pribaltika i kreml', 1940–1953*. Moscow: Rosspen, 2008.

Zuehilke, Mark. *The Gallant Cause: Canadians in the Spanish Civil War, 1936–1939*. Vancouver and Toronto: Whitecap, 1996.

Zveriakov, T. A. *Ot kochev'ia k sotsializmu*. Alma-Ata, 1934.

Zychowicz, Piotr. *Pakt Ribbentrop-Beck, czyli, Jak Polacy mogli u boku III Rzeszy pokonać Związek Sowiecki*. Poznań: Rebis, 2012.

CREDITS

INSERT 1:

INSERT 2:

Page 3, top: Alinari Archives / Getty Images; bottom: Central Press / Hulton Archive / Getty Images

Page 4, top: Popperfoto / Getty Images

Pages 5, top; 11, top; 12: RGASPI

Page 6, top: Hoover Institution Archives

Page 7, top: Corbis Historical / Getty Images; bottom; 8, bottom; 15, middle: ullstein bild / Getty Images

Page 8, top: SVF2 / Universal Images Group / Getty Images

Page 10, bottom: Galerie Bilderwelt / Hulton Archive / Getty Images

Page 11, bottom: Topical Press Agency / Hulton Archive / Getty Images

Page 13, top: Sueddeutsche Zeitung Photo / Alamy Stock Photo; bottom: The Asahi Shimbun / Getty Images

Page 16: Author's personal collection

INDEX